English Tourism Council

The only OFFICIAL Guide to

BED AND BREAKFAS

GUEST ACCOMMODATON

There's something different around every corner

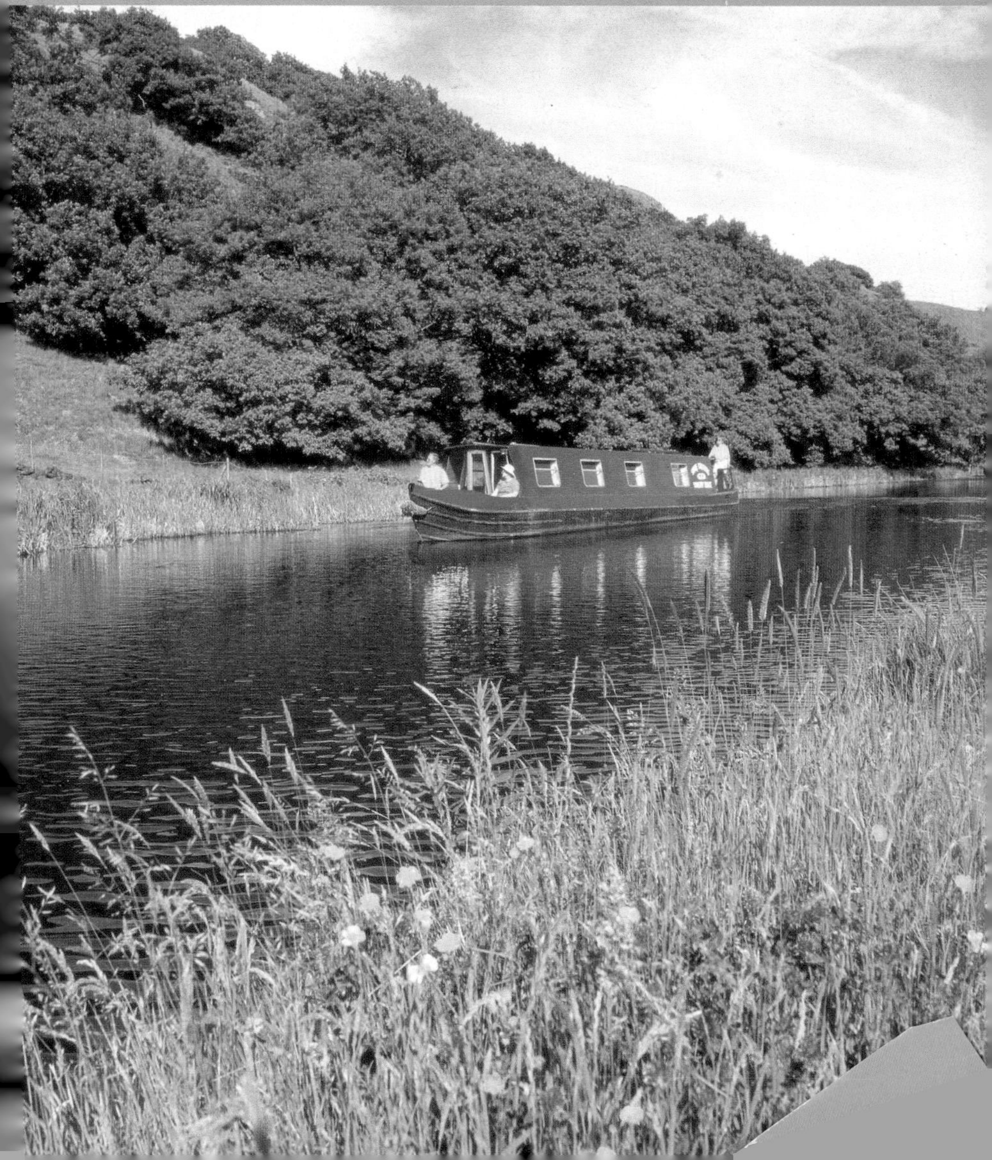

The English Tourism Council

English Tourism Council is the national body for English Tourism. Its mission is to drive forward the quality, competitiveness and wise growth of England's tourism by providing intelligence, setting standards, creating partnerships and ensuring coherence. ETC sets out: to provide leadership and support for the industry – creating the right framework for tourism to flourish and providing a clear focus for tourism policy and promotion; to raise the quality of English tourism – ensuring consumers expectations are met and that tourism contributes to the quality of life; to improve the competitiveness of the industry; to ensure the wise growth of tourism – helping the tourism industry to take better account of the natural and built environment and the communities within which it operates.

Important:
The information contained in this guide has been published in good faith on the basis of information submitted to the English Tourism Council by the proprietors of the premises listed, who have paid for their entries to appear. The English Tourism Council cannot guarantee the accuracy of the information in this guide and accepts no responsibility for any error or misrepresentation. All liability for loss, disappointment, negligence or other damage caused by reliance on the information contained in this guide, or in the event of bankruptcy, or liquidation, or cessation of trade of any company, individual or firm mentioned, is hereby excluded. Please check carefully all prices and other details before confirming a reservation.

Back Cover Pictures:

(Top) Moat Cottage, Corby, Northamptonshire
(Bottom) Virginia Lodge Guest House, Stratford-upon-Avon, Warwickshire

Photo Credits:

Cumbria - Cumbria Tourist Board
Northumbria - Northumbria Tourist Board, Graeme Peacock, Mike Kipling, Colin Cuthbert and Michael Busselle
North West - North West Tourist Board, Cheshire County Council, Lancashire County Council, Marketing Manchester
Yorkshire - Yorkshire Tourist Board
Heart of England - Heart of England Tourist Board
East of England - East of England Tourist Board Collection
South West - South West Tourism
South of England - Southern Tourist Board, Peter Titmuss, Chris Cove-Smith and Iris Buckley
South East England - South East England Tourist Board, Chris Parker and Iris Buckley

Published by: The English Tourism Council, Thames Tower, Black's Road, Hammersmith, London W6 9EL.
ISBN 0 86143 271 1

Publishing Manager: Michael Dewing
Production Manager: Iris Buckley
Compilation, Design & Production: www.jacksonlowe.com
Typesetting: Tradespools Ltd, Somerset and Jackson Lowe Marketing, Lewes
Maps: © Maps In Minutes™ (1999)
Printing and Binding: Mozzon Giutina S.p.A, Florence and Officine Grafiche De Agostini S.p.A, Novara.
Advertisement Sales: Jackson Lowe Marketing, 173 High Street, Lewes, East Sussex BN7 1YE. (01273) 487487

Contents

Where to Stay in England 2003

WELCOME TO WHERE TO STAY

How to find your way around the guide including colour maps

PLACES TO STAY AND THINGS TO DO

Accommodation entries, places to visit, regional tourist board contact details and travel

URTHER INFORMATION

etailed information on accommodation ratings, guidance n how to book, events and more

EY TO SYMBOLS

key to symbols can be found on the inside back cover. Keep it open for easy reference.

a warm welcome

Welcome to this new, fully updated edition of *Where to Stay*, the official guide to quality accommodation in England.

Whether you're looking for country style, seaside splendour or city chic, you'll find nearly 10,00 places to stay here, all Diamond rated and with a range of prices for all pockets. Detailed entri and pictures help you make the right choice. There's also advice on making a booking and a explanation of accommodation ratings and awards, handy location maps plus ideas on what t do and see in each region.

Everything
you need to know for
a great English break.

How to use the guide

The guide is divided into the 10 English Regional Tourist Board regions (these are shown on page 20). These regional sections give you all the information you need on the area: accommodation, places to visit, tourist information centres, travel and publications for further information.

Guest Accommodation is listed alphabetically in order of place name. If you would like to know more about the city, town or village in which you wish to stay, you will find brief descriptions at the end of each regional section. Or you can contact the local Tourist Information Centre - the telephone number can be found next to the town name on the accommodation entry pages.

Finding your accommodation

Whether you know exactly where you want to stay or only have an idea of the area you wish to visit, it couldn't be easier to find accommodation:

BY PLACE if you know the town or village look in the index at the back.

BY AREA if you know the area look at the full colour maps starting on page 22. All the places in black offer accommodation featured in this guide.

BY REGION if you know which part of England look in the relevant regional section. These are colour coded at the top of each page. A map showing the regions can be found on page 20.

BY COUNTY if you know which county look at the listing on page 21 to find the region it is in.

Types of accommodation

Guest accommodation is featured in this guide which includes Guesthouses, Small Hotels, Bed and Breakfast, Farmhouses and Inns. We also include Campus accommodation (see opposite page). Within each entry you will find a brief description of each property and facilities available. (We publish a separate guide for hotel accommodation). See also 'A note on Hotels' on page 733.

Accommodation entries explained

Each accommodation entry contains detailed information to help you decide if it is right for you. This information has been provided by the proprietors themselves, and our aim has been to ensure that it is as objective and factual as possible. To the left of the establishment name you will find the Diamond rating and quality award, if appropriate.

At-a-glance symbols at the end of each entry give you additional information on services and facilities - a key can be found on the back cover flap. Keep this open to refer to as you read.

A sample entry is shown below.

1. Listing under town or village with map reference
2. ETC Diamond rating (plus Gold and Silver Awards where applicable)
3. Colour picture for enhanced entries
4. Accessible rating where applicable
5. Description - standard entries 25 words; enhanced entries 50 words
6. At-a-glance facility symbols
7. Establishment name, address, telephone and fax numbers, e-mail and web site address
8. Prices for bed and breakfast (B&B) and half board (HB) accommodation
9. Shows establishment is open all year.
10. Accommodation details including credit cards accepted
11. Special promotions and themed breaks

Campus Accommodation explained

During 2002 the English Tourism Council introduced a new Star rating standard for Campus accommodation such as universities and colleges with sleeping accommodation in halls of residence or student village complexes, available for individuals, families or groups. For details of the Campus accommodation ratings and accommodation available, see pages 500 to 501.

Guest Accommodation Ratings & Awards

English Tourism Council ratings and awards are an indication of quality which will help you find the most suitable Guest Accommodation to meet your needs and expectations. You'll find several in this guide:

DIAMOND RATINGS FOR QUALITY

The English Tourism Council's national quality assurance standard awards One to Five Diamonds giving you reliable information about the quality of the accommodation you can expect. (See opposite). You'll find something to suit all budgets and tastes.

SPECIAL AWARDS FOR EXCELLENCE

Gold and Silver Awards - Part of the English Tourism Council scheme, Gold and Silver Awards are given to establishments achieving the highest levels of quality in areas guests have identified as a priority. So if you're looking for somewhere special, turn to page 12 for a list of Gold Award holders which have an entry in the regional sections of this guide. Silver award holders are too numerous to list, but they are clearly indicated in the accommodation entries.

The annual Excellence in England awards are the Oscars of the tourism industry. Winners will be announced in Spring 2003 (see page 17).

NATIONAL ACCESSIBLE SCHEME FOR SPECIAL NEEDS

Establishments which have a National Accessible rating provide access and facilities for guests with hearing, mobility and visual impairment. Turn to page 14 for further details.

How do we arrive at a Diamond rating

The English Tourism Council has more than 50 trained assessors throughout England who visit properties annually, generally staying overnight as an anonymous guest. They award ratings based on the overall experience of their stay, and there are strict guidelines to ensure every property is assessed to the same criteria. High standards of housekeeping are a major requirement; heating, lighting, comfort and convenience are also part of the assessment.

THE ASSESSOR'S ROLE - GUEST, ASSESSOR AND ADVISOR

An assessor books their accommodation as a 'normal' guest. He or she will take into account all aspects of the visiting experience, from how the telephone enquiry is dealt with to the quality of the service and facilities on offer.

During their stay the assessor will try to experience as many things as possible including the quality of food, the knowledge of staff and services available. They will even check under the bed!

After paying the bill the assessor reveals who they are and ask to look round the rest of the establishment. The assessor will then advise the proprietor of the Diamond rating they have awarded, discussing the reasons why, as we[ll] as suggesting areas for improvement.

So you can see it's a very thorough process to ensure that when you book accommodation with a particular Diamon[d] rating you can be confident it will meet your expectations. After all, meeting customer expectations is what makes happy guests.

Ratings you can trust

When you're looking for a place to stay, you need a rating system you can trust. The English Tourism Council's ratings give a clear guide to what to expect, in an easy-to-understand form. Properties are visited annually by trained, impartial assessors, so you can have the confidence that your accommodation has been thoroughly checked and rated for quality before you make your booking.

DIAMOND RATINGS

Ratings are awarded from One to Five Diamonds. The more Diamonds, the higher the level of quality and customer care. The brief explanations of the Diamond ratings outlined here show what is included at each rating level (note that each rating also includes what is provided at a lower Diamond rating).

♦ An acceptable overall level of quality and helpful service. Accommodation offering, as a minimum, a full cooked or continental breakfast. Other meals, if provided, will be freshly prepared. Towels are provided and heating and hot water will be available at reasonable times.

♦♦ A good overall level of quality and comfort, with greater emphasis on guest care in all areas.

♦♦♦ A very good overall level of quality in areas such as comfortable bedrooms, well maintained, practical decor, a good choice of quality items at breakfast, customer care and all-round comfort. Where other meals are provided these will be freshly cooked from good quality ingredients.

♦♦♦♦ An excellent level of quality in all areas. Customer care showing very good attention to your needs.

♦♦♦♦♦ An exceptional overall level of quality - for example, ample space with a degree of luxury, a high quality bed and furniture, excellent interior design and customer care which anticipates your needs. Breakfast offering a wide choice of high quality fresh ingredients. Where other meals are provided these will feature fresh, seasonal, and often local ingredients.

Inspiring ideas for a short break

> Parachuting, Rokerby Guest House, Salisbury

Short breaks are always popular and good for mind, body and soul. Where to Stay is full of great ideas - look out for special promotions and offers highlighted in red in the accommodation entries. There's such a variety of activities and interests you can pursue, from cooking to parachuting. And if you need to de-stress go for total relaxation. Here is just a small selection to whet your appetite.

From watercolours to witchcraft

Artistic travellers are spoilt for choice – 2-or 3-day watercolour courses are held at **Trevinhurst Lodge, Eastbourne** where professional tuition is offered in a friendly and informal environment. Landscapes anc seascapes are the topic for summer courses run by Tony Hogan from the **Bosville Arms Country Hotel Bridlington.** Studio-based life and still-life winter courses are held in Tony's own 1,000 sq ft gallery.

Adventure enthusiasts can try the Landrover Experience at the 4x4 off-road driving centre based on site at **Wessington Farm, Honiton.** Or experience the thrill of a tandem parachute descent with a qualified instructor when staying at **The Rokeby Guest House, Salisbury.**

> Watercolour course, Trevinhurst Lodge, Eastbourn

> The Landrover Experience, Wessington Farm, Honiton

West Vale Country House, Sawrey is a great base fc a spot of fishing where free passes are available durin the season. Or for something more unusual go and ge spooked on a weekend of witchcraft at **The Hill Hous Ross-on-Wye!**

Entertainment of a different kind

Enjoy a classical, in-house concert featuring top performers from around the world at **Yewfield Vegetarian Guest House, Hawkshead.**

> The National Space Centre, Leicester

Murder and mystery are on the menu at **Manor Farm Oast, Rye.** Have a really fun evening with no actors and lots of red herrings. Eat, drink and be merry at **Bolebroke Castle, Hartfield** where you can step back in time and experience a medieval banquet hosted by minstrels.

> Bolebroke Castle, Hartfield

Or discover the world beyond - **Spindle Lodge Hotel, Leicester** offers 2-night breaks which include a complimentary day pass to the National Space Centre.

Tempt your tastebuds

For a working holiday in beautiful surroundings consider the start-up business courses for would-be proprietors, or learn how to cook perfect food on an Aga at **Blaven Homestay, Kendal.** If food is your passion stay at **Holmwood House Hotel, York** and experience the Gourmet Extravaganza! Eat out at a different, top-class restaurant every night for 3 nights, or enjoy a 2- or 3-night break with dinner at the same top restaurant each night. Gourmet food weekends are also run throughout the year at **The Willow House, Watton.**

Relax and revive

Champagne and chocolates make a short break a special occasion. Look out for the many offers throughout the guide.

And, for a change of pace, relax and unwind on a Stress-Busting break at **Embleton House Bed & Breakfast, Cavendish.** Therapies, including massage, lymphatic drainage and Indian head massage, are tailored to individual needs. Two-day, mid-week breaks include a free therapy.

For further details of the offers mentioned on these pages, please contact the establishments directly.
These offers are correct at time of publication but may be subject to change without notice.

Guest Accommodation Gold Awards 2003

The English Tourism Council marks the achievement by Guest Accommodation of exceptional levels of quality with special Gold and Silver Awards. While Diamond ratings are based on overall quality and customer care, there are areas of comfort and service visitors have identified as priorities. These include quality of bedrooms and bathrooms (furniture, fixtures and fittings), their comfort and ease of use, and the service received and its efficiency. There is no master checklist to work through in order for Guest Accommodation to achieve an Award. Recommendations are made during assessment and ETC's assessor will recognise where the highest levels of quality have been reached in the areas identified by guests as being really important to them.

Guest Accommodation featured in the regional sections of this Where to Stay guide which have achieved a Gold Award are listed opposite. Use the Town Index at the back of this guide to find the page numbers for their full entry.

Guest Accommodation with a Silver Award are too numerous to list here but these Awards are also indicated in the regional sections. The listings at the back of this guide shows all Guest Accommodation in ETC's scheme in receipt of a Gold or Silver Award.

> Burr Bank, Pickering

> The Salty Monk, Sidmouth

> Garden Cottages, Kidderminster

> Monkshill, Bath

> Mile Hill Barn, Yoxford

> Bracken House Country Hotel, Bratton Fleming

> Alden Cottage, Stonyhurst

> Lakeshore House, Windermere

Alden Cottage, Stonyhurst, Lancashire

Ayrlington Hotel, Bath, Bath and North East Somerset

Blounts Court Farm, Devizes, Wiltshire

Bracken House Country Hotel, Bratton Fleming, Devon

Burhill Farm, Broadway, Worcestershire

Burr Bank, Pickering, North Yorkshire

Coniston Lodge, Coniston, Cumbria

The Cottage, Bishop's Stortford, Hertfordshire

Cotteswold House, Bibury, Gloucestershire

Efford Cottage, Lymington, Hampshire

Felton House, Hereford, Herefordshire

Field House, Hindringham, Norfolk

Garden Cottages, Kidderminster, Worcestershire

Glencot House, Wells, Somerset

Hazel Bank Country House, Borrowdale, Cumbria

Hill House Farm, Ely, Cambridgeshire

Lakeshore House, Windermere, Cumbria

Magnolia House, Canterbury, Kent

Manor Farm Oast, Rye, East Sussex

M'Dina Courtyard, Chipping Campden, Gloucestershire

Mile Hill Barn, Yoxford, Suffolk

Monkshill, Bath, Bath and North East Somerset

Number Twenty Eight, Ludlow, Shropshire

The Old Coach House, Blackpool, Lancashire

Oldstead Grange, Helmsley, North Yorkshire

The Paddock, Leominster, Herefordshire

Peacock House, Beetley, Norfolk

The Salty Monk, Sidmouth, Devon

The Temple, Longhope, Gloucestershire

Thanington Hotel, Canterbury, Kent

The Three Lions, Fordingbridge, Hampshire

Tor Cottage, Tavistock, Devon

Tower House, Hastings, East Sussex

Victoria Villa, Whitstable, Kent

Villa Magdala Hotel, Bath, Bath and North East Somerset

The White House, Stratford-upon-Avon, Warwickshire

Websters, Salisbury, Wiltshire

National Accessible Scheme

The English Tourism Council's new National Accessible Scheme for accommodation includes standards for hearing and visually impaired guests in addition to standards for guests with mobility impairment.

Accommodation taking part in the National Accessible Scheme, and which appear in the regional sections of this guide are listed on page 16. Use the Town Index at the back to find the page numbers for their full entries.

The English Tourism Council has a variety of accessible accommodation in its scheme, and the different accessible ratings will help you choose the one that best suits your needs. When you see one of the following symbols, you can be sure that the accommodation has been thoroughly assessed against demanding criteria. If you have additional needs or special requirements we strongly recommend that you make sure these can be met by your chosen establishment before you confirm your booking. The criteria the English Tourism Council and National and Regional Tourist Boards have adopted do not necessarily conform to British Standards or to Building Regulations. They reflect what the Boards understand to be acceptable to meet the practical needs of wheelchair users.

National Accessible Scheme ratings are also shown on the full list of ETC-assessed Guest Accommodation in the listings at the back of this guide.

The National Accessible Scheme forms part of the Tourism for All Campaign that is being promoted by the English Tourism Council and National and Regional Tourist Boards. Additional help and guidance on finding suitable holiday accommodation for those with special needs can be obtained from:

Holiday Care,
2nd Floor, Imperial Buildings,
Victoria Road,
Horley, Surrey RH6 7PZ

Tel: (01293) 774535
Fax: (01293) 784647
Email: holiday.care@virgin.net
Internet: www.holidaycare.org.uk
Minicom: (01293) 776943

Access Symbols

MOBILITY

Level 1 – Typically suitable for a person with sufficient mobility to climb a flight of steps but who would benefit from points of fixtures and fittings to aid balance.

Level 2 – Typically suitable for a person with restricted walking ability and for those that may need to use a wheelchair some of the time.

Level 3 – Typically suitable for a person who depends on the use of a wheelchair and transfers unaided to and from the wheelchair in a seated position.

Level 4 – Typically suitable for a person who depends on the use of a wheelchair in a seated position. They can require personal/mechanical assistance to aid transfer (eg carer, hoist).

HEARING IMPAIRMENT

Level 1 – Minimum entry requirements to meet the National Accessible Standards for guests with hearing impairment, from mild hearing loss to profoundly deaf.

Level 2 – Recommended (Best Practice) additional requirements to meet the National Accessible Standards for guests with hearing impairment, from mild hearing loss to profoundly deaf.

VISUAL IMPAIRMENT

Level 1 – Minimum entry requirements to meet the National Accessible Standards for visually impaired guests.

Level 2 – Recommended (Best Practice) additional requirements to meet the National Accessible Standards for visually impaired guests.

Details of participating establishments can be found on the next page.

Accessible Accommodation

At the time of going to press the following establishments had been assessed under the new National Accessible Scheme. Their details can be found in the regional sections of the guide.

MOBILITY LEVEL 1

Ashbourne, Derbyshire - **Mona Villas Bed & Breakfast**
Boscastle, Cornwall - **The Old Coach House**
Bratton Fleming, Devon - **Bracken House Country Hotel**
Otterburn, Northumberland - **Redesdale Arms Hotel**
Skipton, North Yorkshire - **Craven Heifer Inn**
Weston-super-Mare, North Somerset - **Moorlands Country Guesthouse**

MOBILITY LEVEL 2

Salisbury, Wiltshire - **Websters**
Sudbury, Suffolk - **Fiddlesticks**

Additional accommodation participating in the National Accessible Scheme can be found in the complete list of ETC-assessed Guest Accommodation at the back of this guide.

The Excellence in England AWARDS 2003

The Safeway Excellence in England Awards are all about blowing English tourism's trumpet and telling the world what a fantastic place England is to visit, whether it's for a day trip, a weekend break or a fortnight's holiday.

The Awards, now in their 14th year, are run by the English Tourism Council in association with England's ten regional tourist boards. This year there are 12 categories including B&B of the Year, Hotel of the Year and Visitor Attraction of the Year. New for 2003 is an award for the best tourism website.

Winners of the 2003 awards will receive their trophies at a fun and festive event to be held on St George's Day (23 April) in London. The day will not only celebrate excellence in tourism but also Englishness in all its diversity.

The winners of the 2002 Safeway Excellence in England B&B of the Year Award are:
Gold winner: Clow Beck House, Croft-on-Tees, Darlington
Silver winners: Lakeshore House, Windermere, Cumbria and The Old Lock-Up, Wirksworth, Derbyshire

For more information about the Excellence in England Awards visit **www.englishtourism.org.uk**

Safeway is the 4th largest supermarket in the UK and has over 470 stores; 150 petrol stations; 50 BP/Safeway petrol stations and over 85,000 employees nationwide. Safeway's vision is to be the first choice food retailer for its customers, by having the best fresh products and best deals sold by the most well informed, friendly and responsive staff. **www.safeway.co.uk**

Hoseasons is the UK's leading self-catering specialist offering over 12,000 places to stay in coastal and countryside settings. Holiday accommodation ranges from holiday parks to country cottages throughout Britain and Ireland as well as narrowboats and cruisers on British waterways. **www.hoseasons.co.uk**

Tourist information Centres

When it comes to your next England break, the first stage of your journey could be closer than you think. You've probably got a Tourist Information Centre nearby which is there to serve the local community – as well as visitors. Knowledgeable staff will be happy to help you, wherever you're heading.

Many Tourist Information Centres can provide you with maps and guides, and sometimes it's even possible to book your accommodation, too.

Across the country, there are more than 550 Tourist Information Centres. You'll find the address of your nearest Tourist Information Centre in your local Phone Book.

Making a booking

Please remember that changes may occur after the guide is printed. When you have found a suitable plac to stay we advise you to contact the establishment to check availability, also to confirm prices and specifi facilities which may be important to you. Further advice on how to make a booking can be found at th back of this guide, together with information about deposits and cancellations. It is always advisable t confirm your booking in writing.

In 2003 the English Tourism Council launches a new range of training recognition awards for commitment to improving customer service for all types of accommodation and other tourism organisations.

Where you find the Welcome to Excellence plaque, you can be assured of a commitment to:

- achieve excellence in customer service
- exceed guest needs and expectations
- provide an environment where courtesy, helpfulness and a warm welcome are standard
- focus and develop individual skills.

Those displaying the plaque meet a special charter and have at least 50% of staff trained to the required standards.

Visitor Attraction Quality Assurance

The English Tourism Council's Visitor Attraction Quality Assurance Service is a new national quality assurance standard. Participating attractions are visited annually by trained, impartial assessors who look at all aspects of the visit, from customer services to catering, retail and toilet facilities plus all aspects of the 'visitor experience', including interpretation and activities such as tours, rides, or film shows. Only those attractions which have been assessed by the English Tourism Council and meet the standard receive the quality marque, your sign of a 'Quality Assured Visitor Attraction'.

Look out for the English Tourism Council marque and visit with confidence.

Regional Tourist Board Areas

This Where to Stay guide is divided into 10 regional sections as shown on the map below. To identify each regional section and its page number, please refer to the key below. The county index overleaf indicates in which regional section you will find a particular county.

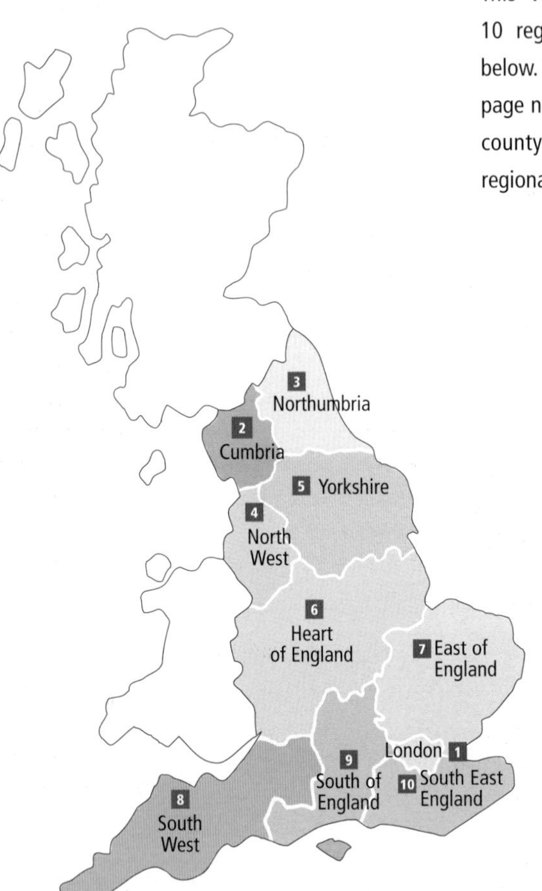

Each of the 10 English regions shown here has a Regional Tourist Board which can give you information about things to see or do locally. Contact details are given both at the beginning and end of each regional section.

Colour location maps showing all the cities, towns and villages with accommodation in the regional sections of this guide can be found on pages 22-34. Turn to the Town Index at the back of this guide for the page number on which you can find the relevant accommodation.

In which region is the county I wish to visit?

COUNTY/UNITARY AUTHORITY	REGION
Bath & North East Somerset	South West
Bedfordshire	East of England
Berkshire	South of England
Bristol	South West
Buckinghamshire	South of England
Cambridgeshire	East of England
Cheshire	North West
Cornwall	South West
Cumbria	Cumbria
Derbyshire	Heart of England
Devon	South West
Dorset (Eastern)	South of England
Dorset (Western)	South West
Durham	Northumbria
East Riding of Yorkshire	Yorkshire
East Sussex	South East England
Essex	East of England
Gloucestershire	Heart of England
Greater London	London
Greater Manchester	North West
Hampshire	South of England
Herefordshire	Heart of England
Hertfordshire	East of England
Isle of Wight	South of England
Isles of Scilly	South West
Kent	South East England
Lancashire	North West
Leicestershire	Heart of England
Lincolnshire	Heart of England
Merseyside	North West
Norfolk	East of England
North East Lincolnshire	Yorkshire
North Lincolnshire	Yorkshire
North Somerset	South West
North Yorkshire	Yorkshire
Northamptonshire	Heart of England
Northumberland	Northumbria
Nottinghamshire	Heart of England
Oxfordshire	South of England
Rutland	Heart of England
Shropshire	Heart of England
Somerset	South West
South Gloucestershire	South West
South Yorkshire	Yorkshire
Staffordshire	Heart of England
Suffolk	East of England
Surrey	South East England
Tees Valley	Northumbria
Tyne & Wear	Northumbria
Warwickshire	Heart of England
West Midlands	Heart of England
West Sussex	South East England
West Yorkshire	Yorkshire
Wiltshire	South West
Worcestershire	Heart of England
York	Yorkshire

UNITARY AUTHORITIES

Please note that many new unitary authorities have been formed - for example Brighton & Hove and Bristol - and are officially separate from the county in which they were previously located. To aid the reader we have only included the major unitary authorities in the list above and on the colour maps.

A B

Location Maps

Every place name featured in the regional accommodation sections of this Where to Stay guide has a map reference to help you locate it on the maps which follow. For example, to find Colchester, Essex, which has 'Map ref 3B2', turn to Map 3 and refer to grid square B2.

All place names appearing in the regional sections are shown in black type on the maps. This enables you to find other places in your chosen area which may have suitable accommodation - the Town Index (at the back of this guide) gives page numbers.

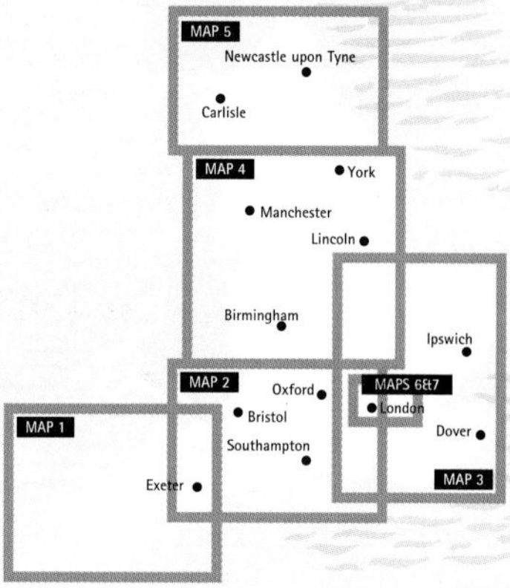

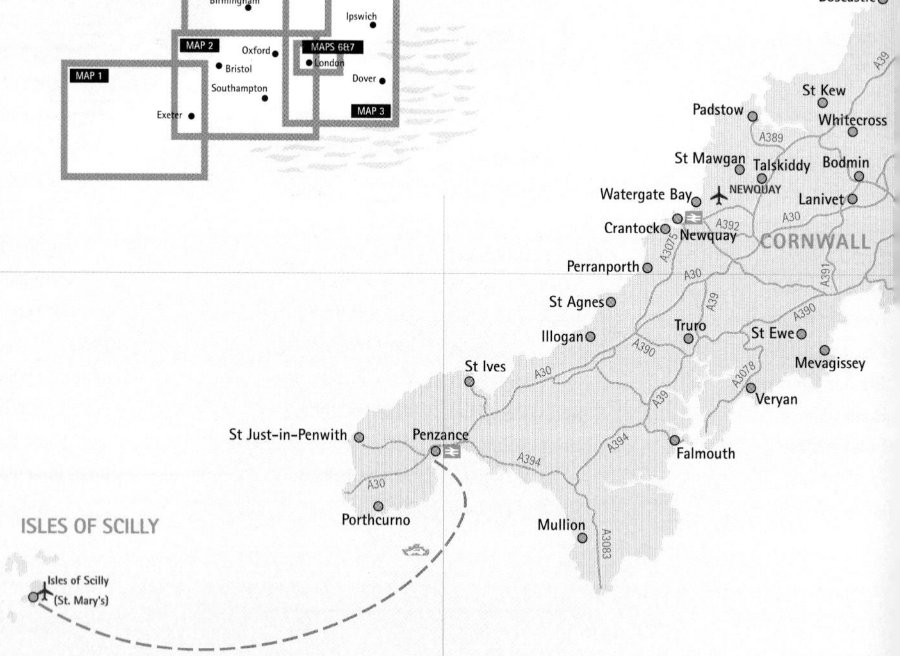

Key to regions: South West

place names in black offer accommodation in this guide.

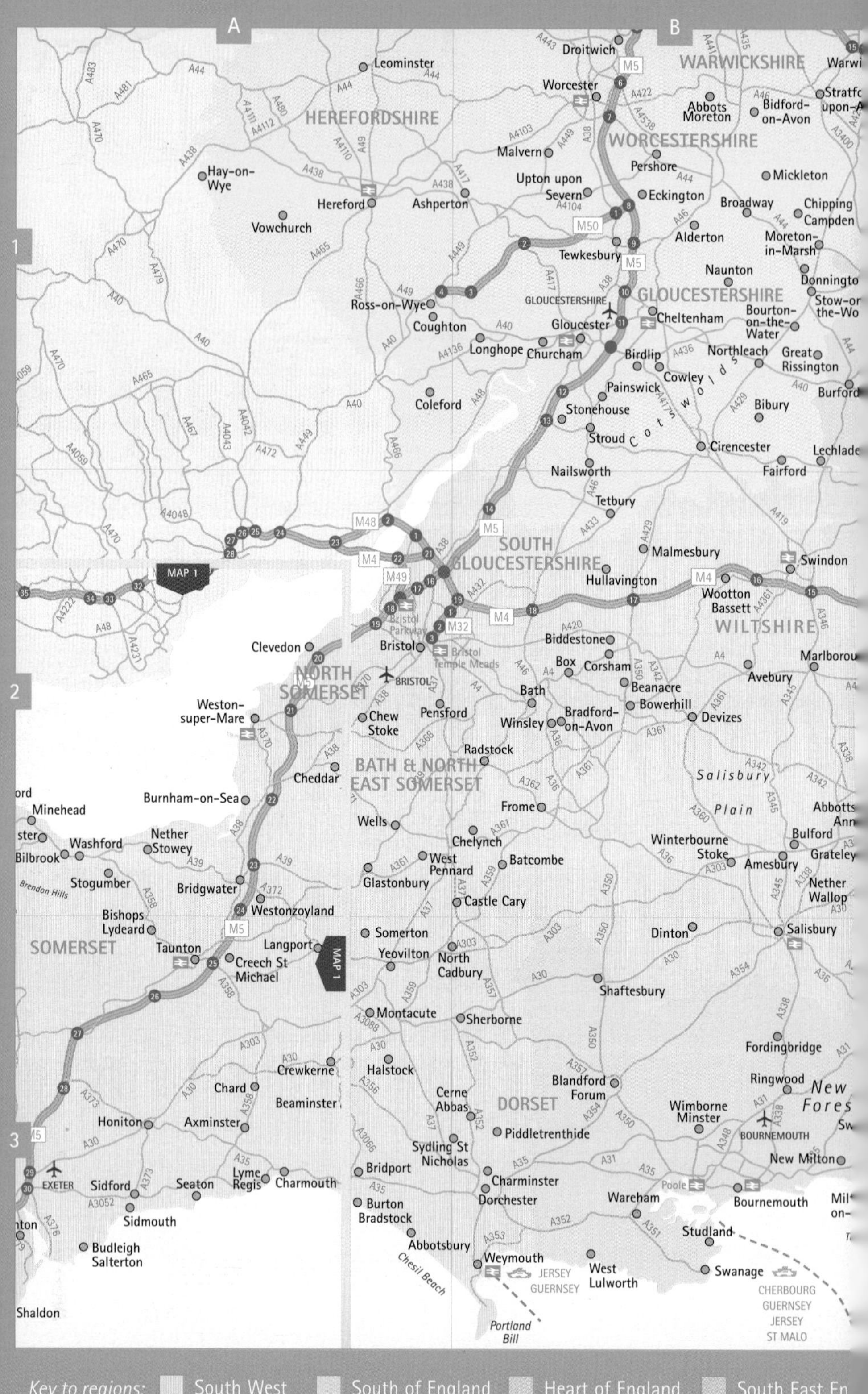

Key to regions: South West South of England Heart of England South East En

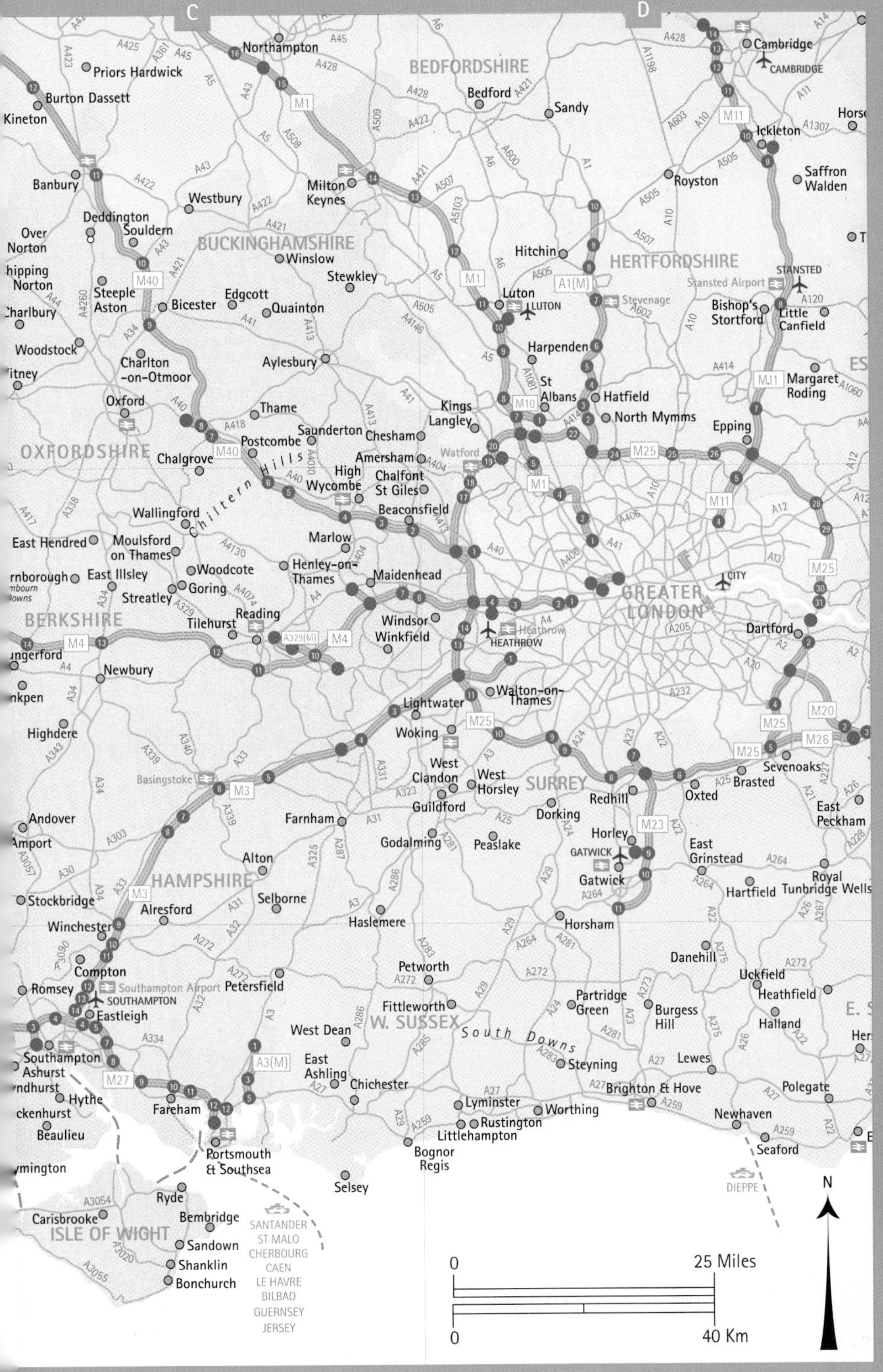

All place names in black offer accommodation in this guide.

Key to regions: London East of England Heart of England South East Engla

place names in black offer accommodation in this guide.

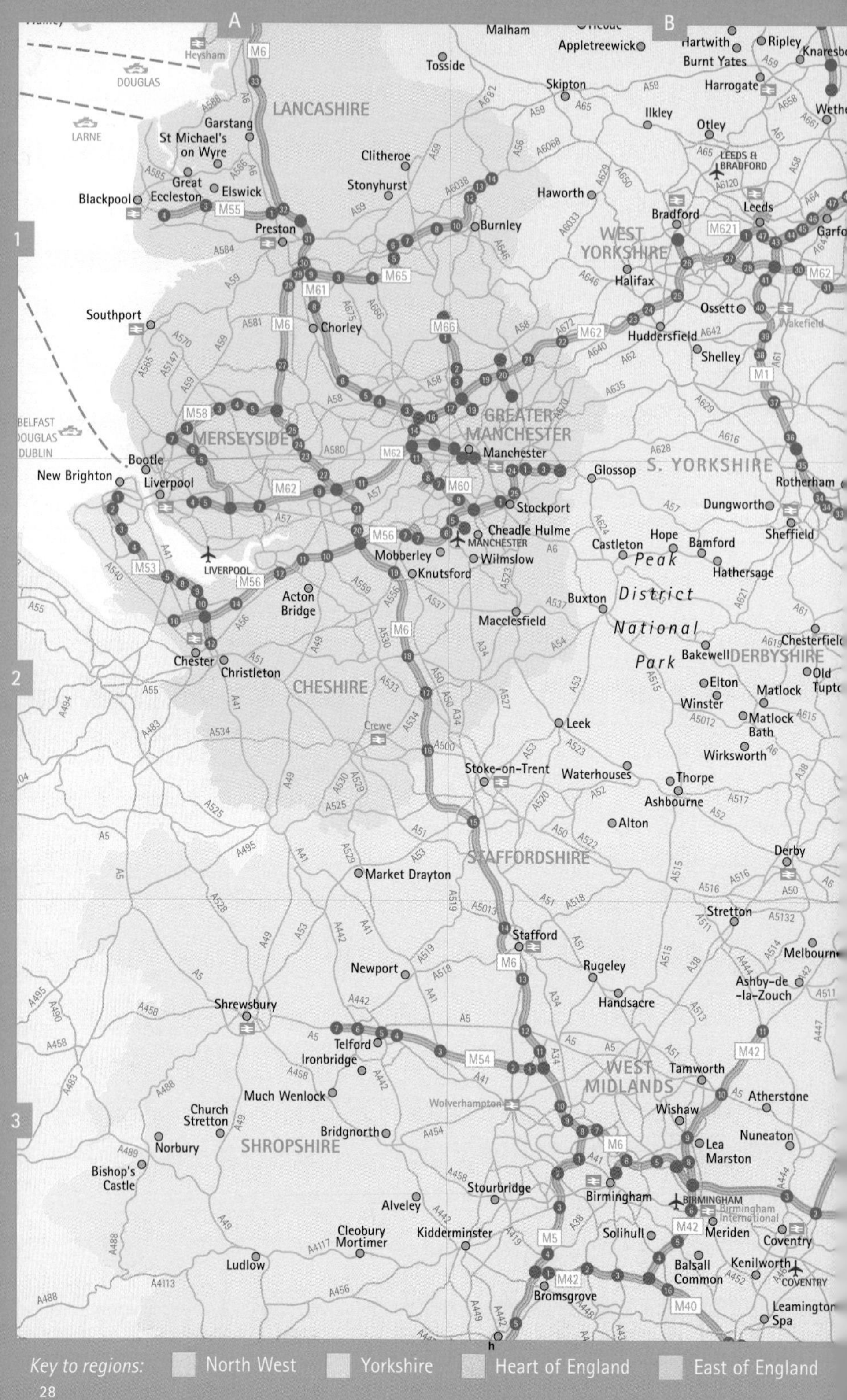

Key to regions: North West Yorkshire Heart of England East of England

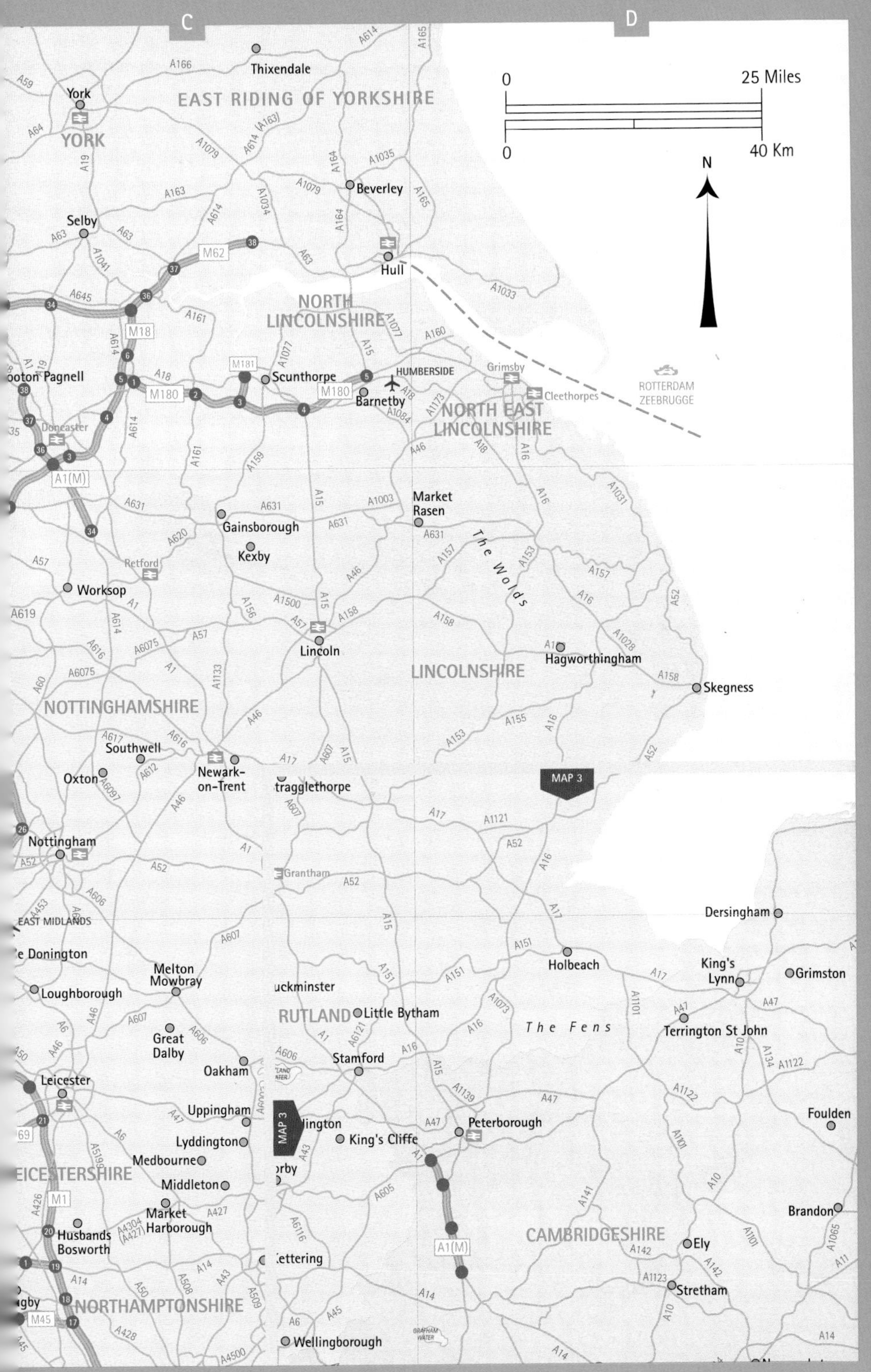

place names in black offer accommodation in this guide.

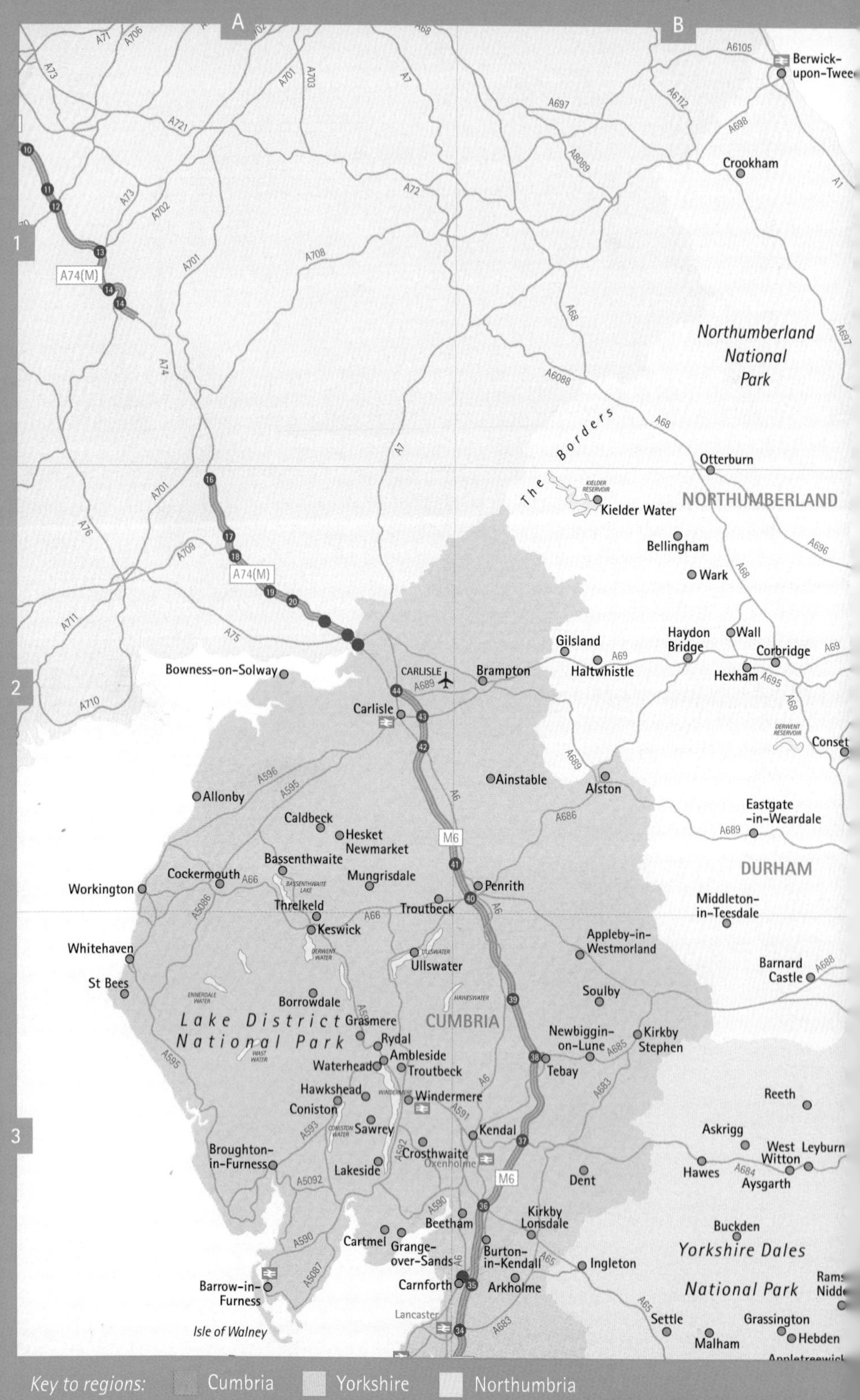
A
B
1
2
3
A71
A706
A73
A701
A703
A7
A68
A6105
Berwick-upon-Tweed
A6112
A697
A698
A721
A6089
Crookham
A1
A72
A73
A702
A708
A701
A74(M)
A68
Northumberland National Park
A697
A74
A6088
The Borders
A68
A7
Otterburn
A701
Kielder Reservoir
Kielder Water
NORTHUMBERLAND
A76
A709
A74(M)
Bellingham
A696
Wark
A68
A711
A75
Gilsland
Haydon Bridge
Wall
Corbridge
A69
Bowness-on-Solway
CARLISLE
A689
Brampton
Haltwhistle
A69
Hexham
A695
A710
Carlisle
A68
Derwent Reservoir
Consett
A689
Alston
A596
Ainstable
Allonby
A595
A6
A686
Eastgate-in-Weardale
Caldbeck
Hesket Newmarket
M6
A689
Bassenthwaite
DURHAM
Cockermouth
A66
Mungrisdale
Penrith
Workington
Bassenthwaite Lake
A5086
Threlkeld
Troutbeck
A6
Middleton-in-Teesdale
A66
Keswick
Whitehaven
Derwent Water
Ullswater
Appleby-in-Westmorland
Ullswater
Barnard Castle
A688
St Bees
Ennerdale Water
Borrowdale
Haweswater
Soulby
Lake District National Park
Grasmere
CUMBRIA
Rydal
Newbiggin-on-Lune
A685
Kirkby Stephen
A595
Wast Water
Waterhead
Ambleside
Troutbeck
Tebay
A6
A683
Hawkshead
Windermere
Windermere
Reeth
Coniston
A591
Sawrey
Coniston Water
A593
Kendal
Askrigg
Broughton-in-Furness
A592
Crosthwaite
West Witton
Leyburn
Oxenholme
Lakeside
M6
Hawes
A684
Aysgarth
A5092
Dent
A590
Beetham
Kirkby Lonsdale
Buckden
A590
Cartmel
Grange-over-Sands
Burton-in-Kendall
A65
Yorkshire Dales National Park
Ingleton
A5087
Barrow-in-Furness
Carnforth
Arkholme
Lancaster
A65
Settle
Grassington
Malham
Hebden
Isle of Walney
A683
Key to regions:
Cumbria
Yorkshire
Northumbria

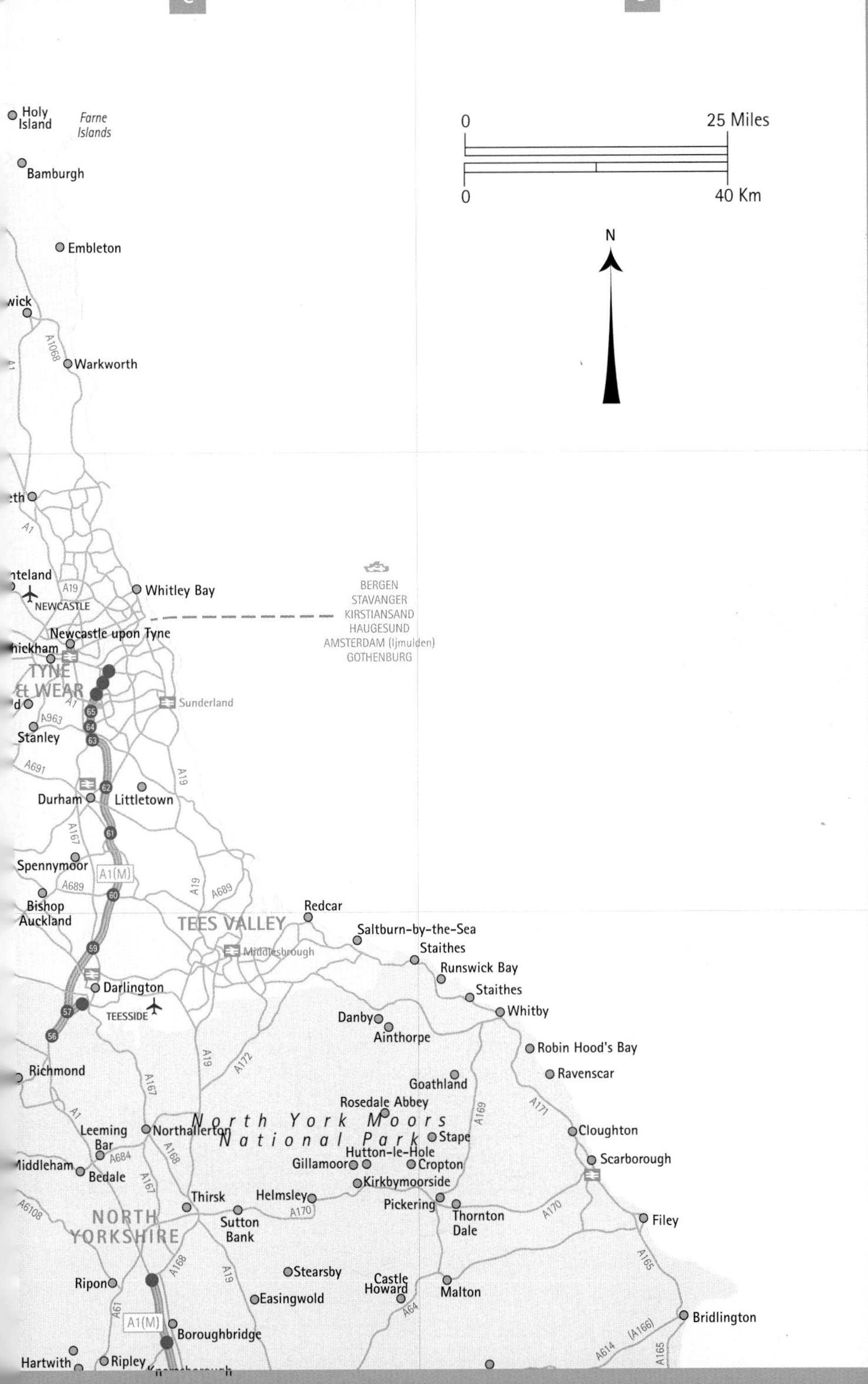

lace names in black offer accommodation in this guide.

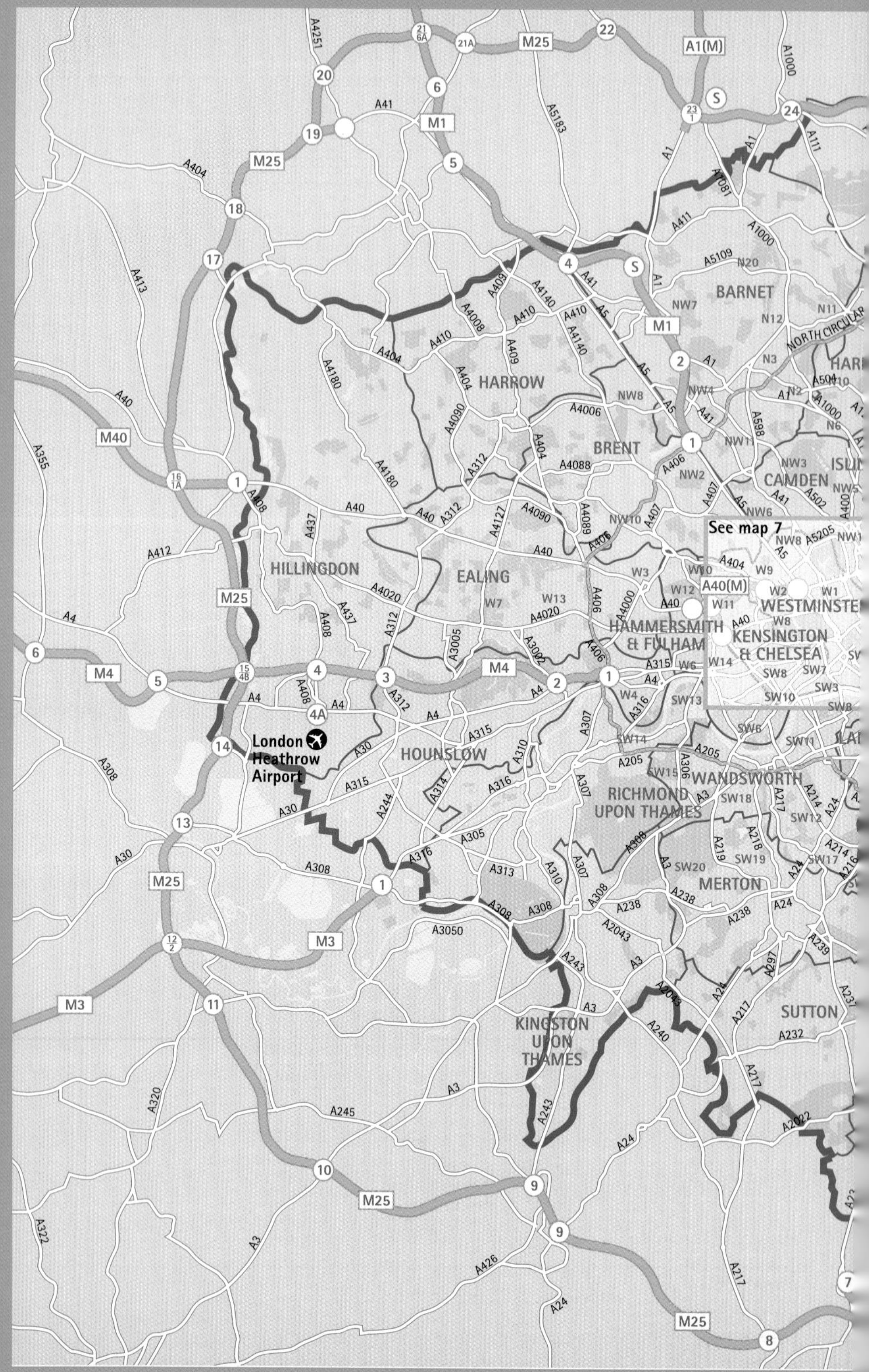
HARROW
BRENT
BARNET
CAMDEN
HILLINGDON
EALING
HAMMERSMITH & FULHAM
KENSINGTON & CHELSEA
WESTMINSTER
HOUNSLOW
RICHMOND UPON THAMES
WANDSWORTH
MERTON
KINGSTON UPON THAMES
SUTTON
London Heathrow Airport
See map 7
NORTH CIRCULAR
M25
M1
M40
M4
M3
A1(M)
A40(M)

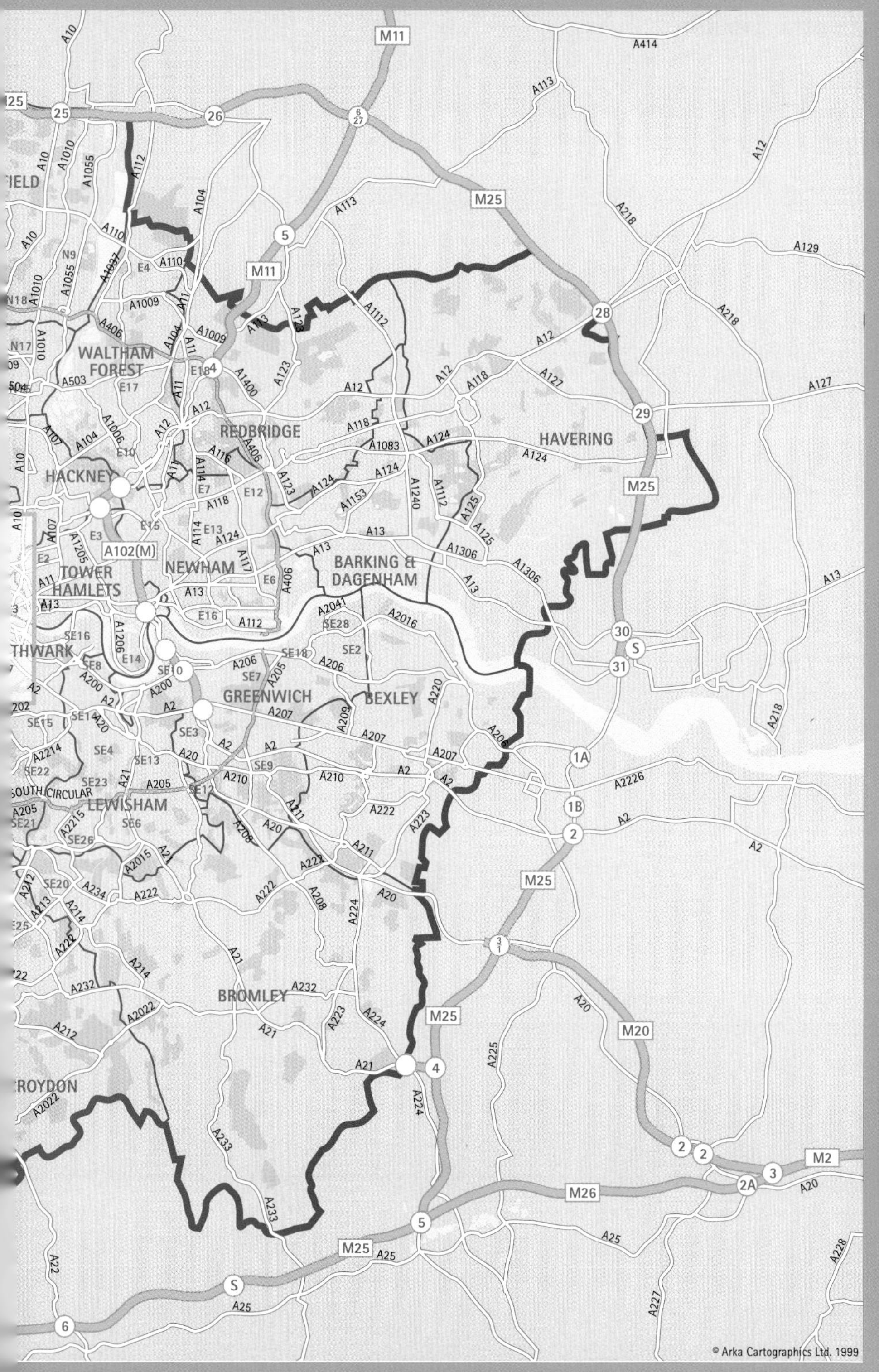

WALTHAM FOREST
REDBRIDGE
HAVERING
HACKNEY
NEWHAM
TOWER HAMLETS
BARKING & DAGENHAM
GREENWICH
BEXLEY
LEWISHAM
BROMLEY
CROYDON
M11
M25
M20
M26
M2
A102(M)
© Arka Cartographics Ltd. 1999

Central London
HOXTON
FINSBURY
EC1
EC2
EC3
EC4
CLERKENWELL
N1
PENTONVILLE
BLOOMSBURY
WC1
WC2
HOLBORN
ST. PANCRAS
SOMERS TOWN
CITY
SOHO
W1
MAYFAIR
SOUTHWARK
THE BOROUGH
SE1
SE11
SE15
SE17
NEWINGTON
BERMONDSEY
WALWORTH
CAMBERWELL
KENNINGTON
LAMBETH
WESTMINSTER
SW1
PIMLICO
SW8
BELGRAVIA
CHELSEA
SW3
BROMPTON
SW7
SOUTH KENSINGTON
SW10
SW5
EARLS COURT
WEST BROMPTON
W8
KENSINGTON
W14
WEST KENSINGTON
W11
NOTTING HILL
W2
BAYSWATER
REGENT'S PARK
NW1
NW8
ST. JOHN'S WOOD
MARYLEBONE
MAIDA VALE
MAIDA HILL
W9
KILBURN
WEST KILBURN
KENSAL TOWN
WESTBOURNE GREEN
Regent's Park
Primrose Hill
Hyde Park
Kensington Gardens
Green Park
St James's Park
Holland Park
RIVER THAMES
King's Cross
St. Pancras
Euston
Marylebone
Paddington
Liverpool Street
Fenchurch Street
Cannon Street
London Bridge
Moorgate
Barbican
Farringdon
City Thameslink
Blackfriars
Waterloo
Waterloo East
Charing Cross
Victoria
Vauxhall
Elephant and Castle
West Brompton
Kensington (Olympia)
Kilburn High Road
Queen's Park
King's Cross Thameslink
COMMERCIAL ST
BISHOPSGATE
ALDGATE
TOWER BRIDGE
TOOLEY ST
BERMONDSEY ST
GRANGE RD
LONG LANE
GT DOVER ST
NEW KENT RD
WALWORTH ROAD
CAMBERWELL
KENNINGTON PARK RD
KENNINGTON LANE
KENNINGTON ROAD
LONDON BRIDGE
SOUTHWARK BRIDGE
BLACKFRIARS BRIDGE
BLACKFRIARS ROAD
WATERLOO BRIDGE
WATERLOO RD
WESTMINSTER BRIDGE
WESTMINSTER BRIDGE RD
LAMBETH BRIDGE
LAMBETH PALACE RD
ALBERT EMBANKMENT
VAUXHALL BRIDGE
VAUXHALL BRIDGE RD
VICTORIA EMBANKMENT
CHELSEA EMBANKMENT
CHELSEA BRIDGE ROAD
MILLBANK
HORSEFERRY ROAD
OLD ST
EAST ROAD
CITY ROAD
GOSWELL ROAD
ALDERSGATE
MOORGATE
LONDON WALL
CHEAPSIDE
CANNON STREET
UPPER THAMES
FLEET ST
STRAND
ALDWYCH
KINGSWAY
HIGH HOLBORN
FARRINGDON ROAD
GRAY'S INN ROAD
CALEDONIAN RD
YORK WAY
PENTONVILLE RD
LIVERPOOL RD
UPPER STREET
EUSTON ROAD
PANCRAS ROAD
WOBURN PLACE
GUILFORD ST
BLOOMSBURY ST
GOWER ST
TOTTENHAM COURT RD
NEW OXFORD STREET
CHARING CROSS RD
OXFORD STREET
OXFORD CIRCUS
REGENT STREET
NEW BOND STREET
OLD BOND STREET
PICCADILLY
PALL MALL
THE MALL
WHITEHALL
BIRDCAGE WALK
CONSTITUTION HILL
BUCKINGHAM PALACE RD
GROSVENOR PL
BELGRAVE PL
UPPER BELGRAVE ST
EBURY STREET
SLOANE SQUARE
SLOANE STREET
SLOANE AVE
KING'S RD
ROYAL HOSPITAL RD
KNIGHTSBRIDGE
BROMPTON ROAD
KENSINGTON ROAD
EXHIBITION RD
QUEEN'S GATE
CROMWELL ROAD
OLD BROMPTON ROAD
FULHAM ROAD
REDCLIFFE GDNS
FINBOROUGH RD
EARLS COURT ROAD
WARWICK RD
LILLIE ROAD
NORTH END ROAD
TALGARTH ROAD
HAMMERSMITH ROAD
ADDISON ROAD
HOLLAND ROAD
KENSINGTON HIGH STREET
KENSINGTON CHURCH ST
HOLLAND PARK AVE
NOTTING HILL GATE
BAYSWATER ROAD
QUEENSWAY
WESTBOURNE GROVE
WESTBOURNE PARK RD
LADBROKE GROVE
PARK LANE
MARBLE ARCH
EDGWARE ROAD
BAKER STREET
GLOUCESTER PLACE
MARYLEBONE ROAD
WIGMORE STREET
GT PORTLAND ST
PORTLAND PL
ALBANY STREET
OUTER CIRCLE
CAMDEN HIGH ST
CAMDEN ST
EVERSHOLT STREET
HAMPSTEAD ROAD
PRINCE ALBERT RD
AVENUE RD
PARK ROAD
LISSON GROVE
WELLINGTON RD
GROVE END ROAD
ABBEY RD
CARLTON VALE
MAIDA VALE
ELGIN AVENUE
SUTHERLAND AVENUE
HARROW ROAD
WESTWAY
A40(M)
WARWICK AVE
PRAED ST
SUSSEX GDNS
EASTBOURNE TER
GLOUCESTER TERR
FERNHEAD ROAD
KILBURN LANE
HARVIST ROAD
BRONDESBURY ROAD
LADBROKE GROVE
THE RING

LONDON

A dynamic mix of history and heritage, cool and contemporary. Great museums, stunning art collections, royal palaces, hip nightlife and stylish shopping, from ritzy Bond Street to cutting-edge Hoxton.

classic sights

St Paul's Cathedral – Wren's famous church

Tower of London – 900 years of British history

London Eye – spectacular views from the world's highest 'big wheel'

arts for all

National Gallery – Botticelli, Rembrandt, Turner and more

Tate Modern – 20thC art in a former power station

Victoria & Albert Museum – decorative arts

city lights

Theatre: musicals – West End; drama – Royal Court and National Theatre;
Music: classical – Wigmore Hall and Royal Festival Hall;
azz – Ronnie Scott's; ballet & opera – Royal Opera House

insider london

Dennis Severs's House, E1 – candlelit tours of this authentically 18thC house

Greater London, comprising the 32 London Boroughs

FOR MORE INFORMATION CONTACT:
London Tourist Board
1 Warwick Row,
London SW1E 5ER
Telephone enquiries - see London Line on page 40
Internet: www.londontouristboard.com

The Pictures: 1 London by night, Piccadilly Circus 2 Royal Guard 3 Houses of Parliament

PLACES to visit

You will find hundreds of interesting places to visit during your stay, just some of which are listed in these pages. Contact any Tourist Information Centre in and around London for more ideas on days out.

1 2 3

Awarded ETC's new 'Quality Assured Visitor Attraction' marque at time of going to press. **(See page 19).**

Bank of England Museum

Threadneedle Street, EC2R 8AH

Tel: (020) 7601 5545 www.bankofengland.co.uk

The museum is housed within the Bank of England. It traces the history of the bank from its foundation by Royal Charter in 1694 to its role today as the nation's central bank.

British Airways London Eye

Jubilee Gardens, South Bank, SE1

Tel: (0870) 5000 600 www.ba-londoneye.com

The British Airways London Eye is the world's largest observation wheel. Take in over 55 of London's most famous landmarks in just 30 minutes!

British Library

96 Euston Road, NW1 2DB

Tel: (020) 7412 7332 www.bl.uk

Exhibition galleries, bookshop and piazza displaying Magna Carta, Gutenberg Bible, Shakespeare's First Folio and illuminated manuscripts as well as temporary exhibitions.

Cabinet War Rooms

Clive Steps, King Charles Street, SW1A 2AQ

Tel: (020) 7930 6961 www.iwm.org.uk

The underground headquarters used by Winston Churchill and the British Government during World War II. Includes Cabinet Room, Transatlantic Telephone Room and Map Room.

Chessington World of Adventures

Leatherhead Road, Chessington, KT9 2NE

Tel: (01372) 729560 www.chessington.com

Fun, family adventures with the 'fang-tastic' Vampire ride, Tomb Blaster, an action-packed adventure ride and a mischievous attraction in Beanoland.

Hampton Court Palace

Hampton Court, East Molesey, KT8 9AU

Tel: (020) 8781 9500 www.hrp.org.uk

The oldest Tudor palace in England with many attractions including the Tudor kitchens, tennis courts, maze, State Apartments and King's Apartments.

HMS Belfast

Morgan's Lane, Tooley Street, SE1 2JH

Tel: (020) 7940 6300 www.iwm.org.uk

World War II cruiser weighing 11,500 tonnes, now a floating naval museum, with nine decks to explore.

Imperial War Museum

Lambeth Road, SE1 6HZ

Tel: (020) 7416 5320 www.iwm.org.uk

Museum tells the story of 20thC war from Flanders to Bosnia. Special features include the Blitz Experience, the Trench Experience and the World of Espionage.

Kensington Palace State Apartments

Kensington Gardens, W8 4PX

Tel: (020) 7937 9561 www.hrp.org.uk

Furniture and ceiling paintings from Stuart-Hanoverian periods, rooms from Victorian era and works of art from the Royal Collection. Also Royal Ceremonial Dress Collection.

Kew Gardens (Royal Botanic Gardens)

Kew, Richmond, TW9 3AB

Tel: (020) 8940 1171 www.kew.org

Three hundred acres (121ha) containing living collections of over 40,000 varieties of plants. Seven spectacular glasshouses, two art galleries, Japanese and rock garden.

London Aquarium

County Hall, Riverside Building, SE1 7PB

Tel: (020) 7967 8000 www.londonaquarium.co.uk

Dive down deep beneath the Thames and submerge yourself in one of Europe's largest displays of aquatic life.

London Dungeon

28-34 Tooley Street, SE1 2SZ

Tel: (020) 7403 7221 www.thedungeons.com

The London Dungeon is the historic horror experience dispensing fun and fear. Relive the Great Fire of London, unmask Jack the Ripper and take the Judgement Day ride.

London Planetarium

Marylebone Road, NW1 5LR

Tel: (0870) 400 3000 www.london-planetarium.com

Visitors can experience a virtual reality trip through space and wander through the interactive Space Zones before the show.

London Transport Museum

Covent Garden Piazza, WC2E 7BB

Tel: (020) 7379 6344 www.ltmuseum.co.uk

The history of transport for everyone, from spectacular vehicles, special exhibitions, actors and guided tours to film shows, gallery talks and children's craft workshops.

Madame Tussaud's

Marylebone Road, NW1 5LR

Tel: (0870) 400 3000 www.madame-tussauds.com

World-famous collection of wax figures in themed settings which include The Garden Party, 200 Years, Superstars, The Grand Hall, The Chamber of Horrors and the Spirit of London.

Museum of London

150 London Wall, EC2Y 5HN

Tel: (020) 7600 3699 www.museumoflondon.org.uk

Discover over 2,000 years of the capital's history, from prehistoric to modern times. Regular temporary exhibitions and lunchtime lecture programmes.

National Army Museum

Royal Hospital Road, Chelsea, SW3 4HT

Tel: (020) 7730 0717

www.national-armymuseum.ac.uk

The story of the British soldier in peace and war, through five centuries. Exhibits range from paintings to uniforms and from the English Civil War to Kosovo.

National Gallery

Trafalgar Square, WC2N 5DN

Tel: (020) 7747 2885 www.nationalgallery.org.uk

Gallery displaying Western European paintings from about 1250-1900. Includes work by Botticelli, Leonardo da Vinci, Rembrandt, Gainsborough, Turner, Renoir, Cezanne.

> The Pictures: 1 Tower Bridge 2 Piccadilly Circus 3 Buckingham Palace 4 Harrods 5 London skyline

National Maritime Museum

Romney Road, SE10 9NF

Tel: (020) 8858 4422 www.nmm.ac.uk

This national museum explains Britain's worldwide influence through its explorers, traders, migrants and naval power. Features on ship models, costume, and ecology of the sea.

Royal Air Force Museum

Grahame Park Way, Hendon, NW9 5LL

Tel: (020) 8205 2266 www.rafmuseum.com

The museum displays a world-class collection of over 70 aircraft, aviation memorabilia and artefacts.

Royal Mews

Buckingham Palace, SW1A 1AA

Tel: (020) 7321 2233

www.the-royal-collection.org.uk

Her Majesty The Queen's carriage horses, carriages and harness used on State occasions (Coronation Coach built 1761).

Royal Observatory Greenwich

Greenwich Park, SE10 9NF

Tel: (020) 8858 4422 www.nmm.ac.uk

Museum of time and space and site of the Greenwich Meridian. Working telescopes and planetarium, timeball, Wren's Octagon Room and intricate clocks and computer simulations.

St Paul's Cathedral

St Paul's Churchyard, EC4M 8AD

Tel: (020) 7236 4128 www.stpauls.co.uk

Wren's famous cathedral church of the diocese of London incorporating the Crypt, Ambulatory and Whispering Gallery.

Science Museum

Exhibition Road, SW7 2DD

Tel: (0870) 870 4868 www.sciencemuseum.org.uk

See, touch and experience the major scientific advances of the last 300 years at the largest museum of its kind in the world.

Shakespeare's Globe Exhibition and Tour

New Globe Walk, Bankside, SE1 9DT

Tel: (020) 7401 9919 www.shakespeares-globe.org

Against the historical background of Elizabethan Bankside, the City of London's playground in Shakespeare's time, the exhibition focuses on actors, architecture and audiences.

Tate Modern

Bankside, 25 Sumner Street, SE1 9TG

Tel: (020) 7887 8000 www.tate.org.uk

Tate Modern is Britain's national museum of Modern Art, and displays the Tate collection of international modern art from 1900 to the present day.

Theatre Museum

Russell Street, WC2E 7PA

Tel: (020) 7943 4700 www.theatremuseum.org

Five galleries illustrating the history of performance inthe United Kingdom. The collection includes displays on theatre, ballet, dance, musical stage, rock and pop music.

Tower Bridge Experience

Tower Bridge, SE1 2UP

Tel: (020) 7403 3761 www.towerbridge.org.uk

Exhibition explaining the history of the bridge and how it operates. Original steam-powered engines on view. Panoramic views from fully-glazed walkways. Gift shop.

Tower of London

Tower Hill, EC3N 4AB

Tel: (020) 7709 0765 www.hrp.org.uk

Home of the 'Beefeaters' and ravens, the building spans 900 years of British history. On display are the nation's Crown Jewels, regalia and armoury robes.

Victoria and Albert Museum

Cromwell Road, SW7 2RL

Tel: (020) 7942 2000 www.vam.ac.uk

The V&A holds one of the world's largest and most diverse collections of the decorative arts, dating from 3000BC to the present day.

Vinopolis, City of Wine

1 Bank End, SE1 9BU

Tel: (0870) 241 4040 www.vinopolis.co.uk

Vinopolis is London's wine-tasting visitor attraction. For anyone who enjoys a glass of wine it is one of the few attractions where guests grow merrier as they walk through!

Westminster Abbey

Parliament Square, SW1P 3PA

Tel: (020) 7222 5152 www.westminster-abbey.org

One of Britain's finest Gothic buildings. Scene of the coronation, marriage and burial of British monarchs. Nave and cloisters, Royal Chapels and Undercroft Museum.

Find out more about London

1 > London Eye

LONDON TOURIST BOARD

London Tourist Board and Convention Bureau
1 Warwick Row, London SW1E 5ER
www.londontouristboard.com

TOURIST INFORMATION CENTRES

INNER LONDON

- **Britain Visitor Centre,** 1 Regent Street, Piccadilly Circus, SW1Y 4XT. Open: Mon 0930-1830,Tue-Fri 0900-1830, Sat & Sun 1000-1600; Jun-Oct, Sat 0900-1700.
- **Camden Direct Information Centre,** Town Hall, Argyle Street, WC1H 8NN. Tel: 020 7974 5974; Fax: 020 7974 3210. Open: Mon-Fri 0900-1700.
- **Greenwich TIC,** Pepys House, 2 Cutty Sark Gardens, Greenwich SE10 9LW. Tel: 0870 608 2000; Fax: 020 8853 4607. Open: Daily 1000-1700.
- **Lewisham TIC,** Lewisham Library, 199-201 Lewisham High Street, SE13 6LG. Tel: 020 8297 8317; Fax: 020 8297 9241. Open: Mon 1000-1700, Tue-Fri 0900-1700, Sat 1000-1600.
- **Liverpool Street Underground Station,** EC2M 7PM Open: Mon-Fri 0800-1800, Sat 0800-1730, Sun 0900-1730
- **Southwark Information Centre,** London Bridge, 6 Tooley Street, SE1 2SY. Tel: 020 7403 8299; Fax: 020 7357 6321. Open: Easter-31 Oct, Mon-Sat 1000-1800, Sun 1100-1800; 1 Nov-Easter, Mon-Sat 1000-1600.
- **London Visitors Centre,** Arrivals Hall, Waterloo International Terminal, SE1 7LT. Open: Daily 0830-2230.
- **Victoria Station Forecourt,** SW1V 1JU Open: Jan-Feb, Mon-Sat 0800-1900; Mar-May, Mon-Sat 0800-2000; Jun-Sep, Mon-Sat, 0800-2100, Oct-Dec, Mon-Sat 0800-2000, Sun 0800-1815

OUTER LONDON

- **Bexley Hall Place TIC,** Bourne Road, Bexley, Kent, DA5 1PQ. Tel: 01322 558676; Fax 01322 522921. Open: Mon-Sat 1000-1630, Sun 1400-1730.
- **Croydon TIC,** Katharine Street, Croydon, CR9 1ET. Tel: 020 8253 1009; Fax: 020 8253 1008. Open: Mon-Wed & Fri 0900-1800, Thu 0930-1800, Sat 0900-1700, Sun 1400-1700.
- **Harrow TIC,** Civic Centre, Station Road, Harrow, HA1 2XF. Tel: 020 8424 1103; Fax: 020 8424 1134. Open: Mon-Fri 0900-1700.
- **Heathrow Terminals 1,2,2** Underground Station, Concourse, Heathrow Airport, TW6 2JA. Open: Daily 0800-1800.
- **Hillingdon TIC,** Central Library, 14-15 High Street, Uxbridge, UB8 1HD. Tel: 01895 250706; Fax: 01895 239794. Open: Mon, Tue & Thu 0930-2000, Wed 0930-1730, Fri 1000-1730, Sat 0930-1600.
- **Hounslow TIC,** The Treaty Centre, High Street, Hounslow, TW3 1ES. Tel: 020 8583 2929; Fax: 020 8583 4714. Open: Mon, Wed, Fri & Sat 0930-1730, Tue & Thu 0930-2000.
- **Kingston TIC,** Market House, Market Place, Kingston upon Thames, KT1 1JS. Tel: 020 8547 5592; Fax: 020 8547 5594. Open: Mon-Sat 1000-1700.
- **Richmond TIC,** Old Town Hall, Whittaker Avenue; Richmond, TW9 1TP. Tel: 020 8940 9125; Fax: 020 8332 0802. Open: Mon-Sat 1000-1700; Easter Sun-end Sep, Sun 1030-1330.
- **Swanley TIC,** London Road, BR8 7AE. Tel: 01322 614660; Fax: 01322 666154. Open: Mon-Thur 0930-1730, Fri 0930-1800, Sat 0900-1600.
- **Twickenham TIC,** The Atrium, Civic Centre, York Street, Twickenham, Middlesex, TW1 3BZ. Tel: 020 8891 7272; Fax: 020 8891 7738. Open: Mon-Thu 0900-1715, Fri 0900-1700.

INFORMATION PACK

For a London information pack call 0870 240 4326. Calls are charged at national rate.

LONDON LINE

London Tourist Board's recorded telephone information service provides information on museums, galleries, attractions, riverboat trips, sightseeing tours, accommodation, theatre, what's on, changing the Guard, children's London, shopping, eating out and gay and lesbian London.

Available 24 hours a day. Calls cost 60p per minute as at July 2002. Call 09068 663344.

ARTSLINE

London's information and advice service for disabled people on arts and entertainment. Call (020) 7388 2227.

HOTEL ACCOMMODATION SERVICE

Accommodation reservations can be made throughout London. Call the London Tourist Board's Telephone Accommodation Service on (020) 7932 2020 with your requirements and MasterCard/Visa/Switch details or email your request on book@londontouristboard.co.uk

Reservations on arrival are handled at the Tourist Information Centres at Victoria Station, Heathrow Underground, Liverpool Street Station and Waterloo International. Go to any of them on the day when you need accommodation. A communication charge and a refundable deposit are payable when making a reservation.

WHICH PART OF LONDON?

The majority of tourist accommodation is situated in the central parts of London and is therefore very convenient for most of the city's attractions and nightlife.

However, there are many hotels in outer London which provide other advantages, such as easier parking. In the 'Where to Stay' pages which follow, you will find accommodation listed under INNER LONDON (covering the E1 to W14 London Postal Area) and OUTER LONDON (covering the remainder of Greater London). Colour maps 6 and 7 at the front of the guide show place names and London Postal Area codes and will help you to locate accommodation in your chosen area of London.

Getting to London

BY ROAD: Major trunk roads into London include: A1, M1, A5, A10, A11, M11, A13, A2, M2, A23, A3, M3, A4, M4, A40, M40, A41, M25 (London orbital).

London Transport is responsible for running London's bus services and the underground rail network. (020) 7222 1234 (24 hour telephone service; calls answered in rotation).

BY RAIL: Main rail termini:
Victoria/Waterloo/Charing Cross - serving the South/South East;
King's Cross - serving the North East; Euston - serving the North West/Midlands;
Liverpool Street - serving the East; Paddington - serving the Thames Valley/West

> The Pictures: 1 China Town 2 The Tower of Lond

LONDON INDEX

If you are looking for accommodation in a particular establishment in London and you know its name, this index will give you the page number of the full entry in the guide.

Where to stay in London

Accommodation entries in this region are listed under Inner London (covering the postcode areas E1 to W14) and Outer London (covering the remainder of Greater London) - please refer to the colour location maps 6 and 7 at the front of this guide.

At-a-glance symbols at the end of each accommodation entry give useful information about services and facilities. A key to symbols can be found inside the back cover flap. Keep this open for easy reference.

A complete listing of all the English Tourism Council assessed accommodation covered by this guide appears at the back of the guide.

INNER LONDON

LONDON E4

Silver Award

AUCKLANDS
25 Eglington Road,
North Chingford, London E4 7AN
T: (020) 8529 1140
F: (020) 8529 9288
E: drumandhelen@amserve.net

Bedrooms: 2 double/twin

Lunch available
Evening meal available

B&B per night:
S Min £35.00
D Min £70.00

OPEN All Year except Christmas

Comfortable Edwardian period family home with exclusive facilities in quiet suburb, easy access to City. Solar-heated swimming pool in landscaped garden.

12

LONDON E7

FOREST VIEW HOTEL
227 Romford Road, Forest Gate,
London E7 9HL
T: (020) 8534 4844
F: (020) 8534 8959
I: www.forestviewhotel.net

Bedrooms: 8 single, 15 double/twin, 5 triple/multiple
Bathrooms: 4 en suite, 11 private

Evening meal available
CC: Delta, Mastercard, Switch, Visa

B&B per night:
S £39.50
D £58.20–£69.80

HB per person:
DY £46.00–£52.30

OPEN All Year

Catering for business and tourist clientele. En suite rooms with tea/coffee-making facilities, direct-dial telephone and TV. Full English breakfast. Warm and friendly atmosphere.

2 P

IMPORTANT NOTE Information on accommodation listed in this guide has been supplied by the proprietors. As changes may occur you are advised to check details at the time of booking.

LONDON E15

◆◆

PARK HOTEL

81 Portway, Stratford, London
E15 3QJ
T: (0208) 2579034
F: (0208) 2798094

Bedrooms: 2 single, 10 double/twin, 2 triple/multiple; permanent suite(s)
Bathrooms: 9 en suite

Lunch available
Evening meal available
CC: Delta, Mastercard, Switch, Visa

Quality budget hotel situated in East London. Conveniently located for Docklands, city, West End and transport links at City and Stansted Airports. Convenient for A406, M25 and M11.

P

B&B per night:
S £30.00–£50.00
D £40.00–£60.00

HB per person:
DY £40.00–£60.00

OPEN All Year

LONDON N1

◆◆◆

KANDARA GUEST HOUSE

68 Ockendon Road, London
N1 3NW
T: (020) 7226 5721 & 7226 3379
F: (020) 7226 3379
E: admin@kandara.co.uk
I: www.kandara.co.uk

Bedrooms: 4 single, 3 double/twin, 4 triple/multiple

CC: Delta, Mastercard, Visa

Small family-run guesthouse near the Angel, Islington. Free street parking and good public transport to West End and City.

B&B per night:
S £41.00–£49.00
D £51.00–£62.00

OPEN All Year

LONDON N8

◆◆◆

WHITE LODGE HOTEL

1 Church Lane, Hornsey, London
N8 7BU
T: (020) 8348 9765
F: (020) 8340 7851

Bedrooms: 7 single, 6 double/twin, 3 triple/multiple
Bathrooms: 8 en suite

Evening meal available
CC: Mastercard, Visa

Small, friendly, family hotel offering personal service. Easy access to all transport, for sightseeing and business trips.

B&B per night:
S £30.00–£32.00
D £40.00–£48.00

OPEN All Year except Christmas

LONDON N10

◆◆◆

THE MUSWELL HILL HOTEL

73 Muswell Hill Road, London
N10 3HT
T: (020) 8883 6447
F: (020) 8883 5158
E: reception@muswellhillhotel.co.uk
I: www.muswellhillhotel.co.uk

Bedrooms: 4 single, 7 double/twin, 3 triple/multiple
Bathrooms: 10 en suite

CC: Mastercard, Switch, Visa

A comfortable 3 storey Edwardian corner property, close to Muswell Hill and Alexandra Palace offering a warm, friendly service.

P

B&B per night:
S £35.00–£40.00
D £55.00–£60.00

OPEN All Year

LONDON N22

◆◆

PANE RESIDENCE

154 Boundary Road, Wood Green, London N22 6AE
T: (020) 8889 3735

Bedrooms: 1 single, 2 double/twin

In a pleasant location 6 minutes' walk from Turnpike Lane underground station and near Alexandra Palace. Kitchen facilities available.

1 P

B&B per night:
S £23.00–£25.00
D £34.00–£38.00

OPEN All Year

LONDON NW3

◆◆

DILLONS HOTEL

21 Belsize Park, Hampstead, London
NW3 4DU
T: (020) 7794 3360
F: (020) 7431 7900
E: desk@dillonshotel.com
I: www.dillonshotel.com

Bedrooms: 1 single, 8 double/twin, 4 triple/multiple
Bathrooms: 8 en suite

CC: Delta, Mastercard, Switch, Visa

Victorian stucco-fronted house, convenient for central London and just 6 minutes from either Swiss Cottage or Belsize Park tube stations. Most rooms have private shower/wc.

B&B per night:
S £32.00–£44.00
D £48.00–£62.00

OPEN All Year

Good value accommodation

Looking for accommodation in London that's comfortable, convenient and ***great value for money.*** Look no further than Abbey Court and Westpoint Hotels. We couldn't be easier to find.

EASY TO REACH

Whether you arrive by Eurostar or plane rail or tube our hotels are accessible and easy to reach.

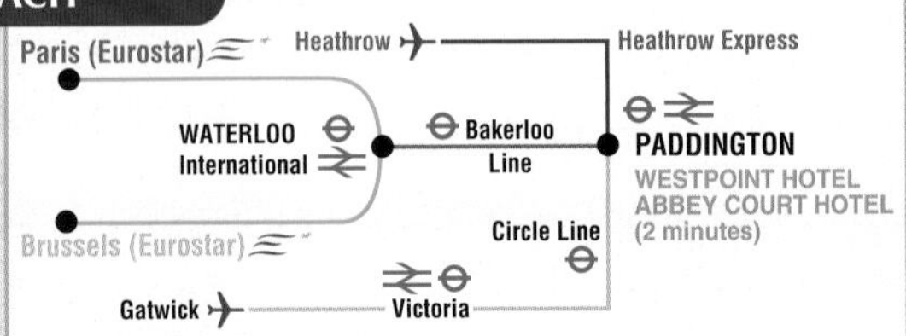

EASY TO FIND

Our hotels are just two minutes from Paddington station for Heathrow Express, British Rail, excellent bus and taxi services and four tube lines (Bakerloo, Circle, District, Hammersmith & City).

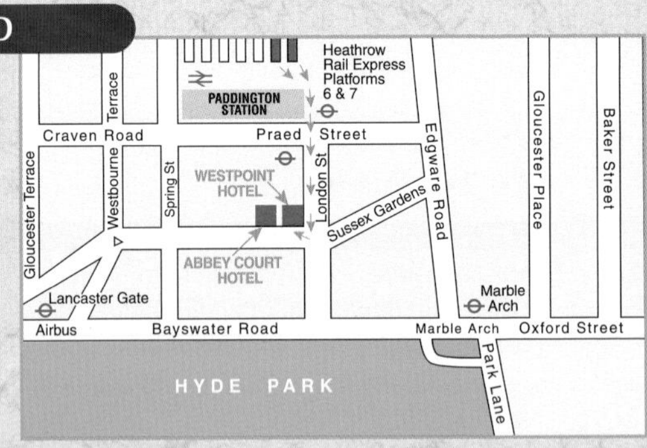

CONVENIENT AND CENTRAL

We are right at the heart of London, just a few minutes by direct tube from Oxford Circus, Piccadilly Circus and Embankment for sightseeing, shopping, restaurants, theatreland and the River Thames.

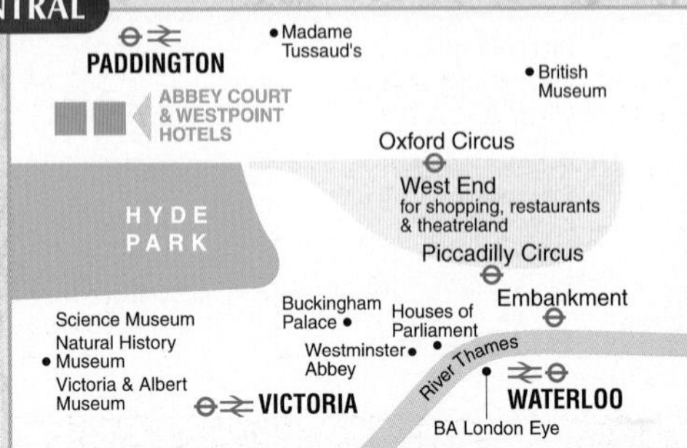

maps not to scale

LONDON NW6

♦♦♦♦

CAVENDISH GUEST HOUSE
24 Cavendish Road, London
NW6 7XP
T: (020) 8451 3249
F: (020) 8451 3249

Bedrooms: 2 single, 2 double/twin, 2 triple/multiple
Bathrooms: 3 en suite

In a quiet residential street, 5 minutes' walk from Kilburn underground station, 15 minutes' travelling time to the West End. Easy access to Wembley Stadium, Heathrow, Gatwick.

P

B&B per night:
S £33.00–£46.00
D £52.00–£58.00

OPEN All Year

LONDON NW10

J AND T GUEST HOUSE
98 Park Avenue North, Willesden Green,
London NW10 1JY
T: (020) 8452 4085
F: (020) 8450 2503
E: jandthome@aol.com
I: www.jandtguesthouses.com

J and T Guest House, situated in a quiet residential area of Willesden Green, is only a few minutes' walk from the underground station and buses. In 10-15 minutes you are in the heart of the West End with shops, restaurants, theatres, and close to all major tourist attractions. Free parking.

Bedrooms: 1 single, 4 double/twin, 1 triple/multiple
Bathrooms: 6 en suite

CC: Amex, Delta, Mastercard, Switch, Visa

P

B&B per night:
S £42.00–£45.00
D £52.00–£62.00

OPEN All Year

LONDON SE3

♦♦♦

THE GROVERS
96 Merriman Road, London
SE3 8RZ
T: (020) 8488 7719 & 07730 877 656
F: (020) 8488 7719

Bedrooms: 1 single, 2 double/twin

A friendly, family house in residential road with off-street parking. Close to shops, pub, restaurant and buses. Two miles to Greenwich centre. Use of garden.

2 P

B&B per night:
S £27.50
D £55.00

OPEN All Year except Christmas

♦♦

3 TILBROOK ROAD
3 Tilbrook Road, Kidbrooke, London
SE3 9QD
T: (020) 8319 8843

Bedrooms: 1 single, 1 double/twin

Semi-detached house, 8 minutes from Eltham Street station by bus and 20 minutes to Greenwich. Central London is 20 minutes by train. Easy access to major roads.

8 P

B&B per night:
S £22.50–£25.00
D £45.00–£50.00

OPEN All Year except Christmas

LONDON SE6

♦♦♦

TULIP TREE HOUSE
41 Minard Road, Catford, London
SE6 1NP
T: (020) 8697 2596
F: (020) 8698 2020

Bedrooms: 1 single, 2 double/twin

Evening meal available

English home in quiet residential area off A205 South Circular Road. 10 minutes' walk to Hither Green station for 20-minute journey to central London.

P

B&B per night:
S £25.00
D £46.00–£48.00

HB per person:
DY £32.00

OPEN All Year

LONDON SE9

BENVENUTI

217 Court Road, Eltham, London SE9 4TG
T: (020) 8857 4855
F: (020) 8265 5635
E: val-alan@benvenuti-guesthouse.co.uk
I: www.benvenuti-guesthouse.co.uk

Friendly, family-run B&B within the London Borough of Greenwich, four minutes' walk from train station. Central London 20 minutes by train. Very convenient for the M25, M20, A20, A2 and M2. No-smoking establishment.

Bedrooms: 2 double/twin, 1 triple/multiple

5 P

B&B per night:
S £30.00–£40.00
D £45.00–£60.00

OPEN All Year except Christmas

♦

WESTON HOUSE

8 Eltham Green, Eltham, London SE9 5LB
T: (020) 8850 5191
F: (020) 8850 0030
E: reservation@westonhousehotel.co.uk
I: www.westonhousehotel.co.uk

Bedrooms: 3 single, 5 double/twin, 2 triple/multiple
Bathrooms: 8 en suite

CC: Delta, Mastercard, Switch, Visa

Victorian hotel set in quiet conservation area. Close to Maritime Greenwich, City Airport, Canary Wharf. Easy access to central London (20 minutes by train) and A2, M2, A20, M20, M25.

P

B&B per night:
S £40.00–£45.00
D £50.00–£58.00

OPEN All Year

LONDON SE10

♦♦♦

THE CORNER HOUSE

28 Royal Hill, Greenwich, London SE10 8RT
T: (020) 8692 3023
F: (020) 8692 3023
E: joannacourtney@aol.com

Bedrooms: 1 single, 2 double/twin
Bathrooms: 2 private

A warm welcome awaits in this highly upgraded period property in the heart of the Greenwich conservation area. Fluent Italian spoken. Special diets catered for.

B&B per night:
S £35.00–£45.00
D £55.00–£65.00

OPEN All Year

♦♦♦

MITRE INN

291 Greenwich High Road, London SE10 8NA
T: (020) 8355 6760 & 8293 0037
F: (020) 8355 6761

Bedrooms: 2 single, 12 double/twin
Bathrooms: 14 en suite

Lunch available
CC: Delta, Mastercard, Switch, Visa

The Mitre is a traditional English inn, catering for bed and breakfast guests. It has 2 main bars plus an Irish theme bar. It also has a function room for private or business groups with a capacity for 60 to 80 people.

P

B&B per night:
S £59.50
D £75.50

OPEN All Year except Christmas

LONDON SE20

♦♦♦♦

MELROSE HOUSE

89 Lennard Road, London SE20 7LY
T: (020) 8776 8884 & 07956 357714
F: (020) 8325 7636
E: melrose.hotel@virgin.net
I: www.guesthouseaccommodation.co.uk

Bedrooms: 4 double/twin; permanent suite(s)
Bathrooms: 3 en suite, 1 private

CC: Delta, Mastercard, Switch, Visa

Superb, friendly accommodation in Victorian house with spacious en suite bedrooms. Easy access to West End. Quiet, respectable and welcoming. Disabled facilities.

12 P

B&B per night:
S £35.00–£50.00
D £50.00–£65.00

OPEN All Year except Christmas

CONFIRM YOUR BOOKING
You are advised to confirm your booking in writing.

LONDON SW1

◆◆

AIRWAYS HOTEL, LONDON

29-31 St George's Drive, Victoria, London SW1V 4DG
T: (020) 7834 0205 & 7834 3567
F: (020) 7932 0007
E: sales@airways-hotel.com
I: www.airways-hotel.com

Bedrooms: 5 single, 20 double/twin, 15 triple/multiple
Bathrooms: 40 en suite

CC: Amex, Delta, Mastercard, Switch, Visa

B&B per night:
S £45.00–£60.00
D £60.00–£80.00

OPEN All Year

Family-run hotel, within walking distance of Buckingham Palace and Westminster Abbey. Convenient for Harrods and theatreland. Friendly, personal service. Full English breakfast.

◆◆◆

HANOVER HOTEL

30-32 St George's Drive, London SW1V 4BN
T: (020) 7834 0367 & 7834 7617
F: (020) 7976 5587
E: reservations@hanoverhotel.co.uk
I: www.hanoverhotel.co.uk

Bedrooms: 8 single, 15 double/twin, 16 triple/multiple
Bathrooms: 38 en suite

CC: Amex, Delta, Diners, Mastercard, Switch, Visa

B&B per night:
S £27.00–£55.00
D £40.00–£75.00

OPEN All Year

The hotel is within 15 minutes' walk of main tourist attractions, 5 minutes' walk from Victoria, and Gatwick and Stansted Airports are within 45 minutes by train or coach.

◆◆◆◆

KNIGHTSBRIDGE GREEN HOTEL

159 Knightsbridge, London SW1X 7PD
T: (020) 7584 6274
F: (020) 7225 1635
E: thekghotel@aol.com
I: www.thekghotel.co.uk

Bedrooms: 7 single, 9 double/twin, 12 triple/multiple; permanent suite(s)
Bathrooms: 28 en suite

CC: Amex, Diners, Mastercard, Visa

B&B per night:
S £103.50–£110.50
D £152.00–£191.00

OPEN All Year

Small, family-owned hotel close to Harrods, offering spacious accommodation at competitive rates. Finalist in 1997 and 1998 London Tourism Awards.

◆◆◆

MELITA HOUSE HOTEL

35 Charlwood Street, Victoria, London SW1V 2DU
T: (020) 7828 0471 & 7834 1387
F: (020) 7932 0988
E: reserve@melitahotel.com
I: www.melitahotel.com

Bedrooms: 2 single, 9 double/twin, 8 triple/multiple
Bathrooms: 19 en suite

CC: Amex, Delta, Diners, Mastercard, Switch, Visa

B&B per night:
S £55.00–£70.00
D £60.00–£90.00

OPEN All Year

Elegant, family-run hotel in excellent location close to Victoria station. Rooms have extensive modern facilities. Warm, friendly welcome, full English breakfast included.

◆◆

STANLEY HOUSE HOTEL

19-21 Belgrave Road, London SW1V 1RB
T: (020) 7834 5042 & 7834 7292
F: (020) 7834 8439
E: cmahotel@aol.com
I: www.londonbudgethotels.co.uk

B&B per night:
S £35.00–£45.00
D £45.00–£55.00

OPEN All Year

In elegant Belgravia, only a few minutes' walk from Victoria station and with easy access to West End. All rooms en suite, with colour TV, direct-dial telephone, hairdryer. Friendly, relaxing atmosphere at affordable rates.

Bedrooms: 4 single, 30 double/twin, 10 triple/multiple
Bathrooms: 44 en suite

CC: Amex, Delta, Diners, Mastercard, Switch, Visa

CREDIT CARD BOOKINGS If you book by telephone and are asked for your credit card number it is advisable to check the proprietor's policy should you cancel your reservation.

LONDON SW1 continued

♦♦♦♦
Silver Award

WINDERMERE HOTEL

142-144 Warwick Way, Victoria, London SW1V 4JE
T: (020) 7834 5163 & 7834 5480
F: (020) 7630 8831
E: reservations@windermere-hotel.co.uk
I: www.windermere-hotel.co.uk

An ideal location, within minutes' walk of Buckingham Palace, Westminster Abbey and Tate Britain, combined with a very warm and personal welcome. All rooms are individually designed and include king, queen, double, twin and family rooms. Dinner is served in the relaxed atmosphere of our licensed restaurant, the Pimlico Room.

Bedrooms: 4 single, 15 double/twin, 3 triple/multiple
Bathrooms: 20 en suite

Evening meal available
CC: Amex, Delta, Mastercard, Switch, Visa

B&B per night:
S £69.00–£96.00
D £89.00–£139.00

OPEN All Year

LONDON SW5

♦♦

HOTEL EARLS COURT

28 Warwick Road, Earls Court, London SW5 9UD
T: (020) 7373 7079 & 7373 0302
F: (020) 7912 0582
E: res@hotelearlscourt.com
I: www.hotelearlscourt.com

Bedrooms: 6 single, 6 double/twin, 5 triple/multiple
Bathrooms: 6 private

CC: Amex, Diners, Mastercard, Visa

B&B per night:
S £30.00–£49.00
D £49.00–£60.00

OPEN All Year

A friendly, clean and comfortable, centrally located bed and breakfast, opposite Earl's Court Exhibition Hall and 50 yards from Earl's Court underground station (Warwick Road exit).

10

♦♦

LORD JIM HOTEL

23-25 Penywern Road, London SW5 9TT
T: (020) 7370 6071 & 07957 167081
F: (020) 7373 8919
E: Ljh@Lgh-hotels.com
I: www.lgh-hotels.com

A good-quality hotel for both business travellers and tourists. Bedrooms are modern and mostly en suite, with colour TVs, telephone and hairdryers. Two minutes' walk from Earls Court station which is directly linked to Heathrow and Gatwick Airports (via Victoria). Earls Court and Olympia exhibition halls within walking distance.

Bedrooms: 8 single, 19 double/twin, 18 triple/multiple
Bathrooms: 38 en suite

Special discounts available in low seasons.

CC: Amex, Delta, Diners, Mastercard, Switch, Visa

B&B per night:
S £35.00–£55.00
D £45.00–£68.00

OPEN All Year

AT-A-GLANCE SYMBOLS

Symbols at the end of each accommodation entry give useful information about services and facilities. A key to symbols can be found inside the back cover flap. Keep this open for easy reference.

LONDON SW5 continued

LORD KENSINGTON HOTEL

38 Trebovir Road, Earls Court, London SW5 9NJ
T: (0207) 373 7331 & 373 9248
F: (0207) 460 3524
E: lkh@lgh-hotels.com
I: www.lgh-hotels.com

A brand-new hotel in the heart of Kensington. The hotel has undergone extensive refurbishment. All en suite rooms with colour TVs, direct-dial telephones, PC modems, tea and coffee. Only 2 minutes from Earls Court station. Earls Court and Olympia exhibition halls within walking distance.

Bedrooms: 2 single, 7 double/twin, 14 triple/multiple; permanent suite(s)
Bathrooms: 18 en suite, 5 private

CC: Amex, Delta, Diners, Mastercard, Switch, Visa

B&B per night:
S £55.00–£75.00
D £60.00–£95.00

OPEN All Year

♦♦

MERLYN COURT HOTEL

2 Barkston Gardens, London SW5 0EN
T: (020) 7370 1640
F: (020) 7370 4986
E: london@merlyncourt.demon.co.uk
I: www.merlyncourthotel.com

Quiet, non-smoking, family-run, good-value hotel in quiet Edwardian square with bright, airy rooms. Family rooms available. Close to Earl's Court and Olympia. Direct underground link to Heathrow, the West End and rail stations. Easy access to motorways and airports. Car park nearby.

Bedrooms: 4 single, 8 double/twin, 5 triple/multiple
Bathrooms: 11 en suite

CC: Delta, Mastercard, Switch, Visa

Nov-Mar: 2/3-night stays at reduced rates on application.

B&B per night:
S £30.00–£45.00
D £55.00–£75.00

OPEN All Year

♦♦

HOTEL OLIVER

198 Cromwell Road, London SW5 0SN
T: (020) 7370 6881
F: (020) 7370 6556
E: reservations@hoteloliver.freeserve.co.uk
I: www.hoteloliver.co.uk

All rooms en suite with colour TV, hairdryer, telephone and trouser press. Full central heating, lift to all floors. Two minutes' walk to Earls Court underground station. Exhibition Centres, Harrods and shopping centre close by. Bus stop outside the hotel.

Bedrooms: 20 single, 22 double/twin, 6 triple/multiple
Bathrooms: 48 en suite

CC: Amex, Diners, Mastercard, Switch, Visa

B&B per night:
S £35.00–£55.00
D £50.00–£75.00

OPEN All Year

♦♦

OLIVER PLAZA HOTEL

33 Trebovir Road, Earl's Court, London SW5 9NF
T: (020) 7373 7183
F: (020) 7244 6021
E: oliverplaza@capricornhotels.co.uk
I: www.capricornhotels.co.uk

Bedrooms: 3 single, 27 double/twin, 8 triple/multiple
Bathrooms: 38 en suite

CC: Amex, Delta, Diners, Mastercard, Switch, Visa

B&B per night:
S £35.00–£50.00
D £50.00–£85.00

OPEN All Year

Friendly hotel with emphasis on efficiency of service and comfort for guests. Fully refurbished in 1999. Good access to public transport and shopping facilities.

LONDON SW5 continued

◆◆◆

HOTEL PLAZA CONTINENTAL

9 Knaresborough Place, Earls Court, London SW5 0TP
T: (020) 7370 3246
F: (020) 7373 9571
E: hpc@lgh-hotels.com
I: www.lgh-hotels.com

Good-quality hotel, recently refurbished, for the needs of both business travellers and tourists. Only 2 minutes' walk from Earls Court station and within walking distance of Earls Court and Olympia exhibition halls. Favourably positioned within easy reach of London's West End and Theatreland, Hyde Park and museums.

Bedrooms: 6 single, 12 double/twin, 3 triple/multiple
Bathrooms: 21 en suite

CC: Amex, Delta, Diners, Mastercard, Switch, Visa

Special discounts when mentioning this guide.

B&B per night:
S £40.00–£72.00
D £50.00–£85.00

OPEN All Year

◆◆

RAMSEES HOTEL

32-36 Hogarth Road, Earl's Court, London SW5 0PU
T: (020) 7370 1445
F: (020) 7244 6835
E: ramsees@rasool.demon.co.uk
I: www.ramseeshotel.com

Our friendly staff are here to make your stay comfortable. Ideally located in fashionable Kensington, close to the heart of the city. One minute's walk Earl's Court station, making major shopping areas of Knightsbridge, Oxford Street and tourist attractions of Buckingham Palace, Tower of London and museums within easy reach.

Bedrooms: 15 single, 39 double/twin, 13 triple/multiple
Bathrooms: 56 en suite

CC: Amex, Delta, Diners, Mastercard, Switch, Visa

B&B per night:
S £33.00–£42.00
D £48.00–£55.00

OPEN All Year

◆◆

RASOOL COURT HOTEL

19-21 Penywern Road, Earl's Court, London SW5 9TT
T: (020) 7373 8900
F: (020) 7244 6835
E: rasool@rasool.demon.co.uk
I: www.rasoolcourthotel.com

Family-run hotel ideally located in fashionable Kensington within 1 minute's walk of Earl's Court station, making the shopping areas of Knightsbridge and Oxford Street and the tourist attractions of Buckingham Palace, the Tower of London and museums within easy reach. The immediate area has a variety of restaurants and shops for your convenience.

Bedrooms: 25 single, 24 double/twin, 8 triple/multiple
Bathrooms: 38 en suite

CC: Amex, Delta, Diners, Mastercard, Switch, Visa

B&B per night:
S £36.00–£45.00
D £48.00–£57.00

OPEN All Year

ACCESSIBILITY

Look for the symbols which indicate National Accessible Scheme standards for hearing and visually impaired guests in addition to standards for guests with mobility impairment. Additional participants are shown in the listings at the back.

LONDON SW5 continued

SWISS HOUSE HOTEL

171 Old Brompton Road, London SW5 0AN
T: (020) 7373 2769 & 7373 9383
F: (020) 7373 4983
E: recep@swiss-hh.demon.co.uk
I: www.swiss-hh.demon.co.uk

B&B per night:
S £54.00–£75.00
D £93.00–£109.00

OPEN All Year

The Swiss House Hotel is located in the heart of South Kensington, one of London's smartest and most fashionable districts, and is close to most of London's main attractions. Whether your visit is for business or pleasure, the Swiss House extends a warm welcome and ensures a comfortable stay.

Bedrooms: 5 single, 7 double/twin, 4 triple/multiple
Bathrooms: 15 en suite

CC: Amex, Delta, Diners, Mastercard, Switch, Visa

Children under 4 stay for free. 5% discount for more than 5-day stay during winter time.

♦

See ad on page 53

WINDSOR HOUSE

12 Penywern Road, London SW5 9ST
T: (020) 7373 9087
F: (020) 7385 2417
E: bookings@windsor-house-hotel.com
I: www.windsor-house-hotel.com

B&B per night:
S £28.00–£48.00
D £42.00–£72.00

OPEN All Year

Central London. Friendly, family-run bed and breakfast. Beautiful Victorian building. Excellent budget standard. Spacious, comfortable rooms. Children welcome – the more the merrier! Use of new hotel kitchen for preparing own teas/meals. Super garden. NCP parking.

Bedrooms: 1 single, 8 double/twin, 9 triple/multiple
Bathrooms: 12 en suite

CC: Delta, Mastercard, Switch, Visa

Super-special savers for stays of 3 nights or more. Discounts for children. 3/4/5-bedroom family rooms from £14-£26pppn.

LONDON SW7

FIVE SUMNER PLACE HOTEL

5 Sumner Place, South Kensington, London SW7 3EE
T: (020) 7584 7586
F: (020) 7823 9962
E: reservations@sumnerplace.com
I: www.sumnerplace.com

B&B per night:
S £85.00–£100.00
D £120.00–£153.00

OPEN All Year

Awarded 'best small hotel'. In South Kensington, one of the most stylish and sought-after locations in London, the hotel brings the charm and elegance of a former age to the 20thC. Ideally placed for visiting the sights. This family-owned and run hotel offers excellent service and personal attention.

Bedrooms: 3 single, 10 double/twin
Bathrooms: 13 en suite

CC: Amex, Mastercard, Switch, Visa

Special offers available Jan-Feb.

QUALITY ASSURANCE SCHEME
Diamond ratings and awards were correct at the time of going to press but are subject to change. Please check at the time of booking.

LONDON SW8

♦♦♦♦

COMFORT INN LONDON

87 South Lambeth Road, London SW8 1RN
T: (020) 7735 9494
F: (020) 7735 1001
E: stay@comfortinnvx.co.uk
I: www.comfortinnvx.co.uk

B&B per night:
S £69.00–£95.00
D £69.00–£95.00

OPEN All Year

This newly built, modern, award-winning hotel offers en suite and well-equipped rooms located in the heart of London close to major tourist attractions, famous shopping areas and public transport access. Offers excellent value for money. Theatres, restaurants and wine bars are all within easy reach of the hotel.

Bedrooms: 78 double/twin, 16 triple/multiple; permanent suite(s)
Bathrooms: 94 en suite

CC: Amex, Delta, Diners, Mastercard, Switch, Visa

Special and promotional rates available for online bookings only on www.comfortinnvx.co.uk

LONDON SW14

♦♦♦

THE PLOUGH INN

42 Christchurch Road, East Sheen, London SW14 7AF
T: (020) 8876 7833 & 8876 4533
F: (020) 8392 8801
E: ploughthe@hotmail.com

Bedrooms: 1 single, 6 double/twin, 1 triple/multiple
Bathrooms: 8 en suite

Lunch available
Evening meal available
CC: Amex, Delta, Mastercard, Switch, Visa

B&B per night:
S £65.00–£70.00
D £85.00–£95.00

HB per person:
DY £75.00–£80.00

OPEN All Year

Delightful old pub, part 16thC, next to Richmond Park. En suite accommodation, traditional ales, home-cooked food.

RATING All accommodation in this guide has been rated, or is awaiting a rating, by a trained English Tourism Council assessor.

LONDON W1

◆◆◆

BLANDFORD HOTEL

80 Chiltern Street, London W1U 5AF
T: (020) 7486 3103
F: (020) 7487 2786
E: blandfordhotel@dial.pipex.com
I: www.capricornhotels.co.uk

Bedrooms: 8 single, 14 double/twin, 11 triple/multiple
Bathrooms: 33 en suite

CC: Amex, Delta, Mastercard, Switch, Visa

B&B per night:
S £40.00–£70.00
D £50.00–£90.00

OPEN All Year

Centrally located hotel, close to Baker Street underground station and Madame Tussauds. Oxford Street and other attractions in the West End are within walking distance.

◆◆

LINCOLN HOUSE HOTEL - CENTRAL LONDON

33 Gloucester Place, London W1U 8HY
T: (020) 7486 7630
F: (020) 7486 0166
E: reservations@lincoln-house-hotel.co.uk
I: www.lincoln-house-hotel.co.uk

Built in the days of King George III, this hotel offers Georgian charm and character. En suite rooms with modern comforts. Competitively priced. Located in the heart of London's West End, next to Oxford Street and most famous shopping attractions, close to theatreland. Ideal for business and leisure. Freephone 0500 007 208.

Bedrooms: 8 single, 10 double/twin, 4 triple/multiple
Bathrooms: 22 en suite

CC: Amex, Delta, Diners, Mastercard, Switch, Visa

Long-stay discounts on request; most Sundays discounted. For other special offers visit our website.

B&B per night:
S £59.00–£79.00
D £69.00–£89.00

OPEN All Year

◆◆◆

WYNDHAM HOTEL

30 Wyndham Street, London W1H 1EB
T: (020) 7723 7204 & 7723 9400
F: (020) 7724 2893
E: wyndhamhotel@talk21.com
I: www.lhghotels.co.uk

Inexpensive and typically British, family-run hotel where many of our visitors choose to repeat their vacations in the friendly and comfortable atmosphere. All rooms have private shower, TV, coffee/tea-making facilities, minibar and telephone.

Bedrooms: 3 single, 6 double/twin, 1 triple/multiple
Bathrooms: 10 private

CC: Amex, Delta, Diners, Mastercard, Switch, Visa

B&B per night:
S £40.00–£49.00
D £58.00–£67.00

OPEN All Year

QUALITY ASSURANCE SCHEME

For an explanation of the quality and facilities represented by the Diamonds please refer to the front of this guide. A more detailed explanation can be found in the information pages at the back.

LONDON W2

◆◆

BARRY HOUSE HOTEL

12 Sussex Place, London W2 2TP
T: (020) 7723 7340
F: (020) 7723 9775
E: hotel@barryhouse.co.uk
I: www.barryhouse.co.uk

We believe in family-like care. Comfortable en suite rooms with TV, telephone and hospitality tray. Located close to Hyde Park, the West End, Paddington Station and many tourist attractions. We offer tourist information, sightseeing and tours arranged, theatre tickets and taxis booked.

Bedrooms: 4 single, 11 double/twin, 3 triple/multiple
Bathrooms: 15 en suite

CC: Amex, Delta, Diners, Mastercard, Switch, Visa

B&B per night:
S £38.00–£54.00
D £78.00–£95.00

OPEN All Year

◆◆

DYLAN HOTEL

14 Devonshire Terrace,
Lancaster Gate, London W2 3DW
T: (020) 7723 3280
F: (020) 7402 2443
E: booking@dylan-hotel.com
I: www.dylan-hotel.com

Bedrooms: 4 single, 11 double/twin, 3 triple/multiple
Bathrooms: 7 en suite

CC: Amex, Delta, Diners, Mastercard, Switch, Visa

Small hotel in central location, 4 minutes from Paddington and Lancaster Gate underground stations. Marble Arch, Hyde Park and Oxford Street close by. Not just a hotel, a home from home.

B&B per night:
S £32.00–£48.00
D £52.00–£72.00

OPEN All Year

◆

HYDE PARK ROOMS HOTEL

137 Sussex Gardens, Hyde Park,
London W2 2RX
T: (020) 7723 0225 & 7723 0965

Bedrooms: 5 single, 7 double/twin, 2 triple/multiple
Bathrooms: 6 en suite

CC: Amex, Diners, Mastercard, Visa

Small centrally located private hotel with personal service. Clean, comfortable and friendly. Within walking distance of Hyde Park and Kensington Gardens. Car parking available.

P

B&B per night:
S £30.00–£45.00
D £45.00–£60.00

OPEN All Year except Christmas

◆◆◆

KINGSWAY PARK HOTEL HYDE PARK

139 Sussex Gardens, Hyde Park, London W2 2RX
T: (020) 7723 5677 & 7724 9346
F: (020) 7402 4352
E: kingswaypark@hotmail.com
I: www.kingswaypark-hotel.com

The hotel is situated in the heart of London, 3 minutes from Paddington station and Hyde Park and 10 minutes' walk to Marble Arch and Oxford Street. Completely refurbished to a high standard, all rooms have en suite facilities, direct-dial telephone, tea/coffee-making facilities, hairdryer, Sky TV and ironing facilities. 24-hour reception.

Bedrooms: 4 single, 7 double/twin, 11 triple/multiple
Bathrooms: 22 en suite

Evening meal available
CC: Amex, Delta, Diners, Mastercard, Switch, Visa

10% discount on weekly bookings.

P

B&B per night:
S £45.00–£60.00
D £60.00–£85.00

OPEN All Year

GOLD & SILVER AWARDS

These exclusive ETC awards are given to establishments achieving the highest levels of quality and service. Further information can be found at the front of the guide and additional accommodation achieving these awards are shown in the listing at the back of this guide.

LONDON W2 continued

◆◆◆

LONDON GUARDS HOTEL
36-37 Lancaster Gate, London W2 3NA
T: (020) 7402 1101
F: (020) 7262 2551
E: info@londonguardshotel.co.uk
I: www.londonguardshotel.co.uk

Bedrooms: 2 single, 25 double/twin, 13 triple/multiple
Bathrooms: 40 en suite

Evening meal available
CC: Amex, Delta, Diners, Mastercard, Switch, Visa

B&B per night:
S £85.00–£120.00
D £95.00–£138.00

OPEN All Year

Close to Hyde Park, 6 minutes' walk to Heathrow Express, in a quiet residential area of Lancaster Gate. Bar and speciality restaurant.

◆

MANOR COURT HOTEL
7 Clanricarde Gardens, London W2 4JJ
T: (020) 7727 5407 & 7792 3361
F: (020) 7229 2875

Bedrooms: 5 single, 11 double/twin, 4 triple/multiple
Bathrooms: 12 en suite, 3 private

CC: Amex, Delta, Diners, Mastercard, Switch, Visa

B&B per night:
S £30.00–£45.00
D £45.00–£55.00

OPEN All Year

Bed and breakfast hotel within walking distance of Hyde Park and Kensington Gardens. Near Notting Hill Gate underground and Airbus stop. All rooms have colour TV and telephone.

◆◆◆

RHODES HOUSE HOTEL
195 Sussex Gardens, London W2 2RJ
T: (020) 7262 5617 & 7262 0537
F: (020) 7723 4054
E: chris@rhodeshotel.com
I: www.rhodeshotel.com

B&B per night:
S £50.00–£60.00
D £65.00–£80.00

OPEN All Year

All rooms with private facilities, air-conditioning, satellite TV, telephone, refrigerator, hairdryer, tea/coffee-making facilities and free internet access. Friendly atmosphere. Families especially welcome. Excellent transport for sightseeing and shopping.

Bedrooms: 3 single, 6 double/twin, 9 triple/multiple
Bathrooms: 18 en suite

CC: Mastercard, Switch, Visa

◆◆◆

ROSE COURT HOTEL
1-3 Talbot Square, London W2 1TR
T: (020) 7723 5128 & 7723 8671
F: (020) 7723 1855
E: rosehotel@aol.com
I: www.rosecourthotel.com

Bedrooms: 7 single, 25 double/twin, 11 triple/multiple
Bathrooms: 41 en suite

CC: Amex, Delta, Diners, Mastercard, Switch, Visa

B&B per night:
S £42.00–£60.00
D £52.00–£80.00

OPEN All Year

Privately-run Victorian townhouse in a quiet garden square. Close to Paddington and the West End.

◆◆

ST DAVID'S AND NORFOLK COURT HOTEL
16 Norfolk Square, Hyde Park, London W2 1RS
T: (020) 7723 3856
F: (020) 7402 9061
E: info@stdavidshotels.com
I: www.stdavidshotels.com

Bedrooms: 6 single, 10 double/twin, 34 triple/multiple
Bathrooms: 44 en suite

CC: Amex, Delta, Diners, Mastercard, Switch, Visa

B&B per night:
S £38.00–£50.00
D £58.00–£68.00

OPEN All Year

Recently refurbished. Situated in front of a quiet garden square, minutes from Paddington Station/Heathrow Express. Same ownership for over 20 years. Excellent English breakfast and service included.

IMPORTANT NOTE Information on accommodation listed in this guide has been supplied by the proprietors. As changes may occur you are advised to check details at the time of booking.

LONDON W2 continued

SPRINGFIELD HOTEL

154 Sussex Gardens, London W2 1UD
T: (020) 7723 9898
F: (020) 7723 0874
E: info@springfieldhotellondon.co.uk
I: www.springfieldhotellondon.co.uk

B&B per night:
S £35.00–£38.00
D £65.00–£70.00

OPEN All Year

Family-run bed and breakfast in excellent location close to Hyde Park, Marble Arch, Paddington and Oxford Street. All rooms are en suite with colour satellite TV, telephone, hairdryer, tea/coffee facilities and full central heating. Generous full English breakfast.

Bedrooms: 2 single, 12 double/twin, 6 triple/multiple
Bathrooms: 20 en suite

CC: Amex, Delta, Mastercard, Switch, Visa

1 child free under 14, Oct-Apr. 3 nights for price of 2 (must include Sunday), Nov-Mar.

P

LONDON W4

◆◆◆

CHISWICK LODGE

104 Turnham Green Terrace, London W4 1QN
T: (020) 8994 9926 & 8994 1712
F: (020) 8742 8238
E: chishot@clara.net
I: www.chiswick-hotel.co.uk

Bedrooms: 9 double/twin
Bathrooms: 9 en suite

CC: Amex, Delta, Diners, Mastercard, Switch, Visa

B&B per night:
S £50.00–£58.00
D £70.00–£78.00

OPEN All Year

New, high-quality accommodation, furnished to a high standard. All rooms are en suite.

P

◆◆

FOUBERT'S HOTEL

162-166 Chiswick High Road, London W4 1PR
T: (020) 8994 5202 & 8995 6743

Bedrooms: 15 single, 13 double/twin, 3 triple/multiple
Bathrooms: 31 en suite

Lunch available
Evening meal available
CC: Mastercard, Visa

B&B per night:
S £50.00–£55.00
D £65.00–£75.00

OPEN All Year

Family-run hotel, close to central London and Heathrow Airport. Fully licensed cafe/restaurant open daily 8am to 11pm. Children welcome.

◆◆◆

CHISWICK GUEST HOUSE

40 Spencer Road, Chiswick, London W4 3SP
T: (020) 8994 0876
E: bdoneill159@aol.com

Bedrooms: 1 single, 1 triple/multiple

B&B per night:
S £34.00–£43.00
D £45.00–£59.00

OPEN All Year except Christmas

Family run, overlooking fields, unrestricted parking. Easy access to central London/Heathrow Airport. Waterloo 20 minutes by rail. Rooms adapted to single, double, triple/family.

14 P

LONDON W5

◆◆

ABBEY LODGE HOTEL

51 Grange Park, Ealing, London W5 3PR
T: (020) 8567 7914
F: (020) 8579 5350
E: enquiries@londonlodgehotels.com
I: www.londonlodgehotels.com

Bedrooms: 10 single, 3 double/twin, 3 triple/multiple
Bathrooms: 16 en suite

CC: Delta, Diners, Mastercard, Switch, Visa

B&B per night:
S £45.00–£49.00
D £57.00–£62.00

OPEN All Year except Christmas

All rooms en suite, with colour TV, tea/coffee-making facilities and radio alarm clocks. Very close to 3 underground lines. Midway central London and Heathrow.

LONDON W5 continued

♦♦♦

GRANGE LODGE HOTEL

48-50 Grange Road, London W5 5BX
T: (020) 8567 1049
F: (020) 8579 5350
E: enquiries@londonlodgehotels.com
I: www.londonlodgehotels.com

Bedrooms: 8 single, 3 double/twin, 3 triple/multiple
Bathrooms: 9 en suite

CC: Delta, Diners, Mastercard, Switch, Visa

B&B per night:
S £45.00–£49.00
D £57.00–£62.00

OPEN All Year except Christmas

Quiet, comfortable hotel, close to 3 underground stations. Midway central London and Heathrow. Colour TV, tea/coffee-making facilities, radio/alarm, most rooms en suite.

LONDON W6

♦♦♦

NEW CENTURY INN

112 Shepherds Bush Road, Hammersmith, London W6 7PD
T: (020) 7751 1200 & 7603 5634
F: (020) 7751 1002
E: reservations@newcenturyinn.co.uk
I: www.newcenturyinn.co.uk

Bedrooms: 3 single, 6 double/twin, 3 triple/multiple
Bathrooms: 12 en suite

CC: Amex, Delta, Diners, Mastercard, Switch, Visa

B&B per night:
S £46.00–£54.00
D £66.00–£76.00

OPEN All Year

New, clean and comfortable B&B. Good-quality furnishings and fittings enhance your stay. The inn's good location enhances its overall package, including a good breakfast.

♦♦

HOTEL ORLANDO

83 Shepherds Bush Road, Hammersmith, London W6 7LR
T: (020) 7603 4890
F: (020) 7603 4890
E: hotelorlando@btconnect.com
I: www.hotelorlando.co.uk

Bedrooms: 4 single, 6 double/twin, 4 triple/multiple
Bathrooms: 14 en suite

CC: Amex, Delta, Mastercard, Switch, Visa

B&B per night:
S £40.00–£48.00
D £52.00–£60.00

OPEN All Year

Recently decorated, Italian family-run business for the last 22 years. Situated near Hammersmith tube station, ideal for easy connection to central London.

LONDON W8

HOTEL ATLAS-APOLLO

18-30 Lexham Gardens, London W8 5JE
T: (020) 7835 1155 & 7835 1133
F: (020) 7370 4853
E: reservations@atlas-apollo.com
I: www.atlas-apollo.com

B&B per night:
S £75.00–£80.00
D £90.00–£100.00

OPEN All Year

Friendly, long-established hotel, situated close to Earl's Court and Olympia exhibition centres and the shopping areas of Knightsbridge and Kensington High Street. Spacious, well-furnished bedrooms all with colour TV, direct-dial telephone and en suite bathroom.

Bedrooms: 28 single, 51 double/twin, 14 triple/multiple
Bathrooms: 93 en suite

CC: Amex, Delta, Mastercard, Switch, Visa

♦♦

CLEARLAKE HOTEL

18-19 Prince of Wales Terrace, Kensington, London W8 5PQ
T: (020) 7937 3274
F: (020) 7376 0604
E: clearlake@talk21.com
I: www.clearlakehotel.co.uk

Bedrooms: 2 single, 6 double/twin, 6 triple/multiple
Bathrooms: 14 en suite

CC: Amex, Diners, Mastercard, Visa

B&B per night:
S £40.00–£50.00
D £55.00–£75.00

OPEN All Year

Comfortable rooms in a hotel in a quiet cul-de-sac, with view of Hyde Park. Self-catering apartments also available. Close to shops and transport.

LONDON W14

AVONMORE HOTEL

66 Avonmore Road, Kensington, London W14 8RS
T: (020) 7603 3121 & 7603 4296
F: (020) 7603 4035
E: reservations@avonmorehotel.co.uk
I: www.avonmorehotel.co.uk

Award-winning, privately owned and run hotel with friendly atmosphere. Refurbished to highest standards, with all in-room facilities. Ideally situated for sights of London and Olympia and Earl's Court exhibition centres. Excellent value for money. Small enough to provide that personal touch.

Bedrooms: 1 single, 5 double/twin, 3 triple/multiple; permanent suite(s)
Bathrooms: 7 en suite

CC: Amex, Delta, Diners, Mastercard, Switch, Visa

B&B per night:
S £73.00–£95.00
D £90.00–£105.00

OPEN All Year

LONDON WC1

CRESCENT HOTEL

49-50 Cartwright Gardens, Bloomsbury, London WC1H 9EL
T: (020) 7387 1515
F: (020) 7383 2054
E: General.Enquiries@CrescentHotelofLondon.com
I: www.CrescentHotelofLondon.com

Comfortable, elegant, family-run hotel in quiet Georgian crescent, with private garden square and tennis courts. All rooms have colour TV, tea/coffee tray and direct-dial telephone, most en suite. The individually prepared English breakfast will sustain you for the best part of the day.

Bedrooms: 12 single, 5 double/twin, 10 triple/multiple
Bathrooms: 18 en suite

CC: Delta, Mastercard, Switch, Visa

10% discount on stays of 3 nights, to include Sun and Mon (excl Christmas and New Year).

B&B per night:
S £44.00–£74.00
D £85.00–£89.00

OPEN All Year

♦

GOWER HOUSE HOTEL

57 Gower Street, London WC1E 6HJ
T: (020) 7636 4685
F: (020) 7636 4685
E: info@gowerhousehotel.co.uk
I: www.gowerhousehotel.co.uk

Bedrooms: 2 single, 7 double/twin, 4 triple/multiple
Bathrooms: 6 en suite

CC: Mastercard, Switch, Visa

Friendly bed and breakfast hotel within easy walking distance of the British Museum, shops, theatres and restaurants. Near Goodge Street underground station and Euston station.

B&B per night:
S £40.00–£50.00
D £55.00–£75.00

OPEN All Year except Christmas

♦

ST ATHANS HOTEL

20 Tavistock Place, Russell Square, London WC1H 9RE
T: (020) 7837 9140 & 7837 9627
F: (020) 7833 8352
E: stathans@ukonline.co.uk
I: www.stathanshotel.com

Bedrooms: 14 single, 28 double/twin, 6 triple/multiple
Bathrooms: 8 en suite

CC: Amex, Diners, Mastercard, Visa

Simple, small but clean family-run hotel offering bed and breakfast.

B&B per night:
S £30.00–£38.00
D £40.00–£48.00

OPEN All Year

CREDIT CARD BOOKINGS If you book by telephone and are asked for your credit card number it is advisable to check the proprietor's policy should you cancel your reservation.

LONDON WC1 continued

♦♦♦♦

STAUNTON HOTEL

13-15 Gower Street, Bloomsbury, London WC1E 6HE
T: (020) 7580 2740
F: (020) 7580 3554
E: enquiries@stauntonhotel.com
I: www.stauntonhotel.com

Grade II Listed Georgian townhouse boasting luxurious decor and warm atmosphere. Only a few minutes' walk to British Museum, Oxford Street, theatreland, Covent Garden etc. All rooms en suite.

Bedrooms: 1 single, 16 double/twin; permanent suite(s)
Bathrooms: 17 en suite

CC: Amex, Delta, Diners, Mastercard, Switch, Visa

B&B per night:
S £70.00–£99.00
D £110.00–£140.00

OPEN All Year

16

LONDON WC2

♦♦

ROYAL ADELPHI HOTEL

21 Villiers Street, London
WC2N 6ND
T: (020) 7930 8764
F: (020) 7930 8735
E: info@royaladelphi.co.uk
I: www.royaladelphi.co.uk

Bedrooms: 20 single, 25 double/twin, 2 triple/multiple
Bathrooms: 34 en suite

Lunch available
Evening meal available
CC: Amex, Delta, Diners, Mastercard, Switch, Visa

B&B per night:
S £55.00–£75.00
D £78.00–£100.00

OPEN All Year except Christmas

Centrally located and ideal for theatreland, near Embankment and Charing Cross underground. All rooms with colour TV, hairdryer, tea/coffee facilities. Most rooms have private bathrooms.

OUTER LONDON
CROYDON *Tourist Information Centre Tel: (020) 8253 1009*

♦♦

ALPHA GUEST HOUSE

99 Brigstock Road, Thornton Heath
CR7 7JL
T: (020) 8684 4811 & 8665 0032
F: (020) 8405 0302

Bedrooms: 5 single, 5 double/twin, 1 triple/multiple
Bathrooms: 6 en suite

B&B per night:
S £30.00–£35.00
D £45.00–£50.00

OPEN All Year except Christmas

Modern, family-run residence in ideal location near Croydon (20 minutes from Victoria station). Tea and coffee-making facilities, satellite TV, free parking and varied breakfasts.

P

♦♦♦

CROYDON FRIENDLY GUESTHOUSE

16 St Peter's Road, Croydon
CR0 1HD
T: (020) 8680 4428 & 07989 924 988
F: (020) 8658 5385
E: bilal@bhasan.fsnet.co.uk

Bedrooms: 5 single, 1 double/twin
Bathrooms: 2 en suite

B&B per night:
S £25.00–£30.00

OPEN All Year

Detached house with comfortable, well-appointed rooms, all with private facilities. Friendly, family atmosphere with ample off-road parking. Perfect base for London or Croydon.

1 P

♦♦♦

CROYDON HOTEL

112 Lower Addiscombe Road, Croydon CR0 6AD
T: (020) 8656 7233
F: (020) 8655 0211
I: www.croydonhotel.co.uk

Bedrooms: 1 single, 5 double/twin, 2 triple/multiple
Bathrooms: 7 en suite

CC: Delta, Mastercard, Visa

B&B per night:
S £35.00–£55.00
D £55.00–£70.00

OPEN All Year

Close to central Croydon (route A222) and 10 minutes' walk from East Croydon station. Opposite shops and restaurants. Frequent direct trains to Victoria and Gatwick Airport.

P

ACCESSIBILITY

Look for the symbols which indicate National Accessible Scheme standards for hearing and visually impaired guests in addition to standards for guests with mobility impairment. Additional participants are shown in the listings at the back.

CROYDON continued

♦♦♦

FOXLEY MOUNT

44 Foxley Lane, Purley CR8 3EE
T: (020) 8660 9751
F: (020) 8645 9368
E: enquiries@foxleymount.co.uk
I: www.foxleymount.co.uk

Bedrooms: 1 single, 1 double/twin, 1 triple/multiple

B&B per night:
S £25.00–£30.00
D £45.00

HB per person:
DY £25.00–£30.00

OPEN All Year except Christmas

Large Edwardian house, family-run bed and breakfast. Walking distance to Purley station. Twenty minutes to Gatwick or central London by train.

5 P

HARROW

CRESCENT HOTEL

58-62 Welldon Crescent, Harrow HA1 1QR
T: (020) 8863 5491
F: (020) 8427 5965
E: jivraj@crsnthtl.demon.co.uk
I: www.crsnthtl.demon.co.uk

Bedrooms: 10 single, 8 double/twin, 2 triple/multiple
Bathrooms: 16 en suite

CC: Amex, Delta, Diners, Mastercard, Switch, Visa

B&B per night:
S £40.00–£50.00
D £55.00–£65.00

HB per person:
DY £58.00–£68.00

OPEN All Year

Modern, friendly hotel with full facilities in the heart of Harrow. Five minutes to underground, easy access to Wembley, West End, Heathrow and major motorways.

P

HINDES HOTEL

8 Hindes Road, Harrow HA1 1SJ
T: (020) 8427 7468 & 8427 7272
F: (020) 8424 0673
E: reception@hindeshotel.com
I: www.hindeshotel.com

Bedrooms: 4 single, 10 double/twin
Bathrooms: 7 en suite

CC: Amex, Delta, Diners, Mastercard, Switch, Visa

B&B per night:
S £39.00–£49.00
D £50.00–£59.00

OPEN All Year

Situated near the M4 and M1. West End 15 minutes by underground. Convenient for Wembley Stadium and Heathrow Airport (25 minutes). Tube and train 5 minutes' walk.

P

HEATHROW AIRPORT

See under Hounslow

HOUNSLOW *Tourist Information Centre Tel: (020) 8572 8279*

LAMPTON PARK GUESTHOUSE

4 Lampton Park Road, Hounslow TW3 4HS
T: (020) 8572 8622
E: michael.duff1@virgin.net

Bedrooms: 2 single, 2 double/twin
Bathrooms: 2 en suite

B&B per night:
S £35.00–£40.00
D £60.00

OPEN All Year except Christmas

Large converted family house in quiet cul-de-sac, close to shops, amenities and only 35 minutes to London's West End by tube.

2 P

SHALIMAR HOTEL

215-221 Staines Road, Hounslow TW3 3JJ
T: (020) 8577 7070 & 0500 238239
F: (020) 8569 6789
E: shalimarhotel@aol.com
I: www.s-h-systems.co.uk/hotels/shalimar.html

B&B per night:
S Max £55.00
D Max £65.00

OPEN All Year

Located in centre of Hounslow, close to underground, M4, M25, M3 and 3 miles from Heathrow. Fantastic shopping centre within walking distance. En suite rooms, colour TV, tea/coffee bar. Beautiful illuminated large lawn and garden. TV lounge and bar.

Bedrooms: 14 single, 27 double/twin, 5 triple/multiple
Bathrooms: 30 en suite

Evening meal available
CC: Amex, Delta, Diners, Mastercard, Switch, Visa

P

HALF BOARD PRICES Half board prices are given per person, but in some cases these may be based on double/twin occupancy.

ILFORD

◆◆◆

PARK HOTEL

327 Cranbrook Road, Ilford IG1 4UE
T: (020) 8554 9616 & 8554 7187
F: (020) 8518 2700
E: parkhotelilford@netscapeonline.co.uk
I: www.the-park-hotel.co.uk

Bedrooms: 9 single, 9 double/twin, 2 triple/multiple
Bathrooms: 17 en suite, 1 private

Evening meal available
CC: Delta, Mastercard, Switch, Visa

B&B per night:
S £33.50–£49.50
D £46.50–£80.00

OPEN All Year except Christmas

Homely, comfortable establishment opposite park and within walking distance of underground and train stations.

P

MORDEN

◆◆

28 MONKLEIGH ROAD

Morden SM4 4EW
T: (020) 8542 5595 & 8287 7494

Bedrooms: 1 single, 1 double/twin

B&B per night:
S £17.50–£18.00
D £35.00–£36.00

OPEN All Year except Christmas

Clean and comfortable family-run bed and breakfast. With easy access to main London attractions and Wimbledon tennis. Approximately 45 minutes to Heathrow or Gatwick.

5

RICHMOND *Tourist Information Centre Tel: (020) 8940 9125*

◆◆◆

IVY COTTAGE

Upper Ham Road, Ham Common, Richmond TW10 5LA
T: (020) 8940 8601
F: (020) 8940 3865
E: taylor@dbta.freeserve.co.uk
I: www.dbta.freeserve.co.uk

Bedrooms: 1 double/twin, 1 triple/multiple
Bathrooms: 2 private

Evening meal available

B&B per night:
S £25.00–£30.00
D £45.00–£50.00

OPEN All Year

Charming, Wisteria-clad Georgian home offering exceptional views over Ham Common. Period features dating from 1760. Large garden. Self-catering an option. Good bus route and parking.

◆◆◆

PRO KEW GARDENS B & B

15 Pensford Avenue, Kew Gardens, Richmond TW9 4HR
T: (020) 8876 3354
E: info@prokewbandb.demon.co.uk

B&B per night:
S £25.00–£32.50
D £50.00–£65.00

OPEN All Year except Christmas

Quiet, detached Edwardian house close to Kew Gardens, Public Records Office and underground station. Unrestricted parking on-street. The rooms on the first floor are for exclusive use of guests and are non-smoking. Hospitable welcome, continental breakfast. Minimum stay 2 nights.

Bedrooms: 2 single, 2 double/twin
Bathrooms: 1 en suite

Reduction of £20 for stays of 7 nights.

5

◆◆◆

QUINNS HOTEL

48 Sheen Road, Richmond TW9 1AW
T: (020) 8940 5444
F: (020) 8940 1828
E: enquiries@quinnshotel.com
I: www.quinnshotel.com

Bedrooms: 6 single, 31 double/twin, 1 triple/multiple
Bathrooms: 23 en suite

Evening meal available
CC: Amex, Delta, Diners, Mastercard, Switch, Visa

B&B per night:
S £70.00
D £90.00

HB per person:
DY £62.50–£87.50

OPEN All Year

Ideally located for business or pleasure, within easy reach of central London, airports and local places of interest.

P

VISITOR ATTRACTIONS For ideas on places to visit refer to the introduction at the beginning of this section. Look out too for the ETC's Quality Assured Visitor Attraction signs.

RICHMOND continued

THE RED COW

59 Sheen Road, Richmond TW9 1YJ
T: (020) 8940 2511
F: (020) 8940 2581
E: tom@redcowpub.com

B&B per night:
S £60.00–£70.00
D £70.00–£80.00

OPEN All Year

Traditional Victorian inn that has retained some lovely original features. Just a short walk from Richmond town centre, river, Royal parks and rail links to London. Tom and Carmel Dillon welcome you to their friendly, local inn.

Bedrooms: 4 double/twin
Bathrooms: 4 en suite

Lunch available
Evening meal available
CC: Delta, Mastercard, Switch, Visa

THE ROSE OF YORK

Petersham Road, Richmond TW10 6UY
T: (020) 8948 5867
F: (020) 8332 6986
E: roseofyork@compuserve.com

B&B per night:
S £85.00
D £95.00–£120.00

OPEN All Year

You will find The Rose of York situated on the lower slopes of leafy Richmond Hill, overlooking Petersham Meadows of the River Thames. Converted to a fine traditional pub, it offers a warm welcome and comfortable stay. English Carvery and food available throughout the year to enhance the general atmosphere of a traditional country inn.

Bedrooms: 10 double/twin, 2 triple/multiple; permanent suite(s)
Bathrooms: 12 en suite

Lunch available
Evening meal available
CC: Amex, Delta, Mastercard, Switch, Visa

Weekend breaks (incl Fri) from £150 per double standard room, minimum 2 nights. Group or coach bookings available.

P

UPMINSTER

CORNER FARM

Corner Farm, Fen Lane,
North Ockendon, Upminster
RM14 3RB
T: (01708) 851310
F: (01708) 852025
E: corner.farm@virgin.net

Bedrooms: 1 single, 2 double/twin, 1 triple/multiple
Bathrooms: 1 en suite

CC: Mastercard, Visa

B&B per night:
S £25.00–£35.00
D £35.00–£40.00

OPEN All Year

Attractive detached bungalow in rural setting. Breakfast served in farmhouse conservatory (30 metres). No public transport. Friendly atmosphere. Parking. No smoking, children under 10 or pets.

P

WEMBLEY

ADELPHI HOTEL

4 Forty Lane, Wembley HA9 9EB
T: (020) 8904 5629 & 89085629
F: (020) 8908 5314
E: adel@dial.pipex.com
I: www.hoteladelphi.co.uk

Bedrooms: 4 single, 7 double/twin, 2 triple/multiple
Bathrooms: 9 en suite

CC: Amex, Delta, Diners, Mastercard, Switch, Visa

B&B per night:
S £35.00–£42.00
D £45.00–£55.00

OPEN All Year

Close to Wembley Stadium and Wembley Park underground, 15 minutes from West End. Attractive decor. TV lounge, tea/coffee in rooms.

P

QUALITY ASSURANCE SCHEME

Diamond ratings and awards were correct at the time of going to press but are subject to change. Please check at the time of booking.

WORCESTER PARK

◆◆◆

THE GRAYE HOUSE
24 The Glebe, Worcester Park
KT4 7PF
T: (020) 8330 1277 &
07733 150621
F: (020) 8255 7850
E: graye.house@virgin.net
I: www.smoothhound.co.uk

Bedrooms: 4 double/
twin, 2 triple/multiple
Bathrooms: 4 en suite

B&B per night:
S £30.00–£35.00
D £50.00–£55.00

OPEN All Year

A modern, comfortable townhouse which serves as a family home. Rooms are en suite. Close to stations and amenities. Annexe with 4 larger rooms also available.

P

CUMBRIA

Cumbria's dramatic and breathtaking landscapes, from the famous Lakes to the rugged mountains and fells, have inspired poets and artists for hundreds of years.

classic sights

Hadrian's Wall – a reminder of Roman occupation
Lake Windermere – largest lake in England

coast & country

Scafell Pike – England's highest mountain
Whitehaven – historic port

literary links

William Wordsworth – the poet's homes: Wordsworth House, Dove Cottage and Rydal Mount
Beatrix Potter – her home, Hill Top; her watercolours at the Beatrix Potter Gallery and the tales at The World of Beatrix Potter

distinctively different

The Gondola – sail Coniston Water aboard the opulent 1859 steam yacht Gondola
Cars of the Stars Museum – cars from TV and film, including Chitty Chitty Bang Bang and the Batmobile

The county of Cumbria

FOR MORE INFORMATION CONTACT:
Cumbria Tourist Board
Ashleigh, Holly Road, Windermere,
Cumbria LA23 2AQ
Tel: (015394) 44444 Fax: (015394) 44041
Email: info@golakes.co.uk
Internet: www.golakes.co.uk

The Pictures: 1 Bluebells at Brantwood, Coniston 2 Hound trailing 3 Old jetty on Derwentwater

PLACES TO VISIT - see pages 66-69 > WHERE TO STAY - see pages 70-104

PLACES to visit

You will find hundreds of interesting places to visit during your sta just some of which are listed in these pages. Contact any Touris Information Centre in the region for more ideas on days out.

Awarded ETC's new 'Quality Assured Visitor Attraction' marque at time of going to press. (See page 19).

Aquarium of the Lakes

Lakeside, Newby Bridge, Ulverston
Tel: (015395) 30153
www.aquariumofthelakes.co.uk
Britain's leading freshwater aquarium featuring the UK's largest collection of freshwater fish. A unique experience for all ages. Open all year. Coffee shop and gift shops.

The Beacon

West Strand, Whitehaven
Tel: (01946) 592302 www.copelandbc.gov.uk
Award-winning attraction and museum superbly situated overlooking the Georgian harbour of Whitehaven, one of Englands 'gem towns'.

Birdoswald Roman Fort

Gilsland, Brampton
Tel: (016977) 47602
www.birdoswaldromanfort.org
Remains of Roman fort on one of the best parts of Hadrian's Wall with excellent views of the Irthing Gorge. Exhibition, shop, tearoom and excavations.

Cars of the Stars Motor Museum

Standish Street, Keswick
Tel: (017687) 73757 www.carsofthestars.com
Features TV and film vehicles including the Batmobile, Chitty Chitty Bang Bang, the James Bond collection, Herbie, FAB 1, plus many other famous cars and motorcycles.

The Dock Museum

North Road, Barrow-in-Furness
Tel: (01229) 894444 www.dockmuseum.org.uk
Spectacular modern museum built over an original Victorian graving dock. Galleries include multi-media interactives and impressive ship models.

Dove Cottage and Wandsworth Museum

Town End, Grasmere, Ambleside
Tel: (015394) 35544 www.wordsworth.org.uk
Wordsworth's home from 1799-1808. Museum with manuscripts, farmhouse reconstruction, paintings and drawings, poet's possessions. Special events throughout the year.

English Heritage Furness Abbey

Barrow-in-Furness
Tel: (01229) 823420
Ruins of 12thC Cistercian abbey, the second-wealthiest ir England. Extensive remains include transepts, choir and west tower of church, canopied seats, arches, church.

Gleaston Water Mill

Gleaston, Ulverston
Tel: (01229) 869244 www.watermill.co.uk
Water-driven corn mill in working order. Impressive wooden machinery and water-wheel. Farm equipment and tools display. Craft workshop, craft videos and rare breeds.

Heron Glass Ltd

The Lakes Glass Centre, Oubas Hill, Ulverston,
Tel: (01229) 581121 www.herongiftware.com
Heron Glass Ltd and Cumbria Crystal: handblown glass-making demonstrations, giftware, lead crystal, Lighthouse cafe and restaurant, Gateway to Furness exhibition.

Hollywood Park Leisure Complex

Hindpool Road, Barrow-in-Furness
Hollywood Park is an exciting leisure facility with restaurants, shops, cinema, health club, superbowl and bingo. Adjacent is the Owl and Pussycat with its large Wacky Warehouse Playbarn.

Jennings Brothers plc

The Castle Brewery, Cockermouth
Tel: (01900) 821011 www.jenningsbrewery.co.uk
Guided tours of Jennings traditional brewery and sampling of the ales in the Old Cooperage Bar.

K Village Outlet Centre

Lound Road, Netherfield, Kendal
Tel: (01539) 732363 www.kvillage.co.uk
Famous-name brands such as K-shoes, Van Heusen, Denby, National Trust Shop, Tog24 and Ponden Mill all discounted. Open seven days a week with full disabled access.

The Lake District Visitor Centre

Brockhole, Windermere
Tel: (015394) 46601 www.lake-district.gov.uk
Brockhole is an Edwardian house on the shores of Windermere with extensive landscaped gardens, superb views, lake cruises, adventure playground, walks, events and activities.

Lakeland Motor Museum, Holker Hall & Gardens

Holker Hall, Cark in Cartmel, Grange-over-Sands
Tel: (015395) 58509 www.holker-hall.co.uk
Over 10,000 exhibits including rare motoring automobilia. A 1930's garage re-creation and the Campbell Legend Bluebird Exhibition. Formal and woodland garden, deer park, adventure playground, cafe, gift shop.

Lakeland Sheep and Wool Centre

Egremont Road, Cockermouth
Tel: (01900) 822673 www.shepherdshotel.co.uk
Live farm show including cows, sheep, dogs and ducks, all displaying their working qualities. Large gift shop and licensed cafe/restaurant. All-weather attraction.

Lakeland Wildlife Oasis

Hale, Milnthorpe
Tel: (015395) 63027 www.wildlifeoasis.co.uk
A wildlife exhibition where both living animals and inanimate hands-on displays are used to illustrate evolution in the animal kingdom. Includes gift shop and cafe.

Lakeside and Haverthwaite Railway

Haverthwaite Station, Ulverston
Tel: (015395) 31594
Standard-gauge steam railway operating a daily seasonal service through the beautiful Leven Valley. Steam and diesel locomotives on display

Levens Hall

Levens, Kendal
Tel: (015395) 60321 www.levenshall.co.uk
Elizabethan home of the Bagot family incorporating 13thC pele tower. World-famous topiary gardens, Bellingham Buttery, Potting Shed Gift Shop, plant centre and play area.

> The Pictures: 1 Lake Windermere
2 St Nicholas Church, Whitehaven
3 Steam train at Haverthwaite Station
4 Fell Foot National Trust Park, Windermere
5 Waterfall in the Dudden Valley

National Trust Hill Top

Near Sawrey, Ambleside
Tel: (015394) 36269 www.nationaltrust.org.uk
Beatrix Potter wrote many of her popular Peter Rabbit stories and other books in this charming little house which still contains her own china and furniture.

National Trust Sizergh Castle

Kendal
Tel: (015395) 60070 www.nationaltrust.org.uk
Strickland family home for 750 years, now National Trust owned. With 14thC pele tower, 15thC great hall, 16thC wings. Stuart connections. Rock garden, rose garden, daffodils.

National Trust Steam Yacht Gondola

Pier Cottage, Coniston
Tel: (015394) 41962 www.nationaltrust.org.uk
Victorian steam-powered vessel, now National Trust owned and completely renovated with an opulently upholstered saloon. Superb way to appreciate the beauty of Coniston Water.

Rheged - The Village in the Hill

Redhills, Penrith
Tel: (01768) 868000 www.rheged.com
Europe's largest grass-covered building, Rheged shows three movies daily on a giant screen and is home to Helly Hanson Mountaineering Exhibition.

The Rum Story

27 Lowther Street, Whitehaven
Tel: (01946) 592933 www.rumstory.co.uk
An authentic, heritage-based experience depicting the unique story of the UK rum trade in the original Jefferson's wine-merchant premises.

Rydal Mount and Gardens

Ambleside
Tel: (015394) 33002 www.wordsworthlakes.co.uk
The 'most beloved' home of William Wordsworth from 1813-1850, nestling between the majestic fells, Lake Windermere and Rydal Water.

Sellafield Visitor Centre

Sellafield, Seascale
Tel: (019467) 27027
The centre has undergone major refurbishment and contains exhibits on the energy debate including the exhibition 'sparking reaction' which was designed and installed by the Science Museum in London. Visit the immersion cinema where you can interact with the film via a touch-screen terminal.

Senhouse Roman Museum

The Battery, Sea Brows, Maryport
Tel: (01900) 816168
Once the headquarters of Hadrian's coastal defence system. UK's largest group of Roman altar stones and inscriptions on one site.

South Lakes Wild Animal Park Ltd

Crossgates, Dalton-in-Furness
Tel: (01229) 466086 www.wildanimalpark.co.uk
Wild zoo park in over 17 acres (7ha) of grounds with over 120 species of animals from around the world including giraffe, rhino, lion and tiger. Miniature railway, toilets, car/coach park.

South Tynedale Railway

Railway Station, Alston
Tel: (01434) 381696 www.strps.org.uk
Narrow-gauge railway operating along 2.25-mile (3.6-km) line from Alston to Kirkhaugh through scenic South Tyne Valley with preserved steam and diesel engines.

Tullie House Museum and Art Gallery

Castle Street, Carlisle
Tel: (01228) 534781 www.tulliehouse.co.uk
Georgian mansion housing magnificent pre-Raphaelite collection and Victorian childhood gallery.

Ullswater 'Steamers'

13 Maude Street, Kendal
Tel: (017684) 82229 www.ullswater-steamers.co.uk
Relax and enjoy a beautiful Ullswater cruise with walks and picnic areas. Boat services operating all year round.

Windermere Lake Cruises

Lakeside, Newby Bridge, Ulverston
Tel: (015395) 31188
www.windermere-lakecruises.co.uk
Steamers and launches sail between Ambleside, Bowness and Lakeside. Forty-minute cruises operate daily from Bowness. Timetables, public services. Private charters available.

The World of Beatrix Potter

The Old Laundry, Crag Brow, Bowness-on-Windermere
Tel: (015394) 88444 www.hop-skip-jump.com
The life and works of Beatrix Potter presented on a nine-screen video wall.

Find out more about Cumbria

1

Further information about holidays and attractions in Cumbria is available from:

CUMBRIA TOURIST BOARD

Ashleigh, Holly Road, Windermere, Cumbria LA23 2AQ.

Tel: (015394) 44444 Fax: (015394) 44041

Email: info@golakes.co.uk

Internet: www.golakes.co.uk

The following publications are available from Cumbria Tourist Board:

Cumbria Tourist Board Holiday Guide (free) Tel: 08705 133059

Events Listings (free)

Cumbria The Lake District Touring Map
including tourist information and touring caravan and camping parks - £3.95

Laminated Poster - £4.50

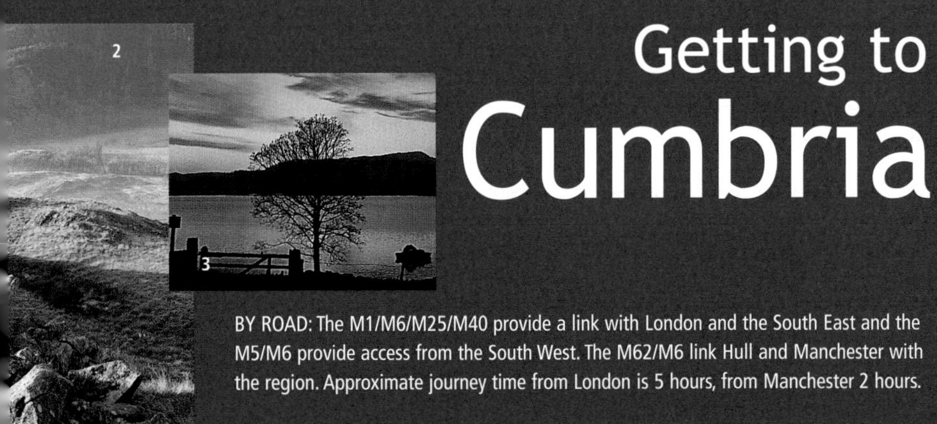

Getting to Cumbria

BY ROAD: The M1/M6/M25/M40 provide a link with London and the South East and the M5/M6 provide access from the South West. The M62/M6 link Hull and Manchester with the region. Approximate journey time from London is 5 hours, from Manchester 2 hours.

BY RAIL: From London (Euston) to Oxenholme (Kendal) takes approximately 3 hours 30 minutes. From Oxenholme (connecting station for all main line trains) to Windermere takes approximately 20 minutes. From Carlisle to Barrow-in-Furness via the coastal route, with stops at many of the towns in between, takes approximately 2 hours. Trains from Edinburgh to Carlisle take 1 hour 45 minutes. The historic Settle-Carlisle line also runs through the county bringing passengers from Yorkshire via the Eden Valley.

www.travelcumbria.co.uk

> The Pictures: 1 Ullswater 2 Thirlmere Valley, Lake District 3 Lake Windermere

Where to stay in Cumbria

Accommodation entries in this region are listed in alphabetical order of place name, and then in alphabetical order of establishment.

Map references refer to the colour location maps at the front of this guide. The first number indicates the map to use; the letter and number which follow refer to the grid reference on the map.

At-a-glance symbols at the end of each accommodation entry give useful information about services and facilities. A key to symbols can be found inside the back cover flap. Keep this open for easy reference.

A brief description of the towns and villages offering accommodation in the entries which follow, can be found at the end of this section.

A complete listing of all the English Tourism Council assessed accommodation covered by this guide appears at the back of the guide.

AINSTABLE, Cumbria Map ref 5B2

♦♦♦♦

BELL HOUSE
Ainstable, Carlisle CA4 9RE
T: (01768) 896255 & 07767 888636
F: (01768) 896255
E: mrobinson@bellhouse.fsbusiness.co.uk

Bedrooms: 1 double/twin
Bathrooms: 1 en suite

12-acre mixed farm. Situated in own grounds with breathtaking views. Excellent accommodation in the Eden Valley. Ideal for walking, riding or exploring Cumbria.

P

B&B per night:
S £22.50
D £45.00

OPEN All Year

ALLONBY, Cumbria Map ref 5A2

SHIP HOTEL
Main Street, Allonby, Maryport CA15 6QF
T: (01900) 881017
F: (01900) 881017
E: theshipallonby@aol.com

Bedrooms: 1 single, 4 double/twin, 4 triple/multiple; permanent suite(s)
Bathrooms: 5 en suite, 1 private

Lunch available
Evening meal available
CC: Mastercard, Visa

A 17thC Grade II Listed coaching inn where Charles Dickens and Wilkie Collins stayed in 1857. Situated on the Solway coastline, close to Lake District.

P

B&B per night:
S £20.00–£35.00
D £50.00–£75.00

OPEN All Year

GOLD & SILVER AWARDS

These exclusive ETC awards are given to establishments achieving the highest levels of quality and service. Further information can be found at the front of the guide and additional accommodation achieving these awards are shown in the listing at the back of this guide.

ALSTON, Cumbria Map ref 5B2

◆◆◆

BROWNSIDE HOUSE
Leadgate, Alston CA9 3EL
T: (01434) 382169 & 382100
E: brownside_hse@hotmail.com
I: www.cumbria1st.com/brown_side/index.htm

Bedrooms: 3 double/twin

Evening meal available
CC: Delta, Mastercard, Switch, Visa

Brownside House (dated 1849) is set in the countryside just outside Alston, with superb views of the South Tyne Valley. Easy reach Lake District/Hadrian's Wall.

P

B&B per night:
S £18.00
D £36.00

HB per person:
DY £24.50

OPEN All Year

AMBLESIDE, Cumbria Map ref 5A3 *Tourist Information Centre Tel: (015394) 32582*

◆◆◆◆◆
Silver Award

AMBLESIDE COUNTRY HOTEL – GREY FRIAR LODGE

Clappersgate, Ambleside LA22 9NE
T: (01539) 433158
F: (01539) 433158
E: greyfriar@veen.freeserve.co.uk
I: www.cumbria-hotels.co.uk

A warm welcome awaits visitors to Pamela and David Veen's country house. This delightful former vicarage enjoys magnificent views of the Brathay River and fells. The house is tastefully furnished with antiques and bric-a-brac. Most en suite bedrooms have antique or 4-poster beds. Good traditional cooking is enjoyed by all.

Bedrooms: 9 double/twin
Bathrooms: 7 en suite, 1 private

Evening meal available
CC: Delta, Mastercard, Switch, Visa

3-and 7-day break rates.

12 P

B&B per night:
S £38.00–£68.00
D £56.00–£105.00

HB per person:
DY £48.00–£68.00

◆◆◆

BROADVIEW
Low Fold, Lake Road, Ambleside LA22 0DN
T: (01539) 432431
E: enquiries@broadviewguesthouse.co.uk
I: www.broadviewguesthouse.co.uk

Bedrooms: 4 double/twin, 2 triple/multiple
Bathrooms: 3 en suite, 1 private

CC: Amex, Delta, Mastercard, Switch, Visa

Quality, friendly Victorian guesthouse near lake and village. Some rooms en suite with lovely views. Great breakfasts and a warm welcome. Non-smoking establishment.

B&B per night:
S £20.00–£38.00
D £36.00–£50.00

OPEN All Year

◆◆◆

CLAREMONT HOUSE
Compston Road, Ambleside LA22 9DJ
T: (01539) 433448
F: (01539) 433448
E: enquiries@claremontambleside.co.uk
I: www.claremontambleside.co.uk

Bedrooms: 1 single, 5 double/twin, 1 triple/multiple
Bathrooms: 6 en suite

CC: Amex, Delta, Diners, Mastercard, Switch, Visa

All rooms have colour TV, tea/coffee-making facilites and most have en suite facilities. Cycles secured at night.

B&B per night:
S £20.00–£27.50
D £40.00–£55.00

OPEN All Year

◆◆◆◆

THE DOWER HOUSE
Wray Castle, Ambleside LA22 0JA
T: (01539) 433211

Bedrooms: 3 double/twin
Bathrooms: 3 en suite

Evening meal available

The house overlooks Lake Windermere, 3 miles from Ambleside. Situated through the main gates of Wray Castle and up the drive. A bird-watcher's paradise.

5 P

B&B per night:
S £27.00–£28.00
D £52.00–£54.00

HB per person:
DY £40.00

OPEN All Year except Christmas

SYMBOLS The symbols in each entry give information about services and facilities. A key to these symbols appears at the back of this guide.

AMBLESIDE continued

♦♦♦♦

ELDER GROVE
Lake Road, Ambleside LA22 0DB
T: (01539) 432504
F: (01539) 432251
E: info@eldergrove.co.uk
I: www.eldergrove.co.uk

Bedrooms: 2 single, 7 double/twin, 1 triple/multiple
Bathrooms: 10 en suite

CC: Delta, Mastercard, Switch, Visa

Enjoy quality accommodation and service in our Victorian house. Pretty bedrooms with private bathrooms, relaxing bar and lounge, hearty Cumbrian breakfast, car park. Non-smoking.

B&B per night:
S £25.50–£33.00
D £51.00–£70.00

OPEN All Year except Christmas

♦♦♦

FERN COTTAGE
6 Waterhead Terrace, Ambleside LA22 0HA
T: (01539) 433007

Bedrooms: 3 double/twin

Homely Lakeland-stone cottage on edge of village. Two minutes to head of Lake Windermere and steamer pier. Friendly atmosphere, hearty breakfast. Non-smoking.

B&B per night:
S £20.00–£22.00
D £32.00–£36.00

OPEN All Year except Christmas

♦♦♦

FERNDALE HOTEL
Lake Road, Ambleside LA22 0DB
T: (01539) 432207
E: info@ferndalehotel.com
I: www.ferndalehotel.com

Bedrooms: 1 single, 9 double/twin
Bathrooms: 10 en suite

CC: Delta, Mastercard, Switch, Visa

Small, family-run hotel in the heart of the Lakes, offering comfortable accommodation and traditional English fare. En suite bedrooms, some with views of the surrounding mountains and fells.

B&B per night:
S £22.00–£26.00
D £42.00–£52.00

OPEN All Year except Christmas

♦♦♦♦

GHYLL HEAD HOTEL
Waterhead, Ambleside LA22 0HD
T: (01539) 432360
F: (01539) 434062
E: ghyllhead@btopenworld.com
I: www.hotelscumbria.com

Splendidly situated Lakeland hotel in its own grounds overlooking Lake Windermere and the rolling fells and mountains beyond, just a short stroll from Ambleside town. All spacious bedrooms have en suite facilities and colour TVs. Private parking available.

Bedrooms: 10 double/twin, 2 triple/multiple; permanent suite(s)
Bathrooms: 12 en suite

Evening meal available
CC: Mastercard, Switch, Visa

B&B per night:
D £85.00–£130.00

OPEN All Year

LAUREL VILLA
Lake Road, Ambleside LA22 0DB
T: (01539) 433240
F: (01539) 433240
E: laurelvilla_ambleside@hotmail.com

Substantial detached Victorian house once visited by children's author Beatrix Potter. Spacious en suite bedrooms, some with 4-poster beds and jacuzzi, decorated in William Morris style, with fell views. Within easy walking distance of Lake Windermere and 1 minute's walk from Ambleside village. Accessible private car park.

Bedrooms: 10 double/twin, 2 triple/multiple
Bathrooms: 12 en suite

B&B per night:
S £25.00–£35.00
D £50.00–£70.00

OPEN All Year

AMBLESIDE continued

♦♦♦ **LYNDHURST HOTEL**
Wansfell Road, Ambleside LA22 0EG
T: (01539) 432421
F: (01539) 432421
E: lyndhurst@amblesidehotels.co.uk
I: www.amblesidehotels.co.uk

Bedrooms: 8 double/twin
Bathrooms: 8 en suite

Evening meal available

B&B per night:
S £30.00–£37.50
D £40.00–£60.00

OPEN All Year except Christmas

Small, attractive Lakeland-stone hotel with private car park. Quietly situated for town and lake. Pretty rooms, delicious food – a delightful experience.

♦♦♦♦ **RIVERSIDE HOTEL**

Under Loughrigg, Rothay Bridge,
Ambleside LA22 9LJ
T: (01539) 432395
F: (01539) 432440
E: info@riverside-at-ambleside.co.uk
I: www.riverside-at-ambleside.co.uk

Riverside is a beautiful and stylish Victorian country house and gardens, situated on the River Rothay on a quiet lane within 10 minutes' walk of the village. Riverside provides high-quality bed and breakfast and is ideally situated for easy access to all Lake District attractions.

Bedrooms: 4 double/twin, 1 triple/multiple
Bathrooms: 5 en suite

CC: Delta, Mastercard, Visa

Up to 10% discount for stays of 3 nights or more. Special rates for anniversary and special occasions.

B&B per night:
S £25.00–£40.00
D £50.00–£80.00

OPEN All Year except Christmas

♦♦♦ **THE RYSDALE HOTEL**
Rothay Road, Ambleside LA22 0EE
T: (01539) 432140 & 433999
F: (01539) 433999
E: info@rysdalehotel.co.uk
I: www.rysdalehotel.co.uk

Bedrooms: 4 single, 3 double/twin, 3 triple/multiple
Bathrooms: 8 en suite, 2 private

B&B per night:
S £25.00–£40.00
D £42.00–£80.00

Family-run hotel with magnificent views over park and fells. Good food, licensed bar. Friendly, personal service. Ideal walking base. No smoking.

♦♦♦♦ **THORNEYFIELD GUEST HOUSE**
Compston Road, Ambleside
LA22 9DJ
T: (01539) 432464
F: (08701) 671968
E: info@thorneyfield.co.uk
I: www.thorneyfield.co.uk

Bedrooms: 3 double/twin, 3 triple/multiple
Bathrooms: 6 en suite

CC: Delta, Diners, Mastercard, Switch, Visa

B&B per night:
D £36.00–£55.00

OPEN All Year

Elegant, family-run guesthouse in village centre, with friendly and helpful service. Close to park, miniature golf, tennis, lakes and fells. Large family rooms available.

♦♦♦♦ **TOCK HOW FARM**
High Wray, Ambleside LA22 0JF
T: (01539) 436106 & 436294
F: (01539) 436294
E: info@tock-how-farm.com
I: www.tock-how-farm.com

Bedrooms: 2 double/twin, 1 triple/multiple
Bathrooms: 3 en suite

B&B per night:
S £30.00–£35.00
D £40.00–£50.00

OPEN All Year except Christmas

Family-run farm with spectacular views overlooking Blelham Tarn and towards Ambleside. Comfortable accommodation with traditional farmhouse breakfast. All rooms en suite and centrally heated. Log fires.

CHECK THE MAPS

The colour maps at the front of this guide show all the cities, towns and villages for which you will find accommodation entries. Refer to the town index to find the page on which they are listed.

AMBLESIDE continued

WANSLEA GUEST HOUSE

Lake Road, Ambleside LA22 0DN
T: (01539) 433884
F: (01539) 433884
E: wanslea.guesthouse@virgin.net
I: www.wansleaguesthouse.co.uk

We look forward to welcoming you to Wanslea. Just a short stroll from the centre of Ambleside and Lake Windermere, it is the ideal base for walking, cycling or a more relaxing break. We offer spacious, comfortable rooms, a good Cumbrian breakfast and friendly service. Families welcome. Pets by arrangement.

Bedrooms: 1 single, 2 double/twin, 4 triple/multiple
Bathrooms: 4 en suite

Evening meal available
CC: Delta, Mastercard, Switch, Visa

4 nights for 3 Oct-Mar (excl school holidays, Christmas and New Year). Ring for other current promotions.

B&B per night:
S £20.00–£30.00
D £37.00–£60.00

APPLEBY-IN-WESTMORLAND, Cumbria Map ref 5B3 *Tourist Information Centre Tel: (017683) 51177*

♦♦♦

BROOM HOUSE

Long Marton, Appleby-in-Westmorland CA16 6JP
T: (01768) 361318
F: (01768) 361318
E: sandra@bland01.freeserve.co.uk
I: www.theuktourist.com/members.lasso?id=5038

Bedrooms: 1 double/twin, 1 triple/multiple

B&B per night:
S £25.00
D £40.00–£45.00

HB per person:
DY £33.00–£35.50

Former farmhouse with large garden, lovely views of the Pennines and countryside. Appleby is 2.5 miles, easy access to A66 and M6.

BARROW-IN-FURNESS, Cumbria Map ref 5A3 *Tourist Information Centre Tel: (01229) 894784*

♦♦♦♦

ARLINGTON HOUSE HOTEL AND RESTAURANT

200-202 Abbey Road, Barrow-in-Furness LA14 5LD
T: (01229) 831976
F: (01229) 870990
E: arlington@tinyworld.co.uk
I: www.arlingtonhousehotel.co.uk

Bedrooms: 8 double/twin
Bathrooms: 8 en suite

Evening meal available
CC: Amex, Mastercard, Visa

B&B per night:
S Min £65.00
D Min £88.00

OPEN All Year except Christmas

Relaxed hotel with an elegant restaurant. In the town, yet not far away from the Lakes and sea.

BASSENTHWAITE, Cumbria Map ref 5A2

♦♦♦♦
Silver Award

HIGH SIDE FARMHOUSE

Embleton, Cockermouth CA13 9TN
T: (01768) 776893
F: (01768) 776893
E: highside@winstanley38.freeserve.co.uk

Bedrooms: 2 double/twin
Bathrooms: 2 en suite

B&B per night:
S £30.00–£32.00
D £50.00–£54.00

OPEN All Year

17thC farmhouse in peaceful location with glorious views. Ideal base for touring. Sitting room with log fire. Home-cooked food. Relaxed and friendly atmosphere.

AT-A-GLANCE SYMBOLS

Symbols at the end of each accommodation entry give useful information about services and facilities. A key to symbols can be found inside the back cover flap. Keep this open for easy reference.

BASSENTHWAITE LAKE, Cumbria Map ref 5A2

LINK HOUSE

Bassenthwaite Lake, Cockermouth
CA13 9YD
T: (01768) 776291
F: (01768) 776670
E: linkhouse@lineone.net
I: www.link-house.co.uk

An interesting, inviting, late-Victorian house enjoying lovely views, set in rural location near Keswick and Cockermouth. This well-maintained house offers spotlessly clean and comfortable accommodation. Bedrooms of varying sizes are equipped with en suite showers or baths. A homely atmosphere is maintained by friendly, helpful hosts.

Bedrooms: 3 single, 5 double/twin, 1 triple/multiple
Bathrooms: 8 en suite, 1 private

Evening meal available
CC: Delta, Mastercard, Switch, Visa

Winter breaks – 3 nights' B&B, £69pp (excl Christmas, New Year and Public Holidays), from 1 Nov-1 Mar only. Bargain breaks – 2 nights' DB&B, £75pp (subject to availabilty).

B&B per night:
S £23.00–£30.00
D £55.00–£58.00

HB per person:
DY £38.00–£44.00

OPEN All Year

BEETHAM, Cumbria Map ref 5B3

BARN CLOSE/BEETHAM NORTH WEST BIRDS

Beetham, Milnthorpe LA7 7AL
T: (01539) 563191 & 07752 620658
F: (01539) 563191
E: anne@nwbirds.co.uk
I: www.nwbirds.co.uk

Bedrooms: 2 double/twin
Bathrooms: 1 en suite, 1 private

Large, comfortable and spacious family house set in 1.75 acres of mature garden. Situated on edge of Beetham village, 4 miles jct 35 M6. Bird-watching holidays.

B&B per night:
S £22.00–£30.00
D £36.00–£50.00

OPEN All Year except Christmas

BORROWDALE, Cumbria Map ref 5A3

Silver Award

GREENBANK COUNTRY HOUSE HOTEL

Borrowdale, Keswick CA12 5UY
T: (01768) 777215
E: jeanwwood@lineone.net
I: www.greenbankcountryhousehotel.co.uk

A refurbished Victorian country house, Greenbank is the friendliest hotel in the Lake District. It stands in an acre of garden high up on the wooded slopes in the heart of Borrowdale. Superb walking and touring area. En suite bedrooms, log fires, restaurant licence. Excellent home-cooked food from local produce.

Bedrooms: 1 single, 8 double/twin, 1 triple/multiple
Bathrooms: 10 en suite

Evening meal available
CC: Delta, Mastercard, Switch, Visa

Nov-Mar (excl Easter): 3 nights' B&B for the price of 2, 4 nights' B&B for the price of 3.

B&B per night:
S £30.00–£35.00
D £60.00–£70.00

HB per person:
DY £47.00–£52.00

QUALITY ASSURANCE SCHEME

For an explanation of the quality and facilities represented by the Diamonds please refer to the front of this guide. A more detailed explanation can be found in the information pages at the back.

BORROWDALE continued

◆◆◆◆◆
Gold Award

HAZEL BANK COUNTRY HOUSE

Rosthwaite, Borrowdale, Keswick CA12 5XB
T: (01768) 777248
F: (01767) 877373
E: enquiries@hazelbankhotel.co.uk
I: www.hazelbankhotel.co.uk

HB per person:
DY £52.50–£77.50

OPEN All Year except Christmas

Exquisite Victorian country house set in 4-acre grounds. Peaceful, idyllic location, superb views of central Lakeland Fells. Bedrooms all en suite. Award-winning cuisine using local produce. Puddings and sauces a speciality, vegetarians welcome. Ideal base for walking. Non-smokers only. No pets. Self-catering cottage for 2 in grounds.

Bedrooms: 8 double/twin; permanent suite(s)
Bathrooms: 8 en suite

Evening meal available
CC: Delta, Mastercard, Switch, Visa

Discounts available when bookings are made more than 3 months in advance of arrival.

BOWNESS-ON-SOLWAY, Cumbria Map ref 5A2

WALLSEND

The Old Rectory, Church Lane, Bowness-on-Solway, Carlisle CA7 5AF
T: (016973) 51055
F: (016973) 52543
E: wallsend@btinternet.com
I: www.wallsend.net

B&B per night:
S £22.00–£25.00
D £40.00

OPEN All Year except Christmas

Peaceful old rectory located in own wooded grounds at end of Hadrian's Wall in Solway, an Area of Outstanding Natural Beauty. All rooms en suite. Picturesque village on Solway Firth with local pub/restaurant 150 yards away. Easy access to/from historic city of Carlisle, North Lakes and Scotland. Ideal for walkers, cyclists and just 'getting away'. Warm welcome and relaxing atmosphere.

Bedrooms: 2 single, 2 double/twin, 1 triple/multiple
Bathrooms: 5 en suite

4 nights or more: 10% reduction.

BRAMPTON, Cumbria Map ref 5B2

VALLUM BARN

Irthington, Carlisle CA6 4NN
T: (01697) 742478
E: vallumbarn@tinyworld.co.uk
I: www.vallumbarn.co.uk

B&B per night:
S £24.00–£26.00
D £40.00–£44.00

OPEN All Year except Christmas

Relax and unwind in our spacious converted barn, easily accessible from M6 and only 5 minutes' walk from country pub serving evening meals. Comfortable guest lounge with open fire, ground floor bedroom suitable for disabled guests, hospitality tray with homemade biscuits. Enjoy a good, hearty breakfast using local produce before exploring this lovely area.

Bedrooms: 2 triple/multiple
Bathrooms: 2 en suite

Lunch available
Evening meal available

3 nights for price of 2 Oct-Mar. Reduced summer rate for 3 nights or more.

PRICES
Please check prices and other details at the time of booking.

BRAMPTON continued

WALTON HIGH RIGG

Walton, Brampton CA8 2AZ
T: (01697) 72117
F: (01697) 741697
E: mounsey-highrigg-@hotmail.com
I: www.waltonhighrigg.co.uk

250-acre mixed farm. 18thC Listed farmhouse on roadside, 1 mile from Walton and Roman Wall, 3.5 miles from Brampton. Family-run with pedigree cattle and sheep, farm trail to waterfall. Friendly atmosphere, delicious food. Good stop-over or holiday base. Ideal centre for walking, fishing, golf and horse-riding.

Bedrooms: 1 triple/multiple
Bathrooms: 1 private

Evening meal available

Discounts for 3 days or more. Children half price.

B&B per night:
S £20.00–£23.00
D £38.00–£40.00

HB per person:
DY £30.00–£32.00

OPEN All Year except Christmas

BROUGHTON-IN-FURNESS, Cumbria Map ref 5A3

BROOM HILL

New Street, Broughton-in-Furness LA20 6JD
T: (01229) 716358 & 0797 4135971
F: (01229) 716358

Bedrooms: 3 double/twin
Bathrooms: 2 en suite, 1 private

Beautiful Georgian country mansion with secluded grounds and magnificent views, yet within walking distance of the centre of this unspoilt village.

B&B per night:
S £25.00
D £50.00

BURTON-IN-KENDAL, Cumbria Map ref 5B3

ROYAL HOTEL

Main Street, Burton-in-Kendal, Kendal LA6 1LY
T: (01524) 781261
F: (01524) 781261

Bedrooms: 1 single, 2 double/twin, 1 triple/multiple
Bathrooms: 4 en suite

Lunch available
Evening meal available
CC: Amex, Delta, Mastercard, Switch, Visa

The Royal Hotel is an 18thC coaching inn, an ideal base for touring the Lakes and Yorkshire Dales. We serve good food and fine ales.

B&B per night:
S £22.00–£27.00
D £36.00–£45.00

OPEN All Year

CALDBECK, Cumbria Map ref 5A2

THE BRIARS

Friar Row, Caldbeck, Wigton CA7 8DS
T: (01697) 478633

Bedrooms: 1 single, 2 double/twin
Bathrooms: 1 en suite

140-acre mixed farm. In lovely village of Caldbeck overlooking Caldbeck Fells. Ideal for touring Lakes and Scottish Borders. Right on Cumbria Way route.

B&B per night:
S £20.00–£25.00
D £40.00–£42.00

OPEN All Year except Christmas

CARLISLE, Cumbria Map ref 5A2 *Tourist Information Centre Tel: (01228) 625600*

ASHLEIGH HOUSE

46 Victoria Place, Carlisle CA1 1EX
T: (01228) 521631

Bedrooms: 1 single, 3 double/twin, 3 triple/multiple
Bathrooms: 7 en suite

CC: Delta, Mastercard, Switch, Visa

Well-appointed guesthouse close to city amenities, bus and rail stations. Convenient for the Lakes, Scottish Borders, Hadrian's Wall and Settle line.

3

B&B per night:
S £25.00–£30.00
D £40.00–£45.00

OPEN All Year except Christmas

CORNERWAYS GUEST HOUSE

107 Warwick Road, Carlisle CA1 1EA
T: (01228) 521733

Bedrooms: 4 single, 4 double/twin, 2 triple/multiple
Bathrooms: 3 en suite

Five minutes to rail and bus stations and city centre. M6 exit 43. Colour TV, central heating in all bedrooms. Tea and coffee facilities. Lounge, payphone.

B&B per night:
S £16.00–£19.00
D £30.00–£36.00

OPEN All Year except Christmas

CARLISLE continued

◆◆◆

CROFT END
Hurst, Ivegill, Carlisle CA4 0NL
T: (01768) 484362 & 07762 346349

Bedrooms: 2 double/twin

Rural bungalow situated midway between jcts 41 and 42 of M6, 4 miles west of Southwaite service area. Ideal stop-over for northbound or southbound travellers.

B&B per night:
S £17.00–£20.00
D £34.00–£40.00

OPEN All Year

CARTMEL, Cumbria Map ref 5A3

◆◆◆◆◆ Silver Award

HILL FARM

Cartmel, Grange-over-Sands LA11 7SS
T: (01539) 536477
F: (01539) 536636
E: pafoulerton@talk21.com

B&B per night:
S £25.00–£35.00
D £50.00–£70.00

Top-quality accommodation for country lovers in enchanting atmosphere of historic Tudor house with superb views and peaceful grounds near monastic village just south of Lake Windermere. Ideal base for exploring Lake District/Yorkshire Dales. Close to M6 (jct 36). Self-contained en suite guest accommodation, log fires.

Bedrooms: 1 single, 2 double/twin
Bathrooms: 3 en suite

COCKERMOUTH, Cumbria Map ref 5A2 *Tourist Information Centre Tel: (01900) 822634*

◆◆◆◆

ROSE COTTAGE

Lorton Road, Cockermouth CA13 9DX
T: (01900) 822189
F: (01900) 822189
E: bookings@rosecottageguest.co.uk
I: www.rosecottageguest.co.uk

B&B per night:
S £30.00–£35.00
D £47.00–£55.00

HB per person:
DY £40.00–£50.00

OPEN All Year

In a pleasant position and only a 10-minute walk from the town, this family-run guesthouse is within easy reach of the Lakes and the coast. Home cooking. Large private car park. An ideal base for walking or touring.

Bedrooms: 1 single, 5 double/twin, 2 triple/multiple
Bathrooms: 8 en suite

Evening meal available
CC: Amex, Delta, Mastercard, Switch, Visa

Mid-week or weekend breaks available all year (min 2 nights). Family group packages also available all year (min 12 people).

CONISTON, Cumbria Map ref 5A3

◆◆◆◆

BANK GROUND

East of Lake, Coniston LA21 8AA
T: (01539) 441264
F: (01539) 441900
E: info@bankground.com
I: www.bankground.com

B&B per night:
S £25.00–£45.00
D £40.00–£80.00

OPEN All Year

'Storybook' location, with Arthur Ransome's 'Swallows and Amazons' being both written and filmed here. A mere 150 yards from the property's own 0.5-mile stretch of Coniston shoreline, there are uninterrupted views over the lake to Coniston village and its magnificent backdrop of Lakeland fells. Ideal for all outdoor activities.

Bedrooms: 8 double/twin, 5 triple/multiple
Bathrooms: 7 en suite, 1 private

Evening meal available
CC: Delta, Mastercard, Switch, Visa

CONISTON continued

♦♦♦♦♦ Gold Award

CONISTON LODGE
Station Road, Coniston LA21 8HH
T: (01539) 441201
F: (01539) 441201
E: info@coniston-lodge.com
I: www.coniston-lodge.com

Bedrooms: 6 double/twin
Bathrooms: 6 en suite

Evening meal available
CC: Amex, Delta, Mastercard, Switch, Visa

Small, family-run hotel in beautiful surroundings, offering superior accommodation and good home cooking. Non-smoking.

10 P

B&B per night:
S £42.50–£52.00
D £75.00–£90.00

HB per person:
DY £57.50–£65.00

OPEN All Year except Christmas

♦♦♦♦

CROWN HOTEL

Coniston LA21 8EA
T: (01539) 441243
F: (01539) 441804
E: enntiidus@crown-hotel-coniston.com
I: www.crown-hotel-coniston.com

The Crown Hotel has been completely refurbished to a very high standard to ensure the comfort of all our guests. Enjoy the delights of Coniston and the lake where Donald Campbell attempted to break the world water speed record. All our bedrooms are en suite with central heating, colour TV, direct-dial telephone, hairdryer and tea/coffee-making facilities.

Bedrooms: 11 double/twin, 1 triple/multiple
Bathrooms: 12 en suite

Lunch available
Evening meal available
CC: Amex, Delta, Diners, Mastercard, Switch, Visa

2-day break for only £180 for 2 people, all meals included. 4-day break from Sun-Thu morning, only £320 for 2 people, all meals included.

P

B&B per night:
S £40.00–£60.00
D £70.00–£90.00

HB per person:
DY £50.00–£80.00

OPEN All Year except Christmas

♦♦♦♦

OAKLANDS
Yewdale Road, Coniston LA21 8DX
T: (01539) 441245
F: (01539) 441245
E: judithzeke@oaklandsguesthouse.fsnet.co.uk
I: www.oaklandsguesthouse.fsnet.co.uk

Bedrooms: 1 single, 3 double/twin
Bathrooms: 2 en suite, 1 private

Spacious 100-year-old Lakeland house, village location, mountain views. Quality breakfast, special diets, owner's personal attention. Parking. Non-smoking.

P

B&B per night:
S £22.00–£25.00
D £44.00–£50.00

OPEN All Year except Christmas

♦♦♦

WILSON ARMS

Torver, Coniston LA21 8BB
T: (01539) 441237
F: (01539) 441590

In the small village of Torver, 2.5 miles from Coniston. Ideal walking area. Well-stocked bar, log fire on cooler days. Good central location for touring the lakes. Meals prepared with local fresh produce. Surrounded by beautiful fells.

Bedrooms: 1 single, 5 double/twin, 2 triple/multiple
Bathrooms: 7 en suite, 1 private

Lunch available
Evening meal available
CC: Amex, Delta, Diners, Mastercard, Switch, Visa

Mid-week breaks of 2 or more nights from £25pp.

P

B&B per night:
S £30.00–£40.00
D £54.00–£60.00

OPEN All Year except Christmas

SPECIAL BREAKS

Many establishments offer special promotions and themed breaks. These are highlighted in red. (All such offers are subject to availability.)

CROSTHWAITE, Cumbria Map ref 5A3

◆◆◆◆

CROSTHWAITE HOUSE

Crosthwaite, Kendal LA8 8BP
T: (01539) 568264
F: (01539) 568264
E: bookings@crosthwaitehouse.co.uk
I: www.crosthwaitehouse.co.uk

Bedrooms: 1 single, 5 double/twin
Bathrooms: 6 en suite

Evening meal available

Mid-18thC building with unspoilt views of the Lyth and Winster valleys, 5 miles from Bowness and Kendal. Family atmosphere and home cooking. Self-catering cottages also available.

B&B per night:
S £22.00–£25.00
D £44.00–£50.00

HB per person:
DY £37.00–£40.00

◆◆◆◆

THE PUNCH BOWL INN

Crosthwaite, Kendal LA8 8HR
T: (01539) 568237
F: (01539) 568875
E: enquiries@punchbowl.fsnet.co.uk
I: www.punchbowl.fsnet.co.uk

Bedrooms: 3 double/twin
Bathrooms: 3 en suite

Lunch available
Evening meal available
CC: Delta, Mastercard, Switch, Visa

Coaching inn with 3 double bedrooms, all with private facilities. Adjacent to Crosthwaite Church in the Lyth Valley, 5 miles from Windermere and Kendal.

B&B per night:
S £37.50–£40.00
D £55.00–£60.00

HB per person:
DY £47.50–£57.50

OPEN All Year

DENT, Cumbria Map ref 5B3

GEORGE AND DRAGON HOTEL

Main Street, Dent, Sedbergh LA10 5QL
T: (01539) 625256

Newly refurbished with full en suite facilities, the George and Dragon lies in the centre of Dent's network of cobbled streets. Gourmet meals and special 'themed' food weekends are complemented by craft beers from the small, local brewery.

Bedrooms: 8 double/twin, 2 triple/multiple
Bathrooms: 10 en suite

Lunch available
Evening meal available
CC: Delta, Mastercard, Switch, Visa

B&B per night:
S £40.00
D £49.00–£70.00

OPEN All Year except Christmas

SUN INN

Main Street, Dent, Sedbergh LA10 5QL
T: (01539) 625208
E: thesun@dentbrewery.co.uk
I: www.dentbrewery.co.uk

Pretty 17thC inn at the top of Dent's famous cobbled street. Original beams, log fire and award-winning beers from the small, local brewery make this the ideal place for a cosy weekend away from it all.

Bedrooms: 3 double/twin

Lunch available
Evening meal available
CC: Delta, Mastercard, Switch, Visa

B&B per night:
D £39.00

OPEN All Year except Christmas

MAP REFERENCES The map references refer to the colour maps at the front of this guide. The first figure is the map number; the letter and figure which follow indicate the grid reference on the map.

GILSLAND, Cumbria Map ref 5B2

BUSH NOOK

Upper Denton, Gilsland, Brampton CA8 7AF
T: (01697) 747194
F: (01697) 747790
E: info@bushnook.co.uk
I: www.bushnook.co.uk

B&B per night:
S £20.00–£26.00
D £48.00–£52.00

HB per person:
DY £33.00–£44.00

OPEN All Year

18thC former farmhouse set in open countryside overlooking Birdoswall Fort on Hadrian's Wall. Spectacular views on all sides, peaceful, charming and restful accommodation easily accessed from the M6 or A1. Award-winning home cooking is our speciality. Ideal base for exploring Roman Wall country and the North Pennines.

Bedrooms: 1 single, 3 double/twin; permanent suite(s)
Bathrooms: 2 en suite, 1 private

Evening meal available
CC: Delta, Diners, Mastercard, Switch, Visa

Any 3 nights for price of 2, Oct-Mar (excl Christmas and New Year). 3 nights or more discount all year.

♦♦♦♦

THE HILL

Gilsland, Brampton CA8 7DA
T: (01697) 747214
F: (01697) 747214
E: info@hadrians-wallbedandbreakfast.com
I: http://www.hadrians-wallbedandbreakfast.com

B&B per night:
S £25.00–£30.00
D £45.00–£50.00

HB per person:
DY £32.50–£37.50

OPEN All Year

A 16thC farmhouse in 1 acre of gardens with outstanding views over the Irthing Valley and Hadrian's Wall at Birdoswald Roman fort. Spacious guest bedrooms/lounge. A splendid situation in the greatest of comfort. Delicious home cooking. Ideal centre for walking/touring/stopover for Scotland. Ample parking.

Bedrooms: 3 double/twin
Bathrooms: 2 en suite, 1 private

Lunch available
Evening meal available

3 nights for price of 2 Oct-Mar (excl Christmas and New Year). Other offers available – please call for details.

GRANGE-OVER-SANDS, Cumbria Map ref 5A3 *Tourist Information Centre Tel: (015395) 34026*

ELTON HOTEL

Windermere Road, Grange-over-Sands LA11 6EQ
T: (01539) 532838
F: (01539) 532838
E: chris.crane@btclick.com

B&B per night:
S £26.00–£30.00
D £42.00–£50.00

HB per person:
DY £33.00–£37.00

Our superior rooms have all the little extras to make them 'home from home', with the emphasis on clean and comfortable. Good home cooking a speciality. Two minutes on level to all amenities. Ground floor rooms. Ideal location for touring Lakes. Come and enjoy a warm welcome from Ian and Christine.

Bedrooms: 6 double/twin, 1 triple/multiple
Bathrooms: 5 en suite

Evening meal available

IMPORTANT NOTE Information on accommodation listed in this guide has been supplied by the proprietors. As changes may occur you are advised to check details at the time of booking.

GRANGE-OVER-SANDS continued

GREENACRES COUNTRY GUESTHOUSE

Lindale, Grange-over-Sands LA11 6LP
T: (01539) 534578
F: (01539) 534578
I: www.smoothhound.co.uk/hotels/greenacres.html

The very best of friendly hospitality, food and accommodation awaits you in our attractive guesthouse for non-smokers. Four well-equipped bedrooms with spacious en suite bathrooms, comfortable lounge with log fire, and conservatory too. An ideal base for Lakeland attractions, Morecambe Bay and the Yorkshire Dales.

Bedrooms: 3 double/twin, 1 triple/multiple
Bathrooms: 4 en suite

Evening meal available
CC: Delta, Mastercard, Switch, Visa

B&B per night:
S £30.00–£34.00
D £50.00–£58.00

HB per person:
DY £39.00–£44.00

OPEN All Year except Christmas

GRASMERE, Cumbria Map ref 5A3

ASH COTTAGE GUEST HOUSE

Red Lion Square, Grasmere, Ambleside LA22 9SP
T: (01539) 435224

Bedrooms: 1 single, 6 double/twin, 1 triple/multiple
Bathrooms: 8 en suite

Evening meal available

Detached guesthouse with comfortable en suite bedrooms, personal attention and fine home cooking. Licensed. Pleasant award-winning garden. Private parking.

B&B per night:
S £25.00–£30.00
D £46.00–£60.00

HB per person:
DY £36.00–£42.00

OPEN All Year except Christmas

Rating Applied For

FOREST SIDE HOTEL

Grasmere, Ambleside LA22 9RN
T: (01539) 435250
F: (01539) 435947
E: hotel@forestsidehotel.com
I: www.forestsidehotel.com

Victorian mansion nestling at the base of wooded fell. Forest Side occupies a secluded and much-envied position with magnificent views and grounds to explore. Close to picturesque Grasmere village and Wordsworth Trust. Ideal for walking, relaxing or visiting nearby attractions. Forest Side is at the heart of Lakeland.

Bedrooms: 10 single, 22 double/twin, 1 triple/multiple
Bathrooms: 25 en suite

Lunch available
Evening meal available

Conferences and wedding receptions catered for – contact us for details.

B&B per night:
S £20.00–£40.00
D £60.00–£90.00

HB per person:
DY £35.00–£55.00

OPEN All Year

♦♦♦

THE HARWOOD

Red Lion Square, Grasmere, Ambleside LA22 9SP
T: (01539) 435248
F: (01539) 435545
E: harwoodlan@aol.com
I: www.harwoodhotel.co.uk

Bedrooms: 6 double/twin
Bathrooms: 4 en suite, 2 private

Lunch available
CC: Delta, Mastercard, Switch, Visa

Traditional Lakeland-stone Victorian hotel in the heart of Grasmere. Comfortable rooms all with private facilities and TV. Friendly and welcoming, speciality Cumbrian breakfasts.

B&B per night:
S £19.50–£35.00
D £39.00–£70.00

OPEN All Year except Christmas

REGIONAL TOURIST BOARD The symbol in an establishment entry indicates that it is a Regional Tourist Board member.

GRASMERE continued

♦♦♦

HOW FOOT LODGE

Town End, Grasmere, Ambleside
LA22 9SQ
T: (015394) 35366
F: (015394) 35268
E: info@howfoot.co.uk
I: www.howfoot.co.uk

Bedrooms: 6 double/twin
Bathrooms: 6 en suite

CC: Delta, Mastercard, Switch, Visa

B&B per night:
S £35.00
D £52.00–£58.00

Beautiful Victorian house in peaceful surroundings. Spacious rooms with lovely views. Ideal base for walking and exploring the Lake District.

LAKE VIEW COUNTRY HOUSE

Lake View Drive, Grasmere, Ambleside
LA22 9TD
T: (015394) 35384
E: wts@lakeview-grasmere.com
I: www.lakeview-grasmere.com

Set in peaceful, magnificent surroundings overlooking the lake and fells amidst large and attractive garden with private lakeshore access. Guests are assured of a very warm welcome and delicious English breakfasts. Dinner available by arrangement. Non-smoking. Pets welcome in some rooms. One room with jacuzzi bath.

Bedrooms: 3 double/twin, 1 triple/multiple
Bathrooms: 4 en suite

Evening meal available
CC: Delta, Mastercard, Switch, Visa

Mid-week breaks and winter DB&B breaks.

B&B per night:
D £45.00–£73.00

HB per person:
DY £38.45–£52.45

OPEN All Year

♦♦♦

RAISE VIEW HOUSE

White Bridge, Grasmere, Ambleside
LA22 9RQ
T: (01539) 435215
F: (01539) 435126
E: john@grasmere-raiseview.co.uk
I: www.grasmere-raiseview.co.uk

Traditional Lakeland-stone house situated at the northern edge of Grasmere. Uninterrupted views of Easedale, easy access to many fine walks. Comfortably furnished, en suite rooms. Cosy lounge with roaring log fires. Residential licence. Candlelit evening supper available at certain times. A warm and friendly welcome awaits you.

Bedrooms: 1 single, 6 double/twin
Bathrooms: 7 en suite

Evening meal available
CC: Amex, Delta, Diners, Mastercard, Switch, Visa

Autumn, winter and early spring 3-day DB&B breaks available.

B&B per night:
S £26.00–£30.00
D £56.00–£60.00

HB per person:
DY £42.00–£46.00

OPEN All Year

TRAVELLERS REST

Grasmere, Ambleside LA22 9RR
T: (015394) 35604 & 0870 011 2152
I: www.lakelandinns.com

Located on the edge of Grasmere village, this 16thC former coaching inn is renowned for its food and hospitality. Cosy and welcoming, with real fires in winter, beer gardens surrounded by stunning views for summer days. Ideal base for exploring the Lake District.

Bedrooms: 8 double/twin
Bathrooms: 7 en suite, 1 private

Lunch available
Evening meal available
CC: Delta, Mastercard, Switch, Visa

B&B per night:
S £34.00–£40.00
D £68.00–£80.00

OPEN All Year

GRASMERE continued

WOODLAND CRAG GUEST HOUSE

How Head Lane, Grasmere, Ambleside LA22 9SG
T: (01539) 435351
F: (01539) 435351
E: woodlandcrag@aol.com
I: www.woodlandcrag.com

B&B per night:
S £25.00–£30.00
D £45.00–£65.00

OPEN All Year except Christmas

Traditional Lakeland-stone Victorian country house in secluded location, a short walk from village centre. Dove Cottage (William Wordsworth) 200 metres. Lovely lake and fell views. One acre woodland garden. Tastefully decorated rooms. Drying room. Enclosed parking. Vegetarians catered for. Ideal for touring. Many walks radiate from here.

Bedrooms: 2 single, 3 double/twin
Bathrooms: 3 en suite

CC: Delta, Mastercard, Switch, Visa

10% discount for 3 nights or more. 3 nights for the price of 2, 1 Nov-28 Feb.

12 P

HAWKSHEAD, Cumbria Map ref 5A3

Silver Award

BETTY FOLD COUNTRY HOUSE

Hawkshead Hill, Ambleside LA22 0PS
T: (01539) 436611
E: holidays@bettyfold.freeserve.co.uk
I: www.bettyfold.co.uk

B&B per night:
D £52.00–£68.00

HB per person:
DY £39.00–£48.00

This unique, spacious, award-winning house has an elevated position with fine views from all rooms. Noted for its peaceful, friendly atmosphere. Set in 3 acres of natural garden, rich in wildlife. Ideally located for walking, touring and outdoor pursuits. Excellent food, freshly prepared from traditional recipes.

Bedrooms: 3 double/twin
Bathrooms: 3 en suite

Evening meal available

10% reduction for members of the Royal Scottish Country Dancing Society.

8 P

♦♦♦♦

WALKER GROUND MANOR

Vicarage Lane, Hawkshead, Ambleside LA22 0PD
T: (01539) 436219
E: info@walkerground.co.uk
I: www.walkerground.co.uk

B&B per night:
S £27.50–£37.50
D £40.00–£56.00

HB per person:
DY £39.50–£50.00

OPEN All Year except Christmas

A 16thC traditional Lakeland house with extensive landscaped gardens. Full of charm and character, with many original features, it combines a high standard of accommodation with a relaxed and friendly family atmosphere. Walker Ground offers a quiet and relaxing experience. An ideal base for visiting the whole of South Lakeland.

Bedrooms: 3 double/twin
Bathrooms: 3 en suite

Evening meal available

Autumn, Winter, Spring breaks available including long weekends – £70pppn. Mid-week breaks – £60pppn – both minimum of 3 nights.

P

www.travelengland.org.uk
Log on for information and inspiration. The latest information on places to visit, events and quality assessed accommodation.

HAWKSHEAD continued

YEWFIELD VEGETARIAN GUEST HOUSE

Yewfield, Hawkshead, Ambleside LA22 0PR
T: (01539) 436765
F: (01539) 436096
E: derek.yewfield@btinternet.com
I: www.yewfield.co.uk

B&B per night:
S £27.00–£35.00
D £44.00–£74.00

A peaceful and quiet retreat in the heart of the Lakes, perfect for lovely walking holidays, an impressive Gothic vegetarian-run guesthouse set in its own 30-acre organic gardens and grounds. All rooms individually appointed to a very high standard with en suite bath and shower. Completely non-smoking.

Bedrooms: 3 double/twin
Bathrooms: 3 en suite

CC: Delta, Mastercard, Switch, Visa

Classical concerts throughout the year. See website for dates.

12 P

HESKET NEWMARKET, Cumbria Map ref 5A2

DENTON HOUSE

Hesket Newmarket, Wigton
CA7 8JG
T: (016974) 78415
E: dentonhnm@aol.com

Bedrooms: 1 single, 3 double/twin, 2 triple/multiple
Bathrooms: 4 en suite, 2 private

Evening meal available

B&B per night:
S £20.00–£25.00
D £40.00–£45.00

HB per person:
DY £30.00–£34.00

OPEN All Year

A friendly atmosphere welcomes everyone to this family-run guesthouse. En suite facilities available. Ideal base for touring the Lakes or travelling to and from Scotland.

P

KENDAL, Cumbria Map ref 5B3 *Tourist Information Centre Tel: (01539) 725758*

Silver Award

BLAVEN HOMESTAY

Middleshaw, Old Hutton, Kendal LA8 0LZ
T: (01539) 734894 & 740490
F: (01539) 727447
E: enquiries@blavenhomestay.co.uk
I: www.blavenhomestay.co.uk

B&B per night:
S £39.50–£46.00
D £59.00–£72.00

HB per person:
DY £46.50–£62.00

OPEN All Year

Peacefully located beside a pretty Lakeland trout stream, this beautifully appointed, sympathetically converted barn is convenient for the M6 and touring the Lake District and Yorkshire Dales. Amiable, welcoming hosts Janet and Barry offer gourmet meals, fine wine and every comfort to guests. Local walks, wood fires, lovely garden, safe parking.

Bedrooms: 1 double/twin, 1 triple/multiple
Bathrooms: 2 en suite

Evening meal available
CC: Delta, Mastercard, Switch, Visa

Business course – 'Running a Bed and Breakfast' – and cookery demonstration – 'Innovative Breakfast and Brunch Cookery' – twice monthly.

P

BURROW HALL

Plantation Bridge, Kendal LA8 9JR
T: (01539) 821711
F: (01539) 821711
E: info@burrowhall.fsnet.co.uk
I: www.burrowhall.co.uk

Bedrooms: 3 double/twin
Bathrooms: 3 en suite

CC: Delta, Mastercard, Switch, Visa

B&B per night:
S Min £35.00
D £45.00–£52.00

Tastefully furnished, 17thC Lakeland house enjoying modern-day comforts. Sits peacefully in idyllic South Lakeland countryside between Kendal and Windermere, on A591.

12 P

CREDIT CARD BOOKINGS If you book by telephone and are asked for your credit card number it is advisable to check the proprietor's policy should you cancel your reservation.

KENDAL continued

◆◆◆

FAIRWAYS GUEST HOUSE
102 Windermere Road, Kendal
LA9 5EZ
T: (01539) 725564
E: mp@fairways1.fsnet.co.uk

Bedrooms: 3 double/twin
Bathrooms: 3 en suite

On the main Kendal-Windermere road. Victorian guesthouse with en suite facilities. TV, tea and coffee in all rooms. 4-poster bedrooms. Private parking.

B&B per night:
S £20.00–£30.00
D £38.00–£44.00

OPEN All Year except Christmas

◆◆◆

LAKELAND NATURAL VEGETARIAN GUESTHOUSE

Low Slack, Queens Road, Kendal LA9 4PH
T: (01539) 733011
F: (01539) 733011
E: relax@lakelandnatural.co.uk
I: www.lakelandnatural.co.uk

Unwind in our spacious Victorian home, with stunning views overlooking Kendal and the surrounding fells. Adjacent woodland walks and golf course. Only 5 minutes' walk from the town centre. Non-smoking. Safe, off-street parking. Children and dogs welcome. Brilliant breakfasts and imaginative evening meals using largely organic produce. Licensed.

Bedrooms: 3 double/twin, 1 triple/multiple
Bathrooms: 4 en suite

Lunch available
Evening meal available
CC: Delta, Mastercard, Switch, Visa

B&B per night:
S £35.00
D £60.00

HB per person:
DY £45.95–£50.95

OPEN All Year

KESWICK, Cumbria Map ref 5A3 *Tourist Information Centre Tel: (017687) 72645*

◆◆◆◆

ABACOURT HOUSE
26 Stanger Street, Keswick
CA12 5JU
T: (017687) 72967
E: abacourt@btinternet.com
I: www.abacourt.co.uk

Bedrooms: 5 double/twin
Bathrooms: 5 en suite

Victorian townhouse, lovingly restored to the highest of standards. Beautifully furnished, fully double glazed. Superior en suites in all bedrooms. Central, quiet, cosy and friendly. Brochure available.

B&B per night:
D £48.00

OPEN All Year except Christmas

◆◆◆◆
Silver Award

ACORN HOUSE HOTEL
Ambleside Road, Keswick CA12 4DL
T: (01768) 772553
E: info@acornhousehotel.co.uk
I: www.acornhousehotel.co.uk

Bedrooms: 8 double/twin, 2 triple/multiple
Bathrooms: 9 en suite, 1 private

CC: Delta, Mastercard, Switch, Visa

Elegant Georgian house set in colourful garden. All bedrooms tastefully furnished, some 4-poster beds. Cleanliness guaranteed. Close to town centre. Good off-street parking. Strictly non-smoking.

6

B&B per night:
S £35.00–£50.00
D £56.00–£66.00

OPEN All Year except Christmas

◆◆◆◆

THE ANCHORAGE
14 Ambleside Road, Keswick
CA12 4DL
T: (01768) 772813
E: anchorage.keswick@btopenworld.com
I: www.anchorage-keswick.co.uk

Bedrooms: 1 single, 3 double/twin, 2 triple/multiple
Bathrooms: 6 en suite

Evening meal available

Small guesthouse with friendly owners. All rooms en suite with tea/coffee-making facilities. Five minutes' walk to town centre, close to lake and parks.

5

B&B per night:
S £22.00–£25.00
D £44.00–£50.00

OPEN All Year except Christmas

MAP REFERENCES

Map references apply to the colour maps at the front of this guide.

KESWICK continued

♦♦♦♦ Silver Award

ANWORTH HOUSE

27 Eskin Street, Keswick CA12 4DQ
T: (01768) 772923
I: www.anworthhouse.co.uk

B&B per night:
S £30.00
D £46.00–£54.00

OPEN All Year except Christmas

Ideally situated for the town centre, theatre, lakes and fells. Each of the 5 en suite bedrooms is individually co-ordinated and tastefully furnished to the highest standards. A relaxed atmosphere and excellent home cooking. Special diets catered for. For the comfort of guests, Anworth House is a no-smoking establishment.

Bedrooms: 5 double/twin
Bathrooms: 5 en suite

CC: Mastercard, Switch, Visa

Special winter breaks Nov-Mar (excl Christmas and New Year).

♦♦♦♦

AVONDALE GUEST HOUSE

20 Southey Street, Keswick CA12 4EF
T: (01768) 772735
F: (01768) 775431
E: enquiries@avondaleguesthouse.com
I: www.avondaleguesthouse.com

B&B per night:
S £23.00–£24.50
D £46.00–£49.00

OPEN All Year except Christmas

High-quality Victorian guesthouse with well-appointed en suite rooms. Close to town centre, theatre, lake and parks. Excellent English and vegetarian breakfasts. In our comfortable guest lounge you can just relax and chat to fellow guests or read from the choice of books and magazines. Non-smokers only please.

Bedrooms: 1 single, 5 double/twin
Bathrooms: 6 en suite

CC: Delta, Mastercard, Switch, Visa

Weekly B&B rate £151.

12

♦♦♦♦

BADGERS WOOD

30 Stanger Street, Keswick CA12 5JU
T: (01768) 772621
E: enquiries@badgers-wood.co.uk
I: www.badgers-wood.co.uk

B&B per night:
S £18.00
D £48.00

Spacious, friendly guesthouse on quieter side of town. All our bedrooms have mountain views, soft towels, white cotton sheets. Our 'Welcome Host' and 'Heartbeat' awards assure you of our ongoing commitment to our guests' comfort and enjoyment.

Bedrooms: 2 single, 4 double/twin
Bathrooms: 4 en suite

12

♦♦♦

BONSHAW GUEST HOUSE

20 Eskin Street, Keswick CA12 4DG
T: (01768) 773084
E: sylviasanderson@compuserve.com
I: www.bonshaw.co.uk

Bedrooms: 3 single, 4 double/twin
Bathrooms: 4 en suite

Evening meal available
CC: Delta, Mastercard, Switch, Visa

B&B per night:
S £16.50–£21.00
D £18.50–£23.00

HB per person:
DY £29.00–£35.50

OPEN All Year except Christmas

Small, friendly, comfortable guesthouse, providing good home cooking. Convenient for town centre and all amenities. En suite rooms available. Private car park. Non-smoking.

5 P

KESWICK continued

◆◆◆◆

GLENCOE GUEST HOUSE
21 Helvellyn Street, Keswick
CA12 4EN
T: (01768) 771016
E: enquiries@glencoeguesthouse.co.uk
I: www.glencoeguesthouse.co.uk

Bedrooms: 1 single, 5 double/twin
Bathrooms: 4 en suite, 1 private

Lunch available
Evening meal available

Victorian townhouse of character. Decorated to high standard with quality fittings. Conveniently situated for town and all amenities. Friendly welcome, excellent service guaranteed. Quiet.

P

B&B per night:
S £18.50–£21.00
D £40.00–£50.00

HB per person:
DY £32.00–£35.00

OPEN All Year

◆◆◆◆

GREYSTONES HOTEL
Ambleside Road, Keswick CA12 4DP
T: (01768) 773108
E: greystones@keslakes.freeserve.co.uk
I: www.greystones.tv

Greystones enjoys an enviable, tranquil location with splendid mountain views, yet the hotel is only a short walk from Lake Derwentwater and the historic Market Square with its restaurants, traditional pubs and craft shops. The accommodation is stylish and comfortable. Private car park.

Bedrooms: 1 single, 7 double/twin
Bathrooms: 7 en suite, 1 private

Mid-week special rates available.

CC: Mastercard, Visa

10 P

B&B per night:
S £23.00–£27.00
D £46.00–£54.00

OPEN All Year except Christmas

◆◆◆◆

HAZELDENE HOTEL
The Heads, Keswick CA12 5ER
T: (01768) 772106
F: (01768) 775435
E: info@hazeldene-hotel.co.uk
I: www.hazeldene-hotel.co.uk

At Hazeldene Hotel our aim is simple: to provide our guests with exceptional quality and value accommodation in an outstanding location. Large and well-furnished, en suite bedrooms, excellent food and a peaceful, relaxed atmosphere combine to make Hazeldene Hotel a perfect haven for your visit to the Lake District.

Bedrooms: 2 single, 13 double/twin, 3 triple/multiple
Bathrooms: 17 en suite

Evening meal available
CC: Delta, Mastercard, Switch, Visa

P

B&B per night:
S £25.00–£35.00
D £50.00–£90.00

HB per person:
DY £43.00–£63.00

◆◆◆◆

HUNTERS WAY GUEST HOUSE
4 Eskin Street, Keswick CA12 4DH
T: (01768) 772324

Bedrooms: 2 single, 3 double/twin, 1 triple/multiple
Bathrooms: 4 en suite

Lunch available
Evening meal available
CC: Delta, Mastercard, Switch, Visa

Victorian guest house, warm and friendly welcome. Five minutes' walk from town centre, ten minutes' walk from Derwentwater and theatre.

5

B&B per night:
S £19.00–£20.00
D £46.00–£48.00

HB per person:
DY £28.00–£35.00

OPEN All Year

◆◆◆

LITTLETOWN FARM
Newlands, Keswick CA12 5TU
T: (01768) 778353
F: (01768) 778437
I: www.littletownfarm.co.uk

Bedrooms: 1 single, 6 double/twin, 2 triple/multiple
Bathrooms: 6 en suite

Evening meal available
CC: Mastercard, Visa

150-acre mixed farm in the beautiful, unspoilt Newlands Valley. Comfortable residents' lounge, dining room and cosy bar. Traditional 4-course dinner 6 nights a week.

P

B&B per night:
S £30.00–£34.00
D £60.00–£68.00

HB per person:
DY £40.00–£46.00

KESWICK continued

LYNWOOD HOUSE

35 Helvellyn Street, Keswick CA12 4EP
T: (01768) 772398
F: (01768) 774090
E: info@lynwoodhouse.net
I: www.lynwoodhouse.net

Situated in a quiet, residential area, our family-run Victorian guesthouse is a 5-minute stroll from Keswick town centre. Each room has TV and tea/coffee facilities, while a comfortable lounge with extensive collection of books is available for your relaxation. Breakfast menu options include traditional, vegetarian and organic dishes. Welcome Host holder.

Bedrooms: 1 single, 2 double/twin, 1 triple/multiple
Bathrooms: 1 en suite

B&B per night:
S £19.00–£19.50
D £17.50–£21.50

OPEN All Year except Christmas

♦♦♦♦

SANDON GUESTHOUSE

13 Southey Street, Keswick
CA12 4EG
T: (01768) 773648
E: enquiries@sandonguesthouse.com
I: www.sandonguesthouse.com

Bedrooms: 2 single, 3 double/twin, 1 triple/multiple
Bathrooms: 4 en suite

Evening meal available

Charming Lakeland-stone Victorian guesthouse, conveniently situated for town, theatre or lake. Friendly, comfortable accommodation. Ideal base for walking or cycling holidays. Superb English breakfast.

B&B per night:
S £19.00–£20.00
D £44.00–£46.00

OPEN All Year except Christmas

♦♦♦

WATENDLATH GUEST HOUSE

15 Acorn Street, Keswick CA12 4EA
T: (01768) 774165
F: (01768) 74165
E: linda@watendlathguesthouse.co.uk
I: www.watendlathguesthouse.co.uk

Bedrooms: 2 double/twin, 2 triple/multiple
Bathrooms: 4 en suite

Within easy walking distance of the lake, hills and town centre. We offer a warm and friendly welcome and traditional English breakfast.

B&B per night:
D £40.00–£48.00

KIRKBY LONSDALE, Cumbria Map ref 5B3 *Tourist Information Centre Tel: (015242) 71437*

♦♦

THE COPPER KETTLE

3-5 Market Street, Kirkby Lonsdale,
Carnforth LA6 2AU
T: (01524) 271714
F: (01524) 271714

Bedrooms: 3 double/twin, 1 triple/multiple
Bathrooms: 3 en suite

Lunch available
Evening meal available
CC: Amex, Delta, Diners, Mastercard, Switch, Visa

Part of an old manor house, built in 1610, on the border between the Yorkshire Dales and the Lakes.

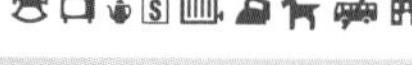

B&B per night:
S £23.00
D £36.00–£42.00

HB per person:
DY £25.00–£28.00

OPEN All Year

USE YOUR *i*s

There are more than 550 Tourist Information Centres throughout England offering friendly help with accommodation and holiday ideas as well as suggestions of places to visit and things to do. You'll find TIC addresses in the local Phone Book.

KIRKBY STEPHEN, Cumbria Map ref 5B3 *Tourist Information Centre Tel: (017683) 71199*

WESTVIEW

Ravenstonedale, Kirkby Stephen CA17 4NG
T: (01539) 623415
E: Enquiries@westview-cumbria.co.uk
I: www.enquiries@westview-cumbria.co.uk

Westview is a 16thC farmhouse overlooking the village green in the unspoiled village of Ravenstonedale. There are 2 pubs, 3 churches and a small golf course all within minutes of Westview, also an excellent walking area. Westview is an ideal base for touring the Lakes, Eden Valley and Yorkshire Dales.

Bedrooms: 3 double/twin
Bathrooms: 2 en suite, 1 private

Evening meal available

B&B per night:
S £27.00–£30.00
D £42.00–£48.00

HB per person:
DY £31.00–£34.00

OPEN All Year except Christmas

LAKESIDE, Cumbria Map ref 5A3

THE KNOLL COUNTRY HOUSE

Lakeside, Newby Bridge LA12 8AU
T: (01539) 531347
F: (01539) 530850
E: info@theknoll-lakeside.co.uk
I: www.theknoll-lakeside.co.uk

The Knoll is a traditional Victorian country house set in its own grounds surrounded by wooded countryside at the southern tip of Lake Windermere. The house is beautifully appointed with large, en suite bedrooms. A relaxing rural retreat with open fires offering a warm welcome, excellent cuisine and fine wines.

Bedrooms: 8 double/twin; permanent suite(s)
Bathrooms: 8 en suite

Evening meal available
CC: Delta, Mastercard, Switch, Visa

B&B per night:
S £40.00–£70.00
D £60.00–£95.00

HB per person:
DY £45.00–£65.00

OPEN All Year except Christmas

MUNGRISDALE, Cumbria Map ref 5A2

♦♦♦

MOSEDALE END FARM

Mungrisdale, Penrith CA11 0XQ
T: (017687) 79605
E: armstrong@awmcmanus.screaming.net
I: www.smoothhound.co.uk/hotels/mosedale.html

Bedrooms: 1 double/twin, 1 triple/multiple
Bathrooms: 2 en suite

A 17thC farmhouse in a peaceful location surrounded by mountains, rivers and green fields in the Central Lakes.

B&B per night:
S £20.00–£24.00
D £40.00–£46.00

OPEN All Year except Christmas

NEWBIGGIN-ON-LUNE, Cumbria Map ref 5B3

TRANNA HILL

Newbiggin-on-Lune,
Kirkby Stephen CA17 4NY
T: (015396) 23227 & 07989 892368
E: trannahill@hotmail.com

Bedrooms: 2 double/twin
Bathrooms: 2 en suite

Evening meal available

Beautifully situated Victorian house with views of Howgill Fells yet only minutes from M6 (jct 38). Ideal base for exploring, walking or breaking your journey.

B&B per night:
S £20.00–£25.00
D £38.00–£40.00

HB per person:
DY £28.00–£30.00

ACCESSIBILITY

Look for the symbols which indicate National Accessible Scheme standards for hearing and visually impaired guests in addition to standards for guests with mobility impairment. Additional participants are shown in the listings at the back.

PENRITH, Cumbria Map ref 5B2 *Tourist Information Centre Tel: (01768) 867466*

Rating Applied For

ALBANY HOUSE

5 Portland Place, Penrith CA11 7QN
T: (01768) 863072
F: (01768) 895527
E: info@albany-house.org.uk
I: www.albany-house.org.uk

Bedrooms: 1 double/twin, 4 triple/multiple
Bathrooms: 2 en suite

Large Victorian terraced house run by proprietress and providing good facilities. Ideal for Lake District and stop-over to or from Scotland. Children welcome, special diets on request.

B&B per night:
D £36.00–£45.00

OPEN All Year except Christmas

◆◆◆

BLUE SWALLOW GUESTHOUSE

11 Victoria Road, Penrith CA11 8HR
T: (01768) 866335
E: blueswallows@lineone.net
I: www.blueswallow.co.uk

Bedrooms: 2 double/twin, 3 triple/multiple
Bathrooms: 3 en suite

Family-run, mid-Victorian townhouse, comfortable and well-appointed throughout. Situated in Eden Valley, 5 minutes from Lakeland. Hearty breakfast and cleanliness assured.

B&B per night:
S £25.00–£32.00
D £38.00–£44.00

OPEN All Year except Christmas

◆◆◆

BRANDELHOW GUEST HOUSE

1 Portland Place, Penrith CA11 7QN
T: (01768) 864470

Bedrooms: 1 single, 1 double/twin, 3 triple/multiple
Bathrooms: 3 en suite

Victorian house with spacious, comfortable accommodation and friendly, personal attention. Ideal base for touring Lakes and Border country.

B&B per night:
S £20.00–£35.00
D £47.00–£60.00

OPEN All Year

GLENDALE

4 Portland Place, Penrith CA11 7QN
T: (01768) 862579
F: (01768) 867934
E: glendale@lineone.net
I: www.glendaleguesthouse.net

Julie, Mike and Gabriella invite you to enjoy a relaxing break in this family-run guesthouse set in a Victorian townhouse overlooking pleasant gardens. Built in the 1860s, it is a property of considerable charm which we hope provides a homely atmosphere. Children and pets are especially welcome.

Bedrooms: 1 single, 2 double/twin, 4 triple/multiple
Bathrooms: 4 en suite

B&B per night:
S £30.00–£35.00
D £40.00–£50.00

OPEN All Year except Christmas

Silver Award

ROUNDTHORN COUNTRY HOUSE

Beacon Edge, Penrith CA11 8SJ
T: (01768) 863952
F: (01768) 864100
E: enquiries@roundthorn.co.uk
I: www.roundthorn.co.uk

Grade II Listed Georgian mansion, set in landscaped grounds, from which there are panoramic views of the Eden Valley, Pennines and Lakeland fells. All rooms are en suite and have TV and tea/coffee-making facilities. The house is fully licensed and rates include a hearty Cumbrian breakfast.

Bedrooms: 8 double/twin, 2 triple/multiple
Bathrooms: 10 en suite

Evening meal available
CC: Amex, Delta, Diners, Mastercard, Switch, Visa

B&B per night:
S £45.00–£55.00
D £60.00–£75.00

OPEN All Year except Christmas

RYDAL, Cumbria Map ref 5A3

NAB COTTAGE GUEST HOUSE

Nab Cottage, Rydal, Ambleside LA22 9SD
T: (01539) 435311
F: (01539) 435493
E: ell@nab.dial.lakesnet.co.uk
I: www.kencomp.net/homepages/ell/nab/

Grade II Listed 16thC cottage overlooking Rydal Water. Former home of Thomas de Quincey with many literary associations. Friendly service, informal atmosphere, homemade bread, log fires, great walking, lake views. Somewhere to let go...

Bedrooms: 1 single, 5 double/twin, 1 triple/multiple
Bathrooms: 4 en suite

Evening meal available

B&B per night:
S £25.00–£30.00
D £50.00–£56.00

HB per person:
DY £37.00–£42.00

OPEN All Year except Christmas

SAWREY, Cumbria Map ref 5A3

◆◆◆◆

BUCKLE YEAT GUEST HOUSE

Sawrey, Ambleside LA22 0LF
T: (01539) 436446 & 436538
F: (01539) 436446
E: info@buckle-yeat.co.uk
I: www.buckle-yeat.co.uk

Bedrooms: 1 single, 6 double/twin
Bathrooms: 6 en suite, 1 private

CC: Amex, Delta, Mastercard, Switch, Visa

17thC oak-beamed cottage, famous for its connections with Beatrix Potter, provides a warm, friendly and centrally located base, and excellent value for money.

B&B per night:
S £27.50–£30.00
D £55.00–£60.00

OPEN All Year except Christmas

◆◆◆

TOWER BANK ARMS

Near Sawrey, Ambleside LA22 0LF
T: (01539) 436334
F: (01539) 436448
E: sales@towerbankarms.fsnet.co.uk

Bedrooms: 3 double/twin
Bathrooms: 3 en suite

Lunch available
Evening meal available
CC: Amex, Delta, Mastercard, Switch, Visa

Next door to Hill Top, the former home of Beatrix Potter. It features in the tale of Jemima Puddleduck.

B&B per night:
S Min £38.00
D Min £55.00

OPEN All Year except Christmas

WEST VALE COUNTRY HOUSE

Far Sawrey, Hawkshead, Ambleside LA22 0LQ
T: (01539) 442817
F: (01539) 45302
E: enquiries@westvalecountryhouse.co.uk
I: www.westvalecountryhouse.co.uk

An elegant Victorian stone-built house, renovated to a high standard and complemented by fine antique furnishings and prints. This, together with superb fell views from all the spacious en suite bedrooms and excellent food and wine, makes West Vale an ideal base to relax or explore the Lake District.

Bedrooms: 5 double/twin, 1 triple/multiple; permanent suite(s)
Bathrooms: 5 en suite, 1 private

Evening meal available
CC: Amex, Delta, Mastercard, Switch, Visa

Take advantage of our free fishing weekend. Hire a small country house for the weekend. Winter-warmer weekends.

B&B per night:
D £66.00–£76.00

HB per person:
DY £55.00–£60.00

OPEN All Year except Christmas

QUALITY ASSURANCE SCHEME

Diamond ratings and awards were correct at the time of going to press but are subject to change. Please check at the time of booking.

ST BEES, Cumbria Map ref 5A3

♦♦♦

FAIRLADIES BARN GUEST HOUSE

Main Street, St Bees CA27 0AD
T: (01946) 822718
F: (01946) 825838
E: info@fairladiesbarn.co.uk
I: www.fairladiesbarn.co.uk

Bedrooms: 9 double/twin, 1 triple/multiple
Bathrooms: 8 en suite

B&B per night:
S £20.00–£25.00
D £36.00–£42.00

OPEN All Year

17thC, converted sandstone barn situated in a small coastal village. Ideal base to visit the Lakes and to see the many local attractions.

P

SOULBY, Cumbria Map ref 5B3

♦♦♦♦

RIDDLESAY FARM

Soulby, Kirkby Stephen CA17 4PX
T: (017683) 71474 & 0772 0811611
F: (017683) 71483
E: mrarmstrong@btinternet.com

B&B per night:
D £40.00–£44.00

OPEN All Year except Christmas

Warm and friendly farmhouse in the Eden Valley, 1 mile north of Kirkby Stephen (A66) on the A685. Double and twin room, both en suite, TV, tea/coffee-making facilities, hairdryer, radio, decorated to high standard. Enjoy a hearty breakfast to start your day. Dog-friendly kennels. Ideal for Pennines and The Lake District.

Bedrooms: 2 double/twin
Bathrooms: 2 en suite

Evening meal available

P

TEBAY, Cumbria Map ref 5B3

PRIMROSE COTTAGE

Orton Road, Tebay, Penrith CA10 3TL
T: (01539) 624791 & 07778 520930
E: info@primrosecottagecumbria.co.uk
I: www.primrosecottagecumbria.co.uk

Bedrooms: 5 double/twin
Bathrooms: 2 en suite, 3 private

Evening meal available

B&B per night:
S £25.00–£35.00
D £45.00–£50.00

OPEN All Year

Close to M6, jct 38. Overnight stops/short breaks. North Lakes and Yorkshire Dales nearby. Excellent facilities include 4-poster bed, jacuzzi bath. Also self-catering flat and bungalow.

P

THRELKELD, Cumbria Map ref 5A3

SCALES FARM COUNTRY GUESTHOUSE

Scales, Threlkeld, Keswick CA12 4SY
T: (017687) 79660
F: (017687) 79510
E: scales@scalesfarm.com
I: www.scalesfarm.com

B&B per night:
S £30.00–£32.00
D £54.00–£58.00

OPEN All Year except Christmas

Stunning views and a warm welcome await you at our tastefully modernised 17thC farmhouse set at the base of Blencathra. Our en suite bedrooms are centrally heated with tea/coffee-making facilites, colour TV and fridges. Separate entrance from private car park allows guests access to rooms, private dining room and traditional lounge.

Bedrooms: 5 double/twin, 1 triple/multiple
Bathrooms: 6 en suite

CC: Delta, Mastercard, Switch, Visa

P

QUALITY ASSURANCE SCHEME

Diamond ratings and awards are explained at the back of this guide.

TROUTBECK, Cumbria Map ref 5A2

GILL HEAD FARM

Troutbeck, Penrith CA11 0ST
T: (01768) 779652
F: (01768) 779130
E: enquiries@gillheadfarm.co.uk
I: www.gillheadfarm.co.uk

Stay in our lovely 17thC farmhouse set against the dramatic backdrop of the northern fells, where a warm welcome and traditional hospitality is assured. Relax in the comfort of our attractive, en suite rooms, log fires in our cosy oak-beamed sitting room and, of course, lots of delicious home cooking!

Bedrooms: 5 double/twin
Bathrooms: 5 en suite

Evening meal available

Discounts for group bookings.

B&B per night:
S £22.00
D £22.00

HB per person:
DY £30.00

OPEN All Year except Christmas

TROUTBECK, Cumbria Map ref 5A3

HIGH GREEN LODGE

High Green, Troutbeck, Windermere
LA23 1PN
T: (01539) 433005

Here all mornings are magical. En suite king-size rooms in peaceful lodge with fantastic views down to Valley Lake/Garbon Pass. Also 'Hill Top Studios', state-of-the-art with 4-poster/French sleigh beds, steam showers, jacuzzi baths, DVDs and TVs, water fountains, drink coolers etc. Truly fabulous!

Bedrooms: 3 double/twin
Bathrooms: 3 en suite

CC: Delta, Mastercard, Switch, Visa

B&B per night:
S £40.00–£60.00
D £60.00–£120.00

OPEN All Year except Christmas

ULLSWATER, Cumbria Map ref 5A3

BANK HOUSE FARM

Matterdale End, Penrith CA11 0LF
T: (01768) 482040
E: tjnhargreaves@aol.com

Set above the small Lakeland hamlet of Matterdale End with magnificent views of the Ullswater Fells, this delightful farmhouse offers a peaceful, tranquil base from which to explore the National Park. Comfortable surroundings, Aga-cooked breakfasts and 7 acres to relax in make this the perfect holiday location.

Bedrooms: 3 double/twin
Bathrooms: 3 en suite

Evening meal available

Short breaks of 3 or more nights available at special rates, Jan-Mar.

B&B per night:
S £30.00
D £60.00

OPEN All Year except Christmas

GOLD & SILVER AWARDS

These exclusive ETC awards are given to establishments achieving the highest levels of quality and service. Further information can be found at the front of the guide and additional accommodation achieving these awards are shown in the listing at the back of this guide.

ULLSWATER continued

◆◆◆

KNOTTS MILL COUNTRY LODGE

Watermillock, Penrith CA11 0JN
T: (017684) 86699
F: (017684) 86190
E: relax@knottsmill.com
I: www.knottsmill.com

A country lodge offering quality, serviced accommodation and delicious home-cooked food. In private grounds set in magnificent scenery around Ullswater with stunning views of the surrounding hills. Ideal for walking, touring, bird-watching and sailing. Relaxed, welcoming atmosphere in a peaceful setting, yet only 10 minutes from the M6.

Bedrooms: 6 double/twin, 3 triple/multiple
Bathrooms: 9 en suite

Evening meal available
CC: Delta, Mastercard, Switch, Visa

Off-peak discounts, e.g. 7 for 6. 'Special Occasion Breaks'. Ullswater Steamers and Rheged discount vouchers. All inclusive, guided walking holidays.

B&B per night:
S £25.00–£37.50
D £45.00–£55.00

HB per person:
DY £34.50–£42.45

OPEN All Year

P

◆◆◆

LAND ENDS COUNTRY LODGE

Watermillock, Ullswater, Penrith CA11 0NB
T: (01768) 486438
F: (01768) 486959
E: infolandends@btinternet.com
I: www.landends.co.uk

A haven of peace and quiet, set in 25 acres with 2 pretty lakes, ducks, red squirrels and wonderful birdlife, our traditional farmhouse has been tastefully restored providing en suite bedrooms, 1 with 4-poster. Light snacks available evenings. Cosy lounge and bar. Close to lake, Ullswater and high fells.

Bedrooms: 2 single, 6 double/twin
Bathrooms: 8 en suite

Evening meal available

3 nights for 2 on specific dates.

B&B per night:
S £31.00–£33.00
D £54.00–£70.00

P

◆◆◆

MOSS CRAG

Eagle Road, Glenridding, Penrith CA11 0PA
T: (01768) 482500 & 0789 9777419
F: (01768) 482500
E: info@mosscrag.co.uk
I: www.mosscrag.co.uk

Small, friendly, family-run guesthouse overlooking Glenridding Beck, and close to Ullswater shore. Individually, tastefully decorated rooms await your arrival. All rooms have TV, hospitality tray etc. A good wholesome breakfast will start your day, whether walking, climbing, fishing, sailing or just touring the area.

Bedrooms: 6 double/twin
Bathrooms: 4 en suite

Lunch available
Evening meal available
CC: Delta, Mastercard, Switch, Visa

B&B weekly breaks from £139-£189. DB&B from £240-£290. B&B 3-day breaks from £60-£81 (excl Bank Holidays).

B&B per night:
S £30.00–£35.00
D £44.00–£60.00

HB per person:
DY £38.00–£46.00

5 P

CHECK THE MAPS

The colour maps at the front of this guide show all the cities, towns and villages for which you will find accommodation entries.
Refer to the town index to find the page on which they are listed.

ULLSWATER continued

NETHERDENE GUEST HOUSE

Troutbeck, Penrith CA11 0SJ
T: (01768) 483475 & 483475
F: (01768) 483475
E: netherdene@aol.com
I: www.netherdene.co.uk

Bedrooms: 1 single, 3 double/twin, 1 triple/multiple
Bathrooms: 5 en suite

Traditional country house in its own quiet grounds, with extensive mountain views, offering comfortable well-appointed rooms and personal attention. Ideal base for touring Lakeland.

B&B per night:
S £20.00–£25.00
D £40.00–£50.00

OPEN All Year except Christmas

WATERHEAD, Cumbria Map ref 5A3

WATERHEAD COUNTRY GUEST HOUSE

Waterhead, Ambleside LA21 8AJ
T: (01539) 441442
F: (01539) 441476
E: waterheadsteve@aol.com
I: www.waterheadguesthouse.co.uk

Bedrooms: 1 single, 4 double/twin
Bathrooms: 4 en suite

CC: Delta, Mastercard, Switch, Visa

In its own grounds with views of the mountains and only 100 yards from the lake and 0.5 miles from Coniston village.

B&B per night:
S £25.00–£30.00
D £50.00–£60.00

OPEN All Year except Christmas

WHITEHAVEN, Cumbria Map ref 5A3 *Tourist Information Centre Tel: (01946) 852939*

CORKICKLE GUEST HOUSE

1 Corkickle, Whitehaven CA28 8AA
T: (01946) 692073
F: (01946) 692073
E: corkickle@tinyworld.co.uk

Bedrooms: 2 single, 4 double/twin
Bathrooms: 4 en suite, 2 private

Evening meal available

Elegant Georgian townhouse close to town centre, offering high standards of comfort. Ideal base for business or leisure visitors.

B&B per night:
S £22.50–£35.00
D £45.00–£50.00

OPEN All Year except Christmas

Silver Award

MORESBY HALL

Moresby, Whitehaven CA28 6PJ
T: (01946) 696317
F: (01946) 694385
E: etc@moresbyhall.co.uk
I: www.moresbyhall.co.uk

Moresby Hall is a historical, 16thC, Grade I Listed building, one of the oldest residences in Cumbria. Semi-rural, walled gardens, good parking. Near Whitehaven, a Georgian harbour town. Delightful, well-equipped, spacious rooms. Renowned for our delicious breakfasts and imaginative dinners. Fully licensed. Lakes, fells, golf, cultural and tourist locations close by.

Bedrooms: 4 double/twin
Bathrooms: 4 en suite

Evening meal available
CC: Amex, Delta, Diners, Mastercard, Switch, Visa

Murder Mystery weekends during autumn/winter months. 2 nights' DB&B for the price of 1 Nov-Mar (excl Christmas and New Year).

B&B per night:
S £40.00–£60.00
D £65.00–£90.00

HB per person:
DY £52.50–£65.00

OPEN All Year

TOWN INDEX

This can be found at the back of the guide. If you know where you want to stay, the index will give you the page number listing accommodation in your chosen town, city or village.

WINDERMERE, Cumbria Map ref 5A3 *Tourist Information Centre Tel: (015394) 46499*

♦♦♦♦

APHRODITES THEMED ACCOMMODATION

Longtail Hill, Bowness-on-Windermere, Windermere LA23 2EQ
T: (01539) 446702
E: enquiries@aphroditeslodge.co.uk
I: www.aphroditeslodge.co.uk

The highest-quality rooms, all with suites, giant spa baths, fabulous garden views and glimpses of the lake, some with private patios. Outstanding gardens, outdoor swimming pool. Near restaurants and village centre.

Bedrooms: 5 double/twin; permanent suite(s)
Bathrooms: 5 private

CC: Delta, Mastercard, Switch, Visa

Half-price, mid-week breaks, low season.

P

B&B per night:
D £60.00–£140.00

OPEN All Year

♦♦♦

APPLEGARTH HOTEL

College Road, Windermere LA23 1BU
T: (01539) 443206
F: (01539) 446636
E: enquiries@applegarthhotel.com
I: www.applegarthhotel.com

Detached, elegant Victorian mansion house in quiet area of central Windermere. Large, comfortable bar, sun lounge, car park, fell views, 4-poster rooms. Warm welcome and excellent service. Free leisure facilities nearby.

Bedrooms: 4 single, 11 double/twin, 3 triple/multiple
Bathrooms: 18 en suite

Evening meal available
CC: Delta, Mastercard, Switch, Visa

3 nights mid-week from £66pp, weekend from £75pp.

10 P

B&B per night:
S £22.00–£35.00
D £25.00–£40.00

OPEN All Year except Christmas

♦♦♦

APPLETHWAITE HOUSE

1 Upper Oak Street, Windermere LA23 2LB
T: (01539) 444689
E: applethwaitehouse@btinternet.com
I: www.btinternet.com/~applethwaitehouse

We offer you a warm welcome and a hearty breakfast in our family-run guesthouse. Clean, comfortable rooms with colour TV and complimentary hot drinks. Situated in a quiet cul-del-sac just minutes from the village centre. Garage for cycle storage. Families, vegetarians and pets all most welcome.

Bedrooms: 1 double/twin, 3 triple/multiple
Bathrooms: 3 en suite, 1 private

CC: Delta, Diners, Mastercard, Switch, Visa

10% discount on mid-week bookings of 2 or more nights (excl Jun-Sep).

B&B per night:
S £18.00–£40.00
D £36.00–£52.00

OPEN All Year

♦♦♦♦

THE ARCHWAY

13 College Road, Windermere LA23 1BU
T: (01539) 445613 & 445328
F: (01539) 445613
E: archway@btinternet.com
I: www.communiken.com/archway

Bedrooms: 4 double/twin
Bathrooms: 4 en suite

Evening meal available

Comfortable Victorian guesthouse, entirely non-smoking. Mountain views and a breakfast worth getting up for. Evening meals available by arrangement. An ideal touring base.

10 P

B&B per night:
S £25.00–£40.00
D £40.00–£60.00

HB per person:
DY £35.00–£45.00

OPEN All Year

COLOUR MAPS Colour maps at the front of this guide pinpoint all places under which you will find accommodation listed.

WINDERMERE continued

◆◆◆

AUTUMN LEAVES GUEST HOUSE

29 Broad Street, Windermere
LA23 2AB
T: (01539) 448410
E: autumnleaves@nascr.net
I: www.autumnleaves.gbr.cc

Bedrooms: 1 single, 4 double/twin, 1 triple/multiple
Bathrooms: 3 en suite

CC: Delta, Mastercard, Switch, Visa

B&B per night:
S £16.00–£21.00
D £34.00–£48.00

OPEN All Year

A comfortable Victorian guesthouse located in the heart of Windermere, providing an excellent quality of service and friendly atmosphere. Five minutes' walk from train/bus station.

◆◆◆

BOWFELL COTTAGE

Middle Entrance Drive, Storrs Park,
Bowness-on-Windermere,
Windermere LA23 3JY
T: (01539) 444835

Bedrooms: 2 double/twin, 1 triple/multiple
Bathrooms: 2 en suite

Evening meal available

B&B per night:
S £20.00–£25.00
D £40.00–£45.00

HB per person:
DY £31.50–£34.00

OPEN All Year

Cottage in a delightful setting, about 1 mile south of Bowness just off the A5074, offering traditional Lakeland hospitality. Secluded parking in own grounds.

P

◆◆◆

BROOKLANDS

Ferry View, Bowness-on-Windermere, Windermere LA23 3JB
T: (01539) 442344
E: brooklandsferryview@btinternet.com
I: www.smoothhound.co.uk/hotels/brooklands

Bedrooms: 1 single, 3 double/twin, 2 triple/multiple
Bathrooms: 5 en suite, 1 private

Evening meal available
CC: Delta, Mastercard, Switch, Visa

B&B per night:
S £25.00–£35.00
D £40.00–£60.00

HB per person:
DY £30.00–£45.00

OPEN All Year

Comfortable guesthouse in rural setting on the outskirts of Bowness, with fine views of the lake and Cumbrian fells. Close to Lake Windermere marina and shops. Golf nearby. Car parking.

P

◆◆◆◆

COLLEGE HOUSE

15 College Road, Windermere LA23 1BU
T: (01539) 445767 & 0798 0000992
E: clghse@aol.com
I: www.college-house.com

B&B per night:
S £20.00–£28.00
D £36.00–£56.00

OPEN All Year

Quiet, comfortable Victorian family house offering a warm and friendly welcome. Close to village centre and bus/railway station. Front rooms have superb mountain views, all are en suite and have colour TV, tea/coffee-making facilities and full central heating. Delicious breakfast choice. Colourful, sunny garden. Non-smoking. Private parking.

Bedrooms: 3 double/twin
Bathrooms: 3 en suite

6 P

◆◆◆

CROMPTON HOUSE

Lake Road, Windermere LA23 2EQ
T: (01539) 443020
F: (01539) 443020
E: westlake@clara.net
I: www.cromptonhouse.com

Bedrooms: 5 double/twin, 2 triple/multiple
Bathrooms: 7 en suite

Evening meal available

B&B per night:
S £30.00–£45.00
D £40.00–£76.00

HB per person:
DY £35.00–£53.00

OPEN All Year

Small, friendly hotel near lake, restaurants. All rooms en suite with colour TV, tea/coffee, hairdryer. 4-poster, deluxe doubles, lounge, car parking. English/continental breakfast.

5 P

CONFIRM YOUR BOOKING

You are advised to confirm your booking in writing.

WINDERMERE continued

◆◆◆◆ Silver Award

FAIR RIGG

Ferry View, Bowness-on-Windermere
LA23 3JB
T: (01539) 443941
E: rtodd51257@aol.com
I: www.fairrigg.co.uk

B&B per night:
S £32.00–£60.00
D £52.00–£68.00

OPEN All Year

In a superb rural setting just a few minutes' walk from Bowness and the lakeshore, this former Victorian gentleman's residence has been lovingly refurbished to provide high-quality, well-proportioned guest house accommodation. A fine view is enjoyed by most of the rooms. Comfort and relaxation. Personal service. Private parking. No smoking.

Bedrooms: 6 double/twin
Bathrooms: 6 en suite

P

◆◆◆◆

THE FAIRFIELD

Brantfell Road, Bowness-on-Windermere, Windermere LA23 3AE
T: (01539) 446565
F: (01539) 446565
E: Ray&barb@the-fairfield.co.uk
I: www.the-fairfield.co.uk

B&B per night:
S £27.00–£34.00
D £54.00–£68.00

Small, friendly, family-run, 200-year-old Lakeland guesthouse for non-smokers. Set in a peaceful garden environment, close to Bowness village and lakeshore. Well-appointed and tastefully furnished bedrooms all with TV, hairdryers, welcome tray etc. Breakfasts are a speciality. Leisure club facilities nearby. Genuine hospitality and a warm welcome.

Bedrooms: 1 single, 6 double/twin, 2 triple/multiple
Bathrooms: 8 en suite, 1 private

CC: Delta, Mastercard, Switch, Visa

Reduced prices for 2, 3 or more nights.

P

◆◆◆◆

FIR TREES

Lake Road, Windermere LA23 2EQ
T: (01539) 442272
F: (01539) 442512
E: enquiries@firtrees.com
I: www.fir-trees.com

B&B per night:
S £37.00–£57.00
D £52.00–£72.00

OPEN All Year

Built in 1888 as a Victorian gentleman's residence and offering elegant accommodation. Situated between Windermere village and the lake. Lovely bedrooms, scrumptious breakfasts and warm hospitality at exceptional value for money. Guests staying 2 nights or more have free use of Parklands Country Club leisure facilities.

Bedrooms: 7 double/twin, 1 triple/multiple
Bathrooms: 8 en suite

CC: Amex, Delta, Mastercard, Switch, Visa

Mid-week special offers Nov-Mar (excl Christmas and New Year).

P

SPECIAL BREAKS

Many establishments offer special promotions and themed breaks. These are highlighted in red. (All such offers are subject to availability.)

WINDERMERE continued

♦♦♦

FIRGARTH

Ambleside Road, Windermere LA23 1EU
T: (01539) 446974
F: (01539) 442384
E: thefirgarth@KTDinternet.com

B&B per night:
S £19.00–£26.50
D £37.00–£48.00

OPEN All Year except Christmas

Elegant Victorian country house offering good breakfast, friendly atmosphere, ample private parking and close to a lake viewpoint. Ideally situated for touring all areas of Lakeland. A number of attractions are within easy reach, including riding stables opposite to Firgarth. There is a good selection of restaurants nearby.

Bedrooms: 1 single, 3 double/twin, 4 triple/multiple
Bathrooms: 8 en suite

CC: Delta, Mastercard, Switch, Visa

4 P

♦♦♦♦

HAZEL BANK

Hazel Street, Windermere LA23 1EL
T: (01539) 445486
F: (01539) 445486
E: enquiries@hazelbank.co.uk
I: www.hazelbank-guesthouse.co.uk

B&B per night:
S £30.00–£35.00
D £45.00–£30.00

OPEN All Year except Christmas

Elegant, detached Victorian house with matured walled garden and own private car park; situated in a quiet cul-de-sac close to the centre of Windermere village. En suite bedrooms (including 4-poster) are spacious and individually decorated. Non-smoking.

Bedrooms: 3 double/twin
Bathrooms: 3 en suite

Please enquire about spring, autumn, pre-Christmas and New Year breaks and offers.

S P

♦♦♦♦ Silver Award

HIGH VIEW

Sun Hill Lane, Troutbeck Bridge, Windermere LA23 1HJ
T: (01539) 444618 & 442731
F: (01539) 444618
E: info@accommodationlakedistrict.com
I: www.accommodationlakedistrict.com

Bedrooms: 1 double/twin, 1 triple/multiple
Bathrooms: 2 en suite

B&B per night:
S £22.00–£24.00
D £40.00–£48.00

OPEN All Year

A delightful bungalow in an elevated position overlooking Lake Windermere. Within walking distance of Troutbeck, Windermere and Bowness. Breakfast a real speciality.

S P

♦♦♦♦

HILTON HOUSE

New Road, Windermere LA23 2EE
T: (01539) 443934
F: (01539) 443934
E: enquiries@hiltonhouse-guesthouse.co.uk
I: hiltonhouse-guesthouse.co.uk

Bedrooms: 6 double/twin, 1 triple/multiple
Bathrooms: 7 en suite

B&B per night:
S £25.00–£35.00
D £40.00–£60.00

OPEN All Year except Christmas

A stunning detached Edwardian 'gentleman's' residence set in lovely garden. Tastefully decorated throughout with interesting pictures, books and furniture. Warm hospitality and delicious breakfasts.

6 S P

RATING All accommodation in this guide has been rated, or is awaiting a rating, by a trained English Tourism Council assessor.

WINDERMERE continued

HOLLY LODGE

6 College Road, Windermere LA23 1BX
T: (01539) 443873
F: (01539) 443873
E: doyle@hollylodge20.fsnet.co.uk
I: www.hollylodge20.fsnet.co.uk

B&B per night:
S £19.00–£27.00
D £38.00–£54.00

OPEN All Year except Christmas

Traditional Lakeland, family-run guesthouse in a quiet location close to shops, restaurants, buses and trains. Friendly atmosphere. Hearty English breakfast with varied menu. Each bedroom is individually furnished and has a refreshment tray. Separate lounge with open fire. Advice is readily available to make your stay with us memorable.

Bedrooms: 7 double/twin, 3 triple/multiple
Bathrooms: 6 en suite

CC: Delta, Mastercard, Switch, Visa

Winter breaks: 4 nights for the price of 3.

HOLLY-WOOD

Holly Road, Windermere LA23 2AF
T: (01539) 442219
F: (01539) 442219
I: www.hollywoodguesthouse.co.uk

B&B per night:
S £19.00–£29.00
D £35.00–£52.00

Comfortable Victorian house in a quiet position, 3-minute walk from village centre. En suite and budget rooms available, all with TV, hairdryer, clock/radio and tea/coffee-maker. Central heating and cosy residents' lounge. Off-street parking, free bus/rail station transfer (please ask when booking).

Bedrooms: 5 double/twin, 1 triple/multiple
Bathrooms: 4 en suite

Reduced rates for 3-day breaks and longer stays (excl Bank Holidays).

◆◆◆

HOLMLEA

Kendal Road, Bowness-on-Windermere, Windermere LA23 3EW
T: (01539) 442597

Bedrooms: 2 single, 4 double/twin
Bathrooms: 4 en suite

B&B per night:
S £19.00–£26.00
D £38.00–£54.00

OPEN All Year except Christmas

Friendly, comfortable guesthouse in quiet location 3 minutes' walk from lake and amenities. Car park, generous breakfast, warm welcome assured.

◆◆◆◆

KAYS COTTAGE

7 Broad Street, Windermere LA23 2AB
T: (01539) 444146
E: kayscottage@freenetname.co.uk
I: www.kayscottage.co.uk

Bedrooms: 2 double/twin, 2 triple/multiple
Bathrooms: 4 en suite

CC: Delta, Mastercard, Switch, Visa

B&B per night:
D £44.00–£52.00

OPEN All Year except Christmas

Small friendly-run guest house, ideally situated, with well decorated en suite bedrooms. Colour TVs, hairdryers, tea and coffee facilities, toiletries and generous breakfasts.

◆◆◆

KENILWORTH GUEST HOUSE

Holly Road, Windermere LA23 2AF
T: (01539) 444004
E: busby@kenilworth-lake-district.co.uk

Bedrooms: 1 single, 4 double/twin, 1 triple/multiple
Bathrooms: 3 en suite

CC: Amex, Delta, Mastercard, Switch, Visa

B&B per night:
S £18.00–£20.00
D £36.00–£44.00

OPEN All Year except Christmas

Grand Victorian house in secluded, yet central location. Hearty breakfast with vegetarian alternatives. Private parking. Free station transfer (Windermere). Non-smoking throughout.

WINDERMERE continued

◆◆◆◆◆ Gold Award

LAKESHORE HOUSE

Ecclerigg, Windermere LA23 1LJ
T: (01539) 433202
F: (01539) 433213
E: lakeshore@lakedistrict.uk.com
I: www.lakedistrict.uk.com

B&B per night:
S £75.00–£112.50
D £130.00–£170.00

OPEN All Year except Christmas

Fine lodgings in a haven of peace and tranquillity for the discerning on the shores of Lake Windermere. Unsurpassed comfort in glorious surroundings – with simply the best view in England. Highest standard bed/breakfast with own private access. Breakfast is served in Lakeshore's 45-foot-long, carpeted conservatory/pool.

Bedrooms: 3 double/twin; permanent suite(s)
Bathrooms: 3 en suite

CC: Mastercard, Switch, Visa

◆◆◆

LANGDALE VIEW GUEST HOUSE

114 Craig Walk, Off Helm Road, Bowness-on-Windermere, Windermere LA23 3AX
T: (01539) 444076
E: enquiries@langdaleview.co.uk
I: www.langdaleview.co.uk

B&B per night:
S £22.00–£30.00
D £44.00–£60.00

HB per person:
DY £39.00–£47.00

OPEN All Year except Christmas

Exclusively for non-smokers, our family-run, mid-19thC house is located away from traffic noise, yet is only a minute's walk from the shops, restaurants and cinema in Bowness. The steamer piers on the lake are just seven minutes' walk away. All rooms have private facilities, mostly en suite.

Bedrooms: 1 single, 4 double/twin
Bathrooms: 3 en suite, 2 private

Evening meal available
CC: Delta, Mastercard, Switch, Visa

Weekly B&B rates from £140 to £160. Discounts for mid-week breaks in Winter.

◆◆◆◆

LAUREL COTTAGE

St Martin's Square, Kendal Road, Bowness-on-Windermere, Windermere LA23 3EF
T: (01539) 445594
F: (01539) 445594
E: enquiries@laurelcottage-bnb.co.uk
I: www.laurelcottage-bnb.co.uk

B&B per night:
S £20.00–£28.00
D £42.00–£68.00

OPEN All Year

Charming, early-17thC cottage (1613), originally the village grammar school, located one minute's stroll from the lake at Bowness Bay. Ideally situated for all local attractions and amenities. Whilst the cottage retains many original features we continue to give all our guests the comforts of the present. Free membership of local leisure club.

Bedrooms: 2 single, 10 double/twin, 2 triple/multiple
Bathrooms: 11 en suite, 1 private

CC: Delta, Mastercard, Switch, Visa

MAP REFERENCES The map references refer to the colour maps at the front of this guide. The first figure is the map number; the letter and figure which follow indicate the grid reference on the map.

WINDERMERE continued

LINDISFARNE HOUSE

Sunny Bank Road, Windermere LA23 2EN
T: (01539) 446295 & 0775 9925528

Traditional, detached Lakeland house in quiet location conveniently situated between Windermere and Bowness, close to lake, shops and scenic walks. Comfortable, friendly atmosphere, good healthy home-cooked English breakfasts. Off-road parking. Non-smoking.

Bedrooms: 2 double/twin, 2 triple/multiple
Bathrooms: 2 en suite, 2 private

B&B per night:
D £40.00–£50.00

OPEN All Year except Christmas

♦♦♦♦

LINGWOOD

Birkett Hill, Bowness-on-Windermere, Windermere LA23 3EZ
T: (01539) 444680
F: (01539) 448154
E: enquiries@lingwood-guesthouse.co.uk
I: www.lingwood-guesthouse.co.uk

Small, friendly, family-run guesthouse set in own gardens but within 400 yards of lake shore, shops and restaurants. Hearty breakfast provided. With ample private car parking and safe storage for bicycles, Lingwood is ideally placed for exploring both the Lake District and surrounding areas.

Bedrooms: 3 double/twin, 3 triple/multiple
Bathrooms: 4 en suite, 2 private

CC: Delta, Mastercard, Switch, Visa

Mid-week breaks available (excl Bank Holidays).

B&B per night:
S £25.00–£35.00
D £40.00–£56.00

OPEN All Year

♦♦♦♦

1 PARK ROAD

Windermere LA23 2AW
T: (01539) 442107
F: (01539) 448997
E: mark.soden@btinternet.com
I: www.1parkroad.com

Bedrooms: 3 double/twin, 3 triple/multiple
Bathrooms: 6 en suite

Evening meal available
CC: Amex, Delta, Mastercard, Switch, Visa

Beautiful, recently renovated Victorian property with spacious en suite rooms. Five minutes from the pubs, shops, rail/coach stations. Licensed bar and car parking on site.

B&B per night:
S £40.00–£50.00
D £50.00–£70.00

HB per person:
DY £40.00–£60.00

OPEN All Year

RAYRIGG VILLA GUEST HOUSE

Ellerthwaite Square, Windermere LA23 1DP
T: (01539) 488342
E: rayriggvilla@nascr.net
I: www.rayriggvilla.co.uk

Lakeland-stone detached guesthouse built in 1873 as the home for a prosperous corn merchant. Ideally situated on edge of Windermere village, facing Library Gardens. All bedrooms have en suite or private facilities. Extensive full English breakfast with alternatives. Private parking. Convenient for buses and trains. A warm welcome assured.

Bedrooms: 6 double/twin, 1 triple/multiple
Bathrooms: 5 en suite, 2 private

CC: Delta, Mastercard, Switch, Visa

Reductions available for breaks of 3 nights or more (excl Bank Holiday periods).

B&B per night:
S £25.00–£35.00
D £45.00–£60.00

OPEN All Year except Christmas

WINDERMERE continued

ST JOHN'S LODGE

Lake Road, Windermere LA23 2EQ
T: (01539) 443078
F: (01539) 488054
E: mail@st-johns-lodge.co.uk
I: www.st-johns-lodge.co.uk

B&B per night:
S £23.00–£35.00
D £38.00–£64.00

OPEN All Year except Christmas

Attractive Lakeland guesthouse between Windermere village and lake. Close to all amenities. Well known for excellent quality and choice of breakfasts. Comfortable, spotlessly clean en suite bedrooms. Offering a relaxed atmosphere, good service, a little bit of humour and excellent value for money. Free use nearby leisure club. Free internet access.

Bedrooms: 2 single, 9 double/twin, 3 triple/multiple
Bathrooms: 12 en suite, 2 private

CC: Delta, Mastercard, Switch, Visa

3-day breaks (price per person): low season from £54, mid season from £63, high season from £75.

◆◆◆◆

TARN RIGG

Thornbarrow Road, Windermere LA23 2DG
T: (01539) 488777
E: stay@tarnrigg-guesthouse.co.uk
I: www.tarnrigg-guesthouse.co.uk

B&B per night:
S £35.00–£50.00
D £45.00–£65.00

OPEN All Year

Welcome to the Lake District. Built in 1903, Tarn Rigg is situated in an ideal position midway between Windermere and Bowness. Panoramic Langdale Pike views. Quiet, convenient location, ample parking, beautiful 0.75 acre grounds. Spacious en suite rooms with excellent modern facilities. Rooms with lake views available.

Bedrooms: 3 double/twin, 2 triple/multiple
Bathrooms: 5 en suite

CC: Delta, Mastercard, Switch, Visa

◆◆◆

WATERMILL INN

Ings, Staveley, Kendal LA8 9PY
T: (01539) 821309
F: (01539) 822309
E: all@watermillinn.co.uk
I: www.watermillinn.co.uk

Bedrooms: 1 single, 3 double/twin, 3 triple/multiple
Bathrooms: 7 en suite

Lunch available
Evening meal available
CC: Delta, Mastercard, Switch, Visa

B&B per night:
S £28.00–£35.00
D £50.00–£65.00

OPEN All Year except Christmas

A traditional Lakeland inn converted from a watermill. Specialising in real ales, home-cooked food and accommodation at moderate prices. Two miles east of Windermere.

WORKINGTON, Cumbria Map ref 5A2 *Tourist Information Centre Tel: (01900) 606699*

◆◆◆

MORVEN GUEST HOUSE

Siddick Road, Siddick, Workington CA14 1LE
T: (01900) 602118
F: (01900) 602118
E: cnelsonmorven@aol.com

Bedrooms: 2 single, 4 double/twin
Bathrooms: 6 en suite

Lunch available
Evening meal available

B&B per night:
S £24.00–£27.00
D £40.00–£46.00

OPEN All Year

Detached house north-west of town. Ideal base for western Lakes and coast. Start of coast-to-coast cycleway. Car park, cycle storage.

IMPORTANT NOTE Information on accommodation listed in this guide has been supplied by the proprietors. As changes may occur you are advised to check details at the time of booking.

A brief guide to the main Towns and Villages offering accommodation in Cumbria

A ALLONBY, CUMBRIA - Small village on Solway Firth with good sandy beaches, once famous for its herring fishing and as a fashionable resort for Victorian gentry. Good views across the Firth to Criffel and the Galloway mountains.

• **ALSTON, CUMBRIA** - Alston is the highest market town in England, set amongst the highest fells of the Pennines and close to the Pennine Way in an Area of Outstanding Natural Beauty. Mainly 17thC buildings and steep, cobbled streets.

• **AMBLESIDE, CUMBRIA** - Market town situated at the head of Lake Windermere and surrounded by fells. The historic town centre is now a conservation area, and the country around Ambleside is rich in historic and literary associations. Good centre for touring, walking and climbing.

• **APPLEBY-IN-WESTMORLAND, CUMBRIA** - Former county town of Westmorland, at the foot of the Pennines in the Eden Valley. The castle was rebuilt in the 17thC, except for its Norman keep, ditches and ramparts. It now houses a Rare Breeds Survival Trust Centre. Good centre for exploring the Eden Valley.

B BARROW-IN-FURNESS, CUMBRIA - On the Furness Peninsula in Morecambe Bay, an industrial and commercial centre with sandy beaches and nature reserves on Walney Island. Ruins of 12thC Cistercian Furness Abbey. The Dock Museum tells the story of the area, and Forum 28 houses a modern theatre and arts centre.

• **BASSENTHWAITE LAKE, CUMBRIA** - The northernmost and only true "lake" in the Lake District. Visited annually by many species of migratory birds.

• **BORROWDALE, CUMBRIA** - Stretching south of Derwentwater to Seathwaite in the heart of the Lake District, the valley is walled by high fellsides. It can justly claim to be the most scenically impressive valley in the Lake District. Excellent centre for walking and climbing.

• **BOWNESS-ON-SOLWAY, CUMBRIA** - Coastal village near the site of the Roman fort Maia at the western end of Hadrian's Wall.

• **BRAMPTON, CUMBRIA** - Excellent centre for exploring Hadrian's Wall. Wednesday is market day around the Moot Hall in this delightful sandstone-built town. Wall plaque marks the site of Bonnie Prince Charlie and his Jacobite army headquarters whilst they laid siege to Carlisle Castle in 1745.

• **BROUGHTON-IN-FURNESS, CUMBRIA** - Old market village whose historic charter to hold fairs is still proclaimed every year on the first day of August in the market square. Good centre for touring the pretty Duddon Valley.

C CALDBECK, CUMBRIA - Quaint limestone village lying on the northern fringe of the Lake District National Park. John Peel, the famous huntsman who is immortalised in song, is buried in the churchyard. The fells surrounding Caldbeck were once heavily mined, being rich in lead, copper and barytes.

• **CARLISLE, CUMBRIA** - Cumbria's only city is rich in history. Attractions include the small red sandstone cathedral and 900-year-old castle with magnificent view from the keep. Award-winning Tullie House Museum and Art Gallery brings 2,000 years of Border history dramatically to life. Excellent centre for shopping.

• **CARTMEL, CUMBRIA** - Picturesque conserved village based on a 12thC priory with a well-preserved church and gatehouse. Just half a mile outside the Lake District National Park, this is a peaceful base for walking and touring, with historic houses and beautiful scenery.

• **CONISTON, CUMBRIA** - The 803-m fell, Coniston Old Man, dominates the skyline to the east of this village at the northern end of Coniston Water. Arthur Ransome set his "Swallows and Amazons" stories here. Coniston's most famous resident was John Ruskin, whose home, Brantwood, is open to the public. Good centre for walking.

• **CROSTHWAITE, CUMBRIA** - Small village in the picturesque Lyth Valley off the A5074.

D DENT, CUMBRIA - Very picturesque village with narrow cobbled streets, lying within the boundaries of the Yorkshire Dales National Park.

G GRANGE-OVER-SANDS, CUMBRIA - Set on the beautiful Cartmel Peninsula, this tranquil resort, known as Lakeland's Riviera, overlooks Morecambe Bay. Pleasant seafront walks and beautiful gardens. The bay attracts many species of wading birds.

• **GRASMERE, CUMBRIA** - Described by William Wordsworth as "the loveliest spot that man hath ever found", this village, famous for its gingerbread, is in a beautiful setting overlooked by Helm Grag. Wordsworth lived at Dove Cottage. The cottage and museum are open to the public.

H HAWKSHEAD, CUMBRIA - Lying near Esthwaite Water, this village has great charm and character. Its small squares are linked by flagged or cobbled alleys and the main square is dominated by the market house, or Shambles, where the butchers had their stalls in days gone by.

K KENDAL, CUMBRIA - The "Auld Grey Town" lies in the valley of the River Kent with a backdrop of limestone fells. Situated just outside the Lake District National Park, it is a good centre for touring the Lakes and surrounding country. Ruined castle, reputed birthplace of Catherine Parr.

• **KESWICK, CUMBRIA** - Beautifully positioned town beside Derwentwater and below the mountains of Skiddaw and Blencathra. Excellent base for walking, climbing, watersports and touring. Motor-launches operate on Derwentwater, and motor boats, rowing boats and canoes can be hired.

• **KIRKBY LONSDALE, CUMBRIA -** Charming old town of narrow streets and Georgian buildings, set in the superb scenery of the Lune Valley. The Devil's Bridge over the River Lune is probably 13thC.

• **KIRKBY STEPHEN, CUMBRIA -** Old market town close to the River Eden, with many fine Georgian buildings and an attractive market square. St Stephen's Church is known as the "Cathedral of the Dales". Good base for exploring the Eden Valley and the Dales.

L LAKESIDE, CUMBRIA - Lakeside lies at the foot of Lake Windermere and is the linking point between the Lakeside and Haverthwaite Railway and the Windermere steamers, both of which run during the summer months.

M MUNGRISDALE, CUMBRIA - Set in an unspoilt valley, this hamlet has a simple, white church with a 3-decker pulpit and box pews.

P PENRITH, CUMBRIA - Ancient and historic market town, the northern gateway to the Lake District. Penrith Castle was built as a defence against the Scots. Its ruins, open to the public, stand in the public park. High above the town is the Penrith Beacon, made famous by William Wordsworth.

S SAWREY, CUMBRIA - Far Sawrey and Near Sawrey lie near Esthwaite Water. Both villages are small but Near Sawrey is famous for Hill Top Farm, home of Beatrix Potter, now owned by the National Trust and open to the public.

T TEBAY, CUMBRIA - Village lying amongst high fells at the north end of the Lune Gorge.

• **THRELKELD, CUMBRIA -** This village is a centre for climbing the Saddleback range of mountains, which tower high above it.

• **TROUTBECK, CUMBRIA -** Most of the houses in this picturesque village are 17thC; some retain their spinning galleries and oak-mullioned windows. At the south end of the village is Townend, owned by the National Trust and open to the public, an excellently preserved example of a yeoman farmer's or statesman's house.

U ULLSWATER, CUMBRIA - This beautiful lake, which is over 7 miles long, runs from Glenridding to Pooley Bridge. Lofty peaks ranging around the lake make an impressive background. A steamer service operates along the lake between Pooley Bridge, Howtown and Glenridding in the summer.

W WHITEHAVEN, CUMBRIA - Historic Georgian port on the west coast. The town was developed in the 17thC and many fine buildings have been preserved. The Beacon Heritage Centre includes a Meteorological Office Weather Gallery. Start or finishing point of Coast to Coast, Whitehaven to Sunderland cycleway.

• **WINDERMERE, CUMBRIA -** Once a tiny hamlet before the introduction of the railway in 1847, it now adjoins Bowness which is on the lakeside. Centre for sailing and boating. A good way to see the lake is a trip on a passenger steamer. Steamboat Museum has a fine collection of old boats.

• **WORKINGTON, CUMBRIA -** A deep-water port on the west Cumbrian coast. There are the ruins of the 14thC Workington Hall, where Mary Queen of Scots stayed in 1568.

1

Romans, sailors and industrial pioneers have all left their mark here. Northumbria's exciting cities, castle-studded countryside and white-sanded coastline make it an undiscovered gem.

classic sights

Lindisfarne Castle – on Holy Island

Housesteads Roman Fort – the most impressive Roman fort on Hadrian's Wall

2

coast & country

Kielder Water and Forest Park – perfect for walking, cycling and watersports

Saltburn – beach of broad sands

Seahouses – picturesque fishing village

maritime history

HMS Trincomalee – magnificent 1817 British warship

Captain Cook – birthplace museum and replica of his ship, *Endeavour*

Grace Darling – museum commemorating her rescue of shipwreck survivors in 1838

arts for all

Angel of the North – awe-inspiring sculpture by Antony Gormley

distinctively different

St Mary's lighthouse – great views from the top

3

The counties of County Durham, Northumberland, Tees Valley and Tyne & Wear

FOR MORE INFORMATION CONTACT:
Northumbria Tourist Board
Aykley Heads, Durham DH1 5UX
Tel: (0191) 375 3010 Fax: (0191) 386 0899
Internet: www.visitnorthumbria.com

The Pictures: 1 Walkers on the Northumbrian Coast 2 Hartlepool Historic Quay 3 The Angel of the North, Gateshead

PLACES TO VISIT - see pages 108-111 > WHERE TO STAY - see pages 112-126

PLACES to visit

1

You will find hundreds of interesting places to visit during your stay, just some of which are listed in these pages. Contact any Tourist Information Centre in the region for more ideas on days out.

2 3

Awarded ETC's new 'Quality Assured Visitor Attraction' marque at time of going to press. (See page 19).

Auckland Castle

Bishop Auckland

Tel: (01388) 601627 www.auckland-castle.co.uk

Historically the Prince Bishop's country residence, home to the Bishop of Durham. Visit St Peter's Chapel, state rooms and deer park.

Bede's World

Church Bank, Jarrow

Tel: (0191) 489 2106 www.bedesworld.co.uk

Discover the exciting world of the Venerable Bede, greatest scholar of early medieval Europe. Church, monastic site, museum with exhibitions and re-created Anglo-Saxon farm.

Belsay Hall, Castle and Gardens

Belsay, Newcastle-upon-Tyne

Tel: (01661) 881636

House of the Middleton family for 600 years set in 30 acres (12ha) of landscaped gardens and winter garden. 14thC castle, ruined 17thC manor house and neo-classical hall.

Blue Reef Aquarium

Grand Parade, Tynemouth

Tel: (0191) 258 1031 www.bluereefaquarium.co.uk

More than 30 hi-tech displays provide encounters with dozens of sea creatures. Journey beneath the North Sea and discover thousands of amazing creatures.

Bowes Museum

Barnard Castle

Tel: (01833) 690606

www.bowesmuseum.org.uk

French-style chateau housing art collections of national importance and archaeology of South West Durham.

Captain Cook Birthplace Museum

Stewart Park, Marton, Middlesbrough

Tel: (01642) 311211

Early life and voyages of Captain Cook and the countries he visited. Temporary exhibitions. One person free with every group of 10 visiting.

Cherryburn: Thomas Bewick Birthplace Museum

Station Bank, Mickley, Stocksfield

Tel: (01661) 843276

Birthplace cottage (1700) and farmyard. Printing house using original printing blocks. Introductory exhibition of the life, work and countryside.

Chillingham Castle

Chillingham, Wooler

Tel: (01668) 215359 www.chillingham-castle.com

Medieval fortress with Tudor additions, torture chamber, dungeon, shop, tearoom, woodland walks, furnished rooms and topiary garden.

Cragside House, Gardens and Estate

Rothbury, Morpeth

Tel: (01669) 620333 www.nationaltrust.org.uk

House built 1864-84 for the first Lord Armstrong, Tyneside industrialist. Cragside was the first house to be lit by electricity generated by water power.

Discovery Museum

Blandford Square, Newcastle-upon-Tyne

Tel: (0191) 232 6789

Discovery Museum offers a wide variety of experiences for all the family to enjoy. Explore Live Wires and Science Factory, Great City, Fashion Works and maritime history.

Dunstanburgh Castle

Craster, Alnwick

Tel: (01665) 576231 www.english-heritage.org.uk

Romantic ruins of extensive 14thC castle in dramatic coastal situation on 100-ft (30.5-km) cliffs. Built by Thomas, Earl of Lancaster. Remains include gatehouse and curtain wall.

Durham Cathedral

The Chapter Office, The College, Durham

Tel: (0191) 386 4266 www.durhamcathedral.co.uk

Durham Cathedral is thought by many to be the finest example of Norman church architecture in England. Contains the tombs of St Cuthbert and the Venerable Bede.

Gisborough Priory

Church Street, Guisborough

Tel: (01287) 633801

Remains of a priory for Augustinian canons, founded by Robert de Brus in AD1119, in the grounds of Guisborough Hall. Main arch and window of east wall virtually intact.

Hall Hill Farm

Lanchester, Durham

Tel: (01388) 730300 www.hallhillfarm.co.uk

Family fun in attractive countryside with an opportunity to see and touch the animals at close quarters. Trailer ride, riverside walk, teashop and play area.

Hartlepool Historic Quay

Maritime Avenue, Hartlepool

Tel: (01429) 860006

www.thisishartlepool.com

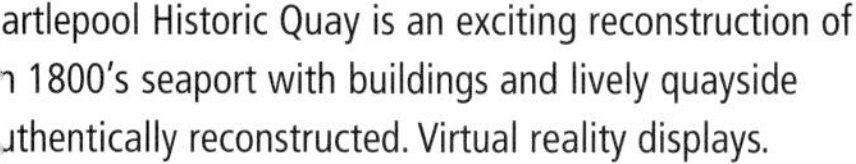

Hartlepool Historic Quay is an exciting reconstruction of an 1800's seaport with buildings and lively quayside authentically reconstructed. Virtual reality displays.

Housesteads Roman Fort (Vercovicium)

Hadrian's Wall, Haydon Bridge, Hexham

Tel: (01434) 344363

Best-preserved and most impressive of the Roman forts, Vercovicium was a 5-acre (2-ha) fort for an extensive 800-strong civil settlement. Only example of a Roman hospital.

Killhope, The North of England Lead Mining Museum

Weardale, Cowshill, Bishop Auckland

Tel: (01388) 537505

www.durham.gov.uk/killhope

Most complete lead-mining site in Great Britain. Mine tours available. 34ft- (10m-) diameter waterwheel, reconstruction of Victorian machinery, miners' lodging, woodland walks.

Kirkleatham Museum

Kirkleatham, Redcar

Tel: (01642) 479500

Displays depicting local life, industry, commerce, history, sea rescue, artists, social and natural history and the story of Kirkleatham.

> The Pictures:: 1 Lindisfarne Castle, Holy Island 2 Hadrian's Wall, Northumberland 3 Durham Castle 4 Bamburgh Castle 5 Town Crier, Alnwick Fair 6 Bridges over the Tyne, Newcastle

Laing Art Gallery

New Bridge Street, Newcastle-upon-Tyne
Tel: (0191) 232 7734
Paintings, including watercolours by Northumbrian-born artist John Martin. Award-winning interactive displays, 'Art on Tyneside' and 'Children's Gallery'. Cafe and shop.

Life Interactive World

Times Square, Scotswood Road, Newcastle-upon-Tyne
Tel: (0191) 243 8210
www.lifeinteractiveworld.co.uk
Life Interactive World is an amazing action-packed journey. Experience the longest motion ride in the world, magical 3D, theatre shows, virtual games and interactives.

Lindisfarne Castle

Holy Island, Berwick upon Tweed
Tel: (01289) 389244
Fort converted into a private home for Edward Hudson by the architect Sir Edwin Lutyens in 1903.

National Glass Centre

Liberty Way, Sunderland
Tel: (0191) 515 5555
www.nationalglasscentre.com
A unique visitor attraction presenting the best in contemporary glass. Master craftspeople will demonstrate glass-making techniques. Classes and workshops available.

Nature's World at the Botanic Centre

Ladgate Lane, Acklam, Middlesbrough
Tel: (01642) 594895 www.naturesworld.org.uk
Demonstration gardens, wildlife pond, white garden, environmental exhibition hall, shop, tearoom, River Tees model. Hydroponicum and visitor exhibition centre.

Newcastle Cathedral Church of St Nicholas

St Nicholas Street, Newcastle-upon-Tyne
Tel: (0191) 232 1939
www.newcastle-ang-cathedral-stnicholas.org.uk
Thirteenth and 14thC church, added to in 18th-20thC. Famous lantern tower, pre-reformation font and font cover, and 15thC stained glass roundel in the side chapel.

The North of England Open Air Museum

Beamish
Tel: (0191) 370 4000 www.beamish.org.uk
Visit the town, colliery village, working farm, Pockerley Manor and 1825 railway, re-creating life in the North East in the early 1800s and 1900s.

Otter Trust's North Pennines Reserve

Vale House Farm, Bowes, Barnard Castle
Tel: (01833) 628339
A branch of the famous Otter Trust. Visitors can see Asian and British otters, red and fallow deer and several rare breeds of farm animals in this 230-acre (93-ha) wildlife reserve.

Raby Castle

Staindrop, Darlington
Tel: (01833) 660202 www.rabycastle.com
This medieval castle, home of Lord Barnard's family since 1626, includes a 200-acre (81-ha) deer park, walled gardens, carriage collection, adventure playground, shop and tearoom.

South Shields Museum and Art Gallery

Ocean Road, South Shields
Tel: (0191) 456 8740
Discover how the area's development has been influenced by its natural and industrial past through lively hands-on displays. Exciting programme of temporary exhibitions.

Vindolanda (Chesterholm)

Chesterholm Museum, Bardon Mill, Hexham
Tel: (01434) 344277 www.vindolanda.com
Visitors may inspect the remains of the Roman fort and settlement and see its extraordinary finds in the superb museum. Full-scale replicas of Roman buildings.

Wallington House, Walled Garden and Grounds

Wallington, Cambo, Morpeth
Tel: (01670) 773600 www.nationaltrust.org.uk
Built 1688 on site of earlier medieval castle and altered in the 1740s. Interior has plasterwork, porcelain, furniture, pictures, needlework and dolls houses. Walled garden.

Washington Old Hall

The Avenue, District 4, Washington
Tel: (0191) 416 6879
The home of George Washington's direct ancestors from 1183 to 1399, remaining in the family until 1613. The manor, from which the family took its name, was restored in 1936.

Wet 'N Wild

Rotary Way, Royal Quays, North Shields
Tel: (0191) 296 1333 www.wetnwild.co.uk
Tropical indoor water park. A fun water playground providing the wildest and wettest indoor rapid experience. Whirlpools, slides and meandering lazy river.

Find out more about Northumbria

Dunstanburgh Castle

Further information about holidays and attractions in Northumbria is available from:

NORTHUMBRIA TOURIST BOARD
Aykley Heads, Durham DH1 5UX.
Tel: (0191) 375 3010 Fax: (0191) 386 0899
Internet: www.visitnorthumbria.com

The following publications are available from Northumbria Tourist Board unless otherwise stated:

Northumbria 2003
nformation on the region, including hotels, bed and breakfast and self-catering accommodation, aravan and camping parks, attractions, shopping, eating and drinking

Going Places
nformation on where to go, what to see and what to do. Combined with the award-winning Powerpass romotion which offers 2-for-1 entry into many of the region's top attractions

Group Travel Directory
uide designed specifically for group organisers, detailing group accommodation providers, laces to visit, suggested itineraries, coaching information and events

Educational Visits
formation to help plan educational visits within the region. Uncover a wide variety of places o visit with unique learning opportunities

Discover Northumbria on two wheels
formation on cycling in the region including an order form allowing the reader to order maps/leaflets om a central ordering point

Discover Northumbria on two feet
formation on walking in the region including an order form allowing the reader to order maps/leaflets om a central ordering point

Getting to Northumbria

ROAD: The north/south routes on the A1 and A19 thread the region as does the A68. East/west routes like the A66 d A69 easily link with the western side of the country. Within Northumbria you will find fast, modern terconnecting roads between all the main centres, a vast network of scenic, traffic-free country roads to make otoring a pleasure and frequent local bus services operating to all towns and villages.

RAIL: London to Edinburgh InterCity service stops at Darlington, Durham, Newcastle and Berwick upon Tweed. 26 ains daily make the journey between London and Newcastle in just under 3 hours. The London to Middlesbrough urney takes 3 hours. Birmingham to Darlington 3 hours 15 minutes. Bristol to Durham 5 hours and Sheffield to ewcastle just over 2 hours. Direct services operate to Newcastle from Liverpool, Manchester, Glasgow, Stranraer and rlisle. Regional services to areas of scenic beauty operate frequently, allowing the traveller easy access. The Tyne & ear Metro makes it possible to travel to many destinations within the Tyneside area, such as Gateshead, South ields, Whitley Bay and Newcastle International Airport, in minutes.

Where to stay in Northumbria

Accommodation entries in this region are listed in alphabetical order of place name, and then in alphabetical order of establishment.

Map references refer to the colour location maps at the front of this guide. The first number indicates the map to use; the letter and number which follow refer to the grid reference on the map.

At-a-glance symbols at the end of each accommodation entry give useful information about services and facilities. A key to symbols can be found inside the back cover flap. Keep this open for easy reference.

A brief description of the towns and villages offering accommodation in the entries which follow, can be found at the end of this section.

A complete listing of all the English Tourism Council assessed accommodation covered by this guide appears at the back of the guide.

ALNWICK, Northumberland Map ref 5C1 *Tourist Information Centre Tel: (01665) 510665*

◆◆◆

BONDGATE HOUSE HOTEL
20 Bondgate Without, Alnwick
NE66 1PN
T: (01665) 602025
F: (01665) 602025
E: aclarvin@aol.com
I: www.bondgatehouse.ntb.org.uk

Bedrooms: 1 single, 4 double/twin, 3 triple/multiple
Bathrooms: 5 en suite

Evening meal available
CC: Delta, Mastercard, Switch, Visa

B&B per night:
S £25.00–£30.00
D £47.00–£49.00

OPEN All Year except Christmas

Small family-run hotel near the medieval town gateway and interesting local shops. Well-placed for touring. Most rooms are en suite.

◆◆◆◆

CHARLTON HOUSE
2 Aydon Gardens, Alnwick
NE66 2NT
T: (01665) 605185
I: www.s-h-systems.co.uk/hotels/charlt2.html

Bedrooms: 1 single, 4 double/twin
Bathrooms: 5 en suite

B&B per night:
S £21.00–£30.00
D £42.00–£48.00

OPEN All Year except Christmas

Victorian townhouse on the edge of historic Alnwick, where a warm welcome awaits. Beautiful en suite bedrooms, TV, hospitality tray. Breakfasts to suit all tastes.

◆◆◆

THE OAKS HOTEL
South Road, Alnwick NE66 2PN
T: (01665) 510014
F: (01665) 603219
I: www.theoakshotel.co.uk

Bedrooms: 2 single, 8 double/twin, 1 triple/multiple
Bathrooms: 11 en suite

Lunch available
Evening meal available
CC: Amex, Delta, Mastercard, Switch, Visa

B&B per night:
S Min £40.00
D Min £60.00

OPEN All Year

A small family-run hotel with excellent bar and restaurant facilities. All rooms recently refurbished and all en suite.

ALNWICK continued

ROCK MIDSTEAD FARM HOUSE

Rock Midstead Organic Farm, Rock, Alnwick NE66 2TH
T: (01665) 579225 & 579326
E: ian@rockmidstead.freeserve.co.uk

B&B per night:
D £54.00

HB per person:
DY £44.50–£54.50

OPEN All Year

Comfortable, spacious, family farmhouse set in peaceful organic dairy farm with extensive views of surrounding countryside. Ideal for walking or cycling. Excellent home cooking, fresh-baked bread daily, afternoon tea on the lawn. Log fires. En suite rooms with colour TV and radio. Perfect base for exploring coastline, castles, hills and historic houses.

Bedrooms: 3 double/twin
Bathrooms: 2 en suite, 1 private

Lunch available
Evening meal available

BAMBURGH, Northumberland Map ref 5C1

GLENANDER GUEST HOUSE

27 Lucker Road, Bamburgh NE69 7BS
T: (01668) 214336
F: (01668) 214695
E: johntoland@tiscali.co.uk
I: www.glenander.com

B&B per night:
S £25.00–£35.00
D £50.00–£55.00

OPEN All Year

Glenander has comfortable double/twin rooms which are available throughout the year. Each bedroom is individually and tastefully furnished in modern design. Amenities include hospitality tray, hairdryer, colour TV and en suite facilities. There is a spacious ground floor guest lounge complete with TV and video.

Bedrooms: 3 double/twin
Bathrooms: 3 en suite

BARNARD CASTLE, Durham Map ref 5B3 *Tourist Information Centre Tel: (01833) 690909*

EGGLESTONE HALL

Barnard Castle DL12 0AG
T: (01833) 650553
F: (01833) 650553
E: willgray@globalnet.co.uk
I: www.egglestonhall.co.uk

B&B per night:
S £50.00–£75.00
D £50.00–£75.00

Egglestone Hall is a Georgian country house situated in upper Teesdale. Enjoy homemade cakes, a glorious log fire and breathtaking views of the River Tees. Facilities include a tennis court, private woodland walks, croquet and boules. All bedrooms are well-appointed and are individually decorated to a high standard.

Bedrooms: 5 double/twin; permanent suite(s)
Bathrooms: 4 en suite, 1 private

CC: Delta, Mastercard, Switch, Visa

BARNARD CASTLE continued

MOORCOCK INN

Hill Top, Gordon Bank, Eggleston,
Barnard Castle DL12 0AU
T: (01833) 650395
F: (01833) 650052
E: zach1@talk21.com
I: www.moorcock-Inn.co.uk

Country inn with scenic views over Teesdale. Ideal walking country. Cosy en suite bedrooms, open log fire in lounge bar. Over 50 malt whiskies and a selection of real ales. Excellent home-cooked food using local produce. Our speciality is Teesdale lamb and locally produced beef and pork. Also, extensive fish menu.

Bedrooms: 2 single, 5 double/twin
Bathrooms: 4 en suite

Lunch available
Evening meal available
CC: Delta, Mastercard, Switch, Visa

B&B per night:
S £20.00–£25.00
D £32.00–£37.00

OPEN All Year

BELLINGHAM, Northumberland Map ref 5B2 *Tourist Information Centre Tel: (01434) 220616*

◆◆◆◆

LYNDALE GUEST HOUSE

Bellingham, Hexham NE48 2AW
T: (01434) 220361 & 03778 925479
F: (01434) 220361
E: ken&joy@lyndalegh.fsnet.co.uk
I: www.SmoothHound.co.uk/hotels/lyndale.html

Bedrooms: 3 double/twin
Bathrooms: 2 en suite, 1 private

Lunch available
Evening meal available
CC: Delta, Mastercard, Visa

Close to Hadrian's Wall, Kielder Water, borders and Pennine Way. Relax in the walled garden or sun lounge. Excellent dinners/good breakfasts. Walking, biking, watersports, golf.

B&B per night:
S £25.00
D £50.00

HB per person:
DY £37.50

OPEN All Year except Christmas

◆◆◆◆

WESTFIELD HOUSE

Bellingham NE48 2DP
T: (01434) 220340
F: (01434) 220356
E: westfield.house@btinternet.com
I: www.westfield-house.net

Bedrooms: 2 double/twin, 1 triple/multiple
Bathrooms: 3 en suite

Evening meal available
CC: Delta, Mastercard, Switch, Visa

Large Victorian residence in private grounds, set in the rolling hills of the North Tyne Valley. Beautiful rooms, good food and genuine hospitality.

B&B per night:
S Min £32.00
D £56.00

HB per person:
DY Min £44.00

OPEN All Year except Christmas

BERWICK-UPON-TWEED, Northumberland Map ref 5B1 *Tourist Information Centre Tel: (01289) 330733*

◆◆◆

COBBLED YARD HOTEL

40 Walkergate, Berwick-upon-Tweed TD15 1DJ
T: (01289) 308407
F: (01289) 330623
E: cobbledyardhotel@berwick35.fsnet.co.uk
I: www.cobbledyardhotel.com

Bedrooms: 2 double/twin, 3 triple/multiple
Bathrooms: 5 en suite

Lunch available
Evening meal available
CC: Delta, Diners, Mastercard, Switch, Visa

Two minutes from town centre, within town walls, close to beach, golf course and railway station. Family-run hotel, good food. Car park.

B&B per night:
S £35.00–£55.00
D £55.00

HB per person:
DY £75.00

OPEN All Year

◆◆◆

LADYTHORNE HOUSE

Cheswick, Berwick-upon-Tweed TD15 2RW
T: (01289) 387382
F: (01289) 387073
E: valparker@ladythorneguesthouse.freeserve.co.uk
I: www.ladythorneguesthouse.freeserve.co.uk

Bedrooms: 1 single, 3 double/twin, 2 triple/multiple

Grade II Listed Georgian house dated 1721. Magnificent views of the countryside, close to unspoilt beaches. Large garden, families welcome. Meals available within 5 minutes' drive.

B&B per night:
S £17.00–£20.00
D £34.00–£40.00

OPEN All Year

BERWICK-UPON-TWEED continued

ROB ROY

Dock Road, Tweedmouth, Berwick-upon-Tweed TD15 2BE
T: (01289) 306428
F: (01289) 303629
E: therobroy@btinternet.com
I: www.therobroy.co.uk

Stone-built pub with cosy bar and log fire. One mile to Berwick centre from our riverside location. Our restaurant and bar menus offer choice local seafood, lobster, oysters, scallops. Visit Northumbria's beautiful coastline and castles, walk the Cheviots or the beautiful Tweed Valley. Or just enjoy Rob Roy hospitality.

Bedrooms: 2 double/twin
Bathrooms: 2 en suite

Lunch available
Evening meal available
CC: Amex, Delta, Diners, Mastercard, Switch, Visa

Reduced out of season offers. Nov-May deals on website.

B&B per night:
S £28.00–£33.00
D £45.00–£52.00

OPEN All Year except Christmas

BISHOP AUCKLAND, Durham Map ref 5C2 *Tourist Information Centre Tel: (01388) 604922*

FIVE GABLES GUEST HOUSE

Binchester, Bishop Auckland DL14 8AT
T: (01388) 608204
F: (01388) 663092
E: book.in@fivegables.co.uk
I: www.fivegables.co.uk

Bedrooms: 1 single, 1 double/twin, 1 triple/multiple
Bathrooms: 3 en suite

Evening meal available
CC: Delta, Mastercard, Switch, Visa

Victorian country house, 3 miles from Bishop Auckland, 15 minutes from Durham. Self-catering cottage available.

B&B per night:
S £28.00–£30.00
D £48.00–£50.00

OPEN All Year except Christmas

CONSETT, Durham Map ref 5B2

◆◆◆

BEE COTTAGE FARM

Castleside, Consett DH8 9HW
T: (01207) 508224

Bedrooms: 1 single, 5 double/twin, 2 triple/multiple; permanent suite(s)
Bathrooms: 3 en suite

Lunch available
Evening meal available

Quiet, pleasant walks, unspoilt views in peaceful surroundings. Ideal base for Beamish Museum, Durham Cathedral, Hadrian's Wall. Some ground floor rooms. You will be very welcome.

B&B per night:
S £28.00–£35.00
D £44.00–£80.00

CORBRIDGE, Northumberland Map ref 5B2

FELLCROFT

Station Road, Corbridge NE45 5AY
T: (01434) 632384
F: (01434) 633918
E: tove.brown@ukonline.co.uk

Bedrooms: 1 double/twin, 1 triple/multiple
Bathrooms: 1 en suite, 1 private

Evening meal available

Well-appointed stone-built Edwardian house with full private facilities. Quiet road in country setting, half a mile south of market square. Non-smokers only, please.

B&B per night:
S £21.00–£23.00
D £35.00–£38.00

HB per person:
DY £27.50–£31.00

OPEN All Year except Christmas

CHECK THE MAPS

The colour maps at the front of this guide show all the cities, towns and villages for which you will find accommodation entries. Refer to the town index to find the page on which they are listed.

CORBRIDGE continued

THE HAYES

Newcastle Road, Corbridge NE45 5LP
T: (01434) 632010
F: (01434) 632010
E: stay@hayes-corbridge.co.uk
I: www.hayes-corbridge.co.uk

B&B per night:
S £21.00–£35.00
D £44.00–£50.00

OPEN All Year except Christmas

Well-appointed, family-run accommodation in fine country house overlooking Tyne Valley. Five minutes from Corbridge with its excellent specialist shops, old inns and eating houses. Eighteen miles Newcastle and airport. Ready access to rail and A69 road links. Ideal centre for Roman Wall, Northumbrian castles, Kielder Water, Durham and Lindisfarne.

Bedrooms: 1 single, 1 double/twin, 2 triple/multiple
Bathrooms: 2 en suite, 2 private

2-night special offer: 2 people £90 B&B.

◆◆◆◆

LOW FOTHERLEY FARMHOUSE BED AND BREAKFAST

Riding Mill NE44 6BB
T: (01434) 682277
F: (01434) 682277
E: hugh@lowfotherley.fsnet.co.uk
I: www.westfarm.freeserve.co.uk

B&B per night:
S £25.00–£27.50
D £45.00–£50.00

OPEN All Year except Christmas

Built in the 19thC, Low Fotherley is an impressive Victorian farmhouse full of character and history situated close to the A68 with outstanding views. Spacious, comfortable house with full central heating. Quality bedrooms with TV and hospitality tray. Close to Hexham, Hadrian's Wall and Durham. Aga breakfast, homemade bread and preserves.

Bedrooms: 2 double/twin
Bathrooms: 1 en suite, 1 private

Special breaks Nov-Mar £19pppn.

CROOKHAM, Northumberland Map ref 5B1

◆◆◆◆

THE COACH HOUSE AT CROOKHAM

Cornhill-on-Tweed TD12 4TD
T: (01890) 820293
F: (01890) 820284
E: stay@coachhousecrookham.com
I: www.coachhousecrookham.com

Bedrooms: 2 single, 7 double/twin
Bathrooms: 6 en suite, 1 private

Evening meal available
CC: Mastercard, Visa

B&B per night:
S £27.00–£47.00
D £54.00–£86.00

HB per person:
DY £46.50–£66.50

Spacious rooms, arranged around a courtyard, in rolling country near the Scottish border. Home-cooked, quality fresh food. Rooms specially equipped for disabled guests.

DARLINGTON, Durham Map ref 5C3 *Tourist Information Centre Tel: (01325) 388666*

◆◆◆

BOOT & SHOE

Church Row, Darlington DL1 5QD
T: (01325) 287501 & 362121
F: (01325) 287501
E: sueemcgee@hotmail.com

Bedrooms: 9 double/twin
Bathrooms: 7 en suite, 2 private

CC: Delta, Mastercard, Switch, Visa

B&B per night:
S £25.00–£35.00
D £40.00–£50.00

OPEN All Year

A Grade II Listed building situated on Darlington's busy market-place, fully refurbished in 2000. Only minutes away from train and bus station and A1.

DARLINGTON continued

◆◆◆

HAREWOOD LODGE

40 Grange Road, Darlington DL1 5NP
T: (01325) 358152
E: harewood.lodge@ntlworld.com

Bedrooms: 2 single, 2 double/twin
Bathrooms: 3 en suite, 1 private

Victorian townhouse on outskirts of town. Short walk to town centre and golf course. Rooms en suite or private facilities.

B&B per night:
S £25.00
D £45.00

OPEN All Year

DURHAM, Durham Map ref 5C2 *Tourist Information Centre Tel: (0191) 384 3720*

◆◆◆

THE AUTUMN LEAVES GUEST HOUSE

Dragonville, Durham DH1 2DX
T: (0191) 386 3394
E: irene@autumnleaves.freeserve.co.uk
I: www.autumnleavesguesthouse.co.uk

Bedrooms: 5 double/twin
Bathrooms: 5 en suite

Built in 1853. Decorated to a very high standard.

B&B per night:
S £28.00–£33.00
D £38.00–£45.00

OPEN All Year

◆◆◆◆

CASTLE VIEW GUEST HOUSE

4 Crossgate, Durham DH1 4PS
T: (0191) 386 8852
F: (0191) 386 8852
E: castle_view@hotmail.com
I: www.castle-view.net

Bedrooms: 1 single, 5 double/twin
Bathrooms: 6 en suite

CC: Delta, Mastercard, Switch, Visa

Two-hundred-and-fifty-year-old, Listed building in the heart of the old city, with woodland and riverside walks and a magnificent view of the cathedral and castle.

2

B&B per night:
S £45.00
D £60.00

OPEN All Year except Christmas

◆◆◆

CASTLEDENE

37 Nevilledale Terrace, Durham DH1 4QG
T: (0191) 384 8386 & 07710 425921
F: (0191) 384 8386
E: lornabyrne@tinyworld.co.uk

Bedrooms: 2 double/twin

Edwardian end-of-terrace house 0.5 miles west of the market place. Within walking distance of the riverside, cathedral and castle.

7

B&B per night:
S Min £25.00
D Min £40.00

OPEN All Year except Christmas

◆◆◆◆

HILLRISE GUEST HOUSE

13 Durham Road West, Bowburn, Durham DH6 5AU
T: (0191) 377 0302
F: (0191) 377 0898
E: hillrise.guesthouse@btinternet.com
I: www.hill-rise.com

Bedrooms: 4 double/twin, 1 triple/multiple
Bathrooms: 5 en suite

CC: Delta, Mastercard, Switch, Visa

Conveniently placed 200 yards from jct 61 A1(M). Family, twin and double rooms with en suite facilities. Friendly atmosphere and a high standard of cleanliness.

B&B per night:
S £20.00–£30.00
D £50.00–£60.00

OPEN All Year

COUNTRY CODE Always follow the Country Code · Enjoy the countryside and respect its life and work · Guard against all risk of fire · Fasten all gates · Keep your dogs under close control · Keep to public paths across farmland · Use gates and stiles to cross fences, hedges and walls · Leave livestock, crops and machinery alone · Take your litter home · Help to keep all water clean · Protect wildlife, plants and trees · Take special care on country roads · Make no unnecessary noise

DURHAM continued

ST AIDAN'S COLLEGE

University of Durham, Windmill Hill, Durham DH1 3LJ
T: (0191) 374 3269
F: (0191) 374 4749
E: aidans.conf@durham.ac.uk
I: www.st-aidans.org.uk

B&B per night:
S £20.00–£32.00
D £38.00–£64.00

Set in landscaped gardens, overlooking the magnificent cathedral, which has proved to be Britain's best-loved visitor attraction. Single/twin en suite bedrooms and a spacious, airy dining room. We are an ideal venue for anyone wishing to visit the many and varied museums/castles to be found in the area.

Bedrooms: 72 single, 24 double/twin
Bathrooms: 96 en suite

Lunch available
Evening meal available
CC: Delta, Mastercard, Switch, Visa

Durham Delights: 3-night/4-day short-break holidays for groups. DB&B, special guided tours. Minimum number of 25.

EASTGATE-IN-WEARDALE, Durham Map ref 5B2

Silver Award

ROSE HILL FARM BED AND BREAKFAST

Rose Hill Farm, Eastgate-in-Weardale, Bishop Auckland DL13 2LB
T: (01388) 517209 & 07808 402425
E: june@rosehillfarm.fsnet.co.uk
I: www.rosehillfarmholidays.co.uk

B&B per night:
S £30.00
D £45.00–£50.00

HB per person:
DY £35.00–£37.50

OPEN All Year

Converted from former barns, this spacious accommodation enjoys panoramic views of Weardale from its large gardens. Five en suite bedrooms including 2 on ground floor. Large residents' lounge with centrepiece inglenook fireplace. Ideal base for visiting Beamish, Durham City, Barnard Castle and Hexham, or walking in the north Pennines.

Bedrooms: 3 double/twin, 2 triple/multiple
Bathrooms: 5 en suite

Evening meal available

EMBLETON, Northumberland Map ref 5C1

BLUE BELL INN

Embleton, Alnwick NE66 3UP
T: (01665) 576573 & 576639

Bedrooms: 3 double/twin
Bathrooms: 3 en suite

B&B per night:
S £25.00–£35.00
D £45.00–£50.00

OPEN All Year

Comfortable and friendly country inn situated in picturesque village of Embleton within walking distance of beach and golf course.

AT-A-GLANCE SYMBOLS

Symbols at the end of each accommodation entry give useful information about services and facilities. A key to symbols can be found inside the back cover flap. Keep this open for easy reference.

HALTWHISTLE, Northumberland Map ref 5B2 *Tourist Information Centre Tel: (01434) 322002*

Silver Award

ASHCROFT

Lantys Lonnen, Haltwhistle NE49 0DA
T: (01434) 320213
F: (01434) 321641
E: enquiries@ashcroftguesthouse.freeserve.co.uk
I: www.ashcroftguesthouse.co.uk

Elegantly furnished former vicarage in beautiful terraced gardens with private parking. Warm welcome and extensive breakfast choice. Non-smoking. Conveniently situated on the southern edge of town, yet only 100 metres from town facilities. The perfect base to explore Hadrian's Wall and surrounding area. Colour brochure available.

Bedrooms: 1 single, 5 double/twin, 1 triple/multiple
Bathrooms: 7 en suite

CC: Mastercard, Visa

10% reduction for stays of 3 nights or more.

B&B per night:
S £25.00–£35.00
D £50.00–£56.00

OPEN All Year except Christmas

HAMSTERLEY FOREST

See under Barnard Castle, Bishop Auckland

HAYDON BRIDGE, Northumberland Map ref 5B2

HADRIAN LODGE

Hindshield Moss, North Road, Haydon Bridge, Hexham NE47 6NF
T: (01434) 684867
F: (01434) 684867
E: hadrianlodge@hadrianswall.co.uk
I: www.hadrianswall.co.uk

Bedrooms: 1 single, 5 double/twin, 3 triple/multiple
Bathrooms: 7 en suite

Evening meal available
CC: Amex, Mastercard, Switch, Visa

Idyllic rural location, overlooking lakes (fishing available), near Housesteads Roman Fort and Hadrian's Wall. Cosy residents' bar, delicious home-cooked meals. Warm welcome. Write/ring for brochure.

B&B per night:
S £25.00–£29.50
D £45.00–£49.50

HB per person:
DY £30.85–£35.35

HEXHAM, Northumberland Map ref 5B2

Silver Award

BLACK HALL

Black Hall, Juniper, Hexham NE47 0LD
T: (01434) 673218
F: (01434) 673218
E: nblackhall@lineone.net
I: www.blackhall-hexham.co.uk

Black Hall is a peaceful Grade II Listed country house set in its own parkland. Spacious, warm, south-facing rooms with open views over our fields and woods. We are 5 miles south of Hexham within easy reach of Hadrian's Wall and the many attractions of Northumberland.

Bedrooms: 2 double/twin
Bathrooms: 2 private

Evening meal available
CC: Delta, Mastercard, Switch, Visa

B&B per night:
D £49.00–£56.00

HB per person:
DY £44.50–£53.00

OPEN All Year except Christmas

CREDIT CARD BOOKINGS If you book by telephone and are asked for your credit card number it is advisable to check the proprietor's policy should you cancel your reservation.

HEXHAM continued

DUKESFIELD HALL FARM

Steel, Hexham NE46 1SH
T: (01434) 673634
F: (01434) 673170
E: cath@dukesfield.supanet.com

Charming Grade II Listed farmhouse set in 300 acres, 5 miles south of Hexham and ideally situated for walking, cycling, touring or just relaxing. Charming en suite bedrooms and a delightful guest lounge, with a friendly atmosphere. Local country pub 1.5 miles.

Bedrooms: 2 double/twin
Bathrooms: 2 en suite

B&B per night:
S £20.00–£25.00
D £40.00–£50.00

OPEN All Year

♦♦♦♦

HETHERINGTON
Wark-on-Tyne, Wark, Hexham NE48 3DR
T: (01434) 230260
F: (01434) 230260
E: a_nichol@hotmail.com

Bedrooms: 3 double/twin
Bathrooms: 2 en suite, 1 private

B&B per night:
S £20.00
D £50.00–£56.00

Northumbrian farmhouse on 400-acre mixed farm on a public road. Stabling available. Excellent facilities. Ideal walking and touring area – the Pennine Way runs through the farm.

♦♦♦

ROSE AND CROWN INN
Main Street, Slaley, Hexham NE47 0AA
T: (01434) 673263
F: (01434) 673305
E: rosecrowninn@supanet.com
I: www.smoothhound.co.uk/hotels/rosecrowninn.html

Bedrooms: 1 single, 2 double/twin
Bathrooms: 3 en suite

Lunch available
Evening meal available
CC: Amex, Delta, Mastercard, Switch, Visa

B&B per night:
S £29.50–£35.00
D £45.00–£50.00

OPEN All Year

Warm, friendly, family-run business with good wholesome home cooking and a la carte restaurant. All bedrooms en suite in this 200-year-old Listed village freehouse in Slaley.

HOLY ISLAND, Northumberland Map ref 5C1

♦♦♦

BRITANNIA
Britannia House, Holy Island, Berwick-upon-Tweed TD15 2RX
T: (01289) 389218

Bedrooms: 2 double/twin, 1 triple/multiple
Bathrooms: 1 en suite

B&B per night:
S £21.00–£25.00
D £40.00–£45.00

Comfortable, friendly bed and breakfast in centre of Holy Island. Tea-making facilities in all rooms. TV lounge. En suite available.

KIELDER FOREST

See under Bellingham, Wark

QUALITY ASSURANCE SCHEME

For an explanation of the quality and facilities represented by the Diamonds please refer to the front of this guide. A more detailed explanation can be found in the information pages at the back.

KIELDER WATER, Northumberland Map ref 5B2

THE PHEASANT INN (BY KIELDER WATER)

Stannersburn, Falstone, Hexham NE48 1DD
T: (01434) 240382
F: (01434) 240382
E: thepheasantinn@kielderwater.demon.co.uk
I: www.thepheasantinn.com

Charming 16thC inn, retaining its character while providing comfortable, modern en suite accommodation. Features include stone walls and low-beamed ceilings in the bars, antique artefacts and open fires. Emphasis on traditional home cooking, using fresh vegetables, served in bar or dining room. Sunday roasts are renowned for their quality. Ten double/twin with en suite. One family room with en suite.

Bedrooms: 10 double/twin, 1 triple/multiple
Bathrooms: 11 en suite

Lunch available
Evening meal available
CC: Delta, Mastercard, Switch, Visa

Reduced rates Oct-May, DB&B £45pppn.

B&B per night:
S £35.00–£40.00
D £55.00–£65.00

OPEN All Year except Christmas

LITTLETOWN, Durham Map ref 5C2

LITTLETOWN LODGE

Front Street, Littletown, Durham DH6 1PZ
T: 0771 3322667 & (0191) 3723712
E: littletownlodge@aol.com
I: www.littletownlodge.co.uk

A warm welcome awaits you in this traditional country guesthouse situated in a tranquil rural setting only minutes from Durham City centre. Beautiful 4-poster rooms are available for that extra-special break. It is an ideal base for walking, cycling or touring, with collection and delivery service available.

Bedrooms: 3 double/twin, 2 triple/multiple
Bathrooms: 5 en suite

Lunch available
Evening meal available
CC: Mastercard, Visa

Romantic weekend (2 nights) in one of our 4-poster room suites available from £120 per room, including complimentary bottle of champagne.

B&B per night:
S £25.00–£30.00
D £45.00

OPEN All Year

MIDDLETON-IN-TEESDALE, Durham Map ref 5B3

BELVEDERE HOUSE

54 Market Place, Middleton-in-Teesdale, Barnard Castle DL12 0QH
T: (01833) 640884
F: (01833) 640884
E: belvedere@thecoachhouse.net
I: www.thecoachhouse.net

Bedrooms: 3 double/twin
Bathrooms: 3 en suite

18thC house, centrally situated in Dales village. Enjoy a warm welcome and great breakfast. Explore Teesdale's beautiful countryside and places of historic interest. Magnificent waterfalls.

B&B per night:
S £18.00
D £34.00

OPEN All Year except Christmas

♦♦♦

BLUEBELL HOUSE

Market Place, Middleton-in-Teesdale, Barnard Castle DL12 0QG
T: (01833) 640584
E: enquiries@bluebellhouse.co.uk
I: www.bluebellhouse-teesdale.co.uk

Bedrooms: 4 double/twin
Bathrooms: 3 en suite, 1 private

Former coaching inn, offering en suite/private facilities. Some ground floor rooms. Tea, coffee, TV in rooms. Guests' lounge. Ideal for walking. Cycle hire avaliable.

B&B per night:
S £21.00–£25.00
D £30.00–£34.00

OPEN All Year except Christmas

MORPETH, Northumberland Map ref 5C2 *Tourist Information Centre Tel: (01670) 511323*

◆◆◆

COTTAGE VIEW GUEST HOUSE

6 Staithes Lane, Morpeth NE61 1TD
T: (01670) 518550
F: (01670) 510840
E: cottageview.morpeth@virgin.net
I: www.cottageview.co.uk

B&B per night:
S £27.50–£32.50
D £38.50–£43.50

OPEN All Year

Centrally situated, family-run guest house. Private car parking, reception bar, 2 lounges (1 private), e-mail and fax facilities (small charge made). Night porter available for late arrivals/early departures. We can accommodate over 50 people – ideal for wedding guests. So don't delay, book today!

Bedrooms: 20 double/twin, 5 triple/multiple
Bathrooms: 19 en suite

CC: Amex, Delta, Diners, Mastercard, Switch, Visa

Child discounts available.

NEWCASTLE UPON TYNE, Tyne and Wear Map ref 5C2 *Tourist Information Centre Tel: (0191) 277 8000*

◆◆◆

CHIRTON HOUSE HOTEL

46 Clifton Road,
Off Grainger Park Road,
Newcastle upon Tyne NE4 6XH
T: (0191) 273 0407 & 273 3454
F: (0191) 273 0407

Bedrooms: 3 single, 5 double/twin, 3 triple/multiple
Bathrooms: 6 en suite

CC: Delta, Mastercard, Switch, Visa

B&B per night:
S £26.00–£36.00
D £39.00–£49.00

OPEN All Year

Comfortable, elegant country-style house in private grounds and car park. Close to the city, central for travel, sightseeing and shopping.

◆◆◆

JESMOND PARK HOTEL

74-76 Queens Road, Jesmond,
Newcastle upon Tyne NE2 2PR
T: (0191) 281 2821 & 281 1913
F: (0191) 281 0515
E: vh@jespark.fsnet.co.uk
I: www.jesmondpark.com

Bedrooms: 8 single, 5 double/twin, 5 triple/multiple
Bathrooms: 13 en suite

Evening meal available
CC: Amex, Delta, Mastercard, Switch, Visa

B&B per night:
S £26.00–£38.00
D £44.00–£52.00

OPEN All Year

Clean and friendly hotel offering good English breakfast. Residents' bar, free parking, close to city centre and handy for MetroCentre and Hadrian's Wall.

◆◆

UNIVERSITY OF NORTHUMBRIA CLAUDE GIBB HALLS OF RESIDENCE

Room 107, Ellison Terrce, Ellison Place,
Newcastle upon Tyne NE1 8ST
T: (0191) 227 4024 & 227 4403
F: (0191) 227 3197
E: rc.conferences@northumbria.ac.uk
I: www.northumbria.ac.uk/conferences

B&B per night:
S £22.00–£28.00

Our central location is ideal for day meetings or weekends away. Adjacent to Newcastle's shopping and entertainment, 15 minutes' walk from Central Station and 30 minutes by the Metro line direct to the airport. In the city, our traditonal Halls of Residence has 200 single bedrooms.

Bedrooms: 200 single

Lunch available
Evening meal available
CC: Mastercard, Switch, Visa

12

ACCESSIBILITY

Look for the symbols which indicate National Accessible Scheme standards for hearing and visually impaired guests in addition to standards for guests with mobility impairment. Additional participants are shown in the listings at the back.

OTTERBURN, Northumberland Map ref 5B1 *Tourist Information Centre Tel: (01830) 520093*

BUTTERCHURN GUEST HOUSE

Main Street, Otterburn, Northumberland NE19 1NP
T: (01830) 520585
E: keith@butterchurn.freeserve.co.uk
I: www.butterchurn.freeserve.co.uk

Excellent family-run guesthouse in quiet village location renowned for its welcome, quality of service and ambience. Situated in Northumberland National Park, on the scenic route to Scotland. Central for Hadrian's Wall, Kielder Water, coast and castles. Everyone welcome in the county known as the 'Land of Far Horizons'.

Bedrooms: 4 double/twin, 3 triple/multiple
Bathrooms: 7 en suite

CC: Delta, Mastercard, Visa

B&B per night:
S £25.00–£30.00
D £45.00–£50.00

OPEN All Year

REDESDALE ARMS HOTEL
Rochester, Newcastle upon Tyne NE19 1TA
T: (01830) 520668
F: (01830) 520063
E: redesdalehotel@hotmail.com
I: www.redesdale-hotel.co.uk

Bedrooms: 7 double/twin, 3 triple/multiple
Bathrooms: 10 en suite

Lunch available
Evening meal available
CC: Amex, Delta, Mastercard, Switch, Visa

Family-run old coaching inn with log fires and fine food. Central for Hadrian's Wall and the Kielder Forest. Beautiful en suite country bedrooms.

B&B per night:
S £38.00–£43.00
D £60.00–£70.00

HB per person:
DY £45.00–£53.00

OPEN All Year except Christmas

PONTELAND, Northumberland Map ref 5C2

Silver Award

HAZEL COTTAGE

Eachwick, Dalton, Newcastle upon Tyne NE18 0BE
T: (01661) 852415
F: (01661) 854797
E: hazelcottage@eachwick.fsbusiness.co.uk
I: www.hazel-cottage.co.uk

A warm welcome awaits you in our comfortable, traditional Northumbrian farmhouse, set in a lovely, tranquil rural area. Delightful en suite bedrooms with TV, tea-making facilities and everything for your comfort. Freshly prepared evening meals and splendid breakfasts. Newcastle, Hexham, Hadrian's Wall and MetroCentre within easy reach. Non-smoking.

Bedrooms: 4 double/twin
Bathrooms: 4 en suite

Evening meal available
CC: Mastercard, Visa

B&B per night:
S £28.00
D £45.00

OPEN All Year except Christmas

REDCAR, Tees Valley Map ref 5C3 *Tourist Information Centre Tel: (01642) 471921*

FALCON HOTEL
13 Station Road, Redcar TS10 1AH
T: (01642) 484300

Bedrooms: 8 single, 8 double/twin, 3 triple/multiple
Bathrooms: 12 en suite

Evening meal available

Licensed hotel in centre of town with recent extension of en suite twins and singles. Within easy reach of the Cleveland Hills.

B&B per night:
S £17.00–£25.00
D £30.00–£40.00

HB per person:
DY £24.00–£32.00

OPEN All Year

HALF BOARD PRICES Half board prices are given per person, but in some cases these may be based on double/twin occupancy.

SALTBURN-BY-THE-SEA, Tees Valley Map ref 5C3 *Tourist Information Centre Tel: (01287) 622422*

◆◆◆◆

THE ROSE GARDEN
20 Hilda Place, Saltburn-by-the-Sea
TS12 1BP
T: (01287) 622947
F: (01287) 622947
E: enquiries@therosegarden.co.uk
I: www.therosegarden.co.uk

Bedrooms: 3 double/twin
Bathrooms: 2 en suite, 1 private

Evening meal available

B&B per night:
S £22.00–£32.00
D £55.00

Large Victorian terraced house with small front garden. Well situated for all amenities in a charming seaside town. Homemade preserves a speciality. Mainly organic produce.

Rating Applied For

THE SPA HOTEL

Saltburn Bank, Saltburn-by-the-Sea
TS12 1HH
T: (01287) 622544
F: (01287) 625870
E: reservations@spahotels.co.uk
I: www.spahotels.co.uk

B&B per night:
S £20.00–£39.50
D £40.00–£60.00

HB per person:
DY £25.00–£70.00

OPEN All Year

Unrivalled views overlooking North Sea and Huntcliffe. Traditionally restored, fully en suite bedrooms, most with sea views. Disabled facilities. Family rooms available. Home-cooked food is our speciality. Menu with over 100 meals, all day every day, including our famous 4-meat carvery. Friendly, helpful staff assure you of a warm welcome and a memorable stay.

Bedrooms: 31 double/twin
Bathrooms: 31 en suite

CC: Amex, Delta, Diners, Mastercard, Switch, Visa

3 nights for the price of 2; weekend breakaways; themed weekends. Weekly rates also available.

SPENNYMOOR, Durham Map ref 5C2

THE GABLES

10 South View, Middlestone Moor,
Spennymoor DL16 7DF
T: (01388) 817544
F: (01388) 812533
E: thegablesghouse@aol.com
I: www.thegables.ntb.org.uk

B&B per night:
S £35.00–£38.00
D £46.00–£50.00

OPEN All Year except Christmas

The Gables is a spacious, detatched house in a quiet residential area 7 miles from historic Durham City. Ground floor, en suite rooms available. Private, off-road parking for 6 cars. Ideal touring base for the North East. The Gables is completely non-smoking. Pets welcome.

Bedrooms: 6 double/twin
Bathrooms: 3 en suite

CC: Amex, Delta, Mastercard, Switch, Visa

USE YOUR *i*s

There are more than 550 Tourist Information Centres throughout England offering friendly help with accommodation and holiday ideas as well as suggestions of places to visit and things to do. You'll find TIC addresses in the local Phone Book.

SPENNYMOOR continued

IDSLEY HOUSE

4 Green Lane, Spennymoor DL16 6HD
T: (01388) 814237

B&B per night:
S £32.00–£35.00
D £48.00

OPEN All Year except Christmas

Detached Victorian residence in quiet area at junction of A167/A688, opposite council offices. Just 8 minutes south of Durham City. Tastefully furnished, spacious bedrooms. Recommended breakfasts served in conservatory overlooking mature garden. Safe parking in walled garden. Northern family with lots of local knowledge with genealogy interest. Central location for touring area.

Bedrooms: 1 single, 3 double/twin, 1 triple/multiple
Bathrooms: 4 en suite, 1 private

CC: Amex, Delta, Mastercard, Switch, Visa

10 P

STANLEY, Durham Map ref 5C2

BUSHBLADES FARM

Harperley, Stanley DH9 9UA
T: (01207) 232722

B&B per night:
S £25.00–£30.00
D £37.00–£42.00

OPEN All Year except Christmas

60-acre livestock farm. Georgian house with large garden in rural setting. All rooms are spacious with colour TV, tea/coffee facilities and comfortable chairs. Ideal base or stopover. A1M 10 minutes. Easy reach of Durham City, Beamish Museum, Hadrian's Wall and the Northumberland Coast. Ample parking.

Bedrooms: 3 double/twin
Bathrooms: 1 en suite

12 P

TANFIELD, Durham Map ref 5C2

♦♦♦

TANFIELD GARDEN LODGE

Tanfield Lane, Tanfield, Stanley DH9 9QF
T: (01207) 282821 & 0797 039 8890
F: (01207) 282821

Bedrooms: 1 double/twin, 2 triple/multiple
Bathrooms: 2 en suite, 1 private

B&B per night:
S Min £35.00
D Min £50.00

Guesthouse in private grounds offering first-class accommodation. Close to Beamish Museum and MetroCentre. Also within easy reach of Durham and Newcastle. Private parking.

P

WALL, Northumberland Map ref 5B2

♦♦♦

THE HADRIAN HOTEL

Wall, Hexham NE46 4ER
T: (01434) 681232
E: david.lindsay13@btinternet.com
I: www.hadrianhotel.com

Bedrooms: 6 double/twin
Bathrooms: 4 en suite

Lunch available
Evening meal available
CC: Delta, Mastercard, Switch, Visa

B&B per night:
S £25.00–£40.00
D £45.00–£50.00

OPEN All Year

Situated close to Hadrian's Wall, the Hadrian Hotel has quiet, tranquil views of the countryside whilst being close to Hexham.

P

VISITOR ATTRACTIONS For ideas on places to visit refer to the introduction at the beginning of this section. Look out too for the ETC's Quality Assured Visitor Attraction signs.

WARK, Northumberland Map ref 5B2

BATTLESTEADS HOTEL

Wark, Hexham NE48 3LS
T: (01434) 230209
F: (01434) 230730
E: Info@Battlesteads-Hotel.co.uk
I: www.Battlesteads-Hotel.co.uk

18thC inn, formerly a farmhouse, in the heart of rural Northumberland, close to the Roman Wall and Kielder Water. An ideal centre for exploring Border country and for relaxing, walking, cycling or horse-riding. Collection and delivery service operated for walkers and cyclists.

Bedrooms: 1 single, 7 double/twin, 2 triple/multiple
Bathrooms: 10 en suite

Please see website.

Lunch available
Evening meal available
CC: Amex, Delta, Mastercard, Switch, Visa

B&B per night:
S £35.00–£40.00
D £60.00–£70.00

HB per person:
DY £47.95–£85.90

OPEN All Year

WARKWORTH, Northumberland Map ref 5C1

NORTH COTTAGE

Birling, Warkworth, Morpeth
NE65 0XS
T: (01665) 711263
E: edithandjohn@another.com
I: www.accta.co.uk/north

Bedrooms: 1 single, 3 double/twin
Bathrooms: 3 en suite

Attractive cottage with ground floor, en suite, non-smoking rooms. Extensive gardens with patio where visitors are welcome to relax. Off-street parking.

B&B per night:
S £22.00–£24.00
D £44.00–£48.00

OPEN All Year except Christmas

WHICKHAM, Tyne and Wear Map ref 5C2

Silver Award

EAST BYERMOOR GUEST HOUSE

Fellside Road, Whickham,
Newcastle upon Tyne NE16 5BD
T: (01207) 272687
F: (01207) 272145
E: eastbyermoor-gh.arbon@virgin.net

Bedrooms: 6 double/twin
Bathrooms: 5 en suite, 1 private

Evening meal available
CC: Delta, Mastercard, Switch, Visa

Large, stone, former farmhouse in open countryside, convenient for Gateshead MetroCentre, Newcastle, Durham and Sunderland. Comfortable guests' lounge, quiet reading room, landscaped garden. Christian proprietors.

B&B per night:
S £25.00
D £50.00

OPEN All Year

WHITLEY BAY, Tyne and Wear Map ref 5C2 *Tourist Information Centre Tel: (0191) 200 8535*

MARLBOROUGH HOTEL

20-21 East Parade, The Promenade,
Whitley Bay NE26 1AP
T: (0191) 251 3628
F: (0191) 252 5033
E: reception@marlborough-hotel.com
I: www.marlborough-hotel.com

Bedrooms: 6 single, 7 double/twin, 3 triple/multiple
Bathrooms: 12 en suite

Evening meal available
CC: Amex, Delta, Mastercard, Switch, Visa

Seaside hotel with fine sea views. Comfortable, modern accommodation with friendly service. Close to MetroCentre and ferry terminal.

B&B per night:
S £22.00–£38.00
D £45.00–£65.00

OPEN All Year except Christmas

TOWN INDEX

This can be found at the back of the guide. If you know where you want to stay, the index will give you the page number listing accommodation in your chosen town, city or village.

A brief guide to the main Towns and Villages offering accommodation in Northumbria

A **ALNWICK, NORTHUMBERLAND** - Ancient and historic market town, entered through the Hotspur Tower, an original gate in the town walls. The medieval castle, the second biggest in England and still the seat of the Dukes of Northumberland, was restored from ruin in the 18thC.

B **BAMBURGH, NORTHUMBERLAND** - Village with a spectacular red sandstone castle standing 150 ft above the sea. On the village green the magnificent Norman church stands opposite a museum containing mementoes of the heroine Grace Darling.

• **BARNARD CASTLE, DURHAM** - High over the Tees, a thriving market town with a busy market square. Bernard Baliol's 12thC castle (now ruins) stands nearby. The Bowes Museum, housed in a grand 19thC French chateau, holds fine paintings and furniture. Nearby are some magnificent buildings.

• **BELLINGHAM, NORTHUMBERLAND** - Set in the beautiful valley of the North Tyne close to the Kielder Forest, Kielder Water and lovely moorland below the Cheviots. The church has an ancient stone wagon roof fortified in the 18thC with buttresses.

• **BERWICK-UPON-TWEED, NORTHUMBERLAND** - Guarding the mouth of the Tweed, this is England's northernmost town with the best 16thC city walls in Europe. The handsome Guildhall and barracks date from the 18thC. Three bridges cross to Tweedmouth, the oldest built in 1634.

• **BISHOP AUCKLAND, DURHAM** - Busy market town on the bank of the River Wear. The Bishop's Palace, a castellated Norman manor house altered in the 18thC, stands in beautiful gardens. Entered from the market square by a handsome 18thC gatehouse, the park is a peaceful retreat of trees and streams.

C **CONSETT, DURHAM** - Former steel town on the edge of rolling moors. Modern development includes the shopping centre and a handsome Roman Catholic church, designed by a local architect. To the west, the Derwent Reservoir provides water sports and pleasant walks.

• **CORBRIDGE, NORTHUMBERLAND** - Small town on the River Tyne. Close by are extensive remains of the Roman military town Corstopitum, with a museum housing important discoveries from excavations. The town itself is attractive with shady trees, a 17thC bridge and interesting old buildings, notably a 14thC vicarage.

D **DARLINGTON, DURHAM** - Largest town in County Durham, standing on the River Skerne and home of the earliest passenger railway which first ran to Stockton in 1825. Now the home of a railway museum. Originally a prosperous market town occupying the site of an Anglo-Saxon settlement, it still holds an open market.

• **DURHAM, DURHAM** - Ancient city with its Norman castle and cathedral, now a World Heritage site, set on a bluff high over the Wear. A market and university town and regional centre, spreading beyond the market-place on both banks of the river.

H **HALTWHISTLE, NORTHUMBERLAND** - Small market town with interesting 12thC church, old inns and blacksmith's smithy. North of the town are several important sites and interpretation centres of Hadrian's Wall. Ideal centre for archaeology, outdoor activity or touring holidays.

• **HAYDON BRIDGE, NORTHUMBERLAND** - Small town on the banks of the South Tyne with an ancient church built of stone from sites along the Roman Wall just north. Ideally situated for exploring Hadrian's Wall and the Border country.

• **HEXHAM, NORTHUMBERLAND** - Old coaching and market town near Hadrian's Wall. Since pre-Norman times a weekly market has been held in the centre with its market-place and abbey park, and the richly furnished 12thC abbey church has a superb Anglo-Saxon crypt.

• **HOLY ISLAND, NORTHUMBERLAND** - Still an idyllic retreat, a tiny island and fishing village and cradle of northern Christianity. It is approached from the mainland at low water by a causeway. The clifftop castle (National Trust) was restored by Sir Edwin Lutyens.

K **KIELDER WATER, NORTHUMBERLAND** - A magnificent man-made lake, the largest in Northern Europe, with over 27 miles of shoreline. On the edge of the Northumberland National Park and near the Scottish border, Kielder can be explored by car, on foot or by ferry.

M **MIDDLETON-IN-TEESDALE, DURHAM** - Small stone town of hillside terraces overlooking the river, developed by the London Lead Company in the 18thC. Five miles up-river is the spectacular 70-ft waterfall, High Force.

• **MORPETH, NORTHUMBERLAND** - Market town on the River Wansbeck. There are charming gardens and parks, among them Carlisle Park which lies close to the ancient remains of Morpeth Castle. The chantry building houses the Northumbrian Craft Centre and the Bagpipe Museum.

N **NEWCASTLE UPON TYNE, TYNE AND WEAR** - Commercial and cultural centre of the North East, with a large indoor shopping centre, Quayside market, museums and theatres which offer an annual six-week season by the Royal Shakespeare Company. Norman castle keep, medieval alleys, old Guildhall.

CONFIRM YOUR BOOKING

You are advised to confirm your booking in writing.

O **OTTERBURN, NORTHUMBERLAND** - Small village set at the meeting of the River Rede with Otter Burn, the site of the Battle of Otterburn in 1388. A peaceful tradition continues in the sale of Otterburn tweeds in this beautiful region, which is ideal for exploring the Border country and the Cheviots.

P **PONTELAND, NORTHUMBERLAND** - A place of great antiquity, now a dormitory town for Newcastle. The fine Norman church, fortified rectory, Vicar's Pele and old inn, formerly a 17thC manor house, make this town particularly interesting.

S **SALTBURN-BY-THE-SEA, CLEVELAND** - Set on fine cliffs just north of the Cleveland Hills, a gracious Victorian resort with later developments and wide, firm sands. A handsome Jacobean mansion at Marske can be reached along the sands.

- **SPENNYMOOR, DURHAM** - Booming coal and iron town from the 18thC until early in the 20thC when traditional industry gave way to lighter manufacturing, and trading estates were built. On the moors south of the town there are fine views of the Wear Valley.

- **STANLEY, DURHAM** - Small town on the site of a Roman cattle camp. At the Beamish North of England Open Air Museum numerous set-pieces and displays recreate industrial and social conditions prevalent during the area's past.

W **WARK, NORTHUMBERLAND** - Set in the beautiful North Tyne Valley amid the Northumbrian fells, old village just above the meeting of Warks Burn with the North Tyne. Grey stone houses surround the green with its shady chestnut trees, and an iron bridge spans the stream. The mound of a Norman castle occupies the riverbank.

- **WARKWORTH, NORTHUMBERLAND** - A pretty village overlooked by its medieval castle. A 14thC fortified bridge across the wooded Coquet gives a superb view of 18thC terraces climbing to the castle. Upstream is a curious 14thC Hermitage and in the market square is the Norman church of St Lawrence.

- **WHITLEY BAY, TYNE AND WEAR** - Traditional seaside resort with long beaches of sand and rock and many pools to explore. St Mary's lighthouse is open to the public.

Welcome *to* Excellence

In 2003 the English Tourism Council launches a new range of training recognition awards for commitment to improving customer service for all types of accommodation and other tourism organisations.

Where you find the Welcome to Excellence plaque, you can be assured of a commitment to:

- achieve excellence in customer service
- exceed guest needs and expectations
- provide an environment where courtesy, helpfulness and a warm welcome are standard
- focus and develop individual skills.

Those displaying the plaque meet a special charter and have at least 50% of staff trained to the required standards.

NORTH WEST

Home of pop stars, world-famous football teams, Blackpool Tower and Coronation Street, he great North West has vibrant cities, idyllic countryside and world-class art collections oo.

classic sights

Blackpool Tower & Pleasure Beach – unashamed razzamatazz
ootball – museums and tours at Manchester United and Liverpool ootball clubs
he Beatles – The Beatles Story, Magical Mystery Tour Bus and Macca's former home

coast & country

he Ribble Valley – unchanged rolling landscapes
ormby – a glorious beach of sand dunes and pine woods
Vildfowl & Wetlands Trust, near Ormskirk – 120 types of birds ncluding flamingoes

arts for all

he Tate Liverpool – modern art
he Lowry – the world's largest collection of LS Lowry paintings

The counties of Cheshire, Greater Manchester, Lancashire, Merseyside and the High Peak District of Derbyshire

FOR MORE INFORMATION CONTACT:

North West Tourist Board
Swan House, Swan Meadow Road,
Wigan Pier, Wigan WN3 5BB
Tel: 0845 600 6040 Fax: (01942) 820002
Internet: www.visitnorthwest.com

he Pictures: 1 Rochdale Canal 2 Blackpool Pleasure Beach

PLACES TO VISIT - see pages 130-133 > WHERE TO STAY - see pages 134-145

PLACES to visi

You will find hundreds of interesting places to visit during your sta just some of which are listed in these pages. Contact any Touri Information Centre in the region for more ideas on days out.

Awarded ETC's new 'Quality Assured Visitor Attraction' marque at time of going to press. (See page 19).

1 2 3

Albert Dock, The Albert Dock Company Ltd

Edward Pavilion, Albert Dock, Liverpool
Tel: (0151) 708 7334 www.albertdock.com
Britain's largest Grade I Listed historic building. Restored four-sided dock including shops, bars, restaurants, entertainment, marina and the Maritime Museum.

Arley Hall and Gardens

Arley, Northwich
Tel: (01565) 777353
www.arleyestate.zuunet.co.uk
Early Victorian building set in 12 acres (5ha) of magnificent gardens with a 15thC tithe barn. Plant nursery, gift shop and restaurant. A plantsman's paradise!

Astley Hall Museum and Art Gallery

Astley Park, Chorley
Tel: (01257) 515555 astleyhall.co.uk
Astley Hall dates from 1580 with subsequent additions. Unique collections of furniture including a fine Elizabethan bed and the famous Shovel Board Table.

The Beatles Story Ltd

Britannia Vaults, Albert Dock, Liverpool
Tel: (0151) 709 1963
Liverpool's award-winning visitor attraction with a replica of the original Cavern Club. Available for private parties

Beeston Castle

Beeston, Tarporley
Tel: (01829) 260464
A ruined 13thC castle situated on top of the Peckforton Hills with views of the surrounding countryside. Exhibitions are held featuring the castle's history.

Blackpool Pleasure Beach

Ocean Boulevard, South Shore, Blackpool
Tel: 0870 444 5577
www.blackpoolpleasurebeach.co.uk
Europe's greatest show and amusement park, Blackpoo Pleasure Beach offers over 145 rides and attractions, pl spectacular shows.

Blackpool Sea Life Centre

The Promenade, Blackpool
Tel: (01253) 622445 www.sealife.co.uk
Tropical sharks up to 8ft (2.5m) housed in a 100,000-gallon (454,609-litre) water display, with an underwater walkway. The new 'Lost City of Atlantis' is back with the feature exhibition.

Blackpool Tower and Circus

The Promenade, Blackpool
Tel: (01253) 622242
www.blackpoollive.com
Inside Blackpool Tower you will find the UK's best circu world-famous Tower Ballroom, children's entertainmen Jungle Jim's Playground, Tower Top Ride and Undersea World.

Bridgemere Garden World

Bridgemere, Nantwich
Tel: (01270) 520381
Twenty-five fascinating acres (10ha) of plants, gardens, greenhouses, shop, coffee shop, restaurant and over 20 different display gardens in the Garden Kingdom.

Chester Zoo

Upton-by-Chester, Chester
Tel: (01244) 380280
www.chesterzoo.org.uk

Chester Zoo is one of Europe's leading conservation zoos with over 5,000 animals in spacious and natural enclosures. Now featuring the new 'Twilight Zone'.

Croxteth Hall and Country Park

Croxteth Hall Lane, Liverpool
Tel: (0151) 228 5311 www.croxteth.co.uk
An Edwardian stately home set in 500 acres (202ha) of countryside (woodlands and pasture), featuring a Victorian walled garden and animal collection.

East Lancashire Railway

Bolton Street Station, Bury
Tel: (0161) 764 7790 www.east-lancs-rly.co.uk
ight miles (13km) of preserved railway, operated rincipally by steam. Traction Transport Museum close by.

Gawsworth Hall

Gawsworth, Macclesfield
Tel: (01260) 223456 www.gawsworthhall.com
Gawsworth Hall is a Tudor half-timbered manor house with tilting ground. Featuring pictures, sculpture and urniture and an open-air theatre.

Gulliver's World Family Theme Park

ff Shackleton Close, Warrington
el: (01925) 444888
theme park with rides for the young and old.

Imperial War Museum North

afford Park, Manchester
el: (0161) 836 4000 www.iwm.org.uk
IWM North has a stunning exterior and is clad in uminium. Inside, the main exhibition gallery ovides a spectacular setting in which to xplore the internationally renowned llections.

Jodrell Bank Science Centre, Planetarium and Arboretum

Lower Withington, Macclesfield
Tel: (01477) 571339 www.jb.man.ac.uk/scicen
Exhibition and interactive exhibits on astronomy, space, energy and the environment. Planetarium and the world-famous Lovell telescope, plus a 35-acre (14-ha) arboretum.

Knowsley Safari Park

Prescot
Tel: (0151) 430 9009 www.knowsley.com
A 5-mile (8-km) safari through 500 acres (202ha) of rolling countryside and the world's wildest animals roaming free - that's the wonderful world of freedom you'll find at the park.

Lady Lever Art Gallery

Port Sunlight Village, Higher Bebington, Wirral
Tel: (0151) 478 4136
www.ladyleverartgallery.org.uk
The first Lord Leverhulme's magnificent collection of British paintings dated 1750-1900, British furniture, Wedgewood pottery and oriental porcelain.

> The Pictures: 1 Imperial War Museum North, Salford Quays, Manchester
2 Blackpool Tower
3 Bridgewater Hall, Manchester
4 Liverpool waterfront
5 Chester Clock

Lancaster Castle

Shire Hall, Castle Parade, Lancaster
Tel: (01524) 64998
www.lancashire.gov.uk/resources/ps/castle/index.htm
Shire Hall has a collection of coats of arms, a crown court, a grand jury room, a 'drop room' and dungeons. Also external tour of castle.

Macclesfield Silk Museum

The Heritage Centre, Roe Street, Macclesfield
Tel: (01625) 613210 www.silk-macclesfield.org
The museum presents the story of silk in Macclesfield by audio-visual means. Exhibitions feature textiles, garments, models and room settings. Gift shop and coffee shop.

Merseyside Maritime Museum

Albert Dock, Liverpool
Tel: (0151) 478 4499
www.merseysidemaritimemuseum.org.uk
The Merseyside Maritime Museum, set in the heart of Liverpool's historic waterfront, holds craft demonstrations, working displays and permanent galleries.

The Museum of Science & Industry in Manchester

Liverpool Road, Castlefield, Manchester
Tel: (0161) 832 1830 www.msim.org.uk
The Museum of Science and Industry in Manchester is based in the world's oldest passenger railway station with galleries that amaze, amuse and entertain.

The National Football Museum

Deepdale Stadium, Preston
Tel: (01772) 908442
www.nationalfootballmuseum.com
The National Football Museum exists to explain how and why football has become 'the people's game'.

Pleasureland Theme Park

Marine Drive, Southport
Tel: 08702 200204 www.pleasureland.uk.com
A traditional amusement park with a wide variety of thrilling family rides.

Quarry Bank Mill

Styal, Wilmslow
Tel: (01625) 527468
www.rmplc.co.uk/orgs/quarrybankmill
A Georgian, water-powered cotton-spinning mill with four floors of displays and demonstrations and 300 acres (121ha) of parkland surroundings.

Rufford Old Hall

Rufford, Ormskirk
Tel: (01704) 821254 www.nationaltrust.org.uk
One of the finest 16thC buildings in Lancashire with a magnificent hall, particularly noted for its immense moveable screen.

Smithills Hall

Smithills Dean Road, Bolton
Tel: (01204) 332377 www.smithills.org
Smithills Hall is a fascinating example of the growth of a great house, mirroring the changes in fashion and living conditions from the 14thC.

Southport Zoo and Conservation Trust

Princes Park, Southport
Tel: (01704) 538102 www.southportzoo.co.uk
Zoological gardens and conservation trust. Southport Zo has been run by the Petrie family since 1964. Talks on natural history are held in the schoolroom.

Stapeley Water Gardens & Palms Tropical Oasis

London Road, Stapeley, Nantwich
Tel: (01270) 623868
www.stapeleywatergardens.com
Large water garden centre filled with display lakes, pool fountains, trees, shrubs, pot plants, gifts, garden sundries and pets. Thousands of items on display.

Tate Liverpool

Albert Dock, Liverpool
Tel: (0151) 702 7400 www.tate.org.uk/liverpool/
Tate Liverpool exhibits the National Collection of Moder Art.

Wigan Pier

Trencherfield Mill, Wigan
Tel: (01942) 323666 www.wiganmbc.gov.uk
Wigan Pier combines interaction with displays and reconstructions and the Wigan Pier Theatre Company. Facilities include shops and a cafe.

Wildfowl and Wetland Trust Martin Mere

Burscough, Ormskirk
Tel: (01704) 895181 www.wwt.org.uk
Martin Mere Wildfowl and Wetland Centre is home to over 1,600 ducks, geese and swans.

Find out more about the North West

Further information about holidays and attractions in the North West is available from:

NORTH WEST TOURIST BOARD
Swan House, Swan Meadow Road, Wigan Pier, Wigan WN3 5BB.
Tel: 0845 600 6040 Fax: (01942) 820002
Internet: www.visitnorthwest.com

The following publications are available from North West Tourist Board:

Best of England's North West
a guide to information on the region

Great Days Out in England's North West
a non-accommodation guide, A1 (folded to A4) map including list of visitor attractions, what to see and where to go

Freedom
forming part of a family of publications about camping and caravan parks in the north of England

Stay on a Farm
a guide to farm accommodation in the north of England

Group Travel Planner
a guide to choosing the right accommodation, attraction or venue for group organisers

Getting to the North West

BY ROAD:
Motorways intersect within the region which has the best road network in the country. Travelling north or south use the M6, and east or west the M62.

BY RAIL:
Most North West coastal resorts are connected to InterCity routes with trains from many parts of the country, and there are through trains to major cities and towns.

The Pictures: 1 Walkers on Kinder Scout, Derbyshire 2 The Lowry, Salford Quays, Manchester

Where to stay in the North West

Accommodation entries in this region are listed in alphabetical order of place name, and then in alphabetical order of establishment.

Map references refer to the colour location maps at the front of this guide. The first number indicates the map to use; the letter and number which follow refer to the grid reference on the map.

At-a-glance symbols at the end of each accommodation entry give useful information about services and facilities. A key to symbols can be found inside the back cover flap. Keep this open for easy reference.

A brief description of the towns and villages offering accommodation in the entries which follow, can be found at the end of this section.

A complete listing of all the English Tourism Council assessed accommodation covered by this guide appears at the back of the guide.

ACTON BRIDGE, Cheshire Map ref 4A2

MANOR FARM

Cliff Road, Acton Bridge, Northwich
CW8 3QP
T: (01606) 853181
F: (01606) 853181
E: terri.mac.manorfarm@care4free.net

B&B per night:
S £24.00–£27.00
D £48.00–£54.00

OPEN All Year except Christmas

Peaceful, elegantly furnished country house. Open views from all rooms. Situated down long, private drive, above wooded banks of the River Weaver. Large garden provides access to private path through woodland into the picturesque valley. In central Cheshire, ideal location for business or pleasure, convenient for Chester, Merseyside and motorways.

Bedrooms: 1 single, 2 double/twin
Bathrooms: 1 en suite, 2 private

Babies 0-3 free, children 3-5 £5.00, 5-12 half price. Long distance or circular walks on Delamere Way and sandstone trail.

QUALITY ASSURANCE SCHEME

Diamond ratings and awards were correct at the time of going to press but are subject to change. Please check at the time of booking.

ARKHOLME, Lancashire Map ref 5B3

REDWELL INN

Kirkby Lonsdale Road, Arkholme,
Carnforth LA6 1BQ
T: (015242) 21240
F: (015242) 21107
E: julie@redwellinn.co.uk
I: www.redwellinn.co.uk

A 17thC coaching inn set in the beautiful Lune Valley. Fabulous food served all day – great value for money. Superior rooms, all en suite. Nice views over rolling countryside. Close to jct 35 on M6.

Bedrooms: 1 single, 3 double/twin, 1 triple/multiple; permanent suite(s)
Bathrooms: 5 en suite

Lunch available
Evening meal available
CC: Amex, Delta, Diners, Mastercard, Switch, Visa

Stay 3 nights or more at last year's rates – £150 for 3 nights double room B&B, £300 per week, double room B&B.

B&B per night:
S £39.50–£59.50
D £49.50–£59.50

HB per person:
DY £40.00–£50.00

OPEN All Year

BLACKPOOL, Lancashire Map ref 4A1 *Tourist Information Centre Tel: (01253) 478 222*

♦♦♦

ASHCROFT HOTEL

42 King Edward Avenue,
North Shore, Blackpool FY2 9TA
T: (01253) 351538 & 07765 542306
E: dave@ashcroftblackpool.freeserve.co.uk
I: www.smoothhound.co.uk/hotels/ashcroft.html

Bedrooms: 3 single, 5 double/twin, 2 triple/multiple
Bathrooms: 7 en suite

Evening meal available

Small, friendly, licensed hotel off Queens Promenade, 2 minutes from sea and Gynn Gardens. Offering personal service. Non-smoking dining room. Cleanliness assured.

B&B per night:
S £21.00–£23.00
D £42.00–£46.00

HB per person:
DY £28.00–£30.00

OPEN All Year except Christmas

♦♦♦

BARICIA

40-42 Egerton Road, Blackpool
FY1 2NW
T: (01253) 623130
E: TKBariciahotel@aol.com

Bedrooms: 2 single, 7 double/twin, 3 triple/multiple
Bathrooms: 8 en suite

Evening meal available

Eight bedrooms with full en suite facilites. Four bedrooms semi en suite with own toilet/washbasin. No supplement for illuminations. Close to town centre.

B&B per night:
S £15.00–£20.00
D £30.00–£40.00

OPEN All Year except Christmas

♦♦♦

BEVERLEY HOTEL

25 Dean Street, Blackpool FY4 1AU
T: (01253) 344426
E: beverley.hotel@virgin.net
I: www.beverleyhotel-blackpool.co.uk

Bedrooms: 1 single, 6 double/twin, 4 triple/multiple
Bathrooms: 11 en suite

Evening meal available
CC: Delta, Diners, Mastercard, Switch, Visa

Licensed family-run hotel, with good home-cooked food. All rooms en suite. Adjacent promenade, Pleasure Beach and swimming complex, with local shopping facilities nearby.

B&B per night:
S £20.00–£30.00
D £38.00–£46.00

HB per person:
DY £26.00–£30.00

OPEN All Year

CHECK THE MAPS

The colour maps at the front of this guide show all the cities, towns and villages for which you will find accommodation entries. Refer to the town index to find the page on which they are listed.

◆◆◆

BOLTONIA HOTEL

124-126 Albert Road, Blackpool FY1 4PN
T: (01253) 620248
F: (01253) 299064
E: info@boltoniahotel.co.uk
I: www.boltoniahotel.co.uk

Family-run and owned establishment. Ideal for holiday or mini-breaks and illuminations. Close to conference centre, dance festival venues, theatres and shops. All bedrooms are en suite with colour TV, complimentary tea/coffee facilities, hairdyers and shaver points. This small, licensed hotel also benefits from its own private car park.

Bedrooms: 6 single, 12 double/twin, 3 triple/ multiple
Bathrooms: 21 en suite

Evening meal available
CC: Amex, Delta, Diners, Mastercard, Switch, Visa

Any 4 nights' B&B plus early dinner £95, any 4 nights' B&B £84, from 4 Nov 2002 to 5 Sep 2003 (excl Christmas, New Year and Bank Holidays).

B&B per night:
S £21.00–£30.00
D £42.00–£60.00

HB per person:
DY £25.00–£35.00

OPEN All Year

◆◆◆◆

COLLINGWOOD HOTEL

8-10 Holmfield Road, North Shore, Blackpool FY2 9SL
T: (01253) 352929
F: (01253) 352929
E: enquiries@collingwoodhotel.co.uk
I: www.collingwoodhotel.co.uk

Family supervised hotel, established for 25 years, in a select area just off Queens Promenade, near Gynn Gardens. Decorated and furnished to the highest standard with all the comforts of a modern hotel. Fine restaurant with plenty of choice. A warm and friendly welcome assured. Excellence is our standard. Private car park.

Bedrooms: 2 single, 11 double/twin, 4 triple/ multiple
Bathrooms: 17 en suite

Evening meal available
CC: Amex, Delta, Diners, Mastercard, Switch, Visa

Tinsel and Turkey weekends, Theatre weekends, over 55s offers, early season special, Christmas and New Year house party.

B&B per night:
S £20.00–£27.00
D £40.00–£54.00

HB per person:
DY £24.00–£33.00

OPEN All Year

◆◆

LLANRYAN HOUSE

37 Reads Ave, Blackpool FY1 4DD
T: (01253) 628446
E: keith@llanryanguesthouse.co.uk
I: www.llanryanguesthouse.co.uk

Bedrooms: 2 single, 3 double/twin, 3 triple/ multiple
Bathrooms: 6 en suite

Evening meal available
CC: Delta, Mastercard, Switch, Visa

Convenient for the many attractions of Blackppol. Just a few minutes' walk from the town centre, Tower, Winter Gardens, theatres and working men's clubs.

B&B per night:
S £13.50–£17.50
D £27.00–£35.00

HB per person:
DY £18.00–£22.00

OPEN All Year

◆◆

MANOR GROVE HOTEL

24 Leopold Grove, Blackpool FY1 4LD
T: (01253) 625577
F: (01253) 625577
E: lyndon@evans2ooo.freeserve.co.uk
I: www.manorgrovehotel.com

Bedrooms: 4 single, 2 double/twin, 3 triple/ multiple
Bathrooms: 9 en suite

Evening meal available
CC: Amex, Delta, Diners, Mastercard, Switch, Visa

Lovely, bright, clean, modern rooms. Family-run guest house, central location behind the Winter Gardens. All rooms en suite, TV, direct dial telephones and hairdryers.

B&B per night:
S £20.00–£24.99
D £36.00–£50.00

HB per person:
DY £25.00–£32.00

OPEN All Year except Christmas

SYMBOLS The symbols in each entry give information about services and facilities. A key to these symbols appears at the back of this guide.

BLACKPOOL continued

♦♦♦

MAY-DENE LICENSED HOTEL

10 Dean Street, Blackpool FY4 1AU
T: (01253) 343464
F: (01253) 401424
E: may_dene_hotel@hotmail.com

Bedrooms: 6 double/twin, 4 triple/multiple
Bathrooms: 7 en suite, 1 private

Evening meal available
CC: Amex, Delta, Diners, Mastercard, Switch, Visa

In a sun-trap area close to South Promenade, Sandcastle, Pleasure Beach, markets and pier. Clean and friendly. Good food prepared by C&G-qualified cooks.

B&B per night:
S £30.00–£60.00
D £42.00–£60.00

HB per person:
DY £28.00–£38.00

OPEN All Year

♦♦♦♦♦
Gold Award

THE OLD COACH HOUSE

50 Dean Street, Blackpool FY4 1BP
T: (01253) 349195
E: blackpool@theoldcoachhouse.freeserve.co.uk
I: www.theoldcoachhouse.freeserve.co.uk

Bedrooms: 11 double/twin
Bathrooms: 11 en suite

Evening meal available
CC: Delta, Mastercard, Switch, Visa

A large detached house set in beautiful gardens. Situated near the promenade and the South Pier. Superior rooms with 4-poster beds and baths also available.

B&B per night:
S £50.00–£80.00
D £70.00–£90.00

HB per person:
DY £54.95–£69.95

OPEN All Year

SUNNYMEDE HOTEL

50 King Edward Avenue, Blackpool FY2 9TA
T: (01253) 352877
E: enquiries@sunnymedehotel.co.uk
I: www.sunnymedehotel.co.uk

B&B per night:
S £18.00–£22.00
D £36.00–£44.00

HB per person:
DY £23.00–£27.00

OPEN All Year

The Sunnymede offers you a warm and friendly welcome, and endeavors to make your stay feel like home from home. We provide good-quality home cooking and are happy to cater for special diets. We are situated adjacent to the prom, close to Gynn Gardens and the golf course.

Bedrooms: 1 single, 5 double/twin, 3 triple/multiple
Bathrooms: 9 en suite

Evening meal available

Special rates for over fifties and stays of 7 days or more.

SUNNYSIDE HOTEL

36 King Edward Avenue, North Shore, Blackpool FY2 9TA
T: (01253) 352031
F: (01253) 354255
E: stuart@sunnysidehotel.com
I: www.sunnysidehotel.com

B&B per night:
S £18.50–£26.00
D £32.00–£44.00

HB per person:
DY £25.00–£32.00

OPEN All Year except Christmas

Small hotel, BIG welcome, situated adjacent to promenade in a select, quiet area of North Shore yet near the town centre attractions. South-facing sun lounge, bar lounge, spacious dining area with varied menu to suit your needs. All bedrooms are en suite. Unrestricted street parking, and private parking for 4 cars.

Bedrooms: 1 single, 3 double/twin, 4 triple/multiple
Bathrooms: 8 en suite

Evening meal available

Early-season savers (excl Bank Holidays), Feb-Jun.

THE WINDSOR HOTEL

21 King Edward Avenue, North Shore, Blackpool FY2 9TA
T: (01253) 353735
F: (01253) 353735

Bedrooms: 3 single, 5 double/twin, 1 triple/multiple
Bathrooms: 9 en suite

Evening meal available
CC: Delta, Mastercard, Switch, Visa

Furnishings and decoration of the highest quality. Specialising in homemade British cuisine. Varied daily menu. Many special offers, Christmas and New Year packages available.

B&B per night:
S £20.00–£22.50
D £40.00–£45.00

HB per person:
DY £27.50–£29.50

OPEN All Year

BLACKPOOL continued

WOODLEIGH HOTEL

32 King Edward Ave, North Shore, Blackpool FY2 9TA
T: (01253) 593624
E: bookings@woodleighhotel.freeserve.co.uk
I: blackpool-holidays.com/Woodleigh.htm

Bedrooms: 1 single, 6 double/twin, 3 triple/multiple
Bathrooms: 9 en suite, 1 private

Evening meal available

B&B per night:
S £16.00–£22.50
D £32.00–£45.00

HB per person:
DY £22.00–£28.50

OPEN All Year

On select North Shore. Highest standards of cleanliness, comfortable and friendly. Traditional home-cooked food. Caters specifically for over 50s, but younger couples also welcome.

BOOTLE, Merseyside Map ref 4A2

REGENT MARITIME HOTEL

58-62 Regent Road, Liverpool L20 8DB
T: (0151) 922 4090
F: (0151) 922 6308
E: regent_maritime_hotel@hotmail.com
I: www.regentmaritimehotel.co.uk

Bedrooms: 5 single, 10 double/twin, 4 triple/multiple
Bathrooms: 4 en suite

Lunch available
Evening meal available
CC: Amex, Delta, Diners, Mastercard, Switch, Visa

B&B per night:
S £28.50
D £28.50–£57.00

OPEN All Year

Regent Maritime Hotel is situated approximately 3 miles north along the riverside road (Dock Road) from the city centre. M62 and M58 4 miles from hotel.

BURNLEY, Lancashire Map ref 4B1 *Tourist Information Centre Tel: (01282) 664421*

◆◆◆

ORMEROD HOTEL

121-123 Ormerod Road, Burnley BB11 3QW
T: (01282) 423255

Bedrooms: 4 single, 4 double/twin, 2 triple/multiple
Bathrooms: 10 en suite

B&B per night:
S £26.00–£29.00
D £42.00–£44.00

OPEN All Year

Small bed and breakfast hotel in quiet, pleasant surroundings facing local parks. Recently refurbished, all en suite facilities. 5 minutes from town centre.

CARNFORTH, Lancashire Map ref 5B3

◆◆◆◆

GRISEDALE FARM

Leighton, Carnforth LA5 9ST
T: (01524) 734360

Bedrooms: 2 double/twin

B&B per night:
D £40.00

OPEN All Year except Christmas

Working family farm set in an Area of Outstanding Natural Beauty. Leighton Moss RSPB 300 yards. Convenient for Lakes and Dales. Ten minutes from M6.

LONGLANDS HOTEL

Tewitfield, Carnforth LA6 1JH
T: (01524) 781256
F: (01524) 781004
E: info@thelonglandshotel.co.uk

B&B per night:
S £25.00–£30.00
D £50.00–£60.00

OPEN All Year

Old world coaching inn, on the A6070 0.5 miles from M6 exit 35A. Convenient for the Lakes, Yorkshire Dales, the seaside resort of Morecambe and historic Lancaster. Regular live entertainment. Bar snacks and a la carte restaurant. All bedrooms en suite. A warm welcome guaranteed.

Bedrooms: 2 single, 3 double/twin, 1 triple/multiple
Bathrooms: 6 en suite

Lunch available
Evening meal available
CC: Delta, Mastercard, Switch, Visa

PRICES
Please check prices and other details at the time of booking.

CHEADLE HULME, Greater Manchester Map ref 4B2

♦♦♦

SPRING COTTAGE GUEST HOUSE
60 Hulme Hall Road,
Cheadle Hulme, Cheadle SK8 6JZ
T: (0161) 485 1037

Bedrooms: 1 single, 5 double/twin
Bathrooms: 3 en suite

CC: Delta, Mastercard, Switch, Visa

B&B per night:
S £25.00–£31.00
D £41.00–£45.00

OPEN All Year

Beautifully furnished Victorian house, in historic part of Cheadle Hulme. Convenient for airport, rail station and variety of local restaurants.

P

CHESTER, Cheshire Map ref 4A2 *Tourist Information Centre Tel: (01244) 402111*

♦♦♦

BAWN LODGE
10 Hoole Road, Chester CH2 3NH
T: (01244) 324971
F: (01244) 310951
E: enquiries@bawnlodge.co.uk
I: www.bawnlodge.co.uk

Bedrooms: 2 single, 8 double/twin, 7 triple/multiple
Bathrooms: 15 en suite

CC: Amex, Delta, Diners, Mastercard, Switch, Visa

B&B per night:
S £20.00–£45.00
D £40.00–£60.00

OPEN All Year

Delightful Victorian building in own grounds with large private car park, 1 mile from M53, 0.5 miles to city centre.

P

♦♦♦

CHEYNEY LODGE HOTEL
77-79 Cheyney Road, Chester
CH1 4BS
T: (01244) 381925

Bedrooms: 1 single, 6 double/twin, 1 triple/multiple
Bathrooms: 8 en suite

Lunch available
Evening meal available
CC: Delta, Mastercard, Switch, Visa

B&B per night:
S £30.00–£36.00
D £48.00–£56.00

HB per person:
DY £34.95–£38.95

OPEN All Year except Christmas

Small, friendly hotel of unusual design, featuring indoor garden and fish pond. Ten minutes' walk from city centre and on main bus route. Personally supervised, emphasis on good food.

P

♦♦♦

GROSVENOR PLACE GUEST HOUSE
2-4 Grosvenor Place, Chester
CH1 2DE
T: (01244) 324455 & 400225
F: (01244) 400225

Bedrooms: 3 single, 4 double/twin, 3 triple/multiple
Bathrooms: 6 en suite

CC: Delta, Mastercard, Switch, Visa

B&B per night:
S £27.00–£35.00
D £38.00–£48.00

OPEN All Year except Christmas

City centre guesthouse within the walls, two minutes from famous Rows, surrounded by restaurants, in quiet cul-de-sac. Most rooms en suite.

♦♦♦♦

GROVE HOUSE

Holme Street, Tarvin, Chester CH3 8EQ
T: (01829) 740893
F: (01829) 741769
E: helen_s@btinternet.com

B&B per night:
S £30.00–£40.00
D £60.00–£70.00

OPEN All Year except Christmas

Warm welcome in relaxing environment. Spacious, comfortable rooms, attractive garden. Ample parking. Within easy reach of Chester (4 miles) and major North West and North Wales tourist attractions. NWTB 'Place to Stay' Award 1996 and 1997. Closed Christmas and New Year.

Bedrooms: 1 single, 2 double/twin
Bathrooms: 2 en suite, 1 private

12 P

GOLD & SILVER AWARDS

These exclusive ETC awards are given to establishments achieving the highest levels of quality and service. Further information can be found at the front of the guide and additional accommodation achieving these awards are shown in the listing at the back of this guide.

CHESTER continued

♦♦♦♦ Silver Award

THE LIMES

12 Hoole Road, Hoole, Chester CH2 3NJ
T: (01244) 328239
F: 07968 404105
E: limeschester@btinternet.com
I: www.limeschester.btinternet.co.uk

B&B per night:
S £48.00–£50.00
D £70.00–£90.00

OPEN All Year except Christmas

A warm welcome awaits you at The Limes, which is under the personal supervision of the resident proprietors, Howard and Christine Braydon. Originally a fine Victorian gentleman's residence, The Limes is furnished to the highest standard. For your added comfort we operate a no-smoking policy.

Bedrooms: 2 single, 3 double/twin, 2 triple/multiple
Bathrooms: 7 en suite

CC: Delta, Mastercard, Switch, Visa

Winter breaks: 20% discount on stays of 3 nights or more.

12 P

CHORLEY, Lancashire Map ref 4A1

PARR HALL FARM

Parr Lane, Eccleston, Chorley PR7 5SL
T: (01257) 451917
F: (01257) 453749
E: parrhall@talk21.com

B&B per night:
S £30.00–£35.00
D £50.00–£60.00

OPEN All Year

Georgian farmhouse built in 1721 and tastefully restored. Quiet, rural location within easy walking distance of good public houses, restaurants and village amenities. Conveniently situated for Lancashire coast and countryside, Lake District and Yorkshire Dales. Manchester Airport 45 minutes, M6 jct 27 5 miles north on B5250.

Bedrooms: 1 single, 3 double/twin
Bathrooms: 4 en suite

CC: Delta, Mastercard, Switch, Visa

P

CLITHEROE, Lancashire Map ref 4A1 *Tourist Information Centre Tel: (01200) 425566*

♦♦♦♦

RAKEFOOT FARM

Thornley Road, Chaigley, Nr Clitheroe BB7 3LY
T: (01995) 61332 & 07889 279063
F: (01995) 61296
E: info@rakefootfarm.co.uk
I: www.rakefootfarm.co.uk

Bedrooms: 6 double/twin, 3 triple/multiple
Bathrooms: 6 en suite, 3 private

Lunch available
Evening meal available

B&B per night:
S £17.00–£30.00
D £34.00–£50.00

HB per person:
DY £29.00–£45.00

OPEN All Year

Family farm, 17thC farmhouse and traditional stone barn, original features. En suite, ground floor available. Panoramic views. Forest of Bowland between Clitheroe and Chipping. Home cooking. Also self-catering.

P

♦♦♦♦

SELBORNE GUEST HOUSE

Back Commons, Kirkmoor Road, Clitheroe BB7 2DX
T: (01200) 423571 & 422236
F: (01200) 423571
E: selbornehouse@lineone.net
I: selbornehouse@lineone.net

Bedrooms: 4 double/twin
Bathrooms: 4 en suite

Evening meal available

B&B per night:
S £25.00–£27.50
D £45.00–£50.00

OPEN All Year

Detached house on quiet lane giving peace and tranquillity but within walking distance of the town, bus and rail interchange. Private parking. Open all year.

P

REGIONAL TOURIST BOARD The symbol in an establishment entry indicates that it is a Regional Tourist Board member.

ELSWICK, Lancashire Map ref 4A1

THORNTON HOUSE

High Street, Elswick, Preston
PR4 3ZB
T: (01995) 671863
F: (01995) 671863
E: john@thorntonhouse.biz
I: www.thorntonhouse.biz

Bedrooms: 3 double/twin
Bathrooms: 3 en suite

B&B per night:
S Min £24.00
D Min £39.00

OPEN All Year except Christmas

Comfortable, friendly home, spacious rooms, king-size beds. Situated in the Fylde countryside. Ideal base for exploring west coast resorts and many Fylde golf courses.

P

GARSTANG, Lancashire Map ref 4A1 *Tourist Information Centre Tel: (01995) 602125*

◆◆◆

GUY'S THATCHED HAMLET

Canalside, St Michael's Road, Bilsborrow, Garstang, Preston PR3 0RS
T: (01995) 640010 & 640020
F: (01995) 640141
E: guyshamlet@aol.com
I: www.guysthatchedhamlet.co.uk

Friendly, family-run thatched canalside hamlet, with restaurant, flagged floored Tavern Pizzeria, en suite lodgings, craft shops, cricket ground and thatched pavilion (all-weather wicket), crown green bowling (special events, corporate days), conference centre. Blackpool, Lake District, Yorkshire Dales within easy reach. Off jct 32 of M6, then 3 miles north on A6 to Garstang.

Bedrooms: 48 double/twin, 5 triple/multiple
Bathrooms: 53 en suite

Lunch available
Evening meal available
CC: Amex, Delta, Diners, Mastercard, Switch, Visa

Champagne weekends. Oyster Festival 6-11 Sept. International Jazz Festival 12-15 Sept.

B&B per night:
S £46.50–£65.00
D £50.25–£70.50

OPEN All Year except Christmas

P

GREAT ECCLESTON, Lancashire Map ref 4A1

◆◆◆

CARTFORD HOTEL

Cartford Lane, Little Eccleston, Preston PR3 0YP
T: (01995) 670166
F: (01995) 671785

Bedrooms: 1 single, 5 double/twin
Bathrooms: 6 en suite

Lunch available
Evening meal available
CC: Delta, Mastercard, Switch, Visa

B&B per night:
S £36.95–£39.95
D £48.95–£52.95

OPEN All Year except Christmas

Country riverside pub and coaching inn, CAMRA 'Pub of the Year' winner. Hosts on-site Hart Brewery. Easy access to Blackpool and the Lake District.

P

KNUTSFORD, Cheshire Map ref 4A2 *Tourist Information Centre Tel: (01565) 632611*

◆◆◆

MOAT HALL MOTEL

Chelford Road, Marthall, Knutsford WA16 8SU
T: (01625) 860367 & 07747 796730
F: (01625) 861136
E: val@moathall.fsnet.co.uk

Bedrooms: 3 single, 3 double/twin
Bathrooms: 6 en suite

CC: Amex, Mastercard, Switch, Visa

B&B per night:
S £35.00–£50.00
D £45.00–£70.00

OPEN All Year

Modern accommodation on Cheshire farm, 6 miles from Manchester Airport. Knutsford 3 miles (M6 jct 19). All rooms en suite with microwave and fridge. Suitable for business and touring guests.

P

LIVERPOOL, Merseyside Map ref 4A2

HOLME LEIGH GUEST HOUSE

93 Woodcroft Road, Wavertree, Liverpool L15 2HG
T: (0151) 734 2216 & 726 9980
F: (0151) 728 9521
E: bridges01@blueyonder.co.uk

Bedrooms: 4 single, 6 double/twin
Bathrooms: 6 en suite

CC: Amex, Mastercard, Switch, Visa

B&B per night:
S £15.00–£25.00
D £30.00–£45.00

OPEN All Year

Victorian red brick 3-storey corner dwelling and fashion shop, facing on to Lawrence Road. Just 2.5 miles from city centre, 2 miles from M62.

5

MACCLESFIELD, Cheshire Map ref 4B2 *Tourist Information Centre Tel: (01625) 504114*

◆◆◆

MOORHAYES HOUSE HOTEL

27 Manchester Road, Tytherington, Macclesfield SK10 2JJ
T: (01625) 433228
F: (01625) 429878
E: helen@moorhayes.co.uk
I: www.smoothhound.co.uk/hotels/moorhaye

Bedrooms: 1 single, 6 double/twin, 1 triple/multiple
Bathrooms: 8 en suite

CC: Delta, Mastercard, Switch, Visa

B&B per night:
S £35.00–£40.00
D £55.00

OPEN All Year

Warm welcome, comfortable house with gardens and parking. 0.5 miles from town centre. Hearty breakfasts. Rooms en suite with tea/coffee, TV and telephone.

◆◆◆

SANDPIT FARM

Messuage Lane, Marton, Macclesfield SK11 9HS
T: (01260) 224254

Bedrooms: 3 double/twin
Bathrooms: 2 en suite

B&B per night:
S £23.00–£25.00
D £46.00–£50.00

OPEN All Year

A friendly welcome to our 300-year-old oak-beamed farmhouse. Excellent touring centre for Peak District, Potteries, Chester, stately homes. Manchester Airport 14 miles.

3 P

MANCHESTER, Greater Manchester Map ref 4B1 *Tourist Information Centre Tel: (0161) 234 3157*

◆◆◆

LUTHER KING HOUSE

Brighton Grove, Wilmslow Road, Manchester M14 5JP
T: (0161) 224 6404
F: (0161) 248 9201
E: reception@lkh.co.uk
I: www.lkh.co.uk

Bedrooms: 8 single, 14 double/twin, 3 triple/multiple
Bathrooms: 25 en suite

Lunch available
Evening meal available
CC: Delta, Mastercard, Switch, Visa

B&B per night:
S £25.50
D £36.50

OPEN All Year except Christmas

A peaceful oasis, set in 2 acres only minutes from the city centre. Offering quality accommodation, good food and a warm welcome.

◆◆◆

REMBRANDT HOTEL

33 Sackville Street, Manchester M1 3LZ
T: (0161) 236 1311 & 236 2435
F: (0161) 236 4257
E: rembrandthotel@aol.com
I: www.rembrandtmanchester.com

Bedrooms: 19 double/twin, 1 triple/multiple
Bathrooms: 14 en suite

Lunch available
Evening meal available
CC: Amex, Delta, Diners, Mastercard, Switch, Visa

B&B per night:
S £35.00–£75.00
D £45.00–£95.00

HB per person:
DY £50.00–£70.00

OPEN All Year

Small, friendly hotel in city centre, adjacent to main coach station and near main railway station. In the vibrant gay village.

MANCHESTER AIRPORT

See under Cheadle Hulme, Knutsford, Manchester, Mobberley, Stockport, Wilmslow

MOBBERLEY, Cheshire Map ref 4A2

◆◆◆◆
Silver Award

THE HINTON

Town Lane, Mobberley, Knutsford WA16 7HH
T: (01565) 873484
F: (01565) 873484
I: www.hinton.co.uk

B&B per night:
S Min £44.00
D Min £58.00

OPEN All Year

Award-winning bed and breakfast for both business and private guests. Within easy reach of M6, M56, Manchester Airport and InterCity rail network. Ideal touring base, on the B5085 between Knutsford and Wilmslow. Beautifully appointed rooms with many extras. All good home cooking.

Bedrooms: 2 single, 2 double/twin, 1 triple/multiple
Bathrooms: 5 en suite

Evening meal available
CC: Amex, Diners, Mastercard, Visa

NEW BRIGHTTON, Merseyside Map ref 4A2

♦♦♦

SHERWOOD GUEST HOUSE

55 Wellington Road, New Brighton, Wirral CH45 2ND
T: (0151) 639 5198
F: (0151) 639 9079
E: sheila@sherwood-guest-house.co.uk

Bedrooms: 1 single, 3 double/twin, 2 triple/multiple
Bathrooms: 3 en suite

Evening meal available

Family guesthouse facing promenade and Irish Sea. Close to station and M53. Ideal centre for Chester, North Wales, Lakes and Liverpool (15 minutes).

B&B per night:
S £16.00–£19.00
D £30.00–£35.00

HB per person:
DY £23.00–£26.00

OPEN All Year except Christmas

PRESTON, Lancashire Map ref 4A1 *Tourist Information Centre Tel: (01772) 253731*

♦♦♦

ASHWOOD HOTEL

11-13 Fishergate Hill, Preston PR1 8JB
T: (01772) 203302
F: (01772) 203302

Bedrooms: 7 single, 6 double/twin, 2 triple/multiple
Bathrooms: 8 en suite

CC: Delta, Mastercard, Switch, Visa

Warm and comfortable family-run hotel. En suite facilities. Five minutes' walk from town centre, railway station and university. Tea/coffee facilities and colour TV in all bedrooms.

B&B per night:
S £23.00–£28.00
D £40.00–£45.00

OPEN All Year except Christmas

RIBBLE VALLEY

See under Clitheroe

ST MICHAEL'S ON WYRE, Lancashire Map ref 4A1

COMPTON HOUSE

Garstang Road, St Michael's on Wyre, Preston PR3 0TE
T: (01995) 679378
F: (01995) 679378
E: dave@compton-hs.co.uk
I: www.compton-hs.co.uk

Bedrooms: 3 double/twin
Bathrooms: 3 en suite

Well-furnished country house in own grounds in a picturesque village, near M6 and 40 minutes from Lake District. Fishing in the Wyre. 'Best-Kept Guesthouse' award 1995, 1996 and 2001.

B&B per night:
S £25.00
D £40.00

OPEN All Year except Christmas

SOUTHPORT, Merseyside Map ref 4A1 *Tourist Information Centre Tel: (01704) 533333*

LEICESTER HOTEL

24 Leicester Street, Southport PR9 0EZ
T: (01704) 530049
F: (01704) 545561
E: leicester.hotel@mail.cybase.co.uk
I: www.leicesterhotelsouthport.co.uk

Bedrooms: 3 single, 4 double/twin
Bathrooms: 5 en suite

Evening meal available
CC: Mastercard, Visa

Family-run hotel with personal attention, clean and comfortable, close to all amenities. Car park. Licensed bar. TV in all rooms. En suite available.

B&B per night:
S £20.00–£25.00
D £50.00

OPEN All Year except Christmas

ROSEDALE HOTEL

11 Talbot Street, Southport PR8 1HP
T: (01704) 530604
F: (01704) 530604
E: info@rosedalehotelsouthport.co.uk
I: www.rosedalehotelsouthport.co.uk

Bedrooms: 3 single, 4 double/twin, 2 triple/multiple
Bathrooms: 8 en suite, 1 private

CC: Delta, Mastercard, Switch, Visa

Centrally located, well-established, family-run, private hotel. Ideally placed for beach, parks, quality restaurants, entertainment and the famous Lord Street.

B&B per night:
S £25.00–£28.00
D £50.00–£56.00

OPEN All Year except Christmas

MAP REFERENCES

Map references apply to the colour maps at the front of this guide.

SOUTHPORT continued

SANDY BROOK FARM

52 Wyke Cop Road, Scarisbrick,
Southport PR8 5LR
T: (01704) 880337
F: (01704) 880337
E: sandybrookfarm@lycos.co.uk

Bedrooms: 1 single, 2 double/twin, 3 triple/multiple
Bathrooms: 6 en suite

B&B per night:
S £23.00
D £37.00

OPEN All Year except Christmas

27-acre arable farm. Comfortable accommodation in converted farm buildings in rural area of Scarisbrick, 3.5 miles from Southport. Special facilities for disabled guests.

STOCKPORT, Greater Manchester Map ref 4B2 *Tourist Information Centre Tel: (0161) 474 4444*

NEEDHAMS FARM

Uplands Road, Werneth Low,
Gee Cross, Hyde SK14 3AG
T: (0161) 368 4610
F: (0161) 367 9106
E: charlotte@needhamsfarm.co.uk
I: www.needhamsfarm.co.uk

Bedrooms: 2 single, 4 double/twin, 1 triple/multiple
Bathrooms: 6 en suite, 1 private

Evening meal available
CC: Mastercard, Visa

B&B per night:
S £20.00–£22.00
D £36.00–£40.00

HB per person:
DY £28.00–£30.00

OPEN All Year

30-acre, non-working farm. Five-hundred-year-old farmhouse with exposed beams and open fire in bar/dining room. Excellent views. Well placed for Manchester city and airport.

STONYHURST, Lancashire Map ref 4A1

Gold Award

ALDEN COTTAGE

Kemple End, Birdy Brow, Stonyhurst,
Clitheroe BB7 9QY
T: (01254) 826468
F: (01254) 826468
E: carpenter@aldencottage.f9.co.uk
I: http://fp.aldencottage.f9.co.uk

B&B per night:
S £28.00–£34.00
D £52.00–£56.00

OPEN All Year except Christmas

Quality accommodation in idyllic country cottage, situated in in an Area of Outstanding Natural Beauty overlooking the Ribble and Hodder Valleys. Charmingly furnished rooms with all modern comforts, fresh flowers etc. Private facilities include jacuzzi bath. Ribble Valley Design and Conservation Award winner.

Bedrooms: 3 double/twin
Bathrooms: 1 en suite, 1 private

5% discount for 3 or more nights, 10% discount for 7 or more nights (based on 2 people sharing).

TOSSIDE, Lancashire Map ref 4A1

DOG AND PARTRIDGE

Tosside, Skipton BD23 4SQ
T: (01729) 840668

B&B per night:
S Max £18.50
D Max £37.00

HB per person:
DY £20.50–£24.50

OPEN All Year except Christmas

The highest hotel in Ribble Valley nestling in the quiet hamlet of Tosside. It is only a short distance from Clitheroe, Settle, Skipton, Cumbria and the Yorkshire Dales. Magnificent views looking to the Forest of Bowland. Ideal for walking, cycling or touring. A cosy atmosphere with delicious home-cooked food.

Bedrooms: 3 double/twin, 1 triple/multiple

Lunch available
Evening meal available

QUALITY ASSURANCE SCHEME

Diamond ratings and awards are explained at the back of this guide.

WILMSLOW, Cheshire Map ref 4B2

◆◆◆◆

HOLLOW BRIDGE GUEST HOUSE
90 Manchester Road, Wilmslow
SK9 2JY
T: (01625) 537303
F: (01625) 528718
E: lynandjack@hollowbridge.com
I: www.hollowbridge.com

Bedrooms: 2 single, 2 double/twin
Bathrooms: 4 en suite

CC: Delta, Mastercard, Visa

Recently refurbished house, en suite bedrooms, garden room dining, reading room. Off-road parking. Manchester Airport and motorway 10 minutes, Wilmslow centre 5 minutes.

B&B per night:
S £38.00
D £50.00

OPEN All Year

◆◆◆◆

MARIGOLD HOUSE
132 Knutsford Road, Wilmslow
SK9 6JH
T: (01625) 584414 & 0793 9514609

Bedrooms: 3 double/twin
Bathrooms: 3 en suite

18thC period house with oak beams, flagged floors and antique furnishings. Log fires in winter. Private sitting room and dining room. Courtesy car to airport.

B&B per night:
S £35.00
D £45.00

OPEN All Year except Christmas

WIRRAL

See under New Brighton

COUNTRY CODE

Always follow the Country Code ♣ Enjoy the countryside and respect its life and work ♣ Guard against all risk of fire ♣ Fasten all gates ♣ Keep your dogs under close control ♣ Keep to public paths across farmland ♣ Use gates and stiles to cross fences, hedges and walls ♣ Leave livestock, crops and machinery alone ♣ Take your litter home ♣ Help to keep all water clean ♣ Protect wildlife, plants and trees ♣ Take special care on country roads ♣ Make no unnecessary noise ♣

A brief guide to the main Towns and Villages offering accommodation in the North West

A ACTON BRIDGE, CHESHIRE - Village with old farmsteads and cottages on a picturesque section of the River Weaver. Riverside walks pass the great Dutton Viaduct on the former Grand Junction Railway and shipping locks on the Weaver Navigation Canal.

B BLACKPOOL, LANCASHIRE - Britain's largest fun resort, with Blackpool Pleasure Beach, three piers and the famous Tower. Host to the spectacular autumn illuminations.

• **BURNLEY, LANCASHIRE** - A town amidst the Pennines. Towneley Hall has fine period rooms and is home to Burnley's art gallery and museum. The Kay-Shuttleworth collection of lace and embroidery can be seen at Gawthorpe Hall (National Trust). Burnley Mechanics Arts Centre is a well-known jazz and blues venue.

C CARNFORTH, LANCASHIRE - Carnforth station was the setting for the film "Brief Encounter". Nearby are Borwick Hall, an Elizabethan manor house, and Leighton Hall which has good paintings and Gillow furniture and is open to the public.

• **CHEADLE HULME, GREATER MANCHESTER** - Residential area near Manchester with some older buildings dating from the 19thC, once occupied by merchants and industrialists from surrounding towns. Several fine timber-framed houses, shopping centre and easy access to Manchester Airport.

• **CHESTER, CHESHIRE** - Roman and medieval walled city rich in treasures. Black and white buildings are a hallmark, including 'The Rows' - two-tier shopping galleries. 900-year-old cathedral and the famous Chester Zoo.

• **CHORLEY, LANCASHIRE** - Set between the Pennine moors and the Lancashire Plain, Chorley has been an important town since medieval times, with its covered markets. The rich heritage includes Astley Hall and Park, Hoghton Tower, Rivington Country Park and the Leeds-Liverpool Canal.

• **CLITHEROE, LANCASHIRE** - Ancient market town with an 800-year-old castle keep and a wide range of award-winning shops. Good base for touring Ribble Valley, Trough of Bowland and Pennine moorland. Country market on Tuesdays and Saturdays.

G GARSTANG, LANCASHIRE - Market town. The gateway to the fells, it stands on the Lancaster Canal and is a popular cruising centre. Close by are the remains of Greenhalgh Castle (no public access) and the Bleasdale Circle. Discovery Centre shows history of Over Wyre and Bowland fringe areas.

K KNUTSFORD, CHESHIRE - Delightful town with many buildings of architectural and historic interest. The setting of Elizabeth Gaskell's "Cranford". Annual May Day celebration and decorative "sanding" of the pavements are unique to the town. Popular Heritage Centre.

L LIVERPOOL, MERSEYSIDE - Vibrant city which became prominent in the 18thC as a result of its sugar, spice and tobacco trade with the Americas. Today the historic waterfront is a major attraction. Home to the Beatles, the Grand National, two 20thC cathedrals and many museums and galleries.

M MACCLESFIELD, CHESHIRE - Cobbled streets and quaint old buildings stand side by side with modern shops and three markets. Centuries of association with the silk industry; museums feature working exhibits and social history. Stunning views of the Peak District National Park.

• **MANCHESTER, GREATER MANCHESTER** - The Gateway to the North, offering one of Britain's largest selections of arts venues and theatre productions, a wide range of chain stores and specialist shops, a legendary, lively nightlife, spectacular architecture and a plethora of eating and drinking places.

N NEW BRIGHTON, MERSEYSIDE - This resort on the Mersey Estuary has seven miles of coastline, with fishing off the sea wall and pleasant walks along the promenade. Attractions include New Palace Amusements, Floral Pavilion Theatre, ten pin bowling and good sports facilities.

P PRESTON, LANCASHIRE - Scene of decisive Royalist defeat by Cromwell in the Civil War and later of riots in the Industrial Revolution. Local history exhibited in Harris Museum. Famous for i Guild and the celebration that takes plac every 20 years.

CHECK THE MAPS

The colour maps at the front of this guide show all the cities, towns and villages for which you will find accommodation entries. Refer to the town index to find the page on which they are listed.

S ST MICHAEL'S ON WYRE, LANCASHIRE - Village near Blackpool with interesting 13thC church of St Michael containing medieval stained-glass window depicting sheep shearing, and clock tower bell made in 1548.

• **SOUTHPORT, MERSEYSIDE** - Delightful Victorian resort noted for gardens, sandy beaches and 6 golf-courses, particularly Royal Birkdale. Attractions include the Atkinson Art Gallery, Southport Railway Centre, Pleasureland and the annual Southport Flower Show. Excellent shopping, particularly in Lord Street's elegant boulevard.

• **STOCKPORT, GREATER MANCHESTER** - Once an important cotton-spinning and manufacturing centre, Stockport has an impressive railway viaduct, a shopping precinct built over the River Mersey and a new leisure complex. Lyme Hall and Vernon Park Museum nearby.

T TOSSIDE, LANCASHIRE - Small hillside hamlet with village school, church, public house and early 18thC Congregational Chapel. In beautiful countryside on the edge of the Forest of Bowland, close to the Stocks Reservoir.

W WILMSLOW, CHESHIRE - Nestling in the valleys of the Rivers Bollin and Dane, Wilmslow retains an intimate village atmosphere. Easy-to-reach attractions include Quarry Bank Mill at Style. Lindow Man was discovered on a nearby common. A Romany caravan sits in a memorial garden.

Ratings you can trust

When you're looking for a place to stay, you need a rating system yo can trust. The **English Tourism Council's** ratings are your clear guid to what to expect, in an easy-to-understand form. Properties are visite annually by our trained, impartial assessors, so you can hav confidence that your accommodation has been thoroughly checke and rated for quality before you make a booking.

Using a simple One to five Diamond rating, the system put great emphasis on quality and is based on research which show exactly what consumers are looking for when when choosin accommodation.

"Guest Accommodation" covers a wide variety of serviced accommodation for which England is renowne including guesthouses, bed and breakfasts, ,inns and farmhouses. Establishments are rated from One to Fiv Diamonds. Progressively higher levels of quality and customer care must be provided for each of the One to Fiv Diamond ratings. The rating reflects the unique character of Quest Accommodation, and covers areas such a cleanliness, service and hospitality, bedrooms, bathrooms and food quality.

Look out, too for the English Tourism Council's Gold and Silver Awards, which are awarded to thos establishments which not only achieve the overall quality required for their Diamond rating, but also reach th highest levels of quality in those specific areas which guests identify as being really important for them. The will reflect the quality of comfort and cleanliness you'll find in the bedrooms and bathrooms and the quality service you'll enjoy throughout your stay.

The ratings are you sign of quality assurance, giving you the confidence to book the accommodati that meets your expectations.

Yorkshire combines wild and brooding moors with historic cities, elegant spa towns and a varied coastline of traditional resorts and working fishing ports.

classic sights

Fountains Abbey & Studley Royal – 12thC Cistercian abbey and Georgian water garden

Nostell Priory – 18thC house with outstanding art collection

York Minster – largest medieval Gothic cathedral north of the Alps

coast & country

The Pennines – dramatic moors and rocks

Whitby – unspoilt fishing port, famous for jet (black stone)

literary links

Bronte parsonage, Haworth – home of the Bronte sisters; inspiration for 'Wuthering Heights' and 'Jane Eyre'

arts for all

National Museum of Photography, Film and Television, Bradford – hi-tech and hands-on

distinctively different

The Original Ghost Walk of York – spooky tours every night

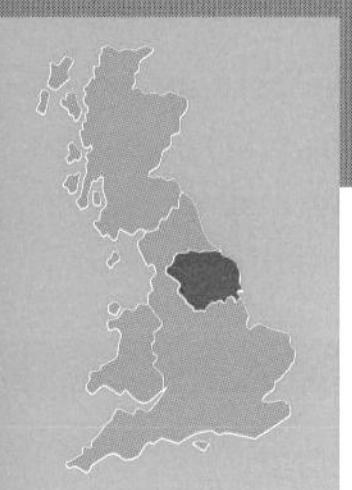

The counties of North, South, East and West Yorkshire, and Northern Lincolnshire

FOR MORE INFORMATION CONTACT:

Yorkshire Tourist Board
312 Tadcaster Road, York YO24 1GS
Tel: (01904) 707070 (24-hour brochure line) Fax: (01904) 701414
Email: info@ytb.org.uk Internet: www.yorkshirevisitor.com

The Pictures: 1 Castle Howard, North Yorkshire 2 Flamborough, East Riding of Yorkshire 3 Red post box, Whitby, North Yorkshire

> PLACES TO VISIT - see pages 150-153 > WHERE TO STAY - see pages 154-197

PLACES to visit

You will find hundreds of interesting places to visit during your stay, just some of which are listed in these pages. Contact any Tourist Information Centre in the region for more ideas on days out.

Awarded ETC's new 'Quality Assured Visitor Attraction' marque at time of going to press. (See page 19).

2

3

Beningbrough Hall & Gardens

Beningbrough, York
Tel: (01904) 470666
Handsome Baroque house built in 1716 with 100 pictures from the National Portrait Gallery, Victorian laundry, potting shed and restored walled garden.

Bolton Abbey Estate

Bolton Abbey, Skipton
Tel: (01756) 718009 www.boltonabbey.com
Ruins of 12thC priory in a park setting by the River Wharfe. Tearooms, catering, nature trails, fishing, fell walking and picturesque countryside.

Eden Camp Modern History Theme Museum

Malton
Tel: (01653) 697777 www.edencamp.co.uk
Modern history theme museum depicting civilian way of life during World War II. Millennium features.

Eureka! The Museum for Children

Discovery Road, Halifax
Tel: (01422) 330069 www.eureka.org.uk
Eureka! is the first museum of its kind designed especially for children up to the age of 12 with over 400 hands-on exhibits.

Flamingo Land Theme Park, Zoo and Holiday Village

Kirby Misperton, Malton
Tel: (01653) 668287 www.flamingoland.co.uk
One-price family funpark with over 100 attractions, 7 shows and Europe's largest privately owned zoo. Europe's only triple-looping coaster, Magnum Force.

Fountains Abbey and Studley Royal

Studley Park, Ripon
Tel: (01765) 608888
www.fountainsabbey.org.uk
Largest monastic ruin in Britain founded by Cistercian monks in 1132. Landscaped garden laid between 1720-40 with lake, formal water garden, temples and deer park.

Helmsley Castle

Helmsley, York
Tel: (01439) 770442 www.english-heritage.org.uk
Great ruined keep dominates the town. Other remains include a 16thC domestic range with original panelling and plasterwork. Spectacular earthwork defences.

Hornsea Freeport Ltd

Rolston Road, Hornsea
Tel: (01964) 534211
Set in 25 acres (10ha) of landscaped gardens with over 40 quality high-street names all selling stock with discounts of up to 50%. Licensed restaurant, leisure attractions.

Jorvik - The Viking City

Coppergate, York

Tel: (01904) 643211 www.vikingjorvik.com

Technology of the 21stC transports visitors back to Viking-age York for a truly multi-sensory experience of life in the 10thC.

Last Of the Summer Wine Exhibition (Compo's House)

30 Huddersfield Road, Holmfirth, Huddersfield

Tel: (01484) 681408

Collection of photographs and memorabilia connected with the television series 'Last of the Summer Wine'.

Leeds City Art Gallery

The Headrow, Leeds

Tel: (0113) 247 8248

www.leeds.gov.uk/tourinfo/attract/museums/artgall.html

Art gallery containing British paintings, sculptures, prints and drawings of the 19th/20thC. Henry Moore gallery with permanent collection of 20thC sculpture.

Lightwater Valley Theme Park

North Stainley, Ripon

Tel: 0870 4580060 www.lightwatervalley.net

Set in 175 acres (71ha) of parkland, Lightwater Valley features a number of white-knuckle rides and attractions for all the family, shopping, a restaurant and picnic areas.

Magna

Sheffield Road, Templeborough, Rotherham

Tel: (01709) 720002 www.magnatrust.org.uk

Magna is the UK's first science adventure centre set in the vast Templeborough steelworks in Rotherham. Fun is unavoidable here with giant interactives.

Mother Shipton's Cave & Petrifying Well

Prophesy House, High Bridge, Knaresborough

Tel: (01423) 864600 www.mothershipton.co.uk

Mother Shipton's Cave and Petrifying Well are the oldest tourist attractions in Britain, opened in 1630. Cave, well, museum, playground and 12 acres (5ha) of riverside grounds.

National Centre for Early Music

t Margarets Church, Walmgate, York

Tel: (01904) 645738 www.yorkearlymusic.org

The National Centre for Early Music provides a unique combination of music, heritage and new technology and offers a perfect venue for music-making, drama, recordings and conferences.

National Fishing Heritage Centre

Alexandra Dock, Grimsby

Tel: (01472) 323345 www.welcome.to/NFHCentre

A journey of discovery - experience the reality of life on a deep-sea trawler. Interactive games and displays, children's area.

National Railway Museum

Leeman Road, York

Tel: (01904) 621261 www.nrm.org.uk

Discover the story of the train in a great day out for all the family. The National Railway Museum mixes fascination and education with hours of fun and - best of all - it's free!

Newby Hall & Gardens

Ripon

Tel: (01423) 322583 www.newbyhall.com

Late 17thC house with additions, interior by Robert Adam. Classical sculpture, Gobelins tapestries, 25 acres (10ha) of gardens, miniature railway, children's adventure garden.

> The Pictures: 1 Yorkshire Dales
2 North Yorkshire Moors, Westerdale
3 Thixendale in the Wolds, East Yorkshire
4 Worsbrough Mill Museum, South Yorkshire
5 North Yorkshire Moors, Railway Steam Train
6 Staithes, North Yorkshire

North Yorkshire Moors Railway

Pickering Station, Park Street, Pickering
Tel: (01751) 472508 www.nymr.demon.co.uk
Evening and Sunday lunchtime dining-service trains offer a unique and nostalgic experience with a wonderful selection of menus to suit all tastes.

Nunnington Hall

Nunnington, York
Tel: (01439) 748283
Large 17thC manor house situated on banks of River Rye with hall, bedrooms, nursery, maid's room (haunted) and Carlisle collection of miniature rooms. National Trust shop.

Piece Hall

Halifax
Tel: (01422) 358087 www.calderdale.gov.uk
Built in 1779 and restored in 1976, this Grade I Listed building forms a unique and striking monument to the wealth and importance of the wool trade.

Ripley Castle

Ripley, Harrogate
Tel: (01423) 770152 www.ripleycastle.co.uk
Ripley Castle, home to the Ingilby family for over 26 generations, is set in the heart of a delightful estate with Victorian walled gardens, deer park and pleasure grounds.

Royal Armouries Museum

Armouries Drive, Leeds
Tel: 0870 5106666 www.armouries.org.uk
Experience more than 3,000 years of history covered by over 8,000 spectacular exhibits and stunning surroundings. Arms and armour.

Ryedale Folk Museum

Hutton-le-Hole, York
Tel: (01751) 417367
Reconstructed local buildings including cruck-framed long-houses, Elizabethan manor house, furnished cottages, craftsmen's tools and household/agricultural implements.

Sea Life and Marine Sanctuary

Scalby Mills, Scarborough
Tel: (01723) 376125 www.sealife.co.uk
At the Sea Life Centre you have the opportunity to meet creatures that live in and around the oceans of the British Isles, ranging from starfish and crabs to rays and seals.

Sheffield Botanical Gardens

Clarkehouse Road, Sheffield
Tel: (0114) 250 0500 www.sbg.org.uk
Extensive gardens with over 5,500 species of plants and Grade II Listed garden pavillion (now closed).

Skipton Castle

Skipton
Tel: (01756) 792442
www.skiptoncastle.co.uk
Fully-roofed Skipton Castle is in excellent condition. It is one of the most complete and well-preserved medieval castles in England.

Thirsk Museum

14-16 Kirkgate, Thirsk
Tel: (01845) 527707 www.thirskmuseum.org
Exhibits of local life and industry and cricket memorabilia. The building was the home of Thomas Lord, founder of Lords cricket ground in London.

Vintage Carriages Trust - Museum of Rail Travel

Ingrow Railway Station, Ingrow, Keighley
Tel: (01535) 680425 www.neotek.demon.co.uk/vct/
Collection of historic railway coaches plus elderly steam locomotives. Some used occasionally by Worth Valley Railway, also for filming.

York Dungeon

12 Clifford Street, York
Tel: (01904) 632599 www.thedungeons.com
Set in dark, musty, atmospheric cellars and featuring life-size tableaux of Dark Age deaths, medieval punishments and the persecution/torture of heretics.

York Minster

Deangate, York
Tel: (01904) 557200 www.yorkminster.org
York Minster is the largest medieval Gothic cathedral north of the Alps. Museum of Roman/Norman remains. Chapter house.

1

Find out more about Yorkshire

Further information about holidays and attractions in Yorkshire is available from:

YORKSHIRE TOURIST BOARD
312 Tadcaster Road, York YO24 1GS.
Tel: (01904) 707070 (24-hour brochure line)
Fax: (01904) 701414
Email: info@ytb.org.uk
Internet: www.yorkshirevisitor.com

The following publications are available from Yorkshire Tourist Board:

Yorkshire Visitor Guide 2003
information on the region, including hotels, self-catering, camping and caravan parks. Also attractions, shops, restaurants and major events

Yorkshire - A Great Day Out
non-accommodation A5 guide listing where to go, what to see and where to eat, the list goes on! Including map

Bed & Breakfast Touring Map
forming part of a 'family' of maps covering England, this guide provides information on bed and breakfast establishments in Yorkshire

Heritage Yorkshire
more great houses, castles, abbeys and gardens than any other region of England

Walk Yorkshire
a walking pack tailored to meet the individual's needs according to the area they are interested in

Hidden Yorkshire
a guide to Yorkshire's less well known haunts

On Screen Guide
a guide to Yorkshire's TV, Movie, and Literary heritage

2

Getting to Yorkshire

BY ROAD: Motorways: M1, M62, M606, M621, M18, M180, M181, A1(M). Trunk roads: A1, A19, A57, A58, A59, A61, A62, A63, A64, A65, A66.

BY RAIL: InterCity services to Bradford, Doncaster, Harrogate, Kingston upon Hull, Leeds, Sheffield, Wakefield and York. Frequent regional railway services city centre to city centre including Manchester Airport service to Scarborough, York and Leeds.

> The Pictures: 1 Whitby, North Yorkshire 2 Swaledale, Yorkshire

Where to stay in Yorkshire

Accommodation entries in this region are listed in alphabetical order of place name, and then in alphabetical order of establishment.

Map references refer to the colour location maps at the front of this guide. The first number indicates the map to use; the letter and number which follow refer to the grid reference on the map.

At-a-glance symbols at the end of each accommodation entry give useful information about services and facilities. A key to symbols can be found inside the back cover flap. Keep this open for easy reference.

A brief description of the towns and villages offering accommodation in the entries which follow, can be found at the end of this section.

A complete listing of all the English Tourism Council assessed accommodation covered by this guide appears at the back of the guide.

AINTHORPE, North Yorkshire Map ref 5C3

THE FOX & HOUNDS INN
45 Brook Lane, Ainthorpe, Whitby YO21 2LD
T: (01287) 660218
F: (01287) 660030
E: ajbfox@globalnet.co.uk
I: www.foxandhounds-ainthorpe.com

Bedrooms: 6 double/twin, 1 triple/multiple
Bathrooms: 7 en suite

Lunch available
Evening meal available
CC: Amex, Delta, Diners, Mastercard, Switch, Visa

B&B per night:
S £35.00
D £60.00

OPEN All Year

16thC former coaching inn, now a high quality residential country inn and restaurant. Set amidst the beautiful North York Moors National Park.

APPLETREEWICK, North Yorkshire Map ref 4B1

KNOWLES LODGE
Appletreewick, Skipton BD23 6DQ
T: (01756) 720228
F: (01756) 720381
E: pam@knowleslodge.com
I: www.knowleslodge.com

Bedrooms: 3 double/twin
Bathrooms: 3 en suite

Evening meal available
CC: Amex, Delta, Mastercard, Switch, Visa

B&B per night:
S £33.00
D £56.00

HB per person:
DY £46.00

OPEN All Year

In a spectacular setting of garden, meadow and woodland, Knowles Lodge overlooks River Wharfe. Accommodation comprises 3 stylishly appointed bedrooms, each with en suite bathrooms.

CHECK THE MAPS

The colour maps at the front of this guide show all the cities, towns and villages for which you will find accommodation entries.
Refer to the town index to find the page on which they are listed.

ASKRIGG, North Yorkshire Map ref 5B3

♦♦♦♦ Silver Award

THE APOTHECARY'S HOUSE

Market Place, Askrigg, Leyburn DL8 3HT
T: (01969) 650626

B&B per night:
S £32.00
D £46.00–£50.00

OPEN All Year except Christmas

A 3-storey Geogian house in the centre of the quiet village of Askrigg. Built around 1756 by the apothecary, a Mr James Lightfoot. Unlike him, we don't claim to cure your ills, but we can provide comfortable, individually styled accommodation ensuring you get the most from your stay in the Yorkshire Dales.

Bedrooms: 3 double/twin
Bathrooms: 2 en suite, 1 private

8 P

♦♦♦

HOME FARM

Stalling Busk, Askrigg, Leyburn DL8 3DH
T: (01969) 650360

B&B per night:
D £38.00

HB per person:
DY £30.00

OPEN All Year

Situated amidst breathtaking scenery overlooking Semerwater Lake in Wensleydale. The 17thC beamed farmhouse with log fires is beautifully furnished with antiques, brass beds, patchwork quilts etc. Bed and breakfast with optional evening meal. Traditional cooking and homemade bread are the order of the day. Licensed.

Bedrooms: 3 double/twin

Evening meal available

P

AYSGARTH, North Yorkshire Map ref 5B3

♦♦♦

WENSLEYDALE FARMHOUSE

Aysgarth, Leyburn DL8 3SR
T: (01969) 663534
F: (01969) 663534
E: wykesarego@aol.com

B&B per night:
S £26.00–£28.00
D £44.00–£48.00

HB per person:
DY £56.00–£60.00

OPEN All Year except Christmas

A few hundred yards from Aysgarth Falls. Lovely views of the surrounding hills and wonderful church. Ideal for exploring the Dales by foot, bike or car. Pleasant rooms with en suite. Open fire in dining room. Evening dinner by prior arrangement. Offering home-cooked food. A warm welcome is guaranteed.

Bedrooms: 2 double/twin
Bathrooms: 2 en suite

Evening meal available

Try a mid-week break. With 3 or more nights' stay we offer a 10% discount.

5 P

SPECIAL BREAKS

Many establishments offer special promotions and themed breaks. These are highlighted in red. (All such offers are subject to availability.)

AYSGARTH continued

♦♦♦

WHEATSHEAF HOTEL

Carperby, Leyburn DL8 4DF
T: (01969) 663216
F: (01969) 663019
E: wheatsheaf@paulmit.globalnet.co.uk
I: www.wheatsheafinwensleydale.co.uk

Bedrooms: 1 single, 8 double/twin
Bathrooms: 7 en suite

Lunch available
Evening meal available
CC: Delta, Mastercard, Switch, Visa

Delightful dales country hotel made famous when the real-life James Herriot spent his honeymoon here. Log fires in winter. Cosy panelled dining room. Some 4-poster beds.

B&B per night:
S Min £27.50
D £55.00–£65.00

HB per person:
DY £35.00–£40.00

OPEN All Year except Christmas

BARNETBY, North Lincolnshire Map ref 4C1

♦♦♦♦

REGINALD HOUSE

27 Queens Road, Barnetby
DN38 6JH
T: (01652) 688566
F: (01652) 688510

Bedrooms: 1 single, 2 double/twin
Bathrooms: 3 en suite

Evening meal available

Quiet, family-run guesthouse in Barnetby village. Five minutes from M180 and railway station, 3 miles from Humberside Airport. Near to Grimsby, Scunthorpe and Hull.

B&B per night:
S £22.50–£25.00
D £40.00

OPEN All Year

BEDALE, North Yorkshire Map ref 5C3

♦♦♦♦

THE CASTLE ARMS INN

Snape, Bedale DL8 2TB
T: (01677) 470270
F: (01677) 470837
E: castlearms@aol.com

A family-run 14thC inn which has been completely refurbished. Nine en suite twin/double bedrooms have been added, all furnished to an exceptional standard and including TV and tea/coffee-making facilities. A warm welcome awaits you, with open fires, traditional ales and real home cooking.

Bedrooms: 9 double/twin
Bathrooms: 9 en suite

Lunch available
Evening meal available
CC: Delta, Mastercard, Switch, Visa

Special seasonal rates available Oct-Mar.

B&B per night:
S £47.50
D £62.50

HB per person:
DY £38.00–£47.00

OPEN All Year

♦♦♦♦♦

ELMFIELD COUNTRY HOUSE

Arrathorne, Bedale DL8 1NE
T: (01677) 450558
F: (01677) 450557
E: stay@elmfieldhouse.freeserve.co.uk
I: www.elmfieldhouse.co.uk

Bedrooms: 7 double/twin, 2 triple/multiple
Bathrooms: 9 en suite

Evening meal available
CC: Delta, Mastercard, Switch, Visa

Country house in own grounds with special emphasis on standards and home cooking. All rooms en suite. Bar, games room, solarium. Ample secure parking.

B&B per night:
S £37.00–£40.00
D £55.00–£65.00

HB per person:
DY £42.50–£55.00

OPEN All Year

AT-A-GLANCE SYMBOLS

Symbols at the end of each accommodation entry give useful information about services and facilities. A key to symbols can be found inside the back cover flap. Keep this open for easy reference.

BEDALE continued

◆◆◆◆◆ Silver Award

MILL CLOSE FARM

Patrick Brompton, Bedale DL8 1JY
T: (01677) 450257
F: (01677) 450585
E: millclosefarm@btopenworld.com
I: www.smoothhound.co.uk/hotels/millclosefarm

17thC farmhouse at the foothills of Yorkshire Dales. Exceptional views. Charming en suite bedrooms, one with jacuzzi. Large beds, TV and video, tea tray, fridge with complimentary fruit, mineral water and chocolates. Walled garden with pond and waterfall. Delicious farmhouse breakfasts. Excellent local pubs. Colour brochure.

Bedrooms: 2 double/twin
Bathrooms: 2 en suite

B&B per night:
D £20.00–£30.00

BEVERLEY, East Riding of Yorkshire Map ref 4C1 *Tourist Information Centre Tel: (01482) 867430*

◆◆◆

EASTGATE GUEST HOUSE

7 Eastgate, Beverley HU17 0DR
T: (01482) 868464
F: (01482) 871899

Family-run Victorian guesthouse, established and run by the same proprietor for 31 years. Close to town centre, Beverley Minster, Museum of Army Transport and railway station. Fifteen minutes to Hull city centre and The Deep. Excellent central location for exploring the surrounding Wolds.

Bedrooms: 5 single, 8 double/twin, 3 triple/multiple
Bathrooms: 7 en suite

B&B per night:
S £18.00–£35.00
D £30.00–£49.00

OPEN All Year

◆◆◆◆

RUDSTONE WALK COUNTRY ACCOMMODATION AND COTTAGES

South Cave, Beverley HU15 2AH
T: (01430) 422230
F: (01430) 424552
E: office@rudstone-walk.co.uk
I: www.rudstone-walk.co.uk

Nestled in its own corner of the Yorkshire Wolds with magnificent views, Rudstone Walk provides a relaxing retreat with luxury en suite bed and breakfast and self-catering accommodation. Fully licensed. Superb home-cooked food is served in the beautiful 400-year-old farmhouse. Ideal for Beverley, York, coast and moors. Colour brochure on request.

Bedrooms: 7 single, 7 double/twin; permanent suite(s)
Bathrooms: 14 en suite

Evening meal available
CC: Amex, Delta, Diners, Mastercard, Switch, Visa

B&B per night:
S £40.00–£47.00
D £55.00–£59.00

HB per person:
DY Min £65.00

OPEN All Year

BOLTON PERCY, North Yorkshire Map ref 4C1

◆◆◆◆

GLEBE FARM
Bolton Percy, York YO23 7AL
T: (01904) 744228

Bedrooms: 1 double/twin
Bathrooms: 1 en suite

225-acre mixed farm. Excellent accommodation in self-contained en suite annexe on family-run farm. Conservatory, garden, ample parking.

B&B per night:
S £22.00–£28.00
D £44.00–£56.00

BOROUGHBRIDGE, North Yorkshire Map ref 5C3

◆◆◆

BURTON GRANGE

Helperby, York YO61 2RY
T: (01423) 360825
E: burton_grange@hotmail.com

Bedrooms: 2 double/twin
Bathrooms: 2 private

18thC farmhouse in the beautiful Vale of York. Working farm offering a peaceful and comfortable stay. Close to A1 at Boroughbridge.

B&B per night:
S Min £22.00
D Min £40.00

OPEN All Year except Christmas

BRADFORD, West Yorkshire Map ref 4B1 *Tourist Information Centre Tel: (01274) 753678*

◆◆

IVY GUEST HOUSE

3 Melbourne Place, Bradford BD5 0HZ
T: (01274) 727060
F: (01274) 306347
E: nickbaggio@aol.com

Bedrooms: 2 single, 8 double/twin

CC: Amex, Delta, Diners, Mastercard, Switch, Visa

Large, detached, Listed Yorkshire-stone house. Close to city centre, National Museum of Photography, Film and Television, Alhambra Theatre and the University of Bradford.

B&B per night:
S £20.00
D £34.00

OPEN All Year

◆◆◆

NEW BEEHIVE INN

171 Westgate, Bradford BD1 3AA
T: (01274) 721784
F: (01274) 375092

Bedrooms: 2 single, 3 double/twin, 3 triple/multiple
Bathrooms: 8 en suite

Lunch available
CC: Delta, Mastercard, Switch, Visa

Edwardian gaslit oak-panelled inn, full of character, close to centre of Bradford. Antique furniture and individually furnished bedrooms.

B&B per night:
S £26.00–£31.00
D £42.00–£48.00

OPEN All Year

BRIDLINGTON, East Riding of Yorkshire Map ref 5D3 *Tourist Information Centre Tel: (01262) 673474*

◆◆◆

A recently modernised, licensed hotel providing very comfortable bedrooms and lounges. Situated in Bridlington town centre close to the beach, shops and harbour. The hotel offers high-quality accommodation, service and food, in a no-smoking environment, beer garden, bar snacks and 5-course dinner cooked by a Master Chef.

BALMORAL PRIVATE HOTEL

21 Marshall Avenue, Bridlington YO15 2DT
T: (01262) 676678
F: (01262) 676678
E: hotel@balmoral-bridlington.co.uk
I: www.balmoral-hotel.net

Bedrooms: 2 single, 5 double/twin, 2 triple/multiple
Bathrooms: 2 en suite

Lunch available
Evening meal available
CC: Amex, Delta, Mastercard, Switch, Visa

Book 2 nights or more for 5% discount, book 5 nights or more for 10% discount.

B&B per night:
S £20.00–£24.00
D £40.00–£66.00

HB per person:
DY £26.00–£40.00

OPEN All Year

◆◆◆

Family-run country motel with village pub and quality restaurant. All rooms en suite. Located in beautiful historic Wolds village, only minutes from coast and golf courses. Art breaks with resident artist available. Quality accommodation, good food and fine ale, in a friendly country village.

BOSVILLE ARMS COUNTRY HOTEL

High Street, Rudston, Driffield YO25 4UB
T: (01262) 420259
F: (01262) 420259
E: hogan@bosville.freeserve.co.uk
I: www.bosville.freeserve.co.uk

Bedrooms: 3 double/twin, 3 triple/multiple
Bathrooms: 6 en suite

Lunch available
Evening meal available
CC: Delta, Mastercard, Switch, Visa

Residential art breaks with Yorkshire artist Tony Hogan. Small groups. All media and abilities catered for. All year round.

B&B per night:
S £29.50–£39.50
D £54.50–£67.50

OPEN All Year

BRIDLINGTON continued

THE WHITE ROSE

123 Cardigan Road, Bridlington YO15 3LP
T: (01262) 673245 & 07860 159208
F: (01262) 401362
E: c.a.young@tesco.net
I: www.smoothhound.co.uk/hotels/thewhiterose

Bedrooms: 4 double/twin, 1 triple/multiple
Bathrooms: 4 en suite, 1 private

Lunch available
Evening meal available
CC: Mastercard, Visa

B&B per night:
S £20.00–£25.00
D £40.00–£44.00

HB per person:
DY £27.50–£32.00

OPEN All Year

Personal attention with warm, friendly hospitality and emphasis on food. No hidden extras. Near the South Beach, spa and harbour. Special pensioners' weeks at discount prices.

WINSTON HOUSE HOTEL

5-6 South Street, Bridlington YO15 3BY
T: (01262) 670216
F: (01262) 670216
E: bob.liz@winstonhouse.fsnet.co.uk
I: www.winston-house.co.uk

B&B per night:
S £20.00
D £38.00–£46.00

HB per person:
DY £26.00–£30.00

OPEN All Year

Quietly situated minutes from the glorious South Beach, harbour and town. En suite accommodation with family room and 4-poster for that special occasion, all with beverage tray and Sky movies. Enjoy a varied and generous home-cooked menu. Ideal for touring the moors and Wolds and 'Heartbeat' country.

Bedrooms: 3 single, 7 double/twin, 1 triple/multiple
Bathrooms: 9 en suite

Evening meal available
CC: Amex, Delta, Diners, Mastercard, Switch, Visa

Special rates for short breaks, Senior Citizens and children. Holiday flat also available.

BUCKDEN, North Yorkshire Map ref 5B3

THE WHITE LION INN

Cray, Skipton BD23 5JB
T: (01756) 760262
F: (01756) 761024
E: admin.whitelion@btinternet.com
I: www.whitelioncray.com

B&B per night:
S £30.00–£37.50
D £45.00–£65.00

HB per person:
DY £30.00–£55.00

OPEN All Year

Located in Upper Wharfedale, you are assured a warm welcome to our traditional 17thC Dales inn. Relax in the friendly atmosphere and enjoy the country charm of stone-flagged floors, roaring log fire, quality home-prepared foods and real ales. Idyllic location with excellent walks direct from our door!

Bedrooms: 8 double/twin, 1 triple/multiple
Bathrooms: 8 en suite, 1 private

Lunch available
Evening meal available
CC: Delta, Mastercard, Switch, Visa

3 nights for the price of 2, subject to eating from the full evening menu every night (one main course per person).

BURNT YATES, North Yorkshire Map ref 4B1

THE NEW INN HOTEL

Burnt Yates, Harrogate HG3 3EG
T: (01423) 771070
F: (01423) 771070
E: enquiries@newinnburntyates.co.uk
I: www.newinnburntyates.co.uk

Bedrooms: 1 single, 6 double/twin
Bathrooms: 7 en suite

Lunch available
Evening meal available
CC: Amex, Delta, Mastercard, Switch, Visa

B&B per night:
S £50.00–£55.00
D £60.00–£75.00

OPEN All Year

Once a farm, The New Inn still retains its old world charm amidst the beautiful countryside at the gateway to the Yorkshire Dales.

COLOUR MAPS Colour maps at the front of this guide pinpoint all places under which you will find accommodation listed.

CASTLE HOWARD, North Yorkshire Map ref 5C3

◆◆◆

LOWRY'S RESTAURANT AND GUEST HOUSE

Malton Road, Slingsby, York
YO62 4AF
T: (01653) 628417
E: dgwilliams@onetel.net.uk

Bedrooms: 3 double/twin, 1 triple/multiple
Bathrooms: 2 en suite

Lunch available
Evening meal available
CC: Delta, Mastercard, Switch, Visa

Friendly, family-run guesthouse 2 miles from Castle Howard, 8 miles from Yorkshire Moors. Ideal location for touring the area. Excellent home-cooked food.

B&B per night:
S £25.00
D £40.00

OPEN All Year

CLOUGHTON, North Yorkshire Map ref 5D3

COBER HILL

Newlands Road, Cloughton, Scarborough YO13 0AR
T: (01723) 870310
F: (01723) 870271
E: enquiries@coberhill.co.uk
I: www.coberhill.co.uk

Bedrooms: 22 single, 28 double/twin, 13 triple/multiple
Bathrooms: 63 en suite

Lunch available
Evening meal available
CC: Delta, Mastercard, Visa

Conference, holiday and education centre in a beautiful location between Scarborough and Whitby, on the edge of the North York Moors and Heritage Coast.

B&B per night:
S Max £35.00

HB per person:
DY Max £50.00

OPEN All Year

CROPTON, North Yorkshire Map ref 5C3

Silver Award

HIGH FARM

Cropton, Pickering YO18 8HL
T: (01751) 417461
F: (01751) 417807
E: highfarmcropton@aol.com
I: www.hhml.com/bb/highfarmcropton.htm

B&B per night:
S £27.00
D £44.00

OPEN All Year

Relax in the friendly atmosphere of this elegant Victorian farmhouse surrounded by beautiful gardens, on the edge of quiet, unspoilt village and overlooking North Yorkshire Moors National Park. Peaceful base for walkers, nature/garden lovers. Steam railway and Castle Howard nearby. Village inn has own brewery. A warm welcome awaits.

Bedrooms: 3 double/twin
Bathrooms: 3 en suite

CC: Delta, Mastercard, Switch, Visa

10

DANBY, North Yorkshire Map ref 5C3

DUKE OF WELLINGTON INN

Danby, Whitby YO21 2LY
T: (01287) 660351
E: landlord@dukeofwellington.freeserve.co.uk
I: www.danby-dukeofwellington.co.uk

B&B per night:
S £33.00–£50.00
D £60.00

HB per person:
DY £40.00–£43.00

OPEN All Year except Christmas

An ivy-clad, traditional 18thC inn located in the tranquil village of Danby at the heart of the North Yorkshire Moors. Enjoy our home-cooked food, real ales, interesting wines and malt whiskies whilst seated by the open fire. An ideal base for exploring the Moors, Whitby and coast.

Bedrooms: 3 single, 5 double/twin, 1 triple/multiple
Bathrooms: 9 en suite

Lunch available
Evening meal available
CC: Delta, Mastercard, Switch, Visa

Winter breaks Jan-Apr.

MAP REFERENCES The map references refer to the colour maps at the front of this guide. The first figure is the map number; the letter and figure which follow indicate the grid reference on the map.

DUNGWORTH, South Yorkshire Map ref 4B2

THE ROYAL HOTEL

Main Road, Dungworth, Bradfield, Sheffield S6 6HF
T: (0114) 285 1213
F: (0114) 285 1723
E: reception@royalhotel-dungworth.co.uk
I: www.royalhotel-dungworth.co.uk

The Royal Hotel is a 19thC, family-run public house on the edge of the Peak Park yet only 6 miles from the centre of Sheffield and Meadowhall/M1. Located on the hillside overlooking the Vale of Bradfield in idyllic countryside for walking, with fishing and golfing close by.

Bedrooms: 3 double/twin
Bathrooms: 3 en suite

Lunch available
Evening meal available
CC: Mastercard, Switch, Visa

B&B per night:
S £35.00–£40.00
D £50.00–£60.00

OPEN All Year

EASINGWOLD, North Yorkshire Map ref 5C3

◆◆◆

YEOMAN'S COURSE HOUSE

Thornton Hill, Easingwold, York YO61 3PY
T: (01347) 868126
F: (01347) 868129
E: chris@yeomanscourse.fsnet.co.uk

Bedrooms: 3 double/twin

Built c1800 as part of Newburgh Priory Estate. Set in the Howardian Hills overlooking the Vale of York and beyond.

12

B&B per night:
S £20.00–£22.00
D £40.00–£44.00

FILEY, North Yorkshire Map ref 5D3

◆◆◆

SEAFIELD HOTEL

9-11 Rutland Street, Filey YO14 9JA
T: (01723) 513715

Bedrooms: 2 single, 4 double/twin, 9 triple/multiple
Bathrooms: 14 en suite

Evening meal available
CC: Delta, Mastercard, Visa

Small, friendly and comfortable hotel in the centre of Filey, close to the beach and all amenities. Car park. Family rooms.

B&B per night:
S £18.50–£20.50
D £37.00–£41.00

HB per person:
DY £24.00–£26.00

OPEN All Year except Christmas

GARFORTH, West Yorkshire Map ref 4B1

◆◆◆

MYRTLE HOUSE

31 Wakefield Road, Garforth, Leeds LS25 1AN
T: (0113) 286 6445

Bedrooms: 1 single, 2 double/twin, 3 triple/multiple

Spacious Victorian terraced house between M62 and A1 (M1, jct 47). All rooms have tea and coffee making facilities, TV, vanity basins and central heating.

B&B per night:
S £19.00–£21.50
D £38.00–£43.00

OPEN All Year except Christmas

GILLAMOOR, North Yorkshire Map ref 5C3

◆◆◆

ROYAL OAK INN

Main Street, Gillamoor, York YO62 7HX
T: (01751) 431414
F: (01751) 431414

Bedrooms: 6 double/twin
Bathrooms: 6 en suite

Lunch available
Evening meal available
CC: Delta, Mastercard, Switch, Visa

Relax at our 17thC inn situated in the North York Moors National Park. Log fires and excellent cuisine complemented by fine wines and ales.

B&B per night:
S £26.00–£30.00
D £52.00–£60.00

HB per person:
DY £43.00–£47.50

OPEN All Year except Christmas

CONFIRM YOUR BOOKING
You are advised to confirm your booking in writing.

GOATHLAND, North Yorkshire Map ref 5D3

◆◆◆

BARNET HOUSE GUEST HOUSE

Goathland, Whitby YO22 5NG
T: (01947) 896201
F: (01947) 896201
E: barnethouse@hotmail.com
I: www.barnethouse.co.uk

Bedrooms: 1 single, 5 double/twin
Bathrooms: 4 en suite

CC: Delta, Mastercard, Switch, Visa

B&B per night:
S £22.50–£23.50
D £45.00–£55.00

OPEN All Year except Christmas

Stone-built house in large garden on edge of village overlooking North Yorkshire Moors Railway. Magnificent views of surrounding moors.

◆◆◆

FAIRHAVEN COUNTRY HOTEL

The Common, Goathland, Nr Whitby YO22 5AN
T: (01947) 896361
F: (01947) 896099
E: royellis@thefairhavenhotel.co.uk
I: www.thefairhavenhotel.co.uk

Bedrooms: 2 single, 4 double/twin, 3 triple/multiple
Bathrooms: 8 en suite, 1 private

Evening meal available
CC: Delta, Mastercard, Switch, Visa

B&B per night:
S £26.00–£37.00
D £56.00

HB per person:
DY £40.00–£51.00

OPEN All Year

Edwardian country house with superb moorland views in centre of village. Warm hospitality and fine food in a relaxed atmosphere. Families welcome. Dogs by arrangement.

◆◆◆◆
Silver Award

PRUDOM GUEST HOUSE

Goathland, Whitby YO22 5AN
T: (01947) 896368
F: (01947) 896030
E: info@prudomhouse.co.uk
I: www.prudomhouse.co.uk

B&B per night:
S £27.50–£32.50
D £55.00–£65.00

A warm welcome awaits you at our cosy, family-owned, 18thC farmhouse in the village of Goathland. Situated opposite the church and surrounded by magnificent moorland views. Perfect for walking and touring. Quality accommodation, log fires, pretty cottage gardens and excellent food using local produce.

Bedrooms: 1 single, 5 double/twin
Bathrooms: 6 en suite

GRASSINGTON, North Yorkshire Map ref 5B3 *Tourist Information Centre Tel: (01756) 752774*

◆◆◆

FORESTERS ARMS HOTEL

20 Main Street, Grassington, Skipton BD23 5AA
T: (01756) 752349
F: (01756) 753633
E: theforesters@totalise.co.uk

Bedrooms: 5 double/twin, 2 triple/multiple
Bathrooms: 7 en suite

Lunch available
Evening meal available
CC: Delta, Mastercard, Switch, Visa

B&B per night:
S £30.00–£45.00
D £60.00–£75.00

OPEN All Year except Christmas

Formerly an old coaching inn, situated in picturesque village, serving lunch and evening meals. Hand-pulled ales and en suite accommodation.

◆◆◆◆

NEW LAITHE HOUSE

Wood Lane, Grassington, Skipton BD23 5LU
T: (01756) 752764
E: enquiries@newlaithehouse.co.uk
I: www.newlaithehouse.co.uk

Bedrooms: 5 double/twin, 1 triple/multiple
Bathrooms: 4 en suite, 1 private

B&B per night:
D £48.00–£54.00

Situated in a quiet location. An ideal base for walking or fishing and for visiting the many historic towns in North and West Yorkshire.

RATING All accommodation in this guide has been rated, or is awaiting a rating, by a trained English Tourism Council assessor.

GRASSINGTON continued

TOWN HEAD GUEST HOUSE

1 Low Lane, Grassington, Skipton BD23 5AU
T: (01756) 752811

Bedrooms: 4 double/twin
Bathrooms: 4 en suite

Small, modern guesthouse in the heart of beautiful countryside. Ideal centre for walking and touring the Dales.

B&B per night:
D £52.00–£55.00

OPEN All Year except Christmas

HALIFAX, West Yorkshire Map ref 4B1 *Tourist Information Centre Tel: (01422) 368725*

Silver Award

ROSE COTTAGE

Shibden Fold, Halifax HX3 6XP
T: (01422) 365437
F: (01422) 323376
E: welcome@shibden-fold.co.uk
I: www.shibden-fold.co.uk

Spacious, comfortable accommodation in a lovely private home. Built in the 16thC in rural surroundings. Beautifully decorated, en suite bedrooms and visitors' study. Excellent walking and sightseeing, Eureka! Children's Museum and Shibden Hall are very close. Enjoy the gardens, streams and 15 acres with good food and personal service.

Bedrooms: 2 double/twin
Bathrooms: 2 en suite

Evening meal available
CC: Mastercard, Visa

B&B per night:
S £30.00–£35.00
D £50.00–£55.00

HB per person:
DY £45.00–£50.00

OPEN All Year

HARROGATE, North Yorkshire Map ref 4B1 *Tourist Information Centre Tel: (01423) 537300*

ALAMAH

88 Kings Road, Harrogate HG1 5JX
T: (01423) 502187
F: (01423) 566175

Bedrooms: 2 single, 4 double/twin, 1 triple/multiple
Bathrooms: 6 en suite

CC: Delta, Mastercard, Visa

Comfortable rooms, personal attention, friendly atmosphere and full English breakfast. Three hundred metres from town centre, 150 metres from Exhibition Centre. Garages/parking.

B&B per night:
S £28.00–£35.00
D £54.00–£60.00

OPEN All Year except Christmas

Silver Award

THE ALEXANDER

88 Franklin Road, Harrogate HG1 5EN
T: (01423) 503348
F: (01423) 540230
E: thealexander@amserve.net

Bedrooms: 2 single, 2 double/twin, 3 triple/multiple
Bathrooms: 5 en suite

Friendly, family-run, elegant Victorian guesthouse with some en suite facilities. Ideal for conference centre and Harrogate town. Good touring centre for dales. Non-smokers only, please.

B&B per night:
S £27.00–£30.00
D £50.00–£55.00

OPEN All Year except Christmas

ASHLEY HOUSE HOTEL

36-40 Franklin Road, Harrogate HG1 5EE
T: (01423) 507474
F: (01423) 560858
E: ron@ashleyhousehotel.com
I: www.ashleyhousehotel.com

Bedrooms: 5 single, 13 double/twin
Bathrooms: 18 en suite

CC: Amex, Delta, Diners, Mastercard, Switch, Visa

Close to town centre and numerous excellent restaurants. Friendly atmosphere. Delightful bar with extensive selection of whiskies. Delicious breakfasts.

B&B per night:
S £45.00–£80.00
D £65.00–£90.00

OPEN All Year

HARROGATE continued

◆◆◆◆

CAVENDISH HOTEL
3 Valley Drive, Harrogate HG2 0JJ
T: (01423) 509637
F: (01423) 504434

Bedrooms: 3 single, 6 double/twin
Bathrooms: 9 en suite

CC: Delta, Mastercard, Visa

B&B per night:
S £35.00–£45.00
D £55.00–£70.00

OPEN All Year

Overlooking the beautiful Valley Gardens in a quiet location yet close to conference centre and extensive shopping area. Ideal for business or pleasure.

◆◆◆◆ Silver Award

CENTRAL HOUSE FARM
Haverah Park, Harrogate HG3 1SQ
T: (01423) 566050
F: (01423) 709152
E: jayne-ryder@lineone.net

Bedrooms: 3 double/twin
Bathrooms: 3 en suite

B&B per night:
S £35.00
D £47.00–£50.00

OPEN All Year except Christmas

Traditional farmhouse in picturesque rural location. Close to Harrogate and its amenities. York 30 miles, Leeds 20 miles. All rooms are en suite.

P

◆◆◆◆

GARDEN HOUSE HOTEL
14 Harlow Moor Drive, Harrogate HG2 0JX
T: (01423) 503059
F: (01423) 503059
E: gardenhouse@harrogate.com
I: www.harrogate.com/gardenhouse

Bedrooms: 3 single, 4 double/twin
Bathrooms: 5 en suite

CC: Delta, Mastercard, Switch, Visa

B&B per night:
S Min £25.00
D Min £55.00

OPEN All Year except Christmas

Small, family-run, Victorian hotel overlooking Valley Gardens, in a quiet location with unrestricted parking. Non-smokers only please.

2

◆◆◆◆

GRAFTON HOTEL
1-3 Franklin Mount, Harrogate HG1 5EJ
T: (01423) 508491
F: (01423) 523168
E: enquiries@graftonhotel.co.uk
I: www.graftonhotel.co.uk

Bedrooms: 6 single, 8 double/twin, 3 triple/multiple
Bathrooms: 17 en suite

Lunch available
Evening meal available
CC: Amex, Delta, Diners, Mastercard, Switch, Visa

B&B per night:
S £30.00–£35.00
D £50.00–£60.00

OPEN All Year except Christmas

This fine Victorian resdience, which has been tastefully modernised, is quietly situated close to the town centre and restaurants. We offer comfort and personal attention.

P

◆◆

HALF MOON INN
Main Street, Pool in Wharfedale, Otley LS21 1LH
T: (0113) 284 2878
F: (0113) 203 7895

Bedrooms: 5 double/twin
Bathrooms: 5 en suite

Lunch available
Evening meal available
CC: Delta, Mastercard, Switch, Visa

B&B per night:
S £35.00–£45.00
D £45.00–£55.00

OPEN All Year

Situated within the heart of the beautiful Wharfedale Valley within easy reach of Harrogate, Leeds and Bradford. High class accommodation, home cooking, real ales and family hospitality.

P

◆◆◆

SCOTIA HOUSE HOTEL
66-68 Kings Road, Harrogate HG1 5JR
T: (01423) 504361
F: (01423) 526578
E: info@scotiahotel.harrogate.net
I: www.scotiahotel.harrogate.net

Bedrooms: 6 single, 8 double/twin, 1 triple/multiple
Bathrooms: 12 en suite

CC: Amex, Delta, Mastercard, Switch, Visa

B&B per night:
S £28.00–£40.00
D £58.00–£68.00

OPEN All Year

Award-winning, warm, friendly hotel opposite conference centre and close to town and amenities. Individually styled bedrooms offering colour TV, telephone, beverage tray, modem point etc.

7 P

IMPORTANT NOTE Information on accommodation listed in this guide has been supplied by the proprietors. As changes may occur you are advised to check details at the time of booking.

HARTWITH, North Yorkshire Map ref 4B1

♦♦♦♦

BRIMHAM LODGE

Brimham Rocks Road, Burnt Yates, Harrogate HG3 3HE
T: (01423) 771770
F: (01423) 770370
E: neil.clarke@virgin.net
I: www.farmhousesbedandbreakfast.com

Bedrooms: 2 double/twin
Bathrooms: 2 private

350-acre dairy farm. Brimham Lodge is close to Brimham Rocks and Harrogate on the Nidderdale Way. Features include oak beams, open fires and friendly surroundings.

B&B per night:
D £40.00–£50.00

OPEN All Year except Christmas

HAWES, North Yorkshire Map ref 5B3 *Tourist Information Centre Tel: (01969) 667450*

♦♦♦♦

COCKETTS HOTEL AND RESTAURANT

Market Place, Hawes DL8 3RD
T: (01969) 667312
F: (01969) 667162
E: enquiries@cocketts.co.uk
I: www.cocketts.co.uk

Bedrooms: 7 double/twin, 1 triple/multiple
Bathrooms: 8 en suite

Lunch available
Evening meal available
CC: Delta, Mastercard, Switch, Visa

17thC stone-built hotel in the market place. Ideally situated for touring the Dales. English and French cuisine.

10

B&B per night:
S £35.00–£45.00
D £48.00–£69.00

HB per person:
DY £39.95–£50.45

OPEN All Year except Christmas

♦♦♦

EBOR GUEST HOUSE

Burtersett Road, Hawes DL8 3NT
T: (01969) 667337
F: (01969) 667337
E: gwen@eborhouse.freeserve.co.uk

Bedrooms: 3 double/twin
Bathrooms: 2 en suite

Small, friendly, centrally located and family run. Walkers and cyclists catered for with drying facilities and under-cover bike store, hearty breakfasts and packed lunches.

B&B per night:
D £40.00–£46.00

OPEN All Year except Christmas

♦♦♦

LABURNUM HOUSE

The Holme, Hawes DL8 3QR
T: (01969) 667717
F: (01969) 667041
E: janetbatty@hotmail.com
I: www.stayatlaburnumhouse.co.uk

18thC Dales House in Hawes, central for walking and touring. Warm welcome, hearty breakfast.

Bedrooms: 2 double/twin, 1 triple/multiple
Bathrooms: 3 en suite

B&B per night:
D Min £44.00

OPEN All Year

♦♦♦

WHITE HART INN

Main Street, Hawes DL8 3QL
T: (01969) 667259
F: (01969) 667259
E: whitehart@wensleydale.org
I: www.wensleydale.org

Bedrooms: 1 single, 6 double/twin

Lunch available
Evening meal available
CC: Delta, Diners, Mastercard, Switch, Visa

17thC coaching inn with a friendly welcome, offering traditional fare. Open fires, Yorkshire ales. Central for exploring the dales.

B&B per night:
S £23.00–£30.00
D £44.00–£46.00

OPEN All Year except Christmas

HAWORTH, West Yorkshire Map ref 4B1 *Tourist Information Centre Tel: (01535) 642329*

◆◆◆

THE APOTHECARY GUEST HOUSE

86 Main Street, Haworth, Keighley
BD22 8DA
T: (01535) 643642
F: (01535) 643642
E: apot@sisley86.freeserve.co.uk
I: www.sisley86.freeserve.co.uk

Bedrooms: 1 single, 5 double/twin, 1 triple/multiple
Bathrooms: 6 en suite, 1 private

Lunch available
CC: Mastercard, Visa

B&B per night:
S £20.00–£25.00
D £40.00–£45.00

OPEN All Year

At the top of Haworth Main Street opposite the famous Bronte church, 1 minute from the Parsonage and moors. Ten minutes' walk from steam railway.

P

◆◆

BRONTE HOTEL

Lees Lane, Haworth, Keighley
BD22 8RA
T: (01535) 644112
F: (01535) 646725
E: Brontehotel@btinternet.com
I: www.bronte-hotel.co.uk

Bedrooms: 3 single, 5 double/twin, 3 triple/multiple
Bathrooms: 8 en suite

Lunch available
Evening meal available
CC: Amex, Mastercard, Switch, Visa

B&B per night:
S £23.00–£35.00
D £45.00–£60.00

OPEN All Year except Christmas

On the edge of the Moors, 5 minutes' walk from the station and 15 minutes' walk to the Parsonage, the former home of the Brontes.

P

HEBDEN, North Yorkshire Map ref 5B3

◆◆◆

COURT CROFT

Church Lane, Hebden, Skipton
BD23 5DX
T: (01756) 753406

Bedrooms: 2 double/twin

Lunch available

B&B per night:
S £20.00–£23.00
D £36.00–£46.00

OPEN All Year

500-acre livestock farm. Newly-built farmhouse in village location. Close to the Dales Way.

P

HELMSLEY, North Yorkshire Map ref 5C3

◆◆◆◆◆
Gold Award

OLDSTEAD GRANGE

Oldstead, Coxwold, York YO61 4BJ
T: (01347) 868634
E: oldsteadgrange@yorkshireuk.com
I: www.yorkshireuk.com

B&B per night:
D £56.00–£70.00

OPEN All Year

17thC farmhouse offering exceptional luxury amidst superb quiet country location. Spacious en suite rooms with really comfortable king-size beds, warm towels and robes, fresh flowers and homemade chocolates. Special 4-poster suite. Wide choice of traditional and speciality breakfasts. Renowned eating places in local picturesque villages.

Bedrooms: 3 double/twin
Bathrooms: 3 en suite

CC: Delta, Mastercard, Visa

Call for up to 20% discount, current Special Breaks and brochure (lots of pictures including bedrooms). See all details on our website!

10 P

◆◆◆◆

STILWORTH HOUSE

1 Church Street, Helmsley, York
YO62 5AD
T: (01439) 771072
E: carol@stilworth.co.uk
I: www.stilworth.co.uk

Bedrooms: 4 double/twin, 1 triple/multiple
Bathrooms: 5 en suite

B&B per night:
S £35.00–£45.00
D £46.00–£60.00

OPEN All Year except Christmas

Comfortable, relaxed atmosphere in elegant Georgian townhouse off the market square of Helmsley. Pretty en suite rooms with colour TV, hairdryer, tea/coffee facilities. Private car park.

P

HALF BOARD PRICES Half board prices are given per person, but in some cases these may be based on double/twin occupancy.

HOOTON PAGNELL, South Yorkshire Map ref 4C1

♦♦♦

ROCK FARM
Hooton Pagnell, Doncaster DN5 7BT
T: (01977) 642200 & 07785 916186

Bedrooms: 1 single, 1 double/twin, 1 triple/multiple
Bathrooms: 1 en suite

B&B per night:
S Min £19.00
D Min £40.00

OPEN All Year except Christmas

200-acre mixed farm. Traditional farmhouse in an unspoilt, picturesque stone village on the B6422, 6 miles north-west of Doncaster and 1.5 miles west of the A1.

P

HUDDERSFIELD, West Yorkshire Map ref 4B1 *Tourist Information Centre Tel: (01484) 223200*

♦♦♦

CAMBRIDGE LODGE
4 Clare Hill, Huddersfield HD1 5BS
T: (01484) 519892
F: (01484) 534534
E: cambridge.lodge@ntlworld.com
I: www.huddersfield.co.uk/cambridgelodge

Bedrooms: 22 double/twin
Bathrooms: 22 en suite

CC: Amex, Delta, Diners, Mastercard, Switch, Visa

B&B per night:
S £25.00–£30.00
D £30.00–£35.00

OPEN All Year

We have 22 en suite bedrooms, all rooms double sized, twin rooms with tea/coffee-making facilities, telephone and colour TV in all rooms. Ample free parking and CCTV coverage.

10 P

♦♦♦

THE MALLOWS GUEST HOUSE
55 Spring Street, Springwood, Huddersfield HD1 4AZ
T: (01484) 544684

Bedrooms: 1 single, 5 double/twin
Bathrooms: 3 en suite

B&B per night:
S £19.50–£29.50
D £35.00–£40.00

OPEN All Year except Christmas

An elegant, impeccably maintained Listed building with tastefully furnished, spacious bedrooms. Close to town centre, 1.5 miles from M62.

P

HULL, East Riding of Yorkshire Map ref 4C1 *Tourist Information Centre Tel: (01482) 223559 (Paragon Street)*

♦♦♦♦

CONWAY-ROSEBERRY HOTEL
86 Marlborough Avenue, Hull HU5 3JT
T: (01482) 445256 & 07909 517328
F: (01482) 343215
I: www.SmoothHound.co.uk/hotels/conway.html

Bedrooms: 1 single, 2 double/twin, 1 triple/multiple
Bathrooms: 3 en suite

CC: Mastercard, Visa

B&B per night:
S £19.00–£30.00
D £38.00–£42.00

OPEN All Year

Comfortable guesthouse in quiet conservation area. Emphasis on good food, cleanliness and service, in a friendly atmosphere.

HUTTON-LE-HOLE, North Yorkshire Map ref 5C3

♦♦♦♦
Silver Award

Award-winning Georgian guesthouse in one of England's prettiest villages situated within the Moors National Park, ideal for exploring Yorkshire's natural beauty, historical sites and coast. Relax by log fires or in the tranquillity of our beautiful streamside garden. Enjoy sumptuous breakfasts, deep armchairs, tea, cake, a game of croquet or tennis, and memorable dinners.

MOORLANDS OF HUTTON-LE-HOLE

Hutton-le-Hole, North Yorkshire Moors YO62 6UA
T: (01751) 417548
F: (01751) 417760
E: stay@moorlandshouse.com
I: www.moorlandshouse.com

Bedrooms: 3 double/twin
Bathrooms: 3 en suite

Evening meal available
CC: Amex, Delta, Mastercard, Switch, Visa

Special Christmas and New Year breaks; fun 'learning' breaks; museum/arts/crafts packages, murder mystery dinners, self-guided trails.

B&B per night:
S £40.00
D £65.00

HB per person:
DY £50.50–£58.00

OPEN All Year

15 P

VISITOR ATTRACTIONS For ideas on places to visit refer to the introduction at the beginning of this section. Look out too for the ETC's Quality Assured Visitor Attraction signs.

ILKLEY, West Yorkshire Map ref 4B1

GROVE HOTEL

66 The Grove, Ilkley LS29 9PA
T: (01943) 600298
F: 0870 706 5587
E: info@grovehotel.org
I: www.grovehotel.org

This very well cared for, friendly hotel offers thoughtfully equipped bedrooms together with a cosy lounge and small bar. Breakfast is served in the bright dining room. The hotel is convenient for several local restaurants and shops. Complimentary use for hotel guests of the private health club adjacent to the hotel.

Bedrooms: 4 double/twin, 2 triple/multiple
Bathrooms: 6 en suite

CC: Amex, Delta, Diners, Mastercard, Switch, Visa

B&B per night:
S £47.00–£54.00
D £64.00–£69.00

OPEN All Year except Christmas

Rating Applied For

STAR HOTEL

1 Leeds Road, Ilkley LS29 8DH
T: (01943) 605438

Public house fully refurbished in 2002 situated in the centre of Ilkley. Spacious and comfortable en suite rooms. Close to all amenities and bus/railway stations. Two minutes' walk from the River Wharfe and the start of the Dales Way. Nearby public swimming pool, outdoor pool, tennis, bowls and putting.

Bedrooms: 1 double/twin, 5 triple/multiple; permanent suite(s)
Bathrooms: 5 en suite, 1 private

Lunch available
Evening meal available
CC: Delta, Mastercard, Switch, Visa

B&B per night:
S £32.50
D £55.00

OPEN All Year

♦♦♦

SUMMERHILL GUEST HOUSE
24 Crossbeck Road, Ilkley LS29 9JN
T: (01943) 607067

Bedrooms: 2 single, 3 double/twin
Bathrooms: 1 en suite

Elegant Victorian villa with beautiful garden opening onto Ilkley Moor. Quiet position, lovely views, private parking. Easy walking distance to town.

B&B per night:
S £20.00–£30.00
D £40.00–£46.00

OPEN All Year except Christmas

INGLETON, North Yorkshire Map ref 5B3

FERNCLIFFE COUNTRY GUEST HOUSE

55 Main Street, Ingleton, Carnforth LA6 3HJ
T: (01524) 242405
E: ferncliffe@hotmail.com

Ferncliffe is a Victorian, dales-style, detached house on the edge of Ingleton. A warm welcome is assured from your hosts Susan and Peter Ring. An ideal base to explore the Yorkshire Dales and South Lakes area. The comfortable rooms are en suite, with beverage tray and colour TV.

Bedrooms: 5 double/twin
Bathrooms: 5 en suite

Evening meal available
CC: Mastercard, Visa

B&B per night:
S £29.00–£30.00
D £46.00–£50.00

INGLETON continued

◆◆◆◆

INGLEBOROUGH VIEW GUEST HOUSE

Main Street, Ingleton, Carnforth
LA6 3HH
T: (01524) 241523
E: anne@ingleboroughview.co.uk
I: www.ingleboroughview.co.uk

Bedrooms: 3 double/twin, 1 triple/multiple
Bathrooms: 2 en suite, 2 private

Attractive Victorian house with picturesque riverside location. All rooms have superb views. Highly recommended for food, comfort and hospitality. Ideally situated for local walks/touring Dales.

P

B&B per night:
S £25.00–£30.00
D £40.00–£44.00

OPEN All Year except Christmas

◆◆◆

RIVERSIDE LODGE

24 Main Street, Ingleton, Carnforth
LA6 3HJ
T: (015242) 41359
E: info@riversideingleton.co.uk
I: www.riversideingleton.co.uk

Splendid Victorian house overlooking River Greta. Delightful terraced gardens leading down to river bank. Rooms available on ground floor. Sauna and games room. Home-cooked evening meals available upon request. All rooms en suite. Nearby waterfalls' walk and caves. Ideal base for walkers and for touring Yorkshire Dales and Lake District.

Bedrooms: 8 double/twin
Bathrooms: 8 en suite

Evening meal available
CC: Delta, Mastercard, Visa

P

B&B per night:
S £34.00
D £42.00–£50.00

HB per person:
DY £33.00–£37.00

OPEN All Year

◆◆◆

SPRINGFIELD COUNTRY HOUSE HOTEL

Main Street, Ingleton, Carnforth LA6 3HJ
T: (01524) 241280
F: (01524) 241280
I: www.destination-england.co.uk.springfield

Detached Victorian villa, large garden with patio down to River Greta. Home-grown vegetables in season, home cooking. Private fishing. Pets welcome. All credit cards are accepted.

Bedrooms: 4 double/twin, 1 triple/multiple
Bathrooms: 5 en suite

Evening meal available
CC: Amex, Delta, Diners, Mastercard, Switch, Visa

Special terms for 2 or more days: single £22, double £44. Weekly terms also available.

P

B&B per night:
S £25.00–£28.00
D £44.00–£48.00

HB per person:
DY £55.00–£59.00

OPEN All Year except Christmas

KIRKBYMOORSIDE, North Yorkshire Map ref 5C3

Rating Applied For

BRICKFIELDS FARM

Kirby Mills, Kirkbymoorside, York
YO62 6NS
T: (01751) 433074

Bedrooms: 3 double/twin; permanent suite(s)
Bathrooms: 3 en suite

Evening meal available

Newly renovated, comfortable accommodation in a private location near North York Moors. Quiet, informal atmosphere with a warm and friendly welcome assured. Opening late 2002.

10 P

B&B per night:
S £35.00–£40.00
D £58.00

HB per person:
DY £44.00

OPEN All Year

CREDIT CARD BOOKINGS If you book by telephone and are asked for your credit card number it is advisable to check the proprietor's policy should you cancel your reservation.

KIRKBYMOORSIDE continued

Rating Applied For

THE CORNMILL

Kirby Mills, Kirkbymoorside, York YO62 6NP
T: (01751) 432000
F: (01751) 432300
E: cornmill@kirbymills.demon.co.uk
I: www.kirbymills.demon.co.uk

B&B per night:
D £55.00–£65.00

Converted 18thC watermill and Victorian farmhouse providing luxury bed and breakfast accommodation on the River Dove. Bedrooms (some with 4-posters and one for wheelchairs), lounge, bar, woodburning stove and bootroom are in the farmhouse. Sumptuous breakfasts and pre-booked group dinners are served in the mill, with viewing panel in the floor.

Bedrooms: 5 double/twin
Bathrooms: 5 en suite

Evening meal available
CC: Mastercard, Visa

◆◆◆

THE LION INN

Blakey Ridge, Kirkbymoorside, York YO62 7LQ
T: (01751) 417320
F: (01751) 417717
E: dkc@lionblakey.freeserve.co.uk
I: www.lionblakey.co.uk

B&B per night:
S £17.50–£36.50
D £50.00–£64.00

OPEN All Year

Family-run, 16thC freehouse at the highest point of the North Yorkshire Moors offering spectacular views over Rosedale and Farndale. Eight real ales, bar meals served all day. Candlelit a la carte restaurant open every evening and for Sunday lunch. Conference facilities.

Bedrooms: 7 double/twin, 3 triple/multiple
Bathrooms: 8 en suite

Lunch available
Evening meal available
CC: Delta, Mastercard, Switch, Visa

Oct-Apr: book for more than 1 night and receive 25% discount on subsequent nights (excl Fri and Sat).

KNARESBOROUGH, North Yorkshire Map ref 4B1

◆◆◆

BAY HORSE INN

York Road, Green Hammerton, York YO26 8BN
T: (01423) 330338 & 331113
F: (01423) 331279
E: Thebayhorseinn@aol.com
I: www.thebayhorse.com

Bedrooms: 1 single, 9 double/twin
Bathrooms: 10 en suite

Lunch available
Evening meal available
CC: Delta, Mastercard, Switch, Visa

B&B per night:
S £40.00
D £55.00–£60.00

HB per person:
DY £50.00–£60.00

OPEN All Year

Village inn 10 miles from York and Harrogate on the A59 and 3 miles off the A1. Restaurant and bar meals. Weekly rates on request.

8

◆◆◆

EBOR MOUNT

18 York Place, Knaresborough HG5 0AA
T: (01423) 863315
F: (01423) 863315

Bedrooms: 1 single, 5 double/twin, 2 triple/multiple
Bathrooms: 8 en suite

CC: Delta, Mastercard, Switch, Visa

B&B per night:
S £22.00–£40.00
D £44.00

Charming 18thC townhouse with private car park, providing bed and breakfast accommodation in recently refurbished rooms. Ideal touring centre.

5

ACCESSIBILITY

Look for the symbols which indicate National Accessible Scheme standards for hearing and visually impaired guests in addition to standards for guests with mobility impairment. Additional participants are shown in the listings at the back.

KNARESBOROUGH continued

♦♦♦♦

NEWTON HOUSE HOTEL
5-7 York Place, Knaresborough
HG5 0AD
T: (01423) 863539
F: (01423) 869748
E: newtonhouse@btinternet.com
I: www.newtonhousehotel.com

Bedrooms: 1 single, 10 double/twin
Bathrooms: 10 en suite, 1 private

Evening meal available
CC: Delta, Mastercard, Switch, Visa

B&B per night:
S £40.00–£70.00
D £60.00–£70.00

Charming, family-run, 17thC former coaching inn, 2 minutes' walk from the market square, castle and river. Spacious and comfortable accommodation. Ideal Harrogate, York, Dales.

WATERGATE LODGE

Watergate Haven, Ripley Road,
Knaresborough HG5 9BU
T: (01423) 864627
F: (01423) 861087
E: info@watergatehaven.com
I: www.watergatehaven.com

B&B per night:
S £39.50–£49.50
D £49.50–£59.50

OPEN All Year

Comfortable en suite bedrooms, ideal for business or holidays. Tastefully appointed with many personal touches. Spectacular setting with woodland walks to River Nidd, Knaresborough and the beautiful Nidd Gorge. Good travel links to all areas. Many nearby attractions. Convenient for Harrogate, York and the Yorkshire Dales. Also self-catering apartments.

Bedrooms: 3 double/twin, 1 triple/multiple; permanent suite(s)
Bathrooms: 4 en suite

CC: Delta, Mastercard, Visa

Weekend breaks – Sun night free (min 2 persons, 3 nights). 10% discount for stays of more than 4 nights.

LEEDS, West Yorkshire Map ref 4B1 *Tourist Information Centre Tel: (0113) 242 5242*

♦♦

AINTREE HOTEL
38 Cardigan Road, Headingley,
Leeds LS6 3AG
T: (0113) 275 8290 & 275 7053
F: (0113) 275 8290

Bedrooms: 5 single, 6 double/twin
Bathrooms: 6 en suite

Evening meal available
CC: Delta, Mastercard, Switch, Visa

B&B per night:
S £27.00–£37.00
D £39.00–£47.00

HB per person:
DY £39.00–£49.00

OPEN All Year

Small, comfortable, licensed family hotel overlooking Headingley Cricket Ground. Close to amenites, public transport, Headingley shopping centre, 1.5 miles from city centre.

GLENGARTH HOTEL

162 Woodsley Road, Leeds LS2 9LZ
T: (0113) 245 7940
F: (0113) 216 8033

B&B per night:
S £28.00–£40.00
D £40.00–£60.00

HB per person:
DY £33.00–£45.00

OPEN All Year

Attractive, clean family-run hotel close to city centre, university and city hospital. 20 minutes from Leeds City Airport. Easy access to M1 and M62. Most of the rooms have en suite facilities and colour TVs.

Bedrooms: 8 single, 2 double/twin, 4 triple/multiple
Bathrooms: 10 en suite

Lunch available
Evening meal available
CC: Mastercard, Switch, Visa

Special discount for group bookings.

♦♦

MANXDENE PRIVATE HOTEL
154 Woodsley Road, Leeds LS2 9LZ
T: (0113) 243 2586
E: manxdene@dial.pipex.com

Bedrooms: 6 single, 3 double/twin, 3 triple/multiple

Evening meal available
CC: Delta, Mastercard, Switch, Visa

B&B per night:
S £25.00–£35.00
D £40.00–£50.00

OPEN All Year except Christmas

A family-run, friendly hotel in a Victorian house. Convenient for city centre, universities, hospitals, football and Yorkshire cricket. A warm, comfortable welcome awaits you.

LEEDS continued

◆◆◆

ST MICHAEL'S TOWER HOTEL

5 St Michael's Villas, Cardigan Road, Headingley, Leeds LS6 3AF
T: (0113) 275 5557 & 275 6039
F: (0113) 230 7491

Bedrooms: 8 single, 14 double/twin, 2 triple/multiple
Bathrooms: 13 en suite

Evening meal available
CC: Delta, Mastercard, Switch, Visa

Comfortable, licensed hotel, 1.5 miles from city centre and close to Headingley Cricket Ground and university. Easy access to Yorkshire countryside. Warm welcome from friendly staff.

B&B per night:
S £25.00–£33.00
D £39.00–£44.00

HB per person:
DY £22.00–£29.50

OPEN All Year except Christmas

LEEDS/BRADFORD AIRPORT

See under Bradford, Leeds, Otley

LEEMING BAR, North Yorkshire Map ref 5C3

Silver Award

LITTLE HOLTBY

Leeming Bar, Northallerton DL7 9LH
T: (01609) 748762
F: (01609) 748822
E: littleholtby@yahoo.co.uk
I: www.littleholtby.co.uk

Bedrooms: 3 double/twin
Bathrooms: 1 en suite

Evening meal available

Recently restored old farmhouse retaining many features, including open fires, old beams, polished floors, and furnished with antiques. Beautiful views.

B&B per night:
S £30.00
D £50.00–£55.00

HB per person:
DY £37.50–£40.00

OPEN All Year except Christmas

LEYBURN, North Yorkshire Map ref 5B3 *Tourist Information Centre Tel: (01969) 623069*

Silver Award

PARK GATE HOUSE

Constable Burton, Leyburn DL8 5RG
T: (01677) 450466 & 450466
E: parkgatehouse@freenet.co.uk

18thC house of character and charm, conveniently situated in Lower Wensleydale. Attractively furnished to a high standard with low oak beams, inglenook fireplace and cottage gardens. Each bedroom is decorated in country style with pretty fabrics and old pine furniture. Private facilities, TV and refreshment tray.

Bedrooms: 4 double/twin
Bathrooms: 3 en suite, 1 private

Evening meal available
CC: Mastercard, Visa

Any 2 nights DB&B £40pp (excl Bank Holidays) Oct-May inclusive.

B&B per night:
S £33.00–£38.00
D £56.00–£68.00

HB per person:
DY £40.00–£45.00

OPEN All Year except Christmas

MALHAM, North Yorkshire Map ref 5B3

BECK HALL GUEST HOUSE

Malham, Skipton BD23 4DJ
T: (01729) 830332

Bedrooms: 1 single, 11 double/twin, 2 triple/multiple
Bathrooms: 10 en suite, 1 private

Lunch available
Evening meal available
CC: Delta, Mastercard, Switch, Visa

Family-run guesthouse set in a spacious riverside garden. Homely atmosphere, 4-poster beds, log fires, large car park.

B&B per night:
S £20.00–£29.00
D £40.00–£58.00

HB per person:
DY Min £29.00

OPEN All Year

MALTON, North Yorkshire Map ref 5D3 *Tourist Information Centre Tel: (01653) 600048*

THE WENTWORTH ARMS

111 Town Street, Old Malton, Malton YO17 7HD
T: (01653) 692618
F: (01653) 600061
E: wentwortharms@btinternet.com

Bedrooms: 5 double/twin
Bathrooms: 4 en suite, 1 private

Lunch available
Evening meal available
CC: Delta, Mastercard, Switch, Visa

Former coaching inn offering a central base to explore York, the east coast and North York Moors. Excellent food available in our restaurant or bar.

B&B per night:
S £23.00–£28.00
D £46.00–£56.00

OPEN All Year

MIDDLEHAM, North Yorkshire Map ref 5C3

THE PRIORY
West End, Middleham, Leyburn
DL8 4QG
T: (01969) 623279

Bedrooms: 2 single, 4 double/twin, 2 triple/multiple
Bathrooms: 4 en suite, 1 private

B&B per night:
S £27.00
D £50.00–£54.00

Friendly, family-run Georgian property opposite Richard III castle. Local amenities and ideal centre for walking, golfing and touring in surrounding beautiful dales countryside. Brochure.

8 P

NORTHALLERTON, North Yorkshire Map ref 5C3 *Tourist Information Centre Tel: (01609) 776864*

ALVERTON GUEST HOUSE
26 South Parade, Northallerton
DL7 8SG
T: (01609) 776207
F: (01609) 776207
E: alverton.26@talk21.com

Bedrooms: 2 single, 2 double/twin, 1 triple/multiple
Bathrooms: 3 en suite

B&B per night:
S £22.00–£27.00
D £40.00–£45.00

OPEN All Year except Christmas

Family-run guesthouse convenient for county town facilities and ideal for touring the Dales, moors and coastal areas.

P

Silver Award

ELMSCOTT

10 Hatfield Road, Northallerton DL7 8QX
T: (01609) 760575
E: elmscott@freenet.co.uk
I: www.elmscottbedandbreakfast.co.uk

B&B per night:
S £30.00–£40.00
D £50.00–£60.00

OPEN All Year except Christmas

Elmscott is a charming property set in a delightful landscaped garden giving seclusion yet situated close to the centre of this thriving market town, which is located midway between the North Yorkshire Moors and Yorkshire Dales' National Parks. There are 2 attractive bedrooms both with en suite bathrooms. Private parking. Non-smoking.

Bedrooms: 2 double/twin
Bathrooms: 2 en suite

Discounts for longer stays.

P

OSSETT, West Yorkshire Map ref 4B1

HEATH HOUSE

Chancery Road, Ossett WF5 9RZ
T: (01924) 260654 & 07870 488874
F: (01924) 260654
E: jo.holland@amserve.net
I: www.heath-house.co.uk

B&B per night:
S £25.00–£35.00
D £40.00–£48.00

OPEN All Year

Set in spacious gardens, a warm welcome awaits you at Heath House. Our family home for over half a century, we take great pleasure in sharing it with our guests. Ideally situated 1.5 miles west of jct 40 M1 on the A638. Leeds, Bradford, Wakefield and Dewsbury easily accessible.

Bedrooms: 1 single, 3 double/twin, 1 triple/multiple
Bathrooms: 5 en suite

CC: Mastercard, Visa

P

QUALITY ASSURANCE SCHEME

Diamond ratings and awards were correct at the time of going to press but are subject to change. Please check at the time of booking.

OTLEY, West Yorkshire Map ref 4B1 *Tourist Information Centre Tel: (0113) 247 7707*

◆◆◆

PADDOCK HILL

Norwood, Otley LS21 2QU
T: (01943) 465977
E: cheribeaumont@connectfree.co.uk

Bedrooms: 2 single, 2 double/twin

B&B per night:
S £17.00–£18.00
D £34.00–£36.00

OPEN All Year except Christmas

Converted farmhouse on B6451. Open fires, lovely views; quiet, rural setting. Convenient for 'Emmerdale' and 'Heartbeat' country and for the Dales. Leeds 16 miles, York 28 miles.

P

PICKERING, North Yorkshire Map ref 5D3 *Tourist Information Centre Tel: (01751) 473791*

◆◆◆◆◆
Gold Award

BURR BANK

Cropton, Pickering YO18 8HL
T: (01751) 417777 & 0776 884 2233
F: (01751) 417789
E: bandb@burrbank.com
I: www.burrbank.com

B&B per night:
S £29.00
D £58.00

HB per person:
DY £47.00

OPEN All Year

Winner of 'Guest Accommodation of the Year'. Comfortable, quiet and spacious with home cooking and personal attention. Two-acre garden, 80-acre grounds. Wonderful views of moors and forest. Close to York, moors, dales, coast. Excursions and route plans. Local golf, fishing and riding.

Bedrooms: 2 double/twin
Bathrooms: 2 en suite

Evening meal available

P

◆◆◆◆

FOX AND HOUNDS COUNTRY INN

Sinnington, Nr Pickering YO62 6SQ
T: (01751) 431577
F: (01751) 432791
E: foxhoundsinn@easynet.co.uk

B&B per night:
S £44.00–£49.00
D £50.00–£80.00

OPEN All Year except Christmas

Family-run inn with relaxed, friendly atmosphere. Our priority is good food, fine wine and excellent service. Comfort and exceptional cuisine in one of Yorkshire's prettiest villages.

Bedrooms: 1 single, 9 double/twin
Bathrooms: 10 en suite

Lunch available
Evening meal available
CC: Amex, Mastercard, Switch, Visa

2-night breaks often available throughout the year. Telephone for last-minute offers.

P

◆◆◆

GIVENDALE HEAD FARM

Ebberston, Scarborough YO13 9PU
T: (01723) 859383
F: (01723) 859383
E: sue.gwilliam@talk21.com
I: www.givendaleheadfarm.co.uk

B&B per night:
S £22.00–£25.00
D £40.00–£44.00

OPEN All Year except Christmas

A warm welcome awaits at our family-run, mixed farm on the edge of Dalby Forest. An ideal place to relax, walk, bike or tour the area (Castle Howard, York, Moors, coast etc). Take breakfast in the conservatory and enjoy our outstanding views of the Yorkshire countryside.

Bedrooms: 3 double/twin
Bathrooms: 3 en suite

Evening meal available

P

PICKERING continued

◆◆

THE STATION HOTEL

11 Park Street, Pickering YO18 7AJ
T: (01751) 472171
F: (01751) 477416
E: huntagri@supanet.com

Bedrooms: 2 single, 5 double/twin, 1 triple/multiple
Bathrooms: 6 en suite

Evening meal available
CC: Mastercard, Visa

Friendly, family-run pub/hotel close to coast, moors, 'Heartbeat' country, Flamingoland and many other visitor attractions.

B&B per night:
S £25.00–£30.00
D £50.00–£70.00

OPEN All Year

RAMSGILL IN NIDDERDALE, North Yorkshire Map ref 5B3

◆◆◆◆

COVILL BARN

Bouthwaite, Ramsgill in Nidderdale, Harrogate HG3 5RW
T: (01423) 755306
F: (01423) 755306
E: sales@jandsenterprises.co.uk
I: www.jandsenterprises.co.uk

Covill Barn lies on the Nidderdale Way, overlooking Gouthwaite Nature Reserve. A sympathetic conversion of an 18thC Dales barn and granary enhanced by many original features whilst complemented by modern facilities. An ideal location for walking or exploring the wonderful countryside, stately homes or nearby market towns of the Dales.

Bedrooms: 2 double/twin; permanent suite(s)
Bathrooms: 2 en suite

B&B per night:
S Min £35.00
D £48.00–£60.00

RAVENSCAR, North Yorkshire Map ref 5D3

SMUGGLERS ROCK COUNTRY HOUSE

Staintondale Road, Ravenscar, Scarborough YO13 0ER
T: (01723) 870044
E: info@smugglersrock.co.uk
I: www.smugglersrock.co.uk

Georgian country house, reputedly a former smugglers' haunt, with panoramic views over National Park and sea. In open countryside with wonderful walks. Ideal country holiday area – located at southern end of Robin Hood's Bay. Whitby, Scarborough and 'Heartbeat' country within easy reach. Self-catering cottages also available.

Bedrooms: 1 single, 4 double/twin, 3 triple/multiple
Bathrooms: 8 en suite

CC: Delta, Mastercard, Visa

B&B per night:
S £27.00–£31.00
D £48.00–£54.00

REETH, North Yorkshire Map ref 5B3

◆◆◆

ELDER PEAK

Arkengarthdale Road, Reeth, Richmond DL11 6QX
T: (01748) 884770

Bedrooms: 2 double/twin

Quiet, comfortable family home, within easy walking distance of village centre. Panoramic views across the valley.

B&B per night:
S Min £20.00
D Min £34.00

RIPLEY, North Yorkshire Map ref 4B1

◆◆◆

SLATE RIGG FARM

Birthwaite Lane, Ripley, Harrogate HG3 3JQ
T: (01423) 770135

Bedrooms: 1 double/twin, 1 triple/multiple

Secluded mixed 190-acre working farm with views over Lower Nidderdale. One mile north of historic village of Ripley and 10 minutes from Harrogate.

B&B per night:
S £25.00–£35.00
D £40.00–£50.00

OPEN All Year except Christmas

RIPON, North Yorkshire Map ref 5C3

♦♦♦

BISHOPTON GROVE HOUSE

Bishopton, Ripon HG4 2QL
T: (01765) 600888
E: wimpress@bronco.co.uk

Bedrooms: 3 double/twin
Bathrooms: 3 en suite

Restored Georgian (pink) house in a lovely rural corner of Ripon, near the River Laver and Fountains Abbey. Ten minutes' walk to town centre.

B&B per night:
S £20.00–£30.00
D £36.00–£45.00

OPEN All Year

♦♦♦♦

MOOR END FARM

Knaresborough Road, Littlethorpe, Ripon HG4 3LU
T: (01765) 677419
E: pspensley@ukonline.co.uk
I: www.yorkshirebandb.co.uk

Bedrooms: 3 double/twin
Bathrooms: 2 en suite, 1 private

Relax in the friendly, peaceful atmosphere of this Victorian farmhouse. Well furnished and decorated. Delicious breakfast. Pleasant garden. Safe parking. Excellent meals found locally. Non-smoking.

B&B per night:
S £35.00–£45.00
D £46.00–£52.00

OPEN All Year except Christmas

ROBIN HOOD'S BAY, North Yorkshire Map ref 5D3

♦♦♦♦

FLASK INN & FLASK INN TRAVEL LODGE

Robin Hood's Bay, Whitby YO22 4QH
T: (01947) 880305 & 880692
F: (01947) 880592
E: flaskinn@aol.com
I: www.flaskinn.com

Originally a 17thC coaching inn, situated on the A171 Scarborough to Whitby road in the North York Moors National Park. Adjoining the inn is the Travel Lodge. All rooms are on the ground floor. Coffee house serving homemade cakes and snacks.

Bedrooms: 1 single, 8 double/twin, 3 triple/multiple
Bathrooms: 12 en suite

Lunch available
Evening meal available
CC: Delta, Mastercard, Switch, Visa

B&B per night:
S £30.00–£35.00
D £50.00–£60.00

OPEN All Year

ROSEDALE ABBEY, North Yorkshire Map ref 5C3

Silver Award

SEVENFORD HOUSE

Rosedale Abbey, Pickering YO18 8SE
T: (01751) 417283
F: (01751) 417505
E: sevenford@aol.com
I: www.sevenford.com

In the heart of the North York Moors National Park lies the picturesque village of Rosedale Abbey. Nestling halfway up the valleyside, Sevenford House sits in 4 acres of grounds overlooking the village and moorland. Expect a warm welcome at this former Victorian vicarage which offers modern, comfortable accommoation with outstanding views.

Bedrooms: 2 double/twin, 1 triple/multiple
Bathrooms: 3 en suite

B&B per night:
S £30.00–£35.00
D £45.00–£50.00

OPEN All Year except Christmas

GOLD & SILVER AWARDS

These exclusive ETC awards are given to establishments achieving the highest levels of quality and service. Further information can be found at the front of the guide and additional accommodation achieving these awards are shown in the listing at the back of this guide.

ROTHERHAM, South Yorkshire Map ref 4B2

◆◆◆

FITZWILLIAM ARMS HOTEL

Taylors Lane, Parkgate, Rotherham
S62 6EE
T: (01709) 522744
F: (01709) 710110

Bedrooms: 1 single, 17 double/twin; permanent suite(s)
Bathrooms: 18 en suite

Lunch available
Evening meal available
CC: Delta, Mastercard, Switch, Visa

Public house/hotel with 18 en suite bedrooms. Children's area with video games and pool tables. Function room available. Extensive car parking facilities.

B&B per night:
S £30.00–£35.00
D £43.00–£53.00

HB per person:
DY £35.00–£40.00

OPEN All Year

RUNSWICK BAY, North Yorkshire Map ref 5D3

◆◆◆◆

THE FIRS

26 Hinderwell Lane, Runswick Bay, Saltburn-by-the-Sea TS13 5HR
T: (01947) 840433
F: (01947) 841616
E: mandy.shackleton@talk21.com
I: www.the-firs.co.uk

Bedrooms: 1 single, 6 double/twin, 4 triple/ multiple
Bathrooms: 11 en suite

Evening meal available

In a coastal village, 8 miles north of Whitby. All rooms en suite, with colour TV, tea/coffee facilities. Private parking. Children and dogs welcome.

B&B per night:
S £30.00–£40.00
D £50.00–£60.00

HB per person:
DY Min £43.50

SCARBOROUGH, North Yorkshire Map ref 5D3 *Tourist Information Centre Tel: (01723) 373333*

◆◆◆◆

The Arlington Private Hotel is a lovely old Victorian house, successfully modernised to provide greater comfort and efficiency without altering its inherent charm. Every room has been tastefully refurbished and beautifully decorated. For good food, good company and tasteful surroundings The Arlington is highly recommended by many of our guests as being a hotel of distinction.

ARLINGTON PRIVATE HOTEL

42 West Street, South Cliff, Scarborough
YO11 2QP
T: (01723) 503600
F: (01723) 506762
E: alex@arlingtonhotel.fsnet.co.uk
I: www.smoothhound.co.uk/hotels/arlingtonhotel/html

Bedrooms: 2 single, 6 double/twin, 2 triple/ multiple
Bathrooms: 10 en suite

Evening meal available

Reductions for stays of 1 week or more.
Discretionary rates may apply for Senior Citizens.

B&B per night:
S £24.00–£25.00
D £44.00–£46.00

HB per person:
DY £34.00–£35.00

OPEN All Year

◆◆◆

BRINCLIFFE EDGE HOTEL

105 Queens Parade, Scarborough
YO12 7HY
T: (01723) 364834
E: brincliffeedgehotel@yahoo.co.uk
I: www.brincliffeedgehotel.co.uk

Bedrooms: 2 single, 5 double/twin, 3 triple/ multiple
Bathrooms: 7 en suite

Evening meal available
CC: Delta, Mastercard, Switch, Visa

Welcoming hotel overlooking North Bay. Car park, sea views, en suites available. Home cooking, separate tables. Cleanliness assured. Comfortable walking distance from most attractions and shops.

5 P

B&B per night:
S Max £23.00
D Max £50.00

◆◆◆

FALCON INN

Whitby Road, Cloughton, Scarborough YO13 0DY
T: (01723) 870717
I: www.yorkshirecoast.co.uk/falcon

Bedrooms: 6 double/ twin
Bathrooms: 6 en suite

Lunch available
Evening meal available
CC: Delta, Mastercard, Switch, Visa

Family-run coaching inn. Traditional ales, home-cooked bar meals, garden seating area, ample parking, open log fire (winter). 'Twixt Scarborough/Whitby. Ideal touring and walking.

B&B per night:
D £50.00–£60.00

OPEN All Year except Christmas

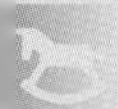

SYMBOLS The symbols in each entry give information about services and facilities. A key to these symbols appears at the back of this guide.

SCARBOROUGH continued

◆◆◆◆

HILLCREST PRIVATE HOTEL
2 Peasholm Avenue, Scarborough
YO12 7NE
T: (01723) 361981
E: peacock@hillcresthotel.fsnet.co.uk
I: www.hillcresthotel.fsnet.co.uk

Bedrooms: 2 single, 4 double/twin, 1 triple/multiple
Bathrooms: 7 en suite

Evening meal available

Small, detached, non-smoking hotel with emphasis on food, friendliness, comfort and service. Close to Peasholm Park and all other attractions.

B&B per night:
S £23.00–£28.00
D £41.00–£46.00

HB per person:
DY £32.00–£34.00

OPEN All Year

◆◆◆◆

HOWDALE HOTEL

121 Queens Parade, Scarborough
YO12 7HU
T: (01723) 372696 & (01771) 8761864
F: (01723) 372696
E: maria_keith_howdalehotel@yahoo.co.uk
I: www.howdalehotel.moonfruit.com

Beautifully situated overlooking North Bay and Scarborough Castle, yet close to town. We are renowned for cleanliness and the friendly, efficient service we provide in a comfortable atmosphere. Our substantial breakfasts are deservedly famous. Thirteen of our excellent bedrooms are en suite, many have sea views. All have TVs, tea/coffee facilities, hairdryers etc.

Bedrooms: 1 single, 13 double/twin, 1 triple/multiple
Bathrooms: 13 en suite

CC: Delta, Mastercard, Switch, Visa

Mini-breaks (3 nights minimum) from Mar-Jul and Sep-Nov, £20pppn.

B&B per night:
S £19.00–£21.00
D £44.00–£48.00

◆◆◆

NORLANDS HOTEL

10 Weydale Avenue, Scarborough
YO12 6BA
T: (01723) 362606
F: (01723) 372884
E: atkinsonhun@tinyworld.co.uk

The Norlands is a friendly, family-run hotel located in the picturesque North Bay of Scarborough. The beach, parks, gardens, children's activities, Country Cricket, golf and the famous Stephen Joseph Theatre are all within walking distance of the hotel. Many famous attractions are easily reached by bus or car.

Bedrooms: 2 single, 12 double/twin, 2 triple/multiple
Bathrooms: 16 en suite

Evening meal available
CC: Amex, Delta, Mastercard, Switch, Visa

Three nights B&B for the price of 2, Oct-Mar (excl Christmas).

B&B per night:
S £25.00–£28.00
D £50.00–£56.00

HB per person:
DY £33.00–£36.00

OPEN All Year except Christmas

◆◆◆

PARMELIA HOTEL
17 West Street, Southcliff,
Scarborough YO11 2QN
T: (01723) 361914
E: parmeliahotel@btinternet.com
I: parmeliahotel.co.uk

Bedrooms: 2 single, 8 double/twin, 4 triple/multiple
Bathrooms: 11 en suite, 1 private

Evening meal available

Spacious, licensed hotel with emphasis on comfort, quality and home cooking. On the South Cliff near the Esplanade Gardens, the cliff lift to the Spa and the beach.

B&B per night:
S £19.50–£27.50
D Min £43.00

CHECK THE MAPS

The colour maps at the front of this guide show all the cities, towns and villages for which you will find accommodation entries.
Refer to the town index to find the page on which they are listed.

SCARBOROUGH continued

VILLA MARINA

59 Northstead Manor Drive, Scarborough
YO12 6AF
T: (01723) 361088

Detatched, non-smoking hotel in a beautiful location, overlooking Peasholm Park and close to North Bay holiday attractions. Car parking available. Ideal base for touring surrounding area including 'Heartbeat' country and North Yorkshire Moors railway.

Bedrooms: 8 double/twin, 2 triple/multiple
Bathrooms: 10 en suite

Evening meal available
CC: Mastercard, Visa

3-night special from £64pp, 4-night special from £86pp.

B&B per night:
S £23.00–£25.00
D £46.00–£50.00

HB per person:
DY £60.00–£64.00

♦♦♦♦

WHARNCLIFFE HOTEL

26 Blenheim Terrace, Scarborough
YO12 7HD
T: (01723) 374635
E: dandawharncliffe@aol.com

Bedrooms: 8 double/twin, 4 triple/multiple
Bathrooms: 12 en suite

CC: Delta, Mastercard, Switch, Visa

Non-smoking, friendly, family-run licensed hotel with panoramic views of North Bay. Comfortable bedrooms with en suite facilities. A great breakfast to start your day!

B&B per night:
S £28.00–£35.00
D £46.00–£54.00

OPEN All Year

SCUNTHORPE, North Lincolnshire Map ref 4C1

♦♦♦

BEVERLEY HOTEL

55 Old Brumby Street, Scunthorpe
DN16 2AJ
T: (01724) 282212
F: (01724) 270422

Bedrooms: 5 single, 8 double/twin, 2 triple/multiple
Bathrooms: 15 en suite

Evening meal available
CC: Delta, Mastercard, Switch, Visa

In the pleasant, quiet residential district of Old Brumby off the A18, close to Scunthorpe town centre and M180 motorway.

B&B per night:
S Min £39.50
D Min £49.50

OPEN All Year except Christmas

SELBY, North Yorkshire Map ref 4C1 *Tourist Information Centre Tel: (01757) 703263*

♦♦♦

HAZELDENE GUEST HOUSE

34 Brook Street, Doncaster Road,
Selby YO8 4AR
T: (01757) 704809
E: selbystay@breathe.com
I: www.smoothhound.co.uk/hotels/hazel.html

Bedrooms: 2 single, 5 double/twin
Bathrooms: 5 en suite

CC: Delta, Mastercard, Visa

Victorian townhouse in a pleasant market town location, 12 miles south of York. On the A19 with easy access to the A1 and M62 motorways.

B&B per night:
S £30.00–£34.00
D £44.00–£47.00

OPEN All Year except Christmas

SETTLE, North Yorkshire Map ref 5B3 *Tourist Information Centre Tel: (01729) 825192*

♦♦♦♦

ARBUTUS GUEST HOUSE

Riverside, Clapham, Lancaster
LA2 8DS
T: (01524) 251240
F: (01524) 251197
E: info@arbutus.co.uk
I: www.arbutus.co.uk

Bedrooms: 1 single, 3 double/twin, 2 triple/multiple
Bathrooms: 5 en suite, 1 private

Evening meal available

Situated in the heart of the beautiful village of Clapham. Country guesthouse offering traditional home cooking and a friendly atmosphere. Ideal for touring, walking and relaxing.

B&B per night:
S £20.00–£21.50
D £49.00–£52.00

HB per person:
DY £40.00–£41.50

OPEN All Year

PRICES
Please check prices and other details at the time of booking.

SETTLE continued

SCAR CLOSE FARM

Feizor, Austwick, Lancaster LA2 8DF
T: (01729) 823496

High-standard, en suite accommodation and food in a farmhouse in one of the quietest and most picturesque hamlets in the Yorkshire Dales. Popular walking and touring centre. TV and tea-makers in all rooms. Free evening transport to local pub if required. Double, twin and family rooms.

Bedrooms: 2 double/twin, 2 triple/multiple
Bathrooms: 4 en suite

Evening meal available

B&B per night:
S £30.00–£32.00
D £50.00–£52.00

HB per person:
DY £37.50–£38.50

OPEN All Year except Christmas

♦♦♦

WHITEFRIARS COUNTRY GUEST HOUSE

Church Street, Settle BD24 9JD
T: (01729) 823753
E: info@Whitefriars-settle.co.uk
I: www.whitefriars-settle.co.uk

17thC family home standing in 0.75 acres of secluded gardens, 50 yards from the town's central market place. This delightful guest house offers traditional, pleasantly furnished accommodation. Two lounges together with a beamed dining room, where good home cooking is served. The house is fully non-smoking.

Bedrooms: 1 single, 6 double/twin, 2 triple/multiple
Bathrooms: 5 en suite, 1 private

Evening meal available

B&B per night:
S Min £19.50
D £39.00–£50.00

HB per person:
DY £33.00–£39.00

OPEN All Year except Christmas

SHEFFIELD, South Yorkshire Map ref 4B2 *Tourist Information Centre Tel: (0114) 221 1900*

♦♦♦

BEIGHTON BED & BREAKFAST

48-50 High St, Beighton, Sheffield S20 1EA
T: (01142) 692004
F: (01142) 692004
E: beightonbandb@talk21.com

Bedrooms: 3 single, 3 double/twin
Bathrooms: 6 en suite

Located just off M1 jct 31 within easy reach of town centre, Meadowhall and Arena. Supertram park and ride nearby.

B&B per night:
S Min £18.00
D £32.00–£34.00

OPEN All Year

♦♦♦

ETRURIA HOUSE HOTEL

91 Crookes Road, Broomhill, Sheffield S10 5BD
T: (0114) 266 2241 & 267 0853
F: (0114) 267 0853
E: etruria@waitrose.com

Bedrooms: 4 single, 5 double/twin, 1 triple/multiple
Bathrooms: 6 en suite

CC: Mastercard, Visa

Small, family-run hotel, giving personal service. Five minutes from the city centre/hospitals/universities. Peak District easily accessible.

B&B per night:
S £32.00–£40.00
D £46.00–£54.00

OPEN All Year

♦♦♦

HILLSIDE

28 Sunningdale Mount, Ecclesall, Sheffield S11 9HA
T: (0114) 2620833

Bedrooms: 1 single, 1 double/twin

CC: Mastercard, Switch, Visa

Modern detached property in quiet, select rural area. Homely atmosphere extended to all our guests.

B&B per night:
S £19.00
D £38.00

OPEN All Year

SHEFFIELD continued

RIVERSIDE COURT HOTEL

4 Nursery Street, Sheffield S3 8GG
T: (0114) 273 1962 & 0800 0352228
F: (0114) 272 3619
E: enquiries@riversidecourt.co.uk
I: www.riversidecourt.co.uk

City centre family-run hotel within walking distance of City Hall, Ponds Forge, Crucible and Lyceum Theatres, bus and train stations, Sheffield and Hallam Universities and all popular city centre pubs, clubs and restaurants. All bedrooms en suite, colour TV etc. Self-catering facilities if required. Residents-only bar with satellite TV and snooker table. Guest gymnasium.

Bedrooms: 6 single, 12 double/twin, 17 triple/multiple
Bathrooms: 35 en suite

CC: Delta, Mastercard, Switch, Visa

B&B per night:
S £32.50
D £46.00

OPEN All Year except Christmas

SHELLEY, West Yorkshire Map ref 4B1

THREE ACRES INN AND RESTAURANT

Roydhouse, Shelley, Huddersfield HD8 8LR
T: (01484) 602606
F: (01484) 608411
E: 3acres@globalnet.co.uk
I: www.3acres.com

Bedrooms: 6 single, 14 double/twin
Bathrooms: 20 en suite

Lunch available
Evening meal available
CC: Amex, Delta, Mastercard, Switch, Visa

An attractive country inn conveniently situated for all of Yorkshire's major conurbations and motorway networks. Restaurant. Traditional beers.

B&B per night:
S £55.00–£60.00
D £75.00–£80.00

OPEN All Year except Christmas

SKIPTON, North Yorkshire Map ref 4B1 *Tourist Information Centre Tel: (01756) 792809*

CRAVEN HEIFER INN

Grassington Road, Skipton BD23 3LA
T: (01756) 792521 & 07767 476077
F: (01756) 794442
E: philandlynn@cravenheifer.co.uk
I: www.cravenheifer.co.uk

Traditional country inn, serving cask ale and excellent home-cooked food, all day every day. Bar food or enjoy a meal in our restaurant overlooking the Yorkshire Dales. Excellent car parking. Most rooms ground floor. Non-smoking restaurant. Non-smoking rooms available. Prices shown are per room (max 2 people) including buffet breakfast.

Bedrooms: 1 single, 15 double/twin, 4 triple/multiple
Bathrooms: 17 en suite

Lunch available
Evening meal available
CC: Delta, Mastercard, Switch, Visa

B&B per night:
S £44.95
D £44.95

OPEN All Year

STAITHES, North Yorkshire Map ref 5C3

BROOKLYN

Brown's Terrace, Staithes, Saltburn-by-the-Sea TS13 5BG
T: (01947) 841396

Bedrooms: 3 double/twin

Sea-Captain's house in picturesque historic fishing village. Comfortable, individually decorated rooms with view of Cowbar cliffs. Pets and children welcome.

B&B per night:
S £20.00
D £40.00

OPEN All Year except Christmas

REGIONAL TOURIST BOARD The symbol in an establishment entry indicates that it is a Regional Tourist Board member.

STAITHES continued

THE ENDEAVOUR RESTAURANT

1 High Street, Staithes, Saltburn-by-the-Sea TS13 5BH
T: (01947) 840825
E: theendeavour@ntlworld.com
I: www.endeavour-restaurant.co.uk

The Endeavour Restaurant nestles in a cobbled street at the heart of this old fishing village. All 3 rooms are fully en suite. Private parking. The restaurant specialises in local seafood, with meat and vegetarian alternatives. Breakfast menu also offers oak-smoked kippers, or kedgeree.

Bedrooms: 3 double/twin
Bathrooms: 3 en suite

Lunch available
Evening meal available
CC: Delta, Mastercard, Switch, Visa

3 nights for the price of 2, Oct-Mar (excl Christmas and New Year).

B&B per night:
S £40.00–£45.00
D £55.00–£65.00

HB per person:
DY £55.00–£65.00

OPEN All Year

STAPE, North Yorkshire Map ref 5D3

RAWCLIFFE HOUSE FARM

Stape, Pickering YO18 8JA
T: (01751) 473292
F: (01751) 473766
E: office@yorkshireaccommodation.com
I: www.yorkshireaccommodation.com

Luxury, en suite, ground floor rooms with open beamed ceilings, every convenience and comfort. Own key in annexed room situated around a south-facing courtyard. Set in 42 acres of North Yorkshire Moors. Aga-cooked breakfast, using local produce, taken in adjacent farmhouse where a warm welcome awaits you

Bedrooms: 3 double/twin
Bathrooms: 3 en suite

B&B per night:
S £31.50–£33.50
D £53.00–£57.00

OPEN All Year except Christmas

STEARSBY, North Yorkshire Map ref 5C3

Silver Award

THE GRANARY

Stearsby, York YO61 4SA
T: (01347) 888652
F: (01347) 888652
E: robertturl@thegranary.org.uk
I: www.thegranary.org.uk

18thC converted granary set in beautiful 1-acre garden. Surrounded by woodland, yet only 12 miles from York. Ideally located for York, Yorkshire Dales, North Yorkshire Moors and Herriot country. En suite rooms with own sitting rooms in barn annexe, en suite double in main house. Breakfast in south-facing conservatory overlooking the pool.

Bedrooms: 3 double/twin; permanent suite(s)
Bathrooms: 3 en suite

3 nights for price of 2 for mid-week stays (Mon-Thu) Apr-Jun and Sep-Oct.

B&B per night:
S Min £30.00
D Min £50.00

SPECIAL BREAKS

Many establishments offer special promotions and themed breaks. These are highlighted in red. (All such offers are subject to availability.)

SUTTON BANK, North Yorkshire Map ref 5C3 *Tourist Information Centre Tel: (01845) 597426*

♦♦

COTE FAW
Hambleton Cottages, Sutton Bank, Thirsk YO7 2EZ
T: (01845) 597363

Bedrooms: 1 single, 2 double/twin

Comfortable cottage in National Park, midway between Thirsk/Helmsley on Cleveland Way and national cycle route. Central for visiting all of North Yorkshire and beyond.

B&B per night:
S £17.00–£18.00
D £34.00–£36.00

OPEN All Year except Christmas

THIRSK, North Yorkshire Map ref 5C3 *Tourist Information Centre Tel: (01845) 522755*

♦♦♦♦
Silver Award

LABURNUM HOUSE
31 Topcliffe Road, Thirsk YO7 1RX
T: (01845) 524120
I: www.SmoothHound.co.uk/hotels/laburnumhse.html

Bedrooms: 3 double/twin
Bathrooms: 2 en suite, 1 private

Spacious, comfortable detached house on the edge of town, overlooking Hambleton Hills and playing fields. Furnished with antiques and traditional furniture. English and vegetarian breakfasts.

5

B&B per night:
D £45.00

TOWN PASTURE FARM
Boltby, Thirsk YO7 2DY
T: (01845) 537298

Bedrooms: 1 double/twin, 1 triple/multiple
Bathrooms: 2 en suite

Evening meal available

180-acre mixed farm. Farmhouse, with views of the Hambleton Hills, in picturesque Boltby village within the boundary of the North York Moors National Park.

B&B per night:
S £21.00–£24.00
D Min £40.00

HB per person:
DY Min £32.00

OPEN All Year except Christmas

THIXENDALE, North Yorkshire Map ref 4C1

THE CROSS KEYS
Thixendale, Malton YO17 9TG
T: (01377) 288272

Bedrooms: 3 double/twin
Bathrooms: 3 en suite

Lunch available
Evening meal available
CC: Amex, Delta, Mastercard, Switch, Visa

Traditional village pub renowned locally for its hand-pulled beers and home-made and home-cooked food. Facilities available for storing cycles and drying.

14

B&B per night:
S Min £20.00
D Min £40.00

OPEN All Year except Christmas

THORNTON DALE, North Yorkshire Map ref 5D3

THE BUCK HOTEL
Chestnut Avenue, Thornton Dale, Pickering YO18 7RW
T: (01751) 474212
F: (01751) 474212
E: buckhotel.tld@btopenworld.com

Bedrooms: 3 double/twin, 1 triple/multiple
Bathrooms: 4 en suite

Lunch available
Evening meal available

In the beautiful village of Thornton Dale, a comfortable, family-run hotel with excellent en suite accommodation. Village inn atmosphere. Quality food. Open all year.

B&B per night:
D £45.00

OPEN All Year

QUALITY ASSURANCE SCHEME

For an explanation of the quality and facilities represented by the Diamonds please refer to the front of this guide. A more detailed explanation can be found in the information pages at the back.

WEST WITTON, North Yorkshire Map ref 5B3

THE OLD VICARAGE

Main Street, West Witton, Leyburn DL8 4LX
T: (01969) 622108
E: info@dalesbreaks.co.uk
I: www.dalesbreaks.co.uk

B&B per night:
S £20.00–£25.00
D £38.00–£42.00

OPEN All Year

En suite rooms and all facilities provided in this charming Grade II Listed former Dales Vicarage in 2 acres of gardens, with wonderful views right across Wensleydale. Spacious private car parking. Centrally placed for visiting the Dales, Lake District, Whitby or York. Friends old and new most welcome.

Bedrooms: 1 single, 4 double/twin
Bathrooms: 4 en suite, 1 private

Stay 4 nights for the price of 3, Sun-Thu, Sep-Mar inclusive (mention 'Where to Stay' guide offer).

12 P

WETHERBY, West Yorkshire Map ref 4B1 *Tourist Information Centre Tel: (0113) 247 7251*

◆◆

PROSPECT HOUSE
8 Caxton Street, Wetherby
LS22 6RU
T: (01937) 582428

Bedrooms: 2 single, 4 double/twin
Bathrooms: 4 en suite

B&B per night:
S Min £25.00
D Min £50.00

OPEN All Year

Established 40 years. En suite rooms available. Near York, Harrogate, Dales, Herriot country. Midway London/Edinburgh. Restaurants nearby. Pets welcome.

P

WHITBY, North Yorkshire Map ref 5D3 *Tourist Information Centre Tel: (01947) 602674*

◆◆◆◆

GLENDALE GUEST HOUSE
16 Crescent Avenue, Whitby
YO21 3ED
T: (01947) 604242

Bedrooms: 1 single, 5 double/twin
Bathrooms: 5 en suite

Evening meal available

B&B per night:
S £20.00
D £48.00

HB per person:
DY £35.00

Family-run Victorian guesthouse. On the West Cliff, offering good food and cleanliness. Rooms are attractively decorated and have excellent facilities. Private parking, pets welcome.

P

◆◆◆

HIGH TOR

7 Normanby Terrace, Whitby YO21 3ES
T: (01947) 602507
E: hightorguesthouse@hotmail.com
I: www.hightorguesthouse.co.uk

B&B per night:
D £44.00–£48.00

OPEN All Year

An elegant Victorian townhouse situated on the West Cliff close to the centre of historic Whitby and its beautiful beach and harbour, near to the Yorkshire Moors. Attractive en suite rooms have all been recently refurbished. Family run, we offer style and comfort at affordable prices. No smoking or pets.

Bedrooms: 3 double/twin, 2 triple/multiple
Bathrooms: 4 en suite, 1 private

CC: Delta, Mastercard, Switch, Visa

3 nights for the price of 2, Dec, Jan and Feb (excl Christmas and New Year).

◆◆◆

LANSBURY GUEST HOUSE
29 Hudson Street, Whitby YO21 3EP
T: (01947) 604821
I: www.whitbyonline.co.uk/lansburyhse.html

Bedrooms: 1 single, 6 double/twin, 1 triple/multiple
Bathrooms: 6 en suite

B&B per night:
S £20.00–£22.50
D £40.00–£45.00

OPEN All Year except Christmas

Comfortable Victorian house on West Cliff, 3 minutes' walk to the beach. Homely atmosphere and good food. Colour TV, hospitality tray, radio and hairdryer in all rooms.

WHITBY continued

MORNINGSIDE HOTEL

10 North Promenade, West Cliff, Whitby
YO21 3JX
T: (01947) 602643 & 604030

B&B per night:
S £35.00
D £50.00–£64.00

HB per person:
DY £40.00–£45.00

Within easy distance of sports ground, indoor swimming pool, Spa Theatre and Pavilion, and 0.5 miles to the 18-hole golf course. Set in quiet location overlooking the sea. All rooms en suite with TV and welcome tray. Table d'hote menu using fresh, local produce. Senior Citizens' reductions. Hospitable staff guarantee a warm welcome.

Bedrooms: 1 single, 14 double/twin, 1 triple/multiple
Bathrooms: 16 en suite

Evening meal available
CC: Mastercard, Visa

Mid-week breaks from £69pp for 3 nights, and £92pp for 4 nights (excl Aug and Bank Holidays).

♦♦♦

PARTRIDGE NEST FARM

Eskdaleside, Sleights, Whitby
YO22 5ES
T: (01947) 810450 & 811412
F: (01947) 811413
E: Barbara@partridgenestfarm.com
I: www.partridgenestfarm.com

Bedrooms: 2 triple/multiple

B&B per night:
S Max £20.00
D Max £32.00

OPEN All Year except Christmas

Farmhouse B&B with 2 double rooms with unbeatable views and informal, friendly, relaxed atmosphere. Farm is also a working equestrian centre. TVs in rooms.

ROSSLYN HOUSE

11 Abbey Terrace, Whitby YO21 3HQ
T: (01947) 604086
E: rosslynhouse@bushinternet.com
I: www.guesthousewhitby.co.uk

B&B per night:
S £25.00
D £40.00–£45.00

HB per person:
DY £30.00–£35.00

OPEN All Year except Christmas

Characteristic Victorian guesthouse with a good standard of accommodation to make your visit comfortable and enjoyable. All bedrooms are en suite with colour TVs and hot-drink trays. Close to all amenities. We are favoured by many returning guests. For further information and quality colour brochure please freephone 0800 298 5254.

Bedrooms: 1 single, 3 double/twin, 2 triple/multiple
Bathrooms: 6 en suite

Evening meal available
CC: Delta, Mastercard, Switch, Visa

3 nights for the price of 2, mid-Oct-Apr, available Sun-Thurs (excl Christmas and New Year).

SEACLIFFE HOTEL

12 North Promenade, West Cliff, Whitby
YO21 3JX
T: (01947) 603139 & 08000 191747
F: (01947) 603139
E: julie@seacliffe.fsnet.co.uk
I: www.seacliffe.co.uk

B&B per night:
S £39.50–£49.50
D £69.00–£73.00

OPEN All Year

Whitby's premier family hotel overlooking the sea. All rooms en suite. Wine and dine in our candle lit a la carte restaurant. Local seafood a speciality. Golf course nearby. Tee-off times may be booked through the hotel.

Bedrooms: 1 single, 15 double/twin, 4 triple/multiple
Bathrooms: 20 en suite

Evening meal available
CC: Amex, Delta, Diners, Mastercard, Switch, Visa

Yorkshire Rose break: 2 nights' DB&B £99pp.

WHITBY continued

♦♦♦♦

WHEELDALE HOTEL

11 North Promenade, Whitby YO21 3JX
T: (01947) 602365 & 07710 994277
E: wheeldale_hotel@lineone.net
I: www.wheeldale-hotel.co.uk

B&B per night:
D £50.00–£64.00

HB per person:
DY £40.00–£47.00

Premier non-smoking, seafront hotel in quiet, peaceful location. Tastefully decorated and furnished. All bedrooms en suite with courtesy trays and colour TV. Central heating. Beautiful sea view lounge/bar and dining room. Vegetarians catered for. Private car park. Personally run by proprietors Liz and Ian. Autumn and spring breaks.

Bedrooms: 9 double/twin
Bathrooms: 9 en suite

Evening meal available
CC: Delta, Mastercard, Visa

Spring and autum mid-week breaks. 3 nights' B&B for the price of 2 – Mon-Thu (excl Bank Holidays).

P

YORK, North Yorkshire Map ref 4C1 *Tourist Information Centre Tel: (01904) 621756*

Rating Applied For

132

132 The Mount, York YO24 1AS
T: (01904) 600060
F: (01904) 676132
E: enquiries@one3two.co.uk
I: one3two.co.uk

B&B per night:
D £75.00–£140.00

OPEN All Year except Christmas

An elegant Georgian townhouse restored as a chic bed and breakfast hotel offering the very best in modern luxury with a touch of old-fashioned glamour. There are 5 sensational bedrooms, huge teak beds and stunning marble bathrooms. Only a short walk to the city centre, racecourse and station.

Bedrooms: 5 double/twin
Bathrooms: 5 en suite

CC: Delta, Mastercard, Switch, Visa

P

♦♦♦♦
Silver Award

THE ACER HOTEL

52 Scarcroft Hill, York YO24 1DE
T: (01904) 653839 & 677017
F: (01904) 677017
E: info@acerhotel.co.uk
I: www.acerhotel.co.uk

B&B per night:
S £40.00
D £60.00–£80.00

OPEN All Year except Christmas

Winner of York Tourism 'Guest Accommodation of the Year' award 2001. Elegant, multi-award-winning hotel. Superior en suite accommodation and service provided in a relaxed and pleasant atmosphere. Beautiful 4-poster room. Celebration packages of champagne, chocolates and flowers available. Highly acclaimed breakfasts. Convenient for attractions, railway station and racecourse.

Bedrooms: 2 double/twin, 1 triple/multiple
Bathrooms: 3 en suite

CC: Amex, Delta, Mastercard, Switch, Visa

CONFIRM YOUR BOOKING
You are advised to confirm your booking in writing.

YORK continued

◆◆◆◆◆ Silver Award

ALEXANDER HOUSE
94 Bishopthorpe Road, York
YO23 1JS
T: (01904) 625016 & 07799 490484
E: info@alexanderhouseyork.co.uk
I: www.alexanderhouseyork.co.uk

Bedrooms: 4 double/twin
Bathrooms: 4 en suite

CC: Delta, Mastercard, Switch, Visa

B&B per night:
D £55.00–£69.00

OPEN All Year except Christmas

Totally refurbished Victorian townhouse, only 5 minutes' walk to city centre. Warm, friendly welcome. Hearty breakfasts. Sparkling new en suite bedrooms. Car parking.

10 P

◆◆◆◆

ASCOT HOUSE

80 East Parade, York YO31 7YH
T: (01904) 426826
F: (01904) 431077
E: j&k@ascot-house-york.demon.co.uk
I: www.ascothouseyork.com

B&B per night:
S £22.00–£50.00
D £44.00–£60.00

OPEN All Year except Christmas

A family-run, 15-bedroomed Victorian villa, built in 1869, with en suite rooms of character and many 4-poster or canopy beds. Delicious traditional English breakfasts. Fifteen minutes' walk to city centre, Jorvik Viking Museum or York Minster. Residential licence and residents' lounge, sauna, private enclosed car park.

Bedrooms: 1 single, 11 double/twin, 3 triple/multiple
Bathrooms: 12 en suite, 1 private

CC: Delta, Diners, Mastercard, Switch, Visa

P

◆◆◆◆

ASHBOURNE HOUSE

139 Fulford Road, York YO10 4HG
T: (01904) 639912
F: (01904) 631332
E: ashbourneh@aol.com

B&B per night:
S £35.00–£45.00
D £40.00–£60.00

OPEN All Year except Christmas

Charming, family-run Victorian private house on the main route into York from the south. Licensed, with a small bar in a comfortable guest lounge. En suite bedrooms furnished in a contemporary style and fully equipped. Within walking distance of city centre. Close to university and golf course. Car parking.

Bedrooms: 5 double/twin, 2 triple/multiple
Bathrooms: 6 en suite, 1 private

CC: Amex, Delta, Diners, Mastercard, Switch, Visa

5 P

◆◆◆

THE BAR CONVENT ENTERPRISES LTD
17 Blossom Street, York YO24 1AQ
T: (01904) 643238 & 464902
F: (01904) 631792
E: info@bar-convent.org.uk
I: www.bar-convent.org.uk

Bedrooms: 8 single, 7 double/twin
Bathrooms: 1 en suite

Lunch available
Evening meal available
CC: Delta, Mastercard, Switch, Visa

B&B per night:
S £24.00–£26.00
D £45.00–£48.00

The oldest Catholic convent in the UK, housed in a Georgian building dating from 1767. Museum, shop and conference venue. See web site.

MAP REFERENCES The map references refer to the colour maps at the front of this guide. The first figure is the map number; the letter and figure which follow indicate the grid reference on the map.

YORK continued

Rating Applied For

BARBICAN HOUSE

20 Barbican Road, York YO10 5AA
T: (01904) 627617
F: (01904) 647140
E: info@barbicanhouse.com
I: www.barbicanhouse.com

B&B per night:
S £50.00–£54.00
D £58.00–£62.00

OPEN All Year except Christmas

Small, friendly, family-run Victorian residence of charm and character, lovingly restored. Overlooking medieval city walls. Leave your car in our floodlit car park and take a short stroll to most city centre attractions. The Barbican Centre is a 2-minute walk away. Yorkshire University is 10 minutes away.

Bedrooms: 6 double/twin
Bathrooms: 6 en suite

CC: Amex, Delta, Mastercard, Switch, Visa

12 P

◆◆◆

BEDFORD HOTEL

108-110 Bootham, York YO30 7DG
T: (01904) 624412
F: (01904) 632851
E: info@bedfordhotelyork.co.uk
I: www.bedfordhotel.york.co.uk

B&B per night:
S £40.00–£50.00
D £54.00–£70.00

HB per person:
DY £39.00–£47.00

Enjoy a relaxing stay in this tastefully converted Victorian house where the resident owners assure you of a warm welcome and comfortable stay. Licensed hotel, all bedrooms en suite and non-smoking. Car park. Five minutes' walk along historic Bootham to the famous York Minster and city centre. Traditional, home-cooked evening meals available.

Bedrooms: 2 single, 10 double/twin, 5 triple/multiple
Bathrooms: 17 en suite

Evening meal available
CC: Amex, Delta, Diners, Mastercard, Switch, Visa

P

◆◆◆

BEECH HOUSE

6-7 Longfield Terrace, Bootham, York YO30 7DJ
T: (01904) 634581
I: www.beech-house-york.co.uk

B&B per night:
S £31.00–£35.00
D £52.00–£56.00

Beech House is centrally situated in a quiet tree-lined street about 5 minutes' walk from York Minster and the city centre. You can stroll through the museum gardens or along the riverside. All rooms have en suite, shower, toilet, colour TV, clock/radio, hairdryer, tea-making facilities and direct-dial telephone.

Bedrooms: 1 single, 9 double/twin
Bathrooms: 10 en suite

CC: Mastercard, Visa

10 P

NB

IMPORTANT NOTE Information on accommodation listed in this guide has been supplied by the proprietors. As changes may occur you are advised to check details at the time of booking.

YORK continued

♦♦♦

BLAKENEY HOTEL
180 Stockton Lane, York YO31 1ES
T: (01904) 422786
F: (01904) 422786
E: reception@blakeneyhotel-york.co.uk
I: www.blakeneyhotel-york.co.uk

Bedrooms: 2 single, 9 double/twin, 6 triple/multiple
Bathrooms: 9 en suite, 1 private

Lunch available
Evening meal available
CC: Amex, Delta, Mastercard, Switch, Visa

Comfortable, family-run hotel located within easy reach of the city centre and attractions. Ground floor en suite rooms. Restaurant, bar and lounge. Car park. Brochure available.

B&B per night:
S £30.00–£37.50
D £52.00–£60.00

HB per person:
DY £37.00–£50.00

OPEN All Year except Christmas

♦♦♦

BRIAR LEA GUEST HOUSE
8 Longfield Terrace, Bootham, York YO30 7DJ
T: (01904) 635061 & 07703 344302
F: (01904) 330356
E: briargh8l@aol.com

Bedrooms: 4 double/twin, 2 triple/multiple
Bathrooms: 6 en suite

CC: Delta, Mastercard, Switch, Visa

Victorian house with all rooms en suite, 6 minutes' walk from the city centre and railway station.

B&B per night:
S £25.00–£35.00
D £46.00–£50.00

OPEN All Year except Christmas

♦♦♦

THE CAVALIER
39 Monkgate, York YO31 7PB
T: (01904) 636615
F: (01904) 636615
E: julia@cavalierhotel.co.uk
I: www.cavalierhotel.co.uk

Georgian, family-run hotel close to the city centre, only yards from the ancient Bar Walls, Minster and many of York's famous historic landmarks. High standards, traditional English breakfast, sauna and private parking ensure the comfort of our guests. Please phone for a map and brochure.

Bedrooms: 2 single, 6 double/twin, 2 triple/multiple
Bathrooms: 7 en suite

CC: Delta, Mastercard, Switch, Visa

B&B per night:
S £35.00–£55.00
D £50.00–£75.00

OPEN All Year

♦♦♦♦
Silver Award

CITY GUEST HOUSE
68 Monkgate, York YO31 7PF
T: (01904) 622483
E: info@cityguesthouse.co.uk
I: www.cityguesthouse.co.uk

Bedrooms: 1 single, 4 double/twin, 2 triple/multiple
Bathrooms: 6 en suite, 1 private

CC: Amex, Delta, Mastercard, Switch, Visa

Small, friendly, family-run guesthouse in attractive Victorian townhouse. Five minutes' walk to York Minster, close to attractions. Private parking. Cosy en suite rooms. Restaurants nearby. Non-smoking.

B&B per night:
S £30.00–£35.00
D £54.00–£58.00

OPEN All Year except Christmas

♦♦♦

CLARENCE GARDENS HOTEL
Haxby Road, York YO31 8JS
T: (01904) 624252
F: (01904) 671293
E: clarencehotel@hotmail.com
I: www.clarencegardenhotel.com

Just 10 minutes' walk to the historic and beautiful city of York. This 18-bedroomed hotel offers all en suite rooms, licensed bar, restaurant, telephone in all rooms, large car park with adjacent bowling green and children's park.

Bedrooms: 4 double/twin, 15 triple/multiple
Bathrooms: 19 en suite

Evening meal available
CC: Amex, Delta, Mastercard, Switch, Visa

Our luxurious dorm is now available for group bookings – hen/stag parties, shopping trips, sports groups etc.

B&B per night:
S £35.00–£47.50
D £55.00–£70.00

HB per person:
DY £40.00–£50.00

OPEN All Year except Christmas

YORK continued

♦♦♦

COOK'S GUEST HOUSE
120 Bishopthorpe Road, York
YO23 1JX
T: (01904) 652519 & 07946 577247
F: (01904) 652519
E: jslcook@hotmail.com

Bedrooms: 1 double/twin, 1 triple/multiple
Bathrooms: 2 en suite

CC: Visa

B&B per night:
S £25.00–£35.00
D £44.00–£50.00

OPEN All Year

Featured on TV's 'This Morning'. Small, friendly and comfortable guesthouse with unique decor. 10 minutes' walk to city, railway station and racecourse.

7

♦♦♦

CUMBRIA HOUSE
2 Vyner Street, Haxby Road, York
YO31 8HS
T: (01904) 636817
E: clark@cumbriahouse.freeserve.co.uk
I: www.cumbriahouse.com

Bedrooms: 1 single, 3 double/twin, 2 triple/multiple
Bathrooms: 2 en suite

CC: Delta, Mastercard, Switch, Visa

B&B per night:
S £21.00–£25.00
D £42.00–£50.00

OPEN All Year

Family-run guesthouse, warm welcome assured, 12 minutes' walk from York Minster. En suites available. Easily located from ring road. Private car park. Brochure.

2 P

♦♦♦♦

CURZON LODGE AND STABLE COTTAGES

23 Tadcaster Road, Dringhouses, York
YO24 1QG
T: (01904) 703157
F: (01904) 703157
I: www.smoothhound.co.uk/hotels/curzon.html

Bedrooms: 1 single, 7 double/twin, 2 triple/multiple
Bathrooms: 10 en suite

CC: Delta, Mastercard, Switch, Visa

B&B per night:
S £39.00–£49.00
D £49.00–£70.00

OPEN All Year except Christmas

Charming 17thC Listed house and former stables in a conservation area overlooking York racecourse. Ten comfortable en suite rooms, some with 4-poster or brass beds. Country antiques, books, prints, fresh flowers and complimentary sherry lend traditional ambience. Delicious breakfasts. Warm relaxed atmosphere with restaurants a minute's walk. Entirely non-smoking. Parking in grounds.

8 P

♦♦♦

FAIRTHORNE
356 Strensall Road, Earswick, York
YO32 9SW
T: (01904) 768609
F: (01904) 768609

Bedrooms: 1 double/twin, 1 triple/multiple
Bathrooms: 2 en suite

B&B per night:
S Max £25.00
D Max £20.00

OPEN All Year except Christmas

Detached dormer bungalow with spacious gardens, 4 miles from York city centre. Family-run guesthouse with private car parking and en suite.

P

USE YOUR *i*s

There are more than 550 Tourist Information Centres throughout England offering friendly help with accommodation and holiday ideas as well as suggestions of places to visit and things to do. You'll find TIC addresses in the local Phone Book.

YORK continued

♦♦♦

FARTHINGS HOTEL

5 Nunthorpe Avenue, York YO23 1PF
T: (01904) 653545
F: (01904) 628355
E: farthings@york181.fsbusiness.co.uk
I: www.farthingsyork.co.uk

B&B per night:
S £25.00–£35.00
D £40.00–£60.00

OPEN All Year

Bill and Barbara Dickson extend a warm welcome to their guests. Ideally situated in a quiet cul-de-sac 10 minutes' stroll to city centre. The Farthings is a charming Victorian residence. Selection of quality rooms including en suite, all fully equipped. Breakfast freshly cooked including vegetarian. Unrestricted street parking. Non-smoking throughout.

Bedrooms: 1 single, 6 double/twin, 2 triple/multiple
Bathrooms: 5 en suite

CC: Delta, Mastercard, Switch, Visa

Winter breaks and mid-week packages available – prices on request. (Excl Bank Hols, Christmas and New Year).

♦♦♦

FEVERSHAM LODGE INTERNATIONAL GUEST HOUSE

No 1 Feversham Crescent,
Off Wigginton Road, York YO31 8HQ
T: (01904) 623882
F: (01904) 623882
E: bookings@fevershamlodge.co.uk
I: www.fevershamlodge.co.uk

B&B per night:
S £25.00–£45.00
D £50.00–£70.00

OPEN All Year except Christmas

Nick and Yan speak Japanese/Chinese/Italian/French and offer you a warm welcome in their former 19thC Methodist manse. Lovely large en suite rooms, including Laura Ashley-style rooms with honeymoon 4-poster or canopy bed. Walking distance to city centre. Fresh home-cooked full English/vegetarian breakfast. Acupuncture and acupressure massage clinic. Car-parking.

Bedrooms: 4 double/twin, 1 triple/multiple
Bathrooms: 5 en suite

CC: Delta, Mastercard, Switch, Visa

3 nights for the price of 2, Oct-Mar (excl Saturday). 10% discount for acupuncture and acupressure massage.

P

♦♦♦

FOSS BANK GUEST HOUSE

16 Huntington Road, York YO31 8RB
T: (01904) 635548
I: www.fossbank.co.uk

B&B per night:
S £23.00–£25.00
D £42.00–£52.00

OPEN All Year except Christmas

Overlooking the River Foss, this Victorian townhouse provides comfortable accommodation in individually furnished rooms. Our private car park allows you to leave your car and take a 10-minute stroll into the city via Monkgate Bar, one of the original stone gateways through the city walls.

Bedrooms: 1 single, 3 double/twin, 1 triple/multiple
Bathrooms: 2 en suite

Reduction for 3 nights or more, all year round.

6 P

YORK continued

♦♦♦

Your hosts Shirley and Gary welcome you to their Victorian villa. Enjoy the comfort and luxury of our 4-poster beds. Start the day with the house speciality 'a hearty English breakfast'. Ten minutes' walk to the city centre, close to The Barbican Centre, Fulford Golf Course and York University. Licensed. Car park.

FOURPOSTER LODGE HOTEL

68-70 Heslington Road, Barbican Road, York YO10 5AU
T: (01904) 651170
F: (01904) 651170
E: fourposter.lodge@virgin.net
I: www.fourposterlodgehotel.co.uk

Bedrooms: 1 single, 7 double/twin, 2 triple/multiple
Bathrooms: 9 en suite, 1 private

Evening meal available
CC: Amex, Delta, Mastercard, Switch, Visa

Reduction for 3 nights or more, all year round.

B&B per night:
S £35.00–£50.00
D £55.00–£80.00

HB per person:
DY £45.00–£95.00

OPEN All Year except Christmas

♦♦♦

GREENSIDE

124 Clifton, York YO30 6BQ
T: (01904) 623631
F: (01904) 623631

Charming, detached, conservation, owner-run guesthouse fronting onto Clifton Green. Ideally situated, 10 minutes' walk from the city walls and all York's attractions. Offers many facilities, including an enclosed, locked car park. All types of ground/first floor bedrooms are available in a warm, homely atmosphere.

Bedrooms: 1 single, 5 double/twin, 2 triple/multiple
Bathrooms: 3 en suite

Evening meal available

B&B per night:
S Min £20.00
D Min £40.00

HB per person:
DY Min £29.50

OPEN All Year

♦♦♦♦
Silver Award

THE HAZELWOOD

24-25 Portland Street, York YO31 7EH
T: (01904) 626548
F: (01904) 628032
E: Reservations@thehazelwoodyork.com
I: www.thehazelwoodyork.com

Situated in the very heart of York in an extremely quiet residential area only 400 yards from York Minster. Elegant Victorian townhouse with private car park providing high-quality accommodation in individually designed, en suite bedrooms. Wide choice of delicious breakfasts catering for all tastes including vegetarian. Completely non-smoking.

Bedrooms: 1 single, 11 double/twin, 2 triple/multiple
Bathrooms: 14 en suite

CC: Delta, Mastercard, Switch, Visa

B&B per night:
S £35.00–£95.00
D £75.00–£110.00

OPEN All Year

CREDIT CARD BOOKINGS If you book by telephone and are asked for your credit card number it is advisable to check the proprietor's policy should you cancel your reservation.

YORK continued

HILLCREST GUEST HOUSE

110 Bishopthorpe Road, York YO23 1JX
T: (01904) 653160
E: hillcrest@accommodation.gbr.fm
I: www.accommodation.gbr.fm

B&B per night:
S £20.00–£28.00
D £38.00–£56.00

OPEN All Year except Christmas

Spaciously, elegant Victorian townhouse 10 minutes' walk from city centre and racecourse. Next to Rowantree Park. Private car park. Highly complimented, generous breakfast selection. Special diets catered for. En suite ground floor room available. Enjoy comfort, cleanliness and personal attention in a relaxed and homely atmosphere. Non-smoking.

Bedrooms: 3 single, 7 double/twin, 3 triple/multiple
Bathrooms: 7 en suite

CC: Delta, Mastercard, Visa

Bargain breaks Nov-Mar.

P

◆◆◆◆

HOLLY LODGE

206 Fulford Road, York YO10 4DD
T: (01904) 646005
I: www.thehollylodge.co.uk

B&B per night:
S £58.00–£78.00
D £58.00–£78.00

OPEN All Year except Christmas

Beautifully appointed Georgian Grade II Listed building where you are assured of a warm welcome. 10 minutes' riverside stroll to centre, conveniently located for all York's attractions including Barbican and university. All rooms individually furnished, each overlooking garden or terrace. On-site parking, easy to find. Booking recommended.

Bedrooms: 4 double/twin, 1 triple/multiple
Bathrooms: 5 en suite

CC: Delta, Mastercard, Visa

7 P

HOLMWOOD HOUSE HOTEL

114 Holgate Road, York YO24 4BB
T: (01904) 626183
F: (01904) 670899
E: holmwood.house@dial.pipex.com
I: www.holmwoodhousehotel.co.uk

B&B per night:
S £35.00–£68.00
D £60.00–£105.00

OPEN All Year

Elegant Victorian house with a secure car park. Carefully restored and furnished with antiques. Five minutes' walk from the city walls, 10 minutes' walk from the station. Two family suites available.

Bedrooms: 13 double/twin, 1 triple/multiple
Bathrooms: 14 en suite

CC: Amex, Delta, Mastercard, Switch, Visa

Gourmet breaks with York's top restaurants from £110pp for 2 nights. 3 nights for price of 2 offers, mid-week, off-peak.

8 P

ACCESSIBILITY

Look for the symbols which indicate National Accessible Scheme standards for hearing and visually impaired guests in addition to standards for guests with mobility impairment. Additional participants are shown in the listings at the back.

YORK continued

◆◆◆

Linden Lodge is a friendly, licensed hotel, with a warm welcome. All rooms have remote-control colour TV, welcome tray and hairdryer. Choice of singles, twins, doubles and family rooms, en suite or standard. Situated 10 minutes' walk from city centre, railway station and racecourse. Unrestricted parking.

LINDEN LODGE

6 Nunthorpe Avenue, Scarcroft Road, York YO23 1PF
T: (01904) 620107
F: (01904) 620985
E: bookings@lindenlodge.yorks.net
I: www.yorkshirenet.co.uk/stayat/lindenlodge

Bedrooms: 2 single, 9 double/twin, 2 triple/multiple
Bathrooms: 10 en suite

CC: Amex, Delta, Mastercard, Switch, Visa

B&B per night:
S £25.00–£27.50
D £50.00–£52.00

OPEN All Year

◆◆◆◆
Silver Award

NUNMILL HOUSE

85 Bishopthorpe Road, York
YO23 1NX
T: (01904) 634047
F: (01904) 655879
E: info@nunmill.co.uk
I: www.nunmill.co.uk

Bedrooms: 7 double/twin, 1 triple/multiple
Bathrooms: 7 en suite, 1 private

Splendid Victorian house with well-appointed rooms, 4-poster beds. Just outside the medieval walls, convenient for the racecourse and railway station. Walking distance to all attractions.

P

B&B per night:
S £45.00–£50.00
D £50.00–£65.00

◆◆◆

PARK VIEW GUEST HOUSE

34 Grosvenor Terrace, Bootham, York YO30 7AG
T: (01904) 620437
F: (01904) 620437
E: park_view@talk21.com

Bedrooms: 1 single, 2 double/twin, 3 triple/multiple
Bathrooms: 5 en suite, 1 private

Family-run Victorian house with views of York Minster, close to city centre off the A19. Reductions for children sharing.

B&B per night:
S £27.50–£35.00
D £46.00–£55.00

OPEN All Year except Christmas

◆◆◆

QUEEN ANNE'S GUEST HOUSE

24 Queen Anne's Road, Bootham, York YO30 7AA
T: (01904) 629389
F: (01904) 619529
E: info@queenannes.fsnet.co.uk
I: www.s-h-systems.co.uk/hotels/queenann

Bedrooms: 1 single, 5 double/twin, 1 triple/multiple
Bathrooms: 5 en suite

CC: Mastercard, Visa

Spick and span. Warm and friendly. Five minutes' walk to city centre. All rooms with TV, tea and coffee, most en suite. Hearty English breakfast.

3 P

B&B per night:
S £18.00–£22.00
D £38.00–£44.00

OPEN All Year

◆◆◆

Charming B&B on banks of River Ouse. A 450-yard riverside walk to city and 5 minutes' walk to York Minster, rail/bus stations and all main attractions. Quiet location, private car park. All rooms en suite, no smoking. Tearooms open daily.

RIVERSIDE WALK GUEST HOUSE

9 Earlsborough Terrace, Marygate, York YO30 7BQ
T: (01904) 620769 & 646249
F: (01904) 671743
E: riverside@rsummers.cix.co.uk
I: www.bedandbreakfastyork.co.uk

Bedrooms: 2 single, 10 double/twin
Bathrooms: 10 en suite, 2 private

CC: Delta, Mastercard, Switch, Visa

P

B&B per night:
S £35.00–£42.00
D £52.00–£62.00

OPEN All Year except Christmas

YORK continued

ROMLEY GUEST HOUSE

2 Millfield Road, Scarcroft Road, York YO23 1NQ
T: (01904) 652822
E: info@romleyhouse.co.uk
I: www.romleyhouse.co.uk

B&B per night:
S £20.00–£22.00
D £40.00–£56.00

OPEN All Year except Christmas

Family-run guesthouse, few minutes' walk from city centre and all attractions, offers happy atmosphere, hearty breakfast, home comforts. All rooms are well-appointed (en suite available) with colour TV, clock radio alarms, tea/coffee-making facilities. Comfortable residents' lounge with licensed bar.

Bedrooms: 1 single, 3 double/twin, 2 triple/multiple
Bathrooms: 2 en suite

CC: Delta, Mastercard, Visa

23 ST MARYS

Bootham, York YO30 7DD
T: (01904) 622738
F: (01904) 628802
E: stmarys23@hotmail.com
I: www.23stmarys.co.uk

B&B per night:
S £36.00–£40.00
D £60.00–£80.00

OPEN All Year except Christmas

Large Victorian terraced house peacefully set within 5 minutes' stroll of city centre. Spacious rooms, antique furnishings, en suite bedrooms of different sizes and character. Extensive breakfast menu in elegant surroundings. Julie and Chris will offer you a warm welcome to their home.

Bedrooms: 2 single, 7 double/twin, 1 triple/multiple
Bathrooms: 9 en suite

CC: Delta, Mastercard, Switch, Visa

Third night at 50% reduction (excl peak periods).

ST RAPHAEL GUEST HOUSE

44 Queen Anne's Road, Bootham, York YO30 7AF
T: (01904) 645028 & 658788
F: (01904) 658788
E: straphael2000@yahoo.co.uk

B&B per night:
S £21.00–£35.00
D £40.00–£70.00

OPEN All Year except Christmas

Enjoy a peaceful and relaxing stay in the friendly and informal mock Tudor 1890's guesthouse, only 5 minutes from the city walls and York Minster, close to the rail station and historic sites. All rooms en suite. Traditional English breakfast provided.

Bedrooms: 1 single, 2 double/twin, 3 triple/multiple
Bathrooms: 6 en suite

CC: Amex, Delta, Mastercard, Switch, Visa

4 nights for the price of 3 Sep-Mar (excl Bank Holidays). Children under 12 sharing: 50% reduction.

♦♦♦

SAXON HOUSE HOTEL

Fishergate, 71-73 Fulford Road, York YO10 4BD
T: (01904) 622106
F: (01904) 633764
E: saxon@househotel.freeserve.co.uk
I: www.saxonhousehotel.co.uk

Bedrooms: 2 single, 7 double/twin, 5 triple/multiple
Bathrooms: 14 en suite

CC: Delta, Mastercard, Switch, Visa

B&B per night:
S £30.00–£50.00
D £40.00–£70.00

OPEN All Year except Christmas

Victorian hotel offering a friendly welcome and personal service. Close to all city-centre attractions, golf course, race course, university, Barbican leisure centre and Designer Outlet.

YORK continued

◆◆◆

THE STEER INN
Hull Road, Wilberfoss, York
YO41 5PE
T: (01759) 380600
F: (01759) 388904
E: kevin@steerinn.co.uk
I: www.steerinn.co.uk

Bedrooms: 12 double/twin, 2 triple/multiple
Bathrooms: 14 private

Lunch available
Evening meal available
CC: Delta, Mastercard, Switch, Visa

B&B per night:
S £35.00
D £49.00

OPEN All Year

Traditional interior, family-run hotel, bar and restaurant in rural setting, yet situated 15 minutes from York city centre.

P

◆◆◆

TREE TOPS
21 St Mary's, Bootham, York
YO30 7DD
T: (01904) 658053
F: (01904) 658053
E: treetops.guesthouse@virgin.net
I: business.thisisyork.co.uk/treetops

Bedrooms: 1 single, 5 double/twin, 1 triple/multiple
Bathrooms: 7 en suite

CC: Mastercard, Visa

B&B per night:
S £29.00–£35.00
D £50.00–£56.00

Tastefully decorated period house, 5 minutes' walk from Minster, located in quiet side street. Rooms available with views of Minster. Private car park. Continental breakfast available.

12 **P**

◆◆◆

TYBURN HOUSE HOTEL
11 Albemarle Road, The Mount, York YO23 1EN
T: (01904) 655069
F: (01904) 655069
E: york@tyburnhotel.freeserve.co.uk

Bedrooms: 2 single, 6 double/twin, 5 triple/multiple
Bathrooms: 12 en suite, 1 private

B&B per night:
S £32.00–£49.99
D £64.00–£100.00

Family-owned and run guesthouse overlooking the racecourse. In a quiet and beautiful area, close to the city centre and railway station.

◆◆◆

WARRENS GUEST HOUSE

30 Scarcroft Road, York YO23 1NF
T: (01904) 643139
F: (01904) 658297
I: www.warrens.ndo.co.uk

B&B per night:
S £35.00–£50.00
D £50.00–£65.00

A prominent hotel set in secluded gardens overlooking twin Gothic arches. Free resident parking. A few minutes' walk from city centre. Conveniently situated on A19 on south side of city within easy reach of outer and inner ring roads.

Bedrooms: 3 double/twin, 3 triple/multiple
Bathrooms: 6 en suite

Reductions for 3 or more days Sun–Thu inclusive (excl Bank Holidays and race days).

P

◆◆◆

WATERS EDGE

5 Earlsborough Terrace, Marygate, York
YO30 7BQ
T: (01904) 644625
E: julie@watersedgeyork.co.uk
I: www.watersedgeyork.co.uk

B&B per night:
S £45.00
D £50.00–£65.00

OPEN All Year

Quiet position on river bank, 450 yards from city wall. 4-poster rooms, all en suite. Totally non-smoking. Terrace garden. Free parking. Five minutes' walk to rail station and all main attractions.

Bedrooms: 4 double/twin, 1 triple/multiple
Bathrooms: 5 en suite

CC: Delta, Mastercard, Switch, Visa

4-poster rooms overlooking the river.

8 **P**

YORK continued

♦♦♦

WOLD VIEW HOUSE HOTEL

171-175 Haxby Road, York
YO31 8JL
T: (01904) 632061
F: (01904) 632061
E: enquiries@woldviewhousehotel.co.uk
I: www.woldviewhousehotel.co.uk

Bedrooms: 2 single, 8 double/twin
Bathrooms: 10 en suite

B&B per night:
S £23.00–£30.00
D £52.00–£65.00

OPEN All Year

The Wold View House Hotel is situated 15 minutes' walk from York Minster. With a licensed bar and en suite rooms a friendly welcome awaits.

A brief guide to the main Towns and Villages offering accommodation in Yorkshire

A AINTHORPE, NORTH YORKSHIRE - Eskdale village on the banks of the River Esk, in the picturesque North York Moors National Park.

- **APPLETREEWICK, NORTH YORKSHIRE** - Wharfedale village below the craggy summit of "Simon's Seat". Halfway through the village of Monks Hall stands High Hall, former home of the Craven family.

- **ASKRIGG, NORTH YORKSHIRE** - The name of this Dales village means "ash tree ridge". It is centred on a steep main street of high, narrow, three-storey houses and thrived on cotton and later wool in the 18thC. Once famous for its clock making.

- **AYSGARTH, NORTH YORKSHIRE** - Famous for its beautiful falls - a series of three cascades extending for half a mile on the River Ure in Wensleydale. There is a coach and carriage museum at Yore Mill and a National Park Centre. A single-arched Elizabethan bridge spans the River Ure.

B BEDALE, NORTH YORKSHIRE - Ancient church of St Gregory and Georgian Bedale Hall occupy commanding positions over this market town situated in good hunting country. The hall, which contains interesting architectural features including great ballroom and flying-type staircase, now houses a library and museum.

- **BEVERLEY, NORTH HUMBERSIDE** - Beverley's most famous landmark is its beautiful medieval minster dating from 1220, with Percy family tomb. Many attractive squares and streets, notably Wednesday and Saturday Market and North Bar Gateway. Famous racecourse. Market cross dates from 1714.

- **BOLTON PERCY, NORTH YORKSHIRE** - Secluded village of limestone with red-brick buildings. Exceptional 15thC parish church contains medieval stained glass and monument to Fairfaxes. 15thC half-timbered gatehouses with carved timber-work.

- **BOROUGHBRIDGE, NORTH YORKSHIRE** - On the River Ure, Boroughbridge was once an important coaching centre with 22 inns and, in the 18thC, a port for Knaresborough's linens. It has fine old houses, many trees and a cobbled square with market cross. Nearby stand three megaliths known as the Devil's Arrows.

- **BRADFORD, WEST YORKSHIRE** - City founded on wool, with fine Victorian and modern buildings. Attractions include the cathedral, city hall, Cartwright Hall, Lister Park, Moorside Mills Industrial Museum and National Museum of Photography, Film and Television.

- **BRIDLINGTON, EAST RIDING OF YORKSHIRE** - Lively seaside resort with long sandy beaches, Leisure World and busy harbour with fishing trips in cobles. Priory church of St Mary whose Bayle Gate is now a museum. Mementoes of flying pioneer, Amy Johnson, in Sewerby Hall. Harbour Museum and Aquarium.

C CLOUGHTON, NORTH YORKSHIRE - Village north of Scarborough, close to the east coast and North York Moors.

- **CROPTON, NORTH YORKSHIRE** - Moorland village at the top of a high ridge with stone houses, some of cruck construction, a Victorian church and the remains of a 12thC moated castle. Cropton Forest and Cropton Brewery nearby.

D DANBY, NORTH YORKSHIRE - Eskdale village 12 miles west of Whitby. Visit the Moors Centre at Danby Lodge, a former shooting lodge in 13 acres of grounds including woodland and riverside meadow. Remains of medieval Danby Castle.

E EASINGWOLD, NORTH YORKSHIRE - Market town of charm and character with a cobbled square and many fine Georgian buildings.

F FILEY, NORTH YORKSHIRE - Resort with elegant Regency buildings along the front and six miles of sandy beaches bounded by natural breakwater, Filey Brigg. Starting point of the Cleveland Way. St Oswald's church, overlooking a ravine, belonged to Augustinian canons until the Dissolution.

G GARFORTH, WEST YORKSHIRE - Town seven miles east of Leeds, between Temple Newsam Estate and Lotherton Hall. Old coal-mining district of Leeds.

- **GILLAMOOR, NORTH YORKSHIRE** - Village much admired by photographers for its views of Farndale, including "Surprise View" from the churchyard.

- **GOATHLAND, NORTH YORKSHIRE** - Spacious village with several large greens grazed by sheep, an ideal centre for walking the North York Moors. Nearby are several waterfalls, among them Mallyan Spout. Plough Monday celebrations held in January. Location for filming of TV "Heartbeat" series.

- **GRASSINGTON, NORTH YORKSHIRE** - Tourists visit this former lead-mining village to see its "smiddy", antique and craft shops and Upper Wharfedale Museum of country trades. Popular with fishermen and walkers. Cobbled market square, numerous prehistoric sites. Grassington Feast in October. National Park Centre.

H HALIFAX, WEST YORKSHIRE - Founded on the cloth trade, and famous for its building society, textiles, carpets and toffee. Most notable landmark is Piece Hall where wool merchants traded, now restored to house shops, museums and ar gallery. Home also to Eureka! The Museu for Children.

- **HARROGATE, NORTH YORKSHIRE** - Major conference, exhibition and shoppir centre, renowned for its spa heritage and award-winning floral displays, spacious parks and gardens. Famous for antiques, toffee, fine shopping and excellent tea shops, also its Royal Pump Rooms and Baths. Annual Great Yorkshire Show in July.

• **HAWES, NORTH YORKSHIRE** - The capital of Upper Wensleydale on the famous Pennine Way, Yorkshire's highest market town and renowned for great cheeses. Popular with walkers. Dales National Park Information Centre and Folk Museum. Nearby is spectacular Hardraw Force waterfall.

• **HAWORTH, WEST YORKSHIRE** - Famous since 1820 as home of the Bronte family. The Parsonage is now a Bronte Museum where furniture and possessions of the family are displayed. Moors and Bronte waterfalls nearby, and steam trains on the Keighley and Worth Valley Railway pass through.

• **HEBDEN, NORTH YORKSHIRE** - Situated between Grassington and Pateley Bridge. The present bridge across the ravine was built in 1827, but the old stone bridge can still be seen. Close by is Scala Force. Abundant remains of lead-mining activity.

• **HELMSLEY, NORTH YORKSHIRE** - Delightful small market town with red roofs, warm stone buildings and cobbled market square, on the River Rye at the entrance to Ryedale and the North York Moors. Remains of 12thC castle, several inns and All Saints' Church.

• **HUDDERSFIELD, WEST YORKSHIRE** - Founded on wool and cloth, the town has a famous choral society. Town centre redeveloped, but several good Victorian buildings remain, including railway station, St Peter's Church, Tolson Memorial Museum, art gallery and nearby Colne Valley Museum.

• **HULL, EAST RIDING OF YORKSHIRE** - Busy seaport with a modern city centre and excellent shopping facilities. Maritime traditions in the town, docks museum, and the home of William Wilberforce, the slavery abolitionist, whose house is now a museum. The Humber Bridge is five miles west.

• **HUTTON-LE-HOLE, NORTH YORKSHIRE** - Listed in the Domesday Book, this pretty village of red-tiled stone cottages situated around Hutton Beck became a refuge for persecuted Quakers in the 17thC. Ryedale Folk Museum.

I **ILKLEY, WEST YORKSHIRE** - Former spa with an elegant shopping centre and famous for its ballad. The 16thC manor house, now a museum, displays local prehistoric and Roman relics. Popular walk leads up Heber's Ghyll to Ilkley Moor, with the mysterious Swastika Stone and White Wells, 18thC plunge baths.

• **INGLETON, NORTH YORKSHIRE** - Thriving tourist centre for fell-walkers, climbers and pot-holers. Popular walks up beautiful Twiss Valley to Ingleborough Summit, Whernside, White Scar Caves and waterfalls.

K **KIRKBYMOORSIDE, NORTH YORKSHIRE** - Attractive market town with remains of Norman castle. Good centre for exploring Moors. Nearby are wild daffodils of Farndale.

• **KNARESBOROUGH, NORTH YORKSHIRE** - Picturesque market town on the River Nidd. The 14thC keep is the best-preserved part of John of Gaunt's castle, and the manor house, with its chequerboard walls, was presented by James I to his son Charles as a fishing lodge. Prophetess Mother Shipton's cave. Boating on river.

L **LEEDS, WEST YORKSHIRE** - Large city with excellent modern shopping centre and splendid Victorian architecture. Museums and galleries including Temple Newsam House (the Hampton Court of the North), Tetley's Brewery Wharf and the Royal Armouries Museum; also home of Opera North.

• **LEYBURN, NORTH YORKSHIRE** - Attractive Dales market town where Mary Queen of Scots was reputedly captured after her escape from Bolton Castle. Fine views over Wensleydale from nearby.

M **MALHAM, NORTH YORKSHIRE** - Hamlet of stone cottages amid magnificent rugged limestone scenery in the Yorkshire Dales National Park. Malham Cove is a curving, sheer white cliff 240 ft high. Malham Tarn, one of Yorkshire's few natural lakes, belongs to the National Trust. National Park Centre.

• **MALTON, NORTH YORKSHIRE** - Thriving farming town on the River Derwent with large livestock market. Famous for racehorse training. The local museum has Roman remains and the Eden Camp Modern History Theme Museum transports visitors back to wartime Britain. Castle Howard within easy reach.

• **MIDDLEHAM, NORTH YORKSHIRE** - Town famous for racehorse training, with cobbled squares and houses of local stone. Norman castle, once principal residence of Warwick the Kingmaker and later Richard III. Ancient stronghold of the Neville family, it was taken over by the Crown after the Battle of Barnet in 1471.

N **NORTHALLERTON, NORTH YORKSHIRE** - Formerly a staging post on coaching route to the north and later a railway town. Today a lively market town and administrative capital of North Yorkshire. Parish church of All Saints dates from 1200. Dickens stayed at The Fleece.

O **OSSETT, WEST YORKSHIRE** - Small town lying just off the M1 west of Dewsbury. Noted for its textiles, engineering and coal mining. World coal-carrying championship takes place every Easter Monday.

• **OTLEY, WEST YORKSHIRE** - Charming market and small manufacturing town in Lower Wharfedale, the birthplace of Thomas Chippendale, painted by Turner. Old inns, medieval 5-arched bridge, local history museum, maypole, historic All Saints' Church. Beautiful countryside. Annual carnival.

AT-A-GLANCE SYMBOLS

Symbols at the end of each accommodation entry give useful information about services and facilities. A key to symbols can be found inside the back cover flap. Keep this open for easy reference.

P **PICKERING, NORTH YORKSHIRE** - Market town and tourist centre on edge of North York Moors. Parish church has complete set of 15thC wall paintings depicting lives of saints. Part of 12thC castle still stands. Beck Isle Museum. The North York Moors Railway begins here.

R **RAVENSCAR, NORTH YORKSHIRE** - Splendidly positioned small coastal resort with magnificent views over Robin Hood's Bay. Its Old Peak is the end of the famous Lyke Wake Walk or "corpse way".

• **REETH, NORTH YORKSHIRE** - Once a market town and lead-mining centre, Reeth today serves holidaymakers in Swaledale with its folk museum and 18thC shops and inns lining the green at High Row.

• **RIPON, NORTH YORKSHIRE** - Ancient city with impressive cathedral containing Saxon crypt which houses church treasures from all over Yorkshire. Charter granted in 886 by Alfred the Great. "Setting the Watch" tradition kept nightly by horn-blower in Market Square. Fountains Abbey nearby.

• **ROBIN HOOD'S BAY, NORTH YORKSHIRE** - Picturesque village of red-roofed cottages with main street running from cliff top down ravine to seashore, a magnet for artists. Scene of much smuggling and shipwrecks in 18thC. Robin Hood is reputed to have escaped to the continent by boat from here.

• **ROSEDALE ABBEY, NORTH YORKSHIRE** - Sturdy hamlet built around Cistercian nunnery in the reign of Henry II, in the middle of Rosedale, largest of the moorland valleys. Remains of 12thC priory. Disused lead mines on the surrounding moors.

• **ROTHERHAM, SOUTH YORKSHIRE** - In the Don Valley, Rotherham became an important industrial town in the 19thC with the discovery of coal and the development of the iron and steel industry by Joshua Walker who built Clifton House, now the town's museum. Magnificent 15thC All Saints Church is town's showpiece.

• **RUNSWICK BAY, NORTH YORKSHIRE** - Holiday and fishing village on the west side of Runswick Bay.

S **SCARBOROUGH, NORTH YORKSHIRE** - Large, popular East Coast seaside resort, formerly a spa town. Beautiful gardens and two splendid sandy beaches. Castle ruins date from 1100; fine Georgian and Victorian houses. Scarborough Millennium depicts 1,000 years of town's history. Sea Life Centre.

• **SCUNTHORPE, NORTH LINCOLNSHIRE** - Consisted of five small villages until 1860 when extensive ironstone beds were discovered. Today an industrial "garden town" with some interesting modern buildings. Nearby Normanby Hall contains fine examples of Regency furniture.

• **SELBY, NORTH YORKSHIRE** - Small market town on the River Ouse, believed to have been birthplace of Henry I, with a magnificent abbey containing much fine Norman and Early English architecture.

• **SETTLE, NORTH YORKSHIRE** - Town of narrow streets and Georgian houses in an area of great limestone hills and crags. Panoramic view from Castleberg Crag which stands 300 ft above town.

• **SHEFFIELD, SOUTH YORKSHIRE** - Local iron ore and coal gave Sheffield its prosperous steel and cutlery industries. The modern city centre has many interesting buildings - cathedral, Cutlers' Hall, Crucible Theatre, Graves and Mappin Art Galleries. Meadowhall Shopping Centre nearby.

• **SHELLEY, WEST YORKSHIRE** - West Yorkshire village south of Huddersfield and close to Kirklees Light Railway.

• **SKIPTON, NORTH YORKSHIRE** - Pleasant market town at gateway to dales, with farming community atmosphere, a Palladian Town Hall, parish church and fully roofed castle at the top of the High Street. The Clifford family motto, "Desoramis", is sculpted in huge letters on the parapet over the castle gateway.

• **STAITHES, NORTH YORKSHIRE** - Busy fishing village until growth of Whitby, Staithes is a maze of steep, cobbled streets packed with tall houses of red brick and bright paintwork. Smuggling was rife in 18thC. Cotton bonnets worn by fisherwomen can still be seen. Strong associations with Captain Cook.

T **THIRSK, NORTH YORKSHIRE** - Thriving market town with cobbled square surrounded by old shops and inns. St Mary's Church is probably the best example of Perpendicular work in Yorkshire. House of Thomas Lord - founder of Lord's Cricket Ground - is now a folk museum.

• **THORNTON DALE, NORTH YORKSHIRE** - Picturesque village with Thorntondale Beck, traversed by tiny stone footbridges at the edge of pretty cottage gardens.

W **WETHERBY, WEST YORKSHIRE** - Prosperous market town on the River Wharfe, noted for horse-racing.

• **WHITBY, NORTH YORKSHIRE** - Holiday town with narrow streets and steep alleys at the mouth of the River Esk. Captain James Cook, the famous navigator, lived in Grape Lane. 199 steps lead to St Mary's Church and St Hilda's Abbey overlooking harbour. Dracula connections. Gothic weekend every April.

Y **YORK, NORTH YORKSHIRE** - Ancient walled city nearly 2,000 years old, containing many well-preserved medieval buildings. Its Minster has over 100 stained glass windows and is the largest Gothic cathedral in England. Attractions include Castle Museum, National Railway Museum, Jorvik Viking Centre and York Dungeon.

GOLD & SILVER AWARDS

These exclusive ETC awards are given to establishments achieving the highest levels of quality and service. Further information can be found at the front of the guide and additional accommodation achieving these awards are shown in the listing at the back of this guide.

HEART of England

The home of Shakespeare, fine china and the grandest palaces in Britain, the region is full of surprises, from the thriving multicultural cities of Birmingham and Nottingham to countryside, both dramatic and picturesque.

classic sights

Hardwick Hall – probably Britain's greatest Elizabethan house

Pottery & porcelain – factory tours of Royal Crown Derby, Wedgwood, Spode and more

Ironbridge Gorge – the world's first cast-iron bridge

country

The Cotswolds – picturebook England

The Peak District – moorland, limestone gorges and ancient woodlands

literary links

Stratford-upon-Avon – Royal Shakespeare Company; the homes of Shakespeare and his family

Nottingham – DH Lawrence Birthplace Museum

arts for all

Walsall – The New Art Gallery

Wightwick Manor – arts & crafts masterpiece

Arts Festivals – Bromsgrove, Malvern and Cheltenham

distinctively different

Cadbury World – Chocaholic heaven

The counties of Derbyshire, Gloucestershire, Herefordshire, Leicestershire, Lincolnshire, Northamptonshire, Nottinghamshire, Rutland, Shropshire, Staffordshire, Warwickshire, Worcestershire and West Midlands

FOR MORE INFORMATION CONTACT:

Heart of England Tourist Board
Larkhill Road, Worcester WR5 2EZ
Tel: (01905) 761100 Fax: (01905) 763450
Internet: www.visitheartofengland.com

The Pictures: 1 Stokesay Castle, Shropshire 2 Cotswold village

PLACES TO VISIT - see pages 202-206 > WHERE TO STAY - see pages 207-273

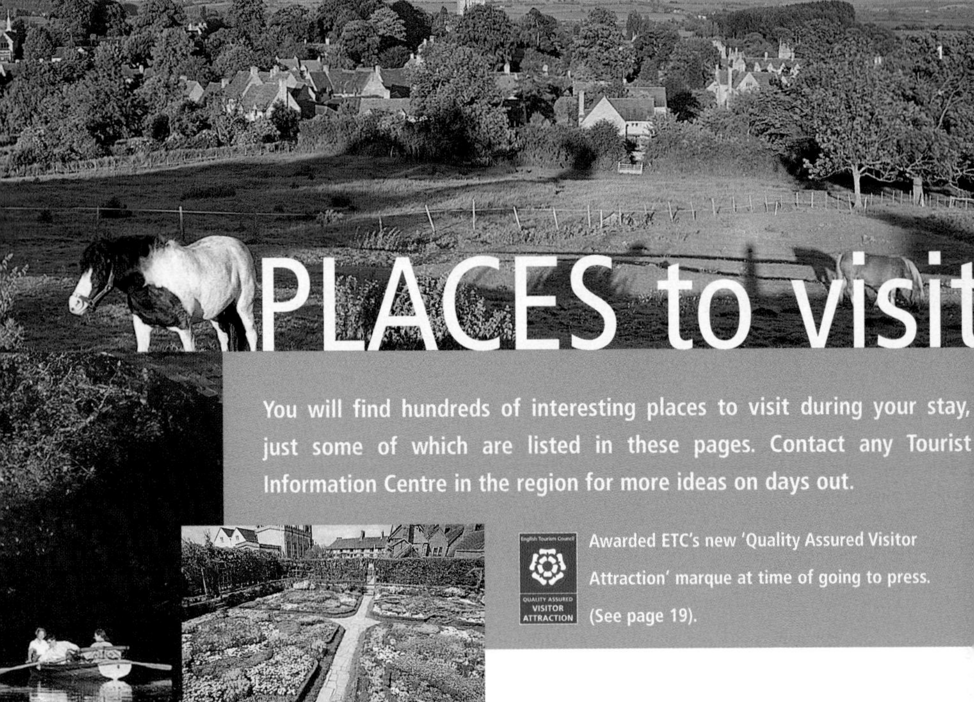

You will find hundreds of interesting places to visit during your stay, just some of which are listed in these pages. Contact any Tourist Information Centre in the region for more ideas on days out.

2

Awarded ETC's new 'Quality Assured Visitor Attraction' marque at time of going to press. (See page 19).

Acton Scott Historic Working Farm

Wenlock Lodge, Acton Scott, Church Stretton
Tel: (01694) 781306 www.actonscotmuseum.co.uk
Acton Scott Historic Working Farm demonstrates farming and rural life in South Shropshire at the close of the 19thC.

Alton Towers Theme Park

Alton, Stoke-on-Trent
Tel: 0870 5204060 www.altontowers.com
Theme Park with over 125 rides and attractions including Oblivion, Nemesis, Haunted House, Runaway Mine Train, Congo River Rapids, Log Flume and many children's rides.

The American Adventure

Ilkeston
Tel: 0845 3302929
www.americanadventure.co.uk
The American Adventure has action and entertainment for all ages including The Missile white-knuckle rollercoaster, Europe's tallest skycoaster and the world's wettest log flume.

Belton House, Park and Gardens

Belton, Grantham
Tel: (01476) 566116 www.nationaltrust.org.uk
The crowning achievement of restoration country house architecture, built in 1685-88 for Sir John Brownlow with alterations by James Wyatt in 1777.

Belvoir Castle

Estate Office, Belvoir, Grantham
Tel: (01476) 870262 www.belvoircastle.com
The present castle is the fourth to be built on this site and dates from 1816. Art treasures include works by Poussin, Rubens, Holbein and Reynolds. Queen's Royal Lancers display.

Birmingham Botanical Gardens and Glasshouses

Westbourne Road, Edgbaston, Birmingham
Tel: (0121) 454 1860
www.birminghambotanicalgardens.org.uk
Fifteen acres (6ha) of ornamental gardens and glasshouses. Widest range of plants in the Midlands from tropical rainforest to arid desert. Aviaries with exotic birds, children's play area.

Black Country Living Museum

Tipton Road, Dudley
Tel: (0121) 557 9643 www.bclm.co.uk
A warm welcome awaits you at Britain's friendliest open air museum. Wander around original shops and houses, or ride on fair attractions and take a look down the min

Blenheim Palace

Woodstock, Oxford

Tel: (01993) 811325

Home of the 11th Duke of Marlborough, birthplace of Sir Winston Churchill. Designed by Vanbrugh in the English baroque style. Park landscaped by 'Capability' Brown.

Butlins

Roman Bank, Skegness

Tel: (01754) 762311 www.butlins.co.uk

Butlins has a skyline pavilion, toyland, sub-tropical waterworld, tenpin bowling and entertainment centre with live shows.

Cadbury World

Linden Road, Bournville, Birmingham

Tel: (0121) 451 4180 www.cadburyworld.co.uk

Story of Cabdury's chocolate includes chocolate-making demonstration and attractions for all ages, with free samples.

Chatsworth House, Garden, Farmyard & Adventure Playground

Chatsworth, Bakewell

Tel: (01246) 582204 www.chatsworth.org

Chatsworth is one of the great treasure houses of England with gardens, adventure playground and farmyard.

Cotswold Farm Park

Guiting Power, Cheltenham

Tel: (01451) 850307 www.cotswoldfarmpark.co.uk

Collection of rare breeds of British farm animals. Pets' corner, adventure playground, tractor school, picnic area, gift shop, cafe and seasonal farming displays.

Crich Tramway Village

Crich, Matlock

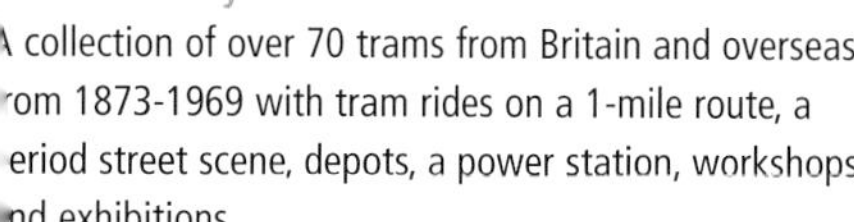

Tel: (01773) 852565

www.tramway.co.uk

A collection of over 70 trams from Britain and overseas from 1873-1969 with tram rides on a 1-mile route, a period street scene, depots, a power station, workshops and exhibitions.

Drayton Manor Family Theme Park

Tamworth

Tel: (01827) 287979 www.draytonmanor.co.uk

A major theme park with over 100 rides and attractions plus children's rides, zoo, farm, museums and the new live 'Popeye Show'.

The Elgar Birthplace Museum

Crown East Lane, Lower Broadheath, Worcester

Tel: (01905) 333224 www.elgar.org

Country cottage, birthplace of Sir Edward Elgar. The Elgar Centre gives a fascinating insight into his life, music, family, friends and inspirations.

The Galleries of Justice

Shire Hall, High Pavement, Lace Market, Nottingham

Tel: (0115) 952 0555 www.galleriesofjustice.org.uk

An atmospheric experience of justice over the ages located in and around an original 19thC courthouse and county gaol, brought to life by live actors.

The Heights of Abraham Cable Cars, Caverns and Hilltop Park

Matlock Bath, Matlock

Tel: (01629) 582365 www.heights-of-abraham.co.uk

A spectacular cable-car ride takes you to the summit. There is a wide variety of attractions for young and old alike within the grounds. Gift shop and coffee shop.

> The Pictures: 1 Chipping Campden
2 River Avon, Warwick
3 Knott Garden, New Place, Stratford-upon-Avon
4 Chatsworth House, Derbyshire
5 Robin Hood Statue, Nottingham

Ikon Gallery

1 Oozells Square, Brindleyplace, Birmingham

Tel: (0121) 248 0708 www.ikongallery.co.uk

Ikon Gallery is one of Europe's foremost galleries for presenting the work of living artists within an innovative, educational framework.

Ironbridge Gorge Museum

Ironbridge, Telford

Tel: (01952) 433522 www.ironbridge.org.uk

World's first cast-iron bridge, Museum of the Gorge Visitor Centre, Tar Tunnel, Jackfield Tile Museum, Coalport China Museum, Rosehill House, Blists Hill Museum and Museum of Iron.

Lincoln Castle

Castle Hill, Lincoln

Tel: (01522) 511068

A medieval castle including towers and ramparts with a Magna Carta exhibition, a prison chapel experience, reconstructed Westgate and popular events throughout the summer.

Midland Railway Centre

Butterley Station, Ripley

Tel: (01773) 747674

Over 50 locomotives and over 100 items of historic rolling stock of Midland and LMS origin with a steam-hauled passenger service, a museum site, country and farm park.

Museum of British Road Transport

Hales Street, Coventry

Tel: (024) 7683 2425 www.mbrt.co.uk

Two hundred cars and commercial vehicles from 1896 to date, 200 cycles from 1818 to date, 90 motorcycles from 1920 to date and the 'Thrust 2' land-speed story.

National Sea Life Centre

The Water's Edge, Brindleyplace, Birmingham

Tel: (0121) 633 4700 www.sealife.co.uk

Over 55 fascinating displays. The opportunity to come face-to-face with literally hundreds of fascinating sea creatures, from sharks to shrimps.

Nottingham Industrial Museum

Courtyard Buildings, Wollaton Park, Nottingham

Tel: (0115) 915 3910 www.nottinghamcity.gov.uk

An 18thC stables presenting the history of Nottingham's industries: printing, pharmacy, hosiery and lace. There is also a Victorian beam engine, a horse gin and transport.

Peak District Mining Museum

The Pavilion, Matlock Bath, Matlock

Tel: (01629) 583834 www.peakmines.co.uk

A large exhibition on 3,500 years of lead mining with displays on geology, mines and miners, tools and engines. The climbing shafts make it suitable for children as well.

Rockingham Castle

Rockingham, Market Harborough

Tel: (01536) 770240

www.rockinghamcastle.com

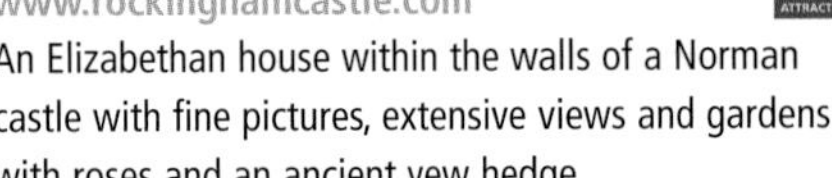

An Elizabethan house within the walls of a Norman castle with fine pictures, extensive views and gardens with roses and an ancient yew hedge.

Rugby School Museum

10 Little Church Street, Rugby

Tel: (01788) 556109

Rugby School Museum tells the story of the school, scene of 'Tom Brown's Schooldays', and contains the earlier memorabilia of the game, which was invented on the school close.

Severn Valley Railway

The Railway Station, Bewdley

Tel: (01299) 403816 www.svr.co.uk

Preserved standard-gauge steam railway running 16 miles (26km) between Kidderminster, Bewdley and Bridgnorth. Collection of locomotives and passenger coaches.

Shakespeare's Birthplace

Henley Street, Stratford-upon-Avon

Tel: (01789) 204016 www.shakespeare.org.uk

The world-famous house where William Shakespeare was born in 1564 and where he grew up. See the highly acclaimed Shakespeare Exhibition.

Shugborough Estate

Shugborough, Milford, Stafford

Tel: (01889) 881388 www.staffordshire.gov.uk

18thC mansion house with fine collection of furniture. Gardens and park contain beautiful neo-classical monuments.

Skegness Natureland Seal Sanctuary

North Parade, The Promenade, Skegness

Tel: (01754) 764345

www.skegnessnatureland.co.uk

Collection of performing seals, baby seals, penguins, aquarium, crocodiles, snakes, terrapins, scorpions, tropical birds, butterflies (April-October) and pets.

Snibston Discovery Park

Ashby Road, Coalville, Leicester

Tel: (01530) 278444 www.leics.gov.uk/museums

An all-weather and award-winning science and industrial heritage museum.

Spode Visitor Centre

Spode, Church Street, Stoke-on-Trent

Tel: (01782) 744011 www.spode.co.uk

Visitors are shown the various processes in the making of bone china. Visitors can have a go themselves in the craft demonstration area.

The Tales of Robin Hood

30-38 Maid Marian Way, Nottingham

Tel: (0115) 948 3284

Join the world's greatest medieval adventure. Ride through the magical green wood and play the Silver Arrow game in the search for Robin Hood.

Twycross Zoo

Twycross, Atherstone

Tel: (01827) 880250 www.twycrosszoo.com

A zoo with gorillas, orang-utans, chimpanzees, a modern gibbon complex, elephants, lions, giraffes, reptile house, pets' corner and rides.

Walsall Arboretum

Lichfield Street, Walsall

Tel: (01922) 653148 www.walsallarboretum.co.uk

Picturesque Victorian park with over 79 acres (32ha) of gardens, lakes and parkland.

Warwick Castle

Warwick

Tel: 0870 4422000 www.warwick-castle.co.uk

Set in 60 acres (24ha) of grounds with state rooms, armoury, dungeon, torture chamber, clock tower, A Royal Weekend Party 1898 and Kingmaker - a preparation for battle.

The Wedgwood Story Visitor Centre

Barlaston, Stoke-on-Trent

Tel: (01782) 204218 www.thewedgwoodstory.com

This £4.5 million visitor centre exhibits centuries of craftsmanship on a plate. Audio-guided tour includes exhibition and demonstration areas. Shop and restaurants.

The Wildfowl and Wetlands Trust Slimbridge

Slimbridge, Gloucester

Tel: (01453) 890333 www.wwt.org.uk

Tropical house, hides, heated observatory, exhibits, shop, restaurant, children's playground, pond zone.

Worcester Cathedral

10a College Green, Worcester

Tel: (01905) 611002 www.cofe-worcester.org.uk

Norman crypt and chapter house, King John's tomb, Prince Arthur's chantry, medieval cloisters and buildings. Touch- and hearing-control visually impaired facilities available.

> The Pictures: 1 Rutland Water
2 Black Country Museum, Dudley

Find out more about HEART of England

1

Further information about holidays and attractions in Heart of England is available from:

HEART OF ENGLAND TOURIST BOARD
Larkhill Road, Worcester WR5 2EZ.
Tel: (01905) 761100 Fax: (01905) 763450
Internet: www.visitheartofengland.com

The following publications are available free from the Heart of England Tourist Board:

Bed & Breakfast Touring Map including Camping and Caravan Parks
Escape to the Heart 2003/4
Great Places to Visit in the Heart of England

Getting to the HEART of England

2

BY ROAD: Britain's main motorways (M1/M6/M5) meet in the Heart of England; the M40 links with the M42 south of Birmingham while the M4 provides fast access from London to the south of the region. These road links ensure that the Heart of England is more accessible by road than any other region in the UK.

BY RAIL: The Heart of England lies at the centre of the country's rail network. There are direct trains from London and other major cities to many towns and cities within the region.

> The Pictures: 1 River Avon, Evesham 2 Shrewsbury Castle

Where to stay in the Heart of England

Accommodation entries in this region are listed in alphabetical order of place name, and then in alphabetical order of establishment. As West Oxfordshire and Cherwell are promoted in both Heart of England and South of England, places in these areas with accommodation are lsted in this section. See South of England for full West Oxfordshire and Cherwell entries.

Map references refer to the colour location maps at the front of this guide. The first number indicates the map to use; the letter and number which follow refer to the grid reference on the map.

At-a-glance symbols at the end of each accommodation entry give useful information about services and facilities. A key to symbols can be found inside the back cover flap. Keep this open for easy reference.

A brief description of the towns and villages offering accommodation in the entries which follow, can be found at the end of this section.

A complete listing of all the English Tourism Council assessed accommodation covered by this guide appears at the back of the guide.

ABBOTS MORTON, Worcestershire Map ref 2B1

◆◆◆◆

THE COTTAGE APARTMENT
The Cottage,
Gooms Hill, Abbots Morton Manor,
Abbots Morton, Worcester WR7 4LT
T: (01386) 792783
F: (01386) 792783
E: cottage@bedbrek.fsnet.co.uk
I: www.bedbrek.co.uk

Bedrooms: 1 double/twin
Bathrooms: 1 en suite

B&B per night:
S £30.00–£35.00
D £50.00–£60.00

OPEN All Year

Beautiful apartment in grounds of timber-framed cottage c1455. Malvern views. Set in peaceful countryside with fabulous walks, pubs and history. Central for all tourist sites.

P

ALDERTON, Gloucestershire Map ref 2B1

GANTIER
12 Church Road, Alderton,
Tewkesbury GL20 8NR
T: (01242) 620343
F: (01386) 442415
E: johnandsueparry@yahoo.co.uk
I: www.gantier.co.uk

Bedrooms: 2 double/twin
Bathrooms: 1 en suite, 1 private

B&B per night:
S £25.00–£35.00
D £45.00–£55.00

OPEN All Year except Christmas

Lovely views over pastureland to Cotswold Hills. Peaceful, relaxing and a warm welcome. Good food locally, and an ideal, central location for touring or sightseeing.

P

QUALITY ASSURANCE SCHEME

Diamond ratings and awards were correct at the time of going to press but are subject to change. Please check at the time of booking.

ALTON, Staffordshire Map ref 4B2

♦♦♦

ADMIRALS HOUSE

Mill Road, Oakamoor, Stoke-on-Trent ST10 3AG
T: (01538) 702187
F: (01538) 702957
E: admiralshouse@btinternet.com
I: www.admiralshouse.co.uk

Bedrooms: 2 double/twin, 6 triple/multiple
Bathrooms: 8 en suite

Evening meal available
CC: Delta, Mastercard, Switch, Visa

B&B per night:
S £30.00–£45.00
D £50.00–£65.00

OPEN All Year except Christmas

Originally a coaching inn, now a peaceful country guesthouse and restaurant. Riverside location. Range of comfortable, fully-equipped en suite rooms. One and a half miles from Alton Towers.

P

♦♦♦♦

BRADLEY ELMS FARM

Alton Road, Threapwood, Cheadle ST10 4RB
T: (01538) 753135 & 750202
F: (01538) 750202

B&B per night:
S £32.00
D £46.00

Nine tastefully converted farm buildings all with en suite facilities, colour TV and tea/coffee. Residents' lounge, children's play area, excellent car parking. Three miles to Alton Towers. Within easy reach of The Potteries and the Peak District. Ideal for walkers and cyclists. Full English or continental breakfast included.

Bedrooms: 6 double/twin, 3 triple/multiple
Bathrooms: 9 en suite

Evening meal available

P

♦♦♦

BULLS HEAD INN

High Street, Alton, Stoke-on-Trent ST10 4AQ
T: (01538) 702307
F: (01538) 702065
E: janet@alton.freeserve.co.uk
I: www.thebullsheadinn.freeserve.co.uk

Bedrooms: 3 double/twin, 2 triple/multiple
Bathrooms: 5 en suite

Lunch available
Evening meal available
CC: Delta, Mastercard, Switch, Visa

B&B per night:
S £25.00–£45.00
D £55.00–£60.00

OPEN All Year

In the village of Alton close to Alton Towers, an 18thC inn with real ale, home cooking and a friendly atmosphere.

P

♦♦♦♦

CHURCH GRANGE

Bradley in the Moors, Alton, Stoke-on-Trent ST10 4DF
T: (01889) 507525
F: (01889) 590399
E: cdmasalt.chgrange@btinternet.com
I: www.staffordshire.gov.uk/tourism/chgrange.htm

Bedrooms: 1 double/twin, 3 triple/multiple
Bathrooms: 3 en suite, 1 private

CC: Delta, Mastercard, Switch, Visa

B&B per night:
S £22.50–£25.00
D £45.00–£50.00

OPEN All Year

Recently converted former 18thC coach house set amidst peaceful countryside with splendid views. Lawns to front and rear.

P

CHECK THE MAPS

The colour maps at the front of this guide show all the cities, towns and villages for which you will find accommodation entries. Refer to the town index to find the page on which they are listed.

ALTON continued

◆◆◆◆ Silver Award

FIELDS FARM

Chapel Lane, Threapwood, Alton, Stoke-on-Trent ST10 4QZ
T: (01538) 752721 & 07850 310381
F: (01538) 757404
E: pat.massey@ukonline.co.uk

B&B per night:
S £23.00–£27.00
D £34.00–£41.00

HB per person:
DY £24.00–£32.00

OPEN All Year except Christmas

Traditional farmhouse hospitality and comfort in the picturesque Churnet Valley, 10 minutes from Alton Towers. Near Peak Park and within easy reach of Potteries and many stately homes. Stabling available. Ideal for walking, cycling, riding and fishing. Dogs by arrangement. Proprietor Pat Massey.

Bedrooms: 3 double/twin
Bathrooms: 2 en suite, 1 private

Evening meal available

◆◆◆

HILLSIDE FARM AND COTTAGES

Alton Road, Denstone, Uttoxeter ST14 5HG
T: (01889) 590760
I: www.smoothhound.co.uk/hotels/hillside.html

Bedrooms: 1 double/twin, 3 triple/multiple
Bathrooms: 1 en suite, 1 private

B&B per night:
S £18.00–£22.00
D £34.00–£40.00

Victorian farmhouse with extensive views to the Weaver Hills and Churnet Valley. Situated 2 miles south of Alton Towers on B5032.

ALVELEY, Shropshire Map ref 4A3

◆◆◆◆ Silver Award

ARNSIDE BED AND BREAKFAST

Arnside, Kidderminster Road, Alveley, Bridgnorth WV15 6LL
T: (01746) 780007
F: (01746) 780007
E: Terry@ptah.freeserve.co.uk
I: www.virtual-shropshire.co.uk/arnside

Bedrooms: 2 double/twin, 1 triple/multiple
Bathrooms: 3 en suite

B&B per night:
S £30.00–£35.00
D £40.00–£48.00

OPEN All Year except Christmas

An impressive bungalow set in 1.5 acres of lawns containing 3 double rooms including a twin and family room. All are en suite. Situated in the beautiful Severn Valley 6 miles south of Bridgnorth, Shropshire.

ASHBOURNE, Derbyshire Map ref 4B2 *Tourist Information Centre Tel: (01335) 343666*

◆◆◆

THE BLACK HORSE INN

Main Road, Hulland Ward, Ashbourne DE6 3EE
T: (01335) 370206
F: (01335) 370206

B&B per night:
S £40.00–£50.00
D £60.00–£70.00

HB per person:
DY £35.00–£48.00

OPEN All Year

Dating from the 1690s and personally run by owners. 4-poster, en suite accommodation. Home-cooked food, vegetarian options, traditional Sunday carvery. Guest beers, bar games, beer garden. Set in Derbyshire Dales on edge of Peak District National Park, 4 miles Ashbourne. Ideal for Carsington Water, Alton Towers, Chatsworth and Dovedale.

Bedrooms: 4 double/twin
Bathrooms: 4 en suite

Lunch available
Evening meal available
CC: Delta, Mastercard, Switch, Visa

QUALITY ASSURANCE SCHEME

Diamond ratings and awards are explained at the back of this guide.

ASHBOURNE continued

♦♦♦♦

CROSS FARM

Main Road, Ellastone, Ashbourne DE6 2GZ
T: (01335) 324668
F: (01335) 324039
E: janecliffe@hotmail.com

Bedrooms: 2 double/twin, 1 triple/multiple
Bathrooms: 3 en suite

B&B per night:
S £19.00–£25.00
D £36.00–£38.00

OPEN All Year

19thC farmhouse near Alton Towers, Potteries, National Trust properties. Good accommodation and traditional Aga cooking in village location. Pub within walking distance.

P

♦♦♦

MONA VILLAS BED AND BREAKFAST

1 Mona Villas, Church Lane, Mayfield, Ashbourne DE6 2JS
T: (01335) 343773
F: (01335) 343773

Bedrooms: 3 double/twin
Bathrooms: 3 en suite

B&B per night:
S £25.00–£30.00
D £40.00–£50.00

OPEN All Year except Christmas

A warm, friendly welcome to our Edwardian home with new purpose-built en suite accommodation. Beautiful views over open countryside. Near Alton Towers, Dovedale etc.

P

THORPE COTTAGE

Thorpe, Ashbourne DE6 2AW
T: (01335) 350466 & 07711 217475
F: (01335) 350217
I: www.peakdistrict-bandb.com

B&B per night:
S £20.00–£24.00
D £50.00–£60.00

OPEN All Year

Grade II Listed, recently refurbished limestone cottage with antiques. Situated at the edge of conservation village within walking distance of Dovedale. Welcoming, attentive hospitality. Splendid fireside breakfast with the now-rapidly-becoming-famous freshly made muffins! Also separate self-contained cottage with 4-poster bed. Self-catering or bed and breakfast. Short breaks.

Bedrooms: 1 single, 2 double/twin, 1 triple/multiple
Bathrooms: 2 en suite

P

ASHBY-DE-LA-ZOUCH, Leicestershire Map ref 4B3 *Tourist Information Centre Tel: (01530) 411767*

Rating Applied For

QUEENS HEAD HOTEL

79 Market Street, Ashby-de-la-Zouch LE65 1AH
T: (01530) 412780
F: (01530) 412134

Bedrooms: 4 single, 5 double/twin, 1 triple/multiple
Bathrooms: 4 en suite

Lunch available
Evening meal available
CC: Delta, Mastercard, Switch, Visa

B&B per night:
S £25.00–£32.50
D £40.00–£59.95

HB per person:
DY £30.00–£40.00

OPEN All Year except Christmas

A family-run 17thC town centre hotel with bars and restaurant. Friday and Saturday evening night-club. Seven miles from East Midlands Airport.

ASHPERTON, Herefordshire Map ref 2B1

♦♦♦

PRIDEWOOD

Ashperton, Ledbury HR8 2SF
T: (01531) 670416 & 0797 9917573
F: (01531) 670416

Bedrooms: 2 double/twin
Bathrooms: 1 en suite, 1 private

B&B per night:
S £19.00–£30.00
D £38.00–£50.00

OPEN All Year except Christmas

157-acre mixed farm. A working hop farm situated in peaceful surroundings, ideal situation for touring Malvern Hills, Welsh border and local rural town for shopping and sightseeing.

P

COLOUR MAPS Colour maps at the front of this guide pinpoint all places under which you will find accommodation listed.

ATHERSTONE, Warwickshire Map ref 4B3

◆◆◆

MANOR FARM BED AND BREAKFAST

Manor Farm, Ratcliffe Culey,
Atherstone CV9 3NY
T: (01827) 712269 & 716947
E: user880243@aol.com

Bedrooms: 2 double/twin

A bed and breakfast at a working dairy farm in a small village. Within close distance to a public house and 2 miles from a town.

B&B per night:
S £25.00
D £40.00

OPEN All Year

BAKEWELL, Derbyshire Map ref 4B2 *Tourist Information Centre Tel: (01629) 813227*

CASTLE CLIFFE

Monsal Head, Bakewell DE45 1NL
T: (01629) 640258
F: (01629) 640258
E: relax@castle-cliffe.com
I: www.castle-cliffe.com

Stunning position overlooking the beautiful Monsal Dale. Noted for its friendly atmosphere, hearty breakfasts and exceptional views. Drinks in the garden or around open log fire in winter. Centrally situated for Chatsworth, Haddon Hall and other attractions. Choice of dinner venues within an easy stroll. Walks in all directions.

Bedrooms: 4 double/twin, 2 triple/multiple
Bathrooms: 6 en suite

CC: Delta, Mastercard, Switch, Visa

B&B per night:
S £35.00–£40.00
D £47.50–£57.50

OPEN All Year except Christmas

BALSALL COMMON, West Midlands Map ref 4B3

◆◆◆

BLYTHE PADDOCKS

Barston Lane, Balsall Common,
Coventry CV7 7BT
T: (01676) 533050
F: (01676) 533050

Bedrooms: 2 single, 2 double/twin
Bathrooms: 1 en suite

Family home standing in 5 acres. Ten minutes from Birmingham Airport and National Exhibition Centre. NAC Stoneleigh 8 miles. Countryside location. Find us in Birmingham A-Z page 168 square 1D.

B&B per night:
S £20.00–£22.00
D £40.00–£44.00

OPEN All Year

BAMFORD, Derbyshire Map ref 4B2

PIONEER HOUSE

Station Road, Bamford, Hope Valley
S33 0BN
T: (01433) 650638
E: pioneerhouse@yahoo.co.uk
I: www.pioneerhouse.co.uk

Pioneer House is a comfortable Edwardian home with spacious en suite bedrooms, beautifully decorated in turn-of-the-century style but with all modern conveniences. Nestling in the Hope Valley, we are ideally placed for visiting the Peak District and the Derbyshire Dales. Hearty breakfasts in a warm and friendly atmosphere.

Bedrooms: 3 double/twin
Bathrooms: 2 en suite, 1 private

3 nights for the price of 2 during low season.

B&B per night:
D £40.00–£44.00

OPEN All Year

BANBURY

See South of England region for entries

CONFIRM YOUR BOOKING
You are advised to confirm your booking in writing.

BIBURY, Gloucestershire Map ref 2B1

♦♦♦♦
Gold Award

COTTESWOLD HOUSE

Arlington, Bibury, Cirencester GL7 5ND
T: (01285) 740609
F: (01285) 740609
E: cotteswold.house@btclick.com
I: http://home.btclick.com/cotteswold.house

Situated in this picturesque village, Cotteswold House offers high-quality accommodation in a relaxed, friendly atmosphere. Three tastefully furnished bedrooms with en suite facilities, colour TV and tea/coffee. Spacious guest lounge/dining room. Cotteswold House is an ideal centre for touring Cotswolds and surrounding area. No smoking/pets. Private parking.

Bedrooms: 3 double/twin
Bathrooms: 3 en suite

CC: Mastercard, Visa

B&B per night:
S Min £35.00
D Min £48.00

OPEN All Year

BICESTER

See South of England region for entries

BIDFORD-ON-AVON, Warwickshire Map ref 2B1

AVONVIEW HOUSE

Stratford Road, Bidford-on-Avon, Alcester B50 4LU
T: (01789) 778667
F: (01789) 778667
E: avonview@talk21.com

Convenience meets country life at Avonview House. Whether exploring Shakespeare country and the warm heart of England or just passing through, you will be made welcome in our 200-year-old converted stone barn with beamed bedrooms, set in ancient orchard and paddocks. Opposite is a pay-as-you-play golf course.

Bedrooms: 2 double/twin
Bathrooms: 2 private

Evening meal available

4 nights for the price of 3 Nov-Mar.

B&B per night:
S £28.00–£32.00
D £48.00–£52.00

HB per person:
DY £36.00–£41.00

OPEN All Year except Christmas

BROOM HALL INN

Bidford Road, Broom, Alcester B50 4HE
T: (01789) 773757

Family-owned country inn with carvery restaurant and extensive range of bar meals. Close to Stratford-upon-Avon and Cotswolds. Roaring log fires in the winter and a large garden with rare trees to relax in during the summer months.

Bedrooms: 4 single, 8 double/twin
Bathrooms: 9 en suite, 3 private

Lunch available
Evening meal available
CC: Delta, Mastercard, Visa

B&B per night:
S £27.50–£37.50
D £50.00–£60.00

HB per person:
DY £34.50

OPEN All Year

GOLD & SILVER AWARDS

These exclusive ETC awards are given to establishments achieving the highest levels of quality and service. Further information can be found at the front of the guide and additional accommodation achieving these awards are shown in the listing at the back of this guide.

BIRDLIP, Gloucestershire Map ref 2B1

◆◆◆

BEECHMOUNT
Birdlip, Gloucester GL4 8JH
T: (01452) 862262
F: (01452) 862262
E: thebeechmount@breathemail.net
I: www.thebeechmount.co.uk

Bedrooms: 3 double/twin, 3 triple/multiple
Bathrooms: 2 en suite

Evening meal available
CC: Delta, Mastercard, Switch, Visa

B&B per night:
S £20.00–£32.00
D £34.00–£46.00

OPEN All Year

Warm hospitality in family-run guesthouse, ideal centre for the Cotswolds. All rooms individually decorated. Choice of menu for breakfast. Evening meal by arrangement. Unrestricted access.

P

BIRMINGHAM, West Midlands Map ref 4B3 *Tourist Information Centre Tel: (0121) 643 2514*

◆◆◆

ATHOLL LODGE
16 Elmdon Road, Acocks Green, Birmingham B27 6LH
T: (0121) 707 4417
F: (0121) 707 4417
E: davey@which.net

Bedrooms: 6 single, 3 double/twin, 1 triple/multiple
Bathrooms: 4 en suite

Evening meal available
CC: Mastercard, Switch, Visa

B&B per night:
S £23.00–£30.00
D £40.00–£50.00

OPEN All Year except Christmas

Friendly guesthouse in a quiet location on the south side of Birmingham. The National Exhibition Centre, airport and city centre are all within easy reach.

P

◆◆◆

CENTRAL GUEST HOUSE

1637 Coventry Road, South Yardley,
Birmingham B26 1DD
T: (0121) 706 7757
F: (0121) 706 7757
E: mmou826384@aol.com
I: www.centralguesthouse.com

Small, family-run guesthouse with nicely decorated, well-equipped en suite bedrooms. Friendly, attentive service. Freshly cooked full or vegetarian breakfast. Situated on main A45 Coventry road, 4 miles to Birmingham city centre, New Street Station, Birmingham International Airport, international railway station and National Exhibition Centre.

Bedrooms: 1 single, 3 double/twin, 1 triple/multiple
Bathrooms: 4 en suite, 1 private

CC: Mastercard, Switch, Visa

B&B per night:
S £20.00–£25.00
D £40.00–£45.00

OPEN All Year

1 P

◆◆◆

ELMDON GUEST HOUSE
2369 Coventry Road, Sheldon, Birmingham B26 3PN
T: (0121) 742 1626 & 688 1720
F: (0121) 742 1626

Bedrooms: 2 single, 4 double/twin, 1 triple/multiple
Bathrooms: 7 en suite

Lunch available
Evening meal available
CC: Delta, Mastercard, Switch, Visa

B&B per night:
S £32.00–£42.00
D £45.00–£58.00

HB per person:
DY £35.00–£41.50

OPEN All Year

Family-run guesthouse with en suite facilities. TV in all rooms, including Sky. On main A45 close to the National Exhibition Centre, airport, railway and city centre.

P

◆◆◆

HOMELEA
2399 Coventry Road, Sheldon, Birmingham B26 3PN
T: (0121) 742 0017
F: (0121) 688 1879

Bedrooms: 1 single, 2 double/twin
Bathrooms: 2 en suite, 1 private

CC: Delta, Mastercard, Switch, Visa

B&B per night:
S £24.00–£32.00
D £42.00–£46.00

OPEN All Year

A friendly bed and breakfast close to National Exhibition Centre and airport. Comfortable rooms all with TV. Full English breakfast included. Pubs and restaurants within walking distance.

P

RATING All accommodation in this guide has been rated, or is awaiting a rating, by a trained English Tourism Council assessor.

BIRMINGHAM continued

♦♦

ROLLASON WOOD HOTEL

130 Wood End Road, Erdington, Birmingham B24 8BJ
T: (0121) 373 1230
F: (0121) 382 2578
E: rollwood@globalnet.co.uk

Bedrooms: 19 single, 14 double/twin, 4 triple/multiple
Bathrooms: 13 en suite

Evening meal available
CC: Amex, Delta, Diners, Mastercard, Switch, Visa

B&B per night:
S £18.00–£38.00
D £32.00–£49.50

OPEN All Year except Christmas

Friendly, family-run hotel, 1 mile from M6, exit 6. Convenient for city centre, NEC and convention centre. A la carte restaurant and bar.

P

BIRMINGHAM AIRPORT

See under Balsall Common, Birmingham, Coventry, Meriden, Solihull

BISHOP'S CASTLE, Shropshire Map ref 4A3

♦♦♦♦

SHUTTOCKS WOOD

Norbury, Bishop's Castle SY9 5EA
T: (01588) 650433
F: (01588) 650492
E: shuttockswood@btconnect.com
I: www.SmoothHound.co.uk/hotels/shuttock/html

Bedrooms: 4 double/twin
Bathrooms: 4 en suite

CC: Delta, Mastercard, Switch, Visa

B&B per night:
S £30.00–£35.00
D £50.00–£60.00

HB per person:
DY £65.00–£75.00

OPEN All Year

Scandinavian house in woodland setting, within easy travelling distance of Longmynd and Stiperstones Hills. Good base for walking and touring. Ground floor rooms available.

12 P

BOURTON-ON-THE-WATER, Gloucestershire Map ref 2B1 *Tourist Information Centre Tel: (01451) 820211*

♦♦♦

THE COTSWOLD HOUSE

Lansdowne, Bourton-on-the-Water, Cheltenham GL54 2AR
T: (01451) 822373

Bedrooms: 2 double/twin, 2 triple/multiple
Bathrooms: 2 en suite, 2 private

B&B per night:
S £30.00–£50.00
D £40.00–£60.00

OPEN All Year except Christmas

Lovely detached Cotswold-stone house. Elegant hall, curved stairs to galleried landing, spacious en suite rooms overlooking pretty garden. Homely atmosphere. Two minutes village centre.

P

♦♦♦♦

LANSDOWNE HOUSE

Lansdowne, Bourton-on-the-Water, Cheltenham GL54 2AT
T: (01451) 820812
F: (01451) 822484
E: heart@lansdownehouse.co.uk
I: www.lansdownehouse.co.uk

B&B per night:
D £40.00–£45.00

OPEN All Year except Christmas

Large period stone family house. Tastefully furnished en suite accommodation with a combination of old and antique furniture. All rooms have tea/coffee trays and colour TV. There is parking and a garden for guests' use and a good selection of guide books to help you explore the area.

Bedrooms: 2 double/twin, 1 triple/multiple
Bathrooms: 3 en suite

P

♦♦♦

MOUSETRAP INN

Lansdowne, Bourton-on-the-Water, Cheltenham GL54 2AR
T: (01451) 820579
F: (01451) 822393
E: mtinn@waverider.co.uk
I: www.mousetrap-inn.co.uk

Bedrooms: 9 double/twin
Bathrooms: 9 en suite

Lunch available
Evening meal available
CC: Delta, Mastercard, Switch, Visa

B&B per night:
D £45.00–£65.00

HB per person:
DY £35.00–£45.00

OPEN All Year

Small homely inn. All rooms en suite with TV and tea/coffee facilities. Excellent food served in relaxed surroundings. Open fire in the winter.

P

BRIDGNORTH, Shropshire Map ref 4A3 *Tourist Information Centre Tel: (01746) 763257*

◆◆◆

BASSA VILLA BAR AND GRILL

48 Cartway, Bridgnorth WV16 4BG
T: (01746) 763977 & (01952) 691184
F: (01952) 691604
E: sugarloaf@globalnet.co.uk
I: www.SmoothHound.co.uk/hotels/bassavilla.html

Bedrooms: 4 double/twin, 1 triple/multiple
Bathrooms: 5 en suite

Lunch available
Evening meal available
CC: Delta, Mastercard, Switch, Visa

B&B per night:
S £45.00–£60.00
D £55.00–£70.00

HB per person:
DY £55.00–£65.00

OPEN All Year

Very comfortable en suite accommmodation provided in a delightful 16thC riverside inn. Award-winning restaurant, cosy bar offering fine wines and several draught ales. Friendly staff guarantee warm welcome.

◆◆◆◆

BULLS HEAD INN

Chelmarsh, Bridgnorth WV16 6BA
T: (01746) 861469
F: (01746) 862646
E: dave@bullshead.fsnet.co.uk
I: www.virtual-shropshire.co.uk/bulls-head-inn

B&B per night:
S £33.00–£46.00
D £48.00–£70.00

OPEN All Year except Christmas

17thC country inn offering excellent accommodation and country fare, approximately 4 miles from Bridgnorth. All bedrooms are en suite with tea/coffee-making facilities. Three ground floor bedrooms for people with disabilities. Choice of cottages/apartments for self-catering or bed and breakfast. Fishing parties welcome – lock-up store for tackle and bait.

Bedrooms: 1 single, 5 double/twin, 3 triple/multiple
Bathrooms: 9 en suite

Lunch available
Evening meal available
CC: Delta, Mastercard, Switch, Visa

Short breaks Nov-Feb, minimum 2 nights.

◆◆◆

THE CROFT HOTEL

St. Mary's Street, Bridgnorth WV16 4DW
T: (01746) 762416 & 767155
F: (01746) 767431
E: crofthotel@aol.com

Bedrooms: 3 single, 8 double/twin, 1 triple/multiple
Bathrooms: 10 en suite

CC: Amex, Delta, Mastercard, Switch, Visa

B&B per night:
S £25.00–£41.00
D £50.00–£70.00

OPEN All Year

Listed building with a wealth of oak beams, in an old street. Family run and an ideal centre for exploring the delightful Shropshire countryside.

BROADWAY, Worcestershire Map ref 2B1

THE BELL AT WILLERSEY

The Bell Inn, Willersey, Broadway WR12 7PJ
T: (01386) 858405
F: (01386) 853563
E: reservations@bellatwillersey.fsnet.co.uk
I: www.the-bell-willersey.com

B&B per night:
S £40.00–£70.00
D £55.00–£75.00

HB per person:
DY £37.50–£48.50

OPEN All Year

17thC inn overlooking the village green and duck pond. One mile from Broadway, a perfect location for touring. Enjoys a high reputation for home-produced food. Restaurant open lunchtime and evenings. Relax in our brand-new bedrooms situated in our courtyard.

Bedrooms: 3 double/twin, 2 triple/multiple; permanent suite(s)
Bathrooms: 5 en suite

Lunch available
Evening meal available
CC: Delta, Mastercard, Switch, Visa

HALF BOARD PRICES Half board prices are given per person, but in some cases these may be based on double/twin occupancy.

BROADWAY continued

♦♦♦♦♦
Gold Award

BURHILL FARM

Buckland, Broadway WR12 7LY
T: (01386) 858171
F: (01386) 858171
E: burhillfarm@yahoo.co.uk
I: www.burhillfarm.co.uk

B&B per night:
D £45.00–£60.00

OPEN All Year except Christmas

A warm welcome awaits guests at our mainly grass farm lying in the folds of the Cotswolds, just 2 miles south of Broadway. Both guest rooms are en suite and have TV and tea/coffee facilities. The Cotswold Way runs through the middle of the farm providing many lovely walks.

Bedrooms: 2 double/twin
Bathrooms: 2 en suite

5 P

♦♦♦

CROWN AND TRUMPET INN

Church Street, Broadway WR12 7AE
T: (01386) 853202
F: (01386) 834650
E: ascott@cotswoldholidays.co.uk
I: www.cotswoldholidays.co.uk

B&B per night:
D £50.00–£70.00

OPEN All Year

17thC Cotswold-stone inn in picturesque Broadway, gateway to the Cotswolds and an ideal touring base. Extensive menu of seasonal and local dishes, many homemade, and fine selection of traditional beers and seasonal drinks. Oak beams, log fires in winter. Special offers for off-season and extended stays – telephone for details.

Bedrooms: 5 double/twin
Bathrooms: 5 en suite

Lunch available
Evening meal available
CC: Delta, Mastercard, Switch, Visa

3-night stays available Oct-May (excl Christmas, New Year, Easter).

P

♦♦♦♦
Silver Award

LEASOW HOUSE

Laverton Meadow, Broadway WR12 7NA
T: (01386) 584526
F: (01386) 584596
E: leasow@clara.net
I: www.leasow.co.uk

B&B per night:
S £45.00–£55.00
D £55.00–£75.00

OPEN All Year except Christmas

Set in tranquil countryside close to Broadway. Leasow House is a 16thC farmhouse, ideally based for touring the Cotwolds and Shakespeare Country.

Bedrooms: 5 double/twin, 2 triple/multiple
Bathrooms: 7 en suite

CC: Amex, Mastercard, Visa

P

COUNTRY CODE Always follow the Country Code Enjoy the countryside and respect its life and work Guard against all risk of fire Fasten all gates Keep your dogs under close control Keep to public paths across farmland Use gates and stiles to cross fences, hedges and walls Leave livestock, crops and machinery alone Take your litter home Help to keep all water clean Protect wildlife, plants and trees Take special care on country roads Make no unnecessary noise

BROADWAY continued

Silver Award

SHEEPSCOMBE HOUSE

Snowshill, Broadway WR12 7JU
T: (01386) 853769
F: (01386) 853769
E: reservations@snowshill-broadway.co.uk
I: www.broadway-cotswolds.co.uk

Situated in the heart of the Cotswolds, Sheepscombe House is surrounded by beautiful countryside with spectacular views. Accommodation is warm and very comfortable. Good, fresh breakfast, ample parking, ideal touring base for Stratford-upon-Avon. Excellent walking (600 metres to Cotswold Way). Open all year except Christmas.

Bedrooms: 3 double/twin
Bathrooms: 1 en suite

Mid-week breaks: 4 nights for price of 3 for 2 people sharing room (excl July, Aug, Sept and Bank Holidays).

B&B per night:
D £60.00–£75.00

OPEN All Year except Christmas

SOUTHWOLD GUEST HOUSE

Station Road, Broadway WR12 7DE
T: (01386) 853681
F: (01386) 854610
E: sueandnick.southwold@talk21.com

Sue and Nick Smiles invite you to their spacious and tastefully decorated Edwardian house situated in one of the Cotswolds' most picturesque villages. We are 3 minutes' walk from pubs, restaurants and the Cotswolds Way. Well-appointed rooms available with en suites (single with private facilities), hospitality tray, colour TV, hairdryer. Guest lounge.

Bedrooms: 1 single, 6 double/twin, 1 triple/multiple
Bathrooms: 7 en suite, 1 private

CC: Mastercard, Switch, Visa

B&B per night:
S Min £30.00
D Min £50.00

OPEN All Year except Christmas

Silver Award

WHITEACRES

Station Road, Broadway WR12 7DE
T: (01386) 852320
F: (01386) 852674
E: whiteacres@btinternet.com

Bedrooms: 4 double/twin, 1 triple/multiple
Bathrooms: 5 en suite

This beautiful Edwardian property is decorated to a high standard and our aim is to provide a comfortable, happy base for a perfect holiday.

B&B per night:
S £33.00–£45.00
D £50.00–£65.00

OPEN All Year

♦♦♦♦
Silver Award

WINDRUSH HOUSE

Station Road, Broadway WR12 7DE
T: (01386) 853577 & 853790
F: (01386) 853790
E: richard@broadway-windrush.co.uk
I: www.broadway-windrush.co.uk

Bedrooms: 5 double/twin, 1 triple/multiple
Bathrooms: 6 en suite

An outstanding example of Edwardian elegance, located a few minutes' walk from the centre of Broadway. Spacious, relaxed and sophisticated surroundings combine with a homely and welcoming atmosphere.

B&B per night:
S £35.00–£50.00
D £55.00–£70.00

HB per person:
DY £50.00–£85.00

OPEN All Year

VISITOR ATTRACTIONS For ideas on places to visit refer to the introduction at the beginning of this section. Look out too for the ETC's Quality Assured Visitor Attraction signs.

BROMSGROVE, Worcestershire Map ref 4B3 *Tourist Information Centre Tel: (01527) 831809*

♦♦♦♦

BROMSGROVE COUNTRY HOTEL

249 Worcester Road, Stoke Heath, Bromsgrove B61 7JA
T: (01527) 835522
F: (01527) 871257
I: www.smoothhound.co.uk

Bedrooms: 6 double/twin, 3 triple/multiple
Bathrooms: 8 en suite, 1 private

CC: Delta, Mastercard, Switch, Visa

Quiet, elegant, Victorian residence with modern amenities. Close to M6/M42/M5 and historic countryside. A pleasant stay ensured under personal supervision of the proprietors.

B&B per night:
S £49.00
D £55.00

OPEN All Year except Christmas

♦♦♦♦

OVERWOOD BED AND BREAKFAST

Woodcote Lane, Woodcote, Bromsgrove B61 9EE
T: (01562) 777193
F: (01562) 777689
E: info@overwood.net
I: www.overwood.net

Whether on business or pleasure enjoy a relaxing visit to our charming, peaceful cottage set in 3 acres surrounded by farm and woodland. Ideal for touring the Midlands, just 5 miles from M5/M42. Excellent, well-equipped rooms with luxurious beds. Delicious breakfasts using our own free-range eggs. Evening meals by arrangement.

Bedrooms: 3 double/twin
Bathrooms: 2 en suite, 1 private

Lunch available
Evening meal available

Fri-Sun breaks: Apr-Oct 3 nights for the price of 2, Nov-Mar second night half price.

B&B per night:
S Min £30.00
D Min £50.00

OPEN All Year

BUCKMINSTER, Leicestershire Map ref 3A1

♦♦♦♦

THE TOLLEMACHE ARMS

Main Street, Buckminster, Grantham NG33 55A
T: (01476) 860252
F: (01476) 860731
E: info@tollemachearms.co.uk
I: www.tollemachearms.co.uk

Elegant, stone, 19thC coaching inn set in a beautiful countryside village. Excellent restaurant serving wide range of bar snacks plus exquisite a la carte menu. The accommodation comprises en suite rooms and separate residents' lounge. Dogs and horses welcome.

Bedrooms: 1 double/twin, 4 triple/multiple
Bathrooms: 5 en suite

Lunch available
Evening meal available
CC: Delta, Mastercard, Switch, Visa

Special rates for residents staying longer than 1 week.

B&B per night:
S Max £42.00
D Max £50.00

OPEN All Year

BURFORD

See South of England region for entries

AT-A-GLANCE SYMBOLS

Symbols at the end of each accommodation entry give useful information about services and facilities. A key to symbols can be found inside the back cover flap. Keep this open for easy reference.

BURTON DASSETT, Warwickshire Map ref 2C1

Silver Award

THE WHITE HOUSE BED AND BREAKFAST

Burton Dassett, Southam CV47 2AB
T: (01295) 770143 & 0476 458314
E: lisa@whitehouse10.freeserve.co.uk
I: www.thewhitehousebandb.info

B&B per night:
S £35.00–£40.00
D £45.00–£50.00

HB per person:
DY £40.00–£45.00

OPEN All Year

Former farmhouse set in a peaceful, rural location at the top of the Burton Dassett Hills enjoying magnificent views over Warwickshire/Oxfordshire countryside. High standard of accommodation, comfort and service. Homely and welcoming. Tasty, home-cooked breakfasts. Centrally located with easy access to Warwick, Stratford-upon-Avon, Cotswolds, Birmingham, NEC. Please telephone for brochure.

Bedrooms: 3 double/twin
Bathrooms: 3 en suite

BUXTON, Derbyshire Map ref 4B2 *Tourist Information Centre Tel: (01298) 25106*

Silver Award

BUXTON'S VICTORIAN GUESTHOUSE

3A Broad Walk, Buxton SK17 6JE
T: (01298) 78759 & 07801 861227
F: (01296) 74732
E: buxvic@tiscali.co.uk
I: www.smoothhound.co.uk

Bedrooms: 6 double/twin, 2 triple/multiple
Bathrooms: 8 en suite

CC: Delta, Mastercard, Switch, Visa

B&B per night:
S £35.00–£50.00
D £55.00–£75.00

OPEN All Year

Built in 1860, an elegant, Grade II Listed townhouse, recently refurbished in classical Victorian style. On a quiet, tree-lined promenade, overlooking 40-acre park and opera house.

FAIRHAVEN

1 Dale Terrace, Buxton SK17 6LU
T: (01298) 24481
F: (01298) 24481
E: paulandcatherine@fairhavenguesthouse.freeserve.co.uk

Bedrooms: 1 single, 4 double/twin, 1 triple/multiple
Bathrooms: 1 private

Evening meal available
CC: Amex, Delta, Mastercard, Switch, Visa

B&B per night:
S £17.50–£21.00
D £32.00–£37.00

OPEN All Year except Christmas

Within easy reach of the Opera House, Pavilion Gardens, 2 golf courses and the many and varied attractions of Derbyshire's Peak District.

SYMBOLS The symbols in each entry give information about services and facilities. A key to these symbols appears at the back of this guide.

BUXTON continued

Silver Award

GRENDON GUESTHOUSE

Bishops Lane, Buxton SK17 6UN
T: (01298) 78831 & 07711 380143
F: (01298) 79257
E: parkerh1@talk21.com
I: www.grendonguesthouse.co.uk

B&B per night:
S £25.00–£40.00
D £50.00–£70.00

HB per person:
DY £36.00–£46.00

OPEN All Year

Grendon is a beautiful, elegant family home with a stunning rural outlook yet close to Buxton's amenities. No expense spared to offer our guests a memorable visit in deluxe, exceedingly comfortable, spacious and hospitable surroundings. Superb 4-poster suite available.

Bedrooms: 1 single, 3 double/twin
Bathrooms: 3 en suite, 1 private

Evening meal available
CC: Delta, Mastercard, Switch, Visa

A complimentary dinner for longer mid-week stays low/mid season.

Silver Award

HAREFIELD

15 Marlborough Road, Buxton SK17 6RD
T: (01298) 24029
F: (01298) 24029
E: hardie@harefield1.freeserve.co.uk
I: www.harefield1.freeserve.co.uk

B&B per night:
S £23.00–£25.00
D £46.00–£54.00

OPEN All Year except Christmas

Elegant Victorian property set in its own grounds overlooking Buxton. Quiet location just a few minutes' walk from the historic town centre and an ideal base for exploring the beautiful Peak District. Spacious and comfortable accommodation with all bedrooms en suite. Friendly atmosphere, delicious food and lovely gardens to enjoy.

Bedrooms: 1 single, 5 double/twin
Bathrooms: 5 en suite, 1 private

Lunch available
Evening meal available

♦♦♦♦
Silver Award

KINGSCROFT

10 Green Lane, Buxton SK17 9DP
T: (01298) 22757 & 07889 977971
F: (01298) 27858

B&B per night:
S £25.00–£45.00
D £50.00–£60.00

OPEN All Year

Welcome to our Victorian luxury guesthouse. Central yet quiet location. Take a relaxing break in comfortable surroundings with period furnishings. Enjoy our hearty, delicious full English or vegetarian breakfasts. Fully licensed bar. All 8 rooms are en suite with TV/video and well-stocked hospitality tray. Private car park.

Bedrooms: 1 single, 7 double/twin
Bathrooms: 8 en suite

Evening meal available

10% discount on stays of 4 nights or more.

♦♦♦♦

LAKENHAM GUESTHOUSE
11 Burlington Road, Buxton
SK17 9AL
T: (01298) 79209

Bedrooms: 4 double/twin, 2 triple/multiple
Bathrooms: 5 en suite, 1 private

B&B per night:
D £60.00–£70.00

OPEN All Year

Elegant Victorian house in own grounds overlooking Pavilion Gardens. Furnished in Victorian manner and offering personal service in a friendly, relaxed atmosphere.

BUXTON continued

STADEN GRANGE COUNTRY HOUSE

Staden Lane, Staden, Buxton
SK17 9RZ
T: (01298) 24965
F: (01298) 72067
E: enquiries@stadengrange.co.uk
I: www.stadengrange.co.uk

Bedrooms: 4 double/twin
Bathrooms: 4 en suite

CC: Amex, Delta, Mastercard, Switch, Visa

B&B per night:
S £42.50
D £66.00–£85.00

OPEN All Year except Christmas

250-acre beef farm. Spacious residence 1.5 miles from Buxton, in a magnificent scenic area. Carefully extended, uninterrupted views over open farmland. Ground floor rooms available.

CASTLE DONINGTON, Leicestershire Map ref 4C3

Silver Award

CASTLETOWN HOUSE

4 High Street, Castle Donington,
Derby DE74 2PP
T: (01332) 812018 & 814550
F: (01332) 814550
E: enquiry@castletownhouse.fsnet.co.uk
I: www.castletownhouse.com

Bedrooms: 5 double/twin
Bathrooms: 5 en suite

CC: Delta, Mastercard, Switch, Visa

B&B per night:
S £35.00–£38.00
D £50.00–£55.00

OPEN All Year except Christmas

17thC Tudor wood-framed farmhouse in village centre, with wood beams in most rooms. Ample parking. All rooms very spacious. Disabled room available.

CASTLETON, Derbyshire Map ref 4B2

BARGATE COTTAGE

Bargate, Market Place, Castleton,
Hope Valley S33 8WG
T: (01433) 620201
F: (01433) 621739
E: fionasaxon@bargatecottage78.freeserve.co.uk
I: www.peakland.com/bargate

Bedrooms: 3 double/twin
Bathrooms: 3 en suite

B&B per night:
S Min £37.00
D Min £50.00

OPEN All Year except Christmas

Charming, warm, friendly 17thC cottage, quietly situated below Peveril Castle, in picturesque village. An ideal base to explore the many delights of the Peak District.

CHARLBURY

See South of England region for entries

CHARLTON-ON-OTMOOR

See South of England region for entries

CHELTENHAM, Gloucestershire Map ref 2B1 *Tourist Information Centre Tel: (01242) 522878*

IVYDENE GUEST HOUSE

145 Hewlett Road, Cheltenham
GL52 6TS
T: (01242) 521726
F: (01242) 525694
E: jvhopwood@ivydenehouse.freeserve.co.uk
I: www.ivydenehouse.freeserve.co.uk

Bedrooms: 3 single, 4 double/twin, 2 triple/multiple
Bathrooms: 5 en suite, 2 private

CC: Delta, Mastercard, Switch, Visa

B&B per night:
S £27.50–£35.00
D £55.00–£60.00

OPEN All Year except Christmas

A stylish, yet good value, Victorian house close to city centre. 'Themed' en suite rooms (e.g, Tuscan, Greek, Oriental). Hearty English breakfasts.

THE WYNYARDS

Butts Lane, Woodmancote,
Cheltenham GL52 9QH
T: (01242) 673876
E: graham@wynyards1.freeserve.co.uk
I: www.SmoothHound.co.uk/hotels/wynyards.html

Bedrooms: 3 double/twin
Bathrooms: 2 en suite, 1 private

B&B per night:
S £25.00
D £40.00

OPEN All Year except Christmas

Secluded old Cotswold-stone house in elevated position with panoramic views. Set in open countryside on outskirts of small village, 4 miles from Cheltenham.

CHESTERFIELD, Derbyshire Map ref 4B2 *Tourist Information Centre Tel: (01246) 345777*

◆◆◆

ABIGAILS

62 Brockwell Lane, Chesterfield
S40 4EE
T: (01246) 279391 & 07970 777909
F: (01246) 854468
E: gail@abigails.fsnet.co.uk
I: www.abigailsguesthouse.co.uk

Bedrooms: 2 single, 5 double/twin
Bathrooms: 7 en suite

Relax taking breakfast in the conservatory overlooking Chesterfield and surrounding moorlands. Garden with pond and waterfall, private car park. Best B&B winners 2000.

B&B per night:
S £28.00
D £42.00

OPEN All Year

◆◆◆

CLARENDON GUESTHOUSE

32 Clarence Road, West Bars,
Chesterfield S40 1LN
T: (01246) 235004

Bedrooms: 2 single, 3 double/twin
Bathrooms: 4 en suite

Evening meal available

Victorian town residence, near town centre, cricket ground, leisure facilities and Peak District National Park. Special diets catered for. Overnight laundry service.

B&B per night:
S £16.00–£21.00
D £34.00–£36.00

HB per person:
DY £21.50–£28.00

OPEN All Year

◆◆◆

ROSE COTTAGE GUEST HOUSE

Derby Road, Old Tupton,
Chesterfield S42 6LA
T: (01246) 864949
F: (01246) 864949
E: bookings@rosecottagetupton.freeserve.co.uk
I: www.rosecottage-tupton.co.uk

Bedrooms: 3 double/twin
Bathrooms: 2 en suite, 1 private

Stone-built cottage with cottage garden. Traditional pine-furnished en suite bedrooms and comfortable lounge. Close to Peak District, Chatsworth and Chesterfield. Ample parking.

B&B per night:
S Min £28.00
D Min £45.00

OPEN All Year except Christmas

CHIPPING CAMPDEN, Gloucestershire Map ref 2B1

◆◆◆

THE EIGHT BELLS

Church Street, Chipping Campden
GL55 6JG
T: (01386) 840371
F: (01386) 841669
I: www.eightbellsinn.co.uk

An unspoilt 14thC Cotswold inn featuring open fires in winter and candlelit tables all year round. In addition there is a sun-drenched courtyard and terraced beer garden which overlooks the church. All accommodation is en suite, food is of the very highest standard and a friendly but informal welcome awaits you.

Bedrooms: 3 double/twin, 1 triple/multiple
Bathrooms: 4 en suite

Lunch available
Evening meal available
CC: Delta, Mastercard, Switch, Visa

Oct-Mar: 3 nights for the price of 2 (Sun-Thu).

B&B per night:
S Min £40.00
D Min £70.00

OPEN All Year

QUALITY ASSURANCE SCHEME

For an explanation of the quality and facilities represented by the Diamonds please refer to the front of this guide. A more detailed explanation can be found in the information pages at the back.

CHIPPING CAMPDEN continued

♦♦♦♦ Gold Award

M'DINA COURTYARD

Park Road, Chipping Campden GL55 6EA
T: (01386) 841752
F: (01386) 840942
E: barbara@mdina-bandb.co.uk
I: www.mdina-bandb.co.uk

Character Cotswold-stone house, apartment and 250-year-old cottage, in idyllic courtyard setting. Located at the quieter end of Chipping Campden's historic High Street. Extensive breakfast menu using local produce wherever possible. All rooms en suite with colour TV, hairdryer, tea/coffee facilities and much more. Off-road parking.

Bedrooms: 2 double/twin, 1 triple/multiple; permanent suite(s)
Bathrooms: 3 en suite

B&B per night:
S £47.00–£57.00
D £60.00–£75.00

OPEN All Year except Christmas

♦♦♦

THE MALINS
21 Station Road, Blockley, Moreton-in-Marsh GL56 9ED
T: (01386) 700402
F: (01386) 700402
E: johnmalin@btinternet.com
I: www.chippingcampden.co.uk/themalins.htm

Bedrooms: 3 double/twin
Bathrooms: 3 en suite

Beautifully presented Cotswold-stone house on edge of delightful village. Ideal base for touring Cotswolds and Shakespeare country. Tastefully decorated, comfortable, non-smoking accommodation. A warm welcome awaits.

B&B per night:
S Max £32.00
D Max £45.00

OPEN All Year

♦♦♦♦

MANOR FARM

Weston Subedge, Chipping Campden GL55 6QH
T: (01386) 840390 & 07889 108812
F: 08701 640 638
E: lucy@manorfarmbnb.demon.co.uk
I: www.manorfarmbnb.demon.co.uk

A warm, friendly welcome and a hearty full English breakfast are assured for all guests at Manor Farm, a traditional 17thC Cotswold-stone, oak-beamed farmhouse. Excellent base for exploring the Cotswolds and Shakespeare country from our 800-acre working farm. Superb choice of eating houses. 1.5 miles from Chipping Campden.

Bedrooms: 3 double/twin
Bathrooms: 3 en suite

Reductions for stays of 4 nights or more.

B&B per night:
S £35.00–£50.00
D £45.00–£50.00

OPEN All Year

USE YOUR *i*s

There are more than 550 Tourist Information Centres throughout England offering friendly help with accommodation and holiday ideas as well as suggestions of places to visit and things to do. You'll find TIC addresses in the local Phone Book.

CHIPPING CAMPDEN continued

◆◆◆◆ Gold Award

NINEVEH FARM

Campden Road, Mickleton,
Chipping Campden GL55 6PS
T: (01386) 438923
E: stay@ninevehfarm.co.uk
I: www.ninevehfarm.co.uk

18thC farmhouse with oak beams, flagstone floors and a warm welcome. Gardens of 1.5 acres in open countryside just 0.25 miles from village pubs. Ideal for exploring Cotswolds, Stratford-upon-Avon and Warwick. Cream teas and free loan of cycles.

Bedrooms: 4 double/twin, 1 triple/multiple
Bathrooms: 5 en suite

CC: Amex, Delta, Mastercard, Switch, Visa

Details of short breaks on request.

B&B per night:
D £55.00–£60.00

OPEN All Year

CHIPPING NORTON

See South of England region for entries

CHURCH STRETTON, Shropshire Map ref 4A3

◆◆◆◆

BELVEDERE GUEST HOUSE
Burway Road, Church Stretton
SY6 6DP
T: (01694) 722232
F: (01694) 722232
E: belv@bigfoot.com
I: www.belvedereguesthouse.btinternet.co.uk

Bedrooms: 3 single, 5 double/twin, 4 triple/multiple
Bathrooms: 6 en suite

CC: Delta, Mastercard, Switch, Visa

B&B per night:
S £26.00–£34.00
D £52.00–£58.00

OPEN All Year except Christmas

Quiet detached house set in its own grounds, convenient for Church Stretton town centre and Longmynd Hills. Adequate parking.

◆◆◆◆

SAYANG HOUSE

Hope Bowdler, Church Stretton SY6 7DD
T: (01694) 723981
E: madegan@aol.com
I: www.sayanghouse.com

Comfortable house set in 1 acre of landscaped gardens amongst the Shropshire hills 0.5 miles from Church Stretton. Wonderful walking from the door. Within easy access to Ludlow. All rooms en suite with tea/coffee facilities and TV. Homemade meals, fully licensed, guests' own sitting room. Self-catering also available.

Bedrooms: 1 double/twin, 2 triple/multiple
Bathrooms: 3 en suite

Lunch available
Evening meal available

Out-of-season special offers. Reductions for 3-day stays.

B&B per night:
S £27.50–£30.00
D £50.00–£55.00

HB per person:
DY £37.50–£45.00

OPEN All Year except Christmas

TOWN INDEX

This can be found at the back of the guide. If you know where you want to stay, the index will give you the page number listing accommodation in your chosen town, city or village.

CHURCHAM, Gloucestershire Map ref 2B1

THE PINETUM LODGE

Churcham, Gloucester GL2 8AD
T: (01452) 750554
F: (01452) 750402
E: pinetum1@aol.com
I: www.pinetumlodge.ik.com

B&B per night:
S £25.00–£30.00
D £50.00–£60.00

HB per person:
DY £42.50–£47.50

OPEN All Year

Intriguing Victorian hunting lodge in magical setting. 13 acres of beautiful woodland garden planted by Thomas Gambier Parry in 1844. Only 4 miles west of Gloucester. Views across rolling Cotswold hills and Severn Vale. Daffodils, bluebells, nightingales in spring. Easy walks. Haven for wildlife. Heated outdoor pool in the summer.

Bedrooms: 1 single, 2 double/twin
Bathrooms: 2 en suite, 1 private

CC: Mastercard, Visa

Third and fourth night less 10%.

CIRENCESTER, Gloucestershire Map ref 2B1 *Tourist Information Centre Tel: (01285) 654180*

♦♦♦♦ Silver Award

SMERRILL BARNS

Kemble, Cirencester GL7 6BW
T: (01285) 770907
F: (01285) 770706
E: gsopher@smerrillbarns.com
I: www.smerrillbarns.com

B&B per night:
S £45.00–£55.00
D £55.00–£70.00

OPEN All Year except Christmas

Enjoy a friendly welcome at Smerrill Barns, a wonderful old barn dating from the 1700s and sympathetically converted in 1992. The bedroooms are comfortable and well equipped and there is a light and spacious sitting room in which to relax. Breakfasts are excellent and vegetarians are well catered for.

Bedrooms: 6 double/twin, 1 triple/multiple
Bathrooms: 7 en suite

CC: Delta, Mastercard, Switch, Visa

♦♦

THE WHITE LION INN

8 Gloucester Street, Cirencester GL7 2DG
T: (01285) 654053
F: (01285) 641316
E: roylion@aol.com
I: www.white-lion-cirencester.co.uk

Bedrooms: 3 single, 4 double/twin
Bathrooms: 7 en suite

Lunch available
Evening meal available
CC: Amex, Delta, Mastercard, Switch, Visa

B&B per night:
S £39.50–£50.00
D £50.00–£65.00

OPEN All Year

A 17thC coaching inn behind 14thC church in a quiet street.

CLEOBURY MORTIMER, Shropshire Map ref 4A3

♦♦♦♦

THE OLD BAKE HOUSE

46/47 High Street, Cleobury Mortimer, Kidderminster DY14 8DQ
T: (01299) 270193
E: oldbakehouse@amserve.net
I: www.cleobury-mortimer.co.uk

Bedrooms: 2 double/twin
Bathrooms: 2 en suite

Evening meal available

B&B per night:
S £25.00–£27.00
D £50.00–£54.00

HB per person:
DY Min £30.00

OPEN All Year

Grade II Listed townhouse, formerly both a public house and bakery, with 18thC frontage. Home cooking. Vegetarians welcome, special diets by arrangement.

CHECK THE MAPS

The colour maps at the front of this guide show all the cities, towns and villages for which you will find accommodation entries.
Refer to the town index to find the page on which they are listed.

COLEFORD, Gloucestershire Map ref 2A1 *Tourist Information Centre Tel: (01594) 812388*

♦♦♦

GRAYGILL
Duke of York Road, Staunton, Coleford GL16 8PD
T: (01600) 712536 & 07769 738961
E: barbara.bond@ukonline.co.uk

Bedrooms: 2 double/twin
Bathrooms: 2 en suite

Secluded family house set in 11 acres of pasture adjoining forestry, offering en suite bed and breakfast accommodation. Ideal for walking, cycling and touring.

B&B per night:
S Min £19.50
D Min £39.00

OPEN All Year except Christmas

CORBY, Northamptonshire Map ref 3A1 *Tourist Information Centre Tel: (01536) 407507*

♦♦♦♦

MOAT COTTAGE

18 Little Oakley, Corby NN18 8HA
T: (01536) 745013
F: (01536) 745013
E: enquiries@moat-cottage.fsbusiness.co.uk
I: www.moat-cottage.fsbusiness.co.uk

16thC beamed, thatched cottage in the centre of a quiet conservation village in the heart of rural Northamptonshire, yet only 4 miles from Rockingham speedway. Two private suites with own seating area in beautiful south-facing garden. Locally sourced organic produce used wherever possible, regional British dishes our speciality.

Bedrooms: 2 double/twin
Bathrooms: 2 en suite

Weekly breaks: self-catering in the Lavender Barn, sleeps 2, en suite shower, own kitchen/sitting room. £150 low season, £250 high season.

B&B per night:
S £35.00–£40.00
D £45.00–£50.00

OPEN All Year except Christmas

WHITE SWAN
Seaton Road, Harringworth, Corby NN17 3AF
T: (01572) 747543
F: (01572) 747323
E: thewhite-swan@fsmail.net
I: www.thewhite-swan.com

Bedrooms: 1 single, 5 double/twin
Bathrooms: 6 en suite

Lunch available
Evening meal available
CC: Amex, Delta, Diners, Mastercard, Switch, Visa

15thC coaching inn offering en suite accommodation, in the delightful village of Harringworth, close to many historic sites. Home-cooked food and real ales.

B&B per night:
S £40.00
D £60.00

OPEN All Year

COTSWOLDS

See under Alderton, Bibury, Birdlip, Bourton-on-the-Water, Broadway, Cheltenham, Chipping Campden, Cirencester, Cowley, Donnington, Fairford, Gloucester, Great Rissington, Lechlade, Mickleton, Moreton-in-Marsh, Nailsworth, Naunton, Northleach, Painswick, Stonehouse, Stow-on-the-Wold, Stroud, Tetbury, Tewkesbury

See also Cotswolds in South of England region

COUGHTON, Herefordshire Map ref 2A1

COUGHTON HOUSE
Coughton, Ross-on-Wye HR9 5SF
T: (01989) 562612
E: jenny.balchin@bigwig.net

Bedrooms: 3 double/twin
Bathrooms: 1 en suite, 1 private

A large Georgian country house within its own walled gardens situated 1.5 miles from the historic market town of Ross-on- Wye. Rolling hills offer beautiful walks, views over 8 or more counties and exceptional wildlife.

B&B per night:
S £30.00–£34.00
D £44.00–£48.00

OPEN All Year except Christmas

SPECIAL BREAKS

Many establishments offer special promotions and themed breaks. These are highlighted in red. (All such offers are subject to availability.)

COVENTRY, West Midlands Map ref 4B3

◆◆◆

ABIGAIL GUESTHOUSE
39 St. Patrick's Road, Coventry
CV1 2LP
T: (024) 7622 1378
F: (024) 7622 1378
E: ag002a@netgates.co.uk
I: www.abigailuk.com

Bedrooms: 3 single, 2 double/twin, 1 triple/multiple

Family-run establishment in centre of city, very clean and friendly. Convenient for station, cathedral and city centre shopping, also NEC and NAC.

P

B&B per night:
S £20.00–£25.00
D £40.00–£45.00

OPEN All Year except Christmas

◆◆◆

ASHDOWNS GUEST HOUSE

12 Regent Street, Earlsdon, Coventry
CV1 3EP
T: (024) 7622 9280

Family-run guesthouse offering quality accommodation. Convenient for city centre, rail and bus services, NEC, NAC, university and Birmingham International Airport. A warm welcome awaits you in this relaxed, non-smoking family home. Private car park at rear.

Bedrooms: 2 single, 5 double/twin, 1 triple/multiple
Bathrooms: 7 en suite

Long-stay and short-break offers, weddings and parties.

5 P

B&B per night:
S £25.00–£36.00
D £42.00–£45.00

HB per person:
DY £45.00–£50.00

OPEN All Year

◆◆◆

ASHLEIGH HOUSE
17 Park Road, Coventry CV1 2LH
T: (024) 7622 3804
F: (024) 76223804

Bedrooms: 5 single, 5 triple/multiple
Bathrooms: 10 en suite

Recently renovated guesthouse only 100 yards from the railway station. All city amenities within 5 minutes' walk. Licensed, evening meals.

P

B&B per night:
S £25.00–£27.50
D £40.00–£46.00

OPEN All Year

◆◆◆◆◆
Silver Award

BARNACLE HALL

Shilton Lane, Shilton, Coventry CV7 9LH
T: (024) 76612629

A beautifully restored 16thC farmhouse offering accommodation of the very highest order. The bedrooms are spacious, tastefully decorated and very comfortable. Surrounded by an attractive garden, the house is set in a rural location but with easy access to the motorway network, the NEC, Coventry and mid-Warwickshire.

Bedrooms: 3 double/twin
Bathrooms: 2 en suite, 1 private

P

B&B per night:
S £30.00–£33.00
D £47.00–£52.00

OPEN All Year except Christmas

◆◆◆◆

BROOKFIELDS
134 Butt Lane, Allesley, Coventry
CV5 9FE
T: (024) 7640 4866
F: (024) 7640 2022

Bedrooms: 2 single, 2 double/twin
Bathrooms: 4 en suite

Small, friendly guesthouse offering quality accommodation and service. Convenient city centre, National Exhibition Centre, Birmingham International Airport, Jaguar Cars/museum, NAC Stoneleigh. Ample parking.

5 P

B&B per night:
S £30.00–£35.00
D £55.00–£60.00

OPEN All Year

COVENTRY continued

◆◆◆

CHESTER HOUSE
3 Chester Street, Coventry CV1 4DH
T: (024) 7622 3857

Bedrooms: 1 single, 3 double/twin, 2 triple/multiple
Bathrooms: 1 en suite

B&B per night:
S £18.00–£30.00
D £36.00–£45.00

OPEN All Year except Christmas

Large white stone house with double bays, the first house off the main Holyhead road.

◆◆

HIGHCROFT GUEST HOUSE
65 Barras Lane, Coundon, Coventry CV1 4AQ
T: (024) 7622 8157
F: (024) 7663 1609
E: deepak8@btopenworld.com

Bedrooms: 2 single, 4 double/twin, 1 triple/multiple
Bathrooms: 3 en suite

B&B per night:
S £18.00–£20.00
D £32.00

OPEN All Year

Large detached guesthouse close to the city centre. A family-run business that endeavours to make guests feel at home. Discounts available.

COWLEY, Gloucestershire Map ref 2B1

Rating Applied For

BUTLERS HILL FARM
Cockleford, Cowley, Cheltenham GL53 9NW
T: (01242) 870455
F: (01242) 870455
E: butlershill@aol.com

Bedrooms: 2 double/twin
Bathrooms: 2 private

B&B per night:
S £20.00–£25.00
D £20.00–£25.00

HB per person:
DY £35.00–£40.00

150-acre mixed farm. A spacious, modern farmhouse in a quiet, unspoilt river valley with attractive walks.

10

DEDDINGTON

See South of England region for entries

DERBY, Derbyshire Map ref 4B2 *Tourist Information Centre Tel: (01332) 255802*

◆◆◆◆

BONEHILL FARM

Etwall Road, Mickleover, Derby DE3 5DN
T: (01332) 513553
E: bonehillfarm@hotmail.com

B&B per night:
S £22.00–£25.00
D £40.00–£48.00

OPEN All Year except Christmas

A 120-acre mixed farm. Comfortable Georgian farmhouse in rural setting, 3 miles from Derby. Alton Towers, Peak District, historic houses and The Potteries within easy reach. Peaceful location.

Bedrooms: 2 double/twin, 1 triple/multiple
Bathrooms: 2 en suite

DONNINGTON, Gloucestershire Map ref 2B1

◆◆

HOLMLEIGH
Donnington, Moreton-in-Marsh GL56 0XX
T: (01451) 830792

Bedrooms: 1 double/twin
Bathrooms: 1 private

CC: Visa

B&B per night:
S £14.50–£15.00
D £29.00–£30.00

15-acre dairy farm. Farmhouse with friendly welcome. In a peaceful setting with own private lane from the village of Donnington, 1 mile from Stow-on-the-Wold. Safe car parking.

5

MAP REFERENCES The map references refer to the colour maps at the front of this guide. The first figure is the map number; the letter and figure which follow indicate the grid reference on the map.

DROITWICH, Worcestershire Map ref 2B1 *Tourist Information Centre Tel: (01905) 774312*

◆◆

RICHMOND GUEST HOUSE

3 Ombersley St. West, Droitwich
WR9 8HZ
T: (01905) 775722
F: (01905) 794642
I: www.infotel.co.uk/hotels/36340.htm

Bedrooms: 6 single, 2 double/twin, 4 triple/multiple

B&B per night:
S £22.00–£24.00
D £36.00–£38.00

OPEN All Year except Christmas

Homely Victorian guesthouse in the town centre, 5 minutes from the railway station/bus routes. Thirty minutes from the NEC via M5/M42. Full English breakfast.

ECKINGTON, Worcestershire Map ref 2B1

◆◆◆

THE ANCHOR INN AND RESTAURANT

Cotheridge Lane, Eckington,
Pershore WR10 3BA
T: (01386) 750356
F: (01386) 750356
E: anchoreck@aol.com
I: www.anchoreckington.co.uk

Bedrooms: 5 double/twin
Bathrooms: 5 en suite

Lunch available
Evening meal available
CC: Mastercard, Visa

B&B per night:
S £35.00–£45.00
D £45.00–£55.00

OPEN All Year

Traditional village inn off the main road, comfortable lounge, separate restaurant. Chef-prepared cuisine. Central for Worcester, Evesham, Cheltenham and Tewkesbury.

ELTON, Derbyshire Map ref 4B2

Silver Award

HAWTHORN COTTAGE

Well Street, Elton, Matlock DE4 2BY
T: (01629) 650372
I: www.hawthorncottage-elton.co.uk

B&B per night:
D £48.00

OPEN All Year

Delightful 17thC farm cottage in conservation village offering a luxurious ground floor private suite comprising double en suite bedroom and lounge/dining room. Secluded, sunny patios and garden with unrivalled views over miles of open countryside. Hearty breakfasts and a warm welcome assured. Ten minutes from Chatsworth and Haddon Hall.

Bedrooms: 1 double/twin; permanent suite(s)
Bathrooms: 1 en suite

10% reduction on visits of 5 nights or more.

HOMESTEAD FARM

Main Street, Elton, Matlock
DE4 2BW
T: (01629) 650359

Bedrooms: 1 double/twin
Bathrooms: 1 private

Evening meal available

B&B per night:
S £18.00–£20.00
D £36.00–£40.00

HB per person:
DY £25.00–£27.00

OPEN All Year

Homely farmhouse B&B. En suite bathroom, private toilet, colour TV, private dining/lounge. Well-behaved pets welcome. We aim for value for money.

FAIRFORD, Gloucestershire Map ref 2B1

MILTON FARM

Fairford GL7 4HZ
T: (01285) 712205
F: (01285) 711349
E: milton@farmersweekly.net
I: www.milton-farm.co.uk

Bedrooms: 2 double/twin, 1 triple/multiple
Bathrooms: 3 en suite

B&B per night:
S £25.00–£30.00
D £40.00–£50.00

OPEN All Year except Christmas

Impressive Georgian farmhouse with large, en suite bedrooms and comfortable guest lounge. Pleasant outlook on edge of most attractive Cotswold market town.

PRICES
Please check prices and other details at the time of booking.

FAIRFORD continued

◆◆

WAITEN HILL FARM
Fairford GL7 4JG
T: (01285) 712652
F: (01285) 712652

Bedrooms: 3 double/twin
Bathrooms: 2 en suite

350-acre mixed farm. Imposing 19thC farmhouse, overlooking River Coln, old mill and famous church. Short walk to shops, pubs, restaurants. Ideal for touring Cotswolds and water parks.

B&B per night:
S £20.00–£25.00
D £35.00–£40.00

OPEN All Year

FOREST OF DEAN

See under Coleford

GAINSBOROUGH, Lincolnshire Map ref 4C2

◆◆◆

THE BECKETT ARMS
25 High Street, Corringham, Gainsborough DN21 5QP
T: (01427) 838201

Bedrooms: 1 double/twin, 3 triple/multiple
Bathrooms: 4 en suite

Lunch available
Evening meal available
CC: Delta, Mastercard, Switch, Visa

Warm, welcoming country pub with good facilities close to Lincoln, Hemswell, Gainsborough, Scunthorpe. Ideal centre for walkers, bikers, tourists etc.

B&B per night:
S £25.00–£27.50
D £40.00–£45.00

OPEN All Year

GLOSSOP, Derbyshire Map ref 4B2 *Tourist Information Centre Tel: (01457) 855920*

◆◆◆

PEELS ARMS
6-12 Temple Street, Padfield, Glossop SK13 1EX
T: (01457) 852719
F: (01457) 860536
E: robert.astle@btopenworld.com

Bedrooms: 4 double/twin
Bathrooms: 1 en suite

Lunch available
Evening meal available
CC: Delta, Mastercard, Switch, Visa

Traditional 19thC country inn with log fires and oak beams. Hand-poured ales, fine food and a warm welcome await you.

B&B per night:
S £25.00–£35.00
D £40.00–£50.00

OPEN All Year

GLOUCESTER, Gloucestershire Map ref 2B1

BROOKTHORPE LODGE

Stroud Road, Brookthorpe, Gloucester GL4 0UQ
T: (01452) 812645
F: (01452) 812645
E: enq@brookthorpelodge.demon.co.uk
I: www.brookthorpelodge.demon.co.uk

Licensed, family-run, spacious and comfortable Georgian detached house on the outskirts of Gloucester (3.5 miles). Set in lovely countryside at the foot of the Cotswold escarpment. Close to ski-slope and golfing facilities. Excellent walking country. Ideal base for visiting the Cotswolds, Cheltenham, Bath and nearby WWT reserve at Slimbridge.

Bedrooms: 3 single, 5 double/twin, 2 triple/multiple
Bathrooms: 6 en suite

Evening meal available
CC: Delta, Mastercard, Switch, Visa

Special discounts on 3-day weekend and 5-day, mid-week breaks.

B&B per night:
S £23.50–£35.00
D £45.00–£55.00

HB per person:
DY £35.00–£45.00

OPEN All Year

◆

GEORGIAN GUEST HOUSE
85 Bristol Road, Gloucester GL1 5SN
T: (01452) 413286
F: (01452) 413286

Bedrooms: 2 single, 3 double/twin, 4 triple/multiple
Bathrooms: 5 en suite

On the main Bristol Road, 20 minutes' walk from Gloucester city centre.

B&B per night:
S £15.00
D £33.00

OPEN All Year

IMPORTANT NOTE Information on accommodation listed in this guide has been supplied by the proprietors. As changes may occur you are advised to check details at the time of booking.

GLOUCESTER continued

♦♦♦♦

All ground floor quality rural accommodation, within a conservation area. Colour TV, tea tray, radio in all bedrooms. Most are en suite. Grade II Listed Chartist smallholding (c1848) keeping free-range hens which provide excellent eggs for breakfast. Ample parking. Ideally situated for walking countryside or touring Cotswolds, Forest of Dean, Malvern Hills.

KILMORIE SMALL HOLDING

Gloucester Road, Corse, Snigs End, Staunton, Gloucester GL19 3RQ
T: (01452) 840224
F: (01452) 840224
E: sheila-barnfield@supanet.com
I: www.SmoothHound.co.uk/hotels/kilmorie.html

Bedrooms: 1 single, 3 double/twin, 1 triple/multiple
Bathrooms: 3 en suite, 2 private

Lunch available
Evening meal available

Reduced rates on stays of 4 nights, further reduced on stays of 7 nights, reduced rates children 5-12 years.

B&B per night:
S £20.00–£25.00
D Min £38.00

HB per person:
DY Min £27.00

♦♦♦

Licensed, family-run detached house, close to ski-slope and golfing facilities. Ideal base for Cotswolds, Gloucester Docks and cathedral. Near south and north M5 junctions. All bedrooms are attractively decorated. You have the choice of en suite rooms or rooms with showers. Come as guests, leave as friends.

PEMBURY GUEST HOUSE

9 Pembury Road, St. Barnabas, Gloucester GL4 6UE
T: (01452) 521856
F: (01452) 303418

Bedrooms: 1 single, 7 double/twin, 2 triple/multiple
Bathrooms: 6 en suite

Evening meal available
CC: Delta, Mastercard, Switch, Visa

B&B per night:
S £22.00–£30.00
D £38.00–£44.00

OPEN All Year

GREAT DALBY, Leicestershire Map ref 4C3

♦♦♦

A warm welcome awaits in our working dairy farm 3 miles south of Melton Mowbray, 7 miles from Oakham and Rutland Water, 40 minutes from Leicester and Nottingham. Brilliant walks and bridle rides close by – bring your own horse or hire. Good pub food in the village.

DAIRY FARM

8 Burrough End, Great Dalby, Melton Mowbray LE14 2EW
T: (01664) 562783

Bedrooms: 3 double/twin; permanent suite(s)
Bathrooms: 2 en suite, 1 private

Cheaper rates for long stays available.

B&B per night:
S £20.00–£22.00
D £36.00–£40.00

OPEN All Year

GREAT RISSINGTON, Gloucestershire Map ref 2B1

STEPPING STONE

Rectory Lane, Great Rissington, Cheltenham GL54 2LL
T: (01451) 821385
E: stepping-stone-b-b@excite.com

B&B per night:
S £27.50–£35.00
D £55.00–£70.00

OPEN All Year except Christmas

Set in large garden at the edge of a picturesque village, providing quiet and comfortable accommodation for B&B and longer stays (two self-contained doubles). Located 3 miles from Bourton-on-the-Water and just 200 metres from The Lamb restaurant and bar. Open all year.

Bedrooms: 1 single, 4 double/twin; permanent suite(s)
Bathrooms: 3 en suite, 2 private

CC: Delta, Mastercard, Visa

Special offers: 10% off for stays of 3 nights or more mid-week. Winter specials Nov-1 Mar: 3 nights for the price of 2.

12 P

HAGWORTHINGHAM, Lincolnshire Map ref 4D2

Silver Award

WHITE OAK GRANGE

Hagworthingham, Spilsby PE23 4LX
T: (01507) 588376
F: (01507) 588377
I: whiteoakgrange.com

B&B per night:
S £25.00–£30.00
D £50.00–£55.00

HB per person:
DY £40.00–£45.00

OPEN All Year

A fine country house standing in landscaped gardens enjoying spectacular views over the beautiful Lincolnshire Wolds. Open log fires and generous hospitality ensure a warm welcome for every guest. Home cooking is a speciality using fresh garden vegetables and local produce. Private trout fishing available. Wonderful walks through Tennyson country.

Bedrooms: 3 double/twin
Bathrooms: 3 en suite

Lunch available
Evening meal available

10% discount for 4 nights or more.

10 P

HANDSACRE, Staffordshire Map ref 4B3

THE OLDE PECULIAR

The Green, Handsacre, Rugeley WS15 4DP
T: (01543) 491891
F: (01543) 493733

Bedrooms: 2 double/twin
Bathrooms: 2 en suite

Lunch available
Evening meal available
CC: Mastercard, Switch, Visa

B&B per night:
S £29.50
D £42.00

OPEN All Year

A traditional village pub serving real ales and homemade food. Situated 4 miles from Lichfield city centre on the A513.

P

CHECK THE MAPS

The colour maps at the front of this guide show all the cities, towns and villages for which you will find accommodation entries. Refer to the town index to find the page on which they are listed.

HATHERSAGE, Derbyshire Map ref 4B2

♦♦♦♦ Silver Award

THE PLOUGH INN

Leadmill Bridge, Hathersage, Hope Valley
S32 1BA
T: (01433) 650319 & 650180
F: (01433) 651049

B&B per night:
S £49.50
D £69.50–£99.50

OPEN All Year except Christmas

17thC stone-built inn, formerly a farmhouse, standing in 9 acres of land bounded by the River Derwent. Situated in the Peak District National Park, an ideal base for visiting the stately homes of Chatsworth House and Haddon Hall. The inn is noted for its excellent food and warm atmosphere.

Bedrooms: 6 double/twin; permanent suite(s)
Bathrooms: 6 en suite

Lunch available
Evening meal available
CC: Delta, Mastercard, Switch, Visa

3 nights for the price of 2, Oct-Mar (excl Christmas and New Year).

HAY ON WYE, Herefordshire Map ref 2A1

♦♦♦♦

HAIE BARN VEGETARIAN B&B
The Bage, Dorstone, Hereford
HR3 5SU
T: (01497) 831729
E: goodfood@haie-barn.co.uk
I: www.golden-valley.co.uk/haiebarn

Bedrooms: 3 double/twin
Bathrooms: 1 en suite

Evening meal available

B&B per night:
S £25.00–£30.00
D £38.00–£48.00

Relax in our adults-only, converted barn on edge of small hamlet. Savour the flavours of Herefordshire in our sumptuous vegetarian breakfasts. Four and a half miles from Hay-on-Wye.

HEREFORD, Herefordshire Map ref 2A1 *Tourist Information Centre Tel: (01432) 268430*

♦♦♦♦

THE BOWENS COUNTRY HOUSE

Fownhope, Hereford HRI 4PS
T: (01432) 860430
F: (01432) 860430
E: Thebowenshotel@AOL.com
I: www.Thebowenshotel.co.uk

B&B per night:
S £32.50
D £50.00–£65.00

HB per person:
DY £47.50–£50.00

OPEN All Year

Delightful Georgian house set in peaceful Wye Valley village, midway Hereford and Ross-on-Wye (B4224). Well-appointed, en suite rooms (including ground floor, single and family rooms). All home-cooked meals using local produce. Vegetarians welcome. Fully licensed bar, good wine list. Large garden, putting green and grass tennis court (summer only).

Bedrooms: 2 single, 6 double/twin, 2 triple/multiple
Bathrooms: 10 en suite

Lunch available
Evening meal available
CC: Delta, Mastercard, Switch, Visa

DB&B short breaks available all year.

COUNTRY CODE Always follow the Country Code · Enjoy the countryside and respect its life and work · Guard against all risk of fire · Fasten all gates · Keep your dogs under close control · Keep to public paths across farmland · Use gates and stiles to cross fences, hedges and walls · Leave livestock, crops and machinery alone · Take your litter home · Help to keep all water clean · Protect wildlife, plants and trees · Take special care on country roads · Make no unnecessary noise

HEREFORD continued

CEDAR GUEST HOUSE

123 Whitecross Road, Whitecross, Hereford HR4 0LS
T: (01432) 267235
F: (01432) 267235
E: info@cedarguesthouse.com
I: www.cedarguesthouse.com

Former Victorian gentleman's residence, retaining many of the original features. Family run, offering spacious accommodation, within easy walking distance of Hereford's historic city centre. Situated on major tourist route, also close to the excellent coarse angling on River Wye.

Bedrooms: 3 double/twin, 3 triple/multiple
Bathrooms: 3 en suite

Evening meal available
CC: Delta, Mastercard, Switch, Visa

B&B per night:
S £26.00–£36.00
D £39.00–£46.00

HB per person:
DY £32.00–£47.00

OPEN All Year

♦♦♦♦
Gold Award

FELTON HOUSE

Felton, Hereford HR1 3PH
T: (01432) 820366
F: (01432) 820366
E: bandb@ereal.net
I: www.smoothhound.co.uk/hotels/felton.html

Romantic country house in 4-acre tranquil gardens. Comfort assured in 4-poster and antique beds. Highest level of hospitality and service (ETC Gold Award). Fresh, pure, local produce used in large breakfast menu. Herefordshire Best Breakfast Award. Just 20 minutes Hereford, Leominster, Bromyard, Ledbury.

Bedrooms: 1 single, 3 double/twin
Bathrooms: 2 en suite, 2 private

B&B per night:
S £27.00
D £54.00

OPEN All Year except Christmas

♦♦♦♦

HEDLEY LODGE

Belmont Abbey, Abergavenny Road, Hereford HR2 9RZ
T: (01432) 374747
F: (01432) 277318
E: hedleylodge@aol.com
I: www.hedleylodge.com

Set in lovely grounds of Belmont Abbey (above), this friendly, modern guesthouse offers 17 bedrooms comfortably appointed with en suite facilities, TV and telephone. Our licensed restaurant offers a wide selection of snacks or main meals. Located 2.5 miles from Hereford off A465, an ideal venue for visiting the Wye Valley.

Bedrooms: 16 double/twin, 1 triple/multiple
Bathrooms: 17 en suite

Lunch available
Evening meal available
CC: Delta, Mastercard, Switch, Visa

B&B per night:
S Min £35.00
D Min £55.00

HB per person:
DY £37.00–£44.50

OPEN All Year

♦♦♦

HERON HOUSE BED & BREAKFAST

Heron House,
Canon Pyon Road, Portway,
Burghill, Hereford HR4 8NG
T: (01432) 761111
F: (01432) 760603
E: info@theheronhouse.com
I: www.theheronhouse.com

Bedrooms: 2 double/twin
Bathrooms: 1 en suite

Country location with panoramic view, 4 miles north of Hereford city. Off-road parking. Excellent centre for country pursuits and places of historic interest. No smoking.

10

B&B per night:
S £19.00
D £22.00

OPEN All Year

HEREFORD continued

◆◆◆◆

MONTGOMERY HOUSE

12 St Owen Street, Hereford
HR1 2PL
T: (01432) 351454 & 07971 649787
F: (01432) 344463
E: lizforbes@lineone.net
I: www.montgomeryhousehereford.com

Bedrooms: 2 double/twin
Bathrooms: 2 en suite

Lunch available

B&B per night:
S £45.00
D £60.00

OPEN All Year except Christmas

Elegant accommodation in Georgian Grade II Listed townhouse in centre of Hereford. Spacious en suite facilities, king-size beds and luxury linen. Hearty breakfasts include award-winning local produce.

HOLBEACH, Lincolnshire Map ref 3A1

◆◆

THE BULL INN

Old Main Road,
Fleet Hargate, Holbeach, Spalding
PE12 8LH
T: (01406) 426866

Bedrooms: 3 double/twin

Lunch available
Evening meal available
CC: Mastercard, Switch, Visa

B&B per night:
S £18.00–£20.00
D £30.00–£40.00

OPEN All Year

Ancient coaching inn on the road round The Wash. Grade II Listed building, site of archaeological interest. Bar, restaurant, rooms, car park and beer garden.

Silver Award

CACKLE HILL HOUSE

Cackle Hill Lane, Holbeach, Spalding
PE12 8BS
T: (01406) 426721 & 07930 228755
F: (01406) 426721
E: cacklehillhouse@farming.co.uk

Bedrooms: 3 double/twin
Bathrooms: 2 en suite, 1 private

B&B per night:
S Min £28.00
D £44.00–£46.00

OPEN All Year except Christmas

We welcome you to our farm situated in a rural position just off the A17. Spacious accommodation, tea/coffee facilities, excellent traditional breakfasts.

HOPE, Derbyshire Map ref 4B2

◆◆◆

CAUSEWAY HOUSE

Back Street, Castleton, Hope Valley
S33 8WE
T: (01433) 623291 & (0114) 236 8574
E: susanbridget@aol.com
I: www.causewayhouse.co.uk

Bedrooms: 1 single, 4 double/twin
Bathrooms: 3 en suite, 1 private

B&B per night:
S Min £30.00
D £40.00–£65.00

OPEN All Year except Christmas

Our cottage, right in the middle of Castleton village, is a cruck cottage with exposed beams and open log fires. Some parts are 17thC.

6

UNDERLEIGH HOUSE

Off Edale Road, Hope, Hope Valley S33 6RF
T: (01433) 621372 & 621324
F: (01433) 621324
E: underleigh.house@btinternet.com
I: www.underleighhouse.co.uk

B&B per night:
S £40.00–£49.00
D £64.00–£69.00

OPEN All Year except Christmas

Secluded cottage and barn conversion near the village of Hope with magnificent countryside views. Ideal for walking and exploring the Peak District. Delicious breakfasts featuring local and homemade specialities, served in flagstoned dining hall. Welcoming and relaxing atmosphere with a log fire on chilly evenings in the charming, beamed lounge.

Bedrooms: 6 double/twin; permanent suite(s)
Bathrooms: 6 en suite

CC: Delta, Mastercard, Switch, Visa

Low season 3-night breaks: £50 B&B per room per night (excl Saturday night).

12

REGIONAL TOURIST BOARD The symbol in an establishment entry indicates that it is a Regional Tourist Board member.

HUSBANDS BOSWORTH, Leicestershire Map ref 4C3

◆◆

MRS ARMITAGE'S

31-33 High Street,
Husbands Bosworth, Lutterworth
LE17 6LJ
T: (01858) 880066

Bedrooms: 1 single, 1 double/twin, 1 triple/multiple

B&B per night:
S £16.00–£18.00
D £32.00–£36.00

OPEN All Year

Village centre home of character on A4304/A427, with wholesome cooking and warm welcome. Good choice of reasonably priced evening meals at local inns.

P

IRONBRIDGE, Shropshire Map ref 4A3 *Tourist Information Centre Tel: (01952) 432166*

◆◆◆◆◆

Silver Award

BRIDGE HOUSE

Buildwas, Telford TF8 7BN
T: (01952) 432105
F: (01952) 432105
E: janethedges@talk21.com
I: www.smoothhound.co.uk/hotels/bridgehs.html

B&B per night:
S £42.00–£45.00
D £65.00–£70.00

Charming 17thC country house situated by the River Severn and close to the famous Ironbridge. A house full of character and charm. Beautiful rooms all individually decorated and en suite, with a breakfast to be remembered. In all, the place to stay when visiting the famous Ironbridge Gorge.

Bedrooms: 3 double/twin, 1 triple/multiple; permanent suite(s)
Bathrooms: 4 en suite

P

◆◆◆◆

BRIDGE VIEW

10 Tontine Hill, Ironbridge, Telford
TF8 7AL
T: (01952) 432541
F: (01952) 433405
I: www.ironbridgeview.co.uk

Bedrooms: 4 double/twin, 1 triple/multiple
Bathrooms: 4 en suite, 1 private

CC: Delta, Mastercard, Switch, Visa

B&B per night:
S £35.00–£45.00
D £45.00–£55.00

OPEN All Year

Right in the heart of Ironbridge with breathtaking views of the bridge. All rooms with en suite or private bathroom, colour TV, beverage tray. English breakfast. Private car park.

P

◆◆◆◆

THE GOLDEN BALL INN

Newbridge Road, Ironbridge, Telford
TF8 7BA
T: (01952) 432179
F: (01952) 433123
E: matrowland@hotmail.com
I: www.goldenballinn.com

Bedrooms: 3 double/twin
Bathrooms: 3 en suite

Lunch available
Evening meal available
CC: Delta, Mastercard, Switch, Visa

B&B per night:
S £42.00–£50.00
D £50.00–£65.00

OPEN All Year

Ironbridge's oldest and finest inn, specialising in guest ale, wine and freshly prepared restaurant and bar meals. Friendly and informal atmosphere. Open every day.

P

◆◆

LORD HILL GUEST HOUSE

Duke Street, Broseley TF12 5LU
T: (01952) 884270 & 580792

Bedrooms: 2 single, 5 double/twin
Bathrooms: 2 en suite, 1 private

B&B per night:
S £20.00–£24.00
D £40.00–£44.00

OPEN All Year except Christmas

Former public house. Friendly atmosphere, full English breakfast, parking. Easy access to Ironbridge, Bridgnorth, Shrewsbury and Telford.

8 P

CREDIT CARD BOOKINGS If you book by telephone and are asked for your credit card number it is advisable to check the proprietor's policy should you cancel your reservation.

KENILWORTH, Warwickshire Map ref 4B3

♦♦♦♦

ENDERLEY GUEST HOUSE

20 Queens Road, Kenilworth
CV8 1JQ
T: (01926) 855388
F: (01926) 850450
E: enderleyguesthouse@supanet.com

Bedrooms: 1 single, 4 double/twin, 1 triple/multiple
Bathrooms: 6 en suite

B&B per night:
S £27.00–£30.00
D £45.00–£50.00

OPEN All Year

Family-run guesthouse, quietly situated near town centre and convenient for Warwick, Stratford-upon-Avon, Stoneleigh, Warwick University and National Exhibition Centre.

P

♦♦♦♦

THE OLD BAKERY HOTEL

12 High Street, Kenilworth CV8 1LZ
T: (01926) 864111
F: (01926) 864127
E: info@theoldbakeryhotel.co.uk
I: www.theoldbakeryhotel.co.uk

B&B per night:
S £50.00–£60.00
D £65.00–£75.00

OPEN All Year except Christmas

The Old Bakery Hotel is ideally situated for tourists and business people alike. Birmingham International Airport, National Exhibition Centre, National Agricultural Centre, Warwick, Leamington Spa and Stratford are all within easy reach. Superb modern accommodation, all en suite, has been blended into authentic Elizabethan surroundings. Hospitable staff guarantee personal service.

Bedrooms: 1 single, 10 double/twin, 1 triple/multiple; permanent suite(s)
Bathrooms: 12 en suite

CC: Delta, Mastercard, Switch, Visa

P

♦♦♦♦

VICTORIA LODGE HOTEL

180 Warwick Road, Kenilworth
CV8 1HU
T: (01926) 512020
F: (01926) 858703
E: info@victorialodgehotel.co.uk
I: www.victorialodgehotel.co.uk

Bedrooms: 1 single, 7 double/twin, 1 triple/multiple
Bathrooms: 9 en suite

CC: Amex, Delta, Mastercard, Switch, Visa

B&B per night:
S £42.00–£52.00
D Min £64.00

OPEN All Year except Christmas

Prestigious small hotel with a warming ambience. Luxurious bedrooms, with individual appeal and character, complemented by traditional hospitality. Non-smoking.

12 P

KETTERING, Northamptonshire Map ref 3A2 *Tourist Information Centre Tel: (01536) 410266*

♦♦♦♦

DAIRY FARM

Cranford St Andrew, Kettering
NN14 4AQ
T: (01536) 330273

Bedrooms: 4 double/twin
Bathrooms: 3 en suite, 1 private

Evening meal available

B&B per night:
S £22.00–£38.00
D £44.00–£76.00

HB per person:
DY £40.00–£56.00

OPEN All Year except Christmas

350-acre mixed farm. 17thC thatched house with inglenook fireplaces and a garden with an ancient circular dovecote and mature trees. Good food.

P

KEXBY, Lincolnshire Map ref 4C2

♦♦♦

THE GRANGE

Kexby, Gainsborough DN21 5PJ
T: (01427) 788265

Bedrooms: 1 single, 1 double/twin
Bathrooms: 1 private

Lunch available
Evening meal available

B&B per night:
S £18.00
D £36.00

OPEN All Year

650-acre mixed farm. Victorian farmhouse offering warm welcome. 4 miles from Gainsborough. Convenient for Lincoln, Hemswell Antique Centre and Wolds. Double room has private bathroom.

P

MAP REFERENCES

Map references apply to the colour maps at the front of this guide.

KIDDERMINSTER, Worcestershire Map ref 4B3

◆◆◆

COLLINGDALE PRIVATE HOTEL
197 Comberton Road,
Kidderminster DY10 1UE
T: (01562) 515460 & 862839
E: collingdale@sharvell.fsnet.co.uk
I: mysite.freeserve.com/collingdalehotel

Bedrooms: 1 single, 6 double/twin, 2 triple/multiple
Bathrooms: 4 en suite, 1 private

B&B per night:
S £25.00–£34.00
D £42.00–£52.00

OPEN All Year except Christmas

Extended, roomy, Regency-type house with gallery landing. Corner position with walled garden facing south. Small car park (6 cars) at rear of hotel.

◆◆◆◆
Gold Award

GARDEN COTTAGES

Crossway Green, Hartlebury, Kidderminster DY13 9SJ
T: (01299) 250626
F: (01299) 250626
E: mamod@btinternet.com
I: gardencottages.co.uk

B&B per night:
S £30.00
D £55.00

HB per person:
DY £65.00–£70.00

OPEN All Year except Christmas

A comfortable, oak-beamed country cottage. Ample off-road parking. Close to the main roads and motorways. All rooms have en suite or private facilities, colour TV, clock radio, hospitality tray, hairdryer, iron. Evening meal available if booked in advance. Plenty of good pubs, and restaurant close by.

Bedrooms: 1 single, 2 double/twin, 1 triple/multiple
Bathrooms: 3 en suite, 1 private

Lunch available
Evening meal available

KINETON, Warwickshire Map ref 2C1

◆◆◆

THE CASTLE
Edgehill, Kineton, Warwick
OX15 6DJ
T: (01295) 670255
F: (01295) 670521
E: castleedgehill@btopenworld.com
I: www.thecastle-edgehill.co.uk

Bedrooms: 1 double/twin, 2 triple/multiple; permanent suite(s)
Bathrooms: 3 en suite

Lunch available
Evening meal available
CC: Amex, Delta, Diners, Mastercard, Switch, Visa

B&B per night:
D Min £57.50

OPEN All Year

'Folly' built by Sanderson-Miller. Copy of Guy's Tower at Warwick Castle. Erected to commemorate 100th aniversary of Battle of Edgehill (1642) traditionally where King Charles I stood.

KING'S CLIFFE, Northamptonshire Map ref 3A1

19 WEST STREET

King's Cliffe, Peterborough PE8 6XB
T: (01780) 470365
F: (01780) 470623
E: kjhl_dixon@hotmail.com
I: www.kingjohnhuntinglodge.com

B&B per night:
S £25.00
D £40.00–£45.00

HB per person:
DY £12.00–£18.00

OPEN All Year

Grade II Listed 500-year-old stone house, beautiful walled garden, reputedly one of King John's hunting lodges. Situated in centre of unspoilt stone village near Stamford. Rooms have private bathroom and colour TV. Dinner on request. Central location for many stately homes and a number of other attractions. Secure parking.

Bedrooms: 1 single, 2 double/twin
Bathrooms: 3 private

Lunch available
Evening meal available

QUALITY ASSURANCE SCHEME
Diamond ratings and awards are explained at the back of this guide.

LEA MARSTON, West Midlands Map ref 4B3

♦♦♦♦

REINDEER PARK LODGE

Kingsbury Road, Lea Marston, Sutton Coldfield B76 0DE
T: (01675) 470811 & 470710
F: (01675) 470710

Bedrooms: 1 single, 4 double/twin, 1 triple/multiple
Bathrooms: 6 en suite

CC: Amex, Delta, Diners, Mastercard, Switch, Visa

B&B per night:
S £37.50–£39.50
D £47.50–£57.50

Property is set in 50 acres with woodland walks, 6 deluxe rooms all en suite with lovely views. We have the only reindeer herd in England!

LEAMINGTON SPA, Warwickshire Map ref 4B3 *Tourist Information Centre Tel: (01926) 742762*

♦♦♦♦
Silver Award

8 CLARENDON CRESCENT

Leamington Spa CV32 5NR
T: (01926) 429840
F: (01926) 424641
E: lawson@lawson71.fsnet.co.uk
I: www.shakespeare-country.co.uk

Bedrooms: 1 single, 3 double/twin
Bathrooms: 3 en suite, 1 private

B&B per night:
S £35.00–£40.00
D £60.00

OPEN All Year except Christmas

Grade II Listed Regency house overlooking private dell, in quiet backwater of Leamington Spa with its many shops and restaurants. Elegantly furnished with antiques. Individually designed en suite bedrooms. Five minutes' walk town centre, convenient for Warwick, Stratford, Royal Agricultural Centre and NEC.

♦♦♦♦

THE COACH HOUSE

Snowford Hall Farm, Hunningham, Leamington Spa CV33 9ES
T: (01926) 632297
F: (01926) 633599
E: the_coach_house@lineone.net
I: lineone.net/~the_coach_house

Bedrooms: 3 double/twin
Bathrooms: 2 en suite, 1 private

B&B per night:
S £32.00–£36.00
D £42.00–£46.00

OPEN All Year except Christmas

200-acre arable farm. Converted barn farmhouse off the Fosse Way, on the edge of Hunningham village. On elevated ground overlooking quiet surrounding countryside.

♦♦♦♦

HILL FARM

Lewis Road, Radford Semele, Leamington Spa CV31 1UX
T: (01926) 337571
E: rebecca@hillfarm3000.fsnet.co.uk

Bedrooms: 4 double/twin
Bathrooms: 3 en suite, 1 private

B&B per night:
S £25.00–£30.00
D £50.00

OPEN All Year except Christmas

350-acre mixed farm. Farmhouse set in large attractive garden, 2 miles from Leamington town centre and close to Warwick Castle and Stratford-upon-Avon.

♦♦♦♦

VICTORIA PARK HOTEL

12 Adelaide Road, Leamington Spa CV31 3PW
T: (01926) 424195
F: (01926) 421521
E: info@victoriaparkhotelleamingtonspa.co.uk
I: www.victoriaparkhotelleamingtonspa.co.uk

Bedrooms: 6 single, 7 double/twin, 7 triple/multiple
Bathrooms: 20 en suite

Lunch available
Evening meal available
CC: Amex, Delta, Mastercard, Switch, Visa

B&B per night:
S £39.50–£45.00
D £60.00

OPEN All Year except Christmas

Victorian house close to bus and railway stations and town centre. Park, Pump Room, gardens, bowls, tennis and river all 3 minutes' walk away.

COLOUR MAPS Colour maps at the front of this guide pinpoint all places under which you will find accommodation listed.

LECHLADE, Gloucestershire Map ref 2B1

♦♦♦♦

CAMBRAI LODGE
Oak Street, Lechlade GL7 3AY
T: (01367) 253173 & 07860 150467

Bedrooms: 2 single, 5 double/twin; permanent suite(s)
Bathrooms: 5 en suite

B&B per night:
S £30.00–£40.00
D £50.00–£60.00

OPEN All Year

Friendly, family-run guesthouse, recently modernised, close to River Thames. Ideal base for touring the Cotswolds. 4-poster bedroom, garden and ample parking.

LEEK, Staffordshire Map ref 4B2 *Tourist Information Centre Tel: (01538) 483741*

♦♦♦♦

PROSPECT HOUSE
334 Cheadle Road, Cheddleton, Leek ST13 7BW
T: (01782) 550639 & 07973 179478
E: prospect@talk21.com
I: www.prospecthouseleek.co.uk

Bedrooms: 1 single, 2 double/twin, 2 triple/multiple
Bathrooms: 5 en suite

Evening meal available
CC: Delta, Mastercard, Switch, Visa

B&B per night:
S £22.00–£23.00
D £44.00–£46.00

HB per person:
DY £35.00–£36.00

OPEN All Year

A 19thC converted coach house in a tranquil courtyard setting, offering superior accommodation and a personal service tailored to your individual needs.

LEICESTER, Leicestershire Map ref 4C3 *Tourist Information Centre Tel: (0906) 294 1113 (Premium rate)*

Rating Applied For

ABINGER GUEST HOUSE
175 Hinckley Road, Leicester LE3 0TF
T: (0116) 255 4674
F: (0116) 255 4674
E: bobwel1234@aol.com

Bedrooms: 1 single, 5 double/twin, 2 triple/multiple
Bathrooms: 1 en suite, 1 private

CC: Amex, Delta, Diners, Mastercard, Switch, Visa

B&B per night:
S Min £24.00
D £36.00–£38.00

OPEN All Year

Extensively modernised guest house situated a mile from Leicester city centre. Friendly staff, great breakfasts and extremely comfortable beds. TVs in every room.

♦

GLENFIELD LODGE HOTEL

4 Glenfield Road, Leicester LE3 6AP
T: (0116) 262 7554

B&B per night:
S £20.00
D £35.00

OPEN All Year except Christmas

Small, friendly hotel with an interesting ornamental courtyard, home-cooked food and cosy, relaxed surroundings. Close to city centre.

Bedrooms: 6 single, 7 double/twin, 2 triple/multiple

Evening meal available

♦♦♦

SPINDLE LODGE HOTEL

2 West Walk, Leicester LE1 7NA
T: (0116) 233 8801
F: (0116) 233 8804
E: spindlelodgeleicester@orange.net
I: www.smoothhound.co.uk/hotels/spindle.html

B&B per night:
S £27.50–£50.00
D £46.00–£65.00

OPEN All Year except Christmas

Located in a tree-lined conservation area and built in 1876, charming Spindle Lodge is in a quiet location, yet centrally positioned. A family-run Victorian house with a friendly atmosphere, within easy walking distance of city centre, railway station, universities, civic and entertainment centres.

Bedrooms: 6 single, 5 double/twin, 2 triple/multiple
Bathrooms: 8 en suite

Evening meal available
CC: Delta, Mastercard, Switch, Visa

Complimentary tickets for a family of 3 to visit the National Space Centre if you stay 2 nights or more.

CONFIRM YOUR BOOKING
You are advised to confirm your booking in writing.

LEOMINSTER, Herefordshire Map ref 2A1 *Tourist Information Centre Tel: (01568) 616460*

♦♦♦♦ Gold Award

THE PADDOCK

Shobdon, Leominster HR6 9NQ
T: (01568) 708176
F: (01568) 708829
E: thepaddock@talk21.com

B&B per night:
S £35.00–£37.00
D £46.00–£50.00

HB per person:
DY £39.00–£51.00

Delightful ground floor accommodation set in beautiful countryside bordering Wales. All rooms en suite. Large garden and patio, ample off-road parking. Guests' lounge and dining room. We offer delicious home-cooked food and a very warm welcome. Telephone for brochure.

Bedrooms: 5 double/twin
Bathrooms: 5 en suite

Evening meal available

♦♦♦

TYN-Y-COED
Shobdon, Leominster HR6 9NY
T: (01568) 708277
F: (01568) 708277
E: jandrews@shobdondesign.kc3.co.uk

Bedrooms: 2 double/twin
Bathrooms: 1 en suite, 1 private

B&B per night:
S £20.00
D £40.00

Country house in large garden on Mortimer Trail, close to Croft Castle and Berrington Hall (National Trust). Convenient for Leominster, Ludlow and Presteigne.

10 P

LINCOLN, Lincolnshire Map ref 4C2

♦♦♦♦

DAMON'S MOTEL
997 Doddington Road, Lincoln LN6 3ES
T: (01522) 887733
F: (01522) 887734

Bedrooms: 47 double/twin
Bathrooms: 47 en suite

Lunch available
Evening meal available
CC: Amex, Delta, Diners, Mastercard, Switch, Visa

B&B per night:
S £49.25–£52.25
D £55.00–£58.00

OPEN All Year

Purpose-built, 2-storey motel on the Lincoln ring road. Adjacent restaurant, indoor pool, gym, solarium. Satellite TV.

P

♦♦♦

NEWPORT GUEST HOUSE
26-28 Newport, Lincoln LN1 3DF
T: (01522) 528590
F: (01522) 542868
E: info@newportguesthouse.co.uk
I: www.newportguesthouse.co.uk

Bedrooms: 2 single, 4 double/twin, 2 triple/multiple
Bathrooms: 8 en suite

CC: Amex, Delta, Diners, Mastercard, Switch, Visa

B&B per night:
S £28.00–£35.00
D £40.00–£50.00

OPEN All Year except Christmas

A Victorian double-fronted property, walking distance from historic centre of Lincoln. Own off-street parking for guests.

8 P

♦♦♦

73 STATION ROAD
Branston, Lincoln LN4 1LG
T: (01522) 828658 & 07932 162940

Bedrooms: 2 double/twin; permanent suite(s)
Bathrooms: 1 en suite, 1 private

B&B per night:
S Min £25.00
D Min £40.00

OPEN All Year except Christmas

Bed and breakfast 3 miles from the city of Lincoln. Two bedrooms on ground floor overlooking attractive gardens. Off-street parking.

5 P

♦♦♦♦

TENNYSON HOTEL
7 South Park, Lincoln LN5 8EN
T: (01522) 521624
F: (01522) 521355
E: tennyson.hotel@virgin.net
I: www.tennysonhotel.com

Bedrooms: 2 single, 6 double/twin
Bathrooms: 8 en suite

CC: Delta, Mastercard, Switch, Visa

B&B per night:
S £33.00–£37.00
D £45.00–£47.00

OPEN All Year except Christmas

Hotel with a comfortable atmosphere, overlooking the South Park, 1 mile from the city centre. Personally supervised.

P

LINCOLN continued

WELBECK COTTAGE

Meadow Lane, South Hykeham, Lincoln LN6 9PF
T: (01522) 692669 & 07799 741000
F: (01522) 692669
E: mad@wellbeck1.demon.co.uk

Bedrooms: 2 double/twin
Bathrooms: 2 en suite

Lunch available
Evening meal available

Friendly welcome to semi-detached cottage in pleasant rural location. Near historic city of Lincoln. Evening meal available on request.

B&B per night:
S £20.00
D £38.00

HB per person:
DY £26.00–£28.50

OPEN All Year

LITTLE BYTHAM, Lincolnshire Map ref 3A1

THE WILLOUGHBY ARMS

Station Road, Little Bytham, Grantham NG33 4RA
T: (01780) 410276
F: (01780) 410190
E: willo@willoughbyarms.co.uk
I: www.willoughbyarms.co.uk

Great rural pub in beautiful countryside, just north of historic town of Stamford. Built by Lord Willoughby in 1853, originally called The Steam Plough Inn, perfect balance between traditional pub and eating house, serving local community and travellers from further afield. Specialises in home cooking and real ales from micro-breweries.

Bedrooms: 1 single, 1 double/twin, 1 triple/multiple
Bathrooms: 2 en suite, 1 private

Lunch available
Evening meal available
CC: Delta, Mastercard, Switch, Visa

B&B per night:
S £30.00–£50.00
D £50.00–£70.00

OPEN All Year except Christmas

LONGHOPE, Gloucestershire Map ref 2B1

♦♦♦♦

THE OLD FARM

Barrel Lane, Longhope GL17 0LR
T: (01452) 830252 & 0790 568 3029
F: (01452) 830255
E: wheretostay@the-old-farm.co.uk
I: www.the-old-farm.co.uk

Charming 16thC farmhouse with a wealth of character. A peaceful haven in idyllic rural location, yet convenient for Gloucester, the Wye Valley and the Royal Forest of Dean. Comfortable, well-equipped, en suite rooms including a 4-poster. Relax in front of the fire or in the sunny garden. Wonderful walks. Dogs welcome.

Bedrooms: 3 double/twin
Bathrooms: 3 en suite

CC: Delta, Mastercard, Switch, Visa

3 nights for 2, Nov-Mar. Stay 4 nights and receive a 10% discount, Apr-Oct. Both offers exclude Bank Holidays.

B&B per night:
S £29.00
D £42.00–£54.00

OPEN All Year except Christmas

AT-A-GLANCE SYMBOLS

Symbols at the end of each accommodation entry give useful information about services and facilities. A key to symbols can be found inside the back cover flap. Keep this open for easy reference.

LONGHOPE continued

◆◆◆◆◆ Gold Award

THE TEMPLE

Old Monmouth Road, Longhope GL17 0NZ
T: (01452) 831011
F: (01452) 831776
E: tricia.ferguson@virgin.net
I: www.thetemple-longhope.co.uk

B&B per night:
S £50.00
D £65.00–£80.00

OPEN All Year except Christmas

Run by Tricia and Keith Ferguson formerly from Collin House, Broadway. The Temple is a fine Georgian house in over an acre of formal gardens. It is beautifully furnished and ideally situated for Cheltenham, Gloucester, Wye Valley and the Royal Forest of Dean. Delicious home cookery using local produce. Licensed.

Bedrooms: 2 double/twin
Bathrooms: 1 en suite, 1 private

Lunch available
Evening meal available

3 nights for the price of 2 (excl Bank Holidays, Fri and Sat) Nov-Mar.

P

LOUGHBOROUGH, Leicestershire Map ref 4C3 *Tourist Information Centre Tel: (01509) 218113*

◆◆◆◆

CHARNWOOD LODGE

136 Leicester Road, Loughborough LE11 2AQ
T: (01509) 211120
F: (01509) 211121
E: charnwoodlodge@charwat.freeserve.co.uk
I: www.charnwoodlodge.com

B&B per night:
S £35.00–£45.00
D £45.00–£55.00

HB per person:
DY £42.50–£47.50

OPEN All Year

Elegant Victorian licensed guesthouse in pretty gardens with private parking. Peaceful, yet close to town centre, steam railway, university and Charnwood Forest. Spacious, comfortable interior with very attractive en suite rooms including a 4-poster suite. Ideal base for Leicester, Nottingham, Derby, East Midlands Airport and Donington Racecourse. Warm, friendly service assured.

Bedrooms: 1 single, 5 double/twin, 2 triple/multiple
Bathrooms: 7 en suite

Lunch available
Evening meal available
CC: Delta, Diners, Mastercard, Switch, Visa

P

◆◆◆

DEMONTFORT HOTEL

88 Leicester Road, Loughborough LE11 2AQ
T: (01509) 216061
F: (01509) 233667
E: thedemontforthotel@amserve.com
I: thedemontforthotel.co.uk

Bedrooms: 1 single, 5 double/twin, 3 triple/multiple
Bathrooms: 6 en suite

Lunch available
Evening meal available
CC: Amex, Delta, Diners, Mastercard, Switch, Visa

B&B per night:
S £35.00
D £45.00–£50.00

OPEN All Year

Family-run hotel in Victorian house, with beautifully decorated rooms and warm, friendly atmosphere. Close to town centre, Steam Trust, Bell Foundry, University.

QUALITY ASSURANCE SCHEME

For an explanation of the quality and facilities represented by the Diamonds please refer to the front of this guide. A more detailed explanation can be found in the information pages at the back.

LOUGHBOROUGH continued

◆◆◆

FOREST RISE HOTEL LTD

55-57 Forest Road, Loughborough
LE11 3NW
T: (01509) 215928
F: (01509) 210506

B&B per night:
S £25.00–£55.00
D £50.00–£75.00

OPEN All Year except Christmas

Family-run establishment, friendly personal service, excellent standards throughout. Short walking distance to the town centre, university. Easy access to M1, M42, airport, Donington Park, Prestwold and Beaumanour Halls. Ample secure car parking, large garden and patio to the rear. En suite bedrooms including executive, bridal, family and 4-poster rooms. All prices include full English breakfast.

Bedrooms: 8 single, 11 double/twin, 4 triple/multiple
Bathrooms: 19 en suite

Evening meal available
CC: Delta, Diners, Mastercard, Switch, Visa

◆◆◆◆

THE MOUNTSORREL HOTEL

217 Loughborough Road, Mountsorrel, Loughborough LE12 7AR
T: (01509) 412627 & 416105
F: (01509) 416105
E: info@mountsorrelhotel.co.uk
I: www.mountsorrelhotel.co.uk

B&B per night:
S £35.00–£45.00
D £45.00–£65.00

HB per person:
DY £47.50–£65.00

OPEN All Year

A small, friendly, family-run hotel in secluded grounds off the old A6, midway between Leicester and Loughborough. The Great Central Railway is on the doorstep, and the River Soar runs through the village. There is ample car parking in our own private drive surrounded by shrubs and trees.

Bedrooms: 4 single, 9 double/twin, 1 triple/multiple; permanent suite(s)
Bathrooms: 14 en suite

Lunch available
Evening meal available
CC: Amex, Delta, Mastercard, Switch, Visa

LUDLOW, Shropshire Map ref 4A3 *Tourist Information Centre Tel: (01584) 875053*

◆◆◆

BULL HOTEL

14 The Bull Ring, Ludlow SY8 1AD
T: (01584) 873611
F: (01584) 873666
E: info@bull-ludlow.co.uk
I: www.bull-ludlow.co.uk

Bedrooms: 3 double/twin, 1 triple/multiple
Bathrooms: 4 en suite

Lunch available
CC: Amex, Delta, Mastercard, Visa

B&B per night:
S £32.50–£50.00
D £50.00

OPEN All Year except Christmas

Situated in town centre. Oldest pub in Ludlow, earliest mention c1343. Was known as Peter of Proctor's House and probably dates back to c1199.

◆◆◆

CECIL GUEST HOUSE

Sheet Road, Ludlow SY8 1LR
T: (01584) 872442
F: (01584) 872442

Bedrooms: 2 single, 6 double/twin, 1 triple/multiple
Bathrooms: 4 en suite

Evening meal available
CC: Delta, Mastercard, Visa

B&B per night:
S £21.00–£37.00
D £44.00–£58.00

HB per person:
DY £38.50–£54.50

OPEN All Year

Attractive guesthouse 15 minutes' walk from town centre and station. Freshly cooked food from local produce. Residents' bar and lounge. Off-street parking.

ACCESSIBILITY

Look for the symbols which indicate National Accessible Scheme standards for hearing and visually impaired guests in addition to standards for guests with mobility impairment. Additional participants are shown in the listings at the back.

LUDLOW continued

◆◆◆

HENWICK HOUSE
Gravel Hill, Ludlow SY8 1QU
T: (01584) 873338 & 07951 642159

Bedrooms: 3 double/twin
Bathrooms: 2 en suite, 1 private

Warm, comfortable Georgian coach house, friendly, informal atmosphere, good traditional English breakfast, easy walking distance from town centre and local inns. TV and tea/coffee-making facilities.

P

B&B per night:
S £22.00
D £44.00

◆◆◆

LONGLANDS
Woodhouse Lane, Richards Castle, Ludlow SY8 4EU
T: (01584) 831636
E: iankemsley@aol.com
I: www.ludlow.org.uk/longlands

Bedrooms: 2 double/twin; permanent suite(s)
Bathrooms: 1 en suite, 1 private

Centrally located in 35 acres of grassland with extended rural views. Home-grown produce. Convenient for Ludlow, Mortimer Forest and Croft Castle.

P

B&B per night:
S £26.00–£28.00
D £48.00–£50.00

HB per person:
DY £35.00–£40.00

OPEN All Year except Christmas

◆◆◆◆◆
Gold Award

NUMBER TWENTY EIGHT

28 Lower Broad Street, Ludlow SY8 1PQ
T: (01584) 876996 & 0800 0815000
F: (01584) 876860
E: ross@no28.co.uk
I: www.no28.co.uk

Period houses of great charm in old Ludlow town. Each bedroom individually furnished providing superb en suite accommodation (suites available). More Michelins within walking distance than one can shake a knife and fork at! Come therefore to Ludlow to eat as lords and Number Twenty Eight to stay like them! The place where guests come first.

Bedrooms: 9 double/twin; permanent suite(s)
Bathrooms: 9 en suite

CC: Delta, Mastercard, Switch, Visa

No special offers – just very reasonable rack rates!

B&B per night:
S £65.00–£90.00
D £80.00–£98.00

OPEN All Year

◆◆◆◆

THE WHEATSHEAF INN
Lower Broad Street, Ludlow SY8 1PQ
T: (01584) 872980
F: (01584) 877990
E: karen.wheatsheaf@tinyworld.co.uk

Bedrooms: 5 double/twin
Bathrooms: 5 en suite

Lunch available
Evening meal available
CC: Delta, Mastercard, Switch, Visa

Family-run mid-17thC beamed inn, 100 yards from the town centre, nestling under Ludlow's historic 13thC Broad Gate, the last remaining of 7 town gates.

B&B per night:
S £30.00–£50.00
D £45.00–£50.00

OPEN All Year

LYDDINGTON, Rutland Map ref 4C3

◆◆◆◆

LYDBROOKE
2 Colley Rise, Lyddington, Oakham LE15 9LL
T: (01572) 821471
F: (01572) 821471
E: lydbrookebb@hotmail.com

Bedrooms: 1 single, 2 double/twin
Bathrooms: 2 en suite, 1 private

En suite accommodation, with excellent breakfasts, is offered in the peaceful setting of comfortable, detached home in picturesque, historic village of Lyddington.

P

B&B per night:
S Min £27.50
D £45.00–£50.00

OPEN All Year except Christmas

RATING All accommodation in this guide has been rated, or is awaiting a rating, by a trained English Tourism Council assessor.

MALVERN, Worcestershire Map ref 2B1 *Tourist Information Centre Tel: (01684) 892289*

HARCOURT COTTAGE

252 West Malvern Road, West Malvern, Malvern WR14 4DQ
T: (01684) 574561
F: (01684) 574561
E: harcourtcottage@aol.com

Bedrooms: 3 double/twin
Bathrooms: 3 en suite

Evening meal available

Nestling on the west side of the Malvern Hills, well placed for walking holidays or as a base for touring. English and French cuisine.

B&B per night:
S £30.00
D £44.00

HB per person:
DY £34.50–£42.50

OPEN All Year except Christmas

MARKET DRAYTON, Shropshire Map ref 4A2 *Tourist Information Centre Tel: (01630) 652139*

HEATH FARM BED AND BREAKFAST

Heath Farm, Wellington Road, Hodnet, Market Drayton TF9 3JJ
T: (01630) 685570
F: (01630) 685570
E: adrysdale@telco4u.net
I: www.freeweb.telco4u.net/heathfarm

Bedrooms: 3 double/twin

60-acre mixed farm. Traditional farmhouse welcome. Situated 1.5 miles south of Hodnet off A442, approached by private drive. Easy access for Hodnet Hall, Hawkstone, Potteries, Ironbridge,Shrewsbury.

B&B per night:
S £20.00–£22.00
D £40.00–£44.00

OPEN All Year except Christmas

MARKET HARBOROUGH, Leicestershire Map ref 4C3 *Tourist Information Centre Tel: (01858) 821270*

HUNTERS LODGE

Gumley, Market Harborough LE16 7RT
T: (0116) 279 3744
F: (0116) 279 3855
E: info@hunterslodgefoxton.co.uk
I: www.hunterslodgefoxton.co.uk

Bedrooms: 1 double/twin, 1 triple/multiple
Bathrooms: 2 en suite

CC: Delta, Mastercard, Switch, Visa

Attractive bungalow set in open countryside a short walk from Foxton Locks, convenient for many local attractions. Comfortable, new, en suite rooms, separate dining/sitting room and patio.

B&B per night:
S Min £27.99
D Min £43.99

OPEN All Year except Christmas

MARKET RASEN, Lincolnshire Map ref 4D2

♦♦♦♦

BEECHWOOD GUESTHOUSE

54 Willingham Road, Market Rasen LN8 3DX
T: (01673) 844043
E: beechwoodgh@aol.com
I: www.beechwoodguesthouse.co.uk

'Genuine hospitality' is our aim at Beechwood, an elegant, period guesthouse set off the road in mature gardens. Quality accommodation including one ground floor en suite room. Non-smoking bedrooms are available. Situated on the edge of the Wolds we are an ideal base for cycling, walking and exploring the county.

Bedrooms: 5 double/twin
Bathrooms: 3 en suite

Evening meal available
CC: Mastercard, Visa

Short breaks: 3-night and 7-night DB&B packages available.

B&B per night:
S £25.00–£30.00
D £40.00–£45.00

HB per person:
DY £28.60–£42.00

OPEN All Year

QUALITY ASSURANCE SCHEME

Diamond ratings and awards were correct at the time of going to press but are subject to change. Please check at the time of booking.

MARKET RASEN continued

◆◆◆◆

WAVENEY COTTAGE GUESTHOUSE

Willingham Road, Market Rasen LN8 3DN
T: (01673) 843236
F: (01673) 843236
E: vacancies@waveneycottage.co.uk
I: www.waveneycottage.co.uk

Bedrooms: 3 double/twin
Bathrooms: 3 en suite

Evening meal available

B&B per night:
S £23.00–£25.00
D £40.00–£45.00

HB per person:
DY Min £29.50

OPEN All Year

Charming cottage offering a warm welcome. Clean, comfortable en suite accommodation. Home cooking our speciality. Close to local amenities, Lincolnshire Wolds and National Cycle Route.

MATLOCK, Derbyshire Map ref 4B2 *Tourist Information Centre Tel: (01629) 583388*

◆◆◆

HOME FARM

Ible, Grange Mill, Matlock DE4 4HS
T: (01629) 650349

Bedrooms: 1 double/twin, 1 triple/multiple
Bathrooms: 2 en suite

Evening meal available

B&B per night:
S £20.00–£22.00
D £32.00–£36.00

HB per person:
DY £23.00–£25.00

OPEN All Year except Christmas

A retired farm, but still a few animals. Plenty of walks and places to visit, and a warm welcome to all.

◆◆◆

JACKSON TOR HOUSE HOTEL

76 Jackson Road, Matlock DE4 3JQ
T: (01629) 582348
F: (01629) 582348
E: jacksontorhotel@uk2.net
I: www.jacksontorhotel.co.uk

Bedrooms: 11 single, 15 double/twin, 3 triple/multiple
Bathrooms: 13 en suite

Evening meal available
CC: Delta, Mastercard, Switch, Visa

B&B per night:
S £20.00–£30.00
D £39.00–£65.00

HB per person:
DY £30.00–£45.00

OPEN All Year

A family hotel overlooking Matlock, ideal for touring the National Park, historic houses and the picturesque countryside.

MATLOCK BATH, Derbyshire Map ref 4B2

◆◆

ASHDALE

92 North Parade, Matlock Bath, Matlock DE4 3NS
T: (01629) 57826 & 07714 106402
E: ashdale@matlockbath.fsnet.co.uk
I: www.ashdaleguesthouse.co.uk

Bedrooms: 2 double/twin, 2 triple/multiple; permanent suite(s)
Bathrooms: 4 en suite

CC: Amex, Delta, Diners, Mastercard, Switch, Visa

B&B per night:
S £25.00–£30.00
D £45.00–£50.00

OPEN All Year

A Grade II Listed Georgian villa situated in the centre of Matlock Bath. Large comfortable rooms, level walking to local amenities and station.

HODGKINSONS HOTEL

150 South Parade, Matlock Bath, Matlock DE4 3NR
T: (01629) 582170
F: (01629) 584891
E: enquiries@hodgkinsons-hotel.co.uk
I: www.hodgkinsons-hotel.co.uk

Grade II Listed Georgian hotel dating from 1770, overlooking River Derwent in former spa town. Beautifully restored with original features and open fires. All rooms individually decorated and furnished with en suite facilities. Imaginative dinners prepared with best of local produce. Car parking available.

Bedrooms: 1 single, 6 double/twin
Bathrooms: 7 en suite

Evening meal available
CC: Amex, Delta, Mastercard, Switch, Visa

Bargain breaks – DB&B £54.50pp, minimum 2 nights.

B&B per night:
S £45.00–£65.00
D £68.00–£95.00

HB per person:
DY £63.50–£72.00

OPEN All Year except Christmas

MEDBOURNE, Leicestershire Map ref 4C3

Silver Award

HOMESTEAD HOUSE

5 Ashley Road, Medbourne,
Market Harborough LE16 8DL
T: (01858) 565724
F: (01858) 565324

In an elevated position overlooking the Welland Valley on the outskirts of Medbourne, a picturesque village dating back to Roman times. Surrounded by open countryside and within easy reach of many places of interest. Three tastefully decorated bedrooms with rural views. A warm welcome awaits you.

Bedrooms: 3 double/twin
Bathrooms: 3 en suite

CC: Mastercard, Switch, Visa

B&B per night:
S Min £25.00
D Min £45.00

OPEN All Year

MELBOURNE, Derbyshire Map ref 4B3

BURDETT HOUSE

Derby Road, Melbourne, Derby
DE73 1DE
T: (01332) 862105
E: jjvglaze@btinternet.com

Bedrooms: 3 double/twin; permanent suite(s)
Bathrooms: 3 en suite

Evening meal available

Former pub. En suite rooms. Close to East Midlands Airport, Castle Donnington racetrack and National Trust properties. Off-road parking. Special price for 3 days.

B&B per night:
S Min £20.00
D Min £30.00

OPEN All Year except Christmas

MELTON MOWBRAY, Leicestershire Map ref 4C3 *Tourist Information Centre Tel: (01664) 480992*

Rating Applied For

HALL FARM

1 Main Street, Holwell,
Melton Mowbray LE14 4SZ
T: (01664) 444275
F: (01664) 444731

Bedrooms: 1 double/twin
Bathrooms: 1 en suite

Friendly welcome to a working farm in the conservation village of Holwell. One twin en suite bedroom. Non-smoking. Open all year.

B&B per night:
S £22.50–£25.00
D £44.00–£45.00

OPEN All Year

MERIDEN, West Midlands Map ref 4B3

◆◆

BONNIFINGLAS GUEST HOUSE

3 Berkswell Road, Meriden,
Coventry CV7 7LB
T: (01676) 523193 & 07900 20116
F: (01676) 523193

Bedrooms: 2 single, 5 double/twin, 1 triple/multiple
Bathrooms: 8 en suite

Country house, all rooms en suite with TV. Several pubs and restaurants within walking distance. Fire certificate. Large, off-road car park. 5 minutes NEC.

B&B per night:
S Max £25.00
D Max £40.00

OPEN All Year except Christmas

MICKLETON, Gloucestershire Map ref 2B1

Silver Award

MYRTLE HOUSE

High Street, Mickleton,
Chipping Campden GL55 6SA
T: (01386) 430032 & 07971 938085
E: kate@myrtlehouse.co.uk
I: www.myrtlehouse.co.uk

Bedrooms: 4 double/twin, 1 triple/multiple
Bathrooms: 5 en suite

Evening meal available
CC: Delta, Mastercard, Switch, Visa

A Georgian house situated between Stratford and the Cotswolds, with full en suite facilities, TV, tea and coffee. Open-fire, non-smoking property with a safe, walled garden.

B&B per night:
S £37.50–£45.00
D £55.00–£75.00

OPEN All Year

GOLD & SILVER AWARDS

These exclusive ETC awards are given to establishments achieving the highest levels of quality and service. Further information can be found at the front of the guide and additional accommodation achieving these awards are shown in the listing at the back of this guide.

MIDDLETON, Northamptonshire Map ref 4C3

VALLEY VIEW

3 Camsdale Walk, Middleton, Market Harborough LE16 8YR
T: (01536) 770874

Bedrooms: 2 double/twin

Elevated, stone-built house with panoramic views of the Welland Valley. Within easy distance of Market Harborough, Corby and Rockingham raceway.

B&B per night:
S £20.00
D £38.00–£40.00

OPEN All Year

MORETON-IN-MARSH, Gloucestershire Map ref 2B1

◆◆◆

THE BELL INN

High Street, Moreton-in-Marsh GL56 0AF
T: (01608) 651688
F: (01608) 652195
E: keith.pendry@virgin.net
I: bellinncotswold.com

Traditional Cotswold inn, with en suite bedrooms, converted from original barn. Homemade food, cask ales, enclosed courtyard and impressive beer garden. Railway station 0.25 miles.

Bedrooms: 2 double/twin, 3 triple/multiple
Bathrooms: 5 en suite

Lunch available
Evening meal available
CC: Amex, Delta, Mastercard, Switch, Visa

Book 2,3 or 4 nights (Sun-Thu incl) at our special mid-week break tariff – includes 1 evening meal with house wine.

B&B per night:
S £40.00–£60.00
D £60.00–£80.00

HB per person:
DY £50.00–£65.00

OPEN All Year

◆◆◆

BLUE CEDAR HOUSE

Stow Road, Moreton-in-Marsh GL56 0DW
T: (01608) 650299
E: gandsib@dialstart.net

Bedrooms: 1 single, 2 double/twin, 1 triple/multiple
Bathrooms: 2 en suite

Evening meal available

Attractive detached residence set in 0.5 acre garden in the Cotswolds, with pleasantly decorated, well-equipped accommodation and garden room. Complimentary tea/coffee. Close to village centre.

B&B per night:
S Min £23.00
D Min £45.00

HB per person:
DY Min £34.00

DITCHFORD FARMHOUSE

Stretton on Fosse, Moreton-in-Marsh GL56 9RD
T: (01608) 663307 & 07812 415357
E: randb@ditchford-farmhouse.co.uk
I: www.ditchford-farmhouse.co.uk

Bedrooms: 4 double/twin, 2 triple/multiple
Bathrooms: 3 en suite, 3 private

1000-acre arable farm. Secluded 200-year-old Georgian farmhouse, 1 mile from road. Lovely countryside walks. Close to all attractions. Open all year.

B&B per night:
S £27.00–£32.00
D £46.00–£50.00

OPEN All Year except Christmas

◆◆◆

NEW FARM

Dorn, Moreton-in-Marsh GL56 9NS
T: (01608) 650782
F: (01608) 652704
E: cath.righton@amserve.net
I: www.smoothhound.co.uk/hotels/newfa.html

Guests can enjoy first-class accommodation at very competitive terms in this old farmhouse. Beautiful double 4-poster bed and very pretty twin room. All rooms spacious with colour TV, coffee/tea, private facilities and furnished with antiques. Dining room has large, impressive fireplace. Breakfast served with hot, crispy bread.

Bedrooms: 3 double/twin
Bathrooms: 2 en suite, 1 private

B&B per night:
S £22.00–£25.00
D £40.00–£42.00

OPEN All Year

MORETON-IN-MARSH continued

OLD FARM

Dorn, Moreton-in-Marsh GL56 9NS
T: (01608) 650394
F: (01608) 650394
E: simon@righton.freeserve.co.uk
I: www.oldfarmdorn.co.uk

Enjoy the delights of a 15thC farmhouse on a 250-acre mixed farm surrounded by beautiful Cotswold countryside. Spacious en suite double bedrooms including 4-poster, twin room available. Croquet on lawn. Children welcome. Peaceful setting for relaxing break, ideal base for visiting Cotswolds/Stratford and only 1 mile from Moreton.

Bedrooms: 3 double/twin
Bathrooms: 2 en suite

B&B per night:
D £40.00–£46.00

OPEN All Year except Christmas

♦♦♦♦

TREETOPS

London Road, Moreton-in-Marsh GL56 0HE
T: (01608) 651036
F: (01608) 651036
E: treetops1@talk21.com

Bedrooms: 5 double/twin, 1 triple/multiple
Bathrooms: 6 en suite

CC: Delta, Mastercard, Switch, Visa

Family guesthouse on the A44, set in half an acre of secluded gardens. 5 minutes' walk from the village centre.

B&B per night:
S Min £35.00
D £45.00–£50.00

OPEN All Year except Christmas

MUCH WENLOCK, Shropshire Map ref 4A3

THE GASKELL ARMS HOTEL

Much Wenlock TF13 6AQ
T: (01952) 727212
F: (01952) 728505
E: maxine@gaskellarms.co.uk
I: www.smoothhound.co.uk/hotels/gaskell.html

A charming 17thC coaching inn, situated in the historic town of Much Wenlock, central for the World Heritage site of Ironbridge, Shrewsbury, Bridgnorth and Ludlow. A family- owned freehouse provides an extensive bar and restaurant menu. All bedrooms are delightfully decorated and en suite. Log fires, beer garden, private car park.

Bedrooms: 10 double/twin, 2 triple/multiple
Bathrooms: 7 en suite

Lunch available
Evening meal available
CC: Delta, Mastercard, Switch, Visa

Weekend break £86-£100pp DB&B (Mar-Oct). 10% discount for 3 nights or more.

B&B per night:
S £38.00–£50.00
D £60.00–£80.00

HB per person:
DY £48.00–£60.00

OPEN All Year

NAILSWORTH, Gloucestershire Map ref 2B1

♦♦♦♦

AARON FARM

Nympsfield Road, Nailsworth, Stroud GL6 0ET
T: (01453) 833598
F: (01453) 833626
E: aaronfarm@aol.com
I: www.aaronfarm-bedandbreakfast.co.uk

Bedrooms: 3 double/twin
Bathrooms: 3 en suite

Former farmhouse, with large en suite bedrooms and panoramic views of the Cotswolds. Ideal touring centre. Many walks and attractions. Home cooking. Brochure on request.

B&B per night:
S £30.00–£32.00
D £42.00–£44.00

OPEN All Year

HALF BOARD PRICES Half board prices are given per person, but in some cases these may be based on double/twin occupancy.

NAUNTON, Gloucestershire Map ref 2B1

NAUNTON VIEW GUESTHOUSE

Naunton, Cheltenham GL54 3AS
T: (01451) 850482
F: (01451) 850482

B&B per night:
S £30.00–£35.00
D £45.00–£50.00

OPEN All Year

Recently opened family-run guesthouse in picturesque village near Bourton-on-the-Water. Good base for touring the Cotswolds and within easy reach of Bath and Stratford as well as having excellent walks in the area. All rooms en suite with TV and tea-making facilities. Good views over the village and plenty of safe off-road parking.

Bedrooms: 3 double/twin
Bathrooms: 3 en suite

CC: Delta, Mastercard, Switch, Visa

NEWARK, Nottinghamshire Map ref 4C2 *Tourist Information Centre Tel: (01636) 655765*

♦♦♦♦

THE BOOT AND SHOE INN

Main Street, Flintham, Newark NG23 5LA
T: (01636) 525246

B&B per night:
S Min £35.00
D Min £50.00

OPEN All Year

A 17thC village pub recently renovated to a high standard. All rooms en suite. Situated in an unspoilt conservation area at the edge of the Vale of Belvoir, 6 miles from Newark. Easy access off A46 to Nottingham, Leicester and Lincoln.

Bedrooms: 1 single, 3 double/twin, 1 triple/multiple
Bathrooms: 5 en suite

Lunch available
Evening meal available
CC: Delta, Mastercard, Switch, Visa

NEWPORT, Shropshire Map ref 4A3

Silver Award

LANE END FARM

Chetwynd, Newport TF10 8BN
T: (01952) 550337 & 0777 1632255
F: (01952) 550337
I: www.virtual-shropshire.co.uk/lef

Bedrooms: 3 double/twin
Bathrooms: 2 en suite, 1 private

Evening meal available

Delightful period farmhouse in lovely countryside, on A41 near Newport. Ideal for business/leisure, with good local walks. Reductions for 3 nights or more.

B&B per night:
S £25.00–£30.00
D £40.00–£44.00

HB per person:
DY £31.00–£41.00

OPEN All Year

NEWPORT continued

NORWOOD HOUSE HOTEL AND RESTAURANT

Pave Lane, Newport TF10 9LQ
T: (01952) 825896
F: (01952) 825896
I: www.norwoodhse.freeserve.co.uk

Bedrooms: 1 single, 3 double/twin, 1 triple/multiple
Bathrooms: 5 en suite

Lunch available
Evening meal available
CC: Delta, Mastercard, Switch, Visa

Family-run hotel of character, just off the A41 Wolverhampton to Whitchurch road. Close to Lilleshall National Sports Centre, RAF Cosford and Ironbridge Gorge.

B&B per night:
S Max £39.00
D Max £49.00

OPEN All Year

NORTHAMPTON, Northamptonshire Map ref 2C1 *Tourist Information Centre Tel: (01604) 622677*

Rating Applied For

HASELBECH HOUSE FARM

Haselbech Hill, Northampton NN6 9LL
T: (01604) 686266
F: (01604) 686544
E: lesueur@haselbech.freeserve.co.uk

Comfortable, elegantly decorated, friendly family home surrounded by very beautiful countryside. Ideal for family walking, cycling, riding and peace and quiet. Within 10 minutes of stately homes, gardens and sporting venues. Character villages and pubs abound.

Bedrooms: 2 double/twin

Evening meal available

B&B per night:
S Min £40.00
D Min £60.00

HB per person:
DY £55.00–£65.00

OPEN All Year except Christmas

◆◆◆◆

POPLARS HOTEL

Cross Street, Moulton, Northampton NN3 7RZ
T: (01604) 643983
F: (01604) 790233
E: thepoplars.hotel@btopenworld.com

Bedrooms: 1 single, 4 double/twin, 7 triple/multiple
Bathrooms: 12 en suite

Evening meal available
CC: Delta, Mastercard, Switch, Visa

Personal attention is given at this small country hotel in the heart of Northamptonshire. Within easy reach of many tourist attractions.

B&B per night:
S £30.00–£55.00
D £55.00–£79.00

HB per person:
DY £45.00–£70.00

OPEN All Year except Christmas

NORTHLEACH, Gloucestershire Map ref 2B1

◆◆◆◆ Silver Award

NORTHFIELD BED AND BREAKFAST

Cirencester Road (A429), Northleach, Cheltenham GL54 3JL
T: (01451) 860427
F: (01451) 860820
E: nrthfield0@aol.com

Detached family house with large gardens and home-grown produce. Evening meals available. Excellent centre for visiting the Cotswolds. A warm welcome awaits you.

Bedrooms: 2 double/twin, 1 triple/multiple
Bathrooms: 3 en suite

Evening meal available
CC: Amex, Delta, Mastercard, Switch, Visa

B&B per night:
S £30.00–£40.00
D £48.00–£54.00

HB per person:
DY £36.00–£45.00

OPEN All Year except Christmas

◆◆◆

WHEATSHEAF HOTEL

Northleach, Cheltenham GL54 3EZ
T: (01451) 860244
F: (01451) 861037
E: bookings@wheatsheafinn.org.uk
I: www.wheatsheafinn.org.uk

Bedrooms: 7 double/twin, 1 triple/multiple
Bathrooms: 8 en suite

Lunch available
Evening meal available
CC: Delta, Mastercard, Switch, Visa

Set in the heart of the Cotswolds, this 16thC inn offers a picturesque garden, comfortable en suite bedrooms and fine dining in a relaxed atmosphere of affordable luxury.

B&B per night:
S £45.00–£65.00
D £55.00–£75.00

HB per person:
DY £45.00–£55.00

OPEN All Year

NOTTINGHAM, Nottinghamshire Map ref 4C2 *Tourist Information Centre Tel: (0115) 915 5330*

♦♦♦

ANDREWS PRIVATE HOTEL

310 Queens Road, Beeston, Nottingham NG9 1JA
T: (0115) 925 4902
F: (0115) 917 8839
E: andrews.hotel@ntlworld.com

Bedrooms: 4 single, 5 double/twin, 1 triple/ multiple
Bathrooms: 3 en suite

With a friendly atmosphere and within easy reach of Robin Hood country, Nottingham University, the tennis centre and Central TV with secure parking for guests.

P

B&B per night:
S £25.00–£30.00
D £40.00–£45.00

OPEN All Year except Christmas

NUNEATON, Warwickshire Map ref 4B3 *Tourist Information Centre Tel: (024) 7634 7006*

♦♦

LA TAVOLA CALDA

70 Midland Road, Abbey Green, Nuneaton CV11 5DY
T: (024) 7638 3195 & 07747 010702
F: (024) 7638 1816

Bedrooms: 1 single, 5 double/twin, 2 triple/ multiple
Bathrooms: 8 en suite

Evening meal available
CC: Amex, Delta, Diners, Mastercard, Switch, Visa

Family-run Italian restaurant and hotel.

P

B&B per night:
S £20.00–£25.00
D £35.00

OPEN All Year

♦♦♦♦♦

LEATHERMILL GRANGE

Leathermill Lane, Caldecote, Nuneaton CV10 0RX
T: (01827) 714637
F: (01827) 716422
E: davidcodd@leathermillgrange.co.uk
I: www.leathermillgrange.co.uk

Beautifully refurbished 19thC Victorian farmhouse set in 5 acres of ground with landscaped gardens and lake, surrounded by farmland. Spacious and elegant interior with high-quality decor and furnishing. Bedrooms, including one 4-poster, have en suite shower rooms. Home cooking and attention to detail is our speciality. A non-smoking house.

Bedrooms: 3 double/ twin
Bathrooms: 3 en suite

Evening meal available
CC: Delta, Mastercard, Switch, Visa

4 nights for the price of 3 Oct–Mar. Free bottle of champagne to honeymoon and wedding anniversary couples.

P

B&B per night:
S £60.00–£70.00
D £80.00–£90.00

OPEN All Year except Christmas

OAKHAM, Rutland Map ref 4C3 *Tourist Information Centre Tel: (01572) 724329*

♦♦♦

HALL FARM

Cottesmore Road, Exton, Oakham LE15 8AN
T: (01572) 812271 & 07711 979628
F: (01572) 812271

25-acre arable and horses farm. Early 19thC Grade II Listed stone farmhouse in open countryside. Approximately 2 miles from Rutland Water north shore and 1 mile from Geoff Hamilton's TV gardens. TV, hairdryer and hot drinks in all rooms. Many of our guests are now making frequent return visits. Reduced prices for children.

Bedrooms: 2 double/ twin, 1 triple/multiple
Bathrooms: 1 en suite

P

B&B per night:
S £20.00–£24.50
D £35.00–£44.00

OPEN All Year except Christmas

CHECK THE MAPS

The colour maps at the front of this guide show all the cities, towns and villages for which you will find accommodation entries.
Refer to the town index to find the page on which they are listed.

OAKHAM continued

THE TITHE BARN

Clatterpot Lane, Cottesmore, Oakham
LE15 7DW
T: (01572) 813591
F: (01572) 812719
E: jpryke@thetithebarn.co.uk
I: www.tithebarn-rutland.co.uk

17thC converted tithe barn. Outstanding original dovecote. Spacious and comfortable en suite rooms with a wealth of original features. Panelled dining room and attractive garden. In the heart of unspoilt Rutland, 5 minutes from Rutland Water, Geoff Hamilton's Barnsdale Gardens, Stamford, Oakham and A1. Children and dogs welcome.

Bedrooms: 3 double/twin, 1 triple/multiple
Bathrooms: 3 en suite, 1 private

CC: Delta, Mastercard, Switch, Visa

B&B per night:
S £20.00–£35.00
D £40.00–£50.00

OPEN All Year

OVER NORTON

See South of England region for entries

OXTON, Nottinghamshire Map ref 4C2

FAR BAULKER FARM

Oxton, Southwell NG25 0RQ
T: (01623) 882375 & 0797 1087605
F: (01623) 882375
E: j.esam@virgin.net
I: www.farbaulkerfarm.info

Bedrooms: 3 double/twin
Bathrooms: 2 en suite

B&B per night:
S £20.00–£30.00
D £36.00–£40.00

OPEN All Year

300-acre mixed farm. Attractive farmhouse with pleasant gardens. Situated in peaceful, rural environment in the heart of Sherwood, yet within easy reach of Nottingham, Newark and Mansfield.

PAINSWICK, Gloucestershire Map ref 2B1

◆◆◆◆

CARDYNHAM HOUSE

The Cross, Painswick, Stroud
GL6 6XX
T: (01452) 814006
F: (01452) 812321
E: info@cardynham.co.uk
I: www.cardynham.co.uk

Bedrooms: 6 double/twin, 3 triple/multiple
Bathrooms: 8 en suite, 1 private

Evening meal available
CC: Delta, Mastercard, Switch, Visa

B&B per night:
S £47.00–£75.00
D £69.00–£135.00

OPEN All Year

Rooms of great character, each with a different theme and style. All with 4-poster beds and 1 room with its own heated pool.

PEAK DISTRICT

See under Ashbourne, Bakewell, Bamford, Buxton, Castleton, Calver, Glossop, Hathersage, Hope, Thorpe, Winster

PERSHORE, Worcestershire Map ref 2B1

Silver Award

ALDBURY HOUSE

George Lane, Wyre Piddle, Pershore
WR10 2HX
T: (01386) 553754
F: (01386) 553754
E: aldbury@onetel.net.uk

Bedrooms: 3 double/twin
Bathrooms: 3 en suite

B&B per night:
S £30.00–£35.00
D £44.00–£50.00

OPEN All Year

Quietly situated, comfortable rooms, guests' lounge, off-road parking. Nearby, riverside catering pub. Ideal base for visits to Worcester, Stratford, the Cotswolds and Malverns. Warm welcome.

VISITOR ATTRACTIONS For ideas on places to visit refer to the introduction at the beginning of this section. Look out too for the ETC's Quality Assured Visitor Attraction signs.

PERSHORE continued

◆◆◆◆ Silver Award

ARBOUR HOUSE

Main Road, Wyre Piddle, Pershore
WR10 2HU
T: (01386) 555833
F: (01386) 555833
E: lizbrownsdon@hotmail.com
I: www.smoothhound.co.uk/hotels/arbourhouse.html

A fine Grade II Listed character home with oak beams, overlooking Bredon Hill and close to the River Avon. Comfortable accommodation and good food in a relaxed, friendly atmosphere. Excellent riverside pub opposite. An ideal base for visiting the Cotswolds, Stratford, Worcester and Malvern.

Bedrooms: 3 double/twin
Bathrooms: 3 en suite

10 P

B&B per night:
S £26.00–£36.00
D £48.00–£55.00

OPEN All Year

PRIORS HARDWICK, Warwickshire Map ref 2C1

◆◆◆

HILL FARM

Priors Hardwick, Southam
CV47 7SP
T: (01327) 260338 & 07740 853085
E: simon.darbishire@farming.co.uk
I: www.farmstayuk.co.uk

Bedrooms: 2 double/twin

We offer an ideal rural retreat! Relax, and take in outstanding westerly views, beautiful sunsets over peaceful countryside. Excellent location for M40 jct 12, Stratford, Warwick, Banbury.

P

B&B per night:
S Min £25.00
D Min £40.00

OPEN All Year except Christmas

ROSS-ON-WYE, Herefordshire Map ref 2A1 *Tourist Information Centre Tel: (01989) 562768*

◆◆◆

THE ARCHES

Walford Road, Ross-on-Wye
HR9 5PT
T: (01989) 563348
F: (01989) 563348
E: the.arches@which.net

Bedrooms: 4 double/twin, 1 triple/multiple
Bathrooms: 5 en suite

CC: Delta, Mastercard, Switch, Visa

Small, family-run guesthouse, 10 minutes' walk from town centre. Warm, friendly atmosphere. All rooms with views of the garden. Victorian-style conservatory, 0.5-acre lawned garden to enjoy in summer.

P

B&B per night:
S £25.00
D £50.00

OPEN All Year

◆◆◆

THE FALCON GUEST HOUSE

How Caple, Hereford HR1 4TF
T: (01989) 740223
F: (01989) 740223
E: falconguesthouse@tinyworld.co.uk

Bedrooms: 3 double/twin, 1 triple/multiple
Bathrooms: 4 en suite

Evening meal available

Delightful Georgian house set in Wye Valley between Hereford and Ross-on-Wye. Excellent base for walking, bird-watching and historic attractions. Close to M50.

P

B&B per night:
S £25.00
D £39.00

HB per person:
DY £26.50–£39.00

OPEN All Year

USE YOUR *i*s

There are more than 550 Tourist Information Centres throughout England offering friendly help with accommodation and holiday ideas as well as suggestions of places to visit and things to do. You'll find TIC addresses in the local Phone Book.

ROSS-ON-WYE continued

THE HILL HOUSE

Howle Hill, Ross-on-Wye HR9 5ST
T: (01989) 562033
E: thehillhouse2000@hotmail.com
I: www.thehowlinghillhouse.com

B&B per night:
S £20.00–£30.00
D £30.00–£50.00

HB per person:
DY £22.00–£37.00

OPEN All Year

Something different: secluded, private, woodland setting on Wye Valley walk. Spectacular views, close to Ross and the Forest of Dean. Local organic food, friendly ghosts, sauna. Amazing rooms including 'the Dryad suite' with 7-foot 4-poster bed and sheepskin rugs in front of woodburning stove. Perfect for naughty and good weekends. Relax!

Bedrooms: 2 double/twin, 1 triple/multiple
Bathrooms: 3 en suite

Evening meal available
CC: Delta, Mastercard, Switch, Visa

Special-interest themed weekends, all inclusive prices, long list including: witchcraft, painting, poetry, storytelling, canoeing, nature walks, poker school, stress management.

♦♦♦♦

THE OLD RECTORY

Hope Mansell, Ross-on-Wye
HR9 5TL
T: (01989) 750382
F: (01989) 750382
E: rectory@mansell.wyenet.co.uk

Bedrooms: 3 double/twin
Bathrooms: 1 private

B&B per night:
S £24.50–£29.50
D £49.00

OPEN All Year except Christmas

Georgian house in beautiful rural surroundings near Ross-on-Wye. Friendly atmosphere, comfortable rooms with period furniture. Lovely mature gardens, tennis court, children's play facilities.

♦♦♦♦

THATCH CLOSE

Llangrove, Ross-on-Wye HR9 6EL
T: (01989) 770300
E: thatch.close@virgin.net

B&B per night:
D £40.00–£50.00

HB per person:
DY £34.00–£40.00

OPEN All Year

13-acre mixed farm. Secluded, peaceful and homely Georgian country farmhouse midway between Ross-on-Wye and Monmouth. Home-produced vegetables and meat. Ideal for country lovers of any age. Guests welcome to help with animals. Map sent on request. Ordnance Survey: 51535196.

Bedrooms: 3 double/twin
Bathrooms: 2 en suite, 1 private

Lunch available
Evening meal available

RUGBY, Warwickshire Map ref 4C3 *Tourist Information Centre Tel: (01788) 534970*

♦♦♦

WHITE LION INN

Coventry Road, Pailton, Rugby
CV23 0QD
T: (01788) 832359
F: (01788) 832359
I: www.whitelionpailton.co.uk

Bedrooms: 9 double/twin
Bathrooms: 5 en suite

Lunch available
Evening meal available
CC: Delta, Mastercard, Switch, Visa

B&B per night:
S £24.00–£34.00
D £44.00–£54.00

HB per person:
DY £30.00–£46.00

OPEN All Year

17thC coaching inn, recently refurbished but retaining all old world features. Close to Rugby, Coventry and Stratford. Within 4 miles of motorways. Home-cooked food served daily.

SPECIAL BREAKS

Many establishments offer special promotions and themed breaks. These are highlighted in red. (All such offers are subject to availability.)

RUGELEY, Staffordshire Map ref 4B3

♦♦♦

PARK FARM

Hawkesyard, Armitage Lane, Rugeley WS15 1ED
T: (01889) 583477
F: (01889) 583477

Bedrooms: 2 triple/multiple; permanent suite(s)
Bathrooms: 2 en suite

40-acre livestock farm. While convenient for towns and attractions in the area, Park Farm is quietly tucked away in scenic hills.

B&B per night:
S £20.00–£24.00
D £40.00–£45.00

OPEN All Year except Christmas

RUTLAND WATER *Tourist Information Centre Tel: (01572) 653026*

See under Oakham

SHERWOOD FOREST

See under Newark, Oxton, Southwell, Worksop

SHREWSBURY, Shropshire Map ref 4A3 *Tourist Information Centre Tel: (01743) 281200*

♦♦♦

ABBEY COURT HOUSE

134 Abbey Foregate, Shrewsbury SY2 6AU
T: (01743) 364416
F: (01743) 358559
E: info@abbeycourt.org
I: www.abbeycourt.org

B&B per night:
S £23.00–£25.00
D £40.00–£48.00

OPEN All Year except Christmas

Quality accommodation in a Grade II Listed building. Close to town centre and abbey. We have off-road parking, and a regular bus service is available outside the front door. Very comfortable rooms, all with hospitality trays, teletext TVs, direct dial telephones. Ground floor rooms available. Good choice of breakfasts, including vegetarian.

Bedrooms: 2 single, 6 double/twin, 2 triple/multiple; permanent suite(s)
Bathrooms: 4 en suite

CC: Amex, Delta, Mastercard, Switch, Visa

Discounted rates available for longer stays.

10

♦♦♦♦ Silver Award

ASHTON LEES

Dorrington, Shrewsbury SY5 7JW
T: (01743) 718378

B&B per night:
S £21.00–£24.00
D £42.00–£48.00

For many years we have welcomed guests to our family home. On winter evenings, roaring fires entice you to curl up and read a book, with a drink purchased from our small licensed bar. In summer we serve teas in the tree-shaded garden. A place of relaxation and tranquillity.

Bedrooms: 3 double/twin
Bathrooms: 2 en suite, 1 private

♦♦♦

CHATFORD HOUSE

Bayston Hill, Shrewsbury SY3 0AY
T: (01743) 718301

Bedrooms: 3 double/twin

Comfortable farmhouse built in 1776, 5.5 miles south of Shrewsbury off A49. Through Bayston Hill, take third right (Stapleton) then right to Chatford.

B&B per night:
S £17.00
D £34.00

MAP REFERENCES The map references refer to the colour maps at the front of this guide. The first figure is the map number; the letter and figure which follow indicate the grid reference on the map.

SKEGNESS, Lincolnshire Map ref 4D2 *Tourist Information Centre Tel: (01754) 764821*

◆◆◆

CHATSWORTH HOTEL

North Parade, Skegness PE25 2UB
T: (01754) 764177
F: (01754) 761173
E: Altipper@aol.com
I: www.chatsworthskegness.co.uk

Bedrooms: 5 single, 20 double/twin, 3 triple/multiple
Bathrooms: 28 en suite

Lunch available
Evening meal available
CC: Amex, Delta, Diners, Mastercard, Switch, Visa

B&B per night:
S £35.00–£38.00
D £55.00–£61.00

HB per person:
DY £37.00–£43.00

Centrally situated seafront hotel, close to many amenities. Dinner, lunches and snacks available seasonally. Open year round including Christmas and New Year. All rooms en suite.

SOLIHULL, West Midlands Map ref 4B3 *Tourist Information Centre Tel: (0121) 704 6130*

Silver Award

ACORN GUEST HOUSE

29 Links Drive, Solihull B91 2DJ
T: (0121) 7055241
E: acorn.wood@btinternet.com

Bedrooms: 2 single, 3 double/twin
Bathrooms: 1 en suite

B&B per night:
S £22.00–£25.00
D £44.00–£50.00

OPEN All Year except Christmas

Comfortable, quiet family home with ample private facilities, overlooking golf course. Parking and easy access to NEC, airport, M42 and Solihull centre.

CHELSEA LODGE

48 Meriden Road,
Hampton in Arden, Solihull B92 0BT
T: (01675) 442408
F: (01675) 442408
E: chelsealodgebnb@aol.com
I: www.chelsealodgebnb.co.uk

Bedrooms: 3 double/twin
Bathrooms: 2 en suite, 1 private

B&B per night:
S Min £30.00
D £45.00–£55.00

OPEN All Year except Christmas

Comfortable, detached property with delightful gardens. Walking distance to Hampton in Arden station (direct NEC/Birmingham Airport) and village pubs. Village location, 3 miles NEC/Solihull.

SOULDERN

See South of England region for entries

SOUTHWELL, Nottinghamshire Map ref 4C2

ASHDENE

Radley Road, Halam, Southwell NG22 8AH
T: (01636) 812335
E: david@herbert.newsurf.net

B&B per night:
S £25.00–£30.00
D £45.00–£50.00

OPEN All Year

Ashdene is a 16thC Yeoman farmhouse set in extensive gardens which are opened regularly each year in Open Garden Scheme. Ample parking. Guest sitting room with open fire. Children welcome. Ideal centre to explore Southwell Minster, the Dukeries and Lincoln. German and Italian spoken.

Bedrooms: 1 single, 3 double/twin; permanent suite(s)
Bathrooms: 1 en suite, 2 private

Evening meal available

TOWN INDEX

This can be found at the back of the guide. If you know where you want to stay, the index will give you the page number listing accommodation in your chosen town, city or village.

STAFFORD, Staffordshire Map ref 4B3 *Tourist Information Centre Tel: (01785) 619619*

LITTYWOOD HOUSE

Bradley, Stafford ST18 9DW
T: (01785) 780234 & 780770
E: sue@littywood.co.uk

B&B per night:
S £20.00–£35.00
D £42.00–£48.00

OPEN All Year except Christmas

Littywood is a beautiful, double-moated 14thC manor house, set in its own grounds and surrounded by open countryside. Tastefully furnished with antiques and tapestries throughout. We are easily accessible from the M6 motorway, approximately 15 minutes from jct 13. Ideally situated for Alton Towers, Shugborough Hall, Weston Park and The Potteries. Centrally heated.

Bedrooms: 3 double/twin
Bathrooms: 1 en suite, 2 private

Discounts for 3 nights or more.

STAMFORD, Lincolnshire Map ref 3A1 *Tourist Information Centre Tel: (01780) 755611*

♦♦

DOLPHIN GUESTHOUSE

12 East Street, Stamford PE9 1QD
T: (01780) 757515 & 481567
F: (01780) 757515
E: mikdolphin@mikdolphin.demon.co.uk

Bedrooms: 7 double/twin, 1 triple/multiple; permanent suite(s)
Bathrooms: 6 en suite

CC: Delta, Mastercard, Visa

B&B per night:
S £20.00–£35.00
D £40.00–£55.00

OPEN All Year except Christmas

En suite hotel-style accommodation next to the Dolphin Inn, renowned for its cask ales, friendliness and food. Off-road secure car parking and only 100 yards from the town centre.

♦♦♦♦♦ Silver Award

ROCK LODGE

1 Empingham Road, Stamford PE9 2RH
T: (01780) 481758
F: (01780) 481757
E: rocklodge@innpro.co.uk
I: www.innpro.co.uk

Bedrooms: 3 double/twin
Bathrooms: 3 en suite

CC: Delta, Mastercard, Switch, Visa

B&B per night:
S £50.00–£90.00
D £65.00–£90.00

OPEN All Year

Family-run Edwardian townhouse. Individually decorated en suite rooms with fridges. Set in walled garden with off-street parking. Five minutes' walk to town centre.

STEEPLE ASTON

See South of England region for entries

STOKE-ON-TRENT, Staffordshire Map ref 4B2 *Tourist Information Centre Tel: (01782) 236000*

♦♦♦♦♦ Silver Award

THE OLD DAIRY HOUSE

Trentham Park, Stoke-on-Trent ST4 8AE
T: (01782) 641209
F: (01782) 712904
E: olddairyhouse@hotmail.com

B&B per night:
S £40.00
D £50.00–£52.00

OPEN All Year except Christmas

The house, designed by Sir Charles Barry around 1840, is set in 2 acres of secluded wooded grounds on a private road to the golf club. It is adjacent to Trentham Gardens and only 0.5 miles from jct 15 of the M6. Ample parking. Two double en suite with private sitting room.

Bedrooms: 2 double/twin
Bathrooms: 2 en suite

Evening meal available
CC: Mastercard, Visa

STOKE-ON-TRENT continued

♦♦♦

VERDON GUEST HOUSE

44 Charles Street, Hanley, Stoke-on-Trent ST1 3JY
T: (01782) 264244 & 07711 514682
F: (01782) 264244
E: debbie@howlett18.freeserve.co.uk
I: www.verdonguesthouse.co.uk

Bedrooms: 1 single, 6 double/twin, 6 triple/multiple
Bathrooms: 5 en suite

CC: Mastercard, Visa

B&B per night:
S Min £22.00
D £40.00–£44.00

OPEN All Year

Large, friendly guesthouse in town centre close to bus station. Convenient for pottery visits, museum. Alton Towers 20 minutes, M6 10 minutes. All rooms cable TV, some 4-poster beds.

STONEHOUSE, Gloucestershire Map ref 2B1

Rating Applied For

BEACON INN HOTEL

Haresfield Village, Stonehouse GL10 3DX
T: (01452) 728884
F: (01452) 728884

Bedrooms: 3 double/twin, 2 triple/multiple
Bathrooms: 5 en suite

Lunch available
Evening meal available
CC: Delta, Mastercard, Switch, Visa

B&B per night:
S Min £30.00
D £40.00–£60.00

OPEN All Year

Built in 1841 as The Railway Hotel, The Beacon is a family-run and owned traditional public house, welcoming guests throughout the year.

♦♦

MERTON LODGE

8 Ebley Road, Stonehouse GL10 2LQ
T: (01453) 822018

Bedrooms: 3 double/twin
Bathrooms: 1 en suite

B&B per night:
S £19.00–£21.00
D £38.00–£42.00

OPEN All Year

Former gentleman's residence offering a warm welcome. Non-smoking. Three miles from M5 jct 13, over 4 roundabouts. Along Ebley Road, under footbridge.

STOURBRIDGE, West Midlands Map ref 4B3

ST. ELIZABETH'S COTTAGE

Woodman Lane, Clent, Stourbridge DY9 9PX
T: (01562) 883883
F: (01562) 885034
E: st_elizabeth_cot@btconnect.com

Beautiful country cottage with lovely garden and swimming pool. Interior professionally decorated throughout. Close to all motorway links. Destinations within easy reach – Symphony Hall, Convention Centre in Birmingham, Black Country Museum, Stourbridge crystal factories, Severn Valley railway. Twenty-five minutes from NEC and Birmingham Airport.

Bedrooms: 3 double/twin
Bathrooms: 3 en suite

B&B per night:
S £30.00–£32.00
D £56.00–£60.00

OPEN All Year

CHECK THE MAPS

The colour maps at the front of this guide show all the cities, towns and villages for which you will find accommodation entries. Refer to the town index to find the page on which they are listed.

STOW-ON-THE-WOLD, Gloucestershire Map ref 2B1 *Tourist Information Centre Tel: (01451) 831082*

♦♦♦

CORSHAM FIELD FARMHOUSE

Bledington Road, Stow-on-the-Wold, Cheltenham GL54 1JH
T: (01451) 831750

Traditional farmhouse with spectacular views of Cotswold countryside. Peaceful location 1 mile from Stow-on-the-Wold. Ideally situated for exploring all Cotswold villages, Cheltenham, Stratford-on-Avon, Blenheim and Warwick. All rooms centrally heated with TV, tea tray and hairdryer. Relaxing guest lounge/dining room. Excellent pub food 5 minutes' walk.

Bedrooms: 4 double/twin, 4 triple/multiple
Bathrooms: 6 en suite

B&B per night:
S £25.00–£35.00
D £44.00–£50.00

OPEN All Year except Christmas

♦♦♦

MAUGERSBURY MANOR

Stow-on-the-Wold, Cheltenham GL54 1HP
T: (01451) 870902
F: (01451) 870902
E: karen@manorholidays.co.uk
I: www.manorholidays.co.uk

A warm, friendly welcome awaits you at this Jacobean manor house, in the heart of the beautiful Cotswold countryside. Situated near Stow, this is an ideal place to visit picturesque villages and historic towns. Oxford, Cheltenham, Stratford all within easy reach. Quiet, comfortable accommodation. Ample parking and lovely views.

Bedrooms: 3 double/twin; permanent suite(s)
Bathrooms: 2 en suite

B&B per night:
S £30.00–£40.00
D £45.00–£50.00

♦♦♦

SOUTH HILL FARMHOUSE

Fosseway, Stow-on-the-Wold, Cheltenham GL54 1JU
T: (01451) 831888
F: (01451) 832255
E: info@southhill.co.uk
I: www.southhill.co.uk

A friendly, family-run bed and breakfast in a Listed Cotswold-stone farmhouse on the outskirts of Stow-on-the-Wold. Ideally situated for touring, walking or cycling in the Cotswolds. The town square is only 10 minutes' walk away and we have ample parking for guests.

Bedrooms: 1 single, 4 double/twin, 1 triple/multiple
Bathrooms: 5 en suite, 1 private

CC: Delta, Mastercard, Switch, Visa

B&B per night:
S £37.00
D £50.00

OPEN All Year

NB **IMPORTANT NOTE** Information on accommodation listed in this guide has been supplied by the proprietors. As changes may occur you are advised to check details at the time of booking.

STRAGGLETHORPE, Lincolnshire Map ref 3A1

♦♦♦♦ Silver Award

STRAGGLETHORPE HALL

Stragglethorpe, Lincoln LN5 0QZ
T: (01400) 272308
F: (01400) 273816
E: stragglethorpe@compuserve.com
I: www.stragglethorpe.com

B&B per night:
S £35.00–£40.00
D £90.00

OPEN All Year except Christmas

Situated just south of Lincoln, Stragglethorpe is a Grade II Listed Tudor manor set in formal gardens and furnished with antiques. Individually furnished en suites, including 2 4-poster rooms, have all modern amenities. Ideal for touring the country or simply stopping over between York and Cambridge off the A1.

Bedrooms: 3 double/twin
Bathrooms: 3 en suite

Evening meal available

Meals provided for parties of 5 or more.

P

STRATFORD-UPON-AVON, Warwickshire Map ref 2B1 *Tourist Information Centre Tel: (01789) 293127*

♦♦♦

AMELIA LINHILL GUESTHOUSE

35 Evesham Place, Stratford-upon-Avon CV37 6HT
T: (01789) 292879
F: (01789) 299691
E: Linhill@bigwig.net
I: Linhillguesthouse.co.uk

Bedrooms: 1 single, 2 double/twin, 3 triple/multiple
Bathrooms: 3 en suite

Lunch available
Evening meal available
CC: Amex, Delta, Mastercard, Switch, Visa

B&B per night:
S £20.00–£30.00
D £40.00–£60.00

HB per person:
DY £28.00–£35.00

OPEN All Year

Comfortable Victorian guesthouse offering warm welcome and good food. 5 minutes' walk from town centre and theatres and convenient for Cotswolds. Baby-sitting service.

♦♦♦♦

AVONLEA

47 Shipston Road, Stratford-upon-Avon CV37 7LN
T: (01789) 205940
F: (01789) 209115
E: avonlea-stratford@lineone.net
I: www.avonlea-stratford.co.uk

B&B per night:
S £35.00–£45.00
D £50.00–£64.00

OPEN All Year except Christmas

Stylish Victorian townhouse situated only 5 minutes' walk from the theatre and town centre. All rooms are en suite and furnished to the highest quality. Our guests are assured of a warm welcome and friendly atmosphere.

Bedrooms: 1 single, 6 double/twin, 1 triple/multiple
Bathrooms: 7 en suite, 1 private

CC: Mastercard, Switch, Visa

3 nights for the price of 2 from Oct-Mar.

P

♦♦♦

THE BLUE BOAR INN

Temple Grafton, Alcester B49 6NR
T: (01789) 750010
F: (01789) 750635
E: blueboar@covlink.co.uk
I: www.blueboarinn.co.uk

B&B per night:
S £40.00–£45.00
D £50.00–£65.00

OPEN All Year

This family-owned 16thC country inn is ideally located in the heart of rural Warwickshire, within easy reach of the Cotswolds, Birmingham NEC, NAC, Warwick Castle and Shakespeare's Stratford-upon-Avon. It has beautiful gardens, warm fires and is renowned for its good food, real ales and fine wines.

Bedrooms: 10 double/twin, 5 triple/multiple
Bathrooms: 15 en suite

Lunch available
Evening meal available
CC: Amex, Delta, Diners, Mastercard, Switch, Visa

3 nights for the price of 2 (doubles only) from Oct-Feb inclusive.

P

STRATFORD-UPON-AVON continued

♦♦♦♦

BROADLANDS GUEST HOUSE

23 Evesham Place, Stratford-upon-Avon CV37 6HT
T: (01789) 299181
F: (01789) 551382
E: broadlands.com@virgin.net
I: www.stratford-upon-avon.co.uk/broadlands.htm

Bedrooms: 2 single, 4 double/twin
Bathrooms: 5 en suite, 1 private

Elegant, recently refurbished Victorian house in Old Town conservation area. Friendly atmosphere. Private parking. Complimentary refreshment facilities in all rooms. Five to ten minutes' walk town centre/station.

12 P

B&B per night:
S £25.00–£45.00
D £50.00–£70.00

OPEN All Year except Christmas

♦♦♦

CHURCH FARM

Dorsington, Stratford-upon-Avon CV37 8AX
T: (01789) 720471 & 07831 504194
F: (01789) 720830
E: chfarmdorsington@aol.com
I: www.churchfarmstratford.co.uk

Bedrooms: 5 double/twin, 2 triple/multiple
Bathrooms: 6 en suite, 1 private

127-acre mixed farm. Situated on Heart of England Way, in pretty village. Most rooms en suite, TV, tea and coffee facilities. Close Stratford-upon-Avon, Warwick, Cotswolds, Evesham.

P

B&B per night:
S £25.00–£27.00
D £42.00–£45.00

OPEN All Year

Rating Applied for

COURTLAND HOTEL

12 Guild Street, Stratford-upon-Avon CV37 6RE
T: (01789) 292401
F: (01789) 292401
E: dianamoon@ukvacation.com
I: www.uk-vacation.com/courtland

Bedrooms: 2 single, 3 double/twin, 2 triple/multiple
Bathrooms: 4 en suite

CC: Amex, Mastercard, Visa

Elegant Georgian house, rear of Shakespeare's birthplace. Town centre situation. Three minutes from theatre. Free pick-up from station. Full English or continental breakfast included.

P

B&B per night:
S £25.00–£45.00
D £45.00–£60.00

OPEN All Year

♦♦♦♦

DYLAN GUESTHOUSE

10 Evesham Place, Stratford-upon-Avon CV37 6HT
T: (01789) 204819
E: dylanguesthouse@lineone.net
I: www.thedylan.co.uk

Bedrooms: 1 single, 2 double/twin, 2 triple/multiple
Bathrooms: 5 en suite

Ideally situated for touring the Midlands, 5 minutes' walk Royal Shakespeare Theatre and close to town centre. A non-smoking establishment.

7 P

B&B per night:
S £24.00–£28.00
D £48.00–£56.00

OPEN All Year

HIGHCROFT

Banbury Road, Stratford-upon-Avon CV37 7NF
T: (01789) 296293
F: (01789) 415236
E: suedavies_highcroft@hotmail.com
I: www.smoothhound.co.uk

Lovely country house and converted barns in 2 acres of landscaped gardens in the heart of rural Warwickshire but only 2 miles from Stratford-upon-Avon and close to Cotswolds and Warwick. We welcome you with tea and homemade cakes and then ask you to relax and enjoy our home. Rooms both en suite, sitting room with open fire.

Bedrooms: 1 double/twin, 1 triple/multiple
Bathrooms: 2 en suite

P

B&B per night:
S £30.00
D £50.00

OPEN All Year

STRATFORD-UPON-AVON continued

MELITA PRIVATE HOTEL

37 Shipston Road, Stratford-upon-Avon CV37 7LN
T: (01789) 292432
F: (01789) 204867
E: info@melitahotel.co.uk
I: www.melitahotel.co.uk

Once a Victorian home, the Melita is now a warm and friendly hotel managed by caring proprietors. Accommodation and service are of a high standard, and breakfasts are individually prepared to suit guests' requirements. The Melita is only 400 metres from the theatres and town centre and has free, private, on-site car parking.

Bedrooms: 3 single, 7 double/twin, 2 triple/multiple
Bathrooms: 10 en suite, 2 private

CC: Amex, Delta, Mastercard, Switch, Visa

Discounts available Nov-Mar 2003 (excl Sat and locally important dates).

B&B per night:
S £37.00–£59.00
D £52.00–£82.00

OPEN All Year except Christmas

♦♦♦

MOONLIGHT BED & BREAKFAST

144 Alcester Road, Stratford-upon-Avon CV37 9DR
T: (01789) 298213

Bedrooms: 1 single, 2 double/twin, 1 triple/multiple
Bathrooms: 2 en suite

Small family guesthouse near town centre and station, offering comfortable accommodation at reasonable prices. Tea/coffee-making facilities, colour TV. En suite rooms available.

B&B per night:
S £17.00–£19.00
D £34.00–£38.00

OPEN All Year

♦♦♦

PARKFIELD

3 Broad Walk, Stratford-upon-Avon CV37 6HS
T: (01789) 293313
F: (01789) 293313
E: parkfield@btinternet.com
I: www.parkfieldbandb.co.uk

Bedrooms: 1 single, 5 double/twin, 1 triple/multiple
Bathrooms: 6 en suite, 1 private

CC: Mastercard, Visa

Delightful Victorian house. Quiet location, 5 minutes' walk from theatre and town. Most rooms en suite. Colour TV, tea and coffee facilities and parking. Choice of breakfast, including vegetarian. A non-smoking house.

B&B per night:
S £25.00–£26.00
D £46.00–£48.00

OPEN All Year

♦♦♦♦

PENRYN GUESTHOUSE

126 Alcester Road, Stratford-upon-Avon CV37 9DP
T: (01789) 293718 & 07889 486345
F: (01789) 266077
E: penrynhouse@btinternet.com
I: www.penrynguesthouse.co.uk

Bedrooms: 1 single, 4 double/twin, 2 triple/multiple
Bathrooms: 5 en suite

CC: Amex, Delta, Diners, Mastercard, Switch, Visa

On the A422, 5 minutes from the centre of Stratford and Ann Hathaway's cottage. Ample parking space.

B&B per night:
S £25.00–£28.00
D £45.00–£55.00

COUNTRY CODE Always follow the Country Code · Enjoy the countryside and respect its life and work · Guard against all risk of fire · Fasten all gates · Keep your dogs under close control · Keep to public paths across farmland · Use gates and stiles to cross fences, hedges and walls · Leave livestock, crops and machinery alone · Take your litter home · Help to keep all water clean · Protect wildlife, plants and trees · Take special care on country roads · Make no unnecessary noise

STRATFORD-UPON-AVON continued

RAVENHURST

2 Broad Walk, Stratford-upon-Avon
CV37 6HS
T: (01789) 292515
E: ravaccom@waverider.co.uk
I: www.stratford-ravenhurst.co.uk

Victorian townhouse built in 1865, quiet location, a few minutes' walk from town centre, historical buildings and Royal Shakespeare Theatre. Comfortable home. Breakfasts a speciality. Off-street parking available. All bedrooms en suite, non-smoking. Richard Workman and family offer you a warm welcome and a vast amount of local knowledge. Credit cards welcome.

Bedrooms: 5 double/twin
Bathrooms: 5 en suite

CC: Delta, Mastercard, Switch, Visa

B&B per night:
D £44.00–£50.00

OPEN All Year except Christmas

◆◆◆◆

VIRGINIA LODGE GUEST HOUSE

12 Evesham Place, Stratford-upon-Avon
CV37 6HT
T: (01789) 292157 & 266605
F: (01789) 292157
E: pamela83@btinternet.com
I: www.virginialodge.co.uk

Beautiful Victorian house in the centre of Stratford. All bedrooms beautifully designed to a very high standard with en suite, TV, hairdryer, tea/coffee etc. 4-poster rooms, Laura Ashley, country manor. Full English breakfast served with real coffee. Private car park. A non-smoking house.

Bedrooms: 5 double/twin, 1 triple/multiple
Bathrooms: 6 en suite

B&B per night:
D £36.00–£48.00

OPEN All Year except Christmas

◆◆◆◆
Gold Award

THE WHITE HOUSE

Kings Lane, Bishopton, Stratford-upon-Avon CV37 0RD
T: (01789) 294296
E: enquiries@stratfordwhitehouse.co.uk
I: www.stratfordwhitehouse.co.uk

Bedrooms: 3 double/twin
Bathrooms: 2 en suite, 1 private

Country home built early 1900s, retaining many original features. Mellow pine interior, log fires, antique furnishings. Rural location 1.5 miles north of Stratford-upon-Avon.

B&B per night:
S £35.00–£40.00
D £50.00–£55.00

OPEN All Year except Christmas

STRETTON, Staffordshire Map ref 4B3

◆◆◆◆◆
Silver Award

DOVECLIFF HALL

Dovecliff Road, Stretton,
Burton upon Trent DE13 0DJ
T: (01283) 531818
F: (01283) 516546

Bedrooms: 1 single, 6 double/twin
Bathrooms: 7 en suite

Lunch available
Evening meal available
CC: Amex, Delta, Mastercard, Switch, Visa

Magnificent Georgian house, with breathtaking views, overlooking the River Dove and set in 7 acres of landscaped gardens in open countryside. Half a mile from A38.

B&B per night:
S £65.00–£130.00
D £100.00–£130.00

OPEN All Year

STROUD, Gloucestershire Map ref 2B1

◆◆◆

THE CLOTHIER'S ARMS

1 Bath Road, Stroud GL5 3JJ
T: (01453) 763801
F: (01453) 757161
E: luciano@clothiersarms.demon.co.uk
I: www.clothiersarms.co.uk

Bedrooms: 5 double/twin, 2 triple/multiple
Bathrooms: 6 en suite, 1 private

Lunch available
Evening meal available
CC: Delta, Mastercard, Switch, Visa

B&B per night:
S £30.00–£35.00
D Max £55.00

OPEN All Year

Cotswold inn, en suite rooms, restaurant, real ales, beer garden, children's play area. For reservations telephone or visit our website.

P

◆◆◆

DOWNFIELD HOTEL

134 Cainscross Road, Stroud GL5 4HN
T: (01453) 764496
F: (01453) 753150
E: info@downfieldhotel.com
I: www.downfieldhotel.com

B&B per night:
S £28.00–£42.00
D £50.00–£60.00

OPEN All Year

Set in the heart of the beautiful south Cotswolds, this is a favourite for thousands of guests. Whether you are staying for a few days, exploring the surrounding hills and valleys and the numerous attractions or breaking a long journey, you can enjoy warm hospitality, home-cooked food, spacious lounges and cosy bar.

Bedrooms: 4 single, 16 double/twin, 1 triple/multiple
Bathrooms: 11 en suite

Evening meal available
CC: Amex, Delta, Mastercard, Switch, Visa

P

◆◆◆◆

PRETORIA VILLA

Wells Road, Eastcombe, Stroud GL6 7EE
T: (01452) 770435
F: (01452) 770435
E: glynis@gsolomon.freeserve.co.uk

Bedrooms: 1 single, 2 double/twin
Bathrooms: 2 en suite, 1 private

Evening meal available

B&B per night:
S £25.00
D £50.00

HB per person:
DY £40.00

OPEN All Year except Christmas

Cotswold-stone double-fronted detached house, built c1900, with private gardens. In quiet village lane with beautiful views.

P

TAMWORTH, Staffordshire Map ref 4B3 *Tourist Information Centre Tel: (01827) 709581*

◆◆◆◆
Silver Award

THE CHESTNUTS COUNTRY GUEST HOUSE

Watling Street, Grendon, Atherstone CV9 2PZ
T: (01827) 331355
F: (01827) 896951
E: cclLtd@aol.com
I: www.chestnutsguesthouse.com

B&B per night:
S £55.00
D £70.00

OPEN All Year except Christmas

Beautiful 100-year-old character cottage with oak beams and inglenook fireplace. A warm welcome, wine and home-cooked food awaits you. Lovely themed bedrooms, all en suite with TV, radio alarm and courtesy tray. Secure private parking in the grounds. Countryside setting. Ideal business, special occasion or leisure break.

Bedrooms: 2 single, 2 double/twin
Bathrooms: 4 en suite

Lunch available
Evening meal available
CC: Amex, Mastercard, Switch, Visa

Children under 12 free of charge. Off-peak offers.

P

SYMBOLS The symbols in each entry give information about services and facilities. A key to these symbols appears at the back of this guide.

TELFORD, Shropshire Map ref 4A3 *Tourist Information Centre Tel: (01952) 238008*

♦♦♦

FALCON HOTEL

Holyhead Road, Wellington, Telford TF1 2DD
T: (01952) 255011
E: falconhotel@hotmail.com

Bedrooms: 2 single, 8 double/twin, 1 triple/multiple
Bathrooms: 8 en suite, 2 private

Lunch available
Evening meal available
CC: Delta, Mastercard, Visa

Small, family-run 18thC coaching hotel, 10 miles from Shrewsbury, 4 miles from Ironbridge, 18 miles from M6 at the end of M54 (exit 7).

B&B per night:
S £31.00–£42.00
D £39.00–£51.00

HB per person:
DY £37.00–£55.00

OPEN All Year except Christmas

♦♦♦♦

GROVE HOUSE GUESTHOUSE

Stafford Street, St Georges, Telford TF2 9JW
T: (01952) 616140
F: (01952) 616140

Bedrooms: 2 single, 6 double/twin
Bathrooms: 7 en suite, 1 private

Originally built as a hunting lodge. Close to Telford town centre/exhibition centre/Ironbridge. Accessed from jct 4, M54. Centrally situated for Shropshire attractions.

5

B&B per night:
S £22.00–£28.00
D £36.00–£38.00

OPEN All Year except Christmas

♦♦♦♦

THE MILL HOUSE

Shrewsbury Road, High Ercall, Telford TF6 6BE
T: (01952) 770394
F: (01952) 770394
E: mill-house@talk21.com
I: www.virtual-shropshire.co.uk/millhouse

Bedrooms: 2 double/twin, 1 triple/multiple
Bathrooms: 2 en suite, 1 private

A Grade II Listed watermill (no machinery) incorporating a working smallholding and family home, beside River Roden. Convenient for Ironbridge, Shrewsbury and mid-Wales.

B&B per night:
S £30.00–£35.00
D £40.00–£45.00

OPEN All Year

TETBURY, Gloucestershire Map ref 2B2 *Tourist Information Centre Tel: (01666) 503552*

♦♦

FOLLY FARM COTTAGES

Long Newnton, Tetbury GL8 8XA
T: (01666) 502475
F: (01666) 502358
E: info@gtb.co.uk
I: www.gtb.co.uk

Bedrooms: 1 single, 3 double/twin
Bathrooms: 4 en suite

CC: Mastercard, Switch, Visa

220-acre dairy farm. Queen Anne farmhouse, just 3 minutes' walk into Royal Tetbury and close to M4 and M5 motorways. Resident host.

B&B per night:
S £35.00–£45.00
D £45.00

OPEN All Year

TEWKESBURY, Gloucestershire Map ref 2B1 *Tourist Information Centre Tel: (01684) 295027*

♦♦

THE ABBEY HOTEL

67 Church Street, Tewkesbury GL20 5RX
T: (01684) 294247
F: (01684) 297208
E: brian@the-abbey-hotel.co.uk
I: www.the-abbey-hotel.co.uk

Bedrooms: 1 single, 7 double/twin, 5 triple/multiple
Bathrooms: 13 en suite

CC: Delta, Mastercard, Switch, Visa

Warm, family-run hotel offering accommodation at reasonable cost. All rooms en suite, and hotel has a residents' car park. Excellent food served everyday.

B&B per night:
S £40.00–£45.00
D £50.00–£65.00

HB per person:
DY £55.00–£65.00

OPEN All Year except Christmas

♦♦♦

ABBEY ANTIQUES BED AND BREAKFAST

62 Church Street, Tewkesbury GL20 5RZ
T: (01684) 298145
E: brazdys@amserve.net

Bedrooms: 2 double/twin, 1 triple/multiple
Bathrooms: 3 en suite

Comfortable family-run accommodation in charming Grade II Listed townhouse, 50 yards from magnificent Norman abbey and river. Hearty and leisurely breakfast. Beautiful walled gardens.

B&B per night:
S £30.00
D £50.00

OPEN All Year

PRICES
Please check prices and other details at the time of booking.

TEWKESBURY continued

ABBOTS COURT FARM

Church End, Twyning, Tewkesbury
GL20 6DA
T: (01684) 292515
F: (01684) 292515
E: abbotscourt@hotmail.com

450-acre arable and dairy farm. Large, comfortable farmhouse in excellent touring area. Most rooms en suite. Three games rooms, grass tennis court, fishing lakes.

Bedrooms: 1 single, 3 double/twin, 4 triple/multiple
Bathrooms: 6 en suite

B&B per night:
S £21.00–£26.00
D £39.00–£41.00

OPEN All Year except Christmas

◆◆◆

CARRANT BROOK HOUSE

3 Rope Walk, Tewkesbury GL20 5DS
T: (01684) 290355 & 0771 808 5136
E: lorraine@carrantbrookhouse.co.uk

Bedrooms: 1 single, 2 double/twin
Bathrooms: 3 en suite

Evening meal available

Welcoming, clean, friendly Victorian family home. En suite, colour TV, tea/coffee, toiletries, four-course breakfast to die for! Baby-sitting, laundry, evening meal by arrangement.

B&B per night:
S £25.00–£35.00
D £50.00–£55.00

HB per person:
DY £35.00–£45.00

OPEN All Year

THORPE, Derbyshire Map ref 4B2

◆◆◆

HILLCREST HOUSE

Dovedale, Thorpe, Ashbourne
DE6 2AW
T: (01335) 350436
E: hillcresthouse@freenet.co.uk
I: www.ashbourne-towncom/accom/hillcrest

Bedrooms: 1 single, 6 double/twin
Bathrooms: 5 en suite

CC: Delta, Mastercard, Switch, Visa

A former coaching inn on the road to Dovedale. Relax in a quiet, friendly atmosphere, enjoy outstanding views, family run. A home from home.

B&B per night:
D £40.00–£70.00

OPEN All Year except Christmas

UPPINGHAM, Rutland Map ref 4C3

◆◆◆

THE VAULTS

Market Place, Uppingham, Oakham
LE15 9QH
T: (01572) 823259 & 820019
F: (01572) 820019
I: www.rutnet.co.uk

Bedrooms: 3 double/twin, 1 triple/multiple
Bathrooms: 4 en suite

Lunch available
Evening meal available
CC: Amex, Delta, Mastercard, Switch, Visa

In the market place of this delightful Rutland town in the heart of the East Midlands. Convenient for Leicester, Corby, Peterborough, Melton Mowbray and Rutland Water.

B&B per night:
S Min £35.00
D Min £45.00

OPEN All Year

UPTON-UPON-SEVERN, Worcestershire Map ref 2B1 *Tourist Information Centre Tel: (01684) 594200*

◆◆◆◆
Silver Award

TILTRIDGE FARM AND VINEYARD

Upper Hook Road, Upton-upon-Severn,
Worcester WR8 0SA
T: (01684) 592906
F: (01684) 594142
E: sandy@tiltridge.com
I: www.tiltridge.com

Set in vineyards in a peaceful location this tranquil, pretty farmhouse lies near the Malvern Hills and close to the attractive riverside town of Upton-on-Severn. Five minutes from Three Counties Showground. Bumper farmhouse breakfast with our own eggs and homemade preserves and locally sourced bread, apple juice, bacon and sausages.

Bedrooms: 3 double/twin
Bathrooms: 3 en suite

Third night at a cheaper rate. Free wine tasting.

B&B per night:
S £28.00–£30.00
D £46.00–£50.00

OPEN All Year except Christmas

UPTON-UPON-SEVERN continued

WELLAND COURT

Upton-upon-Severn, Worcester
WR8 0ST
T: (01684) 594426
F: (01684) 594426
E: archer@wellandcourt.freeserve.co.uk
I: www.wellandcourt.co.uk

Bedrooms: 3 double/twin
Bathrooms: 3 en suite

B&B per night:
S £35.00–£50.00
D £65.00–£80.00

OPEN All Year except Christmas

Built c1450 and enlarged in the 18thC. Rescued from a dilapidated state and modernised to a high standard. At the foot of the Malvern Hills, an ideal base for touring.

VOWCHURCH, Herefordshire Map ref 2A1

Silver Award

UPPER GILVACH FARM

St. Margarets, Vowchurch, Hereford
HR2 0QY
T: (01981) 510618
F: (01981) 510618
E: ruth@uppergilvach.freeserve.co.uk
I: www.golden-valley.co.uk/gilvach

A warm welcome awaits you on this family farm between the Golden Valley and Black Mountains. The 300-year-old farmhouse offers 3 spacious, attractively furnished bedrooms, all en suite with colour TV and hospitality tray. Delicious evening meals and hearty farmhouse breakfasts using local wines and produce. Plenty of parking. Licensed.

Bedrooms: 1 single, 1 double/twin, 1 triple/multiple
Bathrooms: 2 en suite, 1 private

Evening meal available
CC: Mastercard, Switch, Visa

B&B per night:
S £25.00–£30.00
D Min £50.00

HB per person:
DY Min £40.00

OPEN All Year except Christmas

WARWICK, Warwickshire Map ref 2B1 *Tourist Information Centre Tel: (01926) 492212*

AUSTIN HOUSE

96 Emscote Road, Warwick
CV34 5QJ
T: (01926) 493583
F: (01926) 493679
E: mike@austinhouse96.ntlworld.com
I: www.austinhousewarwick.co.uk

Bedrooms: 1 single, 4 double/twin, 2 triple/multiple; permanent suite(s)
Bathrooms: 5 en suite

CC: Delta, Mastercard, Switch, Visa

B&B per night:
S £20.00–£25.00
D £38.00–£46.00

OPEN All Year except Christmas

Black and white Victorian house 1 mile from Warwick town and Castle. Three miles from Royal Leamington Spa, 8 miles from Stratford-upon-Avon.

AVON GUEST HOUSE

7 Emscote Road, Warwick
CV34 4PH
T: (01926) 491367
E: sue@comphouse.demon.co.uk
I: www.comphouse.demon.co.uk

Bedrooms: 1 single, 3 double/twin, 2 triple/multiple
Bathrooms: 6 en suite

B&B per night:
S £23.00–£30.00
D £46.00–£50.00

OPEN All Year except Christmas

Family-run guesthouse. All rooms en suite with colour TV, tea/coffee facilities and hairdryer. Car park. Five minutes' walk from castle and town centre.

AT-A-GLANCE SYMBOLS

Symbols at the end of each accommodation entry give useful information about services and facilities. A key to symbols can be found inside the back cover flap. Keep this open for easy reference.

♦♦♦♦

THE CROFT GUESTHOUSE

Haseley Knob, Warwick CV35 7NL
T: (01926) 484447
F: (01926) 484447
E: david@croftguesthouse.co.uk
I: www.croftguesthouse.co.uk

A non-smoking, friendly family guesthouse providing high-quality, clean and comfortable, en suite accommodation at reasonable prices. Centrally located (off A4177) for exploring Warwick, Stratford, Coventry and Kenilworth, or for visiting NEC (15 minutes), National Agricultural Centre (15 minutes). Sky TV, fax and e-mail facilities. More details on our website.

Bedrooms: 2 single, 4 double/twin, 3 triple/multiple
Bathrooms: 6 en suite, 3 private

CC: Amex, Delta, Mastercard, Switch, Visa

B&B per night:
S £35.00–£40.00
D £50.00–£55.00

OPEN All Year except Christmas

♦♦♦♦ Silver Award

FORTH HOUSE

44 High Street, Warwick CV34 4AX
T: (01926) 401512
F: (01926) 490809
E: info@forthhouseuk.co.uk
I: www.forthhouseuk.co.uk

Bedrooms: 1 double/twin, 1 triple/multiple; permanent suite(s)
Bathrooms: 2 en suite

CC: Delta, Mastercard, Switch, Visa

Ground floor and first floor guest suites with private sitting rooms and bathrooms. At the back of the house, overlooking peaceful garden, in town centre.

B&B per night:
S £40.00–£50.00
D £65.00–£72.00

OPEN All Year

♦♦♦♦ Silver Award

LOWER ROWLEY

Wasperton, Warwick CV35 8EB
T: (01926) 624937
E: cliffordveasey@lower-rowley.freeserve.co.uk

Bedrooms: 2 double/twin
Bathrooms: 1 en suite, 1 private

Peace and quiet in luxurious non-smoking accommodation, 4 miles from Warwick and 6 miles from Stratford-upon-Avon. Beautiful rural surroundings, with River Avon at bottom of the garden.

10 P

B&B per night:
S £25.00–£35.00
D £45.00–£48.00

OPEN All Year

♦♦♦♦ Silver Award

NORTHLEIGH HOUSE

Five Ways Road, Hatton, Warwick CV35 7HZ
T: (01926) 484203 & 07774 101894
F: (01926) 484006
I: www.northleigh.co.uk

The personal welcome and the individually designed en suite rooms with many thoughtful extras make this the perfect rural retreat. A full English breakfast is freshly cooked to suit each guest. Excellent country pubs nearby, also Stratford-upon-Avon, Warwick and the Exhibition Centres. Please ring Sylvia Fenwick for brochures.

Bedrooms: 1 single, 6 double/twin
Bathrooms: 7 en suite

CC: Delta, Mastercard, Switch, Visa

Weekend discounts: 5% for 2 nights, 7% for 3 nights.

B&B per night:
S £36.00–£43.00
D £53.00–£62.00

CREDIT CARD BOOKINGS If you book by telephone and are asked for your credit card number it is advisable to check the proprietor's policy should you cancel your reservation.

WARWICK continued

◆◆◆◆ Silver Award

SHREWLEY POOLS FARM

Haseley, Warwick CV35 7HB
T: (01926) 484315
E: cathydodd@hotmail.com
I: www.s-h-systems.co.uk/hotels/shrewley.html

Glorious 17thC traditional family farmhouse with log fires, oak floors, beams etc, set in an acre of outstanding garden featuring herbaceous borders and unusual trees and shrubs. Two spacious, en suite bedrooms and own sitting room with books and games. Perfectly situated for numerous attractions. Surrounded by picturesque farmland.

Bedrooms: 1 double/twin, 1 triple/multiple
Bathrooms: 2 en suite

Evening meal available

Stay 3 nights (2 people sharing) and get fishing half price.

B&B per night:
S £30.00–£40.00
D £45.00–£50.00

HB per person:
DY £40.00–£55.00

OPEN All Year except Christmas

◆◆◆◆

THE TILTED WIG

11 Market Place, Warwick CV34 4SA
T: (01926) 410466 & 411740
F: (01926) 495740

Bedrooms: 4 double/twin
Bathrooms: 4 en suite

Lunch available
Evening meal available
CC: Amex, Delta, Diners, Mastercard, Switch, Visa

Grade II Listed building situated comfortably in the market place, blending in with the town's historic architecture. A cafe bar, brasserie, wine bar atmosphere.

B&B per night:
S £58.00
D £58.00

OPEN All Year except Christmas

WATERHOUSES, Staffordshire Map ref 4B2

◆◆◆◆ Silver Award

LEE HOUSE FARM

Leek Road, Waterhouses, Stoke-on-Trent ST10 3HW
T: (01538) 308439

Bedrooms: 3 double/twin
Bathrooms: 3 en suite

Charming 18thC house in centre of a Staffordshire Moorlands village in Peak National Park. Ideal for Derbyshire Dales, Potteries and Alton Towers.

8

B&B per night:
D £20.00–£25.00

OPEN All Year except Christmas

WELLINGBOROUGH, Northamptonshire Map ref 3A2 *Tourist Information Centre Tel: (01933) 276412*

Rating Applied For

THE MANOR HOUSE

1 Orlingbury Road,
Great Harrowden, Wellingborough NN9 5AF
T: (01933) 678505
E: info@harrowdenmanor.com
I: www.harrowdenmanor.com

Bedrooms: 3 double/twin
Bathrooms: 3 en suite

Evening meal available
CC: Visa

16thC country manor house. Beautiful en suite bedrooms, large gardens, village location, centrally situated for undiscovered Northamptonshire market towns and stately homes. Major roads easily accessible.

12

B&B per night:
D Max £88.13

WESTBURY, Northamptonshire Map ref 2C1

◆◆◆

MILL FARM HOUSE

Westbury, Brackley NN13 5JS
T: (01280) 704843
F: (01280) 704843

Bedrooms: 1 single, 1 double/twin, 1 triple/multiple
Bathrooms: 1 en suite

1000-acre mixed farm. Grade II Listed farmhouse, overlooking a colourful garden including a covered heated swimming pool. Situated in the centre of Westbury village.

B&B per night:
S Min £25.00
D £45.00–£50.00

OPEN All Year

ACCESSIBILITY

Look for the symbols which indicate National Accessible Scheme standards for hearing and visually impaired guests in addition to standards for guests with mobility impairment. Additional participants are shown in the listings at the back.

WINSTER, Derbyshire Map ref 4B2

♦♦♦♦

BRAE COTTAGE

East Bank, Winster, Matlock
DE4 2DT
T: (01629) 650375

Bedrooms: 2 double/twin
Bathrooms: 2 en suite

B&B per night:
D £40.00–£60.00

OPEN All Year

18thC cottage in tranquil surroundings. Picturesque village in Peak District National Park. En suite accommodation, separate from cottage, furnished to high standard. Private courtyard parking.

P

WIRKSWORTH, Derbyshire Map ref 4B2

♦♦♦

RED LION

Market Place, Wirksworth, Derby
DE4 4ET
T: (01629) 822214
E: shfarrand@aol.com
I: www.newcenturyinns.com

Bedrooms: 6 triple/multiple
Bathrooms: 4 en suite, 2 private

Lunch available
Evening meal available

B&B per night:
S £30.00–£35.00
D £50.00–£60.00

OPEN All Year

Quality en suite rooms in this delightful 18thC coaching inn with busy public bar, restaurant and function room. Within historic market town close to the Peak District.

5 P

WISHAW, Warwickshire Map ref 4B3

♦♦♦

ASH HOUSE

The Gravel, Wishaw,
Sutton Coldfield B76 9QB
T: (01675) 475782 & 07850 414000
E: kate@rectory80.freeserve.co.uk

Bedrooms: 2 double/twin
Bathrooms: 2 en suite

CC: Delta, Mastercard, Visa

B&B per night:
S £30.00–£40.00
D £50.00–£60.00

OPEN All Year except Christmas

Former rectory with lovely views. Few minutes' walk from Belfry Golf and Leisure Hotel. Half a mile M42, 10 minutes' drive from Birmingham Airport/NEC.

5 P

WITNEY

See South of England region for entries

WOODSTOCK

See South of England region for entries

WORCESTER, Worcestershire Map ref 2B1 *Tourist Information Centre Tel: (01905) 726311*

♦♦

FIVE WAYS HOTEL

Angel Place, Worcester WR1 3QN
T: (01905) 616980
F: (01905) 616344

Bedrooms: 6 double/twin, 1 triple/multiple
Bathrooms: 4 en suite, 1 private

Lunch available
Evening meal available
CC: Amex, Delta, Mastercard, Switch, Visa

B&B per night:
S £29.00–£39.00
D £48.00–£60.00

HB per person:
DY £35.00–£45.00

OPEN All Year

City-centre location, family run, close to all amenities, all rooms en suite.

♦♦♦♦
Silver Award

YEW TREE HOUSE

Norchard, Crossway Green, Stourport-on-Severn DY13 9SN
T: (01299) 250921 & 07971 112621
F: (01299) 253472
E: paul@knightp.swinternet.co.uk
I: www.yewtreeworcester.co.uk

Bedrooms: 4 double/twin, 1 triple/multiple
Bathrooms: 5 en suite

Evening meal available

Discount of 10% for mid-week business use of 3 or more consecutive nights' stay.

B&B per night:
S £31.50–£35.00
D £50.00–£55.00

HB per person:
DY £40.00–£45.00

OPEN All Year

Built in 1754, Yew Tree house has a special ambience permeating through a beautifully furnished home. We also have an Elizabethan annexe to the main house called The Cider House. The whole is set peacefully in secluded gardens but within easy reach of the M5 and numerous excellent eating establishments.

P

WORKSOP, Nottinghamshire Map ref 4C2 *Tourist Information Centre Tel: (01909) 501148*

◆◆◆

SHERWOOD GUESTHOUSE

57 Carlton Road, Worksop S80 1PP
T: (01909) 474209
F: (01909) 476470
E: CHERWOULD@aol.com

Bedrooms: 1 single, 4 double/twin, 1 triple/multiple
Bathrooms: 2 en suite

Evening meal available

B&B per night:
S £21.00
D £42.00–£47.00

OPEN All Year

In Robin Hood country, near M1 and A1. Close to station and town centre. Comfortable rooms with TV and tea/coffee facilities. Accent on 'service'.

P

WYE VALLEY

See under Hereford, Ross-on-Wye

Welcome *to* Excellence

In 2003 the English Tourism Council launches a new range of training recognition awards for commitment to improving customer service for all types of accommodation and other tourism organisations.

Where you find the Welcome to Excellence plaque, you can be assured of a commitment to:

- achieve excellence in customer service
- exceed guest needs and expectations
- provide an environment where courtesy, helpfulness and a warm welcome are standard
- focus and develop individual skills.

Those displaying the plaque meet a special charter and have at least 50% of staff trained to the required standards.

A brief guide to the main Towns and Villages offering accommodation in the

Heart of England

A **ALDERTON, GLOUCESTERSHIRE** - Hillside village with wide views of Evesham Vale. The restored church has a 15thC tower, a broken Saxon font and some medieval glass. Some stone from the previous Norman church has been incorporated into its structure.

• **ALTON, STAFFORDSHIRE** - Alton Castle, an impressive 19thC building, dominates the village which is set in spectacular scenery. Nearby is Alton Towers, a romantic 19thC ruin with innumerable tourist attractions within one of England's largest theme parks in its 800 acres of magnificent gardens.

• **ASHBOURNE, DERBYSHIRE** - Market town on the edge of the Peak District National Park and an excellent centre for walking. Its impressive church with 212-ft spire stands in an unspoilt old street. Ashbourne is well known for gingerbread and its Shrovetide football match.

• **ASHBY-DE-LA-ZOUCH, LEICESTERSHIRE** - Lovely market town with late-15thC church, impressive ruined 15thC castle, an interesting small museum and a wide, sloping main street with Georgian buildings. Twycross Zoo is nearby.

• **ATHERSTONE, WARWICKSHIRE** - Pleasant market town with some 18thC houses and interesting old inns. Every Shrove Tuesday a game of football is played in the streets, a tradition which dates from the 13thC. Twycross Zoo is nearby with an extensive collection of reptiles and butterflies.

B **BAKEWELL, DERBYSHIRE** - Pleasant market town, famous for its pudding. It is set in beautiful countryside on the River Wye and is an excellent centre for exploring the Derbyshire Dales, the Peak District National Park, Chatsworth House and Haddon Hall.

• **BALSALL COMMON, WEST MIDLANDS** - Close to Birmingham NEC and Kenilworth and within easy reach of Coventry.

• **BAMFORD, DERBYSHIRE** - Village in the Peak District near the Upper Derwent reservoirs of Ladybower, Derwent and Howden. An excellent centre for walking.

• **BIBURY, GLOUCESTERSHIRE** - Village on the River Coln with stone houses and the famous 17thC Arlington Row, former weavers' cottages. Arlington Mill is now a folk museum. Trout farm and Barnsley House Gardens nearby are open to the public.

• **BIDFORD-ON-AVON, WARWICKSHIRE** - Attractive village with an ancient 8-arched bridge. Riverside picnic area and a main street with some interesting 15thC houses.

• **BIRDLIP, GLOUCESTERSHIRE** - Hamlet at the top of a very steep descent down to the Gloucester Vale with excellent viewpoint over Crickley Hill Country Park.

• **BIRMINGHAM, WEST MIDLANDS** - Britain's second city, whose attractions include Centenary Square and the ICC with Symphony Hall, the NEC, the City Art Gallery, Barber Institute of Fine Arts, 17thC Aston Hall, science and railway museums, Jewellery Quarter, Cadbury World, two cathedrals and Botanical Gardens.

• **BOURTON-ON-THE-WATER, GLOUCESTERSHIRE** - The River Windrush flows through this famous Cotswold village which has a green, and cottages and houses of Cotswold stone. Its many attractions include a model village, Birdland, a Motor Museum and the Cotswold Perfumery.

• **BRIDGNORTH, SHROPSHIRE** - Red sandstone riverside town in two parts - High and Low - linked by a cliff railway. Much of interest including a ruined Norman keep, half-timbered 16thC houses, Midland Motor Museum and Severn Valley Railway.

• **BROADWAY, WORCESTERSHIRE** - Beautiful Cotswold village called the "Show village of England", with 16thC stone houses and cottages. Near the village is Broadway Tower with magnificent views over 12 counties, and a country park with nature trails and adventure playground.

• **BROMSGROVE, WORCESTERSHIRE** - This market town, near the Lickey Hills, has an interesting museum and craft centre and 14thC church with fine tombs and a Carillon tower. The Avoncroft Museum of Buildings is nearby where many old buildings have been reassembled, having been saved from destruction.

• **BURTON DASSETT, WARWICKSHIRE** - The church tower looks out over the site of the Battle of Edgehill, and it is said that Cromwell himself climbed the tower to watch the fighting. Nearby is a 16thC beacon tower from which news of the battle was sent.

• **BUXTON, DERBYSHIRE** - The highest market town in England and one of the oldest spas, with an elegant crescent, Poole's Cavern, Opera House and attractive Pavilion Gardens. An excellent centre for exploring the Peak District.

C **CASTLE DONINGTON, LEICESTERSHIRE** - A Norman castle once stood here. The world's largest collection of single-seater racing cars is displayed at Donington Park alongside the racing circuit, and an Aeropark Visitor Centre can be seen at nearby East Midlands International Airport.

CREDIT CARD BOOKINGS If you book by telephone and are asked for your credit card number it is advisable to check the proprietor's policy should you cancel your reservation.

• **CHELTENHAM, GLOUCESTERSHIRE -** Cheltenham was developed as a spa town in the 18thC and has some beautiful Regency architecture, in particular the Pittville Pump Room. It holds international music and literature festivals and is also famous for its race meetings and cricket.

• **CHESTERFIELD, DERBYSHIRE -** Famous for the twisted spire of its parish church, Chesterfield has some fine modern buildings and excellent shopping facilities, including a large, traditional, open-air market. Hardwick Hall and Bolsover Castle are nearby.

• **CHIPPING CAMPDEN, GLOUCESTERSHIRE -** Outstanding Cotswold wool town with many old stone gabled houses, a splendid church and 17thC almshouses. Nearby are Kiftsgate Court Gardens and Hidcote Manor Gardens (National Trust).

• **CHURCH STRETTON, SHROPSHIRE -** Church Stretton lies under the eastern slope of the Longmynd surrounded by hills. It is ideal for walkers, with marvellous views, golf and gliding. Wenlock Edge is not far away.

• **CIRENCESTER, GLOUCESTERSHIRE -** "Capital of the Cotswolds", Cirencester was Britain's second most important Roman town with many finds housed in the Corinium Museum. It has a very fine Perpendicular church and old houses around the market place.

• **COLEFORD, GLOUCESTERSHIRE -** Small town in the Forest of Dean with the ancient iron mines at Clearwell Caves nearby, where mining equipment and geological samples are displayed. There are several forest trails in the area.

• **COVENTRY, WEST MIDLANDS -** Modern city with a long history. It has many places of interest including the post-war and ruined medieval cathedrals, art gallery and museums, some 16thC almshouses, St Mary's Guildhall, Lunt Roman fort and the Belgrade Theatre.

D **DERBY, DERBYSHIRE -** Modern industrial city but with ancient origins. There is a wide range of attractions including several museums (notably Royal Crown Derby), a theatre, a concert hall, and the cathedral with fine ironwork and Bess of Hardwick's tomb.

• **DROITWICH, WORCESTERSHIRE -** Old town with natural brine springs, now incorporated into the Brine Baths Health Centre, developed as a spa at the beginning of the 19thC. Of particular interest is the Church of the Sacred Heart with splendid mosaics. Fine parks and a Heritage Centre.

E **ECKINGTON, WORCESTERSHIRE -** Large and expanding village in a fruit-growing and market-gardening area beside the Avon, which is crossed here by a 15thC bridge. Half-timbered houses are much in evidence.

F **FAIRFORD, GLOUCESTERSHIRE -** Small town with a 15thC wool church famous for its complete 15thC stained glass windows, interesting carvings and original wall paintings. It is an excellent touring centre, and the Cotswolds Wildlife Park is nearby.

G **GAINSBOROUGH, LINCOLNSHIRE -** Britain's most inland port has strong connections with the Pilgrim Fathers. Gainsborough Old Hall, where they worshipped, boasts a 15thC manor house with complete kitchens.

• **GLOSSOP, DERBYSHIRE -** Town in dramatic moorland surroundings with views over the High Peak. The settlement can be traced back to Roman times but expanded during the Industrial Revolution.

• **GLOUCESTER, GLOUCESTERSHIRE -** A Roman city and inland port, its cathedral is one of the most beautiful in Britain. Gloucester's many attractions include museums and the restored warehouses in the Victorian docks containing the National Waterways Museum, Robert Opie Packaging Collection and other attractions.

• **GREAT RISSINGTON, GLOUCESTERSHIRE -** One of two villages overlooking the River Windrush near Bourton-on-the-Water.

H **HATHERSAGE, DERBYSHIRE -** Hillside village in the Peak District, dominated by the church with many good brasses and monuments to the Eyre family which provide a link with Charlotte Bronte. Little John, friend of Robin Hood, is said to be buried here.

• **HEREFORD, HEREFORDSHIRE -** Agricultural county town, its cathedral containing much Norman work, a large chained library and the world-famous Mappa Mundi exhibition. Among the city's varied attractions are several museums including the Cider Museum and the Old House.

• **HOLBEACH, LINCOLNSHIRE -** Small town, mentioned in the Domesday Book, has splendid 14thC church with a fine tower and spire. The surrounding villages also have interesting churches, and the area is well known for its bulbfields.

• **HOPE, DERBYSHIRE -** Village in the Hope Valley which is an excellent base for walking in the Peak District and for fishing and shooting. There is a well-dressing ceremony each June, and its August sheep-dog trials are well known. Castleton Caves are nearby.

• **HUSBANDS BOSWORTH, LEICESTERSHIRE -** This village is situated at the crossroads between Lutterworth and Market Harborough and the A50, Northampton/Leicester. Stanford Hall is within easy reach.

I **IRONBRIDGE, SHROPSHIRE -** Small town on the Severn where the Industrial Revolution began. It has the world's first iron bridge built in 1779. The Ironbridge Gorge Museum, of exceptional interest, comprises a rebuilt, turn-of-the-century town, and sites spread over six square miles.

K **KENILWORTH, WARWICKSHIRE -** The main feature of the town is the ruined 12thC castle. It has many royal associations but was damaged by Cromwell. A good base for visiting Coventry, Leamington Spa and Warwick.

• **KIDDERMINSTER, WORCESTERSHIRE -** The town is the centre for carpet manufacturing. It has a medieval church with good monuments and a statue of Sir Rowland Hill, a native of the town and founder of the penny post. West Midlands Safari Park is nearby, also Severn Valley Railway station.

• **KINETON, WARWICKSHIRE -** Attractive old village in rolling countryside one mile from site of famous battle of Edgehill. Medieval church of St Peter.

RATING All accommodation in this guide has been rated, or is awaiting a rating, by a trained English Tourism Council assessor.

L **LEAMINGTON SPA, WARWICKSHIRE** - 18thC spa town with many fine Georgian and Regency houses and the refurbished 19thC Pump Rooms with Heritage Centre. The attractive Jephson Gardens are laid out alongside the river.

• **LECHLADE, GLOUCESTERSHIRE** - Attractive village on the River Thames and a popular spot for boating. It has a number of fine Georgian houses and a 15thC church. Nearby is Kelmscott Manor, with its William Morris furnishings, and 18thC Buscot House (National Trust).

• **LEEK, STAFFORDSHIRE** - Old silk and textile town, with some interesting buildings and a number of inns dating from the 17thC. Its art gallery has displays of embroidery. Brindley Mill, designed by James Brindley, has been restored as a museum.

• **LEICESTER, LEICESTERSHIRE** - Modern industrial city with a wide variety of attractions including Roman remains, ancient churches, Georgian houses and a Victorian clock tower. Excellent shopping precincts, arcades and market, museums, theatres, concert hall and sports and leisure centres.

• **LEOMINSTER, HEREFORDSHIRE** - The town owed its prosperity to wool and has many interesting buildings, notably the timber-framed Grange Court, a former town hall. The impressive Norman priory church has three naves and a ducking stool. Berrington Hall (National Trust) is nearby.

• **LINCOLN, LINCOLNSHIRE** - Ancient city dominated by the magnificent 11thC cathedral with its triple towers. A Roman gateway is still used and there are medieval houses lining narrow, cobbled streets. Other attractions include the Norman castle, several museums and the Usher Gallery.

• **LONGHOPE, GLOUCESTERSHIRE** - Set in beautiful hilly countryside on the edge of the Forest of Dean, this ancient village is mentioned in the Domesday Book. The church is 12thC and other buildings of historic interest include the medieval Harts Barn.

• **LOUGHBOROUGH, LEICESTERSHIRE** - Industrial town famous for its bell foundry and 47-bell Carillon Tower. The Great Central Railway operates steam railway rides of over eight miles through the attractive scenery of Charnwood Forest.

• **LUDLOW, SHROPSHIRE** - Outstandingly interesting border town with a magnificent castle high above the River Teme, two half-timbered old inns and an impressive 15thC church. The Reader's House, with its 3-storey Jacobean porch, should also be seen.

M **MALVERN, WORCESTERSHIRE** - A spa town in Victorian times, its water is today bottled and sold worldwide. six resorts, set on the slopes of the Hills, form part of Malvern. Great Malvern Priory has splendid 15thC windows. It is an excellent walking centre.

• **MARKET DRAYTON, SHROPSHIRE** - Old market town with black and white buildings and 17thC houses, also acclaimed for its gingerbread. Hodnet Hall is in the vicinity with its beautiful landscaped gardens covering 60 acres.

• **MARKET HARBOROUGH, LEICESTERSHIRE** - There have been markets here since the early 13thC, and the town was also an important coaching centre, with several ancient hostelries. The early-17thC grammar school was once the butter market.

• **MARKET RASEN, LINCOLNSHIRE** - Market town on the edge of the Lincolnshire Wolds. The racecourse and the picnic site and forest walks at Willingham Woods are to the east of the town.

• **MATLOCK, DERBYSHIRE** - The town lies beside the narrow valley of the River Derwent surrounded by steep wooded hills. Good centre for exploring Derbyshire's best scenery.

• **MATLOCK BATH, DERBYSHIRE** - 19thC spa town with many attractions including several caverns to visit, a lead-mining museum and a family fun park. There are marvellous views over the surrounding countryside from the Heights of Abraham, to which a cable car gives easy access.

• **MEDBOURNE, LEICESTERSHIRE** - Picturesque village with medieval bridge.

• **MELTON MOWBRAY, LEICESTERSHIRE** - Close to the attractive Vale of Belvoir and famous for its pork pies and Stilton cheese which are the subjects of special displays in the museum. It has a beautiful church with a tower 100 ft high.

• **MERIDEN, WEST MIDLANDS** - Village halfway between Coventry and Birmingham. Said to be the centre of England, marked by a cross on the green.

• **MICKLETON, GLOUCESTERSHIRE** - Mickleton lies in the Vale of Evesham and is close to Hidcote Manor Gardens (National Trust) and to the beautiful Cotswold town of Chipping Campden.

• **MORETON-IN-MARSH, GLOUCESTERSHIRE** - Attractive town of Cotswold stone with 17thC houses, an ideal base for touring the Cotswolds. Some of the local attractions include Batsford Park Arboretum, the Jacobean Chastleton House and Sezincote Garden.

• **MUCH WENLOCK, SHROPSHIRE** - Small town close to Wenlock Edge in beautiful scenery and full of interest. In particular there are the remains of an 11thC priory with fine carving and the black and white 16thC Guildhall.

N **NAILSWORTH, GLOUCESTERSHIRE** - Ancient wool town with several elegant Jacobean and Georgian houses, surrounded by wooded hillsides with fine views.

• **NAUNTON, GLOUCESTERSHIRE** - A high place on the Windrush, renowned for its wild flowers and with an attractive dovecote.

• **NEWARK, NOTTINGHAMSHIRE** - The town has many fine old houses and ancient inns near the large, cobbled market-place. Substantial ruins of the 12thC castle, where King John died, dominate the riverside walk and there are several interesting museums. Sherwood Forest is nearby.

• **NEWPORT, SHROPSHIRE** - Small market town on the Shropshire Union Canal which has a wide High Street and a church with some interesting monuments. Newport is close to Aqualate Mere which is the largest lake in Staffordshire.

• **NORTHAMPTON, NORTHAMPTONSHIRE** - A bustling town and a shoe-manufacturing centre, with excellent shopping facilities, several museums and parks, a theatre and a concert hall. Several old churches include one of only four round churches in Britain

• **NORTHLEACH, GLOUCESTERSHIRE** - Village famous for its beautiful 15thC wool church with its lovely porch and interesting interior. There are also some fine houses including a 17thC wool merchant's house containing Keith Harding's World of Mechanical Music. The Cotswold Countryside Collection is in the former prison.

• **NOTTINGHAM, NOTTINGHAMSHIRE** - Attractive modern city with a rich history. Outside its castle, now a museum, is Robin Hood's statue. Attractions include "The Tales of Robin Hood", the Lace Hall, Wollaton Hall, museums and excellent facilities for shopping, sports and entertainment.

• **NUNEATON, WARWICKSHIRE** - Busy town with an art gallery and museum which has a permanent exhibition of the work of George Eliot. The library also has an interesting collection of material. Arbury Hall, a fine example of Gothic architecture, is nearby.

O **OAKHAM, LEICESTERSHIRE** - Pleasant former county town of Rutland. Fine 12thC Great Hall, part of its castle, with a historic collection of horseshoes. An octagonal Butter Cross stands in the market-place, and Rutland County Museum, Rutland Farm Park and Rutland Water are of interest.

P **PAINSWICK, GLOUCESTERSHIRE** - Picturesque wool town with inns and houses dating from the 14thC. Painswick Rococo Garden is open to visitors from January to November, and the house is a Palladian mansion. The churchyard is famous for its yew trees.

• **PERSHORE, WORCESTERSHIRE** - Attractive Georgian town on the River Avon close to the Vale of Evesham, with fine houses and old inns. The remains of the beautiful Pershore Abbey form the parish church.

• **PRIORS HARDWICK, WARWICKSHIRE** This tiny village is in peaceful Warwickshire countryside beside the Oxford Union Canal and route of the Walk. Situated five miles south-east of Southam within easy reach of the many attractions of Stratford, Leamington Spa and Banbury.

R **ROSS-ON-WYE, HEREFORDSHIRE** - Attractive market town with a 17thC market hall, set above the River Wye. There are lovely views over the surrounding countryside from the Prospect and the town is close to Goodrich Castle and the Welsh border.

• **RUGBY, WARWICKSHIRE** - Town famous for its public school which gave its name to Rugby Union football and which featured in 'Tom Brown's Schooldays'.

• **RUGELEY, STAFFORDSHIRE** - Town close to Cannock Chase which has over 2,000 acres of heath and woodlands with forest trails and picnic sites. Nearby is Shugborough Hall (National Trust) with a fine collection of 18thC furniture and interesting monuments in the grounds.

S **SHREWSBURY, SHROPSHIRE** - Beautiful historic town on the River Severn retaining many fine old timber-framed houses. Its attractions include Rowley's Museum with Roman finds, remains of a castle, Clive House Museum, St Chad's 18thC round church, rowing on the river and the Shrewsbury Flower Show in August.

• **SKEGNESS, LINCOLNSHIRE** - Famous seaside resort with six miles of sandy beaches and bracing air. Attractions include swimming pools, bowling greens, gardens, Natureland Marine Zoo, golfcourses and a wide range of entertainment at the Embassy Centre. Nearby is Gibraltar Point Nature Reserve.

• **SOLIHULL, WEST MIDLANDS** - On the outskirts of Birmingham. Some Tudor houses and a 13thC church remain amongst the new public buildings and shopping centre. The 16thC Malvern Hall is now a school, and the 15thC Chester House at Knowle is now a library.

• **SOUTHWELL, NOTTINGHAMSHIRE** - Town dominated by the Norman minster which has some beautiful 13thC stone carvings in the Chapter House. Charles I spent his last night of freedom in one of the inns. The original Bramley apple tree can still be seen.

• **STAFFORD, STAFFORDSHIRE** - The town has a long history and some half-timbered buildings still remain, notably the 16thC High House. There are several museums in the town and Shugborough Hall and the famous angler Izaak Walton's cottage, now a museum, are nearby.

• **STAMFORD, LINCOLNSHIRE** - Exceptionally beautiful and historic town with many houses of architectural interest, several notable churches and other public buildings all in the local stone. Burghley House, built by William Cecil, is a magnificent Tudor mansion on the edge of the town.

• **STOKE-ON-TRENT, STAFFORDSHIRE** - Famous for its pottery. Factories of several famous makers, including Josiah Wedgwood, can be visited. The City Museum has one of the finest pottery and porcelain collections in the world.

• **STONEHOUSE, GLOUCESTERSHIRE** - Village in the Stroud Valley with an Elizabethan Court, later restored and altered by Lutyens.

• **STOURBRIDGE, WEST MIDLANDS** - Town on the River Stour, famous for its glassworks. Several of the factories can be visited and glassware purchased at the factory shops.

• **STOW-ON-THE-WOLD, GLOUCESTERSHIRE** - Attractive Cotswold wool town with a large market-place and some fine houses, especially the old grammar school. There is an interesting church dating from Norman times. Stow-on-the-Wold is surrounded by lovely countryside and Cotswold villages.

• **STRATFORD-UPON-AVON, WARWICKSHIRE** - Famous as Shakespeare's home town, Stratford's many attractions include his birthplace, New Place, where he died, the Royal Shakespeare Theatre and Gallery and Hall's Croft (his daughter's house).

• **STROUD, GLOUCESTERSHIRE** - This old town, surrounded by attractive hilly country, has been producing broadcloth for centuries; the local museum has an interesting display on the subject. Many of the mills have been converted into craft centres and for other uses.

T **TELFORD, SHROPSHIRE** - New Town named after Thomas Telford, the famous engineer who designed many of the country's canals, bridges and viaducts. It is close to Ironbridge with its monuments and museums to the Industrial Revolution, including restored 18thC buildings.

• **TETBURY, GLOUCESTERSHIRE** - Small market town with 18thC houses and an attractive 17thC Town Hall. It is a good touring centre with many places of interest nearby including Badminton House and Westonbirt Arboretum.

• **TEWKESBURY, GLOUCESTERSHIRE** - Tewkesbury's outstanding possession is its magnificent church, built as an abbey, with a great Norman tower and beautiful 14thC interior. The town stands at the confluence of the Severn and Avon and has many medieval houses, inns and several museums.

U **UPPINGHAM, RUTLAND** - Quiet market town dominated by its famous public school which was founded in 1584. It has many stone houses and is surrounded by attractive countryside.

• **UPTON-UPON-SEVERN, WORCESTERSHIRE** - Attractive country town on the banks of the Severn and a good river-cruising centre. It has many pleasant old houses and inns, and the pepperpot landmark is now the Heritage Centre.

V **VOWCHURCH, HEREFORDSHIRE** - Close to the Welsh border, its church has 15 dedications which were all confirmed in one day in 1348.

W **WARWICK, WARWICKSHIRE** - Castle rising above the River Avon, 15thC Beauchamp Chapel attached to St Mary's Church, medieval Lord Leycester's Hospital almshouses and several museums. Nearby is Ashorne Hall Nickelodeon and the National Heritage Museum at Gaydon.

• **WATERHOUSES, STAFFORDSHIRE** - Village in the valley of the River Hamps, once the terminus of the Leek and Manifold Light Railway, eight miles of which is now a macadamised walkers' path.

• **WELLINGBOROUGH, NORTHAMPTONSHIRE** - Manufacturing town, mentioned in the Domesday Book, with some old buildings and inns, in one of which Cromwell stayed on his way to Naseby. It has attractive gardens in the centre of the town and two interesting churches.

• **WINSTER, DERBYSHIRE** - Village with some interesting old gritstone houses and cottages, including the 17thC stone market hall now owned by the National Trust. It is a former lead-mining centre.

• **WIRKSWORTH, DERBYSHIRE** - Small town which was once the centre of the lead-mining industry in Derbyshire. It has many old buildings of interest, including the church of St Mary, narrow streets and alleys, a Heritage Centre and the National Stone Centre. There is a well-dressing ceremony in May.

• **WISHAW, WARWICKSHIRE** - A village with interesting features in the small church, now well known as the location of the National Golf Centre. Within easy reach of junction 9 of the M42, close to Sutton Coldfield.

• **WORCESTER, WORCESTERSHIRE** - Lovely riverside city dominated by its Norman and Early English cathedral, King John's burial place. Many old buildings including the 15thC Commandery and the 18thC Guildhall. There are several museums and the Royal Worcester porcelain factory.

• **WORKSOP, NOTTINGHAMSHIRE** - Market town close to the Dukeries, where a number of Ducal families had their estates, some of which, like Clumber Park, may be visited. The upper room of the 14thC gatehouse of the priory housed the country's first elementary school in 1628.

AT-A-GLANCE SYMBOLS

Symbols at the end of each accommodation entry give useful information about services and facilities. A key to symbols can be found inside the back cover flap. Keep this open for easy reference.

A region of remote and wild beauty, with vast expanses of open country, unspoilt coastline, sweeping views and big skies. It's renowned for its charming half-timbered towns and villages, ancient sites, historic country houses and nature reserves.

classic sights

Blickling Hall – one of England's great Jacobean houses
Sutton Hoo – important Anglo-Saxon burial site
Hatfield House – childhood home of Queen Elizabeth I

coast & country

Blakeney Point – good for seal- and bird-watching
Hatfield Forest – medieval royal hunting forest
Norfolk Broads – miles of waterways through glorious countryside
The Fens – unique panorama of waterways and Nature Reserves

arts for all

Aldeburgh Festival – classical music in a picturesque setting
Dedham Vale – the landscapes of John Constable; his home and early studio are at East Bergholt. Also the home of Sir Alfred Munnings, famous for his paintings of horses
Sudbury – Gainsborough's house, with fine collection of paintings

delightfully different

Whipsnade Tree Cathedral – unique, 26-acre (10.5-ha) cathedral made of trees

The counties of Bedfordshire, Cambridgeshire, Essex, Hertfordshire, Norfolk and Suffolk

FOR MORE INFORMATION CONTACT:
East of England Tourist Board
Toppesfield Hall, Hadleigh, Suffolk IP7 5DN
Tel: (01473) 822922 Fax: (01473) 823063
Email: jbowers@bta.org.uk
Internet: www.eastofenglandtouristboard.com

The Pictures: 1 Cambridge 2 Lavenham, Suffolk 3 Norwich Cathedral

PLACES to visit

You will find hundreds of interesting places to visit during your stay, just some of which are listed in these pages. Contact any Tourist Information Centre in the region for more ideas on days out.

Awarded ETC's new 'Quality Assured Visitor Attraction' marque at time of going to press. (See page 19).

Audley End House and Park

Audley End, Saffron Walden
Tel: (01799) 522399
A palatial Jacobean house remodelled in the 18th-19thC with a magnificent great hall with 17thC plaster ceilings. Rooms and furniture by Robert Adam and park by 'Capability' Brown.

Banham Zoo

The Grove, Banham, Norwich
Tel: (01953) 887771 www.banhamzoo.co.uk
Wildlife spectacular which will take you on a journey to experience tigers, leopards and zebra and some of the world's most exotic, rare and endangered animals.

Barleylands Farm

Barleylands Road, Billericay
Tel: (01268) 290229 www.barleylandsfarm.co.uk
Visitor centre with a rural museum, animal centre, craft studios, blacksmith's shop, glass-blowing studio with a viewing gallery, miniature steam railway and a restaurant.

Blickling Hall

Blickling, Norwich
Tel: (01263) 738030
www.nationaltrust.org.uk

A Jacobean redbrick mansion with garden, orangery, parkland and lake. There is also a display of fine tapestries and furniture.

Bressingham Steam Experience and Gardens

Bressingham, Diss
Tel: (01379) 687386 www.bressingham.co.uk
Steam rides through four miles (8km) of woodland. Six acres (2ha) of the Island Beds plant centre. Main line locomotives, the Victorian Gallopers and over 50 steam engines.

Bure Valley Railway

Aylsham Station, Norwich Road, Aylsham, Norwich
Tel: (01263) 733858 www.bvrw.co.uk
A 15-inch narrow-gauge steam railway covering nine miles (14.5km) of track from Wroxham, in the heart of the Norfolk Broads, to Aylsham which is a bustling market town.

Colchester Castle

Colchester
Tel: (01206) 282931
www.colchestermuseums.org.uk
A Norman keep on the foundations of a Roman temple. The archaeological material includes much on Roman Colchester (Camulodunum).

Colchester Zoo

Maldon Road, Stanway, Colchester
Tel: (01206) 331292
www.colchester-zoo.co.uk

Zoo with 200 species and some of the best cat and primate collections in the UK, 60 acres (27ha) of gardens and lakes, award-winning animal enclosures and picnic areas.

Ely Cathedral

Chapter House, The College, Ely
Tel: (01353) 667735
www.cathedral.ely.anglican.org.uk
One of England's finest cathedrals with guided tours and tours of the Octagon and West Tower, monastic precincts and also a brass-rubbing centre and stained-glass museum.

Fritton Lake Country World

Fritton, Great Yarmouth
Tel: (01493) 488208 www.frittonlake.co.uk
A 250-acre (101-ha) centre with a children's assault course, putting, an adventure playground, golf, fishing, boating, wildfowl, heavy horses, cart rides, falconry and flying displays.

The Gardens of the Rose

The Royal National Rose Society, Chiswell Green, St Albans
Tel: (01727) 850461 www.roses.co.uk
The Royal National Rose Society's 27-acre (11-ha) garden with trial grounds for new varieties of rose. Roses of all types displayed with 1,700 different varieties.

Hatfield House, Park and Gardens

Hatfield
Tel: (01707) 287010
Magnificent Jacobean house, home of the Marquess of Salisbury. Exquisite gardens, model soldiers and park trails. Childhood home of Queen Elizabeth I.

Hedingham Castle

Hedingham, Halstead
Tel: (01787) 460261 www.hedinghamcastle.co.uk
The finest Norman keep in England, built in 1140 by the deVeres, Earls of Oxford. Visited by Kings Henry VII and VIII and Queen Elizabeth I and besieged by King John.

Holkham Hall

Wells-next-the-Sea
Tel: (01328) 710806 www.holkham.co.uk
A classic 18thC Palladian-style mansion. Part of a great agricultural estate and a living treasure house of artistic and architectural history along with a bygones collection.

Ickworth House, Park and Gardens

The Rotunda, Horringer, Bury St Edmunds
Tel: (01284) 735270 www.nationaltrust.org.uk
An extraordinary oval house with flanking wings, begun in 1795. Fine paintings, a beautiful collection of Georgian silver, an Italian garden and stunning parkland.

Imperial War Museum

Duxford, Cambridge
Tel: (01223) 835000 www.iwm.org.uk

Over 180 aircraft on display with tanks, vehicles and guns, an adventure playground, shops and a restaurant.

Kentwell Hall

Long Melford, Sudbury
Tel: (01787) 310207 www.kentwell.co.uk
A mellow redbrick Tudor manor surrounded by a moat, this family home has been interestingly restored with Tudor costume displays, a 16thC house and mosaic Tudor-rose maze.

Knebworth House, Gardens and Park

Knebworth, Stevenage
Tel: (01438) 812661 www.knebworthhouse.com
Tudor manor house, re-fashioned in the 19thC, housing a collection of manuscripts and portraits. Jacobean banquet hall, formal gardens, parkland and adventure playground.

> The Pictures: 1 River Wensum, Norfolk
2 Burghley Horse Trials, Stamford
3 Punting on the River Cam, Cambridge
4 Ely Cathedral, Cambridge

Leighton Buzzard Railway

Page's Park Station, Billington Road, Leighton Buzzard
Tel: (01525) 373888 www.buzzrail.co.uk
An authentic narrow-gauge light railway, built in 1919, offering a 65-minute return journey into the Bedfordshire countryside.

Marsh Farm Country Park

Marsh Farm Road, South Woodham Ferrers, Chelmsford
Tel: (01245) 321552
www.marshfarmcountrypark.co.uk
A farm centre with sheep, a pig unit, free-range chickens, milking demonstrations, indoor and outdoor adventure play areas, nature reserve, walks, picnic area and pets' corner.

Melford Hall

Long Melford, Sudbury
Tel: (01787) 880286
www.nationaltrust.org.uk/eastanglia
Turreted brick Tudor mansion with 18thC and Regency interiors. Collection of Chinese porcelain, gardens and a walk in the grounds. Dogs on leads, where permitted.

Minsmere Nature Reserve

Westleton, Saxmundham
Tel: (01728) 648281 www.rspb.org.uk
RSPB reserve on Suffolk coast with bird-watching hides and trails, year-round events, guided walk and visitor centre with large shop and welcoming tearoom.

National Horseracing Museum and Tours

99 High Street, Newmarket
Tel: (01638) 667333 www.nhrm.co.uk
Award-winning display of the people and horses involved in racing's amazing history. Minibus tours to gallops, stables and equine pool. Hands-on gallery with horse simulator.

National Stud

Newmarket
Tel: (01638) 663464 www.nationalstud.co.uk
A visit to the National Stud consists of a conducted tour which includes top thoroughbred stallions, mares and foals.

New Pleasurewood Hills Leisure Park

Leisure Way, Corton, Lowestoft
Tel: (01502) 586000 www.pleasurewoodhill.co.uk
Tidal wave watercoaster, log flume, chairlift, 2 railways, pirate ship, parrot/sealion shows, go-karts and rattlesnake coaster, the fantasy boat ride and 100-ft (30.5-m) tower drop.

Norfolk Lavender Limited

Caley Mill, Heacham, King's Lynn
Tel: (01485) 570384 www.norfolk-lavender.co.uk
Lavender is distilled from the flowers and the oil made into a wide range of gifts. There is a slide show when the distillery is not working.

Norwich Cathedral

62 The Close, Norwich
Tel: (01603) 218321 www.cathedral.org.uk
A Norman cathedral from 1096 with 14thC roof bosses depicting bible scenes from Adam and Eve to the Day of Judgement. Cloisters, cathedral close, shop and restaurant.

Oliver Cromwell's House

29 St Marys Street, Ely
Tel: (01353) 662062
www.elyeastcambs.co.uk

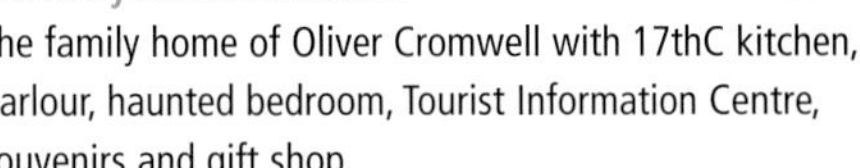

The family home of Oliver Cromwell with 17thC kitchen, parlour, haunted bedroom, Tourist Information Centre, souvenirs and gift shop.

Peter Beales Roses

London Road, Attleborough
Tel: (01953) 454707 www.classicroses.co.uk
Two and a half acres (1 ha) of display rose garden set in rural surroundings.

Pleasure Beach

South Beach Parade, Great Yarmouth
Tel: (01493) 844585 www.pleasure-beach.co.uk
Rollercoaster, Terminator, log flume, twister, monorail, galloping horses, caterpillar, ghost train and fun house. Height restrictions are in force on some rides.

The Royal Air Force Air Defence Radar Museum

RAF Neatishead, Norwich
Tel: (01692) 633309
www.neatishead.raf.mod.uk
History of the development and use of radar in the UK and overseas from 1935 to date. Winner of the Regional Visitor Attraction (under 100,000 visitors). National Silve Award.

Sainsbury Centre for Visual Arts

University of East Anglia, Norwich
Tel: (01603) 593199 www.uea.ac.uk/scva
Housing the Sainsbury collection of works by Picasso, Bacon and Henry Moore alongside many objects of pottery and art. Also a cafe and an art bookshop with activities monthly.

Sandringham

Sandringham, King's Lynn
Tel: (01553) 772675
www.sandringhamestate.co.uk
The country retreat of HM The Queen. A delightful house and 60 acres (24ha) of grounds and lakes. There is also a museum of royal vehicles and royal memorabilia.

Shuttleworth Collection

Old Warden Aerodrome, Biggleswade
Tel: (01767) 627288 www.shuttleworth.org
A unique historical collection of aircraft from a 1909 Bleriot to a 1942 Spitfire in flying condition and cars dating from an 1898 Panhard in running order.

Somerleyton Hall and Gardens

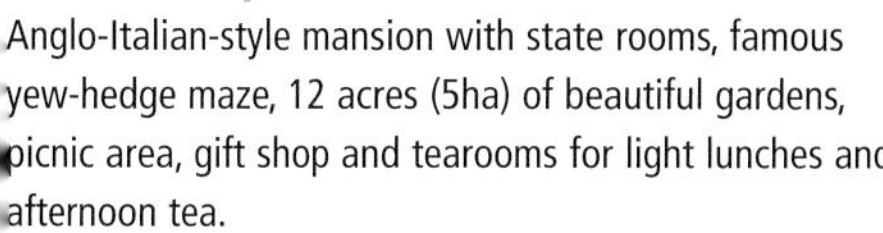

Somerleyton, Lowestoft
Tel: (01502) 730224
www.somerleyton.co.uk
Anglo-Italian-style mansion with state rooms, famous yew-hedge maze, 12 acres (5ha) of beautiful gardens, picnic area, gift shop and tearooms for light lunches and afternoon tea.

Stondon Museum

Station Road, Lower Stondon, Henlow Camp, Henlow
Tel: (01462) 850339 www.transportmuseum.co.uk
A museum with transport exhibits from the early 1900s to the 1980s. The largest private collection in England of bygone vehicles from the beginning of the century.

Thursford Collection

Thursford Green, Thursford, Fakenham
Tel: (01328) 878477
Musical evenings some Tuesdays from mid-July to the end of September. A live musical show with nine mechanical organs and a Wurlitzer show starring Robert Wolfe (daily 29 March to mid-October).

Wimpole Hall and Home Farm

Arrington, Royston
Tel: (01223) 207257 www.wimpole.org
An 18thC house in a landscaped park with a folly and Chinese bridge. There is a plunge bath and yellow drawing room in the house, the work of John Soane. Home Farm has a rare-breeds centre.

Woburn Abbey

Woburn, Milton Keynes
Tel: (01525) 290666 www.woburnabbey.co.uk
An 18thC Palladian mansion, altered by Henry Holland, the Prince Regent's architect, containing a collection of English silver, French and English furniture, and art.

Woburn Safari Park

Woburn, Milton Keynes
Tel: (01525) 290407
www.woburnsafari.co.uk
Drive through the safari park with 30 species of animals in natural groups just a windscreen's width away, plus the action-packed Wild World Leisure Area with shows for all.

> The Pictures: 1 South Raynham, Norfolk
2 Shopping in Cambridge

Find out more about the East of England

Further information about holidays and attractions in the East of England is available from:

EAST OF ENGLAND TOURIST BOARD
Toppesfield Hall, Hadleigh, Suffolk IP7 5DN
Tel: (01473) 822922 Fax: (01473) 823063
Email: jbowers@bta.org.uk
Internet: www.eastofenglandtouristboard.com

The following publications are available from The East of England Tourist Board:

East of England - The Official Guide 2003
an information-packed A5 guide featuring all you need to know about places to visit and things to see and do in the East of England. From historic houses to garden centres, from animal collections to craft centres - the Guide has it all, including film and TV locations, city, town and village information, events, shopping, car tours plus lots more! (£4.50 excl p&p)

England's Cycling Country
the East of England offers perfect cycling country - from quiet country lanes to ancient trackways. This free publication promotes the many Cycling Discovery Maps that are available to buy (£1.50 excl p&p), a well as providing useful information for anyone planning a cycling tour of the region

Getting to the East of England

BY ROAD: The region is easily accessible. From London and the south via the A1, M11, M25, A10, M1, A46 and A12. From the north via the A17, A1, A15, A5, M1 and A6. From the west via the A14, A47, A421, A428, A418, A41 and A427.

BY RAIL: Regular fast trains run to all major cities and towns in the region. London stations which serve the region are Liverpool Street, Kings Cross, Fenchurch Street, Moorgate, St Pancras, London Marylebone and London Euston. Bedford, Luton and St Albans are on the Thameslink line which runs to Kings Cross and on to London Gatwick Airport. There is also a direct link between London Stansted Airport and Liverpool Street. Through the Channel Tunnel, there are trains direct from Paris and Brussels to Waterloo Station, London. A short journey on the Underground will bring passengers to those stations operating services into the East of England. Further information on rail journeys in the East of England can be obtained on (0845) 748 4950.

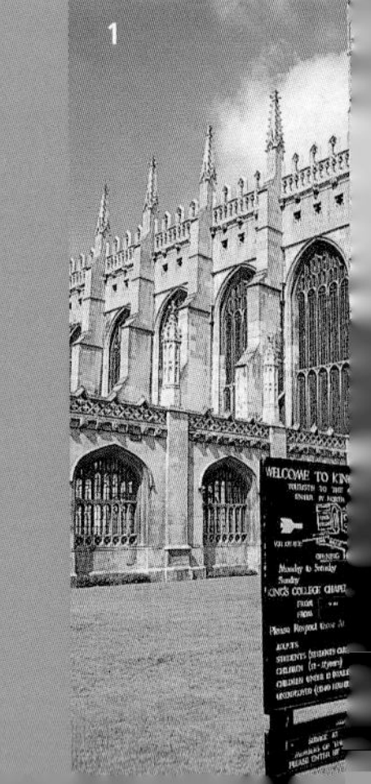

> The Pictures: 1 King's College, Cambridge

Where to stay in the East of England

Accommodation entries in this region are listed in alphabetical order of place name, and then in alphabetical order of establishment.

Map references refer to the colour location maps at the front of this guide. The first number indicates the map to use; the letter and number which follow refer to the grid reference on the map.

At-a-glance symbols at the end of each accommodation entry give useful information about services and facilities. A key to symbols can be found inside the back cover flap. Keep this open for easy reference.

A brief description of the towns and villages offering accommodation in the entries which follow, can be found at the end of this section.

A complete listing of all the English Tourism Council assessed accommodation covered by this guide appears at the back of the guide.

ALDBOROUGH, Norfolk Map ref 3B1

BUTTERFLY COTTAGE
The Green, Aldborough, Norwich NR11 7AA
T: (01263) 768198
F: (01263) 768198
E: butterflycottage@btopenworld.com
I: www.butterflycottage.com

Bedrooms: 1 single, 2 triple/multiple
Bathrooms: 3 en suite

B&B per night:
S £20.00–£25.00
D £40.00–£50.00

OPEN All Year

On the Weavers Way. Comfortable cottage-style, well-equipped, friendly atmosphere. Rooms overlook large garden or village green. Each has own entrance. Car parking.

P

ALDEBY, Norfolk Map ref 3C1

◆◆◆

THE OLD VICARAGE
Rectory Road, Aldeby, Beccles NR34 0BJ
T: (01502) 678229
E: butler@beccles33.freeserve.co.uk

Bedrooms: 2 double/twin, 1 triple/multiple
Bathrooms: 1 en suite, 2 private

B&B per night:
S £19.00–£20.00
D £38.00–£40.00

OPEN All Year except Christmas

Spacious accommodation, quiet rural location. Ground floor suite available. Non-smoking. Convenient for Norfolk Broads boating and bird-watching. Ample off-road parking for cars, bicycles and canoes.

P

QUALITY ASSURANCE SCHEME
Diamond ratings and awards were correct at the time of going to press but are subject to change. Please check at the time of booking.

BATTLESBRIDGE, Essex Map ref 3B3

♦♦

THE COTTAGES GUEST HOUSE

The Cottages, Beeches Road, Battlesbridge, Wickford SS11 8TJ
T: (01702) 232105 & 07753 634933
E: cottage2000@totalise.co.uk

Bedrooms: 1 single, 4 double/twin, 1 triple/multiple
Bathrooms: 1 en suite

CC: Mastercard, Visa

Rural cottage, close to Southend, Chelmsford and Basildon. Good views. Half a mile from Battlesbridge antique centre. Extensive parking. Bridal room and licensed bar.

B&B per night:
S £20.00–£29.00
D £40.00–£49.00

OPEN All Year except Christmas

BECCLES, Suffolk Map ref 3C1

♦♦♦♦

ASHTREE COTTAGE

School Lane, Worlingham, Beccles NR34 7RH
T: (01502) 715206
F: (01502) 711745
E: helen@dhswilcock.freeserve.co.uk

Bedrooms: 1 single, 1 double/twin, 1 triple/multiple

18thC farmhouse set in rural surroundings offering spacious accommodation, close to many places of local interest and the Norfolk and Suffolk coasts.

B&B per night:
D £40.00–£50.00

HB per person:
DY £20.00–£27.00

OPEN All Year

♦♦♦♦

CATHERINE HOUSE

2 Ringsfield Road, Beccles NR34 9PQ
T: (01502) 716428
F: (01502) 716428

Bedrooms: 3 double/twin
Bathrooms: 2 en suite, 1 private

Family home, tastefully decorated to high standard, in quiet position overlooking Waveney Valley. Five minutes' walk to town centre.

B&B per night:
S £20.00–£30.00
D £40.00–£44.00

OPEN All Year

♦♦♦

COLVILLE ARMS MOTEL

Lowestoft Road, Worlingham, Beccles NR34 7EF
T: (01502) 712571
F: (01502) 712571
E: pat@thecolvillearms.freeserve.co.uk
I: www.colville-arms-motel.co.uk

Bedrooms: 2 single, 8 double/twin
Bathrooms: 10 en suite

Lunch available
Evening meal available
CC: Delta, Mastercard, Switch, Visa

Village setting half an hour Lowestoft, Norwich and Yarmouth, 5 minutes to Broads. Excellent fishing, golf, country walks. All rooms en suite with TV, tea-making facilities. Ample parking.

B&B per night:
S £32.50–£37.50
D £47.50–£55.00

HB per person:
DY £40.00–£47.50

OPEN All Year

BEDFORD, Bedfordshire Map ref 2D1 *Tourist Information Centre Tel: (01234) 215226*

Silver Award

CHURCH FARM

41 High Street, Roxton, Bedford MK44 3EB
T: (01234) 870234
F: (01234) 870234
E: churchfarm@amserve.net

Bedrooms: 3 double/twin
Bathrooms: 3 en suite

First-class bed and breakfast accommodation in a historic farmhouse in a lovely village setting. Comfortable bedrooms have en suite bathrooms. Guest lounge for relaxation.

B&B per night:
S £30.00–£35.00
D £50.00–£55.00

OPEN All Year

USE YOUR *i*s

There are more than 550 Tourist Information Centres throughout England offering friendly help with accommodation and holiday ideas as well as suggestions of places to visit and things to do. You'll find TIC addresses in the local Phone Book.

BEETLEY, Norfolk Map ref 3B1

◆◆◆◆ Gold Award

PEACOCK HOUSE

Peacock Lane, Beetley, East Dereham NR20 4DG
T: (01362) 860371 & 0797 9013258
E: PeackH@aol.com
I: www.smoothhound.co.uk/hotels/peacockh.html/

B&B per night:
S £22.00–£28.00
D £44.00–£47.00

OPEN All Year

Beautiful old farmhouse, peacefully situated in lovely garden and grounds. Offering excellent accommodation with all facilities, guests' lounge, open fires, beamed dining room, home cooking and a warm welcome. Centrally situated with Norwich, Sandringham, National Trust houses and the coast all within easy reach, and golf, fishing and swimming all close by.

Bedrooms: 2 double/twin, 1 triple/multiple
Bathrooms: 3 en suite

Evening meal available

◆◆◆

SHILLING STONE

Church Road, Beetley, East Dereham NR20 4AB
T: (01362) 861099 & 07721 306190
F: (01362) 869153
E: jeannepartridge@ukgateway.net
I: www.norfolkshillingstone.co.uk

B&B per night:
S £22.00–£25.00
D £44.00–£48.00

OPEN All Year except Christmas

A large country house on the edge of Beetley. Excellent accommodation with large double and twin rooms, all en suite with colour TV. Full English breakfast. Ideal base for touring Norfolk coast, Broads, Norwich, Sandringham and Gressenhall Rural Life Museum. A warm welcome awaits you. Children and pets welcome. Golf and fishing nearby.

Bedrooms: 3 double/twin
Bathrooms: 3 en suite

Evening meal available
CC: Amex, Delta, Mastercard, Switch, Visa

BISHOP'S STORTFORD, Hertfordshire Map ref 2D1 *Tourist Information Centre Tel: (01279) 655831*

◆◆◆◆ Gold Award

THE COTTAGE

71 Birchanger Lane, Birchanger, Bishop's Stortford, Herts CM23 5QA
T: (01279) 812349
F: (01279) 815045
I: www.thecottagebirchanger.co.uk

B&B per night:
S £40.00–£54.00
D £68.00–£72.00

OPEN All Year except Christmas

The Cottage is a 17thC Listed house with panelled rooms and woodburning stove. Conservatory-style breakfast room overlooks large, mature garden. Quiet and peaceful village setting yet near M11 jct 8, Stansted Airport and Bishop's Stortford. Guest rooms are furnished in a traditional cottage style, all with colour TV and tea/coffee facilities.

Bedrooms: 3 single, 12 double/twin
Bathrooms: 12 en suite, 1 private

CC: Delta, Mastercard, Switch, Visa

GOLD & SILVER AWARDS

These exclusive ETC awards are given to establishments achieving the highest levels of quality and service. Further information can be found at the front of the guide and additional accommodation achieving these awards are shown in the listing at the back of this guide.

BISHOP'S STORTFORD continued

◆◆◆◆

HOMESDALE

Lower Road, Little Hallingbury,
Bishop's Stortford CM22 7QZ
T: (01279) 600647
F: (01279) 600647
E: elfieandsteve@btinternet.com
I: www.homesdale.net

Bedrooms: 1 single,
2 double/twin
Bathrooms: 3 private

Evening meal available
CC: Delta, Mastercard,
Switch, Visa

Situated in delightful rural village, just 15 minutes from Stanstead Airport, this charming and comfortable private home offers all that is best in bed and breakfast.

B&B per night:
S £35.00–£40.00
D £50.00–£60.00

HB per person:
DY £35.00–£45.00

OPEN All Year

PHOENIX LODGE

No. 91 Dunmow Road, Bishop's Stortford
CM23 5HF
T: (01279) 659780
F: (01279) 323958
E: phoenixlodge@ntlworld.com
I: www.phoenixlodge.co.uk

Rooms from £34. Family room en suite available. Five minutes' drive from Stansted airport. Variety of rooms available. Colour TV and en suite facilities. Children welcome. Ten minutes' walk to town and local amenities. All rooms have handwash basin and tea/coffee facilities. No smoking. Long term car park available at small charge.

Bedrooms: 4 single,
2 double/twin, 1 triple/
multiple
Bathrooms: 4 en suite,
3 private

CC: Delta, Mastercard,
Switch, Visa

10% discount Oct-Feb inclusive if 'Where to Stay' is mentioned.

B&B per night:
S £34.00–£39.00
D £55.00–£60.00

OPEN All Year except Christmas

◆◆◆

52 WINDHILL

Bishop's Stortford CM23 2NH
T: (01279) 651712
E: aspence@btinternet.com

Bedrooms: 1 single,
1 triple/multiple

Victorian home within walking distance of all amenities. Close to M11 motorway and Stansted Airport.

B&B per night:
S £25.00–£30.00
D £50.00

OPEN All Year except Christmas

BRADFIELD, Essex Map ref 3B2

◆◆◆

EMSWORTH HOUSE

Ship Hill, Bradfield, Manningtree
CO11 2UP
T: (01255) 870860 & 07767 477771
E: emsworthhouse@hotmail.com
I: www.emsworthhouse.co.uk

Bedrooms: 3 double/
twin
Bathrooms: 1 en suite

Lunch available
Evening meal available

Formerly the vicarage. Spacious rooms with stunning views of the countryside and River Stour. Near Colchester and Harwich. On holiday, business or en route to the continent, it's perfect!

B&B per night:
S £28.00–£45.00
D £44.00–£56.00

OPEN All Year

BRAINTREE, Essex Map ref 3B2 *Tourist Information Centre Tel: (01376) 550066*

◆◆

70 HIGH GARRETT

Braintree CM7 5NT
T: (01376) 345330

Bedrooms: 1 single,
1 double/twin, 1 triple/
multiple

Three-bedroom bed and breakfast situated on main road between Braintree and Halstead. Convenient for Colchester, Chelmsford, Constable country. One hour to London. Non-smokers only.

B&B per night:
S Min £25.00
D Min £50.00

HB per person:
DY Min £25.00

OPEN All Year

CHECK THE MAPS

The colour maps at the front of this guide show all the cities, towns and villages for which you will find accommodation entries.
Refer to the town index to find the page on which they are listed.

BRANDON, Suffolk Map ref 3B2

♦♦♦

THE LAURELS

162 London Road, Brandon
IP27 0LP
T: (01842) 812005

Bedrooms: 2 double/twin
Bathrooms: 1 en suite, 1 private

A cosy welcome awaits you in our comfortable bungalow with tea or coffee on arrival. Close to forest, market town and other places of interest.

B&B per night:
S £18.00–£25.00
D £36.00–£40.00

OPEN All Year

BURY ST EDMUNDS, Suffolk Map ref 3B2 *Tourist Information Centre Tel: (01284) 764667*

♦♦♦♦

BRIGHTHOUSE FARM

Melford Road, Lawshall, Bury St Edmunds
IP29 4PX
T: (01284) 830385 & 07711 829546
F: (01284) 830385
E: brighthousefarm@supanet.com
I: www.brighthousefarm.fsnet.co.uk

A warm welcome awaits you at this 200-year-old Georgian farmhouse. Tastefully presented en suite rooms, outstanding breakfasts served in spacious conservatory. 3 acres of glorious gardens and farm trail to explore. Close to a wealth of interesting places to visit. Good pubs and restaurants nearby. Send SAE for brochure.

Bedrooms: 5 double/twin
Bathrooms: 5 en suite

Reductions for stays of 3 nights or more.

B&B per night:
S £25.00–£40.00
D £45.00–£65.00

OPEN All Year except Christmas

♦♦♦

DUNSTON GUESTHOUSE/HOTEL

8 Springfield Road,
Bury St Edmunds IP33 3AN
T: (01284) 767981
F: (01284) 764574
I: www.dunstonguesthouse.co.uk

Bedrooms: 7 single, 7 double/twin, 3 triple/multiple
Bathrooms: 8 en suite, 3 private

Victorian guesthouse/hotel in a tree-lined road 5-10 minutes' walk from town centre. Comfortable residents' lounge, peaceful sun lounge, gardens, car park. Small groups by arrangement.

B&B per night:
S £25.00–£45.00
D £50.00–£65.00

OPEN All Year except Christmas

♦♦

HILLTOP

22 Bronyon Close, Bury St Edmunds
IP33 3XB
T: (01284) 767066 & 07719 660142
E: bandb@hilltop22br.freeserve.co.uk
I: www.hilltop22br.freeserve.co.uk

Bedrooms: 1 single, 1 double/twin, 1 triple/multiple
Bathrooms: 1 private

Evening meal available

Family home in quiet location, ideal touring centre. Home cooking, homely atmosphere. 'Come as guests – leave as friends'.

B&B per night:
S £18.00–£25.00
D £36.00–£46.00

HB per person:
DY £24.00–£30.00

OPEN All Year except Christmas

CAMBRIDGE, Cambridgeshire Map ref 2D1 *Tourist Information Centre Tel: (01223) 322640*

♦♦♦

ARBURY LODGE GUESTHOUSE

82 Arbury Road, Cambridge
CB4 2JE
T: (01223) 364319 & 566988
F: (01223) 566988
E: arburylodge@ntlworld.com
I: guesthousecambridge.com

Bedrooms: 1 single, 5 double/twin, 1 triple/multiple
Bathrooms: 4 en suite

CC: Amex, Delta, Mastercard, Switch, Visa

Comfortable family-run guesthouse, 1.5 miles north of city centre and colleges. Easy access from A14/M11. Large car park and garden.

B&B per night:
S £28.00–£50.00
D £45.00–£60.00

OPEN All Year except Christmas

REGIONAL TOURIST BOARD The symbol in an establishment entry indicates that it is a Regional Tourist Board member.

◆◆◆

ASHLEY HOTEL
74 Chesterton Road, Cambridge CB4 1ER
T: (01223) 350059
F: (01223) 350900
E: info@arundelhousehotels.co.uk
I: www.arundelhousehotels.co.uk

Bedrooms: 7 double/twin, 3 triple/multiple
Bathrooms: 10 en suite

CC: Mastercard, Visa

Well-appointed recently refurbished small hotel with modern facilities close to city centre. Nearby Arundel House Hotel's facilities available to Ashley residents (under same ownership).

P

B&B per night:
S £49.50–£59.50
D £59.50–£79.50

OPEN All Year except Christmas

◆◆◆◆

AYLESBRAY LODGE GUESTHOUSE

5 Mowbray Road, Cambridge CB1 7SR
T: (01223) 240089
F: (01223) 528678
E: stay@aylesbray.com
I: www.aylesbray.com

All rooms are en suite, tastefully decorated and have complimentary extras. Four-poster rooms, satellite TV. Direct-dial telephones, radio alarm and hairdryer, free car parking. Close to Addenbrookes Hospital and within easy reach of rail station, Colleges and historic city centre. Easy access to M11, A14, A10. Convenient for local businesses.

Bedrooms: 1 single, 2 double/twin, 2 triple/multiple
Bathrooms: 5 en suite

CC: Amex, Delta, Mastercard, Switch, Visa

3 P

B&B per night:
S £30.00–£45.00
D £55.00–£80.00

OPEN All Year

◆◆◆◆

CAMBRIDGE LODGE HOTEL
139 Huntingdon Road, Cambridge CB3 0DQ
T: (01223) 352833
F: (01223) 355166
E: cambridge.lodge@btconnect.com

Bedrooms: 1 single, 14 double/twin
Bathrooms: 12 en suite

Lunch available
Evening meal available
CC: Amex, Delta, Diners, Mastercard, Switch, Visa

Tudor-style hotel with restaurant open to non-residents. Tastefully furnished. Oak-beamed dining room serving an array of freshly prepared foods.

P

B&B per night:
S £66.00–£68.00
D £80.00–£82.50

OPEN All Year except Christmas

◆◆◆

CRISTINAS
47 St Andrews Road, Cambridge CB4 1DH
T: (01223) 365855 & 327700
F: (01223) 365855
E: cristinas.guesthouse@ntlworld.com
I: www.cristinasguesthouse.com

Bedrooms: 8 double/twin, 1 triple/multiple
Bathrooms: 7 en suite

Established in 1986, Cristinas Guest House provides a very warm welcome and a comfortable and contented stay for guests. Walking distance of city centre.

P

B&B per night:
S £38.00–£49.00
D £49.00–£55.00

OPEN All Year

◆◆◆

DRESDEN VILLA GUESTHOUSE
34 Cherry Hinton Road, Cambridge CB1 7AA
T: (01223) 247539
F: (01223) 410640

Bedrooms: 6 single, 5 double/twin, 2 triple/multiple
Bathrooms: 13 en suite

Evening meal available

Family-run guesthouse offering friendly service. All rooms en suite, tea/coffee. Situated approximately 1 mile from city centre and Addenbrookes Hospital.

P

B&B per night:
S £32.00–£36.00
D £50.00–£55.00

HB per person:
DY £45.00–£49.00

OPEN All Year except Christmas

MAP REFERENCES
Map references apply to the colour maps at the front of this guide.

CAMBRIDGE continued

DYKELANDS GUESTHOUSE

157 Mowbray Road, Cambridge CB1 7SP
T: (01223) 244300
F: (01223) 566746
E: dykelands@fsbdial.co.uk
I: www.dykelands.com

Highly recommended guesthouse in south of city, only 1.75 miles from historic city centre. Ideally located for city and for touring. We offer modern, spacious accommodation, most en suite. Two bedrooms on ground floor. A non-smoking establishment. Traditional English breakfast or vegetarian alternatives. Car parking on site.

Bedrooms: 1 single, 5 double/twin, 3 triple/multiple
Bathrooms: 7 en suite

CC: Delta, Mastercard, Switch, Visa

B&B per night:
S Min £30.00
D £40.00–£50.00

OPEN All Year

♦♦♦♦

FINCHES

144 Thornton Road, Girton, Cambridge CB3 0ND
T: (01223) 276653 & 07710 179214
F: (01223) 276653
E: liz.green.b-b@talk21.com
I: www.smoothhound.co.uk/hotels/finches

Bedrooms: 3 double/twin
Bathrooms: 3 en suite

A 3 bedroom bed and breakfast establishment situated on the corner of Huntingdon Road, Cambridge. All en suite.

B&B per night:
S £45.00–£55.00
D £45.00–£55.00

OPEN All Year except Christmas

HAMILTON HOTEL

156 Chesterton Road, Cambridge CB4 1DA
T: (01223) 365664
F: (01223) 314866

Recently refurbished hotel less than 1 mile from centre of city. Easy access from A14 and M11. Most rooms have en suite shower and toilet. All rooms have colour TV, direct-dial telephone and hospitality tray.

Bedrooms: 5 single, 16 double/twin, 4 triple/multiple
Bathrooms: 20 en suite

Evening meal available
CC: Amex, Delta, Diners, Mastercard, Switch, Visa

B&B per night:
S £25.00–£50.00
D £50.00–£70.00

HB per person:
DY £35.00–£59.00

OPEN All Year except Christmas

♦♦♦♦

HILLS GUESTHOUSE

157 Hills Road, Cambridge CB2 2RJ
T: (01223) 214216
F: (01223) 214216

Bedrooms: 2 single, 2 double/twin, 1 triple/multiple
Bathrooms: 5 en suite

CC: Amex, Delta, Mastercard, Switch, Visa

We are a friendly family-run guesthouse. Bedrooms are cosy and spacious. Situated in between Addenbrookes Hospital, railway station and city centre.

B&B per night:
S £35.00–£42.00
D £50.00–£55.00

OPEN All Year except Christmas

♦♦♦♦

HOME FROM HOME

78B Milton Road, Cambridge CB4 1LA
T: (01223) 323555
F: (01223) 563509
E: homefromhome@tesco.net

Bedrooms: 1 double/twin, 1 triple/multiple
Bathrooms: 1 en suite, 1 private

CC: Delta, Mastercard, Switch, Visa

Centrally located near river and colleges. Providing home-from-home hospitality.

B&B per night:
S £40.00–£50.00
D £50.00–£65.00

OPEN All Year

CAMBRIDGE continued

♦♦♦♦

KING'S TITHE

13a Comberton Road, Barton, Cambridge CB3 7BA
T: (01223) 263610
F: (01223) 263610
E: thornebarton@lineone.net

Bedrooms: 2 double/twin

Guests return often to this up-market quiet home. Both rooms with twin beds and countryside views. Excellent breakfasts. Good village pub. Near M11 jct 12 (west A603 to B1046).

B&B per night:
S £35.00–£38.00
D £51.00–£55.00

OPEN All Year except Christmas

♦♦♦

SEGOVIA LODGE

2 Barton Road, Newnham, Cambridge CB3 9JZ
T: (01223) 354105
F: (01223) 323011

Bedrooms: 1 single, 3 double/twin
Bathrooms: 1 en suite, 1 private

A modern house situated on the western side of Cambridge close to M11 (jct 12), A10 and A603, walking distance to city centre. Parking. No credit cards. Non-smoking.

B&B per night:
D £55.00–£58.00

OPEN All Year except Christmas

SOUTHAMPTON GUEST HOUSE

7 Elizabeth Way, Cambridge CB4 1DE
T: (01223) 357780
F: (01223) 314297
E: southamptonhouse@telco4u.net
I: www.southamptonguesthouse.com

Bedrooms: 1 single, 1 double/twin, 3 triple/multiple
Bathrooms: 5 en suite

Victorian property with friendly atmosphere, only 15 minutes' walk along riverside to city centre, colleges and new shopping mall.

B&B per night:
S £35.00–£45.00
D £45.00–£55.00

OPEN All Year

♦♦♦♦

SYCAMORE HOUSE

56 High Street, Great Wilbraham, Cambridge CB1 5JD
T: (01223) 880751 & 07711 845300
F: (01223) 880751
E: barry@thesycamorehouse.co.uk
I: www.thesycamorehouse.co.uk

Bedrooms: 1 single, 2 double/twin

Pleasantly situated detached house in small village with shop and pub. Five miles to Cambridge and Newmarket. Excellent for racing, cycling and touring.

B&B per night:
S £25.00–£30.00
D £50.00–£60.00

OPEN All Year except Christmas

CAVENDISH, Suffolk Map ref 3B2

Silver Award

EMBLETON HOUSE BED & BREAKFAST

Melford Road, Cavendish, Sudbury CO10 8AA
T: (01787) 280447
F: (01787) 282396
E: silverned@aol.com
I: www.smoothhound.co.uk/hotels/embleton

A large, family-run, 1930's house set well back from the road within its own secluded, mature gardens at the eastern edge of Cavendish village. Five spacious, recently appointed en suite bedrooms. Stour Valley views. Suffolk breakfast. Good pub within 8 minutes' walk. Ideal base for exploring Long Melford, Clare, Lavenham and beyond.

Bedrooms: 5 double/twin
Bathrooms: 5 en suite

Evening meal available

Special rates for stays of 3 nights or more. 'Stress Busting' break – holistic therapies, heated pool (May-Sep) and tennis court.

B&B per night:
S £35.00–£50.00
D £55.00–£70.00

OPEN All Year

QUALITY ASSURANCE SCHEME

Diamond ratings and awards are explained at the back of this guide.

CHELMSFORD, Essex Map ref 3B3 *Tourist Information Centre Tel: (01245) 283400*

♦♦♦

BEECHCROFT HOTEL
211 New London Road, Chelmsford CM2 0AJ
T: (01245) 352462 & 250861
F: (01245) 347833
E: enquiries@beechcrofthotel.com
I: www.beechcrofthotel.com

Bedrooms: 11 single, 6 double/twin, 2 triple/multiple
Bathrooms: 13 en suite

CC: Delta, Diners, Mastercard, Switch, Visa

Central hotel offering clean and comfortable accommodation with friendly service. Under family ownership and management. Within walking distance of town centre.

P

B&B per night:
S £36.00–£38.00
D £52.00–£59.00

OPEN All Year

♦♦♦♦

BOSWELL HOUSE HOTEL
118 Springfield Road, Chelmsford CM2 6LF
T: (01245) 287587
F: (01245) 287587
E: SteveBoorman@aol.com

Bedrooms: 5 single, 6 double/twin, 2 triple/multiple
Bathrooms: 13 en suite

Lunch available
Evening meal available
CC: Amex, Delta, Diners, Mastercard, Switch, Visa

Victorian townhouse in central location, offering high-standard accommodation in friendly and informal surroundings. Family atmosphere and home cooking, lounge bar.

P

B&B per night:
S £47.00–£52.00
D £65.00–£70.00

HB per person:
DY £59.00–£64.00

OPEN All Year except Christmas

♦♦♦

TANUNDA HOTEL
217-219 New London Road, Chelmsford CM2 0AJ
T: (01245) 354295 & 258799
F: (01245) 345503

Bedrooms: 8 single, 12 double/twin
Bathrooms: 11 en suite

CC: Amex, Delta, Diners, Mastercard, Switch, Visa

We are on the main road to London and Harwich and 5 minutes from the town centre.

P

B&B per night:
S £36.00–£60.00
D £52.00–£62.00

OPEN All Year except Christmas

CLACTON-ON-SEA, Essex Map ref 3B3 *Tourist Information Centre Tel: (01255) 423400*

♦♦♦

SANDROCK HOTEL
1 Penfold Road, Marine Parade West, Clacton-on-Sea CO15 1JN
T: (01255) 428215
F: (01255) 428215

Bedrooms: 7 double/twin, 1 triple/multiple
Bathrooms: 8 en suite

Lunch available
Evening meal available
CC: Amex, Delta, Diners, Mastercard, Switch, Visa

Private hotel in central position, just off seafront and close to town. Comfortable bedrooms with co-ordinated soft furnishings. Excellent, freshly cooked food. Licensed. Car park.

1 P

B&B per night:
S £35.50–£36.50
D £53.00–£54.00

HB per person:
DY £38.50–£39.95

OPEN All Year

COLCHESTER, Essex Map ref 3B2 *Tourist Information Centre Tel: (01206) 282920*

♦♦♦♦

FRIDAYWOOD FARM

Bounstead Road, Colchester CO2 0DF
T: (01206) 573595
F: (01206) 547011
E: lochorem8@aol.com

Charming period house on working farm. Set in wooded countryside, convenient for bird-watching, Beth Chatto's gardens, walking, cycling and the coast. Enjoy our farmhouse breakfasts and relaxed atmosphere.

Bedrooms: 2 double/twin
Bathrooms: 2 en suite

12 P

B&B per night:
S £30.00–£35.00
D £42.00–£50.00

OPEN All Year

SPECIAL BREAKS

Many establishments offer special promotions and themed breaks. These are highlighted in red. (All such offers are subject to availability.)

COLCHESTER continued

OLD COURTHOUSE INN

Harwich Road, Great Bromley,
Colchester CO7 7JG
T: (01206) 250322 & 251906
F: (01206) 251346
E: oldcourthouseinn@21.com
I: www.theoldcourthouse.com

Bedrooms: 1 single, 3 double/twin, 1 triple/multiple
Bathrooms: 5 en suite

Lunch available
Evening meal available
CC: Amex, Delta, Mastercard, Switch, Visa

17thC inn, all en suite rooms, bar and restaurant. Just off A120, halfway between Harwich and Colchester. Ideally situated for coastal resorts. Beth Chatto garden 2 miles.

B&B per night:
S £35.00–£40.00
D £60.00

HB per person:
DY £40.00–£60.00

OPEN All Year

♦♦

PEVERIL HOTEL

51 North Hill, Colchester CO1 1PY
T: (01206) 574001
F: (01206) 574001

Friendly, family-run hotel with fine restaurant and bar. All rooms have colour TV and all facilities. Some en suite available. We are situated in the centre of Colchester, close to all amenities, and have a weekend and overnight car park.

Bedrooms: 5 single, 12 double/twin
Bathrooms: 6 en suite

Lunch available
Evening meal available
CC: Amex, Delta, Diners, Mastercard, Switch, Visa

20% dicount for weekend bookings of 3 or more nights.

B&B per night:
S £30.00–£50.00
D £42.00–£54.00

HB per person:
DY £40.00–£70.00

OPEN All Year except Christmas

♦♦

SCHEREGATE HOTEL

36 Osborne Street,
via St John's Street, Colchester
CO2 7DB
T: (01206) 573034
F: (01206) 541561

Bedrooms: 11 single, 14 double/twin, 2 triple/multiple
Bathrooms: 10 en suite

CC: Delta, Mastercard, Switch, Visa

Interesting 15thC building, centrally situated, providing accommodation at moderate prices.

B&B per night:
S £24.00–£35.00
D £40.00–£48.00

OPEN All Year except Christmas

COLTISHALL, Norfolk Map ref 3C1

BRIDGE HOUSE

1 High Street, Coltishall, Norwich
NR12 7AA
T: (01603) 737323
F: (01603) 737323
E: bookings@bridge-house.com
I: www.bridge-house.com

Bridge House is a beautiful 18thC former coaching inn standing in delightful gardens with frontage to the River Bure in the pretty Broadland village of Coltishall. Large, comfortable rooms are separate from the house in converted barns, giving freedom and privacy. Ideal for exploring the Broads, coast and Norwich.

Bedrooms: 2 double/twin, 2 triple/multiple
Bathrooms: 4 en suite

B&B per night:
S £35.00
D £49.00

OPEN All Year except Christmas

MAP REFERENCES The map references refer to the colour maps at the front of this guide. The first figure is the map number; the letter and figure which follow indicate the grid reference on the map.

COLTISHALL continued

THE HEDGES GUESTHOUSE

Tunstead Road, Coltishall, Norwich
NR12 7AL
T: (01603) 738361
F: (01603) 738983
E: thehedges@msn.com
I: www.hedgesbandb.co.uk

B&B per night:
S £23.50–£30.00
D £47.00–£49.00

OPEN All Year except Christmas

Hear evening owlsong and the dawn chorus at this friendly family-run guesthouse. Set in large, peaceful gardens surrounded by open countryside, yet convenient for local amenities. Ideal base for exploring the Norfolk Broads, Norwich and Norfolk coast. Families welcome, spacious lounge with log fire, licensed, plenty of parking.

Bedrooms: 3 double/twin, 2 triple/multiple
Bathrooms: 5 en suite

Evening meal available
CC: Delta, Mastercard, Switch, Visa

3 nights for price of 2 Nov-Apr. Quote 342 when booking.

P

TERRA NOVA LODGE

14 Westbourne Road, Coltishall, Norwich
NR12 7HT
T: (01603) 736264

B&B per night:
S £36.00–£38.00
D £42.00–£45.00

OPEN All Year except Christmas

Terranova Lodge offers tranquil accommodation in a lovely Broadland village. Large, en suite rooms, tastefully funished, private entrance for guests, TV and hospitality tray. Full English breakfast served in our conservatory overlooking delightful gardens. Easy access to the coast, the Broads and the fine medieval city of Norwich.

Bedrooms: 2 double/twin
Bathrooms: 2 en suite

5 P

CRETINGHAM, Suffolk Map ref 3B2

Silver Award

THE CRETINGHAM BELL

The Street, Cretingham, Woodbridge
IP13 7BJ
T: (01728) 685419

B&B per night:
S £39.95
D £58.75

OPEN All Year except Christmas

Situated in the quiet village of Cretingham. The Tudor beams, log fires, luxury accommodation, traditional home-cooked food, locally brewed ales and a warm welcome makes The Bell ideal for travellers seeking old world charm, peace and tranquillity.

Bedrooms: 3 double/twin; permanent suite(s)
Bathrooms: 3 en suite

Lunch available
Evening meal available
CC: Delta, Mastercard, Switch, Visa

14 P

NB

IMPORTANT NOTE Information on accommodation listed in this guide has been supplied by the proprietors. As changes may occur you are advised to check details at the time of booking.

CRETINGHAM continued

Silver Award

SHRUBBERY FARMHOUSE

Chapel Hill, Cretingham, Woodbridge IP13 7DN
T: (01473) 737494 & 07860 352317
F: (01473) 737312
E: sm@marmar.co.uk
I: www.shrubberyfarmhouse.co.uk

Charming, part-16thC, Listed Suffolk farmhouse set in some of the most quiet and beautiful countryside in East Anglia. Winter log fires. Al fresco summer breakfasts with fresh eggs from the farmhouse hens make this the ideal base for exploring Suffolk's Heritage Coast. Comfortable bedrooms, gymnasium and tennis court.

Bedrooms: 1 single, 2 double/twin
Bathrooms: 1 en suite, 2 private

Lunch available
Evening meal available

B&B per night:
S £39.00–£49.00
D £59.50–£78.00

HB per person:
DY £45.50–£66.50

OPEN All Year except Christmas

DARSHAM, Suffolk Map ref 3C2

WHITE HOUSE FARM
Main Road, Darsham, Saxmundham IP17 3PP
T: (01728) 668632

Bedrooms: 3 double/twin
Bathrooms: 1 en suite

Small, family-run, modernised farmhouse with pleasant gardens, on edge of village. Easy access to Aldeburgh, Southwold, Dunwich, Minsmere. Large gardens. Hearty farmhouse breakfasts.

B&B per night:
S £25.00–£35.00
D £40.00–£55.00

OPEN All Year except Christmas

DERSINGHAM, Norfolk Map ref 3B1

ASHDENE HOUSE

Dersingham, King's Lynn PE31 6HQ
T: (01485) 540395
I: www3.mistral.co.uk/ashdene

An elegant Victorian house in village centre bordering Royal Estate with woodland walks and close to North Norfolk coastal attractions and nature reserves. Ashdene House is set in a pleasant garden with ample car parking facilities. A warm welcome and friendly personal service is guaranteed.

Bedrooms: 5 double/twin
Bathrooms: 5 en suite

Lunch available
Evening meal available
CC: Delta, Mastercard, Switch, Visa

B&B per night:
S £20.00–£25.00
D £40.00–£48.00

HB per person:
DY £29.50–£31.50

OPEN All Year except Christmas

DISS, Norfolk Map ref 3B2 *Tourist Information Centre Tel: (01379) 650523*

OXFOOTSTONE GRANARY
Low Common, South Lopham, Diss IP22 2JS
T: (01379) 687490
E: paddie@oxfoot.co.uk
I: oxfoot.co.uk

Bedrooms: 2 double/twin
Bathrooms: 2 en suite

Converted barn in open countryside, erected in 1822. Guest rooms are situated in a single-storey wing, formerly cart-sheds, overlooking a large pond with waterfowl.

B&B per night:
S £25.00–£32.00
D £40.00–£45.00

OPEN All Year

EARL SOHAM, Suffolk Map ref 3C2

♦♦♦♦
Silver Award

BRIDGE HOUSE

Earl Soham, Framlingham, Woodbridge IP13 7RT
T: (01728) 685473 & 685289
F: (01728) 685289
E: bridgehouse46@hotmail.com
I: www.jenniferbaker.co.uk

Bedrooms: 3 double/twin
Bathrooms: 3 en suite

Lunch available
Evening meal available

B&B per night:
S Min £28.00
D Min £50.00

HB per person:
DY Min £37.00

OPEN All Year

Bridge House is an attractive, 16thC property near Heritage Coast. A warm welcome and excellent food add charm to well-appointed, comfortable accommodation.

10 P

EARLS COLNE, Essex Map ref 3B2

♦♦♦

RIVERSIDE LODGE

40 Lower Holt Street, Earls Colne, Colchester CO6 2PH
T: (01787) 223487
F: (01787) 223487
E: john+bonnie@riversidelodge-uk.com
I: www.riversidelodge-uk.com

Bedrooms: 5 double/twin
Bathrooms: 5 en suite

Lunch available
Evening meal available
CC: Mastercard, Visa

B&B per night:
S £38.50–£40.50
D £47.00–£51.00

On the A1124 Colchester-Halstead road, single storey en suite chalets on the banks of the River Colne. Restaurants, pubs and village amenities within walking distance.

P

ELY, Cambridgeshire Map ref 3A2 *Tourist Information Centre Tel: (01353) 662062*

♦♦♦♦
Gold Award

HILL HOUSE FARM

9 Main Street, Coveney, Ely CB6 2DJ
T: (01353) 778369
F: (01353) 778369
E: hill_house@madasafish.com

B&B per night:
S £30.00–£40.00
D £48.00–£50.00

OPEN All Year except Christmas

Fine Victorian farmhouse on arable working farm 3 miles west of Ely. First-class breakfast served in traditional dining room. Open views of surrounding countryside. No smoking, no pets, children over 12 welcome. Access from A142 or A10. Situated in the centre of quiet village. Convenient for Ely, Cambridge, Newmarket.

Bedrooms: 3 double/twin
Bathrooms: 3 en suite

CC: Delta, Mastercard, Switch, Visa

10% discount for 3 nights or more Nov-Feb.

12 P

♦♦♦♦

SPINNEY ABBEY

Stretham Road, Wicken, Ely CB7 5XQ
T: (01353) 720971
E: spinney.abbey@tesco.net
I: www.spinneyabbey.co.uk

B&B per night:
D £50.00

OPEN All Year except Christmas

This attractive Georgian Grade II Listed farmhouse, surrounded by pasture fields, stands next to our dairy farm which borders the National Trust Nature Reserve, 'Wicken Fen', on the southern edge of the Fens. Guests are welcome to make full use of spacious garden and all-weather tennis court. All rooms have private facilities.

Bedrooms: 2 double/twin, 1 triple/multiple
Bathrooms: 2 en suite, 1 private

5 P

COLOUR MAPS Colour maps at the front of this guide pinpoint all places under which you will find accommodation listed.

EPPING, Essex Map ref 2D1

◆◆◆

BROOKLANDS

1 Chapel Road, Epping CM16 5DS
T: (01992) 575424
E: abrookland@aol.com
I: www.abrookland@aol.com

Bedrooms: 2 double/twin, 1 triple/multiple
Bathrooms: 2 en suite, 1 private

Quiet central position, short walk to Central Line underground station, shops, pubs and restaurants. Three miles from M11 and M25 motorways.

P

B&B per night:
S £40.00
D £50.00

OPEN All Year except Christmas

EYE, Suffolk Map ref 3B2

◆◆◆

THE WHITE HORSE INN

Stoke Ash, Eye IP23 7ET
T: (01379) 678222
F: (01379) 678557
E: whitehorse@stokeash.fsbusiness.co.uk
I: www.whitehorseinn.fsnet.co.uk

Ideally situated and easy to find on the main A140. Modern, comfortable and quiet double- and twin-bedded accommodation with 24-hour access and many extras. Early check in/out available. The main building is heavily timbered with many period features. Hot food served all day, every day.

Bedrooms: 6 double/twin, 1 triple/multiple
Bathrooms: 7 en suite

Lunch available
Evening meal available
CC: Delta, Mastercard, Switch, Visa

Stay 2 nights, get third night free! (subject to availability) Fri/Sat/Sun. £54.95 per double.

P

B&B per night:
S £39.95
D £54.95

OPEN All Year

FAKENHAM, Norfolk Map ref 3B1

◆◆◆◆◆
Silver Award

HOLLY LODGE

The Street, Thursford Green, Fakenham NR21 0AS
T: (01328) 878465
F: (01328) 878465
E: hollyguestlodge@talk21.com
I: www.hollylodgeguesthouse.co.uk

Warm and welcoming friendly atmosphere at our 18thC house and guest cottages. Picturesque setting, recently renovated, period charm. Stylish, luxurious rooms, all en suite, centrally heated, TV/VCR, tea/coffee facilities, beams, 4-poster, antique furniture. Home-cooked breakfast, car parking. Ideally situated for places of interest, Norfolk Coast and countryside.

Bedrooms: 3 double/twin
Bathrooms: 3 en suite

7 nights for the price of 6.

14 P

B&B per night:
S £45.00–£55.00
D £60.00–£80.00

TOWN INDEX

This can be found at the back of the guide. If you know where you want to stay, the index will give you the page number listing accommodation in your chosen town, city or village.

FEERING, Essex Map ref 3B2

OLD WILLS FARM

Feering, Colchester CO5 9RP
T: (01376) 570259
F: (01376) 570259
E: janecrayston@btconnect.com

Attractive and comfortable Essex farmhouse on a working arable farm with a large garden. Offering homely surroundings and atmosphere. Ideal relaxing base from which to sample the many and varied visitor attractions in the area, including historic sites, coastal regions and good restaurants.

Bedrooms: 1 single, 1 double/twin, 1 triple/multiple
Bathrooms: 1 en suite, 1 private

B&B per night:
S £25.00–£27.50
D Min £45.00

OPEN All Year except Christmas

P

FELIXSTOWE, Suffolk Map ref 3C2 *Tourist Information Centre Tel: (01394) 276770*

◆◆

DOLPHIN HOTEL

41 Beach Station Road, Felixstowe
IP11 2EY
T: (01394) 282261
F: (01394) 278319

Bedrooms: 3 single, 5 double/twin, 1 triple/multiple
Bathrooms: 2 en suite

Lunch available
Evening meal available
CC: Amex, Delta, Mastercard, Switch, Visa

Private hotel, 5 minutes from beach and 10 minutes from town centre. Fully licensed bar, traditional bar menu. Family room.

P

B&B per night:
S £20.00–£30.00
D £34.00–£46.00

OPEN All Year except Christmas

FOULDEN, Norfolk Map ref 3B1

◆◆◆

THE WHITE HART INN

White Hart Street, Foulden,
Thetford IP26 5AW
T: (01366) 328638
E: sylvia.chisholm@virgin.net

Bedrooms: 1 single, 2 double/twin
Bathrooms: 3 en suite

Lunch available
Evening meal available
CC: Delta, Mastercard, Switch, Visa

Traditional country inn with beer garden, conservatory and car park. Home-cooked food and real ale. Accommodation in former barn.

P

B&B per night:
S £35.00
D £45.00

OPEN All Year except Christmas

GARBOLDISHAM, Norfolk Map ref 3B2

◆◆◆◆

INGLENEUK LODGE

Hopton Road, Garboldisham, Diss
IP22 2RQ
T: (01953) 681541
F: (01953) 681138
E: info@ingleneuklodge.co.uk
I: www.ingleneuklodge.co.uk

Bedrooms: 2 single, 6 double/twin
Bathrooms: 8 en suite

Lunch available
Evening meal available
CC: Delta, Mastercard, Switch, Visa

Modern, single-level home, wheelchair friendly, family run. South-facing patio. Friendly, relaxed atmosphere. On B1111, 1 mile south of Garboldisham village.

P

B&B per night:
S £36.00
D £60.00

OPEN All Year

GREAT YARMOUTH, Norfolk Map ref 3C1

◆◆

THE BROMLEY HOTEL

63 Apsley Road, Great Yarmouth
NR30 2HG
T: (01493) 842321
F: (01493) 842322
E: thebromleyhotel@tiscali.co.uk
I: www.smoothhound.co.uk/hotels/bromleyhotel

Bedrooms: 2 single, 6 double/twin, 1 triple/multiple
Bathrooms: 5 en suite

CC: Diners

A fine Regency building adjacent to Brittania Pier, and ideally situated between the seafront, theatres and market place.

P

B&B per night:
S £16.00–£20.00
D £32.00–£40.00

CONFIRM YOUR BOOKING
You are advised to confirm your booking in writing.

GRIMSTON, Norfolk Map ref 3B1

♦♦♦

THE BELL INN

1 Gayton Road, Grimston,
King's Lynn PE32 1BG
T: (01485) 601156 & 07961 304833

Bedrooms: 3 double/twin
Bathrooms: 3 en suite

Lunch available
Evening meal available
CC: Delta, Mastercard, Switch, Visa

A warm and friendly freehouse serving home-cooked food and fine real ales. Close to Sandringham. Ideal for bird-watching, walking and cycling.

14 P

B&B per night:
S £25.50–£33.50
D £36.00–£48.00

HB per person:
DY £31.00–£47.00

OPEN All Year

GRISTON, Norfolk Map ref 3B1

♦♦♦♦
Silver Award

PARK FARM BED & BREAKFAST

Park Farm, Caston Road, Griston,
Thetford IP25 6QD
T: (01953) 483020 & 07974 772485
F: (01953) 483056
E: parkfarm@eidosnet.co.uk
I: www.parkfarmbreckland.co.uk

Bedrooms: 2 double/twin
Bathrooms: 2 en suite

Working arable farm with en suite accommodation in converted outbuildings. Rural location, peaceful surroundings. Large lounge/dining room for residents only. Vist our website.

P

B&B per night:
S £25.00–£30.00
D £40.00–£46.00

HADLEIGH, Suffolk Map ref 3B2

♦♦♦♦

WEAVERS RESTAURANT

25 High Street, Hadleigh, Ipswich
IP7 5AG
T: (01473) 827247 & 823185
F: (01473) 822805
E: cyndymiles@aol.com
I: www.weaversrestaurant.co.uk

Bedrooms: 3 double/twin
Bathrooms: 3 en suite

Lunch available
Evening meal available
CC: Delta, Mastercard, Switch, Visa

Stunning 500-year-old a la carte restaurant and bar with luxury rooms in historic town bordering Constable country. Great food, great ambience, great service!

P

B&B per night:
S £45.00–£70.00
D £55.00–£75.00

HB per person:
DY £65.00–£90.00

OPEN All Year except Christmas

HALESWORTH, Suffolk Map ref 3C2

♦♦♦

FEN-WAY GUEST HOUSE

Fen-Way, School Lane, Halesworth
IP19 8BW
T: (01986) 873574

Bedrooms: 3 double/twin
Bathrooms: 1 en suite

Spacious bungalow in 7 acres of peaceful meadowland. Pets include sheep and lambs. Five minutes' walk from town centre. Convenient for many places including Southwold (9 miles)

5 P

B&B per night:
S £20.00–£25.00
D £36.00–£50.00

OPEN All Year

HARLESTON, Norfolk Map ref 3C2

♦♦♦♦

WESTON HOUSE FARM

Mendham, Harleston IP20 0PB
T: (01986) 782206 & 07803 099203
F: (01986) 782414
E: holden@farmline.com

This peacefully located, 17thC, Grade II Listed farmhouse is set in a one-acre garden and offers comfortable, spacious accommodation on a 600-acre mixed farm on the Norfolk/Suffolk border. It is within easy reach of Suffolk Heritage Coast, Minsmere Nature Reserve, Norfolk Broads, the historic city of Norwich and nearby otter sanctuary.

Bedrooms: 3 double/twin
Bathrooms: 3 en suite

Evening meal available
CC: Amex

P

B&B per night:
S £25.00–£30.00
D £40.00–£50.00

HB per person:
DY £32.00–£42.00

RATING All accommodation in this guide has been rated, or is awaiting a rating, by a trained English Tourism Council assessor.

HARPENDEN, Hertfordshire Map ref 2D1

◆◆◆

MILTON HOTEL
25 Milton Road, Harpenden
AL5 5LA
T: (01582) 762914

Bedrooms: 7 double/twin, 1 triple/multiple
Bathrooms: 8 en suite

CC: Mastercard, Visa

B&B per night:
S Min £50.00
D Min £60.00

OPEN All Year except Christmas

Family-run, comfortable Victorian hotel in residential area close to mainline station, jcts 9/10 of M1 and convenient for M25. Car park.

P

HARWICH, Essex Map ref 3C2 *Tourist Information Centre Tel: (01255) 506139*

◆◆◆◆

NEW FARM HOUSE
Spinnels Lane, Wix, Manningtree
CO11 2UJ
T: (01255) 870365
F: (01255) 870837
E: newfarmhouse@which.net
I: www.newfarmhouse.com

Bedrooms: 2 single, 6 double/twin, 3 triple/multiple
Bathrooms: 9 en suite

Evening meal available
CC: Delta, Mastercard, Switch, Visa

B&B per night:
S £28.00–£38.00
D £46.00–£56.00

OPEN All Year except Christmas

Large, non-working farmhouse in 4 acres of grounds, 10 minutes' drive from Harwich, convenient for Colchester and Constable country. Spacious public rooms. Home cooking, licensed.

P

◆◆◆

PASTON LODGE
1 Una Road, Parkeston, Harwich
CO12 4PP
T: (01255) 551390

Bedrooms: 1 single, 1 double/twin, 1 triple/multiple
Bathrooms: 3 en suite

B&B per night:
S £23.00–£25.00
D £44.00–£46.00

OPEN All Year

Edwardian house offering comfortable en suite bed and breakfast facilities, situated within walking distance of Harwich International port. All rooms are non-smoking.

1 P

◆◆◆◆

WOODVIEW COTTAGE
Wrabness Road, Ramsey, Harwich
CO12 5ND
T: (01255) 886413 & 07714 600134
E: pcohen@cix.co.uk
I: www.woodview-cottage.co.uk

Bedrooms: 1 single, 1 double/twin
Bathrooms: 2 en suite

B&B per night:
S £30.00
D £47.00

OPEN All Year

Spacious homely accommodation in pretty peaceful country cottage adjacent to nature reserve and the beautiful Stour estuary. Four miles from Harwich International.

P

HAUGHLEY, Suffolk Map ref 3B2

◆◆◆◆

RED HOUSE FARM
Station Road, Haughley,
Stowmarket IP14 3QP
T: (01449) 673323
F: (01449) 675413
E: mary@noy1.fsnet.co.uk
I: www.farmstayanglia.co.uk

Bedrooms: 2 single, 2 double/twin
Bathrooms: 4 en suite

B&B per night:
S £30.00
D £50.00

OPEN All Year except Christmas

Attractive farmhouse in rural location on small grassland farm. First class breakfast. Central heating and large garden.

8 P

HETHERSETT, Norfolk Map ref 3B1

◆◆◆

MAGNOLIA HOUSE
Cromwell Close, Hethersett,
Norwich NR9 3HD
T: (01603) 810749
F: (01603) 810749

Bedrooms: 2 single, 2 double/twin
Bathrooms: 4 en suite

B&B per night:
S £26.00–£30.00
D £44.00–£48.00

OPEN All Year

Family-run B&B. All rooms centrally heated, colour TV, hot water, tea/coffee-making facilities. Laundry, public telephone and fax available. Weekend-break discounts. Private car park.

6 P

HEVINGHAM, Norfolk Map ref 3B1

♦♦♦♦

MARSHAM ARMS INN

Holt Road, Hevingham, Norwich NR10 5NP
T: (01603) 754268
F: (01603) 754839
E: nigelbradley@marshamarms.co.uk
I: www.marshamarms.co.uk

Bedrooms: 8 double/twin
Bathrooms: 8 en suite

Lunch available
Evening meal available
CC: Amex, Delta, Mastercard, Switch, Visa

B&B per night:
S £45.00–£50.00
D £65.00–£75.00

OPEN All Year

Set in peaceful Norfolk countryside within reach of Norwich, the Broads and the coast. Comfortable and spacious accommodation, good food and a fine selection of ales.

HINDRINGHAM, Norfolk Map ref 3B1

♦♦♦♦♦
Gold Award

FIELD HOUSE

Moorgate Road, Hindringham, Fakenham NR21 0PT
T: (01328) 878726
F: (01328) 878955
E: wendyfieldhouse@lineone.net
I: www.northnorfolk.co.uk/fieldhouse

B&B per night:
S £40.00–£45.00
D £60.00–£70.00

HB per person:
DY £52.50–£57.50

OPEN All Year except Christmas

Field House stands in lovely gardens on the edge of the peaceful village, close to the North Norfolk coast, and enjoys fine views of the Norfolk countryside. Luxurious bedrooms with many thoughtful extras. Quality cooking, with dinner being a highlight. Relaxing and friendly hospitality. A great place to unwind.

Bedrooms: 3 double/twin
Bathrooms: 3 en suite

Evening meal available

HINTLESHAM, Suffolk Map ref 3B2

♦♦♦♦

COLLEGE FARM

Hintlesham, Ipswich IP8 3NT
T: (01473) 652253
F: (01473) 652253
E: bryce1@agripro.co.uk
I: www.smoothhound.co.uk/hotels/collegefarm

Bedrooms: 1 single, 2 double/twin, 1 triple/multiple
Bathrooms: 1 en suite, 1 private

B&B per night:
S £20.00–£30.00
D £40.00–£48.00

OPEN All Year except Christmas

Peaceful 500-year-old beamed house on 600-acre arable farm near Ipswich. Convenient for 'Constable Country', Sutton Hoo and the coast. Well-appointed, comfortable rooms. Good food locally.

HITCHIN, Hertfordshire Map ref 2D1

THE LORD LISTER HOTEL

1 Park Street, Hitchin SG4 9AH
T: (01462) 432712 & 459451
F: (01462) 438506
E: info@lordlisterhotel.co.uk
I: www.lordlisterhotel.co.uk

Bedrooms: 4 single, 14 double/twin, 2 triple/multiple
Bathrooms: 20 en suite

CC: Amex, Delta, Diners, Mastercard, Switch, Visa

B&B per night:
S £60.00–£70.00
D £70.00–£85.00

OPEN All Year

18thC country-style hotel on the edge of Hitchin town centre. Warm atmosphere with friendly and helpful staff. Individually furnished rooms, all en suite, some non-smoking. Lounge, cosy bar, free car park. Good choice of menu offered for breakfast. 4-poster bedroom for that special occasion.

CREDIT CARD BOOKINGS If you book by telephone and are asked for your credit card number it is advisable to check the proprietor's policy should you cancel your reservation.

HOLT, Norfolk Map ref 3B1

LAWNS HOTEL

Station Road, Holt NR25 6BS
T: (01263) 713390
F: (01263) 710642
E: info@lawnshotel.co.uk
I: www.lawnshotel.co.uk

Situated in North Norfolk's historic town of Holt. Ideal for exploring both the enchanting coastline and scenic countryside, the Lawns is a charming Georgian hotel providing spacious accommodation with tranquil setting and delightful walled gardens. Car park. Much emphasis on hospitality and courteous service. The perfect retreat at any time.

Bedrooms: 1 single, 9 double/twin
Bathrooms: 9 en suite, 1 private

CC: Delta, Mastercard, Switch, Visa

Please ask when booking for out-of-season special offers.

B&B per night:
S £32.50–£42.50
D £65.00–£85.00

OPEN All Year

HORSEHEATH, Cambridgeshire Map ref 3B2

CHEQUER COTTAGE

43 Streetly End, Horseheath, Cambridge CB1 6RP
T: (01223) 891522
F: (01223) 890266
E: debbie@dsills.freeserve.co.uk

Bedrooms: 1 double/twin
Bathrooms: 1 en suite

Luxury self-contained room above a garage with own shower. Take the A1307 between Haverhill and Cambridge. Turn at Horseheath where signed.

B&B per night:
S Min £30.00
D Min £50.00

OPEN All Year except Christmas

HORSEY, Norfolk Map ref 3C1

THE OLD CHAPEL

Horsey Corner, Horsey, Great Yarmouth NR29 4EH
T: (01493) 393498
F: (01493) 393498

The Old Chapel nestles amidst National Trust land, in an Area of Outstanding Natural Beauty. Short stroll to tranquil sandy beach and Horsey Mere, part of Norfolk Broads. Peaceful location, ideal for nature lovers, walkers, bird/seal-watchers. Separate guest accommodation. Sorry, no children or pets. 'Which?' recommended.

Bedrooms: 3 double/twin
Bathrooms: 3 en suite

B&B per night:
S Max £30.00
D £44.00–£48.00

OPEN All Year except Christmas

CHECK THE MAPS

The colour maps at the front of this guide show all the cities, towns and villages for which you will find accommodation entries. Refer to the town index to find the page on which they are listed.

ICKLETON, Cambridgeshire Map ref 2D1

SHEPHERDS COTTAGE

Grange Road, Ickleton, Saffron Walden
CB10 1TA
T: (01799) 531171
E: jcase@nascr.net

B&B per night:
S £25.00–£28.00
D £50.00–£55.00

OPEN All Year except Christmas

Converted from a pair of farm cottages this quiet, comfortable family home is surrounded by open countryside, 0.5 miles from Ickleton, with a pretty garden and private parking. Easy access to M11, jcts 9 and 10. Ideal for visiting Duxford Air Museum, Cambridge, Saffron Walden. Stansted Airport 15 miles.

Bedrooms: 1 double/twin
Bathrooms: 1 private

12 P

KELVEDON, Essex Map ref 3B3

♦♦♦♦

HIGHFIELDS FARM

Kelvedon, Colchester CO5 9BJ
T: (01376) 570334
F: (01376) 570334
E: highfieldsfarm@farmersweekly.net
I: www.highfieldsfarm.20m.com

Bedrooms: 3 double/twin
Bathrooms: 3 en suite

B&B per night:
S £26.00–£28.00
D £46.00–£48.00

OPEN All Year

700-acre arable and horse farm. Timber-framed farmhouse in quiet location in open countryside. Easy access to A12. Heating in all rooms.

P

KING'S LYNN, Norfolk Map ref 3B1 *Tourist Information Centre Tel: (01553) 763044*

♦♦♦

MARANATHA GUESTHOUSE

115-117 Gaywood Road,
King's Lynn PE30 2PU
T: (01553) 774596 & 772331
F: (01553) 763747

Bedrooms: 2 single, 7 double/twin, 2 triple/multiple
Bathrooms: 5 private

Evening meal available
CC: Amex, Delta, Mastercard, Switch, Visa

B&B per night:
S £20.00–£30.00
D £36.00–£44.00

OPEN All Year

Large family-run guesthouse, 10 minutes' walk town centre, Lynnsport and Queen Elizabeth Hospital. Direct road to Sandringham and coast. Special rates for children.

P

KINGS LANGLEY, Hertfordshire Map ref 2D1

WOODCOTE HOUSE

7 The Grove, Whippendell,
Chipperfield, Kings Langley
WD4 9JF
T: (01923) 262077
F: (01923) 266198
E: leveridge@btinternet.com

Bedrooms: 2 single, 2 double/twin
Bathrooms: 4 en suite

Evening meal available

B&B per night:
S £26.00–£30.00
D £46.00–£50.00

OPEN All Year except Christmas

Timber-framed house, sitting in 1 acre of landscaped gardens with quiet rural aspect. Convenient for M1 and M25 and close to Watford and Hemel Hempstead.

P

COUNTRY CODE Always follow the Country Code Enjoy the countryside and respect its life and work Guard against all risk of fire Fasten all gates Keep your dogs under close control Keep to public paths across farmland Use gates and stiles to cross fences, hedges and walls Leave livestock, crops and machinery alone Take your litter home Help to keep all water clean Protect wildlife, plants and trees Take special care on country roads Make no unnecessary noise

KNAPTON, Norfolk Map ref 3C1

CORNERSTONE HOUSE

The Street, Knapton, North Walsham
NR28 0AD
T: (01263) 722884
E: evescornerstone@hotmail.com

B&B per night:
S £22.00–£25.00
D £44.00–£50.00

OPEN All Year

A former 18thC farmhouse situated in rural village. Easy reach of coast, Norwich, Broads and National Trust properties. You can be assured of a warm and friendly welcome. We offer comfortable rooms with TV and tea/coffee-making facilities and pride ourselves on our full English breakfast.

Bedrooms: 3 double/twin
Bathrooms: 2 en suite, 1 private

LAVENHAM, Suffolk Map ref 3B2

BRETT FARM
The Common, Lavenham, Sudbury
CO10 9PG
T: (01787) 248533
E: brettfarm@aol.com
I: www.brettfarm.com

Bedrooms: 3 double/twin
Bathrooms: 2 en suite, 1 private

B&B per night:
S £30.00
D £50.00

OPEN All Year except Christmas

Riverside bungalow set in rural surroundings within walking distance of Lavenham High Street. Three comfortable bedrooms, 2 en suite, 1 private bath. Stabling available.

◆◆◆◆
Silver Award

LAVENHAM GREAT HOUSE HOTEL

Market Place, Lavenham, Sudbury
CO10 9QZ
T: (01787) 247431
F: (01787) 248007
E: info@greathouse.co.uk
I: www.greathouse.co.uk

B&B per night:
S £65.00–£90.00
D £80.00–£150.00

HB per person:
DY £66.95–£110.00

Delightful 16thC house with award-winning restaurant on magnificent Lavenham square. Beautifully decorated, individual bedooms, all furnished with antiques (one 4-poster bedroom). Most have sitting areas and provide every comfort to modern travellers. Daily-changing lunch and dinner (not Saturday) set menus offer excellent value.

Bedrooms: 4 double/twin, 1 triple/multiple; permanent suite(s)
Bathrooms: 5 en suite

Lunch available
Evening meal available
CC: Amex, Delta, Mastercard, Switch, Visa

2/3-night stay from £66.95pppn incl DB&B and full English breakfast. Available Tue-Thu inclusive.

AT-A-GLANCE SYMBOLS

Symbols at the end of each accommodation entry give useful information about services and facilities. A key to symbols can be found inside the back cover flap. Keep this open for easy reference.

LAVENHAM continued

THE OLD CONVENT

The Street, Kettlebaston, Ipswich IP7 7QA
T: (01449) 741557
E: holidays@kettlebaston.fsnet.co.uk
I: www.kettlebaston.fsnet.co.uk

B&B per night:
S £25.00–£32.50
D £50.00–£60.00

OPEN All Year except Christmas

A warm welcome awaits you in our comfortable 17thC Grade II Listed thatched home. We are committed to providing you with a memorable, comfortable stay. Attractive bedrooms with en suite facilities. Exposed beams, seasonal log fires, hearty, imaginative breakfasts. Ample off-street parking. Guests' TV lounge. Centrally located for touring. Colour brochure available.

Bedrooms: 3 double/twin
Bathrooms: 3 en suite

3-night mid-week stay £120/double room Jun, Sep, Oct. 3-night Easter break £160/double room – both B&B basis.

P

LEIGH-ON-SEA, Essex Map ref 3B3

♦♦♦

UNDERCLIFF B & B

52 Undercliff Gardens, Leigh-on-Sea SS9 1EA
T: (01702) 474984 & 07967 788873

Bedrooms: 1 double/twin, 1 triple/multiple

B&B per night:
S £20.00–£25.00
D £40.00

OPEN All Year except Christmas

Cosy accommodation with uninterrupted views of River Thames. Ideal for sightseeing in surrounding area, London 45 minutes by train. Off-street parking on Grand Parade.

P

LITTLE CANFIELD, Essex Map ref 2D1

Silver Award

CANFIELD MOAT

High Cross Lane West, Little Canfield, Dunmow CM6 1TD
T: (01371) 872565 & 07811 165049
F: (01371) 876264
E: falk@canfieldmoat.co.uk
I: www.canfieldmoat.co.uk

B&B per night:
S £40.00–£50.00
D £60.00–£70.00

OPEN All Year except Christmas

A Georgian rectory set in 8 acres including lawns, paddocks, woodland and a small lake. All rooms are spacious and beautifully furnished. Antique furniture and log fires feature in the public rooms. Breakfast includes eggs from our own chickens. Afternoon tea with homemade cakes often available at no extra cost.

Bedrooms: 2 double/twin
Bathrooms: 2 en suite

10 P

LITTLE WALSINGHAM, Norfolk Map ref 3B1

♦♦

ST DAVID'S HOUSE

Friday Market, Little Walsingham, Walsingham NR22 6BY
T: (01328) 820633 & 07710 044452
E: stdavidshouse@amserve.net
I: www.stilwell.co.uk

Bedrooms: 3 double/twin, 2 triple/multiple
Bathrooms: 2 en suite

Lunch available
Evening meal available

B&B per night:
S £28.00–£31.00
D £46.00–£52.00

HB per person:
DY £34.00–£37.00

OPEN All Year

16thC brick house in a delightful medieval village. The village is fully signposted from Fakenham (A148). Four miles from the coast.

ACCESSIBILITY

Look for the symbols which indicate National Accessible Scheme standards for hearing and visually impaired guests in addition to standards for guests with mobility impairment. Additional participants are shown in the listings at the back.

LOWESTOFT, Suffolk Map ref 3C1

♦♦♦♦

ALBANY HOTEL
400 London Road South, Lowestoft
NR33 0BQ
T: (01502) 574394
F: (01502) 581198
E: geoffrey.ward@btclick.com
I: www.albanyhotel-lowestoft.co.uk

Bedrooms: 3 single, 2 double/twin, 3 triple/multiple
Bathrooms: 6 en suite

Evening meal available
CC: Delta, Mastercard, Switch, Visa

B&B per night:
S £21.50–£32.00
D £44.00–£56.00

HB per person:
DY £29.00–£46.95

OPEN All Year

'The small hotel with the BIG welcome' offers standard and luxury accommodation within easy reach of town centre and three minutes from award-winning beach.

♦♦♦♦♦

CHURCH FARM
Corton, Lowestoft NR32 5HX
T: (01502) 730359
F: (01502) 733426
E: medw149227@aol.com
I: www.churchfarmcorton.co.uk

B&B per night:
S £30.00–£35.00
D £45.00–£50.00

Britain's most easterly farm near rural beach and cliff walks. Victorian farmhouse with attractive, high-standard, en suite double-bedded rooms. Generous traditional English breakfast. Non-smoking. German spoken. On A12 from Lowestoft to Great Yarmouth into Stirrups Lane, Church Farm opposite Corton Parish Church.

Bedrooms: 3 double/twin
Bathrooms: 3 en suite

P

♦♦♦

THE SANDCASTLE
35 Marine Parade, Lowestoft
NR33 0QN
T: (01502) 511799
F: (01502) 574720
E: susie@thesandcastle.co.uk
I: www.thesandcastle.co.uk

Bedrooms: 2 double/twin, 2 triple/multiple
Bathrooms: 2 en suite

CC: Amex, Delta, Mastercard, Switch, Visa

B&B per night:
S £20.00–£30.00
D £40.00–£48.00

OPEN All Year except Christmas

A world of comfort, care and Aga cuisine await you and your family at this beautifully appointed Victorian seafront house.

P

LUTON, Bedfordshire Map ref 2D1 *Tourist Information Centre Tel: (01582) 401579*

♦♦

44 SKELTON CLOSE
Barton Hills, Luton LU3 4HF
T: (01582) 495205
F: (01582) 495205

Bedrooms: 1 single, 1 double/twin

B&B per night:
S £25.00
D £36.00

OPEN All Year

Quiet, detached house 4 miles from Luton Airport (good taxi service). Easy reach of M1, A6 and trains to London.

9 P

MALDON, Essex Map ref 3B3 *Tourist Information Centre Tel: (01621) 856503*

♦♦

JOLLY SAILOR
Hythe Quay, Maldon CM9 5HP
T: (01621) 853463
F: (01621) 840253

Bedrooms: 1 single, 2 double/twin, 1 triple/multiple

Lunch available
Evening meal available
CC: Amex, Delta, Mastercard, Switch, Visa

B&B per night:
S £25.00–£30.00
D £40.00–£50.00

OPEN All Year

Riverside pub and bed and breakfast offers lovely views of the River Blackwater. Full restaurant offers pub grub and a la carte. Fresh fish a speciality.

QUALITY ASSURANCE SCHEME

Diamond ratings and awards were correct at the time of going to press but are subject to change. Please check at the time of booking.

MALDON continued

◆◆◆

THE SWAN HOTEL

73 High Street, Maldon CM9 5EP
T: (01621) 853170
F: (01621) 854490
E: info@swanhotel-maldon.co.uk
I: www.swanhotel-maldon.co.uk

Bedrooms: 5 double/twin, 2 triple/multiple
Bathrooms: 5 en suite

Lunch available
Evening meal available
CC: Delta, Mastercard, Switch, Visa

Old coaching inn close to A12 and M25. Centre of town. 5 minutes from beautiful promenade and river views.

B&B per night:
S £30.00–£35.00
D £45.00–£55.00

OPEN All Year except Christmas

MARGARET RODING, Essex Map ref 2D1

◆◆◆◆

GARNISH HALL

Margaret Roding, Dunmow CM6 1QL
T: (01245) 231209
F: (01245) 231224

A 15thC manor house, once moated. Graceful curved staircase. Bedrooms with lovely views of the island. On A1060 Chelmsford road, adjacent to a Norman church which boasts perhaps the most attractive doorway in Essex. Black swans, carp. Tennis court, walled garden. Walking distance of Reid Rooms, popular for the Punchbowl Restaurant.

Bedrooms: 3 double/twin; permanent suite(s)
Bathrooms: 2 en suite, 1 private

Lunch available
Evening meal available

Mid-week breaks – 3 nights for the price of 2 (Mon-Thu).

B&B per night:
S £25.00–£33.00
D £55.00

HB per person:
DY £50.00

OPEN All Year except Christmas

◆◆◆

GREYS

Ongar Road, Margaret Roding, Nr Great Dunmow CM6 1QR
T: (01245) 231509

Bedrooms: 3 double/twin

B&B in old beamed cottage on family arable/sheep farm. A non-smoking house. Turn off A1060 in village at sign to Berners Roding, 0.5 miles along.

10

B&B per night:
S Min £25.00
D Min £45.00

OPEN All Year except Christmas

NAYLAND, Suffolk Map ref 3B2

◆◆◆◆

GLADWINS FARM

Harpers Hill, Nayland, Colchester CO6 4NU
T: (01206) 262261
F: (01206) 263001
E: gladwinsfarm@aol.com
I: www.gladwinsfarm.co.uk

Bedrooms: 1 single, 2 double/twin
Bathrooms: 2 en suite

CC: Delta, Mastercard, Switch, Visa

22-acre smallholding. Timbered farmhouse in peaceful wooded surroundings in Constable country. Entrance on A134. Fishing, tennis, heated indoor pool and sauna. Home and local produce. Colour brochure.

B&B per night:
S Min £25.00
D £60.00–£66.00

OPEN All Year except Christmas

NEATISHEAD, Norfolk Map ref 3C1

◆◆◆

THE BARTON ANGLER COUNTRY INN

Irstead Road, Neatishead, Norwich NR12 8XP
T: (01692) 630740
F: (01692) 631122

Previously an early-Regency rectory, now a country inn with a large garden and mooring to Barton Broad. 4-poster rooms available.

Bedrooms: 3 single, 4 double/twin
Bathrooms: 5 en suite

Lunch available
Evening meal available
CC: Amex, Delta, Mastercard, Switch, Visa

3 nights for price of 2 (Oct-Mar).

B&B per night:
S £25.00–£35.00
D £60.00–£85.00

OPEN All Year except Christmas

NEWMARKET, Suffolk Map ref 3B2 *Tourist Information Centre Tel: (01638) 667200*

THE MEADOW HOUSE

2A High Street, Burwell, Cambridge
CB5 0HB
T: (01638) 741926 & 741354
F: (01638) 743424
E: hilary@themeadowhouse.co.uk
I: www.themeadowhouse.co.uk

Large, well-equipped modern house set in grounds of 2 acres, close to Newmarket Racecourse, Cambridge and Ely. King-size double beds. Family suites available, also coach house available in grounds. Large car park. Generous breakfasts.

Bedrooms: 3 double/twin, 3 triple/multiple
Bathrooms: 4 en suite

B&B per night:
S Min £25.00
D £44.00–£50.00

OPEN All Year except Christmas

NORFOLK BROADS

See under Beccles, Coltishall, Great Yarmouth, Hevingham, Lowestoft, Neatishead, Norwich, South Walsham, Wroxham

NORTH MYMMS, Hertfordshire Map ref 2D1

♦♦

WOOD VIEW

23 Dixon Hill Close, North Mymms, Hatfield AL9 7EF
T: (01707) 263802

Bedrooms: 2 double/twin

A two-bedroom bed and breakfast situated in North Mymms.

B&B per night:
S Max £25.00
D Max £45.00

OPEN All Year

NORWICH, Norfolk Map ref 3C1 *Tourist Information Centre Tel: (01603) 666071*

♦♦♦

BECKLANDS

105 Holt Road, Horsford, Norwich
NR10 3AB
T: (01603) 898582
F: (01603) 754223

Bedrooms: 4 single, 5 double/twin
Bathrooms: 7 en suite, 1 private

CC: Diners, Mastercard, Visa

Quietly located modern house overlooking open countryside 5 miles north of Norwich. Central for the Broads and coastal areas.

B&B per night:
S £25.00–£30.00
D £40.00–£45.00

OPEN All Year

♦♦♦♦

THE BLUE BOAR INN

259 Wroxham Road, Sprowston, Norwich
NR7 8RL
T: (01603) 426802
F: (01603) 487749
E: turnbull101@hotmail.com
I: www.blueboarnorwich.co.uk

Well situated, 10 minutes' drive from the city centre, yet a few minutes from lovely countryside. Broads 15 minutes, coast 25 minutes. Five superb en suite bedrooms, executive standard. Two bars, an all non-smoking restaurant, delicious home-cooked food. Beautiful gardens and great kids' play area.

Bedrooms: 5 double/twin
Bathrooms: 4 en suite, 1 private

Lunch available
Evening meal available
CC: Amex, Delta, Mastercard, Switch, Visa

B&B per night:
S £45.00–£60.00
D £50.00–£70.00

OPEN All Year

♦♦♦

BLUE CEDAR LODGE GUESTHOUSE

391 Earlham Road, Norwich
NR2 3RQ
T: (01603) 458331 & 07836 792659
F: (01603) 458331

Bedrooms: 3 double/twin, 1 triple/multiple
Bathrooms: 2 en suite

Quiet, modern house run by friendly family, set in wooded grounds. Convenient for city centre and University of East Anglia. Close to University Hospital. Fire certificate.

B&B per night:
S £22.00–£30.00
D £39.00–£45.00

OPEN All Year

NORWICH continued

◆◆◆

CAVELL HOUSE
Swardeston, Norwich NR14 8DZ
T: (01508) 578195
F: (01508) 578195

Bedrooms: 1 single, 2 double/twin

Lunch available
Evening meal available

B&B per night:
S £18.00–£20.00
D £38.00–£40.00

OPEN All Year except Christmas

Birthplace of nurse Edith Cavell. Rural Georgian farmhouse on edge of Swardeston village. Off B1113 south of Norwich, 5 miles from centre. Near university, new hospital.

EDMAR LODGE

64 Earlham Road, Norwich NR2 3DF
T: (01603) 615599
F: (01603) 495599
E: edmar@btconnect.com
I: www.edmarlodge.co.uk

B&B per night:
S £30.00–£35.00
D £40.00–£44.00

OPEN All Year

Edmar Lodge is a family-run guesthouse where you will receive a warm welcome from Ray and Sue. We are situated only 10 minutes' walk from the city centre. All rooms have en suite facilities and digital TV. We are well-known for our excellent breakfasts that set you up for the day.

Bedrooms: 4 double/twin, 1 triple/multiple
Bathrooms: 5 en suite

CC: Amex, Delta, Diners, Mastercard, Switch, Visa

Weekend breaks Oct-Mar – special rates including discount on evening meals at local restaurant.

◆◆◆◆

ELM FARM COUNTRY HOUSE
55 Norwich Road, St Faiths
NR10 3HH
T: (01603) 898366
F: (01603) 897129
E: Pmpbelmfarm@aol.com

Bedrooms: 1 single, 6 double/twin, 2 triple/multiple
Bathrooms: 9 en suite

Lunch available
CC: Amex, Delta, Mastercard, Switch, Visa

B&B per night:
S £38.00
D £56.00–£60.00

OPEN All Year

Situated in quiet, pretty village 4 miles north of Norwich. Ideal base for touring Norfolk and Suffolk. En suite chalet bedrooms. Breakfast served in farmhouse dining room. Licensed.

◆◆◆◆

THE GABLES GUESTHOUSE

527 Earlham Road, Norwich NR4 7HN
T: (01603) 456666
F: (01603) 250320

B&B per night:
S £42.00
D £62.00–£67.00

Friendly, family-run, non-smoking guesthouse with very high-quality en suite accommodation and relaxing residents' lounge. Excellent full English breakfast served in our delightful conservatory. Illuminated car park at rear within secluded gardens. Situated within easy walking distance of university and close to Research Park, hospital and city centre.

Bedrooms: 10 double/twin, 1 triple/multiple
Bathrooms: 11 en suite

CC: Delta, Mastercard, Switch, Visa

GOLD & SILVER AWARDS
These exclusive ETC awards are given to establishments achieving the highest levels of quality and service. Further information can be found at the front of the guide and additional accommodation achieving these awards are shown in the listing at the back of this guide.

MANOR BARN HOUSE

Back Lane, Rackheath, Norwich NR13 6NN
T: (01603) 783543
E: jane.roger@manorbarnhouse.co.uk
I: www.manorbarnhouse.co.uk

B&B per night:
S £24.00–£30.00
D £23.00–£52.00

OPEN All Year

Traditional Norfolk barn conversion with exposed beams in quiet setting with pleasant gardens. Just off A1151, two miles from the heart of the Broads, five miles Norwich. Ideally situated for golf (two minutes away), fishing. All rooms are en suite with colour TV, tea/coffee-making facilities. Guest lounge.

Bedrooms: 5 double/twin
Bathrooms: 4 en suite, 1 private

Courtesy break – reductions on a stay of more than one night.

5 P

MARLBOROUGH HOUSE HOTEL

22 Stracey Road, Norwich NR1 1EZ
T: (01603) 628005
F: (01603) 628005

Bedrooms: 9 single, 9 double/twin, 2 triple/multiple
Bathrooms: 12 en suite

Evening meal available

B&B per night:
S £26.00–£36.00
D £46.00–£52.00

HB per person:
DY £41.00–£51.00

OPEN All Year

Long established family hotel, close city centre, new Riverside development, Castle Mall, museum, cathedral. All double, twin and family rooms are en suite. Licensed bar, car park.

P

♦♦♦♦

THE OLD LODGE

New Road, Bawburgh, Norwich NR9 3LZ
T: (01603) 742798
E: peggy@theoldlodge.freeserve.co.uk

B&B per night:
S £25.00–£35.00
D £35.00–£45.00

OPEN All Year

Peaceful, non-smoking country house with conservatory, attractively redeveloped from farm cottages. Tastefully furnished and decorated including 4-poster bed. 1-acre garden, ample off-road parking. Ideally situated (West Norwich outskirts) for hospital, university, Research Park and Norfolk Showground; central for Norfolk Broads and coastline. A warm welcome awaits you.

Bedrooms: 3 double/twin
Bathrooms: 1 en suite

Evening meal available

5 P

Silver Award

THE OLD RECTORY

Hall Road, Framingham Earl, Norwich NR14 7SB
T: (01508) 493590
F: (01508) 495110
E: oldrectory@f-earl.fsnet.co.uk

Bedrooms: 2 double/twin

B&B per night:
S £26.00–£30.00
D £46.00–£54.00

OPEN All Year except Christmas

Beautifully renovated and extended 17thC family house set in 2 acres of country garden. Wealth of beams in lounge and dining room. Village 4.5 miles south-east of Norwich.

P

CHECK THE MAPS

The colour maps at the front of this guide show all the cities, towns and villages for which you will find accommodation entries. Refer to the town index to find the page on which they are listed.

NORWICH continued

◆◆

ROSEDALE
145 Earlham Road, Norwich
NR2 3RG
T: (01603) 453743 & 07949 296542
F: (01603) 259887
E: drcbac@aol.com
I: www.members@aol.com/drcbac

Bedrooms: 2 single, 2 double/twin, 2 triple/multiple

CC: Delta, Mastercard, Switch, Visa

B&B per night:
S £20.00–£25.00
D £40.00–£46.00

OPEN All Year except Christmas

Friendly, family-run, non-smoking Victorian guesthouse, on B1108, 1 mile from city centre. Restaurants, shops and university nearby, convenient for coast and Broads. Cards taken.

PETERBOROUGH, Cambridgeshire Map ref 3A1 *Tourist Information Centre Tel: (01733) 452336*

◆◆◆

THE ANCHOR LODGE

28 Percival Street, Peterborough PE3 6AU
T: (01733) 312724 & 07876 178745

B&B per night:
S £25.00–£35.00
D £40.00–£50.00

OPEN All Year except Christmas

Friendly establishment, 7 minutes' walk from shopping centre and railway. Ten minutes' drive to East of England Showground and A1.

Bedrooms: 2 single, 3 double/twin
Bathrooms: 3 en suite, 2 private

CC: Visa

PETTISTREE, Suffolk Map ref 3C2

◆◆◆

THE THREE TUNS COACHING INN

Main Road, Pettistree, Woodbridge
IP13 0HW
T: (01728) 747979 & 746244
F: (01728) 746244
E: jon@threetuns-coachinginn.co.uk
I: www.threetuns-coachinginn.co.uk

B&B per night:
S £45.00–£49.50
D £65.00–£69.50

HB per person:
DY £42.50–£47.50

OPEN All Year

John and Brenda invite you to visit their enchanting coaching inn, ideally situated for visiting the Suffolk Heritage Coast. All rooms are en suite and fully equipped. After experiencing local ales at the bar and fine food in the restaurant, just relax in the comfortable lounge with its open log fires.

Bedrooms: 1 single, 10 double/twin
Bathrooms: 11 en suite

Lunch available
Evening meal available
CC: Amex, Delta, Mastercard, Switch, Visa

Mid-week/weekend breaks on application.

RAMSHOLT, Suffolk Map ref 3C2

THE RAMSHOLT ARMS

Dock Road, Ramsholt, Woodbridge
IP12 3AB
T: (01394) 411229
F: (01394) 411818
E: ramsholtarms@tinyworld.co.uk
I: www.ramsholtarms.co.uk

B&B per night:
S £35.00–£45.00
D £70.00–£90.00

HB per person:
DY £50.00–£65.00

OPEN All Year

A glorious tidal estuary setting, with a large terrace overlooking the River Deben, a sandy beach and a grassy area between. Surely the most beautiful pub location in Suffolk. Voted the ninth best pub in the country (The Independent). Friendly staff, lovely atmosphere. Excellent food, good local walks, country accommodation.

Bedrooms: 4 double/twin

Lunch available
Evening meal available
CC: Delta, Mastercard, Switch, Visa

Free hire of the marquee in summer.

RIDLINGTON, Norfolk Map ref 3C1

♦♦♦♦ Silver Award

MILL COMMON HOUSE
Mill Common Road, Ridlington, North Walsham NR28 9TY
T: (01692) 650792
F: (01692) 651480
E: johnpugh@millcommon.freeserve.co.uk
I: www.broadland.com/millcommon

Bedrooms: 2 double/twin; permanent suite(s)
Bathrooms: 1 en suite, 1 private

Evening meal available

A Georgian farmhouse set within walled garden in open country/seaside. A warm welcome to comfortable stylish accommodation with large conservatory.

B&B per night:
S Min £36.00
D Min £52.00

HB per person:
DY Min £40.00

OPEN All Year except Christmas

ROYSTON, Hertfordshire Map ref 2D1

♦♦♦♦

HALL FARM
Great Chishill, Royston SG8 8SH
T: (01763) 838263
F: (01763) 838263
E: wisehall@farming.co.uk
I: www.hallfarmbb.co.uk

Bedrooms: 2 double/twin, 1 triple/multiple
Bathrooms: 1 en suite

805-acre arable farm. Beautiful farmhouse accommodation on working farm, in secluded gardens on the highest point in Cambridgeshire. Royston 5 miles, Duxford Museum 4 miles, Cambridge 12 miles.

B&B per night:
S £30.00–£40.00
D £50.00–£60.00

OPEN All Year except Christmas

SAFFRON WALDEN, Essex Map ref 2D1 *Tourist Information Centre Tel: (01799) 510444*

♦♦♦♦♦ Silver Award

THE BONNET
Overhall Lane, Stevington End, Ashdon, Saffron Walden CB10 2JE
T: (01799) 584955
E: thebonnetuk@yahoo.co.uk
I: www.thebonnet.co.uk

Bedrooms: 3 double/twin; permanent suite(s)
Bathrooms: 2 en suite, 1 private

The Bonnet was built in the 16thC with 2 acres of gardens. Ideally located for exploring historic North Essex, Cambridge, Suffolk. Convenient for M11, Stansted.

B&B per night:
S £35.00–£40.00
D £50.00–£60.00

OPEN All Year except Christmas

SAHAM TONEY, Norfolk Map ref 3B1

♦♦♦♦

CRANFORD HOUSE
Ovington Road, Saham Toney, Thetford IP25 7HF
T: (01953) 885292
F: (01953) 885611
E: bookings@cranfordhouse.net
I: www.cranfordhouse.net

Bedrooms: 1 double/twin, 1 triple/multiple
Bathrooms: 2 en suite

Secluded country house set in 2 acres of landscaped gardens and ponds on edge of village overlooking open farmland. Forty mile radius of most East Anglian attractions.

B&B per night:
S £30.00–£33.00
D £44.00–£50.00

OPEN All Year except Christmas

ST ALBANS, Hertfordshire Map ref 2D1 *Tourist Information Centre Tel: (01727) 864511*

♦♦♦♦

TRESCO
76 Clarence Road, St Albans AL1 4NG
T: (01727) 864880
F: (01727) 864880
E: pat.leggatt@talk21.com
I: www.twistedsilicon.co.uk/76/index.htm

Bedrooms: 1 single, 1 double/twin

Spacious Edwardian house with quiet, comfortable rooms and pleasant conservatory. Park nearby. Easy walk to station for fast trains to London (20 minutes).

B&B per night:
S £30.00–£34.00
D £50.00–£54.00

OPEN All Year except Christmas

SPECIAL BREAKS
Many establishments offer special promotions and themed breaks. These are highlighted in red. (All such offers are subject to availability.)

SANDY, Bedfordshire Map ref 2D1 *Tourist Information Centre Tel: (01767) 682728*

♦♦♦♦♦ Silver Award

HIGHFIELD FARM

Great North Road, Sandy SG19 2AQ
T: (01767) 682332
F: (01767) 692503
E: stay@highfield-farm.co.uk

B&B per night:
S £40.00–£50.00
D £55.00–£60.00

OPEN All Year

Beautifully peaceful, welcoming farmhouse plus new barn conversion on attractive arable farm. Wonderful location well back from A1. Bedford, Cambridge, Biggleswade, St Neots, Hitchin and Stevenage all within easy reach. All bedrooms en suite. London just 50 minutes by train. Delightful sitting room for guests' use. Hospitality tray in each bedroom. Safe parking. Most guests return.

Bedrooms: 8 double/twin, 2 triple/multiple
Bathrooms: 9 en suite, 1 private

CC: Delta, Mastercard, Switch, Visa

P

SAXMUNDHAM, Suffolk Map ref 3C2

♦♦♦♦♦ Silver Award

THE GEORGIAN HOUSE

6 North Entrance, Saxmundham IP17 1AY
T: (01728) 603337
E: thegeorgianhse@aol.com

B&B per night:
D £55.00–£80.00

OPEN All Year except Christmas

Explore Suffolk and its Heritage Coast from our beautifully renovated, Grade II Listed guesthouse. Relax in our library. Unwind with a drink in our residents' lounge with its grand piano and open fire. Amble in our walled garden. Enjoy the delights of good home cooking from our kitchen.

Bedrooms: 3 double/twin, 2 triple/multiple
Bathrooms: 5 en suite

Lunch available
Evening meal available
CC: Delta, Mastercard, Switch, Visa

Price reductions for stays of 3 or more nights. Please phone for details.

1 P

♦♦♦

HONEYPOT LODGE

Aldecar Lane, Benhall Green, Saxmundham IP17 1HN
T: (01728) 602449
E: honeypot@freeuk.com
I: www.smoothhound.co.uk/hotels/honeypotlodge.html

Bedrooms: 2 double/twin
Bathrooms: 2 en suite

B&B per night:
S £25.00–£35.00
D £50.00–£60.00

HB per person:
DY £30.00

OPEN All Year except Christmas

An attractive half-rendered and weatherboarded cottage overlooking a swimming pool, beautiful grounds and farmland beyond.

♦♦♦♦

MOAT HOUSE FARM

Rendham Road, Carlton, Saxmundham IP17 2QN
T: (01728) 602228
F: (01728) 602228
E: sally@goodacres.com
I: www.goodacres.com

Bedrooms: 2 double/twin
Bathrooms: 2 en suite

B&B per night:
S £30.00–£35.00
D £50.00–£60.00

OPEN All Year

Detached property set in grounds of 3.5 acres with traditional Suffolk barns. We are surrounded by open farmland. Easy access to the A12 trunk road.

P

HALF BOARD PRICES Half board prices are given per person, but in some cases these may be based on double/twin occupancy.

SCOTTOW, Norfolk Map ref 3C1

◆◆◆◆

HOLMWOOD HOUSE

Tunstead Road, Scottow, Norwich
NR10 5DA
T: (01692) 538386
F: (01692) 538386
E: holmwoodhouse@lineone.net
I: www.norfolkbroads.com/holmwood

Bedrooms: 3 double/twin
Bathrooms: 2 en suite, 1 private

B&B per night:
S £27.00–£30.00
D £38.00–£44.00

OPEN All Year except Christmas

Situated edge of village, rural views, secluded garden, ample parking, en suite/private bathroom. Tea/coffee. TV and hairdryer in all bedrooms. Guests' lounge, full English breakfast .

SHERINGHAM, Norfolk Map ref 3B1

◆◆◆

CAMBERLEY GUESTHOUSE

62 Cliff Road, Sheringham
NR26 8BJ
T: (01263) 823101
F: (01263) 821433
E: graham@camberleyguesthouse.co.uk
I: www.camberleyguesthouse.co.uk

Bedrooms: 2 single, 4 double/twin
Bathrooms: 6 en suite

B&B per night:
S £25.00–£50.00
D £40.00–£54.00

OPEN All Year except Christmas

Friendly, relaxing and spacious guesthouse in a quiet part of Sheringham. Views overlooking sea, town and countryside. All bedrooms en suite. Car parking in grounds.

SIBLE HEDINGHAM, Essex Map ref 3B2

TOCAT HOUSE

9 Potter Street, Sible Hedingham,
Halstead CO9 3RG
T: (01787) 461942

Bedrooms: 3 double/twin

Lunch available
Evening meal available

B&B per night:
S £30.00
D £50.00

HB per person:
DY £46.00–£50.00

OPEN All Year

Victorian Grade II Listed building. Comfortable, elegant family home with 3 tastefully furnished bedrooms. Mature, spacious garden with stunning views.

SOUTH WALSHAM, Norfolk Map ref 3C1

OLD HALL FARM

Newport Road, South Walsham,
Norwich NR13 6DS
T: (01603) 270271 & 270017
F: (01603) 270017
E: veronica@oldhallfarm.co.uk
I: www.oldhallfarm.co.uk

Bedrooms: 3 double/twin
Bathrooms: 3 en suite

B&B per night:
S £21.00–£24.00
D £42.00–£48.00

OPEN All Year except Christmas

Recently restored 17thC thatched farmhouse. Comfortable rooms, all en suite. Wide range of cooked breakfasts. Ideal centre for Norwich coast and Norfolk Broads. Non-smoking.

SOUTHWOLD, Suffolk Map ref 3C2

NORTHCLIFFE GUESTHOUSE

20 North Parade, Southwold
IP18 6LT
T: (01502) 724074
I: www.s-h-systems.co.uk/hotels/northcli.html

Bedrooms: 6 double/twin
Bathrooms: 5 en suite, 1 private

B&B per night:
S £45.00–£60.00
D £60.00–£70.00

OPEN All Year

Select en suite accommodation. Individually designed rooms of a high standard. Panoramic sea views. In quiet location next to beach, close to town centre. Lounge with log fire. Licensed.

MAP REFERENCES The map references refer to the colour maps at the front of this guide. The first figure is the map number; the letter and figure which follow indicate the grid reference on the map.

SOUTHWOLD continued

THE OLD VICARAGE

Wenhaston, Halesworth IP19 9EG
T: (01502) 478339
F: (01502) 478068
E: theycock@aol.com
I: www.southwold.blythweb.co.uk

Our period house in large grounds offers a peaceful stay. Close to Southwold, Minsmere Bird Reserve and Heritage Coast. You will receive a warm welcome and be able to stay in comfortable surroundings, with a full English breakfast in the morning to look forward to.

Bedrooms: 3 double/twin
Bathrooms: 1 private

B&B per night:
S £30.00–£35.00
D £50.00–£65.00

OPEN All Year

P

STOKE-BY-NAYLAND, Suffolk Map ref 3B2

Silver Award

THE ANGEL INN

Polstead Street, Stoke-by-Nayland, Colchester CO6 4SA
T: (01206) 263245
F: (01206) 263373
I: www.angelhotel.com

Bedrooms: 6 double/twin
Bathrooms: 6 en suite

Lunch available
Evening meal available
CC: Delta, Mastercard, Switch, Visa

Beautifully restored freehouse and restaurant in the historic village of Stoke-by-Nayland, in the heart of Constable country.

10 P

B&B per night:
S £54.50
D £69.50

OPEN All Year except Christmas

STRETHAM, Cambridgeshire Map ref 3A2

♦♦♦

THE RED LION

High Street, Stretham, Ely CB6 3JQ
T: (01353) 648132
F: (01353) 648327
E: frank.hayes@gateway.net

A village inn, completely refurbished, with 12 en suite bedrooms, ideally situated for visiting the Fens and other tourist attractions. Four miles from Ely on A10. Cambridge 12 miles, Newmarket 14 miles away. Pets welcome, car park. Non-smoking conservatory restaurant.

Bedrooms: 2 single, 7 double/twin, 3 triple/multiple
Bathrooms: 12 en suite

Lunch available
Evening meal available
CC: Amex, Delta, Diners, Mastercard, Switch, Visa

P

B&B per night:
S Min £42.75
D Min £49.75

OPEN All Year

SUDBOURNE, Suffolk Map ref 3C2

LONG MEADOWS

Gorse Lane, Sudbourne, Woodbridge IP12 2BD
T: (01394) 450269

Bedrooms: 1 single, 2 double/twin
Bathrooms: 1 private

Attractive cottage-style bungalow with show garden in rural location within the village. Consideration to guests' comfort and needs paramount.

12 P

B&B per night:
S £20.00–£21.00
D £42.00–£44.00

OPEN All Year except Christmas

SUDBURY, Suffolk Map ref 3B2 *Tourist Information Centre Tel: (01787) 881320*

FIDDLESTICKS

Pentlow Ridge, Pentlow, Sudbury CO10 7JW
T: (01787) 280154
F: (01787) 280154
E: sarah@fiddlesticks.biz
I: www.fiddlesticks.biz

Bedrooms: 1 single, 1 double/twin; permanent suite(s)
Bathrooms: 2 en suite

Thinking of the needs of the elderly and disabled, there are no steps in this 1960's bungalow. Excellent breakfast and warm welcome.

P

B&B per night:
S £25.00–£40.00
D £60.00

OPEN All Year

SWEFFLING, Suffolk Map ref 3C2

◆◆◆

HALL FARM

Sweffling, Saxmundham IP17 2BT
T: (01728) 663644
F: (01728) 663644
E: stephenmann@suffolkonline.net

Bedrooms: 1 double/twin, 1 triple/multiple

Evening meal available

Set well back from main road in quiet location. Own milk and eggs. Wood fires in season. Always a warm welcome.

B&B per night:
S £25.00–£30.00
D £35.00–£45.00

OPEN All Year except Christmas

TERRINGTON ST JOHN, Norfolk Map ref 3A1

◆◆◆◆

SOMERVILLE HOUSE

Church Road, Terrington St John, Wisbech PE14 7RY
T: (01945) 880952
F: (01945) 880952
E: somervillemc@hotmail.com
I: www.somervillehouse.co.uk

Bedrooms: 1 single, 2 double/twin
Bathrooms: 2 en suite

Lunch available
Evening meal available
CC: Delta, Mastercard, Switch, Visa

Period country house in large, mature gardens. Comfortable, spacious accommodation with licensed fine-dining restaurant. Small, friendly, family-run business.

B&B per night:
S Min £32.50
D Min £55.00

HB per person:
DY £42.45–£47.45

OPEN All Year

THAXTED, Essex Map ref 3B2

Silver Award

CROSSWAYS GUESTHOUSE

32 Town Street, Thaxted, Dunmow CM6 2LA
T: (01371) 830348

Bedrooms: 2 double/twin
Bathrooms: 2 en suite

Elegant 16thC house with Georgian additions, situated on B184 in centre of Thaxted opposite the 600-year-old Guildhall. Good pubs and restaurants in the town.

B&B per night:
S £38.00–£40.00
D £56.00–£58.00

OPEN All Year

THORPENESS, Suffolk Map ref 3C2

THE DOLPHIN INN

Thorpeness, Suffolk IP16 4NA
T: (01728) 454994
F: (01728) 454971
E: info@thorpeness.co.uk
I: www.thorpeness.co.uk

Bedrooms: 3 double/twin
Bathrooms: 3 en suite

Lunch available
Evening meal available
CC: Amex, Delta, Diners, Mastercard, Switch, Visa

Located in the heart of Thorpeness, the Dolphin Inn is a traditional village inn offering good food and award-winning, en suite accommodation.

B&B per night:
S £45.00–£65.00
D £65.00–£85.00

HB per person:
DY £60.00–£80.00

OPEN All Year

TOPPESFIELD, Essex Map ref 3B2

HARROW HILL COTTAGE

Harrow Hill, Toppesfield, Halstead CO9 4LX
T: (01787) 237425

Bedrooms: 1 single, 1 double/twin
Bathrooms: 1 en suite

Evening meal available

A 17thC cottage in a quiet location, set in one acre gardens with outdoor swimming pool, surrounded by pleasant views and farmland.

B&B per night:
S £20.00–£24.00
D £40.00–£48.00

HB per person:
DY £32.50–£36.50

OPEN All Year except Christmas

QUALITY ASSURANCE SCHEME

For an explanation of the quality and facilities represented by the Diamonds please refer to the front of this guide. A more detailed explanation can be found in the information pages at the back.

UPPER SHERINGHAM, Norfolk Map ref 3B1

LODGE COTTAGE

Lodge Hill, Upper Sheringham, Sheringham NR26 8TJ
T: (01263) 821445
E: stay@lodgecottage.co.uk
I: www.lodgecottage.co.uk

B&B per night:
S £35.00–£45.00
D £50.00–£55.00

Pretty, Grade II Listed lodge peacefully situated next to Sheringham Park (National Trust), 1 mile from the sea. Bright, spacious bedrooms, all en suite, and comfortable visitors' sitting room with delightful views. Gracious Upchers restaurant and friendly village pub/bistro, both within 5 minutes' walk. Sorry, no smoking, pets or children.

Bedrooms: 3 double/twin
Bathrooms: 3 en suite

WATTON, Norfolk Map ref 3B1

♦♦♦♦

THE WILLOW HOUSE

2 High Street, Watton, Thetford IP25 6AE
T: (01953) 881181 & (01760) 440760
F: (01953) 885885
E: willowhousewatton@barbox.net
I: www.willowhouse.net

B&B per night:
S £45.00–£50.00
D £50.00–£60.00

HB per person:
DY £40.00–£50.00

OPEN All Year

16thC thatched building with large open fireplaces and low-beamed bedrooms. Seven en suite bedrooms. Quality restaurant with a la carte and table d'hote menus. All food cooked to order using locally sourced produce whenever possible. Family-run with quality service.

Bedrooms: 6 double/twin, 1 triple/multiple
Bathrooms: 7 en suite

Lunch available
Evening meal available
CC: Delta, Mastercard, Switch, Visa

3 nights for price of 2, Oct-Mar (excl Christmas and New Year). Gourmet food weekends.

WIGHTON, Norfolk Map ref 3B1

♦♦♦♦

SHRUBLANDS

Wells Road, Wighton, Wells-next-the-Sea NR23 1PR
T: (01328) 820743
F: (01328) 820088
E: shrublands@shrub-lands.freeserve.co.uk
I: www.shrublandsofwighton.co.uk

Bedrooms: 3 double/twin
Bathrooms: 3 en suite

Evening meal available
CC: Delta, Mastercard, Switch, Visa

B&B per night:
D £48.00–£50.00

HB per person:
DY £34.95–£37.95

OPEN All Year

Country guesthouse, friendly service. Excellent accommodation in picturesque village. Great food, evening meals available. Guest lounge, holiday livery available. Good for coast or country.

USE YOUR *i*s

There are more than 550 Tourist Information Centres throughout England offering friendly help with accommodation and holiday ideas as well as suggestions of places to visit and things to do. You'll find TIC addresses in the local Phone Book.

WINTERTON-ON-SEA, Norfolk Map ref 3C1

CLEVELAND HOUSE

The Lane, Winterton-on-Sea NR29 4BN
T: 07884 117440
F: (01493) 393352
E: cleveland.house@virgin.net

B&B per night:
S £25.00–£35.00
D £50.00–£70.00

OPEN All Year except Christmas

Large Victorian house in beautiful village on edge of National Trust, lovely walks, wildlife and unspoilt beaches in the heart of the Norfolk Broads. TV and video, choice of excellent breakfasts, including homemade bread and preserves. Few minutes' walk from village pub serving excellent food and traditional ales.

Bedrooms: 3 double/twin
Bathrooms: 3 en suite

8 P

WITHAM, Essex Map ref 3B3

CHESTNUTS

8 Octavia Drive, Witham Lodge, Witham CM8 1HQ
T: (01376) 515990
F: (01376) 515990
E: kbmoney2@aol.com

Bedrooms: 1 single, 2 double/twin

Evening meal available

B&B per night:
S £25.00
D £40.00

OPEN All Year except Christmas

Detached, spacious modern house with own parking, reached by private road. Sports centre and golf nearby. Warm welcome assured. Plentiful breakfast with home preserves.

10 P

WOODBRIDGE, Suffolk Map ref 3C2 *Tourist Information Centre Tel: (01394) 382240*

LARK COTTAGE

Shingle Street, Woodbridge IP12 3BE
T: (01394) 411292

Bedrooms: 1 single, 1 double/twin
Bathrooms: 1 private

Lunch available
Evening meal available

B&B per night:
S Min £20.00
D Min £50.00

HB per person:
DY £30.00–£35.00

Beachside shingle bungalow with extended guest accommodation. Country setting, very quiet. Good wildlife and plants. Village with shops 2.5 miles, Woodbridge 9 miles, Snape 14 miles.

5

♦♦♦

SANDPIT HOUSE

Loudham, Wickham Market, Woodbridge IP13 0NW
T: (01728) 747435
E: gilbey@sandpithouse.fsnet.co.uk

Bedrooms: 1 single, 1 double/twin
Bathrooms: 2 private

Evening meal available

B&B per night:
S £25.00–£27.00
D £45.00–£47.00

OPEN All Year except Christmas

17thC house set in 4 acres of meadows and woodland in a delightful secluded position, bounded by the River Deben yet only minutes from Woodbridge.

3 P

WOOLPIT, Suffolk Map ref 3B2

♦♦♦

THE BULL INN & RESTAURANT

The Street, Woolpit, Bury St Edmunds IP30 9SA
T: (01359) 240393
F: (01359) 244216
E: trevor@howling.fsbusiness.co.uk
I: www.bullinnwoolpit.co.uk

Bedrooms: 1 single, 2 double/twin, 1 triple/multiple
Bathrooms: 4 en suite

Lunch available
Evening meal available
CC: Amex, Delta, Mastercard, Switch, Visa

B&B per night:
S Min £27.50
D Min £50.00

HB per person:
DY £32.50–£40.00

OPEN All Year

Public house and restaurant offering good accommodation in centre of pretty village. Large garden, ample parking. Ideal base for touring Suffolk.

2 P

IMPORTANT NOTE Information on accommodation listed in this guide has been supplied by the proprietors. As changes may occur you are advised to check details at the time of booking.

WROXHAM, Norfolk Map ref 3C1

WROXHAM PARK LODGE

142 Norwich Road, Wroxham, Norwich NR12 8SA
T: (01603) 782991
E: prklodge@nascr.net
I: www.smoothhound.co.uk/hotels/wroxhamp.html

B&B per night:
S £22.00–£30.00
D £40.00–£48.00

OPEN All Year

Warm welcome in comfortable Victorian house. All rooms en suite, non-smoking rooms, TV, tea/coffee facilities. Situated in Norfolk Broads' 'capital' of Wroxham. Central for visiting North Norfolk and its coast, Norfolk Broads, Norwich and Bure Valley Railway. Large garden, pets by arrangement, car park.

Bedrooms: 3 double/twin
Bathrooms: 3 en suite

YOXFORD, Suffolk Map ref 3C2

Gold Award

MILE HILL BARN

Main Road, Kelsale, Saxmundham IP17 2RG
T: (01728) 668519
E: richard@milehillbarn.freeserve.co.uk
I: www.mile-hill-barn.co.uk

B&B per night:
D £65.00–£80.00

OPEN All Year except Christmas

Superbly converted Suffolk oak barn. Delightful, ground floor, en suite rooms. Separate access. Private parking. Landscaped grounds and enchanting walled garden. Log fires in beamed and vaulted lounge. Farmhouse Aga cooking for traditional breakfasts and candlelit dinners in winter. Central for Minsmere, Snape, Aldeburgh and Southwold. No smoking, pets or children.

Bedrooms: 3 double/twin; permanent suite(s)
Bathrooms: 3 en suite

Evening meal available

Mid-week winter breaks: Oct-Mar, Tue-Thu 3 nights' DB&B from £135pp.

TOWN INDEX

This can be found at the back of the guide. If you know where you want to stay, the index will give you the page number listing accommodation in your chosen town, city or village.

A brief guide to the main Towns and Villages offering accommodation in the East of England

A **ALDBOROUGH, NORFOLK -** Aldborough is a picturesque village with a large green and winner of 'Best Kept Village '1999. Situated on the "Weaver's Way". The location is ideal for visiting local National Trust properties, Norfolk Broads and the North Norfolk coastal area.

B **BECCLES, SUFFOLK -** Fire destroyed the town in the 16thC and it was rebuilt in Georgian red brick. The River Waveney, on which the town stands, is popular with boating enthusiasts and has an annual regatta. Home of Beccles and District Museum.

• **BEETLEY, NORFOLK -** Rural village close to Dereham with its picturesque pargeted cottages.

• **BISHOP'S STORTFORD, HERTFORDSHIRE -** Fine old town on the River Stort with many interesting buildings, particularly Victorian, and an imposing parish church. The vicarage where Cecil Rhodes was born is now a museum.

• **BRAINTREE, ESSEX -** The Heritage Centre in the Town Hall describes Braintree's former international importance in wool, silk and engineering. St Michael's parish church includes some Roman bricks. Braintree market was first chartered in 1199.

• **BRANDON, SUFFOLK -** Set on the edge of Thetford Forest in an area known as Breckland. Old stone 5-arched bridge links Suffolk with Norfolk. Three miles north-east is Grime's Graves, the largest prehistoric flint mine in Europe.

BURY ST EDMUNDS, SUFFOLK - Ancient market and cathedral town which takes its name from the martyred Saxon king, St Edmund. Bury St Edmunds has many fine buildings including the Athenaeum and Moyses Hall, reputed to be the oldest Norman house in the county.

C **CAMBRIDGE, CAMBRIDGESHIRE -** A most important and beautiful city on the River Cam with 31 colleges forming one of the oldest universities in the world. Numerous museums, good shopping centre, restaurants, theatres, cinema and fine bookshops.

• **CAVENDISH, SUFFOLK -** One of the most picturesque villages in East Anglia, with a number of pretty thatched timber-framed and colour-washed cottages grouped around a large green. Sue Ryder Foundation Museum and coffee room are in the High Street.

• **CHELMSFORD, ESSEX -** The county town of Essex, originally a Roman settlement, Caesaromagus, thought to have been destroyed by Boudicca. Growth of the town's industry can be traced in the excellent museum in Oaklands Park. 15thC parish church has been Chelmsford Cathedral since 1914.

• **CLACTON-ON-SEA, ESSEX -** Developed in the 1870s into a popular holiday resort with pier, pavilion, funfair, theatres and traditional amusements. The Martello Towers on the seafront were built like many others in the early 19thC to defend Britain against Napoleon.

• **COLCHESTER, ESSEX -** Britain's oldest-recorded town standing on the River Colne and famous for its oysters. Numerous historic buildings, ancient remains and museums. Plenty of parks and gardens, extensive shopping centre, theatre and zoo.

• **COLTISHALL, NORFOLK -** On the River Bure, with an RAF station nearby. The village is attractive with many pleasant 18thC brick houses and a thatched church.

D **DARSHAM, SUFFOLK -** Well placed for touring North Suffolk and the coast. The nearby Otter Trust is fascinating to visit.

• **DERSINGHAM, NORFOLK -** Large parish church, mostly of Perpendicular period, with 14thC font and Elizabethan barn dated 1672.

• **DISS, NORFOLK -** Old market town built around three sides of the Mere, a six-acre stretch of water. Although modernised, some interesting Tudor, Georgian and Victorian buildings around the market-place remain. St Mary's church has a fine knapped flint chancel.

E **EARL SOHAM, SUFFOLK -** A good base for visiting Bury St Edmunds, Ipswich and the east of Suffolk. The church of St Mary is notable for its hammerbeam nave roof decorated with angels and its 17thC pulpit with hour-glasses.

• **EARLS COLNE, ESSEX -** In the Colne Valley. Large village with a fine 14thC church and some old houses with interesting pargeting.

• **ELY, CAMBRIDGESHIRE -** Until the 17thC, when the Fens were drained, Ely was an island. The cathedral, completed in 1189, dominates the surrounding area. One particular feature is the central octagonal tower with a fan-vaulted timber roof and wooden lantern.

• **EYE, SUFFOLK -** "Eye" means island, and this town was once surrounded by marsh. The fine church of St Peter and Paul has a tower over 100 ft high, and a carving of the Archangel Gabriel can be seen on the 16thC Guildhall.

F **FAKENHAM, NORFOLK -** Attractive, small market town dates from Saxon times and was a Royal Manor until the 17thC. Its market place has two old coaching inns, both showing traces of earlier work behind Georgian facades, and the parish church has a commanding 15thC tower.

WHERE TO STAY

Please mention this guide when making your booking.

• **FELIXSTOWE, SUFFOLK** - Seaside resort that developed at the end of the 19thC. Lying in a gently curving bay with a two-mile-long beach and backed by a wide promenade of lawns and floral gardens.

G **GREAT YARMOUTH, NORFOLK** - One of Britain's major seaside resorts with five miles of seafront and every possible amenity including an award-winning leisure complex offering a huge variety of all-weather facilities. Busy harbour and fishing centre.

H **HADLEIGH, SUFFOLK** - Former wool town, lying on a tributary of the River Stour. The church of St Mary stands among a remarkable cluster of medieval buildings.

• **HALESWORTH, SUFFOLK** - Small market town which grew firstly with navigation on the Blyth in the 18thC and then with the coming of the railways in the 19thC. Opposite the church, in a beautiful 14thC building, is the Halesworth Gallery.

• **HARLESTON, NORFOLK** - Attractive small town on the River Waveney with two market-places and a museum. Candler's House is an outstanding example of an early Georgian townhouse. At Starston, one mile away, is a restored wind-pump.

• **HARPENDEN, HERTFORDSHIRE** - Delightful country town with many scenic walks through surrounding woods and fields. Harpenden train station provides a fast service into London.

• **HARWICH, ESSEX** - Port where the Rivers Orwell and Stour converge and enter the North Sea. The old town still has a medieval atmosphere with its narrow streets. To the south is the seaside resort of Dovercourt with long sandy beaches.

• **HAUGHLEY, SUFFOLK** - In the heart of Suffolk, very well placed for touring.

• **HETHERSETT, NORFOLK** - Conveniently located for Norwich.

• **HEVINGHAM, NORFOLK** - Located with easy access to Norwich, North Norfolk coast, Broads and Blickling Hall.

• **HITCHIN, HERTFORDSHIRE** - Once a flourishing wool town. Full of interest, with many old buildings around the market square. These include the 17thC almshouses, old inns and the Victorian Corn Exchange.

K **KELVEDON, ESSEX** - Village on the old Roman road from Colchester to London. Many of the buildings are 18thC but there is much of earlier date. The famous preacher Charles Spurgeon was born here in 1834.

• **KINGS LANGLEY, HERTFORDSHIRE** - Between Hemel Hempstead and Watford. The Church of All Saints has parts which date from the 13thC.

• **KING'S LYNN, NORFOLK** - A busy town with many outstanding buildings. The Guildhall and Town Hall are both built of flint in a striking chequer design. Behind the Guildhall in the Old Gaol House the sounds and smells of prison life two centuries ago are recreated.

• **KNAPTON, NORFOLK** - The church is visited for the beauty of its roof and font. The former, dated 1504, is 30 ft wide and adorned with a host of angels. The latter is 13thC, built of Purbeck marble, and has an interesting Decorative cover.

L **LAVENHAM, SUFFOLK** - A former prosperous wool town of timber-framed buildings with the cathedral-like church and its tall tower. The market-place is 13thC and the Guildhall now houses a museum.

• **LEISTON, SUFFOLK** - Centrally placed for visiting the Suffolk Heritage Coast, Leiston is a bustling, working town in a rural setting famous for Leiston Abbey and the award-winning Long Shop Museum.

• **LITTLE WALSINGHAM, NORFOLK** - Little Walsingham is larger than its neighbour Great Walsingham and more important because of its long history as a religious shrine to which many pilgrimages were made. The village has many picturesque buildings of the 16thC and later.

• **LOWESTOFT, SUFFOLK** - Seaside town with wide sandy beaches. Important fishing port with picturesque fishing quarter. Home of the famous Lowestoft porcelain and birthplace of Benjamin Britten. East Point Pavilion's exhibition describes the Lowestoft story.

• **LUTON, BEDFORDSHIRE** - Bedfordshire's largest town with its own airport, several industries and an excellent shopping centre. The town's history is depicted in the museum and art gallery in Wardown Park. Luton Hoo has a magnificent collection of treasures.

M **MALDON, ESSEX** - The Blackwater Estuary has made Maldon a natural base for yachtsmen. Boat-building is also an important industry. Numerous buildings of interest. The 13thC church of All Saints has the only triangular church tower in Britain. Also a museum and maritime centre.

• **MARGARET RODING, ESSEX** - One of the six Rodings, a group of old villages clustered in the rural Roding Valley. The church features some fine Norman work.

N **NEWMARKET, SUFFOLK** - Centre of the English horse-racing world and the headquarters of the Jockey Club and National Stud. Racecourse and horse sales. The National Horse Racing Museum traces the history and development of the Sport of Kings.

• **NORWICH, NORFOLK** - Beautiful cathedral city and county town on the River Wensum with many fine museums and medieval churches. Norman castle, Guildhall and interesting medieval streets. Good shopping centre and market.

www.travelengland.org.uk
Log on for information and inspiration. The latest information on places to visit, events and quality assessed accommodation.

PETERBOROUGH, CAMBRIDGESHIRE - Prosperous and rapidly expanding cathedral city on the edge of the Fens on the River Nene. Catherine of Aragon is buried in the cathedral. City Museum and Art Gallery. Ferry Meadows Country Park has numerous leisure facilities.

ROYSTON, HERTFORDSHIRE - Old town lying at the crossing of the Roman road Ermine Street and the Icknield Way. It has many interesting old houses and inns.

SAFFRON WALDEN, ESSEX - Takes its name from the saffron crocus once grown around the town. The church of St Mary has superb carvings, magnificent roofs and brasses. A town maze can be seen on the common. Two miles south-west is Audley End, a magnificent Jacobean mansion owned by English Heritage.

- **ST ALBANS, HERTFORDSHIRE** - As Verulamium this was one of the largest towns in Roman Britain and its remains can be seen in the museum. The Norman cathedral was built from Roman materials to commemorate Alban, the first British Christian martyr.

- **SANDY, BEDFORDSHIRE** - Small town on the River Ivel on the site of a Roman settlement. Sandy is mentioned in the book 'Domesday'.

- **SAXMUNDHAM, SUFFOLK** - The church of St John the Baptist has a hammer-beam roof and contains a number of good monuments.

- **SHERINGHAM, NORFOLK** - Holiday resort with Victorian and Edwardian hotels and a sand and shingle beach where the fishing boats are hauled up. The North Norfolk Railway operates from Sheringham station during the summer. Other attractions include museums, theatre and Splash Fun Pool.

- **SOUTH WALSHAM, NORFOLK** - Village famous for having two churches in adjoining churchyards. South Walsham Broad consists of an inner and outer section, the former being private. Alongside, the Fairhaven Garden Trust has woodland and water gardens open to the public.

- **SOUTHWOLD, SUFFOLK** - Pleasant and attractive seaside town with a triangular market square and spacious greens around which stand flint, brick and colour-washed cottages. The parish church of St Edmund is one of the greatest churches in Suffolk.

- **STOKE-BY-NAYLAND, SUFFOLK** - Picturesque village with a fine group of half-timbered cottages near the church of St Mary, the tower of which was one of Constable's favourite subjects. In School Street are the Guildhall and the Maltings, both 16thC timber-framed buildings.

- **STRETHAM, CAMBRIDGESHIRE** - On the edge of the Fens, Stretham is noted for its 20-ft-high village cross which dates from around 1400.

THAXTED, ESSEX - Small town rich in outstanding buildings and dominated by its hilltop medieval church. The magnificent Guildhall was built by the Cutlers' Guild in the late 14thC. A windmill built in 1804 has been restored and houses a rural museum.

- **THORPENESS, SUFFOLK** - A planned mock-Tudor seaside resort, built in the early 20thC, with a 65-acre artificial lake. The House in the Clouds was built to disguise a water-tower. The windmill contains an exhibition on Suffolk's Heritage Coast.

WOODBRIDGE, SUFFOLK - Once a busy seaport, the town is now a sailing centre on the River Deben. There are many buildings of architectural merit including the Bell and Angel Inns. The 18thC Tide Mill is now restored and open to the public.

- **WOOLPIT, SUFFOLK** - Village with a number of attractive timber-framed Tudor and Georgian houses. St Mary's Church is one of the most beautiful churches in Suffolk and has a fine porch. The brass eagle lectern is said to have been donated by Elizabeth I.

- **WROXHAM, NORFOLK** - Yachting centre on the River Bure which houses the headquarters of the Norfolk Broads Yacht Club. The church of St Mary has a famous doorway, and the manor house nearby dates back to 1623.

YOXFORD, SUFFOLK - Village given a unique character by the timbered, bow-windowed and balconied houses along the main street. In the surrounding area are Grove Park, Rookery Park and Cockfield Hall, built in 1540, where Katherine Grey, sister of Lady Jane Grey, lived out her last months.

NB **IMPORTANT NOTE** Information on accommodation listed in this guide has been supplied by the proprietors. As changes may occur you are advised to check details at the time of booking.

Finding accommodation is as easy as 1 2 3

Where to Stay makes it quick and easy to find a place to stay. There are several ways to use this guide.

1 Town Index

The town index, starting on page 748, lists all the places with accommodation featured in the regional sections. The index gives a page number where you can find full accommodation and contact details.

2 Colour Maps

All the place names in black on the colour maps at the front have an entry in the regional sections. Refer to the town index for the page number where you will find one or more establishments offering accommodation in your chosen town or village.

3 Accommodation Listing

Contact details for **all** English Tourism Council-assessed accommodation throughout England, together with their national Star rating, are given in the listing section of this guide. Establishments with a full entry in the regional sections are shown in blue. Look in the town index for the page number on which their full entry appears.

SOUTH WEST

A land of myths and legends – and beautiful beaches. The region has cathedral cities, Georgian Bath and maritime Bristol, mysterious castles, evocative country houses and sub tropical gardens to discover, too.

classic sights

Eden Project – plant life from around the world
English Riviera – family-friendly beaches
Dartmoor & Exmoor – wild open moorland, rocky tors and woodland

coast & country

Jurassic Coast – World Heritage Coastline
Runnymede – riverside meadows and woodland
Pegwell Bay & Goodwin Sands – a haven for birds and seals

glorious gardens

Stourhead – 18thC landscaped garden
Westonbirt Arboretum – Over 3,700 different varieties of tree

art for all

Tate Gallery St Ives – modern art and the St Ives School
Arnolfini Gallery, Bristol – contemporary arts

distinctively different

Daphne du Maurier – Cornwall inspired many of her novels
Agatha Christie – follow the trail in Torquay

2

3

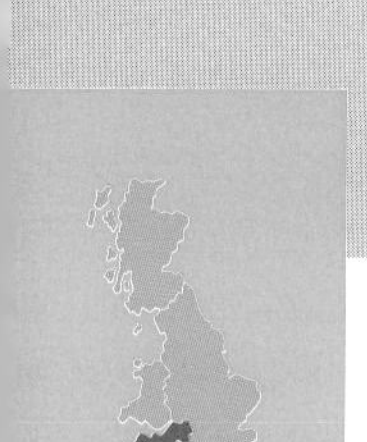

The counties of Bath & Bristol, Cornwall & Isles of Scilly, Devon, Dorset (Western), Gloucestershire South, Somerset and Wiltshire

FOR MORE INFORMATION CONTACT:
South West Tourism
Admail 3186, Exeter EX2 7WH
Tel: (0870) 442 0880 Fax: (0870) 442 0881
Email: info@westcountryholidays.com
Internet: www.westcountrynow.com

The Pictures: 1 Stourhead Gardens, Wiltshire 2 Dartmoor Ponies 3 Water sports in Torquay

PLACES TO VISIT - see pages 326-330 > WHERE TO STAY - see pages 331-399

You will find hundreds of interesting places to visit during your stay, just some of which are listed in these pages. Contact any Tourist Information Centre in the region for more ideas on days out.

Awarded ETC's new 'Quality Assured Visitor Attraction' marque at time of going to press. (See page 19).

At Bristol

Harbourside, Bristol

Tel: (08453) 451235 www.at-bristol.org.uk

A unique destinaton bringing science, nature and art to life on Bristol's historic harbourside. It consists of Explore, Wildwalk and an IMAX Theatre.

Atwell-Wilson Motor Museum Trust

Downside, Stockley Lane, Calne

Tel: (01249) 813119 www.atwell-wilson.org

Motor museum with vintage, post-vintage and classic cars, including American models. Classic motorbikes. A 17thC water-meadow walk. Car clubs welcome for rallies. Play area.

Avebury Manor and Garden

Avebury, Marlborough

Tel: (01672) 539250 www.nationaltrust.org

Manor house, regularly altered and of monastic origins. Present buildings date from the early 16thC with Queen Anne alterations and Edwardian renovations. Gardens.

Babbacombe Model Village

Hampton Avenue, Babbacombe, Torquay

Tel: (01803) 315315
www.babbacombemodelvillage.co.uk

Over 400 models, many with sound and animation, four acres (1.6ha) of award-winning gardens. See modern towns, villages and rural areas. Stunning illuminations.

Bristol City Museum & Art Gallery

Queen's Road, Bristol

Tel: (0117) 922 3571 www.bristol-city.gov.uk/museums

Collection representing applied, oriental and fine art, archaeology, geology, natural history, ethnography and Egyptology.

Bristol Zoo Gardens

Clifton, Bristol

Tel: (0117) 973 8951
www.bristolzoo.org.uk

Enjoy an exciting, real-life experience and see over 300 species of wildlife in beautiful gardens.

Buckland Abbey

Yelverton

Tel: (01822) 853607 www.nationaltrust.org.uk

Originally a Cistercian monastery, then the home of Sir Francis Drake. Ancient buildings, exhibitions, herb garden craft workshops and estate walks. Elizabethan garden.

Cheddar Caves and Gorge

Cheddar

Tel: (01934) 742343 www.cheddarcaves.co.uk

Beautiful caves located in Cheddar Gorge. Gough's Cave with its cathedral-like caverns and Cox's Cave with stalagmites and stalactites. Also 'The Crystal Quest' fantasy adventure.

Combe Martin Motor Cycle Collection

Cross Street, Combe Martin, Ilfracombe
Tel: (01271) 882346
www.motorcycle-collection.co.uk
Collection of motorcylces, scooters and invalid carriages displayed against a background of old petrol pumps, signs and garage equipment. Motoring nostalgia.

Combe Martin Wildlife and Dinosaur Park

Jurassic Hotel, Combe Martin, Ilfracombe
Tel: (01271) 882486
Wildlife park and life-size models of dinosaurs. Light show, butterfly house, the 'T-Rex' show.

Crealy Park

Sidmouth Road, Clyst St Mary, Exeter
Tel: (01395) 233200 www.crealy.co.uk
One of Devon's largest animal farms. Milk a cow, feed a lamb and pick up a piglet. Adventure playgrounds. Dragonfly Lake and farm trails.

Dairyland Farm World

Tresillian Barton, Summercourt, Newquay
Tel: (01872) 510246
www.dairylandfarmworld.com
One hundred and seventy cows milked in a rotary parlour. Heritage centre, farm nature trail, farm park with animals, pets and wildfowl, daily events, conservation area.

Eden Project

Bodelva, St Austell
Tel: (01726) 811911 www.edenproject.com
An unforgettable experience in a breathtaking, epic location. Eden is a gateway into the fascinating world of plants and people.

Exmoor Falconry & Animal Farm

West Lynch Farm, Allerford, Minehead
Tel: (01643) 862816 www.exmoorfalconry.co.uk
Farm animals, rare breeds, pets' corner, birds of prey and owls. Flying displays daily. Historic farm buildings. Short activity breaks.

Flambards Village

Culdrose Manor, Helston
Tel: (01326) 573404 www.flambards.co.uk
Life-size Victorian village with fully stocked shops, carriages and fashions. 'Britain in the Blitz' life-size wartime street, historic aircraft. Science centre and rides.

Heale Garden & Plant Centre

Middle Woodford, Salisbury
Tel: (01722) 782504
Mature, traditional-type garden with shrubs, musk and other roses, and kitchen garden. Authentic Japanese teahouse in water garden. Magnolias. Snowdrops and aconites in winter.

International Animal Rescue

Animal Tracks, Ash Mill, South Molton
Tel: (01769) 550277 www.iar.org.uk
A 60-acre (24-ha) animal sanctuary with a wide range of rescued animals from monkeys to chinchillas and from a shire horse to other horses and ponies. Also rare-plant nursery.

Jamaica Inn Museums (Potters Museum of Curiosity)

Jamaica Inn Courtyard, Bolventor, Launceston
Tel: (01566) 86838
Museums contain lifetime work of Walter Potter, a Victorian taxidermist. Exhibits include 'Kittens' Wedding', 'Death of Cock Robin' and 'The Story of Smuggling'.

> The Pictures: 1 Clifton Suspension Bridge, Bristol
2 Salisbury Cathedral, Wilthshire
3 Sunset at Stonehenge, Wiltshire
4 Land's End, Cornwall
5 Torquay, Devon

Longleat

Estate Office, Longleat, Warminster
Tel: (01985) 844400 www.longleat.co.uk
Elizabethan stately home, safari park and a wonderland of 10 family attractions. World's longest hedge maze, safari boats, pets' corner, Longleat railway.

The Lost Gardens of Heligan

Heligan, Pentewan, St Austell
Tel: (01726) 845100 www.heligan.com
Heligan Gardens is the scene of the largest garden restoration project undertaken since the war. Public access to parts of Home Farm.

Lyme Regis Philpot Museum

Bridge Street, Lyme Regis
Tel: (01297) 443370 www.lymeregismuseum.co.uk
Fossils, geology, local history, literary connections - the story of Lyme in its landscape.

National Marine Aquarium

Rope Walk, Coxside, Plymouth
Tel: (01752) 600301
www.national-aquarium.co.uk
The United Kingdom's only world-class aquarium, located in the heart of Plymouth. Visitor experiences will include a mountain stream and Caribbean reef complete with sharks.

Newquay Zoo

Trenance Park, Newquay
Tel: (01637) 873342
www.newquayzoo.co.uk
A modern, award-winning zoo where you can have fun and learn at the same time. A varied collection of animals, from acouchi to zebra.

Paignton Zoo Environmental Park

Totnes Road, Paignton
Tel: (01803) 697500
www.paigntonzoo.org.uk
One of England's largest zoos with over 1,200 animals in the beautiful setting of 75 acres (30ha) of botanical gardens. The zoo is one of Devon's most popular family days out.

Plant World

St Marychurch Road, Newton Abbot
Tel: (01803) 872939
Four acres (1.6ha) of gardens including the unique 'map of the world' gardens. Cottage garden. Panoramic views. Comprehensive nursery of rare and more unusual plants.

Plymouth Dome

The Hoe, Plymouth
Tel: 01752) 603300
Purpose-built visitor interpretation centre showing the history of Plymouth and its people from Stone Age beginnings to satellite technology. Situated on Plymouth Hoe.

Powderham Castle

The Estate Office, Powderham Castle, Kenton, Exeter
Tel: (01626) 890243 www.powderham.co.uk
Family home of the Courtenays for over 600 years, built c1390 and restored in the 18thC. Georgian interiors, china, furnishings and paintings. Fine views across deer park and River Exe.

Railway Village Museum

34 Faringdon Road, Swindon
Tel: (01793) 466553 www.steam-museum.org.uk
Foreman's house in original Great Western Railway village. Furnished to re-create a Victorian working-class home.

Roman Baths

Pump Room, Abbey Church Yard, Bath
Tel: (01225) 477785 www.romanbaths.co.uk
Two hundred years ago, around Britain's hot springs, the Romans built a vast religious spa that still flows with natural hot water.

St Michael's Mount

Marazion, Penzance
Tel: (01736) 710507
Originally the site of a Benedictine chapel, the castle on its rock dates from the 14thC. Fine views towards Land's End and the Lizard. Reached by foot, or ferry at high tide in summer.

Smugglers Barn

New Barn Road, Abbotsbury, Weymouth
Tel: (01305) 871817 www.abbotsbury.co.uk
Extensive children's farm for the under-11s. Soft, undercover play area with smuggling theme, hand-feeding milk to kids, rabbit and guinea pig cuddling, pony rides (additional charge).

Steam - Museum of the Great Western Railway

Kemble Drive, Churchward, Swindon

Tel: (01793) 466646
www.steam-museum.org.uk
Historic Great Western Railway locomotives, wide range of nameplates, models, illustrations, posters and tickets.

Stonehenge

Amesbury, Salisbury
Tel: (01980) 623108
www.stonehengemasterplan.org
World-famous prehistoric monument built as a ceremonial centre. Started 5,000 years ago and remodelled several times in the following 1,500 years.

Stourhead House and Garden

The Estate Office, Stourton, Warminster
Tel: (01747) 841152 www.nationaltrust.org.uk
Landscaped garden laid out c1741-80 with lakes, temples, rare trees and plants. House, begun in c1721 by Colen Campbell, contains fine paintings and Chippendale furniture.

Tate Gallery St Ives

Porthmeor Beach, St Ives
Tel: (01736) 796226 www.tate.org.uk
Opened in 1993, the gallery offers a unique introduction to modern art. Changing displays focus on the modern movement for which St Ives is famous. Major contemporary exhibitions.

Teignmouth Museum

29 French Street, Teignmouth
Tel: (01626) 777041
http://website.lineone.net/~teignmouth
Exhibits include 16thC cannon, artefacts from Armada wreck and local history. Circa 1920s pier machines and c1877 cannon.

Tintagel Castle

Tintagel
Tel: (01840) 770328 www.english-heritage.org.uk
Medieval ruined castle on wild, wind-swept coast, famous for associations with Arthurian legend. Built largely in 13thC by Richard, Earl of Cornwall. Used as a prison in 14thC.

Totnes Costume Museum - Devonshire Collection of Period Costume

Bogan House, 43 High Street, Totnes
Tel: (01803) 863821
New exhibition of costumes and accessories each season, displayed in one of the historic merchant's houses of Totnes. Bogan House was recently restored by Mitchell Trust.

Woodlands Leisure Park

Blackawton, Totnes
Tel: (01803) 712598
www.woodlandspark.com

All-weather fun guaranteed with unique combination of indoor and outdoor attractions: three watercoasters, toboggan run, indoor adventure centre with rides, falconry and animals.

Wookey Hole Caves and Papermill

Wookey Hole, Wells
Tel: (01749) 672243 www.wookey.co.uk
Spectacular caves and legendary home of the Witch of Wookey. Working Victorian papermill including Old Penny Arcade, Magical Mirror Maze and Cave Diving Museum.

> The Pictures: 1 Selworthy, Somerset 2 Newquay, Cornwall

Find out more about the SOUTH WEST

Further information about holidays and attractions in the South West is available from:

SOUTH WEST TOURISM
Admail 3186, Exeter EX2 7WH.
Tel: (0870) 442 0880
Fax: (0870) 442 0881
Email: info@westcountryholidays.com
Internet: www.westcountrynow.com

The following official guides are available free from South West Tourism:

Quality Bed & Breakfast
Holiday Homes, Cottages & Apartments
Hotels and Guesthouses
Camping and Caravan Touring Map
Attractions and Days Out Touring Map
Trencherman's West Country, Restaurant Guide
South West Walks

Getting to the SOUTH WEST

BY ROAD: Somerset, Devon and Cornwall are well served from the North and Midlands by the M6/M5 which extends just beyond Exeter, where it links in with the dual carriageways of the A38 to Plymouth, A380 to Torbay and the A30 into Cornwall. The North Devon Link Road A361 joins Junction 37 with the coast of North Devon and the A39, which then becomes the Atlantic Highway into Cornwall.

BY RAIL: The main towns in the South West are served throughout the year by fast, direc and frequent rail services from all over the country. Trains operate from London (Paddington) to Chippenham, Swindon, Bath, Bristol, Weston-super-Mare, Taunton, Exete Plymouth and Penzance, and also from Scotland, the North East and the Midlands to the South West. A service runs from London (Waterloo) to Exeter, via Salisbury, Yeovil and Crewkerne. Sleeper services operate between Devon and Cornwall and London as well a between Bristol and Glasgow and Edinburgh. Motorail services operate from strategic points to key South West locations.

> The Pictures: 1 Roman Bath, Bath

Where to stay in the South West

Accommodation entries in this region are listed in alphabetical order of place name, and then in alphabetical order of establishment.

Map references refer to the colour location maps at the front of this guide. The first number indicates the map to use; the letter and number which follow refer to the grid reference on the map.

At-a-glance symbols at the end of each accommodation entry give useful information about services and facilities. A key to symbols can be found inside the back cover flap. Keep this open for easy reference.

A brief description of the towns and villages offering accommodation in the entries which follow, can be found at the end of this section.

A complete listing of all the English Tourism Council assessed accommodation covered by this guide appears at the back of the guide.

ABBOTSBURY, Dorset Map ref 2A3

SWAN LODGE
Rodden Row, Abbotsbury, Weymouth DT3 4JL
T: (01305) 871249
F: (01305) 871249

Bedrooms: 5 double/twin
Bathrooms: 2 en suite

Lunch available
Evening meal available
CC: Mastercard, Visa

B&B per night:
S £33.00–£45.00
D £48.00–£60.00

OPEN All Year

Situated on the B3157 coastal road between Weymouth and Bridport. Swan Inn public house opposite, where food is served all day in season, is under the same ownership.

ALLERFORD, Somerset Map ref 1D1

FERN COTTAGE
Allerford, Minehead TA24 8HN
T: (01643) 862215
F: (01643) 862215
E: ferncottage@bushinternet.com
I: www.exmoor.com/ferncottage

B&B per night:
S £39.00
D £58.00

HB per person:
DY £42.75

OPEN All Year except Christmas

Comfortable, large, traditional Exmoor cottage, c16thC, set in a tiny National Trust village in a wood-fringed vale. Exhilarating walks in dramatic hill and coastal scenery start on doorstep. Noted for fine classic/bistro cooking and comprehensive cellar. A non-smoking house.

Bedrooms: 3 triple/multiple
Bathrooms: 3 en suite

Evening meal available
CC: Amex, Delta, Mastercard, Switch, Visa

The Exmoor break...3 nights' DB&B £122pp (based on 2 people sharing). Single Exmoor break £154.50.

AMESBURY, Wiltshire Map ref 2B2 *Tourist Information Centre Tel: (01980) 622833*

◆◆◆

ENFORD HOUSE
Enford, Pewsey SN9 6DJ
T: (01980) 670414

Bedrooms: 3 double/twin

Evening meal available
CC: Amex

Listed country house with pretty garden. In attractive village 7 miles from Stonehenge. Good food at local village pub. Quiet and comfortable.

B&B per night:
S Min £23.00
D Min £38.00

OPEN All Year except Christmas

◆◆◆

THE OLD BAKERY
Netton, Salisbury SP4 6AW
T: (01722) 782351
E: valahen@aol.com
I: members.aol.com/valahen

Bedrooms: 3 double/twin
Bathrooms: 3 en suite

Pleasantly modernised former bakery in small, quiet, picturesque village. Views over fields and water meadows. Ideal base for Stonehenge/Salisbury. Short walk to local inns.

5

B&B per night:
S £25.00–£30.00
D £36.00–£44.00

OPEN All Year except Christmas

◆◆◆

SOLSTICE FARMHOUSE
39 Holders Road, Amesbury, Salisbury SP4 7PH
T: (01980) 625052 & 07870 593505
E: williamsmc@btinternet.com

Bedrooms: 2 double/twin

Grade II Listed farmhouse boasting a woodburning stove and large, attractive garden with pond and water feature. Comfortable rooms with private en suite showers.

12

B&B per night:
S £30.00–£35.00
D £42.00–£45.00

OPEN All Year except Christmas

◆◆◆

VALE HOUSE
Figheldean, Salisbury SP4 8JJ
T: (01980) 670713

Bedrooms: 1 single, 2 double/twin
Bathrooms: 2 en suite

Secluded house in centre of picturesque village, 4 miles north of Amesbury on A345, 2 miles from Stonehenge. Winchester, Bath, Oxford within easy reach.

B&B per night:
S £22.00
D £40.00

OPEN All Year except Christmas

ASHBURTON, Devon Map ref 1C2

◆◆◆◆
Silver Award

GAGES MILL

Buckfastleigh Road, Ashburton, Newton Abbot TQ13 7JW
T: (01364) 652391
F: (01364) 652391
E: moore@gagesmill.co.uk
I: www.gagesmill.co.uk

14thC former wool mill in over an acre of gardens. A friendly welcome and comfortable accommodation. High standard of cooking. Licensed. One mile from the ancient Stannary town of Ashburton. An ideal base for exploring South Devon, with its many National Trust properties, pretty villages and, of course, Dartmoor.

Bedrooms: 1 single, 7 double/twin
Bathrooms: 7 en suite

Evening meal available

12

B&B per night:
S £22.00–£30.00
D £44.00–£60.00

HB per person:
DY £36.50–£44.50

CHECK THE MAPS

The colour maps at the front of this guide show all the cities, towns and villages for which you will find accommodation entries. Refer to the town index to find the page on which they are listed.

AVEBURY, Wiltshire Map ref 2B2 *Tourist Information Centre Tel: (01672) 539425*

MANOR FARM

Avebury, Marlborough SN8 1RF
T: (01672) 539294
F: (01672) 539294

B&B per night:
S £40.00–£50.00
D £58.00–£70.00

OPEN All Year except Christmas

Listed 18thC farmhouse within the prehistoric stone circle. National Trust manor house, museum and vegetarian restaurant in village. Excellent site for walking and visiting local market towns of Marlborough and Devizes. Bowood House and Corsham Court are nearby. Pub 100 yards. Full breakfast menu and friendly atmosphere!

Bedrooms: 2 double/twin
Bathrooms: 2 private

12 P

AXMINSTER, Devon Map ref 1D2

BECKFORD COTTAGE

Dalwood, Axminster EX13 7HQ
T: (01404) 881641
F: (01404) 881108
E: beckfordcottage@hotmail.com
I: www.beckford-cottage.co.uk

B&B per night:
S £22.00–£25.00
D £44.00–£50.00

HB per person:
DY £37.00–£40.00

OPEN All Year except Christmas

Lovely 17thC thatched cottage set deep in Devon countryside. Very secluded. 9 acres of beautiful gardens with River Yarty running through. Good walking. Close to Dorset Heritage and South Devon Coast. All meals home cooked including bread. Ideal for nature lovers. Many birds and wildlife in garden.

Bedrooms: 2 single, 1 triple/multiple; permanent suite(s)
Bathrooms: 1 en suite, 2 private

Evening meal available

P

CHATTAN HALL

Woodbury Lane, Axminster EX13 5TL
T: (01297) 32365
F: (01297) 32365
E: boston@chattanhall.co.uk
I: www.chattanhall.co.uk

B&B per night:
S £40.00
D £70.00–£80.00

HB per person:
DY £50.00–£60.00

OPEN All Year except Christmas and New Year

Elegant Victorian country house with splendid big rooms set in 2 acres. Wonderful gardens with many specimen trees, shrubs and colourful borders...a garden lover's paradise. Only one couple at a time, unless requested. Guests can enjoy conservatory, gardens, drawing room. Own private balcony with spectacular views. Exclusive, private and secluded.

Bedrooms: 1 double
Bathrooms: 1 private

Evening meal available

10% reduction for 3 or more nights.

12 P

BARNSTAPLE, Devon Map ref 1C1 *Tourist Information Centre Tel: (01271) 375000*

Silver Award

THE SPINNEY

Shirwell, Barnstaple EX31 4JR
T: (01271) 850282
E: thespinney@shirwell.fsnet.co.uk
I: www.thespinneyshirwell.co.uk

B&B per night:
S £19.00–£22.50
D £38.00–£45.00

HB per person:
DY £31.00–£34.00

OPEN All Year

Set in over an acre of grounds with views towards Exmoor, a former rectory. Spacious accommodation, en suite available. Centrally heated. Delicious meals cooked by chef/proprietor, served during summer months in our restored Victorian conservatory under the ancient vine. Residential licence. The Spinney is non-smoking.

Bedrooms: 1 single, 2 double/twin, 2 triple/multiple
Bathrooms: 3 en suite

Evening meal available

BATCOMBE, Somerset Map ref 2B2

♦♦♦

VALLEY VIEW FARM

Batcombe, Shepton Mallet BA4 6AJ
T: (01749) 850302 & 07813 679020
F: (01749) 850302
E: valleyviewfarm@lineone.net

Bedrooms: 2 double/twin, 1 triple/multiple
Bathrooms: 3 en suite

Evening meal available

B&B per night:
S £22.00–£25.00
D £35.00–£40.00

HB per person:
DY £28.00–£35.00

OPEN All Year except Christmas

Set in 1-acre garden. Excellent views, pub nearby. Home-produced eggs and cider. Ideal for Longleat, Stourhead, Salisbury and Bath.

BATH, Bath and North East Somerset Map ref 2B2 *Tourist Information Centre Tel: (01225) 477101*

AQUAE SULIS HOTEL

174/176 Newbridge Road, Bath BA1 3LE
T: (01225) 420061 & 339064
F: (01225) 446077
E: enquiries@aquaesulishotel.com
I: www.aquaesulishotel.com

B&B per night:
S £49.00–£65.00
D £55.00–£95.00

OPEN All Year

Conveniently situated hotel with period charm. Attractive, no-smoking bedrooms, patio and garden with all the extras of a modern hotel. Satellite TV. Bar and smoking/no-smoking lounges. A la carte menu. Large monitored car park. Frequent shuttle or level walk to abbey. Free unlimited golf locally.

Bedrooms: 3 single, 5 double/twin, 5 triple/multiple
Bathrooms: 11 en suite, 2 private

Evening meal available
CC: Amex, Delta, Diners, Mastercard, Switch, Visa

See website or phone for special weekday offers (Sun-Thu) from £39 per room.

♦♦♦♦

ASTOR HOUSE

14 Oldfield Road, Bath BA2 3ND
T: (01225) 429134
F: (01225) 429134
E: astorhouse.visitus@virgin.net

Bedrooms: 6 double/twin, 2 triple/multiple; permanent suite(s)
Bathrooms: 7 en suite, 1 private

CC: Delta, Mastercard, Switch, Visa

B&B per night:
D £50.00–£60.00

OPEN All Year except Christmas

Comfortable, spacious Victorian home with lovely views of the city and countryside yet only a short walk to the centre. Friendly welcome, varied delicious breakfasts.

CREDIT CARD BOOKINGS If you book by telephone and are asked for your credit card number it is advisable to check the proprietor's policy should you cancel your reservation.

BATH continued

♦♦♦♦♦ Silver Award

ATHOLE GUEST HOUSE

33 Upper Oldfield Park, Bath BA2 3JX
T: (01225) 334307
F: (01225) 320000
E: info@atholehouse.co.uk
I: www.atholehouse.co.uk

B&B per night:
S £48.00–£58.00
D £65.00–£78.00

OPEN All Year

Large Victorian home restored to give bright, inviting, quiet bedrooms, sleek furniture, sparkling bathrooms, hotel facilities (mini-bar, laptop connection, satellite TV, safe). Hospitality is old-style, award-winning breakfasts. Relax in our gardens, or let us help you explore the area. Secure parking behind remote-control gates or in garage.

Bedrooms: 2 double/twin, 1 triple/multiple
Bathrooms: 3 en suite

CC: Amex, Delta, Mastercard, Switch, Visa

4 nights (incl 1 night free), all year. 3 nights (incl 1 night free) or 5 nights (incl 2 nights free), Nov-Feb inclusive.

P

♦♦♦♦♦ Gold Award

AYRLINGTON HOTEL

24/25 Pulteney Road, Bath BA2 4EZ
T: (01225) 425495
F: (01225) 469029
E: mail@ayrlington.com
I: www.ayrlington.com

B&B per night:
S £75.00–£155.00
D £75.00–£155.00

OPEN All Year except Christmas

Located within an easy 5-minute level walk of Bath city centre, The Ayrlington is a small, tranquil, non-smoking luxury hotel. Its 12 elegantly appointed rooms boast every modern amenity, and some feature 4-poster beds and spa baths. Private parking. Walled gardens overlooking Bath Abbey.

Bedrooms: 12 double/twin
Bathrooms: 12 en suite

CC: Amex, Delta, Mastercard, Switch, Visa

P

♦♦♦

BAILBROOK LODGE HOTEL

35/37 London Road West, Bath BA1 7HZ
T: (01225) 859090
F: (01225) 852299
E: hotel@bailbrooklodge.co.uk
I: www.bailbrooklodge.co.uk

B&B per night:
S £39.00–£50.00
D £60.00–£89.00

OPEN All Year

Welcome to a fine Georgian house offering 12 bedrooms, all en suite (some 4-posters), with antiques and many original features. The lounge bar and dining room overlook the patio and lawns. Excellently located 1 mile from Bath's centre and close to A46 for M4 and beautiful surrounding countryside. Ample car parking.

Bedrooms: 8 double/twin, 4 triple/multiple
Bathrooms: 12 en suite

Evening meal available
CC: Amex, Delta, Diners, Mastercard, Switch, Visa

Third night half price (excl Sat); 2 nights for the price of 1, Nov-Feb (excl Sat).

P

ACCESSIBILITY

Look for the symbols which indicate National Accessible Scheme standards for hearing and visually impaired guests in addition to standards for guests with mobility impairment. Additional participants are shown in the listings at the back.

BATH continued

◆◆◆◆

CARFAX HOTEL

Great Pulteney Street, Bath BA2 4BS
T: (01225) 462089
F: (01225) 443257
E: reservations@carfaxhotel.co.uk
I: www.carfaxhotel.co.uk

A trio of Georgian houses overlooking Henrietta Park with a view to the surrounding hills. A stroll to the Pump Rooms, Roman baths, canal and river. Recently restored and refurbished, well-appointed rooms. Lift to all floors. Car park for 13 cars. Senior Citizens rates all year.

Bedrooms: 9 single, 22 double/twin, 3 triple/multiple
Bathrooms: 34 en suite

Evening meal available
CC: Amex, Delta, Mastercard, Switch, Visa

4 nights for the price of 3 (excl Christmas). Quote ETB403.

B&B per night:
S £53.50–£70.00
D £76.75–£102.00

HB per person:
DY £48.50–£61.00

OPEN All Year except Christmas

◆◆◆

CHURCH FARM

Monkton Farleigh, Bradford-on-Avon BA15 2QJ
T: (01225) 858583 & 07889 596929
F: (01225) 852474
E: rebecca@tuckerb.fsnet.co.uk
I: www.tuckerb.fsnet.co.uk

Bedrooms: 2 double/twin, 1 triple/multiple
Bathrooms: 3 en suite

Converted farmhouse barn with exceptional views in peaceful, idyllic setting. Ten minutes from Bath, ideal base for touring/walking South West England. Families/dogs welcome.

B&B per night:
S £35.00
D £45.00

OPEN All Year

◆◆◆

EDGAR HOTEL

64 Great Pulteney Street, Bath BA2 4DN
T: (01225) 420619
F: (01225) 466916

Bedrooms: 2 single, 15 double/twin, 1 triple/multiple
Bathrooms: 18 en suite

CC: Delta, Mastercard, Switch, Visa

Georgian townhouse hotel, close to city centre and Roman Baths. Privately run. All rooms with en suite facilities. 4-poster bed available.

B&B per night:
S £35.00–£50.00
D £50.00–£95.00

OPEN All Year except Christmas

◆◆◆

FLAXLEY VILLA

9 Newbridge Hill, Bath BA1 3PW
T: (01225) 313237 & 480574

Bedrooms: 3 double/twin
Bathrooms: 2 en suite

Comfortable Victorian house, just a few minutes by car to city centre and within easy reach of Royal Crescent and main attractions.

B&B per night:
S £22.50–£36.00
D £40.00–£60.00

OPEN All Year

◆◆◆

HENRIETTA HOTEL

32 Henrietta Street, Bath BA2 6LR
T: (01225) 447779
F: (01225) 444150
I: www.SmoothHound.co.uk

Bedrooms: 9 double/twin, 1 triple/multiple
Bathrooms: 10 en suite

CC: Delta, Mastercard, Switch, Visa

Privately run Georgian townhouse hotel, close to city centre and Roman Baths. All rooms with en suite facilities. 4-poster bed available.

B&B per night:
S £35.00–£50.00
D £50.00–£95.00

OPEN All Year except Christmas

◆◆◆

HERMITAGE

Bath Road, Box, Corsham SN13 8DT
T: (01225) 744187
F: (01225) 743447
E: hermitage@telecall.co.uk

Bedrooms: 4 double/twin, 1 triple/multiple
Bathrooms: 5 en suite

16thC house with heated pool in summer. Dining room with vaulted ceiling. Six miles from Bath on A4 to Chippenham, first drive on left by 30 mph sign.

B&B per night:
S £35.00–£40.00
D £45.00–£55.00

OPEN All Year except Christmas

VISITOR ATTRACTIONS For ideas on places to visit refer to the introduction at the beginning of this section. Look out too for the ETC's Quality Assured Visitor Attraction signs.

BATH continued

HIGHFIELDS

207 Bailbrook Lane, Batheaston, Bath BA1 7AB
T: (01225) 859782
E: acham@supanet.com

B&B per night:
S £35.00–£55.00
D £60.00–£70.00

OPEN All Year except Christmas

The perfect place from which to explore Bath and the surrounding area. Peacefully situated with stunning views down the Avon Valley, yet only a few minutes from the city centre. Home from home comforts. A garden with plunge pool to relax in.

Bedrooms: 1 single, 2 double/twin; permanent suite(s)
Bathrooms: 3 private

Discounts on stays of 4 days or more.

♦♦♦♦

THE HOLLIES

Hatfield Road, Wellsway, Bath BA2 2BD
T: (01225) 313366
F: (01255) 313366
E: davcartwright@lineone.net
I: www.visitus.co.uk/bath/hotel.hollies.html

B&B per night:
D £65.00–£75.00

The Hollies was built in 1851 and stands in its own gardens just 15 minutes' walk from Bath centre. Offering peace and quiet, the owners have recently upgraded and redecorated the pretty guest rooms, all with bathrooms. The house is furnished with antiques with your comfort in mind.

Bedrooms: 3 double/twin
Bathrooms: 2 en suite, 1 private

Evening meal available
CC: Delta, Mastercard, Switch, Visa

3 nights or more, 10% discount.

♦♦♦♦♦
Silver Award

HOLLY LODGE

8 Upper Oldfield Park, Bath BA2 3JZ
T: (01225) 424042 & (01255) 339187
F: (01225) 481138
E: stay@hollylodge.co.uk
I: www.hollylodge.co.uk

Bedrooms: 1 single, 6 double/twin
Bathrooms: 7 en suite

CC: Amex, Delta, Diners, Mastercard, Switch, Visa

B&B per night:
S £48.00–£57.00
D £79.00–£97.00

OPEN All Year

Elegant Victorian house set in its own grounds, enjoying magnificent views of the city. Visit my web site for further information.

♦♦♦♦

LAURA PLACE HOTEL

3 Laura Place, Great Pulteney Street, Bath BA2 4BH
T: (01225) 463815
F: (01225) 310222

Bedrooms: 7 double/twin, 1 triple/multiple
Bathrooms: 7 en suite

CC: Amex, Mastercard, Visa

B&B per night:
D £72.00–£95.00

18thC townhouse, centrally located in Georgian square. Two minutes from Roman Baths, Pump Rooms and abbey.

♦♦♦♦

LINDISFARNE GUEST HOUSE

41a Warminster Road, Bathampton, Bath BA2 6XJ
T: (01225) 466342 & 07740 741541
E: lindisfarne-bath@talk21.com
I: www.bath.org/hotel/lindisfarne.htm

Bedrooms: 3 double/twin, 1 triple/multiple
Bathrooms: 4 en suite

CC: Mastercard, Visa

B&B per night:
S £35.00–£39.00
D £50.00–£60.00

OPEN All Year except Christmas

Spacious house with friendly proprietors. Within walking distance of good eating places, about 1.5 miles from Bath city centre. Large car park.

BATH continued

♦♦♦♦

MARLBOROUGH HOUSE
1 Marlborough Lane, Bath BA1 2NQ
T: (01225) 318175
F: (01225) 466127
E: mars@manque.dircon.co.uk
I: www.marlborough-house.net

Bedrooms: 2 single, 4 double/twin, 1 triple/multiple
Bathrooms: 7 en suite

Lunch available
Evening meal available
CC: Amex, Delta, Diners, Mastercard, Switch, Visa

B&B per night:
S £45.00–£75.00
D £65.00–£95.00

HB per person:
DY £45.00–£55.00

OPEN All Year

Enchanting vegetarian-run townhouse in Bath's exquisite centre. Beautiful, antique-filled rooms, 4-poster and brass and iron beds. Unique San Fransisco-style breakfasts and tasty omelettes a speciality.

♦♦♦♦♦
Gold Award

MONKSHILL
Shaft Road, Monkton Combe, Bath BA2 7HL
T: (01225) 833028
F: (01225) 833028
E: monks.hill@virgin.net
I: www.monkshill.com

B&B per night:
S £55.00–£70.00
D £70.00–£85.00

OPEN All Year except Christmas

You are assured of a warm welcome in this secluded and very comfortable country residence surrounded by its own extensive gardens. The emphasis is on luxurious comfort. The individually styled bedrooms are graciously appointed and command excellent views over the garden, with its croquet lawn, the woodland and valley below.

Bedrooms: 3 double/twin
Bathrooms: 2 en suite, 1 private

CC: Amex, Delta, Mastercard, Switch, Visa

♦♦♦♦

NUMBER 30 CRESCENT GARDENS
Bath BA1 2NB
T: (01225) 337393
F: (01225) 337393
E: david.greenwood12@btinternet.com
I: www.numberthirty.co.uk

Bedrooms: 1 single, 5 double/twin
Bathrooms: 5 en suite, 1 private

CC: Mastercard, Switch, Visa

B&B per night:
S £42.00–£60.00
D £75.00–£95.00

OPEN All Year except Christmas

A small, privately owned Victorian house in the centre of Bath. Outstanding housekeeping. Private car parking. Easy walk to shops and to Roman Baths.

2

♦♦♦♦

PARKSIDE
11 Marlborough Lane, Bath BA1 2NQ
T: (01225) 429444
F: (01225) 429444
E: parkside@lynall.freeserve.co.uk
I: www.visitus.co.uk/bath/hotel/parkside.html

Bedrooms: 4 double/twin
Bathrooms: 4 en suite

CC: Delta, Mastercard, Switch, Visa

B&B per night:
S £35.00–£50.00
D £50.00–£65.00

OPEN All Year except Christmas

Edwardian villa by Victoria Park close to Royal Crescent. Pleasant 7-minute walk to town centre. Comfortable bedrooms. Pretty breakfast room. Short breaks.

COUNTRY CODE Always follow the Country Code Enjoy the countryside and respect its life and work Guard against all risk of fire Fasten all gates Keep your dogs under close control Keep to public paths across farmland Use gates and stiles to cross fences, hedges and walls Leave livestock, crops and machinery alone Take your litter home Help to keep all water clean Protect wildlife, plants and trees Take special care on country roads Make no unnecessary noise

BATH continued

ST GEORGES COTTAGE

Bathampton Lane, Bath BA2 6SJ
T: (01225) 466801
F: (01225) 426073
E: stgeorgescottage@aol.com
I: www.stgeorgescottagebath.co.uk

Close to the city centre, St Georges stands in beautiful landscaped gardens overlooking the Avon valley and picturesque Kennet/Avon canal. Only 15 minutes' walk to centre or 10 minutes to local inn. Ample parking, comfortable accommodation and an informal atmosphere make this an ideal base for shopping, sightseeing or just relaxing.

Bedrooms: 3 double/twin; permanent suite(s)
Bathrooms: 2 en suite, 1 private

CC: Amex, Delta, Diners, Mastercard, Switch, Visa

Seasonal breaks Nov-Apr, minimum 2 nights. Weekend £65, mid-week £55.

B&B per night:
D £55.00–£75.00

OPEN All Year

Gold Award

VILLA MAGDALA HOTEL

Henrietta Road, Bath BA2 6LX
T: (01225) 466329
F: (01225) 483207
E: office@villamagdala.co.uk
I: www.villamagdala.co.uk

Ideally situated, this charming Victorian townhouse hotel enjoys a peaceful location overlooking Henrietta Park, only 5 minutes' level walk to the city centre and Roman Baths. The spacious rooms, some with 4-poster beds, all have pleasant views. Private parking is available in the hotel grounds. The Villa Magdala is a non-smoking hotel.

Bedrooms: 2 single, 11 double/twin, 5 triple/multiple
Bathrooms: 18 en suite

CC: Amex, Delta, Mastercard, Switch, Visa

B&B per night:
S £65.00–£95.00
D £80.00–£140.00

OPEN All Year except Christmas

BEAMINSTER, Dorset Map ref 2A3

♦♦♦♦
Silver Award

THE WALNUTS

2 Prout Bridge, Beaminster DT8 3AY
T: (01308) 862211

Bedrooms: 3 double/twin
Bathrooms: 2 en suite

Tastefully refurbished building with very attractive bedrooms. Friendly, family-run establishment. Very well situated within short walk of local inns and tasteful small shops.

B&B per night:
S £28.00–£37.00
D £48.00–£58.00

OPEN All Year except Christmas

BEANACRE, Wiltshire Map ref 2B2

Silver Award

BEECHFIELD HOUSE

Beanacre, Melksham SN12 7PU
T: (01225) 703700
F: (01225) 790118
E: csm@beechfieldhouse.co.uk
I: www.beechfieldhouse.co.uk

A comfortable Victorian country-house hotel set in 8 acres of secluded gardens. Relax and unwind in our elegant and beautifully furnished, family-owned hotel. One mile from the National Trust village of Lacock, 15 miles from Bath and surrounded by beautiful Wiltshire countryside.

Bedrooms: 23 double/twin, 1 triple/multiple
Bathrooms: 24 en suite

Lunch available
Evening meal available
CC: Amex, Delta, Diners, Mastercard, Switch, Visa

DB&B from £60pppn, minimum 2 nights.

B&B per night:
S Min £80.00
D Min £100.00

HB per person:
DY Min £60.00

OPEN All Year except Christmas

BIDDESTONE, Wiltshire Map ref 2B2

THE GRANARY

Cuttle Lane, Biddestone,
Chippenham SN14 7DA
T: (01249) 715077
E: penny.lloyd@virgin.net
I: freespace.virgin.net/penny.lloyd

Bedrooms: 2 double/twin
Bathrooms: 1 en suite, 1 private

B&B per night:
S £20.00–£22.50
D £40.00–£45.00

OPEN All Year except Christmas

You are assured a warm welcome in this comfortable family home. It is well located, 5 miles from M4 and near Bath, Salisbury and the Cotswolds.

P

BIDEFORD, Devon Map ref 1C1 *Tourist Information Centre Tel: (01237) 477676*

♦♦♦♦

THE MOUNT

Northdown Road, Bideford EX39 3LP
T: (01237) 473748
F: (01271) 373813
E: andrew@themountbideford.fsnet.co.uk
I: www.themount1.cjb.net

B&B per night:
S £28.00–£30.00
D £52.00–£56.00

OPEN All Year except Christmas

Elegant Georgian licensed guesthouse, comfortably furnished. All rooms en suite. Peaceful garden for guests' use. Short walk to town centre. Convenient for trips to Lundy, Clovelly, Exmoor, Dartmoor and North Devon coast. No smoking.

Bedrooms: 2 single, 4 double/twin, 1 triple/multiple
Bathrooms: 7 en suite

CC: Amex, Delta, Mastercard, Switch, Visa

2-night break Oct-Mar 10% reduction. Sunday night free if staying 2 days or more.

P

♦♦♦

SUNSET HOTEL

Landcross, Bideford EX39 5JA
T: (01237) 472962
F: (01237) 422520
E: hazellamb@hotmail.com

B&B per night:
S £50.00–£60.00
D £60.00–£65.00

HB per person:
DY £44.00–£48.00

Small, elegant country hotel set in beautiful gardens in a quiet, peaceful location, overlooking spectacular scenery. 1.5 miles from town. Beautifully decorated and spotlessly clean. Highly recommended, quality accommodation. All en suites with colour TV and beverages. Superb cooking, everything homemade. Special needs catered for. Licensed. Private parking. Non-smoking establishment.

Bedrooms: 2 double/twin, 2 triple/multiple
Bathrooms: 4 en suite

Evening meal available
CC: Mastercard, Visa

Reduced rates for 3, 5 and 7 days.

P

BILBROOK, Somerset Map ref 1D1

STEPS FARMHOUSE

Bilbrook, Minehead TA24 6HE
T: (01984) 640974
E: info@stepsfarmhouse.co.uk
I: www.stepsfarmhouse.co.uk

Bedrooms: 2 double/twin, 1 triple/multiple
Bathrooms: 3 en suite

CC: Amex, Delta, Diners, Mastercard, Switch, Visa

B&B per night:
S £25.00–£30.00
D £40.00–£46.00

Traditional 16thC former farmhouse situated near Dunster. En suite accommodation in barn conversions located in beautiful, secluded gardens. Ideal centre for Exmoor and Quantock hills.

P

QUALITY ASSURANCE SCHEME

Diamond ratings and awards were correct at the time of going to press but are subject to change. Please check at the time of booking.

BISHOP'S LYDEARD, Somerset Map ref 1D1

♦♦♦♦

WEST VIEW

Minehead Road, Bishop's Lydeard, Taunton TA4 3BS
T: (01823) 432223
F: (01823) 432223
E: westview@pattemore.freeserve.co.uk

Bedrooms: 3 double/twin
Bathrooms: 2 en suite

B&B per night:
S £21.00–£35.00
D £50.00–£56.00

OPEN All Year

Attractive Victorian house in the village close to the privately-owned West Somerset Steam Railway. Within easy reach of Taunton and the M5.

BODMIN, Cornwall Map ref 1B2 *Tourist Information Centre Tel: (01208) 76616*

BEDKNOBS

Polgwyn, Castle Street, Bodmin PL31 2DX
T: (01208) 77553
F: (01208) 77885
E: gill@bedknobs.co.uk
I: www.bedknobs.co.uk

B&B per night:
S £30.00–£50.00
D £45.00–£70.00

OPEN All Year

A large, rambling Victorian villa in an acre of woodland garden offering comfortable, spacious, en suite accommodation (with Airbath and power showers), a warm welcome and home comforts in abundance. Ideally placed whether visiting for business or pleasure. Close to Bodmin town centre and the A30 with easy access to the whole of Cornwall and The Eden Project.

Bedrooms: 3 double/twin
Bathrooms: 2 en suite, 1 private

CC: Delta, Mastercard, Switch, Visa

11

♦♦♦♦♦
Silver Award

BOKIDDICK FARM

Lanivet, Bodmin PL30 5HP
T: (01208) 831481
F: (01208) 831481
E: gillhugo@bokiddickfarm.co.uk
I: www.bokiddickfarm.co.uk

B&B per night:
S £30.00–£40.00
D £50.00–£60.00

OPEN All Year except Christmas

Welcome to our lovely Georgian farmhouse in central Cornwall. A peaceful location with magnificent views, yet only 2 miles from A30. Close to exciting Eden Project and magnificent National Trust Lanhydrock House and Gardens. Oak beams, wood panelling, pretty en suite bedrooms, delicious Aga-cooked breakfasts. The perfect place for that special break.

Bedrooms: 2 double/twin, 1 triple/multiple
Bathrooms: 3 en suite

3

BOSCASTLE, Cornwall Map ref 1B2

THE OLD COACH HOUSE

Tintagel Road, Boscastle PL35 0AS
T: (01840) 250398
F: (01840) 250346
E: parsons@old-coach.co.uk
I: www.old-coach.co.uk

Bedrooms: 5 double/twin, 3 triple/multiple
Bathrooms: 8 en suite

CC: Delta, Mastercard, Switch, Visa

B&B per night:
S £25.00–£38.00
D £40.00–£44.00

OPEN All Year except Christmas

Relax in beautiful 300-year-old former coach house. All rooms en suite with colour TV, teamaker, hairdryer, etc. Friendly and helpful owners. Good parking.

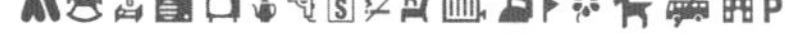

SYMBOLS The symbols in each entry give information about services and facilities. A key to these symbols appears at the back of this guide.

BOSCASTLE continued

ST CHRISTOPHER'S HOTEL
High Street, Boscastle PL35 0BD
T: (01840) 250412

Bedrooms: 2 single, 7 double/twin
Bathrooms: 9 en suite

Evening meal available
CC: Delta, Mastercard, Switch, Visa

Superb Georgian house retaining its character, nestling in this lovely unspoilt village with a wealth of interesting places to visit. A warm welcome awaits.

B&B per night:
S £21.00–£25.00
D £42.00–£50.00

OPEN All Year

TOLCARNE HOUSE HOTEL AND RESTAURANT

Tintagel Road, Boscastle PL35 0AS
T: (01840) 250654
F: (01840) 250654
E: crowntolhouse@eclipse.co.uk
I: www.milford.co.uk/go/tolcarne

A charming Victorian residence, which provides all modern comforts in a peaceful and friendly environment. Our guest rooms are furnished to a high standard and all are en suite. Tolcarne stands in spacious gardens with splendid views of unspoilt countryside and National Trust-owned coastline. Choice of menus. Dogs welcome.

Bedrooms: 1 single, 6 double/twin, 1 triple/multiple
Bathrooms: 8 en suite

Evening meal available
CC: Delta, Mastercard, Switch, Visa

Special tariff for 3 nights or more (excl Fri/Sat).

B&B per night:
S £30.00–£32.00
D £53.00–£68.00

HB per person:
DY £38.50–£46.00

BOVEY TRACEY, Devon Map ref 1D2

BROOKFIELD HOUSE

Challabrook Lane, Bovey Tracey, Newton Abbot TQ13 9DF
T: (01626) 836181
F: (01626) 836182
E: brookfieldh@tinyworld.co.uk
I: www.brookfield-house.com

Spacious early Edwardian residence situated on the edge of Bovey Tracey and Dartmoor. Set in 2 acres with panoramic moor views and bounded by the gently flowing Pottery Leat. Secluded tranquillity yet within easy walking distance of town, local attractions and moorland. Individually decorated bedrooms, all with comfortable seating areas.

Bedrooms: 3 double/twin
Bathrooms: 2 en suite, 1 private

Evening meal available
CC: Amex, Mastercard, Switch, Visa

Special rates on application for stays of 4 nights or more, and also weekly terms.

B&B per night:
S £35.00–£42.00
D £50.00–£64.00

BOX, Wiltshire Map ref 2B2

LORNE HOUSE
London Road, Box, Corsham SN13 8NA
T: (01225) 742597
E: lornehousebandb@aol.com
I: www.lornehouse.net

Bedrooms: 3 double/twin, 1 triple/multiple
Bathrooms: 4 en suite

CC: Delta, Mastercard, Switch, Visa

Listed in guide books in Germany, Canada and America, this Victorian property boasts excellent service and accommodation to discerning travellers. Situated 6 miles from Bath.

B&B per night:
S £30.00–£35.00
D £45.00–£50.00

OPEN All Year except Christmas

GOLD & SILVER AWARDS
These exclusive ETC awards are given to establishments achieving the highest levels of quality and service. Further information can be found at the front of the guide and additional accommodation achieving these awards are shown in the listing at the back of this guide.

BRADFORD-ON-AVON, Wiltshire Map ref 2B2 *Tourist Information Centre Tel: (01225) 865797*

SPRINGFIELDS

182a Great Ashley, Bradford-on-Avon
BA15 2PP
T: (01225) 866125
E: christine.rawlings@farmersweekly.net
I: www.bed-and-breakfast.org

B&B per night:
S £30.00–£35.00
D £45.00–£50.00

OPEN All Year except Christmas

Delightful, quiet country setting in 0.5 acres of cottage gardens between Bradford-on-Avon and Bath. En suite double ground floor accommodation, with adjoining private lounge/dining room. Delicious breakfast, all tastes catered for, home preserves, eggs from our own chickens.

Bedrooms: 1 double/twin; permanent suite(s)
Bathrooms: 1 en suite

Evening meal available

10% reduction on 3 nights or more.

BRATTON FLEMING, Devon Map ref 1C1

Gold Award

BRACKEN HOUSE COUNTRY HOTEL

Bratton Fleming, Barnstaple EX31 4TG
T: (01598) 710320
F: (01598) 710115
E: holidays@brackenhousehotel.com
I: www.brackenhousehotel.com

B&B per night:
D £60.00–£90.00

HB per person:
DY £46.00–£65.00

Charming small country hotel set in 8 peaceful acres of garden, woodland, pond and pasture. Extensive views. Convenient for Rosemoor, Marwood, Arlington, North Devon and Exmoor with its magnificent coastline. Eight en suite bedrooms include two on ground floor. Country-style Aga cooking. Ideal for dogs with well-trained owners.

Bedrooms: 8 double/twin
Bathrooms: 8 en suite

Evening meal available
CC: Delta, Mastercard, Switch, Visa

Reduced tariff for Sun-Sun bookings. Lower prices in August. Reductions for late bookings.

BRIDESTOWE, Devon Map ref 1C2

WAY BARTON BARN

Bridestowe, Okehampton EX20 4QH
T: (01837) 861513
E: Jo.Catling@btopenworld.com

Bedrooms: 3 double/twin; permanent suite(s)
Bathrooms: 2 en suite, 1 private

Evening meal available

B&B per night:
S £20.00–£22.00
D £44.00–£50.00

HB per person:
DY £32.00–£37.00

Lovely old barn set in 12 peaceful acres overlooking Dartmoor. Beams, antiques, 4-poster bed, farmhouse breakfasts. All rooms en suite/private facilities, colour TV, hairdryer.

AT-A-GLANCE SYMBOLS

Symbols at the end of each accommodation entry give useful information about services and facilities. A key to symbols can be found inside the back cover flap. Keep this open for easy reference.

BRIDGWATER, Somerset Map ref 1D1

MODEL FARM

Perry Green, Wembdon, Bridgwater
TA5 2BA
T: (01278) 433999
E: info@modelfarm.com
I: www.modelfarm.com

B&B per night:
S £40.00–£45.00
D £60.00–£70.00

HB per person:
DY £42.00–£58.00

OPEN All Year

Peacefully situated in a rural setting, Model Farm is a licensed, country-house retreat offering spacious, en suite accommodation. A set evening meal is available by prior arrangement, guests being joined by their hosts. A warm welcome and friendly atmosphere awaits all who visit, whether on business or for leisure.

Bedrooms: 3 double/twin
Bathrooms: 3 en suite

Evening meal available
CC: Amex, Delta, Mastercard, Switch, Visa

P

♦♦♦

QUANTOCK VIEW GUEST HOUSE
Bridgwater Road, North Petherton, Bridgwater TA6 6PR
T: (01278) 663309
E: irene@quantockview.freeserve.co.uk
I: www.SmoothHound.co.uk/hotels/quantock.html

Bedrooms: 1 double/twin, 3 triple/multiple
Bathrooms: 4 en suite

Evening meal available
CC: Amex, Delta, Mastercard, Switch, Visa

B&B per night:
S £25.00–£27.00
D £40.00–£44.00

HB per person:
DY £32.50–£35.00

OPEN All Year except Christmas

Comfortable, family-run guesthouse in central Somerset. En suite facilities in all rooms. Close to hills and coast, yet only minutes from M5, jct 24.

P

BRIDPORT, Dorset Map ref 2A3 *Tourist Information Centre Tel: (01308) 424901*

BRITMEAD HOUSE

West Bay Road, Bridport DT6 4EG
T: (01308) 422941
F: (01308) 422516
E: britmead@talk21.com
I: www.britmeadhouse.co.uk

B&B per night:
S £28.00–£44.00
D £46.00–£64.00

OPEN All Year

An elegant Edwardian house situated just off the A35 between the historic market town of Bridport and the harbour at West Bay, the ideal location for exploring the beautiful Dorset countryside. Family-run, en suite accommodation with many thoughtful extras. Ten minutes' walk to harbour, beaches, golf course and the coastal path.

Bedrooms: 5 double/twin, 2 triple/multiple
Bathrooms: 7 en suite

Discounts available on stays of 2 or more nights.

CC: Delta, Mastercard, Switch, Visa

P

♦♦♦♦

CANDIDA HOUSE
Whitchurch Canonicorum DT6 6RQ
T: (01297) 489629
F: (01297) 489629
E: candida@globalnet.co.uk
I: www.holidayaccom.com/candida-house.htm

Bedrooms: 3 double/twin
Bathrooms: 3 en suite

Lunch available
CC: Amex, Delta, Mastercard, Switch, Visa

B&B per night:
S £25.00–£35.00
D £50.00–£60.00

OPEN All Year except Christmas

Comfortable en suite rooms in elegant, spacious Georgian rectory. Peaceful village 2 miles from the sea. Special breakfasts. Warm hospitality and restful ambience.

P

PRICES
Please check prices and other details at the time of booking.

BRISTOL Map ref 2A2 *Tourist Information Centre Tel: (0117) 926 0767*

◆◆◆

THE PADDOCK
Hung Road, Shirehampton, Bristol BS11 9XJ
T: (0117) 9235140

Bedrooms: 1 single, 4 double/twin
Bathrooms: 5 en suite

Modern detached house, set in approximately 1 acre of grounds, offering quality accommodation.

P

B&B per night:
S Max £30.00
D Max £50.00

OPEN All Year except Christmas

◆◆◆

ROWAN LODGE
41 Gloucester Road North, Filton Park, Bristol BS7 0SN
T: (0117) 931 2170
F: (0117) 975 3601

Bedrooms: 1 single, 3 double/twin, 2 triple/multiple
Bathrooms: 3 en suite

CC: Mastercard, Visa

Small family-run establishment in residential suburb on A38. Easy access to M4, M5 and city. Bath, Cotswolds, Welsh Hills within 20-mile radius.

P

B&B per night:
S £26.00–£35.00
D £42.00–£48.00

OPEN All Year except Christmas

◆◆◆

TRICOMO HOUSE B & B
183 Cheltenham Road, Cotham, Bristol BS6 5RH
T: (0117) 9248082
F: (0117) 3735162
E: tricomohouse1@activemail.co.uk

Bedrooms: 1 single, 2 double/twin, 2 triple/multiple

Small, family-run bed and breakfast on A38, 0.5 miles from Bristol centre. Five minutes' drive from Bristol University, BBC. Close to rail and coach stations.

B&B per night:
S £25.00–£35.00
D £45.00–£60.00

HB per person:
DY £25.00–£35.00

OPEN All Year except Christmas

BRIXHAM, Devon Map ref 1D2 *Tourist Information Centre Tel: 0906 680 1268 (Premium rate number)*

◆◆◆

THE SHOALSTONE HOTEL
105 Berry Head Road, Brixham TQ5 9AG
T: (01803) 857919 & 850550
F: (01803) 850540

Bedrooms: 2 single, 7 double/twin
Bathrooms: 9 private

CC: Amex, Delta, Mastercard, Switch, Visa

Family-run bed and breakfast hotel situated on coastal road between Brixham harbour and Berry Head Country Park, overlooking Shoalstone Beach and Lyme Bay.

12 P

B&B per night:
S £27.00–£30.00
D £54.00–£60.00

◆◆◆

WOODLANDS GUEST HOUSE

Parkham Road, Brixham TQ5 9BU
T: (01803) 852040
F: (01803) 852040
E: diparry@aol.com
I: www.dogfriendlyguesthouse.co.uk

Situated close to town centre with panoramic views of Brixham Harbour and close to dog-friendly beaches, parks and woodland walks. En suite rooms. Dogs most welcome and can sleep in your bedroom. Car parks plus unrestricted on-road parking. An ideal holiday base.

Bedrooms: 1 single, 4 double/twin, 1 triple/multiple
Bathrooms: 5 en suite, 1 private

CC: Amex, Delta, Mastercard, Switch, Visa

P

B&B per night:
S £23.00–£25.00
D £46.00–£50.00

OPEN All Year except Christmas

CHECK THE MAPS

The colour maps at the front of this guide show all the cities, towns and villages for which you will find accommodation entries.
Refer to the town index to find the page on which they are listed.

BUDE, Cornwall Map ref 1C2 *Tourist Information Centre Tel: (01288) 354240*

HAREFIELD COTTAGE

Upton, Bude EX23 0LY
T: (01288) 352350
F: (01288) 352712
E: sales@coast-countryside.co.uk
I: www.coast-countryside.co.uk

New stone-built cottage with outstanding coastal views. Luxurious and spacious en suite bedrooms, king-size beds and 4-poster available. Home cooking our speciality. All diets catered for. Personal attention assured at all times. Only 250 yards from the coastal footpath. One mile downhill to the national cycle network. Hot tub available.

Bedrooms: 3 double/twin
Bathrooms: 3 en suite

Evening meal available

Special 3-night walking break including DB&B, packed lunch, transport and professional guide – £100pp.

B&B per night:
S Min £30.00
D Min £44.00

HB per person:
DY Min £64.00

OPEN All Year except Christmas

♦♦♦♦

LINK'S SIDE

7 Burn View, Bude EX23 8BY
T: (01288) 352410
E: linksidebude@hotmail.com
I: www.north-cornwall.co.uk/bude/client/linkside

Bedrooms: 6 double/twin, 1 triple/multiple
Bathrooms: 5 en suite

Town centre location overlooking golf course and within walking distance of beaches and coastal paths.

B&B per night:
S £20.00–£25.00
D £38.00–£46.00

OPEN All Year

♦♦♦

SURF HAVEN

31 Downs View, Bude EX23 8RG
T: (01288) 353923
F: (01288) 353923
E: info@surfhaven.info
I: www.surfhaven.info

Bedrooms: 3 double/twin, 4 triple/multiple
Bathrooms: 7 en suite

CC: Delta, Mastercard, Switch, Visa

Surf Haven is ideally situated 5 minutes' stroll from the beach, town and coastal path. Overlooks the third green of the Bude & North Cornwall Golf Club.

B&B per night:
S £25.00–£30.00
D £40.00–£55.00

OPEN All Year except Christmas

BUDLEIGH SALTERTON, Devon Map ref 1D2 *Tourist Information Centre Tel: (01395) 445275*

Silver Award

LUFFLANDS

Yettington, Budleigh Salterton EX9 7BP
T: (01395) 568422
F: (01395) 568810
E: stay@lufflands.co.uk
I: www.lufflands.co.uk

A warm welcome can be found at Lufflands, a 17thC former farmhouse. All rooms equipped to a high standard, and your breakfast is freshly cooked to order in the guest dining room/lounge with inglenook and bread ovens. Large garden, ample off-street parking. Close to beaches. Excellent walking.

Bedrooms: 1 single, 1 double/twin, 1 triple/multiple
Bathrooms: 2 en suite, 1 private

CC: Delta, Mastercard, Switch, Visa

Short breaks available: Apr-Oct £22pppn, Nov-Mar £20.50pppn. Minimum 3 nights.

B&B per night:
S £21.00–£24.00
D £42.00–£48.00

OPEN All Year

SPECIAL BREAKS

Many establishments offer special promotions and themed breaks. These are highlighted in red. (All such offers are subject to availability.)

BULFORD, Wiltshire Map ref 2B2

THE DOVECOT

Watergate Lane, Bulford, Salisbury
SP4 9DY
T: (01980) 632625
E: hadfields@02.co.uk

B&B per night:
S Min £36.00
D Min £52.00

OPEN All Year except Christmas

Characterful country house based on 18thC dovecot offering comfort, hospitality and relaxation in a superb riverside setting. Quiet location. One mile A303, 4 miles Stonehenge and 10 miles Salisbury. Ideally placed for people wanting to explore Salisbury Plain. Wholesome breakfasts, served in the dovecot, feature our own eggs and preserves.

Bedrooms: 2 double/twin
Bathrooms: 2 en suite

CC: Delta, Mastercard, Switch, Visa

7 P

BURNHAM-ON-SEA, Somerset Map ref 1D1 *Tourist Information Centre Tel: (01278) 787852*

PROSPECT FARM GUEST HOUSE

Strowlands, East Brent, Highbridge TA9 4JH
T: (01278) 760507

B&B per night:
S £20.00–£25.00
D £40.00–£50.00

OPEN All Year except Christmas

17thC Somerset farmhouse with inglenook fireplaces, bread ovens, beamed ceilings and a colourful history. Surrounded by the natural West Country beauty of the Somerset Levels, near legendary Brent Knoll, with remains of Iron Age and Roman settlements. 2 miles jct 22 M5, 3 miles Burnham-on-Sea. Variety of small farm animals and pets. Children welcome.

Bedrooms: 1 double/twin, 2 triple/multiple
Bathrooms: 1 en suite

Stay longer and save. 2-6 nights less 5%. 7-13 nights less 10%. 14 nights less 15%.

P

♦♦♦♦
Silver Award

WALTON HOUSE

148 Berrow Road, Burnham-on-Sea
TA8 2PN
T: (01278) 780034
E: auntflo@dialstart.net

B&B per night:
S £20.00–£25.00
D £40.00–£50.00

OPEN All Year except Christmas

You are assured of a warm and friendly welcome at Walton House. This spacious home provides comfortable accommodation and relaxed atmosphere for those on business, visiting friends or enjoying a holiday break. Close to Burnham and Berrow championship golf course. Walton House is ideally situated for visiting Somerset's many attractions.

Bedrooms: 1 single, 1 double/twin, 1 triple/multiple
Bathrooms: 1 en suite

P

REGIONAL TOURIST BOARD The symbol in an establishment entry indicates that it is a Regional Tourist Board member.

BURTON BRADSTOCK, Dorset Map ref 2A3

♦♦♦♦

PEBBLE BEACH LODGE

Coast Road, Burton Bradstock, Bridport DT6 4RJ
T: (01308) 897428
F: (01308) 897428
E: pebblebeachlodge@supanet.com
I: www.burtonbradstock.org.uk/pebblebeachlodge

Bedrooms: 1 single, 4 double/twin, 4 triple/multiple; permanent suite(s)
Bathrooms: 9 en suite

B&B per night:
S £27.50–£37.50
D £55.00–£60.00

Located on B3157 coast road, affording panoramic views of heritage coastline. Direct access to beach. Spacious and attractive accommodation, large conservatory.

CALLINGTON, Cornwall Map ref 1C2

♦♦♦

GREEN PASTURES

Longhill, Callington PL17 8AU
T: (01579) 382566
E: greenpast@aol.com

Bedrooms: 2 double/twin, 1 triple/multiple
Bathrooms: 2 en suite, 1 private

B&B per night:
S £20.00–£22.00
D £37.00–£44.00

OPEN All Year

Spacious detached bungalow set within 5 acres of pastural land. Large car park. Extensive views towards Dartmoor, Tamar Valley. Cotehele, Morwellam Quay within easy reach.

♦♦♦

HIGHER MANATON

Callington PL17 8PX
T: (01579) 370460
F: (01579) 370460
E: dtrewin@manaton.fsnet.co.uk
I: www.turning-wood.com

B&B per night:
S £20.00–£22.00
D £40.00–£44.00

HB per person:
DY £50.00–£54.00

18thC farmhouse on a working farm. Rooms en suite. Easy access to moors. Eden Project a convenient 28 miles. Historic Plymouth with Hoe and Barbican 16 miles. Launceston 8 miles. National Trust, English Heritage properties and beautiful Tamar Valley nearby. Golf, riding and other country pursuits locally. Ideal for touring.

Bedrooms: 3 double/twin
Bathrooms: 2 en suite, 1 private

Evening meal available

CASTLE CARY, Somerset Map ref 2B2

♦♦♦

THE HORSE POND INN AND MOTEL

The Triangle, Castle Cary BA7 7BD
T: (01963) 350318 & 351762
F: (01963) 351764
E: horsepondinn@aol.com
I: www.horsepondinn.co.uk

Bedrooms: 2 double/twin, 2 triple/multiple; permanent suite(s)
Bathrooms: 4 en suite

Lunch available
Evening meal available
CC: Diners, Mastercard, Switch, Visa

B&B per night:
S £40.00–£45.00
D £50.00–£60.00

HB per person:
DY £50.00–£65.00

OPEN All Year

Nestling at the foot of Castle Cary, centrally located, an ideal base for travelling around Somerset, West Devon, Dorset and Wiltshire either for business or pleasure.

CERNE ABBAS, Dorset Map ref 2B3

♦♦♦♦

BADGER HILL

11 Springfield, Cerne Abbas, Dorchester DT2 7JZ
T: (01300) 341698
F: (01300) 341698

Bedrooms: 2 double/twin
Bathrooms: 1 en suite, 1 private

B&B per night:
S £25.00–£30.00
D £40.00–£50.00

OPEN All Year

Cedarwood bungalow in pleasant wooded area near Cerne Giant-2 minutes to village centre.

10 P

MAP REFERENCES

Map references apply to the colour maps at the front of this guide.

CHARD, Somerset Map ref 1D2 *Tourist Information Centre Tel: (01460) 67463*

♦♦♦♦ Silver Award

YEW TREE COTTAGE
Hornsbury Hill, Chard TA20 3DB
T: (01460) 64735
F: (01460) 68029
E: ytcottage@aol.com
I: www.yewtreecottage.org.uk

Bedrooms: 3 double/twin
Bathrooms: 3 en suite

CC: Delta, Mastercard, Switch, Visa

B&B per night:
S £27.00–£30.00
D £45.00–£48.00

OPEN All Year except Christmas

Comfortable twin and double rooms, fully en suite. Acre of peaceful garden. Ample off-road parking. Close to Chard and Devon/Dorset borders. Non-smoking.

CHARMINSTER, Dorset Map ref 2B3

♦♦♦

THREE COMPASSES INN
Charminster, Dorchester DT2 9QT
T: (01305) 263618

Bedrooms: 1 single, 2 double/twin, 1 triple/multiple
Bathrooms: 2 en suite

Lunch available
Evening meal available

B&B per night:
S £20.00–£25.00
D £40.00–£45.00

OPEN All Year

Traditional village public house/inn with skittle alley, set in village square.

CHARMOUTH, Dorset Map ref 1D2

QUEEN'S ARMES HOTEL
The Street, Charmouth, Bridport DT6 6QF
T: (01297) 560339
F: (01297) 560339

Bedrooms: 2 single, 8 double/twin, 1 triple/multiple; permanent suite(s)
Bathrooms: 10 en suite, 1 private

CC: Delta, Mastercard, Switch, Visa

B&B per night:
S £33.00–£35.00
D £66.00–£70.00

HB per person:
DY £47.00–£50.00

Built around 1500, this former coaching inn with oak beams and wall panels is situated in centre of village on the Heritage Coastline.

CHEDDAR, Somerset Map ref 1D1

BAY ROSE HOUSE

The Bays, Cheddar BS27 3QN
T: (01934) 741377
F: (01934) 741377
E: enquiries@bayrose.co.uk
www.bayrose.co.uk

B&B per night:
S £25.00–£30.00
D £40.00–£50.00

OPEN All Year except Christmas

19thC stone cottage just off the road through Cheddar Gorge. A friendly family home, close to the caves, ideal for touring, cycling and hiking in the Mendips and Somerset Levels. Families welcome, disabled access to ground floor room, extensive breakfast selection including specials, vegetarian options and organic ingredients.

Bedrooms: 3 double/twin
Bathrooms: 2 en suite, 1 private

CC: Amex, Delta, Mastercard, Switch, Visa

Discounts on all stays of 2 or more nights, Nov-Mar. Mid-week breaks available Apr, May, Sep and Oct.

CHELSTON, Devon Map ref 1D2

ELMDENE HOTEL
Rathmore Road, Chelston, Torquay TQ2 6NZ
T: (01803) 294940
F: (01803) 294940
E: elmdenehoteltorq@amserve.net
I: www.s-h-systems.co.uk/hotels/elmdene.html

Bedrooms: 2 single, 5 double/twin, 4 triple/multiple
Bathrooms: 7 en suite

Evening meal available
CC: Amex, Mastercard, Switch, Visa

B&B per night:
S £20.00–£25.00
D £35.00–£50.00

HB per person:
DY £30.00–£35.00

OPEN All Year

A lovely Victorian hotel in rural setting, on the level and close to seafront, Torre Abbey and amenities. Own car park and licensed bar.

QUALITY ASSURANCE SCHEME
Diamond ratings and awards are explained at the back of this guide.

CHELYNCH, Somerset Map ref 2B2

◆◆◆◆

THE OLD STABLES

Hurlingpot Farm, Chelynch,
Shepton Mallet BA4 4PY
T: (01749) 880098 & 07798 600752
E: maureen.keevil@amserve.net
I: www.the-oldstables.co.uk

Bedrooms: 1 double/twin, 1 triple/multiple
Bathrooms: 1 en suite, 1 private

B&B per night:
S £30.00–£35.00
D £45.00–£50.00

Carefully restored Grade II Listed barn offering a high standard of accommodation, set in peaceful country location. Traditional farmhouse breakfast, a warm welcome and ample off-road parking.

CHEW STOKE, Bath and North East Somerset Map ref 2A2

◆◆◆

ORCHARD HOUSE

Bristol Road, Chew Stoke, Bristol
BS40 8UB
T: (01275) 333143
F: (01275) 333754
E: orchardhse@ukgateway.net
I: www.orchardhse.ukgateway.net

Bedrooms: 1 single, 4 double/twin, 1 triple/multiple
Bathrooms: 5 en suite, 1 private

CC: Delta, Mastercard, Switch, Visa

B&B per night:
S £20.00–£27.00
D £40.00–£50.00

OPEN All Year

Comfortable accommodation in a carefully modernised Georgian house and coach house annexe. Good eating in local pubs. Convenient access to Bristol and Bath.

CLEVEDON, Somerset Map ref 1D1

HIGHCLIFFE HOTEL

Wellington Terrace, Clevedon
BS21 7PU
T: (01275) 873250
F: (01275) 873572
E: highcliffehotel@aol.com

Bedrooms: 2 single, 15 double/twin, 2 triple/multiple
Bathrooms: 19 en suite

Evening meal available
CC: Delta, Mastercard, Switch, Visa

B&B per night:
S £39.95–£55.00
D £50.00–£65.00

HB per person:
DY £30.00–£65.50

OPEN All Year except Christmas

Situated in a quiet area overlooking the Bristol Channel near town and pier. Guaranteed a warm welcome with good restaurant and bar.

CLOVELLY, Devon Map ref 1C1

FUCHSIA COTTAGE

Burscott, Clovelly, Bideford
EX39 5RR
T: (01237) 431398
E: curtis@fuchsiacottage.fslife.co.uk
I: www.clovelly-holidays.co.uk

Bedrooms: 1 single, 2 double/twin
Bathrooms: 2 en suite

Evening meal available

B&B per night:
S £17.00
D £40.00

OPEN All Year except Christmas

Fuchsia Cottage has comfortable ground and first floor en suite accommodation. Surrounded by beautiful views of sea and country. Good walking area. Ample parking.

CORSHAM, Wiltshire Map ref 2B2 *Tourist Information Centre Tel: (01249) 714660*

Silver Award

HEATHERLY COTTAGE

Ladbrook Lane, Gastard, Corsham
SN13 9PE
T: (01249) 701402
F: (01249) 701412
E: ladbrook1@aol.com
I: www.smoothhound.co.uk/hotels/heather3.html

Bedrooms: 3 double/twin
Bathrooms: 3 en suite

B&B per night:
S £28.00–£30.00
D £48.00–£52.00

OPEN All Year except Christmas

Delightful 17thC cottage set in 1.5 acres with views over open countryside. Guests' accommodation is in a separate wing of the house with its own front door and staircase. Our attractively furnished rooms are all en suite and have TV and hospitality trays. Many pubs serving food nearby. Bath 9 miles. Ample parking.

CRAFTHOLE, Cornwall Map ref 1C2

◆◆◆

FINNYGOOK INN
Crafthole, Torpoint PL11 3BQ
T: (01503) 230329
I: www.finnygook.co.uk

Bedrooms: 4 double/twin
Bathrooms: 4 en suite

Lunch available
Evening meal available
CC: Delta, Diners, Mastercard, Switch, Visa

16thC coaching inn with 6 en suite bedrooms. Superb food and real ales. This is a fine inn in a wonderful position.

B&B per night:
S £20.00–£40.00
D £45.00

HB per person:
DY £55.00–£60.00

OPEN All Year

CRANTOCK, Cornwall Map ref 1B2

HIGHFIELD LODGE HOTEL

Halwyn Road, Crantock, Newquay TR8 5TR
T: (01637) 830744
F: (01637) 830568
E: highfieldlodge@tinyworld.co.uk
I: www.highfieldlodge.co.uk

Highfield Lodge is a small, friendly, non-smoking hotel in the picturesque coastal village of Crantock. An ideal centre for touring Cornwall with nearby facilities for coarse and sea fishing, riding, surfing and golf. Crantock beach is a mere stroll away. Bar meals available in our cosy, licensed bar.

Bedrooms: 2 single, 8 double/twin, 1 triple/multiple
Bathrooms: 8 en suite

Evening meal available
CC: Delta, Mastercard, Switch, Visa

B&B per night:
S £20.00–£25.00
D £40.00–£50.00

OPEN All Year

CREECH ST MICHAEL, Somerset Map ref 1D1

CURVALION VILLA

Curvalion Road, Creech St Michael, Taunton TA3 5QQ
T: (01823) 444630 & 07711 569589
F: (01823) 444629
E: enquiries@curvalionvilla.co.uk
I: www.curvalionvilla.co.uk

Just 1 mile east off the M5 jct 25. Centrally located for many attractions in the area: Cheddar Gorge, Lyme Regis, West Somerset Steam Rail, Glastonbury, Burnham on Sea, Fleet Air Arm, Minehead Butlins, Somerset Wetlands. The Sustrans Route, Space Walk and River Parrot Trail are close by.

Bedrooms: 3 double/twin
Bathrooms: 1 en suite, 2 private

Lunch available
Evening meal available

B&B per night:
S £27.50–£30.00
D £45.00–£56.00

HB per person:
DY £35.00–£40.00

OPEN All Year

CREWKERNE, Somerset Map ref 1D2

THE GEORGE HOTEL & COURTYARD RESTAURANT
Market Square, Crewkerne TA18 7LP
T: (01460) 73650
F: (01460) 72974
E: eddie@thegeorgehotel.sagehost.co.uk
I: www.thegeorgehotel.sagenet.co.uk

Bedrooms: 3 single, 8 double/twin, 2 triple/multiple
Bathrooms: 8 en suite, 2 private

Lunch available
Evening meal available
CC: Amex, Delta, Diners, Mastercard, Switch, Visa

Recently refurbished 17thC Grade II Listed coaching inn in the market square. Ideally located for touring. Fine food, real ales, warm welcome!

B&B per night:
S £25.00–£50.00
D £50.00–£80.00

OPEN All Year

DARTMOOR

See under Ashburton, Bovey Tracey, Bridestowe, Hexworthy, Moretonhampstead, Okehampton, Tavistock, Yelverton

DARTMOUTH, Devon Map ref 1D3 *Tourist Information Centre Tel: (01803) 834224*

Rating Applied For

HILL VIEW HOUSE

76 Victoria Road, Dartmouth
TQ6 9DZ
T: (01803) 839372
F: (01803) 839372
E: enquire@hillviewdartmouth.co.uk
I: www.hillviewdartmouth.co.uk

Bedrooms: 5 double/twin
Bathrooms: 5 en suite

Evening meal available
CC: Delta, Diners, Mastercard, Switch, Visa

B&B per night:
D £57.00–£79.00

OPEN All Year

Extensively refurbished period townhouse 5 minutes' walk from Dartmouth centre and riverfront. Environmentally friendly, all bedding mite free, quality breakfasts, special diets catered for.

DEVIZES, Wiltshire Map ref 2B2 *Tourist Information Centre Tel: (01380) 729408*

THE ARTICHOKE INN

The Nursery, Bath Road, Devizes
SN10 2AA
T: (01380) 723400
E:avocainns@freddieboxall.co.uk

Bedrooms: 1 single, 2 double/twin
Bathrooms: 3 en suite

Lunch available
Evening meal available
CC: Mastercard, Visa

B&B per night:
S Max £28.00
D Max £56.00

OPEN All Year

One single, 1 twin and 1 double bedroom, all en suite. Lunch and evening meals available. Three minutes from town centre.

♦♦♦♦♦
Gold Award

BLOUNTS COURT FARM

Coxhill Lane, Potterne, Devizes SN10 5PH
T: (01380) 727180
E: caroline@blountscourtfarm.co.uk
I: www.blountscourtfarm.co.uk

B&B per night:
S £32.00–£38.00
D £52.00–£55.00

OPEN All Year

Situated in a peaceful countryside setting of 150 acres with woodland backdrop. Traditional stone-built farmhouse with ground floor guest accommodation in recently converted stables adjoining house. Tastefully furnished rooms including 4-poster bed. Guests' own sitting room. Warm and homely atmosphere. Ideal base to explore this exciting part of Wiltshire.

Bedrooms: 2 double/twin
Bathrooms: 2 en suite

CC: Delta, Mastercard, Switch, Visa

♦♦♦♦

LITTLETON LODGE

Littleton Panell (A360), West Lavington, Devizes SN10 4ES
T: (01380) 813131
F: (01380) 816969
E: stay@littletonlodge.co.uk
I: www.littletonlodge.co.uk

B&B per night:
S £35.00–£40.00
D £55.00–£65.00

OPEN All Year

Lovely Victorian house c1850 in a conservation village. Delightful rural views and large garden backing onto a vineyard. Three good pubs within 5-10 minutes' walk. Private parking. Just 15 minutes north of Stonehenge, 10 minutes from White Horses. Excellent base for exploring Avebury, Bath, Lacock, Longleat, Salisbury, Stourhead and other gardens.

Bedrooms: 3 double/twin
Bathrooms: 3 en suite

CC: Amex, Mastercard, Visa

COLOUR MAPS Colour maps at the front of this guide pinpoint all places under which you will find accommodation listed.

DINTON, Wiltshire Map ref 2B3

♦♦♦

MARSHWOOD FARM B&B
Dinton, Salisbury SP3 5ET
T: (01722) 716334

Bedrooms: 1 double/twin, 1 triple/multiple
Bathrooms: 2 en suite

16thC farmhouse and working farm in Wiltshire countryside. Approximately 10 miles west of Salisbury and 4 miles off A303. Ideal for walking, cycling and pony trekking.

P

B&B per night:
S £30.00–£50.00
D £50.00

OPEN All Year except Christmas

♦♦♦

MORRIS' FARM HOUSE
Baverstock, Dinton, Salisbury
SP3 5EL
T: (01722) 716874
F: (01722) 716874
E: marriott@waitrose.com
I: www.kgp-publishing.co.uk

Bedrooms: 2 double/twin

Small Victorian farmhouse facing south – very light-country view. Attractive garden with patio.

P

B&B per night:
S Min £27.00
D Min £44.00

OPEN All Year except Christmas

DORCHESTER, Dorset Map ref 2B3 *Tourist Information Centre Tel: (01305) 267992*

♦♦♦

CHURCHVIEW GUEST HOUSE

Winterbourne Abbas, Dorchester DT2 9LS
T: (01305) 889296
F: (01305) 889296
E: stay@churchview.co.uk
I: www.churchview.co.uk

Beautiful 17thC guesthouse set in a small village near Dorchester, offers a warm welcome and delicious home-cooked meals. Character bedrooms with hospitality tray, TV and radio. Two comfortable lounges and licensed bar. Your hosts will give every assistance with information to ensure a memorable stay.

Bedrooms: 1 single, 8 double/twin
Bathrooms: 8 en suite, 1 private

Evening meal available
CC: Delta, Mastercard, Switch, Visa

Prices reduced by £2 pp daily, for stays of 2 nights or more with evening meals.

5 P

B&B per night:
S £34.00–£36.00
D £60.00–£64.00

HB per person:
DY £42.00–£46.00

OPEN All Year except Christmas

♦♦♦♦
Silver Award

THE OLD RECTORY

Winterbourne Steepleton, Dorchester
DT2 9LG
T: (01305) 889468
F: (01305) 889737
E: trees@eurobell.co.uk
I: www.trees.eurobell.co.uk

Built 1850 on 1 acre of private ground in a quiet hamlet, surrounded by spectacular walks. Six miles from historic Dorchester, 8 miles from Weymouth's sandy beach. We offer a peaceful stay with a memorable breakfast including many homemade, organic products. Excellent local pubs and restaurants. French spoken.

Bedrooms: 4 double/twin
Bathrooms: 4 en suite

P

B&B per night:
S £45.00–£50.00
D £50.00–£110.00

OPEN All Year except Christmas

DULVERTON, Somerset Map ref 1D1

♦♦♦♦
Silver Award

TOWN MILLS
High Street, Dulverton TA22 9HB
T: (01398) 323124
E: townmills@onetel.net.uk
I: www.townmillsdulverton.co.uk

Bedrooms: 5 double/twin; permanent suite(s)
Bathrooms: 5 en suite

CC: Amex, Delta, Mastercard, Switch, Visa

Our 19thC mill house is secluded but in the centre of Dulverton. We serve you full English breakfast in your spacious room; some have log fires.

P

B&B per night:
D £48.00–£56.00

OPEN All Year

DUNSTER, Somerset Map ref 1D1

◆◆◆◆ Silver Award

SPEARS CROSS HOTEL

1 West Street, Dunster, Minehead TA24 6SN
T: (01643) 821439
E: mjcapel@aol.com
I: www.smoothhound.co.uk/hotels/spearsx.html

Bedrooms: 2 double/twin, 1 triple/multiple
Bathrooms: 3 en suite

Packed lunch available
Evening meal available
CC: Delta, Mastercard, Switch, Visa

B&B per night:
S £30.00–£35.00
D £48.00–£55.00

Pretty 15thC small hotel with old world charm but up-to-date facilities. Situated in picturesque village in the Exmoor National Park. No smoking. Private car parking.

EXETER, Devon Map ref 1D2 *Tourist Information Centre Tel: (01392) 265700*

◆◆◆◆

FAIRWINDS VILLAGE HOUSE HOTEL

Kennford, Exeter EX6 7UD
T: (01392) 832911
E: fairwindshotbun@aol.com

Bedrooms: 5 double/twin, 1 triple/multiple
Bathrooms: 6 en suite

Evening meal available
CC: Mastercard, Visa

B&B per night:
S £39.00–£42.00
D £56.00–£58.00

HB per person:
DY £37.00–£44.00

Friendly little hotel, south of Exeter. Exclusively for non-smokers. Beautiful rural surroundings. Delightful en suite bedrooms (some on ground floor). Delicious homemade food. Bargain breaks available.

◆◆◆◆

THE GRANGE

Stoke Hill, Exeter EX4 7JH
T: (01392) 259723
E: dudleythegrange@aol.com

Bedrooms: 2 double/twin
Bathrooms: 2 en suite

B&B per night:
S £28.00–£31.00
D £40.00–£44.00

OPEN All Year except Christmas

Country house set in 3 acres of woodlands, 1.5 miles from the city centre. Ideal for holidays and off-season breaks. En suite rooms.

◆◆◆◆

ST ANDREWS HOTEL

28 Alphington Road, Exeter EX2 8HN
T: (01392) 276784
F: (01392) 250249

B&B per night:
S £40.00–£54.00
D £55.00–£72.00

OPEN All Year except Christmas

St Andrews is a long-established family-run hotel offering a high standard of comfort and service in a friendly, relaxing atmosphere. Excellent home cooking. Large car park at rear. Weekend breaks. Brochure on request.

Bedrooms: 4 single, 11 double/twin, 2 triple/multiple
Bathrooms: 17 en suite

Lunch available
Evening meal available
CC: Amex, Delta, Diners, Mastercard, Switch, Visa

Weekend breaks all year, must include Sat night. Ideally situated for Christmas shopping or summer touring breaks.

EXMOOR

See under Allerford, Bilbrook, Dulverton, Dunster, Lynmouth, Lynton, Minehead, Porlock, Winsford, Parracombe

QUALITY ASSURANCE SCHEME

For an explanation of the quality and facilities represented by the Diamonds please refer to the front of this guide. A more detailed explanation can be found in the information pages at the back.

FALMOUTH, Cornwall Map ref 1B3 *Tourist Information Centre Tel: (01326) 312300*

♦♦♦♦

APPLE TREE COTTAGE

Laity Moor, Ponsanooth, Truro TR3 7HR
T: (01872) 865047
E: appletreecottage@talk21.com
I: www.cornwall-online.co.uk

Set amid countryside between Falmouth and Truro with a river meandering through the gardens. Rooms are furnished in a country style and guests are offered traditional farmhouse fare cooked on the Aga. Close to superb Cornish gardens and beaches. Non-smoking. Member of Falmouth Hotel Association. For brochure contact Mrs A Tremayne.

Bedrooms: 2 double/twin

B&B per night:
S £30.00
D £50.00

OPEN All Year except Christmas

♦♦♦

CHELSEA HOUSE HOTEL

2 Emslie Road, Falmouth TR11 4BG
T: (01326) 212230
E: enquiries@chelseahousehotel.com
I: www.chelseahousehotel.com

Bedrooms: 4 double/twin, 3 triple/multiple
Bathrooms: 7 en suite

CC: Delta, Mastercard, Switch, Visa

A charming Edwardian house with spacious rooms many with sea views and own balconies. Close to beach, gardens and town.

B&B per night:
S £23.00–£30.00
D £44.00–£56.00

OPEN All Year except Christmas

♦♦♦♦♦
Silver Award

DOLVEAN HOTEL

50 Melvill Road, Falmouth TR11 4DQ
T: (01326) 313658
F: (01326) 313995
E: reservations@dolvean.co.uk
I: www.dolvean.co.uk

Experience the elegance and comfort of our Victorian home where carefully chosen antiques, fine china and fascinating books create an ambience where you can relax and feel at home. Each bedroom has its own character with pretty pictures and lots of ribbon and lace, creating an atmosphere that makes every stay a special occasion.

Bedrooms: 3 single, 8 double/twin
Bathrooms: 11 en suite

CC: Amex, Delta, Mastercard, Switch, Visa

3-night special breaks available in winter, spring and autumn. Check our website for more details.

B&B per night:
S £30.00–£45.00
D £60.00–£90.00

OPEN All Year except Christmas

♦♦♦

HAWTHORNE DENE HOTEL

12 Pennance Road, Falmouth TR11 4EA
T: (01326) 311427
F: (01326) 311994
E: hawthornedene@hotel12.fsbusiness.co.uk

A small Edwardian hotel situated just 5 minutes' walk to the beaches and 10 to town. All rooms are en suite. Our food is local, fresh and mainly organic.

Bedrooms: 2 single, 5 double/twin, 1 triple/multiple
Bathrooms: 8 en suite

Evening meal available
CC: Delta, Mastercard, Switch, Visa

B&B per night:
S £25.00–£30.00
D £50.00–£60.00

HB per person:
DY £35.00–£45.00

OPEN All Year except Christmas

FALMOUTH continued

♦♦♦♦

IVANHOE GUEST HOUSE

7 Melvill Road, Falmouth TR11 4AS
T: (01326) 319083
F: (01326) 319083
E: ivanhoe@enterprise.net
I: www.smoothhound.co.uk/hotels/ivanhoe

Bedrooms: 2 single, 3 double/twin, 1 triple/multiple
Bathrooms: 4 en suite

A warm and comfortable guesthouse with particularly well-equipped en suite rooms. Minutes from the beaches, harbour and town. Off-road parking.

B&B per night:
S £20.00–£24.00
D £48.00–£54.00

OPEN All Year

♦♦♦

WICKHAM GUEST HOUSE

21 Gyllyngvase Terrace, Falmouth TR11 4DL
T: (01326) 311140 & 07977 573575
E: enquiries@wickhamhotel.freeserve.co.uk

Small, friendly, no-smoking guesthouse. Situated between harbour and beach with views over Falmouth Bay, Wickham is the ideal base for exploring Falmouth and South Cornwall's gardens, castles, harbours, coastal footpath and much more. All rooms have TV and tea/coffee facilities, some have sea views.

Bedrooms: 2 single, 2 double/twin, 2 triple/multiple
Bathrooms: 3 en suite

CC: Delta, Mastercard, Visa

B&B per night:
S £19.00–£21.00
D £38.00–£46.00

OPEN All Year except Christmas

FROME, Somerset Map ref 2B2 *Tourist Information Centre Tel: (01373) 467271*

♦♦♦♦

THE LODGE

Monkley Lane, Rode, Frome BA11 6QQ
T: (01373) 830071
E: mcdougal@nildram.co.uk

Bedrooms: 3 double/twin
Bathrooms: 1 en suite, 1 private

Old stone cottage with beautiful gardens and views. Quiet, rural, yet convenient location. Between Trowbridge and Frome. Bath 11 miles. Lovely rooms and warm welcome.

B&B per night:
S £35.00–£40.00
D £50.00–£65.00

OPEN All Year except Christmas

♦♦♦

WADBURY HOUSE

Mells, Frome BA11 3PA
T: (01373) 812359
E: sbrinkmann@btinternet.com

Wadbury is a historic country house with galleried hall, surrounded by gardens and parkland affording complete peace and quiet. Magnificent views, elegant, comfortable rooms, heated outdoor pool for summer, log fires in winter, home produce and a warm welcome. Opportunities for walking, riding and golf. Many places of interest nearby.

Bedrooms: 3 double/twin, 1 triple/multiple
Bathrooms: 3 en suite, 1 private

Lunch available
Evening meal available

B&B per night:
S £28.00–£38.00
D £56.00–£76.00

HB per person:
DY £43.00–£53.00

OPEN All Year

MAP REFERENCES The map references refer to the colour maps at the front of this guide. The first figure is the map number; the letter and figure which follow indicate the grid reference on the map.

GLASTONBURY, Somerset Map ref 2A2 *Tourist Information Centre Tel: (01458) 832954*

MEARE MANOR

60 St Marys Road, Meare, Glastonbury BA6 9SR
T: (01458) 860449
F: (01458) 860449
E: info@mearemanor.co.uk
I: www.mearemanor.co.uk

A 200-year-old manor built by the Abbots of Glastonbury. Imposing, friendly, licensed, parking, gardens. Tea rooms, local walks. All rooms en suite with TV and tea tray. Lift, disabled facilities, dogs welcome. Near Wells and Cheddar, 12 minutes M5. Apartments, suites and rooms.

Bedrooms: 1 single, 4 double/twin, 2 triple/multiple; permanent suite(s)
Bathrooms: 7 en suite

Evening meal available
CC: Delta, Mastercard, Switch, Visa

Book 7 nights for the price of 6, plus a bottle of wine on your arrival.

B&B per night:
S £40.00–£50.00
D £68.50–£80.00

HB per person:
DY £50.00–£80.00

OPEN All Year

HALSTOCK, Dorset Map ref 2A3

QUIET WOMAN HOUSE

Halstock, Yeovil BA22 9RX
T: (01935) 891218
E: quietwomanhouse@ukonline.co.uk

Bedrooms: 2 double/twin, 1 triple/multiple
Bathrooms: 3 en suite

Evening meal available

Three-hundred-year-old former coaching inn offering comfortable and friendly B&B surrounded by beautiful Dorset countryside. We look forward to making you welcome.

B&B per night:
S £25.00–£30.00
D £50.00–£60.00

HB per person:
DY £45.00–£50.00

OPEN All Year

HARTLAND, Devon Map ref 1C1

HARTLAND QUAY HOTEL

Hartland, Bideford EX39 6DU
T: (01237) 441218
F: (01237) 441371

Bedrooms: 2 single, 9 double/twin, 6 triple/multiple
Bathrooms: 15 en suite

Lunch available
Evening meal available
CC: Delta, Mastercard, Switch, Visa

Small family-run hotel overlooking the rugged Atlantic coastline. Coastal walks. Important geological area.

B&B per night:
S £25.00–£27.00
D £50.00–£54.00

HB per person:
DY £37.00–£39.00

OPEN All Year except Christmas

HEXWORTHY, Devon Map ref 1C2

THE FOREST INN

Hexworthy, Dartmoor PL20 6SD
T: (01364) 631211
F: (01364) 631515
E: info@theforestinn.co.uk
I: www.theforestinn.co.uk

A haven for walkers, riders, fishermen or anyone just looking for an opportunity to enjoy the natural beauty of Dartmoor. The restaurant specialises in homemade food using local produce wherever possible. As an alternative, there is an extensive range of meals that can be enjoyed in the more informal setting of the Huccaby room. Dogs and muddy boots welcome.

Bedrooms: 2 single, 8 double/twin
Bathrooms: 7 en suite, 3 private

Lunch available
Evening meal available
CC: Delta, Mastercard, Switch, Visa

Stay any 2 nights (Sun-Wed) and get your third night free.

B&B per night:
S £28.00–£36.00
D £50.00–£60.00

CONFIRM YOUR BOOKING
You are advised to confirm your booking in writing.

HOLBETON, Devon Map ref 1C3

◆◆◆◆ Silver Award

BUGLE ROCKS

The Old School, Battisborough, Holbeton, Plymouth PL8 1JX
T: (01752) 830422
F: (01752) 830558
E: buglerocks@hotmail.com

B&B per night:
S £25.00
D £50.00

Converted coach house and stable block located in an Area of Outstanding Natural Beauty. Formerly part of a gentleman's country residence, in a secluded valley overlooking the sea. Close to the spectacular coastal footpath, 5 minutes from the famous Mothecombe beach.

Bedrooms: 2 double/twin, 1 triple/multiple
Bathrooms: 2 en suite, 1 private

HONITON, Devon Map ref 1D2 *Tourist Information Centre Tel: (01404) 43716*

◆◆◆◆

BIDWELL FARM AND HAYBARTON ANNEXE

Bidwell Farm, Upottery, Honiton EX14 9PP
T: (01404) 861122
F: 08700 554960
E: pat@rbwells.demon.co.uk
I: www.bidwellfarm.co.uk

B&B per night:
S £25.00
D £50.00

OPEN All Year except Christmas

Outstanding views from all windows of this superb farmhouse. Glorious 8-minute walk to the village Inn. All quality bedrooms with en suite/private shower, TV and tea tray. Discount for children. Warm welcome and great breakfasts.

Bedrooms: 6 double/twin
Bathrooms: 3 en suite, 2 private

Free trout fishing in on-stream pond. Child discount: 4 nights for price of 3.

◆◆◆◆

FAIRMILE INN

(on old A40), Fairmile, Ottery St Mary EX11 1LP
T: (01404) 812827
F: (01404) 815806
E: leon.courtney@thefairmileinn.co.uk
I: www.fairmileinn.co.uk

B&B per night:
S £32.50
D £45.00

OPEN All Year

Lovely Grade II East Devon inn, parts of which are 400 years old, privately owned/managed, comfortable en suite accommodation (2 doubles, 1 twin). A la carte restaurant open 7 days a week, good English food, real ales. Half a mile off new A30, free collection Exeter Airport, nearest bus and rail station.

Bedrooms: 3 double/twin
Bathrooms: 3 en suite

Lunch available
Evening meal available
CC: Delta, Mastercard, Switch, Visa

Stay 3 nights pay for 2 (subject to availability). Weekend breaks, Fri night to Mon morning, full board £75pp (excl Bank Holidays).

IMPORTANT NOTE Information on accommodation listed in this guide has been supplied by the proprietors. As changes may occur you are advised to check details at the time of booking.

HONITON continued

Silver Award

WESSINGTON FARM

Awliscombe, Honiton EX14 3NU
T: (01404) 42280
F: (01404) 45271
E: b&b@eastdevon.com
I: www.eastdevon.com/bedandbreakfast

B&B per night:
S £20.00–£30.00
D £40.00–£50.00

OPEN All Year

Elegant Victorian stone farmhouse, on a working stock farm, situated in an Area of Outstanding Natural Beauty, with wonderful panoramic views over open countryside. On A373, 2 miles from Honiton. Picturesque East Devon coastline 20 minutes, World Jurassic Heritage coastline 20 minutes, historic Exeter 16 miles. High-standard rooms, warm, friendly atmosphere, traditional Aga-cooked breakfast.

Bedrooms: 3 double/twin
Bathrooms: 2 en suite, 1 private

Landrover Experience: 4x4 off-road driving centre on site.

HULLAVINGTON, Wiltshire Map ref 2B2

Silver Award

BRADFIELD MANOR

Malmesbury SN14 6EU
T: (01666) 838000
F: (01666) 838200
E: enquiries@bradfieldmanor.co.uk
I: www.bradfieldmanor.co.uk

Bedrooms: 3 double/twin
Bathrooms: 3 en suite

Evening meal available
CC: Amex, Delta, Mastercard, Switch, Visa

B&B per night:
D £90.00–£120.00

OPEN All Year except Christmas

A medieval manor house dating from 1425, Bradfield offers delightful rooms in a historic setting. Close to Malmesbury, Bath and the Cotswolds.

ILFRACOMBE, Devon Map ref 1C1 *Tourist Information Centre Tel: (01271) 863001*

♦♦♦

CAPSTONE HOTEL AND RESTAURANT

St James Place, Ilfracombe EX34 9BJ
T: (01271) 863540
F: (01271) 862277
E: steve@capstone.freeserve.co.uk
I: www.ilfracombe2000.freeserve.co.uk

Bedrooms: 2 single, 7 double/twin, 3 triple/multiple
Bathrooms: 12 en suite

Lunch available
Evening meal available
CC: Amex, Delta, Mastercard, Switch, Visa

B&B per night:
S £19.00–£23.00
D £37.00–£42.00

HB per person:
DY £25.00–£30.00

Family-run hotel, with restaurant on ground floor. Close to harbour and all amenities. Local seafood a speciality.

LYNCOTT HOUSE

56 St Brannock's Road, Ilfracombe EX34 8EQ
T: (01271) 862425
F: (01271) 862425
E: david@ukhotels.com
I: www.lyncottdevon.com

Bedrooms: 1 single, 3 double/twin, 2 triple/multiple
Bathrooms: 6 en suite

Evening meal available

B&B per night:
S £22.00–£25.00
D £44.00–£52.00

HB per person:
DY £36.00–£40.00

OPEN All Year except Christmas

Relax, smoke-free, at elegant, lovingly restored, Victorian Lyncott House. Spacious, individually designed en suite bedrooms. Delicious home-made fare. Near lovely Bicclescombe Park. Private parking.

Silver Award

STRATHMORE HOTEL

57 St Brannocks Road, Ilfracombe EX34 8EQ
T: (01271) 862248
F: (01271) 862243
E: strathmore@ukhotels.com
I: www.strathmore.ukhotels.com

Bedrooms: 2 single, 3 double/twin, 4 triple/multiple; permanent suite(s)
Bathrooms: 9 en suite

Lunch available
Evening meal available
CC: Mastercard, Switch, Visa

B&B per night:
S £35.00–£45.00
D £50.00–£70.00

HB per person:
DY £46.50–£65.00

OPEN All Year

Quality hotel recommended for its superbly prepared home-cooked food, comfort and service. Licensed bar and parking. Close to beautiful beaches and Exmoor. Pets, children welcome.

ILFRACOMBE continued

♦♦♦

THE TOWERS HOTEL

Chambercombe Park Road,
Ilfracombe EX34 9QN
T: (01271) 862809
F: (01271) 879442
E: info@thetowers.co.uk
I: www.thetowers.co.uk

Bedrooms: 1 single, 7 double/twin
Bathrooms: 4 en suite, 1 private

Evening meal available
CC: Delta, Mastercard, Switch, Visa

B&B per night:
S £22.00–£25.00
D £44.00–£50.00

HB per person:
DY £35.00–£38.00

Quiet location, sea views, private parking, family run. Special diets by arrangement. Pets welcome.

♦♦♦♦

WESTAWAY

Torrs Park, Ilfracombe EX34 8AY
T: (01271) 864459 & 07932 032017
F: (01271) 863486
E: westaway55@btopenworld.com
I: www.westaway.net

Bedrooms: 3 double/twin, 3 triple/multiple
Bathrooms: 6 en suite

Evening meal available
CC: Amex, Delta, Mastercard, Switch, Visa

B&B per night:
S £25.00–£37.50
D £50.00–£60.00

HB per person:
DY £37.50–£42.50

OPEN All Year except Christmas

Large detached residence. Car park, bar, dining room, 2 lounges, sun terrace. Five minutes' walk to town centre, seafront and entertainments.

ILLOGAN, Cornwall Map ref 1B3

AVIARY COURT HOTEL

Marys Well, Illogan, Redruth TR16 4QZ
T: (01209) 842256
F: (01209) 843744
E: aviarycourt@connexions.co.uk
I: www.connexions.co.uk/aviarycourt/index.htm

B&B per night:
S £45.00–£47.50
D £65.00–£68.00

HB per person:
DY £47.50–£49.00

OPEN All Year

Charming country house in 2 acres of secluded, well-kept gardens with tennis court. Family-run, personal service, good food. Superior en suite bedrooms with TV, telephone, tea/coffee, fresh fruit. Ideal touring location (coast 5 minutes). St Ives, Tate, Heligan, Eden Project all within easy reach.

Bedrooms: 5 double/twin, 1 triple/multiple
Bathrooms: 6 en suite

Evening meal available
CC: Delta, Mastercard, Switch, Visa

ISLES OF SCILLY Map ref 1A3 *Tourist Information Centre Tel: (01720) 422536*

NUNDEEPS

Rams Valley, St Mary's TR21 0JX
T: (01720) 422517
E: cook@nundeeps.freeserve.co.uk

Bedrooms: 3 double/twin
Bathrooms: 2 en suite, 1 private

B&B per night:
D £56.00–£62.00

OPEN All Year

Situated in a quiet cul-de-sac within easy reach of the town centre and quay, for any boating excursions to the off islands.

USE YOUR *i*s

There are more than 550 Tourist Information Centres throughout England offering friendly help with accommodation and holiday ideas as well as suggestions of places to visit and things to do. You'll find TIC addresses in the local Phone Book.

IVYBRIDGE, Devon Map ref 1C2 *Tourist Information Centre Tel: (01752) 897035*

♦♦♦♦ Silver Award

HILLHEAD FARM

Ugborough, Ivybridge PL21 0HQ
T: (01752) 892674 & 07785 915612
F: (01752) 690111
E: johnshillhead@aol.com
I: www.hillhead-farm.co.uk

Antique furniture and light, sunny rooms combine to create a welcoming atmosphere in this peaceful, friendly farmhouse with lovely views over rolling Devon countryside. Turn off A38 at Wrangaton, turn left, take third right, continue over next crossroads, after 0.75 miles, turn left at Hillheadcross, entrance 75 yards on left.

Bedrooms: 3 double/twin
Bathrooms: 2 en suite, 1 private

Evening meal available

B&B per night:
S £22.00–£24.00
D £44.00–£48.00

HB per person:
DY £33.00–£35.00

OPEN All Year except Christmas

♦♦♦

VENN FARM
Ugborough, Ivybridge PL21 0PE
T: (01364) 73240
F: (01364) 73240
I: www.SmoothHound.co.uk/hotels/vennfarm

Bedrooms: 3 triple/multiple
Bathrooms: 3 en suite

Evening meal available

Only 3 miles from A38. Large, private gardens, streams, lake, wildlife ponds, gypsy caravan, woodland glade, unlimited parking. You will want to return!

B&B per night:
S £24.00–£26.00
D £46.00–£50.00

HB per person:
DY £36.00–£40.00

OPEN All Year

KENTON, Devon Map ref 1D2

♦♦♦

DEVON ARMS
Fore Street, Kenton, Exeter EX6 8LD
T: (01626) 890213
F: (01626) 891678
E: devon.arms@ukgateway.net

Bedrooms: 2 double/twin, 4 triple/multiple
Bathrooms: 6 en suite

Lunch available
Evening meal available
CC: Delta, Mastercard, Switch, Visa

Family-run inn on A379 between Exeter and Dawlish. Adjacent to Powderham Castle. Close to beach. Good base to explore Devon countryside. All rooms en suite.

B&B per night:
D £45.00–£55.00

OPEN All Year except Christmas

KINGSBRIDGE, Devon Map ref 1C3 *Tourist Information Centre Tel: (01548) 853195*

♦♦♦♦

ASHLEIGH HOUSE
Ashleigh Road, Kingsbridge TQ7 1HB
T: (01548) 852893 & 07967 737875
E: reception@ashleigh-house.co.uk
I: www.ashleigh-house.co.uk

Bedrooms: 6 double/twin, 2 triple/multiple
Bathrooms: 8 en suite

Evening meal available
CC: Delta, Mastercard, Switch, Visa

Comfortable, informal, licensed Victorian guesthouse. Edge of town, easy walk. All rooms en suite, colour TV and beverage tray. Sun lounge, bar. Off-road parking.

B&B per night:
S £27.00–£31.00
D £44.00–£52.00

HB per person:
DY £34.00–£40.00

TOWN INDEX

This can be found at the back of the guide. If you know where you want to stay, the index will give you the page number listing accommodation in your chosen town, city or village.

KINGSBRIDGE continued

Silver Award

SOUTH ALLINGTON HOUSE

Chivelstone, Kingsbridge TQ7 2NB
T: (01548) 511272
F: (01548) 511421
E: barbara@sthallingtonbnb.demon.co.uk
I: www.sthallingtonbnb.demon.co.uk

Georgian country house in 4 acres of beautiful grounds, also 140 acres of mixed farm. Abundance of birds, wonderful coastline. Ideal for walking the coastal path. Between Start Point and Prawle Point. If you want peace and quiet, this is just the place for you. Croquet, coarse fishing and tennis court.

Bedrooms: 1 single, 7 double/twin, 1 triple/multiple
Bathrooms: 7 en suite, 2 private

10% reduction for 3-night mid-week bookings May and Jun (excl Bank Holidays). Also Oct-Easter (excl Christmas).

B&B per night:
S £25.50–£26.50
D £50.00–£71.00

OPEN All Year except Christmas

LANGPORT, Somerset Map ref 1D1

THE OLD POUND INN

Aller, Langport TA10 0RA
T: (01458) 250469
F: (01458) 250469

Built in 1571 and upgraded to modern standards with en suite bedrooms, 50-seat dining room and function room for 200. Log fires. Bar meals from £1.95. Ideal for country lovers, walking, fishing, bird-watching. 'Best Pub of the Year' 1999 and 2000.

Bedrooms: 1 single, 4 double/twin, 1 triple/multiple
Bathrooms: 6 en suite

Lunch available
Evening meal available
CC: Amex, Delta, Mastercard, Switch, Visa

B&B per night:
S £35.00
D £55.00

OPEN All Year except Christmas

LANIVET, Cornwall Map ref 1B2

TREMEERE MANOR

Lanivet, Bodmin PL30 5BG
T: (01208) 831513
F: (01208) 832417
E: oliver@tremeeremanor@fwi.co.uk

Bedrooms: 3 double/twin
Bathrooms: 2 en suite, 1 private

A 17thC Listed manor house in pleasant surroundings on working farm, 0.25 miles from Lanivet village. Easy access to coast and moors.

B&B per night:
S £22.00–£26.00
D £36.00–£48.00

OPEN All Year except Christmas

LAUNCESTON, Cornwall Map ref 1C2 *Tourist Information Centre Tel: (01566) 772321/772333*

HILL PARK

St Thomas, Launceston PL15 8SH
T: (01566) 86937
E: barbara_penfold@hotmail.com

Bedrooms: 2 double/twin; permanent suite(s)
Bathrooms: 2 en suite

Evening meal available
CC: Delta, Mastercard, Switch, Visa

Beautiful private rooms with en suite facilities in country lane setting. Peaceful and secluded, but central for walking, beaches and major towns. Open all year.

B&B per night:
S Min £25.00
D £40.00–£50.00

OPEN All Year except Christmas

LAUNCESTON continued

MIDDLE TREMOLLETT FARM

Coad's Green, Launceston PL15 7NA
T: (01566) 782416 & 07974 682603
F: (01566) 782416
E: btrewin@talk21.com
I: www.tremollett.com

19thC Victorian country house set in the heart of Cornwall, where you will find peace and tranquillity and enjoy panoramic views of the open countryside, yet not too far from north/south coasts, Dartmoor, Eden Project, National Trust properties, famous St Mellion golf course and Jamaica Inn.

Bedrooms: 3 double/twin
Bathrooms: 2 en suite, 1 private

Evening meal available
CC: Delta, Mastercard, Switch, Visa

4 nights' B&B for the price of 3, Oct-Mar.

B&B per night:
S £21.00–£24.00
D £40.00–£50.00

HB per person:
DY £28.50–£34.00

OPEN All Year except Christmas

♦♦♦♦

THE OLD GRANARY

North Petherwin, Launceston PL15 8LR
T: (01566) 785593

Bedrooms: 2 double/twin

Evening meal available

Delightfully converted granary set in tranquil garden, in village location, offering comfortable rooms. Well situated for exploring north and south coasts and the many attractions in between.

B&B per night:
S Min £24.50
D £42.00–£45.00

OPEN All Year except Christmas

LEWDOWN, Devon Map ref 1C2

♦♦

STOWFORD GRANGE FARM

Lewdown, Okehampton EX20 4BZ
T: (01566) 783298

Bedrooms: 2 double/twin, 1 triple/multiple

Lunch available
Evening meal available

220-acre mixed farm. Listed building in quiet village. Home-cooked food, fresh vegetables, poultry. Ten miles from Okehampton, 7 miles Launceston. Half a mile from old A30, turn right at Royal Exchange.

B&B per night:
S £16.50–£18.00
D £32.00–£35.00

LISKEARD, Cornwall Map ref 1C2

♦♦♦

HYVUE HOUSE

Barras Cross, Liskeard PL14 6BN
T: (01579) 348175

Bedrooms: 3 double/twin
Bathrooms: 2 en suite, 1 private

Family-run, exclusively for non-smokers, outskirts of town overlooking Bodmin Moor. Providing excellent food and comfort. En suite rooms with tea/coffee and TV. Car park.

B&B per night:
S £25.00–£35.00
D £40.00–£45.00

OPEN All Year

♦♦♦♦

TRECORME BARTON

Quethiock, Liskeard PL14 3SH
T: (01579) 342646
F: (01579) 342646
E: RENFREE@trecormebarton.fsnet.co.uk

Bedrooms: 2 double/twin; permanent suite(s)
Bathrooms: 2 en suite

Comfortable, stone-built farmhouse with wonderful views, in rolling countryside. En suite rooms. Near south coast and moors. Close to Eden. Families most welcome.

B&B per night:
S £30.00–£35.00
D £46.00–£50.00

Silver Award

TREGONDALE FARM

Menheniot, Liskeard PL14 3RG
T: (01579) 342407
F: (01579) 342407
E: tregondale@connectfree.co.uk
I: www.tregondalefarm.co.uk

Bedrooms: 3 double/twin
Bathrooms: 2 en suite, 1 private

Evening meal available
CC: Delta, Diners, Mastercard, Switch, Visa

Superior en suite character farmhouse in beautiful countryside. Local home-produced specialities. Log fires. Tennis court, woodland farm trail. North east of Menheniot between A38/A390.

B&B per night:
S £30.00–£35.00
D £50.00–£60.00

HB per person:
DY Min £40.00

LOOE, Cornwall Map ref 1C3

♦♦♦♦

BARCLAY HOUSE

St Martins Road, Looe PL13 1LP
T: (01503) 262929
F: (01503) 262632
E: info@barclayhouse.co.uk
I: www.barclayhouse.co.uk

B&B per night:
S £45.00–£75.00
D £75.00–£120.00

HB per person:
DY £66.00–£81.00

OPEN All Year

Spacious, relaxing Victorian family villa in terraced grounds giving spectacular views overlooking the Looe River valley and countryside beyond. Each room has its own special charm. Only five minutes' walk to harbour, town and beaches. Private car parking. Heated swimming pool is a suntrap. Wind down to a friendly, unhurried Cornish welcome.

Bedrooms: 2 single, 8 double/twin, 1 triple/multiple; permanent suite(s)
Bathrooms: 11 en suite

Evening meal available
CC: Amex, Delta, Mastercard, Switch, Visa

8 P

♦♦♦♦
Silver Award

BUCKLAWREN FARM

St Martin-by-Looe, Looe PL13 1NZ
T: (01503) 240738
F: (01503) 240481
E: bucklawren@compuserve.com
I: www.bucklawren.co.uk

B&B per night:
S £25.00–£35.00
D £46.00–£50.00

HB per person:
DY £37.00–£40.00

Delightful farmhouse set in glorious countryside with spectacular sea views. Quiet location, situated 1 mile from the beach and 3 miles from the fishing village of Looe. An award-winning farm with all bedrooms en suite. Enjoy dinner in our candle lit restaurant.

Bedrooms: 4 double/twin, 2 triple/multiple
Bathrooms: 6 en suite

Evening meal available
CC: Mastercard, Visa

5 P

♦♦♦

DOWN ENDE COUNTRY HOUSE

Widegates, Looe PL13 1QN
T: (01503) 240213
F: (01503) 240656
E: enquiries@downende.com
I: www.downende.com

Bedrooms: 4 double/twin, 1 triple/multiple; permanent suite(s)
Bathrooms: 5 en suite

CC: Delta, Mastercard, Switch, Visa

B&B per night:
S £30.00–£35.00
D £48.00–£60.00

OPEN All Year

A family-run business specialising in friendly and comfortable accommodation. Minutes from Looe and Polperro, and 30 minutes' drive to Eden Project and Helligan. Large car park.

P

CHECK THE MAPS

The colour maps at the front of this guide show all the cities, towns and villages for which you will find accommodation entries. Refer to the town index to find the page on which they are listed.

LOOE continued

LITTLE LARNICK FARM

Pelynt, Looe PL13 2NB
T: (01503) 262837
F: (01503) 262837
E: littlelarnick@btclick.com

B&B per night:
D £40.00–£50.00

OPEN All Year except Christmas

200-acre dairy farm situated in the beautiful West Looe River valley. The farmhouse and newly converted barn offer peaceful and relaxing character en suite accommodation, including a barn suite and ground floor bedroom. Wonderful walks from the door. Drying room available. Special 'Winter Warmer' breaks.

Bedrooms: 5 double/twin, 1 triple/multiple
Bathrooms: 6 en suite

CC: Amex, Delta, Diners, Mastercard, Switch, Visa

'Winter Warmer' breaks Nov-Mar.

3 P

♦♦♦♦

THE PANORAMA HOTEL

Hannafore Road, Looe PL13 2DE
T: (01503) 262123
F: (01503) 265654
E: stay@looe.co.uk
I: www.looe.co.uk

Bedrooms: 2 single, 3 double/twin, 4 triple/multiple
Bathrooms: 9 en suite

Evening meal available
CC: Delta, Mastercard, Switch, Visa

B&B per night:
S £24.50–£38.50
D £46.00–£77.00

HB per person:
DY £39.00–£53.00

OPEN All Year

Family-run hotel, good food, friendly atmosphere. Magnificent setting overlooking harbour, beach and miles of beautiful coastline.

5 P

Silver Award

TALEHAY

Tremaine, Pelynt, Looe PL13 2LT
T: (01503) 220252
F: (01503) 220252
E: paul@talehay.co.uk
I: www.talehay.co.uk

B&B per night:
S £35.00–£38.00
D £50.00–£56.00

OPEN All Year except Christmas

Quality, en suite B&B on 17thC, non-working farmstead. Provides a high standard of accommodation and delicious breakfasts making use of local produce, the farm's free-range eggs and homemade marmalade. An idael base for exploring the many attractions of Cornwall. Eden Project 20 minutes.

Bedrooms: 2 double/twin
Bathrooms: 2 en suite

CC: Amex, Delta, Diners, Mastercard, Switch, Visa

3 nights for price of 2 Nov-Mar (excl Christmas and New Year).

P

LYME REGIS, Dorset Map ref 1D2 *Tourist Information Centre Tel: (01297) 442138*

CHARNWOOD GUEST HOUSE

21 Woodmead Road, Lyme Regis DT7 3AD
T: (01297) 445281
E: charnwood@lymeregis62.freeserve.co.uk
I: www.lymeregisaccommodation.com

B&B per night:
S £22.00–£26.00
D £44.00–£52.00

OPEN All Year except Christmas

Quaint Edwardian guesthouse in quiet area, 5-10 minutes' walk from main shops/restaurants and the sea. Off-road car parking. Sea views from 3 rooms. We serve an English, vegetarian, or fruit and yoghurt breakfast and can cater for most special requirements. Visit fossil walk or beach – enjoy!

Bedrooms: 1 single, 5 double/twin, 1 triple/multiple
Bathrooms: 7 en suite

CC: Delta, Mastercard, Switch, Visa

Sun to Thu: 5% discount on 3/4 nights, 10% discount on 5 nights. 10% discount on 7 nights or more.

5 P

LYME REGIS continued

♦♦♦

LUCERNE

View Road, Lyme Regis DT7 3AA
T: (01297) 443752
E: lucerne@lineone.net

Bedrooms: 1 single, 4 double/twin
Bathrooms: 4 en suite, 1 private

Private house in quiet residential area. Excellent sea and coastal views. Comfortably furnished, non-smoking. All rooms en suite or private with colour TV, tea/coffee.

B&B per night:
S £23.00–£27.00
D £40.00–£48.00

OPEN All Year except Christmas

♦♦♦♦

OCEAN VIEW

2 Hadleigh Villas, Silver Street, Lyme Regis DT7 3HR
T: (01297) 442567
E: jaybabe@supanet.com
I: www.lymeregis.com/oceanview

Bedrooms: 3 double/twin; permanent suite(s)
Bathrooms: 3 en suite

Edwardian house 200 yards from main street, 3 letting rooms, all en suite, 'home from home' comforts, in a family home. On Dorset's Jurassic coast.

B&B per night:
S Max £36.00
D £48.00–£52.00

OPEN All Year except Christmas

♦♦♦♦

SOUTHERNHAYE

Pound Road, Lyme Regis DT7 3HX
T: (01297) 443077
F: (01297) 443077

Bedrooms: 1 single, 2 double/twin

Distinctive Edwardian house in quiet location with panoramic views over Lyme Bay, about 10 minutes' walk from town and beach. Off-road parking.

B&B per night:
S £21.00–£23.00
D £40.00–£42.00

OPEN All Year except Christmas

♦♦♦

SPRINGFIELD

Woodmead Road, Lyme Regis DT7 3LJ
T: (01297) 443409
F: (01297) 443685
E: springfield@lymeregis.com
I: www.lymeregis.com/springfield

Elegant Georgian house in partly walled garden with conservatory. Well-proportioned rooms, all with far-reaching views over the sea and Dorset coastline. A short walk to the shops and seafront. Close to major footpaths. Concession at local golf course.

Bedrooms: 3 double/twin, 2 triple/multiple
Bathrooms: 4 en suite, 1 private

B&B per night:
D £44.00–£50.00

LYNMOUTH, Devon Map ref 1C1

TREGONWELL THE OLDE SEA-CAPTAINS HOUSE

1 Tors Road, Lynmouth EX35 6ET
T: (01598) 753369
I: www.smoothhound.co.uk/hotels/tregonwl.html

Truly paradise? Romantic, elegant, award-winning, former sea captain's riverside home. Snuggled amidst waterfalls, cascades, wooded valleys, soaring clifftops, rugged beaches. Enchanting harbourside old world smugglers' village ("England's Switzerland"). Devonshire cream teas served in our pretty garden. Beautiful bedrooms, blazing log fires (in cooler seasons), dramatic views. Garaged parking.

Bedrooms: 5 double/twin
Bathrooms: 3 en suite, 2 private

Lunch available

B&B per night:
S £25.00–£35.00
D £50.00–£60.00

OPEN All Year except Christmas

LYNTON, Devon Map ref 1C1 *Tourist Information Centre Tel: (0845) 6603232*

♦♦♦

Homely, friendly guesthouse with spacious rooms, some having en suite facilities. Optional home-cooked evening meals and licensed for diners. The Denes has ample parking and offers baby-sitting by arrangement. Situated at the entrance to the Valley of Rocks, it makes an ideal spot for walking, bird-watching and exploring Exmoor.

THE DENES GUEST HOUSE

15 Longmead, Lynton EX35 6DQ
T: (01598) 753573
F: (01598) 753573
E: j.e.mcgowan@btinternet.com
I: www.thedenes.com

Bedrooms: 2 double/twin, 3 triple/multiple
Bathrooms: 3 en suite

Lunch available
Evening meal available
CC: Delta, Mastercard, Switch, Visa

Beaujolais Nouveau weekend. Christmas and New Year specials. Gift vouchers. 3-night DB&B.

B&B per night:
S £16.50–£24.00
D £33.00–£48.00

HB per person:
DY £29.00–£36.50

OPEN All Year

♦♦♦♦

Ray and Kate run a small and friendly guest house within easy stroll of restaurants and shops yet a short walk to coastal paths, cliff-top views, Lynmouth and Exmoor. Full English breakfast freshly cooked with plenty of choice. All rooms en suite, centrally heated and we have our own car park.

10

FERNLEIGH GUEST HOUSE

Park Street, Lynton EX35 6BY
T: (01598) 753575
F: (01598) 753575
E: bookings@fernleigh.net
I: www.fernleigh.net

Bedrooms: 3 double/twin, 2 triple/multiple
Bathrooms: 5 en suite

CC: Amex, Delta, Mastercard, Switch, Visa

B&B per night:
S £25.00
D £36.00–£50.00

OPEN All Year except Christmas

Delightful Victorian house enjoying sunny position. Walk from the door to the Valley of the Rocks or the famous Cliff Railway. Enjoy traditional home cooking using fresh, local and organic produce whenever possible. All rooms en suite. Comfortable lounge. Licensed. Private parking. A warm welcome awaits.

LEE HOUSE

27 Lee Road, Lynton EX35 6BP
T: (01598) 752364
F: (01598) 752364
E: leehouse@freeuk.com
I: www.smoothhound.co.uk/hotels/lee.html

Bedrooms: 7 double/twin, 1 triple/multiple
Bathrooms: 8 en suite

Evening meal available
CC: Delta, Mastercard, Switch, Visa

B&B per night:
D £42.00–£56.00

HB per person:
DY £35.00–£42.00

OPEN All Year except Christmas

CREDIT CARD BOOKINGS If you book by telephone and are asked for your credit card number it is advisable to check the proprietor's policy should you cancel your reservation.

LYNTON continued

♦♦♦♦ Silver Award

LONGMEAD HOUSE HOTEL

9 Longmead, Lynton EX35 6DQ
T: (01598) 752523
F: (01598) 752523
E: info@longmeadhouse.co.uk
I: www.longmeadhouse.co.uk

Bedrooms: 6 double/twin, 1 triple/multiple
Bathrooms: 6 en suite, 1 private

Evening meal available
CC: Delta, Diners, Mastercard, Switch, Visa

B&B per night:
S £25.00–£30.00
D £40.00–£50.00

HB per person:
DY £30.00–£60.00

One of Lynton's best-kept secrets! Delightful house and gardens quietly situated towards the Valley of the Rocks. Comfortable, relaxed atmosphere with excellent hospitality and cooking.

P

VICTORIA FERNERY

Lydiate Lane, Lynton EX35 6AJ
T: (01598) 752440
F: (01598) 752396
E: info@thefernery.co.uk
I: www.thefernery.co.uk

B&B per night:
S £24.00–£26.00
D £38.00–£42.00

OPEN All Year

Set in the old village, this unique house is steeped in history. Beautiful decor, spacious and comfortable. Delightful walled garden, complete with fernery. Delicious food, friendly and informal atmosphere. Refresh youself with spectacular scenery and miles of unspoilt coastal, moor and tumbling river walks. A very warm welcome awaits you.

Bedrooms: 3 double/twin
Bathrooms: 1 en suite, 2 private

Evening meal available

Special breaks are available (excl Christmas and New Year). Please contact us for details.

12

MALMESBURY, Wiltshire Map ref 2B2 *Tourist Information Centre Tel: (01666) 823748*

♦♦♦

MARSH FARMHOUSE

Crudwell Road, Malmesbury
SN16 9JL
T: (01666) 822208

Bedrooms: 1 single, 7 double/twin
Bathrooms: 8 en suite

B&B per night:
S £25.00–£30.00
D £40.00–£45.00

OPEN All Year

A pleasant farmhouse with en suite rooms. Situated outside England's oldest borough and within reach of M4 and M5 motorways.

P

MARLBOROUGH, Wiltshire Map ref 2B2 *Tourist Information Centre Tel: (01672) 513989*

WESTCOURT BOTTOM

165 Westcourt, Burbage, Marlborough
SN8 3BW
T: (01672) 810924 & 811723
F: (01672) 810924
E: westcourt.b-and-b@virgin.net
I: www.westcourtbottom.co.uk

B&B per night:
S £30.00–£33.00
D £50.00–£56.00

HB per person:
DY £48.00–£51.00

OPEN All Year except Christmas

Large 17thC thatched cottage 5 miles south of Marlborough. The half-timbered bedrooms, sitting room with TV and large garden with swimming pool offer a quiet, relaxed and informal atmosphere. Good local pubs. Ideal base for Ridgeway and Savernake Forest walks, Marlborough, Avebury and Stonehenge. Wonderful free-range breakfasts! Ample parking. Children negotiable.

Bedrooms: 3 double/twin
Bathrooms: 1 en suite, 1 private

Evening meal available

P

RATING All accommodation in this guide has been rated, or is awaiting a rating, by a trained English Tourism Council assessor.

MEVAGISSEY, Cornwall Map ref 1B3

◆◆◆

THE RISING SUN INN

Portmellon Cove, Mevagissey, St Austell PL26 6PL
T: (01726) 843235
F: (01726) 843235
E: cliffnsheila@tiscali.co.uk
I: www.risingsunportmellon.co.uk

B&B per night:
S £42.50–£45.00
D £65.00–£70.00

Beautiful 17thC waterside inn nestled beside a quiet, picturesque cove. Renowned restaurant serving fresh local seafood, Cornish steaks and vegetarian options. Extensive ale and wine selection. Only teenagers and above in restaurant after 6pm. Car park. Ideal for Heligan and Eden Project. Once found, 'keep the secret'!

Bedrooms: 4 double/twin, 3 triple/multiple
Bathrooms: 7 en suite

Lunch available
Evening meal available
CC: Amex, Delta, Diners, Mastercard, Switch, Visa

P

◆◆◆

SEAPOINT HOUSE HOTEL

Battery Terrace, Mevagissey, St Austell PL26 6QS
T: (01726) 842684 & 844627
F: (01726) 842266
E: mevatele@compuserve.com

Bedrooms: 10 double/twin, 2 triple/multiple
Bathrooms: 12 en suite

Lunch available
Evening meal available
CC: Amex, Delta, Mastercard, Switch, Visa

B&B per night:
S £39.00–£58.00
D £60.00–£90.00

HB per person:
DY £52.00–£67.00

OPEN All Year

The only hotel in Mevagissey overlooking both the harbour and bay. Quiet cul-de-sac location. Direct access to Coastal Path. Three minute walk to village. Close to Heligan Gardens and Eden Project.

P

MINEHEAD, Somerset Map ref 1D1 *Tourist Information Centre Tel: (01643) 702624*

◆◆◆◆

DUNKERY LODGE

Townsend Road, Minehead TA24 5RQ
T: (01643) 706170
F: 0870 902 9111
E: book@dunkery-lodge.co.uk
I: www.dunkery-lodge.co.uk

B&B per night:
S £25.00–£28.00
D £44.00–£50.00

HB per person:
DY £32.00–£37.50

OPEN All Year except Christmas

Handsome Edwardian country gentleman's home in secluded grounds close to Minehead centre. Outdoor heated pool. Spacious en suite rooms with all amenities including refrigerator. Separate guest dining room and lounge with log fires. Candlelit dining. Residential licence. Non-smoking. Plenty of private car-parking space. Many original features.

Bedrooms: 3 double/twin; permanent suite(s)
Bathrooms: 3 en suite

Evening meal available
CC: Amex, Mastercard, Switch, Visa

Exmoor Coast and Country Breaks (3 nights): discount on accommodation and evening meals.

12 P

◆◆◆◆

GASCONY HOTEL

The Avenue, Minehead TA24 5BB
T: (01643) 705939
F: (01643) 709926

Bedrooms: 3 single, 6 double/twin, 4 triple/multiple
Bathrooms: 13 en suite

Evening meal available
CC: Delta, Mastercard, Switch, Visa

B&B per night:
S £28.50–£30.50
D £52.00–£55.00

HB per person:
DY £37.00–£39.00

Comfortable and well-appointed Victorian house hotel. Ideally positioned on the level, close to seafront. Home cooking. Large secure car park. Short breaks avaliable.

P

ACCESSIBILITY

Look for the symbols which indicate National Accessible Scheme standards for hearing and visually impaired guests in addition to standards for guests with mobility impairment. Additional participants are shown in the listings at the back.

MONTACUTE, Somerset Map ref 2A3

◆◆◆

MAD HATTERS TEAROOMS

1 South Street, Montacute
TA15 6XD
T: (01935) 823024
E: montacutemuseum@aol.com
I: www.montacutemuseum.com

Bedrooms: 1 single, 2 double/twin
Bathrooms: 2 en suite, 1 private

Lunch available

B&B per night:
S £30.00–£35.00
D £50.00–£55.00

OPEN All Year

Listed Georgian property in the centre of picturesque village. Pubs and restaurants close by. On the Leland trail and South Somerset cycle route. Lovely walks.

MORETONHAMPSTEAD, Devon Map ref 1C2

◆◆◆◆

GREAT DOCCOMBE FARM

Doccombe, Moretonhampstead,
Newton Abbot TQ13 8SS
T: (01647) 440694
E: david.oakey3@btopenworld.com
I: www.greatdoccombefarm.co.uk

Bedrooms: 1 double/twin, 1 triple/multiple
Bathrooms: 2 en suite

B&B per night:
D £40.00–£44.00

OPEN All Year except Christmas

In pretty Dartmoor hamlet, 300-year-old farmhouse in Dartmoor National Park. En suite rooms, farmhouse cooking. Ideal for exploring Dartmoor's delights.

P

◆◆◆◆
Silver Award

GREAT SLONCOMBE FARM

Moretonhampstead, Newton Abbot
TQ13 8QF
T: (01647) 440595
F: (01647) 440595
E: hmerchant@sloncombe.freeserve.co.uk
I: www.greatsloncombefarm.co.uk

Bedrooms: 3 double/twin
Bathrooms: 3 en suite

Evening meal available

B&B per night:
D £24.00–£26.00

HB per person:
DY £38.00–£40.00

OPEN All Year

13thC farmhouse in a magical Dartmoor valley. Meadows, woodland, wild flowers, animals. Farmhouse breakfast with freshly baked bread. Everything provided for an enjoyable break.

8 P

◆◆◆◆

GREAT WOOSTON FARM BED & BREAKFAST

Moretonhampstead, Newton Abbot
TQ13 8QA
T: (01647) 440367 & 07798 670590
F: (01647) 440367
E: info@greatwoostonfarm.com
I: www.greatwoostonfarm.com

Bedrooms: 3 double/twin
Bathrooms: 2 en suite, 1 private

CC: Mastercard, Switch, Visa

B&B per night:
S £23.00–£25.00
D £42.00–£50.00

OPEN All Year except Christmas

Great Wooston is a peaceful haven with views across the moor and walks nearby. Two rooms en suite, one with 4-poster. Excellent breakfast. Quality accommodation.

8 P

MORWENSTOW, Cornwall Map ref 1C2

◆◆◆

CORNAKEY FARM

Morwenstow, Bude EX23 9SS
T: (01288) 331260

Bedrooms: 3 double/twin
Bathrooms: 1 en suite

Evening meal available

B&B per night:
S £20.00–£21.00
D £40.00–£42.00

HB per person:
DY £30.00–£32.00

220-acre mixed farm. Convenient coastal walking area with extensive views of sea and cliffs from bedrooms. Home cooking. Reduced rates for children. Good touring centre.

P

COUNTRY CODE Always follow the Country Code Enjoy the countryside and respect its life and work Guard against all risk of fire Fasten all gates Keep your dogs under close control Keep to public paths across farmland Use gates and stiles to cross fences, hedges and walls Leave livestock, crops and machinery alone Take your litter home Help to keep all water clean Protect wildlife, plants and trees Take special care on country roads Make no unnecessary noise

MULLION, Cornwall Map ref 1B3

Silver Award

COBBLERS COTTAGE

Nantithet, Cury, Helston TR12 7RB
T: (01326) 241342
F: (01326) 241342

Picturesque 17thC rose-clad cottage located in centre of Lizard Peninsula. Former cobblers shop and Kiddlewink, set in an acre of beautiful gardens with meandering stream. Oak beams, all bedrooms en suite. Evening dinner optional. 2.5 miles from beaches, coastal walks and golf course. Highly recommended. No pets or children under 12 years.

Bedrooms: 3 double/twin
Bathrooms: 3 en suite

Evening meal available

B&B per night:
D £46.00–£50.00

HB per person:
DY £35.00–£37.00

OPEN All Year except Christmas

◆◆◆◆

TRENANCE FARMHOUSE

Mullion, Helston TR12 7HB
T: (01326) 240639
F: (01326) 240639
E: info@trenancefarmholidays.co.uk
I: www.trenancefarmholidays.co.uk

Bedrooms: 5 double/twin
Bathrooms: 5 en suite

CC: Mastercard, Visa

B&B per night:
S £21.50–£29.50
D £43.00–£49.00

Lovely Victorian farmhouse with mature gardens, situated between village and Mullion Cove. Footpath across fields to beautiful coastline. Summer pool. Breakfast in our garden room.

NETHER STOWEY, Somerset Map ref 1D1

Silver Award

CASTLE OF COMFORT COUNTRY HOUSE HOTEL & RESTAURANT

Dodington, Nether Stowey, Bridgwater TA5 1LE
T: (01278) 741264 & 07050 642002
F: (01278) 741144
E: reception@castle-of-comfort.co.uk
I: www.castle-of-comfort.co.uk

Bedrooms: 1 single, 4 double/twin, 1 triple/multiple
Bathrooms: 6 en suite

Lunch available
Evening meal available
CC: Delta, Mastercard, Switch, Visa

B&B per night:
S £35.00–£75.00
D £85.00–£118.00

HB per person:
DY £61.00–£86.00

OPEN All Year

16thC country-house hotel and restaurant nestling in the Quantock Hills with 4 acres of grounds. Luxuriously refurbished accommodation of the highest standard.

◆◆

ROSE AND CROWN

St Mary Street, Nether Stowey, Bridgwater TA5 1LJ
T: (01278) 732265
E: rose_crown@netherstowey.freeserve.co.uk

Bedrooms: 3 double/twin, 1 triple/multiple
Bathrooms: 2 en suite

Lunch available
Evening meal available

B&B per night:
S £20.00–£25.00
D £30.00–£35.00

HB per person:
DY £39.00–£55.00

OPEN All Year

A coaching inn written about by John Taylor (the Water Poet) in 1649 when it was old and dirty. Now even older but a lot cleaner!

NEWQUAY, Cornwall Map ref 1B2 *Tourist Information Centre Tel: (01637) 854020*

ALOHA

122 Henver Road, Newquay TR7 3EQ
T: (01637) 878366
E: Alohanewqu@aol.com
I: www.alohanewquay.net

Bedrooms: 1 single, 4 double/twin, 2 triple/multiple
Bathrooms: 6 en suite

CC: Amex, Delta, Diners, Mastercard, Switch, Visa

B&B per night:
S £16.00–£25.00
D £38.00–£50.00

OPEN All Year except Christmas

Friendly and cosy with en suite rooms and home comforts. Well situated for beaches and touring Cornwall. Garden overlooking Trencreek Valley. Ample parking. Close to centre.

NEWQUAY continued

◆

CHICHESTER
14 Bay View Terrace, Newquay TR7 2LR
T: (01637) 874216
F: (01637) 874216
E: sheila.harper@virgin.net
I: http://freespace.virgin.net/sheila.harper

Bedrooms: 2 single, 4 double/twin, 1 triple/multiple
Bathrooms: 5 en suite

Evening meal available

Comfortable, licensed establishment convenient for shops, beaches and gardens. Showers in most bedrooms, many extras. Walking, mineral collecting, archaeology and Cornish heritage holidays in spring and autumn.

B&B per night:
S £16.50
D £33.00

HB per person:
DY £23.00

OPEN All Year except Christmas

◆◆◆◆
Silver Award

THE HARBOUR HOTEL

North Quay Hill, Newquay TR7 1HF
T: (01637) 873040
E: alan@harbourhotel.co.uk
I: www.harbourhotel.co.uk

An outstandingly well situated period building set on the cliff overlooking the picturesque harbour. All the elegant bedrooms are en suite and have balconies with uninterrupted sea views and antique furniture. Peaceful, yet only five minutes' walk to the town centre. This is an idyllic base to relax or explore Cornwall.

Bedrooms: 5 double/twin, 1 triple/multiple
Bathrooms: 6 en suite

Lunch available
Evening meal available
CC: Amex, Mastercard, Visa

B&B per night:
S £55.00–£80.00
D £80.00–£98.00

OPEN All Year except Christmas

NORTH CADBURY, Somerset Map ref 2B3

◆◆◆

THE CATASH INN
North Cadbury, Yeovil BA22 7DH
T: (01963) 440248
F: (01963) 440248
E: clive&sandra@catash.com
I: www.catash.com

Bedrooms: 2 double/twin, 1 triple/multiple
Bathrooms: 2 en suite

Lunch available
Evening meal available
CC: Delta, Mastercard, Switch, Visa

17thC inn with restaurant and large car park, in centre of North Cadbury a mile from A303. Close to Sparkford Motor Museum and Yeovilton Air Base.

B&B per night:
S £25.00–£30.00
D Min £50.00

OPEN All Year except Christmas

OKEHAMPTON, Devon Map ref 1C2

◆◆◆◆

HIGHER CADHAM FARM

Jacobstowe, Okehampton EX20 3RB
T: (01837) 851647
F: (01837) 851410
E: kingscadham@btopenworld.com
I: www.highercadham.co.uk

139-acre mixed farm. For a real Devonshire welcome come to our farm in the secluded Okement Valley near Dartmoor. Famous for our excellent farmhouse food. Plenty of interesting things to amuse the family including farm trail. Well worth the drive out.

Bedrooms: 2 single, 7 double/twin, 3 triple/multiple
Bathrooms: 8 en suite

Lunch available
Evening meal available
CC: Delta, Mastercard, Switch, Visa

B&B per night:
S £20.00–£25.00
D £40.00–£50.00

HB per person:
DY £32.50–£37.50

OPEN All Year except Christmas

OKEHAMPTON continued

Silver Award

THE KNOLE FARM

Bridestowe, Okehampton EX20 4HA
T: (01837) 861241
F: (01837) 861241
E: mavis.bickle@btconnect.com
I: www.knolefarm-dartmoor-holidays.co.uk

Guests return annually for the breathtaking views of Dartmoor, delicious food, a warm welcome and a real countryside holiday. Walking, castles, golfing and pony-trekking are all on the doorstep of this working family farm. En suite rooms (2 doubles, family/twin, 1 single). Closed Christmas and New Year.

Bedrooms: 1 double/twin, 2 triple/multiple
Bathrooms: 3 en suite

Evening meal available

B&B per night:
D £44.00–£46.00

HB per person:
DY £34.00–£36.00

PADSTOW, Cornwall Map ref 1B2 *Tourist Information Centre Tel: (01841) 533449*

TREVONE BAY HOTEL

Dobbin Close, Trevone, Padstow PL28 8QS
T: (01841) 520243
F: (01841) 521195
E: webb@trevonebay.demon.co.uk

Situated in the quiet village of Trevone, with panoramic sea views. Just a short walk from the beach and approximately 2 miles from Padstow. A quiet and tranquil place for you to relax and enjoy the fresh Cornish air, yet within easy reach of many of Cornwall's tourist attractions including the Eden Project.

Bedrooms: 3 single, 7 double/twin, 2 triple/multiple
Bathrooms: 12 en suite

Evening meal available
CC: Delta, Mastercard, Switch, Visa

B&B per night:
S £32.00–£38.00
D £60.00–£78.00

HB per person:
DY £44.95–£53.95

♦♦♦

TREVORRICK FARM
St Issey, Wadebridge PL27 7QH
T: (01841) 540574
F: (01841) 540574
E: info@trevorrick.co.uk
I: www.trevorrick.co.uk

Bedrooms: 3 double/twin
Bathrooms: 3 en suite

CC: Amex, Mastercard, Switch, Visa

Beautiful, peaceful location overlooking creek. Warm welcome and homemade cake. Pub/restaurant 0.5 miles. Ideal for walking/touring. Easy access Camel Trail. Heated indoor pool.

B&B per night:
S £34.00–£37.50
D £48.00–£55.00

OPEN All Year except Christmas

PAIGNTON, Devon Map ref 1D2 *Tourist Information Centre Tel: 0906 680 1268 (Premium rate number)*

♦♦♦

BENBOWS HOTEL
1 Alta Vista Road, Paignton TQ4 6DB
T: (01803) 558128
E: benbowshotel@aol.com
I: www.benbowshotel.co.uk

Bedrooms: 1 single, 7 double/twin, 2 triple/multiple
Bathrooms: 4 en suite

Evening meal available
CC: Amex, Delta, Mastercard, Switch, Visa

Small, friendly, licensed hotel 120 yards from harbour and sandy beaches. Good food, colour TVs, tea-making, en suites and car park. For brochure freephone 0800 0934071.

B&B per night:
S £16.00–£21.00
D £32.00–£42.00

HB per person:
DY £24.50–£29.50

OPEN All Year

QUALITY ASSURANCE SCHEME

Diamond ratings and awards were correct at the time of going to press but are subject to change. Please check at the time of booking.

PAIGNTON continued

DEVON HOUSE HOTEL

20 Garfield Road, Paignton TQ4 6AX
T: (01803) 559371
F: (01803) 550054
E: info@devonhousehotel.com
I: www.devonhousehotel.com

B&B per night:
S £15.00–£20.00
D £30.00–£44.00

HB per person:
DY £23.00–£28.00

OPEN All Year

A spacious hotel, non-smoking throughout. One hundred metres from sea front, opposite Victoria Park, a short walk to town and stations. Licensed bar and TV lounge. Family and en suite rooms avaliable. Tea/coffee facilities and central heating in all rooms. All in a relaxed atmosphere.

Bedrooms: 3 single, 4 double/twin, 3 triple/multiple
Bathrooms: 4 en suite

Evening meal available
CC: Amex, Delta, Mastercard, Switch, Visa

4 nights for the price of 3, B&B only, from Oct-Mar (excl Bank Holidays).

◆◆◆◆

WYNNCROFT HOTEL

2 Elmsleigh Park, Paignton TQ4 5AT
T: (01803) 525728
F: (01803) 526335
E: wynncrofthotel@aol.com
I: www.wynncroft.co.uk

B&B per night:
S £24.00–£28.00
D £48.00–£56.00

HB per person:
DY £36.00–£40.00

Comfort, service and a warm, friendly welcome in our family-run, licensed Victorian hotel. Short level walk from the beach or town. Free transport to coach and railway station. Large free car park. A la carte menu using fresh, local produce. A range of special diets including gluten free.

Bedrooms: 7 double/twin, 2 triple/multiple; permanent suite(s)
Bathrooms: 9 en suite

Lunch available
Evening meal available
CC: Amex, Delta, Mastercard, Switch, Visa

7 nights for the price of 6. 3-night B&B breaks: Jun & Sep £66pp (plus evening meal £99pp). Jul & Aug £76pp (plus evening meal £109pp).

PENSFORD, Bath and North East Somerset Map ref 2A2

◆◆◆

GREEN ACRES

Stanton Wick, Pensford BS39 4BX
T: (01761) 490397
F: (01761) 490397

Bedrooms: 2 single, 3 double/twin
Bathrooms: 1 en suite

Lunch available

B&B per night:
S £22.00–£27.00
D £44.00–£54.00

OPEN All Year

A friendly welcome awaits you in peaceful setting, off A37/A368. Relax and enjoy panoramic views across Chew Valley to Dundry Hills.

PENZANCE, Cornwall Map ref 1A3 *Tourist Information Centre Tel: (01736) 362207*

CARNSON HOUSE HOTEL

2 East Terrace, Penzance TR18 2TD
T: (01736) 365589
F: (01736) 365594
E: carnson@netcomuk.co.uk
I: www.chycor.co.uk/carnson-house

B&B per night:
S £18.50–£21.00
D £37.00–£48.00

OPEN All Year except Christmas

Comfortable, 18thC, granite-built private hotel with friendly atmosphere. Ideally located for rail and coach travellers. All year round we can provide you with a comprehensive tourist information service to give you every opportunity to make the most of your visit to Penzance and West Cornwall.

Bedrooms: 2 single, 5 double/twin
Bathrooms: 2 en suite, 2 private

Evening meal available
CC: Amex, Delta, Mastercard, Switch, Visa

PENZANCE continued

◆◆◆

ESTORIL HOTEL
46 Morrab Road, Penzance
TR18 4EX
T: (01736) 362468 & 367471
F: (01736) 367471
E: estorilhotel@aol.com
I: www.estorilhotel.co.uk

Bedrooms: 1 single, 6 double/twin, 2 triple/multiple
Bathrooms: 9 en suite

Evening meal available
CC: Mastercard, Visa

B&B per night:
S £24.00–£32.00
D £46.00–£64.00

OPEN All Year

Elegant Victorian house with the highest standards of cleanliness, providing comprehensive, smoke-free en suite accommodation and warm, efficient, personal service.

P

◆◆◆

LYNWOOD GUEST HOUSE

41 Morrab Road, Penzance TR18 4EX
T: (01736) 365871
F: (01736) 365871
E: lynwoodpz@aol.com
I: www.lynwood-guesthouse.co.uk

B&B per night:
S £13.50–£21.50
D £27.00–£43.00

OPEN All Year

Lynwood is a well-established, family-run guesthouse. Over the years we have gained an international reputation for a warm welcome, cleanliness and good food. We are located between town centre and promenade. Ideally situated for touring Land's End, Lizard peninsula and nearby St Michael's Mount as well as the Isles of Scilly.

Bedrooms: 2 single, 2 double/twin, 3 triple/multiple
Bathrooms: 4 en suite

CC: Amex, Delta, Diners, Mastercard, Switch, Visa

P

◆◆◆

MENWIDDEN FARM

Ludgvan, Penzance TR20 8BN
T: (01736) 740415

B&B per night:
S Min £18.00
D £36.00–£48.00

HB per person:
DY £25.00–£32.00

Small mixed farm, centrally situated in West Cornwall. Warm, family atmosphere with comfortable beds and good home cooking. Within easy reach of both coasts and Land's End. A warm welcome awaits you. Turn right at Crowlas crossroads on the A30 from Hayle, signposted Vellanoweth on right turn. Last farm on left.

Bedrooms: 1 single, 4 double/twin
Bathrooms: 1 en suite

Evening meal available

P

◆◆◆◆

ROSE FARM
Chyanhal, Buryas Bridge, Penzance
TR19 6AN
T: (01736) 731808
F: (01736) 731808
E: lally@rosefarm.co.uk
I: www.rosefarmcornwall.co.uk

Bedrooms: 2 double/twin, 1 triple/multiple
Bathrooms: 3 en suite

CC: Mastercard, Switch, Visa

B&B per night:
S £32.00–£35.00
D £44.00–£50.00

OPEN All Year except Christmas

25-acre farm with many animals including livestock and horses. Near beaches and shops. Land's End 7 miles, Mousehole 2 miles. Lovely walks. 4-poster bed available. Cosy and relaxing.

P

HALF BOARD PRICES Half board prices are given per person, but in some cases these may be based on double/twin occupancy.

PENZANCE continued

TREVENTON GUEST HOUSE

Alexandra Place, Penzance TR18 4NE
T: (01736) 363521
F: (01736) 361873
I: www.ukholidayaccommodation.com/treventonguesthouse

This elegant Victorian house is situated at the foot of a tree-lined avenue, 200 metres from the sea. Constructed of Cornish granite, it has a restful, spacious atmosphere. Art galleries, antique shops, excellent restaurants nearby. The romantic Lamorna Cove must be visited on one's way to Lands End.

Bedrooms: 1 single, 5 double/twin, 1 triple/multiple
Bathrooms: 4 en suite

B&B per night:
S £16.00–£20.00
D £32.00–£40.00

OPEN All Year except Christmas

WARWICK HOUSE HOTEL

17 Regent Terrace, Penzance TR18 4DW
T: (01736) 363881
F: (01736) 363881
E: jules@warwickhouse.fsworld.co.uk

A warm welcome awaits you in our comfortable Regency house overlooking Mounts Bay. Our pretty bedrooms have stunning sea views. In summer guests can relax on the flower-filled patios. We are an ideal base for exploring the beaches and quaint villages of West Cornwall. Private car parking.

Bedrooms: 3 single, 4 double/twin, 1 triple/multiple
Bathrooms: 5 en suite

CC: Delta, Mastercard, Switch, Visa

3 nights for the price of 2 breaks available low season.

B&B per night:
S £22.00–£26.00
D £45.00–£54.00

OPEN All Year

◆◆◆

WYMERING GUEST HOUSE

15 Regent Square, Penzance TR18 4BG
T: (01736) 362126
F: (01736) 362126
E: wymering@aol.com
I: http://members.aol.com/wymering

Bedrooms: 5 triple/multiple
Bathrooms: 2 en suite, 3 private

Small, select guesthouse situated in a peaceful Regency square, just off the beach. Town centre, promenade, bathing pool, bus, coach and train station all nearby.

B&B per night:
D £32.00–£50.00

OPEN All Year

PERRANPORTH, Cornwall Map ref 1B2

◆◆◆

PONSMERE HOTEL

Ponsmere Road, Perranporth TR6 0BW
T: (01872) 572225 & 572519
F: (01872) 573075
E: info@ponsmere.co.uk
I: www.ponsmere.co.uk

Bedrooms: 8 single, 17 double/twin, 47 triple/multiple
Bathrooms: 72 en suite

Evening meal available
CC: Amex, Delta, Mastercard, Switch, Visa

A seaside hotel on Perranporth's golden beach. Centrally situated and an ideal base for touring Cornwall. Full entertainment programme.

B&B per night:
S £25.00–£33.00
D £42.00–£58.00

HB per person:
DY £31.00–£41.00

GOLD & SILVER AWARDS

These exclusive ETC awards are given to establishments achieving the highest levels of quality and service. Further information can be found at the front of the guide and additional accommodation achieving these awards are shown in the listing at the back of this guide.

PIDDLETRENTHIDE, Dorset Map ref 2B3

♦♦♦♦

THE POACHERS INN

Piddletrenthide, Dorchester DT2 7QX
T: (01300) 348358
F: (01300) 348153
E: thepoachersinn@piddletrenthide.fsbusiness.co.uk
I: www.thepoachersinn.co.uk

Country inn, with riverside garden and swimming pool, within easy reach of all Dorset's attractions. All rooms en suite, restaurant where half board guests choose from our a la carte menu at no extra cost.

Bedrooms: 17 double/twin, 1 triple/multiple
Bathrooms: 18 en suite

Lunch available
Evening meal available
CC: Delta, Mastercard, Switch, Visa

Stay 2 nights (£90pp DB&B) and get third night free (DB&B) – Oct 2002-Apr 2003 (excl Bank Holidays).

B&B per night:
S £35.00
D £60.00

HB per person:
DY £45.00

OPEN All Year except Christmas

PILLATON, Cornwall Map ref 1C2

♦♦♦♦

THE WEARY FRIAR INN

Pillaton, Saltash PL12 6QS
T: (01579) 350238
F: (01579) 350238

Bedrooms: 2 single, 8 double/twin, 1 triple/multiple
Bathrooms: 11 en suite

Lunch available
Evening meal available
CC: Delta, Mastercard, Switch, Visa

Charming country inn noted for its quality food and interesting combination of modern comforts with 12thC character. Ideally placed for exploring inland and coastal areas.

10 P

B&B per night:
S £40.00–£45.00
D £50.00–£55.00

OPEN All Year

PLYMOUTH, Devon Map ref 1C2 *Tourist Information Centre Tel: (01752) 304849/227865*

♦♦♦♦♦
Silver Award

BOWLING GREEN HOTEL

9-10 Osborne Place, Lockyer Street, Plymouth PL1 2PU
T: (01752) 209090 & 667485
F: (01752) 209092
E: dave@bowlinggreenhotel.freeserve.co.uk
I: www.smoothhound.co.uk/hotels/bowling.html

Opposite Drake's bowling green, this elegant Victorian hotel has superbly appointed bedrooms offering all modern facilities. Our friendly and efficient staff will make your stay a memorable one. Centrally situated for the Barbican, Theatre Royal, leisure/conference centre, ferry port, National Marine Aquarium, with Dartmoor only a few minutes away.

Bedrooms: 1 single, 10 double/twin, 1 triple/multiple
Bathrooms: 12 en suite

CC: Amex, Delta, Diners, Mastercard, Switch, Visa

Special weekend breaks Nov-Mar inclusive. Prices on application.

B&B per night:
S £40.00–£48.00
D £54.00–£56.00

OPEN All Year except Christmas

♦♦♦

GABBER FARM

Down Thomas, Plymouth PL9 0AW
T: (01752) 862269
F: (01752) 862269

Bedrooms: 1 single, 2 double/twin, 2 triple/multiple
Bathrooms: 3 en suite

Evening meal available

Courteous welcome at this farm, near coast and Bovisand diving centre. Lovely walks. Special weekly rates, especially for Senior Citizens and children. Directions provided.

P

B&B per night:
S £18.50–£20.50
D £37.00–£41.00

HB per person:
DY £28.50–£30.50

OPEN All Year

♦♦♦

LAMPLIGHTER HOTEL

103 Citadel Road, The Hoe, Plymouth PL1 2RN
T: (01752) 663855
F: (01752) 228139
E: lampligherhotel@ukonline.co.uk

Bedrooms: 7 double/twin, 2 triple/multiple
Bathrooms: 7 en suite, 2 private

CC: Amex, Delta, Mastercard, Visa

Small friendly hotel on Plymouth Hoe, 5 minutes' walk from the city centre and seafront.

P

B&B per night:
S £22.00–£32.00
D £34.00–£42.00

OPEN All Year except Christmas

PLYMOUTH continued

◆◆◆◆

ROSALAND HOTEL

32 Houndiscombe Road, Plymouth PL4 6HQ
T: (01752) 664749
F: (01752) 256984
E: manager@rosalandhotel.com
I: www.rosalandhotel.com

Bedrooms: 4 single, 3 double/twin, 2 triple/multiple
Bathrooms: 4 en suite

CC: Delta, Mastercard, Switch, Visa

B&B per night:
S £19.00–£30.00
D £34.00–£42.00

OPEN All Year

Victorian private hotel in quiet residential area, close to city centre, university and railway station. Well-appointed rooms. Licensed bar. Comfortable lounge. Warm welcome assured.

◆◆◆

WESTWINDS HOTEL

99 Citadel Road, The Hoe, Plymouth PL1 2RN
T: (01752) 601777 & 08007 315717
F: (01752) 662158
E: paul.colman@btinternet.com
I: business.thisisplymouth.co.uk/westwindshotel

Bedrooms: 1 single, 8 double/twin, 1 triple/multiple; permanent suite(s)
Bathrooms: 4 en suite

CC: Amex, Delta, Mastercard, Visa

B&B per night:
S £22.00–£36.00
D £32.00–£44.00

OPEN All Year except Christmas

A family-owned hotel which takes pride in looking after our guests in a professional, friendly and homely environment.

PORLOCK, Somerset Map ref 1D1

MYRTLE COTTAGE

High Street, Porlock, Minehead TA24 8PU
T: (01643) 862978
F: (01243) 862978
E: bob.steer@talk21.com
I: www.smoothhound.co.uk/a12487.html

Bedrooms: 3 double/twin, 2 triple/multiple
Bathrooms: 5 en suite

CC: Delta, Mastercard, Switch, Visa

B&B per night:
S £25.00–£30.00
D £45.00–£50.00

OPEN All Year

Charming 16thC thatched cottage situated in the centre of this picturesque village. Ideal base for walking and exploring Exmoor.

◆◆◆

NUTKIN HOUSE

Toll Road, Porlock, Exmoor TA24 8JH
T: (01643) 863228
E: nutkinhouse@hotmail.com

Bedrooms: 1 single, 2 double/twin

B&B per night:
S £20.00–£25.00
D £40.00–£50.00

OPEN All Year except Christmas

Located in the beautiful Exmoor National Park within easy walking distance of all excellent village amenities. Ideally situated for exploring this truly magical coastal countryside.

PORTHCURNO, Cornwall Map ref 1A3

THE PORTHCURNO HOTEL

The Valley, Porthcurno, St Levan, Penzance TR19 6JX
T: (01736) 810119
F: (01736) 810711
E: mail@porthcurnohotel.co.uk
I: www.porthcurnohotel.co.uk

Bedrooms: 11 double/twin, 1 triple/multiple
Bathrooms: 8 en suite

Lunch available
Evening meal available
CC: Delta, Mastercard, Switch, Visa

B&B per night:
S £38.00–£48.00
D £50.00–£80.00

HB per person:
DY £42.50–£60.00

OPEN All Year

Hotel set in large gardens 600 yards from beach, offering quality accommodation and restaurant. Minack Theatre and Museum of Submarine Telegraphy within 6 minutes' walking distance.

CHECK THE MAPS

The colour maps at the front of this guide show all the cities, towns and villages for which you will find accommodation entries. Refer to the town index to find the page on which they are listed.

RADSTOCK, Bath and North East Somerset Map ref 2B2

THE ROOKERY

Wells Road, Radstock, Bath BA3 3RS
T: (01761) 432626 & 0800 0190070
F: (01761) 432626
E: brandons@therookeryguesthouse.co.uk
I: www.therookeryguesthouse.co.uk

A 200-year-old, family-run property centrally situated for Bath, Wells and the Mendips. We have a relaxing lounge, residents' bar and restaurant and offer the best in service, coupled with an easy-going atmosphere. En suite rooms with hot-beverage facilities, TV, telephone and hairdryer. Large car park.

Bedrooms: 1 single, 8 double/twin, 3 triple/multiple
Bathrooms: 12 en suite

Evening meal available
CC: Delta, Mastercard, Switch, Visa

B&B per night:
S £40.00–£45.00
D £59.00–£70.00

HB per person:
DY £40.00–£55.00

OPEN All Year except Christmas and New Year

ST AGNES, Cornwall Map ref 1B3

PENKERRIS

Penwinnick Road, Penkerris, St Agnes TR5 0PA
T: (01872) 552262
F: (01872) 552262
E: info@penkerris.co.uk
I: www.penkerris.co.uk

Bedrooms: 2 single, 4 double/twin, 2 triple/multiple
Bathrooms: 3 en suite

Evening meal available
CC: Amex, Delta, Mastercard, Switch, Visa

B&B per night:
S £20.00–£35.00
D £30.00–£50.00

OPEN All Year

Attractive B&B hotel with large lawn in unspoilt Cornish village. A home from home offering real food, comfortable bedrooms and log fire in lounge in winter.

ST EWE, Cornwall Map ref 1B3

Silver Award

LOWER BARN

Bosue, St Ewe, St Austell PL26 6EU
T: (01726) 844881
E: janie@bosue.co.uk
I: www.bosue.co.uk

Looking for luxury and tranquillity? Our Mediterranean-style barn is superbly furnished. All en suite, 2 rooms with their own conservatory lounges. Relax in our hot tub whilst overlooking the panoramic views, or why not spoil yourself with the range of therapy treatments we provide. You'll wish you could stay forever!

Bedrooms: 3 double/twin; permanent suite(s)
Bathrooms: 3 en suite

Lunch available
Evening meal available

3 nights including evening meal first night plus wine and chocolates, Nov-Mar.

B&B per night:
S £45.00–£50.00
D £60.00–£80.00

HB per person:
DY £50.00–£55.00

OPEN All Year except Christmas

ST IVES, Cornwall Map ref 1B3 *Tourist Information Centre Tel: (01736) 796297*

THE ANCHORAGE GUEST HOUSE

5 Bunkers Hill, St Ives TR26 1LJ
T: (01736) 797135
F: (01736) 797135
E: james@theanchoragebb.fsnet.co.uk
I: www.theanchoragebb.fsnet.co.uk

Bedrooms: 1 single, 4 double/twin, 1 triple/multiple
Bathrooms: 5 en suite

CC: Amex, Mastercard, Visa

B&B per night:
S £23.00–£26.00
D £40.00–£50.00

OPEN All Year

18thC fisherman's cottage, 30 yards from harbour front and beaches, full of old world charm. Two minutes from Tate Gallery. Open all year.

VISITOR ATTRACTIONS For ideas on places to visit refer to the introduction at the beginning of this section. Look out too for the ETC's Quality Assured Visitor Attraction signs.

ST IVES continued

BLUE HAYES PRIVATE HOTEL

Trelyon Avenue, St Ives TR26 2AD
T: (01736) 797129
F: (01736) 797129
E: malcolm@bluehayes.fsbusiness.co.uk
I: www.bluehayes.co.uk

B&B per night:
S £65.00–£85.00
D £90.00–£130.00

A country house by the sea at St Ives, with ample parking, situated in its own grounds on Porthminster Point, overlooking St Ives bay and harbour, above one of the finest sandy beaches in the country – just a few minutes' walk along the coastal path, from the bottom of the garden. Recently completely refurbished to a high standard.

Bedrooms: 1 single, 6 double/twin; permanent suite(s)
Bathrooms: 7 en suite

Evening meal available
CC: Mastercard, Switch, Visa

ST JUST-IN-PENWITH, Cornwall Map ref 1A3

BOSAVERN HOUSE

St Just-in-Penwith TR19 7RD
T: (01736) 788301
F: (01736) 788301
E: marcol@bosavern.u-net.com
I: www.bosavern.u-net.com

B&B per night:
S £22.00–£30.00
D £44.00–£60.00

OPEN All Year except Christmas

A charming 17thC country house offering the very best in good taste and comfort at an affordable price. All rooms offer en suite facilities, TV, hairdryer and refreshment tray. Relax in our extensive gardens, walk the coastal footpath to an isolated sandy cove or explore West Cornwall. The choice is yours.

Bedrooms: 1 single, 5 double/twin, 2 triple/multiple
Bathrooms: 7 en suite, 1 private

CC: Delta, Mastercard, Switch, Visa

SPECIAL BREAKS

Many establishments offer special promotions and themed breaks. These are highlighted in red. (All such offers are subject to availability.)

ST KEW, Cornwall Map ref 1B2

TREGELLIST FARM

Tregellist, St Kew, Bodmin PL30 3HG
T: (01208) 880537
F: (01208) 881017
E: jillcleave@tregellist.fsbusiness.co.uk

B&B per night:
S Min £30.00
D Min £48.00

HB per person:
DY Min £39.00

OPEN All Year except Christmas

Delightful farmhouse set in pleasant countryside on a 130-acre sheep farm. Delicious home cooking. All bedrooms are en suite with colour TVs and tea/coffee facilities. Some ground floor bedrooms are disabled-friendly. Close to North Cornwall beaches and moors. Camel trail. Within easy reach of Eden Project and Lost Gardens of Heligan. Credit cards accepted.

Bedrooms: 4 double/twin, 1 triple/multiple
Bathrooms: 5 en suite

Evening meal available
CC: Amex, Delta, Diners, Mastercard, Switch, Visa

ST MAWGAN, Cornwall Map ref 1B2

THE FALCON INN

St Mawgan, Newquay TR8 4EP
T: (01637) 860225
F: (01637) 860884
E: enquiries@falconinn.net
I: www.falconinn.net

B&B per night:
S £23.00–£40.00
D £52.00–£70.00

OPEN All Year

16thC, wisteria-covered inn with beautiful gardens in the Vale of Lanherne. Unspoilt, peaceful situation. Quality accommodation and excellent food. Only 20 minutes from Eden Project and the closest inn to Newquay Airport. Log fires, malt whisky and a good wine list enhance the experience.

Bedrooms: 1 single, 3 double/twin
Bathrooms: 2 en suite

Lunch available
Evening meal available
CC: Delta, Diners, Mastercard, Switch, Visa

10% off stays of more than 2 nights.

SALCOMBE, Devon Map ref 1C3 *Tourist Information Centre Tel: (01548) 843927*

♦♦♦♦

TORRE VIEW HOTEL

Devon Road, Salcombe TQ8 8HJ
T: (01548) 842633
F: (01548) 842633
E: boutle@torreview.eurobell.co.uk
I: www.smoothhound.co.uk/hotels/torreview.html

Bedrooms: 7 double/twin, 1 triple/multiple
Bathrooms: 5 en suite, 3 private

Evening meal available
CC: Delta, Mastercard, Visa

B&B per night:
S £28.00–£36.00
D £58.00–£64.00

HB per person:
DY £42.00–£46.00

Detached Victorian residence with every modern comfort, commanding extensive views of the estuary and surrounding countryside yet within reach of the town. No smoking, please.

SALISBURY, Wiltshire Map ref 2B3 *Tourist Information Centre Tel: (01722) 334956*

♦♦♦

THE BELL INN

Warminster Road, South Newton, Salisbury SP2 0QD
T: (01722) 743336
F: (01722) 744202

Bedrooms: 1 single, 2 double/twin
Bathrooms: 3 en suite

Lunch available
Evening meal available
CC: Delta, Mastercard, Switch, Visa

B&B per night:
S Min £30.00
D Min £50.00

OPEN All Year

300-year-old roadside inn offering full en suite facilities. Extensive range of bar meals. Six miles north-west of Salisbury.

SYMBOLS The symbols in each entry give information about services and facilities. A key to these symbols appears at the back of this guide.

SALISBURY continued

◆◆◆

BYWAYS HOUSE

31 Fowlers Road, City Centre, Salisbury SP1 2QP
T: (01722) 328364
F: (01722) 322146
E: byways@bed-breakfast-salisbury.co.uk
I: www.bed-breakfast-salisbury.co.uk

Attractive family-run Victorian house close to cathedral in quiet area of city centre. Large car park. Bedrooms with private bathrooms and colour satellite TV, 4-poster beds. Traditional English and vegetarian breakfasts. From Byways you can walk all around Salisbury. Ideal for Stonehenge and Wilton House.

Bedrooms: 4 single, 10 double/twin, 9 triple/multiple
Bathrooms: 19 en suite

CC: Delta, Mastercard, Switch, Visa

B&B per night:
S £35.00–£65.00
D £50.00–£75.00

OPEN All Year except Christmas

◆◆◆◆

MANOR FARM

Burcombe, Salisbury SP2 0EJ
T: (01722) 742177
F: (01722) 744600
E: sacombes@talk21.com

Comfortable farmhouse, warm and attractively furnished, on 1400-acre mixed farm in a quiet, pretty village 0.25 miles off A30 west of Salisbury. Ideal base for touring this lovely area. Nearby attractions include Wilton House, Salisbury and Stonehenge. Wonderful walks, good riding. Pub with good food nearby. No smoking.

Bedrooms: 2 double/twin
Bathrooms: 2 en suite

CC: Amex, Delta, Diners, Mastercard, Switch, Visa

Reduction for stays of 3 nights or more.

B&B per night:
S £35.00–£40.00
D £44.00–£46.00

◆◆◆◆◆
Silver Award

NEWTON FARM HOUSE

Southampton Road, Whiteparish, Salisbury SP5 2QL
T: (01794) 884416
F: (01794) 884416
E: enquiries@newtonfarmhouse.co.uk
I: www.newtonfarmhouse.co.uk

Historic 16thC farmhouse, once part of the Trafalgar Estate. Delightfully decorated en suite bedrooms, 5 with genuine 4-posters (see our website). Beamed dining room with flagstones, bread oven and Nelson memorabilia. Superb breakfasts include fresh fruits, homemade bread and preserves and free-range eggs. Extensive grounds with swimming pool.

Bedrooms: 5 double/twin, 3 triple/multiple
Bathrooms: 8 en suite

Evening meal available

B&B per night:
S £35.00–£40.00
D £50.00–£70.00

HB per person:
DY £60.00–£65.00

OPEN All Year

MAP REFERENCES The map references refer to the colour maps at the front of this guide. The first figure is the map number; the letter and figure which follow indicate the grid reference on the map.

SALISBURY continued

THE ROKEBY GUEST HOUSE

3 Wain-a-Long Road, Salisbury SP1 1LJ
T: (01722) 329800
F: (01722) 329800
I: www.smoothhound.co.uk/hotels/rokeby.html

Beautiful, nostalgic, Victorian guesthouse, quietly situated, 10 minutes' stroll city centre/cathedral. Large landscaped gardens, summerhouse, elegant 2-storey conservatory, licensed restaurant, gymnasium. Brochure available.

Bedrooms: 4 double/twin, 3 triple/multiple; permanent suite(s)
Bathrooms: 5 en suite, 2 private

Evening meal available

Organised tandem parachute descents with qualified British Parachute Association instructors – ideal for sponsored charity fundraising.

10 P

B&B per night:
S £38.00–£44.00
D £50.00–£55.00

HB per person:
DY £40.00–£55.00

OPEN All Year

♦♦♦♦ Gold Award

WEBSTERS

11 Hartington Road, Salisbury SP2 7LG
T: (01722) 339779
F: (01722) 421903
E: enquiries@websters-bed-breakfast.com
I: www.websters-bed-breakfast.com

Our guests can tell you why Websters is a regional 'Excellence in England' award winner: "wonderful B&B", "the best", "comfortable", "friendly", "helpful", "fantastic", "thank you, we've been thoroughly spoilt". Come and experience excellent hospitality delivered with good humour and find out why so many of our guests return again and again.

Bedrooms: 2 single, 3 double/twin
Bathrooms: 5 en suite

CC: Delta, Mastercard, Switch, Visa

12 P

B&B per night:
S £32.00–£35.00
D £42.00–£45.00

SALISBURY PLAIN

See under Amesbury, Hindon, Salisbury, Winterbourne Stoke

SEATON, Devon Map ref 1D2 *Tourist Information Centre Tel: (01297) 21660*

BEAUMONT

Castle Hill, Seaton EX12 2QW
T: (01297) 20832
F: 0870 0554708
E: tony@lymebay.demon.co.uk
I: www.smoothhound.co.uk/hotels/beaumont.html

Bedrooms: 3 double/twin, 2 triple/multiple
Bathrooms: 5 en suite

Evening meal available

Select Victorian seafront family guesthouse on world Heritage Coast. Two minutes' walk from town. Excellent walks, country parks, attractions and sporting facilities. Unrivalled views over Lyme Bay.

P

B&B per night:
S £25.00
D £50.00

HB per person:
DY £65.00

OPEN All Year except Christmas

IMPORTANT NOTE Information on accommodation listed in this guide has been supplied by the proprietors. As changes may occur you are advised to check details at the time of booking.

SHALDON, Devon Map ref 1D2

POTTERS MOORING

30 The Green, Shaldon, Teignmouth
TQ14 0DN
T: (01626) 873225
F: (01626) 872909
E: mail@pottersmooring.co.uk
I: www.pottersmooring.co.uk

B&B per night:
S £35.00–£45.00
D £65.00–£85.00

OPEN All Year

Potters Mooring was formerly a sea captain's residence and dates from 1625 when Shaldon was a small fishing community. Overlooking the bowling green at the front and the beautiful River Teign at the rear, all rooms, and the family cottage suite, are en suite and furnished to the highest standards.

Bedrooms: 5 double/twin, 3 triple/multiple; permanent suite(s)
Bathrooms: 7 en suite, 1 private

CC: Delta, Mastercard, Switch, Visa

Stay 3 nights or more and enjoy the last night free – Oct-Mar (excl Christmas and New Year).

SHERBORNE, Dorset Map ref 2B3 *Tourist Information Centre Tel: (01935) 815341*

Silver Award

THE ALDERS

Sandford Orcas, Sherborne DT9 4SB
T: (01963) 220666
F: (01963) 220106
E: jonsue@thealdersbb.com
I: www.thealdersbb.com

B&B per night:
D £48.00–£50.00

OPEN All Year

Secluded stone house set in old walled garden, in picturesque conservation village near Sherborne. The house is tastefully furnished, with original watercolour paintings and hand-made pottery. There is a woodburning fire in lounge inglenook fireplace. Good breakfasts served around large farmhouse table. Excellent food available in traditional, friendly village pub.

Bedrooms: 3 double/twin
Bathrooms: 3 en suite

Silver Award

CROMWELL HOUSE

Long Street, Sherborne DT9 3BS
T: (01935) 813352
I: www.smoothhound.co.uk/a53281.html

Bedrooms: 3 double/twin
Bathrooms: 2 en suite, 1 private

CC: Mastercard, Visa

B&B per night:
S £35.00–£40.00
D £55.00–£60.00

OPEN All Year

A charming old manse c1740. Quietly situated in the heart of Sherborne in the conservation area.

AT-A-GLANCE SYMBOLS

Symbols at the end of each accommodation entry give useful information about services and facilities. A key to symbols can be found inside the back cover flap. Keep this open for easy reference.

SHERBORNE continued

◆◆◆◆◆

Listed Victorian Gothic building, elegantly furnished with antiques, set in 3.5 acres of beautiful grounds. The spacious lounge and the dining room afford magnificent views of open country. On Fridays and Saturdays one of the partners, a highly acclaimed chef, prepares dinner. On other nights food can be provided by a pub restaurant 200 yards away.

THE OLD VICARAGE HOTEL

Sherborne Road, Milborne Port, Sherborne DT9 5AT
T: (01963) 251117
F: (01963) 251515
E: theoldvicarage@milborneport.freeserve.co.uk
I: www.milborneport.freeserve.co.uk

Bedrooms: 3 double/twin, 3 triple/multiple
Bathrooms: 6 en suite

Evening meal available
CC: Amex, Delta, Mastercard, Switch, Visa

DB&B for 2 Fri and Sat from £193 (2 nights).

B&B per night:
S £44.00–£74.00
D £56.00–£105.00

HB per person:
DY £46.00–£76.00

SIDMOUTH, Devon Map ref 1D2 *Tourist Information Centre Tel: (01395) 516441*

◆◆◆

CANTERBURY GUEST HOUSE
Salcombe Road, Sidmouth
EX10 8PR
T: (01395) 513373 & 0800 328 1775
E: cgh@eclipse.co.uk

Bedrooms: 5 double/twin, 3 triple/multiple
Bathrooms: 8 en suite

Evening meal available
CC: Amex, Mastercard, Switch, Visa

Old house of charm and character adjacent to River Sid. Close to shops, seafront and National Trust parkland. Non-smoking policy.

B&B per night:
S £18.00–£21.50
D £36.00–£43.00

HB per person:
DY £27.50–£30.00

OPEN All Year

◆◆◆◆
Silver Award

Standing in its own award-winning gardens, Coombe Bank is the perfect choice for your stay in Sidmouth. A choice of seven beautifully appointed rooms awaits you. You are sure to appriciate the 'cooked to order' breakfasts and the spacious, comfortable surroundings.

COOMBE BANK GUEST HOUSE

86 Alexandria Road, Sidmouth EX10 9HG
T: (01395) 514843
F: (01395) 513558
E: info@coombebank.com
I: www.coombebank.com

Bedrooms: 1 single, 5 double/twin, 1 triple/multiple; permanent suite(s)
Bathrooms: 7 en suite

Evening meal available

5% discount for stays of 3 or more nights, 10% discount for stays of 7 or more nights.

B&B per night:
S £22.00–£28.00
D £44.00–£56.00

QUALITY ASSURANCE SCHEME

For an explanation of the quality and facilities represented by the Diamonds please refer to the front of this guide. A more detailed explanation can be found in the information pages at the back.

SIDMOUTH continued

Gold Award

THE SALTY MONK

Church Street, Sidford, Sidmouth EX10 9QP
T: (01395) 513174
F: (01395) 514722
E: andy@saltymonkhotelsidmouth.co.uk
I: www.saltymonkhotelsidmouth.co.uk

B&B per night:
S £49.50–£60.00
D £80.00–£92.00

HB per person:
DY £59.00–£71.25

OPEN All Year

16thC restaurant near the Regency town of Sidmouth, ideal for exploring Dartmoor and Heritage Coastline. Very luxurious and well-appointed en suite rooms, some with spa baths. Award-winning, elegant restaurant overlooking the beautiful gardens. All food is made on the premises by resident chef proprietors using finest, fresh ingredients.

Bedrooms: 5 double/twin; permanent suite(s)
Bathrooms: 5 en suite

Lunch available
Evening meal available
CC: Delta, Mastercard, Switch, Visa

15% off any 3-day break Oct-Mar (excl Christmas and New Year).

SOMERTON, Somerset Map ref 2A3

Silver Award

MILL HOUSE

Barton St. David, Somerton TA11 6DF
T: (01458) 851215
F: (01458) 851372
E: B&B@millhousebarton.co.uk
I: www.MillHouseBarton.co.uk

B&B per night:
S £26.00–£28.00
D £48.00–£56.00

OPEN All Year excep Christmas

Beautifully restored Listed Georgian mill house in a peaceful garden with the mill stream still running through one end of the house. Set in lovely countryside but conveniently accessible from the A303. Elegantly furnished, spacious bedrooms all en suite. Close to Glastonbury and Wells. A warm welcome awaits you.

Bedrooms: 1 single, 2 double/twin; permanent suite(s)
Bathrooms: 3 en suite

CC: Delta, Mastercard, Switch, Visa

10% off 3 nights or more for mid-week bookings and low season.

10 P

SPREYTON, Devon Map ref 1C2

THE TOM COBLEY TAVERN

Spreyton, Crediton EX17 5AL
T: (01647) 231314
F: (01647) 231506
E: fjwfilor@tomcobley.fsnet.co.uk

Bedrooms: 2 single, 2 double/twin

Lunch available
Evening meal available

B&B per night:
S £22.50
D £45.00

HB per person:
DY £35.00–£55.00

OPEN All Year

A small country inn serving the local community. Real ales on draught. Food home-cooked in our kitchen.

USE YOUR *i*s

There are more than 550 Tourist Information Centres throughout England offering friendly help with accommodation and holiday ideas as well as suggestions of places to visit and things to do. You'll find TIC addresses in the local Phone Book.

STOGUMBER, Somerset Map ref 1D1

♦♦♦♦ Silver Award

NORTHAM MILL

Water Lane, Stogumber, Taunton TA4 3TT
T: (01984) 656916 & 656146
F: (01984) 656144
E: bmsspicer@aol.com
I: www.northam-mill.co.uk

Hidden for 300 years. Nestling between the Quantock and Brendon Hills, in 5 acres of picturesque gardens with trout stream. Welcoming and comfortable, log fires and original beams. All rooms en suite including luxury garden suite. Superior, home-cooked food from daily-changing menu. Walking, shooting, fishing and archery. House-party weekends.

Bedrooms: 1 single, 5 double/twin; permanent suite(s)
Bathrooms: 4 en suite, 1 private

Evening meal available
CC: Amex, Delta, Diners, Mastercard, Switch, Visa

B&B per night:
S £35.00
D £58.00–£80.00

HB per person:
DY £42.50–£65.00

OPEN All Year except Christmas

SWINDON, Wiltshire Map ref 2B2 *Tourist Information Centre Tel: (01793) 530328*

♦♦♦♦

COURTLEIGH HOUSE

40 Draycott Road, Chiseldon, Swindon SN4 0LS
T: (01793) 740246

Bedrooms: 2 double/twin
Bathrooms: 1 en suite, 1 private

Large detached village house with downland views, ample parking, tennis court and gardens. Comfortable, relaxing rooms. Easy access to Marlborough, Swindon, M4 and Cotswolds.

B&B per night:
S £25.00–£27.00
D £45.00–£50.00

OPEN All Year except Christmas

SYDLING ST NICHOLAS, Dorset Map ref 2B3

♦♦♦

MAGISTON FARM

Sydling St Nicholas DT2 9NR
T: (01300) 320295

Bedrooms: 2 single, 3 double/twin; permanent suite(s)
Bathrooms: 1 private

Evening meal available

400-acre arable farm. Three-hundred-and-fifty-year-old farmhouse with large garden. Very peaceful, in the heart of Dorset, 5 miles north of Dorchester.

B&B per night:
S £20.00
D £40.00

HB per person:
DY £32.50

OPEN All Year except Christmas

10

TALSKIDDY, Cornwall Map ref 1B2

♦♦♦♦ Silver Award

PENNATILLIE FARM

Talskiddy, St Columb TR9 6EF
T: (01637) 880280
F: (01637) 880280
E: angela@pennatillie.fsnet.co.uk
I: www.cornish-riviera.co.uk/pennatilliefarm.htm

450-acre working dairy farm, set in beautiful countryside. We have 3 spacious guest bedrooms, all with en suite facilities. The Eden Project is only 12 miles away. Wadebridge, Padstow and Truro all nearby along with several National Trust properties. Newquay Airport approximately 6 miles. A warm welcome awaits you.

Bedrooms: 3 double/twin
Bathrooms: 3 en suite

Evening meal available
CC: Amex, Mastercard, Switch, Visa

B&B per night:
S £25.00–£35.00
D £44.00–£50.00

HB per person:
DY £34.00–£37.00

PRICES
Please check prices and other details at the time of booking.

TAUNTON, Somerset Map ref 1D1 *Tourist Information Centre Tel: (01823) 336344*

◆◆◆

PROCKTERS FARM
West Monkton, Taunton TA2 8QN
T: (01823) 412269
F: (01823) 412269

Bedrooms: 2 single, 3 double/twin
Bathrooms: 1 en suite

300-year-old farmhouse on 300-acre mixed farm, 3 miles from M5. Inglenook fireplaces, brass beds, farm antiques. Tea and cake on arrival. Pub walking distance. Farm shop.

P

B&B per night:
S £21.00–£31.00
D £42.00–£46.00

OPEN All Year

◆◆◆

THATCHED COUNTRY COTTAGE AND GARDEN B & B

Pear Tree Cottage, Stapley, Churchstanton, Taunton TA3 7QA
T: (01823) 601224
F: (01823) 601224
E: colvin.parry@virgin.net
I: www.smoothhound.co.uk/hotels/thatch.html

Charming south-facing thatched cottage in idyllic rural location near Devon border in designated Area of Outstanding Natural Beauty. Picturesque countryside of winding lanes with flora and fauna. Central for north/south coasts of Somerset/Devon/Dorset's Jurassic coast. Dartmoor/Exmoor/Cornwall day trips possible. 3.5 acres garden/arboretum. TVs/beverages. Paradise found.

Bedrooms: 1 single, 1 double/twin, 1 triple/multiple
Bathrooms: 1 en suite, 2 private

Evening meal available

P

B&B per night:
S £25.00
D £34.00

HB per person:
DY £29.00–£31.00

OPEN All Year

◆◆◆◆

THE SPINNEY
Curland, Taunton TA3 5SE
T: (01460) 234362 & 234193
F: (01460) 234362
E: bartlett.spinney@zetnet.co.uk
I: www.somerweb.co.uk/spinney-bb

Bedrooms: 1 double/twin, 2 triple/multiple
Bathrooms: 3 en suite

Evening meal available

Modern detached house in quiet countryside. Lovely garden with panoramic views from slopes of Blackdown Hills. Quality en suite accommodation. Evening meals recommended. No smoking throughout.

P

B&B per night:
D £50.00–£54.00

HB per person:
DY £39.00–£41.00

OPEN All Year

TAVISTOCK, Devon Map ref 1C2 *Tourist Information Centre Tel: (01822) 612938*

◆◆◆◆

ACORN COTTAGE
Heathfield, Tavistock PL19 0LQ
T: (01822) 810038
E: viv@acorncot.fsnet.co.uk
I: www.visitbritain.com

Bedrooms: 3 double/twin
Bathrooms: 3 en suite

Evening meal available

17thC Grade II Listed. Many original features, lovely views, peaceful location. Lydford Gorge 3.5 miles and near Brentor medieval church. Central to many activities – bordering Dartmoor. Send for brochure.

5 P

B&B per night:
S £30.00–£40.00
D £35.00–£40.00

OPEN All Year

◆◆◆◆

HARRABEER COUNTRY HOUSE HOTEL

Harrowbeer Lane, Yelverton PL20 6EA
T: (01822) 853302
F: (01822) 853302
E: reception@harrabeer.co.uk
I: www.harrabeer.co.uk

Delightful country house hotel close to the ever-amazing surroundings of Dartmoor. Specialising in food, comfort and service with a smile! Closed week prior to Christmas to week after New Year. Small conferences by arrangement.

Bedrooms: 6 double/twin; permanent suite(s)
Bathrooms: 4 en suite, 2 private

Evening meal available
CC: Amex, Mastercard, Switch, Visa

Special offers for weekly and out-of-season breaks. Visit our website for up-to-date information.

P

B&B per night:
S £27.00–£39.00
D £54.00–£61.00

HB per person:
DY £42.50–£54.50

TAVISTOCK continued

◆◆◆◆◆ Gold Award

TOR COTTAGE

Chillaton, Tavistock PL16 OJE
T: (01822) 860248
F: (01822) 860126
E: info@torcottage.co.uk
I: www.torcottage.co.uk

B&B per night:
S £89.00
D £130.00

National winner of English Tourist Board 'England for Excellence' Gold Award. Tor Cottage has a warm, relaxed atmosphere and nestles in a private valley. Lovely streamside gardens, wildlife hillsides, heated swimming pool. Luxurious en suite bed-sitting rooms, each with log fire, private garden or conservatory. Renowned vegetarian and traditional cuisine. Forty-five minutes Eden Project.

Bedrooms: 4 double/twin; permanent suite(s)
Bathrooms: 4 en suite

CC: Delta, Mastercard, Switch, Visa

Autumn/winter/spring breaks: 3 nights for price of 2. Valentine breaks include special dinners. Honeymoon/anniversary breaks. Gourmet tray suppers to order. 10% discount on 7-night stay.

P

TORQUAY, Devon Map ref 1D2 *Tourist Information Centre Tel: 0906 680 1268 (Premium rate number)*

◆◆◆

AVENUE PARK GUEST HOUSE

3 Avenue Road, Torquay TQ2 5LA
T: (01803) 293902
F: (01803) 293902
E: avenuepark@bushinternet.com
I: www.torbay.gov.uk/tourism/t-hotels/avepark.htm

Bedrooms: 1 single, 3 double/twin, 4 triple/multiple
Bathrooms: 8 en suite

B&B per night:
S £17.00–£21.00
D £34.00–£42.00

OPEN All Year except Christmas

Friendly family-run guesthouse overlooking parkland. Seafront 350 yards, close to town, Riviera Centre, Abbey Gardens. Railway station nearby. Cleanliness and comfort assured.

P

◆◆◆◆

CEDAR COURT HOTEL

3 St Matthew's Road, Chelston, Torquay TQ2 6JA
T: (01803) 607851
F: (01803) 607851
E: enquiries@cedarcourt-hotel.co.uk
I: www.cedarcourt-hotel.co.uk

Bedrooms: 3 single, 5 double/twin, 2 triple/multiple
Bathrooms: 10 en suite

Evening meal available
CC: Amex, Delta, Diners, Mastercard, Switch, Visa

B&B per night:
S £22.00–£28.00
D £44.00–£56.00

HB per person:
DY £36.00–£43.00

OPEN All Year except Christmas

Situated in peaceful surroundings within easy walking distance of seafront, town centre and railway station. All rooms en suite. Quality accommodation and meals. Craft courses.

P

◆◆◆◆◆ Silver Award

CRANBORNE HOTEL

58 Belgrave Road, Torquay TQ2 5HY
T: (01803) 298046
F: (01803) 215477

Bedrooms: 3 single, 6 double/twin, 1 triple/multiple
Bathrooms: 10 en suite

Evening meal available
CC: Delta, Mastercard, Switch, Visa

B&B per night:
D £60.00

Victorian terraced hotel in excellent situation, being close to seafront, town centre and Riviera Centre. Torquay's immaculate 5 Diamond Silver Award hotel.

2 P

◆◆◆◆

THE CRANMORE HOTEL

89 Avenue Road, Torquay TQ2 5LH
T: (01803) 298488
F: (01803) 298488
E: thecranmore@tesco.net
I: www.smoothhound.co.uk/hotels/cranmore.html

Bedrooms: 6 double/twin, 1 triple/multiple; permanent suite(s)
Bathrooms: 7 en suite

Lunch available
CC: Delta, Mastercard, Switch, Visa

B&B per night:
S £23.00–£26.00
D £36.00–£46.00

OPEN All Year

Friendly, family-run hotel. All rooms are en suite, clean, well decorated, warm and comfortable, with all usual facilities. Centrally placed close to all amenities.

P

REGIONAL TOURIST BOARD The symbol in an establishment entry indicates that it is a Regional Tourist Board member.

TORQUAY continued

◆◆◆

THE GARLIESTON HOTEL
Bridge Road, Torquay TQ2 5BA
T: (01803) 294050
E: garliestonhotel@jridewood.fsnet.co.uk

Bedrooms: 1 single, 3 double/twin, 1 triple/multiple
Bathrooms: 3 en suite, 2 private

Evening meal available
CC: Amex, Delta, Mastercard, Switch, Visa

Small, friendly, family-run hotel, few minutes' walk from sea, town centre and Riviera Leisure and Conference Centre. Colour TV, tea-making facilities and central heating in all bedrooms.

B&B per night:
S £15.00–£20.00
D £30.00–£40.00

HB per person:
DY £24.00–£29.00

OPEN All Year

◆◆◆◆◆ Silver Award

KINGSTON HOUSE
75 Avenue Road, Torquay TQ2 5LL
T: (01803) 212760
F: (01803) 201425
E: butto@kingstonhousehotel.co.uk
I: www.kingstonhousehotel.co.uk

Bedrooms: 5 double/twin
Bathrooms: 5 en suite

Evening meal available

Combines Victorian elegance with modern amenities, ensuring a fulfilling, relaxed holiday. Conveniently situated for seafront, harbour, town. Private car park. Favourable weekly terms available.

8 P

B&B per night:
S £24.00–£48.00
D £48.00–£55.00

HB per person:
DY £35.00–£39.00

◆◆◆◆

MAPLE LODGE
36 Ash Hill Road, Torquay TQ1 3JD
T: (01803) 297391
E: TheMapleLodge@aol.com
I: www.themaplelodge.co.uk

Bedrooms: 1 single, 4 double/twin, 2 triple/multiple
Bathrooms: 6 en suite, 1 private

CC: Amex, Delta, Mastercard, Switch, Visa

Detached guesthouse with beautiful views. Relaxed atmosphere, home cooking, en suite rooms. Centrally situated for town and beaches.

P

B&B per night:
S £18.00–£24.00
D £36.00–£48.00

OPEN All Year except Christmas

◆◆◆

THE PINES
19 Newton Road, Torre, Torquay TQ2 5DB
T: (01803) 292882

Bedrooms: 3 double/twin
Bathrooms: 2 en suite, 1 private

A warm welcome awaits you at this family-run, non-smoking guesthouse. Cleanliness and good home cooking assured. Close to all amenities. Quality bedrooms, some en-suite, colour TV and tea/coffee in all rooms. Five-course breakfast, car park.

P

B&B per night:
S £15.00–£20.00
D £30.00–£40.00

OPEN All Year except Christmas

◆◆◆

TRELAWNEY HOTEL
48 Belgrave Road, Torquay TQ2 5HS
T: (01803) 296049
F: (01803) 296049
E: trelawneyhotel@hotmail.com
I: www.trelawneyhotel.net

Bedrooms: 9 double/twin, 3 triple/multiple
Bathrooms: 12 en suite

Evening meal available
CC: Amex, Mastercard, Switch, Visa

Friendly, family-run, licensed hotel. Close to main shops, beaches, theatres, conference/leisure centre. A warm welcome always guaranteed. Highly recommended.

B&B per night:
D £50.00–£70.00

HB per person:
DY £35.00–£45.00

◆◆◆

WHITBURN GUEST HOUSE
St Lukes Road North, Torquay TQ2 5PD
T: (01803) 296719
E: joe@lazenby15.freeserve.co.uk

Bedrooms: 1 double/twin, 4 triple/multiple
Bathrooms: 4 en suite

Cosy, family-run bed and breakfast, no restriction parking, walking distance to beach and town. Rooms have TV, clock radio. Families welcome.

P

B&B per night:
S £12.50–£22.00
D £25.00–£44.00

OPEN All Year

TORRINGTON, Devon Map ref 1C2 *Tourist Information Centre Tel: (01805) 626140*

◆◆◆

WEST OF ENGLAND INN
18 South Street, Torrington
EX38 8AA
T: (01805) 624949

Bedrooms: 3 double/twin, 1 triple/multiple
Bathrooms: 4 en suite

Lunch available
Evening meal available
CC: Delta, Mastercard, Switch, Visa

B&B per night:
S £30.00–£35.00
D £40.00–£50.00

OPEN All Year

Situated in the centre of Torrington in North Devon. Restaurant, bar snacks, real ales. Accommodation in all rooms is en suite. Recently fully refurbished.

TOTNES, Devon Map ref 1D2 *Tourist Information Centre Tel: (01803) 863168*

◆◆◆◆

FOUR SEASONS GUEST HOUSE
13 Bridgetown, Totnes TQ9 5AB
T: (01803) 862146
F: (01803) 867779
E: eecornford@netscapeonline.msn.com

Bedrooms: 1 single, 5 double/twin, 1 triple/multiple
Bathrooms: 7 en suite

Lunch available
Evening meal available

B&B per night:
S £25.00–£30.00
D £44.00–£48.00

HB per person:
DY £35.00–£40.00

OPEN All Year

Close to River Dart and town centre. Ideal base for local attractions. All rooms beverage tray, TV, trouser-press, hairdryer, security safe. Evening meals by arrangement.

◆◆◆◆◆
Silver Award

OLD FOLLATON

Plymouth Road, Totnes TQ9 5NA
T: (01803) 865441
F: (01803) 863597
E: bandb@oldfollaton.co.uk
I: www.oldfollaton.co.uk

B&B per night:
S £40.00–£45.00
D £54.00–£60.00

OPEN All Year

Delightful Georgian country house set in peaceful surroundings and offering accommodation of the highest standard in a friendly and informal atmosphere. It is the ideal location surrounded by a wealth of places to visit, superb coastal and countryside walks and the splendour of Dartmoor.

Bedrooms: 2 double/twin, 1 triple/multiple; permanent suite(s)
Bathrooms: 3 en suite

Evening meal available

4 nights for the price of 3, Nov-Mar (excl Christmas, New Year and Easter).

◆◆◆◆
Silver Award

THE OLD FORGE AT TOTNES

Seymour Place, Totnes TQ9 5AY
T: (01803) 862174
F: (01803) 865385
E: enq@oldforgetotnes.com
I: www.oldforgetotnes.com

B&B per night:
S £44.00–£52.00
D £54.00–£74.00

HB per person:
DY £43.00–£53.00

OPEN All Year except Christmas

A warm welcome assured at this delightful 600-year-old stone building with walled garden and car parking. Whirlpool spa. Extensive breakfast menu. Quiet yet close to town centre and riverside walks. Coast and Dartmoor nearby, Eden Project 1.5 hours. Two-bedroomed cottage suite with private roof terrace.

Bedrooms: 8 double/twin, 2 triple/multiple; permanent suite(s)
Bathrooms: 9 en suite, 1 private

Lunch available
Evening meal available
CC: Amex, Delta, Mastercard, Switch, Visa

3-day breaks (Nov-Mar): £4 off price of room per night.

CREDIT CARD BOOKINGS If you book by telephone and are asked for your credit card number it is advisable to check the proprietor's policy should you cancel your reservation.

TRURO, Cornwall Map ref 1B3 *Tourist Information Centre Tel: (01872) 274555*

♦♦♦♦♦ Silver Award

BISSICK OLD MILL

Ladock, Truro TR2 4PG
T: (01726) 882557
F: (01726) 884057
E: soniav@bissickmill.ndo.co.uk

17thC water mill sympathetically converted to provide well-appointed accommodation with exceptional standards throughout and a relaxing, friendly atmosphere. All bedrooms en suite and well equipped. Candle lit dinners prepared with fresh, quality ingredients and served in a beamed dining room. Ideal base for visiting the Eden Project and Cornwall's beautiful gardens.

Bedrooms: 4 double/twin; permanent suite(s)
Bathrooms: 4 en suite

Evening meal available
CC: Delta, Mastercard, Switch, Visa

B&B per night:
D £54.00–£74.00

♦♦♦♦

MARCORRIE HOTEL
20 Falmouth Road, Truro TR1 2HX
T: (01872) 277374
F: (01872) 241666
E: marcorrie@aol.com
I: www.hotelstruro.com

Bedrooms: 3 single, 5 double/twin, 4 triple/multiple
Bathrooms: 12 en suite

CC: Amex, Delta, Mastercard, Switch, Visa

Victorian townhouse 5 minutes' walk to city centre and cathedral. Country houses and gardens, coastal and river walks. Ample parking. Traditional English cuisine served in period dining room.

B&B per night:
S £39.50–£47.50
D £49.50–£55.00

OPEN All Year except Christmas

♦♦♦♦

TREVISPIAN-VEAN FARM GUEST HOUSE
St Erme, Truro TR4 9AT
T: (01872) 279514
F: (01872) 263730
I: www.guesthousestruro.com

Bedrooms: 4 double/twin, 1 triple/multiple
Bathrooms: 5 en suite

300-acre arable & livestock farm. Beautifully situated 7 miles from coast in heart of the countryside, the farmhouse combines modern comforts with all the charm of a 300-year-old farm.

B&B per night:
S £24.00–£21.00
D £42.00

VERYAN, Cornwall Map ref 1B3

♦♦♦♦

TREVERBYN HOUSE
Pendower Road, Veryan, Truro TR2 5QL
T: (01872) 501201
E: holiday@treverbyn.fsbusiness.co.uk
I: www.cornwall-online.co.uk/treverbyn

Bedrooms: 1 single, 2 double/twin
Bathrooms: 3 en suite

Situated in the centre of Veryan on the Roseland Peninsula, just over one mile from the coast. Near the Eden Project and Heligan Gardens.

B&B per night:
S £25.00
D £45.00

OPEN All Year except Christmas

WASHFORD, Somerset Map ref 1D1

♦♦♦

GREEN BAY
Washford, Watchet TA23 0NN
T: (01984) 640303
E: greenbay@tinyonline.co.uk

Bedrooms: 3 double/twin
Bathrooms: 2 en suite, 1 private

Evening meal available
CC: Delta, Mastercard, Switch, Visa

Charming period cottage. Ideal location near coast, Exmoor, Dunster, Watchet harbour, Cleeve Abbey and steam railway. Friendly hosts, comfortable rooms and good home cooking.

B&B per night:
S £18.00–£20.00
D £36.00–£40.00

HB per person:
DY £25.00–£27.00

OPEN All Year

WATERGATE BAY, Cornwall Map ref 1B2

THE WHITE HOUSE

Watergate Bay, Newquay TR8 4AD
T: (01637) 860119
F: (01637) 860449
E: jenny.vallance@virgin.net
I: www.cornwallwhitehouse.co.uk

B&B per night:
S £20.00–£35.00
D £40.00–£70.00

Quiet, elegant, spacious country house with large gardens, overlooking Watergate Bay and beach for sandcastles and surfing. Beautifully appointed bed and breakfast suites, large, well-equipped family apartments plus a converted chapel for romantic couples. Ideally situated between Padstow and Newquay for touring, walking and sports.

Bedrooms: 2 triple/multiple; permanent suite(s)
Bathrooms: 2 en suite

10 P

WELLS, Somerset Map ref 2A2 *Tourist Information Centre Tel: (01749) 672552*

BURCOTT MILL HISTORIC WATERMILL AND GUESTHOUSE

Wookey, Wells BA5 1NJ
T: (01749) 673118
F: (01749) 677376
E: theburts@burcottmill.com
I: www.burcottmill.com

B&B per night:
S Min £24.00
D £42.00–£64.00

OPEN All Year except Christmas

Authentically restored Victorian watermill dating from Domesday, still stonegrinding flour daily. Enjoy a personal tour with the miller. Families especially welcome: playground, ponies, birds, small animals.Tearoom, craft shops. Opposite country pub for evening meals. Ideal for Cheddar, Wells, Glastonbury. Flexible accommodation. Wheelchair-friendly suite. You won't be disappointed!

Bedrooms: 1 single, 1 double/twin, 4 triple/multiple
Bathrooms: 5 en suite, 1 private

Lunch available
CC: Mastercard, Switch, Visa

10% discount for 2- to 6-night stays. 20% discount for week-long stays. Further reductions for children up to 15.

P

♦♦♦

FRANKLYNS FARM

Chewton Mendip, Bath BA3 4NB
T: (01761) 241372

Bedrooms: 3 double/twin; permanent suite(s)
Bathrooms: 2 en suite, 1 private

B&B per night:
S Min £25.00
D Min £40.00

OPEN All Year

Cosy farmhouse in heart of Mendip. Superb views, peaceful setting. Large garden with tennis court. Offering genuine hospitality and delicious breakfast. Ideal touring Bath, Wells, Cheddar.

P

♦♦♦♦♦
Gold Award

GLENCOT HOUSE

Glencot Lane, Wookey Hole, Wells BA5 1BH
T: (01749) 677160
F: (01749) 670210
E: relax@glencothouse.co.uk
I: www.glencothouse.co.uk

Bedrooms: 3 single, 10 double/twin
Bathrooms: 13 en suite

Evening meal available
CC: Amex, Delta, Diners, Mastercard, Switch, Visa

B&B per night:
S £67.00–£85.00
D £88.00–£114.00

HB per person:
DY £70.00–£83.00

OPEN All Year

Elegantly furnished Victorian mansion set in 18 acres of gardens and parkland with river frontage. High-class accommodation, good food and friendly service. Children and dogs welcome.

P

MAP REFERENCES

Map references apply to the colour maps at the front of this guide.

WELLS continued

♦♦♦♦

LITTLEWELL FARM GUEST HOUSE

Coxley, Wells BA5 1QP
T: (01749) 677914

B&B per night:
S £24.00–£29.00
D £42.00–£52.00

OPEN All Year

Delightful 18thC farmhouse on non-working farm, set in pretty garden and enjoying extensive views over beautiful countryside. Charming en suite bedrooms with antique furniture offer comfort and high standards coupled with personal and thoughtful touches. Our candlelit dinner is skilfully prepared and beautifully presented, using only the best of local produce. One mile south-west of Wells.

Bedrooms: 1 single, 4 double/twin
Bathrooms: 4 en suite, 1 private

Evening meal available

10 P

♦♦♦

THE POUND INN

Burcott Lane, Coxley, Wells BA5 1QZ
T: (01749) 672785
E: poundinnwells@aol.com

B&B per night:
S Min £35.00
D £40.00–£45.00

OPEN All Year except Christmas

Expect a warm welcome at our traditional 17thC village inn 1.5 miles from Wells on A39 to Glastonbury. Varied menu making good use of fresh, local produce with a range of wines and beers to complement, and a high standard of service to match. Convenient base for local tourist attractions.

Bedrooms: 1 double/twin, 1 triple/multiple
Bathrooms: 2 en suite

Lunch available
Evening meal available
CC: Delta, Mastercard, Switch, Visa

10 S P

♦♦♦♦

WORTH HOUSE HOTEL

Worth, Wookey, Wells BA5 1LW
T: (01749) 672041
F: (01749) 672041
E: mblomeley2001@yahoo.co.uk

Bedrooms: 1 single, 5 double/twin, 1 triple/multiple
Bathrooms: 7 en suite

Lunch available
Evening meal available
CC: Delta, Mastercard, Switch, Visa

B&B per night:
S £22.00–£25.00
D £40.00–£44.00

OPEN All Year except Christmas

Small country hotel, dating from the 16thC, 2 miles from Wells on the B3139. Exposed beams and log fires.

S P

WEST PENNARD, Somerset Map ref 2A2

♦♦♦♦
Silver Award

PAGE COTTAGE

West Pennard, Glastonbury
BA6 8NN
T: (01458) 833651

Bedrooms: 1 double/twin
Bathrooms: 1 en suite

B&B per night:
D £42.00–£54.00

OPEN All Year except Christmas

Lovingly renovated cottage in a beautiful country garden, convenient for Glastonbury and surrounding area. Pretty en suite double room with all facilities. Excellent home-cooked breakfast.

6 S P

ACCESSIBILITY

Look for the symbols which indicate National Accessible Scheme standards for hearing and visually impaired guests in addition to standards for guests with mobility impairment. Additional participants are shown in the listings at the back.

WEST PORLOCK, Somerset Map ref 1D1

◆◆◆◆

WEST PORLOCK HOUSE
West Porlock, Minehead TA24 8NX
T: (01643) 862880

Bedrooms: 4 double/twin, 1 triple/multiple
Bathrooms: 2 en suite, 3 private

CC: Delta, Mastercard, Switch, Visa

B&B per night:
S Max £30.00
D £53.00–£58.00

A small licensed country house overlooking the sea and countryside on the road from Porlock to Porlock Weir.

WESTON-SUPER-MARE, Somerset Map ref 1D1 *Tourist Information Centre Tel: (01934) 888800*

◆◆◆

BEACHLANDS HOTEL
17 Uphill Road North, Weston-super-Mare BS23 4NG
T: (01934) 621401
F: (01934) 621966
E: info@beachlandshotel.com
I: www.beachlandshotel.com

Bedrooms: 5 single, 16 double/twin, 3 triple/multiple
Bathrooms: 24 en suite

Lunch available
Evening meal available
CC: Amex, Delta, Diners, Mastercard, Switch, Visa

B&B per night:
S £47.00–£63.50
D £69.00–£89.50

HB per person:
DY £49.50–£66.00

OPEN All Year except Christmas

On the level, overlooking Weston Golf Course and 300 yards from beach. Individually designed bedrooms.

◆◆◆◆

BRAESIDE HOTEL

2 Victoria Park, Weston-super-Mare BS23 2HZ
T: (01934) 626642
F: (01934) 626642
E: braeside@tesco.net
I: www.braesidehotel.co.uk

B&B per night:
S £26.00–£27.00
D £52.00–£54.00

OPEN All Year except Christmas

Fabulous views over Weston Bay; 2 minutes' walk from sandy beach. Quiet location with unrestricted on-street parking. Single rooms always available. Directions: with sea on left, take first right after Winter Gardens, then first left into Lower Church Road. Victoria Park is on the right after the left-hand bend.

Bedrooms: 2 single, 5 double/twin, 2 triple/multiple
Bathrooms: 9 en suite

Stay 2 nights and have a third night free, 1 Nov-end Apr (excl Easter).

◆◆◆

MOORLANDS COUNTRY GUESTHOUSE

Hutton, Weston-super-Mare BS24 9QH
T: (01934) 812283
F: (01934) 812283
E: margaret_holt@email.com
I: www.guestaccom.co.uk/35.htm

B&B per night:
S £21.00–£31.00
D £42.00–£52.00

OPEN All Year

Family-run 18thC house in mature landscaped grounds. The Holts have been at Moorlands for the past 35 years. Hutton is a pretty village with a pub serving meals. Close to hill and country walks and many places of interest easily reached by car. Riding can be arranged for children.

Bedrooms: 3 double/twin, 3 triple/multiple
Bathrooms: 5 en suite

CC: Amex, Diners, Mastercard, Visa

QUALITY ASSURANCE SCHEME
Diamond ratings and awards were correct at the time of going to press but are subject to change. Please check at the time of booking.

WESTONZOYLAND, Somerset Map ref 1D1

◆◆◆◆◆ Silver Award

STADDLESTONES GUEST HOUSE

3 Standards Road, Westonzoyland, Bridgwater TA7 0EL
T: (01278) 691179
F: (01278) 691333
E: staddlestones@euphony.net
I: www.staddlestonesguesthouse.co.uk

Bedrooms: 3 double/twin
Bathrooms: 2 en suite, 1 private

Evening meal available
CC: Delta, Mastercard, Switch, Visa

Elegant, Georgian, converted 17thC farmhouse in centre of village. Comfortable rooms with private facilities. Guest lounge, large garden, parking.

B&B per night:
S £31.00–£35.00
D £52.00–£60.00

HB per person:
DY £41.00–£46.00

OPEN All Year except Christmas

WEYMOUTH, Dorset Map ref 2B3 *Tourist Information Centre Tel: (01305) 785747*

BRUNSWICK GUEST HOUSE

9 Brunswick Terrace, Weymouth DT4 7RW
T: (01305) 785408 & 07776 485600

Enjoy our seafront cul-de-sac position in a picturesque Georgian terrace, with panoramic views of the bay. You are assured of a warm welcome and hearty breakfasts. Walk along the esplanade to the many amenities and attractions. Rail, bus, coach approximately 5 minutes' walk. Full central heating, ideal for out of season breaks.

Bedrooms: 1 single, 4 double/twin, 2 triple/multiple
Bathrooms: 6 en suite, 1 private

CC: Delta, Mastercard, Switch, Visa

B&B per night:
S £20.00–£26.00
D £40.00–£52.00

OPEN All Year except Christmas

◆◆◆◆

CUMBERLAND HOTEL

95 Esplanade, Weymouth DT4 7BA
T: (01305) 785644
F: (01305) 785644
I: www.cumberlandhotel.weymouth.co.uk

Bedrooms: 10 double/twin, 2 triple/multiple
Bathrooms: 12 en suite

Evening meal available
CC: Delta, Mastercard, Switch, Visa

An attractive seafront, licensed hotel offering quality food and good hospitality. We are centrally situated on the Esplanade close to all amenities.

B&B per night:
S £20.00–£50.00
D £40.00–£80.00

HB per person:
DY £26.00–£55.00

OPEN All Year

◆◆◆

THE FRESHFORD HOTEL

3 Grange Road, Weymouth DT4 7PQ
T: (01305) 775862
F: (01305) 775862
E: info@freshfordhotel.co.uk
I: www.freshfordhotel.co.uk

Bedrooms: 2 single, 3 double/twin, 2 triple/multiple
Bathrooms: 1 en suite

Evening meal available
CC: Delta, Mastercard, Visa

Victorian hotel close to seafront, main roads, Jurassic coastline, railway station and coach park. Quiet position. Car park on site. Ferry passengers most welcome.

B&B per night:
S £17.00–£25.00
D £34.00–£50.00

OPEN All Year

◆◆◆

HORIZON GUEST HOUSE

16 Brunswick Terrace, Weymouth DT4 7RW
T: (01305) 784916

Bedrooms: 1 single, 3 double/twin, 1 triple/multiple
Bathrooms: 1 en suite

Evening meal available

Overlooking Weymouth Bay, quiet location, 15 metres to the beach. En suite family room avaliable. Home cooking, vegetarians catered for. Children welcome. Residential licence.

B&B per night:
S £18.00–£24.00
D £34.00–£52.00

HB per person:
DY £25.50–£34.50

OPEN All Year except Christmas

QUALITY ASSURANCE SCHEME

Diamond ratings and awards are explained at the back of this guide.

WEYMOUTH continued

◆◆◆◆

KENORA PRIVATE HOTEL

5 Stavordale Road, Weymouth DT4 0AB
T: (01305) 771215
E: kenora.hotel@wdi.co.uk
I: www.kenorahotel.co.uk

Family-run hotel, aiming to provide good food, with a choice of menu including daily vegetarian choice. Clean, comfortable, well-maintained accommodation and a friendly, relaxed atmosphere where you can enjoy your well-earned holiday. Easy parking, garden to relax in, 700 metres from town, harbour and sandy beach.

Bedrooms: 3 single, 10 double/twin, 2 triple/multiple
Bathrooms: 13 en suite

Evening meal available
CC: Delta, Mastercard, Switch, Visa

Special prices for 3-7-night breaks, Easter, May and last 2 weeks of Sep.

B&B per night:
S £38.00–£42.00
D £63.00–£69.50

HB per person:
DY £43.00–£53.50

◆◆◆

WARWICK COURT

20 Abbotsbury Road, Weymouth DT4 0AE
T: (01305) 783261
F: (01305) 783261
E: sharon@warwickcourt.co.uk

Guests are assured a warm welcome at our family-run hotel just a short walk from the town centre and beach. All bedrooms are comfortable and well equipped. There is a cosy lounge and bar. Choice of breakfasts served in our bright and pleasant dining room.

Bedrooms: 1 single, 4 double/twin, 3 triple/multiple
Bathrooms: 8 en suite

CC: Delta, Mastercard, Switch, Visa

Low season and mid-season deals – please call for more details.

B&B per night:
S £20.00–£27.00
D £36.00–£50.00

OPEN All Year except Christmas

◆◆◆

WEYSIDE GUEST HOUSE

1a Abbotsbury Road, Weymouth DT4 0AD
T: (01305) 772685
E: weysideguesthouse@btinternet.com
I: www.weysideguesthouse.btinternet.co.uk

Bedrooms: 2 double/twin, 2 triple/multiple
Bathrooms: 4 en suite

A well-established guesthouse within walking distance of all attractions. All rooms en suite with television and radio. Catering for families and couples. Own car park.

B&B per night:
S £22.50
D £45.00

WHITECROSS, Cornwall Map ref 1B2

HYCROFT

Whitecross, Wadebridge PL27 7JD
T: (01208) 816568

Bedrooms: 1 single, 2 double/twin
Bathrooms: 1 private

Country-style bungalow opposite Royal Cornwall Showground. Parking for 4 cars. Close to shops, pub and restaurants. Wadebridge 1 mile. Padstow 6 miles.

B&B per night:
S £15.00–£18.00
D £36.00–£40.00

OPEN All Year except Christmas

GOLD & SILVER AWARDS

These exclusive ETC awards are given to establishments achieving the highest levels of quality and service. Further information can be found at the front of the guide and additional accommodation achieving these awards are shown in the listing at the back of this guide.

WINKLEIGH, Devon Map ref 1C2

THE OLD PARSONAGE

Court Walk, Winkleigh EX19 8JA
T: (01837) 83772
F: (01837) 680074

B&B per night:
D £43.00

HB per person:
DY £53.00–£67.50

Typical Devon thatched and cob-walled house. Park-like gardens have many magnificent trees, rhododendrons and azaleas. Comfortable en suite bedrooms with lots of old world charm. Garden gate leads to village square. Five minutes away at Wembworthy we recommend the Lymington Arms for its excellent restaurant and blackboard menus.

Bedrooms: 3 double/twin; permanent suite(s)
Bathrooms: 3 en suite

Evening meal available

5 P

WINSFORD, Somerset Map ref 1D1

KEMPS FARM

Winsford, Minehead TA24 7HT
T: (01643) 851312

B&B per night:
S £19.00
D £38.00

HB per person:
DY £28.00

OPEN All Year except Christmas

Spacious farmhouse with stunning views over Exe Valley. Superb walking, delicious home cooking with local produce. Guests' comfort is paramount. Hostess trays in all rooms.

Bedrooms: 3 double/twin
Bathrooms: 2 en suite, 1 private

Evening meal available

5 P

◆◆◆◆

LARCOMBE FOOT

Winsford, Minehead TA24 7HS
T: (01643) 851306

B&B per night:
S Min £23.00
D Min £23.00

HB per person:
DY Min £37.00

Attractive period house in beautiful, tranquil Exe Valley. Guests' comfort within a warm, happy atmosphere is paramount. Footpath access to the moor and surrounding wildlife make Larcombe Foot an idyllic rural retreat. Dogs welcome.

Bedrooms: 1 single, 2 double/twin
Bathrooms: 1 en suite, 1 private

Evening meal available

6 P

WINSLEY, Wiltshire Map ref 2B2

THE CONIFERS

4 King Alfred Way, Winsley, Bradford-on-Avon BA15 2NG
T: (01225) 722482

Bedrooms: 2 double/twin

B&B per night:
S £20.00–£22.00
D £40.00–£44.00

OPEN All Year

Semi-detached house, 2.25 miles from Bradford-on-Avon, 7 miles from Bath. Quiet area, pleasant outlook. Friendly atmosphere. A short stroll from 'Seven Stars' pub serving good food.

P

WINTERBOURNE STOKE, Wiltshire Map ref 2B2

SCOTLAND LODGE FARM

Winterbourne Stoke, Salisbury
SP3 4TF
T: (01980) 621199
F: (01980) 621188
E: william.lockwood@bigwig.net
I: www.smoothhound.co.uk/hotels/scotlandl.html

Bedrooms: 3 double/twin
Bathrooms: 2 private

CC: Delta, Mastercard, Switch, Visa

Warm welcome at family-run competition yard set in 46 acres of grassland. Lovely views and walks, Stonehenge/Salisbury nearby. Dogs, children and horses welcomed – stabling available on shavings.

B&B per night:
S £27.00–£30.00
D £48.00–£50.00

OPEN All Year

WOOTTON BASSETT, Wiltshire Map ref 2B2

THE HOLLIES

Greenhill, Hook, Wootton Bassett, Swindon SN4 8EH
T: (01793) 770795
F: (01793) 770795

Bedrooms: 2 single, 2 double/twin
Bathrooms: 1 en suite

Lunch available
Evening meal available

In beautiful countryside looking across the valley to the Cotswolds. Large garden, ample parking, non-smoking. One room en suite. Four miles west of Swindon, 8 miles Cotswold Water Park.

B&B per night:
S £21.00–£24.00
D £38.00–£46.00

OPEN All Year except Christmas

YELVERTON, Devon Map ref 1C2

Silver Award

THE OLD ORCHARD

Harrowbeer Lane, Yelverton
PL20 6DZ
T: (01822) 854310
F: (01822) 854310
E: babs@baross.demon.co.uk
I: www.baross.demon.co.uk/theoldorchard

Bedrooms: 2 double/twin
Bathrooms: 1 en suite, 1 private

Select bed and breakfast accommodation on the edge of Dartmoor offering satisfying breakfasts using local and organic produce. You are welcomed by word and deed.

B&B per night:
S Min £25.00
D Min £47.00

OPEN All Year except Christmas

YEOVILTON, Somerset Map ref 2A3

CARY FITZPAINE

Yeovilton, Yeovil BA22 8JB
T: (01458) 223250 & 07932 657140
F: (01458) 223372
E: acrang@aol.com
I: www.caryfitzpaine.com

Bedrooms: 1 single, 2 double/twin, 1 triple/multiple
Bathrooms: 2 en suite, 1 private

CC: Delta, Diners, Mastercard, Switch, Visa

600-acre mixed farm. Elegant Georgian manor farmhouse in idyllic setting. Large gardens. High standard of accommodation, all bedrooms with en suite bath. Four-poster bed.

B&B per night:
S £24.00–£28.00
D £48.00–£52.00

OPEN All Year except Christmas

TOWN INDEX

This can be found at the back of the guide. If you know where you want to stay, the index will give you the page number listing accommodation in your chosen town, city or village.

A brief guide to the main Towns and Villages offering accommodation in the South West

A **ABBOTSBURY, DORSET** - Beautiful village near Chesil Beach, with a long main street of mellow stone and thatched cottages and the ruins of a Benedictine monastery. High above the village on a hill is a prominent 15thC chapel. Abbotsbury's famous swannery and sub-tropical gardens lie just outside the village.

• **ALLERFORD, SOMERSET** - Village with picturesque stone and thatch cottages and a packhorse bridge, set in the beautiful Vale of Porlock.

• **AMESBURY, WILTSHIRE** - Standing on the banks of the River Avon, this is the nearest town to Stonehenge on Salisbury Plain. The area is rich in prehistoric sites.

• **ASHBURTON, DEVON** - Formerly a thriving wool centre and important as one of Dartmoor's four stannary towns. Today's busy market town has many period buildings. Ancient tradition is maintained in the annual ale-tasting and bread-weighing ceremony. Good centre for exploring Dartmoor or the South Devon coast.

• **AVEBURY, WILTSHIRE** - Set in a landscape of earthworks and megalithic standing stones, Avebury has a fine church and an Elizabethan manor. Remains from excavations may be seen in the museum. The area abounds in important prehistoric sites, among them Silbury Hill. Stonehenge stands about 20 miles due south.

• **AXMINSTER, DEVON** - This tree-shaded market town on the banks of the River Axe was one of Devon's earliest West Saxon settlements, but is better known for its carpet making. Based on Turkish methods, the industry began in 1755, declined in the 1830s and was revived in 1937.

B **BARNSTAPLE, DEVON** - At the head of the Taw Estuary, once a ship-building and textile town, now an agricultural centre with attractive period buildings, a modern civic centre and leisure centre. Attractions include Queen Anne's Walk, a charming colonnaded arcade, and Pannier Market.

• **BATCOMBE, SOMERSET** - Village tucked into a fold of the hills, close to the uppermost reaches of the River Alham, giving superb views of the countryside. The church has a splendid 15thC tower.

• **BATH, BATH AND NORTH EAST SOMERSET** - Georgian spa city beside the River Avon. Important Roman site with impressive reconstructed baths, uncovered in 19thC. Bath Abbey built on site of monastery where first king of England was crowned (AD 973). Fine architecture in mellow local stone. Pump Room and museums.

• **BEAMINSTER, DORSET** - Old country town of mellow local stone set amid hills and rural vales. Mainly Georgian buildings; attractive almshouses date from 1603. The 17thC church with its ornate, pinnacled tower was restored inside by the Victorians. Parnham, a Tudor manor house, lies one mile south.

• **BIDEFORD, DEVON** - The home port of Sir Richard Grenville, the town, with its 17thC merchants' houses, flourished as a ship-building and cloth town. The bridge of 24 arches was built about 1460. Charles Kingsley stayed here while writing Westward Ho!

• **BISHOP'S LYDEARD, SOMERSET** - Village five miles north-west of Taunton, the county town. Terminus for the West Somerset steam railway.

• **BODMIN, CORNWALL** - County town south-west of Bodmin Moor with a ruined priory and church dedicated to St Petroc. Nearby are Lanhydrock House and Pencarrow House.

• **BOSCASTLE, CORNWALL** - Small, unspoilt village in Valency Valley. Active as a port until onset of railway era, its natural harbour affords rare shelter on this wild coast. Attractions include spectacular blow-hole, Celtic field strips, part-Norman church. Nearby St Juliot Church was restored by Thomas Hardy.

• **BOVEY TRACEY, DEVON** - Standing by the river just east of Dartmoor National Park, this old town has good moorland views. Its church, with a 14thC tower, holds one of Devon's finest medieval rood screens.

• **BOX, WILTSHIRE** - Village in an Area of Outstanding Natural Beauty, seven miles south-west of Chippenham. It is famed for Box ground stone, used for centuries on buildings of national importance.

• **BRADFORD-ON-AVON, WILTSHIRE** - Huddled beside the river, the buildings of this former cloth-weaving town reflect continuing prosperity from the Middle Ages. There is a tiny Anglo-Saxon church, part of a monastery. The part-14thC bridge carries a medieval chapel, later used as a gaol.

• **BRIDGWATER, SOMERSET** - Former medieval port on the River Parrett, now a small industrial town with mostly 19thC or modern architecture. Georgian Castle Street leads to West Quay and site of 13thC castle razed to the ground by Cromwell. The birthplace of Cromwellian Admiral Robert Blake is now a museum. Arts centre.

• **BRIDPORT, DORSET** - Market town and chief producer of nets and ropes just inland of dramatic Dorset coast. Old, broad streets built for drying and twisting and long gardens for rope-walks. Grand arcaded Town Hall and Georgian buildings. Local history museum has Roman relics.

• **BRISTOL** - Famous for maritime links, historic harbour, Georgian terraces and Brunel's Clifton suspension bridge. Many attractions including SS Great Britain, Bristol Zoo, museums and art galleries and top-name entertainments. Events include Balloon Fiesta and Regatta.

• **BRIXHAM, DEVON** - Famous for its trawling fleet in the 19thC, a steeply built fishing port overlooking the harbour and fish market. A statue of William of Orange recalls his landing here before deposing James II. There is an aquarium and museum. Good cliff views and walks.

• **BUDE, CORNWALL** - Resort on dramatic Atlantic coast. High cliffs give spectacular sea and inland views. Golf-course, cricket pitch, folly, surfing, coarse-fishing and boating. Mother-town Stratton was base of Royalist Sir Bevil Grenville.

• **BUDLEIGH SALTERTON, DEVON** - Small resort with pebble beach on coast of red cliffs, setting for famous Victorian painting "The Boyhood of Raleigh". Sir Walter Raleigh was born at Hayes Barton. A salt-panning village in medieval times, today's resort has some Georgian houses.

• **BURNHAM-ON-SEA, SOMERSET** - Small Victorian resort famous for sunsets and sandy beaches, a few minutes from junction 22 of the M5. Ideal base for touring Somerset, Cheddar and Bath. Good sporting facilities, championship golfcourse.

• **BURTON BRADSTOCK, DORSET** - Lying amid fields beside the River Bride, a village of old stone houses, a 14thC church and a village green. The beautiful coast road from Abbotsbury to Bridport passes by and Iron Age forts top the surrounding hills. The sheltered river valley makes a staging post for migrating birds.

C **CALLINGTON, CORNWALL** - A quiet market town standing on high ground above the River Lynher. The 15thC church of St Mary's has an alabaster monument to Lord Willoughby de Broke, Henry VII's marshal. A 15thC chapel, one mile east, houses Dupath Well, one of the Cornish Holy Wells.

• **CASTLE CARY, SOMERSET** - One of South Somerset's most attractive market towns, with a picturesque winding High Street of golden stone and thatch, market-house and famous round 18thC lock-up.

• **CHARD, SOMERSET** - Market town in hilly countryside. The wide main street has some handsome buildings, among them the Guildhall, court house and almshouses. Modern light industry and dairy produce have replaced 19thC lace making which came at the decline of the cloth trade.

• **CHARMINSTER, DORSET** - Village just north of the county town of Dorchester, with its museums and Maiden Castle Iron Age hillfort. Within easy reach of Thomas Hardy's cottage and the Cerne Giant hillside figure.

• **CHARMOUTH, DORSET** - Set back from the fossil-rich cliffs, a small coastal town where Charles II came to the Queen's Armes when seeking escape to France. Just south at low tide, the sandy beach rewards fossil-hunters; at Black Ven an ichthyosaurus (now in London's Natural History Museum) was found.

• **CHEDDAR, SOMERSET** - Large village at foot of Mendips just south of the spectacular Cheddar Gorge. Close by are Roman and Saxon sites and famous show caves. Traditional Cheddar cheese is still made here.

• **CHEW STOKE, BATH AND NORTH EAST SOMERSET** - Attractive village in the Mendip Hills with an interesting Tudor rectory and the remains of a Roman villa. To the south is the Chew Valley reservoir with its extensive leisure facilities.

• **CLOVELLY, DEVON** - Clinging to wooded cliffs, fishing village with steep cobbled street zigzagging, or cut in steps, to harbour. Carrying sledges stand beside whitewashed, flower-decked cottages. Charles Kingsley's father was rector of the church set high up near the Hamlyn family's Clovelly Court.

• **CORSHAM, WILTSHIRE** - Growing town with old centre showing Flemish influence, legacy of former prosperity from weaving. The church, restored last century, retains Norman features. The Elizabethan Corsham Court, with additions by Capability Brown, has fine furniture.

• **CRANTOCK, CORNWALL** - Pretty village of thatched cottages and seaside bungalows. Village stocks, once used against smugglers, are in the churchyard, and the pub has a smugglers' hideout.

• **CREWKERNE, SOMERSET** - This charming little market town on the Dorset border nestles in undulating farmland and orchards in a conservation area. Built of local sandstone with Roman and Saxon origins. The magnificent St Bartholomew's Church dates from the 15thC; St Bartholomew's Fair is held in September.

D **DARTMOUTH, DEVON** - Ancient port at mouth of Dart. Has fine period buildings, notably town houses near Quay and Butterwalk of 1635. Harbour castle ruin. In 12thC Crusader fleets assembled here. Royal Naval College dominates from hill. Carnival, June; Regatta, August.

• **DEVIZES, WILTSHIRE** - Old market town standing on the Kennet and Avon Canal. Rebuilt Norman castle, good 18thC buildings. St John's church has 12thC work and Norman tower. Museum of Wiltshire's archaeology and natural history reflects wealth of prehistoric sites in the county.

• **DORCHESTER, DORSET** - Busy medieval county town destroyed by fires in 17thC and 18thC. Cromwellian stronghold and scene of Judge Jeffreys' Bloody Assize after Monmouth Rebellion of 1685. The Tolpuddle Martyrs were tried in Shire Hall. The Museum has Roman and earlier exhibits and Hardy relics.

• **DULVERTON, SOMERSET** - Set among woods and hills of south-west Exmoor, a busy riverside town with a 13thC church. The Rivers Barle and Exe are rich in salmon and trout. The information centre at the Exmoor National Park Headquarters at Dulverton is open throughout the year.

• **DUNSTER, SOMERSET** - Ancient town with views of Exmoor. The hilltop castle has been continuously occupied since 1070. Medieval prosperity from cloth built 16thC octagonal Yarn Market and the church. A riverside mill, packhorse bridge and 18thC hilltop folly occupy other interesting corners in the town.

E **EXETER, DEVON** - University city rebuilt after the 1940s around its cathedral. Attractions include 13thC cathedral with fine west front; notable waterfront buildings; Guildhall; Royal Albert Memorial Museum; underground passages; Northcott Theatre.

F **FALMOUTH, CORNWALL** - Busy port and fishing harbour, popular resort on the balmy Cornish Riviera. Henry VIII's Pendennis Castle faces St Mawes Castle across the broad, natural harbour and yacht basin Carrick Roads, which receives seven rivers.

• **FROME, SOMERSET** - Old market town with modern light industry, its medieval centre watered by the River Frome. Above Cheap Street with its flagstones and watercourse is the church showing work of varying periods. Interesting buildings include 18thC wool merchants' houses.

VISITOR ATTRACTIONS For ideas on places to visit refer to the introduction at the beginning of this section. Look out too for the ETC's Quality Assured Visitor Attraction signs.

G **GLASTONBURY, SOMERSET** - Market town associated with Joseph of Arimathea and the birth of English Christianity. Built around its 7thC abbey, said to be the site of King Arthur's burial. Glastonbury Tor, with its ancient tower, gives panoramic views over flat country and the Mendip Hills.

H **HARTLAND, DEVON** - Hamlet on high, wild country near Hartland Point. Just west, the parish church tower makes a magnificent landmark; the light, unrestored interior holds one of Devon's finest rood screens. There are spectacular cliffs around Hartland Point and the lighthouse.

• **HONITON, DEVON** - Old coaching town in undulating farmland. Formerly famous for lace making, it is now an antiques trade centre and market town. Small museum.

I **ILFRACOMBE, DEVON** - Resort of Victorian grandeur set on hillside between cliffs with sandy coves. At the mouth of the harbour stands an 18thC lighthouse, built over a medieval chapel. There are fine formal gardens and a museum. Chambercombe Manor, an interesting old house, is nearby.

• **ILLOGAN, CORNWALL** - Former mining village two miles north-west of Redruth and close to the coast. The Victorian engineer and benefactor, Sir Richard Tangye, was born here in 1833.

• **ISLES OF SCILLY** - Picturesque group of islands and granitic rocks south-west of Land's End. Peaceful and unspoilt, they are noted for natural beauty, romantic maritime history, silver sands, early flowers and sub-tropical gardens on Tresco. Main island is St. Mary's.

• **IVYBRIDGE, DEVON** - Town set in delightful woodlands on the River Erme. Brunel designed the local railway viaduct. South Dartmoor Leisure Centre.

K **KENTON, DEVON** - Village between Exeter and Dawlish, separated from the Exe Estuary by the large estate of Powderham Castle. Fine 14thC church of red sandstone with a massive medieval rood screen and loft.

• **KINGSBRIDGE, DEVON** - Formerly important as a port, now a market town overlooking head of beautiful, wooded estuary winding deep into rural countryside. Summer art exhibitions; Cookworthy Museum.

L **LANGPORT, SOMERSET** - Small market town with Anglo-Saxon origins, sloping to River Parrett. Well known for glove making and, formerly, for eels. Interesting old buildings include some fine local churches.

• **LAUNCESTON, CORNWALL** - Medieval "Gateway to Cornwall", county town until 1838, founded by the Normans under their hilltop castle near the original monastic settlement. This market town, overlooked by its castle ruin, has a square with Georgian houses and an elaborately carved granite church.

• **LEWDOWN, DEVON** - Small village on the very edge of Dartmoor. Lydford Castle is four miles to the east.

• **LISKEARD, CORNWALL** - Former stannary town with a livestock market and light industry, at the head of a valley running to the coast. Handsome Georgian and Victorian residences and a Victorian Guildhall reflect the prosperity of the mining boom. The large church has an early 20thC tower and a Norman font.

• **LOOE, CORNWALL** - Small resort developed around former fishing and smuggling ports occupying the deep estuary of the East and West Looe Rivers. Narrow, winding streets with old inns; museum and art gallery are housed in interesting old buildings. Shark-fishing centre, boat trips; busy harbour.

• **LYME REGIS, DORSET** - Pretty, historic fishing town and resort set against the fossil-rich cliffs of Lyme Bay. In medieval times it was an important port and cloth centre. The Cobb, a massive stone breakwater, shelters the ancient harbour which is still lively with boats.

• **LYNMOUTH, DEVON** - Resort set beneath bracken-covered cliffs and pinewood gorges where two rivers meet and cascade between boulders to the town. Lynton, set on cliffs above, can be reached by a water-operated cliff railway from the Victorian esplanade. Valley of the Rocks, to the west, gives dramatic walks.

• **LYNTON, DEVON** - Hilltop resort on Exmoor coast linked to its seaside twin, Lynmouth, by a water-operated cliff railway which descends from the town hall. Spectacular surroundings of moorland cliffs with steep chasms of conifer and rocks through which rivers cascade.

M **MALMESBURY, WILTSHIRE** - Overlooking the River Avon, an old town dominated by its great church, once a Benedictine abbey. The surviving Norman nave and porch are noted for fine sculptures, 12thC arches and musicians' gallery.

• **MEVAGISSEY, CORNWALL** - Small fishing town, a favourite with holidaymakers. Earlier prosperity came from pilchard fisheries, boat-building and smuggling. By the harbour are fish cellars, some converted, and a local history museum is housed in an old boat-building shed. Handsome Methodist chapel; shark fishing, sailing.

• **MINEHEAD, SOMERSET** - Victorian resort with spreading sands developed around old fishing port on the coast below Exmoor. Former fishermen's cottages stand beside the 17thC harbour; cobbled streets climb the hill in steps to the church. Boat trips, steam railway. Hobby Horse festival 1 May.

• **MONTACUTE, SOMERSET** - Picturesque village named after its "steep hill" and noted for its splendid hamstone Elizabethan mansion. By the church stands the gatehouse of a Cluniac priory, built with stone from the hilltop castle. An 18thC folly now crowns the hill, where the Holy Cross of Waltham Abbey was found.

• **MORETONHAMPSTEAD, DEVON** - Small market town with a row of 17thC almshouses standing on the Exeter road. Surrounding moorland is scattered with ancient farmhouses and prehistoric sites.

N **NETHER STOWEY, SOMERSET** - Winding village below east slopes of Quantocks with attractive old cottages of varying periods. A Victorian clock tower stands at its centre, where a village road climbs the hill beside a small stream. Cottage owned by Coleridge is open to the public.

• **NEWQUAY, CORNWALL** - Popular resort spread over dramatic cliffs around its old fishing port. Many beaches with abundant sands, caves and rock pools; excellent surf. Pilots' gigs are still raced from the harbour and on the headland stands the stone Huer's House from the pilchard-fishing days.

O **OKEHAMPTON, DEVON** - Busy market town near the high tors of northern Dartmoor. The Victorian church, with William Morris windows and a 15thC tower, stands on the site of a Saxon church. A Norman castle ruin overlooks the river to the west of the town. Museum of Dartmoor Life in a restored mill.

P **PADSTOW, CORNWALL** - Old town encircling its harbour on the Camel Estuary. The 15thC church has notable bench-ends. There are fine houses on North Quay and Raleigh's Court House on South Quay. Tall cliffs and golden sands along the coast and ferry to Rock. Famous 'Obby 'Oss Festival on 1 May.

• **PAIGNTON, DEVON** - Lively seaside resort with a pretty harbour on Torbay. Bronze Age and Saxon sites are occupied by the 15thC church, which has a Norman door and font. The beautiful Chantry Chapel was built by local landowners, the Kirkhams.

• **PENSFORD, BATH AND NORTH EAST SOMERSET** - Village six miles south of Bristol and within easy reach of the City of Bath. Chew Valley and Blagdon Lakes close by.

• **PENZANCE, CORNWALL** - Resort and fishing port on Mount's Bay with mainly Victorian promenade and some fine Regency terraces. Former prosperity came from tin trade and pilchard fishing. Grand Georgian-style church by harbour. Georgian Egyptian building at head of Chapel Street and Morrab Gardens.

• **PERRANPORTH, CORNWALL** - Small seaside resort developed around a former mining village. Today's attractions include exciting surf, rocks, caves and extensive sand dunes.

• **PIDDLETRENTHIDE, DORSET** - Situated on the River Piddle, north of Puddletown and Dorchester. Norman church with 15thC towers.

• **PILLATON, CORNWALL** - Peaceful village on the slopes of the River Lynher in steeply wooded country near the Devon border. Within easy reach of the coast and rugged walking country on Bodmin Moor.

• **PLYMOUTH, DEVON** - Devon's largest city, major port and naval base. Old houses on the Barbican and ambitious architecture in modern centre, with new National Marine Aquarium, museum and art gallery, the Dome - a heritage centre on the Hoe. Superb coastal views over Plymouth Sound from the Hoe.

• **PORLOCK, SOMERSET** - Village set between steep Exmoor Hills and the sea at the head of beautiful Porlock Vale. The narrow street shows a medley of building styles. South-westward is Porlock Weir with its old houses and tiny harbour, and further along the shore at Culbone is England's smallest church.

• **PORTHCURNO, CORNWALL** - Beautifully sited village near a beach with white sand and turquoise sea enclosed in granite cliffs. The Minack open-air theatre of concrete and granite slabs, perched 200 ft above the sea, has a good view of Treryn Dinas to the east.

R **RADSTOCK, BATH AND NORTH EAST SOMERSET** - Thriving small town ideally situated for touring the Mendip Hills.

S **ST AGNES, CORNWALL** - Small town in a once-rich mining area on the north coast. Terraced cottages and granite houses slope to the church. Some old mine workings remain, but the attraction must be the magnificent coastal scenery and superb walks. St Agnes Beacon offers one of Cornwall's most extensive views.

• **ST KEW, CORNWALL** - Old village sheltered by trees standing beside a stream. The church is noted for its medieval glass showing the Passion and the remains of a scene of the Tree of Jesse.

• **ST MAWGAN, CORNWALL** - Pretty village of great historic interest, on wooded slopes in the Vale of Lanherne. At its centre, an old stone bridge over the River Menahyl is overlooked by the church with its lofty buttressed tower. Among ancient stone crosses in the churchyard is a 15thC lantern cross with carved figures.

• **ST IVES, CORNWALL** - Old fishing port, artists' colony and holiday town with good surfing beach. Fishermen's cottages, granite fish cellars, a sandy harbour and magnificent headlands typify a charm that has survived since the 19thC pilchard boom. Tate Gallery opened in 1993.

• **ST JUST-IN-PENWITH, CORNWALL** - Coastal parish of craggy moorland scattered with engine houses and chimney stacks of disused mines. The old mining town of St Just has handsome 19thC granite buildings. North of the town are the dramatic ruined tin mines at Botallack.

• **SALCOMBE, DEVON** - Sheltered yachting resort of whitewashed houses and narrow streets in a balmy setting on the Salcombe Estuary. Palm, myrtle and other Mediterranean plants flourish. There are sandy bays and creeks for boating.

• **SALISBURY, WILTSHIRE** - Beautiful city and ancient regional capital set amid water meadows. Buildings of all periods are dominated by the cathedral whose spire is the tallest in England. Built between 1220 and 1258, it is one of the purest examples of Early English architecture.

• **SEATON, DEVON** - Small resort lying near the mouth of the River Axe. A mile-long beach extends to the dramatic cliffs of Beer Head. Annual art exhibition in July.

• **SHALDON, DEVON** - Pretty resort facing Teignmouth from the south bank of the Teign Estuary. Regency houses harmonise with others of later periods; there are old cottages and narrow lanes. On the Ness, a sandstone promontory nearby, a tunnel built in the 19thC leads to a beach revealed at low tide.

• **SHERBORNE, DORSET** - Dorset's "Cathedral City" of medieval streets, golden hamstone buildings and great abbey church, resting place of Saxon kings. Formidable 12thC castle ruins and Sir Walter Raleigh's splendid Tudor mansion and deer park. Street markets, leisure centre, many cultural activities.

• **SIDMOUTH, DEVON** - Charming resort set amid lofty red cliffs where the River Sid meets the sea. The wealth of ornate Regency and Victorian villas recalls the time when this was one of the south coast's most exclusive resorts. Museum; August International Festival of Folk Arts.

• **SOMERTON, SOMERSET** - Old market town, important in Saxon times, situated at a gap in the hills south-east of Sedgemoor. Attractive red-roofed stone houses surround the 17thC octagonal market cross, and among other handsome buildings are the Town Hall and almshouses of about the same period.

• **SPREYTON, DEVON** - Village situated six miles east of Okehampton, just north of the Dartmoor National Park. In 1802, Tom Cobley and his friends travelled from the village to Widecombe Fair.

• **SWINDON, WILTSHIRE** - Wiltshire's industrial and commercial centre, an important railway town in the 19thC, situated just north of the Marlborough Downs. The railway village created in the mid-19thC has been preserved. Railway museum, art gallery, theatre and leisure centre. Designer shopping village.

T **TAUNTON, SOMERSET** - County town, well known for its public schools, sheltered by gentle hill-ranges on the River Tone. Medieval prosperity from wool has continued in marketing and manufacturing and the town retains many fine period buildings. Museum.

• **TAVISTOCK, DEVON** - Old market town beside the River Tavy on the western edge of Dartmoor. Developed around its 10thC abbey, of which some fragments remain, it became a stannary town in 1305 when tin-streaming thrived on the moors. Tavistock Goose Fair, October.

• **TORQUAY, DEVON** - Devon's grandest resort, developed from a fishing village. Smart apartments and terraces rise from the seafront, and Marine Drive along the headland gives views of beaches and colourful cliffs.

• **TORRINGTON, DEVON** - Perched high above the River Torridge, with a charming market square, Georgian Town Hall and a museum. The famous Dartington Crystal Factory, Rosemoor Gardens and Plough Arts Centre are all located in the town.

• **TOTNES, DEVON** - Old market town steeply built near the head of the Dart Estuary. Remains of motte and bailey castle, medieval gateways, a noble church, 16thC Guildhall and medley of period houses recall former wealth from cloth and shipping, continued in rural and water industries.

• **TRURO, CORNWALL** - Cornwall's administrative centre and cathedral city, set at the head of Truro River on the Fal Estuary. A medieval stannary town, it handled mineral ore from West Cornwall; fine Georgian buildings recall its heyday as a society haunt in the second mining boom.

W **WASHFORD, SOMERSET** - Village two miles west of Williton and a good centre for many interesting walks. On the edge of the village is Cleeve Abbey, founded in the 13thC by the Cistercians, and with remarkably complete dormitory and refectory.

• **WATERGATE BAY, CORNWALL** - Beautiful long-board-riders' beach backed by tall cliffs, north-west of Newquay. A small holiday village nestles in a steep river valley making a cleft in the cliffs.

• **WELLS, SOMERSET** - Small city set beneath the southern slopes of the Mendips. Built between 1180 and 1424, the magnificent cathedral is preserved in much of its original glory and, with its ancient precincts, forms one of our loveliest and most unified groups of medieval buildings.

• **WESTON-SUPER-MARE, NORTH SOMERSET** - Large, friendly resort developed in the 19thC. Traditional seaside attractions include theatres and a dance hall. The museum has a Victorian seaside gallery and Iron Age finds from a hill fort on Worlebury Hill in Weston Woods.

• **WEYMOUTH, DORSET** - Ancient port and one of the south's earliest resorts. Curving beside a long, sandy beach, the elegant Georgian esplanade is graced with a statue of George III and a cheerful Victorian Jubilee clock tower. Museum, Sea-Life Centre.

• **WINSFORD, SOMERSET** - Small village in Exmoor National Park, on the River Exe in splendid walking country under Winsford Hill. On the other side of the hill is a Celtic standing stone, the Caratacus Stone, and nearby across the River Barle stretches an ancient packhorse bridge, Tarr Steps.

• **WOOTTON BASSETT, WILTSHIRE** - Small hillside town with attractive old buildings and a 13thC church. The church and the half-timbered town hall were both restored in the 19thC and the stocks and ducking pool are preserved.

Y **YELVERTON, DEVON** - Village on the edge of Dartmoor, where ponies wander over the flat common. Buckland Abbey is two miles south-west, while Burrator Reservoir is two miles to the east.

• **YEOVILTON, SOMERSET** - Village just south of A303. Royal Naval Air Station and Fleet Air Army Museum situated close by.

USE YOUR *i*s

There are more than 550 Tourist Information Centres throughout England offering friendly help with accommodation and holiday ideas as well as suggestions of places to visit and things to do. You'll find TIC addresses in the local Phone Book.

SOUTH of England

A seafaring region with 800 years of nautical heritage to enjoy in its busy harbours and family resorts. For landlubbers there's gentle countryside, Georgian towns, modern cities and outstanding historic houses too.

classic sights

Stonehenge – Wiltshire's ancient and mysterious standing stones
The Round Table – housed in the Great Hall, Winchester and once reputed to be the Round Table of King Arthur
Waddesdon Manor – classic French Renaissance-style chateau

coast & country

The Needles – dramatic chalk pillars extending out into the Solent
Chiltern Hills – tranquil country walks
New Forest – historic wood and heathland

glorious gardens

Savill Garden – a beautiful woodland garden with many royal connections
Mottisfont Abbey – the perfect English rose garden

literary links

Jane Austen – her home in Chawton is now a museum, and she is buried in Winchester Cathedral.
Lewis Carroll – Christ Church, Oxford where Alice in Wonderland was created

maritime history

Portsmouth Historic Dockyard – Henry VIII's Mary Rose, HMS Victory and HMS Warrior 1860

The counties of Berkshire, Buckinghamshire, Dorset (Eastern), Hampshire, Isle of Wight and Oxfordshire

FOR MORE INFORMATION CONTACT:
Southern Tourist Board
40 Chamberlayne Road, Eastleigh,
Hampshire SO50 5JH
Tel: (023) 8062 5505 Fax: (023) 8062 0010
Email: info@southerntb.co.uk
Internet: www.visitbritain.com

The Pictures: 1 Waddesdon Manor, Buckinghamshire 2 Kennet & Avon Canal, Berkshire

> PLACES TO VISIT - see pages 406-409 > WHERE TO STAY - see pages 410-451

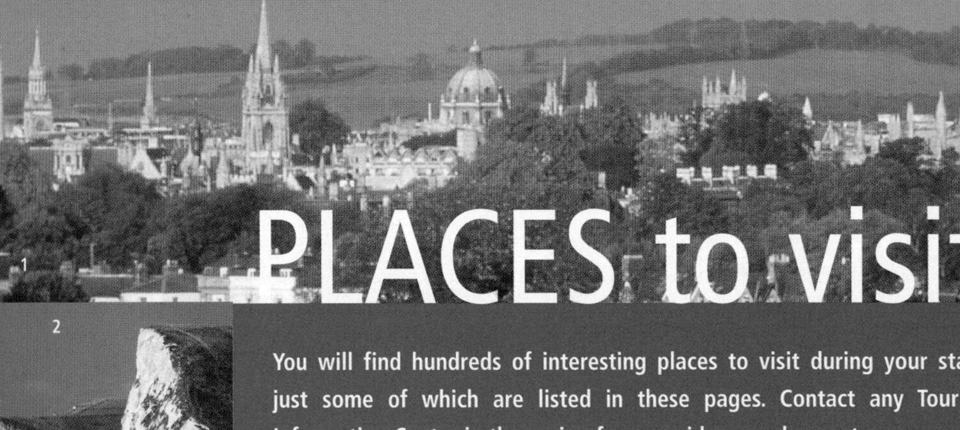

PLACES to visi

You will find hundreds of interesting places to visit during your st just some of which are listed in these pages. Contact any Touri Information Centre in the region for more ideas on days out.

Awarded ETC's new 'Quality Assured Visitor Attraction' marque at time of going to press. (See page 19).

Beale Park (The Child Beale Trust)

Lower Basildon, Reading

Tel: (0118) 984 5172 www.bealepark.co.uk

Beale Park boasts an extraordinary collection of rare birds and animals, a narrow-gauge railway, adventure playground and splash pools. Also nature trails and fishing on day tickets.

Bekonscot Model Village

Warwick Road, Beaconsfield

Tel: (01494) 672919 www.bekonscot.org.uk

The oldest model village in the world, Bekonscot depicts rural England in the 1930s, where time has stood still for 70 years. Narrow-gauge, ride-on railway.

Blenheim Palace

Woodstock

Tel: (01993) 811325 www.blenheimpalace.com

Home of the 11th Duke of Marlborough. Birthplace of Sir Winston Churchill. Designed by Vanbrugh in the English baroque style. Landscaped by 'Capability' Brown.

Breamore House

Breamore, Fordingbridge

Tel: (01725) 512233

Elizabethan manor house of 1583 with fine collection of works of art. Furniture, tapestries, needlework and paintings, mainly 17thC and 18thC Dutch School.

Carisbrooke Castle

Newport

Tel: (01983) 522107 www.english-heritage.org.uk

A splendid Norman castle where Charles I was imprisoned. The governor's lodge houses the county museum. Wheelhouse with wheel operated by donkeys.

Compton Acres

Canford Cliffs Road, Canford Cliffs, Poole

Tel: (01202) 700778 www.comptonacres.co.uk

Eleven separate and distinct gardens of the world including Italian, Japanese, Indian glen and Spanish water garden. Deer sanctuary with treetop lookout.

Cotswold Wildlife Park

Bradwell Grove, Burford, Oxford

Tel: (01993) 823006

www.cotswoldwildlifepark.co.uk

Wildlife park in 200 acres (81ha) of gardens and woodland with a variety of animals from all over the world.

The D-Day Museum and Overlord Embroidery

Clarence Esplanade, Portsmouth

Tel: (023) 9282 7261

www.portsmouthmuseums.co.uk

The magnificent 272ft- (83m-) long Overlord Embroider depicts the allied invasion of Normandy on 6 June 194 Sound guides available in four languages.

Didcot Railway Centre

Great Western Society, Didcot
Tel: (01235) 817200
www.didcotrailwaycentre.org.uk
Living museum recreating the golden age of the Great Western Railway. Steam locomotives and trains, engine shed and small relics museum.

Dinosaur Isle

Culver Parade, Sandown, Isle of Wight
Tel: 01983 404344 www.miwg.freeserve.co.uk
A new museum which takes the visitor from the Ice Age of the recent past, back to the Cretaceous period when dinosaurs lived and includes exciting displays of real fossils, skeletal re-constructions, life sized fleshed re-constructions and an animatronic dinosaur.

Exbury Gardens and Steam Railway

Exbury Estate Office, Exbury, Southampton
Tel: (023) 8089 1203 www.exbury.co.uk.
Over 200 acres (81ha) of woodland garden, including the Rothschild collection of rhododendrons, azaleas, camellias and magnolias. New 12.25-inch narrow-gauge steam railway.

Explosion! Museum of Naval Firepower

Priddy's Hard, Gosport
Tel: (023) 9250 5600 www.explosion.org.uk
An exciting new visitor experience for all the family on the shores of Portsmouth Harbour, Explosion! tells the story of naval firepower from gunpowder to the Exocet. Housed in historic buildings at Priddy's Hard, the Navy's former armaments depot, in Gosport, Hampshire.

The Hawk Conservancy and Country Park

Andover
Tel: (01264) 772252
www.hawk-conservancy.org
Unique to Great Britain: 'Valley of the Eagles' held here daily at 1400. Also 22 acres (9ha) of woodland gardens, butterfly garden and toddlers' play area.

Jane Austen's House

Chawton, Alton
Tel: (01420) 83262
17thC house where Jane Austen lived from 1809-1817 and wrote or revised her six great novels. Letters, pictures, memorabilia, garden with old-fashioned flowers.

Kingston Lacy

Wimborne Minster
Tel: (01202) 883402 www.nationaltrust.org.uk
A 17thC house designed for Sir Ralph Bankes by Sir Roger Pratt and altered by Sir Charles Barry in the 19thC. Collection of paintings, 250-acre (101-ha) wooded park, herd of Devon cattle.

Legoland Windsor

Winkfield Road, Windsor
Tel: 0870 5040404 www.legoland.co.uk
A family park with hands-on activities, rides, themed playscapes and more Lego bricks than you ever dreamed possible!

The Living Rainforest

Hampstead Norreys, Thatcham, Newbury
Tel: (01635) 202444 www.livingrainforest.org
Two under cover tropical rainforests, approximately 20,000sq ft (1,858sq m). Collection of rare and exotic tropical plants together with small representation of wildlife in rainforest.

Marwell Zoological Park

Marwell Zoological Park
Colden Common, Winchester
Tel: (01962) 777407 www.marwell.org.uk
Set in 100 acres (40.5ha) of parkland surrounding Marwell Hall. Venue suitable for all age groups and disabled.

4

5

> The Pictures: 1 The City of Oxford 2 Dorset Coast 3 Windsor Castle 4 Isle of Wight 5 HMS Victory, Portsmouth

National Motor Museum

John Montagu Building, Beaulieu, Brockenhurst
Tel: (01590) 612345 www.beaulieu.co.uk
Motor museum with over 250 exhibits showing history of motoring from 1896. Also Palace House, Wheels Experience, Beaulieu Abbey ruins and a display of monastic life.

Osborne House

Yorke Avenue, East Cowes
Tel: (01983) 200022 www.english-heritage.org.uk
Queen Victoria and Prince Albert's seaside holiday home. Swiss Cottage where royal children learnt cooking and gardening. Victorian carriage service to Swiss Cottage.

The Oxford Story

6 Broad Street, Oxford
Tel: (01865) 728822 www.oxfordstory.co.uk
An excellent introduction to Oxford. Experience 900 years of University history in one hour, from scientists to poets, astronomers to comedians.

Portsmouth Historic Dockyard

Porter's Lodge, 1/7 College Road,
HM Naval Base, Portsmouth
Tel: (023) 9286 1533 www.historicdockyard.co.uk
A fascinating day out: Action Stations, Mary Rose, HMS Victory, HMS Warrior 1860, Royal Naval Museum, 'Warships by water' harbour tours, Dockyard Apprentice exhibition.

River and Rowing Museum

Mill Meadows, Henley-on-Thames
Tel: (01491) 415600 www.rrm.co.uk
A unique, award-winning museum with galleries dedicated to rowing, the River Thames and the town of Henley. Special exhibitions run throughout the year.

The Sir Harold Hillier Gardens and Arboretum

Jermyns House, Jermyns Lane, Ampfield, Romsey
Tel: (01794) 368787 www.hillier.hants.gov.uk/
Established in 1953, The Sir Harold Hillier Gardens and Arboretum comprises the greatest collection of wild and cultivated woody plants in the world.

Staunton Country Park

Middle Park Way, Havant
Tel: (023) 9245 3405
Restored Victorian glasshouses with displays of exotic plants in the charming setting of the historic walled gardens. Ornamental farm with wide range of animals.

Swanage Railway

Station House, Swanage
Tel: (01929) 425800 www.swanagerailway.co.uk
Enjoy a nostalgic steam-train ride on the Purbeck line. Steam trains run every weekend throughout the year with daily running April to October.

The Tank Museum

Bovington, Wareham
Tel: (01929) 405096 www.tankmuseum.co.uk
The world's finest display of armoured fighting vehicles. Experimental vehicles, interactive displays, disabled access and facilities.

Tudor House Museum

St Michael's Square, Bugle Street, Southampton
Tel: (023) 8033 2513
www.southampton.gov.uk/leisure/heritage
Large, half-timbered Tudor house with exhibitions on Tudor, Georgian and Victorian domestic and local history. Unique Tudor garden.

Waddesdon Manor

Waddesdon, Aylesbury
Tel: (01296) 653226
www.waddesdon.org.uk
This French Renaissance-style chateau houses the Rothschild Collection of art treasures. The Victorian garden has a parterre, seasonal displays, aviary, rose and children's gardens.

Whitchurch Silk Mill

28 Winchester Street, Whitchurch
Tel: (01256) 892065 www.whitchurchsilkmill.org.uk
Unique Georgian silk-weaving watermill, now a working museum producing fine silk fabrics on Victorian machinery. Riverside garden, tearoom for light meals, silk gift shop.

Winchester Cathedral

Cathedral Office, 1 The Close, Winchester
Tel: (01962) 857224
www.winchester-cathedral.org.uk
Originally Norman, nave converted to perpendicular with 16thC additions. Old Saxon site adjacent. Tombs, library, medieval wall paintings and Close.

Windsor Castle

Windsor
Tel: (01753) 869898
www.the-royal-collection.org.uk
Official residence of HM The Queen and royal residence for nine centuries. State apartments, Queen Mary's dolls' house

Find out more about the SOUTH of England

Further information about holidays and attractions in the South of England is available from:

SOUTHERN TOURIST BOARD
40 Chamberlayne Road, Eastleigh, Hampshire SO50 5JH.
Tel: (023) 8062 5505 Fax: (023) 8062 0010
Email: info@southerntb.co.uk
Internet: www.visitbritain.com

Getting to the SOUTH of England

> The Pictures:
1 Bournemouth
edene, Buckinghamshire

BY ROAD: A good road network links London and the rest of the UK with major southern destinations. The M27 provides a near-continuous motorway route along the south coast, and the M25/M3/A33 provides a direct route from London to Winchester and Southampton. The scenic A31 stretches from London, through Hampshire and to mid-Dorset, whilst the M40/A34 have considerably cut travelling times from the West Midlands to the South. The M25 has speeded up access to Berkshire on the M4, and Buckinghamshire and Oxfordshire on the M40.

BY RAIL: From London's Waterloo, trains travel to Portsmouth, Southampton and Bournemouth approximately three times an hour. From these stations, frequent trains go to Poole, Salisbury and Winchester. Further information on rail journeys in the South of England can be obtained on 08457 484950.

Where to stay in the South of England

Accommodation entries in this region are listed in alphabetical order of place name, and then in alphabetical order of establishment.

Map references refer to the colour location maps at the front of this guide. The first number indicates the map to use; the letter and number which follow refer to the grid reference on the map.

At-a-glance symbols at the end of each accommodation entry give useful information about services and facilities. A key to symbols can be found inside the back cover flap. Keep this open for easy reference.

A brief description of the towns and villages offering accommodation in the entries which follow, can be found at the end of this section.

A complete listing of all the English Tourism Council assessed accommodation covered by this guide appears at the back of the guide.

ABBOTTS ANN, Hampshire Map ref 2C2

VIRGINIA LODGE
Salisbury Road, Abbotts Ann,
Andover SP11 7NX
T: (01264) 710713
E: b_stuart@talk21.com

Bedrooms: 3 double/twin
Bathrooms: 1 en suite

Genuine welcome at comfortable bungalow (non-smoking). Large gardens. On edge of picturesque Abbotts Ann. On A343, 1 mile from A303, central for Salisbury, Winchester, Stonehenge.

B&B per night:
S £25.00–£35.00
D £40.00–£47.00

OPEN All Year except Christmas

ALRESFORD, Hampshire Map ref 2C2

THE WOOLPACK COUNTRY INN

Totford, Alresford SO24 9TJ
T: (01962) 732101
F: (01962) 732889

Country inn set in the smallest hamlet in England. All 10 bedrooms are en suite with telephone and TV. Fine country restaurant and bar. Ideal for a touring base when visiting Basingstoke, Winchester or Southampton. Situated on the B3046 between Basingstoke and Alresford.

Bedrooms: 10 double/twin
Bathrooms: 10 private

Lunch available
Evening meal available
CC: Amex, Delta, Mastercard, Switch, Visa

B&B per night:
S Min £42.00
D Min £54.00

HB per person:
DY £40.00–£55.00

OPEN All Year except Christmas

ALTON, Hampshire Map ref 2C2 *Tourist Information Centre Tel: (01420) 88448*

♦♦♦♦ Silver Award

BOUNDARY HOUSE BED & BREAKFAST

Gosport Road, Lower Farringdon, Alton GU34 3DH
T: (01420) 587076
F: (01420) 587047
E: BoundaryS@messages.co.uk

Situated on the edge of the Meon Valley and on the boundary of the village of Lower Farringdon. Guests are assured of a warm welcome with comfortable accommodation in a relaxed atmosphere. Lovely garden, excellent breakfast. Ideal touring/walking base. Many places of interest and good pubs/restaurants nearby. Parking.

Bedrooms: 1 single, 2 double/twin
Bathrooms: 1 en suite, 2 private

CC: Delta, Mastercard, Switch, Visa

B&B per night:
S £27.50–£30.00
D £55.00

♦♦♦♦

WEST END FARM

Froyle, Alton GU34 4JG
T: (01420) 22130
F: (01420) 22930
E: cj.butler.farms@farmline.com
I: www.hampshirebedandbreakfast.co.uk

West End Farm offers luxury accommodation in the heart of the countryside. Spacious, comfortable rooms, all with either en suite or private facilities, overlook a lake. Access for walking in the countryside and within easy reach of Winchester, London airports, sea ports and local attractions.

Bedrooms: 2 double/twin, 1 triple/multiple
Bathrooms: 2 en suite, 1 private

3 nights for the price of 2 Nov-Feb.

B&B per night:
S £30.00–£35.00
D £50.00–£55.00

OPEN All Year except Christmas

AMERSHAM, Buckinghamshire Map ref 2D1

♦♦♦♦ Silver Award

39 QUARRENDON ROAD

Amersham HP7 9EF
T: (01494) 727959

Bedrooms: 1 single, 1 double/twin

B&B per night:
S £25.00–£30.00
D £50.00–£60.00

OPEN All Year

Detached house, comfortable, with friendly atmosphere. Residents' lounge, private parking, pleasant garden. One mile to London Underground station, easy reach of M25, M40 and A40.

12

♦♦♦

SARACENS HEAD INN

38 Whielden Street, Old Town, Amersham HP7 0HU
T: (01494) 721958
F: (01494) 725208
E: eamonn@thesaracensheadinn.com
I: www.thesaracensheadinn.com

Bedrooms: 4 double/twin, 1 triple/multiple
Bathrooms: 4 en suite, 1 private

Lunch available
Evening meal available
CC: Amex, Delta, Mastercard, Switch, Visa

B&B per night:
S £50.00
D £60.00–£90.00

OPEN All Year

The inn surrounds a central courtyard, was built in 1530 and is steeped in character. The original stables have been converted into function rooms.

7

CHECK THE MAPS

The colour maps at the front of this guide show all the cities, towns and villages for which you will find accommodation entries. Refer to the town index to find the page on which they are listed.

AMPORT, Hampshire Map ref 2C2

♦♦♦♦

BROADWATER

Amport, Andover SP11 8AY
T: (01264) 772240
F: (01264) 772240
E: carolyn@dmac.co.uk
I: www.dmac.co.uk/carolyn

Listed thatched cottage in delightful secluded garden, providing relaxed and cosy atmosphere in peaceful village setting. Large bedrooms with en suite facilities. Sitting room with open log fire in winter. Excellent stopover for West Country and airport travellers (A303 0.5 miles). Stonehenge only 15 minutes' drive, Salisbury and Winchester 30 minutes.

Bedrooms: 2 double/twin
Bathrooms: 2 en suite

CC: Delta, Mastercard, Switch, Visa

B&B per night:
S £30.00–£35.00
D £60.00–£65.00

OPEN All Year except Christmas

ANDOVER, Hampshire Map ref 2C2 *Tourist Information Centre Tel: (01264) 324320*

♦♦♦

AMBERLEY HOTEL

70 Weyhill Road, Andover
SP10 3NP
T: (01264) 352224 & 364676
F: (01264) 392555
E: amberleyand@fsbdial.co.uk

Bedrooms: 3 single, 9 double/twin, 3 triple/multiple
Bathrooms: 15 en suite

Lunch available
Evening meal available
CC: Amex, Diners, Mastercard, Switch, Visa

Compact 15 bedroom hotel, all en suite. Attractive a la carte and table d'hote restaurant and bar lounge. Private meetings, wedding receptions can be booked in Wightman room.

B&B per night:
S Min £45.00
D Min £60.00

HB per person:
DY Min £40.00

OPEN All Year except Christmas

♦♦♦

AMPORT INN

Amport, Andover SP11 8AE
T: (01264) 710371
F: (01264) 710112

Bedrooms: 7 double/twin, 2 triple/multiple
Bathrooms: 9 en suite

Lunch available
Evening meal available
CC: Mastercard, Switch, Visa

Friendly inn in attractive Hampshire village, with racecourses, riding and fishing nearby. Business people welcome weekdays. Breakaway weekends available. Good food-new restaurant now open.

B&B per night:
S £39.50–£42.50
D £58.00–£61.00

OPEN All Year

♦♦♦♦
Silver Award

MAY COTTAGE

Thruxton, Andover SP11 8LZ
T: (01264) 771241 & 07768 242166
F: (01264) 771770
E: info@maycottage-thruxton.co.uk
I: www.maycottage-thruxton.co.uk

May Cottage dates back to 1740 and is situated in the heart of this picturesque tranquil village. All rooms have en suite/private bathrooms, TV, radio and beverage trays. Guests' own sitting room/dining room. Pretty, secluded garden with stream. Many National Trust and stately homes/gardens within easy reach. Ample private parking. A non-smoking establishment.

Bedrooms: 3 double/twin
Bathrooms: 2 en suite, 1 private

B&B per night:
S £40.00–£45.00
D £60.00–£75.00

OPEN All Year except Christmas

COLOUR MAPS Colour maps at the front of this guide pinpoint all places under which you will find accommodation listed.

ASHURST, Hampshire Map ref 2C3

FOREST GATE LODGE

161 Lyndhurst Road, Ashurst,
Southampton SO40 7AW
T: (023) 8029 3026

Large Victorian house with direct access to New Forest and its attractions – walks, riding, cycling. Pubs and restaurants nearby, Lyndhurst – 'capital of the New Forest' – 5 minutes' drive. Full English breakfast or vegetarian by prior arrangement. Special rates October-March: 3 nights for the price of 2.

Bedrooms: 5 double/twin
Bathrooms: 5 en suite

Special rates: 3 nights for price of 2, weekdays 1 Oct-1 Apr.

B&B per night:
S Min £23.00
D Min £23.00

OPEN All Year

AYLESBURY, Buckinghamshire Map ref 2C1 *Tourist Information Centre Tel: (01296) 330559*

Rating Applied For

LITTLE VENICE B&B

129 Mandeville Road,
Stoke Mandeville, Aylesbury
HP21 8AJ
T: (01296) 339242
F: (01296) 339242
E: littlevenice129@hotmail.com
I: www.littleveniceuk.com

Bedrooms: 2 double/twin, 1 triple/multiple
Bathrooms: 1 en suite, 1 private

Evening meal available
CC: Amex, Delta, Mastercard, Switch, Visa

B&B per night:
S £35.00–£40.00
D £50.00–£75.00

OPEN All Year except Christmas

Enjoys a semi-rural location but within walking distance to Aylesbury town centre. Ideally located for Stoke Mandeville hospital, RAF Halton. Spacious, comfortable interior with very attractive bedrooms.

◆◆◆

THE OLD FORGE BARN

Ridings Way, Cublington,
Leighton Buzzard LU7 0LW
T: (01296) 681194
F: (01296) 681194
E: waples@ukonline.co.uk

Bedrooms: 1 double/twin

B&B per night:
S Max £25.00
D Max £40.00

OPEN All Year except Christmas

Converted barn in village location, close to Aylesbury, Leighton Buzzard, Milton Keynes. Restaurants and pubs serving meals nearby. Friendly welcome.

BANBURY, Oxfordshire Map ref 2C1 *Tourist Information Centre Tel: (01295) 259855*

THE LODGE

Main Road, Middleton Cheney, Banbury
OX17 2PP
T: (01295) 710355

A charming period gatehouse recently extended to provide a comfortable and gracious haven of peace for discerning guests. We welcome you warmly and invite you to relax with all the freedom of home and the enjoyment of our delightful garden. Situated in lovely countryside 1 mile from M40 jct 11.

Bedrooms: 2 double/twin
Bathrooms: 2 en suite

B&B per night:
S £32.00–£34.00
D £56.00–£58.00

OPEN All Year except Christmas

CONFIRM YOUR BOOKING
You are advised to confirm your booking in writing.

BANBURY continued

ST MARTINS HOUSE

Warkworth, Banbury OX17 2AG
T: (01295) 712684
F: (01295) 712838

600-year-old Listed converted barn with galleried dining room. Comfortable en suite rooms with TV. Safe parking, evening meals by arrangement, French and English country cooking.

Bedrooms: 2 double/twin
Bathrooms: 1 en suite, 1 private

Lunch available
Evening meal available

B&B per night:
S £27.50–£30.00
D £55.00–£60.00

HB per person:
DY £45.50–£48.00

OPEN All Year

BEACONSFIELD, Buckinghamshire Map ref 2C2

HIGHCLERE FARM

Newbarn Lane, Seer Green, Beaconsfield HP9 2QZ
T: (01494) 875665 & 874505
F: (01494) 875238

Bedrooms: 1 single, 6 double/twin, 2 triple/multiple
Bathrooms: 9 en suite

CC: Amex, Delta, Diners, Mastercard, Switch, Visa

B&B per night:
S £45.00
D £60.00–£65.00

Comfortable, family-run annexed farm accommodation with all rooms en suite. Two family rooms available. Quiet location, yet within easy reach of Windsor (12 miles) and London.

BEAULIEU, Hampshire Map ref 2C3

DALE FARM HOUSE

Manor Road, Applemore Hill, Dibden, Southampton SO45 5TJ
T: (023) 8084 9632
F: (023) 8084 0285
E: info@dalefarmhouse.co.uk
I: www.dalefarmhouse.co.uk

Beautiful 18thC converted farmhouse in secluded wooded setting with direct access for walks or cycling. Peaceful garden in which to unwind and a bird-watcher's paradise. Excellent food to satisfy your appetite. Barbecues on request. Spoil yourself at this BBC holiday programme-featured bed and breakfast.

Bedrooms: 1 single, 4 double/twin, 1 triple/multiple
Bathrooms: 4 en suite

Evening meal available

10% discount for Christmas breaks on a room-only basis. 3 for 2 weekend breaks Oct-Feb (excl Christmas and New Year).

B&B per night:
S £26.00–£32.00
D £40.00–£52.00

OPEN All Year

BEMBRIDGE, Isle of Wight Map ref 2C3

Silver Award

SEA CHANGE

22 Beachfield Road, Bembridge PO35 5TN
T: (01983) 875558 & 875557
F: (01983) 875667
E: seachangewight@aol.com

Bedrooms: 3 double/twin
Bathrooms: 3 en suite

B&B per night:
S £22.00–£30.00
D £44.00–£50.00

Modern detached home in quiet location on coastal path 100 metres from sea. Three en suite rooms with TV and fridge. Beach cafe, pub restaurant nearby.

SPECIAL BREAKS

Many establishments offer special promotions and themed breaks. These are highlighted in red. (All such offers are subject to availability.)

BICESTER, Oxfordshire Map ref 2C1 *Tourist Information Centre Tel: (01869) 369055*

♦♦♦

BOWSHOT BED AND BREAKFAST

Bowshot Court, 7 Aldergate Road, Bicester OX26 2BJ
T: (01869) 252355
E: reservations@bowshotholidays.com
I: www.bowshotholidays.com

Bedrooms: 1 single, 2 double/twin
Bathrooms: 1 en suite, 2 private

B&B per night:
S £30.00
D £50.00

OPEN All Year except Christmas

Comfortable, friendly accommodation for the business person and holidaymaker in a quiet, pleasant location, yet near the town centre. Parking available. Non-smoking establishment.

10 P

BLANDFORD FORUM, Dorset Map ref 2B3 *Tourist Information Centre Tel: (01258) 454770*

Silver Award

FARNHAM FARM HOUSE

Farnham, Blandford Forum DT11 8DG
T: (01725) 516254
F: (01725) 516306
E: info@farnhamfarmhouse.co.uk
I: www.farnhamfarmhouse.co.uk

A private drive leads to this picturesque 19thC farmhouse nestling in the secluded, rolling slopes of the Cranborne Chase, having flagstone floors, open fires and an acre of tranquil garden. A comfortable and relaxing base, enhanced by the addition of the Sarpenela Treatment Room offering therapeutic massage and holistic therapies.

Bedrooms: 3 double/twin
Bathrooms: 3 en suite

B&B per night:
D £45.00–£50.00

OPEN All Year except Christmas

P

♦♦♦♦
Silver Award

MEADOW HOUSE

Tarrant Hinton, Blandford Forum DT11 8JG
T: (01258) 830498
F: (01258) 830498

Bedrooms: 1 single, 1 double/twin, 1 triple/multiple

B&B per night:
S £20.00–£25.00
D £40.00–£50.00

OPEN All Year except Christmas

Farmhouse set in 4.5 acres. Warm welcome in peaceful, clean and comfortable family home. Noted for delicious home-produced English breakfast. Excellent base for touring.

P

BONCHURCH, Isle of Wight Map ref 2C3

THE LAKE HOTEL

Shore Road, Bonchurch, Ventnor PO38 1RF
T: (01983) 852613
F: (01983) 852613
E: enquiries@lakehotel.co.uk
I: www.lakehotel.co.uk

B&B per night:
D £30.00–£70.00

HB per person:
DY £37.00–£40.00

Charming country-house hotel in 2 acres of beautiful gardens. Located on the seaward side of Bonchurch pond in the old world village of Bonchurch. Run by the same family for over 35 years. We are confident of offering you the best-value accommodation and food on our beautiful island.

Bedrooms: 1 single, 12 double/twin, 7 triple/multiple
Bathrooms: 20 en suite

Evening meal available

4-night special break including breakfast, dinner and car ferry from any port £150 inclusive.

3 P

RATING All accommodation in this guide has been rated, or is awaiting a rating, by a trained English Tourism Council assessor.

BOURNEMOUTH, Dorset Map ref 2B3 *Tourist Information Centre Tel: (0906) 802 0234 (Premium rate)*

♦♦♦♦

ALEXANDER LODGE HOTEL

21 Southern Road, Southbourne, Bournemouth BH6 3SR
T: (01202) 421662
F: (01202) 421662
E: alexanderlodge@yahoo.com
I: www.smoothhound.co.uk/a28852.html

Delightful small hotel offering a friendly welcome, in quiet Bournemouth suburb, 200 yards from Blue Flag sandy beach, cliff-top and lift. Excellent home-cooked meals, comfortable en suite rooms, licensed bar, parking. Low-season specials! Ideal for holidays, short breaks and stopovers. Perfect for visiting Christchurch, New Forest, Bournemouth and Dorset.

Bedrooms: 4 double/twin, 2 triple/multiple
Bathrooms: 5 en suite

Evening meal available
CC: Delta, Mastercard, Switch, Visa

3-night specials available from Sep-Jun. Prices from £61pp B&B, £87pp DB&B.

P

B&B per night:
S Min £30.00
D £40.00–£56.00

OPEN All Year except Christmas

♦♦♦♦
Silver Award

BALINCOURT HOTEL

58 Christchurch Road, Bournemouth BH1 3PF
T: (01202) 552962
F: (01202) 552962
E: rooms@balincourt.co.uk
I: www.balincourt.co.uk

An elegant Victorian residence with luxurious and spacious rooms, where you can be sure of a warm welcome and personal attention. All rooms en suite. Traditional home cooking. Seafront and town centre within a short walk. All modes of public transport close by. Resident proprietors: Alison and Nigel Gandolfi.

Bedrooms: 1 single, 9 double/twin
Bathrooms: 10 en suite

Evening meal available
CC: Delta, Mastercard, Switch, Visa

P

B&B per night:
S £30.00–£45.00
D £70.00–£76.00

HB per person:
DY £42.00–£60.00

OPEN All Year

♦♦♦♦

FAIRMOUNT HOTEL

15 Priory Road, West Cliff, Bournemouth BH2 5DF
T: (01202) 551105
F: (01202) 553210
E: stay@fairmount-hotel.co.uk
I: www.fairmounthotel.co.uk

Clean, comfortable, family-run hotel within 3 minutes of beach, pier, conference centre, main shopping centre and leisure facilities. All rooms with private facilities. Large, secure car/boat park. Renowned cuisine.

Bedrooms: 4 single, 9 double/twin, 7 triple/multiple
Bathrooms: 19 en suite, 1 private

Lunch available
Evening meal available
CC: Delta, Mastercard, Switch, Visa

Discounts available at many local tourist attractions. 3 nights for the price of 2, Oct-Mar (excl Christmas and New Year).

P

B&B per night:
S £27.50–£38.00
D £50.00–£76.00

HB per person:
DY £36.00–£49.00

OPEN All Year except Christmas

MAP REFERENCES The map references refer to the colour maps at the front of this guide. The first figure is the map number; the letter and figure which follow indicate the grid reference on the map.

BOURNEMOUTH continued

◆◆◆◆ Silver Award

MAYFIELD GUEST HOUSE
46 Frances Road,
Knyveton Gardens, Bournemouth
BH1 3SA
T: (01202) 551839
F: (01202) 551839
E: accom@mayfieldhotel.com
I: www.mayfieldhotel.com

Bedrooms: 1 single, 6 double/twin, 1 triple/multiple
Bathrooms: 7 en suite, 1 private

Evening meal available

B&B per night:
S £20.00–£24.00
D £40.00–£48.00

HB per person:
DY £27.00–£31.00

Ideally situated for all amenities, opposite Knyveton Gardens with bowling greens, sensory garden, tennis courts. Handy for rail/coach stations, sea, shops and BIC.

6 P

◆◆◆◆

REDLANDS HOTEL
79 St Michaels Road, West Cliff,
Bournemouth BH2 5DR
T: (01202) 553714
E: enquiries@redlandshotel.co.uk
I: www.redlandshotel.co.uk

Bedrooms: 2 single, 7 double/twin, 3 triple/multiple
Bathrooms: 10 en suite

CC: Delta, Mastercard, Switch, Visa

B&B per night:
S £25.00–£30.00
D £45.00–£60.00

OPEN All Year

A charming Victorian guesthouse in Bournemouth town centre, close to the sea, shops and theatres.

P

◆◆◆

SOUTHERNHAY HOTEL
42 Alum Chine Road, Westbourne,
Bournemouth BH4 8DX
T: (01202) 761251
F: (01202) 761251
E: enquiries@southernhayhotel.co.uk
I: www.southernhayhotel.co.uk

Bedrooms: 1 single, 3 double/twin, 2 triple/multiple
Bathrooms: 4 en suite

B&B per night:
S £18.00–£22.00
D £42.00–£50.00

OPEN All Year

High-standard accommodation, near beach, restaurants and shops. Full English breakfast, rooms with colour TV, radio alarms, hairdryers and tea/coffee facilities. Large car park.

P

◆◆◆

THE VINE HOTEL
22 Southern Road, Southbourne,
Bournemouth BH6 3SR
T: (01202) 428309
F: (01202) 428309
E: thevinehotel@faxvia.net

Bedrooms: 6 double/twin, 2 triple/multiple
Bathrooms: 8 en suite

Evening meal available
CC: Delta, Mastercard, Switch, Visa

B&B per night:
S £20.00–£24.00
D £40.00–£48.00

OPEN All Year

Small family hotel close to local amenities. Superb location 'twixt Bournemouth and Christchurch. Beaches and Hengistbury Head nearby. Residential licence. Parking. Dogs welcome. No smoking.

2 P

BROCKENHURST, Hampshire Map ref 2C3

◆◆

GOLDENHAYES
9 Chestnut Road, Brockenhurst
SO42 7RF
T: (01590) 623743

Bedrooms: 1 double/twin

B&B per night:
S £20.00–£24.00
D £36.00–£40.00

OPEN All Year

Single-storey, owner-occupied home, in central but quiet situation. Close to village, station and open forest. Large garden.

P

BURFORD, Oxfordshire Map ref 2B1 *Tourist Information Centre Tel: (01993) 823558*

◆◆◆◆ Silver Award

BARLEY PARK
Shilton Road, Burford, Oxford
OX18 4PD
T: (01993) 823573
F: (01993) 824220
E: barley_park@hotmail.com
I: www.burford-bed-and-breakfast.co.uk

Bedrooms: 1 double/twin
Bathrooms: 1 private

B&B per night:
S Max £40.00
D £54.00–£60.00

OPEN All Year except Christmas

Immaculate, self-contained annexe with king-size bed, bathroom, fully-equipped dining, kitchen and living room. Excellent breakfast provided with local and/or organic produce.

P

BURFORD continued

THE HIGHWAY

117 High Street, Burford, Oxford OX18 4RG
T: (01993) 822136
F: (01993) 824740
E: rbx20@dial.pipex.com
I: www.oxlink.co.uk/burford

Built circa 1520, The Highway was old when Elizabeth I was on the throne. Today this beamed medieval Cotswold guesthouse offers 9 en suite bedrooms with TV, telephones, hairdryers etc. Perfect base for touring the Cotswolds. Also incorporating the highly acclaimed needlecraft centre.

Bedrooms: 9 double/twin, 2 triple/multiple
Bathrooms: 9 en suite

CC: Amex, Delta, Diners, Mastercard, Switch, Visa

B&B per night:
S £32.00–£55.00
D £55.00–£64.00

OPEN All Year

♦♦♦♦
Silver Award

MANOR LODGE
Shilton, Burford, Oxford OX18 4AS
T: (01993) 841444
F: (01993) 841446
E: enquiries@manorlodgebnb.co.uk
I: www.manorlodgebnb.co.uk

Bedrooms: 3 double/twin
Bathrooms: 3 en suite

Visit our traditional Cotswold house. Beautifully appointed, en suite double and twin accommodation. Situated in a lovely village setting near Burford. Large garden.

B&B per night:
S £39.00–£48.00
D £48.00–£65.00

♦♦♦

ST WINNOW
160 The Hill, Burford, Oxford OX18 4QY
T: (01993) 823843
E: b&b@stwinnow.com
I: www.stwinnow.com

Bedrooms: 1 single, 2 double/twin

Grade II Listed 16thC Cotswold house above the historic high street. Close to restaurants and shops. Garden and parking at rear. Organic/special diets provided.

B&B per night:
S £30.00–£35.00
D £50.00–£55.00

OPEN All Year

♦♦♦

TUDOR COTTAGE
40 Witney Street, Burford, Oxford OX18 4SN
T: (01993) 823251
F: (01993) 823251

Bedrooms: 2 double/twin
Bathrooms: 2 private

Elegant and very beautiful old Cotswold cottage in central Burford. Lovely garden and extremely comfortable en suite rooms. Quiet and peaceful. Ideally situated for all amenities.

12

B&B per night:
S £45.00–£50.00
D £50.00–£55.00

OPEN All Year except Christmas

CARISBROOKE, Isle of Wight Map ref 2C3

♦♦♦

ALVINGTON MANOR FARM
Carisbrooke, Newport PO30 5SP
T: (01983) 523463
F: (01983) 523463

Bedrooms: 3 triple/multiple
Bathrooms: 3 en suite

17thC farmhouse, gardens and parking, 3 en suite double/twin rooms. Ideal base in centre of island for walking, cycling etc.

B&B per night:
S £20.00–£22.50
D £40.00–£45.00

OPEN All Year

CHALFONT ST GILES, Buckinghamshire Map ref 2D2

♦♦♦♦

THE WHITE HART INN
Three Households, Chalfont St Giles HP8 4LP
T: (01494) 872441
F: (01494) 876375
E: whitehartinn@supanet.com

Bedrooms: 2 single, 9 double/twin
Bathrooms: 11 en suite

Lunch available
Evening meal available
CC: Delta, Mastercard, Switch, Visa

One-hundred-year-old village pub with non-smoking restaurant, large gardens and parking. Detached stable conversion accommodation plus new 7-bedroomed lodge.

B&B per night:
S £70.00–£75.00
D £90.00–£110.00

OPEN All Year

CHALGROVE, Oxfordshire Map ref 2C2

◆◆◆

CORNERSTONES

1 Cromwell Close, Chalgrove, Oxford OX44 7SE
T: (01865) 890298
F: (01865) 890298
E: md.cornerstones@amserve.com

Bedrooms: 2 double/twin

B&B per night:
S £25.00
D £40.00

OPEN All Year except Christmas

Bungalow in pretty village with thatched cottages. The Red Lion (0.5 miles away) serves good and reasonably priced food.

P

CHARLBURY, Oxfordshire Map ref 2C1

◆◆◆◆

BANBURY HILL FARM

Enstone Road, Charlbury, Oxford OX7 3JH
T: (01608) 810314
F: (01608) 811891
E: angelawiddows@gfwiddows.f9.co.uk
I: www.charlburyoxfordaccom.co.uk

Bedrooms: 1 single, 6 double/twin, 6 triple/multiple
Bathrooms: 11 en suite

CC: Mastercard, Switch, Visa

B&B per night:
S £22.00–£35.00
D £36.00–£50.00

OPEN All Year except Christmas

54-acre mixed farm. Cotswold-stone farmhouse with extensive views across Evenlode Valley. Ideal touring centre for Blenheim Palace, Oxford and the Cotswolds. Scrumptious breakfasts.

P

CHARLTON-ON-OTMOOR, Oxfordshire Map ref 2C1

◆◆◆

HOME FARM

Mansmoor Lane, Charlton-on-Otmoor, Kidlington OX5 2US
T: (01865) 331267 & 07774 710305
F: (01865) 331267

Bedrooms: 1 single, 1 double/twin

B&B per night:
S £20.00–£25.00
D £40.00–£50.00

OPEN All Year except Christmas

Modern farmhouse on sheep and arable farm. In quiet location 0.5 miles from village. Pets welcome. Stabling available. Central for Bicester, Woodstock, Oxford and Thame.

P

CHESHAM, Buckinghamshire Map ref 2D1

◆◆◆

ROSE COTTAGE

176 Bois Moor Road, Chesham HP5 4SS
T: (01494) 794433
F: (01494) 794444

B&B per night:
S £30.00–£40.00
D £45.00–£60.00

OPEN All Year except Christmas

A pleasant guesthouse on the outskirts of the historic market town of Chesham. All bedrooms are bright and comfortable with en suite facilities. Guests have exclusive use of patio and garden. Deep in the Chiltern countryside, yet central London is only 45 minutes away by tube, and the M25/M40 motorways are nearby.

Bedrooms: 2 double/twin
Bathrooms: 2 en suite

CC: Mastercard, Visa

3 nights for the price of 2 on any weekend throughout the year (excl Christmas and New Year).

CHECK THE MAPS

The colour maps at the front of this guide show all the cities, towns and villages for which you will find accommodation entries. Refer to the town index to find the page on which they are listed.

CHIPPING NORTON, Oxfordshire Map ref 2C1 *Tourist Information Centre Tel: (01608) 644379*

Silver Award

LOWER PARK FARM

Great Tew, Oxford OX7 4DE
T: (01608) 683170
F: (01608) 683859
E: lowerparkfarm@talk21.com
I: www.smoothhound.co.uk/hotels/lowerparkfa.html

This Grade II Listed building, set in the picturesque parkland landscape designed by Loudon, has recently been refurbished to a very high standard and retains many of its original features. Whether you are on business, enjoy walking, bird-watching or wish to explore the Cotswolds, we are the ideal destination.

Bedrooms: 2 double/twin, 1 triple/multiple
Bathrooms: 3 en suite

CC: Delta, Mastercard, Switch, Visa

B&B per night:
S £50.00–£55.00
D £65.00–£75.00

OPEN All Year except Christmas

COMPTON, Hampshire Map ref 2C3

◆◆

MANOR HOUSE

Place Lane, Compton, Winchester
SO21 2BA
T: (01962) 712162

Bedrooms: 1 double/twin

Comfortable country house in a large garden, 8 minutes from Shawford railway station and 2 miles from city of Winchester. Non-smokers preferred.

B&B per night:
S £17.00
D £34.00

OPEN All Year except Christmas

COTSWOLDS

See under Burford, Charlbury, Chipping Norton, Witney, Woodstock

See also Cotswolds in Heart of England region

DEDDINGTON, Oxfordshire Map ref 2C1

STONECROP GUEST HOUSE

Hempton Road, Deddington,
Banbury OX15 0QH
T: (01869) 338335 & 338496
F: (01869) 338505
E: info@stonecropguesthouse.co.uk
I: www.stonecropguesthouse.co.uk

Bedrooms: 1 single, 2 double/twin, 1 triple/multiple

Modern, detached accommodation, close to major roads, shops and places of interest.

B&B per night:
S £18.00–£20.00
D £36.00–£40.00

OPEN All Year except Christmas

EAST HENDRED, Oxfordshire Map ref 2C2

COWDRAYS

Cat Street, East Hendred, Wantage
OX12 8JT
T: (01235) 833313 & 07799 622003
E: cowdrays@virgin.net

A lovely family home situated near centre of this very pretty, historic village, near Didcot, Wantage, Abingdon and Harwell and only 12 miles south of Oxford and north of Newbury. Safe parking in yard.

Bedrooms: 3 double/twin
Bathrooms: 1 en suite, 2 private

B&B per night:
S £30.00–£35.00
D £60.00–£70.00

OPEN All Year

EAST ILSLEY, Berkshire Map ref 2C2

THE STAR INN

High Street, East Ilsley, Newbury RG20 7LE
T: (01635) 281215
F: (01635) 281107

B&B per night:
S £50.00–£70.00
D £60.00–£80.00

OPEN All Year except Christmas

Traditional 15thC country village inn, in the heart of the rolling Berkshire Downs. Ideal for walkers, close to Oxford, very popular with local horse-racing fraternity. Well-appointed, en suite bedrooms full of character and charm. Traditional English pub food, real ales, open fire, patio, beer garden, warm welcome guaranteed.

Bedrooms: 3 single, 5 double/twin, 1 triple/multiple
Bathrooms: 9 en suite

Lunch available
Evening meal available
CC: Delta, Mastercard, Switch, Visa

Special rates for guests staying Newbury Races weekends. Double room £50pn.

P

EASTLEIGH, Hampshire Map ref 2C3

ENDEAVOUR GUEST HOUSE

40 Allbrook Hill, Allbrook, Eastleigh SO50 4LY
T: (023) 8061 3400
F: (023) 8061 4486
E: dcschauffeurs@btconnect.com
I: www.
directchauffeurservices&taxis

Bedrooms: 2 double/twin; permanent suite(s)
Bathrooms: 1 en suite, 1 private

CC: Amex, Diners, Mastercard, Visa

B&B per night:
S Max £50.00
D Max £50.00

OPEN All Year

Situated on the River Itchen navigation canal. Endeavour offers private fishing, gardens and walks. The New Forest is a 15-minute drive. Very private accommodation.

P

EDGCOTT, Buckinghamshire Map ref 2C1

PERRY MANOR FARM

Buckingham Road, Edgcott, Aylesbury HP18 0TR
T: (01296) 770257

Bedrooms: 1 single, 2 double/twin

B&B per night:
S £22.00
D £36.00

OPEN All Year

200-acre working sheep farm, offering peaceful and comfortable accommodation, with en suite toilet and basin. Extensive views over Aylesbury Vale. Walkers welcome. Non-smokers only, please.

P

FAREHAM, Hampshire Map ref 2C3 *Tourist Information Centre Tel: (01329) 221342*

♦♦♦

AVENUE HOUSE HOTEL

22 The Avenue, Fareham PO14 1NS
T: (01329) 232175
F: (01329) 232196

Bedrooms: 2 single, 14 double/twin, 3 triple/multiple
Bathrooms: 19 en suite

Lunch available
Evening meal available
CC: Amex, Delta, Mastercard, Switch, Visa

B&B per night:
S £55.00
D £55.00–£60.00

OPEN All Year

Comfortable, small hotel, with charm and character, set in mature gardens. 5 minutes' walk to town centre, railway station and restaurants.

P

♦♦♦

BRIDGE HOUSE

1 Waterside Gardens, Wallington, Fareham PO16 8SD
T: (01329) 287775 & 07751 674400
F: (01329) 287775
E: maryhb@fish.co.uk

Bedrooms: 2 double/twin
Bathrooms: 1 en suite, 1 private

B&B per night:
S £35.00–£39.00
D £60.00–£70.00

OPEN All Year except Christmas

Comfortable Georgian family home, all facilities, Japanese garden. Full English or continental breakfast. Ample parking. Easy access to M27, jct 11 and town centre.

HALF BOARD PRICES Half board prices are given per person, but in some cases these may be based on double/twin occupancy.

FARNBOROUGH, Hampshire Map ref 2C2

COLEBROOK GUEST HOUSE

56 Netley Street, Farnborough
GU14 6AT
T: (01252) 542269
F: (01252) 542269
E: derekbclark@ukonline.co.uk

Bedrooms: 4 single, 3 double/twin, 2 triple/multiple
Bathrooms: 9 en suite

CC: Amex, Delta, Mastercard, Switch, Visa

B&B per night:
S £25.00–£35.00
D £50.00–£60.00

OPEN All Year except Christmas

Late-Victorian, detached, double-fronted house on 3 floors, in quiet residential area.

FORDINGBRIDGE, Hampshire Map ref 2B3

Silver Award

MERRIMEAD

12 Station Road, Alderholt,
Fordingbridge SP6 3RB
T: (01425) 657544
F: (01425) 650400
E: merrimead@ic24.net
I: www.newforest.demon.co.uk/merrimead.htm

Bedrooms: 2 double/twin
Bathrooms: 1 en suite, 1 private

B&B per night:
S £26.00–£30.00
D £42.00–£50.00

OPEN All Year except Christmas

Family home in small village with easy access to New Forest, Salisbury and Bournemouth. Breakfast by prize-winning cook. Off-street parking. Good pub 3 minutes' walk.

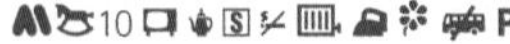

Gold Award

THE THREE LIONS

Stuckton, Fordingbridge SP6 2HF
T: (01425) 652489
F: (01425) 656144
E: the3lions@btinternet.com

Bedrooms: 3 double/twin
Bathrooms: 3 en suite

Lunch available
Evening meal available
CC: Amex, Delta, Mastercard, Switch, Visa

B&B per night:
S £59.00–£75.00
D £65.00–£85.00

Quiet restaurant with rooms, all individually decorated. Wheelchair access. Whirlpool jacuzzi and sauna. English/French cuisine. Rosettes awarded for food.

GORING, Oxfordshire Map ref 2C2

◆◆◆

MILLER OF MANSFIELD

High Street, Goring, Reading
RG8 9AW
T: (01491) 872829
F: (01491) 874200
I: www.millerofmansfield.co.uk

Bedrooms: 2 single, 8 double/twin
Bathrooms: 10 en suite

Lunch available
Evening meal available
CC: Delta, Mastercard, Switch, Visa

B&B per night:
S £54.00–£60.00
D £70.00–£80.00

OPEN All Year except Christmas

Ivy-covered inn with Tudor-style exterior. Interior has original beams, open fires and comfortable bedrooms. Excellent bar and restaurant serving quality food, wines and beers.

GRATELEY, Hampshire Map ref 2C2

Silver Award

GUNVILLE HOUSE

Grateley, Andover SP11 8JQ
T: (01264) 889206
F: (01264) 889060
E: pct@onetel.net.uk
I: www.gunvillehouse.co.uk

B&B per night:
S £30.00–£35.00
D £50.00–£60.00

HB per person:
DY £40.00–£45.00

OPEN All Year

Charming, thatched, beamed family house with lovely views. We pride ourselves on attention to detail. Within easy reach of Salisbury, Stonehenge, Winchester, Marlborough, Bath and Oxford. Local attractions include Hawk Conservancy, Army Air Corps museum, Mottisfont Abbey, Highclere Castle. Fly-fishing, golf and clay-pigeon shooting available locally.

Bedrooms: 1 single, 1 triple/multiple
Bathrooms: 2 en suite

Lunch available
Evening meal available
CC: Mastercard, Switch, Visa

VISITOR ATTRACTIONS For ideas on places to visit refer to the introduction at the beginning of this section. Look out too for the ETC's Quality Assured Visitor Attraction signs.

HENLEY-ON-THAMES, Oxfordshire Map ref 2C2 *Tourist Information Centre Tel: (01491) 578034*

◆◆◆

ABBOTTSLEIGH

107 St Marks Road, Henley-on-Thames RG9 1LP
T: (01491) 572982 & 412666
F: (01491) 572982
E: abbottsleigh@hotmail.com

Bedrooms: 1 single, 1 double/twin, 1 triple/multiple
Bathrooms: 2 en suite, 1 private

B&B per night:
S £38.00–£50.00
D £60.00–£62.00

OPEN All Year

A mature, detached home in quiet location. Ample parking. Comfortable rooms. Walking distance to town centre, river and station. Warm welcome given.

8 P

◆◆◆◆

ALFTRUDIS

8 Norman Avenue, Henley-on-Thames RG9 1SG
T: (01491) 573099 & 07802 408643
F: (01491) 411747
E: b&b@alftrudis.fsnet.co.uk
I: www.alftrudis.co.uk

Bedrooms: 3 double/twin
Bathrooms: 2 en suite, 1 private

B&B per night:
S £45.00–£55.00
D £55.00–£65.00

OPEN All Year

Grade II Listed Victorian home in peaceful tree-lined cul-de-sac a few minutes' level walk from the town centre, station and river.

8 P

◆◆◆

AVALON

36 Queen Street, Henley-on-Thames RG9 1AP
T: (01491) 577829
E: avalon@henleybb.fsnet.co.uk
I: www.henleybb.fsnet.co.uk

Bedrooms: 1 single, 2 double/twin
Bathrooms: 2 en suite

B&B per night:
S £32.00–£45.00
D £55.00–£60.00

OPEN All Year

Spacious Victorian terraced house in a quiet, central location 2 minutes' walk from river, station and town centre.

10 P

◆◆◆◆

COLDHARBOUR HOUSE

3 Coldharbour Close, Henley-on-Thames RG9 1QF
T: (01491) 575229
F: (01491) 575229
E: coldharbourhouse@aol.com

B&B per night:
S £30.00–£45.00
D £55.00–£70.00

OPEN All Year except Christmas

Pretty farmhouse-style home in a quiet close, 15 minutes' walk from the town and river. It has character features and is surrounded by a lovely walled garden. Breakfast is served in the dining room overlooking the garden, and there is a sun lounge for relaxation. Off-street parking.

Bedrooms: 1 single, 2 double/twin
Bathrooms: 1 en suite

P

◆◆◆◆

HOLMWOOD

Shiplake Row, Binfield Heath, Henley-on-Thames RG9 4DP
T: (0118) 947 8747
F: (0118) 947 8637

B&B per night:
S £45.00
D £65.00

OPEN All Year except Christmas

Large, elegant, peaceful Georgian country house with very beautiful gardens and views over the Thames Valley. All bedrooms are large and en suite and furnished with period and antique furnishings. Holmwood is in Binfield Heath, which is signposted off the A4155, equidistant from Henley-on-Thames and Reading.

Bedrooms: 1 single, 4 double/twin
Bathrooms: 5 en suite

CC: Delta, Mastercard, Switch, Visa

12 P

HENLEY-ON-THAMES continued

♦♦♦♦ Silver Award

THE KNOLL

Crowsley Road, Shiplake, Henley-on-Thames RG9 3JT
T: (01189) 402705 & 406538
F: (01189) 402705
E: theknollhenley@aol.com
I: www.theknollhenley.co.uk

Beautifully restored home with every modern convenience, riverside walks and landscaped garden. Good base for Cotswolds, Oxford, Windsor, London and Heathrow. Free internet access and local calls. Winner of the Bed & Breakfast of the Year Award Southern England. Nominated Best British Breakfast.

Bedrooms: 2 double/twin, 1 triple/multiple; permanent suite(s)
Bathrooms: 2 en suite

B&B per night:
S £45.00
D £56.00–£59.00

♦♦♦♦♦

LENWADE

3 Western Road, Henley-on-Thames RG9 1JL
T: (01491) 573468 & 07774 941629
F: (01491) 573468
E: lenwadeuk@aol.com
I: www.w3b-ink.com/lenwade

This beautiful Victorian home is in a quiet residential road within walking distance of town, river and station. Ample parking. Superb, individually cooked breakfasts. Convenient base for Oxford, Heathrow, Windsor. All rooms are en suite or with private bathroom. All have telephone with modem connection.

Bedrooms: 3 double/twin
Bathrooms: 2 en suite, 1 private

B&B per night:
S £45.00–£55.00
D £60.00–£65.00

OPEN All Year except Christmas

♦♦♦♦♦ Silver Award

THAMESMEAD HOUSE HOTEL

Remenham Lane, Remenham, Henley-on-Thames RG9 2LR
T: (01491) 574745
F: (01491) 579944
E: thamesmead@supanet.com
I: www.thamesmeadhousehotel.co.uk

Small, family-owned and managed hotel in a quiet location close to the town and river with the famous regatta course. The rooms are bright, stylish and contemporary. The art and decor is interesting, the ambiance chic, and the atmosphere...totally relaxed.

Bedrooms: 1 single, 5 double/twin
Bathrooms: 6 en suite

Lunch available
CC: Amex, Delta, Mastercard, Switch, Visa

Autumn and winter weekend breaks, stay Sat night and get Sun night half-price.

B&B per night:
S £95.00–£105.00
D £115.00–£140.00

OPEN All Year except Christmas

IMPORTANT NOTE Information on accommodation listed in this guide has been supplied by the proprietors. As changes may occur you are advised to check details at the time of booking.

HIGH WYCOMBE, Buckinghamshire Map ref 2C2 *Tourist Information Centre Tel: (01494) 421892*

AYAM MANOR

Hammersley Lane, High Wycombe
HP10 8HS
T: (01494) 816932
F: (01494) 816338
E: jeansenior@ayammanor.freeserve.co.uk
I: www.ayammanorguesthouse.co.uk

Very large Georgian house, decorated to a high standard, with spacious bedrooms, games room, swimming pool and sitting room. Secure off-road parking. A warm, friendly welcome awaits guests.

Bedrooms: 7 single, 1 double/twin, 2 triple/ multiple
Bathrooms: 9 en suite, 1 private

Lunch available
Evening meal available
CC: Amex, Delta, Diners, Mastercard, Switch, Visa

Book 7 nights pay for 5.

B&B per night:
S £50.00–£67.00
D £65.00–£95.00

HB per person:
DY £60.00–£75.00

OPEN All Year except Christmas

HIGHCLERE, Hampshire Map ref 2C2

HIGHCLERE FARM

Highclere, Newbury RG20 9PY
T: (01635) 255013
E: walshhighclere@newburyweb.net

Bedrooms: 1 double/twin
Bathrooms: 1 en suite

An extremely comfortable converted coach house close to Highclere Castle in an Area of Outstanding Natural Beauty.

B&B per night:
S £35.00–£40.00
D £45.00–£50.00

OPEN All Year

HUNGERFORD, Berkshire Map ref 2C2

◆◆◆◆

ALDERBORNE HOUSE

33 Bourne Vale, Hungerford
RG17 0LL
T: (01488) 683228
E: mail@honeybone.co.uk
I: www.honeybone.co.uk

Bedrooms: 1 single, 2 double/twin

Modern, detached house, quiet location on southern outskirts. Overlooks open countryside, short walk to shops, railway and canal. Ideal stop-over or touring base. Three miles M4 jct 14.

B&B per night:
S £20.00–£25.00
D £37.50–£40.00

OPEN All Year except Christmas

HYTHE, Hampshire Map ref 2C3

◆◆◆◆

CHANGRI-LA

12 Ashleigh Close, Hythe,
Southampton SO45 3QP
T: (023) 8084 6664

Bedrooms: 2 double/twin
Bathrooms: 2 private

Comfortable home on the edge of the New Forest close to Beaulieu, Bucklers Hard, Exbury Gardens, Calshot for sailing, windsurfing etc, and many more places of interest.

B&B per night:
S Min £25.00
D Min £44.00

OPEN All Year except Christmas

INKPEN, Berkshire Map ref 2C2

◆◆◆◆

THE SWAN INN

Inkpen, Hungerford RG17 9DX
T: (01488) 668326
F: (01488) 668306
E: enquiries@theswaninn-organics.co.uk
I: www.theswaninn-organics.co.uk

17thC inn located in an Area of Outstanding Natural Beauty, 1 mile from Coombe Gibbet, the highest point in Southern England (965ft). En suite bedrooms. Owned by local organic beef farmers, the bar food and restaurant use the best fresh organic ingredients. West Berkshire CAMRA 'Pub of the Year' 2000.

Bedrooms: 1 single, 9 double/twin
Bathrooms: 10 en suite

Lunch available
Evening meal available
CC: Delta, Mastercard, Switch, Visa

Weekends (Fri, Sat, Sun): 3 nights for price of 2.

B&B per night:
S £35.00–£65.00
D £70.00–£90.00

HB per person:
DY £45.00–£75.00

OPEN All Year except Christmas

ISLE OF WIGHT

See under Bembridge, Bonchurch, Carisbrooke, Ryde, Sandown, Shanklin

LYMINGTON, Hampshire Map ref 2C3 *Tourist Information Centre Tel: (01590) 689000*

♦♦♦♦♦
Gold Award

EFFORD COTTAGE

Everton, Lymington SO41 0JD
T: (01590) 642315
F: (01590) 641030
E: effordcottage@aol.com
I: www.effordcottage.co.uk

B&B per night:
D £50.00–£65.00

HB per person:
DY £40.00–£65.00

OPEN All Year

Friendly, spacious, Georgian cottage in an acre of garden. Award-winning guesthouse. Elegant bedrooms, luxury facilities. Delicious 4-course breakfast from a wide and varied menu. Homemade bread/preserves. Patricia, a qualified chef, uses home-grown produce for traditional country cooking. Special mid-week winter breaks. 'Your comfort is our concern'.

Bedrooms: 3 double/twin; permanent suite(s)
Bathrooms: 3 en suite

Lunch available
Evening meal available

Christmas, Birthday, Easter and Valentine specials; winter breaks; course and training weekends available on application. Gift certificates available.

14 P

LYNDHURST, Hampshire Map ref 2C3 *Tourist Information Centre Tel: (023) 8028 2269*

♦♦♦♦
Silver Award

BURWOOD LODGE

27 Romsey Road, Lyndhurst SO43 7AA
T: (023) 8028 2445
F: (023) 8028 4104
I: www.burwoodlodge.co.uk

B&B per night:
S £28.00–£35.00
D £48.00–£55.00

OPEN All Year except Christmas

Lovely Edwardian house in 0.5-acre grounds, located just 3 minutes' walk to village high street, 5 minutes from open forest. Guest lounge and separate dining room overlook the gardens, promoting a relaxing environment. Bedrooms tastefully decorated: family, twin, single and a 4-poster room for those special, romantic occasions.

Bedrooms: 1 single, 4 double/twin, 1 triple/multiple
Bathrooms: 6 en suite

P

♦♦♦♦

THE PENNY FARTHING HOTEL

Romsey Road, Lyndhurst SO43 7AA
T: (023) 8028 4422
F: (023) 8028 4488
E: stay@pennyfarthinghotel.co.uk
I: www.pennyfarthinghotel.co.uk

B&B per night:
S £35.00–£45.00
D £59.00–£88.00

OPEN All Year except Christmas

Welcome to our cheerful hotel, conveniently situated a moment's walk from the village centre. Our cosy, centrally heated bedrooms have en suite shower or bath and wc, colour TV, clock, radio and tea/coffee-making facilities. We also provide a residents' bar/lounge, lock-up bicycle store and large, private car park.

Bedrooms: 4 single, 15 double/twin, 2 triple/multiple
Bathrooms: 21 en suite

CC: Amex, Delta, Diners, Mastercard, Switch, Visa

P

SYMBOLS The symbols in each entry give information about services and facilities. A key to these symbols appears at the back of this guide.

LYNDHURST continued

◆◆◆

ROSEDALE BED & BREAKFAST
24 Shaggs Meadow, Lyndhurst
SO43 7BN
T: (023) 8028 3793
E: jenny@theangels.freeserve.co.uk

Bedrooms: 1 double/twin, 1 triple/multiple
Bathrooms: 1 en suite

Evening meal available

Family-run bed and breakfast in the centre of Lyndhurst. We cater for families. Colour TV, tea/coffee facilities. Breakfast served at your convenience. Evening meals by arrangement.

B&B per night:
S £20.00–£22.00
D £48.00–£50.00

HB per person:
DY £34.00–£35.00

OPEN All Year

◆◆◆◆
Silver Award

RUFUS HOUSE HOTEL

Southampton Road, Lyndhurst SO43 7BQ
T: (023) 8028 2930
F: (023) 8028 2930
E: rufushousehotel@dcintra.fsnet.co.uk
I: www.rufushousehotel.co.uk

A family-run hotel, where all our attractive and comfortable bedrooms have views of either forest or fields. Turret bedrooms available for that 'special occasion'. An ideal base for exploring the New Forest. We offer traditional comforts with today's convenience. Visit us to experience our warm, friendly hospitality for yourself.

Bedrooms: 1 single, 10 double/twin
Bathrooms: 11 en suite

CC: Delta, Mastercard, Switch, Visa

B&B per night:
S £35.00–£40.00
D £55.00–£75.00

OPEN All Year

◆◆◆◆

TEMPLE LODGE GUEST HOUSE

Queens Road, Lyndhurst SO43 7BR
T: (023) 8028 2392
F: (023) 8028 2392

Robyn and Eddie Richey invite guests to come and enjoy a break in our gracious Victorian home situated in the heart of the New Forest. We offer en suite accommodation. TV in all rooms, hairdryer and hospitality tray. Choice of breakfasts. Spacious public guest rooms and off-road parking.

Bedrooms: 5 double/twin, 1 triple/multiple
Bathrooms: 6 en suite

CC: Delta, Mastercard, Switch, Visa

B&B per night:
S £30.00–£40.00
D £50.00–£60.00

OPEN All Year

MAIDENHEAD, Berkshire Map ref 2C2 *Tourist Information Centre Tel: (01628) 796502*

◆◆

CARTLANDS COTTAGE
Kings Lane,
Cookham Dean, Cookham,
Maidenhead SL6 9AY
T: (01628) 482196

Bedrooms: 1 triple/multiple
Bathrooms: 1 en suite

Family room in self-contained garden studio. Meals in delightful timbered character cottage with exposed beams. Traditional cottage garden. National Trust common land. Very quiet.

B&B per night:
S £27.50–£35.00
D £40.00–£55.00

OPEN All Year

MAIDENHEAD continued

Silver Award

MOOR FARM

Ascot Road, Holyport, Maidenhead
SL6 2HY
T: (01628) 633761
F: (01628) 636167
E: moorfm@aol.com

B&B per night:
S £45.00–£50.00
D £50.00–£60.00

OPEN All Year

Guests staying at Moor Farm enjoy exclusive use of a wing of this ancient manor house, dating from the early 13thC. Although convenient to jct 8/9 of the M4, Moor Farm enjoys a rural location on the edge of the conservation village of Holyport. Windsor 4 miles, Maidenhead 1 mile, Heathrow 12 miles.

Bedrooms: 2 double/twin
Bathrooms: 1 en suite, 1 private

MARLOW, Buckinghamshire Map ref 2C2 *Tourist Information Centre Tel: (01628) 483597*

ACORN LODGE

79 Marlow Bottom Road, Marlow Bottom, Marlow SL7 3NA
T: (01628) 472197 & 0771 8757601
F: (01628) 472197

B&B per night:
S £40.00–£65.00
D £60.00–£69.00

OPEN All Year except Christmas

Comfortable, peaceful accommodation with well-appointed, spacious rooms backing onto woodland. We offer a warm welcome and a good night's sleep in home from home surroundings. Minutes from motorway access. Perfect for families or for business people needing a restful night and a good breakfast. New Acorn Therapy Centre opposite.

Bedrooms: 3 double/twin; permanent suite(s)
Bathrooms: 2 en suite, 1 private

CC: Amex, Delta, Mastercard, Switch, Visa

♦♦♦♦

THE INN ON THE GREEN LIMITED

The Old Cricket Common, Cookham Dean, Cookham, Maidenhead SL6 9NZ
T: (01628) 482638
F: (01628) 487474
E: enquiries@theinnonthegreen.com
I: www.theinnonthegreen.com

Bedrooms: 6 double/twin, 3 triple/multiple
Bathrooms: 9 en suite

Lunch available
Evening meal available
CC: Amex, Delta, Mastercard, Switch, Visa

B&B per night:
S £100.00–£120.00
D £110.00–£130.00

HB per person:
DY £70.00–£90.00

OPEN All Year

Beautiful restaurant with rooms in heart of the countryside. Freshly prepared modern French/British menu. Stunning al fresco courtyard. Close to Marlow, Windsor, Henley and Cookham.

COUNTRY CODE Always follow the Country Code Enjoy the countryside and respect its life and work Guard against all risk of fire Fasten all gates Keep your dogs under close control Keep to public paths across farmland Use gates and stiles to cross fences, hedges and walls Leave livestock, crops and machinery alone Take your litter home Help to keep all water clean Protect wildlife, plants and trees Take special care on country roads Make no unnecessary noise

MARLOW continued

OLD BARN COTTAGE

Church Road, Little Marlow, Marlow
SL7 3RZ
T: (01628) 483817
F: (01628) 477197
E: falk@globalnet.co.uk

Charming flint and brick period cottage set in an attractive garden situated in a small hamlet near Marlow. River Thames and Chiltern hills are nearby. Easy access to M4, M40 and Heathrow Airport. Spacious and comfortable rooms with en suite facilities.

Bedrooms: 1 double/twin
Bathrooms: 1 en suite

B&B per night:
S £30.00–£35.00
D £45.00–£50.00

OPEN All Year except Christmas

◆◆◆◆

ROSEMARY COTTAGE BED & BREAKFAST

99 Heath End Road, Flackwell Heath,
High Wycombe HP10 9ES
T: (01628) 520635
F: (01628) 520635
E: mike.1@virgin.net
I: www.reservation.co.uk

A charming character cottage with stunning panoramic views across the Thames Valley towards Marlow and Maidenhead. Convenient for London, Windsor, Oxford, access to M40, M25 and M4 motorways. Flackwell Heath is situated in a beautiful part of the Chilterns and is a perfect base for exploring the surrounding area.

Bedrooms: 3 double/twin
Bathrooms: 1 en suite

CC: Delta, Mastercard, Switch, Visa

B&B per night:
S £50.00–£60.00
D £55.00–£65.00

OPEN All Year except Christmas

MILFORD-ON-SEA, Hampshire Map ref 2C3

ALMA MATER

4 Knowland Drive, Milford-on-Sea,
Lymington SO41 0RH
T: (01590) 642811
F: (01590) 642811
E: bandbalmamater@aol.com
I: www.almamater.org.uk

Bedrooms: 3 double/twin
Bathrooms: 2 en suite, 1 private

Evening meal available

Detached, quiet, spacious, non-smoking chalet bunglow with en suite bedrooms overlooking lovely garden. Close to village, beaches, New Forest and IOW. Evening meals by request.

B&B per night:
S £35.00–£38.00
D £45.00–£55.00

HB per person:
DY £37.50–£44.50

OPEN All Year

AT-A-GLANCE SYMBOLS

Symbols at the end of each accommodation entry give useful information about services and facilities. A key to symbols can be found inside the back cover flap. Keep this open for easy reference.

MILFORD-ON-SEA continued

Silver Award

BRIANTCROFT

George Road, Milford-on-Sea, Lymington
SO41 0RS
T: (01590) 644355
F: (01590) 644355
E: florence.iles@lineone.net
I: www.briantcroft.co.uk

Elegant Edwardian house with spacious and luxurious rooms. Leafy lane and peaceful surroundings at the edge of the New Forest. Ten minutes' walk to the beach. Bedrooms have a 3-seater sofa, refreshment tray, colour TV, hairdryer etc. Breakfasts are a gourmet experience with traditional and tempting options using fresh and local produce.

Bedrooms: 2 double/twin, 1 triple/multiple
Bathrooms: 2 en suite, 1 private

Try our mid-week stress-buster in spring and winter – 4 nights (Mon-Thur) for the price of 3!

B&B per night:
S £40.00–£45.00
D £60.00–£65.00

OPEN All Year except Christmas

MILTON KEYNES, Buckinghamshire Map ref 2C1 *Tourist Information Centre Tel: (0870) 1201269*

♦♦♦♦

HAVERSHAM GRANGE

Haversham, Milton Keynes
MK19 7DX
T: (01908) 312389
F: (01908) 312389
E: smithers@haversham-grange.co.uk

Bedrooms: 3 double/twin
Bathrooms: 2 en suite, 1 private

Large 14thC stone house with en suite facilities. Set in own gardens backing onto lakes. Very peaceful, yet only 5 miles from Milton Keynes centre.

B&B per night:
S £33.00–£35.00
D £50.00–£60.00

OPEN All Year except Christmas

♦♦♦♦

THE WHITE HART

1 Gun Lane, Sherington,
Newport Pagnell MK16 9PE
T: (01908) 611953
F: (01908) 618109
E: whitehartresort@aol.com
I: www.whitehartsherington.com

Bedrooms: 4 double/twin
Bathrooms: 4 en suite

Lunch available
Evening meal available
CC: Delta, Mastercard, Switch, Visa

17thC freehouse and restaurant with luxury accomodation in a converted barn across the courtyard from the main building. Three miles from M1 jct 14.

B&B per night:
D £60.00–£80.00

OPEN All Year

MOULSFORD ON THAMES, Oxfordshire Map ref 2C2

♦♦♦♦
Silver Award

WHITE HOUSE

Moulsford on Thames, Wallingford
OX10 9JD
T: (01491) 651397 & 07831 372243
F: (01491) 652560
E: mwatsham@hotmail.com

Bedrooms: 1 single, 2 double/twin

Evening meal available

Beautifully appointed ground floor accommodation in a detached family home surrounded by large garden. Picturesque Thames-side village, convenient for Oxford, Henley and Reading.

B&B per night:
S £30.00–£35.00
D £50.00

HB per person:
DY £45.00–£50.00

OPEN All Year except Christmas

NETHER WALLOP, Hampshire Map ref 2C2

♦♦♦♦

YORK LODGE

Nether Wallop, Stockbridge
SO20 8HE
T: (01264) 781313
F: (01264) 781313
E: bradley@yorklodge.fslife.com
I: www.york-lodge.co.uk

Bedrooms: 2 double/twin
Bathrooms: 2 en suite

Evening meal available

Comfortable, self-contained wing of charming modern house in peaceful, secluded garden on edge of picturesque village. Pub nearby. Easy reach of Stonehenge, Salisbury and Winchester.

B&B per night:
S £30.00–£35.00
D £50.00–£60.00

HB per person:
DY £40.00–£50.00

OPEN All Year

NEW FOREST

See under Ashurst, Beaulieu, Brockenhurst, Fordingbridge, Hythe, Lymington, Lyndhurst, Milford-on-Sea, New Milton, Ringwood, Sway

NEW MILTON, Hampshire Map ref 2B3

◆◆◆◆

FAIRWAYS GUEST HOUSE

Sway Road, Bashley, New Milton
BH25 5QP
T: (01425) 619001
F: (01425) 619001
E: libsfairways@aol.com

Bedrooms: 4 double/twin
Bathrooms: 2 en suite

B&B per night:
S £27.00–£32.00
D £55.00–£62.00

OPEN All Year except Christmas

Edwardian house in wooded setting. Secluded garden with swimming pool. Personal attention in a friendly atmosphere. Five minutes forest and sea.

P

◆◆◆◆

JOBZ-A-GUDN

169 Stem Lane, New Milton
BH25 5ND
T: (01425) 615435 & 07866 881426
F: (01425) 615435
E: jobzagudn@aol.com
I: www.jobzagudn.com

Bedrooms: 1 double/twin
Bathrooms: 1 en suite

Evening meal available

B&B per night:
S £22.00–£25.00
D £40.00–£45.00

HB per person:
DY £25.00–£30.00

OPEN All Year

Lovely family bungalow overlooking farmland. Accommodation of 1 double room with beautiful new en suite. Excellent 4-course breakfast. Close to local beaches and New Forest.

P

◆◆◆

WILLY'S WELL

Bashley Common Road, Wootton,
New Milton BH25 5SF
T: (01425) 616834
E: moyramac2@hotmail.com

B&B per night:
S £30.00
D £50.00

OPEN All Year

A warm welcome awaits you at our mid-1700s Listed thatched cottage standing in 1 acre of mature gardens also available for your enjoyment. We have direct forest access through 6 acres of pasture and are 3 miles from the sea. Ideal for walking, cycling, horse-riding.

Bedrooms: 2 double/twin
Bathrooms: 1 en suite, 1 private

P

NEWBURY, Berkshire Map ref 2C2 *Tourist Information Centre Tel: (01635) 30267*

◆◆◆◆
Silver Award

THE OLD FARMHOUSE

Downend Lane, Chieveley, Newbury
RG20 8TN
T: (01635) 248361 & 07970 583373
E: palletts@aol.com
I: www.smoothhound.co.uk/hotels/oldfarmhouse

B&B per night:
S £35.00–£40.00
D £55.00–£60.00

OPEN All Year

Period farmhouse on edge of village within 2 miles of M4/A34 (jct13), 5 miles north of Newbury. Accommodation in ground floor annexe comprising hall, kitchenette, sitting room (with bed-settee), double bedroom, bathroom. Large gardens overlooking countryside. Oxford, Bath, Windsor and Heathrow Airport within easy reach. London approximately 1 hour.

Bedrooms: 1 double/twin
Bathrooms: 1 en suite

P

PRICES
Please check prices and other details at the time of booking.

NEWBURY continued

THE WHITE HART INN

Kintbury Road, Hamstead Marshall,
Newbury RG20 0HW
T: (01488) 658201
F: (01488) 657192
I: www.thewhitehart-inn.co.uk

B&B per night:
S £60.00–£70.00
D £80.00–£90.00

OPEN All Year except Christmas

Traditional, elegant country inn and restaurant with lovely walled garden and views of open countryside. We offer a relaxed atmosphere and are renowned for our Italian cooking. The stylish bedrooms are peacefully situated in adjacent barn conversion.

Bedrooms: 2 single, 2 double/twin, 2 triple/multiple
Bathrooms: 6 en suite

Lunch available
Evening meal available
CC: Mastercard, Visa

OVER NORTON, Oxfordshire Map ref 2C1

CLEEVES FARM

Over Norton, Chipping Norton OX7 5PH
T: (01608) 645019
F: (01608) 645021
E: tillylamb@hotmail.com

B&B per night:
S Min £25.00
D Min £50.00

Charming, family-run Cotswold farmhouse overlooking small Cotswold town of Chipping Norton. Quiet country atmosphere, amidst arable farm. Excellent walks with easy access to Oxford, Stratford and Burford. Open February-November.

Bedrooms: 2 double/twin, 1 triple/multiple
Bathrooms: 3 en suite

OXFORD, Oxfordshire Map ref 2C1 *Tourist Information Centre Tel: (01865) 726871*

♦♦♦

ACORN GUEST HOUSE

260-262 Iffley Road, Oxford
OX4 1SE
T: (01865) 247998
F: (01865) 247998
E: acorn_gh_oxford@freezone.co.uk

Bedrooms: 4 single, 6 double/twin, 2 triple/multiple
Bathrooms: 5 en suite, 1 private

CC: Amex, Delta, Mastercard, Switch, Visa

B&B per night:
S £27.00–£29.00
D £48.00–£58.00

OPEN All Year except Christmas

Victorian house situated midway between the city centre and the ring-road. Convenient for all local attractions including the river, and more distant places.

♦♦♦

THE BUNGALOW

Cherwell Farm, Mill Lane,
Old Marston, Oxford OX3 0QF
T: (01865) 557171 & 07703 162125

Bedrooms: 3 double/twin
Bathrooms: 1 en suite

B&B per night:
S £28.00–£35.00
D £50.00–£55.00

Modern bungalow set in 5 acres, in quiet location with views over open countryside, 3 miles from city centre. No smoking. No bus route – car essential.

♦♦♦

THE COACH & HORSES INN

Watlington Road, Chiselhampton,
Oxford OX44 7UX
T: (01865) 890255
F: (01865) 891995
E: david-mcphillips@lineone.net
I: www.coachhorsesinn.co.uk

Bedrooms: 9 double/twin
Bathrooms: 9 en suite

Lunch available
Evening meal available
CC: Amex, Delta, Diners, Mastercard, Switch, Visa

B&B per night:
S £49.50–£54.00
D £60.00–£70.00

OPEN All Year

Picturesque 16thC Listed coaching inn with popular beamed restaurant. Rooms with views of the countryside surround a landscaped and cobbled courtyard. South-east of Oxford.

OXFORD continued

♦♦♦

FALCON PRIVATE HOTEL
88-90 Abingdon Road, Oxford
OX1 4PX
T: (01865) 511122
F: (01865) 246642
E: reservations@thefalconhotel.freeserve.co.uk
I: www.oxfordcity.co.uk/hotels/falcon

Bedrooms: 2 single, 7 double/twin, 3 triple/multiple
Bathrooms: 12 en suite

CC: Amex, Delta, Mastercard, Switch, Visa

B&B per night:
S £29.00–£38.00
D £56.00–£68.00

OPEN All Year

Victorian building overlooking Queens College playing fields. Tasetfully decorated and well-maintained en suite rooms. Ten minutes' walk to colleges and city centre. Ample parking.

P

♦♦♦

HIGHFIELD WEST
188 Cumnor Hill, Oxford OX2 9PJ
T: (01865) 863007
E: highfieldwest@msn.com
I: www.oxfordcity.co.uk/accom/highfield-west

Bedrooms: 2 single, 2 double/twin, 1 triple/multiple
Bathrooms: 3 en suite

B&B per night:
S £29.00–£33.00
D £52.00–£57.50

OPEN All Year except Christmas

Comfortable accommodation with good access to city centre and ring road. Large outdoor, heated swimming pool (summer season only). Vegetarians welcome. Non-smoking.

P

♦♦

ISIS GUEST HOUSE
45-53 Iffley Road, Oxford OX4 1ED
T: (01865) 248894 & 242466
F: (01865) 243492
E: isis@herald.ox.ac.uk

Bedrooms: 12 single, 23 double/twin, 2 triple/multiple
Bathrooms: 14 en suite

CC: Mastercard, Switch, Visa

B&B per night:
S £26.00–£35.00
D £52.00–£56.00

Modernised, Victorian, city centre guesthouse within walking distance of colleges and shops. Easy access to ring road.

P

♦♦♦♦

MARLBOROUGH HOUSE HOTEL

321 Woodstock Road, Oxford OX2 7NY
T: (01865) 311321
F: (01865) 515329
E: enquiries@marlbhouse.win-uk.net
I: www.oxfordcity.co.uk/hotels/marlborough

Bedrooms: 2 single, 12 double/twin, 2 triple/multiple
Bathrooms: 16 en suite

CC: Amex, Delta, Diners, Mastercard, Switch, Visa

B&B per night:
S £78.00
D £89.00

OPEN All Year

Immaculate, spacious, privately owned hotel located in attractive leafy area of Victorian houses, 1.5 miles city centre. Bedrooms equipped with a kitchenette containing fridge, microwave, tea/coffee-making facilities, telephone and TV, comfortable chairs, dining table and desk. Restaurants and shops are located within 10 minutes' walk.

5 P

♦♦♦

MILKA'S GUEST HOUSE
379 Iffley Road, Oxford OX4 4DP
T: (01865) 778458
F: (01865) 776477
E: reservations@milkas.co.uk
I: www.milkas.co.uk

Bedrooms: 3 double/twin
Bathrooms: 1 en suite

CC: Amex, Delta, Mastercard, Switch, Visa

B&B per night:
S £35.00–£45.00
D £55.00–£65.00

OPEN All Year

A pleasant, family-run guesthouse on main road, only 1 mile from city centre.

5 P

REGIONAL TOURIST BOARD The symbol in an establishment entry indicates that it is a Regional Tourist Board member.

◆◆◆

MULBERRY GUEST HOUSE
265 London Road, Headington, Oxford OX3 9EH
T: (01865) 767114
F: (01865) 767114
E: reservations@mulberryguesthouse.co.uk
I: www.mulberryguesthouse.co.uk

Bedrooms: 5 double/twin
Bathrooms: 4 en suite, 1 private

CC: Delta, Mastercard, Switch, Visa

B&B per night:
D £60.00–£74.00

OPEN All Year

Detached house close to BMW factory (M40 exit 8), Brookes University and local hospitals. Parking. Bus stops outside for Oxford colleges, Heathrow and Gatwick. Good touring base.

P

◆◆◆

NEWTON HOUSE

82-84 Abingdon Road, Oxford OX1 4PL
T: (01865) 240561
F: (01865) 244647
E: newton.house@btinternet.com
I: www.oxfordcity.co.uk/accom/newton

B&B per night:
S £36.00–£54.00
D £44.00–£68.00

OPEN All Year

Centrally situated. Two handsome Victorian townhouses linked to form a sizable guesthouse, retaining many original features and period furniture. Conveniently located close to the city's restaurants, pubs and shops, university and River Thames (with punting).

Bedrooms: 6 double/twin, 7 triple/multiple
Bathrooms: 11 en suite

CC: Amex, Delta, Mastercard, Switch, Visa

P

◆◆◆

PARK HOUSE
7 St. Bernard's Road, Oxford OX2 6EH
T: (01865) 310824

Bedrooms: 1 single, 1 double/twin

B&B per night:
S £30.00–£35.00
D £50.00–£60.00

OPEN All Year

Traditional Victorian terraced house five minutes' walk from city centre and within easy reach of all amenities.

P

◆◆◆◆

PICKWICKS GUEST HOUSE
15-17 London Road, Headington, Oxford OX3 7SP
T: (01865) 750487
F: (01865) 742208
E: pickwicks@tiscali.co.uk
I: www.oxfordcity.co.uk/accom/pickwicks

Bedrooms: 4 single, 7 double/twin, 4 triple/multiple
Bathrooms: 14 en suite

CC: Amex, Delta, Diners, Mastercard, Switch, Visa

B&B per night:
S £30.00–£45.00
D £65.00–£70.00

OPEN All Year except Christmas

Comfortable guesthouse within five minutes' drive of Oxford ring road and M40 motorway. Nearby coach stop for 24-hour service to central London, Heathrow and Gatwick airports.

P

QUALITY ASSURANCE SCHEME

For an explanation of the quality and facilities represented by the Diamonds please refer to the front of this guide. A more detailed explanation can be found in the information pages at the back.

◆◆◆

RIVER HOTEL

17 Botley Road, Oxford OX2 0AA
T: (01865) 243475
F: (01865) 724306
E: reception@riverhotel.co.uk
I: www.riverhotel.co.uk

B&B per night:
S £57.50–£67.50
D £70.00–£86.00

OPEN All Year except Christmas

Excellent, picturesque location beside Osney bridge on River Thames Walk. Originally a master builder's home built c1870s, run many years as an independent small hotel by proprietor and staff. Like so much of Oxford the property is owned by an Oxford College. Twenty, well-equipped bedrooms, all own bathroom. Car park on site.

Bedrooms: 4 single, 11 double/twin, 5 triple/multiple
Bathrooms: 18 en suite, 2 private

CC: Mastercard, Visa

5 P

◆◆◆

SPORTSVIEW GUEST HOUSE

106-110 Abingdon Road, Oxford OX1 4PX
T: (01865) 244268 & 07798 818190
F: (01865) 249270
E: stay@sportsview.guest-house.freeserve.co.uk
I: www.smoothhound.co.uk/hotels/sportsvi.html

B&B per night:
S £33.00–£40.00
D £46.00–£68.00

OPEN All Year except Christmas

Friendly, family-run Victorian guesthouse overlooking Queens College sports ground, 0.5 miles from city centre. Close to open-air swimming pool. See the colleges and other famous landmarks such as the Sheldonian theatre and Botanical Gardens. Frequent and direct bus services to London and Blenheim Palace.

Bedrooms: 6 single, 9 double/twin, 5 triple/multiple
Bathrooms: 14 en suite

CC: Delta, Mastercard, Switch, Visa

3 P

◆◆◆

STUDLEY LODGE HOTEL

Horton Hill, Horton cum Studley, Oxford OX33 1AY
T: (01865) 351235
F: (01865) 351721
E: res@studleylodge.co.uk
I: www.studleylodge.co.uk

Bedrooms: 1 single, 14 double/twin, 1 triple/multiple
Bathrooms: 16 en suite

Lunch available
Evening meal available
CC: Amex, Delta, Diners, Mastercard, Switch, Visa

B&B per night:
S £52.00–£70.00
D £70.00–£95.00

OPEN All Year

Charming hotel with a unique atmosphere, in a village close to Oxford. Easy access to M40. Excellent restaurant. Themed bedrooms, some with balcony or patio.

P

◆◆◆

TILBURY LODGE PRIVATE HOTEL

5 Tilbury Lane, Eynsham Road, Botley, Oxford OX2 9NB
T: (01865) 862138
F: (01865) 863700
E: tilburylodge@yahoo.co.uk
I: www.oxfordcity.co.uk/hotels/tilbury

Bedrooms: 2 single, 5 double/twin, 2 triple/multiple
Bathrooms: 8 en suite, 1 private

Evening meal available
CC: Delta, Mastercard, Switch, Visa

B&B per night:
S £45.00–£50.00
D £65.00–£70.00

OPEN All Year

Situated in a quiet country lane, only 1.5 miles from city centre. Upmarket B&B with lots of extras including jacuzzi - hospitality at its best.

P

MAP REFERENCES

Map references apply to the colour maps at the front of this guide.

OXFORD continued

THE TOWER HOUSE
15 Ship Street, Oxford OX1 3DA
T: (01865) 246828
F: (01865) 247508
I: www.scoot.co.uk/towerhouse/

Bedrooms: 7 double/twin
Bathrooms: 4 en suite

CC: Amex, Delta, Mastercard, Switch, Visa

B&B per night:
S Min £50.00
D £85.00–£95.00

OPEN All Year except Christmas

17thC guesthouse in university city centre. Renowned for its warm hospitality and good hearty breakfasts. Recently awarded 4 diamonds. Establishment is also of historical interest.

PETERSFIELD, Hampshire Map ref 2C3 *Tourist Information Centre Tel: (01730) 268829*

GREYWALLS HOUSE

London Road, Hillbrow, Liss, Petersfield GU33 7QR
T: (01730) 894246 & 895596
F: (01730) 894865
E: hillbrow.la@lineone.net
I: www.bidbury.co.uk

B&B per night:
S £35.00–£40.00
D £60.00

Stone-built Victorian country house set in extensive, beautiful woodland gardens. Very peaceful yet within 5 minutes of Petersfield and downland. Good golf, walking and riding nearby. Thirty minutes from Winchester, Chichester, Portsmouth and Guildford. Spacious and comfortable lounge with log fire. All bedrooms have private facilities. French spoken.

Bedrooms: 3 double/twin
Bathrooms: 1 en suite, 2 private

◆◆◆

HEATH FARMHOUSE
Heath Road East, Petersfield GU31 4HU
T: (01730) 264709
E: info@heathfarmhouse.co.uk
I: www.heathfarmhouse.co.uk

Bedrooms: 2 double/twin, 1 triple/multiple
Bathrooms: 2 en suite, 1 private

B&B per night:
S Min £25.00
D Min £40.00

OPEN All Year except Christmas

Georgian farmhouse with lovely views and large garden. Surrounded by quiet farmland only 0.75 miles from town centre. Within easy reach of Portsmouth, Chichester, Winchester.

◆◆◆

1 THE SPAIN
Sheep Street, Petersfield GU32 3JZ
T: (01730) 263261 & 261678
F: (01730) 261084
E: allantarver@cwcom.net

Bedrooms: 3 double/twin
Bathrooms: 1 en suite

B&B per night:
S £25.00–£30.00
D £42.00–£46.00

OPEN All Year

18thC house with charming walled garden, in conservation area of Petersfield. Good eating places nearby, lovely walks, plenty to see and do.

PORTSMOUTH & SOUTHSEA, Hampshire Map ref 2C3 *Tourist Information Centre Tel: (023) 9282 6722*

◆◆◆

BEMBELL COURT HOTEL
69 Festing Road, Southsea PO4 0NQ
T: (023) 9273 5915 & 9275 0497
F: (023) 9275 6497
E: keith@bembell.freeserve.co.uk
I: www.bembell.com

Bedrooms: 2 single, 7 double/twin, 3 triple/multiple
Bathrooms: 10 en suite

CC: Amex, Delta, Diners, Mastercard, Switch, Visa

B&B per night:
S £41.50–£44.00
D £54.00–£57.00

OPEN All Year

Friendly, family-run hotel ideally situated in Portsmouth's prime holiday area. A short stroll from shops, restaurants, pubs, boating lake and rose gardens. Close to ferries.

QUALITY ASSURANCE SCHEME
Diamond ratings and awards are explained at the back of this guide.

PORTSMOUTH & SOUTHSEA continued

◆◆◆

THE ELMS GUEST HOUSE

48 Victoria Road South, Southsea PO5 2BT
T: (023) 9282 3924
F: (023) 9282 3924
E: theelmsgh@aol.com
I: www.resort-guide/portsmouth/elms

Bedrooms: 1 double/twin, 4 triple/multiple
Bathrooms: 5 en suite

CC: Delta, Mastercard, Switch, Visa

B&B per night:
S £30.00–£48.00
D £42.00–£48.00

OPEN All Year

Warm, friendly, totally no-smoking guesthouse within 8 minutes' walk of the seafront and restaurants. Close to the maritime attractions and ferry ports.

P

◆◆◆◆

HAMILTON HOUSE

95 Victoria Road North, Southsea, Portsmouth PO5 1PS
T: (023) 9282 3502
F: (023) 9282 3502
E: sandra@hamiltonhouse.co.uk
I: www.hamiltonhouse.co.uk

Bedrooms: 1 single, 5 double/twin, 3 triple/multiple
Bathrooms: 5 en suite

CC: Delta, Mastercard, Switch, Visa

B&B per night:
S £25.00–£45.00
D £44.00–£50.00

OPEN All Year

Delightful Victorian townhouse, many original features. Five minutes to continental/IOW ferry ports, stations, university, historic ships/museums. Ideal touring base. Breakfast served from 6:15am.

P

◆◆◆◆
Silver Award

131 THE HIGH STREET

Old Portsmouth PO1 2HW
T: (02392) 730903

Bedrooms: 2 double/twin
Bathrooms: 1 en suite, 1 private

B&B per night:
S Min £48.00
D Min £58.00

18thC Georgian house near seafront, historic dockyard, station, ferries and restaurants. Offers luxurious bedrooms, breakfast in bed, parking, warm welcome. Non-smokers only.

POSTCOMBE, Oxfordshire Map ref 2C1

◆◆◆◆

BEECH FARM

Salt Lane, Postcombe, Oxford OX9 7EE
T: (01844) 281240
F: (01844) 281632
E: beech.farm@btopenworld.com
I: www.ukworld.net/beechfarm.htm

Bedrooms: 1 single, 2 double/twin
Bathrooms: 2 en suite, 1 private

CC: Mastercard, Switch, Visa

B&B per night:
S £35.00–£45.00
D £50.00–£60.00

OPEN All Year

Quality ground floor accommodation. Working farm, rural location. Excellent walking. One mile jct 6, M40. Handy for Oxford, London by express coach, Henley, Blenheim Palace, Windsor. Heathrow 30 minutes.

P

QUAINTON, Buckinghamshire Map ref 2C1

◆◆◆

WOODLANDS FARMHOUSE

Doddershall, Quainton, Aylesbury HP22 4DE
T: (01296) 770225

Bedrooms: 3 double/twin, 1 triple/multiple
Bathrooms: 4 en suite

B&B per night:
S Min £25.00
D Min £50.00

OPEN All Year

18thC farmhouse offering peaceful accommodation in 11 acres of grounds. Large en suite rooms with individual entrances in barn conversion.

P

READING, Berkshire Map ref 2C2 *Tourist Information Centre Tel: (0118) 956 6226*

◆◆◆

BATH HOTEL

54 Bath Road, Reading RG1 6PG
T: (0118) 957 2019
F: (0118) 950 3203
I: www.destinationsuk.com

Bedrooms: 7 single, 11 double/twin, 3 triple/multiple
Bathrooms: 21 en suite

Lunch available
Evening meal available
CC: Amex, Delta, Mastercard, Switch, Visa

B&B per night:
S £60.00–£75.00
D £70.00–£90.00

HB per person:
DY £75.00–£90.00

OPEN All Year except Christmas

Victorian-built hotel, ideally situated for town centre, M4 and Reading Station. Recently refurbished – all en suite rooms. Weekend special rates. Ample parking.

P

READING continued

◆◆◆

DITTISHAM GUEST HOUSE
63 Tilehurst Road, Reading
RG30 2JL
T: (0118) 956 9483 & 07889 605193
E: dittishamgh@aol.com

Bedrooms: 4 single, 1 double/twin
Bathrooms: 3 en suite

CC: Delta, Mastercard, Switch, Visa

B&B per night:
S £30.00–£37.50
D £37.50–£55.00

OPEN All Year

Renovated Edwardian property with garden, in a quiet but central location. Good value and quality. On bus routes for centre of town. Car park.

◆◆◆

THE OLD FORGE
109 Grovelands Road, Reading
RG30 2PB
T: (0118) 958 2928
F: (0118) 958 2408
E: rees.family@virgin.net

Bedrooms: 4 single, 8 double/twin
Bathrooms: 9 en suite

CC: Delta, Mastercard, Switch, Visa

B&B per night:
S £32.00–£40.00
D £50.00–£60.00

OPEN All Year except Christmas

Family-run guesthouse, approximately 1.5 miles west of Reading town centre. Detached premises, large car park. Comfortable rooms all with tea/coffee and TV.

◆◆

THE ROEBUCK HOTEL
De Hillier Taverns plc, Oxford Road, Tilehurst, Reading RG31 6TG
T: (0118) 942 7517
F: (0118) 941 7629
E: dhtroebuck@aol.com

Bedrooms: 8 double/twin, 3 triple/multiple
Bathrooms: 6 en suite

Lunch available
Evening meal available
CC: Delta, Mastercard, Switch, Visa

B&B per night:
S £45.00–£55.00
D £60.00–£70.00

OPEN All Year

Part 17thC hotel overlooking Thames, with bar and on-site parking. Comfortable bedrooms. Located 3 miles from Reading town centre. Reading's longest running live entertainment venue.

RINGWOOD, Hampshire Map ref 2B3 *Tourist Information Centre Tel: (01425) 470896*

FRASER HOUSE

Salisbury Road, Blashford, Ringwood
BH24 3PB
T: (01425) 473958
F: (01425) 473958
E: fraserhouse@btinternet.com
I: www.fraserhouse.net

Overlooking the Avon Valley, on edge of the New Forest, famous for its ponies, deer and picturesque scenery. Short walk to the market town of Ringwood. Convenient for visiting Stonehenge and the cathedral city of Salisbury. A short drive to Southampton and Poole, or to Christchurch, Bournemouth and the South Coast beaches.

Bedrooms: 1 single, 4 double/twin, 1 triple/multiple
Bathrooms: 6 en suite

CC: Delta, Mastercard, Switch, Visa

B&B per night:
S Min £30.00
D Min £48.00

OPEN All Year

ROMSEY, Hampshire Map ref 2C3 *Tourist Information Centre Tel: (01794) 512987*

◆◆◆◆

3 CHERVILLE MEWS
Romsey SO51 8FY
T: (01794) 830518
F: (01794) 830518
E: patricia.townson@ntlworld.com
I: www.patsbnb.tripod.com

Bedrooms: 1 double/twin; permanent suite(s)
Bathrooms: 1 en suite

B&B per night:
S £30.00–£35.00
D £45.00–£50.00

OPEN All Year

A charming mews cottage hidden away in the old part of Romsey and within walking distance of the Abbey and the town centre.

COLOUR MAPS Colour maps at the front of this guide pinpoint all places under which you will find accommodation listed.

ROMSEY continued

♦♦♦♦

RANVILLES FARM HOUSE

Romsey SO51 6AA
T: (023) 8081 4481
F: (023) 8081 4481
E: info@ranvilles.com
I: www.ranvilles.com

Bedrooms: 1 single, 1 double/twin, 1 triple/multiple
Bathrooms: 3 en suite

B&B per night:
S £35.00–£40.00
D £50.00–£55.00

OPEN All Year except Christmas

A historic farmhouse near Winchester, Salisbury, the New Forest and 1 mile from Romsey. Peaceful situation, set in 5 acres of gardens and paddocks. Extra-large beds.

P

♦♦♦♦

ROSELEA

Hamdown Crescent, East Wellow, Romsey SO51 6BJ
T: (01794) 323262
F: (01794) 323262
E: beds@roselea.info
I: www.roselea.info

Bedrooms: 1 single, 2 double/twin
Bathrooms: 2 en suite

B&B per night:
S £18.00–£25.00
D £40.00–£45.00

HB per person:
DY £30.00–£37.00

OPEN All Year except Christmas

Quiet, ground floor accommodation on the edge of the New Forest. Honey from our own bees, together with home-produced or local food served for breakfast.

8 P

♦♦♦

TREGOYD HOUSE

Crook Hill, Braishfield, Romsey SO51 0QB
T: (01794) 368307
F: (01794) 368307
E: tregoyd@yahoo.co.uk
I: www.geocities.com/eureka/park/2485

Bedrooms: 2 single, 1 double/twin

B&B per night:
S £25.00
D £40.00–£50.00

OPEN All Year except Christmas

Situated 2 miles from Romsey near Hillier Gardens and 8 miles from Winchester. House in 2 acres of attractive gardens with ample parking, on edge of pretty village. We love meeting people – a warm welcome awaits you.

P

RYDE, Isle of Wight Map ref 2C3 *Tourist Information Centre Tel: (01983) 813818*

♦♦♦♦

CLAVERTON

12 The Strand, Ryde PO33 1JE
T: (01983) 613015
F: (01983) 613015
E: clavertonhouse@aol.com

Bedrooms: 1 double/twin, 1 triple/multiple
Bathrooms: 2 en suite

B&B per night:
S £25.00–£30.00
D £40.00–£50.00

OPEN All Year except Christmas

Family run bed and breakfast in a Victorian house providing panoramic views across the Solent. Landscaped garden with pond. Convenient for the town centre and beaches.

P

♦♦♦

THE VINE GUEST HOUSE

16 Castle Street, Ryde PO33 2EG
T: (01983) 566633
F: (01983) 566633
E: vine@guesthouse49.freeserve.co.uk
I: www.thevineguesthouse.co.uk

Bedrooms: 5 double/twin
Bathrooms: 2 en suite

Evening meal available
CC: Diners, Mastercard, Switch, Visa

B&B per night:
S £23.00–£29.00
D £36.00–£48.00

HB per person:
DY £26.00–£37.00

Comfortable, 6 double/twin-bedded guesthouse, close to all amenities. Most rooms have sea views, some en suite. Family rooms available.

SANDOWN, Isle of Wight Map ref 2C3 *Tourist Information Centre Tel: (01983) 813818*

♦♦♦

MONTPELIER HOTEL

Pier Street, Sandown PO36 8JR
T: (01983) 403964
F: (07092) 212734
E: enquiries@montpelier-hotel.co.uk
I: www.montpelier-hotel.co.uk

Bedrooms: 1 single, 3 double/twin, 2 triple/multiple
Bathrooms: 5 en suite, 1 private

CC: Delta, Mastercard, Switch, Visa

B&B per night:
S £20.00–£26.00
D £40.00–£52.00

OPEN All Year

The Montpelier is situated opposite the pier and beaches with the High Street just around the corner.

SAUNDERTON, Buckinghamshire Map ref 2C1

◆◆◆

HUNTERS GATE

Deanfield, Saunderton, Aylesbury
HP14 4JR
T: (01494) 481718
E: dadykes@attglobal.net

Bedrooms: 2 double/twin
Bathrooms: 1 en suite, 1 private

B&B per night:
D £40.00–£45.00

OPEN All Year

A quiet smallholding in the Chilterns, but within easy reach of mainline station to London and close to Oxford and the Thames Valley.

P

SELBORNE, Hampshire Map ref 2C2

◆◆◆◆

8 GOSLINGS CROFT

Selborne, Alton GU34 3HZ
T: (01420) 511285
F: (01420) 587451
E: timothyrouse@hotmail.com

Bedrooms: 1 double/twin
Bathrooms: 1 en suite

B&B per night:
S £20.00
D £40.00

OPEN All Year

Family home, set on edge of historic village, adjacent to National Trust land. Ideal base for walking and touring. Non-smokers only, please.

P

◆◆◆◆

IVANHOE

Oakhanger, Selborne, Alton
GU35 9JG
T: (01420) 473464

Bedrooms: 2 double/twin
Bathrooms: 1 private

B&B per night:
S Min £25.00
D Min £45.00

OPEN All Year except Christmas

Warm welcome in comfortable, homely accommodation with views to open countryside. Ideal touring centre. National Trust properties and walks within easy reach. Good pub nearby.

8 P

SHAFTESBURY, Dorset Map ref 2B3 *Tourist Information Centre Tel: (01747) 853514*

◆◆◆◆

AYSGARTH

Back Street, East Stour, Gillingham
SP8 5JY
T: (01747) 838351
E: aysgarth@lineone.net
I: http://website.lineone.net/~aysgarth

Bedrooms: 3 double/twin
Bathrooms: 2 en suite, 1 private

B&B per night:
S £25.00–£30.00
D £40.00–£45.00

OPEN All Year except Christmas

Chalet bungalow in village location. Some ground floor acommodation. Views over farmland. Good touring base for Dorset, Wiltshire and Somerset. Village inn nearby offering extensive menu.

P

◆◆◆◆

THE RETREAT

47 Bell Street, Shaftesbury SP7 8AE
T: (01747) 850372
F: (01747) 850372
E: at.retreat@virgin.net
I: www.the-retreat.org.uk

Bedrooms: 1 single, 4 double/twin, 5 triple/multiple
Bathrooms: 10 en suite

CC: Mastercard, Switch, Visa

B&B per night:
S £30.00–£40.00
D £55.00–£65.00

OPEN All Year

Perfectly positioned in a quiet street, this Georgian townhouse has light and airy, individually furnished, en suite bedrooms with TV and complimentary tray.

2 P

SHANKLIN, Isle of Wight Map ref 2C3 *Tourist Information Centre Tel: (01983) 813818*

◆◆◆

ATHOLL COURT

1 Atherley Road, Shanklin PO37 7AT
T: (01983) 862414 &
0779 6980 442
F: (01983) 868985
E: info@atholl-court.co.uk
I: www.atholl-court.co.uk

Bedrooms: 3 single, 5 double/twin; permanent suite(s)
Bathrooms: 8 en suite

Lunch available
Evening meal available
CC: Mastercard, Switch, Visa

B&B per night:
S £18.50–£21.50
D £39.00–£47.00

HB per person:
DY £28.50–£33.50

Detached, with own car park. Two minutes from station and 5 minutes from beach. All double rooms en suite. Single and ground floor rooms available.

P

CONFIRM YOUR BOOKING

You are advised to confirm your booking in writing.

◆◆◆◆

CULHAM LODGE HOTEL

31 Landguard Manor Road, Shanklin
PO37 7HZ
T: (01983) 862880
F: (01983) 862880
E: metcalf@culham99.freeserve.co.uk
I: www.isleofwighthotel.biz

Charming hotel in beautiful tree-lined road. Heated swimming pool in secluded garden, conservatory, home cooking and personal service. All rooms have TV with satellite channels, tea-maker and hairdryer. Culham Lodge is well placed for country walks and cycle trails. We can book your ferry crossing and save you money!

Bedrooms: 1 single, 9 double/twin
Bathrooms: 10 en suite

Evening meal available
CC: Delta, Mastercard, Switch, Visa

B&B per night:
S £24.00–£25.00
D £48.00–£50.00

HB per person:
DY £34.00–£35.00

◆◆◆

HAZELWOOD HOTEL

14 Clarence Road, Shanklin
PO37 7BH
T: (01983) 862824
F: (01983) 862824
E: barbara.tubbs@thehazelwood.free-online.co.uk
I: www.thehazelwood.free-online.co.uk

Bedrooms: 1 single, 5 double/twin, 2 triple/multiple; permanent suite(s)
Bathrooms: 8 en suite

Evening meal available
CC: Amex, Diners, Mastercard, Switch, Visa

Detached, friendly, comfortable hotel in a quiet tree-lined road, close to all amenities. Daily bookings taken. Parking available. All rooms en suite, family suites available.

B&B per night:
S £19.00–£21.00
D £38.00–£42.00

HB per person:
DY £27.00–£29.00

OPEN All Year except Christmas

◆◆◆

RYEDALE PRIVATE HOTEL

3 Atherley Road, Shanklin PO37 7AT
T: (01983) 862375 & 07816 812349
F: (01983) 862375
E: ryedale@dottydots.co.uk
I: www.SmoothHound.co.uk/hotels/ryedalep.html

Bedrooms: 1 single, 2 double/twin, 4 triple/multiple
Bathrooms: 4 en suite, 1 private

CC: Amex, Delta, Mastercard, Switch, Visa

Small and friendly hotel, close to all amenities. Free child offer outside school holidays. Discounts in selected local restaurants. Free parking available.

B&B per night:
S £18.50–£23.50
D £37.00–£47.00

◆◆

THE TRITON HOTEL

23 Atherley Road, Shanklin PO37 7AU
T: (01983) 862494
F: (01983) 861281
E: jackie@tritonhotel.freeserve.co.uk
I: www.iow-accommodation.com

Small family-run hotel. Ideal base close to railway, shops, beach and Shanklin old village. Tastefully furnished with attractive and comfortable bedrooms. Home cooking is our speciality. All diets catered for. A very warm welcome awaits from staff and proprietor.

Bedrooms: 4 single, 10 double/twin, 3 triple/multiple
Bathrooms: 9 en suite

Evening meal available
CC: Amex, Delta, Mastercard, Switch, Visa

Christmas package 24th-27th Dec: 3 nights only £210pp FB.

B&B per night:
S £19.00–£24.00
D £38.00–£48.00

HB per person:
DY £27.00–£32.00

OPEN All Year

CREDIT CARD BOOKINGS If you book by telephone and are asked for your credit card number it is advisable to check the proprietor's policy should you cancel your reservation.

SOULDERN, Oxfordshire Map ref 2C1

◆◆◆

TOWER FIELDS

Tusmore Road, Souldern, Bicester
OX27 7HY
T: (01869) 346554
F: (01869) 345157
E: hgould@strayduck.com

Bedrooms: 1 single, 1 double/twin, 1 triple/multiple
Bathrooms: 3 en suite

B&B per night:
S £30.00
D £55.00

OPEN All Year

Converted 18thC cottages and 14-acre smallholding with rare breeds of poultry, sheep and cattle. Small collection of vintage cars.

SOUTHAMPTON, Hampshire Map ref 2C3 *Tourist Information Centre Tel: (023) 8083 3333*

◆◆◆

ASHELEE LODGE

36 Atherley Road, Shirley,
Southampton SO15 5DQ
T: (023) 8022 2095
F: (023) 8022 2095

Bedrooms: 1 single, 2 double/twin, 1 triple/multiple
Bathrooms: 1 en suite

CC: Delta, Mastercard, Switch, Visa

B&B per night:
S £20.00–£22.00
D £40.00–£44.00

OPEN All Year

Homely guesthouse, garden with dip-pool. Half a mile from city centre, near station, M27 and Red Funnel Docks ferryport. Good touring base for New Forest, Salisbury and Winchester. Near university.

◆◆◆

BANISTER HOUSE HOTEL

Banister Road, Southampton
SO15 2JJ
T: (023) 8022 1279 & 8022 5753
F: (023) 8022 6551
E: banisterhotel@btconnect.com
I: www.banisterhotel.co.uk

Bedrooms: 12 single, 8 double/twin, 2 triple/multiple
Bathrooms: 12 en suite

CC: Delta, Mastercard, Switch, Visa

B&B per night:
S £26.00–£34.00
D £46.00–£49.00

OPEN All Year except Christmas

Friendly, warm welcome in this family-run hotel which is central and in a residential area. Off A33 (The Avenue) into Southampton.

Rating Applied For

BRUNSWICK LODGE

100-104 Anglesea Road, Shirley,
Southampton SO15 5QG
T: (023) 8077 4777

Bedrooms: 10 double/twin, 1 triple/multiple
Bathrooms: 6 en suite

Evening meal available
CC: Amex, Mastercard, Visa

B&B per night:
S £22.00–£35.00
D £45.00–£55.00

OPEN All Year except Christmas

Substantial 1832 property under new family ownership. Completely non-smoking. Close M3, M27 and airport. Fifteen minutes' walk to Southampton General Hospital. Large car park.

◆◆◆◆

DORMY HOUSE HOTEL

21 Barnes Lane, Sarisbury Green,
Southampton SO31 7DA
T: (01489) 572626
F: (01489) 573370
E: dormyhousehotel@warsash.globalnet.co.uk
I: www.dormyhousehotel.net

Bedrooms: 3 single, 7 double/twin, 2 triple/multiple
Bathrooms: 12 en suite

Evening meal available
CC: Mastercard, Switch, Visa

B&B per night:
S £44.00–£54.00
D £54.00–£74.00

OPEN All Year except Christmas

A tranquil Victorian house set in an attractive garden, featuring 12 en suite bedrooms, one of which is a superior queen-bedded room. All with tea/coffee-making facilities, direct-dial telephones, hairdryers and remote-control TVs. Close to River Hamble, Portsmouth and local business parks. Eight miles from Southampton.

ACCESSIBILITY

Look for the symbols which indicate National Accessible Scheme standards for hearing and visually impaired guests in addition to standards for guests with mobility impairment. Additional participants are shown in the listings at the back.

SOUTHAMPTON continued

EATON COURT HOTEL

32 Hill Lane, Southampton
SO15 5AY
T: (023) 8022 3081
F: (023) 8032 2006
E: ecourthot@aol.com
I: www.eatoncourtsouthampton.co.uk

Bedrooms: 8 single, 6 double/twin
Bathrooms: 7 en suite

Evening meal available
CC: Amex, Delta, Diners, Mastercard, Switch, Visa

B&B per night:
S £29.00–£37.00
D £42.00–£47.00

HB per person:
DY £40.00–£48.00

OPEN All Year except Christmas

Comfortable, small, owner-run hotel for business or leisure stays. Bedrooms have all amenities and a generous traditional breakfast is served.

SOUTHSEA

See under Portsmouth & Southsea

STEEPLE ASTON, Oxfordshire Map ref 2C1

WESTFIELD FARM MOTEL

Fenway, Steeple Aston, Oxford
OX25 4SS
T: (01869) 340591
F: (01869) 347594
E: info@westfieldmotel.u-net.com
I: www.oxlink.co.uk/accom/westfield-farm/

Bedrooms: 6 double/twin, 3 triple/multiple
Bathrooms: 9 en suite

Evening meal available
CC: Amex, Delta, Diners, Mastercard, Switch, Visa

B&B per night:
S £50.00–£55.00
D £65.00–£75.00

OPEN All Year

Converted stable block with comfortable bedroom units. Combined lounge, dining room and bar. Good touring centre. Fringe of Cotswolds, off A4260, 9 miles Banbury, 5 miles Woodstock.

STEWKLEY, Buckinghamshire Map ref 2C1

◆◆◆

MOUNT PLEASANT FARM

Stewkley, Leighton Buzzard
LU7 0LU
T: (01525) 240451
F: (01525) 240163

Bedrooms: 1 double/twin
Bathrooms: 1 private

B&B per night:
S Min £45.00
D Min £60.00

Annexe extension to farmhouse with own stairs. DIY breakfast provided. Open fields, fishing lake. Good eating in village 1 mile away. Always a friendly welcome. Very restful and comfortable.

STOCKBRIDGE, Hampshire Map ref 2C2

CARBERY GUEST HOUSE

Salisbury Hill, Stockbridge SO20 6EZ
T: (01264) 810771
F: (01264) 811022

B&B per night:
S £30.00–£37.00
D £52.00–£56.00

OPEN All Year except Christmas

Fine old Georgian house in an acre of landscaped gardens and lawns, overlooking the River Test. Games and swimming facilities, riding and fishing can be arranged. Ideal for touring the south coast and the New Forest.

Bedrooms: 4 single, 6 double/twin, 1 triple/multiple
Bathrooms: 8 en suite

Evening meal available
CC: Delta, Mastercard, Switch, Visa

STREATLEY, Berkshire Map ref 2C2

Silver Award

PENNYFIELD

The Coombe, Streatley, Reading
RG8 9QT
T: (01491) 872048 & 07774 946182
F: (01491) 872048
E: mandrvanstone@hotmail.com
I: www.pennyfield.co.uk

Bedrooms: 3 double/twin
Bathrooms: 3 en suite

B&B per night:
S £55.00
D £55.00

OPEN All Year except Christmas

Charming house in beautiful Thames-side village, situated on Thames path, Ridgeway Walk routes. Featuring 4-poster bed and heated spa pool. One mile to rail station.

STUDLAND, Dorset Map ref 2B3

THE BANKES ARMS HOTEL

Manor Road, Studland, Swanage
BH19 3AU
T: (01929) 450225 & 450310
F: (01929) 450307

Award-winning lovely old inn with large gardens, overlooking the sea. Eight real ales, log fires, extensive home-cooked menu (open all day for food during the season). Fresh fish a speciality. Sandy beaches, water sports, golf, riding and coastal walks to start of World Heritage site.

Bedrooms: 1 single, 4 double/twin, 3 triple/multiple
Bathrooms: 6 en suite

Lunch available
Evening meal available
CC: Delta, Diners, Mastercard, Switch, Visa

B&B per night:
S £27.00–£38.00
D £54.00–£80.00

OPEN All Year

SWANAGE, Dorset Map ref 2B3 *Tourist Information Centre Tel: (01929) 423636*

◆◆◆

HEATHER COTTAGE

1 Higher Gardens, Corfe Castle, Wareham BH20 5ES
T: (01929) 480230

Bedrooms: 2 double/twin
Bathrooms: 2 en suite

Modern, Purbeck-stone bungalow with upstairs accommodation situated in the heart of the village down a private road. Views of the Purbeck hills and a warm, friendly welcome.

B&B per night:
S £25.00–£35.00
D £38.00–£44.00

OPEN All Year

SWAY, Hampshire Map ref 2C3

◆◆◆

TIVERTON

9 Cruse Close, Sway, Lymington
SO41 6AY
T: (01590) 683092
F: (01590) 683092
E: ronrowe@talk21.com
I: www.tivertonnewforest.co.uk

Bedrooms: 2 double/twin; permanent suite(s)
Bathrooms: 2 en suite

Quiet friendly accommodation in the village centre. Your suite of rooms includes own private sitting room, with TV, video and fridge. Delicious breakfast. Very relaxing.

B&B per night:
S £35.00–£48.00
D £44.00–£48.00

OPEN All Year except Christmas

THAME, Oxfordshire Map ref 2C1 *Tourist Information Centre Tel: (01844) 212834*

Silver Award

LANGSMEADE HOUSE

Milton Common, Thame OX9 2JY
T: (01844) 278727
F: (01844) 279256
E: CerberusandCo@aol.com
I: www.langsmeadehouse.co.uk

Country house between Thame and Oxford, surrounded by 3.5 acres of mature gardens, with spacious rooms, fireplaces, oak panelling and lovely views from the big terrace onto the Chiltern Hills. The building has housed illustrious people: band leader Jack Hilton and T.E. Lawrence (Lawrence of Arabia). Birthplace of world motorbike champion Mike Hailwood.

Bedrooms: 1 single, 2 double/twin
Bathrooms: 2 private

CC: Delta, Mastercard, Switch, Visa

3 nights for price of 2, Oct-Mar.

B&B per night:
S £35.00–£45.00
D £65.00–£75.00

OPEN All Year

QUALITY ASSURANCE SCHEME

Diamond ratings and awards were correct at the time of going to press but are subject to change. Please check at the time of booking.

WALLINGFORD, Oxfordshire Map ref 2C2 *Tourist Information Centre Tel: (01491) 826972*

◆◆◆

LITTLE GABLES

166 Crowmarsh Hill,
Crowmarsh Gifford, Wallingford
OX10 8BG
T: (01491) 837834 & 07860 148882
F: (01491) 834426
E: jill@stayingaway.com
I: www.stayingaway.com

Bedrooms: 1 single, 2 triple/multiple
Bathrooms: 1 en suite, 2 private

B&B per night:
S £30.00–£40.00
D £50.00–£55.00

OPEN All Year except Christmas

Detached house, close to Ridgeway and Wallingford. Includes single and family room (cot), or twin, double or triple en suite. Tea/coffee-making, colour TV, fridge.

◆◆◆◆◆
Silver Award

NORTH MORETON HOUSE

North Moreton, Nr Wallingford
OX11 9AT
T: (01235) 813283
F: (01235) 511305
E: miles_katie@hotmail.com

Bedrooms: 3 double/twin; permanent suite(s)
Bathrooms: 2 en suite, 1 private

B&B per night:
S £30.00–£38.00
D £50.00–£60.00

OPEN All Year except Christmas

16thC former vicarage nestling in idyllic village with exceptional pub. Heated swimming pool, tennis court. Ideal base for Oxford, Thames, Ridgeway, Cotswolds, Henley, Windsor and London.

WAREHAM, Dorset Map ref 2B3 *Tourist Information Centre Tel: (01929) 552740*

◆◆◆

ANGLEBURY HOUSE

15-17 North Street, Wareham BH20 4AB
T: (01929) 552988
F: (01929) 554665

B&B per night:
S £25.00–£30.00
D £50.00–£60.00

OPEN All Year

Visited by Thomas Hardy and Lawrence of Arabia, the Anglebury has been caring for its patrons for over 200 years. Caring, courteous, family-run, small hotel offering a warm and friendly welcome. Restaurant and coffee shop available for residents and non-residents.

Bedrooms: 1 single, 3 double/twin, 2 triple/multiple
Bathrooms: 5 en suite, 1 private

Lunch available
Evening meal available
CC: Delta, Mastercard, Switch, Visa

WEST LULWORTH, Dorset Map ref 2B3

LULWORTH COVE HOTEL

Main Road, West Lulworth,
Wareham BH20 5RQ
T: (01929) 400333
F: (01929) 400534
E: hotel@lulworth-cove.com
I: www.lulworth-cove.com

Bedrooms: 1 single, 14 double/twin, 2 triple/multiple
Bathrooms: 13 en suite, 1 private

Lunch available
Evening meal available
CC: Amex, Delta, Mastercard, Switch, Visa

B&B per night:
S £27.50–£42.00
D £55.00–£75.00

OPEN All Year

One hundred metres from the cove on the Dorset coastal path. Some sea-view balcony rooms. Wide variety of restaurant and bar meals.

USE YOUR *i*s

There are more than 550 Tourist Information Centres throughout England offering friendly help with accommodation and holiday ideas as well as suggestions of places to visit and things to do. You'll find TIC addresses in the local Phone Book.

WIMBORNE MINSTER, Dorset Map ref 2B3 *Tourist Information Centre Tel: (01202) 886116*

Silver Award

ASHTON LODGE

10 Oakley Hill, Wimborne Minster
BH21 1QH
T: (01202) 883423
F: (01202) 886180
E: ashtonlodge@ukgateway.net
I: www.ashtonlodge.ukgateway.net

Spacious, detached family house with ample off-street parking. Relaxed, friendly atmosphere with all the comforts of home on offer, including a full English breakfast served in the dining room overlooking the attractively laid garden. All bedrooms are centrally heated, tastefully decorated and furnished to a high standard.

Bedrooms: 2 single, 1 double/twin, 2 triple/multiple
Bathrooms: 2 en suite, 1 private

Spring/autumn/winter savers: 10% discount for couples staying 3 nights or more Oct-Mar.

B&B per night:
S Min £25.00
D £50.00–£54.00

OPEN All Year

◆◆◆

TWYNHAM
67 Poole Road, Wimborne Minster
BH21 1QB
T: (01202) 887310

Bedrooms: 3 double/twin

Friendly family home. TV, clock radio, hairdyer and beverages in all rooms. Level walking to town centre, pubs, restaurants and shops.

P

B&B per night:
S £18.00–£20.00
D £36.00–£40.00

OPEN All Year except Christmas

WINCHESTER, Hampshire Map ref 2C3 *Tourist Information Centre Tel: (01962) 840500*

◆◆

12 CHRISTCHURCH ROAD
Winchester SO23 9SR
T: (01962) 854272

Bedrooms: 2 double/twin

Family house, with much old furniture, conservatory and garden. In tree-lined residential area, 10 minutes' walk from the cathedral and city centre.

P

B&B per night:
S £25.00–£30.00
D £35.00–£40.00

OPEN All Year except Christmas

SHAWLANDS

46 Kilham Lane, Winchester SO22 5QD
T: (01962) 861166
F: (01962) 861166
E: kathy@pollshaw.u-net.com

Attractive modern house in a quiet, elevated position overlooking open countryside, 1.5 miles from city centre. Bedrooms are spotlessly clean, bright and attractively decorated. Extra comforts include colour TV, hairdryer and welcome tray with tea and coffee. The inviting breakfast includes homemade bread and preserves with fruit from the garden.

Bedrooms: 4 double/twin, 1 triple/multiple
Bathrooms: 1 en suite

CC: Delta, Mastercard, Switch, Visa

5 P

B&B per night:
S £30.00–£35.00
D £40.00–£52.00

OPEN All Year except Christmas

GOLD & SILVER AWARDS

These exclusive ETC awards are given to establishments achieving the highest levels of quality and service. Further information can be found at the front of the guide and additional accommodation achieving these awards are shown in the listing at the back of this guide.

WINDSOR, Berkshire Map ref 2D2 *Tourist Information Centre Tel: (01753) 743900*

♦♦♦♦

BEAUMONT LODGE
1 Beaumont Road, Windsor
SL4 1HY
T: (01753) 863436 & 07774 841273
F: (01753) 863436
E: bhamshere@beaumontlodge.demon.co.uk
I: www.beaumontlodgeguesthouse.co.uk

Bedrooms: 3 double/twin
Bathrooms: 3 en suite

CC: Delta, Mastercard, Switch, Visa

B&B per night:
S £55.00–£65.00
D £65.00–£75.00

OPEN All Year

All rooms have colour TV, video, clock/radio alarm, tea/coffee facilities and trouser press. Double has spa bath. 'Which?' recommended.

Rating Applied For

BELMONT HOUSE
64 Bolton Road, Windsor SL4 3JL
T: (01753) 860860
F: (01753) 830330
E: bbs@orange.net

Bedrooms: 3 double/twin
Bathrooms: 3 en suite

B&B per night:
S £45.00–£50.00
D £50.00–£55.00

OPEN All Year

Elegant, comfortable and very friendly B&B overlooking Great Windsor Park. All rooms recently refurbished and en suite. Non-smoking. Separate apartment with office facilities located in town centre.

P

♦♦

CLARENCE HOTEL
9 Clarence Road, Windsor SL4 5AE
T: (01753) 864436
F: (01753) 857060
I: www.clarence-hotel.co.uk

B&B per night:
S £50.00–£59.00
D £60.00–£71.00

OPEN All Year except Christmas

Comfortable hotel with licensed bar and steam-sauna. Located near town centre and short walk from Windsor Castle, Eton College and River Thames. All rooms with en suite bathroom, TV, tea/coffee-making facilities, hairdryer and radio alarm. Convenient for Legoland and Heathrow Airport.

Bedrooms: 4 single, 10 double/twin, 6 triple/multiple
Bathrooms: 20 en suite

CC: Amex, Delta, Diners, Mastercard, Switch, Visa

P

♦♦♦

ELANSEY
65 Clifton Rise, Windsor SL4 5SX
T: (01753) 864438

Bedrooms: 1 single, 2 double/twin
Bathrooms: 1 en suite

B&B per night:
S £25.00–£35.00
D £50.00–£60.00

OPEN All Year except Christmas

Quiet, comfortable house. Garden, patio, 0.5 miles town centre. Easy access to M4/M25. Near Windsor racecourse. Excellent breakfasts. Established over 30 years. Highly recommended.

P

♦♦♦

MELROSE HOUSE
53 Frances Road, Windsor SL4 3AQ
T: (01753) 865328 & 07974 454943
F: (01753) 865328
E: m-mellor@supanet.com

Bedrooms: 1 single, 6 double/twin, 2 triple/multiple
Bathrooms: 9 en suite

CC: Delta, Mastercard, Switch, Visa

B&B per night:
S £50.00–£60.00
D £65.00–£70.00

OPEN All Year

Elegant detached Victorian residence 5 minutes' walk to Windsor Castle. TV, telephone, tea/coffee facilities, hairdryer in all rooms. Car park at rear.

10 P

CHECK THE MAPS
The colour maps at the front of this guide show all the cities, towns and villages for which you will find accommodation entries.
Refer to the town index to find the page on which they are listed.

WINDSOR continued

◆◆◆

THE OAST BARN
Staines Road, Wraysbury, Staines TW19 5BS
T: (01784) 481598
F: (01784) 483022
E: B&B@oastbarn.com
I: www.oastbarn.com

Bedrooms: 1 single, 2 double/twin

CC: Delta, Mastercard, Switch, Visa

B&B per night:
S £40.00–£45.00
D £50.00–£60.00

OPEN All Year

Historic house in 1-acre riverside gardens. Quiet, yet close to Heathrow. Comfortable rooms with emphasis on organic and homemade food.

12 P

◆◆◆

OSCAR HOTEL
65 Vansittart Road, Windsor SL4 5DB
T: (01753) 830613
F: (01753) 833744
E: oscarhotel1@hotmail.com
I: www.oscarhotel.com

Bedrooms: 4 single, 5 double/twin, 4 triple/multiple
Bathrooms: 13 en suite

Evening meal available
CC: Amex, Delta, Diners, Mastercard, Switch, Visa

B&B per night:
S £45.00–£60.00
D £60.00–£80.00

OPEN All Year

All rooms en suite with direct-dial telephone, colour TV, tea/coffee facilities. Own car park. Minutes' drive to Legoland and Heathrow. Ten-minute walk to Windsor Castle.

P

WINKFIELD, Berkshire Map ref 2C2

◆◆◆◆

BLUEBELL HOUSE

Lovel Lane, Winkfield, Windsor SL4 2DG
T: (01344) 886828
F: (01344) 893256
E: registrations@bluebellhousehotel.co.uk
I: www.bluebellhousehotel.co.uk

B&B per night:
S £55.00–£75.00
D £65.00–£85.00

Ex-coaching inn dating from 1700 located between Windsor and Ascot. Charming, but with every modern convenience. Large fenced-in garden and heated outdoor pool. Private parking. Ideal base for Windsor, Legoland, Ascot racing, golf at Wentworth and Sunningdale, Polo at Smiths Lawn and Royal Berkshire. En suite and family rooms.

Bedrooms: 2 single, 2 double/twin
Bathrooms: 2 en suite, 1 private

CC: Mastercard, Visa

Reductions for stays over two nights and frequent visitors.

P

WINSLOW, Buckinghamshire Map ref 2C1

◆◆◆

'WITSEND'
9 Buckingham Road, Winslow, Buckingham MK18 3DT
T: (01296) 712503
E: sheila.spatcher@aol.com

Bedrooms: 2 double/twin
Bathrooms: 2 en suite

Evening meal available

B&B per night:
S Min £20.00
D Min £40.00

HB per person:
DY Min £30.00

OPEN All Year except Christmas

Homely semi-detached chalet bungalow with en suite bedrooms. Close to town centre, colour TV, tea/coffee facilities. A warm welcome assured. Great breakfast!

P

WITNEY, Oxfordshire Map ref 2C1 *Tourist Information Centre Tel: (01993) 775802*

◆◆◆

THE COURT INN
43 Bridge Street, Witney OX8 6DA
T: (01993) 703228
F: (01993) 700980
E: info@thecourtinn.co.uk

Bedrooms: 2 single, 7 double/twin, 1 triple/multiple
Bathrooms: 7 en suite

Lunch available
Evening meal available
CC: Delta, Mastercard, Switch, Visa

B&B per night:
S £30.00–£42.00
D £50.00–£60.00

OPEN All Year

Historic inn with dining room and 2 bars. TV and telephone in all bedrooms. Car park. Friendly service.

P

RATING All accommodation in this guide has been rated, or is awaiting a rating, by a trained English Tourism Council assessor.

WITNEY continued

♦♦♦

GREYSTONES LODGE HOTEL

34 Tower Hill, Witney OX8 5ES
T: (01993) 771898
F: (01993) 702064
E: greystoneslodge@aol.com

Bedrooms: 5 single, 4 double/twin, 2 triple/multiple
Bathrooms: 10 en suite, 1 private

Evening meal available
CC: Amex, Delta, Mastercard, Switch, Visa

Family-run hotel close to Cotswolds and Oxford. Ideal location to base yourself while exploring the surrounding area. A friendly welcome awaits your arrival.

P

B&B per night:
S £30.00–£45.00
D £50.00–£60.00

HB per person:
DY £38.00–£57.00

OPEN All Year except Christmas

♦♦♦

QUARRYDENE

17 Dene Rise, Witney OX28 6LU
T: (01993) 772152
F: (01993) 772152
E: jeanniemarshall@quarrydene.fsworld.co.uk

Bedrooms: 2 single, 2 double/twin
Bathrooms: 1 en suite

Evening meal available

Detached home with friendly welcome, a few minutes' walk from town centre, but in quiet area. Good location for Oxford/Cotswolds/Stratford. Long-term bookings welcome.

P

B&B per night:
S Min £26.00
D Min £52.00

HB per person:
DY Min £34.00

OPEN All Year except Christmas

♦♦♦

THE WITNEY HOTEL

7 Church Green, Witney OX28 4AZ
T: (01993) 702137
F: (01993) 705337
E: bookings@thewitneyhotel.co.uk
I: www.thewitneyhotel.co.uk

Bedrooms: 1 single, 7 double/twin, 2 triple/multiple
Bathrooms: 10 en suite

CC: Delta, Mastercard, Switch, Visa

Small, family-run bed and breakfast situated in a Listed building overlooking historic Church Green. Centrally located. Clean and comfortable accommodation at reasonable prices.

B&B per night:
S £37.00
D £54.00–£80.00

OPEN All Year except Christmas

WOODCOTE, Oxfordshire Map ref 2C2

♦♦♦

HEDGES

South Stoke Road, Woodcote, Reading RG8 0PL
T: (01491) 680461
E: Howard-Allen@hedgeswoodcote.freeserve.co.uk

Bedrooms: 2 single, 2 double/twin
Bathrooms: 1 private

Peaceful, rural situation on edge of village. Historic Area of Outstanding Natural Beauty. Good access Henley, Oxford, Reading (Heathrow link), M4, M40.

P

B&B per night:
S £17.00–£19.00
D £34.00–£38.00

OPEN All Year except Christmas

♦♦♦

THE HIGHWAYMAN

Exlade Street, Checkendon, Reading RG8 0UA
T: (01491) 682020
F: (01491) 682229
E: thehighwayman@skyeinnsfsnet.co.uk
I: www.thehighwaymancheckendon.co.uk

Bedrooms: 1 single, 3 double/twin
Bathrooms: 4 en suite

Lunch available
Evening meal available
CC: Amex, Delta, Mastercard, Switch, Visa

A privately owned and run 17thC inn, ideally situated for visiting the Cotswolds, Oxford, Henley-on-Thames and Windsor.

5 P

B&B per night:
S £55.00–£65.00
D £70.00–£75.00

OPEN All Year

WOODSTOCK, Oxfordshire Map ref 2C1 *Tourist Information Centre Tel: (01993) 813276*

♦♦♦

BURLEIGH FARM

Bladon Road, Cassington, Oxford OX29 4EA
T: (01865) 881352
E: j.cook@farmline.com

Bedrooms: 1 double/twin, 1 triple/multiple
Bathrooms: 2 en suite

360-acre farm on Blenheim Estate (home of Duke of Marlborough) at Woodstock. Six miles north-west of Oxford, halfway between Cassington (A40) and Bladon (A4095), south of Woodstock.

P

B&B per night:
S £25.00–£35.00
D £50.00–£55.00

OPEN All Year

WOODSTOCK continued

♦♦♦♦

GORSELANDS HALL

Boddington Lane, North Leigh, Witney OX29 6PU
T: (01993) 882292
F: (01993) 883629
E: hamilton@gorselandshall.com
I: www.gorselandshall.com

Old Cotswold-stone country house with oak beams and flagstone floors. All rooms en suite with colour TV. Large secluded garden. Badminton. Tennis court. Snooker. Quiet rural location. Convenient for Oxford, Blenheim Palace and Cotswolds. Stratford 32 miles, Heathrow 1.25 hours by car and London (Paddington) 1.25 hours by train.

Bedrooms: 5 double/twin, 1 triple/multiple
Bathrooms: 6 en suite

CC: Amex, Delta, Mastercard, Switch, Visa

10% reduction for stays of 4 nights or more. Winter discounts available.

B&B per night:
S £35.00
D £45.00–£50.00

OPEN All Year

♦♦♦♦ Silver Award

THE LAURELS
Hensington Road, Woodstock, Oxford OX20 1JL
T: (01993) 812583
F: (01993) 810041
E: stay@laurelsguesthouse.co.uk
I: www.smoothhound.co.uk/hotels/thelaur.html

Bedrooms: 3 double/twin
Bathrooms: 2 en suite, 1 private

CC: Delta, Mastercard, Switch, Visa

Fine Victorian house, charmingly furnished with an emphasis on comfort and quality. Just off town centre and a short walk from Blenheim Palace.

B&B per night:
S £40.00–£48.00
D £48.00–£58.00

OPEN All Year except Christmas

♦♦♦

THE PUNCHBOWL INN

12 Oxford Street, Woodstock, Oxford OX20 1TR
T: (01993) 811218
F: (01993) 811393
E: info@punchbowl-woodstock.co.uk
I: www.punchbowl-woodstock.co.uk

18thC Grade II Listed traditional inn situated in the centre of Woodstock serving bar meals and afternoon tea/coffee. Ten guest en suite bedrooms are available, residents' car park. Ideal base for visiting Blenheim Palace, Oxford, Stratford-upon-Avon and the Cotswolds.

Bedrooms: 1 single, 9 double/twin
Bathrooms: 9 en suite, 1 private

Lunch available
Evening meal available
CC: Delta, Mastercard, Switch, Visa

B&B per night:
S £50.00–£55.00
D £65.00–£70.00

OPEN All Year

♦♦♦

SHEPHERDS HALL INN
Witney Road, Freeland, Oxford OX29 8HQ
T: (01993) 881256
F: (01993) 883455

Bedrooms: 1 single, 3 double/twin, 1 triple/multiple
Bathrooms: 5 en suite

Lunch available
Evening meal available
CC: Delta, Mastercard, Switch, Visa

Well-appointed inn offering good accommodation. All rooms en suite. Ideally situated for Oxford, Woodstock and the Cotswolds, on the A4095 Woodstock to Witney road.

B&B per night:
S £28.50–£37.50
D £50.00–£55.00

OPEN All Year

SB

SPECIAL BREAKS
Many establishments offer special promotions and themed breaks. These are highlighted in red. (All such offers are subject to availability.)

WOODSTOCK continued

◆◆◆◆

THE TOWNHOUSE
15 High Street, Woodstock, Oxford OX20 1TE
T: (01993) 810843
F: (01993) 810843
E: info@woodstock-townhouse.com
I: www.woodstock-townhouse.com

Bedrooms: 4 double/twin
Bathrooms: 4 en suite

CC: Amex, Mastercard, Switch, Visa

B&B per night:
S £48.00–£52.50
D £68.00–£78.50

OPEN All Year

Character, 18thC stone-built house in centre of historic Woodstock. All rooms en suite. Recently refurbished to high standard. Dining room overlooks charming walled garden.

12

A brief guide to the main Towns and Villages offering accommodation in the South of England

A ALTON, HAMPSHIRE - Pleasant old market town standing on the Pilgrim's Way, with some attractive Georgian buildings. The parish church still bears the scars of bullet marks, evidence of a bitter struggle between the Roundheads and the Royalists.

• **AMERSHAM, BUCKINGHAMSHIRE** - Old town with many fine buildings, particularly in the High Street. There are several interesting old inns.

• **ANDOVER, HAMPSHIRE** - Town that achieved importance from the wool trade and now has much modern development. A good centre for visiting places of interest.

• **ASHURST, HAMPSHIRE** - Small village on the A35, on the edge of the New Forest and three miles north-east of Lyndhurst. Easy access to beautiful forest lawns.

• **AYLESBURY, BUCKINGHAMSHIRE** - Historic county town in the Vale of Aylesbury. The cobbled market square has a Victorian clock tower and the 15thC King's Head Inn (National Trust). Interesting county museum and 13thC parish church.

B BANBURY, OXFORDSHIRE - Famous for its cattle market, cakes, nursery rhyme and Cross. Founded in Saxon times, it has some fine houses and interesting old inns. A good centre for touring Warwickshire and the Cotswolds.

• **BEACONSFIELD, BUCKINGHAMSHIRE** - Former coaching town with several inns still surviving. The old town has many fine houses and an interesting church. Beautiful countryside and beech woods nearby.

• **BEAULIEU, HAMPSHIRE** - Beautifully situated among woods and hills on the Beaulieu river, the village is both charming and unspoilt. The 13thC ruined Cistercian abbey and 14thC Palace House stand close to the National Motor Museum. There is a maritime museum at Bucklers Hard.

• **BEMBRIDGE, ISLE OF WIGHT** - Village with harbour and bay below Bembridge Down - the most easterly village on the island. Bembridge Sailing Club is one of the most important in southern England.

• **BICESTER, OXFORDSHIRE** - Market town with a large army depot and well-known hunting centre with hunt established in the late 18thC. The ancient parish church displays work of many periods. Nearby is the Jacobean mansion of Rousham House with gardens landscaped by William Kent.

• **BLANDFORD FORUM, DORSET** - Almost completely destroyed by fire in 1731, the town was rebuilt in a handsome Georgian style. The church is large and grand and the town is the hub of a rich farming area.

• **BONCHURCH, ISLE OF WIGHT** - Sheltered suburb at the foot of St Boniface Down.

• **BOURNEMOUTH, DORSET** - Seaside town set among the pines with a mild climate, sandy beaches and fine coastal views. The town has wide streets with excellent shops, a pier, a pavilion, museums and conference centre.

• **BRIZE NORTON, OXFORDSHIRE** - Village closely associated with the American Air Force. The medieval church is the only church in England dedicated to St Brice, from whom the village takes its name.

• **BROCKENHURST, HAMPSHIRE** - Attractive village with thatched cottages and a ford in its main street. Well placed for visiting the New Forest.

• **BURFORD, OXFORDSHIRE** - One of the most beautiful Cotswold wool towns with Georgian and Tudor houses, many antique shops and a picturesque High Street sloping to the River Windrush.

C CARISBROOKE, ISLE OF WIGHT - Situated at the heart of the Isle of Wight and an ideal base for touring. Boasts a Norman church, formerly a monastic church, and a castle built on the site of a Roman fortress.

• **CHALFONT ST GILES, BUCKINGHAMSHIRE** - Pretty, old village in wooded Chiltern Hills yet only 20 miles from London and a good base for visiting the city. Excellent base for Windsor, Henley, the Thames Valley, Oxford and the Cotswolds.

• **CHARLBURY, OXFORDSHIRE** - Large Cotswold village with beautiful views of the Evenlode Valley just outside the village and close to the ancient Forest of Wychwood.

• **CHIPPING NORTON, OXFORDSHIRE** - Old market town set high in the Cotswolds and an ideal touring centre. The wide market-place contains many 16thC and 17thC stone houses and the Town Hall and Tudor Guildhall.

D DEDDINGTON, OXFORDSHIRE - On the edge of the Cotswolds and settled since the Stone Age, this is the only village in England to have been granted a full Coat of Arms, displayed on the 16thC Town Hall in the picturesque market square. Many places of interest include the Church of St Peter and St Paul.

E EASTLEIGH, HAMPSHIRE - Town developed around the railway engineering works built there in 1889. The borough stretches from Southampton Water to the Test Valley in the north. Yachting centres at Hamble and Bursledon.

• **EDGCOTT, BUCKINGHAMSHIRE** - Small village within easy reach of Aylesbury, Milton Keynes and Bicester.

SYMBOLS The symbols in each entry give information about services and facilities. A key to these symbols appears at the back of this guide.

F FAREHAM, HAMPSHIRE - Lies on a quiet backwater of Portsmouth Harbour. The High Street is lined with fine Georgian buildings.

• **FARNBOROUGH, HAMPSHIRE** - Home of the Royal Aircraft Establishment and the site of the biennial International Air Show. St Michael's Abbey was built by the Empress Eugenie, wife of Napoleon III of France; they are both buried in the crypt, together with their son.

• **FORDINGBRIDGE, HAMPSHIRE** - On the north-west edge of the New Forest. A medieval bridge crosses the Avon at this point and gave the town its name. A good centre for walking, exploring and fishing.

G GORING, OXFORDSHIRE - Riverside town on the Oxfordshire/Berkshire border, linked by an attractive bridge to Streatley with views to the Goring Gap.

H HENLEY-ON-THAMES, OXFORDSHIRE - The famous Thames Regatta is held in this prosperous and attractive town at the beginning of July each year. The town has many Georgian buildings and old coaching inns and the parish church has some fine monuments.

• **HYTHE, HAMPSHIRE** - Waterside village with spectacular views over Southampton Water. Marina with distinctive "fishing village"-style development, 117-year-old pier, wide range of interesting shops.

L LYMINGTON, HAMPSHIRE - Small, pleasant town with bright cottages and attractive Georgian houses, lying on the edge of the New Forest with a ferry service to the Isle of Wight. A sheltered harbour makes it a busy yachting centre.

• **LYNDHURST, HAMPSHIRE** - The "capital" of the New Forest, surrounded by attractive woodland scenery and delightful villages. The town is dominated by the Victorian Gothic-style church where the original Alice in Wonderland is buried.

M MAIDENHEAD, BERKSHIRE - Attractive town on the River Thames which is crossed by an elegant 18thC bridge and by Brunel's well-known railway bridge. It is a popular place for boating with delightful riverside walks. The Courage Shire Horse Centre is nearby.

• **MARLOW, BUCKINGHAMSHIRE** - Attractive Georgian town on the River Thames, famous for its 19thC suspension bridge. The High Street contains many old houses and there are connections with writers including Shelley and T S Eliot.

• **MILFORD-ON-SEA, HAMPSHIRE** - Victorian seaside resort with shingle beach and good bathing, set in pleasant countryside and looking out over the Isle of Wight. Nearby is Hurst Castle, built by Henry VIII. The school chapel, former abbey church, can be visited.

• **MILTON KEYNES, BUCKINGHAMSHIRE** - Designated a New Town in 1967, Milton Keynes offers a wide range of housing and is abundantly planted with trees. It has excellent shopping facilities and three centres for leisure and sporting activities. The Open University is based here.

N NEW MILTON, HAMPSHIRE - New Forest residential town on the mainline railway.

• **NEWBURY, BERKSHIRE** - Ancient town surrounded by the Downs and on the Kennet and Avon Canal. It has many buildings of interest, including the 17thC Cloth Hall, which is now a museum. The famous racecourse is nearby.

O OXFORD, OXFORDSHIRE - Beautiful university town with many ancient colleges, some dating from the 13thC, and numerous buildings of historic and architectural interest. The Ashmolean Museum has outstanding collections. Lovely gardens and meadows with punting on the Cherwell.

P PETERSFIELD, HAMPSHIRE - Grew prosperous from the wool trade and was famous as a coaching centre. Its attractive market square is dominated by a statue of William III. Close by are Petersfield Heath, with numerous ancient barrows, and Butser Hill with magnificent views.

• **PORTSMOUTH & SOUTHSEA, HAMPSHIRE** - There have been connections with the Navy since early times, and the first dock was built in 1194. HMS Victory, Nelson's flagship, is here and Charles Dickens' former home is open to the public. Neighbouring Southsea has a promenade with magnificent views of Spithead.

Q QUAINTON, BUCKINGHAMSHIRE - Rural village with many 17thC and 18thC monuments, including a large monument which is unsigned. Some Georgian buildings.

R READING, BERKSHIRE - Busy, modern county town with large shopping centre and many leisure and recreation facilities. There are several interesting museums, and the Duke of Wellington's Stratfield Saye is nearby.

• **RINGWOOD, HAMPSHIRE** - Market town by the River Avon comprising old cottages, many of them thatched. Although just outside the New Forest, there is heath and woodland nearby and it is a good centre for horse-riding and walking.

• **ROMSEY, HAMPSHIRE** - The town grew up around the important abbey and lies on the banks of the River Test, famous for trout and salmon. Broadlands House, home of the late Lord Mountbatten, is open to the public.

• **RYDE, ISLE OF WIGHT** - The island's chief entry port, connected to Portsmouth by ferries and hovercraft. Seven miles of sandy beaches with a half-mile pier, esplanade and gardens.

S SANDOWN, ISLE OF WIGHT - The six-mile sweep of Sandown Bay is one of the island's finest stretches, with excellent sands. The pier has a pavilion and sun terrace; the esplanade has amusements, bars, eating places and gardens.

• **SELBORNE, HAMPSHIRE** - Village made famous by Gilbert White, who was a curate here and is remembered for his classic book "The Natural History of Selborne", published in 1788. His house is now a museum.

• **SHAFTESBURY, DORSET** - Hilltop town with a long history. The ancient and cobbled Gold Hill is one of the most attractive in Dorset. There is an excellent small museum containing a collection of buttons for which the town is famous.

• **SHANKLIN, ISLE OF WIGHT** - Set on a cliff with gentle slopes leading down to the beach, esplanade and marine gardens. The picturesque, old thatched village nestles at the end of the wooded chine.

CREDIT CARD BOOKINGS If you book by telephone and are asked for your credit card number it is advisable to check the proprietor's policy should you cancel your reservation.

• **SOUTHAMPTON, HAMPSHIRE** - One of Britain's leading seaports with a long history, now a major container port. In the 18thC it became a fashionable resort with the assembly rooms and theatre. The old Guildhall and the Wool House are now museums. Sections of the medieval wall can still be seen.

• **STOCKBRIDGE, HAMPSHIRE** - Set in the Test Valley which has some of the best fishing in England. The wide main street has houses of all styles, mainly Tudor and Georgian.

• **STREATLEY, BERKSHIRE** - Pretty village on the River Thames, linked to Goring by an attractive bridge. It has Georgian houses and cottages and beautiful views over the countryside and the Goring Gap.

• **STUDLAND, DORSET** - On a beautiful stretch of coast and good for walking, with a National Nature Reserve to the north. The Norman church is the finest in the country, with superb rounded arches and vaulting. Brownsea Island, where the first scout camp was held, lies in Poole Harbour.

• **SWANAGE, DORSET** - Began life as an Anglo-Saxon port, then a quarrying centre of Purbeck marble. Now the safe, sandy beach set in a sweeping bay and flanked by downs is good walking country, making it an ideal resort.

• **SWAY, HAMPSHIRE** - Small village on the south-western edge of the New Forest. It is noted for its 220-ft tower, Peterson's Folly, built in the 1870s by a retired Indian judge to demonstrate the value of concrete as a building material.

T **THAME, OXFORDSHIRE** - Historic market town on the River Thames. The wide, unspoilt High Street has many styles of architecture with medieval timber-framed cottages, Georgian houses and some famous inns.

W **WALLINGFORD, OXFORDSHIRE** - Site of an ancient ford over the River Thames, now crossed by a 900-ft-long bridge. The town has many timber-framed and Georgian buildings, Gainsborough portraits in the 17thC Town Hall and a few remains of a Norman castle.

• **WAREHAM, DORSET** - This site has been occupied since pre-Roman times and has a turbulent history. In 1762 fire destroyed much of the town, so the buildings now are mostly Georgian.

• **WEST LULWORTH, DORSET** - Well known for Lulworth Cove, the almost landlocked circular bay of chalk and limestone cliffs.

• **WESTBURY, BUCKINGHAMSHIRE** - Village close to Buckingham and within easy reach of Milton Keynes and Banbury.

• **WIMBORNE MINSTER, DORSET** - Market town centred on the twin-towered Minster Church of St Cuthberga which gave the town the second part of its name. Good touring base for the surrounding countryside, depicted in the writings of Thomas Hardy.

• **WINCHESTER, HAMPSHIRE** - King Alfred the Great made Winchester the capital of Saxon England. A magnificent Norman cathedral, with one of the longest naves in Europe, dominates the city. Home of Winchester College, founded in 1382.

• **WINDSOR, BERKSHIRE** - Town dominated by the spectacular castle, home of the Royal Family for over 900 years. Parts are open to the public. There are many attractions including the Great Park, Eton and trips on the river.

• **WINSLOW, BUCKINGHAMSHIRE** - Small town with Georgian houses, a little market square and a fine church with 15thC wall-paintings. Winslow Hall, built to the design of Sir Christopher Wren in 1700, is open to the public.

• **WITNEY, OXFORDSHIRE** - Town famous for its blanket making and mentioned in the Domesday Book. The market-place contains the Butter Cross, a medieval meeting place, and there is a green with merchants' houses.

• **WOODCOTE, OXFORDSHIRE** - Town in the Chilterns close to Goring and Henley-on-Thames.

• **WOODSTOCK, OXFORDSHIRE** - Small country town clustered around the park gates of Blenheim Palace, the superb 18thC home of the Duke of Marlborough. The town has well-known inns and an interesting museum. Sir Winston Churchill was born and buried nearby.

SOUTH EAST England

The White Cliffs of Dover, beach huts and piers, yachts at Chichester – this distinctive coast combines with famous gardens and the apples and hops of Kent to make a quintessentially English region.

classic sights

Battle of Hastings – audio tour brings the battle to life

Hever Castle – romantic moated castle, home of Anne Boleyn

coast & country

Runnymede – riverside meadows and woodland

Pegwell Bay & Goodwin Sands – a haven for birds and seals

gorgeous gardens

Sheffield park – great 18thC, Capability Brown-designed landscaped gardens

Leonardslee – rhododendrons and azaleas ablaze with colour in May

literary links

Charles Dickens – Rochester; his home, Gad's Hill Place

Rudyard Kipling – Bateman's, his memento-filled home

Chaucer – The Canterbury Tales

arts for all

Brighton Festival – international performers, artists and writers every May

distinctively different

De la Warr Pavillion, Bexhill – Grade 1 Listed pavillion and theatre. One of the world's finest examples of modernist architecture

The counties of East Sussex, Kent, Surrey and West Sussex

FOR MORE INFORMATION CONTACT:

South East England Tourist Board
The Old Brew House, Warwick Park,
Tunbridge Wells, Kent TN2 5TU
Tel: (01892) 540766 Fax: (01892) 511008
Email: enquiries@seetb.org.uk
Internet: www.SouthEastEngland.uk.com

> The Pictures: 1 South Downs, Sussex 2 Fishing Boats on Hastings beach, East Sussex 3 Picnic at Glyndebourne, East Sussex

> PLACES TO VISIT - see pages 456-459 > WHERE TO STAY - see pages 460-496

PLACES to visit

You will find hundreds of interesting places to visit during your stay, just some of which are listed in these pages. Contact any Tourist Information Centre in the region for more ideas on days out.

Awarded ETC's new 'Quality Assured Visitor Attraction' marque at time of going to press. **(See page 19).**

A Day at the Wells

Corn Exchange, The Pantiles, Royal Tunbridge Wells
Tel: (01892) 546545
With commentary on personal stereos, visitors experience the sights and sounds of 18thC Tunbridge Wells in its heyday as a spa town, escorted by Beau Nash, dandy and MC.

Alfriston Clergy House

The Tye, Alfriston, Polegate
Tel: (01323) 870001 www.nationaltrust.org.uk
A beautiful thatched medieval hall-house, the first building to be acquired by the National Trust in 1896. Pretty cottage garden with a charming gift shop.

Amberley Working Museum

Houghton Bridge, Amberley, Arundel
Tel: (01798) 831370 www.amberleymuseum.co.uk
Open-air industrial history centre in chalk quarry. Working craftsmen, narrow-gauge railway, early buses, working machines and other exhibits. Nature trail/visitor centre.

Anne of Cleves House Museum

52 Southover High Street, Lewes
Tel: (01273) 474610 www.sussexpast.co.uk
A 16thC, timber-framed Wealden hall-house which contains collections of Sussex interest. Displays feature Lewes from the 16thC to the present day.

Arundel Wildfowl and Wetlands Centre

Mill Road, Arundel
Tel: (01903) 883355 www.wwt.org.uk
Set in over 60 acres (24ha). Feed the world's rarest goose and see the only pair of breeding Blue Ducks outside New Zealand. Restaurant, gift shop, lecture theatre and wildlife art gallery.

Basingstoke Canal Visitor Centre

Mytchett Place Road, Mytchett, Camberley
Tel: (01252) 370073 www.basingstoke-canal.co.uk
A canal interpretation centre with an exhibition displaying the history of canals over the past 200 years. Boat trips and boat hire available. Adventure playground.

Battle Abbey and Battlefield

High Street, Battle
Tel: (01424) 773792 www.english-heritage.org.uk
An abbey founded by William the Conqueror on the site of the Battle of Hastings. The church altar is on the spot where King Harold was killed. Battlefield views and exhibition.

Bentley Wildfowl and Motor Museum

Bentley, Halland, Lewes
Tel: (01825) 840573 www.bentley.org.uk
Over 1,000 wildfowl in parkland with lakes. Motor museum with vintage cars, house, children's play facilities and woodland walk.

Borde Hill Garden

Balcombe Road, , Haywards Heath
Tel: (01444) 450326 www.bordehill.co.uk
Garden, park and woodland, something for all the family. A garden of contrasts where botanical interest and garden design play equally important roles. Extended colour througout the year.

The Canterbury Tales Visitor Attraction

St Margaret's Street, Canterbury
Tel: (01227) 479227
www.canterburytales.org.uk
An audio-visual recreation of life in medieval England. Visitors join Chaucer's pilgrims on their journey from London's Tabard Inn to Thomas Becket's shrine at Canterbury.

Chartwell

Mapleton Road, Westerham
Tel: (01732) 866368 www.nationaltrust.org.uk
The home of Sir Winston Churchill with study, studio, museum rooms with gifts, uniforms and photos, garden, Golden Rose Walk, lakes and exhibition.

Chatley Heath Semaphore Tower

Pointers Road, Cobham
Tel: (01372) 458822
A restored historic semaphore tower, set in woodland, displaying the history of overland naval communications in the early 19thC. Working semaphore mast and models.

Dapdune Wharf

Wharf Road, Guildford
Tel: (01483) 561389
www.nationaltrust.org.uk/southern
Dapdune Wharf is the home of 'Reliance', a restored Wey barge, as well as an interactive exhibition which tells the story of the waterway and those who lived and worked on it.

Dover Castle and Secret Wartime Tunnels

Dover
Tel: (01304) 211067 www.english-heritage.org.uk
One of the most powerful medieval fortresses in Western Europe. St Mary-in-Castro Saxon church, Roman lighthouse, secret wartime tunnels, Henry II Great Keep.

Drusillas Park

Alfriston, Polegate
Tel: (01323) 874100 www.drusillas.co.uk
The best small zoo in England with animals in natural habitats. Playland is masses of fun for children from 3-12. Explorers Lagoon.

Eagle Heights

Hulberry Farm, Lullingstone Lane, Eynsford, Dartford
Tel: (01322) 866466 www.eagleheights.co.uk
Bird of prey centre housed under cover where visitors can see eagles, hawks, falcons, owls and vultures from all over the world. Reptile centre, play area and sandpit.

English Wine Centre

Alfriston Roundabout, Alfriston, Polegate
Tel: (01323) 870164 www.weddingwine.co.uk
Large range of English and world wines, fruit wines and cider. Wine-related gifts and locally produced pickles, jams and chocolates. Museum showing history of English wine from Roman times. Tours/tasting.

Goodwood House

Goodwood, Chichester
Tel: (01243) 755040 www.goodwood.co.uk
A magnificent Regency house, home to the Earl of March, extensively refurbished in 1997 and set in a large area of open parkland. Fine furnishings, tapestries and porcelain.

Hastings Castle and 1066 Story

West Hill, Hastings
Tel: (01424) 781112 www.smugglersadventure.co.uk
Fragmentary remains of Norman castle built on West Hill after William the Conqueror's victory at the Battle of Hastings. 1066 Story interpretation centre in siege tent.

> The Pictures: 1 Brighton Pier, East Sussex 2 Guildford Castle, Surrey 3 Brighton Marina, East Sussex 4 Rye, East Sussex 5 Chichester Cathedral 6 Bateman's, East Sussex

Hatchlands Park

East Clandon, Guildford
Tel: (01483) 222482 www.nationaltrust.org.uk/
Built in 1758 and set in a Repton park, Hatchlands has splendid interiors by Robert Adam and houses the Cobbe collection of keyboard musical instruments. Gertrude Jekyll garden.

High Beeches Gardens

Handcross, Haywards Heath
Tel: (01444) 400589 www.highbeeches.com
Twenty-five acres (10ha) of peaceful, landscaped woodland and water gardens with many rare plants, wildflower meadow, spring bulbs and glorious autumn colour.

Kent & East Sussex Railway

Tenterden Town Station, Tenterden
Tel: (01580) 765155 www.kesr.org.uk
Full-size steam railway with restored Edwardian stations at Tenterden and Northiam, 14 steam engines, Victorian coaches and Pullman carriages. Museum and children's play area.

Leeds Castle and Gardens

Leeds, Maidstone
Tel: (01622) 765400 www.leeds-castle.com
A castle built on two islands in a lake, dating from 9thC. Furniture, tapestries, art treasures, dog collar museum, gardens, duckery, aviaries, maze, grotto, vineyard and greenhouses.

Newhaven Fort

Fort Road, Newhaven
Tel: (01273) 517622
www.newhavenfort.org.uk

A Victorian coastal fortress covering 10 acres (4ha) and overlooking Seaford Bay. The fort has barrack rooms housing military and wartime displays and dioramas.

Port Lympne Wild Animal Park, Mansion and Gardens

Port Lympne, Lympne, Hythe
Tel: (01303) 264647 www.howletts.net
A 300-acre (121-ha) wild animal park of rare breeds including gorillas, deer, rhino, tigers, elephants etc. Mansion with art gallery exhibitions, murals and gardens. Trailer rides.

Savill Garden

Windsor Great Park, Wick Lane, Englefield Green, Egham
Tel: (01753) 847518 www.savillgarden.co.uk
Woodland garden with formal gardens and herbaceous borders offering much of great interest and beauty in all seasons. Landscaped Queen Elizabeth temperate house.

Sculpture at Goodwood

Hat Hill Copse, Goodwood, Chichester
Tel: (01243) 538449 www.sculpture.org.uk
A changing collection of contemporary British sculpture set in 20 acres (8ha) of beautiful grounds on the South Downs overlooking Chichester.

South of England Rare Breeds Centre

Highlands Farm, Woodchurch, Ashford
Tel: (01233) 861493 www.rarebreeds.org.uk
Large collection of rare farm breeds on a working farm with children's play activities. Georgian farmstead, woodland walks. See the 'Tamworth Two', the famous pigs who escaped from an abattoir.

Titsey Place and Gardens

Titsey Place, Oxted
Tel: (01273) 407056 www.titsey.com
A guided tour of Titsey Place includes the library, servants' hall, dining room and drawing room. The gardens comprise 10 acres (4ha) of formal gardens and a walled garden.

West Dean Gardens

West Dean Estate, West Dean, Chichester
Tel: (01243) 818210 www.westdean.org.uk

Extensive downland garden with specimen trees, 300-ft (91-m) pergola, rustic summerhouses and restored walled kitchen garden. Walk in parkland and 45-acre (18-ha) arboretum.

Wilderness Wood

Hadlow Down, Uckfield
Tel: (01825) 830509 www.wildernesswood.co.uk
A family-run working woodland of 60 acres (24ha), beautiful in all seasons. There are trails, a bluebell walk, a play area, workshop and a timber barn with exhibition.

Winkworth Arboretum

Hascombe Road, Hascombe, Godalming
Tel: (01483) 208477
www.cornuswwweb.co.uk

One hundred acres (40ha) of hillside planted with rare trees and shrubs. Good views, lakes, newly restored boathouse, azaleas, bluebells, wild spring flowers and autumn colours.

Find out more about SOUTH EAST England

Further information about holidays and attractions in South East England is available from:

SOUTH EAST ENGLAND TOURIST BOARD
The Old Brew House, Warwick Park, Tunbridge Wells, Kent TN2 5TU.
Tel: (01892) 540766 Fax: (01892) 511008
Email: enquiries@seetb.org.uk
Internet: www.SouthEastEngland.uk.com

The following publications are available from the South East England Tourist Board:

South East Breaks
a detailed guide to the region including places to visit and inspected accommodation

Leisure Map and Gazetteer - South East England
produced in conjunction with Estate Publications Ltd, a colourful tourist map of the South East showing roads, railways, hundreds of places to visit and the topography of the region

Favourite Gardens and Garden Stays in South East England
a guide detailing the region's finest garden attractions along with 'garden friendly' accommodation

Walk South East England
a useful guide to the best walking in Hampshire, Kent, Surrey, East and West Sussex

Getting to SOUTH EAST England

BY ROAD: From the north of England - M1/M25; the west and Wales - M4/M25; the east of England - M25; the south of England M3/M25; London - M20 or M2.

BY RAIL: Regular services from London's Charing Cross, Victoria and Waterloo East stations to all parts of South East England.

> The pictures: 1 Bodiam Castle , Kent 2 Arundel, West Sussex

Where to stay in the South East England

Accommodation entries in this region are listed in alphabetical order of place name, and then in alphabetical order of establishment.

Map references refer to the colour location maps at the front of this guide. The first number indicates the map to use; the letter and number which follow refer to the grid reference on the map.

At-a-glance symbols at the end of each accommodation entry give useful information about services and facilities. A key to symbols can be found inside the back cover flap. Keep this open for easy reference.

A brief description of the towns and villages offering accommodation in the entries which follow, can be found at the end of this section.

A complete listing of all the English Tourism Council assessed accommodation covered by this guide appears at the back of the guide.

ASHDOWN FOREST

See under Hartfield

ASHFORD, Kent Map ref 3B4 *Tourist Information Centre Tel: (01233) 629165*

◆◆◆

DEAN COURT FARM
Challock Lane, Westwell, Ashford TN25 4NH
T: (01233) 712924

Bedrooms: 3 double/twin
Bathrooms: 1 en suite, 1 private

Evening meal available

Period farmhouse on working farm with modern amenities. Magnificent views in quiet valley. Comfortable accommodation with separate sitting room for guests.

B&B per night:
S £25.00
D £45.00

HB per person:
DY £37.00–£40.00

OPEN All Year except Christmas

◆◆◆

QUANTOCK HOUSE
Quantock Drive, Ashford TN24 8QH
T: (01233) 638921
E: tucker100@madasafish.com

Bedrooms: 1 single, 1 double/twin, 1 triple/multiple
Bathrooms: 3 en suite

Small, family-run establishment within easy walking distance from town centre with all its facilities, but within a quiet residential area.

B&B per night:
S £25.00–£26.00
D £42.00–£45.00

OPEN All Year except Christmas

MAP REFERENCES The map references refer to the colour maps at the front of this guide. The first figure is the map number; the letter and figure which follow indicate the grid reference on the map.

ASHFORD continued

◆◆◆

WARREN COTTAGE HOTEL AND RESTAURANT

136 The Street, Willesborough, Ashford TN24 0NB
T: (01233) 621905 & 632929
F: (01233) 623400
E: general@warrencottage.co.uk
I: www.warrencottage.co.uk

Bedrooms: 1 single, 4 double/twin, 1 triple/multiple
Bathrooms: 6 en suite

Lunch available
Evening meal available
CC: Delta, Mastercard, Switch, Visa

17thC hotel set in 2.5 acres. All rooms en suite. Large car park. M20 jct 10 and minutes to Ashford International Station and Channel Tunnel.

B&B per night:
S £45.00–£60.00
D £59.90–£89.90

HB per person:
DY £62.00–£77.00

OPEN All Year

BATTLE, East Sussex Map ref 3B4 *Tourist Information Centre Tel: (01424) 773721*

◆◆◆

MOONS HILL FARM

The Green, Ninfield, Battle
TN33 9LH
T: (01424) 892645
F: (01424) 892645
E: june@ive13.fsnet.co.uk

Bedrooms: 3 double/twin
Bathrooms: 3 en suite

10-acre mixed farm. Modernised farmhouse in Ninfield village centre, in the heart of '1066' country. A warm welcome and Sussex home cooking. Pub opposite. Large car park.

B&B per night:
S £20.00–£25.00
D £40.00–£50.00

BETHERSDEN, Kent Map ref 3B4

◆◆◆

THE COACH HOUSE

Oakmead Farm, Bethersden, Ashford
TN26 3DU
T: (01233) 820583
F: (01233) 820583

Comfortable family home, set well back from road, in 5 acres of garden and paddocks. Breakfast of your choice served in the dining room or conservatory, also used as a sitting room for guests. One mile from village – central for ferries, Channel Tunnel, Eurostar, Canterbury, Leeds Castle, Sissinghurst and many tourist attractions. Dutch spoken.

Bedrooms: 3 double/twin
Bathrooms: 2 en suite, 1 private

B&B per night:
S £25.00
D £40.00

BLADBEAN, Kent Map ref 3B4

MOLEHILLS

Bladbean, Canterbury CT4 6LU
T: (01303) 840051 & 07808 639942
E: molehills84@hotmail.com

The house, in large gardens, is situated in a peaceful hamlet within the beautiful Elham Valley. We are within easy reach of Canterbury and the Channel terminals. We produce home-grown vegetables and excellent home cooking. Our comfortable accommodation includes ground floor bedrooms, sitting room with woodburning stove and conservatory.

Bedrooms: 2 double/twin
Bathrooms: 2 en suite

Evening meal available

B&B per night:
S £25.00–£30.00
D £45.00–£50.00

HB per person:
DY £31.00–£40.00

OPEN All Year except Christmas

BOGNOR REGIS, West Sussex Map ref 2C3 *Tourist Information Centre Tel: (01243) 823140*

◆◆◆

JUBILEE GUEST HOUSE

5 Gloucester Road, Bognor Regis PO21 1NU
T: (01243) 863016 & 07702 275967
F: (01243) 868017
E: jubileeguesthouse@breathemail.net
I: www.jubileeguesthouse.com

Bedrooms: 2 single, 1 double/twin, 3 triple/multiple
Bathrooms: 2 en suite

CC: Delta, Mastercard, Switch, Visa

B&B per night:
S £22.00–£35.00
D £44.00–£70.00

OPEN All Year except Christmas

Family-run business, 75 yards from seafront and beach. Ideal for visiting 'Butlin's family entertainment resort', Chichester, Goodwood, Fontwell, Arundel, Portsmouth and IOW.

3 P

◆◆◆

REGIS LODGE

3 Gloucester Road, Bognor Regis PO21 1NU
T: (01243) 827110 & 07768 117770
F: (01243) 827110
E: frank@regislodge.fsbusiness.co.uk
I: www.regislodge.co.uk

Bedrooms: 2 single, 2 double/twin, 8 triple/multiple
Bathrooms: 12 en suite

B&B per night:
S £25.00–£35.00
D £40.00–£55.00

Family-run guesthouse, friendly atmosphere, comfortable rooms. 40 yards from beach, opposite South Coast World. Close to town centre, shops, restaurants, park, leisure centre, Goodwood and Fontwell.

5 P

BRASTED, Kent Map ref 2D2

◆◆◆◆

THE MOUNT HOUSE

Brasted, Westerham TN16 1JB
T: (01959) 563617
F: (01959) 561296
E: jpaulco@webspeed.net

Bedrooms: 1 single, 2 double/twin
Bathrooms: 1 en suite

B&B per night:
S £25.00
D £50.00–£60.00

OPEN All Year except Christmas

Large, early-Georgian family residence in centre of village. Listed Grade II. Convenient for Knole, Hever, Penshurst and fast trains to London from Sevenoaks.

10 P

BRENZETT, Kent Map ref 3B4

◆◆◆

BEBA FARMS BRENZETT

Brenzett Place, Ivychurch Road, Brenzett, Romney Marsh TN29 0EE
T: (01797) 344621
F: (01797) 344172
E: apcbeba@lineone.net
I: www.kent-esites.co.uk/bebafarmsbrenzett

Bedrooms: 3 double/twin

B&B per night:
S £25.00
D £50.00

HB per person:
DY £20.00

OPEN All Year

Peaceful refuge on working farm. Large rooms and excellent service. David and Anne Beba look forward to welcoming you.

P

BRIDGE, Kent Map ref 3B3

◆◆◆

HARROW COTTAGE

2 Brewery Lane, Bridge, Canterbury CT4 5LD
T: (01227) 830218
F: (01227) 830218
E: pamela@phooker.fsbusiness.co.uk

Bedrooms: 2 double/twin
Bathrooms: 2 en suite

B&B per night:
S £25.00
D £40.00

OPEN All Year

Situated in quiet cul-de-sac, in village setting. Three miles from Canterbury and 12 miles from Dover, off the A2.

P

BRIGHTON & HOVE, East Sussex Map ref 2D3

◆◆◆

AEGEAN HOTEL

5 New Steine, Brighton BN2 1PB
T: (01273) 686547
F: (01273) 625613

Bedrooms: 4 single, 2 double/twin, 4 triple/multiple
Bathrooms: 7 en suite

CC: Amex, Diners, Mastercard, Visa

B&B per night:
S £30.00–£37.00
D £62.00–£72.00

Family-run hotel where you can be sure of a warm welcome and satisfaction for your long or short stay.

2

BRIGHTON & HOVE continued

◆◆◆◆

AINSLEY HOUSE HOTEL
28 New Steine, Brighton BN2 1PD
T: (01273) 605310
F: (01273) 688604
E: ahhotel@fastnet.co.uk
I: www.ainsleyhotel.com

Bedrooms: 3 single, 7 double/twin
Bathrooms: 8 en suite

CC: Amex, Delta, Diners, Mastercard, Switch, Visa

B&B per night:
S £27.00–£35.00
D £48.00–£82.00

OPEN All Year except Christmas

Regency townhouse on garden square, overlooking the sea. All rooms comfortably furnished, some non-smoking. Close to all amenities. Extensive breakfast menu, warm welcome guaranteed.

AMBASSADOR HOTEL

22 New Steine, Marine Parade, Brighton BN2 1PD
T: (01273) 676869
F: (01273) 689988
E: ambassadorhoteluk@hotmail.com
I: www.ambassadorhotelbrighton.com

B&B per night:
S £30.00–£40.00
D £65.00–£80.00

OPEN All Year except Christmas

Family-run, licensed hotel in a seafront garden square, overlooking the sea and Palace Pier. Close to Royal Pavilion, shops, conference halls and entertainments. All rooms en suite with colour TV, direct-dial telephone, radio, hospitality tray. Ground floor and no-smoking rooms available.

Bedrooms: 7 single, 7 double/twin, 9 triple/multiple
Bathrooms: 23 en suite

CC: Amex, Delta, Diners, Mastercard, Switch, Visa

Silver Award

ARLANDA HOTEL

20 New Steine, Brighton BN2 1PD
T: (01273) 699300
F: (01273) 600930
E: arlanda@brighton.co.uk
I: www.arlandahotel.co.uk

B&B per night:
S £30.00–£48.00
D £60.00–£120.00

OPEN All Year except Christmas

Charming Grade II Listed Regency townhouse, situated in a garden square adjacent to the seafront. The hotel provides a peaceful and relaxing base for exploring historic Brighton, the countryside and outstanding coastline. Whether your journey is for business or pleasure you are assured of a warm welcome and a clean and comfortable stay.

Bedrooms: 4 single, 9 double/twin, 1 triple/multiple
Bathrooms: 14 en suite

CC: Amex, Delta, Diners, Mastercard, Switch, Visa

◆◆◆

ATLANTIC HOTEL
16 Marine Parade, Brighton BN2 1TL
T: (01273) 695944
F: (01273) 695944

Bedrooms: 1 single, 6 double/twin, 3 triple/multiple
Bathrooms: 10 en suite

Lunch available
Evening meal available
CC: Amex, Diners, Mastercard, Visa

B&B per night:
S £25.00–£30.00
D £50.00–£60.00

OPEN All Year

Attractive family-run hotel facing seafront. Sea Life Centre, Palace Pier, historic Royal Pavilion and famous Lanes are just down the road. Brighton Centre nearby.

◆◆◆◆

AYMER
13 Aymer Road, Hove, Brighton BN3 4GB
T: (01273) 271165 & 07770 488764
F: (01273) 321653
I: www.aymerguesthouse.co.uk

Bedrooms: 3 double/twin
Bathrooms: 3 en suite

B&B per night:
S £40.00–£45.00
D £60.00–£70.00

OPEN All Year except Christmas

Elegant Edwardian house situated in quiet surroundings just off seafront. Conveniently close to Brighton and Hove centre. Free on-street parking.

BRIGHTON & HOVE continued

◆◆◆

THE BEACH HOTEL
2-4 Regency Square, Brighton
BN1 2GP
T: (01273) 323776
F: (01273) 747028
E: beachhotelbrighton@hotmail.com
I: www.beachotel.co.uk

Bedrooms: 1 single, 24 double/twin, 5 triple/multiple
Bathrooms: 30 en suite

Evening meal available
CC: Amex, Delta, Diners, Mastercard, Switch, Visa

B&B per night:
S £35.00–£70.00
D £50.00–£95.00

OPEN All Year

In Regency Square, by seafront, few minutes' walk from major tourist attractions, conference centre, main shopping centre and 'The Lanes'. All rooms face the sea.

◆◆◆◆

CLAREMONT HOUSE HOTEL

Second Avenue, Hove, Brighton BN3 2LL
T: (01273) 735161
F: (01273) 735161
E: claremonthove@aol.com
I: www.claremonthousehotel.co.uk

Claremont House Hotel is an elegantly presented Victorian villa, situated just 250 metres from the seafront and minutes from the centre of Brighton. The spacious, individually decorated rooms are very comfortably furnished and retain many period features; all have en suite facilities. Dinner/lunch parties catered for. Bar available.

Bedrooms: 5 single, 5 double/twin, 2 triple/multiple
Bathrooms: 12 en suite

Lunch available
Evening meal available
CC: Amex, Delta, Mastercard, Switch, Visa

Offers available Oct-Apr. See website or call for details.

B&B per night:
S £40.00–£60.00
D £65.00–£130.00

OPEN All Year

◆◆

DIANA HOUSE
25 St Georges Terrace, Brighton
BN2 1JJ
T: (01273) 605797
E: diana@enterprise.net
I: www.dianahouse.co.uk

Bedrooms: 1 single, 9 double/twin, 1 triple/multiple
Bathrooms: 6 en suite

CC: Delta, Mastercard, Switch, Visa

B&B per night:
S £24.00–£27.00
D £48.00–£54.00

OPEN All Year except Christmas

Large, friendly guesthouse close to sea, town and conference centre. All rooms have TV, hospitality tray, clock/radio, shaver point. Some rooms en suite. 24-hour access.

◆◆◆◆

DOVE HOTEL

18 Regency Square, Brighton BN1 2FG
T: (01273) 779222
F: (01273) 746912
E: dovehotel@dovehotelfree-online.co.uk

Seafront-square hotel, 10 bright bedrooms, all en suite, newly redecorated inside and out, cotton bed linen, freshly cooked breakfast, genuine warm welcome.

Bedrooms: 2 single, 7 double/twin, 1 triple/multiple
Bathrooms: 10 en suite

CC: Amex, Delta, Mastercard, Switch, Visa

B&B per night:
S £37.00–£45.00
D £59.00–£120.00

OPEN All Year

IMPORTANT NOTE Information on accommodation listed in this guide has been supplied by the proprietors. As changes may occur you are advised to check details at the time of booking.

BRIGHTON & HOVE continued

FYFIELD HOUSE

26 New Steine, Brighton BN2 1PD
T: (01273) 602770
F: (01273) 602770
E: fyfield@aol.com
I: www.brighton.co.uk/hotels/fyfield

B&B per night:
S £25.00–£45.00
D £65.00–£90.00

OPEN All Year except Christmas

Excellent, clean, home-from-home private hotel, where Anna and Peter have welcomed their guests for over 30 years. Central to all attractions in and out of town. All rooms are tastefully decorated and most have en suite facilities. Superb breakfast menu, from the traditional to the homemade vegetarian sausage.

Bedrooms: 4 single, 5 double/twin
Bathrooms: 7 en suite

CC: Amex, Delta, Diners, Mastercard, Switch, Visa

Low season: reduced rates available, Sun-Thu.

◆◆◆

RUSSELL GUEST HOUSE

19 Russell Square, Brighton
BN1 2EE
T: (01273) 327969
F: (01273) 821535
E: russell.brighton@btinternet.com

Bedrooms: 4 double/twin, 4 triple/multiple
Bathrooms: 8 en suite

CC: Amex, Delta, Mastercard, Switch, Visa

B&B per night:
S £40.00–£60.00
D £55.00–£85.00

OPEN All Year except Christmas

Five-storey town-centre guesthouse in pleasant garden square. Close to the Brighton Centre, seafront and main shopping area. Unrestricted access. Theatres, cinemas and nightclubs all nearby.

2

◆◆

SANDPIPER GUEST HOUSE

11 Russell Square, Brighton
BN1 2EE
T: (01273) 328202
F: (01273) 329974
E: sandpiper@brighton.co.uk

Bedrooms: 3 single, 2 double/twin, 1 triple/multiple

CC: Amex, Delta, Mastercard, Switch, Visa

B&B per night:
S £18.00–£30.00
D £36.00–£60.00

OPEN All Year

Newly refurbished guesthouse, 2 minutes from conference centre, shopping area, leisure centres and seafront. All rooms have central heating, colour TV, tea/coffee. Unrestricted access.

BROADSTAIRS, Kent Map ref 3C3 *Tourist Information Centre Tel: (01843) 865650*

BAY TREE HOTEL

12 Eastern Esplanade, Broadstairs
CT10 1DR
T: (01843) 862502
F: (01843) 860589

B&B per night:
S £30.00–£34.00
D £60.00–£68.00

HB per person:
DY £45.00–£49.00

OPEN All Year except Christmas

Situated on the lovely Eastern Esplanade overlooking Stone Bay, the hotel enjoys panoramic sea views across the English Channel. Minutes from the town centre and sandy beaches. A warm welcome awaits you at this family-run hotel.

Bedrooms: 1 single, 9 double/twin
Bathrooms: 10 en suite

Evening meal available
CC: Delta, Mastercard, Switch, Visa

10 P

◆◆◆

COPPERFIELDS VEGETARIAN GUEST HOUSE

11 Queens Road, Broadstairs
CT10 1NU
T: (01843) 601247
E: jroger600@aol.com
I: www.copperfieldsbb.co.uk

Bedrooms: 3 double/twin
Bathrooms: 2 en suite

Evening meal available

B&B per night:
S £28.00–£30.00
D £40.00–£50.00

OPEN All Year

Exclusively vegetarian, non-smoking, cycle friendly. Minutes from beach and all amenities. Beautiful en suite rooms, Vegans welcome, evening meals available. Use of patio and garden.

BROADSTAIRS continued

◆◆◆◆

THE VICTORIA

23 Victoria Parade, Broadstairs CT10 1QL
T: (01843) 871010
F: (01843) 860888
E: mullin@thevictoriabroadstairs.co.uk
I: www.thevictoriabroadstairs.co.uk

Bedrooms: 6 double/twin
Bathrooms: 6 en suite

CC: Mastercard, Visa

B&B per night:
S £25.00–£90.00
D £60.00–£100.00

OPEN All Year

Spacious, elegant, well appointed rooms. Some with panoramic views over Viking Bay and Broadstairs Harbour.

12

BURGESS HILL, West Sussex Map ref 2D3 *Tourist Information Centre Tel: (01444) 238202*

◆◆◆◆

THE HOMESTEAD

Homestead Lane, Valebridge Road, Burgess Hill RH15 0RQ
T: (01444) 246899
F: (01444) 241407
E: homestead@burgess-hill.co.uk
I: www.burgess-hill.co.uk

Bedrooms: 1 single, 2 double/twin, 1 triple/multiple
Bathrooms: 4 en suite

CC: Delta, Mastercard, Visa

B&B per night:
S £25.00–£30.00
D £55.00–£60.00

OPEN All Year

Family home in 7.5 acres close to mainline station. Rooms en suite, 2 ground floor. Wheelcahir access to house. Leisure complex with jacuzzi. Unlimited parking.

12 P

CANTERBURY, Kent Map ref 3B3 *Tourist Information Centre Tel: (01227) 378100*

◆◆◆

ABBERLEY HOUSE

115 Whitstable Road, Canterbury CT2 8EF
T: (01227) 450265
F: (01227) 478626

B&B per night:
S £25.00–£28.00
D £42.00–£48.00

OPEN All Year except Christmas

Comfortable, bright, family-run guesthouse in pleasant residential area. Parking. Easy walk to city centre, cathedral, shops and attractions. Tea/coffee-making facilities and TV in rooms. Situated on the A290 just north of town centre. We are a non-smoking house for your comfort. A good centre for exploring East Kent.

Bedrooms: 3 double/twin
Bathrooms: 1 en suite

P

◆◆◆

ALICANTE GUEST HOUSE

4 Roper Road, Canterbury CT2 7EH
T: (01227) 766277
F: (01227) 766277

Bedrooms: 1 single, 5 double/twin, 1 triple/multiple; permanent suite(s)
Bathrooms: 6 en suite, 1 private

B&B per night:
S £25.00–£50.00
D £45.00–£65.00

HB per person:
DY £75.00–£100.00

OPEN All Year

A warm welcome awaits you at our attractive Victorian guesthouse situated near West Station. The cathedral, Marlow Theatre and a good selection of restaurants and bars close by.

◆◆◆◆
Silver Award

BOWER FARM HOUSE

Stelling Minnis, Canterbury CT4 6BB
T: (01227) 709430
E: anne@bowerbb.freeserve.co.uk
I: www.kentac.co.uk/bowerfm

Bedrooms: 2 double/twin
Bathrooms: 1 en suite, 1 private

B&B per night:
S £30.00
D £45.00

OPEN All Year except Christmas

Delightful heavily beamed 17thC farmhouse between the villages of Stelling Minnis and Bossingham. Canterbury and Hythe are approximately 7 miles away.

P

CANTERBURY continued

♦♦♦

CATHEDRAL GATE HOTEL

36 Burgate, Canterbury CT1 2HA
T: (01227) 464381
F: (01227) 462800
E: cgate@cgate.demon.co.uk
I: www.cathgate.co.uk

B&B per night:
S £24.00–£58.00
D £46.50–£88.00

OPEN All Year

Pilgrims slept here! This 1438 building, with massive beams, sloping floors and low doorways, offers modern comfort and is centrally situated at the main cathedral gateway. Our rooms have telephone, TV, welcome tray. Quiet lounge, bar and home-cooked meals in our bow-window dining room. Continental breakfast included, cooked breakfast extra.

Bedrooms: 6 single, 16 double/twin, 5 triple/multiple
Bathrooms: 12 en suite

Evening meal available
CC: Amex, Delta, Diners, Mastercard, Switch, Visa

Special DB&B breaks (full English breakfast), minimum 2 nights.

♦♦♦♦

CHAUCER LODGE

62 New Dover Road, Canterbury CT1 3DT
T: (01227) 459141
F: (01227) 459141
E: wchaucerldg@aol.com
I: www.thechaucerlodge.co.uk

B&B per night:
S £24.00–£30.00
D £42.00–£50.00

HB per person:
DY £35.00–£50.00

OPEN All Year

Alistair and Maria Wilson extend a very warm welcome to their family-run guesthouse. The highest standards of cleanliness and service are provided in a friendly and relaxed atmosphere. Large, well-appointed, quiet, elegantly decorated en suite bedrooms. Ideally situated close to city centre, cathedral, bus, coach and railway station.

Bedrooms: 1 single, 3 double/twin, 2 triple/multiple
Bathrooms: 6 en suite

Evening meal available
CC: Delta, Mastercard, Visa

20% discount for 3 nights Nov-Mar (excl Christmas and New Year).

♦♦♦♦
Silver Award

CLARE-ELLEN GUEST HOUSE

9 Victoria Road, Wincheap, Canterbury CT1 3SG
T: (01227) 760205
F: (01227) 784482
E: loraine.williams@clareellenguesthouse.co.uk
I: www.clareellenguesthouse.co.uk

B&B per night:
S £28.00–£30.00
D £50.00–£58.00

OPEN All Year

A warm welcome and bed and breakfast in style. Large, quiet, elegant, en suite rooms all with colour TV, clock/radio, hairdryer and tea/coffee-making facilities. Full English breakfast. Vegetarian and special diets on request. Six minutes' walk to city centre, 5 minutes to Canterbury East train station. Car park/garage available.

Bedrooms: 1 single, 2 double/twin, 2 triple/multiple
Bathrooms: 5 en suite

CC: Delta, Mastercard, Switch, Visa

Discounts for 2/3-night stay Nov-Mar (excl Christmas and New Year).

CANTERBURY continued

◆◆◆

Home of Agnes Wickfield from Charles Dickens' novel 'David Copperfield', this friendly hotel combines the atmosphere of bygone days with modern comforts. All rooms en suite.

THE DICKENS INN AT HOUSE OF AGNES HOTEL

71 St Dunstan's Street, Canterbury CT2 8BN
T: (01227) 472185
F: (01227) 464527
E: enq@dickens-inn.co.uk
I: www.dickens-inn.co.uk

Bedrooms: 2 single, 6 double/twin, 2 triple/multiple
Bathrooms: 10 en suite

Lunch available
Evening meal available
CC: Delta, Diners, Mastercard, Switch, Visa

B&B per night:
S £39.50–£59.50
D £65.00–£85.00

HB per person:
DY £25.00–£35.00

OPEN All Year

◆◆◆

THE KINGS HEAD
204 Wincheap, Canterbury CT1 3RY
T: (01227) 462885
F: (01227) 459627

Bedrooms: 3 double/twin
Bathrooms: 3 en suite

Lunch available
Evening meal available
CC: Amex, Delta, Diners, Mastercard, Switch, Visa

15thC oak-beamed public house and restaurant 10 minutes from city centre. Excellent reputation for food and real ales.

3 ... P

B&B per night:
S £38.00–£45.00
D £48.00

OPEN All Year except Christmas

◆◆◆◆◆
Gold Award

Charming, late-Georgian house in quiet residential street, a 10-minute stroll from the city centre. Bedrooms, individually co-ordinated, have every facility for an enjoyable stay. Varied breakfasts are served overlooking the attractive walled garden, where you are welcome to relax after a busy day's sightseeing. Evening meals available November to February by prior arrangement.

MAGNOLIA HOUSE

36 St Dunstans Terrace, Canterbury CT2 8AX
T: (01227) 765121 & 07885 595970
F: (01227) 765121
E: magnolia_house_canterbury@yahoo.com
I: http://freespace.virgin.net/magnolia.canterbury

Bedrooms: 1 single, 6 double/twin
Bathrooms: 7 en suite

Evening meal available
CC: Amex, Delta, Diners, Mastercard, Switch, Visa

12 ... P

B&B per night:
S £48.00–£65.00
D £85.00–£125.00

OPEN All Year

◆◆◆◆

OAK COTTAGE
Elmsted, Ashford TN25 5JT
T: (01233) 750272 & 750543
F: (01233) 750543
E: nichols@oakcottage.invictanet.co.uk

Bedrooms: 2 single, 1 double/twin
Bathrooms: 3 private

An attractive 17thC cottage with independent guest wing, own TV, conservatory and beautiful garden set in unspoilt, wooded countryside. Equidistant Canterbury, Folkestone and Ashford (9 miles).

B&B per night:
D Max £50.00

OPEN All Year except Christmas

CREDIT CARD BOOKINGS If you book by telephone and are asked for your credit card number it is advisable to check the proprietor's policy should you cancel your reservation.

CANTERBURY continued

◆◆◆◆◆ Gold Award

THANINGTON HOTEL

140 Wincheap, Canterbury CT1 3RY
T: (01227) 453227
F: (01227) 453225
E: thanington@lineone.net
I: www.thanington-hotel.co.uk

B&B per night:
S £55.00–£68.00
D £73.00–£110.00

OPEN All Year

Enjoy the peace and comfort of this elegant Georgian bed and breakfast hotel, just a short stroll from the city centre. Beautiful bedrooms including 4-posters and ground floor rooms. Indoor heated swimming pool and pretty sun-trap garden. Convenient for Channel Tunnel, ports and historic castle and gardens of Kent.

Bedrooms: 13 double/twin, 2 triple/multiple
Bathrooms: 15 en suite

CC: Amex, Delta, Diners, Mastercard, Switch, Visa

Special 2-night breaks availale Oct-Mar.

◆◆◆◆

WALTHAM COURT HOTEL

Kake Street, Petham, Canterbury CT4 5SB
T: (01227) 700413
F: (01227) 700127
E: enquiries@walthamcourthotel.co.uk
I: www.walthamcourthotel.co.uk

Bedrooms: 5 double/twin, 1 triple/multiple; permanent suite(s)
Bathrooms: 6 en suite

Evening meal available
CC: Amex, Delta, Mastercard, Switch, Visa

B&B per night:
S £40.00–£50.00
D £65.00–£75.00

HB per person:
DY £55.00–£80.00

OPEN All Year except Christmas

Located in beautiful countryside and 10 minutes from Canterbury. Spacious, refurbished en suite bedrooms. Restaurant offering modern British cooking with reputation for vegetarian and vegan food.

◆◆◆◆

THE WHITE HOUSE

6 St Peters Lane, Canterbury CT1 2BP
T: (01227) 761836
E: whwelcome@aol.com
I: www.smoothhound.co.uk/hotels/thewhitehouse/html

B&B per night:
S £30.00–£40.00
D £50.00–£60.00

OPEN All Year

Regency house situated in quiet location within city walls by the Marlowe Theatre. Superior family-run accommodation, all rooms en suite. Two minutes' walk to a charming mix of shops, restaurants, pretty parks and rivers. Cathedral and other major attractions also close by. Excellent English or vegetarian breakfast.

Bedrooms: 1 single, 6 double/twin, 2 triple/multiple
Bathrooms: 9 en suite

CHECK THE MAPS

The colour maps at the front of this guide show all the cities, towns and villages for which you will find accommodation entries. Refer to the town index to find the page on which they are listed.

CHICHESTER, West Sussex Map ref 2C3 *Tourist Information Centre Tel: (01243) 775888*

THE COACH HOUSE

Binderton, Chichester PO18 0JS
T: (01243) 539624 & 07710 536085
F: (01243) 539624
E: spightling@aol.com
I: www.sussexlive.com

B&B per night:
S £25.00–£27.50
D £50.00–£55.00

OPEN All Year

Converted flint and brick coach house of 17thC origin, peacefully set in 2 acres of walled gardens overlooking the unspoilt Lavant Valley on the slopes of the South Downs. Ten minutes' drive to Chichester, Goodwood and West Dean Gardens. Convenient for country walks, local pub. Recently updated, spacious accommodation, delicious English breakfast.

Bedrooms: 1 double/twin, 1 triple/multiple
Bathrooms: 1 private

P

♦♦♦

DRAYMANS

112 St Pancras, Chichester PO19 7LH
T: (01243) 789872
F: (01243) 785474
E: liz@jaegerl.freeserve.co.uk
I: www.jaegerl.freeserve.co.uk

B&B per night:
S £23.00–£25.00
D £46.00–£50.00

OPEN All Year

A warm welcome to Draymans, a Georgian house centrally situated with unrestricted street parking and within easy walking distance of railway and bus stations. Three centrally heated bedrooms: double with en suite bathroom, double and single sharing bathroom with shower. Breakfast is served in a sunny room overlooking a courtyard garden.

Bedrooms: 1 single, 2 double/twin
Bathrooms: 1 en suite

P

♦♦♦

KIA-ORA NURSERY

Main Road, Nutbourne, Chichester PO18 8RT
T: (01243) 572858
F: (01243) 572858
E: ruthiefp@aol.com

Bedrooms: 1 double/twin
Bathrooms: 1 en suite

B&B per night:
S £25.00
D £40.00

OPEN All Year except Christmas

Views to Chichester harbour. Warm welcome in comfortable family house. Large garden. Restaurants and country pubs within walking distance.

COUNTRY CODE Always follow the Country Code · Enjoy the countryside and respect its life and work · Guard against all risk of fire · Fasten all gates · Keep your dogs under close control · Keep to public paths across farmland · Use gates and stiles to cross fences, hedges and walls · Leave livestock, crops and machinery alone · Take your litter home · Help to keep all water clean · Protect wildlife, plants and trees · Take special care on country roads · Make no unnecessary noise

CHICHESTER continued

WOODSTOCK HOUSE HOTEL

Charlton, Chichester PO18 0HU
T: (01243) 811666
F: (01243) 811666
E: info@woodstockhousehotel.co.uk
I: www.woodstockhousehotel.co.uk

Converted from an old farmhouse, our licensed bed and breakfast hotel is set in the heart of the magnificent South Downs. All bedrooms are en suite with full modern amenities. Area rich in spectacular walks with Goodwood's many attractions, The Weald and Downland museum and many National Trust properties.

Bedrooms: 2 single, 10 double/twin
Bathrooms: 12 en suite

CC: Amex, Delta, Mastercard, Switch, Visa

3 nights for price of 2 Sun-Thu (excl Jul and Aug).

B&B per night:
S £45.00–£50.00
D £68.00–£94.00

OPEN All Year except Christmas

12 P

CLIFTONVILLE, Kent Map ref 3C3

♦♦

OCEAN VIEW HOTEL

8-10 Ethelbert Terrace, Cliftonville, Margate CT9 1RX
T: (01843) 220641
F: (01843) 571045
E: info@oceanviewhotel.co.uk
I: www.oceanviewhotel.co.uk

Bedrooms: 11 single, 9 double/twin, 5 triple/multiple; permanent suite(s)
Bathrooms: 19 en suite, 5 private

Evening meal available
CC: Amex, Delta, Mastercard, Switch, Visa

B&B per night:
S £22.00–£25.00
D £45.00–£60.00

HB per person:
DY £28.00–£32.00

OPEN All Year

Seafront, licensed, close to all amenities. Lifts to all floors. Tea-making, colour TV, entertainment, pool room, darts facilities, outdoor pool, covered whirlpool. Easy parking.

P

CRANBROOK, Kent Map ref 3B4

♦♦♦♦

SWATTENDEN RIDGE

Swattenden Lane, Cranbrook TN17 3PR
T: (01580) 712327
F: (01580) 712327

Bedrooms: 2 double/twin
Bathrooms: 1 en suite, 1 private

Lunch available
Evening meal available

B&B per night:
S Min £36.00
D Min £46.00

Modern quiet farmhouse. Wonderful views and ancient woodlands. 15 miles from Hastings, Maidstone and Tunbridge Wells. Outdoor pool for summer use. Evening meals by arrangement.

7 P

DANEHILL, East Sussex Map ref 2D3

♦♦♦♦

NEW GLENMORE

Sliders Lane, Furners Green, Uckfield TN22 3RU
T: (01825) 790783
E: alan.robinson@bigfoot.com

Bedrooms: 1 double/twin, 1 triple/multiple
Bathrooms: 1 en suite, 1 private

B&B per night:
S £40.00–£50.00
D £40.00–£50.00

OPEN All Year except Christmas

Spacious bungalow set in 6 acres of grounds. Rural location close to Bluebell Steam Railway and Sheffield Park. Breakfast includes our own eggs, honey and home-baked bread.

P

DARTFORD, Kent Map ref 2D2

♦♦

CHASHIR

3 Tynedale Close, Fleet Estate, Dartford DA2 6LL
T: (01322) 227886

Bedrooms: 1 single, 1 double/twin

B&B per night:
S Min £21.00
D Min £42.00

OPEN All Year except Christmas

Three bedroomed semi-detached house – adjacent to A225 – 1 mile from M25, 2 miles from Dartford Bridge and 2 miles to Dartford town centre.

1 P

ACCESSIBILITY

Look for the symbols which indicate National Accessible Scheme standards for hearing and visually impaired guests in addition to standards for guests with mobility impairment. Additional participants are shown in the listings at the back.

DEAL, Kent Map ref 3C4 *Tourist Information Centre Tel: (01304) 369576*

◆◆◆◆

ILEX COTTAGE
Temple Way, Worth, Deal CT14 0DA
T: (01304) 617026
F: (01304) 620890
E: info@ilexcottage.com
I: www.ilexcottage.com

Bedrooms: 3 double/twin
Bathrooms: 3 en suite

CC: Delta, Mastercard, Switch, Visa

Renovated 1736 house with lovely conservatory and country views. Secluded yet convenient village location north of Deal. Sandwich 5 minutes, Canterbury, Dover and Ramsgate 25 minutes.

B&B per night:
S £30.00–£35.00
D £50.00–£55.00

OPEN All Year except Christmas

DORKING, Surrey Map ref 2D2

◆◆◆

DENBIES FARMHOUSE B&B

Denbies Wine Estate, London Road, Dorking RH5 6AA
T: (01306) 876777
F: (01306) 876777
E: info@denbiesvineyard.co.uk
I: www.denbiesvineyard.co.uk

Denbies Farmhouse B&B is located in the heart of England's largest vineyard on the beautiful North Downs of Surrey. Tastefully converted from the original farmhouse it offers 5 double en suite bedrooms, all with TV, tea/coffee facilities and trouser press. Spectacular scenery makes it a favourite with walkers, wine lovers and artists.

Bedrooms: 5 double/twin; permanent suite(s)
Bathrooms: 5 en suite

Lunch available
CC: Mastercard, Visa

B&B per night:
S Min £60.00
D Max £65.00

OPEN All Year

◆◆◆

FAIRDENE GUEST HOUSE
Moores Road, Dorking RH4 2BG
T: (01306) 888337
E: zoe@fairdene5.freeserve.co.uk

Bedrooms: 6 double/twin, 1 triple/multiple
Bathrooms: 2 en suite

Late-Victorian house in convenient location, close to town centre, Gatwick Airport and North Downs Way. Friendly and homely atmosphere. Off-street parking.

B&B per night:
S £35.00–£50.00
D £50.00–£65.00

OPEN All Year

DOVER, Kent Map ref 3C4 *Tourist Information Centre Tel: (01304) 205108*

◆◆◆◆

BLAKES OF DOVER

52 Castle Street, Dover CT16 1PJ
T: (01304) 202194 & 211263
F: (01304) 202194
E: j.j.t@btinternet.com

Situated in the shadow of Dover Castle, close to town centre, yet a few minutes from the ferry and cruise terminals. Offering 5 beautifully furnished and decorated en suite rooms, an internationally renowned restaurant serving locally caught fish, steaks and vegetarian dishes. Unquestionably the perfect location for business or pleasure.

Bedrooms: 2 double/twin, 3 triple/multiple; permanent suite(s)
Bathrooms: 5 en suite

Lunch available
Evening meal available
CC: Delta, Mastercard, Switch, Visa

Early Bird evening menu, 6-7.30pm daily May-Oct. 2 courses and wine £10.80pp.

B&B per night:
S £40.00
D £45.00–£55.00

HB per person:
DY £52.50–£57.50

OPEN All Year

QUALITY ASSURANCE SCHEME

Diamond ratings and awards were correct at the time of going to press but are subject to change. Please check at the time of booking.

DOVER continued

◆◆◆

CLEVELAND GUEST HOUSE
2 Laureston Place,
off Castle Hill Road, Dover
CT16 1QX
T: (01304) 204622
F: (01304) 211598
E: albetcleve@aol.com
I: www.albetcleve.homestead.com

Bedrooms: 4 double/twin, 2 triple/multiple
Bathrooms: 6 en suite

Evening meal available
CC: Amex, Delta, Mastercard, Switch, Visa

B&B per night:
S £25.00–£40.00
D £40.00–£45.00

OPEN All Year except Christmas

Family-run quietly situated property a few minutes' walking distance to castle, town centre and ferries.

COLRET HOUSE

The Green, Coldred, Dover CT15 5AP
T: (01304) 830388
F: (01304) 830388
E: jackie.colret@evnet.co.uk

B&B per night:
S £25.00–£30.00
D £50.00–£60.00

OPEN All Year

An early-Edwardian property with modern, purpose-built, en suite garden rooms, standing in extensive, well-maintained grounds. Situated beside the village green in a conservation area on downs above Dover. Ideally situated for overnight stays when travelling by ferries or shuttle. Close to Canterbury and Sandwich. Ample secure parking.

Bedrooms: 2 double/twin
Bathrooms: 2 en suite

Evening meal available

LODDINGTON HOUSE HOTEL
14 East Cliff,
(Seafront - Marine Parade), Dover
CT16 1LX
T: (01304) 201947 & 225031
F: (01304) 201947

Bedrooms: 1 single, 5 double/twin
Bathrooms: 4 en suite, 2 private

Evening meal available
CC: Amex, Delta, Mastercard, Switch, Visa

B&B per night:
S £45.00–£50.00
D £54.00–£60.00

OPEN All Year except Christmas

Well-positioned small hotel in Georgian terrace overlooking harbour. Quality food and wine – prices on request. Yards from east ferry terminal.

◆◆◆

LONGFIELD GUEST HOUSE

203 Folkestone Road, Dover CT17 9SL
T: (01304) 204716
F: (01304) 204716
E: res@longfieldguesthouse.co.uk
I: www.longfieldguesthouse.co.uk

B&B per night:
S £18.00–£25.00
D £35.00–£45.00

OPEN All Year except Christmas

A clean and highly recommended guesthouse, 2 minutes from Dover Priory station, Hoverport and town centre, 10 minutes from Channel Tunnel. Single, double, twin and family rooms, some en suite, one ground floor room, with colour TV, tea/coffee facilities, washbasins and central heating. Large car park and lock-up garage.

Bedrooms: 6 single, 2 double/twin, 2 triple/multiple
Bathrooms: 2 en suite

Evening meal available
CC: Delta, Mastercard, Switch, Visa

GOLD & SILVER AWARDS

These exclusive ETC awards are given to establishments achieving the highest levels of quality and service. Further information can be found at the front of the guide and additional accommodation achieving these awards are shown in the listing at the back of this guide.

DOVER continued

♦♦♦♦ Silver Award

OWLER LODGE

Alkham Valley Road, Alkham, Dover CT15 7DF
T: (01304) 826375
F: (01304) 829372
E: owlerlodge@aol.com
I: www.owlerlodge.co.uk

B&B per night:
S £36.00–£39.00
D £46.00–£54.00

OPEN All Year except Christmas

Small guesthouse situated in the beautiful Alkham Valley between Dover and Folkestone, 3 miles from Channel Tunnel, 4 miles from Dover Docks. Ideal base for touring East Kent. All rooms have en suite shower, toilet, colour TV, clock/radio, hairdryer and tea-making facilities. Beautiful garden with our Koi ponds. Off-street parking. A non-smoking residence.

Bedrooms: 2 double/twin, 1 triple/multiple
Bathrooms: 3 en suite

Lunch available
Evening meal available

5 P

♦♦♦♦ Silver Award

THE PARK INN

1-2 Park Place, Ladywell, Dover CT16 1DQ
T: (01304) 203300
F: (01304) 203324
E: theparkinn@aol.com
I: www.theparkinnatdover.co.uk

B&B per night:
S £35.00–£45.00
D £54.00–£74.00

OPEN All Year

The feel of Victorian England immediately embraces guests on arrival at the Park Inn. An extremely high standard of finish in decor, furnishings and fittings prevails in our en suite rooms which complement our successful inn and restaurant. All our rooms are cosy and comfortable and contain many facilities.

Bedrooms: 1 single, 3 double/twin, 1 triple/multiple
Bathrooms: 5 en suite

Lunch available
Evening meal available
CC: Amex, Delta, Diners, Mastercard, Switch, Visa

♦♦♦

SWINGATE INN AND HOTEL

Deal Road, Dover CT15 5DP
T: (01304) 204043
F: (01304) 204043
E: terry@swingate.com
I: www.swingate.com

Bedrooms: 9 double/twin, 2 triple/multiple
Bathrooms: 11 en suite

Lunch available
Evening meal available
CC: Amex, Delta, Mastercard, Switch, Visa

B&B per night:
S Min £42.00
D Min £50.00

OPEN All Year

Country inn hotel and restaurant situated just outside Dover, yet convenient for the docks and main roads.

P

AT-A-GLANCE SYMBOLS

Symbols at the end of each accommodation entry give useful information about services and facilities. A key to symbols can be found inside the back cover flap. Keep this open for easy reference.

DYMCHURCH, Kent Map ref 3B4

WATERSIDE GUEST HOUSE

15 Hythe Road, Dymchurch, Romney Marsh TN29 0LN
T: (01303) 872253
F: (01303) 872253
E: info@watersideguesthouse.co.uk
I: www.watersideguesthouse.co.uk

Cottage-style house offering comfortable rooms and attractive gardens, ideally situated for Channel crossings and touring historic Romney Marsh countryside by foot or transport. Experience the RH&D railway, visit Port Lympne Wild Animal Park or stroll along nearby sandy beaches, finally enjoying a drink or meal from our varied menu.

Bedrooms: 4 double/twin, 1 triple/multiple
Bathrooms: 5 en suite

Evening meal available
CC: Delta, Mastercard, Switch, Visa

Two, 3 or 4 day short breaks (DB&B). Also Christmas specials – contact for details.

B&B per night:
S £25.00–£30.00
D £40.00–£45.00

HB per person:
DY £28.50–£37.50

OPEN All Year

EAST ASHLING, West Sussex Map ref 2C3

♦♦♦♦

HORSE & GROOM

East Ashling, Chichester PO18 9AX
T: (01243) 575339
F: (01243) 575560
E: horseandgroomea@aol.com
I: www.horseandgroom.sageweb.co.uk

Bedrooms: 11 double/twin
Bathrooms: 11 en suite

Lunch available
Evening meal available
CC: Amex, Delta, Mastercard, Switch, Visa

B&B per night:
S £40.00–£45.00
D £55.00–£100.00

OPEN All Year

A traditional 17thC inn with en suite accommodation. Friendly country-style inn with fine cuisine, real ales and cast-iron range.

EAST GRINSTEAD, West Sussex Map ref 2D2

♦♦♦

CRANSTON HOUSE

Cranston Road, East Grinstead RH19 3HW
T: (01342) 323609
F: (01342) 323609
E: stay@cranstonhouse.screaming.net
I: www.cranstonehouse.co.uk

Bedrooms: 7 double/twin
Bathrooms: 6 en suite, 1 private

Evening meal available
CC: Delta, Mastercard, Switch, Visa

B&B per night:
S £28.00–£35.00
D £40.00–£50.00

OPEN All Year

Attractive detached house in quiet location near town centre and station, 15 minutes' drive from Gatwick. Spacious, high-quality en suite accommodation. Ample off-road parking.

♦♦♦

THE STAR INN

Church Road, Lingfield RH7 6AH
T: (01342) 832364
F: (01342) 832364
E: thestarinn@breathemail.net
I: www.starinnlingfield.co.uk

Bedrooms: 6 double/twin, 1 triple/multiple
Bathrooms: 7 en suite

Lunch available
Evening meal available
CC: Amex, Delta, Mastercard, Switch, Visa

B&B per night:
S Min £40.00
D £41.00–£60.00

OPEN All Year

Situated in the oldest part of the village, this traditional English inn offers a warm friendliness, real comfort, excellent food, ales and wines and a room for the night.

♦♦

TOWN HOUSE

6 De La Warr Road, East Grinstead RH19 3BN
T: (01342) 300310
F: (01342) 315122

Bedrooms: 3 double/twin

B&B per night:
S Min £25.00
D £40.00–£60.00

OPEN All Year

Cosy, friendly, quiet, very clean, en suite rooms. Five minutes from train, town centre, 2 minutes from shops, restaurants, 15 minutes from Gatwick. English breakfast.

HALF BOARD PRICES Half board prices are given per person, but in some cases these may be based on double/twin occupancy.

EAST PECKHAM, Kent Map ref 2D2

◆◆◆

ROYDON HALL

Roydon Hall Road, East Peckham, Tonbridge TN12 5NH
T: (01622) 812121
F: (01622) 813959
E: roydonhall@btinternet.com
I: www.tourismsoutheast.com/member/webpages/A5224.htm

Bedrooms: 5 single, 12 double/twin, 2 triple/multiple
Bathrooms: 7 en suite

Lunch available
Evening meal available
CC: Delta, Mastercard, Switch, Visa

B&B per night:
S £30.00–£50.00
D £40.00–£65.00

HB per person:
DY £38.00–£58.00

16thC Tudor manor set in 10 acres of gardens, terraces and woodlands. Commanding a fine view of Weald of Kent.

EASTBOURNE, East Sussex Map ref 3B4 *Tourist Information Centre Tel: (01323) 411400*

◆◆◆◆
Silver Award

BRAYSCROFT HOTEL

13 South Cliff Avenue, Eastbourne BN20 7AH
T: (01323) 647005
F: (01323) 720705
E: brayscroft@hotmail.com
I: www.brayscrofthotel.co.uk

Elegant, award-winning, small hotel, one of only a handful in Eastbourne with coveted ETC 4 Diamonds – Silver Award for 'outstanding accommodation and hospitality'. Superb position less than a minute from seafront in fashionable Meads district and ideally situated for South Downs, theatres, restaurants and town centre. Totally non-smoking.

Bedrooms: 1 single, 4 double/twin
Bathrooms: 5 en suite

Lunch available
Evening meal available
CC: Amex, Delta, Mastercard, Switch, Visa

Upgrade from single room to double/twin at no extra cost except at peak holiday times. 4-night and weekly breaks.

B&B per night:
S £27.00–£31.50
D £54.00–£63.00

HB per person:
DY £40.00–£44.50

OPEN All Year

14

◆◆◆

GLADWYN HOTEL

16 Blackwater Road, Eastbourne BN21 4JD
T: (01323) 733142
E: gladwynhotel@aol.com
I: www.gladwynhotel.com

Bedrooms: 2 single, 7 double/twin, 1 triple/multiple
Bathrooms: 10 en suite

Lunch available
Evening meal available
CC: Delta, Mastercard, Switch, Visa

B&B per night:
S £23.50–£25.50
D £47.00–£51.00

OPEN All Year

Family-run hotel overlooking Devonshire Park. Close to sea, shops and theatres. Residential licence. TV and tea/coffee-making facilities in en suite bedrooms. Special weekly rates available.

◆◆◆◆

LITTLE FOXES

24 Wannock Road, Eastbourne BN22 7JU
T: (01323) 640670
F: (01323) 640670
E: chris@foxholes55.freeserve.co.uk

Bedrooms: 1 single, 1 double/twin; permanent suite(s)
Bathrooms: 2 en suite

B&B per night:
S £19.00–£27.00
D £38.00–£54.00

OPEN All Year

Personally run B&B. Close to beach and 1 kilometre town centre. En suite facilities. Guests' lounge with Sky TV. All ages welcome. No smoking.

◆◆◆◆

ST OMER HOTEL

13 Royal Parade, Eastbourne BN22 7AR
T: (01323) 722152
F: (01323) 723400
E: st.omer@lineone.net
I: www.st-omer.co.uk

Bedrooms: 7 double/twin, 1 triple/multiple
Bathrooms: 7 en suite

Evening meal available
CC: Delta, Mastercard, Switch, Visa

B&B per night:
S £22.00–£25.00
D £44.00–£50.00

HB per person:
DY £32.00–£35.00

OPEN All Year except Christmas

Friendly, non-smoking hotel situated on the seafront close to pier. Licensed. En suite bedrooms with colour TV and tea/coffee-making facilities. Seniors' discount. No single supplement.

12

EASTBOURNE continued

SHERWOOD HOTEL

7 Lascelles Terrace, Eastbourne BN21 4BJ
T: (01323) 724002
F: (01323) 439989
E: sherwood-hotel@supanet.com
I: www.sherwood-hotel-eastbourne.co.uk

B&B per night:
S £22.00–£35.00
D £44.00–£70.00

HB per person:
DY £32.00–£42.00

OPEN All Year except Christmas

Cosy Victorian townhouse hotel, 100 yards from seafront, theatres, conference centre and tennis courts. All rooms en suite with colour TV and tea-making facilities, some with sea views. Family rooms, 4-poster room. Licensed bar. Small functions catered for. Home-cooked food. Very nicely appointed. Friendly, courteous service. Value for money.

Bedrooms: 5 single, 6 double/twin, 3 triple/multiple
Bathrooms: 12 en suite, 2 private

Evening meal available
CC: Amex, Delta, Diners, Mastercard, Switch, Visa

Three nights for the price of two in our lovely 4-poster room with sea view, Oct-May (excl Bank Holidays) £115.

TREVINHURST LODGE

10 Baslow Road, Meads, Eastbourne BN20 7UJ
T: (01323) 410023
F: (01323) 643238
E: enquiries@trevinhurstlodge.com
I: www.trevinhurstlodge.com

B&B per night:
S £39.00–£59.00
D £58.00–£78.00

HB per person:
DY £59.00–£79.00

OPEN All Year

A warm welcome awaits those looking for a discerning break in a non-smoking, relaxed, informal atmosphere. With attractive, spacious bedrooms we can guarantee the individual attention you would expect. Fine food offered in our elegant dining room completes the picture.Speciality watercolour courses are also available.

Bedrooms: 3 double/twin
Bathrooms: 2 en suite, 1 private

Evening meal available

Proprietor Brian Smith, a professional artist, offers weekend or mid-week residential watercolour courses for small groups.

FARNHAM, Surrey Map ref 2C2 *Tourist Information Centre Tel: (01252) 715109*

ANNE'S COTTAGE

Green Cross Lane, Churt, Farnham GU10 2ND
T: (01428) 714181 & 714020

B&B per night:
S £25.00–£30.00
D £50.00–£55.00

OPEN All Year except Christmas

Pre-dating 1447, when Fareham's manorial role records the rent unpaid due possibly to 'The Black Death', this cosy, low-beamed cottage is a quiet haven. Furnishings are traditional, the plumbing modern. Local produce and homemade preserves are used and the welcome is warm, ensuring every comfort and care.

Bedrooms: 1 single, 2 double/twin
Bathrooms: 1 en suite, 1 private

Evening meal available

Honeymoon and anniversary weekends (2 nights minimum).

CHECK THE MAPS

The colour maps at the front of this guide show all the cities, towns and villages for which you will find accommodation entries.
Refer to the town index to find the page on which they are listed.

FARNHAM continued

♦♦♦

KERNEL COTTAGE
14 Nutshell Lane, Upper Hale, Farnham
T: (01252) 710147
F: (01252) 710147

Bedrooms: 2 double/twin
Bathrooms: 2 private

B&B per night:
S £22.00–£28.00
D £35.00–£43.00

OPEN All Year

Home in peaceful lane very close to Farnham Park offers 2 twins with guest-only shower room – all set apart upstairs. Non-smokers only.

P

FAVERSHAM, Kent Map ref 3B3 *Tourist Information Centre Tel: (01795) 534542*

♦♦♦

BARNSFIELD
Fostall, Hernhill, Faversham ME13 9JH
T: (01227) 750973 & 07889 836259
F: (01227) 273098
E: barnsfield@yahoo.com
I: www.barnsfield.co.uk

Bedrooms: 3 double/twin
Bathrooms: 1 en suite

Evening meal available

B&B per night:
S £14.00–£30.00
D £28.00–£60.00

OPEN All Year

Grade II Listed country cottage accommodation, just off A299, set in 3 acres of orchards, 6 miles from Canterbury. Convenient for ports and touring.

P

♦♦♦♦
Silver Award

PRESTON LEA

Canterbury Road, Faversham ME13 8XA
T: (01795) 535266
F: (01795) 533388
E: preston.lea@which.net
I: homepages.which.net/~alan.turner10

B&B per night:
S £35.00–£40.00
D £55.00–£60.00

OPEN All Year

A unique and elegant Victorian Gothic house with turrets set in large, secluded gardens. Spacious, sunny bedrooms with garden views and antique furniture. Beautiful guest drawing room, panelled dining room and delicious breakfasts. Only 15 minutes from Canterbury, 35 minutes from ports, Eurotunnel, 70 minutes by train to London.

Bedrooms: 3 double/twin
Bathrooms: 2 en suite, 1 private

CC: Delta, Mastercard, Switch, Visa

P

FITTLEWORTH, West Sussex Map ref 2D3

♦♦♦♦
Silver Award

SWAN INN

Lower Street, Fittleworth, Pulborough RH20 1EN
T: (01798) 865429
F: (01798) 865721
E: hotel@swaninn.com
I: www.swaninn.com

B&B per night:
S £30.00–£40.00
D £60.00–£75.00

HB per person:
DY £43.95–£56.75

OPEN All Year

Listed 14thC coaching inn, well placed for visiting many of the historic houses and places of interest in the area. Public bar with welcoming log fires in the winter. Large garden. Cosy oak-beamed restaurant serving homemade food with a fine selection of fresh fish, meat and poultry dishes.

Bedrooms: 3 single, 12 double/twin
Bathrooms: 15 en suite

Lunch available
Evening meal available
CC: Amex, Delta, Mastercard, Switch, Visa

Special DB&B breaks available, minimum 2 nights.

P

SPECIAL BREAKS

Many establishments offer special promotions and themed breaks. These are highlighted in red. (All such offers are subject to availability.)

FOLKESTONE, Kent Map ref 3B4 *Tourist Information Centre Tel: (01303) 258594*

◆◆◆

BEACHBOROUGH PARK

Newington, Folkestone CT18 8BW
T: (01303) 275432
F: (01843) 845131
I: www.kentaccess.org.uk

Bedrooms: 6 double/twin, 2 triple/multiple
Bathrooms: 8 en suite

Lunch available
Evening meal available
CC: Mastercard, Switch, Visa

B&B per night:
S £25.00–£27.50
D £41.00–£50.00

OPEN All Year

Beautiful setting, ideal for sightseeing and very convenient for tunnel and ferries. Very comfortable for both active people and those just seeking peace and quiet.

P

◆◆◆

THE ROB ROY GUEST HOUSE

227 Dover Road, Folkestone CT19 6NH
T: (01303) 253341
F: (01303) 770060
E: RobRoyFolkestone@aol.com
I: www.therobroyguesthouse.co.uk

Bedrooms: 6 double/twin, 1 triple/multiple
Bathrooms: 3 en suite

CC: Delta, Mastercard, Switch, Visa

B&B per night:
S £23.00–£26.00
D £35.00–£40.00

OPEN All Year except Christmas

Attractive guesthouse with good, comfortable accommodation, close to sandy beach and town centre. Views of surrounding hills. Channel Tunnel only 10 minutes, Dover 20 minutes.

P

GATWICK, West Sussex Map ref 2D2

◆◆◆

COLLENDEAN BARN

Collendean Lane, Norwood Hill, Horley RH6 0HP
T: (01293) 862433
F: (01293) 863102
E: collendean.barn@amserve.net

Bedrooms: 1 double/twin, 1 triple/multiple
Bathrooms: 2 en suite

B&B per night:
S Min £30.00
D Min £50.00

OPEN All Year

Bed and breakfast in a self-contained, converted barn with en suite, on a 16thC farm in lovely countryside, 3 miles from Gatwick and trains. Outdoor spa bath.

P

◆◆◆◆

THE CORNER HOUSE

72 Massetts Road, Horley RH6 7ED
T: (01293) 784574
F: (01293) 784620
E: info@thecornerhouse.co.uk
I: www.thecornerhouse.co.uk

B&B per night:
S £36.00–£42.00
D £55.00–£63.00

OPEN All Year except Christmas

Family-run guesthouse offering quality accommodation. Bar/restaurant, en suite rooms with tea/coffee facilities. Holiday parking, 24-hour transfers to and from Gatwick. Let us take the strain out of getting you to the plane.

Bedrooms: 7 single, 12 double/twin, 6 triple/multiple
Bathrooms: 23 en suite

Lunch available
Evening meal available
CC: Amex, Delta, Diners, Mastercard, Switch, Visa

P

◆◆◆

GAINSBOROUGH LODGE

39 Massetts Road, Horley RH6 7DT
T: (01293) 783982 & 430830
F: (01293) 785365
E: enquiries@gainsborough-lodge.co.uk
I: www.gainsborough-lodge.co.uk

Bedrooms: 7 single, 15 double/twin, 4 triple/multiple
Bathrooms: 24 en suite

CC: Diners, Mastercard, Switch, Visa

B&B per night:
S £35.00–£41.00
D Min £55.00

OPEN All Year

Family-run house set in attractive garden. Gatwick 5 minutes in courtesy bus (every 30 minutes), long-term parking. Central London 35 minutes by train.

P

MAP REFERENCES The map references refer to the colour maps at the front of this guide. The first figure is the map number; the letter and figure which follow indicate the grid reference on the map.

GATWICK continued

SOUTHBOURNE GUEST HOUSE GATWICK

34 Massetts Road, Horley RH6 7DS
T: (01293) 771991
F: (01293) 820112
E: reservations@southbournegatwick.com
I: www.southbournegatwick.com

A warm welcome awaits you in our family-run guesthouse. Ideally located for Gatwick Airport, and exploring Surrey, Sussex and London. Five minutes' walk from Horley train station, restaurants, shops and pubs and 30 minutes by train from London. Five minutes' drive from Gatwick with free courtesy transport from 0930-2130.

Bedrooms: 2 single, 5 double/twin, 2 triple/multiple
Bathrooms: 2 en suite

CC: Delta, Mastercard, Switch, Visa

B&B per night:
S £30.00–£40.00
D £45.00–£55.00

OPEN All Year except Christmas

GATWICK AIRPORT

See under East Grinstead, Gatwick, Horley, Horsham, Redhill

GODALMING, Surrey Map ref 2D2

HEATH HALL FARM

Bowlhead Green, Godalming
GU8 6NW
T: (01428) 682808
F: (01428) 684025
E: heathhallfarm@btinternet.com

Bedrooms: 1 single, 2 double/twin
Bathrooms: 2 en suite, 1 private

Farmhouse on the edge of hamlet. Converted stable courtyard. Free-range fowl, sheep and horse. Tennis court. Farmhouse atmosphere. Single pet welcome if under control.

B&B per night:
S £25.00–£30.00
D £50.00

OPEN All Year except Christmas

GUILDFORD, Surrey Map ref 2D2 *Tourist Information Centre Tel: (01483) 444333*

◆◆◆

CHALKLANDS

Beech Avenue, Effingham,
Leatherhead KT24 5PJ
T: (01372) 454936
F: (01372) 459569
E: rreilly@onetel.net.uk

Bedrooms: 3 double/twin
Bathrooms: 2 en suite, 1 private

Evening meal available

Detached house backing onto Effingham golf course. Thirty minutes from Heathrow/Gatwick Airports, 35 minutes from London Waterloo station. Excellent pub food nearby.

B&B per night:
S £30.00–£35.00
D £50.00–£55.00

OPEN All Year except Christmas

◆◆◆

HIGH EDSER

Shere Road, Ewhurst, Cranleigh
GU6 7PQ
T: (01483) 278214 & 0777 5865125
F: (01483) 278200
E: franklinadams@highedser.demon.co.uk

Bedrooms: 3 double/twin

Early 16thC family home in Area of Outstanding Natural Beauty. Ten miles from Guildford and Dorking, easy reach airports and many tourist attractions. Non-smokers only, please.

B&B per night:
S £25.00–£35.00
D £55.00–£60.00

OPEN All Year except Christmas

Rating Applied For

JOANNAS BED & BREAKFAST

30 Nightingale Road, Guildford
GU1 1ER
T: (01483) 568873

Bedrooms: 3 double/twin

CC: Mastercard

Ten minutes from town centre and Spectrum Sports Centre, Stoke Park is one minute away. Some of the rooms have spectacular views.

B&B per night:
D Min £40.00

OPEN All Year except Christmas

VISITOR ATTRACTIONS For ideas on places to visit refer to the introduction at the beginning of this section. Look out too for the ETC's Quality Assured Visitor Attraction signs.

GUILDFORD continued

♦♦♦

LITTLEFIELD MANOR
Littlefield Common, Guildford
GU3 3HJ
T: (01483) 233068 & 07860 947439
F: (01483) 233686
E: john@littlefieldmanor.co.uk
I: www.littlefieldmanor.co.uk

Bedrooms: 2 double/twin
Bathrooms: 2 en suite

Evening meal available
CC: Amex, Delta, Mastercard, Switch, Visa

B&B per night:
S Max £45.00
D Max £65.00

OPEN All Year except Christmas

120-acre mixed farm. 17thC Listed manor house with Tudor origins. Enjoy the walled rose garden in summer or the blazing log fire in winter.

HALLAND, East Sussex Map ref 2D3

♦♦♦♦
Silver
Award

TAMBERRY HALL

Eastbourne Road, Halland, Lewes BN8 6PS
T: (01825) 880090
F: (01825) 880090
E: bedandbreakfast@tamberryhall.fsbusiness.co.uk

B&B per night:
S £35.00–£45.00
D £55.00–£65.00

OPEN All Year except Christmas

Delightful country house in 3 acres. Comfortable, friendly atmosphere, exposed beams and inglenook fireplace in guests' lounge. Central for touring this Area of Outstanding Natural Beauty, the coast, gardens, National Trust properties. Glyndebourne and golf nearby, restaurant and pub within walking distance. Self-catering annexe. Vegetarian cooking a speciality. Mid-week special breaks.

Bedrooms: 2 double/twin, 1 triple/multiple
Bathrooms: 3 en suite

Mid-week breaks: Double en suite – 3 nights £135, 4 nights £170. 'Weekend Plus': double en suite – 3 nights £165, 4 nights £210. All prices per room.

HARTFIELD, East Sussex Map ref 2D2

♦♦♦♦

BOLEBROKE CASTLE LTD

Edenbridge Road, Hartfield TN7 4JJ
T: (01892) 770061
F: (01892) 771041
E: bolebroke@btclick.com
I: www.bolebrokecastle.co.uk

B&B per night:
D £52.00–£79.00

OPEN All Year

Henry VIII's hunting lodge set in a stunningly beautiful location on 30-acre estate away from main roads and noise. Two lakes, woodlands, views to Ashdown Forest, original beamed ceilings, second largest fireplace in England, 4-poster suite, TV, tea/coffee. Tunbridge Wells 5 miles, Brighton 30 miles.

Bedrooms: 6 double/twin
Bathrooms: 5 en suite, 1 private

CC: Amex, Delta, Mastercard, Switch, Visa

Regular medieval banquets with entertainment provided by minstrels.

HASLEMERE, Surrey Map ref 2C2

♦♦♦

SHEPS HOLLOW
Henley Common, Haslemere
GU27 3HB
T: (01428) 653120

Bedrooms: 2 single, 2 double/twin
Bathrooms: 2 en suite

Lunch available
Evening meal available

B&B per night:
S £30.00–£35.00
D £60.00–£70.00

HB per person:
DY £38.00–£40.00

OPEN All Year

Charming 500-year-old cottage in a rural setting. TV with Sky and video channels. Small barn for holiday lets.

SYMBOLS The symbols in each entry give information about services and facilities. A key to these symbols appears at the back of this guide.

HASTINGLEIGH, Kent Map ref 3B4

CRABTREE FARM

Tamley Lane, Hastingleigh, Ashford TN25 5HW
T: (01233) 750327 & 750507

Bedrooms: 2 double/twin
Bathrooms: 2 en suite

Evening meal available

Crabtree farmhouse, c1745, is very pretty with lovely views and great walks around the North Downs Way. Roz, the proprietor, is a Canterbury Cathedral and City Guide.

10

B&B per night:
S £24.00
D £40.00–£48.00

HB per person:
DY £32.00–£36.00

OPEN All Year except Christmas

HASTINGS, East Sussex Map ref 3B4 *Tourist Information Centre Tel: (01424) 781111*

♦♦♦♦

EAGLE HOUSE HOTEL

12 Pevensey Road, St Leonards-on-Sea, Hastings TN38 0JZ
T: (01424) 430535 & 441273
F: (01424) 437771
E: info@eaglehousehotel.com
I: www.eaglehousehotel.com

You are assured of a warm welcome at the Eagle House Hotel. The charm and style of a bygone age is reflected in the spacious Victorian reception rooms. Our competitive rates include full English breakfast and free parking. Few minutes' walk from Warrior Square railway station.

Bedrooms: 16 double/twin, 2 triple/multiple
Bathrooms: 18 en suite

Lunch available
Evening meal available
CC: Amex, Delta, Diners, Mastercard, Switch, Visa

5

B&B per night:
S £30.00–£33.00
D £48.00–£52.00

HB per person:
DY £54.00–£57.00

OPEN All Year

Gold Award

TOWER HOUSE

26-28 Tower Road West, St Leonards, Hastings TN38 0RG
T: (01424) 427217
F: (01424) 427217
E: reservations@towerhousehotel.com
I: www.towerhousehotel.com

Bedrooms: 1 single, 8 double/twin, 1 triple/multiple
Bathrooms: 9 en suite

Evening meal available
CC: Amex, Delta, Mastercard, Switch, Visa

Elegant Victorian house situated half a mile from seafront. Pleasant gardens. Separate licensed bar leading to garden patio. Freshly-cooked meals. Ample parking.

B&B per night:
S £45.00–£55.00
D £60.00–£70.00

HB per person:
DY £47.50–£62.50

OPEN All Year except Christmas

HEATHFIELD, East Sussex Map ref 2D3

Silver Award

IWOOD B&B

Mutton Hall Lane, Heathfield TN21 8NR
T: (01435) 863918 & 07768 917816
F: (01435) 868575
E: iwoodbb@aol.com
I: www.iwoodbb.co.uk

Secluded chalet bungalow in lovely gardens with distant views of South Downs and sea. Situated within coastal towns including 1066 attractions around Hastings and historic towns of Battle, Rye, Lewes and Tunbridge Wells. Excellent standards maintained to ensure a comfortable stay. Be prepared for an excellent breakfast!

Bedrooms: 1 single, 2 double/twin
Bathrooms: 1 en suite, 2 private

Concessionary rates in excess 7 nights' stay.

B&B per night:
S £22.00–£25.00
D £42.00–£48.00

OPEN All Year except Christmas

PRICES
Please check prices and other details at the time of booking.

HERSTMONCEUX, East Sussex Map ref 3B4

♦♦♦♦

SANDHURST

Church Road, Herstmonceux, Hailsham BN27 1RG
T: (01323) 833088
F: (01323) 833088
E: junerussell@compuserve.com

Bedrooms: 1 double/twin, 2 triple/multiple
Bathrooms: 3 en suite

Large bungalow with plenty of off-road parking. Within walking distance of Herstmonceux village and close to Herstmonceux Castle. Twenty minutes' drive to sea. No smoking.

B&B per night:
S £30.00–£40.00
D £50.00–£60.00

OPEN All Year except Christmas

HOLLINGBOURNE, Kent Map ref 3B3

♦♦♦♦

WOODHOUSES

49 Eyhorne Street, Hollingbourne, Maidstone ME17 1TR
T: (01622) 880594
F: (01622) 880594
E: woodhouses@supanet.com

Bedrooms: 3 double/twin
Bathrooms: 3 en suite

Lunch available

17thC Listed building with walled garden. Close to Leeds Castle, village pubs and restaurants. Residents' lounge, TV and tea-making facilities. Direct trains to London.

12

B&B per night:
S £24.00
D £44.00–£46.00

OPEN All Year

HORLEY, Surrey Map ref 2D2

♦♦♦♦
Silver Award

THE LAWN GUEST HOUSE

30 Massetts Road, Gatwick RH6 7DF
T: (01293) 775751
F: (01293) 821803
E: info@lawnguesthouse.co.uk
I: www.lawnguesthouse.co.uk

Imposing Victorian house in pretty gardens. Five minutes Gatwick. Two minutes' walk Horley. Station 300 yards. London 40 minutes. Bedrooms all en suite. Full English breakfast and continental for early departures. Guests' ice machine. On-line residents' computer for e-mails. Overnight/long-term parking. Airport transfers by arrangement.

Bedrooms: 6 double/twin, 6 triple/multiple
Bathrooms: 12 en suite

CC: Amex, Delta, Mastercard, Switch, Visa

B&B per night:
S £40.00–£45.00
D £55.00

OPEN All Year

♦♦♦♦

ROSEMEAD GUEST HOUSE

19 Church Road, Horley RH6 7EY
T: (01293) 784965
F: (01293) 430547
E: info@rosemeadguesthouse.co.uk
I: www.rosemeadguesthouse.co.uk

Edwardian guesthouse, non-smoking throughout, 5 minutes from Gatwick, close to pubs, restaurants and shops. All rooms are centrally heated with colour TV, beverage trays and private bathrooms with a host of extras to make your stay comfortable. Full English breakfast is served in our refurbished dining room.

Bedrooms: 2 single, 2 double/twin, 2 triple/multiple
Bathrooms: 5 en suite, 1 private

CC: Amex, Delta, Mastercard, Switch, Visa

B&B per night:
S £35.00–£40.00
D £50.00–£55.00

OPEN All Year except Christmas

IMPORTANT NOTE Information on accommodation listed in this guide has been supplied by the proprietors. As changes may occur you are advised to check details at the time of booking.

HORSHAM, West Sussex Map ref 2D2 *Tourist Information Centre Tel: (01403) 211661*

◆◆◆

THE WIRRALS
1 Downsview Road, Horsham
RH12 4PF
T: (01403) 269400 & 0787 6631779
F: (01403) 269400
E: p.archibald@lineone.net
I: website.lineone.net/~p.archibald/webba.htm

Bedrooms: 1 single, 1 double/twin

B&B per night:
S £23.00–£24.50
D £40.00–£45.00

OPEN All Year except Christmas

Attractive home with welcoming atmosphere and comfortable accommodation. Located within easy access of the town centre, Gatwick Airport, M23, the South Downs and coast.

P

HOVE

See under Brighton & Hove

LEEDS, Kent Map ref 3B4

◆◆◆

FURTHER FIELDS
Caring Lane, Leeds, Maidstone
ME17 1TJ
T: (01622) 861288

Bedrooms: 1 single, 1 double/twin

Evening meal available

B&B per night:
S Min £23.00
D Min £45.00

A warm welcome in comfortable bungalow. Spectacular views of the Downs. Quiet countryside location, yet minutes from M20. Traditional home cooking using home-grown produce.

1 P

LEWES, East Sussex Map ref 2D3 *Tourist Information Centre Tel: (01273) 483448*

◆◆◆

THE CROWN INN
High Street, Lewes BN7 2NA
T: (01273) 480670
F: (01273) 480679
E: sales@crowninn-lewes.co.uk
I: www.crowninn-lewes.co.uk

Bedrooms: 7 double/twin, 1 triple/multiple
Bathrooms: 6 en suite

Lunch available
CC: Amex, Delta, Mastercard, Switch, Visa

B&B per night:
S £38.00–£50.00
D £60.00–£80.00

OPEN All Year

Family-run inn at the centre of historic town offering traditional food. Licensed bar open all day. Most rooms en suite. Meeting room available.

◆◆◆

13 HILL ROAD
Lewes BN7 1DB
T: (01273) 477723 & 07775 688017
F: (01273) 486032
E: kmyles@btclick.com

Bedrooms: 1 double/twin
Bathrooms: 1 en suite

B&B per night:
D £50.00

OPEN All Year

House with self-contained flat which is the only part to be let. Property positioned on a hill with far-reaching views.

P

LIGHTWATER, Surrey Map ref 2C2

◆◆◆◆

CARLTON GUEST HOUSE
63-65 Macdonald Road, Lightwater, Camberley GU18 5XY
T: (01276) 473580 & 07951 475593
F: (01276) 453595
E: ds@carltongh.co.uk
I: www.carltongh.co.uk

Bedrooms: 6 single, 7 double/twin
Bathrooms: 13 en suite

CC: Delta, Mastercard, Switch, Visa

B&B per night:
S £40.00–£60.00
D £50.00–£70.00

OPEN All Year

Conveniently situated off jct 3 of M3. Easy access to M4 and M25. Quality service to business and private guests. Relaxed, friendly atmosphere. Guest lounge/conservatory.

P

LITTLEHAMPTON, West Sussex Map ref 2D3

◆◆◆

ARUN SANDS
84 South Terrace, Seafront, Littlehampton BN17 5LJ
T: (01903) 732489
F: (01903) 732489
E: info@arun-sands.co.uk
I: www.arun-sands.co.uk

Bedrooms: 1 single, 3 double/twin, 4 triple/multiple
Bathrooms: 8 en suite

CC: Mastercard, Visa

B&B per night:
S Min £25.00
D Min £45.00

Friendly, family-run seafront guesthouse. All rooms en suite with colour TV, tea/coffee facilities, hairdryer, clock radio alarm, bedtime story book and teddy bear.

3

LYMINSTER, West Sussex Map ref 2D3

♦♦♦♦

SANDFIELD HOUSE

Lyminster, Littlehampton BN17 7PG
T: (01903) 724129
F: (01903) 715041
E: thefbs@aol.com

Bedrooms: 2 double/twin

Spacious country-style family house in 2 acres. Between Arundel and sea, near Area of Outstanding Natural Beauty. Tourist Board Blue Badge Guide available.

B&B per night:
S £15.00–£30.00
D £40.00–£50.00

OPEN All Year

MAIDSTONE, Kent Map ref 3B3 *Tourist Information Centre Tel: (01622) 602169*

51 BOWER MOUNT ROAD

Maidstone ME16 8AX
T: (01622) 762948
F: (01622) 202753
E: sylviabnb@compuserve.com

Bedrooms: 2 double/twin

Comfortable Edwardian semi-detached house. TV and tea and coffee-making facilities in all rooms. Within walking distance of the town and easy access to the M20.

B&B per night:
S £22.00–£25.00
D £34.00–£38.00

OPEN All Year except Christmas

GROVE HOUSE BED & BREAKFAST

Grove Green Road, Weavering Street, Maidstone ME14 5JT
T: (01622) 738441
F: (01622) 735927
E: gelco@supanet.com

Attractive, comfortable home in quiet surroundings close to Leeds Castle, Kent County Showground and places of interest. Pubs and restaurant nearby. Double en suite, double and twin rooms, with colour TV, tea/coffee facilities, bathrobes. Full English breakfast.

Bedrooms: 3 double/twin
Bathrooms: 1 en suite

B&B per night:
S £35.00
D £45.00–£50.00

OPEN All Year except Christmas

RAIGERSFELD HOUSE

Mote Park, Ashford Road, Maidstone ME14 4AE
T: (01622) 685211 & 687377
F: (01622) 691013
E: chipdbs@aol.com

Bedrooms: 3 double/twin, 2 triple/multiple

Four/five hundred-year-old farmhouse, inside Mote Park (400+ acres) plus lake. Near leisure centre, town centre. Leeds Castle 4 miles.

B&B per night:
S £20.00–£22.50
D £35.00–£42.50

OPEN All Year

♦♦♦♦♦
Silver Award

THE RINGLESTONE INN & FARMHOUSE HOTEL

Ringlestone Hamlet, Harrietsham, Maidstone ME17 1NX
T: (01622) 859900 & 07973 612261
F: (01622) 859966
E: bookings@ringlestone.com
I: www.ringlestone.com

On the tranquil North Downs, just 10 minutes from Leeds Castle, this character Kentish farmhouse is luxuriously furnished in rustic oak throughout, including a canopied 4-poster bed. Opposite, the famous 16thC Ringlestone Inn is recommended for interesting Kentish fare incorporating English fruit wines in the traditional recipes.

Bedrooms: 2 double/twin, 1 triple/multiple; permanent suite(s)
Bathrooms: 3 en suite

Lunch available
Evening meal available
CC: Amex, Delta, Diners, Mastercard, Switch, Visa

Third night free if booking 2 plus nights to include a Sunday.

B&B per night:
S £104.00–£140.00
D £114.00–£140.00

OPEN All Year except Christmas

MARDEN, Kent Map ref 3B4

◆◆◆◆

TANNER HOUSE
Tanner Farm, Goudhurst Road, Marden, Tonbridge TN12 9ND
T: (01622) 831214
F: (01622) 832472
E: enquiries@tannerfarmpark.co.uk
I: www.tannerfarmpark.co.uk

Bedrooms: 3 double/twin
Bathrooms: 3 en suite

CC: Delta, Mastercard, Switch, Visa

150-acre arable farm. Tudor farmhouse in centre of attractive family farm. Inglenook dining room. Off B2079. Car essential. Shire horses bred on farm. Also camping.

12 P

B&B per night:
D £45.00–£50.00

OPEN All Year except Christmas

NETTLESTEAD, Kent Map ref 3B4

◆◆◆◆

ROCK FARM HOUSE

Gibbs Hill, Nettlestead, Maidstone ME18 5HT
T: (01622) 812244
F: (01622) 812244
I: www.rockfarmhousebandb.co.uk

Delightful 18thC Kentish farmhouse situated in a quiet and idyllic postion on a farm with extensive views and surrounded by 2 acres of beautiful garden developed by Sue Corfe, a professional horticulturalist, and opened to the public through the National Gardens Scheme. Well-furnished, spacious, light and airy rooms with en suite or sole-use facilities.

Bedrooms: 3 double/twin
Bathrooms: 2 en suite, 1 private

P

B&B per night:
S Min £35.00
D Min £60.00

OPEN All Year except Christmas and New Year

NEWHAVEN, East Sussex Map ref 2D3

◆

NEWHAVEN LODGE GUEST HOUSE

12 Brighton Road, Newhaven BN9 9NB
T: (01273) 513736 & 07776 293398
F: (01273) 734619
E: newhavenlodge@aol.com

A comfortable, bright, family-run establishment located close to the Newhaven/Dieppe ferry terminal. Newhaven Lodge also caters for visitors to nearby Brighton and Lewes who wish to take advantage of the South Downs. The establishment motto is 'Arrive as a guest and leave as a friend'.

Bedrooms: 2 single, 1 double/twin, 4 triple/multiple
Bathrooms: 1 en suite

CC: Amex, Mastercard, Switch, Visa

Discounts given to groups of 10 or more who are willing to share family rooms.

P

B&B per night:
S £18.50–£25.00
D £39.00–£50.00

OPEN All Year

OXTED, Surrey Map ref 2D2

◆◆◆

ARAWA
58 Granville Road, Limpsfield, Oxted RH8 0BZ
T: (01883) 714104 & 0800 298 5732
F: (01883) 714104
E: david@davidgibbs.co.uk

Bedrooms: 2 double/twin
Bathrooms: 1 en suite, 1 private

Family home near North Downs Way, Chartwell and Hever. Near rail service to London and 30 minutes to Gatwick by car. Friendly and comfortable. Enjoy your stay!

P

B&B per night:
S £25.00–£35.00
D £50.00–£70.00

OPEN All Year

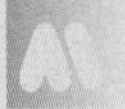

REGIONAL TOURIST BOARD The symbol in an establishment entry indicates that it is a Regional Tourist Board member.

OXTED continued

◆◆◆

THE NEW BUNGALOW

Old Hall Farm, Tandridge Lane, Oxted RH8 9NS
T: (01342) 892508
F: (01342) 892508
E: don.nunn@tesco.net

Bedrooms: 3 double/twin
Bathrooms: 1 en suite

Spacious, modern bungalow set in green fields and reached by a private drive. 5 minutes' drive from M25. London easily accessible by train.

P

B&B per night:
S £25.00–£32.00
D £40.00–£45.00

OPEN All Year except Christmas

PARTRIDGE GREEN, West Sussex Map ref 2D3

◆◆◆

POUND COTTAGE BED & BREAKFAST

Mill Lane, Littleworth, Partridge Green, Horsham RH13 8JU
T: (01403) 710218 & 711285
F: (01403) 711337
E: poundcottagebb@amserve.net
I: www.horsham.co.uk/poundcottage.html

Bedrooms: 1 single, 2 double/twin

Pleasant country house in quiet surroundings, 8 miles from Horsham, 25 minutes from Gatwick. Just off the B2135 West Grinstead to Steyning road.

P

B&B per night:
S £22.00–£23.00
D £44.00–£46.00

OPEN All Year

PEASLAKE, Surrey Map ref 2D2

◆◆◆

THE GARDEN ROOM

Coltsfoot, Peaslake, Guildford GU5 9PE
T: (01306) 737088
E: brimar@coltsfoot0.freeserve.co.uk

Bedrooms: 1 double/twin
Bathrooms: 1 en suite

Village location in beautiful Surrey hills. Self-contained annexe comprising double bedroom, en suite shower room and own lounge. Varied continental-style breakfast provided.

P

B&B per night:
S Min £30.00
D Min £50.00

PETWORTH, West Sussex Map ref 2D3

◆◆◆

BURTON PARK FARM

Petworth GU28 0JT
T: (01798) 342431

Bedrooms: 2 double/twin
Bathrooms: 2 en suite

250-acre arable farm. Relax here with comfort, good food, off-road parking. Excellent pubs nearby.

P

B&B per night:
S £23.00–£25.00
D £46.00–£50.00

OPEN All Year except Christmas

◆◆◆◆

EEDES COTTAGE

Bignor Park Road, Bury Gate, Pulborough RH20 1EZ
T: (01798) 831438
F: (01798) 831942
I: www.sussexlive.com

Bedrooms: 3 double/twin
Bathrooms: 1 en suite

Quiet country house surrounded by farmland. Convenient main roads to Arundel, Chichester and Brighton. Dogs, horses accommodated. TV in all rooms.

P

B&B per night:
S £30.00
D £50.00–£55.00

OPEN All Year

POLEGATE, East Sussex Map ref 2D3

◆◆◆◆

THE COTTAGE

Dittons Road, Polegate BN26 6HS
T: (01323) 482011
F: (01323) 482011

Bedrooms: 3 double/twin

The Cottage is situated on the rural outskirts of Polegate. Ample, well-lit parking available and easy access to the A27.

P

B&B per night:
S £25.00–£30.00
D £40.00–£45.00

OPEN All Year except Christmas

MAP REFERENCES

Map references apply to the colour maps at the front of this guide.

RAMSGATE, Kent Map ref 3C3 *Tourist Information Centre Tel: (01843) 583333*

♦♦♦♦

GLENDEVON GUEST HOUSE

8 Truro Road, Ramsgate CT1 8DB
T: (01843) 570909 & 0800 0352110
F: (01843) 570909
E: adrian.everix@btopenworld.com
I: www.glendevon-guesthouse.co.uk

Bedrooms: 4 double/twin, 2 triple/multiple
Bathrooms: 6 en suite

CC: Amex, Delta, Mastercard, Switch, Visa

B&B per night:
S £22.00–£24.00
D £36.00–£40.00

OPEN All Year

Delightful converted Victorian house near beach, harbour and town. Very comfortable rooms, all en suite and each containing attractive feature of modern kitchen/dining area.

REDHILL, Surrey Map ref 2D2

♦♦♦♦

ASHLEIGH HOUSE HOTEL

39 Redstone Hill, Redhill RH1 4BG
T: (01737) 764763
F: (01737) 780308

Bedrooms: 1 single, 5 double/twin, 2 triple/multiple
Bathrooms: 6 en suite

CC: Mastercard, Visa

B&B per night:
S £40.00–£55.00
D £56.00–£60.00

OPEN All Year except Christmas

Friendly, family-run early Edwardian house with most rooms en suite. Five hundred yards from railway station, London 30 minutes, Gatwick Airport 15 minutes.

ROCHESTER, Kent Map ref 3B3 *Tourist Information Centre Tel: (01634) 843666*

♦♦♦

KING CHARLES HOTEL

Brompton Road, Gillingham
ME7 5QT
T: (01634) 830303
F: (01634) 829430
E: enquiries@kingcharleshotel.co.uk
I: www.kingcharleshotel.co.uk

Bedrooms: 1 single, 54 double/twin, 31 triple/multiple
Bathrooms: 86 en suite

Lunch available
Evening meal available
CC: Amex, Delta, Diners, Mastercard, Switch, Visa

B&B per night:
S £36.00
D £42.00

OPEN All Year

Friendly, modern hotel run by family, catering for all requirements at very reasonable rates in comfortable accommodation. Ideal for groups.

♦♦♦

ST MARTIN

104 Borstal Road, Rochester
ME1 3BD
T: (01634) 848192
E: icolvin@stmartin.freeserve.co.uk

Bedrooms: 3 double/twin

Evening meal available

B&B per night:
S £19.00
D Min £38.00

HB per person:
DY Min £27.00

OPEN All Year except Christmas

Victorian family home overlooking the River Medway, close to city centre. Ideal for North Downs Way.

ROYAL TUNBRIDGE WELLS, Kent Map ref 2D2 *Tourist Information Centre Tel: (01892) 515675*

♦♦♦♦

BLUNDESTON

Eden Road, Royal Tunbridge Wells TN1 1TS
T: (01892) 513030
F: (01892) 540255
E: daysblundeston@excite.co.uk

B&B per night:
S £35.00–£45.00
D £48.00–£54.00

OPEN All Year except Christmas

A typical Kentish period house and gardens with a delightful, relaxing atmosphere. Situated in the village area of Tunbridge Wells in a private road within minutes of the shops, station and Pantiles. Private drive with parking.

Bedrooms: 2 double/twin
Bathrooms: 2 en suite

QUALITY ASSURANCE SCHEME
Diamond ratings and awards are explained at the back of this guide.

ROYAL TUNBRIDGE WELLS continued

◆◆◆

HADLEIGH
69 Sandown Park,
Royal Tunbridge Wells TN2 4RT
T: (01892) 822760
F: (01892) 823170

Bedrooms: 2 double/twin
Bathrooms: 2 private

Quiet comfortable house within easy reach of Royal Tunbridge Wells, the Kent countryside, Gatwick Airport and M25. Off-street parking.

B&B per night:
S £22.00–£25.00
D £44.00

OPEN All Year except Christmas

◆◆◆

MANOR COURT FARM

Ashurst, Royal Tunbridge Wells TN3 9TB
T: (01892) 740279 & 740210
F: (01892) 740919
E: jsoyke@jsoyke.freeserve.co.uk
I: www.manorcourtfarm.co.uk

B&B per night:
S £24.00–£30.00
D £48.00–£60.00

OPEN All Year

Georgian farmhouse with friendly atmosphere, spacious rooms and lovely views of Medway Valley. 350-acre mixed farm, many animals. Good base for walking. Penshurst Place, Hever Castle, Chartwell, Sissinghurst etc all within easy reach by car. London 50 minutes by train from Tonbridge. Guest lounge. Excellent camping facilities. On A264 0.5 miles east of Ashurst village.

Bedrooms: 3 double/twin

Reductions for longer stays. Reductions for children.

◆◆◆

NUMBER TEN

Modest Corner, Southborough,
Royal Tunbridge Wells TN4 0LS
T: (01892) 522450
F: (01892) 522450
E: modestanneke@lineone.net

B&B per night:
D £45.00–£55.00

OPEN All Year except Christmas

Number Ten is situated in a lovely tranquil hamlet on the edge of Tunbridge Wells, with easy access to M25 and a host of historic places. A warm welcome is assured in this attractive home, where the owner's artistic touches can be seen throughout.

Bedrooms: 3 double/twin
Bathrooms: 3 private

Evening meal available

RUSTINGTON, West Sussex Map ref 2D3

◆◆◆◆
Silver Award

KENMORE

Claigmar Road, Rustington, Littlehampton BN16 2NL
T: (01903) 784634
F: (01903) 784634
E: kenmoreguesthouse@amserve.net
I: www.kenmoreguesthouse.co.uk

B&B per night:
S £25.00–£31.50
D £50.00–£55.00

Secluded Edwardian house in a garden setting in the heart of the village and close to sea. Attractive en suite rooms, individually decorated and comfortably furnished. Private parking. Ideal for touring historic towns, castles, cathedrals and stately homes. Sylvia and Ray Dobbs offer a warm and friendly welcome.

Bedrooms: 1 single, 2 double/twin, 4 triple/multiple
Bathrooms: 7 en suite

CC: Amex, Mastercard, Visa

RYE, East Sussex Map ref 3B4 *Tourist Information Centre Tel: (01797) 226696*

♦♦♦

AT WISTERIA CORNER
47 Ferry Road (Sloane Terrace), Rye
TN31 7DJ
T: (01797) 225011
E: mmpartridge@lineone.net

Bedrooms: 2 double/twin

Our small B&B is only two minutes' walk from the ancient town centre of Rye. Sandy beach and scenic countryside walks are within easy reach.

B&B per night:
S £20.00–£22.00
D £32.00

OPEN All Year except Christmas

♦♦♦♦♦
Silver Award

DURRANT HOUSE HOTEL

2 Market Street, Rye TN31 7LA
T: (01797) 223182
F: (01797) 226940
E: kingslands@compuserve.com
I: www.durranthouse.com

A charming Listed building located in the centre of ancient Rye. Comfortable and individually decorated bedrooms, including 4-poster and triple rooms, all en suite and equipped to a high standard. The hotel offers an informal and friendly atmosphere, wholesome food and is the perfect location for a relaxing break.

Bedrooms: 4 double/twin, 2 triple/multiple
Bathrooms: 6 en suite

Evening meal available
CC: Delta, Mastercard, Switch, Visa

Dec-Easter: Sun-Fri mini-breaks – 2 nights 10% discount, 3 nights or more 15% discount, based on 2 people sharing a room.

B&B per night:
S £45.00–£60.00
D £40.00–£85.00

♦♦♦♦♦
Silver Award

JEAKE'S HOUSE

Mermaid Street, Rye TN31 7ET
T: (01797) 222828
F: (01797) 222623
E: jeakeshouse@btinternet.com
I: www.jeakeshouse.com

Ideally located historic house on winding, cobbled street in the heart of ancient medieval town. Individually restored rooms provide traditional luxury combined with all modern facilities. A book-lined bar and cosy parlours. Extensive breakfast menu to suit all tastes. Easy walking distance to restaurants and shops. Private car park.

Bedrooms: 1 single, 8 double/twin, 3 triple/multiple; permanent suite(s)
Bathrooms: 9 en suite, 1 private

CC: Delta, Mastercard, Switch, Visa

Reductions for a stay of 4 or more nights. Mid-week winter breaks.

12

B&B per night:
S £34.00–£70.00
D £68.00–£110.00

HB per person:
DY £34.00–£55.00

OPEN All Year

♦♦♦

KIMBLEY COTTAGE
Main Street, Peasmarsh, Rye
TN31 6UL
T: (01797) 230514
F: (01797) 230850
E: kimbley@clara.co.uk

Bedrooms: 3 double/twin
Bathrooms: 3 en suite

Friendly country house with rural views. Excellent pubs/restaurants in village. Three miles from Rye on A268, 45 minutes to Dover. Non-smoking, off-road parking.

P

B&B per night:
S £27.00–£29.00
D £45.00–£48.00

OPEN All Year except Christmas

RYE continued

◆◆◆◆ Silver Award

LAYCES BED & BREAKFAST

Chitcombe Road, Broad Oak Brede, Rye TN31 6EU
T: (01424) 882836
F: (01424) 882281
E: stephens@layces.co.uk
I: www.layces.co.uk

Bedrooms: 3 double/ twin
Bathrooms: 3 en suite

CC: Amex, Delta, Mastercard, Switch, Visa

B&B per night:
S £27.00
D £40.00

OPEN All Year

Comfortable family home in heart of 1066 country. Beautiful views. Large gardens. Ample parking. Excellent pub/ restaurant nearby.

P

◆◆◆◆◆ Silver Award

LITTLE ORCHARD HOUSE

West Street, Rye TN31 7ES
T: (01797) 223831
F: (01797) 223831
I: www.littleorchardhouse.com

Bedrooms: 2 double/ twin
Bathrooms: 2 en suite

CC: Delta, Mastercard, Switch, Visa

B&B per night:
D £64.00–£90.00

OPEN All Year

Georgian townhouse in centre of Rye. Antique furnishings and large walled garden give country-house atmosphere. 4-poster beds, generous free-range/organic breakfast. Parking available.

12 P

Gold Award

MANOR FARM OAST

Workhouse Lane, Icklesham, Winchelsea TN36 4AJ
T: (01424) 813787
F: (01424) 813787
E: manor.farm.oast@lineone.net

B&B per night:
S £40.00–£45.00
D £64.00–£74.00

HB per person:
DY £54.50–£59.50

OPEN All Year

Three-roundel oast house in the heart of 1066 country. Quiet and secluded in orchards, close to Rye, Battle and Hastings. Beautiful walled garden for romantic breaks, wedding receptions and honeymoons. All rooms are tastefully furnished, the original round room particularly restful. Home-cooked dinners exceptionally good using local produce.

Bedrooms: 3 double/ twin
Bathrooms: 2 en suite, 1 private

Lunch available
Evening meal available
CC: Delta, Mastercard, Switch, Visa

Group Murder Mystery dinners. Honeymoon breaks. Romantic dinners. Bed & Breakfast of the Year 2000 for South East.

12 P

THE OLD VICARAGE

Rye Harbour, Rye TN31 7TT
T: (01797) 222088
F: (01797) 229620
E: jonathan@oldvicarageryeharbour.fsnet.co.uk

Bedrooms: 2 double/ twin

B&B per night:
D £40.00–£58.00

OPEN All Year except Christmas

Imposing Victorian former vicarage, quietly situated close to sea and nature reserve. Antique furniture and open fires. Magnificent English breakfast. Classic excellence and old- fashioned hospitality.

P

QUALITY ASSURANCE SCHEME

For an explanation of the quality and facilities represented by the Diamonds please refer to the front of this guide. A more detailed explanation can be found in the information pages at the back.

RYE continued

♦♦♦♦ Silver Award

THE STRAND HOUSE

Tanyard's Lane, Winchelsea, Nr. Rye
TN36 4JT
T: (01797) 226276
F: (01797) 224806
E: strandhouse@winchelsea98.fsnet.co.uk
I: www.smoothhound.co.uk/hotels/strand.html

A warm welcome awaits in the 15thC old world charm of Winchelsea's old workhouse. Now Grade II Listed with many original beams and inglenooks. Well-furnished rooms. Overlooking National Trust pastureland. 4-poster bedroom. Residents' bar. Traditional breakfasts utilising local produce served in the heavily beamed dining room. Log fires. Pretty gardens.

Bedrooms: 9 double/twin, 1 triple/multiple
Bathrooms: 9 en suite, 1 private

CC: Delta, Mastercard, Switch, Visa

Winter weekend breaks (2 nights min). Special rates off-season mid-week (3 nights min).

B&B per night:
S £34.00–£42.00
D £52.00–£76.00

OPEN All Year except Christmas

RYE FOREIGN, East Sussex Map ref 3B4

♦♦♦

THE HARE & HOUNDS

Rye Road, Rye Foreign, Rye
TN31 7ST
T: (01797) 230483

Bedrooms: 4 double/twin
Bathrooms: 4 en suite

Lunch available
Evening meal available
CC: Delta, Mastercard, Switch, Visa

16thC freehouse set in 3 acres of grounds with 4 double en suite bedrooms in converted barn adjacent to inn.

B&B per night:
S £35.00
D £55.00

OPEN All Year

SEAFORD, East Sussex Map ref 2D3 *Tourist Information Centre Tel: (01323) 897426*

♦♦♦♦

THE SILVERDALE

21 Sutton Park Road, Seaford BN25 1RH
T: (01323) 491849
F: (01323) 891131
E: silverdale@mistral.co.uk
I: www.mistral.co.uk/silverdale/silver.htm

Small, expertly run house-hotel in the centre of peaceful Edwardian seaside town. Beautifully prepared food and a host of English wines. Over 120 single-malt whiskies. Only a few minutes' walk from the seaside, the antique shops and the friendly local pubs. We'd love to meet you!

Bedrooms: 1 single, 5 double/twin, 2 triple/multiple; permanent suite(s)
Bathrooms: 6 en suite

Lunch available
Evening meal available
CC: Amex, Delta, Diners, Mastercard, Switch, Visa

Special 2-night theatre breaks and many others. Contact us for a more detailed list.

B&B per night:
S £28.00–£45.00
D £38.00–£65.00

HB per person:
DY £30.00–£55.00

OPEN All Year

SELSEY, West Sussex Map ref 2C3

♦♦♦♦

ST ANDREWS LODGE

Chichester Road, Selsey, Chichester
PO20 0LX
T: (01243) 606899
F: (01243) 607826
E: info@standrewslodge.co.uk
I: www.standrewslodge.co.uk

Bedrooms: 1 single, 5 double/twin, 4 triple/multiple; permanent suite(s)
Bathrooms: 10 en suite

Evening meal available
CC: Delta, Diners, Mastercard, Switch, Visa

Family-run, friendly relaxed atmosphere, licensed. En suite bedrooms, cosy lounge, log fire, peaceful suntrap garden. Close to natural beaches and countryside, south of Chichester.

B&B per night:
S £30.00–£45.00
D £58.00–£85.00

OPEN All Year except Christmas

COLOUR MAPS Colour maps at the front of this guide pinpoint all places under which you will find accommodation listed.

SEVENOAKS, Kent Map ref 2D2 *Tourist Information Centre Tel: (01732) 450305*

◆◆◆

THE MOORINGS HOTEL

97 Hitchen Hatch Lane, Sevenoaks TN13 3BE
T: (01732) 452589 & 742323
F: (01732) 456462
E: theryans@mooringshotel.co.uk
I: www.mooringshotel.co.uk

Bedrooms: 5 single, 16 double/twin, 2 triple/multiple
Bathrooms: 23 en suite

Lunch available
Evening meal available
CC: Amex, Delta, Diners, Mastercard, Switch, Visa

Friendly family hotel offering high-standard accommodation for tourists and business travellers. Thirty minutes from London. Close to station.

B&B per night:
S £47.00–£57.00
D £69.00–£79.00

HB per person:
DY £89.00–£99.00

OPEN All Year

◆◆◆

ROBANN

5 Vestry Cottages, Old Otford Road, Sevenoaks TN14 5EH
T: (01732) 456272

Bedrooms: 1 triple/multiple
Bathrooms: 1 en suite

Evening meal available

Mid-terrace, 19thC house in a cobbled road just off the Old Otford Road. The property faces south with a large garden.

B&B per night:
D £50.00–£80.00

OPEN All Year except Christmas

SHEERNESS, Kent Map ref 3B3

◆

SHEPPEY GUEST HOUSE

214 Queenborough Road, Halfway, Minster-in-Sheppey, Sheerness ME12 3DF
T: (01795) 665950
F: (01795) 661200
E: mallas@btopenworld.com

Bedrooms: 1 single, 3 double/twin, 5 triple/multiple; permanent suite(s)
Bathrooms: 9 en suite

Lunch available
Evening meal available

Family-run establishment in a semi-rural location. Large parking area, indoor swimming pool. All rooms en suite, Sky TV. Table licence. Large gardens.

B&B per night:
S £20.00
D Min £30.00

HB per person:
DY £22.95–£26.00

OPEN All Year

SITTINGBOURNE, Kent Map ref 3B3

◆◆◆◆◆

HEMPSTEAD HOUSE

London Road, Bapchild, Sittingbourne ME9 9PP
T: (01795) 428020
F: (01795) 436362
E: info@hempsteadhouse.co.uk
I: www.hempsteadhouse.co.uk

Exclusive, privately owned Victorian country-house hotel and restaurant situated in rural location, but on the main A2 between Canterbury and Sittingbourne. Set in 3 acres of beautifully landscaped gardens, we offer superbly appointed accommodation, fine cuisine, prepared solely from fresh, local produce, elegant reception rooms and friendly hospitality.

Bedrooms: 12 double/twin, 3 triple/multiple
Bathrooms: 15 en suite

Lunch available
Evening meal available
CC: Amex, Delta, Diners, Mastercard, Switch, Visa

B&B per night:
S £75.00
D £85.00

HB per person:
DY £62.00–£94.50

OPEN All Year

STELLING MINNIS, Kent Map ref 3B4

◆◆◆◆
Silver Award

GREAT FIELD FARM

Misling Lane, Stelling Minnis, Canterbury CT4 6DE
T: (01227) 709223
F: (01227) 709223
E: Greatfieldfarm@aol.com

Bedrooms: 3 double/twin; permanent suite(s)
Bathrooms: 3 en suite

CC: Delta, Mastercard, Switch, Visa

Delightful farmhouse amidst beautiful countryside, gardens and paddocks. Enjoy peace and privacy in our suites, B&B or self-catering. 10 minutes Canterbury/Channel Tunnel.

B&B per night:
S £30.00–£45.00
D £45.00–£50.00

OPEN All Year

CONFIRM YOUR BOOKING
You are advised to confirm your booking in writing.

STEYNING, West Sussex Map ref 2D3

CHEQUER INN

41 High Street, Steyning BN44 3RE
T: (01903) 814437
F: (01903) 879707
E: chequerinn@btinternet.com

B&B per night:
S Min £35.00
D Min £45.00

OPEN All Year

A fine historic hostelry in the heart of picturesque Steyning. The Chequer Inn is over 500 years old with open fires and many original features. En suite rooms are comfortably appointed and the inn offers fine food and an excellent cellar. A perfect base to explore the beauty of Sussex.

Bedrooms: 3 double/twin
Bathrooms: 3 en suite

Lunch available
Evening meal available
CC: Amex, Delta, Mastercard, Switch, Visa

TENTERDEN, Kent Map ref 3B4

COLLINA HOUSE HOTEL

East Hill, Tenterden TN30 6RL
T: (01580) 764852 & 764004
F: (01580) 762224
E: enquiries@collinahousehotel.co.uk
I: www.collinahousehotel.co.uk

Bedrooms: 1 single, 6 double/twin, 7 triple/multiple
Bathrooms: 14 en suite

Lunch available
Evening meal available
CC: Delta, Mastercard, Switch, Visa

B&B per night:
S £35.00–£55.00
D £45.00–£75.00

HB per person:
DY £50.00–£80.00

OPEN All Year except Christmas

Edwardian house overlooking orchards and garden, within walking distance of picturesque town. Swiss-trained proprietors offering both English and continental cooking.

TUNBRIDGE WELLS

See under Royal Tunbridge Wells

UCKFIELD, East Sussex Map ref 2D3

Silver Award

OLD MILL FARM

High Hurstwood, Uckfield
TN22 4AD
T: (01825) 732279
F: (01825) 732279

Bedrooms: 1 single, 1 double/twin, 1 triple/multiple
Bathrooms: 2 en suite, 1 private

B&B per night:
S £24.00–£30.00
D £48.00–£60.00

OPEN All Year

Sussex barn and buildings converted to a comfortable home, situated in the quiet village of High Hurstwood, off A26. Ashdown Forest nearby.

WALMER, Kent Map ref 3C4

HARDICOT GUEST HOUSE

Kingsdown Road, Walmer, Deal CT14 8AW
T: (01304) 373867 & 389234
F: (01304) 389234
E: guestboss@talk21.com
I: www.smoothhound.co.uk/hotels/hardicot.html

B&B per night:
S £25.00
D £46.00–£50.00

OPEN All Year except Christmas

Large, quiet, detached Victorian house with Channel views and secluded garden, situated 100 yards from the beach. Guests have unrestricted access to rooms. Close to 3 championship golf courses, ferries and the Channel Tunnel. Ideal centre for cliff walks and exploring Canterbury and the castles and gardens of East Kent.

Bedrooms: 3 double/twin
Bathrooms: 1 en suite, 2 private

7 nights for the price of 6.

WALTON-ON-THAMES, Surrey Map ref 2D2

◆◆◆

BEECH TREE LODGE

7 Rydens Avenue, Walton-on-Thames KT12 3JB
T: (01932) 242738 & 886667
E: joanspiteri@aol.com
I: www.smoothhound.co.uk/hotels

Bedrooms: 2 double/twin, 1 triple/multiple

Friendly Edwardian house in quiet avenue near station (25 minutes London), pubs and restaurants. Convenient Hampton Court, Windsor. French, Italian and Spanish spoken. Ample parking.

B&B per night:
S £30.00–£44.00
D £44.00–£48.00

OPEN All Year except Christmas

WEST CLANDON, Surrey Map ref 2D2

◆◆◆◆

WAYS COTTAGE

Lime Grove, West Clandon, Guildford GU4 7UT
T: (01483) 222454

Bedrooms: 2 double/twin
Bathrooms: 1 en suite

Evening meal available

Rural detached house with delightful garden, in quiet location 5 miles from Guildford. Easy reach of A3 and M25. Close to station on Waterloo/Guildford line.

B&B per night:
S £27.00–£29.00
D £38.00–£42.00

HB per person:
DY £39.50–£45.50

OPEN All Year

WEST DEAN, West Sussex Map ref 2C3

◆◆◆

LODGE HILL FARM

West Dean, Chichester PO18 0RT
T: (01243) 535245

Bedrooms: 3 double/twin
Bathrooms: 1 private

Flint farmhouse built in 1813 on the South Downs, superb views, near Goodwood, 15 minutes to Chichester, ideal for walkers.

B&B per night:
S £20.00–£25.00
D £40.00–£50.00

OPEN All Year except Christmas

WEST HORSLEY, Surrey Map ref 2D2

◆◆◆

BRINFORD

off Shere Road, West Horsley, Leatherhead KT24 6EJ
T: (01483) 283636

Bedrooms: 1 single, 2 double/twin
Bathrooms: 1 en suite

Modern house in peaceful, rural location with panoramic views across the countryside. Easy reach of Guildford, A3, M25 and London. Several National Trust properties nearby.

B&B per night:
S £28.00–£38.00
D £46.00–£54.00

OPEN All Year

WESTMARSH, Kent Map ref 3C3

◆◆◆

THE WAY OUT INN

Westmarsh, Canterbury CT3 2LP
T: (01304) 812899
F: (01304) 813181

Bedrooms: 3 double/twin
Bathrooms: 3 en suite

Separate lodge house set in remote village. Ideal for country walks. Close to Channel crossings and major towns. Twelve miles city of Canterbury.

B&B per night:
S Min £30.00
D Min £45.00

OPEN All Year

USE YOUR *i*s

There are more than 550 Tourist Information Centres throughout England offering friendly help with accommodation and holiday ideas as well as suggestions of places to visit and things to do. You'll find TIC addresses in the local Phone Book.

WHITSTABLE, Kent Map ref 3B3 *Tourist Information Centre Tel: (01227) 275482*

◆◆◆◆
Gold Award

VICTORIA VILLA

Victoria Street, Whitstable CT5 1JB
T: (01227) 779191
F: (01227) 779191
E: victoria-villa@i12.com
I: www.victoria-villa@i12.com

B&B per night:
S £65.00–£85.00
D £75.00–£105.00

OPEN All Year

Unrivalled 4 diamond accommodation with a coveted Gold Award, just a stone's throw from the beach in the heart of the conservation area. The tastefully furnished period villa comprises just 2 guest rooms with private or en suite shower rooms. Breakfast is served in the courtyard garden or the elegant dining room.

Bedrooms: 2 double/twin
Bathrooms: 1 en suite, 1 private

5 nights for 2 people with full English breakfast – normally £475, offer price £300. From end Sep 2003 to end Mar 2004.

12 P

WOKING, Surrey Map ref 2D2

◆◆◆

GRANTCHESTER

Boughton Hall Avenue, Send, Woking GU23 7DF
T: (01483) 225383
F: (01483) 596490
E: gary@hotpotmail.com

B&B per night:
S £25.00–£30.00
D £48.00–£55.00

OPEN All Year except Christmas

Attractive family house with large, superbly kept garden. Situated 4 minutes from Guildford and Woking town centres. Close to M25 and A3 motorways. Parking available. Long stays welcome. Close to Heathrow and Gatwick Airports, Wisley Gardens and Clandon Park.

Bedrooms: 2 double/twin

P

WORTHING, West Sussex Map ref 2D3 *Tourist Information Centre Tel: (01903) 210022*

◆◆◆

WOODLANDS GUEST HOUSE
20 Warwick Gardens, Worthing BN11 1PF
T: (01903) 233557 & 0800 096 7103
F: (01903) 536925
E: woodlandsghse@cwcom.net
I: www.woodlands20-22.freeserve.co.uk

Bedrooms: 1 single, 4 double/twin, 1 triple/multiple
Bathrooms: 5 en suite, 1 private

CC: Delta, Mastercard, Switch, Visa

B&B per night:
S £30.00–£38.00
D £50.00–£65.00

OPEN All Year

Edwardian guesthouse providing excellent food and comfortable accommodation. Quiet area close to town and seafront. Honeymoon suite. Ideal touring base for Sussex. Free parking.

P

WYE, Kent Map ref 3B4

◆◆◆

MISTRAL
3 Oxenturn Road, Wye, Ashford TN25 5BH
T: (01233) 813011
F: (01233) 813011
E: geoff@chapman.invictanet.co.uk
I: www.wye.org

Bedrooms: 1 single, 1 double/twin

B&B per night:
S £25.00
D £50.00

OPEN All Year except Christmas

Small bed and breakfast offering high quality food and facilities in a central but secluded part of Wye village. Parking is available by arrangement.

A brief guide to the main Towns and Villages offering accommodation in South East England

A ASHFORD, KENT - Once a market centre, the town has a number of Tudor and Georgian houses and a museum. Eurostar trains stop at Ashford International station.

B BATTLE, EAST SUSSEX - The Abbey at Battle was built on the site of the Battle of Hastings, when William defeated Harold II and so became the Conqueror in 1066. The museum has a fine collection relating to the Sussex iron industry, and there is a social history museum - Buckleys Yesterday's World.

• **BETHERSDEN, KENT** - Typical Wealden village with plenty of weatherboarded houses. Famous in the Middle Ages for its marble, used in Canterbury and Rochester Cathedrals.

• **BOGNOR REGIS, WEST SUSSEX** - Five miles of firm, flat sand has made the town a popular family resort. Well supplied with gardens.

• **BRASTED, KENT** - Standing in a park adjoining the village is 18thC Brasted Place (not open to visitors). The work of Robert Adam, this fine house was once the home of Napoleon III.

• **BRIGHTON & HOVE, EAST SUSSEX** - Brighton's attractions include the Royal Pavilion, Volks Electric Railway, Sea Life Centre and Marina Village, Conference Centre, "The Lanes" and several theatres.

• **BROADSTAIRS, KENT** - Popular seaside resort with numerous sandy bays. Charles Dickens spent his summers at Bleak House where he wrote parts of 'David Copperfield". The Dickens Festival s held in June, when many people wear ickensian costume.

C CANTERBURY, KENT - Place of ilgrimage since the martyrdom of Becket n 1170 and the site of Canterbury Cathedral. Visit St Augustine's Abbey, St 1artin's (the oldest church in England), oyal Museum and Art Gallery and the Canterbury Tales. Nearby is Howletts Wild Animal Park. Good shopping centre.

• **CHICHESTER, WEST SUSSEX** - The county town of West Sussex with a beautiful Norman cathedral. Noted for its Georgian architecture but also has modern buildings like the Festival Theatre. Surrounded by places of interest, including Fishbourne Roman Palace, Weald and Downland Open-Air Museum and West Dean Gardens.

• **COMPTON, WEST SUSSEX** - Brick and flint village on the West Sussex/Hampshire border, with mainly Victorian church.

• **CRANBROOK, KENT** - Old town, a centre for the weaving industry in the 15thC. The 72-ft-high Union Mill is a three-storey windmill, still in working order. Sissinghurst Gardens (National Trust) nearby.

D DEAL, KENT - Coastal town and popular holiday resort. Deal Castle was built by Henry VIII as a fort, and the museum is devoted to finds excavated in the area. Also the Time-Ball Tower museum. Angling available from both beach and pier.

• **DORKING, SURREY** - Ancient market town and a good centre for walking, delightfully set between Box Hill and the Downs. Denbies Wine Estate - England's largest vineyard - is situated here.

• **DOVER, KENT** - A Cinque Port and busiest passenger port in the world. Still a historic town and seaside resort beside the famous White Cliffs. The White Cliffs Experience attraction traces the town's history through the Roman, Saxon, Norman and Victorian periods.

• **DYMCHURCH, KENT** - For centuries the headquarters of the Lords of the Level, the local government of this area. Probably best known today because of the fame of its fictional parson, the notorious Dr Syn, who has inspired a regular festival.

E EAST GRINSTEAD, WEST SUSSEX - A number of fine old houses stand in the High Street, one of which is Sackville College, founded in 1609.

• **EASTBOURNE, EAST SUSSEX** - One of the finest, most elegant resorts on the south-east coast situated beside Beachy Head. Long promenade, well-known Carpet Gardens on the seafront, Devonshire Park tennis and indoor leisure complex, theatres, Towner Art Gallery, "How We Lived Then" Museum of Shops and Social History.

F FARNHAM, SURREY - Town noted for its Georgian houses. Willmer House (now a museum) has a facade of cut and moulded brick with fine carving and panelling in the interior. The 12thC castle has been occupied by Bishops of both Winchester and Guildford.

• **FAVERSHAM, KENT** - Historic town, once a port, dating back to prehistoric times. Abbey Street has more than 50 Listed buildings. Roman and Anglo-Saxon finds and other exhibits can be seen in a museum in the Maison Dieu at Ospringe. Fleur de Lys Heritage Centre.

• **FITTLEWORTH, WEST SUSSEX** - Quiet village that attracts artists and anglers. Groups of cottages can be found beside the narrow lanes and paths in the woodlands near the River Rother.

• **FOLKESTONE, KENT** - Popular resort. The town has a fine promenade, the Leas, from where orchestral concerts and other entertainments are presented. Horse-racing at Westenhanger Racecourse nearby.

G GODALMING, SURREY - Several old coaching inns are reminders that the town was once a staging point. The old Town Hall is now the local-history museum. Charterhouse School moved here in 1872 and is dominated by the 150-ft Founder's Tower.

• **GUILDFORD, SURREY** - Bustling town with Lewis Carroll connections and many historic monuments, one of which is the Guildhall clock jutting out over the old High Street. The modern cathedral occupies a commanding position on Stag Hill.

H HARTFIELD, EAST SUSSEX - Pleasant village in Ashdown Forest, the setting for A A Milne's "Winnie the Pooh" stories.

- **HASLEMERE, SURREY** - Town set in hilly, wooded countryside, much of it in the care of the National Trust. Its attractions include the educational museum and the annual music festival.

- **HASTINGS, EAST SUSSEX** - Ancient town which became famous as the base from which William the Conqueror set out to fight the Battle of Hastings. Later became one of the Cinque Ports, now a leading resort. Castle, Hastings Embroidery, inspired by the Bayeux Tapestry, and Sea Life Centre.

- **HEATHFIELD, EAST SUSSEX** - Old Heathfield is a pretty village which was one of the major centres of the Sussex iron industry.

- **HERSTMONCEUX, EAST SUSSEX** - Pleasant village noted for its woodcrafts and the beautiful 15thC moated Herstmonceux Castle with its Science Centre and gardens open to the public. The only village where traditional Sussex trug baskets are still made.

- **HOLLINGBOURNE, KENT** - Pleasant village near romantic Leeds Castle in the heart of orchard country at the foot of the North Downs. Some fine, half-timbered houses and a flint and ragstone church.

- **HORLEY, SURREY** - Town on the London to Brighton road, just north of Gatwick Airport, with an ancient parish church and 15thC inn.

- **HORSHAM, WEST SUSSEX** - Busy town with much modern development but still retaining its old character. The museum in Causeway House is devoted chiefly to local history and the agricultural life of the county.

L LEWES, EAST SUSSEX - Historic county town with Norman castle. The steep High Street has mainly Georgian buildings. There is a folk museum at Anne of Cleves House, and the archaeological museum is in Barbican House.

- **LITTLEHAMPTON, WEST SUSSEX** - Ancient port at the mouth of the River Arun, now a popular holiday resort, offering flat, sandy beaches, sailing, fishing and boat trips. The Sussex Downs are a short walk inland.

- **LYMINSTER, WEST SUSSEX** - Links up with Littlehampton looking inland, and across the watermeadows to the churches and towers of Arundel. There is a vineyard here.

M MAIDSTONE, KENT - Busy county town of Kent on the River Medway has many interesting features and is an excellent centre for excursions. Museum of Carriages, Museum and Art Gallery, Mote Park.

- **MARDEN, KENT** - The village is believed to date back to Saxon times, though today more modern homes surround the 13thC church.

N NEWHAVEN, EAST SUSSEX - The town has the terminal of a car-ferry service to Dieppe in France. Paradise Park family attraction and indoor ski-slope.

O OXTED, SURREY - Pleasant town on the edge of National Trust woodland and at the foot of the North Downs. Chartwell (National Trust), the former home of Sir Winston Churchill, is close by.

P PARTRIDGE GREEN, WEST SUSSEX - Small village between Henfield and Billingshurst.

- **PETWORTH, WEST SUSSEX** - Town known as an antique centre and dominated by Petworth House (National Trust), the great 17thC mansion, set in 2,000 acres of parkland laid out by Capability Brown. The house contains wood-carvings by Grinling Gibbons.

- **POLEGATE, EAST SUSSEX** - Polegate used to be an important junction for the London, Brighton and South Coast Railway. Polegate Windmill and Milling Museum can be visited.

R RAMSGATE, KENT - Popular holiday resort with good sandy beaches. At Pegwell Bay is a replica of a Viking longship.

- **REDHILL, SURREY** - Part of the borough of Reigate and now the commercial centre with good shopping facilities. Gatwick Airport is three miles to the south.

- **ROCHESTER, KENT** - Ancient cathedral city on the River Medway. Has many places of interest connected with Charles Dickens (who lived nearby) including the fascinating Dickens Centre. Also massive castle overlooking the river and Guildhall Museum.

- **ROYAL TUNBRIDGE WELLS, KENT** - This "Royal" town became famous as a spa in the 17thC and much of its charm is retained, as in the Pantiles, a shaded walk lined with elegant shops. Heritage attraction "A Day at the Wells". Excellent shopping centre.

- **RUSTINGTON, WEST SUSSEX** - Village with thatched cottages and a medieval church.

- **RYE, EAST SUSSEX** - Cobbled, hilly streets and fine old buildings make Rye, once a Cinque Port, a most picturesque town. Noted for its church with ancient clock, potteries and antique shops. Town Model Sound and Light Show gives a good introduction to the town.

S SEAFORD, EAST SUSSEX - The town was a bustling port until 1579 when the course of the River Ouse was diverted. The downlands around the town make good walking country, with fine views of the Seven Sisters cliffs.

- **SELSEY, WEST SUSSEX** - Almost surrounded by water, with the English Channel on two sides and an inland lake, once Pagham Harbour, and the Brook on the other two. Ideal for yachting, swimming, fishing and wildlife.

- **SEVENOAKS, KENT** - Set in pleasant wooded country, with a distinctive character and charm. Nearby is Knole (National Trust), home of the Sackville family and one of the largest houses in England, set in a vast deer park.

NB **IMPORTANT NOTE** Information on accommodation listed in this guide has been supplied by the proprietors. As changes may occur you are advised to check details at the time of booking.

• **SITTINGBOURNE, KENT** - The town's position and its ample supply of water make it an ideal site for the paper-making industry. Delightful villages and orchards lie round about.

• **STELLING MINNIS, KENT** - Off the Roman Stone Street, this quiet, picturesque village lies deep in the Lyminge Forest, south of Canterbury.

• **STEYNING, WEST SUSSEX** - An important market town and thriving port before the Norman Conquest, lying at the foot of the South Downs. Retains a picturesque charm with fascinating timber-framed and stone buildings.

TENTERDEN, KENT - Most attractive market town with a broad main street full of 16thC houses and shops. The tower of the 15thC parish church is the finest in Kent. Fine antiques centre.

UCKFIELD, EAST SUSSEX - Once a medieval market town and centre of the iron industry, Uckfield is now a busy country town on the edge of the Ashdown Forest.

WALTON-ON-THAMES, SURREY - Busy town beside the Thames, retaining a distinctive atmosphere despite being only 12 miles from central London. Close to Hampton Court Palace, Sandown Park racecourse and Claremont Landscape Garden (National Trust), Esher.

• **WEST CLANDON, SURREY** - Home of the Clandon Park (National Trust), the Palladian mansion built in the early 1730s and home of the Queen's Royal Surrey Regiment Museum.

• **WHITSTABLE, KENT** - Seaside resort and yachting centre on Kent's north shore. The beach is shingle, and there are the usual seaside amenities and entertainments and a museum.

• **WOKING, SURREY** - One of the largest towns in Surrey which developed with the coming of the railway in the 1830s. Old Woking was a market town in the 17thC and still retains several interesting buildings. Large arts and entertainment centre.

• **WORTHING, WEST SUSSEX** - Town in the West Sussex countryside and by the south coast, with excellent shopping and many pavement cafes and restaurants. Attractions include the award-winning Museum and Art Gallery, beautiful gardens, pier, elegant townhouses, Cissbury Ring hill fort and the South Downs.

• **WYE, KENT** - Well known for its agricultural and horticultural college. The Olantigh Tower, with its imposing front portico, is used as a setting for part of the Stour Music Festival held annually in June.

Campus Accommodation

ETC has a separate rating scheme of One to Five Stars for Campus Accommodation which includes educational establishments such as universities and colleges with sleeping accommodation in halls of residence or student village complexes available for individuals, families and groups. Availability is mainly during the academic vacation during the summer from June to September, Easter and some Christmas availability. Some universities provide accommodation throughout the year and there is often a wide choice of recreational facilities, with most venues providing TV rooms, bars and restaurants and a variety of sporting and special interest holidays.

Establishments meet a minimum requirement for both the provision of facilities and services, including fixtures, fittings, furnishings, décor. Progressively higher levels of quality and customer care are provided for each of the Star ratings. Quite simply, the more Stars, the higher the overall level of quality you can expect.

What standards to expect at each rating level:

*	Acceptable
**	Good
***	Very Good
****	Excellent
*****	Exceptional

This Campus rating scheme was introduced during 2002. At time of going to press it has only been possible to include the full entries on the next page.

In addition to the symbols shown inside the back cover flap, the following also appear:

Non smokers only	Cycle hire	Regular evening entertainment
Foodshop on site	Business facilities	Spa bath/jacuzzi
Laundrette	Public telephone	Vegetarians catered for
Cooking facilities	Children's play area	Solarium

HATFIELD, Hertfordshire Map ref 2D1 *Tourist Information Centre Tel: (01727) 864511*

★★

UNIVERSITY OF HERTFORDSHIRE

Fielder Centre,
Hatfield Avenue, Hatfield, AL10 9FL
T: (01707) 284841 F: (01707) 268407
E: sales@fieldercentre.co.uk
I: www.fieldercentre.co.uk

Excellent value for money residential accommodation. 4-6 bedroom student flats share a large kitchen, two showers and three w.c.s; single bedrooms contain a wash handbasin. Conference and sports facilities on site. Available for groups, conferences and B&B in June-September. Self catering houses for 6 and traditional halls of residence for group bookings also available.

P

Bedrooms: 350 singles, 196 halls, 14 houses
Total no. of beds: 630
Max group size: 200

Special rates for groups

Meals: Breakfast, lunch & evening meals available
Payment: Visa, Delta, Switch, Mastercard

Per person per night
Bed only £24.00
B&B £29.00

Groups POA

Self-catering per person per week
£90.00

OPEN
June 16 - Sept 14

OXFORD, Oxfordshire Map ref 2C3 *Tourist Information Centre Tel: (01865) 726 871*

Rating Applied For

ST HUGH'S COLLEGE

Rachel Trickett Building
St Margarets Road
Oxford, OX2 6LE
T: (01865) 274921 F: (01865) 274912
E: conferences@st-hughs.ox.ac.uk

Bedrooms: 60 singles
Total no. of beds: 60
Bathrooms: 60 ensuite

Meals: Breakfast available
Payment: Mastercard, Visa, Switch, Travellers Cheques

Per person per night
B&B £47.00

OPEN
Mar - Apr
July - Sept

Erected in 1992, the building boasts full ensuite accommodation with shower, toilet and wash-hand basin in 60 single study bedrooms.

P 12

READING, Berkshire Map ref 2C2 *Tourist Information Centre Tel: (0118) 956 6226*

★★★★

READING STUDENT VILLAGE

Sherfield Drive,
Reading, RG2 7EZ
T: 0870 712 5003 F: 020 701 78273
E: sjennie.bellotto@jarvis-uk.com
I: www.thestudentvillage.com

Just one mile from the heart of Reading, the village is a completely modern complex in landscaped surrounds. Facilities include a cafe, launderette and limited parking. The ensuite rooms are newly finished to a high standard and each flat contains its own fully equipped kitchen. Groups, familes and individuals welcome.

P

Bedrooms: 240 singles, 8 doubles
Total no. of beds: 256
Bathrooms: 256 ensuite

Special rates for students, groups and longer term stayers

Meals: Breakfast, lunch & evening meals available
Payment: Visa, Delta, Switch, Vectron, Mastercard, JCB and Maestro

Per person per night
Bed only
£26.00-£38.00

OPEN
July 25 - Sept 20

English Tourism Council assessed Accommodation

On the following pages you will find an exclusive listing of all Guest Accommodation in England that has been assessed for quality by the English Tourism Council.

Campus Accommodation is listed separately at the end of this section.

The information includes brief contact details for each place to stay, together with its Diamond rating, and quality award if appropriate. The listing also shows if an establishment has a National Accessible rating (see the front of the guide for further information).

More detailed information on all the places shown in blue can be found in the regional sections (where establishments have paid to have their details included). To find these entries please refer to the appropriate regional section, or look in the town index at the back of this guide.

The list which follows was compiled slightly later than the regional sections. For this reason you may find that, in a few instances, a Diamond rating and quality award may differ between the two sections. This list contains the most up-to-date information and was correct at the time of going to press.

LONDON

INNER LONDON

E4

Aucklands
◆◆◆◆ SILVER AWARD
25 Eglington Road, North Chingford, London E4 7AN
T: (020) 8529 1140
F: (020) 8529 9288
E: drumandhelen@amserve.net

Ridgeway Hotel Limited ◆◆◆
115-117 The Ridgeway LTD, North Chingford, London E4 6QU
T: (020) 8529 1964
F: (020) 8542 9130

E7

Forest View Hotel ◆
227 Romford Road, Forest Gate, London E7 9HL
T: (020) 8534 4844
F: (020) 8534 8959
I: www.forestviewhotel.net

E15

Park Hotel ◆◆
81 Portway, Stratford, London E15 3QJ
T: (020) 8257 9034
F: (020) 8279 8094

N1

Kandara Guest House ◆◆◆
68 Ockendon Road, Islington, London N1 3NW
T: (020) 7226 5721
F: (020) 7226 3379
E: admin@kandara.co.uk
I: www.kandara.co.uk

N4

Costello Palace Hotel ◆◆
374 Seven Sisters Road, Finsbury Park, London N4 2PG
T: (020) 8802 6551
F: (020) 8802 9461
E: costellopalacehotel@ukonline.co.uk
I: www.costellopalacehotel.co.uk

Spring Park Hotel ◆◆
400 Seven Sisters Road, London N4 2LX
T: (020) 8800 6030
F: (020) 8802 5652
E: sphotel400@aol.com
I: www.springparkhotel.co.uk

N7

Europa Hotel ◆◆◆
60-62 Anson Road, London N7 0AA
T: (020) 7607 5935
F: (020) 7607 5909

Five Kings Guest House ◆◆
59 Anson Road, Tufnell Park, London N7 0AR
T: (020) 7607 3996
F: (020) 7609 5554
I: www.hotelregister.co.uk/hotel/fivekings.asp

Queens Hotel ◆◆
33 Anson Road, Tufnell Park, London N7 0RB
T: (020) 7607 4725
F: (020) 7697 9725
E: queens@stavrouhotels.co.uk

N8

White Lodge Hotel ◆◆◆
1 Church Lane, Hornsey, London N8 7BU
T: (020) 8348 9765
F: (020) 8340 7851

N10

The Muswell Hill Hotel ◆◆◆
73 Muswell Hill Road, Muswell Hill, London N10 3HT
T: (020) 8883 6447
F: (020) 8883 5158
E: reception@muswellhillhotel.co.uk
I: www.muswellhillhotel.co.uk

N20

The Corner Lodge ◆◆◆◆
9 Athenaeum Road, Whetstone, London N20 9AA
T: (020) 8446 3720
F: (020) 8446 3720

N22

Pane Residence ◆◆
154 Boundary Road, Wood Green, London N22 6AE
T: (020) 8889 3735

NW1

Americana Hotel ◆◆◆
172 Gloucester Place, Regent's Park, London NW1 6DS
T: (020) 7723 1452
F: (020) 7723 4641
E: manager@americanahotel.demon.co.uk
I: www.americanahotel.activehotels.com

NW3

Dillons Hotel ◆◆
21 Belsize Park, Hampstead, London NW3 4DU
T: (020) 7794 3360
F: (020) 7431 7900
E: desk@dillonshotel.com
I: www.dillonshotel.com

NW6

Cavendish Guest House ◆◆◆◆
24 Cavendish Road, London NW6 7XP
T: (020) 8451 3249
F: (020) 8451 3249

Dawson House Hotel ◆◆◆◆
72 Canfield Gardens, London NW6 3ED
T: (020) 7624 0079
F: (020) 7644 6321
E: dawsonhtl@aol.com
I: www.dawsonhouse.com

NW10

Aran Guest House ◆◆
21 Holland Road, Kensal Green, London NW10 5AH
T: (020) 8968 6402

J and T Guest House ◆◆◆
98 Park Avenue North, Willesden Green, London NW10 1JY
T: (020) 8452 4085
F: (020) 8450 2503
E: jandthome@aol.com
I: www.jandtguesthouses.com

NW11

Anchor-Nova Hotel ◆◆◆
10 West Heath Drive, Golders Green, London NW11 7QH
T: (020) 8458 8764
F: (020) 8455 3204
E: enquir@anchor-hotel.co.uk
I: www.anchor-hotel.co.uk

SE3

64 Beaconsfield Road ◆◆
Blackheath, London SE3 7LG
T: (020) 8858 1685

The Grovers ◆◆◆
96 Merriman Road, London SE3 8RZ
T: (020) 8488 7719
F: (020) 8488 7719

Hill Crest Guesthouse ◆◆
2 Hardy Road, Blackheath, London SE3 7NR
T: (020) 8305 0120
F: (020) 8305 0120
E: hillcrest@dial.pipex.com
I: ds.dial.pipex.com/town/drive/xsd11/

59a Lee Road ◆◆
Blackheath, London SE3 9EN
T: (020) 8318 7244
E: angecall@blackheath318.freeserve.co.uk

59 Lee Terrace ◆◆
Blackheath, London SE3 9TA
T: (020) 8852 6334
E: susan.bedbreakfast@virgin.net

Mrs Dove's ◆◆
68 Wricklemarsh Road, Blackheath, London SE3 8DS
T: (020) 8856 1331
F: (020) 8480 6653
E: mrsdove@cwcom.net
I: www.mrsdove.co.uk

Number Nine Blackheath Limited ◆◆◆◆
9 Charlton Road, Blackheath, London SE3 7EU
T: (020) 8858 4175
F: (020) 8858 4175
E: derek@numbernineblackheath.com
I: www.numbernineblackheath.com

3 Tilbrook Road ◆◆
3 Tilbrook Road, Kidbrooke, London SE3 9QD
T: (020) 8319 8843

SE4

Crofton Park Holdenby ◆◆
28 Holdenby Road, Crofton Park, London SE4 2DA
T: (020) 8694 0011
E: savitri.gaines@totalise.co.uk

66 Geoffrey Road ◆◆
London SE4 1NT
T: (020) 8691 3887
F: (020) 8691 3887
E: andrea.dechamps@btclick.com

SE6

The Heathers ◆◆◆
71 Verdant Lane, Catford, London SE6 1JD
T: (020) 8698 8340
F: (020) 8461 3980
E: berylheath@yahoo.co.uk
I: http://theheathersbb.com

Thornsbeach ◆◆◆
122 Bargery Road, Catford, London SE6 2LR
T: (020) 8695 6544
F: (020) 8695 9577
E: helen@thornsbeach.co.uk
I: www.thornsbeach.co.uk

Tulip Tree House ◆◆◆
41 Minard Road, Catford, London SE6 1NP
T: (020) 8697 2596
F: (020) 8698 2020

SE7

Old Rectory Guest House ◆◆◆
80 Maryon Road, London SE7 8DL
T: (020) 8317 9694

SE8

M B Guest House ◆◆
7 Bolden Street, Deptford, London SE8 4JF
T: (020) 8692 7030
F: (020) 8691 6241

SE9

Abigail House ◆◆◆
68 Dunvegan Road, Eltham, London SE9 1SB
T: (020) 8859 3924

Benvenuti ◆◆◆◆
217 Court Road, Eltham, London SE9 4TG
T: (020) 8857 4855
F: (020) 8265 5635
E: val-alan@benvenuti-guesthouse.co.uk
I: www.benvenuti-guesthouse.co.uk

Boru House ◆◆
70 Dunevegan Road, Eltham, London SE9 1SB
T: (020) 8850 0584

80 Rennets Wood Road ◆◆◆
Eltham, London SE9 2NH
T: (020) 8850 1829

Weston House ◆
8 Eltham Green, Eltham, London SE9 5LB
T: (020) 8850 5191
F: (020) 8850 0030
E: reservation@westonhousehotel.co.uk
I: www.westonhousehotel.co.uk

SE10

The Corner House ◆◆◆
28 Royal Hill, Greenwich, London SE10 8RT
T: (020) 8692 3023
F: (020) 8692 3023
E: joannacourtney@aol.com

Greenwich Parkhouse Hotel
◆◆
1-2 Nevada Street, Greenwich, London SE10 9JL
T: (020) 8305 1478
E: B&B@greenwich-parkhouse-hotel.co.uk
I: www.greenwich-parkhouse-hotel.co.uk

81 Greenwich South Street
◆◆◆◆ SILVER AWARD
London SE10 8NT
T: (020) 8293 3121
E: matilda.wade@btopenworld.com

Mitre Inn ◆◆◆
291 Greenwich High Road, London SE10 8NA
T: (020) 8355 6760
F: (020) 8355 6761

16 St Alfeges
Rating Applied For
16 St Alfege Passage, Greenwich, London SE10 9JS
T: (020) 8853 4337
E: nicmesure@yahoo.co.uk
I: www.st-alfeges.co.uk

White Swan Hotel ◆◆
13 Blackheath Road, Greenwich, London SE10 8PE
T: (020) 8692 8855

SE13

Manna House ◆◆◆
320 Hither Green Lane, Lewisham, London SE13 6TS
T: (020) 8461 5984
F: (020) 8695 5316
E: mannahouse@aol.com
I: members.aol.com/mannahouse

13 Wellmeadow Road ◆◆◆
Hither Green, London SE13 6SY
T: (020) 8697 1398
F: (020) 8697 1398

8 Yeats Close ◆◆
Eliot Park, London SE13 7ET
T: (020) 8318 3421
F: (020) 8318 3421
E: pathu@tesco.net

SE18

268 Shooters Hill Road ◆
Blackheath, London SE18 4LX
T: (020) 8319 2699

SE20

Melrose House ◆◆◆◆
89 Lennard Road, London SE20 7LY
T: (020) 8776 8884
F: (020) 8325 7636
E: melrose.hotel@virgin.net
I: www.guesthouseaccommodation.co.uk

SE22

Shepherd's London ◆◆◆◆
39 Marmora Road, London SE22 0RX
T: (020) 8693 4355
F: (020) 8693 7954
E: dulwichdragon@hotmail.com
I: www.shepherdslondon.co.uk

SW1

Airways Hotel, London ◆◆
29-31 St George's Drive, Victoria, London SW1V 4DG
T: (020) 7834 0205
F: (020) 7932 0007
E: sales@airways-hotel.com
I: www.airways-hotel.com

Blair Victoria Hotel ◆◆
78-84 Warwick Way, London SW1V 1RZ
T: (020) 7828 8603
F: (020) 7976 6536
E: sales@blairvictoria.com
I: www.blairvictoria.com

Carlton Hotel ◆◆
90 Belgrave Road, Victoria, London SW1V 2BJ
T: (020) 7976 6634
F: (020) 7821 8020
E: info@cityhotelcarlton.co.uk
I: www.cityhotelcarlton.co.uk

Caswell Hotel ◆◆
25 Gloucester Street, London SW1V 2DB
T: (020) 7834 6345
E: manager@hotellondon.co.uk
I: www.hotellondon.co.uk

Central House Hotel ◆◆
39 Belgrave Road, London SW1V 2BB
T: (020) 7834 8036
F: (020) 7834 1854
E: info@centralhousehotel.co.uk
I: www.centralhousehotel.co.uk

Colliers Hotel ◆
97 Warwick Way, London SW1V 1QL
T: (020) 7834 6931
F: (020) 7834 8439
E: cmahotel@aol.com
I: www.affordablehotel.com

Collin House ◆◆◆
104 Ebury Street, London SW1W 9QD
T: (020) 7730 8031
F: (020) 7730 8031
E: booking@collinhouse.co.uk
I: www.collinhouse.co.uk

Dover Hotel ◆◆
44 Belgrave Road, London SW1V 1RG
T: (020) 7821 9085
F: (020) 7834 6425
E: reception@dover-hotel.co.uk
I: www.dover-hotel.co.uk

Elizabeth Hotel ◆◆◆
37 Eccleston Square, Victoria, London SW1V 1PB
T: (020) 7828 6812
F: (020) 7828 6814
E: info@elizabethhotel.com
I: www.elizabethhotel.com

Georgian House Hotel ◆◆
35-39 St George's Drive, London SW1V 4DG
T: (020) 7834 1438
F: (020) 7976 6085
E: reception@georgianhousehotel.co.uk
I: www.georgianhousehotel.co.uk

Hanover Hotel ◆◆◆
30-32 St George's Drive, London SW1V 4BN
T: (020) 7834 0367
F: (020) 7976 5587
E: reservations@hanoverhotel.co.uk
I: www.hanoverhotel.co.uk

Huttons Hotel ◆
55 Belgrave Road, London SW1V 2BB
T: (020) 7834 3726
F: (020) 7834 3389
E: reservations@huttons-hotel.co.uk
I: www.huttons-hotel.co.uk

Knightsbridge Green Hotel
◆◆◆◆
159 Knightsbridge, London SW1X 7PD
T: (020) 7584 6274
F: (020) 7225 1635
E: thekghotel@aol.com
I: www.thekghotel.co.uk

Luna-Simone Hotel ◆◆
47 Belgrave Road, London SW1V 2BB
T: (020) 7834 5897
F: (020) 7828 2474
E: lunasimone@talk21.com
I: www.lunasimone.com

Melita House Hotel ◆◆◆
35 Charlwood Street, Victoria, London SW1V 2DU
T: (020) 7828 0471
F: (020) 7932 0988
E: reserve@melitahotel.com
I: www.melitahotel.com

Oxford House Hotel ◆◆
92 Cambridge Street, Victoria, London SW1V 4QG
T: (020) 7834 6467
F: (020) 7834 0225
E: oxfordhousehotel@hotmail.com

Stanley House Hotel ◆◆
19-21 Belgrave Road, Victoria, London SW1V 1RB
T: (020) 7834 5042
F: (020) 7834 8439
E: cmahotel@aol.com
I: www.londonbudgethotels.co.uk

Vandon House Hotel ◆◆◆
1 Vandon Street, London SW1H 0AH
T: (020) 7799 6780
F: (020) 7799 1464
E: info@vandonhouse.com
I: www.vandonhouse.com

Victor Hotel ◆◆◆
51 Belgrave Road, London SW1V 2BB
T: (020) 7592 9853
F: (020) 7592 9854
I: www.victorhotel.co.uk

The Victoria Inn London ◆◆◆
65-67 Belgrave Road, London SW1V 2BG
T: (020) 7834 6721
F: (020) 7931 0201
E: welcome@victoriainn.co.uk
I: www.victoriainn.co.uk

Windermere Hotel
◆◆◆◆ SILVER AWARD
142-144 Warwick Way, Victoria, London SW1V 4JE
T: (020) 7834 5163
F: (020) 7630 8831
E: reservations@windermere-hotel.co.uk
I: www.windermere-hotel.co.uk

SW5

The Albany Hotel ◆◆◆
4-12 Barkston Gardens, London SW5 0EN
T: (020) 7370 6116
F: (020) 7244 8024

The Ambassadors Hotel X
◆◆◆
16 Collingham Road, London SW5 0LX
T: (020) 7373 1075
F: (020) 7244 8375

Beaver Hotel ◆◆◆
57-59 Philbeach Gardens, London SW5 9ED
T: (020) 7373 4553
F: (020) 7373 4555
E: hotelbeaver@hotmail.com
I: www.beaverhotel.co.uk

Comfort Inn Earl's Court ◆◆
11-13 Penywern Road, Earl's Court, London SW5 9TT
T: (020) 7373 6514
F: (020) 7370 3639
E: info@comfortinnearlscourt.co.uk
I: www.comfortinnearlscourt.co.uk

Hotel Earls Court ◆◆
28 Warwick Road, Earls Court, London SW5 9UD
T: (020) 7373 7079
F: (020) 7912 0582
E: res@hotelearlscourt.com
I: www.hotelearlscourt.com

Kensington Court Hotel ◆◆◆
33 Nevern Place, London SW5 9NP
T: (020) 7370 5151
F: (020) 7370 3499
E: kensington_court_hotel@visit.uk.com
I: www.visit.uk.com

Kensington International Inn
◆◆◆
4 Templeton Place, London SW5 9LZ
T: (020) 7370 4333
F: (020) 7244 7873
E: hotel@kensingtoninternationalinn.com
I: www.kensingtoninternationalinn.com

London Town Hotel ◆◆◆
15 Penywern Road, Earl's Court, London SW5 9TT
T: (020) 7370 4356
F: (020) 7370 7923
E: londontownhotel@tiscali.co.uk
I: www.londontownhotel.com

Lord Jim Hotel ◆◆
23-25 Penywern Road, London SW5 9TT
T: (020) 7370 6071
F: (020) 7373 8919
E: ljh@lgh-hotels.com
I: www.lgh-hotels.com

Lord Kensington Hotel ♦♦♦
38 Trebovir Road, Earls Court, London SW5 9NJ
T: (0207) 373 7331
F: (0207) 460 3524
E: lkh@lgh-hotels.com
I: www.lgh-hotels.com

Maranton House Hotel ♦♦♦
14 Barkston Gardens, Earls Court, London SW5 0EN
T: (020) 7373 5782
F: (020) 7244 9543
E: marantonhotel@hotmail.com

Mayflower Hotel ♦♦
26-28 Trebovir Road, Earls Court, London SW5 9NJ
T: (020) 7370 0991
F: (020) 7370 0994
E: mayfhotel@aol.com
I: www.mayflower-group.co.uk

Merlyn Court Hotel ♦♦
2 Barkston Gardens, London SW5 0EN
T: (020) 7370 1640
F: (020) 7370 4986
E: london@merlyncourt.demon.co.uk
I: www.merlyncourthotel.com

Mowbray Court Hotel ♦♦
28-32 Penywern Road, Earl's Court, London SW5 9SU
T: (020) 7370 2316
F: (020) 7370 5693
E: mowbraycrthot@hotmail.com
I: www.m-c-hotel.mcmail.com

Hotel Oliver ♦♦
198 Cromwell Road, London SW5 0SN
T: (020) 7370 6881
F: (020) 7370 6556
E: reservations@hoteloliver.freeserve.co.uk
I: www.hoteloliver.co.uk

Oliver Plaza Hotel ♦♦
33 Trebovir Road, Earl's Court, London SW5 9NF
T: (020) 7373 7183
F: (020) 7244 6021
E: oliverplaza@capricornhotels.co.uk
I: www.capricornhotels.co.uk

Hotel Plaza Continental ♦♦♦
9 Knaresborough Place, Earls Court, London SW5 0TP
T: (020) 7370 3246
F: (020) 7373 9571
E: hpc@lgh-hotels.com
I: www.lgh-hotels.com

Ramsees Hotel ♦♦
32-36 Hogarth Road, Earl's Court, London SW5 0PU
T: (020) 7370 1445
F: (020) 7244 6835
E: ramsees@rasool.demon.co.uk
I: www.ramseeshotel.com

Rasool Court Hotel ♦♦
19-21 Penywern Road, Earl's Court, London SW5 9TT
T: (020) 7373 8900
F: (020) 7244 6835
E: rasool@rasool.demon.co.uk
I: www.rasoolcourthotel.com

Swiss House Hotel ♦♦♦
171 Old Brompton Road, London SW5 0AN
T: (020) 7373 2769
F: (020) 7373 4983
E: recep@swiss-hh.demon.co.uk
I: www.swiss-hh.demon.co.uk

Windsor House ♦
12 Penywern Road, London SW5 9ST
T: (020) 7373 9087
F: (020) 7385 2417
E: bookings@windsor-house-hotel.com
I: www.windsor-house-hotel.com

SW7

Aster House
♦♦♦♦♦ SILVER AWARD
3 Sumner Place, London SW7 3EE
T: (020) 7581 5888
F: (020) 7584 4925
E: AsterHouse@btinternet.com
I: www.AsterHouse.com

Five Sumner Place Hotel ♦♦♦♦
5 Sumner Place, South Kensington, London SW7 3EE
T: (020) 7584 7586
F: (020) 7823 9962
E: reservations@sumnerplace.com
I: www.sumnerplace.com

Hotel Number Sixteen ♦♦♦♦♦
16 Sumner Place, London SW7 3EG
T: (020) 7589 5232
F: (020) 7584 8615
E: reservations@numbersixteenhotel.co.uk
I: www.numbersixteenhotel.co.uk

SW8

Comfort Inn London ♦♦♦♦
87 South Lambeth Road, Vauxhall, London SW8 1RN
T: (020) 7735 9494
F: (020) 7735 1001
E: stay@comfortinnvx.co.uk
I: www.comfortinnvx.co.uk

SW11

Lavender Guest House ♦♦♦
18 Lavender Sweep, London SW11 1HA
T: (020) 7585 2767
F: (020) 7924 6274

SW14

106 East Sheen Avenue ♦♦♦
London SW14 8AU
T: (020) 8255 1900
F: (020) 8876 8084
E: rpratt@easynet.co.uk

The Plough Inn ♦♦♦
42 Christchurch Road, East Sheen, London SW14 7AF
T: (020) 8876 7833
F: (020) 8392 8801
E: ploughthe@hotmail.com

The Victoria ♦♦♦
10 West Temple Sheen, London SW14 7RT
T: (020) 8876 4238
F: (020) 8878 3464
E: mark@thevictoria.net
I: www.thevictoria.net

SW16

The Konyots ♦
95 Pollards Hill South, London SW16 4LS
T: (020) 8764 0075

SW18

The Brewers Inn ♦♦♦
147 East Hill, Wandsworth, London SW18 2QB
T: (020) 8874 4128
F: (020) 8877 1953
E: brewersinn@youngs.co.uk
I: www.youngs.co.uk

2 Melrose Road ♦♦♦
London SW18 1NE
T: (020) 8871 3259

SW19

Trochee Hotel ♦♦
21 Malcolm Road, Wimbledon, London SW19 4AS
T: (020) 8946 3924
F: (020) 8946 1579
E: info@trocheehotel.co.uk
I: www.trocheehotel.co.uk

Trochee Hotel Annexe ♦♦
52 Ridgway Place, Wimbledon, London SW19 4SW
T: (020) 8946 9425
F: (020) 8946 1579
E: info@trocheehotel.co.uk

W1

Bentinck House Hotel ♦♦
20 Bentinck Street, London W1U 2EU
T: (020) 7935 9141
F: (020) 7224 5903
E: b.hh@virgin.net

Blandford Hotel ♦♦♦
80 Chiltern Street, London W1U 5AF
T: (020) 7486 3103
F: (020) 7487 2786
E: blandfordhotel@dial.pipex.com
I: www.capricornhotels.co.uk

The Edward Lear Hotel ♦♦
30 Seymour Street, Marble Arch, London W1H 7JB
T: (020) 7402 5401
F: (020) 7706 3766
E: edwardlear@aol.com
I: www.edlear.com

Hallam Hotel ♦♦♦
12 Hallam Street, Portland Place, London W1W 6JF
T: (020) 7580 1166
F: (020) 7323 4527

Lincoln House Hotel - Central London♦♦
33 Gloucester Place, Marble Arch, London W1U 8HY
T: (020) 7486 7630
F: (020) 7486 0166
E: reservations@lincoln-house-hotel.co.uk
I: www.lincoln-house-hotel.co.uk

Marble Arch Inn ♦♦
49-50 Upper Berkeley Street, Marble Arch, London W1H 5QR
T: (020) 7723 7888
F: (020) 7723 6060
E: sales@marblearch-inn.co.uk
I: www.marblearch-inn.co.uk

Hotel La Place ♦♦♦
17 Nottingham Place, London W1V 5LG
T: (020) 7486 2323
F: (020) 7486 4335
E: reservations@hotellaplace.com
I: www.hotellaplace.com

St.George Hotel ♦♦♦♦
49 Gloucester Place, London W1H 3PE
T: (020) 7486 8586
F: (020) 7486 6567
E: reservations@stgeorge-hotel.net
I: www.stgeorge-hotel.net

Ten Manchester Street ♦♦♦♦
10 Manchester Street, London W1U 4DG
T: (020) 7486 6669
F: (020) 7224 0348
E: stay@10manchesterstreet.fsnet.co.uk
I: www.10manchesterstreet.com

Wigmore Court Hotel ♦♦♦
23 Gloucester Place, Portman Square, London W1U 8HS
T: (020) 7935 0928
F: (020) 7487 4254
E: info@wigmore-court-hotel.co.uk
I: www.wigmore-court-hotel.co.uk

Wyndham Hotel ♦♦♦
30 Wyndham Street, London W1H 1EB
T: (020) 7723 7204
F: (020) 7724 2893
E: wyndhamhotel@talk21.com
I: www.lhghotels.co.uk

W2

Abbey Court & Westpoint Hotel ♦♦
170-174 Sussex Gardens, London W2 1TP
T: (020) 7402 0281
F: (020) 7224 9114
E: info@abbeycourt.com
I: www.abbeycourt.com

Admiral Hotel ♦♦
143 Sussex Gardens, Hyde Park, London W2 2RY
T: (020) 7723 7309
F: (020) 7723 8731
E: frank@admiral143.demon.co.uk
I: www.admiral-hotel.com

Allandale Hotel ♦♦
3 Devonshire Terrace, Lancaster Gate, London W2 3DN
T: (020) 7723 8311
F: (020) 7723 8311
E: info@allandalehotel.co.uk
I: www.allandalehotel.co.uk

Apollo Hotel ♦♦♦
64 Queensborough Terrace, London W2 3SH
T: (020) 7727 3066
F: (020) 7727 2800
E: apollohotel@btinternet.com
I: www.hotelapollo.com

Ashley Hotel ♦♦
15 Norfolk Square, London W2 1RU
T: (020) 7723 3375
F: (020) 7723 0173
E: ashhot@btinternet.com
I: www.ashleyhotels.com

Athena Hotel ◆◆◆
110-114 Sussex Gardens,
London W2 1UA
T: (020) 7706 3866
F: (020) 7262 6143
E: athena@stavrouhotels.co.uk
I: www.stavrouhotels.co.uk

Barry House Hotel ◆◆
12 Sussex Place, London W2 2TP
T: (020) 7723 7340
F: (020) 7723 9775
E: hotel@barryhouse.co.uk
I: www.barryhouse.co.uk

The Brunel Hotel ◆◆◆
78-81 Gloucester Terrace,
Bayswater, London W2 3HB
T: (020) 7262 4481
F: (020) 7706 3611
E: brunel.hotel@visit.uk.com
I: www.visit.uk.com

Caring Hotel ◆◆
24 Craven Hill Gardens, London
W2 3EA
T: (020) 7262 8708
F: (020) 7262 8590
E: caring@lineone.net
I: www.caringhotel.co.uk

Crownwall Hotel ◆◆
10/11 Craven Terrace, Hyde Park,
London W2 3QD
T: (020) 7262 9977
F: (020) 7262 5542
E: info@crownwallhotel.com
I: www.crownwallhotel.com

Dylan Hotel ◆◆
14 Devonshire Terrace, Lancaster
Gate, London W2 3DW
T: (020) 7723 3280
F: (020) 7402 2443
E: booking@dylan-hotel.com
I: www.dylan-hotel.com

Euro-UK Investments Ltd T/As Tria Hotel◆◆
35-37 St Stephens Gardens,
London W2 5NA
T: (020) 7221 0450
F: (020) 7229 6717

Europa House Hotel ◆◆
151 Sussex Gardens, London
W2 2RY
T: (020) 7723 7343
F: (020) 7224 9331
E: europahouse@enterprise.net
I: www.europahousehotel.com

Gower Hotel ◆◆
129 Sussex Gardens, Hyde Park,
London W2 2RX
T: (020) 7262 2262
F: (020) 7262 2006
E: gower@stavrouhotels.co.uk
I: www.stavrouhotels.co.uk

Hyde Park House ◆
48 St Petersburgh Place,
Queensway, London W2 4LD
T: (020) 7229 9652

Hyde Park Radnor Hotel ◆◆◆◆
7-9 Sussex Place, Paddington,
London W2 2SX
T: (020) 7723 5969
F: (020) 7262 8955
I: www.hydeparkradnor.com

Hyde Park Rooms Hotel ◆
137 Sussex Gardens, Hyde Park,
London W2 2RX
T: (020) 7723 0225

Kensington Gardens Hotel ◆◆◆
9 Kensington Gardens Square,
Bayswater, London W2 4BH
T: (020) 7221 7790
F: (020) 7792 8612
E: info@kensingtongardenshotel.co.uk
I: www.kensingtongardenshotel.co.uk

Kings Arms Hotel ◆◆
254 Edgware Road, Paddington,
London W2 1DS
T: (020) 7262 8441
F: (020) 7258 0556
E: kingsarmshotel@compuserve.com

Kingsway Hotel ◆◆
27 Norfolk Square, Hyde Park,
London W2 1RX
T: (020) 7723 5569
F: (020) 7723 7317
E: kingswayhotel@hotmail.com
I: www.kingswayhotel.net

Kingsway Park Hotel Hyde Park ◆◆◆
139 Sussex Gardens, Hyde Park,
London W2 2RX
T: (020) 7723 5677
F: (020) 7402 4352
E: kingswaypark@hotmail.com
I: www.kingswaypark-hotel.com

Kyriad Princes Square Hotel ◆◆◆◆
23-25 Princes Square, Off
Ilchester Gardens, London
W2 4NJ
T: (020) 7229 9876
F: (020) 7229 4664
E: info@princessquarehotel.co.uk
I: www.princessquarehotel.co.uk

London Guards Hotel ◆◆◆
36-37 Lancaster Gate, London
W2 3NA
T: (020) 7402 1101
F: (020) 7262 2551
E: info@londonguardshotel.co.uk
I: www.londonguardshotel.co.uk

Manor Court Hotel ◆
7 Clanricarde Gardens, London
W2 4JJ
T: (020) 7727 5407
F: (020) 7229 2875

Oxford Hotel ◆◆◆
13-14 Craven Terrace,
Paddington, London W2 3QD
T: (020) 7402 6860
F: (020) 7262 7574
E: info@oxfordhotellondon.co.uk
I: www.oxfordhotellondon.co.uk

Park Lodge Hotel ◆◆◆
73 Queensborough Terrace,
Bayswater, London W2 3SU
T: (020) 7229 6424
F: (020) 7221 4772
E: info@hotelparklodge.com
I: www.hotelparklodge.com

Parkwood Hotel ◆◆
4 Stanhope Place, London
W2 2HB
T: (020) 7402 2241
F: (020) 7402 1574
E: pkwdhotel@aol.com
I: www.parkwoodhotel.com

Pembridge Palace Hotel ◆◆◆
52-57 Prince's Square, London
W2 4PX
T: (020) 7229 6262
F: (020) 7792 3868
E: london@pembridgehotel.co.uk
I: www.pembridgehotel.co.uk

The Piccolino Hotel ◆◆◆
14 Sussex Place, London W2 2TP
T: (020) 7402 4439
F: (020) 7402 4439
E: nick@piccolino.fsnet.co.uk

Prince William Hotel ◆◆◆
42-44 Gloucester Terrace,
London W2 3DA
T: (020) 7724 7414
F: (020) 7706 2411
E: info@princewilliamhotel.co.uk
I: www.princewilliamhotel.co.uk

Reem Hotel ◆◆◆
50-51 Princes Square,
Bayswater, London W2 4PX
T: (0207) 2438516
F: (0207) 2296821
E: reem_hotel@visit.uk.com
I: www.visit.uk.com

Rhodes House Hotel ◆◆◆
195 Sussex Gardens, London
W2 2RJ
T: (020) 7262 5617
F: (020) 7723 4054
E: chris@rhodeshotel.com
I: www.rhodeshotel.com

Rose Court Hotel ◆◆◆
1-3 Talbot Square, London
W2 1TR
T: (020) 7723 5128
F: (020) 7723 1855
E: rosehotel@aol.com
I: www.rosecourthotel.com

St David's and Norfolk Court Hotel ◆◆
16 Norfolk Square, Hyde Park,
London W2 1RS
T: (020) 7723 3856
F: (020) 7402 9061
E: info@stdavidshotels.com
I: www.stdavidshotels.com

Springfield Hotel ◆◆
154 Sussex Gardens, London
W2 1UD
T: (020) 7723 9898
F: (020) 7723 0874
E: info@springfieldhotellondon.co.uk
I: www.springfieldhotellondon.co.uk

Westland Hotel ◆◆◆◆
154 Bayswater Road, London
W2 4HP
T: (020) 7229 9191
F: (020) 7727 1054
E: reservations@westlandhotel.co.uk
I: www.westlandhotel.co.uk

W4

Chiswick Guest House ◆◆◆
40 Spencer Road, Chiswick,
London W4 3SP
T: (0208) 994 0876
E: bdoneill159@aol.com

Chiswick Lodge ◆◆◆
104 Turnham Green Terrace,
London W4 1QN
T: (020) 8994 9926
F: (020) 8742 8238
E: chishot@clara.net
I: www.chiswick-hotel.co.uk

Foubert's Hotel ◆◆
162-166 Chiswick High Road,
London W4 1PR
T: (020) 8994 5202

Ivy Gate House ◆◆
6 Temple Road, Chiswick,
London W4 5NW
T: (020) 8994 8618
E: thejones@ivygatehouse.co.uk
I: www.ivygatehouse.co.uk

W5

Abbey Lodge Hotel ◆◆
51 Grange Park, Ealing, London
W5 3PR
T: (020) 8567 7914
F: (020) 8579 5350
E: enquiries@londonlodgehotels.com
I: www.londonlodgehotels.com

Creffield Lodge c/o RJ London West ◆◆
2-4 Creffield Road, Ealing,
London W5 3HN
T: (020) 8993 2284
F: (020) 8992 7082
E: jiealing.rs@jarvis.co.uk

Grange Lodge Hotel ◆◆◆
48-50 Grange Road, Ealing,
London W5 5BX
T: (020) 8567 1049
F: (020) 8579 5350
E: enquiries@londonlodgehotels.com
I: www.londonlodgehotels.com

W6

New Century Inn ◆◆◆
112 Shepherds Bush Road,
Hammersmith, London W6 7PD
T: (020) 7751 1200
F: (020) 7751 1002
E: reservations@newcenturyinn.co.uk
I: www.newcenturyinn.co.uk

Hotel Orlando ◆◆
83 Shepherds Bush Road,
Hammersmith, London W6 7LR
T: (020) 7603 4890
F: (020) 7603 4890
E: hotelorlando@btconnect.com
I: www.hotelorlando.co.uk

St Peters Hotel ◆◆◆
407-411 Goldhawk Road,
London W6 0SA
T: (020) 8741 4239
F: (020) 8748 3845

W7

Boston Manor Hotel ◆◆◆
146-152 Boston Road, Hanwell,
London W7 2HJ
T: (020) 8566 1534
F: (020) 8567 9510
E: bmh@bostonmanor.com
I: www.bostonmanor.com

W8

Hotel Atlas-Apollo ◆◆◆
18-30 Lexham Gardens, London
W8 5JE
T: (020) 7835 1155
F: (020) 7370 4853
E: reservations@atlas-apollo.com
I: www.atlas-apollo.com

Clearlake Hotel ♦♦
18-19 Prince of Wales Terrace, Kensington, London W8 5PQ
T: (020) 7937 3274
F: (020) 7376 0604
E: clearlake@talk21.com

W11

Kensington Guest House ♦♦
72 Holland Park Avenue, Kensington, London W11 3QZ
T: (020) 7229 9233
F: (020) 7221 1077
E: HoteLondon@aol.com
I: www.HoteLondon.co.uk

W14

Avonmore Hotel ♦♦♦♦
66 Avonmore Road, Kensington, London W14 8RS
T: (020) 7603 3121
F: (020) 7603 4035
E: reservations@avonmorehotel.co.uk
I: www.avonmorehotel.co.uk

Holland Court Hotel ♦♦♦
31-33 Holland Road, Kensington, London W14 8HJ
T: (020) 7371 1133
F: (020) 7602 9114
E: reservations@hollandcourthotel.com
I: www.hollandcourthotel.com

WC1

Arran House Hotel ♦♦
77 Gower Street, London WC1E 6HJ
T: (020) 7636 2186
F: (020) 7436 5328
E: arran@dircon.co.uk
I: www.london-hotel.co.uk

Hotel California Rating Applied For
4-8 Belgrove Street, Kings Cross, London WC1H 8AB
T: (020) 7837 7629
F: (020) 7278 5836
E: enquiries@californiahotel.co.uk
I: www.californiahotel.co.uk

Comfort Inn Kings Cross ♦♦♦
2/5 St Chads Street, Kings Cross, London WC1H 8BD
T: (020) 7837 1940
F: (020) 7278 5033
E: reception@midhot.demon.co.uk
I: www.comfortinnkingscross.co.uk

Crescent Hotel ♦♦♦
49-50 Cartwright Gardens, Bloomsbury, London WC1H 9EL
T: (020) 7387 1515
F: (020) 7383 2054
E: General.Enquiries@CrescentHotelofLondon.com
I: www.CrescentHotelofLondon.com

Euro Hotel ♦♦♦
53 Cartwright Gardens, London WC1H 9EL
T: (020) 7387 4321
F: (020) 7383 5044
E: Reception@eurohotel.co.uk
I: www.eurohotel.co.uk

George Hotel ♦♦♦
58-60 Cartwright Gardens, London WC1H 9EL
T: (020) 7387 8777
F: (020) 7387 8666
E: ghotel@aol.com
I: www.georgehotel.com

Gower House Hotel ♦
57 Gower Street, London WC1E 6HJ
T: (020) 7636 4685
F: (020) 7636 4685
E: info@gowerhousehotel.co.uk
I: www.gowerhousehotel.co.uk

St Athans Hotel ♦
20 Tavistock Place, Russell Square, London WC1H 9RE
T: (020) 7837 9140
F: (020) 7833 8352
E: stathans@ukonline.co.uk
I: www.stathanshotel.com

Staunton Hotel ♦♦♦♦
13-15 Gower Street, Bloomsbury, London WC1E 6HE
T: (020) 7580 2740
F: (020) 7580 3554
E: enquiries@stauntonhotel.com
I: www.stauntonhotel.com

WC2

Royal Adelphi Hotel ♦♦
21 Villiers Street, London WC2N 6ND
T: (020) 7930 8764
F: (020) 7930 8735
E: info@royaladelphi.co.uk
I: www.royaladelphi.co.uk

BEXLEY

66 Arcadian Avenue ♦♦♦
Bexley, DA5 1JW
T: (020) 8303 5732

Buxted Lodge Bed and Breakfast ♦♦
40 Parkhurst Road, Bexley, DA5 1AS
T: (01322) 554010
F: (01322) 550870
E: buxted.lodge@cwcom.net

BEXLEYHEATH

Vivenda House ♦♦♦♦
1 Ferndale Close, Bexleyheath, DA7 4ES
T: (020) 8304 5486
E: francisvivenda@aol.com
I: www.vivendahouse.co.uk

BRENTFORD

Kings Arms ♦♦♦
19 Boston Manor Road, Brentford, TW8 8EA
T: (020) 8560 5860
F: (020) 8847 4416

BROMLEY

Avondale House ♦♦♦♦
56 Avondale Road, Bromley, BR1 4EP
T: (020) 8402 0844
E: fortis@ukonline.co.uk
I: www.avondale-house.co.uk

Glendevon House Hotel ♦♦♦
80 Southborough Road, Bickley, Bromley, BR1 2EN
T: (020) 8467 2183
F: (020) 8295 0701

Westfields ♦♦♦
78 Hayes Lane, Bromley, BR2 9EE
T: (020) 8462 5591

CHEAM

St Margarets Guest House ♦♦♦
31 Devon Road, Cheam, Sutton SM2 7PP
T: (0208) 643 0164
F: (0208) 643 0717
E: margarettrotman@hotmail.com

CROYDON

63 Addington Road ♦♦♦
Sanderstead, South Croydon, CR2 8RD
T: (020) 8657 8776
F: (020) 8657 8776

Alpha Guest House ♦♦
99 Brigstock Road, Thornton Heath, CR7 7JL
T: (020) 8684 4811
F: (020) 8405 0302

Bramley ♦♦♦
7 Green Court Avenue, Shirley Park, Croydon, CR0 7LD
T: (020) 8654 6776
F: (020) 8654 6776

70 Chelsham Road Rating Applied For
70 Chelsham Road, Croydon, CR2 6HY
T: (020) 8649 9116
E: mikeaf@lineone.net

Croydon Court Hotel ♦♦
597-603 London Road, Croydon, CR7 6AY
T: (020) 8684 3947
F: (020) 8664 9293
E: bookings@croydencourthotel.co.uk
I: www.croydencourthotel.co.uk

Croydon Friendly Guesthouse ♦♦♦
16 St Peter's Road, Croydon, CR0 1HD
T: (020) 8680 4428
E: bilal@bhasan.fsnet.co.uk

Croydon Hotel ♦♦♦
112 Lower Addiscombe Road, Croydon, CR0 6AD
T: (020) 8656 7233
F: (020) 8655 0211
I: www.croydonhotel.co.uk

Foxley Mount ♦♦♦
44 Foxley Lane, Purley, CR8 3EE
T: (020) 8660 9751
F: (020) 8645 9368
E: enquiries@foxleymount.co.uk
I: www.foxleymount.co.uk

Ginetta Guest House ♦♦
32 Rylandes Road, Selsdon, South Croydon, CR2 8EA
T: (020) 8657 3132

Owlets ♦♦♦
112 Arundel Avenue, South Croydon, CR2 8BH
T: (020) 8657 5213
F: (020) 8657 5213

Stocks ♦♦♦
51 Selcroft Road, Purley, CR8 1AJ
T: (020) 8660 3054
F: (020) 8660 3054
E: joycestock@ukonline.co.uk

Woodstock Hotel ♦♦♦
30 Woodstock Road, Croydon, CR0 1JR
T: (020) 8680 1489
F: (020) 8667 1229
E: woodstockhotel@croydon-surrey.fsworld.co.uk
I: www.woodstockhotel.co.uk

ENFIELD

1 Chinnery Close ♦♦♦
Enfield, EN1 4AX
T: (020) 8363 3887
F: (020) 8366 5496

HAMPTON

Friars Cottage ♦♦♦
2B Priory Road, Hampton, TW12 2NR
T: (020) 8287 4699

14 Nightingale Road ♦♦♦♦
Hampton, TW12 3HX
T: (020) 8979 8074

Riverine ♦♦♦
Taggs Island, Hampton Court Road, Hampton, TW12 2HA
T: (020) 8979 2266
F: (020) 8255 4001
E: malcolm@cootpoint.freeserve.co.uk
I: www.feedtheducks.com

HARROW

Central Hotel ♦♦
6 Hindes Road, Harrow, HA1 1SJ
T: (020) 8427 0893
F: (020) 8424 8797
E: central@hindeshotel.com

Crescent Hotel ♦♦♦
58-62 Welldon Crescent, Harrow, HA1 1QR
T: (020) 8863 5491
F: (020) 8427 5965
E: jivraj@crsnthtl.demon.co.uk
I: www.crsnthtl.demon.co.uk

Hindes Hotel ♦♦♦
8 Hindes Road, Harrow, HA1 1SJ
T: (020) 8427 7468
F: (020) 8424 0673
E: reception@hindeshotel.com
I: www.hindeshotel.com

HAYES

Shepiston Lodge ♦♦♦
31 Shepiston Lane, Hayes, UB3 1LJ
T: (020) 8573 0266
F: (020) 8569 2536
E: shepistonlodge@aol.com
I: www.shepistonlodge.co.uk

HOUNSLOW

Abbeyglade Villa Rating Applied For
51 Heath Road, Hounslow, TW3 2NJ
T: (020) 8737 2717
F: (020) 8737 0228
E: nilruparelia@hotmail.com

Civic Guest House ♦♦
87-93 Lampton Road, Hounslow, TW3 4DP
T: (020) 8572 5107
F: (020) 8814 0203
E: enquiries@civicguesthouse.freeserve.co.uk
I: www.civicguesthouse.freeserve.co.uk

Lampton Park Guesthouse ◆◆◆
4 Lampton Park Road, Hounslow, TW3 4HS
T: (020) 8572 8622
E: michael.duff1@virgin.net

Shalimar Hotel ◆◆
215-223 Staines Road, Hounslow, TW3 3JJ
T: (020) 8577 7070
F: (020) 8569 6789
E: shalimarhotel@aol.com
I: www.s-h-systems.co.uk/hotels/shalimar.html

Skylark Bed & Breakfast ◆◆
297 Bath Road, Hounslow, TW3 3DB
T: (020) 8577 8455
F: (020) 8577 8741
E: info@skylark-bb.com
I: www.skylark-bb.com

ILFORD

Park Hotel ◆◆◆
327 Cranbrook Road, Ilford, IG1 4UE
T: (020) 8554 9616
F: (020) 8518 2700
E: parkhotelilford@netscapeonline.co.uk
I: www.the-park-hotel.co.uk

ISLEWORTH

80 Bassett Gardens ◆◆◆
Osterley, Isleworth, TW7 4QY
T: (020) 8570 8362

Harewood Lodge ◆◆◆
43 Harewood Road, Isleworth, TW7 5HN
T: (020) 8560 3627
F: (020) 8758 2105
E: harewoodlodge@hotmail.com

The Swans Nest ◆◆◆
The Swan Inn, 1 Swan Street, Isleworth, TW7 6RJ
T: (020) 8560 5457
F: (020) 8560 4835

KENLEY

Appledore ◆◆◆
6 Betula Close, Kenley, CR8 5ET
T: (020) 8668 4631
F: (020) 8668 4631

KEW

35 Beechwood Avenue ◆◆◆◆
Kew, Richmond TW9 4DD
T: (020) 8878 0049
F: (020) 8878 0049

1 Chelwood Gardens ◆◆◆
Kew, Richmond TW9 4JG
T: (020) 8876 8733
F: (020) 8255 0171
E: MrsLJGray@aol.com

11 Leyborne Park ◆◆◆◆
Kew, Richmond TW9 3HB
T: (020) 8948 1615
F: (020) 8255 1141
E: mary@stay-in-kew.com
I: www.stay-in-kew.com

40 Marksbury Avenue ◆◆◆
Kew, Richmond TW9 4JF
T: (020) 8878 9572

Melbury ◆◆◆
33 Marksbury Avenue, Kew, Richmond TW9 4JE
T: (020) 8876 3930
F: (020) 8876 3930

West Lodge ◆◆◆
179 Mortlake Road, Kew, Richmond TW9 4AW
T: (020) 8876 0584
F: (020) 8876 0584
E: westlodge@thakria.demon.co.uk

29 West Park Road ◆◆◆◆
Kew, Richmond TW9 4DA
T: (020) 8878 0505
E: alanbrooklands@aol.uk

KINGSTON UPON THAMES

40 The Bittoms ◆◆
Kingston upon Thames, KT1 2AP
T: (020) 8541 3171

26 Eaton Drive
Rating Applied For
Kingston upon Thames, KT2 7QT
T: (020) 8547 1200

8 St Albans Road ◆◆◆
Kingston upon Thames, KT2 5HQ
T: (020) 8549 5910

MORDEN

28 Monkleigh Road ◆◆
Morden, SM4 4EW
T: (020) 8542 5595

NORTHOLT

Brenda & Bertie Woosters Guesthouse ◆◆◆
5 Doncaster Drive, Northolt, UB5 4AS
T: (020) 8423 5072

PINNER

Delcon ◆◆
468 Pinner Road, Pinner, HA5 5RR
T: (020) 8863 1054
F: (020) 8863 1054

PURLEY

Arcadia ◆◆
212 Brighton Road, Purley, CR8 4HB
T: (020) 8668 2486

Conifers ◆◆◆
214 Brighton Road, Purley, CR8 4HB
T: (020) 8668 6580
E: ursula@theconifers.net
I: www.theconifers.net

Guest House ◆◆
The Nook Guest House, 12 Grasmere Road, Purley, CR8 1DU
T: (020) 8660 1742
E: agmandrews@callnet.uk.com

The Maple House ◆◆◆
174 Foxley Lane, Purley, CR8 3NF
T: (020) 8407 5123
F: (020) 8405 3918
E: tobrugger@aol.com

Purley Cross Guest House ◆◆◆
50 Brighton Road, Purley, CR8 2LG
T: (020) 8668 4964
F: (020) 8407 2133
E: bookings@purleycross.com

Woodlands ◆◆◆
2 Green Lane, Purley, CR8 3PG
T: (020) 8660 3103

RICHMOND

8 Cardigan Mansions ◆◆
19 Richmond Hill, Richmond, TW10 6RD
T: (020) 8940 1654

Chalon House
◆◆◆◆◆ GOLD AWARD
8 Spring Terrace, Paradise Road, Richmond, TW9 1LW
T: (020) 8332 1121
F: (020) 8332 1131
E: virgilioz@aol.com

Doughty Cottage
◆◆◆◆◆ GOLD AWARD
142a Richmond Hill, Richmond, TW10 6RN
T: (020) 8332 9434
F: (020) 8332 9434
E: deniseoneill425@aol.com
I: www.doughtycottage.com

Dukes Head Inn ◆◆◆
42 The Vineyards, Richmond, TW10 6AW
T: (020) 8948 4557
F: (020) 8948 4557
E: thedukeshead@yahoo.com
I: www.dukeshead.com

Hobart Hall Hotel ◆◆◆
43-47 Petersham Road, Richmond, TW10 6UL
T: (020) 8940 0435
F: (020) 8332 2996
E: hobarthall@aol.com
I: www.smoothhound.co.uk/hotels/hobarthall.html

Ivy Cottage ◆◆◆
Upper Ham Road, Ham Common, Richmond, TW10 5LA
T: (020) 8940 8601
F: (020) 8940 3865
E: taylor@dbta.freeserve.co.uk
I: www.dbta.freeserve.co.uk

195 Mortlake Road ◆◆◆
Kew Gardens, Richmond, TW9 4EW
T: (020) 8878 7018
F: (020) 8487 2748
E: alees.home@virgin.net

Pro Kew Gardens B & B ◆◆◆
15 Pensford Avenue, Kew Gardens, Richmond, TW9 4HR
T: (020) 8876 3354
E: info@prokewbandb.demon.co.uk

Quinns Hotel ◆◆◆
48 Sheen Road, Richmond, TW9 1AW
T: (020) 8940 5444
F: (020) 8940 1828
E: enquiries@quinnshotel.com
I: www.quinnshotel.com

The Red Cow ◆◆◆
59 Sheen Road, Richmond, TW9 1YJ
T: (020) 8940 2511
F: (020) 8940 2581
E: tom@redcowpub.com

Reston Lodge ◆◆◆◆
Petersham Road, Petersham, Richmond, TW10 7AD
T: (020) 8332 9350

Richmond Inn Hotel ◆◆◆◆
50-56 Sheen Road, Richmond, TW9 1UG
T: (020) 8940 0171
F: (020) 8332 2596

Richmond Park Hotel ◆◆◆
3 Petersham Road, Richmond, TW10 6UH
T: (020) 8948 4666
F: (020) 8940 7376
E: richmdpk@globalnet.co.uk

Riverside Hotel ◆◆◆
23 Petersham Road, Richmond, TW10 6UH
T: (020) 8940 1339
F: (020) 8948 0967
E: riversidehotel@yahoo.com
I: www.smoothhound.co.uk/hotels/riversid.html

The Rose of York ◆◆◆
Petersham Road, Richmond, TW10 6UY
T: (020) 8948 5867
F: (020) 8332 6986
E: roseofyork@compuserve.com

248 Sandycombe Road ◆◆◆
Kew, Richmond, TW9 3NP
T: (020) 8940 5970

9 Selwyn Court ◆◆
Church Road, Richmond, TW10 6LR
T: (020) 8940 3309

454 Upper Richmond Road West ◆◆◆
Richmond, TW10 5DY
T: (020) 8876 0327

West Park Gardens ◆◆◆
105 Mortlake Road, Kew, Richmond TW9 4AA
T: (020) 8876 6842
F: (020) 8876 6842
E: edwardsnjdr@aol.com

ROMFORD

The Orchard Guest House ◆◆◆
81 Eastern Road, Romford, RM1 3PB
T: (01708) 744099
F: (01708) 768881
E: johnrt@globalnet.co.uk

SIDCUP

The Chimneys ◆◆◆
6 Clarence Road, Sidcup, DA14 4DL
T: (020) 8309 1460
F: (020) 83065177

Hilbert House ◆◆◆
Halfway Street, Sidcup, DA15 8DE
T: (020) 8300 0549

SOUTH CROYDON

Waldenbury ◆◆◆
33 Crossways, Selsdon, South Croydon, CR2 8JQ
T: (020) 8657 7791
F: (020) 8657 7791
E: waldenbury@tesco.net

SOUTH HARROW

4 Shaftesbury Avenue ◆◆
South Harrow, Harrow HA2 0PH
T: (020) 8357 2548
E: mckeefourguests@bushinternet.com

SURBITON

26 St Matthews Avenue ◆◆◆
Surbiton, KT6 6JQ
T: (020) 8399 6603
E: andyw7@aol.com

Villiers Lodge Bed and Breakfast
Rating Applied For
1 Cranes Park, Surbiton, KT5 8AB
T: (020) 8399 6000

TEDDINGTON

93 Clarence Road ◆◆◆◆
Teddington, TW11 0BN
T: (020) 8977 3459
F: (020) 8943 1560

Glenhurst ♦♦♦
93 Langham Road, Teddington, TW11 9HG
T: (020) 8977 6962
F: (020) 8977 6962
E: lesley@stayinteddington.com
I: www.stayinteddington.com

6 Grove Gardens ♦♦♦
Teddington, TW11 8AP
T: (020) 8977 6066

Hazeldene ♦♦♦♦
58 Hampton Road, Teddington, TW11 0JX
T: (020) 8286 8500
E: glasslisa58@hotmail.com

King Edwards Grove ♦♦♦
Teddington, TW11 9LY
T: (020) 8977 7251

126 Kingston Road ♦♦♦
Teddington, TW11 9JA
T: (020) 8943 9302

187 Kingston Road ♦♦♦
Teddington, TW11 9JN
T: (020) 8977 3392
F: 0870 1352140
E: teddingtonaccom@aol.com
I: www.members.aol.com/teddingtonaccom

Polly's Bed and Breakfast ♦♦♦
166 High Street, Teddington, TW11 8HU
T: (020) 8287 1188
E: b&b@mypolly.net

THORNTON HEATH

The Lloyd's House ♦♦
41 Moffat Road, Thornton Heath, CR7 8PY
T: (020) 8768 1827

TWICKENHAM

Avalon Cottage ♦♦♦
50 Moor Mead Road, St Margarets, Twickenham, TW1 1JS
T: (020) 8744 2178
F: (020) 8891 2444
E: avalon@mead99.freeserve.co.uk

136 London Road ♦♦♦
Twickenham, TW1 1HD
T: (020) 8892 3158
E: jenniferjfinnerty@hotmail.com

11 Spencer Road ♦♦♦
11 Spencer Road, Strawberry Hill, Twickenham, TW2 5TH
T: (020) 8894 5271
F: (020) 8994 4751
E: bruceduff@hotmail.com

Susi Lever ♦♦
St Georges Lodge, 27 The Avenue, Twickenham, TW1 1QP
T: (020) 8892 7679
F: (020) 8892 5596

3 Waldegrave Gardens ♦♦♦
Strawberry Hill, Twickenham, TW1 4PQ
T: (020) 8892 3523

UPMINSTER

Corner Farm ♦♦♦
Corner Farm, Fen Lane, North Ockendon, Upminster RM14 3RB
T: (01708) 851310
F: (01708) 852025
E: corner.farm@virgin.net

WELLING

De + Dees B & B ♦♦♦♦
91 Welling Way, Welling, DA16 2RW
T: (020) 8319 1592
F: (020) 8319 1592

WEMBLEY

Adelphi Hotel ♦♦♦
4 Forty Lane, Wembley, HA9 9EB
T: (020) 8904 5629
F: (020) 8908 5314
E: adel@dial.pipex.com
I: www.hoteladelphi.co.uk

Arena Hotel ♦♦♦
6 Forty Lane, Wembley, HA9 9EB
T: (020) 8908 0670
F: (020) 8908 2007
E: enquiry@arenahotel.fsnet.co.uk
I: www.arena-hotel.co.uk

Elm Hotel ♦♦♦
1-7 Elm Road, Wembley, HA9 7JA
T: (020) 8902 1764
F: (020) 8903 8365
E: elm.hotel@virgin.net
I: www.elmhotel.co.uk

WORCESTER PARK

The Graye House ♦♦♦
24 The Glebe, Worcester Park, KT4 7PF
T: (020) 8330 1277
F: (020) 8255 7850
E: graye.house@virgin.net
I: www.smoothhound.co.uk

CUMBRIA

AINSTABLE Cumbria

Bell House ♦♦♦♦
Ainstable, Carlisle CA4 9RE
T: (01768) 896255
F: (01768) 896255
E: mrobinson@bellhouse.fsbusiness.co.uk

ALLONBY Cumbria

Ship Hotel ♦♦♦
Main Street, Allonby, Maryport CA15 6QF
T: (01900) 881017
F: (01900) 881017
E: theshipallonby@aol.com

ALSTON Cumbria

Brownside House ♦♦♦
Leadgate, Alston, CA9 3EL
T: (01434) 382169
F: (01434) 382100
E: brownside_hse@hotmail.com
I: www.cumbria1st.com/brown_side/index.htm

Greycroft ♦♦♦♦ SILVER AWARD
Middle Park, The Raise, Alston, CA9 3AR
T: (01434) 381383
E: enquiry@greycroft.co.uk
I: www.greycroft.co.uk

AMBLESIDE Cumbria

Ambleside Country Hotel – Grey Friar Lodge ♦♦♦♦♦ SILVER AWARD
Clappersgate, Ambleside, LA22 9NE
T: (01539) 433158
F: (01539) 433158
E: greyfriar@veen.freeserve.co.uk
I: www.cumbria-hotels.co.uk

Amboseli Lodge ♦♦♦♦
Rothay Road, Ambleside, LA22 0EE
T: (01539) 431110
F: (01539) 431110
E: enquiries@amboselilodge.co.uk
I: www.amboselilodge.co.uk

Anchorage Guest House ♦♦♦
The Anchorage, Rydal Road, Ambleside, LA22 9AY
T: (01539) 432046
E: info@anchorageguesthouse.ltd.uk
I: www.anchorageguesthouse.ltd.uk

Barnes Fell Guest House ♦♦♦♦ SILVER AWARD
Low Gale, Ambleside, LA22 0BB
T: (01539) 433311
F: (01539) 43493

Brantfell House ♦♦♦♦
Rothay Road, Ambleside, LA22 0EE
T: (01539) 432239
F: (01539) 432239
E: brantfell@kencomp.net

Broadview ♦♦♦
Low Fold, Lake Road, Ambleside, LA22 0DN
T: (01539) 432431
E: enquiries@broadviewguesthouse.co.uk
I: www.broadviewguesthouse.co.uk

3 Cambridge Villas ♦♦♦
Church Street, Ambleside, LA22 9DL
T: (01539) 432307
E: cambridgevillas3@aol.com

Claremont House ♦♦♦
Compston Road, Ambleside, LA22 9DJ
T: (01539) 433448
F: (01539) 433448
E: enquiries@claremontambleside.co.uk
I: www.claremontambleside.co.uk

Compston House American-Style B&B ♦♦♦♦
Compston Road, Ambleside, LA22 9DJ
T: (01539) 432305
E: compston@globalnet.co.uk
I: www.compstonhouse.co.uk

The Dower House ♦♦♦♦
Wray Castle, Ambleside, LA22 0JA
T: (015394) 33211
F: (015394) 33211

Elder Grove ♦♦♦♦
Lake Road, Ambleside, LA22 0DB
T: (01539) 432504
F: (01539) 432251
E: info@eldergrove.co.uk
I: www.eldergrove.co.uk

Far Nook ♦♦♦♦♦ SILVER AWARD
Rydal Road, Ambleside, LA22 9BA
T: (01539) 431605
F: (01539) 431605
E: farnook@tiscali.co.uk

Fern Cottage ♦♦♦
6 Waterhead Terrace, Ambleside, LA22 0HA
T: (01539) 433007

Ferndale Hotel ♦♦♦
Lake Road, Ambleside, LA22 0DB
T: (01539) 432207
E: ferndalehotel@btconnect.com
I: www.ferndalehotel.com

Fisherbeck Garden ♦♦♦
Old Lake Road, Ambleside, LA22 0DH
T: (015394) 33088
E: janice@fisherbeck.net1.co.uk

Foxghyll ♦♦♦♦
Under Loughrigg, Ambleside, LA22 9LL
T: (01539) 433292
E: foxghyll@hotmail.com
I: www.foxghyll.co.uk

Freshfields ♦♦♦♦ SILVER AWARD
Wansfell Road, Ambleside, LA22 0EG
T: (01539) 434469
F: (01539) 434469
E: info@freshfieldsguesthouse.co.uk
I: www.freshfieldsguesthouse.co.uk

The Gables Rating Applied For
Church Walk, Ambleside, LA22 9DJ
T: (015394) 33272
E: info@gables.f9.co.uk
I: www.gables.f9.co.uk

Ghyll Head Hotel ♦♦♦♦
Waterhead, Ambleside LA22 0HD
T: (01539) 432360
F: (01539) 434062
E: ghyllhead@btopenworld.com
I: www.hotelscumbria.com

Glenside Rating Applied For
Old Lake Road, Ambleside, LA22 0DP
T: (015394) 32635

Greenbank
♦♦♦♦ SILVER AWARD
Skelwith Bridge, Ambleside
LA22 9NW
T: (01539) 433236
E: info@visitgreenbank.co.uk
I: www.visitgreenbank.co.uk

High Wray Farm ♦♦♦♦
High Wray, Ambleside LA22 0JE
T: (01539) 432280
E: sheila@highwrayfarm.co.uk
I: www.highwrayfarm.co.uk

Highfield
Rating Applied For
Lake Road, Ambleside, LA22 0DB
T: (015394) 32671
E: t.m.wright@talk21.com

Hillsdale ♦♦♦♦
Church Street, Ambleside,
LA22 0BT
T: (01539) 433174
F: (01539) 431226
E: stay@hillsdaleguesthouse.co.uk
I: www.hillsdaleguesthouse.co.uk

Holmeshead Farm ♦♦♦♦
Skelwith Fold, Ambleside,
LA22 0HU
T: (01539) 433048
E: info@holmesheadfarm.co.uk
I: www.amblesideonline.co.uk/adverts/holmeshead/main.html

Kent House
♦♦♦♦ SILVER AWARD
Lake Road, Ambleside, LA22 0AD
T: (01539) 433279
F: (01539) 433279
E: info@kent-house.com
I: www.kent-house.com

Lattendales Guest House ♦♦♦
Compston Road, Ambleside,
LA22 9DJ
T: (01539) 432368
E: info@lattendales.co.uk
I: www.lattendales.co.uk

Laurel Villa ♦♦♦
Lake Road, Ambleside, LA22 0DB
T: (01539) 433240
F: (01539) 433240
E: laurelvilla_ambleside@hotmail.com

Lyndale ♦♦♦
Low Fold, Lake Road, Ambleside,
LA22 0DN
T: (01539) 434244
E: wendy@lyndale-guesthouse.co.uk
I: www.lyndale-guesthouse.co.uk

Lyndhurst Hotel ♦♦♦
Wansfell Road, Ambleside,
LA22 0EG
T: (01539) 432421
F: (01539) 432421
E: lyndhurst@amblesidehotels.co.uk
I: www.amblesidehotels.co.uk

Meadowbank ♦♦♦
Rydal Road, Ambleside,
LA22 9BA
T: (01539) 432710
F: (01539) 432710
E: enquiries@meadowbank.org.uk
I: www.meadowbank.org.uk

Melrose ♦♦♦
Church Street, Ambleside,
LA22 0BT
T: (01539) 432500
F: (01539) 431495
E: info@melrose-guesthouse.co.uk
I: www.melrose-guesthouse.co.uk

Norwood House ♦♦♦
Church Street, Ambleside,
LA22 0BT
T: (01539) 433349
F: (01539) 434938
E: mail@norwoodhouse.net
I: www.norwoodhouse.net

The Old Vicarage ♦♦♦♦
Vicarage Road, Ambleside,
LA22 9DH
T: (01539) 433364
F: (01539) 434734
E: the.old.vicarage@kencomp.net
I: www.oldvicarageambleside.co.uk

Red Bank
♦♦♦♦ SILVER AWARD
Wansfell Road, Ambleside,
LA22 0EG
T: (01539) 434637
F: (01539) 434637
E: info@red-bank.co.uk
I: www.red-bank.co.uk

Riverside Hotel ♦♦♦♦
Under Loughrigg, Rothay Bridge,
Ambleside, LA22 9LJ
T: (01539) 432395
F: (01539) 432440
E: info@riverside-at-ambleside.co.uk
I: www.riverside-at-ambleside.co.uk

Rowanfield Country Guesthouse
♦♦♦♦♦ SILVER AWARD
Kirkstone Road, Ambleside,
LA22 9ET
T: (01539) 433686
F: (01539) 431569
E: email@rowanfield.com
I: www.rowanfield.com

The Rysdale Hotel ♦♦♦
Rothay Road, Ambleside,
LA22 0EE
T: (01539) 432140
F: (01539) 433999
E: info@rysdalehotel.co.uk
I: www.rysdalehotel.co.uk

Stepping Stones Country House ♦♦♦♦
Under Loughrigg, Ambleside,
LA22 9LN
T: (01539) 433552
F: (01539) 433552
E: info@steppingstonesambleside.com
I: www.steppingstonesambleside.com

Thorneyfield Guest House ♦♦♦♦
Compston Road, Ambleside,
LA22 9DJ
T: (01539) 432464
F: 0870 1671968
E: info@thorneyfield.co.uk
I: www.thorneyfield.co.uk

Tock How Farm ♦♦♦♦
High Wray, Ambleside, LA22 0JF
T: (01539) 436106
F: (01539) 436294
E: info@tock-how-farm.com
I: www.tock-how-farm.com

Walmar Hotel ♦♦♦
Lake Road, Ambleside, LA22 0DB
T: (01539) 432454

Wanslea Guest House ♦♦♦♦
Lake Road, Ambleside, LA22 0DN
T: (01539) 433884
E: wanslea.guesthouse@virgin.net
I: www.wansleaguesthouse.co.uk

Wateredge Inn ♦♦♦♦
Waterhead Bay, Ambleside,
LA22 0EP
T: (01539) 432332
F: (01539) 431878
E: contact@wateredgeinn.co.uk
I: www.wateredgeinn.co.uk

APPLEBY-IN-WESTMORLAND
Cumbria

Broom House ♦♦♦
Long Marton, Appleby-in-Westmorland CA16 6JP
T: (01768) 361318
F: (01768) 361318
E: sandra@bland01.freeserve.co.uk
I: www.theuktourist.com/members.lasso?id=5038

ARNSIDE
Cumbria

Willowfield Hotel ♦♦♦♦
The Promenade, Arnside,
Carnforth LA5 0AD
T: (01524) 761354
E: info@willowfield.net1.co.uk
I: www.willowfield.uk.com

BAILEY
Cumbria

Cleughside Farm ♦♦♦
Bailey, Newcastleton TD9 0TR
T: (01697) 748634
F: (01697) 748634
E: alicewhy@aol.com
I: www.cleughside.freeserve.co.uk

BARROW-IN-FURNESS
Cumbria

Arlington House Hotel and Restaurant♦♦♦♦
200-202 Abbey Road, Barrow-in-Furness, LA14 5LD
T: (01229) 831976
F: (01229) 870990
E: arlington@tinyworld.co.uk
I: www.arlingtonhousehotel.co.uk

King Alfred Hotel
Rating Applied For
Ocean Road, Walney Island,
Barrow-in-Furness, LA14 3DU
T: (01229) 474717
F: (01229) 474717
E: kingalfred@walney4.fsnet.co.uk

BASSENTHWAITE
Cumbria

Dalton Cottage ♦♦♦♦
Bassenthwaite, Keswick
CA12 4QG
T: (01768) 776952
F: (01768) 776952
E: deborah@daltoncottage.co.uk
I: www.daltoncottage.co.uk

High Side Farmhouse
♦♦♦♦ SILVER AWARD
Embleton, Cockermouth
CA13 9TN
T: (01768) 776893
F: (01768) 776893
E: highside@winstanley38.freeserve.co.uk

BASSENTHWAITE LAKE
Cumbria

Herdwick Croft Guest House ♦♦♦♦
Bassenthwaite, Keswick
CA12 4RD
T: (01768) 776241
E: stayinthelakes@BTconnect.com
I: www.stayinthelakes.co.uk

Kiln Hill Barn ♦♦♦
Bassenthwaite, Keswick
CA12 4RG
T: (01768) 776454
F: (01768) 776454
E: ken@kilnhillbarn.freeserve.co.uk
I: www.kilnhillbarn.co.uk

Lakeside ♦♦♦♦
Dubwath, Bassenthwaite Lake,
Cockermouth CA13 9YD
T: (01768) 776358
F: (01768) 776163

Link House ♦♦♦♦
Bassenthwaite Lake,
Cockermouth CA13 9YD
T: (01768) 776291
F: (01768) 776670
E: linkhouse@lineone.net
I: www.link-house.co.uk

Ravenstone Lodge ♦♦♦♦
Bassenthwaite, Keswick
CA12 4QG
T: (01768) 776629
F: (01768) 776629
E: ravenstone.lodge@talk21.com
I: www.ravenstonelodge.co.uk

Robin Hood House ♦♦♦♦
Bassenthwaite, Keswick
CA12 4RJ
T: (01768) 776296

BEETHAM
Cumbria

Barn Close/North West Birds ♦♦♦
Beetham, Milnthorpe LA7 7AL
T: (01539) 563191
F: (01539) 563191
E: anne@nwbirds.co.uk
I: www.nwbirds.co.uk

BIRKBY
Cumbria

The Retreat Hotel and Restaurant ♦♦♦♦
Birkby, Maryport CA15 6RG
T: (01900) 814056
E: enquiries@retreathotel.co.uk
I: www.retreathotel.co.uk

BOLTON
Cumbria

Eden Grove Farm House
♦♦♦♦ SILVER AWARD
Bolton, Appleby-in-Westmorland CA16 6AX
T: (01768) 362321
E: edengrovecumbria@aol.com
I: www.ukworld.net/edengrove

Glebe House ♦♦♦
Bolton, Appleby-in-Westmorland CA16 6AW
T: (017683) 61125
E: derick.cotton@btinternet.com
I: www.glebeholidays.co.uk

Tarka House ♦♦♦
Bolton, Appleby-in-Westmorland CA16 6AW
T: (01768) 361422
F: (01768) 361422
E: mmpip80@hotmail.com

BOOT
Cumbria

The Burnmoor Inn ♦♦♦
Boot, Holmrook CA19 1TG
T: 0845 1306224
F: (019467) 23337
E: stay@burnmoor.co.uk
I: www.burnmoor.co.uk

BORROWDALE
Cumbria

Greenbank Country House Hotel ♦♦♦♦ SILVER AWARD
Borrowdale, Keswick CA12 5UY
T: (01768) 777215
E: jeanwwood@lineone.net
I: www.greenbankcountryhousehotel.co.uk

Hazel Bank Country House
♦♦♦♦♦ GOLD AWARD
Rosthwaite, Borrowdale, Keswick CA12 5XB
T: (01768) 777248
F: (01767) 877373
E: enquiries@hazelbankhotel.co.uk
I: www.hazelbankhotel.co.uk

Seatoller House ♦♦♦
Borrowdale, Keswick CA12 5XN
T: (01768) 77218
F: (01768) 77189
E: seatollerhouse@btconnect.com
I: www.seatollerhouse.co.uk

BOWLAND BRIDGE
Cumbria

Hare and Hounds Country Inn
Rating Applied For
Bowland Bridge, Grange-over-Sands LA11 6NN
T: (01539) 568333
F: (01539) 568993

BOWNESS-ON-SOLWAY
Cumbria

Maia Lodge ♦♦♦
Bowness-on-Solway, Carlisle CA7 5BH
T: (01697) 351955
E: d.chettle@virgin.net

Wallsend ♦♦♦♦
The Old Rectory, Church Lane, Bowness-on-Solway, Carlisle CA7 5AF
T: (016973) 51055
F: (016973) 52543
E: wallsend@btinternet.com
I: www.wallsend.net

BRAITHWAITE
Cumbria

Coledale Inn ♦♦♦
Braithwaite, Keswick CA12 5TN
T: (01768) 778272
F: (01768) 778416
E: info@coledale-inn.co.uk
I: www.coledale-inn.co.uk

Maple Bank ♦♦♦♦
Braithwaite, Keswick CA12 5RY
T: (01768) 778229
F: (01768) 778000
E: maplebank@aol.com
I: www.maplebank.co.uk

BRAMPTON
Cumbria

Blacksmiths Arms Hotel ♦♦♦
Talkin Village, Brampton, CA8 1LE
T: (01697) 73452
F: (01697) 73396
E: blacksmithsarmstalkin@yahoo.co.uk
I: www.blacksmithsarmstalkin.co.uk

Howard House Farm
♦♦♦♦ SILVER AWARD
Gilsland, Brampton CA8 7AJ
T: (016977) 47285
F: (016977) 47996

Langthwaite ♦♦♦
Lanercost Road, Brampton, CA8 1EN
T: (01697) 72883
E: anneharding@nicetoseeyou.co.uk

Low Rigg Farm ♦♦♦
Walton, Brampton, CA8 2DX
T: (01697) 73233
E: lowrigg@tiscali.co.uk
I: www.smoothhound.co.uk/hotels/lowrigg.html

New Mills House ♦♦♦
Brampton, CA8 2QS
T: (01697) 73376
F: (01697) 73457
E: newmills@btinternet.com
I: www.info@newmillshouse.co.uk

Oakwood Park Hotel ♦♦♦
Longtown Road, Brampton, CA8 2AP
T: (01697) 72436
F: (01697) 72436
E: donal.collier@amserve.net

South View ♦♦♦
Banks, Brampton, CA8 2JH
T: (01697) 72309
E: sandrahodgson@southviewbanks.f9.co.uk
I: www.southviewbanks.f9.co.uk

Vallum Barn ♦♦♦♦
Irthington, Carlisle CA6 4NN
T: (01697) 742478
E: vallumbarn@tinyworld.co.uk
I: www.vallumbarn.co.uk

Walton High Rigg ♦♦♦
Walton, Brampton CA8 2AZ
T: (01697) 72117
F: (01697) 741697
E: mounsey.highrigg@hotmail.com
I: www.waltonhighrigg.co.uk

Windyhaugh ♦♦♦♦
Station Road, Brampton, CA8 1EZ
T: (016977) 3248
F: (016977) 42830
E: irobertsw@aol.com

BRIGSTEER
Cumbria

Low Plain ♦♦♦♦
Brigsteer, Kendal LA8 8AX
T: (01539) 568464
F: (01539) 568916
E: farmhouse@lowplain.co.uk
I: www.lowplain.co.uk

BRISCO
Cumbria

Crossroads House ♦♦♦♦
Brisco, Carlisle CA4 0QZ
T: (01228) 528994
F: (01228) 528994
E: viv@crossroadshouse.co.uk
I: www.crossroadshouse.co.uk

BROUGH
Cumbria

River View ♦♦♦
Brough, Kirkby Stephen CA17 4BZ
T: (01768) 341894
F: (01768) 341894
E: riverviewbb@btinternet.com
I: riverview.moonfruit.com

BROUGHTON-IN-FURNESS
Cumbria

Broom Hill ♦♦♦♦
New Street, Broughton-in-Furness, LA20 6JD
T: (01229) 716358
F: (01229) 716358

The Dower House ♦♦♦
High Duddon, Duddon Bridge, Broughton-in-Furness LA20 6ET
T: (01229) 716279
E: rozanne.nichols@ukgateway.net

Middlesyke
♦♦♦♦ SILVER AWARD
Church Street, Broughton-in-Furness, LA20 6ER
T: (01229) 716549

Oak Bank ♦♦
Ulpha, Broughton-in-Furness LA20 6DZ
T: (01229) 716393
I: www.duddonvalley.co.uk

The Workshop Studios ♦♦♦♦
Church Street, Broughton-in-Furness, LA20 6HJ
T: (01229) 716159
F: (01229) 716159
E: workshop.accom@virgin.net
I: www.theworkshopstudios.com

BURTON-IN-KENDAL
Cumbria

Kings Arms Hotel ♦♦♦♦
Main Street, Burton-in-Kendal, Kendal LA6 1LR
T: (01524) 781409
E: roger@kingsarmshotel.net
I: www.kingsarmshotel.net

Royal Hotel ♦♦♦
Main Street, Burton-in-Kendal, Kendal LA6 1LY
T: (01524) 781261
F: (01524) 781261

CALDBECK
Cumbria

The Briars ♦♦♦
Friar Row, Caldbeck, Wigton CA7 8DS
T: (01697) 478633

Gate House ♦♦♦
Caldbeck, Wigton CA7 8EL
T: (01697) 478092
E: ray@caldbeckgatehouse.co.uk
I: www.caldbeckgatehouse.co.uk

Swaledale Watch ♦♦♦♦
Whelpo, Caldbeck, Wigton CA7 8HQ
T: (01697) 478409
F: (01697) 478409
E: nan.savage@talk21.com

CARLETON
Cumbria

River Forge Bed and Breakfast
♦♦♦♦
River Forge, Carleton, Carlisle CA4 0AA
T: (01228) 523569

CARLISLE
Cumbria

Abbey Court ♦♦♦♦
24 London Road, Carlisle, CA1 2EL
T: (01228) 528696
F: (01228) 528696

Ashleigh House ♦♦♦♦
46 Victoria Place, Carlisle, CA1 1EX
T: (01228) 521631

Avondale ♦♦♦♦
3 St Aidan's Road, Carlisle, CA1 1LT
T: (01228) 523012
F: (01228) 523012
E: info@bed-breakfast-carlisle.co.uk
I: www.bed-breakfast-carlisle.co.uk

Bessiestown
♦♦♦♦♦ SILVER AWARD
Catlowdy, Longtown, Carlisle CA6 5QP
T: (01228) 577219
F: (01228) 577019
E: info@bessiestown.co.uk
I: bessiestown.co.uk

Brooklyn House ♦♦♦
42 Victoria Place, Carlisle, CA1 1EX
T: (01228) 590002

Caldew View ♦♦♦
Metcalfe Street, Denton Holme, Carlisle, CA2 5EU
T: (01228) 595837

Calreena Guest House ♦♦
123 Warwick Road, Carlisle, CA1 1JZ
T: (01228) 525020

Cartref Guest House ♦♦♦
44 Victoria Place, Carlisle, CA1 1EX
T: (01228) 522077

Claremont Guest House ♦♦♦
30 London Road, Carlisle, CA1 2EL
T: (01228) 524691
F: (01228) 524691
E: enquiries@claremontguesthouse.com
I: www.claremontguesthouse.com

Establishments printed in blue have a detailed entry in this guide

Corner House ◆◆◆
4 Grey Street, Off London Road, Carlisle, CA1 2JP
T: (01228) 533239
F: (01228) 546628
E: bcartner@aol.com

Cornerways Guest House ◆◆◆◆
107 Warwick Road, Carlisle, CA1 1EA
T: (01228) 521733

Courtfield House ◆◆◆◆ SILVER AWARD
169 Warwick Road, Carlisle, CA1 1LP
T: (01228) 522767
F: (01228) 522767
E: mdawes@courtfieldhouse.fsnet.co.uk

Croft End ◆◆◆
Hurst, Ivegill, Carlisle CA4 0NL
T: (01768) 484362

Dalroc ◆◆◆
411 Warwick Road, Carlisle, CA1 2RZ
T: (01228) 542805
E: margaret@dalroc.fsnet.co.uk
I: www.dalroc.co.uk

East View Guest House ◆◆◆
110 Warwick Road, Carlisle, CA1 1JU
T: (01228) 522112
F: (01228) 522112
I: www.guesthousecarlisle.co.uk

Fern Lee Guest House ◆◆◆◆
9 St Aidans Road, Carlisle, CA1 1LT
T: (01228) 511930
F: (01228) 511930

Hazeldean Guest House ◆◆◆
Orton Grange, Wigton Road, Carlisle, CA5 6LA
T: (01228) 711953

Howard Lodge Guesthouse ◆◆◆
90 Warwick Road, Carlisle, CA1 1JU
T: (01228) 529842

Ivy House ◆◆◆◆
101 Warwick Road, Carlisle, CA1 1EA
T: (01228) 530432
F: (01228) 530432

Kates Guest House ◆◆◆
Lazonby Terrace, London Road, Harraby Green, Carlisle, CA1 2PZ
T: (01228) 539577
E: katesguesthouse@hotmail.com

angleigh Guest House
Rating Applied For
Howard Place, Carlisle, CA1 1HR
: (01228) 530440
: (01228) 530440
: langleighhouse@aol.com

ynebank House ◆◆◆◆
Westlinton, Carlisle CA6 6AA
(01228) 792820
(01228) 792820
jan@lynebank.co.uk
www.lynebank.co.uk

archmain House ◆◆◆ SILVER AWARD
51 Warwick Road, Carlisle, A1 1LU
(01228) 529551
(01228) 529551

Naworth Guest House ◆◆◆◆
33 Victoria Place, Carlisle, CA1 1HP
T: (01228) 521645
E: stay@naworth.com
I: www.naworth.com

New Pallyards ◆◆◆◆
Hethersgill, Carlisle CA6 6HZ
T: (01228) 577308
F: (01228) 577308
E: info@newpallyards.freeserve.co.uk
I: www.newpallyards.freeserve.co.uk

Newfield Grange Hotel ◆◆◆◆
Newfield Drive, Kingstown, Carlisle CA3 0AF
T: (01228) 819926
F: (01228) 546323
E: bb@newfield53.freeserve.co.uk
I: www.newfield53.freeserve.co.uk

Number Thirty One ◆◆◆◆◆ GOLD AWARD
31 Howard Place, Carlisle, CA1 1HR
T: (01228) 597080
F: (01228) 597080
E: bestpep@aol.com
I: number31.freeservers.com

Stratheden ◆◆◆◆
93 Warwick Road, Carlisle, CA1 1EB
T: (01228) 520192
E: sue.stratheden@tiscali.co.uk

Townhouse Bed & Breakfast ◆◆◆
153 Warwick Road, Carlisle, CA1 1LU
T: (01228) 598782
E: townhouse@christine60.freeserve.co.uk
I: www.townhouse-bandb.com

Vallum House Garden Hotel ◆◆◆
Burgh Road, Carlisle, CA2 7NB
T: (01228) 521860

Warren Guesthouse ◆◆◆
368 Warwick Road, Carlisle, CA1 2RU
T: (01228) 533663
F: (01228) 533663

White Lea Guest House ◆◆◆
191 Warwick Road, Carlisle, CA1 1LP
T: (01228) 533139
F: (01228) 533139

CARTMEL
Cumbria

Bank Court Cottage ◆◆◆
The Square, Cartmel, Grange-over-Sands LA11 6QB
T: (01539) 536593
F: (01539) 536593

Hill Farm ◆◆◆◆◆ SILVER AWARD
Cartmel, Grange-over-Sands LA11 7SS
T: (01539) 536477
F: (01539) 536636
E: pafoulerton@talk21.com

Prior's Yeat ◆◆◆◆
Aynsome Road, Cartmel, Grange-over-Sands LA11 6PR
T: (01539) 535178
E: priorsyeat@hotmail.com

CARTMEL FELL
Cumbria

Lightwood Farmhouse Country Guesthouse ◆◆◆◆
Cartmel Fell, Grange-over-Sands LA11 6NP
T: (01539) 531454
F: (01595) 31454
E: enquiries@lightwoodguesthouse.co.uk
I: www.lightwoodguesthouse.co.uk

COCKERMOUTH
Cumbria

The Melbreak Hotel ◆◆◆◆
Winscales Road, Little Clifton, Workington CA14 1XS
T: (01900) 61443
F: (01900) 606589

Rose Cottage ◆◆◆◆
Lorton Road, Cockermouth, CA13 9DX
T: (01900) 822189
F: (01900) 822189
E: bookings@rosecottageguest.co.uk
I: www.rosecottageguest.co.uk

CONISTON
Cumbria

Bank Ground ◆◆◆◆
East of Lake, Coniston, LA21 8AA
T: (01539) 441264
F: (01539) 441900
E: info@bankground.com
I: www.bankground.com

Beech Tree Guest House ◆◆◆◆
Yewdale Road, Coniston, LA21 8DX
T: (015394) 41717
F: (015394) 41717

Brigg House ◆◆◆◆
Torver, Coniston LA21 8AY
T: (01539) 441592
F: (01539) 441092
E: brigg.house@virgin.net
I: www.brigghouse.co.uk

Coniston Lodge ◆◆◆◆◆ GOLD AWARD
Station Road, Coniston, LA21 8HH
T: (01539) 441201
F: (01539) 441201
E: info@coniston-lodge.com
I: www.coniston-lodge.com

Crown Hotel ◆◆◆◆
Coniston, LA21 8EA
T: (01539) 441243
F: (01539) 441804
E: enntiidus@crown-hotel-coniston.com
I: www.crown-hotel-coniston.com

Cruachan ◆◆◆◆
Collingwood Close, Coniston, LA21 8DZ
T: (01539) 441628
F: (01539) 441628
E: cruachan21@lineone.net

How Head Cottage ◆◆◆
East of Lake, Coniston, LA21 8AA
T: (01539) 441594
E: howhead@lineone.net
I: www.howheadcottages.co.uk

Lakeland House ◆◆◆
Tilberthwaite Avenue, Coniston, LA21 8ED
T: (01539) 441303
E: reservations@lakelandhouse.com
I: www.lakelandhouse.com

Oaklands ◆◆◆◆
Yewdale Road, Coniston, LA21 8DX
T: (01539) 441245
F: (01539) 441245
E: judithzeke@oaklandsguesthouse.fsnet.co.uk
I: www.geocities.com/oaklandsguesthouse

Old Rectory Hotel ◆◆◆◆ SILVER AWARD
Torver, Coniston LA21 8AX
T: (01539) 441353
F: (01539) 441156
E: enquiries@theoldrectoryhotel.com
I: www.theoldrectoryhotel.com

Shepherds Villa ◆◆◆
Tilberthwaite Avenue, Coniston, LA21 8ED
T: (01539) 441337
F: (01539) 441337

Sunny Brae Cottage ◆◆◆
Haws Bank, Coniston, LA21 8AR
T: (01539) 441654
F: (01539) 441532
E: sunnybraecottage@aol.com
I: www.sunnybraecottage.co.uk

Thwaite Cottage ◆◆◆◆
Waterhead, Coniston LA21 8AJ
T: (01539) 441367
E: m@thwaitcot.freeserve.co.uk
I: www.thwaitcot.freeserve.co.uk

Townson Ground ◆◆◆◆
East of Lake Road, Coniston, LA21 8AA
T: (01539) 441272
E: info@townsonground.co.uk
I: www.townsonground.co.uk

Wheelgate Country Guesthouse ◆◆◆◆◆ SILVER AWARD
Little Arrow, Coniston, LA21 8AU
T: (01539) 441418
F: (01539) 441114
E: wheelgate@conistoncottages.co.uk
I: www.wheelgate.co.uk

Wilson Arms ◆◆◆
Torver, Coniston LA21 8BB
T: (01539) 441237
F: (01539) 441590

COWGILL
Cumbria

Hillfarm House ◆◆◆◆
Cowgill, Sedbergh LA10 5RF
T: (01539) 625144
I: homepage.ntlworld.com/r.metcalfe2

CROOK
Cumbria

Mitchelland House ◆◆◆◆
Steeles Lane, Crook, Kendal LA8 8LL
T: (01539) 448589
E: marie.mitchelland@talk21.com

CROSBY-ON-EDEN
Cumbria

Crosby House ♦♦♦♦
Crosby-on-Eden, Carlisle
CA6 4QZ
T: (01228) 573239
F: (01228) 573338
E: enquiries@norbyways.demon.co.uk
I: www.northumbria-byways.com/crosby

CROSTHWAITE
Cumbria

Crosthwaite House ♦♦♦♦
Crosthwaite, Kendal LA8 8BP
T: (01539) 568264
F: (01539) 568264
E: bookings@crosthwaitehouse.co.uk
I: www.crosthwaitehouse.co.uk

The Punch Bowl Inn ♦♦♦♦
Crosthwaite, Kendal LA8 8HR
T: (01539) 568237
F: (01539) 568875
E: enquiries@punchbowl.fsnet.co.uk
I: www.punchbowl.fsnet.co.uk

CULGAITH
Cumbria

The Black Swan Inn ♦♦♦♦
Culgaith, Penrith CA10 1QW
T: (01768) 88223
F: (01768) 88223

CUMREW
Cumbria

Cumrew House
♦♦♦♦ SILVER AWARD
Cumrew, Heads Nook, Carlisle
CA8 9DD
T: (01768) 896115
E: rabduff@aol.com
I: www.countrysport-lodge.com

DALEMAIN
Cumbria

Park House Farm ♦♦♦
Dalemain, Penrith CA11 0HB
T: (01768) 486212
F: (01768) 486212
E: stay@parkhousedalemain.co.uk
I: www.eden-in-cumbria.co.uk/parkhouse

DALTON-IN-FURNESS
Cumbria

Black Dog Inn ♦♦
Holmes Green, Broughton Road, Dalton-in-Furness, LA15 8JP
T: (01229) 462561
F: (01229) 468036
E: jack@blackdoginn.freeserve.co.uk

Park Cottage
Rating Applied For
Park, Dalton-in-Furness,
LA15 8JZ
T: (01229) 462850
E: nicholson.parkcottage@quista.net
I: www.parkcottagedalton.co.uk

DENT
Cumbria

George and Dragon Hotel
♦♦♦
Main Street, Dent, Sedbergh
LA10 5QL
T: (01539) 625256

Smithy Fold ♦♦♦
Whernside, Dent, Sedbergh
LA10 5RE
T: (01539) 625368
E: cheetham@smithyfold.co.uk
I: www.smithyfold.co.uk

Stone Close Tea Shop ♦♦♦
Main Street, Dent, Sedbergh
LA10 5QL
T: (01539) 625231
F: (01539) 726567
E: accommodation@stoneclose.co.uk
I: www.stoneclose.co.uk

DRUMBURGH
Cumbria

The Grange
Rating Applied For
Drumburgh, Carlisle CA7 5DW
T: (01228) 576551
E: messrs.hodgson@tesco.net
I: www.thegrangecottage.co.uk

ELTERWATER
Cumbria

Elterwater Park ♦♦♦♦
Skelwith Bridge, Ambleside
LA22 9NP
T: (01539) 432227
F: (01539) 431768
E: enquiries@elterwater.com
I: www.elterwater.com

ESKDALE
Cumbria

Brook House Inn ♦♦♦♦
Boot, Holmrook CA19 1TG
T: (01946) 723288
F: (01946) 723160
E: stay@brookhouseinn.co.uk
I: www.brookhouseinn.co.uk

Forest How ♦♦♦
Eskdale Green, Holmrook
CA19 1TR
T: (01946) 723201
F: (01946) 723190
E: fcarter@easynet.co.uk
I: www.foresthow-eskdale-cumbria.co.uk/

The Gatehouse Outward Bound
♦♦♦
Eskdale, Holmrook CA19 1TE
T: (01946) 723281
F: (01946) 723393
E: professional@outwardbound-uk.org
I: www.outwardbound-uk.org

Woolpack Inn ♦♦♦
Boot, Eskdale, Holmrook
CA19 1TH
T: (01946) 723230
F: (01946) 723230
E: woolpack@eskdale.dial.lakesnet.co.uk
I: www.insites.co.uk/guide//cumbria/accom/woolpack

GARRIGILL
Cumbria

High Windy Hall Hotel and Restaurant♦♦♦♦
Middleton-in-Teesdale Road, Garrigill, Alston CA9 3EZ
T: (01434) 381547
F: (01434) 382477
E: sales@hwh.u-net.com
I: www.hwh.u-net.com

GILSLAND
Cumbria

Bush Nook ♦♦♦♦
Upper Denton, Gilsland,
Brampton CA8 7AF
T: (01697) 747194
F: (01697) 747790
E: info@bushnook.co.uk
I: www.bushnook.co.uk

The Hill ♦♦♦♦
Gilsland, Brampton CA8 7DA
T: (01697) 747214
F: (01697) 747214
E: info@hadrians-wallbedandbreakfast.com
I: www.hadrians-wallbedandbreakfast.com

Slack House Farm ♦♦♦
Gilsland, Brampton CA6 7DB
T: (016977) 47351
F: (016977) 21100
E: slackhousefarm@lineone.net
I: www.slackhousefarm.co.uk

GRANGE-OVER-SANDS
Cumbria

Birchleigh Guest House
♦♦♦♦
Kents Bank Road, Grange-over-Sands, LA11 7EY
T: (01539) 532592
F: (01539) 532592

Corner Beech Guest House
♦♦♦
1 Methven Terrace, Kents Bank Road, Grange-over-Sands,
LA11 7DP
T: (01539) 533088
E: info@cornerbeech.co.uk
I: www.cornerbeech.co.uk

Elton Hotel ♦♦♦♦
Windermere Road, Grange-over-Sands, LA11 6EQ
T: (01539) 532838
F: (01539) 532838
E: chris.crane@btclick.com

Greenacres Country Guesthouse ♦♦♦♦
Lindale, Grange-over-Sands
LA11 6LP
T: (01539) 534578
F: (01539) 534578
I: www.smoothhound.co.uk/hotels/greenacres.html

The Laurels Bed and Breakfast
♦♦♦♦
Berriedale Terrace, Lindale Road, Grange-over-Sands, LA11 6ER
T: (01539) 535919
F: (01539) 535919
E: gml@thelaurels71.freeserve.co.uk

Mayfields ♦♦♦♦
3 Mayfield Terrace, Kents Bank Road, Grange-over-Sands,
LA11 7DW
T: (01539) 534730
I: www.accommodata.co.uk/010699.htm

Methven Hotel ♦♦♦♦
Kents Bank Road, Grange-over-Sands, LA11 7DU
T: (01539) 532031

Somerset House ♦♦♦
Kents Bank Road, Grange-over-Sands, LA11 7EY
T: (01539) 532631

GRASMERE
Cumbria

Ash Cottage Guest House
♦♦♦♦
Red Lion Square, Grasmere,
Ambleside LA22 9SP
T: (01539) 435224

Beck Allans ♦♦♦♦
College Street, Grasmere,
Ambleside LA22 9SZ
T: (01539) 435563
F: (01539) 435563
E: mail@beckallans.com
I: www.beckallans.com

Chestnut Villa ♦♦♦
Keswick Road, Grasmere,
Ambleside LA22 9RE
T: (015394) 35218

Dunmail House ♦♦♦♦
Keswick Road, Grasmere,
Ambleside LA22 9RE
T: (015394) 35256
E: enquiries@dunmailhouse.freeserve.co.uk
I: www.dunmailhouse.com

Forest Side Hotel
Rating Applied For
Forest Side, Grasmere,
Ambleside LA22 9RN
T: (01539) 435250
F: (01539) 435947
E: hotel@forestsidehotel.com
I: www.forestsidehotel.com

The Harwood ♦♦♦
Red Lion Square, Grasmere,
Ambleside LA22 9SP
T: (01539) 435248
F: (01539) 435545
E: enquiries@harwoodhotel.co.uk
I: www.harwoodhotel.co.uk

How Foot Lodge ♦♦♦
Town End, Grasmere, Ambleside
LA22 9SQ
T: (01539) 435366
F: (01539) 435268
E: info@howfoot.co.uk
I: www.howfoot.co.uk

Lake View Country House
♦♦♦♦
Lake View Drive, Grasmere,
Ambleside LA22 9TD
T: (01539) 435384
F: (01539) 435384
E: michelleking@buryend.freeserve.co.uk
I: www.lakeview-grasmere.com

Raise View House ♦♦♦
White Bridge, Grasmere,
Ambleside LA22 9RQ
T: (01539) 435215
F: (01539) 435126
E: john@grasmere-raiseview.co.uk
I: www.grasmere-raiseview.co.uk

Redmayne Cottage ♦♦♦♦
Grasmere, Ambleside LA22 9QY
T: (01539) 435635
I: www.redmayne-grasmere.co.uk

Silver Lea Guest House ♦♦♦♦
Easedale Road, Grasmere,
Ambleside LA22 9QE
T: (01539) 435657
F: (01539) 435657

Titteringdales Guest House ♦♦♦♦
Pye Lane, Grasmere, Ambleside LA22 9RQ
T: (01539) 435439
E: titteringdales@grasmere.net
I: www.grasmere.net

Travellers Rest ♦♦♦
Grasmere, Ambleside LA22 9RR
T: (015394) 35604
I: www.lakelandinns.com

Woodland Crag Guest House ♦♦♦♦
How Head Lane, Grasmere, Ambleside LA22 9SG
T: (01539) 435351
F: (01539) 435351
E: woodlandcrag@aol.com
I: www.woodlandcrag.com

GRAYRIGG Cumbria

Grayrigg Hall Farm ♦♦♦
Grayrigg, Kendal LA8 9BU
T: (01539) 824689

Punchbowl House ♦♦♦♦ SILVER AWARD
Grayrigg, Kendal LA8 9BU
T: (01539) 824345
F: (01539) 824345
E: enquiries@punchbowlhouse.co.uk
I: www.punchbowlhouse.co.uk

GREAT CLIFTON Cumbria

The Clifton Hotel ♦♦♦♦
2 Moor Road, Great Clifton, Workington CA14 1TS
T: (01900) 64616
F: (01900) 873384
E: sales@cliftonhotel.com
I: www.cliftonhotel.com

HAWKSHEAD Cumbria

Betty Fold Country House ♦♦♦♦ SILVER AWARD
Hawkshead Hill, Ambleside LA22 0PS
T: (01539) 436611
E: holidays@bettyfold.freeserve.co.uk
I: www.bettyfold.co.uk

Borwick Lodge Rating Applied For
Outgate, Ambleside LA22 0PU
T: (015394) 36332
F: (015394) 36332
E: borwicklodge@talk21.com
I: www.borwicklodge.com

The Drunken Duck Inn ♦♦♦♦ SILVER AWARD
Barngates, Ambleside, LA22 0NG
T: (01539) 436347
F: (01539) 436781
E: info@drunkenduckinn.co.uk
I: www.drunkenduckinn.co.uk

Grizedale Lodge Hotel ♦♦♦♦ SILVER AWARD
The Hotel In the Forest, Grizedale, Ambleside LA22 0QL
T: (01539) 436532
F: (01539) 436572
E: enquiries@grizedale-lodge.com
I: www.grizedale-lodge.com

High Grassings ♦♦♦♦
Sunny Brow, Outgate, Ambleside LA22 0PU
T: (01539) 436484
F: (01539) 436140
E: info@highgrassings.com
I: www.highgrassings.com

Walker Ground Manor ♦♦♦♦
Vicarage Lane, Hawkshead, Ambleside LA22 0PD
T: (01539) 436219
E: info@walkerground.co.uk
I: www.walkerground.co.uk

Yewfield Vegetarian Guest House ♦♦♦♦
Yewfield, Hawkshead, Ambleside LA22 0PR
T: (01539) 436765
F: (01539) 436096
E: derek.yewfield@btinternet.com
I: www.yewfield.co.uk

HEADS NOOK Cumbria

Sirelands ♦♦♦
Heads Nook, Carlisle CA8 9BT
T: (01228) 670389
F: (01228) 670389

HESKET NEWMARKET Cumbria

Denton House ♦♦♦
Hesket Newmarket, Wigton CA7 8JG
T: (016974) 78415
E: dentonhnm@aol.com

HIGH LORTON Cumbria

Swinside End Farm ♦♦♦♦
Scales, High Lorton, Cockermouth CA13 9UA
T: (01900) 85134
F: (01900) 85410

Terrace Farm ♦♦♦♦
Lorton, Cockermouth CA13 9TX
T: (01900) 85278
I: www.terracefarm.co.uk

HOLME Cumbria

Marwin House ♦♦
Duke Street, Holme, Carnforth LA6 1PY
T: (01524) 781144
F: (01524) 781144

HOUGHTON Cumbria

The Steadings ♦♦♦
Townhead Farm, Houghton, Carlisle CA6 4JB
T: (01228) 523019
F: (01228) 590178

IREBY Cumbria

Daleside Farm ♦♦♦♦
Ireby, Carlisle CA5 1EW
T: (016973) 71268
E: info@dalesidefarm.co.uk
I: www.dalesidefarm.co.uk

KENDAL Cumbria

Beech House Hotel ♦♦♦♦♦
40 Greenside, Kendal, CA9 4LD
T: (01539) 720385
F: (01539) 724082
E: hilary.claxton@virgin.net
I: www.beechhouse-kendal.co.uk

Blaven Homestay ♦♦♦♦♦ SILVER AWARD
Middleshaw, Old Hutton, Kendal LA8 0LZ
T: (01539) 734894
F: (01539) 727447
E: enquiries@blavenhomestay.co.uk
I: www.blavenhomestay.co.uk

Burrow Hall ♦♦♦♦
Plantation Bridge, Kendal, LA8 9JR
T: (01539) 821711
F: (01539) 821711
E: info@burrowhall.fsnet.co.uk
I: www.burrowhall.co.uk

Cragg Farm ♦♦♦
New Hutton, Kendal LA8 0BA
T: (01539) 721760
E: knowles.cragg@ukgateway.net
I: www.craggfarm.com

Fairways Guest House ♦♦♦
102 Windermere Road, Kendal, LA9 5EZ
T: (01539) 725564
E: mp@fairways1.fsnet.co.uk

Fell View ♦♦♦
100 Windermere Road, Kendal, LA9 5EZ
T: (01539) 728431

The Glen ♦♦♦
Oxenholme, Kendal LA9 7RF
T: (01539) 726386
E: greenintheglen@btinternet.com
I: www.smoothhound.co.uk/hotels/glen2.html

Hillside Guest House ♦♦♦
4 Beast Banks, Kendal, LA9 4JW
T: (01539) 722836

Hollin Root Farm ♦♦♦♦
Garth Row, Kendal, LA8 9AW
T: (01539) 823638
E: b-and-b@hollin-root-farm.freeserve.co.uk
I: www.hollinrootfarm.co.uk

Kendal Arms and Hotel ♦♦♦
72 Milnthorpe Road, Kendal, LA9 5HG
T: (01539) 720956
F: (01539) 724851

Lakeland Natural Vegetarian Guesthouse ♦♦♦
Low Slack, Queens Road, Kendal, LA9 4PH
T: (01539) 733011
F: (01539) 733011
E: relax@lakelandnatural.co.uk
I: www.lakelandnatural.co.uk

Newalls Country House ♦♦♦♦
Skelsmergh, Kendal LA9 6NU
T: (01539) 723202

Riversleigh ♦♦♦
49 Milnthorpe Road, Kendal, LA9 5QG
T: (01539) 726392

Sonata ♦♦♦
19 Burneside Road, Kendal, LA9 4RL
T: (01539) 732290
F: (01539) 732290
E: chris@sonataguesthouse.freeserve.co.uk
I: www.sonataguesthouse.co.uk

7 Thorny Hills ♦♦♦♦
Kendal, LA9 7AL
T: (01539) 720207
E: martyn.jowett@btinternet.com

Union Tavern ♦♦♦
159 Stricklandgate, Kendal, LA9 4RF
T: (01539) 724004
E: uniontavern@edirectory.co.uk
I: www.edirectory.co.uk/uniontavern

KESWICK Cumbria

Abacourt House ♦♦♦♦
26 Stanger Street, Keswick, CA12 5JU
T: (017687) 72967
E: abacourt@btinternet.com
I: www.abacourt.co.uk

Acorn House Hotel ♦♦♦♦ SILVER AWARD
Ambleside Road, Keswick, CA12 4DL
T: (01768) 772553
F: (01768) 775332
E: info@acornhousehotel.co.uk
I: www.acornhousehotel.co.uk

Amble House Guest House ♦♦♦♦
23 Eskin Street, Keswick, CA12 4DQ
T: (01768) 773288
F: (01768) 780220
E: info@amblehouse.co.uk
I: www.amblehouse.co.uk

The Anchorage ♦♦♦♦
14 Ambleside Road, Keswick, CA12 4DL
T: (01768) 772813
E: anchorage.keswick@btopenworld.com
I: www.anchorage-keswick.co.uk

Anworth House ♦♦♦♦ SILVER AWARD
27 Eskin Street, Keswick, CA12 4DQ
T: (01768) 772923
I: www.anworthhouse.co.uk

Avondale Guest House ♦♦♦♦
20 Southey Street, Keswick, CA12 4EF
T: (01768) 772735
F: (01768) 775431
E: enquiries@avondaleguesthouse.com
I: www.avondaleguesthouse.com

Badgers Wood ♦♦♦♦
30 Stanger Street, Keswick, CA12 5JU
T: (01768) 772621
E: enquiries@badgers-wood.co.uk
I: www.badgers-wood.co.uk

Beckstones Farm Guest House ♦♦♦
Thornthwaite, Keswick CA12 5SQ
T: (01768) 778510
E: beckstones@lineone.net
I: www.lineone.net/~beckstones

Berkeley Guest House ♦♦♦♦
The Heads, Keswick, CA12 5ER
T: (017687) 74222
E: berkeley@tesco.net
I: www.berkeley-keswick.homepage.com

Birkrigg Farm ♦♦♦
Newlands, Keswick CA12 5TS
T: (017687) 78278

Bonshaw Guest House ♦♦♦
20 Eskin Street, Keswick, CA12 4DG
T: (01768) 773084
E: sylviasanderson@compuserve.com
I: www.bonshaw.co.uk

Bowfell House ♦♦♦
Chestnut Hill, Keswick, CA12 4LR
T: (01768) 774859
E: bowfell.keswick@easicom.com
I: www.stayinkeswick.co.uk

Braemar
♦♦♦♦ SILVER AWARD
21 Eskin Street, Keswick, CA12 4DQ
T: (01768) 773743
E: enquires@braemar-guesthouse.co.uk
I: www.braemar-guesthouse.co.uk

The Cartwheel ♦♦♦
5 Blencathra Street, Keswick, CA12 4HW
T: (01768) 773182
E: info@thecartwheel.co.uk
I: www.thecartwheel.co.uk

Castle Head House
Rating Applied For
Borrowdale Road, Keswick, CA12 5DD
T: (017687) 72082
F: (017687) 74650

Charnwood Guest House ♦♦♦♦
6 Eskin Street, Keswick, CA12 4DH
T: (01768) 774111

Charnwood Lodge ♦♦♦
Thrushwood, Keswick, CA12 4PG
T: (01768) 771318

Cherry Trees ♦♦♦♦
16 Eskin Street, Keswick, CA12 4DQ
T: (01768) 771048
E: cherry.trees@virgin.net
I: www.cherrytrees-keswick.co.uk

Clarence House ♦♦♦♦
14 Eskin Street, Keswick, CA12 4DQ
T: (01768) 773186
F: (01768) 772317
E: clarenceho@aol.com
I: www.clarencehousekeswick.co.uk

The Cottage in the Wood
Rating Applied For
Whinlatter Pass, Braithwaite, Keswick CA12 5TW
T: (017687) 78409
F: (017687) 78064
E: cottage@whinlatter.fsnet.co.uk
I: www.lake-district.net/cottage

Cragwood ♦♦♦
44 Blencathra Street, Keswick, CA12 4HT
T: (01687) 773792
E: cragwood@btopenworld.com
I: www.cragwood-keswick.co.uk

Cumbria House ♦♦♦♦
1 Derwentwater Place, Ambleside Road, Keswick, CA12 4DR
T: (01768) 773171
F: (01768) 773171
E: ctb@cumbriahouse.co.uk
I: www.cumbriahouse.co.uk

Dalegarth House Country Hotel ♦♦♦♦
Portinscale, Keswick CA12 5RQ
T: (01768) 772817
F: (01768) 772817
E: john@dalegarth-house.co.uk
I: www.dalegarth-house.co.uk

Derwentdale Guesthouse ♦♦♦
8 Blencathra Street, Keswick, CA12 4HP
T: (01768) 774187
E: liz@derwentdale.co.uk
I: www.derwentdage.co.uk

Dolly Waggon ♦♦♦
17 Helvellyn Street, Keswick, CA12 4EN
T: (01768) 773593
E: gjosborn@aol.com
I: www.dwkeswick.co.uk

Dunsford Guest House ♦♦♦♦
16 Stanger Street, Keswick, CA12 5JU
T: (01768) 775059
E: enquiries@dunsford.net
I: www.dunsford.net

The Easedale Hotel ♦♦♦
Southey Street, Keswick, CA12 4EG
T: (01768) 772710
F: (01768) 771127
E: easedaleh@aol.com
I: www.milford.co.uk/go/easedale.html

Eden Green Guest House ♦♦♦
20 Blencathra Street, Keswick, CA12 4HP
T: (017687) 72077
F: (017687) 80870
E: sue.plant@edengreen.co.uk
I: www.edengreenguesthouse.com

Ellas Crag ♦♦♦♦
Stair, Keswick CA12 5TT
T: (017687) 78217
F: (017687) 78105
E: ellascrag@talk21.com
I: http://ellascrag.golakes.co.uk

Ellergill Guest House ♦♦♦♦
22 Stanger Street, Keswick, CA12 5JU
T: (01768) 773347
E: stay@ellergill.uk.com
I: www.ellergill.uk.com

Fell House ♦♦♦♦
28 Stranger Street, Keswick, CA12 5JU
T: (017687) 72669
F: (017687) 72669
E: info@fellhouse.co.uk
I: www.fellhouse.co.uk

Glencoe Guest House ♦♦♦♦
21 Helvellyn Street, Keswick, CA12 4EN
T: (01768) 771016
E: enquiries@glencoeguesthouse.co.uk
I: www.glencoeguesthouse.co.uk

Glendale Guest House ♦♦♦
7 Eskin Street, Keswick, CA12 4DH
T: (01768) 773562
F: (01768) 780668
E: info@glendalekeswick.co.uk
I: www.glendalekeswick.co.uk

The Grange Country House
♦♦♦♦♦ SILVER AWARD
Manor Brow, Ambleside Road, Keswick, CA12 4BA
T: (01768) 772500
E: info@grangekeswick.com
I: www.grangekeswick.com

Grassmoor Guest House ♦♦
10 Blencathra Street, Keswick, CA12 4HP
T: (01768) 774008
E: grassmoor.keswick@ukonline.co.uk
I: www.grassmoor-keswick.co.uk

Greystones Hotel ♦♦♦♦
Ambleside Road, Keswick, CA12 4DP
T: (01768) 773108
E: greystones@keslakes.freeserve.co.uk
I: www.greystones.tv

Hazeldene Hotel ♦♦♦♦
The Heads, Keswick, CA12 5ER
T: (01768) 772106
F: (01768) 775435
E: info@hazeldene-hotel.co.uk
I: www.hazeldene-hotel.co.uk

Hedgehog Hill Guesthouse ♦♦♦
18 Blencathra Street, Keswick, CA12 4HP
T: (01768) 774386
F: (01768) 780622
E: etc@hedgehoghill.co.uk
I: www.hedgehoghill.co.uk

Howe Keld Lakeland Hotel ♦♦♦♦
5-7 The Heads, Keswick, CA12 5ES
T: (017687) 72417
F: (017687) 72417
E: david@howekeld.co.uk
I: www.howekeld.co.uk

Hunters Way Guest House ♦♦♦♦
4 Eskin Street, Keswick, CA12 4DH
T: (01768) 772324

Kalgurli Guest House ♦♦♦
33 Helvellyn Street, Keswick, CA12 4EP
T: (01768) 772935
E: info@kalgurli.co.uk
I: www.kalgurli.co.uk

Keskadale Farm ♦♦♦♦
Newlands Valley, Keswick, CA12 5TS
T: (017687) 78544
F: (017687) 78150
E: keskadale.b.b@kencomp.net

Langdale Guest House
Rating Applied For
14 Leonard Street, Keswick, CA12 4EL
T: (017687) 73977

Latrigg House ♦♦♦♦
St Herbert Street, Keswick, CA12 4DF
T: (01768) 773068
F: (01768) 772801
E: latrigghse@aol.com
I: www.latrigghouse.com

Leonard's Field House ♦♦♦
3 Leonard Street, Keswick, CA12 4EJ
T: (01768) 774170
E: leonardsfieldhouse@talk21.com
I: www.leonardsfieldhouse.com

Lincoln Guest House ♦♦♦
23 Stanger Street, Keswick, CA12 5JX
T: (01768) 772597
F: (01768) 772597
E: joan@lincoln-guesthouse.fsnet.co.uk
I: www.lincoln-guesthouse.fsnet.co.uk

Lindisfarne ♦♦♦♦
21 Church Street, Keswick, CA12 4DX
T: (01768) 773218
I: www.lindisfarnehouse.com

Linnett Hill ♦♦♦
4 Penrith Road, Keswick, CA12 4HF
T: (01768) 773109
E: Pete@linnetthill.info
I: www.linnetthill.info

Littlebeck ♦♦♦♦
Chestnut Hill, Keswick, CA12 4LT
T: (01768) 772972
E: littlebeck@btinternet.com

Littletown Farm ♦♦♦
Newlands, Keswick CA12 5TU
T: (01768) 778353
F: (01768) 778437
I: www.littletownfarm.co.uk

Loch Villa ♦♦♦
34 Blencartha Street, Keswick, CA12 4HP
T: (01768) 773226

Lynwood ♦♦♦♦
12 Ambleside Road, Keswick, CA12 4DL
T: (01768) 772081
E: info@lynwood-keswick.co.uk
I: www.lynwood-keswick.co.uk

Lynwood House ♦♦♦♦
35 Helvellyn Street, Keswick, CA12 4EP
T: (017687) 72398
E: info@lynwoodhouse.net
I: www.lynwoodhouse.net

Melbreak House ♦♦♦
29 Church Street, Keswick, CA12 4DX
T: (01768) 773398
F: (01768) 773398
E: melbreakhouse@btinternet.com
I: www.melbreakhouse.co.uk

The Paddock ♦♦♦♦
Wordsworth Street, Keswick, CA12 4HU
T: (01768) 772510
E: val@thepaddock.info
I: www.thepaddock.info

Parkfield Guesthouse
♦♦♦♦ SILVER AWARD
The Heads, Keswick, CA12 5ES
T: (01768) 772328
F: (01768) 771396
E: enquiries@parkfieldkeswick.com
I: www.parkfieldkeswick.com

Ravensworth Hotel
♦♦♦♦ SILVER AWARD
29 Station Street, Keswick, CA12 5HH
T: (01768) 772476
F: (01768) 775287
E: info@ravensworth-hotel.co.uk
I: www.ravensworth-hotel.co.uk

Rickerby Grange ♦♦♦♦
Portinscale, Keswick CA12 5RH
T: (01768) 772344
F: (01768) 775588
E: val@ricor.co.uk
I: www.ricor.co.uk

Sandon Guesthouse ♦♦♦♦
13 Southey Street, Keswick, CA12 4EG
T: (01768) 773648
E: enquiries@sandonguesthouse.com
I: www.sandonguesthouse.com

Seymour House ♦♦♦
36 Lake Road, Keswick, CA12 5DQ
T: (017687) 72764
F: (017687) 71289
E: andy042195@aol.com
I: www.seymour-house.com

Shemara Guest House ♦♦♦♦
27 Bank Street, Keswick, CA12 5JZ
T: (017687) 73936
F: (017687) 80785
E: info@shemara.uk.com
I: www.shemara.uk.com/

The Silverdale Hotel ♦♦♦
17-19 Blencathra Street, Keswick, CA12 4HT
T: (01768) 772294
E: mandy@mdowson.fsnet.co.uk
I: www.silverdalehotelkeswick.co.uk

Skiddaw Grove Country Guest House ♦♦♦♦
Vicarage Hill, Keswick, CA12 5QB
T: (01768) 773324
F: (01768) 773324
E: info@skiddawgrove.demon.co.uk

Stonegarth ♦♦♦♦
Eskin Street, Keswick, CA12 4DH
T: (01768) 772436
E: info@stonegarth.com
I: www.stonegarth.com

Strathmore Guest House ♦♦♦
St John's Terrace, Ambleside Road, Keswick, CA12 4DP
T: (01768) 772584
F: (01768) 772584
E: pbrown@strathmore-lakes.demon.co.uk
I: www.keswick.net/strathmore.com

Sunnyside Guest House ♦♦♦
Southey Street, Keswick, CA12 4EF
T: (01768) 772446
E: enquiries@sunnysideguesthouse.com

Swinside Farmhouse ♦♦♦
Newlands Farmhouse, Keswick, CA12 5UE
T: (01768) 778363
E: swinside.farmhouse@btopenworld.com

Swinside Inn ♦♦♦
Newlands, Keswick, CA12 5UE
T: (01768) 778253
F: (01768) 778253
E: info@theswinsideinn.com
I: www.theswinsideinn.com

Tarn Hows ♦♦♦♦
3-5 Eskin Street, Keswick, CA12 4DH
T: (01768) 773217
F: (01768) 773217
E: info@tarnhows.co.uk
I: www.tarnhows.co.uk

Watendlath Guest House ♦♦♦
15 Acorn Street, Keswick, CA12 4EA
T: (01768) 774165
F: (01768) 74165
E: linda@watendlathguesthouse.co.uk
I: www.watendlathguesthouse.co.uk

West View Guest House ♦♦♦♦
The Heads, Keswick, CA12 5ES
T: (01768) 773638

Whitehouse Guest House
♦♦♦♦ SILVER AWARD
15 Ambleside Road, Keswick, CA12 4DL
T: (01768) 773176
F: (01768) 773176
E: whitehousekeswick@hotmail.com
I: www.whitehousekeswick.co.uk

KIRKBY LONSDALE
Cumbria

Capernwray House
♦♦♦♦ SILVER AWARD
Borrans Lane, Capernwray, Carnforth LA6 1AE
T: (01524) 732363
F: (01524) 736895
E: thesmiths@capernwrayhouse.com
I: www.capernwrayhouse.com

The Copper Kettle ♦♦
3-5 Market Street, Kirkby Lonsdale, Carnforth LA6 2AU
T: (01524) 271714
F: (01524) 271714

Tossbeck Farm ♦♦♦
Middleton, Kirkby Lonsdale, Carnforth LA6 2LZ
T: (015242) 76214
E: postmaster@tossbeck.f9.co.uk
I: www.tossbeck.co.uk

KIRKBY STEPHEN
Cumbria

Ing Hill Lodge ♦♦♦♦
nr Outhgill, Mallerstang Dale, Kirkby Stephen, CA17 4JT
T: (017683) 71153
F: (017683) 72710
E: inghill@fsbdial.co.uk

Jolly Farmers Guest House ♦♦♦♦
63 High Street, Kirkby Stephen, CA17 4SH
T: (017683) 71063
F: (017683) 71063
E: jollyf@cumbria.com
I: www.cumbria.com/jollyf/

West View ♦♦♦♦
Ravenstonedale, Kirkby Stephen CA17 4NG
T: (01539) 623415
E: enquiries@westview-cumbria.co.uk
I: www.enquiries@westview-cumbria.co.uk

KIRKLINTON
Cumbria

Clift House Farm ♦♦♦
Kirklinton, Carlisle CA6 6DE
T: (01228) 675237
F: (01228) 675237

Fergushill ♦♦♦
Kirklinton, Carlisle CA6 6DA
T: (01228) 675785
F: (01228) 675785
E: info@fergushill.co.uk
I: www.fergushill.co.uk

LAKESIDE
Cumbria

The Knoll Country House
♦♦♦♦ SILVER AWARD
Lakeside, Newby Bridge, Ulverston LA12 8AU
T: (01539) 531347
F: (01539) 530850
E: info@theknoll-lakeside.co.uk
I: www.theknoll-lakeside.co.uk

LANERCOST
Cumbria

Abbey Bridge Inn
Rating Applied For
Lanercost, Brampton CA8 2HG
T: (01697) 72224
F: (01697) 742184
E: tim@abbeybridge.co.uk
I: abbeybridge.co.uk

LAZONBY
Cumbria

Banktop House ♦♦♦
Lazonby, Penrith CA10 1AQ
T: (01768) 898268
F: (01768) 898851
E: hartsop@globalnet.co.uk

LONGTOWN
Cumbria

Briar Lea House ♦♦♦♦
Brampton Road, Longtown, Carlisle CA6 5TN
T: (01228) 791538
F: (01228) 791538
E: info@briarleahouse.co.uk
I: www.briarleahouse.co.uk

Craigburn ♦♦♦♦
Catlowdy, Longtown, Carlisle CA6 5QP
T: (01228) 577214
F: (01228) 577014
E: louiselawson@hotmail.com
I: www.craigburnfarmhouse.co.uk

LOWESWATER
Cumbria

Askhill Farm ♦♦♦
Loweswater, Cockermouth CA13 0SU
T: (01946) 861640

LOWICK
Cumbria

Garth Row ♦♦♦
Lowick Green, Ulverston LA12 8EB
T: (01229) 885633
E: b&b@garthrow.freeserve.co.uk
I: www.garthrow.co.uk

LOWICK GREEN
Cumbria

The Farmers Arms Hotel ♦♦♦
Lowick Green, Ulverston, LA12 8DT
T: (01229) 861277
F: (01229) 861853
E: bookings@farmersarms.co.uk
I: www.farmersarmslowick.co.uk

MAULDS MEABURN
Cumbria

Trainlands Bed & Breakfast ♦♦♦
Maulds Meaburn, Penrith CA10 3HX
T: (017683) 51249
F: (017683) 53983
E: bousfield@trainlands.u-net.com

MILBURN
Cumbria

Low Howgill Farm ♦♦♦♦
Low Howgill, Milburn, Penrith CA10 1TL
T: (01768) 361595
F: (01768) 361598
E: holidays@low-howgill.co.uk
I: www.low-howgill.f9.co.uk

Slakes Farm ♦♦♦
Knock, Appleby-in-Westmorland CA16 6DP
T: (01768) 361385
E: oakleaves5491@aol.com

MILLOM
Cumbria

The Duddon Pilot Hotel ♦♦♦♦
Devonshire Road, Millom, LA18 4JT
T: (01229) 774116
F: (01229) 774116

MILNTHORPE
Cumbria

The Cross Keys Hotel ♦♦♦♦
1 Park Road, Milnthorpe, LA7 7AD
T: (01539) 562115
F: (01539) 562445
E: infocrosskeys@aol.com
I: www.thecrosskeyshotel.co.uk

MOSEDALE
Cumbria

Mosedale House ♦♦♦♦
Mosedale, Penrith CA11 0XQ
T: (01768) 779371
E: mosedale@northlakes.co.uk
I: www.mosedalehouse.co.uk
♿

MUNGRISDALE
Cumbria

Mosedale End Farm ♦♦♦
Mungrisdale, Penrith CA11 0XQ
T: (017687) 79605
E: armstrong@awmcmanus.screaming.net
I: www.smoothhound.co.uk/hotels/mosedale.html

Near Howe Hotel ♦♦♦
Mungrisdale, Penrith CA11 0SH
T: (01768) 779678
F: (01768) 779678
E: nearhowe@btopenworld
I: www.nearhowe.co.uk

NEWBIGGIN-ON-LUNE
Cumbria

Tranna Hill ♦♦♦♦
Newbiggin-on-Lune, Kirkby Stephen CA17 4NY
T: (015396) 23227
E: trannahill@hotmail.com

NEWBY BRIDGE
Cumbria

Old Barn Farm ♦♦♦♦
Fiddler Hall, Newby Bridge, Ulverston, LA12 8NQ
T: (01539) 531842

NEWLANDS
Cumbria

Uzzicar Farm ♦♦♦
Newlands, Keswick CA12 5TS
T: (017687) 78367
F: (017687) 78367
E: csimpson@ktdinternet.com

OUTGATE
Cumbria

Bracken Fell ♦♦♦
Outgate, Ambleside LA22 0NH
T: (01539) 436289
F: (01539) 436142
E: hart.brackenfell@virgin.net
I: www.brackenfell.com

OXENHOLME
Cumbria

Station Inn ♦♦♦♦
Oxenholme, Kendal LA9 7RF
T: (01539) 724094
F: (01539) 724094

PATTERDALE
Cumbria

Deepdale Hall ♦♦♦♦
Patterdale, Penrith CA11 0NR
T: (01768) 482369
F: (01768) 482608
E: brown@deepdalehall.freeserve.co.uk
I: www.deepdalehall.co.uk

PENRITH
Cumbria

Albany House Rating Applied For
5 Portland Place, Penrith, CA11 7QN
T: (01768) 863072
F: (01768) 895527
E: info@albany-house.org.uk
I: www.albany-house.org.uk

Beacon Bank Hotel ♦♦♦♦
Beacon Edge, Penrith, CA11 7BD
T: (01768) 862633
F: (01768) 899055
E: beaconbank.hotel@virgin.net
I: www.smoothhound.co.uk

Blue Swallow Guesthouse ♦♦♦
11 Victoria Road, Penrith, CA11 8HR
T: (01768) 866335
E: blueswallows@tiscali.co.uk
I: www.blueswallow.co.uk

Brandelhow Guest House ♦♦♦
1 Portland Place, Penrith, CA11 7QN
T: (01768) 864470

The Friarage ♦♦♦♦
Friargate, Penrith, CA11 7XR
T: (01768) 863635
F: (01768) 863635

Glendale ♦♦♦♦
4 Portland Place, Penrith, CA11 7QN
T: (01768) 862579
F: (01768) 867934
E: glendale@lineone.net
I: www.glendaleguesthouse.net

Hornby Hall Country Guest House ♦♦♦♦
Hornby Hall, Brougham, Penrith CA10 2AR
T: (01768) 891114
F: (01768) 891114
E: enquiries@hornbyhall.co.uk
I: www.hornbyhall.co.uk

Limes Country Hotel ♦♦♦
Redhills, Penrith, CA11 0DT
T: (01768) 863343
F: (01768) 867190
E: jdhanton@aol.com
I: www.members.aol.com/jdhanton/index.htm

Little Blencowe Farm ♦♦♦
Blencowe, Penrith, CA11 0DG
T: (017684) 83338
F: (017684) 83054
E: bart.fawcett@ukgateway.net

Queen's Head Inn ♦♦
Tirril, Penrith CA10 2JF
T: (01768) 863219
F: (01768) 863243
E: bookings@queensheadinn.co.uk
I: www.queensheadinn.co.uk

Roundthorn Country House ♦♦♦♦ SILVER AWARD
Beacon Edge, Penrith, CA11 8SJ
T: (01768) 863952
F: (01768) 864100
E: enquiries@roundthorn.co.uk
I: www.roundthorn.co.uk

POOLEY BRIDGE
Cumbria

Sun Inn ♦♦♦
Pooley Bridge, Penrith CA10 2NN
T: (01768) 486205
F: (01768) 486913

PORTINSCALE
Cumbria

Derwent Cottage ♦♦♦♦♦ GOLD AWARD
Portinscale, Keswick CA12 5RF
T: (01768) 774838
E: enquires@dercott.demon.co.uk
I: www.dercott.demon.co.uk

RAVENSTONEDALE
Cumbria

The Stables Bed & Breakfast ♦♦♦♦
The Stables, Coldbeck, Ravenstonedale, Kirkby Stephen CA17 4LW
T: (01539) 623641
F: (01539) 623641
E: info@coldbeckstables.com
I: www.coldbeckstables.com

RYDAL
Cumbria

Nab Cottage Guest House ♦♦♦
Nab Cottage, Rydal, Ambleside LA22 9SD
T: (01539) 435311
F: (01539) 435493
E: ell@nab.dial.lakesnet.co.uk
I: www.kencomp.net/homepages/ell/nab/

ST BEES
Cumbria

Fairladies Barn Guest House ♦♦♦
Main Street, St Bees, CA27 0AD
T: (01946) 822718
F: (01946) 825838
E: info@fairladiesbarn.co.uk
I: www.fairladiesbarn.co.uk

SANDSIDE
Cumbria

Plantation Cottage ♦♦♦♦
Arnside Road, Sandside, Milnthorpe LA7 7JU
T: (01524) 762069

SATTERTHWAITE
Cumbria

Town End ♦♦♦♦
Satterthwaite, Ulverston LA12 8LN
T: (01229) 860936

SAWREY
Cumbria

Beechmount Country House ♦♦♦
Near Sawrey, Ambleside LA22 0JZ
T: (01539) 436356
E: beechmount@supanet.com
I: www.beechmountcountryhouse.co.uk

Buckle Yeat Guest House ♦♦♦♦
Sawrey, Ambleside LA22 0LF
T: (01539) 436446
E: info@buckle-yeat.co.uk
I: www.buckle-yeat.co.uk

High Green Gate Guest House ♦♦♦
Near Sawrey, Ambleside LA22 0LF
T: (01539) 436296
E: highgreengate@amserve.net

Lakefield ♦♦♦♦
Sawrey, Ambleside LA22 0JZ
T: (01539) 436635
F: (01539) 436635

Tower Bank Arms ♦♦♦
Near Sawrey, Ambleside LA22 0LF
T: (01539) 436334
F: (01539) 43448
E: sales@towerbankarms.fsnet.co.uk

West Vale Country House ♦♦♦♦
Far Sawrey, Hawkshead, Ambleside LA22 0LQ
T: (01539) 442817
F: (01539) 45302
E: enquiries@westvalecountryhouse.co.uk
I: www.westvalecountryhouse.co.uk

SCOTBY
Cumbria

Windsover ♦♦♦♦
Lambley Bank, Scotby, Carlisle CA4 8BX
T: (01228) 513550
E: jimcallaghan@tinyworld.co.uk
I: www.windsover.co.uk

SEASCALE
Cumbria

Victoria Villa Hotel and Egloff's Eating House ♦♦♦♦
58 Gosforth Road, Seascale, CA20 1JG
T: (01946) 727309
F: (01946) 727158
I: www.egloffeatinghouse.co.uk

SEDBERGH
Cumbria

Ash Hining Farm ♦♦♦
Howgill, Sedbergh LA10 5HU
T: (01539) 620957
F: (01539) 620957

Bridge House ♦♦♦♦
Brigflatts, Sedbergh, LA10 5HN
T: (01539) 621820
F: (01539) 621820

Bull Hotel ♦♦♦♦
Main Street, Sedbergh, LA10 5BL
T: (01539) 620264
F: (01539) 620212
E: bullhotel@btinternet.com
I: www.bullatsedbergh.co.uk

Dalesman Country Inn ♦♦♦♦
Main Street, Sedbergh, LA10 5BN
T: (01539) 621183
F: (01539) 621311
E: info@thedalesman.co.uk
I: www.thedalesman.co.uk

St Mark's ♦♦♦♦
Cautley, Sedbergh, LA10 5LZ
T: (01539) 620287
F: (01539) 621585
E: st.marks@talk21.com

SELSIDE
Cumbria

Hollowgate Farm ♦♦♦
Hollowgate, Selside, Kendal LA8 9LG
T: (01539) 823258
E: hollowgate@talk21.com

SOULBY
Cumbria

Riddlesay Farm ♦♦♦♦
Soulby, Kirkby Stephen CA17 4PX
T: (017683) 71474
F: (017683) 71483
E: mrarmstrong@btinternet.com

STANWIX
Cumbria

Aldingham House Townhouse B&B ♦♦♦♦♦ SILVER AWARD
Aldingham House, 1 Eden Mount, Carlisle, CA3 9LZ
T: (01228) 522554
F: (01228) 527089
E: enquiries@aldinghamhouse.co.uk
I: www.aldinghamhouse.co.uk

STAVELEY
Cumbria

Eagle and Child Hotel ♦♦♦
Kendal Road, Staveley, Kendal
LA8 9LP
T: (01539) 821320
E: eaglechildinn@btinternet.com
I: www.eaglechildinn.co.uk

Tarn House ♦♦♦♦
18 Danes Road, Staveley, Kendal
LA8 9PW
T: (01539) 821656

TALKIN
Cumbria

Hullerbank ♦♦♦♦
Talkin, Brampton CA8 1LB
T: (016977) 46668
F: (016977) 46668
E: info@hullerbank.freeserve.co.uk
I: www.smoothhound.co.uk/hotels/huller.html

TEBAY
Cumbria

Primrose Cottage ♦♦♦♦
Orton Road, Tebay, Penrith
CA10 3TL
T: (01539) 624791
E: info@primrosecottagecumbria.co.uk
I: www.primrosecottagecumbria.co.uk

THORNTHWAITE
Cumbria

Jenkin Hill Cottage
♦♦♦♦ SILVER AWARD
Thornthwaite, Keswick
CA12 5SG
T: (017687) 78443
F: (017687) 78445
E: quality@jenkinhill.co.uk
: www.jenkinhill.co.uk

Thornthwaite Grange ♦♦♦
hornthwaite, Keswick
CA12 5SA
: (01768) 778205
: joan_berwick@hotmail.com
: www.thornthwaite-grange.
o.uk

THRELKELD
Cumbria

cales Farm Country
uesthouse ♦♦♦♦
cales, Threlkeld, Keswick
A12 4SY
: (01768) 779660
: (01768) 779510
: scales@scalesfarm.com.
www.scalesfarm.com

TROUTBECK
Cumbria

ill Head Farm ♦♦♦
outbeck, Penrith CA11 0ST
(01768) 779652
(01768) 779130
enquiries@gillheadfarm.co.uk
www.gillheadfarm.co.uk

gh Fold Farm ♦♦♦♦
outbeck, Windermere
A23 1PG
(01539) 432200
enquiries@highfoldfarm.
.uk
www.highfoldfarm.co.uk

gh Green Lodge ♦♦♦♦
gh Green, Troutbeck,
indermere LA23 1PN
(01539) 433005

Lane Head Farm Guest House
♦♦♦♦
Troutbeck, Penrith CA11 0SY
T: (01768) 779220
F: (01768) 779220
E: info@laneheadfarm.freeserve.co.uk
I: www.laneheadfarm.co.uk

Troutbeck Inn ♦♦♦♦
Troutbeck, Penrith CA11 0SJ
T: (01768) 483635
F: (01768) 483928
E: enquiries@troutbeck-inn.com
I: www.troutbeck_inn.com

ULLSWATER
Cumbria

Bank House Farm ♦♦♦♦
Matterdale End, Penrith
CA11 0LF
T: (01768) 482040
E: tjnhargreaves@aol.com

Elm House
♦♦♦♦ SILVER AWARD
Pooley Bridge, Penrith
CA10 2NH
T: (01768) 486334
F: (01768) 486851
E: b&b@elmhouse.demon.co.uk
I: www.elmhouse.demon.co.uk

Knotts Mill Country Lodge
♦♦♦
Ullswater, Watermillock, Penrith
CA11 0JN
T: (017684) 86699
F: (017684) 86190
E: relax@knottsmill.com
I: www.knottsmill.com

Land Ends Country Lodge
♦♦♦
Watermillock, Ullswater, Penrith
CA11 0NB
T: (01768) 486438
F: (01768) 486959
E: infolandends@btinternet.com
I: www.landends.co.uk

Moss Crag ♦♦♦
Eagle Road, Glenridding, Penrith
CA11 0PA
T: (01768) 482500
F: (01768) 482500
E: info@mosscrag.co.uk
I: www.mosscrag.co.uk

Netherdene Guest House ♦♦♦
Troutbeck, Penrith CA11 0SJ
T: (01768) 483475
F: (01768) 483475
E: netherdene@aol.com
I: www.netherdene.co.uk

Tymparon Hall ♦♦♦♦
Newbiggin, Stainton, Penrith
CA11 0HS
T: (01768) 483236
F: (01768) 483236
E: margaret@tymparon.freeserve.co.uk
I: www.tymparon.freeserve.co.uk

Ullswater House ♦♦♦
Pooley Bridge, Penrith
CA10 2NN
T: (01768) 486259

Whitbarrow Farm ♦♦♦
Berrier, Penrith CA11 0XB
T: (01768) 483366
F: (01768) 483179
E: mary@whitebarrowfarm.co.uk
I: www.whitebarrowfarm.co.uk

ULVERSTON
Cumbria

Trinity House Hotel
Rating Applied For
Princess Street, Ulverston,
LA12 7NB
T: (01229) 588889
F: (01229) 588552
E: traininghotel@aol.com

Virginia House Hotel ♦♦♦♦
24 Queen Street, Ulverston,
LA12 7AF
T: (01229) 584844
F: (01229) 588565
E: virginia@ulverstonhotels.co.uk
I: www.ulverstonhotels.com

UNDERBARROW
Cumbria

High Gregg Hall Farm ♦♦♦
Underbarrow, Kendal LA8 8BL
T: (01539) 568318

Tranthwaite Hall ♦♦♦♦
Underbarrow, Kendal LA8 8HG
T: (01539) 568285
E: tranthwaitehall@aol.com
I: www.tranthwaitehall.co.uk

Tullythwaite House
♦♦♦♦ SILVER AWARD
Underbarrow, Kendal LA8 8BB
T: (01539) 568397

WALTON
Cumbria

Town Head Farm ♦♦♦
Walton, Brampton CA8 2DJ
T: (01697) 72730
E: armstrong_townhead@hotmail.com
I: www.town-head-farm.co.uk

WARWICK BRIDGE
Cumbria

Brookside Bed and Breakfast
♦♦♦♦
Warwick Bridge, Carlisle
CA4 8RE
T: (01228) 560250
E: brookside@contactme.co.uk
I: www.brooksidebedandbreakfast.homestead.com

WATERHEAD
Cumbria

Waterhead Country Guest
House ♦♦♦
Waterhead, Ambleside LA21 8AJ
T: (01539) 441442
F: (01539) 441476
E: waterheadsteve@aol.com
I: www.waterheadguesthouse.co.uk

WHITEHAVEN
Cumbria

Corkickle Guest House ♦♦♦♦
1 Corkickle, Whitehaven,
CA28 8AA
T: (01946) 692073
F: (01946) 692073
E: corkickle@tinyworld.co.uk

The Cottage Bed and Breakfast
♦♦
The Cottage, Mirehouse Road,
Whitehaven, CA28 9UD
T: (01946) 695820

Glenfield ♦♦♦
Corkickle, Whitehaven, CA28 7TS
T: (01946) 691911
E: glenfield_hotel@talk21.com
I: www.whitehaven.org.uk/glenfield.html

Moresby Hall
♦♦♦♦ SILVER AWARD
Moresby, Whitehaven, CA28 6PJ
T: (01946) 696317
F: (01946) 694385
E: etc@moresbyhall.co.uk
I: www.moresbyhall.co.uk

WINDERMERE
Cumbria

Acton House ♦♦♦
41 Craig Walk, Windermere,
LA23 2HB
T: (015394) 45340

Almaria House ♦♦♦
17 Broad Street, Windermere,
LA23 2AB
T: (015394) 43026

Aphrodites Themed
Accommodation ♦♦♦♦
Longtail Hill, Bowness-on-Windermere, Windermere
LA23 2EQ
T: (01539) 446702
E: enquiries@aphroditeslodge.co.uk
I: www.aphroditeslodge.co.uk

Applegarth Hotel ♦♦♦
College Road, Windermere,
LA23 1BU
T: (01539) 443206
F: (01539) 446636
E: enquiries@applegarthhotel.com
I: www.applegarthhotel.com

Applethwaite House ♦♦♦
1 Upper Oak Street, Windermere,
LA23 2LB
T: (015394) 44689
E: applethwaitehouse@btinternet.com
I: www.btinternet.com/~applethwaitehouse

The Archway ♦♦♦♦
13 College Road, Windermere,
LA23 1BU
T: (01539) 445613
F: (01539) 445613
E: archway@btinternet.com
I: www.communiken.com/archway

Ashleigh Guest House ♦♦♦♦
11 College Road, Windermere,
LA23 1BU
T: (01539) 442292
F: (01539) 442292
E: enquiries@ashleighhouse.com
I: www.ashleighhouse.com

Aspen Cottage ♦♦
6 Havelock Road, Windermere,
LA23 1EH
T: (01539) 443946

Autumn Leaves Guest House
♦♦♦
29 Broad Street, Windermere,
LA23 2AB
T: (01539) 448410
E: autumnleaves@nascr.net
I: www.autumnleaves.gbr.cc

The Beaumont
Rating Applied For
Holly Road, Windermere,
LA23 2AF
T: (015394) 47075
F: (015394) 47075
E: thebeaumonthotel@btinternet.com
I: www.lakesbeaumont.co.uk

Beaumont ♦♦♦♦
Thornbarrow Road, Windermere,
LA23 2DG
T: (01539) 445521
F: (01539) 446267
E: etc@beaumont-holidays.co.uk
I: www.beaumont-holidays.co.uk

Beckmead House ♦♦♦
5 Park Avenue, Windermere,
LA23 2AR
T: (015394) 42757
F: (015394) 42757

Beckside Cottage
Rating Applied For
4 Park Road, Windermere,
LA23 2AW
T: (015394) 42069
E: beckside-cottage@hotmail.com

Beechwood Private Hotel
♦♦♦♦ SILVER AWARD
South Craig, Beresford Road,
Bowness-on-Windermere,
Windermere LA23 2JG
T: (015394) 43403
F: (015394) 43403

Belsfield House ♦♦♦♦
4 Belsfield Terrace, Kendal Road,
Bowness-on-Windermere,
Windermere LA23 3EQ
T: (01539) 445823
I: www.belsfieldhouse.co.uk

Boston House
♦♦♦♦ SILVER AWARD
4 The Terrace, Windermere,
LA23 1AJ
T: (01539) 443654
E: info@bostonhouse.co.uk
I: www.bostonhouse.co.uk

Bowfell Cottage ♦♦♦
Middle Entrance Drive, Storrs
Park, Bowness-on-Windermere,
Windermere LA23 3JY
T: (01539) 444835

Braemount House ♦♦♦♦
Sunny Bank Road, Windermere,
LA23 2EN
T: (01539) 445967
F: (01539) 445967
E: enquiries@braemount-house.co.uk
I: www.braemount-house.co.uk

Brook House ♦♦♦
30 Ellerthwaite Road,
Windermere, LA23 2AH
T: (01539) 444932

Brooklands ♦♦♦
Ferry View, Bowness-on-Windermere, Windermere
LA23 3JB
T: (01539) 442344
E: brooklandsferryview@btinternet.com
I: www.smoothhound.co.uk/hotels/brooklands

Cambridge House
Rating Applied For
9 Oak Street, Windermere,
LA23 1EN
T: (01539) 443846
F: (01539) 446662
E: reservations@cambridge-house.fsbusiness.co.uk
I: www.cambridge-house.fsbusiness.co.uk

Clifton House ♦♦♦
28 Ellerthwaite Road,
Windermere, LA23 2AH
T: (01539) 444968
E: info@cliftonhse.co.uk
I: www.cliftonhse.co.uk

College House ♦♦♦♦
15 College Road, Windermere,
LA23 1BU
T: (01539) 445767
E: clghse@aol.com
I: www.college-house.com

The Common Farm ♦♦♦
Windermere, LA23 1JQ
T: (01539) 443433

The Cottage ♦♦♦
Elleray Road, Windermere,
LA23 1AG
T: (01539) 444796
F: (01539) 444721
E: janetfox@thecottageguesthouse.com
I: www.thecottageguesthouse.com

Craig Wood Guest House ♦♦♦
119 Craig Walk, Bowness-on-Windermere, Windermere
LA23 3AX
T: (015394) 44914
F: (015394) 44914
E: fennix@globalnet.com

Crompton House ♦♦♦
Lake Road, Windermere,
LA23 2EQ
T: (01539) 443020
F: (01539) 443020
E: westlake@clara.net
I: www.cromptonhouse.com

Dene Crest ♦♦♦
Woodland Road, Windermere,
LA23 2AE
T: (015394) 44979
E: denecrest@btinternet.com
I: www.denecrest.gbr.cc

Denehurst Guest House
♦♦♦♦
40 Queens Drive, Windermere,
LA23 2EL
T: (015394) 44710
F: (015394) 44710
E: denehurst@btconnect.com
I: www.denehurst-guesthouse.co.uk

Dunvegan Guest House ♦♦♦
Broad Street, Windermere,
LA23 2AB
T: (01539) 443502
F: (01539) 447721
E: bryan.twaddle@btinternet.com
I: www.smoothhound.co.uk/hotels/dunvegan

Eastbourne ♦♦♦♦
Biskey Howe Road, Bowness-on-Windermere, Windermere
LA23 2JR
T: (01539) 443525
F: (01539) 443525
E: mail@eastbourne-guesthouse.co.uk
I: www.eastbourne-guesthouse.co.uk

Elim Lodge ♦♦♦
Biskey Howe Road, Bowness-on-Windermere, Windermere
LA23 2JP
T: (01539) 447299
E: enquiries@elimlodge.co.uk
I: www.elimlodge.co.uk

Fair Rigg
♦♦♦♦ SILVER AWARD
Ferry View, Bowness-on-Windermere, Windermere
LA23 3JB
T: (015394) 43941
E: rtodd51257@aol.com
I: www.fairrigg.co.uk

The Fairfield ♦♦♦♦
Brantfell Road, Bowness-on-Windermere, Windermere
LA23 3AE
T: (01539) 446565
F: (01539) 446565
E: ray&barb@the-fairfield.co.uk
I: www.the-fairfield.co.uk

Fir Trees ♦♦♦♦
Lake Road, Windermere,
LA23 2EQ
T: (01539) 442272
F: (01539) 442512
E: enquiries@firtrees.com
I: www.fir-trees.com

Firgarth ♦♦♦
Ambleside Road, Windermere,
LA23 1EU
T: (01539) 446974
F: (01539) 442384
E: thefirgarth@KTDinternet.com

Glenville Hotel ♦♦♦♦
Lake Road, Windermere,
LA23 2EQ
T: (01539) 443371
F: (01539) 443371
E: glenville1@btinternet.com
I: www.glenvillehotel.co.uk

Greenriggs Guest House ♦♦♦
8 Upper Oak Street, Windermere,
LA23 2LB
T: (01539) 442265
E: greenriggs@talk21.com
I: www.greenriggs.co.uk

Hazel Bank ♦♦♦♦
Hazel Street, Windermere,
LA23 1EL
T: (01539) 445486
F: (01539) 445486
E: enquiries@hazelbank.co.uk
I: www.hazelbank-guesthouse.co.uk

Heather Cottage Guest House
Rating Applied For
11 Broad Street, Windermere,
LA23 2AB
T: (015394) 44616
F: (015394) 44616
E: bookings@heather-cottage.co.uk
I: www.heather-cottage.co.uk

Heatherbank Guest House
♦♦♦
13 Birch Street, Windermere,
LA23 1EG
T: (01539) 446503
F: (01539) 446503
E: heatherbank@btinternet.com
I: www.heatherbank.com

High View
♦♦♦♦ SILVER AWARD
Sun Hill Lane, Troutbeck Bridge,
Windermere LA23 1HJ
T: (01539) 444618
F: (01539) 444618
E: info@accommodationlakedistrict.com
I: www.accommodationlakedistrict.com

Hilton House ♦♦♦♦
New Road, Windermere,
LA23 2EE
T: (01539) 443934
F: (01539) 443934
E: enquiries@hiltonhouse-guesthouse.co.uk
I: hilton-guesthouse.co.uk

Holly Lodge ♦♦♦
6 College Road, Windermere,
LA23 1BX
T: (01539) 443873
F: (01539) 443873
E: doyle@hollylodge20.fsnet.co.uk
I: www.hollylodge20.fsnet.co.uk

Holly-Wood ♦♦♦♦
Holly Road, Windermere,
LA23 2AF
T: (015394) 42219
F: (015394) 42219
I: www.hollywoodguesthouse.co.uk

Holmlea ♦♦♦
Kendal Road, Bowness-on-Windermere, Windermere
LA23 3EW
T: (01539) 442597

Ivy Bank ♦♦♦♦
Holly Road, Windermere,
LA23 2AF
T: (015394) 42601
E: ivybank@clara.co.uk
I: www.ivybank.clara.co.uk

Kays Cottage ♦♦♦♦
7 Broad Street, Windermere,
LA23 2AB
T: (01539) 444146
E: kayscottage@freenetname.co.uk
I: www.kayscottage.co.uk

Kenilworth Guest House ♦♦♦
Holly Road, Windermere,
LA23 2AF
T: (015394) 44004
E: busby@kenilworth-lake-district.co.uk

Kirkwood Guest House ♦♦♦
Prince's Road, Windermere,
LA23 2DD
T: (01539) 443907
F: (01539) 443907
E: info@kirkwood51.co.uk
I: www.kirkwood51.co.uk

Lakes Hotel ♦♦♦
1 High Street, Windermere,
LA23 1AF
T: (015394) 42751
F: (015394) 46026
E: admin@lakes-hotel.com
I: www.lakes-hotel.com

Lakeshore House
♦♦♦♦♦ GOLD AWARD
Ecclerigg, Windermere, LA23 1LJ
T: (01539) 433202
F: (01539) 433213
E: lakeshore@lakedistrict.uk.com
I: www.lakedistrict.uk.com

Langdale View Guest House
♦♦♦
114 Craig Walk, Off Helm Road, Bowness-on-Windermere, Windermere LA23 3AX
T: (015394) 44076
E: enquiries@langdaleview.co.uk
I: www.langdaleview.co.uk

Latimer House ♦♦♦
Lake Road, Bowness-on-Windermere, Windermere LA23 2JJ
T: (01539) 446888
F: (01539) 446888
E: latimerhouse@hotmail.com
I: www.latimerhouse.co.uk

Laurel Cottage ♦♦♦♦
St Martin's Square, Kendal Road, Bowness-on-Windermere, Windermere LA23 3EF
T: (01539) 445594
F: (01539) 445594
E: enquiries@laurelcottage-bnb.co.uk
I: www.laurelcottage-bnb.co.uk

Laurel Cottage ♦♦♦♦
8 Park Road, Windermere, LA23 2BJ
T: (01539) 443053
E: wendy@laurelcottage8.freeserve.co.uk
I: www.laurelcottagewindermere.co.uk

Lindisfarne House ♦♦♦
Sunny Bank Road, Windermere, LA23 2EN
T: (015394) 46295

Lingwood ♦♦♦♦
Birkett Hill, Bowness-on-Windermere, Windermere LA23 3EZ
: (01539) 444680
: (01539) 448154
: enquiries@lingwood-guesthouse.co.uk
: www.lingwood-guesthouse.co.uk

Little Longtail ♦♦♦
Ferry view, Bowness-on-Windermere, Windermere LA23 3JB
: (01539) 443884

The Lonsdale ♦♦♦
Lake Road, Bowness-on-Windermere, Windermere LA23 2JJ
: (015394) 43348
: (015394) 43348
: lonsdale@fsbdial.co.uk
www.south-lakes.com

Lowfell ♦♦♦♦ SILVER AWARD
Ferney Green, Bowness-on-Windermere, Windermere LA23 3ES
T: (01539) 445612
F: (01539) 448411
E: lowfell@talk21.com
I: www.low-fell.co.uk

Lynwood Guest House ♦♦♦♦
Broad Street, Windermere, LA23 2AB
T: (01539) 442550
F: (01539) 442550
E: enquiries@lynwood-guest-house.co.uk
I: www.lynwood-guest-house.co.uk

Meadfoot Guest House ♦♦♦♦
New Road, Windermere, LA23 2LA
T: (01539) 442610
F: (01539) 445280
E: enquiries@meadfoot-guesthouse.co.uk
I: www.meadfoot-guesthouse.co.uk

Melbourne Guest House ♦♦♦
2-3 Biskey Howe Road, Bowness-on-Windermere, Windermere LA23 2JP
T: (01539) 443475
F: (01539) 442475
E: info@melbournecottage.co.uk
I: www.melbournecottage.co.uk

Mount View Guest House
♦♦♦
New Road, Windermere, LA23 2LA
T: (015394) 45548

Mylne Bridge House ♦♦♦
Brookside, Lake Road, Windermere, LA23 2BX
T: (01539) 443314
F: (01539) 448052
E: mylnebridgehouse@talk21.com
I: www.s-h-systems.co.uk/hotels/mylne.html

Oakbank House Hotel
♦♦♦♦♦
Helm Road, Bowness-on-Windermere, Windermere LA23 3BU
T: (015394) 43386
F: (015394) 47965
E: enquiries@oakbankhousehotel.co.uk
I: www.oakbankhousehotel.co.uk

Oldfield House ♦♦♦♦
Oldfield Road, Windermere, LA23 2BY
T: (01539) 488445
E: thewants@uk4free.net
I: www.oldfieldhouse.co.uk

Park Beck ♦♦♦
3 Park Road, Windermere, LA23 2AW
T: (01539) 444025
E: parkbeck@supanet.com

1 Park Road ♦♦♦♦
1 Park Road, Windermere, LA23 2AW
T: (01539) 442107
F: (01539) 448997
E: mark.soden@btinternet.com
I: www.1parkroad.com

Rayrigg Villa Guest House
♦♦♦♦
Ellerthwaite Square, Windermere, LA23 1DP
T: (01539) 488342
E: rayriggvilla@nascr.net
I: www.rayriggvilla.co.uk

Rocklea ♦♦♦♦
Brookside, Lake Road, Windermere, LA23 2BX
T: (01539) 445326
F: (01539) 445326
E: info@rocklea.co.uk
I: www.rocklea.co.uk

St John's Lodge ♦♦♦
Lake Road, Windermere, LA23 2EQ
T: (01539) 443078
F: (01539) 488054
E: mail@st-johns-lodge.co.uk
I: www.st-johns-lodge.co.uk

Sandown ♦♦♦
Lake Road, Bowness-on-Windermere, Windermere LA23 2JF
T: (01539) 445275
F: (01539) 445275

Squirrel Bank
Rating Applied For
Ferry View, Bowness-on-Windermere, Windermere LA23 3JB
T: (015394) 43329
E: soar@squirrelbank.co.uk
I: www.squirrelbank.co.uk

Storrs Gate House ♦♦♦♦
Longtail Hill, Bowness-on-Windermere, Windermere LA23 3JD
T: (01539) 443272
E: enquiries@storrsgatehouse.co.uk
I: www.storrsgatehouse.co.uk

Tarn Rigg ♦♦♦♦
Thornbarrow Road, Windermere, LA23 2DG
T: (015394) 88777
E: stay@tarnrigg-guesthouse.co.uk
I: www.tarnrigg-guesthouse.co.uk

Thornbank House ♦♦♦
4 Thornbarrow Road, Windermere, LA23 2EW
T: (01539) 443724
F: (01539) 443724

Tudor House ♦♦
60 Main Street, Ellerthwaite Square, Windermere, LA23 1DP
T: (01539) 442363

Villa Lodge Guest House
♦♦♦♦
25 Cross Street, Windermere, LA23 1AE
T: (01539) 443318
F: (01539) 443318
E: rooneym@btconnect.com
I: www.villa-lodge.co.uk

Watermill Inn ♦♦♦
Ings, Staveley, Kendal LA8 9PY
T: (01539) 821309
F: (01539) 822309
E: all@watermillinn.co.uk
I: www.watermill-inn.demon.co.uk

Westbourne Hotel ♦♦♦♦
Biskey Howe Road, Bowness-on-Windermere, Windermere LA23 2JR
T: (01539) 443625
F: (01539) 443625
E: westbourne@btinternet.com
I: www.milford.co.uk

Westbury House ♦♦♦
27 Broad Street, Windermere, LA23 2AB
T: (01539) 446839
F: (01539) 442784
E: tonybaker@aol.com

White Lodge Hotel ♦♦♦♦
Lake Road, Windermere, LA23 2JJ
T: (01539) 443624
F: (01539) 444749
E: enquiries@whitelodgehotel.com
I: www.whitelodgehotel.com

White Rose ♦♦♦
Broad Street, Windermere, LA23 2AB
T: (01539) 445180
F: (01539) 445180
E: whiteroselakes@lineone.net
I: www.whiteroselakes.co.uk

The Windermere Hotel ♦♦♦
Kendal Road, Windermere, LA23 1AL
T: (01539) 442251
F: (01539) 488903
E: gm.win@barbox.net
I: www.shearingsholidays.com

WORKINGTON
Cumbria

Morven Guest House ♦♦♦
Siddick Road, Siddick, Workington CA14 1LE
T: (01900) 602118
F: (01900) 602118
E: cnelsonmorven@aol.com

NORTHUMBRIA

ACOMB
Northumberland

The Sun Inn ♦♦♦♦
Main Street, Acomb, Hexham
NE46 4PW
T: (01434) 602934
F: (01434) 606635
E: alanmcjannet@aol.com

ALLENDALE
Northumberland

Oakey Dene ♦♦♦♦
Allendale, Hexham NE47 9EL
T: (01434) 683572

Struthers Farm ♦♦♦
Catton, Allendale, Hexham
NE47 9LP
T: (01434) 683580

Thornley House ♦♦♦♦
Allendale, Hexham NE47 9NH
T: (01434) 683255
E: e.finn@ukonline.co.uk
I: web.ukonline.co.uk/e.finn

ALNMOUTH
Northumberland

B&B with Beaches Restaurant Rating Applied For
57 Northumberland Street,
Alnmouth, Alnwick NE66 2RS
T: (01665) 830443
F: (01665) 830443
E: le.chef@breathe.com

Beech Lodge ♦♦♦♦
8 Alnwood, Alnmouth, Alnwick
NE66 3NN
T: (01665) 830709

Bilton Barns Farmhouse ♦♦♦♦ SILVER AWARD
Alnmouth, Alnwick NE66 2TB
T: (01665) 830427
F: (01665) 830063
E: dorothy@biltonbarns.co.uk
I: www.biltonbarns.co.uk

The Grange – Alnmouth Rating Applied For
Northumberland Street,
Alnmouth, Alnwick NE66 2RJ
T: (01665) 830401
F: (01665) 830401
E: enquiries@thegrange-alnmouth.com
I: www.thegrange-alnmouth.com

High Buston Hall ♦♦♦♦♦ GOLD AWARD
High Buston, Alnmouth, Alnwick
NE66 3QH
T: (01665) 830606
F: (01665) 830707
E: highbuston@aol.com
I: www.highbuston.com

Hipsburn Farm ♦♦♦♦
Alnmouth, Alnwick NE66 3PY
T: 07710 896430
F: (01665) 830206

Hope and Anchor Hotel ♦♦♦
44 Northumberland Street,
Alnmouth, Alnwick NE66 2RA
T: (01665) 830363
F: (01665) 603082
E: debbiephilipson@hopeandanchorholiday.fsnet.co.uk
I: www.hopeandanchorholidays.co.uk

Red Lion Inn ♦♦♦
22 Northumberland Street,
Alnmouth, Alnwick NE66 2RJ
T: (01665) 830584

Westlea Guest House Rating Applied For
29 Riverside Road, Alnmouth,
Alnwick NE66 2SD
T: (01665) 830730
E: janiceedwards@totalise.co.uk

ALNWICK
Northumberland

Aln House ♦♦♦♦
South Road, Alnwick, NE66 2NZ
T: (01665) 602265
E: bill@alnhousealnwick.worldonline.co.uk

Alndyke Farmhouse Rating Applied For
Alnmouth Road, Alnwick,
NE66 3PB
T: (01665) 510252

Aydon House ♦♦♦
South Road, Alnwick, NE66 2NT
T: (01665) 602218

Bondgate House Hotel ♦♦♦
20 Bondgate Without, Alnwick,
NE66 1PN
T: (01665) 602025
F: (01665) 602025
E: aclarvin@aol.com
I: www.bondgatehouse.ntb.org.uk

21 Boulmer Village ♦♦♦♦
Alnwick, NE66 3BS
T: (01665) 577262

Charlton House ♦♦♦♦
2 Aydon Gardens, South Road,
Alnwick, NE66 2NT
T: (01665) 605185
I: www.s-h-systems.co.uk/hotels/charlt2.html

Crosshills House ♦♦♦♦
40 Blakelaw Road, Alnwick,
NE66 1BA
T: (01665) 602518

East Cawledge Park Farm ♦♦♦
Alnwick, NE66 2HB
T: (01665) 605705
F: (01665) 605963

Hawkhill Farmhouse ♦♦♦♦ SILVER AWARD
Lesbury, Alnwick NE66 3PG
T: (01665) 830380
F: (01665) 830093

Lilburn Grange ♦♦♦
West Lilburn, Alnwick, NE66 4PP
T: (01668) 217274

Limetree Cottage ♦♦♦♦
38 Eglingham Village, Alnwick,
NE66 2TX
T: (01665) 578322

Masons Arms ♦♦♦♦
Stamford, Rennington, Alnwick,
NE66 3RX
T: (01665) 577275
F: (01665) 577894
E: masonsarms@lineone.net
I: www.masonsarms.net

Norfolk ♦♦♦♦ SILVER AWARD
41 Blakelaw Road, Alnwick,
NE66 1BA
T: (01665) 602892
I: www.norfolk.ntb.org.uk

The Oaks Hotel ♦♦♦
South Road, Alnwick, NE66 2PN
T: (01665) 510014
F: (01665) 603219
I: www.theoakshotel.co.uk

Reighamsyde ♦♦♦♦
The Moor, Alnwick, NE66 2AJ
T: (01665) 602535

Rock Midstead Farm House ♦♦♦
Rock Midstead Organic Farm,
Rock, Alnwick NE66 2TH
T: (01665) 579225
E: ian@rockmidstead.freeserve.co.uk

Rooftops ♦♦♦♦ SILVER AWARD
14 Blakelaw Road, Alnwick,
NE66 1AZ
T: (01665) 604201
E: rooftops.alnwick@talk21.com
I: www.rooftops.ntb.org.uk

Roseworth ♦♦♦♦
Alnmouth Road, Alnwick,
NE66 2PR
T: (01665) 603911
E: bowden@roseworthann.freeserve.co.uk

Tower Guest Rooms ♦♦♦♦
10 Bondgate Within, Alnwick,
NE66 1TD
T: (01665) 603888
F: (01665) 603222
E: hotspurtower@aol.com
I: www.hotspur-tower.com

AMBLE
Northumberland

Marine House Rating Applied For
20 Marine Road, Amble,
Morpeth NE65 0BB
T: (01665) 711965

AMBLE-BY-THE-SEA
Northumberland

Bisley Place ♦♦♦
37 Bisley Road, Amble, Morpeth
NE65 0NP
T: (01665) 710473

Coquetside ♦♦♦♦
16 Broomhill Street, Amble,
Morpeth NE65 0AN
T: (01665) 710352
I: coquetside.future.easyspace.com

The Hollies ♦♦♦♦
3 Riverside Park, Amble,
Morpeth NE65 0YR
T: (01665) 712323
E: terrihollies@clara.co.uk
I: www.the-hollies-amble.co.uk

Togston Hall Farmhouse ♦♦♦
North Togston, Morpeth
NE65 0HR
T: (01665) 712699
F: (01665) 712699

BAMBURGH
Northumberland

Broome ♦♦♦♦
22 Ingram Road, Bamburgh,
NE69 7BT
T: (01668) 214287
E: mdixon4394@aol.com
I: www.member.xoom.com/bamburgh

Glenander Bed & Breakfast ♦♦♦♦
27 Lucker Road, Bamburgh,
NE69 7BS
T: (01668) 214336
F: (01668) 214695
E: johntoland@tiscali.co.uk
I: www.glenander.com

Green Gates ♦♦♦
34 Front Street, Bamburgh,
NE69 7BJ
T: (01668) 214535
E: bamburgh.sunset@talk21.com
I: www.greengatesbamburgh.co.uk

Hillcrest House ♦♦♦♦
29 Lucker Road, Bamburgh,
NE69 7BS
T: (01668) 214639
E: desmy0410@aol.com

Hillside Bed & Breakfast ♦♦♦♦ SILVER AWARD
25 Lucker Road, Bamburgh,
NE69 7BS
T: (01668) 214674
F: (01668) 214674
I: www.hillside-bamburgh.com

Squirrel Cottage ♦♦♦♦
1 Friars Court, Bamburgh,
NE69 7AE
T: (01668) 214494
E: theturnbulls2k@btinternet.com
I: www.geocities.com/thetropics/bay/3021

BARDON MILL
Northumberland

Carrsgate East ♦♦♦♦
Bardon Mill, Hexham NE47 7EX
T: (01434) 344376
F: (01434) 344011
E: lesley@armstrongrl.freeserve.co.uk
I: carrsgate-east.com

Gibbs Hill Farm ♦♦♦
Once Brewed, Bardon Hill,
Hexham, Once Brewed,
NE47 7AP
T: (01434) 344030
F: (01434) 344030
E: val@gibbshillfarm.co.uk
I: www.gibbshillfarm.co.uk

Montcoffer ♦♦♦♦♦ GOLD AWARD
Bardon Mill, Hexham NE47 7HZ
T: (01434) 344138
F: (01434) 344730
E: john-dehlia@talk21.com
I: www.montcoffer.co.uk

Strand Cottage Bed and Breakfast ♦♦♦♦
Main Road (A69), Bardon Mill,
Hexham NE47 7BH
T: (01434) 344643
E: strandcottage@aol.com
I: www.strand-cottage.co.uk

Vallum Lodge Hotel ♦♦♦♦
Military Road, Twice Brewed,
Bardon Mill, Hexham NE47 7AN
T: (01434) 344248
F: (01434) 344488
E: vallum.lodge@ukonline.co.uk
I: www.vallumlodge.ntb.org.uk

BARNARD CASTLE
Durham

Bowes Moor Hotel ♦♦♦
Bowes Moor, Barnard Castle,
DL12 9RH
T: (01833) 628331
F: (01833) 628331
E: bowesmoorhotel@
btopenworld.com
I: www.barnard-castle.
co.uk/accommodation/
bowes_moor_hotel.html

Bowfield Farm ♦♦
Scargill, Barnard Castle
DL12 9SU
T: (01833) 638636

Cloud High
♦♦♦♦ GOLD AWARD
Eggleston, Barnard Castle
DL12 0AU
T: (01833) 650644
F: (01833) 650644
E: cloudhigh@btinternet.com
: www.cloud-high.co.uk

Demesnes Mill
♦♦♦♦♦ GOLD AWARD
Barnard Castle, DL12 8PE
T: (01833) 637929
F: (01833) 637974
E: millbb2@ic24.net
: www.webproze.com/millbb

Egglestone Hall ♦♦♦♦♦
Eggleston, Barnard Castle
DL12 0AG
: (01833) 650553
: (01833) 650553
: willgray@globalnet.co.uk
: www.egglestonhall.co.uk

Greta House
♦♦♦♦ GOLD AWARD
9 Galgate, Barnard Castle,
L12 8ES
: (01833) 631193
: (01833) 631193
: gretahousebc@btclick.com

he Homelands
♦♦♦ SILVER AWARD
5 Galgate, Barnard Castle,
L12 8ES
: (01833) 638757
: homelands@barnard-castle.
net.co.uk
www.barnard-castle.
.uk/accommodation

Harwood House ♦♦♦♦
3 Galgate, Barnard Castle,
L12 8BJ
(01833) 637493
(01833) 637493
john&sheila@kilgarriff.
mon.co.uk
www.kilgarriff.demon.co.uk

ontalbo Hotel ♦♦♦
ontalbo Road, Barnard Castle,
12 8BP
(01833) 637342
(01833) 637342
suzannethomas@
ontalbohotel.co.uk
www.montalbohotel.co.uk

Moorcock Inn ♦♦♦
Hill Top, Gordon Bank,
Eggleston, Barnard Castle
DL12 0AU
T: (01833) 650395
F: (01833) 650052
E: zach1@talk21.com
I: www.moorcock-Inn.co.uk

33 Newgate ♦♦♦
Barnard Castle, DL12 8NJ
T: (01833) 690208
E: peter.whittaker@tinyworld.
co.uk
I: www.barnard-castle.
co.uk/accommodation/
whittaker.html

Raygill Farm ♦♦♦
Lartington, Barnard Castle
DL12 9DG
T: (01833) 690118
F: (01833) 690118
E: anne@raygillriding.co.uk
I: www.raygillriding.co.uk

Spring Lodge ♦♦♦
Newgate, Barnard Castle,
DL12 8NW
T: (01833) 638110
F: (01833) 630389
E: ormston@telinco.co.uk
I: www.smoothhound.
co.uk/hotels/springlodge

Strathmore Lawn East ♦♦♦
81 Galgate, Barnard Castle,
DL12 8ES
T: (01833) 637061
E: strathmoreebb@talk21.co.uk

Wilson House ♦♦♦♦
Barningham, Richmond
DL11 7EB
T: (01833) 621218
F: (01833) 621110

BARRASFORD
Northumberland

Barrasford Arms ♦♦♦
Barrasford, Hexham NE48 4AA
T: (01434) 681237
F: (01434) 681237

BEADNELL
Northumberland

Beach Court
♦♦♦♦ SILVER AWARD
Harbour Road, Beadnell, Chathill
NE67 5BJ
T: (01665) 720225
F: (01665) 721499
E: info@beachcourt.com
I: www.beachcourt.com

Beadnell House Hotel ♦♦♦
Beadnell, Chathill NE67 5AT
T: (01665) 721380
F: (01665) 720217
E: enquiries@beadnellhouse.
co.uk
I: www.beadnellhouse.co.uk

Low Dover Beadnell Bay
♦♦♦♦ SILVER AWARD
Harbour Road, Beadnell, Chathill
NE67 5BJ
T: (01665) 720291
F: (01665) 720291
E: kathandbob@lowdover.co.uk
I: www.lowdover.co.uk

The New Beadnell Towers
Hotel ♦♦♦♦ SILVER AWARD
Beadnell, Chathill NE67 5AU
T: (01665) 721211
F: (01665) 720424
E: beadnell@towers.fsnet.co.uk

Shepherds Cottage ♦♦♦♦
Beadnell, Chathill NE67 5AD
T: (01665) 720497
F: (01665) 720497
I: www.shepherdscottage.ntb.
org.uk

BEAL
Northumberland

Brock Mill Farmhouse ♦♦♦
Brock Mill, Beal, Berwick-upon-
Tweed TD15 2PB
T: (01289) 381283
F: (01289) 381283
E: brockmillfarmhouse@
btopenworld.com

West Mains House ♦♦♦
Beal, Berwick-upon-Tweed
TD15 2PD
T: (01289) 381227

BEAMISH
Durham

The Beamish Mary Inn
Rating Applied For
Beamish, Stanley DH9 0QH
T: (0191) 370 0237
F: (0191) 370 0091
E: beamishmary@hotmail.com
I: www.beamishmary.co.uk

The Coach House ♦♦♦♦
High Urpeth, Beamish, Stanley
DH9 0SE
T: (0191) 370 0309
F: (0191) 370 0046
E: coachhouse@foreman25.
freeserve.co.uk
I: www.coachhousebeamish.ntb.
org.uk

Malling House ♦♦♦
1 Oakdale Terrace, Newfield,
Chester-le-Street DH2 2SU
T: (0191) 370 2571
F: (0191) 370 1391
E: heather@mallingguesthouse.
co.uk
I: www.mallinghouse.com

No Place House Bed & Breakfast ♦♦
Beamish, Stanley DH9 0QH
T: (0191) 370 0891
E: gaz@nobeam.fsnet.co.uk
I: www.noplace.co.uk

BELFORD
Northumberland

Detchant Farm ♦♦♦
Belford, NE70 7PF
T: (01668) 213261
F: (01668) 219261
E: detchant@farming.co.uk

Easington Farm
♦♦♦♦ SILVER AWARD
Belford, NE70 7EG
T: (01668) 213298

The Farmhouse Guest House
♦♦♦♦
24 West Street, Belford,
NE70 7QE
T: (01668) 213083

Fenham-le-Moor ♦♦♦♦
Belford, NE70 7PN
T: (01668) 213247
F: (01668) 213247
E: katie@fenhamlemoor.com

Oakwood House
♦♦♦♦ GOLD AWARD
3 Cragside Avenue, Belford,
NE70 7NA
T: (01668) 213303
E: maureenatoakwood@talk21.
com

BELLINGHAM
Northumberland

Bridgeford Farm ♦♦♦♦
Bridgeford, Bellingham, Hexham
NE48 2HU
T: (01434) 220940

The Cheviot Hotel ♦♦♦
Bellingham, Hexham NE48 2AU
T: (01434) 220696
F: (01434) 220696

Ivy Cottage ♦♦♦
Lanehead, Tarset, Hexham
NE48 1NT
T: (01434) 240337
F: (01434) 240073

Lyndale Guest House ♦♦♦♦
Bellingham, Hexham NE48 2AW
T: (01434) 220361
F: (01434) 220361
E: ken&joy@lyndalegh.fsnet.
co.uk
I: www.SmoothHound.
co.uk/hotels/lyndale.html

Westfield House ♦♦♦♦
Bellingham, Hexham NE48 2DP
T: (01434) 220340
F: (01434) 220356
E: westfield.house@btinternet.
com
I: www.westfield-house.net

BELMONT
Durham

Moor End House Bed and Breakfast ♦♦♦
7-8 Moor End Terrace, Belmont,
Durham DH1 1BJ
T: (0191) 384 2796
F: (0191) 3842796

BERWICK-UPON-TWEED
Northumberland

Alannah House
♦♦♦♦ SILVER AWARD
84 Church Street, Berwick-
upon-Tweed, TD15 1DU
T: (01289) 307252
I: www.alannahhouse.co.uk

Bridge View ♦♦♦♦
14 Tweed Street, Berwick-upon-
Tweed, TD15 1NG
T: (01289) 308098

Castlegate ♦♦♦
32 Castlegate, Berwick-upon-
Tweed, TD15 1JJ
T: (01289) 306120

The Cat Inn ♦♦♦
Great North Road, Cheswick,
Berwick-upon-Tweed, TD15 2RL
T: (01289) 387251
F: (01289) 387251

Cear Urfa ♦♦♦♦
15 Springfield Park, East Ord,
Berwick-upon-Tweed, TD15 2FD
T: (01289) 303528

Clovelly House
♦♦♦♦ SILVER AWARD
58 West Street, Berwick-upon-Tweed, TD15 1AS
T: (01289) 302337
F: (01289) 302052
E: vivroc@clovelly53.freeserve.co.uk
I: www.clovelly53.freeserve.co.uk

Cobbled Yard Hotel ♦♦♦
40 Walkergate, Berwick-upon-Tweed, TD15 1DJ
T: (01289) 308407
F: (01289) 330623
E: cobbledyardhotel@berwick35.fsnet.co.uk
I: www.cobbledyardhotel.com

Dervaig Guest House
♦♦♦♦ SILVER AWARD
1 North Road, Berwick-upon-Tweed, TD15 1PW
T: (01289) 307378
F: (01289) 307378
E: dervaig@talk21.com
I: www.dervaig-guesthouse.co.uk

Eastfield House ♦♦♦♦
6 North Road, Berwick-upon-Tweed, TD15 1PL
T: (01289) 308949
E: info@eastfieldhouse-berwick.co.uk
I: www.eastfieldhouse-berwick.co.uk

Fairholm ♦♦♦♦
East Ord, Berwick-upon-Tweed, TD15 2NS
T: (01289) 305370

Four North Road
♦♦♦♦ SILVER AWARD
4 North Road, Berwick-upon-Tweed, TD15 1PL
T: (01289) 306146
F: (01289) 306146
E: sandra@thorntonfour.freeserve.co.uk
I: www.fournorthroad.co.uk

The Friendly Hound ♦♦♦♦
Ford Common, Berwick-upon-Tweed, TD15 2QD
T: (01289) 388554
E: friendlyhound@talk21.com

Heron's Lee
♦♦♦♦ SILVER AWARD
Thornton, Berwick-upon-Tweed, TD15 2LP
T: (01289) 382000
F: (01289) 382000
E: john_burton@btconnect.com
I: www.northumbandb.co.uk

High Letham Farmhouse
♦♦♦♦♦ SILVER AWARD
High Letham, Berwick-upon-Tweed, TD15 1UX
T: (01289) 306585
F: (01289) 304194
E: hlf-b@fantasyprints.co.uk
I: www.ntb.org.uk

Ladythorne House ♦♦♦
Cheswick, Berwick-upon-Tweed, TD15 2RW
T: (01289) 387382
F: (01289) 387073
E: valparker@ladythorneguesthouse.freeserve.co.uk
I: www.ladythorneguesthouse.freeserve.co.uk

Meadow Hill Guest House
♦♦♦♦
Duns Road, Berwick-upon-Tweed, TD15 1UB
T: (01289) 306325
F: (01289) 306325
E: barryandhazel@meadow-hill.co.uk
I: www.meadow-hill.co.uk

Middle Ord Manor House
♦♦♦♦♦ GOLD AWARD
Middle Ord Farm, Berwick-upon-Tweed, TD15 2XQ
T: (01289) 306323
F: (01289) 308423
E: joan@middleordmanor.co.uk
I: www.middleordmanor.co.uk

No 1 Sallyport
♦♦♦♦ SILVER AWARD
Bridge Street, Berwick-upon-Tweed, TD15 1EZ
T: (01289) 308827
F: (01289) 308827
E: info@1sallyport-bedandbreakfast.com
I: www.1sallyport-bedandbreakfast.com

The Old Vicarage Guest House
♦♦♦♦
24 Church Road, Tweedmouth, Berwick-upon-Tweed TD15 2AN
T: (01289) 306909
F: (01289) 309052
E: stay@oldvicarageberwick.co.uk
I: www.oldvicarageberwick.co.uk

Orkney House ♦♦
37 Woolmarket, Berwick-upon-Tweed, TD15 1DH
T: (01289) 331710

6 Parade ♦♦♦
Berwick-upon-Tweed, TD15 1DF
T: (01289) 308454
F: (01289) 308454

40 Ravensdowne
♦♦♦♦ SILVER AWARD
Berwick-upon-Tweed, TD15 1DQ
T: (01289) 306992
F: (01289) 301606
E: petedot@dmuckle.freeserve.co.uk
I: www.secretkingdom.com/40/ravensdowne.htm

Rob Roy ♦♦♦♦
Dock Road, Tweedmouth, Berwick-upon-Tweed TD15 2BE
T: (01289) 306428
F: (01289) 303629
E: therobroy@btinternet.com
I: www.therobroy.co.uk

Whyteside House
♦♦♦♦ SILVER AWARD
46 Castlegate, Berwick-upon-Tweed, TD15 1JT
T: (01289) 331019
F: (01289) 331419
E: albert@whyteside100.freeserve.co.uk
I: www.secretkingdom.com/whyte/side.htm

BISHOP AUCKLAND
Durham

Albion Cottage Hotel ♦♦♦
Albion Terrace, Bishop Auckland, DL14 6EL
T: (01388) 602217
F: (01388) 602217
E: albionbookings@aol.com
I: www.smoothhound.co.uk/hotels/albion.html

Five Gables Guest House
♦♦♦♦
Binchester, Bishop Auckland DL14 8AT
T: (01388) 608204
F: (01388) 663092
E: book.in@fivegables.co.uk
I: www.fivegables.co.uk

The Old Farmhouse ♦♦♦♦
Grange Hill, Bishop Auckland, DL14 8EG
T: (01388) 602123
F: (01388) 602123

BOWBURN
Durham

Prince Bishop Guest House
♦♦♦
1 Oxford Terrace, Bowburn, Durham DH6 5AX
T: (0191) 377 8703
E: enquiries@durhamguesthouse.co.uk
I: www.durhamguesthouse.co.uk

BRANCEPETH
Durham

Nafferton Farm ♦♦♦
Brancepeth, Durham DH7 8EF
T: (0191) 378 0538
F: (0191) 378 0538
E: sndfell@aol.com

BRIGNALL
Durham

Lily Hill Farm ♦♦♦
Brignall, Barnard Castle DL12 9SF
T: (01833) 627254

BYWELL
Northumberland

The Old Vicarage
♦♦♦♦ SILVER AWARD
Bywell, Stocksfield NE43 7AD
T: (01661) 842521
F: (01661) 842521
E: strachan@oldvicaragebywell.fsnet.co.uk
I: www.oldvicaragebywell.fsnet.co.uk

CAMBO
Northumberland

Shieldhall ♦♦♦♦
Wallington, Morpeth, NE61 4AQ
T: (01830) 540387
F: (01830) 540490
E: robinson.gay@btinternet.com

CASTLESIDE
Durham

Deneview ♦♦♦
15 Front Street, Castleside, Consett DH8 9AR
T: (01207) 502925
E: cyndyglancy@lineone.net

CHATHILL
Northumberland

North Charlton Farm
♦♦♦♦♦ GOLD AWARD
Chathill, NE67 5HP
T: (01665) 579443
F: (01665) 579407
E: ncharlton1@agricplus.net
I: www.northcharlton.com

CHATTON
Northumberland

South Hazelrigg Farmhouse
♦♦♦♦
South Hazelrigg, Chatton, Alnwick NE66 5RZ
T: (01668) 215216
E: sdodds@farmhousebandb.co.uk
I: www.farmhousebandb.co.uk

CHESTER-LE-STREET
Durham

Hollycroft ♦♦♦♦
11 The Parade, Chester-le-Street, DH3 3LR
T: (0191) 388 7088
E: cutter@hollycroft11.freeserve.co.uk

Low Urpeth Farm House
♦♦♦♦
Ouston, Chester-le-Street, DH2 1BD
T: (0191) 410 2901
F: (0191) 410 0088
E: stay@lowurpeth.co.uk
I: www.lowurpeth.co.uk

CHESTER MOOR
Durham

Church Mouse, Inkeepers Lodge Durham ♦♦♦♦
Great North Road, Chester Moor, Chester-le-Street DH2 3RJ
T: (0191) 3892628
F: (0191) 3871298
I: www.innkeeperslodge.com

CHOPPINGTON
Northumberland

The Anglers Arms ♦♦♦
Sheep Wash Bank, Choppington NE62 5NB
T: (01670) 822300

The Swan Hotel ♦♦♦
Choppington, NE62 5TG
T: (01670) 826060
F: (01670) 531143

CONSETT
Durham

Bee Cottage Farm ♦♦♦
Castleside, Consett DH8 9HW
T: (01207) 508224

CORBRIDGE
Northumberland

Dilston Mill ♦♦♦♦
Corbridge, NE45 5QZ
T: (01434) 633493
F: (01434) 633513
E: susan@dilstonmill.com
I: www.dilstonmill.com

Dilston Plains ♦♦♦
Corbridge, NE45 5RE
T: (01434) 602785

Fellcroft ♦♦♦♦
Station Road, Corbridge, NE45 5AY
T: (01434) 632384
F: (01434) 633918
E: tove.brown@ukonline.co.uk

The Hayes ♦♦♦
Newcastle Road, Corbridge, NE45 5LP
T: (01434) 632010
F: (01434) 632010
E: stay@hayes-corbridge.co.uk
I: www.hayes-corbridge.co.uk

Holmlea ◆◆◆
Station Road, Corbridge,
NE45 5AY
T: (01434) 632486

Low Fotherley Farmhouse Bed and Breakfast◆◆◆◆
Riding Mill, NE44 6BB
T: (01434) 682277
F: (01434) 682277
E: hugh@lowfotherley.fsnet.co.uk
I: www.westfarm.freeserve.co.uk

Priorfield
◆◆◆◆ SILVER AWARD
Hippingstones Lane, Corbridge,
NE45 5JA
T: (01434) 633179
F: (01434) 633179
E: nsteenberg@btinternet.com

Riverside Guest House ◆◆◆◆
Main Street, Corbridge,
NE45 5LE
T: (01434) 632942
F: (01434) 633883
E: david@theriversideguesthouse.co.uk
I: www.theriversideguesthouse.co.uk

Town Barns ◆◆◆◆
Off Trinity Terrace, Corbridge,
NE45 5HP
T: (01434) 633345

COTHERSTONE
Durham

Glendale ◆◆◆
Cotherstone, Barnard Castle
DL12 9UH
T: (01833) 650384
I: www.barnard-castle.co.uk/accommodation/glendale.html

CRASTER
Northumberland

Cottage Inn ◆◆◆
Dunstan Village, Craster,
Alnwick NE66 3SZ
T: (01665) 576658
F: (01665) 576788
E: enquiry@cottageinnhotel.co.uk
I: www.cottageinnhotel.co.uk

Howick Scar Farmhouse ◆◆◆
Craster, Alnwick NE66 3SU
T: (01665) 576665
F: (01665) 576665
E: howick.scar@virgin.net
I: www.howickscar.co.uk

Stonecroft
◆◆◆◆ SILVER AWARD
Dunstan, Craster, Alnwick
NE66 3SZ
T: (01665) 576433
F: (01665) 576311
E: sally@stonestaff.freeserve.co.uk
I: www.stonecroft.ntb.org.uk

CRESSWELL
Northumberland

Cresswell House ◆◆◆◆
Morpeth, NE61 5LA
T: (01670) 861302

CROOKHAM
Northumberland

The Coach House at Crookham ◆◆◆◆
Cornhill-on-Tweed, TD12 4TD
T: (01890) 820293
F: (01890) 820284
E: stay@coachhousecrookham.com
I: www.coachhousecrookham.com

CROXDALE
Durham

Croxdale Inn ◆◆◆
Front Street, Croxdale, Durham
DH6 5HX
T: (01388) 815727
F: (01388) 815368
E: croxdale@talk21.com

DALTON PIERCY
Tees Valley

The Dalton Lodge Hotel ◆◆◆
Dalton Piercy, Hartlepool
TS27 3HN
T: (01429) 267142
F: (01429) 222629
I: www.turtle_uk.com

DARLINGTON
Durham

Aberlady Guest House ◆◆◆◆
51 Corporation Road,
Darlington, DL3 6AD
T: (01325) 461449

Boot & Shoe ◆◆◆
Church Row, Darlington,
DL1 5QD
T: (01325) 287501
F: (01325) 287501
E: sueemcgee@hotmail.com

The Chequers Inn ◆◆◆
Darlington, DL2 2NT
T: (01325) 721213
F: (01325) 722357

Clow-Beck House
◆◆◆◆◆ GOLD AWARD
Monk End Farm, Croft,
Darlington DL2 2SW
T: (01325) 721075
F: (01325) 720419
E: david@clowbeckhouse.co.uk
I: www.clowbeckhouse.co.uk

Greenbank Guest House ◆◆◆
90 Greenbank Road, Darlington,
DL3 6EL
T: (01325) 462624
F: (01325) 250233

Harewood Lodge ◆◆◆
40 Grange Road, Darlington,
DL1 5NP
T: (01325) 358152
E: Harewood.Lodge@NTLWorld.com

DURHAM
Durham

60 Albert Street ◆◆◆◆
Western Hill, Durham, DH1 4RJ
T: (0191) 386 0608
F: (0191) 370 9739
E: laura@sixtyalbertstreet.co.uk
I: www.sixtyalbertstreet.co.uk

The Anchorage ◆◆◆
25 Langley Road, Newton Hall,
Durham, DH1 5LR
T: (0191) 386 2323
F: (0191) 386 8315
E: anchorageb@aol.com

The Autumn Leaves Guest House ◆◆◆
Dragonville, Durham, DH1 2DX
T: (0191) 386 3394
E: irene@autumnleaves.freeserve.co.uk
I: www.autumnleavesguesthouse.co.uk

12 The Avenue ◆◆◆
Durham, DH1 4ED
T: (0191) 384 1020
E: janhanim@aol.com

The Avenue Inn ◆
Avenue Street, High Shincliffe,
Durham DH1 2PT
T: (0191) 386 5954
F: (0191) 375 7415
E: wenmah@aol.com

Bay Horse Inn ◆◆◆
Brandon Village, Durham,
DH7 8ST
T: (0191) 378 0498

Belle Vue Guest House ◆◆◆
4 Belle Vue Terrace, Gilesgate
Moor, Durham, DH1 2HR
T: (0191) 386 4800

Broom Farm Guest House ◆◆◆◆
Broom Farm, Broom Park Village,
Durham, DH7 7QX
T: (0191) 386 4755

Castle View Guest House ◆◆◆◆
4 Crossgate, Durham, DH1 4PS
T: (0191) 386 8852
F: (0191) 386 8852
E: castle_view@hotmail.com
I: www.castle-view.net

Castledene ◆◆◆
37 Nevilledale Terrace, Durham,
DH1 4QG
T: (0191) 384 8386
F: (0191) 384 8386
E: lornabyrne@tinyworld.co.uk

Cathedral View Guest House ◆◆◆◆
212 Gilesgate, Durham,
DH1 1QN
T: (0191) 386 9566
E: cathedralview@hotmail.com

College of Saint Hild and Saint Bede Guest Rooms◆
St Hild's Lane, Durham, DH1 1SZ
T: (0191) 374 3069
F: (0191) 374 4740
E: l.c.hugill@durham.ac.uk
I: www.dur.ac.uk/HildBede

Collingwood College Cumbrian Wing ◆◆◆
South Road, Durham, DH1 3LT
T: (0191) 374 4567
F: (0191) 374 4595
E: collingwood_college.conference@durham.ac.uk

Durham University Conference & Tourism Ltd◆◆◆
Trevelyan College (Macaulay Wi,
Elvet Hill Road, Durham,
DH1 3LN
T: (0191) 374 3765
F: (0191) 374 3789
E: trev.coll@durham.ac.uk
I: www.dur.ac.uk/~dtr0www/conference.html

Farnley Tower
◆◆◆◆ SILVER AWARD
The Avenue, Durham, DH1 4DX
T: (0191) 375 0011
F: (0191) 383 9694
E: enquiries@farnley-tower.co.uk
I: www.farnley-tower.co.uk

The Georgian Town House ◆◆◆◆
10 Crossgate, Durham, DH1 4PS
T: (0191) 386 8070
F: (0191) 386 8070
E: enquiries@georgian-townhouse.fsnet.com

10 Gilesgate ◆◆
Durham, DH1 1QW
T: (0191) 386 2026
F: (0191) 386 2026

14 Gilesgate ◆◆
Top of Claypath, Durham,
DH1 1QW
T: (0191) 384 6485
F: (0191) 386 5173
E: bb@nimmins.co.uk
I: www.nimmins.co.uk

The Gilesgate Moor Hotel ◆◆◆
Teasdale Terrace, Gilesgate,
Durham DH1 2RN
T: (0191) 386 6453
F: (0191) 386 6453

Grey College ◆◆
South Road, Durham, DH1 3LG
T: (0191) 374 2900
F: (0191) 374 2992
E: joyce.dover@durham.ac.uk
I: www.dur.ac.uk/GreyCollege

Hatfield College, Jevons ◆◆
North Bailey, Durham, DH1 3RQ
T: (0191) 374 3164
F: (0191) 374 7472
E: a.m.ankers@durham.ac.uk
I: www.dur.ac.uk/Hatfield/college/confrnce.html

Hillrise Guest House ◆◆◆◆
13 Durham Road West,
Bowburn, Durham DH6 5AU
T: (0191) 377 0302
F: (0191) 377 0898
E: hillrise.guesthouse@btinternet.com
I: www.hill-rise.com

Knights Rest ◆◆◆
1 Anchorage Terrace, Durham,
DH1 3DL
T: (0191) 386 6229
F: (0191) 386 6229

The Newton Grange Hotel ◆◆
Finchal Road, Brasside, Durham
DH1 5SA
T: (0191) 386 0872
F: (0191) 386 0872

O'Neills Inn ◆
91a Claypath, Durham, DH1 1RG
T: (0191) 383 6951

St Aidan's College ◆◆◆
University of Durham, Windmill
Hill, Durham, DH1 3LJ
T: (0191) 374 3269
F: (0191) 374 4749
E: aidans.conf@durham.ac.uk
I: www.st-aidans.org.uk

St Chad's College ♦♦
18 North Bailey, Durham, DH1 3RH
T: (0191) 374 3364
F: (0191) 374 3309
E: St-Chads.www@durham.ac.uk
I: www.dur.ac.uk/StChads/

Saint Cuthberts Society ♦♦
12 South Bailey, Durham, DH1 3EE
T: (0191) 374 3464
F: (0191) 374 4753
E: i.d.barton@durham.ac.uk
I: www.dur.ac.uk/st-cuthberts.society

St Johns College ♦♦
3 South Bailey, Durham, DH1 3RJ
T: (0191) 374 3598
F: (0191) 374 3573
E: enquiries@stjohnscollege-durham.com
I: www.stjohnscollege-durham.com

Seven Stars Inn ♦♦♦
Shincliffe Village, Durham, DH1 2NU
T: (0191) 384 8454
F: (0191) 386 0640

Three Horse Shoes Inn ♦♦♦
Running Waters, Sherburn House, Durham DH1 2SR
T: (0191) 372 0286
F: (0191) 372 3386
E: m.s.parkinson@threehorseshoes.fsbusiness.co.uk
I: www.smoothhound.co.uk/

Triermayne ♦♦♦♦
Nevilles Cross Bank, Durham, DH1 4JP
T: (0191) 384 6036

Van Mildert College (Tunstall Stairs) ♦♦♦
Mill Hill Lane, Durham, DH1 3LH
T: (0191) 374 3900
F: (0191) 374 3974
E: van-mildert.college@durham.ac.uk
I: www.dur.ac.uk/VanMildert/Conferences/together.htm

Victoria Inn ♦♦♦
86 Hallgarth Street, Durham, DH1 3AS
T: (0191) 386 5269
F: (0191) 386 0465

Waterside
♦♦♦♦ SILVER AWARD
Elvet Waterside, Durham, DH1 3BW
T: (0191) 384 6660
F: (0191) 384 6996

EASINGTON
Tees Valley

The Grapes ♦♦♦
Scaling Dam, Easington, Saltburn-by-the-Sea TS13 4TP
T: (01287) 640461
E: mark79@kenny7997.freeserve.co.uk
I: www.touristnetuk.com/ne/grapes/

EAST ORD
Northumberland

Inverleacainn ♦♦♦♦
4 Springfield Park, East Ord, Berwick-upon-Tweed TD15 2FD
T: (01289) 304627

Tweed View House ♦♦♦♦
East Ord, Berwick-upon-Tweed TD15 2NS
T: (01289) 332378
F: (01289) 332378
E: khdobson@aol.com
I: www.tweedview@8k.com

EASTGATE
Durham

Rose Hill Farm Bed and Breakfast
♦♦♦♦ SILVER AWARD
Rose Hill Farm, Eastgate-in-Weardale, Bishop Auckland DL13 2LB
T: (01388) 517209
E: june@rosehillfarm.fsnet.co.uk
I: www.rosehillfarmholidays.co.uk

EGLINGHAM
Northumberland

Ash Tree House ♦♦♦♦
The Terrace, Eglingham, Alnwick NE66 2UA
T: (01665) 578533
E: prudence@ukpc.net
I: www.ashtreehouse.com

EMBLETON
Northumberland

Blue Bell Inn ♦♦♦
Embleton, Alnwick NE66 3UP
T: (01665) 576573

The Sportsman ♦♦♦
Sea Lane (6), Embleton, Alnwick NE66 3XF
T: (01665) 576588
F: (01665) 576524

ESCOMB
Durham

The Gables ♦♦♦
3 Lane Ends, Escomb, Bishop Auckland DL14 7SR
T: (01388) 604745

FALSTONE
Northumberland

The Blackcock Inn ♦♦♦
Falstone, Hexham NE48 1AA
T: (01434) 240200
E: blackcock@falstone.fsbusiness.co.uk
I: www.smoothhound.co.uk/hotels/black.html

High Yarrow Farm ♦♦♦
Falstone, Hexham NE48 1BG
T: (01434) 240264

Woodside ♦♦♦♦
Yarrow, Falstone, Hexham NE48 1BG
T: (01434) 240443

FELTON
Northumberland

Cook and Barker Inn
♦♦♦♦ SILVER AWARD
Newton-on-the-Moor, Felton, Morpeth NE65 9JY
T: (01665) 575234
F: (01665) 575234

FENHAM
Tyne and Wear

The Brighton ♦♦
47-49 Brighton Grove, Fenham, Newcastle upon Tyne NE4 5NS
T: (0191) 273 3600
F: (0191) 226 0563

FIR TREE
Durham

Duke of York Inn
♦♦♦♦ SILVER AWARD
Fir Tree, Crook DL15 8DG
T: (01388) 762848

FORD
Northumberland

The Estate House
♦♦♦♦ SILVER AWARD
Ford, Berwick-upon-Tweed TD15 2PX
T: (01890) 820668
F: (01890) 820672
E: theestatehouse@supanet.com

Hay Farm Farmhouse ♦♦♦♦
Ford, Berwick-upon-Tweed TD12 4TR
T: (01890) 820647
F: (01890) 820659
E: tinahayfarm@tiscali.co.uk
I: www.hayfarm.co.uk

The Old Post Office ♦♦♦
2 Old Post Office Cottages, Ford, Berwick-upon-Tweed TD15 2QA
T: (01890) 820286
E: jwait309139627@aol.com
I: www.secretkingdom.com

FOURSTONES
Northumberland

8 St Aidans Park ♦♦♦♦
Fourstones, Hexham NE47 5EB
T: (01434) 674073
F: (01434) 674073
E: info@8staidans.co.uk
I: www.8staidans.co.uk

FROSTERLEY
Durham

High Laithe ♦♦♦
10A Hill End, Frosterley, Bishop Auckland DL13 2SX
T: (01388) 526421

GATESHEAD
Tyne and Wear

The Bewick Hotel ♦♦♦
145 Prince Consort Road, Gateshead, NE8 4DS
T: (0191) 477 1809
F: (0191) 477 6146
E: bewickenquiries@145bewick.fsnet.co.uk
I: www.bewickhotel.co.uk

Shaftesbury Guest House ♦♦♦
245 Prince Consort Road, Gateshead, NE8 4DT
T: (0191) 478 2544
F: (0191) 478 2544

GREAT TOSSON
Northumberland

Tosson Tower Farm
♦♦♦♦ GOLD AWARD
Great Tosson, Morpeth NE65 7NW
T: (01669) 620228
F: (01669) 620228
E: ann@tossontowerfarm.com
I: www.tossontowerfarm.com

GREENHEAD
Northumberland

Four Wynds ♦♦♦
Longbyre, Greenhead, Brampton CA8 7HN
T: (01697) 747330
F: (01697) 747330
E: rozhadrianswall@aol.com
I: www.bed-breakfast-hadrianswall.com

Holmhead Guest House ♦♦♦♦
Thirlwall Castle Farm, Hadrian's Wall, Greenhead, Brampton CA8 7HY
T: (016977) 47402
F: (016977) 47402
E: Holmhead@hadrianswall.freeserve.co.uk
I: www.bandbhadrianswall.com

GRETA BRIDGE
Durham

The Coach House
♦♦♦♦♦ SILVER AWARD
Greta Bridge, Barnard Castle DL12 9SD
T: (01833) 627201
E: info@coachhousegreta.co.uk
I: www.coachhousegreta.co.uk

HALTWHISTLE
Northumberland

Ald White Craig Farm ♦♦♦♦
Near Hadrian's Wall, Shield Hill, Haltwhistle, NE49 9NW
T: (01434) 320565
F: (01434) 322004
E: info@hadrianswallholidays.com
I: www.hadrianswallholidays.com

Ashcroft
♦♦♦♦ SILVER AWARD
Lantys Lonnen, Haltwhistle, NE49 0DA
T: (01434) 320213
F: (01434) 321641
E: enquiries@ashcroftguesthouse.freeserve.co.uk
I: www.ashcroftguesthouse.co.uk

Brookside House Bed and Breakfast ♦♦♦♦
Brookside House, Town Foot, Haltwhistle, NE49 0ER
T: (01434) 322481
E: brooksidehse-b-and-b@ntlworld.com
I: website.lineone.net/~billstapleton

Broomshaw Hill Farm
♦♦♦♦♦ GOLD AWARD
Willia Road, Haltwhistle, NE49 9NP
T: (01434) 320866
F: (01434) 320866
E: broomshaw@msn.com
I: www.broomshaw.co.uk

Doors Cottage Bed and Breakfast ♦♦♦
Shield Hill, Haltwhistle, NE49 9NW
T: (01434) 322556
E: doors-cottage@supanet.com

The Grey Bull Hotel ♦♦♦
Main Street, Haltwhistle,
NE49 0DL
T: (01434) 321991
F: (01434) 320770
E: PamGreyB@aol.com

Hall Meadows ♦♦♦
Main Street, Haltwhistle,
NE49 0AZ
T: (01434) 321021
F: (01434) 321021

The Mount ♦♦♦
Comb Hill, Haltwhistle,
NE49 9NS
T: (01434) 321075
E: the-mount@talk21.com

Oaky Knowe Farm ♦♦♦
Haltwhistle, NE49 0NB
T: (01434) 320648
F: (01434) 320648

Saughy Rigg Farm ♦♦♦
Twice Brewed, Haltwhistle,
NE49 9PT
T: (01434) 344120
E: kathandbrad@aol.com
I: www.saughyrigg.co.uk

The Spotted Cow Inn ♦♦♦
Castle Hill, Haltwhistle,
NE49 0EN
T: (01434) 320327
F: (01434) 320009

Spring House
♦♦♦♦ SILVER AWARD
Comb Hill, Haltwhistle,
NE49 9NS
T: (01434) 320334

HAMSTERLEY
Durham

Dryderdale Hall ♦♦♦♦
Hamsterley, Bishop Auckland
DL13 3NR
T: (01388) 488494
F: (01388) 488494

HARBOTTLE
Northumberland

The Byre Vegetarian B&B
♦♦♦♦
Harbottle, Morpeth NE65 7DG
T: (01669) 650476
E: rosemary@the-byre.co.uk
I: www.the-byre.co.uk

HARTFORD BRIDGE
Northumberland

Woodside
♦♦♦♦ SILVER AWARD
Hartford Bridge Farm, Hartford
Bridge, Bedlington NE22 6AL
T: (01670) 822035

HARTLEPOOL
Tees Valley

Brafferton Guest House ♦♦
161 Stockton Road, Hartlepool,
TS25 1SL
T: (01429) 273875
E: braffertonguesthouse@
yahoo.co.uk

The Oakroyd Hotel ♦♦♦
133 Park Road, Hartlepool,
TS26 9HT
T: (01429) 864361
F: (01429) 890535
E: mandyoakroydhotel@
hotmail.com

The York Hotel ♦♦♦
185 York Road, Hartlepool,
TS26 9EE
T: (01429) 867373
F: (01429) 867220
E: info@theyorkhotel.co.uk
I: www.theyorkhotel.co.uk

HAYDON BRIDGE
Northumberland

Hadrian Lodge ♦♦♦
Hindshield Moss, North Road,
Haydon Bridge, Hexham
NE47 6NF
T: (01434) 684867
F: (01434) 684867
E: hadrianlodge@hadrianswall.
co.uk
I: www.hadrianswall.co.uk

Railway Hotel ♦♦♦
Church Street, Haydon Bridge,
Hexham NE47 6JG
T: (01434) 684254

West Mill Hills ♦♦♦
Haydon Bridge, Hexham
NE47 6JR
T: (01434) 684387

HEXHAM
Northumberland

10 Alexandra Terrace ♦♦♦
Hexham, NE46 3JQ
T: (01434) 601954
E: davesue@onetel.net.uk
I: www.hexham.lookscool.com

Anick Grange ♦♦♦
Hexham, NE46 4LP
T: (01434) 603807

The Beeches ♦♦♦♦
40 Leazes Park, Hexham,
NE46 3AY
T: (01434) 605900

Black Hall
♦♦♦♦ SILVER AWARD
Black Hall, Juniper, Hexham
NE47 0LD
T: (01434) 673218
F: (01434) 673218
E: nblackhall@lineone.net
I: www.blackhall-hexham.co.uk

The County Hotel ♦♦♦
Priestpopple, Hexham, NE46 1PS
T: (01434) 603601
F: (01434) 603616
E: the-county-hotel-hexham@
supanet.com

Dene House
♦♦♦♦ SILVER AWARD
Juniper, Hexham, NE46 1SJ
T: (01434) 673413
F: (01434) 673413
E: margaret@
denehouse-hexham.co.uk
I: www.denehouse-hexham.
co.uk

Dukesfield Hall Farm ♦♦♦♦
Steel, Hexham NE46 1SH
T: (01434) 673634
F: (01434) 673170
E: cath@dukesfield.supanet.
com

The Fairway ♦♦♦♦
4 Shaws Park, Hexham,
NE46 3BJ
T: (01434) 604846
E: gailcowley@aol.com

Hetherington ♦♦♦♦
Wark-on-Tyne, Wark, Hexham
NE48 3DR
T: (01434) 230260
F: (01434) 230260
E: a_nichol@hotmail.com

High Reins ♦♦♦♦
Leazes Lane, Hexham, NE46 3AT
T: (01434) 603590
E: walton45@hotmail.com
I: www.highreins.co.uk

Kitty Frisk House
♦♦♦♦ SILVER AWARD
Corbridge Road, Hexham,
NE46 1UN
T: (01434) 601533
F: (01434) 601533
E: alan@kittyfriskhouse.co.uk
I: www.kittyfriskhouse.co.uk

Laburnum House ♦♦♦♦
23 Leazes Crescent, Hexham,
NE46 3JZ
T: (01434) 601828
E: laburnum.house@virgin.net.
co.uk

Number 18 Hextol Terrace
♦♦♦
Hexham, NE46 2DF
T: (01434) 602265

Peth Head Cottage
♦♦♦♦ SILVER AWARD
Juniper, Hexham NE47 0LA
T: (01434) 673286
F: (01434) 673038
E: tedliddle@compuserve.com
I: www.peth-head-cottage.co.uk

Queensgate House ♦♦♦
Cockshaw, Hexham, NE46 3QU
T: (01434) 605592

Rose and Crown Inn ♦♦♦
Main Street, Slaley, Hexham
NE47 0AA
T: (01434) 673263
F: (01434) 673305
E: rosecrowninn@supanet.com
I: www.smoothhound.
co.uk/hotels/rosecrowninn.html

Rye Hill Farm ♦♦♦♦
Slaley, Hexham NE47 0AH
T: (01434) 673259
F: (01434) 673259
E: enquiries@consult-courage.
co.uk
I: www.ryehillfarm.co.uk

Topsy Turvy ♦♦♦♦
9 Leazes Lane, Hexham,
NE46 3BA
T: (01434) 603152
E: topsy.turvy@ukonline.co.uk

West Close House
♦♦♦♦ GOLD AWARD
Hextol Terrace, Hexham,
NE46 2AD
T: (01434) 603307

West Wharmley ♦♦♦♦
Hexham, NE46 2PL
T: (01434) 674227

Woodley Field ♦♦♦♦
Allendale Road, Hexham,
NE46 2NB
T: (01434) 601600
I: www.woodleyfield.co.uk

HIGH SHINCLIFFE
Durham

Shincliffe Station House ♦♦♦
High Shincliffe, Durham
DH1 2TE
T: (0191) 384 6906
F: (0191) 386 7415
E: joan@shincliffe.demon.co.uk
I: www.shincliffe.demon.co.uk

HOLY ISLAND
Northumberland

Britannia ♦♦♦
Britannia House, Holy Island,
Berwick-upon-Tweed TD15 2RX
T: (01289) 389218

The Bungalow ♦♦♦♦
Holy Island, Berwick-upon-
Tweed TD15 2SE
T: (01289) 389308
E: bungalow@lindisfarne.org.uk
I: www.lindisfarne.org.
uk/bungalow

Crown & Anchor Hotel ♦♦♦
Market Place, Holy Island,
Berwick-upon-Tweed TD15 2RX
T: (01289) 389215
F: (01289) 389215

Open Gate ♦♦♦♦
Marygate, Holy Island, Berwick-
upon-Tweed TD15 2SD
T: (01289) 389222
E: info@theopengate.ndo.uk
I: www.lindisfarne.org.
uk-accommodation

The Ship ♦♦♦
Marygate, Holy Island, Berwick-
upon-Tweed TD15 2SJ
T: (01289) 389311
F: (01289) 389316
E: theship@
lindisfarneaccommodate.com
I: www.
lindisfarneaccommodate.com

HORSLEY
Northumberland

Belvedere ♦♦♦♦
Harlow Hill, Horsley, Newcastle
upon Tyne NE15 0QD
T: (01661) 853689
E: pat.carr@btinternet.com
I: www.belvederehouse.co.uk

HOUSESTEADS
Northumberland

Moss Kennels Farm ♦♦♦♦
Housesteads, NE47 9NL
T: (01434) 344016
F: (01434) 344016
E: tim.mosskennels@virgin.net

HOWICK
Northumberland

The Old Rectory ♦♦♦♦
Howick, Alnwick NE66 3LE
T: (01665) 577139
F: (01665) 576004

HUMSHAUGH
Northumberland

Greencarts Farm ♦♦♦
Humshaugh, Hexham NE46 4BW
T: (01434) 681320

JARROW
Tyne and Wear

Bedeswell Guest House ♦♦♦
146 Bede Burn Road, Jarrow,
NE32 5AV
T: (0191) 428 4794
F: (0191) 483 7743
E: bedeswell@yahoo.com
I: www.where2stay.co.uk

KIELDER
Northumberland

Deadwater Farm ♦♦♦♦
Kielder, Hexham NE48 1EW
T: (01434) 250216

KIELDER WATER
Northumberland

The Pheasant Inn (by Kielder Water) ♦♦♦♦
Stannersburn, Falstone, Hexham NE48 1DD
T: (01434) 240382
F: (01434) 240382
E: thepheasantinn@kielderwater.demon.co.uk
I: www.thepheasantinn.com

KIRKWHELPINGTON
Northumberland

Cornhills Farmhouse
♦♦♦♦ SILVER AWARD
Cornhills, Kirkwhelpington, Newcastle upon Tyne NE19 2RE
T: (01830) 540232
F: (01830) 540388
E: cornhills@northumberlandfarmhouse.co.uk
I: www.northumberlandfarmhouse.co.uk

LANCHESTER
Durham

Maiden Hall Farmhouse Bed and Breakfast♦♦♦
Maiden Law, Lanchester, Durham DH7 0QX
T: (01207) 520796

LITTLETOWN
Durham

Littletown Lodge ♦♦♦
Front Street, Littletown, Durham DH6 1PZ
T: 0771 3322667
F: (0191) 3723712
E: littletownlodge@aol.com
I: www.littletownlodge.co.uk

LONGFRAMLINGTON
Northumberland

The Angler's Arms ♦♦♦♦
Weldon Bridge, Longframlington, Morpeth NE65 8AX
T: (01665) 570655
F: (01665) 570041
I: www.anglersarms.com

Lee Farm ♦♦♦♦ GOLD AWARD
Rothbury, Morpeth NE65 8JQ
T: (01665) 570257
F: (01665) 570257
E: enqs@leefarm.co.uk
I: www.leefarm.co.uk

LONGHORSLEY
Northumberland

The Baronial ♦♦♦
Cross Cottage, Longhorsley, Morpeth NE65 8TD
T: (01670) 788378
F: (01670) 788378

Kington ♦♦♦
East Linden, Longhorsley, Morpeth NE65 8TH
T: (01670) 788554
F: (01670) 788747
E: clive@taylor-services.freeserve.co.uk

Thistleyhaugh Farm
♦♦♦♦♦ SILVER AWARD
Longhorsley, Morpeth NE65 8RG
T: (01665) 570629
F: (01665) 570629
I: www.thistleyhaugh.co.uk

LOWICK
Northumberland

Black Bull Inn ♦♦♦♦
Main Street, Lowick, Berwick-upon-Tweed TD15 2UA
T: (01289) 388228
E: tom@blackbullowick.freeserve.co.uk

The Old Manse ♦♦♦♦
5 Cheviot View, Lowick, Berwick-upon-Tweed TD15 2TY
T: (01289) 388264
E: glenc99@aol.com

MARLEY HILL
Tyne and Wear

Hedley Hall
♦♦♦♦ SILVER AWARD
Hedley Lane, Marley Hill, Newcastle upon Tyne NE16 5EH
T: (01207) 231835
E: sfr1008452@aol.com

MIDDLETON
Northumberland

East Shaftoe Hall ♦♦♦♦
Middleton, Morpeth NE61 4EA
T: (01830) 530249
F: (01830) 530249
E: charlotterobson@shaftoe.fsbusiness.co.uk
I: www.s-h-systems.co.uk/hotels/eastshaf.html

MIDDLETON-IN-TEESDALE
Durham

Belvedere House ♦♦♦♦
54 Market Place, Middleton-in-Teesdale, Barnard Castle DL12 0QH
T: (01833) 640884
F: (01833) 640884
E: belvedere@thecoachhouse.net
I: www.thecoachhouse.net

Bluebell House ♦♦♦
Market Place, Middleton-in-Teesdale, Barnard Castle DL12 0QG
T: (01833) 640584
F: (01833) 640584
E: enquiries@bluebellhouse.co.uk
I: www.bluebellhouse-teesdale.co.uk

Brunswick House ♦♦♦♦
55 Market Place, Middleton-in-Teesdale, Barnard Castle DL12 0QH
T: (01833) 640393
F: (01833) 640393
E: enquiries@brunswickhouse.net
I: www.brunswickhouse.net

Grove Lodge ♦♦♦♦
Hude, Middleton-in-Teesdale, Barnard Castle DL12 0QW
T: (01833) 640798

Ivy House ♦♦♦
Stanhope Road, Middleton-in-Teesdale, Barnard Castle DL12 0RT
T: (01833) 640603

Lonton South Farm ♦♦♦
Middleton-in-Teesdale, Barnard Castle DL12 0PL
T: (01833) 640409

Marketplace Guest House ♦♦♦
16 Market Place, Middleton-in-Teesdale, Barnard Castle DL12 0QG
T: (01833) 640300

Snaisgill Farm ♦♦♦
Middleton-in-Teesdale, Barnard Castle DL12 0RP
T: (01833) 640343

Wemmergill Hall Farm ♦♦♦♦
Lunedale, Middleton-in-Teesdale, Barnard Castle DL12 0PA
T: (01833) 640379
E: wemmergill@freenet.co.uk
I: www.wemmergill-farm.co.uk

MORPETH
Northumberland

Cottage View Guest House ♦♦♦
6 Staithes Lane, Morpeth, NE61 1TD
T: (01670) 518550
F: (01670) 510840
E: cottageview.morpeth@virgin.net
I: www.cottageview.co.uk

Cotting Burn House ♦♦♦
40 Bullers Green, Morpeth, NE61 1DE
T: (01670) 503195
F: (01670) 503195
I: www.cottingburn.co.uk

Elder Cottage
♦♦♦♦ SILVER AWARD
High Church, Morpeth, NE61 2QT
T: (01670) 517664
F: (01670) 517644
E: cook@eldercot.freeserve.co.uk
I: www.eldercottage.co.uk

Newminster Cottage ♦♦♦
High Stanners, Morpeth, NE61 1QL
T: (01670) 503124

Riverside Guest House ♦♦♦
77 Newgate Street, Morpeth, NE61 1BX
T: (01670) 515026
F: (01670) 514647
E: elaine.riverside@virgin.net
I: www.riverside-guesthouse.co.uk

NEW BRANCEPETH
Durham

Alum Waters Guest House ♦♦♦♦
Unthank Farmhouse, Alum Waters, New Brancepeth, Durham DH7 7JJ
T: (0191) 373 0628
F: (0191) 373 0628
E: tony@alumwaters.freeserve.co.uk

NEWBIGGIN-BY-THE-SEA
Northumberland

Seaton House ♦♦♦
20 Seaton Avenue, Newbiggin-by-the-Sea, NE64 6UX
T: (01670) 816057

NEWBROUGH
Northumberland

Allerwash Farmhouse
♦♦♦♦♦ GOLD AWARD
Newbrough, Hexham NE47 5AB
T: (01434) 674574
F: (01434) 674574

Newbrough Park
♦♦♦♦ SILVER AWARD
Newbrough, Hexham NE47 5AR
T: (01434) 674545
F: (01434) 674544
E: newbroughpark@aol.com

NEWCASTLE UPON TYNE
Tyne and Wear

Avenue Hotel ♦♦♦
2 Manor House Road, Jesmond, Newcastle upon Tyne NE2 2LU
T: (0191) 281 1396
F: (0191) 281 6588

Chirton House Hotel ♦♦♦
46 Clifton Road, Off Grainger Park Road, Newcastle upon Tyne, NE4 6XH
T: (0191) 273 0407
F: (0191) 273 0407

Eldon Hotel ♦♦
24 Akenside Terrace, Jesmond, Newcastle upon Tyne NE2 1TN
T: (0191) 281 2562
F: (0191) 213 0546

Elm Cottage
♦♦ SILVER AWARD
37 Sunniside Road, Sunnise, Newcastle upon Tyne, NE16 5NA
T: (0191) 496 0156

Jesmond Park Hotel ♦♦♦
74-76 Queens Road, Jesmond, Newcastle upon Tyne NE2 2PR
T: (0191) 281 2821
F: (0191) 281 0515
E: vh@jespark.fsnet.co.uk
I: www.jesmondpark.com

The Keelman's Lodge ♦♦♦♦
Grange Road, Newburn, Newcastle upon Tyne NE15 8NL
T: (0191) 267 1689
F: (0191) 499 0041
E: admin@petersen-stainless.co.uk
I: www.petersen-stainless.co.uk

The Lynnwood ♦♦♦
1 Lynwood Terrace, Newcastle upon Tyne, NE4 6UL
T: (0191) 273 3497
F: (0191) 273 3497

University of Northumbria Claude Gibb Halls of Residence ♦♦
Room 107, Ellison Terrce, Ellison Place, Newcastle upon Tyne, NE1 8ST
T: (0191) 227 4024
F: (0191) 227 3197
E: rc.conferences@northumbria.ac.uk
I: www.northumbria.ac.uk/conferences

Westland Hotel ♦♦♦
27 Osborne Avenue, Jesmond, Newcastle upon Tyne NE2 1JR
T: (0191) 281 0412
F: (0191) 281 5005
I: www.westland-hotel.co.uk

NEWTON
Northumberland

Crookhill Farm ♦♦♦
Newton, Stocksfield NE43 7UX
T: (01661) 843117
F: (01661) 844702

NORHAM
Northumberland

Dromore House ♦♦♦
12 Pedwell Way, Norham, Berwick-upon-Tweed TD15 2LD
T: (01289) 382313

Threeways ♦♦♦♦
Norham, Berwick-upon-Tweed TD15 2JZ
T: (01289) 382795

NORTH HYLTON
Tyne and Wear

The Shipwrights Hotel ♦♦♦
Ferry Boat Lane, North Hylton, Sunderland SR5 3HW
T: (0191) 549 5139
F: (0191) 549 7464
E: tony@theshipwrights.freeserve.co.uk

NORTON
Tees Valley

Grange Guest House ♦♦♦
33 Grange Road, Norton, Stockton-on-Tees TS20 2NS
T: (01642) 552541
I: www.shlwell.co.uk

OTTERBURN
Northumberland

Butterchurn Guest House ♦♦♦♦
Main Street, Otterburn, Newcastle upon Tyne NE19 1NP
T: (01830) 520585
F: (01830) 520874
E: keith@butterchurn.freeserve.co.uk
I: www.butterchurn.freeserve.co.uk

Dunns Houses Farmhouse Bed and Breakfast♦♦♦♦
Dunns Houses, Otterburn, Newcastle upon Tyne NE19 1LB
T: (01830) 520677
F: (01830) 520677
E: dunnshouses@hotmail.com
I: www.northumberlandfarmholidays.co.uk

Redesdale Arms Hotel ♦♦♦♦
Rochester, Newcastle upon Tyne NE19 1TA
T: (01830) 520668
F: (01830) 520063
E: redesdalehotel@hotmail.com
I: www.redesdale-hotel.co.uk

Woolaw Farm
Rating Applied For
Rochester, Newcastle upon Tyne NE19 1TB
T: (01830) 520686
F: (01830) 520686
E: fww.chapman@btopenworld.com

OVINGTON
Northumberland

Southcroft ♦♦♦♦
Ovington, Prudhoe NE42 6EE
T: (01661) 830651
F: (01661) 834312

PIERCEBRIDGE
Durham

The Bridge House ♦♦♦
Piercebridge, Darlington DL2 3SG
T: (01325) 374727
E: ceformstone@virgin.net

Holme House ♦♦♦
Piercebridge, Darlington DL2 3SY
T: (01325) 374280
F: (01325) 374280
E: graham@holmehouse22.freeserve.co.uk
I: www.destinationengland.co.uk/holmehousse.html

PITY ME
Durham

The Lambton Hounds Inn ♦♦♦
Front Street, Pity Me, Durham DH1 5DE
T: (0191) 386 4742
F: (0191) 375 0805
E: lambtonhounds@aol.com

PLAWSWORTH
Durham

Lilac Cottage ♦♦
Wheatley Well Lane, Plawsworth, Chester-le-Street DH2 3LD
T: (0191) 371 2969

PONTELAND
Northumberland

Hazel Cottage
♦♦♦♦ SILVER AWARD
Eachwick, Ponteland, Newcastle upon Tyne NE18 0BE
T: (01661) 852415
F: (01661) 854797
E: hazelcottage@eachwick.fsbusiness.co.uk
I: www.hazel-cottage.co.uk

Stone Cottage ♦♦♦
Prestwick Road End, Ponteland, Newcastle upon Tyne NE20 9BX
T: (01661) 823957
E: klee@euphony.net
I: www.stonecottageguesthouse.com

Stonehaven Lodge ♦♦♦
Prestwick Road End, Ponteland, Newcastle upon Tyne NE20 9BX
T: (01661) 872363
E: brenanderson@ncletw.freeserve.co.uk

QUEBEC
Durham

Hamsteels Hall ♦♦♦♦
Hamsteels Lane, Quebec, Durham DH7 9RS
T: (01207) 520388
F: (01207) 520388
E: June@hamsteelshall.co.uk
I: www.hamsteelshall.co.uk

RAMSHAW
Northumberland

The Bridge Inn ♦♦
1 Gordon Lane, Ramshaw, Bishop Auckland DL14 0NS
T: (01388) 832509
F: (01388) 832509
E: bridgeinnramshaw@barbox.com

REDCAR
Tees Valley

A 2 Z Guest House
Rating Applied For
71 Station Road, Redcar, TS10 1RD
T: (01642) 775533
F: (01642) 484790

All Welcome In
Rating Applied For
81 Queen Street, Redcar, TS10 1BQ
T: (01642) 484790

Clarendon Hotel
Rating Applied For
2 High Street, Redcar, TS10 3DU
T: (01642) 484301
F: (01642) 775819
E: fitzyone44618340@:aol.com

Claxton Hotel ♦♦♦
196 High Street, Redcar, TS10 3AW
T: (01642) 486745
F: (01642) 486522
E: enquiries@claxtonhotel.co.uk
I: www.claxtonhotel.co.uk

Falcon Hotel ♦♦♦
13 Station Road, Redcar, TS10 1AH
T: (01642) 484300

The Kastle Hotel
Rating Applied For
55 Newcomen Place, Redcar, TS10 1DB
T: (01642) 489313

Ocean View Guest House
Rating Applied For
32 Arthur Street, Redcar, TS10 1BW
T: (01642) 489536

O'Gradys
Rating Applied For
20 Queen Street, Redcar, TS10 1AE
T: (01642) 477624
F: (01642) 482059
E: mankguard@o-gradys.fsnet.co.uk
I: www.o-gradys.co.uk

Red Barns Hotel
Rating Applied For
31 Kirkleatham Street, Redcar, TS10 1QH
T: (01642) 477622
F: (01642) 493346

RIDING MILL
Northumberland

Broomley Fell Farm ♦♦♦
Riding Mill, NE44 6AY
T: (01434) 682682
F: (01434) 682728
E: enquiries@broomleyfell.co.uk
I: www.broomleyfell.co.uk

Woodside House ♦♦♦♦
Sandy Bank, Riding Mill, NE44 6HS
T: (01434) 682306

ROMALDKIRK
Durham

Mill Riggs Cottage ♦♦♦
Romaldkirk, Barnard Castle DL12 9EW
T: (01833) 650392

ROOKHOPE
Durham

High Brandon ♦♦♦♦
Rookhope, Bishop Auckland DL13 2AF
T: (01388) 517673
E: highbrandonbb@aol.com
I: members.aol.com/highbrandonbb

ROTHBURY
Northumberland

The Chirnells ♦♦♦♦
Thropton, Morpeth NE65 7JE
T: (01669) 621507

Farm Cottage Guest House
♦♦♦♦ SILVER AWARD
Thropton, Morpeth NE65 7NA
T: (01669) 620831
F: (01669) 620831
E: joan@farmcottageguesthouse.co.uk
I: www.farmcottageguesthouse.co.uk

The Haven ♦♦♦♦
Backcrofts, Rothbury, Morpeth NE65 7YA
T: (01669) 620577
F: (01669) 620766
E: the.haven.rothbury@talk21.com

Katerina's Guest House
♦♦♦♦ SILVER AWARD
Sun Buildings, High Street, Rothbury, Morpeth NE65 7TQ
T: (01669) 620691
F: (01669) 620691
E: cath@katerinasguesthouse.co.uk
I: www.katerinasguesthouse.co.uk

Lorbottle West Steads ♦♦♦
Thropton, Morpeth NE65 7JT
T: (01665) 574672
F: (01665) 574672
E: helen.farr@farming.co.uk
I: www.cottageguide.co.uk/lorbottle.html

Newcastle Hotel ♦♦♦
Rothbury, Morpeth NE65 7UT
T: (01669) 620334
F: (01669) 620334

Orchard Guest House ♦♦♦♦
High Street, Rothbury, Morpeth NE65 7TL
T: (01669) 620684
E: jpickard@orchardguesthouse.co.uk
I: www.orchardguesthouse.co.uk

The Queens Head Hotel ♦♦♦
Townfoot, Rothbury, Morpeth NE65 7SR
T: (01669) 620470
E: enqs@queensheadrothbury.com

Silverton House ♦♦♦♦
Silverton Lane, Rothbury, Morpeth NE65 7RJ
T: (01669) 621395
E: silverton_house@lineone.net
I: www.silvertonhouse.co.uk

Silverton Lodge
♦♦♦♦♦ SILVER AWARD
Silverton Lane, Rothbury, Morpeth NE65 7RJ
T: (01669) 620144
F: (01669) 621920
E: info@silvertonlodge.co.uk
I: www.silvertonlodge.co.uk

Wagtail Farm ♦♦♦♦
Rothbury, Morpeth NE65 7PL
T: (01669) 620367
E: wagtail@tinyworld.co.uk
I: www.wagtailfarm.info

Whitton Farmhouse Hotel ♦♦♦♦
Whitton, Rothbury, Morpeth NE65 7RL
T: (01669) 620811
F: (01669) 620811
E: whittonfarmhotel@supanet.com
I: www.smoothhound.co.uk/hotels

RUSHYFORD
Durham

Garden House ♦♦♦♦
Windlestone Park, Windlestone, Rushyford, Ferryhill DL17 0LZ
T: (01388) 720217

RYTON
Tyne and Wear

Hedgefield House ♦♦♦
Stella Road, Ryton, NE21 4LR
T: (0191) 413 7373
F: (0191) 413 7373

ST JOHN'S CHAPEL
Durham

Low Chesters Guesthouse Rating Applied For
St John's Chapel, Bishop Auckland DL13 1QP
T: (01388) 537406

SALTBURN-BY-THE-SEA
Tees Valley

Amble Guest House ♦♦♦
2 Bath Street, Saltburn-by-the-Sea, TS12 1BJ
T: (01287) 622314

Diamond Quay Rating Applied For
9 Diamond Street, Saltburn-by-the-Sea, TS12 1EB
T: (01287) 203149
F: (01287) 203149
E: diamondquay@aol.com

The Rose Garden ♦♦♦♦
20 Hilda Place, Saltburn-by-the-Sea, TS12 1BP
T: (01287) 622947
F: (01287) 622947
E: enquiries@therosegarden.co.uk
I: www.therosegarden.co.uk

The Spa Hotel Rating Applied For
Saltburn Bank, Saltburn-by-the-Sea, TS12 1HH
T: (01287) 622544
F: (01287) 625870
E: reservations@spahotels.co.uk
I: www.spahotels.co.uk

'Merhba' Bed & Breakfast ♦♦♦
11 Dundas Street West, Saltburn-by-the-Sea, TS12 1BL
T: (01287) 622566
E: pcookmerhba@ntlworld.co.uk

SEAHOUSES
Northumberland

Braidstone Lodge ♦♦♦
1 Braidstone Square, Seahouses, NE68 7RP
T: (01665) 720055

Fairfield ♦♦♦
102 Main Street, Seahouses, NE68 7TP
T: (01665) 721736
E: jen2col@fairfield.fsnet.co.uk

Kingsway ♦♦♦♦
19 Kings Street, Seahouses, NE68 7XW
T: (01665) 720449
F: (01665) 720449
I: www.kingsway-guesthouse.co.uk

Leeholme ♦♦♦
93 Main Street, Seahouses, NE68 7TS
T: (01665) 720230

Railston House ♦♦♦♦ SILVER AWARD
133 Main Street, North Sunderland, Seahouses NE68 7TS
T: (01665) 720912

Rowena ♦♦♦
99 Main Street, Seahouses, NE68 7TS
T: (01665) 721309

St Aidan Hotel ♦♦♦♦
1 St Aidans, Seafield Road, Seahouses, NE68 7SR
T: (01665) 720355
F: (01665) 721989
E: enquiries@staidanhotel.co.uk
I: www.staidanhotel.co.uk

Springwood ♦♦♦♦
South Lane, Seahouses, NE68 7UL
T: (01665) 720320
F: (01665) 720146
E: ian@slatehall.freeserve.co.uk
I: www.slatehallridingcentre.com

Stoneridge ♦♦♦
15 Quarry Field, Seahouses, NE68 7TB
T: (01665) 720835

Union Cottage Guest House ♦♦♦♦
11 Union Street, Seahouses, NE68 7RT
T: (01665) 720521
F: (01665) 720521
E: carruthers@unioncottage.freeserve.co.uk
I: www.unioncottage.freeserve.co.uk

Westfield Farmhouse ♦♦♦♦
North Sunderland, Seahouses, NE68 7UR
T: (01665) 720161
F: (01665) 720713
E: westfield@theforsyths.com

Wyndgrove House ♦♦♦
156 Main Street, North Sunderland, Seahouses NE68 7UA
T: (01665) 720658

SEATON CAREW
Tees Valley

Altonlea Lodge Guest House ♦♦♦
19 The Green, Seaton Carew, Hartlepool TS25 1AT
T: (01429) 271289
E: enquiries@altonlea.co.uk
I: www.altonlea.co.uk

Durham Hotel Rating Applied For
38-39 The Front, Seaton Carew, Hartlepool TS25 1DA
T: (01429) 236502

SEDGEFIELD
Durham

Forge Cottage ♦♦♦
2 West End, Sedgefield, Stockton-on-Tees TS21 2BS
T: (01740) 622831
F: (01740) 622831
E: forgecottage@lineone.net

Glower-Oer-Him Farm ♦♦
Sedgefield, Stockton-on-Tees TS21 3HO
T: (01740) 622737

Todds House Farm ♦♦♦
Sedgefield, Stockton-on-Tees TS21 3EL
T: (01740) 620244
F: (01740) 620244
E: edgoosej@aol.com
I: www.toddshousefarm.co.uk

SHINCLIFFE
Durham

The Bracken Hotel ♦♦♦♦ SILVER AWARD
Bank Foot, Shincliffe, Durham DH1 2PD
T: (0191) 386 2966
F: (0191) 384 5423

SHOTLEY BRIDGE
Durham

The Manor House Inn ♦♦♦♦ SILVER AWARD
Carterway Heads, Shotley Bridge, Consett DH8 9LX
T: (01207) 255268
F: (01207) 255268
I: www.scoot.co.uk/manor.house/

SIMONBURN
Northumberland

Simonburn Guest House ♦♦♦
1 The Mains, Simonburn, Hexham NE48 3AW
T: (01434) 681321

SKELTON
Tees Valley

Westerland's Guest House ♦♦♦♦
27 East Parade, Skelton, Saltburn-by-the-Sea TS12 2BJ
T: (01287) 650690

The Wharton Arms ♦♦
133 High Street, Skelton, Saltburn-by-the-Sea TS12 2DY
T: (01287) 650618

SLALEY
Northumberland

Flothers Farm ♦♦♦
Slaley, Hexham NE47 0BJ
T: (01434) 673240
F: (01434) 673240
E: dart@flothers.fsnet.co.uk
I: www.flothers.co.uk

The Strothers ♦♦♦♦ SILVER AWARD
Slaley, Hexham NE47 0AA
T: (01434) 673417
F: (01434) 673417
E: ednahardy@the-strothers.co.uk
I: www.the-strothers.co.uk

Travellers Rest ♦♦♦♦ SILVER AWARD
Slaley, Hexham NE47 1TT
T: (01434) 673231
F: (01434) 673906
E: enq@travellersrest.sagehost.co.uk
I: www.travellersrest.sagesite.co.uk

SOUTH SHIELDS
Tyne and Wear

Ainsley Guest House ♦♦♦
59 Ocean Road, South Shields, NE33 2JJ
T: (0191) 454 3399
F: (0191) 454 3399
E: ainsleyguesthouse@hotmail.com

Aquarius Guest House ♦♦♦
61 Ocean Road, South Shields, NE33 2JJ
T: (0191) 422 3340
F: (0191) 422 3340

Britannia Guesthouse Rating Applied For
54/56 Julian Avenue, South Shields, NE33 2EW
T: (0191) 456 0896
F: (0191) 456 3203
E: britimports@aol.com

Dunlin Guest House ♦♦♦
11 Urfa Terrace, South Shields, NE33 2ES
T: (0191) 456 7442
F: (0191) 456 7442

Forest Guest House ♦♦♦♦
117 Ocean Road, South Shields, NE33 2JL
T: (0191) 454 8160
F: (0191) 454 8160
E: enquiries@forestguesthouse.com
I: www.forestguesthouse.com

The Kingsmere ♦♦♦
9 Urfa Terrace, South Shields, NE33 2ES
T: (0191) 456 0234
F: (0191) 425 5026

Marina Guest House ♦♦♦
32 Seaview Terrace, South Shields, NE33 2NW
T: (0191) 456 1998
F: (0191) 456 1998
E: austin@marina32.fsnet.co.uk

North View ♦♦♦
12 Urfa Terrace, South Shields, NE33 2ES
T: (0191) 454 4950
F: (0191) 454 4950

Ravensbourne Guest House ♦♦♦
106 Beach Road, South Shields, NE33 2NE
T: (0191) 456 5849
F: (0191) 456 5849
I: www.sanddancers.co.uk

River's End Guest House ♦♦♦
41 Lawe Road, South Shields, NE33 2EU
T: (0191) 456 4229
F: (0191) 456 4229
E: Brian@riversend.fsnet.co.uk
I: www.riversend.fsnet.co.uk

Saraville Guest House ♦♦♦
103 Ocean Road, South Shields, NE33 2JL
T: (0191) 454 1169
F: (0191) 454 1169
E: Emma@saraville.freeserve.co.uk
I: www.geocities.com/saravillehouse

Sir William Fox Hotel ♦♦♦
5 Westoe Village, South Shields, NE33 3D2
T: (0191) 456 4554
F: (0191) 427 6312
I: www.sirwilliamfox.co.uk

South Shore ♦♦♦
115 Ocean Road, South Shields, NE33 2JL
T: (0191) 454 4049
F: (0191) 454 4049

SPENNYMOOR
Durham

The Gables ♦♦♦
10 South View, Middlestone Moor, Spennymoor DL16 7DF
T: (01388) 817544
F: (01388) 812533
E: thegablesghouse@aol.com
I: www.thegables.ntb.org.uk

Highview Country House ♦♦♦♦
Kirkmerrington, Spennymoor, DL16 7JT
T: (01388) 811006

Idsley House ♦♦♦♦
4 Green Lane, Spennymoor, DL16 6HD
T: (01388) 814237

SPITTAL
Northumberland

All Seasons ♦♦♦
46 Main Street, Spittal, Berwick-upon-Tweed TD15 1QY
T: (01289) 308452

The Roxburgh ♦♦
117 Main Street, Spittal, Berwick-upon-Tweed TD15 1RP
T: (01289) 306266

STAINDROP
Durham

Grove Farm
Rating Applied For
Staindrop, Darlington DL2 3LN
T: (01833) 660327
F: (01833) 660886
E: info@grovefarmbreaks.fsnet.co.uk
I: www.grovefarmbreaks.co.uk

Malvern House ♦♦♦
7 Front Street, Staindrop, Darlington DL2 3LZ
T: (01833) 660846
F: (01833) 660846
E: malvernhousebookings@lineone.net
I: website.lineone.net/~meridlin

STAINTON
Tees Valley

Stainton House
♦♦♦♦♦ SILVER AWARD
2 Hemlington Road, Stainton, Middlesbrough TS8 9AJ
T: (01642) 594221

STAMFORDHAM
Northumberland

The Stamfordham Bay Horse Inn ♦♦♦♦
Southside, Stamfordham, Newcastle upon Tyne NE18 0PB
T: (01661) 886244
E: stay@stamfordham-bay.co.uk
I: www.stamfordham-bay.co.uk

STANHOPE
Durham

Horsley Hall
♦♦♦♦♦ SILVER AWARD
Eastgate, Stanhope, Bishop Auckland DL13 2LJ
T: (01388) 517239
F: (01388) 517608
E: hotel@horsleyhall.co.uk
I: www.horsleyhall.co.uk

STANLEY
Durham

Bushblades Farm ♦♦♦
Harperley, Stanley DH9 9UA
T: (01207) 232722

Harperley Hotel ♦♦♦
Harperley, Stanley DH9 9TY
T: (01207) 234011
F: (01207) 232325
E: harperley-hotel@supernet.com

STANNERSBURN
Northumberland

Spring Cottage ♦♦♦♦
Stannersburn, Hexham NE48 1DD
T: (01434) 240388
E: springcottage2000@yahoo.co.uk

STANNINGTON
Northumberland

Cheviot View Farmhouse Bed & Breakfast♦♦♦♦
North Shotton Farm, Stannington, Morpeth NE61 6EU
T: (01670) 789231
E: julia.philipson1@btopenworld.com

STOCKSFIELD
Northumberland

Old Ridley Hall ♦♦♦
Stocksfield, NE43 7RU
T: (01661) 842816
E: oldridleyhall@talk21.com

Wheelbirks Farm ♦♦♦♦
Stocksfield, NE43 7HY
T: (01661) 843378
F: (01661) 842613
I: www.wheelbirks.ndo.co.uk

STOCKTON-ON-TEES
Tees Valley

Four Seasons Guest House ♦♦♦
314 Norton Road, Stockton-on-Tees, TS20 2PU
T: (01642) 554826
F: (01642) 554826

SUNDERLAND
Tyne and Wear

Abingdon and Belmont Guest House ♦♦♦
5 St George's Terrace, Roker, Sunderland, SR6 9LX
T: (0191) 567 2438
E: belmontguesthouse@hotmail.com
I: www.belmontguesthouse.com

Acorn Guest House ♦♦
10 Mowbray Road, Hendon, Sunderland SR2 8EN
T: (0191) 514 2170
E: theacornguesthouse@hotmail.com

Anchor Lodge Guest House ♦♦♦
16 Roker Terrace, Roker Seafront, Sunderland, SR6 9NB
T: (0191) 567 4154

April Guest House ♦♦♦♦
12 Saint Georges Terrace, Roker, Sunderland, SR6 9LX
T: (0191) 565 9550
F: (0191) 565 9550
E: ghunter@aprilguesthouse.freeserve.co.uk and gary@aprilguesth
I: www.aprilguesthouse.com

Areldee Guest House ♦♦♦
18 Roker Terrace, Sunderland, SR6 9NB
T: (0191) 514 1971
F: (0191) 514 0678
E: peter@areldeeguesthouse.freeserve.co.uk
I: www.abbeyandareldeeguesthouses.co.uk

The Ashborne ♦♦♦
7 St George's Terrace, Roker, Sunderland, SR6 9LX
T: (0191) 565 3997
F: (0191) 565 3997

The Balmoral Guest House ♦♦♦
3 Roker Terrace, Roker, Sunderland, SR6 9NB
T: (0191) 565 9217
E: thebalmoral@supanet.com
I: www.thebalmoral.supanet.com

Beach View ♦♦♦
15 Roker Terrace, Sunderland, SR6 9NB
T: (0191) 567 0719

Braeside Holiday Guest House ♦♦
26 Western Hill, (Beside University), Sunderland, SR2 7PH
T: (0191) 565 4801
F: (0191) 552 4198
E: george@the20thhole.co.uk
I: www.the20thhole.co.uk

Brookside Bed and Breakfast ♦♦♦
6 Brookside Terrace, Tunstall Road, Sunderland, SR2 7RN
T: (0191) 565 6739

The Chaise Guest House ♦♦♦
5 Roker Terrace, Roker Seafront, Sunderland, SR6 9NB
T: (0191) 565 9218
F: (0191) 565 9218
E: thechaise@aol.com

Felicitations ♦♦♦
94 Ewesley Road, High Barnes, Sunderland, SR4 7RJ
T: (0191) 522 0960
F: (0191) 551 8915
E: felicitations_uk@talk21.com

Lemonfield Hotel ♦♦♦
Sea Lane, Seaburn, Sunderland, SR6 8EE
T: (0191) 529 3018
F: (0191) 529 5952
E: ian@lemonfield.fsnet.co.uk

Mayfield Hotel ♦♦♦
Sea Lane, Seaburn, Sunderland, SR6 8EE
T: (0191) 529 3345
F: (0191) 529 3345

Terrace Guest House
Rating Applied For
2 Roker Terrace, Sunderland, SR6 9NB
T: (0191) 565 0132
F: (0191) 565 0132

SWALWELL
Tyne and Wear

The Angel Guest House ♦♦♦
6 Front Street, Swalwell, Newcastle upon Tyne NE16 3DW
T: (0191) 496 0186
F: (0191) 496 0186
E: angel@swalwell.freeserve.com

SWARLAND
Northumberland

Swarland Old Hall
♦♦♦♦ GOLD AWARD
Swarland, Morpeth NE65 9HU
T: (01670) 787642
E: proctor@swarlandoldhall.fsnet.co.uk
I: www.swarlandoldhall.com

TANFIELD
Durham

Tanfield Garden Lodge ♦♦♦
Tanfield Lane, Tanfield, Stanley DH9 9QF
T: (01207) 282821
F: (01207) 282821

Tanfield Lane Farm ♦♦♦
Tanfield, Stanley DH9 9QE
T: (01207) 232739

TANTOBIE
Durham

Oak Tree Inn ♦♦
Tantobie, Stanley DH9 9RF
T: (01207) 235445
F: (01207) 235445
E: anne@dorbiere.co.uk

THROPTON
Northumberland

Three Wheat Heads ♦♦♦
Main Street, Thropton, Morpeth NE65 7LR
T: (01669) 620262
F: (01669) 621281

TOW LAW
Durham

Bracken Hill Weardale
♦♦♦♦ SILVER AWARD
Thornley, Tow Law, Bishop Auckland DL13 4PQ
T: (01388) 731329
E: farrow@bracken-hill.com
I: www.bracken-hill.com

TWEEDMOUTH
Northumberland

Westsunnyside House ♦♦♦♦
Tweedmouth, Berwick-upon-Tweed TD15 2QH
T: (01289) 305387

TYNEMOUTH
Tyne and Wear

Martineau Guest House
♦♦♦♦ SILVER AWARD
57 Front Street, Tynemouth, North Shields NE30 4BX
T: (0191) 296 0746
E: martineau.house@ukgateway.net
I: www.martineau-house.co.uk

WALL
Northumberland

Blossom Hill Bed & Breakfast ♦♦♦♦
Blossom Hill, High Brunton, Wall, Hexham NE46 4E
T: (01434) 681274
F: (01434) 681274
E: jproudlock@lineone.net

The Hadrian Hotel ♦♦♦
Wall, Hexham NE46 4ER
T: (01434) 681232
E: david.lindsay13@btinternet.com
I: www.hadrianhotel.com

St Oswalds Farm ♦♦
Wall, Hexham NE46 4HB
T: (01434) 681307
E: ereay@fish.co.uk

WALLSEND
Tyne and Wear

Imperial Guest House ♦♦♦♦
194 Station Road, Wallsend, NE28 8RD
T: (0191) 236 9808
F: (0191) 236 9808
E: enquiries@imperialguesthouse.co.uk
I: www.imperialguesthouse.co.uk

WARK
Northumberland

Battlesteads Hotel ♦♦♦
Wark, Hexham NE48 3LS
T: (01434) 230209
F: (01434) 230730
E: Info@Battlesteads-Hotel.co.uk
I: www.Battlesteads-Hotel.co.uk

WARKWORTH
Northumberland

Beck 'N' Call ♦♦♦♦
Birling West Cottage, Warkworth, Morpeth NE65 0XS
T: (01665) 711653
E: beck-n-call@lineone.net
I: www.beck-n-call.co.uk

Bide A While ♦♦♦
4 Beal Croft, Warkworth, Morpeth NE65 0XL
T: (01665) 711753

North Cottage ♦♦♦♦
Birling, Warkworth, Morpeth NE65 0XS
T: (01665) 711263
E: edithandjohn@another.com
I: www.accta.co.uk/north

The Old Manse ♦♦♦♦
20 The Butts, Warkworth, Morpeth NE65 0SS
T: (01665) 710850
F: (01665) 710850

WASHINGTON
Tyne and Wear

Willow Lodge ♦♦♦♦
12 The Willows, Washington, NE38 8JE
T: (0191) 419 4363
F: (0191) 419 4363
E: glover@nobrad.demon.co.uk

Ye Olde Cop Shop ♦♦♦♦
6 The Green, Washington Village, Washington, NE38 7AB
T: (0191) 416 5333
E: yeoldecopshop@btinternet.com

WATERHOUSES
Durham

Ivesley ♦♦♦♦
Waterhouses, Durham DH7 9HB
T: (0191) 373 4324
F: (0191) 373 4757
E: ivesley@msn.com
I: www.ridingholidays-ivesley.co.uk

WEST AUCKLAND
Durham

Wheatside Hotel ♦♦
Bildershaw Bank, West Auckland, Bishop Auckland DL14 9PL
T: (01388) 832725
F: (01388) 832485

WEST WOODBURN
Northumberland

Bay Horse Inn ♦♦♦♦
West Woodburn, Hexham NE48 2RX
T: (01434) 270218
F: (01434) 270118

Plevna House ♦♦♦♦ SILVER AWARD
West Woodburn, Hexham NE48 2RA
T: (01434) 270369
F: (01434) 270179
E: bookings@plevnahouse.fsnet.co.uk
I: www.plevnahouse.ntb.org.uk

WESTGATE-IN-WEARDALE
Durham

Lands Farm ♦♦♦♦ SILVER AWARD
Westgate-in-Weardale, Bishop Auckland DL13 1SN
T: (01388) 517210
F: (01388) 517210

WHICKHAM
Tyne and Wear

East Byermoor Guest House ♦♦♦♦ SILVER AWARD
Fellside Road, Whickham, Newcastle upon Tyne NE16 5BD
T: (01207) 272687
F: (01207) 272145
E: eastbyermoor-gh.arbon@virgin.net

WHITLEY BAY
Tyne and Wear

Caprice Hotel ♦♦♦
14-16 South Parade, Whitley Bay, NE26 2RG
T: (0191) 253 0141
F: (0191) 252 3329
E: stay@caprice-hotel.co.uk
I: www.caprice-hotel.co.uk

The Cara ♦♦
9 The Links, Whitley Bay, NE26 1PS
T: (0191) 253 0172
I: www.thecara.co.uk

Chedburgh Hotel ♦♦♦
12 The Esplanade, Whitley Bay, NE26 1AH
T: (0191) 253 0415
F: (0191) 253 0415
E: chedburghhotel@aol.com
I: www.SmoothHound.co.uk

The Glen Esk Guest House ♦♦♦
8 South Parade, Whitley Bay, NE26 2RG
T: (0191) 253 0103
F: (0191) 253 0103
E: the.glenesk@talk21.com

Marlborough Hotel ♦♦♦♦
20-21 East Parade, The Promenade, Whitley Bay, NE26 1AP
T: (0191) 251 3628
F: (0191) 252 5033
E: reception@marlborough-hotel.com
I: www.marlborough-hotel.com

Shan-Gri-La ♦
29 Esplanade, Whitley Bay, NE26 2AL
T: (0191) 253 0230

York House Hotel & Studios Ltd ♦♦♦♦
30 Park Parade, Whitley Bay, NE26 1DX
T: (0191) 252 8313
F: (0191) 251 3953
E: reservations@yorkhousehotel.com
I: www.yorkhousehotel.com

WHITTINGHAM
Northumberland

Callaly Cottage Bed and Breakfast ♦♦♦♦
Callaly, Alnwick NE66 4TA
T: (01665) 574684
E: callaly@alnwick.org.uk
I: www.callaly.alnwick.org.uk

WITTON GILBERT
Durham

The Coach House ♦♦♦♦
Stobbilee House, Witton Gilbert, Durham DH7 6TW
T: (0191) 373 6132
F: (0191) 373 6711
E: suzanne.cronin@btinternet.com
I: www.stobbilee.com

WOLSINGHAM
Durham

Bradley Hall Rating Applied For
Wolsingham, Bishop Auckland DL13 3JH
T: (01388) 527280
F: 08701 374975
E: cjs@bradleyhall.net
I: www.bradleyhall.net

Holywell Farm ♦♦♦♦
Wolsingham, Bishop Auckland DL13 3HB
T: (01388) 527249
F: (01388) 527249

WOOLER
Northumberland

The Old Manse ♦♦♦♦♦ GOLD AWARD
New Road, Chatton, Alnwick NE66 5PU
T: (01668) 215343
E: chattonbb@aol.com
I: www.oldmansechatton.co.uk

Ryecroft Hotel Rating Applied For
28 Ryecroft Way, Wooler, NE71 6AB
T: (01668) 281459
F: (01668) 282214
E: ryecrofthtl@aol.com
I: www.ryecroft-hotel.com

Saint Hilliers ♦♦♦
6 Church Street, Wooler, NE71 6DA
T: (01668) 281340
E: mhugall@onetel.net.uk

Tilldale House ♦♦♦♦
34-40 High Street, Wooler, NE71 6BG
T: (01668) 281450
E: tilldalehouse@freezone.co.uk
I: www.tilldalehouse.com

West Weetwood Farmhouse ♦♦♦♦
West Weetwood, Wooler, NE71 6AQ
T: (01668) 281497
F: (01668) 281497

Winton House ♦♦♦
39 Glendale Road, Wooler, NE71 6DL
T: (01668) 281362
F: (01668) 281362
E: winton.house@virgin.net
I: www.wintonhouse.ntb.org.uk

WYLAM
Northumberland

Wormald House ♦♦♦♦
Main Street, Wylam, NE41 8DN
T: (01661) 852529
F: (01661) 852529
E: john.craven3@btinternet.com

NORTH WEST

ABBEYSTEAD
Lancashire

Greenbank Farmhouse ♦♦♦
Abbeystead, Lancaster LA2 9BA
T: (01524) 792063
F: (01524) 792063
E: tait@greenbankfarmhouse.freeserve.co.uk
I: www.greenbankfarmhouse.co.uk

ACCRINGTON
Lancashire

Horizons Hotel and Restaurant Traders Brasserie♦♦♦
The Globe Centre, St James Square, Accrington, BB5 0RE
T: (01254) 602020
F: (01254) 602021
E: horizons@theglobe111.fsnet.co.uk

Norwood Guest House ♦♦♦♦
349 Whalley Road, Accrington, BB5 5DF
T: (01254) 398132
F: (01254) 398132
E: stuart@norwoodguesthouse.co.uk
I: www.norwoodguesthouse.co.uk

ACTON BRIDGE
Cheshire

Manor Farm ♦♦♦♦
Cliff Road, Acton Bridge, Northwich CW8 3QP
T: (01606) 853181
F: (01606) 853181
E: terri.mac.manorfarm@care4free.net

AINTREE
Merseyside

Church View Guest House ♦♦
7 Church Avenue, Aintree, Liverpool L9 4SG
T: (0151) 525 8166

ALPRAHAM
Cheshire

Tollemache Arms ♦♦♦
Chester Road, Alpraham, Tarporley CW6 9JE
T: (01829) 260030
F: (01829) 260030

ALSAGER
Cheshire

Sappho Cottage ♦♦♦♦
118 Crewe Road, Alsager, Stoke-on-Trent ST7 2JA
T: (01270) 882033
F: (01270) 883556
E: reception@sappho-cottage.demon.co.uk
I: www.sappho-cottage.demon.co.uk

ALTRINCHAM
Greater Manchester

Belvedere Guest House Rating Applied For
58 Barrington Road, Altrincham, WA14 1HY
T: (0161) 941 5996
E: paddykel@aol.com

APPLETON
Cheshire

Birchdale Hotel ♦♦♦
Birchdale Road, Appleton, Warrington WA4 5AW
T: (01925) 263662
F: (01925) 860607
E: rfw@birchdalehotel.co.uk
I: www.birchdalehotel.co.uk

ARKHOLME
Lancashire

Redwell Inn ♦♦♦
Kirkby Lonsdale Road, Arkholme, Carnforth LA6 1BQ
T: (01524) 221240
F: (01524) 221107
E: julie@redwellinn.co.uk
I: www.redwellinn.co.uk

The Tithe Barn Rating Applied For
Main Street, Arkholme, Carnforth LA6 1AU
T: (015242) 22236
F: (015242) 22207
E: tithebarn@btopenworld.com
I: www.mailerassoc.co.uk

ASHLEY
Greater Manchester

Birtles Farm ♦♦♦♦
Ashley, Altrincham WA14 3QH
T: (0161) 928 0458

ASHTON-IN-MAKERFIELD
Greater Manchester

Cranberry Hotel ♦♦
Wigan Road, Ashton-in-Makerfield, Wigan WN4 0BZ
T: (01942) 243519
F: (01942) 820677
E: cranberryhotel@netscapeonline.co.uk

ASHTON-UNDER-LYNE
Greater Manchester

Lynwood Hotel ♦♦♦
3 Richmond Street, Ashton-under-Lyne, OL6 7TX
T: (0161) 330 5358
F: (0161) 330 5358

BACUP
Lancashire

Pasture Bottom Farm ♦♦♦
Bacup, OL13 9UZ
T: (01706) 873790
F: (01706) 873790
E: ha.isherwood@zen.co.uk
I: www.smoothhound.co.uk/hotels/pasture.html

BARLEY
Lancashire

The Pendle Inn ♦♦♦
Barley, Burnley BB12 9JX
T: (01282) 614808
F: (01282) 695242
E: john@pendleinn.freeserve.co.uk
I: www.pendleinn.freeserve.co.uk

BASHALL EAVES
Lancashire

Hodder House B&B ♦♦♦
Hodder House Farm, Mitton Road, Bashall Eaves, Clitheroe BB7 3LZ
T: (01254) 826328
F: 0870 135 7687
E: heather@hodderhousebb.freeserve.co.uk
I: www.hodderhousebb.freeserve.co.uk

BAY HORSE
Lancashire

Stanley Lodge Farmhouse ♦♦♦
Cockerham Road, Bay Horse, Lancaster LA2 0HE
T: (01524) 791863
F: (01524) 793115
I: www.shortbreaks-uk.co.uk

BILLINGTON
Lancashire

Rosebury ♦♦♦
51 Pasturelands Drive, Billington, Clitheroe BB7 9LW
T: (01254) 822658
E: enquiries@rosebury-guest-house.freeserve.co.uk
I: www.rosebury-guest-house.co.uk

BIRKDALE
Merseyside

Belgravia Hotel ♦♦♦
11 Trafalgar Road, Birkdale, Southport PR8 2EA
T: (01704) 565298
F: (01704) 562728
E: belgravias@aol.com
I: www.hotelsouthport.com

BIRKENHEAD
Merseyside

Shrewsbury Lodge Hotel and Restaurant♦♦♦
31 Shrewsbury Road, Oxton, Birkenhead, CH43 2JB
T: (0151) 652 4029
F: (0151) 653 4079
E: info@shrewsbury-hotel.com
I: www.shrewsbury-hotel.com

Sleepstation ♦♦♦
24-28 Hamilton Street, Birkenhead, CH41 1AL
T: (0151) 647 1047
F: (0151) 650 1155
E: info@sleepstation.co.uk
I: www.sleepstation.co.uk

Villa Venezia ♦♦♦
14-16 Prenton Road West, Birkenhead, CH42 9PN
T: (0151) 608 9212
F: (0151) 608 6671

BISPHAM
Lancashire

Cliff Head Hotel ♦♦
174 Queens Promenade, Bispham, Blackpool, Blackpool FY2 9JN
T: (01253) 591086
F: (01253) 590952

Cliff Head Hotel ♦♦
174 Queens Promenade, Bispham, Blackpool, Blackpool FY2 9JN
T: (01253) 591086
F: (01253) 590952

BLACKBURN
Lancashire

The Fernhurst & Star Lodge ♦♦♦
466 Bolton Road, Blackburn, BB2 4JP
T: (01254) 693541
F: (01254) 695004

Shalom ♦♦♦♦ SILVER AWARD
531b Livesey Branch Road, Blackburn, BB2 5DF
T: (01254) 209032
F: (01254) 209032
E: paul@shalomblackburn.co.uk

BLACKPOOL
Lancashire

Abbey Hotel Rating Applied For
31 Palatine Road, Blackpool, FY1 4BX
T: (01253) 624721
F: (01253) 624721
E: abbeybpool@aol.com
I: abbeyhotel-blackpool.co.uk

Adelaide House Hotel ♦♦♦
66-68 Adelaide Street, Blackpool, FY1 4LA
T: (01253) 625172
F: (01253) 625172

Alderley Hotel ♦♦♦
581 South Promenade, Blackpool, FY4 1NG
T: (01253) 342173

Allendale Hotel ♦♦♦
104 Albert Road, Blackpool, FY1 4PR
T: (01253) 623268

Ardsley Hotel ♦♦
20 Woodfield Road, Blackpool, FY1 6AX
T: (01253) 345419
F: (01253) 345419

Arncliffe Hotel ♦♦♦
24 Osborne Road, Blackpool, FY4 1HJ
T: (01253) 345209
F: (01253) 345209
E: arncliffehotel@talk21.com
I: www.blackpool-internet.co.uk/HOMEarncliffe.html

Ashcroft Hotel ♦♦♦
42 King Edward Avenue, North Shore, Blackpool, FY2 9TA
T: (01253) 351538
E: dave@ashcroftblackpool.freeserve.co.uk
I: www.smoothhound.co.uk/hotels/ashcroft.html

Astoria Guest house ♦♦
50 Park Road, Blackpool, FY1 4HT
T: (01253) 622377
F: (01253) 291321
E: astoriablackpool@aol.com
I: members.aol.com/astoriablackpool/

Astoria Hotel ♦♦♦
118-120 Albert Road, Blackpool, FY1 4PN
T: (01253) 621321
E: abnw15916@blueyonder.co.uk
I: www.blackpool.com/accom/hotels.html

Baricia ♦♦♦
40-42 Egerton Road, Blackpool, FY1 2NW
T: (01253) 623130
E: TKBariciahotel@aol.com

Baron Hotel ♦♦♦♦
296 North Promenade, Blackpool, FY1 2EY
T: (01253) 622729
F: (01253) 297165
E: baronhotel@btinternet.com

Beachcomber Hotel ♦♦♦
78 Reads Avenue, Blackpool, FY1 4DE
T: (01253) 621622
F: (01253) 299254
E: beachcomber@.net
I: www.beachcomberhotel.net

Beauchief Hotel ♦♦♦
48 King Edward Avenue, Blackpool, FY2 9TA
T: (01253) 353314
F: (01253) 353314
E: beauchiefhotel@blackpool.net
I: www.fyldecoast.co.uk/beauchief

The Beaucliffe Hotel ♦♦♦
20-22 Holmfield Road, Blackpool, FY2 9TB
T: (01253) 351663
E: don.siddall@talk21.com
I: members.netscapeonline.co.uk/beaucliffe

Belvedere Hotel ♦♦♦
91 Albert Road, Blackpool, FY1 4PW
T: (01253) 628029
F: (01253) 297069
E: belvedere91@btopenworld.com
I: www.blackpoolhotels.org.uk

Berwick Hotel ♦♦♦
23 King Edward Avenue, North Shore, Blackpool, FY2 9TA
T: (01253) 351496
E: chris@berwickhotel.fsnet.co.uk
I: www.smoothhound.co.uk/hotels/berwickpriv.html

Berwyn Hotel ♦♦♦♦
1 Finchley Road, Gynn Square, Blackpool, FY1 2LP
T: (01253) 352896
F: (01253) 594391
I: www.blackpool-holidays.com

Beverley Hotel ♦♦♦
25 Dean Street, South Shore, Blackpool, FY4 1AU
T: (01253) 344426
E: beverley.hotel@virgin.net
I: www.beverleyhotel-blackpool.co.uk

Boltonia Hotel ♦♦♦
124-126 Albert Road, Blackpool, FY1 4PN
T: (01253) 620248
F: (01253) 299064
E: info@boltoniahotel.co.uk
I: www.boltoniahotel.co.uk

Bona Vista Hotel ♦♦♦
104-106 Queens Promenade, Blackpool, FY2 9NX
T: (01253) 351396
F: (01253) 594985
E: bona.vista@talk21.com
I: www.bonavistahotel.com

Braeside Hotel ♦♦♦
6 Willshaw Road, Gynn Square, Blackpool, FY2 9SH
T: (01253) 351363
I: www.blackpoolholidays-braeside.co.uk

The Brayton ♦♦♦
7-8 Finchley Road, Gynn Square, Blackpool, FY1 2LP
T: (01253) 351645
F: (01253) 595500
E: brayton@btinternet.com
I: www.brayton.btinternet.co.uk

Briny View ♦♦
2 Woodfield Road, Blackpool, FY1 6AX
T: (01253) 346584

Canasta Hotel ♦♦♦♦
288 North Promenade, Blackpool, FY1 2EY
T: (01253) 290501
F: (01253) 290501
E: canasta@blackpool.net
I: www.ontheprom.com

Cardoh Lodge ♦♦♦
21 Hull Road, Blackpool, FY1 4QB
T: (01253) 627755
F: (01253) 295634
E: cardoh.lodge@btinternet.com
I: www.cardohlodge.co.uk

Chequers Hotel ♦♦♦
24 Queens Promenade, Blackpool, FY2 9RN
T: (01253) 500076
E: sales@chequers-hotel.com
I: www.chequers-hotel.com

The Cheslyn ♦♦♦
21 Moore Street, Blackpool, FY4 1DA
T: (01253) 349672

Clifton Court Hotel
Rating Applied For
12 Clifton Drive, Blackpool, FY4 1NX
T: (01253) 342385
F: (01253) 342358
E: enquiries@clifton-court-hotel.co.uk
I: www.clifton-court-hotel.co.uk

Collingwood Hotel ♦♦♦♦
8-10 Holmfield Road, North Shore, Blackpool, FY2 9SL
T: (01253) 352929
F: (01253) 352929
E: enquiries@collingwoodhotel.co.uk
I: www.collingwoodhotel.co.uk

Colris Hotel ♦♦♦
209 Central Promenade, Blackpool, FY1 5DL
T: (01253) 625461
E: stew1@skynow.net

The Commodore Hotel ♦♦♦
246 Queens Promenade, Northshore, Blackpool, FY2 9HA
T: (01253) 351440

Courtneys of Gynn Square ♦♦♦♦
1 Warbreck Hill Road, Blackpool, FY2 9SP
T: (01253) 352179
F: (01253) 352179

The Cresta ♦♦♦
85 Withnell Road, Blackpool, FY4 1HE
T: (01253) 343866
E: john@snelly.co.uk
I: www.snelly.co.uk

Denely Private Hotel ♦♦♦
15 King Edward Avenue, Blackpool, FY2 9TA
T: (01253) 352757

Derwent Private Hotel ♦♦♦
42 Palatine Road, Blackpool, FY1 4BY
T: (01253) 620004
F: (01253) 620004
E: welcome@blackpoolderwenthotel.co.uk
I: www.blackpoolderwenthotel.co.uk

Elgin Hotel ♦♦♦
36 - 42 Queens Promenade, Blackpool, FY2 9RW
T: (01253) 351433
F: (01253) 353535
E: info@elginhotel.com
I: www.elginhotel.com

Fairway Hotel ♦♦♦
34-36 Hull Road, Blackpool, FY1 4QB
T: (01253) 623777
F: (01253) 753455
E: bookings@fairway.gb.com
I: www.fairway.gb.com

The Fern Royd Hotel ♦♦♦
35 Holmfield Road, North Shore, Blackpool, FY2 9TE
T: (01253) 351066
E: info@fernroydhotel.co.uk
I: www.fernroydhotel.co.uk

Fylde Hotel ♦♦♦
93 Palatine Road, Blackpool, FY1 4BX
T: (01253) 623735
F: (01253) 622801
E: fyldehotel@talk21.com

Glen ♦♦
25 Barton Avenue, South Shore, Blackpool, FY1 6AP
T: (01253) 346978

Gleneagles Hotel ♦♦♦
75 Albert Road, Blackpool, FY1 4PW
T: (01253) 295266
F: (01253) 295266

The Grand Hotel ♦♦♦
Station Road, Blackpool, FY4 1EU
T: (01253) 343741
F: (01253) 408228
E: max@grandholidayflats.co.uk
I: www.grandholidayflats.co.uk

Granville Hotel ♦♦♦
12 Station Road, Blackpool, FY4 1BE
T: (01253) 343012
F: (01253) 408594
E: wilft@thegranvillehotelfsnet.co.uk
I: www.thegranvillehotel.co.uk

The Grosvenor View Hotel ♦♦♦
7-9 King Edward Avenue, Blackpool, FY2 9TD
T: (01253) 352851
E: grosvenor_view@yahoo.co.uk

Happy Return Hotel ♦♦♦
17-19 Hull Road, Blackpool, FY1 4QB
T: (01253) 622596
F: (01253) 290024
E: happyreturn@yahoo.co.uk

Hartshead Private Hotel ♦♦♦
17 King Edward Avenue, Blackpool, FY2 9TA
T: (01253) 353133
I: www.hartsheadhotel.gbr.cc

The Hatton Hotel ♦♦♦
10 Banks Street, North Shore, Blackpool, FY1 1RN
T: (01253) 624944
E: hattonhotel@hotmail.com
I: www.hattonhotel.com

Hertford Hotel ♦♦♦
18 Lord Street, North Shore, Blackpool, FY1 2BD
T: (01253) 292931
E: ceges@blueyonder.co.uk
I: www.ceges.pwp.blueyonder.co.uk

Holmsdale Hotel ♦♦♦
6-8 Pleasant Street, North Shore, Blackpool, FY1 2JA
T: (01253) 621008
F: 0870 133 1487
E: holmsdale@talk21.com
I: www.blackpool-hotels.co.uk/holmsdale.html

Homecliffe Hotel ♦♦♦
5-6 Wilton Parade, North Promenade, Blackpool, FY1 2HE
T: (01253) 625147
F: (01253) 292667
E: douglas@homecliffe56.freeserve.co.uk

Hornby Villa ♦♦♦
130 Hornby Road, Blackpool, FY1 4QS
T: (01253) 624959
E: hornby.villa@virgin.net
I: www.hornbyvillahotel.com

Hurstmere Hotel ♦♦♦
5 Alexandra Road, Blackpool, FY1 6BU
T: (01253) 345843
F: (01253) 347188

Inglewood Hotel ♦♦♦
18 Holmfield Road, Blackpool, FY2 9TB
T: (01253) 351668
E: patandpaulwest@aol.com
I: www.blackpool-hotels.co.uk/inglewood.html

The Kimberley ♦♦♦
25 Gynn Avenue, Blackpool, FY1 2LD
T: (01253) 352264
E: kimberley@gynnavenue.fsnet.co.uk

Llanryan House ♦♦
37 Reads Ave, Blackpool, FY1 4DD
T: (01253) 628446
E: keith@llanryanguesthouse.co.uk
I: www.llanryanguesthouse.co.uk

Lochinvar Christian Guest House ♦♦♦
14 Chatsworth Avenue, Norbreck, Blackpool, FY2 9AN
T: (01253) 351761
E: lochinvar@cghblackpool.fsnet.co.uk
I: www.lochinvar-christianholidays.co.uk

Manor Grove Hotel ♦♦
24 Leopold Grove, Blackpool, FY1 4LD
T: (01253) 625577
F: (01253) 625577
E: lyndon@evans2ooo.freeserve.co.uk
I: www.manorgrovehotel.com

Manor Private Hotel ♦♦♦
32 Queens Promenade, Blackpool, FY2 9RN
T: (01253) 351446
F: (01253) 355449
E: holidays@manorblackpool.co.uk
I: manorblackpool.co.uk

Marlow Lodge Hotel ♦♦♦
76 Station Road, Blackpool, FY4 1EU
T: (01253) 341580
F: (01253) 408330
E: hotelreception@yahoo.co.uk
I: www.blackpoolmarlowhotel.com

May-Dene Licensed Hotel ♦♦♦
10 Dean Street, Blackpool, FY4 1AU
T: (01253) 343464
F: (01253) 401424
E: may_dene_hotel@hotmail.com

Merecliff Hotel ♦♦
24 Holmfield Road, Blackpool, FY2 9TE
T: (01253) 356858
E: enquiries@merecliffhotel.co.uk
I: www.merecliffhotel.co.uk

Hotel Montclair ♦♦♦
95 Albert Road, Blackpool, FY1 4PW
T: (01253) 625860

Newholme Private Hotel ♦♦♦
2 Wilton Parade, Blackpool, FY1 2HE
T: (01253) 624010
I: www.fyldecoast.co.uk/newholme.

North Crest Hotel ♦♦♦
22 King Edward Avenue, Blackpool, FY2 9TD
T: (01253) 355937

Northlands Hotel ♦♦♦
31-33 Hornby Road, Blackpool, FY1 4QG
T: (01253) 625795
F: (01253) 625795
E: enquiries@northlandshotel.co.uk
I: www.northlandshotel.co.uk

The Old Coach House
♦♦♦♦♦ GOLD AWARD
50 Dean Street, Blackpool, FY4 1BP
T: (01253) 349195
F: (01253) 344330
E: blackpool@theoldcoachhouse.freeserve.co.uk
I: www.theoldcoachhouse.freeserve.co.uk

Pembroke Private Hotel ♦♦♦♦
11 King Edward Avenue, Blackpool, FY2 9TD
T: (01253) 351306
F: (01253) 351306
E: stay@pembrokehotel.com
I: www.pembrokehotel.com

Penrhyn Hotel ♦♦♦
38 King Edward Avenue, Blackpool, FY2 9TA
T: (01253) 352762
E: janetpenrhyn@aol.com

Pickwick Hotel ♦♦♦
93 Albert Road, Blackpool, FY1 4PW
T: (01253) 624229
F: (01253) 624229

Raffles Hotel ♦♦♦♦
73-75 Hornby Road, Blackpool, FY1 4QJ
T: (01253) 294713
F: (01253) 294240
E: enq@raffleshotelblackpool.fsworld.co.uk
I: www.raffleshotelblackpool.co.uk

The Robin Hood Hotel
Rating Applied For
100 Queens Prom, Blackpool, FY2 9NS
T: (01253) 351599
I: www.robinhoodhotel.co.uk

Rosedale Private Hotel ♦♦♦
9 Chatsworth Avenue, Bispham, Blackpool, FY2 9AN
T: (01253) 352661
F: (01253) 352661
E: mail@rosedaleprivatehotel.co.uk
I: www.rosedaleprivatehotel.co.uk

Rowan Hotel ♦♦♦♦
8 Empress Drive, Blackpool, FY2 9SE
T: (01253) 52218

The Royal Seabank Hotel ♦♦♦
219-221 Central Promenade, Blackpool, FY1 5DL
T: (01253) 622717
F: (01253) 295148
E: royalseabank@hotmail.com
I: www.blackpool.net/wwwroyalseabank

Rutland Hotel ♦♦♦
330 North Promenade, Blackpool, FY1 2JG
T: (01253) 622791
F: (01253) 622831
E: tony-morgan@rutland-hotel.co.uk
I: www.rutland-hotel.co.uk

Rutlands Hotel ♦♦♦
13 Hornby Road, Blackpool, FY1 4QG
T: (01253) 623067

St Ives Hotel ♦♦
10 King George Avenue, North Shore, Blackpool, FY2 9SN
T: (01253) 352122
F: (01253) 352122
E: enquiries@stiveshotel-blackpool.co.uk
I: stiveshotel-blackpool.co.uk

Sands Hotel ♦♦♦
485 South Promenade, Blackpool, FY4 1AZ
T: (01253) 349262
F: (01253) 407081

Seabreeze ♦♦♦
1 Gynn Avenue, Blackpool, FY1 2LD
T: (01253) 351427
F: (01253) 310713
E: info@vbreezey.co.uk
I: www.vbreezey.co.uk

Seaforth Hotel ♦♦♦
18 Lonsdale Road, Blackpool, FY1 6EE
T: (01253) 345820
F: (01253) 345820
E: enquiries@seaforthhotel.co.uk
I: www.seaforthhotel.co.uk

Sheron House ♦♦♦♦
21 Gynn Avenue, Blackpool North Shore, Blackpool, FY1 2LD
T: (01253) 354614
E: sheronhouse@amserve.net
I: www.sheronhouse.co.uk

Hotel Skye ♦♦
571-573 New South Promenade, Blackpool, FY4 1NG
T: (01253) 343220
F: (01253) 401244
E: office@blackpool-hotel.co.uk
I: www.blackpool-hotel.co.uk

Somerville Hotel ♦♦♦
72 Station Road, Blackpool, FY4 1EU
T: (01253) 341219
F: (01253) 341219
E: michael.haigh@btclick.com
I: www.somervillehotel.co.uk/

South Lea Hotel ♦♦♦
4 Willshaw Road, Blackpool, FY2 9SH
T: (01253) 351940
F: (01253) 595758
E: southlea@hotmail.com
I: www.blackpool-holidays.com/southlea.htm.

Hotel St Elmo ♦♦♦
20-22 Station Road, South Shore, Blackpool, FY4 1BE
T: (01253) 341820
F: (01253) 347559
I: www.blackpoolhotels.org.uk/stelmo.html

The Strathdon Hotel ♦♦♦
28 St Chads Road, South Shore, Blackpool, FY1 6BP
T: (01253) 343549
E: stay@strathdonhotel.com

Sunnymede Hotel ♦♦♦
50 King Edward Avenue, Blackpool, FY2 9TA
T: (01253) 352877
F: (01253) 352877
E: enquiries@sunnymedehotel.co.uk
I: www.sunnymedehotel.co.uk

Sunnyside Hotel ♦♦♦
36 King Edward Avenue, North Shore, Blackpool, FY2 9TA
T: (01253) 352031
F: (01253) 354255
E: stuart@sunnysidehotel.com
I: www.sunnysidehotel.com

Sussex Hotel
Rating Applied For
14-16 Pleasant St North Shore, Blackpool, FY1 2JA
T: (01253) 627824
F: (01253) 627824

Thorncliffe Hotel ♦♦
63 Dickson Road, Blackpool, FY1 2BX
T: (01253) 622508

Trafalgar Hotel
Rating Applied For
106 Albert Road, Blackpool, FY1 4PR
T: (01253) 625000
E: trafalgarhotel@msn.com

Tudor Rose Original ♦♦♦♦
5 Withnell Road, Blackpool, FY4 1HF
T: (01253) 343485
E: tudororiginal@aol.com

Victoria House ♦♦♦
14 Regent Road, Blackpool, FY1 4LY
T: (01253) 626967
F: (01253) 626967

Vidella Hotel ♦♦♦
80-82 Dickson Road, North Shore, Blackpool, FY1 2BU
T: (01253) 621201
F: (01253) 620319

Waverley Hotel ♦♦♦
95 Reads Avenue, Blackpool, FY1 4DG
T: (01253) 621633
F: (01253) 753581
E: wavehotel@aol.com
I: www.thewaverleyhotel.com

Westdean Hotel ♦♦♦
59 Dean Street, Blackpool, FY4 1BP
T: (01253) 342904
F: (01253) 342926
E: mikeball@westdeanhotel.freeserve.co.uk
I: www.westdeanhotel.com

Wilton Hotel ♦♦♦
108-112 Dickson Road, Blackpool, FY1 2HF
T: (01253) 627763
F: (01253) 295379
E: wiltonhotel@supanet.com

The Windsor Hotel ♦♦♦♦
21 King Edward Avenue, North Shore, Blackpool, FY2 9TA
T: (01253) 353735
F: (01253) 353735

Windsor Park Hotel
Rating Applied For
96 Queens Promenade, North Shore, Blackpool, FY2 9NS
T: (01253) 357025
F: (01253) 357076

Woodleigh Hotel ♦♦♦
32 King Edward Ave, North Shore, Blackpool, FY2 9TA
T: (01253) 593624
E: bookings@woodleighhotel.freeserve.co.uk
I: blackpool-holidays.com/woodleigh.htm

BLUNDELLSANDS
Merseyside

Blundellsands Bed & Breakfast ♦♦♦♦ SILVER AWARD
9 Elton Avenue, Blundellsands, Liverpool L23 8UN
T: (0151) 924 6947
F: (0151) 287 4113
E: liz@bsbb.freeserve.co.uk
I: www.blundellsands.info

BOLTON
Greater Manchester

Archangelos ♦♦♦
82 Pennine Road, Horwich, Bolton, BL6 7HW
T: (01204) 692303
E: enquiries@archangelos.co.uk
I: www.archangelos.co.uk

Ash Woods ♦♦♦
6 Oakenclough Drive, Bolton, BL1 5QY
T: (01204) 492100
F: (01204) 492100
E: neilmags@cwcom.net
I: www.boltonbandb.co.uk

Cheetham Arms ♦♦♦
987 Blackburn Road, Sharples, Bolton, BL1 7LG
T: (01204) 301372
F: (01204) 598209
E: mike@cheethamarms.freeserve.co.uk

Fourways Hotel ♦♦♦
13-15 Bolton Road, Moses Gate, Farnworth, Bolton BL4 7JN
T: (01204) 573661
F: (01204) 862488
E: fourwayshotel@pureasphalt.co.uk

The Grosvenor Guest House ♦♦♦
46 Bradford Street, Bolton, BL2 1JJ
T: (01204) 391616

The Highgrove Guest House ♦♦♦
63 Manchester Road, Bolton, BL2 1ES
T: (01204) 384928

Morden Grange Guest House ♦♦♦
15 Chadwick Street, The Haulgh, Bolton, BL2 1JN
T: (01204) 522000
E: enquiries@mordengrange.co.uk
I: www.mordengrange.co.uk

BOLTON-BY-BOWLAND
Lancashire

Copy Nook Hotel ♦♦♦♦
Bolton-by-Bowland, Clitheroe BB7 4NL
T: (01200) 447205
F: (01200) 447004
E: copynookhotel@btinternet.com
I: www.copynookhotel.com

Middle Flass Lodge ♦♦♦♦
Forest Becks Brow, Settle Road, Bolton-by-Bowland, Clitheroe BB7 4NY
T: (01200) 447259
F: (01200) 447300
E: info@middleflasslodge.fsnet.co.uk
I: www.mflodge.freeservers.com/

BOOTLE
Merseyside

Regent Maritime Hotel ♦♦♦
58-62 Regent Road, Liverpool, L20 8DB
T: (0151) 922 4090
F: (0151) 922 6308
E: regent_maritime_hotel@hotmail.com
I: www.regentmaritimehotel.co.uk

BROMBOROUGH
Merseyside

Dibbinsdale Inn ♦♦
Dibbinsdale Road, Bromborough, Wirral CH63 0HJ
T: (0151) 334 5171
F: (0151) 334 0097

Woodlands Guest House ♦♦♦♦
66 Woodyear Road, Bromborough, Wirral CH62 6AZ
T: (0151) 327 3735
F: (0151) 328 1572

BROMLEY CROSS
Greater Manchester

The Poplars ♦♦♦♦
58 Horseshoe Lane, Bromley Cross, Bolton BL7 0RR
T: (01204) 308001
F: (01204) 308001
E: patricia@v-b-elec.u-net.com
I: www.v-b-elec.u-net.com

BURNLEY
Lancashire

Ormerod Hotel ♦♦♦
121-123 Ormerod Road, Burnley, BB11 3QW
T: (01282) 423255

Thorneyholme Farm Cottage ♦♦♦♦
Barley New Road, Roughlee, Burnley, BB12 9LH
T: (01282) 612452

BURSCOUGH
Lancashire

Martin Inn ♦♦♦
Martin Lane, Burscough, Ormskirk L40 0RT
T: (01704) 892302
F: (01704) 895735

BURY
Greater Manchester

The Rostrevor Hotel ♦♦♦
146-148 Manchester Road, Bury, BL9 0TL
T: (0161) 764 3944
F: (0161) 764 8266
E: michelle@rostrevorhotel.co.uk
I: www.rostrevorhotel.co.uk

CALDY
Merseyside

Cheriton ♦♦♦♦
151 Caldy Road, Caldy, Wirral CH48 1LP
T: (0151) 625 5271
F: (0151) 625 5271
E: cheriton151@hotmail.com
I: www.cheritonguesthouse.co.uk

CAPERNWRAY
Lancashire

New Capernwray Farm ♦♦♦♦♦ SILVER AWARD
Capernwray, Carnforth LA6 1AD
T: (01524) 734284
F: (01524) 734284
E: info@newcapfarm.co.uk
I: www.newcapfarm.co.uk

CARNFORTH
Lancashire

The County Hotel Rating Applied For
Lancaster Road, Carnforth, LA5 9LD
T: (01524) 732469
F: (01524) 720142
E: county@mitchellshotels.co.uk
I: www.mitchellshotels.co.uk

Dale Grove ♦♦♦
162 Lancaster Road, Carnforth, LA5 9EF
T: (01524) 733382
E: cal.craig@ntlworld.com
I: www.dalegrove.co.uk

Galley Hall Farm ♦♦♦♦
Shore Road, Carnforth, LA5 9HZ
T: (01524) 732544

The George Washington ♦♦♦
Main Street, Warton, Carnforth, LA5 9PJ
T: (01524) 732865

Grisedale Farm ♦♦♦♦
Leighton, Carnforth, LA5 9ST
T: (01524) 734360

High Bank ♦♦♦♦
Hawk Street, Carnforth, LA5 9LA
T: (01524) 733827

Longlands Hotel ♦♦♦
Tewitfield, Carnforth LA6 1JH
T: (01524) 781256
F: (01524) 781004
E: info@thelonglandshotel.co.uk

CHEADLE
Greater Manchester

Curzon House ♦♦♦
3 Curzon Road, Heald Green, Cheadle, SK8 3LN
T: (0161) 436 2804
E: curzonhouse@aol.com

CHEADLE HULME
Greater Manchester

Spring Cottage Guest House ♦♦♦
60 Hulme Hall Road, Cheadle Hulme, Cheadle SK8 6JZ
T: (0161) 485 1037
F: (0161) 485 1037

CHELFORD
Cheshire

Astle Farm East ♦♦♦
Chelford, Macclesfield SK10 4TA
T: (01625) 861270
E: gill.farmhouse@vision.net

CHESTER
Cheshire

Alton Lodge Hotel ♦♦♦
78 Hoole Road, Chester, CH2 3NT
T: (01244) 310213
F: (01244) 319206
E: enquiries@altonlodge.co.uk
I: www.altonlodge.co.uk

Arden Guest House ♦♦
17 Victoria Road, Chester, CH2 2AX
T: (01244) 390898
F: (01244) 380805
E: abbotsfordcourt@hotmail.com

Bawn Lodge ♦♦♦
10 Hoole Road, Chester, CH2 3NH
T: (01244) 324971
F: (01244) 310951
E: enquiries@bawnparkhotel.co.uk
I: www.bawnparkhotel.co.uk

Belgrave Hotel ♦♦
61 City Road, Chester, CH1 3AE
T: (01221) 324951

Bowman Lodge ♦♦♦
52 Hoole Road, Chester, CH2 3NL
T: (01244) 342208
E: cig.davies@virgin.net
I: freespace.virgin.net/cig.davies/bowman.htm

Buckingham House ♦♦♦
38 Hough Green, Chester, CH4 8JQ
T: (01244) 678885
F: (01244) 671028
E: terrigrayca@yahoo.com

Castle House ♦♦♦
23 Castle Street, Chester, CH1 2DS
T: (01244) 350354
F: (01244) 350354

Cheyney Lodge Hotel ♦♦♦
77-79 Cheyney Road, Chester, CH1 4BS
T: (01244) 381925

Chippings ♦♦♦♦
10 Cranford Court, Chester, CH4 7LN
T: (01244) 679728
F: (01244) 659470

City Road Apartments ♦
18 City Road, Chester, CH1 3AE
T: (01244) 313651
F: (01244) 817067
E: cityroad@deesideinsurance.co.uk
I: www.stay-at-chester.co.uk

Comfort Inn Chester ♦♦♦♦
74 Hoole Road, Chester, CH2 3NL
T: (01244) 327542
F: (01244) 344889
E: comfortinn@chestergb.u-net.com
I: www.comfortinnchester.com

The Commercial Hotel ♦♦♦
St Peters Churchyard, Chester, CH1 2HG
T: (01244) 320749
F: (01244) 348318
I: www.stayhereuk.com

Dee Hills Lodge ♦♦♦♦
7 Dee Hills Park, Boughton, Chester, CH3 5AR
T: (01244) 325719

Derry Raghan Lodge ♦♦♦
54 Hoole Road, Chester, CH2 3NL
T: (01244) 318740
I: www.derryraghanlodge.co.uk

Establishments printed in blue have a detailed entry in this guide

Eastern Guest House ♦♦♦
1 Eastern Pathway, Queens Park, Handbridge, Chester, CH3 7AQ
T: (01244) 680104

Eaton House ♦♦♦
36 Eaton Road, Handbridge, Chester, CH4 7EN
T: (01244) 680349
F: (01244) 659021
E: grahamd@aol.com

Edwards House Hotel ♦♦♦
61-63 Hoole Road, Chester, CH2 3NJ
T: (01244) 318055
F: (01244) 310948
E: steanerob@supanet.com
I: www.smoothhound.co.uk/hotels/edwardhou.html

Golborne Manor ♦♦♦♦
Platts Lane, Hatton Heath, Chester CH3 9AN
T: (01829) 770310
F: (01829) 770370
E: ann.ikin@golbornemanor.co.uk

The Golden Eagle Pub/Hotel ♦♦♦
18 Castle Street, Chester, CH1 2DS
T: (01244) 321098
F: (01244) 321098

Greenwalls Bed & Breakfast ♦♦♦
Whitchurch Road, Waverton, Chester, CH3 7PB
T: (01244) 336799
F: (01244) 332124
I: www.bedandbreakfastnationwide.com

Grosvenor Place Guest House ♦♦♦
2-4 Grosvenor Place, Chester, CH1 2DE
T: (01244) 324455
F: (01244) 400225

Grove House ♦♦♦♦
Holme Street, Tarvin, Chester CH3 8EQ
T: (01829) 740893
F: (01829) 741769
E: helen_s@btinternet.com

Grove Villa ♦♦♦
18 The Groves, Chester, CH1 1SD
T: (01244) 349713
E: Grove.Villa@tesco.net

Halcyon House ♦♦♦
18 Eaton Road, Handbridge, Chester, CH4 7EN
T: (01244) 676159
F: (01244) 676159

Hameldaeus ♦♦♦
9 Lorne Street, Chester, CH1 4AE
T: (01244) 374913
E: joyce33@brunton81.freeserve.co.uk

Holly House ♦♦♦
41 Liverpool Road, Chester, CH2 1AB
T: (01244) 383484
E: fjb5@tutor.open.ac.uk

Homeleigh Guest House ♦♦♦
14 Hough Green, Chester, CH4 8JG
T: (01244) 676761
F: (01244) 679977
I: www.scoot.co.uk/homeleigh_guest_house/

Kent House ♦♦
147 Boughton, Chester, CH3 5BH
T: (01244) 324171
F: (01244) 319758
E: kent-house@turner10101.freeserve.co.uk

The Kings Guest House ♦♦♦
14 Eaton Road, Handbridge, Chester, CH4 7EN
T: (01244) 671249

Laburnum House ♦♦♦
2 St Anne Street, Chester, CH1 3HS
T: (01244) 380313
F: (01244) 380313
E: laburnumhouse@bushinternet.com

Latymer Hotel ♦♦♦
82 Hough Green, Chester, CH4 8JW
T: (01244) 675074
F: (01244) 683413
E: info@latymerhotel.com
I: www.latymerhotel.com

Laurels ♦♦♦♦
14 Selkirk Road, Curzon Park, Chester, CH4 8AH
T: (01244) 697682
E: howell@ellisroberts.freeserve.co.uk

The Laurels Guest House ♦♦♦
61 Tarvin Road, Boughton, Chester, CH3 5DY
T: (01244) 346292
E: carlton40@btinternet.com

The Limes
♦♦♦♦ SILVER AWARD
12 Hoole Road, Hoole, Chester CH2 3NJ
T: (01244) 328239
F: 07968 404105
E: limeschester@btinternet.com
I: www.limeschester.btinternet.co.uk

Mitchells of Chester Guest House ♦♦♦♦ SILVER AWARD
28 Hough Green, Chester, CH4 8JQ
T: (01244) 679004
F: (01244) 659567
E: mitoches@dialstart.net
I: www.mitchellsofchester.com

Newton Hall ♦♦♦♦
Newton Lane, Tattenhall, Chester CH3 9NE
T: (01829) 770153
F: (01829) 770655
E: newton.hall@farming.co.uk

Recorder Hotel ♦♦♦
19 City Walls, Chester, CH1 1SB
T: (01244) 326580
F: (01244) 401674
E: reservations@recorderhotel.co.uk
I: www.recorderhotel.co.uk

Rowland House ♦♦♦
No 2 Chichester Street, Chester, CH1 4AD
T: (01244) 390967
F: (01244) 390967
E: rowlandhousechester@hotmail.com
I: www.rowlandhouse.chester.co.uk

Strathearn Guest House ♦♦♦
38 Hoole Road, Chester, CH2 3NL
T: (01244) 321522
F: (01244) 321522
E: strathearn@breathemail.net

Ten The Groves ♦♦♦
10 The Groves, Chester, CH1 1SD
T: (01244) 317907
E: ten-the-groves@freeuk.com

Tentry Heys ♦♦
Queens Park Road, Chester, CH4 7AD
T: (01244) 677857
F: (01244) 659439
E: njarthur@btconnect.com

Tower House ♦♦♦♦
14 Dee Hills Park, Chester, CH3 5AR
T: (01244) 341936
E: sueheather62@hotmail.com

Walpole House ♦♦♦♦
26 Walpole Street, Chester, CH1 4HG
T: (01244) 373373
F: (01244) 373373
E: walphse@aol.com

CHILDWALL
Merseyside

Childwall Abbey Hotel ♦♦♦
Score Lane, Childwall, Liverpool L16 5EY
T: (0151) 722 5293
F: (0151) 722 0438

The Real McCoy ♦♦♦
126 Childwall Park Avenue, Childwall, Liverpool L16 0JH
T: (0151) 722 7116
F: (0151) 722 7116

CHOLMONDELEY
Cheshire

Manor Farm ♦♦♦♦
Egerton, Malpas SY14 8AW
T: (01829) 720261

CHORLEY
Lancashire

Parr Hall Farm ♦♦♦♦
Parr Lane, Eccleston, Chorley PR7 5SL
T: (01257) 451917
F: (01257) 453749
E: parrhall@talk21.com

CLAUGHTON
Lancashire

The Old Rectory ♦♦♦♦
Claughton, Lancaster LA2 9LA
T: (01524) 221150
F: (01524) 221098
E: info@rectorylancs.co.uk
I: www.rectorylancs.co.uk

CLAYTON-LE-MOORS
Lancashire

Maple Lodge Hotel ♦♦♦
70 Blackburn Road, Clayton-le-Moors, Accrington BB5 5JH
T: (01254) 301284
F: (01254) 388152
E: maplelod@aol.com
I: www.maplelodgehotel.co.uk

CLEVELEYS
Lancashire

Briardene Hotel ♦♦♦♦
56 Kelso Avenue, Cleveleys, Blackpool FY5 3JG
T: (01253) 852312
F: (01253) 851190

CLITHEROE
Lancashire

Brooklands ♦♦♦
9 Pendle Road, Clitheroe, BB7 1JQ
T: (01200) 422797
F: (01200) 422797
E: kenandjean@tesco.net
I: www.ribblevalley.gov.uk/hotel/brooklan/index.htm

Don Dino ♦♦♦♦
78-82 Whalley Road, Clitheroe, BB7 1EE
T: (01200) 424450

Lower Standen Farm
Rating Applied For
Whalley Road, Clitheroe, BB7 1PP
T: (01200) 424176
F: (01200) 424176

Rakefoot Farm ♦♦♦♦
Thornley Road, Chaigley, Clitheroe BB7 3LY
T: (01995) 61332
F: (01995) 61296

Selborne Guest House ♦♦♦♦
Back Commons, Kirkmoor Road, Clitheroe, BB7 2DX
T: (01200) 423571
F: (01200) 423571
E: selbornehouse@lineone.net
I: www.selbornehouse.co.uk

The Swan & Royal ♦♦♦
26 Castle Street, Clitheroe, BB7 2BX
T: (01200) 423130
F: (01200) 444351
I: www.jenningsbrewery.co.uk

Timothy Cottage ♦♦♦
Whalley Road, Hurst Green, Clitheroe, BB7 9QJ
T: (01254) 826337
F: (01254) 826737
E: jgordon@dial.pipex.com

COLNE
Lancashire

Blakey Hall Farm ♦♦♦
Red Lane, Colne, BB8 9TD
T: (01282) 863121

Higher Wanless Farm ♦♦♦♦
Red Lane, Colne, BB8 7JP
T: (01282) 865301
F: (01282) 865823
E: wanlessfarm@bun.com
I: www.stayinlancs.co.uk

Middle Beardshaw Head Farm ♦♦♦
Burnley Road, Trawden, Colne BB8 8PP
T: (01282) 865257
F: (01282) 865257
E: ursula@mann1940.freeserve.co.uk

Reedymoor Farm ♦♦♦♦
Reedymoor Lane, Foulridge, Colne, BB8 7LJ
T: (01282) 865074

Wickets ♦♦♦♦
148 Keighley Road, Colne, BB8 0PJ
T: (01282) 862002
F: (01282) 859675
E: wickets@colne148.fsnet.co.uk

CONGLETON
Cheshire

The Plough at Eaton ♦♦♦♦
Macclesfield Road, Eaton, Congleton CW12 2NR
T: (01260) 280207
F: (01260) 298377
E: trev@plough76.fsnet.co.uk

Sandhole Farm ♦♦♦♦
Hulme Walfield, Congleton, CW12 2JH
T: (01260) 224419
F: (01260) 224766
E: veronica@sandholefarm.co.uk
I: www.sandholefarm.co.uk

The Woodlands ♦♦♦♦
Quarry Wood Farm, Wood Street, Mow-Cop, Congleton, ST7 3PF
T: (01782) 518877
F: (01782) 518877

Yew Tree Farm ♦♦♦♦
North Rode, Congleton, CW12 2PF
T: (01260) 223569
F: (01260) 223328
E: yewtreebb@hotmail.com
I: www.yewtreebb.co.uk

COPSTER GREEN
Lancashire

The Brown Leaves Country Hotel ♦♦♦
Longsight Road, Copster Green, Blackburn BB1 9EU
T: (01254) 249523
F: (01254) 245240
I: www.brownleavescountry.hotel.co.uk

CREWE
Cheshire

Balterley Green Farm ♦♦♦♦
Deans Lane, Balterley Green, Crewe, CW2 5QJ
T: (01270) 820214
E: greenfarm@balterley.fsnet.co.uk
I: www.greenfarm.freeserve.co.uk

Coole Hall Farm ♦♦♦♦
Hankelow, Crewe, CW3 0JD
T: (01270) 811232
E: goodwin200@hotmail.com

CULCHETH
Cheshire

99 Hob Hey Lane ♦♦♦♦
Culcheth, Warrington WA3 4NS
T: (01925) 763448
F: (01925) 763448

DARWEN
Lancashire

The Lychgate
Rating Applied For
Lower Sunnyhurst Farm, Sunnyhurst, Darwen, BB3 1JX
T: (01254) 775632
F: (01254) 775632
E: natalie@thelychgate.fsbusiness.co.uk
I: www.the-lychgate.co.uk

DISLEY
Cheshire

The Grey Cottage ♦♦♦♦
20 Jacksons Edge Road, Disley, Stockport SK12 2JE
T: (01663) 763286
E: carol.greycottage@talk21.com

DUKINFIELD
Greater Manchester

Barton Villa Guest House ♦♦♦
Crescent Road, Dukinfield, SK16 4EY
T: (0161) 330 3952
F: (0161) 285 8488
E: enquiries@bartonvilla.co.uk
I: www.bartonvilla.co.uk

DUNSOP BRIDGE
Lancashire

Wood End Farm ♦♦♦♦
Dunsop Bridge, Clitheroe BB7 3BE
T: (01200) 448223
E: spencers@beatrix-freeserve.co.uk
I: www.members.tripod.co.uk/Woodend

ELSWICK
Lancashire

Thornton House ♦♦♦♦
High Street, Elswick, Preston PR4 3ZB
T: (01995) 671863
F: (01995) 671863
E: john@thortonhouse.biz
I: www.thorntonhouse.biz

FARNWORTH
Greater Manchester

Fernbank Guest House ♦♦♦♦
61 Rawson Street, Farnworth, Bolton BL4 7RJ
T: (01204) 708832
E: sandlan@openworld.com
I: www.fernbankguesthouse.co.uk

FOULRIDGE
Lancashire

Bankfield Guest House ♦♦♦
Skipton Road, Foulridge, Colne BB8 7PY
T: (01282) 863870
F: (01282) 863870
E: estaatbankfield@aol.com

Hare And Hounds Inn ♦♦♦
Old Skipton Road, Foulridge, Colne BB8 7PD
T: (01282) 864235
F: (01282) 865966
E: hareandhounds1@hotmail.com
I: www.hareandhoundsinn.com

FULWOOD
Lancashire

Kiwi House ♦♦♦♦
6 Sharoe Green Park, Fulwood, Preston PR2 8HW
T: (01772) 719873
F: (01772) 719873

GARSTANG
Lancashire

Ashdene ♦♦♦
Parkside Lane, Nateby, Garstang, Preston PR3 0JA
T: (01995) 602676
F: (01995) 602676
E: ashdene@supanet.com
I: www.ashdenebedandbreakfast.gbr.cc

Guy's Thatched Hamlet ♦♦♦
Canalside, St Michael's Road, Bilsborrow, Garstang, Preston PR3 0RS
T: (01995) 640010
F: (01995) 640141
E: guyshamlet@aol.com
I: www.guysthatchedhamlet.co.uk

Woodacre Hall Farm ♦♦♦
Scorton, Preston PR3 1BN
T: (01995) 602253
F: (01995) 602253

GARSTON
Merseyside

Aplin House Hotel ♦♦
35 Clarendon Road, Garston, Liverpool L19 6PJ
T: (0151) 427 5047

GOODSHAW
Lancashire

The Old White Horse ♦♦♦♦
211 Goodshaw Lane, Goodshaw, Rossendale BB4 8DD
T: (01706) 215474
E: johnandmaggie54@hotmail.com
I: www.211oldwhitehorse.freeserve.co.uk

GOOSNARGH
Lancashire

Isles Field Barn ♦♦♦
Syke, Goosnargh, Preston PR3 2EN
T: (01995) 640398
E: susanmchugh@tetinco.co.uk
I: www.islesfieldbarn.com

GREAT ECCLESTON
Lancashire

Cartford Hotel ♦♦♦
Cartford Lane, Little Eccleston, Preston PR3 0YP
T: (01995) 670166
F: (01995) 671785

HALE
Greater Manchester

Clovelly Court ♦♦♦♦
224 Ashley Road, Hale, Altrincham WA15 9SR
T: (0161) 927 7027

HARTFORD
Cheshire

The Coachman ♦♦♦
Chester Road, Hartford, Northwich CW8 1QU
T: (01606) 871359
F: (01606) 871359

HEATH CHARNOCK
Lancashire

The Coach House at 'The Ridges' ♦♦♦
Weavers Brow, Limbrick, Heath Charnock, Chorley PR6 9EB
T: (01257) 279981
F: (01257) 279984
E: barlow.ridges@virgin.net
I: www.smoothhound.co.uk/hotels/thechoachhse.html

HESKIN
Lancashire

Farmers Arms ♦♦♦
85 Wood Lane, Heskin, Chorley PR7 5NP
T: (01257) 451276
F: (01257) 453958
E: andy@farmersarms.co.uk
I: www.farmersarms.co.uk

HEYSHAM
Lancashire

It'l Do ♦♦♦
15 Oxcliffe Road, Heysham, LA3 1PR
T: (01524) 850763

HIGHER BEBINGTON
Merseyside

The Bebington Hotel ♦♦♦
24 Town Lane, Higher Bebington, Wirral CH63 5JG
T: (0151) 645 0608
E: veghena@aol.com

HOLMES CHAPEL
Cheshire

Bridge Farm Bed and Breakfast ♦♦♦
Blackden, Jodrell Bank, Holmes Chapel, Crewe CW4 8BX
T: (01477) 571202
E: stay@bridgefarm.com
I: www.bridgefarm.com

Padgate Guest House ♦♦♦♦
Twemlow Lane, Cranage, Middlewich CW4 8EX
T: (01477) 534291
F: (01477) 544726
E: lynda@padgate.freeserve.co.uk

HOOLE
Cheshire

Glann Hotel ♦♦♦
2 Stone Place, Hoole, Chester CH2 3NR
T: (01244) 344800
E: glannhot@supanet.com

Hamilton Court Hotel ♦♦♦
5-7 Hamilton Street, Hoole, Chester CH2 3JG
T: (01244) 345387
F: (01244) 317404
E: hamiltoncourth@aol.com
I: www.smoothhound.co.uk

Holly House Guest House ♦♦♦
1 Stone Place, Hoole, Chester CH2 3NR
T: (01244) 328967
E: runcas@hotmail.com

Oaklea Guest House ♦♦
63 Oaklea Avenue, Hoole, Chester CH2 3RG
T: (01244) 340516

HORWICH
Greater Manchester

Highercroft ♦♦♦
1 Foxholes Road, Horwich, Bolton BL6 6AS
T: (01204) 691323
F: 07941 989887
E: highercroft@linone.net
I: www.highercroft.8m.net

HOYLAKE
Merseyside

Crestwood ♦♦♦
25 Drummond Road, Hoylake, Wirral CH47 4AU
T: (0151) 632 2937
E: elainehowe@totalise.co.uk

HUXLEY
Cheshire

Higher Huxley Hall
♦♦♦♦ SILVER AWARD
Red Lane, Huxley, Chester
CH3 9BZ
T: (01829) 781484
F: (01829) 781142
E: info@huxleyhall.co.uk
I: www.huxleyhall.co.uk

KIRKBY
Merseyside

Greenbank ♦♦
193 Rowan Drive, Westvale,
Kirkby, Liverpool L32 0SG
T: (0151) 546 9971
F: (0151) 546 9971
E: patricia@greenbank193.fsnet.co.uk

KNUTSFORD
Cheshire

The Dog Inn ♦♦♦
Well Bank Lane, Over Peover,
Knutsford, WA16 8UP
T: (01625) 861421
F: (01625) 864800

Laburnum Cottage Guest House ♦♦♦♦
Knutsford Road, Mobberley,
Knutsford WA16 7PU
T: (01565) 872464
F: (01565) 872464

Moat Hall Motel ♦♦♦
Chelford Road, Marthall,
Knutsford WA16 8SU
T: (01625) 860367
F: (01625) 861136
E: val@moathall.fsnet.co.uk

Wash Lane Farm ♦♦♦
Allostock, Knutsford, WA16 9JP
T: (01565) 722215
F: (01565) 722215

LACH DENNIS
Cheshire

Melvin Holme Farm ♦♦♦
Pennys Lane, Lach Dennis,
Northwich CW9 7SJ
T: (01606) 330008

LANCASTER
Lancashire

Castle Hill Bed and Breakfast ♦♦♦
27 St Mary's Parade, Castle Hill,
Lancaster, LA1 1YX
T: (01524) 849137
F: (01524) 849137
E: gsutclif@aol.com.uk

Farmhouse Tavern ♦♦♦
Morecambe Road, Lancaster,
LA1 5JB
T: (01524) 69255
F: (01524) 845823

Lancaster Town House ♦♦♦
11-12 Newton Terrace, Caton
Road, Lancaster, LA1 3PB
T: (01524) 65527
F: (01524) 383148
E: hedge-holmes@talk21.com
I: www.lancastertownhouse.co.uk

Low House Farm ♦♦♦
Claughton, Lancaster, LA2 9LA
T: (01524) 221260
F: (01524) 221260
E: shirley@lunevalley.freeserve.co.uk
I: www.lowhousefarm.co.uk

Middle Holly Cottage ♦♦♦
Middle Holly Lane, Forton,
Preston PR3 1AH
T: (01524) 792399

The Old Station House ♦♦♦
25 Meeting House Lane,
Lancaster, LA1 1TX
T: (01524) 381060

Railton Hotel ♦
2 Station Road, Lancaster,
LA1 5SJ
T: (01524) 388364
F: (01524) 388364

Shakespeare Hotel ♦♦♦♦
96 St Leonardgate, Lancaster,
LA1 1NN
T: (01524) 841041

Wagon and Horses ♦♦♦
27 St Georges Quay, Lancaster,
LA1 1RD
T: (01524) 34036

LANGHO
Lancashire

Petre Lodge Country Hotel ♦♦♦♦
Northcote Road, Langho,
Blackburn BB6 8BG
T: (01254) 245506
F: (01254) 245506
E: aslambert@fsbdial.co.uk

LEYLAND
Lancashire

Oxen House Farm ♦♦♦
204 Longmeanygate, Leyland,
Preston PR5 3TB
T: (01772) 423749
E: mal@oxen.fslife.co.uk
I: www.oxenhousefarm.gbr.cc

LITHERLAND
Merseyside

Litherland Park Bed and Breakfast ♦♦♦
34 Litherland Park, Litherland,
Bootle L21 9HP
T: (0151) 928 1085

LITTLEBOROUGH
Greater Manchester

Hollingworth Lake Bed and Breakfast
♦♦♦♦♦ GOLD AWARD
164 Smithy Bridge Road,
Hollingworth Lake,
Littleborough, OL15 0DB
T: (01706) 376583
E: karen@hollingworth.masterflash.co.uk

Swing Cottage ♦♦♦♦
31 Lakebank, Hollingworth Lake
Country Park, Littleborough,
OL15 0DQ
T: (01706) 379094
F: (01706) 379091
E: swingcottage@aol.com
I: www.hollingworthlake.com

LIVERPOOL
Merseyside

Aachen Hotel ♦♦♦
89-91 Mount Pleasant,
Liverpool, L3 5TB
T: (0151) 709 3477
F: (0151) 709 1126
E: enquiries@aachenhotel.co.uk
I: www.aachenhotel.co.uk

Dolby Hotel Liverpool Ltd ♦♦♦
36-42 Chaloner Street, Queen's
Dock, Liverpool, L3 4DE
T: (0151) 708 7272
F: (0151) 708 7266
E: liverpool@dolbyhotels.co.uk
I: www.dolbyhotels.co.uk

Feathers Hotel ♦♦♦
117 Mount Pleasant, Liverpool,
L3 5TF
T: (0151) 709 9655
F: (0151) 709 3838
E: feathershotel@feathers.uk.com
I: www.feathers.uk.com

The Feathers Inn ♦♦
1 Paul Street, Vauxhall Road,
Liverpool, L3 6DX
T: 0870 120 2348
F: 0870 120 2347

Holme Leigh Guest House ♦♦
93 Woodcroft Road, Wavertree,
Liverpool, L15 2HG
T: (0151) 734 2216
F: (0151) 728 9521
E: bridges01@blueyonder.co.uk

The Kensington 189
Rating Applied For
189 Kensington, Liverpool,
L7 2RF
T: (0151) 263 6807
F: (0151) 263 8349

Lord Nelson ♦
Lord Nelson Street, Liverpool,
L3 5PD
T: (0151) 709 4362
F: (0151) 707 1321

Parkland ♦♦♦
38 Coachmans Drive, Croxteth
Park, Liverpool, L12 0HX
T: (0151) 259 1417

Redcroft ♦♦♦
12 Parkfield Road, Sefton Park,
Liverpool, L17 8UH
T: (0151) 727 3723

Woolton Redbourne Hotel
♦♦♦♦ SILVER AWARD
Acrefield Road, Woolton,
Liverpool, L25 5JN
T: (0151) 421 1500
F: (0151) 421 1501
E: wooltonredbourne@cwcom.net

LONGRIDGE
Lancashire

Oak Lea ♦♦♦♦
Clitheroe Road, Knowle Green,
Longridge, Preston PR3 2YS
T: (01254) 878486
F: (01254) 878486

LONGTON
Lancashire

Moorside Villa ♦♦♦♦
Drumacre Lane West, Longton,
Preston PR4 4SB
T: (01772) 616612
E: enquiries@moorsidevilla.gbr.cc
I: www.moorsidevilla.gbr.cc

Willow Cottage ♦♦♦♦
Longton Bypass, Longton,
Preston PR4 4RA
T: (01772) 617570
E: info@lancashirebedandbreakfast.co.uk
I: www.lancashirebedandbreakfast.co.uk

LOWER WHITLEY
Cheshire

Tall Trees Lodge ♦♦♦
Tarporley Road, Lower Whitley,
Warrington WA4 4EZ
T: (01928) 790824
F: (01928) 791330
E: booking@talltreeslodge.co.uk
I: www.talltreeslodge.co.uk

LYTHAM ST ANNES
Lancashire

Clifton Park Hotel ♦♦♦♦
299-301 Clifton Drive South,
Lytham St Annes, FY8 1HN
T: (01253) 725801
F: (01253) 721135
E: info@cliftonpark.co.uk
I: www.cliftonpark.co.uk

Monarch Hotel ♦♦♦
29 St Annes Road East, Lytham
St Annes, FY8 1TA
T: (01253) 720464
E: churchill@monarch91.freeserve.co.uk
I: www.monarch-st-annes.co.uk

Strathmore Hotel ♦♦♦
305 Clifton Drive South, Lytham
St Annes, FY8 1HN
T: (01253) 725478

MACCLESFIELD
Cheshire

Carr House Farm ♦♦♦
Mill Lane, Adlington,
Macclesfield, SK10 4LG
T: (01625) 828337
F: (01625) 828337
E: isobel@carrhousefarm.fsnet.co.uk
I: www.topfarms.co.uk

Moorhayes House Hotel ♦♦♦
27 Manchester Road,
Tytherington, Macclesfield,
SK10 2JJ
T: (01625) 433228
F: (01625) 429878
E: helen@moorhayes.co.uk
I: www.smoothhound.co.uk/hotels/moorhaye

Oldhams Hollow Farm ♦♦♦
Manchester Road, Tytherington,
Macclesfield, SK10 2JW
T: (01625) 424128
F: (01625) 574280
E: brenda@oldhamshollow.go-plus.net
I: www.topfarms.co.uk

Penrose Guest House ♦♦♦♦
56 Birtles Road, Whirley,
Macclesfield, SK10 3JQ
T: (01625) 615323
F: (01625) 432284
E: info@penroseguesthouse.co.uk
I: www.penroseguesthouse.co.uk

Sandpit Farm ♦♦♦
Messuage Lane, Marton,
Macclesfield SK11 9HS
T: (01260) 224254

MAGHULL
Merseyside

Rosedene ♦♦♦
175 Liverpool Road South,
Maghull, Liverpool L31 8AA
T: (0151) 527 1897

MALPAS
Cheshire

Hamilton House Bed and Breakfast ♦♦♦
Station Road, Hampton Heath, Malpas, SY14 8JF
T: (01948) 820421
E: katch&ted@hamiltonhouse.com
I: www.smoothhound.co.uk

MANCHESTER
Greater Manchester

Anbermar ♦♦♦
32 Gibwood Road, Northenden, Manchester, M22 4BS
T: (0161) 998 2375

Bentley Guest House ♦♦♦
64 Hill Lane, Blackley, Manchester M9 6PF
T: (0161) 795 1115

Commercial Hotel ♦♦
125 Liverpool Road, Castlefield, Manchester, M3 4JN
T: (0161) 834 3504
F: (0161) 835 2725

Dolby Hotel Manchester West Ltd ♦♦♦
55 Blackfriars Road, Manchester, M3 7DB
T: (0161) 907 2277
F: (0161) 907 2266
E: manchester@dolbyhotels.co.uk
I: www.dolbyhotels.co.uk

The Kempton House Hotel ♦♦♦
400 Wilbraham Road, Chorlton-cum-Hardy, Manchester, M21 0UM
T: (0161) 881 8766
E: kempton.house@virgin.net

Luther King House ♦♦♦
Brighton Grove, Wilmslow Road, Manchester, M14 5JP
T: (0161) 224 6404
F: (0161) 248 9201
E: reception@lkh.co.uk
I: www.lkh.co.uk

Monroe's ♦
38 London Road, Piccadilly, Manchester, M1 1PE
T: (0161) 236 0564

The Ox Bar Restaurant Hotel ♦♦♦
71 Liverpool Road, Castlefield, Manchester, M3 4NQ
T: (0161) 839 7740
F: (0161) 839 7760
E: david@theox.co.uk
I: www.theox.co.uk

Rembrandt Hotel ♦♦♦
33 Sackville Street, City Centre, Manchester, M1 3LZ
T: (0161) 236 1311
F: (0161) 236 4257
E: rembrandthotel@aol.com
I: www.rembrandtmanchester.com

MELLOR
Lancashire

Old Dad's Barn ♦♦♦
Mellor Lane, Mellor, Blackburn BB2 7EN
T: (01254) 812434

MICKLE TRAFFORD
Cheshire

Manor Guest House ♦♦♦
Mickle Trafford Manor, Warrington Road, Mickle Trafford, Chester CH2 4EA
T: (01244) 300555
F: (01244) 301909

MIDDLEWICH
Cheshire

Hopley House ♦♦♦
Wimboldsley, Middlewich, CW10 0LN
T: (01270) 526292
F: (01270) 526292
E: margery@mreade.freeserve.co.uk
I: www.mreade.freeserve.co.uk

MINSHULL VERNON
Cheshire

Higher Elms Farm ♦♦
Minshull Vernon, Crewe CW1 4RG
T: (01270) 522252
F: (01270) 522252

MOBBERLEY
Cheshire

The Hinton ♦♦♦♦ SILVER AWARD
Town Lane, Mobberley, Knutsford WA16 7HH
T: (01565) 873484
F: (01565) 873484
I: www.hinton.co.uk

MORECAMBE
Lancashire

Ashley Private Hotel ♦♦♦
371 Marine Road East, Morecambe, LA4 5AH
T: (01524) 412034
F: (01524) 421390
E: info@ashleyhotel.co.uk
I: www.ashleyhotel.co.uk

The Balmoral Hotel ♦♦♦
34 Marine Road West, Morecambe, LA3 1BZ
T: (01524) 418526
F: (01524) 418526
E: info@balmoralhotelmorecambe.co.uk
I: www.balmoralhotelmorecambe.co.uk

Belle Vue Hotel ♦♦♦
330 Marine Road, Morecambe, LA4 5AA
T: (01524) 411375
F: (01524) 411375

Berkeley Private Hotel ♦♦♦
39 Marine Road West, Promenade West, Morecambe, LA3 1BZ
T: (01524) 418201

The Broadwater Private Hotel ♦♦
356 Marine Road, Morecambe, LA4 5AQ
T: (01524) 411333
F: (01524) 411 333

Caledonian Hotel ♦♦
60 Marine Road West, Morecambe, LA4 4ET
T: (01524) 418503
F: (01524) 401710

The Clifton Hotel ♦♦
43-46 Marine Road West, Morecambe, LA3 1BZ
T: (01524) 411573
F: (01524) 420839

Craigwell Hotel ♦♦♦
372 Marine Road East, Morecambe, LA4 5AH
T: (01524) 410095
F: (01524) 410095

The Durham Guest House ♦♦♦
73 Albert Road, Morecambe, LA4 4HY
T: (01524) 424790
E: durhamhouse.com@bushinternet.com

Eidsforth Hotel ♦♦♦
317-318 Marine Road Central, Promenade, Morecambe, LA4 5AA
T: (01524) 411691
F: (01524) 832334

Glen Isla Guest House ♦♦
16 Clark Street, Morecambe, LA4 5HR
T: (01524) 418496

Glenthorn Private Hotel ♦♦
24-26 West End Road, Seaview Parade, Morecambe, LA4 4DL
T: (01524) 411640
F: (01524) 411640
E: glenthorn@computerweekly.com
I: www.glenthorn.co.uk

Lakeland View Guest House ♦♦
130 Clarendon Road, Morecambe, LA3 1SD
T: (01524) 415873
I: www.morecambebehta.co.uk

The Marina Hotel ♦♦♦
324 Marine Road Central, Morecambe, LA4 5AA
T: (01524) 423979
F: (01524) 426699
E: marina@marina-hotel.demon.co.uk
I: www.marina-hotel.demon.co.uk

Roxbury Private Hotel ♦♦
78 Thornton Road, Morecambe, LA4 5PJ
T: (01524) 410561
F: (01524) 420286
E: ritall@bigfoot.com
I: www.roxburghhotelmorecambe.com

St Winifred's Hotel ♦♦♦
Marine Road East, Morecambe, LA4 5AR
T: (01524) 412322
F: (01524) 412322

Seacrest ♦♦♦
9-13 West End Road, Morecambe, LA4 4DJ
T: (01524) 411006

Tern Bay Hotel ♦♦♦
43 Heysham Road, Morecambe, LA3 1DA
T: (01524) 421209
F: (01524) 831925
E: info@ternbayhotel.co.uk
I: www.ternbayhotel.co.uk

Trevelyan Private Hotel ♦♦♦
27 West End Road, Morecambe, LA4 4DJ
T: (01524) 412013
F: (01524) 417590
E: thetrevelyan@supanet.com
I: www.thetrevelyan.freeserve.co.uk

Westleigh Hotel ♦♦♦
9 Marine Road, Morecambe, LA3 1BS
T: (01524) 418352
F: (01524) 418352

Yacht Bay View Hotel ♦♦♦
359 Marine Road East, Morecambe, LA4 5AQ
T: (01524) 414481
E: yachtbayview@hotmail.com
I: www.yachtbay.co.uk

MOTTRAM ST ANDREW
Cheshire

Goose Green Farm ♦♦♦
Oak Road, Mottram St Andrew, Macclesfield SK10 4RA
T: (01625) 828814
F: (01625) 828814
E: goosegreenfarm@talk21.com

MUCH HOOLE
Lancashire

The Barn Guest House ♦♦♦
204 Liverpool Old Road, Much Hoole, Preston PR4 4QB
T: (01772) 612654

NANTWICH
Cheshire

Henhull Hall ♦♦♦♦
Welshmans Lane, Nantwich, CW5 6AD
T: (01270) 624158
F: (01270) 624158
E: philip.percival@virgin.net

Stoke Grange Farm ♦♦♦♦
Chester Road, Nantwich, CW5 6BT
T: (01270) 625525
F: (01270) 625525
E: stokegrange@freeuk.com
I: www.smoothhoundstokegrangefarm.com

NATEBY
Lancashire

Bowers Hotel and Brasserie ♦♦♦
Bowers Lane, Nateby, Preston PR3 0JD
T: (01995) 601500
F: (01995) 603770

NELSON
Lancashire

Lovett House Guest House ♦♦♦
6 Howard Street, Off Carr Road, Nelson, BB9 7SZ
T: (01282) 697352
F: (01282) 700186
E: lovetthouse@ntlworld.com
I: www.lovetthouse.co.uk

NETHER ALDERLEY
Cheshire

Millbrook Cottage Guest House ♦♦♦♦
Congleton Road, Nether Alderley, Macclesfield SK10 4TW
T: (01625) 583567
F: (01625) 599556
E: millbrookcottage@hotmail.com
I: www.millbrookcottage.co.uk

NEW BRIGHTON
Merseyside

Sea Level Hotel ♦♦
126 Victoria Road, New Brighton, Wirral CH45 9LD
T: (0151) 639 3408
F: (0151) 639 3408

Sherwood Guest House ♦♦♦
55 Wellington Road, New Brighton, Wirral CH45 2ND
T: (0151) 639 5198
F: (0151) 639 9079
E: sheila@sherwood-guest-house.co.uk

Wellington House Hotel ♦♦♦
65 Wellington Road, New Brighton, Wirral CH45 2NE
T: (0151) 639 6594
F: (0151) 639 6594
I: www.wellington-house-hotel.freeserve.co.uk

NEWTON-LE-WILLOWS
Merseyside

The Pied Bull Hotel and Restaurant
Rating Applied For
54 High Street, Newton-le-Willows, WA12 9SH
T: (01925) 224549
F: (01925) 291929
E: piedbull@btopenworld.com
I: www.piedbull.com

NORTHWICH
Cheshire

Ash House Farm ♦♦♦♦
Chapel Lane, Acton Bridge, Northwich CW8 3QS
T: (01606) 852717
F: (01606) 853752
E: sue_schofield40@hotmail.com

Park Dale Guest House ♦♦♦
140 Middlewich Road, Rudheath, Northwich CW9 7DS
T: (01606) 45228
F: (01606) 331770

OAKENCLOUGH
Lancashire

Calderbank Country Lodge ♦♦♦♦
Calderbank, Oakenclough, Preston PR3 1UL
T: (01995) 604384
I: www.calderbanklodge.com

OLDHAM
Greater Manchester

Boothstead Farm ♦♦♦♦
Rochdale Road, Denshaw, Oldham OL3 5UE
T: (01457) 878622
E: boothsteadfarm@bushinternet.com

Globe Farm Guest House ♦♦♦
Huddersfield Road, Standedge, Delph, Oldham OL3 5LU
T: (01457) 873040
F: (01457) 873040
E: globefarm@amserve.net
I: www.globefarm.co.uk

Temple Bar Farm ♦♦♦♦
Wallhill Road, Dobcross, Oldham OL3 5BH
T: (01457) 870099
F: (01457) 872003
E: info@templebarfarm.co.uk
I: www.templebarfarm.co.uk

ORMSKIRK
Lancashire

The Meadows ♦♦♦♦
New Sutch Farm, Sutch Lane, Ormskirk, L40 4BU
T: (01704) 894048

OVER ALDERLEY
Cheshire

Lower Harebarrow Farm ♦♦
Over Alderley, Macclesfield SK10 4SW
T: (01625) 829882

OVERTON
Lancashire

The Globe Hotel ♦♦♦
40 Main Street, Overton, Morecambe LA3 3HG
T: (01524) 858228
F: (01524) 858 073
E: theglobe@talk21.com

PADIHAM
Lancashire

Windsor House ♦♦
71 Church Street, Padiham, Burnley BB12 8JH
T: (01282) 773271
E: chuchstreetfb@talk21.com

PARBOLD
Lancashire

Red Lion Hotel ♦♦♦
9 Newburgh Village, Parbold, Wigan WN8 7NF
T: (01257) 462336
F: (01257) 462827
I: www.burtonwoodhotels.co.uk

PICTON
Cheshire

The Fox Covert Guest House ♦♦♦♦
Fox Covert Lane, Picton, Chester CH2 4HB
T: (01244) 300363
F: (01244) 300963
E: george.derby@virgin.net
I: www.thefoxcovert.co.uk

PRESTBURY
Cheshire

Artizana Suite
Rating Applied For
The Village, Prestbury, Macclesfield SK10 4DG
T: (01625) 827582
F: (01625) 827582
E: suite@artizana.co.uk

PRESTON
Lancashire

Ashwood Hotel ♦♦♦
11-13 Fishergate Hill, Preston, PR1 8JB
T: (01772) 203302
F: (01772) 203302

Derby Court Hotel ♦♦
1 Pole Street, Preston, PR1 1DX
T: (01772) 202077
F: (01772) 252277

Olde Duncombe House ♦♦♦
Garstang Road, Bilsborrow, Preston PR3 0RE
T: (01995) 640336
F: (01995) 640336
E: oldedunc@aol.com
I: www.geocities.com/oldduncombehouse

Ye Horns Inn ♦♦♦♦
Horns Lane, Goosnargh, Preston, PR3 2FJ
T: (01772) 865230
F: (01772) 864299
E: enquiries@yehornsinn.co.uk
I: www.yehornsinn.co.uk

PRESTWICH
Greater Manchester

Church Inn ♦♦♦
Church Lane, Prestwich, Manchester M25 1AJ
T: (0161) 798 6727
F: (0161) 773 6281
E: tom.gribben@virgin.net

RAWTENSTALL
Lancashire

Lindau Guest House ♦♦
131 Haslingden Old Road, Rawtenstall, Rossendale BB4 8RR
T: (01706) 214592
E: humm@globalnet.co.uk
I: www.lindau-guest-house.co.uk

RUSHTON
Cheshire

Hill House Farm Bed and Breakfast ♦♦♦♦
The Hall Lane, Rushton, Tarporley CW6 9AU
T: (01829) 732238
F: (01829) 733929
E: rayner@hillhousefarm.fsnet.co.uk

SADDLEWORTH
Greater Manchester

Farrars Arms ♦♦
56 Oldham Road, Grasscroft, Oldham OL4 4HL
T: (01457) 872124
F: (01457) 820351

ST MICHAEL'S ON WYRE
Lancashire

Compton House ♦♦♦♦
Garstang Road, St Michael's on Wyre, Preston PR3 0TE
T: (01995) 679378
F: (01995) 679378
E: dave@compton-hs.co.uk
I: www.compton-hs.co.uk

SALFORD
Greater Manchester

Hazeldean Hotel ♦♦♦
467 Bury New Road, Kersal Bar, Salford, M7 3NE
T: (0161) 792 6667
F: (0161) 792 6668

Lyndale Court Accommodation ♦♦♦
1-2 The Drive, Bury New Road, Salford, M7 3ND
T: (0161) 792 7270
E: enquiries@lyndalecourt.co.uk
I: www.lyndalecourt.co.uk

SALTNEY
Cheshire

The Garden Gate Guest House ♦♦♦
8 Chester Street, Saltney, Chester CH4 8BJ
T: (01244) 682306
F: 07769 723128
E: dollywal@msn.com

SEALAND
Cheshire

The Elms Farmhouse Hotel ♦♦
Sealand Road, Sealand, Chester CH1 6BS
T: (01244) 880747
F: (01244) 880920

SIDDINGTON
Cheshire

Golden Cross Farm ♦♦♦
Siddington, Macclesfield SK11 9JP
T: (01260) 224358

SILVERDALE
Lancashire

Silverdale Hotel ♦♦♦
Shore Road, Silverdale, Carnforth LA5 0TP
T: (01524) 701206

SLAIDBURN
Lancashire

Hark to Bounty Inn ♦♦♦
Slaidburn, Clitheroe BB7 3EP
T: (01200) 446246
F: (01200) 446361
E: isobel@hark-to-bounty.co.uk
I: www.hark-to-bounty.co.uk

SLYNE
Lancashire

Slyne Lodge
Rating Applied For
92 Main Road, Slyne, Lancaster LA2 6AZ
T: (01524) 825035
F: (01524) 823467
E: skilshaw@jenningsbrewery.co.uk
I: www.jenningsbrewery.co.uk

SOUTHPORT
Merseyside

Aaron Hotel ♦♦♦
18 Bath Street, Southport, PR9 0DA
T: (01704) 530283
F: (01704) 501055
E: info@aaronhotel.co.uk
I: www.aaronhotel.co.uk

Alhambra Hotel ♦♦♦
41 Bold Street, Southport, PR9 0ED
T: (01704) 534853
E: info@alhambrahotel.co.uk
I: www.alhambrahotel.co.uk

Ambassador Private Hotel ♦♦♦♦
13 Bath Street, Southport, PR9 0DP
T: (01704) 543998
E: ambassador.walton@virgin.net
I: www.ambassadorprivatehotel.co.uk

Brae Mar Private Hotel ♦♦♦
4 Bath Street, Southport, PR9 0DA
T: (01704) 535838
F: (01704) 535838

Carlton Lodge Hotel ♦♦♦♦
43 Bath Street, Southport, PR9 0DP
T: (01704) 542290
F: (01704) 542290
E: benvale@which.net
I: www.smoothhound.co.uk/hotels/carlton

Clifton Villa Hotel ♦♦♦
6 Bath Street, Southport, PR9 0DA
T: (01704) 535780
F: (01704) 549111
E: sales@cliftonvilla.co.uk
I: www.cliftonvilla.co.uk

Crescent House Hotel ♦♦♦
27 Bath Street, Southport,
PR9 0DP
T: (01704) 530339
F: (01704) 530339
E: glynor@creshohotel.freeserve.co.uk
I: www.smoothhound.co.uk/hotels/crescnt.html

Fairfield Private Hotel ♦♦♦
83 Promenade, Southport,
PR9 0JN
T: (01704) 530137

Le Maitre Hotel ♦♦♦♦
69 Bath Street, Southport,
PR9 0DN
T: (01704) 530394
F: (01704) 548755
E: enquiries@hotel-lemaitre.co.uk
I: www.hotel-lemaitre.co.uk

Leicester Hotel ♦♦♦
24 Leicester Street, Southport,
PR9 0EZ
T: (01704) 530049
F: (01704) 545561
E: leicester.hotel@mail.cybase.co.uk
I: www.leicesterhotelsouthport.co.uk

Lynwood Private Hotel ♦♦♦♦
11a Leicester Street, Southport,
PR9 0ER
T: (01704) 540794
F: (01704) 500724
I: www.smoothhound.co.uk/lynwood.html

Rosedale Hotel ♦♦♦♦
11 Talbot Street, Southport,
PR8 1HP
T: (01704) 530604
F: (01704) 530604
E: info@rosedalehotelsouthport.co.uk
I: www.rosedalehotelsouthport.co.uk

Sandy Brook Farm ♦♦♦
52 Wyke Cop Road, Scarisbrick,
Southport, PR8 5LR
T: (01704) 880337
F: (01704) 880337
E: sandybrookfarm@lycos.co.uk

Sidbrook Hotel ♦♦♦
14 Talbot Street, Southport,
PR8 1HP
T: (01704) 530608
F: (01704) 530608
E: sidbrookhotel@tesco.net
I: www.sidbrookhotel.co.uk

Silverdale Hotel ♦♦♦♦
10 Victoria Street, Southport,
PR9 0DU
T: (01704) 536479
F: (01704) 536479

Sunnyside Hotel ♦♦♦
47 Bath Street, Southport,
PR9 0DP
T: (01704) 536521
F: (01704) 539237
E: sunnysidehotel@rapid.co.uk
I: www.sunny-lisa.co.uk

Waterford ♦♦♦♦
37 Leicester Street, Southport,
PR9 0EX
T: (01704) 530559
F: (01704) 542630
E: reception@waterford-hotel.co.uk
I: www.waterford-hotel.co.uk

Whitworth Falls Hotel ♦♦♦
16 Lathom Road, Southport,
PR9 0JH
T: (01704) 530074
E: whitworthfalls@rapid.co.uk
I: www.whitworthfallshotel.co.uk

Windsor Lodge Hotel ♦♦♦
37 Saunders Street, Southport,
PR9 0HJ
T: (01704) 530070

STOCKPORT
Greater Manchester

Hallfield Guest House ♦♦♦
50 Hall Street, Stockport,
SK1 4DA
T: (0161) 429 8977
F: (0161) 429 9017
E: hallfieldhouse@btconnect.com
I: www.hallfieldguesthouse.co.uk

Henry's Hotel ♦♦♦♦
204-206 Buxton Road,
Davenport, Stockport, SK2 7AE
T: (0161) 292 0202
F: (0161) 355 6585
E: enquiries@henryshotel.com
I: www.henryshotel.com

Moss Deeping ♦♦♦
7 Robins Lane, Bramhall,
Stockport, SK7 2PE
T: (0161) 439 1969
F: (0161) 439 9985
E: gbanks7872@aol.com
I: www.mossdeeping.co.uk

Needhams Farm ♦♦♦
Uplands Road, Werneth Low,
Gee Cross, Hyde SK14 3AG
T: (0161) 368 4610
F: (0161) 367 9106
E: charlotte@needhamsfarm.co.uk
I: www.needhamsfarm.co.uk

STONYHURST
Lancashire

Alden Cottage
♦♦♦♦ GOLD AWARD
Kemple End, Birdy Brow,
Stonyhurst, Clitheroe BB7 9QY
T: (01254) 826468
F: (01254) 826468
E: carpenter@aldencottage.f9.co.uk
I: fp.aldencottage.f9.co.uk

TARPORLEY
Cheshire

Foresters Arms ♦♦♦
92 High Street, Tarporley,
CW6 0AX
T: (01829) 733151
F: (01829) 730020

TATTENHALL
Cheshire

Broad Oak Farm ♦♦♦
Birds Lane, Tattenhall, Chester
CH3 9NL
T: (01829) 770325
F: (01829) 771546

Ford Farm ♦♦♦
Newton Lane, Tattenhall,
Chester CH3 9NE
T: (01829) 770307

TIMPERLEY
Greater Manchester

Acorn of Oakmere ♦♦♦
Oakmere, 6 Wingate Drive,
Timperley, Altrincham
WA15 7PX
T: (0161) 980 8391
F: (0161) 980 8391
E: oakmere6@cwctv.net

TORSIDE
Greater Manchester

The Old House ♦♦♦
Woodhead Road, Torside,
Glossop SK13 1HU
T: (01457) 857527
E: oldhouse@torside.co.uk
I: www.oldhouse.torside.co.uk

TOSSIDE
Lancashire

Dog and Partridge ♦♦♦
Tosside, Skipton BD23 4SQ
T: (01729) 840668

WADDINGTON
Lancashire

Peter Barn Country House ♦♦♦♦
Cross Lane, Waddington,
Clitheroe BB7 3JH
T: (01200) 428585
E: jean@peterbarn.fsnet.co.uk

WALLASEY
Merseyside

The Russell Hotel ♦♦♦
44 Church Road, Seacombe,
Wallasey, CH44 7BA
T: (0151) 639 5723
F: (0151) 639 5723
E: mail@russellhotel.fsnet.co.uk

WARTON
Lancashire

Cotestones Farm ♦♦♦
Sand Lane, Warton, Carnforth
LA5 9NH
T: (01524) 732418
F: (01524) 732418

WATERLOO
Merseyside

Marlborough Hotel ♦♦
21 Crosby Road South,
Waterloo, Liverpool L22 1RG
T: (0151) 928 7709
F: (0151) 928 7709

Woodlands Guest House ♦♦♦
10 Haigh Road, Waterloo,
Liverpool L22 3XP
T: (0151) 920 5373

WEST DERBY
Merseyside

Blackmoor ♦♦♦
160 Blackmoor Drive, West
Derby, Liverpool L12 9EF
T: (0151) 291 1407

WEST KIRBY
Merseyside

Caldy Warren Cottage ♦♦♦♦
42 Caldy Road, West Kirby,
Wirral CH48 2HQ
T: (0151) 625 8740
F: (0151) 625 4115
E: office@warrencott.demon.co.uk
I: www.warrencott.demon.co.uk

WESTHOUGHTON
Greater Manchester

Daisy Hill Hotel ♦♦♦
3 Lower Leigh Road, Daisy Hill,
Westhoughton, Bolton BL5 2JP
T: (01942) 812096
F: (01942) 797180
E: daisy.hill@cwcom.net
I: www.daisyhillhotel.co.uk

WESTON
Cheshire

Snape Farm ♦♦♦
Snape Lane, Weston, Crewe
CW2 5NB
T: (01270) 820208
F: (01270) 820208
E: jean@snapefarm.fsnet.co.uk

WHALLEY
Lancashire

Bayley Arms Hotel ♦♦♦
Avenue Road, Hurst Green,
Whalley, Clitheroe BB7 9QB
T: (01254) 826478
F: (01254) 826797

WHITEWELL
Lancashire

The Inn at Whitewell ♦♦♦♦
Whitewell, Clitheroe BB7 3AT
T: (01200) 448222
F: (01200) 448298

WHITWORTH
Lancashire

Hindle Pastures ♦♦♦♦
Highgate Lane, Whitworth,
Rochdale OL12 0TS
T: (01706) 643310
F: (01706) 653846
E: p-marshall@breathemail.net
I: www.smoothhound.co.uk/hotels/hindlepastures

WIGAN
Greater Manchester

Wilden ♦♦♦
11a Miles Lane, Shevington,
Wigan WN6 8EB
T: (01257) 251516
F: (01257) 255622
E: wildenbandb@aol.com

WILMSLOW
Cheshire

Dean Bank Hotel ♦♦♦
Adlington Road, Wilmslow,
SK9 2BT
T: (01625) 524268
F: (01625) 549715
I: www.deanbankhotel.co.uk

Finney Green Cottage ♦♦♦♦
134 Manchester Road,
Wilmslow, SK9 2JW
T: (01625) 533343
I: www.finneygreencottage.co.uk

Hollow Bridge Guest House ♦♦♦♦
90 Manchester Road, Wilmslow,
SK9 2JY
T: (01625) 537303
F: (01625) 528718
E: lynandjack@hollowbridge.com
I: www.hollowbridge.com

King William Hotel ♦♦♦
35 Manchester Road, Wilmslow,
SK0 1BQ
T: (01625) 524022
I: www.kingwilliam20m.com

Establishments printed in blue have a detailed entry in this guide

Marigold House ♦♦♦♦
132 Knutsford Road, Wilmslow, SK9 6JH
T: (01625) 584414

WINCLE
Cheshire

Hill Top Farm ♦♦♦♦
Wincle, Macclesfield SK11 0QH
T: (01260) 227257
E: a.brocklehurst@talk21.com

WINTERLEY
Cheshire

Field Mews ♦♦♦♦
The Fields, 36 Hassall Road, Winterley, Sandbach CW11 4RL
T: (01270) 761858

WISWELL
Lancashire

Pepper Hill ♦♦♦♦
Pendleton Road, Wiswell, Clitheroe BB7 9BZ
T: (01254) 825098

WYCOLLER
Lancashire

Parson Lee Farm ♦♦♦
Wycoller, Colne BB8 8SU
T: (01282) 864747
E: pathodgson@hotmail.com
I: www.parsonleefarm.co.uk

YORKSHIRE

ACKLAM
North Yorkshire

Trout Pond Barn ♦♦♦♦
Acklam, Malton YO17 9RG
T: (01653) 658468
F: (01653) 698688
E: margaret@troutpondbarn.co.uk
I: www.troutpondbarn.co.uk

ADDINGHAM
West Yorkshire

The Crown Inn
Rating Applied For
Main Street, Addingham, Ilkley LS29 0NS
T: (01943) 830278

Ghyll House Farm ♦♦♦
Straight Lane, Addingham, Ilkley LS29 9JX
T: (01943) 830370

Lumb Beck Farmhouse Bed and Breakfast
♦♦♦♦ SILVER AWARD
Moorside Lane, Addingham, Ilkley LS29 9JX
T: (01943) 830400

Walker Acre House B&B ♦♦♦
School Lane, Addingham, Ilkley LS29 0JL
T: (01943) 839950
E: miladymarim@aol.com

AINTHORPE
North Yorkshire

The Fox & Hounds Inn ♦♦♦♦
45 Brook Lane, Ainthorpe, Whitby YO21 2LD
T: (01287) 660218
F: (01287) 660030
E: ajbfox@globalnet.co.uk
I: www.foxandhounds-ainthorpe.com

AIRTON
North Yorkshire

Lindon House ♦♦♦
Malhamdale, Airton, Skipton BD23 4BE
T: (01729) 830418

ALDBROUGH
East Riding of Yorkshire

Wentworth House Hotel
♦♦♦♦
12 Seaside Road, Aldbrough, Hull HU11 4RX
T: (01964) 527246
F: (01964) 527246
E: enquiry@wentworthhouse.fsnet.co.uk
I: www.wentworthhouse.fsnet.co.uk

West Carlton ♦♦♦♦
Carlton Lane, Aldbrough, Hull HU11 4RB
T: (01964) 527724
F: (01964) 527505
E: caroline_maltas@hotmail.com
I: www.west-carlton.co.uk

ALDFIELD
North Yorkshire

Bay Tree Farm
♦♦♦♦ SILVER AWARD
Aldfield, Ripon HG4 3BE
T: (01765) 620394
F: (01765) 620394
E: btfarm@ppcmail.co.uk

ALLERTON
West Yorkshire

Victoria Hotel ♦♦♦
10 Cottingley Road, Sandy Lane, Allerton, Bradford BD15 9JP
T: (01274) 823820
F: (01274) 823820

AMOTHERBY
North Yorkshire

Old Station Farm Country Guest House
♦♦♦♦ GOLD AWARD
High Street, Amotherby, Malton YO17 6TL
T: (01653) 693683
F: (01653) 693683
E: info@oldstationfarm.co.uk
I: www.oldstationfarm.co.uk

AMPLEFORTH
North Yorkshire

Carr House Farm ♦♦♦
Shallowdale, Ampleforth, York YO62 4ED
T: (01347) 868526
E: ampleforth@hotmail.com
I: www.guestaccom.co.uk/912.htm

Daleside ♦♦♦♦
East End, Ampleforth, York YO62 4DA
T: (01439) 788266

Shallowdale House
♦♦♦♦♦ GOLD AWARD
West End, Ampleforth, York YO62 4DY
T: (01439) 788325
F: (01439) 788885
E: stay@shallowdalehouse.demon.co.uk
I: www.shallowdalehouse.demon.co.uk

Spring Cottage ♦♦♦
Ampleforth, York YO62 4DA
T: (01439) 788579

APPERSETT
North Yorkshire

Thorney Mire House ♦♦♦♦
Hawes, DL8 3LU
T: (01969) 667159
E: sylvia@thorneymire.yorks.net
I: www.thorneymire.yorks.net

APPLETREEWICK
North Yorkshire

Knowles Lodge ♦♦♦♦
Appletreewick, Skipton BD23 6DQ
T: (01756) 720228
F: (01756) 720381
E: pam@knowleslodge.com
I: www.knowleslodge.com

ARKENGARTHDALE
North Yorkshire

Chapel Farmhouse ♦♦♦♦
Whaw, Arkengarthdale, Richmond DL11 6RT
T: (01748) 884062
F: (01748) 884062
E: chapelfarmbb@aol.com

The Charles Bathurst Inn
♦♦♦♦
Arkengarthdale, Richmond DL11 6EN
T: (01748) 884567
F: (01748) 884599
E: info@cbinn.co.uk
I: www.cbinn.co.uk

The Ghyll ♦♦♦
Arkle Town, Arkengarthdale, Richmond DL11 6EU
T: (01748) 884353
F: (01748) 884015
E: bookings@theghyll.co.uk
I: www.theghyll.co.uk

ASKRIGG
North Yorkshire

The Apothecary's House
♦♦♦♦ SILVER AWARD
Market Place, Askrigg, Leyburn DL8 3HT
T: (01969) 650626

Bottom Chapel ♦♦♦♦
Askrigg, Leyburn DL8 3HT
T: (01969) 650180

Helm ♦♦♦♦♦ GOLD AWARD
Askrigg, Leyburn DL8 3JF
T: (01969) 650443
F: (01969) 650443
E: holiday@helmyorkshire.com
I: www.helmyorkshire.com

Home Farm ♦♦♦
Stalling Busk, Askrigg, Leyburn DL8 3DH
T: (01969) 650360

Milton House ♦♦♦♦
Askrigg, Leyburn DL8 3HJ
T: (01969) 650217

Stoney End
♦♦♦♦ SILVER AWARD
Worton, Leyburn DL8 3ET
T: (01969) 650652
F: (01969) 650077
E: pmh@stoneyend.co.uk
I: www.stoneyend.co.uk

Thornsgill House ♦♦♦♦
Moor Road, Askrigg, Leyburn DL8 3HH
T: (01969) 650617
E: thornsgill.house@virgin.net

AUSTWICK
North Yorkshire

Dalesbridge House ♦♦♦♦
Austwick, Lancaster LA2 8AZ
T: (01524) 251021
F: (01524) 251051
E: info@dalesbridge.co.uk
I: www.dalesbridge.co.uk

Wood View
Rating Applied For
Austwick, Lancaster LA2 8BB
T: (015242) 57268
F: (015242) 57268
E: jennifersuri@msn.com
I: www.yorkshiredales.com

AYSGARTH
North Yorkshire

Cornlee ♦♦♦
Aysgarth, Leyburn DL8 3AE
T: (01969) 663779
F: (01969) 663779
E: cornlee@tesco.net
I: www.cornlee.co.uk

Field House ♦♦♦♦
East End, Aysgarth, Leyburn DL8 3AB
T: (01969) 663556
E: Ros.evans@voidalimage.com
I: www.wensleydale.org

Stow House Hotel ♦♦♦♦
Aysgarth Falls, Aysgarth, Leyburn DL8 3SR
T: (01969) 663635
E: info@stowhouse.co.uk
I: www.stowhouse.co.uk

Wensleydale Farmhouse ♦♦♦
Aysgarth, Leyburn DL8 3SR
T: (01969) 663534
F: (01969) 663534
E: wykesarego@aol.com

Wheatsheaf Hotel ♦♦♦
Carperby, Leyburn DL8 4DF
T: (01969) 663216
F: (01969) 663019
E: wheatsheaf@paulmit.globalnet.co.uk
I: www.wheatsheafinwensleydale.co.uk

Establishments printed in blue have a detailed entry in this guide

BAILDON
West Yorkshire

Ford House Farm Bed and Breakfast ♦♦♦♦
Buck Lane, Baildon, Shipley
BD177 7R
T: (01274) 584489
F: (01274) 584489
E: mick@mpadley.fsnet.co.uk

BAINBRIDGE
North Yorkshire

Hazel's Roost ♦♦♦
Bainbridge, Leyburn DL8 3EH
T: (01969) 650400

High Force Farm ♦♦♦
Bainbridge, Leyburn DL8 3DL
T: (01969) 650379
F: (01969) 650826
E: highforce@uk4free.net

BAINTON
East Riding of Yorkshire

Bainton Burrows Farm ♦♦♦
Bainton, Driffield YO25 9BS
T: (01377) 217202

BALDERSBY
North Yorkshire

The Barn ♦♦♦
Nemur, Baldersby, Thirsk
YO7 4PE
T: (01765) 640561
E: sthain@zoom.co.uk

BARLOW
North Yorkshire

Berewick House ♦♦♦♦
Park Lane, Barlow, Selby
YO8 8EW
T: (01757) 617051
E: Wilson.Guesthouse@Berewick.co.uk

BARNETBY
South Humberside

Reginald House ♦♦♦♦
27 Queens Road, Barnetby,
DN38 6JH
T: (01652) 688566
F: (01652) 688510

BARROW UPON HUMBER
North Lincolnshire

Glebe Farm ♦♦♦
Cross Street, Barrow upon Humber, DN19 7AL
T: (01469) 531548
F: (01469) 530034
E: glebe_farm@lineone.net

BARTON-LE-STREET
North Yorkshire

Laurel Barn Cottage ♦♦♦
Barton-le-Street, Malton
YO17 6QB
T: (01653) 628329

BARTON-UPON-HUMBER
North Lincolnshire

George Hotel ♦♦
George Street, Barton-upon-Humber, DN18 5ES
T: (01652) 662001
F: (01652) 662002

BECK HOLE
North Yorkshire

Brookwood Farm ♦♦♦♦ SILVER AWARD
Beck Hole, Whitby YO22 5LE
T: (01947) 896402
I: www.brookwoodfarm.co.uk

BEDALE
North Yorkshire

The Castle Arms Inn ♦♦♦♦
Snape, Bedale DL8 2TB
T: (01677) 470270
F: (01677) 470837
E: castlearms@aol.com

Elmfield Country House ♦♦♦♦♦
Arrathorne, Bedale DL8 1NE
T: (01677) 450558
F: (01677) 450557
E: stay@elmfieldhouse.freeserve.co.uk
I: www.elmfieldhouse.co.uk

Georgian Bed and Breakfast ♦♦♦♦
16 North End, Stabann, Bedale,
DL8 1AB
T: (01677) 424454
E: georgian@bedale-town.com

Mill Close Farm ♦♦♦♦♦ SILVER AWARD
Patrick Brompton, Bedale
DL8 1JY
T: (01677) 450257
F: (01677) 450585
E: millclosefarm@btopenworld.com
I: www.smoothhound.co.uk/hotels/millclosefarm.html

BEEFORD
East Riding of Yorkshire

Pinderhill Farm Bed & Breakfast ♦♦♦♦
Pinderhill Farm, Beeford,
Driffield YO25 8AE
T: (01262) 488645

BEESTON
West Yorkshire

Crescent Hotel ♦♦
274 Dewsbury Road, Beeston,
Leeds LS11 6JT
T: (0113) 270 1819
F: (0113) 270 1819

BELL BUSK
North Yorkshire

Tudor House ♦♦♦♦
Bell Busk, Skipton BD23 4DT
T: (01729) 830301
F: (01729) 830301
E: bellbusk.hitch@virgin.net
I: www.tudorbellbusk.co.uk

BEVERLEY
East Riding of Yorkshire

Apple Tree House ♦♦♦♦
31 Norwood, Beverley,
HU17 9HN
T: (01482) 873615
F: (01482) 873615
E: enquiries@appletreehouse.co.uk
I: www.appletreehouse.co.uk

Beck View Guest House ♦♦♦♦
Beck View House, 1a Blucher Lane, Beverley, HU17 0PT
T: (01482) 882332
E: BeckViewHouse@aol.com

Eastgate Guest House ♦♦♦
7 Eastgate, Beverley, HU17 0DR
T: (01482) 868464
F: (01482) 871899

Market Cross Hotel ♦♦♦
14 Lairgate, Beverley, HU17 8EE
T: (01482) 882573

North Bar Lodge ♦♦♦
28 North Bar, Beverley,
HU17 7AB
T: (01482) 881375
F: (01482) 861184

Number One ♦♦♦
Woodlands, Beverley, HU17 8BT
T: (01482) 862752
F: (01482) 862752
E: neilandsarah@mansle.karoo.co.uk
I: www.beverley.net/accommodation/numberone

The Pipe and Glass Inn ♦♦♦
West End, South Dalton,
Beverley, HU17 7PN
T: (01430) 810246
F: (01430) 810246

Rudstone Walk Country Accommodation and Cottages ♦♦♦♦
South Cave, Brough, HU15 2AH
T: (01430) 422230
F: (01430) 424552
E: office@rudstone-walk.co.uk
I: www.rudstone-walk.co.uk

Springdale Bed and Breakfast ♦♦♦
Springdale Stud, Long Lane,
Beverley, HU17 0RN
T: (01482) 888264

The Tudor Rose Hotel & Restaurant ♦♦♦
Wednesday Market, Beverley,
HU17 0DG
T: (01482) 882028

13 Westfield Avenue ♦♦♦
Beverley, HU17 7KA
T: (01482) 860212

Windmill Inn ♦♦
53 Lairgate, Beverley, HU17 8ET
T: (01482) 862817
F: (01482) 870741

BILSDALE WEST
North Yorkshire

Hill End Farm ♦♦♦
Chop Gate, Middlesbrough
TS9 7JR
T: (01439) 798278

BINGLEY
West Yorkshire

Ashley End ♦♦♦
22 Ashley Road, Bingley,
BD16 1DZ
T: (01274) 569679

Five Rise Locks Restaurant and Rooms ♦♦♦♦ SILVER AWARD
Beck Lane, Bingley, BD16 4DD
T: (01274) 565296
F: (01274) 568828
E: info@five-rise-locks.co.uk
I: www.five-rise-locks.co.uk

March Cote Farm ♦♦♦♦
Off Woodside Avenue,
Cottingley, Bingley BD16 1UB
T: (01274) 487433
F: (01274) 561074
E: jean.warin@nevisuk.net
I: www.yorkshirenet.co.uk/accqde/marchcote

BIRKBY
West Yorkshire

Cherry Tree Bed and Breakfast ♦♦♦♦
Stanwell Royd, Birkby Road,
Birkby, Huddersfield HD2 2BX
T: (01484) 546628
F: (01484) 546628
E: hyatt@royd2.fsnet.co.uk

BISHOP THORNTON
North Yorkshire

Bowes Green Farm ♦♦♦♦
Colber Lane, Bishop Thornton,
Harrogate HG3 3JX
T: (01423) 770114
F: (01423) 770114

Dukes Place ♦♦♦♦
Bishop Thornton, Harrogate
HG3 3JY
T: (01765) 620229
F: (01765) 620454
E: jakimoorhouse@onetel.net.uk

BISHOP WILTON
East Riding of Yorkshire

High Belthorpe ♦♦♦
High Belthorpe, Bishop Wilton,
York YO42 1SB
T: (01759) 368238
I: www.holidayswithdogs.com

BOLTBY
North Yorkshire

Willow Tree Cottage Bed and Breakfast ♦♦♦♦
Boltby, Thirsk YO7 2DY
T: (01845) 537406
F: (01845) 537073
E: townsend.sce@virgin.net

BOLTON PERCY
North Yorkshire

Glebe Farm ♦♦♦♦
Bolton Percy, York YO23 7AL
T: (01904) 744228

BOROUGHBRIDGE
North Yorkshire

Burton Grange ♦♦♦
Helperby, York YO61 2RY
T: (01423) 360825
E: burton_grange@hotmail.com

Primrose Cottage ♦♦♦♦
Lime Bar Lane, Grafton, York
YO51 9QJ
T: (01423) 322835
F: (01423) 323985
E: primrosecottage@btinternet.com

BOSTON SPA
West Yorkshire

Crown Hotel ♦♦♦
128 High Street, Boston Spa,
Wetherby LS23 6BW
T: (01937) 842608
F: (01937) 541373

Four Gables ♦♦♦♦ SILVER AWARD
Oaks Lane, Boston Spa,
Wetherby LS23 6DS
T: (01937) 845592
F: (01937) 845592
E: info@fourgables.co.uk
I: www.fourgables.co.uk

BRADFORD West Yorkshire

Brow Top Farm
♦♦♦♦ SILVER AWARD
Baldwin Lane, Clayton, Bradford BD14 6PS
T: (01274) 882178
F: (01274) 882178
E: ruthpriestley@farmersweekly.co.uk
I: www.browtopfarm.co.uk

Carnoustie ♦♦♦
8 Park Grove, Bradford, BD9 4JY
T: (01274) 490561
F: (01274) 490561
E: carnoustie1@activemail.co.uk

Castle Hotel
Rating Applied For
20 Grattan Road, Bradford, BD1 2LU
T: (01274) 393166
F: (01274) 393200
E: rooms@castle-bfd.freeserve.co.uk
I: www.thecastlehotel.britain-uk.com

Hillside House ♦♦♦
10 Hazelhurst Road, Daisy Hill, Bradford, BD9 6BJ
T: (01274) 542621

Ivy Guest House ♦♦
3 Melbourne Place, Bradford, BD5 0HZ
T: (01274) 727060
F: (01274) 306347
E: nickbaggio@aol.com

New Beehive Inn ♦♦♦
171 Westgate, Bradford, BD1 3AA
T: (01274) 721784
F: (01274) 375092

Norland Guest House ♦♦♦
695 Great Horton Road, Bradford, BD7 4DU
T: (01274) 571698
F: (01274) 503290
E: pipin@ic24.net
I: www.norlandguesthouse.gbr.cc

Shaw House ♦♦♦
35 bierley Lane, Bierley, Bradford, BD4 6AD
T: (01274) 682929

Westleigh Hotel ♦♦♦
30 Easby Road, Bradford, BD7 1QX
T: (01274) 727089
F: (01274) 394658
E: info@thewestleighhotel.co.uk
I: www.thewestleighhotel.co.uk

Woodlands Guest House ♦♦♦♦
2 The Grove, Shelf, Halifax HX3 7PD
T: (01274) 677533

BRAMHOPE West Yorkshire

The Cottages
♦♦♦♦ SILVER AWARD
Moor Road, Bramhope, Leeds LS16 9HH
T: (0113) 284 2754
F: (0113) 203 7496

BRIDLINGTON East Riding of Yorkshire

Balmoral Private Hotel ♦♦♦
21 Marshall Avenue, Bridlington, YO15 2DT
T: (01262) 676678
F: (01262) 676678
E: hotel@balmoral-bridlington.co.uk
I: www.balmoral-hotel.net

Bay Court Hotel
♦♦♦♦ SILVER AWARD
35a Sands Lane, Bridlington, YO15 2JG
T: (01262) 676288
E: bay.court@virgin.net
I: www.baycourt.co.uk

Bay Ridge Hotel ♦♦♦
11 Summerfield Road, Bridlington, YO15 3LF
T: (01262) 673425
I: bridlington.net/business/bayridge/index.html

Belmont ♦♦♦
27 Flamborough Road, Bridlington, YO15 2HU
T: (01262) 673808

Blantyre House Hotel ♦♦♦
21 Pembroke Terrace, Bridlington, YO15 3BX
T: (01262) 400660
E: baker@blantyre21.fsnet.co.uk

Bluebell Guest House ♦♦♦
3 St Annes Road, Bridlington, YO15 2JB
T: (01262) 675163
E: judith@mybluebell.com
I: www.mybluebell.com

Bon Accord ♦♦
64 Windsor Crescent, Bridlington, YO15 3JA
T: (01262) 675589

Bosville Arms Country Hotel ♦♦♦
High Street, Rudston, Driffield YO25 4UB
T: (01262) 420259
F: (01262) 420259
E: hogan@bosville.freeserve.co.uk
I: www.bosville.freeserve.co.uk

The Brockton Hotel ♦♦♦
4 Shaftesbury Road, Bridlington, YO15 3NP
T: (01262) 673967
F: (01262) 673967
E: grbrocktonhotel@aol.com

The Chimes
Rating Applied For
9 Wellington Road, Bridlington, YO15 2BA
T: (01262) 401659
F: (01262) 401659
E: sandisbb@aol.com
I: www.smoothhound.co.uk/hotels/chimesgu.html

The Crescent Hotel ♦♦♦
12 The Crescent, Bridlington, YO15 2NX
T: (01262) 401015
F: (01262) 400465

Dulverton Court Hotel ♦♦♦
17 Victoria Road, Bridlington, YO15 2BW
T: (01262) 672600

Edelweiss ♦♦♦
86/88 Windsor Crescent, Bridlington, YO15 3JA
T: (01262) 673822
F: (01262) 673822

The Grantlea Guest House ♦♦♦
2 South Street, Bridlington, YO15 3BY
T: (01262) 400190

Lansdowne Lodge ♦♦♦
14 Lansdowne Crescent, Bridlington, YO15 2QR
T: (01262) 400760

London Hotel ♦♦♦
1 Royal Crescent, York Road, Bridlington, YO15 2PF
T: (01262) 675377

Longcroft Hotel ♦♦♦♦
100 Trinity Road, Bridlington, YO15 2HF
T: (01262) 672180
F: (01262) 608240
E: longcroft53@hotmail.com

The Mayville Guest House ♦♦♦
74 Marshall Avenue, Bridlington, YO15 2DS
T: (01262) 674420
F: (01262) 674420

The Mount Hotel ♦♦♦♦
2 Roundhay Roud, Bridlington, YO15 3JY
T: (01262) 672306
F: (01262) 672306

Newcliffe Hotel ♦♦♦
6 Belgrave Road, Bridlington, YO15 3JR
T: (01262) 674244

Promenade Hotel ♦♦♦
121 Promenade, Bridlington, YO15 2QN
T: (01262) 602949

Queens Hotel ♦♦♦
75/77 High Street, Bridlington, YO16 4PN
T: (01262) 672051

Rags Restaurant & Dyl's Hotel ♦♦♦
South Pier, Southcliff Road, Bridlington, YO15 3AN
T: (01262) 400355
F: (01262) 674729
E: lesdylrags@freedomland.co.uk
I: bridlington.net/accommodation

Rivendell Hotel ♦♦♦
19 Sands Lane, Bridlington, YO15 2JG
T: (01262) 679189

Rosebery House ♦♦♦♦
1 Belle Vue, Tennyson Ave, Bridlington, YO15 2ET
T: (01262) 670336
F: (01262) 608381

St Aubyn's Hotel ♦♦♦
111-113 Cardigan Road, Bridlington, YO15 3LP
T: (01262) 673002

Sandringham House Hotel ♦♦
11 The Crescent, Bridlington, YO15 2NX
T: (01262) 672064
F: (01262) 424631
E: sandringham-hotel@talk21.com

Sandsend Hotel ♦♦
8 Sandslane, Bridlington, YO15 2JE
T: (01262) 673265

Seawinds Guest House ♦♦♦
48 Horsforth Avenue, Bridlington, YO15 3DF
T: (01262) 676330
E: seawinds@btinternet.com

Shellbourne Hotel ♦♦♦
14-16 Summerfield Road, Bridlington, YO15 3LF
T: (01262) 674697

South Dene Hotel ♦♦
94-96 Horsforth Avenue, Bridlington, YO15 3DF
T: (01262) 674436

Spinnaker House Hotel ♦♦♦♦
19 Pembroke Terrace, Bridlington, YO15 3BX
T: (01262) 678440
F: (01262) 678440

Springfield Private Hotel ♦♦♦
12 Trinity Road, Bridlington, YO15 2EY
T: (01262) 672896

Stonmar Guest House ♦♦♦
15 Flamborough Road, Bridlington, YO15 2HU
T: (01262) 674580
F: (01262) 674580

Strathmore Hotel ♦♦♦
63-65 Horsforth Avenue, Bridlington, YO15 3DH
T: (01262) 602828
F: (01262) 602828
E: strathmore_hotel@compuserve.com
I: www.bridlington-ey.freeserve.co.uk

Sunflower Lodge ♦♦♦
24 Flamborough Road, Bridlington, YO15 2HX
T: (01262) 400447

The Tennyson Hotel ♦♦♦♦
19 Tennyson Avenue, Bridlington, YO15 2EU
T: (01262) 604382
I: www.bridlington.net/accommodation/hotels/tennyson

Three Gables Private Hotel ♦♦♦
37 Windsor Crescent, Bridlington, YO15 3HZ
T: (01262) 673826
E: 3gables@web.com

Trinity Hotel ♦♦♦
9 Trinity Road, Bridlington, YO15 2EZ
T: (01262) 670444
F: (01262) 670444
E: trinityhotel@btconnect.com
I: www.trinityhotel.co.uk

Vernon Villa Guesthouse ♦♦♦♦
2 Vernon Road, Bridlington, YO15 2HQ
T: (01262) 670661
E: catherine@sdinardo.freeserve.co.uk

Victoria Hotel ♦♦♦
25/27 Victoria Road, Bridlington, YO15 2AT
T: (01262) 673871
F: (01262) 609431
E: victoria.hotel@virgin.net
I: www.victoriahotelbridlington.co.uk

Waverley Hotel ♦♦♦
105 Cardigan Road, Bridlington, YO15 3LP
T: (01262) 671040
E: waverley.hotel@bridlington.worldonline.co.uk

The White Rose ♦♦♦
123 Cardigan Road, Bridlington, YO15 3LP
T: (01262) 673245
F: (01262) 401362
E: c.a.young@tesco.net
I: www.smoothhound.co.uk/hotels/thewhiterose

Winston House Hotel ♦♦♦
5-6 South Street, Bridlington, YO15 3BY
T: (01262) 670216
F: (01262) 670216
E: bob.liz@winstonhouse.fsnet.co.uk
I: www.winston-house.co.uk

BRIGG
North Lincolnshire

Albert House ♦♦♦♦
23 Bigby Street, Brigg, DN20 8ED
T: (01652) 658081

Arties Mill ♦♦♦♦
Wressle Road, Castlethorpe, Brigg DN20 9LF
T: (01652) 652094
F: (01652) 657107
E: enquiries@artiesmill.com
I: www.artiesmill.com

Holcombe Guest House ♦♦♦
34 Victoria Road, Barnetby, DN38 6JR
T: 07850 764002
F: (01652) 680841
E: holcombe.house@virgin.net
I: www.holcombeguesthouse.co.uk

Lord Nelson Hotel & Hardy's Cafe Bar ♦♦♦
Market Place, Brigg, DN20 8LD
T: (01652) 652127
F: (01652) 658952

The Woolpack Hotel ♦♦
4 Market Place, Brigg, DN20 8HA
T: (01652) 655649
F: (01652) 655649
E: harry@woolpack488.freeserve.co.uk
I: www.woolpack-hotel.co.uk

BRIGSLEY
Lincolnshire

Prospect Farm ♦♦♦♦
Waltham Road, Brigsley, Grimsby DN37 0RQ
T: (01472) 826491
E: prospectfarm@btchick.com
I: www.nelincs.gov.uk

BROUGH
East Riding of Yorkshire

Woldway ♦♦♦
10 Elloughton Road, Brough, HU15 1AE
T: (01482) 667666
I: www.woldway.co.uk

BUCKDEN
North Yorkshire

Low Raisgill ♦♦♦♦
Hubberholme, Skipton BD23 5JQ
T: (01756) 760351

Redmire Farm
♦♦♦♦ SILVER AWARD
Upper Wharfedale, Buckden, Skipton BD23 5JD
T: (01756) 760253

The White Lion Inn ♦♦♦
Cray, Buckden, Skipton BD23 5JB
T: (01756) 760262
F: (01756) 761024
E: admin.whitelion@btinternet.com
I: www.whitelioncray.com

BULMER
North Yorkshire

Grange Farm ♦♦♦
Castle Howard, Bulmer, York YO60 7BN
T: (01653) 618376
F: (01653) 618600
E: foster@grangefarm35.fsnet.co.uk
I: www.grangefarmbulmer.co.uk

Lower Barn ♦♦♦♦
Wandales Lane, Castle Howard, Bulmer, York YO60 7ES
T: (01653) 618575
F: (01653) 618575
E: isabelhall@lowerbarn.fsnet.co.uk
I: www.lowerbarn.fsnet.co.uk

BURLEY IN WHARFEDALE
West Yorkshire

Hillcrest ♦♦♦
24 Hill Crescent, Burley in Wharfedale, Ilkley LS29 7QG
T: (01943) 863258
F: 07801 865609

Upstairs, Downstairs ♦♦♦
3 Elm Grove, Burley in Wharfedale, Ilkley LS29 7PL
T: (01943) 862567

BURNSALL
North Yorkshire

Valley View ♦♦♦♦
Burnsall, Skipton BD23 6BN
T: (01756) 720314
F: (01756) 720314
E: fitton_valley_view@lineone.net

BURNT YATES
North Yorkshire

High Winsley Farm ♦♦♦
Burnt Yates, Harrogate HG3 3EP
T: (01423) 770376
E: highwinsley@aol.com

The New Inn Hotel ♦♦♦♦
Burnt Yates, Harrogate HG3 3EG
T: (01423) 771070
E: enquiries@newinnburntyates.co.uk
I: www.newinnburntyates.co.uk

BURTON AGNES
East Riding of Yorkshire

Park Farm House ♦♦
Main Road, Burton Agnes, Driffield YO25 4NA
T: (01262) 490394
F: (01262) 490394

CARLTON
North Yorkshire

Abbots Thorn ♦♦♦♦
Carlton, Leyburn DL8 4AY
T: (01969) 640620
F: (01969) 640304
E: abbots.thorn@virgin.net
I: www.abbotsthorn.co.uk

Foxwood ♦♦♦
Carr Lane, Carlton, Wakefield WF3 3RT
T: (0113) 282 4786
F: (0113) 282 4786

Middleham House ♦♦♦
Carlton, Leyburn DL8 4BB
T: (01969) 640645
E: trevorw.smith@virgin.net

CARLTON HUSTHWAITE
North Yorkshire

Crofts ♦♦♦♦
Carlton Husthwaite, Thirsk YO7 2BJ
T: (01845) 501325
F: (01845) 501325

CARLTON MINIOTT
North Yorkshire

The Poplars ♦♦♦♦
Carlton Miniott, Thirsk YO7 4LX
T: (01845) 522712
F: (01845) 522712
E: chrischilton.thepoplars@virginnet
I: www.yorkshirebandb.co.uk

CASTLE HOWARD
North Yorkshire

Lowry's Restaurant and Guest House ♦♦♦
Malton Road, Slingsby, York YO62 4AF
T: (01653) 628417
E: dgwilliams@onetel.net.uk

CASTLEFORD
West Yorkshire

Broadleigh House ♦♦♦♦
14 Hillcrest Ave, Townville, Castleford, WF10 3WL
T: (01977) 550102
F: (01977) 550102
E: jeanadamsuk@yahoo.co.uk
I: www.smoothhound.co.uk/hotels/broadleigh

CATTERICK
North Yorkshire

Rose Cottage Guest House ♦♦♦
26 High Street, Catterick, Richmond DL10 7LJ
T: (01748) 811164

CHAPEL ALLERTON
West Yorkshire

Green House ♦♦♦
5 Bank View, Chapel Allerton, Leeds LS7 2EX
T: (0113) 268 1380
E: anniegreen11@hotmail.com

CHAPELTOWN
South Yorkshire

The Norfolk Arms ♦♦♦
White Lane, Chapeltown, Sheffield S35 2YG
T: (0114) 2402016
F: (0114) 2468414
E: norfharri@aol.com

CHERRY BURTON
East Riding of Yorkshire

Burton Mount
♦♦♦♦♦ SILVER AWARD
Malton Road, Cherry Burton, Beverley HU17 7RA
T: (01964) 550541
F: (01964) 551955
E: pg@burtonmount.co.uk
I: www.burtonmount.co.uk

CHOP GATE
North Yorkshire

Beacon Guest Farm ♦♦♦
Chop Gate, Middlesbrough TS9 7JS
T: (01439) 798320
F: (01439) 798320

CLAPHAM
North Yorkshire

Brook House ♦♦♦
Station Road, Clapham, Lancaster LA2 8ER
T: (01524) 251580
E: brookhousecafe@yahoo.co.uk

Flying Horseshoe Hotel ♦♦♦
Clapham Station, Clapham, Lancaster LA2 8ES
T: (01524) 251229

CLEASBY
North Yorkshire

Cleasby House ♦♦♦♦
Cleasby, Darlington DL2 2QY
T: (01325) 350160
E: junehirst@aol.com

CLEETHORPES
North East Lincolnshire

Hotel 77 ♦♦♦
77 Kingsway, Cleethorpes, DN35 0AB
T: (01472) 692035
F: (01472) 692035
E: hotel77@knox24.fsbusiness.comuk

Abbeydale Guest House ♦♦♦
39 Isaacs Hill, Cleethorpes, DN35 8JT
T: (01472) 692248
F: (01472) 311088
E: info@abbeydaleguesthouse.co.uk
I: www.abbeydaleguesthouse.com

Adelaide Hotel ♦♦♦♦
41 Isaacs Hill, Cleethorpes, DN35 8JT
T: (01472) 693594
F: (01472) 329717
E: robertcallison@ntlworld.com
I: www.adelaide-hotel.com

Alpine Guest House ♦♦♦
55 Clee Road, Cleethorpes, DN35 8AD
T: (01472) 690804

Ascot Lodge Guest House ♦♦♦
11 Princes Road, Cleethorpes, DN35 8AW
T: (01472) 290129
F: (01472) 290129
E: ascotclee@aol.com
I: www.ascotlodgeguesthouse.co.uk

Brentwood Guest House ♦♦♦
9 Princes Road, Cleethorpes, DN35 8AW
T: (01472) 693982
E: brentwoodguesthouse@hotmail.com
I: www.brentwoodguesthouse.co.uk/

Brier Parks Guest House ♦♦
27 Clee Road, Cleethorpes, DN35 8AD
T: (01472) 605591
E: a.brierley1@ntlworld.com
I: www.thebrierparks.co.uk

Clee House ♦♦♦♦
31-33 Clee Road, Cleethorpes, DN35 8AD
T: (01472) 200850
F: (01472) 200850
E: david@cleehouse.com
I: www.cleehouse.com

Comat Hotel ♦♦♦♦
26 Yarra Road, Cleethorpes, DN35 8LS
T: (01472) 694791
F: (01472) 592823
E: comat-hotel@ntlworld.com
I: www.comat-hotel.co.uk

Ginnies ♦♦♦
27 Queens Parade, Cleethorpes, DN35 0DF
T: (01472) 694997
F: (01472) 316799
E: kimkwood@aol.com
I: www.ginniesguesthousecleethorpes.co.uk

Gladson Guest House ♦♦♦
43 Isaacs Hill, Cleethorpes, DN35 8JT
T: (01472) 694858
F: (01472) 239642
E: enquiries@gladsonguesthouse.co.uk
I: www.gladsonguesthouse.co.uk

The Saxon House Hotel ♦♦♦♦
70 St Peters Avenue, Cleethorpes, DN35 8HP
T: (01472) 697427
F: (01472) 602696
E: reservations@saxonhouse-hotel.co.uk

Sherwood Guest House ♦♦♦
15 Kingsway, Cleethorpes, DN35 8QU
T: (01472) 692020
F: (01472) 239177
E: sherwood.guesthouse@ntlworld.com
I: www.sherwoodguesthouse.co.uk

Tudor Terrace Guest House ♦♦♦♦
11 Bradford Avenue, Cleethorpes, DN35 0BB
T: (01472) 600800
F: (01472) 501395
E: enquiries.tudorterrace@btinternet.com
I: www.tudorterrace.co.uk

White Rose Guest House ♦♦♦
3 Princes Road, Cleethorpes, DN35 8AW
T: (01472) 695060

CLIFTON
North Yorkshire

Avenue Guest House ♦♦♦
6 The Avenue, Clifton, York YO30 6AS
T: (01904) 620575
E: allen@avenuegh.fsnet.co.uk
I: www.avenuegh.fsnet.co.uk

CLOUGHTON
North Yorkshire

Cober Hill ♦♦♦
Newlands Road, Cloughton, Scarborough YO13 0AR
T: (01723) 870310
F: (01723) 870271
E: enquireis@coberhill.co.uk
I: www.coberhill.co.uk

COTTINGHAM
East Riding of Yorkshire

Kenwood House ♦♦♦
7 Newgate Street, Cottingham, HU16 4DY
T: (01482) 847558

COUNTERSETT
North Yorkshire

Carr End House ♦♦♦♦
Countersett, Askrigg, Leyburn DL8 3DE
T: (01969) 650346

COWESBY
North Yorkshire

Springfield House ♦♦♦♦
Cowesby, Thirsk YO7 2JL
T: (01845) 537063
F: (01845) 537063
E: patti910@yahoo.com

COWLING
North Yorkshire

Woodland House
Rating Applied For
2 Woodland Street, Cowling, Keighley BD22 0BS
T: (01535) 637886
E: susansandybb@hotmail.com
I: www.woodland-house.co.uk

COXWOLD
North Yorkshire

Newburgh House ♦♦♦♦♦
Coxwold, York YO61 4AS
T: (01347) 868177
F: (01347) 868046
E: info@newburghhouse.co.uk
I: www.newburghhouse.co.uk

CRAGG VALE
West Yorkshire

Hinchliffe Arms ♦♦♦
Cragg Vale, Hebden Bridge HX7 5TA
T: (01422) 883256
F: (01422) 886216
E: phil.chaplin@ukonline.co.uk
I: www.hinchliffearms.com

CRAYKE
North Yorkshire

The Hermitage ♦♦♦
Mill Lane, Crayke, York YO61 4TB
T: (01347) 821635

CROFTON
West Yorkshire

Redbeck Motel Ltd ♦♦
Doncaster Road, Crofton, Wakefield WF4 1RR
T: (01924) 862730
F: (01924) 862937
I: www.redbeckmotel.co.uk

CROPTON
North Yorkshire

High Farm
♦♦♦♦ SILVER AWARD
Cropton, Pickering YO18 8HL
T: (01751) 417461
F: (01751) 417807
E: highfarmcropton@aol.com
I: www.hhml.com/bb/highfarmcropton.htm

New Inn and Cropton Brewery ♦♦♦
Cropton, Pickering YO18 8HH
T: (01751) 417330
F: (01751) 417582
E: newinn@cropton.fsbusiness.co.uk
I: www.croptonbrewery.co.uk

CROXTON
North Lincolnshire

Croxton House
Rating Applied For
Croxton, Ulceby DN39 6YD
T: (01652) 688306
F: (01652) 680577
E: k_gallimore@yahoo.co.uk/k_gallimore@yahool.co.uk

CULLINGWORTH
West Yorkshire

The Five Flags Hotel
Rating Applied For
Manywells Height, Cullingworth, Bradford BD13 5EA
T: (01274) 834188
F: (01274) 833340
E: fiveflags@hotmail.com
I: www.fiveflagshotel.com

CUNDALL
North Yorkshire

Cundall Lodge Farm
♦♦♦♦ SILVER AWARD
Cundall, York YO61 2RN
T: (01423) 360203
F: (01423) 360805
E: cundalllodgefarm@hotmail.com
I: www.cundalllodgefarm.free-online.co.uk

DACRE BANKS
North Yorkshire

Dalriada ♦♦♦
Cabin Lane, Dacre Banks, Harrogate HG3 4EE
T: (01423) 780512

Gate Eel Farm ♦♦♦♦
Dacre Banks, Harrogate HG3 4ED
T: (01423) 781707

The Royal Oak Inn ♦♦♦♦
Oak Lane, Dacre Banks, Harrogate HG3 4EN
T: (01423) 780200
F: (01423) 781748
E: enquiries@the royaloak.uk.com
I: www.theroyaloak.uk.com

DALTON
North Yorkshire

Dalton Hall ♦♦♦♦
Dalton, Richmond DL11 7HU
T: (01833) 621339

Throstle Gill Farm ♦♦♦♦
Dalton, Richmond DL11 7HZ
T: (01833) 621363
F: (01833) 621363

Ye Jolly Farmers of Olden Times ♦♦♦
Dalton, Thirsk YO7 3HY
T: (01845) 577359

DANBY
North Yorkshire

Botton Grove Farm ♦♦♦
Danby Head, Danby, Whitby YO21 2NH
T: (01287) 660284
E: judytait@bottongrove.freeserve.co.uk

Crag Farm ♦♦♦♦
Danby, Whitby YO21 2LQ
T: (01287) 660279
F: (01287) 660279
E: sal.b.b.cragfarm.n.y.@ukgateway.net

Crossley Gate Farm House
♦♦♦♦ SILVER AWARD
Crossley Gate Farm, Little Fryup, Danby, Whitby YO21 2NR
T: (01287) 660165

Duke of Wellington Inn ♦♦♦♦
Danby, Whitby YO21 2LY
T: (01287) 660351
E: landlord@dukeofwellington.freeserve.co.uk
I: www.danby-dukeofwellington.co.uk

Rowantree Farm ♦♦♦
Ainthorpe, Whitby YO21 2LE
T: (01287) 660396
E: krbsatindall@aol.com

Stonebeck Gate Farm ♦♦♦
Little Fryup, Danby, Whitby YO21 2NS
T: (01287) 660363
F: (01287) 660363
I: www.stonebeckgatefarm.co.uk

Sycamore House ♦♦♦
Danby Dale, Danby, Whitby YO21 2NW
T: (01287) 660125
F: (01287) 669122
E: sycamore.danby@btinternet.com
I: www.smoothhound.co.uk/hotels/sycamore1.html

DARLEY
North Yorkshire

Brimham Guest house ♦♦♦♦
Brookfield, Silverdale Close, Darley, Harrogate HG3 2PQ
T: (01423) 780948

Elsinglea Guest House ♦♦♦♦
Sheepcote Lane, Darley, Harrogate HG3 2RW
T: (01423) 781069
F: (01423) 780189
I: www.elsingleaguesthouse.homestead.com/homepage.html

DEEPDALE
North Lincolnshire

West Wold Farmhouse ♦♦♦♦
West Wold Farm, Deepdale, Barton-upon-Humber DN18 6ED
T: (01652) 633293
F: (01652) 633293
E: westworldfarm@aol.com

DEIGHTON
North Yorkshire

Grimston House ♦♦♦
Deighton, York YO19 6HB
T: (01904) 728328
F: (01904) 720093
E: grimstonhouse@talk21.com
I: www.grimstonhouse.com

Rush Farm ♦♦♦
Rush Farm, York Road, Deighton, York YO19 6HQ
T: (01904) 728459
E: david@rushfarm.fsnet.co.uk
I: www.rushfarm.fsnet.co.uk

DENBY DALE
West Yorkshire

Eastfield Cottage ♦♦♦♦
248 Wakefield Road, Denby Dale, Huddersfield HD8 8SU
T: (01484) 861562

DONCASTER
South Yorkshire

Ashlea Hotel ♦♦
81 Thorne Road, Doncaster, DN1 2ES
T: (01302) 363374
F: (01302) 760215
E: brigby@ashlea25.freeserve.co.uk

The Balmoral Hotel ♦♦♦
129 Thorne Road, Doncaster, DN2 5BH
T: (01302) 364385
F: (01302) 364385
E: thebalmoralhotel@bt.connect.com
I: www.thebalmoralhotel@bt.connect.com

The Grange Guesthouse
Rating Applied For
Grange Road, Moorends Thorne, Doncaster, DN8 4LS
T: (01405) 815028
F: (01405) 815028
E: cliftonproprerties@btinternet.com

Low Farm
♦♦♦♦♦ SILVER AWARD
The Green, Clayton, Doncaster DN5 7DB
T: (01977) 648433
F: (01977) 640472
E: bar@lowfarm.freeserve.co.uk
I: www.lowfarm.freeserve.co.uk

Lyntone Hotel ♦♦♦
24 Avenue Road, Wheatley, Doncaster, DN2 4AQ
T: (01302) 361586
F: (01302) 361079

DOWNHOLME
North Yorkshire

Walburn Hall
Rating Applied For
Downholme, Richmond DL11 6AF
T: (01748) 822152
F: (01748) 822152
E: walburnhall@farmersweekly.net

DRIFFIELD
East Riding of Yorkshire

Kelleythorpe Farm ♦♦♦
Driffield, YO25 9DW
T: (01377) 252297
E: jhopper@kelleythorpe.fsbusiness.co.uk

DUNFORD BRIDGE
South Yorkshire

Stanhope Arms Inn
Rating Applied For
Windle Edge Road, Dunford Bridge, Sheffield S36 4TF
T: (01226) 763104
F: (01226) 765022
E: stanhopearms@tiscali.co.uk
I: www.stanhopearms.co.uk

DUNGWORTH
South Yorkshire

Rickett Field Farm ♦♦♦
Sidlings Hollow, Dungworth, Bradfield, Sheffield S6 6HA
T: (0114) 285 1218
E: shepherd@rickettlathe.freeserve.co.uk

The Royal Hotel ♦♦♦♦
Main Road, Dungworth, Bradfield, Sheffield S6 6HF
T: (0114) 285 1213
F: (0114) 285 1723
E: reception@royalhotel-dungworth.co.uk
I: www.royalhotel-dungworth.co.uk

EASINGWOLD
North Yorkshire

Allerton House ♦♦♦
34 Uppleby, Easingwold, York YO61 3BB
T: (01347) 821912

The Old Vicarage
♦♦♦♦ GOLD AWARD
Market Place, Easingwold, York YO61 3AL
T: (01347) 821015
F: (01347) 823465
E: kirman@oldvic-easingwold.freeserve.co.uk
I: www.oldvicarage.co.uk

Thornton Lodge Farm
Rating Applied For
Thornton Hill, Easingwold, York YO61 3QA
T: (01347) 821306
F: (01347) 821306
E: sue@loumic.demon.co.uk
I: www.thorntonlodgefarm.co.uk

Yeoman's Course House ♦♦♦
Thornton Hill, Easingwold, York YO61 3PY
T: (01347) 868126
F: (01347) 868129
E: chris@yeomanscourse.fsnet.co.uk

EAST HESLERTON
North Yorkshire

Manor Farm ♦♦♦
East Heslerton, Malton YO17 8RN
T: (01944) 728268
F: (01944) 728277
E: bandb@manorfarmholidays.co.uk
I: www.manorfarmholidays.co.uk

EAST MARTON
North Yorkshire

Drumlins ♦♦♦♦
Heber Drive, East Marton, Skipton BD23 3LS
T: (01282) 843521
I: www.yorkshiredales.net/stayat/drumlins

EASTBY
North Yorkshire

The Masons Arms Inn ♦♦♦
Barden Road, Eastby, Skipton BD23 6SN
T: (01756) 792754

EBBERSTON
North Yorkshire

Foxholm Hotel ♦♦♦
Ebberston, Scarborough YO13 9NJ
T: (01723) 859550
F: (01723) 859550
E: kay@foxholm.freeserve.co.uk
I: www.foxholm.freeserve.co.uk

Littlegarth
♦♦♦♦ SILVER AWARD
High Street, Ebberston, Scarborough YO13 9PA
T: (01723) 850045
F: (01723) 850151

Studley House ♦♦♦♦
67 Main Street, Ebberston, Scarborough YO13 9NR
T: (01723) 859285
F: (01723) 859285
E: ernie@jhodgson.fsnet.co.uk
I: www.studley-house.co.uk

EGTON
North Yorkshire

Flushing Meadow ♦♦♦
Egton, Whitby YO21 1UA
T: (01947) 895395
F: (01947) 895395
E: flushing_meadow_egton@yahoo.co.uk

EGTON BRIDGE
North Yorkshire

Broom House ♦♦♦♦
Broom House Lane, Egton Bridge, Whitby YO21 1XD
T: (01947) 895279
F: (01947) 895657
E: welcome@broomhouseegtonbridge.freeserve.co.uk
I: www.egton/bridge.co.uk

The Postgate ♦♦♦
Egton Bridge, Whitby YO21 1UX
T: (01947) 895241
F: (01947) 895111
I: www.touristnetuk.com/ne/postgate

ELLINGSTRING
North Yorkshire

Holybreen ♦♦♦
Ellingstring, Ripon HG4 4PW
T: (01677) 460216
F: (01677) 460106
E: anne.wright@virgin.net

EMBSAY
North Yorkshire

Bondcroft Farm ♦♦♦♦
Embsay, Skipton BD23 6SF
T: (01756) 793371
F: (01756) 793371
E: bondcroftfarm@bondcroftfarm.yorks.net
I: www.bondcroft.yorks.net

FACEBY
North Yorkshire

Four Wynds Bed and Breakfast ♦♦♦
Whorl Hill, Faceby, Stokesley, Middlesbrough TS9 7BZ
T: (01642) 701315
F: (01642) 701315

FADMOOR
North Yorkshire

Mount Pleasant ♦♦♦
Rudland, Fadmoor, York YO62 7JJ
T: (01751) 431579
E: info@mountpleasantbedandbreakfast.co.uk
I: www.mountpleasantbedandbreakfast.co.uk

FEATHERSTONE
West Yorkshire

Rolands Croft Guest House ♦♦
Waldenhowe Close, Ackton Lane, Featherstone, Pontefract WF7 6ED
T: (01977) 790802
F: (01977) 790802
E: sut3@ail.com
I: www.rolandscroft.co.uk

FILEY
North Yorkshire

Abbot's Leigh Hotel ♦♦♦
7 Rutland Street, Filey, YO14 9JA
T: (01723) 513334
E: barbara_abbots@yahoo.com

Athol Guest House ♦♦♦♦
67 West Avenue, Filey, YO14 9AX
T: (01723) 515189
E: baker@athol67.freeserve.co.uk

Cherries ♦♦♦♦
59 West Avenue, Filey, YO14 9AX
T: (01723) 513299
E: cherriesfiley@hotmail.com

The Edwardian Guest House
Rating Applied For
2 Brooklands, Filey, YO14 9BA
T: (01273) 514557

The Forge
Rating Applied For
23 Rutland Street, Filey, YO14 9JA
T: (01723) 512379
E: mikeforgefiley@aol.com

Gables Guest House ♦♦♦♦
Rutland Street, Filey, YO14 9JB
T: (01723) 514750
E: kate_gables@talk21.com

Seafield Hotel ♦♦♦
9-11 Rutland Street, Filey, YO14 9JA
T: (01723) 513715

'This'll do' Binton Guest House ♦♦♦
25 West Avenue, Filey, YO14 9AX
T: (01723) 513753

FITLING
East Riding of Yorkshire

Westfield Farm Bed & Breakfast ♦♦♦
Fitling, Hull HU12 9AL
T: (01964) 527353
F: (01964) 527353

FREMINGTON
North Yorkshire

Broadlands Bed & Breakfast ♦♦♦
Fremington, Richmond DL11 6AW
T: (01748) 884297
F: (01748) 884297

FRIDAYTHORPE
East Riding of Yorkshire

Manor House Inn and Restaurant ♦♦♦♦
Fridaythorpe, Driffield YO25 9RT
T: (01377) 288221
F: (01377) 288402

FRYUP
North Yorkshire

Crossley Side Farm ♦♦♦♦
Fryup, Danby, Whitby YO21 2NR
T: (01287) 660313
E: ruth.sjsfarm@farmersweekly.net

Furnace Farm ♦♦♦
Fryup, Danby, Whitby YO21 2AP
T: (01947) 897271

FYLINGTHORPE
North Yorkshire

Croft Farm ♦♦♦♦
Church Lane, Fylingthorpe, Whitby YO22 4PW
T: (01947) 880231
F: (01947) 880231

Sunnybrook ♦♦♦
Fylingthorpe, Whitby YO22 4UA
T: (01947) 880980

GANTON
North Yorkshire

Cherry Tree Cottage ♦♦♦
23 Main Street, Ganton, Scarborough YO12 4NR
T: (01944) 710507
E: iris@hallaways.freeserve.co.uk
I: www.gantonholidays.co.uk

GARFORTH
West Yorkshire

Myrtle House ♦♦♦
31 Wakefield Road, Garforth, Leeds LS25 1AN
T: (0113) 286 6445

GARGRAVE
North Yorkshire

The Old Swan Inn ♦♦♦
20 High Street, Gargrave, Skipton BD23 3RB
T: (01756) 749232
F: (01756) 749232

GAYLE
North Yorkshire

Blackburn Farm/Trout Fishery ♦♦♦
Blackburn Farm, Gayle, Hawes DL8 3NX
T: (01969) 667524
E: blackburnfarm@hotmail.com
I: www.dalesaccommodation.com/blackburnfarm

Hunters Hill Bed and Breakfast ♦♦♦♦
Gayle, Hawes DL8 3RZ
T: (01969) 667137
E: clive@firehunter.freeserve.co.uk

Rookhurst Country House Hotel ♦♦♦♦♦ SILVER AWARD
West End, Gayle, Hawes DL8 3RT
T: (01969) 667454
F: (01969) 667128
E: rookhurst@lineone.net
I: www.rookhurst.co.uk

Thimble Cottage ♦♦♦
Gayle Lane, Gayle, Hawes DL8 3RP
T: (01969) 667828

GIGGLESWICK
North Yorkshire

Black Horse Hotel ♦♦♦
Church Street, Giggleswick, Settle BD24 0BE
T: (01729) 822506

The Harts Head Hotel ♦♦♦♦
Belle Hill, Giggleswick, Settle BD24 0BA
T: (01729) 822086
F: (01729) 824992
E: hartshead@hotel52.freeserve.co.uk

GILDERSOME
West Yorkshire

End Lea ♦♦♦♦
39 Town Street, Gildersome, Morley, Leeds LS27 7AX
T: (0113) 252 1661

GILLAMOOR
North Yorkshire

Manor Farm ♦♦♦
Gillamoor, York YO62 7HX
T: (01751) 432695
F: (01751) 432695

Royal Oak Inn ♦♦♦
Main Street, Gillamoor, York YO62 7HX
T: (01751) 431414
F: (01751) 431414

GLAISDALE
North Yorkshire

Egton Banks Farm ♦♦♦♦
Glaisdale, Whitby YO21 2QP
T: (01947) 897289
E: egtonbanksfarm@agriplus.net
I: www.egtonbanksfarm.agriplus.net

Hollins Farm ♦♦♦
Glaisdale, Whitby YO21 2PZ
T: (01947) 897516

London House Farm ♦♦♦
Dale Head, Glaisdale, Whitby YO21 2PZ
T: (01530) 836122
F: (01947) 897166
E: marydanaher@hotmail.com
I: www.londonhousefarm.com

GOATHLAND
North Yorkshire

Barnet House Guest House ♦♦♦
Goathland, Whitby YO22 5NG
T: (01947) 896201
F: (01947) 896201
E: barnethouse@hotmail.com
I: www.barnethouse.co.uk

The Beacon Guest House ♦♦♦♦ SILVER AWARD
The Beacon, Goathland, Whitby YO22 5AN
T: (01947) 896409
F: (01947) 896431
E: stewartkatz@compuserve.com
I: www.touristnetuk.com/ne/beacon.

Fairhaven Country Hotel ♦♦♦
The Common, Goathland, Whitby YO22 5AN
T: (01947) 896361
F: (01947) 896099
E: royellis@thefairhavenhotel.co.uk
I: www.thefairhavenhotel.co.uk

Heatherdene Hotel ♦♦♦♦
The Common, Goathland, Whitby YO22 5AN
T: (01947) 896334
F: (01947) 896334
E: info@heatherdenehotel.co.uk
I: www.heatherdenehotel.co.uk

Heatherlands ♦♦♦
Darnholm, Goathland, Whitby YO22 5LA
T: (01947) 896311
E: keiththompson@yorkcollege.ac.uk

Prudom Guest House ♦♦♦♦ SILVER AWARD
Goathland, Whitby YO22 5AN
T: (01947) 896368
F: (01947) 896030
E: info@prudomhouse.co.uk
I: www.prudomhouse.co.uk

GOLDSBOROUGH
North Yorkshire

Bay Horse Inn ♦♦♦♦
Goldsborough, Knaresborough HG5 8NW
T: (01423) 862212
F: (01423) 862212
E: bayhorseinn@btinternet.com
I: www.edirectory.co.uk/bayhorseinn/

GOXHILL
North Lincolnshire

King's Well ♦♦♦
Howe Lane, Goxhill, Barrow upon Humber DN19 7HU
T: (01469) 532471
F: (01469) 532471

GRASSINGTON
North Yorkshire

Craiglands Guest House ♦♦♦♦
1 Brooklyn, Threshfield, Grassington, Skipton BD23 5ER
T: (01756) 752093
E: craiglands@talk21.com
I: www.craiglands.com

Foresters Arms Hotel ♦♦♦
20 Main Street, Grassington, Skipton BD23 5AA
T: (01756) 752349
F: (01756) 753633
E: theforesters@totalise.co.uk

Grassington Lodge ♦♦♦♦♦ SILVER AWARD
8 Wood Lane, Grassington, Skipton BD23 5LU
T: (01756) 752518
F: (01756) 752518
E: relax@grassingtonlodge.co.uk
I: grassingtonlodge.co.uk

Long Ashes Inn ♦♦♦
Long Ashes Park, Threshfield, Skipton BD23 5PN
T: (01756) 752434
F: (01756) 752937
E: info@longashesinn.co.uk
I: www.longashesinn.co.uk

New Laithe House ♦♦♦♦
Wood Lane, Grassington, Skipton BD23 5LU
T: (01756) 752764
E: enquiries@newlaithehouse.co.uk
I: www.newlaithehouse.co.uk

Raines Close Guest House ♦♦♦♦
Station Road, Grassington, Skipton BD23 5LS
T: (01756) 752678
E: rainesclose@yorks.net
I: www.rainesclose.co.uk

Springroyd House ♦♦♦
8A Station Road, Grassington, Skipton BD23 5NQ
T: (01756) 752473
F: (01756) 752473
E: springroydhouse@hotmail.com
I: www.hotelmaster.co.uk

Station House ♦♦♦
Station Road, Threshfield, Skipton BD23 5ES
T: (01756) 752667
E: peter@station-house.freeserve.co.uk
I: www.yorkshirenet.co.uk/stayat/stationhouse

Town Head Guest House ♦♦♦♦
1 Low Lane, Grassington, Skipton BD23 5AU
T: (01756) 752811

GREAT AYTON
North Yorkshire

Eskdale Cottage ♦♦♦♦
31 Newton Road, Great Ayton, Middlesbrough TS9 6DT
T: (01642) 724306
E: info@mhoughton.co.uk

Food For Thought ♦♦♦
5 Bridge Street, Great Ayton, Middlesbrough TS9 6NP
T: (01642) 725236
F: (01642) 725236

Pinchinthorpe Hall ♦♦♦♦♦
Pinchinthorpe, Guisborough, TS14 8HG
T: (01287) 630200
F: (01287) 630200

Royal Oak Hotel ♦♦♦
High Green, Great Ayton, Middlesbrough TS9 6BW
T: (01642) 722361
F: (01642) 724047

Susie D's B & B ♦♦♦♦
Crossways, 116 Newton Road, Great Ayton, Middlesbrough TS9 6DL
T: (01642) 724351
E: susieD's@crossways26.fsnet.co.uk

The Wheelhouse ♦♦♦
Langbaurgh Grange, Great Ayton, Middlesbrough TS9 6QQ
T: (01642) 724523

GREAT BARUGH
North Yorkshire

White House Farm ♦♦♦♦
Great Barugh, Malton YO17 6XB
T: (01653) 668317

GREAT BUSBY
North Yorkshire

Chestnut Farm ♦♦♦
Great Busby, Middlesbrough TS9 5LB
T: (01642) 710676

GREAT EDSTONE
North Yorkshire

Cowldyke Farm ♦♦♦
Great Edstone, York YO62 6PE
T: (01751) 431242
E: info@cowldyke-farm.co.uk
I: www.cowldyke-farm.co.uk

GRIMSBY
North East Lincolnshire

The Danish Lodge ♦♦♦♦
2-4 Cleethorpes Road, Grimsby, DN31 3LQ
T: (01472) 342257
F: (01472) 344156
E: danishlodge@aol.com
I: www.danishlodge.co.uk

Sunnyview Guesthouse ♦♦♦♦
Carr Lane, Healing, Grimsby DN41 7QR
T: (01472) 885015
F: (01472) 885015
E: starian@btinternet.com

GROSMONT
North Yorkshire

Eskdale ♦♦♦
Grosmont, Whitby YO22 5PT
T: (01947) 895385
E: counsell@supanet.com

GUISELEY
West Yorkshire

Bowood ♦♦♦
Carlton Lane, Guiseley, Leeds LS20 9NL
T: (01943) 874556

Lyndhurst ♦♦♦
Oxford Road, Guiseley, Leeds LS20 9AB
T: (01943) 879985
I: www.guisley.co.uk/lyndhurst

GUNNERSIDE
North Yorkshire

Dalegarth House ♦♦♦
Gunnerside, Richmond DL11 6LD
T: (01748) 886275
E: dalegarth@btinternet.com

HABROUGH
North East Lincolnshire

Church Farm ♦♦♦♦
Immingham Road, Habrough, Immingham DN40 3BD
T: (01469) 576190

The Old Vicarage ♦♦♦♦
Killingholme Road, Habrough, Immingham DN40 3BB
T: (01469) 575051
F: (01469) 577160
E: ken@theoldvicarage.freeserve.co.uk

HACKFORTH
North Yorkshire

Ainderby Myers Farm ♦♦
Hackforth, Bedale DL8 1PF
T: (01609) 748668
F: (01609) 748424

HALIFAX
West Yorkshire

Beech Court ♦♦♦
40 Prescott Street, Halifax, HX1 2QW
T: (01422) 366004

Claytons ♦♦♦♦
146 Pye Nest Road, Halifax, HX2 7HS
T: (01422) 835053

The Elms ♦♦♦
Keighley Road, Illingworth, Halifax HX2 8HT
T: (01422) 244430
E: sylvia@theelms.f9.co.uk

Field House ♦♦♦♦
Staups Lane, Stump Cross, Halifax, HX3 6XW
T: (01422) 355457
E: stayatfieldhouse@yahoo.co.uk
I: www.fieldhouse-bb.co.uk

Heathleigh ♦♦♦♦
124 Skircoat Road, Halifax, HX1 2RE
T: (01422) 323957

Joan's Guest House ♦♦♦
13 Heath Park Avenue, Halifax, HX1 2PP
T: (01422) 369290

Lower Causeway ♦♦♦♦
Raw End Road, Warley, Halifax, HX2 7SS
T: (01422) 882022
F: (01422) 886882
E: sootymel@aol.com

Mozart House ♦♦♦
34 Prescott Street, Halifax, HX1 2QW
T: (01422) 340319
F: (01422) 340319

Rose Cottage
♦♦♦♦ SILVER AWARD
Shibden Fold, Halifax, HX3 6XP
T: (01422) 365437
F: (01422) 323376
E: welcome@shibden-fold.co.uk
I: www.shibden-fold.co.uk

Victoria Hotel ♦♦
31-35 Horton Street, Halifax, HX1 1QE
T: (01422) 351209
F: (01422) 351209

HAMPSTHWAITE
North Yorkshire

Graystone View Farm ♦♦♦♦
Grayston Plain Lane, Hampsthwaite, Harrogate HG3 2LY
T: (01423) 770324
F: (01423) 772536
E: greystoneviewfarm@btinternet.co.uk

Lonsdale House ♦♦♦
Hampsthwaite, Harrogate HG3 2ET
T: (01423) 771311
F: (01423) 772810

HARMBY
North Yorkshire

Sunnyridge ♦♦♦
Argill Farm, Harmby, Leyburn DL8 5HQ
T: (01969) 622478
E: richah@freenet.co.uk

HARPHAM
East Riding of Yorkshire

St Quintin Arms Inn ♦♦♦♦
Main Street, Harpham, Driffield YO25 4QY
T: (01262) 490329
F: (01262) 490329

HARROGATE
North Yorkshire

Acomb Lodge ♦♦♦
6 Franklin Road, Harrogate, HG1 5EE
T: (01423) 563599

Acorn Lodge Hotel ♦♦♦
1 Studley Road, Harrogate, HG1 5JU
T: (01423) 525630
F: (01423) 564413

Alderside Guest House ♦♦♦
11 Belmont Road, Harrogate, HG2 0LR
T: (01423) 529400
F: (01423) 527531

The Alexander
♦♦♦♦ SILVER AWARD
88 Franklin Road, Harrogate, HG1 5EN
T: (01423) 503348
F: (01423) 540230
E: thealexander@amserve.net

Amadeus Hotel ♦♦♦♦
115 Franklin Road, Harrogate, HG1 5EN
T: (01423) 505151
F: (01423) 505151
E: amadeushotel@btinternet.com
I: www.acartha.com/amadeushotel

Argyll House ♦♦♦
80 King's Road, Harrogate, HG1 5JX
T: (01423) 562408
F: (01423) 567166

Ashbrooke House Hotel ♦♦♦♦
140 Valley Drive, Harrogate, HG2 0JS
T: (01423) 564478
F: (01423) 564458
E: ashbrooke@harrogate.com
I: www.harrogate.com/ashbrooke

Ashley House Hotel ♦♦♦♦
36-40 Franklin Road, Harrogate, HG1 5EE
T: (01423) 507474
F: (01423) 560858
E: ron@ashleyhousehotel.com
I: www.ashleyhousehotel.com

Askern Guest House ♦♦♦
3 Dragon Parade, Harrogate, HG1 5BZ
T: (01423) 523057
F: (01423) 523057
E: info@askernhouse.co.uk
I: www.askernhouse.co.uk

Azalea Court Hotel ♦♦♦
56-58 Kings Road, Harrogate, HG1 5JR
T: (01423) 560424
F: (01423) 505662

Barkers Guest House ♦♦♦
202-204 King's Road, Harrogate, HG1 5JG
T: (01423) 568494

Belmont Hotel ♦♦♦♦
86 Kings Road, Harrogate, HG1 5JX
T: (01423) 528086
E: marilyn@thebelmont86.fsnet.co.uk
I: www.smoothhound.co.uk/hotels/belmonthotel.html

Britannia Lodge
♦♦♦♦ SILVER AWARD
16 Swan Road, Harrogate, HG1 2SA
T: (01423) 508482
F: (01423) 526840
E: info@britlodge.co.uk
I: www.britlodge.co.uk

Brookfield House ♦♦♦♦
5 Alexandra Road, Harrogate, HG1 5JS
T: (01423) 506646
F: (01423) 850383
E: brookfieldhouse@hotmail.com
I: www.brookfield-house.co.uk

Brooklands ♦♦♦♦
5 Valley Drive, Harrogate, HG2 0JJ
T: (01423) 564609
E: brooklandsbb@supanet.com

Camberley Hotel ♦♦♦♦
52-54 Kings Road, Harrogate, HG1 5JR
T: (01423) 561618
F: (01423) 536360
E: camberley.hotel@virgin.net
I: www.camberleyhotel.co.uk

Cavendish Hotel ♦♦♦♦
3 Valley Drive, Harrogate, HG2 0JJ
T: (01423) 509637
F: (01423) 504434

Central House Farm
♦♦♦♦ SILVER AWARD
Haverah Park, Harrogate, HG3 1SQ
T: (01423) 566050
F: (01423) 709152
E: jayne-ryder@lineone.net

Claremont House ♦♦♦
8 Westcliffe Grove, Harrogate, HG2 0PL
T: (01423) 502738

Conference View Guest House ♦♦♦♦
74 Kings Road, Harrogate, HG1 5JR
T: (01423) 563075
F: (01423) 563075
E: admin@conferenceview.f9.co.uk
I: www.conferenceview.f9.co.uk

The Coppice ♦♦♦♦
9 Studley Road, Harrogate, HG1 5JU
T: (01423) 569626
F: (01423) 569005
E: coppice@harrogate.com
I: www.harrogate.com/coppice

Craigmoor Manor Hotel ♦♦♦
10 Harlow Moor Drive, Harrogate, HG2 0JX
T: (01423) 523562
F: (01423) 523562

Crescent Lodge ♦♦♦♦
20 Swan Road, Harrogate, HG1 2SA
T: (01423) 503688
F: (01423) 503688
E: peter.humphris@dial.pipex.com

Delaine Hotel
♦♦♦♦ SILVER AWARD
17 Ripon Road, Harrogate, HG1 2JL
T: (01423) 567974
F: (01423) 561723

Dragon House ♦♦♦
6 Dragon Parade, Harrogate, HG1 5DA
T: (01423) 569888

The Franklin ♦♦♦
25 Franklin Road, Harrogate, HG1 5ED
T: (01423) 569028
E: leighrichardson@ntlworld.com
I: www.thefranklin.co.uk

Franklin View
♦♦♦♦ SILVER AWARD
19 Grove Road, Harrogate, HG1 5EW
T: (01423) 541388
F: (01423) 547872
E: jennifer@franklinview.com
I: www.franklinview.com

The Gables Hotel ♦♦♦
2 West Grove Road, Harrogate, HG1 2AD
T: (01423) 505625
F: (01423) 561312
E: gableshotel@quista.net
I: www.harrogategables.co.uk

Garden House Hotel ♦♦♦♦
14 Harlow Moor Drive, Harrogate, HG2 0JX
T: (01423) 503059
F: (01423) 503059
E: gardenhouse@harrogate.com
I: www.harrogate.com/gardenhouse

Geminian Guest House ♦♦♦
11-13 Franklin Road, Harrogate, HG1 5ED
T: (01423) 523347
F: (01423) 523347
E: geminian@talk21.com
I: www.geminian.org.uk

Gillmore Hotel ♦♦♦
98 Kings Road, Harrogate, HG1 5HH
T: (01423) 503699
F: (01423) 563223
E: gillmoregh@aol.com

Grafton Hotel ♦♦♦♦
1-3 Franklin Mount, Harrogate, HG1 5EJ
T: (01423) 508491
F: (01423) 523168
E: enquiries@graftonhotel.co.uk
I: www.graftonhotel.co.uk

Half Moon Inn ♦♦
Main Street, Pool in Wharfedale, Otley LS21 1LH
T: (0113) 284 2878
F: (0113) 203 7895

The Herbitage ♦♦♦♦
71 St Winifred's Avenue West, Harrogate, HG2 8LS
T: (01423) 884830
E: enquiries@theherbitage.co.uk
I: www.theherbitage.co.uk

Hollins House ♦♦♦
17 Hollins Road, Harrogate, HG1 2JF
T: (01423) 503646
F: (01423) 503646
E: hollins_house@lineone.net
I: www.hollinshouse.co.uk

Imbercourt Hotel ♦♦
57 Valley Drive, Harrogate, HG2 0JW
T: (01423) 502513
F: (01423) 562696

Kimberley Hotel ♦♦♦♦
11-19 Kings Road, Harrogate, HG1 5JY
T: (01423) 505613
F: (01423) 530276
E: info@thekimberley.co.uk
I: www.thekimberley.co.uk

Kingsway Hotel ♦♦♦
36 Kings Road, Harrogate, HG1 5JW
T: (01423) 562179
F: (01423) 562179
E: andy.noble@btinternet.com
I: www.kingswayhotel.com

Knabbs Ash
♦♦♦♦ GOLD AWARD
Skipton Road, Felliscliffe, Harrogate HG3 2LT
T: (01423) 771040
F: (01423) 771515
E: colin&sheila@knabbsash.freeserve.co.uk
I: www.yorkshirenet.co.uk/stayat/knabbsash

Lamont House ♦♦♦♦
12 St Mary's Walk, Harrogate, HG2 0LW
T: (01423) 567143
F: (01423) 567143

Oakbrae Guest House ♦♦♦♦
3 Springfield Avenue, Harrogate, HG1 2HR
T: (01423) 567682
F: (01423) 567682
E: oakbrae@nascr.net
I: accommodation.uk.net/oakbrae.htm

Orient Townhouse ♦♦♦♦
51 Valley Drive, Harrogate, HG JH
T: (01423) 565818
F: (01423) 504518
E: rowena@orienttownhouse.com
I: www.orienttownhouse.com

Parnas Hotel
Rating Applied For
98 Franklin Road, Harrogate, HG1 5EN
T: (01423) 564493
F: (01423) 563554
E: info@parnashotel.co.uk
I: www.parnashotel.co.uk

17 Peckfield Close ♦♦♦
Hampsthwaite, Harrogate HG3 2ES
T: (01423) 770765

Royd Mount
♦♦♦♦ GOLD AWARD
4 Grove Road, Harrogate, HG1 5EW
T: (01423) 529525
E: roydmount@btinternet.com

Ruskin Hotel
♦♦♦♦♦ SILVER AWARD
1 Swan Road, Harrogate, HG1 2SS
T: (01423) 502045
F: (01423) 506131
E: ruskin.hotel@virgin.net
I: www.ruskinhotel.co.uk

Scotia House Hotel ♦♦♦
66-68 Kings Road, Harrogate, HG1 5JR
T: (01423) 504361
F: (01423) 526578
E: info@scotiahotel.harrogate.net
I: www.scotiahotel.harrogate.net

Shannon Court Hotel ♦♦♦♦
65 Dragon Avenue, Harrogate, HG1 5DS
T: (01423) 509858
F: (01423) 530606
E: shannon@hotels.harrogate.com
I: www.harrogate.com/shannon

Sherwood ♦♦♦♦
7 Studley Road, Harrogate, HG1 5JU
T: (01423) 503033
F: (01423) 564659
E: sherwood@harrogate.com
I: www.sherwood-hotel.com

Spring Lodge Guest House ♦♦♦
22 Spring Mount, Harrogate, HG1 2HX
T: (01423) 506036
F: (01423) 506036
E: dv22harrogate@aol.com

Staveleigh
♦♦♦♦ SILVER AWARD
20 Ripon Road, Harrogate, HG1 2JJ
T: (01423) 524175
F: (01423) 524178
E: enquiries@staveleigh.co.uk
I: www.staveleigh.co.uk

Valley Hotel ♦♦♦♦
93-95 Valley Drive, Harrogate, HG2 0JP
T: (01423) 504868
F: (01423) 531940
E: valley@harrogate.com
I: www.valleyhotel.co.uk

Wharfedale House ♦♦♦
28 Harlow Moor Drive, Harrogate, HG2 0JY
T: (01423) 522233

HARTWITH
North Yorkshire

Brimham Lodge ♦♦♦♦
Brimham Rocks Road, Burnt Yates, Harrogate HG3 3HE
T: (01423) 771770
F: (01423) 770370
E: neil.clarke@virgin.net
I: www.farmhousesbedandbreakfast.com

HARWOOD DALE
North Yorkshire

The Grainary ♦♦♦♦
Keasbeck Hill Farm, Harwood Dale, Scarborough YO13 0DT
T: (01723) 870026
F: (01723) 870026
E: thesimpsons@grainary.co.uk
I: www.grainary.co.uk

HAWES
North Yorkshire

Bulls Head Hotel ♦♦♦♦
Market Place, Hawes, DL8 3RD
T: (01969) 667437
F: (01969) 667048
E: jeff@bullsheadhotel.com
I: www.bullsheadhotel.com

The Bungalow ♦♦♦
Spring Bank, Hawes, DL8 3NW
T: (01969) 667209

Cocketts Hotel and Restaurant ♦♦♦♦
Market Place, Hawes, DL8 3RD
T: (01969) 667312
F: (01969) 667162
E: enquiries@cocketts.co.uk
I: www.cocketts.co.uk

East House ♦♦♦♦
Gayle, Hawes DL8 3RZ
T: (01969) 667405
E: lornaward@lineone.net
I: www.dalesaccommodation.com/easthouse

Ebor Guest House ♦♦♦
Burtersett Road, Hawes, DL8 3NT
T: (01969) 667337
F: (01969) 667337
E: gwen@eborhouse.freeserve.co.uk

Fairview House ♦♦♦♦
Burtersett Road, Hawes, DL8 3NP
T: (01969) 667348
F: (01969) 667348
E: joan.bill.fairview@tinyonline.co.uk
I: www.wensleydale.org

Herriots Hotel & Restaurant ♦♦♦♦
Main Street, Hawes, DL8 3QW
T: (01969) 667536
F: (01969) 667810
E: herriotshotel@aol.com
I: www.herriots.com

Laburnum House ♦♦♦
The Holme, Hawes, DL8 3QR
T: (01969) 667717
F: (01969) 667 041
E: janetbatty@hotmail.com
I: www.stayatlaburnumhouse.co.uk

Old Station House ♦♦♦♦
Hardraw Road, Hawes, DL8 3NL
T: (01969) 667785
E: alan.watkinson@virgin.net

Pry House ♦♦♦
Hawes, DL8 3LP
T: (01969) 667241
E: B&B@pryhousefarm.co.uk
I: www.pryhousefarm.co.uk

South View ♦♦♦
Gayle Lane, Hawes, DL8 3RW
T: (01969) 667447

Springbank House ♦♦♦
Springbank, Townfoot, Hawes, DL8 3NW
T: (01969) 667376
F: (01969) 667376

White Hart Inn ♦♦♦
Main Street, Hawes, DL8 3QL
T: (01969) 667259
F: (01969) 667259
E: whitehart@wensleydale.org
I: www.wensleydale.org

Widdale Foot ♦♦♦♦
Hawes, DL8 3LX
T: (01969) 667383
F: (01969) 667471
E: widdalefoot@talk21.com
I: www.wensleydale.org

HAWNBY
North Yorkshire

Easterside Farm ♦♦♦
Hawnby, York YO62 5QT
T: (01439) 798277
F: (01439) 798277

HAWORTH
West Yorkshire

Aitches Guest House & Restaurant ♦♦♦♦
11 West Lane, Haworth, Keighley BD22 8QU
T: (01535) 642501
E: aitches@talk21.com
I: www.aitches.co.uk

The Apothecary Guest House ♦♦♦
86 Main Street, Haworth, Keighley BD22 8DA
T: (01535) 643642
F: (01535) 643642
E: apot@sisley86.freeserve.co.uk
I: www.sisley86.freeserve.co.uk

Ashmount ♦♦♦♦ SILVER AWARD
Mytholmes Lane, Haworth, Keighley BD22 8EZ
T: (01535) 645726
F: (01535) 645726
E: ashmounthaworth@aol.com
I: members.aol.com/ashmounthaworth

Blue Lantern Guest House & Restaurant Rating Applied For
81 Main Street, Haworth, Keighley BD22 8DA
T: (01535) 642809
F: (01535) 642809

Bronte Hotel ♦♦
Lees Lane, Haworth, Keighley BD22 8RA
T: (01535) 644112
F: (01535) 646725
E: Brontehotel@btinternet.com
I: www.bronte-hotel.co.uk

Ebor House ♦♦♦
Lees Lane, Haworth, Keighley BD22 8RA
T: (01535) 645869
E: derekbelle@aol.com

Haworth Tea Rooms and Guest House ♦♦♦
68 Main Street, Haworth, Keighley BD22 8DP
T: (01535) 644278

Hole Farm ♦♦♦♦
Dimples Lane, Haworth, Keighley BD22 8QT
T: (01535) 644755
F: (01535) 644755
E: janet@bronteholidays.co.uk
I: www.bronteholidays.co.uk

Kershaw House ♦♦♦♦
90 West Lane, Haworth, Keighley BD22 8EN
T: (01535) 642074
F: (01535) 642074
E: jbrosnan@whsmithnet.com

Moorfield Guest House ♦♦♦
80 West Lane, Haworth, Keighley BD22 8EN
T: (01535) 643689
E: daveandann@moorfieldgh.demon.co.uk
I: www.moorfieldgh.demon.co.uk

The Old Registry ♦♦♦♦
2-4 Main Street, Haworth, Keighley BD22 8DA
T: (01535) 646503
F: (01535) 646503
E: oldregistry.haworth@virgin.net
I: www.oldregistry.com

The Old Silent Inn ♦♦♦
Hob Lane, Stanbury, Keighley BD22 0HW
T: (01535) 647437
F: (01535) 646449

Park Top House ♦♦♦♦
1 Rawdon Road, Haworth, Keighley BD22 8DX
T: (01535) 646102
E: gmilnes@parktophouse.fsnet.co.uk

6 Penistone Mews ♦♦♦♦
Rawdon Road, Haworth, Keighley BD22 8DF
T: (01535) 647412
E: philip@haworth3.freeserve.co.uk

Rosebud Cottage Guest House ♦♦♦
1 Belle Isle Road, Haworth, Keighley BD22 8QQ
T: (01535) 640321
E: rosebudcottage24@hotmail.com
I: www.rosebudcottage.co.uk

Woodlands Grange Private Hotel ♦♦♦
Woodlands Grange, Belle Isle, Haworth, Keighley BD22 8PB
T: (01535) 646814
F: (01535) 648282
E: woodlandsgrange@hotmail.com

HAXEY
North Lincolnshire

Duke William ♦♦♦
Church Street, Haxey, Doncaster DN9 2HY
T: (01427) 752210
F: (01427) 752210

HEADINGLEY
West Yorkshire

Boundary Hotel Express ♦♦♦
42 Cardigan Road, Headingley, Leeds LS6 3AG
T: (0113) 275 7700
F: (0113) 275 7700
E: info@boundaryhotel.co.uk
I: www.boundaryhotel.co.uk

Oak Villa Hotel ♦♦♦
55/57 Cardigan Road, Headingley, Leeds LS6 1DW
T: (0113) 275 8439
F: (0113) 275 8439

HEALAUGH
North Yorkshire

Riddings Farm ♦♦♦
Reeth, Richmond DL11 6UR
T: (01748) 884267

HEALEY
North Yorkshire

The Olive ♦♦♦♦
Healey Mill, Healey, Ripon HG4 4LH
T: (01765) 689774
E: theolive.healeymill@virgin.net

HEBDEN
North Yorkshire

Court Croft ♦♦♦
Church Lane, Hebden, Skipton BD23 5DX
T: (01756) 753406

HEBDEN BRIDGE
West Yorkshire

Angeldale Guest House ♦♦♦
Hangingroyd Lane, Hebden Bridge, HX7 7DD
T: (01422) 847321
E: enq@angeldale.co.uk
I: www.angeldale.co.uk

Badger Fields Farm ♦♦♦♦
Badger Lane, Blackshaw Head, Hebden Bridge, HX7 7JX
T: (01422) 845161
E: enquiries@badgerfields.com
I: www.badgerfields.com

The Grove Inn ♦♦♦
Burnley Road, Brearley, Luddendenfoot, Halifax HX2 6HS
T: (01422) 883235
F: (01422) 883905

Myrtle Grove ♦♦♦♦
Old Lees Road, Hebden Bridge, HX7 8HL
T: (01422) 846078
E: myrtlegrove@btinternet.com

1 Primrose Terrace ♦♦
Hebden Bridge, HX7 6HN
T: (01422) 844747

Prospect End ♦♦♦
8 Prospect Terrace, Savile Road, Hebden Bridge, HX7 6NA
T: (01422) 843586
F: (01422) 843586

Robin Hood Inn ♦♦♦
Keighley Road, Pecket Well, Hebden Bridge HX7 8QR
T: (01422) 842593
F: (01422) 844938
E: info@robinhoodsinn.com
I: www.robinhoodsinn.com

White Lion Hotel ♦♦♦
Bridge Gate, Hebden Bridge, HX7 8EX
T: (01422) 842197
F: (01422) 846619
E: enquiries@whitelionhotelhb.co.uk
I: www.whitelionhotelhb.co.uk

HELMSLEY
North Yorkshire

Argyle House ♦♦♦♦
Ashdale Road, Helmsley, York YO62 5DD
T: (01439) 770590

Carlton Grange ♦♦♦
Helmsley, York YO62 5HH
T: (01439) 770259
I: www.carltongrange.co.uk

Carlton Lodge ♦♦♦♦
Bondgate, Helmsley, York YO62 5EY
T: (01439) 770557
F: (01439) 770623
E: enquiries@carlton-lodge.com
I: www.carlton-lodge.com

Griff Farm Bed & Breakfast ♦♦♦♦
Griff Farm, Helmsley, York YO62 5EN
T: (01439) 771600
F: (01439) 770462
E: j.fairburn@farmline.com

The Hawnby Hotel ♦♦♦
Hill Top, Hawnby, York YO62 5QS
T: (01439) 798202
F: (01439) 798344
E: info@hawnbyhotel.co.uk
I: www.hawnbyhotel.co.uk

High House Farm ♦♦♦
Sutton Bank, Thirsk YO7 2HL
T: (01845) 597557

Laskill Grange ♦♦♦♦
Hawnby, York YO62 5NB
T: (01439) 798268
F: (01439) 798498
E: suesmith@laskillfarm.fsnet.co.uk
I: www.laskillfarm.co.uk

Mount Grace Farm ♦♦♦♦
Cold Kirby, Thirsk YO7 2HL
T: (01845) 597389
F: (01845) 597872
E: joyce@mountgracefarm.com
I: www.mountgracefarm.com

Oldstead Grange ♦♦♦♦♦ GOLD AWARD
Oldstead, Coxwold, York YO61 4BJ
T: (01347) 868634
E: oldsteadgrange@yorkshireuk.com
I: www.yorkshireuk.com

Sproxton Hall ♦♦♦♦
Sproxton, York YO62 5EQ
T: (01439) 770225
F: (01439) 771373
E: info@sproxtonhall.demon.co.uk
I: www.sproxtonhall.co.uk

Stilworth House ♦♦♦♦
1 Church Street, Helmsley, York YO62 5AD
T: (01439) 771072
E: carol@stilworth.co.uk
I: www.stilworth.co.uk

HEPTONSTALL
West Yorkshire

Poppyfields House ♦♦♦
29 Slack Top, Heptonstall, Hebden Bridge HX7 7HA
T: (01422) 843636
F: (01422) 845621

HEPWORTH
West Yorkshire

Uppergate Farm ♦♦♦♦
Hepworth, Holmfirth, Huddersfield HD9 1TG
T: (01484) 681369
F: (01484) 687343
E: stevenal.booth@virgin.net
I: www.uppergatefarm.co.uk

HESSLE
East Riding of Yorkshire

Redcliffe House Luxury B&B ♦♦♦♦
Redcliffe Road, Hessle, HU13 0HA
T: (01482) 648655

Weir Lodge Guest House ♦♦♦♦
Tower Hill, Hessle, HU13 0SG
T: (01482) 648564
I: www.weirlodge.co.uk

HEWORTH
Yorkshire

The Nags Head ♦♦♦
56 Heworth Road, Heworth, York YO3 0AD
T: (01904) 422989

HIGH BENTHAM
North Yorkshire

Fowgill Park ♦♦♦♦
High Bentham, Lancaster
LA2 7AH
T: (01524) 261630

HIGH HAWSKER
North Yorkshire

Grange Farm
Rating Applied For
High Hawsker, Whitby YO22 4LF
T: (01947) 881080
F: (01947) 881080
E: gf@grangefarm.net
I: www.grangefarm.net

HIGH STITTENHAM
North Yorkshire

Hall Farm ♦♦♦♦
High Stittenham, York
YO60 7TW
T: (01347) 878461
F: (01347) 878461
E: hallfarm@btinternet.com
I: www.hallfarm.btinternet.co.uk

HOLMBRIDGE
West Yorkshire

Corn Loft House ♦♦♦
146 Woodhead Road,
Holmbridge, Holmfirth,
Huddersfield HD7 1NL
T: (01484) 683147

HOLMFIRTH
West Yorkshire

Crimes House ♦♦♦♦
Far Lane, Hepworth, Holmfirth,
Huddersfield HD9 1RN
T: (01484) 682395
F: (01484) 682395

Linden Grove Bed and Breakfast ♦♦♦
39 Huddersfield Road,
Holmfirth, Huddersfield
HD9 3JH
T: (01484) 683718

The Old Bridge Bakery ♦♦
15 Victoria Street, Holmfirth,
Huddersfield HD7 1DF
T: (01484) 685807

Red Lion Inn ♦♦♦
Sheffield Road, Jackson Bridge,
Holmfirth, Huddersfield
HD7 7HS
T: (01484) 683499

Springfield House ♦♦♦♦
95 Huddersfield Road,
Holmfirth, Huddersfield HD7 1JA
T: (01484) 683031
E: ann_brook@hotmail.com

HOLMPTON
East Riding of Yorkshire

Elmtree Farm ♦♦♦
Main Road, Holmpton,
Withernsea, HU19 2QR
T: (01964) 630957

HOOTON PAGNELL
South Yorkshire

Rock Farm ♦♦♦
Hooton Pagnell, Doncaster
DN5 7BT
T: (01977) 642200

HORNSEA
East Riding of Yorkshire

Merlstead Private Hotel ♦♦♦
59 Eastgate, Hornsea, HU18 1NB
T: (01964) 533068
F: (01964) 536975
E: doreen.lamb@btopenworld.com

Sandhurst Guest House ♦♦♦
3 Victoria Avenue, Hornsea,
HU18 1NH
T: (01964) 534653
F: (01964) 534653
E: rhodes@hornsea15.fsnet.co.uk

HORTON-IN-RIBBLESDALE
North Yorkshire

Crown Hotel ♦♦♦
Horton-in-Ribblesdale, Settle
BD24 0HF
T: (01729) 860209
F: (01729) 860444
E: minehost@crown-hotel.co.uk
I: www.crown-hotel.co.uk

Middle Studfold Farm ♦♦♦
Horton-in-Ribblesdale, Settle
BD24 0ER
T: (01729) 860236

HUBBERHOLME
North Yorkshire

Church Farm ♦♦♦♦
Hubberholme, Skipton BD23 5JE
T: (01756) 760240
F: (01756) 761091
E: gwhuck@hubberholme.fsnet.co.uk
I: www.yorkshirenet.co.uk/stayat/churchfarm

HUDDERSFIELD
West Yorkshire

Ashfield Hotel ♦♦♦
93 New North Road,
Huddersfield, HD1 5ND
T: (01484) 425916
F: (01484) 537029
E: enquiries@theashfieldhotel.co.uk
I: www.theashfieldhotel.co.uk

Cambridge Lodge ♦♦♦
4 Clare Hill, Huddersfield,
HD1 5BS
T: (01484) 519892
F: (01484) 534534
E: cambridge.lodge@ntlworld.com
I: www.huddersfield.co.uk/cambridgelodge

Croppers Arms ♦♦♦
136 Westbourne Road, Marsh,
Huddersfield, HD1 4LF
T: (01484) 421522
F: (01484) 301300

Ellasley Guest House ♦♦
86 New North Road,
Huddersfield, HD1 5NE
T: (01484) 423995
F: (01484) 432995

Elm Crest
Rating Applied For
2 Queens Road, Edgerton,
Huddersfield, HD2 2AG
T: (01484) 530990
F: (01484) 516227
E: chris@elmcrest.fsnet.co.uk
I: www.elm-crest.co.uk

Holmcliffe Guest House ♦♦♦
16 Mountjoy Road, Edgerton,
Huddersfield, HD1 5PZ
T: (01484) 429598
F: (01484) 429598
E: jwilco@mwfree.net

Laurel Cottage Guest House ♦♦♦
34 Far Dene, Kirkburton,
Huddersfield HD8 0QU
T: (01484) 607907

The Mallows Guest House ♦♦♦
55 Spring Street, Springwood,
Huddersfield, HD1 4AZ
T: (01484) 544684

Manor Mill Cottage ♦♦♦♦
21 Linfit Lane, Kirkburton,
Huddersfield HD8 0TY
T: (01484) 604109
E: manormill@paskham.freeserve.co.uk

The White House ♦♦
Holthead, Slaithwaite,
Huddersfield HD7 5TY
T: (01484) 842245
F: (01484) 842245
E: whthouse@globalnet.co.uk
I: www.whitehouse-hotel.co.uk

HULL
East Riding of Yorkshire

Acorn Guest House ♦♦♦
719 Beverley High Road, Hull,
HU6 7JN
T: (01482) 853248
F: (01482) 853148

The Admiral Guest House ♦♦
234 The Boulevard, Hull,
HU3 3ED
T: (01482) 329664
F: (01482) 329664

The Arches ♦♦♦
38 Saner Street, Hull, HU3 2TR
T: (01482) 211558

Clyde House Hotel ♦♦♦
13 John Street, Hull, HU2 8DH
T: (01482) 214981
F: (01482) 214981

Conway-Roseberry Hotel ♦♦♦♦
86 Marlborough Avenue, Hull,
HU5 3JT
T: (01482) 445256
F: (01482) 343215
I: www.smoothhound.co.uk/hotels/conwayhtml

The Earlsmere Hotel ♦♦♦
76-78 Sunnybank, Off Spring
Bank West, Hull, HU3 1LQ
T: (01482) 341977
F: (01482) 473714
E: su@earlsmerehotel.karoo.co.uk
I: www.earlsmerehotel.karoo.net

West Park Hotel ♦♦♦
405-411 Anlaby Road, Hull,
HU3 6AB
T: (01482) 571888
F: (01482) 351215
E: westparkhotel@mandp.karoo.uk

HUNMANBY
North Yorkshire

Saxdale House Farm ♦♦♦♦
Bartindale Road, Hunmanby,
Filey YO14 0JD
T: (01723) 892346
F: (01723) 892400
E: saxdale.house@virgin.net
I: www.saxdale.co.uk

Sea Cabin ♦♦♦
16 Gap Road, Hunmanby Gap,
Filey, YO14 9QP
T: (01723) 891368

HUTTON CRANSWICK
East Riding of Yorkshire

Londesborough Lodge
Rating Applied For
44 Southgate, Hutton
Cranswick, Driffield YO25 9QX
T: (01377) 271170
E: kate_ottell@hotmail.com

HUTTON-LE-HOLE
North Yorkshire

Barn Hotel and Tea Room ♦♦♦
Hutton-le-Hole, York YO62 6UA
T: (01751) 417311
E: fairhurst@lineone.net

Moorlands of Hutton-le-Hole ♦♦♦♦ SILVER AWARD
Hutton-le-Hole, York YO62 6UA
T: (01751) 417548
F: (01751) 417760
E: stay@moorlandshouse.com
I: www.moorlandshouse.com

Westfield Lodge ♦♦♦
Hutton-le-Hole, York YO62 6UG
T: (01751) 417261
F: (01751) 417876
E: sticklandrw@farmersweekly.net

HUTTON SESSAY
North Yorkshire

Burtree Country House ♦♦♦♦
Burtree House, York Road,
Hutton Sessay, Thirsk YO7 3AY
T: (01845) 501333
F: (01845) 501596
E: dawn@burtreecountryhouse.co.uk
I: www.burtreecountryhouse.co.uk

HUTTONS AMBO
North Yorkshire

High Gaterley Farm ♦♦♦♦
Castle Howard Estate, Huttons
Ambo, York YO60 7HT
T: (01653) 694636
F: (01653) 694636
E: relax@highgaterley.com
I: www.highgaterley.com

IBURNDALE
North Yorkshire

Mill Race Cottage ♦♦♦
8 Mill Lane, Iburndale, Whitby
YO22 5DU
T: (01947) 810009
F: (01947) 810009

ILKLEY
West Yorkshire

Grove Hotel ♦♦♦♦
66 The Grove, Ilkley, LS29 9PA
T: (01943) 600298
F: 0870 706 5587
E: info@grovehotel.org
I: www.grovehotel.org

Ilkley Riverside Hotel ♦♦♦
Riverside Gardens, Bridge Lane,
Ilkley, LS29 9EU
T: (01943) 607338
F: (01943) 607338

One Tivoli Place ♦♦♦♦
Ilkley, LS29 8SU
T: (01943) 600328
F: (01943) 600320
E: tivolipl@aol.com

Roberts Family Bed and Breakfast ♦♦♦
63 Skipton Road, Ilkley, LS29 9HF
T: (01943) 817542
F: (01943) 817542
E: petraroberts1@activemail.co.uk

Star Hotel
Rating Applied For
1 Leeds Road, Ilkley, LS29 8DH
T: (01943) 605438

Summerhill Guest House ♦♦♦
24 Crossbeck Road, Ilkley, LS29 9JN
T: (01943) 607067

Summerhouse ♦♦♦♦
Hangingstone Road, Ilkley, LS29 8RS
T: (01943) 601612
F: (01943) 601612
E: k_towler@talk21.com

ILLINGWORTH
West Yorkshire

Whitehill Lodge ♦♦♦
102 Keighley Road, Illingworth, Halifax HX2 8HF
T: (01422) 240813
F: (01422) 240813
E: lodge102@Pgen.net

INGBIRCHWORTH
South Yorkshire

The Fountain Inn & Rooms ♦♦♦♦
Wellthorne Lane, Ingbirchworth, Penistone, Sheffield S36 7GJ
T: (01226) 763125
F: (01226) 761336
E: reservations@fountain-inn.co.uk
I: www.fountain-inn.co.uk

INGLEBY CROSS
North Yorkshire

Blue Bell Inn ♦
Ingleby Cross, Northallerton DL6 3NF
T: (01609) 882272
E: david.kinsella@tesco.net

INGLEBY GREENHOW
North Yorkshire

Manor House Farm ♦♦♦♦
Ingleby Greeenhow, Great Ayton, Middlesbrough TS9 6RB
T: (01642) 722384
E: mbloom@globalnet.co.uk

INGLETON
North Yorkshire

The Dales Guest House ♦♦♦
Main Street, Ingleton, Carnforth LA6 3HH
T: (015242) 41401
E: dalesgh@hotmail.com

Ferncliffe Country Guest House ♦♦♦♦
55 Main Street, Ingleton, Carnforth LA6 3HJ
T: (01524) 242405
E: ferncliffe@hotmail.com

Gatehouse Farm ♦♦♦♦
Far Westhouse, Ingleton, Carnforth LA6 3NR
T: (01524) 241458

Ingleborough View Guest House ♦♦♦♦
Main Street, Ingleton, Carnforth LA6 3HH
T: (01524) 241523
E: anne@ingleboroughview.co.uk
I: www.ingleboroughview.co.uk

Inglenook Guest House ♦♦♦
20 Main Street, Ingleton, Carnforth LA6 3HJ
T: (01524) 241270
E: inglenook20@hotmail.com
I: www.nebsweb.co.uk/inglenook

New Butts Farm ♦♦♦
High Bentham, Lancaster LA2 7AN
T: (01524) 241238

Pines Country House ♦♦♦♦
Ingleton, Carnforth LA6 3HN
T: (01524) 241252
F: (01524) 241252
E: pineshotel@aol.com
I: www.yorkshirenet.co.uk/stayat/thepines

Riverside Lodge ♦♦♦
24 Main Street, Ingleton, Carnforth LA6 3HJ
T: (015242) 41359
E: info@riversideingleton.co.uk
I: www.riversideingleton.co.uk

Springfield Country House Hotel ♦♦♦
Main Street, Ingleton, Carnforth LA6 3HJ
T: (01524) 241280
F: (01524) 241280
I: www.destination-england.co.uk.springfield

Station Inn ♦♦♦
Ribblehead, Ingleton, Carnforth LA6 3AS
T: (01524) 241274
E: stationinn@btopenworld.com
I: www.smoothhound.co.uk/hotels/station2.html

Thorngarth Country Guest House ♦♦♦♦
New Road, Ingleton, Carnforth LA6 3HN
T: (015242) 41295
F: (015242) 41033
E: Thorngarthcountryguesthouse@btinternet.com
I: www.Thorngarth.co.uk

Wheatsheaf Inn & Hotel ♦♦♦♦
22 High Street, Ingleton, Carnforth LA6 3AD
T: (01524) 241275
F: (01524) 241275
E: randall.d@ingleton01.freeserve.co.uk
I: www.yorkshirenet.co.uk/stayat/thewheatsheaf

KETTLESING
North Yorkshire

Green Acres
♦♦♦♦ GOLD AWARD
Sleights Lane, Kettlesing, Harrogate HG3 2LE
T: (01423) 771524
E: christine@yorkshiredalesbb.com
I: www.yorkshiredalesbb.com

KETTLEWELL
North Yorkshire

Blue Bell Inn ♦♦♦
Kettlewell, Skipton BD23 5QX
T: (01756) 760230
F: (01756) 760230
E: info@bluebellinn.co.uk
I: www.bluebellinn.co.uk

Chestnut Cottage ♦♦♦
Kettlewell, Skipton BD23 5RL
T: (01756) 760804

Lynburn ♦♦♦
Kettlewell, Skipton BD23 5RF
T: (01756) 760803
E: lorna@lthornborrow.fsnet.co.uk

KILBURN
North Yorkshire

Church Farm ♦♦
Kilburn, York YO61 4AH
T: (01347) 868318

The Forresters Arms Hotel ♦♦♦
Kilburn, York YO61 4AH
T: (01347) 868550
F: (01347) 868386
E: forrestersarms@fsnet.co.uk
I: www.destination-england.co.uk/forresters.html

KIRBY HILL
North Yorkshire

Shoulder of Mutton ♦♦♦
Kirby Hill, Richmond, DL11 7JH
T: (01748) 822772
F: (01325) 718936
E: info@shoulderofmutton.net
I: www.shoulderofmutton.net

KIRBY MISPERTON
North Yorkshire

Beansheaf Hotel ♦♦♦
Malton Road, Kirby Misperton, Malton YO17 6UE
T: (01653) 668614
F: (01653) 668370

KIRKBURTON
West Yorkshire

The Woodman Inn ♦♦♦♦
Thunderbridge, Kirkburton, Huddersfield HD8 0PX
T: (01484) 605778
F: (01484) 604110
E: thewoodman@connectfree.co.uk
I: www.woodman-inn.co.uk

KIRKBY
North Yorkshire

Dromonby Hall Farm ♦♦♦
Busby Lane, Kirkby, Stokesley, Middlesbrough TS9 7AP
T: (01642) 712312
F: (01642) 712312
E: b-b@dromonby.co.uk
I: www.dromonby.co.uk

KIRKBY-IN-CLEVELAND
North Yorkshire

Dromonby Grange Farm
Rating Applied For
Kirkby-in-Cleveland, Middlesbrough TS9 7AR
T: (01642) 712227
E: jehugill@aol.com

KIRKBY MALHAM
North Yorkshire

Yeoman's Barn ♦♦♦♦
Kirkby Malham, Skipton BD23 4BL
T: (01729) 830639
E: c_d.turner@virgin.net
I: www.yeomansbarn.co.uk

KIRKBYMOORSIDE
North Yorkshire

Brickfields Farm
Rating Applied For
Kirby Mills, Kirkbymoorside, York YO62 6NS
T: (01751) 433074

Cartoft Lodge ♦♦♦♦
Keldholme, Kirkbymoorside, York YO62 6NU
T: (01751) 431566

The Cornmill
Rating Applied For
Kirby Mills, Kirkbymoorside, York YO62 6NP
T: (01751) 432000
F: (01751) 432300
E: cornmill@kirbymills.demon.co.uk
I: www.kirbymills.demon.co.uk

High Blakey House ♦♦♦♦
Blakey Ridge, Kirkbymoorside, York YO62 7LQ
T: (01751) 417186
E: highblakey.house@virginnet.net
I: freespace.virginnet.co.uk/highblakey.house/

The Lion Inn ♦♦♦
Blakey Ridge, Kirkbymoorside, York YO62 7LQ
T: (01751) 417320
F: (01751) 417717
E: info@lionblakey.co.uk
I: www.lionblakey.co.uk

Red Lion House ♦♦♦♦
Crown Square, Kirkbymoorside, York YO62 6AY
T: (01751) 431815
E: angela.thomson@red-lion-house.freeserve.co.uk

Sinnington Common Farm ♦♦♦♦
Kirkbymoorside, York YO62 6NX
T: (01751) 431719
E: Felicity@scfarm.demon.co.uk
I: www.scfarmdemon.co.uk

White Horse Hotel ♦♦♦
5 Market Place, Kirkbymoorside, York YO62 6AB
T: (01751) 431296

KIRKSTALL
West Yorkshire

Abbey Guest House ♦♦♦♦
44 Vesper Road, Kirkstall, Leeds LS5 3NX
T: (0113) 278 5580
F: (0113) 2787780
E: abbeyleeds@aol.com

KNARESBOROUGH
North Yorkshire

Bay Horse Inn ♦♦♦
York Road, Green Hammerton, York YO26 8BN
T: (01423) 330338
F: (01423) 331279
E: thebayhorseinn@aol.com
I: www.thebayhorse.com

Ebor Mount ♦♦♦
18 York Place, Knaresborough, HG5 0AA
T: (01423) 863315
F: (01423) 863315

Hermitage Guest House & Tea Garden ♦♦♦
10 Waterside, Knaresborough, HG5 9AZ
T: (01423) 863349
I: www.smoothhound.co.uk/hotels/hermitagel.html

Holly Corner ♦♦♦♦
3 Coverdale Drive, High Bond End, Knaresborough, HG5 9BW
T: (01423) 864204
F: (01423) 864204
E: hollycorner@ukhotelguide.net
I: www.hotelmaster.co.uk

Kirkgate House ♦♦♦♦
17 Kirkgate, Knaresborough, HG5 8AD
T: (01423) 862704
F: (01423) 862704
I: www.knaresborough.co.uk/guest-accom.

The Mitre Hotel ♦♦♦
4 Station Road, Knaresborough, HG5 9AA
T: (01423) 863589
F: (01423) 863589
E: the-mitre@bizhosting.com
I: www.the-mitrehotelbizhosting.com

Newton House Hotel ♦♦♦♦
5-7 York Place, Knaresborough, HG5 0AD
T: (01423) 863539
F: (01423) 869748
E: newtonhouse@btinternet.com
I: www.newtonhousehotel.com

Rosedale ♦♦♦
11 Aspin Way, Knaresborough, HG5 8HL
T: (01423) 867210
F: (01423) 860675
I: www.knaresborough.co.uk/guest-accommodation

11a Silver Street ♦♦♦
11a Silver Street, Knaresborough, HG5 8AJ
T: (01423) 863246
F: (01423) 863246
E: john.prudames@btinternet.com

Watergate Lodge ♦♦♦♦
Watergate Haven, Ripley Road, Knaresborough, HG5 9BU
T: (01423) 864627
F: (01423) 861087
E: info@watergatehaven.com
I: www.watergatehaven.com

Yorkshire Lass ♦♦♦
High Bridge, Harrogate Road, Knaresborough, HG5 8DA
T: (01423) 862962
F: (01423) 869091
E: yorkshirelass@knaresborough.co.uk
I: www.knaresborough.co.uk/yorkshirelass

KNOTTINGLEY
West Yorkshire

Wentvale Court ♦♦♦♦
Great North Road, Knottingley, WF11 8PF
T: (01977) 676714
F: (01977) 676714
E: wentvale@aol.com
I: www.wentvalecourt.co.uk

LANGSETT
South Yorkshire

Waggon and Horses ♦♦♦
Langsett, Stocksbridge, Sheffield S36 4GY
T: (01226) 763147
F: (01226) 763147
E: info@langsettinn.com
I: www.langsettinn.com

LANGTOFT
East Riding of Yorkshire

The Ship Inn ♦♦♦
Scarborough Road, Langtoft, Driffield YO25 3TH
T: (01377) 267243

LAYCOCK
West Yorkshire

Far Laithe Farm
♦♦♦♦♦ SILVER AWARD
Laycock, Keighley BD22 0PP
T: (01535) 661993

LEALHOLM
North Yorkshire

The Board Inn ♦♦♦
Village Green, Lealholm, Whitby YO21 2AJ
T: (01947) 897279
F: (01947) 897764
E: theboardinn@amserve.net

High Park Farm ♦♦♦
Lealholm, Whitby YO21 2AQ
T: (01947) 897416
E: jeremywelford@care4free.net

LEEDS
West Yorkshire

Adriatic Hotel ♦♦♦
87 Harehills Avenue, Leeds, LS8 4ET
T: (0113) 262 0115
F: (0113) 262 6071
E: adriatichotel@tiscali.co.uk
I: www.theadriatichotel.co.uk

Aintree Hotel ♦♦
38 Cardigan Road, Headingley, Leeds LS6 3AG
T: (0113) 275 8290
F: (0113) 275 8290

Avalon Guest House ♦♦♦
132 Woodsley Road, Leeds, LS2 9LZ
T: (0113) 243 2545
F: (0113) 242 0649

Beckett's Park Bed & Breakfast ♦♦♦
49 St Chad's Drive, Headingley, Leeds, LS6 3PZ
T: (0113) 275 0703

Broomhurst Hotel ♦♦♦
12 Chapel Lane, Off Cardigan Road, Headingley, Leeds LS6 3BW
T: (0113) 278 6836
F: (0113) 230 7099

Central Hotel ♦♦
35 - 47 New Briggate, Leeds, LS2 8JD
T: (0113) 294 1456
F: (0113) 294 1551
E: reception@central-hotel.freeserve.com.uk

City Centre Hotel ♦♦
51A New Briggate, Leeds, LS2 8JD
T: (0113) 242 9019
F: (0113) 247 1921

Cliff Lawn Hotel LTD ♦♦♦♦
44/45 Cliff Road, Headingley, Leeds, LS6 2ET
T: (0113) 278 5442
F: (0113) 278 5422
E: ian@clifflawn.fsbusiness.co.uk
I: www.clifflawn-hotel.co.uk

17 Cottage Road ♦♦
Headingley, Leeds LS6 4DD
T: (0113) 275 5575

Fairbairn House ♦♦♦
71-75 Clarendon Road, Leeds, LS2 9PL
T: (0113) 343 6633
F: (0113) 343 6914
E: m.a.timm@leeds.ac.uk

7 Glebelands Drive
Rating Applied For
Leeds, LS6 4AG
T: (0113) 275 6621
E: jprudames@aol.com

Glengarth Hotel ♦♦♦
162 Woodsley Road, Leeds, LS2 9LZ
T: (0113) 245 7940
F: (0113) 216 8033

Highbank Hotel & Restaurant ♦♦
83 Harehills Lane, Leeds, LS7 4HA
T: 0870 741 9227
F: 0870 741 4225
E: highbankhotel@hotmail.com
I: www.leedshotel.com

Hilldene Hotel ♦♦
99 Harehills Lane, Leeds, LS8 4DN
T: (0113) 262 1292
F: (0113) 262 1292

Hinsley Hall ♦♦♦
62 Headingley Lane, Leeds, LS6 2BX
T: (0113) 261 8000
F: (0113) 224 2406
E: info@hinsley-hall.co.uk
I: www.hinsley-hall.co.uk

Kirkstall Hall, Trinity and All Saints College ♦♦♦
Brownberrie Lane, Horsforth, Leeds LS18 5HD
T: (0113) 283 7240
F: (0113) 283 7239
E: j_cressey@tasc.ac.uk
I: www.tasc.ac.uk

Manxdene Private Hotel ♦♦
154 Woodsley Road, Leeds, LS2 9LZ
T: (0113) 243 2586
E: manxdene@dial.pipex.com

The Moorlea Hotel ♦♦♦
146 Woodsley Road, Leeds, LS2 9LZ
T: (0113) 243 2653
F: (0113) 246 5393
E: moorleahotel@aol.com

Number 23 ♦♦♦
23 St Chad's Rise, Far Headingley, Leeds, LS6 3QE
T: (0113) 275 7825

St Michael's Tower Hotel ♦♦♦
5 St Michael's Villas, Cardigan Road, Headingley, Leeds LS6 3AF
T: (0113) 275 5557
F: (0113) 230 7491

Sandylands ♦♦♦
44 Lidgett Lane, Leeds, LS8 1PQ
T: (0113) 266 1666
E: stanpackman@hotmail.com

Temple Manor ♦♦♦♦
2 Field End Garth, Temple Newsam, Leeds, LS15 0QQ
T: (0113) 264 1384

Wheelgate Guest House ♦♦♦
7 Kirkgate, Sherburn-In-Elmet, Leeds, LS25 6BH
T: (01977) 682231
F: (01977) 685287

LEEMING BAR
North Yorkshire

Little Holtby
♦♦♦♦ SILVER AWARD
Leeming Bar, Northallerton DL7 9LH
T: (01609) 748762
F: (01609) 748822
E: littleholtby@yahoo.co.uk
I: www.littleholtby.co.uk

LEVISHAM
North Yorkshire

Horseshoe Inn ♦♦♦
Levisham, Pickering YO18 7NL
T: (01751) 460240
F: (01751) 460240

The Moorlands Country House Hotel ♦♦♦♦♦ GOLD AWARD
Levisham, Pickering YO18 7NL
T: (01751) 460229
F: (01751) 460470
E: ronaldoleonardo@aol.com
I: www.moorlandslevisham.co.uk

Rectory Farm House ♦♦♦♦
Levisham, Pickering YO18 7NL
T: (01751) 460491
E: stay@levisham.com
I: www.levisham.com

LEYBURN
North Yorkshire

Clyde House ♦♦♦
5 Railway Street, Leyburn, DL8 5AY
T: (01969) 623941
F: (01969) 623941
E: info@clydehouseleyburn.co.uk
I: www.clydehouseleyburn.co.uk

Craken House Farm ♦♦♦♦
Middleham Road, Leyburn, DL8 5HF
T: (01969) 622204
F: (01969) 622204
E: marjorie@miveson.fsnet.co.uk

Eastfield Lodge Private Hotel ♦♦♦
St Matthews Terrace, Leyburn, DL8 5EL
T: (01969) 623196
F: (01969) 624599

Grove Hotel ◆◆◆
8 Grove Square, Leyburn, DL8 5AE
T: (01969) 622569
E: info@grove-hotel.com
I: www.grove-hotel.com

The Haven ◆◆◆
Market Place, Leyburn, DL8 5BJ
T: (01969) 623814
E: warmwelcome@havenguesthouse.co.uk
I: www.havenguesthouse.co.uk

Hayloft Suite ◆◆◆
Foal Barn, Spennithorne, Leyburn DL8 5PR
T: (01969) 622580

Park Gate House
◆◆◆◆◆ SILVER AWARD
Constable Burton, Leyburn DL8 5RG
T: (01677) 450466
E: parkgatehouse@freenet.co.uk

LINTON
West Yorkshire

Glendales ◆◆◆
Muddy Lane, Linton, Wetherby LS22 4HW
T: (01937) 585915

LITTLE RIBSTON
North Yorkshire

Beck House ◆◆◆◆
Wetherby Road, Little Ribston, Wetherby LS22 4EP
T: (01937) 583362

LOCKTON
North Yorkshire

Farfields Farmhouse ◆◆◆◆
Farfields Farm, Lockton, Pickering YO18 7NQ
T: (01751) 460239
E: farfieldsfarm@btinternet.com

LOFTHOUSE
West Yorkshire

Tall Trees Hotel ◆◆◆◆
188 Leeds Road, Lofthouse, Wakefield WF3 3LS
T: (01924) 827666
F: (01924) 827555
E: gordon304@aol.com
I: www.talltreeshotel.co.uk

LONDESBOROUGH
East Riding of Yorkshire

Towthorpe Grange ◆◆
Towthorpe Lane, Londesborough, York YO43 3LB
T: (01430) 873814

LONDONDERRY
North Yorkshire

Tatton Lodge ◆◆◆
Londonderry, Northallerton DL7 9NF
T: (01677) 422222
F: (01677) 422222
E: enquiries@tattonlodge.co.uk
I: www.tattonlodge.co.uk

LOW ROW
North Yorkshire

Summer Lodge Farm ◆◆◆
Summer Lodge, Low Row, Richmond DL11 6NP
T: (01748) 886504

LUDDENDENFOOT
West Yorkshire

Bankfield Bed and Breakfast ◆◆◆◆
Danny Lane, Luddendenfoot, Halifax HX2 6AW
T: (01422) 883147
E: jenden@bankfieldbb.fsnet.co.uk

2 Lane Ends ◆◆◆◆
Midgley, Luddendenfoot, Halifax HX2 6TU
T: (01422) 883388
E: sandra@lane-ends-b-b.fsnet.co.uk

Rockcliffe West ◆◆◆◆
Burnley Road, Luddendenfoot, Halifax HX2 6HL
T: (01422) 882151
F: (01422) 882151
E: rockcliffe.b.b@virgin.net

LUND
East Riding of Yorkshire

Clematis House, Farmhouse Bed and Breakfast◆◆◆◆
1 Eastgate, Lund, Driffield YO25 9TQ
T: (01377) 217204
F: (01377) 217204
E: clematis@bblund.fsnet.co.uk
I: www.clematisfarm.co.uk

MALHAM
North Yorkshire

Beck Hall Guest House ◆◆◆
Malham, Skipton BD23 4DJ
T: (01729) 830332

Miresfield Farm ◆◆◆
Malham, Skipton BD23 4DA
T: (01729) 830414
E: chris@miresfield.freeserve.co.uk

River House Hotel ◆◆◆◆
Malham, Skipton BD23 4DA
T: (01729) 830315
F: (01729) 830672
E: info@riverhousehotel.co.uk
I: www.riverhousehotel.co.uk

MALTBY
South Yorkshire

The Cottages Guest House ◆◆
1, 3 & 5 Blyth Road, Maltby, Rotherham S66 8HX
T: (01709) 813382

MALTON
North Yorkshire

Barugh House
◆◆◆◆ SILVER AWARD
Great Barugh, Malton, YO17 6UZ
T: (01653) 668615
E: barughhouse@aol.co.uk

Mill House Bed & Breakfast ◆◆◆
Mill House, East Knapton, Malton, YO17 8JA
T: (01944) 728026
E: carol@millhouse822.freeserve.co.uk

The Old Lodge Hotel ◆◆◆◆
Old Maltongate, Malton, YO17 7EG
T: (01653) 690570

The Old Rectory
◆◆◆◆ SILVER AWARD
West Heslerton, Malton YO17 8RE
T: (01944) 728285
F: (01944) 728436
E: bhillas@supanet.com
I: www.theoldrectoryny.co.uk

The Wentworth Arms ◆◆◆◆
111 Town Street, Old Malton, Malton YO17 7HD
T: (01653) 692618
F: (01653) 600061
E: wentwortharms@btinternet.com

MANKINHOLES
West Yorkshire

Cross Farm ◆◆◆◆
Mankinholes, Todmorden OL14 6HB
T: (01706) 813481

MAPPLEWELL
South Yorkshire

The Grange ◆◆◆
29 Spark Lane, Mapplewell, Barnsley S75 6AA
T: (01226) 380078
E: the.grange@telinco.com

MARKET WEIGHTON
East Riding of Yorkshire

Arras Farmhouse ◆◆◆
Arras Farm, Market Weighton, York YO43 4RN
T: (01430) 872404
F: (01430) 872404

MARSDEN
West Yorkshire

Olive Branch Restaurant with Rooms and Bar
◆◆◆◆ SILVER AWARD
Manchester Road, Marsden, Huddersfield HD7 6LU
T: (01484) 844487
E: reservations@olivebranch.uk.com
I: www.olivebranch.uk.com

Throstle Nest Cottage B&B Rating Applied For
3 Old Mount Road, Marsden, Huddersfield HD7 6DU
T: (01484) 846371
F: (01484) 846371

MARTON
North Yorkshire

Wildsmith House
◆◆◆◆ SILVER AWARD
Marton, Sinnington, York YO62 6RD
T: (01751) 432702
E: wildsmithhouse@talk21.com
I: www.pb-design.com/swiftlink/bb/1102.htm

MASHAM
North Yorkshire

Garden House ◆◆◆◆
1 Park Street, Masham, Ripon HG4 4HN
T: (01765) 689989
E: S.Furby@freenet.co.uk
I: www.ukfreenet.co.uk

Haregill Lodge ◆◆◆◆
Ellingstring, Masham, Ripon HG4 4PW
T: (01677) 460272
F: (01677) 460272
E: haregilllodge@freenet.co.uk

Warren House Farm ◆◆◆
High Ellington, Masham, Ripon HG4 4PP
T: (01677) 460244
F: (01677) 460244
E: cath.e.broadley@btopenworld.com

MENSTON
West Yorkshire

Chevin End Guest House ◆◆◆
West Chevin Road, Menston, Ilkley LS29 6DU
T: (01943) 876845
E: chevinend.guesthouse@virgin.net
I: www.chevinendguesthouse.co.uk

MIDDLEHAM
North Yorkshire

The Black Bull Inn ◆◆◆◆
Market Place, Middleham, Leyburn DL8 4NX
T: (01969) 623669
E: blackbull@tinyworld.co.uk

Chapelfields ◆◆◆
East Witton Road, Middleham, Leyburn DL8 4PY
T: (01969) 625075
F: (01765) 689991
E: chapelfieldsuk@aol.com
I: www.chapelfieldsuk.co.uk

Domus ◆◆◆◆
Market Place, Middleham, Leyburn DL8 4NR
T: (01969) 623497
E: domus_2000@yahoo.co.uk

Jasmine House
◆◆◆◆◆ GOLD AWARD
Market Place, Middleham, Leyburn DL8 4NU
T: (01969) 622858
E: enquiries@jasminehouse.net
I: jasminehouse.net

The Priory ◆◆◆
West End, Middleham, Leyburn DL8 4QG
T: (01969) 623279

Richard III Hotel ◆◆◆
Market Place, Middleham, Leyburn DL8 4NP
T: (01969) 623240

17th Century Castle Keep ◆◆◆◆
Castle Hill, Middleham, Leyburn DL8 4QR
T: (01969) 623665
E: tonymaddison@aol.co.uk
I: www.c17castlekeep.com

Yore View ◆◆◆◆
Leyburn Road, Middleham, Leyburn DL8 4PL
T: (01969) 622987

MIDDLETON-ON-THE-WOLDS
East Riding of Yorkshire

Post Cottage ◆◆◆
31 Front Street, Middleton-on-the-Wolds, Driffield YO25 9UA
T: (01377) 217115

MIDGLEY
West Yorkshire

Midgley Lodge Motel ◆◆◆
Bar Lane, Midgley, Wakefield WF4 4JJ
T: (01924) 830069
F: (01924) 830087
I: www.scoot.co.uk/midgley-lodge-motel

MIDHOPESTONES
South Yorkshire

Ye Olde Mustard Pot ♦♦♦♦
Mortimer Road, Midhopestones, Sheffield S36 4GW
T: (01226) 761155
F: (01226) 761161
E: reservations@yeoldemustardpot.co.uk
I: www.yeoldemustardpot.co.uk

MILLINGTON
East Riding of Yorkshire

Laburnum Cottage ♦♦♦
Millington, York YO42 1TX
T: (01759) 303055
E: roger&maureen@labcott.fslife.co.uk
I: www.smoothhound.co.uk/hotels/laburnumcottage.html

MUKER
North Yorkshire

Bridge House
Rating Applied For
Muker, Richmond DL11 6QD
T: (01748) 886461
E: alannichols88@hotmail.com

Hylands ♦♦♦♦
Muker, Richmond DL11 6QQ
T: (01748) 886003
E: jonesr3@btinternet.com

MYTHOLMROYD
West Yorkshire

Redacre Mill
♦♦♦♦ SILVER AWARD
Redacre Mill, Mytholmroyd, Hebden Bridge HX7 5DQ
T: (01422) 885563
F: (01422) 885563
E: peters@redacremill.freeserve.co.uk
I: www.redacremill.freeserve.co.uk

NAWTON
North Yorkshire

Nawton Grange ♦♦♦♦
Gale Lane, Nawton, York YO62 7SD
T: (01439) 771146
E: chrisbaxter@themail.co.uk

NEW WALTHAM
North East Lincolnshire

Peaks Top Farm ♦♦♦
Hewitts Avenue, New Waltham, Grimsby DN36 4RS
T: (01472) 812941
F: (01472) 812941
E: lmclayton@tinyworld.co.uk

NEWBY WISKE
North Yorkshire

Well House ♦♦♦♦
Newby Wiske, Northallerton DL7 9EX
T: (01609) 772253
F: (01609) 772253

NEWTON-ON-OUSE
North Yorkshire

Village Farm Holidays ♦♦♦♦
Cherry Tree Avenue, Newton-on-Ouse, York YO30 2BN
T: (01347) 848064
F: (01347) 848065
E: vfholidays@cs.com
I: www.yorkshirenet.co.uk/stayat/villagefarm

NEWTON-ON-RAWCLIFFE
North Yorkshire

Elm House Farm ♦♦♦♦
Newton-on-Rawcliffe, Pickering YO18 8QA
T: (01751) 473223

Swan Cottage ♦♦♦
Newton-on-Rawcliffe, Pickering YO18 8QA
T: (01751) 472502

NORTH CAVE
East Riding of Yorkshire

Albion House ♦♦
18 Westgate, North Cave, Brough HU15 2NJ
T: (01430) 422958
E: caroline@ccockin.freeserve.co.uk

NORTH FERRIBY
East Riding of Yorkshire

B & B @103 ♦♦♦
103 Ferriby High Road, North Ferriby, HU14 3LA
T: (01482) 633637
E: info@bnb103.co.uk
I: www.bnb103.co.uk

NORTHALLERTON
North Yorkshire

Alverton Guest House ♦♦♦
26 South Parade, Northallerton, DL7 8SG
T: (01609) 776207
F: (01609) 776207
E: alverton.26@talk21.com

The Conifers ♦♦♦
18 Almond Grove, Northallerton, DL7 8RQ
T: (01609) 773361
E: ericpennypop@aol.com

Elmscott
♦♦♦♦ SILVER AWARD
10 Hatfield Road, Northallerton, DL7 8QX
T: (01609) 760575
E: elmscott@freenet.co.uk
I: www.elmscottbedandbreakfast.co.uk

Heyrose Farm ♦♦♦
Lovesome Hill, Northallerton, DL6 2PS
T: (01609) 881554
F: (01609) 881554
E: heyrosefarm@hotmail.com

Lovesome Hill Farm ♦♦♦♦
Lovesome Hill, Northallerton DL6 2PB
T: (01609) 772311
E: pearsonlhf@care4free.net

Masham House Bed And Breakfast ♦♦♦♦
18 South Parade, Northallerton, DL7 8SG
T: (01609) 771541
E: jpbb@ukonline.co.uk

Porch House
♦♦♦♦ GOLD AWARD
68 High Street, Northallerton, DL7 8EG
T: (01609) 779831
F: (01609) 778603

NORTON
North Yorkshire

Lynden ♦♦♦
165 Welham Road, Norton, Malton YO17 9DU
T: (01653) 694236

NORWOOD
North Yorkshire

The Old Primary ♦♦♦♦
Bland Hill, Norwood, Harrogate HG3 1TB
T: (01943) 880472

NUNNINGTON
North Yorkshire

Sunley Court ♦♦♦
Nunnington, York YO62 5XQ
T: (01439) 748233
F: (01439) 748233

OSMOTHERLEY
North Yorkshire

Oak Garth Farm ♦♦
North End, Osmotherley, Northallerton DL6 3BH
T: (01609) 883314

Osmotherley Walking Shop ♦♦♦
4 West End, Osmotherley, Northallerton DL6 3AA
T: (01609) 883818
E: walkingshop@osmotherley.fsbusiness.co.uk
I: www.coast2coast.co.uk/osmotherleywalkingshop

Vane House ♦♦♦
11A North End, Osmotherley, Northallerton DL6 3BA
T: (01609) 883448
F: (01609) 883448
I: www.coast2coast.co.uk/vanehouse

OSSETT
West Yorkshire

Heath House ♦♦♦
Chancery Road, Ossett, WF5 9RZ
T: (01924) 260654
F: (01924) 260654
E: jo.holland@amserve.net
I: www.heath-house.co.uk

Mews Hotel ♦♦♦♦
Dale Street, Ossett, WF5 9HN
T: (01924) 273982
F: (01924) 279389
E: enquiries@mews-hotel.co.uk
I: www.mews-hotel.co.uk

OTLEY
West Yorkshire

11 Newall Mount ♦♦♦
Otley, LS21 2DY
T: (01943) 462898

Paddock Hill ♦♦♦
Norwood, Otley LS21 2QU
T: (01943) 465977
E: cheribeaumont@connectfree.co.uk

Scaife Hall Farm
♦♦♦♦ SILVER AWARD
Hardisty Hill, Blubberhouses, Otley LS21 2PL
T: (01943) 880354
F: (01943) 880374
E: christine.a.ryder@btinternet.com
I: www.scaifehallfarm.co.uk

Wood Top Farm ♦♦♦♦
Off Norwood Edge, Lindley, Otley, LS21 2QS
T: (01943) 464010
F: (01943) 464010
E: mailwoodtop@aol.com

OTTRINGHAM
East Riding of Yorkshire

Highfield Farm ♦♦♦♦
Station Road, Ottringham, Hull HU12 0BJ
T: (01964) 622283
E: sylvia@highfieldfarm.ukf.net
I: www.highfieldfarm.ukf.net

PATELEY BRIDGE
North Yorkshire

Bewerley Hall Farm ♦♦♦
Bewerley, Harrogate HG3 5JA
T: (01423) 711636
E: chris@farmhouseholidays.freeserve.co.uk
I: www.bewerleyhallfarm.co.uk

Bruce House Farm ♦♦♦♦
Top Wath Road, Pateley Bridge, Harrogate HG3 5PG
T: (01423) 711813
F: (01423) 712843
E: brucehse@aol.com
I: members.aol.com/brucehse

Dale View ♦♦♦
Old Church Lane, Pateley Bridge, Harrogate HG3 5LY
T: (01423) 711506
F: (01423) 711506
E: bedandbreakfast@daleview.com

Greengarth ♦♦♦
Greenwood Road, Pateley Bridge, Harrogate HG3 5LR
T: (01423) 711688

Knottside Farm
♦♦♦♦♦ GOLD AWARD
The Knott, Pateley Bridge, Harrogate HG3 5DQ
T: (01423) 712927
F: (01423) 712927

Nidderdale Lodge Farm ♦♦♦
Fellbeck, Harrogate HG3 5DR
T: (01423) 711677

North Pasture Farm
♦♦♦♦ SILVER AWARD
Brimham Rocks, Summer Bridge, Harrogate HG3 4DW
T: (01423) 711470
F: (01423) 711470
I: www.yorkshirenet.co.uk/stayat/northpasturefarm

PATRICK BROMPTON
North Yorkshire

Neesham Cottage
Rating Applied For
Patrick Brompton, Bedale DL8 1LN
T: (01677) 450271
E: info@neeshamcottage.co.uk
I: www.neeshamcottage.co.uk

PENISTONE
South Yorkshire

Cubley Hall Freehouse Pub-Restaurant-Hotel ♦♦♦♦
North Star Hotels Ltd, Mortimer Road, Penistone, Sheffield S36 9DF
T: (01226) 766086
F: (01226) 767335
E: cubley.hall@ukonline.co.uk

PICKERING
North Yorkshire

Barker Stakes Farm ♦♦♦
Lendales Lane, Pickering, YO18 8EE
T: (01751) 476759
F: (01751) 476759

Beech Cottage ♦♦♦
Saintoft, Pickering, YO18 8QQ
T: (01751) 417625

Black Swan Hotel ♦♦♦
18 Birdgate, Pickering, YO18 7AL
T: (01751) 472286
F: (01751) 472928

Bramwood Guest House
♦♦♦♦ SILVER AWARD
19 Hallgarth, Pickering,
YO18 7AW
T: (01751) 474066
I: www.bramwoodguesthouse.co.uk

Bridge House
♦♦♦♦ SILVER AWARD
8 Bridge Street, Pickering,
YO18 8DT
T: (01751) 477234

Burgate House Hotel & Restaurant ♦♦♦♦
17 Burgate, Pickering, YO18 7AU
T: (01751) 473463
E: info@burgatehouse.co.uk
I: www.burgatehouse.co.uk

Burr Bank
♦♦♦♦♦ GOLD AWARD
Cropton, Pickering YO18 8HL
T: (01751) 417777
F: (01751) 417789
E: bandb@burrbank.com
I: www.burrbank.com

Clent House ♦♦♦
15 Burgate, Pickering, YO18 7AU
T: (01751) 477928
E: swiftlink/bb/1315@pb-design.com
I: www.pb-design.com/swiftlink/bb/1315.htm

Costa House
♦♦♦♦ SILVER AWARD
12 Westgate, Pickering,
YO18 8BA
T: (01751) 474291
E: rooms@costahouse.co.uk
I: www.costahouse.co.uk

Eden House
♦♦♦♦ SILVER AWARD
120 Eastgate, Pickering,
YO18 7DW
T: (01751) 472289
F: (01751) 476066
E: edenhouse@breathemail.net
I: www.edenhousebandb.co.uk

Fox and Hounds Country Inn ♦♦♦♦
Sinnington, York YO62 6SQ
T: (01751) 431577
F: (01751) 432791
E: foxhoundsinn@easynet.co.uk

Givendale Head Farm ♦♦♦
Ebberston, Scarborough
YO13 9PU
T: (01723) 859383
F: (01723) 859383
E: sue.gwilliam@talk21.com
I: www.givendaleheadfarm.co.uk

Grindale House ♦♦♦♦
123 Eastgate, Pickering,
YO18 7DW
T: (01751) 476636
F: (01751) 475727

Heathcote House ♦♦♦♦
100 Eastgate, Pickering,
YO18 7DW
T: (01751) 476991
F: (01751) 476991
E: joanlovejoy@lineone.net

Laurel Bank B&B
♦♦♦♦ SILVER AWARD
Middleton Road, Pickering,
YO18 8AP
T: (01751) 476399

Munda Wanga ♦
14 Garden Way, Pickering,
YO18 8BG
T: (01751) 473310

The Old Manse ♦♦♦♦
Middleton Road, Pickering,
YO18 8AL
T: (01751) 476484
F: (01751) 477124
E: valerie-a-gardner@talk21.com

Rains Farm ♦♦♦♦
Allerston, Pickering YO18 7PQ
T: (01723) 859333
E: allan@rainsfarm.freeserve.co.uk
I: www.rains-farm-holidays.co.uk

Rose Folly
♦♦♦♦ SILVER AWARD
112 Eastgate, Pickering,
YO18 7DW
T: (01751) 475057
E: gail@rosefolly.freeserve.co.uk
I: www.rosefolly.freeserve.co.uk

Rosebank Bed & Breakfast ♦♦♦♦
61 Ruffa Lane, Pickering,
YO18 7HN
T: (01751) 472531

The Station Hotel ♦♦
11 Park Street, Pickering,
YO18 7AJ
T: (01751) 472171
F: (01751) 477416
E: huntagri@supanet.com

Vivers Mill ♦♦♦
Mill Lane, Pickering, YO18 8DJ
T: (01751) 473640
E: viversmill@talk21.com
I: www.viversmill.com

POCKLEY
North Yorkshire

West View Cottage
♦♦♦♦ SILVER AWARD
Pockley, York YO62 7TE
T: (01439) 770526
E: westviewcottage@bedbreakfast.freeserve.co.uk
I: www.s-h-systems.co.uk/hotels/westviewcottage

PRESTON
East Riding of Yorkshire

Little Weghill Farm ♦♦♦♦
Weghill Road, Preston, Hull
HU12 8SX
T: (01482) 897650
F: (01482) 897650
E: littleweghillfarm@amserve.net

PUDSEY
West Yorkshire

Heatherlea House ♦♦♦
105 Littlemoor Road, Pudsey,
LS28 8AP
T: (0113) 257 4397
E: heatherlea_pudsey.leeds@excite.co.uk

Lynnwood House ♦♦♦
18 Alexandra Road, Uppermoor,
Pudsey, LS28 8BY
T: (0113) 257 1117

RAMSGILL
North Yorkshire

Covill Barn ♦♦♦♦
Bouthwaite, Harrogate
HG3 5RW
T: (01423) 755306
F: (01423) 755306
E: sales@jandsenterprises.co.uk
I: www.jandsenterprises.co.uk

RASKELF
North Yorkshire

Old Black Bull Inn ♦♦♦
Raskelf, York YO61 3LF
T: (01347) 821431
E: pjacksobbull@bizonline.co.uk

RASTRICK
West Yorkshire

Elder Lea House
♦♦♦♦♦ SILVER AWARD
Clough Lane, Rastrick, Brighouse
HD6 3QH
T: (01484) 717832
E: elderleahouse@amserve.net

RATHMELL
North Yorkshire

The Stables ♦♦♦♦
Field House, Rathmell, Settle
BD24 0LA
T: (01729) 840234
F: (01729) 840775
E: rosehyslop@easynet.co.uk

RAVENSCAR
North Yorkshire

Cliff House ♦♦♦♦
Ravenscar, Scarborough
YO13 0LX
T: (01723) 870889
E: hodgson@cliffhouse.fsbusiness.co.uk
I: www.clifftopstop.com

Smugglers Rock Country House ♦♦♦♦
Staintondale Road, Ravenscar,
Scarborough YO13 0ER
T: (01723) 870044
E: info@smugglersrock.co.uk
I: www.smugglersrock.co.uk

RAVENSWORTH
North Yorkshire

The Bay Horse Inn ♦♦♦
Ravensworth, Richmond
DL11 7ET
T: (01325) 718328

REETH
North Yorkshire

Arkle House ♦♦♦♦
Mill Lane, Reeth, Richmond
DL11 6SJ
T: (01748) 884815
F: (01748) 884942
E: andy@arklehouse.com
I: www.arklehouse.com

2 Bridge Terrace ♦♦♦
Reeth, Richmond DL11 6TP
T: (01748) 884572
E: davidsizer@freenetname.co.uk
I: coast2coast.co.uk/2bridgeterrace

Buck Hotel ♦♦♦
Reeth, Richmond DL11 6SW
T: (01748) 884210
F: (01748) 884802
E: enquiries@buckhotel.co.uk
I: www.buckhotel.co.uk

Elder Peak ♦♦♦
Arkengarthdale Road, Reeth,
Richmond DL11 6QX
T: (01748) 884770

Hackney House ♦♦♦
Reeth, Richmond DL11 6TW
T: (01748) 884302
E: hackneyhse@tinyworld.co.uk

Kernot Court ♦♦
Reeth, Richmond DL11 6SF
T: (01748) 884662

Springfield House ♦♦♦♦
Quaker Close, Reeth, Richmond
DL11 6UY
T: (01748) 884634
E: springfield.house@breathemail.net

RICCALL
North Yorkshire

South Newlands Farm ♦♦♦
Selby Road, Riccall, York
YO19 6QR
T: (01757) 248203
F: (01757) 249450
E: pswann3059@aol.com
I: www.yorkbandb.f9.co.uk

RICHMOND
North Yorkshire

The Buck Inn
Rating Applied For
27-29 Newbiggin, Richmond,
DL10 4DX
T: (01748) 822259

Emmanuel Guest House ♦♦♦
41 Maison Dieu, Richmond,
DL10 7AU
T: (01748) 823584
F: (01748) 821554

66 Frenchgate ♦♦♦
Richmond, DL10 7AG
T: (01748) 823421
E: Paul@66french.freeserve.co.uk

18 Gilling Road ♦♦♦
Richmond, DL10 5AA
T: (01748) 825491
F: (01748) 821847

Holmedale ♦♦♦
Dalton, Richmond DL11 7HX
T: (01833) 621236
F: (01833) 621236
E: David@holmedale.free-online.co.uk

27 Hurgill Road ♦♦
Richmond, DL10 4AR
T: (01748) 824092
F: (01748) 824092

Mount Pleasant Farm ♦♦♦♦
Whashton, Richmond DL11 7JP
T: (01748) 822784
F: (01748) 822784

Nuns Cottage ♦♦♦♦
5 Hurgill Road, Richmond,
DL10 4AR
T: (01748) 822809
E: nunscottage@richmond.org.uk
I: www.richmond.org.uk/business/nunscottage

Pottergate Guest House ♦♦♦
4 Pottergate, Richmond,
DL10 4AB
T: (01748) 823826

The Restaurant on the Green ♦♦♦
5-7 Bridge Street, Richmond, DL10 4RW
T: (01748) 826229
F: (01748) 826229
E: accom.bennett@talk21.com
I: www.coast2coast.co.uk/restaurantonthegreen

Victoria House ♦♦♦♦
49 Maison Dieu, Richmond, DL10 7AU
T: (01748) 824830

West Cottage ♦♦♦
Victoria Road, Richmond, DL10 4AS
T: (01748) 824046
E: kay.gibson@tesco.net

West End Guest House ♦♦♦♦
45 Reeth Road, Richmond, DL10 4EX
T: (01748) 824783
E: westend@richmond.org
I: www.stayatwestend.com

Whashton Springs Farm
♦♦♦♦ SILVER AWARD
(North Yorkshire), Richmond, DL11 7JS
T: (01748) 822884
F: (01748) 826285
E: whashton@turnbullg-f.freeserve.co.uk
I: www.whashtonsprings.co.uk

White Cottage ♦♦♦
Colburn Village, Richmond, DL9 4PD
T: (01748) 833714
E: whitecottage@colburnvillage.fsnet.co.uk
I: www.whitecottage.info

Willance House Guesthouse ♦♦♦
24 Frenchgate, Richmond, DL10 7AG
T: (01748) 824467
F: (01748) 824467
E: willance@bun.com

RIEVAULX
North Yorkshire

Barn Close Farm
Rating Applied For
Rievaulx, York YO62 5LH
T: (01439) 798321

RIPLEY
North Yorkshire

Slate Rigg Farm ♦♦♦
Birthwaite Lane, Ripley, Harrogate HG3 3JQ
T: (01423) 770135

RIPON
North Yorkshire

Bishopton Grove House ♦♦♦
Bishopton, Ripon, HG4 2QL
T: (01765) 600888
E: wimpress@bronco.co.uk

Cowscot House ♦♦♦
Kirkby Malzeard, Ripon HG4 3SE
T: (01765) 658266

Crescent Lodge ♦♦♦♦
42 North Street, Ripon, HG4 1EN
T: (01765) 609589
F: (01765) 609594
E: simpgry@aol.com
I: www.crescentlodge.co.uk

Fremantle House ♦♦♦
35 North Road, Ripon, HG4 1JR
T: (01765) 605819
F: (01765) 601313
E: jcar105462@aol.com
I: www.riponforward.homestead.com/freemantle.html

Mallard Grange
♦♦♦♦♦ SILVER AWARD
Aldfield, Ripon HG4 3BE
T: (01765) 620242
F: (01765) 620242
E: Mallard@Grange@btinternet.com

Middle Ridge
♦♦♦♦♦ GOLD AWARD
42 Mallorie Park Drive, Ripon, HG4 2QF
T: (01765) 690558
F: (01765) 690558
E: john@midrig.demon.co.uk

Moor End Farm ♦♦♦♦
Knaresborough Road, Littlethorpe, Ripon HG4 3LU
T: (01765) 677419
E: pspensley@ukonline.co.uk
I: www.yorkshirebandb.co.uk

Ravencroft B&B
Rating Applied For
Moorside Avenue, Ripon, HG4 1TA
T: (01765) 602543
F: (01765) 606058
E: ravencroftbandb@btopenworld.com
I: www.btopenworld.com?~ravencroftbandb

River Side Guest House ♦♦♦
20-21 Iddesleigh Terrace, Boroughbridge Road, Ripon, HG4 1QW
T: (01765) 603864
F: (01765) 602707
E: christopher-pearson3@virgin-net

The Royal Oak
Rating Applied For
36 Kirkgate, Ripon, HG4 1PB
T: (01765) 602284
F: (01765) 690031

St George's Court ♦♦♦♦
Old Home Farm, Grantley, Ripon HG4 3EU
T: (01765) 620618
F: (01765) 620618
E: stgeorgescourt@bronco.co.uk
I: www.stgeorges-court.co.uk

Sharow Cross House
♦♦♦♦ SILVER AWARD
Dishforth Road, Sharow, Ripon HG4 5BQ
T: (01765) 609866
E: sharowcrosshouse@btinternet.com
I: www.sharowcrosshouse.com

RISPLITH
North Yorkshire

Yeomans Well
♦♦♦♦ SILVER AWARD
Risplith, Ripon HG4 3EP
T: (01765) 620378
E: yeomanswell@hotmail.com
I: www.yorkshirebandb.co.uk

ROBIN HOOD'S BAY
North Yorkshire

Boathouse Bistro ♦♦♦
The Dock, Robin Hood's Bay, Whitby YO22 4SJ
T: (01947) 880099

Flask Inn Travel Lodge ♦♦♦♦
Robin Hood's Bay, Whitby YO22 4QH
T: (01947) 880692
F: (01947) 880592
E: flaskinn@aol.com
I: www.flaskinn.com

Lee-Side ♦♦♦♦
Mount Pleasant South, Robin Hood's Bay, Whitby YO22 4RQ
T: (01947) 881143

Ravenswood Bed and Breakfast ♦♦♦
Ravenswood, Mount Pleasant North, Robin Hood's Bay, Whitby YO22 4RE
T: (01947) 880690
F: (01947) 880690
E: ravenswood@mail.com
I: www.ravenswoodbb.co.uk

Victoria Hotel ♦♦♦♦
Station Road, Robin Hood's Bay, Whitby YO22 4RL
T: (01947) 880205
F: (01947) 881170

ROECLIFFE
North Yorkshire

The Crown at Roecliffe ♦♦♦
Roecliffe, York YO51 9LY
T: (01423) 322578
F: (01423) 324060
E: crownroecliffe@btinternet.com

ROMANBY
North Yorkshire

Bridge End ♦♦
159 Chantry Road, Romanby, Northallerton DL7 8JJ
T: (01609) 772655
F: (01609) 772655

ROSEDALE ABBEY
North Yorkshire

Sevenford House
♦♦♦♦ SILVER AWARD
Rosedale Abbey, Pickering YO18 8SE
T: (01751) 417283
F: (01751) 417505
E: sevenford@aol.com
I: www.sevenford.com

ROTHERHAM
South Yorkshire

Fernlea Hotel ♦♦♦
74 Gerard Road, Moorgate, Rotherham, S60 2PW
T: (01709) 830884
F: (01709) 305951

Fitzwilliam Arms Hotel ♦♦♦
Taylors Lane, Parkgate, Rotherham, S62 6EE
T: (01709) 522744
F: (01709) 710110

Phoenix Hotel ♦♦
1 College Road, Rotherham, S60 1EY
T: (01709) 364611
F: (01709) 511121

RUDSTON
East Riding of Yorkshire

Eastgate Farm Cottage ♦♦♦
Rudston, Driffield YO25 0UX
T: (01262) 420150
F: (01262) 420150
E: ebrudston@aol.com
I: www.eastgatefarmcottage.com

RUNSWICK BAY
North Yorkshire

Cockpit House ♦♦
The Old Village (Nr Whitby), Runswick Bay, Saltburn-by-the-Sea TS13 5HU
T: (01947) 840504

Ellerby Hotel
♦♦♦♦ SILVER AWARD
Ellerby, Saltburn-by-the-Sea YO21 2DE
T: (01947) 840342
F: (01947) 841221
E: relax@ellerbyhotel.co.uk
I: www.ellerbyhotel.co.uk

The Firs ♦♦♦♦
26 Hinderwell Lane, Runswick Bay, Saltburn-by-the-Sea TS13 5HR
T: (01947) 840433
F: (01947) 841616
E: mandy.shackleton@talk21.com
I: www.the-firs.co.uk

Newholme ♦♦♦
8 Hinderwell Lane, Runswick Bay, Saltburn-by-the-Sea TS13 5HR
T: (01947) 840358

The Runswick Bay Hotel ♦♦♦
Runswick Bay, Saltburn-by-the-Sea TS13 5HR
T: (01947) 841010
F: (01947) 841337

RUSWARP
North Yorkshire

Old Hall Hotel ♦♦
High Street, Ruswarp, Whitby YO21 1NH
T: (01947) 602801
F: (01947) 602801
E: info@oldhallhotel.co.uk
I: www.oldhallhotel.co.uk

The Old Station House ♦♦♦♦
Ruswarp, Whitby YO21 1NJ
T: (01947) 825050
E: pipparuswarp@aol.com

SALTERSGATE
North Yorkshire

Newgate Foot Farm ♦♦♦♦
Newgate Foot, Saltersgate, Pickering YO18 7NR
T: (01751) 460215
F: (01751) 460215

SANDSEND
North Yorkshire

The Haven Under The Hill ♦♦♦♦
Sandsend, Whitby YO21 3TG
T: (01947) 893202

Woodlands
Rating Applied For
Sandsend, Whitby YO21 3TG
T: (01947) 893272
I: www.woodlandssandsend.co.uk

SCACKLETON
North Yorkshire

Church Farm ♦♦♦♦
Scackleton, York YO62 4NB
T: (01653) 628403
F: (01653) 628403
E: b&b@churchfarmyork.freeserve.co.uk

SCAGGLETHORPE
North Yorkshire

Scagglethorpe Manor
♦♦♦♦ SILVER AWARD
Main Street, Scagglethorpe,
Malton YO17 8DT
T: (01944) 758909
F: (01944) 758909

SCALBY
North Yorkshire

Holly Croft ♦♦♦♦♦
28 Station Road, Scalby,
Scarborough YO13 0QA
T: (01723) 375376
F: (01723) 360563

SCARBOROUGH
North Yorkshire

Aartswood Guest House ♦♦
27 - 29 Trafalgar Square,
Scarborough, YO12 7PZ
T: (01723) 360689
E: aartswood@btconnect.com
I: www.yorkshirecoast.co.uk/aartswood

Abbey Court Hotel ♦♦♦
19 West Street, South Cliff,
Scarborough, YO11 2QR
T: (01723) 360659

Aberdeen House Hotel ♦♦♦
34 Aberdeen Walk, Scarborough,
YO11 1XW
T: (01723) 371158
F: (01723) 350959

Adene Hotel ♦♦♦
39 Esplanade Road,
Scarborough, YO11 2AT
T: (01723) 373658

Admiral ♦♦♦
13 West Square, Scarborough,
YO11 1TW
T: (01723) 375084
F: (01723) 375084

Airedale Guest House ♦♦♦
23 Trafalgar Square,
Scarborough, YO12 7PZ
T: (01723) 366809
E: shaunatairedale@aol.com

Aldon Hotel ♦♦♦♦
120-122 Columbus Ravine,
Scarborough, YO12 7QZ
T: (01723) 372198

The Alexander Hotel
♦♦♦♦ SILVER AWARD
33 Burniston Road,
Scarborough, YO11 6PG
T: (01723) 363178
F: (01723) 354821
E: alex@atesto.freeserve.co.uk
I: www.atesto.freeserve.co.uk

Hotel Almar ♦♦♦
116 Columbus Ravine,
Scarborough, YO12 7QZ
T: (01723) 372887
F: (01723) 372887

The Anchor Guest Accommodation ♦♦
61 Northstead Manor Drive,
Scarborough, YO12 6AF
T: (01723) 364518
F: (01723) 364518
E: theanchor@hotmail.com

Arlington Private Hotel
♦♦♦♦
42 West Street, South Cliff,
Scarborough, YO11 2QP
T: (01723) 503600
F: (01723) 506762
E: alex@arlington-hotel.fsnet.co.uk
I: www.smoothhound.co.uk/hotels/arlingtonhotel/html

Arran Licensed Hotel ♦♦♦
114 North Marine Road,
Scarborough, YO12 7JA
T: (01723) 364692

Ashburton Hotel ♦♦♦
43 Valley Road, Scarborough,
YO11 2LX
T: (01723) 374382
F: (01723) 374382
E: lindahindhaugh@ashburton43.freeserve.co.uk
I: www.yorkshirecoast.co.uk/ashburton

Atlanta Hotel ♦♦♦
62 Columbus Ravine,
Scarborough, YO12 7QU
T: (01723) 360996
E: atlanta62@aol.com
I: www.atlantahotelscarborough.co.uk

Boston Hotel ♦♦♦
1-2 Blenheim Terrace, North
Bay, Scarborough, YO12 7HF
T: (01723) 360296
F: (01723) 353838
E: suzannewhitton@bostonhotel.freeserve.co.uk
I: www.2000k.com/ta/bostonhotel

Brincliffe Edge Hotel ♦♦♦
105 Queens Parade,
Scarborough, YO12 7HY
T: (01723) 364834
E: brincliffeedgehotel@yahoo.co.uk
I: www.brincliffeedgehotel.co.uk

Hotel Catania ♦♦
141 Queens Parade,
Scarborough, YO12 7HU
T: (01723) 364516
F: (01723) 372640
E: hotelcatania@aol.co.uk

Cavendish Private Hotel
♦♦♦♦
53 Esplanade Road, Southcliff,
Scarborough, YO11 2AT
T: (01723) 362108
E: cavendishhotel@hotmail.com
I: www.s-h-a.dircon.co.uk

Chessington Hotel ♦♦♦
The Crescent, Scarborough,
YO11 2PP
T: (01723) 365207
F: (01723) 375206

Cliffside Hotel ♦♦♦
79-81 Queens Parade,
Scarborough, YO12 7HT
T: (01723) 361087
F: (01723) 366472
E: cliffside@fsmail.net
I: www.yorkshirecoast.co.uk/cliffside

Cordelia Hotel ♦♦♦
51 Esplanade Road, South Cliff,
Scarborough, YO11 2AT
T: (01723) 363393
F: (01723) 363393

Donnington Hotel ♦♦♦
13 Givendale Road,
Scarborough, YO12 6LE
T: (01723) 374394
E: bookings@donningtonhotel.co.uk
I: www.donningtonhotel.co.uk

Earlsmere Hotel
Rating Applied For
5 Belvedere Road, South Cliff,
Scarborough, YO11 2UU
T: (01723) 361340

Hotel Ellenby ♦♦♦
95-97 Queens Parade,
Scarborough, YO12 7HY
T: (01723) 372916
F: (01723) 372916
E: thorn9523@aol.com

Empire Hotel ♦♦
39 Albermarle Crescent,
Scarborough, YO11 1XX
T: (01723) 373564

Esplanade Gardens Hotel ♦♦♦
24 Esplanade Gardens,
Southcliff, Scarborough,
YO11 2AP
T: (01723) 360728
E: hopkin@ntlworld.com
I: www.yorkshirecoast.co.uk/martyns/index.htm

Falcon Inn ♦♦♦
Whitby Road, Cloughton,
Scarborough YO13 0DY
T: (01723) 870717
I: www.yorkshirecoast.co.uk/falcon

Gardens Hotel ♦♦♦
12 Esplanade Gardens, South
Cliff, Scarborough, YO11 2AW
T: (01723) 361800
E: gardenshotel@beetl.com
I: www.gardenshotel.co.uk

Gordon Hotel ♦♦♦♦
Ryndleside, Scarborough,
YO12 6AD
T: (01723) 362177
E: sales@gordonhotel.co.uk
I: www.gordonhotel.co.uk

The Grand Hotel ♦♦♦
St Nicholas Cliff, Scarborough,
YO11 2ET
T: (01723) 375371
F: (01723) 378518
E: reservations@grandhotelscarborough.co.uk
I: www.grandhotelgroup.co.uk

Granville Lodge Hotel ♦♦♦♦
Belmont Road, Scarborough,
YO11 2AA
T: (01723) 367668
F: (01723) 363089
E: granville@scarborough.co.uk
I: www.granville.scarborough.co.uk

Greno Seafront Hotel ♦♦
25 Blenheim Terrace, Queens
Parade, Scarborough, YO12 7HD
T: (01723) 375705
F: (01723) 355512

The Gresham Hotel ♦♦♦
18 Lowdale Avenue, Northstead,
Scarborough, YO12 6JW
T: (01723) 372117
F: (01723) 372117
E: karen.robinson3@tesco.net
I: www.thegreshamhotel.co.uk

Grosvenor Hotel ♦♦♦
51 Grosvenor Road,
Scarborough, YO11 2LZ
T: (01723) 363801
F: (01723) 366936

Harcourt Hotel ♦♦♦♦
45 Esplanade, Scarborough,
YO11 2AY
T: (01723) 373930
E: harcourthotel@netscapeonline.co.uk

Harmony Country Lodge
♦♦♦♦
80 Limestone Road, Burniston,
Scarborough YO13 0DG
T: (01723) 870276
F: (01723) 870276
E: tony@harmonylodge.net
I: www.harmonylodge.net

Harmony Guest House ♦♦♦
13 Princess Royal Terrace, South
Cliff, Scarborough, YO11 2RP
T: (01723) 373562
E: harmonyguesthouse@hotmail.com
I: www.harmonyguesthouse.co.uk

Headlands Hotel ♦♦♦
Weydale Avenue, Scarborough,
YO12 6AX
T: (01723) 373717
F: (01723) 373717

Hotel Helaina ♦♦♦
14 Blenheim Terrace,
Scarborough, YO12 7HF
T: (01723) 375191

Hillcrest Private Hotel ♦♦♦♦
2 Peasholm Avenue,
Scarborough, YO12 7NE
T: (01723) 361981
E: peacock@hillcresthotel.fsnet.co.uk
I: www.hillcresthotel.fsnet.co.uk

Howdale Hotel ♦♦♦♦
121 Queens Parade,
Scarborough, YO12 7HU
T: (01723) 372696
F: (01723) 372696
E: maria_keith_howdalehotel@yahoo.co.uk
I: www.howdalehotel.moonfruit.com

Killerby Cottage Farm ♦♦♦♦
Killerby Lane, Cayton,
Scarborough YO11 3TP
T: (01723) 581236
F: (01723) 585465
E: val@green-glass.demon.co.uk
I: www.yorkshire.co.uk/valgreen

La Baia Hotel ♦♦♦♦
24 Blenheim Terrace,
Scarborough, YO12 7HD
T: (01723) 370780

Langsett Hotel ♦♦♦
108 Columbus Ravine,
Scarborough, YO12 7QZ
T: (01723) 372094
F: (01723) 372094
I: www.s-h-a.dircon.co.uk

Londesborough Arms Hotel
♦♦♦
24 Main Street, Seamer,
Scarborough YO12 4PS
T: (01723) 863230
F: (01723) 863230
E: londesborough@scarborough.co.uk
I: www.londesborough.scarborough.co.uk

Lonsdale Villa Hotel ♦♦♦♦
Lonsdale Road, South Cliff, Scarborough, YO11 2QY
T: (01723) 363383

Lyncris Manor Hotel ♦♦♦
45 Northstead Manor Drive, Scarborough, YO12 6AF
T: (01723) 361052
E: lyncris@manorhotel.fsnet.co.uk
I: www.manorhotel.fsnet.co.uk

Lysander Hotel ♦♦♦
22 Weydale Avenue, Scarborough, YO12 6AX
T: (01723) 373369
E: joy-harry@lysanderhotel.freeserve.co.uk
I: www.lysanderhotel.freeserve.co.uk

Maynard Hotel ♦♦♦
16 Esplanade Gardens, South Cliff, Scarborough, YO11 2AW
T: (01723) 372289

Moorings ♦♦♦♦
3 Burniston Road, Scarborough, YO12 6PG
T: (01723) 373786
F: (01723) 364276
I: www.s-h-a.dircon.co.uk/moorings

Moseley Lodge Private Hotel ♦♦♦♦
26 Avenue Victoria, South Cliff, Scarborough, YO11 2QT
T: (01723) 360564
F: (01723) 363088
I: www.yorkshirenet.co.uk/moseleylodge

Mount House Hotel ♦♦♦♦
33 Trinity Road, South Cliff, Scarborough, YO11 2TD
T: (01723) 362967
E: bookings@mounthouse-hotel.co.uk
I: www.mounthouse-hotel.co.uk

Mountview Private Hotel (Non-Smoking) ♦♦♦
32 West Street, South Cliff, Scarborough, YO11 2QP
T: (01723) 500608
F: (01723) 501385
E: stay@mountview-hotel.co.uk
I: www.mountview-hotel.co.uk

Norbreck Hotel ♦♦♦
Castle Road, Scarborough, YO11 1HY
T: (01723) 366607
F: (01723) 500984
E: gm.nor@barbox.net
I: www.shearingsholidays.com

Norlands Hotel ♦♦♦
10 Weydale Avenue, Scarborough, YO12 6BA
T: (01723) 362606
F: (01723) 372884
E: atkinsonhun@tinyworld.co.uk

The Old Mill Hotel ♦♦♦
Mill Street, Scarborough, YO11 1SZ
T: (01723) 372735
F: (01723) 377190
E: info@windmill-hotel.co.uk
I: www.windmill-hotel.co.uk

Parmelia Hotel ♦♦♦
17 West Street, Southcliff, Scarborough, YO11 2QN
T: (01723) 361914
E: parmeliahotel@btinternet.com
I: parmeliahotel.co.uk

Perry's Court ♦♦♦♦
1 & 2 Rutland Terrace, Queen's Parade, Scarborough, YO12 7JB
T: (01723) 373768
F: (01723) 353274
E: john@perryscourthotel.fsnet.co.uk
I: www.perryscourthotel.com

Philamon ♦♦♦
108 North Marine Road, Scarborough, YO12 7JA
T: (01723) 373107

Philmore Hotel ♦♦♦♦
126 Columbus Ravine, Scarborough, YO12 7QZ
T: (01723) 361516

Powy's Lodge Hotel ♦♦♦
2 Westbourne Road, South Cliff, Scarborough, YO11 2SP
T: (01723) 374019
F: (01723) 374019
E: info@powslodge.co.uk
I: www.powyslodge.co.uk

Princess Court Guest House ♦♦♦
11 Princess Royal Terrace, Scarborough, YO11 2RP
T: (01723) 501922
E: andy@princesscourt.co.uk
I: www.princesscourt.co.uk

Raincliffe Hotel Rating Applied For
21 Valley Road, Scarborough, YO11 2LY
T: (01723) 373541
E: enquiries@raincliffehotel.co.uk
I: www.raincliffehotel.co.uk

Riviera Hotel ♦♦♦
St Nicholas Cliff, Scarborough, YO11 2ES
T: (01723) 372277

Rose Dene Hotel Rating Applied For
106 Columbus Ravine, Scarborough, YO12 7QZ
T: (01723) 374252

The Russell Hotel ♦♦♦
22 Ryndleside, Scarborough, YO12 6AD
T: (01723) 365453
F: (01723) 369029
E: info@russellhotel.net
I: www.russellhotel.net

St Michael's Hotel ♦♦♦
27 Blenheim Terrace, Scarborough, YO12 7HD
T: (01723) 374631
F: (01723) 374631
E: elstop@tiscali.co.uk

Selbourne Hotel ♦♦♦
4 West Street, South Cliff, Scarborough, YO11 2QL
T: (01723) 372822
F: (01723) 372822

Selomar Hotel ♦♦♦♦
23 Blenheim Terrace, Scarborough, YO12 7HD
T: (01723) 364964
F: (01723) 364964

Sylvern Hotel ♦♦♦
25 New Queen Street, Scarborough, YO12 7HJ
T: (01723) 360952
E: sylvernhotel@aol.com
I: www.smoothhound.co.uk/hotels/sylvern.html

The Terrace Hotel ♦♦
69 Westborough, Scarborough, YO11 1TS
T: (01723) 374937
E: theterracehotel@btinternet.com

Victoria Lodge Hotel ♦♦♦
19 Avenue Victoria, Southcliffe, Scarborough, YO11 2QS
T: (01723) 370906

Victoria Seaview Hotel ♦♦♦♦
125 Queen's Parade, Scarborough, YO12 7HY
T: (01723) 362164
E: victoria-seaview-hotel@tinyworld.co.uk

Villa Marina ♦♦♦♦
59 Northstead Manor Drive, Scarborough, YO12 6AF
T: (01723) 361088

The Warren Hotel ♦♦♦
34 Princess Street, Scarborough, YO11 1QR
T: (01723) 367790

Wharncliffe Hotel ♦♦♦♦
26 Blenheim Terrace, Scarborough, YO12 7HD
T: (01723) 374635
E: dandawharncliffe@ad.com

The Whiteley Hotel ♦♦♦♦
99-101 Queens Parade, Scarborough, YO12 7HY
T: (01723) 373514
F: (01723) 373007
E: Whiteley_Hotel@compuserve.com
I: www.s-h-a.dircon.co.uk/thewhiteleyhotel.htm

SCAWBY
North Lincolnshire

The Old School ♦♦♦♦
Church Street, Scawby, Brigg DN20 9AH
T: (01652) 654239

Olivers ♦♦♦
Church Street, Scawby, Brigg DN20 9AM
T: (01652) 650446
E: eileen_harrison@lineone.net

SCHOLES
West Yorkshire

24 The Avenue ♦♦♦
Arthursdale, Scholes, Leeds LS15 4AS
T: (0113) 273 0289
E: ian.mann@virgin.net

The Willows ♦♦♦
Scholes Moor Road, Scholes, Holmfirth, Huddersfield HD9 1SJ
T: (01484) 684231

The Willows ♦♦♦
Scholes Moor Road, Scholes, Holmfirth, Huddersfield HD9 1SJ
T: (01484) 684231

SCOTCH CORNER
North Yorkshire

Vintage Hotel ♦♦♦
Scotch Corner, Richmond DL10 6NP
T: (01748) 824424
F: (01748) 826272

SCUNTHORPE
North Lincolnshire

Beverley Hotel ♦♦♦
55 Old Brumby Street, Scunthorpe, DN16 2AJ
T: (01724) 282212
F: (01724) 270422

The Downs Guest House ♦♦♦
33 Deyne Avenue, Scunthorpe, DN15 7PZ
T: (01724) 850710
F: (01724) 330928
I: www.thedownsguesthouse.co.uk

Elm Field ♦♦
22 Deyne Avenue, Scunthorpe, DN15 7PZ
T: (01724) 869306

Kirks Korner ♦♦
12 Scotter Road, Scunthorpe, DN15 8DR
T: (01724) 855344
E: paul.kirk1@ntlworld.com

Larchwood Hotel ♦♦♦
1-5 Shelford Street, off Mary Street, Scunthorpe, DN15 6NU
T: (01724) 864712
F: (01724) 864712
I: www.thelarchwoodhotel.co.uk

Normanby Hotel ♦♦♦
9-11 Normanby Road, Scunthorpe, DN15 6AR
T: (01724) 289982

SELBY
North Yorkshire

Hazeldene Guest House ♦♦♦
34 Brook Street, Doncaster Road, Selby, YO8 4AR
T: (01757) 704809
E: selbystay@breathe.com
I: www.smoothhound.co.uk/hotels/hazel.html

SETTLE
North Yorkshire

Arbutus Guest House ♦♦♦♦
Riverside, Clapham, Lancaster LA2 8DS
T: (01524) 251240
F: (01524) 251197
E: info@arbutus.co.uk
I: www.arbutus.co.uk

Golden Lion Hotel ♦♦♦♦
Duke Street, Settle, BD24 9DU
T: (01729) 822203
F: (01729) 824103
E: bookings@goldenlion.yorks.net
I: www.yorkshirenet.co.uk/stayat/goldenlion

Husbands Barn ♦♦♦♦ SILVER AWARD
Stainforth, Settle BD24 9PB
T: (01729) 822240
F: (01729) 822240
I: www.husbands.force9.co.uk

Mainsfield ♦♦♦♦
Stackhouse Lane, Giggleswick, Settle BD24 0DL
T: (01729) 823549

Maypole Inn ♦♦♦
Maypole Green, Main Street, Long Preston, Skipton BD23 4PH
T: (01729) 840219
E: landlord@maypole.co.uk
I: www.maypole.co.uk

Oast Guest House ♦♦♦
5 Pen-Y-Ghent View, Settle, BD24 9JJ
T: (01729) 822989
E: king@oast2000.freeserve.co.uk
I: www.theoastguesthouse.co.uk

Ottawa ♦♦♦♦
Station Road, Giggleswick, Settle BD24 0AE
T: (01729) 822757

Penmar Court ♦♦♦♦
Duke Street, Settle, BD24 9AS
T: (01729) 823258
F: (01729) 823258
E: stay@penmarcourt.freeserve.co.uk
I: www.settle.org.uk

Scar Close Farm ♦♦♦♦
Feizor, Austwick, Lancaster LA2 8DF
T: (01729) 823496

Station House ♦♦♦
Settle, BD24 9AA
T: (01729) 822533
E: stationhouse@btinternet.com
I: www.stationhouse.btinternet.co.uk

Whitefriars Country Guest House ♦♦♦
Church Street, Settle, BD24 9JD
T: (01729) 823753
E: info@whitefriars-settle.co.uk
I: www.whitefriars-settle.co.uk

SEWERBY
East Riding of Yorkshire

The Poplars Motel ♦♦♦
45 Jewison Lane, Sewerby, Bridlington YO15 1DX
T: (01262) 677251
F: (01262) 677251

SHAROW
North Yorkshire

Half Moon Inn ♦♦♦
Sharow Lane, Sharow, Ripon HG4 5BP
T: (01765) 600291
E: halfmoon@bronco.co.uk
I: www.ripon.org/webads/halfmoon

SHEFFIELD
South Yorkshire

Abbey View House ♦♦♦
168 Prospect Road, Totley Rise, Sheffield, S17 4HX
T: (0114) 235 1349

Ashford ♦♦♦
44 Westwick Crescent, Beauchief, Sheffield, S8 7DH
T: (0114) 237 5900

Beighton Bed & Breakfast ♦♦♦
48-50 High Street, Beighton, Sheffield, S20 1EA
T: (01142) 692004
F: (01142) 692004
E: beightonbandb@talk21.com

Coniston Guest House ♦♦♦
90 Beechwood Road, Hillsborough, Sheffield, S6 4LQ
T: (0114) 233 9680
F: (0114) 233 9680
E: coniston@freeuk.co.uk
I: www.conistonguest.freeuk.co.uk

Etruria House Hotel ♦♦♦
91 Crookes Road, Broomhill, Sheffield, S10 5BD
T: (0114) 266 2241
F: (0114) 267 0853
E: etruria@waitrose.com

Gulliver's Bed And Breakfast ♦♦♦
167 Ecclesall Road South, Sheffield, S11 9PN
T: (0114) 262 0729

Hardwick House ♦♦♦
18 Hardwick Crescent, Ecclesall, Sheffield, S11 8WB
T: (0114) 266 1509
E: hardwickhouse@hardwickhouse.fsnet.co.uk
I: www.lennox01.freeserve.co.uk

Harvey House ♦♦♦♦
159 Dobcroft Road, Sheffield, S7 2LT
T: (0114) 236 1018

Hillside ♦♦♦
28 Sunningdale Mount, Ecclesall, Sheffield, S11 9HA
T: (0114) 2620833

Ivory House Hotel ♦♦♦
34 Wostenholm Road, Sheffield, S7 1LJ
T: (0114) 255 1853
F: (0114) 255 1578
E: ivoryhousehotel@amserve.com

Lindrick Hotel ♦♦♦
226-230 Chippinghouse Road, Sheffield, S7 1DR
T: (0114) 258 5041
F: (0114) 255 4758
E: reception@thelindrick.co.uk
I: www.thelindrick.co.uk

Lindum Hotel ♦♦♦
91 Montgomery Road, Nether Edge, Sheffield, S7 1LP
T: (0114) 255 2356
F: (0114) 249 4746
E: lindumhotel@freenetname.co.uk

Loadbrook Cottages ♦♦♦♦ SILVER AWARD
Game Lane, Loadbrook, Sheffield, S6 6GT
T: (0114) 233 1619
E: acolver@commontime.com
I: www.smoothhound.co.uk

The Martins Guest House ♦♦
397 Fulwood Road, Sheffield, S10 3GE
T: (0114) 230 8588
F: (0114) 230 2281

Parklands ♦♦
113 Rustlings Road, Sheffield, S11 7AB
T: (0114) 267 0692

Priory Lodge Hotel ♦♦
40 Wostenholm Road, Netheredge, Sheffield, S7 1LJ
T: (0114) 258 4670
F: (0114) 255 6672
I: www.priorylodgehotel.co.uk

Psalter House ♦♦♦♦
17 Clifford Road, Brincliffe, Sheffield, S11 9AQ
T: (0114) 255 7758
F: (0114) 255 7758
E: psalterhouse@waitrose.com
I: www.smoothhound.co.uk/hotels/psalter.html

Riverside Court Hotel ♦♦♦
4 Nursery Street, Sheffield, S3 8GG
T: (0114) 273 1962
F: (0114) 272 3619
E: enquiries@riversidecourt.co.uk
I: www.riversidecourt.co.uk

The Rock Inn Hotel ♦♦♦♦
Cranemoor Road, Cranemoor, Sheffield, S35 7AT
T: (0114) 288 3427
F: (0114) 288 3726
E: reservations@rockinnhotel.com
I: www.rockinn.co.uk

Tyndale ♦♦♦
164 Millhouses Lane, Sheffield, S7 2HE
T: (0114) 236 1660
F: (0114) 236 1660

Whirlow Park Guest House ♦♦♦
20 Whirlow Park Road, Whirlow, Sheffield, S11 9NP
T: (0114) 236 0909
F: (0114) 235 0214
E: julie.bradwell@virgin.net

SHELF
West Yorkshire

Rook Residence ♦♦♦
69 Shelf Hall Lane, Shelf, Halifax HX3 7LT
T: (01274) 601586
F: (01274) 670179
E: rookbnb@btinternet.com

SHELLEY
West Yorkshire

Three Acres Inn and Restaurant ♦♦
Roydhouse, Shelley, Huddersfield HD8 8LR
T: (01484) 602606
F: (01484) 608411
E: 3acres@globalnet.co.uk
I: www.3acres.com

SHERBURN
North Yorkshire

Cherry Tree Cottage ♦♦♦
37 St Hilda's Street, Sherburn, Malton YO17 8PG
T: (01944) 710851
E: cherrybnb@ntlworld.com
I: www.Cherrybnb.co.uk

SHIBDEN
West Yorkshire

Ploughcroft Cottage ♦♦♦
53 Ploughcroft Lane, Shibden, Halifax HX3 6TX
T: (01422) 341205
E: ploughcroft.cottage@Care4free.net
I: www.ploughcroftcottage.com

Staups House ♦♦♦♦
36 Staups Lane, Shibden, Halifax HX3 7AB
T: (01422) 362866

SHIPLEY
West Yorkshire

Beeties of Saltaire ♦♦♦♦
7 Victoria Road, Saltaire Village, Shipley, BD18 3LA
T: (01274) 581718
F: (01274) 582118
E: maureen@beeties.co.uk
I: www.beeties.co.uk

Clifton Lodge Guest House ♦♦♦
75 Kirkgate, Shipley, BD18 3LU
T: (01274) 580509
F: (01274) 580343
E: jaynefoster75@hotmail.com

SILSDEN
West Yorkshire

Dalesbank Holiday Park ♦♦♦
Low Lane, Silsden, Keighley BD20 9JH
T: (01535) 653321

SINNINGTON
North Yorkshire

Green Lea ♦♦♦
Sinnington, York YO62 6SH
T: (01751) 432008

Sinnington Manor ♦♦♦♦
Sinnington, York YO62 6SN
T: (01751) 433296
F: (01751) 433296
E: charles.wilson@sinningtonmanor.fsnet.co.uk

SKEEBY
North Yorkshire

The Old Chapel ♦♦♦♦
Richmond Road, Skeeby, Richmond DL10 5DR
T: (01748) 824170
E: hazel@theoldchapel.fsnet.co.uk

SKIPSEA
East Riding of Yorkshire

The Grainary ♦♦♦
Skipsea Grange, Hornsea Road, Skipsea, Driffield YO25 8SY
T: (01262) 468745
F: (01262) 468840
E: francesdavies@btconnect.com
I: www.the-grainary.co.uk

SKIPTON
North Yorkshire

Bourne House ♦♦♦
22 Upper Sackville Street, Skipton, BD23 2EB
T: (01756) 792633
F: (01756) 701609
E: bournehouse@totalise.co.uk
I: www.bournehouseguesthouse.co.uk

Carlton House ♦♦♦♦
46 Keighley Road, Skipton, BD23 2NB
T: (01756) 700921
F: (01756) 700921
E: carltonhouse@rapidial.co.uk
I: www.guesthouseinskipton.co.uk

Craven Heifer Inn ♦♦♦
Grassington Road, Skipton, BD23 3LA
T: (01756) 792521
F: (01756) 794442
E: philandlynn@cravenheifer.co.uk
I: www.cravenheifer.co.uk

Cravendale Guest House ♦♦♦
57 Keighley Road, Skipton, BD23 2LX
T: (01756) 795129
F: (01756) 795129

Dalesgate Lodge ♦♦♦♦
69 Gargrave Road, Skipton, BD23 1QN
T: (01756) 790672
E: dalesgatelodge@talk21.com

Highfield Hotel ♦♦♦
58 Keighley Road, Skipton, BD23 2NB
T: (01756) 793182
F: (01756) 793182
I: www.highfield-hotel.co.uk

Napier's Restaurant & Accommodation ♦♦♦♦
Chapel Hill, Skipton, BD23 1NL
T: (01756) 799688
F: (01756) 798111
I: www.restaurant-skipton.co.uk

Skipton Park Guest'otel ♦♦♦
2 Salisbury Street, Skipton, BD23 1NQ
T: (01756) 700640
F: (01756) 700641
E: derekchurch@skiptonpark.freeserve.co.uk
I: www.milford.co.uk/go/skiptonpark.html

Spring Gardens Cottage ♦♦♦
20 Queens Street, Skipton, BD23 1HE
T: (01756) 790739

Unicorn Hotel ♦♦♦
Devonshire Place, Keighley Road, Skipton, BD23 2LP
T: (01756) 794146
F: (01756) 793376

SLAITHWAITE
West Yorkshire

Hey Leys Farm ♦♦♦♦
Marsden Lane, Cop Hill, Slaithwaite, Huddersfield HD7 5XA
T: (01484) 845404
F: (01484) 843188
I: www.yorkshireholidays.com

SLEDMERE
North Humberside

Life Hill Farm
Rating Applied For
Sledmere, Driffield YO25 3EU
T: (01377) 236224
F: (01377) 236685
E: paygrace@breathemail.net

The Triton Inn ♦♦♦
Sledmere, Driffield YO25 3XQ
T: (01377) 236644
E: thetritoninn@sledmere.fsbusiness.co.uk
I: www.sledmere.fsbusiness.co.uk

SLEIGHTS
North Yorkshire

Hedgefield ♦♦♦♦
47 Coach Road, Sleights, Whitby YO223 5A
T: (01947) 810647
E: hedgefield@ntlworld.com
I: www.hedgefieldguesthouse.co.uk

The Lawns
♦♦♦♦♦ GOLD AWARD
73 Carr Hill Lane, Sleights, Whitby YO21 1RS
T: (01947) 810310
F: (01947) 810310
E: lorton@onetel.net.uk

The Salmon Leap Hotel ♦♦
6 Coach Road, Sleights, Whitby YO22 5AA
T: (01947) 810233

SOUTH CAVE
East Riding of Yorkshire

Fairways ♦♦♦
Northfield Close, South Cave, Brough HU15 2EW
T: (01430) 421285
E: jewitt@fairwaysfarm.karoo.co.uk
I: www.fairwaysfarm.karoo.net

Turks Trod House ♦♦♦
67a Church Street, South Cave, Brough HU15 2EP
T: (01430) 423931

SOWERBY
North Yorkshire

Long Acre Bed and Breakfast ♦♦♦
Long Acre, 86A Topcliffe Road, Sowerby, Thirsk YO7 1RY
T: (01845) 522360
F: (01845) 527373
E: dawsonlongacre@aol.com

SOWERBY BRIDGE
West Yorkshire

Park Villa Guest House ♦♦♦
141 Park Villas, Bolton Brow, Sowerby Bridge, HX6 2BE
T: (01422) 832179

STADDLEBRIDGE
North Yorkshire

Staddlebridge House ♦♦♦
Staddlebridge Farm, Staddlebridge, Northallerton DL6 3JF
T: (01609) 882264
E: staddlebridgehouse@ntlworld.com

STAINFORTH
North Yorkshire

2 Bridge End Cottage
Rating Applied For
Stainforth, Settle BD24 9PG
T: (01729) 822149

STAINTONDALE
North Yorkshire

Island House ♦♦♦♦
Island Farm, Staintondale, Scarborough YO13 0EB
T: (01723) 870249
E: roryc@tinyworld.co.uk
I: www.islandhousefarm.co.uk

Wellington Lodge ♦♦♦♦
Staintondale, Scarborough YO13 0EL
T: (01723) 871234
F: (01723) 871234
E: b&b@llamatreks.co.uk
I: www.llamatreks.co.uk

STAIRFOOT
South Yorkshire

The Old Coach House Guest House ♦♦♦
255 Doncaster Road, Stairfoot, Barnsley S70 3RH
T: (01226) 290612
F: (01226) 298967

STAITHES
North Yorkshire

Brooklyn ♦♦♦
Brown's Terrace, Staithes, Saltburn-by-the-Sea TS13 5BG
T: (01947) 841396

The Endeavour Restaurant ♦♦♦♦
1 High Street, Staithes, Saltburn-by-the-Sea TS13 5BH
T: (01947) 840825
E: theendeavour@ntlworld.com
I: www.endeavour-restaurant.co.uk

The Giardini Guest House ♦♦♦
Roxby Lane, Staithes, Saltburn-by-the-Sea TS13 5DZ
T: (01947) 840572
F: (01947) 841642

Grinkle Lodge
♦♦♦♦ SILVER AWARD
Snipe Lane, Grinkle, Staithes, Saltburn-by-the-Sea TS13 4UD
T: (01287) 644701
E: grinklelodge@yahoo.co.uk
I: www.yorkshirecoast.co.uk/grinklelodge

Springfields ♦♦♦
42 Staithes Lane, Staithes, Saltburn-by-the-Sea TS13 5AD
T: (01947) 841011

STAMFORD BRIDGE
East Riding of Yorkshire

High Catton Grange ♦♦♦♦
Stamford Bridge, York YO41 1EP
T: (01759) 371374
F: (01759) 371374

STANBURY
West Yorkshire

Ponden House ♦♦♦♦
Stanbury, Keighley BD22 0HR
T: (01535) 644154
E: brenda.taylor@pondenhouse.co.uk
I: www.pondenhouse.co.uk

STAPE
North Yorkshire

Grange Farm ♦♦♦♦
Stape, Pickering YO18 8HZ
T: (01751) 473805
F: (01751) 477805
E: thelma_grange_farm@yahoo.co.uk
I: www.yorkshireholidays.com

Rawcliffe House Farm ♦♦♦♦
Stape, Pickering YO18 8JA
T: (01751) 473292
F: (01751) 473766
E: office@yorkshireaccommodation.com
I: www.yorkshireaccommodation.com

Seavy Slack ♦♦♦♦
Stape, Pickering YO18 8HZ
T: (01751) 473131

STARBOTTON
North Yorkshire

Bushey Lodge Farm
♦♦♦♦ SILVER AWARD
Starbotton, Skipton BD23 5HY
T: (01756) 760424
I: www.yorkshirenet.co.uk/stayat/busheylodgefarm

STEARSBY
North Yorkshire

The Granary
♦♦♦♦ SILVER AWARD
Stearsby, York YO61 4SA
T: (01347) 888652
F: (01347) 888652
E: robertturl@thegranary.org.uk
I: www.thegranary.org.uk

STOKESLEY
North Yorkshire

The Buck Inn ♦♦♦
Chopgate, Stokesley, Middlesbrough TS9 7JL
T: (01642) 778334

Harker Hill Farm ♦♦♦
Harker Hill, Seamer, Stokesley, Middlesbrough TS9 5NF
T: (01642) 710431
F: (01642) 710431
E: harkerhill@freeuk.com
I: www.destination-england.co.uk/harkerhill.html

STONEGRAVE
North Yorkshire

Manor Cottage Bed and Breakfast ♦♦♦♦
Manor Cottage, Stonegrave, York YO62 4LJ
T: (01653) 628599
E: gideon.v@virgin.net
I: business.virgin.net/gideon.v/index.html

STUDLEY ROGER
North Yorkshire

Downing House Farm ♦♦♦♦
Studley Roger, Ripon HG4 3AY
T: (01765) 601014
F: (01765) 601014
E: dickhelen@supanet.com
I: www.downinghousefarm.co.uk

SUTTON BANK
North Yorkshire

Cote Faw ♦♦
Hambleton Cottages, Sutton Bank, Thirsk YO7 2EZ
T: (01845) 597363

Greystones ♦♦♦
Sutton Bank, Thirsk YO7 2HB
T: (01845) 597580

SUTTON-ON-THE-FOREST
North Yorkshire

Goose Farm ♦♦♦
Eastmoor, Sutton-on-the-Forest, York YO61 1ET
T: (01347) 810577
F: (01347) 810577
E: stay@goosefarm.fsnet.co.uk
I: www.yorkshirenet.co.uk/stayat/goosefarm

The Old Village Stores
Rating Applied For
Main Street, Sutton-on-the-Forest, York YO61 1DP
T: (01347) 811376
E: maria.demkowicz@talk21.com
I: www.oldyork.co.uk

SWAINBY
North Yorkshire

Churchview House
♦♦♦♦♦ GOLD AWARD
72 High Street, Swainby, Northallerton DL6 3DG
T: (01642) 706058
F: (01642) 706058
E: churchviewhouse@aol.com
I: www.churchviewhouse.co.uk

SWILLINGTON
West Yorkshire

Bridge Farm Hotel ♦♦♦
Wakefield Road, Swillington, Leeds LS26 8PZ
T: (0113) 282 3718
F: (0113) 282 5135

SWINTON
North Yorkshire

Low Farm Bed & Breakfast ♦♦♦♦
Low Farm, East Street, Swinton, Malton YO17 6SH
T: (01653) 693684
F: (01653) 693684
I: www.lowfarmswinton.co.uk

TERRINGTON
North Yorkshire

Gate Farm ♦♦♦
Ganthorpe, Terrington, York YO60 6QD
T: (01653) 648269
E: millgate001@aol.com

THIMBLEBY
North Yorkshire

Stonehaven ♦♦♦
Thimbleby, Northallerton DL6 3PY
T: (01609) 883689

THIRSK
North Yorkshire

Fourways Guest House ♦♦
Town End, Thirsk, YO7 1PY
T: (01845) 522601
F: (01845) 522131
E: fourways@nyorks.fsbusiness.co.uk

The Gallery Bed And Breakfast ♦♦♦
18 Kirkgate, Thirsk, YO7 1PQ
T: (01845) 523767
F: (01845) 523767
E: jenkin@tesco.net

Laburnum House ♦♦♦♦ SILVER AWARD
31 Topcliffe Road, Thirsk, YO7 1RX
T: (01845) 524120
I: www.smoothhound.co.uk/hotels/laburnumhse.html

Lavender House ♦♦♦
27 Kirkgate, Thirsk, YO7 1PL
T: (01845) 522224
E: susie.dodds@btinternet.com
I: www.lavenderhouse.org

St James House ♦♦♦
36 St James Green, Thirsk, YO7 1AQ
T: (01845) 526565

Station House ♦♦♦
Station Road, Thirsk, YO7 4LS
T: (01845) 522063

Town Pasture Farm ♦♦♦
Boltby, Thirsk YO7 2DY
T: (01845) 537298

Treetops Hotel ♦♦♦
Sutton Road, Thirsk, YO7 2ER
T: (01845) 522293
F: (01845) 522579
E: treetops@chimeira.com
I: www.treetops-hotel.com

THIXENDALE
North Yorkshire

The Cross Keys ♦♦♦
Thixendale, Malton YO17 9TG
T: (01377) 288272

Manor Farm ♦♦♦♦
Thixendale, Malton YO17 9TG
T: (01377) 288315
F: (01377) 288315

THORALBY
North Yorkshire

Pen View ♦♦♦
Thoralby, Leyburn DL8 3SU
T: (01969) 663319
F: (01969) 663319
E: audrey@penview.yorks.net
I: www.penview.yorks.net

THORNTON
West Yorkshire

Ann's Farmhouse ♦♦♦
New Farm, Thornton Road, Thornton, Bradford BD13 3QE
T: (01274) 833214
E: ajdarby@aol.com

THORNTON DALE
North Yorkshire

Banavie ♦♦♦♦
Roxby Road, Thornton Dale, Pickering YO18 7SX
T: (01751) 474616
E: ella@banavie.fsbusiness.co.uk
I: www.smoothhound.co.uk/

Bridgefoot Guest House ♦♦♦
Thornton Dale, Pickering YO18 7RR
T: (01751) 474749

The Buck Hotel ♦♦♦
Chestnut Avenue, Thornton Dale, Pickering YO18 7RW
T: (01751) 474212
F: (01751) 474212
E: buckhotel.tld@btopenworld.com

Hall Farm ♦♦♦
Maltongate, Thornton Dale, Pickering YO18 7SA
T: (01751) 475526
E: hallfarmholidays@amserve.net

Nabgate ♦♦♦♦
Wilton Road, Thornton Dale, Pickering YO18 7QP
T: (01751) 474279

New Inn ♦♦♦♦
Maltongate, Thornton Dale, Pickering YO18 7LF
T: (01751) 474226
F: (01751) 477715
E: newinntld@aol.com

The Old Granary Bed and Breakfast ♦♦♦♦ SILVER AWARD
Top Bridge Farm, Thornton Dale, Pickering YO18 7RA
T: (01751) 477217

Tangalwood ♦♦♦
Roxby Road, Thornton Dale, Pickering YO18 7SX
T: (01751) 474688

THORPE
North Yorkshire

Langerton House Farm ♦♦♦
Cracoe, Thorpe Lane, Thorpe, Skipton BD23 5HN
T: (01756) 730260

THORPE BASSETT
North Yorkshire

The Old School House ♦♦
Thorpe Bassett, Malton YO17 8LU
T: (01944) 758797

THWAITE
North Yorkshire

Kearton Country Hotel ♦♦♦
Thwaite, Richmond DL11 6DR
T: (01748) 886277
F: (01748) 886590
E: idanton@btconnect.com
I: www.keartoncountryhotel.co.uk

THWAITES BROW
West Yorkshire

Golden View Guest House Rating Applied For
21 Golden View Drive, Thwaites Brow, Keighley BD21 4SN
T: (01535) 662138

TODMORDEN
West Yorkshire

Woodleigh Hall ♦♦♦♦
Ewood Lane, Todmorden, OL14 7DF
T: (01706) 814664
F: (01706) 810673

TOLLERTON
North Yorkshire

The Bungalow Farm ♦♦♦
Warehills Lane, Tollerton, York YO61 1RG
T: (01347) 838732
F: (01347) 838732

TRIANGLE
West Yorkshire

The Dene ♦♦♦♦
Triangle, Sowerby Bridge HX6 3EA
T: (01422) 823562
E: knoble@uk2.net

ULCEBY
North Lincolnshire

Gillingham Court ♦♦♦♦
Spruce Lane, Ulceby, DN39 6UL
T: (01469) 588427

UPPER GREETLAND
West Yorkshire

Crawstone Knowl Farm ♦♦♦
Rochdale Road, Upper Greetland, Halifax HX4 8PX
T: (01422) 370470

WALSDEN
West Yorkshire

Birks Clough ♦♦♦
Hollingworth Lane, Walsden, Todmorden OL14 6QX
T: (01706) 814438
F: (01706) 819002
E: mstorah@mwfree.net

Highstones Guest House ♦♦♦
Lane Bottom, Walsden, Todmorden OL14 6TY
T: (01706) 816534

WEAVERTHORPE
North Yorkshire

The Blue Bell Inn ♦♦♦
Main Street, Weaverthorpe, Malton YO17 8EX
T: (01944) 738204
F: (01944) 738204

The Star Country Inn ♦♦♦
Weaverthorpe, Malton YO17 8EY
T: (01944) 738273
E: info@starinn.net
I: www.starinn.net

WEETON
North Yorkshire

Arthington Lodge ♦♦♦♦
Jubilee Farm, Wescoe Hill Lane, Weeton, Leeds LS17 0EZ
T: (01423) 734102

WENSLEYDALE
North Yorkshire

Ivy Dene Country Guesthouse ♦♦♦
Main Street, West Witton, Leyburn DL8 4LP
T: (01969) 622785
F: (01969) 622785

WEST BRETTON
West Yorkshire

The Old Manor House ♦♦♦
19 Sycamore Lane, West Bretton, Wakefield WF4 4JR
T: (01924) 830324
F: (01924) 830150

WEST BURTON
North Yorkshire

The Grange ♦♦♦♦♦
West Burton, Leyburn DL8 4JR
T: (01969) 663348
E: ashfordpaul5@aol.com
I: www.thegrange-yorkshiredales.co.uk

WEST WITTON
North Yorkshire

The Old Star ♦♦♦
West Witton, Leyburn DL8 4LU
T: (01969) 622949
E: theoldstar@amserve.com

WESTOW
North Yorkshire

Blacksmiths Arms Inn ♦♦♦
Westow, York YO60 7NE
T: (01653) 618365
E: blacksmithsinn@hotmail.com

Clifton Farm ♦♦♦
Clifton Farm, Westow, York YO60 7LS
T: (01653) 658557
F: (01653) 658 557
E: lynn@cliftonfarm.co.uk
I: www.cliftonfarm.co.uk

WETHERBY
West Yorkshire

Broadleys ♦♦♦
39 North Street, Wetherby, LS22 6NU
T: (01937) 585866

The Coach House Garden Studio ♦♦♦♦
North Grove Approach, Wetherby, LS22 7GA
T: (01937) 586100
F: (01937) 586100

Lindum Fields ♦♦♦♦
48a Spofforth Hill, Wetherby, LS22 6SE
T: (01937) 520389
F: (01937) 520389
E: p.stretton1@ntlworld.com

Linton Close ♦♦♦♦
2 Wharfe Grove, Wetherby, LS22 6HA
T: (01937) 582711
F: (01937) 588499

Prospect House ♦♦
8 Caxton Street, Wetherby, LS22 6RU
T: (01937) 582428

Swan Guest House ♦♦
38 North Street, Wetherby, LS22 6NN
T: (01937) 582381
F: (01937) 584908
E: info@swanguesthouse.co.uk
I: www.swanguesthouse.co.uk

14 Woodhill View ♦♦♦
Wetherby, LS22 6PP
T: (01937) 581200

WHENBY
North Yorkshire

Deerholme ♦♦♦♦
Main Street, Whenby, York
YO61 4SE
T: (01347) 878116
E: pufinny@aol.com

WHITBY
North Yorkshire

Abbotsleigh ♦♦♦♦
5 Argyle Road, Whitby,
YO21 3HS
T: (01947) 601142
F: (01947) 601142

Anchorage Non Smoking Hotel ♦♦♦
3 Crescent Terrace, Whitby,
YO21 3EL
T: (01947) 821888

Arches Guesthouse ♦♦♦♦
8 Havelock Place, Hudson Street,
Whitby, YO21 3ER
T: (01947) 601880
E: archeswhitby@freeola.com
I: www.whitbyguesthouses.co.uk

Argyle House ♦♦♦♦
18 Hudson Street, Whitby,
YO21 3EP
T: (01947) 602733
E: pat.donegan@ntlworld.com
I: www.argyle-house.co.uk

Ashford Guest House ♦♦♦
8 Royal Crescent, Whitby,
YO21 3EJ
T: (01947) 602138
E: info@ashfordguesthouse.co.uk
I: www.ashfordguesthouse.co.uk

Avalon Hotel ♦♦♦
13-14 Royal Crescent, Whitby,
YO21 3EJ
T: (01947) 820313
F: (01947) 602349
I: www.avalonhotel.freeserve.co.uk

Boulmer ♦♦♦
23 Crescent Avenue, Whitby,
YO21 3ED
T: (01947) 604284

Bramblewick Guest House ♦♦♦♦
3 Havelock Place, Whitby,
YO21 3ER
T: (01947) 604504
E: bramblewick@nfieldhouse.freeserve.co.uk
I: www.bramblewick.co.uk

Bruncliffe Guest House ♦♦♦
9 North Promenade, Whitby,
YO21 3JX
T: (01947) 602428
E: bruncliffewhitby@aol.com
I: www.bruncliffewhitby.co.uk

Chiltern Guest House ♦♦♦♦
13 Normanby Terrace, West
Cliff, Whitby, YO21 3ES
T: (01947) 604981
F: (01947) 604981
E: john@chilternguesthouse.fsnet.co.uk
I: www.chilternwhitby.co.uk

Corner Guest House ♦♦♦♦
3-4 Crescent Place, Whitby,
YO21 3HE
T: (01947) 602444
I: www.thecornerguesthouse.co.uk

Crescent Lodge ♦♦♦♦
27 Crescent Avenue, Whitby,
YO21 3EW
T: (01947) 820073

The Elders B&B ♦♦♦
3 Hanover Terrace, Whitby,
YO21 1QQ
T: (01947) 602587

Elford House ♦♦♦
10 Prospect Hill, Whitby,
YO21 1QE
T: (01947) 602135

Esklet Guest House ♦♦♦
22 Crescent Avenue, West Cliff,
Whitby, YO21 3ED
T: (01947) 605663
E: les@llintott.freserve.co.uk
I: www.eskletguesthouse.co.uk

The Esplanade Hotel ♦♦♦
2 Esplanade, Whitby, YO21 3HH
T: (01947) 605053
F: (01947) 605053

The George Hotel ♦♦♦
Baxtergate, Whitby, YO21 1BN
T: (01947) 602565
F: (01947) 820950

Glendale Guest House ♦♦♦♦
16 Crescent Avenue, Whitby,
YO21 3ED
T: (01947) 604242

Glenora ♦♦♦
8 Upgang Lane, Whitby,
YO21 3EA
T: (01947) 605363
I: glenora.users.btopenworld.com

Grantley House ♦♦♦♦
26 Hudson Street, Whitby,
YO21 3EP
T: (01947) 600895
F: (01947) 600895
E: kevin@thegrantley.freeserve.co.uk
I: www.thegrantley.freeserve.co.uk

Grove Hotel ♦♦♦
36 Bagdale, Whitby, YO21 1QL
T: (01947) 603551
I: www.smoothhound.co.uk/hotels/grove2.html

Havelock Guest House ♦♦♦
30 Hudson Street, West Cliff,
Whitby, YO21 3EP
T: (01947) 602295
F: (01947) 602295

High Tor ♦♦♦
7 Normanby Terrace, Whitby,
YO21 3ES
T: (01947) 602507
E: hightorguesthouse@hotmail.com
I: www.hightorguesthouse.co.uk

Jaydee Guest House ♦♦♦
15 John Street, Whitby,
YO21 3ET
T: (01947) 605422
F: (01947) 605422

The Langley Hotel ♦♦♦♦
Royal Crescent, West Cliff,
Whitby, YO21 3EJ
T: (01947) 604250
F: (01947) 604250
E: langleyhotel@hotmail.co.uk
I: www.langleyhotel.com

Lansbury Guest House ♦♦♦
29 Hudson Street, Whitby,
YO21 3EP
T: (01947) 604821
F: (01947) 604821
I: www.whitbyonline.co.uk/lansburyhse.html

Lavender House ♦♦♦♦
28 Love Lane, Whitby, YO21 3LJ
T: (01947) 602917
F: (01947) 602917
E: dcrichmond@aol.com

Lavinia House ♦♦♦♦
3 East Crescent, Whitby,
YO21 3HD
T: (01947) 602945
F: (01947) 820656
E: tony@lavinia-whitby.freeserve.co.uk

Leeway Guest House ♦♦♦♦
1 Havelock Place, Whitby,
YO21 3ER
T: (01947) 602604
E: linda@leeway.co.uk
I: www.leeway.fsbusiness.co.uk

The Middleham ♦♦
3 Church Square, Whitby,
YO21 3EG
T: (01947) 603423
F: (01947) 603423

Morningside Hotel ♦♦♦♦
10 North Promenade, West Cliff,
Whitby, YO21 3JX
T: (01947) 602643

Netherby House
♦♦♦♦ SILVER AWARD
90 Coach Road, Sleights, Whitby
YO22 5EQ
T: (01947) 810211
F: (01947) 810211
E: info@netherby-house.co.uk
I: www.netherby-house.co.uk

Number Five ♦♦♦
5 Havelock Place, Whitby,
YO21 3ER
T: (01947) 606361
F: (01947) 606361

Number Seven Guest House ♦♦♦♦
7 East Cresent, Whitby,
YO21 3HD
T: (01947) 606019
F: (01947) 606019
E: numberseven@whitbytown.freeserve.co.uk
I: www.1up.co.uk/whitby

The Olde Ford
♦♦♦♦ SILVER AWARD
1 Briggswath, Whitby, YO21 1RU
T: (01947) 810704
E: gray@theoldeford.fsnet.co.uk

Pannett House
Rating Applied For
14 Normanby Terrace, Whitby,
YO21 3ES
T: (01947) 603261

Partridge Nest Farm ♦♦♦
Eskdaleside, Sleights, Whitby
YO22 5ES
T: (01947) 810450
F: (01947) 811413
E: barbara@partridgenestfarm.com
I: www.partridgenestfarm.com

Postgate Farm Holidays ♦♦♦♦
Postgate Farm, Glaisdale, Whitby
YO21 2PZ
T: (01947) 897353
F: (01947) 897353
E: j-m.thompson.bandb@talk21.com
I: www.eskvalley.com/postgate/postgate.html

Prospect Villa Hotel ♦♦♦
13 Prospect Hill, Whitby,
YO21 1QE
T: (01947) 603118
F: (01947) 825445
E: chris@prospectvilla.freeserve.co.uk

Riviera Hotel ♦♦♦
4 Crescent Terrace, West Cliff,
Whitby, YO21 3EL
T: (01947) 602533
F: (01947) 606441
E: info@rivierawhitby.com
I: www.rivierawhitby.com

Rosslyn House ♦♦♦
11 Abbey Terrace, Whitby,
YO21 3HQ
T: (01947) 604086
E: rosslynhouse@bushinternet.com
I: www.guesthousewhitby.co.uk

Rothbury ♦♦♦♦
2 Ocean Road, Whitby,
YO21 3HY
T: (01947) 606282

The Royal Hotel ♦♦♦
East Terrace, West Cliff, Whitby,
YO21 3HA
T: (01947) 602234
F: (01947) 820355
E: gm.whi@barbox.net
I: www.shearingsholidays.com

Ryedale House ♦♦♦♦
156 Coach Road, Sleights,
Whitby YO22 5EQ
T: (01947) 810534
F: (01947) 810534

Sandpiper Guest House ♦♦♦♦
4 Belle Vue Terrace, Whitby,
YO21 3EY
T: (01947) 600246
F: (01947) 600246

Seacliffe Hotel ♦♦♦♦
12 North Promenade, West Cliff,
Whitby, YO21 3JX
T: (01947) 603139
F: (01947) 603139
E: julie@seacliffe.fsnet.co.uk
I: www.seacliffe.co.uk

Seaview ♦♦♦
5 East Crescent, Whitby,
YO21 3HD
T: (01947) 604462

Sneaton Castle Centre ♦♦♦♦
Sneaton Castle, Whitby,
YO21 3QN
T: (01947) 600051
F: (01947) 603490
E: holden@connectfree.co.uk
I: www.sneatoncastle.co.uk

Storrbeck Guest House ♦♦♦♦
9 Crescent Avenue, Whitby, YO21 3ED
T: (01947) 605468
E: storrbeck@bigfoot.com
I: www.storrbeck.fsnet.co.uk

Weardale Guest House ♦♦♦
12 Normanby Terrace, Whitby, YO21 3ES
T: (01947) 820389
F: (01947) 820389
I: www.weardaleguesthouse.co.uk

Wentworth House ♦♦♦
27 Hudson Street, Whitby, YO2 3EP
T: (01947) 602433
E: info@whitbywentworth.co.uk
I: www.whitbywentworth.co.uk

Wheeldale Hotel ♦♦♦♦
11 North Promenade, Whitby, YO21 3JX
T: (01947) 602365
E: wheeldale_hotel@lineone.net
I: www.wheeldale-hotel.co.uk

The Willows ♦♦♦
35 Bagdale, Whitby, YO21 1QL
T: (01947) 600288

York House Hotel ♦♦♦♦
3 Back Lane, High Hawsker, Whitby YO22 4LW
T: (01947) 880314
F: (01947) 880314
E: yorkhtl@aol.com

WICKERSLEY
South Yorkshire

Millstone Farm ♦♦♦♦
Morthen Road, Wickersley, Rotherham S66 1EA
T: (01709) 542382

WIKE
West Yorkshire

Wike Ridge Farm ♦♦♦♦
Wike Ridge Lane, Wike, Leeds LS17 9JF
T: (0113) 266 1190

WILBERFOSS
East Riding of Yorkshire

Cuckoo Nest Farm ♦♦♦
Wilberfoss, York YO41 5NL
T: (01759) 380365

WILSDEN
West Yorkshire

Springhill Bed and Breakfast ♦♦
2 Spring Hill, Wilsden, Bradford BD15 0AW
T: (01535) 275211

WILSILL
North Yorkshire

The Birch Tree Inn ♦♦♦
Wilsill, Harrogate HG3 5EA
T: (01423) 711131

WILTON
North Yorkshire

The Old Forge ♦♦♦♦
Wilton, Pickering YO18 7JY
T: (01751) 477399
F: (01751) 477464
E: theoldforge@themutual.net
I: www.forgecottages.themutual.net/fc.html

WOLD NEWTON
East Riding of Yorkshire

The Wold Cottage ♦♦♦♦♦ SILVER AWARD
Wold Newton, Driffield YO25 3HL
T: (01262) 470696
F: (01262) 470696
E: katrina@woldcottage.com
I: www.woldcottage.com

WOMBLETON
North Yorkshire

Rockery Cottage ♦♦♦♦ SILVER AWARD
Main Street, Wombleton, York YO62 7RX
T: (01751) 432257
E: angela@rockery-cottage.fsnet.co.uk

WORTLEY
South Yorkshire

Wortley Hall Ltd ♦♦
Wortley, Sheffield S35 7DB
T: (0114) 288 2100
F: (0114) 283 0695
E: info@wortleyhall.org.uk
I: www.wortleyhall.org.uk

WRAWBY
North Lincolnshire

Mowden House Rating Applied For
Barton Road, Wrawby, Brigg DN20 8SQ
T: (01652) 652145

Wish 'u' Well Guest House ♦♦♦
Brigg Road, Wrawby, Brigg DN20 8RH
T: (01652) 652301
F: (01652) 652301
E: wishuwell@talk21.com

WRELTON
North Yorkshire

Huntsman Licensed Guesthouse ♦♦♦
Main Street, Wrelton, Pickering YO18 8PG
T: (01751) 472530
F: (01751) 472530
E: howard@thehuntsman.freeserve.co.uk
I: www.europage.co.uk/huntsman

WROOT
North Lincolnshire

Green Garth Country Guest House ♦♦♦♦
High Street, Wroot, Doncaster DN9 2BU
T: (01302) 770416
F: (01302) 770416
E: enquiries@greengarth.co.uk
I: www.greengarth.co.uk

YORK
North Yorkshire

Aaron Guest House ♦♦♦
42 Bootham Crescent, Bootham, York, YO30 7AH
T: (01904) 625927

Abbey Guest House ♦♦♦
14 Earlsborough Terrace, Marygate, York, YO30 7BQ
T: (01904) 627782
F: (01904) 671743
E: abbey@rsummers.cix.co.uk
I: www.bedandbreakfastyork.co.uk

Abbeyfields ♦♦♦♦
19 Bootham Terrace, York, YO30 7DH
T: (01904) 636471
F: (01904) 636471
E: info@abbeyfields.co.uk
I: www.abbeyfields.co.uk

The Abbingdon ♦♦
60 Bootham Crescent, Bootham, York, YO30 7AH
T: (01904) 621761
F: (01904) 610002
E: paula@abbingdon.freeserve.co.uk
I: www.abbingdon.co.uk

The Acer Hotel ♦♦♦♦ SILVER AWARD
52 Scarcroft Hill, York, YO24 1DE
T: (01904) 653839
F: (01904) 677017
E: info@acerhotel.co.uk
I: www.acerhotel.co.uk

Acorn Guest House ♦♦♦
1 Southlands Road, York, YO23 1NP
T: (01904) 620081
F: (01904) 613331
E: acorn.gh@btinternet.com

Acres Dene Guesthouse ♦♦♦
87 Fulford Road, York, YO10 4BD
T: (01904) 647482
F: (01904) 637330
E: acresdene@bigwig.net

Airden House ♦♦♦
1 St Mary's, Bootham, York, YO30 7DD
T: (01904) 638915

Alcuin Lodge ♦♦♦♦
15 Sycamore Place, Bootham, York, YO30 7DW
T: (01904) 632222
F: (01904) 626630
E: alcuinlodg@aol.com

Aldwark Bridge House ♦♦♦
Ouseburn, Boat Lane, York, YO26 9SJ
T: (01423) 331097
F: (01423) 331097
E: bbabh@netscapeonline.co.uk

Alemar Guesthouse Rating Applied For
19 Queen Anne's Road, Bootham, York, YO30 7AA
T: (01904) 652367
E: sugartown5@talk21.com

Alexander House ♦♦♦♦♦ SILVER AWARD
94 Bishopthorpe Road, York, YO23 1JS
T: (01904) 625016
E: info@alexanderhouseyork.co.uk
I: www.alexanderhouseyork.co.uk

Ambleside Guest House ♦♦♦
62 Bootham Crescent, Bootham, York, YO30 7AH
T: (01904) 637165
F: (01904) 637165
E: ambles@globalnet.co.uk
I: www.ambleside-gh.co.uk

Arndale Hotel ♦♦♦♦ SILVER AWARD
290 Tadcaster Road, York, YO24 1ET
T: (01904) 702424
F: (01904) 709800

Arnot House ♦♦♦♦ SILVER AWARD
17 Grosvenor Terrace, Bootham, York, YO30 7AG
T: (01904) 641966
F: (01904) 641966
E: kim.robbins@virgin.net
I: www.arnothouseyork.co.uk

Ascot House ♦♦♦♦
80 East Parade, York, YO31 7YH
T: (01904) 426826
F: (01904) 431077
E: j&k@ascot-house-york.demon.co.uk
I: www.ascothouseyork.com

Ascot Lodge ♦♦♦
112 Acomb Road, York, YO24 4EY
T: (01904) 798234
F: (01904) 786742
E: info@ascotlodge.com
I: www.ascotlodge.com

Ashbourne House ♦♦♦♦
139 Fulford Road, York, YO10 4HG
T: (01904) 639912
F: (01904) 631332
E: ashbourneh@aol.com

Ashbury Hotel ♦♦♦
103 The Mount, York, YO24 1AX
T: (01904) 647339
F: (01904) 647339
E: ashbury@talk21.com

Astley House ♦♦♦
123 Clifton, York, YO30 6BL
T: (01904) 634745
F: (01904) 621327
E: astley123@aol.com
I: www.astley123.co.uk

Avondale Guest House ♦♦♦
61 Bishopthorpe Road, York, YO23 1NX
T: (01904) 633989
E: addyman@avondalehouse.freeserve.co.uk
I: www.avondalehouse.co.uk

The Bar Convent Enterprises Ltd ♦♦♦
17 Blossom Street, York, YO24 1AQ
T: (01904) 643238
F: (01904) 631792
E: info@bar-convent.org.uk
I: www.bar-convent.org.uk

Barbican House Rating Applied For
20 Barbican Road, York, YO10 5AA
T: (01904) 627617
F: (01904) 647140
E: info@barbicanhouse.com
I: www.barbicanhouse.com

Barrington House ♦♦♦
15 Nunthorpe Avenue, Scarcroft Road, York, YO23 1PF
T: (01904) 634539

Bay Tree Guest House ♦♦♦
92 Bishopthorpe Road, York, YO23 1JS
T: (01904) 659462
F: (01904) 659462
E: thomas.hall3@btopenworld.com

Bedford Hotel ♦♦♦
108-110 Bootham, York,
YO30 7DG
T: (01904) 624412
F: (01904) 632851
E: info@bedfordhotelyork.co.uk
I: www.bedfordhotelyork.co.uk

Beech House ♦♦♦
6-7 Longfield Terrace, Bootham,
York, YO30 7DJ
T: (01904) 634581
I: www.beech-house-york.co.uk

Bentley Guest House ♦♦♦♦
25 Grosvenor Terrace, Bootham,
York, YO30 7AG
T: (01904) 644313
F: (01904) 644313
E: bentley.ofyork@btinternet.
com
I: www.bentleyofyork.co.uk

Bishopgarth Guest House ♦♦♦
3 Southlands Road,
Bishopthorpe Road, York,
YO23 1NP
T: (01904) 635220
F: (01904) 635220
E: megspreckley@aol.com
I: www.bishopgarth.co.uk

Bishops Hotel
♦♦♦♦ SILVER AWARD
135 Holgate Road, Holgate,
York, YO24 4DF
T: (01904) 628000
F: (01904) 628181
E: bishops@ukonline.co.uk
I: www.bishopshotel.co.uk

Blakeney Hotel ♦♦♦
180 Stockton Lane, York,
YO31 1ES
T: (01904) 422786
F: (01904) 422786
E: reception@
blakeneyhotel-york.co.uk
I: www.blakeneyhotel-york.co.uk

Blue Bridge Hotel ♦♦♦
Fishergate, York, YO10 4AP
T: (01904) 621193
F: (01904) 671571
E: info@bluebridgehotel.co.uk
I: www.bluebridgehotel.co.uk

Bootham Guest House ♦♦♦
56 Bootham Crescent, York,
YO30 7AH
T: (01904) 672123
F: (01904) 672123
E: bgh@whsmithnet.co.uk

Bootham Park ♦♦♦♦
9 Grosvenor Terrace, Bootham,
York, YO30 7AG
T: (01904) 644262
F: (01904) 645647
E: boothampark@aol.com
I: www.boothampark@aol.com

Brentwood Guest House ♦♦♦
54 Bootham Crescent, Bootham,
York, YO30 7AH
T: (01904) 636419
F: (01904) 636419
E: brentwood@aol.com
I: www.visitus.co.uk

Briar Lea Guest House ♦♦♦
8 Longfield Terrace, Bootham,
York, YO30 7DJ
T: (01904) 635061
F: (01904) 330356
E: briargh8l@aol.com

Bronte Guesthouse ♦♦♦♦
22 Grosvenor Terrace, Bootham,
York, YO30 7AG
T: (01904) 621066
F: (01904) 653434
E: enquires@
bronte-guesthouse.com
I: www.bronte-guesthouse.com/

Bull Lodge Guest House ♦♦♦
37 Bull Lane, Lawrence Street,
York, YO10 3EN
T: (01904) 415522
F: (01904) 415522
E: stay@bulllodge.co.uk
I: www.bulllodge.co.uk

Burton Villa Guest House
Rating Applied For
24 Haxby Road, York, YO31 8JX
T: (01904) 626364
E: burtonvilla@hotmail.com
I: www.burtonvilla.com

Carlton House Hotel ♦♦♦
134 The Mount, York, YO24 1AS
T: (01904) 622265
F: (01904) 637157
E: etb@carltonhouse.co.uk
I: www.carltonhouse.co.uk

Carousel Guest House ♦♦♦
83 Eldon Street, off Stanley
Street, Haxby Road, York,
YO31 7NH
T: (01904) 646709

The Cavalier ♦♦♦
39 Monkgate, York, YO31 7PB
T: (01904) 636615
F: (01904) 636615
E: julia@cavalierhotel.co.uk
I: www.cavalierhotel.co.uk

Chelmsford Place Guest House ♦♦♦
85 Fulford Road, York, YO10 4BD
T: (01904) 624491
F: (01904) 624491
E: chelmsfordplace@btinternet.
com
I: www.chelmsfordplace.co.uk

Chilton Guest House ♦♦♦
1 Claremont Terrace, Gillygate,
York, YO31 7EJ
T: (01904) 612465
F: (01904) 612465

City Guest House
♦♦♦♦ SILVER AWARD
68 Monkgate, York, YO31 7PF
T: (01904) 622483
E: info@cityguesthouse.co.uk
I: www.cityguesthouse.co.uk

Clarence Gardens Hotel ♦♦♦
Haxby Road, York, YO31 8JS
T: (01904) 624252
F: (01904) 671293
E: clarencehotel@hotmail.com
I: www.clarencegardenhotel.
com

Claxton Hall Cottage
♦♦♦♦ SILVER AWARD
Malton Road, York, YO60 7RE
T: (01904) 468697
E: claxcott@aol.com
I: www.claxtonhallcottage.com

Clifton Bridge Hotel
Rating Applied For
Water End, Clifton, York
YO30 6LL
T: (01904) 610510
F: (01904) 640208
E: enquiries@cliftonbridgehotel.
co.uk
I: www.cliftonbridgehotel.co.uk

Cook's Guest House ♦♦♦
120 Bishopthorpe Road, York,
YO23 1JX
T: (01904) 652519
F: (01904) 652519
E: cooks@talk21.com

Cornmill Lodge Vegetarian Guest House ♦♦♦
120 Haxby Road, York, YO31 8JP
T: (01904) 620566
F: (01904) 620566
E: cornmillyork@aol.com
I: www.cornmillyork.co.uk

Crescent Guest House ♦♦
77 Bootham, York, YO30 7DQ
T: (01904) 623216
F: (01904) 623216
I: www.guesthousesyork.net

Crook Lodge
Rating Applied For
26 St Mary's, Bootham, York,
YO30 7DD
T: (01904) 655614
F: (01904) 655614
E: crooklodge@hotmail.com
I: www.crooklodge.co.uk

Crossways Guest House ♦♦♦
23 Wigginton Road, York,
YO31 8HJ
T: (01904) 637250
E: info@crosswaysguesthouse.
freeserve.co.uk
I: www.crosswaysguesthouse.
freeserve.co.uk

Cumbria House ♦♦♦
2 Vyner Street, Haxby Road,
York, YO31 8HS
T: (01904) 636817
E: clark@cumbriahouse.
freeserve.co.uk
I: www.cumbriahouse.com

Curzon Lodge and Stable Cottages ♦♦♦♦
23 Tadcaster Road, Dringhouses,
York YO24 1QG
T: (01904) 703157
F: (01904) 703157
I: www.smoothhound.
co.uk/hotels/curzon.html

Dalescroft Guest House ♦♦♦
10 Southlands Road,
Bishopthorpe Road, York,
YO23 1NP
T: (01904) 626801
E: dalescroftg.h.@aol.com

Eastons ♦♦♦♦
90 Bishopthorpe Road, York,
YO23 1JS
T: (01904) 626646
F: (01904) 626165
E: eastonsbbyork@aol.com
I: members.aol.
com/eastonsbbyork/home.htm

Elliotts ♦♦♦♦
Sycamore Place, Bootham
Terrace, York, YO30 7DW
T: (01904) 623333
F: (01904) 654908
E: elliottshotel@aol.com
I: www.elliottshotel.co.uk

Fairthorne ♦♦♦
356 Strensall Road, Earswick,
York YO32 9SW
T: (01904) 768609
F: (01904) 768609

Farthings Hotel ♦♦♦
5 Nunthorpe Avenue, York,
YO23 1PF
T: (01904) 653545
F: (01904) 628355
E: farthings@york181.
fsbusiness.co.uk
I: www.farthingsyork.co.uk

Feversham Lodge International Guest House ♦♦♦
No 1 Feversham Crescent, Off
Wigginton Road, York,
YO31 8HQ
T: (01904) 623882
F: (01904) 623882
E: feversham@lutyens.
freeserve.co.uk
I: www.
fevershamlodgeguesthouseyork.
co.uk

Five Lions Hotel
Rating Applied For
24 Walmgate, York, YO1 9TJ
T: (01904) 625124

Foss Bank Guest House ♦♦♦
16 Huntington Road, York,
YO31 8RB
T: (01904) 635548
I: www.fossbank.co.uk

Four Seasons Hotel
♦♦♦♦ SILVER AWARD
7 St Peter's Grove, Bootham,
York, YO30 6AQ
T: (01904) 622621
F: (01904) 620976
E: roe@fourseasons.supanet.
com
I: www.fourseasons-hotel.co.uk

Fourposter Lodge Hotel ♦♦♦
68-70 Heslington Road,
Barbican Road, York, YO10 5AU
T: (01904) 651170
F: (01904) 651170
E: fourposter.lodge@virgin.net
I: www.fourposterlodgehotel.
co.uk

Friars Rest Guest House ♦♦♦
81 Fulford Road, York, YO10 4BD
T: (01904) 629823
F: (01904) 629823
E: friarsrest@btinternet.com
I: www.friarsrest.co.uk

Gables Guest House ♦♦
50 Bootham Crescent, Bootham,
York, YO30 7AH
T: (01904) 624381
F: (01904) 624381
I: www.thegablesofyork.co.uk

George Hotel ♦♦♦
6 St George's Place, Tadcaster
Road, York, YO24 1DR
T: (01904) 625056
F: (01904) 625009
E: sixstgeorg@aol.com
I: members.aol.com/sixstgeorg/

Goldsmiths Guest House
Rating Applied For
18 Longfield Terrace, Bootham,
York, YO30 7DJ
T: (01904) 655738

Grange Lodge ♦♦♦
52 Bootham Crescent, Bootham,
York, YO30 7AH
T: (01904) 621137
E: grangeldg@aol.com

Greenside ♦♦♦
124 Clifton, York, YO30 6BQ
T: (01904) 623631
F: (01904) 623631

The Hazelwood
◆◆◆◆ SILVER AWARD
24-25 Portland Street, York, YO31 7EH
T: (01904) 626548
F: (01904) 628032
E: Reservations@thehazelwoodyork.com
I: www.thehazelwoodyork.com

Heworth Guest House ◆◆◆
126 East Parade, Heworth, York YO31 7YG
T: (01904) 426384
F: (01904) 426384
E: chris.thompson1@virgin.net
I: www.yorkcity.co.uk

Hillcrest Guest House ◆◆◆
110 Bishopthorpe Road, York, YO23 1JX
T: (01904) 653160
E: hillcrest@accommodation.gbr.fm
I: www.accommodation.gbr.fm

Holgate Bridge Hotel ◆◆◆
106-108 Holgate Road, York, YO24 4BB
T: (01904) 647288
F: (01904) 670049
E: info@holgatebridge.co.uk
I: www.holgatebridge.co.uk

The Hollies Guest House ◆◆◆
141 Fulford Road, York, YO10 4HG
T: (01904) 634279
F: (01904) 625435
E: enquiries@hollies-guesthouse.co.uk
I: www.hollies-guesthouse.co.uk

Holly Lodge ◆◆◆◆
206 Fulford Road, York, YO10 4DD
T: (01904) 646005
I: www.thehollylodge.co.uk

Holme Lea Manor Guest House ◆◆◆
18 St Peter's Grove, Bootham, York, YO30 6AQ
T: (01904) 623529
F: (01904) 653584
E: holmelea@btclick.com

Holmlea Guest House ◆◆
6-7 Southlands Road, York, YO23 1NP
T: (01904) 621010
F: (01904) 659566
E: steve@holmlea.co.uk
I: www.holmlea.co.uk

Holmwood House Hotel ◆◆◆◆
114 Holgate Road, York, YO24 4BB
T: (01904) 626183
F: (01904) 670899
E: holmwood.house@dial.pipex.com
I: www.holmwoodhousehotel.co.uk

Kirkham Coffee Shop & Guest House ◆◆◆
Station House, Kirkham Abbey, York, YO60 7JS
T: (01653) 618658

The Limes ◆◆◆◆
135 Fulford Road, York, YO10 4HE
T: (01904) 624548
F: (01904) 624944
E: queries@limeshotel.co.uk
I: www.limeshotel.co.uk

Linden Lodge ◆◆◆
6 Nunthorpe Avenue, Scarcroft Road, York, YO23 1PF
T: (01904) 620107
F: (01904) 620985
E: bookings@lindenlodge.yorks.net
I: www.yorkshirenet.co.uk/stayat/lindenlodge

The Manor Country House ◆◆◆◆
Acaster Malbis, York YO23 2UL
T: (01904) 706723
F: (01904) 700737
E: manorhouse@selcom.co.uk
I: www.manorhse.co.uk

Martin's Guest House ◆◆
5 Longfield Terrace, York, YO30 7DJ
T: (01904) 634551
F: (01904) 634551
E: martinsbandb@talk21.com
I: www.smoothhound.co.uk.hotels/martins.html

Meadowcroft Hotel ◆◆◆
84 Bootham, York, YO30 7DF
T: (01904) 655194
F: (01904) 651384
E: mcroftyork@aol.com

Midway House Hotel ◆◆◆
145 Fulford Road, York, YO10 4HG
T: (01904) 659272
E: midway.house@virgin.net
I: www.s-h-systems.co.uk/hotels/midway.html

Minster View Guest House
Rating Applied For
2 Grosvenor Terrace, Bootham, York, YO30 7AG
T: (01904) 655034
F: (01904) 655034

Monkgate Guest House ◆◆◆
65 Monkgate, York, YO31 7PA
T: (01904) 655947
E: jwb@monkgate.swinternet.co.uk
I: www.monkgateguesthouse.co.uk

Moorgarth Guest House ◆◆◆
158 Fulford Road, York, YO10 4DA
T: (01904) 636768
F: (01904) 636768
E: moorgarth@fsbdial.co.uk
I: www.moorgarth-york.co.uk

Moorland House ◆◆◆
1A Moorland Road, Fulford Road, York, YO10 4HF
T: (01904) 629354
F: (01904) 629354

Mowbray House ◆◆◆
34 Haxby Road, York, YO31 8JX
T: (01904) 637710
E: carol@mowbrayhouse.co.uk
I: www.mowbrayhouse.co.uk

Northolme Guest House ◆◆◆
114 Shipton Road, Rawcliffe, York YO30 5RN
T: (01904) 639132
E: g.liddle@tesco.net
I: www.northholmeguesthouse.co.uk

Nunmill House
◆◆◆◆ SILVER AWARD
85 Bishopthorpe Road, York, YO23 1NX
T: (01904) 634047
F: (01904) 655879
E: info@nunmill.co.uk
I: www.nunmill.co.uk

Oaklands Guest House ◆◆◆
351 Strensall Road, Earswick, York YO32 9SW
T: (01904) 768443
E: mavmo@oaklands5.fsnet.co.uk
I: www.holidayguides.com

Olga's Licensed Guest House ◆◆◆
12 Wenlock Terrace, Fulford Road, York, YO10 4DU
T: (01904) 641456
F: (01904) 641456
E: olgasguesthouseyork@talk21.com
I: www.olgas-guesthouse-york.co.uk

One3Two
Rating Applied For
132 The Mount, York, YO24 1AS
T: (01904) 600060
F: (01904) 676132

Orillia House ◆◆◆
89 The Village, Stockton-on-the-Forest, York YO32 9UP
T: (01904) 400600
F: (01904) 400101
E: orillia@globalnet.co.uk
I: www.orilliahouse.co.uk

Palm Court Hotel ◆◆◆◆
17 Huntington Road, York, YO31 8RB
T: (01904) 639387
F: (01904) 639387

Papillon Hotel ◆◆
43 Gillygate, York, YO31 7EA
T: (01904) 636505
F: (01904) 611968
E: papillonhotel@btinternet.com
I: www.btinternet.com/~papillonhotel

Park View Guest House ◆◆◆
34 Grosvenor Terrace, Bootham, York, YO30 7AG
T: (01904) 620437
F: (01904) 620437
E: park_view@talk21.com

Primrose Lodge ◆◆◆
Hull Road, Dunnington, York YO19 5LP
T: (01904) 489140

Priory Hotel & Garth Restaurant ◆◆◆
126-128 Fulford Road, York, YO10 4BE
T: (01904) 625280
F: (01904) 637330
E: reservations@priory-hotelyork.co.uk
I: www.priory-hotelyork.co.uk

Queen Anne's Guest House ◆◆◆
24 Queen Anne's Road, Bootham, York, YO30 7AA
T: (01904) 629389
F: (01904) 619529
E: info@queenannes.fsnet.co.uk
I: www.queen-annes-guesthouse.co.uk

Red Lion Motel and Country Inn ◆◆◆
Boroughbridge Road, Upper Poppleton, York YO26 6PR
T: (01904) 781141
F: (01904) 785143
E: reservations@redlionhotel.com
I: www.redlionhotel.com

Riverside Walk Guest House ◆◆◆
9 Earlsborough Terrace, Marygate, York, YO30 7BQ
T: (01904) 620769
F: (01904) 671743
E: riverside@rsummers.cix.co.uk
I: www.bedandbreakfastyork.co.uk

Romley Guest House ◆◆◆
2 Millfield Road, Scarcroft Road, York, YO23 1NQ
T: (01904) 652822
E: info@romleyhouse.co.uk
I: www.romleyhouse.co.uk

St Deny's Hotel ◆◆◆
51 St Denys Road, York, YO1 9QD
T: (01904) 622207
F: (01904) 624800
E: info@stdenyshotel.co.uk
I: www.stdenyshotel.co.uk

St Mary's Hotel ◆◆◆
17 Longfield Terrace, Bootham, York, YO30 7DJ
T: (01904) 626972
F: (01904) 626972
E: stmaryshotel@talk21.com
I: www.stmaryshotel.co.uk

St Paul's Hotel ◆◆◆
120 Holgate Road, York, YO24 4BB
T: (01904) 611514
F: (01904) 623188
E: normfran@supanet.com

Saxon House Hotel ◆◆◆
Fishergate, 71-73 Fulford Road, York, YO10 4BD
T: (01904) 622106
F: (01904) 633764
E: saxon@househotel.freeserve.co.uk
I: www.saxonhousehotel.co.uk

Skelton Grange Farmhouse ◆◆◆
Orchard View, Skelton, York YO30 1XQ
T: (01904) 470780
F: (01904) 471229
E: info@skelton-farm.co.uk
I: www.skelton-farm.co.uk

Southlands Bed and Breakfast ◆◆◆◆
Huntington Road, Huntington, York YO32 9PX
T: (01904) 766796
F: (01904) 764536
E: southlandsbandb.york@btinternet.com
I: www.southlandsbandb.freeserve.co.uk

Southland's Guest House
Rating Applied For
69 Nunmill Street, South Bank, York, YO23 1NT
T: (01904) 675966
F: (01904) 675965
E: southlands.house@virgin.net
I: www.southlandsguesthouse.co.uk

23 St Marys ♦♦♦♦
Bootham, York, YO30 7DD
T: (01904) 622738
F: (01904) 628802
E: stmarys23@hotmail.com
I: www.23stmarys.co.uk

Stanley House ♦♦♦
Stanley Street, Haxby Road, York, YO31 8NW
T: (01904) 637111
F: (01904) 659599
E: dawson@stanleyhouseyork.co.uk
I: www.stanleyhouseyork.co.uk

Staymor Guest House ♦♦♦
2 Southlands Road, York, YO23 1NP
T: (01904) 626935
E: kathwilson@lineone.net
I: www.staymorguesthouse.com

The Steer Inn ♦♦♦
Hull Road, Wilberfoss, York YO41 5PE
T: (01759) 380600
F: (01759) 388904
E: kevin@steerinn.co.uk
I: www.steerinn.co.uk

Sycamore Guest House ♦♦♦
19 Sycamore Place, Bootham, York, YO30 7DW
T: (01904) 624712
F: (01904) 624712
E: thesycamore@talk21.com
I: www.guesthousesyork.co.uk

Tower Guest House ♦♦♦
2 Feversham Crescent, Wigginton Road, York, YO31 8HQ
T: (01904) 655571
F: (01904) 655571
E: reservations@towerguesthouse.fsnet.co.uk
I: www.towerguesthouse.fsnet.co.uk

Tree Tops ♦♦♦
21 St Mary's, Bootham, York, YO30 7DD
T: (01904) 658053
F: (01904) 658053
E: treetops.guesthouse@virgin.net
I: business.thisisyork.co.uk/treetops

Turnberry House ♦♦♦
143 Fulford Road, York, YO10 4HG
T: (01904) 658435
F: (01904) 658435

Tyburn House Hotel ♦♦♦
11 Albemarle Road, The Mount, York, YO23 1EN
T: (01904) 655069
F: (01904) 655069
E: york@tyburnhotel.freeserve.co.uk

The Victoria Hotel ♦♦♦
1 Heslington Road, York, YO10 5AR
T: (01904) 622295
F: (01904) 677860

Victoria Villa ♦♦
72 Heslington Road, York, YO10 5AU
T: (01904) 631647
F: (01904) 651170
E: vicvilla@fsmail.net
I: www.smoothhound.co.uk/hotels/vicvilla.html

Warrens Guest House ♦♦♦
30 Scarcroft Road, York, YO23 1NF
T: (01904) 643139
F: (01904) 658297
I: www.warrens.ndo.co.uk

Waters Edge ♦♦♦
5 Earlsborough Terrace, Marygate, York, YO30 7BQ
T: (01904) 644625
E: julie@watersedgeyork.co.uk
I: www.watersedgeyork.co.uk

Wellgarth House ♦♦♦
Wetherby Road, Rufforth, York YO23 3QB
T: (01904) 738592
F: (01904) 738595

White Doves ♦♦♦
20 Claremont Terrace, Gillygate, York, YO31 7EJ
T: (01904) 625957

Wold View House Hotel ♦♦♦
171-175 Haxby Road, York, YO31 8JL
T: (01904) 632061
F: (01904) 632061
E: enquiries@woldviewhousehotel.co.uk
I: www.woldviewhousehotel.co.uk

York House
Rating Applied For
62 Heworth Green, York, YO31 7TQ
T: (01904) 427070
F: (01904) 427070

York Lodge Guest House ♦♦♦
64 Bootham Crescent, Bootham, York, YO30 7AH
T: (01904) 654289
F: (01904) 654289
E: liza@moore01.fsnet.co.uk
I: www.yorkshirenet.co.uk/accgde/yorklodge

HEART OF ENGLAND

AB KETTLEBY
Leicestershire

White Lodge Farm ♦♦♦♦
Nottingham Road, Ab Kettleby, Melton Mowbray LE14 3JB
T: (01664) 822286
I: www.farm-holidays.co.uk

ABBOTS BROMLEY
Staffordshire

Crown Inn ♦♦
Market Place, Abbots Bromley, Rugeley WS15 3BS
T: (01283) 840227
F: (01283) 840016

ABBOTS MORTON
Worcestershire

The Cottage Apartment ♦♦♦♦
The Cottage, Gooms Hill, Abbots Morton Manor, Abbots Morton, Worcester WR7 4LT
T: (01386) 792783
F: (01386) 792783
E: cottage@bedbrek.fsnet.co.uk
I: www.bedbrek.co.uk

ABTHORPE
Northamptonshire

Rignall Farm Barns ♦♦♦♦
Handley Park, Abthorpe, Towcester NN12 8PA
T: (01327) 350766
F: (01327) 350766

ACTON BURNELL
Shropshire

Acton Pigot ♦♦♦♦♦ SILVER AWARD
Acton Burnell, Shrewsbury SY5 7PH
T: (01694) 731209
E: acton@farmline.com
I: www.actonpigot.co.uk

ADSTONE
Northamptonshire

Manor Farm ♦♦♦♦
Adstone, Towcester NN12 8DT
T: (01327) 860284
F: (01327) 860685
I: www.manorfarmsports.co.uk

ALBRIGHTON
Shropshire

Parkside Farm ♦♦♦♦ SILVER AWARD
Holyhead Road, Albrighton, Wolverhampton WV7 3DA
T: (01902) 372310
F: (01902) 375013
E: jmshanks@farming.co.uk
I: www.parksidefarm.com

ALCESTER
Warwickshire

The Globe Hotel ♦♦♦♦
54 Birmingham Road, Alcester, B49 5EG
T: (01789) 763287
F: (01789) 763287
E: info@theglobehotel.com
I: www.theglobehotel.com

Orchard Lawns ♦♦♦♦ SILVER AWARD
Wixford, Alcester B49 6DA
T: (01789) 772668
E: margaret.orchardlawns@farmersweekly.net

Sambourne Hall Farm ♦♦♦♦
Wike Lane, Sambourne, B96 6NZ
T: (01527) 852151

ALDERTON
Gloucestershire

Corner Cottage ♦♦♦
Stow Road, Alderton, Tewkesbury GL20 8NH
T: (01242) 620630
F: (01242) 621550
E: cornercottagebb@talk21.com

Gantier ♦♦♦♦
12 Church Road, Alderton, Tewkesbury GL20 8NR
T: (01242) 620343
F: (01386) 442415
E: johnandsueparry@yahoo.co.uk
I: www.gantier.co.uk

Moors Farm House ♦♦♦♦♦ GOLD AWARD
32 Beckford Road, Alderton, Tewkesbury GL20 8NL
T: (01242) 620523
E: moorsfarmhouse@ukworld.net
I: www.ukworld.net/moorsfarmhouse

ALDWARK
Derbyshire

Lydgate Farm ♦♦♦♦
Aldwark, DE4 4HW
T: (01629) 540250
F: (01629) 540250
E: lomas.lydgate@lineone.net
I: www.peakdistrictfarmhols.co.uk

ALDWINCLE
Northamptonshire

Pear Tree Farm ♦♦♦♦
Aldwincle, Kettering NN14 3EL
T: (01832) 720614
F: (01832) 720559
E: beverley@peartreefarm.net

ALFRETON
Derbyshire

Crown Inn ♦♦
73 Sleetmoor Lane, Somercotes, Alfreton, DE55 1RE
T: (01773) 602537

The Spinney Cottage ♦♦♦
Derby Road, Swanwick, Alfreton, DE55 1BG
T: (01773) 609020

ALMELEY
Herefordshire

Almeley House Bed and Breakfast ♦♦♦♦
Almeley House, Almeley, Hereford HR3 6LB
T: (01544) 327269
F: (01544) 328406
E: gwenda@hamesg.freeserve.co.uk

ALTON
Staffordshire

Admirals House ♦♦♦
Mill Road, Oakamoor, Stoke-on-Trent ST10 3AG
T: (01538) 702187
F: (01538) 702957
E: admiralshouse@btinternet.com
I: www.admiralshouse.co.uk

Alverton Motel ♦♦♦♦
Denstone Lane, Alton, Stoke-on-Trent ST10 4AX
T: (01538) 702265
F: (01538) 703284
I: www.alvertonmotel.co.uk

Bradley Elms Farm ♦♦♦♦
Alton Road, Threapwood, Cheadle, ST10 4RB
T: (01538) 753135
F: (01538) 750202

Bramble Cottage ♦♦♦♦
Gallows Green, Alton, Stoke-on-Trent ST10 4BN
T: (01538) 703805

Bulls Head Inn ♦♦♦
High Street, Alton, Stoke-on-Trent ST10 4AQ
T: (01538) 702307
F: (01538) 702065
E: janet@alton.freeserve.co.uk
I: www.thebullsheadinn.freeserve.co.uk

Church Grange ♦♦♦♦
Bradley in the Moors, Alton, Stoke-on-Trent ST10 4DF
T: (01889) 507525
F: (01889) 507282
E: ddeb@lineone.net
I: www.staffordshire.gov.uk/tourism/chgrange.htm

The Cross Inn ♦♦♦
Cauldon Low, Stoke-on-Trent, ST10 3EX
T: (01538) 308338
F: (01538) 308767
E: adrian_weaver@hotmail.com
I: www.crossinn.co.uk

Fernlea Guest House ♦♦♦
Cedar Hill, Alton, Stoke-on-Trent ST10 4BH
T: (01538) 702327

Fields Farm
♦♦♦♦ SILVER AWARD
Chapel Lane, Threapwood, Alton, Stoke-on-Trent ST10 4QZ
T: (01538) 752721
F: (01538) 757404
E: pat.massey@ukonline.co.uk

Hansley Cross Cottage ♦♦♦
Cheadle Road, Alton, Stoke-on-Trent ST10 4DH
T: (01538) 702189
F: (01538) 702189
E: jeanhcross@aol.com
I: www.hansleycrosscottage.co.uk

Hillside Farm and Cottages ♦♦♦
Alton Road, Denstone, Uttoxeter ST14 5HG
T: (01889) 590760
I: www.smoothhound.co.uk/hotels/hillside.html

The Malthouse ♦♦♦♦
Malthouse Road, Alton, Stoke-on-Trent ST10 4AG
T: (01538) 703273
I: www.the-malthouse.gbr.fm/2001/contact.asp

The Old School House
♦♦♦♦♦ SILVER AWARD
Castle Hill Road, Alton, Stoke-on-Trent ST10 4AI
T: (01538) 702151
E: old_school_house@talk21.com
I: www.geocities.com/denniseardley

The Peakstones Inn ♦♦
Cheadle Road, Alton, Stoke-on-Trent ST10 4DH
T: (01538) 755776

Rockhaven ♦♦♦
Smithy Bank, Alton, Stoke-on-Trent ST10 4AA
T: (01538) 702066
F: (01538) 702066

Royal Oak ♦♦
Alton, Stoke-on-Trent ST10 4BH
T: (01538) 702625
E: enq@royaloak-alton.co.uk
I: www.royaloak-alton.co.uk

Trough Ivy House ♦♦♦♦
1 Hay Lane, Farley, Alton, Stoke-on-Trent ST10 3BQ
T: (01538) 702683
F: (01538) 702683
E: bookings@trough-ivy-house.demon.co.uk
I: www.trough-ivy-house.demon.co.uk

Tythe Barn House ♦♦♦
Denstone Lane, Alton, Stoke-on-Trent ST10 4AX
T: (01538) 702852

The Warren ♦♦♦♦
The Dale, Battlesteads, Alton, Stoke-on-Trent ST10 4BG
T: (01538) 702493
F: (01538) 702493

Yoxall Cottage ♦♦♦
Malt House Road, Alton, Stoke-on-Trent ST10 4AG
T: (01538) 702537
F: (01538) 702537
E: bb_yoxallcottage@btopenworld.com

ALVASTON
Derbyshire

Grace Guesthouse ♦♦
1063 London Road, Alvaston, Derby DE24 8PZ
T: (01332) 572522
F: (01332) 341916

ALVECHURCH
Worcestershire

Alcott Farm ♦♦♦
Weatheroak, Alvechurch, Birmingham B48 7EH
T: (01564) 824051
F: (01564) 824051

ALVELEY
Shropshire

Arnside Bed and Breakfast
♦♦♦♦ SILVER AWARD
Arnside, Kidderminster Road, Alveley, Bridgnorth WV15 6LL
T: (01746) 780007
F: (01746) 780007
E: terry@ptah.freeservce.co.uk
I: www.virtual-shropshire.co.uk/arnside

AMBERLEY
Gloucestershire

Dunkirk Manor
Rating Applied For
Amberley, Amberley, Stroud GL5 5AU
T: (01453) 873456
F: (01453) 878518
E: info@dunkirkmanor.com
I: www.dunkirkmanor.com

High Tumps ♦♦♦♦
St Chloe Green, Amberley, Stroud GL5 5AR
T: (01453) 873584
F: (01453) 873587

APPLEBY MAGNA
Leicestershire

Elms Farm
♦♦♦♦ SILVER AWARD
Appleby Magna, Swadlincote DE12 7AP
T: (01530) 270450
F: (01530) 272718

ARLEY
Worcestershire

Tudor Barn
♦♦♦♦ SILVER AWARD
Nib Green, Arley, Bewdley DY12 3LY
T: (01299) 400129
E: tudorbarn@aol.com
I: www.tudor-barn.co.uk

ARMSCOTE
Warwickshire

Willow Corner
♦♦♦♦ SILVER AWARD
Armscote, Stratford-upon-Avon CV37 8DE
T: (01608) 682391
E: willowcorner@compuserve.com
I: www.willowcorner.co.uk

ARNOLD
Nottinghamshire

Rufford Guesthouse ♦♦♦♦
117 Redhill Road, Arnold, Nottingham NG5 8GZ
T: (0115) 926 1759
F: (0115) 926 1759
E: ruffordhouse@hotmail.com
I: www.ruffordhouse.co.uk

ASFORDBY VALLEY
Leicestershire

Valley End ♦♦♦♦
17 North Street, Asfordby Valley, Melton Mowbray LE14 3SQ
T: (01664) 812003

ASH MAGNA
Shropshire

Ash Hall ♦♦♦
Ash Magna, Whitchurch SY13 4DL
T: (01948) 663151

ASHBOURNE
Derbyshire

The Black Horse Inn ♦♦♦
Main Road, Hulland Ward, Ashbourne DE6 3EE
T: (01335) 370206
F: (01335) 370206

Cross Farm ♦♦♦♦
Main Road, Ellastone, Ashbourne DE6 2GZ
T: (01335) 324668
F: (01335) 324039
E: janecliffe@hotmail.com

Cubley Common Farm ♦♦♦♦
Cubley, Ashbourne, DE6 2EX
T: (01335) 330041

Green Gables ♦♦♦♦
107 The Green Road, Ashbourne, DE6 1EE
T: (01335) 342431

Hurtswood ♦♦♦
Buxton Road, Sandybrook, Ashbourne, DE6 2AQ
T: (01335) 342031
F: (01335) 347467
E: gl.hurtswood@virgin.net
I: www.hurtswood.co.uk

The Lilacs ♦♦♦♦
Mayfield Road, Ashbourne, DE6 2BJ
T: (01335) 343749
F: (01335) 343749

Mona Villas Bed and Breakfast ♦♦♦
1 Mona Villas, Church Lane, Mayfield, Ashbourne DE6 2JS
T: (01335) 343773
F: (01335) 343773

Omnia Somnia
♦♦♦♦♦ GOLD AWARD
The Coach House, The Firs, Ashbourne, DE6 1HF
T: (01335) 300145
F: (01335) 300958
E: alan@omniasomnia.co.uk
I: www.omniasomnia.co.uk

Overfield Farm ♦♦♦
Tissington, Ashbourne, DE6 1RA
T: (01335) 390285

Shirley Hall Farm
♦♦♦♦ SILVER AWARD
Shirley, Ashbourne DE6 3AS
T: (01335) 360346
F: (01335) 360346
E: sylviafoster@shirleyhallfarm.com
I: www.shirleyhallfarm.com

Stanshope Hall ♦♦♦♦
Stanshope, Ashbourne DE6 2AD
T: (01335) 310278
F: (01335) 310470
E: naomi@stanshope.demon.co.uk
I: www.stanshope.demon.co.uk

Tan Mill Farm ♦♦♦♦
Mappleton Road, Ashbourne, DE6 2AA
T: (01335) 342387
F: (01335) 342387

Thorpe Cottage ♦♦♦♦
Thorpe, Ashbourne DE6 2AW
T: (01335) 350466
F: (01335) 350217
I: www.peakdistrict-bandb.com

The Wheelhouse ♦♦♦♦
Belper Road, Hulland Ward, Ashbourne, DE6 3EE
T: (01335) 370953
E: samax@supanet.com

White Cottage ♦♦♦♦
Wyaston, Ashbourne DE6 2DR
T: (01335) 345503

ASHBY-DE-LA-ZOUCH
Leicestershire

Church Lane Farm House ♦♦♦♦
Church Lane, Ravenstone, Coalville, Leicester LE67 2AE
T: (01530) 810536
F: (01530) 811299
E: annthorne@ravenstone-guesthouse.co.uk
I: www.ravenstone-guesthouse co.uk

Holywell House Hotel ♦♦
58 Burton Road, Ashby-de-la-Zouch, LE65 2LN
T: (01530) 412005

The Laurels Bed and Breakfast ♦♦♦
17 Ashby Road, Measham, Ashby-de-la-Zouch, DE12 7JR
T: (01530) 272567
F: (01530) 272567
E: evanslaurels@onetel.net.uk
I: www.thelaurelsguesthouse.com

Measham House Farm ♦♦♦♦
Gallows Lane, Measham,
Swadlincote, DE12 7HD
T: (01530) 270465
F: (01530) 270465
E: jjlovett@meashamhouse.freeserve.co.uk
I: www.meashamhouse.co.uk

Queens Head Hotel
Rating Applied For
79 Market Street, Ashby-de-la-Zouch, LE65 1AH
T: (01530) 412780
F: (01530) 412134

ASHBY ST LEDGERS
Northamptonshire

The Olde Coach House Inn ♦♦♦
Main Street, Ashby St Ledgers,
Rugby CV23 8UN
T: (01788) 890349
F: (01788) 891922
E: oldecoachhouse@traditionalfreehouses.co.uk

ASHFORD IN THE WATER
Derbyshire

Chy-an-Dour
♦♦♦♦ SILVER AWARD
Vicarage Lane, Ashford in the Water, Bakewell DE45 1QN
T: (01629) 813162

Gritstone House
♦♦♦♦ SILVER AWARD
Greaves Lane, Ashford in the Water, Bakewell DE45 1QH
T: (01629) 813563
F: (01629) 813563

Marble Cottage
♦♦♦♦ SILVER AWARD
The Dukes Drive, Ashford in the Water, Bakewell DE45 1QP
T: (01629) 813624
F: (01629) 813832
E: marblecottage@aol.com
I: www.cressbrook.co.uk/bakewell/marblecottage

Warlands ♦♦♦
Hill Cross, Ashford in the Water,
Bakewell DE45 1QL
T: (01629) 813736

Woodland View ♦♦♦
John Bank Lane, Ashford in the Water, Bakewell DE45 1PY
T: (01629) 813008
F: (01629) 813008
E: woodview@neilellis.free-online.co.uk
I: www.woodlandviewbandb.co.uk

ASHLEWORTH
Gloucestershire

Ashleworth Court ♦♦♦
Ashleworth, Gloucester
GL19 4JA
T: (01452) 700241
F: (01452) 700411
E: chamberlayne@farmline.com
I: members.farmline.com/chamberlayne

ASHOVER
Derbyshire

Hardwick View ♦♦♦♦
Ashover Road, Littlemoor,
Ashover, Chesterfield S45 0BL
T: (01246) 590876
E: sueworsey@talk21.com

Old School Farm ♦♦♦♦
Uppertown, Ashover,
Chesterfield S45 0JF
T: (01246) 590813

ASHPERTON
Herefordshire

Pridewood ♦♦♦
Ashperton, Ledbury HR8 2SF
T: (01531) 670416
F: (01531) 670416

ASLACKBY
Lincolnshire

The Hayloft ♦♦♦♦
Martins, Temple Road, Aslackby,
Sleaford NG34 0HJ
T: (01778) 440113
F: (01778) 440920
E: jacqueline.cole@talk21.com

ASTLEY
Worcestershire

Woodhampton House ♦♦♦
Weather Lane, Astley, Stourport-on-Severn DY13 0SF
T: (01299) 826510
F: (01299) 827059
E: pete-a@sally-a.freeserve.co.uk

ATHERSTONE
Warwickshire

Hall Farm ♦♦♦♦
The Green, Orton-on-the-Hill,
Atherstone, CV9 3NG
T: (01827) 880350
F: (01827) 881041
E: hallfm101@aol.com

Manor Farm Bed and Breakfast ♦♦♦
Manor Farm, Ratcliffe Culey,
Atherstone, CV9 3NY
T: (01827) 712269
E: user880243@aol.com

Mythe Farm Bed & Breakfast ♦♦♦♦
Pinwall Lane, Sheepy Magna,
Atherstone, CV9 3PF
T: (01827) 712367
F: (01827) 715738
E: bosworth/advertising@connectfree.co.uk

AUDLEY
Staffordshire

The Domvilles Farm ♦♦♦♦
Barthomley Road, Audley,
Stoke-on-Trent ST7 8HT
T: (01782) 720378
F: (01782) 720883

AVON DASSETT
Warwickshire

Crandon House
♦♦♦♦♦ SILVER AWARD
Avon Dassett, Leamington Spa,
CV47 2AA
T: (01295) 770652
F: (01295) 770632
E: crandonhouse@talk21.com
I: www.crandonhouse.co.uk

AWSWORTH
Nottinghamshire

Hog's Head Hotel ♦♦♦
Main Street, Awsworth,
Nottingham NG16 2RN
T: (0115) 938 4095
F: (0115) 945 9718

AYLBURTON
Gloucestershire

Bridge Cottage ♦♦♦
High Street, Aylburton,
Gloucester GL15 6BX
T: (01594) 843527

BADBY
Northamptonshire

Meadows Farm
♦♦♦♦♦ GOLD AWARD
Newnham Lane, Badby,
Daventry NN11 3AA
T: (01327) 703302
F: (01327) 703085

BADSEY
Worcestershire

Orchard House ♦♦♦
99 Bretforton Road, Badsey,
Evesham WR11 5UQ
T: (01386) 831245

BAKEWELL
Derbyshire

Castle Cliffe ♦♦♦
Monsal Head, Bakewell,
DE45 1NL
T: (01629) 640258
F: (01629) 640258
E: relax@castle-cliffe.com
I: www.castle-cliffe.com

Castle Inn ♦♦♦
Castle Street, Bakewell,
DE45 1DU
T: (01629) 812103
F: (01629) 814726

Easthorpe ♦♦♦♦
Buxton Road, Bakewell,
DE45 1DA
T: (01629) 814929
E: easthorpe@supanet.com

Ferndale Mews ♦♦♦♦
Buxton Road, Bakewell,
DE45 1DA
T: (01629) 814339

The Garden Room
♦♦♦♦ SILVER AWARD
1 Park Road, Bakewell, DE45 1AX
T: (01629) 814299
E: the.garden.room@talk21.com
I: www.smoothhound.co.uk/hotels/thegarden.html

Haddon House Farm
♦♦♦♦♦ GOLD AWARD
Haddon Road, Bakewell,
DE45 1BN
T: (01629) 814024
F: (01629) 812759
E: m@great-place.co.uk
I: www.great-place.co.uk

The Haven ♦♦♦♦
Haddon Road, Bakewell,
DE45 1AW
T: (01629) 812113
E: RoseArmstg@aol.com
I: members.aol.com/RoseArmstg

Long Meadow House Bed and Breakfast
♦♦♦♦♦ SILVER AWARD
Coombs Road, Bakewell,
DE45 1AQ
T: (01629) 812500
E: amshowarth@cs.com
I: www.longmeadowhouse.co.uk

Loughrigg
♦♦♦♦ SILVER AWARD
Burton Close Drive, Bakewell,
DE45 1BG
T: (01629) 813173
E: john@bakewell55.freeserve.co.uk
I: www.bakewell55.freeserve.co.uk

2 Lumford Cottages ♦♦♦
Off Holme Lane, Bakewell,
DE45 1GG
T: (01629) 813273
F: (01629) 813273
I: www.cressbrook.co.uk/bakewell/lumford

Mandale House ♦♦♦♦
Haddon Grove, Bakewell,
DE45 1JF
T: (01629) 812416
F: (01629) 812416
E: julia.finney@virginnet.com

Melbourne House ♦♦♦♦
Buxton Road, Bakewell,
DE45 1DA
T: (01629) 815357
E: melbournehouse@supanet.com

River Walk Bed and Breakfast ♦♦♦
River Walk, 3 New Lumford,
Bakewell, DE45 1GH
T: (01629) 812459

Tannery House
♦♦♦♦♦ GOLD AWARD
Matlock Street, Bakewell,
DE45 1EE
T: (01629) 815011
F: (01629) 815327
I: www.tanneryhouse.co.uk

West Lawn Bed and Breakfast ♦♦♦♦
2 Aldern Way, Bakewell,
DE45 1AJ
T: (01629) 812243
I: www.westlawn.co.uk

Willow Croft ♦♦♦
Station Road, Great Longstone,
Bakewell DE45 1TS
E: willowcroftbandb@aol.com

BALSALL COMMON
West Midlands

Avonlea ♦♦
135 Kenilworth Road, Balsall
Common, Coventry CV7 7EU
T: (01676) 533003
F: (01676) 533003

Blythe Paddocks ♦♦♦
Barston Lane, Balsall Common,
Coventry CV7 7BT
T: (01676) 533050
F: (01676) 533050

Camp Farm ♦♦♦
Hob Lane, Balsall Common,
Coventry CV7 7GX
T: (01676) 533804
F: (01676) 533804

BALTERLEY
Staffordshire

Pear Tree Lake Farm ♦♦♦♦
Balterley, Crewe CW2 5QE
T: (01270) 820307
F: (01270) 820868

BAMFORD
Derbyshire

Pioneer House ♦♦♦♦
Station Road, Bamford, Hope
Valley S33 0BN
T: (01433) 650638
E: pioneerhouse@yahoo.co.uk
I: www.pioneerhouse.co.uk

The Snake Pass Inn ♦♦
Ashopton Woodlands, Bamford,
Hope Valley S33 0BJ
T: (01433) 651480
F: (01433) 651480

BARBER BOOTH
Derbyshire

Brookfield Guesthouse ♦♦♦
Brookfield, Barber Booth, Edale, Sheffield S33 7ZL
T: (01433) 670227

BARDNEY
Lincolnshire

The Black Horse ♦♦♦
16 Wragby Road, Bardney, Lincoln LN3 5XL
T: (01526) 398900
F: (01526) 399281
E: black-horse@lineone.net

BARLASTON
Staffordshire

Hurden Hall Farm ♦♦♦
Barlaston, Stoke-on-Trent ST12 9AZ
T: (01782) 372378
F: (01782) 372378

Wedgwood Memorial College ♦♦♦
Station Road, Barlaston, Stoke-on-Trent ST12 9DG
T: (01782) 372105
F: (01782) 372393
E: wedgwood.college@staffordshire.gov.uk.
I: www.aredu.demon.co.uk/wedgwoodcollege

BARLBOROUGH
Derbyshire

Stone Croft Bed and Breakfast ♦♦♦
15 Church Street, Barlborough, Chesterfield S43 4ER
T: (01246) 810974
F: (01246) 810974

BARLOW
Derbyshire

Millbrook
♦♦♦♦ SILVER AWARD
Furnace Lane, Monkwood, Barlow, Dronfield S18 7SY
T: (0114) 2890253
F: (0114) 2891365

Woodview Cottage ♦♦♦♦
Millcross Lane, Barlow, Dronfield S18 7TA
T: (0114) 289 0724
F: (0114) 289 0724

BARNBY MOOR
Nottinghamshire

White Horse Inn and Restaurant ♦♦♦
Great North Road, Barnby Moor, Retford DN22 8QS
T: (01777) 707721
F: (01777) 869445

BARROW-ON-TRENT
Derbyshire

5 Nook Cottages
♦♦♦♦ SILVER AWARD
The Nook, Barrow-on-Trent, Derby DE73 1NA
T: (01332) 702050
F: (01332) 705927
E: nookcottage@nookcottage.com
I: www.nookcottage.com

BARTON UNDER NEEDWOOD
Staffordshire

Fairfield Guest House
♦♦♦♦ SILVER AWARD
55 Main Street, Barton under Needwood, Burton upon Trent DE13 8AB
T: (01283) 716396
F: (01283) 716396
E: hotel@fairfield-uk.fsnet.co.uk
I: www.fairfield-hotel.com

Three Way Cottage ♦♦♦
2 Wales Lane, Barton under Needwood, Burton upon Trent DE13 8JF
T: (01283) 713572
E: marion@threewaycottage.fsnet.co.uk
I: communities.msn.co.uk/threewayscottagebedbreakfast

BASLOW
Derbyshire

Bubnell Cliff Farm ♦♦♦
Wheatlands Lane, Baslow, Bakewell DE45 1RF
T: (01246) 582454
E: c.k.mills@btinternet.com

Nether Croft ♦♦♦♦
Eaton Place, Baslow, Bakewell DE45 1RW
T: (01246) 583564
E: nethercroftB&B@aol.com

The Old School House
♦♦♦♦ SILVER AWARD
School Lane, Baslow, Bakewell DE45 1RZ
T: (01246) 582488
F: (01246) 583323
E: yvonnewright@talk21.com

BAUMBER
Lincolnshire

Baumber Park ♦♦♦♦
Baumber, Horncastle LN9 5NE
T: (01507) 578235
F: (01507) 578417

BAYSTON HILL
Shropshire

Lythwood Hall Bed and Breakfast ♦♦♦
2 Lythwood Hall, Lythwood, Bayston Hill, Shrewsbury SY3 0AD
T: 07074 874747
F: 07074 874747
E: lythwoodhall@amserve.net
I: www.smoothhound.co.uk

BEESTON
Nottinghamshire

The Grove Guesthouse ♦♦
8 Grove Street, Beeston, Nottingham NG9 1JL
T: (0115) 9259854

Hylands Hotel ♦♦♦
307 Queens Road, Beeston, Nottingham NG9 1JB
T: (0115) 925 5472
F: (0115) 922 5574
E: hylands.hotel@telinco.co.uk
I: www.s-h-systems.co.uk/hotels/hylands.html

BELPER
Derbyshire

Amber Hills ♦♦♦♦
Whitehouse Farm, Belper Lane, Belper, DE56 2UJ
T: (01773) 824080
F: (01773) 824080
E: stew@scooke54.fsnet.co.uk

Broadhurst Bed and Breakfast
♦♦♦♦ SILVER AWARD
West Lodge, Bridge Hill, Belper, DE56 2BY
T: (01773) 823596
F: (01773) 880810
E: stel.broadhurst@talk21.com

The Cedars ♦♦♦♦
Field Lane, Belper, DE56 1DD
T: (01773) 824157
F: (01773) 825573
E: enquiries@derbyshire-holidays.com
I: www.derbyshire-holidays.com

Hill Top Farm ♦♦♦♦
80 Ashbourne Road, Cowers Lane, Belper, DE56 2LF
T: (01773) 550338

The Old Shop ♦♦♦
10 Bakers Hill, Heage, Belper DE56 2BL
T: (01773) 856796

32 Spencer Road ♦♦♦♦
Belper, DE56 1JY
T: (01773) 823877

BELTON IN RUTLAND
Rutland

The Old Rectory ♦♦♦
4 New Road, Belton in Rutland, Oakham LE15 9LE
T: (01572) 717279
F: (01572) 717343
E: bb@iepuk.com
I: www.rutnet.co.uk/orb

BENNIWORTH
Lincolnshire

Glebe Farm
♦♦♦♦ SILVER AWARD
Benniworth, Market Rasen LN8 6JP
T: (01507) 313231
F: (01507) 313231
E: info@glebe-farm.com
I: www.glebe-farm.com

BENTHALL
Shropshire

Hilltop House ♦♦♦♦
Bridge Road, Benthall, Broseley TF12 5RB
T: (01952) 884821
E: hilltophouse@ukonline.co.uk
I: www.smoothhound.co.uk/hotels/hilltop.html

BEOLEY
Worcestershire

Windmill Hill ♦♦♦♦
Cherry Pit Lane, Beoley, Redditch B98 9DH
T: (01527) 62284
F: (01527) 64476
E: macotton@tinyworld.co.uk

BERKELEY
Gloucestershire

Pickwick Farm ♦♦♦
A38, Berkeley, GL13 9EU
T: (01453) 810241
E: piclwick@supanet.com

BESTHORPE
Nottinghamshire

Lord Nelson Inn ♦♦♦
Main Road, Besthorpe, Newark NG23 7HR
T: (01636) 892265

BETLEY
Staffordshire

Adderley Green Farm ♦♦♦♦
Heighley Lane, Betley, Crewe CW3 9BA
T: (01270) 820203
F: (01270) 820542
E: adderleygreenfarm@betley.fsbusiness.co.uk

BEWDLEY
Worcestershire

Lightmarsh Farm
♦♦♦♦ SILVER AWARD
Crundalls Lane, Bewdley, DY12 1NE
T: (01299) 404027
I: www.farmstayworcs.co.uk

The Old Farmhouse ♦♦♦♦
Button Bridge, Bewdley, DY12 3AW
T: (01299) 841277
F: (01299) 841277

Sydney Place ♦♦♦
7 Kidderminster Road, Bewdley, DY12 1AQ
T: (01299) 404832

Winbrook Cottage ♦♦♦
Cleobury Road, Bewdley, DY12 2BA
T: (01299) 405686

BIBURY
Gloucestershire

Coln Cottage ♦♦♦♦
Coln Court, Bibury, Cirencester GL7 5NL
T: (01285) 740314
F: (01285) 740314

Cotteswold House
♦♦♦♦ GOLD AWARD
Arlington, Bibury, Cirencester GL7 5ND
T: (01285) 740609
F: (01285) 740609
E: cotteswold.house@btclick.com
I: http://home.btclick.com/cotteswold.house

The William Morris Bed & Breakfast
♦♦♦♦ SILVER AWARD
11 The Street, Bibury, Cirencester GL7 5NP
T: (01285) 740555
F: (01285) 740049
E: info@thewilliammorris.com
I: www.thewilliammorris.com

BICKENHILL
West Midlands

Church Farm Accommodation ♦♦
Church Farm, Church Lane, Bickenhill, Solihull B92 0DN
T: (01675) 442641
F: (01675) 442905

BIDDULPH
Staffordshire

Chapel Croft Bed and Breakfast ♦♦♦
Newtown Road, Biddulph Park, Biddulph, Stoke-on-Trent ST8 7SW
T: (01782) 511013
E: chapelcroft@biddulphpark.freeserve.co.uk
I: www.chapelcroft.com

BIDFORD-ON-AVON
Warwickshire

Avonview House ♦♦♦♦
Stratford Road, Bidford-on-Avon, Alcester B50 4LU
T: (01789) 778667
F: (01789) 778667
E: avonview@talk21.com

Brook Leys Bed and Breakfast ♦♦♦♦
Honeybourne Road, Bidford-on-Avon, Alcester B50 4PD
T: (01789) 772785
E: brookleys@amserve.net
I: www.brookleys.co.uk

Broom Hall Inn ♦♦♦
Bidford Road, Broom, Alcester B50 4HE
T: (01789) 773757

Fosbroke House ♦♦♦♦
4 High Street, Bilford-on-Avon, Warwick, B50 6HU
T: (01789) 772327
F: (01789) 772327
I: ww.smoothhound

The Harbour ♦♦♦♦
Salford Road, Bidford-on-Avon, Alcester B50 4EN
T: (01789) 772975
E: pwarwick@theharbour-gh.co.uk
I: www.theharbour-gh.co.uk

BIGGIN-BY-HARTINGTON
Derbyshire

The Kings at Ivy House ♦♦♦♦ SILVER AWARD
Biggin-by-Hartington, Buxton SK17 0DT
T: (01298) 84709
F: (01298) 84710
E: kings.ivyhouse@lineone.net
I: www.SmoothHound.co.uk/hotels/kingsivy.html

BILLINGHAY
Lincolnshire

Old Mill Crafts ♦♦♦
8 Mill Lane, Billinghay, Lincoln LN4 4ES
T: (01526) 861996

BIRCH VALE
Derbyshire

Spinney Cottage ♦♦♦♦
Spinnerbottom, Birch Vale, High Peak SK22 1BL
T: (01663) 743230

BIRDLIP
Gloucestershire

Beechmount ♦♦♦
Birdlip, Gloucester GL4 8JH
T: (01452) 862262
F: (01452) 862262
E: thebeechmount@breathemail.net
I: www.thebeechmount.co.uk

BIRMINGHAM
West Midlands

Alden ♦♦♦
7 Elmdon Road, Marston Green, Birmingham, B37 7BS
T: (0121) 779 2063
F: (0121) 788 0898

Ashley House ♦♦♦
18 Alcott Lane, Marston Green, Birmingham, B37 7AT
T: (0121) 779 5368
F: (0121) 779 5368

Atholl Lodge ♦♦♦
16 Elmdon Road, Acocks Green, Birmingham, B27 6LH
T: (0121) 707 4417
F: (0121) 707 4417
E: davey@which.net

Central Guest House ♦♦♦
1637 Coventry Road, South Yardley, Birmingham, B26 1DD
T: (0121) 706 7757
F: (0121) 706 7757
E: mmou826384@aol.com
I: www.centralguesthouse.com

Clay Towers ♦♦♦♦
51 Frankley Beeches Road, Northfield, Birmingham, B31 5AB
T: (0121) 6280053
F: (0121) 6280053

Cook House Hotel ♦♦
425 Hagley Road, Edgbaston, Birmingham, B17 8BL
T: (0121) 429 1916

Elmdon Guest House ♦♦♦
2369 Coventry Road, Sheldon, Birmingham, B26 3PN
T: (0121) 742 1626
F: (0121) 7421626

The Glades Guest House ♦♦♦
2469 Coventry Road, Sheldon, Birmingham, B26 3PP
T: (0121) 742 1871
F: (0121) 742 1871

Grasmere Guesthouse ♦♦
37 Serpentine Road, Harborne, Birmingham, B17 9RD
T: (0121) 427 4546
F: (0121) 427 4546

Greenway House Hotel ♦♦
978 Warwick Road, Acocks Green, Birmingham B27 6QG
T: (0121) 706 1361
F: (0121) 706 1361

Homelea ♦♦♦
2399 Coventry Road, Sheldon, Birmingham B26 3PN
T: (0121) 742 0017
F: (0121) 688 1879

Kensington Guest House Hotel ♦♦♦
785 Pershore Road, Selly Park, Birmingham, B29 7LR
T: (0121) 472 7086
F: (0121) 472 5520

Knowle Lodge Hotel ♦♦
423 Hagley Road, Edgbaston, Birmingham B17 8BL
T: (0121) 429 8366

Rollason Wood Hotel ♦♦
130 Wood End Road, Erdington, Birmingham B24 8BJ
T: (0121) 373 1230
F: (0121) 382 2578
E: rollwood@globalnet.co.uk

Woodville House ♦
39 Portland Road, Edgbaston, Birmingham B16 9HN
T: (0121) 454 0274
F: (0121) 454 5965

BISHOP'S CASTLE
Shropshire

Broughton Farm ♦♦♦
Bishop's Castle, SY15 6SZ
T: (01588) 638393

The Castle Hotel ♦♦♦
The Square, Bishop's Castle, SY9 5BN
T: (01588) 638403
F: (01588) 638403
I: www.bishops-castle.co.uk/castlehotel

Old Time ♦♦
29 High Street, Bishop's Castle, SY9 5BE
T: (01588) 638467
F: (01588) 638467
E: jane@oldtime.co.uk
I: www.oldtime.co.uk

Shuttocks Wood ♦♦♦♦
Norbury, Bishop's Castle SY9 5EA
T: (01588) 650433
F: (01588) 650492
E: shuttockswood@btconnect.com
I: www.smoothhound.co.uk/hotels/shuttock.html

The Sun at Norbury ♦♦♦♦
Norbury, Bishop's Castle, SY9 5DX
T: (01588) 650680
E: suninn.norbury@virgin.net
I: freespace.virgin.net/suninn.norbury

BISHOP'S CLEEVE
Gloucestershire

Manor Cottage ♦♦
41 Station Road, Bishop's Cleeve, Cheltenham GL52 8HH
T: (01242) 673537

BLEDINGTON
Gloucestershire

Kings Head Inn and Restaurant ♦♦♦♦
The Green, Bledington, Oxford OX7 6XQ
T: (01608) 658365
F: (01608) 658902
E: kingshead@orr-ewing.com
I: www.kingsheadinn.net

BLOCKLEY
Gloucestershire

Arreton House ♦♦♦♦
Station Road, Blockley, Moreton-in-Marsh GL56 9DT
T: (01386) 701077
F: (01386) 701077
E: bandb@arreton.demon.uk
I: www.arreton.demon.co.uk

Claremont Bed & Breakfast ♦♦♦♦
The Greenway, Blockley, Moreton-in-Marsh GL56 9BQ
T: (01386) 700744
F: (01386) 700412
E: enquiries@claremontbandb.co.uk
I: www.claremontbandb.co.uk

Mill Dene ♦♦♦♦
Mill Dene, Blockley, Moreton-in-Marsh GL56 9HU
T: (01386) 700457
F: (01386) 700526
E: wendy@milldene.co.uk
I: www.milldene.co.uk

The Old Bakery ♦♦♦♦♦ GOLD AWARD
High Street, Blockley, Moreton-in-Marsh GL56 9EU
T: (01386) 700408
F: (01386) 700408

BOBBINGTON
Staffordshire

Blakelands Country Guest House and Restaurant ♦♦♦♦
Halfpenny Green, Bobbington, Stourbridge DY7 5DP
T: (01384) 221000
F: (01384) 221585
E: enquiries@blakelands.com
I: www.blakelands.com

BODENHAM
Herefordshire

The Forge ♦♦♦♦ SILVER AWARD
Bodenham, Hereford HR1 3JZ
T: (01568) 797144
E: stay@bodenhamforge.co.uk
I: www.bodenhamforge.co.uk

BONSALL
Derbyshire

The Old School House Rating Applied For
The Dale, Bonsall, Matlock DE4 2AY
T: (01629) 826017

Townhead Farmhouse ♦♦♦♦
70 High Street, Bonsall, Matlock DE4 2AR
T: (01629) 823762

BOSTON
Lincolnshire

Bramley House ♦♦♦
267 Sleaford Road, Boston, PE21 7PQ
T: (01205) 354538
F: (01205) 354538

The Chestnuts ♦♦♦♦
117 London Road, Boston, PE21 7EZ
T: (01205) 354435
F: (01205) 366662
E: 113015.2032@compuserve.com

Fairfield Guest House ♦♦♦
101 London Road, Boston, PE21 7EN
T: (01205) 362869

Park Lea Guest House ♦♦♦
85 Norfolk Street, Boston, PE21 6PE
T: (01205) 356309
E: park.lea@btinternet.com

BOTTESFORD
Leicestershire

The Thatch Hotel & Restaurant Rating Applied For
26 High Street, Bottesford, Nottingham NG13 0AA
T: (01949) 842330
F: (01949) 844470

BOURNE
Lincolnshire

Mill House ♦♦♦♦
64 North Road, Bourne, PE10 9BU
T: (01778) 422278
F: (01778) 422546
E: millhousebnb@fsbdial.co.uk

BOURTON-ON-THE-WATER
Gloucestershire

Alderley Guesthouse
♦♦♦♦ SILVER AWARD
Rissington Road, Bourton-on-the-Water, Cheltenham GL54 2DX
T: (01451) 822788
F: (01451) 822788
E: alderleyguesthouse@hotmail.com
I: www.AlderleyGuesthouse.com

Broadlands Guest House
♦♦♦♦
Clapton Row, Bourton-on-the-Water, Cheltenham GL54 2DN
T: (01451) 822002
F: (01451) 821776
E: marco@broadlands-guest-house.co.uk
I: www.broadlands-guest-house.co.uk

Chestnuts Bed & Breakfast
♦♦♦
The Chestnuts, High Street, Bourton-on-the-Water, Cheltenham GL54 2AN
T: (01451) 820244
F: (01451) 820558
E: chestnutsbb@aol.com

Coach and Horses ♦♦♦♦
Fosseway, A429, Bourton-on-the-Water, Cheltenham GL54 2HN
T: (01451) 821064
F: (01451) 810570
E: info@coach-horses.co.uk
I: www.coach-horses.co.uk

Coombe House
♦♦♦♦ SILVER AWARD
Rissington Road, Bourton-on-the-Water, Cheltenham GL54 2DT
T: (01451) 821966
F: (01451) 810477
E: coombe.house@virgin.net
I: www.coombehousecotswolds.co.uk

Cotswold Bed and Breakfast Rooftrees♦♦♦♦
Rissington Road, Bourton-on-the-Water, Cheltenham GL54 2DX
T: (01451) 821943
F: (01451) 810614

Cotswold Carp Farm ♦♦♦♦
Bury Barn Lane, Bourton-on-the-Water, Cheltenham GL54 2HB
T: (01451) 821795

The Cotswold House ♦♦♦
Lansdowne, Bourton-on-the-Water, Cheltenham GL54 2AR
T: (01451) 822373

Elvington Bed and Breakfast
♦♦♦♦
Elvington, Rissington Road, Bourton-on-the-Water, Cheltenham GL54 2DX
T: (01451) 822026
F: (01451) 822026
E: the@tuckwells.freeserve.co.uk
I: www.bandb.fsnet.co.uk

Fairlie ♦♦♦
Riverside, Bourton-on-the-Water, Cheltenham GL54 2DP
T: (01451) 821842
F: (01451) 821842

Farncombe ♦♦♦♦
Clapton, Bourton-on-the-Water, Cheltenham GL54 2LG
T: (01451) 820120
F: (01451) 820120
E: jwrightbb@aol.com
I: www.SmoothHound.co.uk/hotels/farncomb.htmlANDhttp://www.farncombecotswolds.com

Holly House
♦♦♦♦ SILVER AWARD
Station Road, Bourton-on-the-Water, Cheltenham GL54 2ER
T: (01451) 821302
E: jenanddave@talk21.com

The Kingsbridge Inn ♦♦♦
Riverside, Bourton-on-the-Water, Cheltenham GL54 2BS
T: (01451) 820371
F: (01451) 810179
E: book@lionheartinns.co.uk
I: www.lionheartinns.co.uk

Lamb Inn ♦♦♦
Great Rissington, Bourton-on-the-Water, Cheltenham GL54 2LP
T: (01451) 820388
F: (01451) 820724
I: www.thelamb-inn.com

Lansdowne House ♦♦♦♦
Lansdowne, Bourton-on-the-Water, Cheltenham GL54 2AT
T: (01451) 820812
F: (01451) 822484
E: heart@lansdownehouse.co.uk
I: www.lansdownehouse.co.uk

Lansdowne Villa Guest House
♦♦♦♦
Lansdowne, Bourton-on-the-Water, Cheltenham GL54 2AR
T: (01451) 820673
F: (01451) 822099
E: lansdownevilla@aol.com
I: www.lansdownevilla.co.uk

Larch House
♦♦♦♦♦ GOLD AWARD
Station Road, Bourton-on-the-Water, Cheltenham GL54 2AA
T: (01451) 821172
F: (01451) 821172
I: www.s-n-systems.co.uk/hotels/larchhse

The Lawns ♦♦♦♦
Station Road, Bourton-on-the-Water, Cheltenham GL54 2ER
T: (01451) 821195
F: (01451) 821195

Manor Close
♦♦♦♦ SILVER AWARD
High Street, Bourton-on-the-Water, Cheltenham GL54 2AP
T: (01451) 820339

Mousetrap Inn ♦♦♦
Lansdowne, Bourton-on-the-Water, Cheltenham GL54 2AR
T: (01451) 820579
F: (01451) 822393
E: mtinn@waverider.co.uk
I: www.mousetrap-inn.co.uk

The Red House Bed and Breakfast ♦♦♦
Station Road, Bourton-on-the-Water, Cheltenham GL54 2EN
T: (01451) 810201
F: (01451) 810201
E: charlie@theredhouse@bourton.co.uk

The Ridge Guesthouse ♦♦♦♦
Whiteshoots Hill, Bourton-on-the-Water, Cheltenham GL54 2LE
T: (01451) 820660
F: (01451) 822448
E: info@theridge-guesthouse.co.uk
I: www.theridge-guesthouse.co.uk

Station Villa ♦♦♦
2 Station Villa, Station Road, Bourton-on-the-Water, Cheltenham GL54 2ER
T: (01451) 810406
F: (01451) 821359
E: rooms@stationvilla.com
I: www.stationvilla.com

Strathspey
♦♦♦♦ SILVER AWARD
Lansdowne, Bourton-on-the-Water, Cheltenham GL54 2AR
T: (01451) 820694
F: (01451) 821466
E: mel@strathspey-bedfsnet.co.uk

Sycamore House ♦♦♦
Lansdowne, Bourton-on-the-Water, Cheltenham GL54 2AR
T: (01451) 821647

Touchstone
♦♦♦♦ SILVER AWARD
Little Rissington, Bourton-on-the-Water, Cheltenham GL54 2ND
T: (01451) 822481
F: (01451) 822481
E: touchstone.bb@lineone.net
I: website.lineone.net/~touchstone.bb

Trevone Bed & Breakfast ♦♦♦
Moore Road, Bourton-on-the-Water, Cheltenham GL54 2AZ
T: (01451) 822852

Upper Farm ♦♦♦♦♦
Clapton on the Hill, Bourton-on-the-Water, Cheltenham GL54 2LG
T: (01451) 820453
F: (01451) 810185
I: www.tuckedup.com/upperfarm.html

Whiteshoots Cottage Bed and Breakfast♦♦♦♦
Whiteshoots Hill, Fosseway, Bourton-on-the-Water, Cheltenham GL54 2LE
T: (01451) 822698
E: whiteshootscottage@talk21.com

Willow Crest ♦♦♦♦
Rissington Road, Bourton-on-the-Water, Cheltenham GL54 2DZ
T: (01451) 822073

BOYLESTONE
Derbyshire

Lees Hall Farm ♦♦♦
Boylestone, Ashbourne DE6 5AA
T: (01335) 330259
F: (01335) 330259

BRACKLEY
Northamptonshire

Astwell Mill ♦♦♦♦
Helmdon, Brackley NN13 5QU
T: (01295) 760507
F: (01295) 768602
E: astwell01@aol.com

Brackley House Private Hotel
♦♦♦♦ SILVER AWARD
Brackley House, 4 High Street, Brackley, NN13 7DT
T: (01280) 701550
F: (01280) 704965
E: sales@brackleyhouse.com
I: www.brackleyhouse.com

Floral Hall Guest House ♦♦
50 Valley Road, Brackley, NN13 7DA
T: (01280) 702950
E: floralhallquesthouse@talk21.com

The Thatches ♦♦♦
Whitfield, Brackley NN13 5TQ
T: (01280) 850358

Walltree House Farm ♦♦♦♦
Steane, Brackley NN13 5NS
T: (01295) 811235
F: (01295) 811147

BRADLEY
Derbyshire

Holly Meadow Farm ♦♦♦♦
Bradley, Ashbourne DE6 1PN
T: (01335) 370261
F: (01335) 370261
I: www.hollymeadowbandb.freeserve.co.uk

Yeldersley Old Hall Farm
♦♦♦♦
Yeldersley Lane, Bradley, Ashbourne DE6 1PH
T: (01335) 344504
F: (01335) 344504
E: janethindsfarm@yahoo.co.uk

BRADNOP
Staffordshire

Middle Farm Guest House
Rating Applied For
Apesford, Bradnop, Leek ST13 7EX
T: (01538) 382839
F: (01538) 382839

BRADWELL
Derbyshire

Stoney Ridge
♦♦♦♦ SILVER AWARD
Granby Road, Bradwell, Hope Valley S33 9HU
T: (01433) 620538
F: (01433) 623154
E: toneyridge@aol.com
I: www.cressbrook.co.uk/hopev/stoneyridge

BRAILES
Warwickshire

Agdon Farm ♦♦♦
Brailes, Banbury OX15 5JJ
T: (01608) 685226
F: (01608) 685226
E: maggie_cripps@hotmail.com

BRAMPTON
Derbyshire

Brampton Guesthouse ♦♦
75 Old Road, Off Chatsworth Road, Brampton, Chesterfield S40 2QU
T: (01246) 276533
F: (01246) 211636
E: guesthouse@bramptonoldroad.freeserve.co.uk

BRAMSHALL
Staffordshire

Bowmore House ◆◆◆
Stone Road, Bramshall,
Uttoxeter ST14 8SH
T: (01889) 564452
F: (01889) 564452
E: glovatt@furoris.com

BRASSINGTON
Derbyshire

Ivy Bank House
◆◆◆◆ SILVER AWARD
Church Street, Brassington,
Matlock DE4 4HJ
T: (01629) 540818
E: june@ivybankhouse.co.uk
I: www.ivybankhouse.co.uk

The Old Barn ◆◆◆◆
Middle Lane, Brassington,
Matlock DE4 4HL
T: (01629) 540317
E: tyler.family@lineone.net

BREAM
Gloucestershire

The Hedgehog Freehouse
◆◆◆
High Street, Bream, Lydney
GL15 6JS
T: (01594) 562358
F: (01594) 564273
E: thehedgehogfreehouse@
btinternet.com

Lindum House Bed and Breakfast ◆◆◆
Oakwood Road, Bream, Lydney
GL15 6HS
T: (01594) 562051
E: lynne@lindumhouse.fsworld.
co.uk
I: www.smoothhound.
co.uk/hotels/lindumhs.html

BREDON
Worcestershire

Royal Oak Inn ◆◆◆◆
Main Road, Bredon, Tewkesbury
GL20 7LW
T: (01684) 772393

BREDON'S NORTON
Worcestershire

Round Bank House ◆◆◆◆
Lampitt Lane, Bredon's Norton,
Tewkesbury GL20 7HB
T: (01684) 772983
F: (01684) 773035

BREDWARDINE
Herefordshire

Old Court Farm ◆◆◆
Bredwardine, Hereford HR3 6BT
T: (01981) 500375
E: whittall@oldcourt74.co.uk

BRETFORTON
Worcestershire

Bretforton House Farm Bed and Breakfast◆◆◆◆
Bretforton House Farm,
Bretforton, Evesham WR11 5JH
T: (01386) 830831
F: (01386) 830831
E: japplebya@aol.com

BREWOOD
Staffordshire

The Blackladies
◆◆◆◆◆ GOLD AWARD
Kiddemore Green Road,
Brewood, Stafford ST19 9BH
T: (01902) 850210
F: (01902) 851782

BRIDGNORTH
Shropshire

The Albynes
◆◆◆◆ SILVER AWARD
Nordley, Bridgnorth WV16 4SX
T: (01746) 762261

Bassa Villa Bar and Grill ◆◆◆
48 Cartway, Bridgnorth,
WV16 4BG
T: (01746) 763977
F: (01952) 691604
E: sugarloaf@globalnet.co.uk
I: www.smoothhound.
co.uk/hotels/bassavilla.html

Bearwood Lodge Hotel ◆◆◆
10 Kidderminster Road,
Bridgnorth, WV15 6BW
T: (01746) 762159
F: (01746) 762159
E: bearlodge@lineone.net

Bulls Head Inn ◆◆◆◆
Chelmarsh, Bridgnorth
WV16 6BA
T: (01746) 861469
F: (01746) 862646
E: dave@bullshead.fsnet.co.uk
I: www.virtual-shropshire.
co.uk/bulls-head-inn

The Croft Hotel ◆◆◆
St. Mary's Street, Bridgnorth,
WV16 4DW
T: (01746) 762416
F: (01746) 767431
E: crofthotel@aol.com

Dinney Farm ◆◆
Chelmarsh, Bridgnorth
WV16 6AU
T: (01746) 861070
F: (01746) 861002
E: hedley.southport@virgin.net
I: www.smoothhound.
co.uk/hotels/dinney.html

The Golden Lion Inn ◆◆◆
83 High Street, Bridgnorth,
WV16 4DS
T: (01746) 762016
F: (01746) 762016

Haven Pasture ◆◆◆◆
Underton, Bridgnorth, WV16 6TY
T: (01746) 789632
F: (01746) 789333
E: havenpasture@underton.
co.uk
I: www.underton.co.uk

Highfields ◆◆◆◆
44 Ludlow Road, Bridgnorth,
WV16 5AF
T: (01746) 763110
F: (01746) 763110
I: www.virtual-shropshire.
co.uk/highfields

Linley Crest
◆◆◆◆ SILVER AWARD
Linley Brook, Bridgnorth,
WV16 4SZ
T: (01746) 765527
F: (01746) 765527
E: linleycrest@easicom.com

Pen-y-Ghent ◆◆◆
7 Sabrina Road, Bridgnorth,
WV15 6DQ
T: (01746) 762880
E: firman.margret@freeuk.com
I: pen-y-ghent.8m.com

Saint Leonards Gate ◆◆◆
6 Church Street, Bridgnorth,
WV16 4EQ
T: (01746) 766647

Sandward Guesthouse ◆◆◆
47 Cartway, Bridgnorth,
WV16 4BG
T: (01746) 765913
E: sandward@amserve.net
I: www.virtual-shropshire.
co.uk/sandward

BRIMPSFIELD
Gloucestershire

Highcroft
◆◆◆◆◆ GOLD AWARD
Brimpsfield, Gloucester GL4 8LF
T: (01452) 862405

BRINGHURST
Leicestershire

Castle View Farm ◆◆◆◆
Bringhurst, Market Harborough
LE16 8RJ
T: (01536) 770408
F: (01536) 771626
E: tommyandsal@hotmail.com

BRINKLOW
Warwickshire

White Lion ◆◆◆
32 Broad Street, Brinklow,
Rugby CV23 0LN
T: (01788) 832579
F: (01788) 833844
E: brinklowlion@aol.com
I: www.thewhitelion-inn.co.uk

BROAD CAMPDEN
Gloucestershire

Marnic House
◆◆◆◆ GOLD AWARD
Broad Campden, Chipping
Campden GL55 6UR
T: (01386) 840014
F: (01386) 840441
E: marnic@zoom.co.uk

BROADWAY
Worcestershire

Barn House
◆◆◆◆ SILVER AWARD
152 High Street, Broadway,
WR12 7AJ
T: (01386) 858633
F: (01386) 858633
E: barnhouse@btinternet.com
I: www.btinternet.
com/~barnhouse/

The Bell at Willersey ◆◆◆◆
The Bell Inn, Willersey, Broadway
WR12 7PJ
T: (01386) 858405
F: (01386) 853563
E: reservations@bellatwillersey.
fsnet.co.uk
I: www.the-bell-willersey.com

Bourne House ◆◆◆
Leamington Road, Broadway,
WR12 7DZ
T: (01386) 853486
E: kate.zuill@virgin.net
I: www.broadwayguesthouse.
co.uk

Burhill Farm
◆◆◆◆◆ GOLD AWARD
Buckland, Broadway WR12 7LY
T: (01386) 858171
F: (01386) 858171
E: burhillfarm@yahoo.co.uk
I: www.burhillfarm.co.uk

Crown and Trumpet Inn ◆◆◆
Church Street, Broadway,
WR12 7AE
T: (01386) 853202
F: (01386) 834650
E: ascott@cotswoldholidays.
co.uk
I: www.cotswoldholidays.co.uk

Dove Cottage ◆◆◆◆
Colletts Fields, Broadway,
WR12 7AT
T: (01386) 859085
I: www.broadway-cotswolds.
co.uk

Highlands Country House Bed and Breakfast◆◆◆◆
Highlands, Fish Hill, Broadway,
WR12 7LD
T: (01386) 858015
F: (01386) 852584
E: sue@adames.demon.co.uk

Knoll Bed and Breakfast
◆◆◆◆
The Knoll, Springfield Lane,
Broadway, WR12 7BT
T: (01386) 858702

Leasow House
◆◆◆◆ SILVER AWARD
Laverton Meadow, Broadway,
WR12 7NA
T: (01386) 584526
F: (01386) 584596
E: leasow@clara.net
I: www.leasow.co.uk

Lowerfield Farm ◆◆◆◆
Willersey, Broadway WR11 5HF
T: (01386) 858273
F: (01386) 854608
E: info@lowerfield-farm.co.uk
I: www.lowerfield-farm.co.uk

Milestone House ◆◆◆◆
Upper High Street, Broadway,
WR12 7AJ
T: (01386) 853432
E: milestone.house@talk21.com
I: www.milestone-broadway.
co.uk

Mount Pleasant Farm ◆◆◆◆
Childswickham, Broadway
WR12 7HZ
T: (01386) 853424
F: (01386) 853424
I: www.broadway-cotswolds.
co.uk/perryhtml

Old Stationhouse Eastbank
◆◆◆◆
Station Drive, Broadway,
WR12 7DF
T: (01386) 852659
F: (01386) 852891
E: trueman@
eastbank-broadway.fsnet.co.uk
I: www.broadway-cotswolds.
co.uk/ebank.html

Olive Branch Guest House
◆◆◆◆
78 High Street, Broadway,
WR12 7AJ
T: (01386) 853440
F: (01386) 859070
E: broadway@theolive-branch.
co.uk
I: www.
theolivebranch-broadway.com

Pathlow House ♦♦♦
82 High Street, Broadway, WR12 7AJ
T: (01386) 853444
F: (01386) 853444
E: pathlow@aol.com
I: www.pathlowguesthouse.co.uk

Sheepscombe House
♦♦♦♦ SILVER AWARD
Snowshill, Broadway, WR12 7JU
T: (01386) 853769
F: (01386) 853769
E: reservations@snowshill-broadway.co.uk
I: www.broadway-cotswolds.co.uk

Shenberrow Hill ♦♦♦♦
Stanton, Broadway, WR12 7NE
T: (01386) 584468
F: (01386) 584468
E: michael.neilan@talk21.com
I: www.cotswold-way.co.uk

Small Talk Lodge ♦♦♦
2 Keil Close, 32 High Street, Broadway, WR12 7DP
T: (01386) 858953
E: kathybarnes@totalise.com
I: www.broadway-cotswolds.co.uk

Southwold Guest House
♦♦♦♦
Station Road, Broadway, WR12 7DE
T: (01386) 853681
F: (01386) 854610
E: sueandnick.southwold@talk21.com

Whiteacres
♦♦♦♦ SILVER AWARD
Station Road, Broadway, WR12 7DE
T: (01386) 852320
F: (01386) 852674
E: whiteacres@btinternet.com

Windrush House
♦♦♦♦ SILVER AWARD
Station Road, Broadway, WR12 7DE
T: (01386) 853577
F: (01386) 853790
E: richard@broadway-windrush.co.uk
I: www.broadway-windrush.co.uk

BROADWELL
Gloucestershire

The White House ♦♦♦
2 South Road, Broadwell, Coleford GL16 7BH
T: (01594) 837069
F: (01594) 833130
I: www.ukworld-int.co.uk

BROMSGROVE
Worcestershire

Bea's Lodge ♦♦
245 Pennine Road, Bromsgrove, B61 0TN
T: (01527) 877613

Bromsgrove Country Hotel
♦♦♦♦
249 Worcester Road, Stoke Heath, Bromsgrove B61 7JA
T: (01527) 835522
F: (01527) 871257
I: www.smoothhound.co.uk

The Durrance ♦♦♦♦
Berry Lane, Upton Warren, Bromsgrove, B61 9EL
T: (01562) 777533
F: (01562) 777533
E: helenhirons@thedurrance.co.uk
I: www.thedurrance.co.uk

Fox Hollies ♦♦♦
78 New Road, Bromsgrove, B60 2LA
T: (01527) 574870

Honeypot ♦♦♦♦
305 Old Birmingham Road, Lickey, Bromsgrove, B60 1HQ
T: (0121) 445 2580
E: ena.stanworth@btopenworld.com

Merrivale ♦♦♦♦
309 Old Birmingham Road, Lickey, Bromsgrove, B60 1HQ
T: (0121) 445 1694
F: (0121) 445 1694
E: smithmerrivale@amserve.net

Overwood Bed and Breakfast
♦♦♦♦
Woodcote Lane, Woodcote, Bromsgrove, B61 9EE
T: (01562) 777193
F: (01562) 777689
E: info@overwood.net
I: www.overwood.net

Sprite House ♦♦♦
58 Stratford Road, Bromsgrove, B60 1AU
T: (01527) 874565
F: (01527) 870935

BROMYARD
Herefordshire

Linton Brook Farm ♦♦♦
Malvern Road, Bringsty, Worcester WR6 5TR
T: (01885) 488875
F: (01885) 488875

Littlebridge House ♦♦♦♦
Tedstone Wafre, Bromyard HR7 4PN
T: (01885) 482471
F: (01885) 482471

The Old Cowshed
♦♦♦♦ SILVER AWARD
Avenbury Court Farm, Bromyard, HR7 4LA
T: (01885) 482384
F: (01885) 482367
E: combes@cowshed.uk.com
I: www.cowshed.uk.com

Park House Hotel ♦♦♦
28 Sherford Street, Bromyard, HR7 4DL
T: (01885) 482294
F: (01885) 482294
E: parkhouse@callnet.uk.com
I: www.bromyard.co.uk/parkhouse

BROOM
Warwickshire

The Arrows
♦♦♦♦ SILVER AWARD
Broom, Alcester B50 4HR
T: (01789) 772260
F: (01789) 772260
E: softly@compuserve.com
I: www.smoothhound.co.uk/hotels/arrows.html

BROSELEY
Shropshire

The Cumberland Hotel ♦♦♦
Jackson Avenue, Broseley, TF12 5NB
T: (01952) 882301
F: (01952) 884438

The Pheasant Inn ♦♦♦
56 Church Street, Broseley, TF12 5BX
T: (01952) 884499
F: (01952) 884499

Rock Dell
♦♦♦♦ SILVER AWARD
30 Ironbridge Road, Broseley, TF12 5AJ
T: (01952) 883054
F: (01952) 883054
E: rockdell@ukgateway.net

BROXWOOD
Herefordshire

Broxwood Court
♦♦♦♦♦ GOLD AWARD
Broxwood, Leominster HR6 9JJ
T: (01544) 340245
F: (01544) 340573
E: mikeanne@broxwood.kc3.co.uk

BUCKMINSTER
Leicestershire

The Tollemache Arms ♦♦♦♦
Main Street, Buckminster, Grantham NG33 55A
T: (01476) 860252
F: (01476) 860731
E: info@tollemachearms.co.uk
I: www.tollemachearms.co.uk

BUCKNELL
Shropshire

The Hall ♦♦♦
Bucknell, SY7 0AA
T: (01547) 530249
F: (01547) 530249
E: thehallbucknell@hotmail.com
I: www.smoothhound.co.uk/hotels/thehall.html

The Willows ♦♦♦♦
Bucknell, Ludlow, SY7 0AA
T: (01547) 530201
E: the_willows@btopenworld.com
I: www.willows-bucknell.co.uk

BUGBROOKE
Northamptonshire

The Byre ♦♦♦♦
2 Church Lane, Bugbrooke, Northampton NN7 3PB
T: (01604) 830319

BULLO PILL
Gloucestershire

Grove Farm ♦♦♦♦
Bullo Pill, Newnham-on-Severn GL14 1DZ
T: (01594) 516304
F: (01594) 516304
E: davidandpennyhill@btopenworld.com

BURLTON
Shropshire

Petton Hall Farm
♦♦♦♦ SILVER AWARD
Petton, Burlton, Shrewsbury SY4 5TH
T: (01939) 270601
F: (01939) 270601
I: www.virtual-shropshire.co.uk/petton-hall-farm

BURTON DASSETT
Warwickshire

The White House Bed and Breakfast
♦♦♦♦ SILVER AWARD
Burton Dassett, Southam CV47 2AB
T: (01295) 770143
E: lisa@whitehouse10.freeserve.co.uk
I: www.thewhitehousebandb.info

BURTON UPON TRENT
Staffordshire

Meadowview ♦♦♦
203 Newton Road, Winshill, Burton upon Trent, DE15 0TU
T: (01283) 564046

New Inn Farm ♦♦♦
Burton Road, Needwood, Burton upon Trent DE13 9PB
T: (01283) 575435

Primrose Bank House ♦♦
194A Newton Road, Burton upon Trent, DE15 0TU
T: (01283) 532569

BUSHLEY
Worcestershire

Shiloh House ♦♦♦
Church End, Bushley, Tewkesbury GL20 6HT
T: (01684) 293435

BUTTERTON
Staffordshire

Black Lion Inn ♦♦♦
Butterton, Leek ST13 7ST
T: (01538) 304232
E: theblacklion@clara.net
I: www.blacklioninn.co.uk

Butterton House ♦♦♦
Park Road, Butterton, Newcastle-under-Lyme ST5 4DZ
T: (01782) 619085
E: buttertonhouse@lineone.net
I: www.touristnetuk.com/wm/butterton

Butterton Moor House
♦♦♦♦ SILVER AWARD
Parsons Lane, Butterton, Leek ST13 7PD
T: (01538) 304506
F: (01538) 304506

Coxon Green Farm ♦♦♦♦
Butterton, Leek, ST13 7TA
T: (01538) 304221

Greenhead Cottage ♦♦♦♦
Pot Hooks Lane, Butterton, Leek ST13 7SY
T: (01538) 304541

Heathy Roods Farm ♦♦♦♦
Butterton, Leek ST13 7SR
T: (01538) 304397

New Hayes Farm ♦♦♦♦
Trentham Road, Butterton, Newcastle-under-Lyme ST5 4DX
T: (01782) 680889
I: www.SmoothHound.co.uk/Hotels/newhayes.html

BUXTON
Derbyshire

Abbey Guesthouse ♦♦♦
43 South Avenue, Buxton, SK17 6NQ
T: (01298) 26419
E: aghbuxton@aol.com

All Seasons Guest House
♦♦♦♦
4 Wye Grove, Buxton, SK17 9AJ
T: (01298) 74628
E: chrisandruss@allseasonsguesthouse.fsnet.co.uk
I: www.allseasonsguesthouse.fsnet.co.uk

Alpine Guesthouse ♦♦♦♦
Thornsett, Hardwick Mount, Buxton, SK17 6PS
T: (01298) 26155
E: exclusively.psandqs@talk21.com

Avalon ♦♦
31 South Avenue, Buxton, SK17 6NQ
T: (01298) 72667
E: AvalonBandB@aol.com

Barn House ♦♦♦♦
itton Mill, Buxton, SK17 8SW
T: (01298) 872751

Braemar ♦♦♦♦
10 Compton Road, Buxton, SK17 9DN
T: (01298) 78050
E: buxtonbraemar@supanet.com
I: www.cressbrook.co.uk/buxton/braemar

Buxton Hilbre Bed & Breakfast
♦♦♦
White Knowle Road, Buxton, SK17 9NH
T: (01298) 22358
E: min@8whiteknowle.fsnet.co.uk

Buxton Lodge Guest House
♦♦♦
8 London Road, Buxton, SK17 9NX
T: (01298) 23522

Buxton Wheelhouse Hotel
♦♦♦♦ SILVER AWARD
9 College Road, Buxton, SK17 9DZ
T: (01298) 24869
F: (01298) 24869
E: lyndsie@buxton-wheelhouse.com
I: www.buxton-wheelhouse.com

Buxton's Victorian Guesthouse
♦♦♦♦ SILVER AWARD
3A Broad Walk, Buxton, SK17 6JE
T: (01298) 78759
F: (01298) 74732
E: buxvic@tiscali.co.uk
I: www.smoothhound.co.uk/hotels/buxtons/html

Compton House Guesthouse
♦♦♦
Compton Road, Buxton, SK17 9DN
T: (01298) 26926
F: (01298) 26926
E: comptonbuxton@aol.com
I: www.cressbrook.co.uk/buxton/compton

Cotesfield Farm ♦♦
rsley Hay, Buxton, SK17 0BD
T: (01298) 83256
F: (01298) 83256

Devonshire Arms ♦♦♦
ak Forest, Buxton SK17 8EJ
T: (01298) 23875
I: www.devarms.com

Devonshire Lodge Guesthouse
♦♦♦♦ SILVER AWARD
2 Manchester Road, Buxton, SK17 6SB
T: (01298) 71487

Fairhaven ♦♦
1 Dale Terrace, Buxton, SK17 6LU
T: (01298) 24481
F: (01298) 24481
E: paulandcatherine@fairhavenguesthouse.freeserve.co.uk

Grendon Guesthouse
♦♦♦♦♦ SILVER AWARD
Bishops Lane, Buxton, SK17 6UN
T: (01298) 78831
F: (01298) 79257
E: parkerh1@talk21.com
I: www.grendonguesthouse.co.uk

Grosvenor House ♦♦♦♦
1 Broad Walk, Buxton, SK17 6JE
T: (01298) 72439
F: (01298) 72439
E: grosvenor.buxton@btinternet.com
I: www.smoothhound.co.uk/hotels/grosvenr.html

Harefield
♦♦♦♦ SILVER AWARD
15 Marlborough Road, Buxton, SK17 6RD
T: (01298) 24029
F: (01298) 24029
E: hardie@harefield1.freeserve.co.uk
I: www.harefield1.freeserve.co.uk

Hawthorn Farm Guesthouse
♦♦♦
Fairfield Road, Buxton, SK17 7ED
T: (01298) 23230
F: (01298) 71322

Kingscroft
♦♦♦♦ SILVER AWARD
10 Green Lane, Buxton, SK17 9DP
T: (01298) 22757
F: (01298) 27858

Lakenham Guesthouse ♦♦♦♦
11 Burlington Road, Buxton, SK17 9AL
T: (01298) 79209

Linden Lodge ♦♦♦♦
31 Temple Road, Buxton, SK17 9BA
T: (01298) 27591
E: info@lindentreelodge.co.uk
I: www.lindentreelodge.co.uk

Lowther Guesthouse ♦♦♦♦
7 Hardwick Square West, Buxton, SK17 6PX
T: (01298) 71479
E: enquires@lowtherguesthouse.co.uk
I: www.lowtherguesthouse.co.uk

Netherdale Guesthouse
♦♦♦♦
16 Green Lane, Buxton, SK17 9DP
T: (01298) 23896
F: (01298) 73771

Nithen Cottage
♦♦♦♦ SILVER AWARD
123 Park Road, Buxton, SK17 6SP
T: (01298) 24679
E: nithencott@netscape.co.uk

The Old Manse Private Hotel
♦♦♦
6 Clifton Road, Silverlands, Buxton, SK17 6QL
T: (01298) 25638
F: (01298) 25638
E: old_manse@yahoo.co.uk
I: www.oldmanse.co.uk

The Queens Head Hotel ♦♦♦
High Street, Buxton, SK17 6EU
T: (01298) 23841
F: (01298) 71238

Roseleigh Hotel ♦♦♦♦
19 Broad Walk, Buxton, SK17 6JR
T: (01298) 24904
F: (01298) 24904
E: enquiries@roseleighhotel.co.uk
I: www.roseleighhotel.co.uk

Staden Grange Country House
♦♦♦
Staden Lane, Staden, Buxton, SK17 9RZ
T: (01298) 24965
F: (01298) 72067
E: enquires@stadengrange.co.uk
I: StadenGrange.co.uk

Stoneridge
♦♦♦♦ SILVER AWARD
9 Park Road, Buxton, SK17 6SG
T: (01298) 26120
E: hoskin@stoneridge.co.uk
I: www.stoneridge.co.uk

Templeton Guesthouse ♦♦
Compton Road, Buxton, SK17 9DN
T: (01298) 25275
F: (01298) 25275
E: tembux@lineone.net

Twelve Trees Guest House
Rating Applied For
Twelve Trees, Burlington Road, Buxton, SK17 9AL
T: (01298) 24371
E: info@buxtonlet.com
I: www.buxtonlet.com

BYFIELD
Northamptonshire

Glebe Farm Bed and Breakfast
♦♦♦
Glebe Farm, 61 Church Street, Byfield, Daventry NN11 6XN
T: (01327) 260512
F: (01327) 260512

CALDECOTE
Warwickshire

Hill House Country Guest House ♦♦♦♦
Off Mancetter Road, Caldecote, Nuneaton CV10 0RS
T: (024) 7639 6685
F: (024) 7639 6685

CALLOW
Herefordshire

Knockerhill Farm ♦♦♦♦
Callow, Hereford HR2 8BP
T: (01432) 268460
F: (01432) 268460

CALLOW END
Worcestershire

Henwick House ♦♦♦♦
Jennett Tree Lane, Callow End, Worcester WR2 4UB
T: (01905) 831736
F: (01905) 831886
E: henwick@lineone.net
I: www.henwickhouse.net

CALMSDEN
Gloucestershire

The Old House
♦♦♦♦ SILVER AWARD
Calmsden, Cirencester GL7 5ET
T: (01285) 831240
F: (01285) 831240
E: baxter@calmsden.freeserve.co.uk

CALVER
Derbyshire

Valley View ♦♦♦♦
Smithy Knoll Road, Calver, Hope Valley S32 3XW
T: (01433) 631407
F: (01433) 631407
E: sue@a-place-2-stay.co.uk
I: www.a-place-2-stay.co.uk

CANON PYON
Herefordshire

Nags Head ♦♦♦
Canon Pyon, Hereford HR4 8NY
T: (01432) 830252

CARDINGTON
Shropshire

Woodside Farm ♦♦♦♦
Cardington, Church Stretton SY6 7LB
T: (01694) 771314

CARSINGTON
Derbyshire

Breach Farm ♦♦♦♦
Carsington, Matlock DE4 4DD
T: (01629) 540265

CASTLE DONINGTON
Leicestershire

Castletown House
♦♦♦♦ SILVER AWARD
4 High Street, Castle Donington, Derby DE74 2PP
T: (01332) 812018
F: (01332) 814550
E: enquiry@castletownhouse.fsnet.co.uk
I: www.castletownhouse.com

Little Chimneys Guesthouse
♦♦♦
19 The Green, Diseworth, Castle Donington, Derby DE74 2QN
T: (01332) 812458
F: (01332) 853336
E: kay@little-chimneys.demon.co.uk
I: www.little-chimneys.demon.co.uk

Scot's Corner Guesthouse Bed and Breakfast ♦♦♦
82 Park Lane, Castle Donington, Derby DE74 2JG
T: (01332) 811226
E: linda.deary@ntlworld.com
I: www.scots-corner.com

CASTLEMORTON
Worcestershire

Hawthorne Cottage ♦♦♦
New Road, Castlemorton, Malvern WR13 6BT
T: (01684) 833266
F: (01684) 833857

CASTLETON
Derbyshire

Bargate Cottage ♦♦♦♦
Bargate, Market Place, Castleton, Hope Valley S33 8WG
T: (01433) 620201
F: (01433) 621739
E: fionasaxon@bargatecottage78.freeserve.co.uk
I: www.peakland.com/bargate

Cryer House ♦♦♦
Castle Street, Castleton, Hope Valley S33 8WG
T: (01433) 620244
E: FleeSkel@aol.com

Dunscar Farm Bed & Breakfast ♦♦♦♦
Dunscar Farm, Castleton, Hope Valley S33 8WA
T: (01433) 620483
I: www.hopenet.co.uk/dunscarfarm

Hillside House ♦♦♦♦
Pindale Road, Castleton, Hope Valley S33 8WU
T: (01433) 620312
F: (01433) 620312

Ramblers Rest ♦♦♦
Mill Bridge, Castleton, Hope Valley S33 8WR
T: (01433) 620125
F: (01433) 621677
E: peter.d.m.gillott@btinternet.com
I: www.peakland.com/ramblersrest

Swiss House Hotel and Nero's Italian Restaurant ♦♦♦
How Lane, Castleton, Hope Valley S33 8WJ
T: (01433) 621098
F: (01433) 623781
E: swisshousehotel@castleton8WJ.fsnet.co.uk

Ye Olde Cheshire Cheese Inn ♦♦♦♦
How Lane, Castleton, Hope Valley S33 8WJ
T: (01433) 620330
F: (01433) 621847
I: www.peakland.com.cheshirecheese

Ye Olde Nags Head Hotel ♦♦♦
Cross Street, Castleton, Hope Valley S33 8WH
T: (01433) 620248

CAUNTON
Nottinghamshire

Knapthorpe Lodge ♦♦♦
Hockerton Road, Caunton, Newark NG23 6AZ
T: (01636) 636262
F: (01636) 636415

CHADDESDEN
Derbyshire

Green Gables ♦♦♦
19 Highfield Lane, Chaddesden, Derby DE21 6PG
T: (01332) 672298
E: us@sallyandtony.fsnet.co.uk
I: www.greengablesuk.com

CHAPEL-EN-LE-FRITH
Derbyshire

The Potting Shed ♦♦♦♦
Bank Hall, Chapel-en-le-Frith, High Peak SK23 9UB
T: (01298) 812656
I: www.thepottingshedhighpeak.com

Slack Hall Farm ♦♦♦
Castleton Road, Chapel-en-le-Frith, High Peak SK23 0QS
T: (01298) 812845

CHARLTON KINGS
Gloucestershire

Glenfall House ♦♦♦
Mill Lane, Charlton Kings, Cheltenham GL54 4EP
T: (01242) 583654
F: (01242) 251314
E: glenfall@surfaid.org
I: www.users.surfaid.org/~glenfall

Orion House ♦♦♦
220 London Road, Charlton Kings, Cheltenham GL52 6HW
T: (01242) 233309
F: (01242) 233309
E: ena@orionhouse.fs.net.co.uk

CHEADLE
Staffordshire

Caverswall Castle ♦♦♦♦♦ GOLD AWARD
Caverswall, Stoke-on-Trent ST11 9EA
T: (01782) 393239
F: (01782) 394590
E: yarsargent@hotmail.com
I: www.caverswallcastle.co.uk

The Church Farm ♦♦♦♦
Holt Lane, Kingsley, Stoke-on-Trent ST10 2BA
T: (01538) 754759
F: (01538) 754759

Ley Fields Farm ♦♦♦♦ SILVER AWARD
Leek Road, Cheadle, ST10 2EF
T: (01538) 752875
F: (01583) 752875
E: kathryn@leyfieldsfarm.freeserve.co.uk

Park Lodge Guest House ♦♦♦
1 Tean Road, Cheadle, ST10 1LG
T: (01538) 753562
E: margaret.mower@amserver.net

Park View Guest House ♦♦♦
15 Mill Road, Cheadle, ST10 1NG
T: (01538) 755412
E: janet@parkviewguesthouse.freeserve.co.uk
I: www.theparkviewguesthouse.com

Woodhouse Farm Country Guesthouse ♦♦♦
Lockwood Road, Near Kingsley Holt, Cheadle, ST10 4QU
T: (01538) 754250
F: (01538) 754470
E: ask@woodhousefarm.net
I: www.woodhousefarm.net

CHEDDLETON
Staffordshire

Brook House Farm ♦♦♦
Brook House Lane, Cheddleton, Leek ST13 7DF
T: (01538) 360296

Choir Cottage and Choir House ♦♦♦♦♦ GOLD AWARD
Ostlers Lane, Cheddleton, Leek ST13 7HS
T: (01538) 360561
E: enquiries@choircottage.co.uk
I: www.choircottage.co.uk

CHEDWORTH
Gloucestershire

The Vicarage ♦♦♦
Chedworth, Cheltenham GL54 4AA
T: (01285) 720392

CHELLASTON
Derbyshire

The Lawns Hotel ♦♦♦
High Street, Chellaston, Derby DE73 1TB
T: (01332) 701553
F: (01332) 690198

CHELMARSH
Shropshire

Hampton House ♦♦♦♦
Hampton Loade, Chelmarsh, Bridgnorth WV16 6BN
T: (01746) 861436

Unicorn Inn ♦♦
Hampton Loade, Chelmarsh, Bridgnorth WV16 6BN
T: (01746) 861515
F: (01746) 861515
E: unicorninn.bridgnorth@virginnet.co.uk
I: freespace.virginnet.co.uk/unicorninn.bridgnorth

CHELMORTON
Derbyshire

Ditch House ♦♦♦♦
Chelmorton, Buxton SK17 9SG
T: (01298) 85719
F: (01298) 85719

Shallow Grange ♦♦♦♦♦ GOLD AWARD
Chelmorton, Buxton SK17 9SG
T: (01298) 23578
F: (01298) 78242
E: holland@shallowgrangefarm.freeserve.co.uk

CHELTENHAM
Gloucestershire

The Abbey Hotel ♦♦♦♦
14-16 Bath Parade, Cheltenham, GL53 7HN
T: (01242) 516053
F: (01242) 513034
E: office@abbeyhotel-cheltenham.com
I: www.abbeyhotel-cheltenham.com

Barn End ♦♦♦♦
23 Cheltenham Road, Bishop's Cleeve, Cheltenham GL52 8LU
T: (01242) 672404
F: (01242) 678320
E: joymerrell@aol.com

The Battledown ♦♦♦
125 Hales Road, Cheltenham, GL52 6ST
T: (01242) 233881
F: (01242) 524198
E: smurth@fsbdial.co.uk

Beaumont House Hotel ♦♦♦♦ SILVER AWARD
Shurdington Road, Cheltenham, GL53 0JE
T: (01242) 245986
F: (01242) 520044
E: rocking.horse@virgin.net
I: www.smoothhound.co.uk/hotels/beauchel.html

Beechcroft B&B and Apartments ♦♦♦
295 Gloucester Road, Cheltenham, GL51 7AD
T: (01242) 519564
F: (01242) 519564
E: beechcroft.cheltenham@dialpipex.com
I: www.geocities.com/beechcroftuk

Beechworth Lawn Hotel ♦♦♦♦
133 Hales Road, Cheltenham, GL52 6ST
T: (01242) 522583
F: (01242) 574800
E: beechworth.lawn@dial.pipex.com
I: www.beechworthlawnhotel.co.uk

Bentleyville ♦♦♦
179 Gloucester Road, Cheltenham, GL51 8NQ
T: (01242) 581476
F: (01242) 700595
E: bentleyville_179@hotmail.com
I: www.bentleyville.co.uk

Bentons ♦♦♦
71 Bath Road, Cheltenham, GL53 7LH
T: (01242) 517417
F: (01242) 527772

Bibury House ♦♦♦
Priory Place, Cheltenham, GL52 6HG
T: (01242) 525014

Brennan Guest House ♦♦♦
21 St Lukes Road, Cheltenham, GL53 7JF
T: (01242) 525904
F: (01242) 525904

Briarfields Motel Rating Applied For
Gloucester Road, Cheltenham, GL51 0SX
T: (01242) 235324
F: (01242) 262216

Bridge House ♦♦♦♦
88 Lansdown Road, Cheltenha GL51 6QR
T: (01242) 583559
F: (01242) 255920
E: bridgehouse@freeuk.com

Central Hotel ♦♦
7-9 Portland Street, Cheltenham, GL52 2NZ
T: (01242) 582172

Crossways Guest House ♦♦♦
Oriel Place, 57 Bath Road, Cheltenham, GL53 7LH
T: (01242) 527683
F: (01242) 577226
E: cross.ways@btinternet.com
I: www.crossways.btinternet.co.uk

Detmore House ♦♦♦
London Road, Charlton Kings,
Cheltenham, GL52 6UT
T: (01242) 582868
F: (01242) 582868

Elm Villa ♦♦
49 London Road, Cheltenham,
GL52 6HE
T: (01242) 231909

Evington Hill Farm
♦♦♦♦ GOLD AWARD
Tewkesbury Road, The Leigh,
Gloucester, GL19 4AQ
T: (01242) 680255

Glencree ♦♦♦♦
80 Lansdown Road, Cheltenham,
GL51 6QW
T: (01242) 260242
F: (01242) 260242
E: jdn.hopkins@virgin.net

Ham Hill Farm
♦♦♦♦ SILVER AWARD
Whittington, Cheltenham
GL54 4EZ
T: (01242) 584415
F: (01242) 222535
E: hamhillfarm@msn.com

Hannaford's ♦♦♦♦
20 Evesham Road, Cheltenham,
GL52 2AB
T: (01242) 524190
F: (01242) 580102
E: sue@hannafords.icom43.net
I: www.hannafords.icom43.net

Home Cottage ♦♦♦
1 Priors Road, Cheltenham,
GL52 5AB
T: (01242) 518144
F: (01242) 518144
E: barrycott@msn.com
: www.homecottage.co.uk

Home Farm
Rating Applied For
Stockwell Lane, Woodmancote,
Cheltenham, GL52 9QE
: (01242) 675816
: (01242) 701319
: info@homefarmbb.co.uk
: www.homefarmbb.co.uk

lope Orchard ♦♦♦
loucester Road, Staverton,
heltenham GL51 0TF
: (01452) 855556
: (01452) 530037
: info@hopeorchard.com
: www.hopeorchard.com

vydene Guest House ♦♦♦
45 Hewlett Road, Cheltenham,
L52 6TS
: (01242) 521726
: (01242) 525694
: jvhopwood@ivydenehouse.
eeserve.co.uk
www.ivydenehouse.freeserve.
o.uk

awn Hotel ♦♦♦
Pittville Lawn, Cheltenham,
L52 2BE
(01242) 526638
(01242) 526638

eeswood ♦♦
4 Montpellier Drive,
heltenham, GL50 1TX
(01242) 524813
(01242) 524813
leeswood@hotmail.com
www.leeswood.org.uk

Lonsdale House ♦♦♦
Montpellier Drive, Cheltenham,
GL50 1TX
T: (01242) 232379
F: (01242) 232379
E: lonsdalehouse@hotmail.com

Milton House
♦♦♦♦♦ GOLD AWARD
12 Bayshill Road, Royal Parade,
Cheltenham, GL50 3AY
T: (01242) 582601
F: (01242) 222326
E: info@miltonhousehotel.co.uk
I: www.miltonhousehotel.co.uk

Montpellier Hotel ♦♦♦
33 Montpellier Terrace,
Cheltenham, GL50 1UX
T: (01242) 526009

The Old Station
Rating Applied For
Westfield, Notgrove,
Cheltenham, GL5 4BU
T: (01451) 850305
E: trolter98@hotmail.com

Parkview ♦♦♦
4 Pittville Crescent, Cheltenham,
GL52 2QZ
T: (01242) 575567
E: jospa@tr250.freeserve.co.uk

Penhill Farm ♦♦♦
Colesbourne, Cheltenham,
GL53 9NS
T: (01242) 870300
F: (01242) 870300
E: pwgilder@farmersweekly.net

Pike House ♦♦♦♦
Fossebridge, Cheltenham,
GL54 3JR
T: (01285) 720223
F: (01285) 720223

Pittville Gate Hotel ♦♦♦
12/14 Pittville Lawn,
Cheltenham, GL52 2BD
T: (01242) 221922
F: (01242) 244687

Saint Cloud ♦♦♦
97 Leckhampton Road,
Cheltenham, GL53 0BZ
T: (01242) 575245

St Michaels
♦♦♦♦ SILVER AWARD
4 Montpellier Drive,
Cheltenham, GL50 1TX
T: (01242) 513587
F: (01242) 513587
E: st_michaels_guesthouse@
yahoo.com
I: st_michaels.future.easyspace.
com

Segrave ♦♦♦
7 Park Place, Cheltenham,
GL50 2QS
T: (01242) 523606

Steyne Cross Bed and Breakfast ♦♦♦
Steyne Cross, Malvern Road,
Cheltenham, GL50 2NU
T: (01242) 255289
F: (01242) 255289
E: sumiko@susumago.f9.co.uk

Stray Leaves ♦♦♦
282 Gloucester Road,
Cheltenham, GL51 7AG
T: (01242) 572303
F: (01242) 572303

Stretton Lodge Hotel
♦♦♦♦ SILVER AWARD
Western Road, Cheltenham,
GL50 3RN
T: (01242) 570771
F: (01242) 528724
E: info@strettonlodge.co.uk
I: www.strettonlodge.co.uk

Westal Court
♦♦♦♦ SILVER AWARD
2 Westal Court, 27 Hatherley
Road, Cheltenham, GL51 6EB
T: (01242) 696679
F: (01242) 696679
E: martinkw@onetel.net.uk
I: web.onetel.net.uk/~martinkw

Westcourt ♦♦♦♦
14 Old Bath Road, Cheltenham,
GL53 7QD
T: (01242) 241777
F: (01242) 228666
E: michael.seston@which.net

Whittington Lodge Farm
♦♦♦♦ SILVER AWARD
Whittington, Cheltenham,
GL54 4HB
T: (01242) 820603
F: (01242) 820603
E: cathy@whittlodgefarm.fslife.
co.uk
I: www.whittlodgefarm.fslife.
co.uk

Wishmoor Guest House
♦♦♦♦ SILVER AWARD
147 Hales Road, Cheltenham,
GL52 6TD
T: (01242) 238504
F: (01242) 226090
E: wishmoor@aol.com

The Wynyards ♦♦♦♦
Butts Lane, Woodmancote,
Cheltenham GL52 9QH
T: (01242) 673876
E: graham@wynyards1.
freeserve.co.uk
I: www.SmoothHound.
co.uk/hotels/wynyards.html

CHESTERFIELD
Derbyshire

Abigails ♦♦♦
62 Brockwell Lane, Chesterfield,
S40 4EE
T: (01246) 279391
F: (01246) 854468
E: gail@abigails.fsnet.co.uk
I: www.abigailsguesthouse.co.uk

Anis Louise Guesthouse ♦♦♦
34 Clarence Road, Chesterfield,
S40 1LN
T: (01246) 235412
E: neil@anislouise.co.uk
I: www.anislouise.co.uk

Batemans Mill
♦♦♦♦ SILVER AWARD
Mill Lane, Old Tupton,
Chesterfield S42 6AE
T: (01246) 862296
F: (01246) 865672
E: info@batemansmill.co.uk
I: www.ukhotel.
com/heart-of-england/
batemans-mill-hotel.htm

Brook House
♦♦♦♦ SILVER AWARD
45 Westbrook Drive, Brookside,
Chesterfield, S40 3PQ
T: (01246) 568535

Clarendon Guesthouse ♦♦♦
32 Clarence Road, West Bars,
Chesterfield, S40 1LN
T: (01246) 235004

Fairfield House ♦♦♦
3 Fairfield Road, Chesterfield,
S40 4TR
T: (01246) 204905
F: (01246) 230155
E: sp8@talk21.com

Locksley ♦♦♦
21 Tennyson Avenue,
Chesterfield, S40 4SN
T: (01246) 273332

The Maylands ♦♦♦
56 Sheffield Road, Chesterfield,
S41 7LS
T: (01246) 233602

Rose Cottage Guest House ♦♦♦
Derby Road, Old Tupton,
Chesterfield S42 6LA
T: (01246) 864949
F: (01246) 864949
E: bookings@
rosecottagetupton.freeserve.
co.uk
I: www.rose-cottage-tupton.
co.uk

The Shoulder at Hardstoft ♦♦♦
Hardstoft, Chesterfield, S45 8AF
T: (01246) 850276
F: (01246) 854760

CHETWYND ASTON
Shropshire

Woodcroft Bed and Breakfast ♦♦♦
Woodcroft, Pitchcroft Lane,
Chetwynd Aston, Newport
TF10 9AU
T: (01952) 812406
E: judith_woodcroft@hotmail.
com
I: www.virtual-shropshire.
co.uk/woodcroft

CHINLEY
Derbyshire

Mossley House Farm ♦♦♦
Maynestone Road, Chinley, High
Peak SK23 6AH
T: (01663) 750240

CHIPPING CAMPDEN
Gloucestershire

Badgers Hall Tearooms
♦♦♦♦ SILVER AWARD
High Street, Chipping Campden,
GL55 6HB
T: (01386) 840839
E: badgershall@talk21.com
I: http://www.chippingcampden.
co.uk/badgershall.htm

The Bantam Tearooms
Rating Applied For
High Street, Chipping Campden,
GL55 6HB
T: (01386) 840386
E: thebantam@hotmail.com

Brymbo ♦♦♦♦
Honeybourne Lane, Mickleton,
Chipping Campden GL55 6PU
T: (01386) 438890
F: (01386) 438113
E: enquiries@brymbo.com
I: www.brymbo.com

Dragon House ♦♦♦♦
High Street, Chipping Campden, GL55 6AG
T: (01386) 840734
F: (01386) 840734
E: valatdragonhouse@btinternet.com
I: www.dragonhouse-chipping-campden.com

The Eight Bells ♦♦♦
Church Street, Chipping Campden, GL55 6JG
T: (01386) 840371
F: (01386) 841669
I: www.eightbellsinn.co.uk

Home Farm House ♦♦♦♦
Ebrington, Chipping Campden, GL55 6NL
T: (01386) 593309
F: (01386) 593309
E: willstanley@farmersweekly.net
I: www.homefarminthecotswolds.co.uk

The Malins ♦♦♦
21 Station Road, Blockley, Moreton-in-Marsh GL56 9ED
T: (01386) 700402
F: (01386) 700402
E: johnmalin@talk21.com
I: http://www.chippingcampden.co.uk/themalins.htm

Manor Farm ♦♦♦♦
Weston Subedge, Chipping Campden GL55 6QH
T: (01386) 840390
F: 08701 640 638
E: lucy@manorfarmbnb.demon.co.uk
I: www.manorfarmbnb.demon.co.uk

M'Dina Courtyard
♦♦♦♦ GOLD AWARD
Park Road, Chipping Campden, GL55 6EA
T: (01386) 841752
F: (01386) 840942
E: barbara@mdina-bandb.co.uk
I: www.mdina-bandb.co.uk

Nineveh Farm
♦♦♦♦ GOLD AWARD
Campden Road, Mickleton, Chipping Campden, GL55 6PS
T: (01386) 438923
E: stay@ninevehfarm.co.uk
I: www.ninevehfarm.co.uk

Sandalwood House ♦♦♦♦
Back-Ends, Chipping Campden, GL55 6AU
T: (01386) 840091
F: (01386) 840091

Weston Park Farm ♦♦♦
Dovers Hill, Chipping Campden, GL55 6UW
T: (01386) 840835
E: jane_whitehouse@hotmail.com

CHURCH EATON
Staffordshire

Slab Bridge Cottage ♦♦♦♦
Little Onn, Church Eaton, Stafford ST20 0AY
T: (01785) 840220
F: (01785) 840220

CHURCH STRETTON
Shropshire

Acton Scott Farm ♦♦♦
Acton Scott, Church Stretton SY6 6QN
T: (01694) 781260
E: edandm@clara.co.uk
I: www.golfgreenfees.com/ActonScottFarm

Belvedere Guest House ♦♦♦♦
Burway Road, Church Stretton, SY6 6DP
T: (01694) 722232
F: (01694) 722232
E: belv@bigfoot.com
I: www.smoothhound.co.uk/hotels/belvedere.html

Brereton's Farm ♦♦♦♦
Church Stretton, SY6 6QD
T: (01694) 781201
F: (01694) 781201

Brook House Farm ♦♦♦
Wall-under-Heywood, Church Stretton, SY6 7DS
T: (01694) 771308

Brookfields Guesthouse ♦♦♦♦
Watling St. North, Church Stretton, SY6 7AR
T: (01694) 722314
F: (01694) 722314
E: paulangie@brookfields51.fsnet.co.uk
I: www.smoothhound.co.uk/hotels/brookfieldsgh.html

The Coates Farm ♦♦♦
Rushbury, Church Stretton SY6 7DZ
T: (01694) 771330
F: (01694) 771330
E: sarah-madeley@excite.co.uk

Cwm Dale Farm Bed and Breakfast ♦♦♦
Cwm Dale Farm, Cwm Dale Valley, Church Stretton, SY6 6JL
T: (01694) 722362
F: (01694) 724656
E: cwmdale@hotmail.com
I: www.churchstretton.co.uk

Gilberries Cottage ♦♦♦♦
Wall-under-Heywood, Church Stretton SY6 7HZ
T: (01694) 771400
F: (01694) 771400
E: griffiths@gilberries.freeserve.co.uk

Highcliffe ♦♦♦
Madeira Walk, Church Stretton, SY6 6JQ
T: (01694) 722908

Jinlye ♦♦♦♦♦ GOLD AWARD
Castle Hill, All Stretton, Church Stretton SY6 6JP
T: (01694) 723243
F: (01694) 723243
E: info@jinlye.co.uk
I: www.jinlye.co.uk

Juniper Cottage ♦♦♦♦
All Stretton, Church Stretton, SY6 6HG
T: (01694) 723427
F: (01694) 722061

Old Rectory House ♦♦♦
Burway Road, Church Stretton, SY6 6DW
T: (01694) 724462
F: (01694) 724799
E: smamos@btinternet.com
I: www.oldrectoryhouse.co.uk

Ragdon Manor ♦♦♦
Ragdon, Church Stretton, SY6 7EZ
T: (01694) 781389

Rheingold ♦♦♦♦
9 The Bridleways, Church Stretton, SY6 7AN
T: (01694) 723969

Sayang House ♦♦♦♦
Hope Bowdler, Church Stretton, SY6 7DD
T: (01694) 723981
E: madegan@aol.com
I: www.sayanghouse.com

Travellers Rest Inn ♦♦♦
Upper Affcot, Church Stretton, SY6 6RL
T: (01694) 781275
F: (01694) 781555
E: reception@travellersrestinn.co.uk
I: www.travellersrestinn.co.uk

Willowfield Country Guesthouse
♦♦♦♦♦ GOLD AWARD
Lower Wood, All Stretton, Church Stretton SY6 6LF
T: (01694) 751471
F: (01694) 751471
I: www.willowfieldguesthouse.co.uk

CHURCHAM
Gloucestershire

The Pinetum Lodge ♦♦♦
Pinetum, Churcham, Gloucester GL2 8AD
T: (01452) 750554
F: (01452) 750402
E: pinetum1@aol.com
I: www.pinetumlodge.ik.com

CIRENCESTER
Gloucestershire

Abbeymead ♦♦♦♦
39a Victoria Road, Cirencester, GL7 1ES
T: (01285) 653740
F: (01285) 652721
E: abbeymead@amserve.net
I: www.smoothhound.co.uk/shs.html

Apsley Villa ♦♦♦
16 Victoria Road, Cirencester, GL7 1ES
T: (01285) 653489

The Black Horse ♦♦♦
17 Castle Street, Cirencester, GL7 1QD
T: (01285) 653187
F: (01285) 659772

Brooklands Farm ♦♦♦
Ewen, Cirencester GL7 6BU
T: (01285) 770487
F: (01285) 770487
I: www.glosfarmhols.co.uk

The Bungalow ♦♦♦
93 Victoria Road, Cirencester, GL7 1ES
T: (01285) 654179
F: (01285) 656159
E: CBEARD7@compuserve.com

Catherine Wheel ♦♦♦
Arlington Bibury, Cirencester, GL7 5ND
T: (01285) 740250
F: (01285) 740779

Chesil Rocks ♦♦♦
Baunton Lane, Stratton, Cirencester, GL7 2LL
T: (01285) 655031

Claremont Villa Bed and Breakfast ♦♦♦
131 Cheltenham Road, Stratton, Cirencester, GL7 2JF
T: (01285) 654759

Coleen Bed and Breakfast ♦♦♦♦
Ashton Road, Siddington, Cirencester, GL7 6HR
T: (01285) 642203
E: bookings@coleen.co.uk
I: www.coleen.co.uk

The Corner House ♦♦♦♦
101A Victoria Road, Cirencester, GL7 1EU
T: (01285) 641958
F: (01285) 640805
E: info@thecornerhouse.info
I: www.thecornerhouse.info

Eliot Arms Hotel Free House ♦♦♦♦
Clarks Hay, South Cerney, Cirencester GL7 5UA
T: (01285) 860215
F: (01285) 861121
E: eliotarms.cirencester@eldridge.pope.co.uk

Greensleeves
♦♦♦♦ SILVER AWARD
Baunton Lane, Cirencester, GL7 2LN
T: (01285) 642516
F: (01285) 642761
E: johnps@tesco.net
I: www.greensleeves4u.co.uk

The Ivy House ♦♦♦
2 Victoria Road, Cirencester, GL7 1EN
T: (01285) 656626
E: info@ivyhousecotswolds.com
I: www.ivyhousecotswolds.com

King's Head Hotel ♦♦♦♦
Market Place, Cirencester, GL7 2NR
T: (01285) 653322
F: (01285) 655103
E: gm.kin@barbox.net

Landage House ♦♦♦♦
Rendcomb, Cirencester, GL7 7H
T: (01285) 831250

The Leauses ♦♦♦♦
101 Victoria Road, Cirencester, GL7 1EU
T: (01285) 653643
F: (01285) 640805
E: the.leauses@virgin.net

Manby's Farm ♦♦♦♦
Oaksey, Malmesbury SN16 9SA
T: (01666) 577399
F: (01666) 577241
E: manbys@oaksey.junglelink.co.uk
I: www.cotswoldbandb.com

The Masons Arms ♦♦♦
High Street, Meysey Hampton, Cirencester, GL7 5JT
T: (01285) 850164
F: (01285) 850164
E: jane@themasonsarms.freeserve.co.uk
I: www.SmoothHound.co.uk/hotels/mason

Millstone
♦♦♦♦ SILVER AWARD
Down Ampney, Cirencester, GL7 5QR
T: (01793) 750475

No 12 ♦♦♦♦
12 Park Street, Cirencester, GL7 2BW
T: (01285) 640232
F: (01285) 640233
E: no12cirencester@ukgateway.net
I: www.no12cirencester.co.uk

Oddfellows Arms ♦♦♦
12-14 Chester Street, Cirencester, GL7 1HF
T: (01285) 641540
F: (01285) 640771
E: mike@oddfellowsfsnet.co.uk
I: www.oddfellowsarms.com

The Old Rectory ♦♦♦♦
Rodmarton, Cirencester, GL7 6PE
T: (01285) 841246
F: (01285) 841246
E: jfitz@globalnet.co.uk
I: www.rodmarton.com

Raydon House Hotel ♦♦♦
3 The Avenue, Cirencester, GL7 1EH
T: (01285) 653485
F: (01285) 653485

Riverside House ♦♦♦
Watermoor, Cirencester, GL7 1LF
T: (01285) 647642
F: (01285) 647615
E: riversidehouse@mitsubishi-cars.co.uk

Smerrill Barns
♦♦♦♦ SILVER AWARD
Kemble, Cirencester, GL7 6BW
T: (01285) 770907
F: (01285) 770706
E: gsopher@smerrillbarns.com
I: www.smerrillbarns.com

Sunset ♦♦♦
Baunton Lane, Cirencester, GL7 2NQ
T: (01285) 654822

The Talbot Inn ♦♦♦♦
14 Victoria Road, Cirencester, GL7 1EN
T: (01285) 653760
F: (01285) 658014
E: info@talbotinncotswolds.co.uk
I: www.talbotinncotswolds.co.uk

The White Lion Inn ♦♦
8 Gloucester Street, Cirencester, GL7 2DG
T: (01285) 654053
F: (01285) 641316
E: roylion@aol.com.
I: www.white-lion-cirencester.co.uk

Willow Pool
♦♦♦♦ SILVER AWARD
Oaksey Road, Poole Keyes, Cirencester, GL7 6DZ
T: (01285) 861485
E: jones.willow@btopenworld.com

Willows ♦♦♦
2 Glebe Lane, Kemble, Cirencester, GL7 6BD
T: (01285) 770667
E: Kamma@Tesco.net

CLAVERDON
Warwickshire

Hither Barn ♦♦♦
Star Lane, Claverdon, Warwick CV35 8LW
T: (01926) 842839
E: bestbandb@btclick.com

CLAVERLEY
Shropshire

Woodman Inn ♦♦♦
Danford, Claverley, Wolverhampton WV5 7DG
T: (01746) 710553
F: (01746) 710566

CLEEVE HILL
Gloucestershire

Malvern View ♦♦♦
Cleeve Hill, Cheltenham GL52 3PR
T: (01242) 672017
F: (01242) 676207
E: vchoak@hotmail.com

CLENT
Worcestershire

The French Hen ♦♦♦
Bromsgrove Road, Clent, Stourbridge DY9 9PY
T: (01562) 883040
F: (01562) 888000
I: www.frenchhen.co.uk

CLEOBURY MORTIMER
Shropshire

Clod Hall ♦♦♦
Milson, Kidderminster, DY14 0BJ
T: (01584) 781421
F: (01584) 781421
I: www.farmstayworcs.co.uk

Cox's Barn ♦♦♦♦
Bagginswood, Cleobury Mortimer, Kidderminster DY14 8LS
T: (01746) 718415
I: www.southshropshire.org.uk

The Old Bake House ♦♦♦♦
46/47 High Street, Cleobury Mortimer, Kidderminster DY14 8DQ
T: (01299) 270193
E: oldbakehouse@amserve.net
I: www.cleobury-mortimer.co.uk

The Old Cider House ♦♦♦♦
1 Lion Lane, Cleobury Mortimer, Kidderminster DY14 8BT
T: (01299) 270304
F: (01299) 270304
E: lennox@old-cider-house.fsnet.co.uk

Woodview
♦♦♦♦ GOLD AWARD
Mawley Oak, Cleobury Mortimer, Kidderminster DY14 9BA
T: (01299) 271422

CLEOBURY NORTH
Shropshire

Cleobury Court
♦♦♦♦♦ SILVER AWARD
Cleobury North, Bridgnorth WV16 6RW
T: (01746) 787005
F: (01746) 787005
E: info@cleoburycourt.co.uk

CLIFFORD
Herefordshire

Cottage Farm ♦♦♦
Middlewood, Clifford, Hereford HR3 5SX
T: (01497) 831496
F: (01497) 831496
E: julie@hgjmjones.freeserve.co.uk
I: www.smoothhound.co.uk/hotels/cottagef.html

CLIFTON
Derbyshire

Stone Cottage ♦♦♦
Green Lane, Clifton, Ashbourne DE6 2BL
T: (01335) 343377
F: (01335) 34117
E: info@stone-cottage.fsnet.co.uk
I: www.stone-cottage.fsnet.co.uk

CLUN
Shropshire

Llanhedric Farm ♦♦♦♦
Clun, Craven Arms SY7 8NG
T: (01588) 640203
F: (01588) 640203
E: llanhedric@21.com

New House Farm
♦♦♦♦♦ GOLD AWARD
Clun, Craven Arms SY7 8NJ
T: (01588) 638314
E: sarah@bishopscastle.co.uk
I: www.new-house-clun.co.uk

The Old Farmhouse ♦♦♦
Woodside, Clun, Craven Arms SY7 0JB
T: (01588) 640695
F: (01588) 640501
E: helen@vuan1.freeserve.co.uk
I: www.tuckedup.com/theoldfarmhouse.html

The Old Stables and Saddlery, Crown House ♦♦♦♦
Church Street, Clun, Craven Arms SY7 8JW
T: (01588) 640780
E: crownhouseclun@talk21.com

Springhill Farm ♦♦♦
Clun, Craven Arms SY7 8PE
T: (01588) 640337
F: (01588) 640337

CLUNGUNFORD
Shropshire

Knock Hundred Cottage
♦♦♦♦ GOLD AWARD
Abcott, Clungunford, Craven Arms SY7 0PX
T: (01588) 660594
F: (01588) 660594

COALBROOKDALE
Shropshire

Fat Frog Restaurant ♦♦♦
10 Wellington Road, Coalbrookdale, Telford TF8 7DX
T: (01952) 433269
F: (01952) 433269
E: frog@fat-frog.co.uk
I: www.fat-frog.co.uk

The Old Vicarage
♦♦♦♦ SILVER AWARD
Church Road, Coalbrookdale, Telford TF8 7NT
T: (01952) 432525
F: (01952) 432544
E: theoldvicarage@tf87nt.freeserve.co.uk

COALEY
Gloucestershire

Silver Street Farmhouse
♦♦♦♦
Silver Street, Coaley, Dursley GL11 5AX
T: (01453) 860514

COALPORT
Shropshire

Thorpe House ♦♦♦
High Street, Coalport, Telford TF8 7HP
T: (01952) 586789
F: (01952) 586789

COALVILLE
Leicestershire

Broadlawns ♦♦♦
98 London Road, Coalville, Leicester LE67 3JD
T: (01530) 836724

St Joseph's
Rating Applied For
Abbey Road, Oaks in Charnwood, Coalville, Leicester LE67 4UA
T: (01509) 503943
E: m.havers@virgin.net

COATES
Gloucestershire

Southfield House ♦♦♦♦
Coates, Cirencester GL7 6NH
T: (01285) 770220
F: (01285) 770177
E: awberry@aol.com

COCKSHUTT
Shropshire

Highfields ♦♦♦♦
Stanwardine, Cockshutt, Ellesmere SY12 0JL
T: (01939) 270659

COLD ASTON
Gloucestershire

Bangup Cottage ♦♦♦♦
Bangup Lane, Cold Aston, Cheltenham GL54 3BQ
T: (01451) 810127
E: chrisarmer@yahoo.com

Grove Farm House ♦♦♦♦♦
Cold Aston, Cheltenham GL54 3BJ
T: (01451) 821801
F: (01451) 821108
E: mstorey@btinternet.com
I: cotswoldbedandbreakfast.com

COLEFORD
Gloucestershire

Forest House Hotel ♦♦♦♦
Cinder Hill, Coleford, GL16 8HQ
T: (01594) 832424
F: (01594) 838030
E: suesparkes@tumphouse.fsnet.co.uk

Graygill ♦♦♦
Duke of York Road, Staunton, Coleford, GL16 8PD
T: (01600) 712536
E: barbara.bond@ukonline.co.uk

Meadow Cottage ♦♦♦
59 Coalway Road, Coleford, GL16 7HL
T: (01594) 833444
F: (01594) 833444

Millend House and Garden ♦♦♦♦
Newland, Coleford, GL16 8NF
T: (01594) 832128
F: (01594) 832128
E: apriljohnt@aol.com

Symonds Yat Rock Lodge ♦♦♦
Hillersland, Coleford, GL16 7NY
T: (01594) 836191
E: enquiries@rocklodge.co.uk
I: www.rocklodge.co.uk

COLEORTON Leicestershire

Zion Cottage ♦♦♦♦
93 Zion Hill, Peggs Green, Coleorton, Leicester LE67 8JP
T: (01530) 223914
F: (01530) 222488
E: zionbnb@aol.com
I: members.aol.com/zionbnb

COLESHILL Warwickshire

The Old Rectory ♦♦♦♦
Church Lane, Maxstoke, Coleshill, Birmingham B46 2QW
T: (01675) 462248
F: (01675) 481615
I: www.SmoothHound.co.uk/hotels/oldrect.html

Packington Lane Farm ♦♦♦♦
Packington Lane, Coleshill, Birmingham B46 3JJ
T: (01675) 462228
F: (01675) 462228

COLLINGHAM Nottinghamshire

Lime Tree Farm ♦♦♦♦
Lunn Lane, Collingham, Nottingham NG23 7LP
T: (01636) 892044

COLSTERWORTH Lincolnshire

The Fox (A1) Ltd ♦♦♦
Great North Road southbound, Colsterworth, Grantham NG33 5LN
T: (01572) 767697
F: (01572) 767977

The Stables ♦♦♦♦
Stainby Road, Colsterworth, Grantham NG33 5JB
T: (01476) 861057
I: www.stablesbandb.co.uk

COLWALL Herefordshire

Brook House ♦♦♦♦♦ SILVER AWARD
Walwyn Road, Colwall, Malvern WR13 6QX
T: (01684) 540604
F: (01684) 540604
E: Maggie@brookhouse.fsnt.co.uk

Old Library Lodge ♦♦♦
Stone Drive, Colwall, Malvern WR13 6QJ
T: (01684) 540077

COLWALL GREEN Herefordshire

Oakley House ♦♦♦
Colwall Green, Malvern WR13 6DX
T: (01684) 540215

CONINGSBY Lincolnshire

The Lea Gate Inn ♦♦♦♦
Leagate Road, Coningsby, Lincoln LN4 4RS
T: (01526) 342370
F: (01526) 345468
E: enquiries@theleagateinn.co.uk
I: www.theleagateinn.co.uk

CONISHOLME Lincolnshire

Wickham House ♦♦♦♦♦ SILVER AWARD
Church Lane, Conisholme, Louth LN11 7LX
T: (01507) 358465
F: (01507) 358465
E: kenmor_wickham@hotmail.com

CORBY Northamptonshire

Moat Cottage ♦♦♦♦
18 Little Oakley, Little Oakley, Corby, NN18 8HA
T: (01536) 745013
F: (01536) 745013
E: enquiries@moat-cottage.fsbusiness.co.uk
I: www.moat-cottage.fsbusiness.co.uk

White Swan ♦♦♦♦
Seaton Road, Harringworth, Corby NN17 3AF
T: (01572) 747543
F: (01572) 747323
E: thewhiteswan@fsmail.net
I: www.thewhite-swan.com

CORELEY Shropshire

Brookfield House ♦♦♦♦
Coreley, Ludlow, SY8 3AS
T: (01584) 890059

CORRINGHAM Lincolnshire

The Old Hall ♦♦♦♦
Field Lane, Corringham, Gainsborough DN21 5QX
T: (01427) 838470
F: (01427) 839333
E: wayneturner@btconnect.com

COSBY Leicestershire

The Vineries ♦♦♦♦
Countesthorpe Road, Cosby, Leicester LE9 1UL
T: (0116) 2750817

COUGHTON Herefordshire

Coughton House ♦♦♦♦
Coughton, Ross-on-Wye HR9 5SF
T: (01989) 562612
E: jenny.balchin@bigwig.net

COVENTRY West Midlands

Abigail Guesthouse ♦♦♦
39 St. Patrick's Road, Coventry, CV1 2LP
T: (024) 7622 1378
F: (024) 76221378
E: ag002a@netgates.co.uk
I: www.abigailuk.com

Aburley ♦♦♦♦
23 St Patricks Road, Cheylesmore, Coventry, CV1 2LP
T: (024) 76251348
F: (024) 76223243

Acacia Guest House ♦♦♦♦
11 Park Road, Coventry, CV1 2LE
T: (02476) 633622
F: (02476) 633622
E: acaciaguesthouse@ukonline.co.uk

Albany Guest House ♦♦♦
121 Holyhead Road, Coundon, Coventry, CV1 3AD
T: (024) 7622 3601
F: (024) 7622 3601

Arlon Guest House ♦♦♦
25 St Patricks Road, Coventry, CV1 2LP
T: (024) 7622 5942

Ashdowns Guest House ♦♦♦
12 Regent Street, Earlsdon, Coventry, CV1 3EP
T: (024) 7622 9280

Ashleigh House ♦♦♦
17 Park Road, Coventry, CV1 2LH
T: (024) 7622 3804
F: (024) 76223804

Barnacle Hall ♦♦♦♦♦ SILVER AWARD
Shilton Lane, Shilton, Coventry CV7 9LH
T: (024) 76612629

Bourne Brook Lodge ♦♦♦♦
Mill Lane, Fillongley, Coventry CV7 8EE
T: (01676) 541898
F: (01676) 541898
E: bournebrooklodge@care4free.net

Brookfields ♦♦♦♦
134 Butt Lane, Allesley, Coventry, CV5 9FE
T: (024) 7640 4866
F: (024) 7640 2022

Chester House ♦♦♦
3 Chester Street, Coventry, CV1 4DH
T: (024) 7622 3857

Crest Guest House ♦♦♦♦ SILVER AWARD
39 Friars Road, Coventry, CV1 2LJ
T: (024) 7622 7822
F: (024) 7622 7244
E: alanharve@aol.com
I: www.SmoothHound.co.uk/hotels/crestgue.html

Fairlight Guest House ♦♦♦
14 Regent Street, Off Queen's Road, Coventry, CV1 3EP
T: (024) 7622 4215
F: (024) 7622 4215
E: k.schofield@btinternet.com

Highcroft Guest House ♦♦
65 Barras Lane, Coundon, Coventry, CV1 4AQ
T: (024) 7622 8157
F: (024) 7663 1609
E: deepak8@btopenworld.com

Lodge Farm House Bed and Breakfast ♦♦♦♦
Westwood Heath Road, Coventry, CV4 8AA
T: (024) 7646 6786
F: (024) 7646 6786
E: lodgefarmhouse@aol.com

Mount Guest House ♦♦♦
9 Coundon Road, Coventry, CV1 4AR
T: (024) 7622 5998
F: (024) 7622 5998
E: enquiries@guesthousecoventry.com
I: www.guesthousecoventry.com

St Mary's Cottage ♦♦♦
107 Kingsbury Road, Coventry, CV6 1PT
T: (024) 7659 1557
F: (024) 7659 1557
E: afoster543@aol.com

Spire View Guest House ♦♦♦♦
36 Park Road(Near Railway Station), Coventry, CV1 2LD
T: (024) 7625 1602
F: (024) 7622 2779
E: j-m@spireviewcov.freeserve.co.uk

Vardre ♦♦
68 Spencer Avenue, Earlsdon, Coventry, CV5 6NP
T: (024) 7671 5154
F: (024) 76715748
E: valvardre@aol.com
I: www.s-h.systems.co.uk

Westwood Cottage ♦♦♦
79 Westwood Heath Road, Westwood Heath, Coventry, CV4 8GN
T: (024) 7647 1084
F: (024) 7647 1084

COWLEY Gloucestershire

Butlers Hill Farm Rating Applied For
Cockleford, Cowley, Cheltenham GL53 9NW
T: (01242) 870455
F: (01242) 870455
E: butlershill@aol.com

CRADLEY Herefordshire

Hollings Hill Farm ♦♦♦♦
Bosbury Road, Cradley, Malvern WR13 5LY
T: (01886) 880203
E: ajgkhollingshill@farmersweekly.net

CRANWELL Lincolnshire

Byards Leap Cottage ♦♦♦
Cranwell, Sleaford NG34 8EY
T: (01400) 261537
F: (01400) 261537

CRAVEN ARMS Shropshire

Castle View ♦♦♦♦
148 Stokesay, Craven Arms, SY7 9AL
T: (01588) 673712

Earnstrey Hill House ♦♦♦♦
Abdon, Shropshire, Craven Arms, SY7 9HU
T: (01746) 712579
F: (01746) 712631
E: hugh.scurfield@smwh.org.uk

The Firs ♦♦♦♦
Norton, Craven Arms, SY7 9LS
T: (01588) 672511
F: (01588) 672511
E: thefirs@go2.co.uk
I: www.go2.co.uk/firs

Glebelands ◆◆◆
25 Knighton Road, Clun, Craven Arms SY7 8JH
T: (01588) 640442
F: (01588) 640442
E: Tourism@clun25.freeserve.co.uk
I: www.clun25.freeserve.co.uk

Groveside ◆◆◆
Shrewsbury Road, Craven Arms, SY7 8BX
T: (01588) 672948

CRESSBROOK
Derbyshire

Cressbrook Hall ◆◆◆◆
Cressbrook, Buxton SK17 8SY
T: (01298) 871289
F: (01298) 871845
E: stay@cressbrookhall.co.uk
I: www.cressbrookhall.co.uk

The Old Toll House ◆◆◆◆
Cressbrook, Buxton SK17 8SY
T: (01298) 872547
E: loy@oldtollhouse.freeserve.co.uk
I: www.oldtollhouse.freeserve.co.uk

CRICH
Derbyshire

Penrose Avista Property Partnership
◆◆◆◆ SILVER AWARD
Sandy Lane, Crich, Matlock DE4 5DE
T: (01773) 852625
E: keith@avista.freeserve.co.uk
I: www.s-h-systems.co.uk/hotels/avista.html

CROPTHORNE
Worcestershire

The Cedars Guest House
◆◆◆◆
Evesham Road, Cropthorne, Pershore WR10 3JU
T: (01386) 860219
E: cedarsguesthouse@ukonline.co.uk

Cropvale Farm Bed and Breakfast
◆◆◆◆ GOLD AWARD
Cropvale Farm, Smokey Lane, Cropthorne, Pershore WR10 3NF
T: (01386) 860237
F: (01386) 860237
E: susan@hutchings22.freeserve.co.uk
I: www.smoothhound.co.uk/hotels/cropvale.html

CROXDEN
Staffordshire

Farriers Cottage and Mews
◆◆◆◆
Woodhouse Farm, Nabb Lane, Croxden, Uttoxeter ST14 5JB
T: (01889) 507507
F: (01889) 507282
E: ddeb@lineone.net
I: www.smoothhound.co.uk/a47700.html

CROXTON KERRIAL
Leicestershire

Peacock at Croxton ◆◆◆◆
Peacock Inn, 1 School Lane, Croxton Kerrial, Grantham NG32 1QR
T: (01476) 870324
F: (01476) 870171
E: peacockcroxton@globalnet.co.uk
I: www.peakcockcroxton.com

CUBBINGTON
Warwickshire

Bakers Cottage ◆◆◆◆
52/54 Queen Street, Cubbington, Leamington Spa CV32 7NA
T: (01926) 772146

Staddlestones Bed and Breakfast ◆◆◆
67 Rugby Road, Cubbington, Leamington Spa CV32 7HY
T: (01926) 740253

CURBAR
Derbyshire

Bridgend ◆◆◆
Dukes Drive, Curbar, Calver, Hope Valley S32 3YP
T: (01433) 630226
E: hunt@g3fwb.freeserve.co.uk

CUTTHORPE
Derbyshire

Cow Close Farm ◆◆◆
Overgreen, Cutthorpe, Chesterfield S42 7BA
T: (01246) 232055
E: cowclosefarm.cottages@virginnet

DAGLINGWORTH
Gloucestershire

Windrush Cottage ◆◆◆
Itlay, Daglingworth, Cirencester GL7 7HZ
T: (01285) 652917

DARLEY ABBEY
Derbyshire

The Coach House ◆◆◆
185A Duffield Road, Darley Abbey, Derby DE22 1JB
T: (01332) 551795

DARLEY BRIDGE
Derbyshire

Square and Compass ◆◆◆
Station Road, Darley Bridge, Matlock DE4 2EQ
T: (01629) 733255

DAVENTRY
Northamptonshire

Drayton Lodge ◆◆◆◆
Staverton Road, Daventry, NN11 4NL
T: (01327) 702449
F: (01327) 872110
E: annspicer@farming.co.uk

Kingsthorpe Guesthouse ◆◆◆
18 Badby Road, Daventry, NN11 4AW
T: (01327) 702752
F: (01327) 301854

Threeways House
◆◆◆◆ SILVER AWARD
Everdon, Daventry NN11 6BL
T: (01327) 361631
F: (01327) 361359
E: elizabethbarwood@hotmail.com
I: threewayshouse.com

DENSTONE
Staffordshire

Denstone Hall Farm ◆◆◆
Denstone, Uttoxeter ST14 5HF
T: (01889) 590253
F: (01889) 590930
E: denstonehallfarm@talk21.com

Manor House Farm
◆◆◆◆ SILVER AWARD
Prestwood, Denstone, Uttoxeter ST14 5DD
T: (01889) 590415
F: (01335) 342198
E: cm_ball@yahoo.co.uk
I: www.4posteraccom.com

Rowan Lodge ◆◆◆◆
Stubwood, Denstone, Uttoxeter ST14 5HU
T: (01889) 590913
E: rowanlodge@hotmail.com
I: www.smoothhound.co.uk/hotels/rowanlodge.html

DERBY
Derbyshire

Alambie ◆◆◆
189 Main Road, Morley, Derby, DE7 6DG
T: (01332) 780349
F: (01332) 780349
E: alambie@beeb.net
I: www.alambieguesthouse.co.uk

Bonehill Farm ◆◆◆◆
Etwall Road, Mickleover, Derby DE3 5DN
T: (01332) 513553
E: bonehillfarm@hotmail.com

Chuckles Guesthouse ◆◆◆
48 Crompton Street, Derby, DE1 1NX
T: (01332) 367193
E: ianfraser@chucklesguesthouse.freeserve.co.uk
I: www.chucklesguesthouse.gbr.cc

The Hill House Hotel ◆◆◆
294 Burton Road, Derby, DE23 6AD
T: (01332) 361523
F: (01332) 361523
E: amandafearn@hillhousehotel.co.uk
I: www.hillhousehotel-derby.co.uk

Red Setters Guesthouse ◆◆◆
85 Curzon Street, Derby, DE1 1LN
T: (01332) 362770
E: yvonne@derbycity.com
I: www.derbycity.com/michael/redset.html

Rose & Thistle Guesthouse
◆◆◆
21 Charnwood Street, Derby, DE1 2GU
T: (01332) 344103
F: (01332) 291006
E: rosethistle@gpanet.co.uk

The Wayfarer Guesthouse
◆◆◆
27 Crompton Street, Derby, DE1 1NY
T: (01332) 348350

DIGBETH
West Midlands

The Works Guesthouse ◆◆◆
29-30 Warner Street, Digbeth, Birmingham B12 0JG
T: (0121) 7723326
F: (0121) 7723326

DIGBY
Lincolnshire

Digby Manor ◆◆◆◆
The Manor, North Street, Digby, Lincoln LN4 3LY
T: (01526) 322064
E: gilltown@lineone.net

Woodend Farm Bed and Breakfast ◆◆◆
Woodend Farm, Digby, Lincoln LN4 3NG
T: (01526) 860347

DONNINGTON
Gloucestershire

Holmleigh ◆◆
Donnington, Moreton-in-Marsh GL56 0XX
T: (01451) 830792

DORRINGTON
Shropshire

Meadowlands ◆◆◆
Lodge Lane, Frodesley, Dorrington, Shrewsbury SY5 7HD
T: (01694) 731350
F: (01694) 731350
E: Meadowlands@talk21.com
I: www.meadowlands.co.uk

DORSTONE
Herefordshire

Westbrook Manor Bed and Breakfast ◆◆◆
Westbrook Manor, Dorstone, Hereford HR3 5SY
T: (01497) 831431
F: (01497) 831431
E: roddyandlibby@nextcall.net
I: www.golden-valley.co.uk/wmamor

DROITWICH
Worcestershire

Foxbrook ◆◆◆◆
238A Worcester Road, Droitwich, WR9 8AY
T: (01905) 772414

Middleton Grange
◆◆◆◆ SILVER AWARD
Ladywood Road, Salwarpe, Droitwich, WR9 0AH
T: (01905) 451678
F: (01905) 453978
E: salli@middletongrange.com
I: www.middletongrange.com

The Old Farmhouse
◆◆◆◆◆ SILVER AWARD
Hadley Heath, Droitwich, WR9 0AR
T: (01905) 620837
F: (01905) 621722
E: judylambe@ombersley.demon.co.uk
I: www.the-old-farmhouse.com

Richmond Guest House ◆◆
3 Ombersley St. West, Droitwich, WR9 8HZ
T: (01905) 775722
F: (01905) 794642
I: www.infotel.co.uk/hotels/36340.htm

Temple Broughton Farm
◆◆◆◆ GOLD AWARD
Broughton Green, Droitwich, WR9 7EF
T: (01905) 391456
F: (01905) 391515
E: suemaccoll@ukonline.co.uk
I: www.templebroughtonfarm.co.uk

DRONFIELD
Derbyshire

Cassita ♦♦♦♦
Off Snape Hill Lane, Dronfield, S18 2GL
T: (01246) 417303
F: (01246) 417303

DUNCHURCH
Warwickshire

Toft Hill ♦♦♦♦
Dunchurch, Rugby CV22 6NR
T: (01788) 810342

DUNTISBOURNE ABBOTS
Gloucestershire

Dixs Barn ♦♦♦
Duntisbourne Abbots, Cirencester GL7 7JN
T: (01285) 821249
E: wilcox@dixsbarn.freeserve.co.uk

DURSLEY
Gloucestershire

Foresters ♦♦♦♦
Chapel Street, Upper Cam Village, Dursley, GL11 5NX
T: (01453) 549996
F: (01453) 548200
E: foresters@freeuk.com
I: www.ibex.freeserve.co.uk/foresters

DUSTON
Northamptonshire

Hopping Hare ♦♦♦♦
18 Hopping Hill Gardens, Duston, Northampton NN5 6PF
T: (01604) 683888
F: (01604) 683889
E: enquiries@mcmanuspub.co.uk
I: www.mcmanuspub.co.uk

DYMOCK
Gloucestershire

Granary ♦♦♦
Lower House Farm, Kempley, Dymock GL18 2BS
T: (01531) 890301
F: (01531) 890301

The White House ♦♦♦
Dymock, GL18 2AQ
T: (01531) 890516

EARDISLAND
Herefordshire

Eardisland Tea Room ♦♦
Church Lane, Eardisland, Leominster HR6 9BP
T: (01544) 388226

The Manor House ♦♦♦♦
Eardisland, Leominster HR6 9BN
T: (01544) 388138

EARL STERNDALE
Derbyshire

Chrome Cottage ♦♦♦
Earl Sterndale, Buxton SK17 0BS
T: (01298) 83360
F: (01298) 83360
E: adgregg@bigwig.net

Fernydale Farm ♦♦♦♦
Earl Sterndale, Buxton SK17 0BS
T: (01298) 83236
F: (01298) 83605
E: jane@jmycock.fsnet.co.uk

EAST BARKWITH
Lincolnshire

Bodkin Lodge
♦♦♦♦♦ GOLD AWARD
Grange Farm, Torrington Lane, East Barkwith, Market Rasen LN8 5RY
T: (01673) 858249
F: (01673) 858249

The Grange
♦♦♦♦ SILVER AWARD
Torrington Lane, East Barkwith, Market Rasen LN8 5RY
T: (01673) 858670
E: sarahstamp@farmersweekly.net
I: www.the-grange.f2s.com

EAST HADDON
Northamptonshire

East Haddon Lodge ♦♦♦
East Haddon, Northampton NN6 8BU
T: (01604) 770240

EAST LANGTON
Leicestershire

The Bell Inn ♦♦♦♦
Main Street, East Langton, Market Harborough LE16 7TW
T: (01858) 545278
F: (01858) 545748
E: achapman@thebellinn.co.uk
I: www.thebellinn.co.uk

EASTCOTE
Northamptonshire

West Farm
♦♦♦♦ SILVER AWARD
Gayton Road, Eastcote, Towcester NN12 8NS
T: (01327) 830310
F: (01327) 830310
E: west.farm@eastcote97.fsnet.co.uk

EASTNOR
Herefordshire

Hill Farmhouse Bed and Breakfast ♦♦
Eastnor, Ledbury HR8 1EF
T: (01531) 632827

EASTWOOD
Nottinghamshire

Horseshoe Cottage ♦♦♦♦
25 Babbington Village, Eastwood, Nottingham NG16 2SS
T: (0115) 930 4769
F: (0115) 930 4769
E: janet@jtserve.force9.co.uk

ECCLESHALL
Staffordshire

Cobblers Cottage ♦♦♦♦
Kerry Lane, Eccleshall, Stafford ST21 6EJ
T: (01785) 850116
F: (01785) 850116
E: cobblerscottage@tinyonline.co.uk

The George Inn ♦♦♦
Castle Street, Eccleshall, Stafford ST21 6DF
T: (01785) 850300
F: (01785) 851452
E: information@thegeorgeinn.freeserve.co.uk
I: www.thegreeninn,freeserve.co.uk

Slindon House Farm ♦♦♦♦
Slindon, Eccleshall, Stafford ST21 6LX
T: (01782) 791237
E: bonsallslindonhouse@supanet.com

ECKINGTON
Worcestershire

The Anchor Inn and Restaurant ♦♦♦
Cotheridge Lane, Eckington, Pershore WR10 3BA
T: (01386) 750356
F: (01386) 750356
E: anchoreck@aol.com
I: www.anchoreckington.co.uk

Lantern House ♦♦♦
Boon Street, Eckington, Pershore WR10 3BL
T: (01386) 750003
E: ann@parker14.freeserve.co.uk

Nafford House ♦♦♦♦
Eckington, Pershore WR10 3DJ
T: (01386) 750233

EDALE
Derbyshire

Mam Tor House ♦♦♦
Edale, Hope Valley S33 7ZA
T: (01433) 670253
E: mam.tor@tiscali.co.uk

Stonecroft
♦♦♦♦ GOLD AWARD
Grindsbrook, Edale, Hope Valley S33 7ZA
T: (01433) 670262
F: (01433) 670262
E: stonecroftedale@aol.com
I: accommodation.uk.net/hotels/stonecroftguesthouse

EDGBASTON
West Midlands

Swiss Cottage Hotel ♦♦
475 Gillott Road, Edgbaston, Birmingham B16 9LJ
T: (0121) 454 0371
F: (0121) 454 0371

EDGE
Gloucestershire

Painswick View ♦♦♦♦
Back Edge Lane, Edge, Stroud GL6 6PE
T: (01452) 813396
E: ascahill@hotmail.com

ELLASTONE
Staffordshire

Chapel House ♦♦♦♦
Wootton, Wootton, DE6 2GW
T: (01335) 324554
F: (01335) 324554
E: lizzy@weaverband.co.uk

ELLERDINE
Shropshire

The Tackroom ♦♦♦
Occupation Lane, Chelmarsh, Ellerdine, Telford WV16 6BE
T: (01746) 861397

ELLESMERE
Shropshire

The Grange ♦♦♦
Grange Road, Ellesmere, SY12 9DE
T: (01691) 623495
F: (01691) 623227
E: rosie@thegrange.uk.com
I: www.thegrange.uk.com

Hordley Hall ♦♦♦
Hordley, Ellesmere SY12 9BB
T: (01691) 622772

Oakhill ♦♦♦♦
Dudleston, Ellesmere, SY12 9LL
T: (01691) 690548

ELMESTHORPE
Leicestershire

Badgers Mount ♦♦♦♦
6 Station Road, Elmesthorpe, Leicester LE9 7SG
T: (01455) 848161
F: (01455) 848161
E: info@badgersmount.com
I: www.badgersmount.com

ELMLEY CASTLE
Worcestershire

The Old Mill Inn ♦♦♦♦
Mill Lane, Elmley Castle, Pershore WR10 3HP
T: (01386) 710407
F: (01386) 710066
E: oldmilin@dircon.co.uk
I: www.elmleymill.com

ELTON
Derbyshire

Elton Guesthouse ♦♦♦
Moor Lane, Elton, Matlock DE4 2DA
T: (01629) 650217

Hawthorn Cottage
♦♦♦♦ SILVER AWARD
Well Street, Elton, Bakewell, DE4 2BY
T: (01629) 650372
I: www.hawthorncottage-elton.co.uk

Homestead Farm ♦♦♦
Main Street, Elton, Matlock DE4 2BW
T: (01629) 650359

ENDON
Staffordshire

Hollinhurst Farm ♦♦♦
Park Lane, Endon, Stoke-on-Trent ST9 9JB
T: (01782) 502633
E: hjball@ukf.net

ENGLISH BICKNOR
Gloucestershire

Dryslade Farm ♦♦♦♦
English Bicknor, Coleford GL16 7PA
T: (01594) 860259
F: (01594) 860259
E: dryslade@agriplus.net
I: www.drysladefarm.co.uk

EVESHAM
Worcestershire

Bredon View Guest House
♦♦♦♦ SILVER AWARD
Village Street, Harvington, Evesham, WR11 5NQ
T: (01386) 871484
F: (01386) 871484
E: b.v.circa1898@bushinternet.com
I: www.bredonview.net

Park View Hotel ♦♦♦
Waterside, Evesham, WR11 6BS
T: (01386) 442639
E: mike.spires@btinternet.com
I: www.superstay.co.uk

Establishments printed in blue have a detailed entry in this guide

EWYAS HAROLD
Herefordshire

The Old Rectory ♦♦♦♦
Ewyas Harold, Hereford HR2 0EY
T: (01981) 240498
F: (01981) 240498

EYAM
Derbyshire

Crown Cottage ♦♦♦♦
Main Road, Eyam, Hope Valley
S32 5QW
T: (01433) 630858
E: crown-cottage@amserve.com
I: www.crown-cottage.co.uk

EYDON
Northamptonshire

Crockwell Farm
♦♦♦♦ SILVER AWARD
Eydon, Daventry NN11 3QA
T: (01327) 361358
F: (01327) 361573
E: info@crockwellfarm.co.uk
I: www.crockwellfarm.co.uk

FAIRFIELD
Derbyshire

Barms Farm
♦♦♦♦ SILVER AWARD
Fairfield Common, Fairfield,
Buxton SK17 7HW
T: (01298) 77723
F: (01298) 78692
E: barmsfarm@highpeak.co.uk
I: www.highpeak.co.uk/barmsfarm

FAIRFORD
Gloucestershire

East End House
♦♦♦♦♦ GOLD AWARD
Fairford, GL7 4AP
T: (01285) 713715
F: (01285) 713505
E: diana.ewart@virgin.net
I: www.eastendhouse.co.uk

Kempsford Manor ♦♦♦
Fairford, GL7 4EQ
T: (01285) 810131
F: (01285) 810131
E: kempsford_manor@acmemail.net
I: members.lycos.co.uk/kempsford_manor/

Milton Farm ♦♦♦♦
Fairford, GL7 4HZ
T: (01285) 712205
F: (01285) 711349
E: milton@farmersweekly.net
I: www.milton-farm.co.uk

Waiten Hill Farm ♦♦
Fairford, GL7 4JG
T: (01285) 712652
F: (01285) 712652

FARNSFIELD
Nottinghamshire

Lockwell House ♦♦♦
Lockwell Hill, Old Rufford Road,
Farnsfield, Newark NG22 8JG
T: (01623) 883067
F: (01623) 883067

FARTHINGHOE
Northamptonshire

Greenfield
♦♦♦♦ SILVER AWARD
Baker Street, Farthinghoe,
Brackley NN13 5PH
T: (01295) 712380
F: (01295) 712380
E: vivwebb@aol.com
I: http://members.aol.com/vivwebb/

FARTHINGSTONE
Northamptonshire

Glebe Farm ♦♦♦♦
Maidford Road, Farthingstone,
Towcester NN12 8HE
T: (01327) 361558
F: (01327) 361558
E: gjbryce.glebefarm@virgin.net

FECKENHAM
Worcestershire

Orchard House
♦♦♦♦ SILVER AWARD
Berrow Hill Lane, Feckenham,
Redditch B96 6QJ
T: (01527) 821497
F: (01527) 821497

The Steps ♦♦♦
6 High Street, Feckenham,
Redditch B96 6HS
T: (01527) 892678
E: jenny@thesteps.co.uk
I: www.thesteps.co.uk

FENNY BENTLEY
Derbyshire

Cairn Grove ♦♦♦♦
Ashes Lane, Fenny Bentley,
Ashbourne DE6 1LD
T: (01335) 350538
E: keith.wheeldon@virgin.net
I: www.cairngrove.co.uk

FENNY DRAYTON
Leicestershire

White Wings
♦♦♦♦♦ SILVER AWARD
Quaker Close, Fenny Drayton,
Nuneaton CV13 6BS
T: (01827) 716100
F: (01827) 717191
E: lloyd@whitewings.freeserve.co.uk

FERNHILL HEATH
Worcestershire

Dilmore House Hotel ♦♦♦♦
Droitwich Road, Fernhill Heath,
Worcester WR3 7UL
T: (01905) 451543
F: (01905) 452015
E: dilmorehouse@ukgateway.net

Heathside ♦♦♦♦
Droitwich Road, Fernhill Heath,
Worcester WR3 7UA
T: (01905) 458245
F: (01905) 458245

FIDDINGTON
Gloucestershire

Hillview B and B ♦♦♦♦
Fiddington, Tewkesbury
GL20 7BJ
T: (01684) 293231
F: (01684) 293231
E: johnhargreaves@aol.com

FILLINGHAM
Lincolnshire

Church Farm
♦♦♦♦ SILVER AWARD
Fillingham, Gainsborough
DN21 5BS
T: (01427) 668279
F: (01427) 668025
E: fillinghambandb@lineone.net

FILLONGLEY
Warwickshire

Manor House Farm
♦♦♦♦ SILVER AWARD
Green End Road, Fillongley,
Coventry CV7 8DS
T: (01676) 540256

FISHMORE
Shropshire

Acorn Place ♦♦♦♦
Fishmore, Ludlow, SY8 3DP
T: (01584) 875295
E: carollomas@acornplaceludlowfsnet.co.uk

FLAXLEY
Gloucestershire

Waldron Farm ♦♦♦♦
Flaxley, Newnham-on-Severn
GL14 1JR
T: (01452) 760581
F: (01452) 760581
E: charlesworth@waldronfarm.fsbusiness.co.uk
I: www.waldronfarm.co.uk

FLYFORD FLAVELL
Worcestershire

Lilyvale Cottage
Rating Applied For
Bishampton Road, Flyford
Flavell, Worcester WR7 4BT
T: (01386) 462337
E: holiday@lilyvale.com
I: www.lilyvale.com

FOOLOW
Derbyshire

Housley Cottage ♦♦♦
Housley, Foolow, S32 5QB
T: (01433) 631505
E: kevin@housley-cottage.freeserve.co.uk

FORTON
Shropshire

The Swan At Forton ♦♦
Eccleshall Road, Forton,
Newport TF10 8BY
T: (01952) 812169
F: (01952) 812722

FOWNHOPE
Herefordshire

The Tan House ♦♦♦
Fownhope, Hereford HR1 4NJ
T: (01432) 860549
F: (01432) 860466
E: vera@ukbu.co.uk

FOXTON
Leicestershire

The Old Manse
♦♦♦♦ SILVER AWARD
Swingbridge Street, Foxton,
Market Harborough LE16 7RH
T: (01858) 545456
F: (01858) 540030
E: theoldmanse37@hotmail.com

FRAMPTON-ON-SEVERN
Gloucestershire

Archway House ♦♦♦♦
The Green, Frampton-on-Severn,
Gloucester GL2 7DY
T: (01452) 740752
F: (01452) 741629
E: mike.brown@archwayhouse.fsnet.co.uk

FRODESLEY
Shropshire

The Haven ♦♦♦♦
Frodesley, Dorrington,
Shrewsbury, SY5 7EY
T: (01694) 731672
E: the-haven@frodesley.fsnet.co.uk
I: www.welcomingyou.co.uk/the-haven

FULBECK
Lincolnshire

The Hare and Hounds Country Inn ♦♦♦
The Green, Fulbeck, Grantham
NG32 3JJ
T: (01400) 272090
F: (01400) 273663

GAINSBOROUGH
Lincolnshire

The Beckett Arms ♦♦♦
25 High Street, Corringham,
Gainsborough DN21 5QP
T: (01427) 838201

Swallow Barn ♦♦♦♦
Sturgate, Gainsborough,
DN21 5PX
T: (01427) 839042
F: (01427) 839043
E: gwen.anselm@ntlworld.com

GARWAY
Herefordshire

The Old Rectory ♦♦♦♦
Garway, Hereford HR2 8RH
T: (01600) 750363
F: (01600) 750364
E: garwayoldrectory@yahoo.co.uk

GAYTON LE MARSH
Lincolnshire

Westbrook House ♦♦♦♦
Gayton le Marsh, Alford
LN13 0NW
T: (01507) 450624
E: westbrook_house@hotmail.com
I: www.smoothhound.co.uk/hotels/westh.html

GEDNEY HILL
Lincolnshire

Sycamore Farmhouse ♦♦♦
6 Station Road, Gedney Hill,
Spalding PE12 0NP
T: (01406) 330445
F: (01406) 330445
E: sycamore.farm@virgin.net
I: www.farmhousebedandbreakfast.freeserve.co.uk

GLOSSOP
Derbyshire

Avondale ♦♦♦♦
28 Woodhead Road, Glossop,
SK13 7RH
T: (01457) 853132
F: (0161) 494 6078
E: avondale.glossop@talk21.com
I: www.cressbrook.co.uk/glossop/avondale

Establishments printed in blue have a detailed entry in this guide

Peels Arms ♦♦♦
6-12 Temple Street, Padfield, Hyde, SK13 1EX
T: (01457) 852719
F: (01457) 860536
E: robert.astle@btopenworld.com

White House Farm ♦♦♦
Padfield Main Road, Hyde, SK13 1ET
T: (01457) 854695
F: (01457) 854695

GLOUCESTER
Gloucestershire

Albert Hotel ♦♦♦
56-58 Worcester Street, Gloucester, GL1 3AG
T: (01452) 502081
F: (01452) 311738
E: enquiries@alberthotel.com
I: www.alberthotel.com

Brookthorpe Lodge ♦♦♦
Stroud Road, Brookthorpe, Gloucester GL4 0UQ
T: (01452) 812645
F: (01452) 812645
E: enq@brookthorpelodge.demon.co.uk
I: www.brookthorpelodge.demon.co.uk

The Chestnuts ♦♦♦♦
9 Brunswick Square, Gloucester, GL1 1UG
T: (01452) 330356
F: (01452) 539571
E: dchampion@blueyonder.co.uk

The Coppins ♦♦♦♦
11c Kenilworth Avenue, Gloucester, GL2 0QN
T: (01452) 302777

Georgian Guest House ♦
85 Bristol Road, Gloucester, GL1 5SN
T: (01452) 413286
F: (01452) 413286

Kilmorie Small Holding ♦♦♦♦
Gloucester Road, Corse, Snigs End, Staunton, Gloucester GL19 3RQ
T: (01452) 840224
F: (01452) 840224
E: sheila-barnfield@supanet.com
I: www.SmoothHound.co.uk/hotels/kilmorie.html

Lulworth ♦♦♦
12 Midland Road, Gloucester, GL1 4UF
T: (01452) 521881
F: (01452) 386149
E: themanager@lulworth.swinternet.co.uk
I: www.lulworth.swinternet.co.uk

Nicki's Hotel & Taverna ♦♦
105-107 Westgate Street, Gloucester, GL1 2PG
T: (01452) 301359

Notley House and The Coach House ♦♦♦
93 Hucclecote Road, Hucclecote, Gloucester GL3 3TR
T: (01452) 611584
E: heyhouse@aol.com
I: ourworld.compuserve.com/homepages/notleyhouse

Pembury Guest House ♦♦♦
9 Pembury Road, St. Barnabas, Gloucester, GL4 6UE
T: (01452) 521856
F: (01452) 303418

Spalite Hotel ♦♦
121 Southgate Street, Gloucester, GL1 1XQ
T: (01452) 380828
E: marsh@spalitehotel.fsnet.co.uk
I: www.spalitehotel.co.uk

The Tailors House ♦♦♦
43-45 Westgate Street, Gloucester, GL1 2NW
T: (01452) 521750
F: (01452) 521750

GNOSALL
Staffordshire

The Leys House ♦♦♦♦
Gnosall, Stafford ST20 0BZ
T: (01785) 822532
F: (01785) 822060

GOADBY
Leicestershire

The Hollies ♦♦♦
Goadby, Leicester LE7 9EE
T: (0116) 259 8301
F: (0116) 2598491
E: j.parr@btinternet.com

GRANGEMILL
Derbyshire

Middle Hills Farm ♦♦♦♦
Grangemill, Derby DE4 4HY
T: (01629) 650368
F: (01629) 650368
E: l.lomas@btinernet.com
I: www.peakdistrictfarmhols.co.uk

GRANTHAM
Lincolnshire

Beechleigh Guesthouse ♦♦♦♦
55 North Parade, Grantham, NG31 8AT
T: (01476) 572213
F: (01476) 566058
E: info@beechleigh.co.uk
I: www.beechleigh.co.uk

The Red House ♦♦♦
74 North Parade, Grantham, NG31 8AN
T: (01476) 579869
F: (01476) 401597
E: redhousebb@aol.com
I: www.smoothhound.co.uk/hotels/theredhouse1.html

GREAT COMBERTON
Worcestershire

Tibbitts Farm ♦♦♦♦
Russell Street, Great Comberton, Pershore WR10 3DT
T: (01386) 710210
F: (01386) 710210
E: pixiefarr@aol.com

GREAT DALBY
Leicestershire

Dairy Farm ♦♦♦
8 Burrough End, Great Dalby, Melton Mowbray LE14 2EW
T: (01664) 562783

GREAT HUCKLOW
Derbyshire

The Old Manse ♦♦♦♦
Great Hucklow, Buxton SK17 8RF
T: (01298) 871262
F: (01298) 872916
E: bedandbreakfast@angus.co.uk
I: www.angus.co.uk/bedandbreakfast/

GREAT RISSINGTON
Gloucestershire

Lower Farmhouse ♦♦♦
Great Rissington, Cheltenham GL54 2LH
T: (01451) 810163
F: (01451) 810187
E: B&B@lowerfarmhouse.co.uk
I: www.lowerfarmhouse.co.uk

Stepping Stone ♦♦♦♦
Rectory Lane, Great Rissington, Cheltenham GL54 2LL
T: (01451) 821385
E: stepping-stone-b-b@excite.com

GREAT WITLEY
Worcestershire

Home Farm ♦♦♦♦ SILVER AWARD
Great Witley, Worcester WR6 6JJ
T: (01299) 896825
F: (01299) 896176
E: homefarm@yescomputers.co.uk
I: www.homefarmbandb.com

GRETTON
Gloucestershire

Elms Farm ♦♦♦
Gretton, Cheltenham GL54 5HQ
T: (01242) 620150
E: rose@elmfarm.demon.co.uk.
I: www.elmfarm.demon.co.uk.

Gretton Court ♦♦♦♦ SILVER AWARD
Church Stretton, Gretton, SY6 7HU
T: (01694) 771630

GRIMSTON
Leicestershire

Gorse House ♦♦♦♦ SILVER AWARD
33 Main Street, Grimston, Melton Mowbray LE14 3BZ
T: (01664) 813537
F: (01664) 813537
E: cowdell@gorsehouse.co.uk
I: www.gorsehouse.co.uk

GRINDLEFORD
Derbyshire

Sir William Hotel ♦♦♦♦
Sir William Hill, Grindleford, Hope Valley S32 2HS
T: (01433) 630303
F: (01433) 639753
E: sirwilliamhotel@btinternet.com

Woodlands ♦♦♦♦
Sir William Hill Road, Grindleford, Hope Valley S32 2HS
T: (01433) 631593

GRINDON
Staffordshire

Summerhill Farm ♦♦♦♦
Grindon, Leek ST13 7TT
T: (01538) 304264

GUILSBOROUGH
Northamptonshire

Lodge Farm ♦♦♦♦ SILVER AWARD
West Haddon Road, Guilsborough, Northampton NN6 8QE
T: (01604) 740392
F: (01604) 740392

GUITING POWER
Gloucestershire

Castlett Bank ♦♦♦♦
Castlett Street, Guiting Power, Cheltenham GL54 5US
T: (01451) 850300
F: (01451) 850300
E: wilderspin.castlettbank@btinternet.com
I: www.SmoothHound.co.uk/hotels/castlett.html

Cobnutt Cottage ♦♦♦
Winchcombe Road, Guiting Power, Cheltenham GL54 5UX
T: (01451) 850658

The Guiting Guest House ♦♦♦♦♦ SILVER AWARD
Post Office Lane, Guiting Power, Cheltenham GL54 5TZ
T: (01451) 850470
F: (01451) 850034
E: info@guitingguesthouse.com
I: www.guitingguesthouse.com

Halfway House ♦♦♦
Kineton, Guiting Power, Cheltenham GL54 5UG
T: (01451) 850344

The Hollow Bottom ♦♦♦
Winchcombe Road, Guiting Power, Cheltenham GL54 5UX
T: (01451) 850392
F: (01451) 850945
E: hollow.bottom@virgin.net
I: www.hollowbottom.com

Tally Ho Guesthouse ♦♦♦♦
1 Tally Ho Lane, Guiting Power, Cheltenham GL54 5TY
T: (01451) 850186
E: tallyhobb@aol.com
I: www.cotswolds-bedandbreakfast.co.uk

GUNBY
Lincolnshire

Brook House ♦♦♦♦
Gunby, Grantham NG33 5LF
T: (01476) 860010
F: (01476) 860010

HACKTHORN
Lincolnshire

Honeyholes ♦♦♦♦
South Farm, Hackthorn, Lincoln LN2 3PW
T: (01673) 861868
F: (01673) 861868

HADNALL
Shropshire

Hall Farm House ♦♦♦
Hadnall, Shrewsbury SY4 4AG
T: (01939) 210269
E: hallfarmhouse1@whsmithnet.co.uk

Saracens ♦♦♦♦
Shrewsbury Road, Hadnall, Shrewsbury SY4 4AG
T: (01939) 210877
F: (01939) 210877
E: saracenshotel@aol.com
I: www.saracenshotel.co.uk

HAGWORTHINGHAM
Lincolnshire

White Oak Grange
♦♦♦♦ SILVER AWARD
Hagworthingham, Spilsby
PE23 4LX
T: (01507) 588376
F: (01507) 588377
I: whiteoakgrange.com

HALSE
Northamptonshire

Hill Farm ♦♦♦
Halse, Brackley NN13 6DY
T: (01280) 703300
F: (01280) 704999
E: jg.robinson@farmline.com

HAMPTON IN ARDEN
West Midlands

The Cottage Guest House
♦♦♦
Kenilworth Road, On A452 to
Balsall Common, Hampton in
Arden, Solihull B92 0LW
T: (01675) 442323
F: (01675) 443323

The Hollies ♦♦♦♦
Kenilworth Road, Hampton in
Arden, Solihull B92 0LW
T: (01675) 442681
F: (01675) 442941
E: thehollies@hotmail.com
I: www.theholliesguesthouse.
co.uk

HANDSACRE
Staffordshire

The Olde Peculiar ♦♦♦
The Green, Handsacre, Rugeley
WS15 4DP
T: (01543) 491891
F: (01543) 493733

HANLEY
Staffordshire

Northwood Hotel Limited
♦♦♦
146 Keelings Road, Northwood,
Hanley, Stoke-on-Trent ST1 6QA
T: (01782) 279729
F: (01782) 207507

HANLEY CASTLE
Worcestershire

The Chestnuts ♦♦♦♦
Gilberts End, Hanley Castle,
Worcester WR8 0AS
T: (01684) 311219
E: heather@hanleyswans.
demon.co.uk

HANLEY SWAN
Worcestershire

Brook Farm ♦♦♦♦
Tyre Hill, Hanley Swan,
Worcester WR8 0EQ
T: (01684) 310796
F: (01684) 310796
E: bandb@brookfarm.org.uk
I: www.brookfarm.org.uk

Meadowbank
♦♦♦♦ SILVER AWARD
Picken End, Hanley Swan,
Worcester WR8 0DQ
T: (01684) 310917
E: dave@meadowbank.
freeserve.co.uk
I: mysite.freeserve.
com/meadowbank

Yew Tree House Bed and Breakfast
♦♦♦♦♦ SILVER AWARD
Yew Tree House, Hanley Swan,
Worcester WR8 0DN
T: (01684) 310736
F: (01684) 311709
E: yewtreehs@aol.com
I: www.yewtreehouse.co.uk

HARDWICK
Herefordshire

The Haven ♦♦♦♦
Hardwick, Hay on Wye, Hereford
HR3 5TA
T: (01497) 831254
F: (01497) 831254
E: robinson@havenhay.demon.
co.uk
I: www.golden-valley.
co.uk/haven

HARLASTON
Staffordshire

The Old Rectory ♦♦♦♦
Churchside, Harlaston,
Tamworth B79 9HE
T: (01827) 383583
F: (01827) 383583

HARLEY
Shropshire

Rowley Farm Hospitality ♦♦♦
Harley, Shrewsbury SY5 6LX
T: (01952) 727348

HARMER HILL
Shropshire

The Red Castle ♦♦
Harmer Hill, Shrewsbury
SY4 3EB
T: (01939) 291071
F: (01939) 291071

HARTINGTON
Derbyshire

Bank Top Farm ♦♦♦
Pilsbury Road, Hartington,
Buxton SK17 0AD
T: (01298) 84205
F: (01298) 84859
E: owenjane@farming.co.uk
I: www.banktophartington.
freeserve.co.uk

Manifold Inn ♦♦♦
Hulme End, Hartington, Buxton,
SK17 0EX
T: (01298) 84537
I: www.themanifoldinn.co.uk

Wolfscote Grange ♦♦♦♦
Hartington, Buxton SK17 0AX
T: (01298) 84342
E: wolfscote@btinternet.com

HASELOR
Warwickshire

Walcote Farm ♦♦♦♦
Walcote, Haselor, Alcester
B49 6LY
T: (01789) 488264
E: john@walcotefarm.co.uk
I: www.walcotefarm.co.uk

HASSOP
Derbyshire

Flatts Farm ♦♦♦♦
Hassop, Bakewell DE45 1NU
T: (01629) 812983

HATHERSAGE
Derbyshire

Cannon Croft
♦♦♦♦ GOLD AWARD
Cannonfields, Hathersage, Hope
Valley S32 1AG
T: (01433) 650005
F: (01433) 650005
E: soates@cannoncroft.
fsbusiness.co.uk
I: www.cannoncroft.fsbusiness.
co.uk

The Plough Inn
♦♦♦♦ SILVER AWARD
Leadmill Bridge, Hathersage,
Hope Valley S32 1BA
T: (01433) 650319
F: (01433) 651049

Sladen ♦♦♦
Jaggers Lane, Hathersage, Hope
Valley S32 1AZ
T: (01433) 650706
F: (01433) 650315

Sladen Cottage ♦♦♦
Castleton Road, Hathersage,
Hope Valley S32 1EH
T: (01433) 650104
E: colley@sladencottage.co.uk

HAY ON WYE
Herefordshire

Haie Barn Vegetarian B&B
♦♦♦♦
The Bage, Dorstone, Hereford
HR3 5SU
T: (01497) 831729
E: goodfood@haie-barn.co.uk
I: www.golden-valley.
co.uk/haiebarn

HENLEY-IN-ARDEN
Warwickshire

Holland Park Farm ♦♦♦
Buckley Green, Henley-in-Arden,
Solihull B95 5QF
T: (01564) 792625
F: (01564) 792625

HEREFORD
Herefordshire

Alberta ♦♦
7-13 Newtown Road, Hereford,
HR4 9LH
T: (01432) 270313
F: (01432) 270313

Ancroft ♦♦♦
10 Cheviot Close, Kings Acre,
Hereford, HR4 0TF
T: (01432) 274394

Aylestone Court Hotel
♦♦♦♦ GOLD AWARD
2 Aylestone Hill, Hereford,
HR1 1HS
T: (01432) 341891
F: (01432) 267691
E: lynxservs@aol.com
I: www.aylestonecourthotel.com

The Bowens Country House
♦♦♦♦
Fownhope, Hereford HRI 4PS
T: (01432) 860430
F: (01432) 860430
E: thebowenshotel@aol.com
I: www.thebowenshotel.co.uk

Brandon Lodge
♦♦♦♦ SILVER AWARD
Ross Road, Grafton, Hereford,
HR2 8BL
T: (01432) 355621
F: (01432) 355621
E: info@brandonlodge.co.uk
I: www.brandonlodge.co.uk

Cedar Guest House ♦♦♦
123 Whitecross Road,
Whitecross, Hereford, HR4 0LS
T: (01432) 267235
F: (01432) 267235
E: info@cedarguesthouse.com
I: www.cedarguesthouse.com

Charades ♦♦♦
34 Southbank Road, Hereford,
HR1 2TJ
T: (01432) 269444

Felton House
♦♦♦♦ GOLD AWARD
Felton, Hereford HR1 3PH
T: (01432) 820366
F: (01432) 820366
E: bandb@ereal.net
I: www.smoothhound.
co.uk/hotels/felton.html

Grafton Villa Farm House
♦♦♦♦ SILVER AWARD
Grafton, Hereford HR2 8ED
T: (01432) 268689
F: (01432) 268689
E: jennielayton@ereal.net
I: www.graftonvilla.co.uk

Hedley Lodge ♦♦♦♦
Belmont Abbey, Abergavenny
Road, Hereford, HR2 9RZ
T: (01432) 277475
F: (01432) 277318
E: hedleylodge@aol.com
I: www.hedleylodge.com

Heron House Bed & Breakfast
♦♦♦
Heron House, Canon Pyon Road,
Portway, Burghill, Hereford
HR4 8NG
T: (01432) 761111
F: (01432) 760603
E: info@theheronhouse.com
I: www.theheronhouse.com

Holly Tree Guest House ♦♦♦
21 Barton Road, Hereford,
HR4 0AY
T: (01432) 357845

Hopbine Hotel ♦♦
The Hopbine, Roman Road,
Hereford, HR1 1LE
T: (01432) 268722
F: (01432) 268722

Montgomery House ♦♦♦♦
12 St Owen Street, Hereford,
HR1 2PL
T: (01432) 351454
F: (01432) 344463
E: lizforbes@lineone.net
I: www.
montgomeryhousehereford.com

Old Rectory
Rating Applied For
Byford, Hereford, Hereford,
HR4 7LD
T: (01981) 590218
F: 07970 512515
E: info@cm-ltd.com
I: www.smoothhpind.
co.uk/hotels/oldrectory2.html

Sink Green Farm ♦♦♦♦
Rotherwas, Hereford HR2 6LE
T: (01432) 870223
E: sinkgreenfarm@email.msn.com

The Somerville ♦♦♦
12 Bodenham Road, Hereford, HR1 2TS
T: (01432) 273991
F: (01432) 268719

HIGH PEAK
Derbyshire

Sycamore Inn ♦♦♦
Sycamore Road, Birch Vale, High Peak, SK22 1AB
T: (01663) 747568
F: (01663) 747382
E: sycamoreinn@aol.com
I: www.sycamoreinn.co.uk

Twiggys ♦♦♦
86 Hague Bar, New Mills, High Peak, SK22 3AR
T: (01663) 745036
F: (01663) 745036
E: enquires@twiggys-bandb.co.uk
I: www.twiggys-bandb.co.uk

HILCOTE
Derbyshire

Hilcote Hall ♦♦
Hilcote Lane, Hilcote, Alfreton DE55 5HR
T: (01773) 812608
F: (01773) 812608

HIMBLETON
Worcestershire

Phepson Farm ♦♦♦♦
Himbleton, Droitwich WR9 7JZ
T: (01905) 391205
F: (01905) 391338
E: havard@globalnet.co.uk
I: www.phepsonfarm.co.uk

HINTON IN THE HEDGES
Northamptonshire

The Old Rectory ♦♦♦
Hinton in the Hedges, Brackley NN13 5NG
T: (01280) 706807
F: (01280) 706809
E: lavinia@lavinia.demon.co.uk
I: www.northamptonshire.co.uk/hotels/oldrectory.htm

HOARWITHY
Herefordshire

Aspen House ♦♦♦♦
Hoarwithy, Hereford HR2 6QP
T: (01432) 840353
F: (01432) 840353
E: hoarwithy@aol.com

Old Mill
♦♦♦♦ SILVER AWARD
Hoarwithy, Hereford HR2 6QH
T: (01432) 840602
F: (01432) 840602

HOCKLEY HEATH
West Midlands

Illshaw Heath Farm ♦♦♦♦
Kineton Lane, Hockley Heath, Solihull B94 6RX
T: (01564) 782214

HOLBEACH
Lincolnshire

The Bull Inn ♦♦
Old Main Road, Fleet Hargate, Holbeach, Spalding PE12 8LH
T: (01406) 426866

Cackle Hill House
♦♦♦♦ SILVER AWARD
Cackle Hill Lane, Holbeach, Spalding PE12 8BS
T: 07930 228755
F: (01406) 426721
E: cacklehillhouse@farming.co.uk

Pipwell Manor
♦♦♦♦ SILVER AWARD
Washway Road, Saracens Head, Holbeach, Spalding PE12 8AL
T: (01406) 423119
F: (01406) 423119
E: honnor@pipwellmanor.freeserve.co.uk
I: www.smoothhound.co.uk/hotels/pipwell.html

HOLBECK
Nottinghamshire

Browns
♦♦♦♦♦ SILVER AWARD
The Old Orchard Cottage, Holbeck, Worksop S80 3NF
T: (01909) 720659
F: (01909) 720659
E: Browns@holbeck.fsnet.co.uk
I: www.brownsholbeck.co.uk

HOLLINGTON
Staffordshire

The Raddle Inn ♦♦♦
Quarry Bank, Hollington, Stoke-on-Trent ST10 4HQ
T: (01889) 507278
F: (01889) 507520
E: peter@logcabin.co.uk
I: www.logcabin.co.uk

Reevsmoor ♦♦♦♦
Hoargate Lane, Hollington, Ashbourne DE6 3AG
T: (01335) 330318
F: (01335) 330978
E: hlivesey@aol.com

HOLMESFIELD
Derbyshire

Carpenter House ♦♦♦
Millthorpe, Holmesfield, Dronfield S18 7WH
T: (0114) 289 0307

HOLYMOORSIDE
Derbyshire

Burnell ♦♦♦♦
Baslow Road, Holymoorside, Chesterfield S42 7HJ
T: (01246) 567570
I: www.geocities.com/burnellbnb

HOPE
Derbyshire

Causeway House ♦♦♦
Back Street, Castleton, Hope Valley S33 8WE
T: (01433) 623291
E: susanbridget@aol.com
I: www.causewayhouse.co.uk

Underleigh House
♦♦♦♦♦ SILVER AWARD
Off Edale Road, Hope, Hope Valley S33 6RF
T: (01433) 621372
F: (01433) 621324
E: underleigh.house@btinternet.com
I: www.underleighhouse.co.uk

HOPE BAGOT
Shropshire

Croft Cottage ♦♦♦♦
Cumberley Lane, Hope Bagot, Ludlow SY8 3LJ
T: (01584) 890664
F: 0870 1299897
E: croft.cottage@virgin.net
I: www.croftcottage.org.uk

HOPE VALLEY
Derbyshire

The Rambler Country House Hotel ♦♦♦
Edale, Hope Valley, S33 7ZA
T: (01433) 670268
F: (01433) 670106
E: theramblers@dorbiere.co.uk
I: www.therambleinn.co.uk

The Rising Sun Hotel ♦♦♦♦
Thornhill Moor, Near Bamford, Hope Valley, S33 0AL
T: (01433) 651323
F: (01433) 651601
E: info@the-riding-sun.org
I: www.the-rising-sun.org

HOPTON CASTLE
Shropshire

Upper House Farm ♦♦♦♦
Hopton Castle, Craven Arms SY7 0QF
T: (01547) 530319
I: www.go2.co.uk/upperhouse

HORSLEY
Derbyshire

Horsley Lodge
♦♦♦♦ SILVER AWARD
Smalley Mill Road, Horsley, Derby DE21 5BL
T: (01332) 780838
F: (01332) 781118
E: enquiries@horsleylodge.co.uk
I: www.horsleylodge.co.uk

HORTON
Staffordshire

Croft Meadows Farm ♦♦♦
Horton, Leek ST13 8QE
T: (01782) 513039

HULME END
Staffordshire

Raikes Farm ♦♦♦
Raikes, Hulme End, Buxton SK17 0HJ
T: (01298) 84344
F: (01298) 84344

Riverside
Rating Applied For
Hulme End, Buxton SK17 0EZ
T: (01298) 84474
F: (01298) 84474
E: roger@riversidevilla.co.uk
I: www.riversidevilla.co.uk

HUMBERSTONE
Leicestershire

The Squirrels ♦♦♦
9 Widford Close, Humberstone, Leicester LE5 0AN
T: (0116) 2202894
F: (0116) 2768424

HUNTLEY
Gloucestershire

Birdwood Villa Farm ♦♦
Main Road, Birdwood, Huntley, Gloucester GL19 3EQ
T: (01452) 750451
E: mking@farmersweekly.net

Forest Gate ♦♦♦
Huntley, Gloucester GL19 3EU
T: (01452) 831192
F: (01452) 831192
E: forest.gate@huntley-glos.demon.co.uk
I: www.huntley-glos.demon.co.uk

The Kings Head Inn ♦♦♦
Birdwood, Huntley, Gloucester GL19 3EF
T: (01452) 750348
F: (01452) 750348

HUSBANDS BOSWORTH
Leicestershire

Mrs Armitage's ♦♦
31-33 High Street, Husbands Bosworth, Lutterworth LE17 6LJ
T: (01858) 880066

IDRIDGEHAY
Derbyshire

Millbank Cottage Bed and Breakfast ♦♦♦♦
Idridgehay, Belper DE56 2SH
T: (01629) 823 161

ILAM
Staffordshire

Beechenhill Farm
♦♦♦♦ SILVER AWARD
Ilam, Ashbourne DE6 2BD
T: (01335) 310274
F: (01335) 310274
E: beechenhill@btinternet.com
I: www.beechenhill.co.uk

Throwley Hall ♦♦♦♦
Ilam, Ashbourne DE6 2BB
T: (01538) 308202
F: (01538) 308243
E: throwleyhall@talk21.com
I: www.throwleyhallfarm.co.uk

INKBERROW
Worcestershire

Bulls Head Inn ♦♦♦
The Village Green, Inkberrow, Worcester WR7 4DY
T: (01386) 792233
F: (01386) 793090

IRONBRIDGE
Shropshire

Bird in Hand Inn ♦♦♦
Waterloo Street, Ironbridge, Telford TF8 7HG
T: (01952) 432226

Bridge House
♦♦♦♦♦ SILVER AWARD
Buildwas, Telford TF8 7BN
T: (01952) 432105
F: (01952) 432105
E: janethedges@talk21.com
I: www.smoothhound.co.uk/hotels/bridgehs.html

Bridge View ♦♦♦♦
10 Tontine Hill, Ironbridge, Telford TF8 7AL
T: (01952) 432541
F: (01952) 433405
I: www.ironbridgeview.co.uk

The Calcutts House ♦♦♦
Jackfield, Ironbridge, Telford TF8 7LH
T: (01952) 882631
F: (01952) 882951
E: alan&linda@calcuttshouse.co.uk
I: www.calcuttshouse.co.uk

Coalbrookdale Villa
♦♦♦♦ SILVER AWARD
Paradise, Coalbrookdale, Ironbridge, Telford TF8 7NR
T: (01952) 433450
F: (01952) 433450
E: coalbrookdalevilla@currantbun.com
I: www.coalbrookdale.f9.co.uk

The Firs Guest House ♦♦♦
32 Buildwas Road, Ironbridge, Telford TF8 7BJ
T: (01952) 432121
F: (01952) 433010

The Golden Ball Inn ♦♦♦♦
Newbridge Road, Ironbridge, Telford TF8 7BA
T: (01952) 432179
F: (01952) 433123
E: matrowland@hotmail.com
I: www.goldenballinn.com

Greenways Guest House
♦♦♦♦
57 High Street, Telford, Madeley, Telford TF7 5AT
T: (01952) 583118
F: (01952) 408777
E: greenwaysguesthouse@hotmail.com
I: www.greenwaysguesthouse.com

The Library House
♦♦♦♦♦ GOLD AWARD
11 Severn Bank, Ironbridge, Telford TF8 7AN
T: (01952) 432299
F: (01952) 433967
E: info@libraryhouse.com
I: www.libraryhouse.com

Lord Hill Guest House ♦♦
Duke Street, Broseley, TF12 5LU
T: (01952) 884270

The Malthouse ♦♦♦♦
The Wharfage, Ironbridge, Telford TF8 7NH
T: (01952) 433712
F: (01952) 433298
E: enquiries@malthousepubs.co.uk
I: malthousepubs.co.uk

Orchard House ♦♦♦
40 King Street, Broseley, TF12 5NA
T: (01952) 882684

Post Office House ♦♦♦
6 The Square, Ironbridge, Telford TF8 7AQ
T: (01952) 433201
F: (01952) 433582
E: Hunter@pohouse-ironbridge.fsnet.co.uk
I: www.pohouse-ironbridge.fsnet.co.uk

The Swan ♦♦♦♦
The Wharfage, Ironbridge, Telford TF8 7NH
T: (01952) 432306
F: (01952) 432994

Tontine Hotel ♦♦♦
The Square, Ironbridge, Telford TF8 7AL
T: (01952) 432127
F: (01952) 432094
E: tontinehotel@netscapeonline.co.uk
I: www.tontine-ironbridge.co.uk

Wharfage Cottage ♦♦♦
17 The Wharfage, Ironbridge, Telford TF8 7AW
T: (01952) 432721
F: (01952) 432639

Ye Olde Robin Hood Inn ♦♦♦
33 Waterloo Street, Ironbridge, Telford TF8 7HQ
T: (01952) 433100

KEGWORTH
Leicestershire

The Coach House
Rating Applied For
35 High Street, Kegworth, Derby DE74 2DA
T: (01509) 674131
I: www.kegworthvillage.com/coachhouse

KEMERTON
Worcestershire

Wings Cottage
♦♦♦♦ GOLD AWARD
Wing Lane, Kemerton, Tewkesbury GL20 7JG
T: (01386) 725273
F: (01386) 725273
E: jway@wingscottage.demon.co.uk
I: www.wingscottage.demon.co.uk/index.html

KEMPSEY
Worcestershire

Anchor Inn ♦♦
69 Main Road, Kempsey, Worcester WR5 3NB
T: (01905) 820411
E: gwenrig@netscapeonline.co.uk

Malbre Hotel ♦♦♦
Baynhall, Kempsey, Worcester WR5 3PA
T: (01905) 820412

KENILWORTH
Warwickshire

Abbey Guest House ♦♦♦♦
41 Station Road, Kenilworth, CV8 1JD
T: (01926) 512707
F: (01926) 859148
E: the-abbey@virgin.net

Avondale B & B ♦♦♦♦
18 Moseley Road, Kenilworth, CV8 2AQ
T: (01926) 859072

Bridgend ♦♦♦♦
15 Farmer Ward Road, Kenilworth, CV8 2DJ
T: (01926) 511995
E: bridgeendbb@hotmail.com

Castle Laurels Hotel
♦♦♦♦ SILVER AWARD
22 Castle Road, Kenilworth, CV8 1NG
T: (01926) 856179
F: (01926) 854954
E: moores22@aol.com
I: www.castlelaurelshotel.co.uk

The Cottage Inn ♦♦♦
36 Stoneleigh Road, Kenilworth, CV8 2GD
T: (01926) 853900
F: (01926) 856032

Enderley Guest House ♦♦♦♦
20 Queens Road, Kenilworth, CV8 1JQ
T: (01926) 855388
F: (01926) 850450
E: enderleyguesthouse@supanet.com

Ferndale Guest House ♦♦♦♦
45 Priory Road, Kenilworth, CV8 1LL
T: (01926) 853214
F: (01926) 858336
E: derekwilson1@canpuserve.com

Howden House ♦♦
170 Warwick Road, Kenilworth, CV8 1HS
T: (01926) 850310

The Old Bakery Hotel ♦♦♦♦
12 High Street, Kenilworth, CV8 1LZ
T: (01926) 864111
F: (01926) 864127
E: info@theoldbakeryhotel.co.uk
I: www.theoldbakeryhotel.co.uk

The Priory Guesthouse ♦♦♦
58 Priory Road, Kenilworth, CV8 1LQ
T: (01926) 856173
F: (01926) 856173

The Quince House ♦♦♦♦
29 Moseley Road, Kenilworth, CV8 2AR
T: (01926) 858652
E: georgina.thomas@ntlworld.com
I: www.balldesi.demon.co.uk/b_b.html

Victoria Lodge Hotel ♦♦♦♦
180 Warwick Road, Kenilworth, CV8 1HU
T: (01926) 512020
F: (01926) 858703
E: info@victorialodgehotel.co.uk
I: www.victorialodgehotel.co.uk

KETTERING
Northamptonshire

Dairy Farm ♦♦♦♦
Cranford St Andrew, Kettering NN14 4AQ
T: (01536) 330273

Hawthorn House (Private) Hotel ♦♦♦
2 Hawthorn Road, Kettering, NN15 7HS
T: (01536) 482513
F: (01536) 513121

Pennels Guesthouse ♦♦♦
175 Beatrice Road, Kettering, NN16 9QR
T: (01536) 481940
F: (01536) 410798
E: pennelsgh@aol.com
I: www.members.aol.com/pennelsgh

2 Wilkie Close
♦♦♦♦ SILVER AWARD
Kettering, NN15 7RD
T: (01536) 310270
F: (01536) 310270
E: roxmere@aol.com

KEXBY
Lincolnshire

The Grange ♦♦♦
Kexby, Gainsborough DN21 5PJ
T: (01427) 788265

KEYWORTH
Nottinghamshire

Flinders Farm Bed & Breakfast
♦♦♦♦
33 Main Street, Keyworth, Nottingham NG12 5HA
T: (0115) 937 2352

KIDDERMINSTER
Worcestershire

Bewdley Hill House ♦♦♦♦
8 Bewdley Hill, Kidderminster, DY11 6BS
T: (01562) 60473
F: (01562) 60473
E: judy-john@bewdleyhillhouse.fsnet.co.uk

Collingdale Private Hotel ♦♦♦
197 Comberton Road, Kidderminster, DY10 1UE
T: (01562) 515460
E: collingdale@sharvell.fsnet.co.uk
I: mysite.freeserve.com/collingdalehotel

Garden Cottages
♦♦♦♦ GOLD AWARD
Crossway Green, Hartlebury, Kidderminster DY13 9SJ
T: (01299) 250626
F: (01299) 250626
E: mamod@btinternet.com
I: gardencottages.co.uk

Hollies Farm Cottage ♦♦♦♦
Hollies Lane, Franche, Kidderminster, DY11 5RW
T: (01562) 745677
F: (01562) 824580
E: pete@top-floor.fsbusiness.co.uk

Victoria Hotel ♦♦♦
15 Comberton Road, Kidderminster, DY10 1UA
T: (01562) 67240
F: (01562) 67240
E: victoriakidderminster@yahoo.co.uk

KILCOT
Gloucestershire

Withyland Heights Bed and Breakfast ♦♦♦
Withyland Heights, Beavans Hill, Kilcot, Newent GL18 1PG
T: (01989) 720582
F: (01989) 720238
E: withyland@farming.co.uk
I: www.withylandheights.co.uk

KILSBY
Northamptonshire

The Hollies Farm ♦♦♦
Main Road, Kilsby, CV23 8XR
T: (01788) 822629

KINETON
Warwickshire

The Castle ♦♦♦
Edgehill, Kineton, Warwick OX15 6DJ
T: (01295) 670255
F: (01295) 670521
E: castleedgehill@btopenworld.com
I: www.thecastle-edgehill.co.uk

Swan Inn ♦♦♦
Banbury Street, Kineton, Kineton, Warwick CV35 0JS
T: (01926) 642517

KING'S CLIFFE
Northamptonshire

19 West Street ♦♦♦♦
King's Cliffe, Peterborough
PE8 6XB
T: (01780) 470365
F: (01780) 470623
E: kjhl-dixon@hotmail.com
I: www.kingjohnhuntinglodge.com

KINGS CAPLE
Herefordshire

Lion House ♦♦♦
Kings Caple, Hereford HR1 4UQ
T: (01432) 840524
E: lionhouse2002@aol.com

Ruxton Farm ♦♦♦♦
Kings Caple, Hereford HR1 4TX
T: (01432) 840493
F: (01432) 840493

KINGSLAND
Herefordshire

The Buzzards ♦♦♦
Kingsland, Leominster HR6 9QE
T: (01568) 708941
E: booking@bakerpovey.co.uk
I: www.bakerpovey.co.uk

The Corners Inn
♦♦♦♦ SILVER AWARD
Kingsland, Leominster HR6 9RY
T: (01568) 708385
F: (01568) 709033
E: enq@cornersinn.co.uk
I: www.cornersinn.co.uk

KINGSTONE
Herefordshire

Mill Orchard
♦♦♦♦ GOLD AWARD
Kingstone, Hereford HR2 9ES
T: (01981) 250326
F: (01981) 250520
E: cleveland@millorchard.co.uk
I: www.millorchard.co.uk

Webton Court Farmhouse ♦♦
Kingstone, Hereford HR2 9NF
T: (01981) 250220
F: (01981) 250220
E: juliet@pudgefsnet.co.uk

KINLET
Worcestershire

Catsley Farm ♦♦
Kinlet, Bewdley DY12 3AP
T: (01299) 841323

KINVER
Staffordshire

Anchor Hotel ♦♦♦
Dark Lane, Kinver, Stourbridge
DY7 6NR
T: (01384) 872085
F: (01384) 878824
E: anchorhotel@kinver2000.freeserve.co.uk
I: www.anchorhotel.com

KISLINGBURY
Northamptonshire

The Elms ♦♦♦
Kislingbury, Northampton
NN7 4AH
T: (01604) 830326

KNOCKDOWN
Gloucestershire

Avenue Farm ♦♦♦
Knockdown, Tetbury GL8 8QY
T: (01454) 238207
F: (01454) 238033
E: sonjames@breathemail.net
I: www.glosfarmhols.co.uk

KNOWLE
West Midlands

Ivy House Guest House ♦♦♦
Warwick Road, Heronfield,
Knowle, Solihull B93 0EB
T: (01564) 770247
F: (01564) 778063
E: email@ivy-guest-house.freeserve.co.uk
I: www.smoothhound.co.uk/hotels/ivyguest.html

LAMBLEY
Nottinghamshire

Magnolia Guest House ♦♦♦♦
22 Spring Lane, Lambley,
Nottingham NG4 4PH
T: (0115) 9314404
F: (0115) 9314582
E: magnoliahouse@lineone.net

LAXTON
Nottinghamshire

Lilac Farm ♦♦♦
Laxton, Newark NG22 0NX
T: (01777) 870376
F: (01777) 870376

Manor Farm ♦♦♦
Moorhouse Road, Laxton,
Newark NG22 0NU
T: (01777) 870417

Spanhoe Lodge
♦♦♦♦ GOLD AWARD
Harringworth Road, Laxton,
Corby NN17 3AT
T: (01780) 450328
F: (01780) 450328
E: jennie.spanhoe@virgin.net
I: www.spanhoelodge.co.uk

LEA
Herefordshire

Forest Edge
♦♦♦♦ GOLD AWARD
4 Noden Drive, Lea, Ross-on-Wye HR9 7NB
T: (01989) 750682
E: don@wood11.freeserve.co.uk
I: www.wood11.freeserve.co.uk

Warren Farm ♦♦♦♦
Warren Lane, Lea, Ross-on-Wye
HR9 7LT
T: (01989) 750272
F: (01989) 750272

LEA MARSTON
West Midlands

Reindeer Park Lodge ♦♦♦♦
Kingsbury Road, Lea Marston,
Sutton Coldfield B76 0DE
T: (01675) 470811
F: (01675) 470710

LEADENHAM
Lincolnshire

George Hotel ♦♦♦
High Street, Leadenham, Lincoln
LN5 0PN
T: (01400) 272251
F: (01400) 272091
E: the-george-hotel@willgoose.freeserve.co.uk

LEAMINGTON SPA
Warwickshire

Adelaide ♦♦♦
15 Adelaide Road, Leamington
Spa, CV31 3PN
T: (01926) 450633
F: (01926) 450633

Almond House ♦♦♦♦
8 Parklands Avenue, Lillington,
Leamington Spa, CV32 7BA
T: (01926) 424052

Avenue Lodge Guest House ♦♦♦
61 Avenue Road, Leamington
Spa, CV31 3PF
T: (01926) 338555
F: (01926) 338555

Buckland Lodge Hotel ♦♦♦
35 Avenue Road, Leamington
Spa, CV31 3PG
T: (01926) 423843
F: (01926) 423843
E: buckland.lodge1@btinternet.com
I: www.Buckland-Lodge.co.uk.

Bungalow Farm ♦♦♦♦
Windmill Hill, Cubbington,
Leamington Spa, CV32 7LW
T: (01926) 423276
E: sheila@lewitt.freeserve.co.uk

Charnwood Guest House ♦♦♦
47 Avenue Road, Leamington
Spa, CV31 3PF
T: (01926) 831074
F: (01926) 831074

8 Clarendon Crescent
♦♦♦♦ SILVER AWARD
Leamington Spa, CV32 5NR
T: (01926) 429840
F: (01926) 424641
E: lawson@lawson71.fsnet.co.uk
I: www.shakespeare-country.co.uk

The Coach House ♦♦♦♦
Snowford Hall Farm,
Hunningham, Leamington Spa,
CV33 9ES
T: (01926) 632297
F: (01926) 633599
E: the_coach_house@lineone.net
I: lineone.net/~the_coach_house

Corkill Bed and Breakfast ♦♦♦
27 Newbold Street, Leamington
Spa, CV32 4HN
T: (01926) 336303
F: (01926) 336303
E: mrscorkill@aol.com

The Dell Guesthouse ♦♦♦
8 Warwick Place, Leamington
Spa, CV32 5BJ
T: (01926) 422784
F: (01926) 422784
E: dellguesthouse@virgin.net
I: www.dellguesthouse.co.uk

5 The Grange ♦♦♦
Cubbington, Leamington Spa,
CV32 7LE
T: (01926) 744762

Hedley Villa Guest House ♦♦♦
31 Russell Terrace, Leamington
Spa, CV31 1EZ
T: (01926) 424504
F: (01926) 745801
E: pat.ashfield@ntlworld.com
I: www.hedleyvilla.freeserve.co.uk

Hill Farm ♦♦♦♦
Lewis Road, Radford Semele,
Leamington Spa CV31 1UX
T: (01926) 337571
E: rebecca@hillfarm3000.fsnet.co.uk

Lansdowne Hotel ♦♦♦♦
87 Clarendon Street,
Leamington Spa, CV32 4PF
T: (01926) 450505
F: (01926) 421313
E: thelansdowne@cwcom.net
I: www.thelansdowne.cwc.net

4 Lillington Road ♦♦♦
Leamington Spa, CV32 5YR
T: (01926) 429244
E: pauline.burton@btinternet.com

Milverton House Hotel ♦♦♦♦
1 Milverton Terrace, Leamington
Spa, CV32 5BE
T: (01926) 428335
F: (01926) 428335

Trendway Guest House ♦♦♦
45 Avenue Road, Leamington
Spa, CV31 3PF
T: (01926) 316644
F: (01926) 337506

Victoria Park Hotel ♦♦♦♦
12 Adelaide Road, Leamington
Spa, CV31 3PW
T: (01926) 424195
F: (01926) 421521
E: info@victoriaparkhotelleamingtonspa.co.uk
I: www.victoriaparkhotelleamingtonspa.co.uk

The Willis ♦♦♦
11 Eastnor Grove, Leamington
Spa, CV31 1LD
T: (01926) 425820

Wymondley Lodge
♦♦♦♦♦ SILVER AWARD
8 Adelaide Road, Leamington
Spa, CV31 3PW
T: (01926) 882669
F: (01926) 882669

York House Hotel ♦♦♦
9 York Road, Leamington Spa,
CV31 3PR
T: (01926) 424671
F: (01926) 832272
E: York1@mwfree.net

LECHLADE
Gloucestershire

Apple Tree Guest House ♦♦♦
Buscot, Faringdon SN7 8DA
T: (01367) 252592
E: emreay@aol.com

Cambrai Lodge ♦♦♦♦
Oak Street, Lechlade, GL7 3AY
T: (01367) 253173

New Inn Hotel ♦♦♦
Market Square, Lechlade-on-Thames, Lechlade, GL7 3AB
T: (01367) 252296
F: (01367) 252315
E: info@newinnhotel.com
I: www.newinnhotel.co.uk

LEDBURY
Herefordshire

Brook House ♦♦♦♦
Birtsmorton, Malvern WR13 6AF
T: (01531) 650664
F: (01531) 650664
E: maryd@lineone.net

Church Farm ♦♦♦
Coddington, Ledbury HR8 1JJ
T: (01531) 640271

The Hopton Arms ♦♦♦
Ashperton, Ledbury, HR8 2SE
T: (01531) 670520
E: peter@hoptonarms.co.uk
I: www.hoptonarms.co.uk

Little Marcle Court ♦♦♦♦
Little Marcle, Ledbury, HR8 2LB
T: (01531) 670936

Mainstone House ♦♦♦
Trumpet, Ledbury, HR8 2RA
T: (01531) 670230

Wall Hills Country Guest House ♦♦♦♦
Hereford Road, Ledbury,
HR8 2PR
T: (01531) 632833
I: www.smoothhound.co.uk/hotels/wallhill.html

LEEK
Staffordshire

Abbey Inn ♦♦♦
Abbey Green Road, Leek,
ST13 8SA
T: (01538) 382865
F: (01538) 398604
E: martin@abbeyinn.co.uk
I: www.abbeyinn.co.uk

Beechfields ♦♦♦♦
Park Road, Leek, ST13 8JS
T: (01538) 372825
E: judith@beech-fields.fsnet.co.uk
I: www.beech-fields.fsnet.co.uk

The Green Man ♦♦♦
38 Compton, Leek, ST13 5NH
T: (01538) 388084
I: www.greenman-guesthouse.co.uk

The Hatcheries ♦♦♦
Church Lane, Leek, ST13 5EX
T: (01538) 399552
F: (01538) 399552
E: the.hatcheries@faxvia.net
I: www.thehatcheries.co.uk

Little Brookhouse Farm ♦♦♦♦
Cheddleton, Leek ST13 7DF
T: (01538) 360350

New House Farm ♦♦♦
Bottomhouse, Leek, ST13 7PA
T: (01538) 304350
F: (01538) 304338
E: newhousefarm@btinternet.com

Peak Weavers Hotel ♦♦♦
21 King Street, Leek, ST13 5NW
T: (01538) 383729
F: (01538) 387475
E: peak.weavers@virgin.net
I: www.peakweavershotel.com

Prospect House ♦♦♦♦
334 Cheadle Road, Cheddleton,
Leek ST13 7BW
T: (01782) 550639
E: prospect@talk21.com
I: www.prospecthouseleek.co.uk

LEICESTER
Leicestershire

Abinger House B&B Rating Applied For
175 Hinckley Road, Leicester,
LE3 0TF
T: (0116) 255 4674
F: (0116) 255 4674
E: bobwel1234@aol.com

Beaumaris Guesthouse ♦♦♦
18 Westcotes Drive, Leicester,
LE3 0QR
T: (0116) 254 0261
E: beaumarisgh@talk21.com

Burlington Hotel ♦♦♦
Elmfield Avenue, Stoneygate,
Leicester, LE2 1RB
T: (0116) 270 5112
F: (0116) 270 4207
E: welcome@burlingtonhotel.co.uk
I: www.burlingtonhotel.co.uk

Croft Hotel ♦♦♦
3 Stanley Road, Leicester,
LE2 1RF
T: (0116) 270 3220
F: (0116) 270 3220
E: crofthotel@hotmail.com

Glenfield Lodge Hotel ♦
4 Glenfield Road, Leicester,
LE3 6AP
T: (0116) 262 7554

Scotia Hotel ♦♦♦
10 Westcotes Drive, Leicester,
LE3 0QR
T: (0116) 254 9200
F: (0116) 254 9200
E: scotiahotel@hotmail.com

South Fork Guesthouse ♦♦♦
464-466 Narborough Road,
Leicester, LE3 2FT
T: (0116) 2999960
F: (0116) 2994332
E: southfork@ntlworld.com

Spindle Lodge Hotel ♦♦♦
2 West Walk, Leicester, LE1 7NA
T: (0116) 233 8801
F: (0116) 233 8804
E: spindlelodgeleicester@orange.net
I: www.smoothhound.co.uk/hotels/spindle.html

LEIGH SINTON
Worcestershire

Chirkenhill ♦♦♦♦
Leigh Sinton, Malvern
WR13 5DE
T: (01886) 832205
E: wenden@eidosnet.co.uk

LEINTWARDINE
Herefordshire

Lower House ♦♦♦♦ SILVER AWARD
Adforton, Leintwardine, Craven
Arms SY7 0NF
T: (01568) 770223
F: (01568) 770592
E: cutler@sy7.com
I: www.sy7.com/lowerhouse

The Wardens ♦♦♦♦
Watling Street, Leintwardine,
Craven Arms SY7 0LL
T: (01547) 540498
F: (01547) 540500
E: janewells@supanet.com
I: www.shropshiretourism.com

LEOMINSTER
Herefordshire

Bedford House ♦♦♦
Dilwyn, Hereford HR4 8JJ
T: (01544) 388260

Bramlea ♦♦♦
Barons Cross Road, Leominster,
HR6 8RW
T: (01568) 613406
F: (01568) 613406
E: lesbramlea@netlineUK.net

Chesfield ♦♦♦
112 South Street, Leominster,
HR6 8JF
T: (01568) 613204

Copper Hall ♦♦♦♦
South Street, Leominster,
HR6 8JN
T: (01568) 611622
E: sccrick@copperhall.freeserve.co.uk

Highfield ♦♦♦♦
Ivington Road, Newtown,
Leominster, HR6 8QD
T: (01568) 613216
E: info@stay-at-highfield.co.uk
I: www.stay-at-highfield.co.uk

Highgate House ♦♦♦♦
29 Hereford Road, Leominster,
HR6 8JS
T: (01568) 614562
F: (01568) 614562
E: highgatehouse@easicom.com

Home Farm ♦♦♦♦
Bircher, Leominster HR6 0AX
T: (01568) 780525

Little Bury Farm ♦♦♦
Luston, Leominster, HR6 0EB
T: (01568) 611575

The Paddock ♦♦♦♦ GOLD AWARD
Shobdon, Leominster, HR6 9NQ
T: (01568) 708176
F: (01568) 708829
E: thepaddock@talk21.com

Rossendale Guesthouse ♦♦♦
46 Broad Street, Leominster,
HR6 8BS
T: (01568) 612464

Tyn-Y-Coed ♦♦♦
Shobdon, Leominster, HR6 9NY
T: (01568) 708277
F: (01568) 708277
E: jandrews@shobdondesign.kc3.co.uk

LICHFIELD
Staffordshire

Altair House ♦♦♦
21 Shakespeare Avenue,
Lichfield, WS14 9BE
T: (01543) 252900

32 Beacon Street ♦♦♦♦
Lichfield, WS13 7AJ
T: (01543) 262378

Chimneys ♦♦♦♦
26 Friary Avenue, Lichfield,
WS13 6QQ
T: (01543) 263370

8 The Close ♦♦♦♦
Lichfield, WS13 7LD
T: (01543) 418483
F: (01543) 418483
E: gilljones@talk21.com
I: www.ldb.co.uk/accommodation.htm

Coppers End Guest House ♦♦♦
Walsall Road, Muckley Corner,
Lichfield WS14 0BG
T: (01543) 372910
F: (01543) 360423
I: www.coppersendguesthouse.co.uk

Davolls Cottage ♦♦♦♦
156 Woodhouses Road,
Burntwood, Lichfield, WS7 9EL
T: (01543) 671250

16 Dimbles Lane ♦♦♦
Lichfield, WS13 7HW
T: (01543) 251107

The Farmhouse ♦♦♦♦ GOLD AWARD
Lysway Lane, Longdon Green,
Stafford, WS15 4PZ
T: (0121) 378 4552
F: (0121) 311 2915
E: jaynetdrury@aol.com
I: www.chez.com/thefarmhouse

Freeford Farm ♦♦♦
Freeford, Lichfield, WS14 9QL
T: (01543) 263330

4 Hayes View ♦♦♦
Lichfield, WS13 7BT
T: (01543) 253725

Holly House Bed and Breakfast ♦♦♦
198 Upper St John Street,
Lichfield, WS14 9EF
T: (01543) 263078

Pauline Duvals Bed and Breakfast ♦♦♦
21-23 Dam Street, The Bogey
Hole, Lichfield, WS13 6AE
T: (01543) 264303

Twenty Three The Close ♦♦♦♦
23 The Close, Lichfield,
WS13 7LD
T: (01543) 306140
E: charles.taylor@lichfield-cathedral.org

The White House ♦♦
Market Lane, Wall, Lichfield,
WS14 0AS
T: (01543) 480384

LINCOLN
Lincolnshire

AA and M Guesthouse ♦♦♦
79 Carholme Road, Lincoln,
LN1 1RT
T: (01522) 543736
F: (01522) 543736

Aaron Whisby Guest House ♦♦♦
262 West Parade, Lincoln,
LN1 1LY
T: (01522) 526930

Allwood Guesthouse ♦♦
258 West Parade, Lincoln,
LN1 1LY
T: (01522) 887868

Damon's Motel ♦♦♦♦
997 Doddington Road, Lincoln,
LN6 3ES
T: (01522) 887733
F: (01522) 887734

Hamilton Hotel ♦♦
2 Hamilton Road, Lincoln,
LN5 8ED
T: (01522) 528243
F: (01522) 528243

Manor Farm Stables ♦♦♦♦
Broxholme, Lincoln, LN1 2NG
T: (01522) 704220
E: pfieldson@lineone.net

Manor House
♦♦♦♦ SILVER AWARD
Bracebridge Heath, Lincoln
LN4 2HW
T: (01522) 520825
F: (01522) 542418
E: mikescoley@farming.co.uk

Mayfield Guest House ♦♦♦
213 Yarborough Road, Lincoln, LN1 3NQ
T: (01522) 533732
F: (01522) 533732
E: stay@mayfieldguesthouse.co.uk
I: www.mayfieldhguesthouse.co.uk

Newport Cottage ♦♦♦♦
21 Newport, Lincoln, LN1 3DQ
T: (01522) 534470

Newport Guest House ♦♦♦
26-28 Newport, Lincoln, LN1 3DF
T: (01522) 528590
F: (01522) 542868
E: info@newportguesthouse.co.uk
I: www.newportguesthouse.co.uk

The Old Bakery Guesthouse
♦♦♦
26-28 Burton Road, Lincoln, LN1 3LB
T: (01522) 576057
E: oldbakery-guesthouse@ntlworld.com
I: www.theold-bakery.co.uk

Savill Guesthouse ♦♦♦♦
203 Yarborough Road, Lincoln, LN1 3NQ
T: (01522) 523261
E: vvn@themail.co.uk
I: www.savillguesthouse.co.uk

73 Station Road ♦♦♦
Branston, Lincoln, LN4 1LG
T: (01522) 828658

Tennyson Hotel ♦♦♦♦
7 South Park, Lincoln, LN5 8EN
T: (01522) 521624
F: (01522) 521355
E: tennyson.hotel@virgin.net
I: www.tennysonhotel.com

Truro House ♦♦♦♦
421 Newark Road, North Hykeham, Lincoln, LN6 9SP
T: (01522) 882073

Welbeck Cottage ♦♦♦
Meadow Lane, South Hykeham, Lincoln LN6 9PF
T: (01522) 692669
F: (01522) 692669
E: mad@wellbeck1.demon.co.uk

LINTON
Derbyshire

The Manor
♦♦♦♦ SILVER AWARD
Hillside Road, Linton, Swadlincote DE12 6RA
T: (01283) 761177
E: themanor@ukonline.co.uk

LITTLE BRINGTON
Northamptonshire

The Saracens Head ♦♦♦♦
Main Street, Little Brington, Northampton NN7 4HS
T: (01604) 770640
F: (01604) 770640

LITTLE BYTHAM
Lincolnshire

The Willoughby Arms ♦♦♦♦
Station Road, Little Bytham, Grantham NG33 4RA
T: (01780) 410276
F: (01780) 410190
E: willo@willoughbyarms.co.uk
I: www.willoughbyarms.co.uk

LITTLE COWARNE
Herefordshire

Three Horseshoes Inn ♦♦♦
Little Cowarne, Bromyard HR7 4RQ
T: (01885) 400276
F: (01885) 400276
I: www.threehorseshoes.co.uk

LITTLE HAYFIELD
Derbyshire

Lantern Pike Inn ♦♦♦
Glossop Road, Little Hayfield, High Peak SK22 2NG
T: (01663) 747590
F: (01663) 749045

LITTLE INKBERROW
Worcestershire

Perrymill Farm ♦♦♦
Little Inkberrow, Worcester WR7 4JX
T: (01386) 792177
F: (01386) 793449
E: alexander@estatesgazette.net

LITTLE SHURDINGTON
Gloucestershire

Sundown ♦♦♦
Whitelands Lane, Little Shurdington,Shurdington, Cheltenham GL51 5TX
T: (01242) 863353

LITTLE WENLOCK
Shropshire

Wenboro Cottage ♦♦♦
Church Lane, Little Wenlock, Telford TF6 5BB
T: (01952) 505573
E: rcarter@wenboro.freeserve.co.uk

LITTON
Derbyshire

Beacon House ♦♦♦♦
Litton, Buxton SK17 8QP
T: (01298) 871752

Hall Farm House ♦♦♦♦
Litton, Buxton SK17 8QP
T: (01298) 872172

LLANGROVE
Herefordshire

Prospect Place ♦♦♦
Llangrove, Ross-on-Wye HR9 6ET
T: (01989) 770596
E: prospectplacehr96et@btinternet.com

LLANWARNE
Herefordshire

The Lawns ♦♦♦♦
Llanwarne, Hereford HR2 8EN
T: (01981) 540351
E: elrah@breathemail.net
I: www.thelawnsbedandbreakfast.co.uk

LONG BUCKBY
Northamptonshire

Murcott Mill ♦♦♦
Murcott, Long Buckby, Northampton NN6 7QR
T: (01327) 842236
F: (01327) 844524
E: bhart6@compuserve.com

LONG CLAWSON
Leicestershire

Elms Farm ♦♦♦♦
East End, Long Clawson, Melton Mowbray LE14 4NG
T: (01664) 822395
F: (01664) 823399
E: elmsfarm@whittard.net
I: www.whittard.net

LONG COMPTON
Warwickshire

Butlers Road Farm ♦♦♦
Long Compton, Shipston-on-Stour CV36 5JZ
T: (01608) 684262
F: (01608) 684262
E: eileenwhittaker@easicom.com

Manor House Hotel & Restaurant ♦♦♦♦
Long Compton, Shipston-on-Stour CV36 5JJ
T: (01608) 684218
F: (01608) 684218
E: themanor@gleneldon.fsbusiness.co.uk
I: www.accofind.com

LONGBOROUGH
Gloucestershire

Luckley Farm Bed and Breakfast ♦♦♦
Luckley Farm, Longborough, Moreton-in-Marsh GL56 0RD
T: (01451) 870885
F: (01451) 831481
E: luckleyholidays@talk21.com
I: www.luckley-holidays.co.uk

LONGDON
Staffordshire

Grand Lodge ♦♦♦♦
Horsey Lane, Longdon, Rugeley WS15 4LW
T: (01543) 686103
F: (01543) 676266
E: grandlodge@edbroemt.demon.co.uk

LONGHOPE
Gloucestershire

New House Farm ♦♦♦
Barrel Lane, Aston Ingham, Longhope, GL17 0LS
T: (01452) 830484
F: (01452) 830484
E: scaldbrain@aol.com
I: www.newhousefarm-accommodation.co.uk

The Old Farm ♦♦♦♦
Barrel Lane, Longhope, GL17 0LR
T: (01452) 830252
F: (01452) 830255
E: lucy@the-old-farm.co.uk
I: www.the-old-farm.co.uk

Royal Spring Farm ♦♦♦♦
(A4136), Longhope, GL17 0PY
T: (01452) 830550

The Temple
♦♦♦♦♦ GOLD AWARD
Old Monmouth Road, Longhope, GL17 0NZ
T: (01452) 831011
F: (01452) 831776
E: tricia.ferguson@virgin.net
I: www.thetemple-longhope.co.uk

LONGNOR
Staffordshire

Crewe and Harpur Arms Hotel
♦♦♦
Longnor, Buxton SK17 0NS
T: (01298) 83205

LONGTOWN
Herefordshire

Olchon Cottage Farm ♦♦♦
Longtown, Hereford HR2 0NS
T: (01873) 860233
F: (01873) 860233
I: www.golden-valley.co.uk/Olchon

LOUGHBOROUGH
Leicestershire

The Beauchief Hotel ♦♦♦
29 Pinfold Gate, Loughborough, LE11 1BE
T: (01509) 268096
F: (01509) 268586
I: www.corushotels.co.uk/thebeauchief

Charnwood Lodge ♦♦♦♦
136 Leicester Road, Loughborough, LE11 2AQ
T: (01509) 211120
F: (01509) 211121
E: charnwoodlodge@charwat.freeserve.co.uk
I: www.charnwoodlodge.com

Demontfort Hotel ♦♦♦
88 Leicester Road, Loughborough, LE11 2AQ
T: (01509) 216061
F: (01509) 233667
E: thedemontforthotel@amserve.com
I: thedemontforthotel.co.uk

Forest Rise Hotel Ltd ♦♦♦
55-57 Forest Road, Loughborough, LE11 3NW
T: (01509) 215928
F: (01509) 210506

Garendon Park Hotel ♦♦♦
92 Leicester Road, Loughborough, LE11 2AQ
T: (01509) 236557
F: (01509) 265559
E: info@garendonparkhotel.co.uk
I: www.garendonparkhotel.co.uk

The Highbury Guesthouse
♦♦♦
146 Leicester Road, Loughborough, LE11 2AQ
T: (01509) 230545
F: (01509) 233086
E: emkhighbury@supanet.com
I: www.thehighburyguesthouse.co.uk

Holywell House ♦♦♦
40 Leicester Road, Loughborough, LE11 2AG
T: (01509) 267891
F: (01509) 214075
E: lezdes@holywellhouse.fsbusiness.co.uk
I: www.holywell.here.co.uk

Lane End Cottage ♦♦♦♦
45 School Lane, Old Woodhouse, Loughborough, LE12 8UJ
T: (01509) 890706
F: (01509) 890246
E: mary.hudson@talk21.com

The Lindens
Rating Applied For
22 Halstead Road, Mountsorrel, Loughborough, LE12 7HF
T: (0116) 2302163
F: (0116) 2302163

Lubcloud Farm Bed & Breakfast
♦♦♦♦ SILVER AWARD
Lubcloud Farm, Oaks In Charnwood, Loughborough, LE12 9YA
T: (01509) 503204
F: (01509) 651267

The Mountsorrel Hotel ♦♦♦♦
217 Loughborough Road, Mountsorrel, Loughborough LE12 7AR
T: (01509) 412627
F: (01509) 416105
E: info@mountsorrelhotel.co.uk
I: www.mountsorrelhotel.co.uk

New Life Guesthouse ♦♦♦
121 Ashby Road, Loughborough, LE11 3AB
T: (01509) 216699
F: (01509) 210020
E: jean-of-newlife@assureweb.com

Peachnook Guest House ♦♦
154 Ashby Road, Loughborough, LE11 3AG
T: (01509) 264390
I: www.SmoothHound.co.uk/hotels/peachnohtml

LOUTH
Lincolnshire

Masons Arms ♦♦♦
Cornmarket, Louth, LN11 9PY
T: (01507) 609525
F: 0870 7066450
E: justin@themasons.co.uk
I: www.themasons.co.uk

LOWER CATESBY
Northamptonshire

The Old Coach House
♦♦♦♦ SILVER AWARD
Lower Catesby, Daventry NN11 6LF
T: (01327) 310390
F: (01327) 312220
E: coachhouse@lowercatesby.co.uk
I: www.lowercatesby.co.uk

LOWER SLAUGHTER
Gloucestershire

Greenfingers ♦♦♦♦
Wyck Rissington Lane, Lower Slaughter, Cheltenham GL54 2EX
T: (01451) 821217

LOXLEY
Warwickshire

Elm Cottage ♦♦♦♦
Stratford Road, Loxley, Warwick CV35 9JW
T: (01789) 840609

LUBENHAM
Leicestershire

The Old Bakehouse ♦♦♦♦
9 The Green, Lubenham, Market Harborough LE16 9TD
T: (01858) 463401

LUDLOW
Shropshire

The Brakes
♦♦♦♦ SILVER AWARD
Downton, Ludlow, SY8 2LF
T: (01584) 856485
F: (01584) 856485
E: thebrakes@cwcom.net
I: www.ludlow.org.uk/brakes

Bull Hotel ♦♦♦
14 The Bull Ring, Ludlow, SY8 1AD
T: (01584) 873611
F: (01584) 873666
E: info@bull-ludlow.co.uk
I: www.bull-ludlow.co.uk

Castle View ♦♦♦
7 Castle View Terrace, Ludlow, SY8 2NG
T: (01584) 875592
F: (01584) 875592

Cecil Guest House ♦♦♦
Sheet Road, Ludlow, SY8 1LR
T: (01584) 872442
F: (01584) 872442

The Crown Inn
♦♦♦♦ SILVER AWARD
Hopton Wafers, Cleobury Mortimer, Kidderminster DY14 0NB
T: (01299) 270372
F: (01299) 271127
E: desk@crownathopton.co.uk
I: www.go2.co.uk/crownathopton

Eight Dinham ♦♦♦♦
Dinham, Ludlow, SY8 1EJ
T: (01584) 875661

Elsich Manor Cottage ♦♦♦
Seifton, Ludlow, SY8 2DL
T: (01584) 861406
F: (01584) 861406

Hen and Chickens Guesthouse ♦♦♦♦
103 Old Street, Ludlow, SY8 1NU
T: (01584) 874318
E: sally@hen-and-chickens.co.uk
I: www.hen-and-chickens.co.uk

Henwick House ♦♦♦
Gravel Hill, Ludlow, SY8 1QU
T: (01584) 873338

Longlands ♦♦♦
Woodhouse Lane, Richards Castle, Ludlow SY8 4EU
T: (01584) 831636
E: iankemsley@aol.com
I: www.ludlow.org.uk/longlands

Lower House Farm
♦♦♦♦ GOLD AWARD
Cleedownton, Ludlow, SY8 3EH
T: (01584) 823648
E: gsblack@talk21.com
I: www.ludlow.org.uk/lowerhouse

Manna Oak ♦♦♦♦
Mill Street, Ludlow, SY8 1BE
T: (01584) 873204

Mill House ♦♦♦
Squirrel Lane, Lower Ledwyche, Ludlow, SY8 4JX
T: (01584) 872837
E: millhousebnb@aol.com

Mr Underhills
♦♦♦♦♦ SILVER AWARD
Dinham Weir, Dinham, Ludlow, SY8 1EH
T: (01584) 874431
F: (01584) 874431
I: www.mr-underhills.co.uk

Mulberry House
Rating Applied For
10 Corve Street, Ludlow, Ludlow, SY8 1DA
T: (01584) 876765
F: (01584) 879871
E: bookings@tencorvestreet.co.uk
I: www.tencorvestreet.co.uk

Nelson Cottage ♦♦♦
Rocks Green, Ludlow, SY8 2DS
T: (01584) 878108
F: (01584) 878108
E: info@ludlow.uk.com
I: www.ludlow.uk.com

Number Twenty Eight
♦♦♦♦♦ GOLD AWARD
28 Lower Broad Street, Ludlow, SY8 1PQ
T: (01584) 876996
F: (01584) 876860
E: ross@no28.co.uk
I: www.no28.co.uk

Pengwern ♦♦♦♦
5 St Julians Avenue, Ludlow, Ludlow, SY8 1ET
T: (01584) 874635
F: (01584) 872649
E: butterdev@aol.com

Ravenscourt Manor
♦♦♦♦ GOLD AWARD
Woofferton, Ludlow SY8 4AL
T: (01584) 711905
F: (01584) 711905
I: www.virtual-shropshire.co.uk/ravenscourt-manor

The Wheatsheaf Inn ♦♦♦♦
Lower Broad Street, Ludlow, SY8 1PQ
T: (01584) 872980
F: (01584) 877990
E: karen.wheatsheaf@tinyworld.co.uk

LUSTON
Herefordshire

Knapp House ♦♦♦
Luston, Leominster HR6 0EB
T: (01568) 615705

Ladymeadow Farm ♦♦♦♦
Luston, Leominster HR6 0AS
T: (01568) 780262
E: ladymeadowfarm@agriplus.net

LUTTERWORTH
Leicestershire

The Greyhound Coaching Inn ♦♦♦
9 Market Street, Lutterworth, LE17 4EJ
T: (01455) 553307
F: (01455) 554558
E: bookings@greyhoundinn.fsnet.co.uk
I: www.greyhoundinn.co.uk

Orchard House ♦♦♦♦
Church Drive, Gilmorton, Lutterworth LE17 5LR
T: (01455) 559487
F: (01455) 553047
E: diholman@hotmail.com

LYDDINGTON
Rutland

Lydbrooke ♦♦♦♦
2 Colley Rise, Lyddington, Oakham, LE15 9LL
T: (01572) 821471
F: (01572) 821471
E: lydbrookebb@hotmail.com

LYONSHALL
Herefordshire

Penrhos Farm ♦♦♦♦
Lyonshall, Kington HR5 3LH
T: (01544) 231467
F: (01544) 340273
E: sallyw@totalise.co.uk
I: www.penrhosfarm.ukfarmers.com

MACKWORTH
Derbyshire

Thames House ♦♦♦♦
6 Thames Close, Mackworth, Derby DE22 4HT
T: (01332) 513526
F: (01332) 513526
E: jswarbrooke@aol.com

MADELEY
Staffordshire

Bar Hill House ♦♦♦♦
Bar Hill, Madeley, Crewe CW3 9QE
T: (01782) 752199
F: (01782) 750981
E: barhillbb@hotmail.com
I: www.touristnet.com

MALTBY LE MARSH
Lincolnshire

Farmhouse Bed and Breakfast ♦♦♦
Grange Farm, Maltby le Marsh, Alford LN13 0JP
T: (01507) 450267
F: (01507) 450180
E: graves_ann@hotmail.co.uk
I: www.grange-farmhouse.co.uk

MALVERN
Worcestershire

Berewe Court ♦♦♦♦
Whiting Lane, Berrow, Malvern WR13 6AY
T: (01531) 650250
E: susanmaryprice@hotmail.com
I: www.ourworcester.net/berewecourt

Cannara ♦♦♦
147 Barnards Green Road, Malvern, WR14 3LT
T: (01684) 564418
F: (01684) 564418

Clevelands ♦♦♦
41 Alexandra Road, Malvern, WR14 1HE
T: (01684) 572164
F: (01684) 576691
E: jonmargstocks@aol.com

Como House ♦♦♦
Como Road, Malvern, WR14 2TH
T: (01684) 561486
E: kevin@como-house.freeserve.co.uk

Cowleigh Park Farm ♦♦♦♦
Cowleigh Road, Malvern, WR13 5HJ
T: (01684) 566750
E: cowleighpark@ukonline.co.uk

Edgeworth ♦♦♦
4 Carlton Road, Malvern, WR14 1HH
T: (01684) 572565

The Firs ♦♦♦
243 West Malvern Road, Malvern, WR14 4BE
T: (01684) 564016
F: (01684) 564016
E: valshearerthefirs@hotmail.com
I: www.smoothhound.co.uk/hotels/firs.html

Guarlford Grange
♦♦♦♦ SILVER AWARD
11 Guarlford Road, Malvern, WR14 3QW
T: (01684) 575996
F: (01684) 575996

Harcourt Cottage ♦♦♦
252 West Malvern Road, West Malvern, Malvern, WR14 4DQ
T: (01684) 574561
F: (01684) 574561
E: harcourtcottage@aol.com

Homestead Lodge ♦♦♦
25 Somers Park Avenue, Malvern, WR14 1SE
T: (01684) 573094
F: (01684) 573094
E: trant@homesteadlodge.freeserve.co.uk
I: www.homesteadlodge.freeserve.co.uk

Mellor Heights ♦♦♦
46A West Malvern Road, Malvern, WR14 4NA
T: (01684) 565105
F: (01684) 565105
E: mellorheights@onetel.net.uk

Montrose Hotel ♦♦♦
23 Graham Road, Malvern, WR14 2HU
T: (01684) 572335
F: (01684) 575 707

Priory Holme ♦♦♦♦
18 Avenue Road, Malvern, WR14 3AR
T: (01684) 568455

Rathlin ♦♦♦♦
1 Carlton Road, Malvern, WR14 1HH
T: (01684) 572491
E: guiver@rathlin-malvern.fsnet.co.uk

The Red Gate
♦♦♦♦ SILVER AWARD
32 Avenue Road, Malvern, WR14 3BJ
T: (01684) 565013
F: (01684) 565013
E: enquires@the-red-gate.co.uk
I: www.SmoothHound.co.uk/shs.html

Rosendale The View ♦♦♦♦
66 Worcester Road, Malvern, WR14 1NU
T: (01684) 566159

Sunnydale
♦♦♦♦ SILVER AWARD
69 Tanhouse Lane, Malvern, WR14 1LQ
T: (01886) 832066

Wyche Keep Country House
♦♦♦♦ SILVER AWARD
22 Wyche Road, Malvern, WR14 4EG
T: (01684) 567018
F: (01684) 892304
E: wychekeep@aol.com
I: www.jks.org/wychekeep

MANSFIELD
Nottinghamshire

Blue Barn Farm ♦♦♦
Nether Langwith, Mansfield NG20 9JD
T: (01623) 742248
F: (01623) 742248
E: ibbotsonbluebarn@netscape-online.co.uk

MARCHINGTON
Staffordshire

Forest Hills ♦♦♦♦
Moisty Lane, Marchington, Uttoxeter ST14 8JY
T: (01283) 820447

MARKET DRAYTON
Shropshire

Crofton ♦♦♦♦
80 Rowan Road, Market Drayton, TF9 1RR
T: (01630) 655484
F: (01630) 655484
E: eric.russell@ci24.net

Heath Farm Bed and Breakfast ♦♦
Heath Farm, Wellington Road, Hodnet, Market Drayton, TF9 3JJ
T: (01630) 685570
F: (01630) 685570
E: adrysdale@telco4u.net
I: www.freeweb.telco4u.net/heathfarm

Milford ♦♦♦♦
Adderley Road, Market Drayton, TF9 3SW
T: (01630) 655249

Millstone ♦♦♦♦
Adderley Road, Market Drayton, TF9 3SW
T: (01630) 657584

Red House Cottage ♦♦♦
31 Shropshire Street, Market Drayton, TF9 3DA
T: (01630) 655206

Stafford Court Hotel ♦♦♦
Stafford Street, Market Drayton, TF9 1HY
T: (01630) 652646
F: (01630) 658496
I: www.staffordcourthotel.co.uk

The Tudor House Hotel and Restaurant♦♦♦
1 Cheshire Street, Market Drayton, TF9 1PD
T: (01630) 657523
F: (01630) 657806
E: sugarloaf@globalnet.co.uk

Willow House ♦♦♦♦
Shrewsbury Road, Tern Hill, Market Drayton, TF9 3PX
T: (01630) 638326
F: (01630) 638326
E: moira@willowhouse.free-online.co.uk

MARKET HARBOROUGH
Leicestershire

The George at Great Oxendon ♦♦♦♦
Great Oxendon, Market Harborough LE16 8NA
T: (01858) 465205
F: (01858) 465205

Hunters Lodge ♦♦♦♦
Gumley, Market Harborough LE16 7RT
T: (0116) 279 3744
F: (0116) 279 3855
E: info@hunterslodgefoxton.co.uk
I: www.hunterslodgefoxton.co.uk

The Old House ♦♦♦
Church Street, Wilbarston, Market Harborough LE16 8QG
T: (01536) 771724
F: (01536) 771622
E: oldhousebb@aol.com.uk

MARKET RASEN
Lincolnshire

Beechwood Guesthouse ♦♦♦♦
54 Willingham Road, Market Rasen, LN8 3DX
T: (01673) 844043
E: beechwoodgh@aol.com
I: www.beechwoodguesthouse.co.uk

The Dell Bed & Breakfast ♦♦♦♦
Private Lane, Normanby by Spital, Market Rasen, LN8 2HF
T: (01673) 878514

Sunnybrow ♦♦♦♦
Ludford Road, Binbrook, Market Rasen LN8 6DR
T: (01472) 398181
E: sunnysggp@btinternet.com
I: www.smoothhound.co.uk

Waveney Cottage Guesthouse ♦♦♦♦
Willingham Road, Market Rasen, LN8 3DN
T: (01673) 843236
F: (01673) 843236
E: vacancies@waveneycottage.co.uk
I: www.waveneycottage.co.uk

MARSTON
Lincolnshire

Gelston Grange Farm ♦♦♦♦
Marston, Grantham NG32 2AQ
T: (01400) 250281
F: (01400) 250281

MARSTON MONTGOMERY
Derbyshire

The Old Barn ♦♦♦♦
Marston Montgomery, Ashbourne DE6 2FF
T: (01889) 590848
F: (01889) 590698

MARTIN HUSSINGTREE
Worcestershire

Knoll Farm Bed and Breakfast ♦♦♦
Knoll Farm, Ladywood Road, Martin Hussingtree, Worcester WR3 7SX
T: (01905) 455565
E: aligriggs@hotmail.com

MARTLEY
Worcestershire

Admiral Rodney Inn ♦♦♦♦
Berrow Green, Martley, Worcester WR6 6PL
T: (01886) 821375
F: (01886) 821375
E: admiral@biimember.net

The Chandlery ♦♦♦♦
Worcester Road, Martley, Worcester WR6 6QA
T: (01886) 888318
F: (01886) 889047
E: john.nicklin@virgin.net
I: www.chandleybandb.co.uk

MATLOCK
Derbyshire

Bank House
Rating Applied For
12 Snitterton Road, Matlock, DE4 3LZ
T: (01629) 56101
F: (01629) 56101
E: jennyderbydales@hotmail.com

Derwent House ♦♦♦
Knowleston Place, Matlock, DE4 3BU
T: (01629) 584681
F: (01629) 55331
E: stay@derwenthouse.co.uk
I: www.derwenthouse.co.uk

Edgemount ♦♦
16 Edge Road, Matlock, DE4 3NH
T: (01629) 584787

Ellen House ♦♦♦♦
37 Snitterton Road, Matlock, DE4 3LZ
T: (01629) 55584

Home Farm ♦♦♦
Ible, Grange Mill, Matlock, DE4 4HS
T: (01629) 650349

Jackson Tor House Hotel ♦♦♦
76 Jackson Road, Matlock, DE4 3JQ
T: (01629) 582348
F: (01629) 582348
E: jacksontorhotel@uk2.net
I: www.jacksontorhotel.co.uk

Riverbank House ♦♦♦♦
Derwent Avenue, (Off Old English Road), Matlock, DE4 3LX
T: (01629) 582593
E: bookings@riverbankhouse.co.uk
I: www.riverbankhouse.co.uk

Robertswood Guesthouse
♦♦♦♦♦ GOLD AWARD
Farley Hill, Matlock, DE4 3LL
T: (01629) 55642
F: (01629) 55642
E: robertswood@supanet.com
I: www.robertswood.com

Sheriff Lodge ♦♦♦♦
51 Dimple Road, Matlock, DE4 3JX
T: (01629) 760760
F: (01629) 760860
E: info@sherifflodge.co.uk
I: www.sherifflodge.co.uk

Establishments printed in blue have a detailed entry in this guide

Warren Carr Barn
♦♦♦♦ SILVER AWARD
Warren Carr, Matlock, DE4 2LN
T: (01629) 733856
E: cherry@warrencarrbarn.freeserve.co.uk
I: www.SmoothHound.co.uk/hotels/warrenca.html

Wayside Farm ♦♦♦
Matlock Moor, Matlock, DE4 5LZ
T: (01629) 582967
I: www.waysidefarm-holiday.co.uk

MATLOCK BATH
Derbyshire

Ashdale ♦♦
92 North Parade, Matlock Bath, Matlock DE4 3NS
T: (01629) 57826
E: ashdale@matlockbath.fsnet.co.uk
I: www.ashdaleguesthouse.co.uk

The Firs ♦♦♦
180 Dale Road, Matlock Bath, Matlock DE4 3PS
T: (01629) 582426
F: (01629) 582426
E: moira@thefirs180.demon.co.uk

Fountain Villa ♦♦♦♦
86 North Parade, Matlock Bath, Matlock DE4 3NS
T: (01629) 56195
F: (01629) 581057
E: enquiries@fountainvilla.co.uk
I: www.fountainvilla.co.uk

Hodgkinsons Hotel ♦♦♦♦
150 South Parade, Matlock Bath, Matlock DE4 3NR
T: (01629) 582170
F: (01629) 584891
E: enquiries@hodgkinsons-hotel.co.uk
I: www.hodgkinsons-hotel.co.uk

Old Museum Guesthouse
♦♦♦
170-172 South Parade, Matlock Bath, Matlock DE4 3NR
T: (01629) 57783
E: lindsayandstewartbailey@tinyworld.co.uk

Sunnybank Guesthouse
♦♦♦♦ SILVER AWARD
37 Clifton Road, Matlock Bath, Matlock DE4 3PW
T: (01629) 584621
E: sunward@lineone.net
I: www.SmoothHound.co.uk/hotels/sunbankgh.html

MAVESYN RIDWARE
Staffordshire

The Old Rectory
♦♦♦♦ SILVER AWARD
Mavesyn Ridware, Rugeley WS15 3QE
T: (01543) 490792

MEDBOURNE
Leicestershire

Homestead House
♦♦♦♦ SILVER AWARD
5 Ashley Road, Medbourne, Market Harborough LE16 8DL
T: (01858) 565724
F: (01858) 565324

MELBOURNE
Derbyshire

Burdett House ♦♦
Derby Road, Melbourne, Derby DE73 1DE
T: (01332) 862105
E: jjvglaze@btinternet.com

MELTON MOWBRAY
Leicestershire

Amberley Gardens B&B
♦♦♦♦
4 Church Lane, Asfordby, Melton Mowbray LE14 3RU
T: (01664) 812314
F: (01664) 813740
E: doris@amberleygardens.net
I: www.amberleygardens.net

Cottage – Tole ♦♦♦♦
10 Main Street, Kirby Bellars, Melton Mowbray LE14 2EA
T: (01664) 812932
E: enquiries@tolecottage-melton.co.uk
I: www.tolecottage-melton.co.uk

Hall Farm
Rating Applied For
1 Main Street, Holwell, Melton Mowbray LE14 4SZ
T: (01664) 444275
F: (01664) 444731

Hillside House ♦♦♦♦
27 Melton Road, Burton Lazars, Melton Mowbray, LE14 2UR
T: (01664) 566312
F: (01664) 501819
E: Hillhs27@aol.com
I: www.hillside-house.co.uk

MELVERLEY
Shropshire

Church House ♦♦♦♦
Melverley, Oswestry SY10 8PJ
T: (01691) 682754
E: melverley@aol.com
I: members.aol.com/melverley

MEOLE BRACE
Shropshire

Meole Brace Hall
♦♦♦♦♦ SILVER AWARD
Church Lane, Meole Brace, Shrewsbury SY3 9HF
T: (01743) 235566
F: (01743) 236886
E: hathaway@meolebracehall.co.uk
I: www.meolebracehall.co.uk

MERIDEN
West Midlands

Barnacle Farm ♦♦♦♦
Back Lane, Meriden, Coventry CV7 7LD
T: (024) 7646 8875
F: (024) 7646 8875

Bonnifinglas Guest House ♦♦
3 Berkswell Road, Meriden, Coventry CV7 7LB
T: (01676) 523193
F: (01676) 523193

Cooperage Farm Bed and Breakfast ♦♦
Old Road, Meriden, Coventry CV7 7JP
T: (01676) 523493
F: (01676) 523876
E: lucy@cooperagefarm.co.uk
I: www.copperagefarm.co.uk

Dumela B&B ♦♦♦♦
Berkswell Road, Meriden, Coventry CV7 7LB
T: (01676) 523118
F: (01676) 523118
E: wadejanice@hotmail.com

Innellan House ♦♦♦
Eaves Green Lane, Meriden, Coventry CV7 7JL
T: (01676) 523005
F: (01676) 523005
E: caroled@innellanhouse.fsnet.co.uk
I: www.smoothhound.co.uk/hotels/innellan.html

MICHAELCHURCH ESCLEY
Herefordshire

The Grove Farm ♦♦♦♦
Michaelchurch Escley, Hereford HR2 0PT
T: (01981) 510229
F: (01981) 510229

MICKLETON
Gloucestershire

Myrtle House
♦♦♦♦ SILVER AWARD
High Street, Mickleton, Chipping Campden GL55 6SA
T: (01386) 430032
E: kate@myrtlehouse.co.uk
I: www.myrtlehouse.co.uk

MIDDLE DUNTISBOURNE
Gloucestershire

Manor Farm ♦♦♦
Middle Duntisbourne, Cirencester GL7 7AR
T: (01285) 658145
F: (01285) 641504
E: tina.barton@farming.co.uk
I: www.smoothhound.co.uk/hotels/manorfar.html

MIDDLETON
Derbyshire

Eastas Gate ♦♦♦♦
18 Main Street, Middleton, Matlock DE4 4LQ
T: (01629) 822790
E: eastasgate@hotmail.com

Middleton House Farm
♦♦♦♦ SILVER AWARD
Tamworth Road, Middleton, Tamworth B78 2BD
T: (01827) 873474
F: (01827) 872246
E: rob.jane@tinyonline.co.uk
I: middletonhousefarm.co.uk

Valley View ♦♦♦
3 Camsdale Walk, Middleton, Market Harborough LE16 8YR
T: (01536) 770874

MIDDLETON-BY-YOULGREAVE
Derbyshire

Castle Farm ♦♦♦♦
Middleton-by-Youlgreave, Bakewell DE45 1LS
T: (01629) 636746

Smerrill Grange ♦♦♦
Middleton-by-Youlgreave, Derby DE45 1LQ
T: (01629) 636232

MILLTHORPE
Derbyshire

Cordwell House ♦♦♦♦
Cordwell Lane, Millthorpe, Holmesfield, Dronfield S18 7WH
T: (0114) 289 0271

MILTON
Nottinghamshire

The Stables
♦♦♦♦ SILVER AWARD
Milton, Newark NG22 0PW
T: (01777) 871920
F: (01777) 871920
E: wellez@hotmail.com

MINSTERLEY
Shropshire

The Callow Inn ♦♦♦
Bromlow, Minsterley, Shrewsbury SY5 0EA
T: (01743) 891933
F: (01743) 891933
E: del@callowinn.freeserve.co.uk
I: www.callowinn.freeserve.co.uk

Cricklewood Cottage ♦♦♦♦
Plox Green, Minsterley, Shrewsbury SY5 0HT
T: (01743) 791229
E: paul.crickcott@bushinternet.com
I: www.smoothhound.co.uk/hotels/crickle

Mandalay Bed and Breakfast
♦♦♦♦
The Grove, Minsterley, Shrewsbury SY5 0AG
T: (01743) 791758

MITCHELDEAN
Gloucestershire

Gunn Mill House
Rating Applied For
Lower Spout Lane, Mitcheldean, GL17 0EA
T: (01594) 827577
F: (01594) 827577
E: info@gunnmillhouse.co.uk
I: www.gunnmillhouse.co.uk

MONNINGTON-ON-WYE
Herefordshire

Dairy House Farm ♦♦♦
Monnington-on-Wye, HR4 7NL
T: (01981) 500143
F: (01981) 500043
E: pearson-greg@clara.co.uk

MONSAL DALE
Derbyshire

Upperdale House ♦♦♦
Monsal Dale, Buxton SK17 8SZ
T: (01629) 640536
F: (01629) 640536
E: bookings@upperdale.fsnet.co.uk
I: www.monsaldale.com

MONYASH
Derbyshire

Chapel View Farm ♦♦♦♦
Chapel Street, Monyash, Bakewell DE45 1JJ
T: (01629) 814317

High Rakes Farm
♦♦♦♦ SILVER AWARD
Rakes Road, Monyash, Bakewell DE45 1JL
T: (01298) 84692

MOORHOUSE
Nottinghamshire

Brecks Cottage Bed and Breakfast ♦♦♦♦
Green Lane, Moorhouse, Newark NG23 6LZ
T: (01636) 822445
F: (01636) 821384
E: BandB@breckscottage.co.uk
I: www.breckscottage.co.uk

MORETON EYE
Herefordshire

Bunns Croft ♦♦♦
Moreton Eye, Leominster
HR6 0DP
T: (01568) 615836
F: (01568) 610620

MORETON-IN-MARSH
Gloucestershire

Acacia ♦♦♦
2 New Road, Moreton-in-Marsh,
GL56 0AS
T: (01608) 650130

The Bell Inn ♦♦♦
High Street, Moreton-in-Marsh,
GL56 0AF
T: (01608) 651688
F: (01608) 652195
E: keith.pendry@virgin.net
I: bellinncotswold.com

Blue Cedar House ♦♦♦
Stow Road, Moreton-in-Marsh,
GL56 0DW
T: (01608) 650299
E: gandsib@dialstart.net

Bran Mill Cottage ♦♦♦
Aston Magna, Moreton-in-Marsh GL56 9QP
T: (01386) 593517
F: (01386) 593 517
E: enquiries@branmillcottage.co.uk
I: www.branmillcottage.co.uk

Ditchford Farmhouse
Stretton on Fosse, Moreton-in-Marsh GL56 9RD
T: (01608) 663307
E: randb@ditchford-farmhouse.co.uk
I: www.ditchford-farmhouse.co.uk

Fosseway Farm B&B ♦♦♦♦
Stow Road, Moreton-in-Marsh,
GL56 0DS
T: (01608) 650503

Fourshires Bed and Breakfast
♦♦♦♦ SILVER AWARD
Fourshires House, Great Wolford Road, Moreton-in-Marsh,
GL56 0PE
T: (01608) 651412
F: (01608) 651412
E: M1aff@aol.com
I: www.fourshires.com

Kymalton House ♦♦♦♦
Todenham Road, Moreton-in-Marsh, GL56 9NJ
T: (01608) 650487

Neighbrook Manor
Rating Applied For
Near Aston Magna, Moreton-in-Marsh, GL56 9QP
T: (01386) 593232
F: (01386) 593500
E: info@neighbrookmanor.com
I: www.neighbrookmanor.com

New Farm ♦♦♦
Dorn, Moreton-in-Marsh
GL56 9NS
T: (01608) 650782
F: (01608) 652704
E: cath.righton@amserve.net
I: www.smoothhound.co.uk

The Old Chequer
♦♦♦♦ SILVER AWARD
Draycott, Moreton-in-Marsh,
GL56 9LB
T: (01386) 700647
F: (01386) 700647
E: g.f.linley@tesco.net
I: www.smoothhound.co.uk/hotels/oldchequer.html

Old Farm ♦♦♦
Dorn, Moreton-in-Marsh
GL56 9NS
T: (01608) 650394
F: (01608) 650394
E: simon@righton.freeserve.co.uk
I: www.oldfarmdorn.co.uk

Staddle Stones Guest House ♦♦♦
Rowborough, Stretton-on-Fosse, Moreton-in-Marsh,
GL56 9RE
T: (01608) 662774

Townend Cottage and Coach House ♦♦♦♦
High Street, Moreton-in-Marsh,
GL56 0AD
T: (01608) 650846
E: townend-cottage@moreton.junglelink.co.uk
I: www.townend-cottage.co.uk

Treetops ♦♦♦♦
London Road, Moreton-in-Marsh, GL56 0HE
T: (01608) 651036
F: (01608) 651036
E: treetops1@talk21.com

Warwick House ♦♦♦
London Road, Moreton-in-Marsh, GL56 0HH
T: (01608) 650773
F: (01608) 650773
E: charlie@warwickhousebnb.demon.co.uk
I: www.snoozeandsizzle.com

MORETON PINKNEY
Northamptonshire

Englands Rose ♦♦♦
Upper Green, Moreton Pinkney,
Daventry NN11 3SG
T: (01295) 760353
F: (01295) 760353
E: sheila@englandsrose.freeserve.co.uk

The Old Vicarage
♦♦♦♦ SILVER AWARD
Moreton Pinkney, Daventry
NN11 3SQ
T: (01295) 760057
F: (01295) 760057
E: tim@tandjeastwood.fsnet.co.uk
I: www.tandjeastwood.fsnet.co.uk

MORVILLE
Shropshire

Hannigans Farm ♦♦♦♦
Morville, Bridgnorth WV16 4RN
T: (01746) 714332
E: Hanningansfarm@btinternet.com

MUCH BIRCH
Herefordshire

The Old School ♦♦♦
Much Birch, Hereford HR2 8HJ
T: (01981) 541317

MUCH MARCLE
Herefordshire

New House Farm ♦♦♦
Much Marcle, Ledbury HR8 2PH
T: (01531) 660674

MUCH WENLOCK
Shropshire

Broadstone Mill
♦♦♦♦♦ GOLD AWARD
Broadstone, Much Wenlock,
TF13 6LE
T: (01584) 841494
F: (01584) 841515
E: hargreaves@broadstones.fsnet.co.uk
I: www.broadstonemill.co.uk

Danywenallt ♦♦♦
Farley Road, Much Wenlock,
TF13 6NB
T: (01952) 727892

The Gaskell Arms Hotel ♦♦♦
Much Wenlock, TF13 6AQ
T: (01952) 727212
F: (01952) 728505
E: maxine@gaskellarms.co.uk
I: www.smoothhound.co.uk/gaskell.html

The Longville Arms ♦♦♦
Longville in the Dale, Much Wenlock, TF13 6DT
T: (01694) 771206
F: (01694) 771742
E: longvillearm@aol.com

Old Quarry Cottage ♦♦♦♦
Brockton, Much Wenlock,
TF13 6JR
T: (01746) 785596
E: rod@brockton.fsbusiness.co.uk

Red House Farm
Rating Applied For
Longville, Much Wenlock,
TF13 6ED
T: (01694) 771224

Rowe Cottage ♦♦♦♦
Rowe Lane, Stanton Long, Much Wenlock, TF13 6LR
T: (01584) 841286
E: rob_cleal@hotmail.com

Seraphique
Rating Applied For
16 Stretton Road, Much Wenlock, TF13 6AS
T: (01952) 728588
F: (01952) 728329
E: malcolm.m-r@ukf.net

Talbot Inn ♦♦♦
Much Wenlock, TF13 6AA
T: (01952) 727077
F: (01952) 728436

MUNSTONE
Herefordshire

Munstone House
Rating Applied For
Munstone, Hereford HR1 3AH
T: (01432) 267122

MYDDLE
Shropshire

Oakfields ♦♦♦
Baschurch Road, Myddle,
Shrewsbury SY4 3RX
T: (01939) 290823

NAILSWORTH
Gloucestershire

Aaron Farm ♦♦♦♦
Nympsfield Road, Nailsworth,
Stroud GL6 0ET
T: (01453) 833598
F: (01453) 833626
E: aaronfarm@aol.com
I: www.aaronfarm-bedandbreakfast.co.uk

Hazelwood Bed & Breakfast ♦♦♦♦
Hazelwood, Church Street,
Nailsworth, Stroud GL6 0BP
T: (01453) 839304
E: alanwheeler@btintemet.com
I: www.hazlewood.cjb.net

Highlands ♦♦♦♦
Shortwood, Nailsworth, Stroud
GL6 0SJ
T: (01453) 832591
F: (01453) 833590

1 Orchard Mead ♦♦♦
Nailsworth, Stroud GL6 0RE
T: (01453) 833581

The Upper House ♦♦♦♦
Spring Hill, Nailsworth, Stroud
GL6 0LX
T: (01453) 836606
F: (01453) 836769

NASSINGTON
Northamptonshire

Fairlands
Rating Applied For
35 Church Street, Nassington,
Peterborough PE8 6QG
T: (01780) 783603
E: marriottann@hotmail.com

Sunnyside ♦♦♦
62 Church Street, Nassington,
Peterborough PE8 6QG
T: (01780) 782864

NAUNTON
Gloucestershire

The Black Horse Inn ♦♦♦
Naunton, Cheltenham GL54 3A[illegible]
T: (01451) 850565

Fox Hill ♦♦♦
Old Stow Road, Naunton,
Cheltenham GL54 5RL
T: (01451) 850496
F: (01451) 850602

Naunton View Guesthouse ♦♦♦
Naunton, Cheltenham GL54 3A[illegible]
T: (01451) 850482
F: (01451) 850482

NAVENBY
Lincolnshire

The Barn Bed and Breakfast
♦♦♦♦ SILVER AWARD
The Barn, North Lane, Navenby
Lincoln LN5 0EH
T: (01522) 810318
F: (01522) 810318
E: gill@barnbb.fsnet.co.uk

NETHER HEYFORD
Northamptonshire

Heyford Bed and Breakfast ♦♦
27 Church Street, Nether Heyford, Northampton NN7 3LH
T: (01327) 340872

NETHER WESTCOTE
Gloucestershire

Cotswold View Guesthouse ♦♦♦
Nether Westcote, Oxford OX7 6SD
T: (01993) 830699
F: (01993) 830699
E: info@cotswoldview-guesthouse.co.uk
I: www.cotswoldview-guesthouse.co.uk

NEW DUSTON
Northamptonshire

Rowena ♦♦♦♦
569 Harlestone Road, New Duston, Northampton NN5 6NX
T: (01604) 755889
F: 0870 1376484
E: info@rowenaBB.co.uk
I: www.rowenaBB.co.uk

NEWARK
Nottinghamshire

The Boot and Shoe Inn ♦♦♦♦
Main Street, Flintham, Newark NG23 5LA
T: (01636) 525246

Crosshill House Bed and Breakfast ♦♦♦♦
Crosshill House, Laxton, Newark, NG22 0NT
T: (01777) 871953
E: roberta@crosshillhouse.freeserve.co.uk
I: www.crosshillhouse.com

NEWCASTLE-UNDER-LYME
Staffordshire

Graythwaite Guest House ♦♦♦
106 Lancaster Road, Newcastle-under-Lyme, ST5 1DS
T: (01782) 612875
E: cooke@graythwaite.fsnet.co.uk
I: www.smoothhound.co.uk/hotels/grayth

NEWENT
Gloucestershire

George Hotel ♦♦♦
Church Street, Newent, GL18 1PU
T: (01531) 820203
F: (01531) 822899
E: enquiries@georgehotel.uk.com
I: www.georgehotel.uk.com

Newent Golf and Lodges ♦♦♦
Newent Golf Course, Coldharbour Lane, Newent, GL18 1DJ
T: (01531) 820478
F: (01531) 820478
E: tomnewentgolf@aol.com
I: www.short-golf-break.com

The Old Winery ♦♦♦♦♦ GOLD AWARD
Welsh House Lane, Dymock, Newent, GL18 1LR
T: (01531) 890824

Sandyway Nurseries Countryside B & B ♦♦♦♦
Redmarley Road, Newent, GL18 1DR
T: (01531) 820693
E: jeansandywaybb@hotmail.com
I: www.visitheartofengland.com/wheretostay/index.htm

Three Ashes House ♦♦♦♦ SILVER AWARD
Ledbury Road, Newent, GL18 1DE
T: (01531) 820226
F: (01531) 820226
E: jrichard.cockroft@tinyworld.co.uk

NEWNHAM-ON-SEVERN
Gloucestershire

Hayden Lea ♦♦♦
Dean Road, Newnham-on-Severn, GL14 1AB
T: (01594) 516626

Swan House ♦♦♦♦
High Street, Newnham-on-Severn, GL14 1BY
T: (01594) 516504
F: (01594) 516177
E: enquiries@swanhousenewham.co.uk
I: www.swanhousenewnham.co.uk

The White House World ♦♦♦
Popes Hill, Newnham-on-Severn, GL14 1LE
T: (01452) 760463
F: (01452) 760776
E: whitehouseworld@talk21.com
I: www.fweb.org.uk/whitehouse

NEWPORT
Shropshire

Lane End Farm ♦♦♦♦ SILVER AWARD
Chetwynd, Newport, TF10 8BN
T: (01952) 550337
F: (01952) 550337
I: www.virtual-shropshire.co.uk/lef

Norwood House Hotel and Restaurant ♦♦♦
Pave Lane, Newport, TF10 9LQ
T: (01952) 825896
F: (01952) 825896
I: www.norwoodhse.freeserve.co.uk

Pear Tree Farmhouse ♦♦♦♦
Farm Grove, Newport, TF10 7PX
T: (01952) 811193
F: (01952) 812115
E: patgreen@peakfarmhouse.co.uk
I: www.peartreefarmhouse.co.uk

Sambrook Manor ♦♦♦
Sambrook, Newport TF10 8AL
T: (01952) 550256

NEWTOWN LINFORD
Leicestershire

Wondai ♦♦♦
47-49 Main Street, Newtown Linford, Leicester LE6 0AE
T: (01530) 242728
E: j_weazel@eggconnect.net

NORBURY
Shropshire

Oulton House Farm ♦♦♦♦
Norbury, Stafford ST20 0PG
T: (01785) 284264
F: (01785) 284264
E: judy@oultonhousefarm.co.uk
I: www.oultonhousefarm.co.uk

NORTH COTES
Lincolnshire

Fleece Inn ♦♦♦
Lock Road, North Cotes, Grimsby DN36 5UP
T: (01472) 388233
F: (01472) 388 233

NORTH HYKEHAM
Lincolnshire

Lakeview Guesthouse ♦♦♦♦
50 Station Road, North Hykeham, Lincoln LN6 9AQ
T: (01522) 680455

NORTH KYME
Lincolnshire

Old Coach House Motel & Cafe ♦♦♦♦
Church Lane, North Kyme, LN4 4DJ
T: (01526) 861465
F: (01526) 861658
E: Barbara@motel-plus.co.uk
I: www.Motel-Plus.co.uk

NORTH SOMERCOTES
Lincolnshire

Pigeon Cottage Bed & Breakfast & LLA Summer Camps ♦♦
Conisholme Road, North Somercotes, Louth LN11 7PS
T: (01507) 359063
F: (01507) 359063
E: lla.hill@ukgateway.net
I: www.lifelongadventure.co.uk

NORTH WINGFIELD
Derbyshire

South View ♦♦♦
95 Church Lane, North Wingfield, Chesterfield S42 5HR
T: (01246) 850091

NORTHAMPTON
Northamptonshire

Aarandale Regent Hotel and Guesthouse ♦♦
6-8 Royal Terrace, Barrack Road (A508), Northampton, NN1 3RF
T: (01604) 631096
F: (01604) 621035
E: info@aarandale.co.uk
I: www.aarandale.co.uk

Abington Park Guesthouse ♦♦♦
407 Wellingborough Road, Abington, Northampton NN1 4EY
T: (01604) 635072

The Gables Guest House ♦♦♦♦
74 Fulford Drive, Links View, Northampton, NN2 7NR
T: (01604) 713858

Haselbech House Farm Rating Applied For
Haselbech Hill, Northampton, NN6 9LL
T: (01604) 686266
F: (01604) 686544
E: lesueur@haselbech.freeserve.co.uk

Poplars Hotel ♦♦♦♦
Cross Street, Moulton, Northampton NN3 7RZ
T: (01604) 643983
F: (01604) 790233
E: thepoplars.hotel@btopenworld.com

NORTHLEACH
Gloucestershire

Cotteswold House ♦♦♦♦ SILVER AWARD
Market Place, Northleach, Cheltenham GL54 3EG
T: (01451) 860493
F: (01451) 860493
E: cotteswoldhouse@talk21.com
I: www.cotteswoldhouse.com

The Eastington Suite ♦♦♦♦♦ GOLD AWARD
Japonica, Upper End Eastington, Northleach, Cheltenham GL54 3PJ
T: (01451) 861117
F: (01451) 861117
I: members.tripod.co.uk/the2eastingtonsuite/

Long Barrow ♦♦♦♦
Farmington, Northleach, Cheltenham GL54 3NQ
T: (01451) 860428
F: (01451) 860166
E: ghowson@longbarrow.fsnet.co.uk

The Mead House ♦♦♦
Sherborne, Cheltenham GL54 3DR
T: (01451) 844239

Northfield Bed and Breakfast ♦♦♦♦ SILVER AWARD
Cirencester Road (A429), Northleach, Cheltenham GL54 3JL
T: (01451) 860427
F: (01451) 860427
E: nrthfield0@aol.com

The Sherborne Arms ♦♦♦
Market Place, Northleach, Cheltenham GL54 3EE
T: (01451) 860241

Wheatsheaf Inn ♦♦♦
Northleach, Cheltenham GL54 3EZ
T: (01451) 860244
F: (01451) 861037
E: bookings@wheatsheafinn.org.uk
I: www.wheatsheafinn.org.uk

NOTTINGHAM
Nottinghamshire

Acorn Hotel ♦♦♦
4 Radcliffe Road, West Bridgford, Nottingham NG2 5FW
T: (0115) 981 1297
F: (0115) 981 7654
E: reservations@acorn-hotel.co.uk

Andrews Private Hotel ♦♦♦
310 Queens Road, Beeston, Nottingham NG9 1JA
T: (0115) 925 4902
F: (0115) 917 8839
E: andrews.hotel@ntlworld.com

Elm Bank Lodge ♦♦♦
Elm Bank, Mapperley Park, Nottingham, NG3 5AJ
T: (0115) 9625493
F: (0115) 9625493
E: stewpot1a@aol.co.uk
I: www.smoothhound.co.uk/hotels/elmbank

Grantham Hotel ♦♦♦
24-26 Radcliffe Road, West Bridgford, Nottingham NG2 5FW
T: (0115) 981 1373
F: (0115) 981 8567
E: granthamhotel@netlineuk.net

Greenwood Lodge City Guesthouse
♦♦♦♦♦ GOLD AWARD
Third Avenue, Sherwood Rise, Nottingham NG7 6JH
T: (0115) 962 1206
F: (0115) 962 1206
E: coolspratt@aol.com
I: www.SmoothHound.co.uk/hotels/greenwo.html

Nelson and Railway Inn ♦♦
Station Road, Kimberley, Nottingham, NG16 2NR
T: (0115) 938 2177
I: www.nelsonandrailway.fsnet.co.uk

Orchard Cottage ♦♦♦♦
The Old Workhouse, Trowell, Nottingham NG9 3PQ
T: (0115) 9280933
F: (0115) 9280933
E: orchardcottage.bandb@virgin.net
I: www.orchardcottages.com

Park Hotel City Centre ♦♦
7 Waverley Street, Nottingham, NG7 4HF
T: (0115) 978 6299
F: (0115) 942 4358
E: enquiries@parkhotelcitycentre.co.uk
I: www.parkhotelcitycentre.co.uk

Yew Tree Grange ♦♦♦♦
2 Nethergate, Clifton Village, Nottingham, NG11 8NL
T: (0115) 984 7562
F: (0115) 984 7562
E: yewtreel@nascr.net
I: www.yewtreegrange.co.uk

NUNEATON
Warwickshire

La Tavola Calda ♦♦
70 Midland Road, Abbey Green, Nuneaton, CV11 5DY
T: (024) 7638 3195
F: (024) 7638 1816

Leathermill Grange ♦♦♦♦♦
Leathermill Lane, Caldecote, Nuneaton CV10 0RX
T: (01827) 714637
F: (01827) 716422
E: davidcodd@leathermillgrange.co.uk
I: www.leathermillgrange.co.uk

Royal Arms ♦♦♦♦
Main Street, Sutton Cheney, Nuneaton, CV13 0AG
T: (01455) 290263
F: (01455) 290124
I: www.royalarms.co.uk

OAKAMOOR
Staffordshire

Bank House
♦♦♦♦♦ GOLD AWARD
Farley Road, Oakamoor, Stoke-on-Trent ST10 3BD
T: (01538) 702810
F: (01538) 702810
E: john.orme@dial.pipex.com
I: www.smoothhound.co.uk/hotels/bank.html

Beehive Guest House ♦♦♦♦
Churnet View Road, Oakamoor, Stoke-on-Trent ST10 3AE
T: (01538) 702420
F: (01538) 702420
E: thebeehiveoakamoor@btinternet.com
I: www.thebeehiveguesthouse.co.uk

Crowtrees Farm ♦♦♦♦
Oakamoor, Stoke-on-Trent ST10 3DY
T: (01538) 702260
F: (01538) 702260
E: crowtrees@fenetre.co.uk.
I: www.touristnetuk.com/wm/crowtrees

The Laurels ♦♦♦♦
Star Bank, Oakamoor, Stoke-on-Trent ST10 3BN
T: (01538) 702629
F: (01538) 702796
E: bbthelaurels@aol.com
I: www.thelaurels.co.uk

The Lord Nelson ♦♦♦
Carr Bank, Oakamoor, Stoke-on-Trent ST10 3DQ
T: (01538) 702242

Ribden Farm ♦♦♦♦
Oakamoor, Stoke-on-Trent ST10 3BW
T: (01538) 702830
F: (01538) 702830
E: ribdenfarm@aol.com
I: www.ribden.fsnet.co.uk

Tenement Farm ♦♦♦♦
Three Lows, Ribden, Oakamoor, Stoke-on-Trent ST10 3BW
T: (01538) 702333
F: (01538) 703603
E: stanleese@aol.com
I: www.tenementfarm.co.uk

OAKENGATES
Shropshire

Chellow Dene ♦♦♦
Park Road, Malinslee, Dawley, Telford TF3 2AY
T: (01952) 505917

OAKHAM
Rutland

Hall Farm ♦♦♦
Cottesmore Road, Exton, Oakham LE15 8AN
T: (01572) 812271
F: (01572) 812271

The Tithe Barn ♦♦♦
Clatterpot Lane, Cottesmore, Oakham, LE15 7DW
T: (01572) 813591
F: (01572) 812719
E: jpryke@thetithebarn.co.uk
I: www.tithebarn-rutland.co.uk

OASBY
Lincolnshire

The Houblon Inn ♦♦♦
Oasby, Grantham NG32 3NB
T: (01529) 455215

The Pinomar ♦♦♦♦
Mill Lane, Oasby, Grantham NG32 3ND
T: (01529) 455400
F: (01529) 455681

OLD
Northamptonshire

Wold Farm
♦♦♦♦ SILVER AWARD
Daventry, NN6 9RJ
T: (01604) 781258
F: (01604) 781258
I: www.woldfarm.co.uk

OMBERSLEY
Worcestershire

Greenlands
♦♦♦♦ SILVER AWARD
Uphampton, Ombersley, Droitwich WR9 0JP
T: (01905) 620873
E: xlandgreenlands@onetel.net.uk

ORLETON
Worcestershire

Hope Cottage Bed and Breakfast ♦♦♦
Hope Cottage, Orleton, Ludlow SY8 4JB
T: (01584) 831674
F: (01584) 831124
E: hopecott@aol.com

Line Farm
♦♦♦♦♦ GOLD AWARD
Tunnel Lane, Orleton, Ludlow SY8 4HY
T: (01568) 780400
F: (01568) 780995
E: linefarm@lineone.net
I: www.virtual-shropshire.co.uk/linefarm

OSGATHORPE
Leicestershire

Royal Oak House ♦♦♦
20 Main Street, Osgathorpe, Loughborough LE12 9TA
T: (01530) 222443

OSWESTRY
Shropshire

Ashfield Farmhouse
♦♦♦♦ SILVER AWARD
Maesbury, Oswestry, SY10 8JH
T: (01691) 653589
F: (01691) 653589
E: marg@ashfieldfarmhouse.co.uk
I: www.ashfieldfarmhouse.co.uk

Bridge House ♦♦♦♦
Llynclys, Oswestry, SY10 8AE
T: (01691) 830496
F: (01691) 830496
E: jenny@llynclys.freeserve.co.uk

5 Llanforda Close ♦♦♦
Oswestry, SY11 1SZ
T: (01691) 655823

Llwyn Guesthouse ♦♦♦
5 Llwyn Terrace, Oswestry, SY11 1HR
T: (01691) 670746
E: llwyn@virtual-shropshire.co.uk
I: www.virtual-shropshire.co.uk/llwyn

Montrose ♦♦♦
Weston Lane, Oswestry, SY11 2BG
T: (01691) 652063
I: www.shropshiretourism.com/placestostay

35 Oak Drive ♦♦♦
Oswestry, SY11 2RX
T: (01691) 655286

The Old Rectory ♦♦♦
Selattyn, Oswestry, SY10 7DH
T: (01691) 659708

Railway Cottage ♦♦♦
51 Gobowen Road, Oswestry, SY11 1HU
T: (01691) 654851
F: (01691) 654851
E: pmull36823@aol.com

Red Lion ♦♦♦♦
Bailey Head, Oswestry, SY11 1PZ
T: (01691) 655459
F: (01691) 655459

Top Farm House
♦♦♦♦ SILVER AWARD
Knockin, Oswestry, SY10 8HN
T: (01691) 682582
F: (01691) 682070
E: p.a.m@knockin.freeserve.co.uk
I: www.topfarmknockin.co.uk

OUNDLE
Northamptonshire

Ashworth House ♦♦♦♦
75 West Street, Oundle, Peterborough PE8 4EJ
T: (01832) 275312
F: (01832) 275312
E: sue@ashworthhouse.co.uk.co.uk
I: www.ashworthhouse.co.uk

2 Benefield Road ♦♦♦♦
Oundle, Peterborough PE8 4ET
T: (01832) 273953
F: (01832) 273953

Castle Farm Guesthouse ♦♦♦♦
Castle Farm, Fotheringhay, Peterborough PE8 5HZ
T: (01832) 226200
F: (01832) 226200

Lilford Lodge Farm ♦♦♦♦
Barnwell, Oundle, Peterborough PE8 5SA
T: (01832) 272230
F: (01832) 272230
E: trudy@lilford-lodge.demon.co.uk
I: www.lilford-lodge.demon.co.uk

OXLYNCH
Gloucestershire

Tiled House Farm ♦♦♦♦
Oxlynch, Stonehouse GL10 3DF
T: (01453) 822363
F: (01453) 822363
E: dmj@ukgateway.net

OXTON
Nottinghamshire

Far Baulker Farm ♦♦♦♦
Oxton, Southwell NG25 0RQ
T: (01623) 882375
F: (01623) 882375
E: j.esam@virgin.net
I: www.farbaulkerfarm.info

PAINSWICK
Gloucestershire

Cardynham House ♦♦♦♦
The Cross, Painswick, Stroud GL6 6XX
T: (01452) 814006
F: (01452) 812321
E: info@cardynham.co.uk
I: www.cardynham.co.uk

Hambutts Mynd ♦♦♦
Edge Road, Painswick, Stroud GL6 6UP
T: (01452) 812352
F: (01452) 813862
E: ewarland@aol.com
I: www.accommodation.uk.net/hambutts.htm

Meadowcote ♦♦♦♦
Stroud Road, Painswick, Stroud GL6 6UT
T: (01452) 813565

Skyrack ♦♦♦
The Highlands, Painswick, Stroud GL6 6SL
T: (01452) 812029
F: (01452) 813846
E: wendyskyrack@hotmail.com
I: www.painswick.co.uk/skyrack

Thorne ♦♦♦
Friday Street, Painswick, Stroud GL6 6QJ
T: (01452) 812476
F: (01458) 10925
I: www.painswick.co.uk.forward/thorne.

Upper Doreys Mill ♦♦♦
Edge, Painswick, Stroud GL6 6NF
T: (01452) 812459
F: (01452) 814756
E: sylvia@painswick.co.uk
I: www.painswick.co.uk/doreys

Wheatleys
♦♦♦♦♦ GOLD AWARD
Cotswold Mead, Painswick, Stroud GL6 6XB
T: (01452) 812167
F: (01452) 814270
E: wheatleys@dial.pipex.com
I: www.wheatleys-b-and-b.co.uk

PANT
Shropshire

The Palms ♦♦♦♦
Pant, Oswestry SY10 8JZ
T: (01691) 830813
F: (01691) 830813

PAPPLEWICK
Nottinghamshire

Forest Farm ♦♦♦
Mansfield Road, Papplewick, Nottingham NG15 8FL
T: (0115) 963 2310

PARKEND
Gloucestershire

Deanfield ♦♦♦
Royal Forest Of Dean, Parkend, Lydney GL15 4JF
T: (01594) 562256
F: (01594) 562524

Edale House ♦♦♦
Folly Road, Parkend, Lydney GL15 4JF
T: (01594) 562835
F: (01594) 564488
E: edale@lineone.net
I: www.edalehouse.co.uk

The Fountain Inn & Lodge
♦♦♦
Fountain Way, Parkend, Lydney GL15 4JD
T: (01594) 562189
F: (01594) 564438
E: thefountaininn@aol.com
I: www.thefoutaininnandlodge.com

PARWICH
Derbyshire

Flaxdale House
♦♦♦♦ SILVER AWARD
Parwich, Ashbourne DE6 1QA
T: (01335) 390252
F: (01335) 390644
E: mike@flaxdale.demon.co.uk
I: www.flaxdale.demon.co.uk

PEMBRIDGE
Herefordshire

Lowe Farm Bed and Breakfast
♦♦♦♦ GOLD AWARD
Lowe Farm, Pembridge, Leominster HR6 9JD
T: (01544) 388395
E: williams_family@lineone.net
I: www.lowe-farm.co.uk

PENTRICH
Derbyshire

Coney Grey Farm ♦♦♦
Chesterfield Road, Pentrich, Ripley DE5 3RF
T: (01773) 833179

PERSHORE
Worcestershire

Aldbury House
♦♦♦♦ SILVER AWARD
George Lane, Wyre Piddle, Pershore WR10 2HX
T: (01386) 553754
F: (01386) 553754
E: aldbury@onetel.net.uk

Arbour House
♦♦♦♦ SILVER AWARD
Main Road, Wyre Piddle, Pershore WR10 2HU
T: (01386) 555833
F: (01386) 555833
E: lizbrownsdon@hotmail.com
I: www.smoothhound.co.uk/hotels/arbourhouse.html

The Barn
♦♦♦♦♦ GOLD AWARD
Pensham Hill House, Pensham, Pershore WR10 3HA
T: (01386) 555270
F: (01386) 552894

Byeways ♦♦♦♦
Pershore Road, Little Comberton, Pershore WR10 3EW
T: (01386) 710203
F: (01386) 710203
E: pwbyeways@aol.com

PILLERTON HERSEY
Warwickshire

The Old Vicarage
♦♦♦♦♦ SILVER AWARD
Pillerton Hersey, Warwick CV35 0QJ
T: (01789) 740185
E: oldvicarage98@hotmail.com

PITCHCOMBE
Gloucestershire

Gable End ♦♦♦
Pitchcombe, Stroud GL6 6LN
T: (01452) 812166
F: (01452) 812719

PITSFORD
Northamptonshire

Ashley House ♦♦♦♦
19 Broadlands, Pitsford, Northampton NN6 9AZ
T: (01604) 880691
F: (01604) 880691

PONTESBURY
Shropshire

Jasmine Cottage
♦♦♦♦ SILVER AWARD
Pontesford, Pontesbury, Shrewsbury SY5 0UA
T: (01743) 792771
E: joyce@jasmine-cottage.fsnet.co.uk
I: www.jasminecottage.net

PONTRILAS
Herefordshire

Station House ♦♦
Pontrilas, Hereford HR2 0EH
T: (01981) 240564
F: (01981) 240564
E: john.pring@tesco.net
I: www.golden-valley.co.uk/stationhouse

POULTON
Gloucestershire

Sprucewood ♦♦♦♦
Elf Meadow, Poulton, Cirencester GL7 5HQ
T: (01285) 851351
F: (01285) 851351

PRIORS HARDWICK
Warwickshire

Hill Farm ♦♦♦
Priors Hardwick, Southam CV47 7SP
T: (01327) 260338
E: simon.darbishire@farming.co.uk
I: www.farmstayuk.co.uk

QUENIBOROUGH
Leicestershire

Three Ways Farm ♦♦♦
Melton Road, Queniborough, Leicester LE7 3FN
T: (0116) 260 0472

RAITHBY
Lincolnshire

The Red Lion Inn ♦♦♦
Main Street, Raithby, Spilsby PE23 4DS
T: (01790) 753727
E: alcaprawn@aol.com

REDDITCH
Worcestershire

Avonhill Lodge Guest House
♦♦♦
Alcester Road, Beoley, Redditch B98 9EP
T: (01564) 742413
F: (01564) 741873

Black Horse Cottage
♦♦♦♦♦ SILVER AWARD
Gorcott Hill, Redditch, B98 9EU
T: (01527) 854124
E: jaynepotter@msn.com

REDMILE
Leicestershire

Peacock Farm Guesthouse and The Feathers Restaurant ♦♦♦
Redmile, Nottingham NG13 0GQ
T: (01949) 842475
F: (01949) 43127
E: peacockfarm@primeuk.net
I: www.peacock-farm.co.uk

Peacock Inn
Rating Applied For
Church Corner, Main Street, Redmile, Nottingham NG13 0GA
T: (01949) 842554
F: (01949) 843746
E: peacock@redmile.fsbusiness.co.uk

RETFORD
Nottinghamshire

The Barns Country Guesthouse
♦♦♦♦
Morton Farm, Babworth, Retford DN22 8HA
T: (01777) 706336
F: (01777) 709773
E: harry@thebarns.co.uk
I: www.Thebarns.co.uk

Bolham Manor
♦♦♦♦ SILVER AWARD
Retford, DN22 9SG
T: (01777) 703528
E: pamandbutch@bolhammanor.com
I: www.bolham-manor.com

The Brick and Tile ♦♦♦
81 Moorgate, Retford, DN22 6RR
T: (01777) 703681
E: elvira.foster@btinternet.com

RIPLEY
Derbyshire

Hellinside ♦♦♦
1-3 Whitegates, Codnor, Ripley, DE5 9QD
T: (01773) 742750
F: 07977 556576
E: hellinside@aol.com

Spinney Lodge Guesthouse
♦♦♦
Coach Road, Butterley Park, Ripley, DE5 3QU
T: (01773) 740168

RIPPLE
Worcestershire

Green Gables ♦♦♦
Ripple, Tewkesbury GL20 6EX
T: (01684) 592740
F: (01684) 592740

ROADE
Northamptonshire

Roade House Restaurant and Hotel ♦♦♦♦ SILVER AWARD
16 High Street, Roade, Northampton NN7 2NW
T: (01604) 863372
F: (01604) 862421
E: chris@roadehousehotel.demon.co.uk

RODBOROUGH
Gloucestershire

Hillview ♦♦♦
104 Kingscourt Lane, Rodborough, Stroud GL5 3PX
T: (01453) 758234

ROSS-ON-WYE
Herefordshire

The Arches ♦♦♦
Walford Road, Ross-on-Wye, HR9 5PT
T: (01989) 563348
F: (01989) 563348
E: the.arches@which.net

Ashe Leigh ♦♦♦
Bridstow, Ross-on-Wye, HR9 6QB
T: (01989) 565020

Beechcroft Bed & Breakfast
♦♦♦♦
Gloucester Road, Ross-on-Wye, HR9 5LR
T: (01989) 566685
E: re.wallis@ntlworld.com

Brookfield House ♦♦♦
Over Ross, Ross-on-Wye, HR9 7AT
T: (01989) 562188
F: (01989) 564053
E: reception@brookfieldhouse.co.uk
I: www.brookfieldhouse.co.uk

The Falcon Guest House ♦♦♦
How Caple, Hereford HR1 4TF
T: (01989) 740223
F: (01989) 740223
E: falconguesthouse@tinyworld.co.uk

Four Seasons ♦♦♦♦
Coughton, Walford, Ross-on-Wye, HR9 5SE
T: (01989) 567884

Haslemere ♦♦♦♦
Ledbury Road, Ross-on-Wye, HR9 7BE
T: (01989) 563046
F: (01989) 563046
E: bandb@rossonwye.fsnet.co.uk

The Hill House ♦♦♦
Howle Hill, Ross-on-Wye, HR9 5ST
T: (01989) 562033
E: thehillhouse2000@hotmail.com
I: www.thehowlinghillhouse.com

Lavender Cottage ♦♦♦
Bridstow, Ross-on-Wye HR9 6QB
T: (01989) 562836
F: (01989) 762129
E: barbara_lavender@yahoo.co.uk

Linden House ♦♦♦♦
14 Church Street, Ross-on-Wye, HR9 5HN
T: (01989) 565373
F: (01989) 565575
I: WWW.LINDENHOUSE.WYENET.CO.UK

Lumleys
♦♦♦♦ SILVER AWARD
Kerne Bridge, Bishopswood, Ross-on-Wye, HR9 5QT
T: (01600) 890040
F: (01600) 891095
E: helen@lumleys.force9.co.uk
I: www.lumleys.force9.co.uk

Lyndor Bed and Breakfast ♦♦♦
Lyndor, Hole-in-the-Wall, Ross-on-Wye, HR9 7JW
T: (01989) 563833

The Mill House ♦♦♦
Walford, Ross-on-Wye, HR9 5QS
T: (01989) 764339
F: (01989) 763231

Norton House
♦♦♦♦ GOLD AWARD
Whitchurch, Ross-on-Wye, HR9 6DJ
T: (01600) 890046
F: (01600) 890045
E: sue@norton.wyenet.co.uk
I: www.Norton-House.com

The Old Rectory ♦♦♦♦
Hope Mansell, Ross-on-Wye HR9 5TL
T: (01989) 750382
F: (01989) 750382
E: rectory@mansell.wyenet.co.uk

Radcliffe Guest House ♦♦♦
Wye Street, Ross-on-Wye, HR9 7BS
T: (01989) 563895
E: Radcliffegh@btinternet.com

Sunnymount Hotel ♦♦♦♦
Ryefield Road, Ross-on-Wye, HR9 5LU
T: (01989) 563880
F: (01989) 566251
E: sunnymount@tinyworld.co.uk

Thatch Close ♦♦♦♦
Llangrove, Ross-on-Wye HR9 6EL
T: (01989) 770300
E: thatch.close@virgin.net

Vaga House ♦♦♦
Wye Street, Ross-on-Wye, HR9 7BS
T: (01989) 563024
E: vagahouse@hotmail.com
I: www.vagahouse.co.uk

Walnut Tree Cottage Hotel
♦♦♦♦ SILVER AWARD
Symonds Yat West, Ross-on-Wye, HR9 6BN
T: (01600) 890828
F: (01600) 890828
E: enquiries@walnuttreehotel.co.uk
I: www.walnuttreehotel.co.uk

Welland House ♦♦♦
Archenfield Road, Ross-on-Wye, HR9 5BA
T: (01989) 566500
F: (01989) 566500
E: wellandhouse@hotmail.com

ROWSLEY
Derbyshire

The Old Station House ♦♦♦♦
4 Chatsworth Road, Rowsley, Matlock DE4 2EJ
T: (01629) 732987
F: (01629) 735169
E: patches@proach.fsnet.co.uk

Vernon House ♦♦♦♦
Bakewell Road, Rowsley, Matlock DE4 2EB
T: (01629) 734294

1 Vicarage Croft ♦♦♦
Church Lane, Rowsley, Rowsley, Matlock DE4 2EA
T: (01629) 735429

RUARDEAN
Gloucestershire

Oakleigh Farm House ♦♦
Crooked End, Ruardean, GL17 9XF
T: (01594) 542284
F: (01594) 543610
E: christine@iconmodel2.demon.co.uk

RUGBY
Warwickshire

The Croft Bed and Breakfast ♦♦♦
69 Rugby Road, Dunchurch, Rugby, CV22 6PQ
T: (01788) 816763
E: tlong79@hotmail.com

Diamond House Hotel ♦♦♦
28-30 Hillmorton Road, Rugby, CV22 5AA
T: (01788) 572701
F: (01788) 572701

Lawford Hill Farm
♦♦♦♦ SILVER AWARD
Lawford Heath Lane, Rugby, CV23 9HG
T: (01788) 542001
F: (01788) 537880
E: lawford.hill@talk21.com
I: www.lawfordhill.co.uk

Marston House
♦♦♦♦ SILVER AWARD
Priors Marston, Southam, CV47 7RP
T: (01327) 260297
F: (01327) 262846
E: kim@mahonand.co.uk
I: www.ivabestbandb.co.uk

The Old Rectory ♦♦♦♦
Main Street, Harborough Magna, Rugby, CV23 0HS
T: (01788) 833151
F: (01788) 833151
E: parkinnen@btopenworld.com
I: www.theoldrectorywarwickshire.co.uk

Village Green Hotel
♦♦♦♦ SILVER AWARD
The Green, Dunchurch, Rugby, CV22 6NX
T: (01788) 813434
F: (01788) 814714
E: info@ughrugby.co.uk
I: www.vghrugby.co.uk

White Lion Inn ♦♦♦
Coventry Road, Pailton, Rugby, CV23 0QD
T: (01788) 832359
F: (01788) 832359
I: www.whitelionpailton.co.uk

RUGELEY
Staffordshire

Park Farm ♦♦♦
Hawkesyard, Armitage Lane, Rugeley, WS15 1ED
T: (01889) 583477
F: (01889) 583477

RUSHWICK
Worcestershire

Laugherne Grange ♦♦♦
Bransford Road, Rushwick, Worcester WR2 5SJ
T: (01905) 428 047

RUSKINGTON
Lincolnshire

Sunnyside Farm ♦♦♦
Leasingham Lane, Ruskington, Sleaford NG34 9AH
T: (01526) 833010

ST OWENS CROSS
Herefordshire

Amberley
♦♦♦♦ SILVER AWARD
Aberhall Farm, St Owens Cross, Hereford HR2 8LL
T: (01989) 730256
F: (01989) 730256
E: freda-davies@ereal.net
I: www.SmoothHound.co.uk/hotels/amberley2.html

SANDHURST
Gloucestershire

Brawn Farm ♦♦♦♦
Sandhurst, Gloucester GL2 9NR
T: (01452) 731010
F: (01452) 731102
E: williams.sally@excite.com

SAXILBY
Lincolnshire

Orchard Cottage ♦♦♦♦
3 Orchard Lane, Saxilby, Lincoln LN1 2HT
T: (01522) 703192
F: (01522) 703192
E: margaretallen@orchardcottage.org.uk
I: www.smoothhound.co.uk/hotels/orchardcot.html

SCALDWELL
Northamptonshire

The Old House ♦♦♦♦
East End, Scaldwell, Northampton NN6 9LB
T: (01604) 880359
F: (01604) 880359
E: mrsv@scaldwell43.fsnet.co.uk
I: www.the-oldhouse.co.uk

SCOTTER
Lincolnshire

Ivy Lodge Hotel ♦♦♦♦
4 Messingham Road, Scotter, Gainsborough DN21 3UQ
T: (01724) 763723
F: (01724) 761698
E: hotel@choxx.co.uk
I: www.SmoothHound.co.uk/hotels/ivylodge.html

SEATON
Rutland

Grange Farm Bed & Breakfast ♦♦♦♦
Seaton Grange, Uppington, Seaton, Oakham LE15 9HT
T: (01572) 747664
E: david.reading@farmline.com

SHEEPSCOMBE
Gloucestershire

Sen Sook ♦♦♦
Far End Lane, Sheepscombe, Stroud GL6 7RL
T: (01452) 812047
E: annehawkins@sensook.freeserve.co.uk

SHEPSHED
Leicestershire

Croft Guesthouse ♦♦♦
21 Hall Croft, Shepshed, Loughborough LE12 9AN
T: (01509) 505657
F: 0870 0522266
E: ray@croftguesthouse.demon.co.uk
I: www.croftguesthouse.demon.co.uk

The Grange Courtyard
♦♦♦♦♦ SILVER AWARD
The Grange, Forest Street, Shepshed, Loughborough LE12 9DA
T: (01509) 600189
E: lindalawrence@thegrangecourtyard.co.uk
I: www.thegrangecourtyard.co.uk

SHIFNAL
Shropshire

Naughty Nell's Limited ♦♦♦
1 Park Street, Shifnal, TF11 9BA
T: (01952) 411412
F: (01952) 463336

Odfellows - The Wine Bar
♦♦♦
Market Place, Shifnal, TF11 9AU
T: (01952) 461517
F: (01952) 463855
E: matt@odley.co.uk

SHIPSTON-ON-STOUR
Warwickshire

Chavignol at The Old Mill
♦♦♦♦♦ GOLD AWARD
Mill Street, Shipston-on-Stour, CV36 4AW
T: (01608) 663888
F: (01608) 663188
E: chavignol@virginbiz.com
I: www.chavignol.co.uk

SHIREBROOK
Derbyshire

The Old School Guesthouse
♦♦♦
80 Main Street, Shirebrook, Mansfield NG20 8DL
T: (01623) 744610
F: (01623) 744610
E: pemiles@oldschoolguesthouse.fsnet.co.uk
I: www.oldschoolguesthouse.co.uk

SHIRLEY
Derbyshire

The Old Byre Guesthouse
♦♦♦♦
Hollington Lane, Shirley, Ashbourne DE6 3AS
T: (01335) 360054
F: (01335) 360054
E: alan@theoldbyre.fsbusiness.co.uk
I: www.theoldbyre.fsbusiness.co.uk

SHOBDON
Herefordshire

Four Oaks ♦♦♦♦
Uphampton, Shobdon, Leominster HR6 9PA
T: (01568) 708039
F: (01568) 708039
E: bandb@fouroaks.plus.com

SHOBY
Leicestershire

Shoby Lodge Farm
♦♦♦♦ SILVER AWARD
Shoby, Melton Mowbray LE14 3PF
T: (01664) 812156

SHREWSBURY
Shropshire

Abbey Court House ♦♦♦
134 Abbey Foregate, Shrewsbury, SY2 6AU
T: (01743) 364416
F: (01743) 358559
E: info@abbeycourt.org
I: www.abbeycourt.org

Abbey Lodge Guest House
♦♦♦
68 Abbey Foregate, Shrewsbury, SY2 6BG
T: (01743) 235832
F: (01743) 235832
E: lindsay.abbeylodge@virgin.net
I: www.abbeylodgeshrewsbury.co.uk

Anton Guest House ♦♦♦♦
1 Canon Street, Monkmoor, Shrewsbury, SY2 5HG
T: (01743) 359275
E: antonhouse@supanet.com
I: www.antonhouse.supanet.com

Ashley House ♦♦♦♦
Crew Green, Shrewsbury, SY5 9AS
T: (01743) 884936

Ashton Lees
♦♦♦♦ SILVER AWARD
Dorrington, Shrewsbury SY5 7JW
T: (01743) 718378

Avonlea ♦♦
33 Coton Crescent, Coton Hill, Shrewsbury, SY1 2NZ
T: (01743) 359398

164 Bed and Continental Breakfast ♦♦♦
164 Abbey Foregate, Shrewsbury, SY2 6AL
T: (01743) 367750
F: (01743) 367750
E: chris@164bedandbreakfast.co.uk
I: www.164bedandbreakfast.co.uk

The Bell Inn ♦♦♦
Old Wenlock Road, Cross Houses, Shrewsbury, SY5 6JJ
T: (01743) 761264

Brambleberry ♦♦♦♦
Halfway House, Shrewsbury, SY5 9DD
T: (01743) 884762

The Burlton Inn
♦♦♦♦ SILVER AWARD
Burlton, Shrewsbury, SY4 5TB
T: (01939) 270284
F: (01939) 270204
E: bean@burltoninn.co.uk
I: www.burltoninn.co.uk

Cardeston Park Farm ♦♦♦
Ford, Shrewsbury SY5 9NH
T: (01743) 884265
F: (01743) 886265

Castlecote ♦♦♦
77 Monkmoor Road, Shrewsbury, SY2 5AT
T: (01743) 245473
F: (01743) 340274
E: btench@castlecote.fsbusiness.co.uk

Chatford House ♦♦♦
Bayston Hill, Shrewsbury, SY3 0AY
T: (01743) 718301

College Hill Guest House ♦♦
11 College Hill, Shrewsbury, SY1 1LZ
T: (01743) 365744
F: (01743) 365744

Eye Manor ♦♦♦♦
Leighton, Shrewsbury, SY5 6SQ
T: (01952) 510066
F: (01952) 510967

Golden Cross Hotel ♦♦♦
14 Princess Street, Shrewsbury, SY1 1LP
T: (01743) 362507

Lyth Hill House
♦♦♦♦ SILVER AWARD
28 Old Coppice, Lyth Hill, Shrewsbury, SY3 0BP
T: (01743) 874660
E: bnb@lythhillhouse.com
I: www.lythhillhouse.com

Noneley Hall ♦♦♦♦
Noneley, Near Wem, Shrewsbury, SY4 5SL
T: (01939) 233271
F: (01939) 233271
E: Noneley Hall@aol.com
I: www.noneleyhall.co.uk

North Farm ♦♦♦♦
Eaton Mascot, Shrewsbury, SY5 6HF
T: (01743) 761031
F: (01743) 761854
E: northfarm@talk21.com
I: www.northfarm.co.uk

The Old Station
♦♦♦♦ SILVER AWARD
Leaton, Bomere Heath, Shrewsbury SY4 3AP
T: (01939) 290905

The Old Vicarage
♦♦♦♦ SILVER AWARD
Leaton, Shrewsbury, SY4 3AP
T: (01939) 290989
F: (01939) 290989
E: m-j@oldvicleaton.com
I: www.oldvicleaton.com

Restawhile ♦♦♦
36 Coton Crescent, Coton Hill, Shrewsbury, SY1 2NZ
T: (01743) 240969
F: (01743) 231841
E: restawhile@breathemail.net
I: www.virtual-shropshire.co.uk/restawhile

Severn Cottage ♦♦♦♦
4 Coton Hill, Shrewsbury, SY1 2DZ
T: (01743) 358467
F: (01743) 340254
E: david.tudor1@virgin.net
I: www.shrewsburynet.com

Shenandoah ♦♦♦
Sparrow Lane, Abbey Forgate, Shrewsbury, SY2 5EP
T: (01743) 363015
F: (01743) 244918

The Stiperstones Guest House
♦♦♦
18 Coton Crescent, Coton Hill, Shrewsbury, SY1 2NZ
T: (01743) 246720
F: (01743) 350303
E: thestiperstones@aol.com
I: www.thestiperstones.com

Sydney House Hotel ♦♦♦
Coton Crescent, Coton Hill, Shrewsbury, SY1 2LJ
T: (01743) 354681
F: (01743) 354681

Trevellion House ♦♦♦
1 Bradford Street, Monkmoor, Shrewsbury, SY2 5DP
T: (01743) 249582
F: (01743) 232096
E: marktaplin@bradfordstreet.junglelink.co.uk

Upper Brompton Farm
♦♦♦♦♦ GOLD AWARD
Brompton, Cross Houses, Shrewsbury SY5 6LE
T: (01743) 761629
F: (01743) 761679
E: upper-brompton.farm@dial.pipex.com
I: www.smoothhound.co.uk/hotels/upperbro.html

Ye Olde Bucks Head Inn ♦♦♦
Frankwell, Shrewsbury, SY3 8JR
T: (01743) 369392
E: jennyhodges@onetel.net.uk

SHUSTOKE
Warwickshire

Ye Olde Station Guest House
♦♦♦
Church Road, Shustoke, Coleshill, Birmingham B46 2AX
T: (01675) 481736
F: (01675) 481736
E: yeoldestationguestho@talk21.com
I: www.yeoldestationguesthouse.activehotels.com/EZS

SKEGNESS
Lincolnshire

Chatsworth Hotel ♦♦♦
North Parade, Skegness, PE25 2UB
T: (01754) 764177
F: (01754) 761173
E: Altipper@aol.com
I: www.chatsworthskegness.co.uk

Clarence House Hotel ♦♦♦
32 South Parade, Skegness, PE25 3HW
T: (01754) 765588
E: colin-rita@lineone.net

Crawford Hotel ♦♦♦
104 South Parade, Skegness, PE25 3HR
T: (01754) 764215
F: (01754) 764215

The Dovedale Hotel ♦♦
118 Drummond Road, Skegness, PE25 3EH
T: (01754) 768676
I: www.dovedale.ccom.co.uk

Eastleigh ♦♦♦
60 Scarbrough Avenue, Skegness, PE25 2TB
T: (01754) 764605
F: (01754) 764605
I: www.eastleigh-skegness.co.uk

Fountaindale Hotel ♦♦♦
69 Sandbeck Avenue, Skegness, PE25 3JS
T: (01754) 762731
I: www.fountaindale.co.uk

Merton Hotel ♦♦♦
14 Firbeck Avenue, Skegness, PE25 3JY
T: (01754) 764423
F: (01754) 766627

North Parade Hotel ♦♦♦
20 North Parade, Skegness, PE25 2UB
T: (01754) 762309
F: (01754) 610949
E: northparadehotel@btinternet.com

Palm Court Hotel ♦♦♦
74 South Parade, Skegness, PE25 3HP
T: (01754) 767711
F: (01754) 767711

Rufford Hotel ♦♦♦
5 Saxby Avenue, Skegness, PE25 3JZ
T: (01754) 763428
F: (01754) 763428
E: a14jrw@aol.com
I: www.ruffordhotel-skegness.com

Savoy Hotel ♦♦♦
12 North Parade, Skegness, PE25 2UB
T: (01754) 763371
F: (01754) 761256
E: info@savoy-skegness.co.uk
I: www.savoy-skegness.co.uk

Saxby Hotel ♦♦♦
12 Saxby Avenue, Skegness, PE25 3LG
T: (01754) 763905
F: (01754) 763905

Stoneleigh Private Hotel ♦♦♦
67 Sandbeck Avenue, Skegness, PE25 3JS
T: (01754) 769138
E: enquiries@stoneleigh-hotel.freeserve.co.uk
I: www.stoneleigh-hotel.freeserve.co.uk

Sun Hotel ♦♦♦
19 North Parade, Skegness, PE25 2UB
T: (01754) 762364
F: (01754) 762364

Sunnybank Hotel ♦♦♦
29 Ida Road, Skegness, PE25 2AU
T: (01754) 762583
E: sunnybank.hotel@amserve.net

Woodthorpe Private Hotel ♦♦
64 South Parade, Skegness, PE25 3HP
T: (01754) 763452

SKILLINGTON
Lincolnshire

Jackson's House ♦♦♦♦
Middle Street, Skillington, Grantham NG33 5EU
T: (01476) 861634

Sproxton Lodge Farm ♦♦
Sproxton Lodge, Sproxton Road, Skillington, Grantham NG33 5HJ
T: (01476) 860307
F: (01476) 860307

SLEAFORD
Lincolnshire

The Tally Ho Inn ♦♦♦
Aswarby, Sleaford NG34 8SA
T: (01529) 455205
F: (01529) 309024
E: tallyhoaswarby@aol.com

SMISBY
Derbyshire

Forest Court Accommodation ♦♦♦
Annwell Place, Smisby, Ashby-de-la-Zouch LE65 2TA
T: (01530) 411711
F: (01530) 411146

Hillside Lodge ♦♦♦♦
Derby Road, Smisby, Ashby-de-la-Zouch LE65 2RG
T: (01530) 416411
E: barbaraball2000@yahoo.co.uk
I: www.hillsidelodge.co.uk

SOLIHULL
West Midlands

Acorn Guest House ♦♦♦♦ SILVER AWARD
29 Links Drive, Solihull, B91 2DJ
T: (0121) 7055241
E: acorn.wood@btinternet.com

Boxtrees Farm ♦♦♦♦
Stratford Road, Hockley Heath, Solihull B94 6EA
T: (01564) 782039
F: (01564) 784661
E: b&b@boxtrees.co.uk
I: boxtrees.co.uk

Cedarwood Guesthouse ♦♦♦
347 Lyndon Road, Cedarwood House, Solihull, B92 7QT
T: (0121) 743 5844
F: (0121) 743 5844
E: mail@cedarwoodguesthouse.co.uk
I: www.cedarwoodguesthouse.co.uk

Chelsea Lodge ♦♦♦♦
48 Meriden Road, Hampton in Arden, Solihull B92 0BT
T: (01675) 442408
F: (01675) 442408
E: chelsealodgebnb@aol.com
I: www.chelsealodgebnb.co.uk

Clovelly Guest House ♦♦♦
Coleshill Heath Road, Marston Green, Solihull, B37 7HY
T: (0121) 779 2886

The Edwardian Guest House ♦♦♦♦
7 St Bernards Road, Olton, Solihull, B92 7AU
T: (0121) 706 2138

The Oaks Bed & Breakfast ♦♦♦
92 Cheswick Way, Shirley, Solihull, B90 4HG
T: (0121) 744 9200
F: (0121) 744 9295
E: oaks92ches@aol.com
I: www.theoaksguesthouse.co.uk

Ravenhurst ♦♦♦
56 Lode Lane, Solihull, B91 2AW
T: (0121) 7055754
F: (0121) 704 0717
E: ravenhurstaccom@aol.com

Shirley Guest House ♦♦♦
967 Stratford Road, Shirley, Solihull B90 4BG
T: (0121) 744 2846
F: (0121) 6240044
E: shirleyguesthouse@post.com
I: www.smoothhound.co.uk/hotels/chalegue.htm

SOUTH HYKEHAM
Lincolnshire

Hall Farm House ♦♦♦
Meadow Lane, South Hykeham, Lincoln LN6 9PF
T: (01522) 686432
F: (01522) 686432
E: ray@surreyors2.freeserve.co.uk

SOUTH NORMANTON
Derbyshire

The Boundary Lodge ♦♦♦♦ SILVER AWARD
Lea Vale, Broadmeadows, South Normanton, Alfreton DE55 3NA
T: (01773) 819066
F: (01773) 819006
E: manager@boundarylodgefs.net.co.uk
I: theboundary.co.uk

SOUTH WINGFIELD
Derbyshire

Platts Farm Guesthouse ♦♦♦
High Road, South Wingfield, Alfreton DE55 7LX
T: (01773) 832280

SOUTH WITHAM
Lincolnshire

Barn Owl House ♦♦♦♦
20 High Street, South Witham, Grantham NG33 5QB
T: (01572) 767688
F: (01572) 767688
E: barnowl.house@btinternet.com
I: www.barnowlhouse.co.uk

The Blue Cow Inn and Brewery ♦♦♦
29 High Street, South Witham, Grantham NG33 5QB
T: (01572) 768432
F: (01572) 768432
E: richard@thirlwell.fslife.co.uk
I: www.thebluecowinn.co.uk

Rose Cottage ♦♦♦♦
7 High Street, South Witham, Grantham NG33 5QB
T: (01572) 767757
F: (01572) 767199
E: bob@vankimmenade.freeserve.co.uk

SOUTHAM
Warwickshire

Wormleighton Hall ♦♦♦♦ SILVER AWARD
Wormleighton, Southam, CV47 2XQ
T: (01295) 770234
F: (01295) 770234
E: wormleightonhall@farming.co.uk
I: www.smoothhound/hotels/wormleighton.html

SOUTHWELL
Nottinghamshire

Ashdene ♦♦♦♦
Radley Road, Halam, Southwell, NG22 8AH
T: (01636) 812335
E: david@herbert.newsurf.net

Church Street Bed and Breakfast ♦♦♦♦
56 Church Street, Southwell, NG25 0HG
T: (01636) 812004
E: ian.wright5@btinternet.com

SPALDING
Lincolnshire

Belvoir House ♦♦♦♦
13 London Road, Spalding, PE11 2TA
T: (01775) 723901
E: belvoir@fsbdial.co.uk

Lavender Lodge ♦♦♦
81 Pinchbeck Road, Spalding, PE11 1QF
T: (01775) 712800

STAFFORD
Staffordshire

Cedarwood ♦♦♦♦ SILVER AWARD
46 Weeping Cross, Stafford, ST17 0DS
T: (01785) 662981

The Foxes ♦♦♦
2A Thorneyfields Lane, Stafford, ST17 9YS
T: (01785) 602589
F: (01785) 602589
E: thefoxes.beech@ntlworld.com

Littywood House ♦♦♦♦
Bradley, Stafford, ST18 9DW
T: (01785) 780234
E: sue@littywood.co.uk

The Old House Bed & Breakfast Rating Applied For
Main Road, Wolseley Bridge, Stafford, ST17 0XJ
T: (01889) 881264
E: oldhousebb@zoom.co.uk

Park Farm ♦♦♦
Weston Road, Stafford, ST18 0BD
T: (01785) 240257
F: (01785) 240257
E: parkfarm12@hotmail.com

Woodhouse Farm ♦♦♦♦
Woodhouse Lane, Haughton, Stafford, ST18 9JJ
T: (01785) 822259

Wyndale Guest House ♦♦
199 Corporation Street, Stafford, ST16 3LQ
T: (01785) 223069

STAMFORD
Lincolnshire

Abbey House and Coach House ♦♦♦♦
West End Road, Maxey, Peterborough PE6 9EJ
T: (01778) 344642
F: (01778) 342706
E: sales@abbeyhouse.co.uk
I: www.abbeyhouse.co.uk

Birch House ♦♦♦
4 Lonsdale Road, Stamford, PE9 2RW
T: (01780) 754876
F: (01780) 754876
E: Birch_House@faxvia.net

4 Camphill Cottages ♦♦♦♦
Little Casterton, Stamford, PE9 4BE
T: (01780) 763661
E: anna.martin@tesco.net

86 Casterton Road ♦♦♦
Stamford, PE9 2UB
T: (01780) 754734

Chestnut View Bed & Breakfas ♦♦♦
Chestnut View, 94 Casterton Road, Stamford, PE9 2UB
T: (01780) 763648
F: (01780) 480 663
E: jstimson@telco4u.net
I: www.angelfire.com/ga3/chestnutview

Dolphin Guesthouse ♦♦
12 East Street, Stamford, PE9 1QD
T: (01780) 757515
F: (01780) 757515
E: mikdolphin@mikdolphin.demon.co.uk

Gwynne House ♦♦♦♦
Kings Road, Stamford, PE9 1HD
T: (01780) 762210
E: john@johnng.demon.co.uk

Martins ♦♦♦♦
20 High Street, Saint Martin's, Stamford, PE9 2LF
T: (01780) 752106
F: (01780) 482691
E: marie@martins-b-b.demon.co.uk

Midstone Farmhouse
♦♦♦♦ SILVER AWARD
Southorpe, Stamford, PE9 3BX
T: (01780) 740136
F: (01780) 749294
E: ahsmidstonehouse@amserve.net

The Oak Inn ♦♦♦
48 Stamford Road, Easton on the Hill, Stamford PE9 3PA
T: (01780) 752286
F: (01780) 756931
E: peter@klippon.demon.co.uk

Rock Lodge
♦♦♦♦♦ SILVER AWARD
1 Empingham Road, Stamford, PE9 2RH
T: (01780) 481758
F: (01780) 481757
E: rocklodge@innpro.co.uk
I: www.innpro.co.uk

5 Rock Terrace ♦♦♦♦
Scotgate, Stamford, PE9 2YJ
T: (01780) 755475
E: averdieckguest@talk21.com

8 Southview Terrace ♦♦
New Cross Road, Stamford, PE9 1QY
T: (01780) 755987

Spires View ♦♦♦
North Street, Stamford, PE9 1AA
T: (01780) 764419

Ufford Farm ♦♦♦
Main Street, Ufford, Stamford, PE9 3BH
T: (01780) 740220
F: (01780) 740220
E: vergette@ufford1.freeserve.co.uk

STANDISH
Gloucestershire

Oaktree Farm ♦♦♦♦
Little Haresfield, Standish, Stonehouse GL10 3DS
T: (01452) 883323
E: Jackie@oaktreefarm.fsnet.co.uk

STANFORD BISHOP
Herefordshire

The Hawkins Farm ♦♦♦
Stanford Bishop, Worcester WR6 5TQ
T: (01886) 884250
F: (01886) 884250

STANTON-BY-BRIDGE
Derbyshire

Ivy House Farm
♦♦♦♦ SILVER AWARD
Stanton-by-Bridge, Derby DE73 1HT
T: (01332) 863152
F: (01332) 863152
E: mary@guesthouse.sbusiness.co.uk
I: www.ivy-house-farm.com

STANTON IN PEAK
Derbyshire

Congreave Farm
♦♦♦♦ SILVER AWARD
Congreave, Stanton in Peak, Matlock DE4 2NF
T: (01629) 732063
E: deborahbettney@congreave.junglelink.co.uk
I: www.matsam16.freeserve.co.uk/congreave/

STANTON-ON-THE-WOLDS
Nottinghamshire

Laurel Farm ♦♦♦
Browns Lane, Stanton-on-the-Wolds, Keyworth, Nottingham NG12 5BL
T: (0115) 937 3488
F: (0115) 9376490
E: laurelfarm@yahoo.com
I: www.s-h-systems.co.uk/laurelfa.html

STAPLETON
Shropshire

Stapleton Cottage ♦♦♦♦
Stapleton, Dorrington, Shrewsbury SY5 7EQ
T: (01743) 718314
F: (01743) 718314
E: wilkinson@ichthusltd.fsnet.co.uk

STIPERSTONES
Shropshire

The Old Chapel ♦♦♦♦
Perkinsbeach Dingle, Stiperstones, SY5 0PE
T: (01743) 791449
E: jean@a-lees.freeserve.co.uk
I: www.s-h-systems.co.uk/hotels/oldchapel.html

STOCKINGFORD
Warwickshire

Aberglynmarch Guest House
♦♦♦
198 Church Road, Stockingford, Nuneaton CV10 8LH
T: (02476) 342793
F: (02476) 342793

STOKE-ON-TRENT
Staffordshire

Cedar Tree Cottage ♦♦♦♦
41 Longton Road, Trentham, Stoke-on-Trent, ST4 8ND
T: (01782) 644751

Flower Pot Hotel ♦
44-46 Snow Hill, Shelton, Stoke-on-Trent, ST1 4LY
T: (01782) 207204
F: (01782) 207204

The Hollies ♦♦♦
Clay Lake, Endon, Stoke-on-Trent ST9 9DD
T: (01782) 503252
F: (01782) 503252
E: theholliesendon@faxvia.net

Holly Trees ♦♦♦♦
Crewe Road, Alsager, Stoke-on-Trent, ST7 2JL
T: (01270) 876847
F: (01270) 883301
E: hollytreeshotel@aol.com
I: www.hollytreeshotel.co.uk

The Limes ♦♦♦
Cheadle Road, Blythe Bridge, Stoke-on-Trent ST11 9PW
T: (01782) 393278

The Old Dairy House
♦♦♦♦♦ SILVER AWARD
Trentham Park, Stoke-on-Trent, ST4 8AE
T: (01782) 641209
F: (01782) 712904
E: olddairyhouse@hotmail.com

Old Vicarage Guesthouse
♦♦♦♦
Birchenwood Road, Newchapel, Stoke-on-Trent ST7 4QT
T: (01782) 785270
E: peter.kent-baguley@birchenwood.freeserve.co.uk

Reynolds Hey ♦♦♦♦
Park Lane, Endon, Stoke-on-Trent ST9 9JB
T: (01782) 502717
E: reynoldshey@hotmail.com

Shaw Gate Farm ♦♦♦
Shay Lane, Foxt, Stoke-on-Trent, ST10 2HN
T: (01538) 266590
F: (01538) 266590
E: Ken_morris@lineone.net
I: www.shawgatefarm.co.uk

Sneyd Arms Hotel ♦♦
Tower Square, Tunstall, Stoke-on-Trent ST6 5AA
T: (01782) 826722
F: (01782) 826722
I: www.thesneydarms.co.uk

Star Hotel ♦♦♦
92 Marsh Street North, Hanley, Stoke-on-Trent ST1 5HH
T: (01782) 207507
F: (01782) 207507

Verdon Guest House ♦♦♦
44 Charles Street, Hanley, Stoke-on-Trent ST1 3JY
T: (01782) 264244
F: (01782) 264244
E: debbie@howlett18.freeserve.co.uk
I: www.verdonguesthouse.co.uk

STONE
Staffordshire

Lock House ♦♦♦♦
74 Newcastle Road, Stone, ST15 8LB
T: (01785) 811551
F: (01785) 286587
E: mbd@fsbdial.co.uk

Mayfield House
Rating Applied For
112 Newcastle Road, Stone, ST15 8LG
T: (01785) 811446

STONEHOUSE
Gloucestershire

Beacon Inn Hotel
Rating Applied For
Haresfield Village, Stonehouse, GL10 3DX
T: (01452) 728884
F: (01452) 728884

The Grey Cottage
♦♦♦♦♦ GOLD AWARD
Bath Road, Leonard Stanley, Stonehouse, GL10 3LU
T: (01453) 822515
F: (01453) 822515

Merton Lodge ♦♦
8 Ebley Road, Stonehouse, GL10 2LQ
T: (01453) 822018

STOTTESDON
Worcestershire

Hardwicke Farm ♦♦♦♦
Stottesdon, Kidderminster DY14 8TN
T: (01746) 718220
E: Hardwickefarm@hotmail.com
I: www.farm-holidays.co.uk

STOULTON
Worcestershire

Caldewell ♦♦♦♦
Pershore Road, Stoulton, Worcester WR7 4RL
T: (01905) 840894
F: (01905) 840894
E: sheila@caldewell.demon.co.uk
I: www.caldewell.com

STOURBRIDGE
West Midlands

St. Elizabeth's Cottage ♦♦♦♦
Woodman Lane, Clent, Stourbridge DY9 9PX
T: (01562) 883883
F: (01562) 885034
E: st_elizabeth_cot@btconnect.com

STOURPORT-ON-SEVERN
Worcestershire

Baldwin House ♦♦♦
8 Lichfield Street, Stourport-on-Severn, DY13 9EU
T: (01299) 877221
F: (01299) 877221
E: baldwinhousebb@aol.com

STOW-ON-THE-WOLD
Gloucestershire

Aston House
♦♦♦♦ SILVER AWARD
Broadwell, Moreton-in-Marsh, GL56 0TJ
T: (01451) 830475
E: fja@netcomuk.co.uk
I: www.netcomuk.co.uk/~nmfa/aston_house.html

The Beeches ♦♦♦
Fosse Lane, Stow-on-the-Wold, Cheltenham GL54 1EH
T: (01451) 870836

Corsham Field Farmhouse
♦♦♦
Bledington Road, Stow-on-the-Wold, Cheltenham GL54 1JH
T: (01451) 831750

The Cotswold Garden Tea Room & B&B. ♦♦♦
Wells Cottage, Digbeth Street, Stow-on-the-Wold, Cheltenham GL54 1BN
T: (01451) 870999

Crestow House ♦♦♦♦
Stow-on-the-Wold, Cheltenham GL54 1JX
T: (01451) 830969
F: (01451) 832129
E: fsimonetti@btinternet.com
I: www.crestow.co.uk

Cross Keys Cottage ♦♦♦
Park Street, Stow-on-the-Wold, Cheltenham GL54 1AQ
T: (01451) 831128
F: (01451) 831128

Fairview Farmhouse
♦♦♦♦ SILVER AWARD
Bledington Road, Stow-on-the-Wold, GL54 1JH
T: (01451) 830279
F: (01451) 830279
E: sdavis0145@aol.com
I: www.smoothHound.co.uk/shs

The Fox Inn ♦♦♦♦
Stow-on-the-Wold, Cheltenham GL56 0UR
T: (01451) 870555
F: (01451) 870669
E: info@foxinn.net
I: www.foxinn.net

The Gate Lodge ♦♦♦♦
Stow Hill, Stow-on-the-Wold, Cheltenham GL54 1JZ
T: (01451) 832103

Honeysuckle Cottage
♦♦♦♦ SILVER AWARD
Kings Arms Lane, The Square, Stow-on-the-Wold, Cheltenham GL54 1AF
T: (01451) 830973
E: hsucklecottage@aol.com

Littlebroom ♦♦♦♦
Maugersbury, Stow-on-the-Wold, Cheltenham GL54 1HP
T: (01451) 830510
E: davidandbrenda@talk21.com
I: www.completely-cotswold.com

Maugersbury Manor ♦♦♦
Stow-on-the-Wold, Cheltenham GL54 1HP
T: (01451) 830581
F: (01451) 870902
E: karen@manorholidays.co.uk
I: www.manorholidays.co.uk

Mount Pleasant Farm ♦♦♦
Oddington Road, Stow-on-the-Wold, Cheltenham GL54 1JJ
T: (01451) 832078
F: (01451) 832078
E: sgaden72@aol.com

Pear Tree Cottage ♦♦♦
High Street, Stow-on-the-Wold, Cheltenham GL54 1DL
T: (01451) 831210
E: peartreecottage@btinternet.com

South Hill Farmhouse ♦♦♦
Fosseway, Stow-on-the-Wold, Cheltenham GL54 1JU
T: (01451) 831888
F: (01451) 832255
E: info@southhill.co.uk
I: www.southhill.co.uk

South Hill Lodge
♦♦♦♦ SILVER AWARD
Fosseway, Stow-on-the-Wold, Cheltenham GL54 1JU
T: (01451) 831083
E: digby@southilllodge.freeserve.co.uk
I: www.SmoothHound.co.uk/hotels/southhill

Tall Trees ♦♦♦♦
Oddington Road, Stow-on-the-Wold, Cheltenham GL54 1AL
T: (01451) 831296
F: (01451) 870049
E: talltreestow@aol.com

White Hart Inn ♦♦♦
The Square, Stow-on-the-Wold, Cheltenham GL54 1AF
T: (01451) 830674
F: (01451) 830090

Wyck Hill Lodge ♦♦♦♦♦
Burford Road, Stow-on-the-Wold, Cheltenham GL54 1HT
T: (01451) 830141
E: gkhwyck@compuserve.com

STOWE-BY-CHARTLEY
Staffordshire

The Plough Inn ♦♦♦
Amerton, Stowe-by-Chartley, Stafford ST18 0LA
T: (01889) 270308
F: (01889) 271131

STRAGGLETHORPE
Lincolnshire

Stragglethorpe Hall
♦♦♦♦ SILVER AWARD
Stragglethorpe, Lincoln LN5 0QZ
T: (01400) 272308
F: (01400) 273816
E: stragglethorpe@compuserve.com
I: www.stragglethorpe.com

STRATFORD-UPON-AVON
Warwickshire

Aberfoyle Guest House ♦♦♦
3 Evesham Place, Stratford-upon-Avon, CV37 6HT
T: (01789) 295703
F: (01789) 295703

Aidan Guest House ♦♦♦♦
11 Evesham Place, Stratford-upon-Avon, CV37 6HT
T: (01789) 292824
F: (01789) 269072
E: john2aidan@aol.com
I: www.aidanhouse.co.uk

All Seasons ♦♦
51 Grove Road, Stratford-upon-Avon, CV37 6PB
T: (01789) 293404
F: (01789) 293404

Amelia Linhill Guesthouse ♦♦♦
35 Evesham Place, Stratford-upon-Avon, CV37 6HT
T: (01789) 292879
F: (01789) 299691
E: Linhill@bigwig.net
I: Linhillguesthouse.co.uk

The Applegarth ♦♦♦
Warwick Road, Stratford-upon-Avon, CV37 6YW
T: (01789) 267388
F: (01789) 267388
E: applegarth@supanet.com

Arden Park Hotel ♦♦♦
6 Arden Street, Stratford-upon-Avon, CV37 6PA
T: (01789) 296072
F: (01789) 296072

Arrandale Guesthouse ♦♦♦
208 Evesham Road, Stratford-upon-Avon, CV37 9AS
T: (01789) 267112

Ashley Court Hotel ♦♦♦
55 Shipston Road, Stratford-upon-Avon, CV37 7LN
T: (01789) 297278
F: (01789) 204453
E: info@ashleycourthotel.co.uk
I: www.ashleycourthotel.co.uk

Avon View Hotel ♦♦♦♦
121 Shipston Road, Stratford-upon-Avon, CV37 7LW
T: (01789) 297542
F: (01789) 292936
E: avon.view@lineone.net

Avonlea ♦♦♦♦
47 Shipston Road, Stratford-upon-Avon, CV37 7LN
T: (01789) 205940
F: (01789) 209115
E: avonlea-stratford@lineone.net
I: www.avonlea-stratford.co.uk

34 Banbury Road ♦♦♦
Stratford-upon-Avon, CV37 7HY
T: (01789) 269714
E: clodagh@lycosmail.com
I: www.smoothhound.co.uk/hotels/34banbur.html

Barbette ♦♦♦
165 Evesham Road, Stratford-upon-Avon, CV37 9BP
T: (01789) 297822

The Blue Boar Inn ♦♦♦
Temple Grafton, Alcester B49 6NR
T: (01789) 750010
F: (01789) 750635
E: blueboar@covlink.co.uk
I: www.blueboarinn.co.uk

Bradbourne House ♦♦♦♦
44 Shipston Road, Stratford-upon-Avon, CV37 7LP
T: (01789) 204178
F: (01789) 262335
E: ian@bradbourne-house.co.uk
I: www.bradbourne-house.co.uk

Brett House ♦♦♦
8 Broad Walk, Stratford-upon-Avon, CV37 6HS
T: (01789) 266374
F: (01789) 414027
E: cyril21@openworld.com
I: www.bretthouse.co.uk

Broadlands Guest House ♦♦♦♦
23 Evesham Place, Stratford-upon-Avon, CV37 6HT
T: (01789) 299181
F: (01789) 551382
E: broadlands.com@virgin.net
I: www.stratford-upon-avon.co.uk/broadlands.htm

Brook Lodge Guest House
♦♦♦♦ SILVER AWARD
192 Alcester Road, Stratford-upon-Avon, CV37 9DR
T: (01789) 295988
F: (01789) 295988
E: brooklodgeguesthouse@btinternet.com
I: www.smoothhound.co.uk/hotels/brooklod.html

Burton Farm ♦♦♦♦
Bishopton, Stratford-upon-Avon CV37 0RW
T: (01789) 293338
F: (01789) 262877

Carlton Guest House ♦♦♦
22 Evesham Place, Stratford-upon-Avon, CV37 6HT
T: (01789) 293548
F: (01789) 293548

Chadwyns Guest House ♦♦♦♦
6 Broad Walk, Stratford-upon-Avon, CV37 6HS
T: (01789) 269077
F: (01789) 298855
E: stay@chadwyns.co.uk
I: www.chadwyns.co.uk

Church Farm ♦♦♦
Long Marston, Stratford-upon-Avon CV37 8RH
T: (01789) 720275
F: (01789) 720275
E: wiggychurchfarm@hotmail.com
I: www.churchfarmhouse.co.uk

Church Farm ♦♦♦
Dorsington, Stratford-upon-Avon CV37 8AX
T: (01789) 720471
F: (01789) 720830
E: chfarmdorsington@aol.com
I: www.churchfarmstratford.co.uk

Courtland Hotel
Rating Applied For
12 Guild Street, Stratford-upon-Avon, CV37 6RE
T: (01789) 292401
F: (01789) 292401
E: dianamoon@ukvacation.com
I: www.uk-vacation.com/courtland

Craig Cleeve House Hotel & Restaurant ♦♦♦♦
67-69 Shipston Road, Stratford-upon-Avon, CV37 7LW
T: (01789) 296573
F: (01789) 299452
E: craigcleev@aol.com

Curtain Call ♦♦♦
142 Alcester Road, Stratford-upon-Avon, CV37 9DR
T: (01789) 267734
F: (01789) 267734
E: curtaincall@btinternet.com
I: www.curtaincallguesthouse.co.uk

Cymbeline House ♦♦♦
24 Evesham Place, Stratford-upon-Avon, CV37 6HT
T: (01789) 292958
F: (01789) 292958

Dylan Guesthouse ♦♦♦♦
10 Evesham Place, Stratford-upon-Avon, CV37 6HT
T: (01789) 204819
E: dylanguesthouse@lineone.net
I: www.thedylan.co.uk

East Bank House ♦♦♦♦
19 Warwick Road, Stratford-upon-Avon, CV37 6YW
T: (01789) 292758
F: (01789) 292758
E: eastbank.house@virgin.net
I: www.east-bank-house.co.uk

Eastnor House Hotel ♦♦♦♦
Shipston Road, Stratford-upon-Avon, CV37 7LN
T: (01789) 268115
F: (01789) 551133
E: enquiries@eastnorhouse.com
I: www.eastnorhouse.com

The Emsley Guest House ♦♦♦♦
4 Arden Street, Stratford-upon-Avon, CV37 6PA
T: (01789) 299557
F: (01789) 299023
E: emsleygh@bigfoot.com
I: www.theemsley.co.uk

Ettington Chase Conference Centre
♦♦♦♦♦ SILVER AWARD
Banbury Road, Ettington, Stratford-upon-Avon, CV37 7NZ
T: (01789) 740000
F: (01789) 740909
E: ettconf@hayleycc.co.uk
I: www.hayley-conf.co.uk

Eversley Bears' Guest House ♦♦♦♦
37 Grove Road, Stratford-upon-Avon, CV37 6PB
T: (01789) 292334
F: (01789) 292334
E: eversleybears@btinternet.com
I: www.stratford-upon-avon.co.uk/eversleybears.htm

Faviere ♦♦♦♦
127 Shipston Road, Stratford-upon-Avon, CV37 7LW
T: (01789) 293764
F: (01789) 269365
E: guestsfaviere@cwcom.net
I: www.faviere.com

Folly Farm Cottage
♦♦♦♦ GOLD AWARD
Back Street, Ilmington, Shipston-on-Stour CV36 4LJ
T: (01608) 682425
F: (01608) 682425
E: slowe@follyfarm.co.uk
I: www.follyfarm.co.uk

Gravelside Barn
♦♦♦♦ SILVER AWARD
Binton, Stratford-upon-Avon CV37 9TU
T: (01789) 750502
F: (01789) 750502
E: denise@gravelside.fsnet.co.uk

Green Gables ♦♦♦
47 Banbury Road, Stratford-upon-Avon, CV37 7HW
: (01789) 205557
: jeankerr@talk21.com
: www.stratford-upon-avon.co.uk/greengables.htm

Green Haven ♦♦♦♦
217 Evesham Road, Stratford-upon-Avon, CV37 9AS
: (01789) 297874
: (01789) 550487
: information@green-haven.co.uk
www.green-haven.co.uk

ampton Lodge Guest House ♦♦♦
8 Shipston Road, Stratford-pon-Avon, CV37 7LP
: (01789) 299374
: (01789) 299374
: hamptonlodgeinfo@aol.com
www.hamptonlodge.co.uk

arvard Private Hotel ♦♦♦
9 Shipston Road, Stratford-pon-Avon, CV37 7LW
(01789) 262623
: (01789) 261354

eron Lodge ♦♦♦
60 Alcester Road, Stratford-pon-Avon, CV37 9JQ
(01789) 299169
(01789) 204463
chrisandbob@heronlodge.m
www.heronlodge.com

Highcroft ♦♦♦
Banbury Road, Stratford-upon-Avon, CV37 7NF
T: (01789) 296293
F: (01789) 415236
E: suedavies_highcroft@hotmail.com
I: www.smoothhound.co.uk

Houndshill House ♦♦♦
Banbury Road, Ettington, Stratford-upon-Avon CV37 7NS
T: (01789) 740267
F: (01789) 740075

Howard Arms
♦♦♦♦♦ SILVER AWARD
Lower Green, Ilmington, Shipston-on-Stour CV36 4LT
T: (01608) 682226
F: (01608) 682226
E: howard.arms@virgin.net
I: www.howardarms.com

Ingon Bank Farm ♦♦♦
Warwick Road, Stratford-upon-Avon, CV37 0NY
T: (01789) 292642
F: (01789) 292642

Kawartha House ♦♦♦
39 Grove Road, Stratford-upon-Avon, CV37 6PB
T: (01789) 204469
F: (01789) 292837
E: kawarthahouse@btopenworld.com
I: www.stratford-upon-avon.co.uk/kawartha.htm

Marlyn Hotel ♦♦♦
3 Chestnut Walk, Stratford-upon-Avon, CV37 6HG
T: (01789) 293752
F: (01789) 293752
E: evansmarlynhotel@aol.com
I: www.marlynhotel.co.uk

Mary Arden Inn ♦♦♦♦
The Green, Wilmcote, Stratford-upon-Avon CV37 9XJ
T: (01789) 267030
F: (01789) 204875

Melita Private Hotel ♦♦♦♦
37 Shipston Road, Stratford-upon-Avon, CV37 7LN
T: (01789) 292432
F: (01789) 204867
E: info@melitahotel.co.uk
I: www.melitahotel.co.uk

Midway ♦♦♦♦
182 Evesham Road, Stratford-upon-Avon, CV37 9BS
T: (01789) 204154
E: mealmg@midway182.fsnet.co.uk
I: www.stratford-upon-avon.co.uk/midway.htm

Mil-Mar ♦♦♦♦
96 Alcester Road, Stratford-upon-Avon, CV37 9DP
T: (01789) 267095
F: (01789) 262205
E: milmar@btinternet.com
I: www.strafford-upon-avon.co.uk/milmar.htm

Minola Guest House ♦♦♦
25 Evesham Place, Stratford-upon-Avon, CV37 6HT
T: (01789) 293573
F: (01789) 551625

Moonlight Bed & Breakfast ♦♦♦
144 Alcester Road, Stratford-upon-Avon, CV37 9DR
T: (01789) 298213

Moss Cottage ♦♦♦♦
61 Evesham Road, Stratford-upon-Avon, CV37 9BA
T: (01789) 294770
F: (01789) 294770
E: pauline_rush@onetel.net.uk

The Myrtles Bed and Breakfast ♦♦♦♦
6 Rother Street, Stratford-upon-Avon, CV37 6LU
T: (01789) 295511

Nando's ♦♦
18-19 Evesham Place, Stratford-upon-Avon, CV37 6HT
T: (01789) 204907
F: (01789) 204907
E: rooms@nandosguesthouse.co.uk

Newlands ♦♦♦♦
7 Broad Walk, Stratford-upon-Avon, CV37 6HS
T: (01789) 298449
F: (01789) 267806
E: newlandslynwalter@hotmail.com
I: www.smoothhound.co.uk/hotels/newlands.html

Oxstalls Farm ♦♦♦
Warwick Road, Stratford-upon-Avon, CV37 0NS
T: (01789) 205277
F: (01789) 205277

Parkfield ♦♦♦
3 Broad Walk, Stratford-upon-Avon, CV37 6HS
T: (01789) 293313
F: (01789) 293313
E: parkfield@btinternet.com
I: www.parkfieldbandb.co.uk

Payton Hotel
♦♦♦♦ SILVER AWARD
6 John Street, Stratford-upon-Avon, CV37 6UB
T: (01789) 266442
F: (01789) 294410
E: info@payton.co.uk
I: www.payton.co.uk

Peartree Cottage
♦♦♦♦ SILVER AWARD
7 Church Road, Wilmcote, Stratford-upon-Avon CV37 9UX
T: (01789) 205889
F: (01789) 262862
E: mander@peartreecot.co.uk
I: www.peartreecot.co.uk

Penryn Guesthouse ♦♦♦♦
126 Alcester Road, Stratford-upon-Avon, CV37 9DP
T: (01789) 293718
F: (01789) 266077
E: penrynhouse@btinternet.com
I: www.penrynguesthouse.co.uk

Penshurst Guesthouse ♦♦♦
34 Evesham Place, Stratford-upon-Avon, CV37 6HT
T: (01789) 205259
F: (01789) 295322
E: karen@penshurst.net
I: www.penshurst.net

The Poplars ♦♦♦
Mansell Farm, Newbold-on-Stour, Stratford-upon-Avon, CV37 8BZ
T: (01789) 450540
F: (01789) 450540
E: juidth@poplars-farmhouse.co.uk
I: www.SmoothHound.co.uk/hotel/poplars2html

The Queens Head ♦♦♦♦
Ely Street, Stratford-upon-Avon, CV37 6LN
T: (01789) 204914
F: (01789) 772983
E: richard@distinctivepubs.freeserve.co.uk
I: www.distinctivepubs.co.uk

Quilt and Croissants ♦♦♦
33 Evesham Place, Stratford-upon-Avon, CV37 6HT
T: (01789) 267629
F: (01789) 551651
E: rooms@quilt-croissants.demon.co.uk
I: www.smoothhound.co.uk/hotels/quilt.html

Ravenhurst ♦♦♦
2 Broad Walk, Stratford-upon-Avon, CV37 6HS
T: (01789) 292515
E: ravaccom@waverider.co.uk
I: www.stratford-ravenhurst.co.uk

Salamander Guest House ♦♦♦
40 Grove Road, Stratford-upon-Avon, CV37 6PB
T: (01789) 205728
F: (01789) 205728

Shakespeare's View
♦♦♦♦♦ GOLD AWARD
Kings Lane, Snitterfield, Stratford-upon-Avon CV37 0QB
T: (01789) 731824
F: (01789) 731824
E: shakespeares.view@btinternet.co.uk
I: www.shakespeares.view.btinternet.co.uk

Stratheden Hotel ♦♦♦
5 Chapel Street, Stratford-upon-Avon, CV37 6EP
T: (01789) 297119
F: (01789) 297119
E: richard@stratheden.fsnet.co.uk
I: www.stratheden.co.uk

Sunnydale Guest House ♦♦♦
64 Shipston Road, Stratford-upon-Avon, CV37 7LP
T: (01789) 295166

Victoria Spa Lodge
♦♦♦♦ SILVER AWARD
Bishopton Lane, Bishopton, Stratford-upon-Avon, CV37 9QY
T: (01789) 267985
F: (01789) 204728
E: ptozer@victoriaspalodge.demon.co.uk
I: www.stratford-upon-avon.co.uk/victoriaspa.htm

Virginia Lodge Guest House ♦♦♦♦
12 Evesham Place, Stratford-upon-Avon, CV37 6HT
T: (01789) 292157
F: (01789) 292157
E: pamela83@btinternet.com
I: www.virginialodge.co.uk

The White House
♦♦♦♦ GOLD AWARD
Kings Lane, Bishopton, Stratford-upon-Avon CV37 0RD
T: (01789) 294296
E: enquiries@stratfordwhitehouse.co.uk
I: www.stratfordwhitehouse.co.uk

Woodstock Guest House
♦♦♦♦ SILVER AWARD
30 Grove Road, Stratford-upon-Avon, CV37 6PB
T: (01789) 299881
F: (01789) 299881
E: woodstockhouse@compuserve.com

STRETTON Staffordshire

Dovecliff Hall
♦♦♦♦♦ SILVER AWARD
Dovecliff Road, Stretton, Burton upon Trent DE13 0DJ
T: (01283) 531818
F: (01283) 516546

STRETTON ON FOSSE Warwickshire

Jasmine Cottage ♦♦♦
Stretton on Fosse, Moreton-in-Marsh GL56 9SA
T: (01608) 661972

STROUD Gloucestershire

Ashleigh House ♦♦♦♦
Bussage, Stroud GL6 8AZ
T: (01453) 883944
F: (01453) 886931
E: etc@ashleighgh.co.uk
I: www.ashleighgh.co.uk

Beechcroft ♦♦♦
Brownshill, Stroud GL6 8AG
T: (01453) 883422
E: jenny@beechcroftbb.fsnet.co.uk

Burleigh Farm
♦♦♦♦ SILVER AWARD
Minchinhampton, Stroud, GL5 2PF
T: (01453) 883112
F: (01453) 883112

The Clothier's Arms ♦♦♦
1 Bath Road, Stroud, GL5 3JJ
T: (01453) 763801
F: (01453) 757161
E: luciano@clothiersarms.demon.co.uk
I: www.clothiersarms.co.uk

Downfield Hotel ♦♦♦
134 Cainscross Road, Stroud, GL5 4HN
T: (01453) 764496
F: (01453) 753150
E: info@downfieldhotel.co.uk
I: www.downfieldhotel.co.uk

Grove Cottage ♦♦♦♦
Browns Hill, Stroud, GL6 8AJ
T: (01453) 882561

Keallasay
Rating Applied For
73 Barrowfield Road, Farmhill, Stroud, GL5 4DG
T: (01453) 765995
E: bakj@waitrose.com

Pretoria Villa ♦♦♦♦
Wells Road, Eastcombe, Stroud GL6 7EE
T: (01452) 770435
F: (01452) 770435
E: glynis@gsolomon.freeserve.co.uk

Threeways ♦♦♦
Lypiatt Hill, Bisley Road, Stroud, GL6 7LQ
T: (01453) 756001

The Yew Tree Bed and Breakfast ♦♦♦♦
Walls Quarry, Brimscombe, Stroud, GL5 2PA
T: (01453) 887594
F: (01453) 883428
E: elizabeth.peters@tesco.net
I: www.uk-bedandbreakfasts.com/Gloucestershire/Stroud

STURTON-BY-STOW Lincolnshire

Ivy Cottage ♦♦♦
Stow Road, Sturton-by-Stow, Lincoln LN1 2BZ
T: (01427) 788023

SULGRAVE Northamptonshire

Rectory Farm ♦♦♦
Little Street, Sulgrave, Banbury OX17 2SG
T: (01295) 760261
F: (01295) 760089
E: rectoryfarm@talk21.com

SUTTON-ON-SEA Lincolnshire

Athelstone Lodge Hotel ♦♦♦
25 Trusthorpe Road, Sutton-on-Sea, Mablethorpe LN12 2LR
T: (01507) 441521
I: www.athelstonelodge.co.uk

Bacchus Hotel ♦♦♦
High Street, Sutton-on-Sea, Mablethorpe LN12 2EY
T: (01507) 441204
F: (01507) 441204

SUTTON-ON-TRENT Nottinghamshire

Fiveways ♦♦♦
Barrel Hill Road, Sutton-on-Trent, Newark NG23 6PT
T: (01636) 822086

Woodbine Farmhouse ♦♦♦
1 Church Street, Sutton-on-Trent, Newark NG23 6PD
T: (01636) 822549
F: (01636) 821716
E: woodbinefmhouse@cs.com

SWADLINCOTE Derbyshire

Ferne Cottage ♦♦♦
5 Black Horse Hill, Appleby Magna, Swadlincote, DE12 7AQ
T: (01530) 271772
F: (01503) 270652

Hurst Farm Guesthouse
♦♦♦♦
Netherseal Road, Chilcote, Swadlincote, DE12 8DQ
T: (01827) 373853
E: suehfgh@aol.com

Manor Farm
Rating Applied For
Coton in the Elms, Swadlincote, DE12 8EP
T: (01283) 760340
F: (01283) 760340

SWANNINGTON Leicestershire

Hillfield House ♦♦♦♦
52 Station Hill, Swannington, Leicester LE67 8RH
T: (01530) 837 414
F: (01530) 458 233
E: molly@hillfieldhouse.co.uk
I: www.hillfieldhouse.co.uk

SWARKESTONE Derbyshire

October House ♦♦♦♦
The Water Meadows, Swarkestone, Derby DE73 1JA
T: (01332) 705849
E: longsons@hotmail.com

SWAYFIELD Lincolnshire

The Royal Oak Inn ♦♦♦
High Street, Swayfield, Grantham NG33 4LL
T: (01476) 550247
F: (01476) 550996

SWINSCOE Staffordshire

Common End Farm ♦♦♦♦
Swinscoe, Ashbourne DE6 2BW
T: (01335) 342342
I: www.spenwith.com/commonendfarm/index.html

SWINSTEAD Lincolnshire

Croake Hill Cottage ♦♦♦
Swinstead, Grantham NG33 4PA
T: (01476) 550210
E: croakehill@croakehill.f9.co.uk

SYMONDS YAT EAST Herefordshire

Garth Cottage
♦♦♦♦ SILVER AWARD
Symonds Yat East, Ross-on-Wye HR9 6JL
T: (01600) 890364
F: (01600) 890364
E: bertie@yateast.fsnet.co.uk
I: www.smoothhound.co.uk/hotels/garthcottage.html

Rose Cottage Tea Gardens
♦♦♦
Symonds Yat East, Ross-on-Wye HR9 6JL
T: (01600) 890514
F: (01600) 890498
E: rose.cottage.s.yat@virgin.net
I: www.SmoothHound.co.uk/hotels/rose2.html

TADDINGTON Derbyshire

Ade House ♦♦♦♦
Taddington, Buxton SK17 9TY
T: (01298) 85203

The Old Bake and Brewhouse
♦♦♦
Blackwell Hall, Blackwell in the Peak, Taddington, Buxton SK17 9TQ
T: (01298) 85271
F: (01298) 85271
E: christine.gregory@btinternet.com
I: www.peakdistrictfarmhols.co.uk

TAMWORTH Staffordshire

Bonehill Farm House ♦♦♦♦
Bonehill Road, Tamworth, B78 3HP
T: (01827) 310797

The Chestnuts Country Guest House ♦♦♦♦ SILVER AWARD
Watling Street, Grendon, Atherstone CV9 2PZ
T: (01827) 331355
F: (01827) 896951
E: cclLtd@aol.com
I: www.chestnutsguesthouse.com

Oak Tree Farm
♦♦♦♦♦ GOLD AWARD
Hints Road, Hopwas, Tamworth, B78 3AA
T: (01827) 56807
F: (01827) 56807

The Peel Hotel ♦♦♦♦
14b Aldergate, Tamworth, B79 7DL
T: (01827) 67676
F: (01827) 69812

TANSLEY Derbyshire

Packhorse Farm ♦♦♦♦
Tansley, Matlock DE4 5LF
T: (01629) 580950
F: (01629) 580950

Packhorse Farm Bungalow
♦♦♦♦
Tansley, Matlock DE4 5LF
T: (01629) 582781

TANWORTH-IN-ARDEN Warwickshire

Grange Farm
Rating Applied For
Forde Hall Lane, Tanworth-in-Arden, Solihull B94 5AX
T: (01564) 74211

TEDDINGTON Gloucestershire

Bengrove Farm ♦♦♦
Bengrove, Teddington, Tewkesbury GL20 8JB
T: (01242) 620332
F: (01242) 620851

TELFORD Shropshire

Albion Inn ♦♦♦
West Street, St Georges, Telford, TF2 9AD
T: (01952) 614193

Allscott Inn ♦♦
Walcot, Wellington, Telford TF6 5EQ
T: (01952) 248484
F: (01952) 222622
E: allscottinn@telfordlife.co.uk

Coppice Heights ♦♦♦
Spout Lane, Little Wenlock, Telford, TF6 5BL
T: (01952) 505655

Falcon Hotel ♦♦♦
Holyhead Road, Wellington, Telford TF1 2DD
T: (01952) 255011
E: falconhotel@hotmail.com

Grove House Guesthouse
♦♦♦♦
Stafford Street, St Georges, Telford, TF2 9JW
T: (01952) 616140
F: (01952) 616140

The Mill House ♦♦♦♦
Shrewsbury Road, High Ercall, Telford, TF6 6BE
T: (01952) 770394
F: (01952) 770394
E: mill-house@talk21.com
I: www.virtual-shropshire.co.uk/millhouse

Old Rectory
♦♦♦♦ SILVER AWARD
Stirchley Village, Telford, TF3 1DY
T: (01952) 596308
F: (01952) 596308
E: hazelmiller@waitrose.com

The Old Vicarage Country House ♦♦♦♦
Church Street, St George's, Telford, TF2 9LZ
T: (01952) 616437
F: (01952) 616952
E: skristian@aol.com
I: www.oldvicarage.uk.com

Stone House ♦♦♦♦
Shifnal Road, Priorslee, Telford TF2 9NN
T: (01952) 290119
F: (01952) 290119
E: dave@stonehouseguesthouse.freeserve.co.uk
I: www.smoothhound.co.uk/hotels/stonehou.html

West Ridge Bed and Breakfast
♦♦♦♦ SILVER AWARD
West Ridge, Kemberton, Shifnal TF11 9LB
T: (01952) 580992
F: (01952) 580992
E: westridge@ntlworld.com
I: www.westridgebb.com

Westbrook House ♦♦
78a Holy Head Road, Ketly, Telford, TF1 5DJ
T: (01952) 615535

Willow House ♦♦♦
137 Holyhead Road, Wellington, Telford TF1 2DH
T: (01952) 223817
F: (01952) 223817

TENBURY WELLS
Worcestershire

Court Farm ♦♦♦♦
Hanley Childe, Tenbury Wells, WR15 8QY
T: (01885) 410265
E: yarnold@courtfarmhanley.fsnet.co.uk

Elliott House Farm ♦♦♦♦
Vine Lane, Kyre, Tenbury Wells, WR15 8RL
T: (01885) 410240
F: (01885) 410240

Peacock Inn ♦♦♦♦
Worcester Road, Boraston, Tenbury Wells WR15 8LL
T: (01584) 810506
F: (01584) 811236
E: juidler@fsbdial.co.uk
I: www.smoothhound.co.uk/hotels/peacockinn.html

TETBURY
Gloucestershire

Folly Farm Cottages ♦♦
Long Newnton, Tetbury, GL8 8XA
T: (01666) 502475
F: (01666) 502358
E: info@gtb.co.uk
I: www.gtb.co.uk

The Old Rectory
♦♦♦♦ GOLD AWARD
Didmarton, Badminton GL9 1DS
T: (01454) 238233
F: (01454) 238909
E: mt@betcentral.com

TEWKESBURY
Gloucestershire

Abbey Antiques Bed and Breakfast ♦♦♦
62 Church Street, Tewkesbury, GL20 5RZ
T: (01684) 298145
E: brazdys@amserve.net

The Abbey Hotel ♦♦
67 Church Street, Tewkesbury, GL20 5RX
T: (01684) 294247
F: (01684) 297208
E: brian@the-abbey-hotel.co.uk
I: www.the-abbey-hotel.co.uk

Abbots Court Farm ♦♦♦
Church End, Twyning, Tewkesbury, GL20 6DA
T: (01684) 292515
F: (01684) 292515
E: abbotscourt@hotmail.com

Alstone Fields Farm
♦♦♦♦♦ GOLD AWARD
Teddington Hands, Stow Road, Tewkesbury, GL20 8NG
T: (01242) 620592
E: alstone.fields@freeuk.com
I: www.alstone.fields.freeuk.com

Carrant Brook House ♦♦♦
3 Rope Walk, Tewkesbury, GL20 5DS
T: (01684) 290355
E: lorraine@carrantbrookhouse.co.uk

The Fleet Inn ♦♦♦♦
Twyning, Tewkesbury, GL20 6DG
T: (01684) 274310
F: (01684) 291612
E: fleetinn@hotmail.com
I: www.fleetinn.co.uk

Jessop House Hotel ♦♦♦♦
65 Church Street, Tewkesbury, GL20 5RZ
T: (01684) 292017
F: (01684) 273076
E: LesThurlow@aol.com
I: www.jessophousehotel.com

Malvern View Guest House ♦♦♦
1 St. Mary's Road, Tewkesbury, GL20 5SE
T: (01684) 292776

Town Street Farm ♦♦♦
Tirley, Gloucester GL19 4HG
T: (01452) 780442
F: (01452) 780890
E: townstreetfarm@hotmail.com
I: www.townstreetfarm.co.uk

Two Back of Avon ♦♦♦
2 Back of Avon, Riverside Walk, Tewkesbury, GL20 5BA
T: (01684) 298935

THORPE
Derbyshire

Hillcrest House ♦♦♦
Dovedale, Thorpe, Ashbourne DE6 2AW
T: (01335) 350436
E: hillcresthouse@freenet.co.uk
I: www.ashbourne-town.com/accom/hilcrest/hillcst.html

The Old Orchard ♦♦♦
Stoney Lane, Thorpe, Ashbourne DE6 2AW
T: (01335) 350410
F: (01335) 350410

THRAPSTON
Northamptonshire

The Poplars ♦♦♦♦
50 Oundle Road, Thrapston, Kettering NN14 4PD
T: (01832) 732499

THURLBY
Lincolnshire

6 The Pingles
♦♦♦♦ SILVER AWARD
Thurlby, Bourne PE10 0EX
T: (01778) 394517

TIBSHELF
Derbyshire

Rosvern House Bed and Breakfast ♦♦♦♦
High Street, Tibshelf, Alfreton DE55 5NY
T: (01773) 874800
F: (01773) 874800

TICKNALL
Derbyshire

The Staff of Life Public House and Restaurant♦♦♦♦
7 High Street, Ticknall, Derby DE73 1JH
T: (01332) 862479
F: (01332) 862479
I: www.thestaffoflife.com

TINWELL
Rutland

The Old Village Hall Rating Applied For
Main Road, Tinwell, Stamford PE9 3UD
T: (01780) 763900

TISSINGTON
Derbyshire

Bassett Wood Farmhouse Bed and Breakfast♦♦♦
Bassett Wood Farm, Tissington, Ashbourne DE6 1RD
T: (01335) 350254
E: janet@bassettwood.freeserve.co.uk
I: www.peakdistrictfarmhols.co.uk

TOTON
Nottinghamshire

Brookfield Cottage ♦♦♦
108 Carrfield Avenue, Toton, Beeston, Nottingham NG9 6FB
T: (0115) 9178046
E: sheila.done@amserve.net

TOWCESTER
Northamptonshire

Brave Old Oak Rating Applied For
Watling Street, Towcester, NN12 6BT
T: (01327) 358255
F: (01327) 352168

Green's Park ♦♦♦♦
Woodend, Towcester, NN12 8SD
T: (01327) 860386
F: (01327) 861003

The Leys ♦♦♦♦
Field Burcote, Towcester, NN12 8AL
T: (01327) 350431
F: (01327) 350431

Monk and Tipster ♦♦♦
36 Watling Street, Towcester, NN12 6AF
T: (01327) 350416

Potcote ♦♦♦♦ SILVER AWARD
Towcester, NN12 8LP
T: (01327) 830224
F: (01327) 830911
E: timbeckbrown@aol.com
I: www.potcote.co.uk

Slapton Manor
♦♦♦♦ SILVER AWARD
Chapel Lane, Slapton, Towcester, NN12 8PF
T: (01327) 860344
F: (01327) 860758

TRUSTHORPE
Lincolnshire

The Ramblers Hotel ♦♦♦
Sutton Road, Trusthorpe, Mablethorpe LN12 2PY
T: (01507) 441171

TUNSTALL
Staffordshire

Victoria Hotel ♦♦♦
4 Roundwell Street, Tunstall, Stoke-on-Trent ST6 5JJ
T: (01782) 835964
F: (01782) 835964
E: victoria-hotel@tunstall51.fsnet.co.uk

TUTBURY
Staffordshire

Woodhouse Farm Bed and Breakfast ♦♦♦
Woodhouse Farm, Tutbury, Burton upon Trent DE13 9HR
T: (01283) 812185
F: (01283) 815743
E: enquiries@tutbury.co.uk
I: www.tutbury.co.uk/woodhouse

TWO DALES
Derbyshire

Hazel House ♦♦♦♦
Chesterfield Road, Two Dales, Matlock DE4 2EZ
T: (01629) 734443
E: adrian.jenny@freewebisp.co.uk
I: www.info@hazel-house.co.uk

Norden House ♦♦♦♦
Chesterfield Road, Two Dales, Matlock DE4 2EZ
T: (01629) 732074
F: (01629) 735805
E: david.a.pope@talk21.com
I: www.nordenhouse.co.uk

UCKINGTON
Gloucestershire

Linthwaite ♦♦♦
3 Homecroft Drive, Uckington, Cheltenham GL51 9SN
T: (01242) 680146

ULLINGSWICK
Herefordshire

The Steppes
♦♦♦♦♦ SILVER AWARD
Ullingswick, Hereford HR1 3JG
T: (01432) 820424
F: (01432) 820042
E: info@steppeshotel.co.uk
I: www.steppeshotel.co.uk

UPPER COBERLEY
Gloucestershire

Upper Coberley Farm
♦♦♦♦ SILVER AWARD
Upper Coberley, Cheltenham GL53 9RB
T: (01242) 870306
E: allen@uppercoberley.freeserve.co.uk

UPPER HULME
Staffordshire

Paddock Farm Bed and Breakfast ♦♦♦♦
Paddock Farm, Upper Hulme, Leek ST13 8TY
T: (01538) 300345

Roaches Hall ♦♦♦♦
Upper Hulme, Leek ST13 8UB
T: (01538) 300115
E: roacheshall@aol.com

UPPER QUINTON
Warwickshire

Winton House
♦♦♦♦ SILVER AWARD
The Green, Upper Quinton, Stratford-upon-Avon CV37 8SX
T: (01789) 720500
E: gail@wintonhouse.com
I: www.wintonhouse.com

UPPER SAPEY
Herefordshire

The Baiting House
Rating Applied For
Stourport Road, Upper Sapey, Worcester WR6 6XT
T: (01886) 853201

UPPINGHAM
Rutland

Garden Hotel ♦♦♦♦
High Street West, Uppingham, Oakham LE15 9QD
T: (01572) 822352
F: (01572) 821156
E: gardenhotel@btinternet.com

The Vaults ♦♦♦
Market Place, Uppingham, Oakham LE15 9QH
T: (01572) 823259
F: (01572) 820019
I: www.rutnet.co.uk

UPTON SNODSBURY
Worcestershire

The French House Inn ♦♦♦
Worcester Road, Upton Snodsbury, Worcester WR7 4NW
T: (01905) 381631
F: (01905) 381635
I: www.frenchhousepub.co.uk

UPTON ST LEONARDS
Gloucestershire

Bullens Manor Farm ♦♦♦♦
Portway, Upton St Leonards, Gloucester GL4 8DL
T: (01452) 616463

UPTON-UPON-SEVERN
Worcestershire

Bridge House
♦♦♦♦ SILVER AWARD
Welland Stone, Upton-upon-Severn, Worcester WR8 0RW
T: (01684) 593046
F: (01684) 593046
E: merrymichael@clara.net
I: www.malvern.net/commerce/bridge-house.htm

Old Street Bed & Breakfast ♦♦
35 Old Street, Upton-upon-Severn, Worcester WR8 0HN
T: (01684) 594242
F: (01684) 594242
E: julieburt@tinyworld.co.uk

Ryall House Farm ♦♦♦♦
Ryall, Upton-upon-Severn, Worcester WR8 0PL
T: (01684) 592013
F: (01684) 592013

Tiltridge Farm and Vineyard
♦♦♦♦ SILVER AWARD
Upper Hook Road, Upton-upon-Severn, Worcester WR8 0SA
T: (01684) 592906
F: (01684) 594142
E: sandy@tiltridge.com
I: www.tiltridge.com

Welland Court ♦♦♦♦
Upton-upon-Severn, Worcester WR8 0ST
T: (01684) 594426
F: (01684) 594426
E: archer@wellandcourt.freeserve.co.uk
I: www.wellandcourt.co.uk

UTTOXETER
Staffordshire

Oldroyd Guest House & Motel ♦♦♦
18-22 Bridge Street, Uttoxeter, ST14 8AP
T: (01889) 562763
F: (01889) 568916
E: jim@oldroyd-guesthouse.com
I: www.oldroyd-guesthouse.com

Troutsdale Bed & Breakfast ♦♦♦♦
Alton Road, Denstone, Uttoxeter, ST14 5DH
T: (01889) 590220
F: 07790 577015
E: cliff@troutsdale.co.uk
I: www.troutsdale.co.uk

VOWCHURCH
Herefordshire

New Barns Farm ♦♦♦♦
Vowchurch, Hereford HR2 0QA
T: (01981) 250250
F: (01981) 250250
E: lloydnewbarns@tesco.net
I: www.golden-valley.co.uk

The Old Vicarage
♦♦♦♦ SILVER AWARD
Vowchurch, Hereford HR2 0QD
T: (01981) 550357
F: (01981) 550357
I: www.golden-valley.co.uk/vicarage

Upper Gilvach Farm
♦♦♦♦ SILVER AWARD
St. Margarets, Vowchurch, Hereford HR2 0QY
T: (01981) 510618
F: (01981) 510618
E: ruth@uppergilvach.freeserve.co.uk
I: www.golden-valley.co.uk/gilvach

WADSHELF
Derbyshire

Temperance House Farm
♦♦♦♦ SILVER AWARD
Bradshaw Lane, Wadshelf, Chesterfield S42 7BT
T: (01246) 566416

WALTERSTONE
Herefordshire

Coed Y Grafel ♦♦
Coed Y Grafel, Walterstone, Hereford HR2 0DJ
T: (01873) 890675
F: (01873) 890600
E: dianapalmer@btinternet.com

Lodge Farm Cottage ♦♦♦
Walterstone Common, Walterstone, Hereford HR2 0DT
T: (01873) 890263

WARWICK
Warwickshire

Agincourt Lodge Hotel ♦♦♦♦
36 Coten End, Warwick, CV34 4NP
T: (01926) 499399
F: (01926) 499399
E: enquires@agincourtlodge.co.uk
I: www.agincourtlodge.co.uk

Apothecary's ♦♦♦♦
The Old Dispensary, Stratford Road, Wellesbourne, Warwick CV35 9RN
T: (01789) 470060
E: apothband@aol.com

Ashburton Guest House ♦♦♦
74 Emscote Road, Warwick, CV34 5QG
T: (01926) 401082
F: (01926) 774642
E: ashburton6h@aol.com
I: www.smoothhound.co.uk

Austin House ♦♦♦
96 Emscote Road, Warwick, CV34 5QJ
T: (01926) 493583
F: (01926) 493679
E: mike.austinhouse96@ntlworld.com
I: www.austinhousewarwick.co.uk

Avon Guest House ♦♦♦♦
7 Emscote Road, Warwick, CV34 4PH
T: (01926) 491367
E: sue@comphouse.demon.co.uk
I: www.comphouse.demon.co.uk

Avonside Cottage
♦♦♦♦♦ GOLD AWARD
1 High Street, Barford, Warwick CV35 8BU
T: (01926) 624779

Brome House
♦♦♦♦ SILVER AWARD
35 Bridge End, Warwick, CV34 6PB
T: (01926) 491069
F: (01926) 491069
E: brome.house@virgin.net
I: www.smoothhound.co.uk/hotel/brome.html

Cambridge Villa Hotel ♦♦
20A Emscote Road, Warwick, CV34 4PP
T: (01926) 491169
F: (01926) 491169

Charter House
♦♦♦♦♦ GOLD AWARD
87-91 West Street, Warwick, CV34 6AH
T: (01926) 496965
F: (01926) 411910
E: penon@charterhouse8.freeserve.co.uk
I: www.smoothhound.co.uk/hotels/charter.html

Cliffe Hill House Bed and Breakfast
♦♦♦♦ SILVER AWARD
37 Coventry Road, Warwick, CV34 5HW
T: (01926) 496431
F: (01926) 496431
E: quirke@cliffehillhouse.freeserve.co.uk
I: www.cliffehillhouse.freeserve.co.uk

The Coach House
♦♦♦♦ SILVER AWARD
Old Budbrooke Road, Budbrooke, Warwick, CV35 7DU
T: (01926) 410893
F: (01926) 490453
E: falcosource@btclick.com

The Croft Guesthouse ♦♦♦♦
Haseley Knob, Warwick CV35 7NL
T: (01926) 484447
F: (01926) 484447
E: david@croftguesthouse.co.uk
I: www.croftguesthouse.co.uk

Crown and Castle Inn ♦♦♦
2-4 Coventry Road, Warwick, CV34 4NT
T: (01926) 492087
F: (01926) 410638

Forth House
♦♦♦♦ SILVER AWARD
44 High Street, Warwick, CV34 4AX
T: (01926) 401512
F: (01926) 490809
E: info@forthhouseuk.co.uk
I: www.forthhouseuk.co.uk

Hill House ♦♦♦♦
Hampton Lucy, Warwick, CV35 8AU
T: (01789) 840329
E: eliz_hunter@hotmail.com
I: www.stratford-upon-avon.co.uk/hillhouse.htm

Jersey Villa Guest House ♦♦♦
69 Emscote Road, Warwick, CV34 5QR
T: (01926) 774607
F: (01926) 774607
E: jerseyvillaguesthouse@emscote.freeserve.co.uk

Longbridge Farm ♦♦♦
Stratford Road, Warwick, CV34 6RB
T: (01926) 401857

Lower Rowley
♦♦♦♦ SILVER AWARD
Wasperton, Warwick, CV35 8EB
T: (01926) 624937
E: cliffordveasey@lower-rowley.freeserve.co.uk

Lower Watchbury Farm
♦♦♦♦
Wasperton Lane, Barford, Warwick CV35 8DH
T: (01926) 624772
F: (01926) 624772
E: eykyn@barford.spacomputers.com
I: www.farmaccommodation.com

Merchant's House ♦♦♦♦♦
Hampton Lucy, Warwick, CV35 8BE
T: (01789) 842280
E: hwaterworth@hotmail.com

Northleigh House
♦♦♦♦ SILVER AWARD
Five Ways Road, Hatton, Warwick CV35 7HZ
T: (01926) 484203
F: (01926) 484006
I: www.northleigh.co.uk

The Old Rectory Hotel ♦♦♦
Vicarage Lane, Sherbourne, Warwick, CV35 8AB
T: (01926) 624562
F: (01926) 624995

Park Cottage ♦♦♦♦
113 West Street, Warwick, CV34 6AH
T: (01926) 410319
F: (01926) 410319
E: Janet@park-cottage.com
I: www.park-cottage.com

Park House Guest House ♦♦♦
17 Emscote Road, Warwick, CV34 4PH
T: (01926) 494359
F: (01926) 494359
E: park.house@ntlworld.com
I: www.parkhousewarwick.co.uk

Peacock Lodge ♦♦♦
97 West Street, Warwick, CV34 6AH
T: (01926) 419480
F: (01926) 411892

Rushbrook Farmhouse ♦♦♦♦
Rushbrook Lane, Tanworth-in-Arden, Solihull B94 5HW
T: (01564) 742281
E: enquiries@rushbrookfarmhouse.co.uk
I: www.rushbrookfarmhouse.co.uk

The Seven Stars Public House
♦♦♦♦
Friars Street, Warwick, CV34 6HD
T: (01926) 492658
F: (01926) 411747
I: www.smoothhound.co.uk

Shrewley Pools Farm
♦♦♦♦ SILVER AWARD
Haseley, Warwick CV35 7HB
T: (01926) 484315
E: cathydodd@hotmail.com
I: www.s-h-systems.co.uk/hotels/shrewley.html

The Tilted Wig ♦♦♦♦
11 Market Place, Warwick, CV34 4SA
T: (01926) 410466
F: (01926) 495740

Tudor House Inn ♦♦
90-92 West Street, Warwick, CV34 6AW
T: (01926) 495447
F: (01926) 492948
I: www.oldenglish.co.uk

Warwick Lodge Guest House
♦♦♦
82 Emscote Road, Warwick, CV34 5QJ
T: (01926) 492927

Westham Guest House ♦♦♦
76 Emscote Road, Warwick, CV34 5QG
T: (01926) 491756
F: (01926) 491756
E: westhamhouse@aol.com
I: www.smoothhound.co.uk/hotels/westham.html

Woodside ♦♦♦
Langley Road, Claverdon, Warwick CV35 8PJ
T: (01926) 842446
F: (01926) 843697
E: ab021@dial.pipex.com

WATERHOUSES
Staffordshire

Broadhurst Farm ♦♦♦
Waterhouses, Stoke-on-Trent ST10 3LQ
T: (01538) 308261
E: enquires@broadhurstfarm.com
I: www.broadhurstfarm.com

Lee House Farm
♦♦♦♦ SILVER AWARD
Leek Road, Waterhouses, Stoke-on-Trent ST10 3HW
T: (01538) 308439

WELDON
Northamptonshire

Thatches on the Green ♦♦♦♦
9 School Lane, Weldon, Corby NN17 3JN
T: (01536) 266681
F: (01536) 266659
E: tom@thatches-on-the-green.fsnet.co.uk
I: www.thatches-on-the-green.fsnet.co.uk

WELFORD
Northamptonshire

West End Farm ♦♦♦♦
5 West End, Welford, Northampton NN6 6HJ
T: (01858) 575226
E: bevin@uklynx.net

WELFORD-ON-AVON
Warwickshire

Bridgend ♦♦♦♦
Binton Road, Welford-on-Avon, Stratford-upon-Avon CV37 8PW
T: (01789) 750900
F: (01789) 750900
E: bridgend.g.house@amserve.net

Mullions
♦♦♦♦ SILVER AWARD
Greenhill, Binton Road, Welford-on-Avon, Stratford-upon-Avon CV37 8PP
T: (01789) 750413
F: (01789) 750413
E: bandbpmw@aol.com

One Acre Guest House ♦♦♦♦
One Acre, Barton Road, Welford-on-Avon, Stratford-upon-Avon CV37 8EZ
T: (01789) 750477
E: ken.clifton@btopenworld.com
I: www.oneacre.co.uk

WELLAND
Worcestershire

The Lovells
♦♦♦♦ SILVER AWARD
Welland, Malvern WR13 6NF
T: (01684) 310795

WELLESBOURNE
Warwickshire

Brook House ♦♦♦♦
9 Chestnut Square, Wellesbourne, Warwick CV35 9QS
T: (01789) 840922

Meadow Cottage Bed and Breakfast ♦♦♦
36 Church Walk, Wellesbourne, Warwick CV35 9QT
T: (01789) 840220
E: robertharland@lineone.net

WELLINGBOROUGH
Northamptonshire

The Manor House
Rating Applied For
1 Orlingbury Road, Great Harrowden, Wellingborough, NN9 5AF
T: (01933) 678505
E: info@harrowdenmanor.com
I: www.harrowdenmanor.com

WELLINGTON
Shropshire

Barnfield House ♦♦♦
5 Barnfield Court, Wellington, Telford TF1 2ET
T: (01952) 223406

Clairmont ♦♦♦
54 Haygate Road, Wellington, Telford TF1 1QN
T: (01952) 414214
F: (01952) 414214

WEM
Shropshire

Aston Lodge ♦♦♦
Souton Road, Wem, Shrewsbury SY4 5BG
T: (01939) 232577
F: (01939) 232577

Forncet ♦♦♦
Soulton Road, Wem, Shrewsbury SY4 5HR
T: (01939) 232996

Lowe Hall Farm
♦♦♦♦ SILVER AWARD
Wem, Shrewsbury SY4 5UE
T: (01939) 232236
F: (01939) 232236
E: bandb@lowehallfarm.demon.co.uk
I: www.lowehallfarm.demon.co.uk

WENLOCK EDGE
Shropshire

The Wenlock Edge Inn
♦♦♦♦ SILVER AWARD
Hilltop, Wenlock Edge, Much Wenlock TF13 6DJ
T: (01746) 785678
F: (01746) 785285
E: info@wenlockedgeinn.co.uk
I: www.wenlockedgeinn.co.uk

WENTNOR
Shropshire

Crown Inn ♦♦♦♦
Wentnor, Bishop's Castle SY9 5EE
T: (01588) 650613
F: (01588) 650436
E: crowninn@wentnor.com
I: www.wentnor.com

WEOBLEY
Herefordshire

Garnstone House ♦♦♦
Weobley, Hereford HR4 8QP
T: (01544) 318943
F: (01544) 318197

The Marshpools Country Inn
♦♦♦
Ledgemoor, Weobley, Hereford HR4 8RN
T: (01544) 318215
F: (01544) 318847
E: enquires@country-inn.co.uk
I: www.country-inn.co.uk

WESSINGTON
Derbyshire

Crich Lane Farm ♦♦♦♦
Moorwood Moor Lane, Wessington, Alfreton, DE55 6DU
T: (01773) 835186

WEST BARKWITH
Lincolnshire

The Manor House
♦♦♦♦ SILVER AWARD
Louth Road, West Barkwith, Market Rasen LN8 5LF
T: (01673) 858253
F: (01673) 858253

WEST BRIDGFORD
Nottinghamshire

The Gallery Hotel ♦♦♦
8-10 Radcliffe Road, West Bridgford, Nottingham NG2 5FW
T: (0115) 981 3651
F: (0115) 981 3732
I: www.yell.co.uk/sites/galleryhotel/

Number 56 ♦♦
56 Melton Road, West Bridgford, Nottingham NG2 7NF
T: (0115) 9821965

WEST HADDON
Northamptonshire

Pear Trees ♦♦♦♦
31 Station Road, West Haddon, Northampton NN6 7AU
T: (01788) 510389
E: peartrees@lineone.net
I: www.pear-trees.co.uk

WESTBURY
Northamptonshire

Mill Farm House ♦♦♦
Westbury, Brackley, NN13 5JS
T: (01280) 704843
F: (01280) 704843

WESTBURY-ON-SEVERN
Gloucestershire

Boxbush Barn
♦♦♦♦♦ GOLD AWARD
Rodley, Westbury-on-Severn
GL14 1QZ
T: (01452) 760949
F: (01452) 760949
E: bed&breakfast@
boxbushbarn.fsnet.co.uk

WESTON
Staffordshire

Canalside Bed and Breakfast
♦♦♦
Bridge Cottage, Green Road,
Weston, Stafford ST18 0HZ
T: (01889) 271403
E: melgodridge@
canalsidebbweston.fsnet.co.uk

WESTON UNDER PENYARD
Herefordshire

Wharton Farm Bed and Breakfast ♦♦♦♦
Wharton Farm, Weston under
Penyard, Ross-on-Wye HR9 5SX
T: (01989) 750255
F: (01989) 750255
E: je.savage@breathemail.net

WETTON
Staffordshire

Croft Cottage ♦♦♦♦
Wetton, Ashbourne DE6 2AF
T: (01335) 310402

The Old Chapel ♦♦♦♦
Wetton, Ashbourne DE6 2AF
T: (01335) 310450
F: (01335) 310089

WHALEY BRIDGE
Derbyshire

Cote Bank Farm
♦♦♦♦ SILVER AWARD
Buxworth, Whaley Bridge, High
Peak SK23 7NP
T: (01663) 750566
F: (01663) 750566
E: cotebank@btinternet.com
I: www.cotebank.co.uk

WHAPLODE
Lincolnshire

Westgate House & Barn
♦♦♦♦ SILVER AWARD
Little Lane, Whaplode, Spalding
PE12 6RU
T: (01406) 370546
E: bandb@westgatehouse.f9.
co.uk
I: www.westgatehouse.f9.co.uk

WHATSTANDWELL
Derbyshire

Meerbrook Farm ♦♦♦
Wirksworth Road,
Whatstandwell, Matlock
DE4 5HU
T: (01629) 824180

Riverdale ♦♦♦♦
Middle Lane, Whatstandwell,
Matlock DE4 5EG
T: (01773) 853905
F: (01773) 853905

WHATTON
Nottinghamshire

The Dell ♦♦♦♦
Church Street, Whatton,
Nottingham NG13 9EL
T: (01949) 850832
E: thedell@bushinternet.com

WHISTON
Staffordshire

Heath House Farm ♦♦♦
Ross Road, Whiston, Stoke-on-
Trent ST10 2JF
T: (01538) 266497
E: heathhousefarm@aol.com
I: www.heathhousefarm.com

WHITCHURCH
Shropshire

Pheasant Walk ♦♦♦
Terrick Road, Whitchurch,
SY13 4JZ
T: (01948) 667118

Roden View ♦♦♦♦
Dobsons Bridge, Whixall,
Whitchurch, SY13 2QL
T: (01948) 710320
F: (01948) 710320
E: rodenview@talk21.com

Wayside ♦♦♦
Whitchurch, Ross-on-Wye,
HR9 JDJ
T: (01600) 890442
F: (01600) 890442
E: info@waysideb-b.co.uk
I: www.waysideb-b.co.uk

Wood Farm
♦♦♦♦ SILVER AWARD
Old Woodhouses, Whitchurch,
SY13 4EJ
T: (01948) 871224

WHITTINGTON
Staffordshire

The Dog Inn ♦♦♦
Main Street, Whittington,
Lichfield WS14 9JU
T: (01543) 432252
F: (01543) 433748

WICKHAMFORD
Worcestershire

Avonwood
♦♦♦♦ GOLD AWARD
30 Pitchers Hill, Wickhamford,
Evesham WR11 7RT
T: (01386) 834271
F: (01386) 834271
E: enquiries@
avonwood-guesthouse.co.uk
I: www.avonwood-guesthouse.
co.uk

WIGMORE
Herefordshire

Compasses Hotel ♦♦
Ford Street, Wigmore,
Leominster HR6 9UN
T: (01568) 770203
F: (01568) 770705

Gotherment House ♦♦♦
Wigmore, Leominster HR6 9UF
T: (01568) 770547
E: blair@gotherment.co.uk
I: www.gotherment.co.uk

Pear Tree Farm ♦♦♦♦
Wigmore, Leominster HR6 9UR
T: (01568) 770140
F: (01568) 770140
E: steveandjill@peartreefarmco.
freeserve.co.uk
I: www.peartreefarmco.
freeserve.co.uk

WILLERSEY
Gloucestershire

Bowers Hill Farm ♦♦♦♦
Bowers Hill, Willersey, Broadway
WR11 5HG
T: (01386) 834585
F: (01386) 830234
E: sarah@bowershillfarm.com
I: www:bowershillfarm.com

WILTON
Herefordshire

Benhall Farm ♦♦♦
Wilton, Ross-on-Wye HR9 6AG
T: (01989) 563900
F: (01989) 563900
E: carol_m_brewer@hotmail.
com

Copperfield House ♦♦♦♦
Wilton Lane, Wilton, Ross-on-
Wye HR9 6AH
T: (01989) 764379
E: fran@copperfieldhouse.co.uk
I: www.copperfieldhouse.co.uk

WINCHCOMBE
Gloucestershire

Blair House ♦♦♦
41 Gretton Road, Winchcombe,
Cheltenham GL54 5EG
T: (01242) 603626
F: (01242) 604214
E: chissurv@aol.com

Cleveley ♦♦♦♦
Wadfield Farm, Corndean Lane,
Winchcombe, Cheltenham
GL54 5AL
T: (01242) 602059
F: (01242) 602059

Gower House ♦♦♦♦
16 North Street, Winchcombe,
Cheltenham GL54 5LH
T: (01242) 602616

Ireley Grounds ♦♦♦♦
Broadway Road, Winchcombe,
Cheltenham GL54 5NY
T: (01242) 603736
F: (01242) 603736
E: mike@ireley.fsnet.co.uk
I: www.ireleygrounds.freeserve.
co.uk/

Manor Farm ♦♦♦♦
Greet, Winchcombe,
Cheltenham GL54 5BJ
T: (01242) 602423
F: (01242) 602423
E: janet@dickandjanet.fsnet.
co.uk

Mercia ♦♦♦♦ SILVER AWARD
Hailes Street, Winchcombe,
Cheltenham GL54 5HU
T: (01242) 602251
F: (01242) 602251
E: jonathanhupton@hotmail.
com
I: www.merciaguesthouse.co.uk

North Farmcote Bed and Breakfast ♦♦♦
North Farmcote, Winchcombe,
Cheltenham GL54 5AU
T: (01242) 602304
F: (01242) 603860

The Old Bakehouse ♦♦♦♦
Castle Street, Winchcombe,
Cheltenham GL54 5JA
T: (01242) 602441
F: (01242) 602441
E: deniseparker@onetel.net.uk

Old Station House ♦♦♦♦
Greet Road, Winchcombe,
Cheltenham GL54 5LB
T: (01242) 602283
F: (01242) 602283
E: old_station_house@hotmail.
com

Parks Farm ♦♦♦♦
Sudeley, Winchcombe,
Cheltenham GL54 5JB
T: (01242) 603874
F: (01242) 603874
E: rosmaryawilson@hotmail.
com

The Plaisterers Arms ♦♦♦
Abbey Terrace, Winchcombe,
Cheltenham GL54 5LL
T: (01242) 602358
F: (01242) 602360
E: plaisterers.arms@btinternet.
com

Postlip Hall Farm
♦♦♦♦ GOLD AWARD
Winchcombe, Cheltenham
GL54 5AQ
T: (01242) 603351
F: (01242) 603351
E: postuphallfarm@tiscali.co.uk
I: www.smoothhound.
co.uk/hotels/postlip.html

Sudeley Hill Farm ♦♦♦♦
Winchcombe, Cheltenham
GL54 5JB
T: (01242) 602344
F: (01242) 602344
E: scudamore4@aol.com

The White Hart Inn and Restaurant ♦♦♦
High Street, Winchcombe,
Cheltenham GL54 5LJ
T: (01242) 602359
F: (01242) 602703
E: enquiries@
the-white-hart-inn.com
I: www.the-white-hart-inn.co.uk

WING
Rutland

Kings Arms Inn ♦♦♦♦
Top Street, Wing, Oakham
LE15 8SE
T: (01572) 737634
F: (01572) 737255
E: neil@thekingsarms-wing.
co.uk
I: www.thekingsarms-wing.co.uk

WINKHILL
Staffordshire

Country Cottage ♦♦♦♦
Back Lane Farm, Winkhill, Leek
ST13 7XZ
T: (01538) 308273
F: (01538) 308098
E: mjb6435@aol.com
I: www.biophysics.umn.
edu/~bent/

WINSLOW
Worcestershire

Munderfield Harold ♦♦
Winslow, Bromyard HR7 4SZ
T: (01885) 483231

WINSTER
Derbyshire

Brae Cottage ♦♦♦♦
East Bank, Winster, Matlock
DE4 2DT
T: (01629) 650375

The Dower House
◆◆◆◆◆ GOLD AWARD
Main Street, Winster, Matlock
DE4 2DH
T: (01629) 650931
F: (01629) 650932
E: fosterbig@aol.com
I: www.SmoothHound.co.uk/hotels/dowerho

Old Shoulder of Mutton
◆◆◆◆
West Bank, Winster, Matlock
DE4 2DQ
T: (01629) 650778
E: brianskyrme@btinternet.com

WIRKSWORTH
Derbyshire

Avondale Farm
◆◆◆◆ SILVER AWARD
Grangemill, Matlock, DE4 4HT
T: (01629) 650820
F: (01629) 650233
E: avondale@tinyworld.co.uk

Old Lock Up
◆◆◆◆◆ GOLD AWARD
North End, Wirksworth, Derby
DE4 4FG
T: (01629) 826272
F: (01629) 826272
E: wheeler@theoldlockup.co.uk
I: www.theoldlockup.co.uk

Red Lion ◆◆◆
Market Place, Wirksworth, Derby
DE4 4ET
T: (01629) 822214
E: shfarrand@aol.com
I: www.newcenturyinns.co.uk

WISHAW
Warwickshire

Ash House ◆◆◆
The Gravel, Wishaw, Sutton
Coldfield B76 9QB
T: (01675) 475782
E: kate@rectory80.freeserve.co.uk

WITCOMBE
Gloucestershire

Crickley Court
◆◆◆◆ SILVER AWARD
Dog Lane, Witcombe, Gloucester
GL3 4UF
T: (01452) 863634
F: (01452) 863634
E: Lispilgrimmorris@yahoo.com

Springfields Farm ◆◆
Little Witcombe, Gloucester,
GL3 4TU
T: (01452) 863532

WITHINGTON
Gloucestershire

Willowside Farm ◆◆◆
Withington, Cheltenham
GL54 4DA
T: (01242) 890362
F: (01242) 890556

WOLLASTON
Northamptonshire

Duckmire ◆◆◆◆
1 Duck End, Wollaston,
Northampton, NN29 7SH
T: (01933) 664249
F: (01933) 664249
E: kerry@foreverengland.freeserve.co.uk

WOLSTANTON
Staffordshire

Whispering Pines
◆◆◆◆◆ GOLD AWARD
11A Milehouse Lane,
Wolstanton, Newcastle-under-Lyme ST5 9JR
T: (01782) 639376
F: (01782) 639376
E: timpriestman@whisperingpinesbb45.freeserve.co.uk
I: www.smoothhound.co.uk/hotels/whisperingpines.ltml

WOLSTON
Warwickshire

The Byre
◆◆◆◆ SILVER AWARD
Lords Hill Farm, Coalpit Lane,
Wolston, Coventry CV8 3GB
T: (024) 7654 2098

WOODCHESTER
Gloucestershire

Southfield Mill ◆◆◆◆
Southfield Road, Woodchester,
Stroud GL5 5PA
T: (01453) 872896
F: (01453) 872896
E: judysutch@hotmail.com

WOODHALL SPA
Lincolnshire

Claremont Guesthouse ◆◆
9-11 Witham Road, Woodhall
Spa, LN10 6RW
T: (01526) 352000

The Dower House Hotel ◆◆◆
The Manor Estate, Woodhall Spa,
LN10 6PY
T: (01526) 352588
F: (01526) 352588
E: cplumb_dowerhouse@yahoo.co.uk
I: www.web-marketing.co.uk/dowerhouse

Newlands ◆◆◆◆
56 Woodland Drive, Woodhall
Spa, LN10 6YG
T: (01526) 352881

Pitchaway Guesthouse ◆◆◆
The Broadway, Woodhall Spa,
LN10 6SQ
T: (01526) 352969
E: barry@pitchaway.fsnet.co.uk

WOONTON
Herefordshire

Rose Cottage
◆◆◆◆ SILVER AWARD
Woonton, Hereford HR3 6QW
T: (01544) 340459
F: (01544) 340459

WORCESTER
Worcestershire

Barbourne ◆◆◆
42 Barbourne Road, Worcester,
WR1 1HU
T: (01905) 27507
F: (01905) 27507

The Boot Inn
◆◆◆◆ SILVER AWARD
Radford Road, Flyford Flavell,
Worcester WR7 4BS
T: (01386) 462658
F: (01386) 462547
E: thebootinn@yahoo.com

City Guest House ◆◆◆
36 Barbourne Road, Worcester,
WR1 1HU
T: (01905) 24695
F: (01905) 24695

The Croft ◆◆◆
25 Station Road, Fernhill Heath,
Worcester, WR3 7UJ
T: (01905) 453482

Five Ways Hotel ◆◆
Angel Place, Worcester,
WR1 3QN
T: (01905) 616980
F: (01905) 616344

Foresters Guest House ◆◆◆
2 Chestnut Walk, Arboretum,
Worcester, WR1 1PP
T: (01905) 20348
F: (01905) 20348

Green Farm ◆◆◆◆
Crowle Green, Crowle,
Worcester WR7 4AB
T: (01905) 381807
F: (01905) 381706
E: lupa@beeb.net
I: www.thegreenfarm.co.uk

Hidelow House
◆◆◆◆ SILVER AWARD
Acton Green, Acton Beauchamp,
Malvern, WR6 5AH
T: (01886) 884547
F: (01886) 884060
E: bta@hidelow.co.uk
I: www.hidelow.co.uk

Hill Farm House
Rating Applied For
Dormston Lane, Dormston,
Worcester, WR7 4JS
T: (01386) 793159
F: (01386) 793239
E: jim@hillfarmhouse.co.uk
I: www.hillfarmhouse.co.uk

Ivy Cottage ◆◆◆◆
Sinton Green, Hallow, Worcester
WR2 6NP
T: (01905) 641123

Little Lightwood Farm ◆◆◆◆
Lightwood Lane, Cotheridge,
Worcester WR6 5LT
T: (01905) 333236
F: (01905) 333236
E: lightwood.holidays@virgin.net

Oaklands ◆◆◆◆
Claines, Worcester WR3 7RR
T: (01905) 458871
F: (01905) 759362
E: barbaragadd@hotmail.com
I: www.ukbed.com/heart-of-england/oaklands.htm

The Old Smithy ◆◆◆◆
Pirton, Worcester WR8 9EJ
T: (01905) 820482
E: welcome@theoldsmithy.co.uk
I: www.smoothhound.co.uk/hotels/oldsmith.html

Oldbury Farm Bed and Breakfast
◆◆◆◆ SILVER AWARD
Oldbury Farm, Lower
Broadheath, Worcester,
WR2 6RQ
T: (01905) 421357

Osborne House ◆◆◆
17 Chestnut Walk, Worcester,
WR1 1PR
T: (01905) 22296
F: (01905) 22296
E: enquiries@osborne-house.freeserve.co.uk
I: www.osborne-housefreeserve.co.uk

Retreat Farm ◆◆◆◆
Camp Lane, Grimley, Worcester,
WR2 6LX
T: (01905) 640266
F: (01905) 641397

Shrubbery Guest House ◆◆◆
38 Barbourne Road, Worcester,
WR1 1HU
T: (01905) 24871
F: (01905) 23620

Sundown ◆◆◆
7 Albert Park Road, Malvern,
WR14 1HL
T: (01684) 893612
F: (01684) 562459
E: sundown@ntlworld.com
I: www.malvern-hills.co.uk

Yew Tree House
◆◆◆◆ SILVER AWARD
Norchard, Crossway Green,
Stourport-on-Severn DY13 9SN
T: (01299) 250921
F: (01299) 253472
E: paul@knightp.swinternet.co.uk
I: www.yewtreeworcester.co.uk

WORKSOP
Nottinghamshire

Carlton Road Guesthouse
◆◆◆
67 Carlton Road, Worksop,
S80 1PP
T: (01909) 483084

Sherwood Guesthouse ◆◆◆
57 Carlton Road, Worksop,
S80 1PP
T: (01909) 474209
F: (01909) 476470
E: CHERWOULD@aol.com

WORMELOW
Herefordshire

Lyston Villa ◆◆◆
Wormelow, Hereford HR2 8EL
T: (01981) 540130
F: (01981) 540130

WOTTON-UNDER-EDGE
Gloucestershire

Falcon Cottage ◆◆◆◆
15 Station Road, Charfield,
Wotton-under-Edge, GL12 8SY
T: (01453) 843528

Hillesley Mill ◆◆◆
Alderley, Wotton-under-Edge,
GL12 7QT
T: (01453) 843258

YARDLEY
West Midlands

Olton Cottage Guest House
◆◆◆◆
School Lane, Old Yardley Village,
Yardley, Birmingham B33 8PD
T: (0121) 783 9249
F: (0121) 789 6545
E: olton.cottage@virgin.net
I: www.olton-cottage.co.uk

Yardley Guesthouse ♦♦♦
330 Church Road, Yardley, Birmingham B25 8XT
T: (0121) 783 6634
F: (0121) 7836634
E: dave@yardleyguesthouse.fsnet.co.uk
I: www.yardleyguesthouse.com

YARKHILL
Herefordshire

Chelwood ♦♦♦♦
Chelwood, Yarkhill, Hereford HR1 3SS
T: (01432) 890387
F: (01432) 890699

YORTON HEATH
Shropshire

Country Bed & Breakfast
♦♦♦♦ SILVER AWARD
Mayfield, Yorton Heath, Shrewsbury SY4 3EZ
T: (01939) 210860
F: (01939) 210860
E: macdonalds@mayfieldyortonheath.freeserve.co.uk
I: www.mayfieldyortonheath.freeserve.co.uk

YOULGREAVE
Derbyshire

Bankside Cottage ♦♦♦
Bankside, Youlgreave, Bakewell DE45 1WD
T: (01629) 636689

Fairview ♦♦♦
Bradford Road, Youlgreave, Bakewell DE45 1WG
T: (01629) 636043
F: (01629) 636043

The Farmyard Inn ♦♦♦
Main Street, Youlgreave, Bakewell DE45 1UW
T: (01629) 636221

The Old Bakery ♦♦♦
Church Street, Youlgreave, Bakewell DE45 1UR
T: (01629) 636887
E: croasdell@oldbakeryyoulgrave.freeserve.co.uk
I: www.cressbrook.co.uk/youlgve/oldbakery

EAST OF ENGLAND

ACTON
Suffolk

Barbie's ♦♦
25 Clayhall Place, Acton, Sudbury CO10 0BT
T: (01787) 373702

Lime Tree House ♦♦♦♦
Lime Tree Green, Acton, Sudbury CO10 0UU
T: (01787) 373551

ALBURY
Hertfordshire

Tudor Cottage
♦♦♦♦ SILVER AWARD
Upwick Green, Albury, Ware SG11 2JX
T: (01279) 771440
E: peterandelphine@onetel.net.uk

ALDBOROUGH
Norfolk

Butterfly Cottage ♦♦♦
The Green, Aldborough, Norwich NR11 7AA
T: (01263) 768198
F: (01263) 768198
E: butterflycottage@btopenworld.com
I: www.butterflycottage.com

ALDBURY
Hertfordshire

Livingston's Bed & Breakfast ♦♦♦
Chimanimani, Toms Hill Road, Aldbury, Tring HP23 5SA
T: (01442) 851527

ALDEBURGH
Suffolk

Faraway ♦♦♦
28 Linden Close, Aldeburgh, IP15 5JL
T: (01728) 452571

Lime Tree House B&B ♦♦♦
Benhall Green, Saxmundham, IP17 1HU
T: (01728) 602149
E: linda.pebody@limetreehouse.demon.co.uk

Margaret's ♦♦♦
50 Victoria Road, Aldeburgh, IP15 5EJ
T: (01728) 453239

Saffron House ♦♦♦♦
Barley Lands, Aldeburgh, IP15 5LW
T: (01728) 454716
F: (01728) 454716

Sanviv ♦♦♦
59 Fairfield Road, Aldeburgh, IP1 5JN
T: (01728) 453107

Wateringfield ♦♦♦♦
Golf Lane, Aldeburgh, IP15 5PY
T: (01728) 453163
E: wateringfield@tesco.net

ALDEBY
Norfolk

The Old Vicarage ♦♦♦
Rectory Road, Aldeby, Beccles NR34 0BJ
T: (01502) 678229
E: butler@beccles33.freeserve.co.uk

ALDHAM
Essex

Old House ♦♦♦
Ford Street, Aldham, Colchester CO6 3PH
T: (01206) 240456
F: (01206) 240456

ALDRINGHAM
Suffolk

Fern House ♦♦♦
6 The Follies, Aldringham, Leiston IP16 4LU
T: (01728) 830759
F: (01728) 830334
E: gallowaymd@aol.com

ALPHETON
Suffolk

Amicus ♦♦♦♦
Old Bury Road, Alpheton, Sudbury CO10 9BT
T: (01284) 828579
F: (01284) 828579
E: stanleybureham@aol.com

ARDLEIGH
Essex

Malting Farm ♦♦♦♦
Malting Farm Lane, Ardleigh, Colchester CO7 7QG
T: (01206) 230207

Old Shields Farm ♦♦♦♦
Waterhouse Lane, Ardleigh, Colchester CO7 7NE
T: (01206) 230251
F: (01206) 231825
E: ruth.marshall@amserve.net

ARKESDEN
Essex

Parsonage Farm ♦♦♦♦
Arkesden, Saffron Walden CB11 4HB
T: (01799) 550306

ASHDON
Essex

Cobblers
♦♦♦♦ SILVER AWARD
Bartlow Road, Ashdon, Saffron Walden CB10 2HR
T: (01799) 584666
E: cobblers@ashdon2000.freeserve.co.uk

ASHILL
Norfolk

Moat Farm G C Pickering and Son ♦♦♦♦
Cressingham Road, Ashill, Thetford IP25 7BX
T: (01760) 440357
F: (01760) 441447

ASPLEY GUISE
Bedfordshire

Chain Guest House
♦♦♦♦ SILVER AWARD
Church Street, Aspley Guise, Milton Keynes MK17 8HQ
T: (01908) 586511
F: (01908) 586511
E: chainhouse@ukgateway.net
I: www.chainhouse.ukgateway.net

The Strawberry Farm ♦♦♦♦
Salford Road, Aspley Guise, Milton Keynes MK17 8HZ
T: (01908) 587070
F: (01908) 587070
E: strawberryfarm@onetel.net.uk
I: www.smoothhound.co.uk/hotels/thestraw.html

ATTLEBOROUGH
Norfolk

Scales Farm ♦♦♦♦
Old Buckenham, Attleborough NR17 1PE
T: (01953) 860324
F: (01953) 860324

AYLMERTON
Norfolk

Felbrigg Lodge
♦♦♦♦♦ GOLD AWARD
Aylmerton, Holt, NR11 8RA
T: (01263) 837588
F: (01263) 838012
E: info@felbrigglodge.co.uk
I: www.felbrigglodge.co.uk

AYLSHAM
Norfolk

The Old Pump House ♦♦♦♦
Holman Road, Aylsham, Norwich NR11 6BY
T: (01263) 733789
F: (01263) 733789

BACTON-ON-SEA
Norfolk

Keswick Hotel ♦♦♦
Walcott Road, Bacton-on-Sea, Norwich NR12 0LS
T: (01692) 650468
F: (01692) 650788
E: bookings@keswickhotelbacton.co.uk
I: www.keswickhotelbacton.co.uk

BADINGHAM
Suffolk

Colston Hall
♦♦♦♦ SILVER AWARD
Badingham, Woodbridge IP13 8LB
T: (01728) 638375
F: (01728) 638084
E: lizjohn@colstonhall.com
I: www.colstonhall.com

BARHAM
Suffolk

The Sorrel Horse Inn Various Ltd ♦♦♦
Old Norwich Road, Barham, Ipswich IP6 0PG
T: (01473) 830327
F: (01473) 833149
E: matt@sorrelhorse.freeserve.co.uk
I: www.sorrelhouse.freeserve.co.uk

Tamarisk House ♦♦♦♦
Sandy Lane, Barham, Ipswich IP6 0PB
T: (01473) 831825
I: www.hotelmaster.co.uk

BARNSTON
Essex

Pear Tree Cottage ♦♦♦♦
Chelmsford Road, Barnston, Dunmow CM6 3PS
T: (01371) 820229
E: admin@peartreebandb.co.uk
I: www.peartreebandb.co.uk

BASILDON
Essex

38 Kelly Road ♦♦♦♦
Bowers Gifford, Basildon, SS13 2HL
T: (01268) 726701
F: (01268) 726701
E: patricia.jenkinson@tesco.net
I: www.uk-visit.co.uk

BATTLESBRIDGE
Essex

The Cottages Guest House ♦♦
The Cottages, Beeches Road, Battlesbridge, Wickford SS11 8TJ
T: (01702) 232105
E: cottage2000@totalise.co.uk

BECCLES
Suffolk

Ashtree Cottage ♦♦♦♦
School Lane, Worlingham, Beccles NR34 7RH
T: (01502) 715206
F: (01502) 711745
E: helen@dhswilcock.freeserve.co.uk

Catherine House ♦♦♦♦
2 Ringsfield Road, Beccles, NR34 9PQ
T: (01502) 716428
F: (01502) 716428

Colville Arms Motel ♦♦♦
Lowestoft Road, Worlingham, Beccles NR34 7EF
T: (01502) 712571
F: (01502) 712571
E: pat@thecolvillearms.freeserve.co.uk
I: www.colville-arms-motel.co.uk

The Kings Head ♦♦♦
New Market, Beccles, NR34 9HA
T: (01502) 712147
F: (01502) 715386
E: kings.head@elizabethhotels.co.uk
I: www.elizabethhotels.co.uk

Plantation House
♦♦♦♦ GOLD AWARD
Rectory Road, Haddiscoe, Beccles, NR14 6PG
T: (01502) 677778
F: (01502) 677778
E: plantationhouse@ukonline.co.uk
I: www.broadland.com/plantationhouse

BEDFORD
Bedfordshire

Church Farm
♦♦♦♦ SILVER AWARD
41 High Street, Roxton, Bedford MK44 3EB
T: (01234) 870234
F: (01234) 870234
E: churchfarm@amserve.net

Cornfields Restaurant and Hotel ♦♦♦♦ SILVER AWARD
Wilden Road, Colmworth, Bedford, MK44 2NJ
T: (01234) 378990
F: (01234) 376370
E: reservations@cornfieldsrestaurant.co.uk
I: www.cornfieldsrestaurant.co.uk

Grafton Hotel ♦♦
141 Midland Road, Bedford, MK40 1DN
T: (01234) 359294
F: (01234) 305402

Robertson's Bed & Breakfast ♦♦♦
4 Winifred Road, Bedford, MK40 4ES
T: (01234) 340803
F: (01234) 340803
E: robertsonsbed_breakfast@hotmail.com

BEESTON
Norfolk

Holmdene Farm ♦♦♦
Beeston, King's Lynn PE32 2NJ
T: (01328) 701284
E: holmdenefarm@farmersweekly.net
I: www.northnorfolk.co.uk/holmdenefarm

BEESTON REGIS
Norfolk

Sheringham View Cottage ♦♦♦♦
Cromer Road, Beeston Regis, Cromer NR26 8RX
T: (01263) 820300

BEETLEY
Norfolk

Peacock House
♦♦♦♦ GOLD AWARD
Peacock Lane, Beetley, East Dereham NR20 4DG
T: (01362) 860371
E: PeackH@aol.com
I: www.smoothhound.co.uk/hotels/peacockh.html/

Shilling Stone ♦♦♦
Church Road, Beetley, East Dereham NR20 4AB
T: (01362) 861099
F: (01362) 869153
E: jeannepartridge@ukgateway.net
I: www.norfolkshillingstone.co.uk

BEIGHTON
Norfolk

Beech House Bed & Breakfast ♦♦♦
Southwood Road, Beighton, Norwich NR13 3AB
T: (01493) 750870
F: (01493) 750870

BELCHAMP ST PAUL
Essex

The Plough
♦♦♦♦ SILVER AWARD
Gages Road, Belchamp St Paul, Sudbury CO10 7BT
T: (01787) 278882
E: info@theplough-belchamp.co.uk
I: www.theplough-belchamp.co.uk

BENHALL
Suffolk

Kiln Farm B&B ♦♦♦♦
Kiln Lane, Benhall, Saxmundham IP17 1HA
T: (01728) 603166

BERKHAMSTED
Hertfordshire

Broadway Farm
♦♦♦♦ SILVER AWARD
Berkhamsted, HP4 2RR
T: (01442) 866541
F: (01442) 866541
E: a.knowles@broadway.nildram.co.uk

BIGGLESWADE
Bedfordshire

Old Warden Guesthouse ♦♦♦
Shop and Post Office, Old Warden, Biggleswade SG18 9HQ
T: (01767) 627201

BILDESTON
Suffolk

The Crown Hotel ♦♦♦
104 High Street, Bildeston, Ipswich IP7 7EB
T: (01449) 740510
F: (01449) 740510
I: www.thecrownbildeston.co.uk

Silwood Barns ♦♦♦
Consent Lane, Bildeston, Ipswich IP7 7SB
T: (01449) 741370
F: (01449) 740819
E: neilashwell@aol.com
I: www.lalaproducts.com

BILLERICAY
Essex

Badgers Rest
♦♦♦♦ SILVER AWARD
2 Mount View, Billericay, CM11 1HB
T: (01277) 625384
F: (01277) 633912

BINHAM
Norfolk

Field House
♦♦♦♦ SILVER AWARD
Field House, Walsingham Road, Binham, Fakenham NR21 0BU
T: (01328) 830639

BISHOP'S STORTFORD
Hertfordshire

Acer Cottage ♦♦♦
17 Windhill, Bishop's Stortford, CM23 2NE
T: (01279) 834797
F: (01279) 834797
E: admill@ntlworld.com

5 Ascot Close ♦♦♦
Bishop's Stortford, CM23 5BP
T: (01279) 652228

6 Ascot Close ♦♦♦
Bishop's Stortford, CM23 5BP
T: (01279) 651027
E: 113714.2346@compuserve.com

Chippendales ♦♦♦
7 Stort Lodge, Off Hadham Road, Bishop's Stortford, CM23 2QL
T: (01279) 656315
E: gorsim@aol.com

The Cottage
♦♦♦♦ GOLD AWARD
71 Birchanger Lane, Birchanger, Bishop's Stortford CM23 5QA
T: (01279) 812349
F: (01279) 815045
I: www.thecottagebirchanger.co.uk

26 Heath Row ♦♦♦♦
Bishop's Stortford, CM23 5DE
T: (01279) 833870
F: (01279) 833870

Homesdale ♦♦♦♦
Lower Road, Little Hallingbury, Bishop's Stortford CM22 7QZ
T: (01279) 600647
F: (01279) 600647
E: elfieandsteve@btinternet.com
I: www.homesdale.net

Lancasters ♦♦♦♦
Castle House, Market Square, Bishop's Stortford, CM23 3UU
T: (01279) 501307
E: lindaevans19@hotmail.com

3 Lindsey Close
Rating Applied For
Bishop's Stortford, CM23 2TB
T: (01279) 653206

Marrianno ♦♦♦
104 Hadham Road, Bishop's Stortford, CM23 2QF
T: (01279) 508568
E: cattolica55@hotmail.com

Phoenix Lodge ♦♦♦
No. 91 Dunmow Road, Bishop's Stortford, CM23 5HF
T: (01279) 659780
F: (01279) 323958
E: phoenixlodge@ntlworld.com
I: www.phoenixlodge.co.uk

Pleasant Cottage ♦♦♦♦
Woodend Green, Henham, Stansted, CM22 6AZ
T: (01279) 850792
F: (01279) 850792
E: george@pleasantcott.fsnet.co.uk
I: www.henham.org/accommodation

Saint Vincent ♦♦♦
24 Elm Road, Bishop's Stortford, CM23 2SS
T: (01279) 658884
E: hilarydave@lineone.net

Tap Hall ♦♦♦
15 The Street, Takeley, Bishop's Stortford CM22 6QS
T: (01279) 871035
F: (01279) 871035

52 Thorley Hill ♦♦♦♦
Bishop's Stortford, CM23 3NA
T: (01279) 658311
F: (01279) 658311

1B Thornbera Road ♦♦♦
Bishop's Stortford, CM23 3NJ
T: (01279) 507900
E: airportbnb@aol.com
I: www.stanstedairportbedandbreakfast.com

32 Wentworth Drive ♦♦♦
Bishop's Stortford, CM23 2PB
T: (01279) 507133

52 Windhill ♦♦♦
Bishop's Stortford, CM23 2NH
T: (01279) 651712
E: aspence@btinternet.com

Woodlands Lodge ♦♦♦♦
Dunmow Road, Bishop's Stortford, CM23 5QX
T: (01279) 504784
F: (01279) 461474
E: lynn_kingsbury@yahoo.com
I: www.woodlandslodge.co.uk

BLAKENEY
Norfolk

Navestock Bed & Breakfast ♦♦♦♦
Cley Road, Blakeney, Holt NR25 7NL
T: (01263) 740998
F: (01263) 740998

BLAXHALL
Suffolk

The Ship Inn ♦♦
Blaxhall, Snape, Saxmundham IP12 2DY
T: (01728) 688316
F: (01728) 688316
E: shipinnblaxhall@aol.com
I: www.shipinnblaxhall.co.uk

BLETSOE
Bedfordshire

North End Barns
♦♦♦♦ SILVER AWARD
North End Farm, Risley Road, Bletsoe, Bedford MK44 1QT
T: (01234) 781320
F: (01234) 781320

BLICKLING
Norfolk

The Buckinghamshire Arms
♦♦♦
Blickling, Norwich NR11 6NF
T: (01263) 732133

BOVINGDON
Hertfordshire

Rose Farm-Accommodation
♦♦♦
Water Lane, Bovingdon, Hemel Hempstead HP3 0NA
T: (01442) 834529
E: fuglylea@aol.com

BOXFORD
Suffolk

Hurrells Farmhouse
♦♦♦♦ SILVER AWARD
Boxford Lane, Boxford, Sudbury CO10 5JY
T: (01787) 210215
F: (01787) 211806
E: hurrellsf@aol.com
I: members.aol.com/hurrellsf/index.htm

BOXTED
Essex

Round Hill House ♦♦♦♦
Parsonage Hill, Boxted, Colchester CO4 5ST
T: (01206) 272392
F: (01206) 272392
E: crispin1@bigfoot.com
I: www.information-britain.co.uk

BRADFIELD
Essex

Emsworth House ♦♦♦
Ship Hill, Bradfield, Manningtree CO11 2UP
T: (01255) 870860
E: emsworthhouse@hotmail.com
I: www.emsworthhouse.co.uk

BRADFIELD COMBUST
Suffolk

Church Farm ♦♦♦♦
Bradfield Combust, Bury St Edmunds IP30 0LW
T: (01284) 386333
F: (01284) 386155
E: paul@williamsonff.freeserve.co.uk

BRADWELL
Essex

Park Farmhouse ♦♦♦
Church Road, Bradwell, Braintree CM7 8EP
T: (01376) 563584

BRAINTREE
Essex

16 Acorn Avenue ♦♦
Braintree, CM7 2LR
T: (01376) 320155

Brook Farm c/o Mrs A Butler
♦♦♦♦
Wethersfield, Braintree CM7 4BX
T: (01371) 850284
F: (01371) 850284

Greengages Bed & Breakfast
♦♦♦♦
268 Broad Road, Braintree, CM7 5NJ
T: (01376) 345868
I: www.greengagesbandb.co.uk

70 High Garrett ♦♦
Braintree, CM7 5NT
T: (01376) 345330

The Old House ♦♦♦
11 Bradford Street, Braintree, CM7 9AS
T: (01376) 550457
F: (01376) 343863
E: old_house@talk21.com
I: theoldhousebraintree.co.uk

BRANCASTER
Norfolk

The Ship Inn ♦♦♦
Main Road, Brancaster, King's Lynn PE31 8AP
T: (01485) 210333
F: (01485) 210333

BRANDON
Suffolk

The Laurels ♦♦♦
162 London Road, Brandon, IP27 0LP
T: (01842) 812005

BRENT ELEIGH
Suffolk

Wroughton Lodge
♦♦♦♦ SILVER AWARD
Brent Eleigh, Sudbury CO10 9PB
T: (01787) 247495
F: (01787) 248462
E: elizabethknight@wroughtonlodge.fsnet.co.uk
I: www.wroughtonlodge.fsnet.co.uk

BRENTWOOD
Essex

Brentwood Guesthouse ♦♦♦
75/77 Rose Valley, Brentwood, CM14 4HJ
T: (01277) 262713
F: (01277) 211146
E: info@brentwoodguesthouse.com
I: www.brentwoodguesthouse.com

Chestnut Tree Cottage ♦♦♦
Great Warley Street, Great Warley Village Green, Brentwood, CM13 3JF
T: (01277) 221727
F: (01277) 221727

BRICKET WOOD
Hertfordshire

Little Oaks ♦♦♦♦
Lye Lane, Bricket Wood, St Albans AL2 3TE
T: (01923) 681299
F: (01923) 681299
E: varleyh@aol.com

BRIGHTLINGSEA
Essex

Paxton Dene ♦♦♦♦
Church Road, Brightlingsea, Colchester CO7 0QT
T: (01206) 304560
F: (01206) 304809
E: holben@btinternet.com
I: www.brightlingsea-town.co.uk/business

BRISLEY
Norfolk

The Brisley Bell Inn and Restaurant
Rating Applied For
The Green, Brisley, East Dereham NR20 5DW
T: (01362) 668686
F: (01362) 668686

Pond Farm ♦♦♦♦
Brisley, East Dereham NR20 5LL
T: (01362) 668332
F: (01362) 668332

BROCKDISH
Norfolk

Grove Thorpe
♦♦♦♦♦ GOLD AWARD
Grove Road, Brockdish, Diss IP21 4JE
T: (01379) 668305
F: (01379) 668305
E: b-b@grovethorpe.co.uk
I: www.grovethorpe.co.uk

BROOKE
Norfolk

Hillside Farm ♦♦♦♦
Welbeck Road, Brooke, Norwich NR15 1AU
T: (01508) 550260
F: (01508) 550260
E: carrieholl@tinyworld.co.uk
I: www.hillside-farm.com

The Old Vicarage
♦♦♦♦ SILVER AWARD
48 The Street, Brooke, Norwich NR15 1JU
T: (01508) 558329

BROXTED
Essex

The Granary ♦♦♦♦
Moor End Farm, Broxted, Dunmow CM6 2EL
T: (01371) 870821
F: (01371) 870821
E: cathy@moorendfarm.com
I: www.moorendfarm.com

BRUNDALL
Norfolk

Braydeston House ♦♦♦♦
9 The Street, Brundall, Norwich NR13 5JY
T: (01603) 713123
E: ann@braydeston.freeserve.co.uk

3 Oak Hill ♦♦♦
Brundall, Norwich NR13 5AQ
T: (01603) 717903

BUNGAY
Suffolk

Castles ♦♦♦♦
35 Earsham Street, Bungay, NR35 1AF
T: (01986) 892283
E: castles@lineone.net

Cleveland House ♦♦♦♦
2 Broad Street, Bungay, NR35 1EE
T: (01986) 896589
F: (01986) 892311

Dove Restaurant ♦♦♦
Holbrook Hill, Alburgh, Harleston IP20 0EP
T: (01986) 788315
F: (01986) 788315
E: thedovenorfolk@freeola.com
I: www.thedovenorfolk.co.uk

Earsham Park Farm
♦♦♦♦ GOLD AWARD
Harleston Road, Earsham, Bungay NR35 2AQ
T: (01986) 892180
F: (01986) 892180
E: watchorn_s@freenet.co.uk
I: www.earsham-parkfarm.co.uk

Manor Farm House ♦♦♦♦
St Margarets Road, Bungay, NR35 1PQ
T: (01986) 896895
F: (01986) 896840

BUNTINGFORD
Hertfordshire

Buckland Bury Farm ♦♦♦♦
Buckland Bury, Buntingford, SG9 0PY
T: (01763) 272958
F: (01763) 274722
E: buckbury@farmersweekly.net

Chipping Hall ♦♦♦♦
Chipping, Buntingford SG9 0PH
T: (01763) 271514
F: (01763) 272833
E: jacquelinenoy@aol.com

BURES
Suffolk

Queen's House ♦♦♦♦
Church Square, Bures, Sudbury, CO8 5AB
T: (01787) 227760
F: (01787) 227082
E: rogerarnold2@aol.com
I: www.queens-house.com

BURGH ST PETER
Norfolk

Shrublands Farm
♦♦♦♦ SILVER AWARD
Burgh St Peter, Beccles NR34 0BB
T: (01502) 677241
F: (01502) 677241

BURNHAM MARKET
Norfolk

Holmesdale
Rating Applied For
Church Walk, Burnham Market, King's Lynn PE31 8DH
T: (01328) 738699
E: veronicagroom@lineone.net

The Lord Nelson Public House
♦♦♦♦
Creake Road, Burnham Market, King's Lynn PE31 8EN
T: (01328) 738321

Wood Lodge
♦♦♦♦ SILVER AWARD
Millwood, Herring's Lane, Burnham Market, King's Lynn PE31 8DP
T: (01328) 730152
F: (01328) 730158

BURNHAM-ON-CROUCH
Essex

Holyrood House ♦♦♦
46 Green Lane, Ostend, Burnham-on-Crouch, CMO 8PU
T: (01621) 784759

The Railway Hotel ♦♦♦♦
Station Road, Burnham-on-Crouch, CMo 8BQ
T: (01621) 786868
F: (01621) 783002

BURNHAM THORPE
Norfolk

Whitehall Farm ♦♦♦♦
Burnham Thorpe, King's Lynn PE31 8HN
T: (01328) 738416
F: (01328) 730937
E: barry.southerland@amserve.net

BURY ST EDMUNDS
Suffolk

Abbotts House Bed & Breakfast ♦♦♦
2 Grove Road, Bury St Edmunds, IP33 3BE
T: (01284) 749660
F: (01284) 749660
E: robert.everitt@talk21.com
I: www.abbottshouse.co.uk

Brighthouse Farm ♦♦♦♦
Melford Road, Lawshall, Bury St Edmunds IP29 4PX
T: (01284) 830385
F: (01284) 830385
E: brighthousefarm@supanet.com
I: www.brighthousefarm.fsnet.co.uk

Clarice House
♦♦♦♦♦ SILVER AWARD
Horringer Court, Horringer Road, Bury St Edmunds, IP29 5PH
T: (01284) 705550
F: (01284) 716120
E: enquiry@clarice-bury.fsnet.co.uk
I: www.clarice.co.uk

Dunston Guesthouse/Hotel ♦♦♦
8 Springfield Road, Bury St Edmunds, IP33 3AN
T: (01284) 767981
F: (01284) 17645174
I: www.dunstonguesthouse.co.uk

The Glen ♦♦♦♦
84 Eastgate Street, Bury St Edmunds, IP33 1YR
T: (01284) 755490
E: rallov@aol.com

Hilltop ♦♦
22 Bronyon Close, Bury St Edmunds, IP33 3XB
T: (01284) 767066
E: bandb@hilltop22br.freeserve.co.uk
I: www.hilltop22br.freeserve.co.uk

Kent House ♦♦♦
20 St Andrews Street North, Bury St Edmunds, IP33 1TH
T: (01284) 769661
E: lizkent@supanet.com
I: www.lizkent.supanet.com

Manorhouse
♦♦♦♦♦ GOLD AWARD
The Green, Beyton, Bury St Edmunds IP30 9AF
T: (01359) 270960
E: manorhouse@beyton.com
I: www.beyton.com

Northgate House ♦♦♦♦♦
8 Northgate Street, Bury St Edmunds, IP33 1HQ
T: (01284) 760469
F: (01284) 724008
E: northgate_hse@hotmail.com
I: www.northgatehouse.com

The Old Bakery ♦♦♦♦
Farley Green, Wickhambrook, Newmarket CB8 8PX
T: (01440) 820852
F: (01440) 820852
E: info@theoldbakery.freeserve.co.uk
I: www.theoldbakery.freeserve.co.uk

Ounce House ♦♦♦♦
Northgate Street, Bury St Edmunds, IP33 1HP
T: (01284) 761779
F: (01284) 768315
E: pott@globalnet.co.uk

Park House ♦♦♦
22A Mustow Street, Bury St Edmunds, IP33 1XL
T: (01284) 703432
F: (01284) 703432

Regency House Hotel ♦♦♦♦
3 Looms Lane, Bury St Edmunds, IP33 1HE
T: (01284) 764676
F: (01284) 725444
I: www.regencyhousehotel.co.uk

South Hill House ♦♦♦♦
43 Southgate Street, Bury St Edmunds, IP33 2AZ
T: (01284) 755650
F: (01284) 752718
E: southill@lineone.net
I: www.southill.cwc.net

Sycamore House ♦♦♦♦
23 Northgate Street, Bury St Edmunds, IP33 1HP
T: (01284) 755828
E: m.chalkley@ntlworld.com
I: www.sycamorehouse.net

Westbank House B&B ♦♦
116A Westley Road, Bury St Edmunds, IP33 3SD
T: (01284) 753874
F: (01284) 725775
E: graham@paske.fs.business.co.uk

BUXTON
Norfolk

Belair ♦♦♦
Crown Road, Buxton, Norwich NR10 5EN
T: (01603) 279637
F: (01603) 279637
E: johnblake1234@aol.com

CAMBRIDGE
Cambridgeshire

Acer House ♦♦♦
3 Dean Drive, Holbrook Road, Cambridge, CB1 7SW
T: (01223) 210404
E: carol.dennett@btinternet.com
I: www.acerhouse.co.uk

Acorn Guesthouse ♦♦♦♦
154 Chesterton Road, Cambridge, CB4 1DA
T: (01223) 353888
F: (01223) 350527
E: info@acornguesthouse.co.uk
I: www.acornguesthouse.co.uk

Alpha Milton Guesthouse ♦♦♦
61-63 Milton Road, Cambridge, CB4 1XA
T: (01223) 311625
F: (01223) 565100

Arbury Lodge Guesthouse ♦♦♦
82 Arbury Road, Cambridge, CB4 2JE
T: (01223) 364319
F: (01223) 566988
E: arburylodge@ntlworld.com
I: www.guesthousecambridge.com

Ashley Hotel ♦♦♦
74 Chesterton Road, Cambridge, CB4 1ER
T: (01223) 350059
F: (01223) 350900
E: info@arundelhousehotels.co.uk
I: www.arundelhousehotels.co.uk

Assisi Guesthouse ♦♦♦
193 Cherry Hinton Road, Cambridge, CB1 7BX
T: (01223) 246648
F: (01223) 412900

Aylesbray Lodge Guesthouse ♦♦♦♦
5 Mowbray Road, Cambridge, CB1 7SR
T: (01223) 240089
F: (01223) 528678
E: stay@aylesbray.com
I: www.aylesbray.com

Brooklands Guesthouse ♦♦♦
95 Cherry Hinton Road, Cambridge, CB1 7BS
T: (01223) 242035
F: (01223) 242035

Cam Guesthouse ♦♦♦
17 Elizabeth Way, Cambridge, CB4 1DD
T: (01223) 354512
F: (01223) 353164
E: camguesthouse@btinternet.com
I: www.camguesthouse.co.uk

Cambridge Lodge Hotel ♦♦♦♦
139 Huntingdon Road, Cambridge, CB3 0DQ
T: (01223) 352833
F: (01223) 355166
E: cambridge.lodge@btconnect.com

Carolina Bed & Breakfast ♦♦♦♦
148 Perne Road, Cambridge, CB1 3NX
T: (01223) 247015
F: (01223) 247015
E: carolina.amabile@tesco.net
I: www.smoothhound.co.uk/hotels/carol.html

Cristinas ♦♦♦
47 St Andrews Road, Cambridge, CB4 1DH
T: (01223) 365855
F: (01223) 365855
E: cristinas.guesthouse@ntlworld.com
I: www.cristinasguesthouse.com

Dresden Villa Guesthouse ♦♦♦
34 Cherry Hinton Road, Cambridge, CB1 7AA
T: (01223) 247539
F: (01223) 410640

Dykelands Guesthouse ♦♦♦
157 Mowbray Road, Cambridge, CB1 7SP
T: (01223) 244300
F: (01223) 566746
E: dykelands@fsbdial.co.uk
I: www.dykelands.com

Finches ♦♦♦♦
144 Thornton Road, Girton, Cambridge CB3 0ND
T: (01223) 276653
F: (01223) 276653
E: liz.green.b-b@talk21.com
I: www.smoothhound.co.uk/hotels/finches

Gransden Lodge Farm ♦♦♦♦
Little Gransden, Longstowe, Cambridge SG19 3EB
T: (01767) 677365
F: (01767) 677647

Hamilton Hotel ♦♦♦
156 Chesterton Road, Cambridge, CB4 1DA
T: (01223) 365664
F: (01223) 314866

Hills Guesthouse ♦♦♦♦
157 Hills Road, Cambridge, CB2 2RJ
T: (01223) 214216
F: (01223) 214216

Home From Home ♦♦♦♦
78B Milton Road, Cambridge, CB4 1LA
T: (01223) 323555
F: (01223) 563509
E: homefromhome@tesco.net

King's Tithe ♦♦♦♦
13a Comberton Road, Barton, Cambridge CB3 7BA
T: (01223) 263610
F: (01223) 263610
E: thornebarton@lineone.net

Lensfield Hotel ♦♦♦♦
53 Lensfield Road, Cambridge, CB2 1EN
T: (01223) 355017
F: (01223) 312022
E: reservations@lensfield.co.uk & enquiries@lensfieldhotel.co.u
I: www.lensfieldhotel.co.uk

Lovell Lodge Hotel ♦♦♦
365 Milton Road, Cambridge, CB4 1SR
T: (01223) 425478
F: (01223) 426581

Segovia Lodge ♦♦♦
2 Barton Road, Newnham, Cambridge, CB3 9JZ
T: (01223) 354105
F: (01223) 323011

Southampton Guest House ♦♦♦
7 Elizabeth Way, Cambridge, CB4 1DE
T: (01223) 357780
F: (01223) 314297
E: southamptonhouse@telco4u.net
I: www.southamptonguesthouse.com

The Suffolk House ♦♦♦♦
69 Milton Road, Cambridge, CB4 1XA
T: (01223) 352016
F: (01223) 566816
E: suffolkhouse@btinternet.com

Sycamore House ♦♦♦♦
56 High Street, Great Wilbraham, Cambridge CB1 5JD
T: (01223) 880751
F: (01223) 880751
E: barry@thesycamorehouse.co.uk
I: www.thesycamorehouse.co.uk

Tudor Cottage ♦♦♦♦
292 Histon Road, Cambridge, CB4 3HS
T: (01223) 565212
F: (01223) 508656
E: tudor.cottage@ntlworld.com

Woodfield House ♦♦♦♦
Madingley Road, Coton, Cambridge CB3 7PH
T: (01954) 210265
F: (01954) 212650
E: wendy-john@wsadler.freeserve.co.uk

Worth House ♦♦♦♦
152 Chesterton Road, Cambridge, CB4 1DA
T: (01223) 316074
F: (01223) 316074
E: enquiry@worth-house.co.uk
I: www.worth-house.co.uk

CAMPSEA ASHE
Suffolk

The Old Rectory
♦♦♦♦♦ GOLD AWARD
Campsea Ashe, Woodbridge IP13 0PU
T: (01728) 746524
F: (01728) 746524

CARBROOKE
Norfolk

White Hall
♦♦♦♦ GOLD AWARD
Carbrooke, Thetford IP25 6SG
T: (01953) 885950
F: (01953) 884420
E: shirleycarr@whitehall.uk.net

CARLETON RODE
Norfolk

Upgate Farm ♦♦♦
Carleton Rode, Norwich NR16 1NJ
T: (01953) 860300
F: (01953) 860300
E: upgatefarm@btinternet.com

CASTLE ACRE
Norfolk

Willow Cottage Tea Rooms ♦♦♦♦
Willow Cottage, Stocks Green, Castle Acre, King's Lynn PE32 2AE
T: (01760) 755551
E: willowcottage@webwise.fm

CASTLE HEDINGHAM
Essex

Fishers ♦♦♦♦
St James Street, Castle Hedingham, Halstead CO9 3EW
T: (01787) 460382
F: (01787) 460382
E: Fishers@hutchingsh.freeserve.co.uk

The Old School House ♦♦♦
St James Street, Castle Hedingham, Halstead CO9 3EW
T: (01787) 461629
E: ccdawson@aol.com

CASTOR
Cambridgeshire

Cobnut Cottage ♦♦♦♦
45 Peterborough Road, Castor, Peterborough PE5 7AX
T: (01733) 380745
F: (01733) 380745
E: huckle.cobnut@talk21.com

The Old Smithy ♦♦♦♦
47 Peterborough Road, Castor, Peterborough PE5 7AX
T: (01733) 380186
F: (01733) 380186
E: julie.e.m.taylor@lineone.net

CAVENDISH
Suffolk

Embleton House
♦♦♦♦ SILVER AWARD
Melford Road, Cavendish, Sudbury CO10 8AA
T: (01787) 280447
F: (01787) 282396
E: silverned@aol.com
I: www.smoothhound.co.uk/hotels/embleton

The Red House Bed and Breakfast
♦♦♦♦ SILVER AWARD
Stour Street, Cavendish, Sudbury CO10 8BH
T: (01787) 280611
F: (01787) 280611
E: mtheaker@btinternet.com
I: www.SmoothHound.co.uk/hotels/theredh.html

CHELMSFORD
Essex

Aarandale ♦♦♦
9 Roxwell Road, Chelmsford, CM1 2LY
T: (01245) 251713
F: (01245) 251713
E: aarandaleuk@aol.com

Almond Lodge ♦♦♦
The Bringey, Great Baddow, Chelmsford CM2 7JW
T: (01245) 471564
E: regnorfolk@btinternet.com

Beechcroft Hotel ♦♦♦
211 New London Road, Chelmsford, CM2 0AJ
T: (01245) 352462
F: (01245) 347833
E: enquiries@beechcrofthotel.com
I: www.beechcrofthotel.com

Boswell House Hotel ♦♦♦♦
118 Springfield Road, Chelmsford, CM2 6LF
T: (01245) 287587
F: (01245) 287587
E: SteveBoorman@aol.com

Brook House
♦♦♦♦ SILVER AWARD
Chelmsford Road, Great Waltham, Chelmsford, CM3 1AQ
T: (01245) 360776

The Chelmer Hotel ♦♦
2-4 Hamlet Road, Chelmsford, CM2 0EU
T: (01245) 353360
F: (01245) 609055
E: collingsnick@hotmail.com

Fitzjohns Farmhouse ♦♦♦
Mashbury Road, Great Waltham, Chelmsford, CM3 1EJ
T: (01245) 360204
F: (01245) 361724
E: RosRenwick@aol.com

Neptune Cafe Motel ♦♦
Burnham Road, Latchingdon, Chelmsford CM3 6EX
T: (01621) 740770

Old Bakery ♦♦♦♦
Waltham Road, Terling, Chelmsford, CM3 2QR
T: (01245) 233363

Pemajero ♦♦♦
Cedar Avenue West, Chelmsford, CM1 2XA
T: (01245) 264679
F: (01245) 264679

Sherwood ♦♦♦
Cedar Avenue West, Chelmsford, CM1 2XA
T: (01245) 257981
F: (01245) 257981
E: jeremy.salter@btclick.com

Silvertrees ♦♦
565 Galleywood Road, Chelmsford, CM2 8AA
T: (01245) 268767

Stump Cross House
♦♦♦♦ SILVER AWARD
Moulsham Street, Chelmsford, CM2 9AQ
T: (01245) 353804

Tanunda Hotel ♦♦♦
217-219 New London Road, Chelmsford, CM2 0AJ
T: (01245) 354295
F: (01245) 345503

Wards Farm ♦♦
Loves Green, Highwood Road, Highwood, Chelmsford CM1 3QJ
T: (01245) 248812
F: (01245) 248812
E: alsnbrtn@aol.com

CHIPPENHAM
Cambridgeshire

The Maltings Yard Cottage Rating Applied For
20 High Street, Chippenham, Ely CB7 5PP
T: (01638) 720110

CLACTON-ON-SEA
Essex

Le'Vere House Hotel ♦♦♦
15 Agate Road, Clacton-on-Sea, CO15 1RA
T: (01255) 423044
F: (01255) 423044

Sandrock Hotel ♦♦♦
1 Penfold Road, Marine Parade West, Clacton-on-Sea, CO15 1JN
T: (01255) 428215
F: (01255) 428215

Stonar Hotel ♦♦♦
19 Agate Road, Clacton-on-Sea, CO15 1RA
T: (01255) 221011
F: (01255) 422973

CLAPHAM
Bedfordshire

Narly Oak Lodge Narly Oak ♦♦♦♦
The Baulk, Green Lane, Clapham, Bedford MK41 6AA
T: (01234) 350353
F: (01234) 350353
E: fostert@csd.bedfordshire.gov.uk

CLARE
Suffolk

The Clare Hotel ♦♦♦
19 Nethergate Street, Clare, Sudbury CO10 8NP
T: (01787) 277449
F: (01787) 277161
E: rhrng@netscapeonline.co.uk

Ship Stores ♦♦♦♦
22 Callis Street, Clare, Sudbury CO10 8PX
T: (01787) 277834
E: shipclare@aol.com
I: www.ship-stores.co.uk

CLEY NEXT THE SEA
Norfolk

Cooke's of Cley ♦♦♦
High Street, Cley next the Sea, Holt NR25 7RX
T: (01263) 740776
F: (01263) 740776
I: www.broadland.com

The George Hotel ♦♦♦
High Street, Cley next the Sea, Holt NR25 7RN
T: (01263) 740652
F: (01263) 741275
E: thegeorge@cleynextthesea.com
I: www.thegeorgehotelcley.com

CLOPHILL
Bedfordshire

Shallmarose Bed & Breakfast ♦♦♦
32 Bedford Road, Clophill, Bedford MK45 4AE
T: (01525) 861565

COLCHESTER
Essex

Apple Blossom House ♦♦♦
8 Guildford Road, Colchester, CO1 2YL
T: (01206) 512303
F: (01206) 870260
E: morleeharris@virgin.net

Athelstan House ♦♦♦♦
201 Maldon Road, Colchester, CO3 3BQ
T: (01206) 548652
E: robert.mackman@ntlworld.com

Four Sevens Guesthouse ♦♦♦
28 Inglis Road, Colchester, CO3 3HU
T: (01206) 546093
F: (01206) 546093
E: calypso1@hotmail.com
I: www.cdemetri.freeserve.com.uk

Fridaywood Farm ♦♦♦♦
Bounstead Road, Colchester, CO2 0DF
T: (01206) 573595
F: (01206) 547011
E: lochorem8@aol.com

Hampton House ♦♦♦
224 Maldon Road, Colchester, CO3 3BD
T: (01206) 579291

11 Harvest End ♦♦♦
Stanway, Colchester, CO3 5YX
T: (01206) 543202

Lemoine ♦♦♦♦
2 Whitefriars Way, Colchester, CO3 4EL
T: (01206) 574710

11a Lincoln Way ♦♦♦
Colchester, CO1 2RL
T: (01206) 867192
F: (01206) 799993
E: j.medwards@easicom.com

Nutcrackers ♦♦♦
6 Mayberry Walk, Colchester, CO2 8PS
T: (01206) 543085
E: jean@aflex.net

Old Courthouse Inn ♦♦♦♦
Harwich Road, Great Bromley, Colchester, CO7 7JG
T: (01206) 250322
F: (01206) 251346
E: oldcourthouseinn@21.com
I: www.theoldcourthouse.com

Pescara House ♦♦♦
88 Manor Road, Colchester, CO3 3LY
T: (01206) 520055
F: (01206) 512127
E: dave@pescarahouse.co.uk
I: www.pescarahouse.co.uk

Peveril Hotel ♦♦
51 North Hill, Colchester, CO1 1PY
T: (01206) 574001
F: (01206) 574001

The Red House
♦♦♦♦ SILVER AWARD
29 Wimpole Road, Colchester, CO1 2DL
T: (01206) 509005
F: (01206) 500311
E: theredhousecolchester@hotmail.com

76 Roman Road ♦♦♦
Colchester, CO1 1UP
T: (01206) 514949

Scheregate Hotel ♦♦
36 Osborne Street, via St John's Street, Colchester, CO2 7DB
T: (01206) 573034
F: (01206) 541561

Seven Arches Farm ♦♦
Chitts Hill, Lexden, Colchester, CO3 5SX
T: (01206) 574896
F: (01206) 574896

Tall Trees ♦♦♦♦
25 Irvine Road, Colchester, CO3 3TP
T: (01206) 576650
E: whitehead.talltrees@ntlworld.com

Telstar ♦♦♦
Layer Breton, Colchester, CO2 0PS
T: (01206) 331642
F: (01206) 330761

4 Wavell Avenue ♦♦
Colchester, CO2 7HP
T: (01206) 571736

COLTISHALL
Norfolk

Bridge House ♦♦♦♦
1 High Street, Coltishall, Norwich NR12 7AA
T: (01603) 737323
F: (01603) 737323
E: bookings@bridge-house.com
I: www.bridge_house.com

The Hedges Guesthouse
♦♦♦♦
Tunstead Road, Coltishall, Norwich NR12 7AL
T: (01603) 738361
F: (01603) 738983
E: thehedges@msn.com
I: www.hedgesbandb.co.uk

Kings Head ♦♦♦
26 Wroxham Road, Coltishall, Norwich NR12 7EA
T: (01603) 737426
F: (01603) 736542

The Old Railway Station ♦♦♦
The Old Railway Station, Station Road, Coltishall, Norwich NR12 7JG
T: (01603) 737069

Terra Nova Lodge ♦♦♦♦
14 Westbourne Road, Coltishall, Norwich NR12 7HT
T: (01603) 736264

CORTON
Suffolk

Barn Owl Lodge ♦♦♦♦
Yarmouth Road, Corton, Lowestoft NR32 5NH
T: (01502) 733105

Holly Cottage ♦♦♦♦
11 Mill Lane, Corton, Lowestoft NR32 5HZ
T: (01502) 731224

COTTENHAM
Cambridgeshire

Denmark House ♦♦♦♦
58 Denmark Road, Cottenham, Cambridge CB4 8QS
T: (01954) 251060
F: (01954) 251629
E: denmark@house33.fsnet.co.uk
I: www.denmarkhouse.fsnet.co.uk

CRANFIELD
Bedfordshire

49 Mill Road ♦♦♦
Cranfield, Bedford MK43 0JG
T: (01234) 750715

The Swan ♦♦
2 Court Road, Cranfield, Bedford MK43 0DR
T: (01234) 750332
F: (01234) 750332
E: theswan.cranfield@virgin.net

CREETING ST MARY
Suffolk

Saint Eia ♦♦♦♦
All Saints Road, Creeting St Mary, Ipswich IP6 8PP
T: (01449) 721977

CRETINGHAM
Suffolk

The Cretingham Bell
♦♦♦♦ SILVER AWARD
The Street, Cretingham, Woodbridge IP13 7BJ
T: (01728) 685419

Shrubbery Farmhouse
♦♦♦♦ SILVER AWARD
Chapel Hill, Cretingham, Woodbridge IP13 7DN
T: (01473) 737494
F: (01473) 737312
E: sm@marmar.co.uk
I: www.shrubberyfarmhouse.co.uk

CROMER
Norfolk

Birch House ♦♦♦
34 Cabbell Road, Cromer, NR27 9HX
T: (01263) 512521

Cambridge House ♦♦♦♦
Sea Front, Cromer, NR27 9HD
T: (01263) 512085
I: www.broadland.com/cambridgehouse

The Grove Guesthouse ♦♦♦
95 Overstrand Road, Cromer, NR27 0DJ
T: (01263) 512412
F: (01263) 513416
E: thegrovecromer@btopenworld.com
I: www.thegrovecromer.co.uk

Knoll Guesthouse ♦♦♦
23 Alfred Road, Cromer, NR27 9AN
T: (01263) 512753
E: ian@knollguesthouse.co.uk
I: www.knollguesthouse.co.uk

Morden House ♦♦♦♦
20 Cliff Avenue, Cromer, NR27 0AN
T: (01263) 513396
E: rosemary@broadland.com
I: www.broadland.com/mordenhouse

Seaspray ♦♦♦♦
1 Cliff Drive, Cromer, NR27 0AW
T: (01263) 512116

Shrublands Farm
♦♦♦♦ SILVER AWARD
Northrepps, Cromer, NR27 0AA
T: (01263) 579297
F: (01263) 579297
E: youngman@farming.co.uk
I: www.broadland.com/shrublands

Stenson ♦♦♦♦
32 Overstrand Road, Cromer, NR27 0AJ
T: (01263) 511308

CULFORD
Suffolk

47 Benyon Gardens ♦♦♦
Culford, Bury St Edmunds IP28 6EA
T: (01284) 728763

DALLINGHOO
Suffolk

Old Rectory ♦♦♦
Dallinghoo, Woodbridge IP13 0LA
T: (01473) 737700

DANBURY
Essex

Southways ♦♦♦
Copt Hill, Danbury, Chelmsford CM3 4NN
T: (01245) 223428

Wych Elm ♦♦♦
Mayes Lane, Danbury, Chelmsford CM3 4NJ
T: (01245) 222674
E: axonwychelm@tinyworld.co.uk

DARSHAM
Suffolk

Priory Farm ♦♦♦
Darsham, Saxmundham IP17 3QD
T: (01728) 668459

White House Farm ♦♦♦
Main Road, Darsham, Saxmundham IP17 3PP
T: (01728) 668632

DEBDEN
Essex

Redbrick House ♦♦♦♦
Deynes Road, Debden, Saffron Walden CB11 3LG
T: (01799) 540221
F: 0870 1643639
E: emma@redbrick-house.co.uk

DEDHAM
Essex

Good Hall
♦♦♦♦ SILVER AWARD
Coggeshall Road, Dedham, Colchester CO7 7LR
T: (01206) 322100
F: (01206) 323902
E: goodhall@ic24.net

May's Barn Farm
♦♦♦♦ SILVER AWARD
May's Lane, Off Long Road West, Dedham, Colchester CO7 6EW
T: (01206) 323191
E: maysbarn@talk21.com
I: www.mays.barn.btinternet.co.uk

DENNINGTON
Suffolk

Grange Farm Bed & Breakfast
♦♦♦
Grange Farm, Dennington, Woodbridge IP13 8BT
T: (01986) 798388
I: www.framlingham.com/grangefarm

DENVER
Norfolk

Westhall Cottages ♦♦♦
20-22 Sluice Road, Denver, Downham Market PE38 0DY
T: (01366) 382987
F: (01366) 385553

DEREHAM
Norfolk

Greenbanks Country Hotel
♦♦♦♦
Swaffham Road, Wendling, Dereham, NR19 2AR
T: (01362) 687742
F: (01362) 687742
E: greenbanks@skynow.net
I: www.greenbankshotel.co.uk

Hill House ♦♦♦♦
26 Market Place, Dereham, NR19 2AP
T: (01362) 699699
E: jvellam@aol.com

Park Farm ♦♦♦♦
Bylaugh, East Dereham NR20 4QE
T: (01362) 688584
E: lakeparkfm@aol.com

DERSINGHAM
Norfolk

Ashdene House ♦♦♦
Dersingham, King's Lynn PE31 6HQ
T: (01485) 540395
I: www3.mistral.co.uk/ashdene

The Corner House
♦♦♦♦ SILVER AWARD
2 Sandringham Road, Dersingham, King's Lynn PE31 6LL
T: (01485) 543532

Dove Lodge ♦♦♦♦
21 Woodside Avenue, Dersingham, King's Lynn PE31 6QB
T: (01485) 540053
F: (01485) 540053
E: dovelodgebb@fsnet.co.uk
I: www.dovelodge.20m.com

Spring Cottage ♦♦♦
11 Fern Hill, Dersingham, King's Lynn PE31 6HT
T: (01485) 541012
E: hillarytuttle@hotmail.com

The White House ♦♦♦
44 Hunstanton Road, Dersingham, King's Lynn PE31 6HQ
T: (01485) 541895
F: (01485) 544880
E: whitehouseguestaccom@ukonline.co.uk

The Willows
Rating Applied For
Post Office Road, Dersingham, King's Lynn PE31 6HR
T: (01485) 543602
F: (01485) 543602
E: thewillowsbandb@hotmail.com

DISS
Norfolk

Abbey Farm ♦♦♦
Great Green, Thrandeston, Diss IP21 4BN
T: (01379) 783422
E: jean.carlisle@virgin.net
I: www.diss.co.uk

Dickleburgh Hall
♦♦♦♦♦ GOLD AWARD
Semere Green Lane, Dickleburgh, Diss, IP21 4NT
T: (01379) 741259
I: www.dickhall.co.uk

Koliba ♦♦♦
8 Louie's Lane, Diss, IP22 3LR
T: (01379) 650046
F: (01379) 650046
E: olgakoliba@aol.com

Oxfootstone Granary ♦♦♦♦
Low Common, South Lopham, Diss, IP22 2JS
T: (01379) 687490
E: paddie@oxfoot.co.uk
I: www.oxfoot.co.uk

South View ♦♦♦
High Road, Roydon, Diss IP22 5RU
T: (01379) 651620

Strenneth ♦♦♦♦
Airfield Road, Fersfield, Diss IP22 2BP
T: (01379) 688182
F: (01379) 688260
E: pdavey@strenneth.co.uk
I: www.strenneth.co.uk

DOCKING
Norfolk

Jubilee Lodge ♦♦♦
Station Road, Docking, King's Lynn PE31 8LS
T: (01485) 518473
F: (01485) 518473
E: eqhoward62@hotmail.com
I: www.jubilee-lodge.co.uk

DOVERCOURT
Essex

Dudley Guesthouse ♦♦
34 Cliff Road, Dovercourt, Harwich CO12 3PP
T: (01255) 504927

Homebay ♦♦♦
9 Bay Road, Dovercourt, Harwich CO12 3JZ
T: (01255) 504428
E: sydie@dialstart.net

Sun View ♦♦♦
42 Cliff Road, Dovercourt, Harwich CO12 3PP
T: (01255) 507816
E: enquiries@sunview.fsworld.co.uk

Tudor Rose ♦♦♦
124 Fronks Road, Dovercourt, Harwich CO12 4EQ
T: (01255) 552398
E: jane@morgan-co12.freeserve.co.uk

DOWNHAM MARKET
Norfolk

Chestnut Villa ♦♦♦
44 Railway Road, Downham Market, PE38 9EB
T: (01366) 384099
E: chestnutvilla@talk21.com

Lion House Licensed Restaurant and Guest House ♦♦♦
Lion House, 140 Lynn Road, Downham Market, PE38 9QF
T: (01366) 382017
E: lionhouse@supanet.com
I: www.lionhouse.supanet.com

DUNSTABLE
Bedfordshire

Cherish End B & B ♦♦♦♦
21 Barton Avenue, Dunstable, LU5 4DF
T: (01582) 606266
F: (01582) 606266
E: dandg4bandb@tinyworld.co.uk

EARITH
Cambridgeshire

Riverview Hotel ♦♦♦
37 High Street, Earith, Huntingdon PE28 3PP
T: (01487) 841405
E: riverviewhotel@tinyworld.co.uk
I: www.riverviewhotel.co.uk

EARL SOHAM
Suffolk

Bridge House
♦♦♦♦ SILVER AWARD
Earl Soham, Framlingham, Woodbridge IP13 7RT
T: (01728) 685473
F: (01728) 685289
E: bridgehouse46@hotmail.com
I: www.jenniferbaker.co.uk

EARLS COLNE
Essex

Chalkney Wood Cottage ♦♦♦♦
Tey Road, Earls Colne, Colchester CO6 2LD
T: (01787) 223522
I: www.chalkneywoodcottage.com

Greenlands Farm ♦♦♦♦
Lamberts Lane, Earls Colne, Colchester CO6 2LE
T: (01787) 224895
E: david@greenlandsfarm.freeserve.co.uk

Riverside Lodge ♦♦♦
40 Lower Holt Street, Earls Colne, Colchester CO6 2PH
T: (01787) 223487
F: (01787) 223487
E: john+bonnie@riversidelodge-uk.com
I: www.riversidelodge-uk.com

EAST BARSHAM
Norfolk

White Horse Inn ♦♦♦
Fakenham Road, East Barsham, Fakenham NR21 0LH
T: (01328) 820645
F: (01328) 820645

EAST BERGHOLT
Suffolk

Rosemary ♦♦♦
Rectory Hill, East Bergholt, Colchester CO7 6TH
T: (01206) 298241
E: s.finch@bcs.org.uk

EAST MERSEA
Essex

Bromans Farm ♦♦♦♦
Mersea Island, East Mersea, Colchester CO5 8UE
T: (01206) 383235
F: (01206) 383235

Mersea Island Vineyard ♦♦♦♦
Rewsalls Lane, East Mersea, Colchester CO5 8SX
T: (01206) 385900
F: (01206) 383600
E: jacqui.barber@merseawine.com
I: www.merseawine.com

EASTON
Suffolk

Atlantis Stud Farm ♦♦♦♦
Framlingham Road, Easton, Woodbridge IP13 0EW
T: (01728) 621553
F: (01728) 621553
E: atlantisbandb@yahoo.co.uk
I: www.eastanglia-bandb.co.uk

ELMSWELL
Suffolk

Elmswell Hall Bed & Breakfast ♦♦♦♦
Elmswell Hall, Elmswell, Bury St Edmunds IP30 9EN
T: (01359) 240215
F: (01359) 240215
E: kate@elmswellhall.freeserve.co.uk
I: www.elmswellhall.co.uk

Kiln Farm ♦♦♦
Kiln Lane, Elmswell, Bury St Edmunds IP30 9QR
T: (01359) 240442
E: barry-sue@kilnfarm.fsnet.co.uk

Mulberry Farm
♦♦♦♦ SILVER AWARD
Ashfield Road, Elmswell, Bury St Edmunds IP30 9HG
T: (01359) 244244
F: (01359) 244244

ELSENHAM
Hertfordshire

Aspens ♦♦♦
Park Road, Elsenham, Bishop's Stortford CM22 6DF
T: (01279) 816281

ELY
Cambridgeshire

Casa Nostra Guesthouse ♦♦♦
6 Black Bank Road, Little Downham, Ely, CB6 2UA
T: (01353) 862495
F: (01353) 862495
E: casanostra@btinternet.com
I: guesthousesinbritain.co.uk

Cathedral House ♦♦♦♦
17 St Mary's Street, Ely, CB7 4ER
T: (01353) 662124
F: (01353) 662124
E: farndale@cathedralhouse.co.uk
I: www.cathedralhouse.co.uk

The Flyer Restaurant, Public House & Hotel ♦♦♦
69 Newnham Street, Ely, CB7 4PQ
T: (01353) 669200
F: (01353) 669100
E: graham@flyerhotel.co.uk
I: www.flyerhotel.co.uk

The Grove
♦♦♦♦ SILVER AWARD
Bury Lane, Sutton Gault, Ely, CB6 2BD
T: (01353) 777196
F: (01353) 777425

Hill House Farm
♦♦♦♦ GOLD AWARD
9 Main Street, Coveney, Ely CB6 2DJ
T: (01353) 778369
F: (01353) 778369
E: hill_house@madasafish.com

Nyton Hotel ♦♦♦
7 Barton Road, Ely, CB7 4HZ
T: (01353) 662459
F: (01353) 666217
E: nytonhotel@yahoo.co.uk

Rosendale Lodge
♦♦♦♦♦ SILVER AWARD
223 Main Street, Witchford, Ely CB6 2HT
T: (01353) 667700
F: (01353) 667799

Spinney Abbey ♦♦♦♦
Stretham Road, Wicken, Ely CB7 5XQ
T: (01353) 720971
E: spinney.abbey@tesco.net
I: www.spinneyabbey.co.uk

Springfields
♦♦♦♦♦ SILVER AWARD
Ely Road, Little Thetford, Ely CB6 3HJ
T: (01353) 663637
F: (01353) 663130
E: springfields@talk21.com
I: www.smoothhound.co.uk/hotels/springfields.html

Sycamore House ♦♦♦♦
91 Cambridge Road, Ely,
CB7 4HX
T: (01353) 662139
F: (01353) 662795
E: sycamore_house@hotmail.com
I: www.sycamorehouse.gb.com

EPPING
Essex

Brooklands ♦♦♦
1 Chapel Road, Epping,
CM16 5DS
T: (01992) 575424
E: abrookland@aol.com
I: www.abrookland@aol.com

Country House Bed & Breakfast ♦♦♦♦
16 Beulah Road, Epping,
CM16 6RH
T: (01992) 576044
F: (01992) 570430
E: epping.accomm@btinternet.com

ERPINGHAM
Norfolk

Saracens Head Inn ♦♦♦
Wolterton, Erpingham, Norwich
NR11 7LX
T: (01263) 768909
F: (01263) 768993
I: www.saracenshead-norfolk.co.uk

EYE
Suffolk

The White Horse Inn ♦♦♦
Stoke Ash, Eye IP23 7ET
T: (01379) 678222
F: (01379) 678557
E: whitehorse@stokeash.fsbusiness.co.uk
I: www.whitehorseinn.fsnet.co.uk

EYKE
Suffolk

Marsh Cottage ♦♦♦
Eyke, Woodbridge IP12 2QT
T: (01394) 460203

The Old House ♦♦♦♦
Eyke, Woodbridge IP12 2QW
T: (01394) 460213

FAKENHAM
Norfolk

Abbott Farm ♦♦♦
Walsingham Road, Binham,
Fakenham, NR21 0AW
T: (01328) 830519
F: (01328) 830519
E: abbot.farm@btinternet.com

Erika's Bed and Breakfast ♦♦♦
3 Gladstone Road, Fakenham,
NR21 9BZ
T: (01328) 863058

Hardlands ♦♦♦♦
East Raynham, Fakenham
NR21 7EQ
T: (01328) 862567
E: harlands@waitrose.com

Highfield Farm ♦♦♦♦
Great Ryburgh, Fakenham
NR21 7AL
T: (01328) 829249
F: (01328) 829422
E: jegshighfield@onet.co.uk
I: www.broadland.com/highfield

Holly Lodge
♦♦♦♦♦ SILVER AWARD
The Street, Thursford Green,
Fakenham, NR21 0AS
T: (01328) 878465
F: (01328) 878465
E: hollyguestlodge@talk21.com
I: www.hollylodgeguesthouse.co.uk

Mulberry Cottage
♦♦♦♦ SILVER AWARD
Green Farm Lane, Thursford
Green, Fakenham, NR21 0RX
T: (01328) 878968

The Old Brick Kilns Guesthouse ♦♦♦♦
Little Barney Lane, Barney,
Fakenham, NR21 0NL
T: (01328) 878305
F: (01328) 878948
E: enquire@old-brick-kilns.co.uk
I: www.old-brick-kilns.co.uk

Southview ♦♦♦♦
Lynn Road, Sculthorpe,
Fakenham NR21 9QE
T: (01328) 851300

FARCET
Cambridgeshire

Red House Farm ♦♦♦
Broadway, Farcet, Peterborough
PE7 3AZ
T: (01733) 243129
F: (01733) 243129
E: gill.emberson@totalise.co.uk

FEERING
Essex

The Old Anchor ♦♦♦♦
132 Feering Hill, Feering,
Colchester CO5 9PY
T: (01376) 572855
F: (01376) 572855

Old Wills Farm ♦♦♦
Feering, Colchester CO5 9RP
T: (01376) 570259
F: (01376) 570259
E: janecrayston@btconnect.com

FELIXSTOWE
Suffolk

Burlington House ♦♦♦♦
7 Beach Road West, Felixstowe,
IP11 2BH
T: (01394) 282051

Dolphin Hotel ♦♦
41 Beach Station Road,
Felixstowe, IP11 2EY
T: (01394) 282261
F: (01394) 278319

Dorincourt Guesthouse ♦♦♦
41 Undercliff Road West,
Felixstowe, IP11 2AH
T: (01394) 270447
F: (01394) 270447

The Grafton Guesthouse ♦♦♦♦
13 Sea Road, Felixstowe,
IP11 2BB
T: (01394) 284881
F: (01394) 279101
E: info@grafton-house.com
I: www.grafton-house.com

Primrose Gate Bed & Breakfast ♦♦♦♦
263 Ferry Road, Felixstowe,
IP11 9RX
T: (01394) 271699
F: (01394) 283614
E: lesley_berry@hotmail.com

FELMINGHAM
Norfolk

Larks Rise ♦♦
North Walsham Road,
Felmingham, North Walsham
NR28 0JU
T: (01692) 403173
I: www.broadland.com/larksrise

FELSTED
Essex

Potash Farm ♦♦♦♦
Cobblers Green, Causeway End
Road, Felsted, Dunmow
CM6 3LX
T: (01371) 820510
F: (01371) 820510
E: rgspotash@compuserve.com

FENSTANTON
Cambridgeshire

Orchard House ♦♦♦
6A Hilton Road, Fenstanton,
Huntingdon PE28 9LH
T: (01480) 469208
F: (01480) 497487
E: ascarrow@aol.com

FINCHAM
Norfolk

Rose Cottage Bed and Breakfast ♦♦♦♦
Downham Road, Fincham, King's
Lynn PE33 9HF
T: (01366) 347426
F: (01366) 347426

FINCHINGFIELD
Essex

The Red Lion Inn ♦♦♦
6 Church Hill, Finchingfield,
Braintree CM7 4NN
T: (01371) 810400
F: (01371) 851062
I: www.red-lion-finchingfield.com

FORNHAM ALL SAINTS
Suffolk

The Three Kings ♦♦♦♦
Hengrave Road, Fornham All
Saints, Bury St Edmunds
IP28 6LA
T: (01284) 766979
F: (01284) 723308
E: c.conway@tinyworld.co.uk
I: www.the-three-kings.com

FOULDEN
Norfolk

The White Hart Inn ♦♦♦
White Hart Street, Foulden,
Thetford IP26 5AW
T: (01366) 328638
E: sylvia.chisholm@virgin.net

FRAMLINGHAM
Suffolk

Fieldway Bed & Breakfast ♦♦♦♦
Saxtead Road, Dennington,
Woodbridge IP13 8AP
T: (01728) 638456
F: (01728) 638456
E: dianaturan@hotmail.com
I: www.framlingham.com/fieldway

High House Farm ♦♦♦
Cransford, Framlingham,
Woodbridge IP13 9PD
T: (01728) 663461
F: (01728) 663409
E: bb@highhousefarm.co.uk
I: www.highhousefarm.co.uk

Shimmens Pightle ♦♦♦
Dennington Road, Framlingham,
Woodbridge IP13 9JT
T: (01728) 724036

FRESSINGFIELD
Suffolk

Elm Lodge ♦♦♦♦
Chippenhall Green, Fressingfield,
Eye IP21 5SL
T: (01379) 586249
E: sheila-webster@elm-lodge.fsnet.co.uk
I: www.elm-lodge.fsnet.co.uk

FRINTON-ON-SEA
Essex

Uplands Guesthouse ♦♦♦
41 Hadleigh Road, Frinton-on-
Sea, CO13 9HQ
T: (01255) 674889
E: info@uplandsguesthouse.freeserve.co.uk
I: www.uplandsguesthouse.com

FRISTON
Suffolk

The Flint House ♦♦♦♦
Aldeburgh Road, Friston,
Saxmundham IP17 1PD
T: (01728) 689123
F: (01728) 687406
E: handsel@eidosnet.co.uk
I: www.soi.city.ac.uk/~sunil/flinthouse

The Old School ♦♦♦♦
Aldeburgh Road, Friston,
Saxmundham IP17 1NP
T: (01728) 688173
E: oldschool@fristonoldschool.freeserve.co.uk

GARBOLDISHAM
Norfolk

Ingleneuk Lodge ♦♦♦♦
Hopton Road, Garboldisham,
Diss IP22 2RQ
T: (01953) 681541
F: (01953) 681138
E: info@ingleneuklodge.co.uk
I: www.ingleneuklodge.co.uk

GOOD EASTER
Essex

Treloyhan Bed & Breakfast ♦♦♦
Treloyhan, Chelmsford Road,
Good Easter, Chelmsford
CM1 4PU
T: (01245) 231425
E: tdellar@btopenworld.com

GOSFIELD
Essex

Rare View ♦♦♦
Shardlones Farm, Gosfield,
Halstead CO9 1PL
T: (01787) 474696

GRANTCHESTER
Cambridgeshire

Honeysuckle Cottage ♦♦♦
38 High Street, Grantchester,
Cambridge CB3 9NF
T: (01223) 845977

GREAT BADDOW
Essex

Homecroft ♦♦♦
Southend Road, Great Baddow,
Chelmsford CM2 7AD
T: (01245) 475070
F: (01245) 475070

Establishments printed in blue have a detailed entry in this guide

Orchard House ♦♦♦
The Bringey, Church Street, Great Baddow, Chelmsford CM2 7JW
T: (01245) 474333

Rothmans ♦♦♦
22 High Street, Great Baddow, Chelmsford CM2 7HQ
T: (01245) 473837
F: (01245) 476833
E: eliz_barron@excite.co.uk
I: www.city2000.com/h/rothmans-b&b.essex-html

GREAT BARTON Suffolk

40 Conyers Way ♦♦♦
Great Barton, Bury St Edmunds IP31 2SW
T: (01284) 787632

GREAT BRICETT Suffolk

Riverside Cottage ♦♦♦♦
The Street, Great Bricett, Ipswich IP7 7DH
T: (01473) 658266
E: chasmhorne@aol.com

GREAT CHESTERFORD Essex

White Gates ♦♦♦♦
School Street, Great Chesterford, Saffron Walden CB10 1NN
T: (01799) 530249
E: margaret-mortimer@lineone.net
I: www.welcometowhitegates.co.uk

GREAT CRESSINGHAM Norfolk

The Vines ♦♦♦♦
The Street, Great Cressingham, Thetford IP25 6NL
T: (01760) 756303
E: stay@thevines.fsbusiness.co.uk
I: www.thevines.info

GREAT DUNMOW Essex

Harwood Guest House
♦♦♦♦ SILVER AWARD
52 Stortford Road, Great Dunmow, CM6 1DN
T: (01371) 874627
F: (01371) 874627

Homelye Farm ♦♦♦♦
Homelye Chase, Braintree Road, Dunmow, CM6 3AW
T: (01371) 872127
F: (01371) 876428
E: homelye@supanet.com
I: www.homelyefarm.co.uk

Mallards ♦♦♦♦
Star Lane, Great Dunmow, CM6 1AY
T: (01371) 872641
F: (01371) 872172
E: millersmallardsdunmow@tesco.net

Rose Cottage ♦♦♦♦
Pharisee Green, Great Dunmow, CM6 1JN
T: (01371) 872254

GREAT ELLINGHAM Norfolk

Home Cottage Farm ♦♦♦
Penhill Road, Great Ellingham, Attleborough NR17 1LS
T: (01953) 483734
E: royandmaureen@mail.com

Manor Farm
♦♦♦♦ SILVER AWARD
Hingham Road, Great Ellingham, Attleborough NR17 1JE
T: (01953) 453388
F: (01953) 453388

GREAT EVERSDEN Cambridgeshire

Red House Farm ♦♦♦♦♦
44 High Street, Great Eversden, Cambridge CB3 7 HW
T: (01223) 262154
F: (01223) 264875
E: pbgtebbit@farmersweekly.net

GREAT FINBOROUGH Suffolk

Dairy Farmhouse
♦♦♦♦ SILVER AWARD
Valley Lane, Great Finborough, Stowmarket IP14 3BE
T: (01449) 615730
F: (01449) 615730

GREAT HOCKHAM Norfolk

Manor Farm Bed & Breakfast ♦♦♦♦
Manor Farm, Vicarage Road, Great Hockham, Thetford IP24 1PE
T: (01953) 498204
F: (01953) 498204
E: manorfarm@ukf.net

GREAT HORKESLEY Essex

Knowles Farm ♦♦♦♦
Great Horkesley, Colchester CO6 4BU
T: (01206) 271110
F: (01206) 273197
E: c.longprice@btinternet.com

GREAT RYBURGH Norfolk

The Boar Inn ♦♦♦
Great Ryburgh, Fakenham NR21 0DX
T: (01328) 829212
I: ourworld.compuserve.com/homepages/boar_inn

GREAT SAMPFORD Essex

Stow Farmhouse
♦♦♦♦ SILVER AWARD
High Street, Great Sampford, Saffron Walden CB10 2RG
T: (01799) 586060
F: (01799) 586060
E: joanne.barratt@lineone.net

GREAT SNORING Norfolk

Top Farm
Rating Applied For
Thursford Road, Great Snoring, Fakenham NR21 0HW
T: (01328) 820351
F: (01328) 820140
E: davidperowne@aol.com

GREAT TEY Essex

The Old Shop ♦♦♦
Chappel Road, Great Tey, Colchester CO6 1JQ
T: (01206) 211556
F: (01206) 211556

GREAT WALDINGFIELD Suffolk

Jasmine Cottage ♦♦♦♦
The Heath, Lavenham Road, Great Waldingfield, Sudbury CO10 0RN
T: (01787) 374665
I: www.jasminecottage-b-and-b.co.uk

GREAT WALSINGHAM Norfolk

Port Hole Cottage ♦♦♦♦
Hindringham Road, Great Walsingham, NR22 6DR
T: (01328) 820157

GREAT YARMOUTH Norfolk

Alexandra Hotel ♦♦♦
9 Kent Square, Great Yarmouth, NR30 2EX
T: (01493) 853115

Barnard House
♦♦♦♦ SILVER AWARD
2 Barnard Crescent, Great Yarmouth, NR30 4DR
T: (01493) 855139
F: (01493) 843143
E: barnardhouse@btinternet.com
I: www.barnardhouse.com

The Bromley Hotel ♦♦
63 Apsley Road, Great Yarmouth, NR30 2HG
T: (01493) 842321
F: (01493) 842322
E: thebromleyhotel@tiscali.co.uk
I: www.smoothhound.co.uk/hotels/bromleyhotel

Carlton Hotel ♦♦♦
Marine Parade, Great Yarmouth, NR30 3JE
T: (01493) 855234
F: (01493) 852220

Cleasewood Private Hotel ♦♦♦
55 Wellesley Road, Great Yarmouth, NR30 1EX
T: (01493) 843960

Concorde Private Hotel ♦♦♦
84 North Denes Road, Great Yarmouth, NR30 4LW
T: (01493) 843709
F: (01493) 843709
E: concordeyarmouth@hotmail.com
I: www.concorde-hotel.co.uk

The Dragons Rest ♦♦
25 St Georges Road, Great Yarmouth, NR30 2JT
T: (01493) 850676
F: (01493) 850676

The Edwardian Hotel ♦♦
18-20 Crown Road, Great Yarmouth, NR30 2JN
T: (01493) 856482
E: sandy@eaglemont.freeserve.co.uk
I: www.edwardianhotel.co.uk

Fjaerland Hotel ♦♦♦
24-25 Trafalgar Road, Great Yarmouth, NR30 2LD
T: (01493) 856339
F: (01493) 856339
I: www.smoothhound.co.uk/hotels/fjaerland.html

Hadleigh Gables Hotel ♦♦♦
6-7 North Drive, Great Yarmouth, NR30 1ED
T: (01493) 843078
F: (01493) 843078
E: mike@hadleigh-gables.co.uk
I: www.hadleigh-gables.co.uk

Midland Hotel ♦♦♦
7-9 Wellesley Road, Great Yarmouth, NR30 2AP
T: (01493) 330046
F: (01493) 330046

Oasis Hotel ♦♦♦
Tower Building, Marine Parade, Great Yarmouth, NR30 2EW
T: (01493) 855281
F: (01493) 330697

Royston House ♦♦
11 Euston Road, Great Yarmouth, NR30 1DY
T: (01493) 844680
F: (01493) 844680

Ryecroft Licensed Guesthouse ♦♦♦♦
91 North Denes Road, Great Yarmouth, NR30 4LW
T: (01493) 844015
F: (01493) 856096
E: theryecroft@aol.com
I: www.ryecroft-guesthouse.co.uk

Sandy Acres ♦♦♦
80-81 Salisbury Road, Great Yarmouth, NR30 4LB
T: (01493) 856553
E: sandyacres@talk21.com
I: www.sandyacres.co.uk

Silverstone House ♦♦♦
29 Wellesley Road, Great Yarmouth, NR30 1EU
T: (01493) 844862

Southern Hotel ♦♦♦
46 Queens Road, Great Yarmouth, NR30 3JR
T: (01493) 843313
F: (01493) 843313
E: southern.hotel@tinyonline.co.uk
I: www.southernhotel.co.uk

Sunnydene Hotel ♦♦♦
83 North Denes Road, Great Yarmouth, NR30 4LW
T: (01493) 843554
F: (01493) 332391
E: greatyarmouthhotel@yahoo.co.uk
I: www.sunnydenehotel.co.uk

Trotwood Private Hotel ♦♦♦
2 North Drive, Great Yarmouth, NR30 1ED
T: (01493) 843971
E: richard@trotwood.fsbusiness.co.uk
I: www.trotwood.fsbusiness.co.uk

The Waverley Hotel ♦♦♦
32-37 Princes Road, Great Yarmouth, NR30 2DG
T: (01493) 842508
F: (01493) 842508
E: malcolm@waverley-hotel.co.uk
I: www.waverley-hotel.co.uk

GRESSENHALL
Norfolk

Wood Hill ♦♦♦♦♦
Gressenhall, East Dereham NR19 2NR
T: (01362) 699186
F: (01362) 699291
E: tania.bullard@btopenworld.com

GRIMSTON
Norfolk

The Bell Inn ♦♦♦
1 Gayton Road, Grimston, King's Lynn PE32 1BG
T: (01485) 601156

GRISTON
Norfolk

Park Farm Bed & Breakfast ♦♦♦♦ SILVER AWARD
Park Farm, Caston Road, Griston, Thetford IP25 6QD
T: (01953) 483020
F: (01953) 483056
E: parkfarm@eidosnet.co.uk
I: www.parkfarmbreckland.co.uk

HADLEIGH
Suffolk

Edgehall Hotel ♦♦♦♦
2 High Street, Hadleigh, Ipswich IP7 5AP
T: (01473) 822458
F: (01473) 827751
E: r.rolfe@edgehall-hotel.co.uk
I: www.edgehall-hotel.co.uk

Odds and Ends House ♦♦♦♦
131 High Street, Hadleigh, Ipswich IP7 5EJ
T: (01473) 822032
F: (01473) 829816
E: oddsandends@fsmail.net

Weavers Restaurant ♦♦♦♦
25 High Street, Hadleigh, Ipswich IP7 5AG
T: (01473) 827247
F: (01473) 822805
E: cyndymiles@aol.com
I: www.weaversrestaurant.co.uk

The White Hart ♦♦♦
46 Bridge Street, Hadleigh, Ipswich IP7 6DB
T: (01473) 822206
F: (01473) 822206
E: enquiries@whiteharthadleight.co.uk
I: www.whiteharthadleigh.co.uk

HALESWORTH
Suffolk

The Angel Hotel ♦♦♦
Thoroughfare, Halesworth, IP19 8AH
T: (01986) 873365
F: (01986) 874891
E: hotel@angel-halesworth.co.uk
I: www.angel-halesworth.co.uk

The Croft ♦♦♦
Ubbeston Green, Halesworth, IP19 0HB
T: (01986) 798502

Fen-Way Guest House ♦♦♦
Fen-Way, School Lane, Halesworth, IP19 8BW
T: (01986) 873574

The Huntsman and Hounds ♦♦♦
Stone Street, Spexhall, Halesworth IP19 0RN
T: (01986) 781341

Stradbroke Town Farm ♦♦♦♦
Westhall, Halesworth IP19 8NY
T: (01502) 575204

HALSTEAD
Essex

The Dog Inn ♦♦♦
37 Hedingham Road, Halstead, CO9 2DB
T: (01787) 477774

Hedingham Antiques Bed & Breakfast ♦♦♦
100 Swan Street, Sible Hedingham, Halstead CO9 3HP
T: (01787) 460360
F: (01787) 469109
E: patriciapatterson@totalise.co.uk
I: www.hedinghamantiques.co.uk

HALVERGATE
Norfolk

School Lodge Country Guesthouse ♦♦♦
Marsh Road, Halvergate, Norwich NR13 3QB
T: (01493) 700111
F: (01493) 700111
E: info@uk.guesthouse.com
I: www.uk.guesthouse.com

HAPPISBURGH
Norfolk

Cliff House Guesthouse Teashop and Restaurant♦♦♦
Beach Road, Happisburgh, Norwich NR12 0PP
T: (01692) 650775

Manor Farmhouse & Manor Barn ♦♦♦♦
Happisburgh, Norwich NR12 0SA
T: (01692) 651262
I: www.northnorfolk.co.uk/manorbarn

HARDWICK
Cambridgeshire

Wallis Farm ♦♦♦♦
98 Main Street, Hardwick, Cambridge CB3 7QU
T: (01954) 210347
F: (01954) 210988
E: wallisfarm@mcmail.com
I: www.wallisfarmhouse.co.uk

HARLESTON
Norfolk

Weston House Farm ♦♦♦♦
Mendham, Harleston IP20 0PB
T: (01986) 782206
F: (01986) 782414
E: holden@farmline.com

HARPENDEN
Hertfordshire

Hall Barn ♦♦♦♦
20 Sun Lane, Harpenden, AL5 4EU
T: (01582) 769700

Holly Dene ♦♦♦♦
Bower Heath, Harpenden, AL5 5EE
T: (01582) 769095

The Laurels Guest House ♦♦♦♦
22 Leyton Road, Harpenden, AL5 2HU
T: (01582) 712226
F: (01727) 712226

Milton Hotel ♦♦♦
25 Milton Road, Harpenden, AL5 5LA
T: (01582) 762914

HARTEST
Suffolk

The Hatch ♦♦♦♦♦ SILVER AWARD
Pilgrims Lane, Cross Green, Hartest, Bury St Edmunds IP29 4ED
T: (01284) 830226
F: (01284) 830226

HARWICH
Essex

New Farm House ♦♦♦♦
Spinnels Lane, Wix, Manningtree CO11 2UJ
T: (01255) 870365
F: (01255) 870837
E: newfarmhouse@which.net
I: www.newfarmhouse.com

Oceanview ♦♦
86 Main Road, Dovercourt, Harwich, CO13 3LH
T: (01255) 554078
F: (01255) 554519
E: oceanview@dovercourt.org.uk
I: www.oceanview.fsbusiness.co.uk

Paston Lodge ♦♦♦
1 Una Road, Parkeston, Harwich CO12 4PP
T: (01255) 551390

Woodview Cottage ♦♦♦♦
Wrabness Road, Ramsey, Harwich CO12 5ND
T: (01255) 886413
E: pcohen@cix.co.uk
I: www.woodview-cottage.co.uk

HATFIELD BROAD OAK
Essex

The Cottage ♦♦♦
Dunmow Road, Hatfield Broad Oak, Bishop's Stortford CM22 7JJ
T: (01279) 718230
E: elizabethbritton@virgin.net

HATFIELD HEATH
Essex

The Barn ♦♦♦
Great Heath Farm, Chelmsford Road, Hatfield Heath, Bishop's Stortford CM22 7BQ
T: (01279) 739093

Friars Farm ♦♦♦♦
Hatfield Heath, Bishop's Stortford CM22 7AP
T: (01279) 730244
F: (01279) 730244

Hunters' Meet Restaurant and Hotel ♦♦♦♦
Chelmsford Road, Hatfield Heath, Bishop's Stortford CM22 7BQ
T: (01279) 730549
F: (01279) 731587
E: info@huntersmeet.co.uk
I: www.huntersmeet.co.uk

Oaklands ♦♦♦♦
Hatfield Heath, Bishop's Stortford CM22 7AD
T: (01279) 730240

HATFIELD PEVEREL
Essex

The Swan Inn ♦♦♦
The Street, Hatfield Peverel, Chelmsford CM3 2DW
T: (01245) 380238
F: (01245) 380238

HAUGHLEY
Suffolk

Red House Farm ♦♦♦♦
Station Road, Haughley, Stowmarket IP14 3QP
T: (01449) 673323
F: (01449) 675413
E: mary@noy1.fsnet.co.uk
I: www.farmstayanglia.co.uk

HEACHAM
Norfolk

Church Farm House Rating Applied For
19 Church Farm Road, Heacham, King's Lynn PE31 7JD
T: (01485) 579015

The Grove ♦♦♦♦
Collins Lane, Heacham, King's Lynn PE31 7DZ
T: (01485) 570513
E: tm.shannon@virgin.net

Holly House ♦♦♦
3 Broadway, Heacham, King's Lynn PE31 7DF
T: (01485) 572935

Saint Annes Guesthouse ♦♦♦
53 Neville Road, Heacham, King's Lynn PE31 7HB
T: (01485) 570021
F: (01485) 570021
I: www.smoothhound.co.uk/

HELLESDON
Norfolk

Cairdean ♦♦♦♦
71 Middletons Lane, Hellesdon, Norwich NR6 5NS
T: (01603) 419041
F: (01603) 423643
E: cairdean-b.b@ukgateway.net

The Old Corner Shop Guesthouse ♦♦♦
26 Cromer Road, Hellesdon, Norwich NR6 6LZ
T: (01603) 419000
F: (01603) 419000

HEMEL HEMPSTEAD
Hertfordshire

47 Crescent Road Rating Applied For
Hemel Hempstead, HP2 4AJ
T: (01442) 255137

The Red House Bed & Breakfast ♦♦♦
34 Alexandra Road, Hemel Hempstead, HP2 5BS
T: (01442) 246665

Establishments printed in blue have a detailed entry in this guide

HETHEL
Norfolk

Old Thorn Barn
♦♦♦♦ SILVER AWARD
Corporation Farm, Wymondham Road, Hethel, Norwich NR14 8EU
T: (01953) 607785
F: 08707 066409
E: enquiries@oldthornbarn.co.uk
I: www.oldthornbarn.co.uk

HETHERSETT
Norfolk

Magnolia House ♦♦♦
Cromwell Close, Hethersett, Norwich NR9 3HD
T: (01603) 810749
F: (01603) 810749

HEVINGHAM
Norfolk

Marsham Arms Inn ♦♦♦♦
Holt Road, Hevingham, Norwich NR10 5NP
T: (01603) 754268
F: (01603) 754839
E: nigelbradley@marshamarms.co.uk
I: www.marshamarms.co.uk

HICKLING
Norfolk

Hickling Broad Bed & Breakfast ♦♦♦♦
Paddock Cottage, Staithe Road, Hickling, Norwich NR12 0YJ
T: (01692) 598259

HIGH EASTER
Essex

Maidens Farm ♦♦♦
High Easter, Chelmsford CM3 1HU
T: (01245) 231515
F: (01245) 231075
E: maidens.farm@talk21.com

HIGH KELLING
Norfolk

Olive Tree Breaks ♦♦♦♦
Lynton, Vale Road, High Kelling, Holt NR25 6RA
T: (01263) 712933
E: lynton@highkelling.fsnet.co.uk
I: www.olivetreebreaks.co.uk

HILGAY
Norfolk

Crosskeys Riverside House ♦♦♦
Bridge Street, Hilgay, Downham Market, PE38 0LD
T: (01366) 387777
F: (01366) 387777

HINDRINGHAM
Norfolk

Field House
♦♦♦♦♦ GOLD AWARD
Moorgate Road, Hindringham, Fakenham NR21 0PT
T: (01328) 878726
F: (01328) 878955
E: stay@fieldhousehindringham.co.uk
I: www.fieldhousehindringham.co.uk

HINTLESHAM
Suffolk

College Farm ♦♦♦♦
Back Road, Hintlesham, Ipswich IP8 3NT
T: (01473) 652253
F: (01473) 652253
E: bryce1@agripro.co.uk
I: www.smoothhound.co.uk/hotels/collegefarm

HITCHIN
Hertfordshire

The Greyhound ♦♦♦
London Road, St Ippolyts, Hitchin, SG4 7NL
T: (01462) 440989

The Lord Lister Hotel ♦♦♦
1 Park Street, Hitchin, SG4 9AH
T: (01462) 432712
F: (01462) 438506
E: info@lordlisterhotel.co.uk
I: www.lordlisterhotel.co.uk

HOLBROOK
Suffolk

Highfield
♦♦♦♦ GOLD AWARD
Harkstead Road, Holbrook, Ipswich IP9 2RA
T: (01473) 328250
F: (01473) 328250

HOLKHAM
Norfolk

Peterstone Cutting Bed & Breakfast ♦♦♦♦
Peterstone Cutting, Peterstone, Holkham, Wells-next-the-Sea NR23 1RR
T: (01328) 730171
F: (01328) 730171
E: thefreesiders@yahoo.co.uk

HOLME NEXT THE SEA
Norfolk

Meadow Springs ♦♦♦♦
15 Eastgate Road, Holme next the Sea, Hunstanton PE36 6LL
T: (01485) 525279

Seagate House ♦♦♦♦
60 Beach Road, Holme next the Sea, Hunstanton PE36 6LG
T: (01485) 525510

HOLT
Norfolk

Hempstead Hall ♦♦♦♦
Holt, NR25 6TN
T: (01263) 712224
F: (01263) 710137
I: www.broadland.com/hempsteadhall

Lawns Hotel ♦♦♦♦
Station Road, Holt, NR25 6BS
T: (01263) 713390
F: (01263) 710642
E: info@lawnshotel.co.uk
I: www.lawnshotel.co.uk

Three Corners ♦♦♦
12 Kelling Close, Holt, NR25 6RU
T: (01263) 713389
E: roncox@supanet.com

The White Cottage ♦♦♦
Norwich Road, Holt, NR25 6SW
T: (01263) 713353

HOLTON
Suffolk

Blythwood House ♦♦♦♦
Beccles Road, Holton, Halesworth IP19 8NQ
T: (01986) 873379
F: (01986) 873379

HOLTON ST MARY
Suffolk

Stratford House ♦♦♦♦
Holton St Mary, Colchester CO7 6NT
T: (01206) 298246
F: (01206) 298246
E: fjs.stratho@brutus.go-plus.net

HONINGTON
Suffolk

North View Guesthouse ♦♦♦
North View, Malting Row, Honington, Bury St Edmunds IP31 1RE
T: (01359) 269423
F: (01359) 269423

HORRINGER
Suffolk

12 The Elms ♦♦♦
Horringer, Bury St Edmunds IP29 5SE
T: (01284) 735400
E: neca56@onetel.net.uk

HORSEHEATH
Cambridgeshire

Chequer Cottage ♦♦♦♦
43 Streetly End, Horseheath, Cambridge CB1 6RP
T: (01223) 891522
F: (01223) 890266
E: debbie@dsills.freeserve.co.uk

HORSEY
Norfolk

The Old Chapel ♦♦♦♦
Horsey Corner, Horsey, Great Yarmouth NR29 4EH
T: (01493) 393498
F: (01493) 393498

HORSFORD
Norfolk

Lower Farm B&B
♦♦♦♦ SILVER AWARD
Lower Farm, Horsford, Norwich NR10 3AW
T: (01603) 891291
E: lowerfarm@lowerfarm.f9.co.uk
I: www.norfolkbroads.com/lowerfarm

HORSTEAD
Norfolk

Beverley Farm ♦♦♦
Norwich Road, Horstead, Norwich NR12 7EH
T: (01603) 737279

HOVETON
Norfolk

The Willows
♦♦♦♦ SILVER AWARD
Marsh Road, Hoveton, Norwich NR12 8UH
T: (01603) 782844
F: (01603) 782 844

HUNSTANTON
Norfolk

Burleigh Hotel ♦♦♦♦
7 Cliff Terrace, Hunstanton, PE36 6DY
T: (01485) 533080

Cambridge House
Rating Applied For
32 Westgate, Hunstanton, PE36 5AL
T: (01485) 535014
F: (01485) 534313

Cobblers Cottage ♦♦♦
3 Wodehouse Road, Old Hunstanton, Hunstanton, PE36 6JD
T: (01485) 534036

Eccles Cottage ♦♦♦
Heacham Road, Sedgeford, Hunstanton, PE36 5LU
T: (01485) 572688
E: mike99.barker@virgin.net

The Gables ♦♦♦♦
28 Austin Street, Hunstanton, PE36 6AW
T: (01485) 532514
E: bbatthegables@aol.com
I: www.thegableshunstanton.co.uk

Garganey House ♦♦♦
46 Northgate, Hunstanton, PE36 6DR
T: (01485) 533269
E: Garganey1.@f.s.net.co.uk

Gate Lodge ♦♦♦♦
2 Westgate, Hunstanton, PE36 5AL
T: (01485) 533549
F: (01485) 533361
E: sagemo2206@talk21.com

Glenberis Bed & Breakfast ♦♦♦♦
6 St Edmunds Avenue, Hunstanton, PE36 6AY
T: (01485) 533663
F: (01485) 533663
E: glenberis.hunstanton@ntlworld.com

Kiama Cottage Guesthouse ♦♦♦
23 Austin Street, Hunstanton, PE36 6AN
T: (01485) 533615
E: kiamacottage@btopenworld.com

Lakeside ♦♦♦
Waterworks Road, Old Hunstanton, Hunstanton, PE36 6JE
T: (01485) 533763

The Linksway Country House Hotel ♦♦♦
Golf Course Road, Old Hunstanton, Hunstanton, PE36 6JE
T: (01485) 532209
F: (01485) 532209
E: linksway-hotel@totalize.co.uk
I: www.linkswayhotel.co.uk

Miramar Guesthouse ♦♦♦
7 Boston Square, Hunstanton, PE36 6DT
T: (01485) 532902
I: www.miramar.co.uk

Neptune Inn ♦♦♦
85 Old Hunstanton Road, Old Hunstanton, Hunstanton, PE36 6HZ
T: (01485) 532122
E: neptune-inn@supanet.com

Peacock House ♦♦♦♦
28 Park Road, Hunstanton, PE36 5BY
T: (01485) 534551
E: peacockhouse@onetel.net.uk
I: web.onetel.net.uk/~peacockhouse

Queensbury House ◆◆◆
18 Glebe Avenue, Hunstanton, PE36 6BS
T: (01485) 534320

Rosamaly Guesthouse ◆◆◆
14 Glebe Avenue, Hunstanton, PE36 6BS
T: (01485) 534187
E: vacancies@rosamaly.co.uk
I: www.rosamaly.co.uk

The Shelbrooke Hotel ◆◆◆
9 Cliff Terrace, Hunstanton, PE36 6DY
T: (01485) 532289
F: (01485) 535385
E: mik@shelbrooke.f9.co.uk
I: www.shelbrooke.force9.co.uk

Sunningdale Hotel ◆◆◆
3-5 Avenue Road, Hunstanton, PE36 5BW
T: (01485) 532562
F: (01485) 534915
E: reception@sunningdalehotel.com
I: www.sunningdalehotel.com

Sunset View
Rating Applied For
3 Alexandra Road, Hunstanton, PE36 5BT
T: (01485) 535246

HUNTINGDON
Cambridgeshire

Grange Hotel ◆◆◆
115 High Street, Brampton, Huntingdon PE28 4RA
T: (01480) 459516
F: (01480) 459391
E: enquiries@grangehotelbrampton.com
I: www.grangehotelbrampton.co.uk

Prince of Wales ◆◆◆◆
Potton Road, Hilton, Huntingdon PE28 9NG
T: (01480) 830257
F: (01480) 830257
E: princeofwales.hilton@talk21.com

HUNTINGFIELD
Suffolk

Huntingfield Arms ◆◆
The Street, Huntingfield, Halesworth IP19 0PU
T: (01986) 798320

ICKLETON
Cambridgeshire

Providence House ◆◆◆◆
6 Frogge Street, Ickleton, Saffron Walden CB10 1SH
T: (01799) 530330

Shepherds Cottage ◆◆◆◆
Grange Road, Ickleton, Saffron Walden CB10 1TA
T: (01799) 531171
E: jcase@nascr.net

ILKETSHALL ST MARGARET
Suffolk

Shoo-Devil Farmhouse ◆◆◆
Low Street, Ilketshall St Margaret, Bungay NR35 1QU
T: (01986) 781303
E: shoo.devil@virgin.net

INGOLDISTHORPE
Norfolk

Pencob House
◆◆◆◆ SILVER AWARD
56 Hill Road, Ingoldisthorpe, King's Lynn PE31 6NZ
T: (01485) 543882
F: (01485) 543882
E: swans.norfolk@virgin.net

IPSWICH
Suffolk

Carlton Hotel ◆◆
41-43 Berners Street, Ipswich, IP1 3LN
T: (01473) 254955
F: (01473) 429811
E: carltonhotel@hotmail.com

The Gatehouse Hotel Ltd
◆◆◆◆◆ SILVER AWARD
799 Old Norwich Road, Ipswich, IP1 6LH
T: (01473) 741897
F: (01473) 744236
E: info@gatehousehotel.co.uk
I: www.gatehousehotel.co.uk

Lattice Lodge Guest House
◆◆◆◆ SILVER AWARD
499 Woodbridge Road, Ipswich, IP4 4EP
T: (01473) 712474
F: (01473) 272239
E: lattice.lodge@btinternet.com
I: www.latticelodge.co.uk

Mockbeggars Hall
◆◆◆◆ SILVER AWARD
Paper Mill Lane, Claydon, Ipswich IP6 0AH
T: (01473) 830239
F: (01473) 832989
E: pru@mockbeggars.co.uk
I: www.mockbeggars.co.uk

Redholme Guesthouse ◆◆◆◆
52 Ivry Street, Ipswich, IP1 3QP
T: (01473) 250018
F: (01473) 238174
E: john@redholmeipswich.co.uk
I: www.redholmeipswich.co.uk

Sidegate Guesthouse
◆◆◆◆ SILVER AWARD
121 Sidegate Lane, Ipswich, IP4 4JB
T: (01473) 728714
F: (01473) 728714
E: sidegate.guesthouse@btinternet.com

Stebbings ◆◆◆◆
Back Lane, Washbrook, Ipswich IP8 3JA
T: (01473) 730216
F: 07989 061088
E: caroline@foxworld.fsnet.co.uk

KEDINGTON
Suffolk

The White House
◆◆◆◆◆ GOLD AWARD
Silver Street, Kedington, Haverhill CB9 7QG
T: (01440) 707731
F: (01440) 707731

KELVEDON
Essex

Highfields Farm ◆◆◆◆
Kelvedon, Colchester CO5 9BJ
T: (01376) 570334
F: (01376) 570334
E: HighfieldsFarm@farmersweekly.net
I: www.highfieldsfarm.20m.com

KERSEY
Suffolk

Red House Farm ◆◆◆
Wickerstreet Green, Kersey, Ipswich IP7 6EY
T: (01787) 210245

KETTLEBASTON
Suffolk

Box Tree Farm ◆◆◆
Kettlebaston, Ipswich IP7 7PZ
T: (01449) 741318
F: (01449) 741318

KETTLEBURGH
Suffolk

Church Farm ◆◆◆
Kettleburgh, Woodbridge IP13 7LF
T: (01728) 723532
E: jbater@suffolkonline.net

KING'S LYNN
Norfolk

The Beeches Guesthouse ◆◆◆
2 Guanock Terrace, King's Lynn, PE30 5QT
T: (01553) 766577
F: (01553) 776664

Fairlight Lodge ◆◆◆◆
79 Goodwins Road, King's Lynn, PE30 5PE
T: (01553) 762234
F: (01553) 770280
E: joella@nash42.freeserve.co.uk

Flint's Hotel ◆◆
73 Norfolk Street, King's Lynn, PE30 1AD
T: (01553) 769400

Maranatha Guesthouse ◆◆◆
115-117 Gaywood Road, King's Lynn, PE30 2PU
T: (01553) 774596
F: (01553) 763747

Marsh Farm ◆◆◆◆
Wolferton, King's Lynn PE31 6HB
T: (01485) 540265
F: (01485) 543143
E: info@marshfarmbedandbreakfast.co.uk
I: www.marshfarmbedandbreakfast.co.uk

The Old Rectory ◆◆◆◆
33 Goodwins Road, King's Lynn, PE30 5QX
T: (01553) 768544
E: clive@theoldrectory-kingslynn.com
I: www.theoldrectory-kingslynn.com

KINGS LANGLEY
Hertfordshire

67 Hempstead Road ◆◆◆
Kings Langley, WD4 8BS
T: (01923) 400453
F: (01923) 400453
E: macpherson1@ntlworld.com

Woodcote House ◆◆◆◆
7 The Grove, Whippendell, Chipperfield, Kings Langley WD4 9JF
T: (01923) 262077
F: (01923) 266198
E: leveridge@btinternet.com

KIRBY CANE
Norfolk

Butterley House ◆◆◆
Leet Hill Farm, Kirby Cane, Bungay NR35 2HJ
T: (01508) 518301
F: (01508) 518301

KNAPTON
Norfolk

Cornerstone House ◆◆◆◆
The Street, Knapton, North Walsham NR28 0AD
T: (01263) 722884
E: evescornerstone@hotmail.com

LANGHAM
Essex

Oak Apple Farm ◆◆◆◆
Greyhound Hill, Langham, Colchester CO4 5QF
T: (01206) 272234
E: rosie@oakapplefarm.fsnet.co.uk
I: www.smoothhound.co.uk/hotels/oak.html

LAVENHAM
Suffolk

Anchor House
◆◆◆◆ SILVER AWARD
27 Prentice Street, Lavenham, Sudbury CO10 9RD
T: (01787) 249018
E: suewade1@aol.com
I: www.anchorhouse.co.uk

Angel Gallery ◆◆◆◆
17 Market Place, Lavenham, Sudbury CO10 9QZ
T: (01787) 248417
F: (01787) 248417
E: angel-gallery@gofornet.co.uk
I: http://www.lavenham.co.uk/angelgallery

Brett Farm ◆◆◆◆
The Common, Lavenham, Sudbury CO10 9PG
T: (01787) 248533
E: brettfarm@aol.co.uk
I: www.brettfarm.co.uk

Hill House Farm
◆◆◆◆ SILVER AWARD
Preston St Mary, Lavenham, Sudbury CO10 9LT
T: (01787) 247571
F: (01787) 247571

The Island House
◆◆◆◆ SILVER AWARD
Lower Road, Lavenham, Sudbury CO10 9QJ
T: (01787) 248181
E: islandhouse@dial.pipex.com
I: lavenham.co.uk/islandhouse/

Lavenham Great House Hotel
◆◆◆◆ SILVER AWARD
Market Place, Lavenham, Sudbury CO10 9QZ
T: (01787) 247431
F: (01787) 248007
E: info@greathouse.co.uk
I: www.greathouse.co.uk

Lavenham Priory
◆◆◆◆◆ GOLD AWARD
Water Street, Lavenham, Sudbury CO10 9RW
T: (01787) 247404
F: (01787) 248472
E: mail@lavenhampriory.co.uk
I: www.lavenhampriory.co.uk

Mortimer's Barn
♦♦♦♦ SILVER AWARD
Preston St Mary, Lavenham, Sudbury CO10 9ND
T: (01787) 248231
F: (01787) 248075
E: mervyn@mortimers.freeserve.co.uk
I: www.diggins.co.uk/mortimers/

The Old Convent ♦♦♦♦
The Street, Kettlebaston, Ipswich IP7 7QA
T: (01449) 741557
E: holidays@kettlebaston.fsnet.co.uk
I: www.kettlebaston.fsnet.co.uk

The Red House ♦♦♦♦
29 Bolton Street, Lavenham, Sudbury CO10 9RG
T: (01787) 248074
I: www.lavenham.co.uk/redhouse

21 Shilling Street
Rating Applied For
Lavenham, Sudbury CO10 9RH
T: (01787) 249046
F: (01787) 249619
E: gdelucy@aol.com

Sunrise Cottage ♦♦♦
32 The Glebe, Sudbury Road, Lavenham, Sudbury CO10 9SN
T: (01787) 248439
E: deallen@talk21.com or derekeallen@hotmail.com

LAXFIELD
Suffolk

The Villa Stables ♦♦♦♦
The Villa, High Street, Laxfield, Woodbridge IP13 8DU
T: (01986) 798019
F: (01986) 798155
E: laxfieldleisure@talk21.com

LEIGH-ON-SEA
Essex

Undercliff B & B ♦♦♦
52 Undercliff Gardens, Leigh-on-Sea, SS9 1EA
T: (01702) 474984

LEISTON
Suffolk

Field End
♦♦♦♦ SILVER AWARD
1 Kings Road, Leiston, IP16 4DA
T: (01728) 833527
F: (01728) 833527
E: pwright@fieldend-guesthouse.co.uk
I: www.fieldend-guesthouse.co.uk

LEVINGTON
Suffolk

Lilac Cottage ♦♦♦♦
Levington Green, Levington, Ipswich IP10 0LE
T: (01473) 659509

LINDSELL
Essex

The Old Vicarage ♦♦♦♦
Church End, Lindsell, Dunmow CM6 3QR
T: (01371) 870349
E: fletcher.oldvicarage@btopenworld.com

LITTLE BADDOW
Essex

Chestnuts ♦♦♦
Chestnut Walk, Little Baddow, Chelmsford CM3 4SP
T: (01245) 223905

LITTLE BEALINGS
Suffolk

10 Michaels Mount ♦♦♦
Little Bealings, Woodbridge IP13 6LS
T: (01473) 610466

Timbers ♦♦♦
Martlesham Road, Little Bealings, Woodbridge IP13 6LY
T: (01473) 622713

LITTLE CANFIELD
Essex

Canfield Moat
♦♦♦♦♦ SILVER AWARD
High Cross Lane West, Little Canfield, Dunmow CM6 1TD
T: (01371) 872565
F: (01371) 876264
E: falk@canfieldmoat.co.uk
I: www.canfieldmoat.co.uk

LITTLE LEIGHS
Essex

Little Leighs Hall ♦♦♦♦
Little Leighs, Chelmsford CM3 1PG
T: (01245) 361462
F: (01245) 361462

LITTLE SAMPFORD
Essex

Bush Farm ♦♦♦
Bush Lane, Little Sampford, Saffron Walden CB10 2RY
T: (01799) 586636
E: aimreso@aol.com

Woodlands
♦♦♦♦ SILVER AWARD
Hawkins Hill, Little Sampford, Saffron Walden CB10 2QW
T: (01371) 810862
E: lynne.jameson@amserve.net

LITTLE WALDINGFIELD
Suffolk

The Swan Inn ♦♦♦
The Street, Little Waldingfield, Sudbury CO10 0SQ
T: (01787) 248584

LITTLE WALSINGHAM
Norfolk

The Black Lion Hotel ♦♦♦♦
Friday Market Place, Little Walsingham, Walsingham NR22 6DB
T: (01328) 820235
F: (01328) 821406
E: blacklionwalsingham@btinternet.com
I: www.blacklionwalsingham.com

The Old Bakehouse
♦♦♦♦ SILVER AWARD
33 High Street, Little Walsingham, Walsingham NR22 6BZ
T: (01328) 820454
F: (01328) 820454
E: chris.padley@btopenworld.com

St David's House ♦♦
Friday Market, Little Walsingham, Walsingham NR22 6BY
T: (01328) 820633
E: stdavidshouse@amserve.net
I: www.stilwell.co.uk

LITTLE WALTHAM
Essex

Little Belsteads ♦♦♦♦
Back Lane, Little Waltham, Chelmsford CM3 3PP
T: (01245) 360249
F: (01245) 360996

Windmill Motor Inn ♦♦♦
Chatham Green, Little Waltham, Chelmsford CM3 3LE
T: (01245) 361188
F: (01245) 362992
E: a131windmill.essex@virgin.net

LODDON
Norfolk

Poplar Farm ♦♦♦♦
Sisland, Loddon, Norwich NR14 6EF
T: (01508) 520706
E: milly@hemmant.myhome.org.uk
I: www.hemmant.myhome.org.uk

LONDON COLNEY
Hertfordshire

The Conifers ♦♦♦
42 Thamesdale, London Colney, St Albans AL2 1TL
T: (01727) 823622

LONG MARSTON
Hertfordshire

The Queens Head ♦♦♦
38 Tring Road, Long Marston, Tring HP23 4QL
T: (01296) 668368
I: http://mysite.freeserve.com/thequeenshead

LONG MELFORD
Suffolk

The Crown Hotel ♦♦♦
Hall Street, Long Melford, Sudbury CO10 9JL
T: (01787) 377666
F: (01787) 379005
E: melfordcrown@btinternet.com

LONG STRATTON
Norfolk

Greenacres Farm ♦♦♦♦
Woodgreen, Long Stratton, Norwich NR15 2RR
T: (01508) 530261
F: (01508) 530261
E: greenacresfarm@tinyworld.co.uk

LOUGHTON
Essex

Forest Edge ♦♦♦
61 York Hill, Loughton, IG10 1HZ
T: (020) 8508 9834
F: (020) 8281 1894
E: arthur@catterallarthur.fsnet.co.uk

9 Garden Way ♦♦♦
Loughton, IG10 2SF
T: (020) 8508 6134

LOWER LAYHAM
Suffolk

Badgers ♦♦♦♦
Rands Road, Lower Layham, Ipswich IP7 5RW
T: (01473) 823396
E: catbadgers@aol.com
I: www.badgersbed.co.uk

LOWESTOFT
Suffolk

Albany Hotel ♦♦♦♦
400 London Road South, Lowestoft, NR33 0BQ
T: (01502) 574394
F: (01502) 581198
E: geoffrey.ward@btclick.com
I: www.albanyhotel-lowestoft.co.uk

All Seasons Guest House ♦♦♦
17 Wellington Esplanade, Lowestoft, NR33 0QQ
T: (01502) 530870
F: (01502) 530875
E: allseasonsgh@aol.com
I: www.allseasons.lowestoft.org.uk

The Blinking Owl ♦♦♦
30 Marine Parade, Lowestoft, NR33 0QN
T: (01502) 563717
F: (01502) 563717
E: paynee35@hotmail.com

Church Farm ♦♦♦♦♦
Corton, Lowestoft NR32 5HX
T: (01502) 730359
F: (01502) 733426
E: medw149227@aol.com
I: www.churchfarmcorton.co.uk

Elizabeth Denes Hotel ♦♦♦
Corton Road, Lowestoft, NR32 4PL
T: (01502) 500679
F: (01502) 565774
E: elizabeth.denes@elizabethhotels.co.uk
I: www.elizabethhotels.co.uk

Hall Farm
Rating Applied For
Jay Lane, Church Lane, Lound, Lowestoft NR32 5LJ
T: (01502) 730415
E: josephashley@compuserve.com

Homelea Guest House ♦♦♦
33 Marine Parade, Lowestoft, NR33 0QN
T: (01502) 511640

Longshore Guesthouse ♦♦♦♦
7 Wellington Esplanade, Lowestoft, NR33 0QQ
T: (01502) 565037
F: (01502) 582032
E: SandraNolan@btconnect.com

Oak Farm ♦♦♦
Market Lane, Blundeston, Lowestoft NR32 5AP
T: (01502) 731622

St Catherines House ♦♦♦
186 Denmark Road, Lowestoft, NR32 2EN
T: (01502) 500951

The Sandcastle ♦♦♦
35 Marine Parade, Lowestoft, NR33 0QN
T: (01502) 511799
F: (01502) 574720
E: susie@thesandcastle.co.uk
I: www.thesandcastle.co.uk

LUTON
Bedfordshire

Adara Lodge ♦♦♦
539 Hitchin Road, Luton, LU2 7UL
T: (01582) 731361

The Pines Hotel ♦♦♦
10 Marsh Road, Luton, LU3 3NH
T: (01582) 651130
F: (01582) 615182
E: pineshotelluton@aol.com
I: www.pineshotel.com

44 Skelton Close ♦♦
Barton Hills, Luton, LU3 4HF
T: (01582) 495205
F: (01582) 495205

MALDON
Essex

Anchor Guesthouse ♦♦♦
7 Church Street, Maldon, CM9 5HW
T: (01621) 855706
F: (01621) 850405

Barges Galore ♦♦♦
28 The Hythe, Maldon, CM9 5HN
T: (01621) 853520

Black Cottage ♦♦♦
Curling Tye Green, Woodham Walter, Maldon, CM9 6LU
T: (01621) 857230

Crystal Motel & Cafe/ Restaurant ♦♦
154 High Street, Maldon, CM9 5BX
T: (01621) 853667
F: (01621) 851850

Home While Away ♦♦♦
25c Spital Road, Maldon, CM9 6DZ
T: (01621) 851470

Jolly Sailor ♦♦
Hythe Quay, Maldon, CM9 5HP
T: (01621) 853463
F: (01621) 840253

The Limes ♦♦♦♦
21 Market Hill, Maldon, CM9 4PZ
T: (01621) 850350
F: (01621) 850350
E: thelimes@ukonline.co.uk
I: www.smoothhound.co.uk

Little Owls ♦♦♦
Post Office Road, Woodham Mortimer, Maldon CM9 6ST
T: (01245) 224355
F: (01245) 224355
E: the.bushes@virgin.net

4 Lodge Road ♦♦♦
Maldon, CM9 6HW
T: (01621) 858736

Star House Bed & Breakfast ♦♦♦
72 Wantz Road, Maldon, CM9 5DE
T: (01621) 853527
F: (01621) 850635
E: star.house@talk21.com

The Swan Hotel ♦♦♦
73 High Street, Maldon, CM9 5EP
T: (01621) 853170
F: (01621) 854490
E: info@swanhotel-maldon.co.uk
I: www.swanhotel-maldon.co.uk

Tatoi Bed & Breakfast ♦♦♦♦
31 Acacia Drive, Maldon, CM9 6AW
T: (01621) 853841
E: diana.rogers@tesco.net

MARGARET RODING
Essex

Garnish Hall ♦♦♦♦
Margaret Roding, Dunmow CM6 1QL
T: (01245) 231209
F: (01245) 231224

Greys ♦♦♦
Ongar Road, Margaret Roding, Great Dunmow, CM6 1QR
T: (01245) 231509

MARKYATE
Hertfordshire

Beechwood Home Farm ♦♦♦
Markyate, St Albans AL3 8AJ
T: (01582) 840209

MARSHAM
Norfolk

Plough Inn ♦♦♦
Old Norwich Road, Marsham, Norwich NR10 5PS
T: (01263) 735000
F: (01263) 735407
E: enquiries@ploughinnmarsham.co.uk
I: www.ploughinnmarsham.co.uk

MARSTON MORETAINE
Bedfordshire

Aldermans Tanglewood B&B ♦♦♦
35 Upper Shelton Road, Marston Moretaine, Bedford MK43 0LT
T: (01234) 768584
F: (01234) 764373

Twin Lodge ♦♦♦
177 Lower Shelton Road, Lower Shelton, Marston Moretaine, Bedford MK43 0LP
T: (01234) 767597
F: (01234) 767597
E: pwillsmore@waitrose.com
I: www.twinlodge.co.uk

The White Cottage ♦♦♦♦ SILVER AWARD
Marston Hill, Cranfield, Bedford MK43 0QJ
T: (01234) 751766
F: (01234) 757823
E: stay@thewhitecottage.fsbusiness.co.uk
I: www.smoothhound.co.uk/hotels/whitecottage

MARTHAM
Norfolk

3 Nursery Close ♦♦♦♦
Bell Meadow, Martham, Great Yarmouth NR29 4UB
T: (01493) 740307
E: davena@vk-bedandbreakfasts.com

MELBOURN
Cambridgeshire

Ari's Inn
Rating Applied For
Flint Cross, Newmarket Road, Melbourn, Royston SG8 7PN
T: (01763) 208272
F: (01763) 208268
E: arisinn@hotmail.com
I: www.arisinn.com

MELTON CONSTABLE
Norfolk

Lowes Farm ♦♦♦♦
Edgefield, Melton Constable, NR24 2EX
T: (01263) 712317

MESSING
Essex

Crispin's Restaurant ♦♦♦♦
The Street, Messing, Colchester CO5 9TR
T: (01621) 815868
E: dine@crispinsrestaurant.co.uk
I: www.crispinsrestaurant.co.uk

MILDENHALL
Suffolk

Oakland House ♦♦♦
9 Mill Street, Mildenhall, Bury St Edmunds IP28 7DP
T: (01638) 717099
F: (01638) 714852
E: lardnerjk@btinternet.com
I: www.oaklandhouse.co.uk

MILTON BRYAN
Bedfordshire

Town Farm ♦♦♦♦
Milton Bryan, Milton Keynes MK17 9HS
T: (01525) 210001
F: (01525) 210001

MUCH HADHAM
Hertfordshire

1 Hall Cottages
Rating Applied For
High Street, Much Hadham, SG10 6BZ
T: (01279) 842640
E: marcusian@aol.com

MUNDESLEY
Norfolk

The Grange ♦♦♦♦
High Street, Mundesley, Norwich NR11 8JL
T: (01263) 722977

Overcliff Lodge ♦♦♦
46 Cromer Road, Mundesley, Norwich NR11 8DB
T: (01263) 720016
E: overcliffodge@btinternet.com
I: www.broadland.com/overclifflodge/

MUNDFORD
Norfolk

Colveston Manor ♦♦♦♦
Mundford, Thetford IP26 5HU
T: (01842) 878218
F: (01842) 879218
I: www.farmstayanglia.co.uk

NARBOROUGH
Norfolk

Park Cottage ♦♦♦
Narford Road, Narborough, King's Lynn PE32 1HZ
T: (01760) 337220

NAYLAND
Suffolk

Gladwins Farm ♦♦♦♦
Harpers Hill, Nayland, Colchester CO6 4NU
T: (01206) 262261
F: (01206) 263001
E: gladwinsfarm@aol.com
I: www.gladwinsfarm.co.uk

The White Hart Inn ♦♦♦♦ SILVER AWARD
High Street, Nayland, Colchester CO6 4JF
T: (01206) 263382
F: (01206) 263638
E: nayhart@aol.com
I: www.whitehart-nayland.co.uk

NEATISHEAD
Norfolk

Allens Farmhouse ♦♦♦♦
School Lane, Neatishead, Norwich NR12 8XW
T: (01692) 630080
E: allensfarmhouse@lineone.net

The Barton Angler Country Inn ♦♦♦
Irstead Road, Neatishead, Norwich NR12 8XP
T: (01692) 630740
F: (01692) 631122

Regency Guesthouse ♦♦♦♦
The Street, Neatishead, Norwich NR12 8AD
T: (01692) 630233
F: (01692) 630233
E: wrigleyregency@talk21.com
I: www.norfolkbroads.com/regency

NEWMARKET
Suffolk

2 Birdcage Walk ♦♦♦♦ GOLD AWARD
Newmarket, CB8 0NE
T: (01638) 669456
F: (01638) 669456

The Meadow House ♦♦♦♦
2A High Street, Burwell, Cambridge CB5 0HB
T: (01638) 741926
F: (01638) 743424
E: hilary@themeadowhouse.co.uk
I: www.themeadowhouse.co.uk

NEWPORT
Essex

The Toll House ♦♦♦♦ SILVER AWARD
Belmont Hill, Newport, Saffron Walden CB11 3RD
T: (01799) 540880
F: (01799) 540880
E: teampoole@rdplus.net
I: www.tollhousebedandbreakfast.co.uk

NORTH FAMBRIDGE
Essex

Ferry Boat Inn ♦♦♦
North Fambridge, Chelmsford CM3 6LR
T: (01621) 740208
F: (01621) 740208
E: sylviaferryboat@aol.com

NORTH LOPHAM
Norfolk

Church Farm House ♦♦♦♦♦ SILVER AWARD
North Lopham, Diss IP22 2LP
T: (01379) 687270
F: (01379) 687270
E: b&b@bassetts.demon.co.uk
I: www.churchfarmhouse.org

NORTH MYMMS
Hertfordshire

Little Gables Guest House ♦♦♦♦
3 Swanland Road, North Mymms, Hatfield AL9 7TG
T: (01707) 660804
F: (020) 8449 3556

Wood View ♦♦
23 Dixon Hill Close, North Mymms, Hatfield AL9 7EF
T: (01707) 263802

NORTH WALSHAM
Norfolk

Dolphin Lodge ♦♦♦
Trunch, North Walsham, NR18 0QE
T: (01263) 720961

Green Ridges ♦♦♦♦
104 Cromer Road, North Walsham, NR28 0HE
T: (01692) 402448
F: (01692) 402448
E: admin@greenridges.com
I: www.greenridges.com

Kings Arms Hotel ♦♦♦
Kings Arms Street, North Walsham, NR28 9JX
T: (01692) 403054
F: (01692) 500095
E: martin@kingsarmshotel.fsnet.co.uk

Pinetrees ♦♦♦♦
45 Happisburgh Road, North Walsham, NR28 9HB
T: (01692) 404213

NORTH WOOTTON
Norfolk

Red Cat Hotel ♦♦♦
Station Road, North Wootton, King's Lynn PE30 3QH
T: (01553) 631244
F: (01553) 631574
E: enquiries@redcathotel.com
I: www.redcathotel.com

NORWICH
Norfolk

The Abbey Hotel ♦♦♦
16 Stracey Road, Thorpe Road, Norwich, NR1 1EZ
T: (01603) 612915
F: (01603) 612915

Arbor Linden Lodge ♦♦♦♦
Linden House, 557 Earlham Road, Norwich, NR4 7HW
T: (01603) 451303
F: (01603) 250641
E: info@guesthousenorwich.com
I: www.guesthousenorwich.com

Aylwyne House ♦♦♦
59 Aylsham Road, Norwich, NR3 2HF
T: (01603) 665798

Becklands ♦♦♦
105 Holt Road, Horsford, Norwich NR10 3AB
T: (01603) 898582
F: (01603) 754223

Hotel Belmonte and Belmonte Restaurant♦♦♦
60-62 Prince of Wales Road, Norwich, NR1 1LT
T: (01603) 622533
F: (01603) 760805
E: bar7seven@yahoo.com
I: www.geocities.com/bar7seven/

The Blue Boar Inn ♦♦♦♦
259 Wroxham Road, Sprowston, Norwich NR7 8RL
T: (01603) 426802
F: (01603) 487749
E: blueboar102@hotmail.com
I: www.blueboarnorwich.co.uk

Blue Cedar Lodge Guesthouse ♦♦♦
391 Earlham Road, Norwich, NR2 3RQ
T: (01603) 458331
F: (01603) 458331

Cavell House ♦♦♦
The Common, Swardeston, Norwich NR14 8DZ
T: (01508) 578195
F: (01508) 578195

Church Farm Guesthouse ♦♦♦
Church Street, Horsford, Norwich NR10 3DB
T: (01603) 898020
F: (01603) 891649
E: churchfarmguesthouse.@btopenworld.com

Conifers Hotel ♦♦♦
162 Dereham Road, Norwich, NR2 3AH
T: (01603) 628737

Earlham Guesthouse ♦♦♦♦
147 Earlham Road, Norwich, NR2 3RG
T: (01603) 454169
F: (01603) 454169
E: earlhamgh@hotmail.com

Eaton Bower
♦♦♦♦ SILVER AWARD
20 Mile End Road, Norwich, NR4 7QY
T: (01603) 462204
E: eaton_bower@hotmail.com
I: www.eatonbower.co.uk

Edmar Lodge ♦♦♦
64 Earlham Road, Norwich, NR2 3DF
T: (01603) 615599
F: (01603) 495599
E: edmar@btconnect.com
I: www.edmarlodge.co.uk

Elm Farm Country House ♦♦♦♦
55 Norwich Road, St Faiths, NR10 3HH
T: (01603) 898366
F: (01603) 897129
E: Pmpbelmfarm@aol.com

309 Fakenham Road ♦♦♦
Taverham, Norwich, NR8 6LF
T: (01603) 860103
E: jeanshepherd@lineone.net

The Gables Guesthouse ♦♦♦♦
527 Earlham Road, Norwich, NR4 7HN
T: (01603) 456666
F: (01603) 250320

Garden House ♦♦♦
Salhouse Road, Rackheath, Norwich NR13 6AA
T: (01603) 720007
F: (01603) 720007
E: gardenhousebandb@aol.com
I: www.thegardenhousehotel.uk.com

Hanover House ♦♦♦♦
60 Earlham Road, Norwich, NR2 3DF
T: (01603) 667402
E: aylmus@clara.com

Harvey House Guesthouse ♦♦♦
50 Harvey Lane, Norwich, NR7 0AQ
T: (01603) 436575
F: (01603) 436575
E: harveyhouse@which.net

The Limes ♦♦
188 Unthank Road, Norwich, NR2 2AH
T: (01603) 454282

Manor Barn House ♦♦♦♦
Back Lane, Rackheath, Norwich NR13 6NN
T: (01603) 783543
E: jane.roger@manorbarnhouse.co.uk
I: www.manorbarnhouse.co.uk

Marlborough House Hotel ♦♦♦
22 Stracey Road, Norwich, NR1 1EZ
T: (01603) 628005
F: (01603) 628005

Mousehold Lodge Guesthouse ♦♦♦
53 Mousehold Lane, Norwich, NR7 8HL
T: (01603) 426026
F: (01603) 424590
E: info@mousehold-lodge.co.uk
I: www.mousehold-lodge.co.uk

The Old Lodge ♦♦♦♦
New Road, Bawburgh, Norwich NR9 3LZ
T: (01603) 742798
E: peggy@theoldlodge.freeserve.co.uk

The Old Rectory
♦♦♦♦ SILVER AWARD
Hall Road, Framingham Earl, Norwich NR14 7SB
T: (01508) 493590
F: (01508) 495110
E: oldrectory@f-earl.fsnet.co.uk

Rosedale ♦♦
145 Earlham Road, Norwich, NR2 3RG
T: (01603) 453743
F: (01603) 259887
E: drcbac@aol.com
I: www.members@aol.com/drcbac

Undici ♦♦♦
Kimberley Road, Bacton, Norwich, NR12 0EN
T: (01692) 651194
F: (01692) 651194

Wedgewood House ♦♦♦
42 St Stephens Road, Norwich, NR1 3RE
T: (01603) 625730
F: (01603) 615035
E: stay@wedgewoodhouse.co.uk
I: www.wedgewoodhouse.co.uk

Witton Hall Farm ♦♦♦
Witton, North Walsham NR13 5DN
T: (01603) 714580
E: wittonhall@yahoo.com

OCCOLD
Suffolk

The Cedars Guesthouse ♦♦♦♦
Church Street, Occold, Eye IP23 7PS
T: (01379) 678439

OLD CATTON
Norfolk

Catton Old Hall
♦♦♦♦♦ SILVER AWARD
Lodge Lane, Old Catton, Norwich NR6 7HG
T: (01603) 419379
F: (01603) 400339
E: enquiries@catton-hall.co.uk
I: www.catton-hall.co.uk

ORTON LONGUEVILLE
Cambridgeshire

Orton Mere Guest House ♦♦♦♦
547 Oundle Road, Orton Longueville, Peterborough PE2 7DH
T: (01733) 708432
F: (01733) 708425

OULTON
Suffolk

Laurel Farm ♦♦♦♦
Hall Lane, Oulton, Lowestoft NR32 5DL
T: (01502) 568724
F: (01502) 568724
E: janethodgkin@laurelfarm.com
I: laurelfarm.com

OVERSTRAND
Norfolk

Cliff Cottage Bed & Breakfast ♦♦♦
Cliff Cottage, 18 High Street, Overstrand, Cromer NR27 0AB
T: (01263) 578179
E: roymin@btinternet.com

Danum House ♦♦♦
22 Pauls Lane, Overstrand, Cromer NR27 0PE
T: (01263) 579327
F: (01263) 579327

OXBOROUGH
Norfolk

Bedingfield Coach House Rating Applied For
Oxborough, King's Lynn PE33 9PS
T: (01366) 328300
F: (01366) 328300

PAKEFIELD
Suffolk

Pipers Lodge Hotel & Motel ♦♦♦
41 London Road, Pakefield, NR33 7AA
T: (01502) 569805
F: (01502) 565383
I: www.piperslodge.co.uk

PALGRAVE
Suffolk

The Paddocks B & B ♦♦♦
3 The Paddocks, Palgrave, Diss IP22 1AG
T: (01379) 642098
F: (01379) 652796
E: rod@rodjones.force9.co.uk
I: www.rodjones.force9.co.uk

PETERBOROUGH
Cambridgeshire

The Anchor Lodge ♦♦♦
28 Percival Street, Peterborough, PE3 6AU
T: (01733) 312724

Aragon House ♦♦♦
75-77 London Road, Peterborough, PE2 9BS
T: (01733) 563718
F: (01733) 563718
E: mail@aragonhouse.co.uk
I: www.aragonhouse.co.uk

Arman Lodge House ♦♦
3 Scotney Street, Newengland, Peterborough, PE1 3NG
T: (01733) 554232
E: rajna@talk21.com
I: www.armanlodgehouse.com

The Brandon ♦♦♦
161 Lincoln Road, Peterborough, PE1 2PW
T: (01733) 568631
F: (01733) 568631
I: www.peterboroughaccommodation.co.uk

Clarks ♦♦♦♦
21 Oundle Road, Peterborough, PE2 9PB
T: (01733) 342482
F: (01733) 553227
E: fiona@clarksguesthouse.com
I: www.clarksguesthouse.com

The Graham Guesthouse ♦♦♦
296 Oundle Road, Peterborough, PE2 9QA
T: (01733) 567824
F: (01733) 567824

Longueville Guesthouse ♦♦♦♦
411 Oundle Road, Orton Longueville, Peterborough, PE2 7DA
T: (01733) 233442
F: (01733) 233442

Montana ♦♦♦
15 Fletton Avenue, Peterborough, PE2 8AX
T: (01733) 567917
F: (01733) 567917
I: www.stilwell.co.uk/www.peterboroughaccomodation.co.uk

Park Road Guesthouse ♦♦
67 Park Road, Peterborough, PE1 2TN
T: (01733) 562220
F: (01733) 344279

Wisteria House ♦♦♦
5 Church Lane, Helpston, Peterborough PE6 7DT
T: (01733) 252272

PETTISTREE
Suffolk

The Three Tuns Coaching Inn ♦♦♦
Main Road, Pettistree, Woodbridge IP13 0HW
T: (01728) 747979
F: (01728) 746244
E: jon@threetuns-coachinginn.co.uk
I: www.threetuns-coachinginn.co.uk

PLESHEY
Essex

Acreland Green ♦♦♦♦
Pleshey, Chelmsford CM3 1HP
T: (01245) 231277
F: (01245) 231277

POLSTEAD
Suffolk

Polstead Lodge ♦♦♦♦
Mill Street, Polstead, Colchester CO6 5AD
T: (01206) 262196
E: polsteadlodge@bushinternet.com

POTTER HEIGHAM
Norfolk

Falgate Inn ♦♦♦
Ludham Road, Potter Heigham, Great Yarmouth NR29 5HZ
T: (01692) 670003
E: malber@cypress72.freeserve.co.uk

Hazelden ♦♦♦♦
Bridge Road, Potter Heigham, Great Yarmouth NR29 5JB
T: (01692) 670511

POTTERS BAR
Hertfordshire

Bruggen Lodge ♦♦♦♦
13 The Drive, Potters Bar, EN6 2AP
T: (01707) 655904
F: (01707) 857287
E: andreaseggie@lineone.net

PULHAM MARKET
Norfolk

The Old Bakery ♦♦♦♦♦ GOLD AWARD
Church Walk, Pulham Market, Diss IP21 4SJ
T: (01379) 676492
F: (01379) 676492
E: jean@theoldbakery.net
I: www.theoldbakery.net

RACKHEATH
Norfolk

Barn Court ♦♦♦
6 Back Lane, Rackheath, Norwich NR13 6NN
T: (01603) 782536
F: (01603) 782536
E: barncourtbb@hotmail.com

RAMSHOLT
Suffolk

The Ramsholt Arms ♦♦♦
Dock Road, Ramsholt, Woodbridge IP12 3AB
T: (01394) 411229
F: (01394) 411818
E: ramsholtarms@tinyworld.co.uk
I: www.ramsholtarms.co.uk

RAVENSDEN
Bedfordshire

Tree Garth ♦♦♦
Church End, Ravensden, Bedford MK44 2RP
T: (01234) 771745
F: (01234) 771745
E: treegarth@ukonline.co.uk
I: treegarth.co.uk

RENDHAM
Suffolk

Rendham Hall ♦♦♦
Rendham, Saxmundham IP17 2AW
T: (01728) 663440
F: (01728) 663245
E: dc.strachan@talk21.com

REPPS WITH BASTWICK
Norfolk

Grove Farm Bed & Breakfast ♦♦♦
Grove Farm, Repps With Bastwick, Great Yarmouth NR29 5JN
T: (01692) 670205
E: jenny@grovefarmholidays.co.uk
I: www.grovefarmholidays.co.uk

REYDON
Suffolk

Broadlands ♦♦♦♦
68 Halesworth Road, Reydon, Southwold IP18 6NS
T: (01502) 724384
F: (01502) 724384

Newlands Country House ♦♦♦♦
72 Halesworth Road, Reydon, Southwold IP18 6NS
T: (01502) 722164
F: (01502) 722762
E: newlandssouthwold@lycos.co.uk
I: www.newlandssouthwold.com

The Randolph Hotel ♦♦♦♦
41 Wangford Road, Reydon, Southwold IP18 6PZ
T: (01502) 723603
F: (01502) 722194
E: enquiries@randolph-hotel.co.uk
I: www.randolph-hotel.co.uk

Ridge Bed & Breakfast ♦♦♦
The Ridge, 14 Halesworth Road, Reydon, Southwold IP18 6NH
T: (01502) 724855
E: jules.heal@ntlworld.com
I: www.southwold.ws/ridge

RIDLINGTON
Norfolk

Mill Common House ♦♦♦♦ SILVER AWARD
Mill Common Road, Ridlington, North Walsham NR28 9TY
T: (01692) 650792
F: (01692) 651480
E: johnpugh@millcommon.freeserve.co.uk
I: www.broadland.com/millcommon

RIVENHALL
Essex

North Ford Farm ♦♦♦♦
Church Road, Rivenhall, Witham CM8 3PG
T: (01376) 583321
F: (01376) 583321

Rickstones Farmhouse Bed & Breakfast ♦♦♦♦
Rickstones Farmhouse, Rickstones Road, Rivenhall, Witham CM8 3HQ
T: (01376) 514351
F: (01376) 514351
E: rickstonesfarmhouse@btinternet.com

ROXWELL
Essex

Cross Keys Inn ♦♦♦
Boyton Cross, Roxwell, Chelmsford CM1 4LP
T: (01245) 248201

ROYSTON
Hertfordshire

Hall Farm ♦♦♦♦
Great Chishill, Royston, SG8 8SH
T: (01763) 838263
F: (01763) 838263
E: wisehall@farming.co.uk
I: www.hallfarmbb.co.uk

RUMBURGH
Suffolk

Rumburgh Farm ♦♦♦♦
Rumburgh, Halesworth IP19 0RU
T: (01986) 781351
F: (01986) 781351
E: binder@rumburghfarm.freeserve.co.uk
I: www.rumburghfarm.freeserve.co.uk

SAFFRON WALDEN
Essex

Archway Guesthouse ♦♦♦♦
Archway House, Church Street, Saffron Walden, CB10 1JW
T: (01799) 501500
F: (01799) 506003

Ashleigh House ♦♦♦
7 Farmadine Grove, Saffron Walden, CB11 3DR
T: (01799) 513611
E: info@ashleighhouse.dabsol.co.uk
I: www.ashleighhouse.dabsol.co.uk

The Bell House ♦♦♦♦
53-55 Castle Street, Saffron Walden, CB10 1BD
T: (01799) 527857

The Bonnet ♦♦♦♦♦ SILVER AWARD
Overhall Lane, Stevington End, Ashdon, Saffron Walden CB10 2JE
T: (01799) 584955
E: thebonnetuk@yahoo.co.uk
I: www.thebonnet.co.uk

The Cricketers ♦♦♦♦
Clavering, Saffron Walden, CB11 4QT
T: (01799) 550442
F: (01799) 550882
E: cricketers@lineone.net
I: www.thecricketers.co.uk

11 Dawson Close ♦♦♦
Saffron Walden, CB10 2AR
T: (01799) 528491

Grimalkins B & B ♦♦♦
49 Castle Street, Saffron Walden, CB10 1BD
T: (01799) 521557
E: gertrud@hill-castle.freeserve.co.uk

1 Gunters Cottages ♦♦♦♦
Thaxted Road, Saffron Walden, CB10 2UT
T: (01799) 522091

30 Lambert Cross ♦♦
Saffron Walden, CB10 2DP
T: (01799) 527287

Oak House ♦♦♦
40 Audley Road, Saffron Walden, CB11 3HD
T: (01799) 523290
E: oakhouse@macunlimited.net

The Plough Inn at Radwinter ◆◆◆
Sampford Road, Radwinter, Saffron Walden CB10 2TL
T: (01799) 599222
F: (01799) 599161

Pudding House ◆◆◆
9a Museum Street, Saffron Walden, CB10 1JL
T: (01799) 522089

Redgates Farmhouse ◆◆◆◆
Redgate Lane, Sewards End, Saffron Walden, CB10 2LP
T: (01799) 516166

Rockells Farm ◆◆◆◆
Duddenhoe End, Saffron Walden CB11 4UY
T: (01763) 838053

Rowley Hill Lodge ◆◆◆◆
Little Walden, Saffron Walden CB10 1UZ
T: (01799) 525975
F: (01799) 516622
E: eh@clara.net

Victoria House ◆◆◆
10 Victoria Avenue, Saffron Walden, CB11 3AE
T: (01799) 525923

Yardley's
◆◆◆◆ SILVER AWARD
Orchard Pightle, Hadstock, Cambridge CB1 6PQ
T: (01223) 891822
F: (01223) 891822
E: yardleys@waitrose.com
I: www.users.waitrose.com/~yardleys/

SAHAM TONEY
Norfolk

Cranford House ◆◆◆◆
Ovington Road, Saham Toney, Thetford IP25 7HF
T: (01953) 885292
F: (01953) 885611
E: bookings@cranfordhouse.net
I: www.cranfordhouse.net

ST ALBANS
Hertfordshire

5 Approach Road ◆◆
St Albans, AL1 1SP
T: (01727) 852471
F: (01727) 847408
E: nigelcocks@compuserve.com

22 Ardens Way ◆◆◆
St Albans, AL4 9UJ
T: (01727) 861986

Ardmore House ◆◆◆
54 Lemsford Road, St Albans, AL1 3PP
T: (01727) 859313
F: (01727) 859313
E: info@ardmorehousehotel.altodigital.co.uk
I: www.ardmorehousehotel.com

Avona ◆◆◆
478 Hatfield Road, St Albans, AL4 0SX
T: (01727) 842216
F: (01727) 857578
E: murchu@ntlworld.com

Black Lion Inn ◆◆◆
198 Fishpool Street, St Albans, AL3 4SB
T: (01727) 851786
F: (01727) 859243
E: info@theblacklioninn.com
I: www.theblacklioninn.com

Braemar House ◆◆◆◆
89 Salisbury Avenue, St Albans, AL1 4TY
T: (01727) 839641
F: (01727) 839641
E: slaters@braemar435.fsnet.co.uk

55 Charmouth Road ◆◆◆
St Albans, AL1 4SE
T: (01727) 860002
E: terry@charmouthfsnet.co.uk

35 Chestnut Drive ◆◆◆
St Albans, AL4 0ER
T: (01727) 833401

5 Cunningham Avenue ◆◆◆
St Albans, AL1 1JJ
T: (01727) 857388

Fern Cottage ◆◆◆◆
116 Old London Road, St Albans, AL1 1PU
T: (01727) 834200
E: dorotheabristow@ntlworld.com
I: www.ferncottage.uk.net

Fleuchary House ◆◆◆◆
3 Upper Lattimore Road, St Albans, AL1 3UD
T: (01727) 766764
E: linda@fleucharyhouse.freeserve.co.uk
I: www.fleucharyhouse.com

32 Gurney Court Road ◆◆◆
St Albans, AL1 4RL
T: (01727) 760250
E: v.salisbury@ntlworld.com

8 Hall Place Gardens ◆◆◆
St Albans, AL1 3SP
T: (01727) 858939

2 The Limes ◆◆◆
Spencer Gate, St Albans, AL1 4AT
T: (01727) 831080
E: hunter.mitchell@virgin.net

178 London Road ◆◆◆◆
St Albans, AL1 1PL
T: (01727) 846726
F: (01727) 831267

Margaret's B&B ◆◆◆
16 Broomleys, St Albans, AL4 9UR
T: (01727) 862421

7 Marlborough Gate ◆◆◆
St Albans, AL1 3TX
T: (01727) 865498
F: (01727) 812965
E: michael.jameson@btinternet.com

Park House ◆◆◆
30 The Park, St Albans, AL1 4RY
T: (01727) 832054

36 Potters Field ◆◆◆
St Albans, AL3 6LJ
T: (01727) 766840
F: (01727) 766840
E: manners_smith@ntlworld.com

Riverside
◆◆◆◆ SILVER AWARD
24 Minister Court, St Albans, AL2 2NF
T: (01727) 758780
F: (01727) 758760
E: Ellispatriciam@aol.com

56 Sandpit Lane ◆◆◆◆
St Albans, AL1 4BW
T: (01727) 856799
F: (01727) 856799

Tresco ◆◆◆◆
76 Clarence Road, St Albans, AL1 4NG
T: (01727) 864880
F: (01727) 864880
E: pat.leggatt@talk21.com
I: www.twistedsilicon.co.uk/76/index.htm

33 Upper Heath Road ◆◆
St Albans, AL1 4DN
T: (01727) 856098

The White House ◆◆
28 Salisbury Avenue, St Albans, AL1 4TU
T: (01727) 861017

Wren Lodge ◆◆◆◆
24 Beaconsfield Road, St Albans, AL1 3RB
T: (01727) 855540
F: (01727) 766674
E: wren.lodge@ntlworld.com
I: www.destination-england.co.uk/wrenlodge.html

16 York Road ◆◆◆
St Albans, AL1 4PL
T: (01727) 853647

ST NEOTS
Cambridgeshire

The Nags Head Hotel ◆◆◆
2 Berkley Street, Eynesbury, St Neots, Huntingdon PE19 2NA
T: (01480) 476812
F: (01480) 391881

SALHOUSE
Norfolk

The Lodge Inn ◆◆◆
Vicarage Road, Salhouse, Norwich NR13 6HD
T: (01603) 782828
E: thelodgeinn@salhouse.f.s.business.co.uk

Oldfield ◆◆◆◆
Vicarage Road, Salhouse, Norwich NR13 6HA
T: (01603) 781080
F: (01603) 781083

SANDY
Bedfordshire

Highfield Farm
◆◆◆◆◆ SILVER AWARD
Tempsford Road, Great North Road, Sandy, SG19 2AQ
T: (01767) 682332
F: (01767) 692503
E: stay@highfield-farm.co.uk

Village Farm ◆◆◆
Thorncote Green, Sandy, SG19 1PU
T: (01767) 627345

SAWBRIDGEWORTH
Hertfordshire

7 Church Walk ◆◆◆
Sawbridgeworth, CM21 9BJ
T: (01279) 723233
E: kent@sawbridgeworth.co.uk

SAWTRY
Cambridgeshire

A1 Bed & Breakfast ◆◆
5 High Street, Sawtry, Huntingdon PE28 5SR
T: (01487) 830201
F: (01487) 830201

SAXLINGHAM
Norfolk

The Map House
◆◆◆◆ GOLD AWARD
The Map House, Smokers Hole, Saxlingham, Holt NR25 7JU
T: (01263) 741304
E: enquiries@maphouse.net
I: www.maphouse.net

SAXLINGHAM THORPE
Norfolk

Foxhole Farm ◆◆◆◆
Windy Lane, Foxhole, Saxlingham Thorpe, Norwich NR15 1UG
T: (01508) 499226
F: (01508) 499226
E: foxholefarm@hotmail.com

SAXMUNDHAM
Suffolk

The Georgian House
◆◆◆◆◆ SILVER AWARD
6 North Entrance, Saxmundham, IP17 1AY
T: (01728) 603337
E: thegeorgianhse@aol.com

Honeypot Lodge ◆◆◆
Aldecar Lane, Benhall Green, Saxmundham IP17 1HN
T: (01728) 602449
E: honeypot@freeuk.com
I: www.smoothhound.co.uk/hotels/honeypotlodge.html

Moat House Farm ◆◆◆◆
Rendham Road, Carlton, Saxmundham IP17 2QN
T: (01728) 602228
F: (01728) 602228
E: sally@goodacres.com
I: www.goodacres.com

Poppy Cottage ◆◆◆
7 Stour Close, Saxmundham, IP17 1XX
T: (01728) 602936
E: sbyard@ntlworld.com

SAXTEAD
Suffolk

Ivy Forge ◆◆◆◆
The Green, Saxtead, Woodbridge IP13 9QG
T: (01728) 685054
F: (01728) 6865054
E: george@ivyforge.freeserve.co.uk

SCOTTOW
Norfolk

Holmwood House ◆◆◆◆
Tunstead Road, Scottow, Norwich NR10 5DA
T: (01692) 538386
F: (01692) 538386
E: holmwoodhouse@lineone.net
I: www.norfolkbroads.com/holmwood

SCULTHORPE
Norfolk

Manor Farm Bed & Breakfast
◆◆◆◆ SILVER AWARD
Manor Farm, Sculthorpe, Fakenham NR21 9NJ
T: (01328) 862185
F: (01328) 862033
E: mddwo2@dial.pipex.com
I: www.manorfarmbandb.com

SHERINGHAM
Norfolk

Achimota ♦♦♦♦
31 North Street, Sheringham, NR26 8LW
T: (01263) 822379
I: www.broadland.com/achimota

Alverstone ♦♦♦
33 The Avenue, Sheringham, NR26 8DG
T: (01263) 825527

Ashcroft House Bed & Breakfast ♦♦♦♦
15 Morris Street, Sheringham, NR26 8JY
T: (01263) 822225
E: ashcrofthouse@tiscali.co.uk

The Bay Leaf Guest House ♦♦♦
10 St Peters Road, Sheringham, NR26 8QY
T: (01263) 823779
F: (01263) 820041
E: thebayleaf@bushinternet.com
I: www.broadland.com/bayleaf

The Burlington Lodge ♦♦♦
5 St Nicholas Place, Sheringham, NR26 8LF
T: (01263) 820931
F: (01263) 820964
E: r.mcdermott@hemscott.net

Camberley Guesthouse ♦♦♦
62 Cliff Road, Sheringham, NR26 8BJ
T: (01263) 823101
F: (01263) 821433
E: graham@camberleyguesthouse.co.uk
I: www.camberleyguesthouse.co.uk

Holly Cottage ♦♦♦♦
14a The Rise, Sheringham, NR26 8QB
T: (01263) 822807
F: (01263) 824822
E: hollyperks@aol.com
I: www.sheringham-network.co.uk

Maison ♦♦♦
9 Cremers Drift, Sheringham, NR26 8HX
T: (01263) 821945

The Melrose ♦♦♦
9 Holway Road, Sheringham, NR26 8HN
T: (01263) 823299
E: jparsonage@btconnect.com
I: www.themelrsosesheringham.co.uk

Olivedale Guesthouse ♦♦♦♦
20 Augusta Street, Sheringham, NR26 8LA
T: (01263) 825871
F: (01263) 821104
E: info@olivedale.co.uk
I: www.olivedale.co.uk

Pentland Lodge ♦♦
51 The Avenue, Sheringham, NR26 8DQ
T: (01263) 823533
F: (01263) 823533
E: janetnolson@aol.co.uk

Priestfields
♦♦♦♦ SILVER AWARD
6B North Street, Sheringham, NR26 8LW
T: (01263) 820305
F: (01263) 820125
E: david.phillips10@which.net

Sheringham Lodge ♦♦♦
Cromer Road, Sheringham, NR26 8RS
T: (01263) 821954
E: mikewalker19@hotmail.com
I: www.sheringhamlodge.co.uk

Squirrels Drey ♦♦♦
27 Holt Road, Sheringham, NR26 8NB
T: (01263) 822982
F: (01263) 822364
E: squirrels_drey@hotmail.com

The Two Lifeboats Hotel ♦♦♦
2 The High Street, Sheringham, NR26 8JR
T: (01263) 822401
F: (01263) 823130
E: info@twolifeboats.co.uk
I: www.twolifeboats.co.uk

Westwater B&B Guest House ♦♦♦
28 Norfolk Road, Sheringham, NR26 8HJ
T: (01263) 822321
F: (01263) 825932
E: bookings@westwater.uk.net
I: www.westwater.uk.net

Willow Lodge ♦♦♦♦
6 Vicarage Road, Sheringham, NR26 8NH
T: (01263) 822204
F: (01263) 822204

SHOTLEY
Suffolk

Hill House Farm
♦♦♦♦ SILVER AWARD
Wades Lane, Shotley, Ipswich IP9 1EW
T: (01473) 787318
F: (01473) 787111
E: richard@rjwrinch.fsnet.co.uk

SHUDY CAMPS
Cambridgeshire

Old Well Cottage ♦♦♦♦
Main Street, Shudy Camps, Cambridge CB1 6RA
T: (01799) 584387
F: (01799) 584486
E: jackiesamvet@aol.com

SIBLE HEDINGHAM
Essex

Brickwall Farm ♦♦♦♦
Queen Street, Sible Hedingham, Halstead CO9 3RH
T: (01787) 460329
F: (01787) 460329
E: brickwallfarm@btinternet.com

Tocat House ♦♦♦♦
9 Potter Street, Sible Hedingham, Halstead CO9 3RG
T: (01787) 461942

SIBTON
Suffolk

Church Farm
♦♦♦♦♦ SILVER AWARD
Yoxford Road, Sibton, Saxmundham IP17 2LX
T: (01728) 660101
F: (01728) 660102
E: dixons@church-farmhouse.demon.co.uk
I: www.church-farmhouse.demon.co.uk

Park Farm ♦♦♦♦
Sibton, Saxmundham IP17 2LZ
T: (01728) 668324
F: (01728) 668564
E: margaret.gray@btinternet.com
I: www.farmstayanglia.co.uk/parkfarm

SNAPE
Suffolk

Flemings Lodge ♦♦♦♦
Gromford Lane, Snape, Saxmundham IP17 1RG
T: (01728) 688502
F: (01728) 688502

SNETTISHAM
Norfolk

The Hollies
♦♦♦♦ SILVER AWARD
12 Lynn Road, Snettisham, King's Lynn PE31 7LS
T: (01485) 541294
F: (01485) 541294

The Rose & Crown ♦♦♦♦
Old Church Road, Snettisham, King's Lynn PE31 7LX
T: (01485) 541382
F: (01485) 543172
I: www.14th-century-inn.co.uk

The Round House ♦♦♦♦
131 Lynn Road, Snettisham, King's Lynn PE31 7QG
T: (01485) 540580
E: ziphac@aol.com

SOHAM
Cambridgeshire

The Fountain ♦♦♦
1 Churchgate Street, Soham, Ely CB7 5DS
T: (01353) 720374
F: (01353) 722103
E: enquiries@thefountain.co.uk
I: www.thefountain.co.uk

SOUTH CREAKE
Norfolk

Valentine House ♦♦♦
62 Back Street, South Creake, Fakenham NR21 9PG
T: (01328) 823413
E: nickhaywood@classic-sheds.fsnet.co.uk

SOUTH LOPHAM
Norfolk

Malting Farm ♦♦♦
Blo' Norton Road, South Lopham, Diss IP22 2HT
T: (01379) 687201
I: www.farmstayanglia.co.uk

SOUTH WALSHAM
Norfolk

Old Hall Farm ♦♦♦♦
Newport Road, South Walsham, Norwich NR13 6DS
T: (01603) 270271
F: (01603) 270017
E: veronica@oldhallfarm.co.uk
I: www.oldhallfarm.co.uk

SOUTHEND-ON-SEA
Essex

Arosa Guest House ♦♦
184 Eastern Esplanade, Southend-on-Sea, SS1 3AA
T: (01702) 585416
F: (01702) 580599
E: jonwilson@arosa184.freeserve.co.uk
I: www.smoothhound.co.uk

Atlantis Guest House ♦♦♦♦
63 Alexandra Road, Southend-on-Sea, SS1 1EY
T: (01702) 332538
F: (01702) 392736

The Bay Guesthouse ♦♦♦♦
187 Eastern Esplanade, Thorpe Bay, Southend-on-Sea, SS1 3AA
T: (01702) 588415
E: thebayguesthouse@hotmail.com
I: http://www.smoothhound.co.uk/hotels/thebayguest

Beaches
♦♦♦♦ SILVER AWARD
192 Eastern Esplanade, Thorpe Bay, Southend-on-Sea, SS1 3AA
T: (01702) 586124
F: (01702) 588377
E: beaches@quista.net
I: www.smoothhound.co.uk/hotels/beaches

Lee Villas Guesthouse ♦
1 & 2 Hartington Place, Southend-on-Sea, SS1 2HP
T: (01702) 317214
E: SMCK764100@aol.com
I: www.leevillas.co.uk

Pebbles Guesthouse ♦♦♦♦
190 Eastern Esplanade, Thorpe Bay, Southend-on-Sea, SS1 3AA
T: (01702) 582329
F: (01702) 582329

Strand Guesthouse ♦♦
165 Eastern Esplanade, Thorpe Bay, Southend-on-Sea, SS1 2YB
T: (01702) 586611

Tower Hotel and Restaurant ♦♦♦
146 Alexandra Road, Southend-on-Sea, SS1 1HE
T: (01702) 348635
F: (01702) 433044

The Waverley Guesthouse ♦♦♦
191 Eastern Esplanade, Thorpe Bay, Southend-on-Sea, SS1 3AA
T: (01702) 585212
F: (01702) 586764
E: waverleyguesthouse@hotmail.com
I: www.waverleyguesthouse.co.uk

SOUTHMINSTER
Essex

New Moor Farm ♦♦♦♦
Tillingham Road, Burnham-on-Crouch, Southminster, CM0 7DS
T: (01621) 772840
F: (01621) 774087

Saxegate Guesthouse ♦♦♦
44 North Street, Southminster, CM0 7DG
T: (01621) 773180
F: (01621) 774116

SOUTHREPPS
Norfolk

Avalon ♦♦♦♦
Lower Southrepps, Southrepps, Norwich NR11 8UJ
T: (01263) 834461
F: (01263) 834461
E: mokies@msn.com

SOUTHWOLD
Suffolk

Acton Lodge ♦♦♦♦
South Green, Southwold, IP18 6HB
T: (01502) 723217

Amber House ♦♦♦
24 North Parade, Southwold, IP18 6LT
T: (01502) 723303
E: spring@amberhouse.fsnet.co.uk
I: www.southwold.blythweb.co.uk/amber_house/index.htm

Avocet House ♦♦♦♦
1 Strickland Place, Southwold, IP18 6HN
T: (01502) 724 720
E: barnett@beeb.net
I: www.southwold.ws/avocet-house

Brenda's ♦♦♦
Wellesley House, 3 Strickland Place, Southwold, IP18 6HN
T: (01502) 722403

Dunburgh Guesthouse ♦♦♦♦
28 North Parade, Southwold, IP18 6LT
T: (01502) 723253
I: www.southwold.ws/dunburgh

No 21 ♦♦♦
North Parade, Southwold, IP18 6LT
T: (01502) 722573
F: (01502) 724326
E: jackie_comrie@onetel.net.uk
I: www.southwold.blythweb.co.uk/north_parade/index.htm

Northcliffe Guesthouse ♦♦♦♦
20 North Parade, Southwold, IP18 6LT
T: (01502) 724074
I: www.s-h-systems.co.uk/hotels/northcli.html

Number Three ♦♦♦♦
3 Cautley Road, Southwold, IP18 6DD
T: (01502) 723611

The Old Vicarage ♦♦♦♦
Wenhaston, Halesworth IP19 9EG
T: (01502) 478339
F: (01502) 478068
E: theycock@aol.com
I: www.southwold.blythweb.co.uk

Prospect Place ♦♦♦♦
33 Station Road, Southwold, IP18 6AX
T: (01502) 722757
E: sally@prospect-place.demon.co.uk
I: www.prospect-place.demon.co.uk

Shanklin House ♦♦♦♦
6 Chester Road, Southwold, IP18 6LN
T: (01502) 724748
E: ratcliffshanklin@aol.com

Ventnor Villas ♦♦♦
4 Hurn Crag Road, Reydon, Southwold, IP18 6RG
T: (01502) 723619
F: (01502) 723619
E: sue@ventnorvillas.co.uk
I: www.ventnorvillas.co.uk

Victoria House ♦♦♦♦
9 Dunwich Road, Southwold, IP18 6LJ
T: (01502) 722317
E: victoria@southwold.info
I: www.victoria.southwold.info

SPELLBROOK
Hertfordshire

Spellbrook Farm B&B ♦♦♦
London Road, Spellbrook, Bishop's Stortford CM23 4AX
T: (01279) 600191
F: (01279) 722758

SPORLE
Norfolk

Corfield House
♦♦♦♦ SILVER AWARD
Sporle, Swaffham, PE32 2EA
T: (01760) 723636
E: corfield.house@virgin.net
I: www.corfieldhouse.co.uk

SPROUGHTON
Suffolk

Finjaro ♦♦♦♦
Valley Farm Drive, Hadleigh Road, Sproughton, Ipswich IP8 3EL
T: 0705 0065465
F: (01473) 652139
E: jan@finjaro.freeserve.co.uk
I: www.s-h-systems.co.uk/hotels/finjaro.html

SPROWSTON
Norfolk

Driftwood Lodge ♦♦♦♦
102 Wroxham Road, Sprowston, Norwich NR7 8EX
T: (01603) 444908
E: johniekate@driftwood16.freeserve.co.uk
I: www.driftwoodlodge.co.uk

STALHAM
Norfolk

Bramble House
♦♦♦♦ SILVER AWARD
Cat's Common, Norwich Road, Smallburgh, Norwich NR12 9NS
T: (01692) 535069
F: (01692) 535069
E: bramblehouse@tesco.net
I: www.norfolkbroads.com/bramblehouse

Chapelfield Cottage ♦♦♦♦
Chapelfield, Stalham, Norwich NR12 9EN
T: (01692) 582173
F: (01692) 583009
E: gary@cinqueportsmarine.freeserve.co.uk
I: www.whiteswan.u-net.com

STANDON
Hertfordshire

Fox and Hounds House ♦♦♦♦
Bromley, Standon, Ware SG11 1NX
T: (01279) 842722
E: timakerz@aol.com
I: www.smoothhound.co.uk/hotels/foxandhounds.html

16 Vicarage Close ♦♦♦
Standon, Ware SG11 1QP
T: (01920) 821065

STANSTED
Essex

High Trees ♦♦♦
Parsonage Road, Takeley, Bishop's Stortford CM22 6QX
T: (01279) 871306
F: (01279) 820569

STANSTED MOUNTFITCHET
Essex

Chimneys ♦♦♦♦
44 Lower Street, Stansted Mountfitchet, Stansted CM24 8LR
T: (01279) 813388
F: (01279) 813388
E: info@chimneysguesthouse.co.uk
I: www.chimneysguesthouse.co.uk

The Laurels Hotel ♦♦♦
84 St Johns Road, Stansted Mountfitchet, Stansted CM24 8JS
T: (01279) 813023
F: (01279) 813023

STEEPLE BUMPSTEAD
Essex

Yew Tree House ♦♦♦♦
15 Chapel Street, Steeple Bumpstead, Haverhill CB9 7DQ
T: (01440) 730364
F: (01440) 730364
E: yewtreehouse@btinternet.com
I: www.haverhill-uk.com/yewtree

STIFFKEY
Norfolk

The Saltings ♦♦♦♦
68 Wells Road, Stiffkey, Wells-next-the-Sea NR23 1AJ
T: (01328) 830194
I: www.thesaltings.com

STOKE-BY-NAYLAND
Suffolk

The Angel Inn
♦♦♦♦ SILVER AWARD
Polstead Street, Stoke-by-Nayland, Colchester CO6 4SA
T: (01206) 263245
F: (01206) 263373
I: www.angelhotel.com

Ryegate House
♦♦♦♦ GOLD AWARD
Stoke-by-Nayland, Colchester CO6 4RA
T: (01206) 263679
E: ryegate@lineone.net
I: www.w-h-systems.co.uk/hotels/ryegate.html

Thorington Hall ♦♦♦
Stoke-by-Nayland, Colchester CO6 4SS
T: (01206) 337329

STOKE HOLY CROSS
Norfolk

Salamanca Farm ♦♦♦
116-118 Norwich Road, Stoke Holy Cross, Norwich NR14 8QJ
T: (01508) 492322
I: www.smoothhound.co.uk/salamanc.html

STOWMARKET
Suffolk

Gipping Heights Hotel ♦♦♦♦
Creeting Road, Stowmarket, IP14 5BT
T: (01449) 675264

The Step House ♦♦♦♦
Hockey Hill, Wetheringsett, Stowmarket, IP14 5PL
T: (01449) 766476
F: (01449) 766476
E: stephouse@talk21.com

Stricklands ♦♦♦
Stricklands Road, Stowmarket, IP14 1AP
T: (01449) 612450
F: (01449) 614944
E: poppy@stricklandshouse.fsnet.co.uk

The Three Bears House Mulberrytree Farm ♦♦♦
Blacksmiths Lane, Middlewood Green, Stowmarket, IP14 5EU
T: (01449) 711707
F: (01449) 711707

Verandah House ♦♦♦♦
29 Ipswich Road, Stowmarket, IP14 1BD
T: (01449) 676104
F: (01449) 616127
E: verandahhs@aol.com
I: www.verandah-house.co.uk

STRADBROKE
Suffolk

Timbers ♦♦♦♦
New Street, Stradbroke, Eye IP21 5JJ
T: (01379) 384920
F: (01379) 384946
E: diana.sharpe@btopenworld.com

STRETHAM
Cambridgeshire

The Red Lion ♦♦♦
High Street, Stretham, Ely CB6 3JQ
T: (01353) 648132
F: (01353) 648327
E: frank.hayes@gateway.net

SUDBOURNE
Suffolk

Long Meadows ♦♦♦
Gorse Lane, Sudbourne, Woodbridge IP12 2BD
T: (01394) 450269

SUDBURY
Suffolk

Fiddlesticks ♦♦♦♦
Pinkuah Lane, Pentlow, Sudbury CO10 7JW
T: (01787) 280154
F: (01787) 280154
E: sarah@fiddlesticks.biz
I: www.fiddlesticks.biz

The Hall ♦♦♦♦
Milden, Lavenham, Sudbury, CO10 9NY
T: (01787) 247235
F: (01787) 247235
E: gjb53@dial.pipex.com
I: www.farmstayanglia.co.uk

Old Bull Hotel and Restaurant ♦♦♦
Church Street, Ballingdon, Sudbury, CO10 2BL
T: (01787) 374120
F: (01787) 379044
E: old-bull.8sudbury@virgin.net
I: www.theoldbullhotel.co.uk

West House ♦♦♦
59 Ballingdon Street, Sudbury, CO10 2DA
T: (01787) 375033

SWAFFHAM
Norfolk

Glebe Bungalow ♦♦♦♦
8a Princes Street, Swaffham, PE37 7BP
T: (01760) 722764
E: doreenmharvey@aol.com

Strattons
♦♦♦♦♦ SILVER AWARD
Strattons, 4 Ash Close, Swaffham, PE37 7NH
T: (01760) 723845
F: (01760) 720458
E: strattonshotel@btinternet.com
I: www.stratton-hotel.co.uk

SWAFFHAM PRIOR
Cambridgeshire

Sterling Farm ♦♦♦
Heath Road, Swaffham Prior, Cambridge CB5 0LA
T: (01638) 741431
F: (01638) 741431

SWEFFLING
Suffolk

Hall Farm ♦♦♦
Sweffling, Saxmundham IP17 2BT
T: (01728) 663644
F: (01728) 663644
E: stephenmann@suffolkonline.net

Wayside Bed and Breakfast ♦♦♦♦
Glemham Road, Sweffling, Saxmundham IP17 2BQ
T: (01728) 663256
E: anthonywilkinson@suffolkonline.net
I: www.wayside-sweffling.co.uk

TAKELEY
Essex

Crossroads B & B ♦♦
2 Hawthorn Close, Takeley, Bishop's Stortford CM22 6SD
T: (01279) 870619
E: ajcaiger884@aol.com

Jan Smiths B&B ♦♦♦
The Cottage, Jacks Lane, Takeley, Bishop's Stortford CM22 6NT
T: (01279) 870603
F: (01279) 870603

Joseph's Drive ♦♦
2 Joseph's Drive, The Street, Takeley, Bishop's Stortford CM22 6QT
T: (01279) 870652
E: ethlyn_king@hotmail.com

Joyners ♦♦♦
The Street, Takeley, Bishop's Stortford CM22 6QU
T: (01279) 870944
F: (01279) 870944
E: andersonsi@joyners99.freeserve.co.uk

Little Bullocks Farm ♦♦♦♦
Hope End, Takeley, Bishop's Stortford CM22 6TA
T: (01279) 870464
F: (01279) 871430
E: julie@waterman-farm.fsnet.co.uk

Pippins ♦♦♦
Smiths Green, Takeley, Bishop's Stortford CM22 6NR
T: (01279) 870369
F: (01279) 871216
E: kevinmatthews@pippinsbandb.co.uk

San Michelle ♦♦♦♦
Jacks Lane, Takeley, Bishop's Stortford CM22 6NT
T: (01279) 870946

TERRINGTON ST JOHN
Norfolk

Somerville House ♦♦♦♦
Church Road, Terrington St John, Wisbech PE14 7RY
T: (01945) 880952
F: (01945) 880952
E: somervillemc@hotmail.com
I: www.somervillehouse.co.uk

THAXTED
Essex

Crossways Guesthouse
♦♦♦♦ SILVER AWARD
32 Town Street, Thaxted, Dunmow CM6 2LA
T: (01371) 830348

The Farmhouse Inn ♦♦♦
Monk Street, Thaxted, Dunmow CM6 2NR
T: (01371) 830864
F: (01371) 831196

THEBERTON
Suffolk

The Alders ♦♦♦
Potters Street, Theberton, Leiston IP16 4RL
T: (01728) 831790
F: (01728) 831790

The Granary ♦♦♦♦
Theberton, Leiston IP16 4RR
T: (01728) 831633
F: (01728) 831633
E: GranaryTheberton@aol.com

THETFORD
Norfolk

East Farm ♦♦♦♦
Euston Road, Barnham, Thetford IP24 2PB
T: (01842) 890231
F: (01842) 890457

The Glebe Country House Bed and Breakfast♦♦♦♦
34 London Road, Thetford, IP24 3TL
T: (01842) 890027
F: (01842) 890027
E: deirdre@jrudderham.freeserve.co.uk

The Wereham House Hotel ♦♦♦
24 White Hart Street, Thetford, IP24 1AD
T: (01842) 761956
F: (01842) 765207
E: wereham@flexnet.co.uk
I: www.werehamhousehotel.co.uk

THOMPSON
Norfolk

The Chequers Inn ♦♦♦♦
Griston Road, Thompson, Thetford IP24 1PX
T: (01953) 483360
F: (01953) 488092
E: themcdowalls@barbox.net
I: www.thompsonchequers.com

THORNDON
Suffolk

Moat Farm ♦♦♦♦
Thorndon, Eye IP23 7LX
T: (01379) 678437
F: (01379) 678023
E: geralde@clara.co.uk
I: www.moatfarm.co.uk

THORNHAM
Norfolk

Rushmeadow ♦♦♦♦
Main Road, Thornham, Hunstanton PE36 6LZ
T: (01485) 512372
F: (01485) 512372
E: rushmeadow@lineone.net
I: www.rushmeadow.com

THORPE MARKET
Norfolk

Manorwood ♦♦♦
Church Road, Thorpe Market, Norwich NR11 8UA
T: (01263) 834938

THORPENESS
Suffolk

The Dolphin Inn ♦♦♦
Thorpeness, Leiston IP16 4NA
T: (01728) 454994
F: (01728) 454971
E: info@thorpeness.co.uk
I: www.thorpeness.co.uk

TOFT
Cambridgeshire

Orchard Farmhouse ♦♦♦♦
56 Comberton Road, Toft, Cambridge CB3 7RY
T: (01223) 262309
F: (01223) 263979
E: tebbit.bxb.toft@talk21.com
I: www.smoothhound.co.uk/hotels/orchfarm.html

TOLLESBURY
Essex

Fernleigh ♦♦♦
16 Woodrolfe Farm Lane, Tollesbury, Maldon CM9 8SX
T: (01621) 868245
F: (01621) 868245
E: gill.willson@ntlworld.com

TOLLESHUNT MAJOR
Essex

Mill Lodge ♦♦♦
Mill Lane, Tolleshunt Major, Maldon CM9 8YF
T: (01621) 860311

Wicks Manor Farm ♦♦♦♦
Witham Road, Tolleshunt Major, Maldon CM9 8JU
T: (01621) 860629
F: (01621) 860629
E: rhowie@aspects.net

TOPPESFIELD
Essex

Harrow Hill Cottage ♦♦♦
Harrow Hill, Toppesfield, Halstead CO9 4LX
T: (01787) 237425

TOTTENHILL
Norfolk

Andel Lodge Hotel & Restaurant ♦♦♦♦
48 Lynn Road, Tottenhill, King's Lynn PE33 0RH
T: (01553) 810256
F: (01553) 811429

TRUNCH
Norfolk

North Barn ♦♦♦♦
Mundesley Road, Trunch, North Walsham NR28 0QB
T: (01263) 722256
F: (01263) 722256
E: richardjelliff@hotmail.com
I: www.north-barn.co.uk

UFFORD
Suffolk

Strawberry Hill ♦♦♦♦
Loudham Lane, Lower Ufford, Ufford, Woodbridge IP13 6ED
T: (01394) 460252
E: strawberryhilly@yahoo.co.uk
I: www.smoothhound.co.uk/hotels/strawber.html

UPPER SHERINGHAM
Norfolk

Lodge Cottage ♦♦♦♦
Lodge Hill, Upper Sheringham, Sheringham NR26 8TJ
T: (01263) 821445
E: stay@lodgecottage.co.uk
I: www.lodgecottage.co.uk

UPWELL
Cambridgeshire

The Olde Mill Hotel
♦♦♦♦ SILVER AWARD
Town Street, Upwell, Wisbech PE14 9AF
T: (01945) 772614
F: (01945) 772614
E: oldemill@lineone.net

WAKES COLNE
Essex

Rosebank Bed and Breakfast ♦♦♦♦
Rosebank Station Road, Wakes Colne, Colchester CO6 2DS
T: (01787) 223552
F: (01787) 220415

WALBERSWICK
Suffolk

The Anchor Inn ♦♦♦
Main Street, Walberswick, Southwold IP18 6UA
T: (01502) 722112
F: (01502) 724464

Dickon ♦♦
Main Street, Walberswick, Southwold IP18 6UX
T: (01502) 724046

WALSHAM-LE-WILLOWS
Suffolk

Wagner Cottage ♦♦
Walsham-le-Willows, Bury St Edmunds IP31 3AA
T: (01359) 259380
E: gill@wagner123.fsnet.co.uk

WANGFORD
Suffolk

Poplar Hall ♦♦♦♦
Frostenden Corner, Frostenden, Wangford, Beccles NR34 7JA
T: (01502) 578549
I: www.southwold.co.uk/poplar-hall/

WANSFORD
Cambridgeshire

The Cross Keys ♦♦♦
21 Elton Road, Wansford, Peterborough PE8 6JD
T: (01780) 782266
F: (01780) 782266

Stoneacre Guest House ♦♦♦♦
Elton Road, Wansford, Peterborough PE8 6JT
T: (01780) 783283
F: (01780) 783283

WASHBROOK
Suffolk

High View ♦♦♦♦
Back Lane, Washbrook, Ipswich IP8 3JA
T: (01473) 730494
E: rosanna.steward@virgin.net

WATERDEN
Norfolk

The Old Rectory
Rating Applied For
Waterden, Walsingham NR22 6AT
T: (01328) 823298

WATTON
Norfolk

The Willow House ♦♦♦♦
2 High Street, Watton, Thetford IP25 6AE
T: (01953) 881181
F: (01953) 885885
E: willowhousewatton@barbox.net
I: www.willowhouse.net

WELLINGHAM
Norfolk

Manor House Farm
♦♦♦♦ SILVER AWARD
Wellingham, King's Lynn PE32 2TH
T: (01328) 838227
F: (01328) 838348
E: libbyellis@farming.co.uk

WELLS-NEXT-THE-SEA
Norfolk

Blenheim House ♦♦♦♦
Theatre Road, Wells-next-the-Sea, NR23 1DJ
T: (01328) 711368
F: (01328) 711368
E: jmarjoram@blenheimhse.freeserve.co.uk

The Cobblers ♦♦♦
Standard Road, Wells-next-the-Sea, NR23 1JU
T: (01328) 710155
E: ina@cobblers.co.uk
I: www.cobblers.co.uk

Corner House ♦♦♦
Staithe Street, Wells-next-the-Sea, NR23 1AF
T: (01328) 710701
E: lmoney@ukonline.co.uk
I: www.cornerhouseatwells.com

Glebe Barn ♦♦♦♦
7a Glebe Road, Wells-next-the-Sea, NR23 1AZ
T: (01328) 711809
E: glebebarn@supanet.com

Hideaway ♦♦♦
Red Lion Yard, Wells-next-the-Sea, NR23 1AX
T: (01328) 710524
F: (01328) 710524
E: hideaway.wells@btinternet.com

Ilex House ♦♦♦
Bases Lane, Wells-next-the-Sea, NR23 1DH
T: (01328) 710556
F: (01328) 710556
E: tommcjay@aol.com
I: www.broadland.com/ilexhouse

Machrimore ♦♦♦♦
Burnt Street, Wells-next-the-Sea, NR23 1HS
T: (01328) 711653
E: dorothy.maccallum@ntlworld.com
I: www.machrimore.co.uk

Mill House Guesthouse ♦♦♦
Mill House, Northfield Lane, Wells-next-the-Sea, NR23 1JZ
T: (01328) 710739
I: www.broadland.com/millhouse

The Normans ♦♦♦♦
Invaders Court, Standard Road, Wells-next-the-Sea, NR23 1JW
T: (01328) 710657
F: (01328) 710468

The Old Custom House ♦♦♦
East Quay, Wells-next-the-Sea, NR23 1LD
T: (01328) 711463
F: (01328) 710277
E: bb@eastquay.co.uk
I: www.eastquay.co.uk

Old Police House ♦♦♦♦
Polka Road, Wells-next-the-Sea, NR23 1ED
T: (01328) 710630
F: (01328) 710630
E: ophwells@yahoo.co.uk
I: www.northnorfolk.co.uk/oldpolicehouse

27 Staithe Street ♦♦
Wells-next-the-Sea, NR23 1AG
T: (01328) 710480
F: (01328) 710480
E: jspinks4@aol.com

WENHASTON
Suffolk

Rowan House ♦♦♦♦
Hall Road, Wenhaston, Halesworth IP19 9HF
T: (01502) 478407
E: rowanhouse@freeuk.com

WEST BERGHOLT
Essex

The Old Post House ♦♦♦
10 Colchester Road, West Bergholt, Colchester CO6 3JG
T: (01206) 240379
F: (01206) 243301

WEST DEREHAM
Norfolk

Bell Barn ♦♦♦♦
Lime Kiln Road, West Dereham, King's Lynn PE33 9RT
T: (01366) 500762
F: (01366) 500762
E: chris@woodbarn.freeserve.co.uk

WEST MERSEA
Essex

Hazel Oak ♦♦♦♦
28 Seaview Avenue, West Mersea, Colchester CO5 8HE
T: (01206) 383030
E: ann.blackmore@btinternet.com
I: www.btinternet.com/~daveblackmore/

WEST RUNTON
Norfolk

The Old Barn ♦♦♦♦
Cromer Road, West Runton, Cromer NR27 9QT
T: (01263) 838285

WEST SOMERTON
Norfolk

Three Acres B&B ♦♦♦♦
Winterton Road, West Somerton, Great Yarmouth NR29 4DR
T: (01493) 393433

White House Farm ♦♦♦♦
The Street, West Somerton, Great Yarmouth NR29 4EA
T: (01493) 393991
E: gc_dobinson@btinternet.com

WESTCLIFF-ON-SEA
Essex

Chilton House ♦♦♦
3 Trinity Avenue, Westcliff-on-Sea, SS0 7PU
T: (01702) 342282
F: (01702) 342282

Pavilion Hotel ♦♦
1 Trinity Avenue, Westcliff-on-Sea, SS0 7PU
T: (01702) 332767
F: (01702) 332767

Retreat Guesthouse ♦♦♦
12 Canewdon Road, Westcliff-on-Sea, SS0 7NE
T: (01702) 348217
F: (01702) 391179
E: retreatguesthouse.co.uk@tinyworld.co.uk
I: www.retreatguesthouse.co.uk

Welbeck Hotel ♦♦♦♦
27 Palmerston Road, Westcliff-on-Sea, SS0 7TA
T: (01702) 347736
F: (01702) 339140
E: welbeck@tinyworld.co.uk

WESTLETON
Suffolk

Pond House ♦♦♦♦
The Hill, Westleton, Saxmundham IP17 3AN
T: (01728) 648773

WHITE RODING
Essex

Marks Hall Farmhouse ♦♦♦♦
Marks Hall, White Roding, Dunmow CM6 1RT
T: (01279) 876438
F: (01279) 876236
E: jane@markshall.fsnet.co.uk
I: www.marks-hall.co.uk

WHITTLESEY
Cambridgeshire

Whitmore House ♦♦♦♦
31 Whitmore Street, Whittlesey, Peterborough PE7 1HE
T: (01733) 203088

WICKHAM BISHOPS
Essex

Meadow Bank
♦♦♦♦ SILVER AWARD
Station Road, Wickham Bishops, Witham CM8 3JN
T: (01621) 892743
F: (01621) 892930
E: james.cravensmith@btinternet.com

WICKHAM MARKET
Suffolk

The Old Pharmacy ♦♦♦♦
72 High Street, Wickham Market, Woodbridge IP13 0QU
T: (01728) 745012
E: juliefiona@talk21.com

WIGHTON
Norfolk

Shrublands ♦♦♦♦
Wells Road, Wighton, Wells-next-the-Sea NR23 1PR
T: (01328) 820743
F: (01328) 820088
E: shrublands@shrub-lands.freeserve.co.uk
I: www.shrub-lands.freeserve.co.uk

WIMBISH
Essex

Blossom Cottage ♦♦♦♦
Rowney Corner, Thaxted road, Wimbish, Saffron Walden CB10 2UZ
T: (01799) 599430
E: cmacpherson@waitrose.com

Newdegate House
♦♦♦♦ SILVER AWARD
Howlett End, Wimbish, Saffron Walden CB10 2XW
T: (01799) 599748
F: (01799) 599748

WINGFIELD
Suffolk

Gables Farm ♦♦♦♦
Earsham Street, Wingfield, Diss IP21 5RH
T: (01379) 586355
F: (01379) 588058
E: gables-farm@ntlworld.com
I: www.gablesfarm.co.uk

WINTERTON-ON-SEA
Norfolk

Cleveland House ♦♦♦♦
The Lane, Winterton-on-Sea, Great Yarmouth NR29 4BN
T: 07884 117440
F: (01493) 393352
E: cleveland.house@virgin.net

WISBECH
Cambridgeshire

Marmion House Hotel ♦♦♦
11 Lynn Road, Wisbech, PE13 3DD
T: (01945) 582822
F: (01945) 475889

WITHAM
Essex

Chestnuts ♦♦♦♦
8 Octavia Drive, Witham Lodge, Witham, CM8 1HQ
T: (01376) 515990
F: (01376) 515990
E: kbmoney2@aol.com

WIX
Essex

Dairy House Farm
♦♦♦♦♦ SILVER AWARD
Bradfield Road, Wix, Manningtree CO11 2SR
T: (01255) 870322
F: (01255) 870186
E: bridgetwhitworth@hotmail.com

WOOD NORTON
Norfolk

Manor Farm Bed and Breakfast
♦♦♦♦ SILVER AWARD
Manor Farm, Hall Lane, Wood Norton, East Dereham NR20 5BE
T: (01362) 683231
F: (01362) 683231

WOODBRIDGE
Suffolk

Deben Lodge ♦♦
Melton Road, Woodbridge, IP12 1NH
T: (01394) 382740
I: www.SmoothHound.co.uk/shs.html

Grove House ♦♦♦
39 Grove Road, Woodbridge, IP12 4LG
T: (01394) 382202
F: (01394) 380652
E: reception@grovehousehotel.com
I: www.grovehousehotel.com

Lark Cottage ♦♦♦♦
Shingle Street, Woodbridge, Suffolk IP12 3BE
T: (01394) 411292

Moat Barn ♦♦♦♦
Bredfield, Woodbridge IP13 6BD
T: (01473) 737520
F: (01473) 737520
I: www.moat-barn.co.uk

Moat Farmhouse ♦♦♦
Dallinghoo Road, Bredfield, Woodbridge IP13 6BD
T: (01473) 737475

Sandpit House ♦♦♦
Loudham, Wickham Market, Woodbridge IP13 0NW
T: (01728) 747435
E: gilbey@sandpithouse@fsnet.co.uk

WOODHAM MORTIMER
Essex

Chase Farm Bed & Breakfast ♦♦♦
Chase Farm, Hyde Chase, Woodham Mortimer, Maldon CM9 6TN
T: (01245) 223268

WOODSTON
Cambridgeshire

White House Guesthouse ♦♦♦
White House, 318 Oundle Road, Woodston, Peterborough PE2 9QP
T: (01733) 566650

WOOLPIT
Suffolk

The Bull Inn & Restaurant ♦♦♦
The Street, Woolpit, Bury St Edmunds IP30 9SA
T: (01359) 240393
F: (01359) 244216
E: trevor@howling.fsbusiness.co.uk
I: www.bullinnwoolpit.co.uk

Grange Farm ♦♦♦♦
Woolpit, Bury St Edmunds IP30 9RG
T: (01359) 241143
F: (01359) 244296
E: grangefarm@btinternet.com
I: www.farmstayanglia.co.uk/grangefarm/

Swan Inn ♦♦♦
The Street, Woolpit, Bury St Edmunds IP30 9QN
T: (01359) 240482

WOOTTON
Bedfordshire

Maple Tree Cottage ♦♦♦♦
Wootton Green, Wootton, Bedford MK43 9EE
T: (01234) 768631
F: (01234) 768631
E: francy.mtc@cwcom.net

WORLINGTON
Suffolk

Worlington Hall Country House Hotel ♦♦♦♦
The Street, Worlington, Bury St Edmunds IP28 8RX
T: (01638) 712237
F: (01638) 712631

WORSTEAD
Norfolk

Hall Farm Guesthouse ♦♦♦♦
Hall Farm, Sloley Road, Worstead, North Walsham NR28 9RS
T: (01692) 536124
E: d.lowe4@tinyworld.co.uk OR j.lowe4@tinyworld.co.uk

Holly Grove House ♦♦♦♦
Lyngate, Worstead, North Walsham NR28 9RQ
T: (01692) 535546
E: michaelhorwood@freenetname.co.uk
I: www.broadland.com/hollygrove

The Ollands ♦♦♦♦
Swanns Loke, Worstead, North Walsham NR28 9RP
T: (01692) 535150
F: (01692) 535150
E: ollands@worstead.freeserve.co.uk

WOTHORPE
Cambridgeshire

Firwood ♦♦♦♦
First Drift, Wothorpe, Stamford PE9 3JL
T: (01780) 765654
F: (01780) 765654

WRENTHAM
Suffolk

The Garden Flat ♦♦♦
68 Southwold Road, Wrentham, Beccles NR34 7JF
T: (01502) 675692
F: (01502) 675692
E: r.ashton@ecosse.net

7 Mill Lane ♦♦♦
Wrentham, Beccles NR34 7JQ
T: (01502) 675489

Southwold Lodge ♦♦♦♦
67 Southwold Road, Wrentham, Beccles NR34 7JE
T: (01502) 676148
F: (01986) 784797
E: qhbfield@aol.com

WRESTLINGWORTH
Bedfordshire

Orchard Cottage ♦♦♦
1 High Street, Wrestlingworth, Sandy SG19 2EW
T: (01767) 631355
F: (01767) 631355

WRITTLE
Essex

Moor Hall ♦♦♦♦ SILVER AWARD
Newney Green, Writtle, Chelmsford CM1 3SE
T: (01245) 420814
E: moorhall@talk21.com

WROXHAM
Norfolk

The Coach House ♦♦♦♦
96 Norwich Road, Wroxham, Norwich NR12 8RY
T: (01603) 784376
F: (01603) 783734
E: bishop@worldonline.co.uk
I: www.coachhousewroxham.co.uk

The Dragon Flies ♦♦♦♦ SILVER AWARD
5 The Avenue, Wroxham, Norwich NR12 8TN
T: (01603) 783822
F: (01603) 783822
E: geoff.g.kimberley@talk21.com

Ridge House ♦♦♦♦
7 The Avenue, Wroxham, Norwich NR12 8TN
T: (01603) 782130

Wroxham Park Lodge ♦♦♦♦
142 Norwich Road, Wroxham, Norwich NR12 8SA
T: (01603) 782991
E: prklodge@nascr.net
I: www.smoothhound.co.uk/hotels/wroxhamp.html

WYMONDHAM
Norfolk

Witch Hazel ♦♦♦♦ SILVER AWARD
Church Lane, Wicklewood, Wymondham NR18 9QH
T: (01953) 602247
F: (01953) 602247

YAXLEY
Suffolk

The Bull Auberge ♦♦♦♦♦ SILVER AWARD
Ipswich Road, Yaxley, Eye IP23 8BZ
T: (01379) 783604
F: (01379) 783604
E: bullauberge@aol.com

YOXFORD
Suffolk

The Griffin ♦♦♦
High Street, Yoxford, Saxmundham IP17 3EP
T: (01728) 668229
E: i.terry@thegriffin.co.uk
I: www.thegriffin.co.uk

Mile Hill Barn ♦♦♦♦♦ GOLD AWARD
Main Road, Kelsale, Saxmundham IP17 2RG
T: (01728) 668519
E: richard@milehillbarn.freeserve.co.uk
I: www.mile-hill-barn.co.uk

The Old Methodist Chapel ♦♦♦♦
High Street, Yoxford, Saxmundham IP17 3EU
T: (01728) 668333
F: (01728) 668333
E: browns@chapelsuffolk.co.uk
I: www.chapelsuffolk.co.uk

SOUTH WEST

ABBOTSBURY
Dorset

Corfe Gate House ♦♦♦♦♦ SILVER AWARD
Coryates, Abbotsbury, Weymouth DT3 4HW
T: (01305) 871483
F: (01305) 264024
E: maureenadams@corfegatehouse.co.uk
I: www.corfegatehouse.co.uk

Linton Cottage ♦♦♦♦ SILVER AWARD
Abbotsbury, Weymouth DT3 4JL
T: (01305) 871339
F: (01305) 871339
E: queenbee@abbotsbury.co.uk
I: www.lintoncottage.co.uk

Swan Lodge ♦♦♦
Rodden Row, Abbotsbury, Weymouth DT3 4JL
T: (01305) 871249
F: (01305) 871249

ADVENT
Cornwall

Higher Trezion ♦♦♦♦
Tresinney, Advent, Camelford PL32 9QW
T: (01840) 213761
F: (01840) 212509
E: highertrezion@virgin.net

ALLERFORD
Somerset

Exmoor Falconry & Animal Farm ♦♦♦
West Lynch Farm, Allerford, Minehead TA24 8HJ
T: (01643) 862816
F: (01643) 862816
E: exmoorfalcon@freenet.co.uk
I: www.exmoorfalconry.co.uk

Fern Cottage ♦♦♦♦
Allerford, Minehead TA24 8HN
T: (01643) 862215
F: (01643) 862215
E: ferncottage@bushinternet.com
I: www.exmoor.com/ferncottage

AMESBURY
Wiltshire

Enford House ♦♦♦
Enford, Pewsey SN9 6DJ
T: (01980) 670414

Fairlawn Hotel ♦♦
42 High Street, Amesbury, Salisbury SP4 7DL
T: (01980) 622103
F: (01980) 624888

Mandalay ♦♦♦♦
15 Stonehenge Road, Amesbury, Salisbury SP4 7BA
T: (01980) 623733
F: (01980) 626642

The Old Bakery ♦♦♦
Netton, Salisbury SP4 6AW
T: (01722) 782351
E: valahen@aol.com
I: members.aol.com/valahen

Solstice Farmhouse ♦♦♦
39 Holders Road, Amesbury, Salisbury SP4 7PH
T: (01980) 625052
E: williams@btinternet.com

Vale House ♦♦♦
Figheldean, Salisbury SP4 8JJ
T: (01980) 670713

ASHBRITTLE
Somerset

Lower Westcott Farm ♦♦♦
Ashbrittle, Wellington TA21 0HZ
T: (01398) 361296
E: lowerwestcott@dot.com

ASHBURTON
Devon

Gages Mill
♦♦♦♦ SILVER AWARD
Buckfastleigh Road, Ashburton, Newton Abbot TQ13 7JW
T: (01364) 652391
F: (01364) 652391
E: moore@gagesmill.co.uk
I: www.gagesmill.co.uk

The Rising Sun ♦♦♦♦
Woodland, Ashburton, Newton Abbot TQ13 7JT
T: (01364) 652544
F: (01364) 654202
E: mail@risingsunwoodland.co.uk
I: www.risingsunwoodland.co.uk

Sladesdown Farm
♦♦♦♦ SILVER AWARD
Landscove, Ashburton, Newton Abbot TQ13 7ND
T: (01364) 653973
F: (01364) 653973
E: sue@sladesdownfarm.co.uk
I: www.sladesdownfarm.co.uk

Wellpritton Farm ♦♦♦♦
Holne, Newton Abbot TQ13 7RX
T: (01364) 631273
E: info@wellprittonfarm.com
I: www.wellprittonfarm.com

ASHTON
Somerset

Ashton Road Farm ♦♦♦
Ashton, Wedmore BS28 4QE
T: (01934) 713462
F: (01934) 713462

ASHTON KEYNES
Wiltshire

Corner Cottage ♦♦♦
Fore Street, Ashton Keynes, Swindon SN6 6NP
T: (01285) 861454

Wheatleys Farm ♦♦♦♦
High Road, Ashton Keynes, Swindon SN6 6NX
T: (01285) 861310
F: (01285) 861310
E: wheatleys.farm@lineone.net
I: www.smoothhound.co.uk

ASKERSWELL
Dorset

Hembury House ♦♦♦♦
Askerswell, Dorchester DT2 9EN
T: (01308) 485297
F: (01308) 485032
E: askers@askers.free-online.co.uk
I: www.freeyellow.com/members5/hembury/page1.html

ATWORTH
Wiltshire

Church Farm ♦♦♦♦
Church Street, Atworth, Melksham SN12 8JA
T: (01225) 702215
F: (01225) 702215
E: churchfarm@tinyonline.co.uk
I: www.churchfarm-atworth.freeserve.co.uk

AVEBURY
Wiltshire

Manor Farm ♦♦♦♦
Avebury, Marlborough SN8 1RF
T: (01672) 539294
F: (01672) 539294

The New Inn ♦♦♦
Winterbourne Monkton, Swindon SN4 9NW
T: (01672) 539240
F: (01672) 539150

AVEBURY TRUSLOE
Wiltshire

Manor Farm ♦♦♦
Avebury Trusloe, Marlborough SN8 1QY
T: (01672) 539243
F: (01672) 539230

AVETON GIFFORD
Devon

Helliers Farm ♦♦♦♦
Ashford, Aveton Gifford, Kingsbridge TQ7 4ND
T: (01548) 550689
F: (01548) 550689
E: helliersfarm@ukonline.co.uk
I: www.helliersfarm.co.uk

AWLISCOMBE
Devon

Birds Farm ♦♦
Awliscombe, Honiton EX14 3PU
T: (01404) 841620

Godford Farm ♦♦♦♦
Awliscombe, Honiton EX14 3PW
T: (01404) 42825
F: (01404) 42825
E: lawrencesally@hotmail.com
I: www.devon-farm-holidays.co.uk

AXBRIDGE
Somerset

Lamb Inn
Rating Applied For
The Square, Axbridge, BS26 2AP
T: (01934) 732253
F: (01934) 733821

Waterside ♦♦♦
Cheddar Road, Axbridge, BS26 2DP
T: (01934) 743182

AXMINSTER
Devon

Beckford Cottage ♦♦♦♦
Dalwood, Axminster EX13 7HQ
T: (01404) 881641
F: (01404) 881108
E: beckfordcottage@hotmail.com
I: www.beckford-cottage.co.uk

Chalfont House ♦♦♦♦
Crewkerne Road, Raymonds Hill, Axminster, EX13 5SX
T: (01297) 33852
E: chalfont.house@btopenworld.com

Chattan Hall ♦♦♦♦♦
Woodbury Lane, Axminster, EX13 5TL
T: (01297) 32365
F: (01297) 32365
E: boston@chattanhall.co.uk
I: www.chatanhall.co.uk

Coaxdon Farm ♦♦♦♦
Axminster, EX13 7LP
T: (01297) 35540

Kerrington House Hotel
♦♦♦♦♦ SILVER AWARD
Musbury Road, Axminster, EX13 5JR
T: (01297) 35333
E: ja.reaney@kerringtonhouse.com

BABBACOMBE
Devon

Astral Palms Hotel
Rating Applied For
2 York Road, Babbacombe, Torquay TQ1 3SG
T: (01803) 327087
F: (01803) 329446
E: enquiries@inter-docs.co.uk
I: www.astralpalms.co.uk

Birch Tor ♦♦♦
315 Babbacombe Road, Babbacombe, Torquay TQ1 3TB
T: (01803) 292707
E: terry@birchtor.co.uk
I: www.birchtor.co.uk

Regency Hotel ♦♦♦♦
33,35 Babbacombe Downs Road, Babbacombe, Torquay TQ1 3LN
T: (01803) 323509
F: (01803) 323509
E: theregency@hotmail.com
I: www.regencytorquay.co.uk

Seabury Hotel ♦♦♦♦
Manor Road, Babbacombe, Torquay TQ1 3JX
T: (01803) 327255
F: (01803) 315321

BACKWELL
North Somerset

Moorlands ♦♦♦♦
Backwell Hill, Backwell, Bristol BS48 3EJ
T: (01275) 462755
E: moorlandsguesthouse@yahoo.co.uk

BAMPTON
Devon

Bampton Gallery ♦♦♦♦
2-4 Brook Street, Bampton, Tiverton EX16 9LY
T: (01398) 331354
F: (01398) 331119
E: bampgall@aol.com
I: www.exmoortourism.org/bamptongallery.htm

Lodfin Farm Bed & Breakfast
♦♦♦♦
Morebath, Bampton, Tiverton EX16 9DD
T: (01398) 331400
F: (01398) 331400
E: lodfin.farm@eclipse.co.uk
I: www.lodfinfarm.com

Manor Mill House
♦♦♦♦ SILVER AWARD
Bampton, Tiverton EX16 9LP
T: (01398) 332211
F: (01398) 332009
E: stay@manormill.demon.co.uk
I: www.manormill.demon.co.uk

BARBROOK
Devon

West Lyn Farmhouse ♦♦♦♦
Barbrook, Lynton EX35 6LD
T: (01598) 753618
F: (01598) 753618
E: info@westlynfarm.co.uk
I: www.westlynfarm.co.uk

BARFORD ST MARTIN
Wiltshire

Briden House ♦♦♦♦
West Street, Barford St Martin, Salisbury SP3 4AH
T: (01722) 743471
F: (01722) 743471
E: bridenhouse@barford25.freeserve.co.uk
I: www.smoothhound.co.uk/hotels/bridenho.html

BARNSTAPLE
Devon

Bradiford Cottage ♦♦♦♦
Bradiford, Barnstaple EX31 4DP
T: (01271) 345039
F: (01271) 345039
E: tony@humesfarm.co.uk
I: www.humesfarm.co.uk

Little Orchard ♦♦♦
Braunton Road, Barnstaple, EX31 1GA
T: (01271) 371714
F: (01271) 342590
E: terrychaplin@accanet.com

The Red House ♦♦♦♦
Brynsworthy, Roundswell, Barnstaple EX31 3NP
T: (01271) 345966
F: (01271) 379966
E: booking@theredhousenorthdevon.co.uk
I: www.theredhousenorthdevon.co.uk

The Spinney
♦♦♦♦ SILVER AWARD
Shirwell, Barnstaple EX31 4JR
T: (01271) 850282
E: thespinny@shirwell.fsnet.co.uk
I: www.thespinneyshirwell.co.uk

Waytown Farm ♦♦♦♦
Shirwell, Barnstaple EX31 4JN
T: (01271) 850396
F: (01271) 850396
E: info@waytownholidays.co.uk
I: www.waytownholidays.co.uk

BASONBRIDGE
Somerset

Merry Farm ♦♦♦♦
Merry Lane, Basonbridge, Highbridge TA9 3PS
T: (01278) 783655
E: janetdearing@aol.com

BATCOMBE
Somerset

Home Farm ♦♦♦♦
Batcombe, Shepton Mallet BA4 6HF
T: (01749) 850303
F: (01749) 850540
E: christopher.frederick@virgin.net

Valley View Farm ♦♦♦
Batcombe, Shepton Mallet BA4 6AJ
T: (01749) 850302
F: (01749) 850302
E: valleyviewfarm@lineone.net

BATH
Bath and North East Somerset

Abbey Rise ♦♦♦♦
97 Wells Road, Bath, BA2 3AN
T: (01225) 316177
F: (01225) 316177
E: b+b@abbeyrise.co.uk

Abbot House ♦♦♦
168 Newbridge Road, Bath, BA1 3LE
T: (01225) 314151
F: (01225) 314151
E: sandra.ashley@btinternet.com
I: www.abbothouseguesthouse.co.uk

The Albany Guest House
♦♦♦♦ SILVER AWARD
24 Crescent Gardens, Upper Bristol Road, Bath, BA1 2NB
T: (01225) 313339
E: the_albany@lineone.net
I: www.bath.org/hotel/albany.htm

Apartment 1 ♦♦♦
60 Great Pulteney Street, Bath, BA2 4DN
T: (01225) 464134
F: (01225) 483663
E: chanloosmith@aptone.fsnet.co.uk

Aquae Sulis Hotel ♦♦♦♦
174/176 Newbridge Road, Bath, BA1 3LE
T: (01225) 420061
F: (01225) 446077
E: enquiries@aquaesulishotel.com
I: www.aquaesulishotel.com

Ashley House ♦♦♦
8 Pulteney Gardens, Bath, BA2 4HG
T: (01225) 425027

Ashley Villa Hotel ♦♦♦♦
26 Newbridge Road, Bath, BA1 3JZ
T: (01225) 421683
F: (01225) 313604
E: ashleyvilla@clearface.co.uk
I: www.ashleyvilla.co.uk

Astor House ♦♦♦♦
14 Oldfield Road, Bath, BA2 3ND
T: (01225) 429134
F: (01225) 429134
E: astorhouse.visitus@virgin.net

Athelney Guest House ♦♦♦
5 Marlborough Lane, Bath, BA1 2NQ
T: (01225) 312031
F: (01225) 312031
E: colin-davies@supanet.com
I: www.bath.org/hotel/athelney.htm

Athole Guest House
♦♦♦♦♦ SILVER AWARD
33 Upper Oldfield Park, Bath, BA2 3JX
T: (01225) 334307
F: (01225) 320000
E: info@atholehouse.co.uk
I: www.atholehouse.co.uk

Avon Guest House ♦♦
1 Pulteney Gardens, Bath, BA2 4HG
T: (01225) 313009
F: (01225) 313009

Ayrlington Hotel
♦♦♦♦♦ GOLD AWARD
24/25 Pulteney Road, Bath, BA2 4EZ
T: (01225) 425495
F: (01225) 469029
E: mail@ayrlington.com
I: www.ayrlington.com

Badminton Villa
♦♦♦♦ SILVER AWARD
10 Upper Oldfield Park, Bath, BA2 3JZ
T: (01225) 426347
F: (01225) 420393
E: badmintonvilla@blueyonder.co.uk
I: www.smoothhound.co.uk/hotels/badmintn.html

Bailbrook Lodge Hotel ♦♦♦
35/37 London Road West, Bath, BA1 7HZ
T: (01225) 859090
F: (01225) 852299
E: hotel@bailbrooklodge.demon.co.uk
I: www.bailbrooklodge.demon.co.uk

Bay Tree House ♦♦♦♦
12 Crescent Gardens, Bath, BA1 2NA
T: (01225) 483699
F: (01225) 483699
E: enquires@bay-tree-house.fsnet.co.uk
I: www.wherenow.net/baytree

The Belmont ♦♦♦
7 Belmont, Lansdown Road, Bath, BA1 5DZ
T: (01225) 423082
E: archie_watson@hotmail.com

The Belvedere Wine Vaults
Rating Applied For
25 Belvedere, Lansdown Road, Bath, BA1 5ED
T: (01225) 330264
E: thebelvedere.bath@virgin.net
I: www.thebelvedere-bath.co.uk

Bloomfield House
♦♦♦♦♦ SILVER AWARD
146 Bloomfield Road, Bath, BA2 2AS
T: (01225) 420105
E: bloomfieldhouse@compuserve.com
I: www.bloomfield-house.co.uk

16 Bloomfield Road ♦♦♦
Bear Flat, Bath, BA2 2AB
T: (01225) 337804

Bridgnorth House ♦♦♦♦
2 Crescent Gardens, Bath, BA1 2NA
T: (01225) 331186

Brinsley Sheridan House
♦♦♦♦
95 Wellsway, Bear Flat, Bath, BA2 4RU
T: (01225) 429562
E: post@sheridan-house.com
I: www.sheridan-house.com

Brompton House ♦♦♦♦
St John's Road, Bath, BA2 6PT
T: (01225) 420972
F: (01225) 420505
E: bromptonhouse@btinternet.com
I: www.bromptonhouse.co.uk

Carfax Hotel ♦♦♦♦
Great Pulteney Street, Bath, BA2 4BS
T: (01225) 462089
F: (01225) 443257
E: reservations@carfaxhotel.co.uk
I: www.carfaxhotel.co.uk

Cherry Tree Villa ♦♦♦
7 Newbridge Hill, Bath, BA1 3PW
T: (01225) 331671

Chesterfield House ♦♦♦
11 Great Pulteney Street, Bath, BA2 4BR
T: (01225) 460953
F: (01225) 448770
E: info@chesterfieldhouse.com
I: www.chesterfieldhouse.com

Church Farm ♦♦♦
Monkton Farleigh, Bradford-on-Avon BA15 2QJ
T: (01225) 858583
F: (01225) 852474
E: rebecca@tuckerb.fsnet.co.uk
I: www.tuckerb.fsnet.co.uk

Corston Fields Farm ♦♦♦♦
Corston, Bath BA2 9EZ
T: (01225) 873305
E: corston.fields@btinternet.com
I: www.corstonfields.com

County Hotel
♦♦♦♦♦ GOLD AWARD
18-19 Pulteney Road, Bath, BA2 4EZ
T: (01225) 425003
F: (01225) 466493
E: reservations@county-hotel.co.uk
I: www.county-hotel.co.uk

Crescent Guest House ♦♦♦
21 Crescent Gardens, Bath, BA1 2NA
T: (01225) 425945

Edgar Hotel ♦♦♦
64 Great Pulteney Street, Bath, BA2 4DN
T: (01225) 420619
F: (01225) 466916

Elgin Villa ♦♦♦♦
6 Marlborough Lane, Bath, BA1 2NQ
T: (01225) 424557
F: (01225) 424557
E: stay@elginvilla.co.uk
I: www.elginvilla.co.uk

The Firs ♦♦♦♦
2 Newbridge Hill, Bath, BA1 3PU
T: (01225) 334575

Flaxley Villa ♦♦♦
9 Newbridge Hill, Bath, BA1 3PW
T: (01225) 313237

Forres House ♦♦♦
172 Newbridge Road, Bath, BA1 3LE
T: (01225) 427698
F: (01225) 338350
E: Jj.forres@btinternet.co.uk
I: www.forreshouse.co.uk

The Gainsborough ♦♦♦♦
Weston Lane, Bath, BA1 4AB
T: (01225) 311380
F: (01225) 447411
E: gainsborough_hotel@compuserve.com
I: www.gainsboroughhotel.co.uk

Glan Y Dwr ♦♦♦
14 Newbridge Hill, Bath, BA1 3PU
T: (01225) 317521
F: (01225) 317521
E: glanydwr@hotmail.com

Glen View ♦♦♦♦
162 Newbridge Road, Bath, BA1 3LE
T: (01225) 421376
F: (01225) 310271
E: info@glenviewbath.co.uk
I: www.glenviewbath.co.uk

Glentworth
♦♦♦♦ SILVER AWARD
12 Marlborough Lane, Bath, BA1 2NQ
T: (01225) 334554
F: (01225) 425239
E: stay@glentworth.co.uk
I: www.glentworthbath.co.uk

Grove Lodge
Rating Applied For
11 Lambridge, Bath, BA1 6BJ
T: (01225) 310860
F: (01225) 429630
E: grovelodge@bath24.fsnet.co.uk

Hatt Farm ♦♦♦♦
Old Jockey, Box, Corsham SN13 8DJ
T: (01225) 742989
F: (01225) 742779
E: hattfarm@netlineuk.net

Haydon House
♦♦♦♦♦ SILVER AWARD
9 Bloomfield Park, Bath, BA2 2BY
T: (01225) 444919
F: (01225) 444919
E: stay@haydonhouse.co.uk
I: www.haydonhouse.co.uk

Henrietta Hotel ♦♦♦
32 Henrietta Street, Bath, BA2 6LR
T: (01225) 447779
F: (01225) 444150
I: www.smoothound.co.uk

Hermitage ♦♦♦
Bath Road, Box, Corsham SN13 8DT
T: (01225) 744187
F: (01225) 743447
E: hermitage@telecall.co.uk

Highfields ♦♦♦♦♦
207 Bailbrook Lane, Batheaston, Bath BA1 7AB
T: (01225) 859782
E: acham@supanet.com

Highways House ♦♦♦♦
143 Wells Road, Bath, BA2 3AL
T: (01225) 421238
F: (01225) 481169
E: stay@highwayshouse.co.uk
I: www.highwayshouse.co.uk

The Hollies ♦♦♦♦
Hatfield Road, Bath, BA2 2BD
T: (01225) 313366
F: (01225) 313366
E: davcartwright@lineone.net
I: www.visitus.co.uk/bath/hotel.hollies.html

Holly Lodge
♦♦♦♦♦ SILVER AWARD
8 Upper Oldfield Park, Bath, BA2 3JZ
T: (01225) 424042
F: (01225) 481138
E: stay@hollylodge.co.uk
I: www.hollylodge.co.uk

Kennard Hotel
♦♦♦♦♦ SILVER AWARD
11 Henrietta Street, Bath, BA2 6LL
T: (01225) 310472
F: (01225) 460054
E: reception@kennard.co.uk
I: www.kennard.co.uk

Kinlet Villa Guest House
♦♦♦♦
99 Wellsway, Bath, BA2 4RX
T: (01225) 420268
F: (01225) 420268
E: kinlet@inbath.freeserve.co.uk
I: www.visitus.co.uk/bath/hotel/kinlet.htm

Lamp Post Villa ♦♦♦
3 Crescent Gardens, Upper Bristol Road, Bath, BA1 2NA
T: (01225) 331221
F: (01225) 426783

Laura Place Hotel ♦♦♦♦
3 Laura Place, Great Pulteney Street, Bath, BA2 4BH
T: (01225) 463815
F: (01225) 310222

Lavender House
♦♦♦♦♦ SILVER AWARD
17 Bloomfield Park, Bath, BA2 2BY
T: (01225) 314500
F: (01225) 448564
E: lavenderhouse@btintenet.com
I: www.lavenderhouse-bath.com

Leighton House
♦♦♦♦♦ GOLD AWARD
139 Wells Road, Bath, BA2 3AL
T: (01225) 314769
F: (01225) 443079
E: welcome@leighton-house.co.uk
I: www.leighton-house.co.uk

Lilac Cottage ♦♦
Gurney Slade, Bath, BA3 4TT
T: (01749) 840469
E: lilaccotbandb@aol.com

Lindisfarne Guest House
♦♦♦♦
41a Warminster Road, Bathampton, Bath BA2 6XJ
T: (01225) 466342
F: (01225) 444062
E: lindisfarne-bath@talk21.com
I: www.bath.org/hotel/lindisfarne.htm

The Manor House ♦♦♦
Mill Lane, Monkton Combe, Bath BA2 7HD
T: (01225) 723128
F: (01225) 722972
E: beth@manorhousebath.co.uk
I: www.manorhousebath.co.uk

Marisha's Guest House ♦♦♦
68 Newbridge Hill, Bath, BA1 3QA
T: (01225) 446881
F: (01225) 446881
E: marishasinbath@amserve.net

Marlborough House ♦♦♦♦
1 Marlborough Lane, Bath, BA1 2NQ
T: (01225) 318175
F: (01225) 466127
E: mars@manque.dircon.co.uk
I: www.marlborough-house.net

Meadowland
♦♦♦♦♦ GOLD AWARD
36 Bloomfield Park, Bath, BA2 2BX
T: (01225) 311079
F: (01225) 311079
E: meadowland@bath92.freeserve.co.uk
I: www.meadowlandbath.co.uk

Membland Guest House ♦♦♦
7 Pulteney Terrace, Pulteney Road, Bath, BA2 4HJ
T: 07958 599572
E: prmoore@wimpey.co.uk

Midway Cottage ♦♦♦♦
Farleigh Wick, Bradford-on-Avon BA15 2PU
T: (01225) 863932
F: (01225) 866836
E: midway_cottage@hotmail.com

Milton Guest House ♦♦♦♦
75 Wellsway, Bear Flat, Bath, BA2 4RU
T: (01225) 335632
E: sue@milton-house.fsnet.co.uk
I: www.milton-house.fsnet.co.uk

Monkshill
♦♦♦♦♦ GOLD AWARD
Shaft Road, Monkton Combe, Bath BA2 7HL
T: (01225) 833028
F: (01225) 833028
E: monks.hill@virgin.net
I: www.monkshill.com

Number 30 Crescent Gardens
♦♦♦♦
Bath, BA1 2NB
T: (01225) 337393
F: (01225) 337393
E: david.greenwood12@btinternet.com
I: www.numberthirty.co.uk

Parkside ♦♦♦♦
11 Marlborough Lane, Bath, BA1 2NQ
T: (01225) 429444
F: (01225) 429444
E: parkside@lynall.freeserve.co.uk
I: www.visitus.co.uk/bath/hotel/parkside.html

Poplar Farm ♦♦♦
Stanton Prior, Bath BA2 9HX
T: (01761) 470382
F: (01761) 470382
E: poplarfarm@talk21.com

Pulteney Hotel ♦♦♦
14 Pulteney Road, Bath, BA2 4HA
T: (01225) 460991
F: (01225) 460991
E: pulteney@tinyworld.co.uk
I: www.pulteneyhotel.co.uk

14 Raby Place ♦♦♦♦
Bathwick Hill, Bath, BA2 4EH
T: (01225) 465120

Radnor Guesthouse ♦♦♦♦
9 Pulteney Terrace, Pulteney Road, Bath, BA2 4HJ
T: (01225) 316159
F: (01225) 319199
E: radnor@bath10.freeserve.co.uk
I: www.bath.org/hotel/radnor.htm

Ravenscroft
♦♦♦♦ SILVER AWARD
Sydney Road, Bath, BA2 6NT
T: (01225) 469267
F: (01225) 448722
E: chmbaker@gatewayuk.net

Roman City Guest House
♦♦♦♦
18 Raby Place, Bathwick Hill, Bath, BA2 4EH
T: (01225) 463668
E: romancityguesthse@amserve.net
I: www.romancityguesthouse.co.uk

Royal Park Guest House ♦♦
16 Crescent Gardens, Upper Bristol Road, Bath, BA1 2NA
T: (01225) 317651
F: (01225) 483950
E: royal@parkb-b.freeserve.co.uk

St Georges Cottage ♦♦♦♦
Bathampton Lane, Bath, BA2 6SJ
T: (01225) 466801
F: (01225) 426073
E: stgeorgescottage@aol.com
I: www.stgeorgescottagebath.co.uk

St Leonards
♦♦♦♦ SILVER AWARD
Warminster Road, Bathampton, Bath BA2 6SQ
T: (01225) 465838
F: (01225) 442800
E: stleon@dircon.co.uk
I: www.smoothhound.co.uk/hotels/stleonar.html

Sampford ♦♦
11 Oldfield Road, Bath, BA2 3ND
T: (01225) 310053
E: robert.dolby@btinternet.com

Stoke Bottom Farm ♦♦
Stoke St Michael, Bath BA3 5HW
T: (01761) 232273

Toghill House Farm ♦♦♦♦
Wick, Bristol BS30 5RT
T: (01225) 891261
F: (01225) 892128
I: www.toghillhousefarm.co.uk

The Town House
♦♦♦♦ SILVER AWARD
7 Bennett Street, Bath, BA1 2QJ
T: (01225) 422505

Villa Magdala Hotel
♦♦♦♦ GOLD AWARD
Henrietta Road, Bath, BA2 6LX
T: (01225) 466329
F: (01225) 483207
E: office@villamagdala.co.uk
I: www.villamagdala.co.uk

Walton Villa ♦♦♦♦
3 Newbridge Hill, Bath, BA1 3PW
T: (01225) 482792
F: (01225) 313093
E: walton.villa@virgin.net
I: www.walton.izest.com

Wellsway Guest House ♦♦
51 Wellsway, Bath, BA2 4RS
T: (01225) 423434

The Wheatsheaf Inn ♦♦♦♦
Combe Hay, Bath BA2 7EG
T: (01225) 833504
F: (01225) 833504
I: www.the-wheatsheaf.freeserve.co.uk

Wheelwrights Arms ♦♦
Monkton Combe, Bath BA2 7HB
T: (01225) 722287
F: (01225) 723029
E: debbie@gillespie.fslife.co.uk
I: www.yell.co.uk/sites/the-wheelwright-arms/

BATHEASTON
Bath and North East Somerset

Brook Lodge ♦♦♦♦
199 London Road East, Batheaston, Bath BA1 7NB
T: (01225) 851158
F: (01225) 851158
E: bobmatthews@netscapeonline.co.uk

BATHFORD
Bath and North East Somerset

Garston Cottage ♦♦♦
28 Ashley Road, Bathford, Bath BA1 7TT
T: (01225) 852510
F: (01225) 852793
E: garstoncot@aol.com
I: www.garstoncottage.freeservers.com

The Lodge Hotel ♦♦♦♦
Bathford Hill, Bathford, Bath BA1 7SL
T: (01225) 858467
F: (01225) 858172
E: lodgethe@aol.com
I: www.lodgehotelbath.co.uk

BATHWICK
Bath and North East Somerset

Greenways ♦♦♦
1 Forester Road, Bathwick, Bath
BA2 6QF
T: (01225) 310132
F: (01225) 310132
E: greenways@supanet.com
I: www.greenwaysbath.co.uk

Ravenscroft
♦♦♦♦ GOLD AWARD
North Road, Bathwick, Bath
BA2 6HZ
T: (01225) 461919
F: (01225) 461919
E: patrick@ravenscroftbandb.co.uk
I: www.ravenscroftbandb.co.uk

BAWDRIP
Somerset

Kings Farm ♦♦♦
10 Eastside Lane, Bawdrip, Bridgwater TA7 8QB
T: (01278) 683233

BEAMINSTER
Dorset

Beam Cottage ♦♦♦♦
16 North Street, Beaminster, DT8 3DZ
T: (01308) 863639
E: margie@beam-cottage.fsnt.co.uk

Jenny Wrens ♦♦♦
1 Hogshill Street, Beaminster, DT8 3AE
T: (01308) 862814
F: (01308) 861191

Kitwhistle Farm ♦♦♦
Beaminster Down, Beaminster, DT8 3SG
T: (01308) 862458
F: (01308) 862 458

North Buckham Farm ♦♦♦
Beaminster, DT8 3SH
T: (01308) 863054
F: (01308) 863054
E: andrew@northbuckham.fsnet.co.uk

Slape Hill Barn ♦♦♦♦
Waytown, Bridport DT6 5LQ
T: (01308) 488429

The Walnuts
♦♦♦♦ SILVER AWARD
2 Prout Bridge, Beaminster, DT8 3AY
T: (01308) 862211

Water Meadow House
♦♦♦♦ SILVER AWARD
Bridge Farm, Hooke, Beaminster
DT8 3PD
T: (01308) 862619
F: (01308) 862619
E: enquiries@watermeadowhouse.co.uk
I: www.watermeadowhouse.co.uk

BEANACRE
Wiltshire

Beechfield House
♦♦♦♦♦ SILVER AWARD
Beanacre, Melksham SN12 7PU
T: (01225) 703700
F: (01225) 790118
E: csm@beechfieldhouse.co.uk
I: www.beechfieldhouse.co.uk

BECKINGTON
Somerset

Eden Vale Farm ♦♦♦
Mill Lane, Beckington, Bath
BA11 6SN
T: (01373) 830371
F: (01373) 831233

BELSTONE
Devon

The Cleave House ♦♦♦♦
Belstone, Okehampton
EX20 1QY
T: (01837) 840055
I: www.caterham.force9.co.uk/cleavehouse.htm

BERROW
Somerset

Berrow Links House
♦♦♦♦ SILVER AWARD
Coast Road, Berrow, Burnham-on-Sea TA8 2QS
T: (01278) 751422

Yew Tree House
♦♦♦♦ SILVER AWARD
Hurn Lane, Berrow, Burnham-on-Sea TA8 2QT
T: (01278) 751382
F: (01278) 751382
E: yewtree@yewtree-house.co.uk
I: www.yewtree-house.co.uk
♿

BERRY POMEROY
Devon

Berry Farm ♦♦♦♦
Berry Pomeroy, Totnes TQ9 6LG
T: (01803) 863231

BERRYNARBOR
Devon

Langleigh House ♦♦♦
The Village, Berrynarbor, Ilfracombe EX34 9SG
T: (01271) 883410
F: (01271) 882396
E: langleigh@hotmail.com

The Lodge ♦♦♦♦
Pitt Hill, Berrynarbor, Ilfracombe
EX34 9SG
T: (01271) 883246
F: (01271) 882984
E: teem.mabin@virgin.net
I: www.thelodgeberrynarbor.co.uk

Mill Park House ♦♦♦♦
Mill Lane, Berrynarbor, Ilfracombe EX34 9SH
T: (01271) 882990
F: (01271) 882682
E: ian_smith@millparkhouse.freeserve.co.uk
I: www.millparkhouse.freeserve.co.uk

BIDDESTONE
Wiltshire

The Granary ♦♦♦
Cuttle Lane, Biddestone, Chippenham SN14 7DA
T: (01249) 715077
E: penny.lloyd@virgin.net
I: freespace.virgin.net/penny.lloyd

Home Farm ♦♦♦♦
Harts Lane, Biddestone, Chippenham SN14 7DQ
T: (01249) 714475
F: (01249) 701488
E: audrey.smith@homefarmbandb.co.uk
I: www.homefarmbandb.co.uk

Home Place ♦♦
The Green, Biddestone, Chippenham SN14 7DG
T: (01249) 712928

BIDEFORD
Devon

Bulworthy Cottage ♦♦♦♦
Stony Cross, Bideford, EX39 4PY
T: (01271) 858441
E: bulworthy@aol.com

The Mount ♦♦♦♦
Northdown Road, Bideford, EX39 3LP
T: (01237) 473748
F: (01271) 342268
E: andrew@themountbideford.fsnet.co.uk
I: www.themount1.cjb.net

The Orchard Hill Hotel ♦♦♦
Orchard Hill, Bideford, EX39 2QY
T: (01237) 472872
F: (01237) 423803
E: info@orchardhillhotel.co.uk
I: www.orchardhillhotel.co.uk

Sunset Hotel ♦♦♦
Landcross, Bideford EX39 5JA
T: (01237) 472962
F: (01237) 422520
E: hazellamb@hotmail.com

BILBROOK
Somerset

Steps Farmhouse ♦♦♦♦
Bilbrook, Minehead TA24 6HE
T: (01984) 640974
E: info@stepsfarmhouse.co.uk
I: www.stepsfarmhouse.co.uk

BINEGAR
Somerset

Mansefield House
♦♦♦♦ SILVER AWARD
Binegar, Shepton Mallet
BA3 4UG
T: (01749) 840568
F: (01749) 840572
E: mansfieldhouse@aol.com

BISHOP SUTTON
Bath and North East Somerset

Centaur ♦♦♦
Ham Lane, Bishop Sutton, Bristol
BS39 5TZ
T: (01275) 332321

Withymede ♦♦♦♦
The Street, Bishop Sutton, Bristol BS39 5UU
T: (01275) 332069

BISHOP'S LYDEARD
Somerset

The Kingfisher ♦♦♦
Taunton Road, Bishop's Lydeard, Taunton TA4 3LR
T: (01823) 432394
E: ivor@kingfisherinn.co.uk
I: www.kingfisherinn.co.uk

The Lethbridge Arms ♦♦♦
Gore Square, Bishop's Lydeard, Taunton TA4 3BW
T: (01823) 432234
F: (01823) 433982
E: phutchings@tinyworld.co.uk

West View ♦♦♦♦
Minehead Road, Bishop's Lydeard, Taunton TA4 3BS
T: (01823) 432223
F: (01823) 432223
E: westview@pattemore.freeserve.co.uk

BISHOPS HULL
Somerset

The Old Mill
♦♦♦♦♦ SILVER AWARD
Roughmoor, Bishops Hull, Taunton TA1 5AB
T: (01823) 289732
F: (01823) 289732

BISHOPSTON
Bristol

Basca Guest House ♦♦♦
19 Broadway Road, Bishopston, Bristol BS7 8ES
T: (0117) 9422182

BLACK DOG
Devon

Hele Barton Farm Guest House
♦♦♦
Black Dog, Crediton EX17 4QJ
T: (01884) 860278
F: (01884) 860278
E: gillbard@eclipse.co.uk
I: www.eclipse.co.uk/helebarton

BLACKAWTON
Devon

The Normandy Arms ♦♦♦♦
Chapel Street, Blackawton, Totnes TQ9 7BN
T: (01803) 712316
F: (01803) 712191
E: normandyarms@hotmail.com

BLUE ANCHOR
Somerset

Camelot ♦♦♦
Carhampton Road, Blue Anchor, Minehead TA24 6LB
T: (01643) 821348
E: d.thrush@btinternet.com

The Langbury ♦♦♦
Blue Anchor, Minehead
TA24 6LB
T: (01643) 821375
F: (01643) 822012
E: post@langbury.co.uk
I: www.langbury.co.uk

BODMIN
Cornwall

Agan Chy ♦♦♦
68 Castle Street, Bodmin, PL31 2DY
T: (01208) 75339
F: (01208) 75339
E: agan.chy@btinternet.com

Bedknobs ♦♦♦♦
Polgwyn, Castle Street, Bodmin, PL31 2DX
T: (01208) 77553
F: (01208) 77885
E: gill@bedknobs.co.uk
I: www.bedknobs.co.uk

Bokiddick Farm
♦♦♦♦♦ SILVER AWARD
Lanivet, Bodmin PL30 5HP
T: (01208) 831481
F: (01208) 831481
E: gillhugo@bokiddickfarm.co.uk
I: www.bokiddickfarm.co.uk

Establishments printed in blue have a detailed entry in this guide

Hotel Casi Casa ♦♦♦
11 Higher Bore Street, Bodmin, PL3 1JS
T: (01208) 77592
F: (01208) 75771
E: casi@casa30.fsnet.co.uk
I: www.cornwall-online.co.uk/casicasa

Colliford Tavern ♦♦♦♦
Colliford Lake, St Neot, Liskeard PL14 6PZ
T: (01208) 821335
F: (01208) 821335
E: colliford@hotmail.com
I: www.colliford.com

Elm Grove ♦♦♦
1 'Elm Grove', Cardell Road, Bodmin, PL31 2NJ
T: (01208) 74044

Higher Windsor Cottage ♦♦♦♦
18 Castle Street, Bodmin, PL31 2DU
T: (01208) 76474
E: johntrishpencheon@tinyworld.co.uk
I: www.higherwindsorcottage.co.uk

The Old School House ♦♦♦♦
Averys Green, Cardinham, Bodmin PL30 4EA
T: (01208) 821303
E: libby@pidcock18.freeserve.co.uk

Priory Cottage Bed & Breakfast ♦♦♦
34 Rhind Street, Bodmin, PL31 2EL
T: (01208) 73064
F: (01208) 73064
E: jackiedingle@yahoo.com

Trebray House ♦♦♦
8 Cross Lane, Bodmin, PL31 2EJ
T: (01208) 73007
F: (01208) 73190
E: beelew@clara.net
I: www.beelew.clara.net/trebray.html

BOLVENTOR
Cornwall

Jamaica Inn ♦♦♦
Bolventor, Launceston PL15 7TS
T: (01566) 86250
F: (01566) 86177
E: jamaicainn@eclipse.co.uk

BOSCASTLE
Cornwall

Bridge House ♦♦♦
Boscastle, PL35 0HE
T: (01840) 250011
F: (01840) 250860

The Harbour Restaurant ♦♦♦♦♦
Riverside Walk, Boscastle, PL35 0HD
T: (01840) 250380

The Old Coach House ♦♦♦♦
Tintagel Road, Boscastle, PL35 0AS
T: (01840) 250398
F: (01840) 250346
E: parsons@old-coach.co.uk
I: www.old-coach.co.uk

Reddivallen Farmhouse ♦♦♦♦
Reddivallen Farm, Trevalga, Boscastle, PL35 0EE
T: (01840) 250854
F: (01840) 250854

St Christopher's Hotel ♦♦♦
High Street, Boscastle, PL35 0BD
T: (01840) 250412

Tolcarne House Hotel and Restaurant ♦♦♦♦
Tintagel Road, Boscastle, PL35 0AS
T: (01840) 250654
F: (01840) 250654
E: crowntolhouse@eclipse.co.uk
I: www.milford.co.uk/go/tolcarne

Trefoil Farm ♦♦♦
Camelford Road, Boscastle, PL35 0AD
T: (01840) 250606

Tregatherall Farm ♦♦♦
Boscastle, PL35 0EQ
T: (01840) 250277

Tremorvah B&B ♦♦♦
Fore Street, Boscastle, PL35 0AU
T: (01840) 250636
F: (01840) 250616
E: jdrawingboard@aol.com
I: www.cornwall-online.co.uk/tremorvah

Trerosewill Farmhouse ♦♦♦♦♦ SILVER AWARD
Paradise, Boscastle, PL35 0BL
T: (01840) 250545
F: (01840) 250545
E: trerosewill@ipl.co.uk
I: www.trerosewill.co.uk

Valency ♦♦♦
Penally Hill, Boscastle, PL35 0HF
T: (01840) 250397

BOSSINGTON
Somerset

Buckley Lodge ♦♦♦♦
Bossington, Minehead TA24 8HQ
T: (01643) 862521
E: bucklodgeuk@yahoo.co.uk

BOVEY TRACEY
Devon

Brookfield House ♦♦♦♦♦
Challabrook Lane, Bovey Tracey, Newton Abbot TQ13 9DF
T: (01626) 836181
F: (01626) 836182
E: brookfieldh@tinyworld.co.uk
I: www.brookfield-house.com

The Cromwell Arms Hotel ♦♦♦♦
Fore Street, Bovey Tracey, Newton Abbot TQ13 9AE
T: (01626) 833473
F: (01626) 836873

Frost Farmhouse ♦♦♦
Frost Farm, Hennock Road, Bovey Tracey, Newton Abbot TQ13 9PP
T: (01626) 833266
F: (01626) 833266
E: linda@frostfarm.co.uk
I: www.frostfarm.co.uk

BOX
Wiltshire

Lorne House ♦♦♦♦
London Road, Box, Corsham SN13 8NA
T: (01225) 742597
E: lornehousebandb@aol.com
I: www.lornehouse.net

Norbin Farmhouse ♦♦♦♦
Box, Corsham SN13 8JJ
T: (01225) 866907
E: gillhillier@yahoo.co.uk

BRADFORD ABBAS
Dorset

Purbeck House ♦♦♦♦
North Street, Bradford Abbas, Sherborne DT9 6SA
T: (01935) 474817

BRADFORD-ON-AVON
Wiltshire

The Beeches Farmhouse ♦♦♦♦♦
Holt Road, Bradford-on-Avon, BA15 1TS
T: (01225) 863475
F: (01225) 863996
E: beeches-farmhouse@netgates.co.uk
I: www.beeches-farmhouse.co.uk

Great Ashley Farm ♦♦♦♦ SILVER AWARD
Ashley Lane, Bradford-on-Avon, BA15 2PP
T: (01225) 864563
F: (01225) 309117
E: greatashleyfarm@farmersweekly.net
I: www.greatashleyfarm.co.uk

The Great Barn Maplecroft Bed and Breakfast Rating Applied For
Leigh Road West, Maplecroft, Bradford-on-Avon, BA15 2RB
T: (01225) 868790
F: (01225) 868858
E: gbarn@freeserve.co.uk

Hillside Lodge Bed & Breakfast ♦♦♦♦♦
Hillside Lodge, Jones Hill, Bradford-on-Avon, BA15 2EE
T: (01225) 866312
F: (01225) 866312
E: barnes@hillsidelodge.fsnet.co.uk

Springfields ♦♦♦♦
182a Great Ashley, Bradford-on-Avon, BA15 2PP
T: (01225) 866125
E: christine.rawlings@farmersweekly.net
I: www.bed-and-breakfast.org

Widbrook Grange ♦♦♦♦♦
Trowbridge Road, Widbrook, Bradford-on-Avon, BA15 1UH
T: (01225) 864750
F: (01225) 862890
E: widgra@aol.com

Woodpeckers ♦♦♦♦
Holt Road, Bradford-on-Avon, BA15 1TR
T: (01225) 865616
F: (01225) 865615
E: b+b@wood-peckers.co.uk
I: www.wood-peckers.co.uk

BRADPOLE
Dorset

Spray Copse Farm ♦♦♦♦♦
Lee Lane, Bradpole, Bridport DT6 4AP
T: (01308) 458510
F: (01308) 421015
E: spraycopse@lineone.net
I: www.spraycopsefarm.com

BRATTON FLEMING
Devon

Bracken House Country Hotel ♦♦♦♦♦ GOLD AWARD
Bratton Fleming, Barnstaple EX31 4TG
T: (01598) 710320
F: (01598) 710115
E: holidays@brackenhousehotel.com
I: www.brackenhousehotel.com

Haxton Down Farm ♦♦♦♦
Bratton Fleming, Barnstaple EX32 7JL
T: (01598) 710275
F: (01598) 710275

BRAUNTON
Devon

Moorsands ♦♦♦
34 Moor Lane, Croyde Bay, Braunton, EX33 1NP
T: (01271) 890781
I: www.croyde-bay.com/moorsands.htm

BRAYFORD
Devon

Rockley Farmhouse ♦♦♦♦ SILVER AWARD
Brayford, Barnstaple EX32 7QR
T: (01598) 710429
F: (01598) 710429
E: info@rockleyfarmhouse.co.uk
I: www.rockleyfarmhouse.co.uk

BREAN
Somerset

Berrow Heath Guest House ♦♦♦
South Road, Brean, Burnham-on-Sea TA8 2RD
T: (01278) 751385
F: (01278) 751542
E: walter@robertprice.freeserve.co.uk

The Old Rectory Motel ♦♦♦
Church Road, Brean, Burnham-on-Sea TA8 2SF
T: (01278) 751447
F: (01278) 751800
I: www.old-rectory.fsbusiness.co.uk

BREMHILL
Wiltshire

Hilltop Farm ♦♦♦
Bremhill, Calne SN11 9HQ
T: (01249) 740620

BRENDON
Devon

Brendon House Hotel ♦♦♦
Brendon, Lynton EX35 6PS
T: (01598) 741206
E: dave@brendonhouse.freeserve.co.uk
I: www.brendonvalley.co.uk

BRENT KNOLL
Somerset

The Hawthorns ♦♦♦♦
Crooked Lane, Brent Knoll, Highbridge TA9 4BQ
T: (01278) 760181

BRIDESTOWE
Devon

Way Barton Barn ♦♦♦
Bridestowe, Okehampton EX20 4QH
T: (01837) 861513
E: jo.catling@btopenworld.com

BRIDGWATER
Somerset

Admirals Rest ♦♦♦
5 Taunton Road, Bridgwater, TA6 3LW
T: (01278) 458580
F: (01278) 458580
E: sueparker@admiralsrest.freeserve.co.uk
I: www.admiralsrest.co.uk

Ash-Wembdon Farm
♦♦♦♦ SILVER AWARD
Hollow Lane, Wembdon, Bridgwater TA5 2BD
T: (01278) 453097
F: (01278) 445856
E: mary.rowe@btinternet.com
I: www.farmaccommodation.co.uk

Brookland Hotel ♦♦♦
56 North Street, Bridgwater, TA6 3PN
T: (01278) 423263
F: (01278) 452988

Cokerhurst Farm ♦♦♦♦
87 Wembdon Hill, Bridgwater, TA6 7QA
T: (01278) 422330
F: (01278) 422330
E: cokerhurst@clara.net
I: www.cokerhurst.clara.net

Manor Farm ♦♦♦
Waterpitts, Broomfield, Bridgwater, TA5 1AT
T: (01823) 451266

Manor Farmhouse ♦♦♦
Wembdon, Bridgwater TA5 2BB
T: (01278) 427913

Model Farm ♦♦♦♦
Perry Green, Wembdon, Bridgwater TA5 2BA
T: (01278) 433999
E: info@modelfarm
I: www.modelfarm.com

Quantock View Guest House ♦♦♦
Bridgwater Road, North Petherton, Bridgwater TA6 6PR
T: (01278) 663309
E: irene@quantockview.freeserve.co.uk
I: www.smoothhound.co.uk/hotels/quantock

BRIDPORT
Dorset

Bridge House Hotel
Rating Applied For
115 East Street, Bridport, DT6 3LB
T: (01308) 423371
F: (01308) 423371
I: www.bridgehousebridport.co.uk

Britmead House ♦♦♦♦
West Bay Road, Bridport, DT6 4EG
T: (01308) 422941
F: (01308) 422516
E: britmead@talk21.com
I: www.britmeadhouse.co.uk

The Bull Hotel ♦♦
34 East Street, Bridport, DT6 3LF
T: (01308) 422878
F: (01308) 422878

Candida House ♦♦♦♦
Whitchurch Canonicorum, DT6 6RQ
T: (01297) 489629
F: (01297) 489629
E: candida@globalnet.co.uk
I: www.holidayaccom.com/candida-house.htm

Durbeyfield Guest House ♦♦♦
10 West Bay, West Bay, Bridport DT6 4EL
T: (01308) 423307
F: (01308) 423307
E: manager@durbeyfield.co.uk
I: www.durbeyfield.co.uk

Eypeleaze
♦♦♦♦ SILVER AWARD
117 West Bay Road, Bridport, DT6 4EQ
T: (01308) 423363
F: (01308) 420228
E: enquiries@eypeleaze.co.uk
I: www.eypeleaze.co.uk

New House Farm ♦♦♦
Mangerton Lane, Bradpole, Bridport DT6 3SF
T: (01308) 422884
F: (01308) 422884
E: jane@mangertonlake.freeserve.co.uk
I: www.mangertonlake.co.uk

Patchwork House ♦♦♦
47 Burton Road, Bridport, DT6 4JE
T: (01308) 456515
E: loveridge1@netlineuk.net

Polly's ♦♦♦♦
22 West Allington, Bridport, DT6 5BG
T: (01308) 458095
F: (01308) 421834
E: mail@hime.org.uk

Rudge Farm
♦♦♦♦♦ SILVER AWARD
Chilcombe, Bridport DT6 4NF
T: (01308) 482630
E: sue@rudgefarm.co.uk
I: www.rudgefarm.co.uk

Southcroft
♦♦♦♦ SILVER AWARD
Park Road, Bridport, DT6 5DA
T: (01308) 423335
F: (01308) 423335
E: info@southcroftguesthouse.com
I: www.southcroftguesthouse.com

Southview ♦♦♦
Whitecross, Netherbury, Bridport, DT6 5NH
T: (01308) 488471
E: southview@beeb.net
I: www.southviewbb.members.beeb.net

Urella ♦♦♦♦
65 Burton Road, Bridport, DT6 4JE
T: (01308) 422450
E: urella_uk@yahoo.co.uk
I: www.sparksoft.net/urella

The Well ♦♦♦
St Andrews Well, Bridport, DT6 3DL
T: (01308) 424156

BRISLINGTON
Bristol

The Beeches ♦♦♦♦
Broomhill Road, Brislington, Bristol BS4 5RG
T: (0117) 972 8778
F: (0117) 971 1968

Kingston House ♦♦
101 Hardenhuish Road, Brislington, Bristol BS4 3SR
T: (0117) 9712456

Woodstock ♦♦♦
534 Bath Road, Brislington, Bristol BS4 3JZ
T: (0117) 987 1613
F: (0117) 987 1613
E: woodstock@blueyonder.co.uk
I: www.homestead.com/wstock/

BRISTOL

A4 Hotel ♦♦♦
511 Bath Road, Brislington, Bristol BS4 3LA
T: (0117) 9715492
F: (0117) 9711791
E: a4hotel@lineone.net

Arches Hotel ♦♦♦
132 Cotham Brow, Cotham, Bristol BS6 6AE
T: (0117) 9247398
F: (0117) 9247398
E: ml@arches-hotel.co.uk
I: www.arches-hotel.co.uk

Cumberland Guest House ♦♦♦
6 Clift House Road, Ashton, Bristol BS3 1RY
T: (0117) 966 0810
F: (0117) 966 0810
E: cumberlandguesthouse@talk21.com

The Hunters Rest ♦♦♦♦
King Lane, Clutton Hill, Bristol, BS39 5QL
T: (01761) 452303
F: (01761) 453308
E: paul@huntersrest.co.uk
I: www.huntersrest.co.uk

Naseby House Hotel ♦♦♦
105 Pembroke Road, Clifton, Bristol BS8 3EF
T: (0117) 9737859
F: (0117) 9737859
I: www.nasebyhousehotel.co.uk

Norfolk House ♦♦
577 Gloucester Road, Horfield, Bristol, BS7 0BW
T: (0117) 9513191
F: (0117) 9513191

Oakfield Hotel ♦♦♦
52 Oakfield Road, Clifton, Bristol BS8 2BG
T: (0117) 973 5556
F: (0117) 974 4141

The Old Court
♦♦♦♦♦ SILVER AWARD
Main Road, Temple Cloud, Bristol BS39 5DA
T: (01761) 451101
F: (01761) 451224
E: oldcourt@gifford.co.uk
I: www.theoldcourt.com

The Paddock ♦♦♦
Hung Road, Shirehampton, Bristol BS11 9XJ
T: (0117) 9235140

Rowan Lodge Hotel ♦♦♦
41 Gloucester Road North, Filton Park, Bristol, BS7 0SN
T: (0117) 931 2170
F: (0117) 975 3601

Treborough ♦♦♦
3 Grove Road, Coombe Dingle, Bristol BS9 2RQ
T: (0117) 968 2712

Tricomo House B & B ♦♦♦
183 Cheltenham Road, Cotham, Bristol BS6 5RH
T: (0117) 9248082
F: (0117) 3735162
E: tricomohouse1@activemail.co.uk

Washington Hotel ♦♦♦
11-15 St Paul's Road, Clifton, Bristol, BS8 1LX
T: (0117) 973 3980
F: (0117) 973 4740
E: washington@cliftonhotels.com
I: www.cliftonhotels.com

BRIXHAM
Devon

Anchorage Guest House ♦♦♦♦
170 New Road, Brixham, TQ5 8DA
T: (01803) 852960
F: (01803) 852960

Black Cottage Guest House ♦♦♦
17 Milton Street, Brixham, TQ5 0BX
T: (01803) 853752

Brioc Hotel ♦♦♦
11 Prospect Road, Brixham, TQ5 8HS
T: (01803) 853540
E: bill@brioc-hotel.fsnet.co.uk
I: www.brioc-hotel.fsnet.co.uk

Lamorna ♦♦♦
130 New Road, Brixham, TQ5 8DA
T: (01803) 853954
E: lamornabrixham@aol.com

Melville Hotel ♦♦♦
45 New Road, Brixham, TQ5 8NL
T: (01803) 852033
E: melvillehotel@brixham45.fsnet.co.uk
I: www.smoothhound.co.uk/hotels.melville2.html

Raddicombe Lodge ♦♦♦♦
Kingswear Road, Brixham, TQ5 0EX
T: (01803) 882125
F: (01803) 882125
E: val-trev@raddicombe-fsbusiness.co.uk

Ranscombe House Hotel ♦♦♦♦
Ranscombe Road, Brixham, TQ5 9UP
T: (01803) 882337
F: (01803) 882337
E: ranscombe@lineone.net
I: www.RanscombeHouseHotel.co.uk

Redlands Hotel ♦♦♦
136 New Road, Brixham, TQ5 8DA
T: (01803) 853813
F: (01803) 853813
E: redlandsbrixham@aol.com
I: www.members.aol.com/redlandsbrixham/index.html

Richmond House Hotel ♦♦♦
Higher Manor Road, Brixham, TQ5 8HA
T: (01803) 882391
F: (01803) 882391
E: juliegiblett@richmondhse.hoteloneman.fsnet.co.uk

Sampford House ♦♦♦
57-59 King Street, Brixham, TQ5 9TH
T: (01803) 857761
F: (01803) 857761
E: carole.boulton@btinternet.com

Sea Tang Guest House ♦♦♦
67 Berry Head Road, Brixham, TQ5 9AA
T: (01803) 854651
F: (01803) 854651
E: seatangguesthouse@yahoo.co.uk
I: www.smoothhound.co.uk/hotels/seatang.html

The Shoalstone Hotel ♦♦♦
105 Berry Head Road, Brixham, TQ5 9AG
T: (01803) 857919
F: (01803) 850540

Tor Haven Hotel ♦♦♦
97 King Street, Brixham, TQ5 9TH
T: (01803) 882281

Westbury Guest House ♦♦♦
51 New Road, Brixham, TQ5 8NL
T: (01803) 851684
E: ann.burt@lineone.net

Woodlands Guest House ♦♦♦
Parkham Road, Brixham, TQ5 9BU
T: (01803) 852040
F: (01803) 852040
E: diparry@aol.com
I: www.dogfriendlyguesthouse.co.uk

BRIXTON
Devon

Venn Farm ♦♦♦♦
Brixton, Plymouth PL8 2AX
T: (01752) 880378
F: (01752) 880378

BROAD CHALKE
Wiltshire

Orchard House Bed & Breakfast ♦♦♦♦
Orchard House, Little London, Broad Chalke, Salisbury SP5 5HL
T: (01722) 780385
E: simon@orchard2.demon.co.uk

The Queens Head Inn ♦♦♦♦
1 North Street, Broad Chalke, Salisbury SP5 5EN
T: (01722) 780344
F: (01722) 780344

BROADHEMBURY
Devon

Lane End Farm ♦♦♦
Broadhembury, Honiton EX14 3LU
T: (01404) 841563
F: (01404) 841563

Stafford Barton Farm ♦♦♦♦♦
Broadhembury, Honiton EX14 3LU
T: (01404) 841403
E: jeanwalters1@tesco.net

BROADOAK
Dorset

Dunster Farm ♦♦♦♦
Broadoak, Bridport DT6 5NR
T: (01308) 424626

BROADWOODWIDGER
Devon

Rexon Cross Farm ♦♦♦
Broadwoodwidger, Lifton PL16 0JJ
T: (01566) 784295
F: (01566) 784295
E: john.worden@btclick.com
I: www.rexoncross.co.uk

BROMHAM
Wiltshire

The Cottage ♦♦♦
Westbrook, Bromham, Chippenham SN15 2EE
T: (01380) 850255
E: rjsteed@cottage16.freeserve.co.uk

Paddock House ♦♦♦
104 Devizes Road, Bromham, Chippenham SN15 2DZ
T: (01380) 850970
F: (01380) 850970
E: mikjan.argue.paddock@virgin.net

BROUGHTON GIFFORD
Wiltshire

Frying Pan Farm ♦♦♦
Broughton Gifford, Melksham SN12 8LL
T: (01225) 702343
F: (01225) 793652
E: fr65@dial.pipex.com
I: www.fryingpanfarm.dial.pipex.com

Honeysuckle Cottage ♦♦♦♦
95 the Common, Broughton Gifford, Melksham SN12 8ND
T: (01225) 782463
E: dmehta@globalnet.co.uk
I: www.users.globalnet.co.uk/~dmehta/index.htm

BRUTON
Somerset

Gants Mill ♦♦♦♦
Gants Mill Lane, Bruton, BA10 0DB
T: (01749) 812393
E: shingler@gantsmill.co.uk
I: www.gantsmill.co.uk

BRYHER
Cornwall

Bank Cottage Guest House ♦♦♦♦
Bryher, TR23 0PR
T: (01720) 422612
F: (01720) 422612
E: macmace@patrol.i-way.co.uk

Soleil D'or ♦♦♦♦
Bryher, TR23 0PR
T: (01720) 422003

BUCKFAST
Devon

Furzeleigh Mill Country Hotel ♦♦♦
Dartbridge, Buckfastleigh, TQ11 0JP
T: (01364) 643476
F: (01364) 643476
E: enquiries@furzeleigh.co.uk
I: www.furzeleigh.co.uk

BUCKLAND NEWTON
Dorset

Holyleas House ♦♦♦♦ SILVER AWARD
Buckland Newton, Dorchester DT2 7DP
T: (01300) 345214
F: (01305) 264488
E: tiabunkall@holyleas.fsnet.co.uk

Rew Cottage ♦♦♦♦
Buckland Newton, Dorchester DT2 7DN
T: (01300) 345467
F: (01300) 345467

Whiteways Farmhouse Accommodation ♦♦♦♦ SILVER AWARD
Bookham, Alton Pancras, Dorchester DT2 7RP
T: (01300) 345511
F: (01300) 345511
E: bookhamfarm@netscapeonline.co.uk
I: www.bookhamcourt.co.uk

BUDE
Cornwall

Atlantic Calm ♦♦♦♦ SILVER AWARD
30 Downs View, Bude, EX23 8RG
T: (01288) 359165
E: atlanticcalm@btinternet.com
I: www.atlanticcalm.co.uk

Bentley House ♦♦♦
Killerton Road, Bude, EX23 8EW
T: (01288) 353698

Brendon Arms ♦♦
Falcon Terrace, Bude, EX23 8SD
T: (01288) 354542
F: (01288) 354542
E: enquiries@brendonarms.co.uk
I: www.brendonarms.co.uk

Cliff Hotel ♦♦♦♦
Crooklets Beach, Bude, EX23 8NG
T: (01288) 353110
F: (01288) 353110
I: www.cliffhotel.co.uk

Edgcumbe Hotel ♦♦♦♦
19 Summerleaze Cres, Bude, EX23 8HJ
T: (01288) 353846
F: (01288) 355256
E: info@edgcumbe-hotel.co.uk
I: www.edgcumbe-hotel.co.uk

The Elms ♦♦♦
37 Lynstone Road, Bude, EX23 8LR
T: (01288) 353429

Grosvenor Hotel Rating Applied For
Summerleaze Cres, Bude, EX23 8HH
T: (01288) 352062
E: bern@peppercombe.fsnet.co.uk

Hallagather Farmhouse ♦♦♦♦
Crackington Haven, Bude EX23 0LA
T: (01840) 230276
F: (01840) 230276

Harefield Cottage ♦♦♦♦
Upton, Bude EX23 0LY
T: (01288) 352350
F: (01288) 352712
E: sales@coast-countryside.co.uk
I: www.coast-countryside.co.uk

Haven Cottage Rating Applied For
35 Killerton Road, Bude, EX23 8EL
T: (01288) 354995

Inn on the Green ♦♦
Crooklets Beach, Bude, EX23 8NF
T: (01288) 356013
F: (01288) 356244
E: info@innonthegreen.info
I: www.innonthegreen.info

Link's Side ♦♦♦♦
7 Burn View, Bude, EX23 8BY
T: (01288) 352410
E: linksidebude@hotmail.com
I: www.north-cornwall.co.uk/bude/client/linkside

Lower Tresmorn ♦♦♦♦ SILVER AWARD
Lower Tresmorn Farm, Crackington Haven, Bude EX23 0LQ
T: (01840) 230667
F: (01840) 230667

Meadow View ♦♦♦
6 Kings Hill Close, Bude, EX23 8RR
T: (01288) 355095

Old Orchard ♦♦♦
Upper Lynstone, Bude, EX23 0LR
T: (01288) 355617

Penleaze Farm Bed and Breakfast ♦♦♦♦ SILVER AWARD
Penleaze, Marham Church, Bude, EX23 0ET
T: (01288) 381226
F: (01288) 381226

Seagulls Guest House ♦♦♦♦
11 Downs View, Bude, EX23 8RF
T: (01288) 352059
F: (01288) 359259
E: contactus@seagullsguesthouse.co.uk
I: www.seagullsguesthouse.co.uk

Stratton Gardens Hotel ♦♦♦♦
Cot Hill, Stratton, Bude
EX23 9DN
T: (01288) 352500
F: (01288) 352256
E: stratton.gardens@which.net
I: www.cornwall-online.co.uk/stratton-gardens

Sunrise Guest House ♦♦♦♦
6 Burn View, Bude, EX23 8BY
T: (01288) 353214
E: kathyandken@sunriseguesthouse.freeserve.co.uk
I: www.sunrise-bude.co.uk

Surf Haven ♦♦♦
31 Downs View, Bude, EX23 8RG
T: (01288) 353923
F: (01288) 353923
E: info@surfhaven.info
I: www.surfhaven.info

Tee-Side Guest House ♦♦♦♦
2 Burn View, Bude, EX23 8BY
T: (01288) 352351
F: (01288) 352351
E: tee_side@hotmail.com
I: www.tee-side.co.uk

Tresillian ♦♦♦♦
10 Killerton Road, Bude, EX23 8EL
T: (01288) 356199

Wyvern House ♦♦♦♦
7 Downs View, Bude, EX23 8RF
T: (01288) 352205
F: (01288) 356802
E: eileen@wyvernhouse.co.uk
I: www.wyvernhouse.co.uk

BUDLEIGH SALTERTON
Devon

Lufflands
♦♦♦♦ SILVER AWARD
Yettington, Budleigh Salterton, EX9 7BP
T: (01395) 568422
F: (01395) 568810
E: stay@lufflands.co.uk
I: www.lufflands.co.uk

BUDOCK WATER
Cornwall

Higher Kergilliack Farm ♦♦♦
Budock Water, Falmouth
TR11 5PB
T: (01326) 372271

The Home Country House Hotel ♦♦♦
Penjerrick, Budock Water, Falmouth TR11 5EE
T: (01326) 250427
F: (01326) 250143

BULFORD
Wiltshire

The Dovecot ♦♦♦♦
Watergate Lane, Bulford, Salisbury SP4 9DY
T: (01980) 632625
E: hadfields@genie.co.uk

BURLAWN
Cornwall

Pengelly Farmhouse ♦♦♦♦
Burlawn, Wadebridge PL27 7LA
T: (01208) 814217

BURNHAM-ON-SEA
Somerset

Alstone Court Farm ♦♦
Alstone Lane, Highbridge, TA9 3DS
T: (01278) 789417
F: (01278) 784582

Ar Dhachaedh ♦♦♦
36 Abingdon Street, Burnham-on-Sea, TA8 1PJ
T: (01278) 783652
E: ardhachaedh@aol.com

Boundrys Edge ♦♦♦
40 Charlestone Road, Burnham-on-Sea, TA8 2AP
T: (01278) 783128
F: (01278) 783128

Dunstan House Inn ♦♦♦
Love Lane, Burnham-on-Sea, TA8 1EU
T: (01278) 784343

Knights Rest ♦♦♦
9 Dunstan Road, Burnham-on-Sea, TA8 1ER
T: (01278) 782318

Priorsmead ♦♦♦
23 Rectory Road, Burnham-on-Sea, TA8 2BZ
T: (01278) 782116
F: (01278) 782116
E: priorsmead@aol.com
I: www.priorsmead.co.uk

Prospect Farm Guest House ♦♦♦
Strowlands, East Brent, Highbridge TA9 4JH
T: (01278) 760507

Sandhills Guest House ♦♦♦
3 Poplar Road, Burnham-on-Sea, TA8 2HD
T: (01278) 781208

Shalimar Guest House ♦♦♦
174 Berrow Road, Burnham-on-Sea, TA8 2JE
T: (01278) 785898

Somewhere House ♦♦♦
68 Berrow Road, Burnham-on-Sea, TA8 2EZ
T: (01278) 795236
E: di@somewherehouse.com
I: www.somewherehouse.com

Walton House
♦♦♦♦ SILVER AWARD
148 Berrow Road, Burnham-on-Sea, TA8 2PN
T: (01278) 780034
E: auntflo@dialstart.net

The Warren Guest House ♦♦♦
29 Berrow Road, Burnham-on-Sea, TA8 2EZ
T: (01278) 786726
F: (01278) 786726
E: TheWarren@compuserve.com
I: www.Thewarrenguesthouse.co.uk

BURTLE
Somerset

The Tom Mogg Inn ♦♦♦
Station Road, Burtle, Bridgwater TA7 8NU
T: (01278) 722399
F: (01278) 722724
E: tommogg@telinco.com

BURTON BRADSTOCK
Dorset

Burton Cliff Hotel ♦♦♦
Cliff Road, Burton Bradstock, Bridport DT6 4RB
T: (01308) 897205
F: (01308) 898111
♿

Pebble Beach Lodge ♦♦♦♦
Coast Road, Burton Bradstock, Bridport DT6 4RJ
T: (01308) 897428
F: (01308) 897428
E: pebblebeachlodge@supanet.com
I: www.burtonbradstock.org.uk/pebblebeachlodge

BUTCOMBE
North Somerset

Butcombe Farm ♦♦♦♦
Aldwick Lane, Butcombe, Bristol BS40 7UW
T: (01761) 462380
F: (01761) 462300
E: info@butcombe-farm.demon.co.uk
I: www.butcombe-farm.demon.co.uk

CADLEY
Wiltshire

Kingstones Farm ♦♦♦♦
Cadley, Marlborough SN8 4NE
T: (01672) 512039
F: (01672) 515947

CALLINGTON
Cornwall

Dozmary ♦♦♦
Tors View Close, Tavistock Road, Callington, PL17 7DY
T: (01579) 383677
E: dozmarybb@aol.com

Green Pastures ♦♦♦
Longhill, Callington, PL17 8AU
T: (01579) 382566
E: greenpast@aol.com

Higher Manaton ♦♦♦
Callington, PL17 8PX
T: (01579) 370460
F: (01579) 370460
E: dtrewin@manaton.fsnet.co.uk
I: www.turning-wood.com

CALNE
Wiltshire

Calstone Bed and Breakfast
♦♦♦♦ SILVER AWARD
Manor House, Manor Farm, Calstone Wellington, Calne SN11 8PY
T: (01249) 816804
F: (01249) 817966
E: calstonebandb@farmersweekly.net
I: www.calstone.co.uk

Chilvester Hill House
♦♦♦♦♦ SILVER AWARD
Calne, SN11 0LP
T: (01249) 813981
F: (01249) 814217
E: gill.dilley@talk21.com
I: www.wolsey-lodges.co.uk

Maundrell House ♦♦♦♦
Horsebrook, The Green, Calne, SN11 8DL
T: (01249) 821267
F: (01249) 821267
E: liz@mundrell.bigwig.net
I: maundrell.bigwig.net

Queenwood Golf Lodge
♦♦♦♦♦ GOLD AWARD
Bowood Golf & Country Club, Derry Hill, Calne, SN11 9PQ
T: (01249) 822228
F: (01249) 822218
E: golfclub@bowood.org
I: www.bowood.org

White Hart Hotel ♦♦
2 London Road, Calne, SN11 0AB
T: (01249) 812413
F: (01249) 812467

CANNINGTON
Somerset

Blackmore Farm
♦♦♦♦♦ SILVER AWARD
Cannington, Bridgwater TA5 2NE
T: (01278) 653442
F: (01278) 653427
E: dyerfarm@aol.com
I: www.dyerfarm.co.uk
♿

The Friendly Spirit ♦♦♦
Brook Street, Cannington, Bridgwater TA5 2HP
T: (01278) 652215
F: (01278) 653636

Gurney Manor Mill ♦♦♦♦
Gurney Street, Cannington, Bridgwater TA5 2HW
T: (01278) 653582
F: (01278) 653993
E: gurneymill@yahoo.co.uk
I: www.gurneymill.freeserve.co.uk

Kings Head Inn ♦♦♦
12-14 High Street, Cannington, Bridgwater TA5 2HE
T: (01278) 652293
F: (01278) 652293

CARBIS BAY
Cornwall

Chy An Gwedhen ♦♦♦♦
St Ives Road, Treloyhan, Carbis Bay, St Ives TR26 2JN
T: (01736) 798684
F: (01736) 798684
E: gwedhen@btinternet.com
I: www.connexions.co.uk/gwedhen

Howards Hotel ♦♦♦
St Ives Road, Carbis Bay, St Ives TR26 2SB
T: (01736) 795651
F: (01736) 795535
E: dmgill@hhotel.fsbusiness.co.uk
I: www.cornwall-online.co.uk/howardshotel

Trelowena Guest House ♦♦♦
27 Richmond Way, Carbis Bay, St Ives TR26 2JY
T: (01736) 798276

CARDINHAM
Cornwall

The Stables ♦♦♦
Welltown, Cardinham, Bodmin PL30 4EG
T: (01208) 821316
E: geraldmoseley@lineone.net

CASTLE CARY
Somerset

Bond's ♦♦♦♦
Ansford Hill, Castle Cary, BA7 7JL
T: (01963) 350464
F: (01963) 350464

Clanville Manor
♦♦♦♦ SILVER AWARD
Clanville, Castle Cary, BA7 7PJ
T: (01963) 350124
F: (01963) 350719
E: info@clanvillemanor.co.uk
I: www.clanvillemanor.co.uk

The Horse Pond Inn and Motel ♦♦♦
The Triangle, Castle Cary, BA7 7BD
T: (01963) 350318
F: (01963) 351764
E: horsepondinn@aol.com
I: www.horsepondinn.co.uk

Orchard Farm ♦♦♦
Cockhill, Castle Cary, BA7 7NY
T: (01963) 350418
F: (01963) 350418
E: boyeroj@talk21.com
I: www.orchardfm.freeuk.com

CASTLE COMBE
Wiltshire

Fosse Farmhouse ♦♦♦♦
Nettleton Shrub, Nettleton, Chippenham SN14 7NJ
T: (01249) 782286
F: (01249) 783066
E: caroncooper@compuserve.com
I: www.fossefarmhouse.8m.com

Goulters Mill Farm ♦♦♦
Goulters Mill, Nettleton, Chippenham SN14 7LL
T: (01249) 782555

Thorngrove Cottage ♦♦♦
Summer Lane, Castle Combe, Chippenham SN14 7LG
T: (01249) 782607
E: chrisdalene@compuserve.com

CATTISTOCK
Dorset

Greystones ♦♦♦
Cattistock, Dorchester DT2 0JB
T: (01300) 320477
E: j_f.fletcher@virgin.net

CAWSAND
Cornwall

Penmillard Farm
♦♦♦♦ SILVER AWARD
Rame, Cawsand, Torpoint PL10 1LG
T: (01752) 822215

CERNE ABBAS
Dorset

Badger Hill ♦♦♦♦
11 Springfield, Cerne Abbas, Dorchester DT2 7JZ
T: (01300) 341698
F: (01300) 341698

CHALLACOMBE
Devon

Twitchen Farm ♦♦♦
Challacombe, Barnstaple EX31 4TT
T: (01598) 763568
F: (01598) 763310
E: holidays@twitchen.co.uk
I: www.twitchen.co.uk

CHARD
Somerset

Ammonite Lodge ♦♦♦♦
43 High Street, Chard, TA20 1QL
T: (01460) 63839
E: steve@hyams43.fsnet.co.uk

Bath House Restaurant and Hotel
Rating Applied For
28 Holyrood Street, Chard, TA20 2AH
T: (01460) 67575
F: (01460) 64106

Bellplot House Hotel ♦♦♦♦♦
High Street, Chard, TA20 1QB
T: (01460) 62600
F: (01460) 62600
E: bellplothousehotel@fsbdial.co.uk
I: www.bellplothouse.co.uk

Home Farm ♦♦♦
Hornsbury Hill, Chard, TA20 3DB
T: (01460) 63731

Hornsbury Mill ♦♦♦♦
Eleighwater, Chard TA20 3AQ
T: (01460) 63317
F: (01460) 63317
E: horsburymill@btclick.com
I: www.hornsburymill.co.uk

Wambrook Farm ♦♦♦
Wambrook, Chard TA20 3DF
T: (01460) 62371
E: wambrookfarm@aol.com

Yew Tree Cottage
♦♦♦♦ SILVER AWARD
Hornsbury Hill, Chard, TA20 3DB
T: (01460) 64735
F: (01460) 68029
E: ytcottage@aol.com
I: www.yewtreecottage.org.uk

CHARLTON HORETHORNE
Somerset

Ashclose Farm ♦♦♦
Blackford Road, Charlton Horethorne, Sherborne DT9 4PG
T: (01963) 220360
F: 08704 034570
E: gooding@ashclosefarm.freeserve.co.uk

Longbar ♦♦♦
Level Lane, Charlton Horethorne, Sherborne DT9 4NN
T: (01963) 220266
E: longbar@tinyworld.co.uk
I: www.longbarfarm.co.uk

CHARMINSTER
Dorset

The Bungalow ♦♦♦
25 Herrison Cottages, Charminster, Dorchester DT2 9RJ
T: (01305) 261694
E: penny.suarez@talk21.com

The Inn For All Seasons ♦♦♦
16 North Street, Charminster, Dorchester DT2 9QZ
T: (01305) 264694
F: (01305) 257824

Slades Farm ♦♦♦♦
North Street, Charminster, Dorchester DT2 9QZ
T: (01305) 265614
F: (01305) 265713
I: www.sladesfarm.co.uk

Three Compasses Inn ♦♦♦
Charminster, Dorchester DT2 9QT
T: (01305) 263618

CHARMOUTH
Dorset

Cardsmill Farm ♦♦♦
Whitchurch Canonicorum, DT6 6RP
T: (01297) 489375
F: (01297) 489375
E: cardsmill@aol.com
I: www.farmhousedorest.com

Fernhill Hotel ♦♦♦♦
Charmouth, Bridport DT6 6BX
T: (01297) 560492
F: (01297) 561159
E: fernhill@tiscali.co.uk
I: fernhill-hotel.co.uk

Queen's Armes Hotel ♦♦♦♦
The Street, Charmouth, Bridport DT6 6QF
T: (01297) 560339
F: (01297) 560339
E: peterm@netcomuk.co.uk

CHEDDAR
Somerset

Applebee South Barns B & B ♦♦
The Hayes, Cheddar, BS27 3AN
T: (01934) 743146
F: (01934) 743146

Bay Rose House ♦♦
The Bays, Cheddar, BS27 3QN
T: (01934) 741377
F: (01934) 741377
E: enquiries@bayrose.co.uk
I: www.bayrose.co.uk

Chedwell Cottage ♦♦♦♦
59 Redcliffe Street, Cheddar, BS27 3PF
T: (01934) 743268
F: (01934) 743268
E: suecriddle@lineone.net
I: www.westcountrynow.com

Constantine ♦♦♦
Lower New Road, Cheddar, BS27 3DY
T: (01934) 741339

Gordons Hotel ♦♦♦
Cliff Street, Cheddar, BS27 3PT
T: (01934) 742497
F: (01934) 742511
E: gordons.hotel@virgin.net
I: www.gordonshotel.co.uk

Market Cross Hotel ♦♦♦
The Cross, Church Street, Cheddar, BS27 3RA
T: (01934) 742264
F: (01934) 741411
E: annfieldhouse@aol.com
I: www.marketcrosshotel.co.uk

Neuholme ♦♦♦♦
The Barrows, Cheddar, BS27 3BG
T: (01934) 742841

Tor Farm ♦♦♦♦
Nyland, Cheddar BS27 3UD
T: (01934) 743710
F: (01934) 743710
E: bcjbkj@aol.com

Wassells House ♦♦♦♦
Upper New Road, Cheddar, BS27 3DN
T: (01934) 744317
E: aflinders@wassells99.freeserve.co.uk

CHEDZOY
Somerset

Apple View
♦♦♦♦ SILVER AWARD
Temple Farm, Chedzoy, Bridgwater TA7 8QR
T: (01278) 423201
F: (01278) 423201
E: temple_farm@hotmail.com

CHELSTON
Devon

Colindale Hotel ♦♦♦♦♦
20 Rathmore Road, Chelston, Torquay TQ2 6NY
T: (01803) 293947
E: bronte@eurobell.co.uk
I: www.colindalehotel.co.uk

Millbrook House Hotel
♦♦♦♦♦ SILVER AWARD
Old Mill Road, Chelston, Torquay TQ2 6AP
T: (01803) 297394
F: (01803) 297394
E: millbrookhotel@virgin.net

Parks Hotel ♦♦♦♦
Rathmore Road, Chelston, Torquay TQ2 6NZ
T: (01803) 292420
F: (01803) 296006
E: enquiries@parks-hotel.co.uk
I: www.parks-hotel.co.uk

Tower Hall Hotel ♦♦♦
Solsbro Road, Chelston, Torquay TQ2 6PF
T: (01803) 605292
E: johnbutler@towerhallhotel.co.uk

CHELYNCH
Somerset

The Old Stables ♦♦♦♦
Hurlingpot Farm, Chelynch, Shepton Mallet BA4 4PY
T: (01749) 880098
E: maureen.keevil@amserve.net
I: www.the-oldstables.co.uk

CHEW MAGNA
Bath and North East Somerset

Valley Farm ♦♦♦♦
Sandy Lane, Stanton Drew, Bristol BS39 4EL
T: (01275) 332723
F: (01275) 332723
E: highmead.gardens@virgin.net
I: www.smoothhound.com

Woodbarn Farm ♦♦♦
Denny Lane, Chew Magna, Bristol BS40 8SZ
T: (01275) 332599
F: (01275) 332599
E: woodbarnfarm@hotmail.com

CHEW STOKE
Bath and North East Somerset

Orchard House ♦♦♦
Bristol Road, Chew Stoke, Bristol BS40 8UB
T: (01275) 333143
F: (01275) 333754
E: orchardhse@ukgateway.net
I: www.orchardhse.ukgateway.net

Establishments printed in blue have a detailed entry in this guide

CHICKERELL
Dorset

Stonebank
◆◆◆◆◆ GOLD AWARD
14 West Street, Chickerell, Weymouth DT3 4DY
T: (01305) 760120
F: (01305) 760871
E: BB@stonebank-chickerell.co.uk
I: www.stonebank-chickerell.co.uk

CHICKLADE
Wiltshire

The Old Rectory ◆◆◆◆
Chicklade, Hindon, Salisbury SP3 5SU
T: (01747) 820226
F: (01747) 820783
E: vbronson@old-rectory.co.uk
I: www.old-rectory.co.uk

CHILSWORTHY
Devon

Ugworthy Barton
◆◆◆◆ SILVER AWARD
Chilsworthy, Holsworthy EX22 7JH
T: (01409) 254435
F: (01409) 254435

CHILTON CANTELO
Somerset

Higher Farm ◆◆◆◆
Chilton Cantelo, Yeovil BA22 8BE
T: (01935) 850213
E: susankerton@tinyonline.co.uk

CHILTON TRINITY
Somerset

Chilton Farm ◆◆◆◆
Chilton Trinity, Bridgwater TA5 2BL
T: (01278) 421864
E: warmt@supanet.com

CHIPPENHAM
Wiltshire

The Bramleys ◆◆◆
73 Marshfield Road, Chippenham, SN15 1JR
T: (01249) 653770

Church Farm ◆◆◆◆
Hartham, Corsham, SN13 0PU
T: (01249) 715180
F: (01249) 715572
E: kmjbandb@aol.com
I: www.churchfarm.cjb.net

Fairfield Farm ◆◆◆◆
Upper Wraxall, Chippenham, SN14 7AG
T: (01225) 891750
F: (01225) 891050
E: mcdonoug@globalnet.co.uk

Glebe House ◆◆◆◆
Chittoe, Chippenham, SN15 2EL
T: (01380) 850864
F: (01380) 850189
E: gscrope@aol.com

London Road Guest House ◆◆◆
122 London Road, Chippenham, SN15 3BA
T: (01249) 660027
E: ron@read122a.fsnet.co.uk

New Road Guest House ◆◆◆
31 New Road, Chippenham, SN15 1HP
T: (01249) 657259
F: (01249) 657259
E: mail@newroadyguesthouse.co.uk
I: www.newroadguesthouse.co.uk

Oakfield Farm ◆◆◆◆
Easton Piercy Lane, Yatton Keynell, Chippenham SN14 6JU
T: (01249) 782355
F: (01249) 783458
E: oakfieldfarm@bushinternet.com

75 Rowden Hill ◆◆
Chippenham, SN15 2AL
T: (01249) 652981

Teresa Lodge (Glen Avon) ◆◆◆
43 Bristol Road, Chippenham, SN15 1NT
T: (01249) 653350
F: (01249) 653 350

CHISELDON
Wiltshire

Norton House ◆◆◆◆
46 Draycott Road, Chiseldon, Swindon SN4 0LS
T: (01793) 741210
F: (01793) 741020
E: sharian@clara.co.uk
I: www.nortonhouse.uk.com

CHITTLEHAMPTON
Devon

Higher Biddacott Farm ◆◆◆
Chittlehampton, Umberleigh EX37 9PY
T: (01769) 540222
F: (01769) 540222
E: waterers.@sosi.net
I: www.heavyhorses.net

CHRISTIAN MALFORD
Wiltshire

Beanhill Farm ◆◆◆
Main Road, Christian Malford, Chippenham SN15 4BS
T: (01249) 720672

The Ferns ◆◆◆
Church Road, Christian Malford, Chippenham SN15 4BW
T: (01249) 720371
E: ault.ferns@amserve.net

CHUDLEIGH
Devon

Farmborough House
◆◆◆◆ SILVER AWARD
Old Exeter Road, Chudleigh, Newton Abbot TQ13 0DR
T: (01626) 853258
F: (01626) 853258
E: holidays@farmborough-house.com
I: www.farmborough-house.com

The Old Coaching House ◆◆◆
25 Fore Street, Chudleigh, Newton Abbot TQ13 0HX
T: (01626) 853270
F: (01626) 852122
E: kelly_townsend@coachinghouse.freeserve.co.uk
I: www.oldcoachinghouse.co.uk

CHUDLEIGH KNIGHTON
Devon

Church House ◆◆◆◆
Chudleigh Knighton, TQ13 0HE
T: (01626) 852123
F: (01626) 852123
E: brandon@churchhouse100.freeserve.co.uk
I: www.smoothhound.co.uk/hotels/churchho.html

CHURCHILL
North Somerset

Clumber Lodge ◆◆◆
New Road, Churchill, Winscombe BS25 5NW
T: (01934) 852078

Hillslee House ◆◆◆◆
New Road, Churchill, Winscombe BS25 5NP
T: (01934) 853035
F: (01934) 852470

CHURCHINFORD
Somerset

The York Inn ◆◆◆◆
Honiton Road, Churchinford, Taunton TA3 7RF
T: (01823) 601333
F: (01823) 601026
E: wdatheyorkinn@aol.com
I: www.the-york-inn.freeserve.co.uk

CLATFORD
Wiltshire

Clatford Park Farm ◆◆◆
Clatford, Marlborough SN8 4DZ
T: (01672) 861646
I: www.clatfordparkfarm.co.uk

CLAWTON
Devon

The Hollies ◆◆◆
Clawton, Holsworthy EX22 6PN
T: (01409) 253770
E: the_hollies_2001@hotmail.com
I: www.TheHolliesFarm.co.uk

The Old Vicarage ◆◆◆◆
Clawton, Holsworthy EX22 6PS
T: (01409) 271100
E: enquiries@oldvicarageclawton.co.uk
I: www.oldvicarageclawton.co.uk/welcome/intro.asp

CLENCH
Wiltshire

Clench Farmhouse ◆◆◆
Clench, Marlborough SN8 4NT
T: (01672) 810264
F: (01672) 811458
E: clarissaroe@btinternet.com
I: www.clenchfarmhouse.co.uk

CLEVEDON
Somerset

Highcliffe Hotel ◆◆◆
Wellington Terrace, Clevedon, BS21 7PU
T: (01275) 873250
F: (01275) 873572
E: highcliffehotel@aol.com

Maybank Guest House ◆◆
4 Jesmond Road, Clevedon, BS21 7SA
T: (01275) 876387

CLIFTON
Bristol

Downs View Guest House ◆◆◆
38 Upper Belgrave Road, Clifton, Bristol BS8 2XN
T: (0117) 973 7046
F: (0117) 973 8169
E: bookings@downsviewguesthouse.co.uk

Number 31 ◆◆◆◆
31 Royal York Crescent, Clifton, Bristol BS8 4JU
T: (0117) 9735330

Rosebery House ◆◆◆
14 Camden Terrace, Clifton, Bristol BS8 4PU
T: (0117) 9149508
F: (0117) 9149508
E: anne@amalindine.freeserve.co.uk
I: www.roseberyhouse.net

CLOVELLY
Devon

Dyke Green Farm ◆◆◆◆
Clovelly, Bideford EX39 5RU
T: (01237) 431699
E: edward@ecjohns.freeserve.co.uk

Fuchsia Cottage ◆◆◆◆
Burscott, Clovelly, Bideford EX39 5RR
T: (01237) 431398
E: curtis@fuchsiacottage.fslife.co.uk
I: www.clovelly-holidays.co.uk

Holloford Farm ◆◆◆◆
Higher Clovelly, Bideford, EX39 5SD
T: (01237) 441275
E: wade@holloford.freeserve.co.uk

CLUTTON
Bath and North East Somerset

Cholwell Hall ◆◆◆◆
Clutton, Bristol BS39 5TE
T: (01761) 452380
I: www.cholwellhall.co.uk

COLLINGBOURNE KINGSTON
Wiltshire

Cum-Bye ◆◆◆
Aughton, Collingbourne Kingston, Marlborough SN8 3RZ
T: (01264) 850256

Manor Farm B & B Rating Applied For
Manor Farm, Collingbourne Kingston, Marlborough SN8 3SD
T: (01264) 850859
F: (01264) 850859
E: stay@manorfm.com
I: www.manorfm.com

COLYFORD
Devon

Hayes Holme ◆◆◆◆◆
2 Kingsholme, Colyford, Colyton EX24 6RJ
T: (01297) 553808
E: www.pathayes@youremail.co.uk

COLYTON
Devon

Smallicombe Farm
♦♦♦♦ SILVER AWARD
Northleigh, Colyton EX24 6BU
T: (01404) 831310
F: (01404) 831431
E: maggie_todd@yahoo.com
I: www.smallicombe.com

COMBE DOWN
Bath and North East Somerset

Beech Wood ♦♦♦♦
Shaft Road, Combe Down, Bath, BA2 7HP
T: (01225) 832242
F: (01225) 836060
E: info@beechwoodbath.co.uk
I: www.beechwoodbath.co.uk

Grey Lodge
♦♦♦♦ SILVER AWARD
Summer Lane, Combe Down, Bath, BA2 7EU
T: (01225) 832069
F: (01225) 830161
E: greylodge@freenet.co.uk
I: www.greylodge.co.uk

COMBE FLOREY
Somerset

Redlands ♦♦♦♦
Trebles Holford, Combe Florey, Taunton TA4 3HA
T: (01823) 433159
E: redlandshouse@hotmail.com
I: www.escapetothecountry.co.uk

COMBE MARTIN
Devon

Channel Vista ♦♦♦
Woodlands, Combe Martin, Ilfracombe, EX34 0AT
T: (01271) 883514
F: (01271) 883963
E: channelvista@freeuk.com

Saffron House Hotel ♦♦♦
King Street, Combe Martin, Ilfracombe EX34 0BX
T: (01271) 883521
E: stay@saffronhousehotel.co.uk
I: www.saffronhousehotel.co.uk

COMBPYNE
Devon

1 Granary Cottage ♦♦♦♦
Combpyne, Axminster EX13 8SX
T: (01297) 442856

COMPTON DANDO
Bath and North East Somerset

Cottage Garden ♦♦♦♦
Tynings Cottage, Fairy Hill, Compton Dando, Bristol BS39 4LH
T: (01761) 490421
F: (01761) 490030
E: vivsands@hotmail.com
I: www.cottage-garden.ukgateway.net/

The Old Chapel ♦♦♦♦
Court Hill, Compton Dando, Bristol BS39 4JZ
T: (01761) 490903
F: (01761) 490903
E: the.oldchapel@btinternet.com
I: www.the.oldchapel.btinternet.co.uk

COMPTON DUNDON
Somerset

Rickham House ♦♦♦♦
Compton Dundon, Somerton TA11 6QA
T: (01458) 445056
F: (01458) 445056
E: rickham.house@talk21.com

COOMBE BISSETT
Wiltshire

Evening Hill ♦♦♦
Blandford Road, Coombe Bissett, Salisbury SP5 4LH
T: (01722) 718561
E: henrys@tesco.net
I: www.smoothhound.co.uk/hotels/eveninghillhtml

CORSHAM
Wiltshire

Boyds Farm
♦♦♦♦♦ SILVER AWARD
Gastard, Corsham SN13 9PT
T: (01249) 713146
F: (01249) 713146
E: dorothyboydsfarm@aol.com
I: www.smoothhound.co.uk/hotels/boydsfarm.html

Heatherly Cottage
♦♦♦♦ SILVER AWARD
Ladbrook Lane, Gastard, Corsham SN13 9PE
T: (01249) 701402
F: (01249) 701412
E: ladbrook1@aol.com
I: www.smoothhound.co.uk/hotels/heather3.html

Pickwick Lodge Farm ♦♦♦♦
Guyers Lane, Corsham, SN13 0PS
T: (01249) 712207
F: (01249) 701904
I: www.pickwickfarm.co.uk

Saltbox Farm ♦♦♦♦
Drewetts Mill, Box, Corsham SN13 8PT
T: (01225) 742608
F: (01225) 742608

Thingley Court Farm ♦♦♦
Corsham, SN13 9QQ
T: (01249) 713617

CORSLEY
Wiltshire

Sturford Mead
♦♦♦♦ SILVER AWARD
Corsley, Warminster BA12 7QT
T: (01373) 832039
F: (01373) 832104
E: bradshaw@sturford.co.uk
I: www.sturford.co.uk

CORTON
Wiltshire

The Dove Inn ♦♦♦♦
Corton, Warminster BA12 0SZ
T: (01985) 850109
F: (01985) 851041
E: info@thedove.co.uk
I: www.thedove.co.uk

COSSINGTON
Somerset

Brookhayes Farm ♦♦♦♦
Bell Lane, Cossington, Bridgwater TA7 8LR
T: (01278) 722559
F: (01278) 722559

COTHAM
Bristol

Farle Villa
♦♦♦♦ SILVER AWARD
45 Sydenham Hill, Cotham, Bristol BS6 5SL
T: (0117) 9420809
F: (0117) 9420809
E: joysyd@farleyvilla.fsnet.co.uk

COVERACK
Cornwall

The Paris Hotel ♦♦♦
Coverack, Helston TR12 6SX
T: (01326) 280258
F: (01326) 280372

CRACKINGTON HAVEN
Cornwall

Venn Park Farm
Rating Applied For
Crackington Haven, Bude EX23 0LB
T: (01840) 230159
F: (01840) 230159

CRAFTHOLE
Cornwall

Finnygook Inn ♦♦♦
Crafthole, Torpoint PL11 3BQ
T: (01503) 230329
I: www.finnygook.co.uk

CRANMORE
Somerset

Lynfield ♦♦♦
Frome Road, Cranmore, Shepton Mallet BA4 4QQ
T: (01749) 880600
E: rsgildo@aol.com
I: www.shepton-mallet.co.uk

CRANTOCK
Cornwall

Highfield Lodge Hotel ♦♦♦♦
Halwyn Road, Crantock, Newquay TR8 5TR
T: (01637) 830744
F: (01637) 830568
I: www.highfieldlodge.co.uk

Tregenna House ♦♦♦♦
West Pentire Road, Crantock, Newquay TR8 5RZ
T: (01637) 830222
F: (01637) 831267
E: dench@cix.compulink.co.uk

Treringey Farm ♦♦
Crantock, Newquay TR8 5EN
T: (01637) 830265

CREDITON
Devon

Great Park Farm ♦♦♦
Crediton, EX17 3PR
T: (01363) 772050

CREECH ST MICHAEL
Somerset

Curvalion Villa ♦♦♦♦
Curvalion Road, Creech St Michael, Taunton TA3 5QQ
T: (01823) 444630
F: (01823) 444629
E: enquiries@curvalionvilla.co.uk
I: www.curvalionvilla.co.uk

CREWKERNE
Somerset

The George Hotel & Courtyard Restaurant ♦♦♦
Market Square, Crewkerne, TA18 7LP
T: (01460) 73650
F: (01460) 72974
E: eddie@thegeorgehotel.sagehost.co.uk
I: www.thegeorgehotel.sagenet.co.uk

Honeydown Farm
Rating Applied For
Seaborough Hill, Crewkerne, TA18 8PL
T: (01460) 72665
F: (01460) 72665
E: cb@honeydown.freeserve.co.uk
I: www.honeydown.freeserve.co.uk

The Manor Arms ♦♦♦
North Perrott, Crewkerne TA18 7SG
T: (01460) 72901
F: (01460) 72901
E: info@manorarmshotel.co.uk
I: www.manorarmshotel.co.uk

CRICKLADE
Wiltshire

Waterhay Farm ♦♦♦♦
Leigh, Leigh, Swindon SN6 6QY
T: (01285) 861253
F: (01285) 861253

The White Lion ♦♦
50 High Street, Cricklade, Swindon SN6 6DA
T: (01793) 750443
E: info@whitelion-inn.com
I: www.whitelion-inn.com

CROCKERTON
Wiltshire

Easter Cottage ♦♦♦♦
Foxholes, Crockerton, Warminster BA12 7DE
T: (01985) 219367
E: askew.easter@btinternet.com

Stoneyside ♦♦♦♦
Potters Hill, Crockerton, Warminster BA12 8AS
T: (01985) 218149

CROWCOMBE
Somerset

Hooks House ♦♦♦♦
Crowcombe, Taunton TA4 4AE
T: (01984) 618691
E: lukemacdd@hookhouse.fsbusiness.co.uk

CROYDE
Devon

Combas Farm ♦♦♦♦
Putsborough, Croyde, Braunton EX33 1PH
T: (01271) 890398
F: (01271) 890398

Denham House ♦♦♦♦
North Buckland, Braunton EX33 1HY
T: (01271) 890297
F: (01271) 890297
E: info@denhamhouse.co.uk
I: www.denhamhouse.co.uk

CROYDE BAY
Devon

West Winds ◆◆◆◆
Moor Lane, Croyde Bay, Braunton EX33 1PA
T: (01271) 890489
F: (01271) 890489
E: chris@croydewestwinds.freeserve.co.uk
I: www.westwindsguesthouse.co.uk

CULLOMPTON
Devon

Upton House
◆◆◆◆◆ GOLD AWARD
Cullompton, EX15 1RA
T: (01884) 33097
F: (01884) 33097

Weir Mill Farm
◆◆◆◆ SILVER AWARD
Jaycroft, Willand, Cullompton EX15 2RE
T: (01884) 820803
F: (01884) 820973
E: parish@weirmillfarm.freeserve.co.uk
I: www.smoothhound.co.uk/hotels/weirmill.html

Wishay ◆◆◆
Trinity, Cullompton, EX15 1PE
T: (01884) 33223
F: (01884) 33223
E: wishaytrinity@hotmail.com

CURRY RIVEL
Somerset

Orchard Cottage
◆◆◆◆ SILVER AWARD
Townsend, Curry Rivel, Langport TA10 0HT
T: (01458) 251511
F: (01458) 251511

DARTMOUTH
Devon

Barrington House
◆◆◆◆ SILVER AWARD
Mount Boone, Dartmouth, TQ6 9HZ
T: (01803) 835545
F: (01803) 835545
E: enquiries@barrington-house.com
I: www.barrington-house.com

Hill View House
Rating Applied For
76 Victoria Road, Dartmouth, TQ6 9DZ
T: (01803) 839372
F: (01803) 839372
E: enquiries@hillviewdartmouth.co.uk
I: www.hillviewdartmouth.co.uk

Nonsuch House
◆◆◆◆◆ GOLD AWARD
Church Hill, Kingswear, Dartmouth TQ6 0BX
T: (01803) 752829
F: (01803) 752357
E: enquiries@nonsuch-house.co.uk
I: www.nonsuch-house.co.uk

Sunnybanks ◆◆◆
1 Vicarage Hill, Dartmouth, TQ6 9EW
T: (01803) 832766
F: (01803) 832766
E: sue@sunnybanks.com
I: www.sunnybanks.com

Westbourne House
◆◆◆◆ SILVER AWARD
4 Vicarage Hill, Dartmouth, TQ6 9EW
T: (01803) 832213
F: (01803) 839209
E: peterwalton@westbourne-house.co.uk
I: www.westbourne-house.co.uk

Woodside Cottage Bed & Breakfast
◆◆◆◆ SILVER AWARD
Blackawton, Totnes TQ9 7BL
T: (01803) 712375
F: (01803) 712375
E: woodside-cottage@lineone.net
I: www.woodside-cottage-devon.co.uk

DAWLISH
Devon

Radfords Country Hotel
◆◆◆◆
Lower Dawlish Water, Dawlish, EX7 0QN
T: (01626) 863322
F: (01626) 888515
E: radfords@eclipse.co.uk
I: www.eclipse.co.uk/radfords

Smallacombe Farm
Rating Applied For
Aller Valley, Dawlish, EX7 0PS
T: (01626) 862536

DENBURY
Devon

Tornewton ◆◆◆◆
Denbury, Newton Abbot TQ12 6EF
T: (01803) 812257
F: (01803) 812257

DEVIZES
Wiltshire

The Artichoke Inn ◆◆◆
The Nursery, Bath Road, Devizes, SN10 2AA
T: (01380) 723400
E: avocainns@freddieboxall.co.uk

Asta ◆◆
66 Downlands Road, Devizes, SN10 5EF
T: (01380) 722546

Blounts Court Farm
◆◆◆◆◆ GOLD AWARD
Coxhill Lane, Potterne, Devizes SN10 5PH
T: (01380) 727180
E: caroline@blountscourtfarm.co.uk
I: www.blountscourtfarm.co.uk

The Chestnuts ◆◆◆◆
Potterne Road, Devizes, SN10 5DD
T: (01380) 724532

Eastcott Manor ◆◆◆
Easterton, Devizes SN10 4PL
T: (01380) 813313

Eastleigh House ◆◆◆◆
3 Eastleigh Road, Devizes, SN10 3EE
T: (01380) 726918
F: (01380) 726918

The Gate House ◆◆◆
Wick Lane, Devizes, SN10 5DW
T: (01380) 725283
F: (01380) 722382
E: laura@gatehouse-b-and-b.freeserve.co.uk

Littleton Lodge ◆◆◆◆
Littleton Panell (A360), West Lavington, Devizes SN10 4ES
T: (01380) 813131
F: (01380) 816969
E: stay@littletonlodge.co.uk
I: www.littletonlodge.co.uk

Longwater ◆◆◆
Lower Road, Erlestoke, Devizes SN10 5UE
T: (01380) 830095
F: (01380) 830095
E: pam.hampton@talk21.com

Melbourne House ◆◆◆◆
Melbourne Place, Devizes, SN10 2AB
T: (01380) 720555
F: (01380) 720777
E: accom@melbhouse.co.uk
I: www.melbhouse.co.uk

The Old Manor ◆◆◆◆
Chirton, Devizes, SN10 3QS
T: (01380) 840777
F: (01380) 840927
E: theoldmanor@talk21.com

DINTON
Wiltshire

Honeysuckle Homestead ◆◆◆
Catherine Ford Road, Dinton, Salisbury SP3 5HA
T: (01722) 717887

Marshwood Farm B&B ◆◆◆
Dinton, Salisbury SP3 5ET
T: (01722) 716334

Morris' Farm House ◆◆◆
Baverstock, Dinton, Salisbury SP3 5EL
T: (01722) 716874
F: (01722) 716874
E: marriott@waitrose.com
I: www.kgp-publishing.co.uk

DITTISHAM
Devon

Red Lion Inn
Rating Applied For
The Level, Dittisham, Dartmouth TQ6 0ES
T: (01803) 722235

DIZZARD
Cornwall

Bears and Boxes ◆◆◆
Penrose, Dizzard, Bude EX23 0NX
T: (01840) 230318
F: (01840) 230318
E: rwfrh@btinternet.com
I: www.4hotels.co.uk/uk/hotels/penrose

DODDISCOMBSLEIGH
Devon

Whitemoor Farm ◆
Doddiscombsleigh, Exeter EX6 7PU
T: (01647) 252423
E: blaceystaffyrescue@easicom.com

DORCHESTER
Dorset

Aquila Heights ◆◆◆
44 Maiden Castle Road, Dorchester, DT1 2ES
T: (01305) 267145
F: (01305) 267145
E: aquila.heights@tiscali.co.uk

The Beagles ◆◆◆
37 London Road, Dorchester, DT1 1NF
T: (01305) 267338
E: joyce.graham@talk21.com

The Casterbridge Hotel ◆◆◆◆
49 High East Street, Dorchester, DT1 1HU
T: (01305) 264043
F: (01305) 260884
E: reception@casterbridgehotel.co.uk
I: www.casterbridgehotel.co.uk

Churchview Guest House ◆◆◆
Winterbourne Abbas, Dorchester DT2 9LS
T: (01305) 889296
F: (01305) 889296
E: stay@churchview.co.uk
I: www.churchview.co.uk

Higher Came Farmhouse
◆◆◆◆
Higher Came, Dorchester, DT2 8NR
T: (01305) 268908
F: (01305) 268908
E: highercame@eurolink.ltd.net
I: www.highercame.co.uk

Hillfort View ◆◆
10 Hillfort Close, Dorchester, DT1 2QT
T: (01305) 268476

5 Little Britain Farmhouse
◆◆◆
Fordington, Dorchester, DT1 1NN
T: (01305) 263431

Maiden Castle Farm
◆◆◆◆ SILVER AWARD
Dorchester, DT2 9PR
T: (01305) 262356
F: (01305) 251085
E: maidencastlefarm@euphony.net
I: www.maidencastlefarm.co.uk

The Old Manor
◆◆◆◆◆ GOLD AWARD
Kingston Maurward, Dorchester, DT2 8PX
T: (01305) 261110
F: (01305) 263734
E: thomson@kingston-maurward.co.uk
I: www.kingston-maurward.co.uk

The Old Rectory
◆◆◆◆ SILVER AWARD
Winterbourne Steepleton, Dorchester DT2 9LG
T: (01305) 889468
F: (01305) 889737
E: trees@eurobell.co.uk
I: www.trees.eurobell.co.uk

Port Bredy
◆◆◆◆ SILVER AWARD
107 Bridport Road, Dorchester, DT1 2NH
T: (01305) 265778
F: (01305) 265778
E: B&Benquires@portbredy.fsnet.co.uk

Sunrise Guest House ◆◆◆◆
34 London Road, Dorchester, DT1 1NE
T: (01305) 262425

Tarkaville ♦♦♦♦
30 Shaston Crescent, Manor Park, Dorchester, DT1 2EB
T: (01305) 266253
E: tarkaville@lineone.net

Victoria Hotel ♦♦♦
33 Maud Road, Dorchester, DT1 2LW
T: (01305) 262808
F: (01305) 262808

Westwood House Hotel ♦♦♦♦
29 High West Street, Dorchester, DT1 1UP
T: (01305) 268018
F: (01305) 250282
E: reservations@westwoodhouse.co.uk
I: www.westwoodhouse.co.uk

The White House ♦♦♦
9 Queens Avenue, Dorchester, DT1 2EW
T: (01305) 266714
E: sandratwh@yahoo.co.uk

Whitfield Farm Cottage ♦♦♦♦ SILVER AWARD
Poundbury Whitfield, Dorchester DT2 9SL
T: (01305) 260233
F: (01305) 260233
E: dc.whitfield@clara.net
I: www.milford.co.uk&www.dc.whitfield.clara.net

Woodwalls House Rating Applied For
Corscombe, Dorchester, DT2 0NT
T: (01935) 891477
F: (01935) 891477

Yalbury Park ♦♦♦♦ SILVER AWARD
Frome Whitfield Farm, Frome Whitfield, Dorchester DT2 7SE
T: (01305) 250336
F: (01305) 260070
E: yalburypark@tesco.net

Yellowham Farm ♦♦♦♦ SILVER AWARD
Yellowham Wood, Dorchester DT2 8RW
T: (01305) 262892
F: (01305) 848155
E: b&b@yellowham.freeserve.co.uk
I: www.yellowham.freeserve.co.uk

DOWNTON
Wiltshire

The Bull ♦♦♦
The Headlands, Downton, Salisbury SP5 3HL
T: (01725) 510374

Witherington Farm ♦♦♦♦♦
Downton, Salisbury SP5 3QT
T: (01722) 710222
F: (01722) 710405
E: band@witheringtonfarm.co.uk
I: www.witheringtonfarm.co.uk

DULOE
Cornwall

Carglonnon Farm ♦♦♦♦
Duloe, Liskeard PL14 4QA
T: (01579) 320210
F: (01579) 320210

DULVERTON
Somerset

Exton House Hotel ♦♦♦♦ SILVER AWARD
Exton, Dulverton TA22 9JT
T: (01643) 851365
F: (01643) 851213

Highercombe Farm ♦♦♦♦ SILVER AWARD
Dulverton, TA22 9PT
T: (01398) 323616
F: (01398) 323616
E: abigail@highercombe.demon.co.uk
I: www.highercombe.demon.co.uk

Penlee ♦♦♦♦
31 Battleton, Dulverton, TA22 9HU
T: (01398) 323798
F: (01398) 323780
E: info@penlee-bnb.co.uk
I: www.penlee-bnb.co.uk

Springfield Farm ♦♦♦♦
Ashwick Lane, Dulverton, TA22 9QD
T: (01398) 323722
F: (01398) 323722
E: info@springfieldfarms.co.uk
I: www.springfieldfarms.co.uk

Town Mills ♦♦♦♦ SILVER AWARD
High Street, Dulverton, TA22 9HB
T: (01398) 323124
E: townmills@onetel.net.uk
I: www.townmillsdulverton.co.uk

Winsbere House ♦♦♦
64 Battleton, Dulverton, TA22 9HU
T: (01398) 323278
I: www.exmoor.tv/winsberehouse.htm

DUNBALL
Somerset

Admiral's Table ♦♦♦
Bristol Road, Dunball, Bridgwater TA6 4TW
T: (01278) 685671
F: (01278) 685672

DUNSFORD
Devon

Oak Lodge ♦♦♦♦ SILVER AWARD
The Court, Dunsford, Exeter EX6 7DD
T: (01647) 252829
E: shirley.hodge@virgin.net
I: www.oaklodge-devon.co.uk

DUNSTER
Somerset

Cobbles Bed & Breakfast ♦♦♦♦
14-16 Church Street, Dunster, Minehead TA24 6SH
T: (01643) 821305
F: (01643) 821305

Conygar House ♦♦♦♦ SILVER AWARD
2A The Ball, Dunster, Minehead TA24 6SD
T: (01643) 821872
F: (01643) 821872
E: bale.dunster@virgin.net
I: homepage.virgin.net/bale.dunster

Exmoor House Hotel ♦♦♦♦
12 West Street, Dunster, Minehead TA24 6SN
T: (01643) 821268

Higher Orchard ♦♦♦♦
30 St Georges Street, Dunster, Minehead TA24 6RS
T: (01643) 821915
E: lamacraft@higherorchard.fsnet.co.uk
I: www.higherorchard.fsnet.co.uk

The Old Bakery ♦♦♦♦ SILVER AWARD
14 West Street, Dunster, Minehead TA24 6SN
T: (01643) 822123
F: (01643) 821139
I: www.dunsterbandb.co.uk

Spears Cross Hotel ♦♦♦♦ SILVER AWARD
1 West Street, Dunster, Minehead TA24 6SN
T: (01643) 821439
E: mjcapel@aol.com
I: www.smoothhound.co.uk/hotels/spearsx.html

EAST ALLINGTON
Devon

Higher Torr Farm ♦♦♦
East Allington, Totnes TQ9 7QH
T: (01548) 521248
F: (01548) 521248
E: helen@hrtorr.freeserve.co.uk

EAST COKER
Somerset

Granary House ♦♦♦♦ SILVER AWARD
East Coker, Yeovil BA22 9LY
T: (01935) 862738
E: granary.house@virgin.net
I: www.granaryhouse.co.uk

EAST TYTHERTON
Wiltshire

Barnbridge ♦♦
East Tytherton, Chippenham SN15 4LT
T: (01249) 740280
F: (01249) 447463
E: bgiffard@aol.com
I: www.smoothhound.co.uk/hotels/barnbrdg.html

EASTON ROYAL
Wiltshire

Follets B & B ♦♦♦♦
Easton Royal, Pewsey SN9 5LZ
T: (01672) 810619
F: (01672) 810619
E: margaretlandless@talk21.com
I: www.folletsbb.com

ENFORD
Wiltshire

Three Horseshoes Cottage ♦♦♦♦
Enford, Pewsey SN9 6AW
T: (01980) 670459

EVERCREECH
Somerset

The Bell Inn ♦♦♦
Bruton Road, Evercreech, Shepton Mallet BA4 6HY
T: (01749) 830287
E: richrewardsltd@ukonline.co.uk

Crossdale Cottage ♦♦♦
Pecking Mill, Evercreech, Shepton Mallet BA4 6PQ
T: (01749) 830293
F: (01749) 830293

EVERLEIGH
Wiltshire

The Crown Hotel ♦♦♦
Everleigh, Marlborough SN8 3EY
T: (01264) 850229
F: (01264) 850819
E: crowner@aol.com
I: www.thecrownhotel.info

EVERSHOT
Dorset

The Acorn Inn ♦♦♦♦
Fore Street, Evershot, Dorchester DT2 0JW
T: (01935) 83228
F: (01935) 83707
E: stay@acorn-inn.co.uk
I: www.acorn-inn.co.uk

EXETER
Devon

Bickham Farmhouse ♦♦♦♦
Kenn, Exeter EX6 7XL
T: (01392) 832206
F: (01392) 832206

Fairwinds Village House Hotel ♦♦♦♦
Kennford, Exeter EX6 7UD
T: (01392) 832911
E: fairwindshotbun@aol.com

The Grange ♦♦♦♦
Stoke Hill, Exeter, EX4 7JH
T: (01392) 259723
E: dudleythegrange@aol.com

Hayne Barton ♦♦♦
Whitestone, Exeter EX4 2JN
T: (01392) 811268
F: (01392) 811343
E: graham@hayne-barton.devon.co.uk
I: www.milvertoncountryholidays.com

Hayne House ♦♦♦
Silverton, Exeter EX5 4HE
T: (01392) 860725
F: (01392) 860725
E: haynehouse@ukonline.co.uk

Park View Hotel ♦♦♦
8 Howell Road, Exeter, EX4 4LG
T: (01392) 271772
F: (01392) 253047
E: philbatho@parkviewhotel.freeserve.co.uk
I: www.parkviewhotel.freeserve.co.uk

Raffles Hotel ♦♦♦♦
11 Blackall Road, Exeter, EX4 4HD
T: (01392) 270200
F: (01392) 270200
E: raffleshtl@btinternet.com
I: www.raffles-exeter.co.uk

Rydon Farm ♦♦♦♦
Woodbury, Exeter EX5 1LB
T: (01395) 232341
F: (01395) 232341
E: sallyglanvill@hotmail.com
I: www.devonbandb.co.uk

St Andrews Hotel ♦♦♦♦
28 Alphington Road, Exeter, EX2 8HN
T: (01392) 276784
F: (01392) 250249

Silversprings
♦♦♦♦♦ SILVER AWARD
12 Richmond Road, St Davids, Exeter, EX4 4JA
T: (01392) 494040
F: 0870 0561615
E: juliet@silversprings.co.uk
I: www.silversprings.co.uk

EXFORD
Somerset

Exmoor Lodge Guesthouse ♦♦♦
Chapel Street, Exford, Minehead TA24 7PY
T: (01643) 831694
E: patricia&larry@exmoorlodge.fsnet.co.uk

Hunters Moon ♦♦♦
Church Hill, Exford, Minehead TA24 7PP
T: (01643) 831695
E: huntersmoon@bushinternet.com
I: www.exmooraccommodation.co.uk

EXMOUTH
Devon

The Imperial ♦♦♦♦
The Esplanade, Exmouth, EX8 2SW
T: (01395) 274761
F: (01395) 265161
I: www.shearingsholidays.com

The Swallows ♦♦♦♦
11 Carlton Hill, Exmouth, EX8 2AJ
T: (01395) 263937
F: (01395) 271040
E: swallows@amserve.net
I: www.exmouth-guide.co.uk/swallows.htm

FALMOUTH
Cornwall

Apple Tree Cottage ♦♦♦♦
Laity Moor, Ponsanooth, Truro TR3 7HR
T: (01872) 865047
E: appletreecottage@talk21.com
I: www.cornwall-online.co.uk

Chelsea House Hotel ♦♦♦
2 Emslie Road, Falmouth, TR11 4BG
T: (01326) 212230
E: enquiries@chelseahousehotel.com
I: www.chelseahousehotel.com

Dolvean Hotel
♦♦♦♦♦ SILVER AWARD
50 Melvill Road, Falmouth, TR11 4DQ
T: (01326) 313658
F: (01326) 313995
E: reservations@dolvean.co.uk
I: www.dolvean.co.uk

Hawthorne Dene Hotel ♦♦♦
12 Pennance Road, Falmouth, TR11 4EA
T: (01326) 311427
F: (01326) 311994
E: hawthornedene@hotel12.fsbusiness.co.uk

Headlands Hotel ♦♦♦
4 Avenue Road, Falmouth, TR11 4AZ
T: (01326) 311141
F: (01356) 311141
E: acoddington@headlands1.freeserve.co.uk
I: www.cornwall-online.co.uk/headlands-falmouth

Ivanhoe Guest House ♦♦♦♦
7 Melvill Road, Falmouth, TR11 4AS
T: (01326) 319083
E: ivanhoe@enterprise.net
I: www.smoothhound.co.uk/hotels/ivanhoe

Poltair ♦♦♦
Emslie Road, Falmouth, TR11 4BG
T: (01326) 313158
I: www.poltair.co.uk

The Trevelyan ♦♦
6 Avenue Road, Falmouth, TR11 4AZ
T: (01326) 311545
F: (01326) 311545
E: gaunt@tre6.freeserve.co.uk
I: www.bedandbreakfastfalmouth.com

Wickham Guest House ♦♦♦
21 Gyllyngvase Terrace, Falmouth, TR11 4DL
T: (01326) 311140
E: enquiries@wickhamhotel.freeserve.co.uk

FARMBOROUGH
Bath and North East Somerset

Barrow Vale Farm ♦♦♦♦
Farmborough, Bath BA2 0BL
T: (01761) 470300
F: (01761) 470300
E: cherilynlangley@hotmail.com
I: www.visitbath.co.uk

FAULKLAND
Somerset

Lime Kiln Farm ♦♦♦♦
Faulkland, Bath BA3 5XE
T: (01373) 834305
E: limekiln@btinternet.com

FENNY BRIDGES
Devon

Skinners Ash Farm ♦♦♦
Fenny Bridges, Honiton EX14 3BH
T: (01404) 850231
F: (01404) 850231
I: www.smoothhound.co.uk/skinnersash/b+b

FLEET
Dorset

Highfield
♦♦♦♦ SILVER AWARD
Fleet, Weymouth DT3 4EB
T: (01305) 776822
E: highfield.fleet@lineone.net

FOWEY
Cornwall

The Old Ferry Inn ♦♦♦♦
Bodinnick, Fowey PL23 1LX
T: (01726) 870237
F: (01726) 870116

FRAMPTON
Dorset

The Stables ♦♦♦
Hyde Crook, Frampton, Dorchester DT2 9NW
T: (01300) 320075

FREMINGTON
Devon

Lower Yelland Farm ♦♦♦♦
Fremington, Barnstaple EX31 3EN
T: (01271) 860101
F: (01271) 860101
E: pday@loweryellandfarm.co.uk
I: www.loweryellandfarm.co.uk

FRESHFORD
Bath and North East Somerset

Longacre ♦♦♦
17 Staples Hill, Freshford, Bath BA3 6EL
T: (01225) 723254
F: (01225) 723254
E: fran.joe@talk21.com

FROME
Somerset

Abergele Guest House ♦♦♦♦
2 Fromefield, Frome, BA11 2HA
T: (01373) 463998

The Full Moon at Rudge ♦♦♦♦
Rudge, Frome BA11 2QF
T: (01373) 830936
F: (01373) 831366
E: fullmoon@lineone.net
I: www.thefullmoon.co.uk

Kozy-Glen
♦♦♦♦ SILVER AWARD
Rooks Lane, Berkley Marsh, Frome, BA11 5JD
T: (01373) 464767

The Lodge ♦♦♦♦
Monkley Lane, Rode, BA11 6QQ
T: (01373) 830071
E: mcdougal@nildram.co.uk

Number Four ♦♦♦
Catherine Street, Frome, BA11 1DA
T: (01373) 455690
F: (01373) 455992
E: pie@tulsli.freeserve.co.uk

Stonewall Manor ♦♦♦♦
Culver Hill, Frome, BA11 4AS
T: (01373) 462131

The Sun Inn ♦♦♦
6 Catherine Street, Frome, BA11 1DA
T: (01373) 471913

Wadbury House ♦♦♦
Wadbury House, Mells, Frome BA11 3PA
T: (01373) 812359
E: sbrinkmann@btinternet.com

GALMPTON
Devon

Rose Cottage ♦♦♦♦
Galmpton, Hope Cove, Kingsbridge TQ7 3EU
T: (01548) 561953
F: (01548) 561953
I: www.rosecottagesalcombe.co.uk

GITTISHAM
Devon

Catshayes Farm ♦♦
Gittisham, Honiton EX14 3AE
T: (01404) 850302
F: (01404) 850302
E: catshayesfarm@aol.com
I: www.farmstay.co.uk

GLASTONBURY
Somerset

ARP ♦♦♦♦
4 Chalice Way, Glastonbury, BA6 8EX
T: (01458) 830794
E: ann@arp-b-and-b.freeserve.co.uk
I: www.arp-b-and-b.freeserve.co.uk

Avalon Barn ♦♦♦♦
Lower Godney, Wells BA5 1RZ
T: (01458) 835005
F: (01458) 835636
E: wigan@ukonline.co.uk

The Barn ♦♦♦
84b Bove Town, Glastonbury, BA6 8JG
T: (01458) 832991

The Bolthole ♦♦♦
32 Chilkwell Street, Glastonbury, BA6 8DA
T: (01458) 832800

46 Bove Town ♦♦♦
Glastonbury, BA6 8JE
T: (01458) 833684

Coig Deug ♦♦
15 Helyar Close, Glastonbury, BA6 9LQ
T: (01458) 835945
E: kath@coigdeug.freeserve.co.uk
I: www.coigdeug.freeserve.co.uk

Divine Light Bed and Breakfast ♦♦♦
16a Magdalene Street, Glastonbury, BA6 9EH
T: (01458) 835909
E: glastonburyrose@lineone.net
I: www.divinelightcentre.co.uk

The Flying Dragon ♦♦♦♦
12 Hexton Road, Glastonbury, BA6 8HL
T: (01458) 830321
E: rench.ness@virgin.net
I: www.flyingdragon.co.uk

Hawthornes Hotel and Restaurant ♦♦
8-12 Northload Street, Glastonbury, BA6 9JJ
T: (01458) 831255
F: (01458) 831255
E: walker@hawthorneshotel.fsnet.co.uk

The Heart Centred Bed & Breakfast with Morning Meditation ♦♦♦
24 Bove Town, Glastonbury, BA6 8JE
T: (01458) 833467
I: www.glastonbury.co.uk/users/mitchell-a.html

The Lightship ♦♦♦
82 Bove Town, Glastonbury, BA6 8JG
T: (01458) 833698
E: roselightship2001@yahoo.co.uk
I: www.lightship.ukf.net

Little Orchard ♦♦♦
Ashwell Lane, Glastonbury, BA6 8BG
T: (01458) 831620
E: the.littleorchard@lineone.net
I: www.smoothhound.co.uk/hotels/orchard.html

Mafeking
♦♦♦♦ SILVER AWARD
67 Wells Road, Glastonbury, BA6 9BY
T: (01458) 833379
E: mafeking@wellsroad.freeserve.co.uk

Meadow Barn
Rating Applied For
Middlewick Holiday Cottages, Wick Lane, Glastonbury, BA6 8JW
T: (01458) 832351
F: (01458) 832351
E: info@middlewickholidaycottages.co.uk
I: www.smoothhound.co.uk/hotels/middlewi.html

Meare Manor ♦♦♦♦
60 St Marys Road, Meare, Glastonbury BA6 9SR
T: (01458) 860449
F: (01458) 860449
E: info@mearemanor.co.uk
I: www.mearemanor.co.uk

Melrose ♦♦♦
Coursing Batch, Glastonbury, BA6 8BH
T: (01458) 834706
F: 07973 108646
E: melrose@underthetor.freeserve.co.uk

Merryall House ♦♦♦
50 Roman Way, Glastonbury, BA6 8AD
T: (01458) 834511
E: francidev@hotmail.com
I: www.merriyallhouse.com

Number Three ♦♦♦♦♦
3 Magdalene Street, Glastonbury, BA6 9EW
T: (01458) 832129
F: (01458) 834227
E: info@numberthree.co.uk
I: www.numberthree.co.uk

The Old Bakery ♦♦♦
84A Bove Town, Glastonbury, BA6 8JG
T: (01458) 833400
E: oldbakery@talk21.com

Pilgrims ♦♦♦
12/13 Norbins Road, Glastonbury, BA6 9JE
T: (01458) 834722
E: pilgrimsbb@hotmail.com
I: www.pigrimsbb.co.uk

Pippin ♦♦♦
4 Ridgeway Gardens, Glastonbury, BA6 8ER
T: (01458) 834262
E: daphne.slater@ukonline.co.uk
I: www.smoothhound.co.uk/hotels/pippin.html

Shambhala Health & Healing Retreat ♦♦♦
Coursing Batch, Glastonbury, BA6 8BH
T: (01458) 831797
F: (01458) 834751
E: findyourself@shambhala.co.uk
I: www.shambhala.co.uk

Tordown Guest House ♦♦♦♦
5 Ashwell Lane, Glastonbury, BA6 8BG
T: (01458) 832287
F: (01458) 831100
E: torangel@aol.com
I: www.tordown.com

Wearyall Hill House ♦♦♦♦
78 The Roman Way, Glastonbury, BA6 8AD
T: (01458) 835510
E: enquiries@wearyallhillhouse.co.uk
I: www.wearyallhillhouse.co.uk

GODNEY
Somerset

Double-Gate Farm
♦♦♦♦ GOLD AWARD
Godney, Wells BA5 1RX
T: (01458) 832217
F: (01458) 835612
E: doublegatefarm@aol.com
I: www.doublegatefarm.com

GOLDSITHNEY
Cornwall

Penleen ♦♦♦
South Road, Goldsithney, Penzance TR20 9LF
T: (01736) 710633
F: (01736) 711171
E: jimblain@penleen.com
I: www.penleen.com

GRAMPOUND
Cornwall

Perran House ♦♦♦
Fore Street, Grampound, Truro TR2 4RS
T: (01726) 882066
F: (01726) 882936

GREAT DURNFORD
Wiltshire

Meadow Croft ♦♦♦♦
Great Durnford, Salisbury SP4 6AY
T: (01722) 782643
F: 07714 158791

GREENHAM
Somerset

The Granary ♦♦♦♦
Bishops Barton, Greenham, Wellington TA21 0JJ
T: (01823) 672969
E: bishopsbarton@talk21.com

Greenham Hall ♦♦♦
Greenham, Wellington TA21 0JJ
T: (01823) 672603
F: (01823) 672307
E: greenhamhall@btopenworld.com
I: www.greenhamhall.co.uk

GRITTLETON
Wiltshire

The Neeld Arms Inn ♦♦♦
The Street, Grittleton, Chippenham SN14 6AP
T: (01249) 782470
F: (01249) 782470
E: neeldarms@genie.co.uk
I: www.neeldarms.co.uk

GULWORTHY
Devon

Colcharton Farm
♦♦♦♦ SILVER AWARD
Gulworthy, Tavistock PL19 8HU
T: (01822) 616435
F: (01822) 616435
E: colchartonfarm@agriplus.net
I: www.visit-dartmoor.co.uk

Hele Farm ♦♦♦♦
Gulworthy, Tavistock PL19 8PA
T: (01822) 833084
F: (01822) 833084

GURNEY SLADE
Somerset

The Old Mendip Coaching Inn ♦♦♦
Gurney Slade, Bath BA3 4UU
T: (01749) 841234
E: floella@tinyonline.co.uk

HALLATROW
Bath and North East Somerset

Tennis Court House ♦♦♦♦
Wells Road, Hallatrow, Bristol BS39 6EJ
T: (01761) 451568

HALSTOCK
Dorset

Quiet Woman House ♦♦♦
Halstock, Yeovil BA22 9RX
T: (01935) 891218
E: quietwomanhouse@ukonline.co.uk

HALWELL
Devon

The Old Inn ♦♦♦♦
Halwell, Totnes TQ9 7JA
T: (01803) 712329

Orchard House
♦♦♦♦♦ SILVER AWARD
Horner, Halwell, Totnes TQ9 7LB
T: (01548) 821448
I: www.orchard-house-halwell.co.uk

HAMBRIDGE
Somerset

Manor Farmhouse ♦♦♦
Manor Farm, Hambridge, Langport TA10 0AY
T: (01460) 281207
F: (01460) 281207
E: manorfm@yahoo.co.uk

HARLYN BAY
Cornwall

The Harlyn Inn ♦♦♦
Harlyn Bay, Padstow PL28 8SB
T: (01841) 520207
F: (01841) 520722
E: harlyninn@aol.com

Polmark Hotel ♦♦♦
Harlyn Bay, Padstow PL28 8SB
T: (01841) 520206
F: (01841) 520206
E: dplum9705@aol.com

St Cadoc Farm ♦♦♦
Harlyn Bay, Padstow, PL28 8SA
T: (01841) 520487
F: (01841) 520487

HARTLAKE
Somerset

Hartlake Farm ♦♦♦♦
Hartlake, Glastonbury BA6 9AB
T: (01458) 835406
F: (01749) 670373
I: www.hartlakebandb.co.uk

HARTLAND
Devon

Elmscott Farm ♦♦♦♦
Hartland, Bideford EX39 6ES
T: (01237) 441276
F: (01237) 441076

Gawlish Farm - Beach & Bracken BO7 ♦♦♦
Hartland, Bideford
T: (01237) 441320

Golden Park
♦♦♦♦♦ GOLD AWARD
Hartland, Bideford EX39 6EP
T: (01237) 441254
E: YEO@gopark.freeserve.co.uk

Hartland Quay Hotel ♦♦♦
Hartland, Bideford EX39 6DU
T: (01237) 441218
F: (01237) 441371

Trutrese ♦♦♦♦
Harton Cross, Hartland, Bideford EX39 6AE
T: (01237) 441274

HATHERLEIGH
Devon

The George ♦♦♦
Market Street, Hatherleigh, Okehampton EX20 3JN
T: (01837) 810454
F: (01837) 810901
E: jfpozzetto@yahoo.co.uk

Seldon Farm ♦♦♦
Monkokehampton, Winkleigh EX19 8RY
T: (01837) 810312

HAWKRIDGE
Somerset

Parsonage Farm Guesthouse ♦♦♦
Parsonage Farm, Hawkridge, Dulverton TA22 9QP
T: (01643) 831503
F: (01643) 831197
E: guests@parsonagefarm.plus.com
I: www.parsonagefarm.plus.com

HAYLE
Cornwall

Penellen Hotel ♦♦♦
Riviere Towans, Hayle, TR27 5AF
T: (01736) 753777
F: (01736) 753777

HELSTON
Cornwall

Longstone Farm ♦♦♦
Coverack Bridges, Trenear, Helston TR13 0HG
T: (01326) 572483
F: (01326) 572483

Lyndale Guest House ♦♦♦
4 Greenbank, Meneage Road, Helston, TR13 8JA
T: (01326) 561082
F: (01326) 565813
E: enquiries@lyndale1.freeserve.co.uk
I: www.lyndale1.freeserve.co.uk

Mandeley Guest House ♦♦♦
Clodgey Lane, Helston, TR13 8PJ
T: (01326) 572550

Strathallan ♦♦♦♦
6 Monument Road, Helston, TR13 8HF
T: (01326) 573683
F: (01326) 565777
E: strathallangh@aol.com
I: www.connexions.co.uk/strathallan

HENLADE
Somerset

Barn Close Nurseries ♦♦♦
Henlade, Taunton TA3 5DH
T: (01823) 443507

HENSTRIDGE
Somerset

Fountain Inn
Rating Applied For
High Street, Henstridge, Templecombe BA8 0RA
T: (01963) 362722
F: (01963) 362722
I: www.fountaininn.fsnet.co.uk

Quiet Corner Farm ♦♦♦♦
Henstridge, Templecombe BA8 0RA
T: (01963) 363045
F: (01963) 363045
E: quietcorner.thompson@virgin.net

HERMITAGE
Dorset

Almshouse Farm
♦♦♦♦ GOLD AWARD
Hermitage, Holnest, Sherborne DT9 6HA
T: (01963) 210296
F: (01963) 210296

HEXWORTHY
Devon

The Forest Inn ♦♦♦♦
Hexworthy, Yelverton PL20 6SD
T: (01364) 631211
F: (01364) 631515
E: info@theforestinn.co.uk
I: www.theforestinn.co.uk

HEYTESBURY
Wiltshire

Red Lion Hotel ♦♦
42a High Street, Heytesbury, Warminster BA12 0EA
T: (01985) 840315

HIGHBRIDGE
Somerset

46 Church Street ♦♦
Highbridge, TA9 3AQ
T: (01278) 788365

Knoll Farm ♦♦♦
Jarvis Lane, East Brent, Highbridge, TA9 4HS
T: (01278) 760227

Sandacre ♦♦♦
75 Old Burnham Road, Highbridge, TA9 3JG
T: (01278) 781221

HIGHWORTH
Wiltshire

Roves Farm ♦♦♦
Sevenhampton, Highworth, Swindon SN6 7QG
T: (01793) 763939
F: (01793) 763939
E: jb@rovesfarm.freeserve.co.uk
I: www.rovesfarm.co.uk

HILMARTON
Wiltshire

Burfoots ♦♦♦♦
The Close, Hilmarton, Calne SN11 8TH
T: (01249) 760492
F: (01249) 760609
E: anncooke@burfoots.co.uk
I: www.burfoots.co.uk

HOLBETON
Devon

Bugle Rocks
♦♦♦♦ SILVER AWARD
The Old School, Battisborough, Holbeton, Plymouth PL8 1JX
T: (01752) 830422
F: (01752) 830558
E: buglerocks@hotmail.com

HOLNE
Devon

Mill Leat Farm ♦♦♦
Holne, Newton Abbot TQ13 7RZ
T: (01364) 631283
F: (01364) 631283

HOLSWORTHY
Devon

Bason Farm ♦♦♦♦
Bradford, Holsworthy, EX22 7AW
T: (01409) 281277
E: info@basonfarmholidays.co.uk
I: www.basonfarmholidays.co.uk

Highbre Crest ♦♦♦♦
Whitstone, Holsworthy, EX22 6UF
T: (01288) 341002
E: lindacole@ukonline.co.uk

Leworthy Farmhouse Bed & Breakfast
♦♦♦♦ SILVER AWARD
Leworthy Farmhouse, Lower Leworthy, Pyworthy, Holsworthy EX22 6SJ
T: (01409) 259469

HONITON
Devon

Barn Park Farm ♦♦♦
Stockland Hill, Honiton, EX14 9JA
T: 0800 3282605
F: (01404) 861297
E: pab@barnparkfarm.fsnet.co.uk
I: www.lymeregis.com

Bidwell Farm and Haybarton Annexe ♦♦♦♦
Bidwell Farm, Upottery, Honiton EX14 9PP
T: (01404) 861122
F: 08700 554960
E: pat@rbwells.demon.co.uk
I: www.bidwellfarm.co.uk

Fairmile Inn ♦♦♦♦
On old A30, Fairmile, Ottery St Mary EX11 1LP
T: (01404) 812827
F: (01404) 815806
E: leon.courtney@thefairmileinn.co.uk
I: www.fairmileinn.co.uk

Lelamarie ♦♦♦
Awliscombe, Honiton EX14 3PP
T: (01404) 44646
F: (01404) 42131

The New Dolphin Hotel ♦♦♦
115 High Street, Honiton, EX14 8LS
T: (01404) 42377
F: (01404) 47662

The Old Vicarage ♦♦♦♦
Yarcombe, Honiton, EX14 9BD
T: (01404) 861594
F: (01404) 861594
E: jonannstockwell@aol.com
I: members.aol.com/Jonannstockwell/

Wessington Farm
♦♦♦♦ SILVER AWARD
Awliscombe, Honiton EX14 3NU
T: (01404) 42280
F: (01404) 45271
E: b&b@eastdevon.com
I: www.eastdevon.com/bedandbreakfast

HORNINGSHAM
Wiltshire

Mill Farm ♦♦♦♦
Horningsham, Warminster BA12 7LL
T: (01985) 844333
E: millfarm_horningsham@yahoo.co.uk

HORRABRIDGE
Devon

Overcombe Hotel ♦♦♦♦
Old Station Road, Horrabridge, Yelverton PL20 7RA
T: (01822) 853501
F: (01822) 853501
E: overcombehotel@horrabridge99.freeserve.co.uk
I: www.overcombehotel.co.uk

HORSINGTON
Somerset

Half Moon Inn ♦♦♦
Horsington, Templecombe BA8 0EF
T: (01963) 370140
F: (01963) 371450
E: halfmoon@horsington.co.uk
I: www.horsington.co.uk

HORTON
Wiltshire

Partacre ♦♦
Horton, Devizes SN10 3NB
T: (01380) 860261

HUISH EPISCOPI
Somerset

Spring View ♦♦♦♦
Wagg Drove, Huish Episcopi, Langport TA10 9ER
T: (01458) 251215
E: ruddockspring@aol.com

Wagg Bridge Cottage ♦♦♦♦
Ducks Hill, Huish Episcopi, Langport TA10 9EN
T: (01458) 251488
F: 0820 4055 2077
E: sandy@waggbridgecottage.freeserve.co.uk
I: www.waggbridgecottage.co.uk

HULLAVINGTON
Wiltshire

Bradfield Manor
♦♦♦♦♦ SILVER AWARD
Malmesbury, SN14 6EU
T: (01666) 838000
F: (01666) 838200
E: enquiries@bradfieldmanor.co.uk
I: www.bradfieldmanor.co.uk

IDDESLEIGH
Devon

Parsonage Farm
♦♦♦♦ SILVER AWARD
Iddesleigh, Winkleigh EX19 8SN
T: (01837) 810318

IFORD
Wiltshire

Dog Kennel Farm Cottage ♦♦
Iford, Bradford-on-Avon BA15 2BB
T: (01225) 723533

ILFRACOMBE
Devon

Cairn House Hotel ♦♦♦
43 St Brannocks Road, Ilfracombe, EX34 8EH
T: (01271) 863911
F: 07070 800630
E: info@cairnhousehotel.co.uk
I: www.cairnhousehotel.co.uk

Capstone Hotel and Restaurant ♦♦♦
St James Place, Ilfracombe, EX34 9BJ
T: (01271) 863540
F: (01271) 862277
E: steve@capstone.freeserve.co.uk
I: www.ilfracombe2000.freeserve.co.uk

The Collingdale Hotel ♦♦♦
Larkstone Terrace, Ilfracombe, EX34 9NU
T: (01271) 863770
F: (01271) 863770
E: collingdale@onet.co.uk
I: www.ilfracombe-guide.co.uk/collingdale.htm

Combe Lodge Hotel ♦♦♦
Chambercombe Park, Ilfracombe, EX34 9QW
T: (01271) 864518
F: (01271) 867628
E: combelodgehotel@tinyworld.co.uk
I: www.members.aol.com/combelodgehotel

Dedes Hotel ♦♦♦
1-4 The Promenade, Ilfracombe, EX34 9BD
T: (01271) 862545
F: (01271) 862234
E: jackie@dedes.fsbusiness.co.uk
I: www.clayshooting-dedes.co.uk

Dilkhusa Grand Hotel ♦♦♦
Wilder Road, Ilfracombe, EX34 9AH
T: (01271) 863505
F: (01271) 864739
I: www.shearingsholidays.com

Dorchester Hotel ♦♦
59 St Brannocks Road, Ilfracombe, EX34 8EQ
T: (01271) 866949

The Epchris Hotel ♦♦♦
Torrs Park, Ilfracombe, EX34 8AZ
T: (01271) 862751
F: (01271) 879077
E: epchris-hotel@ic24.net
I: www.epchrishotel.co.uk

Glen Tor Hotel ♦♦♦♦
Torrs Park, Ilfracombe, EX34 8AZ
T: (01271) 862403
F: (01271) 862403
E: info@glentorhotel.co.uk
I: www.glentorhotel.co.uk

Greyven House ♦♦♦
4 St James Place, Ilfracombe, EX34 9BH
T: (01271) 862505
F: (01271) 862505
E: sandratrevor@greyvenhouse.fsnet.co.uk
I: www.ilfracombe-tourism.co.uk/greyvenhouse

Grosvenor Hotel ♦♦♦
Wilder Road, Ilfracombe, EX34 9AF
T: (01271) 863426
F: (01271) 863714

Laston House Hotel ♦♦♦
Hillsborough Road, Ilfracombe, EX34 9NT
T: (01271) 866557
F: (01271) 867754
E: hilary@lastonhouse.com
I: www.s-h-systems.co.uk/hotels/laston.html

Lyncott House ♦♦♦♦
56 St Brannock's Road, Ilfracombe, EX34 8EQ
T: (01271) 862425
F: (01271) 862425
E: david@ukhotels.com
I: www.lyncottdevon.com

Rivendell Guest House ♦♦♦
28 St Brannocks Road, Ilfracombe, EX34 8EQ
T: (01271) 866852
E: jackie@rivendellguesthouse.co.uk
I: www.rivendellguesthouse.co.uk

Strathmore Hotel
♦♦♦♦♦ SILVER AWARD
57 St Brannocks Road, Ilfracombe, EX34 8EQ
T: (01271) 862248
F: (01271) 862243
E: strathmore@ukhotels.com
I: www.strathmore.ukhotels.com

Sunnymeade Country Hotel ♦♦♦
Dean Cross, West Down, Ilfracombe EX34 8NT
T: (01271) 863668
F: (01271) 863668
E: info@sunnymeade.co.uk
I: www.sunnymeade.co.uk

The Towers Hotel ♦♦♦
Chambercombe Park Road, Ilfracombe, EX34 9QN
T: (01271) 862809
F: (01271) 879442
E: info@thetowers.co.uk
I: www.thetowers.co.uk

Varley House ♦♦♦♦
Chambercombe Park, Ilfracombe, EX34 9QW
T: (01271) 863927
F: (01271) 879299
E: info@varleyhouse.co.uk
I: www.varleyhouse.co.uk

Westaway ♦♦♦♦
Torrs Park, Ilfracombe, EX34 8AY
T: (01271) 864459
F: (01271) 863486
E: westaway55@btopenworld.com
I: www.westaway.net

Wildersmouth Hotel ♦
Sommers Crescent, Ilfracombe, EX34 9DP
T: (01271) 862002
F: (01271) 862803
E: booking@devoniahotel.co.uk
I: www.devoniahotels.co.uk

ILLOGAN
Cornwall

Aviary Court Hotel ♦♦♦♦
Marys Well, Illogan, Redruth TR16 4QZ
T: (01209) 842256
F: (01209) 843744
E: aviarycourt@connexions.co.uk
I: www.connexions.co.uk/aviarycourt/index.htm

ILMINSTER
Somerset

Dillington House
♦♦♦♦ SILVER AWARD
Ilminster, TA19 9DT
T: (01460) 52427
F: (01460) 52433
E: dillington@somerset.gov.uk
I: www.dillington.co.uk

Graden ♦♦♦
Peasmarsh, Ilminster TA19 0SG
T: (01460) 52371
F: (01460) 52371

Hermitage ♦♦♦
29 Station Road, Ilminster, TA19 9BE
T: (01460) 53028
I: www.home.freeuk.net/hermitage

Kent House
Rating Applied For
Barrington, Ilminster, TA19 0JP
T: (01460) 52613
E: jrclushington@yahoo.co.uk

Minster View ♦♦♦♦
8 Butts Road, Ilminster, TA19 0AX
T: (01460) 54619
E: trishlee@freenet.co.uk
I: www.minsterview.co.uk

ISLES OF SCILLY

Hotel Beachcomber ♦♦♦
Thorofare, St Mary's, TR21 0LN
T: (01720) 422682
F: (01720) 422532

Nundeeps ♦♦♦
Rams Valley, St Mary's, TR21 0JX
T: (01720) 422517
E: cook@nundeeps.freeserve.co.uk

Polreath Guest House ♦♦♦
Higher Town, St Martin's, TR25 0QL
T: (01720) 422046
F: (01720) 422046
E: sarah.poat@ntlworld.com

Seaview Moorings
♦♦♦♦♦ SILVER AWARD
The Strand, St Mary's, TR21 0PT
T: (01720) 422327
E: enquiries@islesofscillyestateagents.com
I: www.islesofscillyestateagents.com

IVYBRIDGE
Devon

Hillhead Farm
♦♦♦♦ SILVER AWARD
Ugborough, Ivybridge PL21 0HQ
T: (01752) 892674
F: (01752) 690111
I: www.hillheadfarm.co.uk

Venn Farm ♦♦♦
Ugborough, Ivybridge PL21 0PE
T: (01364) 73240
F: (01364) 73240
I: www.smoothhound.co.uk/hotels/vennfarm

JACOBSTOW
Cornwall

The Old Rectory ♦♦♦♦♦
Jacobstow, Bude EX23 0BR
T: (01840) 230380
F: (01840) 230380
E: johntodd50@hotmail.com

KEA
Cornwall

Nansavallan Farm ♦♦♦
Kea, Truro TR3 6AD
T: (01872) 272350

KEINTON MANDEVILLE
Somerset

Stangray House ♦♦♦♦
Church Street, Keinton Mandeville, Somerton TA11 6ER
T: (01458) 223984
F: (01458) 224 295
E: david.moran@btinternet.com

KELSTON
Bath and North East Somerset

Old Crown ♦♦♦
Kelston, Bath BA1 9AQ
T: (01225) 423032
F: (01225) 480115

KENN
Devon

Lower Thornton Farm ♦♦♦♦
Kenn, Exeter EX6 7XH
T: (01392) 833434
F: (01392) 833434
E: alisonlack@msn.com

KENTISBURY
Devon

Beachborough Country House
Rating Applied For
Beachborough, Kentisbury, Barnstaple EX31 4NH
T: (01271) 882487
F: (01271) 882487
E: viviane@beachborough.freeserve.co.uk
I: www.BeachboroughCountryHouse.co.uk

KENTON
Devon

Devon Arms ♦♦♦
Fore Street, Kenton, Exeter EX6 8LD
T: (01626) 890213
F: (01626) 891678
E: devon.arms@ukgateway.net

KILVE
Somerset

The Old Mill ♦♦♦♦
Kilve, Bridgwater TA5 1EB
T: (01278) 741571

KINGSAND
Cornwall

Halfway House Inn ♦♦♦
Fore Street, Kingsand, PL10 1NA
T: (01752) 822279
F: (01752) 823146
E: info@halfwayinn.biz
I: www.halfwayinn.biz

KINGSBRIDGE
Devon

The Ashburton Arms ♦♦♦
West Charleton, Kingsbridge TQ7 2AH
T: (01548) 531242

Ashleigh House ♦♦♦♦
Ashleigh Road, Kingsbridge, TQ7 1HB
T: (01548) 852893
F: (01548) 854468
E: reception@ashleigh-house.co.uk
I: www.ashleigh-house.co.uk

Combe Farm B & B
♦♦♦♦ SILVER AWARD
Loddiswell, Kingsbridge TQ7 4DT
T: (01548) 550560
F: (01548) 550560
E: Combefarm@Hotmail.com

Coombe Farm ♦♦♦♦
Kingsbridge, TQ7 4AB
T: (01548) 852038
F: (01548) 852038

Globe Inn ♦♦
Frogmore, Kingsbridge TQ7 2NR
T: (01548) 531351
F: (01548) 531351
E: enquiries@theglobeinn.co.uk
I: www.theglobeinn.co.uk

Shute Farm ♦♦♦
South Milton, Kingsbridge TQ7 3JL
T: (01548) 560680
E: luscombe@shutefarm.fsnet.co.uk

Sloop Inn ♦♦♦
Bantham, Kingsbridge TQ7 3AJ
T: (01548) 560489
F: (01548) 561940

South Allington House
♦♦♦♦ SILVER AWARD
Chivelstone, Kingsbridge TQ7 2NB
T: (01548) 511272
F: (01548) 511421
E: barbara@sthallingtonbnb.demon.co.uk
I: www.sthallingtonbnb.demon.co.uk

KINGSBURY EPISCOPI
Somerset

The Retreat ♦♦♦♦
Kingsbury Episcopi, Martock TA12 6AZ
T: (01935) 823500

KINGSKERSWELL
Devon

Harewood Guesthouse ♦♦♦
17 Torquay Road, Kingskerswell, Newton Abbot, TQ12 5HH
T: (01803) 872228

KINGSWEAR
Devon

Coleton Barton Farm ♦♦♦
Brownstone Road, Kingswear, Dartmouth TQ6 0EQ
T: (01803) 752795
F: (01803) 752241
E: carolinehaddock@btconnect.com

KINGTON LANGLEY
Wiltshire

The Moors ♦♦♦
Malmesbury Road, Kington Langley, Chippenham SN14 6HT
T: (01249) 750288
F: (01249) 7508814

KINGWESTON
Somerset

Lower Farm ♦♦♦♦
Kingweston, Somerton
TA11 6BA
T: (01458) 223237
F: (01458) 223276
E: lowerfarm@kingweston.demon.co.uk
I: www.lowerfarm.net

KNOWSTONE
Devon

West Bowden Farm ♦♦♦
Knowstone, South Molton
EX36 4RP
T: (01398) 341224

LACOCK
Wiltshire

King John's Hunting Lodge ♦♦♦♦
21 Church Street, Lacock, Chippenham SN15 2LB
T: (01249) 730313
F: (01249) 730725

Lacock Pottery Bed & Breakfast ♦♦♦♦
1 The Tanyard, Church Street, Lacock, Chippenham SN15 2LB
T: (01249) 730266
F: (01249) 730946
E: simonemcdowell@lacockbedandbreakfast.com
I: www.lacockbedandbreakfast.com

Lower Lodge ♦♦♦
35 Bowden Hill, Lacock, Chippenham SN15 2PP
T: (01249) 730711
F: (01249) 730955

The Old Rectory ♦♦♦♦
Cantax Hill, Lacock, Chippenham SN15 2JZ
T: (01249) 730335
F: (01249) 730166
E: sexton@oldrectorylacock.co.uk
I: www.oldrectorylacock.co.uk

Pen-Y-Brook ♦♦♦
Notton, Lacock, Chippenham SN15 2NF
T: (01249) 730376

Videl ♦♦♦
6A Bewley Lane, Lacock, Chippenham SN15 2PG
T: (01249) 730279

LADOCK
Cornwall

Swallows Court ♦♦♦♦
Treworyan, Ladock, Truro
TR2 4QD
T: (01726) 883488
F: (01726) 882689
E: sarah@swallowscourt.fsnet.co.uk

LAMERTON
Devon

New Court Farm ♦♦♦
Lamerton, Tavistock PL19 8RR
T: (01822) 614319

LAMORNA
Cornwall

Castallack Farm Rating Applied For
Castallack, Lamorna, Penzance
TR19 6NL
T: (01736) 731969
F: (01736) 731969
E: hood@castallackfarm.fsnet.co.uk
I: www.castallackfarm.co.uk

LANDSCOVE
Devon

Thornecroft
♦♦♦♦ SILVER AWARD
Landscove, Ashburton, Newton Abbot TQ13 7LX
T: (01803) 762500
E: tonymatthews@lineone.net
I: www.b&b@thornecroft.co.uk

LANEAST
Cornwall

Stitch Park ♦♦♦♦
Laneast, Launceston PL15 8PN
T: (01566) 86687
E: stitchpark@hotmail.com

LANGFORD
Devon

Newcourt Barton ♦♦♦
Langford, Cullompton EX15 1SE
T: (01884) 277326
F: (01884) 277326
E: newcourtbarton@btinternet.com

LANGPORT
Somerset

Amberley ♦♦♦♦
Martock Road, Long Load, Langport, TA10 9LD
T: (01458) 241542
E: jean.atamberley@talk21.com

The Black Swan ♦♦♦
North Street, Langport,
TA10 9RQ
T: (01458) 250355
F: (01458) 253589

Gothic House ♦♦♦♦
Muchelney, Langport TA10 0DW
T: (01458) 250626
E: joy-thorne@totalserve.co.uk

Muchelney Ham Farm
♦♦♦♦♦ GOLD AWARD
Muchelney, Langport TA10 0DJ
T: (01458) 250737
F: (01458) 250737
I: www.muchelneyhamfarm.co.uk

The Old Pound Inn ♦♦♦
Aller, Langport TA10 0RA
T: (01458) 250469
F: (01458) 250469

LANIVET
Cornwall

St Benet's Abbey ♦♦♦♦
Truro Road, Lanivet, PL30 5HF
T: (01208) 831352
F: (01208) 832052

Tremeere Manor ♦♦♦
Lanivet, Bodmin PL30 5BG
T: (01208) 831513
F: (01208) 832417
E: oliver@tremeeremanor@fwi.co.uk

Willowbrook ♦♦♦♦
Old Coach Road, Lamorick, Lanivet, Bodmin PL30 5HB
T: (01208) 831670
F: (01208) 831670
E: miles.willowbrook@btinternet.com
I: www.bnbirdex.com/willowbrook

LANSALLOS
Cornwall

Lesquite
♦♦♦♦ SILVER AWARD
Lansallos, Looe PL13 2QE
T: (01503) 220315
F: (01503) 220137
E: lesquite@farmersweekly.net
I: www.lesquite-polperro.fsnet.co.uk

West Kellow Farmhouse ♦♦♦
Lansallos, Looe PL13 2QL
T: (01503) 272089
F: (01503) 272089
E: westkellow@aol.com
I: www.westkellow.co.uk

LATTON
Wiltshire

Dolls House ♦♦♦
55 The Street, Latton, Swindon
SN6 6DJ
T: (01793) 750384
F: (01793) 750384
E: gemma-maraffi@bbdollshouse.freeserve.co.uk

LAUNCELLS
Cornwall

Hersham Carpentry ♦♦♦
Launcells, Bude EX23 9LZ
T: (01288) 321369
F: (01288) 321 369
E: tillinghast@ndirect.co.uk

LAUNCESTON
Cornwall

Berrio Bridge House ♦♦♦♦
North Hill, Launceston PL15 7NL
T: (01566) 782714
F: (01566) 782714
E: Helen@berriobridge.freeserve.co.uk

11 Castle Street ♦♦♦♦
Launceston, PL15 8BA
T: (01566) 773873

Glencoe Villa ♦♦♦
13 Race Hill, Launceston,
PL15 9BB
T: (01566) 773012

Hill Park ♦♦♦♦
St Thomas, Launceston,
PL15 8SH
T: (01566) 86937
E: barbara_penfold@hotmail.com

Laneast Barton ♦♦♦
Laneast Barton, Launceston,
PL15 8PN
T: (01566) 880104
F: (01566) 880104
E: affb@totalise.co.uk

Middle Tremollett Farm ♦♦♦♦
Coad's Green, Launceston
PL15 7NA
T: (01566) 782416
F: (01566) 782416
E: btrewin@talk21.com
I: www.tremollett.com

The Old Granary ♦♦♦♦
North Petherwin, Launceston
PL15 8LR
T: (01566) 785593

The Old Vicarage
♦♦♦♦ SILVER AWARD
Treneglos, Launceston PL15 8UQ
T: (01566) 781351
F: (01566) 781351
E: maggie@fancourt.freeserve.co.uk
I: www.fancourt.freeserve.co.uk

Panson Mill Farm ♦♦♦♦
St Giles on the Heath, Launceston, PL15 9SQ
T: (01409) 211306
F: (01409) 211107
E: lizzie.browning@care4free.net

Trethorne Leisure Farm ♦♦♦
Kennards House, Launceston,
PL15 8QE
T: (01566) 86324
F: (01566) 86981
E: trethorneleisure@eclipse.co.uk
I: www.cornwall-online.co.uk/trethorne

Trevadlock Farm
♦♦♦♦ SILVER AWARD
Trevadlock, Congdon Shop, Launceston, PL15 7PW
T: (01566) 782239
F: (01566) 782239
E: trevadlock@farming.co.uk
I: www.trevadlock.co.uk

Wheatley Farm
♦♦♦♦♦ GOLD AWARD
Maxworthy, Launceston
PL15 8LY
T: (01566) 781232
F: (01566) 781232
E: valerie@wheatleyfrm.com
I: www.wheatleyfrm.com

White Hart Hotel ♦♦♦
15 Broad Street, Launceston,
PL15 8AA
T: (01566) 772013
F: (01566) 773668
E: reception@whitehartotellaunceston.co.uk
I: www.whitehartotel-launceston.co.uk

The White Horse Inn ♦♦♦
14 Newport Square, Launceston,
PL15 8EL
T: (01566) 772084
F: (01566) 772090
E: m.howard@talk21.com

LAVERSTOCK
Wiltshire

20 Potters Way ♦♦♦
Laverstock, Salisbury SP1 1PY
T: (01722) 335031
F: (01722) 335031

1 Riverside Close ♦♦♦♦
Laverstock, Salisbury SP1 1QW
T: (01722) 320287
F: (01722) 320287
E: marytucker2001@yahoo.com

The Twitterings ♦♦♦
73 Church Road, Laverstock, Salisbury SP1 1QZ
T: (01722) 321760

LAVERTON
Somerset

Hollytree Cottage ♦♦♦♦
Laverton, Bath BA2 7QZ
T: (01373) 830786
F: (01373) 830786

LEWDOWN
Devon

Stowford Grange Farm ♦♦
Lewdown, Okehampton
EX20 4BZ
T: (01566) 783298

LISKEARD
Cornwall

Elnor Guest House ♦♦♦
1 Russell Street, Station Road, Liskeard, PL14 4BP
T: (01579) 342472
F: (01579) 345673
E: Elnor@btopenworld.com

Hyvue House ♦♦♦
Barras Cross, Liskeard, PL14 6BN
T: (01579) 348175

Lampen Farm ♦♦♦♦
St Neot, Liskeard PL14 6PB
T: (01579) 320284
F: (01579) 320284

Pencubitt Country House Hotel ♦♦♦♦
Station Road, Lamellion Cross, Liskeard, PL14 4EB
T: (01579) 342694
F: (01579) 342694
E: bookings@pencubitt.com
I: www.pencubitt.com

Trecorme Barton ♦♦♦♦
Quethiock, Liskeard PL14 3SH
T: (01579) 342646
F: (01579) 342646
E: RENFREE@trecormebarton.fsnet.co.uk

Tregondale Farm
♦♦♦♦ SILVER AWARD
Menheniot, Liskeard PL14 3RG
T: (01579) 342407
F: (01579) 342407
E: tregondale@connectfree.co.uk
I: www.tregondalefarm.co.uk

Trewint Farm ♦♦♦♦
Menheniot, Liskeard PL14 3RE
T: (01579) 347155
F: (01579) 347155

LITTLE BEDWYN
Wiltshire

Bridge Cottage ♦♦♦
Little Bedwyn, Marlborough
SN8 3JS
T: (01672) 870795
F: (01672) 870795
E: rwdaniel@bridgecott.fsnet.co.uk
I: www.bridgecott.co.uk

LITTLE LANGFORD
Wiltshire

Little Langford Farmhouse
♦♦♦♦♦ GOLD AWARD
Little Langford, Salisbury
SP3 4NR
T: (01722) 790205
F: (01722) 790086
E: bandb@littlelangford.co.uk
I: www.littlelangford.co.uk

LITTLE PETHERICK
Cornwall

Molesworth Manor ♦♦♦
Little Petherick, Padstow, PL27 7QT
T: (01841) 540292
E: molesworthmanor@aol.com
I: www.molesworthmanor.co.uk

LITTLE TORRINGTON
Devon

Smytham Manor Leisure ♦♦♦
Smytham Manor, Little Torrington, Torrington EX38 8PU
T: (01805) 622110
F: (01805) 625451
E: info@smytham.fsnet.co.uk

LITTLEHEMPSTON
Devon

Post Cottage ♦♦♦
Littlehempston, Totnes TQ9 6LU
T: (01803) 868192
F: (01803) 868192
E: hugh.gf@virgin.net
I: www.postcottage.co.uk

LONG BREDY
Dorset

Middle Farm ♦♦♦
Long Bredy, Dorchester
DT2 9HW
T: (01308) 482215
F: (01308) 482215
E: jonchrisscott@aol.com

LONG LOAD
Somerset

Fairlight ♦♦♦♦
Martock Road, Long Load, Langport TA10 9LG
T: (01458) 241323
E: mavisfairlight@eurobell.co.uk

LONGBRIDGE DEVERILL
Wiltshire

The George Inn ♦♦♦♦
Longbridge Deverill, Warminster
BA12 7DG
T: (01985) 840396
F: (01985) 841333
I: www.thegeorgeinnlongbridgedeveril.co.uk

LONGLEAT
Wiltshire

Post Office Farm ♦♦♦
Corsley Heath, Longleat, Warminster BA12 7PR
T: (01373) 832734
F: (01373) 832734
E: kmyoudan@lineone.net

LOOE
Cornwall

Barclay House ♦♦♦♦
St Martins Road, Looe, PL13 1LP
T: (01503) 262929
F: (01503) 262632
E: info@barclayhouse.co.uk
I: www.barclayhouse.co.uk

Bucklawren Farm
♦♦♦♦ SILVER AWARD
St Martin-by-Looe, Looe, PL13 1NZ
T: (01503) 240738
F: (01503) 240481
E: bucklawren@compuserve.com
I: www.bucklawren.co.uk

Coombe Farm Country House Hotel ♦♦♦♦
Widegates, Looe PL13 1QN
T: (01503) 240223
F: (01503) 240895
E: coombe_farm@hotmail.com
I: www.coombefarmhotel.co.uk

Down Ende Country House ♦♦♦
Widegates, Looe, PL13 1QN
T: (01503) 240213
F: (01503) 240656
E: enquiries@downende.com
I: www.downende.com

Little Larnick Farm ♦♦♦♦
Pelynt, Looe PL13 2NB
T: (01503) 262837
F: (01503) 262837
E: littlelarnick@btclick.com

The Panorama Hotel ♦♦♦♦
Hannafore Road, Looe, PL13 2DE
T: (01503) 262123
F: (01503) 265654
E: stay@looe.co.uk
I: www.looe.co.uk

Stonerock Cottage ♦♦♦♦
Portuan Road, Hannafore, West Looe, Looe PL13 2DN
T: (01503) 263651
F: (01503) 263414

Talehay ♦♦♦♦ SILVER AWARD
Tremaine, Pelynt, Looe PL13 2LT
T: (01503) 220252
F: (01503) 220252
E: paul@talehay.co.uk
I: www.talehay.co.uk

Trehaven Manor Hotel
♦♦♦♦ SILVER AWARD
Station Road, Looe, PL13 1HN
T: (01503) 262028
F: (01503) 262028
E: enquiries@trehavenhotel.co.uk
I: www.trehavenhotel.co.uk

Trevanion Hotel ♦♦♦
Hannafore, Looe, PL13 2DE
T: (01503) 262003
F: (01503) 265408
E: hotel@looecornwall.co.uk
I: www.looecornwall.co.uk

LOSTWITHIEL
Cornwall

Atkinson's Service Station ♦♦♦
Carnsews, Lostwithiel, PL22 0LH
T: (01208) 872548

LUSTLEIGH
Devon

Eastwrey Barton ♦♦♦♦
Moretonhampstead Road, Lustleigh, Newton Abbot
TQ13 9SN
T: (01647) 277338
F: (01647) 277133
E: jb@ewbarton.fsnet.co.uk

LYDIARD TREGOZE
Wiltshire

Park Farm ♦♦♦
Hook Street, Lydiard Tregoze, Swindon SN5 3NY
T: (01793) 853608

LYME REGIS
Dorset

Charnwood Guest House ♦♦♦♦
21 Woodmead Road, Lyme Regis, DT7 3AD
T: (01297) 445281
E: charnwood@lymeregis62.freeserve.co.uk
I: www.lymeregisaccommodation.com

Clappentail House
♦♦♦♦♦ SILVER AWARD
Uplyme Road, Lyme Regis, DT7 3LP
T: (01297) 445739
F: (01297) 444794
E: pountain@clappentail.freeserve.co.uk

Cliff Cottage ♦♦♦
Cobb Road, Lyme Regis, DT7 3JE
T: (01297) 443334
E: merry.bolton@btinternet.com

Coombe House ♦♦♦
41 Coombe Street, Lyme Regis, DT7 3PY
T: (01297) 443849
E: dunc@hughduncan.freeserve.co.uk
I: www.coombe-house.co.uk

Devon Hotel ♦♦♦♦
Lyme Road, Uplyme, Lyme Regis
DT7 3TQ
T: (01297) 443231
F: (01297) 445836
E: thedevonhotel@virgin.net
I: www.lymeregis.com/devon-hotel

Devonia Guest House ♦♦♦♦
2 Woodmead Road, Lyme Regis, DT7 3AB
T: (01297) 442869
F: (01297) 442869
E: roysue@fsmail.net.co.uk
I: www.devoniaguest.co.uk

Higher Spence ♦♦♦
Wootton Fitzpaine, Bridport
DT6 6DF
T: (01297) 560556
E: higherspence@eurolink.ltd.net

Kent House hotel ♦♦♦
Silver Street, Lyme Regis, DT7 3HT
T: (01297) 443442
F: (01297) 444626
E: thekenthouse@talk21.com
I: www.kenthousehotel.co.uk

The London Bed and Breakfast ♦♦♦
40 Church Street, Lyme Regis, DT7 3DA
T: (01297) 442083

Lucerne ♦♦♦
View Road, Lyme Regis, DT7 3AA
T: (01297) 443752
E: lucerne@lineone.net

Manaton B & B ♦♦♦♦
Hill Road, Lyme Regis, DT7 3PE
T: (01297) 445138

Mermaid House ♦♦♦♦
32 Coombe Street, Lyme Regis, DT7 3PP
T: (01297) 445351
E: mermaidhouse@talk21.com
I: www.smoothhound.co.uk

Ocean View ♦♦♦♦
2 Hadleigh Villas, Silver Street, Lyme Regis, DT7 3HR
T: (01297) 442567
E: Jaybabe@supanet.com
I: www.lymeregis.com/ocean/view

Old Lyme Guest House ♦♦♦♦ GOLD AWARD
29 Coombe Street, Lyme Regis, DT7 3PP
T: (01297) 442929
E: oldlyme.guesthouse@virgin.net
I: www.oldlymeguesthouse.co.uk

Orchard Country Hotel ♦♦♦♦
Rousdon, Lyme Regis, DT7 3XW
T: (01297) 442972
F: (01297) 443670
E: the.orchard@btinternet.com
I: www.orchardcountryhotel.com

The Red House ♦♦♦♦
Sidmouth Road, Lyme Regis, DT7 3ES
T: (01297) 442055
F: (01297) 442055
E: red.house@virgin.net
I: www.smoothhound.co.uk/hotels/redhous2.html

Rotherfield ♦♦♦
View Road, Lyme Regis, DT7 3AA
T: (01297) 445585
E: rotherfield@lymeregis.com
I: www.lymeregis.com/rotherfield/

Southernhaye ♦♦♦♦
Pound Road, Lyme Regis, DT7 3HX
T: (01297) 443077
F: (01297) 443077

Springfield ♦♦♦
Woodmead Road, Lyme Regis, DT7 3LJ
T: (01297) 443409
F: (01297) 443685
E: springfield@lymeregis.com
I: www.lymeregis.com/springfield

Thatch ♦♦♦♦
Uplyme Road, Lyme Regis, DT7 3LP
T: (01297) 442212
F: (01297) 443485
E: thethatch@lineone.net
I: www.uk-bedandbreakfasts.co.uk

Tudor House Hotel ♦♦♦♦
Church Street, Lyme Regis, DT7 3BU
T: (01297) 442472
E: tudor@eclipse.co.uk
I: www.thetudorhouse.co.uk

Victoria Hotel ♦♦♦
Uplyme Road, Lyme Regis, DT7 3LP
T: (01297) 444801
F: (01297) 442949
E: info@vichotel.co.uk
I: www.vichotel.co.uk

Westwood Guest House ♦♦♦
1 Woodmead Road, Lyme Regis, DT7 3LJ
T: (01297) 442376

LYNMOUTH
Devon

Bonnicott House Hotel ♦♦♦♦♦
Watersmeet Road, Lynmouth, EX35 6EP
T: (01598) 753346
F: (01598) 753724
E: bonnicott@hotmail.com
I: www.bonnicott.com

Coombe Farm ♦♦♦
Countisbury, Lynton EX35 6NF
T: (01598) 741236
F: (01598) 741236

Seaview Villa ♦♦♦♦
6 Summerhouse Path, Lynmouth, EX35 6ES
T: (01598) 753460
F: (01598) 752399
E: seaviewvilla.lynmouth@virgin.net

Tregonwell 'The Olde Sea-Captain's Guesthouse' ♦♦♦
1 Tors Road, Lynmouth, EX35 6ET
T: (01598) 753369
I: www.smoothhound.co.uk/hotels/tregonwl.html

The Village Inn ♦♦♦
19 Lynmouth Street, Lynmouth, EX35 6EH
T: (01598) 752354

LYNTON
Devon

Alford House Hotel ♦♦♦
3 Alford Terrace, Lynton, EX35 6AT
T: (01598) 752359
F: (01598) 752359
E: alfordhouse@btinternet.com
I: www.smoothhound.co.uk/hotels/alford.html

The Denes Guest House ♦♦♦
15 Longmead, Lynton, EX35 6DQ
T: (01598) 753573
F: (01598) 753573
E: j.e.mcgowan@btinternet.com
I: www.thedenes.com

Fernleigh Guest House ♦♦♦♦
Park Street, Lynton, EX35 6BY
T: (01598) 753575
F: (01598) 753575
E: bookings@fernleigh.net
I: www.fernleigh.net

Ingleside Hotel ♦♦♦♦
Lee Road, Lynton, EX35 6HW
T: (01598) 752223
E: johnpauldevon@aol.com
I: www.ingleside-hotel.co.uk

Kingford House ♦♦♦♦ SILVER AWARD
Longmead, Lynton, EX35 6DQ
T: (01598) 752361
E: kingfordhousehotel@compuserve.com
I: www.kingfordhouse.co.uk

Longmead House Hotel ♦♦♦♦ SILVER AWARD
9 Longmead, Lynton, EX35 6DQ
T: (01598) 752523
F: (01598) 752523
E: info@longmeadhouse.co.uk
I: www.longmeadhouse.co.uk

Meadhaven ♦♦♦
12 Crossmead, Lynton, EX35 6DG
T: (01598) 753288

Millslade Country House Hotel ♦♦♦
Brendon, Lynton EX35 6PS
T: (01598) 741322
F: (01598) 741355
E: bobcramp@millslade.freeserve.co.uk
I: www.brendonvalley.co.uk/millslade.htm

North Walk House ♦♦♦♦
North Walk, Lynton, EX35 6HJ
T: (01598) 753372
E: murphynwh@tesco.net

Pine Lodge ♦♦♦♦
Lynway, Lynton, EX35 6AX
T: (01598) 753230
E: info@pinelodgehotel.com
I: www.pinelodgehotel.com

Rockvale Hotel ♦♦♦♦
Lee Road, Lynton, EX35 6HW
T: (01598) 752279
E: JudithWoodland@rockvale.fsbusiness.co.uk
I: www.rockvalehotel.co.uk

Sinai House ♦♦♦♦
Lynway, Lynton, EX35 6AY
T: (01598) 753227
F: (01598) 752633
E: enquiries@sinaihouse.co.uk
I: www.sinaihouse.co.uk

South View Guest House ♦♦♦
23 Lee Road, Lynton, EX35 6BP
T: (01598) 752289
F: (01598) 752289

Southcliffe ♦♦♦♦
34 Lee Road, Lynton, EX35 6BS
T: (01598) 753328
E: info@southcliffe.co.uk
I: www.southcliffe.co.uk

The Turret ♦♦♦
33 Lee Road, Lynton, EX35 6BS
T: (01598) 753284
F: (01598) 753284
I: www.turrethotel.co.uk

Valley of Rocks ♦♦♦
Lee Road, Lynton, EX35 6HS
T: (01598) 752349
F: (01598) 753720
I: www.shearingsholidays.com/hotels/lynton.htm

Victoria Fernery ♦♦♦♦
Lydiate Lane, Lynton, EX35 6AJ
T: (01598) 752440
F: (01598) 752396
E: info@thefernery.co.uk
I: www.thefernery.co.uk

MALMESBURY
Wiltshire

Bremilham House ♦♦♦
Bremilham Road, Malmesbury, SW16 0DQ
T: (01666) 822680

Honeysuckle ♦♦♦
Foxley Road, Malmesbury, SN16 0JQ
T: (01666) 825267

The Kings Arms Hotel ♦♦♦♦
High Street, Malmesbury, SN16 9AA
T: (01666) 823383
F: (01666) 825327
E: kingsarmshotel@malmesburywilts.freeserve.co.uk
I: www.kingsarmshotel.info

Lovett Farm ♦♦♦♦
Little Somerford, Chippenham SN15 5BP
T: (01666) 823268
F: (01666) 823268
E: lovettfarm@btinternet
I: www.lovettfarm.co.uk

Manor Farm ♦♦♦♦
Corston, Malmesbury SN16 0HF
T: (01666) 822148
F: (01666) 826565
E: ross@manorfarmbandb.fsnet.co.uk
I: www.manorfarmbandb.co.uk

Marsh Farmhouse ♦♦♦
Crudwell Road, Malmesbury, SN16 9JL
T: (01666) 822208

Oakwood Farm ♦♦♦
Upper Minety, Malmesbury SN16 9PY
T: (01666) 860286
F: (01666) 860286

The Old Manor House ♦♦
6 Oxford Street, Malmesbury, SN16 9AX
T: (01666) 823494

Rothay ♦♦♦♦
Milbourne Lane, Malmesbury, SN16 9JQ
T: (01666) 823509

Whychurch Farm ♦♦♦♦
Whychurch Hill, Malmesbury, SN16 9JL
T: (01666) 822156
E: chriswhychurch@aol.com

Winkworth Farm ♦♦♦♦
Lea, Malmesbury SN16 9NH
T: (01666) 823267

MANNAMEAD
Devon

Devonshire Guest House ♦♦♦
22 Lockyer Road, Mannamead, Plymouth PL3 4RL
T: (01752) 220726
F: (01752) 220766
E: phil@devshire.demon.co.uk
I: www.devshire.demon.co.uk

MANTON
Wiltshire

Sunrise ♦♦♦
Manton, Marlborough SN8 4HL
T: (01672) 512878
F: (01672) 512878

MARAZION
Cornwall

Chymorvah Private Hotel ♦♦♦
Marazion, TR17 0DQ
T: (01736) 710497
F: (01736) 710508
I: www.smoothhound.co.uk/hotels/chymorva.html

MARK
Somerset

Burnt House Farm ♦♦♦
Yarrow Road, Mark, Highbridge TA9 4LR
T: (01278) 641280
F: (01278) 641280
E: carmen@burnthousefarm.fsnet.co.uk

Laurel Farm ♦♦♦
The Causeway, Mark, Highbridge TA9 4PZ
T: (01278) 641216
F: (01278) 641447

MARLBOROUGH
Wiltshire

Ash Lodge ♦♦♦♦
Choppingknife Lane, Marlborough, SN8 2AT
T: (01672) 516745
E: ashlodge@virgin.co.uk
I: www.ashlodge.co.uk

Cartref ♦♦♦
63 George Lane, Marlborough, SN8 4BY
T: (01672) 512771

Fishermans House ♦♦♦♦
Mildenhall, Marlborough SN8 2LZ
T: (01672) 515390
F: (01672) 519009

The Lamb Inn ♦♦♦
The Parade, Marlborough, SN8 1NE
T: (01672) 512668
F: (01672) 512668

Merlin Hotel ♦♦♦
36/39 High Street, Marlborough, SN8 1LW
T: (01672) 512151
F: (01672) 514656

Wernham Farm ♦♦♦
Clench Common, Marlborough, SN8 4DR
T: (01672) 512236
F: (01672) 515001
E: margglvsf@aol.com

West View ♦♦♦
Barnfield, Marlborough, SN8 2AX
T: (01672) 515583
E: maggiestewart@euphony.net
I: www.westviewb-b.co.uk

Westcourt Bottom ♦♦♦♦
165 Westcourt, Burbage, Marlborough SN8 3BW
T: (01672) 810924
F: (01672) 810924
E: westcourt.b-and-b@virgin.net
I: www.westcourtbottom.co.uk

MARSHGATE
Cornwall

Melrose ♦♦♦
Marshgate, Camelford PL32 9YN
T: (01840) 261744

MARSTON
Wiltshire

Home Farm ♦♦♦♦
Close Lane, Marston, Devizes SN10 5SN
T: (01380) 725484

MARTOCK
Somerset

Bartletts Farm ♦♦♦♦
Isle Brewers, Taunton, TA3 6QN
T: (01460) 281423
F: (01460) 281423
E: sandjpeach@tesco.net
I: www.pcmanyeouil.co.uk/bnb.html

Madey Mills ♦♦
Martock, TA12 6NN
T: (01935) 823268

The Nags Head ♦♦♦
East Street, Martock, TA12 6NF
T: (01935) 823432
E: Thenagschef@aol.com

The White Hart Hotel ♦♦♦♦
East Street, Martock, TA12 6JQ
T: (01935) 822005
F: (01935) 822056
E: mpjc@whiteharthotelmartock.co.uk
I: www.whiteharthotelmartock.co.uk

Wychwood ♦♦♦♦
7 Bearley Road, Wychwood, Martock, TA12 6PG
T: (01935) 825601
F: (01935) 825601
E: wychwoodmartock@yahoo.co.uk
I: www.theaa.co.uk/region8/76883.html

MAWGAN PORTH
Cornwall

Bre-Pen Farm ♦♦♦♦
Mawgan Porth, Newquay TR8 4AL
T: (01637) 860420
E: jill.brake@virgin.net

Trevarrian Lodge
Rating Applied For
Trevarrian, Mawgan Porth, Newquay TR8 4AQ
T: (01637) 860156
F: (01637) 860422
E: trevarrian@aol.com
I: www.trevarrianlodge.co.uk

MEAVY
Devon

Callisham Farm ♦♦♦
Meavy, Yelverton, PL20 6PS
T: (01822) 853901
F: (01822) 853901
E: wills@callishamfarm.fsnet.co.uk
I: www.callishamfarm.fsnet.co.uk

MELKSHAM
Wiltshire

Longhope Guest House ♦♦♦
9 Beanacre Road, Melksham, SN12 8AG
T: (01225) 706737
F: (01225) 706737

The Old Manor ♦♦♦
48 Spa Road, Melksham, SN12 7NY
T: (01225) 793803
F: (01225) 793803
E: theoldmanor@yahoo.co.uk

The Spa Bed & Breakfast ♦♦♦
402 The Spa, Melksham, SN12 6QL
T: (01225) 707984
I: www.melksham.org.uk/thespa

Springfield B & B ♦♦♦♦
403 The Spa, Melksham, SN12 6QL
T: (01225) 703694
F: (01225) 703694
E: springfieldbandb@ukworld.net
I: www.ukworld.net/springfieldbandb

The Town House ♦♦♦
18 Spa Road, Melksham, SN12
T: (01225) 700125
E: 18townhouse@tiscali.co.uk

MELPLASH
Dorset

Mount Meadow Farm ♦♦♦
The Mount, Melplash, Bridport DT6 3TV
T: (01308) 488524
E: rosiegroves@newmail.net
I: www.mountmeadow.co.uk

MERE
Wiltshire

The Beeches ♦♦♦
Chetcombe Road, Mere, Warminster BA12 6AU
T: (01747) 860687

Downleaze ♦♦♦
North Street, Mere, Warminster BA12 6HH
T: (01747) 860876

MERRYMEET
Cornwall

Higher Trevartha Farm ♦♦♦♦
Pengover, Merrymeet, Liskeard PL14 3NJ
T: (01579) 343382

MEVAGISSEY
Cornwall

Kerry Anna Country House ♦♦♦♦
Treleaven Farm, Mevagissey, St Austell PL26 6RZ
T: (01726) 843558
F: (01726) 843558
E: linda.hennah@btinternet.com
I: www.kerryanna.co.uk

Rising Sun Inn ♦♦♦
Portmellon Cove, Mevagissey, St Austell PL26 6PL
T: (01726) 843235
F: (01726) 843235
E: cliffnsheila@tiscali.co.uk
I: www.risingsunportmellon.co.uk

Seapoint House Hotel ♦♦♦
Battery Terrace, Mevagissey, St Austell PL26 6QS
T: (01726) 842684
F: (01726) 844476
E: mevatele@compuserve.com

MIDDLEMARSH
Dorset

White Horse Farm ♦♦♦♦
Middlemarsh, Sherborne DT9 5QN
T: (01963) 210222
F: (01963) 210222
E: enquiries@whitehorsefarm.co.uk
I: www.whitehorsefarm.co.uk

MILLBROOK
Cornwall

Stone Farm Bed and Breakfast ♦♦♦♦ SILVER AWARD
Whitsand Bay, Millbrook, Torpoint PL10 1JJ
T: (01752) 822267
F: (01752) 822267

MILVERTON
Somerset

Cullendown ♦♦
Springrove, Milverton, Taunton TA4 1NL
T: (01823) 400731

MINEHEAD
Somerset

Alcombe Cote Guest House ♦♦♦
19 Manor Road, Alcombe, Minehead TA24 6EH
T: (01643) 703309
F: (01643) 709901
E: collopalcombecote@bushinternet.com

Allington House ♦♦♦♦
30 Ponsford Road, Minehead, TA24 5DY
T: (01643) 703898

Avill House ♦♦♦
Townsend Road, Minehead, TA24 5RG
T: (01643) 704370

Avondale ♦♦♦♦
Martlet Road, Minehead, TA24 5QD
T: (01643) 706931

Bactonleigh Hotel ♦♦♦
20 Tregonwell Road, Minehead, TA24 5DU
T: (01643) 702147

Baytree ♦♦♦
29 Blenheim Road, Minehead, TA24 5PZ
T: (01643) 703374
E: derekcole@onetel.net.uk

Dorchester Hotel ♦♦♦
38 The Avenue, Minehead, TA24 5AZ
T: (01643) 702052
F: (01643) 702052
E: rooms@dorchester-minehead.com
I: www.dorchester-minehead.com

Dunkery Lodge ♦♦♦♦
Townsend Road, Minehead, TA24 5RQ
T: (01643) 706170
F: 0870 902 9111
E: book@dunkery-lodge.co.uk
I: www.dunkery-lodge.co.uk

Fernside ♦♦♦
The Holloway, Minehead, TA24 5PB
T: (01643) 707594
E: colin.cjs@btinternet.com

Field House ♦♦♦
The Parks, Minehead, TA24 8BU
T: (01643) 706958
F: (01643) 704335

Finial ♦♦♦♦
24 Ponsford Road, Minehead, TA24 5DY
T: (01643) 703945
E: greenfinial@lineone.net

Foxes Hotel ♦♦♦
The Esplanade, Minehead, TA24 5PQ
T: (01643) 704450
F: (01643) 708249
E: foxeshotel@aol.com

Gascony Hotel ♦♦♦♦
The Avenue, Minehead, TA24 5BB
T: (01643) 705939
F: (01643) 709926

Higher Rodhuish Farm ♦♦♦
Rodhuish, Minehead TA24 6QL
T: (01984) 640253
F: (01984) 640253

Kingsway Hotel ♦♦♦♦
36 Ponsford Road, Minehead, TA24 5DY
T: (01643) 702313
F: (01643) 702313

Lorna Doone Guesthouse ♦♦♦
26 Tregonwell Road, Minehead, TA24 5DU
T: (01643) 702540
E: lornadooneguesthouse@msn.com

Lyn Valley Guest House ♦♦♦
3 Tregonwell Road, Minehead, TA24 5DT
T: (01643) 703748
F: (01643) 703748

Marston Lodge Hotel ♦♦♦♦
St Michael's Road, North Hill, Minehead, TA24 5JP
T: (01643) 702510
F: (01643) 702510
E: enquiry@marstonlodgehotel.co.uk
I: www.marstonlodgehotel.co.uk

1 Moorlands ♦♦♦
Moor Road, Minehead, TA24 5RT
T: (01643) 703453
E: moorlands@amserve.net

Old Ship Aground ♦♦♦
Quay Street, Minehead, TA24 5UL
T: (01643) 702087
F: (01643) 709066
E: enquiries@oldshipaground.co.uk
I: www.oldshipaground.co.uk

The Parks Guest House ♦♦♦
26 The Parks, Minehead, TA24 8BT
T: (01643) 703547
F: (01643) 703547
E: parksgh@talk21.com

Promenade Hotel ♦♦♦
The Esplanade, Minehead, TA24 5QS
T: (01643) 702572
F: (01643) 702572
E: jgph@globalnet.co.uk
I: www.johngroons.org.uk

Sunfield Private Hotel ♦♦♦
83 Summerland Avenue, Minehead, TA24 5BW
T: (01643) 703565
F: (01643) 705822
E: sunfield@primex.co.uk
I: www.hotelsminehead.com

Tranmere House ♦♦♦
24 Tregonwell Road, Minehead, TA24 5DU
T: (01643) 702647

Wanneroo Farm ♦♦♦
Timberscombe, Minehead, TA24 7TU
T: (01643) 841493
F: (01643) 841693
E: bandb@wanneroo.fslifs.co.uk
I: www.smoothhound.co.uk/hotels/wanneroo.html

Wyndcott Hotel ♦♦♦
Martlett Road, Minehead, TA24 5QE
T: (01643) 704522
F: (01643) 707577
E: march.corp@which.net
I: www.wyndcotthotel.co.uk

MINSTER
Cornwall

Branarth ♦♦♦♦
Minster, Boscastle PL35 0BN
T: (01840) 250102
F: (01840) 250102
E: arthur.bradley1@lineone.net
I: www.cornwall-online.co.uk/branarth

Home Farm ♦♦♦♦
Minster, Boscastle PL35 0BN
T: (01840) 250195
F: (01840) 250195
E: jackie.haddy@btclick.com

MODBURY
Devon

Weeke Farm ♦♦♦
Modbury, Ivybridge PL21 0TT
T: (01548) 830219
F: (01548) 830219

MONKLEIGH
Devon

Annery Barton ♦♦♦
Monkleigh, Bideford EX39 5JL
T: (01237) 473629
F: (01237) 424468

MONTACUTE
Somerset

Carents House ♦♦♦♦
7A Middle Street, Montacute, TA15 6UZ
T: (01935) 824914
E: carentshouse@amserve.net

Mad Hatters Tearooms ♦♦♦
1 South Street, Montacute, TA15 6XD
T: (01935) 823024
E: montacutemuseum@aol.com
I: www.montacutemuseum.com

The Phelips Arms ♦♦♦
The Borough, Montacute, TA15 6XB
T: (01935) 822557
E: thephelipsarms@aol.com

Slipper Cottage ♦♦♦
41 Bishopston, Montacute, TA15 6UX
T: (01935) 823073
F: (01935) 826868
E: sue.weir@totalise.co.uk
I: www.slippercottage.co.uk

MORCOMBELAKE
Dorset

Bullenside Bed and Breakfast ♦♦♦♦
Sun Lane, Morcombelake, Bridport DT6 6DL
T: (01297) 489350
E: bullenside@hotmail.com
I: www.bullenside.co.uk

Wisteria Cottage ♦♦♦
Taylors Lane, Morcombelake, Bridport DT6 6ED
T: (01297) 489019

MORELEIGH
Devon

Island Farm ♦♦♦♦
Moreleigh, Totnes TQ9 7JH
T: (01548) 821441

MORETONHAMPSTEAD
Devon

Cookshayes Country Guest House ♦♦♦
33 Court Street, Moretonhampstead, Newton Abbot TQ13 8LG
T: (01647) 440374
F: (01647) 440374
E: cookshayes@eurobell.co.uk
I: www.cookshayes.co.uk

Great Doccombe Farm ♦♦♦♦
Doccombe, Moretonhampstead, Newton Abbot TQ13 8SS
T: (01647) 440694
E: david.oakey3@btopenworld.com
I: www.greatdoccombefarm.co.uk

Great Sloncombe Farm ♦♦♦♦ SILVER AWARD
Moretonhampstead, Newton Abbot TQ13 8QF
T: (01647) 440595
F: (01647) 440595
E: hmerchant@sloncombe.freeserve.co.uk
I: www.greatsloncombefarm.co.uk

Great Wooston Farm Bed & Breakfast ♦♦♦♦
Moretonhampstead, Newton Abbot TQ13 8QA
T: (01647) 440367
F: (01647) 440367
E: info@greatwoostonfarm.com
I: www.greatwoostonfarm.com

Little Wooston Farm ♦♦♦
Moretonhampstead, Newton Abbot TQ13 8QA
T: (01647) 440551
F: (01647) 440551

Midfields ♦♦♦♦
North Bovey Road, Moretonhampstead, Newton Abbot TQ13 8PB
T: (01647) 440462
F: (01647) 440039
E: sharon@ridgetor.freeserve.co.uk
I: www.midfields.co.uk

Moorcote Guest House ♦♦♦♦
Chagford Cross, Moretonhampstead, Newton Abbot TQ13 8LS
T: (01647) 440966
E: moorcote@smartone.co.uk
I: www.moorcotehouse.co.uk

Yarningale ♦♦♦
Exeter Road, Moretonhampstead, Newton Abbot TQ13 8SW
T: (01647) 440560
F: (01647) 440560
E: sally-radcliffe@virgin.net

MORTEHOE
Devon

Baycliffe Hotel ♦♦♦♦
Chapel Hill, Mortehoe, Woolacombe EX34 7DZ
T: (01271) 870393
F: (01271) 870393
E: jane@baycliffehotel.fsnet.co.uk
I: www.baycliffehotel.co.uk

The Cleeve House ♦♦♦♦ SILVER AWARD
North Morte Road, Mortehoe, Woolacombe EX34 7ED
T: (01271) 870719
F: (01271) 870719
E: info@cleevehouse.co.uk
I: www.cleevehouse.co.uk

Sunnycliffe Hotel ♦♦♦♦
Chapel Hill, Mortehoe, Woolacombe EX34 7EB
T: (01271) 870597
F: (01271) 870597
E: jj@sunnycliffe.freeserve.co.uk

MORWENSTOW
Cornwall

Cornakey Farm ♦♦♦
Morwenstow, Bude EX23 9SS
T: (01288) 331260

Little Bryaton ♦♦♦♦
Morwenstow, Bude EX23 9JU
T: (01288) 331755
E: little.bryan@dial.pipex.com
I: www.little.bryaton.dial.pipex.com

MOSTERTON
Dorset

Yeabridge Farm ♦♦♦♦
Whetley Cross, Mosterton, Beaminster DT8 3HE
T: (01308) 868944
F: (01308) 868944

MOUNT HAWKE
Cornwall

Trenerry Farm ♦♦♦
Mingoose, Mount Hawke, Truro TR4 8BX
T: (01872) 553755

MOUSEHOLE
Cornwall

Kerris Farmhouse ♦♦♦♦
Kerris, Paul, Penzance TR19 6UY
T: (01736) 731309
E: susangiles@btconnect.com
I: www.cornwall-online.co.uk/kerris-farm

MULLION
Cornwall

Cobblers Cottage ♦♦♦♦♦ SILVER AWARD
Nantithet, Cury, Helston TR12 7RB
T: (01326) 241342
F: (01326) 241342

Meaver Farm ♦♦♦♦ SILVER AWARD
Mullion, Helston TR12 7DN
T: (01326) 240128
F: (01326) 240011
E: meaverfarm@eclipse.co.uk
I: www.meaverfarm.co.uk

Polhormon Farm ♦♦♦
Polhormon Lane, Mullion, Helston TR12 7JE
T: (01326) 240304
F: (01326) 240304
E: polhormonfarm@farmersweekly.net

Tregaddra Farm ♦♦♦♦ SILVER AWARD
Cury, Helston TR12 7BB
T: (01326) 240235
F: (01326) 240235
E: holidays@tregaddra.freeserve.co.uk
I: www.tregaddra.freeserve.co.uk

Trenance Farmhouse ♦♦♦♦
Mullion, Helston TR12 7HB
T: (01326) 240639
F: (01326) 240639
E: info@trenancefarmholidays.co.uk
I: www.trenancefarmholidays.co.uk

MUSBURY
Devon

Kate's Farm Bed & Breakfast ♦♦♦
Lower Bruckland Farm, Musbury, Axminster EX13 8ST
T: (01297) 552861

MUTLEY
Devon

The Dudley Hotel ♦♦♦♦
42 Sutherland Road, Mutley, Plymouth PL4 6BN
T: (01752) 668322
F: (01752) 673763
E: whittingdudleyhotel@btopenworld.com

NANCEGOLLAN
Cornwall

Little Pengwedna Farm ♦♦♦♦
Helston, TR13 0AY
T: (01736) 850649
F: (01736) 850649
E: ray@good-holidays.demon.co.uk
I: www.good-holidays.demon.co.uk

NETHER STOWEY
Somerset

Castle of Comfort Country House ♦♦♦♦ SILVER AWARD
Dodington, Nether Stowey, Bridgwater TA5 1LE
T: (01278) 741264
F: (01278) 741144
E: reception@castle-of-comfort.co.uk
I: www.castle-of-comfort.co.uk

Rose and Crown ♦♦
St Mary Street, Nether Stowey, Bridgwater TA5 1LJ
T: (01278) 732265
E: rose_crown@netherstowey.freeserve.co.uk

NETHERBURY
Dorset

Jasmine Cottage ♦♦♦♦ SILVER AWARD
St James Road, Netherbury, Bridport DT6 5LP
T: (01308) 488767

NEW POLZEATH
Cornwall

Cornish Cottage Hotel ♦♦♦
New Polzeath, Wadebridge PL27 6UF
T: (01208) 862213
F: (01208) 862259
E: enquiries@cornish-cottage-hotel.co.uk
I: www.cornish-cottage-hotel.co.uk

NEWBRIDGE
Cornwall

Wheal Buller ♦♦♦♦ SILVER AWARD
North Road, Newbridge, Penzance TR20 8PS
T: (01736) 787999
E: rwrgibson@supanet.com

NEWMILL
Cornwall

Laidback Trailblazers ♦♦♦♦
The Old Barn, Bosulval, Newmill, Penzance TR20 8XA
T: (01736) 367742
F: (01736) 361721
E: info@laidback-trails.co.uk
I: www.laidback-trails.co.uk

NEWQUAY
Cornwall

Alicia Guest House ♦♦♦♦
136 Henver Road, Newquay, TR7 3EQ
T: (01637) 874328
F: (01637) 874328
E: aliciaguesthouse@mlimer.fsnet.co.uk
I: www.alicia-guesthouse.co.uk

Aloha ♦♦♦
122 Henver Road, Newquay, TR7 3EQ
T: (01637) 878366
I: www.alohanewquay.net

Beresford Hotel ♦♦♦
Narrowcliff, Newquay, TR7 2PR
T: (01637) 873238
F: (01637) 851874
I: www.shearingsholidays.com

Chichester ♦
14 Bay View Terrace, Newquay, TR7 2LR
T: (01637) 874216
F: (01637) 874216
E: sheila.harper@virgin.net
I: http://freespace.virgin.net/sheila.harper

Degembris Farmhouse ♦♦♦♦ SILVER AWARD
St Newlyn East, Newquay TR8 5HY
T: (01872) 510555
F: (01872) 510230
E: kathy@degembris.co.uk
I: www.degembris.co.uk

Edwardian Hotel Island Crescent ♦♦♦
3-7 Island Crescent, Newquay, TR7 1DZ
T: (01637) 874087

The Harbour Hotel ♦♦♦♦ SILVER AWARD
North Quay Hill, Newquay, TR7 1HF
T: (01637) 873040
E: alan@harbourhotel.co.uk
I: www.harbourhotel.co.uk

Marina Hotel ♦♦♦♦
Narrowcliff, Newquay, TR7 2PL
T: (01637) 873012
F: (01637) 851273
I: www.shearingsholidays.com

Rose Cottage ♦♦♦♦
Shepherds Farm, Fiddlers Green, St Newlyn East, Newquay TR8 5NW
T: (01872) 540502
F: (01872) 540340

St Andrews Hotel Rating Applied For
Island Crescent, Newquay, TR7 1DZ
T: (01637) 873556
F: (01637) 873556
E: enquiries@standrewsnewquay.co.uk
I: www.standrewsnewquay.co.uk

Tir Chonaill Lodge Hotel ♦♦♦
106 Mount Wise, Newquay, TR7 1QP
T: (01637) 876492
E: tirchonailhotel@talk21.com
I: www.tirchonaill.co.uk

Trevilla ♦♦♦
18 Berry Road, Newquay, TR7 1AR
T: (01637) 871504
E: trevillaguesthouse@hotmail.com

Wenden Guest House ♦♦♦
11 Berry Road, Newquay, TR7 1AU
T: (01637) 872604
F: (01637) 872604
E: wenden@newquay-holidays.co.uk
I: www.newquay-holidays.co.uk

NEWTON ABBOT
Devon

Keyberry Hotel ♦♦♦
17 Kingskerswell Road, Decoy, Newton Abbot, TQ12 1DQ
T: (01626) 352120

The Mount Rating Applied For
Ideford Combe, Newton Abbot, TQ12 3GR
T: (01626) 331418
F: (01626) 331418
E: tom@themountguesthouse.co.uk
I: www.themountguesthouse.co.uk

NEWTON FERRERS
Devon

Broadmoor Farm ♦♦♦♦
Newton Ferrers, Plymouth PL8 2NE
T: (01752) 880407
E: agfarms@hotmail.com

NEWTON ST LOE
Bath and North East Somerset

Pennsylvania Farm ♦♦♦♦
Newton St Loe, Bath BA2 9JD
T: (01225) 314912
F: (01225) 314912
E: info@pennsylvaniafarm.co.uk
I: www.pennsylvaniafarm.co.uk

NORTH BOVEY
Devon

Ring of Bells Rating Applied For
North Bovey, Newton Abbot TQ13 8RB
T: (01647) 440375
F: (01647) 440218
E: ringofbellsinn@compuserve.com
I: www.ourworld.compuserve.com/homepages/ringofbellsinn

NORTH BRADLEY
Wiltshire

49a Church Lane ♦♦♦
North Bradley, Trowbridge BA14 0TA
T: (01225) 762558

NORTH CADBURY
Somerset

Ashlea House ♦♦♦♦ SILVER AWARD
High Street, North Cadbury, Yeovil BA22 7DP
T: (01963) 440891
F: (01963) 440891
E: ashlea@ashleahouse.com
I: www.ashleahouse.co.uk

The Catash Inn ♦♦♦
North Cadbury, Yeovil BA22 7DH
T: (01963) 440248
F: (01963) 440248
E: clive&sandra@catash.com
I: www.catash.com

NORTH PETHERWIN
Cornwall

Stenhill Farm ♦♦♦♦♦ SILVER AWARD
North Petherwin, Launceston PL15 8NN
T: (01566) 785686
F: (01566) 785686
E: e.reddock@btinternet.com
I: www.stenhill.com

West Barton ♦♦♦♦
North Petherivin, Launceston, PL15 8LR
T: (01566) 785710
F: (01566) 785710
E: enquiries@westbarton.co.uk
I: www.westbarton.co.uk

NORTH TAWTON
Devon

Kayden House Hotel ♦♦♦
High Street, North Tawton, EX20 2HF
T: (01837) 82242

Lower Nichols Nymet Farm ♦♦♦♦ SILVER AWARD
Lower Nichols Nymet, North Tawton, EX20 2BW
T: (01363) 82510
F: (01363) 82510
E: pylefarm@btinternet.com
I: www.pyle-farm-holidays.co.uk

Oaklands Farm ♦♦♦
North Tawton, EX20 2BQ
T: (01837) 82340

NORTH WOOTTON
Dorset

Stoneleigh Barn ♦♦♦♦ SILVER AWARD
North Wootton, Sherborne DT9 5JW
T: (01935) 815964
E: stoneleigh@ic24.net

NORTON ST PHILIP
Somerset

George Inn ♦♦♦
High Street, Norton St Philip, Bath BA2 7LH
T: (01373) 834224
F: (01373) 834861

OAKFORD
Devon

Harton Farm ♦♦♦
Oakford, Tiverton EX16 9HH
T: (01398) 351209
F: (01398) 351209
E: lindy@hartonfarm.co.uk

OAKHILL
Somerset

Blakes Farm ♦♦♦
Radstock, Oakhill, Bath BA3 5HY
T: (01749) 840301

The Boltons ♦♦♦
Sumach House, Neighbourne, Oakhill, Bath BA3 5BQ
T: (01749) 840366
F: (01749) 840366
E: sumachhouse@aol.com
I: www.somersetbreak.co.uk

Establishments printed in blue have a detailed entry in this guide

OBORNE
Dorset

The Grange Restaurant and Hotel ◆◆◆◆◆ SILVER AWARD
Oborne, Sherborne DT9 4LA
T: (01935) 813463
F: (01935) 817464

OKEHAMPTON
Devon

Higher Cadham Farm ◆◆◆◆
Jacobstowe, Okehampton
EX20 3RB
T: (01837) 851647
F: (01837) 851410
E: kingscadham@btopenworld.com
I: www.highercadham.co.uk

The Knole Farm
◆◆◆◆ SILVER AWARD
Bridestowe, Okehampton
EX20 4HA
T: (01837) 861241
F: (01837) 861241
E: mavis.buckle@btconnect.com
I: www.knolefarm-dartmoor-holiday.co.uk

The Tuit ◆◆◆
Lewdown, Okehampton,
EX20 4BS
T: (01566) 783301
F: (01566) 783327
E: spooner@thetuit.freeserve.co.uk

Week Farm Country Holidays
◆◆◆◆
Bridestowe, Okehampton
EX20 4HZ
T: (01837) 861221
F: (01837) 861221
E: accom@weekfarmonline.com
I: www.weekfarmonline.com

OLD SODBURY
South Gloucestershire

Dornden Guest House ◆◆◆◆
Church Lane, Old Sodbury,
Bristol BS37 6NB
T: (01454) 313325
F: (01454) 312263
E: dorndenguesthouse@tinyworld.co.uk
I: www.westcountrynow.com

OLD TOWN
Cornwall

Carn Ithen ◆◆◆◆
Trench Lane, Old Town, St Mary's
TR21 0PA
T: (01720) 422917
F: (01720) 422917
E: roz-alfred@carn-ithen.fsnet.co.uk
I: www.scilly-oldtown.com

ORCHESTON
Wiltshire

The Crown Inn ◆◆◆
Stonehenge Park, Orcheston,
Salisbury SP3 4SH
T: (01980) 620304
F: (01980) 621121
E: stp@orcheston.freeserve.co.uk
I: www.orcheston.freeserve.co.uk

OSMINGTON
Dorset

The Briary
Rating Applied For
Main Road, Osmington,
Weymouth DT3 6EH
T: (01305) 835397
F: (01305) 835397

OTTERY ST MARY
Devon

Pitt Farm ◆◆◆◆
Fairmile, Ottery St Mary
EX11 1NL
T: (01404) 812439
F: (01404) 812439
I: www.smoothhound.co.uk/hotels/pittfarm.html

PADSTOW
Cornwall

Althea House
◆◆◆◆◆ SILVER AWARD
64 Church Street, Padstow,
PL28 8BG
T: (01841) 532579

Althea Library Bed and Breakfast
◆◆◆◆◆ SILVER AWARD
27 High Street, Padstow,
PL28 8BB
T: (01841) 532717
F: (01841) 532717
E: enquiries@althealibrary.co.uk
I: www.althealibrary.co.uk

Armsyde B&B ◆◆◆
10 Cross Street, Padstow,
PL28 8AT
T: (01841) 532271
F: (01841) 532271
E: info@armsyde.co.uk
I: www.armsyde.co.uk

Beau Vista ◆◆◆◆
Sarah's Lane, Padstow, PL28 8EL
T: (01841) 533270
F: (01841) 533270
E: beauvista@padstow.uk.com
I: www.padstow.uk.com/beauvista

Cally Croft ◆◆◆◆
26 Raleigh Close, Padstow,
PL28 8BQ
T: (01841) 533726
E: john@cally26.freeserve.co.uk
I: www.padstow-callycroft.co.uk

50 Church Street ◆◆◆◆
Padstow, PL28 8BG
T: (01841) 532121
F: (01841) 532121
E: churchstreet50@hotmail.com

Chy Veor ◆◆◆
24 Hawkins Road, Padstow,
PL28 8EU
T: (01841) 533545
F: (01841) 532630

Chyloweth ◆◆◆
Constatine Bay, Padstow,
PL28 8JQ
T: (01841) 521012
F: (01841) 521012
E: roger.vivian@ukgateway.net

The Dower House
◆◆◆◆◆ GOLD AWARD
Fentonluna Lane, Padstow,
PL28 8BA
T: (01841) 532317
E: dower@btinternet.com
I: www.padstow.uk.com/dowerhouse/

Jane's Bed and Breakfast
◆◆◆◆
Tregudda, 5 Grenville Road,
Padstow, PL28 8EX
T: (01841) 532089
E: janestone11@aol.com

Mena Gwins ◆◆◆◆
6 Raleigh Close, Padstow,
PL28 8BQ
T: (01841) 533896
E: js_vivian@hotmail.com

The Old Mill House ◆◆◆◆
Little Petherick, Wadebridge
PL27 7QT
T: (01841) 540388
F: 0870 056 9360
E: dwalker@oldmillbandb.demon.co.uk
I: www.SmoothHound.co.uk/hotels/theoldmillhouse.html

Petrocstowe ◆◆◆◆
30 Treverbyn Road, Padstow,
PL28 8DW
T: (01841) 532429

12 Raleigh Road
Rating Applied For
Padstow, PL28 8ET
T: (01841) 532701

Sable House
Rating Applied For
76 Sarah's View, Padstow,
PL28 8LU
T: (01841) 533358
F: (01841) 533835
E: info@sablehouse.co.uk
I: www.sablehouse.co.uk

Trealaw ◆◆◆
22 Duke Street, Padstow,
PL28 8AB
T: (01841) 533161
F: (01841) 533161

Tregea Hotel
◆◆◆◆ SILVER AWARD
16-18 High Street, Padstow,
PL28 8BB
T: (01841) 532455
F: (01841) 533542
E: reservations@tregea.co.uk
I: www.tregea.co.uk

Treverbyn House ◆◆◆◆
Station Road, Padstow,
PL28 8AD
T: (01841) 532855
F: (01841) 532855
I: www.treverbynmembers.easyspace.com

Trevone Bay Hotel ◆◆◆◆
Dobbin Close, Trevone, Padstow
PL28 8QS
T: (01841) 520243
F: (01841) 521195
E: webb@trevonebay.demon.co.uk

Trevorrick Farm ◆◆◆
St Issey, Wadebridge PL27 7QH
T: (01841) 540574
F: (01841) 540574
E: info@trevorrick.co.uk
I: www.trevorrick.co.uk

The White Hart ◆◆◆◆
1 New Street, Padstow,
PL28 8EA
T: (01841) 532350
E: whthartpad@aol.com
I: www.padstow.uk.com/whitehart

PAIGNTON
Devon

Arcadia Hotel ◆◆◆
Marine Gardens, Preston,
Paignton, TQ3 2NT
T: (01803) 551039
F: (01803) 551039
E: arcadia.hotel@btinternet.com

Arden House Hotel ◆◆◆
10 Youngs Park Road, Paignton,
TQ4 6BU
T: (01803) 558443
E: stan@ardenhousepaignton.co.uk
I: www.ardenhousepaignton.co.uk

Arrandale ◆◆◆
34 Garfield Road, Paignton,
TQ4 6AX
T: (01803) 552211
I: www.paigntondevon.co.uk/arrandale.htm

Baildon Royd Hotel ◆◆◆◆
4 Marine Park, Paignton,
TQ3 2NW
T: (01803) 550347
E: baildonroydhotel@aol.com
I: www.westcountrynow.com

Bay Sands Hotel ◆◆◆◆
14 Colin Road, Paignton,
TQ3 2NR
T: (01803) 524877
E: enquiries@baysands.co.uk
I: www.baysands.co.uk

Beach House
Rating Applied For
39 Garfield Road, Paignton,
TQ4 6AX
T: (01803) 525742

Beecroft Hotel ◆
10 St. Andrews Road, Paignton,
TQ4 6HA
T: (01803) 558702
F: (01803) 558702
I: www.beecrofthotel.co.uk

Bella Vista Guest House ◆◆◆
5 Berry Square, Paignton,
TQ4 6AZ
T: (01803) 558122
E: bellavista@berrysquare.fsbusiness.co.uk
I: www.english-riviera.co.uk/accommodation/guest-houses/bella-vista/index.htm

Benbows Hotel ◆◆◆
1 Alta Vista Road, Roudham,
Paignton, TQ4 6DB
T: (01803) 558128
E: Benbowshotel@aol.com
I: www.benbowshotel.co.uk

Beresford Hotel
Rating Applied For
5 Adelphi Road, Paignton,
TQ4 6AW
T: (01803) 551560
F: (01803) 552776
E: pat-beresford@lineone.net
I: www.beresfordhotel.co.uk

Birchwood House Hotel
◆◆◆◆ SILVER AWARD
33 St Andrews Road, Paignton,
TQ4 6HA
T: (01803) 551323
F: (01803) 401301
E: birchwoodhouse@aol.com
I: www.birchwoodhouse.net

Birklands Guest House ♦♦♦
33 Garfield Road, Paignton, TQ4 6AX
T: (01803) 556970
F: (01803) 556970

Blue Waters Hotel ♦♦♦
4 Leighon Road, Paignton, TQ3 2BQ
T: (01803) 557749
E: bluewatershtl@aol.com
I: www.bluewaterspaignton.co.uk

Briars Hotel ♦♦♦♦
26 Sands Road, Paignton, TQ4 6EJ
T: (01803) 557729
F: (01803) 557729
E: enquiries@briarshotel.com
I: www.briarshotel.com

Bronte Hotel ♦♦♦♦
7 Colin Road, Paignton, TQ3 2NR
T: (01803) 550254
F: (01803) 391489

Carrington Hotel ♦♦
10 Beach Road, Paignton, TQ4 6AY
T: (01803) 558785

Cherwood Hotel
♦♦♦♦ SILVER AWARD
26 Garfield Road, Paignton, TQ4 6AX
T: (01803) 556515
F: (01803) 555126
E: James-pauline@cherwood-hotel.co.uk
I: www.cherwood-hotel.co.uk

Cleve Court Hotel
♦♦♦♦ SILVER AWARD
3 Cleveland Road, Paignton, TQ4 6EN
T: (01803) 551444
F: (01803) 664617
I: www.clevecourthotel.co.uk

Cliveden ♦♦♦♦
27 Garfield Road, Paignton, TQ4 6AX
T: (01803) 557461
F: (01803) 557461
E: cliveden@lineone.net
I: www.clivedenguesthouse.co.uk

Colin House ♦♦♦♦
2 Colin Road, Paignton, TQ3 2NR
T: (01803) 550609
F: (01803) 550609
E: colin-house@talk21.com
I: www.paigntondevon.co.uk/colinhouse.htm

Craigmore Guest House ♦♦♦
54 Dartmouth Road, Paignton, TQ4 5AN
T: (01803) 557373
F: (01803) 665801
E: bookings@craigmore-guesthouse.fsnet.co.uk
I: www.craigmore-guesthouse.fsnet.co.uk

Dalmary Guest House ♦♦♦
21 Garfield Road, Paignton, TQ4 6AX
T: (01803) 528145

Danethorpe Hotel ♦♦♦♦
23 St Andrews Road, Roundham, Paignton, TQ4 6HA
T: (01803) 551251
F: (01803) 557075

Devon House Hotel ♦♦♦
20 Garfield Road, Paignton, TQ4 6AX
T: (01803) 559371
F: (01803) 550054
E: info@devonhousehotel.com
I: www.devonhousehotel.com

Earlston House Hotel ♦♦♦♦
31 St Andrews Road, Paignton, TQ4 6HA
T: (01803) 558355
F: (01803) 556085
E: earlstonhouse@tinyworld.co.uk
I: www.earlstonhouse.co.uk

Ebor Towers Hotel ♦♦♦
Alta Vista Road, Paignton, TQ4 6DA
T: (01803) 551422
F: (01803) 663661

Esplanade Hotel ♦♦♦
Sands Road, Paignton, TQ4 6EG
T: (01803) 556333
F: (01803) 666786
I: www.shearingsholidays.com

Hotel Fiesta ♦♦♦
2 Kernou Road, Paignton, TQ4 6BA
T: (01803) 521862
F: (01803) 392978
E: mark@hawker55.fsnet.co.uk

Florida Hotel ♦♦♦♦
9 Colin Road, Paignton, TQ3 2NR
T: (01803) 551447
E: lemm@florida44.fsnet.co.uk

Garfield Lodge ♦♦♦♦
30 Garfield Road, Paignton, TQ4 6AX
T: (01803) 557764
E: garfieldlodge@aol.com
I: www.garfieldlodge.co.uk

Greenford Lodge Hotel ♦♦♦
56 Dartmouth Road, Paignton, TQ4 5AN
T: (01803) 553635

Harbour Lodge ♦♦♦
4 Cleveland Road, Paignton, TQ4 6EN
T: (01803) 556932
E: harbourlodge@theseed.net

Kingswinford Hotel ♦♦♦♦
32 Garfield Road, Paignton, TQ4 6AX
T: (01803) 558358
E: kingswinford@garfieldroad.freeserve.co.uk
I: www.kingswinfordhotel.co.uk

The Linton Hotel ♦♦♦♦
7 Elmsleigh Road, Paignton, TQ4 5AX
T: (01803) 558745
F: (01803) 527345

Lyncourt Hotel ♦♦♦
14 Elmsleigh Park, Paignton, TQ4 5AT
T: (01803) 557124

Mandalay Private Hotel ♦♦♦
7 Cleveland Road, Paignton, TQ4 6EN
T: (01803) 525653
F: (01803) 525193
E: mandalayhotel@btconnect.com
I: www.mandalay-hotel.co.uk

Mayfield Hotel ♦♦♦♦
8 Queens Road, Paignton, TQ4 6AT
T: (01803) 556802
F: (01803) 556802
E: mayfieldhotel@supanet.com

Meadowfield Hotel ♦♦♦♦
36 Preston Down Road, Paignton, TQ3 2RW
T: (01803) 522987
F: (01803) 554605
E: rpitchell@aol.com
I: www.meadowfieldhotel.co.uk

Middlepark Hotel ♦♦♦
3 Marine Drive, Paignton, TQ3 2NJ
T: (01803) 559025
F: (01803) 559025

Norbreck ♦♦♦
35 New Street, Paignton, TQ3 3HL
T: (01803) 558033
F: (01803) 665755
E: norbreckguesthouse@hotmail.com
I: www.//members.tripod.co.uk/Norbreck/Bandb.html

Ocean Villa ♦♦♦♦
8 Kernou Road, Paignton, TQ4 6BA
T: (01803) 664121
I: www.oceanvilla.co.uk

Olifants ♦♦♦
32 Highfield Crescent, Paignton, TQ3 3TR
T: (01803) 529440

Paignton Court Hotel ♦♦♦
17-19 Sands Road, Paignton, TQ4 6EG
T: (01803) 553111
E: paigntoncourt@aol.com
I: www.paignton-court-hotel.co.uk

Richmond Guest House ♦♦♦
19 Norman Road, Paignton, TQ3 2BE
T: 0800 074 4754
F: (01803) 558792
E: therichmond@aol.com

Rockview Guest House ♦♦♦
13 Queens Road, Paignton, TQ4 6AT
T: (01803) 556702

Rosemead Guest House ♦♦♦
22 Garfield Road, Paignton, TQ4 6AX
T: (01803) 557944
E: pauldgama@aol.com

Rougemont Hotel ♦♦♦
23 Roundham Road, Paignton, TQ4 6DN
T: (01803) 556570
F: (01803) 556570
E: beds@rougemonthotel.co.uk
I: www.rougemonthotel.co.uk

Roundham Lodge
♦♦♦♦♦ SILVER AWARD
16 Roundham Road, Paignton, TQ4 6DN
T: (01803) 558485
F: (01803) 553090
E: alan@vega68.freeserve.co.uk
I: www.roundham-lodge.co.uk

Rowcroft Private Hotel ♦♦♦♦
14 Youngs Park Road, Paignton, TQ4 6BU
T: (01803) 559420

St Edmund's Hotel ♦♦♦
25 Sands Road, Paignton, TQ4 6EG
T: (01803) 558756
E: stedmunds@currantbun.com
I: www.stedmundshotel.com

St Weonards Private Hotel ♦♦♦
12 Kernou Road, Paignton, TQ4 6BA
T: (01803) 558842
F: (01803) 558842

Hotel San Brelade ♦♦♦
3 Alta Vista Road, Paignton, TQ4 6DB
T: (01803) 553725

The Sands Hotel ♦♦♦
32 Sands Road, Paignton, TQ4 6EJ
T: (01803) 551282
F: (01803) 407269
E: sands.hotel@virgin.net

Sea Spray Hotel ♦♦♦
1 Beach Road, Paignton, TQ4 6AY
T: (01803) 553141
I: www.seasprayhotel.co.uk

Seacroft Guest House ♦♦♦♦
41 Sands Road, Paignton, TQ4 6EG
T: (01803) 523791

Seaford Sands Hotel ♦♦♦
17 Roundham Road, Paignton, TQ4 6DN
T: (01803) 557722
F: (01803) 526071

Sealawn Hotel ♦♦♦
Sea Front, 20 Esplanade Road, Paignton, TQ4 6BE
T: (01803) 559031

Seaways Hotel ♦♦♦♦
30 Sands Road, Paignton, TQ4 6EJ
T: (01803) 551093
F: (01803) 551167
E: seawayshotel@aol.com

Sonachan House Hotel ♦♦♦
35 St Andrews Road, Paignton, TQ4 6HA
T: (01803) 558021

Sundale Hotel ♦♦♦
10 Queens Road, Paignton, TQ4 6AT
T: (01803) 557431
E: sundalehotel@tinyworld.co.uk

Two Beaches Hotel ♦♦♦
27 St Andrews Road, Paignton, TQ4 6HA
T: (01803) 522164
E: 2beaches@Tiscali.co.uk
I: www.TWOBEACHES.co.uk

Wulfruna Hotel
♦♦♦♦ SILVER AWARD
8 Esplanade, Paignton, TQ4 6EB
T: (01803) 555567
F: (01803) 555567
E: julieatwulf@aol.com

Wynncroft Hotel ♦♦♦♦
2 Elmsleigh Park, Paignton, TQ4 5AT
T: (01803) 525728
F: (01803) 526335
E: wynncrofthotel@aol.com
I: www.wynncroft.co.uk

PANBOROUGH
Somerset

Garden End Farm ◆◆◆
Panborough, Wells BA5 1PN
T: (01934) 712414
E: sheila@gardenendfarm.freeserve.co.uk
I: www.gardenendfarm.freeserve.co.uk

PATTERDOWN
Wiltshire

Bennett's ◆◆◆◆
Holywell House, Patterdown, Chippenham SN15 2NP
T: (01249) 652922
E: holywell-house@btinternet.com
I: www.holywell-house.co.uk

PAYHEMBURY
Devon

Yellingham Farm ◆◆◆◆
Payhembury, Honiton EX14 3HE
T: (01404) 850272
F: (01404) 850873
E: JanetEast@compuserve.com

PEDWELL
Somerset

Sunnyside
◆◆◆◆ SILVER AWARD
34 Taunton Road, Pedwell, Bridgwater TA7 9BG
T: (01458) 210097

PELYNT
Cornwall

Bake Farm ◆◆◆
Pelynt, Looe PL13 2QQ
T: (01503) 220244
F: (01503) 220244
E: bakefarm@btopenworld.com

Cardwen Farm ◆◆◆◆
Pelynt, Looe PL13 2LU
T: (01503) 220213
F: (01503) 220213

Penkelly Farm ◆◆◆
Pelynt, Looe PL13 2QH
T: (01503) 220348
I: www.penkellyfarm.co.uk

Trenderway Farm ◆◆◆◆◆
Pelynt, Polperro, Looe PL13 2LY
T: (01503) 272214
F: (01503) 272991
E: trenderwayfarm@hotmail.com
I: www.trenderwayfarm.co.uk

PENDEEN
Cornwall

Field House ◆◆◆◆
8 Trewellard Road, Pendeen, Penzance TR19 7ST
T: (01736) 788097
E: fieldhousetrewellard@talk21.com
I: www.cornwall-online.co.uk/field-house

PENSFORD
Bath and North East Somerset

Green Acres ◆◆◆
Stanton Wick, Pensford, BS39 4BX
T: (01761) 490397
F: (01761) 490397

Leigh Farm ◆◆
Old Road, Pensford, BS39 4BA
T: (01761) 490281
F: (01761) 490281

The Model Farm ◆◆◆
Norton Hawkfield, Pensford, BS39 4HA
T: (01275) 832144
F: (01275) 832144
E: margarethasell@hotmail.com

PENSILVA
Cornwall

Penharget Farm Bed and Breakfast ◆◆◆
Penharget Farm, Pensilva, Liskeard PL14 5RJ
T: (01579) 362221
F: (01579) 363965
E: penhargetfarm@ukonline.co.uk

PENZANCE
Cornwall

Carnson House Hotel ◆◆
2 East Terrace, Penzance, TR18 2TD
T: (01736) 365589
F: (01736) 365594
E: carnson@netcomuk.co.uk
I: www.chycor.co.uk/carnson-house

Con Amore ◆◆◆
38 Morrab Road, Penzance, TR18 4EX
T: (01736) 363423
F: (01736) 363423

Cornerways Guest House ◆◆◆
5 Leskinnick Street, Penzance, TR18 2HA
T: (01736) 364645
F: (01736) 364645
E: enquiries@cornerways-penzance.co.uk
I: www.penzance.co.uk/cornerways

Estoril Hotel ◆◆◆
46 Morrab Road, Penzance, TR18 4EX
T: (01736) 362468
F: (01736) 367471
E: estorilhotel@aol.com
I: www.estorilhotel.co.uk

Glencree Private Hotel ◆◆◆
2 Mennaye Road, Penzance, TR18 4NG
T: (01736) 362026
F: (01736) 362026
E: glencree@btinternet.com
I: www.glencreehotel.co.uk

Halcyon Guest House ◆◆◆◆
6 Chyandour Square, Penzance, TR18 3LW
T: (01736) 366302
F: (01736) 366302
E: pat+bob@halcyon1.co.uk

Lombard House
◆◆◆◆ SILVER AWARD
16 Regent Terrace, Penzance, TR18 4DW
T: (01736) 364897
F: (01736) 364897
E: rita.kruge@talk21.com
I: www.cornwall-online.co.uk/lombard-house

Lynwood Guest House ◆◆◆
41 Morrab Road, Penzance, TR18 4EX
T: (01736) 365871
F: (01736) 365871
E: lynwoodpz@aol.com
I: www.lynwood-guesthouse.co.uk

Menwidden Farm ◆◆◆
Ludgvan, Penzance TR20 8BN
T: (01736) 740415

Richmond Lodge ◆◆◆
61 Morrab Road, Penzance, TR18 4EP
T: (01736) 365560
E: ivor@richmondlodge.fsnet.co.uk
I: www.geocities.com/richmondlodge_uk

Rose Farm ◆◆◆◆
Chyanhal, Buryas Bridge, Penzance TR19 6AN
T: (01736) 731808
F: (01736) 731808
E: lally@rosefarm.co.uk
I: www.rosefarmcornwall.co.uk

Roseudian ◆◆◆◆
Crippas Hill, Kelynack, St. Just, Penzance, TR19 7RE
T: (01736) 788556
E: roseudian@ukgateway.net
I: www.roseudian.ukgateway.net

The Summer House
◆◆◆◆◆ SILVER AWARD
Cornwall Terrace, Penzance, TR18 4HL
T: (01736) 363744
F: (01736) 360959
E: summerhouse@dial.pipex.com
I: www.summerhouse-cornwall.com

Treventon Guest House ◆◆◆
Alexandra Place, Penzance, TR18 4NE
T: (01736) 363521
F: (01736) 361873
I: www.ukholidayaccommodation.com/treventonguesthouse

Trewella Guest House ◆◆◆
18 Mennaye Road, Penzance, TR18 4NG
T: (01736) 363818
F: (01736) 363818
E: shan.dave@lineone.net
I: www.trewella.co.uk

Warwick House Hotel ◆◆◆
17 Regent Terrace, Penzance, TR18 4DW
T: (01736) 363881
F: (01736) 363881
E: jules@warwickhouse.fsworld.co.uk

Wymering Bed and Breakfast ◆◆◆
15 Regent Square, Penzance, TR18 4BG
T: (01736) 362126
F: (01736) 362126
E: wymering@aol.com
I: www.members.aol.com/wymering

PERRANPORTH
Cornwall

Chy-an-Kerensa Guest House ◆◆◆
Cliff Road, Perranporth, TR6 0DR
T: (01872) 572470
F: (01872) 572470

Ponsmere Hotel ◆◆◆
Ponsmere Road, Perranporth, TR6 0BW
T: (01872) 572225
F: (01872) 573075
E: info@ponsmere.co.uk
I: www.ponsmere.co.uk

Trevie Guest House ◆◆◆◆
Mill Road, Bolingey, Perranporth TR6 0AP
T: (01872) 573475
F: (01872) 573475

PIDDLEHINTON
Dorset

Muston Manor
◆◆◆◆ SILVER AWARD
Piddlehinton, Dorchester DT2 7SY
T: (01305) 848242
F: (01305) 848242

Whites Dairy House
◆◆◆◆◆ SILVER AWARD
High Street, Piddlehinton, Dorchester DT2 7TD
T: (01300) 348386
F: (01300) 348368
E: robin.adeney@care4free.web
I: www.whitesdairyhouse.co.uk

PIDDLETRENTHIDE
Dorset

Kingsmead ◆◆◆◆
Piddletrenthide, Dorchester DT2
T: (01300) 348234
F: (01300) 348234

The Poachers Inn ◆◆◆◆
Piddletrenthide, Dorchester DT2 7QX
T: (01300) 348358
F: (01300) 348153
E: thepoachersinn@piddletrenthide.fsbusiness.co.uk
I: www.thepoachersinn.co.uk

PILLATON
Cornwall

Larks Rise ◆◆◆
Pillaton, Saltash PL12 6QS
T: (01579) 350447
F: (01579) 350447

The Weary Friar Inn ◆◆◆◆
Pillaton, Saltash PL12 6QS
T: (01579) 350238
F: (01579) 350238

PILTON
Somerset

Bowermead House ◆◆◆◆
Whitstone Hill, Pilton, Shepton Mallet BA4 4DT
T: (01749) 890744
F: (01749) 890744
E: wsouthcomb@aol.com

PINKNEY
Wiltshire

Home Farm House ◆◆◆
Pinkney, Malmesbury SN16 0NX
T: (01666) 840772
E: elainemilsom@hotmail.com

PLUSH
Dorset

The Old Barn House ◆◆◆
Plush, Dorchester DT2 7RQ
T: (01300) 348730

PLYMOUTH
Devon

Athenaeum Lodge ◆◆◆◆
4 Athenaeum Street, The Hoe, Plymouth, PL1 2RQ
T: (01752) 665005
F: (01752) 665005

Berkeleys of St James ◆◆◆◆
4 St James Place East, The Hoe, Plymouth, PL1 3AS
T: (01752) 221654
F: (01752) 221654
I: www.smoothhound.co.uk/hotels/berkely2html.

Blackhall Lodge ♦♦♦♦
Old Staddiscombe Road, Plymouth, PL9 9NA
T: (01752) 482482
F: (01752) 482482
E: johnm@jboocock.freeserve.co.uk
I: www.jboocock.freeserve.co.uk

Bowling Green Hotel ♦♦♦♦♦ SILVER AWARD
9-10 Osborne Place, Lockyer Street, Plymouth, PL1 2PU
T: (01752) 209090
F: (01752) 209092
E: dave@bowlinggreenhotel.freeserve.co.uk
I: www.smoothhound.co.uk/hotels/bowling.html

Gabber Farm ♦♦♦
Down Thomas, Plymouth PL9 0AW
T: (01752) 862269
F: (01752) 862269

The George Guest House ♦♦♦
161 Citadel Road, The Hoe, Plymouth, PL1 2HU
T: (01752) 661517
F: (01752) 661517
E: georgeguesthouse@talk21.com
I: www.accommodationplymouth.co.uk

Lamplighter Hotel ♦♦♦
103 Citadel Road, The Hoe, Plymouth, PL1 2RN
T: (01752) 663855
F: (01752) 228139
E: lampligherhotel@ukonline.co.uk

Mayflower Guest House ♦♦♦
209 Citadel Road East, The Hoe, Plymouth, PL1 2JF
T: (01752) 667496
F: (01752) 202727
E: info@mayflowerguesthouse.co.uk
I: www.mayflowerguesthouse.co.uk

The Old Pier Guest House ♦♦♦
20 Radford Road, West Hoe, Plymouth, PL1 3BY
T: (01752) 268468
E: enquiries@oldpier.freeserve.co.uk
I: www.oldpier.freeserve.co.uk/oldpier

Osmond Guest House ♦♦♦
42 Pier Street, Plymouth, PL1 3BT
T: (01752) 229705
F: (01752) 269655
E: mike@osmondgh.freeserve.co.uk
I: plymouth-explore.co.uk

Rosaland Hotel ♦♦♦♦
32 Houndiscombe Road, Plymouth, PL4 6HQ
T: (01752) 664749
F: (01752) 256984
E: manager@rosalandhotel.com
I: www.rosalandhotel.com

St Lawrence Guest House ♦♦♦
10 St Lawrence Road, Mutley, Plymouth, PL4 6HN
T: (01752) 667046
F: (01752) 667046
E: StLawrenceGuestHouse@plymouthdevon.fsbusiness.co.uk
I: www.st.lawrenceguesthouse.co.uk

Smeaton's Tower Hotel ♦♦♦♦
40-42 Grand Parade, The Hoe, Plymouth, PL1 3DJ
T: (01752) 221007
F: (01752) 221664
E: info@smeatonstowerhotel.co.uk
I: www.smeatonstowerhotel.co.uk

Squires Guest House ♦♦♦♦
7 St James Place East, The Hoe, Plymouth, PL1 3AS
T: (01752) 261459
F: (01752) 261459
E: pagea8@aol.com
I: www.squiresguesthouse.co.uk

Westwinds Hotel ♦♦♦
99 Citadel Road, The Hoe, Plymouth, PL1 2RN
T: (01752) 601777
F: (01752) 662158
E: paul.colman@btinternet.com
I: business.thisisplymouth.co.uk/westwindshotel

POLBATHIC
Cornwall

Hendra Farm ♦♦♦♦
Polbathic, Torpoint PL11 3DT
T: (01503) 250225
F: (01503) 250225
E: polbathic@ic24.net

POLPERRO
Cornwall

Brent House ♦♦
1 Brent House, Talland Hill, Polperro, Looe PL13 2RY
T: (01503) 272495

POLRUAN
Cornwall

Quayside House ♦♦♦♦
The Quay, Polruan, Fowey PL23 1PA
T: (01726) 870377
E: quayhousepolruan@aol.com

POLZEATH
Cornwall

The White Heron ♦♦♦
Polzeath, Wadebridge PL27 6TJ
T: (01208) 863623
E: info@whiteheronhotel.co.uk
I: www.whiteheronhotel.co.uk

PORLOCK
Somerset

Burley Cottage Guest House ♦♦♦♦
Parsons Street, Porlock, Minehead TA24 8QJ
T: (01643) 862563
F: (01643) 862563
E: burleycottage@aol.com
I: www.Burnleycottage.com

Leys B & B ♦♦♦♦
The Ridge, Off Bossington Lane, Porlock, Minehead TA24 8HA
T: (01643) 862477
F: (01643) 862477

The Lorna Doone Hotel ♦♦♦
High Street, Porlock, Minehead TA24 8PS
T: (01643) 862404
F: (01643) 863018
E: lorna@doone99.freeserve.co.uk

Myrtle Cottage ♦♦♦
High Street, Porlock, Minehead TA24 8PU
T: (01643) 862978
F: (01243) 862978
E: bob.steer@talk21.com
I: www.smoothhound.co.uk

Nutkin House ♦♦♦
Toll Road, Porlock, Minehead TA24 8JH
T: (01643) 863228
E: nutkinhouse@hotmail.com

Seapoint ♦♦♦♦
Upway, Porlock, Minehead TA24 8QE
T: (01643) 862289
F: (01643) 862289

PORT ISAAC
Cornwall

Anchorage ♦♦♦♦
12 The Terrace, Port Isaac, PL29 3SG
T: (01208) 880629

Hathaway ♦♦♦♦
Roscarrock Hill, Port Isaac, PL29 3RG
T: (01208) 880416
E: marion.andrews1@btopenworld.com
I: www.cornwall-online.co.uk/hathaway

The Slipway Hotel & Restaurant ♦♦♦
Harbour Front, Port Isaac, PL29 3RH
T: (01208) 880264
F: (01208) 880408
E: slipwayhotel@portisaac.com
I: www.portisaac.com

PORTESHAM
Dorset

The Old Fountain ♦♦♦♦
36 Front Street, Portesham, Weymouth DT3 4ET
T: (01305) 871278
F: (01305) 871278

PORTH
Cornwall

Porth Cliff Hotel ♦♦♦
Watergate Road, Porth, Newquay TR7 3LX
T: (01637) 872503
F: (01637) 872503
E: enquiry@porthcliffhotel.co.uk
I: www.porthcliffhotel.co.uk

PORTHCURNO
Cornwall

The Porthcurno Hotel ♦♦♦♦
The Valley, Porthcurno, St Levan, Penzance TR19 6JX
T: (01736) 810119
F: (01736) 810711
E: mail@porthcurnohotel.co.uk
I: www.porthcurnohotel.co.uk

PORTHLEVEN
Cornwall

Beacon Crag Guest House ♦♦
Beacon Crag, Porthleven, Helston TR13 9LA
T: (01326) 573789
E: martin@beaconcrag.freeserve.co.uk
I: www.beacon-crag.co.uk

POULSHOT
Wiltshire

Higher Green Farm ♦♦
Poulshot, Devizes SN10 1RW
T: (01380) 828355
F: (01380) 828355

Middle Green Farm ♦♦♦
The Green, Poulshot, Devizes SN10 1RT
T: (01380) 828413
F: (01380) 828826

Poulshot Lodge Farm ♦♦♦
Poulshot, Devizes SN10 1RQ
T: (01380) 828255

POYNTINGTON
Dorset

Welgoer ♦♦♦
Sherborne, DT9 4LF
T: (01963) 220737

PRESTON
Devon

Innisfree Hotel ♦♦♦♦
12 Colin Road, Preston, Paignton TQ3 2NR
T: (01803) 550692
F: (01803) 550692

QUEEN CAMEL
Somerset

Mildmay Arms ♦♦
High Street, Queen Camel, Yeovil BA22 7NJ
T: (01935) 850456
F: (01935) 851610
E: mike@mildmayarms.greatxscape.net
I: www.mildmayarms.greatxscape.net

RADSTOCK
Bath and North East Somerset

The Rookery ♦♦♦♦
Wells Road, Radstock, Bath BA3 3RS
T: (01761) 432626
F: (01761) 432626
E: brandons@therookeryguesthouse.co.uk
I: www.therookeryguesthouse.co.uk

RAMSBURY
Wiltshire

Marridge Hill Cottage ♦♦♦
Marridge Hill, Ramsbury, Marlborough SN8 2HG
T: (01672) 520486

RATTERY
Devon

Knowle Farm ♦♦♦♦ SILVER AWARD
Rattery, South Brent TQ10 9JY
T: (01364) 73914
F: (01364) 73914
E: lynn@knowle-farm.co.uk
I: www.knowle-farm.co.uk/b&b

REDLYNCH
Wiltshire

Orchards Country House Bed & Breakfast ♦♦♦♦
Kiln Road, Redlynch, Salisbury SP5 2HT
T: (01725) 510372
F: (01725) 510372
E: orchardsbandb@hotmail.com
I: www.btinternet.com/~alanjj

Templeman's Old Farmhouse ♦♦♦♦
Redlynch, Salisbury SP5 2JS
T: (01725) 510331
F: (01752) 510331

ROCK
Cornwall

Silvermead ♦♦♦
Rock, Wadebridge PL27 6LB
T: (01208) 862425
F: (01208) 862919
E: barbara@silvermead.freeserve.co.uk

ROOKSBRIDGE
Somerset

Rooksbridge House ♦♦♦♦
Rooksbridge, Axbridge BS26 2UL
T: (01934) 750630

ROWDE
Wiltshire

Lower Foxhangers Farm ♦♦♦
Rowde, Devizes SN10 1SS
T: (01380) 828254
F: (01380) 828254

The Manor House ♦♦♦
High Street, Rowde, Devizes SN10 2ND
T: (01380) 729319

RUSHALL
Wiltshire

Little Thatch ♦♦♦
Rushall, Pewsey SN9 6EN
T: (01980) 635282
F: (01980) 635282

ST AGNES
Cornwall

Covean Cottage ♦♦♦♦
St Agnes, TR22 0PL
T: (01720) 422620
F: (01720) 422620

Penkerris ♦♦
Penwinnick Road, St Agnes, TR5 0PA
T: (01872) 552262
F: (01872) 552262
E: info@penkerris.co.uk
I: www.penkerris.co.uk

ST AUSTELL
Cornwall

Polgreen Farm ♦♦♦♦
London Apprentice, St Austell PL26 7AP
T: (01726) 75151
F: (01726) 75151
E: polgreen.farm@btclick.com

ST BREOCK
Cornwall

Pawton Stream ♦♦♦
St Breock, Wadebridge PL27 7LN
T: (01208) 814845

ST BREWARD
Cornwall

Treswallock Cottage B&B ♦♦♦♦
Treswallock Cottage, St Breward, Bodmin PL30 4PL
T: (01208) 851508
E: pauline@treswallock-cottage.fsnet.co.uk
I: www.treswallock-cottage.fsnet.co.uk

Treswallock Farm ♦♦♦
St Breward, Bodmin PL30 4PL
T: (01208) 850255
E: treswallockfarm@cwcom.net

ST BURYAN
Cornwall

Boskenna Home Farm ♦♦♦♦ SILVER AWARD
St Buryan, Penzance TR19 6DQ
T: (01736) 810705
F: (01736) 810705
E: julia.hosking@btclick.com
I: www.boskenna.co.uk

Tregurnow Farm ♦♦♦♦
St Buryan, Penzance TR19 6BL
T: (01736) 810255
F: (01736) 810255
E: tregurno@eurobell.co.uk
I: www.tregurno.eurobell.co.uk

Trelew Farm ♦♦♦
St Buryan, Penzance TR19 6ED
T: (01736) 810308
F: (01736) 810308
E: trelewfarm@btconnect.co.uk
I: www.cornwall-online.co.uk/trelew-farm

ST EWE
Cornwall

Higher Kestle Farm ♦♦♦♦ SILVER AWARD
St Ewe, Mevagissey, St Austell PL26 6EP
T: (01726) 842001
F: (01726) 842001
E: vicky@higherkestle.freeserve.co.uk

Lower Barn ♦♦♦♦ SILVER AWARD
Bosue, St Ewe, St Austell PL26 6EU
T: (01726) 844881
E: janie@www.bosue.co.uk
I: www.bosue.co.uk

ST ISSEY
Cornwall

Cannallidgey Villa Farm ♦♦♦♦
St Issey, Wadebridge, PL27 7RB
T: (01208) 812276
F: (01208) 812276

ST IVES
Cornwall

The Anchorage Guest House ♦♦♦♦
5 Bunkers Hill, St Ives, TR26 1LJ
T: (01736) 797135
F: (01736) 797135
E: james@theanchoragebb.fsnet.co.uk
I: www.theanchoragebb.fsnet.co.uk

Blue Hayes Private Hotel ♦♦♦♦
Trelyon Avenue, St Ives, TR26 2AD
T: (01736) 797129
F: (01736) 797129
E: malcolm@bluehayes.fsbusiness.co.uk
I: www.bluehayes.co.uk

Carlill ♦♦
9 Porthminster Terrace, St Ives, TR26 2DQ
T: (01736) 796738

Chy-an-Creet ♦♦♦♦
Higher Stennack, St Ives, TR26 2HA
T: (01736) 796559
F: (01736) 796559
E: relax@chy.co.uk
I: www.chy.co.uk

The Countryman at Trink ♦♦♦♦
Old Coach Road, St Ives, TR26 3JQ
T: (01736) 797571
F: (01736) 797571
E: countrymanstives@bushinternet.com
I: www.the-countryman-hotel-stives.co.uk

The Grey Mullet Guest House ♦♦♦
2 Bunkers Hill, St Ives, TR26 1LJ
T: (01736) 796635
E: greymulletguesthouse@lineone.net
I: www.touristnetuk.com/sw/greymullet

Longships Hotel ♦♦♦♦
Talland Road, St Ives, TR26 2DF
T: (01736) 798180
F: (01736) 798180
E: enquiries@longships-hotel.co.uk
I: www.longships-hotel.co.uk

Pierview Guesthouse ♦♦♦♦
32-34 Back Road East, St Ives, TR26 1PD
T: (01736) 794268
F: (01736) 794268
I: www.pierview-stives.co.uk

The Pondarosa ♦♦♦♦
10 Porthminster Terrace, St Ives, TR26 2DQ
T: (01736) 795875
F: (01736) 797811
E: pondarosa.hotel@talk21.com
I: www.cornwall-online.co.uk

Porthmeor Hotel ♦♦♦
Godrevy Terrace, St Ives, TR26 1JA
T: (01736) 796712
F: (01736) 796712
E: info@porthmeor.com
I: www.porthmeor.com

St Ives Bay Hotel ♦♦♦
The Terrace, St Ives, TR26 2BP
T: (01736) 795106
F: (01736) 793216
I: www.shearingsholidays.com/hotels/stives.htm

Tregony Guest House ♦♦♦♦
1 Clodgy View, St Ives, TR26 1JG
T: (01736) 795884
F: (01736) 798942
E: info@tregony.com
I: www.tregony.com

ST JULIOT
Cornwall

Higher Pennycrocker Farm ♦♦♦♦
Boscastle, PL35 0BY
T: (01840) 250488
F: (01840) 250488
E: Jackiefarm@aol.com

The Old Rectory ♦♦♦♦♦ GOLD AWARD
St Juliot, Boscastle PL25 0BT
T: (01840) 250225
F: (01840) 250225
E: sally@stjuliot.com
I: www.stjuliot.com

ST JUST-IN-PENWITH
Cornwall

Bosavern House ♦♦♦
St Just-in-Penwith, TR19 7RD
T: (01736) 788301
F: (01736) 788301
E: marcol@bosavern.u-net.com
I: www.bosavern.u-net.com

Boscean Country Hotel ♦♦♦♦
Boswedden Road, St Just-in-Penwith, TR19 7QP
T: (01736) 788748
F: (01736) 788748
E: boscean@aol.com
I: www.connexions.co.uk/boscean/index.htm

Boswedden House ♦♦♦
Cape Cornwall, St Just-in-Penwith, TR19 7NJ
T: (01736) 788733
F: (01736) 788733
E: relax@boswedden.org.uk
I: www.smoothhound.co.uk/hotels/boswedd.html

ST KEVERNE
Cornwall

Eden House ♦♦♦♦
Lemon Street, St Keverne, Helston TR12 6NE
T: (01326) 280005
E: RobertBOBhughes@aol.com

ST KEW
Cornwall

Tregellist Farm ♦♦♦♦
Tregellist, St Kew, Bodmin PL30 3HG
T: (01208) 880537
F: (01208) 881017
E: jillcleave@tregellist.fsbusiness.co.uk

ST MABYN
Cornwall

Chrismar ♦♦
Wadebridge Road, St Mabyn, Bodmin PL30 3BH
T: (01208) 841518

Cles Kernyk ♦♦♦
Wadebridge Road, St Mabyn, Bodmin PL30 3BH
T: (01208) 841258
E: sue@mabyn.freeserve.co.uk

Treglown House ♦♦♦♦
Haywood Farm, St Mabyn, Bodmin PL30 3BU
T: (01208) 841896
F: (01208) 841896
E: treglownhouse@stmabyn.fsnet.co.uk
I: www.treglownhouse.co.uk

ST MARY'S
Isles of Scilly

Anjeric Guest House ♦♦♦
The Strand, St Mary's, TR21 0PS
T: (01720) 422700
F: (01720) 422700
E: judyarcher@yahoo.co.uk
I: www.scillyonline.co.uk/accomm/anjeric.html

Annet ♦♦♦♦ SILVER AWARD
Porthlow, St Mary's, TR21 0NF
T: (01720) 422441
F: (01720) 422553
E: annet-cottage@lineone.net
I: www.annet-cottage.co.uk

April Cottage
♦♦♦♦ SILVER AWARD
Church Road, St Mary's, TR21 0NA
T: (01720) 422279
F: (01720) 423247

Armeria ♦♦♦
1 Porthloo Terrace, St Mary's, TR21 0NF
T: (01720) 422961

Auriga Guest House ♦♦♦♦
7 Porthcressa Road, St Mary's, TR21 0JL
T: (01720) 422637
E: aurigascilly@aol.com

Beachfield House ♦♦♦♦
Porthloo, St Mary's, TR21 0NE
T: (01720) 422463
F: (01720) 422463
E: whomersley@supanet.com

Belmont ♦♦♦♦
Church Road, St Mary's, TR21 0NA
T: (01720) 423154
F: (01720) 423357
E: enquiries@the-belmont.freeserve.co.uk
I: www.the-belmont.freeserve.co.uk

Blue Carn Cottage ♦♦♦
Old Town, St Mary's, TR21 0NH
T: (01720) 422309

The Boathouse ♦♦♦
Thorofare Hugh Town, St Mary's, TR21 0LN
T: (01720) 422688

Broomfields ♦♦♦
Church Road, St Mary's, TR21 0NA
T: (01720) 422309

Buckingham House ♦♦
The Bank, St Mary's, TR21 0HY
T: (01720) 422543

The Bylet ♦♦♦
Church Road, St Mary's, TR21 0NA
T: (01720) 422479
F: (01720) 422479

Cornerways ♦♦♦♦
Jackson's Hill, St Mary's, TR21 0JZ
T: (01720) 422757
F: (01720) 422797

Crebinick House
♦♦♦♦ SILVER AWARD
Church Street, St Mary's, TR21 0JT
T: (01720) 422968
E: wct@crebinick.co.uk
I: www.crebinick.co.uk

Evergreen Cottage Guest House ♦♦♦♦
The Parade, Hugh Town, St Mary's, TR21 0LP
T: (01720) 422711

Garrison House
♦♦♦♦ SILVER AWARD
Garrison Hill, St Mary's, TR21 0LS
T: (01720) 422972
F: (01720) 422972
E: garrisonhouse@aol.com
I: www.isles-of-scilly.co.uk/guesthouses

Gunners Rock ♦♦♦♦
Jackson's Hill, St Mary's, TR21 0JZ
T: (01720) 422595

Hazeldene ♦♦♦♦
Church Street, St Mary's, TR21 0JT
T: (01720) 422864

High Lanes Farm ♦♦♦
Atlantic View, St Mary's, TR21 0NW
T: (01720) 422684

Higher Trenoweth
♦♦♦♦ SILVER AWARD
St Mary's, TR21 0NS
T: (01720) 422419

Innisidgen Guest House ♦♦♦
Church Street, St Mary's, TR21 0JT
T: (01720) 422899
F: (01720) 422899
E: innisidgen@yahoo.co.uk
I: www.isles-of-scilly.co.uk

Kistvaen ♦♦♦♦
St Mary's, TR21 0JE
T: (01720) 422002
F: (01720) 422002
E: chivy002@aol.com

Lamorna ♦♦♦
Rams Valley, St Mary's, TR21 0JX
T: (01720) 422333

Lynwood ♦♦♦♦
Church Street, St Mary's, TR21 0JT
T: (01720) 423313
F: (01720) 423313

Lyonnesse Guest House ♦♦♦
The Strand, St Mary's, TR21 0PS
T: (01720) 422458

Marine House ♦♦♦
Church Street, Hugh Town, St Mary's, TR21 0JT
T: (01720) 422966
E: peggy@rowe55.freeserve.co.uk

Men-a-Vaur ♦♦♦
Church Road, St Mary's, TR21 0NA
T: (01720) 422245

Morgelyn ♦♦♦
McFarlands Down, St Mary's, TR21 0NS
T: (01720) 422897
E: info@morgelyn.co.uk
I: www.morgelyn.co.uk

Pier House ♦♦♦♦
The Bank, St Mary's, TR21 0HY
T: (01720) 423061

Rose Cottage
♦♦♦♦ SILVER AWARD
The Strand, St Mary's, TR21 0PT
T: (01720) 422078
F: (01720) 423588
E: rosecottage@infinnet.co.uk

St Hellena ♦♦♦♦
13 Garrison Lane, St Mary's, TR21 0JD
T: (01720) 423231

Santa Maria ♦♦♦♦
Sallyport, St Mary's, TR21 0JE
T: (01720) 422687
F: (01720) 422687

Scillonia ♦♦
Bank, St Mary's, TR21 0HY
T: (01720) 422101

Shamrock ♦♦♦♦
High Lanes, St Mary's, TR21 0NW
T: (01720) 423269

Shearwater Guest House ♦♦♦
The Parade, Hugh Town, St Mary's, TR21 0LP
T: (01720) 422402
F: (01720) 422351
E: ianhopkin@aol.com
I: www.shearwater-guest-house.co.uk

Strand House ♦♦♦
The Strand, St Mary's, TR21 0PS
T: (01720) 422808
F: (01720) 423009

Sylina ♦♦♦
McFarlands Downs, St Mary's, TR21 0NS
T: (01720) 422129
F: (01720) 422129

Trelawney Guest House ♦♦♦♦
Church Street, St Mary's, TR21 0JT
T: (01720) 422377
F: (01720) 422377
E: dtownend@netcomuk.co.uk
I: www.trlawney-ios.co.uk

Veronica Lodge ♦♦♦♦
The Garrison, St Mary's, TR21 0LS
T: (01720) 422585
E: veronicalodge@freenetname.co.uk

Westford House ♦♦♦
Church Street, St Mary's, TR21 0JT
T: (01720) 422510
F: (01720) 422510
E: susan@wiosh.fsnet.co.uk

The Wheelhouse ♦♦♦♦
Porthcressa, St Mary's, TR21 0JG
T: (01720) 422719
F: (01720) 422719

Wingletang Guest House ♦♦♦
The Parade, St Mary's, TR21 0LP
T: (01720) 422381

The Withies
♦♦♦♦ SILVER AWARD
Trench Lane, Old Town, St Mary's, TR21 0PA
T: (01720) 422986

ST MARYS
Devon

The Town House
♦♦♦♦ SILVER AWARD
Little Porth, St Mary's, TR21 0JG
T: (01720) 422793
E: scillytownhouse@btclick.com
I: www.isles-of-scilly.co.uk/the-town-house.html

ST MAWES
Cornwall

The Ship and Castle ♦♦♦
The Waterfront, St Mawes, Truro TR2 5DG
T: (01326) 270401
F: (01326) 270152
I: www.shearingsholidays.com

ST MAWGAN
Cornwall

The Falcon Inn ♦♦♦♦
St Mawgan, Newquay TR8 4EP
T: (01637) 860225
F: (01637) 860884
E: enquiries@falconinn.net
I: www.falconinn.net

ST MERRYN
Cornwall

Tregavone Farm ♦♦♦
St Merryn, Padstow PL28 8JZ
T: (01841) 520148

Trewithen Farm ♦♦♦♦
St Merryn, Padstow PL28 8JZ
T: (01841) 520420

ST MINVER
Cornwall

Porteath Barn ♦♦♦
St Minver, Wadebridge PL27 6RA
T: (01208) 863605
F: (01208) 863954
E: mbloor@ukonline.co.uk

ST NEOT
Cornwall

The London Inn ♦♦♦
St Neot, Liskeard PL14 6NG
T: (01579) 320263
F: (01579) 321642
E: jpleisuregroup@cs.com

ST TEATH
Cornwall

Trehannick Farm ♦♦♦
St Teath, Bodmin PL30 3JW
T: (01208) 850312
F: (01208) 850312

ST TUDY
Cornwall

Polrode Mill Cottage
♦♦♦♦♦ SILVER AWARD
Allen Valley, St Tudy, Bodmin PL30 3NS
T: (01208) 850203
E: polrode@tesco.net
I: www.cornwall-online.co.uk/polrode-mill

SALCOMBE
Devon

Burton Farm
♦♦♦♦ SILVER AWARD
Galmpton, Kingsbridge TQ7 3EY
T: (01548) 561210
F: (01548) 561210
I: www.burtonfarm.co.uk

Torre View Hotel ♦♦♦♦
Devon Road, Salcombe, TQ8 8HJ
T: (01548) 842633
F: (01548) 842633
E: bouttle@torreview.eurobell.co.uk
I: www.SmoothHound.co.uk/hotels/torreview.html

SALISBURY
Wiltshire

Avila ♦♦♦
130 Exeter Street, Salisbury, SP1 2SG
T: (01722) 421093

The Avon Brewery Inn ♦♦♦
75 Castle Street, Salisbury, SP1 3SP
T: (01722) 416184
F: (01722) 326219

The Barford Inn ♦♦♦♦
Barford St Martin, Salisbury SP3 4AB
T: (01722) 742242
F: (01722) 743606
E: ido@barfordinn.co.uk
I: www.barfordinn.co.uk

Barlings ♦♦♦♦
41 Gravel Close, Downton, Salisbury SP5 3JQ
T: (01725) 510310

The Bell Inn ♦♦♦
Warminster Road, South Newton, Salisbury SP2 0QD
T: (01722) 743336
F: (01722) 744202

40 Belle Vue Road ♦♦
Salisbury, SP1 3YD
T: (01722) 325773

78 Belle Vue Road ♦♦♦
Salisbury, SP1 3YD
T: (01722) 329477

Bridge Farm
♦♦♦♦ GOLD AWARD
Lower Road, Britford, Salisbury SP5 4DY
T: (01722) 332376
F: (01722) 332376
E: mail@bridgefarmbb.co.uk
I: www.bridgefarmbb.co.uk

Burcombe Manor ♦♦♦
Burcombe, Salisbury, SP2 0E3
T: (01722) 744288

Byways House ♦♦♦
31 Fowlers Road, City Centre, Salisbury, SP1 2QP
T: (01722) 328364
F: (01722) 322146
E: byways@bed-breakfast-salisbury.co.uk
I: www.bed-breakfast-salisbury.co.uk

The Edwardian Lodge ♦♦♦♦
59 Castle Road, Salisbury, SP1 3RH
T: (01722) 413329
F: (01722) 503105
E: richardwhite@edlodge.freeserve.co.uk
I: www.edwardianlodge.co.uk

Farthings ♦♦♦
9 Swaynes Close, Salisbury, SP1 3AE
T: (01722) 330749
F: (01722) 330749
E: farthings@amserve.com
I: www.shammer.freeserve.co.uk

Gerrans House
♦♦♦♦ SILVER AWARD
91 Castle Road, Salisbury, SP1 3RW
T: (01722) 334394
F: (01722) 332508
E: gerranshouse@robinsg.fsnet.co.uk

Glenshee
♦♦♦♦ SILVER AWARD
3 Montague Road, West Harnham, Salisbury, SP2 8NJ
T: (01722) 322620
F: (01722) 322620
E: glenshee@breathemail.net
I: www.smoothhound.co.uk/hotels/glenshee.htm

Griffin Cottage ♦♦♦♦
10 St Edmunds Church Street, Salisbury, SP1 1EF
T: (01722) 328259
F: (01722) 416928
E: mark@brandonasoc.demon.co.uk
I: www.smoothhound.co.uk/hotels/griffinc.html

Highveld ♦♦♦
44 Hulse Road, Salisbury, SP1 3LY
T: (01722) 338172
E: icedawn@amserve.net

Holly Tree House ♦♦
53 Wyndham Road, Salisbury, SP1 3AH
T: (01722) 322955

Holmhurst Guest House ♦♦
Downton Road, Salisbury, SP2 8AR
T: (01722) 410407
F: (01722) 323164
E: holmhurst@talk21.com

Leena's Guest House ♦♦♦
50 Castle Road, Salisbury, SP1 3RL
T: (01722) 335419
F: (01722) 335419

Malvern
♦♦♦♦ SILVER AWARD
31 Hulse Road, Salisbury, SP1 3LU
T: (01722) 327995
F: (01722) 327995
E: malvern_gh@madasafish.com

Manor Farm ♦♦♦♦
Burcombe, Salisbury SP2 0EJ
T: (01722) 742177
F: (01722) 744600
E: sacombes@talk21.com

94 Milford Hill ♦♦♦
Salisbury, SP1 2QL
T: (01722) 322454

Newton Farm House
♦♦♦♦♦ SILVER AWARD
Southampton Road, Whiteparish, Salisbury, SP5 2QL
T: (01794) 884416
F: (01794) 884416
E: enquiries@newtonfarmhouse.co.uk
I: www.newtonfarmhouse.co.uk

Number Eighty Eight ♦♦♦♦
88 Exeter Street, Salisbury, SP1 2SE
T: (01722) 330139
E: enquiries@no88.co.uk
I: www.no88.co.uk

Old Chequers Cottage
♦♦ SILVER AWARD
17 Guilder Lane, Salisbury, SP1 1HW
T: (01722) 325335
F: (01722) 325335
E: old_chequers@onetel.net.uk

The Old Rectory Bed & Breakfast ♦♦♦♦
75 Belle Vue Road, Salisbury, SP1 3YE
T: (01722) 502702
F: (01722) 501135
E: stay@theoldrectory-bb.co.uk
I: www.theoldrectory-bb.co.uk

Pathways ♦♦
41 Shady Bower, Salisbury, SP1 2RG
T: (01722) 324252

The Retreat Inn ♦♦♦
33 Milford Street, Salisbury, SP1 2AP
T: (01722) 338686

Richburn Guest House ♦♦♦
25 Estcourt Road, Salisbury, SP1 3AP
T: (01722) 325189
F: (01722) 325189

The Rokeby Guest House ♦♦♦♦
3 Wain-a-Long Road, Salisbury, SP1 1LJ
T: (01722) 329800
F: (01722) 329800
I: www.smoothhound.co.uk/hotels/rokeby.html

Saddlers ♦♦♦♦
Princes Hill, Redlynch, Salisbury SP5 2HF
T: (01725) 510571
F: (01725) 510571
E: sadd.lers@virgin.net
I: www.s-h-systems.co.uk/hotels/saddlers.html

34 Salt Lane ♦♦
Salisbury, SP1 1EG
T: (01722) 326141

Spire House ♦♦♦♦
84 Exeter Street, Salisbury, SP1 2SE
T: (01722) 339213
F: (01722) 339213
E: lois.faulkner@talk21.com
I: www.smoothhound.co.uk/hotels/spire.html

Stratford Lodge ♦♦♦♦
4 Park Lane, Castle Road, Salisbury, SP1 3NP
T: (01722) 325177
F: (01722) 325177
E: enquiries@stratfordlodge.co.uk
I: www.stratfordlodge.co.uk

Swaynes Firs Farm ♦♦♦
Grimsdyke, Coombe Bissett, Salisbury SP5 5RF
T: (01725) 519240
E: swaynes.firs@virgin.net
I: www.swaynesfirs.co.uk

Tiffany ♦♦♦
2 Bourne Villas, off College Street, Salisbury, SP1 3AW
T: (01722) 332367

Torrisholme ♦♦♦
Stratford Sub Castle, Salisbury SP1 3LQ
T: (01722) 329089
F: (01722) 321363
E: torrisholme@hotmail.com

Victoria Lodge Guest House Rating Applied For
61 Castle Road, Salisbury, SP1 3RH
T: (01722) 320586
F: (01722) 414507
E: mail@viclodge.co.uk
I: www.viclodge.co.uk

Websters
♦♦♦♦ SILVER AWARD
11 Hartington Road, Salisbury, SP2 7LG
T: (01722) 339779
F: (01722) 421903
E: enquiries@webster-bed-breakfast
I: www.websters-bed-breakfast.com

White Horse Inn ♦♦
38 Castle Street, Salisbury, SP1 1BN
T: (01722) 327844
F: (01722) 336226

Wyndham Park Lodge ♦♦♦♦
51 Wyndham Road, Salisbury, SP1 3AB
T: (01722) 416517
F: (01722) 328851
E: enquiries@wyndhamparklodge.co.uk
I: www.wyndhamparklodge.co.uk

SALTASH
Cornwall

Haye Farm ♦♦♦♦
Landulph, Saltash PL12 6QQ
T: (01752) 842786
F: (01752) 842786
I: www.hayefarmcornwall.co.uk

SAMPFORD COURTENAY
Devon

Langdale ♦♦
Sampford Courtenay, Okehampton EX20 2SY
T: (01837) 82433
E: chrisclayton7@lineone.net

Lower Trecott Farm ♦♦♦♦
Sampford Courtenay, Okehampton EX20 2TD
T: (01837) 880118
E: craig@trecott.fsnet.co.uk

SAND
Somerset

Townsend Farm
♦♦♦♦ SILVER AWARD
Sand, Wedmore BS28 4XH
T: (01934) 712342
F: (01934) 712405
E: smewillcox0@farmersweekly.net

SEATON
Devon

Beaumont ♦♦♦♦
Castle Hill, Seaton, EX12 2QW
T: (01297) 20832
F: 0870 0554708
E: tony@lymebay.demon.co.uk
I: www.smoothhound.co.uk/hotels/beaumont.html

Blue Haven ♦♦♦♦
Looe Hill, Seaton, Torpoint PL11 3JQ
T: (01503) 250310
E: bluehaven@btinternet.com
I: www.smoothhound.co.uk/hotels/bluehave.html

Four Seasons ♦♦♦
3 Burrow Road, Seaton, EX12 2NF
T: (01297) 20761
F: (01297) 20761

Gatcombe Farm ♦♦♦♦
Seaton, EX12 3AA
T: (01297) 21235
F: (01297) 23010
E: gatcombefarm@tinyworld.co.uk

Hill House
♦♦♦♦ SILVER AWARD
Highcliffe Crescent, Seaton, EX12 2PS
T: (01297) 20377
E: jphil.beard@lineone.net

Mariners Hotel ♦♦♦♦
The Esplanade, Seaton, EX12 2NP
T: (01297) 20560
F: (01297) 20560

Pinehurst Bed & Breakfast ♦♦♦♦
189 Beer Road, Seaton, EX12 2QB
T: (01297) 21878
E: stay@pinehurst.co.uk
I: www.pinehurst.co.uk

SEMINGTON
Wiltshire

Newhouse Farm ♦♦♦♦
Littleton, Semington, Trowbridge BA14 6LF
T: (01380) 870349

SHALDON
Devon

Glenside House Hotel ♦♦♦
Ringmore Road, Shaldon, Teignmouth TQ14 0EP
T: (01626) 872448
F: (01626) 872448
I: www.smoothhound.co.uk/hotels/glensideho.html

Potters Mooring ♦♦♦
30 The Green, Shaldon, Teignmouth TQ14 0DN
T: (01626) 873225
F: (01626) 872909
E: mail@pottersmooring.co.uk
I: www.pottersmooring.co.uk

SHARCOTT
Wiltshire

The Old Dairy House ♦♦♦♦
Sharcott, Pewsey SN9 5PA
T: (01672) 562287
E: old.dairy@virgin.net
I: business.virgin.net/neville.burrell/sharcott.htm

SHEPTON MALLET
Somerset

Belfield Guest House ♦♦♦
34 Charlton Road, Shepton Mallet, BA4 5PA
T: (01749) 344353
F: (01749) 344353
E: andrea@belfield-house.co.uk
I: www.belfield-house.co.uk

The Bell Hotel ♦♦♦
2 High Street, Shepton Mallet, BA4 5AN
T: (01749) 345593
F: (01749) 347480

Burnt House Farm
♦♦♦♦ SILVER AWARD
Waterlip, West Cranmore, Shepton Mallet BA4 4RN
T: (01749) 880280
F: (01749) 880004

Hillbury House ♦♦♦♦
65 Compton Road, Shepton Mallet, BA4 5QT
T: (01749) 345473
F: (01749) 345473
E: patandjerry@ukonline.co.uk

Hurlingpot Farmhouse
Rating Applied For
Chelynch, Shepton Mallet, BA4 4PY
T: (01749) 880256
I: www.smoothhound.co.uk/hotels/hurling.html

Knapps Farm
♦♦♦♦♦ SILVER AWARD
Doulting, Shepton Mallet BA4 4LA
T: (01749) 880471

Middleton House ♦♦♦♦
68 Compton Road, Shepton Mallet, BA4 5QT
T: (01749) 343720
E: lynandbob@shepton.freeserve.co.uk

Pecking Mill Inn and Hotel ♦♦
A371 Evercreech, Evercreech, Shepton Mallet BA4 6PG
T: (01749) 830336
F: (01749) 831316

Temple House Farm ♦♦♦♦
Doulting, Shepton Mallet BA4 4RQ
T: (01749) 880294
F: (01749) 880688

SHEPTON MONTAGUE
Somerset

Lower Farm
♦♦♦♦ SILVER AWARD
Shepton Montague, Wincanton BA9 8JG
T: (01749) 812253
E: susiedowding@netscapeonline.co.uk
I: www.lowerfarm.org.uk

SHERBORNE
Dorset

The Alders
♦♦♦♦ SILVER AWARD
Sandford Orcas, Sherborne DT9 4SB
T: (01963) 220666
F: (01963) 220106
E: jonsue@thealdersbb.com
I: www.thealdersbb.com

Bridleways ♦♦♦
Oborne Road, Sherborne, DT9 3RX
T: (01935) 814716
F: (01935) 814716

The Britannia Inn ♦♦♦
Westbury, Sherborne, DT9 3EH
T: (01935) 813300

Clatcombe Grange ♦♦♦♦
Bristol Road, Sherborne, DT9 4RH
T: (01935) 814355
F: (01935) 814696

Cromwell House
♦♦♦♦ SILVER AWARD
Long Street, Sherborne, DT9 3BS
T: (01935) 813352
I: www.smoothhound.co.uk/a53281.html

Crown Inn ♦♦♦
Green Hill, Sherborne, DT9 4EP
T: (01935) 812930
F: (01935) 812930

Huntsbridge Farm
♦♦♦♦♦ SILVER AWARD
Batcombe Road, Leigh, Sherborne DT9 6JA
T: (01935) 872150
F: (01935) 872150
E: huntsbridge@lineone.net

The Old Vicarage Hotel
♦♦♦♦♦
Sherborne Road, Milborne Port, Sherborne DT9 5AT
T: (01963) 251117
F: (01963) 251515
E: theoldvicarage@milborneport.freeserve.co.uk
I: www.milborneport.freeserve.co.uk

Village Vacations ♦♦♦
Brookmead, Rimpton, Yeovil BA22 8AQ
T: (01935) 850241
F: (01935) 850241
E: villagevac@aol.com
I: www.villagevacations.co.uk

SHERSTON
Wiltshire

Widleys Farm ♦♦♦
Sherston, Malmesbury SN16 0PY
T: (01666) 840213
F: (01666) 840156

SHIPHAM
Somerset

Herongates ♦♦♦♦
Horseleaze Lane, Shipham, Winscombe BS25 1UQ
T: (01934) 843280
F: (01934) 843280

SHIPTON GORGE
Dorset

Cairnhill
♦♦♦♦♦ GOLD AWARD
Shipton Gorge, Bridport DT6 4LL
T: (01308) 898203
F: (01308) 898203
E: cairnhill@talk21.com

SHREWTON
Wiltshire

Maddington House ♦♦♦♦
Maddington Street, Shrewton, Salisbury SP3 4JD
T: (01980) 620406
F: (01980) 620406
E: rsrobathan@freenet.co.uk

SIDBURY
Devon

Rose Cottage Sidbury ♦♦♦♦
Rose Cottage, Greenhead, Sidbury, Sidmouth EX10 0RH
T: (01395) 597357
F: (01395) 597357
E: lincoln@rosecottagesidbury.co.uk
I: www.rosecottagesidbury.co.uk

SIDMOUTH
Devon

The Barn And Pinn Cottage Guest House♦♦♦♦
Bowd Cross, Sidmouth, EX10 0ND
T: (01395) 513613
E: thebarnandpinncott@amserve.net

Berwick Guest House
Rating Applied For
Salcombe Road, Sidmouth, EX10 8PX
T: (01395) 513621

Canterbury Guest House ♦♦♦
Salcombe Road, Sidmouth, EX10 8PR
T: (01395) 513373
E: cgh@eclipse.co.uk

Coombe Bank Guest House
♦♦♦♦ SILVER AWARD
86 Alexandria Road, Sidmouth, EX10 9HG
T: (01395) 514843
F: (01395) 513558
E: info@coombebank.com
I: www.coombebank.com

Ferndale ♦♦♦♦
92 Winslade Road, Sidmouth, EX10 9EZ
T: (01395) 515495
F: (01395) 515495

Higher Coombe Farm ♦♦♦
Tipton St John, Sidmouth EX10 0AX
T: (01404) 813385
F: (01404) 813385
E: KerstinFarmer@farming.co.uk
I: www.smoothhound.co.uk/hotels/higherco.html

Lower Pinn Farm ♦♦♦♦
Pinn, Sidmouth EX10 0NN
T: (01395) 513733
F: (01395) 513733
E: liz@lowerpinnfarm.co.uk
I: www.lowerpinnfarm.co.uk

Lynstead ♦♦♦♦
Vicarage Road, Sidmouth, EX10 8UQ
T: (01395) 514635
F: (01395) 578954
E: lynstead@aol.com
I: wwwsmoothhound.co.uk/hotels/lynstead.html

Pinn Barton Farm
Rating Applied For
Peak Hill, Pinn Lane, Sidmouth, EX10 0NN
T: (01395) 514004
F: (01395) 514004
I: www.smoothhound.co.uk/hotels/pinn.html

The Salty Monk
♦♦♦♦♦ GOLD AWARD
Church Street, Sidford, Sidmouth EX10 9QP
T: (01395) 513174
F: (01395) 514722
E: andy@saltymonkhotelsidmouth.co.uk
I: www.saltymonkhotelsidmouth.co.uk

Willow Bridge Private Hotel ♦♦♦♦
Millford Road, Sidmouth, EX10 8DR
T: (01395) 513599
F: (01395) 513599
E: willowframing@c.s.com

Wiscombe Linhaye Farm ♦♦♦♦
Southleigh, Colyton EX24 6JF
T: (01404) 871342
F: (01404) 871342
E: rabjohns@btinternet.com

SILVERTON
Devon

Three Tuns Inn ♦♦♦
14 Exeter Road, Silverton, Exeter EX5 4HX
T: (01392) 860352
F: (01392) 860636
I: www.threetuninn.co.uk

SIMONSBATH
Somerset

Emmett's Grange ♦♦♦♦
Simonsbath, Minehead TA24 7LD
T: (01643) 831138
F: (01643) 831093
E: emmetts.grange@virgin.net
I: www.emmettsgrange.co.uk

SKILGATE
Somerset

Chapple Farm ♦
Skilgate, Taunton TA4 2DP
T: (01398) 331364

SLAPTON
Devon

Little Pittaford ♦♦♦♦♦ SILVER AWARD
Slapton, Kingsbridge TQ7 2QG
T: (01548) 580418
F: (01548) 580406
E: LittlePittaford@compuserve.com
I: www.littlepittaford.co.uk

Start House ♦♦♦
Start, Slapton, Kingsbridge TQ7 2QD
T: (01548) 580254

SOMERTON
Somerset

Littleton House ♦♦♦
New Street, Somerton, TA11 7NU
T: (01458) 273072

Mill House ♦♦♦♦♦ SILVER AWARD
Barton St. David, Somerton TA11 6DF
T: (01458) 851215
F: (01458) 851372
E: B&B@millhousebarton.co.uk
I: www.MillHouseBarton.co.uk

SOUTH MOLTON
Devon

Huxtable Farm ♦♦♦♦ SILVER AWARD
West Buckland, Barnstaple EX32 0SR
T: (01598) 760254
F: (01598) 760254
E: info@huxtablefarm.co.uk
I: www.huxtablefarm.co.uk

Kerscott Farm ♦♦♦♦♦ GOLD AWARD
Ash Mill, South Molton EX36 4QG
T: (01769) 550262
F: (01769) 550910
E: kerscott.farm@virgin.net
I: www.devon-bandb.co.uk

Old Coaching Inn ♦♦
Queen Street, South Molton, EX36 3BJ
T: (01769) 572526

SOUTH NEWTON
Wiltshire

Salisbury Old Mill House ♦♦♦♦ SILVER AWARD
Warminster Road, South Newton, Salisbury SP2 0QD
T: (01722) 742458
F: (01722) 742458

SOUTH PERROTT
Dorset

Shepherds Farmhouse ♦♦♦♦
South Perrott, Beaminster DT8 3HU
T: (01935) 891599
F: (01935) 891977
E: shepherds@eclipse.co.uk
I: www.shepherds.eclipse.co.uk

SOUTH PETHERWIN
Cornwall

Oakside Bed and Breakfast ♦♦♦
Oakside Bungalow, South Petherwin, Launceston PL15 7LJ
T: (01566) 86733

SOUTH ZEAL
Devon

Poltimore ♦♦♦
Ramsley, South Zeal, Okehampton EX20 2PD
T: (01837) 840209

SOUTHVILLE
Bristol

the greenhouse ♦♦♦
61 Greenbank Road, Southville, Bristol BS3 1RJ
T: (0117) 902 9166
F: (0117) 902 9007
E: krofc@msn.com

Walmer House ♦♦♦
94 Stackpool Road, Southville, Bristol BS3 1NW
T: (0117) 966 8253
F: (0117) 966 8253

SPREYTON
Devon

The Tom Cobley Tavern ♦♦♦
Spreyton, Crediton EX17 5AL
T: (01647) 231314
F: (01647) 231506
E: fjwfilor@tomcobley.fsnet.co.uk

STANTON DREW
Bath and North East Somerset

Greenlands ♦♦♦♦
Stanton Drew, Bristol BS39 4ES
T: (01275) 333487
F: (01275) 331211

STANTON WICK
Bath and North East Somerset

The Carpenters Arms ♦♦♦♦
Stanton Wick, Pensford, Bristol BS39 4BX
T: (01761) 490202
F: (01761) 490763
E: carpenters@dial.pipex.com
I: www.buccaneer.co.uk

STAPLEFORD
Wiltshire

The Parsonage ♦♦♦♦
Stapleford, Salisbury SP3 4LJ
T: (01722) 790334

STARCROSS
Devon

The Croft Guest House ♦♦♦
Cockwood Harbour, Starcross, Exeter EX6 8QY
T: (01626) 890282
F: (01626) 891768

STATHE
Somerset

Black Smock Inn ♦♦♦
Stathe Road, Stathe, Bridgwater TA7 0JN
T: (01823) 698352
F: (01823) 690138
E: info@blacksmock.co.uk
I: www.blacksmock.co.uk

STAVERTON
Devon

Kingston House ♦♦♦♦♦ SILVER AWARD
Staverton, Totnes TQ9 6AR
T: (01803) 762235
F: (01803) 762444
E: info@kingston-estate.co.uk
I: www.kingston-estate.co.uk

STEEPLE ASHTON
Wiltshire

Church Farm ♦♦♦♦
Steeple Ashton, Trowbridge BA14 6EL
T: (01380) 870518
E: church.farm@farmline.com

Longs Arms Inn ♦♦♦
High Street, Steeple Ashton, Trowbridge BA14 6EU
T: (01380) 870245
F: (01380) 870245
E: chantal@stayatthepub.freeserve.co.uk
I: www.stayatthepub.freeserve.co.uk

STERT
Wiltshire

Orchard Cottage ♦♦♦
Stert, Devizes SN10 3JD
T: (01380) 723103

STIBB
Cornwall

Strands ♦♦♦
Stibb, Bude EX23 9HW
T: (01288) 353514

STICKLEPATH
Devon

Higher Coombe Head House ♦♦♦♦
Sticklepath, Okehampton EX20 1QL
T: (01837) 840240
E: coombehead@btinternet.com

STOGUMBER
Somerset

Hall Farm ♦♦♦
Stogumber, Taunton TA4 3TQ
T: (01984) 656321

Northam Mill ♦♦♦♦ SILVER AWARD
Water Lane, Stogumber, Taunton TA4 3TT
T: (01984) 656916
F: (01984) 656144
E: bmsspicer@aol.com
I: www.northam-mill.co.uk

Wick House ♦♦♦
2 Brook Street, Stogumber, Taunton TA4 3SZ
T: (01984) 656422
E: sheila@wickhouse.fsbusiness.co.uk
I: www.wickhouse.fsbusiness.co.uk

STOKE-IN-TEIGNHEAD
Devon

Deane Thatch Accommodation ♦♦♦
Deane Road, Stoke-in-Teignhead, Newton Abbot TQ12 4QU
T: (01626) 873724
F: (01626) 873724
E: deanethatch@hotmail.com
I: www.deanethatch.co.uk

STOKE ST GREGORY
Somerset

Ashgrove ♦♦♦♦ SILVER AWARD
Meare Green, Stoke St Gregory, Taunton TA3 6HZ
T: (01823) 490209
E: sueperowne@hotmail.com

Meare Green Farm ♦♦♦♦
Meare Green, Stoke St Gregory, Taunton TA3 6HT
T: (01823) 490759
F: (01823) 490759
E: jane.pine@kitesourcing.com

STOKE SUB HAMDON
Somerset

Castle Farm ♦♦♦♦
Stoke sub Hamdon, TA14 6QS
T: (01935) 822231
F: (01935) 822057

STOKENHAM
Devon

Brookfield ♦♦♦
Stokenham, Kingsbridge TQ7 2SL
T: (01548) 580615
F: (01548) 580615
E: heath@brookfield37.freeserve.co.uk

STRATFORD SUB CASTLE
Wiltshire

Carp Cottage ♦♦♦♦
Stratford Sub Castle, Salisbury SP1 3LH
T: (01722) 327219

STRATTON
Cornwall

Cann Orchard ♦♦♦♦
Howard Lane, Stratton, Bude EX23 9TD
T: (01288) 352098
F: (01288) 352098

STRATTON-ON-THE-FOSSE
Somerset

Oval House ♦♦♦
Stratton-on-the-Fosse, Radstock BA3 4RB
T: (01761) 232183
F: (01761) 232183
E: mellotte@clara.co.uk
I: www.mellotte.clara.co.uk

STREET
Somerset

Leigh Nook ♦♦♦♦
Marshalls Elm, Somerton Road, Street, BA16 0TZ
T: (01458) 443511
E: williamavril@leighnook.fsnet.co.uk

Marshalls Elm Farm ♦♦♦
Street, BA16 0TZ
T: (01458) 442878

Old Orchard House ♦♦♦♦
Middle Brooks, Street, BA16 0TU
T: (01458) 442212
E: oldorchardhouse@amserve.net
I: www.oldorchardhouse.co.uk

STRETE
Devon

Skerries Bed & Breakfast
♦♦♦♦ SILVER AWARD
Skerrries, Strete, Dartmouth
TQ6 0PH
T: (01803) 770775
F: (01803) 770950
E: jam.skerries@rya-online.net
I: www.skerriesbandb.co.uk

SUTTON POYNTZ
Dorset

Brookfield ♦♦♦
White Horse Lane, Sutton Poyntz, Weymouth DT3 6LU
T: (01305) 833674

SWINDON
Wiltshire

Courtleigh House ♦♦♦♦
40 Draycott Road, Chiseldon, Swindon SN4 0LS
T: (01793) 740246

Swandown Hotel ♦♦
36/37 Victoria Road, Swindon, SN1 3AS
T: (01793) 536695
F: (01793) 432551
E: swandownhotel@aol.com
I: www.swandownhotel.co.uk

SYDLING ST NICHOLAS
Dorset

Magiston Farm ♦♦♦
Sydling St Nicholas, Dorchester, DT2 9NR
T: (01300) 320295

TALATON
Devon

Larkbeare Farmhouse ♦♦♦♦
Larkbeare, Talaton, Exeter
EX5 2RY
T: (01404) 822069
F: (01404) 823746
E: stay@larkbeare.net
I: www.larkbeare.net

TALSKIDDY
Cornwall

Pennatillie Farm
♦♦♦♦ SILVER AWARD
Talskiddy, St Columb TR9 6EF
T: (01637) 880280
F: (01637) 880280
E: angela@pennatillie.fsnet.co.uk
I: www.cornish-riviera.co.uk/pennatilliefarm

TAUNTON
Somerset

Acorn Lodge ♦♦♦
22 Wellington Road, Taunton, TA1 4EQ
T: (01823) 337613

Close House ♦♦♦
Hatch Beauchamp, Taunton, TA3 6AE
T: (01823) 480424
F: (01823) 480424
E: close.house@talk21.co.uk

Fursdon House ♦♦
88-90 Greenway Road, Taunton, TA2 6LE
T: (01823) 331955

Gatchells ♦♦♦♦
Angersleigh, Taunton TA3 7SY
T: (01823) 421580
E: gatchells@somerweb.co.uk
I: www.somerweb.co.uk/gatchells

Heathercroft ♦♦♦
118 Wellington Road, Taunton, TA1 5LA
T: (01823) 275516

Higher Yarde Farmhouse
♦♦♦♦
Higher Yarde Farm, Staplegrove, Taunton TA2 6SW
T: (01823) 451553
E: anita.hyf@rya-online.net

Lowdens House ♦♦♦
26 Wellington Road, Taunton, TA1 4EQ
T: (01823) 334500

North Down Farm Bed & Breakfast
♦♦♦♦ SILVER AWARD
Pyncombe Lane, Wiveliscombe, Taunton TA4 2BL
T: (01984) 623730
F: (01984) 623730
E: jennycope@tiscali.co.uk

Orchard House
♦♦♦♦ SILVER AWARD
Fons George, Middleway, Taunton, TA1 3JS
T: (01823) 351783
F: (01823) 351785
E: orch-hse@dircon.co.uk
I: www.smoothhound.co.uk/hotels/orchard2.html

Prockters Farm ♦♦♦
West Monkton, Taunton
TA2 8QN
T: (01823) 412269
F: (01823) 412269

Pyrland Farm ♦♦♦♦
Cheddon Road, Taunton, TA2 7QX
T: (01823) 334148

Rumwell Manor Hotel
♦♦♦♦ SILVER AWARD
Rumwell, Taunton, TA4 1EL
T: (01823) 461902
F: (01823) 254861
E: reception@rumwellmanor.co.uk
I: www.rumwellmanor.co.uk

The Spinney ♦♦♦♦
Curland, Taunton TA3 5SE
T: (01460) 234362
F: (01460) 234362
E: bartlett.spinney@zetnet.co.uk
I: www.somerweb.co.uk/spinney-bb

Staplegrove Lodge ♦♦♦♦
Staplegrove, Taunton TA2 6PX
T: (01823) 331153
I: www.staplegrovelodge.co.uk

Thatched Country Cottage and Garden B&B ♦♦♦
Pear Tree Cottage, Stapley, Churchstanton, Taunton
TA3 7QA
T: (01823) 601224
F: (01823) 601224
E: colvin.parry@virgin.net
I: www.best-hotel.com/peartreecottage

Yallands Farmhouse
♦♦♦♦ SILVER AWARD
Staplegrove, Taunton, TA2 6PZ
T: (01823) 278979
F: (01823) 278983
E: mail@yallands.co.uk
I: www.yallands.co.uk

TAVISTOCK
Devon

Acorn Cottage ♦♦♦♦
Heathfield, Tavistock, PL19 0LQ
T: (01822) 810038
E: viv@acorncot.fsnet.co.uk
I: www.visitbritain.com

April Cottage ♦♦♦♦
Mount Tavy Road, Tavistock, PL19 9JB
T: (01822) 613280
F: (01822) 613280

Beera Farmhouse
♦♦♦♦ SILVER AWARD
Milton Abbot, Tavistock
PL19 8PL
T: (01822) 870216
F: (01822) 870216
E: robert.tucker@farming.co.uk
I: www.beerafarmbedandbreakfast.com

Harrabeer Country House Hotel ♦♦♦♦
Harrowbeer Lane, Yelverton, PL20 6EA
T: (01822) 853302
F: (01822) 853302
E: reception@harrabeer.co.uk
I: www.harrabeer.co.uk

Mallards ♦♦♦♦
48 Plymouth Road, Tavistock, PL19 8BU
T: (01822) 615171
E: mallardstavistock@tinyworld.co.uk
I: www.mallardsoftavistock.co.uk

Old Rectory Farm ♦♦♦♦
Mary Tavy, Tavistock PL19 9PP
T: (01822) 810102

Rubbytown Farm ♦♦♦♦
Gulworthy, Tavistock PL19 8PA
T: (01822) 832493

Tor Cottage
♦♦♦♦♦ GOLD AWARD
Chillaton, Lifton PL16 0JE
T: (01822) 860248
F: (01822) 860126
E: info@torcottage.co.uk
I: www.torcottage.co.uk

TEIGNMOUTH
Devon

Belvedere Hotel ♦♦♦
Barn Park Road, Teignmouth, TQ14 8PJ
T: (01626) 774561
E: belvedere.hotel@amserve.net

Leicester House ♦♦♦
2 Winterbourne Road, Teignmouth, TQ14 8JT
T: (01626) 773043

The Moorings ♦♦♦♦
33 Teignmouth Road, Teignmouth, TQ14 8UR
T: (01626) 770400
F: (01626) 770400
E: mickywaters@aol.com

Thomas Luny House
♦♦♦♦♦ GOLD AWARD
Teign Street, Teignmouth, TQ14 8EG
T: (01626) 772976
E: alisonandjohn@thomas-luny-house.co.uk
I: www.thomas-luny-house.co.uk

THE LIZARD
Cornwall

Trethvas Farmhouse ♦♦♦♦
The Lizard, Helston TR12 7AR
T: (01326) 290720
F: (01326) 290720

THORNBURY
Devon

Forda Farm ♦♦♦♦
Thornbury, Holsworthy
EX22 7BS
T: (01409) 261369

THORNE
Somerset

Thorne Cottage ♦♦♦♦
Thorne, Yeovil BA21 3PZ
T: (01935) 421735
E: william.grimster@tesco.net

THORNE ST MARGARET
Somerset

Thorne Manor ♦♦♦♦
Thorne St Margaret, Wellington
TA21 0EQ
T: (01823) 672264
E: thorne.manor@euphony.net

TIMBERSCOMBE
Somerset

The Dell ♦♦♦
Cowbridge, Timberscombe, Minehead TA24 7TD
T: (01643) 841564
E: hcrawford@dellcow.f9.co.uk
I: www.thedellfarmhouse.co.uk

Knowle Manor and Riding Centre ♦♦♦
Timberscombe, Minehead
TA24 6TZ
T: (01643) 841342
F: (01643) 841644
E: knowlemnr@aol.com
I: www.ridingholidaysuk.com

TINHAY
Devon

Tinhay Mill Restaurant ♦♦♦♦
Tinhay, Lifton PL16 0AJ
T: (01566) 784201
F: (01566) 784201

TINTAGEL
Cornwall

9 Atlantic Way ♦♦♦
Tintagel, PL34 0DF
T: (01840) 770732
F: (01840) 770732

Bosayne Guest House ♦♦♦
Atlantic Road, Tintagel, PL34 0DE
T: (01840) 770514
F: (01840) 770514
E: clark@clarky100.freeserve.co.uk
I: www.bosayne.co.uk

Establishments printed in blue have a detailed entry in this guide

Cottage Teashop ♦♦♦♦
Bossiney Road, Tintagel,
PL34 0AH
T: (01840) 770639
E: cotteashop@talk21.com

Pendrin House ♦♦♦♦
Atlantic Road, Tintagel,
PL34 0DE
T: (01840) 770560
F: (01840) 770560
E: pendrin@tesco.co.uk
I: www.pendrinhouse.co.uk

Polkerr Guest House ♦♦♦♦
Molesworth Street, Tintagel,
PL34 0BY
T: (01840) 770382
E: polkerr@tiscali.co.uk

Port William Inn ♦♦♦♦
Trebarwith Strand, Tintagel
PL34 0HB
T: (01840) 770230
F: (01840) 770936
E: william@eurobell.co.uk

The Trewarmett Inn ♦♦
Trewarmett, Tintagel PL34 0ET
T: (01840) 770460

TIVERTON
Devon

Brambles Guesthouse
♦♦♦♦ SILVER AWARD
Whitnage Cottage, Whitnage,
Tiverton, EX16 7DS
T: (01884) 829211
F: (01884) 829211
E: info@bramblesguesthouse.co.uk
I: www.bramblesguesthouse.co.uk

Bridge Guest House ♦♦♦
23 Angel Hill, Tiverton, EX16 6PE
T: (01884) 252804
F: (01884) 252804
I: www.smoothhound.co.uk/hotels/bridgegh.html

Great Bradley Farm ♦♦♦♦
Withleigh, Tiverton EX16 8JL
T: (01884) 256946
F: (01884) 256946
E: hann@agriplus.net
I: www.SmoothHound.co.uk/hotels/gbrad

Lodgehill Farm Hotel ♦♦♦
Tiverton, EX16 5PA
T: (01884) 251200
F: (01884) 242090
E: Lodgehill@dial.pipex.com
I: www.lodgehill.co.uk

Lower Collipriest Farm
♦♦♦♦ SILVER AWARD
Tiverton, EX16 4PT
T: (01884) 252321
F: (01884) 252321
E: linda@lowercollipriest.co.uk
I: www.lowercollipriest.co.uk

TIVINGTON
Somerset

Clements Cottage ♦♦♦
Tivington, Minehead TA24 8SU
T: (01643) 703970
E: clementscottage@exmoorbandb.co.uk
I: www.exmoorbandb.co.uk

TOLLER PORCORUM
Dorset

Barrowlands ♦♦♦
Toller Porcorum, Dorchester
DT2 0DW
T: (01300) 320281
E: jrdovey@ukgateway.net

Colesmoor Farm ♦♦♦♦
Toller Porcorum, Dorchester
DT2 0DU
T: (01300) 320812
F: (01300) 321402
E: rachael@colesmoorfarm.co.uk
I: www.colesmorrfarm.co.uk

Grays Farmhouse ♦♦♦♦
Clift Lane, Toller Porcorum,
Dorchester DT2 0EJ
T: (01308) 485574
E: rosie@farmhousebnb.co.uk
I: www.farmhousebnb.co.uk

The Kingcombe Centre ♦♦
Lower Kingcombe, Toller
Porcorum, Dorchester DT2 0EQ
T: (01300) 320684
F: (01300) 321409
E: nspring@kingcombe-centre.demon.co.uk
I: www.kingcombe-centre.demon.co.uk

The Manor
♦♦♦♦♦ SILVER AWARD
5 Kingcombe Road, Toller
Porcorum, Dorchester DT2 0DG
T: (01300) 320010

TOPSHAM
Devon

The Galley Restaurant with Cabins ♦♦♦♦
41 Fore Street, Topsham, Exeter
EX3 0HY
T: (01392) 876078
F: (01392) 876078
E: fish@galleyrestaurant.co.uk
I: www.galleyrestaurant.co.uk

TORCROSS
Devon

Cove Guest House ♦♦♦
Torcross, Kingsbridge TQ7 2TH
T: (01548) 580350
F: (01548) 580350

TORQUAY
Devon

Abbeyfield Hotel ♦♦♦♦
Bridge Road, Torquay, TQ2 5AX
T: (01803) 294268
F: (01803) 296310

Acorn Lodge ♦♦♦
28 Bridge Road, Torquay,
TQ2 5BA
T: (01803) 296939
F: (01803) 296939
E: acronlodgehotel@aol.com

Alstone Hotel ♦♦♦
22 Bridge Road, Torquay,
TQ2 5BA
T: (01803) 293243
E: alstonehotel@hotmail.com
I: www.english-riviera.co.uk

Arden Court Hotel ♦♦
525 Babbacombe Road, Torquay,
TQ1 1HG
T: (01803) 293498
E: ardencourthotel@tinyworld.co.uk
I: www.english-reviera.com

Ash Wood Grange Hotel ♦♦♦
18 Newton Road, Torquay,
TQ2 5BZ
T: (01803) 212619
F: (01803) 212619
E: stay@ashwoodgrangehotel.co.uk
I: www.ashwoodgrangehotel.co.uk

Ashfield Guest House ♦♦♦
9 Scarborough Road, Torquay,
TQ2 5UJ
T: (01803) 293537

Ashleigh House ♦♦♦
61 Meadfoot Lane, Torquay,
TQ1 2BP
T: (01803) 294660

Ashurst Lodge Hotel ♦
St Efrides Road, Torquay,
TQ2 5SG
T: (01803) 292132

Avenue Park Guest House ♦♦♦
3 Avenue Road, Torquay,
TQ2 5LA
T: (01803) 293902
F: (01803) 293902
E: avenuepark@bushinternet.com
I: www.torbay.gov.uk/tourism/t-hotels/avepark.htm

Bahamas Hotel ♦♦♦
17 Avenue Road, Torquay,
TQ2 5LB
T: (01803) 296005

Beverley House Hotel ♦♦♦♦
9 Clifton Grove, Old Torwood
Road, Torquay, TQ1 1PR
T: (01803) 294626

Blue Haze Hotel
♦♦♦♦♦ SILVER AWARD
Seaway Lane, Torquay, TQ2 6PS
T: (01803) 607186
F: (01803) 607186
E: mail@bluehazehotel.co.uk
I: www.bluehazehotel.co.uk

Braddon Hall Hotel ♦♦♦♦
70 Braddon Hill Road East,
Torquay, TQ1 1HF
T: (01803) 293908
F: (01803) 293908
E: info@braddonhallhotel.co.uk
I: www.braddonhallhotel.co.uk

Brampton Court Hotel ♦♦♦♦
St Luke's Road South, Torquay,
TQ2 5NZ
T: (01803) 294237
F: (01803) 211842
E: stay@bramptoncourt.co.uk
I: www.bramptoncourt.co.uk

Brandize Hotel ♦♦♦
19 Avenue Road, Torquay,
TQ2 5LB
T: (01803) 297798
F: (01803) 297798
E: ted@brandize20.freeserve.co.uk
I: www.brandizehotel.com

Brantwood Hotel ♦♦♦♦
Rowdens Road, Torquay,
TQ2 5AZ
T: (01803) 297241

Brocklehurst Hotel ♦♦♦
Rathmore Road, Torquay,
TQ2 6NZ
T: (01803) 292735
F: (01803) 403204
E: enquiries@brocklehursthotel.co.uk
I: www.brocklehursthotel.co.uk

Brooklands Guest House ♦♦♦
5 Scarborough Road, Torquay,
TQ2 5UJ
T: (01803) 296696

Buckingham Lodge ♦♦♦♦
Falkland Road, Torquay, TQ2 5JP
T: (01803) 293538
F: (01803) 290343
E: bookingbucklodge@aol.com
I: www.buckinghamlodge.co.uk

Capri Hotel ♦♦♦♦
12 Torbay Road, Livermead,
Torquay, TQ2 6RG
T: (01803) 293158
I: www.capri-hotel.co.uk

Cedar Court Hotel ♦♦♦♦
3 St Matthew's Road, Chelston,
Torquay, TQ2 6JA
T: (01803) 607851
F: (01803) 607851
E: enquiries@cedarcourt-hotel.co.uk
I: www.cedarcourt-hotel.co.uk

Charterhouse Hotel ♦♦♦
Cockington Lane, Torquay,
TQ2 6QT
T: (01803) 605804
F: (01803) 690741
E: acb@charterhouse-hotel.co.uk
I: www.charterhouse-hotel.co.uk

Chester Court Hotel ♦♦♦
30 Cleveland Road, Torquay,
TQ2 5BE
T: (01803) 294565
F: (01803) 294565
E: kevin@kpmorris.freeserve.co.uk
I: www.kpmorris.freeserve.co.uk/cch.html

Chesterfield Hotel ♦♦♦♦
62 Belgrave Road, Torquay,
TQ2 5HY
T: (01803) 292318
F: (01803) 293676
E: joannefoskett@tinyworld.co.uk
I: www.chesterfieldhoteltorquay.co.uk

Hotel Cimon ♦♦♦
82 Abbey Road, Torquay,
TQ2 5NP
T: (01803) 294454
F: (01803) 201988
E: englishbrian434@aol.com

Clevedon Hotel ♦♦♦♦
Meadfoot Sea Road, Torquay,
TQ1 2LQ
T: (01803) 294260
E: clevedonhotel@btconnect.com
I: www.smoothhound.co.uk/hotels/clevedon.html

Clovelly Guest House ♦♦♦
91 Avenue Road, Chelston, Torquay, TQ2 5LH
T: (01803) 292286
F: (01803) 242286
E: clovellytorquay@ntlworld.com
I: homepage.ntlworld.com/clovelly.guesthouse

Collingwood Hotel ♦♦♦
38 Braddons Hill Road East, Torquay, TQ1 1HB
T: (01803) 293448
F: (01803) 400221

The Court Hotel
♦♦♦♦ SILVER AWARD
Lower Warberry Road, Torquay, TQ1 1QS
T: (01803) 212011
F: (01803) 292648
E: enq@court-hotel.co.uk
I: www.court-hotel.co.uk

Cranborne Hotel
♦♦♦♦♦ SILVER AWARD
58 Belgrave Road, Torquay, TQ2 5HY
T: (01803) 298046
F: (01803) 215477

The Cranmore ♦♦♦♦
89 Avenue Road, Torquay, TQ2 5LH
T: (01803) 298488
E: thecranmore@tesco.net
I: www.smoothhound.co.uk/hotels/cranmore

Crimdon Dene Hotel ♦♦♦
12 Falkland Road, Torquay, TQ2 5JP
T: (01803) 294651
F: (01803) 294651
E: marjohn@crimdon-dene.freeserve.co.uk

Crown Lodge ♦♦♦♦
83 Avenue Road, Torquay, TQ2 5LH
T: (01803) 298772
F: (01803) 291155
E: crown.lodge@virgin.net

Crowndale Hotel
Rating Applied For
18 Bridge Road, Torquay, TQ2 5BA
T: (01803) 293068
F: (01803) 293068
I: www.torquayhotels.com

Daylesford Hotel ♦♦♦♦
60 Bampfylde Road, Torquay, TQ2 5AY
T: (01803) 294435
I: www.daylesfordhotel.com

The Downs Hotel ♦♦♦
43 Babbacombe Downs Road, Babbacombe, Torquay TQ1 3LN
T: (01803) 328543
F: (01803) 328543
E: manager@downshotel.co.uk
I: www.downshotel.co.uk

Ellington Court Hotel ♦♦♦♦
St Lukes Road South, Torquay, TQ2 5NZ
T: (01803) 294957
F: (01803) 201383
E: stay@ellingtoncourthotel.co.uk
I: www.ellingtoncourthotel.co.uk

Fairmount House Hotel
♦♦♦♦
Herbert Road, Chelston, Torquay TQ2 6RW
T: (01803) 605446
F: (01803) 605446
E: fairmounthouse@aol.com

Fairways ♦♦♦♦
72 Avenue Road, Torquay, TQ2 5LF
T: (01803) 298471
F: (01803) 298471

Ferndale Hotel ♦♦♦♦
22 St Marychurch Road, Torquay, TQ1 3HY
T: (01803) 295311

Fleurie House
♦♦♦♦ SILVER AWARD
50 Bampflyde Road, Torquay, TQ2 5AY
T: (01803) 294869
E: fleuriehouse@virgin.net

Gainsboro Hotel ♦♦♦♦
22 Rathmore Road, Torquay, TQ2 6NY
T: (01803) 292032
F: (01803) 292032
E: gainsboro@freeuk.com

The Garlieston Hotel ♦♦♦
Bridge Road, Torquay, TQ2 5BA
T: (01803) 294050
E: garliestonhotel@jridewood.fsnet.co.uk

Glendower Hotel ♦♦♦
Falkland Road, Torquay, TQ2 5JP
T: (01803) 299988
F: (01803) 403222
E: peter@hoteltorquay.co.uk
I: www.hoteltorquay.co.uk

Glenross Hotel
♦♦♦♦ SILVER AWARD
25 Avenue Road, Torquay, TQ2 5LB
T: (01803) 297517
F: (01803) 297517
E: holiday@glenross-hotel.co.uk
I: www.glenross-hotel.co.uk

Glenroy Hotel ♦♦♦
10 Bampfylde Road, Torquay, TQ2 5AR
T: (01803) 299255
F: (01803) 299255
E: andydawkes@tiscali.co.uk

The Green Park Hotel ♦♦♦
25 Morgan Avenue, Torquay, TQ2 5RR
T: (01803) 293618
E: greenpark@eclipse.co.uk
I: www.greenpark.eclipse.co.uk

Grosvenor House Hotel ♦♦♦♦
Falkland Road, Torquay, TQ2 5JP
T: (01803) 294110
E: grosvenorhse@eurobell.co.uk

The Haven Hotel ♦♦♦
11 Scarborough Road, Belgravia, Torquay, TQ2 5UJ
T: (01803) 293390
E: enquiries@havenhotel.biz
I: www.havenhotel.biz

Heathcliff House Hotel ♦♦♦♦
16 Newton Road, Torquay, TQ2 5BZ
T: (01803) 211580
E: heathcliffhouse@aol.com

The Hotel Newburgh ♦♦
14 Scarborough Road, Torquay, TQ2 5UJ
T: (01803) 293270
E: the-newburgh-torquay@hotels.activebooking.com

Howard Court Hotel ♦♦♦
31 St Efrides Road, Torquay, TQ2 5SG
T: (01803) 295494

Hotel Iona ♦♦♦
5 Cleveland Road, Torquay, TQ2 5BD
T: (01803) 294918
F: (01803) 294918
E: hoteliona@btopenworld.com

Jesmond Dene Hotel ♦♦
85 Abbey Road, Torquay, TQ2 5NN
T: (01803) 293062

Kelvin House Hotel
Rating Applied For
46 Bampfylde Road, Torquay, TQ2 5AY
T: (01803) 209093
F: (01803) 209093

Kings Hotel ♦♦♦♦
44 Bampfylde Road, Torquay, TQ2 5AY
T: (01803) 293108
F: (01803) 201499
E: kingshotel@bigfoot.com
I: www.kingshoteltorquay.co.uk

Kingsholm Hotel ♦♦♦
539 Babbacombe Road, Torquay, TQ1 1HQ
T: (01803) 297794

Kingston House
♦♦♦♦♦ SILVER AWARD
75 Avenue Road, Torquay, TQ2 5LL
T: (01803) 212760
F: (01803) 201425
E: butto@kingstonhousehotel.co.uk

Kingsway Lodge ♦♦♦
95 Avenue Road, Torquay, TQ2 5LH
T: (01803) 295288

Lanscombe House Hotel ♦♦♦
Cockington Village, Torquay, TQ2 6XA
T: (01803) 606938
F: (01803) 607656
E: LanscombeHouse@aol.com

Lee Hotel ♦♦♦
Torbay Road, Livermead, Torquay, TQ2 6RG
T: (01803) 293946
F: (01803) 293946
E: info@leehotel.co.uk
I: www.leehotel.co.uk

Lindens Hotel
Rating Applied For
31 Bampfylde Road, Torquay, TQ2 5AY
T: (01803) 212281

Lindum Hotel ♦♦♦♦
105 Abbey Road, Torquay, TQ2 5NP
T: (01803) 292795
F: (01803) 299358
E: lindum@eurobell.co.uk
I: www.lindum-hotel.co.uk

Maple Lodge Guest House
♦♦♦♦
36 Ash Hill Road, Torquay, TQ1 3JD
T: (01803) 297391
E: TheMapleLodge@aol.com
I: www.themaplelodge.co.uk

The Marstan Hotel ♦♦♦♦♦
Meadfoot Sea Road, Torquay, TQ1 2LQ
T: (01803) 292837
F: (01803) 299202
E: enquiries@marstanhotel.co.uk
I: www.marstanhotel.co.uk

Melba House Hotel ♦♦♦
62 Bampfylde Road, Torquay, TQ2 5AY
T: (01803) 213167
F: (01803) 211953

Melbourne Tower Hotel
♦♦♦♦
Solsbro Road, Chelston, Torquay TQ2 6PF
T: (01803) 607252
F: (01803) 607252
E: wilson@melbournetowerhotel.co.uk
I: www.melbournetowerhotel.co.uk

Mount Edgcombe Hotel
♦♦♦♦
23 Avenue Road, Torquay, TQ2 5LB
T: (01803) 292310
F: (01803) 292310

Mount Nessing Hotel ♦♦♦
St Luke's Road North, Torquay, TQ2 5PD
T: (01803) 294259
F: (01803) 294259
E: mntnessing@hotmail.com
I: www.smoothhound.co.uk

Newlyn Hotel ♦♦♦♦
62 Braddons Hill Road East, Torquay, TQ1 1HF
T: (01803) 295100
F: (01803) 380724
E: Barbara@newlyn-hotel.co.uk
I: www.newlyn-hotel.co.uk

The Pines ♦♦♦
19 Newton Road, Torre, Torquay, TQ2 5DB
T: (01803) 292882

Richwood Hotel ♦♦♦♦
20 Newton Road, Torquay, TQ2 5BZ
T: (01803) 293729
F: (01803) 213632
E: enq@richwood-hotel-torquay.co.uk
I: www.richwood-hotel-torquay.co.uk

Robin Hill International Hotel
♦♦♦♦
74 Braddons Hill Road East, Torquay, TQ1 1HF
T: (01803) 214518
F: (01803) 291410
E: jo@robinhillhotel.co.uk
I: www.robinhillhotel.co.uk

Sandpiper Hotel ♦♦♦♦
Rowdens Road, Torquay, TQ2 5AZ
T: (01803) 292779
E: sandpiper57@home13859.fsnet.co.uk
I: www.sandpiper-hotel.co.uk

Sandpiper Lodge Hotel ♦♦♦
96 Avenue Road, Torquay,
TQ2 5LF
T: (01803) 293293

Seapoint Hotel ♦♦♦
Old Torwood Road, Torquay,
TQ1 1PR
T: (01803) 211808
F: (01803) 211808
E: seapointhotel@hotmail.com

Shirley Hotel ♦♦♦♦
Braddons Hill Road East,
Torquay, TQ1 1HF
T: (01803) 293016
E: shirleyhotel@eurobell.co.uk

Silverlands ♦♦♦
27 Newton Road, Torquay,
TQ2 5DB
T: (01803) 292013

South View Hotel ♦♦♦♦
12 Scarborough Road, Torquay,
TQ2 5UJ
T: (01803) 296029
F: (01803) 296029
E: dianesouthview@aol.com

Southbank Hotel ♦♦♦♦
15/17 Belgrave Road, Torquay,
TQ2 5HU
T: (01803) 296701
F: (01803) 292026

Suite Dreams Hotel
♦♦♦♦ SILVER AWARD
Steep Hill, Maidencombe,
Torquay TQ1 4TS
T: (01803) 313900
F: (01803) 313841
E: suitedreams@suitedreams.co.uk
I: www.suitedreams.co.uk

Sunnymead ♦♦♦
501 Babbacombe Road, Torquay,
TQ1 1HL
T: (01803) 296938

Tor Dean Hotel ♦♦♦
27 Bampfylde Road, Torquay,
TQ2 5AY
T: (01803) 294669
E: tordeanhotel@aol.com

Tor Park Hotel ♦♦♦
24 Vansittart Road, Torquay,
TQ2 5BW
T: (01803) 295151
F: (01803) 200584
I: www.shearingsholidays.com

Torbay Hotel ♦♦♦♦
Torbay Road, Torquay, TQ2 5EY
T: (01803) 295218
F: (01803) 291127
I: www.shearingsholidays.com

Torbay Star Guest House ♦♦♦
73 Avenue Road, Torquay,
TQ2 5LL
T: (01803) 293998
F: (01803) 293998

Trafalgar House Hotel ♦♦♦
30 Bridge Road, Torquay,
TQ2 5BA
T: (01803) 292486
E: s.collett@ntlworld.com
I: www.torquayhotelsuk.com

Tree Tops Hotel ♦♦♦
St Albans Road, Torquay,
TQ1 3NP
T: (01803) 325135

Trelawney Hotel ♦♦♦
48 Belgrave Road, Torquay,
TQ2 5HS
T: (01803) 296049
F: (01803) 296049
E: trelawneyhotel@hotmail.com
I: www.trelawneyhotel.net

Trouville Hotel ♦♦♦
70 Belgave Road, Torquay,
TQ2 5HY
T: (01803) 294979

Villa Marina ♦♦♦♦
Tor Park Road, Torquay, TQ2 5BQ
T: (01803) 292187

The Wayland Hotel & Belgravia Self-Catering Holiday Suites ♦♦♦
31-47 Belgrave Road, Torquay,
TQ2 5HX
T: (01803) 293417
F: (01803) 293417

West Bank Hotel ♦♦♦
54 Bampfylde Road, Torquay,
TQ2 5AY
T: (01803) 295271

Westbourne Hotel ♦♦♦♦
106 Avenue Road, Torquay,
TQ2 5LQ
T: (01803) 292927
F: (01803) 292927

Whitburn Guest House ♦♦♦
St Lukes Road North, Torquay,
TQ2 5PD
T: (01803) 296719
E: joe@lazenby15.freeserve.co.uk

Wilsbrook Guest House ♦♦♦
77 Avenue Road, Torquay,
TQ2 5LL
T: (01803) 298413
E: wilsbrook@amserve.net
I: www.wilsbrook.freeserve.co.uk

TORRINGTON
Devon

Beaford House Hotel ♦♦♦♦
Beaford, Winkleigh EX19 8AB
T: (01805) 603305
F: (01805) 603305
I: www.beafordhousehotel.co.uk

Cavalier Inn
Rating Applied For
Well Street, Torrington,
EX38 8EP
T: (01805) 623832

Locksbeam Farm
♦♦♦♦ SILVER AWARD
Torrington, EX38 7EZ
T: (01805) 623213
F: (01805) 623213
I: www.tarka-country.co.uk/locksbeamfarm

West of England Inn ♦♦♦
18 South Street, Torrington,
EX38 8AA
T: (01805) 624949

TOTNES
Devon

Buckyette Farm ♦♦♦
Buckyette, Totnes, TQ9 6ND
T: (01803) 762638
F: (01803) 762638

The Elbow Room
♦♦♦♦♦ SILVER AWARD
North Street, Totnes, TQ9 5NZ
T: (01803) 863480
E: elbowroomtotnes@AOL.COM

Four Seasons Guest House
♦♦♦♦
13 Bridgetown, Totnes, TQ9 5AB
T: (01803) 862146
F: (01803) 867779
E: eecornford@netscapeonline.msn.com

Great Court Farm
♦♦♦♦ SILVER AWARD
Weston Lane, Totnes, TQ9 6LB
T: (01803) 862326
F: (01803) 862326

The Hungry Horse Restaurant
♦♦♦♦
Old Road, Harbertonford, Totnes
TQ9 7TA
T: (01803) 732441
F: (01803) 732780

Old Follaton
♦♦♦♦♦ SILVER AWARD
Plymouth Road, Totnes,
TQ9 5NA
T: (01803) 865441
F: (01803) 863597
E: bandb@oldfollaton.co.uk
I: www.oldfollaton.co.uk

The Old Forge at Totnes
♦♦♦♦ SILVER AWARD
Seymour Place, Totnes, TQ9 5AY
T: (01803) 862174
F: (01803) 865385
E: enq@oldforgetotnes.com
I: www.oldforgetotnes.com

Steam Packet Inn ♦♦♦♦
4 St. Peter's Quay, Totnes,
TQ9 5EW
T: (01803) 863880
F: (01803) 862754
E: esther@thesteampacketinn.co.uk
I: www.thesteampacketinn-totnes.co.uk

TREATOR
Cornwall

Woodlands Close ♦♦♦
Treator, Padstow PL28 8RU
T: (01841) 533109
E: john@stock65.freeserve.co.uk
I: www.cornwall-online.co.uk/woodlands-close

TREBETHERICK
Cornwall

Daymer House ♦♦♦♦♦
Daymer Bay, Trebetherick,
Wadebridge PL27 6SA
T: (01208) 862639
F: (01208) 813781
E: lindaburrows@genie.co.uk

Elm Cottage ♦♦♦
Trebetherick, Wadebridge
PL27 6SB
T: (01208) 863805
E: h.thwaites@euphony.net

TREGONY
Cornwall

Tregonan ♦♦♦♦
Tregony, Truro TR2 5SN
T: (01872) 530249
F: (01872) 530249
E: tregonan@fwi.co.uk

TREMAINE
Cornwall

Tremaine Chapel ♦♦♦
Tremaine, Launceston PL15 8SA
T: (01566) 781590

TRENALE
Cornwall

Hendra Old Farmhouse ♦♦♦♦
Trenale, Tintagel PL34 0HP
T: (01840) 770975

TRESILLIAN
Cornwall

Polsue Manor Farm ♦♦♦
Tresillian, Truro TR2 4BP
T: (01872) 520234
F: (01872) 520616
E: geraldineholliday@hotmail.com

TREVALGA
Cornwall

Trehane Farm ♦♦♦
Trevalga, Boscastle PL35 0EB
T: (01840) 250510

TREVAUNANCE COVE
Cornwall

Driftwood Spars Hotel ♦♦♦
Trevaunance Cove, St Agnes
TR5 0RT
T: (01872) 552428
F: (01872) 553701
E: driftwoodspars@hotmail.com
I: www.english-inns.co.uk/DriftwoodSpars

TREWARMETT
Cornwall

Melrosa ♦♦♦♦
Trewarmett, Tintagel PL34 0ES
T: (01840) 770360
E: valerie.stephens@btinternet.com

TROWBRIDGE
Wiltshire

Herons Knoll ♦♦
18 Middle Lane, Trowbridge,
BA14 7LG
T: (01225) 752593
F: (01225) 752593

Lion and Fiddle ♦♦♦
Devizes Road, Hilperton,
Trowbridge BA14 7QS
T: (01225) 776392
F: (01225) 774501

Old Manor Hotel ♦♦♦♦♦
Trowle, Bradford-on-Avon,
BA14 9BL
T: (01225) 777393
F: (01225) 765443
E: oldbeams@oldmanorhotel.com
I: www.oldmanorhotel.com

62b Paxcroft Cottages ♦♦♦♦
Devizes Road, Hilperton,
Trowbridge BA14 6JB
T: (01225) 765838
E: paxcroftcottages@hotmail.com

Sue's B & B ♦♦♦
25 Blair Road, Trowbridge,
BA14 9JZ
T: (01225) 764559
E: sue_b_n_b@yahoo.com
I: www.visitbritain.com

Welam House ♦♦♦
Bratton Road, West Ashton,
Trowbridge BA14 6AZ
T: (01225) 755908

TRUDOXHILL
Somerset

Lilac Cottage ♦♦♦
Foghamshire Lane, Trudoxhill, Frome BA11 5DG
T: (01373) 836222
F: (01373) 836222
E: paul@pwacey.freeserve.co.uk

TRULL
Somerset

The Winchester Arms ♦♦♦
Church Road, Trull, Taunton TA3 7LG
T: (01823) 284723
F: (01823) 284723

TRURO
Cornwall

Bissick Old Mill
♦♦♦♦♦ SILVER AWARD
Ladock, Truro TR2 4PG
T: (01726) 882557
F: (01726) 884057
E: sonia.v@bissickmill.ndo.co.uk

Gwel-Tek-Lodge ♦♦
41 Treyew Road, Truro, TR1 2BY
T: (01872) 276843

Marcorrie Hotel ♦♦♦♦
20 Falmouth Road, Truro, TR1 2HX
T: (01872) 277374
F: (01872) 241666
E: marcorrie@aol.com
I: www.hotelstruro.com

Moonfleet House
♦♦♦♦♦ SILVER AWARD
20 St Georges Road, Truro, TR1 3JD
T: (01872) 263105
E: george.fisher@ntlworld.com

Trevispian-Vean Farm Guest House ♦♦♦♦
St Erme, Truro TR4 9AT
T: (01872) 279514
F: (01872) 263730
I: www.guesthousestruro.com

TUNLEY
Somerset

King William IV Inn ♦♦♦
Bath Road, Tunley, Bath BA2 0EB
T: (01761) 470408
F: (01761) 470408
E: welcome@kingwilliaminn.co.uk
I: www.kingwilliaminn.co.uk

UPLODERS
Dorset

Uploders Farm ♦♦♦
Dorchester Road, Uploders, Bridport DT6 4NZ
T: (01308) 423380

UPLYME
Devon

Elton ♦♦♦♦
Lyme Road, Uplyme, Lyme Regis DT7 3TH
T: (01297) 445986
E: mikecawte@aol.com

Hill Barn
♦♦♦♦ SILVER AWARD
Gore Lane, Uplyme, Lyme Regis DT7 3RJ
T: (01297) 445185
F: (01297) 445185
E: jwb@lymeregis-accommodation.com
I: www.lymeregis-accommodation.com

UPOTTERY
Devon

Robins Cottage
♦♦♦♦ SILVER AWARD
Upottery, Honiton EX14 9PL
T: (01404) 861281

UPTON
Cornwall

The Chough Hotel & Restaurant ♦♦♦♦
Marine Drive, Upton, Bude EX23 0LZ
T: (01288) 352386
F: (01288) 352386
E: bull-ji@choughhotel.swinternet.co.uk
I: www.activehotels.com/hotels/index.php3?hotelid=121543&trkref=&searchCount=9

Upton Cross ♦♦♦
Upton, Bude EX23 0LY
T: (01288) 355310

Upton Lodge
♦♦♦♦♦ SILVER AWARD
Upton, Bude EX23 0LY
T: (01288) 354126
E: edwardwhitehouse@onetel.net.uk

UPTON LOVELL
Wiltshire

Prince Leopold ♦♦♦
Upton Lovell, Warminster BA12 0JP
T: (01985) 850460
F: (01985) 850737
E: princeleopold@lineone.net
I: www.princeleopoldinn.co.uk

UPTON NOBLE
Somerset

Kingston House
♦♦♦♦ SILVER AWARD
Upton Noble, Shepton Mallet BA4 6BA
T: (01749) 850805
F: (01749) 850806
E: timstroud220@netscapeonline.co.uk

UPWEY
Dorset

Bankside Cottage ♦♦♦
Church Street, Upwey, Weymouth DT3 5QE
T: (01305) 812320
E: edward.bird@care4free.net

VERYAN
Cornwall

Treverbyn House ♦♦♦♦
Pendower Road, Veryan, Truro TR2 5QL
T: (01872) 501201
E: holiday@treverbyn.fsbusiness.co.uk
I: www.cornwall-online.co.uk/treverbyn

VICTORIA
Cornwall

Auberge Asterisk ♦♦♦
Victoria, Roche, St Austell PL26 8LH
T: (01726) 890863
F: (01726) 890642
E: aubasterisk@hotmail.com
I: www.cornwallconferencecentre.com/asterisk

WADEBRIDGE
Cornwall

Brookfields B & B
Rating Applied For
Hendra Lane, St Kew Highway, Wadebridge, PL30 3EQ
T: (01208) 841698
F: (01208) 841174
E: robbie.caswell@btinternet.com
I: www.brookfields-stkew.co.uk

St Ervan Manor and Country Cottages
Rating Applied For
The Old Rectory, St Ervan, Wadebridge, PL27 7TA
T: (01841) 540255
E: jontiejonce1@hotmail.com

St Giles Cottage ♦♦♦♦
Gonvena Hill, Wadebridge, PL27 6DP
T: (01208) 813695
E: stgilesbb@talk21.com

Spring Gardens
Rating Applied For
Bradfords Quay, Wadebridge, PL27 6DB
T: (01208) 813771
F: (01208) 813771
E: jijen@aol.com

Tregolls Farm ♦♦♦♦
St Wenn, Bodmin PL30 5PG
T: (01208) 812154
F: (01208) 812154
E: tregollsfarm@btclick.com
I: www.tregollsfarm.co.uk

WAMBROOK
Somerset

Woodview ♦♦♦
Wambrook, Chard TA20 3EH
T: (01460) 65368

WARMINSTER
Wiltshire

Bugley Barton
♦♦♦♦♦ SILVER AWARD
Warminster, BA12 7RB
T: (01985) 213389
F: (01985) 300450
E: bugleybarton@aol.com

Sturford Mead Farm ♦♦♦♦
Corsley, Warminster BA12 7QU
T: (01373) 832213
F: (01373) 832213
E: lynn_sturford.bed@virgin.net

WARMLEY
Gloucestershire

Ferndale Guest House ♦♦♦
37 Deanery Road, Warmley, Bristol BS15 9JB
T: (0117) 9858247
F: (0117) 9044855
E: alexandmikewake@yahoo.co.uk

WASHFORD
Somerset

Green Bay ♦♦♦
Washford, Watchet TA23 0NN
T: (01984) 640303
E: greenbay@tinyonline.co.uk

WATCHET
Somerset

Esplanade House ♦♦♦♦
The Esplanade, Watchet, TA23 0AJ
T: (01984) 633444

Wyndham House
♦♦♦♦ SILVER AWARD
4 Sea View Terrace, Watchet, TA23 0DF
T: (01984) 631881
F: (01984) 631881
E: rhv@dialstart.net

WATERGATE BAY
Cornwall

The White House ♦♦♦♦
Watergate Bay, Newquay TR8 4AD
T: (01637) 860119
F: (01637) 860449
E: jenny.vallance@virgin.net
I: www.cornwallwhitehouse.co.uk

WATERROW
Somerset

Handley Farm Accommodation
♦♦♦♦ SILVER AWARD
Handley Farm, Waterrow, Taunton TA4 2BE
T: (01398) 361516
F: (01398) 361516
E: leigh-firbank.george@ntlworld.com
I: www.handleyfarm.co.uk

WELLINGTON
Somerset

Backways Farmhouse ♦♦♦♦
Wellington, TA21 9RN
T: (01823) 660712
E: vanessa.archer@tinyworld.co.uk

WELLS
Somerset

Bay Tree House ♦♦♦♦
85 Portway, Wells, BA5 2BJ
T: (01749) 677933
F: (01749) 678322
E: baytree.house@ukonline.co.uk
I: www.baytree-house.co.uk

Beryl ♦♦♦♦♦
Wells, BA5 3JP
T: (01749) 678738
F: (01749) 670508
E: stay@beryl.co.uk
I: www.beryl-wells.co.uk

Burcott Mill Historic Watermill and Guesthouse ♦♦♦
Wookey Road, Wookey, Wells BA5 1NJ
T: (01749) 673118
F: (01749) 677376
E: theburts@burcottmill.com
I: www.burcottmill.com

Cadgwith ♦♦♦♦
Hawkers Lane, Wells, BA5 3JH
T: (01749) 677799
E: rplettscadgwith@aol.com

Canon Grange ♦♦♦♦
Cathedral Green, Wells, BA5 2UB
T: (01749) 671800
E: canongrange@email.com
I: www.canongrange.co.uk

Carmen B & B
♦♦♦♦ SILVER AWARD
Bath Road, Wells, BA5 3LQ
T: (01749) 677331
E: carmenbandb@tesco.net

Franklyns Farm ♦♦♦
Chewton Mendip, Bath BA3 4NB
T: (01761) 241372

Establishments printed in blue have a detailed entry in this guide

Glencot House
♦♦♦♦♦ GOLD AWARD
Glencot Lane, Wookey Hole, Wells BA5 1BH
T: (01749) 677160
F: (01749) 670210
E: relax@glencothouse.co.uk
I: www.glencothouse.co.uk

Glengarth ♦♦♦♦
7 Glastonbury Road, Wells, BA5 1TW
T: (01749) 673087

Hillside Cottage ♦♦♦
5-6 Keward, Glastonbury Road, Wells, BA5 1TR
T: (01749) 673770
E: hillsidecott@compuserve.com

Littlewell Farm Guest House
♦♦♦♦
Coxley, Wells BA5 1QP
T: (01749) 677914

30 Mary Road ♦♦♦
Wells, BA5 2NF
T: (01749) 674031
F: (01749) 674031
E: triciabailey30@hotmail.com

The Old Stores ♦♦♦♦
Westbury-sub-Mendip, Wells BA5 1HA
T: (01749) 870817
F: (01749) 870980
E: moglin980@aol.com

The Pound Inn ♦♦♦
Burcott Lane, Coxley, Wells BA5 1QZ
T: (01749) 672785
E: poundinnwells@aol.com

Southway Farm ♦♦♦♦
Polsham, Wells BA5 1RW
T: (01749) 673396
F: (01749) 670373
E: southwayfarm@ukonline.co.uk
I: www.southwayfarm.co.uk

Wookey Hole Inn ♦♦♦♦
Wookey Hole, Somerset, Wells, BA5 1BP
T: (01749) 676677
F: (01749) 676677
E: toadhall@lineone.net
I: www.wookeyholeinn.com

Worth House Hotel ♦♦♦♦
Worth, Wookey, Wells BA5 1LW
T: (01749) 672041
F: (01749) 672041
E: mblomeley2001@yahoo.co.uk

WEMBURY
Devon

Bay Cottage ♦♦♦
150 Church Road, Wembury, Plymouth PL9 0HR
T: (01752) 862559
F: (01752) 862559
E: thefairies@aol.com
I: www.bay-cottage.com

WEST ANSTEY
Devon

Greenhills Farm
♦♦♦♦ SILVER AWARD
Yeo Mill, West Anstey, South Molton EX36 3NU
T: (01398) 341300

Jubilee House ♦♦♦♦
Highaton Farm, West Anstey, South Molton EX36 3PJ
T: (01398) 341312
F: (01398) 341323
E: denton@exmoorholiday.co.uk
I: www.exmoorholiday.co.uk

WEST BAY
Dorset

The George Hotel ♦♦♦
West Bay, Bridport DT6 4EY
T: (01308) 423191

Heatherbell Cottage ♦♦♦
Hill Close, West Bay, Bridport DT6 4HW
T: (01308) 422998
E: heatherbell4bnb@onetel.net.uk

WEST BUCKLAND
Somerset

Causeway Cottage ♦♦♦♦
West Buckland, Wellington TA21 9JZ
T: (01823) 663458
F: (01823) 663458
E: orrs@westbuckland.freeserve.co.uk
I: members.tripod.com/~causeway_cottage/causeway.htm

WEST CAMEL
Somerset

The Walnut Tree ♦♦♦♦
Fore Street, West Camel, Yeovil BA22 7QW
T: (01935) 851292
F: (01935) 851292
I: www.thewalnuttreehotel.com

WEST COKER
Somerset

Millbrook House ♦♦♦♦
92 High Street, West Coker, Yeovil BA22 9AU
T: (01935) 862840
F: (01935) 863846

WEST DOWN
Devon

The Long House ♦♦♦♦
The Square, West Down, Ilfracombe EX34 8NF
T: (01271) 863242

WEST HARPTREE
Bath and North East Somerset

The Wellsway Inn ♦♦♦
Harptree Hill, West Harptree, Bristol BS40 6EJ
T: (01761) 221382

WEST HUNTSPILL
Somerset

Greenwood Lodge ♦♦♦♦
76 Main Road, West Huntspill, Highbridge TA9 3QU
T: (01278) 795886
F: (01278) 795886

Ilex House ♦♦♦♦
102 Main Road, West Huntspill, Highbridge TA9 3QZ
T: (01278) 783801
F: (01278) 794254
E: rogwyn@onetel.net.uk

WEST KNIGHTON
Dorset

Church Cottage
♦♦♦♦ SILVER AWARD
West Knighton, Dorchester DT2 8PF
T: (01305) 852243
E: info@church-cottage.com
I: www.church-cottage.com

WEST MONKTON
Somerset

Springfield House ♦♦♦♦
Walford Cross, West Monkton, Taunton TA2 8QW
T: (01823) 412116
E: tina.ridout@btopenworld.com
I: www.springfieldhse.co.uk

WEST OVERTON
Wiltshire

Cairncot ♦♦♦
West Overton, Marlborough SN8 4ER
T: (01672) 861617

WEST PENNARD
Somerset

The Lion At Pennard ♦♦♦
Glastonbury Road, West Pennard, Glastonbury BA6 8NH
T: (01458) 832941
F: (01458) 832941

Page Cottage
♦♦♦♦ SILVER AWARD
West Pennard, Glastonbury BA6 8NN
T: (01458) 833651

WEST PORLOCK
Somerset

West Porlock House ♦♦♦♦
West Porlock, Minehead TA24 8NX
T: (01643) 862880

WEST STAFFORD
Dorset

Keepers Cottage ♦♦♦♦
West Stafford, Dorchester DT2 8AA
T: (01305) 264389
F: (01305) 264389
E: keeperscottage@tinyworld.co.uk
I: www.keeperscottage.net

WESTBURY
Wiltshire

Sherbourne House ♦♦♦
47 Station Road, Westbury, BA13 3JW
T: (01373) 864865

WESTHAY
Somerset

New House Farm
♦♦♦♦ SILVER AWARD
Burtle Road, Westhay, Glastonbury BA6 9TT
T: (01458) 860238
F: (01458) 860568
E: newhousefarm@farmersweekly.net

WESTON
Devon

Higher Weston Farm ♦♦♦♦
Weston, Honiton EX10 0PH
T: (01395) 513741

WESTON-SUPER-MARE
Somerset

Algarve Guest House ♦♦♦
24 Quantock Road, Weston-super-Mare, BS23 4DT
T: (01934) 626128

Ashcombe Court ♦♦♦♦
17 Milton Road, Weston-super-Mare, BS23 2SH
T: (01934) 625104
F: (01934) 625104
E: ashcombecourt@tinyonline.co.uk

Beachlands Hotel ♦♦♦
17 Uphill Road North, Weston-super-Mare, BS23 4NG
T: (01934) 621401
F: (01934) 621966
E: info@beachlandshotel.com
I: www.beachlandshotel.com

Braeside Hotel ♦♦♦♦
2 Victoria Park, Weston-super-Mare, BS23 2HZ
T: (01934) 626642
F: (01934) 626642
E: braeside@tesco.net
I: www.braesidehotel.co.uk

Cornerways ♦♦♦
14 Whitecross Road, Weston-super-Mare, BS23 1EW
T: (01934) 623708

The Grand Atlantic ♦♦♦
Beach Road, Weston-super-Mare, BS23 1BA
T: (01934) 626543
F: (01934) 415048
I: www.shearingsholidays.com

Moorlands Country Guesthouse ♦♦♦
Hutton, Weston-super-Mare BS24 9QH
T: (01934) 812283
F: (01934) 812283
E: margaret_holt@email.comm
I: www.guestaccom.co.uk/35.htm

Orchard House
♦♦♦♦ SILVER AWARD
Summer Lane, West Wick, Weston-super-Mare, BS24 7TF
T: (01934) 520948
F: (01934) 520948

Richmond Hotel
Rating Applied For
14 Park Place, Weston-super-Mare, BS23 2BA
T: (01934) 644722
F: (01934) 644722

Saxonia ♦♦♦
95 Locking Road, Weston-super-Mare, BS23 3EW
T: (01934) 633856
F: (01934) 623141
E: saxonia@lineone.net
I: www.smoothhound.co.uk/hotels/saxonia.html

Spreyton Guest House ♦♦♦
72 Locking Road, Weston-super-Mare, BS23 3EN
T: (01934) 416887

Welbeck Hotel ♦♦♦
Knightstone Road, Marine Parade, Weston-super-Mare, BS23 2BB
T: (01934) 621258
F: (01934) 643585
E: info@weston-welbeck.co.uk
I: www.weston-welbeck.co.uk

WESTONZOYLAND
Somerset

Staddlestones Guest House
♦♦♦♦♦ SILVER AWARD
3 Standards Road, Westonzoyland, Bridgwater TA7 0EL
T: (01278) 691179
F: (01278) 691333
E: staddlestones@euphony.net
I: www.staddlestonesguesthouse.co.uk

WESTROP
Wiltshire

Park Farm Barn ♦♦♦♦
Westrop, Corsham SN13 9QF
T: (01249) 715911
F: (01249) 715911

WESTWARD HO!
Devon

Brockenhurst ♦♦♦
11 Atlantic Way, Westward Ho!, Bideford EX39 1HX
T: (01237) 423346
F: (01237) 423346
E: snowball@brockenhurst1.freeserve.co.uk

WEYMOUTH
Dorset

Aaran House ♦♦
2 The Esplanade, Weymouth, DT4 8EA
T: (01305) 766669

Albatross Hotel ♦♦♦
96 The Esplanade, Weymouth, DT4 7AT
T: (01305) 785191
F: (01305) 785191

Bay Lodge
♦♦♦♦♦ GOLD AWARD
27 Greenhill, Weymouth, DT4 7SW
T: (01305) 782419
F: (01305) 782828
E: barbara@baylodge.co.uk
I: www.baylodge.co.uk

Bay View Hotel ♦♦♦♦
35 The Esplanade, Weymouth, DT4 8DH
T: (01305) 782083
F: (01305) 782083

Beach Guest House ♦♦♦
34 Lennox Street, Weymouth, DT4 7HD
T: (01305) 779212

Beaufort Hotel
Rating Applied For
24 The Esplanade, Weymouth, DT4 8DN
T: (01305) 782088
F: (01305) 782088

Brunswick Guest House ♦♦♦
9 Brunswick Terrace, Weymouth, DT4 7RW
T: (01305) 785408

Cavendale Hotel ♦♦♦
10 The Esplanade, Weymouth, DT4 8EB
T: (01305) 786960
F: (01305) 786960
E: stay@cavendale.co.uk

The Chandlers Hotel
Rating Applied For
4 Westerhall Road, Weymouth, DT4 7SZ
T: (01305) 771341
E: debbiesare@aol.com

The Channel Hotel ♦♦♦
93 The Esplanade, Weymouth, DT4 7AY
T: (01305) 785405
F: (01305) 785405
E: lee@thechannel.freeserve.co.uk
I: www.resort-guide.co.uk/channel

The Chatsworth ♦♦♦♦
14 The Esplanade, Weymouth, DT4 8EB
T: (01305) 785012
F: (01305) 766342
E: david@thechatsworth.co.uk

Crofton Guest House ♦♦♦
36 Lennox Street, Weymouth, DT4 7HD
T: (01305) 785903
F: (01305) 750165
E: stevemerrill1@excite.com

Cumberland Hotel ♦♦♦♦
95 Esplanade, Weymouth, DT4 7BA
T: (01305) 785644
F: (01305) 785644
I: www.cumberlandhotelweymouth.co.uk

Cunard Guest House ♦♦♦
45-46 Lennox Street, Weymouth, DT4 7HB
T: (01305) 771546
F: (01305) 771546
E: cunardhotel@hotmail.com

Double Three ♦♦♦♦
33 Rodwell Road, Weymouth, DT4 8QP
T: (01305) 786259
E: doublethree16762@aol.com

Eastney ♦♦♦♦
15 Longfield Road, Weymouth, DT4 8RQ
T: (01305) 771682
E: eastneyhotel@aol.com
I: www.eastneyhotel.co.uk

Elwell Manor Guest House ♦♦♦♦
70 Rodwell Road, Weymouth, DT3 8QU
T: (01305) 782434
F: (01305) 782434
E: burville@ntlworld.com
I: www.weymouthbedandbreakfast.co.uk

Fairlie House
Rating Applied For
13 Holland Road, Weymouth, DT4 0AL
T: (01305) 783951

Flintstones Guest House ♦♦♦
10 Carlton Road South, Weymouth, DT4 7PJ
T: (01305) 784153

Florian Guest House ♦♦♦
59 Abbotsbury Road, Weymouth, DT4 0AQ
T: (01305) 773836
E: clare@florian-guesthouse.co.uk
I: www.florian-guesthouse.co.uk

Fosters Guest House
Rating Applied For
3 Lennox Street, Weymouth, DT3 7HB
T: (01305) 771685

Frensham Hotel ♦♦♦
70 Abbotsbury Road, Weymouth, DT4 0BJ
T: (01305) 786827
E: micksherry@hotmail.com

The Freshford Hotel ♦♦♦
3 Grange Road, Weymouth, DT4 7PQ
T: (01305) 775862
F: (01305) 775862
E: info@freshfordhotel.co.uk
I: www.freshfordhotel.co.uk

Glenthorne ♦♦♦♦
15 Old Castle Road, Weymouth, DT4 8QB
T: (01305) 777281

Golden Bay Hotel ♦♦
54-55 Esplanade, Weymouth, DT4 8DG
T: (01305) 760868

Green Gables ♦♦♦♦
14 Carlton Road South, Weymouth, DT4 7PJ
T: (01305) 774808
E: greengables@w-a-g.co.uk
I: www.w-a-g.co.uk/greengables

Harbour Lights ♦♦♦
20 Buxton Road, Weymouth, DT4 9PJ
T: (01305) 783273
F: (01305) 783273
E: harbourlights@btconnect.com

Harlequin House Guest House ♦♦♦
9 Carlton Road South, Weymouth, DT4 7PL
T: (01305) 785598

Hazeldene Guest House ♦♦
16 Abbotsbury Road, Weymouth, DT4 0AE
T: (01305) 782579
F: (01305) 761022

Horizon Guest House ♦♦♦
16 Brunswick Terrace, Weymouth, DT4 7RW
T: (01305) 784916

Kelston Guest House ♦♦♦
1 Lennox Street, Weymouth, DT4 7HB
T: (01305) 779378

Kenora Private Hotel ♦♦♦♦
5 Stavordale Road, Weymouth, DT4 0AB
T: (01305) 771215
E: kenora.hotel@wdi.co.uk
I: www.kenorahotel.co.uk

Kimberley Family Run Guest House ♦♦♦
16 Kirtleton Avenue, Weymouth, DT4 7PT
T: (01305) 783333
F: (01305) 839603

Kings Acre Hotel ♦♦♦♦
140 The Esplanade, Weymouth, DT4 7NH
T: (01305) 782534
F: (01305) 782534

The Kingsley Hotel ♦♦♦♦
10 Kirtleton Avenue, Weymouth, DT4 7PT
T: (01305) 777888

Hotel Kinley ♦♦♦
98 The Esplanade, Weymouth, DT4 7AT
T: (01305) 782264
E: hotelkinley@hotmail.com
I: hotelkinley.co.uk

Langham Hotel ♦♦♦
130 The Esplanade, Weymouth, DT4 7EX
T: (01305) 782530

Lichfield House Hotel ♦♦♦
8 Brunswick Terrace, Weymouth, DT4 7RW
T: (01305) 784112

Lilac Villa Guest House ♦♦♦
124 Donchester Road, Weymouth, DT4 7LG
T: (01305) 782670
F: (01305) 782670
E: lilacvilla@lineone.net

Mar June Guest House ♦♦♦
32 Lennox Street, Weymouth, DT4 7HD
T: (01305) 761320

Marina Court Hotel ♦♦♦
142 The Esplanade, Weymouth, DT4 7PB
T: (01305) 782146
F: (01305) 782146

Mayfair Hotel ♦♦♦
99 The Esplanade, Weymouth, DT4 7BE
T: (01305) 782094
F: (01305) 782094

Morven House Hotel ♦♦♦
2 Westerhall Road, Weymouth, DT4 7SZ
T: (01305) 785075

Oaklands Edwardian Guesthouse ♦♦♦♦
1 Glendinning Avenue, Weymouth, DT4 7QF
T: (01305) 767081
F: (01305) 767379
E: vicki@oaklands-guesthouse.co.uk
I: www.oakland-guesthouse.co.uk

Park Edge Guest House ♦♦♦♦
8 Charlton Road South, Weymouth, DT4 7PS
T: (01305) 771325
E: charlene.mullett@btopenworld.com

The Pebbles Guest House ♦♦♦
18 Kirtleton Avenue, Weymouth, DT4 7PT
T: (01305) 784331
F: (01305) 784695
E: blackwoodg@aol.com

Royal Hotel ♦♦♦♦
90-91 The Esplanade, Weymouth, DT4 4AX
T: (01305) 782777
F: (01305) 761088
I: www.shearingsholidays.com

St John's Guest House ♦♦♦
7 Dorchester Road, Weymouth, DT4 7JR
T: (01305) 775523
F: (01305) 775815

Seacrest Guest House ♦♦♦
4 Esplanade, Weymouth, DT4 8EA
T: (01305) 784759

The Seaham
♦♦♦♦ GOLD AWARD
3 Waterloo Place, Weymouth, DT4 7NU
T: (01305) 782010
E: stay@theseaham.co.uk
I: www.theseaham.co.uk

The Sherborne Hotel ♦♦♦♦
117 The Esplanade, Weymouth, DT4 7EH
T: (01305) 777888
F: (01305) 759111

Shirley Hotel ♦♦♦
20 Dorchester Road, Weymouth, DT3
T: (01305) 782123

Southville Guest House ♦♦♦
5 Dortchester Road, Weymouth, DT4 7JR
T: (01305) 770382
E: southvillehotel@aol.com

Spindrift Guest House ♦♦♦
11 Brunswick Terrace, Weymouth, DT4 7RW
T: (01305) 773625
E: stayatspindrift@aol.com
I: www.resort-guide.co.uk/spindrift

Sunbay
Rating Applied For
12 Brunswick Terrace, Weymouth, DT4 7RW
T: (01305) 785992
F: (01305) 785992

Suncroft Hotel ♦♦♦♦
7 The Esplanade, Weymouth, DT4 8EB
T: (01305) 782542
F: (01305) 770071
E: suncroft@cdr-i.net

Hotel Sunnywey ♦♦♦
23 Kirtleton Avenue, Weymouth, DT4 7PS
T: (01305) 786911
F: (01305) 767084

Trevann Guest House ♦♦♦
28 Lennox Street, Weymouth, DT4 7HE
T: (01305) 782604

Warwick Court ♦♦♦
20 Abbotsbury Road, Weymouth, DT4 0AE
T: (01305) 783261
F: (01305) 783261
E: sharon@warwickcourt.co.uk

Weyside Guest House ♦♦♦
1a Abbotsbury Road, Weymouth, DT4 0AD
T: (01305) 772685
E: weysideguesthouse@btinternet.com
I: www.weysideguesthouse.btinternet.co.uk

Whitecliff Guest House ♦♦♦
7 Brunswick Terrace, Weymouth, DT4 7RW
T: (01305) 785554
F: (01305) 785554
E: whitecliff@guest-house.fsnet.co.uk
I: www.whitecliffguesthouse.co.uk

WHEDDON CROSS
Somerset

Cutthorne
♦♦♦♦ GOLD AWARD
Luckwell Bridge, Wheddon Cross, Minehead TA24 7EW
T: (01643) 831255
F: (01643) 831255
E: durbin@cutthorne.co.uk
I: www.cutthorne.co.uk

Exmoor House
♦♦♦♦♦ SILVER AWARD
Wheddon Cross, Minehead TA24 7DU
T: (01643) 841432
F: (01643) 841811
E: exmoorhouse@hotmail.com
I: www.exmoorhotel.co.uk

Little Brendon Hill Farm
♦♦♦♦♦ GOLD AWARD
Wheddon Cross, Minehead TA24 7BG
T: (01643) 841556
F: (01643) 841556
E: info@exmoorheaven.co.uk
I: www.exmoorheaven.co.uk

Little Quarme Farm
♦♦♦♦♦ SILVER AWARD
Wheddon Cross, Minehead TA24 7EA
T: (01643) 841249
F: (01643) 841249
E: info@littlequarme.co.uk
I: www.littlequarme.co.uk

The Rest And Be Thankful Inn
♦♦♦♦ SILVER AWARD
Wheddon Cross, Minehead TA24 7DR
T: (01643) 841222
F: (01643) 841222
E: enquiries@restandbethankful.co.uk
I: www.restandbethankful.co.uk

Sundial Guesthouse
♦♦♦♦ SILVER AWARD
Wheddon Cross, Minehead TA24 7DP
T: (01643) 841188
E: admin@sundialguesthouse.co.uk
I: www.sundialguesthouse.co.uk

WHIDDON DOWN
Devon

Fairhaven Farm ♦♦♦
Gooseford, Whiddon Down, Okehampton EX20 2QH
T: (01647) 231261

WHIMPLE
Devon

Higher Southbrook Farm
♦♦♦♦
Southbrook Lane, Whimple, Exeter EX5 2PG
T: (01404) 823000
E: hsf@currantbun.com

WHITECROSS
Cornwall

Hycroft ♦♦
Whitecross, Wadebridge PL27 7JD
T: (01208) 816568

The Old Post Office ♦♦♦
Whitecross, Wadebridge PL27 7JD
T: (01208) 812620
E: bywaysoldpostoffice@supanet.com

WICK ST LAWRENCE
North Somerset

Icelton Farm ♦♦♦
Wick St Lawrence, Weston-super-Mare BS22 7YJ
T: (01934) 515704
F: (01934) 515704
E: icelton.farm@virgin.net

WIDECOMBE-IN-THE-MOOR
Devon

Higher Venton Farm ♦♦♦
Widecombe-in-the-Moor, Newton Abbot TQ13 7TF
T: (01364) 621235
F: (01364) 621382

Sheena Tower ♦♦♦
Widecombe-in-the-Moor, Newton Abbot TQ13 7TE
T: (01364) 621308
E: sheenatower@compuserve.com

WIDEMOUTH BAY
Cornwall

Bay View Inn ♦♦
Marine Drive, Widemouth Bay, Bude EX23 0AW
T: (01288) 361273
F: (01288) 361273
E: enquiries@bayviewinn.co.uk
I: www.bayviewinn.co.uk

Brocksmoor Hotel ♦♦♦
Widemouth Bay, Bude EX23 0DF
T: (01288) 361207
F: (01288) 361 589

WILCOT
Wiltshire

Wilcot Lodge ♦♦♦♦
Wilcot, Pewsey SN9 5NS
T: (01672) 563465
F: (01672) 569040
E: gmikegswindells@hotmail.com
I: www.bed-breakfast-uk.com/bb-uk-wilts.htm

WILTON
Wiltshire

The Pembroke Arms Hotel
♦♦♦♦
Minster Street, Wilton, Salisbury SP2 0BH
T: (01722) 743328
F: (01722) 744886
E: fleur@pembrokearms.co.uk

WINKLEIGH
Devon

The Old Parsonage ♦♦♦
Court Walk, Winkleigh, EX19 8JA
T: (01837) 83772
F: (01837) 680074

WINSFORD
Somerset

Kemps Farm ♦♦♦
Winsford, Minehead TA24 7HT
T: (01643) 851312

Larcombe Foot ♦♦♦♦
Winsford, Minehead TA24 7HS
T: (01643) 851306

WINSLEY
Wiltshire

The Conifers ♦♦
4 King Alfred Way, Winsley, Bradford-on-Avon BA15 2NG
T: (01225) 722482

Stillmeadow ♦♦♦♦♦
18 Bradford Road, Winsley, Bradford-on-Avon BA15 2HW
T: (01225) 722119
F: (01225) 722633
E: sue.gilby@btinternet.com

WINTERBOURNE STOKE
Wiltshire

Scotland Lodge Farm ♦♦♦♦
Winterbourne Stoke, Salisbury SP3 4TF
T: (01980) 621199
F: (01980) 621188
E: william.lockwood@bigwig.net
I: www.smoothhound.co.uk/hotels/scotlandl.html

WINTERSLOW
Wiltshire

Shiralee Bed & Breakfast ♦♦
Tytherley Road, Winterslow, Salisbury SP5 1PY
T: (01980) 862004
F: (01980) 862004
E: anything@faisa.co.uk
I: www.faisa.co.uk

WITHAM FRIARY
Somerset

Higher West Barn Farm
♦♦♦♦ SILVER AWARD
Witham Friary, Frome BA11 5HH
T: (01749) 850819
E: ea.harrison@tesco.net

WITHERIDGE
Devon

South Coombe Farm ♦♦♦♦
Witheridge, Tiverton EX16 8QL
T: (01884) 860302
F: (01884) 861064
E: holidays@southcoombe.ukf.net

Thelbridge Cross Inn ♦♦♦♦
Thelbridge, Crediton EX17 4SQ
T: (01884) 860316
F: (01884) 861318
E: thelbridgexinn@cwcom.net
I: www.westcountry-hotels.co.uk/thelbridgexinn

WIVELISCOMBE
Somerset

Greenway Farm ♦♦♦
Wiveliscombe, Taunton TA4 2UA
T: (01984) 623359
F: (01984) 624051

Mill Barn ♦♦♦♦
Jews Farm, Maundown, Wiveliscombe, Taunton TA4 2HL
T: (01984) 624739
F: (01984) 624408
E: Tony&Marilyn@mill-barn.freeserve.co.uk
I: www.mill-barn.freeserve.co.uk

WOODBOROUGH
Wiltshire

Well Cottage ♦♦♦
Honey Street, Woodborough, Pewsey SN9 5PS
T: (01672) 851577
E: b_trowbridgewellcottage@yahoo.com

WOODY BAY
Devon

Moorlands ♦♦♦
Woody Bay, Parracombe, Barnstaple EX31 4RA
T: (01598) 763224
E: info@moorlandshotel.freeserve.co.uk
I: www.moorlandshotel.co.uk

WOOKEY HOLE
Somerset

Broadleys
♦♦♦♦ SILVER AWARD
21 Wells Road, Wookey Hole, Wells BA5 1DN
T: (01749) 674746
F: (01749) 674746
E: broadleys.wells@btopenworld.com

Whitegate Cottage ♦♦♦
Milton Lane, Wookey Hole, Wells BA5 1DG
T: (01749) 675326
E: sueandnic@whitegate.freeserve.co.uk

WOOLACOMBE
Devon

Camberley ♦♦♦
Beach Road, Woolacombe, EX34 7AA
T: (01271) 870231
E: camberley@tesco.net
I: www.camberleybandb.co.uk

Castle Hotel ♦♦♦♦
The Esplanade, Woolacombe, EX34 7DJ
T: (01271) 870788
F: (01271) 870788

Gull Rock Hotel ♦♦♦♦
Mortehoe, Woolacombe EX34 7EA
T: (01271) 870534
F: (01271) 870534
E: info@thegullrockhotel.co.uk
I: www.thegullrockhotel.co.uk

Ossaborough House ♦♦♦♦
Ossaborough Lane, Woolacombe, EX34 7HJ
T: (01271) 870297
E: info@ossaboroughhouse.co.uk
I: www.ossaboroughhouse.co.uk

WOOLLEY
Cornwall

East Woolley Farm ♦♦♦♦
Woolley, Bude EX23 9PP
T: (01288) 331525
F: (01288) 331525

WOOLVERTON
Somerset

The Old School House ♦♦♦
Woolverton, Bath BA3 6RH
T: (01373) 830200
F: (01373) 830200

WOOTTON BASSETT
Wiltshire

1 Highgate Cottages ♦♦♦
Brinkworth Road, Wootton Bassett, Swindon SN4 8DU
T: (01793) 848054

The Hollies ♦♦♦
Greenhill, Hook, Wootton Bassett, Swindon SN4 8EH
T: (01793) 770795
F: (01793) 770795

WRAXALL
Somerset

Rose's Farm ♦♦♦♦
Wraxall, Shepton Mallet BA4 6RQ
T: (01749) 860261
F: (01749) 860261

YARCOMBE
Devon

Crawley Farm ♦♦♦
Yarcombe, Honiton EX14 9AX
T: (01460) 64760
F: (01460) 64760
E: info@crawleyfarm.com
I: www.crawleyfarm.com

YELVERTON
Devon

Eggworthy Farm ♦♦♦
Sampford Spiney, Yelverton PL20 6LJ
T: (01822) 852142
F: (01822) 852142
E: bj&llandick@aol.com

The Old Orchard
♦♦♦♦ SILVER AWARD
Harrowbeer Lane, Yelverton, PL20 6DZ
T: (01822) 854310
F: (01822) 854310
E: babs@baross.demon.co.uk
I: www.baross.demon.co.uk/theoldorchard

The Rosemont ♦♦♦♦
Greenbank Terrace, Yelverton, PL20 6DR
T: (01822) 852175
E: office@rosemontgh.fsnet.co.uk
I: www.therosemont.co.uk

Torrfields ♦♦♦♦
Sheepstor, Yelverton PL20 6PF
T: (01822) 852161

YEOVIL
Somerset

Globetrotters Cafe, Bar, Restaurant and Lodge ♦♦♦
73-74 South Street, Yeovil, BA20 1QF
T: (01935) 423328
F: (01935) 411701
E: Reception@globetrotters.co.uk
I: www.theglobetrotters.co.uk

Greystones Court ♦♦♦♦
152 Hendford Hill, Yeovil, BA20 2RG
T: (01935) 426124
F: (01935) 426124
E: rich&isobel@greystones.freeserve.co.uk
I: www.greystones.freeserve.co.uk

Jessops ♦♦♦♦
Vagg Lane, Chilthorne Domer, Yeovil BA22 8RY
T: (01935) 841097
F: (01935) 841097

Royal Oak Farm
Rating Applied For
Hardington Mandeville, Yeovil, BA22 9NW
T: (01935) 862348
F: (01935) 862348
I: www.sommysroyaloak.co.uk

The Sparkford Inn ♦♦♦
High Street, Sparkford, Yeovil BA22 7JN
T: (01963) 440218
F: (01963) 440358
E: sparkfordinn@sparkford.fsbusiness.co.uk

Sunnymede
♦♦♦♦ SILVER AWARD
26 Lower Wraxhill Road, Yeovil, BA20 2JU
T: (01935) 425786

YEOVILTON
Somerset

Cary Fitzpaine ♦♦♦♦
Yeovilton, Yeovil BA22 8JB
T: (01458) 223250
F: (01458) 223372
E: acrang@aol.com
I: www.caryfitzpaine.com

Courtry Farm ♦♦♦
Bridgehampton, Yeovil BA22 8HF
T: (01935) 840327
F: (01935) 840964
E: courtryfarm@hotmail.com

YETMINSTER
Dorset

Bingers Farm
♦♦♦♦ SILVER AWARD
Ryme Road, Yetminster, Sherborne DT9 6JY
T: (01935) 872555
F: (01935) 872555
E: bingersfarm@talk21.com

Old Mill House ♦♦♦♦
Mill Lane, Yetminster, Sherborne DT9 6ND
T: (01935) 873672
F: (01935) 873672
E: theparks@inyetminster.freeserve.co.uk

ZEALS
Wiltshire

Cornerways Cottage ♦♦♦♦
Longcross, Zeals, Warminster BA12 6LL
T: (01747) 840477
F: (01747) 840477
E: cornerways.cottage@btinternet.com
I: www.smoothhound.co.uk/hotels/cornerwa.html

SOUTH OF ENGLAND

ABBOTTS ANN
Hampshire

Carinya Farm ♦♦♦
Cattle Lane, Abbotts Ann, Andover SP11 7DR
T: (01264) 710269
E: carinyafarm@virgin.net
I: www.carinyafarm.co.uk

East Manor House
♦♦♦♦♦ SILVER AWARD
Abbotts Ann, Andover SP11 7BH
T: (01264) 710031

Virginia Lodge ♦♦♦
Salisbury Road, Abbotts Ann, Andover SP11 7NX
T: (01264) 710713
E: b_stuart@talk21.com

ABINGDON
Oxfordshire

Barrows End
Rating Applied For
3 The Copse, Barrows End, Abingdon, OX14 3YW
T: (01235) 523541
F: (01235) 523541
E: dsharm@tesco.net

Dinckley Court ♦♦♦♦
Burcot, Abingdon, OX14 3DP
T: (01865) 407763
F: (01865) 407010
E: annette@dinckleycourt.co.uk
I: www.dinckleycourt.co.uk

ADDERBURY
Oxfordshire

The Bell Inn ♦♦♦
High Street, Adderbury, Banbury OX17 3LS
T: (01295) 810338
F: (01295) 812221
E: tim@thebell-adderbury.com
I: www.thebell@adderbury.com

Le Restaurant Francais at Morgans Orchard ♦♦♦
9 Twyford Gardens, Adderbury, Banbury OX17 3JA
T: (01295) 812047
F: (01295) 812341
E: morgansorchard@aol.com
I: www.banbury-cross.co.uk/morgans

ADSTOCK
Buckinghamshire

The Folly Inn ♦♦
Buckingham Road, Adstock, Buckingham MK18 2HS
T: (01296) 712671
F: (01296) 712671

ALDERHOLT
Dorset

Blackwater House ♦♦♦♦
Blackwater Grove, Alderholt, Fordingbridge SP6 3AD
T: (01425) 653443
E: bandb@blackwater47.fsnet.co.uk
I: www.blackwater47.fsnet.co.uk

ALDERMASTON
Berkshire

Hinds Head ♦♦♦
Wasing Lane, Aldermaston, Reading RG7 4LX
T: (0118) 971 2194

ALDWORTH
West Berkshire

Fieldview Cottage ♦♦♦♦
Bell Lane, Aldworth, Reading RG8 9SB
T: (01635) 578964
E: chunt@fieldview.freeserve.co.uk

ALRESFORD
Hampshire

Haygarth
Rating Applied For
82 Jacklyns Lane, Alresford, SO24 9LJ
T: (01962) 732715

Heronbrook House
♦♦♦♦ SILVER AWARD
New Farm Road, Alresford, SO24 9QH
T: (01962) 738726
F: (01962) 732602
E: jane@heronbrookhouse.co.uk
I: www.heronbrookhouse.co.uk

Tichborne Grange B & B ♦♦♦♦
Grange Farm, Tichborne, Alresford, SO24 0NE
T: (01962) 732120
F: (01962) 732365
E: gussieraimes@hotmail.com

The Woolpack Country Inn ♦♦♦
Totford, Alresford, SO24 9TJ
T: (01962) 732101
F: (01962) 732889

ALTON
Hampshire

Boundary House B & B ♦♦♦♦ SILVER AWARD
Gosport Road, Lower Farringdon, Alton GU34 3DH
T: (01420) 587076
F: (01420) 587047
E: BoundaryS@messages.co.uk

The Vicarage ♦♦♦
East Worldham, Alton GU34 3AS
T: (01420) 82392
F: (01420) 82367
E: wenrose@bigfoot.com
I: www.altonbedandbreakfast.co.uk

West End Farm ♦♦♦♦
Froyle, Alton GU34 4JG
T: (01420) 22130
F: (01420) 22930
E: cj.butler.farms@farmline.co.uk
I: www.hampshirebedandbreakfast.co.uk

ALVERSTOKE
Hampshire

The Old Lodge Hotel ♦♦♦
81 The Avenue, Alverstoke, Gosport PO12 2JX
T: (023) 9258 1865
F: (023) 9252 8104

AMERSHAM
Buckinghamshire

Coldmoreham House ♦♦♦♦
172 High Street, Amersham, HP7 0EG
T: (01494) 725245

The Dacha ♦♦♦♦
118 Chestnut Lane, Amersham, HP6 6DZ
T: (01494) 433063

127 High Street ♦♦♦♦
Amersham, HP7 0DY
T: (01494) 725352

La Fosse ♦♦
Fagnall Lane, Winchmore Hill, Amersham, HP7 0PG
T: (01494) 726546
F: (01494) 726546

Morningside
Rating Applied For
Piggotts Orchard, Amersham, HP7 0JG
T: (01494) 721134

Nita Hurley's Bed & Breakfast ♦♦♦
63 Hundred Acres Lane, Amersham, HP7 9BX
T: (01494) 433095
E: nitahurleybb@hotmail.com
I: www.nitasbnb.co.uk

39 Quarrendon Road ♦♦♦♦ SILVER AWARD
Amersham, HP7 9EF
T: (01494) 727959

Rocquaine House ♦♦♦♦♦
36 Stanley Hill Avenue, Amersham, HP7 9BB
T: (01494) 726671

St Catherins ♦♦♦
9 Parkfield Avenue, Amersham, HP6 6BE
T: (01494) 728125
E: jameselliott8@btopenworld.com

Saracens Head Inn ♦♦♦
38 Whielden Street, Old Town, Amersham, HP7 0HU
T: (01494) 721958
F: (01494) 725208
E: eamonn@thesaracensheadinn.com
I: www.thesaracensheadinn.com

The Vicarage ♦♦♦
70 Sycamore Road, Amersham, HP6 5DR
T: (01494) 729993
F: (01494) 727553

The White House ♦♦♦♦
20 Church Street, Amersham, HP7 0DB
T: (01494) 433015
F: (01494) 433015

AMPFIELD
Hampshire

The Taj ♦♦♦♦
2 Hook Crescent, Ampfield, Romsey SO51 9DE
T: (023) 8027 0810
E: christine@jeaves.freeserve.co.uk

AMPORT
Hampshire

Broadwater ♦♦♦♦
Amport, Andover SP11 8AY
T: (01264) 772240
F: (01264) 772240
E: carolyn@dmac.co.uk
I: www.dmac.co.uk/carolyn

ANDOVER
Hampshire

Amberley Hotel ♦♦♦
70 Weyhill Road, Andover, SP10 3NP
T: (01264) 352224
F: (01264) 392555
E: amberleyand@fsbdial.co.uk

Amport Inn ♦♦♦
Amport, Andover SP11 8AE
T: (01264) 710371
F: (01264) 710112

The Bourne Valley Inn ♦♦♦
St Mary Bourne, Andover SP11 6BT
T: (01264) 738361
F: (01264) 738126
E: bourneinn@aol.com
I: www.townpages.com

Fernihurst ♦♦♦♦
1 Strathfield Road, Andover, SP10 2HH
T: (01264) 361936

Holmdene Guest House ♦♦♦
1 Winchester Road, Andover, SP10 2EG
T: (01264) 365414

Malt Cottage ♦♦♦♦ SILVER AWARD
Upper Clatford, Andover SP11 7QL
T: (01264) 323469
E: info@maltcottage.co.uk
I: www.maltcottage.co.uk

May Cottage ♦♦♦♦ SILVER AWARD
Thruxton, Andover SP11 8LZ
T: (01264) 771241
F: (01264) 771770
E: info@maycottage-thruxton.co.uk
I: www.maycottage-thruxton.co.uk

Old Grange ♦♦♦♦
86 Winchester Road, Andover, SP10 2ER
T: (01264) 352784

Salisbury Road Bed & Breakfast ♦♦♦
99 Salisbury Road, Andover, SP10 2LN
T: (01264) 362638
F: (01264) 396597
E: jenny@mosaicevents.co.uk
I: www.exploretestvalley.com/salisr

Shangri-La Guest House ♦♦♦
Walworth Road, Picket Piece, Andover, SP11 6LU
T: (01264) 354399

Sutherland Guest House ♦♦♦♦
Micheldever Road, Andover, SP10 2BH
T: (01264) 365307
E: mikejkelly@talk21.com

ARDLEY
Oxfordshire

The Old Post Office ♦♦♦
Church Road, Ardley, Bicester OX27 7NP
T: (01869) 345958
F: (01869) 345958

ASCOT
Berkshire

Ascot Corner ♦♦♦♦ SILVER AWARD
Wells Lane, Ascot, SL5 7DY
T: (01344) 627722
F: (01344) 873965
E: susan.powell@easynet.co.uk

Ennis Lodge Private Guest House ♦♦♦
Winkfield Road, Ascot, SL5 7EX
T: (01344) 621009
F: (01344) 621009

Tanglewood ♦♦♦
Birch Lane, off Longhill Road, Chavey Down, Ascot SL5 8RF
T: (01344) 882528
F: (01344) 882528
E: beer.tanglewood@btinternet.com

ASCOTT-UNDER-WYCHWOOD
Oxfordshire

College Farm ♦♦♦♦
Ascott-under-Wychwood, Oxford OX7 6AL
T: (01993) 831900
F: (01993) 831900
E: walkers@collegefarmbandb.fsnet.co.uk

The Mill ♦♦♦
Ascott-under-Wychwood, Oxford OX7 6AP
T: (01993) 831282
F: (01993) 831282
E: Mill@auwoxon32.freeserve.co.uk

ASHENDON
Buckinghamshire

The Gatehangers ♦♦♦
Lower End, Ashendon, Aylesbury HP18 0HE
T: (01296) 651296
F: (01296) 651340

ASHEY
Isle of Wight

Little Upton Farmhouse ♦♦♦♦♦
Little Upton Farm, Gatehouse Road, Ashey, Ryde PO33 4BS
T: (01983) 563236
F: (01983) 563236
E: alison@littleuptonfarm.co.uk
I: www.littleuptonfarm.co.uk

ASHLEY HEATH
Dorset

Yorkland ♦♦♦♦
12 Ashley Drive West, Ashley Heath, Ringwood BH24 2JW
T: (01425) 472869
E: garethbeau@btinternet.com

ASHMORE
Dorset

Glebe Cottage Farm ♦♦♦♦
Ashmore, Shaftesbury, DT5 5AE
T: (01747) 811974
F: (01747) 811104
E: all@glebe.force9.co.uk

ASHURST
Hampshire

Forest Gate Lodge ♦♦♦♦
161 Lyndhurst Road, Ashurst, Southampton SO40 7AW
T: (023) 8029 3026

Kingswood Cottage ♦♦♦♦ SILVER AWARD
10 Woodlands Road, Ashurst, Southampton SO40 7AD
T: (023) 8029 2582
F: (023) 8029 3435

ASTON ABBOTTS
Buckinghamshire

The Royal Oak Inn ♦♦
Wingrave Road, Aston Abbotts, Aylesbury HP22 4LT
T: (01296) 681262
E: moulty.towers@btinternet.com

Windmill Hill Barns ♦♦♦♦
Moat Lane, Aston Abbotts, Aylesbury HP22 4NF
T: (01296) 681714

ASTON CLINTON
Buckinghamshire

Baywood Guest House ♦♦
98 Weston Road, Aston Clinton, Aylesbury HP22 5EJ
T: (01296) 630612

ASTON ROWANT
Oxfordshire

Tower Cottage ♦♦♦
Chinnor Road, Aston Rowant, Oxford OX49 5SN
T: (01844) 354676
F: (01844) 355999

ASTON UPTHORPE
Oxfordshire

Middle Fell ♦♦♦♦
Moreton Road, Aston Upthorpe, Didcot OX11 9ER
T: (01235) 850207
F: (01235) 850207
E: middlefell@ic24.net

AWBRIDGE
Hampshire

Crofton Country Bed & Breakfast
♦♦♦♦ SILVER AWARD
Kents Oak, Awbridge, Romsey
SO51 0HH
T: (01794) 340333
F: (01794) 340333
E: pauline@crofton-ca.fsnet.co.uk

AYLESBURY
Buckinghamshire

Amber Court ♦
116 Bierton Road, Aylesbury, HP20 1EN
T: (01296) 432184

Bay Lodge Guest House
Rating Applied For
47 Tring Road, Aylesbury, HP20 1LD
T: (01296) 331404
F: (01296) 331404
E: blodge47@hotmail.com
I: www.bay-lodge.co.uk

Dovedale Court Guest House ♦♦
46 Wendover Road, Aylesbury, HP21 9LB
T: (01296) 339400
F: (01296) 429364
E: campions@btopenworld.com

74 Friarscroft Way
Rating Applied For
Aylesbury, HP20 2TF
T: (01296) 489439

Little Venice B&B
Rating Applied For
129 Mandeville Road, Aylesbury, HP21 8AJ
T: (01296) 339242
F: (01296) 339242
E: littlevenice129@hotmail.com
I: www.littleveniceuk.com

Oakridge House B & B
Rating Applied For
263 Wendover Road, Aylesbury, HP21 9PB
T: (01296) 437926

The Old Forge Barn ♦♦♦
Ridings Way, Cublington, Leighton Buzzard LU7 0LW
T: (01296) 681194
F: (01296) 681194
E: waples@ukonline.co.uk

Spindleberries ♦♦♦♦
331 Tring Road, Aylesbury, HP20 1PJ
T: (01296) 424012

Wallace Farm ♦♦♦
Dinton, Aylesbury HP17 8UF
T: (01296) 748660
F: (01296) 748851
E: jackiecook@wallacefarm.freeserve.co.uk
I: www.wallacefarm.co.uk

BAMPTON
Oxfordshire

Chimney Farm House ♦♦♦♦
Chimney, Bampton OX18 2EH
T: (01367) 870279
F: (01367) 870279
I: www.country-accom.co.uk/chimneyfarmhouse

The Granary ♦♦♦
Main Street, Clanfield, Bampton OX18 2SH
T: (01367) 810266

BANBURY
Oxfordshire

Amberley Guest House ♦♦
151 Middleton Road, Banbury, OX16 8QS
T: (01295) 255797
F: (01295) 255797

Ark Guest House
Rating Applied For
120 Warwick Road, Banbury, OX16 2AN
T: (01295) 254498
F: (01295) 254498

Ashlea Guest House ♦♦
58 Oxford Road, Banbury, OX16 9AN
T: (01295) 250539
F: (01295) 250539
E: johnatstandrews@btinternet.com

Avonlea Guest House ♦♦
41 Southam Road, Banbury, OX16 7EP
T: (01295) 267837
F: (01295) 271 946

Aynho Fields ♦♦♦
Aynho, Banbury, OX17 3AU
T: (01869) 810288

Banbury Cross Bed & Breakfast ♦♦♦♦
1 Broughton Road, Banbury, OX16 9QB
T: (01295) 266048
F: (01295) 266698

College Farmhouse ♦♦♦♦
Kings Sutton, Banbury, OX17 3PS
T: (01295) 811473
F: (01295) 812505
E: sallday@aol.com
I: www.banburytown.co.uk/accom/collegefarm/

Cotefields Bed & Breakfast ♦♦
Opposite Bodicote Park, Banbury, OX15 4AQ
T: (01295) 264977
F: (01295) 264977
E: tony.stockford@ic24.net

Fernleigh Guest House ♦♦♦
67 Oxford Road, Banbury, OX16 9AJ
T: (01295) 250853
F: (01295) 269349
E: a.cumberlidge@btinternet.com

George & Dragon ♦♦♦
Silver Street, Chacombe, Banbury, OX17 2JR
T: (01295) 711500
F: (01295) 758827

The Glebe House ♦♦♦♦
Village Road, Warmington, Banbury, OX17 1BT
T: (01295) 690642

The Lodge ♦♦♦♦
Main Road, Middleton Cheney, Banbury, OX17 2PP
T: (01295) 710355

Prospect House Guest House ♦♦♦
70 Oxford Road, Banbury, OX16 9AN
T: (01295) 268749
F: (01295) 268749

St Martins House ♦♦♦
Warkworth, Banbury OX17 2AG
T: (01295) 712684
F: (01295) 712838

Treetops Guest House ♦♦
28 Dashwood Road, Banbury, OX16 8HD
T: (01295) 254444

BARTLEY
Hampshire

Bartley Farmhouse ♦♦♦♦
Ringwood Road, Bartley, Southampton SO40 7LD
T: (023) 8081 4194
F: (023) 8081 4117

BARTON ON SEA
Hampshire

Cleeve House ♦♦♦♦
58 Barton Court Avenue, Barton on Sea, New Milton BH25 7HG
T: (01425) 615211
F: (01425) 615211
I: www.2stay.com/uk/hotels/cleeveho.html

Everglades ♦♦♦♦
81 Sea Road, Barton on Sea, New Milton BH25 7ND
T: (01425) 617350

Hotel Gainsborough ♦♦♦♦
Marine Drive East, Barton on Sea, New Milton BH25 7DX
T: (01425) 610541

Laurel Lodge ♦♦♦
48 Western Avenue, Barton on Sea, New Milton BH25 7PZ
T: (01425) 618309

Westbury House ♦♦♦
12 Greenacre, Barton on Sea, New Milton BH25 7BS
T: (01425) 620935
E: les@westbury-house.freeserve.co.uk
I: www.westbury-house.freeserve.co.uk

BARTON STACEY
Hampshire

The Swan Inn ♦♦♦
High Street, Barton Stacey, Winchester SO21 3RL
T: (01962) 760470

BASINGSTOKE
Hampshire

Fernbank Hotel ♦♦♦♦
4 Fairfields Road, Basingstoke, RG21 3DR
T: (01256) 321191
F: (01256) 321191
E: availability@fernbankhotel.co.uk
I: www.fernbankhotel.co.uk

Street Farm House ♦♦♦♦
The Street, South Warnborough, Hook, RG29 1RS
T: (01256) 862225
F: (01256) 862225
E: streetfarmhouse@btinternet.com

96 Worting Road ♦♦♦
Basingstoke, RG21 8TT
T: (01256) 320136

BEACONSFIELD
Buckinghamshire

Beacon House ♦♦♦
113 Maxwell Road, Beaconsfield, HP9 1RF
T: (01494) 672923
F: (01494) 672923
E: Ben.Dickinson@Tesco.net
I: www.beaconhouse.org.uk

Highclere Farm ♦♦♦♦
Newbarn Lane, Seer Green, Beaconsfield HP9 2QZ
T: (01494) 875665
F: (01494) 875238

BEAULIEU
Hampshire

Dale Farm House ♦♦♦
Manor Road, Applemore Hill, Dibden, Southampton SO45 5TJ
T: (023) 8084 9632
F: (023) 8084 0285
E: info@dalefarmhouse.co.uk
I: www.dalefarmhouse.co.uk

Leygreen Farm House ♦♦♦
Lyndhurst Road, Beaulieu, Brockenhurst SO42 7YP
T: (01590) 612355
F: (01590) 612355
I: www.newforest.demon.co.uk/leygreen.htm

Old School House ♦♦♦♦
High Street, Beaulieu, Brockenhurst SO42 7YD
T: (01590) 612062
F: (01590) 612062
E: jeanie@eurolink.ltd.net

BEDHAMPTON
Hampshire

Cherry Trees ♦♦♦♦
23 Parkside, Bedhampton, Havant PO9 3PJ
T: (023) 9248 2480

BEMBRIDGE
Isle of Wight

The Crab and Lobster ♦♦♦♦
32 Forelands Field Road, Bembridge, PO35 5TR
T: (01983) 872244
F: (01983) 873495

Harbour Farm ♦♦♦♦
Embankment Road, Bembridge, PO35 5NS
T: (01983) 872610
F: (01983) 874080
E: deirdremhicks@aol.com
I: www.harbourfarm.co.uk

Sea Change
♦♦♦♦ SILVER AWARD
22 Beachfield Road, Bembridge, PO35 5TN
T: (01983) 875558
F: (01983) 875667
E: seachangewight@aol.com

BENSON
Oxfordshire

Brookside ♦♦♦
Brook Street, Benson, Wallingford OX10 6LJ
T: (01491) 838289
F: (01491) 838289

The Crown Inn ♦♦♦
52 High Street, Benson, Wallingford OX10 6RP
T: (01491) 838247

Fyfield Manor
♦♦♦♦ SILVER AWARD
Benson, Wallingford OX10 6HA
T: (01491) 835184
F: (01491) 825635
E: ffbrown@fifield-software.demon.co.uk

BENTLEY
Hampshire

Pittersfield ♦♦♦
Bentley, Farnham GU10 5LT
T: (01420) 22414
F: (01420) 22414

BERE REGIS
Dorset

The Dorsetshire Golf Lodge ♦♦♦♦
The Dorset Golf & Country Club, Bere Regis, Wareham BH20 7NT
T: (01929) 472244
F: (01929) 471294
E: thedorset@dorsetshiregolf.co.uk

BICESTER
Oxfordshire

Bowshot Bed and Breakfast ♦♦♦
Bowshot Court, 7 Aldergate Road, Bicester, OX26 2BJ
T: (01869) 252355
E: reservations@bowshotholidays.com
I: www.bowshotholidays.com

Manor Farm Bed & Breakfast ♦♦♦
Poundon, Bicester OX27 9BB
T: (01869) 277212
E: jeannettecollett@aol.com
I: www.smoothhound.co.uk/hotels/manor3.html

Oxford Terrace B&B ♦♦
28 Kings End, Bicester, OX26 2AA
T: (01869) 248739
E: rmorgans@ntlworld.com

Priory House ♦♦♦
86 Chapel Street, Bicester, OX26 6BD
T: (01869) 325687
E: anderson@prioryhouse.fsnet.co.uk
I: mysite.freeserve.com/prioryhouse/

BINSTEAD
Isle of Wight

Elm Close Cottage ♦♦♦♦
Ladies Walk, Church Road, Binstead, Ryde PO33 3SY
T: (01983) 567161
E: elm_cottage@hotmail.com

Newnham Farm Bed & Breakfast
♦♦♦♦♦ SILVER AWARD
Newnham Lane, Binstead, Ryde PO33 4ED
T: (01983) 882423
F: (01983) 882423
E: newnhamfarm@talk21.com
I: www.newnhamfarm.co.uk

BISHOP'S WALTHAM
Hampshire

Post Mead
♦♦♦♦ SILVER AWARD
Shore Lane, Bishop's Waltham, Southampton SO32 1DY
T: (01489) 895795
F: (01489) 895795

BIX
Oxfordshire

The Barn ♦♦♦♦
Bix, Henley-on-Thames RG9 4RS
T: (01491) 414062
E: tgb@btinternet.com
I: www.thebarnbix.btinternet.co.uk

Meadow Corner ♦♦♦
Bix, Henley-on-Thames RG9 6BU
T: (01491) 578456

BLACKTHORN
Oxfordshire

Lime Trees Farm ♦♦♦♦
Lower Road, Blackthorn, Bicester OX25 1TG
T: (01869) 248435
F: (01869) 325843
E: keithcrampton@tiscali.co.uk
I: www.smoothhound.co.uk/hotels/limetrees.html

BLANDFORD FORUM
Dorset

Farnham Farm House
♦♦♦♦ SILVER AWARD
Farnham, Blandford Forum DT11 8DG
T: (01725) 516254
F: (01725) 516306
E: info@farnhamfarmhouse.co.uk
I: www.farnhamfarmhouse.co.uk

Meadow House
♦♦♦♦ SILVER AWARD
Tarrant Hinton, Blandford Forum DT11 8JG
T: (01258) 830498
F: (01258) 830498

St Leonards Farmhouse ♦♦♦♦
Wimborne Road, Blandford Forum, DT11 7SB
T: (01258) 456635
F: (01258) 455598
E: jodi@brittours.com
I: www.brittours.com/st.leonard/st.leonards.htm.htm

BLEDLOW
Buckinghamshire

Cross Lanes Guest House ♦♦♦♦
Cross Lanes Cottage, Bledlow, Aylesbury HP27 9PF
T: (01844) 345339
F: (01844) 274165
E: ronaldcoul@aol.com

BLEDLOW RIDGE
Buckinghamshire

Old Callow Down Farm ♦♦♦♦
Wigans Lane, Bledlow Ridge, High Wycombe HP14 4BH
T: (01844) 344416
F: (01844) 344703
E: oldcallow@aol.com
I: www.chilternscottage.co.uk

BLEWBURY
Oxfordshire

The Barley Mow ♦♦♦
London Road, Blewbury, Didcot OX11 9NU
T: (01235) 850296
F: (01235) 850296

BLOXHAM
Oxfordshire

Brook Cottage ♦♦♦
Little Bridge Road, Bloxham, Banbury OX15 4PU
T: (01295) 721089

Rowan Court ♦♦♦♦
Milton Road, Bloxham, Banbury OX15 4HD
T: (01295) 722566
F: (01295) 722566
E: enquiries@rowancourt.co.uk
I: ww.rowancourt.com

BOLDRE
Hampshire

Kingston Cottage ♦♦♦
Lower Sandy Down, Boldre, Lymington SO41 8PP
T: (01590) 623051

Pinecroft ♦♦
Coxhill, Boldre, Lymington SO41 8PS
T: (01590) 624260
F: (01590) 624025
E: enquiries@pinecroftbandb.co.uk
I: www.pinecroftbandb.co.uk

The Well House ♦♦♦♦
Southampton Road, Boldre, Lymington SO41 8PT
T: (01590) 689055
F: (01590) 688993
E: thewellhouse@btinternet.com
I: www.thewellhouse.bnb.com

BONCHURCH
Isle of Wight

The Lake Hotel ♦♦♦♦
Shore Road, Bonchurch, Ventnor PO38 1RF
T: (01983) 852613
F: (01983) 852613
E: enquiries@lakehotel.co.uk
I: www.lakehotel.co.uk

Under Rock Country House Bed & Breakfast ♦♦♦
Shore Road, Bonchurch, Ventnor PO38 1RF
T: (01983) 855274
E: enquiries@under-rock.co.uk
I: www.under-rock.co.uk

BOSCOMBE
Dorset

Aloha Wyvern Hotel ♦♦♦♦
24 Glen Road, Boscombe, Bournemouth BH5 1HR
T: (01202) 397543
F: (01202) 256175

Au-Levant Hotel ♦♦♦
15 Westby Road, Boscombe, Bournemouth BH5 1HA
T: (01202) 394884

Audmore Hotel ♦♦♦
3 Cecil Road, Boscombe, Bournemouth BH5 1DU
T: (01202) 395166
I: www.audmorehotel.co.uk

Bramcote Hall Hotel ♦♦♦
1 Glen Road, Boscombe, Bournemouth BH5 1HR
T: (01202) 395555
F: (01202) 398623
E: bramcotehall@lineone.net

Denewood Hotel ♦♦♦
1 Percy Road, Boscombe, Bournemouth BH5 1JE
T: (01202) 394493
F: (01202) 391155
E: peteer@denewood.co.uk
I: www.denewood.co.uk

The Marven Hotel ♦♦♦
5 Watkin Road, Boscombe, Bournemouth BH5 1HP
T: (01202) 397099

Rosemount Hotel ♦♦♦♦
11 Argyll Road, Boscombe, Bournemouth BH5 1EB
T: (01202) 395460
F: (01202) 385461

Siena Private Hotel ♦♦♦♦
17 Cecil Road, Boscombe, Bournemouth BH5 1DU
T: (01202) 394159
F: (01202) 309798
E: barbara_hall16@yahoo.com

Hotel Sorrento ♦♦♦
16 Owls Road, Boscombe, Bournemouth BH5 1AG
T: (01202) 394019
F: (01202) 394019
E: mail@hotelsorrento.co.uk
I: www.hotelsorrento.co.uk

BOTLEY
Hampshire

Steeple Court Farm ♦♦♦
Church Lane, Botley, Southampton SO30 2EQ
T: (01489) 798824
E: theblue.room@btinternet.com

BOTOLPH CLAYDON
Buckinghamshire

Hickwell House ♦♦♦♦
40 Botyl Road, Botolph Claydon, Buckingham MK18 2LR
T: (01296) 712217
F: (01296) 712217

BOURNE END
Buckinghamshire

Hollands Farm ♦♦♦♦
Hedsor Road, Bourne End, SL8 5EE
T: (01628) 520423
F: (01628) 531602

BOURNEMOUTH
Dorset

Alexander Lodge Hotel ♦♦♦♦
21 Southern Road, Southbourne, Bournemouth BH6 3SR
T: (01202) 421662
F: (01202) 421662
E: alexanderlodge@yahoo.com
I: www.smoothhound.co.uk/a28852.html

Balincourt Hotel
♦♦♦♦ SILVER AWARD
58 Christchurch Road, Bournemouth, BH1 3PF
T: (01202) 552962
F: (01202) 552962
E: rooms@balincourt.co.uk
I: www.balincourt.co.uk

Bonnington Hotel ♦♦♦
44 Tregonwell Road, Bournemouth, BH2 5NT
T: (01202) 553621
F: (01202) 317797
E: bonnington.bournemouth@btinternet.com
I: www.bonnington-hotel.com

Cairnsmore Hotel ♦♦♦
37 Beaulieu Road, Alum Chine, Bournemouth, BH4 8HY
T: (01202) 763705
E: ritacoombs@hotmail.com

Carisbrooke Hotel ♦♦♦♦
42 Tregonwell Road, Bournemouth, BH2 5NT
T: (01202) 290432
F: (01202) 310499
E: all@carisbrooke58.freeserve.co.uk
I: www.carisbrooke.co.uk

Coniston Hotel ♦♦♦
27 Studland Road, Alum Chine, Bournemouth, BH4 8HZ
T: (01202) 765386
E: coniston.hotel@virgin.net

Cransley Hotel ♦♦♦♦
11 Knyveton Road, East Cliff, Bournemouth, BH1 3QG
T: (01202) 290067
F: 07092 381721
E: info@cransley.com
I: www.cransley.com

Crosbie Hall Hotel ♦♦♦
21 Florence Road, Boscombe, Bournemouth BH5 1HJ
T: (01202) 394714
F: (01202) 394714
E: david@crosbiehall.fsnet.co.uk
I: www.crosbiehall.fsnet.co.uk

Earlham Lodge ♦♦♦♦
91 Alumhurst Road, Alum Chine, Bournemouth, BH4 8HR
T: (01202) 761943
F: (01202) 768223
E: info@earlhamlodge.com
I: www.earlhamlodge.com

East Cliff Cottage Hotel ♦♦♦
57 Grove Road, Bournemouth, BH1 3AT
T: (01202) 552788
F: (01202) 556400
E: len@l.wallen.freeserve.co.uk
I: www.smoothhound.co.uk/hotels/eastcliff.html

Fairmount Hotel ♦♦♦♦
15 Priory Road, West Cliff, Bournemouth, BH2 5DF
T: (01202) 551105
F: (01202) 553210
E: stay@fairmount-hotel.co.uk
I: www.fairmounthotels.co.uk

Gervis Court Hotel ♦♦♦
38 Gervis Road, Bournemouth, BH1 3DH
T: (01202) 556871
F: (01202) 467066
E: enquiries@gerviscourthotel.co.uk
I: www.gerviscourthotel.co.uk

Glenbourne Hotel ♦♦♦♦
81 Alumhurst Road, Alum Chine, Bournemouth, BH4 8HR
T: (01202) 761607
F: (01202) 762837
E: enquiries@theglenbournehotel.com
I: www.theglenbournehotel.com

The Inverness Hotel ♦♦♦♦
26 Tregonwell Road, Bournemouth, BH2 5NS
T: (01202) 554968
F: (01202) 294197
E: inverness.hotel@tesco.net
I: www.hotelsbournemouth.uk.com

Kings Langley Hotel ♦♦♦
1 West Cliff Road, Bournemouth, BH2 5ES
T: (01202) 557349
F: (01202) 789739
E: john@kingslangleyhotel.com
I: www.kingslangleyhotel.com

Lawnswood Hotel ♦♦♦
22A Studland Road, Alum Chine, Bournemouth, BH4 8JA
T: (01202) 761170
F: (01202) 761170
E: lawnswood_hotel_uk@yahoo.com
I: www.lawnswoodhotel.co.uk

Majestic Hotel ♦♦♦♦
34 Derby Road, East Cliff, Bournemouth, BH1 3QE
T: (01202) 294771
F: (01202) 310962

Mayfield Guest House
♦♦♦♦ SILVER AWARD
46 Frances Road, Knyveton Gardens, Bournemouth, BH1 3SA
T: (01202) 551839
F: (01202) 551839
E: accom@mayfieldhotel.com
I: www.mayfieldhotel.com

Oxford Hall Hotel ♦♦♦♦
6 Sandbourne Road, Bournemouth, BH4 8JH
T: (01202) 761016
F: (01202) 540465
E: oxfordhall@eurolinkltd.net

Parklands Hotel ♦♦♦♦
4 Rushton Crescent, Bournemouth, BH3 7AF
T: (01202) 552529
F: (01202) 249013
E: parklandshotel@redhotant.com
I: www.parklandshotel.redhotant.com

Redlands Hotel ♦♦♦♦
79 St Michaels Road, West Cliff, Bournemouth, BH2 5DR
T: (01202) 553714
E: enquiries@redlandshotel.co.uk
I: www.redlandshotel.co.uk

Rosedene Cottage Hotel ♦♦♦
St Peter's Road, Bournemouth, BH1 2LA
T: (01202) 554102
F: (01202) 246995
E: enquiries@rosedenecottagehotel.co.uk
I: www.rosedenecottagehotel.co.uk

St Winifrides Hotel
♦♦♦♦ SILVER AWARD
1 Studland Road, Alum Chine, Bournemouth, BH4 8HZ
T: (01202) 761829
E: infa@stwinifrideshotel.co.uk
I: www.stwinifrideshotel.co.uk

Shoreline Hotel ♦♦♦♦
7 Pinecliffe Avenue, Southbourne, Bournemouth BH6 3PY
T: (01202) 429654
F: (01202) 429654
E: timjonshorelinebb@amserve.net

Silver How Hotel ♦♦♦♦
5 West Cliff Gardens, Bournemouth, BH2 5HL
T: (01202) 551537
F: (01202) 551456
E: reservations@silverhowhotel.co.uk
I: www.silverhowhotel.co.uk

Southernhay Hotel ♦♦♦
42 Alum Chine Road, Westbourne, Bournemouth, BH4 8DX
T: (01202) 761251
F: (01202) 761251
E: enquiries@southernhayhotel.co.uk
I: www.southernhayhotel.co.uk

Trelawny Guest House ♦♦♦♦
34 Wellington Road, Bournemouth, BH8 8JW
T: (01202) 554015
F: (01202) 554015
E: trelawny34@talk21.com
I: trelawnyguesthouse.co.uk

The Twin Tops
♦♦♦♦ SILVER AWARD
33 Wheelers Lane, Bournemouth, BH11 9QQ
T: (01202) 570080
F: (01202) 570080
E: twintops@btinternet.com
I: www.thetwintops.com

The Ventura Hotel ♦♦♦♦
1 Herbert Road, Bournemouth, BH4 8HD
T: (01202) 761265
F: (01202) 757673
E: enquiries@venturahotel.co.uk
I: www.venturahotel.co.uk

The Vine Hotel ♦♦♦
22 Southern Road, Southbourne, Bournemouth BH6 3SR
T: (01202) 428309
F: (01202) 428309
E: thevinehotel@faxvia.net

West Cliff Sands Hotel ♦♦
9 Priory Road, Bournemouth, BH2 5DF
T: (01202) 557013
F: (01202) 557013
E: wst.clff-sds@virgin.net
I: www.westcliffsands.sageweb.co.uk

45 Wheelers Lane ♦♦♦
Bearwood, Bournemouth, BH11 9QQ
T: (01202) 572760

Whitley Court Hotel ♦♦♦
West Cliff Gardens, Bournemouth, BH2 5HL
T: (01202) 551302
F: (01202) 551302

Willowdene Hotel
♦♦♦♦ SILVER AWARD
43 Grand Avenue, Southbourne, Bournemouth BH6 3SY
T: (01202) 425370
F: (01202) 425 370
E: willowdenehotel@aol.com
I: www.willowdenehotel.co.uk

Winter Dene Hotel ♦♦♦♦
11 Durley Road South, West Cliff, Bournemouth, BH2 5JH
T: (01202) 554150
F: (01202) 555426
E: info@winterdenehotel.com
I: www.winterdenehotel.com

Wood Lodge Hotel ♦♦♦♦
10 Manor Road, East Cliff, Bournemouth, BH1 3EY
T: (01202) 290891
F: (01202) 290892

The Woodlands Hotel
Rating Applied For
28 Percy Road, Boscombe Manor, Bournemouth, BH5 1JG
T: (01202) 396499
F: (01202) 396499
E: thewoodlandshotel@tinyworld.co.uk

Woodside Private Hotel ♦♦♦♦
29 Southern Road, Southbourne, Bournemouth BH6 3SR
T: (01202) 427213
F: (01202) 417609
E: ann.jeff@btinternet.com
I: www.smoothhound.co.uk/hotels/woodsid3.html

Wrenwood Hotel ♦♦♦
11 Florence Road, Boscombe, Bournemouth BH5 1HH
T: (01202) 395086
F: (01202) 396511
E: bookings@wrenwood.co.uk
I: www.wrenwood.co.uk

Wychcote Hotel ♦♦♦♦
2 Somerville Road, West Cliff, Bournemouth, BH2 5LH
T: (01202) 557898
E: info@wychcote.co.uk
I: www.wychcote.co.uk

BRACKNELL
Berkshire

Elizabeth House ♦♦♦
Wokingham Road, Bracknell, RG42 1PB
T: (01344) 868480
F: (01344) 648453
E: rooms@elizabeth-house.freeserve.co.uk
I: www.elizabeth-house.freeserve.co.uk

22 Evedon ♦♦
Birch Hill, Bracknell, RG12 7NF
T: (01344) 450637

BRADWELL COMMON
Buckinghamshire

Central
Rating Applied For
25 Clapham Place, Bradwell Common, Milton Keynes MK13 8ES
T: (01908) 661248

BRANKSOME PARK
Dorset

Grovefield Manor Hotel
♦♦♦♦ SILVER AWARD
18 Pinewood Road, Branksome Park, Poole BH13 6JS
T: (01202) 766798

BRANSGORE
Hampshire

The Corner House ♦♦♦♦
Betsy Lane, Bransgore, Christchurch BH23 8AQ
T: (01425) 673201
E: aerominx35@aol.com

Wiltshire House ♦♦♦♦
West Road, Bransgore, Christchurch BH23 8BD
T: (01425) 672450
F: (01425) 672450
E: hooper@wiltshirehouse.freeserve.co.uk
I: www.smoothhound.co.uk/hotels/wiltshirehouse.html

BRAZIERS END
Buckinghamshire

Braziers Well
Rating Applied For
Oak Lane, Braziers End, Chesham HP5 2UL
T: (01494) 758956
E: jjhardie@compuserve.com

BRIGHSTONE
Isle of Wight

Chilton Farm ♦♦♦
Chilton Lane, Brighstone, Newport PO30 4DS
T: (01983) 740338
F: (01983) 741370
E: info@chiltonfarm.co.uk
I: www.chiltonfarm.co.uk

Moortown Cottage ♦♦♦
Moortown Lane, Brighstone, Newport PO30 4AN
T: (01983) 741428
E: denise_moortown@beeb.net

BRILL
Buckinghamshire

Laplands Farm ♦♦♦♦
Ludgershall Road, Brill, Aylesbury HP18 9TZ
T: (01844) 237888
F: (01844) 238870
E: enquiries@intents-marquees.co.uk
I: www.intents-marquees.co.uk

BRIZE NORTON
Oxfordshire

Anvil Croft ♦♦♦
64 Station Road, Brize Norton, Carterton OX18 3QA
T: (01993) 843655
F: (01993) 843655
E: judyleckyt@aol.com

Carpenters ♦♦♦
96 Station Road, Brize Norton, Carterton, OX18 3QA
T: (01993) 844222
E: BonnieHgh@aol.com

Foxbury Farmhouse ♦♦♦
Burford Road, Brize Norton, Carterton OX18 3NX
T: (01993) 844141
F: (01993) 844141
E: foxburyfarm@cs.com
I: foxburyfarm.co.uk

The Long Barn ♦♦♦♦
26 Carterton Road, Brize Norton, Carterton OX18 3LY
T: (01993) 843309
F: (01993) 843309
E: kgillians@the-long-barn.co.uk
I: www.the-long-barn.co.uk

The Willows ♦♦♦♦
Quarry Dene, Burford Road, Brize Norton, Carterton OX18 3NN
T: (01993) 842437
E: willowsbbbrize@aol.com

BROADSTONE
Dorset

Honey Lodge ♦♦♦♦
41 Dunyeats Road, Broadstone, BH18 8AB
T: (01202) 694247

Tarven ♦♦♦
Corfe Lodge Road, Broadstone, BH18 9NF
T: (01202) 694338
E: browning@tarvencorfe.fsnet.co.uk

Weston Cottage ♦♦♦♦
6 Macaulay Road, Broadstone, BH18 8AR
T: (01202) 699638
F: (01202) 699638
E: westoncot@aol.com

BROCKENHURST
Hampshire

Annerley
Rating Applied For
Waters Green, Brockenhurst, SO42 7RG
T: (01590) 624536
F: (01590) 624536

Briardale ♦♦♦
11 Noel Close, Brockenhurst, SO42 7RP
T: (01590) 623946
F: (01590) 623946
E: briardale@brockenhurst.fsbusiness.co.uk
I: www.brockenhurst.fsbusiness.co.uk

The Filly Inn ♦♦♦
Lymington Road, Setley, Brockenhurst, SO42 7UF
T: (01590) 623449
F: (01590) 623449
E: pub@fillyinn.co.uk
I: www.fillyinn.co.uk

Garlands Cottage ♦♦♦♦
2 Garlands Cottage, Lyndhurst Road, Brockenhurst, SO42 7RH
T: (01590) 623250
E: garlandscottage@hotmail.com

Goldenhayes ♦♦
9 Chestnut Road, Brockenhurst, SO42 7RF
T: (01590) 623743

Jacmar Cottage ♦♦♦
Mill Lane, Brockenhurst, SO42 7UA
T: (01590) 622019
E: jacmarcottage@aol.com

Mansfield ♦♦♦♦
Partridge Road, Brockenhurst, SO42 7RZ
T: (01590) 623877
E: chippie.lorri@btinternet.com

BUCKINGHAM
Buckinghamshire

5 Bristle Hill ♦♦♦
Buckingham, MK18 1EZ
T: (01280) 814426
F: (01280) 814426

The Britannia Inn
Rating Applied For
Gawcott Road, Buckingham, MK18 1DR
T: (01280) 822338
F: (01280) 822338

Churchwell ♦♦♦
23 Church Street, Buckingham, MK18 1BY
T: (01280) 815415
F: (01280) 815415
I: www.churchwell.co.uk

Folly Farm ♦♦♦
Padbury, Buckingham MK18 2HS
T: (01296) 712413
F: (01296) 714923

Huntsmill House B&B ♦♦♦♦
Huntsmill Farm, Shalstone, Buckingham MK18 5ND
T: (01280) 704852
F: (01280) 704852
E: fiona@huntsmill.com
I: www.huntsmill.com

Radclive Dairy Farm ♦♦♦♦
Radclive Road, Gawcott, Buckingham MK18 4AA
T: (01280) 813433
F: (01280) 813433

BURFORD
Oxfordshire

Barley Park
♦♦♦♦ SILVER AWARD
Shilton Road, Burford, Oxford OX18 4PD
T: (01993) 823573
F: (01993) 824220
E: barley_park@hotmail.com
I: www.burford-bed-and-breakfast.co.uk

Burford House Hotel
♦♦♦♦♦ GOLD AWARD
99 High Street, Burford, Oxford OX18 4QA
T: (01993) 823151
F: (01993) 823240
E: stay@burfordhouse.co.uk
I: www.burfordhouse.co.uk

The Fox Inn ♦♦♦
Great Barrington, Burford, Oxford OX18 4TB
T: (01451) 844385

The Highway ♦♦♦
117 High Street, Burford, Oxford OX18 4RG
T: (01993) 822136
F: (01993) 824740
E: rbx20@dial.pipex.com
I: www.oxlink.co.uk/burford

Jonathan's at The Angel
♦♦♦♦♦ GOLD AWARD
14 Witney Street, Burford, Oxford OX18 4SN
T: (01993) 822714
F: (01993) 822069
E: jo@theangel-uk.com
I: www.theangel-uk.com

Manor Lodge
♦♦♦♦ SILVER AWARD
Shilton, Burford, Oxford OX18 4AS
T: (01993) 841444
F: (01993) 841446
E: enquiries@manorlodgebnb.co.uk
I: www.manorlodgebnb.co.uk

Merryfield ♦♦♦
High Street, Fifield, Oxford OX7 6HL
T: (01993) 830517
E: jpmgtd@freeuk.com
I: www.merryfieldbandb.co.uk

The Old Bell Foundry ♦♦♦♦
45 Witney Street, Burford, Oxford OX18 4RX
T: (01993) 822234
E: barguss@ukgateway.net

Potters Hill Farm ♦♦♦
Leafield, Burford, Oxford OX8 5QB
T: (01993) 878018
F: (01993) 878018
E: k.stanley@virgin.net
I: www.country-accom.co.uk/potters-hill-farm

St Winnow ♦♦♦
160 The Hill, Burford, Oxford OX18 4QY
T: (01993) 823843
E: b&b@stwinnow.com
I: www.stwinnow.com

Tudor Cottage ♦♦♦
40 Witney Street, Burford, Oxford OX18 4SN
T: (01993) 823251
F: (01993) 823251

Willow Cottage ♦♦♦♦
Shilton, Burford, Oxford OX18 4AB
T: (01993) 842456
F: (01993) 842456
I: www.smoothhound.co.uk/hotels/willowcot.html

BURLEY
Hampshire

Bay Tree House ♦♦♦
1 Clough Lane, Burley, Ringwood BH24 4AE
T: (01425) 403215
F: (01425) 403215
E: Baytreehousebandb@burleyhants.freeserve.co.uk

Burbush Farm
♦♦♦♦♦ GOLD AWARD
Pound Lane, Burley, Ringwood BH24 4EF
T: (01425) 403238
F: (01425) 403238
I: www.burbush-farm.co.uk

Forest Teahouse ♦♦♦
Forest Cottage, Pound Lane, Burley, Ringwood BH24 4ED
T: (01425) 402305

Great Wells House
♦♦♦♦♦ GOLD AWARD
Beechwood Lane, Burley, Ringwood BH24 4AS
T: (01425) 402302
F: (01425) 402302
E: chrisstewart@compuserve.com

Holmans
♦♦♦♦ SILVER AWARD
Bisterne Close, Burley, Ringwood BH24 4AZ
T: (01425) 402307
F: (01425) 402307

Little Deeracres ♦♦♦
Bisterne Close, Burley, Ringwood BH24 4BA
T: (01425) 402477
F: (01425) 402477

The White Buck Inn
Rating Applied For
Bisterne Close, Burley, Ringwood BH24 4AT
T: (01425) 402264

BUSCOT WICK
Oxfordshire

Weston Farm ♦♦♦♦
Buscot Wick, Faringdon SN7 8DJ
T: (01367) 252222
F: (01367) 252230
E: westonfarmjean@amserve.net
I: www.country-accom.co.uk/weston-farm

CADMORE END
Buckinghamshire

South Fields ♦♦♦
Cadmore End, High Wycombe HP14 3PJ
T: (01494) 881976
F: (01494) 883765
E: crichtons@crichtonville.freeserve.co.uk
I: www.crichtonville.freeserve.co.uk

CADNAM
Hampshire

Kingsbridge House ♦♦♦
Southampton Road, Cadnam, Southampton SO40 2NH
T: (023) 8081 1161

CARISBROOKE
Isle of Wight

Alvington Manor Farm ♦♦♦
Carisbrooke, Newport PO30 5SP
T: (01983) 523463
F: (01983) 523463

CASHMOOR
Dorset

Cashmoor House ♦♦♦
Cashmoor, Blandford Forum DT11 8DN
T: (01725) 552339
F: (01725) 552219
E: spencer.jones@ukonline.co.uk
I: www.cashmoorhouse.cjb.net

CASSINGTON
Oxfordshire

St Margaret's Lodge ♦♦♦
The Green, Cassington, Oxford OX8 1DN
T: (01865) 880361
F: (01865) 731314

CASTLETHORPE
Buckinghamshire

Balney Grounds
♦♦♦♦ SILVER AWARD
Home Farm, Hanslope Road, Castlethorpe, Milton Keynes MK19 7HD
T: (01908) 510208
F: (01908) 516119
E: mary.stacey@tesco.net
I: www.lets-stay-mk.co.uk

CHALE
Isle of Wight

Little Atherfield Farm ♦♦♦♦
Chale, Ventnor PO38 2LQ
T: (01983) 551363
F: (01983) 551033
E: david's.farm@virgin.net

CHALFONT ST GILES
Buckinghamshire

Gorelands Corner ♦♦♦♦
Gorelands Lane, Chalfont St Giles, HP8 4HQ
T: (01494) 872689
F: (01494) 872689
E: bickfordcsg@onetel.net.uk

Holmdale ♦♦♦♦
Cokes Lane, Little Chalfont, Amersham, HP8 4TX
T: (01494) 762527
F: (01494) 764701
E: judy@holmdalebb.freeserve.co.uk
I: www.smoothhand.co.uk/hotels/holmdale.html

The White Hart Inn ♦♦♦♦
Three Households, Chalfont St Giles, HP8 4LP
T: (01494) 872441
F: (01494) 876375
E: whitehartinn@supanet.com

CHALFONT ST PETER
Buckinghamshire

Whitewebbs ♦♦♦♦
Grange Road, Off Lower Road, Chalfont St Peter, Gerrards Cross SL9 9AQ
T: (01753) 884105
F: (01753) 884105

CHALGROVE
Oxfordshire

Cornerstones ♦♦♦
1 Cromwell Close, Chalgrove, Oxford OX44 7SE
T: (01865) 890298
F: (01865) 890298
E: md.cornerstones@amserve.com

CHANDLERS FORD
Hampshire

Blackbird Hill ♦♦♦
24 Ashbridge Rise, Chandlers Ford, Eastleigh SO53 1SA
T: (023) 8026 0398
E: dotsid@onetel.net.uk

Landfall ♦♦♦
133 Bournemouth Road, Chandlers Ford, Eastleigh SO53 3HA
T: (023) 8025 4801
F: (023) 8025 4801

Monks House
♦♦♦♦♦ GOLD AWARD
111 Hocombe Road, Chandlers Ford, Eastleigh SO53 5QD
T: (023) 8027 5986
F: (023) 8027 1505
E: info@monkshouse.com
I: www.monkshouse.com

Thornbury ♦♦♦♦
243 Winchester Road, Chandlers Ford, Eastleigh SO53 2DX
T: (023) 8026 0703

CHARLBURY
Oxfordshire

Banbury Hill Farm ♦♦♦♦
Enstone Road, Charlbury, Oxford OX7 3JH
T: (01608) 810314
F: (01608) 811891
E: angelawiddows@gfwiddows.f9.co.uk
I: www.charlburyoxfordaccom.co.uk

Tanyer's House ♦♦♦♦
Hundley Way, Charlbury, Oxford OX7 3QX
T: (01608) 811711
E: jrose@charlburybb.co.uk
I: www.charlburybb.co.uk

CHARLTON
Hampshire

Acer ♦♦♦
16 Foxcotte Close, Charlton, Andover SP10 4AS
T: (01264) 363286

CHARLTON MARSHALL
Dorset

Keston House
♦♦♦♦ SILVER AWARD
314 Bournemouth Road, Charlton Marshall, Blandford Forum DT11 9NQ
T: (01258) 451973
F: (01258) 451973
E: bandb@kestonhouse.co.uk
I: www.kestonhouse.co.uk

CHARLTON-ON-OTMOOR
Oxfordshire

Home Farm ♦♦♦
Mansmoor Lane, Charlton-on-Otmoor, Kidlington OX5 2US
T: (01865) 331267
F: (01865) 331267

CHECKENDON
Oxfordshire

Larchdown Farm
♦♦♦♦ SILVER AWARD
Whitehall Lane, Checkendon, Reading RG8 0TT
T: (01491) 682282
F: (01491) 682282
E: larchdown@onetel.net.uk

CHERITON
Hampshire

Brandy Lea
Rating Applied For
Cheriton, Alresford SO24 0QQ
T: (01962) 771534

Old Kennetts Cottage ♦♦♦♦
Cheriton, Alresford SO24 0PX
T: (01962) 771863

CHESHAM
Buckinghamshire

49 Lowndes Avenue ♦♦
Chesham, HP5 2HH
T: (01494) 792647

May Tree House Bed and Breakfast ♦♦♦♦
32 Hampden Avenue, Chesham, HP5 2HL
T: (01494) 784019
F: (01494) 776896

Rose Cottage ♦♦♦
176 Bois Moor Road, Chesham, HP5 4SS
T: (01494) 794433
F: (01494) 794444

CHESTERTON
Oxfordshire

Larchmont ♦♦♦
Alchester Road, Chesterton, Bicester OX6 8UN
T: (01869) 245033
F: (01869) 245033

CHIEVELEY
Berkshire

19 Heathfields ♦♦♦
Chieveley, Newbury RG20 8TW
T: (01635) 248179
F: (01635) 248799
E: ingandco@aol.com

CHILBOLTON
Hampshire

Sycamores ♦♦♦
Meadow View, Chilbolton, Stockbridge SO20 6AZ
T: (01264) 860380
E: maureen@sycamoresbb.freeserve.co.uk
I: www.sycamoresbb.freeserve.co.uk/sycamores2

CHILCOMB
Hampshire

Complyns ♦♦♦♦
Chilcomb, Winchester SO21 1HT
T: (01962) 861600

CHILDREY
Oxfordshire

Ridgeway House
♦♦♦♦ SILVER AWARD
West Street, Childrey, Wantage OX12 9UL
T: (01235) 751538
E: robertsfamily@compuserve.com

CHIPPING NORTON
Oxfordshire

The Bell Inn ♦♦
56 West Street, Chipping Norton, OX7 5ER
T: (01608) 642521
F: 07000 783864

Kings Arms Hotel ♦♦♦
18 West Street, Chipping Norton, OX7 5AA
T: (01608) 642668
F: (01608) 646673

Lower Park Farm
♦♦♦♦ SILVER AWARD
Great Tew, Oxford OX7 4DE
T: (01608) 683170
F: (01608) 683859
E: lowerparkfarm@talk21.com
I: members.lycos.co.uk/lowerparkfarm/

The Old Vicarage ♦♦♦
5 Church Street, Chipping Norton, OX7 5NT
T: (01608) 641562
E: anthony.ross@virgin.net

Southcombe Lodge Guest House ♦♦♦
Southcombe, Chipping Norton OX7 5QH
T: (01608) 643068
F: (01608) 642948
E: georgefinlysouthcombelodge@tinyworld.co.uk

CHOLDERTON
Hampshire

Parkhouse Motel ♦♦♦♦
Cholderton, Salisbury SP4 0EG
T: (01980) 629256
F: (01980) 629256

CHOLSEY
Oxfordshire

The Well Cottage ♦♦♦
Caps Lane, Cholsey, Wallingford OX10 9HQ
T: (01491) 651959
F: (01491) 651675
E: joanna@thewellcottage.com
I: www.thewellcottage.co.uk

CHRISTCHURCH
Dorset

The Beech Tree ♦♦♦♦
2 Stuart Road, Highcliffe, BH23 5JS
T: (01425) 272038

Belvedere Guest House ♦♦
3 Twynham Avenue, Christchurch, BH23 1QU
T: (01202) 485978
F: (01202) 485978
E: belvedere@eurolink.ltd.net

Beverly Glen Guest House ♦♦♦♦
1 Stuart Road, Highcliffe, BH23 5JS
T: (01425) 273811

Cafe 39 – The Pines Hotel ♦♦♦
39 Mudeford, Christchurch, BH23 3NQ
T: (01202) 475121
F: (01202) 487666
E: pineshotelcafe39@ic24.net
I: www.mudeford.com

Druid House ♦♦♦♦♦
26 Sopers Lane, Christchurch, BH23 1JE
T: (01202) 485615
F: (01202) 473484
E: reservations@druid-house.co.uk
I: www.druid-house.co.uk

Salmons Reach Guest House ♦♦♦
28 Stanpit, Christchurch, BH23 3LZ
T: (01202) 477315
F: (01202) 477315

Seawards ♦♦♦♦
13 Avon Run Close, Friars Cliff, Christchurch, BH23 4DT
T: (01425) 273188

Stour Lodge Guest House ♦♦♦
54 Stour Road, Christchurch, BH23 1LW
T: (01202) 486902
E: kcat@stourlodge.fsnet.co.uk

The White House ♦♦♦♦
428 Lymington Road, Highcliffe, BH23 5HF
T: (01425) 271279
F: (01425) 276900
E: thewhitehouse@themail.co.uk
I: www.thewhite-house.co.uk

CHURCHILL
Oxfordshire

The Forge ♦♦♦♦
Churchill, Oxford OX7 6NJ
T: (01608) 658173
F: (01608) 659262
E: jon@theforge.co.uk
I: www.theforge.co.uk

CLANVILLE
Hampshire

Flinty Cottage ♦♦♦♦
Clanville, Andover SP11 9HZ
T: (01264) 773307

COLD ASH
Berkshire

2 Woodside ♦♦♦♦
Cold Ash, Thatcham RG18 9JF
T: (01635) 860028
E: anita.rhiggs@which.net

COLE HENLEY
Hampshire

Long Barrow House ♦♦♦♦
Cole Henley, Whitchurch, RG28 7QJ
T: (01256) 895980
E: info@longbarrowhouse.co.uk
I: www.longbarrowhouse.co.uk

COLEHILL
Dorset

Long Lane Farmhouse ♦♦♦♦
Long Lane, Colehill, Wimborne Minster BH21 7AQ
T: (01202) 887829
E: paddysmyth@aol.com
I: www.eastdorsetdc.gov.uk/tourism

COLWELL BAY
Isle of Wight

Chine Cottage ♦♦♦
Colwell Chine Road, Colwell Bay, PO40 9NP
T: (01983) 752808
E: enq1999@hotmail.com

Rockstone Cottage ♦♦♦♦ SILVER AWARD
Colwell Chine Road, Colwell Bay, PO40 9NR
T: (01983) 753723
F: (01983) 753721
E: enquiries@rockstonecottage.co.uk
I: www.rockstonecottage.co.uk

Shorefield House ♦♦♦♦ SILVER AWARD
Madeira Lane, Colwell Bay, PO40 9SP
T: (01983) 752232
E: shorefield.house@btinternet.com

COMPTON
Hampshire

Manor House ♦♦
Place Lane, Compton, Winchester SO21 2BA
T: (01962) 712162

COMPTON ABBAS
Dorset

The Old Forge ♦♦♦
Fanners Yard, Compton Abbas, Shaftesbury SP7 0NQ
T: (01747) 811881
F: (01747) 811881
E: theoldforge@hotmail.com
I: www.smoothhound.co.uk/

COOKHAM
Berkshire

Wylie Cottage ♦♦♦
School Lane, Cookham, Maidenhead SL6 9QJ
T: (01628) 520106
F: (01628) 520106
E: crowegc@btopenworld.com

COOMBE KEYNES
Dorset

Highfield ♦♦♦
Coombe Keynes, Wareham BH20 5PS
T: (01929) 463208
F: (01929) 463208
E: jmitchell@coombekeynes.freeserve.co.uk
I: www.highfield-bb.co.uk

CORFE CASTLE
Dorset

Bankes Hotel ♦♦♦
East Street, Corfe Castle, Wareham BH20 5ED
T: (01929) 480206
F: (01929) 480186
E: bankescorfe@aol.com
I: www.dorset-hotel.co.uk

Bradle Farmhouse ♦♦♦♦ SILVER AWARD
Bradle Farm, Church Knowle, Wareham BH20 5NU
T: (01929) 480712
F: (01929) 481144
E: bradkefarmhouse@farmersweekly.net
I: www.smoothhound.co.uk/hotels/bradle.html

Knitson Old Farmhouse Rating Applied For
Corfe Castle, Wareham BH20 5JB
T: (01929) 422836
E: mark@knitson.freeserve.co.uk

COWES
Isle of Wight

Comforts Gate ♦♦
108 Pallance Road, Northwood, Cowes, PO31 8LS
T: (01983) 290342
F: (01983) 297810

Halcyone Villa ♦♦♦
Grove Road, Cowes, PO31 7JP
T: (01983) 291334
E: sandra@halcyone.freeserve.co.uk
I: www.halcyonevilla.freeuk.com

CRANBORNE
Dorset

Chaseborough Farm ♦♦♦
Gotham, Cranborne, Wimborne Minster BH21 5QY
T: (01202) 813166
E: jim@ghinn.fsnet.co.uk

The Fleur de Lys ♦♦♦
5 Wimborne Street, Cranborne, Wimborne Minster BH21 5PP
T: (01725) 517282
F: (01725) 517945
E: fleurdelys@btinternet.com
I: www.fleurdelys-cranborne.co.uk

La Fosse at Cranborne ♦♦♦♦
London House, The Square, Cranborne, Wimborne Minster BH21 5PR
T: (01725) 517604
F: (01725) 517778
E: mac@la-fosse.com
I: www.la-fosse.com

CROPREDY
Oxfordshire

Poplars Farm ♦♦♦♦ SILVER AWARD
Claydon Road, Cropredy, Banbury OX17 1JP
T: (01295) 750561
E: colkathpoplars@supanet.com

DAMERHAM
Hampshire

The Compasses Inn ♦♦♦
Damerham, Fordingbridge SP6 3HQ
T: (01725) 518231
F: (01725) 518880

DATCHET
Berkshire

Chaseside ♦♦♦
71 The Myrke, Datchet, Slough SL3 9AB
T: (01753) 574354

DEDDINGTON
Oxfordshire

Hill Barn ♦♦
Milton Gated Road, Deddington, Banbury OX15 0TS
T: (01869) 338631
F: (01869) 338631
E: hillbarn-bb@supanet.com

Stonecrop Guest House ♦♦
Hempton Road, Deddington, Banbury OX15 0QH
T: (01869) 338335
F: (01869) 338505
E: info@stonecropguesthouse.co.uk
I: www.stonecropguesthouse.co.uk

The Unicorn Inn ♦♦♦
Market Place, Deddington, Banbury OX15 0SE
T: (01869) 338838
F: (01869) 338592
E: unicorninn@deddigton.fsbusiness.co.uk

DENMEAD
Hampshire

Bellchamber House ♦♦♦
80 Anmore Road, Denmead, Waterlooville PO7 6NT
T: (023) 9236 0978

DIBDEN PURLIEU
Hampshire

Ashdene Guest House ♦♦♦
Beaulieu Road, Dibden Purlieu, Southampton SO45 4PT
T: (023) 8084 6073
F: (023) 8087 9146
I: www.ashdenehouse.co.uk

DINTON
Buckinghamshire

Dinton Cottage ♦♦♦
Dinton, Aylesbury HP17 8UH
T: (01296) 748270
F: (01296) 748585
E: scribe@blankpage.freeserve.co.uk
I: www.amicitiam.com

Perryfield ♦♦♦♦
New Road, Dinton, Aylesbury HP17 8UT
T: (01296) 748265
F: (01296) 747765
E: caroline@perryfield.co.uk
I: www.perryfield.co.uk

DUMMER
Hampshire

Oakdown Farm Bungalow ♦♦♦
Oakdown Farm, Dummer, Basingstoke RG23 7LR
T: (01256) 397218

EAST COWES
Hampshire

Crossways House ♦♦♦
Crossways Road, East Cowes, PO32 6LJ
T: (01983) 298282
F: (01983) 298282

The Doghouse ♦♦♦♦
Crossways Road, East Cowes, PO32 6LJ
T: (01983) 293677
E: timindoghouse@beeb.net

EAST END
Oxfordshire

The Leather Bottel Guest House ♦♦♦
East End, North Leigh, Witney OX29 6PX
T: (01993) 882174
F: (01993) 882174

EAST HENDRED
Oxfordshire

Cowdrays ♦♦♦
Cat Street, East Hendred, Wantage OX12 8JT
T: (01235) 833313
E: cowdrays@virgin.net

EAST ILSLEY
Berkshire

The Star Inn ♦♦♦♦
High Street, East Ilsley, Newbury RG20 7LE
T: (01635) 281215
F: (01635) 281107

EAST MEON
Hampshire

Drayton Cottage
♦♦♦♦ SILVER AWARD
East Meon, Petersfield GU32 1PW
T: (01730) 823472
E: draytoncottage@btinternet.com
I: www.SmoothHound.co.uk/hotels/drayton.html

Dunvegan Cottage ♦♦♦♦
Frogmore Lane, East Meon, Petersfield GU32 1QJ
T: (01730) 823213
F: (01730) 823858
E: dunvegan@btinternet.com

EAST STOUR
Dorset

The Glen B & B ♦♦♦
Fern Hill, East Stour, Gillingham SP8 5ND
T: (01747) 839819
F: 08701 371170
E: b&b@theglen-dorset.co.uk
I: www.theglen-dorset.co.uk

EAST WELLOW
Hampshire

Country Views B & B ♦♦♦♦
Willowbend, Dunwood Hill, Shootash, Romsey SO51 6FD
T: (01794) 514735
F: (01794) 521867
E: sue@countryviewsbandb.freeserve.co.uk
I: www.countryviewsbandb.freeserve.co.uk

EASTLEIGH
Hampshire

Carinya B & B ♦♦♦
38 Sovereign Way, Boyatt Wood, Eastleigh, SO50 4SA
T: (023) 8061 3128
F: (023) 8061 3128

Endeavour Guest House ♦♦♦♦
40 Allbrook Hill, Allbrook, Eastleigh, SO50 4LY
T: (023) 8061 3400
F: (023) 8061 4486
E: dcschauffeurs@btconnect.com
I: www.directchauffeurservices&taxis

EDGCOTT
Buckinghamshire

Perry Manor Farm ♦♦
Buckingham Road, Edgcott, Aylesbury HP18 0TR
T: (01296) 770257

EMBERTON
Buckinghamshire

Ekeney House ♦♦♦
Wood Farm, Emberton, Olney MK46 5JH
T: (01234) 711133
F: (01234) 711133

EMSWORTH
Hampshire

Apple Blossom ♦♦♦
19A Bosmere Gardens, Emsworth, PO10 7NP
T: (01243) 372201
E: neilandann@lanchbury.co.uk

Bunbury Lodge ♦♦♦♦
10 West Road, Emsworth, PO10 4JT
T: (01243) 432030
F: (01243) 432030
E: Bunbury.Lodge@breathemail.net
I: www.guestaccom.co.uk

The Merry Hall Hotel ♦♦♦
73 Horndean Road, Emsworth, PO10 7PU
T: (01243) 431377
F: (01243) 431411

EPWELL
Oxfordshire

Yarnhill Farm ♦♦♦
Epwell, Banbury OX15 6JA
T: (01295) 780250
F: (01295) 780250

ETON
Berkshire

The Crown & Cushion Inn ♦♦
84 High Street, Eton, Windsor SL4 6AF
T: (01753) 861531
E: sylvieglinister@yahoo.com

EWELME
Oxfordshire

Mays Farm ♦♦♦♦
Ewelme, Oxford OX10 6QF
T: (01491) 641294
F: (01491) 641697
E: passmore@farmersweekly.net

EYNSHAM
Oxfordshire

Grange House ♦♦♦
Station Road, Eynsham, Oxford OX29 4HX
T: (01865) 880326
F: (01865) 880326
E: bookings@grangehouse.co.uk
I: www.grangehouse.co.uk

FAREHAM
Hampshire

Avenue House Hotel ♦♦♦
22 The Avenue, Fareham, PO14 1NS
T: (01329) 232175
F: (01329) 232196

Bridge House ♦♦♦
1 Waterside Gardens, Wallington, Fareham, PO16 8SD
T: (01329) 287775
F: (01329) 287775
E: maryhb@fish.co.uk

Catisfield Cottage Guest House ♦♦
1 Catisfield Lane, Catisfield, Fareham, PO15 5NW
T: (01329) 843301
F: (01329) 841652

Seven Sevens Guest House ♦♦♦
56 Hill Head Road, Hill Head, PO14 3JL
T: (01329) 662408

Springfield Hotel ♦♦♦♦
67 The Avenue, Fareham, PO14 1PE
T: (01329) 828325

FARINGDON
Oxfordshire

Ashen Copse Farm ♦♦♦
Coleshill, Faringdon, SN6 7PU
T: (01367) 240175
F: (01367) 241418
E: pat@hodd.demon.co.uk
I: www.hodd.demon.co.uk

Gallery Cottage ♦♦♦
21 London Street, Faringdon, SN7 7AG
T: (01367) 244853

Portwell House Hotel ♦♦♦
Market Place, Faringdon, SN7 7HU
T: (01367) 240197
F: (01367) 244330
E: enquiries@portwellhouse.com

The Trout At Tadpole Bridge ♦♦♦♦
Buckland Marsh, Faringdon, SN7 8RF
T: (01367) 870382

FARNBOROUGH
Hampshire

Colebrook Guest House ♦♦♦
56 Netley Street, Farnborough, GU14 6AT
T: (01252) 542269
F: (01252) 542269
E: derekbclark@ukonline.co.uk

The Oak Tree Guest House ♦♦♦
112 Farnborough Road, Farnborough, GU14 6TN
T: (01252) 545491
F: (01252) 545491

The White Residence Town House Hotel
♦♦♦♦ GOLD AWARD
Farnborough Park, 76 Avenue Road, Farnborough, GU14 7BG
T: (01252) 375510
F: (01252) 655567
E: info@countyapartments.com
I: www.whiteresidence.co.uk

FAWLEY
Hampshire

Walcot House ♦♦♦
Blackfield Road, Fawley, Southampton SO45 1ED
T: (023) 8089 1344

FERNDOWN
Dorset

Woodridings ♦♦♦♦
73 Beaufoys Avenue, Ferndown, BH22 9RN
T: (01202) 876729

FIFEHEAD ST QUINTON
Dorset

Lower Fifehead Farm ♦♦♦♦
Fifehead St Quinton, Sturminster Newton DT10 2AP
T: (01258) 817335
F: (01258) 817335

FIFIELD
Berkshire

Victoria Cottage
Rating Applied For
2 Victoria Cottages, Fififield Road, Fifield, Maidenhead SL6 2NZ
T: (01628) 623564
F: (01628) 623564

FILKINS
Oxfordshire

The Five Alls ♦♦♦
Filkins, Lechlade GL7 3JQ
T: (01367) 860306
F: (01367) 860776

FLEET
Hampshire

Copperfield ♦♦♦
16 Glen Road, Fleet, GU13 9QR
T: (01252) 616140

FORDINGBRIDGE
Hampshire

The Augustus John ♦♦♦♦
116 Station Road, Fordingbridge, SP6 1DG
T: (01425) 652098
E: peter@augustusjohn.com
I: www.augustusjohn.com

Broomy ♦♦♦♦
Ogdens, Fordingbridge SP6 2PY
T: (01425) 653264

The Crown Inn ♦♦♦
62 High Street, Fordingbridge, SP6 1AX
T: (01425) 652552
F: (01425) 655752
E: candmbell@ukgateway.net

Drummond House ♦♦♦♦
Bowerwood Road, Fordingbridge, SP6 1BL
T: (01425) 653165
E: drumbb@btinternet.com
I: www.newforest.demon.co.uk/drummond.htm

Hillbury ♦♦♦
2 Fir Tree Hill, Camel Green Road, Alderholt, Fordingbridge SP6 3AY
T: (01425) 652582
F: (01425) 657587
I: www.newforest.demon.co.uk/hillbury.htm

Merrimead
♦♦♦♦ SILVER AWARD
12 Station Road, Alderholt, Fordingbridge SP6 3RB
T: (01425) 657544
F: (01425) 650400
E: merrimead@ic24.net
I: www.newforest.demon.co.uk/merrimead.htm

Noarlunga ♦♦♦♦
16 Broomfield Drive, Alderholt, Fordingbridge SP6 3HY
T: (01425) 650491

Primrose Cottage ♦♦♦♦
Newgrounds, Godshill, Fordingbridge SP6 2LJ
T: (01425) 650447
F: (01425) 650447
E: ann@blake98.freeserve.co.uk

The Ship Inn ♦♦♦
68 High Streeet, Fordingbridge, SP6 1AX
T: (01425) 651820
F: (01425) 651825
E: shipinn@supanet.com

The Three Lions
♦♦♦♦♦ GOLD AWARD
Stuckton, Fordingbridge SP6 2HF
T: (01425) 652489
F: (01425) 656144
E: the3lions@btinternet.com

FREELAND
Oxfordshire

Malvern Villas Bed & Breakfast ♦♦♦
1 Malvern Villas, Witney Road, Freeland, Oxford OX29 8HG
T: (01993) 880019
E: lburge@malvernvillas.fsnet.co.uk
I: www.malvernvillas.co.uk

FRESHWATER
Isle of Wight

Brookside Forge Hotel ♦♦♦
Brookside Road, Freshwater, PO40 9ER
T: (01983) 754644

Cherry Trees ♦♦♦♦
29 School Green Road, Freshwater, PO40 9AW
T: (01983) 756000
F: (01983) 752681
E: cherrytrees@cuemedianet.com
I: www.islandbreaks.co.uk/cherrytrees

Field House Bed & Breakfast
♦♦♦♦ GOLD AWARD
Pound Green, Freshwater, PO40 9HG
T: (01983) 754190
E: alisson.smith@virgin.net
I: www.fieldhouseiow.co.uk

Royal Standard Hotel ♦♦♦
School Green Road, Freshwater, PO40 9AJ
T: (01983) 753227
E: sue@stephenson84.freeserve.co.uk

Seahorses ♦♦♦♦
Victoria Road, Freshwater, PO40 9PP
T: (01983) 752574
F: (01983) 752574
E: lanterncom@aol.com

Traidcraft ♦♦
119 School Green Road, Freshwater, PO40 9AZ
T: (01983) 752451

FRESHWATER BAY
Isle of Wight

Wighthaven ♦♦♦♦
Afton Road, Freshwater Bay, PO40 9TT
T: (01983) 753184
E: wighthaven@btinternet.com

FRITHAM
Hampshire

Fritham Farm ♦♦♦♦
Fritham, Lyndhurst SO43 7HH
T: (023) 8081 2333
F: (023) 8081 2333
E: frithamfarm@supanet.com

FROGHAM
Hampshire

Wayside Bed & Breakfast
♦♦♦♦ SILVER AWARD
Wayside, Frogham, Fordingbridge SP6 2HN
T: (01425) 650372
F: (01425) 653648
E: mark@rosanegra.fsnet.co.uk

FROXFIELD GREEN
Hampshire

The Trooper Inn and Hotel ♦♦♦♦
Alton Road, Froxfield Green, Petersfield GU32 1BD
T: (01730) 827293
F: (01730) 827103
E: troopersec@aol.com
I: www.trooperinn.com

GARSINGTON
Oxfordshire

Hill Copse Cottage ♦♦♦
Wheatley Road, Garsington, Oxford OX44 9DT
T: (01865) 361478
F: (01865) 361478

GATCOMBE
Isle of Wight

Little Gatcombe Farm ♦♦♦♦
New Barn Lane, Gatcombe, Newport PO30 3EQ
T: (01983) 721580
E: littlegatcombefarm@gatcombelow.fsnet.co.ukl
I: www.littlegatcombefarm.co.uk

GERRARDS CROSS
Buckinghamshire

15 Howards Wood Drive ♦♦♦
Gerrards Cross, SL9 7HR
T: (01753) 884911
F: (01753) 884911
E: j.crosby@ntlworld.com

GIFFARD PARK
Buckinghamshire

Giffard House ♦♦♦
10 Broadway Avenue, Giffard Park, Milton Keynes MK14 5QF
T: (01908) 618868
F: (01908) 618868
E: lizziemm@btinternet.com

GILLINGHAM
Dorset

Ansty Rose Cottage
Rating Applied For
Wyke Road, Gillingham, SP8 4NH
T: (01747) 825379
E: kasworks@pottery82.freeserve.co.uk

Bugley Court Farm
Rating Applied For
Gillingham, SP8 5RA
T: (01747) 823242

GODSHILL
Hampshire

Croft Cottage ♦♦♦
Southampton Road, Godshill, Fordingbridge SP6 2LE
T: (01425) 657955
I: www.croftcottagenewforest.co.uk

Vennards Cottage ♦♦♦
Newgrounds, Godshill, Fordingbridge SP6 2LJ
T: (01425) 652644
E: gillian.bridgeman@virgin.net

GORING
Oxfordshire

The John Barleycorn ♦
Manor Road, Goring, Reading RG8 9DP
T: (01491) 872509

Miller of Mansfield ♦♦♦
High Street, Goring, Reading RG8 9AW
T: (01491) 872829
F: (01491) 874200
I: www.millerofmansfield.co.uk

GOSPORT
Hampshire

West Wind Guest House ♦♦♦♦
197 Portsmouth Road, Lee on the Solent, PO13 9AA
T: (023) 9255 2550
F: (023) 9255 4657
E: maggie@west-wind.co.uk
I: www.west-wind.co.uk

GRATELEY
Hampshire

Gunville House
♦♦♦♦ SILVER AWARD
Grateley, Andover SP11 8JQ
T: (01264) 889206
F: (01264) 889060
E: pct@onetel.net.uk
I: www.gunvillehouse.co.uk

GREAT KINGSHILL
Buckinghamshire

Hatches Farm ♦♦
Hatches Lane, Great Kingshill, High Wycombe HP15 6DS
T: (01494) 713125
F: (01494) 714666

GREAT MISSENDEN
Buckinghamshire

Margaret Cottage
Rating Applied For
122 High Street, Great Missenden, HP16 OB6
T: (01494) 868105

GURNARD
Isle of Wight

Hillbrow Private Hotel ♦♦♦♦
Tuttons Hill, Gurnard, Cowes PO31 8JA
T: (01983) 297240
F: (01983) 297240

The Woodvale Hotel ♦♦♦♦
1 Princes Esplanade, Gurnard, Cowes PO31 8LE
T: (01983) 292037
F: (01983) 292037
E: woodvaleparkin@aol.com
I: www.the-woodvale.co.uk

HADDENHAM
Buckinghamshire

The Majors ♦♦♦♦♦
19-21 Townside, Haddenham, Aylesbury HP17 8BQ
T: (01844) 292654
F: (01844) 299050

HAMBLE
Hampshire

Farthings Bed & Breakfast
♦♦♦♦ SILVER AWARD
Farthings, School Lane, Hamble, Southampton SO31 4JD
T: (023) 8045 2009
F: (023) 8045 2613
E: strakers@hamble2.fsnet.co.uk
I: www.farthingsinhamble.co.uk

HAMBLEDON
Hampshire

Cams ♦♦♦
Hambledon, Waterlooville PO7 4SP
T: (023) 9263 2865
F: (023) 9263 2691

HAMWORTHY
Dorset

Harbourside Guest House ♦♦♦
195 Blandford Road, Hamworthy, Poole BH15 4AX
T: (01202) 673053
F: (01202) 673053

Holes Bay B & B ♦♦♦
365 Blandford Road, Hamworthy, Poole BH15 4JL
T: (01202) 672069

Individual Touristik Poole ♦♦♦♦
53 Branksea Avenue, Hamworthy, Poole BH15 4DP
T: (01202) 673419
F: (01202) 667260
E: johnrenate@lineone.net

Seashells ♦♦♦
4 Lake Road, Hamworthy, Poole BH15 4LH
T: (01202) 671921
F: (01202) 671921

HANSLOPE
Buckinghamshire

Cuckoo Hill Farm ♦♦
Hanslope, Milton Keynes MK19 7HQ
T: (01908) 510748
F: (01908) 511669

Woad Farm ♦♦♦
Tathall End, Hanslope, Milton Keynes MK19 7NE
T: (01908) 510985
F: (01908) 510985
E: mail@sarahstacey.freeserve.co.uk

HAVANT
Hampshire

High Towers ♦♦♦
14 Portsdown Hill Road, Bedhampton, Havant PO9 3JY
T: (023) 9247 1748

HAYLING ISLAND
Hampshire

Ann's Cottage ♦♦♦
45 St Andrews Road, Hayling Island, PO11 9JN
T: (023) 9246 7048
E: ann.jay@virgin.net

16 Charleston Close ♦♦♦
Hayling Island, Hayling Island, PO11 0JY
T: (023) 9246 2527

The Coach House ♦♦♦♦
Church Lane, Northney Village, Hayling Island, PO11 0SB
T: (023) 9246 6266

Maidlings ♦♦♦
55 Staunton Avenue, Hayling Island, PO11 0EW
T: (023) 9246 6357

The Nook ♦♦♦♦
11 Fishery Lane, Hayling Island, PO11 9NP
T: (023) 9246 6248
E: valerie.nagle@ntlworld.com
I: http://homepage.ntlworld.com/gerald.nagle

The Rook Hollow ♦♦♦
84 Church Road, Hayling Island, PO11 0NX
T: (023) 9246 7080

The Shallows ♦♦♦♦
Woodgaston Lane, Hayling Island, PO11 0RL
T: (023) 9246 3713

Tide Reach ♦♦♦
214 Southwood Road, Hayling Island, PO11 9QQ
T: (023) 9246 7828
F: (023) 9246 7828
E: welcome@tidereach.fsnet.co.uk

White House ♦♦♦♦
250 Havant Road, Hayling Island, PO11 0LN
T: (023) 9246 3464

HEADBOURNE WORTHY
Hampshire

Upper Farm ♦♦♦
Headbourne Worthy, Winchester SO23 7LA
T: (01962) 882240
F: (01962) 886144

HEADINGTON
Oxfordshire

Red Mullions ♦♦♦
23 London Road, Headington, Oxford OX3 7RE
T: (01865) 742741
F: (01865) 769944
E: redmullion@aol.com
I: www.oxfordcity.co.uk/accom/redmullions

HEDGE END
Hampshire

Montana Guest House ♦♦♦
90 Lower Northam Road, Hedge End, Southampton SO30 4FT
T: (01489) 782797

HEELANDS
Buckinghamshire

Butter's Guest House ♦♦
51 Langcliffe Drive, Heelands, Milton Keynes MK13 7LA
T: (01908) 312166

Rovers Return ♦♦
49 Langcliffe Drive, Heelands, Milton Keynes MK13 7LA
T: (01908) 310465

HENLEY-ON-THAMES
Oxfordshire

Abbottsleigh ♦♦♦
107 St Marks Road, Henley-on-Thames, RG9 1LP
T: (01491) 572982
F: (01491) 572982
E: abbottsleigh@hotmail.com

Alftrudis ♦♦♦♦
8 Norman Avenue, Henley-on-Thames, RG9 1SG
T: (01491) 573099
F: (01491) 411747
E: b&b@alftrudis.fsnet.co.uk
I: www.alftrudis.co.uk

Apple Ash ♦♦♦♦
Woodlands Road, Harpsden Woods, Henley-on-Thames, RG9 4AB
T: (01491) 574198
F: (01491) 578183

Avalon ♦♦♦
36 Queen Street, Henley-on-Thames, RG9 1AP
T: (01491) 577829
E: avalon@henleybb.fsnet.co.uk
I: www.henleybb.fsnet.co.uk

Azalea House ♦♦♦
55 Deanfield Road, Henley-on-Thames, RG9 1UU
T: (01491) 576407
F: (01491) 576407
E: masseyp@globalnet.co.uk

Bank Farm ♦♦
The Old Road, Pishill, Henley-on-Thames RG9 6HS
T: (01491) 638601
F: (01491) 638601
E: bankfarm@btinternet.com

16 Baronsmead ♦♦♦♦
Henley-on-Thames, RG9 2DL
T: (01491) 578044

4 Coldharbour Close ♦♦♦
Henley-on-Thames, RG9 1QF
T: (01491) 575297
F: (01491) 575297
E: jenny_bower@email.com
I: www.henley-bb.freeserve.co.uk

Coldharbour House ♦♦♦♦
3 Coldharbour Close, Henley-on-Thames, RG9 1QF
T: (01491) 575229
F: (01491) 575229
E: coldharbourhouse@aol.com

Denmark House ♦♦♦
2 Northfield End, Henley-on-Thames, RG9 2HN
T: (01491) 572028
F: (01491) 572458

Gablehurst ♦♦♦
34 Cromwell Road, Henley-on-Thames, RG9 1JH
T: (01491) 575876
F: (01491) 575876
E: gablehurst@rg91jh.free-online.co.uk

26 Hart Street
Rating Applied For
Henley-on-Thames, RG9 2AU
T: (01491) 579031
F: (01491) 579031
E: pkmckenna@aol.com
I: www.26hartst.co.uk

Henley House ♦♦♦
School Lane, Medmenham, Marlow SL7 2HJ
T: (01491) 576100
E: admin@henley-house.com
I: www.crownandanchor.co.uk

Holmwood ♦♦♦♦
Shiplake Row, Binfield Heath, Henley-on-Thames RG9 4DP
T: (0118) 947 8747
F: (0118) 947 8637

The Knoll
♦♦♦♦ SILVER AWARD
Crowsley Road, Shiplake, Henley-on-Thames RG9 3JT
T: (01189) 402705
F: (01189) 402705
E: theknollhenley@aol.com
I: www.theknollhenley.co.uk

Lenwade ♦♦♦♦♦
3 Western Road, Henley-on-Thames, RG9 1JL
T: (01491) 573468
F: (01491) 573468
E: lenwadeuk@aol.com
I: www.w3b-ink.com/lenwade

Little Parmoor Farm ♦♦♦♦
Frieth, Henley-on-Thames RG9 6NL
T: (01494) 881600
F: (01494) 883634
E: francesemmett@waitrose.com
I: www.parmoor.co.uk

Little White Hart Hotel
Rating Applied For
Riverside, Henley-on-Thames, RG9 2LJ
T: (01491) 574145
F: (01491) 411772
E: phil-iwhart@msn.com

New Lodge ♦♦♦
Henley Park, Henley-on-Thames, RG9 6HU
T: (01491) 576340
F: (01491) 576340
E: newlodge@mail.com

Old School House ♦♦♦♦
Off Hart Street, Henley-on-Thames, RG9 2AU
T: (01491) 573929
F: (01491) 411148
E: adrian.lake@btinternet.com

The Old Wood ♦♦
197 Greys Road, Henley-on-Thames, RG9 1QU
T: (01491) 573930
F: (01491) 576285
E: janice@janicejones.co.uk

Park View Farm ♦♦
Lower Assendon, Henley-on-Thames RG9 6AN
T: (01491) 414232
F: (01491) 577515
E: thomasmartin@globalnet.co.uk
I: www.thomasmartin.co.uk

Pennyford House ♦♦
Peppard Common, Henley-on-Thames RG9 5JE
T: (01491) 628272
F: (01491) 628779

The Rise ♦♦♦♦
Rotherfield Road, Henley-on-Thames, RG9 1NR
T: (01491) 579360
F: (01491) 579360

Silver Birches ♦♦♦
6 Elizabeth Road, Henley-on-Thames, RG9 1RG
T: (01491) 575727
E: clarktandh@aol.com

Slaters Farm ♦♦♦
Peppard Common, Henley-on-Thames RG9 5JL
T: (01491) 628675
F: (01491) 628675

Somewhere to Stay ♦♦♦♦
c/o Loddon Acres, Bath Road, Twyford, Reading RG10 9RU
T: (0118) 934 5880
F: (0118) 934 5880
E: reservations@somewhere-tostay.com
I: www.somewhere-tostay.com

Stag Hall ♦♦♦
Peppard, Henley-on-Thames, RG9 5NX
T: (01491) 680338
F: (01491) 680338

Thamesmead House Hotel
♦♦♦♦♦ SILVER AWARD
Remenham Lane, Remenham, Henley-on-Thames RG9 2LR
T: (01491) 574745
F: (01491) 579944
E: thamesmead@supanet.com
I: www.thamesmeadhousehotel.co.uk

Vine Cottage ♦♦♦
53 Northfield Road, Henley-on-Thames, RG9 2JJ
T: (01491) 573545
F: (01491) 410707

Windy Brow ♦♦♦♦
204 Victoria Road, Wargrave, Reading RG10 8AJ
T: (0118) 940 3336
F: (0118) 940 1260
E: heathcar@aol.com

HERMITAGE
Berkshire

Eling Farm ♦♦♦♦
Hermitage, Thatcham RG18 9XR
T: (01635) 200021
F: (01635) 201105
E: eling.farm@farmline.com

HETHE
Oxfordshire

Manor Farm ♦♦♦♦
Hethe, Bicester OX27 8ES
T: (01869) 277602
F: (01869) 278376
E: chrmanor@aol.com

HIGH WYCOMBE
Buckinghamshire

Ayam Manor ♦♦♦
Hammersley Lane, High Wycombe, HP10 8HS
T: (01494) 816932
F: (01494) 816338
E: jeansenior@ayammanor.freeserve.co.uk
I: www.ayammanorguesthouse.co.uk

The Birches ♦♦
30 Lucas Road, High Wycombe, HP13 6QG
T: (01494) 533547

Bird in Hand ♦♦♦
81 West Wycombe Road, High Wycombe, HP11 2LR
T: (01494) 523502
F: (01494) 459449

31 Green Road ◆◆◆
High Wycombe, HP13 5BD
T: (01494) 522625
F: (01494) 522625

P Smails Guest Accommodation ◆◆◆
106 Green Hill, High Wycombe, HP13 5QE
T: (01494) 524310
E: pauline@smails.fsnet.co.uk

9 Sandford Gardens ◆◆◆
Daws Hill, High Wycombe, HP11 1QT
T: (01494) 441723

Sunnydale ◆◆◆
425 Amersham Road, Hazlemere, High Wycombe, HP15 7JG
T: (01494) 711439

HIGHCLERE
Hampshire

Highclere Farm ◆◆◆
Highclere, Newbury RG20 9PY
T: (01635) 255013
E: walshhighclere@newburyweb.net

HIGHCLIFFE
Dorset

10 Brook Way ◆◆◆
Friars Cliff, Highcliffe, BH23 4HA
T: (01425) 276738
E: midgefinn@hotmail.com

Castle Lodge ◆◆◆◆
173 Lymington Road, Highcliffe, BH23 4JS
T: (01425) 275170
F: (01425) 275170
E: chard_family@hotmail.com
I: www.four-runner.com/castlelodge

The Close ◆◆◆
12 Shelley Close, Highcliffe, BH23 4HW
T: (01425) 273559

Sea Corner Guest House & Angolo Del Mare Italian Restaurant◆◆◆◆
397 Waterford Road, Highcliffe, BH23 5JN
T: (01425) 272731
F: (01425) 272077
E: marlene@seacorner.fsnet.co.uk

HINTON ST MARY
Dorset

The Old Post Office Guest House ◆◆◆◆
Hinton St Mary, Sturminster Newton DT10 1NG
T: (01258) 472366
F: (01258) 472173
E: sofields@aol.com

HINTON ST MICHAEL
Hampshire

The East Close Country Hotel ◆◆
Lyndhurst Road, Hinton St Michael, BH23 7EF
T: (01425) 672404
F: (01425) 674315
E: eastclosecountryhotel@yahoo.co.uk
I: www.eastclosecountryhotel.co.uk

HOLTON
Oxfordshire

Home Farm House ◆◆◆◆
Holton, Oxford OX33 1QA
T: (01865) 872334
F: (01865) 876220
E: sonjab@btinternet.com

HOOK
Hampshire

Cherry Lodge Guest House ◆◆◆
Reading Road, Hook, RG27 9DB
T: (01256) 762532
F: (01256) 766068
E: cherrylodge@btinternet.com

Oaklea Guest House ◆◆◆
London Road, Hook, RG27 9LA
T: (01256) 762673
F: (01256) 762150

HOOK NORTON
Oxfordshire

Manor Farm ◆◆◆
Hook Norton, Banbury OX15 5LU
T: (01608) 737204
E: jdyhughes@aol.com

HORDLE
Hampshire

Long Acre Farm ◆◆◆
Vaggs Lane, Hordle, Lymington SO41 0FP
T: (01425) 610443
F: (01425) 613026
E: long.acre@amserve.net

HORLEY
Oxfordshire

Sor Brook House Farm ◆◆◆◆
Horley, Banbury OX15 6BL
T: (01295) 738121

HORNDEAN
Hampshire

Rosedene ◆◆◆◆
63 Rosemary Way, Horndean, Waterlooville PO8 9DQ
T: (023) 9261 5804
F: (023) 9242 3948
E: pbbatt@aol.com

The Ship & Bell Hotel ◆◆◆
6 London Road, Horndean, Waterlooville PO8 0BZ
T: (02392) 592107

HORNTON
Oxfordshire

The Yews ◆◆◆
Church Lane, Hornton, Banbury OX15 6BY
T: (01295) 670460

HORTON
Dorset

The Horton Inn
Rating Applied For
Cranborne Road, Horton, Wimborne Minster BH21 5AD
T: (01258) 840252
F: (01258) 841400
I: www.activehotels.com

HUNGERFORD
Berkshire

Alderborne House ◆◆◆◆
33 Bourne Vale, Hungerford, RG17 0LL
T: (01488) 683228
E: mail@honeybone.co.uk
I: www.honeybone.co.uk

Anne's B & B ◆◆◆
59 Priory Avenue, Hungerford, RG17 0AS
T: (01488) 682290
F: (01488) 686993
E: anne@hungerfordberks.co.uk
I: www.hungerfordberks.co.uk

Fishers Farm ◆◆◆◆
Ermin Street, Shefford Woodlands, Hungerford RG17 7AB
T: (01488) 648466
F: (01488) 648706
E: mail@fishersfarm.co.uk
I: www.fishersfarm.co.uk

Marshgate Cottage Hotel ◆◆◆◆
Marsh Lane, Hungerford, RG17 0QX
T: (01488) 682307
F: (01488) 685475
E: reservations@marshgate.co.uk
I: www.marshgate.co.uk

Wilton House
◆◆◆◆ SILVER AWARD
33 High Street, Hungerford, RG17 0NF
T: (01488) 684228
F: (01488) 685037
E: welfares@hotmail.com
I: www.wiltonhouse.freeserve.com

HURN
Dorset

Avon Causeway Inn ◆◆◆
Hurn, Christchurch BH23 6AS
T: (01202) 482714
F: (01202) 477416
E: avoncauseway@wadworth.co.uk
I: www.avoncausewayhotel.co.uk

HYTHE
Hampshire

Changri-La ◆◆◆◆
12 Ashleigh Close, Hythe, Southampton SO45 3QP
T: (023) 8084 6664

IBTHORPE
Hampshire

Staggs Cottage ◆◆◆
Windmill Hill, Ibthorpe, Andover SP11 0BP
T: (01264) 736235
F: (01264) 736597
E: staggscottage@aol.com

INKPEN
Berkshire

The Crown & Garter ◆◆◆◆
Great Common, Inkpen, Hungerford RG17 9QR
T: (01488) 668325
F: (01488) 669072
I: www.crownandgarter.com

The Swan Inn ◆◆◆◆
Inkpen, Hungerford RG17 9DX
T: (01488) 668326
F: (01488) 668306
E: enquiries@theswaninn-organics.co.uk
I: www.theswaninn-organics.co.uk

ITCHEN ABBAS
Hampshire

Hatch End
Rating Applied For
Main Road, Itchen Abbas, Winchester SO21 1AT
T: (01962) 779279

The Trout ◆◆◆◆
Itchen Abbas, Winchester SO21 1BQ
T: (01962) 779537
F: (01962) 791046
E: thetroutinn@freeuk.com

IVINGHOE
Buckinghamshire

Bull Lake B&B ◆◆◆◆
Bull Lake Farm, Ivinghoe, Leighton Buzzard LU7 9EA
T: (01296) 668834
F: (01296) 668175

The Old Forge ◆◆◆◆
5 High Street, Ivinghoe, Leighton Buzzard LU7 9EP
T: (01296) 668122
F: (01296) 668122
I: www.ivinghoe.co.uk

IWERNE MINSTER
Dorset

Cleff House
◆◆◆◆◆ GOLD AWARD
Brookmans Valley, Iwerne Minster, Blandford Forum DT11 8NG
T: (01747) 811129
F: (01747) 811112

JORDANS
Buckinghamshire

Old Jordans Guest House & Conference Centre◆◆◆
Jordans Lane, Jordans, Beaconsfield HP9 2SW
T: (01494) 879700
F: (01494) 875657
E: info@oldjordans.org.uk
I: www.oldjordans.org.uk

KELMSCOTT
Oxfordshire

Bradshaws Farmhouse
◆◆◆◆ SILVER AWARD
Kelmscott, Lechlade GL7 3HD
T: (01367) 252519
F: (01367) 244800
E: bradshawsfarmhouse@hotmail.com
I: www.bradshawsfarmhouse.co.uk

KIDLINGTON
Oxfordshire

Breffni House ◆◆◆
9 Lovelace Drive, Kidlington, OX5 2LY
T: (01865) 372569

Colliers B & B ◆◆◆
55 Nethercote Road, Tackley, Kidlington, OX5 3AT
T: (01869) 331255
F: (01869) 331670

Warsborough House ◆◆◆
52 Mill Street, Kidlington, OX5 2EF
T: (01865) 370316
F: (01865) 370316
E: elizabethmair@lycos.co.uk
I: www.warsboroughhouse.co.uk

Wise Alderman Inn ◆◆◆
249 Banbury Road, Kidlington, OX5 1BF
T: (01865) 372281
F: (01865) 370153

KIMMERIDGE
Dorset

Kimmeridge Farmhouse ◆◆◆◆ GOLD AWARD
Kimmeridge, Wareham BH20 5PE
T: (01929) 480990
F: (01929) 481503
E: kimmeridgefarmhouse@hotmail.com

KINGHAM
Oxfordshire

The Plough Inn ◆◆◆
17 The Green, Kingham, Oxford OX7 6YD
T: (01608) 658327

The Tollgate Hotel ◆◆◆◆
Church Street, Kingham, Oxford OX7 6YA
T: (01608) 658389
F: (01608) 659467
E: info@the-tollgate.com
I: www.the-tollgate.com

KINGSLEY
Hampshire

The Cricketers Inn ◆◆◆
Main Road, Kingsley, Bordon GU35 9ND
T: (01420) 476730
F: (01420) 477871

KINGSTON
Hampshire

Greenacres Farmhouse ◆◆◆◆
Christchurch Road, Kingston, Ringwood BH24 3BJ
T: (01425) 480945
F: (01425) 480945
E: paddy@strongarm.freeserve.co.uk

Kingston Country Courtyard ◆◆◆◆
Greystone Court, Kingston, Corfe Castle, Wareham BH20 5LR
T: (01929) 481066
F: (01929) 481256
E: annfry@kingstoncountrycourtyard.co.uk
I: www.kingstoncountrycourtyard.co.uk

KINGTON MAGNA
Dorset

Kington Manor Farm ◆◆◆◆
Church Hill, Kington Magna, Gillingham SP8 5EG
T: (01747) 838371
F: (01747) 838371
E: gosney@aol.com

KINTBURY
Berkshire

Holt Lodge ◆◆◆◆
Kintbury, Hungerford RG17 9SX
T: (01488) 668244
F: (01488) 668244
E: johnfreeland@holtlodge.freeserve.co.uk
I: www.holt-lodge.co.uk

KIRTLINGTON
Oxfordshire

Vicarage Farm House ◆◆◆◆
Kirtlington, Oxford OX5 3JY
T: (01869) 350254
F: (01869) 350254
E: jahunter@talk21.co.uk,jahunter1@talk21.co.uk
I: www.country-accom.co.uk/vicaragefarm

LAKE
Isle of Wight

Ashleigh House Hotel ◆◆◆◆
81 Sandown Road, Lake, Sandown PO36 9LE
T: (01983) 402340

Cliff Lodge ◆◆◆
13 Cliff Path, Lake, Sandown PO36 8PL
T: (01983) 402963

Haytor Lodge ◆◆◆◆
16 Cliff Path, Lake, Sandown PO36 8PL
T: (01983) 402969

Osterley Lodge ◆◆◆◆
62 Sandown Road, Lake, Sandown PO36 9JX
T: (01983) 402017
F: (01983) 402854
E: osterleylodge@netguides.co.uk
I: www.netguides.co.uk/wight/basic/osterley.html

Piers View Guest House ◆◆◆
20 Cliff Path, Lake, Sandown PO36 8PL
T: (01983) 404646
E: piers-view@zoom.co.uk

LANGTON LONG
Dorset

The Old Brew House ◆◆◆◆◆ SILVER AWARD
Langton Long, Blandford Forum DT11 9HR
T: (01258) 452861
F: (01258) 450718

LEAFIELD
Oxfordshire

Greenside Cottage ◆◆◆
The Ridings, Leafield, Oxford OX29 9NN
T: (01993) 878368
F: (01993) 878368

Langley Farm ◆◆◆
Langley, Oxford OX29 9QD
T: (01993) 878686

Pond View ◆◆◆
Fairspear Road, Leafield, Oxford OX8 9NT
T: (01993) 878133

LECKHAMPSTEAD
Berkshire

Catslide Cottage ◆◆◆◆
Hill Green, Leckhampstead, Newbury RG20 8RB
T: (01635) 247098
F: (01635) 247098
E: 101756.1607@compuserve.com

Weatherhead Farm ◆◆◆◆
Leckhampstead, Buckingham MK18 5NP
T: (01280) 860502
F: (01280) 860535
E: ed@cgurney.fsnet.co.uk

LEE ON THE SOLENT
Hampshire

Apple Tree Cottage ◆◆◆
159 Portsmouth Road, Lee on the Solent, PO13 9AD
T: (023) 9255 1176
F: (023) 9235 2492
E: lmgell@aol.com

Avon Manor Guest House ◆◆◆
12 South Place, Lee on the Solent, PO13 9AS
T: (023) 9255 2773
E: karen@avonmanor.fsnet.co.uk
I: www.avonmanor.fsnet.co.uk

Chester Lodge ◆◆◆
20 Chester Crescent, Lee on the Solent, PO13 9BH
T: (023) 9255 0894
F: (023) 9255 6291

LETCOMBE REGIS
Oxfordshire

Regis Bed & Breakfast ◆◆◆◆
2 Court Road, Letcombe Regis, Wantage OX12 9JH
T: (01235) 762860
F: (01235) 769975
E: millerastall@aol.com

LEWKNOR
Oxfordshire

Moorcourt Cottage ◆◆◆◆
Weston Road, Lewknor, Oxford OX49 5RU
T: (01844) 351419
F: (01844) 351419
E: p.hodgson@freeuk.com

LIPHOOK
Hampshire

The Bailiff's Cottage ◆◆◆
Hollycombe, Liphook GU30 7LR
T: (01428) 722171
F: (01428) 729394
E: jenner@bailiffs.fsnet.co.uk

LITTLE CHESTERTON
Oxfordshire

Cover Point ◆◆◆◆
Little Chesterton, Bicester OX6 8PD
T: (01869) 252500
F: (01869) 252500
E: lamb@coverpoint100.freeserve.co.uk

LITTLE MARLOW
Buckinghamshire

The Crooked Cottage ◆◆◆
Sheepridge Lane, Little Marlow, Marlow SL7 3SG
T: (01628) 521130

LITTLETON
Hampshire

The Furlongs ◆◆◆◆
18 North Drive, Littleton, Winchester SO22 6QA
T: (01962) 880320
F: 0870 134 9332

The Garden Flat
Rating Applied For
7A Bercote Close, Littleton, Winchester SO22 6PX
T: (01962) 883660
E: d.elsmore@virgin.net
I: www.garden-flat.com

LONG HANBOROUGH
Oxfordshire

The Close Guest House ◆◆◆
Witney Road, Long Hanborough, Oxford OX29 8HF
T: (01993) 882485
F: (01993) 883819

Old Farmhouse ◆◆◆◆
Station Hill, Long Hanborough, Oxford OX8 8JZ
T: (01993) 882097
E: old.farm@virgin.net

LONG WITTENHAM
Oxfordshire

Witta's Ham Cottage ◆◆◆◆
High Street, Long Wittenham, Abingdon OX14 4QH
T: (01865) 407686
F: (01865) 407469
E: martin.meller@sjpp.co.uk

LONGPARISH
Hampshire

Yew Cottage Bed & Breakfast ◆◆◆
Yew Cottage, Longparish, Andover SP11 6QE
T: (01264) 720325
E: yewcottage@ukgateway.net

LOUDWATER
Buckinghamshire

Trevona ◆◆◆
7 Derehams Lane, Loudwater, High Wycombe HP10 9RH
T: (01494) 526715
E: ssmith4739@aol.com

LOWER ASSENDON
Oxfordshire

Orchard Dene Cottage ◆◆◆◆
Lower Assendon, Henley-on-Thames RG9 6AG
T: (01491) 575490
F: (01491) 575490
E: orcharddene@freeuk.com
I: www.orcharddene.freeuk.com

LYMINGTON
Hampshire

Birchcroft ◆◆◆
Westfield Road, Lymington, SO41 3QB
T: (01590) 688844
F: (01590) 688766

Britannia House ◆◆◆◆◆ GOLD AWARD
Mill Lane, Lymington, SO41 9AY
T: (01590) 672091
E: enquiries@britannia-house.com
I: www.britannia-house.com

Dolphins ◆◆◆◆
6 Emsworth Road, Lymington, SO41 9BL
T: (01590) 676108
F: (01590) 676108
E: dolphins@easynet.co.uk
I: www.dolphinsnewforestbandb.co.uk

Durlston Guest House ◆◆◆
Durlston House, Gosport Street, Lymington, SO41 9EG
T: (01590) 677364

Efford Cottage ◆◆◆◆◆ GOLD AWARD
Everton, Lymington SO41 0JD
T: (01590) 642315
F: (01590) 641030
E: effcottage@aol.com
I: www.effordcottage.co.uk

Gleneagles ♦♦♦♦
34 Belmore Road, Lymington, SO41 3NT
T: (01590) 675958
F: (01590) 675958
E: gleneagles34@hotmail.com

Gorse Meadow Guest House ♦♦♦
Gorse Meadow, Sway Road, Lymington, SO41 8LR
T: (01590) 673354
F: (01590) 673336
E: mrs.tee@newforestguesthouse.com
I: www.newforestguesthouse.com

Hideaway ♦♦♦
Middle Common Road, Pennington, Lymington SO41 8LE
T: (01590) 676974
F: (01590) 676974
I: www.newforest.demon.co.uk/hideaway.htm

The Hillsman House ♦♦♦♦♦ SILVER AWARD
74 Milford Road, Lymington, SO41 8DP
T: (01590) 674737
E: caroline@hillsman-house.co.uk
I: www.newforest.demon.co.uk/hillsman.htm

Monks Pool ♦♦♦♦
Waterford Lane, Lymington, SO41 3PS
T: (01590) 678850
F: (01590) 678850
E: cam@monkspool.swinternet.co.uk
I: www.camandjohn.com

Moonraker Cottage ♦♦♦♦
62 Milford Road, Lymington, SO41 8DU
T: (01590) 678677
F: (01590) 678677

Our Bench ♦♦♦♦
9 Lodge Road, Pennington, Lymington, SO41 8HH
T: (01590) 673141
F: (01590) 673141
E: enquiries@ourbench.co.uk
I: www.ourbench.co.uk

Pennavon House ♦♦♦♦ SILVER AWARD
Lower Pennington Lane, Lymington, SO41 8AL
T: (01590) 673984

Rosefield House ♦♦♦♦♦ GOLD AWARD
Sway Road, Lymington, SO41 8LR
T: (01590) 671526
F: (01590) 689007

The Rowans ♦♦♦♦
76 Southampton Road, Lymington, SO41 9GZ
T: (01590) 672276
F: (01590) 688610
E: the.rowans@totalise.co.uk

40 Southampton Road ♦♦♦♦
40 Southampton Road, Lymington, SO41 9GG
T: (01590) 672237
F: (01590) 673592

Tranmere House ♦♦♦♦ GOLD AWARD
Tranmere Close, Lymington, SO41 3QQ
T: (01590) 671983
E: tranmere.house@tesco.net
I: www.tranmere_house.com

LYNDHURST Hampshire

Burwood Lodge ♦♦♦♦ SILVER AWARD
27 Romsey Road, Lyndhurst, SO43 7AA
T: (023) 8028 2445
F: (023) 8028 4104
I: www.burwoodlodge.co.uk

Englefield ♦♦♦♦
Chapel Lane, Lyndhurst, SO43 7FG
T: (023) 8028 2685

Forest Cottage ♦♦♦♦ SILVER AWARD
High Street, Lyndhurst, SO43 7BH
T: (023) 8028 3461
I: www.forestcottage.i12.com

Hurst End ♦♦♦
Clayhill, Lyndhurst, SO43 7DE
T: (023) 8028 2606
F: (023) 8028 2606

Little Hayes ♦♦♦♦
43 Romsey Road, Lyndhurst, SO43 7AR
T: (023) 8028 3816

Lyndhurst House ♦♦♦♦ SILVER AWARD
35 Romsey Road, Lyndhurst, SO43 7AR
T: (023) 8028 2230
F: (023) 8028 3190
E: lyndhursthouse@aol.com
I: www.lyndhursthousebandb.co.uk

Pen Cottage ♦♦♦
Bournemouth Road, Swan Green, Lyndhurst, SO43 7DP
T: (023) 8028 2075

The Penny Farthing Hotel ♦♦♦♦
Romsey Road, Lyndhurst, SO43 7AA
T: (023) 8028 4422
F: (023) 8028 4488
E: stay@pennyfarthinghotel.co.uk
I: www.pennyfarthinghotel.co.uk

Reepham House ♦♦♦♦ SILVER AWARD
12 Romsey Road, Lyndhurst, SO43 7AA
T: (023) 8028 3091
F: (023) 8028 3091

Rose Cottage ♦♦♦♦
Chapel Lane, Lyndhurst, SO43 7FG
T: (023) 8028 3413
F: (023) 8028 3413
E: cindy@rosecottageb-b.freeserve.co.uk
I: www.rosecottageb-b.freeserve.co.uk/

Rosedale Bed & Breakfast ♦♦♦
24 Shaggs Meadow, Lyndhurst, SO43 7BN
T: (023) 8028 3793
E: jenny@theangels.freeserve.co.uk

Rufus House Hotel ♦♦♦♦ SILVER AWARD
Southampton Road, Lyndhurst, SO43 7BQ
T: (023) 8028 2930
F: (023) 8028 2930
E: rufushousehotel@dcintra.fsnet.co.uk
I: www.rufushousehotel.co.uk

Southview ♦♦♦
Gosport Lane, Lyndhurst, SO43 7BL
T: (023) 8028 2224
E: gburbidge@virgin.net

Temple Lodge Guest House ♦♦♦♦
Queens Road, Lyndhurst, SO43 7BR
T: (023) 8028 2392
F: (023) 8028 4590

MAIDENHEAD Berkshire

Braywick Grange Rating Applied For
100 Braywick Road, Maidenhead, SL6 1DJ
T: (01628) 625915
F: (01628) 626222

Cartlands Cottage ♦♦
Kings Lane, Cookham Dean, Cookham, Maidenhead SL6 9AY
T: (01628) 482196

Clifton Guest House ♦♦♦
21 Crauford Rise, Maidenhead, SL6 7LR
T: (01628) 623572
F: (01628) 623572
E: clifton@aroram.freeserve.co.uk
I: www.cliftonguesthouse.co.uk

Gilbraiths ♦♦♦
36 The Binghams, Maidenhead, SL6 2ES
T: (01628) 630400
E: gilbraiths@aol.com
I: www.maidenhead.net/gilbraiths

Moor Farm ♦♦♦♦ SILVER AWARD
Ascot Road, Holyport, Maidenhead SL6 2HY
T: (01628) 633761
F: (01628) 636167
E: moorfm@aol.com

Sheephouse Manor ♦♦♦
Sheephouse Road, Maidenhead, SL6 8HJ
T: (01628) 776902
F: (01628) 625138
E: info@sheephousemanor.co.uk
I: www.sheephousemanor.co.uk

MARLOW Buckinghamshire

Acha Pani ♦♦♦
Bovingdon Green, Marlow, SL7 2JL
T: (01628) 483435
F: (01628) 483435
E: mary@achapani.freeserve.co.uk

Acorn Lodge ♦♦♦
79 Marlow Bottom Road, Marlow Bottom, Marlow SL7 3NA
T: (01628) 472197
F: (01628) 472197

32 Barnhill Road ♦♦♦♦
Marlow, SL7 3EY
T: (01628) 484770
E: alisonsm32@postmanpat.org.uk

The Boundary ♦♦♦♦
Seymour Plain, Marlow, SL7 3DA
T: (01628) 476674

The Chequers Inn Rating Applied For
High Street, Marlow, SL7 1BA
T: (01628) 482053
F: (01628) 898386

The Country House ♦♦♦♦
Bisham, Marlow, SL7 1RP
T: (01628) 890606
F: (01628) 890983
I: www.countryhousemarlow.com

Four Winds ♦♦♦♦
18 Bovingdon Heights, Marlow, SL7 2JS
T: (01628) 476567
F: (01628) 481711
E: gooding@globalnet.co.uk

Glade End ♦♦♦♦
2 Little Marlow Road, Marlow, SL7 1HD
T: (01628) 471334
E: sue@gladeend.com
I: www.gladeend.com

Granny Anne's ♦♦♦
54 Seymour Park Road, Marlow, SL7 3EP
T: (01628) 473086
F: (01628) 472721
E: retaylor@nildram.co.uk

Holly Tree House ♦♦♦♦
Burford Close, Marlow Bottom, Marlow SL7 3NE
T: (01628) 891110
F: (01628) 481278
E: hollytreeaccommodation@yahoo.co.uk

The Inn on the Green ♦♦♦♦
The Old Cricket Common, Cookham Dean, Cookham, Maidenhead SL6 9NZ
T: (01628) 482638
F: (01628) 487474
E: enquiries@theinnonthegreen.com
I: www.theinnonthegreen.com

31 Institute Road ♦♦♦
Marlow, SL7 1BJ
T: (01628) 485662

10 Lock Road ♦♦♦
Marlow, SL7 1QP
T: (01628) 473875

Merrie Hollow ♦♦♦
Seymour Court Hill, Marlow Road, Marlow, SL7 3DE
T: (01628) 485663
F: (01628) 485663

Nia Roo ♦♦♦
4 Pound Crescent, Marlow, SL7 2BG
T: (01628) 486679
F: (01628) 486679

Oak Lodge ♦♦♦
29 Oaktree Road, Marlow, SL7 3ED
T: (01628) 472145

Old Barn Cottage ♦♦♦♦
Church Road, Little Marlow, Marlow SL7 3RZ
T: (01628) 483817
F: (01628) 477197
E: falk@globalnet.co.uk

Old Kiln House ♦♦♦
Marlow Common, Marlow, SL7 2QP
T: (01628) 475615
F: (01628) 475615

The Prince of Wales ♦♦♦
1 Mill Road, Marlow, SL7 1PX
T: (01628) 482970
F: (01628) 482970

Red Barn Farm ♦♦♦
Marlow Road, Marlow, SL7 3DQ
T: (01494) 882820
F: (01494) 883545

Riverdale ♦♦♦
Marlow Bridge Lane, Marlow, SL7 1RH
T: (01628) 485206
E: chrisrawlings@onetel.net.uk

18 Rookery Court
♦♦♦♦ SILVER AWARD
Marlow, SL7 3HR
T: (01628) 486451
F: (01628) 486451
E: gillbullen@compuserve.com

Rosemary Cottage Bed & Breakfast ♦♦♦♦
99 Heath End Road, Flackwell Heath, High Wycombe HP10 9ES
T: (01628) 520635
F: (01628) 520635
E: mike.1@virgin.net
I: www.reservation.co.uk

53 Stapleton Close ♦♦♦
Marlow, SL7 1TZ
T: (01628) 482183

MARLOW BOTTOM
Buckinghamshire

61 Hill Farm Road ♦♦♦
Marlow Bottom, Marlow SL7 3LX
T: (01628) 475145
F: (01628) 475775
E: paul.simmons8@btinternet.com

63 Hill Farm Road ♦♦
Marlow Bottom, Marlow SL7 3LX
T: (01628) 472970

T J O'Reillys ♦♦♦
61 Marlow Bottom Road, Marlow Bottom, Marlow SL7 3NA
T: (01628) 891187
F: (01628) 484926

MARNHULL
Dorset

Moorcourt Farm
Rating Applied For
Moorside, Marnhull, Sturminster Newton DT10 1HH
T: (01258) 820271
F: (01258) 820271

The Old Bank ♦♦♦
Burton Street, Marnhull, Sturminster Newton DT10 1PH
T: (01258) 821019
F: (01258) 821019

Yew House Farm
♦♦♦♦ SILVER AWARD
Husseys, Marnhull, Sturminster Newton DT10 1PD
T: (01258) 820412
F: (01258) 821044
E: yewfarmhouse@aol.com

MARSH GIBBON
Buckinghamshire

Judges Close ♦♦♦
West Edge, Marsh Gibbon, Bicester OX27 0HA
T: (01869) 278508
F: (01869) 277189
E: royllambourne1@farmersweekly.net

MEDSTEAD
Hampshire

Woodfield Bed & Breakfast
Rating Applied For
Windsor Road, Medstead, Alton GU34 5EF
T: (01420) 563308
F: (01420) 561495
E: tonydrake@compuserve.com
I: www.vinntec.co.uk/woodfield

MELCOMBE BINGHAM
Dorset

Badgers Sett ♦♦♦♦
Cross Lanes, Melcombe Bingham, Dorchester DT2 7NY
T: (01258) 880006
F: (01258) 880697
E: seasteeluk@btinternet.com
I: www.badgers_sett.freeserve.co.uk

MENTMORE
Buckinghamshire

The Orchard ♦♦♦
Mentmore, Leighton Buzzard LU7 0QF
T: (01296) 668976
F: (01296) 662189
E: jan.hc@virgin.net

MERSTONE
Isle of Wight

Redway Farm ♦♦♦♦
Merstone, Newport PO30 3DJ
T: (01983) 865228
F: (01983) 865228
E: redway@wightfarmholidays.co.uk
I: www.redway-farm.co.uk

MIDDLE ASTON
Oxfordshire

Home Farm House ♦♦♦
Middle Aston, Oxford OX25 5PX
T: (01869) 340666
F: (01869) 347789
E: carolineparsons@tiscali.co.uk
I: www.country-accom.co.uk/home-farm-house

MIDDLE WALLOP
Hampshire

The George Inn – Middle Wallop ♦♦♦♦ SILVER AWARD
The Crossroads, Middle Wallop, Stockbridge SO20 8EG
T: (01264) 781224

MILFORD-ON-SEA
Hampshire

Alma Mater ♦♦♦♦
4 Knowland Drive, Milford-on-Sea, Lymington SO41 0RH
T: (01590) 642811
F: (01590) 642811
E: bandbalmamater@aol.com
I: www.almamater.org.uk

Briantcroft
♦♦♦♦♦ SILVER AWARD
George Road, Milford-on-Sea, Lymington SO41 0RS
T: (01590) 644355
F: (01590) 644355
E: florence.iles@lineone.net
I: www.briantcroft.co.uk

Compton Hotel ♦♦♦
59 Keyhaven Road, Milford-on-Sea, Lymington SO41 0QX
T: (01590) 643117
F: (01590) 643117
E: dbembo@talk21.com

Laburnum Cottage ♦♦♦
19 Carrington Lane, Milford-on-Sea, Lymington SO41 0RA
T: (01590) 644225
I: www.simplybedandbreakfast.com/laburnum/index.htm

Sun Cottage ♦♦♦♦
Barnes Lane, Milford-on-Sea, Lymington SO41 0RR
T: (01590) 644840
F: (01590) 642064

MILTON ABBAS
Dorset

Dunbury Heights ♦♦♦♦
Milton Abbas, Blandford Forum DT11 0DH
T: (01258) 880445

MILTON COMMON
Oxfordshire

Byways ♦♦♦♦
Old London Road, Milton Common, Oxford OX9 2JR
T: (01844) 279386
F: (01844) 279386
I: www.byways-oxfordshire.co.uk

MILTON KEYNES
Buckinghamshire

A City Central B & B ♦♦♦♦
37 Mitcham Place, Bradwell Common, Milton Keynes, MK13 8BX
T: (01908) 663750

Chantry Farm ♦♦♦
Pindon End, Hanslope, Milton Keynes MK19 7HL
T: (01908) 510269
F: (01908) 510269

Conifers Bed & Breakfast ♦♦
29 William Smith Close, Woolstone, Milton Keynes MK15 0AN
T: (01908) 674506
F: (01908) 550628

The Croft ♦♦♦
Little Crawley, Newport Pagnell, MK16 9LT
T: (01234) 391296

Furtho Manor Farm ♦♦♦
Old Stratford, Milton Keynes, MK19 6NR
T: (01908) 542139
F: (01908) 542139
E: dsansome@farming.co.uk

The Grange Stables ♦♦♦
Winslow Road, Great Horwood, Milton Keynes MK17 0QN
T: (01296) 712051
F: (01296) 714991
E: grangestables@suncheck.demon.co.uk

Haversham Grange ♦♦♦♦
Haversham, Milton Keynes MK19 7DX
T: (01908) 312389
F: (01908) 312389
E: smithers@haversham-grange.co.uk

Kingfishers ♦♦♦
9 Rylstone Close, Heelands, Milton Keynes MK13 7QT
T: (01908) 310231
F: (01908) 318601
E: sheila-derek@m-keynes.freeserve.co.uk
I: www.smoothhound.co.uk/hotels/kingfishers.html

Manor Farm House ♦♦♦
South Street, Castlethorpe, Milton Keynes MK19 7EL
T: (01908) 510216
F: (01908) 510216
E: manorfarmhouse@aol.com

Milford Leys Farm ♦♦♦
Castlethorpe, Milton Keynes MK19 7HH
T: (01908) 510153

Mill Farm ♦♦♦
Gayhurst, Newport Pagnell MK16 8LT
T: (01908) 611489
F: (01908) 611489
E: adamsmillfarm@aol.com

Spinney Lodge Farm ♦♦♦
Forest Road, Hanslope, Milton Keynes MK19 7DE
T: (01908) 510267

Vignoble ♦♦♦
2 Medland, Woughton Park, Milton Keynes MK6 3BH
T: (01908) 666804
F: (01908) 666626
E: vignoblegh@aol.com

The White Hart ♦♦♦♦
1 Gun Lane, Sherington, Newport Pagnell MK16 9PE
T: (01908) 611953
F: (01908) 618109
E: whitehartresort@aol.com
I: www.whitehartsherington.com

MINSTEAD
Hampshire

Grove House ♦♦
Newtown, Minstead, Lyndhurst SO43 7GG
T: (023) 8081 3211

The Trusty Servant ♦♦♦
Minstead, Lyndhurst SO43 7FY
T: (023) 8081 2137

MINSTER LOVELL
Oxfordshire

Hill Grove Farm ♦♦♦♦
Crawley Road, Minster Lovell, Oxford OX29 0NA
T: (01993) 703120
F: (01993) 700528
E: kbrown@eggconnect.net

MONKS RISBOROUGH
Buckinghamshire

26 Little Ham Lane ♦
Monks Risborough, Aylesbury HP27 9JW
T: (01844) 345410

MORETON
Oxfordshire

Elm Tree Farmhouse ♦♦♦♦
Moreton, Thame OX9 2HR
T: (01844) 213692
F: (01844) 215369
E: wendy@elmtreefarmhouse.co.uk
I: www.elmtreefarmhouse.co.uk

MOTCOMBE
Dorset

The Coppleridge Inn ◆◆◆
Elm Hill, Motcombe, Shaftesbury SP7 9HW
T: (01747) 851980
F: (01747) 851858
E: thecoppleridgeinn@btinternet.com
I: www.coppleridge.com

Shorts Green Farm
◆◆◆◆ SILVER AWARD
Motcombe, Shaftesbury SP7 9PA
T: (01747) 852260
F: (01747) 852260

MOULSFORD ON THAMES
Oxfordshire

White House
◆◆◆◆ SILVER AWARD
Moulsford on Thames, Wallingford OX10 9JD
T: (01491) 651397
F: (01491) 652560
E: mwatsham@hotmail.com

MUDEFORD
Dorset

Seahaze
◆◆◆◆ SILVER AWARD
4 Rook Hill Road, Friars Cliff, Mudeford, Christchurch BH23 4DZ
T: (01425) 270866
F: (01425) 278285
E: seahaze@eggconnect.net

MURSLEY
Buckinghamshire

Fourpenny Cottage ◆◆◆◆
23 Main Street, Mursley, Milton Keynes MK17 0RT
T: (01296) 720544
F: (01296) 720906
E: fourpennycottage@tinyworld.co.uk

NAPHILL
Buckinghamshire

Woodpeckers ◆◆◆
244 Main Road, Naphill, High Wycombe HP14 4RX
T: (01494) 563728
E: angela.brand@virgin.net

NETHER WALLOP
Hampshire

Halcyon ◆◆◆
Church Hill, Nether Wallop, Stockbridge SO20 8EY
T: (01264) 781348

York Lodge ◆◆◆◆
Nether Wallop, Stockbridge SO20 8HE
T: (01264) 781313
F: (01264) 781313
E: bradley@yorklodge.fslife.com
I: www.york-lodge.co.uk

NETTLEBED
Oxfordshire

Parkcorner Farm House ◆◆◆
Park Corner, Nettlebed, Henley-on-Thames RG9 6DX
T: (01491) 641450
E: parkcorner_farmhouse@hotmail.com

NEW MILTON
Hampshire

Fairways Guest House ◆◆◆◆
Sway Road, Bashley, New Milton, BH25 5QP
T: (01425) 619001
F: (01425) 619001
E: libsfairways@aol.com

Jobz-A-Gudn ◆◆◆◆
169 Stem Lane, New Milton, BH25 5ND
T: (01425) 615435
F: (01425) 615435
E: jobzagudn@aol.com
I: www.jobzagudn.com

St Ursula ◆◆◆
30 Hobart Road, New Milton, BH25 6EG
T: (01425) 613515

Taverners Cottage ◆◆◆◆
Bashley Cross Road, Bashley, New Milton, BH25 5SZ
T: (01425) 615403
F: (01425) 632177
E: jbaines@supanet.com
I: www.taverners.cottage.bandb.baines.com

Willy's Well ◆◆◆
Bashley Common Road, Wootton, New Milton, BH25 5SF
T: (01425) 616834
E: moyramac2@hotmail.com

NEWBRIDGE
Isle of Wight

Homestead Farmhouse ◆◆◆
Newbridge, Yarmouth PO41 0TZ
T: (01983) 531270
F: (01983) 531270

NEWBURY
Berkshire

Little Paddocks ◆◆◆
Woolhampton Hill, Woolhampton, Reading RG7 5SY
T: (0118) 971 3451
F: (0118) 971 3451
E: annie_pat@gardner38.freeserve.co.uk

Livingstone House ◆◆◆
48 Queens Road, Newbury, RG14 7PA
T: (01635) 45444
F: (01635) 45444

The Old Farmhouse
◆◆◆◆ SILVER AWARD
Downend Lane, Chieveley, Newbury RG20 8TN
T: (01635) 248361
E: palletts@aol.com
I: www.smoothhound.co.uk/hotels/oldfarmhouse

The Paddock ◆◆◆
Midgham Green, Reading, RG7 5TT
T: (0118) 971 3098
F: (0118) 971 2925
E: david.cantwell@virgin.net
I: http://freespace.virgin.net/david.cantwell

Rookwood Farmhouse ◆◆◆◆
Stockcross, Newbury RG20 8JX
T: (01488) 608676
F: (01488) 657961

St Ann's
Rating Applied For
32 Craven Road, Newbury, RG14 5NE
T: (01635) 41353

White Cottage ◆◆◆
Newtown, Newbury, RG20 9AP
T: (01635) 43097
F: (01635) 43097
E: ellie@p-p-i.fsnet.co.uk

The White Hart Inn ◆◆◆◆
Kintbury Road, Hamstead Marshall, Newbury RG20 0HW
T: (01488) 658201
F: (01488) 657192
I: www.thewhitehart-inn.co.uk

NEWINGTON
Oxfordshire

Hill Farm ◆◆◆
Newington, Wallingford OX10 7AL
T: (01865) 891173

NEWPORT
Isle of Wight

Castle Lodge ◆◆◆
54 Castle Road, Newport, PO30 1DP
T: (01983) 527862
F: (01983) 527862
E: wcastlelodge@aol.com

L'Abri ◆◆◆
8 Ulster Crescent, Newport, PO30 5RU
T: (01983) 520596

Litten Park Guest House ◆◆◆
48 Medina Avenue, Newport, PO30 1EL
T: (01983) 526836

Newport Quay Hotel ◆◆◆
41 Quay Street, Newport, PO30 5BA
T: (01983) 528544
F: (01983) 527143
E: keith@newportquayhotel.freeserve.co.uk

Wheatsheaf Hotel ◆◆◆
St Thomas Square, Newport, PO30 1SG
T: (01983) 523865
F: (01983) 528255
E: information@wheatsheaf-iow.co.uk
I: www.wheatsheaf-iow.co.uk

NEWPORT PAGNELL
Buckinghamshire

The Limes
◆◆◆◆◆ SILVER AWARD
North Square, Newport Pagnell, MK16 8EP
T: (01908) 617041
F: (01908) 217292
E: royandruth@8thelimes.freeserve.co.uk

Rectory Farm ◆◆◆
North Crawley, Newport Pagnell MK16 9HH
T: (01234) 391213

Rosemary House ◆◆◆
7 Hill View, Wolverton Road, Newport Pagnell, MK16 8BE
T: (01908) 612198
F: (01908) 612198

5 Walnut Close ◆◆
Newport Pagnell, MK16 8JH
T: (01908) 611643
F: (01908) 611643
E: shirleyderek.clitheroe@btinternet.com

NORTH GORLEY
Hampshire

The Gorley Tea Rooms ◆◆◆◆
Ringwood Road, North Gorley, Fordingbridge SP6 2PB
T: (01425) 653427
F: (01425) 653720

NORTH LEIGH
Oxfordshire

Elbie House
◆◆◆◆ SILVER AWARD
East End, North Leigh, Witney OX29 6PX
T: (01993) 880166
E: mandy@cotswoldbreak.co.uk
I: www.cotswoldbreak.co.uk

Forge Cottage ◆◆
East End, North Leigh, Woodstock, Oxford OX8 6PZ
T: (01993) 881120
E: jill.french@talk21.com
I: www.country-accom.co.uk (Forge Cottage)

NORTH MORETON
Oxfordshire

Stapleton's Chantry
◆◆◆◆ SILVER AWARD
Long Wittenham Road, North Moreton, Didcot OX11 9AX
T: (01235) 818900
F: (01235) 818555
E: stapletonchantry@aol.com

NORTH NEWINGTON
Oxfordshire

The Blinking Owl Country Inn ◆◆◆
Main Street, North Newington, Banbury OX15 6AE
T: (01295) 730650

La Madonette Country Guest House ◆◆◆◆
North Newington Road, North Newington, Banbury OX15 6AA
T: (01295) 730212
F: (01295) 730363
E: lamadonett@aol.com
I: www.lamadonette.co.uk

NURSLING
Hampshire

Conifers ◆◆◆
6 Nursling Street Cottages, Nursling, Southampton SO16 0XH
T: (023) 8034 9491
F: (023) 8034 9491
E: barbara.hinton@lineone.net

OAKDALE
Dorset

Heathwood Guest House ◆◆◆◆
266 Wimborne Road, Oakdale, Poole BH15 3EF
T: (01202) 679176
F: (01202) 679176
I: www.heathwoodhotel.co.uk

OAKLEY
Buckinghamshire

New Farm ◆◆◆
Oxford Road, Oakley, Aylesbury HP18 9UR
T: (01844) 237360

OAKLEY GREEN
Berkshire

Rainworth Guest House
Rating Applied For
Oakley Green Road, Oakley Green, Windsor SL4 5UL
T: (01753) 856749
F: (01753) 859192

OLNEY
Buckinghamshire

Colchester House ◆◆◆◆
26 High Street, Olney, MK46 4BB
T: (01234) 712602
F: (01234) 240564
I: www.olneybucks.co.uk

The Lindens ♦♦♦
30A High Street, Olney,
MK46 4BB
T: (01234) 712891
E: thelindens@amserve.net
I: www.thelindens.com

OVER NORTON
Oxfordshire

Cleeves Farm ♦♦♦
Over Norton, Chipping Norton
OX7 5PH
T: (01608) 645019
F: (01608) 645021
E: tillylamb@hotmail.com

Woodhaven Cottage ♦♦♦
The Green, Over Norton,
Chipping Norton OX7 5PT
T: (01608) 646265

OWER
Hampshire

Octagon Lodge ♦♦♦♦
Romsey Road, Ower, Romsey
SO51 6AH
T: (023) 8081 4233
F: (023) 8081 4233
E: octagonlodge@tinyworld.
co.uk

OWLSMOOR
Berkshire

De-Rosen
Rating Applied For
43 Cambridge Road, Owlsmoor,
Sandhurst GU47 0TA
T: (01344) 776400
F: (01344) 776400

OXFORD
Oxfordshire

Acorn Guest House ♦♦♦
260-262 Iffley Road, Oxford,
OX4 1SE
T: (01865) 247998
F: (01865) 247998
E: acorn_gh_oxford@freezone.
co.uk

Adams Guest House ♦♦
302 Banbury Road,
Summertown, Oxford, OX2 7ED
T: (01865) 556118
F: (01865) 514066

Arden Lodge ♦♦♦
34 Sunderland Avenue, off
Banbury Road, Oxford, OX2 8DX
T: (01865) 552076

Beaumont Guest House ♦♦♦
234 Abingdon Road, Oxford,
OX1 4SP
T: (01865) 241767
F: (01865) 241767
E: info@beaumont.sagehost.
co.uk
I: www.oxfordcity.
co.uk/accom/beaumont

Becket House ♦
5 Becket Street, Oxford, OX1 7PP
T: (01865) 724675
F: (01865) 724675

Brenal Guest House ♦♦♦
307 Iffley Road, Oxford,
OX4 4AG
T: (01865) 721561
F: (01865) 435814
E: brenalguesthouse@yahoo.
co.uk

Brown's Guest House ♦♦♦
281 Iffley Road, Oxford,
OX4 4AQ
T: (01865) 246822
F: (01865) 246822
E: brownsgh@hotmail.com

The Bungalow ♦♦♦
Cherwell Farm, Mill Lane, Old
Marston, Oxford OX3 0QF
T: (01865) 557171

Casa Villa Guest House ♦♦
388 Banbury Road,
Summertown, Oxford, OX2 7PW
T: (01865) 512642
F: (01865) 512642
E: stoya@casavilla.fsnet.co.uk
I: www.casavilla.fsnet.co.uk

Chestnuts ♦♦♦
72 Cumnor Hill, Oxford,
OX2 9HU
T: (01865) 863602

Chestnuts Guest House
♦♦♦♦♦ SILVER AWARD
45 Davenant Road, Off
Woodstock Road, Oxford,
OX2 8BU
T: (01865) 553375
F: (01865) 553375
E: stay@chestnutsguesthouse.
co.uk

The Coach & Horses Inn ♦♦♦
Watlington Road,
Chiselhampton, Oxford
OX44 7UX
T: (01865) 890255
F: (01865) 891995
E: david-mcphillips@lineone.
net
I: www.coachhorsesinn.co.uk

Cock and Camel ♦♦♦♦
24-26 George Street, Oxford,
OX1 2AE
T: (01865) 203705
F: (01865) 792130
E: cockandcamel@youngs.co.uk
I: www.youngs.co.uk

College Guest House ♦♦♦
103-105 Woodstock Road,
Oxford, OX2 6HL
T: (01865) 552579
F: (01865) 311244
E: r.pal@ukonline.co.uk

Conifer Lodge ♦♦♦
159 Eynsham Road, Botley,
Oxford OX2 9NE
T: (01865) 862280

Cornerways Guest House ♦♦♦
282 Abingdon Road, Oxford,
OX1 4TA
T: (01865) 240135
F: (01865) 247652
E: jeakings@btinternet.com

Cotswold House ♦♦♦♦♦
363 Banbury Road, Oxford,
OX2 7PL
T: (01865) 310558
F: (01865) 310558
E: d.r.walker@talk21.com
I: www.house363.freeserve.co.uk

Dial House ♦♦♦
25 London Road, Headington,
Oxford OX3 7RE
T: (01865) 769944
F: (01865) 769944
E: dialhouse@aol.com
I: www.oxfordcity.
co.uk/accom/dialhouse

Earlmont Guest House ♦♦♦
322-324 Cowley Road, Oxford,
OX4 2AF
T: (01865) 240236
F: (01865) 434903
E: beds@earlmont.prestel.co.uk
I: www.oxfordcity.
co.uk/accom/earlmont.html

Euro Bar & Hotel Oxford ♦♦♦
48 George Street, Oxford,
OX1 2AQ
T: (01865) 725087
F: (01865) 243367
E: eurobarox@aol.com
I: www.oxfordcity.
co.uk/accom/eurobar/

Falcon Private Hotel ♦♦♦
88-90 Abingdon Road, Oxford,
OX1 4PX
T: (01865) 511122
F: (01865) 246642
E: reservations@thefalconhotel.
freeserve.co.uk
I: www.oxfordcity.
co.uk/hotels/falcon

Five Mile View Guest House
♦♦♦
528 Banbury Road, Oxford,
OX2 8EG
T: (01865) 558747
F: (01865) 558747
E: fivemileview@aol.com
I: www.oxfordpages.
co.uk/fivemileview

Gables ♦♦♦♦ SILVER AWARD
6 Cumnor Hill, Oxford, OX2 9HA
T: (01865) 862153
F: (01865) 864054
E: stay@gables-oxford.co.uk
I: www.oxfordcity.
co.uk/accom/gables/

Green Gables ♦♦♦
326 Abingdon Road, Oxford,
OX1 4TE
T: (01865) 725870
F: (01865) 723115
E: green.gables@virgin.net
I: www.greengables.uk.com

Head of the River ♦♦♦♦
Folly Bridge, St Aldates, Oxford,
OX1 4LB
T: (01865) 721600
F: (01865) 726158

Highfield West ♦♦♦
188 Cumnor Hill, Oxford,
OX2 9PJ
T: (01865) 863007
E: highfieldwest@msn.com
I: www.oxfordcity.
co.uk/accom/highfield-west

Hollybush Guest House ♦♦♦
530 Banbury Road, Oxford,
OX2 8EG
T: (01865) 554886
F: (01865) 554886
E: heather@hollybush.
fsbusiness.co.uk
I: www.angelfire.
com/on/hollybush

Homelea Guest House ♦♦♦♦
356 Abingdon Road, Oxford,
OX1 4TQ
T: (01865) 245150
F: (01865) 245150
E: homelea@talk21.com
I: www.guesthouseoxford.com

Isis Guest House ♦♦
45-53 Iffley Road, Oxford,
OX4 1ED
T: (01865) 248894
F: (01865) 243492
E: isis@herald.ox.ac.uk

Lakeside Guest House ♦♦♦
118 Abingdon Road, Oxford,
OX1 4PZ
T: (01865) 244725
F: (01865) 244725

21 Lincoln Road ♦♦♦♦
Oxford, OX1 4TB
T: (01865) 246944
F: (01865) 246944
E: gbaleham@hotmail.com

The Lodge ♦♦♦
Horton Hill, Horton cum Studley,
Oxford OX33 1AY
T: (01865) 351235
F: (01865) 351721
E: res@studleylodge.com
I: www.studleylodge.com

Lonsdale Guest House ♦♦♦
312 Banbury Road, Oxford,
OX2 7ED
T: (01865) 554872
F: (01865) 554872

Marlborough House Hotel
♦♦♦♦
321 Woodstock Road, Oxford,
OX2 7NY
T: (01865) 311321
F: (01865) 515329
E: enquiries@marlbhouse.
win-uk.net
I: www.oxfordcity.
co.uk/hotels/marlborough

Milka's Guest House ♦♦♦
379 Iffley Road, Oxford,
OX4 4DP
T: (01865) 778458
F: (01865) 776477
E: reservations@milkas.co.uk
I: www.milkas.co.uk

Mulberry Guest House ♦♦♦
265 London Road, Headington,
Oxford OX3 9EH
T: (01865) 767114
F: (01865) 767114
E: reservations@
mulberryguesthouse.co.uk
I: www.mulberryguesthouse.
co.uk

Newton House ♦♦♦
82-84 Abingdon Road, Oxford,
OX1 4PL
T: (01865) 240561
F: (01865) 244647
E: newton.house@btinternet.
com
I: www.oxfordcity.
co.uk/accom/newton

The Old Black Horse Hotel
♦♦♦
102 St Clements, Oxford,
OX4 1AR
T: (01865) 244691
F: (01865) 242771
E: info@
theoldblackhorsehoteloxford.
co.uk
I: www.
theoldblackhorsehoteloxford.
co.uk

Park House ♦♦♦
7 St. Bernard's Road, Oxford,
OX2 6EH
T: (01865) 310824

Parklands Hotel ♦♦♦♦
100 Banbury Road, Oxford, OX2 6JU
T: (01865) 554374
F: (01865) 559860
E: theparklands@freenet.co.uk
I: www.oxfordcity.co.uk/hotels/parklands

Pembroke House ♦♦♦♦♦
379 Woodstock Road, Oxford, OX2 8AA
T: (01865) 310782
F: (01865) 310649
E: gaynordean@aol.co.uk

Pickwicks Guest House ♦♦♦♦
15-17 London Road, Headington, Oxford OX3 7SP
T: (01865) 750487
F: (01865) 742208
E: pickwicks@tiscali.co.uk
I: www.oxfordcity.co.uk/accom/pickwicks

Pine Castle Hotel ♦♦♦
290-292 Iffley Road, Oxford, OX4 4AE
T: (01865) 241497
F: (01865) 727230
E: stay@pinecastle.co.uk
I: www.oxfordcity.co.uk/hotels/pinecastle

The Ridings ♦♦♦
280 Abingdon Road, Oxford, OX1 4TA
T: (01865) 248364
F: (01865) 251348
E: ringsoxi@aol.com

River Hotel ♦♦♦
17 Botley Road, Oxford, OX2 0AA
T: (01865) 243475
F: (01865) 724306
E: info@southerntb.co.uk
I: www.riverhotel.co.uk

Royal Oxford Hotel ♦♦♦♦
Park End Street, Oxford, OX1 1HR
T: (01865) 248432
F: (01865) 250049
E: frontdesk@royaloxfordhotel.co.uk
I: www.royaloxfordhotel.co.uk

Ryan's Guest House ♦♦♦
164 Banbury Road, Summertown, Oxford, OX2 7BU
T: (01865) 558876
F: (01865) 558876
E: ryansguesthouse@yahoo.co.uk

Sportsview Guest House ♦♦♦
106-110 Abingdon Road, Oxford, OX1 4PX
T: (01865) 244268
F: (01865) 249270
E: stay@sportsview.guest-house.freeserve.co.uk
I: www.smoothhound.co.uk/hotels/sportsvi.html

Tilbury Lodge ♦♦♦
5 Tilbury Lane, Botley, Oxford OX2 9NB
T: (01865) 862138
F: (01865) 863700
E: tilburylodge@yahoo.co.uk
I: www.oxfordcity.co.uk/hotels/tilbury/

The Tower House ♦♦♦♦
15 Ship Street, Oxford, OX1 3DA
T: (01865) 246828
F: (01865) 247508
I: www.scoot.co.uk/towerhouse

West Farm ♦♦♦
Eaton, Appleton, Abingdon OX13 5PR
T: (01865) 862908
F: (01865) 865512

The Westgate Hotel ♦♦
1 Botley Road, Oxford, OX2 0AA
T: (01865) 726721
F: (01865) 722078

Whitehouse View ♦♦
9 Whitehouse Road, Oxford, OX1 4PA
T: (01865) 721626

PADWORTH COMMON
Berkshire

Lanteglos House ♦♦
Rectory Road, Padworth Common, Reading RG7 4JD
T: (01189) 700333

PANGBOURNE
Berkshire

Weir View House ♦♦♦
9 Shooters Hill, Pangbourne, Reading RG8 7DZ
T: (01189) 842120
F: (01189) 842120

PARK GATE
Hampshire

Four Winds Guest House ♦♦♦
17 Station Road, Park Gate, Southampton SO31 7GJ
T: (01489) 584433
F: (01489) 584433
E: mags@fourwindsguesthouse.com
I: www.fourwindsguesthouse.com

Little Park Lodge ♦♦♦
5 Bridge Road, Park Gate, Southampton SO31 7GD
T: (01489) 600500
F: (01489) 605231
E: julie@manicmike.com
I: www.manicmike.com

60 Southampton Road ♦♦♦
Park Gate, Southampton SO31 6AF
T: (01489) 573994

PARKSTONE
Dorset

Casa Ana Guest House ♦♦♦
93 North Road, Parkstone, Poole BH14 0LT
T: (01202) 741367

Danecourt Lodge ♦♦♦♦
58 Danecourt Road, Parkstone, Poole BH14 0PQ
T: (01202) 730957

Toad Hall ♦♦♦♦
30 Church Road, Parkstone, Poole BH14 0NS
T: (01202) 733900
F: (01202) 746814
E: toadhallguesthouse@btinternet.com
I: www.smoothhound.co.uk/hotels/toadhall.html

Viewpoint Guest House ♦♦♦♦ SILVER AWARD
11 Constitution Hill Road, Parkstone, Poole BH14 0QB
T: (01202) 733586
F: (01202) 733586
E: heather@viewpoint-gh.co.uk
I: www.viewpoint-gh.co.uk

PENN
Buckinghamshire

Little Penn Farmhouse ♦♦♦♦
Penn Bottom, Penn, High Wycombe HP10 8PJ
T: (01494) 813439
F: (01494) 817740
E: sally@saundersharris.co.uk

Little Twyford ♦♦♦
Hammersley Lane, Penn, High Wycombe HP10 8HG
T: (01494) 816934
F: (01494) 816934
E: tandt@twyford.freeserve.co.uk

PETERSFIELD
Hampshire

Beaumont ♦♦♦♦
22 Stafford Road, Petersfield, GU32 2JG
T: (01730) 264744
F: (01730) 264744
E: jenny.bewes@btinternet.com

Border Cottage ♦♦♦
4 Heath Road, Petersfield, GU31 4DU
T: (01730) 263179
E: ll@bordercottage.co.uk
I: www.bordercottage.co.uk

Greywalls House ♦♦♦♦
London Road, Hillbrow, Liss, GU33 7QR
T: (01730) 894246
F: (01730) 894865
E: hillbrow.la@lineone.net
I: www.bidbury.co.uk

Heath Farmhouse ♦♦♦
Heath Road East, Petersfield, GU31 4HU
T: (01730) 264709
E: info@heathfarmhouse.co.uk
I: www.heathfarmhouse.co.uk

Heathside ♦♦♦
36 Heath Road East, Petersfield, GU31 4HR
T: (01730) 262337
F: (01730) 262337

The Holt ♦♦♦
60 Heath Road, Petersfield, GU31 4EJ
T: (01730) 262836

Pipers ♦♦♦
1 Oaklands Road, Petersfield, GU32 2EY
T: (01730) 262131

Ridgefield ♦♦
Station Road, Petersfield, GU32 3DE
T: (01730) 261402
E: john.west@hants.gov.uk
I: www.ridgefieldguesthouse.co.uk

Rose Cottage ♦♦♦
1 The Mead, Liss, GU33 7DU
T: (01730) 892378

South Gardens Cottage ♦♦♦
South Harting, Petersfield, GU31 5QJ
T: (01730) 825040
F: (01730) 825040
E: rogerandjulia@beeb.net

1 The Spain ♦♦♦
Sheep Street, Petersfield, GU32 3JZ
T: (01730) 263261
F: (01730) 261084
E: allantarver@cwcom.net

PICKET PIECE
Hampshire

Cherry Trees ♦♦♦
Picket Piece, Andover SP11 6LY
T: (01264) 334891
F: (01264) 334 891

PIDDINGTON
Oxfordshire

Hill Farm House ♦♦♦♦
Hill Farm, Piddington, Bicester OX25 1QB
T: (01844) 238311

PILLEY
Hampshire

Mistletoe Cottage ♦♦♦♦ SILVER AWARD
3 Jordans Lane, Pilley Bailey, Pilley, Lymington SO41 5QW
T: (01590) 676361

PISHILL
Oxfordshire

Orchard House ♦♦♦
Pishill, Henley-on-Thames RG9 6HJ
T: (01491) 638351
F: (01491) 638351

PITT
Hampshire

Enmill Barn ♦♦♦♦♦
Pitt, Winchester SO22 5QR
T: (01962) 856740
F: (01962) 854219

POOLE
Dorset

Annelise ♦♦♦
41 Danecourt Road, Lower Parkstone, Poole, BH14 0PG
T: (01202) 744833
F: (01202) 744833

Ashdell ♦♦
85 Dunyeats Road, Broadstone, BH18 8AF
T: (01202) 692032
E: ian@ashdell.fsnet.co.uk
I: www.ashdell.co.uk

Corkers ♦♦♦♦ SILVER AWARD
1 High Street, The Quay, Poole, BH15 1AB
T: (01202) 681393
F: (01202) 667393
E: corkers@corkers.co.uk
I: www.corkers.co.uk/corkers

Fernway ♦♦♦
56 Fernside Road, Poole, BH15 2JJ
T: (01202) 252044
F: (01202) 666587
E: dave.way@sequencecontrols.co.uk
I: www.fernway.co.uk

Fleetwater Guest House ♦♦♦
161 Longfleet Road, Poole, BH15 2HS
T: (01202) 682509

The Golden Sovereign Hotel ♦♦♦♦
97 Alumhurst Road, Alum Chine, Bournemouth, BH4 8HR
T: (01202) 762088
F: (01202) 762088
E: goldensov@aol.com

The Grange Guest House ♦♦♦
1 Linthorpe Road, Poole, BH15 2JS
T: (01202) 671336

Harlequins B & B ♦♦♦♦ SILVER AWARD
134 Ringwood Road, Poole, BH14 0RP
T: (01202) 677624
F: (01202) 677624
E: harlequins@tinyworld.com
I: www.harlequins.freeuk.com

Highways ♦♦♦
29 Fernside Road, Poole, BH15 2QU
T: (01202) 677060

Laurel Cottages ♦♦♦♦
41 Foxholes Road, Poole, BH15 3NA
T: (01202) 730894
F: (01202) 730894
E: anne.howarth@cwcom.net
I: www.laurel-cottages.cwc.net

Lytchett Mere ♦♦♦♦ SILVER AWARD
191 Sandy Lane, Upton, Poole, BH16 5LU
T: (01202) 622854

The Mariners Guest House ♦♦♦
26 Sandbanks Road, Poole, BH14 8AQ
T: (01202) 247218

Minster Bed & Breakfast ♦♦♦
826 Ringwood Road, Bournemouth, BH11 8NF
T: (01202) 249977
E: friggs@cwctv.net

Quay House ♦♦♦
3A Thames Street, Poole, BH15 1JN
T: (01202) 686335
E: goodeypoolequay@cwctv.net
I: www.poole-bed-and-breakfast.com

The Saltings ♦♦♦♦
5 Salterns Way, Lilliput, Poole, BH14 8JR
T: (01202) 707349
F: (01202) 701435
E: saltings_poole@yahoo.co.uk
I: www.thesaltingsfsnet.co.uk

Sarnia Cherie ♦♦♦♦
375 Blandford Road, Hamworthy, Poole BH15 4JL
T: (01202) 679470
F: (01202) 679470
E: criscollier@aol.com

The Shah of Persia ♦♦♦♦
173 Longfleet Road, Poole, BH15 2HS
T: (01202) 676587
F: (01202) 679327

Tatnam Farm ♦♦♦♦
82 Tatnam Road, Poole, BH15 2DS
T: (01202) 672969
F: (01202) 682732
E: helenbishop@jrb.netkonect.co.uk

Vernon ♦♦
96 Blandford Road North, Beacon Hill, Poole BH16 6AD
T: (01202) 625185

PORCHFIELD
Isle of Wight

Youngwoods Farm ♦♦♦
Whitehouse Road, Porchfield, Newport PO30 4LJ
T: (01983) 522170
F: (01983) 522170
E: judith@youngwoods.com
I: www.youngwoods.com

PORTCHESTER
Hampshire

Harbour View ♦♦
85 Windmill Grove, Portchester, Fareham PO16 9HH
T: (023) 9237 6740

PORTMORE
Hampshire

A Thatched House ♦♦♦
Hundred Lane, Portmore, Lymington SO41 5RG
T: (01590) 679977
F: (01590) 679977

Cherry Tree ♦♦♦♦
Hundred Lane, Portmore, Lymington SO41 5RG
T: (01590) 672990
E: cherry.tree@lineone.net

PORTSMOUTH & SOUTHSEA
Hampshire

Abbey Lodge ♦♦♦
30 Waverley Road, Southsea, PO5 2PW
T: (023) 9282 8285
F: (023) 9287 2943
E: linda@abbeylodge.co.uk
I: www.abbeylodge.co.uk

The Albatross Guest House ♦♦♦♦
51 Waverley Road, Southsea, PO5 2PJ
T: (023) 9282 8325

Aquarius Court Hotel ♦♦♦
34 St Ronans Road, Southsea, PO4 0PT
T: (023) 9282 2872
F: (023) 9261 9065
E: enquiries@aquariuscourt.freeserve.co.uk
I: www.aquariuscourt.com

Arden Guest House ♦♦♦
14 Herbert Road, Southsea, PO4 0QA
T: (023) 9282 6409
F: (023) 9282 6409

Avarest Guest House ♦♦
10 Waverley Grove, Southsea, PO4 0PZ
T: (023) 9282 9444

Bembell Court Hotel ♦♦♦
69 Festing Road, Southsea, PO4 0NQ
T: (023) 9273 5915
F: (023) 9275 6497
E: keith@bembell.freeserve.co.uk
I: www.bembell.com

Birchwood ♦♦♦♦
44 Waverley Road, Southsea, PO5 2PP
T: (023) 9281 1337
E: ged@birchwood.uk.com
I: www.birchwood.uk.com

The Canterbury Hotel ♦♦♦
27-29 St Simons Road, Southsea, PO5 2PE
T: (023) 9229 3136
F: (023) 9283 2211
E: stay@canterburyhotelgroup.com
I: www.canterburyhotelgroup.com

The Dorcliffe ♦♦♦
42 Waverley Road, Southsea, PO5 2PP
T: (023) 9282 8283
E: dorcliffe@supanet.com

The Elms Guest House ♦♦♦
48 Victoria Road South, Southsea, PO5 2BT
T: (023) 9282 3924
F: (023) 9282 3924
E: theelmsgh@aol.com
I: script.ftech.net/~theguide/portsmouth/elms/

Esk Vale Guest House ♦♦♦
39 Granada Road, Southsea, PO4 0RD
T: (023) 9286 2639
F: (023) 9235 5589
I: www.eskvaleguesthouse.co.uk

Everley Guest House ♦♦♦
33 Festing Road, Southsea, PO4 0NG
T: (023) 9273 1001
F: (023) 9278 0995

Fortitude Cottage ♦♦♦♦
51 Broad Street, Spice Island, Portsmouth, PO1 2JD
T: (023) 9282 3748
F: (023) 9282 3748
E: fortcott@aol.com
I: www.fortitudecottage.co.uk

Gainsborough House ♦♦
9 Malvern Road, Southsea, PO5 2LZ
T: (023) 9282 2604

Granada House Hotel ♦♦♦
29 Granada Road, Southsea, PO4 0RD
T: (023) 9286 1575
F: (023) 9271 8343

Greenacres Guest House ♦♦♦
12 Marion Road, Southsea, PO4 0QX
T: (023) 9235 3137

Hamilton House ♦♦♦♦
95 Victoria Road North, Southsea, Portsmouth, PO5 1PS
T: (023) 9282 3502
F: (023) 9282 3502
E: sandra@hamiltonhouse.co.uk
I: www.hamiltonhouse.co.uk

131 The High Street ♦♦♦♦
SILVER AWARD
Portsmouth, PO1 2HW
T: (023) 9273 0903

Hillside Lodge ♦♦♦
1 Blake Road, Farlington, Portsmouth PO6 1ET
T: (023) 9237 2687

Homestead Guest House ♦♦♦
11 Bembridge Crescent, Southsea, PO4 0QT
T: (023) 9273 2362

Kilbenny Guest House ♦♦♦
2 Malvern Road, Southsea, PO5 2NA
T: (023) 9286 1347

Lamorna Guest House ♦♦
23 Victoria Road South, Southsea, PO5 2BX
T: (023) 9281 1157
F: (023) 9281 1157

Langdale Guest House ♦♦♦
13 St Edwards Road, Southsea, PO5 3DH
T: (023) 9282 2146
F: (023) 9282 2152
E: langdalegh@btinternet.com
I: www.smoothhound.co.uk/hotels/langdal.html

Marmion Lodge Guest House ♦♦♦♦
71 Marmion Road, Southsea, PO5 2AX
T: (023) 9282 2150
F: (023) 9282 2150
E: marmionlodge@btinternet.com
I: www.marmionlodge.co.uk

Oakleigh Guest House ♦♦♦
48 Festing Grove, Southsea, PO4 9QD
T: (023) 9281 2276
E: dwillett@cwtv.net
I: www.oakleighguesthouse.co.uk

Rees Hall University of Portsmouth ♦♦♦
Southsea Terrace, Southsea, PO5 3AP
T: (023) 9284 3884
F: (023) 9284 3888
E: reservation@port.ac.uk
I: www.port.ac.uk

The Rowans ♦♦♦♦
43 Festing Grove, Southsea, PO4 9QB
T: (023) 9273 6614
F: (023) 9282 3711

Sally Port Inn ♦♦♦
57-58 High Street, Portsmouth, PO1 2LU
T: (023) 9282 1860
F: (023) 9282 1293

Uplands Hotel ♦♦♦
34 Granada Road, Southsea, PO4 0RH
T: (023) 9282 1508
F: (023) 9283 2211
E: andy@canterburyhotelgroup.com
I: www.canterburyhotelgroup.com

Victoria Court ♦♦♦
29 Victoria Road North, Southsea, PO5 1PL
T: (023) 9282 0305
F: (023) 9283 8277
E: stay@victoriacourt.co.uk
I: www.victoriacourt.co.uk

Waverley Park Lodge Guest House ♦♦♦♦
99 Waverley Road, Southsea, PO5 2PL
T: (023) 9273 0402
I: www.waverleyparklodge.co.uk

Wolverton Guest House ♦♦♦
22 Granada Road, Southsea, PO4 0RH
T: (023) 9273 2819
F: (023) 814234

Woodville Hotel ♦♦♦
6 Florence Road, Southsea, PO5 2NE
T: (023) 9282 3409
F: (023) 9234 6089
E: woodvillehotel@cwcom.net

POSTCOMBE
Oxfordshire

Beech Farm ♦♦♦♦
Salt Lane, Postcombe, Oxford OX9 7EE
T: (01844) 281240
F: (01844) 281632
E: beech.farm@btopenworld.com
I: www.ukworld.net/beechfarm.htm

PRINCES RISBOROUGH
Buckinghamshire

Solis Ortu ♦♦♦
Aylesbury Road, Askett, Princes Risborough, Aylesbury HP27 9LY
T: (01844) 344175
F: (01844) 343509

QUAINTON
Buckinghamshire

The White Hart ♦♦♦
4 The Strand, Quainton, Aylesbury HP22 4AS
T: (01296) 655234

Woodlands Farmhouse ♦♦♦
Doddershall, Quainton, Aylesbury HP22 4DE
T: (01296) 770225

RADNAGE
Buckinghamshire

Highlands ♦♦♦♦
26 Green Lane, Radnage, High Wycombe HP14 4DN
T: (01494) 484835
F: (01494) 482633
E: janekhighlands@aol.com
I: www.country-accom.co.uk

RAMSDEN
Oxfordshire

Ann's Cottage ♦♦♦
Lower End, Ramsden, Oxford OX7 3AZ
T: (01993) 868592
E: foxwoodfamily@lineone.net

READING
Berkshire

Abadair House ♦♦
46 Redlands Road, Reading, RG1 5HE
T: (0118) 986 3792
F: (0118) 986 3792
E: abadair@globalnet.co.uk
I: www.smoothhound.co.uk/hotels/abadair/.html

Bath Hotel ♦♦♦
54 Bath Road, Reading, RG1 6PG
T: (0118) 957 2019
F: (0118) 950 3203
I: www.destinationsuk.com

Caversham Lodge ♦♦
133a Caversham Road, Reading, RG1 8AS
T: (01189) 573529

Crescent Hotel ♦♦♦
35 Coley Avenue, Reading, RG1 6LL
T: (01189) 507980
F: (01189) 574299

Dittisham Guest House ♦♦♦
63 Tilehurst Road, Reading, RG30 2JL
T: (0118) 956 9483
E: dittishamgh@aol.com

The Elms ♦♦
Gallowstree Road, Rotherfield Peppard, Henley-on-Thames RG9 5HT
T: (0118) 972 3164
F: (0118) 972 4594

Greystoke Guest House ♦♦♦♦
10 Greystoke Road, Caversham, Reading RG4 5EL
T: (01189) 475784
E: greystoke.guesthouse@freedomland.co.uk

The Old Forge ♦♦♦
109 Grovelands Road, Reading, RG30 2PB
T: (0118) 958 2928
F: (0118) 958 2408
E: rees.family@virgin.net

The Roebuck Hotel ♦♦
De Hillier Taverns plc, Oxford Road, Tilehurst, Reading RG31 6TG
T: (0118) 942 7517
F: (0118) 941 7629
E: dhtroebuck@aol.com

The Six Bells ♦♦♦
Beenham Village, Beenham, Reading RG7 5NX
T: (0118) 971 3368

Warren Dene Hotel ♦♦♦
1017 Oxford Road, Tilehurst, Reading RG31 6TL
T: (0118) 942 2556
F: (0118) 945 1096
E: wdh@globalnet.co.uk

RINGWOOD
Hampshire

The Auld Kennels ♦♦♦
215 Christchurch Road, Moortown, Ringwood, BH24 3AN
T: (01425) 475170
F: (01425) 461577
E: auldkennels@aol.com

Fraser House ♦♦♦
Salisbury Road, Blashford, Ringwood BH24 3PB
T: (01425) 473958
F: (01425) 473958
E: fraserhouse@btinternet.com
I: www.fraserhouse.net

Old Stacks ♦♦♦♦
154 Hightown Road, Ringwood, BH24 1NP
T: (01425) 473840
F: (01425) 473840
E: oldstacksbandb@aol.com
I: www.smoothhound.co.uk/hotels/oldstacks.html

Picket Hill House
♦♦♦♦ SILVER AWARD
Picket Hill, Ringwood, BH24 3HH
T: (01425) 476173
F: (01425) 470022
E: b&b@pickethill.freeserve.co.uk
I: www.pickthill.co.uk

Torre Avon
♦♦♦♦ SILVER AWARD
21 Salisbury Road, Ringwood, BH24 1AS
T: (01425) 472769
F: (01425) 472769
E: b&b@torreavon.freeserve.co.uk
I: www.torreavon.freeserve.co.uk

ROMSEY
Hampshire

Abbey Hotel ♦♦♦
11 Church Street, Romsey, SO51 8BT
T: (01794) 513360
F: (01794) 524318
E: di@abbeyhotelromsey.co.uk
I: www.abbeyhotelromsey.co.uk

Aylwards Bottom ♦♦♦♦
Top Green, Lockerley, Romsey, SO51 0JP
T: (01794) 340864

The Chalet Guest House ♦♦♦
Botley Road, Whitenap, Romsey, SO51 5RQ
T: (01794) 517299
E: b-and-b@the-chalet.freeserve.co.uk
I: www.homepage.ntlworld.com/obrian

3 Cherville Mews ♦♦♦♦
Romsey, SO51 8FY
T: (01794) 830518
F: (01794) 830518
E: patricia.townson@ntlworld.com
I: www.patsbnb.tripod.com

79 Mercer Way ♦♦♦
Romsey, SO51 7PH
T: (01794) 502009
F: (01794) 503009

Pauncefoot House ♦♦♦♦
Pauncefoot Hill, Romsey, SO51 6AA
T: (01794) 513139
F: (01794) 513139
E: lendupont@aol.com

Pillar Box Cottage ♦♦♦
Toothill, Romsey, SO51 9LN
T: (023) 8073 2390

Pyesmead Farm ♦♦♦
Plaitford, Romsey SO51 6EE
T: (01794) 323386
F: (01794) 323386
E: pyesmead@talk21.com

Ranvilles Farm House ♦♦♦♦
Ower, Romsey, SO51 6AA
T: (023) 8081 4481
F: (023) 8081 4481
E: inro@ranvilles.com
I: www.ranvilles.com

Roselea ♦♦♦♦
Hamdown Crescent, East Wellow, Romsey SO51 6BJ
T: (01794) 323262
F: (01794) 323262
E: beds@roselea.info
I: www.roselea.info

Southernwood ♦♦
Plaitford Common, Salisbury Road, Plaitford, Romsey SO51 6EE
T: (01794) 323255

Stoneymarsh Bed & Breakfast ♦♦♦
Stoneymarsh Cottage, Stoneymarsh, Romsey, SO51 0LB
T: (01794) 368867
F: (01794) 368867
E: mmmoran@btinternet.com

The Sun Inn ♦♦♦♦
116 Winchester Road, Romsey, SO51 7JG
T: (01794) 512255
F: (01794) 521887

Toad Hall ♦♦♦♦♦
66 Mill Lane, Romsey, SO51 8EQ
T: (01794) 512350

Tregoyd House ♦♦♦
Crook Hill, Braishfield, Romsey SO51 0QB
T: (01794) 368307
F: (01794) 368307
E: tregoyd@yahoo.co.uk
I: www.geocities.com/eureka/park/2485

RYDE
Isle of Wight

Claverton ♦♦♦♦
12 The Strand, Ryde, PO33 1JE
T: (01983) 613015
F: (01983) 613015
E: clavertonhouse@aol.com

The Dorset Hotel ♦♦♦
31 Dover Street, Ryde, PO33 2BW
T: (01983) 564327
F: (01983) 614635
E: hoteldorset@aol.com
I: www.thedorsethotel.co.uk

The Elmfield ♦♦♦
18 Marlborough Close, Elmfield, Ryde, PO33 1AP
T: (01983) 614131
E: jeanlewis18@hotmail.com

Fern Cottage ♦♦♦♦
8 West Street, Ryde, PO33 2NW
T: (01983) 565856
F: (01983) 565856
E: sandra@psdferguson.freeserve.co.uk

Kemphill Farm
♦♦♦♦ SILVER AWARD
Stroudwood Road, Upton, Ryde, PO33 4BZ
T: (01983) 563880
F: (01983) 563880
E: ron.holland@farming.me.uk
I: www.kemphill.com

Royal Esplanade Hotel ♦♦♦
16 The Esplanade, Ryde, PO33 2ED
T: (01983) 562549
F: (01983) 563918
I: www.shearingsholidays.com

Sea View ♦♦♦
8 Dover Street, Ryde, PO33 2AQ
T: (01983) 810976

Seahaven Hotel ♦♦♦
36 St Thomas Street, Ryde, PO33 2DL
T: (01983) 563069
F: (01983) 563570
E: seahaven@netguides.co.uk

Seaward Guest House ♦♦♦
14-16 George Street, Ryde, PO33 2EW
T: (01983) 563168
F: (01983) 563168
E: seaward@fsbdial.co.uk

Sillwood Acre ♦♦♦♦
Church Road, Binstead, Ryde PO33 3TB
T: (01983) 563553
E: sillwood.acre@virgin.net

Stonelands ♦♦♦♦
Binstead Road, Binstead, Ryde PO33 3NJ
T: (01983) 616947
F: (01983) 812857
E: stone.lands@tiscali.co.uk

Trentham Guest House ♦♦♦
38 The Strand, Ryde, PO33 1JF
T: (01983) 563418
F: (01983) 563418

The Vine Guest House ♦♦♦
16 Castle Street, Ryde, PO33 2EG
T: (01983) 566633
F: (01983) 566633
E: vine@guesthouse49.freeserve.co.uk
I: www.thevineguesthouse.co.uk

ST CROSS
Hampshire

Dolphin House Studios Rating Applied For
3 Compton Road, St Cross, Winchester SO23 9SL
T: (01962) 853284
F: (01962) 853284

ST LAWRENCE
Isle of Wight

Lisle Combe ♦♦♦
Bank End Farm, Undercliff Drive, St Lawrence, Ventnor PO38 1UW
T: (01983) 852582
E: lislecombe@yahoo.com
I: www.lislecombe.co.uk

Little Orchard ♦♦♦♦
Undercliff Drive, St Lawrence, Ventnor PO38 1YA
T: (01983) 731106

SALFORD
Oxfordshire

Rectory Farm ♦♦♦♦♦
Rectory Farm, Salford, Chipping Norton OX7 5YZ
T: (01608) 643209
F: (01608) 643209
E: colston@rectoryfarm75.freeserve.co.uk

SANDFORD
Isle of Wight

The Barn ♦♦♦♦
Pound Farm, Shanklin Road, Sandford, Ventnor PO38 3AW
T: (01983) 840047
F: (01983) 840047
E: barnpoundfarm@barnpoundfarm.free-online.co.uk

SANDLEHEATH
Hampshire

Sandleheath Post Office & Stores ♦♦♦
Sandleheath, Fordingbridge SP6 1PP
T: (01425) 652230
F: (01425) 652230
E: sue@sandleheath.com
I: www.sandleheath.com

SANDOWN
Isle of Wight

The Belgrave Hotel ♦♦
14-16 Beachfield Road, Sandown, PO36 8NA
T: (01983) 404550
F: (01983) 407257

Belmore Private Hotel ♦♦♦
101 Station Avenue, Sandown, PO36 8HD
T: (01983) 404189
F: (01983) 405942
E: lowbelmore@talk21.com
I: www.islandbreaks.co.uk/belmore

Bernay Hotel ♦♦♦
24 Victoria Road, Sandown, PO36 8AL
T: (01983) 402205
F: (01983) 402205
E: bernayhotel@btconnect.com
I: www.bernay-hotel.co.uk

Bertram Lodge ♦♦♦
3 Leed Street, Sandown, PO36 9DA
T: (01983) 402551
E: gazz@blodge.fslife.co.uk

Carisbrooke House Hotel ♦♦♦
11 Beachfield Road, Sandown, PO36 8NA
T: (01983) 402257
E: carisbrookehotel@aol.com

Cavalier Guest House ♦♦♦
9 Carter Street, Sandown, PO36 8BL
T: (01983) 403269

The Danebury ♦♦♦
26 Victoria Road, Sandown, PO36 8AL
T: (01983) 403795
E: danebury@madasafish.com

Denewood Hotel ♦♦♦♦
7 Victoria Road, Sandown, PO36 8AL
T: (01983) 402980
F: (01983) 402980

Heathfield House Hotel ♦♦♦
52 Melville Street, Sandown, PO36 8LF
T: (01983) 400002
F: (01983) 400002
E: mike.sollis@ic24.net
I: www.netguides.co.uk/wight/heathfieldhouse.html

Homeland Private Hotel ♦♦♦
38 Grove Road, Sandown, PO36 8HH
T: (01983) 404305

Inglewood Guest House ♦♦♦
15 Avenue Road, Sandown, PO36 8BN
T: (01983) 403485

Iona Guest House ♦♦♦
44 Sandown Road, Lake, Sandown PO36 9JT
T: (01983) 402741
F: (01983) 402741
E: ionahotel@supanet.com

Lanowlee ♦♦♦
99 Station Avenue, Sandown, PO36 8HD
T: (01983) 403577

Lyndhurst Hotel ♦♦♦
8 Royal Crescent, Sandown, PO36 8LZ
T: (01983) 403663
F: (01983) 403663

Montpelier Hotel ♦♦♦
Pier Street, Sandown, PO36 8JR
T: (01983) 403964
F: 07092 212734
E: enquiries@montpelier-hotel.co.uk
I: www.montpelier-hotel.co.uk

Rooftree Hotel ♦♦♦♦
26 Broadway, Sandown, PO36 9BY
T: (01983) 403175
F: (01983) 407354
E: rooftree@netguides.co.uk

St Catherines Hotel ♦♦♦♦
1 Winchester Park Road, Sandown, PO36 8HJ
T: (01983) 402392
F: (01983) 402392
E: stcathhotel@hotmail.com
I: www.isleofwight-holidays.co.uk

St Michaels Hotel ♦♦♦♦
33 Leed Street, Sandown, PO36 8JE
T: (01983) 403636

Sandhill Hotel ♦♦♦
6 Hill Street, Sandown, PO36 9DB
T: (01983) 403635
F: (01983) 403695
E: sandhill.hotel@ukgateway.net or sandhill@btconnect.com
I: www.sandhill-hotel.com

Shachri ♦♦♦
31 Avenue Road, Sandown, PO36 8BN
T: (01983) 405718

Shangri-La Hotel ♦♦♦
30 Broadway, Sandown, PO36 9BY
T: (01983) 403672
F: (01983) 403672
E: shangrilahotel0@aol.com
I: www.shangrilahotel.co.uk

Westfield Hotel ♦♦♦♦
17 Broadway, Sandown, PO36 9BY
T: (01983) 403802
F: (01983) 408225

SAUNDERTON
Buckinghamshire

Hunters Gate ♦♦♦
Deanfield, Saunderton, Aylesbury HP14 4JR
T: (01494) 481718
E: dadykes@attglobal.net

SEAVIEW
Isle of Wight

1 Cluniac Cottages ♦♦♦♦
Priory Road, Seaview, PO34 5BU
T: (01983) 812119
E: bill.elfenjay@virgin.net
I: www.cluniaccottages.fsnet.co.uk/

Maple Villa ♦♦♦
Oakhill Road, Seaview, PO34 5AP
T: (01983) 614826
E: mail@maplevilla.co.uk
I: www.maplevilla.co.uk

SELBORNE
Hampshire

8 Goslings Croft ♦♦♦♦
Selborne, Alton GU34 3HZ
T: (01420) 511285
F: (01420) 587451
I: timothyrouse@hotmail.com

Ivanhoe ♦♦♦♦
Oakhanger, Selborne, Alton GU35 9JG
T: (01420) 473464

The Queen's & The Limes ♦♦♦
High Street, Selborne, Alton GU34 3JJ
T: (01420) 511454
F: (01420) 511272
E: enquiries@queens-selborne.co.uk
I: www.queens-selborne.co.uk

Seale Cottage ♦♦♦
Gracious Street, Selborne, Alton GU34 3JE
T: (01420) 511396
E: cw.gibson@virgin.net

Thatched Barn House ♦♦♦♦
Grange Farm, Gracious Street, Selborne, Alton GU34 3JG
T: (01420) 511007
F: (01420) 511008
E: bandb@bobt.dircon.co.uk
I: www.bobt.dircon.co.uk

SHAFTESBURY
Dorset

Aysgarth ♦♦♦♦
Back Street, East Stour, Gillingham SP8 5JY
T: (01747) 838351
E: aysgarth@lineone.net
I: website.lineone.net/~aysgarth

Cliff House ♦♦♦♦♦ SILVER AWARD
Breach Lane, Shaftesbury, SP7 8LF
T: (01747) 852548
F: (01747) 852548
E: dianaepow@aol.com
I: www.cliff-house.co.uk

The Grove Arms Inn ♦♦♦♦
Ludwell, Shaftesbury SP7 9ND
T: (01747) 828328
F: (01747) 828960
I: www.grovearms.com

The Kings Arms Inn ♦♦♦♦
East Stour Common, East Stour, Gillingham SP8 5NB
T: (01747) 838325
E: jenny@kings-arms.fsnet.co.uk

The Knoll ♦♦♦♦ SILVER AWARD
Bleke Street, Shaftesbury, SP7 8AH
T: (01747) 855243
E: pickshaftesbury@compuserve.com
I: www.pick-art.org.uk

The Retreat ♦♦♦♦
47 Bell Street, Shaftesbury, SP7 8AE
T: (01747) 850372
F: (01747) 850372
E: at.retreat@virgin.net
I: www.the-retreat.org.uk

SHALFLEET
Isle of Wight

Hebberdens ♦♦♦
Yarmouth Road, Shalfleet, Newport PO30 4NB
T: (01983) 531364
F: (01983) 531364
E: hebberdens@fsmail-net
I: www.hebberdens.com

The Old Malthouse ♦♦
1 Mill Road, Shalfleet, Newport PO30 4NE
T: (01983) 531329
E: b&b@oldmalthouse.demon.co.uk

SHALSTONE
Buckinghamshire

Barnita ♦♦♦
Wood Green, Shalstone,
Buckingham MK18 5DZ
T: (01280) 850639
I: www.aylesburyvale.net/buckingham/barnita.htm

SHANKLIN
Isle of Wight

Atholl Court ♦♦♦
1 Atherley Road, Shanklin,
PO37 7AT
T: (01983) 862414
F: (01983) 868985
E: info@atholl-court.co.uk
I: www.atholl-court.co.uk

Birkdale Hotel ♦♦♦♦
Grange Road, Shanklin,
PO37 6NN
T: (01983) 862949
F: (01983) 862949
E: enq@birkdalehoteliowfsnet.co.uk

Braemar Hotel ♦♦♦
1 Grange Road, Shanklin,
PO37 6NN
T: (01983) 863172
F: (01983) 863172

Brooke House Hotel ♦♦♦
2 St Pauls Avenue, Shanklin,
PO37 7AL
T: (01983) 863162
E: mike@brookehouse.fsnet.co.uk
I: www.brookehouse.fsnet.co.uk

Cedar Lodge Hotel ♦♦♦
28 Arthurs Hill, Shanklin,
PO37 6EX
T: (01983) 863268
F: (01983) 863268

Chestnuts Hotel ♦♦♦
Hope Road, Shanklin, PO37 6EA
T: (01983) 862162

Claremont Guest House ♦♦♦♦
4 Eastmount Road, Shanklin,
PO37 6DN
T: (01983) 862083

Clifton Hotel ♦♦♦
1 Queens Road, Shanklin,
PO37 6AN
T: (01983) 863015
F: (01983) 865911
E: info@cliftonhotel-shanklin.co.uk
I: www.cliftonhotel-shanklin.co.uk

Cliftonville Hotel ♦♦♦
6 Hope Road, Shanklin,
PO37 6EA
T: (01983) 862197
F: (01983) 862197
E: cliftonvillehotel@talk21.com

Courtlands Hotel ♦♦♦
Paddock Road, Shanklin,
PO37 6PA
T: (01983) 862167
F: (01983) 863308
E: simon@courtlandshotel.co.uk
I: www.courtlandshotel.co.uk

Culham Lodge Hotel ♦♦♦♦
31 Landguard Manor Road,
Shanklin, PO37 7HZ
T: (01983) 862880
F: (01983) 862880
E: metcalf@culham99.freeserve.co.uk
I: www.isleofwight-hotel.biz

The Edgecliffe Hotel ♦♦♦♦
7 Clarence Gardens, Shanklin,
PO37 6HA
T: (01983) 866199
F: (01983) 868841
E: edgecliffehtl@aol.com
I: www.wightonline.co.uk/edgecliffehotel

The Empress of the Sea Hotel ♦♦♦♦♦ SILVER AWARD
Luccombe Road, Shanklin,
PO37 6RQ
T: (01983) 862178
F: (01983) 868636
E: empress.sea@virgin.net
I: www.empressofthesea.com

Esplanade Hotel ♦♦
33 The Esplanade, Shanklin,
PO37 6BG
T: (01983) 863001
F: (01983) 863001

Farringford Hotel ♦♦♦♦
19 Hope Road, Shanklin,
PO37 6EA
T: (01983) 862176
E: farringford@excite.com
I: www.farringfordhotel.com

Fawley Guest House ♦♦♦
12 Hope Road, Shanklin,
PO37 6EA
T: (01983) 868898

Foxhills ♦♦♦♦♦ GOLD AWARD
30 Victoria Avenue, Shanklin,
PO37 6LS
T: (01983) 862329
F: (01983) 866666
E: info@foxhillshotel.co.uk
I: www.foxhillshotel.co.uk

The Glen Hotel ♦♦♦
4 Avenue Road, Shanklin,
PO37 7BG
T: (01983) 862154
E: theglenshanklin@totalise.co.uk

Grange Bank Hotel ♦♦♦♦
Grange Road, Shanklin,
PO37 6NN
T: (01983) 862337
F: (01983) 862737
E: Grangebankhotel@aol.com
I: www.grangebank.co.uk

The Havelock Hotel ♦♦♦♦ SILVER AWARD
2 Queens Road, Shanklin,
PO37 6AN
T: (01983) 862747

Hazelwood Hotel ♦♦♦
14 Clarence Road, Shanklin,
PO37 7BH
T: (01983) 862824
F: (01983) 862824
E: barbara.tubbs@thehazelwood.free-online.co.uk
I: www.thehazelwood.free-online.co.uk

Hope Lodge Hotel ♦♦♦♦ SILVER AWARD
21 Hope Road, Shanklin,
PO37 6EA
T: (01983) 863140
F: (01983) 863140
E: janetwf@aol.com
I: placestostay.com

Kenbury Hotel ♦♦♦♦
Clarence Road, Shanklin,
PO37 7BH
T: (01983) 862085
E: kenbury@isleofwighthotel.co.uk
I: www.isleofwighthotel.co.uk

The Lincoln Hotel ♦♦♦♦
30 Littlestairs Road, Shanklin,
PO37 6HS
T: (01983) 861171
F: (01983) 861171
E: enquiries@thelincolnhotel.org.uk
I: www.thelincolnhotel.org.uk

Miclaran Hotel ♦♦♦
37 Littlestairs Road, Shanklin,
PO37 6HS
T: (01983) 862726
F: (01983) 862726

Mount House Hotel ♦♦♦
20 Arthurs Hill, Shanklin,
PO37 6EE
T: (01983) 862556
F: (01983) 867551
E: mounthouse@netguides.co.uk
I: www.netguides.co.uk

Overstrand Hotel ♦♦♦♦
5 Howard Road, Shanklin,
PO37 6HD
T: (01983) 862100
F: (01983) 862100

Palmerston Hotel ♦♦♦
Palmerston Road, Shanklin,
PO37 6AS
T: (01983) 865547
F: (01983) 868008
E: info@palmerston-hotel.co.uk
I: www.palmerston-hotel.co.uk

Parkway Hotel ♦♦♦
6 Park Road, Shanklin, PO37 6AZ
T: (01983) 862740
E: malcolm@parkwayhotel.flyer.co.uk
I: www.parkwayhotel.flyer.co.uk

Pink Beach Hotel Rating Applied For
20 The Esplanade, Shanklin,
PO37 6BN
T: (01983) 862501

The Roseglen Hotel ♦♦♦♦
12 Palmerston Road, Shanklin,
PO37 6AS
T: (01983) 863164
F: (01983) 862271
E: david@roseglen.co.uk
I: www.roseglen.co.uk

The Royson ♦♦♦♦
26 Littlestairs Road, Shanklin,
PO37 6HS
T: (01983) 862163
F: (01983) 865403
E: theroyson@lineone.net
I: www.theroyson.co.uk

Rozelle Hotel ♦♦♦
Atherley Road, Shanklin,
PO37 7AT
T: (01983) 862745
F: (01983) 862745

Ryedale Private Hotel ♦♦♦
3 Atherley Road, Shanklin,
PO37 7AT
T: (01983) 862375
F: (01983) 862375
E: ryedale@dottydots.co.uk
I: www.smoothhound.co.uk/hotels/ryedalep.html

St Brelades Hotel ♦♦♦
15 Hope Road, Shanklin,
PO37 6EA
T: (01983) 862967
E: julie@st-brelades-hotel.co.uk
I: www.st-brelades-hotel.co.uk

St George's House Hotel ♦♦♦
St George's Road, Shanklin,
PO37 6BA
T: (01983) 863691
F: (01983) 861597
E: info@stgeorgesiow.com
I: www.stgeorgesiow.com

St Leonards Hotel ♦♦♦♦ SILVER AWARD
22 Queens Road, Shanklin,
PO37 6AW
T: (01983) 862121
F: (01983) 868895
E: info@wight-breaks.co.uk
I: www.wight-breaks.co.uk

Seamer House ♦♦♦♦
30 Atherley Road, Shanklin,
PO37 7AT
T: (01983) 864926
F: (01983) 864926
E: seamerhouse@tinyworld.co.uk

Somerville Hotel ♦♦♦
14 St Georges Road, Shanklin,
PO37 6BA
T: (01983) 862821

The Steamer Inn ♦♦♦
18 The Esplanade, Shanklin,
PO37 6BS
T: (01983) 862641
F: (01983) 862741

Suncliffe Private Hotel ♦♦♦
8 Hope Road, Shanklin,
PO37 6EA
T: (01983) 863009
F: (01983) 864868
E: suncliffe@pmorter.tcp.co.uk
I: www.homepages.tcp.co.uk/~pmorter

Swiss Cottage Hotel ♦♦♦
10 St Georges Road, Shanklin,
PO37 6BA
T: (01983) 862333
F: (01983) 862333
E: mail@swiss-cottage.co.uk
I: www.swiss-cottage.co.uk

The Triton Hotel ♦♦
23 Atherley Road, Shanklin,
PO37 7AU
T: (01983) 862494
F: (01983) 861281
E: jackie@tritonhotel.freeserve.co.uk
I: www.iow-accommodation.com

Willow Bank Hotel ♦♦♦♦
36 Atherley Road, Shanklin,
PO37 7AU
T: (01983) 862482
F: (01983) 862486
E: willowbank.hotel@virgin.net
I: www.willowbankhotel.com

SHAWFORD
Hampshire

Greenmead Cottage
Rating Applied For
Fairfield Road, Shawford, Winchester SO21 2DA
T: (01962) 713172
F: (01962) 711903
E: junetice@amserve.net

SHENINGTON
Oxfordshire

Sugarswell Farm ♦♦♦♦
Shenington, Banbury OX15 6HW
T: (01295) 680512
F: (01295) 688149

Top Farm House ♦♦♦
Shenington, Banbury OX15 6LZ
T: (01295) 670226
F: (01295) 678170
E: info@topfarmhouse.co.uk
I: www.topfarmhouse.co.uk

SHENLEY CHURCH END
Buckinghamshire

3 Selby Grove ♦♦♦♦
Shenley Church End, Milton Keynes MK5 6BN
T: (01908) 504663
E: ceyesmk@aol.com

SHERBORNE ST JOHN
Hampshire

Fairfield
Rating Applied For
16 Aldermaston Road, Sherborne St John, Basingstoke, RG24 9JY
T: (01256) 850308
E: jackie-elsley@hotmail.com
I: www.fairfields.org.uk

Manor Farm Stables
Rating Applied For
Vyne Road, Sherborne St John, Tadley RG24 9HX
T: (01256) 851324
F: (01256) 855006

SHILLINGFORD
Oxfordshire

The Kingfisher Inn ♦♦♦♦
27 Henley Road, Shillingford, Wallingford OX10 7EL
T: (01865) 858595
F: (01865) 858286
E: enquiries@kingfisher-inn.co.uk
I: www.kingfisher-inn.co.uk

Marsh House ♦♦♦
7 Court Drive, Shillingford, Wallingford OX10 7ER
T: (01865) 858496
F: (01865) 858496
E: marsh.house@talk21.com

SHIPTON-UNDER-WYCHWOOD
Oxfordshire

Court Farm
♦♦♦♦ SILVER AWARD
Mawles Lane, Shipton-under-Wychwood, Oxford OX7 6DA
T: (01993) 831515
F: (01993) 831813
E: belinda@courtfarmbb.fsnet.co.uk

Courtlands ♦♦♦♦
6 Courtlands Road, Shipton-under-Wychwood, Oxford OX7 6DF
T: (01993) 830551
E: j-jfletcher@which.net
I: www.cotswoldsbandb.com

Garden Cottage ♦♦♦
Fiddlers Hill, Shipton-under-Wychwood, Oxford OX7 6DR
T: (01993) 830640
E: charmian@ukgateway.net

Lodge Cottage ♦♦♦
Shipton-under-Wychwood, Oxford OX7 6DG
T: (01993) 830811
F: (01993) 830811
E: h.a.savill@btopenworld.com

SHIRRELL HEATH
Hampshire

Highdown ♦♦♦♦
Twynhams Hill, Shirrell Heath, Southampton SO32 2JL
T: (01329) 835876
F: (01329) 835876
E: highdown2000@hotmail.com
I: www.highdown.net

SHORWELL
Isle of Wight

Bucks Farm ♦♦♦♦
Shorwell, Newport PO30 3LP
T: (01983) 551206
F: (01983) 551206

Northcourt ♦♦♦♦
Main Road, Shorwell, Newport PO30 3JG
T: (01983) 740415
F: (01983) 740409
E: john@north-court.demon.co.uk

Westcourt Farm ♦♦♦♦
Limerstone Road, Shorwell, Newport PO30 3LA
T: (01983) 740233
E: julie@westcourt-farm.co.uk
I: www.westcourt-farm.co.uk

SHOTTESWELL
Oxfordshire

Slated Barn Guest House
♦♦♦♦
Slated Barn, Warwick Road, Shotteswell, Banbury OX17 1UA
T: (01295) 738999
F: (01295) 738807

SHROTON
Dorset

The Cricketers
♦♦♦♦ SILVER AWARD
Main Street, Shroton, Blandford Forum DT11 8QD
T: (01258) 860421
F: (01258) 861800

SKIRMETT
Buckinghamshire

The Old Bakery ♦♦♦
Skirmett, Henley-on-Thames RG9 6TD
T: (01491) 638309
F: (01491) 638086
E: lizroach@euphony.net

SLOUGH
Berkshire

Upton Park Guest House ♦♦♦
41 Upton Park, Slough, SL1 2DA
T: (01753) 528797
F: (01753) 550208
E: p.jones2370@aoc.com

SONNING
Oxfordshire

The Bull Inn ♦♦♦
High Street, Sonning on Thames, Sonning, Reading RG4 6UP
T: (01189) 693901

SONNING COMMON
Oxfordshire

21 Red House Drive ♦♦♦
Sonning Common, Reading RG4 9NT
T: (0118) 972 2312
F: (0118) 972 2312

SOULDERN
Oxfordshire

The Fox Inn ♦♦
Fox Lane, Souldern, Bicester OX27 7JW
T: (01869) 345284
F: (01869) 345667

Tower Fields ♦♦♦
Tusmore Road, Souldern, Bicester OX27 7HY
T: (01869) 346554
F: (01869) 345157
E: hgould@strayduck.com

SOUTH GORLEY
Hampshire

Hucklesbrook Farm
♦♦♦♦ SILVER AWARD
South Gorley, Fordingbridge SP6 2PN
T: (01425) 653180
E: dh.sampson@btinternet.com

SOUTH LEIGH
Oxfordshire

Stow Cottage ♦♦♦
Station Road, South Leigh, Witney OX29 6XN
T: (01993) 704005
F: (01993) 704005

SOUTHAMPTON
Hampshire

Alcantara Guest House ♦♦♦
20 Howard Road, Shirley, Southampton, SO15 5BN
T: (023) 8033 2966
F: (023) 8049 6163
E: alcantara@supanet.com
I: www.alcantaraguesthouse.co.uk

Argyle Lodge ♦♦♦
13 Landguard Road, Shirley, Southampton, SO15 5DL
T: (023) 8022 4063
F: (023) 8033 3688

Ashelee Lodge ♦♦♦
36 Atherley Road, Shirley, Southampton, SO15 5DQ
T: (023) 8022 2095
F: (023) 8022 2095

Banister House Hotel ♦♦♦
Banister Road, Southampton, SO15 2JJ
T: (023) 8022 1279
F: (023) 8022 6551
E: banisterhotel@btconnect.com
I: www.banisterhotel.co.uk

The Bosun's Locker ♦♦
Castle Square, Upper Bugle Street, Southampton, SO14 2EE
T: (02380) 333364
F: (02380) 333364

Brunswick Lodge
Rating Applied For
100-104 Anglesea Road, Shirley, Southampton, SO15 5QG
T: (02380) 774777

Carmel Guest House ♦♦♦
306 Winchester Road, Shirley, Southampton, SO16 6TU
T: (023) 8077 3579

Dormy House Hotel ♦♦♦♦
21 Barnes Lane, Sarisbury Green, Southampton SO31 7DA
T: (01489) 572626
F: (01489) 573370
E: dormyhousehotel@warsash.globalnet.co.uk
I: www.dormyhousehotel.net

Eaton Court Hotel ♦♦♦
32 Hill Lane, Southampton, SO15 5AY
T: (023) 8022 3081
F: (023) 8032 2006
E: ecourthot@aol.com
I: www.eatoncourtsouthampton.co.uk

Ellenborough House ♦♦♦
172 Hill Lane, Shirley, Southampton, SO15 5DB
T: (023) 8022 1716
F: (023) 8034 8486

Fenland Guest House ♦♦♦
79 Hill Lane, Southampton, SO15 5AD
T: (023) 8022 0360
F: (023) 8022 6574

Linden Guest House ♦♦♦
51-53 The Polygon, Southampton, SO15 2BP
T: (023) 8022 5653
F: (023) 8063 0808

The Lodge ♦♦♦
No 1 Winn Road, The Avenue, Southampton, SO17 1EH
T: (023) 8055 7537
F: (023) 8055 3586
E: lodgehotel@faxvia.net
I: www.yell.co.uk/siteslodgeso17

Madison House ♦♦♦
137 Hill Lane, Southampton, SO15 5AF
T: (023) 8033 3374
F: (023) 8033 1209
E: foley@madisonhouse.co.uk
I: www.madisonhouse.co.uk

The Mayfair Guest House
♦♦♦♦
11 Landguard Road, Shirley, Southampton, SO15 5DL
T: (023) 8022 9861
F: (023) 8021 1552

Rivendell ♦♦♦
19 Landguard Road, Shirley, Southampton, SO15 5DL
T: (02380) 223240
E: rivendellbb@amserve.net

SOUTHBOURNE
Dorset

Acorns Hotel ♦♦♦♦
14 Southwood Avenue, Southbourne, Bournemouth BH6 3QA
T: (01202) 422438
F: (01202) 418384
E: acornshotel@hotmail.com

Hawkesmore Hotel ♦♦♦
Pine Avenue, Southbourne, Bournemouth BH6 3ST
T: (01202) 426787

Newpoint Hotel ♦♦♦♦
25 Pinecliffe Avenue, Southbourne, Bournemouth BH6 3PY
T: (01202) 425047

Pennington Hotel ♦♦♦♦
26 Southern Road, Southbourne, Bournemouth BH6 3SS
T: (01202) 428653
F: (01202) 428653
E: vranderton@btinternet.co.uk

Shearwater Hotel ♦♦♦
61 Grand Avenue, Southbourne, Bournemouth BH6 3TA
T: (01202) 423396
E: shearwaterbb@hotmail.com
I: www.theshearwater.freeserve.co.uk

Sherbourne House Hotel ♦♦♦♦
14 Southern Road, Southbourne, Bournemouth BH6 3SR
T: (01202) 425680
F: (01202) 257423
E: ian@sherbournehousehotel.co.uk
I: www.sherbournehousehotel.co.uk

Sun Haven Guest House Rating Applied For
39 Southern Road, Southbourne, Bournemouth, BH6 3SS
T: (01202) 427560

STANDLAKE
Oxfordshire

Pinkhill Cottage ♦♦♦♦ SILVER AWARD
45 Rack End, Standlake, Witney OX29 7SA
T: (01865) 300544
E: pinkhill@madasafish.com

STANFORD IN THE VALE
Oxfordshire

Stanford Park House ♦♦♦
Park Lane, Stanford in the Vale, Faringdon SN7 8PF
T: (01367) 710702
F: (01367) 710329
E: gjd34@dial.pipex.com
I: www.stanfordpark.co.uk

STANTON ST JOHN
Oxfordshire

The Talkhouse ♦♦♦
Wheatley Road, Stanton St John, Oxford, OX33 1EX
T: (01865) 351648
F: (01865) 351085

STEEPLE
Dorset

Blackmanston Farm Rating Applied For
Steeple, Wareham BH20 5NZ
T: (01929) 480743
F: (01929) 480743

STEEPLE ASTON
Oxfordshire

Westfield Farm Motel ♦♦♦♦
Fenway, Steeple Aston, Oxford OX25 4SS
T: (01869) 340591
F: (01869) 347594
E: info@westfieldmotel.u-net.com
I: www.oxlink.co.uk/accom/westfield-farm/

STEVENTON
Oxfordshire

Tethers End ♦♦♦
Abingdon Road, Steventon, Abingdon OX13 6RW
T: (01235) 834015
F: (01235) 862990
E: peterdmiller@btinternet.com
I: www.millerbandb.co.uk

STEWKLEY
Buckinghamshire

Mount Pleasant Farm ♦♦♦
Stewkley, Leighton Buzzard LU7 0LU
T: (01525) 240451
F: (01525) 240163

Oak Tree Cottage Rating Applied For
6 Ivy Lane, Stewkley, Leighton Buzzard LU7 0EN
T: (01525) 242225
E: karalynsparkes@hotmail.co.uk

STOCKBRIDGE
Hampshire

Carbery Guest House ♦♦♦
Salisbury Hill, Stockbridge, SO20 6EZ
T: (01264) 810771
F: (01264) 811022

The White Hart Inn ♦♦♦♦
High Street, Stockbridge, SO20 6HF
T: (01264) 810663
F: (01264) 810268

STOKENCHURCH
Buckinghamshire

Hallbottom Farm ♦♦♦♦
Park Lane, Stokenchurch, High Wycombe HP14 3TQ
T: (01494) 482520
E: deborah@hallbottomfarm.co.uk
I: www.smoothhound.co.uk/hotels/hallbottom.html

STOURTON CAUNDLE
Dorset

Golden Hill Cottage ♦♦♦♦
Stourton Caundle, Sturminster Newton DT10 0JW
T: (01963) 362109
F: (01963) 364205
E: andrew@oliver.net
I: www.goldenhillcottage.co.uk

STRATTON AUDLEY
Oxfordshire

The Old School ♦♦♦
Mill Road, Stratton Audley, Bicester OX6 9BJ
T: (01869) 277371
E: sawertheimer@euphony.net
I: www.old-school.co.uk

West Farm ♦♦♦♦
Launton Road, Stratton Audley, Bicester OX27 9AS
T: (01869) 278344
F: (01869) 278344
E: sara.westfarmbb@virgin.net
I: www.westfarmbb.co.uk

STREATLEY
Berkshire

Pennyfield ♦♦♦♦ SILVER AWARD
The Coombe, Streatley, Reading RG8 9QT
T: (01491) 872048
F: (01491) 872048
E: mandrvanstone@hotmail.com
I: www.pennyfield.co.uk

STUDLAND
Dorset

The Bankes Arms Hotel ♦♦♦
Manor Road, Studland, Swanage BH19 3AU
T: (01929) 450225
F: (01929) 450307

Fairfields Hotel ♦♦♦♦
Swanage Road, Studland, Swanage BH19 3AE
T: (01929) 450224
F: (01929) 450571

Shell Bay Cottage Rating Applied For
The Glebe, Studland, Swanage BH19 3AS
T: (01929) 450249
F: (01929) 450249

STURMINSTER NEWTON
Dorset

Hazeldean Bed & Breakfast ♦♦♦♦
Bath Road, Sturminster Newton, DT10 1DS
T: (01258) 472224
F: (01258) 472224
E: sarah_grounds@hotmail.com
I: www.hazeldeanbnb.co.uk

The Homestead ♦♦♦
Hole House Lane, off Glue Hill, Sturminster Newton, DT10 2AA
T: (01258) 471390
F: (01258) 471090
E: townsend@dircon.co.uk
I: www.townsend.dircon.co.uk

SULHAMSTEAD
Berkshire

The Old Manor ♦♦♦♦♦ SILVER AWARD
Whitehouse Green, Sulhamstead, Reading RG7 4EA
T: (0118) 983 2423
F: (0118) 983 6262
E: rags-r@theoldmanor.fsbusiness.co.uk

SUNNINGDALE
Berkshire

Beaufort House ♦♦♦♦
Broomfield Park, Sunningdale, Ascot SL5 0JT
T: (01344) 622991
F: (01344) 873705

SWANAGE
Dorset

Amberlea ♦♦♦♦
36 Victoria Avenue, Swanage, BH19 1AP
T: (01929) 426213
E: amberlea-swanage@yahoo.co.uk

Bella Vista Hotel ♦♦♦♦
Burlington Road, Swanage, BH19 1LS
T: (01929) 422873
F: (01929) 426220
E: mail@bellavista-hotel.com
I: www.bellavista-hotel.com

The Castleton Hotel ♦♦♦♦ SILVER AWARD
1 Highcliffe Road, Swanage, BH19 1LW
T: (01929) 423972
F: (01929) 422901
E: castletonhotel@aol.com
I: www.swanagecastletonhotel.com

Caythorpe House ♦♦♦
7 Rempstone Road, Swanage, BH19 1DN
T: (01929) 422892

Easter Cottage ♦♦♦♦
9 Eldon Terrace, Swanage, BH19 1HA
T: (01929) 427782
F: (01929) 427782
E: eastercottage@amserve.com
I: www.eastercottage.co.uk

Firswood ♦♦♦
29 Kings Road West, Swanage, BH19 1HF
T: (01929) 422306
E: firswood@aol.com
I: www.firswoodguesthouse.co.uk

Glenlee Hotel ♦♦♦♦
6 Cauldon Avenue, Swanage, BH19 1PQ
T: (01929) 425794
F: (01929) 421530
E: info@glenleehote.co.uk
I: www.glenleehotel.co.uk

Goodwyns ♦♦♦♦
2 Walrond Road, Swanage, BH19 1PB
T: (01929) 421088

Heather Cottage ♦♦♦
1 Higher Gardens, Corfe Castle, Wareham BH20 5ES
T: (01929) 480230

Horseshoe House Hotel Rating Applied For
9 Cliff Avenue, Swanage, BH19 1LX
T: (01929) 422194
E: horseshoehotel@aol.com

The Limes Hotel ♦♦♦♦
48 Park Road, Swanage, BH19 2AE
T: (01929) 422664
F: 0870 054 8794
E: info@limeshotel.demon.co.uk
I: www.limeshotel.demon.co.uk

Millbrook Guest House ♦♦♦
56 Kings Road West, Swanage, BH19 1HR
T: (01929) 423443
E: bob.millbrook@virgin.net
I: freespace.virgin.net/bob.millbrook

The Oxford Hotel ♦♦♦
3-5 Park Road, Swanage, BH19 2AA
T: (01929) 422247
F: (01929) 475707

Perfick Piece ♦♦♦
Springfield Road, Swanage, BH19 1HD
T: (01929) 423178
F: (01929) 423558
E: perfick-piece@supanet.com
I: www.perfick-piece.co.uk

St Michael ♦♦♦♦
31 Kings Road, Swanage, BH19 1HF
T: (01929) 422064

Sandhaven Guest House Rating Applied For
5 Ulwell Road, Swanage, BH19 1LE
T: (01929) 422322

Sandringham Hotel ♦♦♦
20 Durlston Road, Swanage, BH19 2HX
T: (01929) 423076
F: (01929) 423076
E: silk@sandhot.fsnet.co.uk

White Lodge Hotel ♦♦♦♦
Grosvenor Road, Swanage, BH19 2DD
T: (01929) 422696
F: (01929) 425510
E: whitelodge.hotel@virgin.net
I: www.whitelodgehotel.co.uk

SWAY
Hampshire

Little Arnewood Cottage ♦♦♦
Linnies Lane, Sway, Lymington SO41 6ES
T: (01590) 682920
E: littlearnewoodcottage@eurolink.ltd.net

Little Purley Farm ♦♦♦
Chapel Lane, Sway, Lymington SO41 6BS
T: (01590) 682707
F: (01590) 682707

Manor Farm ♦♦♦
Coombe Lane, Sway, Lymington SO41 6BP
T: (01590) 683542

The Nurse's Cottage
♦♦♦♦♦ GOLD AWARD
Station Road, Sway, Lymington SO41 6BA
T: (01590) 683402
F: (01590) 683402
E: nurses.cottage@lineone.net
I: www.nursescottage.co.uk

The Old Chapel ♦♦♦♦
Chapel House, Coombe Lane, Sway, Lymington SO41 6BP
T: (01590) 683382
F: (01590) 682979

Squirrels ♦♦♦
Broadmead, (off Silver Street), Sway, Lymington SO41 6DH
T: (01590) 683163
E: jean.killford@lineone.net
I: www.newforest.demon.co.uk/squirrels.htm

Tiverton ♦♦♦
9 Cruse Close, Sway, Lymington SO41 6AY
T: (01590) 683092
F: (01590) 683092
E: ronrowe@talk21.com
I: www.tivertonnewforest.co.uk

TAPLOW
Buckinghamshire

Bridge Cottage Guest House ♦♦♦
Bath Road, Taplow, Maidenhead SL6 0AR
T: (01628) 626805
F: (01628) 788785

TARRANT HINTON
Dorset

Old South Farmhouse
Rating Applied For
Tarrant Hinton, Blandford Forum DT11 8JA
T: (01258) 830659
F: (01258) 830692

TARRANT LAUNCESTON
Dorset

Ramblers Cottage ♦♦♦♦
Tarrant Launceston, Blandford Forum DT11 8BY
T: (01258) 830528
E: sworrall@ramblerscottage.fsnet.co.uk
I: www.ramblerscottage.fsnet.co.uk

TASTON
Oxfordshire

Hill Farm ♦♦♦♦♦
Taston, Oxford OX7 3JL
T: (01608) 811258
F: (01608) 811258

TETSWORTH
Oxfordshire

Little Acre ♦♦♦♦
4 High Street, Tetsworth, Oxford OX9 7AT
T: (01844) 281423
F: (01844) 281423
E: julia@little-acre.co.uk
I: www.little-acre.co.uk

THAME
Oxfordshire

The Dairy
♦♦♦♦♦ GOLD AWARD
Moreton, Thame OX9 2HX
T: (01844) 214075
F: (01844) 214075
E: thedairy@freeuk.com
I: www.thedairy.freeuk.com

Field Farm ♦♦♦♦
Rycote Lane, Thame, OX9 2HQ
T: (01844) 215428

Langsmeade House
♦♦♦♦ SILVER AWARD
Milton Common, Thame, OX9 2JY
T: (01844) 278727
F: (01844) 279256
E: CerberusandCo@aol.com
I: www.langsmeadehouse.co.uk

The Mole (& Chicken) ♦♦♦♦
Easington Terrace, Easington, Thame, HP18 9EY
T: (01844) 208387
F: (01844) 208250
E: shanepellis@hotmail.com
I: ww.moleandchicken.co.uk

Oakfield ♦♦♦♦
Thame Park Road, Thame, OX9 3PL
T: (01844) 213709

THATCHAM
Berkshire

33 Green Lane ♦♦♦
Thatcham, RG19 3RG
T: (01635) 863116
F: (01635) 863116

Manor Farm House
Rating Applied For
Church Street, Hampstead Norreys, Thatcham, RG18 0TD
T: (01635) 201276
F: (01635) 201035

THREE LEGGED CROSS
Dorset

Thatch Cottage ♦♦♦♦
Ringwood Road, Three Legged Cross, Wimborne Minster BH21 6QY
T: (01202) 822042
F: (01202) 821888
E: dthatchcottage@aol.com
I: www.thatch-cottage.co.uk

TILEHURST
Berkshire

2 Cotswold Way ♦♦
Tilehurst, Reading RG31 6SH
T: (0118) 9413286

TITCHFIELD
Hampshire

Posbrook Gardens B & B
♦♦♦♦ SILVER AWARD
Posbrook Gardens, Titchfield, Fareham PO14 4HD
T: (01329) 843267
F: (01329) 843267
E: bdlatham@supanet.com
I: www.posbrookgardens.co.uk

Westcote Bed & Breakfast ♦♦♦♦
325 Southampton Road, Titchfield, Fareham PO14 4AY
T: (01329) 846297
F: (01329) 846297

TOTLAND BAY
Isle of Wight

Chart House ♦♦♦♦
Madeira Road, Totland Bay, PO39 0BJ
T: (01983) 755091

Frenchman's Cove ♦♦♦
Alum Bay Old Road, Totland Bay, PO39 0HZ
T: (01983) 752227
F: (01983) 755125
E: boatfield@frenchmanscove.co.uk
I: www.frenchmanscove.co.uk

Littledene Lodge ♦♦♦
Granville Road, Totland Bay, PO39 0AX
T: (01983) 752411
F: (01983) 752411

Sandford Lodge ♦♦♦♦
61 The Avenue, Totland Bay, PO39 0DN
T: (01983) 753478
F: (01983) 753478
E: sandfordlodge@cwcom.net

Sandy Lane Guest House ♦♦♦♦
Colwell Common Road, Totland Bay, PO39 0DD
T: (01983) 752240
F: (01983) 752240
E: jane@sandylaneguesthouse.fsnet.co.uk

TOTTON
Hampshire

Colbury Manor
♦♦♦♦ SILVER AWARD
Jacobs Gutter Lane, Eling, Totton, Southampton SO40 9FY
T: (023) 8086 2283
F: (023) 8086 5545
E: colburymanor@breathemail.net

Ivy Lawn ♦♦♦♦
Eling Hill, Totton, Southampton SO40 9HE
T: (023) 8066 0925
I: www.ivylawn.co.uk

TWYFORD
Berkshire

Chesham House ♦♦♦
79 Wargrave Road, Twyford, Reading RG40 9PE
T: (0118) 932 0428
E: maria.ferguson@virgin.net

Highfield Cottage
Rating Applied For
Old Rectory Lane, Twyford, Winchester SO21 1NS
T: (01962) 712921
F: (01962) 712921
E: cjrees@estatesgazette.net

UFTON NERVET
Berkshire

Hill Cottage ♦♦♦♦
Church Lane, Ufton Nervet, Reading RG7 4HQ
T: (0118) 983 2248
F: (0118) 983 2248

UPPER BUCKLEBURY
Berkshire

Brockley ♦♦♦
Little Lane, Upper Bucklebury, Reading RG7 6QX
T: (01635) 869742
E: prue.matchwick@ukonline.co.uk

UPTON
Oxfordshire

The White House ♦♦♦
Reading Road, Upton, Didcot OX11 9HP
T: (01235) 850289

VENTNOR
Isle of Wight

Bellevue House ♦♦♦♦
Bellevue Road, Ventnor, PO38 1DB
T: (01983) 855047
F: (01983) 854862
E: jdonne1631@aol.com
I: www.wightonline.co.uk/bellevue

Bermuda Guest House ♦♦♦
3 Alexandra Gardens, Ventnor, PO38 1EE
T: (01983) 852349

Cornerways ♦♦♦
39 Madeira Road, Ventnor, PO38 1QS
T: (01983) 852323
I: www.cornerwaysventnor.co.uk

Delamere Guest House ♦♦♦♦
Bellevue Road, Ventnor, PO38 1DB
T: (01983) 852322
F: (01983) 852322
E: kk@delamere1.co.uk
I: www.delamere1.co.uk

VERNEY JUNCTION
Buckinghamshire

The White Cottage ♦♦♦
Verney Junction, Buckingham MK18 2JZ
T: (01296) 714416

VERNHAM DEAN
Hampshire

Upton Cottage ♦♦♦
Vernham Dean, Andover SP11 0JY
T: (01264) 737640
F: (01264) 737640

WADDESDON
Buckinghamshire

The Georgian Doll's Cottage ♦♦♦♦
High Street, Waddesdon, Aylesbury HP18 0NE
T: (01296) 655553

The Old Dairy ♦♦♦
4 High Street, Waddesdon, Aylesbury HP18 0JA
T: (01296) 658627
E: gconyard@btinternet.com

WALKFORD
Dorset

Acorns ♦♦♦
37 Walkford Road, Walkford, Christchurch BH23 5QD
T: (01425) 270903
F: (01425) 270476
E: kevin.prouten@virgin.net

WALLINGFORD
Oxfordshire

Fords Farm ♦♦♦♦
Ewelme, Wallingford, OX10 6HU
T: (01491) 839272
E: fordsfarm@callnetuk.com

Little Gables ♦♦♦
166 Crowmarsh Hill, Crowmarsh Gifford, Wallingford OX10 8BG
T: (01491) 837834
F: (01491) 834426
E: jill@stayingaway.com
I: www.stayingaway.com

North Farm
♦♦♦♦ SILVER AWARD
Shillingford Hill, Wallingford OX10 8NB
T: (01865) 858406
F: (01865) 858519
E: northfarm@compuserve.com
I: www.country-accom.co.uk/north-farm/

North Moreton House
♦♦♦♦♦ SILVER AWARD
North Moreton, Didcot OX11 9AT
T: (01235) 813283
F: (01235) 511305
E: miles_katie@hotmail.com

WAREHAM
Dorset

Anglebury House ♦♦♦
15/17 North Street, Wareham, BH20 4AB
T: (01929) 552988
F: (01929) 554665

Ashcroft
Rating Applied For
64 Furzebrook Road, Wareham, BH20 5AX
T: (01929) 552392
F: (01929) 552422
E: cake@ashcroft-b-and-b.freeserve.co.uk
I: www.ashcroft-b-and-b.freeserve.co.uk

The Old Granary
♦♦♦♦ SILVER AWARD
West Holme Farm, Wareham, BH20 6AQ
T: (01929) 552972
F: (01929) 551616
E: venngoldsack@lineone.net

The Old Granary ♦♦♦
The Quay, Wareham, BH20 4LP
T: (01929) 552010
F: (01929) 552482

WARGRAVE
Berkshire

Appletree Cottage
♦♦♦♦ SILVER AWARD
Backsideans, Wargrave, Reading RG10 8JS
T: (0118) 940 4306
E: trishlangham@appletreecottage.co.uk
I: www.appletreecottage.co.uk

WARRINGTON
Buckinghamshire

Home Farm ♦♦♦♦♦
Warrington, Olney MK46 4HN
T: (01234) 711655
F: (01234) 711855
E: ruth@oldstonebarn.co.uk
I: www.oldstonebarn.co.uk

WARSASH
Hampshire

Solent View Hotel ♦♦♦♦
33 Newtown Road, Warsash, Southampton SO31 9FY
T: (01489) 572300
F: (01489) 572300

WATER STRATFORD
Buckinghamshire

The Rolling Acres ♦♦♦♦
Water Stratford, Buckingham MK18 5DX
T: (01280) 847302
E: david.abbotts@talk21.com

WATERLOOVILLE
Hampshire

Clibdens
♦♦♦♦ SILVER AWARD
Chalton, Waterlooville, PO8 0BG
T: (023) 9259 2172

Holly Dale ♦♦♦
11 Lovedean Lane, Waterlooville, PO8 8HH
T: (023) 9259 2047

WATERSTOCK
Oxfordshire

Park Farm House ♦♦♦♦
Waterstock, Oxford OX33 1JT
T: (01844) 339469
F: (01844) 338890

WATLINGTON
Oxfordshire

Huttons ♦♦♦
Britwell Salome, Watlington, Oxford OX49 5LH
T: (01491) 614389
F: (01491) 614993
E: jbowater@etonwell.com

Woodgate Orchard Cottage
♦♦♦♦
Howe Road, Watlington, Oxford OX49 5EL
T: (01491) 612675
F: (01491) 612675
E: mailbox@wochr.freeserve.co.uk

WENDOVER
Buckinghamshire

Dunsmore Edge ♦♦♦
London Road, Wendover, Aylesbury HP22 6PN
T: (01296) 623080
E: uron@lineone.net.uk

Field Cottage
♦♦♦♦ SILVER AWARD
St Leonards, Tring HP23 6NS
T: (01494) 837602
F: (01494) 837137
E: susan_jepson@hotmail.com
I: www.smoothhound.co.uk/hotels/field.html

46 Lionel Avenue ♦♦♦
Wendover, Aylesbury HP22 6LP
T: (01296) 623426

WEST LULWORTH
Dorset

Abbots Orchard
Rating Applied For
West Road, West Lulworth, Wareham BH20 5RY
T: (01929) 400592
E: theorchard@1c24.net

Gatton House ♦♦♦♦
West Lulworth, Wareham BH20 5RU
T: (01929) 400252
F: (01929) 400252
E: avril@gattonhouse.co.uk
I: gattonhouse.co.uk

Graybank ♦♦♦
Main Road, West Lulworth, Wareham BH20 5RL
T: (01929) 400256

Lulworth Cove Hotel ♦♦♦
Main Road, West Lulworth, Wareham BH20 5RQ
T: (01929) 400333
F: (01929) 400534
E: hotel@lulworth-cove.com
I: www.lulworth-cove.com

The Old Barn ♦♦♦
Lulworth Cove, West Lulworth, Wareham BH20 5RL
T: (01929) 400305
F: (01929) 400516

West Down Farm
Rating Applied For
West Lulworth, Wareham BH20 5RY
T: (01929) 400308
F: (01929) 400308

WEST WELLOW
Hampshire

Lukes Barn ♦♦♦
Maury's Lane, West Wellow, Romsey SO51 6DA
T: (01794) 324431
F: (01794) 324431

WESTON-ON-THE-GREEN
Oxfordshire

Weston Grounds Farm ♦♦♦
Weston-on-the-Green, Bicester OX25 3QX
T: (01869) 351168
F: (01869) 350887

WESTON TURVILLE
Buckinghamshire

Brickwall Farm Cottage ♦♦♦
Mill Lane, Weston Turville, Aylesbury HP22 5RG
T: (01296) 612656
F: (01296) 614017
E: enquiries@brickwallfarmcottage.co.uk
I: www.brickwallfarmcottage.co.uk

The Hideaway ♦♦♦
Main Street, Weston Turville, Aylesbury HP22 5RR
T: (01296) 612604
F: (01296) 615705

Loosley House ♦♦♦♦
87 New Road, Weston Turville, Aylesbury HP22 5QT
T: (01296) 428285
F: (01296) 428285

WEYHILL
Hampshire

Juglans ♦♦♦♦
Red Post Lane, Weyhill, Andover SP11 0PY
T: (01264) 772651

WHERWELL
Hampshire

May Cottage ♦♦♦♦
Fullerton Road, Wherwell, Andover SP11 7JS
T: (01264) 860412
F: (01264) 860791
E: wildgoose_projects@attglobal.net

New House Bed & Breakfast
♦♦♦♦
New House, Fullerton Road, Wherwell, Andover SP11 7JS
T: (01264) 860817
E: DiWoodWherwell@aol.com
I: www.newhousebnb.co.uk

WHITCHURCH
Hampshire

Peak House Farm ♦♦♦
Cole Henley, Whitchurch, RG28 7QJ
T: (01256) 892052
F: (01256) 892052
E: peakhousefarm@tesco.net

White Hart Hotel ♦♦
Newbury Street, Whitchurch, RG28 7DN
T: (01256) 892900
F: (01256) 896628
E: adrian@white-hart.fsnet.co.uk
I: www.whitehart-hotel.co.uk

WHITWELL
Isle of Wight

The Old Rectory
♦♦♦♦ SILVER AWARD
Ashknowle Lane, Whitwell, Ventnor PO38 2PP
T: (01983) 731242
F: (01983) 731288
E: rectory@ukonline.co.uk
I: www.wightonline.co.uk/oldrectory

WICKHAM
Hampshire

Chiphall Acre
Rating Applied For
Droxford Road (A32), Wickham, Fareham PO17 5AY
T: (01329) 833188
F: (01329) 833188
E: mavis.stevens@zoom.co.uk
I: www.smoothhound.co.uk/hotels/chiphall.html

WIDLEY
Hampshire

Roughay ♦♦♦
96 The Brow, Widley, Waterlooville PO7 5DA
T: (023) 9237 9341
E: gillcross@lineone.net
I: www.roughay.co.uk

WIDMER END
Buckinghamshire

The White House ♦♦♦
North Road, Widmer End, High Wycombe HP15 6ND
T: (01494) 712221
F: (01494) 712221
E: vaughanjane@hotmail.com

WIMBORNE MINSTER
Dorset

Ashton Lodge
♦♦♦♦ SILVER AWARD
10 Oakley Hill, Wimborne Minster, BH21 1QH
T: (01202) 883423
F: (01202) 886180
E: ashtonlodge@ukgateway.net
I: www.ashtonlodge.ukgateway.net

Crab Apple Corner ♦♦♦
40 Lacy Drive, Wimborne Minster, BH21 1DG
T: (01202) 840993
E: andrew.curry@virgin.net

Hemsworth Manor Farm
♦♦♦♦
Witchampton, Wimborne Minster BH21 5BN
T: (01258) 840216
F: (01258) 841278

Henbury Farm ♦♦♦♦
Dorchester Road, Sturminster Marshall, Wimborne Minster BH21 3RN
T: (01258) 857306
F: (01258) 857928
E: henburyfarm@aol.com
I: www.henburyfarm.co.uk

Homestay ♦♦♦
22 West Borough, Wimborne Minster, BH21 1NF
T: (01202) 849015
F: (01202) 849819

Hopewell
♦♦♦♦ SILVER AWARD
Little Lonnen, Colehill, Wimborne Minster BH21 7BB
T: (01202) 880311
E: hopewell.wimborne@ntlworld.com

Lantern Lodge
♦♦♦♦ GOLD AWARD
47 Gravel Hill, Merley, Wimborne Minster, BH21 1RW
T: (01202) 884183

The Old George ♦♦♦♦
2 Corn Market, Wimborne Minster, BH21 1JL
T: (01202) 888510
F: (01202) 888513

Old Merchant's House ♦♦♦♦
44 West Borough, Wimborne Minster, BH21 1NQ
T: (01202) 841955

Pear Tree Cottage ♦♦
248 Wimborne Road West, Stapehill, Wimborne Minster, BH21 2DZ
T: (01202) 890174
E: ca.whiteman@ntlworld.com

Silvertrees ♦♦♦
Merley House Lane, Wimborne Minster, BH21 3AA
T: (01202) 880418
F: (01202) 881415
E: fionashammick@aol.com

Twynham ♦♦♦
67 Poole Road, Wimborne Minster, BH21 1QB
T: (01202) 887310

96 West Borough ♦♦♦
Wimborne Minster, BH21 1NH
T: (01202) 884039

38 Wimborne Road West
♦♦♦
Wimborne Minster, BH21 2DP
T: (01202) 889357

Woodlands ♦♦♦♦
29 Merley Ways, Wimborne Minster, BH21 1QN
T: (01202) 887625
E: stevemaggietopliss.woodlands@virgin.net

WINCHESTER
Hampshire

Acacia ♦♦♦♦ SILVER AWARD
44 Kilham Lane, Winchester, SO22 5PT
T: (01962) 852259
F: (01962) 852259
E: eric.buchanan@mcmail.com
I: www.btinternet.com/~eric.buchanan

15B Bereweeke Avenue
♦♦♦♦
Winchester, SO22 6BH
T: (01962) 877883
F: (01962) 841616

12 Christchurch Road ♦♦
Winchester, SO23 9SR
T: (01962) 854272

85 Christchurch Road
♦♦♦♦ SILVER AWARD
Winchester, SO23 9QY
T: (01962) 868661
F: (01962) 868661
E: dilke@waitrose.com

Church Cottage ♦♦♦
20 St Johns Street, Winchester, SO23 0HF
T: (01962) 865058
E: junerowlands@petuchio.freeserve.co.uk

5 Clifton Terrace ♦♦♦♦
Winchester, SO22 5BJ
T: (01962) 890053
F: (01962) 626566
E: chrissiejohnston@hotmail.com
I: www.smoothhound.co.uk/hotels/cliftonterrace.html

5 Compton Road ♦♦♦
Winchester, SO23 9SL
T: (01962) 869199
E: vicb@csma-netlink.co.uk
I: www.winchester.gov.uk

38 Courtenay Road
Rating Applied For
Winchester, SO23 7ER
T: (01962) 855314
E: tom_belshaw@lineone.net

Dawn Cottage
♦♦♦♦ SILVER AWARD
Romsey Road, Winchester, SO22 5PQ
T: (01962) 869956
F: (01962) 869956
E: dawncottage@hotmail.com

East View ♦♦♦♦
16 Clifton Hill, Winchester, SO22 5BL
T: (01962) 862986

The Farrells ♦♦♦
5 Ranelagh Road, St Cross, Winchester SO23 9TA
T: (01962) 869555
F: (01962) 869555
E: thefarrells@easicom.com

The Lilacs ♦♦♦♦
1 Harestock Close, Off Andover Road North, Winchester, SO22 6NP
T: (01962) 884122
F: (01962) 884122
E: susan@rbpell.freeserve.co.uk
I: www.smoothhound.co.uk/hotels/lilacs.html

Mallard Cottage ♦♦♦♦
64 Chesil Street, Winchester, SO23 0HX
T: (01962) 853002
F: (01962) 820430
E: mallardsimpkin@aol.com
I: www.geocities.com/mallardcottageuk

The Old Blue Boar ♦♦♦♦
25 St John's Street, Winchester, SO23 0HF
T: (01962) 865942
E: julietsurridge@aol.com

The Old Coach House Inn
Rating Applied For
156-157 High Street, Winchester, SO23 9BA
T: (01962) 852985

53A Parchment Street
Rating Applied For
Winchester, SO23 8BA
T: (01962) 849962
E: saraby@onetel.net.uk
I: www.accom.finder.co.uk

Portland House ♦♦♦♦
63 Tower Street, Winchester, SO23 8TA
T: (01962) 865195
F: (01962) 865195
E: tony@knightworld.com

21 Rosewarne Court
Rating Applied For
Hyde Street, Winchester, SO23 7HL
T: (01962) 863737

9 Rosewarne Court ♦♦♦
Hyde Street, Winchester, SO23 7HL
T: (01962) 864077

St John's Croft
Rating Applied For
St John's Street, Winchester, SO23 0HF
T: (01962) 859976

St Margaret's ♦♦♦
3 St Michael's Road, Winchester, SO23 9JE
T: (01962) 861450
E: brigid.brett@amserve.net
I: www.winchesterbandb.com

8 Salters Acres ♦♦♦♦
Winchester, SO22 5JW
T: (01962) 856112
E: accommodation@8salters.freeserve.co.uk

Shawlands ♦♦♦♦
46 Kilham Lane, Winchester, SO22 5QD
T: (01962) 861166
F: (01962) 861166
E: kathy@pollshaw.u-net.com

54 St Cross Road ♦♦♦♦
Winchester, SO23 9PS
T: (01962) 852073
F: (01962) 852073
E: mcblockley@tcp.co.uk

Sullivan's
Rating Applied For
29 Stockbridge Road, Winchester, SO22 6RW
T: (01962) 862027

Sycamores ♦♦♦♦
4 Bereweeke Close, Winchester, SO22 6AR
T: (01962) 867242
F: (01962) 620300
E: sycamores.b-and-b@virgin.net

152 Teg Downs Meads ♦♦♦
Winchester, SO22 5NS
T: (01962) 862628
F: (01962) 862628
E: alfred.chalk@talk21.com

Windy Ridge
Rating Applied For
99 Andover Road, Winchester, SO22 6AX
T: (01962) 882527
E: awestall@compuserve.com

The Wykeham Arms
♦♦♦♦ SILVER AWARD
75 Kingsgate Street, Winchester, SO23 9PE
T: (01962) 853834
F: (01962) 854411

WINDRUSH
Oxfordshire

Dellwood ♦♦♦
Quarry Lane, Windrush, Oxford OX18 4TR
T: (01451) 844268

WINDSOR
Berkshire

9 Albany Road ♦♦♦
Windsor, SL4 1HL
T: (01753) 865564

Alma House ♦♦♦
56 Alma Road, Windsor, SL4 3HA
T: (01753) 862983
F: (01753) 862983
E: info@almahouse.co.uk
I: www.almahouse.co.uk

The Arches
Rating Applied For
9 York Road, Windsor, SL4 3NX
T: (01753) 869268
F: (01753) 869268

Barbara Clemens
Rating Applied For
49 Longmead, Windsor, SL4 5PZ
T: (01753) 866019
F: (01753) 830964

Barbara's Bed & Breakfast
Rating Applied For
16 Maidenhead Road, Windsor, SL4 5EQ
T: (01753) 840273
E: bbandb@btinternet.com

Beaumont Lodge ♦♦♦♦
1 Beaumont Road, Windsor, SL4 1HY
T: (01753) 863436
F: (01753) 863436
E: bhamshere@beaumontlodge.demon.co.uk
I: www.beaumontlodgeguesthouse.co.uk

Belmont House
Rating Applied For
64 Bolton Road, Windsor,
SL4 3JL
T: (01753) 860860
F: (01753) 830330
E: bbs@orange.net

Clarence Hotel ♦♦
9 Clarence Road, Windsor,
SL4 5AE
T: (01753) 864436
F: (01753) 857060
I: www.clarence-hotel.co.uk

The Dorset Hotel ♦♦♦♦
4 Dorset Road, Windsor,
SL4 3BA
T: (01753) 852669
F: (01753) 852669

Elansey ♦♦♦
65 Clifton Rise, Windsor,
SL4 5SX
T: (01753) 864438

Halcyon House ♦♦♦
131 Clarence Road, Windsor,
SL4 5AR
T: (01753) 863262
F: (01753) 863262
E: halcyonhouse@hotmail.com

Honeysuckle Cottage ♦♦♦
61 Fairfield Approach,
Wraysbury, Windsor, TW19 5DR
T: (01784) 482519
F: (01784) 482305
E: rooms@hotelswindsor.com
I: www.hotelswindsor.com

Jeans ♦♦
1 Stovell Road, Windsor, SL4 5JB
T: (01753) 852055
F: (01753) 842932

Melrose House ♦♦♦
53 Frances Road, Windsor,
SL4 3AQ
T: (01753) 865328
F: (01753) 865328
E: m-mellor@supanet.com

Morton Lodge
Rating Applied For
135 Clarence Road, Windsor,
SL4 5AR
T: (01753) 840439
F: (01753) 620375

The Oast Barn ♦♦♦
Staines Road, Wraysbury,
Staines TW19 5BS
T: (01784) 481598
F: (01784) 483022
E: theoastbarn@netscapeonline.co.uk
I: www.smoothhound.co.uk/hotels/oastbarn.html

Oscar Hotel ♦♦♦
65 Vansittart Road, Windsor,
SL4 5DB
T: (01753) 830613
F: (01753) 833744
E: info@oscarhotel.com
I: www.oscarhotel.com

Riverview ♦♦♦♦
7 Stovell Road, Windsor, SL4 5JB
T: (01753) 863628
F: (01753) 863628
E: janetn.riverview@virgin.net

The Trooper ♦♦♦
97 St Leonards Road, Windsor,
SL4 3BZ
T: (01753) 670123
F: (01753) 670124

22 York Avenue ♦♦♦
Windsor, SL4 3PD
T: (01753) 865775

3 York Road
Rating Applied For
Windsor, SL4 3NX
T: (01753) 861741
F: (01753) 861741
E: kerrin@tiscali.co.uk

WINFRITH NEWBURGH
Dorset

Wynards Farm ♦♦♦♦
Winfrith Newburgh, Dorchester
DT2 8DQ
T: (01305) 852660
F: (01305) 854094
E: canaven@hotmail.com
I: www.dorset-info.co.uk/wynardsfarm

WINKFIELD
Berkshire

Bluebell House ♦♦♦♦
Lovel Lane, Winkfield, Windsor
SL4 2DG
T: (01344) 886828
F: (01344) 893256
E: registrations@bluebellhousehotel.co.uk
I: www.bluebellhousehotel.co.uk

WINKTON
Dorset

Fisherman's Haunt Hotel ♦♦♦
Salisbury Road, Winkton,
Christchurch BH23 7AS
T: (01202) 477283
F: (01202) 478883

WINSLOW
Buckinghamshire

The Congregational Church ♦♦♦
15 Horn Street, Winslow,
Buckingham MK18 3AP
T: (01296) 715717
F: (01296) 715717

The Old Manse ♦♦
9 Horn Street, Winslow,
Aylesbury MK18 3AP
T: (01296) 712048

Puzzletree ♦♦♦♦
3 Buckingham Road, Winslow,
Buckingham MK18 3DT
T: (01296) 712437
F: (01296) 712437
E: puzzletree@hotmail.com

'Witsend' ♦♦♦
9 Buckingham Road, Winslow,
Buckingham MK18 3DT
T: (01296) 712503
E: sheila.spatcher@aol.com

WINSOR
Hampshire

Trees ♦♦♦
Tatchbury Lane, Winsor,
Southampton SO40 2HA
T: (023) 8081 3128
F: (023) 8081 3128

WINTERBORNE STICKLAND
Dorset

Stickland Farmhouse
♦♦♦♦ SILVER AWARD
Stickland Farmhouse,
Winterborne Stickland,
Blandford Forum DT11 0NT
T: (01258) 880119
F: (01258) 880119
E: sticklandfarmhouse@sticklanddorset.fsnet.co.uk

WINTERBORNE ZELSTON
Dorset

Brook Farm ♦♦♦
Winterborne Zelston, Blandford
Forum DT11 9EU
T: (01929) 459267
F: (01929) 459267

Rainbow View Farm ♦♦♦
Winterborne Zelston, Blandford
Forum DT11 9EU
T: (01929) 459529
F: (01929) 145216

WITNEY
Oxfordshire

The Court Inn ♦♦♦
43 Bridge Street, Witney,
OX8 6DA
T: (01993) 703228
F: (01993) 700980
E: info@thecourtinn.co.uk

Crofters Guest House ♦♦♦♦
29 Oxford Hill, Witney, OX28 3JU
T: (01993) 778165
F: (01993) 778165
E: crofers.ghouse@virgin.net

Ducklington Farm ♦♦♦
Coursehill Lane, Ducklington,
Witney OX8 7YG
T: (01993) 772175
I: www.country-accom.co.uk

Field View
♦♦♦♦ SILVER AWARD
Wood Green, Witney, OX28 1DE
T: (01993) 705485
E: jsimpson@netcomuk.co.uk
I: www.netcomuk.co.uk/~kearse/index.html

Greystones Lodge Hotel ♦♦♦
34 Tower Hill, Witney, OX8 5ES
T: (01993) 771898
F: (01993) 702064
E: greystoneslodge@aol.com

Hawthorn House ♦♦♦
79 Burford Road, Witney,
OX28 6DR
T: (01993) 772768
F: (01993) 772768
E: jdonohoe33@aol.com
I: www.hawthornguesthouse.co.uk

North Leigh Guest House ♦♦♦♦
28 Common Road, North Leigh,
Witney OX8 6RA
T: (01993) 881622

Quarrydene ♦♦♦
17 Dene Rise, Witney, OX28 6LU
T: (01993) 772152
F: (01993) 772152
E: jeanniemarshall@quarrydene.fsworld.co.uk

Springhill Farm Bed & Breakfast ♦♦♦
Cogges, Witney, OX29 6UL
T: (01993) 704919

The Witney Hotel ♦♦♦
7 Church Green, Witney,
OX28 4AZ
T: (01993) 702137
F: (01993) 705337
E: bookings@thewitneyhotel.co.uk
I: www.thewitneyhotel.co.uk

WOBURN SANDS
Buckinghamshire

The Old Stables ♦♦♦♦
Woodleys Farm, Bow Brickhill
Road, Woburn Sands, Milton
Keynes MK17 8DE
T: (01908) 281340
F: (01908) 584812

WOODCOTE
Oxfordshire

Hedges ♦♦♦
South Stoke Road, Woodcote,
Reading RG8 0PL
T: (01491) 680461
E: howard-allen@hedgeswoodcote.freeserve.co.uk

The Highwayman ♦♦♦
Exlade Street, Checkendon,
Reading RG8 0UA
T: (01491) 682020
F: (01491) 682229
E: thehighwayman@skyeinnsfsnet.co.uk
I: www.thehighwaymancheckendon.co.uk

WOODFALLS
Hampshire

The Woodfalls Inn ♦♦♦♦
The Ridge, Woodfalls, Salisbury
SP5 2LN
T: (01725) 513222
F: (01725) 513220
E: woodfallsi@aol.com
I: www.woodfallsinn.co.uk

WOODSTOCK
Oxfordshire

Blenheim Guest House & Tea Rooms ♦♦♦♦
17 Park Street, Woodstock,
Oxford OX20 1SJ
T: (01993) 813814
F: (01993) 813810
E: Theblenheim@aol.com
I: www.theblenheim.com

Burleigh Farm ♦♦♦
Bladon Road, Cassington, Oxford
OX29 4EA
T: (01865) 881352
E: j.cook@farmline.com

Gorselands Hall ♦♦♦♦
Boddington Lane, North Leigh,
Witney OX29 6PU
T: (01993) 882292
F: (01993) 883629
E: hamilton@gorselandshall.com
I: www.gorselandshall.com

The Kings Head Inn ♦♦♦♦
Chapel Hill, Wootton,
Woodstock, Oxford OX20 1DX
T: (01993) 811340
E: t.fay@kings-head.co.uk
I: www.kings-head.co.uk

The Laurels
♦♦♦♦ SILVER AWARD
Hensington Road, Woodstock,
Oxford OX20 1JL
T: (01993) 812583
F: (01993) 810041
E: stay@laurelsguesthouse.co.uk
I: www.smoothhound.co.uk/hotels/thelaur.html

The Lawns ♦♦
2 Flemings Road, Woodstock, Oxford OX20 1NA
T: (01993) 812599
F: (01993) 812599
E: thelawns@amserve.com
I: www.thelawns.co.uk

Plane Tree House
♦♦♦♦ SILVER AWARD
48 Oxford Street, Woodstock, Oxford OX20 1TT
T: (01993) 813075

The Punchbowl Inn ♦♦♦
12 Oxford Street, Woodstock, Oxford OX20 1TR
T: (01993) 811218
F: (01993) 811393
E: info@punchbowl-woodstock.co.uk
I: www.punchbowl-woodstock.co.uk

Shepherds Hall Inn ♦♦♦
Witney Road, Freeland, Oxford OX29 8HQ
T: (01993) 881256
F: (01993) 883455

Shipton Glebe
♦♦♦♦♦ GOLD AWARD
Woodstock, Oxford OX20 1QQ
T: (01993) 812688
F: (01993) 813142
E: stay@shipton-glebe.com
I: www.shipton-glebe.com

The Townhouse ♦♦♦♦
15 High Street, Woodstock, Oxford OX20 1TE
T: (01993) 810843
F: (01993) 810843
E: info@woodstock-townhouse.com
I: www.woodstock-townhouse.com

WOOL
Dorset

Fingle Bridge ♦♦♦
Duck Street, Wool, Wareham BH20 6DE
T: (01929) 462739
E: colin.j.baker@tesco.net
I: www.finglebridge.co.uk

WOOLHAMPTON
Berkshire

Mulberry House ♦♦♦
Carbinswood Lane, Woolhampton, Reading RG7 5TS
T: (01189) 710220
F: (01189) 713117
E: glover-horne@mulberry.00.fsnet.co.uk

River View House ♦♦♦♦
Station Road, Woolhampton, Reading RG7 5SF
T: (0118) 971 3449
F: (0118) 971 3475

WOOLSTONE
Buckinghamshire

Ediths Cottage ♦♦♦♦
21 Newport Road, Woolstone, Milton Keynes MK15 0AB
T: (01908) 604916
E: edithcott@biinternet.com

WOOTTON
Oxfordshire

Killingworth Castle Inn ♦♦♦
Glympton Road, Wootton, Woodstock, Oxford OX20 1EJ
T: (01993) 811401
E: wwigiscastle@aol.com
I: www.killingworthcastle.tablesir.com

WOOTTON BRIDGE
Isle of Wight

Grange Farm ♦♦♦♦
Staplers Road, Wootton Bridge, Ryde PO33 4RW
T: (01983) 882147
F: (01983) 882147

Island Charters Sea Urchin ♦♦
26 Barge Lane, Wootton Creek, Wootton Bridge, Ryde PO33 4LB
T: (01983) 882315
F: (01983) 882315

WORMINGHALL
Buckinghamshire

Crabtree Barn ♦♦♦♦
Field Farm, Worminghall, Aylesbury HP18 9JY
T: (01844) 339719
F: (01844) 339719
E: issymcguinness@crabtreebarn.co.uk

WROXALL
Isle of Wight

The Grange ♦♦♦♦
Wroxall, Ventnor PO38 3DA
T: (01983) 857424
E: thegrange@mcgeoch.com
I: www.mcgeoch.com/thegrange

Little Span Farm ♦♦♦
Rew Lane, Wroxall, Ventnor PO38 3AU
T: (01983) 852419
F: (01983) 852419
E: info@spanfarm.co.uk
I: www.spanfarm.co.uk

YARMOUTH
Isle of Wight

Medlars ♦♦♦
Halletts Shute, Yarmouth, PO41 0RH
T: (01983) 761541
F: (01983) 761541
E: grey@lineone.net
I: www.milford.co.uk/go/medlars.html

Rosemead ♦♦
Tennyson Road, Yarmouth, PO41 0PX
T: (01983) 761078
E: barbara_boon@hotmail.com

YARNTON
Oxfordshire

Eltham Villa Guest House
♦♦♦♦
148 Woodstock Road, Yarnton, Kidlington OX5 1PW
T: (01865) 376037
F: (01865) 376037

Kings Bridge Guest House
♦♦♦
Woodstock Road, Yarnton, Kidlington OX5 1PH
T: (01865) 841748
F: (01865) 849662

YATELEY
Hampshire

Carisbrooke Cottage ♦♦♦
Millmere, Mill Lane, Yateley, GU46 7TQ
T: (01252) 409526

SOUTH EAST ENGLAND

ABINGER COMMON
Surrey

Leylands Farm ♦♦♦♦
Leylands Lane, Abinger Common, Dorking RH5 6JU
T: (01306) 730115
F: (01306) 731675
E: annieblf@btopenworld.com

Park House Farm ♦♦♦♦
Hollow Lane, Abinger Common, Dorking RH5 6LW
T: (01306) 730101
F: (01306) 730643
E: peterwallis@msn.com
I: www.smoothhound.co.uk/hotels/parkhous.html

ACRISE
Kent

Ladwood Farm ♦♦♦
Acrise, Folkestone CT18 8LL
T: (01303) 891328
F: (01303) 891427
E: mail@ladwood.com
I: www.ladwood.com

ALBURY
Surrey

Barn Cottage ♦♦♦♦
Brook Hill, Farley Green, Albury, Guildford GU5 9DN
T: (01483) 202571

ALDINGBOURNE
West Sussex

Limmer Pond House ♦♦♦
Church Road, Aldingbourne, Chichester PO20 6TU
T: (01243) 543210

ALDINGTON
Kent

Hogben Farm ♦♦♦♦
Church Lane, Aldington, Ashford TN25 7EH
T: (01233) 720219
F: (01233) 720285
E: ros.martin@talk21.com

ALFRISTON
East Sussex

Meadowbank ♦♦♦♦
Sloe Lane, Alfriston, Polegate BN26 5UR
T: (01323) 870742

Riverdale House ♦♦♦♦
Seaford Road, Alfriston, Polegate BN26 5TR
T: (01323) 871038
F: (01323) 871038

Russets ♦♦♦♦ SILVER AWARD
14 Deans Road, Alfriston, Polegate BN26 5XJ
T: (01323) 870626
F: (01323) 870626
E: russets@yahoo.co.uk

ALKHAM
Kent

Alkham Court ♦♦♦♦
Meggett Lane, South Alkham, Alkham, Dover CT15 7DG
T: (01303) 892056
E: alkhamcourt@aol.com

AMBERLEY
West Sussex

Amberley House
Rating Applied For
Church Street, Amberley, Arundel BH18 9NF
T: (01798) 839507
F: (01798) 839020
E: relax@waterspirit.co.uk
I: www.waterspirit.co.uk

The Sportsman ♦♦♦
Rackham Road, Amberley, Arundel B18 9NR
T: (01798) 831787
F: (01798) 831787
E: mob.club@virgin.net
I: www.thesportsmanamberley.co.uk

ANSTY
West Sussex

Netherby ♦♦♦♦
Bolney Road, Ansty, Haywards Heath RH17 5AW
T: (01444) 455888
F: (01444) 455888
E: susan@gilbert58.freeserve.co.uk

ARDINGLY
West Sussex

Stonelands West Lodge ♦♦♦
Ardingly Road, West Hoathly, East Grinstead RH19 4RA
T: (01342) 715372

ARPINGE
Kent

Pigeonwood House ♦♦♦♦
Grove Farm, Arpinge, Folkestone CT18 8AQ
T: (01303) 891111
F: (01303) 891019
E: samandmary@aol.com
I: www.pigeonwood.com

ARUNDEL
West Sussex

Arundel House ♦♦♦
11 High Street, Arundel, BN18 9AD
T: (01903) 882136
E: arundelhouse@btinternet.com
I: www.btinternet.com/~arundelhouse/

Houghton Farm ♦♦♦♦
Amberley, Arundel, BN18 9LW
T: (01798) 831327
F: (01798) 831183
E: rosemarylock@ukonline.co.uk

Medlar Cottage ♦♦♦
Poling Street, Poling, Arundel BN18 9PT
T: (01903) 883106
F: (01903) 883106

Mill Lane House ♦♦♦
Slindon, Arundel BN18 0RP
T: (01243) 814440
F: (01243) 814436

Pindars ♦♦♦♦ SILVER AWARD
Lyminster, Littlehampton BN17 7QF
T: (01903) 882628
F: (01903) 882628

Swan Hotel ♦♦♦
27-29 High Street, Arundel, BN18 9AG
T: (01903) 882314
F: (01903) 883759
E: info@swan-hotel.co.uk
I: www.swan-hotel.co.uk

Woodpeckers ♦♦♦♦
15 Dalloway Road, Arundel, BN18 9HJ
T: (01903) 883948

ASH
Kent

Nine Acres Bed & Breakfast ♦♦♦
Billet Hill, Ash, Sevenoaks TN15 7HG
T: (01474) 872253
F: (01474) 872253

ASHFORD
Kent

Beaver Guest House ♦♦♦
100 Beaver Road, Ashford, TN23 7ST
T: (01233) 733569
F: (01233) 732193
E: eurotunnel.town@amserve.net

Croft Hotel ♦♦♦
Canterbury Road, Kennington, Ashford TN25 4DU
T: (01233) 622140
F: (01233) 635271
E: crofthotel@btconnect.com
I: www.crofthotel.com

Dalmeny House
Rating Applied For
18 Magazine Road, Ashford, TN24 8NN
T: (01233) 627596

Dean Court Farm ♦♦♦
Challock Lane, Westwell, Ashford TN25 4NH
T: (01233) 712924

Glenmoor ♦♦♦
Maidstone Road, Ashford, TN25 4NP
T: (01233) 634767

New Flying Horse Inn ♦♦♦
Upper Bridge Street, Wye, Ashford TN25 5AN
T: (01233) 812297
F: (01233) 813487
E: newflyhorse@shepherd-neame.co.uk
I: www.shepherd-neame.co.uk

Quantock House ♦♦♦
Quantock Drive, Ashford, TN24 8QH
T: (01233) 638921
E: tucker100@madasafish.com

20 Spelthorne Lane ♦♦♦
Ashford, Sunbury TW15 1UJ
T: (01784) 420256

Warren Cottage Hotel and Restaurant ♦♦♦
136 The Street, Willesborough, Ashford, TN24 0NB
T: (01233) 621905
F: (01233) 623400
E: general@warrencottage.co.uk
I: www.warrencottage.co.uk

AYLESFORD
Kent

Wickham Lodge ♦♦♦♦
The Quay, High Street, Aylesford, ME20 7AY
T: (01622) 717267
F: (01622) 792855
E: wickhamlodge@aol.com
I: www.wickhamlodge.com

BALCOMBE
West Sussex

Rocks Lane Cottage ♦♦♦
Rocks Lane, Balcombe, Haywards Heath RH17 6JG
T: (01444) 811245
E: kpa@fsbdial.co.uk

BARCOMBE
East Sussex

The Anchor Inn ♦♦♦
Anchor Lane, Barcombe, Lewes BN8 5BS
T: (01273) 400414
F: (01273) 401029
I: www.anchorinnandboating.co.uk

BARNHAM
West Sussex

Downhills ♦♦♦
87 Barnham Road, Barnham, Bognor Regis PO22 0EQ
T: (01243) 553104

Todhurst Farm ♦♦♦
Lake Lane, Barnham, Bognor Regis PO22 0AL
T: (01243) 551959
E: nigelsedg@aol.com

BATTLE
East Sussex

The Abbey Hotel ♦♦♦
84 High Street, Battle, TN33 0AQ
T: (01424) 772755
F: (01424) 773378

Abbey View Bed & Breakfast ♦♦♦♦ SILVER AWARD
Caldbec Hill, Battle, TN33 0JS
T: (01424) 775513
F: (01424) 775513

Acacia House ♦♦♦♦
Starrs Green Lane, Battle, TN33 0TD
T: (01424) 772416

The Gateway Restaurant ♦♦♦
78 High Street, Battle, TN33 0AG
T: (01424) 772856

The George Hotel ♦♦♦♦
23 The High Street, Battle, TN33 0EA
T: (01424) 775512
F: (01424) 774853

High Hedges ♦♦♦♦
28 North Trade Road, Battle, TN33 0HB
T: (01424) 774140
E: gloria.jones@btinternet.com

Kelklands ♦♦♦
Off Chain Lane, Battle, TN33 0HG
T: (01424) 773013

Little Hemingfold Hotel ♦♦♦
Telham, Battle, TN33 0TT
T: (01424) 774338
F: (01424) 775351

Moons Hill Farm ♦♦♦
The Green, Ninfield, Battle, TN33 9LH
T: (01424) 892645
F: (01424) 892645
E: june@ive13.fsnet.co.uk

BEAN
Kent

Black Horse Cottage ♦♦♦
High Street, Bean, Dartford DA2 8AS
T: (01474) 704962

BEARSTED
Kent

88 Ashford Road ♦♦♦
Bearsted, Maidstone ME14 4LT
T: (01622) 738278
F: (01622) 738346

BECKLEY
East Sussex

Woodlands ♦♦♦
Whitebread Lane, Beckley, Rye TN31 6UA
T: (01797) 260486
E: ericrobson99@hotmail.com
I: www.woodlandsrye.co.uk

BELLS YEW GREEN
East Sussex

Rushlye Barn ♦♦♦
Bells Yew Green, Royal Tunbridge Wells TN3 9AP
T: (01892) 750398
E: rushlyebarn@tinyworld.co.uk
I: www.rushlyebarn.tripod.com

BENENDEN
Kent

The Bull At Benenden ♦♦♦♦
The Street, Benenden, Cranbrook TN17 4DE
T: (01580) 240054
E: thebull@thebullatbenenden.co.uk
I: www.thebullatbenenden.co.uk

BEPTON
West Sussex

Park House Hotel ♦♦♦♦♦ SILVER AWARD
Bepton, Midhurst GU29 0JB
T: (01730) 819000
F: (01730) 819099
I: www.Freepages.co.uk/parkhouse_hotel/

BERWICK
East Sussex

Lower Claverham Farm ♦♦♦
Berwick, Polegate BN26 6TJ
T: (01323) 811267
F: (01323) 811267
E: paul.rossi@talk21.com

BETHERSDEN
Kent

Cloverlea ♦♦♦
Hothfield Road, Bethersden, Ashford TN26 3DU
T: (01233) 820353
F: (01233) 820353
E: pam.mills@amserve.net

The Coach House ♦♦♦
Oakmead Farm, Bethersden, Ashford TN26 3DU
T: (01233) 820583
F: (01233) 820583

Little Hodgeham ♦♦♦♦ SILVER AWARD
Smarden Road, Bethersden, Ashford TN26 3HE
T: (01233) 850323
F: (01233) 850006
E: little.hodgeham@virgin.net
I: www.littlehodgeham.co.uk

The Old Stables ♦♦♦♦
Wissenden, Bethersden, Ashford TN26 3EL
T: (01233) 820597
F: (01233) 820199
E: pennygillespie@theoldstables.co.uk
I: www.theoldstables.co.uk

Potters Farm ♦♦♦
Bethersden, Ashford TN26 3JX
T: (01233) 820341
F: (01233) 820469
E: ianmcanderson@cs.com
I: www.smoothhound.co.uk/hotels/potters.html

BEXHILL
East Sussex

The Arosa Hotel ♦♦♦♦ SILVER AWARD
6 Albert Road, Bexhill, TN40 1DG
T: (01424) 212574
F: (01424) 212574

Barkers Bed and Breakfast ♦♦♦
16 Magdalen Road, Bexhill, TN40 1SB
T: (01424) 218969

Barrington B & B ♦♦♦♦
14 Wilton Road, Bexhill, TN40 1HY
T: (01424) 210250
E: mick@barrington14.freeserve.co.uk
I: www.barrington14.freeserve.co.uk

Buenos Aires Guest House ♦♦♦♦
24 Albany Road, Bexhill, TN40 1BZ
T: (01424) 212269
F: (01424) 212269
E: buenosairesguesthouse@hotmail.com

Collington Lodge Guest House ♦♦♦
41 Collington Avenue, Bexhill, TN39 3PX
T: (01424) 210024
F: (01424) 210024
E: info@collington.co.uk
I: www.collington.co.uk

Hartfield House
♦♦♦♦ SILVER AWARD
27 Hartfield Road, Cooden, Bexhill, TN39 3EA
T: (01424) 845715
F: (01424) 845715
E: mansi@hartfieldhouse.free-online.co.uk
I: www.hartfield-house.co.uk

Linden Lodge ♦♦♦
31 Linden Road, Bexhill, TN40 1DN
T: (01424) 225005
F: (01424) 222895
E: lindenlodge@hotmail.com

Little Marabou Mansions ♦♦
58-60 Devonshire Road, Bexhill, TN40 1AX
T: (01424) 215052
E: lexioouk@yahoo.co.uk

Manor Barn ♦♦♦
Lunsford Cross, Bexhill, TN39 5JJ
T: (01424) 893018
F: (01424) 893018

Mulberry
♦♦♦♦ SILVER AWARD
31 Warwick Road, Bexhill, TN39 4HG
T: (01424) 219204

Park Lodge Hotel ♦♦♦♦
16 Egerton Road, Bexhill, TN39 3HH
T: (01424) 216547
F: (01424) 217460

Sackville Hotel
♦♦♦♦ SILVER AWARD
De La Warr Parade, Bexhill-on-Sea, Bexhill, TN40 1LS
T: (01424) 224694
F: (01424) 734132

Sunshine Guest House ♦♦♦
Sandhurst Lane, Little Common, Bexhill, TN39 4RH
T: (01424) 842009

Westwood Farm ♦♦♦
Stonestile Lane, Hastings, TN35 4PG
T: (01424) 751038
F: (01424) 751038
E: york@westwood-farm.fsnet.co.uk

BIDDENDEN
Kent

Birchley House West ♦♦♦♦
Fosten Green, Biddenden, Ashford TN27 8DZ
T: (01580) 291124
F: (01580) 291416
E: birchley@globalnet.co.uk
I: www.birchleywest.co.uk

Bishopsdale Oast ♦♦♦♦
Biddenden, Ashford TN27 8DR
T: (01580) 291027
F: (01580) 292321
E: drysdale@bishopsdaleoast.co.uk
I: www.bishopsdaleoast.co.uk

Heron Cottage ♦♦♦♦
Biddenden, Ashford TN27 8HH
T: (01580) 291358

Tudor Cottage ♦♦♦♦
25 High Street, Biddenden, Ashford TN27 8AL
T: (01580) 291913
E: suemorris.biddenden@virgin.net
I: freespace.virgin.net/suemorris.biddenden

BILLINGSHURST
West Sussex

Groom Cottage ♦♦♦
Station Road, Billingshurst, RH14 9RF
T: (01403) 782285

BILSINGTON
Kent

Willow Farm ♦♦♦
Stone Cross, Bilsington, Ashford TN25 7JJ
T: (01233) 720484
F: (01233) 720484
E: renee@willow-farm.freeserve.co.uk

BIRCHINGTON
Kent

Greenview ♦♦♦♦
28 Canute Road, Minnis Bay, Birchington, CT7 9QJ
T: (01843) 844737
F: (01843) 844737

BIRDHAM
West Sussex

The Red House ♦♦♦♦
Lock Lane, Birdham Pool, Birdham, Chichester PO20 7BB
T: (01243) 512488
F: (01243) 514563
E: susie.redhouse@ukonline.co.uk
I: www.redhousehideaway.co.uk

BIRLING
Kent

The Stable Block ♦♦♦
25 Ryarsh Road, Birling, West Malling, ME19 5JW
T: (01732) 873437
F: (01732) 849320
E: carolinemoorhead1@hotmail.com

BLADBEAN
Kent

Molehills ♦♦♦♦
Bladbean, Canterbury CT4 6LU
T: (01303) 840051
E: molehills84@hotmail.com

BOGNOR REGIS
West Sussex

Alancourt Hotel ♦♦♦
Marine Drive West, Bognor Regis, PO21 2QA
T: (01243) 864844
F: (01243) 864844

Homestead Guest House ♦♦♦
90 Aldwick Road, Bognor Regis, PO21 2PD
T: (01243) 823443
F: (01243) 823443

Jubilee Guest House ♦♦♦
5 Gloucester Road, Bognor Regis, PO21 1NU
T: (01243) 863016
F: (01243) 868017
E: jubileeguesthouse@breathemail.net
I: www.jubileeguesthouse.com

The Maltings
♦♦♦♦ SILVER AWARD
199 Pagahm Road, Nyetimber, Bognor Regis, PO21 4NJ
T: (01243) 261168
F: (01243) 262382
E: info@themaltings.org.uk
I: www.themaltings.org.uk

Regis Lodge ♦♦♦
3 Gloucester Road, Bognor Regis, PO21 1NU
T: (01243) 827110
F: (01243) 827110
E: frank@regislodge.fsbusiness.co.uk
I: www.regislodge.tripod.com

St Albans ♦♦♦♦
The Esplanade, Bognor Regis, PO21 1NY
T: (01243) 860516

Sea Crest Private Hotel ♦♦♦
19 Nyewood Lane, Bognor Regis, PO21 2QB
T: (01243) 821438

Swan Guest House ♦♦♦♦
17 Nyewood Lane, Bognor Regis, PO21 2QB
T: (01243) 826880
F: (01243) 826880
E: swanhse@globalnet.co.uk
I: www.users.globalnet.co.uk/~swanhse

Tudor Cottage Guest House
♦♦♦♦
194 Chichester Road, Bognor Regis, PO21 5BJ
T: (01243) 821826
F: (01243) 862189
E: tudorcottage@supernet.com

BOLNEY
West Sussex

Broxmead Paddock ♦♦♦♦
Broxmead Lane, Bolney, Cuckfield, Haywards Heath RH17 5RG
T: (01444) 881458
F: (01444) 881491
E: broxmeadpaddock@hotmail.com

Colwood Manor West ♦♦♦♦
Spronketts Lane, Bolney, Haywards Heath RH17 5SA
T: (01444) 461331
E: dmartin@ricsonline.org

New Farm House ♦♦♦♦
Nyes Hill, Wineham Lane, Bolney, Haywards Heath RH17 5SD
T: (01444) 881617
F: (01444) 881850
E: newfarmhouse@btinternet.com
I: www.newfarmhouse.co.uk

BOROUGH GREEN
Kent

Yew Tree Barn ♦♦♦♦
Long Mill Lane, Crouch, Borough Green, Sevenoaks TN15 8QB
T: (01732) 883107
F: (01732) 883107
E: yewtreebarnbb@hotmail.com

BOSHAM
West Sussex

Crede Farmhouse
♦♦♦♦ SILVER AWARD
Crede Lane, Bosham, Chichester PO18 8NX
T: (01243) 574929
E: lesley@credefarmhouse.fsnet.co.uk

Good Hope ♦♦♦♦
Delling Lane, Bosham, Chichester PO18 8NR
T: (01243) 572487
F: (01243) 530760

Govers ♦♦♦
Crede Lane, Bosham, Chichester PO18 8NX
T: (01243) 573163

Hatpins
♦♦♦♦♦ SILVER AWARD
Bosham Lane, Old Bosham, Chichester, PO18 8HG
T: (01243) 572644
F: (01243) 572644
E: mary@hatpins.co.uk
I: www.hatpins.co.uk

BOUGH BEECH
Kent

Bank View ♦♦♦
Chequers Hill, Bough Beech, Edenbridge TN8 7PD
T: (01732) 700315
F: (01732) 700786
E: t.dalladay@btopenworld.com

BOUGHTON
Kent

Brenley Farm House ♦♦♦
Brenley Lane, Boughton, Faversham ME13 9LY
T: (01227) 751203
F: (01227) 751203
E: maggie@brenley.freeserve.co.uk
I: www.brenley.co.uk

10 Horselees Road ♦♦♦
Boughton under Blean, Boughton, Faversham ME13 9TG
T: (01227) 751332
F: (01227) 751332
E: keyway@bigfoot.com

Wellbrook Farmhouse ♦♦♦♦
South Street, Boughton, Faversham ME13 9NA
T: (01227) 750941
F: (01227) 750807
E: reservations@wellbrookfarmhouse.co.uk
I: www.wellbrookfarmhouse.co.uk

BOUGHTON MONCHELSEA
Kent

Hideaway ♦♦♦
Heath Road, Boughton Monchelsea, Maidstone ME17 4JD
T: (01622) 747453
F: (01622) 747453

Wierton Hall Farm ♦♦♦
East Hall Hill, Boughton Monchelsea, Maidstone ME17 4JU
T: (01622) 743535
F: (01622) 743535
E: phipps@jackie.68383.fsnet.co.uk

BOXGROVE
West Sussex

The Brufords ♦♦♦♦
66 The Street, Boxgrove, Chichester, PO18 0EE
T: (01243) 774085
F: (01243) 781235
E: brendan@bjcoffey.freeserve.co.uk
I: www.sussexlive.com

BOXLEY
Kent

Barn Cottage ♦♦♦
Harbourland, Boxley, Maidstone ME14 3DN
T: (01622) 675891
F: (01622) 675891

BRAMLEY
Surrey

The Granary ♦♦♦♦
Chinthurst Farmhouse, Chinthurst Lane, Bramley, Guildford GU5 0DR
T: (01483) 898623
F: (01483) 898623

Highpoint
♦♦♦♦ SILVER AWARD
Munstead View Road, Bramley, Guildford GU5 0DA
T: (01483) 893566
F: (01483) 894205
E: chriscard@compuserve.com
I: www.come.to/highpoint

Old Timbers ♦♦♦
Snowdenham Links Road, Bramley, Guildford GU5 0BX
T: (01483) 893258
E: jpold_timbers@hotmail.com

BRASTED
Kent

Lodge House ♦♦♦
High Street, Brasted, Westerham TN16 1HS
T: (01959) 562195
F: (01959) 562195
E: lodgehouse@brastedbb.freeserve.co.uk

The Mount House ♦♦♦♦
Brasted, Westerham TN16 1JB
T: (01959) 563617
F: (01959) 561296
E: jpaulco@webspeed.net

The Orchard House ♦♦♦
Brasted Chart, Westerham, TN16 1LR
T: (01959) 563702
E: david.godsal@tesco.net

BREDE
East Sussex

Brede Court Country House ♦♦♦♦
Brede Hill, Brede, Rye TN31 6EJ
T: (01424) 883105
F: (01424) 883104
E: bredecrt@globalnet.co.uk
I: www.english-training.com

2 Stonelink Cottages ♦♦♦
Stubb Lane, Brede, Rye TN31 6BL
T: (01424) 882943
F: (01424) 883052
E: stonelinkc@aol.com

BRENCHLEY
Kent

Woodlands Cottage ♦♦♦♦
Fairmans Road, Brenchley, Tonbridge TN12 7BB
T: (01892) 722707
F: (01892) 724946
E: chris.omalley@virgin.net

BRENZETT
Kent

Beba Farms Brenzett ♦♦♦
Brenzett Place, Ivychurch Road, Brenzett, Romney Marsh TN29 0EE
T: (01797) 344621
F: (01797) 344172
E: apabeba@lineone.net
I: www.kent-esites.co.uk/bebafarmsbrenzett

BRIDGE
Kent

East Bridge Country Hotel ♦♦♦♦
Bridge Hill, Bridge, Canterbury CT4 5AS
T: (01227) 830808
F: (01227) 832181
E: eastbridgehotel@btinternet.com
I: www.eastbridgehotel.btinternet.co.uk

Harrow Cottage ♦♦♦
2 Brewery Lane, Bridge, Canterbury CT4 5LD
T: (01227) 830218
F: (01227) 830218
E: pamela@phooker.fsbusiness.co.uk

BRIGHTLING
East Sussex

Orchard Barn ♦♦♦
3 Twelve Oaks Cottages, Brightling, Robertsbridge TN32 5HS
T: (01424) 838263

Swallowfield Farm ♦♦♦♦
Brightling, Battle, TN32 5HB
T: (01424) 838225
F: (01424) 838885
E: jssp@swallowfieldfarm.freeserve.co.uk
I: www.swallowfieldfarm.co.uk

BRIGHTON & HOVE
East Sussex

Adelaide Hotel
♦♦♦♦ SILVER AWARD
51 Regency Square, Brighton, BN1 2FF
T: (01273) 205286
F: (01273) 220904
E: adelaide@pavilion.co.uk

Aegean Hotel ♦♦♦
5 New Steine, Brighton, BN2 1PB
T: (01273) 686547
F: (01273) 625613

Ainsley House Hotel ♦♦♦♦
28 New Steine, Brighton, BN2 1PD
T: (01273) 605310
F: (01273) 688604
E: ahhotel@fastnet.co.uk
I: www.ainsleyhotel.com

Ambassador Hotel ♦♦♦♦
22 New Steine, Marine Parade, Brighton, BN2 1PD
T: (01273) 676869
F: (01273) 689988
E: ambassadorhoteluk@hotmail.com
I: www.ambassadorhotelbrighton.com

Andorra Hotel ♦
15-16 Oriental Place, Brighton, BN1 2LJ
T: (01273) 321787
F: (01273) 721418

Aquarium Guest House ♦♦
13 Madeira Place, Brighton, BN2 1TN
T: (01273) 605761

Arlanda Hotel
♦♦♦♦ SILVER AWARD
20 New Steine, Brighton, BN2 1PD
T: (01273) 699300
F: (01273) 600930
E: arlanda@brighton.co.uk
I: www.arlandahotel.co.uk

Atlantic Hotel ♦♦♦
16 Marine Parade, Brighton, BN2 1TL
T: (01273) 695944
F: (01273) 695944

Aymer ♦♦♦♦
13 Aymer Road, Hove, Brighton BN3 4GB
T: (01273) 271165
F: (01273) 321653
I: www.aymerguesthouse.co.uk

The Beach Hotel ♦♦♦
2-4 Regency Square, Brighton, BN1 2GP
T: (01273) 323776
F: (01273) 747028
E: beachhotelbrighton@hotmail.com
I: www.beachotel.co.uk

Beynon House ♦♦♦
24 St George's Terrace, Brighton, BN2 1JJ
T: (01273) 681014
F: (01273) 681014
E: beynonhouse@hotmail.com
I: www.beynonhouse.co.uk

Brighton House Hotel ♦♦♦♦
52 Regency Square, Brighton, BN1 2FF
T: (01273) 323282
E: enquiries@brightonhousehotel.co.uk
I: www.brightonhousehotel.co.uk

Brighton Marina House Hotel ♦♦♦
8 Charlotte Street, Marine Parade, Brighton, BN2 1AG
T: (01273) 605349
F: (01273) 679484
E: rooms@jungs.co.uk
I: www.brighton-mh-hotel.co.uk

Brighton Twenty One Hotel ♦♦♦♦
21 Charlotte Street, Marine Parade, Brighton, BN2 1AG
T: (01273) 686450
F: (01273) 695560
E: the21@pavilion.co.uk
I: www.s-h-systems.co.uk/hotels/21

Brunswick Square Hotel ♦♦
11 Brunswick Square, Hove, Brighton BN3 1EH
T: (01273) 205047
F: (01273) 205047
E: brunswick@brighton.co.uk
I: www.brighton.co.uk/hotels/brunswick

C Breeze Hotel ♦♦♦
12a Upper Rock Gardens, Brighton, BN2 1QE
T: (01273) 602608
F: (01273) 677894

Cavalaire Hotel ♦♦♦♦
34 Upper Rock Gardens, Brighton, BN2 1QF
T: (01273) 696899
F: (01273) 600504
E: welcome@cavalaire.co.uk
I: www.cavalaire.co.uk

Chatsworth Hotel ♦♦
9 Salisbury Road, Hove, Brighton BN3 3AB
T: (01273) 737360
F: (01273) 737360

Churchill Guest House ♦♦♦
44 Russell Square, Brighton, BN1 2EF
T: (01273) 700777
F: (01273) 700887
E: enquiries@churchillguesthouse.com
I: www.churchillguesthouse.com

Claremont House Hotel ♦♦♦♦
Second Avenue, Hove, Brighton BN3 2LL
T: (01273) 735161
F: (01273) 735161
E: claremonthove@aol.com
I: www.claremonthousehotel.co.uk

Cosmopolitan Hotel ♦♦♦
31 New Steine, Marine Parade, Brighton, BN2 1PD
T: (01273) 682461
F: (01273) 622311
E: enquire@cosmopolitanhotel.co.uk
I: www.cosmopolitanhotel.co.uk

Diana House ♦♦
25 St Georges Terrace, Brighton, BN2 1JJ
T: (01273) 605797
E: diana@enterprise.net
I: www.dianahouse.co.uk

Dove Hotel ♦♦♦♦
18 Regency Square, Brighton, BN1 2FG
T: (01273) 779222
F: (01273) 746912
E: dovehotel@dovehotelfree-online.co.uk

Dudley House ♦♦♦
10 Madeira Place, Brighton, BN2 1TN
T: (01273) 676794
E: office@dudleyhousebrighton.com

Funchal Guest House ♦♦♦
17 Madeira Place, Brighton, BN2 1TN
T: (01273) 603975
F: (01273) 603975

Fyfield House ♦♦♦♦
26 New Steine, Brighton, BN2 1PD
T: (01273) 602770
F: (01273) 602770
E: fyfield@aol.com
I: www.brighton.co.uk/hotels/fyfield

Georjan Guest House ♦♦♦
27 Upper Rock Gardens, Brighton, BN2 1QE
T: (01273) 694951
F: (01273) 694951
E: georjan.gh@virgin.net

Granada House ♦♦♦
35 Walsingham Road, Hove, Brighton BN3 4FE
T: (01273) 723855
F: (01273) 723855

Harveys ♦♦♦
1 Broad Street, Brighton, BN2 1TJ
T: (01273) 699227
F: (01273) 699227

Hudsons Guest House ♦♦♦
22 Devonshire Place, Brighton, BN2 1QA
T: (01273) 683642
F: (01273) 696088
E: hudsons@brighton.co.uk
I: brighton.co.uk/hotels/hudsons

The Kelvin Guest House ♦♦♦
9 Madeira Place, Brighton, BN2 1TN
T: (01273) 603735
F: (01273) 603735

Kingsway Hotel
♦♦♦♦ SILVER AWARD
2 St Aubyns, Hove, Brighton BN3 2TB
T: (01273) 722068
F: (01273) 778409
E: admin@kingswayent.demon.co.uk
I: www.kingsway-hotel.co.uk

Leona House ♦♦♦
74 Middle Street, Brighton, BN1 1AL
T: (01273) 327309

Lichfield House ♦♦♦
30 Waterloo Street, Hove, Brighton BN3 1AN
T: (01273) 777740
E: feelgood@lichfieldhouse.freeserve.co.uk
I: www.lichfieldhouse.freeserve.co.uk

Madeira Guest House ♦♦♦
14 Madeira Place, Brighton, BN2 1TN
T: (01273) 681115
F: (01273) 681115
I: www.madeiraguesthouse.co.uk

Miami Hotel ♦♦♦
22 Bedford Square, Brighton, BN1 2PL
T: (01273) 730169
F: (01273) 730169
E: themiami@pavilion.co.uk
I: www.brighton.co.uk/hotels/miami

New Madeira Hotel ♦♦♦
19-23 Marine Parade, Brighton, BN2 1TL
T: (01273) 698331
F: (01273) 606193
E: info@newmadeirahotel.com
I: www.newmadeirahotel.com

Oriental Hotel ♦♦♦
9 Oriental Place, Brighton, BN1 2LJ
T: (01273) 205050
F: (01273) 821096
E: info@orientalhotel.co.uk
I: www.orientalhotel.co.uk

The Palace Hotel ♦♦♦
10-12 Grand Junction Road, Brighton, BN1 1PN
T: (01273) 202035
F: (01273) 202034
E: palacehotel@connectfree.co.uk
I: www.palacebrighton.co.uk

Pavilion Guest House ♦♦♦
12 Madeira Place, Brighton, BN2 1TN
T: (01273) 683195

Penny Lanes ♦♦♦
11 Charlotte Street, Brighton, BN2 1AG
T: (01273) 603197
F: (01273) 689408
E: welcome@pennylanes.co.uk
I: www.pennylanes.co.uk

Russell Guest House ♦♦♦
19 Russell Square, Brighton, BN1 2EE
T: (01273) 327969
F: (01273) 821535
E: russell.brighton@btinternet.com

Sandpiper Guest House ♦♦
11 Russell Square, Brighton, BN1 2EE
T: (01273) 328202
F: (01273) 329974
E: sandpiper@brighton.co.uk

Sea Spray ♦♦♦
25 New Steine, Marine Parade, Brighton, BN2 1PD
T: (01273) 680332
E: seaspray@brighton.co.uk
I: www.seaspraybrighton.co.uk

Hotel Seafield ♦♦♦
23 Seafield Road, Hove, Brighton BN3 2TP
T: (01273) 735912
F: (01273) 323525
I: www.brighton.co.uk/hotels/seafield/

Strawberry Fields Hotel ♦♦♦
6-7 New Steine, Brighton, BN2 1PB
T: (01273) 681576
F: (01273) 693397
E: strawberryfields@pavilion.co.uk
I: www.brighton.co.uk/hotels/strawberryfields

Valentine House Hotel ♦♦♦
38 Russell Square, Brighton, BN1 2EF
T: (01273) 700800
F: (01273) 707606
E: stay@valentinehousehotel.com
I: www.valentinehousehotel.com

The White House ♦♦♦♦
6 Bedford Street, Brighton, BN2 1AN
T: (01273) 626266
E: info@whitehousebrighton.com

BROAD OAK
East Sussex

Fairacres ♦♦♦♦
Udimore Road, Broad Oak, Rye TN31 6DG
T: (01424) 883236

BROADSTAIRS
Kent

Anchor House ♦♦♦♦
10 Chandos Road, Broadstairs, CT10 1QP
T: (01843) 863347
F: (01843) 863347
E: joscott@ukonline.co.uk
I: www.anchorhouse.net

Bay Tree Hotel ♦♦♦♦
12 Eastern Esplanade, Broadstairs, CT10 1DR
T: (01843) 862502
F: (01843) 860589

Cintra Hotel ♦♦♦
24 Victoria Parade, Broadstairs, CT10 1QL
T: (01843) 862253

Copperfields Vegetarian Guest House ♦♦♦
11 Queens Road, Broadstairs, CT10 1NU
T: (01843) 601247
E: jroger600@aol.com
I: www.copperfieldsbb.co.uk

Devonhurst Hotel ♦♦♦♦
Eastern Esplanade, Broadstairs, CT10 1DR
T: (01843) 863010
F: (01843) 868940
E: info@devonhurst.co.uk
I: www.devonhurst.co.uk

Dundonald House Hotel ♦♦♦
43 Belvedere Road, Broadstairs, CT10 1PF
T: (01843) 862236
E: info@dundonaldhousehotel.co.uk
I: www.dundonaldhousehotel.co.uk

East Horndon Hotel ♦♦♦
4 Eastern Esplanade, Broadstairs, CT10 1DP
T: (01843) 868306
E: easthorndon@hotmail.com

16 Eastern Esplanade
Rating Applied For
Broadstairs, CT10 1DR
T: (01843) 861324
F: (01843) 861324

Gull Cottage Hotel ♦♦♦♦
5 Eastern Esplanade, Broadstairs, CT10 1DP
T: (01843) 861936

Hanson Hotel ♦♦♦
41 Belvedere Road, Broadstairs, CT10 1PF
T: (01843) 868936
E: hotelhanson@aol.com

Merriland Hotel ♦♦♦♦
The Vale, Broadstairs, CT10 1RB
T: (01843) 861064
F: (01843) 861064

Oakfield Private Hotel ♦♦♦♦
11 The Vale, Broadstairs, CT10 1RB
T: (01843) 862506
F: (01843) 600659
E: info@oakfield-hotel.com
I: www.oakfield-hotel.com

The Queens Hotel ♦♦♦
31 Queens Road, Broadstairs, CT10 1PG
T: (01843) 861727
F: (01843) 600993
E: enquiries@queenshotel.org
I: www.queenshotel.org

Seaview Cottage ♦♦♦♦
1 Seaview Cottages, Crundale Way, Broadstairs, CT10 3RY
T: (01843) 604784

Velindre Hotel ♦♦♦
10 Western Esplanade, Broadstairs, CT10 1TG
T: (01843) 601081

The Victoria ♦♦♦♦
23 Victoria Parade, Broadstairs, CT10 1QL
T: (01843) 871010
F: (01843) 860888
E: mullin@thevictoriabroadstairs.co.uk
I: www.thevictoriabroadstairs.co.uk

BROOKLAND
Kent

Walland Cottage ♦♦♦♦
Brookland, Romney Marsh TN29 9QZ
T: (01797) 344703

BURGESS HILL
West Sussex

Daisy Lodge B&B ♦♦♦
26 Royal George Road, Burgess Hill, RH15 9SE
T: (01444) 870570
F: (01444) 870571
E: daisylodge@btinternet.com

49 Ferndale Road ♦♦♦
Burgess Hill, RH15 0EZ
T: (01444) 241778
E: marlenwatsonbnb@hotmail.com

The Homestead ♦♦♦♦
Homestead Lane, Valebridge Road, Burgess Hill, RH15 0RQ
T: (01444) 246899
F: (01444) 241407
E: homestead@burgess-hill.co.uk
I: www.burgess-hill.co.uk

87 Meadow Lane ♦♦♦
Burgess Hill, RH15 9JD
T: (01444) 248421
F: (01444) 248421
E: bsayers@onetel.net.uk

Roselands ♦♦♦
3 Upper St Johns Road, Burgess Hill, RH15 8HB
T: (01444) 870491

St Owens ♦♦♦♦
11 Silverdale Road, Burgess Hill, RH15 0ED
T: (01444) 236435
E: n.j.baker@amserve.net

Wellhouse ♦♦♦♦
Wellhouse Lane, Burgess Hill, RH15 0BN
T: (01444) 233231
F: (01444) 233231

BURMARSH
Kent

Dolly Plum Cottage ♦♦♦♦
Burmarsh Road, Burmarsh, Romney Marsh TN29 0JT
T: (01303) 874558
F: (01303) 874558

Stable Cottage ♦♦♦♦
Donkey Street, Burmarsh, Romney Marsh TN29 0JN
T: (01303) 872335
E: janjohn@tiscali.co.uk

BURPHAM
West Sussex

Anderton House ♦♦♦
51 Marlyns Drive, Guildford, GU4 7LU
T: (01483) 826951
F: (01483) 826951
E: mrsdmkelly@yahoo.co.uk

Establishments printed in blue have a detailed entry in this guide

CAMBERLEY
Surrey

Abacus ♦♦♦
7 Woodside, Blackwater, Camberley, GU17 9JJ
T: (01276) 38339
E: abacus@amserve.net

CANTERBURY
Kent

Abberley House ♦♦♦
115 Whitstable Road, Canterbury, CT2 8EF
T: (01227) 450265
F: (01227) 478626

Acacia Lodge & Tanglewood ♦♦♦♦
39-40 London Road, Canterbury, CT2 8LF
T: (01227) 769955
F: (01227) 478960
E: michaelcain@lineone.net

Alexandra House ♦♦♦♦
1 Roper Road, Canterbury, CT2 7EH
T: (01227) 767011
F: (01227) 786617

Alicante Guest House ♦♦♦
4 Roper Road, Canterbury, CT2 7EH
T: (01227) 766277
F: (01227) 766277

Anns House ♦♦♦
63 London Road, Canterbury, CT2 8JZ
T: (01227) 768767
F: (01227) 768172

Ashley Guest House ♦♦
9 London Road, Canterbury, CT2 8LR
T: (01227) 455863

Ashton House ♦♦♦♦
129 Whitstable Road, Canterbury, CT2 8EQ
T: (01227) 455064
E: ashtonbnb@hotmail.com

Bower Farm House
♦♦♦♦ SILVER AWARD
Stelling Minnis, Canterbury, CT4 6BB
T: (01227) 709430
E: anne@bowerbb.freeserve.co.uk
I: www.kentac.co.uk/bowerfm

Carena ♦♦♦
250 Wincheap, Canterbury, CT1 3TY
T: (01227) 765630
F: (01227) 765630

Castle Court Guest House ♦♦
8 Castle Street, Canterbury, CT1 2QF
T: (01227) 463441
F: (01227) 463441
E: guesthouse@castlecourt.fsnet.co.uk
I: www.SmoothHound.co.uk/hotels/castlecourt.html

Cathedral Gate Hotel ♦♦♦
36 Burgate, Canterbury, CT1 2HA
T: (01227) 464381
F: (01227) 462800
E: cgate@cgate.demon.co.uk
I: www.cathgate.co.uk

Charnwood B & B ♦♦♦
64 New Dover Road, Canterbury, CT1 3DT
T: (01227) 451712
F: (01227) 451712
E: charnwood.bb@btinternet.com

Chaucer Lodge ♦♦♦♦
62 New Dover Road, Canterbury, CT1 3DT
T: (01227) 459141
F: (01227) 459141
E: wchaucerldg@aol.com
I: www.thechaucerlodge.co.uk

Clare-Ellen Guest House
♦♦♦♦ SILVER AWARD
9 Victoria Road, Wincheap, Canterbury, CT1 3SG
T: (01227) 760205
F: (01227) 784482
E: loraine.williams@clareellenguesthouse.co.uk
I: www.clareellenguesthouse.co.uk

The Dickens Inn at House of Agnes Hotel ♦♦♦
71 St Dunstan's Street, Canterbury, CT2 8BN
T: (01227) 472185
F: (01227) 464527
E: enq@dickens-inn.co.uk
I: www.dickens-inn.co.uk

Four Seasons ♦♦♦
77 Sturry Road, Canterbury, CT1 1BU
T: (01227) 787078
E: fourseasonsbnb@aol.com
I: members.aol.com/fourseasonsbnb

The Green House ♦♦♦
86 Wincheap, Canterbury, CT1 3RS
T: (01227) 453338
F: (01227) 452185
E: chrismac@greenhouse48.fsnet.co.uk
I: www.bednbreakfastkent.co.uk

Greyfriars House ♦♦♦
6 Stour Street, Canterbury, CT1 2NR
T: (01227) 456255
F: (01227) 455233
E: christine@greyfriars-house.co.uk
I: www.greyfriars-house.co.uk

Harriet House
♦♦♦♦ SILVER AWARD
3 Broad Oak Road, Canterbury, CT2 7PL
T: (01227) 457363
F: (01227) 788214

Iffin Farmhouse ♦♦♦♦
Iffin Lane, Canterbury, CT4 7BE
T: (01227) 462776
F: (01227) 762660
E: iffin.farmhouse@care4free.net

The Kings Head ♦♦♦
204 Wincheap, Canterbury, CT1 3RY
T: (01227) 462885
F: (01227) 459627

Kingsbridge Villas ♦♦♦
15 Best Lane, Canterbury, CT1 2JB
T: (01227) 766415

Kingsmead House ♦♦♦
68 St Stephen's Road, Canterbury, CT2 7JF
T: (01227) 760132
E: john.clarke52@btopenworld.com

London Guest House ♦♦♦
14 London Road, Canterbury, CT2 8LR
T: (01227) 765860
F: (01227) 456721
E: londonguesthousecabnkz@supanet.com

Magnolia House
♦♦♦♦♦ GOLD AWARD
36 St Dunstans Terrace, Canterbury, CT2 8AX
T: (01227) 765121
F: (01227) 765121
E: magnolia_house_canterbury@yahoo.com
I: freespace.virgin.net/magnolia.canterbury

Oak Cottage ♦♦♦♦
Elmsted, Ashford TN25 5JT
T: (01233) 750272
F: (01233) 750543
E: nichols@oakcottage.invictanet.co.uk

Peregrine House ♦♦♦
18 Hawks Lane, Canterbury, CT1 2NU
T: (01227) 472153
F: (01227) 455233
E: christine@greyfriars-house.co.uk
I: www.cantweb.co.uk/peregrine

The Plantation ♦♦♦♦
Iffin Lane, Canterbury, CT4 7BD
T: (01227) 472104
E: plantation@lycos.co.uk
I: www.media-p.co.uk/plantation/

Raemore House ♦♦♦
33 New Dover Road, Canterbury, CT1 3AS
T: (01227) 769740
F: (01227) 769432
E: tom@raemore.demon.co.uk

Renville Oast ♦♦♦♦
Bridge, Canterbury CT4 5AD
T: (01227) 830215
F: (01227) 830215
E: renville.oast@virgin.net
I: www.renvilleoast.co.uk

St Lawrence Guest House ♦♦♦
183 Old Dover Road, Canterbury, CT1 3EP
T: (01227) 451336
F: (01227) 451148
E: stlawrence@ic24.net
I: www.stlawrenceguesthouse.co.uk

St Stephens Guest House ♦♦♦
100 St Stephens Road, Canterbury, CT2 7JL
T: (01227) 767644
F: (01227) 767644
E: info@st-stephens.fsnet.co.uk
I: www.come.to/st-stephens

Thanington Hotel
♦♦♦♦♦ GOLD AWARD
140 Wincheap, Canterbury, CT1 3RY
T: (01227) 453227
F: (01227) 453225
E: enquiries@thanington-hotel.co.uk
I: www.thanington-hotel.co.uk

Tudor House ♦♦♦
6 Best Lane, Canterbury, CT1 2JB
T: (01227) 765650

Twin Mays
♦♦♦♦ GOLD AWARD
Plumpudding Lane, Dargate, Faversham ME13 9EX
T: (01227) 751346
E: janetm@harper128.freeserve.co.uk
I: www.harper128.freeserve.co.uk

Waltham Court Hotel ♦♦♦♦
Kake Street, Petham, Canterbury CT4 5SB
T: (01227) 700413
F: (01227) 700127
E: enquiries@walthamcourthotel.co.uk
I: www.walthamcourthotel.co.uk

White Horse Inn ♦♦♦♦
Boughton, Faversham ME13 9AX
T: (01227) 751700
F: (01227) 751090
E: whitehorse@shepherd-neame.co.uk
I: www.shepherd-neame.co.uk

The White House ♦♦♦♦
6 St Peters Lane, Canterbury, CT1 2BP
T: (01227) 761836
E: whwelcome@aol.com
I: www.smoothhound.co.uk/hotels/thewhitehouse/html

Wincheap Guest House ♦♦♦
94 Wincheap, Canterbury, CT1 3RS
T: (01227) 762309
F: (01227) 762309
E: joe@wincheapguesthouse.co.uk
I: www.wincheapguesthouse.co.uk

Woodlands Farm ♦♦♦
The Street, Adisham, Canterbury CT3 3LA
T: (01304) 840401
F: (01304) 841985
E: woodlands.farm@btinternet.com
I: www.accommodationatwoodlandsfarm.co.uk

The Woolpack Inn ♦♦♦♦
High Street, Chilham, Canterbury CT4 8DL
T: (01227) 730208
F: (01227) 731053
E: woolpack@shepherd-neame.co.uk
I: www.shepherd-neame.co.uk

Yorke Lodge ♦♦♦♦
50 London Road, Canterbury, CT2 8LF
T: (01227) 451243
F: (01227) 462006
E: yorke-lg@dircon.co.uk
I: www.users.dircon.co.uk/~yorke-lg

CAPEL
Surrey

Nightless Copse
Rating Applied For
Rusper Road, Capel, Dorking
RH5 5HE
T: (01306) 713247
F: (01306) 711765
E: bb@nightlesscopse.co.uk
I: www.nightlesscopse.co.uk

CHARING
Kent

Barnfield ◆◆◆
Charing, Ashford TN27 0BN
T: (01233) 712421
F: (01233) 712421

Royal Oak Inn ◆◆◆
5 High Street, Charing, Ashford
TN27 0HU
T: (01233) 712612
F: (01233) 713355
E: royal-oak.charingtn27@barbox.net

CHART SUTTON
Kent

White House Farm ◆◆◆
Green Lane, Chart Sutton,
Maidstone ME17 3ES
T: (01622) 842490
F: (01622) 842490
E: sue.spain@totalise.co.uk

CHARTHAM
Kent

Stour Farm ◆◆◆◆
Riverside, Chartham, Canterbury
CT4 7NX
T: (01227) 731977
F: (01227) 731977
E: info@stourfarm.co.uk
I: www.stourfarm.co.uk

CHATHAM
Kent

Normandy House ◆◆◆
143 Maidstone Road, Chatham,
ME4 6JE
T: (01634) 843047

Officers Hill
◆◆◆◆ SILVER AWARD
7 College Road, Historic
Dockyard, Chatham, ME4 4QW
T: (01634) 828436
F: (01634) 828735
E: carol.chambers@ukgateway.net

10 Officers Terrace ◆◆◆◆
Historic Dockyard, Chatham,
ME4 4LJ
T: (01634) 847512
E: sandrawsparks@aol.com

Roslin Cottage
◆◆◆◆ SILVER AWARD
294 Maidstone Road, Chatham,
ME4 6JJ
T: (01634) 401501

Ship & Trades ◆◆◆
Maritime Way, Chatham,
ME4 3ER
T: (01634) 895200
F: (01634) 895201

CHELWOOD GATE
East Sussex

Holly House ◆◆◆◆
Beaconsfield Road, Chelwood
Gate, Haywards Heath RH17 7LF
T: (01825) 740484
F: (01825) 740172
E: deebirchell@hollyhousebnb.demon.co.uk
I: hollyhousebnb.demon.co.uk

Laurel Cottage ◆◆◆
3 Laurel Cottage, Baxters Lane,
Chelwood Gate, Haywards
Heath RH17 7LU
T: (01825) 740547
F: (01825) 740057
E: smartin@chelwood.fsnet.co.uk

CHEVENING
Kent

Crossways House ◆◆◆◆
Chevening, Sevenoaks TN14 6HF
T: (01732) 456334
F: (01732) 452312
E: info@cheveningconferences.co.uk
I: www.cheveningconferences.co.uk

CHICHESTER
West Sussex

Abelands Barn
◆◆◆◆ SILVER AWARD
Bognor Road, Merston,
Chichester PO20 6DY
T: (01243) 533826
F: (01243) 784474
I: www.accomodata.co.uk/170998.htm

Anna's ◆◆◆
27 Westhampnett Road,
Chichester, PO19 4HW
T: (01243) 788522
F: (01243) 783135
E: nick@annas.freeserve.co.uk
I: www.annasofchichester.co.uk

Bayleaf ◆◆◆
16 Whyke Road, Chichester,
PO19 7AN
T: (01243) 774330

21 Brandy Hole Lane ◆◆◆
Chichester, PO19 4RL
T: (01243) 528201
F: (01243) 528201
E: anneparry@anneparry.screaming.net

The Chichester Inn ◆◆◆
38 West Street, Chichester,
PO19 1RP
T: (01243) 783185
E: churchills@chichester38.fsnet.co.uk

3 Clyesdale Avenue ◆◆◆◆
Chichester, PO19 2LW
T: (01243) 531397

The Coach House ◆◆◆◆
Binderton, Chichester, PO18 0JS
T: (01243) 539624
F: (01243) 539624
E: spightling@aol.com
I: www.sussexlive.com

The Cottage ◆◆◆
22B Westhampnett Road,
Chichester, PO19 4HW
T: (01243) 774979
E: mbc.techincal@virgin.net

Draymans ◆◆◆
112 St Pancras, Chichester,
PO19 7LH
T: (01243) 789872
F: (01243) 785474
E: liz@jaegerl.freeserve.co.uk
I: www.jaegerl.freeserve.co.uk

Encore ◆◆◆◆
11 Clydesdale Avenue,
Chichester, PO19 2LW
T: (01243) 528271

Englewood ◆◆◆◆
East Ashling, Chichester
PO18 9AS
T: (01243) 575407
F: (01243) 575407
E: sjenglewood@tinyworld.co.uk

Finisterre ◆◆◆◆
9 Albert Road, Chichester,
PO19 3JE
T: (01243) 532680
F: (01243) 532680
E: finisterre@albert-road-9.fsnet.co.uk
I: www.sussexlive.com

Forge Hotel
◆◆◆◆◆ SILVER AWARD
High Street, Chilgrove,
Chichester, PO18 9HX
T: (01243) 535333
F: (01243) 535363
E: reservations@forgehotel.com
I: www.forgehotel.com

Friary Close
◆◆◆◆ SILVER AWARD
Friary Lane, Chichester,
PO19 1UF
T: (01243) 527294
F: (01243) 533876
E: friaryclose@btinternet.com

Home Farm House
◆◆◆◆ GOLD AWARD
Elms Lane, West Wittering,
Chichester PO20 8LW
T: (01243) 514252
F: (01243) 512804

Kia-ora Nursery ◆◆◆
Main Road, Nutbourne,
Chichester PO18 8RT
T: (01243) 572858
F: (01243) 572858
E: ruthiefp@aol.com

4 The Lane
◆◆◆◆ SILVER AWARD
Summersdale, Chichester,
PO19 4PY
T: (01243) 527293
E: ynyo5@dial.pipex.com

Litten House ◆◆◆◆
148 St Pancras, Chichester,
PO19 7SH
T: (01243) 774503
F: (01243) 539187
E: victoria@littenho.demon.co.uk
I: www.littenho.demon.co.uk

5A Little London ◆◆◆
Chichester, PO19 1PH
T: (01243) 788405

Longmeadow Guest House
◆◆◆
Pine Grove, Chichester,
PO19 3PN
T: (01243) 782063
E: bbeeching@lineone.net
I: www.longmeadowguesthouse.com

1 Maplehurst Road
◆◆◆◆ SILVER AWARD
Chichester, PO19 4QL
T: (01243) 528467
F: (01243) 528467
E: philandsuespooner@talk21.com

The Old Store Guest House
◆◆◆◆
Stane Street, Halnaker,
Chichester PO18 0QL
T: (01243) 531977
E: theoldstore4@aol.com
I: www.smoothhound.co.uk/hotels/store.html

Palm Tree Cottage ◆◆◆◆
110 Fishbourne West,
Fishbourne, Chichester PO19 3JR
T: (01243) 782110
F: (01243) 785285

Primrose Cottage ◆◆◆
Old Broyle Road, West Broyle,
Chichester, PO19 3PR
T: (01243) 788873

Riverside Lodge ◆◆◆
7 Market Avenue, Chichester,
PO19 1JU
T: (01243) 783164
E: tregeardavid@hotmail.com
I: www.riverside-lodge-chichester.co.uk

University College Chichester
◆◆◆
Bishop Otter Campus, College
Lane, Chichester, PO19 4PE
T: (01243) 816070
F: (01243) 816068
E: conference@ucc.ac.uk
I: www.ucc.ac.uk

Woodstock House Hotel
◆◆◆◆
Charlton, Chichester, PO18 0HU
T: (01243) 811666
F: (01243) 811666
E: info@woodstockhousehotel.co.uk
I: www.woodstockhousehotel.co.uk

CHIDDINGFOLD
Surrey

Combe Ridge ◆◆◆
Pook Hill, Chiddingfold,
Godalming GU8 4XR
T: (01428) 682607
F: (01428) 682607
E: brendaessex@onetel.co.uk

Greenaway ◆◆◆◆
Pickhurst Road, Chiddingfold,
Godalming GU8 4TS
T: (01428) 682920
F: (01428) 685078
E: jfvmarsh@nildram.co.uk
I: www.greenaway.nildram.co.uk

CHIDDINGSTONE
Kent

Hoath House ◆◆◆
Chiddingstone Hoath,
Edenbridge TN8 7DB
T: (01342) 850362
E: jstreatfield@hoath-house.freeserve.co.uk
I: www.hoath_house.freeserve.co.uk

CHILHAM
Kent

Folly House ◆◆◆◆
Chilham, Canterbury CT4 8DU
T: (01227) 738669
F: (01227) 730425

The Old Alma ♦♦♦
Canterbury Road, Chilham,
Canterbury CT4 8DX
T: (01227) 731913
F: (01227) 731078
E: oldalma@aol.com

Woodchip House ♦♦♦
Maidstone Road, Chilham,
Canterbury CT4 8DD
T: (01227) 730386
F: (01227) 730685
E: woodchip@talk21.com

CHIPSTEAD
Kent

Chevers ♦♦♦♦
Moat Close, Homedean Road,
Chipstead, Sevenoaks TN13 2HZ
T: (01732) 779144
E: japarish@supanet.com

Windmill Farm ♦♦♦♦
Chevening Road, Chipstead,
Sevenoaks TN13 2SA
T: (01732) 452054

CLIFTONVILLE
Kent

Carnforth Hotel ♦♦♦♦
103 Norfolk Road, Cliftonville,
Margate CT9 2HX
T: (01843) 292127

Debenham Lodge Hotel ♦♦♦
25 Norfolk Road, Cliftonville,
Margate CT9 2HU
T: (01843) 292568

Lynton House Hotel ♦♦
24-26 Sweyn Road, Cliftonville,
Margate CT9 2DH
T: (01843) 292046

Marsdon Hotel ♦♦♦
7 Ethelbert Crescent, Cliftonville,
Margate CT9 2AY
T: (01843) 220175
F: (01843) 280920
E: enquiries@marsdon.
freeserve.co.uk
I: www.marsdon.freeserve.co.uk

Ocean View Hotel ♦♦
8-10 Ethelbert Terrace,
Cliftonville, Margate CT9 1RX
T: (01843) 220641
F: (01843) 571045
E: info@oceanviewhotel.co.uk
I: www.oceanviewhotel.co.uk

St Malo Hotel
Rating Applied For
54 Surrey Road, Cliftonville,
Margate CT9 2LA
T: (01843) 224931

COBHAM
Kent

Burleigh Farmhouse ♦♦♦♦
Sole Street Road, Cobham,
Gravesend DA12 3AR
T: (01474) 814321
F: (01474) 813843

Roxena ♦♦♦
34 Manor Road, Sole Street,
Cobham, Gravesend DA13 9BN
T: (01474) 814174

COLEMANS HATCH
East Sussex

Gospel Oak ♦♦♦
Sandy Lane, Colemans Hatch,
Hartfield TN7 4ER
T: (01342) 823840

COMPTON
West Sussex

Compton Farmhouse ♦♦♦
Church Lane, Compton,
Chichester PO18 9HB
T: (023) 9263 1597

Little Polsted ♦♦♦♦
Polsted Lane, Compton,
Guildford GU3 1JE
T: (01483) 810398
F: (01483) 810398
E: cwalkinshaw@lineone.net

COOKSBRIDGE
East Sussex

Lower Tulleys Wells Farm ♦♦♦
Beechwood Lane, East
Chiltington Road, Cooksbridge,
Lewes BN7 3QG
T: (01273) 472622

COOLHAM
West Sussex

Selsey Arms ♦♦♦
Coolham, Horsham RH13 8QJ
T: (01403) 741536

COWBEECH
East Sussex

Batchelors ♦♦♦♦
Cowbeech Hill, Cowbeech,
Hailsham BN27 4JB
T: (01323) 832215
I: www.batchelors-bb.co.uk

The Mill
♦♦♦♦ SILVER AWARD
Trolliloes Lane, Cowbeech,
Hailsham BN27 4JG
T: (01323) 833952
F: (01323) 833750
E: sales@massystems.net

COWDEN
Kent

Becketts Bed & Breakfast ♦♦♦♦
Pylegate Farm, Hartfield Road,
Cowden, Edenbridge TN8 7HE
T: (01342) 850514
F: (01342) 851281
E: bed-breakfast.becketts@
tinyworld.co.uk
I: www.becketts-bandb.co.uk

Southernwood House ♦♦♦♦
(The Old Rectory), Church Street,
Cowden, Edenbridge TN8 7JE
T: (01342) 850880

COWFOLD
West Sussex

Coach House ♦♦♦
Horsham Road, Cowfold,
Horsham RH13 8BT
T: (01403) 864247
F: (01403) 865329
E: coachhousecowfold@talk21.
com
I: www.sussexlive.com

CRANBROOK
Kent

Bargate House ♦♦♦♦
Angley Road, Cranbrook,
TN17 2PQ
T: (01580) 714254

Bull Farm Oast ♦♦♦
Corner of Hawkhurst Road &
Bishops Lan, Cranbrook,
TN17 2ST
T: (01580) 714140
F: 0870 055 7698
E: b+b@mixx.demon.co.uk
I: www.mixx.demon.co.uk

Guernsey Cottage ♦♦♦
Wilsley Green, Cranbrook,
TN17 2LG
T: (01580) 712542

Hallwood Farm House ♦♦♦
Hallwood Farm, Cranbrook,
TN17 2SP
T: (01580) 713204
F: (01580) 713204

Old Rectory
♦♦♦♦ SILVER AWARD
The Old Rectory, Frittenden,
Cranbrook TN17 2DG
T: (01580) 852313
F: (01580) 852313

Sissinghurst Castle Farm ♦♦♦♦
Sissinghurst, Cranbrook,
TN17 2AB
T: (01580) 712885
F: (01580) 712601

Swattenden Ridge ♦♦♦♦
Swattenden Lane, Cranbrook,
TN17 3PR
T: (01580) 712327
F: (01580) 712327

Tolehurst Barn ♦♦♦♦
Cranbrook Road, Frittenden,
Cranbrook TN17 2BP
T: (01580) 714385
F: (01580) 714385
E: info@tolehurstbarn.co.uk
I: www.tolehurstbarn.co.uk

CRANLEIGH
Surrey

Pathstruie ♦♦♦
Stovolds Hill, Cranleigh, GU6 8LE
T: (01483) 273551

CRAWLEY
West Sussex

Little Foxes Hotel ♦♦♦♦
Charlwood Road, Ifield Wood,
Crawley, RH11 0JY
T: (01293) 529206
F: (01293) 551434
E: info@littlefoxeshotel.co.uk
I: www.littlefoxeshotel.co.uk

The Manor House ♦♦♦
Bonnetts Lane, Ifield, Crawley
RH11 0NY
T: (01293) 510000
F: (01293) 518046
E: info@manorhouse-gatwick.
co.uk
I: www.manorhouse-gatwick.
co.uk

Three Bridges Lodge ♦♦♦
190 Three Bridges Road,
Crawley, RH10 1LN
T: (01293) 612190
F: (01293) 553078
E: nisangah@yahoo.com

CROWBOROUGH
East Sussex

Bathurst ♦♦♦♦
Fielden Road, Crowborough,
TN6 1TR
T: (01892) 665476
F: (01892) 654189
E: bathurst@aslender.freeserve.
co.uk

Braemore ♦♦♦♦
Eridge Road, Steel Cross,
Crowborough, TN6 2SS
T: (01892) 665700

Bryher Patch ♦♦♦
18 Hydehurst Close,
Crowborough, TN6 1EN
T: (01892) 663038

Hope Court ♦♦♦♦
Rannoch Road, Crowborough,
TN6 1RA
T: (01892) 654017

CUXTON
Kent

27 James Road
Rating Applied For
Cuxton, Rochester ME2 1DH
T: (01634) 715154

DANEHILL
East Sussex

New Glenmore ♦♦♦♦
Sliders Lane, Furners Green,
Uckfield TN22 3RU
T: (01825) 790783
E: alan.robinson@bigfoot.com

DARTFORD
Kent

Chashir ♦♦
3 Tynedale Close, Fleet Estate,
Dartford, DA2 6LL
T: (01322) 227886

DEAL
Kent

Cannongate House ♦♦♦
26 Gilford Road, Deal, CT14 7DJ
T: (01304) 375238

The Hole in the Roof Hotel ♦♦♦
42-44 Queen Street, Deal,
CT14 6EY
T: (01304) 374839
F: (01304) 373768

Ilex Cottage ♦♦♦♦
Temple Way, Worth, Deal
CT14 0DA
T: (01304) 617026
F: (01304) 620890
E: info@ilexcottage.com
I: www.ilexcottage.com

Keep House ♦♦♦
1 Deal Castle Road, Deal,
CT14 7BB
T: (01304) 368162
F: (01304) 368162
E: keephouse@talk21.com
I: www.keephouse.co.uk

Kings Head Public House ♦♦♦
9 Beach Street, Deal, CT14 7AH
T: (01304) 368194
F: (01304) 364182

The Malvern ♦♦♦
5-7 Ranelagh Road, Deal,
CT14 7BG
T: (01304) 372944
F: (01304) 372944

Richmond Villa Guest House ♦♦♦♦
1 Ranelagh Road, Deal,
CT14 7BG
T: (01304) 366211
E: reservations@richmondvilla.
co.uk
I: www.richmondvilla.co.uk

The Roast House Lodge ♦♦♦
224 London Road, Deal,
CT14 9PW
T: (01304) 380824
F: (01304) 380824

DENSOLE
Kent

Garden Lodge ♦♦♦♦
324 Canterbury Road, Densole, Folkestone CT18 7BB
T: (01303) 893147
F: (01303) 894581
E: stay@garden-lodge.com
I: www.garden-lodge.com

DETLING
Kent

East Lodge ♦♦♦♦
Harple Lane, Detling, Maidstone ME14 3ET
T: (01622) 734205
F: (01622) 735500

DODDINGTON
Kent

Palace Farmhouse ♦♦♦
Chequers Hill, Doddington, Sittingbourne ME9 0AU
T: (01795) 886820

DORKING
Surrey

Bulmer Farm ♦♦♦♦
Holmbury St Mary, Dorking RH5 6LG
T: (01306) 730210

Claremont Cottage ♦♦♦
Rose Hill, Dorking, RH4 2ED
T: (01306) 885487
F: (01306) 885487

Denbies Farmhouse B&B ♦♦♦
Denbies Wine Estate, London Road, Dorking, RH5 6AA
T: (01306) 876777
F: (01306) 888930
E: info@denbiesvineyard.co.uk
I: www.denbiesvineyard.co.uk

Fairdene Guest House ♦♦♦
Moores Road, Dorking, RH4 2BG
T: (01306) 888337
E: zoe@fairdene5.freeserve.co.uk

Kerne Hus ♦♦♦♦
Walliswood, Dorking, RH5 5RD
T: (01306) 627548
E: kerne_hus@lineone.net

Sturtwood Farm ♦♦♦
Partridge Lane, Newdigate, Dorking RH5 5EE
T: (01306) 631308
F: (01306) 631908
E: sturtwoodfarm@btopenworld.com

Torridon Guest House ♦♦♦
Longfield Road, Dorking, RH4 3DF
T: (01306) 883724
F: (01306) 880759

DOVER
Kent

Amanda Guest House ♦♦
4 Harold Street, Dover, CT16 1SF
T: (01304) 201711
E: amandaguesthouse@hotmail.com
I: www.amandaguesthouse.homestead.com

Blakes of Dover ♦♦♦♦
52 Castle Street, Dover, CT16 1PJ
T: (01304) 202194
F: (01304) 202194
E: blakes-of-dover@hotels.activebooking.com

Castle Guest House ♦♦♦
10 Castle Hill Road, Dover, CT16 1QW
T: (01304) 201656
F: (01304) 210197
E: dimechr@aol.com
I: www.castle-guesthouse.co.uk

Chrislyn's Guest House ♦♦♦♦
104 Maison Dieu Road, Dover, CT16 1RU
T: (01304) 203317
F: (01304) 212593

Clare Guest House ♦♦♦
167 Folkestone Road, Dover, CT17 9SJ
T: (01304) 204553

Cleveland Guest House ♦♦♦
2 Laureston Place, off Castle Hill Road, Dover, CT16 1QX
T: (01304) 204622
F: (01304) 211598
E: albetcleve@aol.com
I: www.albetcleve.homestead.com

Colret House ♦♦♦♦
The Green, Coldred, Dover CT15 5AP
T: (01304) 830388
F: (01304) 830388
E: jackie.colret@evnet.co.uk

The Dell Guest House ♦♦♦
233 Folkestone Road, Dover, CT17 9SL
T: (01304) 202422
F: (01304) 204816
E: mail@dell-guesthouse.co.uk
I: www.dell-guesthouse.co.uk

Frith Lodge ♦♦♦
14 Frith Road, Dover, CT16 2PY
T: (01304) 208139

Gladstone Guest House ♦♦♦♦
3 Laureston Place, Dover, CT16 1QX
T: (01304) 208457
F: (01304) 208457
E: kkd3gladstone@aol.com
I: www.doveraccommodation.co.uk/gladstone.htm

Le Clermont ♦♦♦
15 Park Avenue, Dover, CT16 1ES
T: (01304) 202302
F: (01304) 202302
E: sally@leclermont32.freeserve.co.uk

Linden Guest House ♦♦♦♦
231 Folkestone Road, Dover, CT17 9SL
T: (01304) 205449
F: (01304) 212499
E: Lindenrog@aol.com
I: www.smoothhound.co.uk/hotels/linden.html

Loddington House Hotel ♦♦♦♦
14 East Cliff, (Seafront - Marine Parade), Dover, CT16 1LX
T: (01304) 201947
F: (01304) 201947

Longfield Guest House ♦♦♦
203 Folkestone Road, Dover, CT17 9SL
T: (01304) 204716
F: (01304) 204716
E: res@longfieldguesthouse.co.uk
I: www.longfieldguesthouse.co.uk

Maison Dieu Guest House ♦♦♦
89 Maison Dieu Road, Dover, CT16 1RU
T: (01304) 204033
F: (01304) 242816
E: lawrie@brguest.co.uk
I: www.brguest.co.uk

The Norman Guest House ♦♦♦
75 Folkestone Road, Dover, CT17 9RZ
T: (01304) 207803

Owler Lodge ♦♦♦♦ SILVER AWARD
Alkham Valley Road, Alkham, Dover CT15 7DF
T: (01304) 826375
F: (01304) 829372
E: owlerlodge@aol.com
I: www.owlerlodge.co.uk

The Park Inn ♦♦♦♦ SILVER AWARD
1-2 Park Place, Ladywell, Dover, CT16 1DQ
T: (01304) 203300
F: (01304) 203324
E: theparkinn@aol.com
I: www.theparkinnatdover.co.uk

St Brelades Guest House ♦♦♦
80-82 Buckland Avenue, Dover, CT16 2NW
T: (01304) 206126
F: (01304) 211486
E: stbrelades@compuserve.com
I: www.stbrelades-dover.co.uk

St Margaret's Holiday Park Hotel ♦♦♦♦
Reach Road, St-Margarets-at-Cliffe, Dover CT15 6AE
T: (01304) 853262
F: (01304) 853434

Swingate Inn and Hotel ♦♦♦
Deal Road, Dover, CT15 5DP
T: (01304) 204043
F: (01304) 204043
E: terry@swingate.com
I: www.swingate.com

Talavera House ♦♦♦♦
275 Folkestone Road, Dover, CT17 9LL
T: (01304) 206794
F: (01304) 207067
E: john-jan@talavera-house.freeserve.co.uk
I: www.smoothhound.co.uk/hotels/talavera

Victoria Guest House ♦♦♦♦
1 Laureston Place, Dover, CT16 1QX
T: (01304) 205140
F: (01304) 205140
E: WHam101496@aol.com
I: www.dover-victoria-guest-house.co.uk

Westbank Guest House ♦♦♦♦
239-241 Folkestone Road, Dover, CT17 9LL
T: (01304) 201061
F: (01304) 214718
E: WSEbnk111@netscapeonline.co.uk
I: www.westbankguesthouse.co.uk

Whitmore Guest House ♦♦♦
261 Folkestone Road, Dover, CT17 9LL
T: (01304) 203080
F: (01304) 240110
E: whitmoredover@aol.com
I: www.smoothhound.co.uk/hotels/whitmore.html.

DUDDLESWELL
East Sussex

Duddleswell Manor ♦♦♦♦
Duddleswell, Uckfield TN22 3JL
T: (01825) 712701
F: (01825) 712701
E: davidsmith@crosscastle.fsnet.co.uk

DUNTON GREEN
Kent

Lilac Cottage ♦♦♦
15 Pounsley Road, Dunton Green, Sevenoaks TN13 2XP
T: (01732) 469898

DYMCHURCH
Kent

The Ship Inn ♦♦
118 High Street, Dymchurch, Romney Marsh TN29 0LD
T: (01303) 872122
F: (01303) 872311
E: bookings@theshipinn.co.uk
I: www.theshipinn.co.uk

Waterside Guest House ♦♦♦♦
15 Hythe Road, Dymchurch, Romney Marsh TN29 0LN
T: (01303) 872253
F: (01303) 872253
E: info@watersideguesthouse.co.uk
I: www.watersideguesthouse.co.uk

EARNLEY
West Sussex

Millstone ♦♦♦♦ GOLD AWARD
Clappers Lane, Earnley, Chichester PO20 7JJ
T: (01243) 670116
E: michaelharrington@btinternet.com
I: www.sussexlive.com

EAST ASHLING
West Sussex

Horse & Groom ♦♦♦♦
East Ashling, Chichester PO18 9AX
T: (01243) 575339
F: (01243) 575339
E: horseandgroomea@aol.com
I: www.horseandgroom.sageweb.co.uk

EAST GRINSTEAD
West Sussex

Cranston House ♦♦♦
Cranston Road, East Grinstead, RH19 3HW
T: (01342) 323609
F: (01342) 323609
E: stay@cranstonhouse.screaming.net
I: www.cranstonehouse.co.uk

Moat House ♦♦♦♦
Moat Road, East Grinstead, RH19 3JZ
T: (01342) 326785
F: (01342) 303235

The Star Inn ♦♦♦
Church Road, Lingfield, RH7 6AH
T: (01342) 832364
F: (01342) 832364
E: thestarinn@breathemail.net
I: www.starinnlingfield.co.uk

Town House ♦♦
6 De La Warr Road, East Grinstead, RH19 3BN
T: (01342) 300310
F: (01342) 315122

EAST LAVANT
West Sussex

The Flint House
♦♦♦♦♦ SILVER AWARD
Pook Lane, East Lavant, Chichester PO18 0AS
T: (01243) 773482
E: theflinthouse@ukonline.co.uk

EAST PECKHAM
Kent

Roydon Hall ♦♦♦
Seven Mile Lane, East Peckham, Tonbridge TN12 5NH
T: (01622) 812121
F: (01622) 813959
E: roydonhall@btinternet.com
I: www.tourismsoutheast.com/member/webpages/A5224.htm

EAST PRESTON
West Sussex

Roselea Cottage ♦♦♦
2 Elm Avenue, East Preston, Littlehampton BN16 1HJ
T: (01903) 786787
F: (01903) 770220
E: roselea.cottage@tesco.net

EASTBOURNE
East Sussex

The Alfriston Hotel ♦♦♦
16 Lushington Road, Eastbourne, BN21 4LL
T: (01323) 725640
F: (01323) 725640
E: alfristonhotel@yahoo.co.uk

Bay Lodge Hotel ♦♦♦
61-62 Royal Parade, Eastbourne, BN22 7AQ
T: (01323) 732515
F: (01323) 735009
E: Beryl@mnewson.freeserve.co.uk
I: eastbourne.org/hotels//bay_lodge_frameset.htm

Bella Vista ♦♦♦♦
30 Redoubt Road, Eastbourne, BN22 7DH
T: (01323) 724222

Birling Gap Hotel ♦♦♦
Birling Gap, Seven Sisters Cliffs, East Dean, Eastbourne BN20 0AB
T: (01323) 423197
F: (01323) 423030
E: info@birlinggaphotel.co.uk
I: www.birlinggaphotel.co.uk

Brayscroft Hotel
♦♦♦♦ SILVER AWARD
13 South Cliff Avenue, Eastbourne, BN20 7AH
T: (01323) 647005
F: (01323) 720705
E: brayscroft@hotmail.com
I: www.brayscrofthotel.co.uk

Cambridge House ♦♦♦
6 Cambridge Road, Eastbourne, BN22 7BS
T: (01323) 721100

Cornerways Hotel ♦♦♦
60 Royal Parade, Eastbourne, BN21 7AQ
T: (01323) 721899
F: (01323) 724422

Cromwell Private Hotel
♦♦♦♦
23 Cavendish Place, Eastbourne, BN21 3EJ
T: (01323) 725288
F: (01323) 725288
E: cromwell-hotel@lineone.net
I: www.SmoothHound.co.uk/hotels/cromwell

Davington House
♦♦♦♦ SILVER AWARD
6 Silverdale Road, Meads, Eastbourne, BN20 7AL
T: (01323) 646618
F: (01323) 648705
E: davingtonhouse@aol.com
I: www.davingtonhouse.co.uk

Edelweiss Guest House ♦♦♦
12 Elms Avenue, Eastbourne, BN21 3DN
T: (01323) 732071
F: (01323) 732071
E: peterbutler@fsbdial.co.uk

Gladwyn Hotel ♦♦♦
16 Blackwater Road, Eastbourne, BN21 4JD
T: (01323) 733142
E: gladwynhotel@aol.com
I: www.gladwynhotel.com

Hanburies Hotel ♦♦♦
4 Hardwick Road, Eastbourne, BN21 4NY
T: (01323) 730698
F: (01323) 730698

Little Foxes ♦♦♦♦
24 Wannock Road, Eastbourne, BN22 7JU
T: (01323) 640670
F: (01323) 640670
E: chris@foxholes55.freeserve.co.uk

Loriston Guest House ♦♦♦
17 St Aubyns Road, Eastbourne, BN22 7AS
T: (01323) 726193

The Lynwood Hotel ♦♦♦
31-33 Jevington Gardens, Eastbourne, BN21 4HP
T: (01323) 638716
F: (01323) 412646
E: gm.@lyn.barbox.net
I: www.shearingsholidays.com

Majestic Hotel ♦♦♦
26-34 Royal Parade, Eastbourne, BN22 7AN
T: (01323) 730311
I: www.shearingsholidays.com

Nirvana Private Hotel ♦♦♦
32 Redoubt Road, Eastbourne, BN22 7DL
T: (01323) 722603

Pinnacle Point
♦♦♦♦♦ GOLD AWARD
Foyle Way, Upper Duke's Drive, Eastbourne, BN20 7XL
T: (01323) 726666
F: (01323) 643946
E: info@pinnaclepoint.co.uk
I: www.pinnaclepoint.co.uk

St Omer Hotel ♦♦♦♦
13 Royal Parade, Eastbourne, BN22 7AR
T: (01323) 722152
F: (01323) 723400
E: st.omer@lineone.net
I: www.st-omer.co.uk

Sea Beach House Hotel ♦♦♦♦
39-40 Marine Parade, Eastbourne, BN22 7AY
T: (01323) 410458
F: (01323) 410458
E: enquiries@seabeachhousehotel.com
I: www.seabeachhousehotel.com

Sherwood Hotel ♦♦♦
7 Lascelles Terrace, Eastbourne, BN21 4BJ
T: (01323) 724002
F: (01323) 439989
E: sherwood-hotel@supanet.com
I: www.sherwoodhotel.com

Southcroft Hotel
♦♦♦♦ SILVER AWARD
15 South Cliff Avenue, Eastbourne, BN20 7AH
T: (01323) 729071
E: southcroft@eastbourne34.freeserve.co.uk
I: www.southcrofthotel.co.uk

Stratford Hotel & Restaurant
♦♦
59 Cavendish Place, Eastbourne, BN21 3RL
T: (01323) 724051
F: (01323) 726391

Trevinhurst Lodge
♦♦♦♦ SILVER AWARD
10 Baslow Road, Meads, Eastbourne, BN20 7UJ
T: (01323) 410023
F: (01323) 643238
E: enquiries@trevinhurstlodge.com
I: www.trevinhurstlodge.com

EASTCHURCH
Kent

Dunmow House ♦♦♦
9 Church Road, Eastchurch, Sheerness ME12 4DG
T: (01795) 880576
F: (01795) 880 230
E: mepordage@msn.com

EASTERGATE
West Sussex

Eastmere House ♦♦♦
Eastergate Lane, Eastergate, Chichester PO20 6SJ
T: (01243) 544204

EDENBRIDGE
Kent

Mowshurst Farm House
♦♦♦♦ SILVER AWARD
Swan Lane, Edenbridge, TN8 6AH
T: (01732) 862064

Shoscombe ♦♦♦♦
Mill Hill, Edenbridge, TN8 5DA
T: (01732) 866781
F: (01732) 867807
E: shoscombe@onetel.net.uk

Ye Old Crown Inn ♦♦♦♦
74-76 The High Street, Edenbridge, TN8 5AR
T: (01732) 867896
F: (01732) 868316
I: www.lionheartinns.co.uk

ELHAM
Kent

Abbot's Fireside Hotel
♦♦♦♦ SILVER AWARD
High Street, Elham, Canterbury CT4 6TD
T: (01303) 840265
F: (01303) 840852
E: info@abbotsfireside.com
I: www.abbotsfireside.com

The Rose and Crown ♦♦♦
High Street, Elham, Canterbury CT4 6TD
T: (01303) 840226
F: (01303) 840141
E: info@roseandcrown.co.uk
I: www.roseandcrown.co.uk

ELSTED
West Sussex

Three Elsted ♦♦♦
Elsted, Midhurst GU29 0JY
T: (01730) 825065
E: rh@rhill.ftech.co.uk

ENGLEFIELD GREEN
Surrey

Bulkeley House
Rating Applied For
Middlehill, Englefield Green, Egham TW20 0JU
T: (01784) 431287
F: (01784) 431287

The Old Parsonage
Rating Applied For
2 Parsonage Road, Englefield Green, Egham TW20 0JW
T: (01784) 436706
F: (01784) 436706
E: the.old.parsonage@talk21.com
I: www.theoldparsonage.com

EPSOM
Surrey

105 Great Tattenhams ♦♦♦
Epsom Downs, Epsom, KT18 5RB
T: (01737) 350456

White House Hotel ♦♦♦♦
Downs Hill Road, Epsom, KT18 5HW
T: (01372) 722472
F: (01372) 744447
E: hopkins.epsom@virgin.net

ESHER
Surrey

The Bear Inn ♦♦♦
71 High Street, Esher, KT10 9LQ
T: (01372) 469786
F: (01372) 468378

Clare House ♦♦♦
22 Claremont Avenue, Esher, KT10 9JD
T: (01372) 464242
F: (01372) 470870
E: clarehouse@aol.com

EWHURST
Surrey

Malricks ♦♦♦
The Street, Ewhurst, Cranleigh GU6 7RH
T: (01483) 277575

Sixpenny Buckle ♦♦♦♦
Gransden Close, Ewhurst, Cranleigh GU6 7RL
T: (01483) 273988
E: patriciamortimoreol@genie.co.uk
I: my.genie.co.uk/patriciamortimore01

Yard Farm ♦♦♦
Ewhurst, Cranleigh GU6 7SN
T: (01483) 276649
F: (01483) 276649

FAIRLIGHT
East Sussex

Fairlight Cottage ♦♦♦♦
Warren Road, (Via Coastguard Lane), Fairlight, Hastings
TN35 4AG
T: (01424) 812545
F: (01424) 812545
E: fairlightcottage@supanet.com

FAIRWARP
East Sussex

Broom Cottage ♦♦♦♦
Browns Brook, Fairwarp, Uckfield TN22 3BY
T: (01825) 712942

FARNHAM
Surrey

Anne's Cottage
♦♦♦♦ SILVER AWARD
Green Cross Lane, Churt, Farnham GU10 2ND
T: (01428) 714181

High Wray ♦♦♦
73 Lodge Hill Road, Farnham, GU10 3RB
T: (01252) 715589
F: (01252) 715746
E: crawford@highwray73.co.uk

Mala Strana ♦♦♦♦
66 Boundstone Road, Farnham, GU10 4TR
T: (01252) 793262

Kernel Cottage ♦♦♦
14 Nutshell Lane, Farnham
T: (01252) 710147
F: (01252) 710147

FAVERSHAM
Kent

Barnsfield ♦♦♦
Fostall, Hernhill, Faversham
ME13 9JH
T: (01227) 750973
F: (01227) 273098
E: barnsfield@yahoo.com
I: www.barnsfield.co.uk

Fairlea ♦♦♦♦
27 Preston Avenue, Faversham, HE13 8NH
T: (01795) 539610

Heronsmere, 19 Nobel Court ♦♦♦
Faversham, ME13 7SD
T: (01795) 536767
E: griffithskeith@lineone.net

Leaveland Court ♦♦♦♦
Leaveland, Faversham, ME13 0NP
T: (01233) 740596
F: (01233) 740015
I: www.leavelandcourt.co.uk

March Cottage ♦♦♦
5 Preston Avenue, Faversham, ME13 8NH
T: (01795) 536514

Owens Court Farm ♦♦♦
Selling, Faversham ME13 9QN
T: (01227) 752247
F: (01227) 752247
E: enquiries@owenscourt.com
I: www.owenscourt.com

Preston Lea
♦♦♦♦ SILVER AWARD
Canterbury Road, Faversham, ME13 8XA
T: (01795) 535266
F: (01795) 533388
E: preston.lea@which.net
I: homepages.which.net/~alan.turner10

FAYGATE
West Sussex

The Willows
♦♦♦♦ SILVER AWARD
Wimlands Lane, Faygate, Horsham RH12 4SP
T: (01293) 851030
F: (01293) 852466
E: stay@the-willows.co.uk
I: www.the-willows.co.uk

FIRLE
East Sussex

New House Farm ♦♦♦♦
Firle, Lewes BN8 6ND
T: (01273) 858242
F: (01273) 858242
E: hecks@farming.co.uk

FISHBOURNE
West Sussex

The Byre ♦♦♦♦
Salthill Park, Salthill Road, Fishbourne, Chichester
PO19 3PS
T: (01243) 537943
F: (01243) 537943

FITTLEWORTH
West Sussex

Fleet Bungalow ♦♦♦
The Fleet, Fittleworth, Pulborough RH20 1HS
T: (01798) 865634
F: (01798) 865 634
E: linda.wagstaff@ntlworld.com
I: www.the-fleet.co.uk

The Old Post Office ♦♦♦♦
Lower Street, Fittleworth, Pulborough RH20 1JE
T: (01798) 865315
E: sue.moseley@ukgateway.net

Swan Inn
♦♦♦♦ SILVER AWARD
Lower Street, Fittleworth, Pulborough RH20 1EN
T: (01798) 865429
F: (01798) 865721
E: hotel@swaninn.com
I: www.swaninn.com

FIVE OAK GREEN
Kent

Ivy House ♦♦♦
Five Oak Green, Tonbridge
TN12 6RB
T: (01892) 832041
F: (01892) 832041

FLETCHING
East Sussex

The Griffin Inn
♦♦♦♦ SILVER AWARD
High Street, Fletching, Uckfield
TN22 3SS
T: (01825) 722890
F: (01825) 722810
E: nigelpullan@thegriffininn.co.uk
I: www.thegriffininn.co.uk

FOLKESTONE
Kent

Banque Hotel ♦♦♦
4 Castle Hill Avenue, Folkestone, CT20 2QT
T: (01303) 253797
F: (01303) 253797
E: banquehotel4@hotmail.com
I: www.banquehotel.com

Beachborough Park ♦♦♦
Newington, Folkestone
CT18 8BW
T: (01303) 275432
F: (01843) 845131
I: www.kentaccess.org.uk

Chandos Guest House ♦♦♦
77 Cheriton Road, Folkestone, CT20 1DG
T: (01303) 851202
F: (01303) 272073
E: don@chandosguesthouse.com
I: www.chandosguesthouse.com

Chilton House Hotel ♦♦♦
14-15 Marine Parade, Folkestone, CT20 1PX
T: (01303) 249786
F: (01303) 247525
E: chiltonhousehotel@btinternet.com
I: www.chiltonhousehotel.co.uk

Cliffside ♦♦♦♦
Radnor Cliff Crescent, Folkestone, CT20 2JH
T: (01303) 248328
F: (01303) 240115
E: hilary@cliffside303.fsnet.co.uk
I: www.cliff-side.co.uk

Granada Guest House ♦♦♦
51 Cheriton Road, Folkestone, CT20 1DF
T: (01303) 254913

Harbourside Hotel
♦♦♦♦♦ GOLD AWARD
13-14 Wear Bay Road, Folkestone, CT19 6AT
T: (01303) 256528
F: (01303) 241299
E: joy@harboursidehotel.com
I: www.harboursidehotel.com

Kentmere Guest House ♦♦♦
76 Cheriton Road, Folkestone, CT20 1DG
T: (01303) 259661
F: (01303) 259661
E: enquiries@kentmere-guesthouse.co.uk
I: www.kentmere-guesthouse.co.uk

The Rob Roy Guest House ♦♦♦
227 Dover Road, Folkestone, CT19 6NH
T: (01303) 253341
F: (01303) 770060
E: RobRoyFolkestone@aol.com
I: www.therobroyguesthouse.co.uk

Seacliffe ♦♦♦
3 Wear Bay Road, Folkestone, CT19 6AT
T: (01303) 254592

Windsor Hotel ♦♦
5-6 Langhorne Gardens, Folkestone, CT20 2EA
T: (01303) 251348
E: williams.windsor@virginnet.co.uk

FONTWELL
West Sussex

Woodacre ♦♦♦♦
Arundel Road, Fontwell, Arundel
BN18 0SD
T: (01243) 814301
F: (01243) 814344
E: wacrebb@aol.com
I: www.woodacre.co.uk

FOREST ROW
East Sussex

Brambletye Hotel ♦♦♦
The Square, Forest Row, RH18 5EZ
T: (01342) 824144
F: (01342) 824833

FOUR ELMS
Kent

Oak House Barn ♦♦♦♦♦
Mapleton Road, Four Elms, Edenbridge TN8 6PL
T: (01732) 700725

FRAMFIELD
East Sussex

Beggars Barn
♦♦♦♦ SILVER AWARD
Barn Lane, Framfield, Uckfield
TN22 5RX
T: (01825) 890869
F: (01825) 890868
E: caroline@beggarsbarn.co.uk
I: www.beggarsbarn.co.uk

The Old Farmhouse
♦♦♦♦ GOLD AWARD
Honey's Green, Framfield, Uckfield TN22 5RE
T: (01825) 841054
F: 0870 122 9055
E: stay@honeysgreen.com
I: www.honeysgreen.com

FRENSHAM
Surrey

The Mariners Hotel ♦♦
Millbridge, Frensham, Farnham
GU10 3DJ
T: (01252) 792050
F: (01252) 792649
I: www.themarinershotel.co.uk

FRISTON
East Sussex

Forest Lodge ♦♦♦♦
Friston, Eastbourne BN20 0AN
T: (01323) 423990
F: (01323) 423991
E: forest.lodgebb@aol.com
I: www.forestlodgebb.co.uk

FUNTINGTON
West Sussex

High Walls ♦♦♦♦♦
5 Weston Lane, Funtington, Chichester PO18 9LT
T: (01243) 576823
F: (01243) 576823

GATWICK
West Sussex

Brooklyn Manor Hotel ♦♦♦
Bonnetts Lane, Ifield, Crawley, RH11 0NY
T: (01293) 546024
F: (01293) 510366

Collendean Barn ♦♦♦
Collendean Lane, Norwood Hill, Horley RH6 0HP
T: (01293) 862433
F: (01293) 863102
E: collendean.barn@amserve.net

The Corner House ♦♦♦♦
72 Massetts Road, Horley, RH6 7ED
T: (01293) 784574
F: (01293) 784620
E: info@thecornerhouse.co.uk
I: www.thecornerhouse.co.uk

Gainsborough Lodge ♦♦♦
39 Massetts Road, Horley, RH6 7DT
T: (01293) 783982
F: (01293) 785365
E: enquiries@gainsborough-lodge.co.uk
I: www.gainsborough-lodge.co.uk

Southbourne Guest House Gatwick ♦♦
34 Massetts Road, Horley, RH6 7DS
T: (01293) 771991
F: (01293) 820112
E: reservations@southbournegatwick.com
I: www.southbournegatwick.com

GILLINGHAM
Kent

Mayfield Guest House ♦♦
34 Kingswood Road, Gillingham, ME7 1DZ
T: (01634) 852606

Ramsey House ♦♦♦
228A Barnsole Road, Gillingham, ME7 4JB
T: (01634) 854193

GLYNDE
East Sussex

Ranscombe House ♦♦♦♦
Ransombe Lane, Glynde, Lewes BN8 6AA
T: (01273) 858538

GODALMING
Surrey

Heath Hall Farm ♦♦♦
Bowlhead Green, Godalming GU8 6NW
T: (01428) 682808
F: (01428) 684025
E: heathhallfarm@btinternet.com

GODMERSHAM
Kent

Waggoners Lodge ♦♦♦
Eggarton Lane, Godmersham, Canterbury CT4 7DY
T: (01227) 731118
F: (01227) 730292
E: maud@waggoners.freeserve.co.uk
I: www.angelfire.com/wy/Waggoners

GODSTONE
Surrey

The Godstone Hotel ♦♦♦
The Green, Godstone, RH9 8DT
T: (01883) 742461
F: (01883) 742461
I: www.godstonehotel.com

GOODWOOD
West Sussex

1 Pilleygreen Lodge ♦♦♦♦
Goodwood, Chichester PO18 0QE
T: (01243) 811467
F: (01243) 811408
E: coachouse@pilleygreen.demon.co.uk
I: www.sussexlive@enta.net

GORING-BY-SEA
West Sussex

Highdown Hotel & Restaurant ♦♦♦
Littlehampton Road, Goring-by-Sea, Worthing BN12 6PF
T: (01903) 700152
F: (01903) 507518
I: www.highdown-towers.com

GOUDHURST
Kent

Mill House ♦♦♦♦
Church Road, Goudhurst, Cranbrook TN17 1BN
T: (01580) 211703
E: therussellsuk@yahoo.com
I: www.goudhurst-online.freeserve.co.uk

Mount House ♦♦♦♦
Ranters Lane, Goudhurst, Cranbrook TN17 1HN
T: (01580) 211230
F: (01580) 212373
E: DavidMargaretSargent@compuserve.com

GRAFFHAM
West Sussex

Brook Barn
♦♦♦♦♦ SILVER AWARD
Selham Road, Graffham, Petworth GU28 0PU
T: (01798) 867356
E: jollands@lineone.net

GRAFTY GREEN
Kent

Who'd A Thought It ♦♦♦
Headcorn Road, Grafty Green, Maidstone ME17 2AR
T: (01622) 858951
F: (01622) 858078

GRAVESEND
Kent

48 Clipper Crescent ♦♦♦
Riverview Park, Gravesend, DA12 4NN
T: (01474) 365360

Dot's B & B ♦♦♦
23 St James' Road, Gravesend, DA11 0HF
T: (01474) 332193
E: dotriley@agassiz.worldonline.co.uk

Eastcourt Oast ♦♦♦♦
14 Church Lane, Chalk, Gravesend, DA12 2NL
T: (01474) 823937
F: (01474) 823937
E: mary.james@lineone.net
I: www.eastcourtoast.co.uk

GREAT BOOKHAM
Surrey

Selworthy ♦♦♦
310 Lower Road, Great Bookham, Leatherhead KT23 4DW
T: (01372) 453952
F: (01372) 453952
E: bnb@selworthy.fslife.co.uk

GREATSTONE
Kent

Holm-Lea ♦♦♦
66 Coast Drive, Greatstone, New Romney TN28 8NR
T: (01797) 364677

White Horses Cottage ♦♦♦♦
180 The Parade, Greatstone, New Romney TN28 8RS
T: (01797) 366626

GROOMBRIDGE
East Sussex

Burrswood Chapel House ♦♦♦♦
Burrswood, Bird in Hand Lane, Groombridge, Royal Tunbridge Wells TN3 9PY
T: (01892) 863637
F: (01892) 862597
E: admin@burrswood.org.uk
I: www.burrswood.org.uk

GUESTLING
East Sussex

Mount Pleasant Farm ♦♦♦♦
White Hart Hill, Guestling, Hastings TN35 4LR
T: (01424) 813108
F: (01424) 813818
E: angelajohn@mountpleasantfarm.fsbusiness.co.uk
I: www.mountpleasantfarm.fsbusiness.co.uk

GUILDFORD
Surrey

Abeille House
Rating Applied For
119 Stoke Road, Guildford, GU1 1ET
T: (01483) 532200
F: (01483) 821220

Albany House B & B
Rating Applied For
21 South Hill, Guildford, GU1 3SY
T: (01483) 450732
F: (01483) 874641
E: albany.house@ntlworld.com

Amberley ♦♦♦
Maori Road, Guildford, GU1 2EL
T: (01483) 573198
E: m.tf.joyner@talk21.com

Beevers Farm ♦♦♦
Chinthurst Lane, Bramley, Guildford GU5 0DR
T: (01483) 898764
F: (01483) 898764
E: beevers@onetel.net.uk

Bluebells ♦♦♦
21 Coltsfoot Drive, Burpham, Guildford, GU1 1YH
T: (01483) 826124
E: hughes.a@ntlworld.com

9 Boxgrove Lane ♦♦♦
9 Boxgrove Lane, Guildford, GU1 2TE
T: (01483) 565524

Cedar Cottage Bed & Breakfast ♦♦♦
4 Boxgrove Road, Guildford, GU1 2LX
T: (01483) 302920
F: (01483) 302920

Chalklands ♦♦♦
Beech Avenue, Effingham, Leatherhead KT24 5PJ
T: (01372) 454936
F: (01372) 459569
E: rreilly@onetel.net.uk

Crawford House Hotel ♦♦♦
73 Farnham Road, Guildford, GU2 5PF
T: (01483) 579299
F: (01483) 579299

Field Villa ♦♦♦
Liddington New Road, Guildford, GU3 3AH
T: (01483) 233961
F: (01483) 234045

The Foxes
Rating Applied For
27 Worplesdon Road, Guildford, GU2 6RW
T: (01483) 566663

Hampton ♦♦♦♦
38 Poltimore Road, Guildford, GU2 7PN
T: (01483) 572012
F: (01483) 572012
E: vgmorris@aol.com
I: www.hampton-bedandbreakfast.co.uk

High Edser ♦♦♦
Shere Road, Ewhurst, Cranleigh, GU6 7PQ
T: (01483) 278214
F: (01483) 278200
E: franklinadams@highedser.demon.co.uk

Holroyd Arms Pubotel ♦♦
36 Aldershot Road, Guildford, GU2 8AF
T: (01483) 560215
F: (01483) 531912

Joannas Bed & Breakfast
Rating Applied For
30 Nightingale Road, Guildford, GU1 1ER
T: (01483) 568873

The Laurels
Rating Applied For
23 Dagden Road, Shalford, Guildford, GU4 8DD
T: (01483) 565753

Littlefield Manor ♦♦♦
Littlefield Common, Guildford, GU3 3HJ
T: (01483) 233068
F: (01483) 233686
E: john@littlefieldmanor.co.uk
I: www.littlefieldmanor.co.uk

4 Longdown Road ♦♦♦♦
Guildford, GU4 8PP
T: (01483) 567417

Matchams ♦♦♦
35 Boxgrove Avenue, Guildford, GU1 1XQ
T: (01483) 567643
F: (01483) 567643

The Old Malt House ♦♦♦
Bagshot Road, Worplesdon, Guildford GU3 3PT
T: (01483) 232152

4 Park Chase
Rating Applied For
Guildford, GU1 1ES
T: (01483) 566482
E: jill.nicolson@ntlworld.com

Patcham ♦♦♦
44 Farnham Road, Guildford, GU2 4LS
T: (01483) 570789
F: (01483) 570789

Plaegan House ♦♦♦♦
96 Wodeland Avenue, Guildford, GU2 4LD
T: (01483) 822181
E: roxanne@plaegan.fsnet.co.uk

Quietways ◆◆◆
29 Liddington Hall Drive, Guildford, GU3 3AE
T: (01483) 232347
E: bill.white@amserve.net

Stoke House ◆◆
113 Stoke Road, Guildford, GU1 1ET
T: (01483) 453025
F: (01483) 453023
E: stokehouse@supanet.com

Three Gates Bed & Breakfast ◆◆
26 Worplesdon Road, Guildford, GU2 9RS
T: (01483) 578961
F: (01483) 578961

Westbury Cottage ◆◆◆◆
1 Waterden Road, Guildford, GU1 2AN
T: (01483) 822602
F: (01483) 822602
E: smythe.smythe@ntlworld.com

Weyview ◆◆◆
Upper Guildown Road, Guildford, GU2 4EZ
T: (01483) 564724

HADLOW
Kent

Leavers Oast ◆◆◆◆
Stanford Lane, Hadlow, Tonbridge TN11 0JN
T: (01732) 850924
F: (01732) 850924
E: denis@leavers-oast.freeserve.co.uk

HAILSHAM
East Sussex

Longleys Farm Cottage ◆◆◆
Harebeating Lane, Hailsham, BN27 1ER
T: (01323) 841227
F: (01323) 841227

Windesworth ◆◆◆◆
Carters Corner, Hailsham, BN27 4HT
T: (01323) 847178
F: (01323) 440696
E: windesworth.bedandbreakfast@virginnet

HALLAND
East Sussex

Halland Forge ◆◆◆
Halland, Lewes BN8 6PW
T: (01825) 840456
F: (01825) 840773

Shortgate Manor Farm ◆◆◆◆ SILVER AWARD
Halland, Lewes BN8 6PJ
T: (01825) 840320
F: (01825) 840320
E: ewalt@shortgate.co.uk
I: www.shortgate.co.uk

Tamberry Hall ◆◆◆◆ SILVER AWARD
Eastbourne Road, Halland, Lewes BN8 6PS
T: (01825) 880090
F: (01825) 880090
E: bedandbreakfast@tamberryhall.fsbusiness.co.uk

HALNAKER
West Sussex

Veronica Cottage ◆◆◆◆
Halnaker, Chichester PO18 0NG
T: (01243) 774929
F: (01243) 774929

HAMBROOK
West Sussex

Ridge Farm ◆◆◆◆
Scant Road (East), Hambrook, Chichester PO18 8UB
T: (01243) 575567
F: (01243) 576798
E: philip@medlams.co.uk

Willowbrook Riding Centre ◆◆◆
Hambrook Hill South, Hambrook, Chichester PO18 8UJ
T: (01243) 572683

HARRIETSHAM
Kent

Homestay ◆◆◆
14 Chippendayle Drive, Harrietsham, Maidstone ME17 1AD
T: (01622) 858698
F: (01622) 858698
E: 4homestay@lineone.net
I: www.kent-homestay.info

HARTFIELD
East Sussex

Bolebroke Castle Ltd ◆◆◆◆
Edenbridge Road, Hartfield, TN7 4JJ
T: (01892) 770061
F: (01892) 771041
E: bolebroke@btclick.com
I: www.bolebrokecastle.co.uk

HARTLEY
Kent

Squirrels Haunt ◆◆◆
Gorsewood Road, Hartley, Longfield DA3 7DE
T: (01474) 702352
F: (01474) 702352

HASLEMERE
Surrey

Little Hoewyck ◆◆◆◆
Lickfold Road, Fernhurst, Haslemere, GU27 3JH
T: (01428) 653059
E: suehodge@hoewyck.freeserve.co.uk

Sheps Hollow ◆◆◆
Henley Common, Haslemere, GU27 3HB
T: (01428) 653120

Strathire ◆◆◆◆
Grayswood Road, Haslemere, GU27 2BW
T: (01428) 642466
F: (01428) 656708

Town House ◆◆◆◆
High Street, Haslemere, GU27 2JY
T: (01428) 643310
F: (01428) 641080

HASSOCKS
West Sussex

New Close Farm ◆◆◆◆
London Road, Hassocks, BN6 9ND
T: (01273) 843144
E: sharon.ballard@newclosefarm.co.uk
I: www.newclosefarm.co.uk

HASTINGLEIGH
Kent

Crabtree Farm ◆◆◆
Tamley Lane, Hastingleigh, Ashford TN25 5HW
T: (01233) 750327

HASTINGS
East Sussex

Amberlene Guest House ◆◆◆
12 Cambridge Gardens, Hastings, TN34 1EH
T: (01424) 439447

Apollo Guest House ◆◆◆
25 Cambridge Gardens, Hastings, TN34 1EH
T: (01424) 444394
F: (01424) 444394
E: jim@apollogh.freeserve.co.uk
I: www.apolloguesthouse.co.uk

Beechwood Hotel ◆◆◆
59 Baldslow Road, Hastings, TN34 2EY
T: (01424) 420078
F: (01424) 435655
E: beechwoodhastings@talk21.com

Bell Cottage ◆◆◆◆
Vinehall Road, Robertsbridge, Hastings, TN32 5JN
T: (01580) 881164
F: (01580) 880519
E: patricia.lowe@tesco.net
I: www.bellcottage.co.uk

Bryn-Y-Mor ◆◆◆◆◆ GOLD AWARD
12 Godwin Road, Hastings, TN35 5JR
T: (01424) 722744
F: (01424) 445933
E: karen-alun@brynymor.ndirect.co.uk
I: www.smoothhound.co.uk

Churchills Hotel ◆◆◆
3 St Helens Crescent, Hastings, TN34 2EN
T: (01424) 439359
E: churchills.hotel@btinternet.com

Croft Place ◆◆◆◆
2 The Croft, Hastings, TN34 3HH
T: (01424) 433004
E: lorraine@croftplace.co.uk
I: www.croftplace.co.uk

Eagle House Hotel ◆◆◆◆
12 Pevensey Road, St Leonards-on-Sea, Hastings, TN38 0JZ
T: (01424) 430535
F: (01424) 437771
E: info@eaglehousehotel.com
I: www.eaglehousehotel.com

The Elms ◆◆◆
9 St Helens Park Road, Hastings, TN34 2ER
T: (01424) 429979

Emerydale ◆◆◆◆
6 King Edward Avenue, Hastings, TN34 2NQ
T: (01424) 437915
F: (01424) 444124

Europa Hotel ◆◆◆
2 Carlisle Parade, Hastings, TN34 1JG
T: (01424) 717329
F: (01424) 717329

The Gallery ◆◆◆◆
19 Fearon Road, Hastings, TN34 2DL
T: (01424) 718110
E: info@thegallerybnb.freeserve.co.uk
I: www.thegallerybnb.freeserve.co.uk

Grand Hotel ◆◆◆
Grand Parade, St Leonards, Hastings, TN38 0DD
T: (01424) 428510
F: (01424) 428510

64 High Street ◆◆◆
Old Town, Hastings, TN34 3EW
T: (01424) 712584

Holyers ◆◆◆
1 Hill Street, Old Town, Hastings, TN34 3HU
T: (01424) 430014
E: max@holyers.co.uk
I: www.holyers.co.uk

Lavender & Lace Guest House ◆◆◆◆
106 All Saints Street, Old Town, Hastings, TN34 3BE
T: (01424) 716290
F: (01424) 716290

Lionsdown House ◆◆◆◆
116 High Street, Old Town, Hastings, TN34 3ET
T: (01424) 420802
F: (01424) 420802
E: sharonlionsdown@aol.com
I: www.lionsdownhouse.co.uk

Millifont Guest House ◆◆◆
8-9 Cambridge Gardens, Hastings, TN34 1EH
T: (01424) 425645
F: (01424) 425645

The Pines ◆◆◆
50 Baldslow Road, Hastings, TN34 2EY
T: (01424) 435838
F: (01424) 435838
E: robert-jean@beeb.net

Pissarro's ◆◆
9/10 South Terrace, Hastings, TN34 1SA
T: (01424) 421363
F: (01424) 729264
E: information@pissarros.co.uk
I: www.pissarros.co.uk

Sea Spray Guest House ◆◆◆◆
54 Eversfield Place, St Leonards, Hastings TN37 6DB
T: (01424) 436583
F: (01424) 436583
E: seaspraybb@faxvia.net
I: www.seaspraybb.co.uk

South Riding Guest House ◆◆◆
96 Milward Road, Hastings, TN34 3RT
T: (01424) 420805

Summerfields House ◆◆◆◆
Bohemia Road, Hastings, TN34 1EX
T: (01424) 718142
F: (01424) 718142
E: liz.orourke@totalise.co.uk

Tower House ◆◆◆◆ GOLD AWARD
26-28 Tower Road West, St Leonards, Hastings TN38 0RG
T: (01424) 427217
F: (01424) 427217
E: reservations@towerhousehotel.com
I: www.towerhousehotel.com

West Hill Cottage ◆◆◆
Exmouth Place, Old Town, Hastings, TN34 3JA
T: (01424) 716021

Woodhurst Lodge ♦♦♦
Ivyhouse Lane, Hastings, TN35 4NN
T: (01424) 754147
F: (01424) 754147

HAWKHURST
Kent

Conghurst Farm
♦♦♦♦♦ SILVER AWARD
Conghurst Lane, Hawkhurst, Cranbrook TN18 4RW
T: (01580) 753331
F: (01580) 754579
E: rosa@conghurst.co.uk

Patricks ♦♦♦♦
Horns Hill, Hawkhurst, Cranbrook TN18 4XH
T: (01580) 752143
F: (01580) 754649
E: elliotpat@aol.com

The Wren's Nest
♦♦♦♦ GOLD AWARD
Hastings Road, Hawkhurst, Cranbrook TN18 4RT
T: (01580) 754919
F: (01580) 754919

HAWKINGE
Kent

Braeheid Bed & Breakfast
♦♦♦♦
2 Westland Way, Hawkinge, Folkestone CT18 7PW
T: (01303) 893928
E: bill@forrest68.fsnet.co.uk

Terlingham Manor Farm
♦♦♦♦
Gibraltar Lane, Hawkinge, Folkestone CT18 7AE
T: (01303) 894141
F: (01303) 894144
E: diana@terlinghammanor.co.uk
I: www.terlinghammanor.co.uk

HAYWARDS HEATH
West Sussex

Copyhold Hollow Bed & Breakfast
♦♦♦♦ SILVER AWARD
Copyhold Lane, Borde Hill, Haywards Heath, RH16 1XU
T: (01444) 413265
E: 2@copyholdhollow.freeserve.co.uk
I: www.copyholdhollow.freeserve.co.uk

HEADCORN
Kent

Four Oaks ♦♦♦
Four Oaks Road, Headcorn, Ashford TN27 9PB
T: (01622) 891224
F: (01622) 890630
E: info@fouroaks.uk.com
I: www.fouroaks.uk.com

HEATHFIELD
East Sussex

The Cottage
Rating Applied For
Rushlake Green, Heathfield TN21 9QH
T: (01435) 830348
F: (01435) 830715
E: kcook@btinternet.com

Iwood B & B
♦♦♦♦ SILVER AWARD
Mutton Hall Lane, Heathfield, TN21 8NR
T: (01435) 863918
F: (01435) 868575
E: iwoodbb@aol.com
I: www.iwoodbb.co.uk

Spicers Bed & Breakfast
♦♦♦♦
21 Spicers Cottages, Cade Street, Heathfield TN21 9BS
T: (01435) 866363
F: (01435) 868171
E: beds@spicersbb.co.uk
I: www.spicersbb.co.uk

HEMPSTEAD
Kent

4 The Rise ♦♦♦
Hempstead, Gillingham ME7 3SF
T: (01634) 388156
F: (01634) 388156

HENFIELD
West Sussex

1 The Laurels ♦♦♦♦
Martyn Close, Henfield, BN5 9RQ
T: (01273) 493518
E: malc.harrington@lineone.net
I: www.no1thelaurels.co.uk

HERSHAM
Surrey

Bricklayers Arms ♦♦♦♦
6 Queens Road, Hersham, Walton-on-Thames KT12 5LS
T: (01932) 220936
F: (01932) 230400

HERSTMONCEUX
East Sussex

Conquerors
♦♦♦♦ SILVER AWARD
Stunts Green, Herstmonceux, Hailsham BN27 4PR
T: (01323) 832446
F: (01323) 831578
E: Conquerors@ukgateway.net

Sandhurst ♦♦♦♦
Church Road, Herstmonceux, Hailsham BN27 1RG
T: (01323) 833088
F: (01323) 833088
E: junerussell@compuserve.com

The Stud Farm ♦♦♦
Bodle Street Green, Herstmonceux, Hailsham BN27 4RJ
T: (01323) 833201
F: (01323) 833201
E: philippa@miroted.freeserve.co.uk

Waldernheath Country House
♦♦♦♦
Amberstone Corner, Herstmonceux, Hailsham BN27 1PJ
T: (01323) 442259
F: (01323) 442259
E: waldernheath@lineone.net

HEYSHOTT
West Sussex

Little Hoyle ♦♦♦♦
Hoyle Lane, Heyshott, Midhurst GU29 0DX
T: (01798) 867359
F: (01798) 867359

HIGH HALDEN
Kent

Badgers ♦♦♦♦
Ashford Road, High Halden, Ashford TN26 3LY
T: (01233) 850158
E: wendy@badgers-bb.co.uk
I: www.badgers-bb.co.uk

HIGH HURSTWOOD
East Sussex

Chillies Granary ♦♦♦♦
Chillies Lane, High Hurstwood, Uckfield TN6 3TB
T: (01892) 655560
F: (01892) 655560

Huckleberry ♦♦♦♦
Perrymans Lane, High Hurstwood, Uckfield, TN22 4AG
T: (01825) 733170

The Orchard ♦♦♦♦
Rocks Lane, High Hurstwood, Uckfield TN22 4BN
T: (01825) 732946
F: (01825) 732946
E: turtonorchard@aol.com
I: www.theorchardbandb.co.uk

HIGHAM
Kent

Kinsale ♦♦♦
1A School Lane, Mid Higham, Higham, Rochester ME3 7AT
T: (01474) 822106

Upshire House ♦♦♦
1 Hermitage Road, Higham, Rochester ME3 7DA
T: (01474) 822134
E: upshire.house@lineone.net

HILDENBOROUGH
Kent

148 Tonbridge Road ♦♦
Hildenborough, Tonbridge TN11 9HW
T: (01732) 838894

HOLLINGBOURNE
Kent

Woodhouses ♦♦♦♦
49 Eyhorne Street, Hollingbourne, Maidstone ME17 1TR
T: (01622) 880594
F: (01622) 880594
E: woodhouses@supanet.com

HOLMBURY ST MARY
Surrey

Holmbury Farm ♦♦♦♦
Holmbury St Mary, Dorking RH5 6NB
T: (01306) 621443
F: (01306) 621498
E: randvlloyd@holmbury100.fsnet.co.uk

Woodhouse Copse ♦♦♦
Horsham Road, Holmbury St Mary, Dorking RH5 6NL
T: (01306) 730956
F: (01306) 730136

HORAM
East Sussex

Oak Mead Bed & Breakfast
♦♦♦
Oak Mead Nursery, Cowden Hall Lane, Horam, Heathfield TN21 9ED
T: (01435) 812962

Wimbles Farm ♦♦♦
Vines Cross, Horam, Heathfield TN21 9HA
T: (01435) 812342
F: (01435) 813603
E: susan_ramsay@madasafish.com
I: www.sussexcountry.com

HORLEY
Surrey

The Beeches ♦♦♦♦
60 Massetts Road, Horley, RH6 7DS
T: (01293) 823457
F: (01293) 415595

Berrens Guest House ♦♦♦
62 Massetts Road, Horley, RH6 7DS
T: (01293) 786125
F: (01293) 786125

Gatwick House ♦♦♦
3 Brighton Road, Horley, RH6 7HH
T: (01293) 782738
F: (01293) 776106
E: info@gatwickhouse.com
I: www.gatwickhouse.com

Glenalmond Guest House
Rating Applied For
64 Massetts Road, Horley, RH6 7DS
T: (01293) 773564
F: (01293) 421728
E: glenalmondguesthouse@hotmail.com
I: glenalmondguesthouse.co.uk

The Lawn Guest House
♦♦♦♦ SILVER AWARD
30 Massetts Road, Gatwick, RH6 7DF
T: (01293) 775751
F: (01293) 821803
E: info@lawnguesthouse.co.uk
I: www.lawnguesthouse.co.uk

Masslink House ♦♦♦
70 Massetts Road, Horley, RH6 7ED
T: (01293) 785798
F: (01293) 783279

Melville Lodge Guest House
♦♦
15 Brighton Road, Horley, Gatwick, RH6 7HH
T: (01293) 784951
F: (01293) 785669
E: melvillelodge.guesthouse@tesco.net

Prinsted Guest House ♦♦♦
Oldfield Road, Horley, RH6 7EP
T: (01293) 785233
F: (01293) 820624
E: kendall@prinsteadguesthouse.co.uk
I: www.prinsteadguesthouse.co.uk

Rosemead Guest House
♦♦♦♦
19 Church Road, Horley, RH6 7EY
T: (01293) 784965
F: (01293) 430547
E: info@rosemeadguesthouse.co.uk
I: www.rosemeadguesthouse.co.uk

Springwood Guest House ◆◆◆
58 Massetts Road, Horley, RH6 7DS
T: (01293) 775998
F: (01293) 823103
E: ernest@springwood58.u-net.com
I: www.networkclub.co.uk/springwood

Trumbles Guest House ◆◆◆◆
Stanhill, Charlwood, Horley RH6 0EP
T: (01293) 863418
F: (01293) 862925
E: info@trumbles.co.uk
I: www.trumbles.co.uk

The Turret Guest House ◆◆◆
48 Massetts Road, Horley, RH6 7DS
T: (01293) 782490
F: (01293) 431492
E: info@theturret.com
I: www.theturret.com

HORSHAM
West Sussex

49 Broadwood Close ◆◆◆
Horsham, RH12 4JY
T: (01403) 263651

The Deans ◆◆◆◆
8 Wimblehurst Road, Horsham, RH12 2ED
T: (01403) 268166
F: (01403) 268166
E: contact@thedeans.co.uk
I: www.thedeans.co.uk

The Larches ◆◆◆
28 Rusper Road, Horsham, RH12 4BD
T: (01403) 263392
F: (01403) 249980

The Studio
Rating Applied For
The Hermitage, Tower Hill, Horsham, RH13 7JS
T: (01403) 270808

The Wirrals ◆◆◆
1 Downsview Road, Horsham, RH12 4PF
T: (01403) 269400
F: (01403) 269400
E: p.archibald@lineone.net
I: website.lineone.net/~p.archibald/webba.htm

HUNSTON
West Sussex

Spire Cottage ◆◆◆
Church Lane, Hunston, Chichester PO20 6AJ
T: (01243) 778937

HURSTPIERPOINT
West Sussex

Wickham Place ◆◆◆◆
Wickham Drive, Hurstpierpoint, Hassocks BN6 9AP
T: (01273) 832172
F: (01273) 832172
E: stay@wickham-place.co.uk

HYTHE
Kent

Fern Lodge Hotel ◆◆◆
87 Seabrook Road, Hythe, CT21 5QP
T: (01303) 267315

Little Orchard ◆◆◆◆
71 North Road, Hythe, CT21 5DX
T: (01303) 266197
E: anita@little-orchard.net
I: www.little-orchard.net

Moyle Cottage ◆◆◆
The Fairway, South Road, Hythe, CT21 6AU
T: (01303) 262106
F: (01303) 262106
E: msmunge@globalnet.co.uk

Seabrook House
◆◆◆◆ SILVER AWARD
81 Seabrook Road, Hythe, CT21 5QW
T: (01303) 269282
F: (01303) 237822
E: info@seabrook-house.co.uk
I: www.smoothhound.co.uk/hotels/seabrook.html

The Shrubsoles B&B ◆◆◆
62 Brockhill Road, Saltwood, Hythe, CT21 4AG
T: (01303) 238832
E: marion_shrubsole@lineone.net

The Swan Hotel ◆◆◆
59 High Street, Hythe, CT21 5AD
T: (01303) 266236
F: (01303) 262584
I: www.theswanhotelhythe.co.uk

Watersedge ◆◆◆
The Watersedge, Red Lion Square, Hythe, CTZ1 5AU
T: (01303) 266686
F: (01303) 269877

ISFIELD
East Sussex

Farm Place ◆◆◆◆
Lewes Road, Isfield, Uckfield TN22 5TY
T: (01825) 750485
F: (01825) 750411

ITCHENOR
West Sussex

Itchenor Park House ◆◆◆◆
Itchenor, Chichester PO20 7DN
T: (01243) 512221
E: susie.green@lineone.net

KINGSDOWN
Kent

Blencathra Country Guest House ◆◆◆
Kingsdown Hill, Kingsdown, Deal CT14 8EA
T: (01304) 373725
E: blencathra2000@hotmail.com

Sparrow Court ◆◆◆
Chalk Hill Road, Kingsdown, Deal CT14 8DP
T: (01304) 389253
F: (01304) 389016
I: www.farmstaykent.com

LADDINGFORD
Kent

The Chequers ◆◆◆◆
The Street, Laddingford, Maidstone ME18 6BP
T: (01622) 871266
F: (01622) 873115

LAMBERHURST
Kent

Chequers Oast ◆◆◆
The Broadway, Lamberhurst, Royal Tunbridge Wells TN3 8DB
T: (01892) 890579
F: (01892) 890579
E: avrilandterry@yahoo.co.uk

LANCING
West Sussex

Edelweiss Guest House ◆◆◆
17 Kings Road, Lancing, BN15 8EB
T: (01903) 753412
F: (01903) 527424

LAUGHTON
East Sussex

Holly Cottage ◆◆◆◆
Lewes Road, Laughton, Lewes BN8 6BL
T: (01323) 811309
F: (01323) 811106
E: hollycottage@tinyworld.co.uk

Spences Farm ◆◆◆
Laughton, Lewes BN8 6BX
T: (01825) 840489
F: (01825) 840760

LAVANT
West Sussex

Flint Cottages ◆◆◆◆
47 Mid Lavant, Lavant, Chichester PO18 0AA
T: (01243) 785883
F: (01243) 785883

LEEDS
Kent

Further Fields ◆◆◆
Caring Lane, Leeds, Maidstone ME17 1TJ
T: (01622) 861288

West Forge ◆◆◆
Back Street, Leeds, Maidstone ME17 1TF
T: (01622) 861428

LEIGH
Surrey

Herons Head Farm ◆◆◆◆
Mynthurst, Leigh, Reigate, RH2 8QD
T: (01293) 862475
F: (01293) 863350
E: heronshead@clara.net
I: www.seetb.org.uk/heronshead

LENHAM
Kent

Bramley Knowle Farm ◆◆◆
Eastwood Road, Ulcombe, Maidstone, ME17 1ET
T: (01622) 858878
F: (01622) 851121
E: diane@bramleyknowlefarm.co.uk
I: www.bramleyknowlefarm.co.uk

The Dog & Bear Hotel ◆◆◆
The Square, Lenham, Maidstone ME17 2PG
T: (01622) 858219
F: (01622) 859415
E: dogbear@shepherd-neame.co.uk
I: www.shepherd-neame.co.uk

East Lenham Farm
◆◆◆◆ SILVER AWARD
Lenham, Maidstone ME17 2DP
T: (01622) 858686
F: (01622) 859474
E: eastlenham@farmline.com
I: www.eastlenhamfarm.co.uk

LEWES
East Sussex

The Crown Inn ◆◆◆
High Street, Lewes, BN7 2NA
T: (01273) 480670
F: (01273) 480679
E: sales@crowninn-lewes.co.uk
I: www.crowninn-lewes.co.uk

Downsview ◆◆◆
15 Montacute Road, Lewes, BN7 1EW
T: (01273) 472719

Eckington House
◆◆◆◆ SILVER AWARD
Ripe Lane, Ripe, Lewes BN8 6AR
T: (01323) 811274
E: sue@eckingtonhouse.co.uk
I: www.eckingtonhouse.co.uk

Hale Farm House ◆◆◆◆
Chiddingly, Lewes BN8 6HQ
T: (01825) 872619
F: (01825) 872619
E: s.burrough@virgin.net
I: www.halefarmhouse.co.uk

13 Hill Road ◆◆◆
Lewes, BN7 1DB
T: (01273) 477723
F: (01273) 486032
E: kmyles@btclick.com

Number 6 ◆◆◆◆
6 Gundreda Road, Lewes, BN7 1PX
T: (01273) 472106
F: (01273) 472106
E: jacquelinelucas@yahoo.co.uk
I: www.stayinlewes.co.uk

Number Seven ◆◆◆◆
7 Prince Edwards Road, Lewes, BN7 1BJ
T: (01273) 487038
E: numberseven@lewesbedandbreakfast.com
I: www.lewesbedandbreakfast.com

Racecourse House ◆◆◆◆
Old Lewes Racecourse, Lewes, BN7 1UR
T: (01273) 480804
F: (01273) 486478
E: a.heyes@btinternet.com

Settlands ◆◆◆◆
Wellgreen Lane, Kingston, Lewes BN7 3NP
T: (01273) 472295
F: (01273) 472295
E: diana-a@solutions-inc.co.uk

Sussex Countryside Accommodation
◆◆◆◆ SILVER AWARD
Crink House, Barcombe Mills, Lewes, BN8 5BJ
T: (01273) 400625
E: crinkhouse@hgaydon.fsnet.co.uk

Whitesmith Barn
◆◆◆◆ SILVER AWARD
Whitesmith, Lewes, BN8 6HA
T: (01825) 872867
E: snellings@whitesmith.fsnet.co.uk

LIGHTWATER
Surrey

Carlton Guest House ♦♦♦♦
63-65 Macdonald Road, Lightwater, Camberley GU18 5XY
T: (01276) 473580
F: (01276) 453595
E: ds@carlton.co.uk
I: www.carltongh.co.uk

LINDFIELD
West Sussex

Little Lywood ♦♦♦
Ardingly Road, Lindfield, Haywards Heath RH16 2QX
T: (01444) 892571
E: nick@littlelywood.freeserve.co.uk

LINGFIELD
Surrey

Long Acres Farm Rating Applied For
Newchapel Road, Lingfield, RH7 6LE
T: (01342) 833205
F: (01622) 735038

LITTLEBOURNE
Kent

King William IV ♦♦♦
4 High Street, Littlebourne, Canterbury CT3 1UN
T: (01227) 721244
F: (01227) 721244

LITTLEHAMPTON
West Sussex

Arun Sands ♦♦♦
84 South Terrace, Seafront, Littlehampton, BN17 5LJ
T: (01903) 732489
F: (01903) 732489
E: info@arun-sands.co.uk
I: www.arun-sands.co.uk

Arun View Inn ♦♦
Wharf Road, Littlehampton, BN17 5DD
T: (01903) 722335
F: (01903) 722335

Quayside Guest House ♦♦♦
36 Pier Road, Littlehampton, BN17 5LW
T: (01903) 721958
F: (01903) 721958

Racing Greens ♦♦♦
70 South Terrace, Littlehampton, BN17 5LQ
T: (01903) 732972
F: (01903) 732932
E: urban.surfer@easynet.co.uk

Sharoleen Guest House ♦♦♦
85 Bayford Road, Littlehampton, BN17 5HW
T: (01903) 713464
F: (01903) 713464

Tudor Lodge Guest House ♦♦♦
2 Horsham Road, Littlehampton, BN17 6BU
T: (01903) 716203
F: (01903) 716203

LONGFIELD
Kent

The Rising Sun Inn ♦♦♦
Fawkham Green, Longfield, DA3 8NL
T: (01474) 872291
F: (01474) 872291

LOOSE
Kent

Vale House ♦♦♦♦
Old Loose Hill, Loose, Maidstone ME15 0BH
T: (01622) 743339
F: (01622) 743103
E: vansegethin@hotmail.com

LOWER BEEDING
West Sussex

The Village Pantry ♦♦♦
Handcross Road, Plummers Plain, Lower Beeding, Horsham RH13 6NU
T: (01403) 891319
F: (01403) 891319
E: bill@rh136nu.sfnet.co.uk

LYMINSTER
West Sussex

Sandfield House ♦♦♦♦
Lyminster, Littlehampton BN17 7PG
T: (01903) 724129
F: (01903) 715041
E: thefbs@aol.com

MAIDSTONE
Kent

The Bower House Rating Applied For
64 Tonbridge Road, Maidstone, ME16 8SE
T: (01622) 763448
E: afarrellfamily@aol.com

51 Bower Mount Road ♦♦♦
Maidstone, ME16 8AX
T: (01622) 762948
F: (01622) 202753
E: sylviabnb@compuserve.com

Conway House ♦♦♦♦
12 Conway Road, Maidstone, ME16 0HD
T: (01622) 688287
F: (01622) 662589
E: conwayhouse@ukgateway.net
I: www.conwayhouse.ukgateway.net

Elm Trees ♦♦♦
55 Upper Fant Road, Maidstone, ME16 8BU
T: (01622) 693620

Grove House Bed & Breakfast ♦♦♦♦
Grove Green Road, Weavering Street, Maidstone ME14 5JT
T: (01622) 738441
F: (01622) 735927
E: gelco@supanet.com

The Hazels ♦♦♦♦
13 Yeoman Way, Bearsted, Maidstone ME15 8PQ
T: (01622) 737943
E: ianbuse@hotmail.com
I: www.redrival.com/thehazels

The Howard Hotel ♦♦
22-24 London Road, Maidstone, ME16 8QL
T: (01622) 758778
F: (01622) 609984

King Street Hotel ♦♦♦♦
74 King Street, Maidstone, ME14 1BH
T: (01622) 663266
F: (01622) 663123
E: reservations@kingstreethotelmaidstone.co.uk
I: www.kingstreethotelmaidstone.co.uk

The Limes ♦♦♦♦
118 Boxley Road, Maidstone, ME14 2BD
T: (01622) 750629
F: (01622) 691266

39 Marston Drive ♦♦♦
Vinters Park, Maidstone, ME14 5NE
T: (01622) 202196
E: steveandlesley@steleybrown.freeserve.co.uk

54 Mote Avenue ♦♦
Maidstone, ME15 7ST
T: (01622) 754016

Raigersfeld House ♦♦
Mote Park, Ashford Road, Maidstone, ME14 4AE
T: (01622) 685211
F: (01622) 691013
E: chipdbs@aol.com

The Ringlestone Inn & Farmhouse Hotel ♦♦♦♦♦ SILVER AWARD
Ringlestone Hamlet, Harrietsham, Maidstone ME17 1NX
T: (01622) 859900
F: (01622) 859966
E: bookings@ringlestone.com
I: www.ringlestone.com

Rock House Hotel ♦♦♦
102 Tonbridge Road, Maidstone, ME16 8SL
T: (01622) 751616
F: (01622) 756119

Rose Cottage ♦♦♦
10 Fant Lane, Maidstone, ME16 8NL
T: (01622) 729883

Roslin Villa ♦♦♦
11 St Michael's Road, Maidstone, ME16 8BS
T: (01622) 758301
F: (01622) 761459

West Belringham ♦♦♦
Chart Road, Sutton Valence, Maidstone ME17 3AW
T: (01622) 843995
E: west.belringham@tesco.net
I: www.travelengland.org.uk

4 White Rock Court ♦♦♦
White Rock Place, Maidstone, ME16 8HX
T: (01622) 753566
F: (01622) 753566
E: catnap.farnham@amserve.net

Wits End Guest House ♦♦♦
78 Bower Mount Road, Maidstone, ME16 8AT
T: (01622) 752684
F: (01622) 752684
E: mail@thewitsend.co.uk
I: www.thewitsend.co.uk

MARDEN
Kent

Tanner House ♦♦♦♦
Tanner Farm, Goudhurst Road, Marden, Tonbridge TN12 9ND
T: (01622) 831214
F: (01622) 832472
E: enquiries@tannerfarmpark.co.uk
I: www.tannerfarmpark.co.uk

MARGATE
Kent

Burlington Hotel ♦♦
8 Buenos Ayres, Margate, CT9 5AE
T: (01843) 292817

Luxor Hotel ♦♦
23 Fort Crescent, Margate, CT9 1HX
T: (01843) 290889
F: (01843) 290889
E: admin@luxorhotel.co.uk
I: luxorhotel.co.uk

MARK CROSS
East Sussex

Houndsell Cottage ♦♦♦
Mark Cross, Crowborough TN6 3PF
T: (01892) 782292

Rose Cottage ♦♦♦♦
Mill Lane, Mark Cross, Crowborough TN6 3PJ
T: (01892) 852592
F: (01892) 853268

MARSHBOROUGH
Kent

Honey Pot Cottage ♦♦♦♦
Marshborough Road, Marshborough, Sandwich CT13 0PQ
T: (01304) 813374
F: (01304) 813374
E: honeypotcottage@lycos.com
I: www.honeypotcottage.co.uk

MEOPHAM
Kent

Lamplights ♦♦♦
Wrotham Road, Meopham, Gravesend DA13 0QW
T: (01474) 813869
F: (0208) 306 1189

Nurstead Court ♦♦
Meopham, Gravesend DA13 9AD
T: (01474) 812121
F: (01474) 815133

MICKLEHAM
Surrey

Old House Cottage ♦♦♦
London Road, Mickleham, Dorking RH5 6EH
T: (01372) 375050

MIDHURST
West Sussex

10 Ashfield Close ♦♦♦♦
Midhurst, GU29 9RP
T: (01730) 814858

Carron Dune ♦♦♦
Carron Lane, Midhurst, GU29 9LD
T: (01730) 813558

20 Guillards Oak ♦♦♦♦
Midhurst, GU29 9JZ
T: (01730) 812550
F: (01730) 816765
E: coljen@tinyworld.co.uk

Oakhurst Cottage ♦♦♦
Carron Lane, Midhurst, GU29 9LF
T: (01730) 813523

Pear Tree Cottage ♦♦♦
Lamberts Lane, Midhurst, GU29 9EF
T: (01730) 817216

18 Pretoria Avenue ♦♦♦
Midhurst, GU29 9PP
T: (01730) 814868
F: (01730) 814868
E: eric@estratford.freeserve.co.uk

Severals House ♦♦♦♦
Severals Wood, Midhurst, GU29 0LX
T: (01730) 812771

Ye Olde Tea Shoppe ♦♦♦
North Street, Midhurst, GU29 9DY
T: (01730) 817081
F: (01730) 810228

MILFORD
Surrey

Holly Tree Cottage ♦♦♦
Mousehill Lane, Milford, Godalming GU8 5BH
T: (01483) 426578
F: (01483) 420677
E: rlidbury@btinternet.com

MILSTEAD
Kent

The Cottage ♦♦♦♦
Frinsted Road, Milstead, Sittingbourne ME9 0SA
T: (01795) 830367

MINSTER-IN-SHEPPEY
Kent

Glen Haven ♦♦♦
Lower Road, Minster-on-Sea, Sheerness, ME12 3ST
T: (01795) 877064
F: (01795) 871746
E: johnstanford@btinternet.com

Mia Crieff ♦♦♦♦
Mill Hill, Chequers Road, Minster-in-Sheppey, Sheerness ME12 3QL
T: (01795) 870620

NETTLESTEAD
Kent

Rock Farm House ♦♦♦♦
Gibbs Hill, Nettlestead, Maidstone ME18 5HT
T: (01622) 812244
F: (01622) 812244
I: www.rockfarmhousebandb.co.uk

NEW ROMNEY
Kent

Martinfield Manor ♦♦♦♦
Lydd Road, New Romney, TN28 8HB
T: (01797) 363802

Warren Lodge Motel ♦♦♦
Dymchurch Road, New Romney, TN28 8UE
T: (01797) 362138
F: (01797) 367377
E: admin@warrenlodge.co.uk
I: www.warrenlodge.co.uk

NEWHAVEN
East Sussex

Newhaven Lodge Guest House ♦
12 Brighton Road, Newhaven, BN9 9NB
T: (01273) 513736
F: (01273) 734619
E: newhavenlodge@aol.com

NEWICK
East Sussex

Firle Cottage ♦♦♦
High Street, Newick, Lewes BN8 4LG
T: (01825) 722392

Holly Lodge ♦♦♦
Oxbottom Lane, Newick, Lewes BN8 4RA
T: (01825) 722738
F: (01825) 723624

NINFIELD
East Sussex

Hollybank House ♦♦♦
Lower Street, Ninfield, Battle TN33 9EA
T: (01424) 892052
F: (01424) 892052

London House ♦♦♦♦
Manchester Road, Ninfield, Battle TN33 9JX
T: (01424) 893532
F: (01424) 893595

NORTH BERSTED
West Sussex

Lorna Doone Bed & Breakfast ♦♦♦♦
58 Sandymount Avenue, North Bersted, Bognor Regis PO22 9EP
T: (01243) 822203
F: (01243) 822203
E: joan@lornadoone.freeserve.co.uk
I: www.lornadoone.freeserve.co.uk

Willow Rise ♦♦♦
131 North Bersted Street, North Bersted, Bognor Regis PO22 9AG
T: (01243) 829544
F: (01243) 829544

NORTH MUNDHAM
West Sussex

The Cottage
♦♦♦♦ SILVER AWARD
Church Road, North Mundham, Chichester PO20 6JU
T: (01243) 784586
E: lambrinudi-bandb@supanet.com

NORTHFLEET
Kent

The Nook ♦♦♦
3 Falcon Mews, Vale Road, Northfleet, Gravesend DA11 8BW
T: (01474) 350748

NUTFIELD
Surrey

Hillside Cottage ♦♦♦
Coopers Hill Road, Nutfield, Redhill RH1 4HX
T: (01737) 822916
F: (01737) 822916
E: jurgen@hillsidecott.co.uk
I: www.hillsidecott.co.uk

NUTLEY
East Sussex

The Court House ♦♦♦♦
School Lane, Nutley, Uckfield TN22 3PG
T: (01825) 713129
F: (01825) 712650
E: execrelocation@compuserve.com

West Meadows ♦♦♦♦
Bell Lane, Nutley, Uckfield TN22 3PD
T: (01825) 712434
F: (01825) 712434
E: alex.everett@virgin.net

OARE
Kent

Mount House ♦♦♦
Mount Pleasant, Oare, Faversham ME13 0PZ
T: (01795) 534735

OCKLEY
Surrey

The Kings Arms Inn ♦♦♦♦
Stane Street, Ockley, Dorking RH5 5TP
T: (01306) 711224
F: (01306) 711224

OTFORD
Kent

Darenth Dene ♦♦♦♦
Shoreham Road, Otford, Sevenoaks TN14 5RP
T: (01959) 522293

The Garden Room ♦♦♦
3 Darnetsfield, Otford, Sevenoaks TN14 5LB
T: (01959) 522521
E: gardenroom@otford.org
I: www.otford.org/garden-room

9 Warham Road ♦♦
Otford, Sevenoaks TN14 5PF
T: (01959) 523596

OUTWOOD
Surrey

The Coach House
♦♦♦♦ SILVER AWARD
Millers Lane, Outwood, Redhill RH1 5PZ
T: (01342) 843193
F: (01342) 842544
E: coachselgw@aol.com

OXTED
Surrey

Arawa ♦♦♦
58 Granville Road, Limpsfield, Oxted RH8 0BZ
T: (01883) 714104
F: (01883) 714104
E: david@davidgibbs.co.uk

Meads ♦♦♦♦
23 Granville Road, Oxted, RH8 0BX
T: (01883) 730115
E: Holgate@meads9.fsnet.co.uk

The New Bungalow ♦♦♦
Old Hall Farm, Tandridge Lane, Oxted, RH8 9NS
T: (01342) 892508
F: (01342) 892508
E: don.nunn@tesco.net

PARTRIDGE GREEN
West Sussex

Pound Cottage Bed & Breakfast ♦♦♦
Mill Lane, Littleworth, Partridge Green, Horsham RH13 8JU
T: (01403) 710218
F: (01403) 711337
E: poundcottagebb@amserve.net
I: www.horsham.co.uk/poundcottage.html

PEASLAKE
Surrey

The Garden Room ♦♦♦
Coltsfoot, Peaslake, Guildford GU5 9PE
T: (01306) 737088
E: brimar@coltsfoot0freeserve.co.uk

PEMBURY
Kent

Gates House ♦♦♦
5 Lower Green Road, Pembury, Royal Tunbridge Wells TN2 4DZ
T: (01892) 822866
F: (01892) 824626
E: simon@s.galway.freeserve.co.uk
I: www.ukworld.net/gates

PETHAM
Kent

South Wootton House ♦♦♦
Capel Lane, Petham, Canterbury CT4 5RG
T: (01227) 700643
F: (01227) 700613
E: mountfrances@farming.co.uk

PETT
East Sussex

Pendragon Lodge
♦♦♦♦♦ SILVER AWARD
Watermill Lane, Pett, Hastings TN35 4HY
T: (01424) 814051
F: (01424) 812499
E: pendragon_lodge@hotmail.com
I: www.pendragonlodge.co.uk

PETWORTH
West Sussex

Badgers Tavern ♦♦♦♦
Coultershaw Bridge, Petworth, GU28 0JF
T: (01798) 342651
F: (01798) 343649

Burton Park Farm ♦♦♦
Petworth, GU28 0JT
T: (01798) 342431

Eedes Cottage ♦♦♦♦
Bignor Park Road, Bury Gate, Pulborough, RH20 1EZ
T: (01798) 831438
F: (01798) 831942
I: www.sussexlive.com

Halfway Bridge Inn ♦♦♦♦
Halfway Bridge, Petworth, GU28 9BP
T: (01798) 861281
F: (01798) 861878

The Old Railway Station ♦♦♦♦♦
Coultershaw Bridge, Petworth, GU28 0JF
T: (01798) 342346
F: (01798) 342346
E: mlr@old-station.co.uk
I: www.old-station.co.uk

Rectory Cottage ♦♦♦
Rectory Lane, Petworth, GU28 0DB
T: (01798) 342380
E: dcradd@aol.com

White Horse Inn ♦♦♦
The Street, Sutton, Pulborough RH20 1PS
T: (01798) 869221
F: (01798) 869291

Establishments printed in blue have a detailed entry in this guide

PEVENSEY BAY
East Sussex

The Sandcastle
Rating Applied For
46 Val Prinseps Road, Pevensey Bay, Pevensey BN24 6JG
T: (01323) 743706
F: (01323) 743706
E: sandcastlebay@aol.com

PILTDOWN
East Sussex

The Piltdown Man Free House ♦♦♦
Piltdown, Uckfield TN22 5XL
T: (01825) 723563
F: (01825) 721087
E: enquiries@thepiltdownman.com
I: www.thepiltdownman.com

PLAYDEN
East Sussex

The Corner House ♦♦♦
Playden, Rye TN31 7UL
T: (01797) 280439
E: yvonne@thecornerhouse-bed-breakfast.co.uk
I: www.thecornerhouse-bed-breakfast.co.uk

Houghton Farm ♦♦♦♦
Houghton Green Lane, Playden, Rye TN31 7PJ
T: (01797) 280175

PLUMMERS PLAIN
West Sussex

Cinnamon Cottage ♦♦♦
Handcross Road, Plummers Plain, Horsham RH13 6NZ
T: (01444) 400539

POLEGATE
East Sussex

The Cottage ♦♦♦♦
Dittons Road, Polegate, BN26 6HS
T: (01323) 482011
F: (01323) 482011

PULBOROUGH
West Sussex

Barn House Lodge ♦♦♦♦
Barn House Lane, Pulborough, RH20 2BS
T: (01798) 872682
F: (01798) 872682

Hurston Warren ♦♦♦
Golf Club Lane, Wiggonholt, Pulborough, RH20 2EN
T: (01798) 875831
F: (01798) 874989
E: kglazier@btinternet.com
I: www.sussexlive.com

Moseleys Barn
♦♦♦♦ SILVER AWARD
Hardham, Pulborough RH20 1LB
T: (01798) 872912
F: (01798) 872912
I: www.smoothhound.co.uk/hotels/moseleys

RAINHAM
Kent

Abigails ♦♦♦
17 The Maltings, Rainham, Gillingham ME8 8JL
T: (01634) 365427

Sans Souci ♦♦♦♦
43 Wakeley Road, Rainham, Gillingham ME8 8HD
T: (01634) 370847

RAMSGATE
Kent

Abbeygail Guest House ♦♦♦
17 Penshurst Road, Ramsgate, CT11 8EG
T: (01843) 594154
F: (01843) 594154
E: lindi.groom@ukf.net
I: www.abbeygail.co.uk

Glendevon Guest House ♦♦♦♦
8 Truro Road, Ramsgate, CT11 8DB
T: (01843) 570909
F: (01843) 570909
E: adrian.everix@btopenworld.com
I: www.glendevon-guesthouse.co.uk

Glenholme ♦♦♦
6 Crescent Road, Ramsgate, CT11 9QU
T: (01843) 595149

The Jalna Hotel ♦♦♦
49 Vale Square, Ramsgate, CT11 9DA
T: (01843) 593848
F: (01843) 593848

The Royale Guest House ♦♦♦
7 Royal Road, Ramsgate, CT11 9LE
T: (01843) 594712
F: (01843) 594712
E: theroyaleguesthouse@talk21.com

Sealan Hotel ♦♦
6 Avenue Road, Ramsgate, CT11 8ET
T: (01843) 593044
F: (01843) 593044

Sion Hill Hotel ♦♦
2 Sion Hill, Ramsgate, CT11 9HZ
T: (01843) 591908
F: (01843) 850283

Spencer Court Hotel ♦♦♦
37 Spencer Square, Ramsgate, CT11 9LD
T: (01843) 594582
F: (01843) 594582

Sunnymede ♦♦♦
10 Truro Road, Ramsgate, CT11 8DP
T: (01843) 593974
F: (01843) 594327
E: sunnymede@tinyworld.co.uk

REDHILL
Surrey

Ashleigh House Hotel ♦♦♦♦
39 Redstone Hill, Redhill, RH1 4BG
T: (01737) 764763
F: (01737) 780308

REIGATE
Surrey

Highview ♦♦♦
78 Woodcrest Walk, Reigate, RH2 0JL
T: (01737) 768294
F: (01737) 760433
E: highview@creative-eye.demon.co.uk
I: www.creative-eye.demon.co.uk/highview.html

RHODES MINNIS
Kent

Monsoon Lodge ♦♦♦
Rhodes Minnis, Canterbury CT4 6XX
T: (01303) 863272
F: (01303) 863272
E: jm@farmersweekly.net
I: www.monsoonlodge.co.uk

RINGMER
East Sussex

Bethany ♦♦♦
25 Ballard Drive, Ringmer, Lewes BN8 5NU
T: (01273) 812025
F: (01273) 812025
E: dybethany@aol.com

Bryn-Clai ♦♦♦
Uckfield Road (A26), Ringmer, Lewes BN8 5RU
T: (01273) 814042

Drove Park ♦♦♦♦
Half Mile Drove, Ringmer, Lewes BN8 5NL
T: (01273) 814470
F: (01273) 814470
E: pru@drovepark.com
I: www.drovepark.com

Gote Farm ♦♦♦♦
Gote Lane, Ringmer, Lewes BN8 5HX
T: (01273) 812303
F: (01273) 812303
E: janecraig@ukgateway.net

RIVER
Kent

Woodlands ♦♦♦
29 London Road, River, Dover CT17 0SF
T: (01304) 823635

ROBERTSBRIDGE
East Sussex

Glenferness ♦♦♦♦
Brightling Road, Robertsbridge, Battle, TN32 5DP
T: (01580) 881841
E: ktwright@ukonline.co.uk
I: www.ktwright.ukonline.co.uk

ROCHESTER
Kent

10 Abbotts Close ♦♦♦♦
Priestfields, Rochester, ME1 3AZ
T: (01634) 811126

Ambleside Lodge ♦♦♦
12 Abbotts Close, Priestfields, Rochester, ME1 3AZ
T: (01634) 815926
F: (01634) 815926
E: bryan@mills19.fsnet.co.uk

The Cottage
Rating Applied For
66 Borstal Road, Rochester, ME1 3BD
T: (01634) 403888

King Charles Hotel ♦♦♦
Brompton Road, Gillingham, ME7 5QT
T: (01634) 830303
F: (01634) 829430
E: enquiries@kingcharleshotel.co.uk
I: www.kingcharleshotel.co.uk

Linden House ♦♦♦
10 Nag's Head Lane, Rochester, ME1 1BB
T: (01634) 819438
E: carolyn@cpidgeon.freeserve.co.uk

Longley House ♦♦♦
Boley Hill, Rochester, ME1 1TE
T: (01634) 819108
F: (01634) 819108
E: margherita@jtq.globalnet.co.uk
I: www.users.globalnet.co.uk/~jtq

North Downs Barn ♦♦♦♦
Bush Road, Rochester, ME2 1HF
T: (01634) 296829
F: (01634) 296829

St Martin ♦♦♦
104 Borstal Road, Rochester, ME1 3BD
T: (01634) 848192
E: icolvin@stmartin.freeserve.co.uk

ROGATE
West Sussex

Mayfield House ♦♦♦♦
Rogate, GU31 5HN
T: (01730) 821916

ROLVENDEN
Kent

Duck & Drake Cottage ♦♦♦
Sandhurst Lane, Rolvenden, Cranbrook TN17 4PQ
T: (01580) 241533
F: (01580) 241533
E: duckanddrake@supanet.com

ROWLEDGE
Surrey

Borderfield Farm ♦♦♦
Boundary Road, Rowledge, Farnham GU10 4EP
T: (01252) 793985

ROYAL TUNBRIDGE WELLS
Kent

Ash Tree Cottage ♦♦♦♦
7 Eden Road, Royal Tunbridge Wells, TN1 1TS
T: (01892) 541317
F: (01892) 616770
E: rogersashtree@excite.com

Badgers End ♦♦♦
47 Thirlmere Road, Royal Tunbridge Wells, TN4 9SS
T: (01892) 533176

Bankside ♦♦♦
6 Scotts Way, Royal Tunbridge Wells, TN2 5RG
T: (01892) 531776

4 Bedford Terrace ♦♦♦
Royal Tunbridge Wells, TN1 1YJ
T: (01892) 532084

Blundeston ♦♦♦♦
Eden Road, Royal Tunbridge Wells, TN1 1TS
T: (01892) 513030
F: (01892) 540255
E: daysblundeston@excite.com

Braeside ♦♦♦
7 Rusthall Road, Royal Tunbridge Wells, TN4 8RA
T: (01892) 521786
F: (01892) 521786
E: itucker@eggconnect.net

Cheviots ♦♦♦
Cousley Wood, Wadhurst, TN5 6HD
T: (01892) 782952
E: b&b@cheviots99.freeserve.co.uk
I: www.cheviots99.freeserve.co.uk

Clarken Guest House ♦♦♦
61 Frant Road, Royal Tunbridge Wells, TN2 5LH
T: (01892) 533397
F: (01892) 617121
E: barrykench@virgin.net

Danehurst
♦♦♦♦♦ SILVER AWARD
41 Lower Green Road, Rusthall, Royal Tunbridge Wells TN4 8TW
T: (01892) 527739
F: (01892) 514804
E: info@danehurst.net
I: www.smoothhound.co.uk/hotels/danehurst.html

Ephraim Lodge
♦♦♦♦♦ GOLD AWARD
The Common, Royal Tunbridge Wells, TN4 8BX
T: (01892) 523053
F: (01892) 523053

Ford Cottage ♦♦♦♦
Linden Park Road, Royal Tunbridge Wells, TN2 5QL
T: (01892) 531419
E: fordcottage@tinyworld.co.uk

Hadleigh ♦♦♦
69 Sandown Park, Royal Tunbridge Wells, TN2 4RT
T: (01892) 822760
F: (01892) 823170

Hawkenbury Farm ♦♦♦♦
Hawkenbury Road, Royal Tunbridge Wells, TN3 9AD
T: (01892) 536977
F: (01892) 536200

Hazelwood House ♦♦♦
Bishop's Down Park Road, Royal Tunbridge Wells, TN4 8XS
T: (01892) 545924
E: judith02@globalnet.co.uk

Manor Court Farm ♦♦♦
Ashurst, Royal Tunbridge Wells TN3 9TB
T: (01892) 740279
F: (01892) 740919
E: jsoyke@jsoyke.freeserve.co.uk
I: www.manorcourtfarm.co.uk

Nightingales ♦♦♦
London Road, Southborough, Royal Tunbridge Wells TN4 0UJ
T: (01892) 528443
F: (01892) 511376
E: the_nightingales@bigfoot.com
I: www.bcity.com/the_nightingales

Number Ten ♦♦♦
Modest Corner, Southborough, Royal Tunbridge Wells TN4 0LS
T: (01892) 522450
F: (01892) 522450
E: modestanneke@lineone.net

80 Ravenswood Avenue ♦♦
Royal Tunbridge Wells, TN2 3SJ
T: (01892) 523069

Rosnaree ♦♦♦
189 Upper Grosvenor Road, Royal Tunbridge Wells, TN1 2EF
T: (01892) 524017
E: david@rosnaree.freeserve.co.uk

Studley Cottage
♦♦♦♦ SILVER AWARD
Bishops Down Park Road, Royal Tunbridge Wells, TN4 8XX
T: (01892) 539854
E: cookhouse28@hotmail.com

191 Upper Grosvenor Road ♦♦♦
Royal Tunbridge Wells, TN1 2EF
T: (01892) 537305

Vale Royal Hotel ♦♦♦
54-57 London Road, Royal Tunbridge Wells, TN1 1DS
T: (01892) 525580
F: (01892) 526022
E: reservations@valeroyalhotel.co.uk
I: www.valeroyalhotel.co.uk

40 York Road ♦♦♦
Royal Tunbridge Wells, TN1 1JY
T: (01892) 531342
F: (01892) 531342
I: www.wolsey-lodge.co.uk

RUDGWICK
West Sussex

The Mucky Duck Inn ♦♦♦
Loxwood Road, Tismans Common, Rudgwick, Horsham RH12 3BW
T: (01403) 822300
F: (01403) 822300
E: mucky_duck_pub@msn.com
I: www.mucky-duck-inn.co.uk

RUSTINGTON
West Sussex

Kenmore
♦♦♦♦ SILVER AWARD
Claigmar Road, Rustington, Littlehampton BN16 2NL
T: (01903) 784634
F: (01903) 784634
E: kenmoreguesthouse@amserve.net
I: www.kenmoreguesthouse.co.uk

RYE
East Sussex

Ascham House ♦♦♦
4 The Grove, Rye, TN31 7ND
T: (01797) 223911
E: tommeyer@jempsons.co.uk
I: www.rye-tourism.co.uk/ascham

At Wisteria Corner ♦♦♦
47 Ferry Road (Sloane Terrace), Rye, TN31 7DJ
T: (01797) 225011
E: mmpartridge@lineone.net

Aviemore Guest House ♦♦♦
28-30 Fishmarket Road, Rye, TN31 7LP
T: (01797) 223052
F: (01797) 223052
E: aviemore@lineone.net
I: www.SmoothHound.co.uk/hotels/aviemore.html

Benson Hotel
♦♦♦♦♦ SILVER AWARD
15 East Street, Rye, TN31 7JY
T: (01797) 225131
F: (01797) 225512
E: info@bensonhotel.co.uk
I: www.bensonhotel.co.uk

Cinque Ports Hotel ♦♦♦
Cinque Ports Street, Rye, TN31 7AN
T: (01797) 222319
F: (01797) 224184
E: elaine@wickhamrobinson.freeserve.co.uk
I: www.rye.org.uk

Culpeppers
♦♦♦♦ SILVER AWARD
15 Love Lane, Rye, TN31 7NE
T: (01797) 224411
F: (01797) 224411
E: peppersrye@aol.com
I: www.culpeppers-rye.com

Durrant House Hotel
♦♦♦♦♦ SILVER AWARD
2 Market Street, Rye, TN31 7LA
T: (01797) 223182
F: (01797) 226940
E: kingslands@compuserve.com
I: www.durranthouse.com

Four Seasons
♦♦♦♦ SILVER AWARD
96 Udimore Road, Rye, TN31 7DX
T: (01797) 224305
F: (01797) 229450
E: coxsam@btinternet.com

Glencoe Farm ♦♦♦♦
West Undercliff, Rye, TN31 7DX
T: (01797) 224347
F: (01797) 224347

11 High Street ♦♦♦
Rye, TN31 7JF
T: (01797) 223952

The Hope Anchor Hotel ♦♦♦♦
Watchbell Street, Rye, TN31 7HA
T: (01797) 222216
F: (01897) 223796

Jeake's House
♦♦♦♦♦ SILVER AWARD
Mermaid Street, Rye, TN31 7ET
T: (01797) 222828
F: (01797) 222623
E: jeakeshouse@btinternet.com
I: www.jeakeshouse.com

Kimbley Cottage ♦♦♦
Main Street, Peasmarsh, Rye TN31 6UL
T: (01797) 230514
F: (01797) 230850
E: kimbley@onetel.net.uk

Layces Bed & Breakfast
♦♦♦♦ SILVER AWARD
Chitcombe Road, Broad Oak, Rye TN31 6EU
T: (01424) 882836
F: (01424) 882281
E: stephens@layces.co.uk
I: www.layces.co.uk

Little Orchard House
♦♦♦♦♦ SILVER AWARD
West Street, Rye, TN31 7ES
T: (01797) 223831
F: (01797) 223831
I: www.littleorchardhouse.com

Manor Farm Oast
♦♦♦♦♦ GOLD AWARD
Workhouse Lane, Icklesham, Winchelsea TN36 4AJ
T: (01424) 813787
F: (01424) 813787
E: manor.farm.oast@lineone.net

The Old Vicarage ♦♦♦
Rye Harbour, Rye, TN31 7TT
T: (01797) 222088
F: (01797) 229620
E: jonathan@oldvicarageryeharbour.fsnet.co.uk

Owlet ♦♦♦
37 New Road, Rye, TN31 7LS
T: (01797) 222544
E: owlet-rye@amserve.net

The Queens Head Hotel ♦♦♦
19 Landgate, Rye, TN31 7LH
T: (01797) 222181
F: (01797) 229180

The Rise
♦♦♦♦ SILVER AWARD
82 Udimore Road, Rye, TN31 7DY
T: (01797) 222285
E: therise@bb-rye.freeserve.co.uk

St Margarets ♦♦♦
Dumbwomans Lane, Udimore, Rye TN31 6AD
T: (01797) 222586

Ship Inn ♦♦♦
The Strand, Rye, TN31 7DB
T: (01797) 222233
F: (01797) 222715
E: shipinn@zoom.co.uk

Simmons of the Mint
Rating Applied For
68-69 The Mint, Rye, TN31 7EW
T: (01797) 226862
F: (01797) 226862

The Strand House
♦♦♦♦ SILVER AWARD
Tanyard's Lane, Winchelsea, TN36 4JT
T: (01797) 226276
F: (01797) 224806
E: strandhouse@winchelsea98.fsnet.co.uk
I: www.s-h-systems.co.uk/hotels/strand.html

Thacker House ♦♦♦
Old Brickyard, Rye, TN31 7EE
T: (01797) 226850
F: (01797) 226850
E: abb25@supanet.com

Tidings ♦♦♦♦
26A Military Road, Rye, TN31 7NY
T: (01797) 223760

Top o'The Hill at Rye ♦♦♦
Rye Hill, Rye, TN31 7NH
T: (01797) 223284
F: (01797) 227030

Tower House ♦♦♦♦
(The Old Dormy), Hilders Cliff, Rye, TN31 7LD
T: (01797) 226865
F: (01797) 226865

Vine Cottage ♦♦♦
25a Udimore Road, Rye, TN31 7DS
T: (01797) 222822

White Vine House
♦♦♦♦♦ SILVER AWARD
24 High Street, Rye, TN31 7JF
T: (01797) 224748
F: (01797) 223599
E: irene@whitevinehouse.freeserve.co.uk

The Windmill Guest House ♦♦♦
Mill Lane, (off Ferry Road), Rye, TN31 7DW
T: (01797) 224027
F: (01797) 227212
I: www.rye-tourism.co.uk/windmill

Wish House ♦♦♦
Wish Ward, Rye, TN31 7DH
T: (01797) 223672
E: wishhouse@zoom.com

Woodpeckers ♦♦♦
West Undercliff, Rye, TN31 7DX
T: (01797) 223013
F: (01797) 222264
E: shirley@caresigns.com

RYE FOREIGN
East Sussex

The Hare & Hounds ♦♦♦
Rye Road, Rye Foreign, Rye TN31 7ST
T: (01797) 230483

Rumples Inn ♦♦♦
Peasmarsh Road, Rye Foreign, Rye TN3L 7SY
T: (01797) 230494

ST LEONARDS
East Sussex

Ashton House ♦♦♦
381 Battle Road, St Leonards on Sea, St Leonards, Hastings TN37 7BE
T: (01424) 853624

Hollington Croft ♦♦♦
272 Battle Road, St Leonards-on-Sea, St Leonards, Hastings TN37 7BA
T: (01424) 851795

Marina Lodge ♦♦♦
123 Marina, St Leonards-on-Sea, St Leonards, Hastings TN38 0BN
T: (01424) 715067
E: marinalodge@lineone.net
I: www.marinalodge.co.uk

May Tree House ♦♦♦
41 Albany Road, St Leonards, Hastings TN38 0LJ
T: (01424) 421760
F: (01424) 421760
E: maytreehouse@hotmail.com

Melrose Guest House ♦♦♦
18 De Cham Road, St Leonards, Hastings TN37 6JP
T: (01424) 715163
F: (01424) 432773
E: melrose18@fsmail.net

Rutland Guest House ♦♦♦
17 Grosvenor Cres, St Leonards, Hastings TN38 0AA
T: (01424) 714720
F: (01424) 714720

Sherwood Guest House ♦♦♦
15 Grosvenor Crescent, St Leonards-on-Sea, St Leonards, Hastings TN38 0AA
T: (01424) 433331
F: (01424) 433331

The Windsor Hotel ♦♦♦
9 Warrior Square, St Leonards-on-Sea, St Leonards, Hastings TN37 6BA
T: (01424) 422709
F: (01424) 422709

ST MARY IN THE MARSH
Kent

Star Inn ♦♦♦
St Mary in the Marsh, Romney Marsh TN29 0BX
T: (01797) 362139
E: marc@star-inn-the-marsh.co.uk
I: www.star-inn-the-marsh.co.uk

ST MICHAELS
Kent

Forge House ♦♦♦♦
Biddenden Road, St Michaels, Tenterden TN30 6SX
T: (01233) 850779
E: forgehouse@email.com
I: pages.eidosnet.co.uk/~forgehouse

Whitelands Farm ♦♦♦
Grange Road, St Michaels, Tenterden TN30 6TJ
T: (01580) 765971
E: whitelandsfarm@tinyonline.co.uk

SALTDEAN
East Sussex

Grand Ocean Hotel ♦♦♦
Longridge Avenue, Saltdean, Brighton BN2 8RP
T: (01273) 302291
F: (01273) 304255
I: www.grandhotelgroup.co.uk

SANDGATE
Kent

Royal Norfolk Hotel ♦♦
7 Sandgate High Street, Sandgate, Folkestone CT20 3BD
T: (01303) 248262
F: (01303) 248262
E: coasthosts@cwctv.net
I: www.southcoastholiday.co.uk/hotel

SANDHURST
Kent

Hope Barn ♦♦♦♦
Crouch Lane, Sandhurst, Cranbrook TN18 5PD
T: (01580) 850689
F: (01580) 850689
I: www.hopebarn.co.uk

SANDWICH
Kent

Durlock Lodge ♦♦♦
Durlock, Minster-in-Thanet, Ramsgate CT12 4HD
T: (01843) 821219
E: david@durlocklodge.co.uk
I: www.durlocklodge.co.uk

Fleur De Lis Hotel Inn & Restaurant ♦♦♦
6-8 Delf Street, Sandwich, CT13 9BZ
T: (01304) 611131
F: (01304) 611199
E: thefleur@verinitaverns.co.uk
I: www.verinitaverns.co.uk

SARRE
Kent

Crown Inn (The Famous Cherry Brandy House)♦♦♦♦
Ramsgate Road, Sarre, Birchington CT7 0LF
T: (01843) 847808
F: (01843) 847914
E: crown@shepherd-neame.co.uk
I: www.shepherd-neame.co.uk

SEAFORD
East Sussex

Copperfields ♦♦♦♦
12 Connaught Road, Seaford, BN25 2PU
T: (01323) 492152
F: (01323) 872311
E: sally.green@btinternet.com

Cornerways ♦♦♦
10 The Covers, Seaford, BN25 1DF
T: (01323) 492400

Holmes Lodge ♦♦♦
72 Claremont Road, Seaford, BN25 2BJ
T: (01323) 898331
F: (01323) 491346
E: holmes.lodge@freemail.co.uk
I: www.seaford.co.uk/holmes/holmes.htm

Malvern House ♦♦♦
Alfriston Road, Seaford, BN25 3QG
T: (01323) 492058
F: (01323) 492000
E: MalvernBandB@aol.com
I: www.seaford.co.uk/malvern/

Oasis Clearview Hotel ♦♦
36-38 Claremont Road, Seaford, BN25 2BD
T: (01323) 890138
F: (01323) 896534
E: reservations@oasisclearview.com
I: www.oasisclearview.com

The Silverdale ♦♦♦♦
21 Sutton Park Road, Seaford, BN25 1RH
T: (01323) 491849
F: (01323) 891131
E: silverdale@mistral.co.uk
I: www.mistral.co.uk/silverdale/silver.htm

Tudor Manor Hotel
♦♦♦♦ SILVER AWARD
Eastbourne Road, Seaford, BN25 4DB
T: (01323) 896006
F: (01323) 896006
E: tudormanortl@aol.com
I: www.tudormanor.co.uk

SEDLESCOMBE
East Sussex

Lower Marley Farm ♦♦♦
New Road, Sedlescombe, Battle TN33 0RG
T: (01424) 871416

SELSEY
West Sussex

Compass House ♦♦♦♦
18 Beacon Drive, Selsey, Chichester PO20 0TW
T: (01243) 601439
F: (01243) 601439
E: sue.trotman@amsetue.net

Greenacre ♦♦♦♦
5 Manor Farm Court, Selsey, Chichester PO20 0LY
T: (01243) 602912
E: greenacre@zoom.co.uk

Ivy House B & B ♦♦♦
71 Hillfield Road, Selsey, Chichester PO20 0LF
T: (01243) 601444
F: (01243) 603806
E: ivyhousebb@hotmail.com

The Lodge ♦♦♦♦
21a Clayton Road, Selsey, Chichester PO20 9DB
T: (01243) 601217
F: (01243) 605282
E: m.valmas@freenet.co.uk

Norton Lea ♦♦♦
Upper Norton, Selsey, Chichester PO20 9EA
T: (01243) 605454
F: (01243) 605456
E: 100013.3142@compuserve.com

St Andrews Lodge ♦♦♦♦
Chichester Road, Selsey, Chichester PO20 0LX
T: (01243) 606899
F: (01243) 607826
E: info@standrewslodge.co.uk
I: www.standrewslodge.co.uk

SEND
Surrey

Sommerhay Barn ♦♦♦♦
Church Lane, Send, Woking GU23 7JL
T: (01483) 210107
F: (01483) 211945
E: angey_watson@hotmail.com

SEVENOAKS
Kent

Beechcombe ♦♦♦♦
4 Vine Lodge Court, Holly Bush Lane, Sevenoaks, TN13 3XY
T: (01732) 741643
F: (01732) 741643
E: anthonytait@hotmail.com

Burley Lodge ♦♦♦
Rockdale Road, Sevenoaks, TN13 1JT
T: (01732) 455761
F: (01732) 458178
E: dilatter@aol.com

75 Clarendon Road ♦♦♦
Sevenoaks, TN13 1ET
T: (01732) 456000
F: (01732) 456000
E: info@chocolateshop.uk.com

Crofters ♦♦♦♦
67 Oakhill Road, Sevenoaks, TN13 1NU
T: (01732) 460189
F: (01732) 460189
E: ritamarfry@talk21.com

56 The Drive ♦♦♦
Sevenoaks, TN13 3AF
T: (01732) 453236
E: jwlloydsks@aol.com

Garden House ♦♦♦♦
Solefields Road, Sevenoaks, TN13 1PJ
T: (01732) 457225

Hornshaw House ♦♦♦♦
47 Mount Harry Road, Sevenoaks, TN13 3JN
T: (01732) 465262
E: embates@hornshaw47.freeserve.co.uk
I: www.hornshaw-house.co.uk

Legh House ♦♦♦♦
Woodland Rise, Sevenoaks, TN15 0HZ
T: (01732) 761587

The Moorings Hotel ♦♦♦
97 Hitchen Hatch Lane, Sevenoaks, TN13 3BE
T: (01732) 452589
F: (01732) 456462
E: theryans@mooringshotel.co.uk
I: www.mooringshotel.co.uk

The Old Police House ♦♦♦♦
18 Shenden Way, Sevenoaks, TN13 1SE
T: (01732) 457150
F: (01732) 457150

The Pightle ♦♦♦♦
21 White Hart Wood, Sevenoaks, TN13 1RS
T: (01732) 451678
F: (01732) 464905
E: miketessa@pightle21.fsnet.co.uk
I: www.pightle21.fsnet.co.uk

Robann ♦♦♦
5 Vestry Cottages, Old Otford Road, Sevenoaks, TN14 5EH
T: (01732) 456272

40 Robyns Way ♦♦♦
Sevenoaks, TN13 3EB
T: (01732) 452401
E: ingram7oaks@onetel.net.uk

Welford ♦♦♦
6 Crownfields, Sevenoaks, TN13 1EE
T: (01732) 452689
F: (01732) 455422
E: rcjollye@aol.com

Wendy Wood ♦♦♦♦
86 Childsbridge Lane, Seal, Sevenoaks TN15 0BW
T: (01732) 763755
E: wendywood@freeuk.com
I: www.wendywood.co.uk

SHALFORD
Surrey

2 Northfield ♦♦♦
Summersbury Drive, Shalford, Guildford GU4 8JN
T: (01483) 570431
E: tonymorden@freeuk.com

SHARPTHORNE
West Sussex

Coach House ♦♦♦
Courtlands, Chilling Street, Sharpthorne, East Grinstead RH19 4JF
T: (01342) 810512
F: (01342) 810512
I: www.sussexlive.com

Saxons ♦♦♦♦
Horsted Lane, Sharpthorne, East Grinstead RH19 4HY
T: (01342) 810821
E: aliexcol@aol.com

SHEERNESS
Kent

Kingsferry House Bed and Breakfast ♦♦
247 Queenborough Road, Halfway, Sheerness, ME12 3EW
T: (01795) 663606

Sheppey Guest House ♦
214 Queenborough Road, Halfway, Minster-in-Sheppey, Sheerness ME12 3DF
T: (01795) 665950
F: (01795) 661200
E: mallas@btinternet.com

SHEPPERTON
Surrey

Splash Cottage ♦♦♦
91 Watersplash Road, Shepperton, TW17 0EE
T: (01932) 229987
F: (01932) 229987
E: info@lazy-river.co.uk
I: www.lazy-river.co.uk

SHERE
Surrey

Lockhurst Hatch Farm Rating Applied For
Lockhurst Hatch Lane, Shere, Guildford GU5 9JN
T: (01483) 202689

SHIPLEY
West Sussex

Goffsland Farm ♦♦♦♦
Shipley, Horsham RH13 7BQ
T: (01403) 730434
F: (01403) 730434

SHOLDEN
Kent

The Sportsman
♦♦♦♦ GOLD AWARD
23 The Street, Sholden, Deal CT14 0AL
T: (01304) 374973
F: (01304) 374973
E: sportsmansholden@aol.com

SHOREHAM
Kent

Church House
♦♦♦♦ SILVER AWARD
Church Street, Shoreham, Sevenoaks TN14 7SB
T: (01959) 522241
F: (01959) 522241
E: katehowie@compuserve.com
I: www.intacom.co.uk/shore/churchouse.htm

Preston Farmhouse ♦♦♦♦
Preston Farm, Shoreham, Sevenoaks TN14 7UD
T: (01959) 522029

SISSINGHURST
Kent

1 Hillview Cottage ♦♦♦
Starvenden Lane, Sissinghurst, Cranbrook TN17 2AN
T: (01580) 712823

The Oast House
♦♦♦♦ SILVER AWARD
Buckhurst Farm, Sissinghurst, Cranbrook TN17 2AA
T: (01580) 720044
F: (01580) 720022

SITTINGBOURNE
Kent

Hempstead House ♦♦♦♦♦
London Road, Bapchild, Sittingbourne ME9 9PP
T: (01795) 428020
F: (01795) 436362
E: info@hempsteadhouse.co.uk
I: www.hempsteadhouse.co.uk

Scuttington Manor Guest House ♦♦♦♦
Dully Road, Dully, Sittingbourne, ME9 9PA
T: (01795) 521316
F: (01795) 521316

Woodstock Guest House ♦♦♦♦
25 Woodstock Road, Sittingbourne, ME10 4HJ
T: (01795) 421516
F: (01795) 421516
E: woodstockbnb@aol.com

SMARDEN
Kent

Chequers Inn ♦♦♦♦
The Street, Smarden, Ashford TN27 8QA
T: (01233) 770217
F: (01233) 770623

Hereford Oast ♦♦♦♦
Smarden, Ashford TN27 8PA
T: (01233) 770541
F: (01233) 770045
E: peter@hill5050.fsnet.co.uk

SOUTHWATER
West Sussex

Meadow House ♦♦♦
Church Lane, Bonfire Hill, Southwater, Horsham RH13 7BT
T: (01403) 730324
F: (01403) 730324

ST-MARGARETS-AT-CLIFFE
Kent

Holm Oaks ♦♦♦♦
Dover Road, St-Margarets-at-Cliffe, Dover CT15 6EP
T: (01304) 852990
F: (01304) 853433
E: holmoaks@hotmail.com

Merzenich Guest House ♦♦♦
Station Road, St-Margarets-at-Cliffe, Dover CT15 6AY
T: (01304) 852260
F: (01304) 852167
E: robclaringbould@lineone.net
I: www.smoothhound.co.uk/hotels/merzen.html

STANSTED
Kent

The Black Horse ♦♦♦♦
Tumblefield Road, Stansted, Sevenoaks TN15 7PR
T: (01732) 822355
F: (01732) 824415

STAPLEHURST
Kent

Overbridge Barn ♦♦♦♦
Marden Road, Staplehurst, Tonbridge TN12 0JH
T: (01580) 890189
F: (01580) 893164
E: paula@overbridge.co.uk
I: www.overbridge.co.uk

The White Cottage ♦♦♦♦
Hawkenbury Road, Hawkenbury, Staplehurst, Tonbridge TN12 0DU
T: (01580) 892554
F: (01580) 891553
E: batten.j.@talk21.com

STEDHAM
West Sussex

Meadowhills ♦
Stedham, Midhurst GU29 0PT
T: (01730) 812609
I: www.meadowhills.co.uk

STELLING MINNIS
Kent

Great Field Farm
♦♦♦♦ SILVER AWARD
Misling Lane, Stelling Minnis, Canterbury CT4 6DE
T: (01227) 709223
F: (01227) 709223
E: Greatfieldfarm@aol.com

STEYNING
West Sussex

Chequer Inn ♦♦♦
41 High Street, Steyning, BN44 3RE
T: (01903) 814437
F: (01903) 879707
E: chequerinn@btinternet.com

STONE-IN-OXNEY
Kent

Tighe Farmhouse ♦♦♦♦
Stone-in-Oxney, Tenterden TN30 7JU
T: (01233) 758251
F: (01233) 758054
I: www.ryetourism.co.uk

STONELEIGH
Surrey

Number Sixty Two ♦♦♦♦
62 Newbury Gardens, Stoneleigh, Epsom KT19 0NX
T: (020) 8393 5227
F: (020) 8393 5885
E: b&b@number62.fsbusiness.co.uk
I: www.number62.biz

STORRINGTON
West Sussex

Chardonnay ♦♦♦♦
Hampers Lane, Storrington, Pulborough RH20 3HZ
T: (01903) 746688
E: annsearancke@bigfoot.com
I: www.sussexlive.co.uk

STROOD
Kent

Cedars Hotel ♦♦♦
38 London Road, Strood, Rochester ME2 3HU
T: (01634) 290277
F: (01634) 290277

Redwood House ♦♦♦
84 Goddington Road, Strood, Rochester ME2 3DE
T: (01634) 725880
F: (01034) 725880
E: junejmprior@aol.com

The White Cottage ♦♦♦
41 Rede Court Road, Strood, Rochester ME2 3SP
T: (01634) 719988

SUTTON AT HONE
Kent

Hamilton ♦♦♦
Arnolds Lane, Sutton at Hone, Dartford DA4 9HE
T: (01322) 272535
F: (01322) 284856

SUTTON VALENCE
Kent

Sparks Oast Farm ♦♦♦
Forsham lane, Sutton Valence, Maidstone ME17 3EW
T: (01622) 842213
E: sparks-oast@supanet.com
I: www.s-h-systems.co.uk/hotels/sparksoa.html

TENTERDEN
Kent

Collina House Hotel ♦♦♦♦
East Hill, Tenterden, TN30 6RL
T: (01580) 764852
F: (01580) 762224
E: enquiries@collinahousehotel.co.uk
I: www.collinahousehotel.co.uk

11 East Hill ♦♦♦
Tenterden, TN30 6RL
T: (01580) 766805

Eight Bells Public House ♦♦♦
43 High Street, Tenterden, TN30 6BJ
T: (01580) 762788
F: (01580) 766070

Old Burren ♦♦♦
25 Ashford Road, Tenterden, TN30 6LL
T: (01580) 764442
E: poo@burren.fsbusiness.co.uk
I: www.oldburren.co.uk

The Tower House ♦♦♦
Ashford Road, Tenterden, TN30 6LL
T: (01580) 761920
F: (01580) 764664

White Cottage ♦♦♦
London Beach, St Michaels, Tenterden TN30 6SR
T: (01233) 850583
I: www.smoothhound.co.uk/shs.html

White Lion Hotel ♦♦♦♦
High Street, Tenterden, TN30 6BD
T: (01580) 765077
F: (01580) 764157

THURNHAM Kent

Court Farm Farmhouse ♦♦♦♦
Thurnham Lane, Thurnham, Maidstone ME14 3LH
T: (01622) 737305
F: (01622) 737305
E: monleggo1@agriplus.net
I: www.courtfarmfarmhouse.co.uk

TICEHURST East Sussex

The Bull Inn ♦♦♦
Three Leg Cross, Ticehurst, Wadhurst TN5 7HH
T: (01580) 200586
F: (01580) 201289
E: michael@thebullinn.co.uk
I: www.thebullinn.co.uk

Cherry Tree Inn ♦♦♦
Dale Hill, Ticehurst, Wadhurst TN5 7DG
T: (01580) 201229
F: (01580) 201325

TILMANSTONE Kent

Plough and Harrow ♦♦
Dover Road, Tilmanstone, Deal Ct14 0HX
T: (01304) 617582

TONBRIDGE Kent

Brown Bear's Den ♦♦♦
95 Barden Road, Tonbridge, TN9 1UR
T: (01732) 351195
E: brownbearsden@aol.com

9 The Crescent ♦♦♦
Tonbridge, TN9 1JH
T: (01732) 366919

86 Hadlow Road ♦♦
Tonbridge, TN9 1PA
T: (01732) 357332

Hogswell Bed and Breakfast ♦♦♦♦
Hogswell, Three Elm Lane, Tonbridge, TN11 0AD
T: (01732) 850283
F: (01732) 850283
E: richard.morley@dial.pipex.com
I: www.hogswell.dial.pipex.com

Lodge Oast ♦♦♦♦
Horns Lodge Lane, Shipbourne Road, Tonbridge, TN11 9NJ
T: (01732) 833976
F: (01732) 838394
E: maryann@lodgeoast.freeserve.co.uk
I: www.lodgeoast.electricfence.co.uk

Marigolds ♦♦♦
19 Old Hadlow Road, Tonbridge, TN10 4EY
T: (01732) 356539
E: jmtn10@aol.com
I: www.tonbridge-kent.com

Masters ♦♦♦
Matfield Green, Tonbridge, TN12 7LA
T: (01892) 722126
F: (01892) 722126

70 The Ridgeway ♦♦♦
Tonbridge, TN10 4NN
T: (01732) 366459
F: (01732) 366459

30 Stacey Road ♦♦♦
Tonbridge, TN10 3AR
T: (01732) 358027

TOYS HILL Kent

Corner Cottage
Rating Applied For
Puddledock Lane, Toys Hill, Westerham TN16 1PY
T: (01732) 750362
F: (01959) 561911
E: olszowskiathome@jshmanco.com

UCKFIELD East Sussex

Hooke Hall
♦♦♦♦♦ GOLD AWARD
250 High Street, Uckfield, TN22 1EN
T: (01825) 761578
F: (01825) 768025
E: a.percy@virgin.net
I: www.hookehall.co.uk

Old Mill Farm
♦♦♦♦ SILVER AWARD
High Hurstwood, Uckfield TN22 4AD
T: (01825) 732279
F: (01825) 732279

The Old Oast ♦♦♦♦
Underhill, Maresfield, Uckfield, TN22 3AY
T: (01825) 768886

South Paddock
♦♦♦♦♦ SILVER AWARD
Maresfield Park, Uckfield, TN22 2HA
T: (01825) 762335

UPCHURCH Kent

Suffield House
♦♦♦♦ SILVER AWARD
The Street, Upchurch, Sittingbourne ME9 7EU
T: (01634) 230409

WADHURST East Sussex

Best Beech Inn ♦♦♦
Best Beech, Mayfield Lane, Wadhurst, TN5 6JH
T: (01892) 782046
F: (01892) 785092
I: www.bestbeechinn.com

Four Keys ♦♦
Station Road, Wadhurst, TN5 6RZ
T: (01892) 782252
F: (01892) 784113

Spring Cottage ♦♦♦
Best Beech Hill, Wadhurst, TN5 6JH
T: (01892) 783896
F: (01892) 784866
E: enquiries@southerncrosstravel.co.uk

WALBERTON West Sussex

Felsted Cottage ♦♦♦♦
Arundel Road, Walberton, Arundel BN18 0QP
T: (01243) 814237
E: felstedcott.bandb@btopenworld.com

Longacre Bed & Breakfast ♦♦♦
The Street, Walberton, Arundel BN18 0PY
T: (01243) 543542
F: (01243) 543342
E: longacreb&b@hotmail.com

Oaks Lodge ♦♦♦♦
Yapton Lane, Walberton, Arundel BN18 0LS
T: (01243) 552865
F: (01243) 553862

WALMER Kent

Hardicot Guest House ♦♦♦♦
Kingsdown Road, Walmer, Deal CT14 8AW
T: (01304) 373867
F: (01304) 389234
E: guestboss@talk21.com
I: www.smoothhound.co.uk/hotels/hardicot.html

WALTHAM Kent

Beech Bank
♦♦♦♦ SILVER AWARD
Duckpit Lane, Waltham, Canterbury CT4 5QA
T: (01227) 700302
F: (01227) 700302

WALTON-ON-THAMES Surrey

Beech Tree Lodge ♦♦♦
7 Rydens Avenue, Walton-on-Thames, KT12 3JB
T: (01932) 242738
E: joanspiteri@aol.com
I: www.smoothhound.co.uk/hotels

WARLINGHAM Surrey

Glenmore ♦♦♦
Southview Road, Warlingham, Oxted CR6 9JE
T: (01883) 624530
F: (01883) 624199
E: thirzapayne@hotmail.co.uk

WARNHAM West Sussex

Nowhere House ♦♦♦
Dorking Road, Horsham, RH12 3RZ
T: (01306) 627272
F: (01306) 627190

WATERSFIELD West Sussex

Beacon Lodge B & B ♦♦♦♦
London Road, Watersfield, Arundel, RH20 1NH
T: (01798) 831026
F: (01798) 831026
E: beaconlodge@hotmail.com
I: www.beaconlodge.co.uk

WEST BRABOURNE Kent

Bulltown Farmhouse Bed & Breakfast ♦♦♦
Bulltown Lane, West Brabourne, Ashford TN25 5NB
T: (01233) 813505
F: (01227) 709544
E: wiltons@bulltown.fsnet.co.uk

WEST CHILTINGTON West Sussex

New Barn Cottage ♦♦♦♦
New Barn Lane, off Harborough Hill, West Chiltington, Pulborough RH20 2PP
T: (01798) 813231
F: (01798) 813231
I: www.sussexlive.com

WEST CLANDON Surrey

The Oaks ♦♦♦
Highcotts Lane, West Clandon, Guildford GU4 7XA
T: (01483) 222531
F: (01483) 224454
E: catherinebroad@callnetuk.com

Ways Cottage ♦♦♦♦
Lime Grove, West Clandon, Guildford GU4 7UT
T: (01483) 222454

WEST DEAN West Sussex

Lodge Hill Farm ♦♦♦
West Dean, Chichester PO18 0RT
T: (01243) 535245

WEST HARTING West Sussex

Three Quebec ♦♦♦♦
West Harting, Petersfield GU31 5PG
T: (01730) 825386
F: (01730) 826652
E: stevens@threequebec.co.uk
I: www.threequebec.co.uk

WEST HORSLEY Surrey

Brinford ♦♦♦
off Shere Road, West Horsley, Leatherhead KT24 6EJ
T: (01483) 283636

Silkmore ♦♦♦♦
Silkmore Lane, West Horsley, Leatherhead KT24 6JQ
T: (01483) 282042
F: (01483) 284109
E: kimpton@leporello.free-online.co.uk

Woolgars House ♦♦♦♦
Blakes Lane, West Horsley, Leatherhead KT24 6EA
T: (01483) 222915
F: (01483) 222431
E: barry.lester@virgin.net

WEST MALLING
Kent

Appledene ♦♦♦♦
164 Norman Road, West Malling, ME19 6RW
T: (01732) 842071
F: (01732) 842071
E: appledene@westmalling.freeserve.co.uk

Westfields Farm ♦♦♦
St Vincents Lane, Addington, West Malling ME19 5BW
T: (01732) 843209

WEST WITTERING
West Sussex

The Beach House ♦♦♦
Rookwood Road, West Wittering, Chichester PO20 8LT
T: (01243) 514800
F: (01243) 514798
E: info@beachhse.co.uk
I: www.beachhse.co.uk

Thornton Cottage
♦♦♦♦ SILVER AWARD
Chichester Road, West Wittering, Chichester PO20 8QA
T: (01243) 512470
F: (01243) 512470
E: thornton@b-and-b.fsbusiness.co.uk

WESTCOTT
Surrey

Corner House Bed & Breakfast ♦♦
Guildford Road, Westcott, Dorking RH4 3QE
T: (01306) 888798

WESTERHAM
Kent

Worples Field ♦♦♦♦
Farley Common, Westerham, TN16 1UB
T: (01959) 562869
E: marr@worplesfield.com
I: www.worplesfield.com

WESTFIELD
East Sussex

Four Winds ♦♦♦♦
Parsonage Lane, Westfield, Hastings TN35 4SH
T: (01424) 752585
F: (01424) 762828
E: stewarts@4-winds.fsnet.co.uk
I: www.4-winds.org

WESTGATE ON SEA
Kent

Seacroft ♦♦♦
108 St Mildreds Road, Westgate on Sea, Margate CT8 8RL
T: (01843) 833334

White Lodge Guest House ♦♦♦
12 Domneva Road, Westgate on Sea, Margate CT8 8PE
T: (01843) 831828
E: whitelodge.thanet@btinternet.com
I: www.whitelodge.thanet.btinternet.co.uk

WESTMARSH
Kent

The Way Out Inn ♦♦♦
Westmarsh, Canterbury CT3 2LP
T: (01304) 812899
F: (01304) 813181

WHITSTABLE
Kent

Alliston House ♦♦♦
1 Joy Lane, Whitstable, CT5 4LS
T: (01227) 779066
F: (01227) 779066
E: allistonhouse@aol.com

The Cherry Garden ♦♦♦
62 Joy Lane, Whitstable, CT5 4LT
T: (01227) 266497

Hotel Continental ♦♦♦
29 Beach Walk, Whitstable, CT5 2BP
T: (01227) 280280
F: (01227) 280257
I: www.oysterfishery.co.uk

Copeland House ♦♦♦
4 Island Wall, Whitstable, CT15 1EP
T: (01227) 266207
F: (01227) 266207

Marine ♦♦♦
Marine Parade, Tankerton, Whitstable, CT5 2BE
T: (01227) 272672
F: (01227) 264721
E: marine@shepherd-neame.co.uk
I: www.shepherd-neame.co.uk

Marine Lodge ♦♦♦
82 Marine Parade, Tankerton, Whitstable, CT5 2BA
T: (01227) 273707
E: christine.tilley@tesco.net

Victoria Villa
♦♦♦♦ GOLD AWARD
Victoria Street, Whitstable, CT5 1JB
T: (01227) 779191
F: (01227) 779191
E: victoria-villa@i12.com
I: www.victoria-villa.i12.com

Windyridge Guest House ♦♦♦♦
Wraik Hill, Whitstable, CT5 3BY
T: (01227) 263506
F: (01227) 771191

WILLESBOROUGH
Kent

Rosemary House ♦♦♦
94 Church Road, Willesborough, Ashford TN24 0JG
T: (01233) 625215

WILMINGTON
Kent

66 Tredegar Road ♦♦♦
Wilmington, Dartford DA2 7AZ
T: (01322) 270659

WINCHELSEA
East Sussex

The New Inn ♦♦♦
German Street, Winchelsea, TN36 4EN
T: (01797) 226252
E: newinnwsea@aol.com

St Anthonys ♦♦♦♦
Castle Street, Winchelsea, TN36 4EL
T: (01797) 226255

Wickham Manor ♦♦♦
Pannel Lane, Winchelsea, TN36 4AG
T: (01797) 226216
F: (01797) 226216

Winchelsea Lodge Motel & Restaurant ♦♦♦♦
Hastings Road (A259), Winchelsea, TN36 4AD
T: (01797) 226211
F: (01797) 226312
E: orlandoatwinchelsealodge@tinyworld.co.uk
I: winchelsea-lodge-motel.co.uk

WINGHAM
Kent

Dambridge Oast ♦♦♦♦
Staple Road, Wingham, Canterbury CT3 1LU
T: (01227) 720082
F: (01227) 720082
E: info@pagoast.co.uk
I: www.pagoust.co.uk

WISBOROUGH GREEN
West Sussex

Lower Sparr Farm ♦♦♦♦
Skiff Lane, Wisborough Green, Billingshurst RH14 0AA
T: (01403) 820465
F: (01403) 820678
E: sclater@lowersparrbb.f9.co.uk
I: www.lowersparrbb.f9.co.uk

WOKING
Surrey

Amberhurst ♦♦♦
Hollybank Road, Hook Heath, Woking, GU22 0JN
T: (01483) 762748
F: (01483) 762748

Grantchester ♦♦♦
Boughton Hall Avenue, Send, Woking, GU23 7DF
T: (01483) 225383
F: (01483) 596490
E: gary@hotpotmail.com

St Columba's House ♦♦
Maybury Hill, Woking, GU22 8AB
T: (01483) 766498
F: (01483) 740441
E: retreats@st.columba.org.uk
I: www.stcolumbashouse.org.uk

Swallow Barn ♦♦♦
Milford Green, Chobham, Woking, GU24 8AU
T: (01276) 856030
F: (01276) 856030
E: swallowbarn@compuserve.com
I: www.bestbandb.co.uk

WOODCHURCH
Kent

Shirkoak Farm
♦♦♦♦ SILVER AWARD
Bethersden Road, Woodchurch, Ashford TN26 3PZ
T: (01233) 860056
F: (01233) 861402
E: shirkoakfarm@aol.com
I: www.shirkoakfarm.com

WORPLESDON
Surrey

Hillside ♦♦♦♦
Perry Hill, Worplesdon, Guildford GU3 3RF
T: (01483) 232051
F: (01483) 232051
I: www.thehillsidehotel.com

Maytime ♦♦♦
43 Envis Way, Fairlands, Worplesdon, Guildford GU3 3NJ
T: (01483) 235025
E: e.m.warby@amserve.net

WORTHING
West Sussex

The Acacia
Rating Applied For
5-7 Warwick Gardens, Worthing, BN11 1PE
T: 0870 710 7313
F: (01903) 210068

Angel Lodge ♦♦♦♦
19 Malvern Close, Worthing, BN11 2HE
T: (01903) 233002
F: (01903) 233002
E: angellodge19@aol.com
I: www.angellodge.co.uk

The Beacons Hotel ♦♦♦♦
18 Shelley Road, Worthing, BN11 1TU
T: (01903) 230948
F: (01903) 230948
I: www.smoothhound.com/worthing

Beechwood Hall Hotel ♦♦♦
Wykeham Road, Worthing, BN11 4JD
T: (01903) 205049

Blair House Hotel
Rating Applied For
11 St Georges Road, Worthing, BN11 2DS
T: (01903) 234071
F: (01903) 234071
E: stay@blairhousehotel.freeserve.co.uk
I: www.blairhousehotel.co.uk

Bonchurch House ♦♦♦♦
1 Winchester Road, Worthing, BN11 4DJ
T: (01903) 202492
F: (01903) 202492
E: bonchurch@enta.net
I: www.smoothhound.co.uk/hotels/bonchurc.html

Brooke House
♦♦♦♦ SILVER AWARD
6 Westbrooke, Worthing, BN11 1RE
T: (01903) 600291
F: (01903) 600291

The Brunswick ♦♦
Thorn Road, Worthing, BN11 3ND
T: (01903) 202141
E: b&b@brunswick.freeserve.co.uk
I: www.brunswick.fsnet.co.uk

Bute House ♦♦♦♦
325 Brighton Road, Worthing, BN11 2HP
T: (01903) 210247
F: (01903) 208109

Camelot House ♦♦♦
20 Gannon Road, Worthing, BN11 2DT
T: (01903) 204334
F: (01903) 207006
E: stay@camelotguesthouse.co.uk
I: www.camelotguesthouse.co.uk

Delmar Hotel ♦♦♦
1-2 New Parade, Worthing, BN11 2BQ
T: (01903) 211834
F: (01903) 219052
I: www.SmoothHound.co.uk/hotels/delmar.html

Haytor Guest House ♦♦♦
5 Salisbury Road, Worthing, BN11 1RB
T: (01903) 235287

Heenefields Guest House ♦♦♦♦
98 Heene Road, Worthing, BN11 3RE
T: (01903) 538780
E: heenefields.guesthouse@virgin.net
I: www.heenefields.com

High Beach ♦♦♦♦
201 Brighton Road, Worthing, BN11 2EX
T: (01903) 236389
F: (01903) 213399
E: highbeach@hotmail.com

High Trees Guest House ♦♦♦♦
2 Warwick Gardens, Worthing, BN11 1PE
T: (01903) 236668
F: (01903) 601688
E: bill@hightreesguesthouse.co.uk
I: www.hightreesguesthouse.co.uk

Marcroft ♦♦♦
17 St Georges Road, Worthing, BN11 2DS
T: (01903) 233626
E: marcroftguesthouse@talk21.com

Marine View Hotel ♦♦♦
111 Marine Parade, Worthing, BN11 3QG
T: (01903) 238413
F: (01903) 238630
E: marineviewhotel@talk21.com

Merton House ♦♦♦♦
96 Broadwater Road, Worthing, BN14 8AW
T: (01903) 238222
F: (01903) 238222
E: stay@mertonhouse.freeserve.co.uk
I: www.mertonhouse.co.uk

The Moorings Hotel ♦♦♦♦
4 Selden Road, Worthing, BN11 2LL
T: (01903) 208882
F: (01903) 236878
E: annette@mooringshotel.fsnet.co.uk

Oakville Guest House ♦♦♦♦
13 Wyke Avenue, Worthing, BN11 1PB
T: (01903) 205026
F: (01903) 205026
E: oakville@denyert.fsbusiness.co.uk
I: www.worthingnet.com/oakville

Olinda Guest House ♦♦♦♦
199 Brighton Road, Worthing, BN11 2EX
T: (01903) 206114
F: (01903) 206114
E: info@olindaguesthouse.co.uk
I: www.olindaguesthouse.co.uk

Pebble Beach ♦♦♦
281 Brighton Road, Worthing, BN11 2HG
T: (01903) 210766
F: (01903) 210766
E: pebblebeach281@aol.com
I: www.worthingnet.com/pebblebeach

Queens Lodge ♦♦♦♦
2 Queens Road, Worthing, BN11 3LX
T: (01903) 205519
E: enquiries.queenslodge@virgin.net

The Rose Garden
Rating Applied For
46 Offington Avenue, Worthing, BN14 0PJ
T: (01903) 263095
F: (01903) 263095

Rosedale House ♦♦♦♦
12 Bath Road, Worthing, BN11 3NU
T: (01903) 233181
E: rosedale@amserve.net

St Albans Guest House ♦♦♦♦
143 Brighton Road, Worthing, BN11 2EU
T: (01903) 206623
F: (01903) 525597
E: suemurraywha@aol.com

School House ♦♦♦♦
11 Ambrose Place, Worthing, BN11 1PZ
T: (01903) 206823
F: (01903) 821902

Sea Lodge ♦♦♦
183 Brighton Road, Worthing, BN11 2EX
T: (01903) 201214
F: (01903) 201214

Southdene Guest House ♦♦
41 Warwick Gardens, Worthing, BN11 1PF
T: (01903) 232909

Tamara Guest House ♦♦♦
19 Alexandra Road, Worthing, BN11 2DX
T: (01903) 520332

Tudor Guest House ♦♦♦
5 Windsor Road, Worthing, BN11 2LU
T: (01903) 210265
F: (01903) 210265
E: stay@tudor-worthing.co.uk
I: www.tudor-worthing.co.uk

Woodlands Guest House ♦♦♦
20 Warwick Gardens, Worthing, BN11 1PF
T: (01903) 233557
F: (01903) 536925
E: woodlandsghse@cwcom.net
I: www.woodlands20-22.freeserve.co.uk

WROTHAM
Kent

Hillside House ♦♦♦
Gravesend Road, Wrotham, Sevenoaks TN15 7JH
T: (01732) 822564
E: clive@broteham.freeserve.co.uk

WYE
Kent

Mistral ♦♦♦
3 Oxenturn Road, Wye, Ashford TN25 5BH
T: (01233) 813011
F: (01233) 813011
E: geoff@chapman.invictanet.co.uk
I: www.wye.org

CAMPUS ACCOMMODATION

BRADFORD
West Yorkshire

Bradford College
Rating Applied For
Margaret McMillan Hall of Residence, Easby Road, Bradford BD7 1QZ
T: (01274) 733291
F: (01274) 741358
E: andrewa@bilk.ac.uk
I: www.bilk.ac.uk

University of Bradford
Rating Applied For
Laiseridge Lane, Dennis Bellamy Hall, Bradford BD5 0NH
T: (01274) 234898
F: (01274) 234881
E: j.humphreys/x11905@bradford.ac.uk
I: bradford.ac.uk

BRIGHTON
East Sussex

University of Sussex
Rating Applied For
Student Services, Bramber House, Falmer, Brighton BN1 9QU
T: (01273) 877412
F: (01273) 877366
E: P.M.Knight@sussex.ac.uk

CANTERBURY
Kent

Christ Church University College
★ - ★★★
North Holmes Road, Canterbury CT1 1QU
T: (01227) 782225
F: (01227) 782528

UKC Hospitality
★★ - ★★★
Tanglewood, The University, Canterbury CT2 7LX
T: (01227) 828000
F: (01227) 828019
E: hospitality-enquiry@ukc.ac.uk
I: www.ukc.ac.uk/hospitality/

EGHAM
Surrey

Royal Holloway University of London
Rating Applied For
Egham Hill, Egham TW20 0EX
T: (01784) 443045
F: (01784) 443797
E: sales-office@rhul.ac.uk
I:www.rhul.ac.uk/rc

HATFIELD
Hertfordshire

University of Hertfordshire
★★
Fielder Centre, Hatfield Avenue, Hatfield AL10 9FL
T: (01707) 284841
F: (01707) 268407
E: sales@fieldercentre.co.uk
I: www.fieldercentre.co.uk

NOTTINGHAM
Nottinghamshire

University of Nottingham
Rating Applied For
C52 Portland Building, University Park, Nottingham NG7 2RD
E: uncc@nottongham.au.uk
I: uncc.co.uk

OXFORD
Oxfordshire

St Hugh's College
Rating Applied For
Rachel Trickett Building, St Margarets Road, Oxford OX2 6LE
T: (01865) 274921
F: (01865) 274912
I: www.conferences@st-hughs.ox.ac.uk

READING
Berkshire

Reading Student Village
★★★★
Sherfield Drive, Reading RG2 7EZ
T: 0870 12 5003
F: (0207) 017 8273
E: sjennie.bellotto@jarvis-uk.com
I: www.thestudentvillage.com

SOUTHBOROUGH
Kent

Salomons
★★★
David Salomons Estate, Broomhill Road, Southborough, Royal Tunbridge Wells TN3 0TG
T: (01892) 515152
F: (01892) 539102
E: m.salomonson@salomons.org.uk
I: www.salomonscentre.org.uk

Establishments printed in blue have a detailed entry in this guide

Information

The National Quality Assurance Standards

A rating you can trust

When you're looking for a place to stay, you need a rating system you can trust. The English Tourism Council's ratings are your clear guide to what to expect, in an easy-to-understand form. Properties are visited annually by our trained impartial assessors, so you can have confidence that your accommodation has been thoroughly checked and rated for quality before you make a booking.

Using a simple One to Five Diamond rating, the system puts a much greater emphasis on quality and is based on research which shows exactly what consumers are looking for when choosing accommodation.

'Guest Accommodation' covers a wide variety of serviced accommodation for which England is renowned, including guesthouses, bed and breakfasts, inns and farmhouses. Establishments are rated from one to five Diamonds. The same minimum requirement for facilities and services applies to all Guest Accommodation from One to Five Diamonds. Progressively higher levels of quality and customer care must be provided for each of the One to Five Diamond ratings. The rating reflects the unique character of Guest Accommodation, and covers areas such as cleanliness, service and hospitality, bedrooms, bathrooms and food quality.

Look out, too, for the English Tourism Council's Gold and Silver Awards, which are awarded to those establishments which not only achieve the overall quality required for their Diamond rating, but also reach the highest levels of quality in those specific areas which guests identify as being really important for them. They will reflect the quality of comfort and cleanliness you'll find in the bedrooms and bathrooms and the quality of service you'll enjoy throughout your stay.

Diamond ratings are your sign of quality assurance, giving you the confidence to book the accommodation that meets your expectations.

What to expect at each rating level

The Diamond ratings for Guest Accommodation reflect visitor expectations of this sector. The quality of what is provided is more important to visitors than a wide range of facilities and services. Therefore, the same minimum requirement for facilities and services applies to all Guest Accommodation from One to Five Diamonds, while progressively higher levels of quality and customer care must be provided for each of the One to Five Diamond ratings.

- **At One Diamond Guest Accommodation, you will find:**

An acceptable overall level of quality and helpful service. Accommodation offering, as a minimum, a full cooked or continental breakfast. Other meals, where provided, will be freshly prepared. You will have a comfortable bed, with clean bed linen and towels and fresh soap. Adequate heating and hot water available at reasonable times for baths or showers at no extra charge.

- **At Two Diamond Guest Accommodation, you will find (in addition to what is provided at One Diamond):**

A good overall level of quality and comfort, with a greater emphasis on guest care in all areas.

- **At Three Diamond Guest Accommodation, you will find (in addition to what is provided at Two Diamond):**

A very good overall level of quality. For example, good quality, comfortable bedrooms; well maintained, practical décor; a good choice of quality items available for breakfast; other meals, where provided, will be freshly cooked from good quality ingredients. A greater degree of comfort provided for you, with good levels of customer care.

- **At Four Diamond Guest Accommodation, you will find (in addition to what is provided at Three Diamond):**

An excellent overall level of quality in all areas and customer care showing very good levels of attention to your needs.

- **At Five Diamond Guest Accommodation, you will find** **(in addition to what is provided at Four Diamond):**

An exceptional overall level of quality. For example, ample space with a degree of luxury, an excellent quality bed, high quality furniture, excellent interior design. Breakfast offering a wide choice of high quality fresh ingredients; other meals, where provided, featuring fresh, seasonal, and often local ingredients. Excellent levels of customer care, anticipating your needs.

NB. En suite and private bathrooms contribute to the quality score at all Diamond levels. Please check when booking or see entry details.

Awaiting confirmation of rating

At the time of going to press some establishments featured in this guide had not yet been assessed for their rating for the year 2003 and so their new rating could not be included.
For your information, the most up-to-date information regarding these establishments' ratings is in the listings pages at the back of this guide.

General Advice & Information

MAKING A BOOKING

When enquiring about accommodation, make sure you check prices and other important details. You will also need to state your requirements, clearly and precisely - for example:

- **Arrival and departure dates,** with acceptable alternatives if appropriate.
- **The type of accommodation you need;** for example, room with twin beds, private bathroom.
- **The terms you want;** for example, room only, bed and breakfast, half board, full board.
- **If you have children with you;** their ages, whether you want them to share your room or be next door, any other special requirements, such as a cot.
- **Particular requirements you may have,** such as a special diet.

Booking by letter

Misunderstandings can easily happen over the telephone, so we strongly advise you to confirm your booking in writing if there is time.

Please note that the English Tourism Council does not make reservations - you should write direct to the accommodation.

DEPOSITS

If you make your reservation weeks or months in advance, you will probably be asked for a deposit. The amount will vary according to the time of year, the number of people in your party and how long you plan to stay. The deposit will then be deducted from the final bill when you leave.

PAYMENT ON ARRIVAL

Some establishments may ask you to pay for your room on arrival if you have not booked it in advance. This is especially likely to happen if you arrive late and have little or no luggage.

If you are asked to pay on arrival, it is a good idea to see your room first, to make sure it meets your requirements.

CANCELLATIONS

Legal contract

When you accept accommodation that is offered to you, by telephone or in writing, you enter a legally binding contract with the proprietor.

This means that if you cancel your booking, fail to take up the accommodation or leave early, the proprietor may be entitled to compensation if he or she cannot re-let for all or a good part of the booked period. You will probably forfeit any deposit you have paid, and may well be asked for an additional payment.

The proprietor cannot make a claim until after the booked period, however, and during that time every effort should be made by the proprietor to re-let the accommodation.

If there is a dispute it is sensible for both sides to seek legal advice on the matter.

If you do have to change your travel plans, it is in your own interests to let the proprietors know in writing as soon as possible, to give them a chance to re-let your accommodation.

And remember, if you book by telephone and are asked for your credit card number, you should check whether the proprietor intends charging your credit card account should you later cancel your reservation.
A proprietor should not be able to charge your credit card account with a cancellation unless he or she has made this clear at the time of your booking and you have agreed. However, to avoid later disputes, we suggest you check with the proprietor whether he or she intends to charge your credit card account if you cancel.

INSURANCE

A travel or holiday insurance policy will safeguard you if you have to cancel or change your holiday plans. You can arrange a policy quite cheaply through your insurance company or travel agent. Some hotels also offer their own insurance schemes.

ARRIVING LATE

If you know you will be arriving late in the evening, it is a good idea to say so when you book. If you are delayed on your way, a telephone call to say that you will be late will help prevent any problems when you arrive.

SERVICE CHARGES AND TIPPING

These days many places levy service charges automatically. If they do, they must clearly say so in their offer of accommodation, at the time of booking. Then the service charge becomes part of the legal contract when you accept the offer of accommodation.

If a service charge is levied automatically, there is no need to tip the staff, unless they provide some exceptional service. The usual tip for meals is ten per cent of the total bill.

TELEPHONE CHARGES

Guest Accommodation establishments can set their own charges for telephone calls made through their switchboard or from direct-dial telephones in bedrooms. These charges are often much higher than telephone companies' standard charges (to defray the cost of providing the service).

Comparing costs

It is a condition of the national quality assurance standard, that unit charges for using the telephone are on display, by the phones or with the room information. But in practice it is not always easy to compare these charges with standard telephone rates. Before using the telephone for long-distance calls, you may decide to ask how the charges compare.

SECURITY OF VALUABLES

You can deposit your valuables with the proprietor or manager during your stay, and we recommend you do this as a sensible precaution. Make sure you obtain a receipt for them.

Some places do not accept articles for safe custody, and in that case it is wisest to keep your valuables with you.

Disclaimer

Some proprietors put up a notice which disclaims liability for property brought on to their premises by a guest. In fact, they can only restrict their liability to a minimum laid down by law (The Hotel Proprietors Act 1956).

Under that Act, a proprietor is liable for the value of the loss or damage to any property (except a motor car or its contents) of a guest who has engaged overnight accommodation, but if the proprietor has the notice on display as prescribed under that Act, liability is limited to £50 for one article and a total of £100 for any one guest. The notice must be prominently displayed in the reception area or main entrance. These limits do not apply to valuables you have deposited with the proprietor for safe-keeping, or to property lost through the default, neglect or wilful act of the proprietor or his staff.

BRINGING PETS TO ENGLAND

The quarantine laws have changed in England, and a Pet Travel Scheme (PETS) is currently in operation. Under this scheme pet dogs and cats are able to come into Britain from over 50 countries via certain sea, air and rail routes into England.

Dogs and cats that have been resident in these countries for more than six months may enter the UK under the Scheme, providing they are accompanied by the appropriate documentation. Pet dogs and cats from other countries will still have to undergo six months' quarantine.

For dogs and cats to be able to enter the UK without quarantine under the PETS Scheme they will have to meet certain conditions and travel with the following documents: the official PETS certificate, a certificate of treatment against tapeworm and ticks and a declaration of residence.

For details of participating countries, routes, operators and further information about the PETS scheme please contact the PETS Helpline, DEFRA (Department for Environment, Food and Rural Affairs), 1a Page Street, London SW1P 4PQ - Tel: +44 (0) 870 241 1710
Fax: +44 (0) 20 7904 6834

Email: pets.helpline@defra.gsi.gov.uk, or visit their web site at www.defra.gov.uk/animalh/quarantine

CODE OF CONDUCT

The operator/manager is required to observe the following Code of Conduct:

- To maintain standards of guest care, cleanliness and service appropriate to the type of establishment;
- To describe accurately in any advertisement, brochure, or other printed or electronic media, the facilities and services provided;
- To make clear to visitors exactly what is included in all prices quoted for accommodation, including taxes and any other surcharges. Details of charges for additional services/facilities should also be made clear;
- To give a clear statement of the policy on cancellations to guests at the time of booking, i.e. by telephone, fax or email, as well as information given in a printed format;
- To adhere to, and not to exceed prices quoted at the time of booking for accommodation and other services;
- To advise visitors at the time of booking, and subsequently of any change, if the accommodation offered is in an unconnected annexe or similar, and to indicate the location of such accommodation and any difference in comfort and/or amenities from accommodation in the establishment;
- To give each visitor, on request, details of payments due and a receipt, if required;
- To deal promptly and courteously with all enquiries, requests, bookings and correspondence from visitors;
- Ensure complaint-handling procedures are in place and that complaints received are investigated promptly and courteously and that the outcome is communicated to the visitor;
- To give due consideration to the requirements of visitors with special needs, and to make suitable provision where applicable;
- To provide public liability insurance or comparable arrangement and to comply with applicable planning, safety and other statutory requirements;
- To allow an ETC representative reasonable access to the establishment, on request, to confirm the Code of Conduct is being observed.

COMMENTS AND COMPLAINTS

Guest accommodation and the law

Places that offer accommodation have legal and statutory responsibilities to their customers, such as providing information about prices, providing adequate fire precautions and safeguarding valuables. Like other businesses, they must also abide by the Trades Description Acts 1968 and 1972 when they describe their accommodation and facilities.

All the places featured in this guide have declared that they do fulfil all applicable statutory obligations.

Information

The proprietors themselves supply the descriptions of their establishments and other information for the entries, and they pay to be included in the regional sections of the guide. All the acommodation featured in this guide has also been assessed or has applied for assessment under the new national quality assurance scheme.

The English Tourism Council cannot guarantee accuracy of information in this guide, and accepts no responsibility for any error or misrepresentation. All liability for loss, disappointment, negligence or other damage caused by reliance on the information contained in this guide, or in the event of bankruptcy or liquidation or cessation of trade of any company, individual or firm mentioned, is hereby excluded.

We strongly recommend that you carefully check prices and other details when you book your accommodation.

Problems

Of course, we hope you will not have cause for complaint, but problems do occur from time to time.

If you are dissatisfied with anything, make your complaint to the management immediately. Then the management can take action at once to investigate the matter and put things right. The longer you leave a complaint, the harder it is to deal with it effectively.

In certain circumstances, the English Tourism Council may look into complaints. However, the Council has no statutory control over establishments or their methods of operating. The Council cannot become involved in legal or contractual matters.

If you do have problems that have not been resolved by the proprietor and which you would like to bring to our attention, please write to: Quality Standards Department, English Tourism Council, Thames Tower, Black's Road, Hammersmith, London W6 9EL.

About the Guide Entries

LOCATIONS

Places to stay are listed under the town, city or village where they are located. If a place is out in the countryside, you will find it listed under the nearest village or town.

Town names are listed alphabetically within each regional section of the guide, along with the name of the county or unitary authority they are in (see note on page 21), and their map reference.

MAP REFERENCES

These refer to the colour location maps at the front of the guide. The first figure shown is the map number, the following letter and figure indicate the grid reference on the map.

Some entries were included just before the guide went to press, so they do not appear on the maps.

ADDRESSES

County names, which appear in the town headings, are not repeated in the entries. When you are writing, you should of course make sure you use the full address and postcode.

TELEPHONE NUMBERS

Telephone numbers are listed below the accommodation address for each entry. Area codes are shown in brackets.

PRICES

The prices shown in Where to Stay 2003 are only a general guide; they were supplied to us by proprietors in summer 2002. Remember, changes may occur after the guide goes to press, so we strongly advise you to check prices when you book your accommodation.

Prices are shown in pounds sterling and include VAT where applicable. Some places also include a service charge in their standard tariff, so check this when you book.

Standardised method

There are many different ways of quoting prices for accommodation. We use a standardised method in the guide to allow you to compare prices.

For example, when we show:
Bed and breakfast, the prices shown are for overnight accommodation with breakfast, for single and double rooms.
The double-room price is for two people. If a double room is occupied by one person there is sometimes a reduction in price.
Halfboard, the prices shown are for room, breakfast and evening meal, per person per day, and are usually based on two people sharing a room.

Some places provide only a continental breakfast in the set price, and you may have to pay extra if you want a full English breakfast.

Checking prices

According to the law, hotels and guest accommodation with at least four bedrooms or eight beds must display their overnight accommodation charges in the reception area or entrance. In your own interests, do make sure you check prices and what they include.

Children's rates

You will find that many places charge a reduced rate for children, especially if they share a room with their parents.

Some places charge the full rate, however, when a child occupies a room which might otherwise have been let to an adult.

The upper age limit for reductions for children varies from one hotel to another, so check this when you book.

Seasonal packages and special promotions

Prices often vary through the year, and may be significantly lower outside peak holiday weeks. Many places offer special package rates - fully inclusive weekend breaks, for example - in the autumn, winter and spring. A number of establishments have included, in their enhanced entry information, any special offers, themed breaks etc that are available.

You can get details of other bargain packages that may be available from the establishment themselves, the Regional Tourist Boards or your local Tourist Information Centre (TIC).

Your local travel agent may also have information, and can help you make bookings.

BATHROOMS

Each accommodation entry shows you the number of en suite and private bathrooms available, the number of private showers and the number of public bathrooms.

'En suite bathroom' means the bath or shower and WC are contained behind the main door of the bedroom. 'Private bathroom' means a bath or shower and WC solely for the occupants of one bedroom, on the same floor, reasonably close and with a key provided. 'Private shower' means a shower en suite with the bedroom but no WC.

Public bathrooms normally have a bath, sometimes with a shower attachment. If the availability of a bath is important to you, remember to check when you book.

MEALS

If an establishment serves evening meals, you will find the starting time and the last order times shown in the entry; some smaller places may ask you at breakfast or at midday whether you want an evening meal.

The prices shown in each entry are for bed and breakfast or half board, but many places also offer lunch, as you will see indicated in the entry.

OPENING PERIOD

If an entry does not state 'Open All Year' please check opening period direct with the Guest Accommodation.

SYMBOLS

The at-a-glance symbols included at the end of each entry show many of the services and facilities available at each place. You will find the key to these symbols on the back-cover flap. Open out the flap and you can check the meanings of the symbols as you go.

ALCOHOLIC DRINKS

Many places listed in the guide are licensed to serve alcohol. The licence may be restricted - to diners only, for example - so you may want to check this when you book. If they have a bar this is shown by the 🍷 symbol.

SMOKING

Many places provide non-smoking areas - from no-smoking bedrooms and lounges to no-smoking sections of the restaurant. Some places prefer not to accommodate smokers, and in such cases the descriptions and symbols in each entry makes this clear.

A NOTE ABOUT 'HOTELS'

There is no restriction on any property that provides serviced accommodation using the word Hotel in the title. Hotels with a Star rating meet all the requirements for the 1 Star hotel standard and will usually have a drinks licence and offer meals in addition to breakfast. 'Hotel' establishments in the Guest Accommodation Guide meet the minimum entry requirements for the Guest Accommodation standard but do not automatically meet the Hotel 1 Star requirements

PETS

Many places accept guests with dogs, but we do advise that you check this when you book, and ask if there are any extra charges or rules about exactly where your pet is allowed. The acceptance of dogs is not always extended to cats, and it is strongly advised that cat owners contact the establishment well in advance. Some establishments do not accept pets at all. Pets are welcome where you see this symbol 🐕.

The quarantine laws have changed in England, and pet dogs and cats are able to come into Britain from over 50 countries. For details of the Pet Travel Scheme (PETS) please turn to page 730.

CREDIT AND CHARGE CARDS

The credit and charge cards accepted by a place are listed in the entry following the letters CC.

If you do plan to pay by card, check that the establishment will take your card before you book.

Some proprietors will charge you a higher rate if you pay by credit card rather than cash or cheque. The difference is to cover the percentage paid by the proprietor to the credit card company.

If you are planning to pay by credit card, you may want to ask whether it would, in fact, be cheaper to pay by cheque or cash. When you book by telephone, you may be asked for your credit card number as 'confirmation'. But remember, the proprietor may then charge your credit card account if you cancel your booking. See under Cancellations on page 729.

CONFERENCES AND GROUPS

Places which cater for conferences and meetings are marked with the symbol 🝖. Rates are often negotiable, depending on the time of year, numbers of people involved and any special requirements you may have.

Distance Chart

The distances between towns on the chart below are given to the nearest mile, and are measured along routes based on the quickest travelling time, making maximum use of motorways or dual-carriageway roads. The chart is based upon information supplied by the Automobile Association.

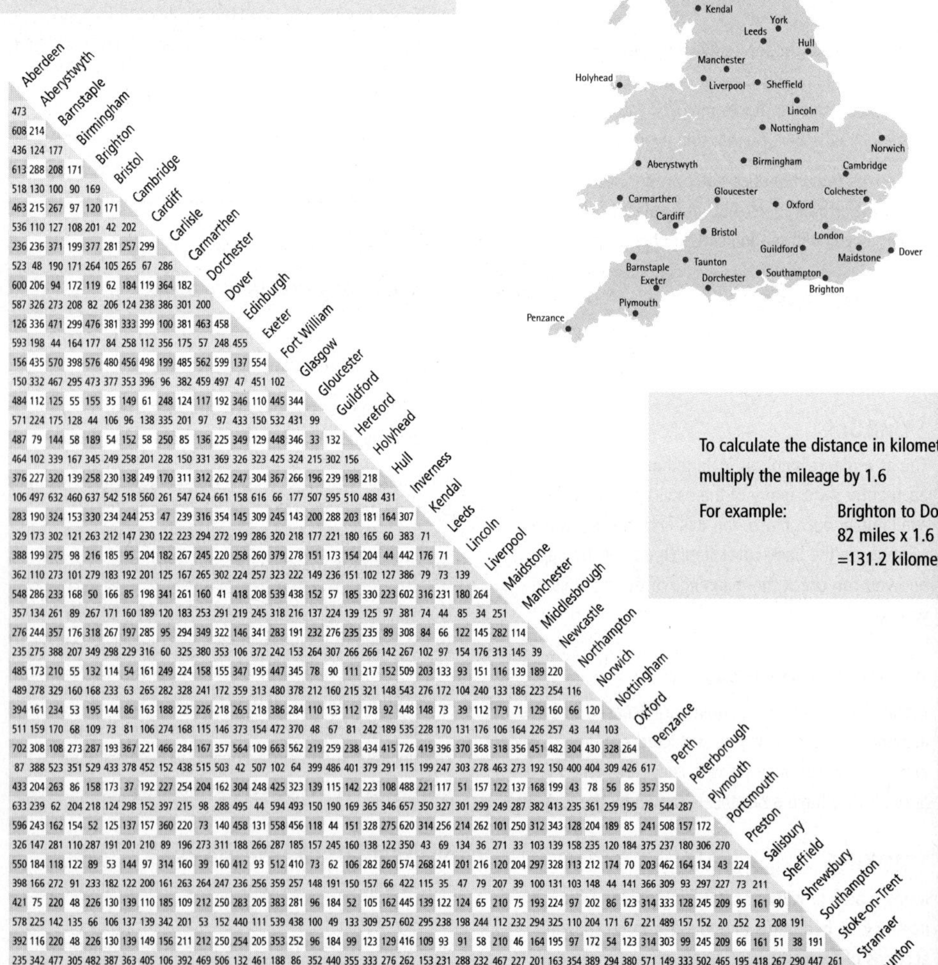

	Aberdeen	Aberystwyth	Barnstaple	Birmingham	Brighton	Bristol	Cambridge	Cardiff	Carlisle	Carmarthen	Dorchester	Dover	Edinburgh	Exeter	Fort William	Glasgow	Gloucester	Guildford	Hereford	Holyhead	Hull	Inverness	Kendal	Leeds	Lincoln	Liverpool	Maidstone	Manchester	Middlesbrough	Newcastle	Northampton	Norwich	Nottingham	Oxford	Penzance	Perth	Peterborough	Plymouth	Portsmouth	Preston	Salisbury	Sheffield	Shrewsbury	Southampton	Stoke-on-Trent	Stranraer	Taunton	Wick	York
Aberystwyth	473
Barnstaple	608	214
Birmingham	436	124	177
Brighton	613	288	208	171
Bristol	518	130	100	90	169
Cambridge	463	215	267	97	120	171
Cardiff	536	110	127	108	201	42	202
Carlisle	236	236	371	199	377	281	257	299
Carmarthen	523	48	190	171	264	105	265	67	286
Dorchester	600	206	94	172	119	62	184	119	364	182
Dover	587	326	273	208	82	206	124	238	386	301	200
Edinburgh	126	336	471	299	476	381	333	399	100	381	463	458
Exeter	593	198	44	164	177	84	258	112	356	175	57	248	455
Fort William	156	435	570	398	576	480	456	498	199	485	562	599	137	554
Glasgow	150	332	467	295	473	377	353	396	96	382	459	497	47	451	102
Gloucester	484	112	125	55	155	35	149	61	248	124	117	192	346	110	445	344
Guildford	571	224	175	128	44	106	96	138	335	201	97	97	433	150	532	431	99
Hereford	487	79	144	58	189	54	152	58	250	85	136	225	349	129	448	346	33	132
Holyhead	464	102	339	167	345	249	258	201	228	150	331	369	326	323	425	324	215	302	156
Hull	376	227	320	139	258	230	138	249	170	311	312	262	247	304	367	266	196	239	198	218
Inverness	106	497	632	460	637	542	518	560	261	547	624	661	158	616	66	177	507	595	510	488	431
Kendal	283	190	324	153	330	234	244	253	47	239	316	354	145	309	245	143	200	288	203	181	164	307
Leeds	329	173	302	121	263	212	147	230	122	223	294	272	199	286	320	218	177	221	180	165	60	383	71
Lincoln	388	199	275	98	216	185	95	204	182	267	245	220	258	260	379	278	151	173	154	204	44	442	176	71
Liverpool	362	110	273	101	279	183	192	201	125	167	265	302	224	257	323	222	149	236	151	102	127	386	79	73	139
Maidstone	548	286	233	168	50	166	85	198	341	261	160	41	418	208	539	438	152	57	185	330	223	602	316	231	180	264
Manchester	357	134	261	89	267	171	160	189	120	183	253	291	219	245	318	216	137	224	139	125	97	381	74	44	85	34	251
Middlesbrough	276	244	357	176	318	267	197	285	95	294	349	322	146	341	283	191	232	276	235	235	89	308	84	66	122	145	282	114
Newcastle	235	275	388	207	349	298	229	316	60	325	380	353	106	372	242	153	264	307	266	266	142	267	102	97	154	176	313	145	39
Northampton	485	173	210	55	132	114	54	161	249	224	158	155	347	195	447	345	78	90	111	217	152	509	203	133	93	151	116	139	189	220
Norwich	489	278	329	160	168	233	63	265	282	328	241	172	359	313	480	378	212	160	215	321	148	543	276	172	104	240	133	186	223	254	116
Nottingham	394	161	234	53	195	144	86	163	188	225	226	218	265	218	386	284	110	153	112	178	92	448	148	73	39	112	179	71	129	160	66	120
Oxford	511	159	170	68	109	73	81	106	274	168	115	146	373	154	472	370	48	67	81	242	189	535	228	170	131	176	106	164	226	257	43	144	103
Penzance	702	308	108	273	287	193	367	221	466	284	167	357	564	109	663	562	219	259	238	434	415	726	419	396	370	368	318	356	451	482	304	430	328	264
Perth	87	388	523	351	529	433	378	452	152	438	515	503	42	507	102	64	399	486	401	379	291	115	199	247	303	278	463	273	192	150	400	404	309	426	617
Peterborough	433	204	263	86	158	173	37	192	227	254	204	162	304	248	425	323	139	115	142	223	108	488	221	117	51	157	122	137	168	199	43	78	56	86	357	350
Plymouth	633	239	62	204	218	124	298	152	397	215	98	288	495	44	594	493	150	190	169	365	346	657	350	327	301	299	249	287	382	413	235	361	259	195	78	544	287
Portsmouth	596	243	162	154	52	125	137	157	360	220	73	140	458	131	558	456	118	44	151	328	275	620	314	256	214	262	101	250	312	343	128	204	189	85	241	508	157	172
Preston	326	147	281	110	287	191	201	210	89	196	273	311	188	266	287	185	157	245	160	138	122	350	43	69	134	36	271	33	103	139	158	235	120	184	375	237	180	306	270
Salisbury	550	184	118	122	89	53	144	97	314	160	39	160	412	93	512	410	73	62	106	282	260	574	268	241	201	216	120	204	297	328	113	212	174	70	203	462	164	134	43	224
Sheffield	398	166	272	91	233	182	122	200	161	263	264	247	236	256	359	257	148	191	150	157	66	422	115	35	47	79	207	39	100	131	103	148	44	141	366	309	93	297	227	73	211
Shrewsbury	421	75	220	48	226	130	139	110	185	109	212	250	283	205	383	281	96	184	52	105	162	445	139	122	124	65	210	75	193	224	97	202	86	123	314	333	128	245	209	95	161	90
Southampton	578	225	142	135	66	106	137	139	342	201	53	152	440	111	539	438	100	49	133	309	257	602	295	238	198	244	112	232	294	325	110	204	171	67	221	489	157	152	20	252	23	208	191
Stoke-on-Trent	392	116	220	48	226	130	139	149	156	211	212	250	254	205	353	252	96	184	99	123	129	416	109	93	91	58	210	46	164	195	97	172	54	123	314	303	99	245	209	66	161	51	38	191
Stranraer	235	342	477	305	482	387	363	405	106	392	469	506	132	461	188	86	352	440	355	333	276	262	153	231	288	232	467	227	201	163	354	389	294	380	571	149	333	502	465	195	418	267	290	447	261
Taunton	560	165	50	131	160	51	225	79	323	142	45	224	422	34	521	419	77	126	96	291	272	584	277	253	228	226	185	214	309	340	162	287	186	121	144	471	214	75	114	234	70	224	172	94	172	429
Wick	207	598	733	561	738	643	618	661	362	648	725	762	259	717	166	278	608	696	611	589	532	104	409	487	543	487	723	482	410	368	610	645	550	636	827	216	589	758	721	451	674	523	546	703	517	362	684
York	323	202	314	134	275	224	155	243	117	251	306	280	194	299	314	213	190	233	193	193	38	377	91	24	80	102	240	72	50	89	146	181	86	183	408	239	126	339	269	96	254	58	150	251	121	223	266	478
L	551	239	216	121	59	120	59	152	314	215	128	79	413	200	512	410	102	30	136	282	186	575	268	198	143	216	40	204	254	285	68	118	131	56	310	462	86	241	74	225	88	169	163	80	161	420	167	676	211

To calculate the distance in kilomet
multiply the mileage by 1.6

For example: Brighton to Dov
82 miles x 1.6
=131.2 kilomet

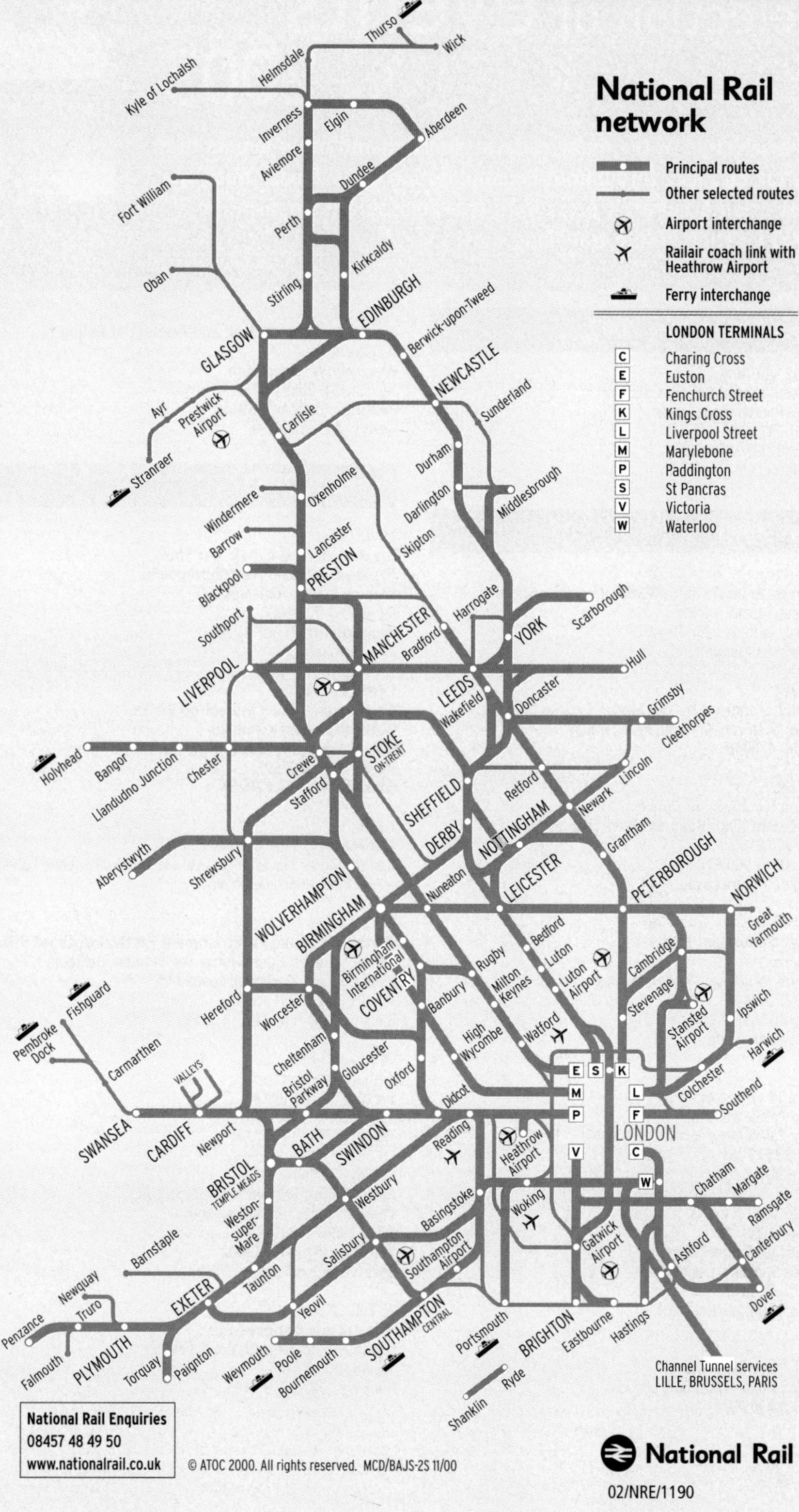
National Rail network
Principal routes
Other selected routes
Airport interchange
Railair coach link with Heathrow Airport
Ferry interchange
LONDON TERMINALS
C Charing Cross
E Euston
F Fenchurch Street
K Kings Cross
L Liverpool Street
M Marylebone
P Paddington
S St Pancras
V Victoria
W Waterloo
Thurso
Wick
Helmsdale
Kyle of Lochalsh
Inverness
Elgin
Aberdeen
Aviemore
Dundee
Fort William
Perth
Kirkcaldy
Oban
Stirling
EDINBURGH
GLASGOW
Berwick-upon-Tweed
NEWCASTLE
Sunderland
Ayr
Prestwick Airport
Carlisle
Stranraer
Durham
Oxenholme
Darlington
Middlesbrough
Windermere
Barrow
Lancaster
Skipton
PRESTON
Blackpool
Harrogate
Scarborough
Southport
MANCHESTER
Bradford
YORK
LIVERPOOL
Hull
LEEDS
Wakefield
Doncaster
Grimsby
Cleethorpes
Holyhead
Bangor
Llandudno Junction
Chester
Crewe
Stafford
STOKE ON-TRENT
SHEFFIELD
Retford
Lincoln
Newark
DERBY
NOTTINGHAM
Grantham
Aberystwyth
Shrewsbury
WOLVERHAMPTON
Nuneaton
LEICESTER
PETERBOROUGH
NORWICH
Great Yarmouth
BIRMINGHAM
Birmingham International
COVENTRY
Rugby
Bedford
Luton
Luton Airport
Cambridge
Milton Keynes
Banbury
Stevenage
Stansted Airport
Ipswich
Fishguard
Pembroke Dock
Hereford
Worcester
Carmarthen
Cheltenham
Gloucester
Bristol Parkway
Oxford
High Wycombe
Watford
Harwich
VALLEYS
SWANSEA
CARDIFF
Newport
Didcot
Colchester
Southend
LONDON
BATH
SWINDON
Reading
Heathrow Airport
BRISTOL TEMPLE MEADS
Westbury
Basingstoke
Woking
Chatham
Margate
Ramsgate
Weston-super-Mare
Salisbury
Southampton Airport
Gatwick Airport
Ashford
Canterbury
Barnstaple
Taunton
Dover
Newquay
Truro
EXETER
Yeovil
Penzance
Falmouth
PLYMOUTH
Torquay
Paignton
Weymouth
Poole
Bournemouth
SOUTHAMPTON CENTRAL
Portsmouth
BRIGHTON
Eastbourne
Hastings
Ryde
Shanklin
Channel Tunnel services
LILLE, BRUSSELS, PARIS
National Rail Enquiries
08457 48 49 50
www.nationalrail.co.uk
© ATOC 2000. All rights reserved. MCD/BAJS-2S 11/00
National Rail
02/NRE/1190

A selection of events for 2003

This is a selection of the many cultural, sporting and other events that will be taking place throughout England during 2003. Please note, as changes often occur after press date, it is advisable to confirm the date and location before travelling.

October 2002 - May 2003

5 Oct 2002 - 17 May
Leeds International Concert Season
Town Hall, The Headrow, Leeds
Tel: (0113) 247 8332
Bookings: (0113) 247 3801
www.leedsconcertseason.com

January 2003

1 Jan
Wood Green Animal Shelter Exemption Dog Show
Wood Green Animal Shelter
King's Bush Farm, London Road,
Godmanchester, Huntingdon

3 Jan - 4 Jan
Exeter Trial organised by The Motor Cycling Club
Around South Devon, finishing near Torquay
Tel: (01308) 420706

9 Jan - 2 Feb
Holiday on Ice 2003 : In Concert
Brighton Centre, Kings Road, Brighton, East Sussex
Tel: 0870 900 9100
Bookings: 0870 900 9100
www.brightoncentre.co.uk

10 Jan - 12 Jan
Whittlesey Straw Bear Festival
Various venues
Town centre, Whittlesey, Peterborough
Tel: (01733) 208245
Bookings: (01733) 208245
www.strawbear.org.uk

12 Jan
Antique and Collectors' Fair
Alexandra Palace and Park
Alexandra Palace Way, London
Tel: (020) 8883 7061
www.allypally-uk.com

18 Jan - 19 Jan
Motorbike 2003
Springfields Exhibition Centre
Camelgate, Spalding, Lincolnshire
Tel: (01775) 724843
www.springfields.mistral.co.uk

26 Jan
Charles I Commemoration
Banqueting House, Whitehall, London
Tel: (01430) 430695

30 Jan - 7 Feb
Wakefield Rhubarb Trail and Festival of Rhubarb
Various venues
Wakefield, West Yorkshire
Tel: (01924) 305911
Bookings: (01924) 305911
www.wakefield.gov.uk

February 2003

1 Feb - 2 Feb
The 24th Bristol Classic Car Show
The Royal Bath and West Showground
Shepton Mallet, Somerset
Tel: (0117) 907 1000
Bookings: (0117) 907 1000
www.nwe.co.uk

1 Feb - 28 Feb
Walsingham Abbey Snowdrop Walks
Walsingham Abbey Grounds
Little Walsingham, Walsingham, Norfolk
Tel: (01328) 820259
Bookings: (01328) 820259

2 Feb
Chinese New Year Celebrations
Gerrard Street, Leicester Square and Trafalgar Square, London
www.chinatownchinese.com

9 Feb
Youth Brass Band Entertainment Festival of Great Britain
Winter Gardens, Opera House and Empress Ballroom
Church Street, Blackpool, Lancashire
Tel: (01706) 373911 x213
Bookings: (01706) 373911 x213

14 Feb - 25 Feb
King's Lynn Mart
Tuesday Market Place
King's Lynn, Norfolk
Tel: (01508) 471772

15 Feb - 22 Feb
Jorvik Viking Festival - Jolablot 2003
Various venues throughout York
Tel: (01904) 643211
Bookings: (01904) 543402
www.vikingjorvik.com

25 Feb - 2 Mar
Fine Art and Antiques Fair
Olympia, Hammersmith Road, London
Tel: 0870 736 3105
Bookings: 0870 739 3105

March 2003

1 Mar - 8 Mar
Bedfordshire Festival of Music, Speech and Drama
Corn Exchange, St Paul's Square, Bedford
Tel: (01234) 720481

6 Mar - 9 Mar
Crufts 2003
National Exhibition Centre
Birmingham, West Midlands
Tel: (020) 7518 1069
Bookings: 0870 909 4133
www.crufts.org.uk

9 Mar
Antique and Collectors' Fair
Alexandra Palace and Park
Alexandra Palace Way, London
Tel: (020) 8883 7061
www.allypally-uk.com

11 Mar - 13 Mar
Cheltenham Gold Cup National Hunt Racing Festival
Cheltenham Racecourse, Prestbury Park, Cheltenham, Gloucestershire
Tel: (01242) 513014
Bookings: (01242) 226226
www.cheltenham.co.uk

12 Mar - 6 Apr
Daily Mail Ideal Home Show
Earls Court Exhibition Centre, Warwick Road, London
Tel: 0870 606 6080
Bookings: 0870 606 6080

14 Mar - 16 Mar
IAAF World Indoor Championships
National Indoor Arena, King Edwards Road, Birmingham, West Midlands
Tel: 0870 909 4144
Bookings: 0870 909 4144
www.necgroup.co.uk

14 Mar - 17 Mar*
St Patrick's Festival and Carnival Parade
Various venues
Downpatrick, County Down
Tel: (028) 44612233
Bookings: (028) 4461 2233
www.downdc.gov.uk

15 Mar - 16 Mar
Ambleside Daffodil and Spring Flower Show
The Kelsick Centre
St Mary's Lane, Ambleside, Cumbria
Tel: (015394) 32252
www.ambleside-show.org.uk

19 Mar
Trafalgar Day Parade - The Sea Cadet Corps
Trafalgar Square, London
Tel: (020) 7928 8978

22 Mar - 23 Mar
Spring Craft Fair
Ragley Hall, Alcester, Warwickshire
Tel: (0161) 860 0755
Bookings: (0161) 860 0755
www.mgafairs.co.uk

23 Mar - 7 Apr
Easter Family Trail
Nunnington Hall (NT)
Nunnington, York
Tel: (01439) 748283
Bookings: (01439) 748283

30 Mar
Barleylands Babies Day
Barleylands Farm
Barleylands Road, Billericay, Essex
Tel: (01268) 290229
Bookings: (01268) 290219
www.barleylandsfarm.co.uk

April 2003

3 Apr - 5 Apr
Horse-racing: Martell Grand National Festival
Aintree Racecourse
Ormskirk Road, Aintree, Liverpool, Merseyside
Tel: (0151) 523 2600
Bookings: (0151) 522 2929
www.aintree.co.uk

5 Apr
Oxford and Cambridge Boat Race
River Thames, London
Tel: (020) 7611 3500
www.theboatrace.org

10 Apr - 15 Apr
Isle of Man Food and Drink Festival
Various venues on the Island, Douglas, Isle of Man
Tel: (01624) 686801
www.isleofman.com

13 Apr
Flora London Marathon
Greenwich Park, London
Tel: (020) 7902 0189
www.london-marathon.co.uk

18 Apr
Old Custom: Pace Egg Plays
Upper Calder Valley
Various venues: Hebden Bridge, Heptonstall, Hebden Bridge; West Yorkshire
Tel: (01422) 843831

19 Apr - 23 Apr
Harrogate International Youth Music Festival
Various venues
Harrogate, North Yorkshire
Tel: (01306) 744360
Bookings: (01423) 537230
www.performeurope.co.uk

20 Apr
Trigg Morris Men's Easter Monday Tour
Various venues starting in the Market Square, Launceston
Tel: (01637) 880394
www.triggmorris.freeserve.co.uk

21 Apr
London Harness Horse Parade
Battersea Park, London

24 Apr - 27 Apr
Harrogate Spring Flower Show
Great Yorkshire Showground, Harrogate, North Yorkshire
Tel: (01423) 561049
Bookings: (01423) 561049
www.flowershow.org.uk

* provisional at time of going to press

May 2003

1 May - 4 May*
Badminton Horse Trials
Badminton House Grounds
Badminton, Avon
Tel: (01454) 218272
Bookings: (01454) 218272
www.badminton-horse.co.uk

1 May - 31 May*
Royal Windsor Horse Show
Home Park, Windsor Castle, Windsor
Tel: 0870 121 5370
Bookings: 0870 121 5370
www.royal-windsor-horse-show.co.uk

1 May - 31 May*
International Kite Flying Festival
Museum of Army Flying Explorers' World
Middle Wallop, Stockbridge, Hampshire
Tel: (01980) 674421

3 May - 25 May*
Brighton Festival
Various venues, Brighton
Tel: (01273) 700747
Bookings: (01273) 709709
www.brighton-festival.org.uk

10 May - 17 May
Wharfedale Music Festival
Various venues, Ilkley
West Yorkshire
Tel: (01943) 872067

11 May
Antique and Collectors' Fair
Alexandra Palace and Park
Alexandra Palace Way, London
Tel: (020) 8883 7061
www.allypally-uk.com

14 May - 18 May*
Royal Windsor Horse Show
Windsor Home Park, Datchet Road, Windsor, Berkshire
Tel: (01753) 860633
Bookings: (020) 7370 8206
www.royal-windsor-horse-show.co.uk

15 May - 17 May
Devon County Show
Westpoint Exhibition Centre
Devon County Showground
Clyst St Mary, Exeter, Devon
Tel: (01392) 446000
Bookings: (01392) 446000

16 May - 1 Jun
Bath International Music Festival
Various venues in Bath
Tel: (01225) 463362
Bookings: (01225) 463362
www.bathfestivals.org.uk

19 May - 21 May*
Jennings Keswick Jazz Festival
Various venues, Keswick, Cumbria
Tel: (01900) 602122
Bookings: (01900) 602122

19 May - 31 Aug*
Glyndebourne Festival Opera
Glyndebourne Opera House
Glyndebourne, Glynde, Lewes, East Sussex
Tel: (01273) 815000
Bookings: (01273) 815000
www.glyndebourne.co.uk

20 May - 23 May
Chelsea Flower Show
Royal Hospital Chelsea
Royal Hospital Road, Chelsea, London
Bookings: 0870 906 3781

24 May - 26 May
Orange WOW
North Shields Fishquay and Town Centre
North Shields, Tyne and Wear
Tel: (0191) 200 5415
www.orangewow.co.uk

24 May - 6 Jun*
Isle of Man TT Motorcycle Festival
Various venues, Isle of Man, Douglas, Isle of Man

26 May
Northumberland County Show
Tynedale Park, Corbridge, Northumberland
Tel: (01697) 747848
Bookings: (01749) 813899
www.northcountyshow.co.uk

28 May - 29 May
Suffolk Show
Suffolk Showground, Bucklesham Road, Ipswich
Tel: (01473) 726847
Bookings: (01473) 726847

28 May - 31 May
The Royal Bath and West Show
The Royal Bath and West Showground
Shepton Mallet, Somerset
Tel: (01749) 822200
Bookings: (01749) 822200
www.bathandwest.co.uk

30 May - 1 Jun*
Dickens Festival
Various venues, Rochester, Kent
Tel: (01634) 843666
www.medway.gov

June 2003

1 Jun - 30 Jun*
Cheshire County Show
The Showground, Tabley, Knutsford, Cheshire
Tel: (01829) 760020
Bookings: (01829) 760020
www.cheshireshow.co.uk

1 Jun - 30 Jun*
Goodwood Festival of Speed
Goodwood Motor Circuit, Goodwood, Chichester, West Sussex
Tel: (01243) 755055
Bookings: (01243) 755055
www.goodwood.co.uk

5 Jun - 7 Jun
Royal Cornwall Show
Royal Cornwall Showground, Wadebridge, Cornwall
Tel: (01208) 812183
Bookings: (01208) 812183
www.royalcornwall.co.uk

6 Jun - 7 Jun
The Keswick Beer Festival
Keswick Rugby Club
Davidson Park, Keswick, Cumbria
Tel: (017687) 73591
Bookings: (017687) 75414
keswickbeerfestival.com

6 Jun - 7 Jun*
Vodafone Derby Horse Race Meeting
Epsom Racecourse, Epsom, Surrey
Tel: (01372) 470047
Bookings: (01372) 470047
www.epsomderby.co.uk

13 Jun - 15 Jun
The East of England Country Show
East of England Showground
Alwalton, Peterborough
Bookings: (01733) 234451

14 Jun
Trooping the Colour - The Queen's Birthday Parade
Horse Guards Parade, London
Tel: (020) 7414 2479
Bookings: (020) 7414 2479

14 Jun - 21 Jun
Tennis: Britannic Asset Management International Championships
International Lawn Tennis Centre
Devonshire Park, College Road, Eastbourne, East Sussex
Tel: (01323) 411555
Bookings: (01323) 411555
www.eastbourne.org/events/britannic_tennis.asp

17 Jun - 20 Jun*
Racing at Ascot: The Royal Meeting
Ascot Racecourse, Ascot, Berkshire
Tel: (01344) 876876
Bookings: (01344) 876876
www.ascot.co.uk

18 Jun - 19 Jun
Corpus Christi Carpet of Flowers and Floral Festival
Cathedral of Our Lady and St Philip Howard
London Road, Arundel, West Sussex
Tel: (01903) 882297
www.arundelcathedral.org

19 Jun - 22 Jun*
Blenheim Palace Flower Show
Blenheim Palace, Woodstock, Oxfordshire
Tel: (01737) 379911
Bookings: (0115) 912 9188
www.bpfs2002.co.uk

20 Jun - 29 Jun
Newcastle Hoppings
Town Moor, Grandstand Road, Newcastle upon Tyne
Tel: (0191) 232 8520

21 Jun
Otley Carnival
Otley Town Centre, Otley, West Yorkshire
Tel: (01943) 463266

21 Jun*
Round the Island Race
Isle of Wight Coast
c/o Island Sailing Club
70 High Street, Cowes, Isle of Wight
Tel: (01983) 296621
www.island.org.uk

23 Jun - 6 Jul
Wimbledon Lawn Tennis Championships
All England Lawn Tennis & Croquet Club
Church Road, London
Tel: (020) 8946 2244
Bookings: (020) 8946 2244

25 Jun - 26 Jun
Royal Norfolk Show 2003
The Showground, New Costessey, Norwich
Tel: (01603) 748931
Bookings: (01603) 748931
www.royalnorfolkshow.co.uk

25 Jun - 29 Jun*
Covent Garden Flower Festival
Covent Garden Piazza, London
Tel: 09064 701 777 (60p per minute)
www.cgff.co.uk

29 Jun - 5 Jul
Alnwick Fair
Market Square, Alnwick
Northumberland
Tel: (01665) 711397
www.fair01.freeserve.co.uk/index.html

30 Jun - 3 Jul
Royal Show
National Agricultural Centre, Stoneleigh Park, Warwickshire
Tel: (024) 7669 6969
Bookings: (024) 766 96969
www.royalshow.org.uk

* provisional at time of going to press

30 Jun - 19 Jul
Chester Mystery Plays
Cathedral Green, Chester
Tel: (01244) 682617

July 2003

1 Jul - 31 Jul*
The Merseyside International Street Festival
Various venues, Liverpool
Tel: (0151) 709 3334
www.brouhaha.uk.com

1 Jul - 31 Jul*
Royal Lancashire Show
Astley Park, Chorley
Tel: (01254) 813769
Bookings: (01254) 813769
www.rlas.co.uk

5 Jul - 6 Jul*
Ocean FM Balloon & Flower Festival
Southampton Common, The Avenue, Southampton
Tel: (023) 8083 2525
www.southampton.gov.uk

5 Jul - 6 Jul
Sunderland International Festival of Kites, Music and Dance
Northern Area Playing Fields, Stephenson
Washington, Tyne and Wear
Tel: (0191) 514 1235

8 Jul - 13 Jul*
Hampton Court Palace Flower Show
Hampton Court Palace, Hampton Court, East Molesey, Surrey
Tel: (020) 7649 1885
Bookings: 0870 906 3791
www.rhs.org.uk

9 Jul - 13 Jul*
Henley Festival
Stewards Enclosure of Henley Royal Regatta
Stewards Enclosure, Henley Royal Regatta, Henley-on-Thames
Oxfordshire
Tel: (01491) 843400
Bookings: (01491) 843404
www.henley-festival.co.uk

12 Jul
World Pea Shooting Championships and Village Fair
Village Green, Witcham, Ely, Cambridgeshire
Bookings: (01353) 777906

17 Jul - 20 Jul*
Golf: The Open Championship
Royal St George's Golf Club, Sandwich, Kent
Tel: (01334) 460000
Bookings: (01334) 460000
www.opengolf.com

18 Jul - 20 Jul
Ripley Castle Antiques Fair
Ripley Castle, Ripley, Harrogate, North Yorkshire
Tel: (01423) 522122
Bookings: (01423) 522122
www.gallowayfairs.co.uk

18 Jul - 13 Sep
The Proms
Royal Albert Hall, Kensington Gore, London
Tel: (020) 7765 5575
Bookings: (020) 7589 8212

20 Jul*
FIA Formula 1 British Grand Prix
Octagan Motorsports Ltd, Silverstone, Towcester, Northamptonshire
Bookings: (01327) 850260

25 Jul - 27 Jul*
Netley Marsh Steam and Craft Show
Meadow Farm, Ringwood Road, Netley Marsh, Southampton
Tel: (023) 8086 7882

25 Jul - 27 Jul
Weymouth National Beach Volleyball
The Beach, Weymouth, Dorset
Tel: (01305) 785747
www.weymouth.gov.uk

26 Jul - 27 Jul*
Gateshead Summer Flower Show
Gateshead Central Nurseries, Whickham Highway, Lobley Hill, Gateshead, Tyne and Wear
Tel: (0191) 433 3838
Bookings: (0191) 433 3838

26 Jul - 27 Jul
Sunderland International Air Show
Promenade, Sea Front, Seaburn, Sunderland
Tel: (0191) 553 2002

29 Jul - 31 Jul
New Forest and Hampshire County Show
New Park, The Showground, New Park, Brockenhurst, Hampshire
Tel: (01590) 622400
Bookings: (023) 8071 1818
www.newforestshow.co.uk

29 Jul - 2 Aug
Horse Racing: July Festival Meeting
Goodwood Racecourse, Goodwood, Chichester, West Sussex
Tel: (01243) 755022
Bookings: (01243) 755022 x2408
www.goodwood.co.uk

30 Jul
Nantwich and South Cheshire Show
Dorfold Hall, Nantwich, Cheshire
Tel: (01270) 780306
Bookings: (01270) 780306
www.nantwichshow.co.uk

31 Jul
Ambleside Traditional Lakeland Sports
Rydal Park, Rydal Road, Rydal, Ambleside, Cumbria
Tel: (015394) 34087
Bookings: (015394) 34087

1 Aug - 3 Aug
'Crowning Glory' Flower Festival
Saint Edmundsbury Cathedral
The Cathedral Office, Angel Hill, Bury St Edmunds, Suffolk
Tel: (01284) 754933
Bookings: (01284) 754933
www.stedscathedral.co.uk

1 Aug - 8 Aug
Sidmouth International Festival
Various venues, Sidmouth, Devon
Tel: (01296) 433669
Bookings: (01296) 433669
www.mrscasey.co.uk/sidmouth

August 2003

1 Aug - 31 Aug*
Woodvale International Rally
Woodvale, Southport, Merseyside
Tel: (01704) 578816
Bookings: (01704) 876283
www.woodvale-rally.org.uk

2 Aug - 9 Aug
Alnwick International Music Festival
Market-place, Alnwick, Northumberland
Tel: (01665) 510417
Bookings: (01665) 510785
www.alnwickfestival.com

2 Aug - 9 Aug
Skandia Life Cowes Week 2003
The Solent, Cowes, Isle of Wight
Tel: (01983) 293303

7 Aug
Honiton Agricultural Show
The Showground, Honiton, Devon
Tel: (01404) 871504

7 Aug - 10 Aug
Bristol Balloon Fiesta
Ashton Court Estate
Long Ashton, Bristol
Tel: (0117) 953 5884
www.bristolfiesta.co.uk

8 Aug - 10 Aug
11th International Jazz Festival
Hilton Isle of Man, Central Promenade
Douglas, Isle of Man
Tel: (01624) 686801
Bookings: (01624) 686766
www.visitisleofman.com

9 Aug - 16 Aug
Billingham International Folklore Festival
John Whitehead Park
Billingham, Cleveland
Tel: (01642) 651060
Bookings: (01642) 552663
www.billinghamfestival.co.uk

14 Aug - 15 Aug*
Jersey Battle of Flowers
Victoria Avenue, St Helier, Jersey, Channel Islands
Tel: (01534) 639000
Bookings: (01534) 639000
www.battleofflowers.com

15 Aug - 17 Aug
Northampton Hot-Air Balloon Festival
Northampton Racecourse, St George's Avenue, Northampton
Tel: (01604) 238791
Bookings: (01604) 238791
www.northampton.gov.uk

16 Aug - 22 Aug 2003
Whitby Folk Week
Various venues, Whitby, North Yorkshire
Tel: (01757) 708424
Bookings: (01757) 708424

20 Aug - 25 Aug 2003
International Beatles Festival
Various venues, Liverpool
Bookings: (0151) 236 9091

* provisional at time of going to press

24 Aug*
Grasmere Lakeland Sports and Show
Sports Field, Stock Lane, Grasmere, Ambleside, Cumbria
Tel: (015394) 32127
Bookings: (015394) 32127

24 Aug - 25 Aug
Notting Hill Carnival
Streets around Ladbroke Grove
London
Tel: (020) 8964 0544

25 Aug
Corsley Show
Corsley Showfield, Corsley, Warminster, Wiltshire
Tel: (01373) 832418
Bookings: (01373) 832418

27 Aug - 31 Aug*
Great Dorset Steam Fair
South Down Farm, Tarrant Hinton, Blandford Forum, Dorset
Tel: (01258) 860361
Bookings: (01258) 488928
www.steam-fair.co.uk

28 Aug - 30 Aug
Port of Dartmouth Royal Regatta
Various venues, Dartmouth, Devon
Tel: (01803) 832435
www.dartmouthregatta.co.uk

29 Aug - 2 Nov
Blackpool Illuminations
Blackpool Promenade, Blackpool
Tel: (01253) 478222
www.blackpooltourism.com

September 2003

1 Sep - 30 Sep*
Goodwood Revival Meeting
Goodwood Motor Circuit, Goodwood, Chichester, West Sussex
Tel: (01243) 755055
Bookings: (01243) 755055
www.goodwood.co.uk

12 Sep - 21 Sep*
Southampton International Boat Show
Western Esplanade, Southampton
Tel: (01784) 223600
Bookings: (0115) 912 9130
www.bigblue.org.uk

13 Sep - 14 Sep*
Beaulieu International Autojumble and Automart
National Motor Museum, John Montagu Building, Beaulieu
Brockenhurst, Hampshire
Tel: (01590) 614614
Bookings: (01590) 612888
www.beaulieu.co.uk

18 Sep
Battle of Britain Air Display
St Peter Port, Guernsey, Channel Islands
Tel: (01481) 723552
www.guernseytouristboard.com

20 Sep - 21 Sep
Mayor's Thames Festival, River Thames, London
Tel: (020) 7928 0960
www.ThamesFestival.org

20 Sep - 21 Sep*
The Royal County of Berkshire Show
Newbury Showground, Priors Court, Hermitage, Thatcham
Berkshire
Tel: (01635) 247111
Bookings: (01635) 247111
www.newburyshowground.co.uk

21 Sep
Antique and Collectors' Fair
Alexandra Palace and Park, Alexandra Palace Way, London
Tel: (020) 8883 7061
www.allypally-uk.com

21 Sep - 27 Sep*
Egremont Crab Fair and Sports
Baybarrow Sports Field, Orgill, Egremont, Cumbria
Tel: (01946) 821554
Bookings: (01946) 820564
crabfair.homestead.com/mainpage.html

October 2003

10 Oct - 18 Oct
Hull Fair
Walton Street Fairground, Walton Street, Hull
Tel: (01482) 615625

10 Oct - 19 Oct
Cheltenham Festival of Literature
Town Hall, Imperial Square, Cheltenham, Gloucestershire
Bookings: (01242) 22979

11 Oct - 25 Oct
Canterbury Festival
Various venues, Canterbury, Kent
Tel: (01227) 452853
Bookings: (01227) 455600

November 2003

1 Nov - 2 Nov
Complementary Medicine Festival
Kings Hall & Winter Gardens
Station Road, Ilkley, West Yorkshire
Tel: (01943) 609454
Bookings: (01943) 609454

1 Nov - 30 Nov*
International Guitar Festival of Great Britain
Various venues, Wirral, Merseyside
Tel: (0151) 666 5060
Bookings: (0151) 666 5023
www.bestguitarfest.com

5 Nov
Old Custom: Rolling of the Tar Barrels
Town Centre, Ottery St Mary, Devon
Tel: (01404) 813964
www.cosmic.org.uk

7 Nov
Bridgwater Guy Fawkes Carnival
Town Centre, Bridgwater, Somerset
Tel: (01278) 421795
www.bridgwatercarnival.org.uk

8 Nov
Cambridge Music Festival
Cambridge Concert Halls, Cambridge
Tel: (01223) 350544
Bookings: (01223) 357851
www.cammusic.co.uk

16 Nov
Antique and Collectors' Fair
Alexandra Palace and Park, Alexandra Palace Way, London
Tel: (020) 8883 7061
www.allypally-uk.com

December 2003

6 Dec - 7 Dec*
Dickensian Christmas
Various venues, Rochester, Kent
Tel: (01634) 843666
www.medway.gov.uk

11 Dec - 14 Dec
York Early Music Christmas Festival
Various venues, York
Tel: (01904) 645738
Bookings: (01904) 658338
www.yorkearlymusic.org

18 Dec - 22 Dec
Olympia International Showjumping Championships
Olympia, Hammersmith Road, London
Tel: (020) 7370 8206
Bookings: (020) 7370 8206
www.olympia-show-jumping.co.uk

* provisional at time of going to press

Calendar 2003

JANUARY

M	T	W	T	F	S	S
		1	2	3	4	5
6	7	8	9	10	11	12
13	14	15	16	17	18	19
20	21	22	23	24	25	26
27	28	29	30	31		

FEBRUARY

M	T	W	T	F	S	S
					1	2
3	4	5	6	7	8	9
10	11	12	13	14	15	16
17	18	19	20	21	22	23
24	25	26	27	28		

MARCH

M	T	W	T	F	S	S
					1	2
3	4	5	6	7	8	9
10	11	12	13	14	15	16
17	18	19	20	21	22	23
24	25	26	27	28	29	30
31						

APRIL

M	T	W	T	F	S	S
	1	2	3	4	5	6
7	8	9	10	11	12	13
14	15	16	17	**18**	19	20
21	22	23	24	25	26	27
28	29	30				

MAY

M	T	W	T	F	S	S
			1	2	3	4
5	6	7	8	9	10	11
12	13	14	15	16	17	18
19	20	21	22	23	24	25
26	27	28	29	30	31	

JUNE

M	T	W	T	F	S	S
						1
2	3	4	5	6	7	8
9	10	11	12	13	14	15
16	17	18	19	20	21	22
23	24	25	26	27	28	29
30						

JULY

M	T	W	T	F	S	S
	1	2	3	4	5	6
7	8	9	10	11	12	13
14	15	16	17	18	19	20
21	22	23	24	25	26	27
28	29	30	31			

AUGUST

M	T	W	T	F	S	S
				1	2	3
4	5	6	7	8	9	10
11	12	13	14	15	16	17
18	19	20	21	22	23	24
25	26	27	28	29	30	31

SEPTEMBER

M	T	W	T	F	S	S
1	2	3	4	5	6	7
8	9	10	11	12	13	14
15	16	17	18	19	20	21
22	23	24	25	26	27	28
29	30					

OCTOBER

M	T	W	T	F	S	S
		1	2	3	4	5
6	7	8	9	10	11	12
13	14	15	16	17	18	19
20	21	22	23	24	25	26
27	28	29	30	31		

NOVEMBER

M	T	W	T	F	S	S
					1	2
3	4	5	6	7	8	9
10	11	12	13	14	15	16
17	18	19	20	21	22	23
24	25	26	27	28	29	30

DECEMBER

M	T	W	T	F	S	S
1	2	3	4	5	6	7
8	9	10	11	12	13	14
15	16	17	18	19	20	21
22	23	24	**25**	**26**	27	28
29	30	31				

Calendar 2004

JANUARY

M	T	W	T	F	S	S
			1	2	3	4
5	6	7	8	9	10	11
12	13	14	15	16	17	18
19	20	21	22	23	24	25
26	27	28	29	30	31	

FEBRUARY

M	T	W	T	F	S	S
						1
2	3	4	5	6	7	8
9	10	11	12	13	14	15
16	17	18	19	20	21	22
23	24	25	26	27	28	29

MARCH

M	T	W	T	F	S	S
1	2	3	4	5	6	7
8	9	10	11	12	13	14
15	16	17	18	19	20	21
22	23	24	25	26	27	28
29	30	31				

APRIL

M	T	W	T	F	S	S
			1	2	3	4
5	6	7	8	**9**	10	11
12	13	14	15	16	17	18
19	20	21	22	23	24	25
26	27	28	29	30		

MAY

M	T	W	T	F	S	S
					1	2
3	4	5	6	7	8	9
10	11	12	13	14	15	16
17	18	19	20	21	22	23
24	25	26	27	28	29	30
31						

JUNE

M	T	W	T	F	S	S
	1	2	3	4	5	6
7	8	9	10	11	12	13
14	15	16	17	18	19	20
21	22	23	24	25	26	27
28	29	30				

JULY

M	T	W	T	F	S	S
			1	2	3	4
5	6	7	8	9	10	11
12	13	14	15	16	17	18
19	20	21	22	23	24	25
26	27	28	29	30	31	

AUGUST

M	T	W	T	F	S	S
						1
2	3	4	5	6	7	8
9	10	11	12	13	14	15
16	17	18	19	20	21	22
23	24	25	26	27	28	29
30	31					

SEPTEMBER

M	T	W	T	F	S	S
		1	2	3	4	5
6	7	8	9	10	11	12
13	14	15	16	17	18	19
20	21	22	23	24	25	26
27	28	29	30			

OCTOBER

M	T	W	T	F	S	S
				1	2	3
4	5	6	7	8	9	10
11	12	13	14	15	16	17
18	19	20	21	22	23	24
25	26	27	28	29	30	31

NOVEMBER

M	T	W	T	F	S	S
1	2	3	4	5	6	7
8	9	10	11	12	13	14
15	16	17	18	19	20	21
22	23	24	25	26	27	28
29	30					

DECEMBER

M	T	W	T	F	S	S
		1	2	3	4	5
6	7	8	9	10	11	12
13	14	15	16	17	18	19
20	21	22	23	24	**25**	**26**
27	28	29	30	31		

Notes

Notes

Notes

TOWN INDEX

The following cities, towns and villages all have accommodation listed in this guide. If the place where you wish to stay is not shown, the location maps (starting on page 22) will help you to find somewhere suitable in the same area.

Y PAGE